THE LAW OF SCOTLAND

THE LAW OF SCOTLAND

by

The Late W.M. GLOAG, KC, LLD
and
The Late R. CANDLISH HENDERSON, QC, LLD

THIRTEENTH EDITION

General Editors
Professor Hector L. MacQueen, LLB, PhD, FBA, FRSE
*Professor of Private Law, University of Edinburgh,
Scottish Law Commissioner*

The Rt Hon. Lord Eassie
Senator of the College of Justice

Assistant Editors
Douglas Bain, BA, LLB, Dip. LP, LLM
Teaching Fellow, University of Aberdeen

David Cabrelli, LLB, Dip. LP
Solicitor, Lecturer in Commercial Law, University of Edinburgh

Gordon Cameron, LLB, MSc
Senior Lecturer, University of Dundee

Professor D.L. Carey-Miller, BA, LLB, LLM, PhD, FRSE
Emeritus Professor of Property Law, University of Aberdeen

Malcolm M. Combe, LLB, Dip. LP
Solicitor, Lecturer, University of Aberdeen

W.C.H. Ervine, BA, LLB, LLM
Honorary Teaching Fellow, University of Dundee

Nicholas Grier, MA, LLB, WS
Solicitor, Senior Lecturer in Law, Edinburgh Napier University

David Irvine, LLB, Dip. LP
Solicitor

Simone Lamont-Black, Assessorin, Doktor der Rechte (Dr Jur)
Lecturer in International Trade Law, University of Edinburgh

Dr Catherine Ng, B.Comm., LLB, LLM, D.Phil
Senior Lecturer in Law, University of Aberdeen

Dr David Nichols, MA, PhD, WS
School of Law, University of Edinburgh

Professor Roderick Paisley, LLB, Dip. LP, NP, PhD
Professor of Commercial Property Law, University of Aberdeen

Morag Wise QC, LLB, LLM, LLP
Advocate

W. GREEN   THOMSON REUTERS

First published 1927
Second edition 1933
Third edition 1939
Fourth edition 1946
Fifth edition 1952
Sixth edition 1956
Seventh edition 1968
Eighth edition 1980
Ninth edition 1987
Tenth edition 1995
Eleventh edition 2001
Twelfth edition 2007
Thirteenth edition 2012

Published in 2012 by W. Green, 21 Alva Street,
Edinburgh EH2 4PS
Part of Thomson Reuters (Professional) UK Limited
(Registered in England & Wales, Company No 1679046.
Registered Office and address for service:
Aldgate House, 33 Aldgate High Street, London EC3N 1DL)

10 0899529 0

Typeset by LBJ Typesetting Ltd, Kingsclere
Printed and bound in the UK by CPI Group (UK) Ltd, Croydon, CR0 4YY

No natural forests were destroyed to make this product;
only farmed timber was used and replanted.

A CIP catalogue record for this title is available from the British Library

ISBN 978-0-414-01818-1

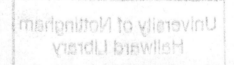

PREFACE TO THIRTEENTH EDITION

The previous edition of this book coincided with the tercentenary of the Anglo-Scottish Union of 1707 and the election to Government in Scotland of a political party committed to ending that union. This edition appears as the same party, re-elected to Government in 2011 with an overall majority in the Scottish Parliament, laid the ground for a referendum on the question of Scottish independence from the United Kingdom, probably to be held in 2014. If the appearance of a comprehensive work on Scots private and commercial law seemed important in 2007, this new and fully updated version will be even more important in the years that follow its publication in 2012, whatever results the political process may throw up. Against this background we and our fellow editors have endeavoured to provide an account of the private and commercial law of Scotland as it stood on June 1 that year, while also taking account of still later developments where possible. In some instances we have even been able to anticipate possible changes in the law: most notably with the Bankruptcy and Diligence etc (Scotland) Act 2007, much of which has still to be brought into force five years after its Parliamentary passage, and the Land Registration etc (Scotland) Act 2012, the entry of which into force should be less sluggish. The suggestions for further reading which accompany each chapter also refer the reader to law reform proposals in relation to the chapter topic, on the basis that during the lifetime of this edition these proposals may become law, or influence the way in which the courts interpret the law.

At the end of the process of producing this edition, we and our fellow editors are left with the feeling of the enormous difficulty of knowing or finding out what is the law in force, and of keeping abreast of the flow of legislation and regulation, not only from Holyrood and Westminster, but also from the European Union; while meantime the courts too remain ever active in the creation and development of precedent. We hope that we have provided at least a useful starting point for the person in search of what the law is, while asking our readers to recognise that the task of keeping *Gloag & Henderson* up-to-date and comprehensive is one that will never end. The recent re-painting of the Forth Bridge, it has been said, means that no further re-painting of the structure will be needed for at least 25 years. We suspect that it will not be so long before there is a need for another edition of this book.

Lord Eassie   Hector L. MacQueen

October 4, 2012

PREFACE TO FIRST EDITION

Since its publication in 1754 Erskine's *Principles*, as revised and brought up to date by various editors, has held a leading place as a textbook in the classes of Scots Law in the Universities. The latest edition, issued in 1911 under the editorship of Sir John Rankine, is now out of print: and, accordingly, in order to meet the requirements of students, it became necessary to consider the preparation of either another edition or of an entirely new book.

On the whole it appeared to us that it would be unwise to attempt a new edition. In the later editions Erskine's original work had been extensively altered by the inclusion of new material rendered necessary by the development of the law: and the addition of this new material in a book within the compass of a student's text-book was possible only at the cost of such compression as to make it extremely difficult for the readers at the outset of their legal studies. As the present book is less comprehensive in its scope, we have been enabled to treat more fully the subjects embraced.

We have confined our work to those branches of the law which are usually dealt with in classes of Scots and of Mercantile Law. Conveyancing, Evidence and Procedure, Private International and Administrative Law are, therefore, only incidentally referred to.

It is hoped that few of the leading decisions have been omitted, but no attempt has been made at such fullness of citation as the practitioner, as distinguished from the student, might expect.

We have to acknowledge the preparation of the work given by Mr. N. M. L. Walker and Mr. T. B. Simpson, Advocates.

W.M.G.
R.C.H.

October, 1927

CONTENTS

TABLE OF CASES

l   *Table of Cases*

Table of Cases

TABLE OF UK STATUTES

TABLE OF SCOTTISH STATUTES

TABLE OF STATUTORY INSTRUMENTS

TABLE OF SCOTTISH STATUTORY INSTRUMENTS

PART I

THE LEGAL SYSTEM

CHAPTER 1

STRUCTURE AND SOURCES OF SCOTS LAW

I. STRUCTURE OF SCOTS PRIVATE LAW

Introduction—This chapter has four main purposes; namely (a) to provide an 1.01
indication of and a guide to the contents of this book, (b) to introduce some basic
legal concepts and terms, (c) to place Scots law in relation to other legal systems
of the world, and (d) to describe the sources of the law of Scotland, that is, to
explain where authoritative statements of the law can be found.

The significance of structure (taxonomy) in a legal system—A legal system 1.02
such as the law of Scotland is not simply a collection of arbitrary rules, but has
some unity and underlying structure. This structure is important because it assists
in seeing how different branches of the law fit together and avoid inconsistencies
between them. For the purposes of exposition, it is necessary to divide the legal
system into sections or chapters, but few of the classifications which may be made
for this purpose are absolutely watertight and developments in any part of the
system may have an impact on other parts of it. In consequence, any division into
chapters may be in part arbitrary. One of the objectives of a general textbook is to
present the law in the way which best represents the underlying structure and
makes it easiest to understand how the parts of it relate to one another. For this
purpose, the first broad distinction to be made is between public law, which is
only dealt with occasionally and incidentally in this book, and private law, which
is its main subject matter.

Public law—The expression "public law" is not capable of precise definition, but 1.03
has been described as the law relating to the state in all its manifestations, and to
its relationship with its citizens and other persons within its borders.[1] Public law,
therefore, is generally thought of as including administrative law,[2] constitutional
law, criminal law, public international law and the law relating to human rights.
However, some of the relationships between the state, or departments of it, and
private citizens are governed by private law, for example when the state enters
into a contract with an individual or company.

Private law—Private law is the branch of law that determines the rights and 1.04
duties of natural and legal persons with each other, as well as those of public and

---

[1] See C.M.G. Himsworth and C.M. O'Neill, *Scotland's Constitution: Law and Practice* (London:
LexisNexis, 2003); J. Munro, *Public Law*, 2nd edn (Edinburgh: W. Green, 2007); *Stair Memorial
Encyclopaedia* (Reissues: "Administrative Law" and "Constitutional Law").
[2] But see Lord Clyde and D. Edwards, *Judicial Review* (Edinburgh: W. Green, 1999), para.8–19;
West v Secretary of State for Scotland, 1992 S.C. 385.

governmental agencies in so far as they do not enjoy any special position under public law.[3] Private law, in turn, can be classified in various ways according to its subject matter. One traditional classification is into the law of obligations, the law of property, the law of persons and the law of actions or legal procedure, and that system is broadly followed in this book, except that the law of actions is only dealt with incidentally. The Scotland Act 1998 adopts a similar but more detailed description by defining "private law" (over which the Scottish Parliament established under the Act has legislative competence) as: (a) the general principles of private law (including private international law); (b) the law of persons (including natural persons, legal persons and unincorporated bodies); (c) the law of obligations (including obligations arising from contract, unilateral promise, delict, unjustified enrichment and *negotiorum gestio*); (d) the law of property (including heritable and moveable property, trust and succession); (e) the law of actions (including jurisdiction, remedies, evidence, procedure, diligence, recognition and enforcement of court orders, limitation of actions and arbitration); and judicial review of administrative action.[4]

1.05 The branches of private law: 1. The law of obligations[5]—

"An obligation may be defined in our law, as it was by the Roman, as a legal tie by which one is bound to pay or perform something to another."[6]

The creditor (obligee) in a personal right or obligation has a right of action against the debtor (obligor, obligant). In the exercise of that right he may compel the debtor (or, if deceased, his representatives) to fulfil that obligation. But the personal right gives him no right in a subject which the debtor is obliged to transfer to him.[7] The right in the subject itself is a right of a different character. It belongs to the law of property, and it is known as a real right.[8] Obligations are brought into existence in various ways. They have been said to fall into two main groups: those which are created by the parties' own free will, of which the leading example is contract; and those imposed by the law regardless of the parties' will, which deal, by and large, with mishaps or departures from the ordinary course of things.[9] For present purposes, however, they may be classified into: (1) obligations arising from force of law; (2) obligations arising from a wrongful act; and (3) obligations arising from the will of the obligor.[10]

---

[3] D.M. Walker, *Principles of Scottish Private Law*, 4th edn (Oxford: Clarendon Press, 1988), Vol.1, p.3; see also *Davidson v Scottish Ministers*, 2006 S.C. (HL) 41, per Lord Rodger of Earlsferry at [77].

[4] Scotland Act 1998 s.126(4). Strictly, judicial review of administrative action belongs to public rather than private law but is sometimes used in the regulation of what are otherwise private law relations (e.g. voluntary associations, see Ch.49; below, see further para.2.05, below). Private international law deals with the relationships of different legal systems as they affect private persons and is a subject for which reference should be made to specialised works.

[5] See Ch.3, below.

[6] Erskine, III, 1, 2.

[7] Erskine, III, 1, 2.

[8] See paras 1.09–1.10, below.

[9] H.L. MacQueen and J.M. Thomson, *Contract Law in Scotland*, 2nd edn (Edinburgh: Bloomsbury Professional, 2007), paras 1.42–1.51.

[10] T.B. Smith, *A Short Commentary on the Law of Scotland* (Edinburgh: W. Green, 1962), p.281; *Stair Memorial Encyclopaedia*, Vol.15, "Obligations", para.1.

Obligations arising from force of law—Obligations which fall into this category **1.06** arise by force of law alone. Their existence comes about in a way that is independent of any agreement, promise or other engagement by the party who is bound by the obligation, or of any wrongful act on his part. These include the obligations which arise between persons because of their relationship to each other, such as that of a parent to support his children,[11] the obligations which arise in cases of unjustified enrichment,[12] the obligation of *negotiorum gestio*,[13] and the obligations arising from average and salvage in shipping law.[14]

Obligations arising from a wrongful act—Into this category falls the obligation **1.07** to make reparation to another for loss, injury or damage caused by the party's fault or other wrongful act. Intentional wrongdoing as well as negligence is covered by it. Obligations which fall into this category are described as "delictual" obligations because they depend upon the law relating to delict.[15] But not all wrongful acts are delictual. Wrongs which arise from a breach of contact or a breach of trust are classified differently. The remedies and obligations arising from a breach of contract belong to the law of voluntary obligations.[16] The remedies and obligations arising from a breach of trust belong to the law of trusts, a separate branch of law developed in Scots law under the influence of English law.[17]

Voluntary obligations—A voluntary obligation is created by the will of the **1.08** creditor. It arises when he expresses an intention to be bound by it, which is communicated to the debtor. This may be done by entering into a contract, by which the parties to it express their mutual intention to be bound by it to each other, and voluntary obligations are created on both sides. This is the area of law known as the law of contract.[18] Or it may arise through an expression of will or promise by one party unilaterally, which is communicated to the other in circumstances where the obligor indicates his intention to be bound by it. This is the unilateral promise, which is an undertaking by one party to perform that does not require the agreement of the beneficiary to be enforceable.[19] Consideration, that is to say some counterpart or reciprocal obligation lying upon the creditor, is not required in order to constitute an obligation which is binding in Scots law.

The branches of private law: 2. Property law[20]—The distinction between the **1.09** law of obligations and the law of property is fundamental to the operation of our law.[21] The essential difference is between rights that affect a subject itself, which are called real rights, and those which are founded upon obligation, which are called personal rights. A real right entitles the person in whom it is vested to possess the subject as his own or, if it is in the possession of another, to demand it from him in consequence of the right which he has in the subject itself. A creditor

---

[11] See paras 44.38–44.52, below.
[12] See Ch.24, below.
[13] See paras 24.24–24.28, below.
[14] See paras 22.34–22.48, below.
[15] See generally Chs 25–29, below.
[16] See Ch.10, below.
[17] See Ch.41, below.
[18] See generally Chs 5–11, below.
[19] See paras 5.01–5.02, below.
[20] See generally Chs 30–36, below.
[21] *Sharp v Thomson*, 1995 S.C. 455 at 463. See also *Burnett's Trustee v Grainger*, 2004 S.C. (HL) 19.

in a personal right, on the other hand, has no more than a right of action against the debtor or his representatives, by which he may compel them to fulfil the obligation.[22] It has been suggested that one way of characterising the difference between real rights and personal rights is to say that, while in general a real right is a right to use or to prevent others from using a thing, a personal right is a right to make a person perform some act or to prevent him from performing some act.[23] Scots law does not recognise a right which lies between the real right on the one hand and the personal right on the other.[24] Property law therefore is the law of things, in so far as they are capable of giving rise to rights in them which can be held by persons,[25] and is concerned with real rights[26] which include rights of ownership, lease and security. The content of the right depends partly upon the type of right which is involved and partly on the type of thing in which the right exists.

1.10 **Classification of real rights**—The principal rights which are classified as real rights in Scots law are rights of ownership, rights under a lease, rights in security, rights of possession and servitudes.[27] The right of ownership was described by Erskine[28] as the right of using and disposing of a subject as our own, except in so far as we are restrained by law or paction.[29] The right under a lease is to possess land or other heritable property in exchange for a periodic payment known as the rent.[30] This right does not extend to the possession of moveable property under a contract of hire, which is attributable only to a personal right against the owner of the moveables.[31] Rights in security include the rights which a creditor acquires under a pledge, a standard security and a floating charge. A pledge is a security over corporeal moveables. A standard security is a security over heritable property. A floating charge is a security over property of all kinds owned by a company.[32] The possession of property, as by a squatter, confers the right not to be dispossessed of the property without consent or the order of a court.[33] A servitude is a right which a person enjoys in his capacity as the owner of land over other land which is not in his ownership.[34]

1.11 **Classification of things**—Scots law has adopted the classification of the Roman law, by which things were classified in two different ways. Things are either corporeal or incorporeal; and they are either heritable or moveable. Corporeal things are articles that have a physical presence and are tangible. Incorporeal things are rights, which have no physical presence and are not tangible. Heritable property consists mainly of land. For the purposes of private international law, the term "immoveable" is normally used to describe what

---

[22] Erskine, III, 1, 2.

[23] K.G.C. Reid, *The Law of Property in Scotland* (Edinburgh: Butterworths, 1996), para.3; see also *Stair Memorial Encyclopaedia*, Vol.18, "Property", para.3.

[24] *Sharp v Thomson*, 1995 S.C. 455 at 468.

[25] Reid, *The Law of Property in Scotland* (1996), para.3.

[26] Reid, *The Law of Property in Scotland* (1996), para.3.

[27] For a full list, see Reid, *The Law of Property in Scotland* (1996), para.5.

[28] Erskine, II, 1, 1.

[29] See further Ch.30, below.

[30] See further Ch.35, below.

[31] See further Ch.13, below.

[32] See further Ch.36, below.

[33] See further para.30.09, below.

[34] See further paras 34.39–34.50, below.

in Scots law is called heritable property.[35] Moveable property consists mainly of things other than land. The result of this system of classification is that there are, in effect, four separate classes of property in Scots law: corporeal heritable property, incorporeal heritable property, corporeal moveable property and incorporeal moveable property. The distinction is between tangible things of each description on the one hand and rights of each description on the other. But it has been suggested that, as the division of rights into heritable rights and moveable rights is largely artificial except in relation to legal rights in succession and the law of diligence, property law is concerned for practical purposes with three classes of property only: corporeal heritable property, corporeal moveable property and rights.[36]

Succession and trusts—Succession is a distinct branch of property law which deals with the disposal of the estate of a deceased person.[37] As for the law of trusts, the English concept of divided ownership between the legal ownership of the trustee and the beneficial or equitable ownership of the beneficiary has not been adopted in Scotland. In Scots law, full and undivided ownership of trust property is held by the trustee, while the right of the beneficiary is simply a personal right to call upon the trustee to implement the trust purposes.[38] Consequently, the law of trusts in Scots law is regulated by the ordinary principles of the law of obligations and of property law.[39] **1.12**

The branches of private law: 3. Persons—A legal person is an entity recognised by the law as one to which rights and obligations can be attached. The law of persons can be divided into two parts: that relating to natural persons and that relating to non-natural persons. Natural persons are human beings and the law relating to natural persons deals with various aspects of their relationship.[40] Much of it consists of family law, which includes the law relating to husband and wife, parent and child and guardianship. The relationships between natural persons which are recognised by law were until quite recently closely regulated by reference to the legal consequences of marriage. But a regular marriage is no longer the dominant criterion, as can be seen from the gradual extension of rights to cohabiting couples and the abolition of the concept of illegitimacy. Family law has undergone significant reform in recent years and has been substantially codified by statute.[41] Non-natural persons are entities such as companies, partnerships and trade unions. The law relating to non-natural persons is largely concerned with how they come into, and go out of, existence, and how their affairs are conducted while they exist. It includes company law, the law of partnership and the law relating to voluntary associations such as clubs and societies. Again, much of this law has been codified by statute.[42] **1.13**

---

[35] The word "heritable", as Reid explains (*The Law of Property in Scotland* (1996), para.11), derives from the fact that under the old law of succession property of this description was inherited by the heir-at-law.

[36] Reid, *The Law of Property in Scotland* (1996), para.11.

[37] See further Chs 37–40, below.

[38] Reid, *The Law of Property in Scotland* (1996), para.40.

[39] See further Ch.41, below.

[40] See further Ch.43, below.

[41] See further Ch.44, below.

[42] See further Chs 45–47, below.

1.14 The law of actions—This part of the legal scheme is concerned with the enforcement of rights. It includes the law of civil remedies, the law of diligence and the
law of insolvency. This area of law has been described as consequential to the
rules relating to various kinds of rights in the law of persons and the law of things
because they contain the secondary rules as to remedies for infringement of
primary rights, as to diligence for the enforcement of claims and as to the distribution of the property of an insolvent.[43] The substantive rules which are comprised
in the law relating to civil remedies include the rules of civil procedure, pleading
and practice, and the law of evidence. They are beyond the scope of this book. But
the book does cover the law of diligence and the law of insolvency, as these are
concerned not just with the forms and methods of procedure, but are closely
related to aspects of the law relating to property.[44]

1.15 The place of Scots law among world systems—There are two principal families
of legal systems in the legal world. These are the civil law system and the Anglo-
American common law system. The civil law system, which has its stronghold in
Continental Europe, is derived from the *ius commune* which in its turn was derived
from Roman law and medieval canon law. The systems of law which are to be
found in Continental Europe have now, almost without exception, been codified.
The Anglo-American common law system has its origins in the common law of
England. It was exported to the colonies and now forms the basis for the legal
systems that have been developed throughout large parts of the Commonwealth
and the United States of America.

1.16 Family of mixed systems—Scotland belongs to a third legal family whose
systems of law are composed of a mixture of the civil law and the common law.[45]
The expression "mixed system" is used by comparative lawyers to describe those
systems in which there are combined major features from these two legal traditions, which are generally thought to represent opposed ways of looking at law.[46]
The legal systems of most members of this family have their origins in the civil
law. They have become mixed because, for one reason or another, their development has been influenced by the common law but not completely overtaken by it.
The family of mixed systems includes such diverse jurisdictions as Louisiana,
Quebec, Sri Lanka, South Africa and Israel. Scotland is the oldest member of this
family, as it was already a mixed system before the Union in 1707. Apart from
Israel, which became mixed by choice after it achieved independence in 1948
following the end of the British mandate, Scotland is the only one of these systems
that became a mixed system by indigenous development. All of the others were the
result of a transfer of sovereignty from a civilian to a common law colonial power.

1.17 Convergence and diversity—Useful though this division of systems into
different families is, it should not be thought that there is a precise separation

---

[43] Walker, *Principles of Scottish Private Law* (1988), Vol.1, p.4.
[44] See further Chs 48–49, below.
[45] See R. Zimmermann and D. Visser, *Southern Cross* (Oxford: Clarendon Press, 1996), pp.2–4;
K.G.C. Reid and R. Zimmermann, *A History of Private Law in Scotland* (Oxford: Oxford University
Press, 2000), pp.1–13; V.V. Palmer, *Mixed Jurisdictions Worldwide: The Third Legal Family*
(Cambridge: Cambridge University Press, 2001); R. Zimmermann, D. Visser and K.G.C. Reid, *Mixed
Legal Systems in Comparative Perspective: Property and Obligations in Scotland and South Africa*
(Oxford: Oxford University Press, 2005).
[46] H.L. MacQueen and J.M. Thomson, *Contract Law in Scotland*, 3rd edn (Haywards Heath:
Bloomsbury Professional, 2012), para.1.1.

between them, or that there is uniformity within each family. It has been pointed out that England was never entirely isolated from the rest of Europe and that ongoing intellectual contact over the centuries has left a definitive and characteristic mark on English law.[47] The common law was written about and taught by jurists who were familiar with Roman law and its structure, and attempts have been made to revive interest in this structure, in order to give the common law a more coherent voice in Europe.[48] Differences on either side, within Europe at least, are in the process of being worn away. Diversity between the civil law systems should not be underrated.[49] Each of the mixed systems also has distinct characteristics, so that it may be hard to find a justification for grouping them all together in one family, except for the fact that their place is at the intersection of civil law and common law.

Three elements—For the purpose of assessing the importance of civil and common law influences, Scots private law can be regarded as falling into three distinct parts or elements. These are: (1) private law relating to persons, obligations and property; (2) commercial law, which used to be more commonly referred to as mercantile law or, yet earlier, the law merchant; and (3) the law governing landownership and the creation and transfer of rights over land. Scots private law relating to persons, obligations and property is mainly civilian in origin, and it still retains significant civilian elements. It is this part of its law that qualifies it for inclusion as a member of the family of mixed systems. As for commercial law, both Scots and English mercantile law drew substantially on the law merchant of Continental Europe. But after the Union of 1707, Scots law was increasingly harmonised with English mercantile law, with which it has now for the most part been assimilated by statute. The principal components in this element are banking law, bills of exchange, carriage by land, sea and air, company law, sale of goods, insurance and partnership.[50] Scottish land law developed from the medieval feudal system, and although not entirely uninfluenced by Roman law concepts, cannot be classified either with civilian or with common law systems.[51] **1.18**

Interaction between public law and private law—Although this book does not attempt to deal with any of the topics which fall within the area of public law, a description of the structure of Scots private law would not be complete without some mention of the extent to which public law interacts with private law. This occurs where the state involves itself in relationships between private individuals for reasons of domestic, social or economic policy, or as a consequence of its treaty obligations in international law. Examples of the former can be found in the law of persons, for example in regard to the law relating to adoption,[52] and in property law, for example in regard to the law relating to protected tenancies.[53] It also occurs where government agencies or nationalised industries have been privatised. This involves the more or less complete departure of a legal entity from the protective umbrella of the public sector and its acquisition instead of the **1.19**

---

[47] Zimmermann and Visser, *Southern Cross* (1996), p.2.

[48] P. Birks, *English Private Law* (Oxford: Oxford University Press, 2000), Vol.1, pp.xxxv–xlvii.

[49] Reid and Zimmermann, *A History of Private Law in Scotland* (2000), p.3.

[50] See generally Chs 12–23, 45–47, below.

[51] W.M. Gordon, *Scottish Land Law*, 3rd edn (Edinburgh: W. Green, 2009), Ch.2; J. Rankine, *The Law of Landownership in Scotland*, 4th edn (Edinburgh: W. Green, 1909), Ch.1.

[52] See paras 44.49–44.51, below.

[53] See paras 35.61–35.64, below.

characteristics of a body which is regulated only by private law. Cases falling into the former category do not alter the underlying structure of the law in the fields which are affected by them. The relevant legislation tends to make use of that structure and to change it only where particular cases make this necessary. The latter category, which is where laws are passed in order to implement treaty obligations in international law, may be more far-reaching in its effects. This is so particularly in the case of the obligations owed by the state under European Union law and in regard to the Convention rights flowing from the European Human Rights Convention. This is a source of law which has been, and is, of growing significance.

1.20 **European Union law**—The name which until recently was given to the body of law created by or under the three Treaties which established the European Communities (the European Coal and Steel Community, the European Economic Community and the European Atomic Energy Community) and various subsequent treaties, conventions and agreements, including the Treaty of European Union (the Maastricht Treaty) and the Treaty of Amsterdam was "Community Law".[54] But the Treaty of Lisbon, which came into force on December 1, 2009, made substantial amendments to both the Treaty on European Union and the Treaty establishing the European Community in consequence of which the term "Community Law" is effectively replaced by the term "European Union Law". Put shortly, the primary sources of European Union law are now contained essentially in the amended version of the Treaty on European Union — "TEU"— and the amended terms of the Treaty establishing the European Community, which was, by such amendment, re-named as the Treaty on the Functioning of the European Union — "TFEU". A consolidated version of the TEU and the TFEU as so amended was published by the Commission of the European Union[55] and in practice that consolidation constitutes the legislative texts upon which one may proceed. The United Kingdom became a Member State of what were then termed the Communities on January 1, 1973. European Union law, previously termed Community law, is to be applied and enforced as part of the law of the United Kingdom.[56] European Union law is an important source of law.[57] A considerable volume of secondary legislation has been made by the European Institutions to give effect to the Treaties.[58] The Scottish Parliament and the Scottish Government (formerly the Scottish Executive),[59] have no power to do anything which is incompatible with European Union law.[60]

1.21 **European Union law and private law**—The importance of EU law for the structure of Scots private law lies in the fact that it is no longer possible to look upon the content of private law as the concern of one single jurisdiction. From time immemorial parties from different jurisdictions have been entering into contracts with

---

[54] *Stair Memorial Encyclopaedia*, Vol.10, "European Community Law and Institutions", para.1.
[55] May 9, 2008 – Official Journal 2008; OJ C115/1.
[56] European Communities Act 1972 s.2(1).
[57] See further para.1.29, below.
[58] See art.288 TFEU—formerly art.249 of the EC Treaty.
[59] The Scotland Act 1998 employs the term "Scottish Executive" but after the Scottish National Party assumed administration in 2007, the Scottish Executive adopted the term "Scottish Government". This change of name was given statutory recognition in s.12 of the Scotland Act 2012, which substitutes references to the Scottish Government for Scottish Executive in the 1998 Act.
[60] Scotland Act 1998 ss.29(2), 57(2).

one another. The problems to which this gives rise lie in the field of international private law. Parliament could of course always choose to enact legislation to give domestic effect to international conventions.[61] But it is only since 1973 that the content of Scots private law has been open to direct change as a result of treaty obligations entered into with the other Member States. This has led to reform of the law relating to consumer contracts,[62] for example, and to a wider recognition of the emerging principle of good faith.[63] There has also been significant impact in areas of commercial law such as agency[64] and in employment law (for example, in the field of equal pay claims, working time[65] and protection of employee rights on the transfer of the employer's business). Many of the regulations on health and safety in the workplace now derive from requirements of EU law.[66]

Convention rights—Convention rights are the rights and freedoms set out in the **1.22** Convention for the Protection of Human Rights and Fundamental Freedoms as agreed by the Council of Europe on November 4, 1950. The United Kingdom is a member of the Council of Europe. It ratified the Convention in 1951, and the Convention itself came into force on September 3, 1953. As a matter of international law, it creates rights against the contracting states and not against private individuals. In 1966 the United Kingdom granted the right of individual petition to enable individual litigants to obtain redress in international law where their Convention rights had been infringed by the state and no adequate remedy could be provided by the domestic courts. In 1998, following a manifesto commitment to bring human rights home by incorporating the Convention into domestic law, Parliament enacted the Human Rights Act 1998.[67] The Convention rights referred to in that Act were also incorporated into the Scotland Act 1998 as limitations on the powers or competencies of the Scottish Parliament and the Scottish Government, which have no power to do anything which is incompatible with Convention rights.[68] Although the application of the law relating to Convention rights lies mainly in the field of public law, private law is not unaffected. Most of the provisions of the 1998 Act are concerned with the acts and omissions of public authorities. But the courts and tribunals are included within the definition of "public authority".[69] The result of this is that courts and tribunals will be acting unlawfully when adjudicating on cases between private individuals if they do not interpret legislation and develop the law in a way which is compatible with Convention rights.[70] It appears, therefore, that the 1998 Act has not only a "vertical" application in disputes between individuals and the state, but also a "horizontal" effect between private litigants. The impact of this approach on Scots

---

[61] See, e.g. the Carriage of Goods by Road Act 1965, giving effect to the CMR Convention.

[62] See, e.g. Unfair Terms in Consumer Contracts Regulations 1999, discussed in para.9.25, below.

[63] See para.3.02, below. For an example of the application of the principle of good faith in Jersey (a civilian jurisdiction whose private law has not been codified), see *Snell v Beadle* [2001] 2 A.C. 304.

[64] See paras 18.33–18.39, below.

[65] See, for example, *Russell v Transocean International Resources* [2010] CSIH 82; 2011 S.C. 175; 2012 S.C. (UKSC) 250.

[66] By way of example, the Provision and Use of Work Equipment Regulations 1998 (SI 1998/2306) implement Council Directive 89/655/EEC on work equipment.

[67] The majority of its provisions were brought into force on October 2, 2000: SI 2000/1851.

[68] Scotland Act 1998 ss.29(2), 57(2); these provisions were brought into force on May 6, 1999 (s.57(2)) and July 1, 1999 (s.29): SI 1999/3178.

[69] Human Rights Act 1998 s.6(3).

[70] Human Rights Act 1998 ss.3(1) and 6(1); see R. Clayton and H. Tomlinson, *The Law of Human Rights* (Oxford: Oxford University Press, 2000), para.5.93.

private law is most likely to be felt in the areas protected by art.8 (right to respect for private and family life), art.10 (freedom of expression) and art.1 of the First Protocol (protection of property).[71]

1.23 Looking to the future—Finally, mention should be made of the phenomenon of electronic commerce on the internet. This too is of growing significance, particularly in regard to cross-border transactions. Differences in the legal rules observed by different legal systems are likely to become increasingly difficult to maintain in what is rapidly becoming a global economy. It has long been the practice for states to enter into agreements for the creation of regimes of law to regulate transactions which have an international character,[72] and for corresponding measures to be enacted into domestic law.[73] Strong pressures are likely to develop for the law in the areas most affected to be further harmonised. Thus, for example, the European Commission has proposed an "optional instrument" on sale of goods and digital products, to be available as an alternative choice of law in cross-border transactions.[74] This is drawn from an earlier "Draft Common Frame of Reference" for private law in Europe, which embraces the law of obligations (including particular contracts) and certain aspects of the law of property such as transfer and trusts.[75] Scottish lawyers, drawing upon their experience of a mixed system, are well placed to play an important role in this debate.

SOURCES OF LAW

1.24 Enacted law—The law of Scotland consists partly of enacted law, which has the authority of some body having legislative powers, and partly of common law, which is recognised by the courts as binding on some ground other than express enactment. Enacted law may include: (i) an Act of the Parliament of the United Kingdom or an Act of the Scottish Parliament[76]; (ii) regulations made by a Secretary of State, or the Scottish Ministers, by way of a "statutory instrument" made pursuant to legislative powers delegated by the relevant primary legislature; (iii) a provision of a European Union or Community treaty[77]; (iv) a regulation, directive or decision of the Council of Ministers or the Commission of the European Union (formerly the European Community); (v) an Act of Sederunt promulgated by the Court of Session; (vi) an Act of Adjournal promulgated by the High Court of Justiciary; and (vii) a by-law or regulation issued by a local authority or body having statutory powers to make such by-laws or regulations.

---

[71] See further Boyle et al., *Human Rights and Scots Law* (Oxford: Hart Publishing, 2002), especially Chs 8–13; A.J. Bowen, "Fundamental Rights in Private Law", 2000 S.L.T. (News) 157; and *Karl Construction v Palisade Properties Plc*, 2002 S.C. 270; *Advocate General v Taylor*, 2004 S.C. 339; and *Gillespie v Toondale*, 2006 S.C. 304. Cf. also *Axa General Insurance Co Ltd v Lord Advocate*, [2011] UKSC 46; 2012 S.C. (UKSC) 122; 2011 S.L.T. 1061.

[72] e.g. the Geneva Convention on Contracts for the International Carriage of Goods by Road 1956; the Warsaw Convention Relating to International Carriage by Air 1929. See on these Chs 22–24, below.

[73] e.g. Contracts (Applicable Law) Act 1990, which gives effect to the Rome Convention on Contractual Obligations 1980.

[74] Proposal for a Regulation on a Common European Sales Law, COM (2011) 635 final.

[75] See C. von Bar, E. Clive and H. Schulte-Nölke, *Draft Common Frame of Reference: Principles, Definitions and Model Rules of European Private Law* (Munich: Sellier, 2009).

[76] The Scottish Parliament was set up under the Scotland Act 1998, see para.1.27, below.

[77] See para 1.20, above.

While no longer of great importance in practice, enacted law also includes provisions made by the Crown by way of proclamation or order in council in the exercise of the Royal Prerogative. Since on one view the Crown may be seen as being at the apex of the legislative hierarchy, the nature of the Royal Prerogative is considered first.

Legislative authority of the Crown—Apart from powers which are delegated to **1.25** the Crown[78] or its Ministers[79] pursuant to statute, various "residual powers" belong to the Crown due to the Royal Prerogative.[80] Whilst considerable uncertainty surrounds the scope of the Royal Prerogative[81], it is clear that there is no general legislative power to change "the law of the land". Legislation made using the Royal Prerogative relates to Crown colonies and servants of the Crown, as well as powers concerning legislation in times of national emergency.[82] These powers, which are part of the common law,[83] can be altered by statute, and will be superseded by statutory powers dealing with the particular area in question[84]; but where statutory provisions are not yet in force, those provisions cannot exclude pre-existing prerogative powers which remain.[85] Proceedings for judicial review can now be brought concerning the exercise of prerogative powers.[86]

Acts of the UK Parliament—A statute may be either a public general statute or **1.26** a local or personal Act. Modern statutes invariably contain provisions defining the extent of their territorial application as respects the constituent parts of the United Kingdom. In the absence of such a defining provision there is, however, a general presumption that a public general statute passed by the Parliament of the United Kingdom applies generally to Great Britain and Northern Ireland, but the extent to which the presumption will apply in relation to matters devolved to the Scottish Parliament remains to be seen.[87] The presumption may be rebutted, and the statute held not to be applicable to Scotland, either on the ground that it is expressed as an amendment of a statute in which any application to Scotland was expressly excluded[88]; or, with less force, that it is expressed in technical terms of English law without an interpretation clause giving the equivalents in the law of Scotland.[89]

---

[78] In *Re M* [1994] 1 A.C. 377 at 395, Lord Templeman noted that there were "two meanings" of "the Crown: the monarch and the executive", but that "Parliament . . . [had] supremacy over" both of them.

[79] This includes "Scottish Ministers" in the Scottish Parliament (as defined in s.44(2) of the Scotland Act 1998). Under the 1998 Act, the Royal Prerogative is not a "reserved matter", see s.29(2) and para.2(1)(a) of Sch.5. Note s.53(2) of the 1998 Act, which allows Scottish Ministers to exercise the Royal Prerogative.

[80] See C.R. Munro, *Studies in Constitutional Law*, 2nd edn (Oxford: Oxford University Press, 1999), p.258.

[81] cf. *Burmah Oil Co (Burma Trading) Ltd v Lord Advocate*, 1964 S.C. (HL) 117.

[82] Note however the Civil Contingencies Act 2004. Note also the Terrorism Act 2000, the Anti-Terrorism, Crime and Security Act 2001, the Prevention of Terrorism Act 2005 (passed following *A v Secretary of State for the Home Department* [2005] 2 A.C. 68) and the Terrorism Act 2006.

[83] See Munro, *Studies in Constitutional Law* (1999), p.256.

[84] *Att Gen. v De Keyser's Royal Hotel Ltd* [1920] A.C. 508; *R. v Secretary of State for Foreign and Commonwealth Affairs, Ex p. Rees-Mogg* [1994] Q.B. 552 at 567; *R. v Secretary of State for the Home Department, Ex p. Fire Brigades Union* [1995] A.C. 513.

[85] *R. v Secretary of State for the Home Department, Ex p. Fire Brigades Union* [1995] A.C. 513 at 553.

[86] *Council of Civil Service Unions v Minister for the Civil Service* [1985] A.C. 374. In Scotland see *Davidson v Scottish Ministers*, 2006 S.C. (HL) 41.

[87] See para.1.27, below.

[88] *Levy v Jackson* (1903) 5 F. 646.

[89] *Scottish Drug Depot v Fraser* (1905) 7 F. 646, per Lord Low (Ordinary). In certain instances such matters may come within the competence of the Scottish Parliament.

A provision that the statute shall not apply to Ireland is a strong indication that it does apply to Scotland.[90] Even before the Scotland Act 1998, Acts of the Parliament of the United Kingdom usually indicated expressly if there were particular provisions which applied specifically to Scotland, e.g. the Sale and Supply of Goods Act 1994, which amended the Sale of Goods Act 1979 by, inter alia, introducing specifically Scottish provisions (ss.15B and 53A).[91] Statutes passed by the old Scots Parliament prior to the Union in 1707 (usually termed "Scots Acts") are binding in Scotland if not repealed or in desuetude.[92] Statutes of the English Parliament prior to 1707 are of no authority in Scotland, unless, as in the case of the Treason Act 1351, they have been applied to Scotland by a later Act.[93] The date at which a statute comes into force is generally stated; if not, it comes into force on the day when it receives the Royal Assent.[94] Commonly, a statute may provide that it will come into force on a date or dates to be appointed by a Minister by means of a statutory instrument, namely a commencement order.

1.27 **Acts of the Scottish Parliament**—Under the settlement embodied in the Scotland Act 1998,[95] the power to legislate on certain matters is devolved to the Scottish Parliament and Government. The UK Parliament retains the power to make legislation applying to Scotland without restriction as to subject matter, but there is now a well-established constitutional convention, known as the Sewell Convention, under which the UK Parliament and Government will not legislate on devolved matters without the consent of the Scottish Parliament. Under s.28 of the Act, the Scottish Parliament can pass primary legislation—called Acts of the Scottish Parliament[96]—in relation to Scotland, but subject to restrictions specified in s.29.[97] The three restrictions are: (i) the Scottish Parliament cannot legislate on matters defined as "reserved" (i.e. areas reserved for the Westminster Parliament)[98]; (ii) it cannot modify certain "protected enactments" including arts 4 and 6 of the Treaty of Union, certain provisions of the European Communities Act 1972 and the Human Rights Act 1998[99]; and (iii) it cannot make legislation which is incompatible[100] with any of the Convention rights (i.e. being the rights and fundamental freedoms set out in the various Articles of the European Convention on Human Rights contained in Sch.1 to the Human Rights Act 1998[101]) or with European

---

[90] *Scottish Drug Depot v Fraser* (1905) 7 F. 646.

[91] Sale of Goods Act 1979 ss.15B and 53A were introduced by s.5(1), (3) of the 1994 Act. See further Ch.12, below.

[92] See para.1.34 below.

[93] See Treason Act 1708.

[94] Interpretation Act 1978 (c.30) s.4.

[95] Thus, the basis of the Scottish Parliament's "existence and powers" is statutory, see *Whaley v Lord Watson of Invergowrie*, 2000 S.C. 340 at 349, per Lord President Rodger.

[96] Scotland Act 1998 s.28(1).

[97] The exceptions are set out in Scotland Act 1998 s.29; see also s.57(1) concerning the continuation by "a Minister of the Crown" of the United Kingdom Parliament of "any function" he exercised concerning "Scotland for the purposes specified in s.2(2) of the European Communities Act 1972".

[98] See Scotland Act 1998 s.29(2)(b) and Sch.5. Sch.5 was amended by the Scotland Act (Modification of Schedule 5) Order 2001 (SI 2001/1456).

[99] Scotland Act 1998 s.29(2)(c) and Sch.4.

[100] It has been said that "[t]he essence of the word 'incompatible' is that there is an inconsistency between one thing and another", see Lord Hope of Craighead in *Montgomery v HM Advocate*, 2001 S.C. (PC) 1 at 18B.

[101] "Convention rights" are defined in Scotland Act 1998 s.126(1) as having the same meaning as under the Human Rights Act 1998 s.1.

Union law.[102] While the Acts of the Scottish Parliament are subject to judicial review on those grounds, they are not subject to such review on common law grounds of irrationality or unreasonableness or arbitrariness.[103] The matters reserved to the Westminster Parliament are listed under eleven heads.[104] Included in the reserved matters are: financial services[105]; business associations[106]; insolvency[107]; competition; intellectual property[108]; employment[109]; and consumer protection[110] (e.g. sale and supply of goods,[111] trading stamps,[112] consumer credit[113] and package holidays[114]). However, floating charges and receivers,[115] except in relation to preferential debts, regulation of insolvency practitioners and co-operation of insolvency courts, are not reserved matters.[116] A dispute as to whether an Act of the Scottish Parliament falls within the Parliament's legislative competence, is a "devolution issue"[117] and is justiciable.[118] The final appellate Court for such matters was formerly the Judicial Committee of the Privy Council but under the Constitutional Reform Act 2005 that final appellate jurisdiction was transferred to the Supreme Court of the United Kingdom.[119] The Scotland Act 1998[120] sets out the ways "devolution issues" can come before the Supreme Court

---

[102] Scotland Act 1998 s.29(2)(d). Under the Scotland Act 1998 s.57(2), a member of the Scottish Executive cannot make subordinate legislation (as defined in s.126(1)) which is incompatible with Convention rights or Community law. "Community law" is defined in the Scotland Act 1998 s.126(9). Under s.34, a reference for a preliminary ruling can be made to the European Court of Justice.

[103] *Axa General Insurance Ltd v Lord Advocate* [2011] UKSC 46; 2012 S.C. (UKSC) 122; 2011 S.L.T. 1061.

[104] The classification of reserved matters depended to some extent on the administrative arrangements existing before 1998 and is not necessarily logical. However, provision is made for amendment of the reserved matters under s.30(2) of the Act and for transfer of functions by s.63. There are potential difficulties in the application of the provisions of s.29(2) and Sch.5: see C. Himsworth and C. Munro, *The Scotland Act 1998*, 2nd edn (Edinburgh: W. Green, 2000), pp.37 et seq. Further complication may arise from the provisions of Sch.4—see *Martin v Most* [2010] UKSC 10; 2010 S.C. (UKSC) 40.

[105] Head A3—Financial and Economic Matters in Sch.5.

[106] Head C1—Trade and Industry in Sch.5. As to partnership and company law generally, see Chs 47 and 48 hereof respectively. However, the Westminster Parliament has devolved certain powers to the Scottish Parliament in relation to limited liability partnerships under ss.14(1),(3), 15, 16 and 17(1),(3) of the Limited Liability Partnerships Act 2000 (c.12): see the Limited Liability Partnerships (Scotland) Regulations 2001 (SI 2001/128), passed pursuant to those provisions of the 2000 Act.

[107] Head C2 in Sch.5. As to insolvency generally, see Ch.46 on company law. Insolvency does not include bankruptcy (as to which see Ch.49 hereof).

[108] Head C4 in Sch.5. See, generally, Ch.33 hereof.

[109] Head H in Sch.5. See, generally, Ch.17 hereof.

[110] Head C7 in Sch.5. See, generally, Ch.14 hereof.

[111] Head C7 in Sch.5. See, generally, Ch.12 hereof.

[112] Head C7 in Sch.5. The Trading Stamps Act 1964 was repealed by the Regulatory Reform (Trading Stamps) Order 2005 (SI 2005/871).

[113] Head C7 in Sch.5. See, generally, Ch.15 hereof.

[114] Head C7 in Sch.5. See, generally, Ch.14 hereof.

[115] Floating charges and receivers are dealt with in respectively Ch.36 hereof on rights in security and Ch.46 hereof on company law.

[116] Head C2 in Sch.5.

[117] "Devolution issues" is defined in Scotland Act 1998 s.98 and Sch.6 Pt I para.1. Devolution issues also include acts or omissions of a member of the Scottish Executive, see Scotland Act 1998 s.57(2). "Scottish Executive" is defined in Scotland Act 1998 s.44(1); "Scottish Ministers" is defined in s.44(2); and "Scottish Law Officers" is defined in s.48.

[118] As to the raising of devolution issues, see Scotland Act 1998 Sch.6 Pt II paras 4–6. See also Ch.25A of the Rules of the Court of Session 1994 (SI 1994/1443), which was introduced by Act of Sederunt (Devolution Issues Rules) 1999 (SI 1999/1345).

[119] As defined in Scotland Act 1998 s.32(4). The Privy Council's "devolution issue" jurisdiction was transferred to the Supreme Court of the United Kingdom under, s.40(4)(b) and Sch.9 Pt 2 of the Constitutional Reform Act 2005.

[120] Scotland Act 1998 s.98 and Sch.6 Pt II paras 7–12. See also Pts III and IV of Sch.6.

of the United Kingdom and formerly before the Privy Council. The UK Supreme Court "has no original jurisdiction" to decide a devolution issue which has not been canvassed before the supreme courts in Scotland.[121] In relation to interpreting Acts of the Scottish Parliament and subordinate legislation which may breach legislative competence, the courts, under the Scotland Act 1998, are to interpret any such legislation as restrictively as may be necessary to avoid that legislative measure being ultra vires, if this can be done.[122]

1.28 **Private Legislation Procedure Acts**—Local and personal, also called private, Acts are statutes conferring powers on a local authority, body or company, or regulating the rights or status of a private individual. By the Private Legislation Procedure (Scotland) Act 1936,[123] where any public authority or persons desire a private Act, they may apply to the Secretary of State for Scotland for a provisional order to obtain Parliamentary powers.[124] However, where the granting of such powers is wholly within the Scottish Parliament's legislative competence, that Act does not apply.[125] If, after advertisement, no opposition is offered, the provisional order, after certain procedure detailed in the Act, will be issued; if objections are lodged, a local inquiry is held by commissioners. If their report is favourable, the provisional order is issued. A provisional order has no legislative force and it has to be confirmed by a Confirmation Act.[126] Provisions, for which reference must be made to the Act, are made excluding procedure by provisional order in projects which do not relate exclusively to Scotland or raise questions of public policy of novelty and importance.[127] A private Act cannot be impugned on the ground that Parliament, in passing it, was misled by fraud.[128] Under the Scotland Act 1998, there is provision for private legislation.[129]

1.29 **European Communities Act**—The European Communities Act 1972,[130] s.2(1), provides that:

> "All such rights, powers, liabilities, obligations and restrictions from time to time created or arising by or under the Treaties, and all such remedies and procedures from time to time provided for by or under the Treaties, as in accordance with the Treaties are without further enactment to be given legal effect or used in the United Kingdom shall be recognised and available in law, and be enforced, allowed and followed accordingly."

---

[121] *Follen v HM Advocate*, 2001 S.L.T. 774 at 776, per Lord Hope of Craighead at [9].

[122] Scotland Act 1998 s.101. This may give rise to conflict between different approaches to interpretation: see *DS v HM Advocate*, 2007 S.C.C.R. 222 (PC). For other decisions deploying s.101 see: *Anderson v Scottish Ministers*, 2001 S.C. 1; *Adams v Scottish Ministers*, 2003 S.C. 171; *HM Advocate v R*, 2003 S.C. (PC) 21.

[123] 26 Geo. v & 1 Edw. VIII, c.52 (as amended by Scotland Act 1998 s.125 and Sch.8 para.5).

[124] Private Legislation Procedure (Scotland) Act (the "1936 Act") s.1.

[125] 1936 Act s.1(5) (added by Scotland Act 1998 s.125 and Sch.8 para.5).

[126] 1936 Act ss.8, 9.

[127] 1936 Act s.2.

[128] *British Railways Board v Pickin* [1974] A.C. 765.

[129] Scotland Act 1998 s.36(3) and Ch.9A of the Scottish Parliament's Standing Orders. As to the Scottish Parliament's power to make standing orders, see Scotland Act 1998 s.22 and Sch.3. See too the Scotland Act 1998 (Transitory and Transitional Provisions) (Standing Orders and Parliamentary Publications) Order 1999 (SI 1999/1095).

[130] As amended.

"The Treaties" are those specified in Pt I of Sch.1 to the Act ("pre-accession treaties") and those specified in s.1(2) (as amended from time to time, either by Order in Council made by authority of s.1(3) or by Act of Parliament). The first effect of this enactment is that the provisions of the treaties are part of the law of the United Kingdom, and any of them which is clear and unconditional—which can

> "be construed as establishing . . . a precise and unconditional principle which is sufficiently operational to be applied by a national court and which is therefore capable of governing the legal position of individuals"[131]

—creates, in terms of EU law, a "directly effective" right or, in United Kingdom statutory terms, an "enforceable EU right"[132] which must be applied and given effect in British courts. Whilst most such provisions are intended to create obligations for, and so may be enforced against, the Member State (read very broadly),[133] some are "horizontally directly effective"—that is, they give rise to enforceable rights as between private persons; this applies (at present) to arts 101 and 102 of the Treaty on the Functioning of the European Union ("TFEU") relating to competition,[134] art.157 relating to equal pay,[135] art.45 relating to the freedom of movement of workers[136] and art.49 relating to the right of natural or juristic persons to establish themselves in the territory of another member state.[137] Secondly, directly applicable rules of EU law "must be fully and uniformly applied in all the Member States" and "by their entry into force render automatically inapplicable any conflicting provisions of current national law".[138] This is an articulation of the principle of the primacy of EU law, as a result of which

> "it [is] the duty of a United Kingdom court, when delivering final judgment, to override any rule of national law found to be in conflict with any directly enforceable rule of Community [now EU] law"[139];

---

[131] *R. v Secretary of State for the Home Department, Ex p. Gloszczuk* (C-63/99) [2001] E.C.R. I-6369, para.38.

[132] European Communities Act 1972 s.2(1). Prior to the amendment effected by the European Union (Amendment) Act 2008 the term used was "enforceable Community right".

[133] There are numerous decisions as to what entities are to be regarded as the State (or "emanation of the State") for these purposes. See, e.g. *Marshall v Southampton and South West Hampshire Area Health Authority (Teaching) (No.1)* (152/84) [1986] E.C.R. 723; *Foster v British Gas Plc* (C-188/89) [1990] E.C.R. I-3313; [1991] 2 A.C. 306; *Johnston v Chief Constable of the Royal Ulster Constabulary* [1987] Q.B. 129; *Doughty v Rolls Royce Plc* [1992] 1 C.M.L.R. 1045; *Griffin v South West Water Services* [1995] I.R.L.R. 15; *National Union of Teachers v Governing Body of St Mary's Church of England (Aided) Junior School* [1997] 3 C.M.L.R. 630; *R. v Durham County Council, Ex p. Huddleston* [2000] Eu.L.R. 514.

[134] *Belgische Radio en Televisie v S.A.B.A.M.* (127/73) [1974] E.C.R. 313; *Garden Cottage Foods Ltd v Milk Marketing Board* [1984] A.C. 130; *Argyll Group plc v Distillers Co Plc*, 1987 S.L.T. 514; *Millar & Bryce Ltd v Keeper of the Registers of Scotland*, 1997 S.L.T. 1000.

[135] See *Defrenne v SABENA (No.2)* (43/75) [1976] E.C.R. 455; *Garland v British Rail Engineering Ltd* [1983] 2 A.C. 751; *R. v Secretary of State for Employment, Ex p. Equal Opportunities Commission* [1995] 1 A.C. 1; *Preston v Wolverhampton NHS Trust (No.2)* [2001] 2 A.C. 455.

[136] *Angonese v Cassa di Risparmio di Bolzano* (C-281/98) [2000] E.C.R. I-4139.

[137] *Viking Line Abp v International Transport Workers' Union* [2005] EWHC 1222 (Comm.); [2005] 1 C.L.C. 951; *International Transport Workers' Union v Viking Line Abp* (C-438/05) [2007] E.C.R. I-10779.

[138] *Amministrazione delle Finanze dello Stato v Simmenthal SpA* (106/77) [1978] E.C.R. 629 at [14] and [17]. See also the Scotland Act 1998 (c.46) s.29(1), (2)(d) whereby an Act of the Scottish Parliament, if incompatible with Community law, "is not law".

[139] *R. v Secretary of State for Transport, Ex p. Factortame Ltd (No.2)* [1991] 1 A.C. 603 at 659, per Lord Bridge.

"anything in our substantive law inconsistent with any of these rights and obligations is abrogated or must be modified in order to avoid the inconsistency. This is true even where the inconsistent municipal provision is contained in primary legislation".[140]

A court may even have to give interim relief by suspending the operation of a UK statute.[141] As it is generally

"for the domestic legal system of each Member State to designate the courts having jurisdiction and to determine the procedural conditions governing actions at law intended to ensure the protection of the rights which citizens have from the direct effect of Community [EU] law"[142]

a pursuer would normally seek judicial review (interdict, declarator), an order under the Court of Session Act 1988 s.45(b) or proceed by ordinary action, as appropriate.[143] But available remedies must comply with the principles of "equivalence" and "effectiveness", i.e. they are no less favourable than those relating to similar domestic actions and are not such as to render virtually impossible or excessively difficult the exercise of the EU right.[144] Where the operation of national law or the conduct of a public authority deprives an individual of the effective exercise of an EU law right, he may claim reparation from the state if three conditions are met: (i) the relevant rule of EU law is one which is intended to confer rights on individuals[145]; (ii) the breach is "sufficiently serious"; and (iii) there is a direct causal link between the breach of the obligation borne by the state and the loss or injury suffered.[146] Damages may be sought in judicial review if it is necessary to invoke the supervisory jurisdiction of the Court of Session, other-

---

[140] *Thoburn v Sunderland City Council* [2002] EWHC 195 (Admin); [2002] 4 All E.R. 156 at 187–8, per Laws J.

[141] *Factortame Ltd v Secretary of State for Transport* [1990] 2 A.C. 85; *R. v Secretary of State for Transport, Ex p. Factortame Ltd* (C-213/89) [1990] E.C.R. I-2433; *R. v Secretary of State for Transport, Ex p. Factortame Ltd (No.2)* [1991] 1 A.C. 603.

[142] *Rewe-Zentralfinanz eG v Landwirtschaftskammer für das Saarland* (33/76) [1976] E.C.R. 1989 at [5].

[143] See, e.g. *Gibson v Lord Advocate*, 1975 S.C. 136 (declarator); *Argyll Group Plc v Distillers Co Plc*, 1987 S.L.T. 514 (interim interdict); *Millar & Bryce Ltd v Keeper of the Registers of Scotland*, 1997 S.L.T. 1000 (interdict, order ad factum praestandum pronounced); *Booker Aquaculture Ltd v Secretary of State for Scotland*, 2000 S.C. 9 (declarator); *ABNA Ltd v Scottish Ministers*, 2004 S.L.T. 176 (interim suspension).

[144] *Amministrazione delle Finanze dello Stato v SpA San Giorgio* (199/82) [1983] E.C.R. 3595; *Unibet (London) Ltd v Justitiekanslern* (C-432/05) [2007] 2 C.M.L.R. 30, ECJ; *Swan v Secretary of State for Scotland (No.1)*, 1998 S.C. 479 at 488, per Lord President Rodger.

[145] "Individuals" is here used in its normal, if misleading, Community law sense of both natural and juristic person. The quality of a legal measure which confers rights on individuals is a construct derived from German principles of Schutznormtheorie.

[146] Joined Cases C-46 and 48/93 *Brasserie du Pêcheur v Germany* and *R. v Secretary of State for Transport, Ex p. Factortame Ltd (No.3)* [1996] E.C.R. I-1029. As to the meaning of "sufficiently serious" see *Brasserie du Pêcheur* at [55]-[64]; *R. v HM Treasury, Ex p. British Telecommunications Plc* (C-392/93) [1996] E.C.R. I-1631; *R. v Minister of Agriculture, Fisheries and Food, Ex p. Hedley Lomas (Ireland) Ltd* (C-5/94) [1996] E.C.R. I-2553; *R. v Secretary of State for Transport, Ex p. Factortame Ltd* [1998] 1 C.M.L.R. 1353, affd [1998] 3 C.M.L.R. 192. Liability of the state may arise even where loss is caused by judicial error, in the "exceptional case" in which a court of final instance (the authorities have not spoken to the conduct of lower courts) has "manifestly infringed the applicable law"; *Köbler v Austria* (C-224/01) [2003] E.C.R. I-10239; *Traghetti del Mediterraneo SpA v Italy* (C-173/03) [2006] E.C.R. I-5177.

wise damages may be sought in an ordinary action.[147] Damages are also available for loss caused by a competitor's, or supplier's, infringement of EU competition rules.[148] The institutions created by the Treaties may adopt legislation in varying forms:[149] regulations, which have general application, are binding in their entirety and are directly applicable in all Member States; directives, which are binding as to the result to be achieved upon each Member State to which they are addressed but leave the choice of form and methods to the national authorities; and decisions, which are binding in their entirety upon those to whom they are addressed. Depending upon their terms, each may produce enforceable EU rights. However, a directive which provides for unconditional and sufficiently precise obligations but which has been inadequately (or not at all) implemented by a competent national authority may be relied on by an individual against a public authority once the time limit for its adoption has passed,[150] but not (horizontally) against another individual.[151] Inadequate transposition which, through that inadequacy, deprives an individual of rights he ought to have enjoyed under the directive may give rise to a right of reparation against the state.[152] Where a question as to the correct interpretation of a provision of EU law arises before a national court, that court may sist proceedings and seek a preliminary ruling on the matter from the European Court of Justice[153]; if a court of final instance, it must do so unless the matter in dispute has already been decided by the Court of Justice or the correct interpretation of EU law is so obvious as to leave no scope for any reasonable doubt (*acte clair*).[154] The Court of Justice may review the legality of any EU measure capable of producing legal effects and declare it void[155]; proceedings

---

[147] See, by analogy, *W.M. Fotheringham and Son v The British Limousin Cattle Society*, 2004 S.L.T. 485.

[148] *Courage Ltd v Crehan* (C-453/99) [2001] E.C.R. I-6297; Joined Cases C-295-298/04 *Manfredi v Lloyd Adriatico Assicurazioni SpA* [2006] E.C.R. I-6619; *Inntrepreneur Pub Co (CPC) v Crehan* [2006] UKHL 38; [2007] 1 A.C. 333. Note the Competition Act 1998 (c. 41) s.47A, which provides for claims in damages to be awarded by the Competition Appeal Tribunal against a party having been found to have infringed arts 81 or 82 of the EC Treaty.

[149] art.288 TFEU.

[150] *van Duyn v Home Office* (41/74) [1974] E.C.R. 1337; *Rutili v Minister of the Interior* (36/75) [1975] E.C.R. 1219; *Becker v Finanzamt Münster-Innenstadt* (8/81) [1982] E.C.R. 53; *Kincardine and Deeside District Council v Forestry Commissioners*, 1992 S.L.T. 1180 at 1186; *English v North Lanarkshire Council*, 1999 S.C.L.R. 310 at 319; *Marks and Spencer Plc v Customs and Excise Commissioners* [2000] S.T.C. 16.

[151] *Marshall v Southampton and South West Hampshire Area Health Authority (Teaching) (No.1)* (152/84) [1986] E.C.R. 723.

[152] Joined Cases C-6 and 9/90 *Francovich & Bonifaci v Italy* [1991] E.C.R. I-5357; *R. v HM Treasury, Ex p. British Telecommunications Plc* (C-392/93) [1996] E.C.R. I-1631; *R. v Minister of Agriculture, Fisheries and Food, Ex p. Hedley Lomas (Ireland) Ltd* (C-5/94) [1996] E.C.R. I-2553; *Robins v Secretary of State for Work and Pensions* (C-278/05) [2007] I.R.L.R. 270; *Evans v Secretary of State for the Environment, Transport and the Regions* [2006] EWHC 322.

[153] art.267 TFEU. There have been only thirteen such references from Scottish courts under art.267 since accession in 1973, one from the House of Lords, three from the High Court of Justiciary, seven from the Court of Session and two from the sheriff court. Compare the much greater enthusiasm from Austrian courts, having lodged 288 references from their accession in 1995 to the end of 2006.

[154] *Srl CILFIT v Ministero della Sanità* (283/81) [1982] E.C.R. 3415. On the House of Lords' view of when a question is so clear from doubt as to absolve it from the duty to refer see *Henn and Darby v DPP* [1981] A.C. 850; *Consorzio del Prosciutto di Parma v Asda Stores Ltd* [2001] UKHL 7; [2001] 1 C.M.L.R. 1103; *Marks & Spencer Plc v HM Commissioners of Customs and Excise* [2005] UKHL 53; [2005] S.T.C. 1254; *Percy v Board of National Mission of the Church of Scotland* [2005] UKHL 73; [2006] 2 A.C. 28 at 69, per Lord Hope; *Russell v Transocean International Resources Ltd* [2011] UKSC 57; 2012 S.C. (UKSC) 250. On the view of the High Court of Justiciary see *Orr & Stewart v HM Advocate*, 1998 S.C.C.R. 59; *Jardine v Crowe (PF Hamilton)*, 1999 S.C.C.R. 52.

[155] arts 263 and 264 TFEU.

(an "action of annulment") must be instituted within two months of the publication of the measure, or of its notification to the pursuer or, in the absence thereof, of the day on which it came to his knowledge.[156] However, there are very strict rules on locus standi under this procedure[157] so that an aggrieved person seeking reduction of a Community measure is normally required to raise an action first in a national court, aver the illegality of the measure and urge the court to seek a preliminary ruling from the Court of Justice under art.267 TFEU with a view to having it declared "invalid". As the Court of Justice alone has jurisdiction definitively to declare a Community measure invalid,[158] the national court may satisfy itself that the measure is lawful and so refuse to refer the matter, but if it has doubts it must refer seeking the definitive answer only the Court of Justice is competent to determine.[159]

1.30 Statutory Instruments: The UK Parliament—A great deal of legislation, often referred to as, "delegated or "subordinate" or "secondary" legislation, is promulgated by authorities other than the UK Parliament under powers conferred on those other authorities by the UK Parliament. Such delegated or secondary or subordinate legislation may take the form of Orders in Council, orders by Ministers, rules of procedure made by courts, and by-laws by local authorities and other corporations.[160] Where an Act gives a power to Her Majesty in Council, exercisable by Order in Council, or to a Minister, exercisable by "statutory instrument", any document by which the power is exercised is a "statutory instrument".[161] Thus, Orders in Council made under the Royal Prerogative[162] and some subordinate legislation made by Ministers[163] are not statutory instruments. But statutory instruments—usually described as regulations—are the most common form of delegated legislation. A statutory instrument containing regulations or other orders made by a Minister may be challenged as being ultra vires.[164]

1.31 Statutory Instruments: Scotland Act 1998—The Scotland Act 1998 defines subordinate legislation as having the same meaning as that in the Interpretation Act 1978 and as including an instrument made under an Act of the Scottish Parliament.[165] Part VI of the Act contains detailed provisions for the making, amending and revocation of subordinate legislation, including the forms in which

---

[156] art.264 TFEU, final alinéa.

[157] art.264 TFEU, fifth alinéa.

[158] *Foto-Frost v Hauptzollamt Lübeck-Ost* (314/85) [1987] E.C.R. 4199.

[159] See *Booker Aquaculture Ltd v Secretary of State for Scotland*, 2000 S.C. 9 at 27, per Lord President Rodger.

[160] See *Macmillan v McConnell*, 1917 J.C. 43; *Herkes v Dickie*, 1958 J.C. 51.

[161] Statutory Instruments Act 1946 (9 & 10 Geo. VI, c.36); see J.D.B. Mitchell, *Constitutional Law* (Edinburgh: W. Green, 1964), pp.273 et seq.

[162] e.g. Territorial Waters Order in Council 1964 (*Post Office v Estuary Radio Ltd* [1968] 2 Q.B. 740: but see Territorial Sea Act 1987 s.1(4)).

[163] e.g. Breath Analysis Devices (Approval) (Scotland) Order 1983 (see *Annan v Mitchell*, 1984 S.C.C.R. 32; *R. v Clarke* [1969] 2 Q.B. 91).

[164] *Alexander & Sons v Minister of Transport*, 1936 S.L.T. 553; *Islay Estates v Agricultural Executive Committee for South Argyll*, 1942 S.L.T. 174; *Forster v Polmaise Patent Fuel Co*, 1947 J.C. 56; *City of Edinburgh District Council v Secretary of State for Scotland*, 1985 S.C. 261; *Air 2000 Ltd v Secretary of State for Transport*, 1990 S.L.T. 335. See also *F. Hoffman-La Roche & Co A.G. v Secretary of State for Trade and Industry* [1975] A.C. 295, and, as to orders under the Royal Prerogative, see *Council of Civil Service Unions v Minister for the Civil Service* [1985] A.C. 374.

[165] Scotland Act 1998 s.126(1). See also Scotland Act 1998 (Transitory and Transitional Provisions) (Statutory Instruments) Order 1999 (SI 1999/1096).

the legislation is to be made and the person or persons who are to exercise the legislative function. A statutory instrument of the Scottish Ministers is to be called a Scottish Statutory Instrument ("SSI").[166] The Scottish Executive can make statutory instruments in relation to pre-commencement enactments[167] (i.e. broadly speaking, legislation which was made before or at the same session as the Scotland Act 1998, or which came into effect before s.53[168]). Acts of the Scottish Parliament may, of course, confer powers to make delegated or subordinate legislation.

Acts of Sederunt and Acts of Adjournal—Acts of Sederunt are rules passed by **1.32** the Court of Session, under powers originally conferred at its foundation.[169] Currently, the Court of Session has power under the Court of Session Act 1988[170] "to regulate and prescribe" its own procedures.[171] In the seventeenth and eighteenth centuries, the court took a wide view of its powers and promulgated Acts of Sederunt amounting to general legislation, e.g. ordaining parties to a strike to resume work.[172] In modern times, Acts of Sederunt relate exclusively to procedure, and are usually passed in virtue of a specific authority in some particular statute. In such cases, the repeal of the statute impliedly repeals the Acts of Sederunt which have been passed under it.[173] If the provisions of the statute admit of two interpretations, that consistent with the Act of Sederunt must be adopted but otherwise in the event of conflict the statute prevails.[174] The Acts of Sederunt relating to procedure have been collected and codified from time to time. The current Rules of the Court of Session were enacted in 1994,[175] but have been repeatedly amended. Under r.2.1, the court has power to relieve any party from the consequences of failure to comply with the rules due to mistake, oversight or other cause, not being wilful non-observance. The House of Lords indicated it would be very reluctant to interfere with the Court of Session's practice and procedure[176] and would "leave it to the Court of Session to decide what changes, if any, should be made to its own rules".[177] An Act of Adjournal is an Act passed by the High Court of Justiciary for regulating procedure in that court and in inferior criminal courts. The present source of the High Court of Justiciary's power is s.305 of the Criminal Procedure (Scotland) Act 1995.[178] In 1996, the court introduced new, consolidated criminal procedure rules by an Act of Adjournal which

---

[166] See s.27 of the Interpretation and Legislative Reform (Scotland) Act 2010. Prior to the entry into force of that Act, the matter was governed by paras 2 and 4 of Scotland Act 1998 (Transitory and Transitional Provisions) (Statutory Instruments) Order 1999 (SI 1999/1096).

[167] Scotland Act 1998 s.118.

[168] Scotland Act 1998 s.53(3).

[169] College of Justice Act 1532. The Law Reform (Miscellaneous Provisions) (Scotland) Act 1966 s.10 provided that Acts of Sederunt and Acts of Adjournal made after that Act under enabling statutes enacted after the commencement of the Statutory Instruments Act 1946 are to be statutory instruments, unless the enabling statute provides to the contrary.

[170] Court of Session Act 1988 s.5.

[171] *Girvan v Inverness Farmers Dairy*, 1998 S.C. (HL) 1 at 21, per Lord Hope of Craighead.

[172] A.S. 1725. See W. Alexander, *Acts of Sederunt* (London: A. & C. Black, 1838).

[173] *Inglis's Trs v Macpherson*, 1910 S.C. 46.

[174] *Tonner v Baird & Co*, 1927 S.C. 870; *Carron Co v Hislop*, 1931 S.C. (HL) 75.

[175] Act of Sederunt (Rules of the Court of Session 1994) (SI 1994/1443).

[176] *Girvan v Inverness Farmers Dairy*, 1998 S.C. (HL) 1.

[177] *Girvan v Inverness Farmers Dairy*, 1998 S.C. (HL) 1 at 21.

[178] The 1995 Act has been amended, most recently by the Criminal Proceedings etc. (Reform) (Scotland) Act 2007.

repealed the previous rules.[179] These rules have been subsequently amended in various respects, including provision for devolution issues.[180]

1.33 Orders and by-laws—If a by-law passed by a local authority or by a company has legislative force, it must derive that force from a statute by which power to make by-laws is conferred. So a by-law issued by a company registered under the Companies Acts may be binding on the shareholders; if so, it is binding on principles of contract and because they have agreed to be bound by it, whereas a company founded on statute may have power to issue by-laws which have legislative force, and are binding on the general public as well as on the shareholders. The exact degree of legislative force possessed by an order or by-law depends on the terms of the statute by which the power to issue it was conferred. If it is there enacted that the by-law, when passed, is to be read as part of the statute, it is still open to the objection that it is inconsistent with a section of the statute, or that the official empowered to make the by-law has gone completely beyond his province; any objections less weighty are excluded.[181] If there is a mere power to make by-laws for some particular object, these, when made, are valid only if they are intra vires, i.e. if they relate to the object referred to[182]; if they are reasonable[183]; and if they are not repugnant to the general law of the country.[184] There is, however, a strong presumption in favour of the validity of a by-law passed by a local authority, especially if it has been confirmed, in accordance with the provisions of the statute, by some public official, such as the Secretary of State for Scotland or the sheriff.[185] In such a case, the function of the confirming authority is to determine the expediency of the by-law and not merely to consider its legality.[186] A by-law falls if the statute authorising it is repealed.[187]

1.34 Repeal of statutes: Desuetude—A statute may be repealed by a later Act, either expressly or by the enactment of provisions inconsistent with it.[188] Repeal is not to be presumed if, consistently with the later statute, it is possible to give any reasonable meaning to the earlier.[189] The repeal of a repealing statute does not revive the statute repealed.[190] Statute Law Revision Acts, providing for the express repeal of statutes or sections impliedly repealed, have been passed at various dates. A statute may also be impliedly repealed by falling into desuetude, with the result that if appealed to, the courts will decline to give effect to it. This rule,

---

[179] Act of Adjournal (Criminal Procedure Rules) 1996 (SI 1996/513) (as frequently amended).
[180] Act of Adjournal (Devolution Issues Rules) 1999 (SI 1999/1346).
[181] *The King v Minister of Health* [1931] A.C. 494, explaining *Institute of Patent Agents v Lockwood* (1894) 21 R. (HL) 61. And see *McEwen's Trs v Church of Scotland General Trs*, 1940 S.L.T. 357, as to validity of a "scheme" made under an Act of Parliament; *Cheyne v Architects' Registration Council*, 1943 S.C. 468.
[182] *Shepherd v Howman*, 1918 J.C. 78; *McAlister v Forth Pilotage Authority*, 1944 S.L.T. 109; *Stewart v Perth* and *Kinross Council*, 2004 S.C. (HL) 71.
[183] *Saunders v South-Eastern Ry* (1880) 5 Q.B.D. 456; *De Prato v Magistrates of Partick*, 1907 S.C. (HL) 5.
[184] *Dunsmore v Lindsay* (1903) 6 F. (J.) 14.
[185] *Aldred v Miller*, 1925 J.C. 21; *Baird v Glasgow Corp*, 1935 S.C. (HL) 21. See Local Government (Scotland) Act 1973 (c.65) ss.201–204 (as amended).
[186] *Glasgow Corp v Glasgow Churches Council*, 1944 S.C. 97.
[187] *Watson v Winch* [1916] 1 K.B. 688.
[188] See, e.g. *Angus County Council v Magistrates of Montrose*, 1933 S.C. 505.
[189] *Lang v Munro* (1892) 19 R. (J.) 53.
[190] Interpretation Act 1978 s.15.

probably, is only applicable to Scots Acts[191]; at least there is no case where a statute passed since 1707 has been held to have fallen into desuetude,[192] and no analogous rule is recognised in England.[193] Mere age is not a sufficient ground for holding an Act to be in desuetude; it requires, in addition, the consideration that there is no recent case reported in which the Act has been given effect to, that it has for a long period been disregarded in practice, or that its provisions are out of accord with modern conditions.[194] A large number of Scots Acts have been repealed by various Statute Law Revision Acts, the first being passed in 1906, and there is a presumption, not conclusive, that Scots Acts not so repealed are still in observance.[195] The Statute Law Revision (Scotland) Act 1964[196] not only repealed a number of Scots Acts which were obsolete, spent or unnecessary, or had been superseded, and deleted obsolete matter from many others but it also provided short titles for the remaining Acts, which may be used without prejudice to any other mode of citation.[197] In deciding whether a statute has fallen into desuetude, the effect, if any, of the Statute Law Revision (Scotland) Acts is an important consideration[198]; and where a party argues that desuetude applies to a statute the onus of proof is on that party.[199]

Interpretation of statutes: Scots Acts—The general rules applicable to the inter- **1.35**
pretation of statutes are not applicable to Scots Acts. These, expressed in nearly all cases briefly and without detailed provisions, have been interpreted in a very liberal spirit, sometimes in terms which cannot be reconciled with the words of the Act. In their construction, it is a recognised rule that, whatever the literal meaning of the statutory words, they are to be read as interpreted by decisions pronounced shortly after the Act was passed.[200]

Interpretation: General principles—The object of interpretation is to find the **1.36**
intention of Parliament from the words it has chosen to enact: "We are seeking not what Parliament meant but the true meaning of what they said."[201] In modern

---

[191] See *McSkimming v The Royal Bank of Scotland*, 1997 S.L.T. 516 at 517C.

[192] For recent examples of Scots statutes held not to be in desuetude (owing to amendment by various Statute Law Repeal (Scotland) Acts), see *Britton v Britton's Curator Bonis*, 1996 S.C. 178 (Curator's Act 1585 (c.25)); and *McSkimming v The Royal Bank of Scotland*, 1997 S.L.T. 516 (Breach of Arrestment Act 1581).

[193] See opinion of Lord Deas, *Bute v More* (1870) 9 M. 180.

[194] *McAra v Magistrates of Edinburgh*, 1913 S.C. 1059; *Brown v Magistrates of Edinburgh*, 1931 S.L.T. 456; *McSkimming v The Royal Bank of Scotland*, 1997 S.L.T. 516 at 517D–E. See also *Britton v Britton's Curator Bonis*, 1996 S.C. 178.

[195] *Brown v Magistrates of Edinburgh*, 1931 S.L.T. 456.

[196] Statute Law Revision (Scotland) Act 1964 (c.80). This was repealed by the Statute Law (Repeals) Act 1995 (c.44) Sch.1 Pt IV.

[197] s.2 and Sch.2. Further repeals were made by the Statute Law Repeals Act 1973 Sch.1 Pt XIII and the Statute Law (Repeals) Act 1993 (c.50) Sch.1 Pt XI. Various "Scottish Local Acts" were repealed by the Statute Law (Repeals) Act 1998 (c.43) Sch.1 Pt VII.

[198] *McSkimming v The Royal Bank of Scotland*, 1997 S.L.T. 516 at 517E–F, per Lord Gill, applying *Brown v Magistrates of Edinburgh*, 1931 S.L.T. 456 at 457–458.

[199] *Brown v Magistrates of Edinburgh*, 1931 S.L.T. 456 at 458; *McSkimming v The Royal Bank of Scotland*, 1997 S.L.T. 516 at 517D.

[200] *Fergusson v Skirving* (1852) 1 Macq. 232; *Heriot's Trust v Paton's Trs*, 1912 S.C. 1123 at 1135, per Lord President Dunedin. But cf. *HM Advocate v L* [2008] HCJAC 77; 2009 S.L.T. 127.

[201] *Black-Clawson International Ltd v Papierwerke Waldhof-Aschaffenburg A.G.* [1975] A.C. 591 at 613, per Lord Reid; see also *Salomon v A. Salomon & Co Ltd* [1897] A.C. 22; *R. v Secretary of State for Environment etc. Ex p. Spath Holmes Ltd* [2001] 2 A.C. 349.

statutes,[202] the most general rule is that if the meaning of the statute is plain and unambiguous it should normally receive effect. Arguments as to resulting inconvenience or injustice or anomaly[203] are irrelevant. If injustice would result from a statute, it is the province of the legislature, not the court, to amend it.[204] The rule yields to cases where a literal interpretation would result in positive absurdity.[205] "Nothing short of impossibility should allow a judge to declare a statute unworkable."[206] Any ambiguity will admit of the construction of the statute in a sense which will not render it nugatory, or result in obvious injustice or inconvenience, although it may not be the most obvious meaning of the words used.[207] Legislation which is intended to implement an "EU obligation"[208] should be given a purposive construction so that it is in conformity with the obligation.[209] Legislation which was not intended to implement an EU obligation, including legislation which was passed before the EU obligation was adopted, must be construed, as far as possible, so that it complies with the obligation.[210] Under the Scotland Act 1998, if a provision in an Act of the Scottish Parliament (or a Bill) might be interpreted as being ultra vires that Parliament's legislative competence, then this provision should be construed, if it can, as restrictively as necessary so that it is not ultra vires.[211]

1.37 Statutory definitions—A general statute, the Interpretation Act 1978,[212] gives the meaning of a number of expressions in common use, such as "person", "month", "Rules of Court", "writing". The statutory meaning is to apply "unless the contrary intention appears". In relation to Acts of the Scottish Parliament, similar general definitions were initially set out in the Scotland Act 1998 (Transitory and Transitional Provisions) (Publication and Interpretation etc. of Acts of the Scottish Parliament) Order 1999[213] but are now to be found in the

---

[202] See P. St. J. Langan (ed.), *Maxwell on the Interpretation of Statutes* (London: Sweet and Maxwell, 1969); *Craies on Legislation*, 8th edn (London: Sweet & Maxwell, 2004); *Bennion on Statutory Interpretation*, 5th edn (London: LexisNexis, 2007); R. Cross, *Statutory Interpretation*, 3rd edn (Oxford: Oxford University Press, 1995).

[203] *Stock v Frank Jones (Tipton) Ltd* [1978] 1 W.L.R. 231; *Anderson v Gibb*, 1993 S.L.T. 726 at 728, per Lord Penrose, approving this statement in the 9th edn of this work.

[204] *Lord Advocate v Earl of Moray's Trs* (1905) 7 F. (HL) 116; *Lawrie v Banknock Colliery Co*, 1912 S.C. (HL) 20, per Lord Shaw; *Feeney v Miller*, 1925 J.C. 65. See, however, para.1.48, Casus Omissus, where, in very limited circumstances, a court will correct drafting mistakes in a statute.

[205] *Cal. Ry v N.B. Ry* (1881) 8 R. (HL) 23 at 30, per Lord Blackburn.

[206] *Murray v Inland Revenue*, 1918 S.C. (HL) 111 at 124, per Lord Dunedin. A similar approach seems to have been taken in *K. v Craig*, 1999 S.C. (HL) 1. In *Dumfries and Maxwelltown Co-operative Society v Williamson*, 1950 J.C. 76, a statutory provision was found unworkable.

[207] *Inland Revenue v Luke*, 1963 S.C. (HL) 65; *Paterson v Ardrossan Harbour Co*, 1926 S.C. 442.

[208] "EU obligation" is defined in the European Communities Act 1972 Sch.1 Pt II.

[209] *Pickstone v Freemans plc* [1989] A.C. 66; *Litster v Forth Dry Dock & Engineering Co Ltd*, 1989 S.C. 96; *Von Colson and Kamann v Land Nordrhein-Westfalen* [1984] E.C.R. 1891; *NUPE v Secretary of State for Employment*, 1993 G.W.D. 14-942; *English v North Lanarkshire Council*, 1999 S.C.L.R. 310 at 319; *Roy v M.R. Pearlman*, 1999 S.C. 459 at 465-6; *King v T. Tunnock Ltd*, 2000 S.C. 424 at 432 and 434; *Centresteel Srl v Adipol GmbH* [2000] 3 C.M.L.R. 711, ECJ.

[210] *Marleasing S.A. v La Comercial Internacional de Alimentacion S.A.* [1991] E.C.R. 4135. Cf. *Duke v Reliance Systems Ltd* [1988] A.C. 618; *Finnegan v Clowney Youth Training Programme Ltd* [1990] 2 A.C. 407; *Webb v EMO Air Cargo (UK) Ltd* [1992] 1 C.M.L.R. 793; *Centrosteel Srl. v Adipol GmbH* [2000] 3 C.M.L.R. 711, ECJ.

[211] Scotland Act 1998 s.101(2). See *Anderson v Scottish Ministers*, 2001 S.C. 1; *Adams v Scottish Ministers*, 2003 S.C. 171; *HM Advocate v R*, 2003 S.C. (PC) 21; *DS v HM Advocate*, 2007 S.C.C.R. 222 (PC); *Somerville v Scottish Ministers* [2007] UKHL 44.

[212] Consolidating the Interpretation Act 1889 and other enactments.

[213] SI 1999/1379; and Scotland Act 1998 s.126.

Interpretation and Legislative Reform (Scotland) Act 2010. Most statutes now contain an interpretation section, giving the meaning to be assigned to expressions used in the Act. If the meaning of the word is defined, that meaning, though it may exclude the ordinary meaning, must be taken, unless the context plainly shows that this was not intended. If defined expressions are used in a context in which the definition will not fit, then the words may be interpreted according to their ordinary meaning.[214] Modern statutes frequently contain provisions that something is to be "deemed" to be something else. If it is declared that a particular word shall "include" something, the result is to enlarge the scope of the word, but not to exclude its ordinary meaning[215]; sometimes, however, "includes" is equivalent to "means and includes" and it then gives an exhaustive definition.[216]

Meaning in context—If a word is not defined in a particular Act, it should be given the natural and ordinary meaning it had at the time the Act was passed.[217] Reference may be made to a dictionary,[218] and especially to a judicial dictionary.[219] It is not permissible to lead evidence as to the meaning of an ordinary English word,[220] but when a word is used in the technical sense it bears in a trade or industry, evidence of persons skilled in the trade or industry is competent.[221] It is important that the word should be read in its context: **1.38**

> "Few words in the English language have a natural or ordinary meaning in the sense that they must be so read that their meaning is entirely independent of their context."[222]

Where a word is included in a list of words of greater precision in which some common characteristic can be discerned, the word should be given a meaning which shares the common characteristic — this is the principle *noscitur a sociis*.[223]

The wider context—The word must also be considered in the context of the whole Act: "A statute must, like any other continuous document, be read as a whole—optimus statuti interpres statutum ipsum"[224]—the best interpreter of a statute is the **1.39**

---

[214] *Strathern v Padden*, 1926 J.C. 9, per Lord Justice-General Clyde.

[215] *Ex p. Ferguson* (1871) L.R. 6 Q.B. 280.

[216] *Dilworth v Stamps Commissioners* [1899] A.C. 99; *Inland Revenue v Joiner* [1975] 1 W.L.R. 1701.

[217] *Peart v Stewart* [1983] 2 A.C. 109; *Sharpe v Wakefeld* (1888) 22 Q.B.D. 239; *Scottish Cinema v Ritchie*, 1929 S.C. 350. Cf. *Dyson Holdings Ltd v Fox* [1976] Q.B. 503. A word may apply to something which did not exist at the time the Act was passed: *Leadbetter v Hutchison*, 1934 J.C. 70; *Barker v Wilson* [1980] 1 W.L.R. 884.

[218] *Baldwin & Francis v Patents Appeal Tribunal* [1959] R.P.C. 221 at 231, per Lord Reid; *Inland Revenue v Russell*, 1955 S.L.T. 255.

[219] *Haigh v Charles W. Ireland Ltd*, 1974 S.C. (HL) 1.

[220] *Marquess Camden v I.R.C.* [1914] 1 K.B. 641; *Cozens v Brutus* [1973] A.C. 854.

[221] *L. & N.E. Ry. v Berriman* [1946] A.C. 278; *Unwin v Hanson* [1891] 2 Q.B. 115.

[222] *Re Bidie* [1949] Ch. 121 at 129, per Lord Greene M.R.

[223] *Ong Ah Chuan v Public Prosecutor* [1981] A.C. 648; *Griffith v Scottish Gas Board*, 1963 S.L.T. 286; cf. *Customs and Excise Commissioners v Viva Gas Appliances Ltd* [1983] 1 W.L.R. 1445.

[224] *Magistrates of Buckie v Dowager Countess of Seafield's Trs*, 1928 S.C. 525 at 529, per Lord President Clyde. See also *Att Gen. v Prince Ernest Augustus of Hanover* [1957] A.C. 436 at 461, per Viscount Simonds, and at 465, per Lord Normand; *McArthur v Strathclyde R.C.*, 1994 S.C.L.R. 752; *K. v Craig*, 1999 S.C. (HL) 1 at 1, per Lord Hope of Craighead.

statute itself. The purpose and effect of other sections of the Act must be examined.[225] The title,[226] and the preamble[227] (usually omitted in recent statutes) may be referred to as determining the scope of the statute, though neither can override an express provision. It is permissible to refer to the marginal or side notes, but they must not be given equal weight with the words of the Act.[228] It has been said in the Outer House that "[i]n modern draftsmanship the sidenote is no more than a brief guide to the content of the section", but, as sidenotes can be "of variable accuracy", they are, "on the whole 'a poor guide' to the scope of the section".[229] Where a statute is divided into parts by specific headings, the heading limits the application of the sections which follow.[230] If a statute contains contradictory provisions, the later sections override the earlier, but nothing in a schedule can overcome a provision in an enacting clause.[231] Other statutes in *pari materia* should be examined,[232] and regard should be had to the social and political situation when the Act was passed and the state of the law at that time.[233] The mischief which the Act was intended to remedy should also be considered[234]; the court should ascertain the social ends the Act was intended to achieve and the practical means by which it was expected to achieve them:

> "Meticulous linguistic analysis of words and phrases used in different contexts in particular sections of the Act should be subordinate to this purposive approach."[235]

The report of a Royal Commission or departmental committee on which the statute followed can be examined to ascertain the mischief aimed at and the state of the law as it was then understood to be,[236] and it now seems to be permissible to consider the recommendations made in the report or a draft Bill annexed to the report.[237] It

---

[225] *Jennings v Kelly* [1940] A.C. 206 at 218, per Viscount Maugham.

[226] *Ayr v St. Andrew's Ambulance Association*, 1918 S.C. 158; *Magistrates of Buckie v Dowager Countess of Seafield's Trs*, 1928 S.C. 525; *R. v Secretary of State for Foreign and Commonwealth Affairs, Ex p. Rees-Mogg* [1994] Q.B. 552 at 565, per Lloyd L.J.

[227] *Att Gen. v Prince Ernest Augustus of Hanover* [1957] A.C. 436. In EU legislation the recitals in the preamble are often lengthy and an important aid to the interpretation of the operative provisions.

[228] *R. v Schildkamp* [1971] A.C. 1 at 10, per Lord Reid; *Maxwell on the Interpretation of Statutes* (1969), p.49; *Alexander v Mackenzie*, 1947 J.C. 155, 166; *Eunson v The Braer Corp.*, 1999 S.L.T. 1405 at 1408C-E. Cf. *Nelson v McPhee* (1889) 17 R. (J.) 1; *Magistrates of Buckie*, 1928 S.C. 525, opinion of Lord President Clyde; *Chandler v DPP* [1964] A.C. 763 at 789, per Lord Reid.

[229] *Eunson v The Braer Corp*, 1999 S.L.T. 1405 at 1408C-E, per Lord Gill.

[230] *Nelson* (1889) 17 R. (J.) 1; *Inglis v Robertson & Baxter* (1898) 25 R. (HL) 70; *Magistrates of Buckie*, 1928 S.C. 525. Cf. *R. v Schildkamp* [1971] A.C. 1.

[231] *Jacobs v Hart* (1900) 2 F. (J.) 33; *Kerr v HM Advocate*, 1986 J.C. 41.

[232] *R. v Loxdale* (1758) 1 Burr. 445. Cf. *Fane v Murray*, 1995 S.L.T. 567, concerning the use of similar or equivalent English statutes as an aid to interpretation of Scottish Statutes.

[233] *Inland Revenue v Hinchy* [1960] A.C. 748 at 763, per Viscount Kilmuir L.C.; *Ealing L.B.C. v Race Relations Board* [1972] A.C. 342; *Henretty v Hart* (1885) 13 R. (J.) 9; *R. v Secretary of State for the Environment, Transport and the Regions, Ex p. Spath Holme Ltd* [2001] 2 A.C. 349.

[234] *Heydon's Case* (1584) 3 Co. Rep. 7a; *Black-Clawson International Ltd v Papierwerke Waldhof-Aschaffenburg A.G.* [1975] A.C. 591 at 614, per Lord Reid.

[235] *R. v National Insurance Commissioner, Ex p. Hudson* [1972] A.C. 944 at 1005, per Lord Diplock. See also *Kammins Ballrooms Co Ltd v Zenith Investments (Torquay) Ltd* [1971] A.C. 850; *Fothergill v Monarch Airlines Ltd* [1981] A.C. 251; *R. v Cuthbertson* [1981] A.C. 470.

[236] *Black-Clawson v Papierwerke Waldhof-Aschaffenburg A.G.* [1975] A.C. 591; *McIntyre v Armitage Shanks Ltd*, 1980 S.C. (HL) 46 at 57, per Lord Hailsham L.C.; *Pepper v Hart* [1993] A.C. 593 at 635, per Lord Browne-Wilkinson.

[237] *R. v Secretary of State for Transport, Ex p. Factortame* [1990] 2 A.C. 85 at 149, per Lord Bridge of Harwich; *Short's Trs v Keeper of the Registers of Scotland*, 1994 S.C. 122 at 137–8, per Lord Hope of Craighead (this view was not doubted on a reclaiming motion, see 1996 S.C. (HL) 14). Cf. *Pepper v Hart* [1993] A.C. 593 at 630–631 and 635, per Lord Browne-Wilkinson.

appears that a White Paper can be used in the same general way.[238] The Inner House has expressed

> "some doubt as to whether it is legitimate . . . to use Scottish Law Commission Reports unless the statute was ambiguous or if there was any doubt about the construction to be placed upon the statutory language".[239]

Law Commission reports may be used to identify the "mischief" to which the statute is directed.[240]

Extrinsic sources: Parliamentary materials, Conventions and Treaties— 1.40
Once an ambiguity has been established, it becomes permissible to have regard to a wider range of materials. Recourse can be had to the legislative history of the subject[241] but not to the course of the Parliamentary proceedings relating to the particular statute.[242] At one time, reference to Parliamentary debates was strictly prohibited.[243] However, now "Parliamentary materials" can be examined

> "where: (a) legislation is ambiguous or obscure or leads to absurdity; (b) the material relied upon consists of one or more statements by a Minister or other promoter of the Bill, together, if necessary, with such other Parliamentary material as is necessary to understand such statements and their effect; and (c) the statements relied upon are clear".[244]

Relatively recent dicta in the House of Lords indicated resistance to a broader approach than that stated above[245] but in practice there is a tendency to adopt a slightly more relaxed approach. In certain circumstances, *travaux préparatoires* have been used to construe an international convention which has been given the

---

[238] *Duke v Reliance Systems Ltd* [1988] A.C. 618 at 631, per Lord Templeman; *Att Gen.'s Reference (No.1 of 1988)* [1989] A.C. 971 at 992, per Lord Lowry; *Pepper v Hart* [1993] A.C. 593 at 635B-C, per Lord Browne-Wilkinson.

[239] *Barratt Scotland Ltd v Keith*, 1993 S.C. 142 at 154D, per Lord Justice-Clerk Ross, Lord Kirkwood agreeing. See too the Outer House in *Archer Car Sales (Airdrie) Ltd v Gregory's Trustee*, 1993 S.L.T. 223, which said such reports could be an "aid to construction", but not where no ambiguity existed. Cf. the Outer House in *McWilliams v Lord Advocate*, 1992 S.L.T. 1045 at 1046J; *Rehman v Ahmad*, 1993 S.L.T. 741 at 745F; *MacDonald Estates Plc v Regenesis (2005) Dunfermline Ltd*, 2007 S.L.T. 791 at [152]–[158].

[240] See, e.g. *Macdonald v Pollocks* [2012] CSIH 12 and the authorities there mentioned.

[241] *Lilley v Public Tr.* [1981] A.C. 839 at 846; cf. *Grant v DPP* [1982] A.C. 190 at 201.

[242] *Cramas Properties Ltd v Connaught Fur Trimmings Ltd* [1965] 1 W.L.R. 892 at 899, per Lord Reid. Similarly, it is not permissible to look at subsequent amending legislation to aid interpretation, see *A.I.B. Finance Ltd v Bank of Scotland*, 1995 S.L.T. 2.

[243] *Davis v Johnson* [1979] A.C. 264.

[244] *Pepper v Hart* [1993] A.C. 593 at 640, per Lord Browne-Wilkinson. See also *R. v Warwickshire C.C., Ex p. Johnson* [1993] A.C. 583; *Stubbings v Webb* [1993] A.C. 498; *Chief Adjudication Officer v Foster* [1993] 2 W.L.R. 292; *Short's Tr. v Keeper of the Registers of Scotland*, 1994 S.C. 122; 1996 S.C. (HL) 14; *R. v Secretary of State for Foreign and Commonwealth Affairs, Ex p. Rees-Mogg* [1994] Q.B. 552; *Buchanan v Secretary of State for Trade and Industry*, 1995 G.W.D. 11-600; *Monckton v Lord Advocate*, 1995 S.L.T. 1201; *Stirling District Council v Allan*, 1995 S.C. 420; *Melluish v B.M.I. Ltd (No.3)* [1996] A.C. 454; *R. v Secretary of State for the Environment, Transport and the Regions, Ex p. Spath Holme Ltd* [2001] 2 A.C. 349 at 391–2 per Lord Bingham of Cornhill.

[245] *Melluish v B.M.I. Ltd (No.3)* [1996] A.C. 454, per Lord Browne-Wilkinson at 481–2; *R. v Secretary of State for the Environment, Transport and the Regions, Ex p. Spath Holme Ltd* [2001] 2 A.C. 349, per Lord Bingham of Cornhill at 391–3; *Wilson v First County Trust (No.2)* [2004] 1 A.C. 816; *McDonnell (FC) v Congregation of Christian Brothers Trustees* [2004] 1 A.C. 1101.

force of law in the United Kingdom.[246] Earlier[247] and later[248] statutes can be
examined. An ambiguity in a consolidation statute justifies resort to the consolidated statutes.[249] Where the language of a statute has received judicial interpretation, and Parliament again uses the same language in a subsequent statute
dealing with the same subject matter, there is a presumption that Parliament
intended that the language so used by it in the subsequent statute should be
given the meaning which meantime had been judicially attributed to it.[250] It
seems that, in some circumstances, subordinate legislation made under powers
contained in the statute can be used to construe the statute.[251] Where the
statute has, apparently, been passed to implement the obligations of the United
Kingdom under an international convention, there is a presumption that Parliament
did not intend to act in breach of specific treaty obligations and where there
is ambiguity a meaning should be attached to the legislation consonant with
the obligations assumed under the convention.[252] If the convention is not
referred to in the body of the statute, it can be looked at only if the statute is
ambiguous and there is cogent evidence that the enactment was intended to give
effect to the particular convention[253]; however, the Outer House has said that a
statute giving effect to a convention should not be interpreted "in a broader
and more liberal way than it otherwise would".[254] If the Act gives effect to the
convention, as set forth, in English, in a schedule, it is permissible to resolve
doubt or ambiguity by examining a text of the convention in another language
which is stated to be the authentic text,[255] or to be an equally authentic text.[256]
In interpreting EU legislation all of the official language versions are equally
authentic and, subject to the limitations imposed by the linguistic abilities of
the bench, should be considered. Before the Human Rights Act 1998 was passed,
making the European Convention on Human Rights (of which the French text
is equally authentic with the English text) part of UK law,[257] the Inner House
held, overruling earlier authority, that the Convention could be used as an aid to

---

[246] *Fothergill v Monarch Airlines Ltd* [1981] A.C. 251; *Gatoil International Inc. v Arkwright-Boston Manufacturers Mutual Insurance Co*, 1985 S.C. (HL) 1.

[247] *Earl of Lonsdale v Att Gen.* [1982] 1 W.L.R. 887.

[248] *Kirkness v John Hudson & Co Ltd* [1955] A.C. 696.

[249] *Farrell v Alexander* [1977] A.C. 59; *R. v Secretary of State for the Environment, Transport and the Regions, Ex p. Spath Holme Ltd* [2001] 2 A.C. 349. Cf. *Johnson v Moreton* [1980] A.C. 37.

[250] *Barras v Aberdeen Trawling Co*, 1933 S.C. (HL) 21; cf. *Haigh v Charles W. Ireland Ltd*, 1974 S.C. (HL) 1; *Kelly v MacKinnon*, 1982 S.C.C.R. 205.

[251] *British Amusements Catering Trades Association v Westminster Council* [1989] A.C. 147; *Hanlon v Law Society* [1981] A.C. 124. Cf. *Jackson v Hall* [1980] A.C. 854.

[252] *Post Office v Estuary Radio* [1968] 2 Q.B. 740; *T., Petitioner*, 1997 S.L.T. 724 at 734C–D, per Lord President Hope.

[253] *Ellerman Lines v Murray* [1931] A.C. 126, where, in the absence of ambiguity in the section under construction, the House of Lords refused to refer to the draft convention mentioned in the preamble and set forth in a schedule to the Act; *Salomon v Commissioners of Customs and Excise* [1967] 2 Q.B. 116; *Stirling District Council v Allan*, 1995 S.L.T. 1255; *P. & O. Scottish Ferries Ltd v The Braer Corp*, 1999 S.C.L.R. 540.

[254] *Skerries Salmond Ltd v Braer Group*, 1999 S.L.T. 1196 at 1200J–K, per Lord Gill; who affirmed this view in *P. & O. Scottish Ferries Ltd v The Braer Group*, 1999 S.C.L.R. 540 at 545.

[255] *Fothergill v Monarch Airlines* [1981] A.C. 251. In *Corocraft v Pan American Airways* [1969] 1 Q.B. 616, the Court of Appeal proceeded on the ambiguous French text rather than the unambiguous English version.

[256] *James Buchanan & Co v Babco Forwarding and Shipping (UK)* [1978] A.C. 141.

[257] Human Rights Act 1998 (c.42). See paras 1.42–1.44, below.

construction[258]; this conformed with the view taken by the House of Lords in English decisions.[259]

Human Rights Act 1998: Interpretation—Pursuant to s.3(1) of the Human **1.41** Rights Act 1998, primary legislation[260] and subordinate legislation[261] must be read and given effect in a way which is compatible[262] with the Convention rights as far as this can be done. Convention rights are the rights and fundamental freedoms set out in the various Articles of the European Convention on Human Rights contained in Sch.1 to the Act[263]; the Act applies to acts by public authorities (which include courts and tribunals[264]) that are incompatible with Convention rights. Section 3 has retroactive effect, as it concerns legislation whenever enacted, but does not invalidate such legislation.[265] Nor can it affect the application of pre-Human Rights Act legislation to facts and circumstances occurring before the section came into force.[266] Section 3 may apply even if on ordinary principles of interpretation the meaning of the legislation appears to be clear.[267] The power of the courts is limited by what is possible given the purpose and principles of the legislation; the judges are not empowered to amend it.[268]

Human Rights Act 1998: Incompatibility—Where a prescribed court[269] is of **1.42** the opinion that legislation is not compatible with Convention rights and cannot be rescued by the interpretive mechanisms provided by s.3 of the Act, it may make a declaration of incompatibility under s.4, after first giving the Crown notice of its intention under s.5.[270] Nonetheless, "a declaration of incompatibility" does not mean that the offending legislation is invalid or of no force or effect[271]; once a declaration has been made, it is then up to Parliament to "take remedial action"[272] to amend the legislation.[273] This may be contrasted with the position of legislation of the Scottish Parliament found to be incompatible with Convention rights.

---

[258] *T., Petitioner*, 1997 S.L.T. 724 at 734C–D, per Lord President Hope, overruling *Kaur v Lord Advocate*, 1980 S.C. 349.

[259] See, e.g. *Re M and H (Minors)* [1990] 1 A.C. 686 at 721, per Lord Brandon; *R. v Home Secretary, Ex p. Brind* [1991] 1 A.C. 696 at 747, per Lord Bridge.

[260] See the definition in s.21(1) of the Human Rights Act 1998.

[261] Human Rights Act 1988 s.21(1).

[262] It has been said that "[t]he essence of the word 'incompatible' is that there is an inconsistency between one thing and another", see Lord Hope of Craighead in *Montgomery v HM Advocate*, 2001 S.C. (PC) 1 at 18B.

[263] Human Rights Act 1998 s.1. See the definition of "the Convention" in s.21 of the 1998 Act. Several Articles of the Convention have been omitted from Sch.1 to the Human Rights Act 1998.

[264] Human Rights Act 1998 s.6(3)(a).

[265] Human Rights Act 1998 s.3(2).

[266] *Wilson v First County Trust Ltd (No.2)* [2004] 1 A.C. 816.

[267] See, e.g. *R. v Lambert* [2002] 2 A.C. 545.

[268] *Ghaidan v Godin-Mendoza* [2004] 2 A.C. 557. See also *Somerville v Scottish Ministers*, 2007 S.C. 140; revd [2007] UKHL 44; 2007 S.C. (HL) 45.

[269] A list of courts able to make such a declaration is set out in Human Rights Act 1998 s.4(5). In Scotland only the Court of Session or the High Court of Justiciary sitting as an appeal court may make such a declaration; see too *R. v Director of Public Prosecutions, Ex p. Kebilene* [2000] 2 A.C. 326. In *Smith v Scott*, 2007 S.C. 345 the Registration Appeal Court was held able to act under this provision as part of the Court of Session.

[270] See, e.g. *Smith v Scott*, 2007 S.C. 345 (declaration of incompatibility of Representation of the People Act 1983 s.3(1) with Convention rights).

[271] Human Rights Act 1998 s.4(6).

[272] Human Rights Act 1998 s.10.

[273] See Human Rights Act 1998 and Sch.2 thereof (which refers to "remedial orders"). As to "orders" made by a "Minister of the Crown" (as defined in s.21 of the 1998 Act), see s.20 of that Act.

Subject to the court's power to limit the temporal extent of its finding of incompatibility, that incompatibility has the consequence that the legislative provision in issue is "not law".[274]

1.43 Human Rights Act 1998: Factors in applying Convention rights—In determining a question of Convention rights, courts and tribunals, so far as considered relevant, must take into account the so-called "Strasbourg jurisprudence"[275] (both the decisions of the European Court of Human Rights and, to a limited extent, the former European Commission of Human Rights)[276] While a UK court will normally follow any clear and settled principles contained in that jurisprudence, the jurisprudence is not binding on a UK court under the 1998 Act.[277] The Strasbourg jurisprudence has indicated that the Convention "is plainly a living instrument".[278] One aspect of that jurisprudence which is applicable is the "proportionality principle", which involves considering whether there is "a fair balance"

> "between the general interest of the community in the realisation of . . . [a legitimate] aim [in the public interest] and the protection of the fundamental rights of the individual".[279]

However, the so-called "margin of appreciation", concerning the giving of a certain "discretion" to Member States in relation to the implementation of legislation due to variations in "local needs and conditions",[280] which "is an integral part of the supervisory jurisdiction" of the European Court of Human Rights,[281] is not available to national courts.[282] Nonetheless, in interpreting the Convention, national courts should see it "as an expression of fundamental principles rather

---

[274] Scotland Act 1998 s.29; see, e.g. *Cameron v Procurator Fiscal, Livingston* [2012] HCJAC 19 (finding of "not law") and [2012] HCJAC 31 (restricting the scope of the finding).

[275] See, e.g. Lord Hope of Craighead in *Millar v Dickson*, 2002 S.C. (PC) 30 at 52, [58], who uses this phrase.

[276] See Human Rights Act 1998 s.2(1).

[277] Human Rights Act 1998 s.2. See, importantly, *R v Horncastle* [2009] UKSC 14; [2010] 2 A.C. 373; *R. (Alconbury) v Secretary of State for the Environment, Transport and the Regions, Ex p. Holding and Barnes Plc* [2003] 2 A.C. 295 at [26], per Lord Slynn, and at [76], per Lord Hoffmann; and also Laws L.J. in *Regina (M) v Commissioner of Police of the Metropolis* [2001] EWHC Admin 553, who refers to creating "a municipal jurisprudence of human rights" (at [11]).

[278] *Brown v Stott*, 2001 S.C. (PC) 43 at 81, per Lord Clyde; *R. v Director of Public Prosecutions, Ex p. Kebilene* [2000] 2 A.C. 326 at 380, per Lord Hope of Craighead. See too Lord Bingham of Cornhill in *Brown v Stott*, 2001 S.C. (PC) 43 at 59, referring to implying terms into the Convention.

[279] per Lord Hope of Craighead in *Brown v Stott*, 2001 S.C. (PC) 43 at 75, referring to art.6 of the Convention. See also Lord Bingham of Cornhill in *Brown v Stott*, 2001 S.C. 43 at 60; Lord Hope of Craighead in *R. v Lambert* [2002] 2 A.C. 545 at [88]; and Lord Clyde in *de Freitas v Permanent Secretary* [1999] 1 A.C. 69 at 80, PC, quoting Gubbay C.J. in *Nyambira v National Social Security Authority* [1996] 1 L.R.C. 64; the judgment of Lord Clyde was cited with approval by Lord Steyn in *R. v Secretary of State for Home Department, Ex p. Daly* [2001] 2 A.C. 532 at 547.

[280] See Lord Hope of Craighead in *R. v Director of Public Prosecutions, Ex p. Kebilene* [2000] 2 A.C. 326 at 380. See also Lord Bingham of Cornhill in *Brown v Stott*, 2001 S.C. 43 at 59. See also J. Beatson, S. Groz, T. Hickman, R. Singh with S. Palmer, *Human Rights: Judicial Protection in the United Kingdom* (London: Sweet & Maxwell, 2008), paras 2–133—2–147; and R. Clayton and H. Tomlinson, *The Law of Human Rights,* 2nd edn (Oxford: Oxford University Press, 2009), Vol.1, paras 6.42–6.62.

[281] *R. v Director of Public Prosecutions, Ex p. Kebilene* [2000] 2 A.C. 326 at 380, per Lord Hope of Craighead.

[282] *R. v Director or Public Prosecutions, Ex p. Kebilene* [2000] 2 A.C. 326. See also Buxton L.J. in *R. v Stratford Justices, Ex p. Imbert* (1999) 2 Cr. App. R. 276 at 286–7; and Lord Bingham of Cornhill in *Brown v Stott*, 2001 S.C. 43 at 59; see too Lord Hoffmann in *Montgomery v HM Advocate*, 2001 S.C. (PC) 1 at 9; Beatson et al, *Human Rights: Judicial Protection in the United Kingdom* (2008), para.1–60.

than a set of mere rules."[283] In considering such "principles", the courts are frequently involved in a balancing process between competing interests and issues of proportionality. The executive or the legislature too may also have a balancing exercise regarding an individual's rights and society's needs when framing legislation, which could involve difficult choices. Consequently, in certain situations, the courts, on democratic grounds, will defer to "the considered opinion of the elected body or person whose act or decision is said to be incompatible with the Convention". This is called the "discretionary area of judgment", and is an analogous doctrine to the margin of appreciation.[284]

Presumptions—There are various presumptions which apply to the interpretation **1.44** of statutes, which include the following. First, there is a general presumption that a statute is not retrospective,[285] unless it expressly bears to be declaratory of the meaning of a prior Act, when the meaning so declared will apply to all pending questions, though not to cases already decided. The rationale for the presumption is the principle of legal certainty.[286] The presumption is stronger in criminal matters than in civil.[287] There are different degrees of retroactivity. Not infrequently legislation may affect existing relationships — for example contracts of lease, or indeed marriage — but only prospectively and the presumption does not generally apply to such legislation. On similar lines, a partial exception to the presumption is that statutes introducing new forms of procedure apply to cases already in court.[288] And it may be a necessary inference from the language of the Act, even though there is no express enactment, that it was intended to be retrospective.[289] Secondly, as

"Parliament does not lightly delegate to the executive the power to amend primary legislation, such a provision should be narrowly and strictly construed and any doubt resolved in favour of the narrower rather than broader interpretation",

but only if "genuine doubt" exists concerning a section of a statute.[290] Thirdly, it is presumed there is no intention that a Consolidating Act should change the

---

[283] *R. v Director of Public Prosecutions, Ex p. Kebilene* [2000] 2 A.C. 326 at 380–1, per Lord Hope of Craighead.

[284] See further *Ghaidan v Godin-Mendoza* [2004] 2 A.C. 557; *DS v HM Advocate*, 2007 S.C. (PC) 1; 2007 S.C.C.R. 222.

[285] *Gardner v Lucas* (1878) 5 R. (HL) 105; *Henshall v Porter* [1923] 2 K.B. 193; *Sunshine Porcelain Potteries Pty Ltd v Nash* [1961] A.C. 927 at 938, per Lord Reid; *Yew Bon Tew v Kenderaan Bas Mara* [1983] 1 A.C. 553 at 558, per Lord Brightman; *Arnold v Central Electricity Generating Board* [1988] A.C. 228 at 272; *Marsal v Apong* [1998] 1 W.L.R. 674. See also *L'Office Cherifien des Phosphates v Yamashita-Shinnihon Steamship Co Ltd* [1994] 1 A.C. 486 at 524–5, per Lord Mustill, who noted the strong "disposition" against retrospectivity, but expressed "reservations" about "generalised presumptions" in construing statutes; and *Westminster City Council v Haywood (No.2)* [2000] 2 All E.R. 634 at 634–44.

[286] *L'Office Cherifien des Phosphates v Yamashita-Shennihon Steamship Co Ltd* [1994] 1 A.C. 486 at 524–5; *Westminster City Council v Haywood (No.2)* [2000] 2 All E.R. 634 at 643; *Axa General Insurance Ltd, Petitioners* [2011] UKSC 46; 2011 S.L.T. 1061, per Lord Reed at [118ff].

[287] cf. ECHR art.7 in respect of criminal law.

[288] *Ballinten v Connor* (1852) 14 D. 927. Cf. *Yew Bon Tew v Kenderaan Bas Mara* [1983] 1 A.C. 553; and *L'Office Cherifien des Phosphates v Yamashita-Shinnihon Steamship Co Ltd* [1994] 1 A.C. 486 at 527; *Marsal v Apong* [1998] 1 W.L.R. 674.

[289] *Wilson v Wilson*, 1939 S.C. 102; *R. v Covernor of Pentonville Prison, Ex p. Azam* [1974] A.C. 18; *L'Office Cherifen des Phosphates v Yamashita-Shinnihon Steamship Co Ltd* [1994] 1 A.C. 486; *Westminster City Council v Haywood (No.2)* [2000] 2 All E.R. 634.

[290] *R. v Secretary of State for the Environment, Transport and the Regions, Ex p. Spath Holme Ltd* [2001] 2 A.C. 349 at 382, per Lord Bingham of Cornhill.

law.[291] Fourthly, there is a presumption that a palpable injustice, such as enabling a party to profit by his own wrong or breach of contract, was not intended.[292] It has been laid down that

> "an intention to take away the property of a subject without giving him a legal right to compensation for the loss of it is not to be attributed to the Legislature, unless that intention is expressed in unequivocal terms",[293]

and "if there was any reasonable doubt the subject should have the benefit of it".[294] The matter would now be subject to the Human Rights Act 1998, in particular art.1 of Protocol 1 to the ECHR. If, however, the intention to take away property is clear, any claim to compensation must be founded on the terms of the statute.[295] Subordinate rules of construction are that the exclusion of the jurisdiction of the Court of Session is not to be presumed[296]; that where alternative constructions are equally open, that alternative is to be chosen which will be consistent with the smooth working of the system which the statute purports to be regulating[297]; and that the Crown (including departments of state) is not bound by a statute of the UK Parliament, unless mentioned expressly[298] or by necessary implication.[299] Conversely, the Crown is bound by the terms of a statute of the Scottish Parliament unless the statute provides otherwise.[300]

1.45 Ample and restrictive interpretation—The theory that certain statutes should receive a beneficial, or ample interpretation, and others a restrictive interpretation,[301] is in modern law discredited, and it is held that the duty of the court is to interpret a statute according to its terms, without any bias. There are still, however, certain cases in which a statute is read, *in dubio*, in a restrictive sense, i.e. in the narrowest sense which the words will bear. This applies to statutes extending the criminal law.[302] Offences are not to be created by implication, unless the implication is so plain as to be equivalent to express enactment.[303] In construing revenue statutes,

---

[291] *Maunsell v Olins* [1975] A.C. 373 at 392–3, per Lord Diplock; *Harvey v McTaggart & Mickel Ltd*, 2000 S.C. 137 at 140 et seq., per Lord McCluskey.

[292] *Malins v Freeman* (1838) 4 Bing. N.C. 395.

[293] per Lord Atkinson, *Central Board v Cannon Brewery Co* [1919] A.C. 744. See *Marshall v Blackpool Corp* (1932) 49 T.L.R. 148; *Westminster Bank Ltd v Minister of Housing and Local Government* [1971] A.C. 508 at 529; *R. v Secretary of State for the Environment, Transport and the Regions, Ex p. Spath Holme Ltd* [2001] 2 A.C. 349 at 383. Such legislation would now be subject to the Human Rights Act 1998, particularly art.1 of the First Protocol to the European Convention on Human Rights, contained in Pt II of Sch.1 to the Act.

[294] *Westminster Bank Ltd v Minister of Housing and Local Government* [1971] A.C. 508 at 529, per Lord Reid; *R. v Secretary of State for the Environment, Transport and the Regions, Ex p. Spath Holme Ltd* [2001] 2 A.C. 349 at 383, per Lord Bingham of Cornhill.

[295] *Hammersmith Ry v Brand* (1869) L.R. 4 H.L. 171; *Cal. Ry v Walker's Trs* (1882) 9 R. (HL) 19; *Scott-Plummer v Board of Agriculture*, 1916 S.C. (HL) 94, per Lords Haldane and Parmoor.

[296] *Dunbar & Co v Scottish County Investment Co Ltd*, 1920 S.C. 210 at 217, per Lord Salvesen.

[297] *Shannon Realties Ltd v Ville de St Michel* [1924] A.C. 185 at 192, per Lord Shaw; *Hynd's Tr. v Hynd's Trs*, 1955 S.C. (HL) 1 at 10, per Viscount Kilmuir L.C.

[298] *Lord Advocate v Dumbarton D.C.*, 1990 S.C. (HL) 1 (in which dicta of Lord Dunedin in *Magistrates of Edinburgh v Lord Advocate*, 1912 S.C. 1085 were disapproved).

[299] *Province of Bombay v Municipal Corp of Bombay* [1947] A.C. 58.

[300] Interpretation and Legislative Reform (Scotland) Act 2010 s.20.

[301] Erskine, I, 1, 53.

[302] See *Friel v Initial Contract Services Ltd*, 1994 S.L.T. 1216 at 1221H-I, per Lord McCluskey, that "doubt or ambiguity . . . be construed in favour of the liberty of the subject".

[303] *Barty v Hill*, 1907 S.C. (J.) 36; *Remmington v Larchin* [1921] 3 K.B. 404.

while considerations of hardship or apparent injustice are irrelevant if the meaning of the statute is clear,[304] it is a recognised rule that no one is to be subjected to taxation unless his case comes within the letter of the law,[305] and that no one can claim exemption from a general tax unless his case is expressly provided for.[306] A Private Act of Parliament, obtained by a public body or company, is to be read as a contract between them and the public, expressed in terms which they have chosen and, therefore, subject to the rule of construction *verba interpretanda sunt contra proferentes*, so that no privilege or right is conferred, unless the words founded on as conferring it are unambiguous.[307]

Ejusdem generis rule—When a list of things to which the statute is to apply is **1.46** given followed by words of wide general import, the normal rule of construction, known as the rule of construction ejusdem generis (literally "of the same kind"), is that the general words apply only to things of the same kind as those in the preceding list. So where betting was prohibited "in any house, office, room or other place" it was held, construing the term "other place" as a place of the same kind as a house, office or room, that the Act did not apply to a racecourse.[308] This rule of construction is a presumption only and may yield to the argument that the statutory provision was intended to be general, and that the list was given merely as an illustration.[309] It does not apply unless the things mentioned have some common and dominant feature. Where it was provided that a landlord, on certain specified conditions, might resume possession of the subjects let for "building, feuing, planting or other purposes", it was held that as building, feuing and planting could not be ascribed to any one genus there was no ground for limiting the generality of the words "or other purposes".[310]

Permissive words—When the words of a statute are permissive, where, for **1.47** instance, it is provided that a party "may" perform a certain act, or that "it shall be lawful" for him to perform it, the general construction is, in accordance with the maxim *cuilibet licet renunciare juri pro se introducto* (anyone can renounce a right conceived in his own favour), that an option is conferred, and no obligation imposed.[311] But if such words are employed in a statute dealing with a matter in which the general public have an interest, permissive words may be read as imperative. So where a statute authorised road trustees to make and keep highways 20 feet in width it was held that an obligation to keep highways of that width was

---

[304] *Duncan v Inland Revenue*, 1923 S.C. 388.

[305] *Coltness Iron Co v Black* (1881) 8 R. (HL) 67 at 72, per Lord Blackburn; *Tennant v Smith* (1892) 19 R. (HL) 1; *Scottish Milk Marketing Board v Ferrier*, 1936 S.C. (HL) 39.

[306] *Gillanders v Campbell* (1884) 12 R. 309.

[307] *Countess of Rothes v Kirkcaldy Water Works* (1882) 9 R. (HL) 108; *Milligan v Ayr Harbour Trustees*, 1915 S.C. 937; *North British Ry v Birrell's Trs*, 1918 S.C. (HL) 33 at 52; *Holburnhead Salmon Fishing Co v Scrabster Harbour Trs*, 1982 S.C. 65.

[308] *Henretty v Hart* (1885) 13 R. (J.) 9; cf. *Dawson v Wright*, 1924 J.C. 121; *Murray v Keith* (1894) 22 R. (J.) 16; *Chernack v Mill*, 1938 J.C. 39; English cases are referred to in Cross, *Statutory Interpretation* (1995) and in Bennion, *Statutory Interpretation* (2007).

[309] *Symington v Symington's Quarries* (1905) 8 F. 121; *Baird v Lees*, 1924 S.C. 83. See *Quazi v Quazi* [1980] A.C. 744 at 823, per Lord Scarman; *Cormack v Crown Estate Commissioners*, 1985 S.L.T. 426.

[310] *Crichton Stuart v Ogilvie*, 1914 S.C. 888; see also *Clark's Tr., Noter*, 1993 S.L.T. 667 and *Secretary of State for Social Security v McSherry*, 1995 S.L.T. 371.

[311] *Julius v Bishop of Oxford* (1880) 5 App. Cas. 214; *Fleming & Ferguson v Burgh of Paisley*, 1948 S.C. 547.

inferred.[312] Where a discretionary power is conferred on a court or on a public body, the statute, however absolute its terms may be, is to be construed subject to the implied limitation that the power is to be exercised in a judicial spirit, and under the conditions observed in judicial proceedings.[313]

1.48 *Casus omissus* **and** *casus improvisus*—Circumstances may arise which show that a particular case has been overlooked by the framers of a statute. It is permissible for the court "in discharging its interpretative function" to "add words, or omit words or substitute words" where there are "plain cases of drafting mistakes".[314] The power is to be exercised with "considerable caution" to avoid "the appearance of judicial legislation".[315] It will be applied where a court is

> "abundantly sure of three matters: (1) the intended purpose of the statute or provision in question; (2) that by inadvertence the draftsman and Parliament failed to give effect to that purpose in the provision in question; and (3) the substance of the provision Parliament would have made, although not necessarily the precise words Parliament would have used, had the error in the Bill been noticed".[316]

However, the satisfaction of these necessary conditions does not mean that the court will always act if "the insertion . . . [is] too big, or too much at variance with the language used by legislature", or the statute requires "strict interpretation", e.g. a penal statute.[317] However, in non-contentious procedure, an application to the Court of Session under the *nobile officium*, or equitable power, may get over the difficulty caused by a *casus improvisus* (an unforeseen case) in a statute. Thus, the court has power to dispense with a statutory formality in a case where, owing to circumstances overlooked in the statute, its observance has been found to be impossible.[318] Though there was no statutory provision for the resuscitation of a company more than two years after its dissolution, it was held to be within the power of the court,[319] and where there was no statutory power to recall a sequestration the court declared it at an end.[320] The limits of the power of the Court of Session in virtue of its *nobile officium* have not been determined, but if a statutory right is given to certain specified persons it cannot, even in a case where there is no opposition, be extended to others.[321]

---

[312] *Gray v St Andrew's District Committee*, 1911 S.C. 266; cf. *Julius v Bishop of Oxford* (1880) 5 App. Cas. 214. See Maxwell, *Interpretation of Statutes* (1969), p.234.

[313] *Macbeth v Ashley* (1874) 1 R. (HL) 14; *Goodall v Bilsland*, 1909 S.C. 1152; *Sharp v Wakefeld* [1891] A.C. 173.

[314] *Inco Europe Ltd v First Choice Distribution (a firm)* [2000] 1 W.L.R. 586 at 592, per Lord Nicholls of Birkenhead. See too *McDermott v Owners of S.S. Tintorento* [1911] A.C. 35; *Bradley v Motherwell District Council*, 1994 S.L.T. 739 at 741–742, applying *Tinkham v Perry* [1951] 1 T.L.R. 91 at 92. See, however, *Piggins & Rix Ltd v Montrose Port Authority*, 1995 S.L.T. 418, where a plea of casus omissus failed.

[315] *Inco Europe Ltd v First Choice Distribution (a firm)* [2000] 1 W.L.R. 586 at 592, per Lord Nicholls of Birkenhead. In *Scottish Water v Clydecare Ltd*, 2003 S.C. 330 and *BP Oil (UK) Ltd v City of Edinburgh Licensing Board* [2011] CSIH 29; 2011 S.C. 632 the court recognised the principle but refused to rectify.

[316] *Inco Europe* [2000] 1 W.L.R. 586 at 592.

[317] *Inco Europe* [2000] 1 W.L.R. 586.

[318] *Roberts* (1901) 3 F. 779; *Train & McIntyre*, 1923 S.C. 291. In *Murray v Comptroller General of Patents*, 1932 S.C. 726, an Outer House judge took similar action.

[319] *Forth Shipbreaking Co*, 1924 S.C. 489.

[320] *Craig & Co*, 1946 S.C. 19.

[321] *Crichton Stuart's Tutrix*, 1921 S.C. 840. See opinions in *Gibson's Trs, Petrs*, 1933 S.C. 190.

Sources of common law—Rules of law which are not referable to any legislative **1.49** enactment constitute the common law. It is spoken of by Lord Stair as "our ancient and immemorial customs", in which he includes the law of succession,[322] and the law, in so far as not affected by statute, of feudal conveyancing.[323] The origin of these customs is not in every case ascertainable; but it is clear that the common law of Scotland is in considerable measure derived from the civil law; to a lesser extent but in important particulars, from the canon law.[324] Though there was probably no period at which the civil law was accounted part of the law of Scotland, that law, as explained and in some respects amended by the Dutch and French commentators of the sixteenth and seventeenth centuries, is the basis of the Scots law of contract and of property, apart from feudal conveyancing.[325] Before the Reformation, much of the judicial business of Scotland was carried on in the ecclesiastical courts with an ultimate appeal to the Papal Court at Rome, and the canon law as the law there administered. By the Act 1567, cap.31, the authority of the canon law was expressly repudiated, but its influence remained especially in the law relating to marriage and the domestic relations.[326] For over 150 years, the chief external factor, apart from legislation, in the development of the law of Scotland has been the law of England, although the effect of EU Law is of increasing importance. The development of the common law may also be affected by the ECHR and the courts' duty as public authorities to act in accordance with Convention rights.[327]

Custom as forming law—Custom may still be recognised as a source of law, **1.50** whether in the form of usage of trade,[328] or of local custom affecting rights of property,[329] or of usage sanctioning some particular method of government in a burgh,[330] or determining the jurisdiction of a particular court[331] but the invocation of rights based on custom as a source of law is rare in modern times.

"Broadly speaking, custom may be said to be the product of generally accepted usage and practice. It has no formal sanction or authority behind it other than the general consensus of opinion within the community."[332]

Usage amounting to a rule of law is distinguishable from the more common case where it is appealed to as importing an unexpressed term into a contract. There, as its recognition is based on implied agreement, knowledge or notice of the usage must be brought home to the party against whom it is pleaded[333]; whereas if the

---

[322] As to the origin of the law of succession in moveables, see *Sommervill v Murray's Creditors* (1744) Mor. 3902.

[323] Stair, I, 1, 16.

[324] See further, Reid and Zimmermann, *History of Private Law in Scotland* (2000), Vols I ("Introduction and Property") and II ("Obligations").

[325] See, as to contrast with English law, *Cantiere San Rocco v Clyde Shipbuilding Co*, 1923 S.C. (HL) 105; *Sinclair v Brougham* [1914] A.C. 398, opinion of Lord Dunedin.

[326] *Collins v Collins* (1884) 11 R. (HL) 19; *Purves's Trs v Purves* (1895) 22 R. 513.

[327] Human Rights Act 1998 s.6; and see above, para.1.22.

[328] *Bechaunaland Exploration Co v London Trading Bank* [1898] 2 Q.B. 658; *Clydesdale Bank Nominees v Snodgrass*, 1939 S.C. 805 (Stock Exchange); *Wilkie v Scottish Aviation*, 1956 S.C. 198.

[329] *Learmonth v Sinclair's Trs* (1878) 5 R. 548.

[330] *Gardner v Magistrates of Kilrenny* (1828) 6 S. 693; *Magistrates of Dunbar v Duchess of Roxburghe* (1835) 1 Shaw and McL. 134 at 195; Erskine, I, 1, 20.

[331] *Neilson v Vallance* (1828) 7 S. 182; *Duncan v Lodijensky* (1904) 6 F. 408.

[332] *Snell v Beadle* [2001] 2 A.C. 304 at 312, [17], per Lord Hope of Craighead.

[333] See below, para.6.18.

usage has acquired the force of law it falls under the general rule that everyone is supposed to know the law, and knowledge or notice is immaterial.[334] Thus,

> "as soon as custom is changed into formal or positive law by judicial decision or by statute it ceases to be custom. Authority is given to the law by the decision of the court or by the statute."[335]

It is not possible to formulate exact rules as to the cases where a custom will be recognised as part of the common law. It need not be universal throughout Scotland; a special form of land tenure, prevailing in one locality only, has been recognised.[336] It cannot prevail against the express terms of a statute,[337] though it may be of material importance when the plea is taken that a statute is in desuetude.[338] A usage of trade that the transfer of a document of title to goods gives a real right to the goods has been uniformly held to be a misunderstanding of a general principle of law, to which no effect could be given.[339] The court refused to sanction, on the plea of customary law, a local usage, under which a certain class of creditors, without resort to legal process, satisfied their debts by seizing the property of their debtors.[340] And a usage must be reasonably fair. So it was held that a custom, proved to exist in Shetland, by which landlords claimed a third of the proceeds of whales killed on shore, had not the force of law, in respect that it amounted to an exaction for which no return was given.[341]

1.51　Authorities—The question whether a particular rule is recognised as part of the common law must be determined, except in the case where appeal is made to a custom or usage hitherto unrecognised, by consideration of the authorities. The authorities may be statements by legal writers, or reports of decided cases. The works of certain authors, usually referred to as the institutional writers, are, in Scotland, treated with exceptional respect. Of these, the chief ones, in questions of general law, are: Viscount Stair, Lord Bankton, Erskine and Bell; in the special sphere of criminal law: Hume[342] and Alison. The authority of decisions as establishing a rule of law was at one time not fully recognised. Erskine lays it down that a decision, even of the House of Lords, is not binding when the same question is raised between different parties, though he admits that a series of decisions should be respected.[343] And there is relatively modern sanction for the statement that a case is an authority only for what it actually decides, not for a proposition which may seem to follow logically from it.[344] In practice, however, more deference is

---

[334] *Learmonth v Sinclair's Trs* (1878) 5 R. 548.

[335] *Snell v Beadle* [2001] 2 A.C. 304 at 312, [18], per Lord Hope of Craighead.

[336] Kindly Tenants of Lochmaben. See J. Rankine, *The Law of Leases in Scotland*, 3rd edn (Edinburgh: W. Green, 1916), p.153; *Marquis of Queensberry v Wright* (1838) 16 S. 439; *Royal Four Towns Fishing Association v Dumfries Assessor*, 1956 S.C. 379. Not all local law is customary, however; the relics of udal law, especially udal tenure in Shetland, are attributable to the ancient connection with Norway, see *Lord Advocate v University of Aberdeen*, 1963 S.C. 533.

[337] See *Walker Trs v Lord Advocate*, 1912 S.C. (HL) 12.

[338] See above, para.1.34.

[339] *Anderson v McCall* (1866) 4 M. 765; *Dobell v Neilson* (1904) 7 F. 281.

[340] *Brodie v Watson* (1714) Mor. 14757.

[341] *Bruce v Smith* (1890) 17 R. 1000.

[342] Hume's Lectures, published posthumously and not prepared for publication by him, are not regarded as books of institutional authority: *Fortington v Lord Kinnaird*, 1942 S.C. 239.

[343] Erskine, I, 1, 17. And see *Sugden v HM Advocate*, 1934 J.C. 127, where Lord Murray doubts whether the modern rule of stare decisis binds the High Court of Justiciary.

[344] *Quinn v Leathem* [1901] A.C. 495, opinion of Lord Chancellor Halsbury.

paid to authority than these statements would suggest. A case two centuries old has been held binding in the Outer House[345] and decisions of the House of Lords, however elderly, will also be followed.[346] The authority of a case depends upon the jurisdiction of the court by which it was pronounced. The decision of a sheriff principal is not binding outside his sheriffdom; the decision of the Court of Session is not binding on the House of Lords, though a decision which has ruled practice for a number of years will not readily be overturned merely because it is thought to be unfounded.[347] The decision of a single judge in the High Court of Justiciary is binding on a sheriff, it seems,[348] and it has been suggested that, by analogy, an Outer House decision binds a sheriff.[349] A decision of the UK Supreme Court, as with a decision of the House of Lords, in a Scots appeal, is binding on all courts in Scotland. A decision of the House of Lords in such an appeal was also binding on the House itself, in so far as Scots law is concerned.[350] The House of Lords resolved however, that it might depart from a previous decision when it appears right to do so.[351] In establishing the UK Supreme Court, the Constitutional Reform Act 2005 provided that in devolution matters the Supreme Court was not bound by its earlier decisions but is otherwise silent on the matter. It may be that the Supreme Court will follow the former practice of the House of Lords. The power to depart from an earlier decision was exercised sparingly, and according to stated principles, but the fact that a case cannot be brought within the formulae used in other cases was not fatal to exercise of the power.[352] There normally had to have been some change of circumstances.[353] This discretion to depart would only be exercised in rare cases, such as in questions relating to the construction of statutes[354] and in matters of commercial law where there is a special need for certainty, consistency and continuity.[355] The power was also been exercised in relation to the evolution of the law of negligence.[356] A decision of the House of Lords in an English appeal not turning on the interpretation of a statute applicable to both countries is not binding in Scotland, though if it proceeded on grounds of general jurisprudence and not on any specialty of English law, it ought to be treated with great respect.[357] With the exception of devolution issues, the

---

[345] *American Express Europe Ltd v Royal Bank of Scotland Plc (No.2)*, 1989 S.L.T. 650.

[346] See, e.g. *Little Cumbrae Estate Ltd v Island of Little Cumbrae Ltd* [2007] CSIH 35; 2007 S.C. 525.

[347] *Kirkpatrick's Trs v Kirkpatrick* (1874) 1 R. (HL) 37, qualified in *Nicol's Trs v Sutherland*, 1951 S.C. (HL) 21.

[348] *Jessop v Stevenson*, 1988 J.C. 17.

[349] *Cromarty Leasing Ltd v Turnbull*, 1988 S.L.T. (Sh. Ct) 62; *Chalmers v Trs of the Harbours of Peterhead*, 1991 S.L.T. 98 at 101. Cf. *Farrell v Farrell*, 1990 S.C.L.R. 717; G. Maher, "Precedent, the Sheriff Court, and Colleges of Justice", 1988 S.L.T. (News) 209.

[350] *London Street Tramways Co v London C.C.* [1898] A.C. 375. The House of Lords, in an English appeal, may apply Scots law, if that is the proper law, even though the Scots law has not been proved in the court below; see *Elliot v Joicey*, 1935 S.C. (HL) 57.

[351] *Practice Statement (Judicial Precedent)* [1966] 1 W.L.R. 1234. See, e.g. *Dick v Burgh of Falkirk*, 1976 S.C. (HL) 1.

[352] *Vestey v I.R.C.* [1980] A.C. 1148.

[353] *Miliangos v George Frank (Textiles) Ltd* [1976] A.C. 443; *Fitzleet Estates Ltd v Cherry* [1977] 1 W.L.R. 1345; *Hesperides Hotels Ltd v Muftizade* [1979] A.C. 508.

[354] *R. v National Insurance Commissioner, Ex p. Hudson* [1972] A.C. 944.

[355] *Paal Wilson & Co A/S v Partenreederei Hannah Blumenthal* [1983] 1 A.C. 854.

[356] *Murphy v Brentwood District Council* [1991] 1 A.C. 398 (overruling *Anns v Merton London Borough Council* [1978] A.C. 728); *Hall (Arthur J.S.) & Co (a firm) v Simons* [2002] 1 A.C. 615 (overruling *Rondel v Worsley* [1969] 1 A.C. 191).

[357] *Orr Ewing's Trs v Orr Ewing* (1885) 13 R. (HL) 1 at 3, per Lord Chancellor Selborne; but see *Glasgow Corp v Central Land Board*, 1956 S.C. (HL) 1. See *Dalgleish v Glasgow Corp*, 1976 S.C. 32 at 51–53, per Lord Justice-Clerk Wheatley.

constitution of the UK Supreme Court maintains the rule that it sits as the Supreme Court in the legal system of the constituent part of the UK from which the appeal comes.[358] Following the Scotland Act 1998, and until the establishment of the UK Supreme Court, the Judicial Committee of the Privy Council[359] was the final appellate court on "devolution issues",[360] and formed part of the Scottish legal system.[361] An opinion by a judge on a point not necessary to the judgment (obiter dictum) has an authority varying with the reputation of the judge and the standing of the court. A decision clearly in point may be challenged on the ground that it is inconsistent with prior authorities which were not brought to the notice of the court[362]; that it proceeded upon views of morality, political economy, or religious observance which are no longer held in esteem[363]; that it had as its basis some theory of physical fact which modern science has shown to be baseless[364]; or that a statutory alteration of the law has altered the basis on which the previous decision rested.[365]

FURTHER READING

Bankton, *Institute* (1753), I, 1.

Beatson, J., Groz, S., Hickman, T., Singh, R. with Palmer, S., *Human Rights: Judicial Protection in the United Kingdom* (London: Sweet and Maxwell, 2008).

Bennion, F.A.R., *Statutory Interpretation: A Code*, 5th edn (London: LexisNexis, 2007).

Birks, P., *English Private Law*, edited by Burrows, A., 2nd edn, 2 vols (Oxford: Oxford University Press, 2007).

Boyle, A., Himsworth, C., Loux, A., and MacQueen, H., *Human Rights and Scots Law* (Oxford: Hart, 2002).

Craies Legislation: A Practitioner's Guide to the Nature, Process, Effect and Interpretation of Legislation, 9th edn (London: Sweet and Maxwell, 2008).

Brealey, M. and Hoskins, M., *Remedies in EC Law*, 2nd edn (London: Sweet and Maxwell,1998).

Brent, R., *Directive: Rights and Remedies in English and Community Law* (London: Sweet and Maxwell, 2001).

Clayton, R., and Tomlinson, H., *The Law of Human Rights*, 2nd edn (Oxford: Oxford University Press, 2009).

Clyde, Lord and Edwards, D., *Judicial Review in Scotland* (Edinburgh: W. Green, 2000).

Cooper, Lord, Meston, M.C., Sellar, W.D.H., *The Scots Legal Tradition,* edited by Styles, S. (Saltire Society, 1991).

---

[358] Constitutional Reform Act 2005 s.40(2).

[359] See Scotland Act 1998 s.32(4) and s.103 concerning the composition of the Judicial Committee.

[360] See Scotland Act 1998 s.98 and Sch.6.

[361] *Montgomery v HM Advocate*, 2001 S.C. (PC) 1 at 13, per Lord Hope of Craighead.

[362] *Mitchell v Mackersy* (1905) 8 F. 198.

[363] *Bowman v Secular Society* [1917] A.C. 406; *Commerzbank Aktiengesellschaft v Large*, 1977 S.C. 375.

[364] *Welldon v Butterley Coal Co* [1920] 1 Ch. 130.

[365] *Beith's Trs v Beith*, 1950 S.C. 66; *Douglas-Hamilton v Duke & Duchess of Hamilton's Trs*, 1961 S.C. 205 at 217, per Lord President Clyde. The course of subsequent development of the common law is not such a ground; see *Weir v J.M. Hodge & Son*, 1990 S.L.T. 266.

Cross, R., Bells, J., Engele, G., *Statutory Interpretation*, 3rd edn (Oxford: Oxford University Press, 1995).

Erskine, *Institute* (1772, edited by Nicolson, 1871), I, 1.

Gordon, R., Ward, T., Eicke, T., *The Strasbourg Case Law: Leading Cases from the European Human Rights Reports* (London: Sweet and Maxwell, 2001).

Gordon, W.M., *Scottish Land Law*, 3rd edn (Edinburgh: W. Green, 2009).

Himsworth, C.M.G. and Munro, C.R., *The Scotland Act 1998*, 2nd edn (Edinburgh: W. Green, 2000).

Himsworth, C.M.G. and O'Neill, C.M., *Scotland's Constitution: Law and Practice*, 3rd edn (London: Bloomsbury, 2009).

Jarvis, M.A., *The Application of EC Law to National Courts* (Oxford: Oxford University Press, 1998).

Lester, Lord of Herne Hill and Pannick, D. (eds), *Human Rights Law and Practice*, 2nd edn (Butterworths, 2004).

McFadden, J. and Lazarowicz, L., *The Scottish Parliament: An Introduction*, 4th edn (Bloomsbury, 2010).

MacQueen, H.L. and Thomson, J., *Contract Law in Scotland*, 3rd edn ((Haywards Heath: Bloomsbury Professional, 2012).

Munro, C.R., *Studies in Constitutional Law*, 2nd edn (Oxford: Oxford University Press, 1999).

Munro, J., *Public Law*, 2nd edn (Edinburgh: W. Green, 2007).

Page, A., Reid, C. and Ross, A., *A Guide to the Scotland Act 1998* (Edinburgh: Butterworths, 1999).

Palmer, V.V., *Mixed Jurisdictions Worldwide: The Third Legal Family* (Cambridge: Cambridge University Press, 2001).

Reed, Lord and Murdoch, J., *Human Rights Law in Scotland* (Edinburgh: Bloomsbury, 2011).

Reid, K.G.C, *The Law of Property in Scotland* (Edinburgh: Butterworths, 1995).

Reid, K.G.C. and Zimmermann, R., *A History of Private Law in Scotland*, Vols I ("Introduction and Property") and II ("Obligations") (Oxford: Oxford University Press, 2000).

Smith, T.B., *Short Commentary on the Law of Scotland* (Edinburgh: W. Green, 1962).

Sources and Literature of Scots Law (Edinburgh: Stair Society, 1936).

Stair, *Institutions of the Law of Scotland* (1681, edited by More, 1832), I, 1.

Stair Memorial Encyclopaedia, Vol.22, paras 35–393.

Walker, D.M., *Principles of Scottish Private Law*, 4th edn, 4 vols (Oxford: Clarendon Press, 1988).

Walker, D.M., *The Scottish Legal System*, 8th edn (London: Sweet and Maxwell, 2001).

Weatherill, S. and Beaumont, P., *EU Law*, 3rd edn (Penguin, 1999).

Zimmermann, R. and Visser, D., *Southern Cross: Civil Law and Common Law in South Africa* (Oxford: Clarendon Press, 1996).

Zimmermann, R., Visser, D. and Reid, K.G.C., *Mixed Legal Systems in Comparative Perspective: Property and Obligations in Scotland and South Africa* (Oxford: Oxford University Press, 2004).

CHAPTER 2

COURTS AND JURISDICTION: ARBITRATION

I. COURTS AND TRIBUNALS

Final courts of appeal: Historical—Prior to the establishment of the Supreme **2.01**
Court of the United Kingdom and its commencing hearing appeals in October
2009, the House of Lords was the ultimate court of appeal in a civil case originating in Scotland. The House of Lords inherited the jurisdiction recognised in
the Claim of Right 1689, whereby the litigant might petition the King and
Parliament for "remeed of law", which had been exercised by the Scots Parliament
prior to the Union in 1707.[1] Until 1876 there was no definite distinction between
the House of Lords as a legislative and as a judicial body. By the Appellate
Jurisdiction Act 1876, provision was made for the appointment of judicial officers,
known as Lords of Appeal in Ordinary, and no appeal could be heard unless
three of those were present. There was no appeal to the House of Lords from
the High Court of Justiciary.[2] Prior to the Scotland Act 1998, the Judicial
Committee of the Privy Council exercised judicial functions in Scottish cases
only under a limited number of particular statutes.[3] During the interval of approxi-
mately a decade between the entry into force of the Scotland Act and the coming
into operation of the Supreme Court of the United Kingdom, the Judicial
Committee of the Privy Council had jurisdiction to hear and determine "devolution issues" arising under the Scotland Act. That jurisdiction was transferred to
the UK Supreme Court by virtue of s.40(4)(b) of and Sch.9 to the Constitutional
Reform Act 2005.

The Supreme Court of the United Kingdom—As already indicated, Pt 3 of the **2.02**
Constitutional Reform Act 2005 provided for the replacement of the appellate
jurisdiction of the House of Lords and the devolution issues jurisdiction of the
Privy Council by a new Supreme Court of the United Kingdom.[4] The court came
into practical existence in October 2009, and is located in the former Middlesex
Guildhall opposite the Houses of Parliament in Westminster. The persons who
immediately before the commencement of the court were Lords of Appeal in
Ordinary became judges of the Supreme Court, and are styled "Justices of the
Supreme Court". Those appointed to the Court after its inception are accorded the
courtesy title of "Lord" or "Lady" as the case may be. The senior and second

---

[1] For a discussion of the controversy leading to the Claim of Right 1689, see *Stair Memorial Encyclopaedia*, Vol.6, "Courts and Competency", paras 808–9.
[2] Criminal Procedure (Scotland) Act 1995 s.124(2); *Mackintosh v Lord Advocate* (1876) 3 R. (HL) 34; *Hoekstra v HM Advocate (No.5)*, 2001 S.C. (PC) 37.
[3] For example, Medical Act 1983 s.40; *McAllister v General Medical Council* [1993] A.C. 388.
[4] See Constitutional Reform Act 2005 ss.23, 40 and Sch.9.

senior Lords of Appeal in Ordinary became respectively the President and Deputy President of the court.[5] The court consists of 12 judges, although there is provision for the appointment of supplementary judges.[6] It is duly constituted for any proceedings only if there is an uneven number of judges (three or more), of whom more than half are permanent judges.[7] The Act states that the court is "a superior court of record".[8] A decision of the court on appeal from a Scottish court other than on devolution issues is to be regarded as a decision of a Scottish court; but a decision on a devolution matter is binding in all legal proceedings save those before the court itself when making a decision on such a matter.[9]

2.03 Appeals to the Supreme Court of the United Kingdom—The Constitutional Reform Act 2005 s.40(3) provides that an appeal lies to the Supreme Court from any order or judgment of a court in Scotland if an appeal lay from that court to the House of Lords immediately before the commencement of the section. Accordingly, the scope for appeal from a court in Scotland to the new UK Supreme Court continues the pre-existing scope of appeal to the House of Lords. Therefore—with the exception of "devolution issues"—no appeal lies to the UK Supreme Court from decisions of the High Court of Justiciary.[10] As respects civil cases, any final judgment of the Court of Session is subject to appeal, except in cases where appeal is excluded by statute,[11] or where the question is one of expenses only.[12] If the Court of Session, on an appeal from the sheriff court, has made findings-in-fact, appeal to the House of Lords was—and thus to the UK Supreme Court is—restricted to questions of law.[13] If the Court of Session has made alterations to the sheriff's findings-in-fact, consideration may be given to the opinion of the Court of Session in order to resolve any ambiguity in the findings in fact.[14] An interlocutory judgment (i.e. one which does not dispose of the whole cause) may be appealed if the judges were not unanimous, or, in any case, with the leave of the court.[15] Leave to appeal may also be required under particular statutes.[16] Leave will not normally be granted by the Court of Session if the appellant proposes to make a legal submission which was not made before the Inner

---

[5] Constitutional Reform Act 2005 ss.23, 24.

[6] Constitutional Reform Act 2005 ss.23(2), 39.

[7] Constitutional Reform Act 2005 s.42.

[8] Constitutional Reform Act 2005 s.40(1). The statement appears to be of no significance in the context of Scots law—see *Eba v Advocate General for Scotland* [2011] UKSC 29; 2012 S.C. (UKSC) 1; 2011 S.L.T 768, per Lord Hope at [16].

[9] Constitutional Reform Act 2005 s.41.

[10] Criminal Procedure (Scotland) Act 1995 s.124(2); *Mackintosh v Lord Advocate* (1876) 3 R. (HL) 34; *Hoekstra v HM Advocate (No.5)*, 2001 S.C. (PC) 37.

[11] e.g. Agricultural Holdings (Scotland) Act 1991 Sch.7 para.21; Children (Scotland) Act 1995 s.51; *John G. McGregor (Contractors) Ltd v Grampian R.C. (No.2)*, 1991 S.C. (HL) 1.

[12] *Caledonian Ry v Barrie* (1903) 5 F. (HL) 10.

[13] Court of Session Act 1988 s.32(5); *Bogota v Alconda*, 1924 S.C. (HL) 66; *Crerar v Bank of Scotland*, 1922 S.C. (HL) 137; *Sutherland v Glasgow Corp*, 1951 S.C. (HL) 1; *Marshall v William Sharp & Sons Ltd*, 1991 S.L.T. 114; *Laing v Scottish Grain Distillers Ltd*, 1992 S.C. (HL) 65; *Wilson v Jaymarke Estates Ltd* [2007] UKHL 29; 2007 S.C. (HL) 135.

[14] *Martinez v Grampian Health Board*, 1996 S.C. (HL) 1; 1996 S.L.T. 69.

[15] Court of Session Act 1988 s.40(1); *Ross v Ross*, 1927 S.C. (HL) 4; *Adelphi Hotel (Glasgow) v Walker & Eglinton Hotels (Scotland)*, 1960 S.C. 182 (interlocutor granting interim interdict). An appeal now lies, without leave, from an interlocutor granting a motion for a new trial (1988 Act s.40(2)).

[16] e.g. Tribunals and Inquiries Act 1992 s.11(7)(d) (as amended by the Constitutional Reform Act 2005 Sch.9 Pt I para.59); Transport Act 1985 s.9(9).

House.[17] The scope for appeal in respect of devolution issues may be summarised thus. An appeal to the UK Supreme Court may be made from a decision of the Inner House without leave.[18] An appeal from two or more judges sitting in the High Court of Justiciary, or from a court from which there is no appeal to the Supreme Court, can be made, but only with leave of the original court or of the UK Supreme Court.[19] Devolution issues may also be referred to the UK Supreme Court from the Inner House, High Court of Justiciary, the Courts of Appeal in England and Wales and in Northern Ireland, and by the Law Officers.[20] A decision of the UK Supreme Court in relation to proceedings under the 1998 Act is binding in all legal proceedings.[21] Where leave is required to be sought from the UK Supreme Court[22] the application for permission is required to be made within 28 days. Where leave is not required, the time for lodging the appeal is 42 days.[23]

The Court of Session—The Court of Session was established in 1532, super- **2.04** seding the jurisdiction of the Lords Auditors, a committee of Parliament, and courts known as the Session and the Daily Council, of which little is known.[24] As originally constituted, it consisted of 14 ordinary judges, with a President. The King had power to nominate Extraordinary Lords, who might sit and vote, but this power was abolished by 10 Geo. I, c.19. Until 1808 all the judges sat together in the Inner House as a *collegium*, sending by rotation one of their body, known as a Lord Ordinary, to hear cases as a judge of first instance in the Outer House. In 1808 and in 1825 the court was reorganised.[25] It was divided into the First Division, presided over by the Lord President; the Second Division, presided over by the Lord Justice-Clerk, these two divisions constituting the Inner House; and the permanent Lords Ordinary. Ten judges, including the Lord President and Lord Justice-Clerk, are allocated to the two Divisions of the Inner House,[26] and the remainder sit as Lords Ordinary in the Outer House. The maximum number of judges—also known as "Senators of the College of Justice"—that may be appointed is now 34,[27] and the retirement age is 70.[28] Temporary judges can be appointed to the Court of Session and their tenure does not conflict with the European Convention on Human Rights.[29] The Court of Session, as now existing, is a combination of two courts—the Inner House, with a jurisdiction mainly appellate, and the Outer House, a court of first instance. For detailed information as to the jurisdiction and procedure of the Court of Session, works devoted to

---

[17] *Strathclyde R.C. v Gallagher*, 1995 S.L.T. 747.

[18] Scotland Act 1998 Sch.6 para.12.

[19] Scotland Act 1998 Sch.6 para.13; *Follen v HM Advocate*, 2001 S.C. (PC) 105.

[20] Scotland Act 1998 Sch.6 paras 10, 11, 22, 30, 32, 33 and 34.

[21] Constitutional Reform Act 2005 s.41(3)(b); cf. Scotland Act 1998 s.103.

[22] Supreme Court Rules 2009 (SI 2009/1603) r.11

[23] Supreme Court Rules 2009 r.19.

[24] See J.W. Cairns, in *Stair Society Miscellany V* (Edinburgh: Stair Society, 2006); A.M. Godfrey, *Civil Justice in Renaissance Scotland: The Origins of a Central Court (Medieval Law and its Practice)* (Leiden: Brill, 2009).

[25] 48 Geo. III, c.151; 6 Geo. IV, c.120.

[26] Number of Inner House Judges (Variation) Order 2001 (SSI 2001/41); in practice, it is now unusual for more than three judges to sit in a Division.

[27] Court of Session Act 1988 s.1(1) as amended by the Maximum Number of Judges (Scotland) Order 2004 (SSI 2004/499).

[28] Judicial Pensions and Retirement Act 1993 s.26 (subject to transitional provisions).

[29] Law Reform (Miscellaneous Provisions) (Scotland) Act 1990 s.35(3); *Clancy v Caird (No.2)*, 2000 S.C. 441.

procedure must be consulted.[30] Speaking generally, the Inner House sits as a court of appeal from the judgments of the Lords Ordinary or of any inferior civil court,[31] except in actions where the value, exclusive of interest and expenses, does not exceed £5,000[32] or where the inferior court is by statute declared to be final.[33] It also sits as a court of appeal from various statutory tribunals. In the Outer House, actions may be brought originally, with the exception of actions where the value, exclusive of interest and expenses, does not exceed £5,000[34] and excluding certain actions where special statutory procedure is enjoined.[35] The criminal jurisdiction of the Court of Session, which at one time included cases of forgery, is in modern times confined to the imposition of penalties for breach of interdict or other contempt of court. The High Court of Admiralty (1681–1830), the Court of Exchequer (1707–1854)[36] and the Jury Court (1815–1830) are now merged in the Court of Session. The Registration Appeal Court is part of the Court of Session for the purpose of making a declaration of legislative incompatibility under s.4 of the Human Rights Act 1998.[37]

2.05 Court of Session: Judicial review—In addition to its ordinary functions, the Court of Session has a general power to review, by suspension or reduction, the judgments of inferior courts or persons vested with judicial or administrative authority, on the ground that they have exceeded the jurisdiction committed to them, have contravened the principles of natural justice, or have been guilty of error in procedure so fundamental as to make their decision a nullity.[38]

> "Wherever any inferior tribunal or any administrative body has exceeded the powers conferred upon it by statute to the prejudice of the subject, the jurisdiction of the Court to set aside such excess of power as incompetent and illegal is not open to dispute."[39]

---

[30] See A.J.G. Mackay, *The Practice of the Court of Session*, 2 Vols (Edinburgh: T & T Clark, 1877–79); A.J.G. Mackay, *Manual of Practice in the Court of Session* (Edinburgh: William Green & Sons, 1893); J.A. Maclaren, *Court of Session Practice* (Edinburgh: W. Green & Son Ltd, 1916); D. Maxwell, *The Practice of the Court of Session* (Scottish Courts Admnistration, 1980); D.J.D. Macfadyen (ed.), *Court of Session Practice* (Bloomsbury Professional).

[31] Erskine, I, iii, 20; *Jeffray v Angus*, 1909 S.C. 400.

[32] Sheriff Courts (Scotland) Act 1907 s.7, as most recently amended by the Sheriff Courts (Scotland) Act 1971 (Privative Jurisdiction and Summary Cause) Order 2007 (SSI 2007/507). See also para.2.08, below. As to what is meant by "value", see *Brady v Napier*, 1944 S.C. 18.

[33] *Adair v Colville*, 1926 S.C. (HL) 51; *Arcari v Dumbartonshire County Council*, 1948 S.C. 62; *Neill's Tr. v Macfarlane's Trs*, 1952 S.C. 356.

[34] Sheriff Courts (Scotland) Act 1971 s.31 as amended; cf. fn.54, below.

[35] Questions involving important patrimonial interests in Church matters may be outside the purview of the Court of Session: see *Ballantyne v Presbytery of Wigtown*, 1936 S.C. 625; *Logan v Presbytery of Dumbarton*, 1995 S.L.T. 1228.

[36] See *Inland Revenue v Barrs*, 1961 S.C. (HL) 22.

[37] *Smith v Scott*, 2007 S.C. 345.

[38] The nature and history of the supervisory jurisdiction of the Court of Session are fully discussed in the important case of *West v Secretary of State for Scotland*, 1992 S.C. 385. See also *Stair Memorial Encyclopaedia*, Reissue, "Administrative Law", paras 4 and 5; Clyde and Edwards, *Judicial Review in Scotland* (Edinburgh: W. Green, 2000); cf. *McDonald v Lanarkshire Fire Brigade Joint Committee*, 1959 S.C. 141; *Brown v Hamilton District Council*, 1983 S.L.T. 397; *Tehrani v Home Secretary*, 2007 S.C. (HL) 1.

[39] *Moss's Empires v Assessor for Glasgow*, 1917 S.C. (HL) 1 at 6, per Lord Kinnear. See *Cheyne v Architects' Registration Council*, 1943 S.C. 468. The main principles respecting possible grounds of review are set out in *Council of Civil Service Unions v Minister for the Civil Service* [1985] A.C. 374; see also *West v Secretary of State for Scotland*, 1992 S.C. 385.

The view at one time judicially expounded that a mere error of law, if intra vires, did not entitle the court to intervene with the decision of a body exercising a statutory jurisdiction[40] has now been disapproved in the UK Supreme Court.[41] In considering whether a tribunal has contravened the principles of natural justice, the question before the court is not whether the tribunal has arrived at a fair result, but whether it has dealt fairly and equally with the parties before it in arriving at that result.[42] Before recourse is had to the Court of Session, it must usually be shown that any remedy provided by the statute by which the tribunal or administrative jurisdiction is founded is inapplicable,[43] but there may be special circumstances which will justify a petitioner proceeding with a judicial review despite his failure to exhaust a statutory remedy.[44] The effect of statutory provisions that the decision of a particular body shall be final is not free from doubt. It is conceived that a statute may confer finality on the proceedings of an inferior court or of a statutory body in terms so wide as to exclude any interference by the Court of Session,[45] but in most cases finality clauses are read as applicable exclusively to procedure which is intra vires and regular and do not affect jurisdiction in cases of what have been termed "constitutional nullities".[46] Applications to the supervisory jurisdiction of the court are now made by means of a petition for judicial review and on such an application the court may make such order in relation to the decision in question as it thinks fit, being an order which could be made in any action or petition and including an order for reduction, suspension, declarator, interdict, implement, restitution and payment.[47] The Court of Session has the power to declare that a provision of primary legislation is incompatible with the European Convention on Human Rights.[48]

The High Court of Justiciary—The High Court of Justiciary, as a supreme crim- **2.06** inal court, was established by the Courts Act 1672 (c.16).[49] As now constituted, it consists of the Lord Justice-General, the Lord Justice-Clerk and the other judges of the Court of Session.[50] Its permanent session is in Edinburgh, but provision is made for sittings elsewhere in Scotland.[51] The High Court of Justiciary has a universal jurisdiction as a court of first instance in all cases of crime, except where, in the case of minor offences, its original jurisdiction is excluded by

---

[40] *Watt v Lord Advocate*, 1979 S.C. 120.

[41] *Eba v Advocate General for Scotland* [2011] UKSC 29; 2012 S.C. (UKSC) 1; 2011 S.L.T. 768.

[42] *Barrs v British Wool Marketing Board*, 1957 S.C. 72 at 82, per Lord President Clyde.

[43] *Crawford v Lennox* (1852) 14 D. 1029; *Lang v Presbytery of Irvine* (1846) 2 M. 823; *British Railways Board v Glasgow Corp*, 1976 S.C. 224 (application to the court incompetent where statutory appeal procedure had not been exhausted and question raised could have been decided by statutory appeal); *Ingle v Ingle's Trs*, 1999 S.L.T. 650.

[44] *Mensah v Secretary of State for the Home Department*, 1992 S.L.T. 177; *Choi v Secretary of State for the Home Department*, 1996 S.L.T. 590.

[45] See *Adair v Colville*, 1926 S.C. (HL) 51.

[46] *Manson v Smith* (1871) 9 M. 492 (Small Debt Court); *Walsh v Magistrates of Pollokshaws*, 1907 S.C. (HL) 1, and *Goodall v Bilsland*, 1909 S.C. 1152 (Licensing Court); *Moss's Empires v Assessor for Glasgow*, 1917 S.C. (HL) 1 (Valuation Court); see also Tribunals and Inquiries Act 1992 s.12(1) and Clyde and Edwards, *Judicial Review in Scotland* (2000), Ch.11.

[47] Rules of the Court of Session 1994 (SI 1994/1443) Ch.58; *West v Secretary of State for Scotland*, 1992 S.C. 385.

[48] Human Rights Act 1998 s.4; *Smith v Scott*, 2007 S.C. 345.

[49] History in Hume, *Commentaries*, ii, 1.

[50] Criminal Procedure (Scotland) Act 1995 (the "1995 Act") s.1(2).The offices of Lord Justice General and Lord President are held by the same person. The technical title of the other judges is "Lord Commissioner of Justiciary" as opposed to their civil judicial title of "Senator of the College of Justice", the High Court of Justiciary being a court wholly separate from the Court of Session.

[51] 1995 Act s.2.

statute. It possesses a paramount and overriding authority which has been described as similar to the *nobile officium* of the Court of Session.[52] When sitting in Edinburgh the court has, at common law, jurisdiction to review the decisions of inferior criminal courts where the proceedings have been initiated by complaint and not by indictment.[53] This jurisdiction has been extended by statute,[54] but a power which previously existed to bring proceedings on indictment in the sheriff court under review by bill of suspension has been abolished.[55] There is an appeal to the High Court, sitting as a court of appeal, by a person convicted on indictment, against conviction or sentence or both, and any alleged miscarriage of justice may be brought under review by such appeal.[56] The Lord Advocate has no right of appeal against the decision of the jury but he may appeal against the sentence or disposal of the case.[57] The Lord Advocate may refer a point of law which has arisen in solemn proceedings to the High Court for its opinion, but the opinion does not affect the acquittal or conviction of the accused.[58] The High Court has in respect of its *nobile officium* the power of interfering in extraordinary circumstances, for instance where no other procedure is available for review.[59] Three judges of the High Court constitute the court of appeal, other than in appeals against sentence when the court may be quorate with two judges.[60] Other than in the case of a devolution issue, there is no appeal to the UK Supreme Court, as formerly there was no appeal to the House of Lords.[61] A devolution issue in a criminal case can be appealed, with leave, to the UK Supreme Court.[62] Devolution issues can be referred to the High Court by lower courts.[63] The High Court, sitting in an appellate capacity, has power to declare a provision of primary legislation incompatible with the European Convention on Human Rights.[64] The High Court also deals with referrals from the Scottish Criminal Cases Review Commission in suspected cases of miscarriage of justice.[65]

2.07 European Union courts—The term "Court of Justice of the European Union" includes three distinct judicial tribunals, namely the "Court of Justice", the "General Court", and any "specialised courts" established under the Treaty on the

---

[52] *Milne v McNicol*, 1944 J.C. 151; *Wan Ping Nam v Minister of Justice of German Federal Republic*, 1972 J.C. 43; *Beck, Petitioner* [2010] HCJAC 8; 2010 S.L.T. 519.

[53] Proceedings initiated by complaint are triable summarily by a sheriff or justice of the justice of the peace court sitting alone. Proceedings on indictment (solemn procedure) are, on a plea of not guilty, tried by a jury. The common law methods of review, preserved by ss.191 and 192(4) of the 1995 Act, are advocation, suspension, and suspension and liberation. Suspension is not competent in proceedings instituted on indictment in the sheriff court (s.130).

[54] 1995 Act s.175 (as amended by the Protection of Children (Scotland) Act 2003 s.16(7)(f)), which enables, inter alia, a limited review of the merits of a conviction by way of stated case, and appeal by note of appeal by accused or prosecutor against sentence.

[55] 1995 Act s.130, re-enacting Criminal Appeal (Scotland) Act 1926 s.13; see *George Outram & Co Ltd v Lees*, 1992 S.L.T. 32.

[56] 1995 Act s.106.

[57] 1995 Act s.108.

[58] 1995 Act s.123. See *Lord Advocate's Reference (No.1 of 1983)*, 1984 J.C. 52; *Lord Advocate's Reference (No.1 of 2000)*, 2001 J.C. 143; *Lord Advocate's Reference (No.1 of 2001)*, 2002 S.L.T. 466.

[59] *Wylie v HM Advocate*, 1966 S.L.T. 149; *Rae, Petitioner*, 1982 S.L.T. 233; *Beck, Petitioner* [2010] HCJAC 8; 2010 S.L.T. 519.

[60] 1995 Act s.103(2) and (3).

[61] *Mackintosh v Lord Advocate* (1876) 3 R. (HL) 34; 1995 Act s.124(2); Constitutional Reform Act 2005 s.40(3).

[62] See para.2.03, above.

[63] Scotland Act 1998 Sch.6 para.9.

[64] Human Rights Act 1998 s.4.

[65] Criminal Procedure (Scotland) Act 1995 ss.194B, C and E.

Functioning of the European Union ("TFEU") art.270.[66] Currently the only specialised court consists of a special tribunal to hear and determine actions brought by a civil servant or employee of an EU institution in respect of an employment matter arising under the staff regulations. The "General Court" was formerly known as the "Court of First Instance". It has essentially a first instance jurisdiction in respect of direct actions brought by natural or legal persons against acts or failures of an EU institution but an appellate jurisdiction in respect of decisions of a specialised court. From its decisions an appeal on a point of law lies to the "Court of Justice". The General Court may also refer matters of difficulty to the Court of Justice. The General Court consists of 27 judges, who sit in chambers of varying size. There are no advocates-general within the membership of the General Court. The tribunal at the apex of the "Court of Justice of the European Union", namely the "Court of Justice", also consists of 27 judges, but they are assisted by eight advocates-general, who are also members of the Court of Justice. One of the judges is elected President. The Court of Justice may sit in chambers of three or five judges, or in a Grand Chamber or as a full court.[67] The "Court of Justice of the European Union"—that is to say, the aggregation of the courts—has jurisdiction in the following: (1) actions brought by the Commission or a Member State against another Member State in respect of a failure to fulfil an obligation under the EC Treaty[68]; (2) actions to review the legality of acts adopted jointly by the European Parliament and the Council, of acts of the Council of Ministers, the Commission and of the European Central Bank other than recommendations and opinions[69]; (3) actions brought by the Member States or the other institutions against the European Parliament, Council or the Commission for failure to act when required to do so in terms of the Treaty[70]; (4) references by municipal courts and tribunals for preliminary rulings concerning the interpretation of the Treaty, the validity and interpretation of acts of the institutions of the European Union (including the European Central Bank) and the interpretation of the statutes of bodies established by an act of the Council, where those statutes so provide[71]; (5) actions to enforce the contractual or non-contractual liability of the Union[72]; (6) disputes between the European Union and its servants[73]; (7) disputes relating to the European Investment Bank and national central banks[74]; (8) matters submitted to arbitration under a contract concluded by or on behalf of the Union[75]; and (9) disputes between Member States submitted under an agreement between the parties.[76] In addition, the court has jurisdiction to interpret the Jurisdiction and

---

[66] TEU art.19.

[67] TFEU art.251.

[68] TFEU arts 258 and 259.

[69] TFEU art.263 The legality of an act adopted by the European Council or the Council under TEU art.7 (breach by a Member State of the values set out in TEU art.2 or serious breach of Treaty obligations) may be reviewed under TFEU art.269 at the request of the Member State concerned and solely in respect of the procedural stipulations in that art.7.

[70] TFEU art.265.

[71] TFEU art.267; European Communities Act 1972 s.3; Rules of the Court of Session 1994 (SI 1994/1443) Ch.65; Sheriff Court Ordinary Cause Rules (SI 1993/1956) Ch.38. See *Mehlich v Mackenzie*, 1984 S.L.T. 449; *Hamilton v Whitelock* [1987] 3 C.M.L.R. 190; *Walkingshaw v Marshall*, 1992 S.L.T. 1167; *Brown v Secretary of State*, 1989 S.L.T. 402; *Wither v Cowie*, 1994 S.L.T. 363; *Booker Aquaculture Ltd v Secretary of State for Scotland*, 2000 S.C. 9.

[72] TFEU art.268.

[73] TFEU art.270.

[74] TFEU art.271.

[75] TFEU art.272.

[76] TFEU art.273.

Judgments Convention[77] and to provide preliminary rulings on the interpretation of the EC Convention on the Law Applicable to Conventional Obligations,[78] but this jurisdiction conferred by protocols to the two conventions is of diminishing importance since the conventions have been largely superseded by directly applicable EU regulations.[79] The court may be called upon to give an opinion as to whether an agreement between the European Union and one or more states or an international organisation is compatible with the Treaty.[80]

2.08 Sheriff court—The sheriff, as a ministerial and judicial officer, appears in the records of the law of Scotland from the twelfth century. By the eighteenth century the office had in most cases become hereditary. Hereditary jurisdictions were abolished by the Heritable Jurisdictions (Scotland) Act 1747,[81] under which, though sheriffs could be appointed by the Crown for a period not exceeding one year, their duties were to be performed by a new officer, the sheriff-depute, who had to be an advocate of at least three years' standing, and was to hold office *ad vitam aut culpam*.[82] Sheriffs-substitute were appointed by the sheriffs-depute until 1877[83] but since 1787 had been definitely recognised as judicial officers paid by the Crown. The use of the title "sheriff" was authorised for the sheriff-depute by the Sheriff Courts (Scotland) Act 1825[84] and in 1971 he was, in accordance with what had become common usage, designated "sheriff principal".[85] At the same time, the title of "sheriff-substitute", for long a misnomer, was replaced by "sheriff".[86] No one may be appointed to the office of sheriff principal or sheriff unless he is an advocate or solicitor of at least 10 years' standing.[87] The word "sheriff" includes sheriff principal unless otherwise provided or the context is repugnant to the construction.[88] All resident sheriffs within a sheriffdom have jurisdiction throughout the sheriffdom.[89] Sheriffs principal and sheriffs are required to retire at the age of 70.[90] The post of temporary sheriff was held to be incompatible with the European Convention on Human Rights because temporary sheriffs did not enjoy sufficient security of tenure to give them the appearance of impartiality.[91] A new position of part-time sheriff with security of tenure was created under the Bail, Judicial Appointments etc. (Scotland) Act 2000.

2.09 Sheriff court: Civil jurisdiction—The civil jurisdiction, or competence, of the sheriff court extends to nearly all types of action. The leading exceptions are certain actions involving status (e.g. declarator of marriage), reduction of deeds, contracts, decisions or decrees, petitions for judicial review, petitions for the

---

[77] See para.2.19, below.

[78] See Contracts (Applicable Law) Act 1990 Schs 1 and 3; Rules of the Court of Session 1994 (SI 1994/1443) r.65(1)(c).

[79] Council Regulation (EC) 44/2001 on jurisdiction and recognition and enforcement of judgments in civil and commercial matters; Council Regulation (EC) 593/2008 on the law applicable to contractual obligations.

[80] TFEU art.218(11).

[81] Heritable Jurisdictions (Scotland) Act 1747 s.5.

[82] Heritable Jurisdictions (Scotland) Act 1747 s.29.

[83] Sheriff Courts (Scotland) Act 1877 s.4.

[84] See also Circuit Courts (Scotland) Act 1828.

[85] Sheriff Courts (Scotland) Act 1971 (the "1971 Act") s.4(1).

[86] 1971 Act s.4(1).

[87] 1971 Act s.5(1).

[88] Interpretation Act 1978 Sch.1; Interpretation and Legislative Reform (Scotland) Act 2010 Sch.1.

[89] Sheriff Courts (Scotland) Act 1971 s.7; *Spence v Davie*, 1993 S.L.T. 217.

[90] Judicial Pensions and Retirement Act 1993 s.26 (subject to transitional provisions).

[91] *Starrs v Ruxton*, 2000 J.C. 208; see further *Millar v Dickson*, 2002 S.C. (PC) 30.

winding up of a company if the paid-up capital exceeds £120,000,[92] suspension of charges upon decrees of the Court of Session,[93] and actions of proving the tenor of a lost document.[94] Actions of divorce and actions of declarator of nullity of marriage, and, to the very limited extent to which they may still be competent[95], actions for declarator of legitimacy, legitimation or illegitimacy, all formerly competent only in the Court of Session, may now be brought in the sheriff court, as also may actions for declarator of parentage or non-parentage and for declarator of death.[96] The sheriff's jurisdiction over actions of debt or damages is without pecuniary limit. In actions which are competent in the sheriff court and where the value, exclusive of interest and expenses, does not exceed £5000, the jurisdiction of the sheriff is privative, i.e. such cases cannot be brought originally in the Court of Session.[97]

Sheriff court: Summary causes and small claims—"Summary cause" proce- **2.10** dure is applicable to all actions for payment of money not exceeding £5000, exclusive of interest and expenses, to multiplepoindings, furthcomings and sequestrations for rent where the subject matter does not exceed £5000 in value, and to actions *ad factum praestandum* and actions for the recovery of heritable or moveable property unless there is an alternative or additional crave for payment of a sum exceeding £5000.[98] If required to do so on joint motion of the parties, the sheriff is to direct that an ordinary cause be treated as a summary cause or a summary cause as an ordinary cause and he may make the latter direction on the motion of any party if he is of the opinion that the importance or difficulty of the cause makes it appropriate to do so.[99] A "small claim" is a form of process used for summary cause proceedings where the value does not exceed £3000.[100] Small claims are exempt from rules relating to admissibility or corroboration of evidence. Expenses are awarded only where the value of the claim exceeds £200, and expenses may not exceed £150 where the value of the claim is £1500 or less or 10 per cent of the value of the claim where that value exceeds £1500.[101] The sheriff also has jurisdiction to deal in a summary manner with a wide range of common law and statutory applications to which the "summary application"

---

[92] Insolvency Act 1986 s.120 (as amended by Insolvency Act 1986 (Amendment) (No.2) Regulations 2002 (SI 2002/1240) reg.7).

[93] Sheriff Courts (Scotland) Act 1907 s.5(5).

[94] *Dunbar v Scottish County Investment Co*, 1920 1 S.L.T. 136.

[95] Subject to certain savings, the status of illegitimacy, and accordingly actions for declarator of illegitimacy, legitimacy and legitimation, were abolished by the Family Law (Scotland) Act 2006 s.21. See the Law Reform (Parent and Child) (Scotland) Act 1986 ss.1, 7 and 9 as amended by the 2006 Act and also SSI 2006/212 art.10.

[96] Divorce Jurisdiction, Court Fees and Legal Aid (Scotland) Act 1983 s.1, amending Sheriff Courts (Scotland) Act 1907 s.5; Law Reform (Parent and Child) (Scotland) Act 1986 s.7; Presumption of Death (Scotland) Act 1977 Sch.1; Family Law (Scotland) Act 2006 s.4.

[97] Sheriff Courts (Scotland) Act 1907 s.7, as amended by the 1971 Act ss.31, 35 and 41 and as most recently amended (from January 14, 2008) by the Sheriff Courts (Scotland) Act 1971 (Privative Jurisdiction and Summary Cause) Order 2007 (SSI 2007/507).

[98] 1971 Act ss.35(1) and 41 and SSI 2007/507.

[99] 1971 Act s.37(1) and (2), as amended by the Law Reform (Miscellaneous Provisions) (Scotland) Act 1980 s.16(a); *Butler v Thom*, 1982 S.L.T. (Sh. Ct) 57.

[100] Law Reform (Miscellaneous Provisions) (Scotland) Act 1985 s.18, amending ss.35–38 of the 1971 Act; Small Claims (Scotland) Order 1988 (SI 1988/1999), as amended by the Small Claims (Scotland) Order 2007 (SSI 2007/496).

[101] Small Claims (Scotland) Order 1988 art.4, as substituted by the Small Claims (Scotland) Amendment Order 2007 (SSI 2007/496 (but see also 1971 Act s.36B(3)).

procedure applies.[102] This procedure is entirely distinct from, and unconnected with, the "summary cause".

2.11 Sheriff court: Appeals—The judgment of a sheriff in the ordinary court may be appealed to the sheriff principal unless such appeal is excluded by statute. If the cause is not a summary cause or application, the appeal may be either to the sheriff principal, from whom an appeal lies to the Court of Session, or directly to the Inner House of the Court of Session.[103] To render an appeal to the Court of Session competent, the judgment of the sheriff principal[104] or sheriff must either be final, or be an interlocutor granting interim decree for payment of money other than a decree for expenses, or sisting an action, or refusing a reponing note. In other cases, the leave of the sheriff principal or sheriff, as the case may be, to appeal is required.[105] In summary causes, appeal is competent only against a final judgment and only on a point of law.[106] The appeal from the sheriff is to the sheriff principal from whose judgment there may be an appeal to the Court of Session only if he certifies the cause as suitable.[107] There is no appeal to the Court of Session in a small claim.[108] In a summary application at common law, appeal to the sheriff principal and, subject to the value or privative jurisdiction rule, to the Court of Session is competent, but in statutory summary applications review is often restricted or excluded by the statute under which the application is brought.[109] In the case of any ordinary cause, the sheriff may, on the motion of any of the parties to the cause, remit the cause to the Court of Session if he is of the opinion that the importance or difficulty of the cause makes it appropriate to do so.[110]

2.12 Sheriff court: Criminal jurisdiction—In criminal matters, the sheriff principal or sheriff is a competent judge in all crimes except treason, murder, attempt to murder, rape and breach of duty by magistrates.[111] The sheriff court and the High Court have between them an inherent universal jurisdiction which can only be restricted or excluded by the express provision or clear implication of a statute.[112] In respect that a sheriff cannot inflict a penalty exceeding five[113] years' imprisonment, it is mainly a question of the gravity of the alleged offence whether criminal proceedings should be taken in the sheriff court or in the High Court of Justiciary.

---

[102] 1907 Act ss.3(p), 50; Act of Sederunt (Summary Applications, Statutory Applications and Appeals etc. Rules) 1999 (SI 1999/929) as amended by subsequent acts of sederunt; see also G. Jamieson, *Summary Applications and Suspensions* (Edinburgh: W. Green, 2000).

[103] 1907 Act ss.27 and 28.

[104] Appeal to the Court of Session will, however, be subject to the value rule respecting the privative jurisdiction of the sheriff court (see above, para.2.04).

[105] Sheriff Courts (Scotland) Act 1907 s.28 as amended by Sheriff Courts Act 1913.

[106] 1971 Act s.38; there are conflicting decisions on whether an incompetent interlocutor may be the subject of an appeal even though the interlocutor is not a final judgment; *City of Glasgow District Council v McAleer*, 1992 S.L.T. (Sh. Ct) 41; cf. *City of Edinburgh District Council v Robbin*, 1994 S.L.T. (Sh. Ct) 51.

[107] 1971 Act s.38.

[108] 1971 Act s.38 as amended.

[109] See Macphail, *Sheriff Court Practice* (Edinburgh: W. Green, 2006), paras 26.29–26.47.

[110] 1971 Act s.37(1)(b), as amended by the Law Reform (Miscellaneous Provisions) (Scotland) Act 1980 s.16(a); *Mullan v Anderson*, 1993 S.L.T. 835. For actions of divorce, custody or adoption, cf. s.37(2A).

[111] Criminal Procedure (Scotland) Act 1995 s.3(6).

[112] See *Blythswood Taxis v Adair*, 1944 J.C. 135 at 140; *Wilson v Hill*, 1943 J.C. 124.

[113] Criminal Procedure (Scotland) Act 1995 s.3 (as amended by the Crime and Punishment (Scotland) Act 1997 s.13).

The decision is for the prosecutor, but the sheriff has a power to remit to the High Court of Justiciary, should he consider his sentencing powers inadequate.

Justice of the Peace courts—The former Justice of the Peace Courts, Burgh **2.13** Courts and Police Courts (which exercised a petty criminal jurisdiction, and, in the case of the justices of the peace, also a very limited civil jurisdiction) were abolished by the District Courts (Scotland) Act 1975 and replaced by district courts.[114] The district courts have, in their turn, now been replaced by new justice of the peace—or "JP"—courts established pursuant to Pt 4 of the Criminal Proceedings etc. (Reform)(Scotland) Act 2007. Whereas the district courts were in large measure a continuation of a longstanding tradition of courts of minor criminal jurisdiction forming an adjunct of municipal or local government administration, the provisions of the 2007 Act seek to integrate the JP courts within the structures of the sheriff court system. Thus JP courts are established by reference to a particular sheriff court district[115] and the territorial jurisdiction of a JP court extends to the sheriff court district within which it is located and any other district in the same sheriffdom.[116] The sheriff principal has responsibility for the efficient administration of any JP court located in the sheriffdom.[117] A JP is appointed on behalf of and in name of Her Majesty, by instrument under the hand of the Scottish Ministers, and he or she is appointed, for a renewable term of five years, to a given sheriffdom.[118] The 2007 Act contains, in Pt 4, various provisions respecting the appointment, training and appraisal of JPs and their removal from office. Whereas a JP is a lay magistrate, the 2007 Act also makes continuing provision for the appointment of a stipendiary magistrate, who must be an advocate or solicitor of at least five years' standing.[119] The jurisdiction (in a non-territorial sense) and powers enjoyed by the JP courts are those possessed by the former courts[120] and are restricted to the trial of offences summarily. But s.7(8)(b) of the Criminal Procedure (Scotland) Act 1995 gives a list of offences, covering most common law offences other than those of a minor character, which are excluded from the competence of the JP court. And it is a general principle that statutory offences cannot be tried by courts such as the JP court, unless jurisdiction is conferred upon that court by statute, either expressly or by implication.[121] The maximum sentence which can be imposed is 60 days' imprisonment and a fine not exceeding £2,500.[122] These restrictions, however, only apply to the court when it is composed of lay justices. A stipendiary magistrate has the summary criminal jurisdiction and powers of a sheriff.[123] It is not contrary to the European Convention on Human Rights for the legally qualified clerk who assists the lay justices to have private communications with the lay justices.[124]

---

[114] District Courts (Scotland) Act 1975 s.1.

[115] Criminal Proceedings etc. (Reform) (Scotland) Act 2007 (the "2007 Act") s.59(2).

[116] 2007 Act s.62(1) and (2).

[117] 2007 Act s.61.

[118] 2007 Act s.67.

[119] 2007 Act ss.74 and 75

[120] Criminal Procedure (Scotland) Act 1995 s.7(1). The civil jurisdiction of the former Justice of the Peace Courts and quarter sessions is, however, excluded.

[121] *Macpherson v Boyd*, 1907 S.C. (J.) 42.

[122] Criminal Procedure (Scotland) Act 1995 s.7.

[123] Criminal Procedure (Scotland) Act 1995 s.7(5). The Criminal Proceedings etc. (Reform) (Scotland) Act 2007 s.46, gives Scottish Ministers power to amend the maximum penalties available to the JP courts.

[124] *Clark v Kelly*, 2003 S.C. (PC) 77.

2.14 The Court of the Lord Lyon—The Lord Lyon King of Arms has jurisdiction, subject to appeal to the Court of Session and the House of Lords, in questions of heraldry and the right to bear arms.[125] It is a matter of some uncertainty whether Lyon has jurisdiction to determine rights of precedence,[126] or to decide a disputed question of chiefship or chieftainship.[127] Ministerial or administrative functions of Lyon may be subject to judicial review.[128]

2.15 The Scottish Land Court—This court was set up in 1911 with judicial functions under the statutes which relate to agricultural land and small holdings and crofts.[129] It consists of a legally qualified chairman, who has the status of a judge of the Court of Session, and a panel of lay members who are experienced in agriculture; one of the members must be a Gaelic speaker.[130]

2.16 The Lands Valuation Appeal Court—This court sits to dispose of appeals on rating questions from local valuation appeal committees and the Lands Tribunal for Scotland. It consists of three judges of the Court of Session (although there is provision for one judge to sit in certain circumstances).[131] Appeals are limited to questions of value and the role of the Land Valuation Appeal Court is to determine whether the Committee has drawn the proper conclusion from the facts found proved.[132] The decision of the Lands Valuation Appeal Tribunal is final as to valuation and no appeal lies on the decision to either the Court of Session or the House of Lords.

2.17 Church courts—Kirk Sessions, Presbyteries, and the General Assembly of the Church of Scotland are established courts of the realm.[133] They now, however, have only a domestic jurisdiction over members of the Church on matters affecting Church discipline, membership, doctrine and ritual.

2.18 The European Court of Human Rights—The European Court of Human Rights is set up under the European Convention on Human Rights 1950. There is a single permanent Court which replaced the former Commission and Court.[134] The Grand Chamber of the Court consists of 17 judges. Chambers consist of seven judges. Committees of three judges consider admissibility issues. Contrary to a frequent popular impression, the Court is not an appellate court forming part of the judicial structures of the Contracting States. Applications to the Court are made either by

---

[125] *Hunter v Weston* (1882) 9 R. 492; *Mackenzie v Mackenzie*, 1920 S.C. 764, affd 1922 S.C. (HL) 39.

[126] *Royal College of Surgeons v Royal College of Physicians*, 1911 S.C. 1054; but see *Law Society of Scotland*, 1955 S.L.T. (Lyon Ct) 2 and *Stair Memorial Encyclopaedia*, Vol.6, para.1018.

[127] *Maclean of Ardgour v Maclean*, 1938 S.L.T. 49; 1941 S.C. 613; but see explanation of this case in *Captain Alwyne Farquharson of Invercauld*, 1950 S.L.T. (Lyon Ct) 13; and *Stair Memorial Encyclopaedia*, Vol.6, para.1018.

[128] *Kerr of Ardgowan v Lord Lyon King of Arms*, 2009 S.L.T. 759

[129] See paras 35.51–35.60, below.

[130] Scottish Land Court Act 1993 s.1. For a history of the Scottish Land Court, see W. Mercer, *No Ordinary Court* (Edinburgh: Avizandum, 2012).

[131] See *Armour on Valuation for Rating*, 5th edn, (Edinburgh: W. Green), para.5–40; Valuation of Lands (Scotland) Amendment Act 1879, as amended by the Rating and Valuation (Amendment) (Scotland) Act 1984 s.13.

[132] *Armour on Valuation for Rating*, paras 5–41 and 5–53.

[133] Church of Scotland Act 1921; *Wight v Presbytery of Dunkeld* (1870) 8 M. 921; *Ballantyne v Wigtown Presbytery*, 1936 S.L.T. 436; *Logan v Presbytery of Dumbarton*, 1995 S.L.T. 1228.

[134] European Convention art.19, as amended by Protocol 11, dated May 11, 1998.

other Contracting States[135] or by any person, non-governmental organisation or group of individuals claiming to be the victim of a violation of the Convention by a Contracting State.[136] The Court is obliged to place itself at the disposal of the parties with a view to securing a friendly settlement.[137] The Court may afford a just satisfaction to an aggrieved party against a Member State.[138] The enactment of the Human Rights Act 1998 enables possible incompatibilities between the Convention and national legislative or executive measures to be dealt with by the national courts in the United Kingdom, thereby reducing the extent to which the United Kingdom might ultimately be held to be in breach of its Convention obligations.

Children's hearings[139]—Children's hearings were created by the Social Work **2.19** (Scotland) Act 1968 but most of the legislative provisions for their functioning were re-enacted in the Children (Scotland) Act 1995. The law relating to children's hearings was amended by and re-stated in the Children's Hearings (Scotland) Act 2011. One of the changes effected by the 2011 Act was a measure of centralisation of the organisation of children's hearings through the creation of an officer known as the National Convener of Children's Hearings Scotland and a body corporate known as Children's Hearings Scotland.[140] The provisions of the 2011 Act are in the process of being brought into force. The National Convener has responsibility for recruiting and appointing members of the Children's Panel[141] and for selecting from the panel members three persons, who must include both male and female, to constitute a children's hearing.[142] So far as practicable, the members of a children's hearing should live or work in the local authority area of the child who is the subject of the hearing. Children's hearings have no power to determine disputed questions of law or fact but are entrusted with the determination of whether children referred to them are in need of compulsory measures of supervision, which may include measures taken for the protection, guidance, treatment or control of the child. In a supervision requirement—in the parlance of the 2011 Act, a compulsory supervision order[143]—such conditions may be imposed as the hearing thinks fit, including a residential condition, and the child may be required to reside in a school or other institution registered with the local authority or Secretary of State for the purposes of the Act. The hearings also have certain advisory functions in relation to children and young persons brought before courts. A child may be in need of compulsory measures of care if any of the grounds mentioned in s.52 of the 1995 Act[144] are satisfied. These grounds include the commission of an offence by the child, as well as those which formerly fell

---

[135] European Convention art.33.

[136] European Convention art.34.

[137] European Convention art.38.

[138] European Convention art.41.

[139] See Children (Scotland) Act 1995 ss.39 et seq and the Children's Hearings (Scotland) Act 2011 (the "2011 Act"); *Kennedy v B*, 1973 S.L.T. 38; *H v McGregor*, 1973 S.L.T. 110; *D v Sinclair*, 1973 S.L.T. (Sh. Ct) 47; *D. v Kennedy*, 1974 S.L.T. 168; *H. v Mearns*, 1974 S.L.T. 184; *K. v Finlayson*, 1974 S.L.T. (Sh. Ct) 51; *McGregor v T*, 1975 S.L.T. 76; *Principal Reporter v K* [2010] UKSC 56; 2011 S.C. (UKSC) 91.

[140] 2011 Act ss.1 and 2.

[141] 2011 Act s.4 and Sch.2.

[142] 2011 Act ss.5 and 6.

[143] The term is defined in s.83 of the 2011 Act, and may include a number of specific types of condition defined in the succeeding sections of that Act.

[144] For the catalogue of grounds under the 2011 Act, see s.67.

within the care and protection jurisdiction of juvenile courts, and the hearings have, accordingly, since 1968 very largely replaced the functions of the courts so far as the measures to be adopted in the case of juvenile offenders are concerned. The decision on whether to refer a child to a hearing is taken by an officer known as the Principal Reporter.[145] If, at the children's hearing, the grounds on which the child is referred are disputed by a "relevant person" — broadly one having parental responsibilities[146] by the child — the hearing, unless it discharges the referral, must direct the reporter to apply to the sheriff for a finding on whether the grounds are established.[147] An application can be made to the sheriff to review a finding that a ground of referral has been established.[148] An appeal lies to the sheriff at the instance of the child or its parents against any decision of a children's hearing.[149] A further appeal can be taken from the sheriff's decision on appeal, or on a finding as to whether the grounds of referral are established, or from the sheriff's decision on an application for review of the grounds of referral. Such an appeal lies at the instance of the child, its parents or the reporter, to the sheriff principal or Court of Session by way of stated case on a point of law, or in respect of any irregularity in the conduct of the case. If an appeal is initially taken to the sheriff principal, leave is required for a further appeal to the Court of Session. There is no appeal to the UK Supreme Court from the Court of Session. In one case, the parents successfully petitioned the *nobile officium* for a rehearing of the grounds of referral.[150] The procedures before children's hearings have been declared generally compliant with the right to a fair trial under the European Convention on Human Rights.[151]

2.20 **Tribunals**—The legislature has long since found it necessary to set up statutory tribunals to determine particular disputes in many different but specified fields. Many tribunals were set up to deal with disputes between the citizen and the State, such as disputes as to tax liabilities or entitlement to social security benefits; but others were instituted to deal with disputes between citizens, such as, for example, certain differences between employer and employee, which were confided originally to industrial tribunals, now known as employment tribunals. Within a given domain, the tribunal system created by the legislature might provide for an appellate statutory tribunal. Thus, in employment matters a decision of an employment tribunal may be subject of an appeal on a point of law to the employment appeal tribunal. Commonly, the legislature would provide for an ultimate appeal, almost invariably on a point of law, to a court, usually the Court of Session. The number of tribunals and the varying and disparate nature of their constitution

---

[145] The office of Principal Reporter was established by s.127 (1) of the Local Government (Scotland) Act 1994 and is continued by s.14 of the 2011 Act.

[146] 2011 Act s.200; but the provisions may have to be read as also embracing a person "who appears to have established family life with the child with which the decision of a children's hearing may interfere" — see *Principal Reporter v K* [2010] UKSC 56; 2011 S.C. (UKSC) 91, in which the judgment was delivered after the 2011 Act had been passed by the Scottish Parliament.

[147] Children (Scotland) Act 1995 s.65; cf. the 2011 Act s.93. As to the standard of proof, corroboration and hearsay, see *Harris v F*, 1991 S.L.T. 242.

[148] Children (Scotland) Act 1995 s.85; cf. the 2011 Act s.110.

[149] Children (Scotland) Act 1995 s.51; cf. the 2011 Act s.154. See *Sloan v B*, 1991 S.L.T. 530.

[150] *L, Petrs (No.1)*, 1993 S.L.T. 1310; see also *H, Petrs*, 1997 S.L.T. 3; *R, Petr*, 1993 S.L.T. 910.

[151] art.6. See *S v Miller*, 2001 S.C. 977; *S v Miller (No.2)*, 2001 S.L.T. 1304, in which it was held that the non-compliant rule that legal aid was unavailable for proceedings before children's hearings could be cured by Scottish Ministers in terms of the Legal Aid (Scotland) Act 1986 s.29 (since amended by the Legal Profession and Legal Aid (Scotland) Act s.72(4)–(6)). See also Pt 19 of the 2011 Act respecting legal aid and advice. But see also *Principal Reporter v K* [2010] UKSC 56; [2011] S.C. (UKSC) 91.

and procedures, including the available appellate mechanisms, led in England and Wales to the publication in 2001 by the Department for Constitutional Affairs of the Leggatt Report[152] which, put shortly, advocated rationalisation of most of the various tribunals into a unified structure which would be more judicially structured. The proposals in the report ultimately resulted in the restructuring enacted in Pt 1 of the Tribunals, Courts and Enforcement Act 2007 ("TCEA"). In brief outline, that restructuring set up a two-level system of tribunals, namely the "First-tier tribunal" and the "Upper Tribunal", the latter being an appellate tribunal, to which system the Lord Chancellor might (to varying extent) transfer the functions of the tribunals listed in Sch.6 to the TCEA. While many of the tribunals subject to restructuring by the TCEA had a territorial jurisdiction confined to England, or England and Wales, others had jurisdiction throughout the United Kingdom. Equally, a number of tribunals existed in Scotland, usually established under legislation applying only to Scotland, and dealing with devolved matters. In the result, and broadly speaking, so far as Scotland is concerned the two tier system established under the TCEA applies only as respects tribunals which formerly had a UK-wide jurisdiction and decisions of the initial decision taker which relate only to reserved matters. In practice, the areas of dispute affecting Scotland most commonly falling within the TCEA system are social security, taxation and immigration and asylum. Outwith that system, the tribunal systems of principal practical importance for the areas of private law covered by this work are those applying in the field of employment law and land law. As part of the TCEA re-structuring the former Council on Tribunals, which had advisory and consultative functions in relation to tribunals, was replaced by the Administrative Justice and Tribunals Council.[153]

The First-tier Tribunal—The members of the First-tier Tribunal comprise two **2.21** classes, namely "judges" and "other members", the former being legally qualified.[154] A number of office holders in the tribunals whose functions passed to the First-tier tribunal were "transferred in" to the tribunal. Power is given[155] to the Lord Chancellor, with the concurrence of the Senior President of Tribunals,[156] to make provision for the organisation of the tribunal in chambers. The First-tier Tribunal is currently organised in six chambers. Two of these, namely the "War Pensions and Armed Forces Compensation" chamber and the "Health, Education and Social Care" chamber, do not extend to Scotland. Three, namely the "Tax" chamber (covering inter alia the former jurisdiction of the general and special commissioners for income tax and the VAT and Duties Tribunal), the "Social Entitlement" chamber (dealing with social security, child support, criminal injuries compensation and asylum support matters) and the "Immigration and Asylum" chamber do extend to Scotland. The remaining chamber, the "General Regulatory" chamber, embraces a variety of former tribunal jurisdictions, including such jurisdictions as the former Transport Tribunal and the Consumer Credit Appeals Tribunal. Some, but not all, of its functions extend to Scotland. Power is given to the First-tier Tribunal to review its decisions either on

---

[152] Department for Constitutional Affairs, *Tribunals for users — One System, One Service* (The Stationery Office, 2001) ("the Leggatt Report").
[153] Tribunals, Courts and Enforcement Act 2007 ("TCEA") ss.44, 45.
[154] TCEA s.4 and Sch.3.
[155] TCEA s.7.
[156] See TCEA s.2 respecting the office of Senior President of Tribunals.

application by a party or of its own initiative.[157] A decision of the First-tier Tribunal may be appealed, with permission granted either by that tribunal or the Upper Tribunal, on a point of law.[158]

2.22 The Upper Tribunal—The membership of the Upper Tribunal similarly consists of two classes, namely "judges", who are legally qualified, and "other members". There is a similar provision for "transfer-in", and the transfer of senior members of the Asylum and Immigration Tribunal and Social Security Commissioners.[159] Most professional, salaried holders of judicial office in the United Kingdom — in the case of Scotland, senators of the College of Justice and sheriffs — are ex officio judges of both the Upper Tribunal and also the First-tier Tribunal.[160] The Upper Tribunal is also organized in chambers, those being currently the "Administrative Appeals" chamber, which as respects Scotland, deals with, among others, matters formerly dealt with by the social security and child support commissioners and some matters affecting Scotland dealt with by the "General Regulatory" chamber of the First-tier Tribunal; the "Tax and Chancery" chamber; the "Asylum and Immigration "chamber; and the "Lands "chamber, which has no application to any Scottish matter. Provision is made for the transfer to the Upper Tribunal of a petition to the Court of Session for the exercise, by judicial review of its supervisory jurisdiction, but transfer may only be made if the application to the court seeks only the exercise of the supervisory jurisdiction and only relates to a reserved, i.e. non-devolved, matter other than immigration or nationality.[161] Transfer is discretionary unless the application to the Court of Session falls within a class prescribed by Act of Sederunt.[162] The only class currently prescribed are applications for judicial review of procedural decisions of the First-tier tribunal.[163] A right of appeal lies from the Upper Tribunal to the "relevant appellate court" — that court being a matter for designation by the Upper Tribunal (being either the Court of Session or the Court of Appeal in Northern Ireland or England and Wales) but only with leave of the tribunal or the relevant appellate court.[164]

2.23 Employment tribunals—These were first set up under the Industrial Training Act 1964 as "industrial" tribunals but their name was later changed to the more appropriate term "employment" tribunals. They hear and decide at first instance a wide variety of disputes between employer and employee. Their initial remit has been greatly extended and their jurisdiction now embraces, among others, claims for redundancy payments, for re-instatement or compensation in respect of unfair dismissal, for equal pay, and complaints of sexual, racial or disability discrimination in the workplace. An employment tribunal consists of a legally qualified chairman – now styled an "employment judge" — who must be an advocate, barrister or solicitor of at least seven years' standing, and two lay members, one of whom is chosen from a panel of persons nominated after consultation with organisations representative of employers and the other after similar consultation

---

[157] TCEA s.9.
[158] TCEA s.11.
[159] TCEA s.5.
[160] TCEA s.6.
[161] TCEA ss.20 and 21.
[162] TCEA s.20(1) and (3).
[163] Act of Sederunt (Transfer of Judicial Review Applications from the Court of Session) 2008 (SSI 2008/357).
[164] TCEA s.13.

with organisations representative of employed persons. For some purposes, however, an employment tribunal may be constituted by the employment judge sitting alone. An appeal lies from a decision of an employment tribunal to the Employment Appeal Tribunal.

The Employment Appeal Tribunal—Originally set up under the Employment **2.24** Protection Act 1975, the Tribunal has in all matters incidental to its jurisdiction the like powers, rights, privileges and authority as the Court of Session.[165] It consists of a judge of the Court of Session and judges of the High Court in England and Wales nominated for the purpose and of appointed members with special knowledge or experience of industrial relations as representatives of either employers or workers. Appeals are heard by a judge with two or four appointed members from employment tribunals on questions of law and from the Certification Officer under Trade Union legislation. The Tribunal also acts as a court of first instance in claims for compensation by a person denied admission to a trade union after a declaration of unfair exclusion by an employment tribunal,[166] and in applications relating to vexatious proceedings.[167] A further appeal lies on a question of law to the Court of Session and thereafter to the UK Supreme Court.

The Lands Tribunal for Scotland—Its membership consists partly of legally **2.25** qualified persons (one of whom is President) and partly of persons with experience in the valuation of land. It was set up by the Lands Tribunal Act 1949 with the principal function of deciding disputes respecting the assessment of compensation for compulsory purchase of land. As a valuation tribunal it later acquired functions in respect of valuation for rating purposes. In 1970 the jurisdiction of the Tribunal was extended to include deciding applications for the variation and discharge of obligations affecting land.[168] That jurisdiction was replaced by a further expanded jurisdiction in respect of title conditions on the abolition of feudal tenure on November 28, 2004.[169] In rating matters, appeal lies to the Lands Valuation Appeal Court; otherwise appeal, on a point of law, is to the Court of Session.

II. JURISDICTION

Jurisdiction over persons—Jurisdiction, in relation to the persons over whom it **2.26** is exercised, has been defined as "a power conferred on a judge or magistrate to determine debatable questions according to law, and to carry his sentences into execution".[170] It is not, however, an absolute rule that the Scottish courts will refuse to pronounce a decree which cannot be carried into execution[171]; and in many cases they exercise their jurisdiction where their decree can be enforced

---

[165] See now Employment Tribunals Act 1996 s.39.

[166] Trade Union and Labour Relations (Consolidation) Act 1992 ss.67 and 176.

[167] Employment Tribunals Act 1996 s.33.

[168] Conveyancing and Feudal Reform (Scotland) Act 1970 ss.1 and 2.

[169] Title Conditions (Scotland) Act 2003 Pt 9; see also Abolition of Feudal Tenure (Scotland) Act 2000 s.20.

[170] Erskine, I, 2, 2. For a discussion of the basic concepts involved in jurisdiction see G. Maher and B. Rodger, *Civil Jurisdiction in the Scottish Courts* (Edinburgh: W. Green, 2010), Ch.1. See also P. Beaumont and P. McEleavy, *Anton's Private International Law*, 3rd edn (Edinburgh: W. Green, 2011), paras 8.01, 8.02.

[171] *Sons of Temperance Friendly Society*, 1926 S.C. 418.

only by proceedings in the courts of some other country.[172] The maxim *actor sequitur forum rei* (a pursuer follows the forum of the defender) imports that no actions can be entertained unless the court has jurisdiction over the defender, but there may be jurisdiction without power to enforce the decree. It is competent to sue the Crown for damages in respect of the negligence of its servants.[173] There are now substantial exceptions to the former rule that no Scottish court has jurisdiction to entertain a case against a foreign sovereign state, unless its immunity is departed from.[174] The immunity of ambassadors and other members of a diplomatic mission[175] includes the chief representatives of Commonwealth countries and their staffs, and now extends to chief representatives of states or provinces of a country within the Commonwealth, to certain consular officers and persons in the service of Commonwealth governments or the government of the Republic of Ireland performing duties of a consular nature, and to other persons on whom it may be conferred by Order in Council.[176] It may also be conferred by Order in Council on certain international organisations and persons connected with them.[177] Under the Visiting Forces Act 1952, restrictions are placed on the power of UK courts to try members of visiting forces, as defined.

2.27 The Civil Jurisdiction and Judgments Act 1982—The principal reason for the enactment of the Civil Jurisdiction and Judgments Act 1982 was to give effect in domestic law within the United Kingdom of the Brussels Convention of September 27, 1968 on Jurisdiction and Enforcement of Judgments in Civil and Commercial Matters. The Convention had been concluded among the six original Member States of the EEC and following the accession of the UK, Denmark and Ireland to the EEC the Convention (and the interpretation protocol) was amended and adapted to take account of the new Member States.[178] The purpose of the Convention was to assist the functioning of the common market by harmonising the jurisdiction rules in the Contracting States and by simplifying the procedures for enforcing in one Contracting State a judgment obtained in another such State. The 1982 Act provided that the Convention, the English text of which was contained in Sch.1 to the Act, should have the force of law in the UK. The 1982 Act also made provision, by means of a modified version of the jurisdiction rules

---

[172] e.g. when jurisdiction is founded on arrestments to found jurisdiction, below, para.2.32.

[173] Crown Proceedings Act 1947 s.2 (as amended).

[174] State Immunity Act 1978; *Government of the Republic of Spain v National Bank of Scotland*, 1939 S.C. 413; *Grangemouth and Forth Towing Co v Netherlands E.I. Govt*, 1942 S.L.T. 228; *Forth Tugs Ltd v Wilmington Trust Company*, 1985 S.C. 317; *Coreck Maritime GmbH v Sevrybokholodflot*, 1994 S.L.T. 893.

[175] Diplomatic Privileges Act 1964, which gave effect to the Vienna Convention on Diplomatic Privileges, 1961. Note that members of the administrative and technical staff are liable civilly, and members of the service staff are liable both criminally and civilly, for acts performed outside the course of their duties.

[176] Consular Relations Act 1968 as amended by Diplomatic and Other Privileges Act 1971. Cf. Diplomatic Immunities (Conferences with Commonwealth Countries and Republic of Ireland) Act 1961. Reference must be made to the statutes for details of the extent of immunity, the conferral and withdrawal of which are, in some cases, subject to resolution by Order in Council.

[177] International Organisations Acts 1968 and 1981.

[178] Convention of Accession of October 9, 1978 (OJ L304 October 30, 1978, p.1). The Brussels Convention—and the text of it contained in the Schedule to the 1982 Act—was successively amended on the later accession of other new Member States—see Macfadyen, *Court of Session Practice* (Bloomsbury Professional), para.B[103].

in the Convention,[179] for the allocation of jurisdiction among the constituent parts of the United Kingdom and the opportunity was taken to enact, in Sch.8 to the Act, a new, but not comprehensive, code of rules for jurisdiction in Scotland. In its application to Scotland the 1982 Act thus put in place a three-part scheme of rules, namely: (a) the Convention rules, which determined whether the courts of the UK, as opposed to another Contracting State, had jurisdiction over the defender; (b) the intra- UK rules, for determining which part of the UK might have jurisdiction; and (c) the Scottish rules, which, while largely reflective of the Convention grounds of jurisdiction, also contain grounds (e.g. arrestment of moveable property) not admissible under the Convention but potentially applicable as respects a defender not domiciled in a Contracting State. The Scottish rules also serve to allocate jurisdiction as between sheriff courts. The 1982 Act was subsequently amended by the Civil Jurisdiction and Judgments Act 1991 to give effect within the UK of the Lugano Convention of 16 September 1988 on Jurisdiction and Enforcement of Judgments.[180] The Lugano Convention was concluded among the Member States of the then European Community and the European Free Trade Area. The text of the Lugano Convention was closely aligned with that of the Brussels Convention. It comes into play where the defender is domiciled in an EFTA State, or where the jurisdiction of the courts of such a State is exclusive or has been prorogated, or where, in questions of litispendency, one of the proceedings is in such a State. A revised version of the Lugano Convention was concluded on October 30, 2007 between the European Community, the EFTA States (Iceland, Norway and Switzerland) and Denmark. Unlike the original convention, it is directly applicable. The revised version closely followed the text of Council Regulation (EC) 44/2001, which, as discussed in the next paragraph, had largely replaced the Brussels Convention.

Regulation 44/2001: The "Brussels I" Regulation—Following the making of **2.28** provision in the EC Treaty for an appropriate legislative power, a decision was taken in the Council of Ministers to replace the Brussels Convention with a European regulation. This was done in Council Regulation (EC) 44/2001 on Jurisdiction and the Recognition and Enforcement of Judgments in Civil and Commercial Matters.[181] The regulation is commonly referred to as the "Brussels I" regulation.[182] Since it takes the form of a regulation, this instrument is directly applicable in the legal systems of the Member States of the EU without the need for any national implementing measure. There was thus no need to amend the 1982 Act to give effect to it — indeed such a legislative exercise would have been contrary to basic rules of EU law. Subject to temporal transitional provisions, the Brussels I regulation thus essentially supersedes the Brussels Convention and, consequently, those provisions of the 1982 Act directed to giving the Brussels Convention force of law in the UK. One peculiarity respecting Denmark may be mentioned. Denmark declined to participate in Brussels I and consequently the definition in the regulation of "Member State" excludes Denmark. To at least that limited Danish extent, the Brussels Convention lived on for a time, but Denmark later concluded an agreement with the EU applying the terms of Brussels I to

---

[179] Sch.4 to the Civil Jurisdiction and Judgments Act 1982.
[180] OJ L319, November 25, 1988, p.9.
[181] OJ L12, January 16, 2001, p.1.
[182] The description of Brussels I follows from the later promulgation in the field of family law of further EU Regulations, commonly referred to as Brussels II or Brussels II bis.

Denmark subject to some very minor variations.[183] The text of the Brussels I regulation followed in large measure the structure and the wording of the Brussels Convention but subject to various amendments or adjustments to particular provisions. Subject to such qualifications as flow from those adjustments or amendments, decisions of the Court of Justice of the European Communities— now the Court of Justice of the European Union—interpreting the Brussels Convention are applicable to the corresponding provisions of the Brussels I regulation.[184]

2.29 **The scope of the Brussels I Regulation and the 1982 Act**—The Brussels I and UK rules are specifically stated to apply only to civil and commercial matters.[185] Not only criminal, but also revenue, customs and administrative cases are excluded. In addition, the Convention and Brussels I rules do not apply where the matter in issue concerns[186]:

(1) status or legal capacity in natural persons;
(2) rights in property arising out of a matrimonial relationship;
(3) wills and succession;
(4) bankruptcy;
(5) winding up of insolvent companies or other legal persons, judicial arrangements, compositions and analogous proceedings;
(6) social security; and
(7) arbitration.

The UK rules have the same list of exclusions as the Brussels I rules with the following additions[187]:

(1) Proceedings for the winding up of a company under the Insolvency Act 1986 (whether or not the company be insolvent) or proceedings relating to a company as respects which jurisdiction is conferred on the court having winding-up jurisdiction under the Act.
(2) Proceedings concerned with the registration or validity of patents, trademarks, designs or other similar rights required to be deposited or registered.
(3) Proceedings under s.6 of the Protection of Trading Interests Act 1980.
(4) Proceedings on appeal from, or for review of decisions of, tribunals.
(5) Proceedings for or relating to maintenance and similar payments to local and other public authorities.
(6) Proceedings brought in pursuance of any statutory provision or rule of law which implements a convention relating to specific matters overriding the general rules of the 1968 Convention.

---

[183] The Agreement, which came into operation on July 1, 2007, is given effect within the UK by the Civil Jurisdiction and Judgments Regulations 2007 (SI 2007/1655). For highly technical reasons, the Brussels Convention still applies respecting the French overseas territories of New Caledonia and Mayotte and the Netherlands overseas territory of Aruba.

[184] See, for example, *Verein für Konsumerinformation v Henkel* (C-167/00) [2002] E.C.R. I-8111; *Falco Privatstiftung v Weller-Lindhorst* (C-533/07) [2009] E.C.R. I-3327.

[185] Brussels I art.1; Civil Jurisdiction and Judgments Act 1982 s.16(1).

[186] Brussels I art.1.

[187] Civil Jurisdiction and Judgments Act 1982 ss.16(1) and 17(1) and Sch.5.

(7) Proceedings in an Admiralty cause where the jurisdiction of the court is based on *arrestment in rem* or *ad fundandam jurisdictionem* of a ship, cargo or freight.

(8) Proceedings for the rectification of the Register of Aircraft Mortgages kept by the Civil Aviation Authority.

(9) Proceedings in pursuance of an order under s.11 of the Petroleum Act 1998.

(10) Proceedings such as are mentioned in s.415 of the Financial Services and Markets Act 2000.

(11) Proceedings under any enactment which confers jurisdiction on a Scottish court in respect of a specific subject matter on specific grounds.[188]

The scope of the Scottish rules is defined in terms different from the Brussels I and UK rules, although the broad effect is similar. It embraces civil proceedings[189] and although commercial cases are not specifically mentioned, as they are in the Brussels I and the UK rules, they can be taken to be included. Criminal cases are thereby excluded, but there is no exclusion of administrative, customs or revenue matters or of matrimonial property, wills and succession, social security or arbitration.[190] Otherwise, the list of specific exceptions excludes from the Scottish rules all the matters which are excluded from the Brussels I and the UK rules and it is made clear that separation proceedings concern status and thus are excluded from the scope of the Scottish rules, as also are actions regulating the custody of children. Whereas r.2(e) in Sch.8 formerly made plain that actions of affiliation and aliment were within the scope of the rules, that rule has been repealed.[191] The following further matters fall outwith the scope of the Scottish rules:

(1) proceedings relating to parental responsibilities and rights under the Children (Scotland) Act 1995;

(2) guardianship of children and the management of the affairs of any incapax;

(3) commissary matters;

(4) remedies which are not in substance actions for decree against any person; and

(5) jurisdiction conferred by any enactment in respect of a specific subject matter on specific grounds.[192]

Domicile under Brussels I and the 1982 Act—Repeating the primary ground of 2.30 jurisdiction under the Brussels Convention, the Brussels I rules set out in art.2 (1) that, subject to other provisions of the Regulation providing for exceptions to that ground — "persons domiciled in a Member State shall, whatever their nationality, be sued in the courts of that Member State." But "domicile", at least so far as an individual is concerned, is not an autonomous European concept since art.59 (1) of Brussels I provides that in order to determine whether a party is domiciled in the Member State whose courts are seised of a matter, the court shall apply its internal law. Against that background a key jurisdictional concept of the 1982 Act

---

[188] Civil Jurisdiction and Judgments Act 1982 s.17(1).

[189] Civil Jurisdiction and Judgments Act 1982 s.20(1).

[190] *Lord Advocate v West End Construction*, 1990 S.C.L.R. 777 (Sh. Ct).

[191] The Civil Jurisdiction and Judgments (Maintenance) Regulations 2011 (SI 2011/1484) Sch.4 para.13.

[192] Civil Jurisdiction and Judgments Act 1982 s.21(1)(a) and Sch.9.

is understandably domicile. Domicile is not to be understood here in the sense in which it is encountered in international private law rules of status and succession ("the domicile of succession") but, in the case of an individual, is defined in the 1982 Act in a manner which is in a sense akin to what has been called the domicile of citation. For the purposes of the Act, a person is domiciled in the United Kingdom or in a part of the United Kingdom, or in a state other than a Contracting State if, and only if, he is resident in the United Kingdom or in a part of the United Kingdom, or in a state other than a Contracting State, as the case may be, and the nature and circumstances of his residence indicate that he has a substantial connection therewith.[193] He is domiciled in a particular place in the United Kingdom if, and only if, he is domiciled in the part of the United Kingdom in which that place is situated and is resident in that place.[194] Three months' residence in the United Kingdom, or part of it, gives rise to a presumption of substantial connection.[195] If a person is not by those rules domiciled in the United Kingdom and a question arises of whether he is domiciled in another Member State, the court is to apply the law of that state in order to determine whether he is domiciled there.[196]

In contrast to the Brussels Convention, the Brussels I Regulation does address the domicile of a legal or juristic person. Article 60(1) provides that such a legal person is domiciled at the place where it has its (a) statutory seat, or (b) central administration, or (c) principal place of business. For the purposes of the United Kingdom and Ireland, art.60(2) states that "statutory seat" means the registered office, or, if there is no such office anywhere, the place of incorporation or, if there is no such place anywhere, the place under the law of which the formation took place.[197] These provisions intermesh, though possibly not in absolute harmony, with the provisions of the 1982 Act which, in summary, provide that the seat of a corporation or association is treated as its domicile.[198] It may have a seat in more than one place. If (a) a company or an association was incorporated or formed under the law of any part of the United Kingdom and has its registered office or some other official address in the United Kingdom, or (b) its central management and control is exercised in the United Kingdom, it will have a seat in any part of, or place in, the United Kingdom in which (i) it has its registered office or some other official address, (ii) its central management and control is exercised, or (iii) it has a place of business.[199] A company or association has its seat in a state other than the United Kingdom if, and only if, it was incorporated or formed under the law of that state and has its registered office or some other official address in that state or its central management and control is exercised there,[200] but it is not to be regarded as having its seat in a Contracting State if it would not be so regarded by the courts of that state.[201] These rules for ascertaining the domicile of a company or association are subject to some modification in cases in which the court has an exclusive jurisdiction in relation to the company or association and also in certain other cases affecting company or association affairs.[202]

---

[193] Civil Jurisdiction and Judgments Act 1982 s.41(1), (2), (3) and (7).
[194] Civil Jurisdiction and Judgments Act 1982 s.41(4).
[195] Civil Jurisdiction and Judgments Act 1982 s.41(6).
[196] Brussels I art.59(2).
[197] art.60 extends also to partnerships and unincorporated associations.
[198] Civil Jurisdiction and Judgments Act 1982 s.42(1).
[199] Civil Jurisdiction and Judgments Act 1982 s.42(3), (4) and (5).
[200] Civil Jurisdiction and Judgments Act 1982 s.42(6).
[201] Civil Jurisdiction and Judgments Act 1982 s.42(7).
[202] Civil Jurisdiction and Judgments Act 1982 s.43.

Grounds of jurisdiction: The Scottish rules of the 1982 Act—The Scottish 2.31
rules provide a code of jurisdiction where they are not in conflict with the Brussels
I rules or the UK rules. In determining whether a Scottish court has jurisdiction, it
is necessary to have recourse to the Brussels I Regulation and the UK rules only
to ascertain whether there is such a conflict. The central principle of the Scottish
rules is that persons, whether legal or natural, are to be sued in the courts for the
place where they are domiciled.[203] That principle reflects corresponding provisions of the Brussels I rules and the UK rules and is not in conflict with them.
Unless the special rules relating to exclusive jurisdiction regardless of domicile
apply, any person domiciled in Scotland may therefore be sued in the Scottish
courts and, subject to any rules regulating the jurisdiction of the Court of Session
or the sheriff court on the basis of subject matter or value of the cause, any such
person may be sued either in the Court of Session or the sheriff court. The sheriff
court in which jurisdiction vests is that for the particular place within Scotland in
which the defender is domiciled. Domicile, although the principal, is not the only
ground of jurisdiction. In a variety of types of proceedings and circumstances,
there is under the Scottish rules independently of jurisdiction on grounds of domicile, special jurisdiction in courts other than those of the defender's domicile.[204]
Some of those grounds coincide or are compatible with the Brussels I rules and
others are not. There appears to be no case of conflict with the UK rules. Where
there is coincidence or compatibility and no rule of exclusive jurisdiction is trans-
gressed, the Scottish courts will have jurisdiction even if the defender is domiciled
in a Member State other than the United Kingdom. Where the rules of special
jurisdiction apply, there is jurisdiction in the Court of Session and also in the
sheriff court for the place in question unless the Court of Session alone is expressly
indicated as having jurisdiction. The following Scottish rules of jurisdiction other
than domicile coincide or are compatible with the Convention rules[205]:

(1) Where the person sued has no fixed residence, there is jurisdiction in
the court within whose jurisdiction he is personally cited. This ground
of jurisdiction does not coincide with any of the Brussels I or UK rules
but is compatible with them because a person who has no fixed
residence cannot be domiciled in another Member State or another
part of the United Kingdom except in the case, probably rare, in which
the law of a Member State so provides.

(2) In matters relating to a contract,[206] there is jurisdiction in the courts for
the place of performance of the "obligation in question". That obligation is that which corresponds to the contractual right upon which the
pursuing party's action is based.[207] Where the action is based on more
than one contractual obligation, it may be possible to identify a principal obligation, to which the other claims are truly ancillary, but in

---

[203] Civil Jurisdiction and Judgments Act 1982 Sch.8 para.1.
[204] Civil Jurisdiction and Judgments Act 1982 Sch.8 para.2.
[205] Civil Jurisdiction and Judgments Act 1982 Sch.8 para.2; cf. Sch.1 art.5; Sch.8 para.5; cf. Sch.1
arts 17 and 18.
[206] "Matters relating to a contract" is an independent concept which is to be given a "Community
meaning": *Peters v ZNAV* [1983] E.C.R. 987. A claim for restitution of money paid under a contract
void ab initio is not a matter relating to a contract — see *Kleinwort Benson Ltd v Glasgow City Council*
[1999] 1 A.C. 153. On the other hand, "the place of performance of the obligation" is to be determined
by the law governing the obligation under the conflict rules of the court before which the matter is
brought: *Tessili v Dunlop* [1976] E.C.R. 1473. See *Engdiv Ltd v G. Percy Trentham Ltd*, 1990 S.C. 53.
[207] *De Bloos v Bouyer* (C-59/77) [1976] E.C.R. 1497.

others there may be no proper scope for such an approach of accession to the principal and in that event the pursuing party has to resort to the fundamental ground of jurisdiction on the basis of domicile.[208] A claim for repayment of money paid under a contract void ab initio has been held not to be a matter relating to contract.[209] Having identified the obligation in question it is then necessary to identify its place of performance. Article 5(1)(b) of Brussels I stipulates that, unless otherwise agreed, in the case of a contract for the sale of goods the place of performance in a Member State is that at which the goods were, or should have been, delivered; and, similarly, in the case of provision of services, the place at which the services were or should have been provided. Subject to that provision, which is not found in the equivalent UK or Scottish rule, identifying the place of performance is governed by the contract's applicable law.[210] The place must be one at which the creditor in the obligation may insist on performance, but it is immaterial that there may be more than one such place.[211] In the case of a negative obligation it may be that the geographical scope is such that no particular place may be identified.[212]

The Brussels I rules[213] and the Scottish rules[214] also provide that, in matters relating to contract, if the action may be combined with an action against the same defender in matters relating to rights in rem in immoveable property, a person may be sued in the court of the place in which the property is situated.

(3) Special rules exist in the case of consumer and employment contracts and—under Brussels I alone—in relation to contracts of insurance. Under r.3 of the Scottish rules, mirroring art.15 (1) of Brussels I, to be a consumer a person must have concluded the contract for a purpose outwith his trade or profession. Additionally, the contract must be either a contract for the sale of goods on instalment credit terms; or a contract for a loan repayable by instalments or some other form of credit to finance the sale of goods; or, in any other case, a contract concluded with a person who pursues commercial or professional activities in Scotland or directs such activities to Scotland and the contract falls within the scope of those activities. Contracts for transport are excluded. Essentially the consumer may sue either in the courts for his domicile or those for the defender's domicile. But the consumer may be sued only in the courts of his domicile. There are restrictions on departing from those provisions by agreement.[215] In the case of an individual contract of employment, the employee may be sued only in the courts for his domicile. But the employer may be sued either in the courts of his domicile; or in the courts for the place where the employee

---

[208] See *Shenevai v Kreischer* (C-266/85) [1987] E.C.R. 239; *Leathertext Divisione Sintetici SpA v Bodotext BVBA* (C-420/97) [1999] E.C.R. I-6747.

[209] *Kleinwort Benson v City of Glasgow Council* [1999] A.C. 153.

[210] *Industrie Tessili Italiana Como v Dunlop AG* (C-12/76) [1976] E.C.R. 1473.

[211] *Bank of Scotland v Seitz*, 1990 S.L.T. 584.

[212] *Besix SA v Wasserreinigungsbau Alfred Kretschmar GmbH & Co KG* (C-256/00) [2002] E.C.R. I-1699.

[213] Brussels I art.6(4).

[214] Civil Jurisdiction and Judgments Act 1982 Sch.8 r.2(p).

[215] Civil Jurisdiction and Judgments Act 1982 Sch.8 r.3(6).

habitually carries out his work, or the place where he last did so; or, if the employee does not or did not habitually carry out his work in any one place, in the courts for the place where the business which engaged the employee is, or was, situated.[216] The rules respecting actions involving insurers are set out in arts 8–14 of Brussels I and, in general terms, provide some measures of protection for the insured.

(4) In matters relating to delict or quasi-delict,[217] there is jurisdiction in the courts for the place where the harmful event occurred or may occur. The notion of the place where the harmful event occurred covers both the place at which the damage occurred and that at which the event giving rise to the damage took place.[218] However, indirect financial consequences may not be taken into account for this purpose.[219] Claims for restitution or unjust enrichment have been held not to be matters relating to delict or quasi-delict.[220]

(5) A court has jurisdiction in matters relating to maintenance if it is the court for the place where the maintenance creditor is domiciled or habitually resident, or if the maintenance claim is ancillary to proceedings before it concerning the status of a person and it has jurisdiction to entertain those proceedings. Provisions to that effect were contained in r.2(e) of the Scottish rules and stemmed from art.5(2) of Brussels I. However, r.2(e) was repealed on June 18, 2011.[221] Article 5(2) is effectively replaced by the provisions contained in Council Regulation (EC) No. 4/2009—"the Maintenance Regulation".[222] A number of different grounds are provided for in the Maintenance Regulation. The principal rule is to be found in art.3, which provides for jurisdiction in the courts for the place where either the creditor or the defender is habitually resident; or in the court which, by its own law, has jurisdiction concerning the status of the person concerned or which, by its own law, has jurisdiction to entertain proceedings concerning parental responsibility provided that (i) maintenance is ancillary to the question of status or parental responsibility, as the case may be, with which the court is primarily concerned and (ii) that jurisdiction as respects the principal issue of status or parental responsibility is not based on nationality, or, in the case of the UK, domicile in the traditional common law sense.[223] Among other provisions of the Maintenance Regulation concerning jurisdiction are rules respecting the extent to which parties may prorogate jurisdiction, jurisdiction by submission

---

[216] cf. *Weber v Universal Ogden Services Ltd* (C-37/00) [2002] E.C.R. I-2013.

[217] "Delict or quasi-delict" must be given an independent meaning: *Kalfelis v Schroder, Munchmeyer, Hengst & Co* [1988] E.C.R. 5565. A statutory claim against insurers is not a matter relating to delict or quasi-delict: *Davenport v Corinthian Motor Policies at Lloyds*, 1991 S.C. 372.

[218] *Bier BV v Mines de Potasse d'Alsace* (21/76) [1976] E.C.R. 1735; see also *Shevill v Press Alliance S.A.* [1996] A.C. 959.

[219] *Dumez France SA and Tracoba SARL v Hessische Landesbank* (220/88) [1990] E.C.R. I-49; *Marinari v Lloyds Bank Plc* (C-364/93) [1995] E.C.R. I-2719; *Kronhofer v Maier* (C-168/02) [2004] E.C.R. I-6009.

[220] *Kleinwort Benson Ltd v Glasgow City Council* [1999] A.C. 153; *Compagnie Commercial Andre S.A. v Artibell Shipping Co Ltd*, 1999 S.L.T. 1051.

[221] Civil Jurisdiction and Judgments (Maintenance) Regulations 2011 (SI 2011/1484) Sch.4 para.13.

[222] Council Regulation (EC) No. 4/2009 of December 18, 2008 on jurisdiction, applicable law and enforcement of decisions and cooperation in matters relating to maintenance obligations ([2009] OJ L7, p.1).

[223] See art.2(3) and recital 18 of the preamble to the Regulation.

and subsidiary jurisdiction.[224] The provisions of the Maintenance Regulation are adapted by Sch.6 of the Civil Jurisdiction and Judgments (Maintenance) Regulations 2011[225] to apply as between the different parts of the UK.

(6) As regards a dispute arising out of the operation of a branch, agency or other establishment, there is jurisdiction in the courts for the place in which the branch, agency or other establishment is situated.[226]

(7) Where a person is sued in his capacity as settlor, trustee or beneficiary of a trust domiciled in Scotland, and created by the operation of statute, or by a written instrument, or created orally and evidenced in writing, there is jurisdiction in the Court of Session or the appropriate sheriff court within the meaning of s.24A of the Trusts (Scotland) Act 1921.[227]

(8) In proceedings concerning an arbitration which is conducted in Scotland or in which the procedure is governed by Scots law, there is jurisdiction in the Court of Session.[228] This ground of jurisdiction is compatible with the Convention rules because arbitration is expressly excluded from the scope of those rules.

(9) In proceedings which have as their object the decision of an organ of a company or other legal person or of an association of natural or legal persons, there is jurisdiction in the courts for the place where that company, legal person or association has its seat.[229]

(10) Where the person sued is one of a number of defenders, there is jurisdiction in the courts for the place where any one of them is domiciled, provided that the claims are so closely connected that it is expedient to hear and determine them together to avoid the risk of irreconcilable judgments resulting from separate proceedings.[230]

(11) Where a person is sued as a third party in an action on a warranty or guarantee or in any other third party proceedings, there is jurisdiction in the courts seized of the original proceedings unless these were instituted solely with the object of removing him from the jurisdiction of the court which would be competent in his case.[231]

(12) On a counterclaim arising from the same contract or facts on which the original claim was based, there is jurisdiction in the court in which the original claim is pending.[232]

(13) Jurisdiction also exists where the defender has agreed to prorogate the jurisdiction of the court. An agreement between parties to prorogate the jurisdiction of a court is subject to conditions respecting its either being in, or evidenced by, writing or being in a form which accords with certain practices or commercial usages.[233] A defender may also

---

[224] arts 4, 5 and 6.

[225] SI 2011/1484.

[226] Civil Jurisdiction and Judgments Act 1982 Sch.8 r.2(f); cf. *Somafer v Saar-Ferngas* (C-3/78) [1978] E.C.R. 2183.

[227] Civil Jurisdiction and Judgments Act 1982 Sch.8 r.2(g).

[228] Civil Jurisdiction and Judgments Act 1982 Sch.8 r.2 (m). See also the Arbitration (Scotland) Act 2010.

[229] Civil Jurisdiction and Judgments Act 1982 Sch.8 r.2(l).

[230] Civil Jurisdiction and Judgments Act 1982 Sch.8 r.2(o)(i); cf. *Réunion Européenne v Spliethoffs Bevrachtingskantoor BV* (C-51/97) [1998] E.C.R. I-6511; *Roche Nederland BV v Primus* (C-539/03) [2006] E.C.R. I-6535.

[231] Civil Jurisdiction and Judgments Act 1982 Sch.8 r.2(o)(ii).

[232] Civil Jurisdiction and Judgments Act 1982 Sch.8 r.2(o)(iii). See also para.2.42, below.

[233] Civil Jurisdiction and Judgments Act 1982 Sch.8 r.6.

prorogate the jurisdiction of a court by submission to it. Submission is effected by entering appearance, unless appearance was entered to contest jurisdiction.[234]

Where a ground of jurisdiction under the Scottish rules is incompatible with the Brussels I rules, that ground may not be invoked against a defender who is domiciled in another Member State or where the Brussels I rules otherwise indicate a jurisdiction outside Scotland. Certain of the Scottish rules fall into that category. Subject to the ground of jurisdiction being excluded on that account, the Scottish courts have jurisdiction in the following further circumstances[235]:

(1) Where the person sued is not domiciled in the United Kingdom, there is jurisdiction in the courts for any place where (a) any moveable property belonging to him has been arrested, or (b) any immoveable property in which he has any beneficial interest is situated. Arrestment to found jurisdiction is further discussed below.[236]

(2) In proceedings which have been brought to assert, declare or determine proprietary or possessory rights or rights of security in or over moveable property or to obtain authority to dispose of moveable property, there is jurisdiction in the courts for the place where the property is situated.

(3) In proceedings for interdict, there is jurisdiction in the courts for the place where it is alleged that the wrong is likely to be committed.[237]

(4) In proceedings concerning a debt secured over immoveable property, there is jurisdiction in the courts for the place where the property is situated.

(5) In proceedings principally concerned with the registration in the United Kingdom or the validity in the United Kingdom of patents, trademarks, designs or other similar rights required to be deposited or registered, there is jurisdiction in the Court of Session.

Exclusive jurisdiction under the Scottish Rules of the 1982 Act—The Scottish **2.32** rules, reflecting in large measure the Brussels I rules, provide that in certain classes of proceedings a court shall have exclusive jurisdiction regardless of domicile or any other jurisdictional rule.[238] The classes of exclusive jurisdiction are as follows:

(1) In proceedings which have as their object rights in rem in, or tenancies of, immoveable property, there is exclusive jurisdiction in the courts for the place where the property is situated. The Brussels I and Scottish rules qualify that rule by providing that where the tenancy is for temporary private use for a maximum period of six consecutive months, the courts of the defendant's domicile shall also have jurisdiction, if the landlord and tenant are natural persons domiciled in the same country.

(2) In proceedings which have as their object the validity of the constitution, the nullity or the dissolution of companies or other legal persons or associations of natural or legal persons, there is exclusive jurisdiction in

---

[234] Civil Jurisdiction and Judgments Act 1982 Sch.8 r.7.
[235] Civil Jurisdiction and Judgments Act 1982 Sch.8 r.2(h), (j), (k) and (n).
[236] See para.2.41, below.
[237] Jurisdiction in actions of interdict may also be available under r.2(c) of the Scottish rules and Brussels I art.5 (3), the former having been amended to include the words referring to the place where the harmful event *may* occur which were included in the latter and which indicate that the provision may cover interdict. See also *Verein für Konsumenteninformation v Henkel* (C-167/00) [2002] E.C.R. I-8111.
[238] Brussels I art.22; Civil Jurisdiction and Judgments Act 1982 Sch.8 rr.5 and 6.

the courts for the place where the company, legal person or association has its seat.

(3) In proceedings which have as their object the validity of entries in public registers, there is exclusive jurisdiction in the courts for the place where the register is kept.

(4) In proceedings concerned with the enforcement of judgments, there is exclusive jurisdiction in the courts for the place where the judgment has been or is to be enforced.

(5) Where parties have prorogated the jurisdiction of a particular court, there is exclusive jurisdiction in that court.[239]

2.33 Actions involving status—Proceedings concerning status, being excluded from the scope of the Civil Jurisdiction and Judgments Act 1982, are subject to distinct jurisdictional rules. With effect from August 1, 2004, Council Regulation (EC) No. 2201/2003, commonly known as "Brussels II bis"[240] introduced a scheme for jurisdiction and the recognition of judgments in certain actions of status.[241] The Regulation contains jurisdictional rules for actions of divorce, legal separation and annulment of marriage. In addition, it deals with parental responsibility over a child.[242] The principal basis for jurisdiction is habitual residence. The Regulation does not cover all cases, so it is also necessary to consider other statutory and common law rules on the subject.

2.34 Marriage and divorce—In matters relating to divorce, legal separation or marriage annulment, jurisdiction is conferred on the courts of the Member State[243] in which: (i) both spouses are habitually resident; (ii) the spouses were last habitually resident insofar as one of them still resides there; (iii) the respondent is habitually resident; (iv) on a joint application, either spouse is habitually resident; or (v) the applicant has been habitually resident for at least one year prior to the application being made, or (vi) for six months coupled with nationality or a domicile in the same country. A further basis for jurisdiction is conferred by nationality or, in the United Kingdom and Ireland, by the domicile of both spouses.[244] In the Brussels II bis regulation the term domicile does not mean domicile as defined in the 1982 Act but connotes the traditional common law concept of a permanent relationship to a legal system.[245] The Court of Session enjoys jurisdiction in actions of divorce or separation if jurisdiction is conferred under the Brussels II

---

[239] But note *McGowan v Summit at Lloyds*, 2002 S.C. 638.

[240] Council Regulation (EC) No. 2201/2003 of November 27, 2003 on Jurisdiction and Recognition and Enforcement of Judgments in Matrimonial Matters and the Matters of Parental Responsibility ([2003] OJ L338, p.1) The description of the regulation "Brussels II bis" results from the fact that it repealed an earlier family law regulation, namely Council Regulation (EC) No. 1347/2000 which had been known as "Brussels II".

[241] The European Communities (Matrimonial and Parental Responsibility Jurisdiction and Judgments) (Scotland) Regulations 2005 (SSI 2005/42) amend other domestic legislation to make it consistent with and clarify their relationship to the Regulation.

[242] EU Council Regulation "Brussels II bis" ss.1 and 2.

[243] In the Brussels II bis Regulation "Member State" is defined, in art.2(3), as not including Denmark.

[244] art.3 of the Regulation. See on parental responsibilities in divorce, legal separation and annulment cases art.12 (below, paras 2.37 and 2.38).

[245] See, by way of example, *Singh v Singh*, 2005 S.L.T. 749. For a summary of the common law concept of domicile, see *Court of Session Practice*, para.B[602] and for a fuller exposition reference may be made to Beaumont and McEleavy, *Anton's Private International Law* (2011), Ch.7.

bis Regulation[246] or, where no court of another Member State has jurisdiction under the Regulation (i.e. the action would be an "excluded action"[247]), if either party to the marriage is domiciled in Scotland when the action commences.[248] Likewise, the Regulation provides the principal ground for jurisdiction in actions for declarator of nullity of marriage with a residual jurisdictional basis on the ground of domicile of either party to the marriage where the Regulation is inapplicable.[249] Actions for declarator of freedom and putting to silence and actions for declarator of marriage are not covered by the Regulation. Such actions may be raised in the Court of Session if either party is domiciled in Scotland when the action is commenced or if either party has been habitually resident in Scotland for one year prior to commencement.[250] In actions for declarator of marriage, a further basis of jurisdiction exists based on the domicile or habitual residence of a party who has died before the action was commenced. In actions of divorce or separation the sheriff court has jurisdiction if the requirements of domicile and habitual residence in Scotland are satisfied (including the non-contravention of the Regulation) and either party to the marriage was resident in the sheriffdom for 40 days preceding the raising of the action, or was so resident for a period of at least 40 days ending within 40 days of the raising of the action and has, when the action is raised, no known residence in Scotland.[251] The Family Law (Scotland) Act 2006 s.4 amended the Sheriff Courts (Scotland) Act 1907 to remove the incompetency of actions of nullity of marriage in the sheriff court, but made no provision for any jurisdictional requirements.

Civil partnerships—The Court of Session and the sheriff court have jurisdiction **2.35** to entertain actions for the dissolution of a civil partnership or for separation of the parties to such a partnership.[252] Only the Court of Session may entertain an action for declarator of nullity of a civil partnership.[253] In all cases, jurisdiction will exist in relation to the dissolution or annulment of a civil partnership or for the separation of civil partners where: (1) both civil partners are habitually resident in Scotland; (2) both civil partners were last habitually resident in Scotland and one of the civil partners continues to reside there; (3) the defender is habitually resident in Scotland; (4) the pursuer is habitually resident in Scotland and has resided there for at least one year immediately preceding the date on which the action is begun; or (5) the pursuer is domiciled and habitually resident in Scotland and has resided there for at least six months immediately preceding the date on which the action is begun.[254] In cases of dissolution or separation, no other court must have or be recognised as having jurisdiction under the preceding rules, and either civil

---

[246] Domicile and Matrimonial Proceedings Act 1973 (the "1973 Act") s.7(2A)(a) as introduced by the European Communities (Matrimonial Jurisdiction and Judgments) (Scotland) Regulations 2001 (SSI 2001/36, now revoked).

[247] As defined in the 1973 Act s.12(5)(d).

[248] 1973 Act s.7(2A)(b).

[249] 1973 Act s.7(3A) and (3B).

[250] 1973 Act s.7(2) and (3).

[251] 1973 Act s.8, as amended by Divorce Jurisdiction, Court Fees and Legal Aid (Scotland) Act 1983 Sch.1 para.18; and European Communities (Matrimonial Jurisdiction and Judgments) (Scotland) Regulations 2001 (SSI 2001/36) and the European Communities (Matrimonial and Parental Responsibility Jurisdiction and Judgments) (Scotland) Regulations 2005 (SSI 2005/42).

[252] See generally Civil Partnership Act 2004 s.225.

[253] Civil Partnership Act 2004 s.225(3).

[254] Civil Partnership (Jurisdiction and Recognition of Judgments) (Scotland) Regulations 2005 (SSI 2005/629) reg.4 (made under the Civil Partnership Act 2004 s.219).

partner must be domiciled in Scotland on the date proceedings begin. For the sheriff court either civil partner must be resident in the sheriffdom for a period of 40 days ending with the date the action begins, or be so resident for a period of not less than 40 days ending not more than 40 days before that date and have no known residence in Scotland at that date.[255] The Court of Session may exercise jurisdiction in dissolution or separation cases only if the civil partnership was registered in Scotland and it appears to the court to be in the interests of justice to assume jurisdiction in the case.[256] The same rules apply in cases of nullity; alternatively, the Court of Session has jurisdiction if either of the ostensible civil partners is either domiciled in Scotland on the date proceedings begin, or died before that date and either was at death domiciled in Scotland or had been habitually resident in Scotland throughout the year ending with the date of death.[257]

2.36 Parentage and death—In declarators of parentage, non-parentage, and to the limited extent that such declarators may still be competent,[258] declarators of legitimacy, legitimation or illegitimacy, the Court of Session has jurisdiction if the child was born in Scotland or if (a) the alleged or presumed parent, or (b) the child, was domiciled in Scotland when the action was raised, or was habitually resident in Scotland for not less than one year immediately preceding that date.[259] If the parent or child is dead the jurisdictional requirements apply to the date of death. In declarators of death, there is jurisdiction if the missing person was domiciled in Scotland on the date on which he was last known to be alive, or had been habitually resident there throughout the preceding year, or if, in an action at the instance of his spouse, the spouse is at the date of raising the action domiciled in Scotland or has been habitually resident there throughout the preceding year.[260] In actions of declarator of parentage, non-parentage, legitimacy, legitimation or illegitimacy, there is jurisdiction if the child was born in the sheriffdom or if one of the grounds for Court of Session jurisdiction is satisfied and the parent or child was habitually resident in the sheriffdom at the date the action was raised or at the date of his death.[261] There is jurisdiction in declarators of death if any of the grounds for vesting jurisdiction in the Court of Session is satisfied and, in addition, the pursuer has been resident in the sheriffdom for a period of not less than 40 days ending with the date of raising the action.[262]

2.37 Parental responsibility: Regulation cases—The Brussels II bis Regulation is also relevant in matters of parental responsibility for children. "Parental responsibility" means all rights and duties relating to the person or property of a child given to a natural or legal person by judgment, operation of law, or agreement having legal effect.[263] The courts of a Member State have jurisdiction in relation to such matters over a child who is habitually resident in that Member State when

---

[255] Civil Partnership Act 2004 s.225(2).
[256] Civil Partnership Act 2004 s.225(1)(c).
[257] Civil Partnership Act 2004 s.225(3).
[258] Subject to certain savings, the status of illegitimacy, and accordingly actions for declarator of illegitimacy, legitimacy and legitimation, were abolished by the Family Law (Scotland) Act 2006 s.21. See the Law Reform (Parent and Child) (Scotland) Act ss.1, 7 and 9 as amended by the 2006 Act and also SSI 2006/212 art.10.
[259] Law Reform (Parent and Child) (Scotland) Act 1986 s.7(2).
[260] Presumption of Death (Scotland) Act 1977 s.1(3).
[261] Law Reform (Parent and Child) (Scotland) Act 1986 s.7(3).
[262] Presumption of Death (Scotland) Act 1977 s.1(4).
[263] EU Council Regulation No. 2201/2003 art.2(7).

the court is seised of the case.[264] This is subject to rules on when a child moves lawfully to a new habitual residence in another Member State; the courts of the Member State of the child's former habitual residence retain jurisdiction for a three-month period following the move for the purpose of modifying judgments on access rights given in that Member State before the child's move, so long as the holder of those access rights continues to have his or her habitual residence in that Member State.[265] There are also rules to deal with cases of child abduction: the courts of the Member State of the abducted child's habitual residence retain jurisdiction until the child has acquired habitual residence in another Member State, and either all persons having custody rights have acquiesced in the removal or retention, or the child has been resident for one year and become settled in the other Member State after the person with custody rights knew or should have known of the child's whereabouts, and at least one of four conditions spelled out in the legislation has been met.[266] The courts of a Member State exercising jurisdiction on an application for divorce, legal separation or marriage annulment have jurisdiction in any matter relating to parental responsibility connected with that application where at least one of the spouses has parental responsibility in relation to the child and the jurisdiction of the court has been accepted expressly or otherwise in an unequivocal manner by the spouses and by the holders of parental responsibility at the time the court is seised, and the jurisdiction is in the superior interests of the child.[267] Where this last rule does not determine a court's jurisdiction, and a child's habitual residence cannot be established, the court of the Member State where the child is present has jurisdiction.[268]

Parental responsibilities: Non-regulation cases—In actions relating to parental **2.38** responsibilities which are not subject to the Brussels II bis Regulation, jurisdiction exists where (1) the child is habitually resident in Scotland, or (2) is present in Scotland and is not habitually resident in any part of the United Kingdom,[269] unless, in either case, matrimonial proceedings are continuing in a court in any part of the United Kingdom in respect of the marriage of the parents of the child.[270] Where it has jurisdiction in an action of divorce, separation, declarator of marriage or declarator of nullity, it has jurisdiction in questions relating to the custody of children.[271] It may also assume jurisdiction where the child is present in Scotland and the court considers that, for the protection of the child, it is necessary to make such an order immediately.[272] In cases relating to parental responsibilities, the sheriff has a jurisdiction on similar principles to those applying to the Court of Session.[273]

Actions not involving status and outwith the 1982 Act: The Court of Session— 2.39 With the exception of proceedings concerning status, in proceedings which by

---

[264] EU Council Regulation No. 2201/2003 art.8(1).

[265] EU Council Regulation No. 2201/2003 art.9.

[266] EU Council Regulation No. 2201/2003 art.10. Art.11 gives rules on proceedings for return of a child under the Hague Convention 1980 on the Civil Aspects of International Child Abduction.

[267] EU Council Regulation No. 2201/2003 art.12.

[268] EU Council Regulation No. 2201/2003 art.13. This rule also applies to refugee or internationally displaced children.

[269] Family Law Act 1986 ss.9, 10.

[270] Family Law Act 1986 s.11.

[271] See *Battaglia v Battaglia*, 1967 S.L.T. 49; 1973 Act s.10 and Sch.2 Pt I para.4; Family Law Act 1986 s.13.

[272] Family Law Act 1986 s.12.

[273] Family Law Act 1986 ss.8–13.

reason of their nature or subject matter fall outwith the scope of the Civil Jurisdiction and Judgments Act 1982 neither domicile in the sense of that Act nor domicile of succession is, as a general rule, relevant to jurisdiction. In such cases the rules of jurisdiction which before the 1982 Act were generally applicable to such proceedings remain in force. Two of the main grounds on which the Court of Session has been wont to assert jurisdiction over persons, and which may still be invoked where the 1982 Act does not apply, and no question of status is in issue, are (1) that the defender is resident is Scotland, or (2) that he is the owner of heritable property in Scotland. Residence is a ground of jurisdiction over all persons ordinarily resident in Scotland, or persons who have been resident for 40 days.[274] Residence means actual and not constructive residence.[275] In the case of a partnership or company the equivalent to residence is having a place of business[276] in Scotland, not merely having an agent there if that agent has no power to bind his principal.[277] Jurisdiction is established over a friendly society if its rules are registered in Scotland or if it is incorporated and has a registered office in Scotland.[278] Ownership of, or a leasehold interest in, heritable property in Scotland will subject the owner to the jurisdiction of the Court of Session although the action may have no relation to that property.[279] Jurisdiction may also be founded by arrestment, by reconvention and by prorogation.[280] The Court of Session has jurisdiction to entertain an action for reduction of any decree granted by a Scottish court.[281]

2.40 Actions not involving status and outwith the 1982 Act: The sheriff court— The jurisdiction of the sheriff court is largely statutory. The principal rules, other than those already noticed for actions concerning status,[282] are contained in s.6 of the Sheriff Courts (Scotland) Act 1907 as amended by the Sheriff Courts (Scotland) Act 1913 and later legislation. These rules now receive effect subject to the Brussels I rules and the Civil Jurisdiction and Judgments Act 1982[283] and are in part superseded by that Act. The following rules remain in force for cases to which the 1982 Act does not apply. A sheriff has jurisdiction, in actions competent in the sheriff court, (a) where the defender (or where there are several defenders over each of whom a sheriff court has jurisdiction in terms of the Act, where one of them) resides[284] within the jurisdiction, or, having resided there for at least 40 days, has ceased to reside there for less than 40 days, and has no known residence in Scotland, (b) where the defender carries on business, and has a place of business, within the jurisdiction, and is cited either personally or at such place

---

[274] Erskine, I, 2, 16; *Joel v Gin* (1859) 21 D. 929; *Martin v Szyszka*, 1943 S.C. 203. The jurisdiction afforded by 40 days' residence ceases immediately on the defender's ceasing to reside in Scotland: see Maclaren, *Court of Session Practice* (1916), p.36; *Carter v Allison*, 1967 S.L.T. 17.

[275] *Findlay v Donachie*, 1944 S.C. 306; *Carter v Allison* 1967 S.L.T. 17.

[276] See *O'Brien v Davies & Son*, 1961 S.L.T. 85.

[277] *Laidlaw Provident, etc. Insurance Co* (1890) 17 R. 544.

[278] *Sons of Temperance Friendly Society*, 1926 S.C. 418; Friendly Societies Act 1992.

[279] *Ferrie v Woodward* (1831) 9 S. 854; *Fraser v Fraser & Hibbert* (1870) 8 M. 400; *Smith v Stuart* (1894) 22 R. 130; *Thorburn v Dempster* (1900) 2 F. 583; *Forth Tugs Ltd v Wilmington Trust Company*, 1985 S.C. 317.

[280] See paras 2.41, 2.42 and 2.43, below.

[281] Law Reform (Miscellaneous Provisions) (Scotland) Act 1980 s.20.

[282] See para.2.34, above.

[283] Civil Jurisdiction and Judgments Act 1982 s.20(3).

[284] There must be actual residence: *Findlay v Donachie*, 1944 S.C. 306; *McCord v McCord*, 1946 S.C. 198. The material date for determining the question of jurisdiction is the date of citation: *McNeill v McNeill*, 1960 S.C. 30.

of business,[285] (c) where the defender is a person not otherwise subject to the jurisdiction of the courts of Scotland and a ship or vessel of which he is owner or part owner or master, or goods, debts, money or other moveable property belonging to him have been arrested within the jurisdiction,[286] (d) where the defender is the owner or part owner or tenant or joint tenant, whether individually or as a trustee, of heritable property within the jurisdiction, and the action relates to such property or to his interest therein; (g) where in an action of furthcoming or multiplepoinding the fund or subject *in medio* is situated within the jurisdiction; or the arrestee or holder of the fund is subject to the jurisdiction of the court, (h) where the party sued is the pursuer in any action pending within the jurisdiction against the party suing[287] and (j) where the defender prorogates the jurisdiction of the court.[288]

Arrestments to found jurisdiction—The mere possession of moveable property **2.41** in Scotland does not afford jurisdiction.[289] But, under the process known as arrestment to found jurisdiction, if moveable property belonging to the defender (e.g. a ship) or a debt due to him in Scotland is arrested under a warrant from the Court of Session or from the sheriff court, he is subjected to the jurisdiction of the courts in Scotland in the action in respect of which the arrestments are used.[290] This applies only to actions with conclusions for payment of money or delivery of an article, not to actions affecting status, nor to a bare declarator or reduction.[291] Nor is it a process which will found jurisdiction in a petition for sequestration.[292] An arrestment to found jurisdiction has no effect except to found jurisdiction in the particular case; it does not give any nexus over the subject arrested, nor does it interpel the arrestee from paying the debt.[293] But the subject arrested must be one which could be arrested in execution.[294] This ground of jurisdiction is preserved by the Scottish rules of the 1982 Act but is not available against a defender who is domiciled in the United Kingdom; and it is incompatible with the Brussels I rules and so is not available against a defender who is domiciled in a Member State.[295] In the sheriff court, jurisdiction may be founded on arrestment only where the defender is not otherwise subject to the jurisdiction of the Scottish courts.[296]

Reconvention—Where a party raises an action in the Court of Session he thereby **2.42** submits himself to its jurisdiction in any counter action relating to the same dispute, as, for instance, in the case of cross-actions arising from a collision

---

[285] *Bruce v British Motor Trading Co*, 1924 S.C. 908; *Hay's Trs v London and N.W. Ry*, 1909 S.C. 707.

[286] See below, para.2.41.

[287] As to reconvention, of which this is an extension, see below, para.2.42. As to the limits of this statutory provision see *Kitson v Kitson*, 1945 S.C. 434.

[288] See below, para.2.34: *McGowan v Summit at Lloyds*, 2002 S.C. 638.

[289] See paras 2.36 and 2.37, above.

[290] See form of warrants in Maclaren, *Court of Session Practice* (1916), Ch.II. A right to expenses may be arrested to found jurisdiction: *Agnew v Norwest Construction Co*, 1935 S.C. 771; *Ladgroup Ltd v Euroeast Lines S.A.*, 1997 S.L.T. 916.

[291] *Morley v Jackson* (1888) 16 R. 78; *Williams v Royal College* (1897) 5 S.L.T. 208.

[292] *Croil, Petr* (1863) 1 M. 509.

[293] *Leggat Bros v Gray*, 1908 S.C. 67; *Fraser-Johnston Engineering Co v Jeffs*, 1920 S.C. 222.

[294] *Leggat Bros v Gray*, 1908 S.C. 67; as to arrestability, see para.48.04, below.

[295] See para.2.29, above.

[296] See para.2.40, above.

between two ships.[297] He does not subject himself to the jurisdiction in an action relating to a separate question.[298] Reconvention will apply even although the action by the foreigner may not be the first in date.[299] It is not pleadable after the *actio conventionis* has been finally decided, though it may technically still be in court.[300] In order that jurisdiction may be founded on reconvention the foreigner must have sought the Scottish courts voluntarily. Where an English woman, not otherwise subject to the jurisdiction, brought a suspension of a threatened charge on a bill, it was held that she had not subjected herself to the jurisdiction of the Court of Session in an action for payment of the amount due on the bill, in respect that her proceedings were not voluntary but taken in self-defence.[301] The principle of reconvention is preserved by Brussels I and the 1982 Act to the extent that, on a counterclaim arising from the same contract or facts on which the original claim was based, there is jurisdiction in the court in which the original claim is pending.[302]

2.43 Prorogation—Jurisdiction may arise from prorogation. If a person submits himself to a court, either by express prior agreement,[303] or by appearing in answer to a citation without taking the plea of no jurisdiction before the record is closed,[304] he cannot afterwards take the objection that the court in question has no jurisdiction over him. Prorogation will not obviate the objection of want of jurisdiction in an action of divorce.[305] In any case, prorogation only meets the objection that the court has no jurisdiction over the particular defender, not the objection that the case is one which the court, at common law or by statute, has no power to entertain. "No parties can convey to a Court jurisdiction which does not belong to it."[306] It has been held in the Outer House that the court might decline to accept jurisdiction, founded on a clause of prorogation, in an undefended case where neither the parties nor the matter in dispute had any connection with Scotland.[307] Any provision in a contract for the sale of an article whereby any party prorogates the jurisdiction of a particular sheriff court is void.[308] The same result is achieved in the case of consumer credit agreements,[309] including hire purchase agreements,[310] and consumer hire agreements[311] by the Consumer Credit Act 1974 which provides that no court, other than the sheriff court where the debtor or hirer resides

---

[297] *Morrison & Milne v Massa* (1866) 5 M. 130. Even a sovereign state by invoking the Scottish court exposes itself to any lawful defence: see *Government of the Republic of Spain v National Bank of Scotland*, 1939 S.C. 413, and cases there cited.

[298] *Thompson v Whitehead* (1862) 24 D. 331. But see *Clydedock Engineering Ltd v Cliveden Compania Naviera S.A.*, 1987 S.L.T. 762, OH.

[299] *Morrison & Milne v Massa* (1866) 5 M. 130.

[300] *Hurst, Nelson & Co v Whatley*, 1912 S.C. 1041.

[301] *Davis v Cadman* (1897) 24 R. 297; see also *Macaulay v Hussain*, 1967 S.L.T. 311.

[302] See para.2.31 (subhead (12)), above.

[303] *Elderslie S.S. Co v Burrell* (1895) 22 R. 389; *Lawrence v Taylor*, 1934 S.L.T. 76 (prorogation by agreement to arbitrate in Scotland).

[304] *Fraser-Johnston Engineering Co v Jeffs*, 1920 S.C. 222.

[305] *Fraser, Husband and Wife*, ii, 1294; but see *A.B. v C.D.*, 1957 S.C. 415 (cross-actions of nullity and declarator of marriage).

[306] per Lord Brougham in *Forest v Harvey* (1845) 4 Bell's App. 197.

[307] *Styring v Borough of Oporovec*, 1931 S.L.T. 493.

[308] Law Reform (Miscellaneous Provisions) (Scotland) Act 1940 s.4; cf. *English v Donnelly*, 1958 S.C. 494.

[309] Consumer Credit Act 1974 s.8(2).

[310] Consumer Credit Act 1974 ss.8(2) and 9(3).

[311] Consumer Credit Act 1974 s.15.

or carries on business, shall have jurisdiction to enforce at the instance of the creditor or owner such an agreement or any security relating to it or to enforce against the debtor or hirer or his relative any linked transactions.[312] The principle of prorogation is preserved by Brussels I and the 1982 Act. A clause which seeks to prorogate exclusive jurisdiction must be clear and precise.[313]

Forum non conveniens—Subject to restrictions in a case covered by Brussels **2.44** I, either the Court of Session or the sheriff court may decline to exercise jurisdiction in a particular case on the plea of forum non conveniens, which developed from the plea of *forum non competens*. The proper English equivalent of the term is, it has been laid down, "appropriate".[314] The issue is thus not one of simple convenience. For the success of the plea it is in the first place necessary to show that some other court, in a civilised country, has concurrent jurisdiction.[315] The principles underlying the plea were described in *Spiliada Maritime Corporation v Cansulex Ltd*,[316] in which the House of Lords applied the Scots doctrine of forum non conveniens to English law. That description has been accepted as applicable in Scotland.[317] No rule has been laid down as to the grounds on which a court should hold that it is not the appropriate one to try a case where it has jurisdiction, except in the very general form that the court has

> "to consider how best the ends of justice in the case in question and on the facts before it, so far as they can be measured in advance, can be respectively ascertained and served".[318]

Appropriateness will, however, involve examining how real and substantial is the connexion between the dispute and the court, and the alternative court said to be *forum conveniens*. Elements of weight, but not necessarily conclusive, are that the question raised is one of foreign law, that the proof must be by foreign witnesses, that neither party is resident in Scotland, or that litiscontestation occurred earlier in this country.[319] It is irrelevant to consider on what grounds the jurisdiction of the Scottish court arises.[320] Where both the parties to an action were carrying on business in France, the question involved a claim for damages for unseaworthiness of a French ship, and all the witnesses were resident either in France or in England, the plea of forum non conveniens was sustained in reference to the sheriff court of Dumbarton, where, with jurisdiction established by arrestments, the action had been brought.[321] The appropriate course if the plea of forum non conveniens is sustained is to sist the cause.[322] However, the plea of forum non

---

[312] Consumer Credit Act 1974 s.141(3) and (3A).

[313] *Morrison v Panic Link Ltd*, 1994 S.L.T. 232; *Compagnie Commercial Andre S.A. v Artibell Shipping Co Ltd*, 1999 S.L.T. 1051: *McGowan v Summit at Lloyds*, 2002 S.C. 638.

[314] per Lord Dunedin in *Société du Gaz v Armateurs Francais*, 1926 S.C. (HL) 13.

[315] *Clements v Macaulay* (1866) 4 M. 583.

[316] *Spiliada Maritime Corporation v Cansulex Ltd* [1987] 1 A.C. 460, per Lord Goff at 476–478.

[317] *RAB v MIB*, 2009 S.C. 58.

[318] *Société du Gaz v Armateurs Francais*, 1926 S.C. (HL) 13 at [22], per Lord Sumner.

[319] *Sim v Robinow* (1892) 19 R. 665; *Société du Gaz*, 1926 S.C. (HL) 13; *Woodbury v Sutherland's Trs*, 1938 S.C. 689; *Argyllshire Weavers Ltd v A. Macaulay (Tweeds) Ltd*, 1962 S.C. 388; *L v L*, 2000 S.L.T. (Sh. Ct) 12. Cf. *Credit Chimique v James Scott Engineering Group*, 1979 S.C. 406; 1982 S.L.T. 131; *Mitchell v Mitchell*, 1992 S.C. 372; *Sokha v Secretary of State for the Home Department*, 1992 S.L.T. 1049.

[320] per Lord Shaw, *Société du Gaz v Armateurs Francais*, 1926 S.C. (HL) 13 at [18].

[321] *Société du Gaz v Armateurs Francais* 1926 S.C. (HL) 13.

[322] *De Mulder v Jadranska Linijska*, 1989 S.L.T. 269, OH.

conveniens is not consistent with the principles of the Brussels I rules and where jurisdiction is based on a ground contained in those rules, for example the domicile of the defender in the Member State concerned, the court cannot decline jurisdiction on the basis of forum non conveniens, irrespective whether the alternative forum said to be the more appropriate forum is in a Member State or outwith the European Union.[323]

2.45 Declinature—In any particular case, the exercise of jurisdiction may be excluded by the declinature of the judge. This may be either on the ground of relationship to one of the parties, or of interest in the matters in the case. The Scots Acts[324] dealing with relationship have now been repealed[325] and the matter is dealt with administratively. Where the objection is that of interest in the cause, any pecuniary interest will disqualify, such as that of holding shares in a company which is a party to the action.[326] But a judge is not prevented from sitting by virtue of his being a taxpayer or a ratepayer and liable to contribute to or benefit from the public exchequer in question[327] Where the interest is not pecuniary it must be shown to be substantial, especially in cases where declinature would result in public inconvenience.[328] In practice, declinature, in cases where the interest is not really substantial, is elided by consent of parties; but if no such consent is given, or if the grounds of objection are not discovered until after decree, the decree will be reducible.[329] A challenge to a judge on the grounds of interest in the cause may also be based on art.6 of the European Convention on Human Rights.[330]

III. ARBITRATION

2.46 Arbitration—Arbitration is a longstanding method of dispute resolution whereby, in preference to having their dispute decided by the courts, parties agree, either in advance of any dispute arising (by, for example, including an arbitration clause in their contract) or after the dispute has arisen, that the dispute should be decided by a private tribunal, whether constituted by one or more individuals, chosen by them, or failing agreement in the selection of the tribunal, an arbiter or arbiters selected by some third party (usually, the holder for the time being of an office in an institution or professional association). In principle, such an agreement excludes the jurisdiction of the courts, if either party insists on the agreement to go to arbitration. The courts will normally enforce that agreement by declining to hear and determine the dispute and leaving matters to the arbitration tribunal. But it has been generally recognised, perhaps to varying extents, that it may be necessary to temper observance of that principle by allowing access to the judicial

---

[323] *Owusu v Jackson* (C-281/02) [2005] E.C.R. I-1383.

[324] Declinature Act 1594 (c.22); Declinature Act 1681 (c.13).

[325] Court of Session Act 1988 s.52(2), Sch.2. The repeal of the 1681 Act is only so far as regarding the Court of Session.

[326] *Sellar v Highland Ry*, 1919 S.C. (HL) 19. See also *R. v Bow Street Magistrates ex parte Pinochet (No.2)* [2000] 1 A.C. 119.

[327] Court of Session Act 1988 s.4.

[328] *Wildridge v Anderson* (1897) 25 R. (J.) 27. See also *Rae v Hamilton* (1904) 6 F. (J.) 42. But cf. *Pinochet* [2000] 1 A.C. 119.

[329] *Ommanney v Smith* (1851) 13 D. 678; *Sellar v Highland Ry*, 1919 S.C. (HL) 19; see also *R. v Bow Street Metropolitan Stipendiary Magistrate, Ex p. Pinochet (No.2)* [2000] 1 A.C. 119.

[330] Human Rights Act 1998 Sch.1; see also *Hoekstra v HM Advocate (No.1)*, 2000 S.L.T. 602; *Hoekstra v HM Advocate (No.2)*, 2000 S.L.T. 605.

system to set aside arbitration decisions which may be outwith the scope of what was referred to the arbiter for decision or which are vitiated by improper behaviour on the part of the arbiter, such as failure to accord natural justice. A more difficult issue for a legal system is the extent to which the arbitration tribunal's understanding of the law may be guided or corrected by the judiciary. While arbitration usually proceeds upon the agreement of the parties, legislation sometimes stipulates that disputes or questions of a particular kind must be determined by arbitration. For example, disputes respecting variation of agricultural rents are required by statute to be settled by arbitration.[331]

The Arbitration (Scotland) Act 2010—This important Act restates, with amend- **2.47** ments, most of the pre-existing law on arbitration in Scotland. In many respects it codifies the law of arbitration and provides a modern statutory framework for the conduct of arbitrations in Scotland. The Act has been drafted with the aim of being consistent with the UNCITRAL Model Law on International Commercial Arbitration[332] and the UNCITRAL Arbitration Rules.[333] The Act applies to domestic arbitration; to arbitration between parties residing or carrying on business anywhere in the UK; and to international arbitration.[334] It also applies to statutory arbitrations,[335] (but the provisions of the Act have not yet been brought into force as respects statutory arbitrations). The Act sets out, in s.1, the "founding principles", to which regard is to be had in construing the Act, namely that (a) the object of arbitration is to resolve disputes fairly, impartially and without unnecessary delay or expense; (b) parties should be free to agree how to resolve disputes subject only to such safeguards as are necessary in the public interest; and (c) the court should not intervene in an arbitration except as provided by the Act. Express provision is made[336] to the effect that where the subject matter of any legal proceedings is covered by an arbitration agreement (whether or not a Scottish arbitration), the court must, on the application of a party to the proceedings, sist—i.e. suspend—the proceedings. However, the right to insist on arbitration will be lost if that party has taken any step in the proceedings to answer any substantive claim against him or otherwise acted in the proceedings in a manner indicating a wish to have the matter decided in those legal proceedings.[337] The Act does not set out any formal requirements for an arbitration agreement. Where the agreement on arbitration forms part of a larger agreement (for example, an arbitration clause in a building contract), the arbitration agreement is treated as distinct and is not invalid or unenforceable merely because the principal agreement is invalid or unenforceable and a dispute about the validity of the principal agreement may be decided in accordance with the arbitration agreement.[338] With the exception of their application to statutory arbitrations, the provisions of the Act were brought into force on June 7, 2010.[339] They do not apply to any arbitration begun before that date; but they do apply to an arbitration arising under an

---

[331] Agricultural Holdings (Scotland) Act 1991 s.13.
[332] Adopted by the United Nations Commission on International Trade Law on June 21, 1985, and amended in 2006.
[333] Adopted by UNCITRAL on April 28, 1976.
[334] The Arbitration (Scotland) Act 2010 (the "2010 Act") s.2(1).
[335] 2010 Act s.16.
[336] 2010 Act s.10.
[337] 2010 Act s.10(1)(d).
[338] 2010 Act s.5.
[339] The Arbitration (Scotland) Act 2010 (Commencement No.1 and Transitional Provisions Order 2010 (SSI 195/2010).

arbitration agreement made before that date unless the parties agree that the Act is not to apply to that arbitration.[340] The Act also makes provision for the enforcement by the court of arbitral awards[341] and for the recognition and enforcement of foreign arbitral awards made in a State which is party to the New York Convention on the Recognition and Enforcement of Foreign Arbitral Awards.[342] An arbitral award, and any other act or omission of the arbitral tribunal, is not open to review or appeal other than as provided in the Scottish Arbitration Rules.[343]

2.48 The Scottish Arbitration Rules—A central part of the arrangements put in place by the 2010 Act is the code for the conduct of arbitration contained in Sch.1 to the Act and titled "Scottish Arbitration Rules". The rules govern any arbitration which is "seated in Scotland".[344] In terms of s.3 of the Act, an arbitration is seated in Scotland if (a) the parties, or any third party to whom the parties have given the requisite power, designate Scotland as the juridical seat of the arbitration; or (b) in the absence of such a designation, if the arbitration tribunal (a sole arbitrator or a panel of arbitrators as the case may be) designates Scotland as the seat; or (c) in the absence of any such designation, if the court determines that Scotland is to be the juridical seat of the arbitration. The fact that an arbitration is seated in Scotland does not, however, affect the substantive law applying to the dispute.[345] The arbitration rules fall into two categories, namely the mandatory rules, which cannot be modified or disapplied by agreement between parties or by any other means, and default rules. A default rule applies only in so far as the parties have not agreed to modify or disapply the rule (or any part of it), which they may do either in the arbitration agreement or by any other means before or after the arbitration has begun.[346] The mandatory rules are listed in s.8 of the Act. They include among others the rule designed to address failures in the procedure for appointment of the arbitration tribunal; the rules designed to ensure the impartiality of the arbitrator, his removal where that is provided for, and his right to resign; the rules respecting the jurisdiction of the arbitrator and procedures for objecting to and appealing from the arbitration tribunal's ruling on its jurisdiction; certain of the rules permitting recourse to the court by way of challenge to the award; and the rules providing for the tribunal's having power to award payment, including payment of damages and interest upon the sum awarded.[347]

2.49 Appointment of the arbitration tribunal—Only an individual who is aged 16 years or older and who is not an incapable adult may act as an arbitrator.[348] Where there is no agreement on the number of arbitrators, the tribunal will consist of a sole arbitrator.[349] Selection of the members of the arbitration tribunal is

---

[340] 2010 Act s.36(1)–(3). Scottish Ministers are given in s.36(4) power by order to set a cut-off date (not before June 7, 2015) after which parties will no longer be able to agree that the Act should not apply to an arbitration arising under a pre-commencement arbitration agreement.

[341] 2010 Act s.12.

[342] 2010 Act ss.18–22.

[343] 2010 Act s.13

[344] 2010 Act s.7.

[345] 2010 Act s.3(2).

[346] 2010 Act s.9.

[347] Historically, the power of an arbiter to award damages and interest in the absence of an express power to do so in the deed of submission has been a matter of controversy. That controversy is now settled.

[348] Scottish Arbitration Rules (2010 Act Sch.1) rr.3 and 4.

[349] Scottish Arbitration Rules r.5.

primarily a matter for agreement between the parties, but they may agree an appointment procedure whereby in default of agreement the arbitrator may be selected by a third party, e.g. the office holder of a professional association. Absent any such mechanism, either party to the dispute may refer the matter to "an arbitral appointments referee".[350] An arbitral appointments referee is a person appointed by order of the Scottish Ministers under s.24 of the 2010 Act.[351] Unless objection is taken within seven days to the referee selected by the referring party, the referee may make the appointment. In the event of objection to the referee or a failure by the referee to appoint an arbitrator within 21 days, appointment of the arbitrator falls to be made by the court.[352] Under certain conditions a senator of the College of Justice may act as an arbitrator or umpire.[353]

Jurisdiction of the arbitral tribunal—The tribunal is empowered to rule upon **2.50** the validity of the arbitration agreement, whether the tribunal is properly constituted, and what matters have been submitted to arbitration in accordance with the arbitration agreement.[354] A party may take objection before the tribunal that the tribunal does not have jurisdiction, or has exceeded its jurisdiction, in relation to any matter and the tribunal has power to decide the merits of that objection either at the time when the objection is taken or, after deferral of a ruling, when making its award on the merits of the dispute.[355] An objection to the jurisdiction of the tribunal should be taken before, or as soon as is reasonably practicable after, the matter to which it relates is raised in the arbitration, but a later objection may be allowed by the tribunal if it considers that circumstances justify a later objection; however, objection may not be made after the tribunal has made its final award.[356] Where the tribunal does not reserve its decision on an objection to its jurisdiction until its award on the merits but gives its decision in the ongoing course of the arbitration proceedings, a party may appeal that decision to the Court of Session, where the appeal will be heard by a Lord Ordinary, whose decision is final.[357] It is also possible, pursuant to r.22 of the Scottish Arbitration Rules, for a question relating to the tribunal's jurisdiction to be referred to the Court of Session for decision by a Lord Ordinary, whose decision is final. Since r.22 is a default rule, parties may opt to exclude it. However, the conditions attaching to a referral by a party under r.22 are contained in r.23, which is mandatory. Such a referral to the court is only valid if either the parties have agreed that it should be made or the arbitral tribunal has consented to its being made and in the latter event, additionally, the court must be satisfied that determining the jurisdictional question is likely to produce substantial savings in expense; that the application has been made without delay; and that there is good reason why the question should be determined by the court.

Powers of the court respecting arbitral proceedings—Additionally to the **2.51** procedure under rr.22 and 23 for referring a question as to the tribunal's

---

[350] Scottish Arbitration Rules r.7(2).
[351] The Arbitral Appointments Referee (Scotland) Order 2010 (SSI 2010/196) specifies certain professional bodies or officeholders in them.
[352] Scottish Arbitration Rules r.7(6).
[353] 2010 Act s.25.
[354] Scottish Arbitration Rules r.19.
[355] Scottish Arbitration Rules r.20.
[356] Scottish Arbitration Rules r.20(3).
[357] Scottish Arbitration Rules r.21; the time limit for appeal is 14 days.

jurisdiction to the court, r.41 of the Scottish Arbitration Rules enables any party to an arbitration to apply to the Outer House of the Court of Session for a determination of any point of Scots law arising in the arbitration. But, as with r.22, r.41 is a default rule and accordingly the power to refer a point of law to the court may similarly be excluded by the parties. The conditions attaching to and the procedure to be followed on an application under r.41 are likewise mandatory[358] and are similar to those under r.23. A referral of a point of Scots law to the court is thus only admissible if either the parties have agreed that it should be made or the tribunal has consented to its being made and in the latter event, additionally, the court must be satisfied that determining the question is likely to produce substantial savings in expense; that the application has been made without delay; and that there is good reason why the question should be determined by the court.[359] The decision of the Lord Ordinary both as to the validity of the referral and the point of law to be determined is final.[360] In addition to the power to determine any point of Scots law arising in the arbitration, the Arbitration Rules also confer on the court powers which are more procedural in nature. Thus power is given to the court to vary any time limit which may have been agreed by the parties either in the arbitration agreement or otherwise.[361] This is also an optional power, being covered by a default rule, but the conditions for making application and the procedure to be followed are similarly mandatory.[362] By virtue of r.46 — a default rule — parties may accept the court's being able to entertain an application for the exercise of various powers which it has in respect of civil litigation such as the grant of warrant for arrestment or inhibition on the dependence of the claim. In all cases the court may, on the application of any party or the arbitral tribunal, order the attendance of witnesses before the arbiter or the disclosure of documents or other evidence.[363]

2.52 **The arbitral award**—Part 6 of the Scottish Arbitration Rules contains a number of provisions respecting arbitral awards. The provisions conferring power to order, in an award, payment of money, including damages, and to order interest to be payable thereon are mandatory.[364] Also mandatory are the provisions concerning the tribunal's rights to withhold delivery of its award where its fees and expenses have not been paid in full.[365] The other rules in Pt 6 are default rules and largely deal with such matters as the form of awards; the making of provisional and part awards; the issuing of draft awards; and correction of awards. Rule 47 (a default rule) contains however provisions relating to the substance of an arbitral award. In short, the dispute must be decided in accordance with the applicable law and not on the basis of "general considerations of justice, fairness or equity" unless such considerations form part of the relevant law or the parties otherwise agree. The tribunal must also have regard to the provisions of any contract relating to the substance of the dispute; the normal commercial or trade usage of any undefined

---

[358] Scottish Arbitration Rules r.42 and s.8.

[359] Scottish Arbitration Rules r.42.

[360] Scottish Arbitration Rules r.42(4).

[361] Scottish Arbitration Rules r.43.

[362] Scottish Arbitration Rules r.44.

[363] Scottish Arbitration Rules r.45, which is a mandatory rule.

[364] Scottish Arbitration Rules rr.48 and 50.

[365] Scottish Arbitration Rules r.56. Arbitrators' fees and expenses are covered by r.60, which is a mandatory rule. In the absence of agreement, there is provision for such fees and expenses to be determined by the Auditor of the Court of Session.

terms in any such contract; any established commercial or trade customs or practices relevant to the dispute; and any other matter agreed by parties to be relevant.

Challenging the award—Three forms of challenge are provided for in Pt 8 of the **2.53** Scottish Arbitration Rules and s.13 of the 2010 Act lays down that a tribunal's award is not subject to review or appeal except as provided for in Pt 8 of the rules. Those forms of challenge are, first, a "jurisdictional appeal" (r.67); secondly, a "serious irregularity appeal" (r.68); and thirdly, a "legal error appeal" (r.69). The provisions respecting a jurisdictional appeal and a serious irregularity appeal are mandatory, but since r.69, concerning a legal error appeal, is a default rule it is open to parties to exclude such an appeal.[366] The court in which any of those forms of challenge may be made is the Court of Session. The basis for a jurisdictional appeal is that the tribunal did not have jurisdiction to make the award. The court may decide a jurisdictional appeal by (a) confirming the award; (b) varying the award (or part of it); or (c) wholly or partially setting aside the award. A "serious irregularity" is an irregularity of any of the kinds listed in r.68(2) which has caused, or will cause, substantial injustice to the appellant. Some eleven kinds of irregularity are listed. They are essentially failures in procedural requirements, such as failure on the part of the tribunal to conduct the arbitration in accordance with the arbitration agreement or the applicable Scottish Arbitration Rules, or lack of impartiality and independence in an arbitrator, or unfair treatment of the parties by an arbitrator, or the award being contrary to public policy or having been obtained by fraud or in a way which is contrary to public policy. The court may decide a serious irregularity appeal by (a) confirming the award; or (b) ordering reconsideration or partial reconsideration of the award; or (c) setting aside the award, wholly or in part. In certain circumstances it may also make orders respecting the tribunal's entitlement to payment of its fees and expenses.[367] The ground for a legal error appeal is that in making its award the tribunal erred on a point of Scots law. A legal error appeal is, however, subject to further, mandatory conditions for its admissibility.[368] It may only be made with the agreement of parties, which failing with leave of the Lord Ordinary. Leave may only be granted by the Lord Ordinary if satisfied (i) that deciding the point of law will substantially affect a party's rights; (ii) that the tribunal was asked to decide the point; and (iii) that on its findings in fact[369], the tribunal's decision was "obviously wrong" or, where the point is considered by the court "to be of general importance", the decision is" open to serious doubt". The decision of the Lord Ordinary on whether leave should be granted is final.[370] On hearing a legal error appeal the court has the same powers of disposal by way of confirmation of the award, ordering reconsideration of the award, or setting aside the award as apply in a serious irregularity appeal. All of the three modes of challenge lie to the "Outer House". Appeal from a decision of the Lord Ordinary on any such challenge is restricted. It requires the leave of the Lord Ordinary. But that restriction is further tightened in that the Lord Ordinary may grant leave only if he considers "(a) that the proposed appeal would

---

[366] Since the rule relating to referral to the court on a point of Scots law (r.41) is also a default rule, parties can thus confine the law (as well as the facts) entirely to the arbitral tribunal's judgment.
[367] Scottish Arbitration Rules r.68(4).
[368] Scottish Arbitration Rules r.70. See also *Arbitration Application No.3 of 2011* [2011] CSOH 164.
[369] Including any facts "treated as established"—typically where the decision proceeds on the basis of relevancy of averment.
[370] Scottish Arbitration Rules r.70(6).

raise an important point of principle or practice or (b) that there is another compelling reason for the Inner House to consider the appeal".[371] The decision of the Lord Ordinary whether those criteria for the grant of leave are met is final.

2.54 Adjudication—Adjudication is a process for the resolution of disputes under certain forms of building contract, established under the Housing Grants, Construction and Regeneration Act 1996. A party to a building contract has the right to refer a dispute to adjudication under a statutory scheme.[372] Adjudication has some resemblance to arbitration but is a sui generis means of dispute resolution. The decision of an adjudicator is provisional only and does not oust the jurisdiction of the courts or of an arbiter. Its primary purpose is to regulate a dispute ad interim.[373]

FURTHER READING

Anton, A.E. and Beaumont, P.R., *Civil Jurisdiction in Scotland*, 2nd edn (Edinburgh: W. Green, 1995).

Davidson, F., *Arbitration*, 2nd edn (Edinburgh: W. Green, 2012).

Graham, K.H.R., *Scottish Land Court Practice and Procedure* (Edinburgh: Butterworths, 1993).

Jamieson, G., *Summary Applications and Suspensions* (Edinburgh: W. Green, 2000).

Macfadyen, D.J.D (ed.), *Court of Session Practice* (looseleaf) (Bloomsbury Professional).

Mackay, A.J.G., *Court of Session Practice* (Edinburgh: T.&T. Clark, 1877–79).

Mackay, A.J.G., *Manual* (Edinburgh: William Green & Sons, 1893).

Maclaren, J.A., *Court of Session Practice* (Edinburgh: W. Green, 1916).

Macphail's Sheriff Court Practice, 3rd edn (Edinburgh: W. Green, 2006).

Maher, G. and Rodger, B., *Civil Jurisdiction in the Scottish Courts* (Edinburgh: W. Green, 2010).

Maxwell, D., *The Practice of the Court of Session* (Scottish Courts Administration, 1980).

McBryde, W.W. and Dowie, N., *Petition Procedure in the Court of Session*, 2nd edn (Edinburgh: W. Green, 1988).

Mercer, W., *No Ordinary Court* (Edinburgh: Avizandum, 2012).

Stair Memorial Encyclopaedia, Vol.6, paras 801–1160.

---

[371] This formulation is similar to that of the "second appeals" test introduced in appeals to the Court of Appeal in England and Wales in s.55 of the Access to Justice Act 1999 and discussed judicially in *Tanfern Ltd v Cameron-MacDonald* [2000] 1 W.L.R. 1311; *Uphill v BRB (Residuary) Ltd* [2005] EWCA Civ 60; and *PR (Sri Lanka) v Secretary of State for the Home Department* [2011] EWCA Civ 988.

[372] See Scheme for Construction Contracts (Scotland) Regulations 1998 (SI 1998/647). As to time for the adjudicator to deliver his decision, see *Ritchie Bros. (PWC) Ltd v David Philp (Commercials) Ltd*, 2005 S.C. 384.

[373] *Diamond v PJW Enterprises Ltd*, 2004 S.C. 430; *Ritchie Bros. (PWC) Ltd. v David Philp (Commercials) Ltd*, 2005 S.C. 384.

PART II

OBLIGATIONS

CHAPTER 3

GENERAL LAW OF OBLIGATIONS

Scope of chapter—The first chapter of this book deals with the meaning and **3.01** principal sources of "obligations" in Scots law, and also discusses the crucial distinction between real rights of property and the personal rights which constitute the law of obligations.[1] This chapter therefore concerns itself with more specific issues arising across the law of obligations, whether the obligation arises in contract, promise, delict or unjustified enrichment. These include concepts of good faith, the fiduciary obligation, personal bar, conditional obligations, multi-party obligations, concurrency of obligations and extinction of obligations (excluding prescription, impossibility and frustration, which are the subject of separate later chapters). The party with a right under the obligation may be described as the creditor or obligee, while the one subject to a duty may be called the debtor, the obligor or the obligant.

Good faith—Good faith in obligations is not just the basically subjective good **3.02** faith familiar in property law, concerned with knowledge of facts or events, or the absence of knowledge.[2] It is also about the imposition of certain standards of behaviour, requiring honesty, cooperation and fair dealing between parties.[3] But Lord Hope has said:

> "Good faith in Scottish contract law . . . is generally an underlying principle of an explanatory and legitimating rather than an active or creative nature."[4]

In other words, the concept underpins existing rules of law and otherwise exists more to exclude bad faith than independently to impose standards of conduct beyond the scope of those existing rules.[5] Many of the rules discussed in later paragraphs and chapters of this book can be seen as examples of good faith expressed in a more specific way: for example, the doctrine of personal bar,[6] or the implication that each party to a contract agrees to do all needing to be done to carry out something which cannot be done unless both parties concur in doing it.[7] It may also help to explain the rare cases of pre-contractual liability under

---

[1] Above, paras 1.05–1.11.

[2] See K.G.C. Reid, *The Law of Property in Scotland* (Edinburgh: Butterworths, 1996), para.132. Note that there is an element of objectivity in the concept of constructive knowledge.

[3] See generally, A.D.M. Forte (ed.), *Good Faith in Contract and Property* (Oxford: Hart, 1999).

[4] *R. v Immigration Officer at Prague Airport, Ex p. European Roma Rights Centre* [2005] 2 A.C. 1 at [60].

[5] See also W.W. McBryde, *The Law of Contract in Scotland*, 3rd edn (Edinburgh: W. Green, 2007), paras 5.57–5.67, 17.23–17.34.

[6] Below, paras 3.04 et seq.

[7] *Mackay v Dick & Stevenson* (1881) 8 R. (HL) 37; 6 App. Cas. 251, speech of Lord Blackburn; below, para.3.12.

Walker v Milne,[8] and those where one party's knowledge of the other's uninduced error as to the contract gives rise to reduction.[9] In *Smith v Bank of Scotland*, however, Lord Clyde spoke of "the broad principle in the field of contract law of fair dealing in good faith" and good faith was used positively and innovatively to require banks to take certain steps before guarantees granted in their favour by the spouse of the debtor would be valid.[10] But the principle of good faith has not received much other such overt recognition in modern Scots law. It does not go so far as the fiduciary principle described in the next paragraph in requiring one party to put another's interest before his own.[11] The bad faith of an enriched person has sometimes been a basis for the imposition of an obligation to restore or give up the enrichment, or to deny recovery of enrichment arising from improvements made to another's property, or to prevent use of the equitable change of position defence.[12] European Directives are also introducing the concept on a statutory basis[13]; it remains to be seen what effect this will have upon the development of the common law.[14]

3.03   **Fiduciary obligations**—A fiduciary obligation is one under which as a matter of law a party (the fiduciary) is bound to prefer to his own interests those of another (the principal), for whose benefit he is exercising particular powers or undertaking particular transactions. The obligations contrast with those arising in ordinary or "arm's-length" transactions, in which each party is entitled to consider only its own interests; and even where there is an obligation of good faith, that does not require a party to put another's interests ahead of its own. The classical relationships in which fiduciary obligations arise in Scots law are those of trustee and beneficiary,[15] agent and principal,[16] partners in a partnership,[17] and director and company.[18] In each of these cases, the first-named party will be subject to fiduciary obligations. But the categories of fiduciary relationships are not closed, and may arise wherever one party is entrusted with powers for the benefit of another in circumstances giving rise to the principal's reasonable expectation that

---

    [8] See para.5.13, below.
    [9] See para.7.25, below.
    [10] *Smith v Bank of Scotland,* 1997 S.C. (HL) 111 at 121. For this case, see paras 7.15, 16.15–16.17, below.
    [11] See para.3.03, below.
    [12] See paras 24.06, 24.17, 24.21, below.
    [13] Council Directive 86/653/EEC, implemented by the Commercial Agents Regulations 1993 (SI 1993/3053); see Pt II of the Regulations, for which see para.19.33; Council Directive 93/13/EEC, now implemented by the Unfair Terms in Consumer Contracts 1999 (SI 1999/2083): see reg.5(1), discussed at para.9.25; European Parliament and Council Directive 97/7/EC, implemented by the Consumer Protection (Distance Selling) Regulations 2000 (SI 2000/2334) (see reg.7(2), discussed at para.14.03 below); European Parliament and Council Directive 2005/29/EC (the Unfair Commercial Practices Directive), art.2(h), implemented without giving rise to individual civil rights and without reference to 'good faith' by the Consumer Protection from Unfair Trading Regulations 2008 (SI 2008/1277).
    [14] See Forte (ed.), *Good Faith in Contract and Property* (1999); F. Brand and D. Brodie, "Good Faith in Contract Law" in R. Zimmermann, D. Visser and K.G.C. Reid (eds), *Mixed Legal Systems in Comparative Perspective* (Oxford: Oxford University Press, 2004); H.L. MacQueen, "Good Faith" in H.L. MacQueen and R. Zimmermann (eds), *European Contract Law: Scots and South African Perspectives* (Edinburgh: Edinburgh University Press, 2006).
    [15] See para.41.15, below.
    [16] See para.18.04, below.
    [17] See para.45.18, below.
    [18] See para.46.33, below.

its interests will be given priority by the other party.[19] More specific consequences of the obligation to prefer the interests of the principal include the duties to avoid conflicts of interest,[20] not to misuse for one's own benefit information acquired as a fiduciary, and not to make secret profits from a fiduciary position. The obligation is therefore more negative than positive in character and does not impose a duty to act in the principal's best interests in all respects. The obligation may be discharged by making appropriate disclosure to the principal and receiving its fully informed consent. Breach of a fiduciary obligation may make any resultant transaction voidable at the principal's instance and renders the fiduciary liable to account to the principal for any personal gain made from the transaction.[21] The fairness or otherwise of the transaction impugned, or the existence of a loss to the principal, is irrelevant. The principal may, however, homologate or adopt the transaction. It should be noted that fiduciary obligations may co-exist alongside other duties in a relationship: for example, a company director also owes duties of care and skill to the company. Liability for breaches of such other duties is distinct from that for breach of the fiduciary obligation.

Personal bar—The capacity of controlling the rights of others, either in the exercise of a real right in property or as the creditor in an obligation, may in particular circumstances be limited or abrogated by the operation of a principle known as personal bar.[22] In many cases the assertion of a right might conflict with ordinary conceptions of justice, either owing to the method by which the right was acquired or owing to the conduct of the party vested with it, and the principle of personal bar underlies many of the established rules of law. Inconsistency on the part of the person barred, and unfairness, are therefore the fundamentals of the doctrine, as expressed in the following framework.[23] (A) Inconsistency: (1) A person claims to have a right, the exercise of which the obligor alleges is barred. (2) To the obligor's knowledge, the obligee has behaved in a way which is inconsistent with the exercise of the right. Inconsistency may take the form of words, actions, or inaction. (3) At the time of so behaving the obligee knew about the right. (4) Nonetheless the obligee now seeks to exercise the right. (5) Its exercise will affect the obligor. (B) Unfairness: In the light of the obligee's inconsistent conduct, it **3.04**

---

[19] The imposition of fiduciary obligations over and above those already expressed in a contract was resisted in *Lothian v Jenolite*, 1969 S.C. 111 and *Raymond Harrison & Co's Tr. v North West Securities*, 1989 S.L.T. 718.

[20] *Aberdeen Ry Co v Blaikie Bros* (1854) 1 Macq. 461. Note, however, that it does not follow that, because a party is subject to a conflict of interest, therefore it has a fiduciary obligation in these circumstances.

[21] For discussion of how far this liability to account should be seen as involving "constructive trust" and a priority for the principal in the fiduciary's insolvency, see G.L. Gretton, "Constructive Trusts I and II" (1997) 1 Edin. L.R. 281, 408 (two parts); P. Hood, "What Is So Special About Being a Fiduciary?" (2000) 4 Edin. L.R. 308. In *Commonwealth Oil & Gas Co Ltd v Baxter* [2009] CSIH 75; 2010 S.C. 156 it was held that a third party recipient of property from a dishonest fiduciary may be liable for "knowing receipt", without clarification as to whether the liability was personal (e.g. in unjustified enrichment) or proprietary in nature. See further the critical commentary by D.J. Carr, "Equity Rising? Commonwealth Oil & Gas Co Ltd v Baxter" (2010) 14 Edin. L.R. 273.

[22] On this subject, see now E.C. Reid and J.W.G. Blackie, *Personal Bar* (Edinburgh: W. Green, 2006). The leading work on the equivalent English doctrine of estoppel is *Spencer-Bower and Turner: Estoppel By Representation*, 4th edn (London: LexisNexis, 2004); see also E. Cooke, *The Modern Law of Estoppel* (Oxford: Oxford University Press, 2000); S. Wilken, *The Law of Waiver, Variation and Estoppel*, 2nd edn (Oxford: Oxford University Press, 2002).

[23] The framework follows that set out in Reid and Blackie, *Personal Bar* (2006) p.lxv and Chs 2–5. The learned authors prefer the terminology of "rightholder" and "obligant" to that of obligee and obligor used here.

would be unfair if the right were now to be exercised. Any of the following is an indicator of unfairness: (1) The obligee's conduct was blameworthy. (2) The obligor reasonably believed that the right would not be exercised. (3) As a result of that belief the obligor acted, or omitted to act, in a way which is proportionate. (4) The exercise of the right would cause prejudice to the obligor which would not have occurred but for the inconsistent conduct. (5) The value of the right barred is proportionate to the inconsistency. This framework is explored in greater detail in the two paragraphs below.

3.05 **Inconsistency**—In order to determine whether the person allegedly barred has acted inconsistently, all of the following elements must be shown to be present. (1) A person claims to have a right, the exercise of which the obligor alleges is barred. Personal bar is irrelevant unless there is a pre-existing right. The right may be actual, or it may be claimed, in that one may be barred from asserting a right which would ultimately have been found to be invalid. (2) To the obligor's knowledge, the person barred has behaved in a way which is inconsistent with the exercise of the right allegedly barred. The obligor's pleadings must disclose the inconsistent conduct upon which bar is allegedly based, whether in the form of words, actions, or inactions. In practice, direct verbal representations are found relatively seldom as the basis of bar, and the plea of bar is made more commonly in relation to positive conduct, or silence or inaction where intervention would have been expected. However, while an unequivocal representation that a right will not be exercised may readily be regarded as supporting bar, where the allegedly inconsistent conduct is constituted by inaction, bar is recognised only where the indicators of unfairness, discussed below, are strongly present. (3) At the time of so behaving the person barred must have known about the right; one cannot be barred from asserting a right of which one has been ignorant, and in this respect personal bar differs from prescription. There are two aspects to be considered in establishing the requisite level of knowledge. In almost all cases,[24] the obligee must have been aware of the factual background supporting the right now allegedly barred. In addition, bar requires that the person barred should have understood the legal implications of that background as they affected him or her.[25] However, the requisite level of knowledge is normally presumed except in exceptional circumstances, such as where the person allegedly barred is clearly disadvantaged relative to the obligor,[26] or where he or she is a private individual with little experience of the law and with limited resources.[27] (4) The fourth element of inconsistency is that the obligee has now sought to exercise the right allegedly barred. (5) The fifth is that the exercise of the right would affect the obligor.

---

[24] There is a statutory exception to the requirement of knowledge. The Requirements of Writing (Scotland) Act 1995 s.1(3)–(5) provides that a contract for which formal writing is required will not fail for lack of formal validity where it has been followed by significant actings by one party in which the other party has acquiesced (para.5.31, below). However, the statute does not stipulate that the party acquiescing must be aware of the specific grounds of invalidity, or that the contract is invalid, before he or she can be said so to have acquiesced. See further Reid and Blackie, *Personal Bar* (2006), para.7.19.

[25] *Lauder v Millars* (1859) 21 D. 1353, per Lord Justice-Clerk Inglis at 1357; *Porteous' Trs v Porteous*, 1991 S.L.T. 129; *Strathclyde R.C. v Persimmon Hones (Scotland) Ltd*, 1996 S.L.T. 176.

[26] See, e.g. *Lauder v Millars* (1859) 21 D. 1353.

[27] See, e.g. *McIntyre and Hogg v Orr and McNaught*, (1868) 41 Sc. Jur. 112; *McDonagh v MacLellan* (1886) 13 R. 1000; *King v East Ayrshire Council*, 1998 S.C. 182.

Unfairness—A plea of bar is sustained only where, in addition to the person **3.06** barred having acted inconsistently, there is clear evidence that it would be unfair for the right allegedly barred now to be exercised. A combination of any of the following factors may indicate unfairness for this purpose, but all five need not be present in any given case. Since unfairness depends upon context, there is no uniform test which can be applied in all of the multifarious circumstances in which bar may arise. The weight attributed to the five different indicators of unfairness (discussed below) varies from case to case, and individual indicators may have special relevance in particular contexts. It is essential, therefore, to consider the unfairness requirement as it has been applied to other cases arising in similar factual circumstances.[28] For example, in cases where a verbal representation is alleged to form the basis of bar, it is normally required that the person to whom that representation was made should have relied upon it to his or her prejudice[29] (factors (3) and (4) below). In cases of encroachment, on the other hand, the decisive factor may be prejudice to the person seeking to enforce bar (factor (4) below), but not necessarily reliance (factor (3) below). Moreover, unfairness cannot be assessed in isolation from the mode of the allegedly inconsistent conduct. Generally speaking, the unfairness requirement may be readily satisfied if the conduct upon which bar is based is clearly inconsistent with an assertion of the right in question: for example, an attempt to renege on an express representation. If, on the other hand, the inference drawn from the conduct is relatively weak—in particular if bar allegedly arises from failure to assert a right—then the indicators of unfairness require to be strongly present. In judging unfairness, regard is had to the following indicators: (1) The first is that the conduct of the person allegedly barred was blameworthy.[30] A person who has misled by an express representation,[31] is more likely to be regarded to have acted culpably, than where the conduct was not deliberate. However, even silence may be regarded as culpable where there was a relationship of trust between the parties, as in contracts uberrimae fidei. In such cases the silent party may have had access to information not readily available to the other, and a "duty to speak"[32] may be identified. (2) The second indicator of unfairness is that the obligor reasonably believed that the right in question would not be exercised. If there is no such belief, or if the belief was unreasonable, then it is unlikely that the inconsistent conduct can be regarded as unfair. In *Gatty v Maclaine*, for example, Lord Birkenhead stipulated that A's conduct should have "justified B in believing in a certain state of facts".[33] There is no reasonable belief if the person seeking to enforce bar made extravagant assumptions, or disregarded facts which were known or could easily have been ascertained.[34] Thus good faith, or, more specifically, lack of bad faith, is a necessary concomitant of bar in almost all contexts. (3) It may also be relevant to consider whether, as a result of the belief discussed at (2), the person seeking to enforce bar acted, or omitted to act, in a particular way. The shorthand often used

---

[28] For detailed analysis of the unfairness requirement as it arises in different factual contexts see Reid and Blackie, *Personal Bar* (2006), Chs 6–22.

[29] *Cairncross v Lorimer* (1860) 3 Macq. 827 per Lord Campbell L.C. at 829.

[30] *Grundt v Great Boulder Pty Gold Mines Ltd* (1937) 59 C.L.R. 641, per Dixon J. at 675.

[31] See *Spencer-Bower and Turner: Estoppel by Representation* (2004), para.III.5.1.

[32] See *William Grant v Glen Catrine Bonded Warehouse*, 2001 S.C. 901, per Lord President Rodger at [49].

[33] *Gatty v Maclaine*, 1921 S.C. (HL) 1 at 7.

[34] See, e.g. remarks by Lord Kingarth in *Saunders v Royal Insurance*, 1999 S.L.T. 358 at 362 (representation made in letter two years previously).

for this criterion is "reliance". There is no such reliance if the actions are otherwise motivated, as for example by the person's own unforced error.[35] Expenditure which would be wasted if the right were to be insisted upon is perhaps the most persuasive example of actings in reliance. However, the strength of reliance as an indicator varies from case to case, and indeed in some cases it need not be present at all.[36] Where personal bar is alleged to have been constituted by silence or inaction on the part of the person barred it may be inappropriate to look for a specific response by the person seeking to enforce bar. An example may be found in the cases of the landowner who acquiesces in a structure built partly on his or her land by a neighbour. Unless the encroachment was preceded by negotiation, the encroacher cannot be said to have relied on the attitude struck by his or her neighbour in embarking upon construction. Yet the neighbour may be barred from insisting on removal if there has been significant outlay on the encroaching works by the time of the eventual challenge.[37] Proportionality is an important consideration, however, in that bar is not applied if reliance was disproportionate. In *Houldsworth v Burgh of Wishaw*,[38] for example, the pursuer was found effectively to have tolerated the construction by the local authority of certain drainage works on his land. However, it was an "extravagant"[39] assumption on the part of the latter that he consented to receiving the steadily increasing sewage of the burgh on an indefinite basis. (4) The fourth, and often crucial,[40] indicator of unfairness is whether the exercise of the right would cause prejudice to the obligor which would not have occurred but for the inconsistent conduct. However, the rules as to whether prejudice is necessary for bar vary widely from context to context. When the inconsistent conduct is constituted purely by inaction, prejudice is usually required.[41] In other situations prejudice may merit little consideration in that it is self-evident that it would occur. Where the inconsistency lies in delay in asserting a procedural right, for example, prejudice to the other party may sometimes be assumed without express deliberation. In a further category of cases, prejudice is found, but only by an interpretation which strains the natural meaning of the word. Where, for example, a petition for judicial review has been presented after a delay, prejudice to an affected third party also represented in proceedings may readily be measured in financial loss, wasted expenditure, administrative inconvenience or even loss of an opportunity; but if no third party is involved, prejudice may be identified solely in terms of detriment to good administration of the public authority involved, and it is deemed "unnecessary to find any specific harm flowing from the specific delay in a specific way".[42] (5) The final consideration in determining unfairness is whether the value of the right barred is proportionate to the inconsistency. If the right is of little value, personal bar may be inferred in circumstances which would otherwise leave room for doubt. But if the right is of great value, bar is not readily imposed.[43]

---

[35] e.g *Cantors Ltd v Swears and Wells*, 1978 S.C. 310.

[36] *Armia Ltd v Daejan Developments Ltd*, 1979 S.C. (HL) 56, per Lord Fraser at 68–9.

[37] Reid and Blackie, *Personal Bar* (2006), paras 6.20–6.21.

[38] *Houldsworth v Burgh of Wishaw* (1887) 14 R. 920.

[39] *Houldsworth v Burgh of Wishaw* (1887) 14 R. 920, per Lord Young at 927.

[40] See *Gatty v Maclaine*, 1921 S.C. (HL) 1, per Lord Birkenhead at 7.

[41] e.g. *William Grant v Glen Catrine Bonded Warehouse*, 2001 S.C. 901.

[42] *Reside v North Ayrshire Council*, 2001 S.L.T. 6, per Lord Prosser at 10.

[43] *William Grant v Glen Catrine Bonded Warehouse*, 2001 S.C. 901; *Macdonald v Newall* (1898) 1 F. 68, per Lord Adam at 73; also *Youell v Bland Welch & Co Ltd (The "Superhulls Cover" Case) (No.2)* [1990] 2 Lloyd's Rep. 431, per Phillips J. at 450.

Mora, acquiescence and waiver as instances of personal bar—It has been 3.07
suggested that the pleas of mora, taciturnity, acquiescence and waiver, often
distinguished from each other in texts and judicial decisions, are all instances
of the more general principle of personal bar outlined in the previous
paragraphs.[44]

Mora, taciturnity and acquiescence—The plea of mora, taciturnity and acquies- 3.08
cence is a plea to the merits.[45] It applies to the case where the defender maintains
that some act of his, involving an invasion of the pursuer's rights, unjustifiable
and not easily remediable, was done with the knowledge of and without objection
from the pursuer, and infers that the latter is barred from now insisting on the right
invaded.[46] The vagueness of the plea makes it difficult to summarise the cases in
which it is applicable.[47] It necessarily imports knowledge by the pursuer of the
defender's act, and also power to intervene. So the plea of acquiescence cannot be
sustained merely because the pursuer did not intervene while the defender was
incurring expenditure on work which he was entitled to carry out, for example
alterations on a mill with a view to taking and using an increased quantity of water
from a river, even though it may have been obvious that the work and expenditure
would be useless unless followed by the aggression of which the pursuer
complains.[48]

Acquiescence is not a method by which the title to heritable property can be
altered, and therefore if A builds on B's land, the fact that B was aware of his
proceedings and took no objection does not operate as a conveyance of the land to
A.[49] But it may bar B's right to insist on the removal of the building in a case
where A acted in good faith and the invasion was due to a mistake as to the
boundary between his own land and that of B.[50] And acquiescence in operations
involving considerable expenditure may bar the right to object to such acts as the
unjustifiable withdrawal of water from a river,[51] or the heightening of a building
in contravention of a servitude *non altius tollendi*.[52] The bar raised by acquiescence is, except in special circumstances, personal to the person who acquiesced
and his heirs, and will not bar a singular successor in the title.[53] If the relations of
the parties are regulated by a written contract the fact that one party has been
allowed to disregard its terms, to the knowledge of and without objection from the
other, though it may bar an action of damages for what has been done in the past,

---

[44] Reid and Blackie, *Personal Bar* (2006), Ch.3. See also above, paras 3.04–3.06, for the general principles of personal bar.

[45] See J.A. Maclaren, *Court of Session Practice* (Edinburgh: W. Green, 1916), p.403; *Tonner v Reiach and Hall* [2007] CSIH 48; 2008 S.C. 1 at [111].

[46] The distinction between failure to intervene while an act is in progress and failure to take timely objection after it has been done is drawn in *De Bussche v Alt* (1878) 8 Ch.D. 286. As to "waiver", see para.3.09, below.

[47] See J. Rankine, *Treatise on the Law of Personal Bar in Scotland* (Edinburgh: W. Green, 1921), p.54; and see further Reid and Blackie, *Personal Bar* (2006), paras 3.04–3.05.

[48] *Earl of Kintore v Pirie* (1903) 5 F. 818, affd. (on other grounds) (1905) 8 F. (HL) 16.

[49] *Nicol v Hope* (1663) Mor. 5627; *Melville v Douglas's Trs* (1830) 8 S. 841.

[50] *Duke of Buccleuch v Magistrates of Edinburgh* (1865) 3 M. 528; *Wilson v Pottinger*, 1908 S.C. 580.

[51] *Cowan v Lord Kinnaird* (1865) 4 M. 236; *Bicket v Morris* (1866) 4 M. (HL) 44, opinion of Lord Chelmsford.

[52] *Muirhead v Glasgow Highland Society* (1864) 2 M. 420; *Grahame v Magistrates of Kirkcaldy* (1882) 9 R. (HL) 91.

[53] *Brown v Baty*, 1957 S.C. 351; Reid and Blackie, *Personal Bar* (2006), paras 5.02–5.06.

will not infer any licence for the future.[54] To amount to such a licence—in effect, to alter the terms of the contract—an agreement for such alteration, though it may be merely verbal, must be proved.[55] In a case where an employee had regularly accepted his salary and given unqualified receipts, he was held to have acquiesced in payment of that salary, and he was not allowed to prove, in support of his contention that he was entitled to a higher salary, that he had frequently protested against the amounts paid.[56] A creditor may be held to have acceded to a private trust deed, and therefore to be barred from using independent diligence, if he takes no objection to proceedings following on it which are being done with his knowledge[57]; and a son, or the trustee in his sequestration, may be barred from claiming legitim by acquiescing in family arrangements for carrying out the provisions of his father's will.[58] No acquiescence was found in a passing off case where the defender had exploited a trade name associated with the pursuer, not because they believed the latter had consented, but because they believed they had a historical right to use the name. Further, acquiescence was being invoked to bar action in respect of future wrongs (i.e. continued passing off), but the evidence did not justify an inference that the pursuer had consented irrevocably to the defender passing off their products as the pursuer's in the future. Knowledge was not the same as acquiescence.[59]

3.09 Waiver—Waiver is the voluntary abandonment of a right for all time, so that the right is extinguished.[60] Waiver may be express or implied,[61] and the party waiving the right must have prior knowledge of its existence.[62] It is unclear whether in the case of an implied waiver the party relying on the waiver must have conducted his affairs on the basis of the waiver.[63]

3.10 Delay in enforcement and mora—In the case of obligations which have no definite period, the effect of lapse of time depends upon whether the obligation in question was definitely constituted or whether it requires to be established by proof. In the former case the mere fact that the creditor in the obligation has not chosen to enforce it for any period short of the negative prescription[64] has no legal effect.

---

[54] *Carron Co v Henderson's Trs* (1896) 23 R. 1042; see also *British Coal Corp v South of Scotland Electricity Board (No.2)*, 1993 S.L.T. 38 at 40.

[55] *Bargaddie Coal Co v Wark* (1859) 3 Macq. 467; *Kirkpatrick v Allanshaw Coal Co* (1880) 8 R. 327.

[56] *Davies v City of Glasgow Friendly Society*, 1935 S.C. 224; *Eunson v Johnson & Grieg*, 1940 S.C. 49.

[57] *Marianski v Wiseman* (1871) 9 M. 673.

[58] *Bell's Tr. v Bell's Tr.*, 1907 S.C. 872.

[59] *William Grant & Sons Ltd v Glen Catrine Bonded Warehouse Ltd*, 2001 S.C. 901; noted by E.C. Reid, "Acquiescence in the Air: *William Grant v Glen Catrine Bonded Ware*", 2001 Jur. Rev. 191.

[60] Reid and Blackie, *Personal Bar* (2006), paras 3.08–3.48; McBryde, *The Law of Contract in Scotland* (2007), paras 25.15–25.20.

[61] *Armia Ltd v Daejan Developments Ltd*, 1979 S.C. (HL) 56; *Cumming v Quartzag Ltd*, 1980 S.C. 276; *Lousada & Co Ltd v J.E. Lesser (Properties) Ltd*, 1990 S.L.T. 823; *British Coal Corp v South of Scotland Electricity Board (No.2)*, 1993 S.L.T. 38; *James Howden & Co Ltd v Taylor Woodrow Property Co Ltd*, 1998 S.C. 853.

[62] *Porteous' Trs v Porteous*, 1991 S.L.T. 129. Knowledge may be imputed when a party is put on inquiry: *Murray v Scottish Boatowners Mutual Insurance Association*, 1986 S.L.T. 329.

[63] Reid and Blackie, *Personal Bar* (2006), para.3.17; McBryde, *The Law of Contract in Scotland* (2007), paras 25.16–25.18; *Moodiesburn House Hotel Ltd v Norwich Union Insurance Ltd*, 2002 S.L.T. 1069.

[64] As to prescription, see Ch.4, below.

"I am not aware of anything short of prescription or express discharge which can cut off a liquid debt standing on a written contract. Delay in making a claim may be fatal if the claim depends on the ascertainment of facts, and the opposite party's case on the facts is prejudiced by the delay."[65]

So a bond has been held to be enforceable although no action had been taken upon it until one day before the expiry of the years of prescription.[66] In the case of obligations which require to be constituted by proof, the plea of mora and taciturnity may be put forward, but delay per se is no bar to an action.[67] If the obligation is in origin contractual, e.g. a claim for damages for breach of contract, or a demand for payment for work done without any definite agreement,[68] the law would appear to be, as in the case of the reduction of a contract, that mere lapse of time short of the prescriptive period does not extinguish the obligation, but increases the onus of proof which lies upon the party asserting the claim.[69] The same rule applies to belated claims on a trust or executry estate.[70] Excessive delay in intimating a claim for reparation or in instituting an action of reparation may appear from the pleadings to have affected the quantity or quality of the evidence available to such an extent as to render proof preferable to jury trial as the means of ascertaining the truth.[71] Unexplained delay may result in a pursuer being ordained to find caution for expenses.[72] After proceedings have been commenced, delay in their prosecution which is both inordinate and inexcusable and which is productive of unfairness to the defender, preventing a fair determination, may justify the dismissal of the proceedings.[73]

Obligations: Pure, future, contingent—An obligation may be pure, future or **3.11** contingent.[74] An obligation is pure when, as in the case of a debt instantly payable, fulfilment is due at once. The term "liquid" as applied to a debt imports that it is pure, and also that it is either admitted, or constituted in such a form, as by a bill, bond or decree, that diligence can at once proceed. An obligation is termed future (as opposed to contingent) when it will become exigible either on a fixed date, or on the occurrence of some event (e.g. the death of some person) which is certain to happen. The maxim *dies statim cedit, sed non venit* means that, in the case of a future debt, the debt exists but cannot be enforced until the day of payment arrives. An obligation is contingent when it is subject either to a suspensive or a resolutive condition. There is a suspensive condition, also termed a condition precedent, when the obligation will arise only on the occurrence of an event which may or may not happen, or at some period (e.g. the attainment by the creditor of a certain

---

[65] *Alexander's Trs v Muir* (1903) 5 F. 406, per Lord Stormonth-Darling.

[66] *Graham v Veitch* (1823) 2 S. 594; *Cunninghame v Boswell* (1868) 6 M. 890.

[67] See Maclaren, *Court of Session Practice* (1916), p.403; also *Halley v Watt*, 1956 S.C. 370.

[68] *Mackison v Burgh of Dundee*, 1910 S.C. (HL) 27.

[69] *Bain v Assets Co* (1905) 7 F. (HL) 104; opinion of Lord President Dunedin in *Bishop v Bryce*, 1910 S.C. 426; *McKenzie's Exrx v Morrison's Trs*, 1930 S.C. 830. And see para.4.05, below.

[70] *Robson v Bywater* (1870) 8 M. 757; *Miller's Exrx v Miller's Trs*, 1922 S.C. 150.

[71] See cases cited in D.M. Walker, *Law of Delict in Scotland,* 2nd edn (Edinburgh: W. Green, 1981), p.439, also *Conetta v Central S.M.T. Co Ltd*, 1966 S.L.T. 302. As to limitation of actions, see paras 25.44–25.45, below.

[72] *G. v H.* (1899) 1 F. 701.

[73] *Tonner v Reiach and Hall* [2007] CSIH 48; 2008 S.C. 1; *Hepburn v Royal Alexandra Hospital* [2010] CSIH 71; 2011 S.C. 20.

[74] See Stair, I, 3, 7; Erskine, III, 1, 6; J.M. Thomson, "Suspensive and Resolutive Conditions in the Scots Law of Contract", in *Obligations in Context*, edited by A.J. Gamble (Edinburgh: W. Green, 1990), p.126; *Costain Building & Civil Engineering Ltd v Scottish Rugby Union Plc*, 1994 S.L.T. 573 at 576–577, per Lord President Hope.

age) which may never arrive. There is a resolutive condition in the exceptional case of an obligation which is at once exigible but which will cease to be exigible on the occurrence of an uncertain event. Thus, where interim execution was authorised of a decree for expenses while the question between the parties was under appeal to the House of Lords, it was held that the claim for expenses was a contingent debt, in respect that although immediately exigible it would cease to be exigible if the judgment of the Court of Session was reversed.[75] A resolutive condition is also exemplified by a provision, in a disposition of property, that, on the occurrence of an uncertain event, the property shall revert to the disponer, or, a provision not uncommon in entails, shall pass to some third party.

3.12 Conditions—A condition is termed potestative when it may be purified by an act which one or other of the parties has the power to do; casual, when the condition depends upon chance, or the action of third parties; mixed, when the concurrence of a potestative and a casual event is required. It is a general rule in the construction of wills that if a legacy is given on a condition which is partly potestative, it is held to be purified if the legatee has done all that he could to purify it, though he has failed. Thus if a legacy is given to A on the condition of his marriage with B, it is due if he had asked B to marry him and been refused.[76] In spite of a dictum of Erskine, it is conceived that this rule (grounded on the presumed intention of the testator) has no application to contracts, and that a party who has undertaken a conditional liability is not liable unless the condition is actually purified.[77] A party who has undertaken a conditional obligation impliedly undertakes that he will do nothing to impede the occurrence of the event on which the condition would be purified. So where A was a creditor in a bond which was not exigible by him for eight years provided that he remained the director of a particular company, it was held that he did not acquire the right to immediate payment by the voluntary resignation of his directorship.[78] And if the scheme of a contract imports that something shall be done which cannot be done unless both parties concur in doing it, the construction of the contract is that each agrees to do all that is necessary to be done on his part for the carrying out of that thing, though there may be no express words to that effect.[79] So when a machine was sold on the condition that it should satisfy a certain test, to be carried out on the premises of the buyer, it was held that he had impliedly agreed to give facilities for the test.[80] An agreement to sell goods at a time to be mutually agreed upon is not defeated by the fact that one party refuses to agree; the court will fix a reasonable time.[81] When goods were sold at a time when, to the knowledge of both parties, the sale could not be carried out unless the seller obtained a permit, it was held that the seller, though he had not guaranteed that he would obtain a permit, had impliedly undertaken to do all that he could to obtain one.[82] But questions of this kind turn on the interpretation of each contract; there is no absolute rule that because a man has undertaken a liability conditional on the performance of an act which he has the power to

---

[75] *Forbes v Whyte* (1890) 18 R. 182; another example is *Hardy v Sime*, 1938 S.L.T. 18.

[76] Erskine, III, 3, 8, founding on Roman law; *Simpson v Roberts*, 1931 S.C. 259.

[77] See W.M. Gloag, *Law of Contract*, 2nd edn (Edinburgh: W. Green, 1929), p.279.

[78] *Pirie v Pirie* (1873) 11 M. 941. See also *Dowling v Methven*, 1921 S.C. 948; *Leith School Board v Clerk-Rattray's Trs*, 1918 S.C. 94. See Rodger, 1991 S.L.T. (News) 253.

[79] See speech of Lord Blackburn, *Mackay v Dick & Stevenson* (1881) 8 R. (HL) 37; 6 App.Cas. 251.

[80] *Mackay v Dick* (1881) 8 R. (HL) 37.

[81] *Pearl Mill Co v Ivy Tannery Co* [1919] 1 K.B. 78; *Henry v Seggie*, 1922 S.L.T. 5.

[82] *Re Anglo-Russian Merchant Traders and Batt* [1917] 2 K.B. 679.

perform he has come under any implied obligation to perform it. When a railway company undertook to purchase lands if they constructed a certain line, it was held that the construction of the line remained a matter within their option, and that they were not in breach of their contract when they failed to construct it during the period within which they had statutory powers.[83] If a party adds to his offer or acceptance a condition which is purely in his own interest, he is entitled to waive compliance with it and insist on implement of the contract; whether a condition is purely in the interest of one party is a question of interpretation of the contract.[84]

Obligations by co-debtors—When an obligation is undertaken by more than one **3.13** person, the liability of each obligor in a question with the creditor may be either in solidum (or several), for the whole debt, or only pro rata (or joint), for his proportionate share. When the matter is regulated by contract there is no doubt that if the parties are taken bound jointly and severally, or as principals and full debtors, the liability of each is in solidum. An obligation undertaken jointly, or conjunctly, involves liability only pro rata.[85] Where there is no express provision there is a general presumption in favour of liability pro rata.[86] This holds in bonds, cautionary obligations,[87] and as to the liability of underwriters in marine insurance.[88] But the exceptions are numerous and important. All the parties to a bill or promissory note are liable in solidum. Each partner is liable for the whole debts of the firm.[89] When an order is given for goods or work by several persons acting in concert, though not partners, each is liable for the whole account.[90] And when the obligation is not for payment of money, but to do a particular act (*ad factum praestandum*), e.g. to return an article hired, the obligation is joint and several, so that, if the obligation is not fulfilled, each is liable for the whole amount awarded as damages.[91]

Rights of relief [92]—When a contractual obligation is joint and several there is a **3.14** general legal implication, without any express agreement to that effect, that if one debtor pays the whole debt, or more than his pro rata share, he has a right of relief against the others. This right may be fortified by an assignation of the debt from the creditor, but exists without it.[93] It was extended to the case where one of two

---

[83] *Philip v Edinburgh, etc. Ry* (1857) 2 Macq. 514; *Maconochie Welwood v Midlothian County Council* (1894) 22 R. 56; *Paterson v McEwan's Trs* (1881) 8 R. 646; *Coranta Corporation Ltd v Morse Business Applications Ltd* Unreported July 11, 2007 Glasgow Sheriff Court.

[84] Gloag, *Law of Contract* (1929), p.42; *Dewar and Finlay v Blackwood*, 1968 S.L.T. 196, OH; *Ellis and Sons Second Amalgamated Properties v Pringle*, 1974 S.C. 200, OH; *Imry Property Holdings Ltd v Glasgow YMCA*, 1979 S.L.T. 261; *Gilchrist v Payton*, 1979 S.C. 380.

[85] *Coats v Union Bank*, 1929 S.C. (HL) 114; see also *Moss v Penman*, 1993 S.C. 300 at 303, per Lord President Hope.

[86] Stair, I, 17, 20; Bell, *Principles*, s.51.

[87] Bell, *Principles*, s.267.

[88] Marine Insurance Act 1906 s.67(2).

[89] Partnership Act 1890 s.9.

[90] *Walker v Brown* (1803) Mor. App. Solidum et pro rata, 1. See also Tenements (Scotland) Act 2004 s.28(7) on the joint and several liability of co-owners of a tenement flat for common repairs. As to the competency of suing one obligor without calling the other, see *Neilson v Wilson* (1890) 17 R. 608.

[91] *Darlington v Gray* (1836) 15 S. 197; *Rankine v Logie Den Land Co* (1902) 4 F. 1074.

[92] As to joint wrongdoers, see para.25.46, below.

[93] Stair, I, 8, 9; Erskine, III, 3, 74; see also *Moss v Penman*, 1993 S.C. 300 at 303–4, per Lord President Hope, approving, inter alios, Stair and Erskine. See also the opinion of Lord President Rodger in *Caledonia North Sea Ltd v London Bridge Engineering Ltd*, 2000 S.L.T. 1123 at 1141–5.

cautioners for an insolvent contractor completed the contract work at his own expense. He was entitled to recover half of the expenses incurred from the other.[94] If the obligation is pro rata, and the whole debt is exacted, no one has paid more or less than his share, and there can be no right of relief. But if less than the sum in the obligation is found to be due, one who has paid more than his share has a right of relief against others bound pro rata with him.[95] Where a party who has paid the whole debt claims relief, either on the general implication of law or in virtue of an assignation from the creditor, he cannot claim against any one of his co-debtors more than that co-debtor's pro rata share, but in computing the number of co-debtors those who are insolvent are not counted.[96] It has been said that the obligation of relief depends upon the principle of recompense.[97] But this may only be an analogy rather than a substantive point. In relief the pursuer recovers what he has spent rather than what the defender has gained, while it has not been suggested that the defender in an action of relief has all the equitable defences available in a claim for recompense.[98]

3.15 Signatures of all obligors necessary—It is a rule largely founded on the existence of the right of relief that when an obligation bears ex facie to be by more than one obligor, each who signs it does so on the implied condition that all the others will sign, and incurs no liability unless the signatures of all are obtained. This is an established rule in cautionary obligations,[99] with a doubtful exception in the case of judicial bonds of caution.[100] So, where a party whose debt to a bank was guaranteed forged the name of one of the guarantors, it was held that the bank could not enforce the guarantee against the others.[101] The rule applies to analogous cases. When three persons had agreed to accept a lease, and one refused to sign, the other two, who had already signed, were held entitled to resile.[102]

3.16 Assignation by creditor—Where one of several co-obligors, bound jointly and severally, pays the whole debt he has a right to receive from the creditor an assignation of the debt, and of any securities which any of the other co-obligors may have granted for it.[103] This is a right which arises only on full payment; not where an obligor is bankrupt and the creditor has ranked for the whole debt and received a dividend.[104] But the creditor may refuse to assign if the assignation would conflict with any legitimate interest of his own. This, when an assignation merely of the debt is demanded, can be the case in exceptional circumstances only[105]; if an assignation of securities also is demanded the creditor's interest may be that he holds a prior security over the same subjects for a separate debt. He is not entitled

---

[94] *Marshall v Pennycook*, 1908 S.C. 276.

[95] *Dering v Lord Winchelsea* (1787) 1 Cox 318; *Ellesmere Brewery Co v Cooper* [1896] 1 Q.B. 75; Bell, *Commentaries*, I, 367.

[96] *Buchanan v Main* (1900) 3 F. 215.

[97] *Moss v Penman*, 1993 S.C. 300; *Christie's Exx. v Armstrong*, 1996 S.C. 295; *Caledonian North Sea Ltd v London Bridge Engineering Ltd*, 2000 S.L.T. 1123 at 1141F–G.

[98] See paras 24.21 et seq, below and *Trades House of Glasgow v Ferguson*, 1979 S.L.T. 187 at 192; *Ross Harper & Murphy v Banks*, 2000 S.C. 500 at 505.

[99] *Paterson v Bonar* (1844) 6 D. 987; *Ellesmere Brewery Co v Cooper* [1896] 1 Q.B. 75.

[100] *Simpson v Fleming* (1860) 22 D. 679.

[101] *Scottish Provincial Assurance Co v Pringle* (1858) 20 D. 465.

[102] *York Buildings Co v Baillie* (1724) Mor. 8435; *Gordon's Exrs v Gordon* (1918) 55 S.L.R. 497.

[103] Bell, *Principles*, s.255.

[104] *Ewart v Latta* (1865) 3 M. (HL) 36.

[105] See *Bruce v Scottish Amicable*, 1907 S.C. 637.

to refuse an assignation on the ground that he has made subsequent advances on the same security.[106]

Effect of discharge of one co-obligor—A creditor is not entitled to do anything **3.17** which would prejudice the right of relief possessed by co-obligors who are jointly and severally bound to him. He does so if he discharges one obligor without the consent of the others. The result, if the co-obligors are co-cautioners, is, by statute, that the others are discharged[107]; if they are not cautioners, the other obligors are relieved only in so far as their rights of relief are prejudiced, and therefore they remain liable for their own share of the debt.[108] But a *pactum de non petendo*, by which a creditor, without discharging an obligor, undertakes not to sue him, does not prejudice the rights of relief of the other obligors, and therefore does not affect their liability.[109] And if there is an express reservation of the creditor's right against the other co-obligors a discharge will be read as a *pactum de non petendo*, which neither bars the right of relief nor affects the liability of the other obligors. Thus, where a creditor acceded to a trust deed granted by one of his debtors, and to a discharge following thereon, reserving his rights against the other debtor, it was held the latter remained liable for the debt, and that his right of relief against the debtor who had been discharged was not affected.[110] It is provided by the Bankruptcy (Scotland) Act 1985[111] that a creditor in a sequestration may assent to the discharge of the bankrupt, with or without a composition, without prejudicing his rights against the bankrupt's co-obligors.

Creditors giving up securities—It is probably the general law, though the **3.18** authorities have all related to the effect on a cautionary obligation of the release of securities granted by the principal debtor, that if a creditor gives up a security granted by one co-debtor he thereby releases the others in so far as their rights of relief are prejudiced.[112]

Concurrent obligations—Concurrent obligations occur when the same act or **3.19** omission gives rise to liability in more than one of the categories of obligations (contract, delict, unjustified enrichment, etc.). The liability under the various obligations may be owed to the same person or to different persons. The pursuer in cases where concurrency is permitted has a choice of action, and may pursue each in the alternate, but may not recover twice in respect of the same loss. Space precludes detailed treatment here, and the reader is referred to the under-noted work for full discussion[113]; but the following general points may usefully be made. Concurrency will be allowed between contract and delict unless there is some good reason to deny it.[114] Contracting parties may by their contract exclude

---

[106] *Sligo v Menzies* (1840) 2 D. 1478.
[107] Mercantile Law Amendment (Scotland) Act 1856 s.9.
[108] *Smith v Harding* (1877) 5 R. 147.
[109] *Muir v Crawford* (1875) 2 R. (HL) 148.
[110] *Morton's Trs v Robertson's Judicial Factor* (1892) 20 R. 72.
[111] Bankruptcy (Scotland) Act 1985 s.60.
[112] *Marshall v Pennycook*, 1908 S.C. 276; *Taylor v Bank of New South Wales* (1886) 11 App. Cas. 596.
[113] See generally M. Hogg, *Obligations*, 2nd edn (Edinburgh: Avizandum, 2006).
[114] *Robertson v Bannigan*, 1965 S.C. 20; *Junior Books Ltd v Veitchi Co Ltd*, 1982 S.C. (HL) 244; *Scott Lithgow Ltd v GEC Electrical Projects Ltd*, 1989 S.C. 412. See also *Henderson v Merrett Syndicates Ltd* [1995] 2 A.C. 145; and see generally Hogg, *Obligations* (2006), Ch.3.

delictual liability between themselves and to third parties.[115] A claim in unjustified enrichment is excluded where there is in place between the parties a valid subsisting contract in terms of which the enriched party has received the benefit in question, since the contract provides the cause, or legal justification, of the enrichment.[116] But a contracting party who is disabled from making a claim on the contract—for example because he is in material breach or because the contract is frustrated—is allowed to claim for any unjustified enrichment of the other party.[117] There is no general concurrency between delict and unjustified enrichment, although there are specific examples of the court granting gain-based remedies in respect of delicts,[118] and enrichment claims arise when unjustified interference with the pursuer's rights has benefited the defender. But such interference need not constitute a delict; the concept is a free-standing one in enrichment law.[119]

3.20 Extinction of obligations—An obligation may be extinguished by a discharge by the creditor; by performance or payment; by compensation; by novation; by confusion; and by lapse of time. Prescription and the results of impossibility of performance and frustration are considered in later chapters.[120]

3.21 Acceptilation and discharge—Acceptilation is the technical term applicable when the creditor discharges his right without payment or performance. There are no longer restrictions as to the method of proof of the acceptilation.[121] The terms of an agreement and the circumstances in which it was made may give rise to an implication of a mutual surrender of rights.[122] It is always a question of construction as to what debts are covered by a discharge. If the discharge was in general terms, without reference to any particular debt, or class of debts, the normal construction is that the debtor is freed from any claim of which the creditor was then aware, e.g. from a debt in which the debtor was merely cautioner.[123] If a list of debts is given, followed by general words of discharge, no debts of a different kind from those enumerated are included.[124] If it turns out that there existed a debt of which the creditor, at the time of granting the discharge was not aware, a general discharge may be reducible on the ground that, so far as relates to the debt in question, it was gratuitous, and granted under error.[125] Fitted accounts, i.e. accounts rendered by one party and docqueted as correct by the other,[126] do not preclude proof that some item or items have been omitted or entered incorrectly, but they lay the onus of proof on the party who challenges their accuracy.[127] The rule applies to entries made by a banker in his customer's pass-book; proof that

---

[115] Hogg, *Obligations* (2006), paras 3.204–3.219.

[116] *Dollar Land (Cumbernauld) Ltd v C.I.N. Properties Ltd*, 1998 S.C. (HL) 90.

[117] *Graham v United Turkey Red Co Ltd*, 1922 S.C. 533; *Cantiere San Rocco S.A. v Clyde Shipbuilding and Engineering Co Ltd*, 1923 S.C. (HL) 105.

[118] *Levin v Caledonian Produce (Holdings) Ltd*, 1975 S.L.T. (Notes) 69 (breach of confidence).

[119] See below, para.24.20.

[120] See below, Chs 4 (prescription) and 11 (impossibility and frustration).

[121] See Requirements of Writing (Scotland) Act 1995 s.11. For a statement of the previous law, see M.L. Ross and J.P. Chalmers, *Walker and Walker: The Law of Evidence in Scotland*, 3rd edn (Tottel, 2009), para.125. There is still the possibility of "waiver" by actings: for which see para.3.09, above.

[122] *Evenoon Ltd v Jackel & Co Ltd*, 1982 S.L.T. 83.

[123] *British Linen Co v Esplin* (1849) 11 D. 1104.

[124] *Greenock Banking Co v Smith* (1844) 6 D. 1340; *McAdam v Scott* (1913) 50 S.L.R. 264.

[125] *Dickson v Halbert* (1854) 16 D. 586; *Purdon v Rowat's Tr.* (1856) 19 D. 206.

[126] *Fell v Rattray* (1869) 41 Sc. Jurist 236.

[127] *Laing v Laing* (1862) 24 D. 1362; *Struthers v Smith*, 1913 S.C. 1116.

the banker never received the money is competent.[128] Fitted accounts, or even a formal discharge, do not preclude a subsequent demand by a client for the taxation of his solicitor's account.[129]

Performance—The question whether any obligation has been performed is one **3.22** of fact in each case. Proof may be *prout de jure*.[130] The onus of proof is on the party alleging performance.[131] Although it has been said to be unclear whether unauthorised performance by a third party can discharge an obligation,[132] the preponderance of authority is in favour of discharge where the performance is due and demanded, or where a penal effect arises from delay, or where the creditor has no interest in demanding performance by the proper debtor.[133] In sum, third-party performance can only be declined where both creditor and debtor object to it.

Proof of payment—Proof of payment was, at common law, restricted in certain **3.23** cases to writ or oath. This restriction has now disappeared as a result of the Requirements of Writing (Scotland) Act 1995.[134]

Presumption of payment—In certain cases, there is a legal presumption of **3.24** payment. Counsel's fees are presumed to be paid. It is conceived that no action is competent against the client, but counsel may recover from the agent fees which the latter has actually received.[135] The onus of proof that a hotel bill has not been paid after the guest has left lies on the hotel-keeper.[136]

Apocha trium annorum **(discharges for three years)**—The production of **3.25** receipts for three consecutive instalments of any termly payment, such as rent, feu-duty, interest, salaries or wages, raises a presumption that all prior instalments have been paid.[137] It is open to the creditor to prove, and by parole evidence, that payment has not in fact been made.[138] The presumption is not raised, and the onus of proof therefore remains with the debtor, if there is only one receipt, though for

---

[128] *Couper's Trs v National Bank* (1889) 16 R. 412.

[129] *Macfarlane v Macfarlane's Trs* (1897) 24 R. 574.

[130] See Requirements of Writing (Scotland) Act 1995.

[131] See *Svendborg v Love & Stewart*, 1916 S.C. (HL) 187; *Carruthers v Macgregor*, 1927 S.C. 816.

[132] See *Caledonia North Sea Ltd v London Bridge Engineering Ltd*, 2000 S.L.T. 1123, per Lord President Rodger at 1144L–1145A.

[133] Bankton, I, 24, 2; Bell, *Principles*, s.557; *Reid v Lord Ruthven* (1918) 55 S.L.Rep. 616 (citing Justinian, Inst., 3.29 proemium); *Stair Memorial Encyclopaedia*, Vol.15 (1996), para.97; cf. Lord Kames, *Principles of Equity*, 5th edn (Edinburgh, 1825), pp.330–1; Hume, *Lectures*, III, 16-17. See further, H.L. MacQueen, "Payment of another's debt", in D. Johnston and R. Zimmermann (eds), *Unjustified Enrichment: Key Issues in Comparative Perspective* (Cambridge: Cambridge University Press, 2002). An example of third party performance discharging debts may be found in the law of benevolent intervention (*negotiorum gestio*): *Stair Memorial Encyclopaedia*, Vol.15, para.97; para.24.25, below. In *Whitbread Group Plc v Goldapple Ltd (No.2)*, 2005 S.L.T. 281 a third party payment was held to discharge the debt on the basis of "ad hoc" agency, but this seems to have been decided without awareness of the above cited material. The party performing the obligation will have a claim against the discharged debtor in either unjustified enrichment or negotiorum gestio: paras 24.18, 24.25, below. See further L.J. Macgregor and N.R. Whitty, "Payment of Another's Debt, Unjustified Enrichment and ad hoc Agency" (2011) 15 Edin. L.R. 57.

[134] Requirements of Writing (Scotland) Act 1995 s.11.

[135] *Batchelor v Pattison & Mackersy* (1876) 3 R. 914.

[136] *Barnet v Colvil* (1840) 2 D. 337.

[137] Erskine, III, 4, 10; Bell, *Principles*, s.567; *Walker and Walker: The Law of Evidence in Scotland* (2001), para.64.

[138] *Cameron v Panton's Trs* (1891) 18 R. 728; *Stenhouse v Stenhouse's Trs* (1899) 6 S.L.T. 368.

several instalments.[139] Nor do receipts for three instalments raise any presumption that a bill, granted for prior arrears, has been paid.[140]

3.26 Document of debt in debtor's hands—The maxim *chirographum apud debitorem repertum praesumitur solutum* imports that the fact that a document of debt is in the possession of the debtor raises a presumption that the debt has been paid. Parole evidence is admissible to prove the contrary.[141] It is competent to prove by parole that a receipt which is in the hands of the debtor was given without payment.[142]

3.27 Ascription of payments—Where a party owing more than one debt makes payments without ascribing them to any particular debt, it is open to the creditor to ascribe them so as to diminish or extinguish any debt he pleases.[143] He cannot, however, thereby preclude the challenge of the validity of any debt.[144] Where there is a continuous account, such as that between banker and customer, the rule, usually termed the rule in *Clayton's Case*,[145] is that the earliest credit item wipes out the earliest debit item. This principle, immaterial in questions solely between the debtor and creditor, is of importance where there are parties subsidiarily liable. Thus, where a cautioner is liable for a fixed period, and after that period the account is allowed to go on without any settlement, any payments subsequently made by the principal debtor, being applied, on the rule in *Clayton's Case*, to wipe out the earliest debit items, will extinguish pro tanto the debt for which the cautioner is liable, even though payments are made to the principal debtor which preserve the debit balance against him.[146] The rule is not applicable to a tradesman's account,[147] nor, probably, to any account except that of banker and customer, or other parties whose relationship is substantially the same.[148] Nor can the rule be applied where two separate accounts are kept with a bank.[149] Moreover, the rule does not apply where the parties' dealings reveal that it was not intended to do so.[150] Provision for the appropriation of payments in respect of two or more regulated agreements with the same person is made by the Consumer Credit Act 1974.[151]

3.28 Mode of payment: Legal tender—A creditor, in the absence of any agreement to the contrary, is entitled to insist on payment in legal tender. Gold coins complying with any minimum weight specification are legal tender for payment of any amount.[152] The £1 and £2 coins are also legal tender for any amount. Cupro-nickel

---

[139] W.G. Dickson, *A Treatise on the Law of Evidence in Scotland* (Bell and Bradfute, 1864), p.177.

[140] *Patrick v Watt* (1859) 21 D. 637.

[141] Bell, *Principles*, s.566; Walker, *The Law of Evidence in Scotland* (2001), p.66.

[142] *Henry v Miller* (1844) 11 R. 713.

[143] Bell, *Principles*, s.563. A mere uncommunicated intention of the debtor will not suffice: *Leeson v Leeson* [1936] 2 K.B. 156.

[144] *Dougall v Lornie* (1899) 1 F. 1187.

[145] *Devaynes v Noble (Clayton's Case)* (1816) 1 Merivale 529, 572.

[146] *Royal Bank v Christie* (1841) 2 Robinson 118; *Cuthill v Strachan* (1894) 21 R. 549; *Deeley v Lloyds Bank* [1912] A.C. 756.

[147] *Dougall v Lornie* (1899) 1 F. 1187.

[148] *Cory Bros v Owners of the Mecca* [1897] A.C. 286; *Hay v Torbet*, 1908 S.C. 781; *Macdonald, Fraser & Co v Cairns' Exrs*, 1932 S.C. 699.

[149] *Bradford Old Bank v Sutcliffe* [1918] 2 K.B. 833.

[150] *Thomas Montgomery & Sons v Gallacher*, 1982 S.L.T. 138.

[151] Consumer Credit Act 1974 s.81.

[152] Coinage Act 1971 ss.1, 2 (as substituted by the Currency Act 1983 s.1(1), (3)); Royal Proclamation of April 20, 1983.

or silver coins of denominations of more than 10p are legal tender for payments up to a maximum of £10; and if 10p or less up to a maximum of £5. Bronze coins are legal tender for payments no greater than 20p.[153] By Royal Proclamation other coins (e.g. the thirteenth Commonwealth Games £2 coin) may be declared legal tender.[154] Bank of England notes for £5 or more are not legal tender in Scotland, although such notes may be circulated in the country.[155] Bank notes issued by a Scottish bank are not legal tender.[156] Normally, a gold clause in a contract, the proper law of which is English, is interpreted as meaning that payment will be made in the sterling equivalent of the gold's value.[157] Decree for payment in a foreign currency may be granted in appropriate circumstances.[158] A cheque, if accepted, is conditional payment. The condition is resolutive, so that the debt is extinguished but revives if the cheque is dishonoured.[159] Payment by a credit card is not conditional upon it being paid by the credit card company.[160] If payment is made in any unusual or unbusinesslike way, any loss by theft or fraud will fall upon the debtor.[161]

Duty of debtor to tender payment—It is the duty of the debtor to tender payment, **3.29** at the creditor's residence or place of business,[162] on the appointed date. Once the date of payment has arrived the creditor is within his rights in taking legal proceedings or using diligence without any formal demand. He must stop his proceedings or diligence on tender of payment in full and expenses, but is not bound to accept a tender of the debt without the expenses of the legal proceedings which he has taken.[163]

Bona fide payments—Payment to a person honestly and reasonably believed to **3.30** be the creditor is good, as, for instance, payment to the original creditor after he has assigned the debt but before intimation has been made. The rule holds even if payment is made before it is due.[164] But a tenant who pre-pays his rent may have to pay again to a party to whom the subjects have been sold, though not to the trustee in the landlord's sequestration.[165] A banker granting a deposit receipt is bound to pay according to his contract, and incurs no liability if the payee (a trustee) should embezzle the money.[166] But where a deposit receipt was paid to a

---

[153] Coinage Act 1971 s.2(1A) (as substituted by the Currency Act 1983 s.1(3)(a)).

[154] Royal Proclamation of December 18, 1985.

[155] Currency and Bank Notes Act 1954 s.1. No Bank of England notes under £5 are now in circulation.

[156] T.B. Smith, *A Short Commentary on the Law of Scotland* (Edinburgh: W. Green, 1962), p.842.

[157] *Feist v Societe Intercommunale Belge* [1934] A.C. 161; *New Brunswick Ry Co v British and French Trust Corp* [1939] A.C. 1. Cf. *Treseder-Griffin v Co-operative Insurance Soc.* [1956] 2 Q.B. 127.

[158] *Commerzbank Aktiengesellschaft v Large*, 1977 S.C. 375.

[159] *Leggat Bros v Gray*, 1908 S.C. 67; *Bolt & Nut Co (Tipton) v Rowlands Nicholls & Co* [1964] 2 Q.B. 10.

[160] *Re Charge Card Services Ltd* [1987] Ch. 150; [1989] Ch. 497; *Customs and Excise Commrs v Diners Club Ltd* (1989) 1 W.L.R. 1196.

[161] *Robb v Gow* (1905) 8 F. 90; *Mitchell Henry v Norwich, etc. Assurance Co* [1918] 2 K.B. 67.

[162] *Bank of Scotland v Seitz*, 1990 S.L.T. 584 at 588–9, per Lord President Hope, approving Gloag, *Law of Contract* (1929), p.709. Note also *Arab Bank Ltd v Barclays Bank (Dominion, Colonial and Overseas)* [1954] A.C. 495 at 531, per Lord Reid.

[163] *Pollock v Goodwin's Trs* (1898) 25 R. 1051.

[164] Bell, *Principles*, s.561.

[165] *Davidson v Boyd* (1868) 7 M. 77.

[166] *Dickson v National Bank*, 1917 S.C. (HL) 50.

person who alleged he was the depositor's brother, and presented the deposit receipt and a letter of authority, it was held, on proof that he had stolen the documents, that the bank could not rely on the payment as a discharge.[167] Payment made to the creditor's agent is good if in fact he had authority to receive it, or if he was in a line of business such as to give ostensible authority.[168] A solicitor has ostensible authority to receive payment of a sum sued for,[169] or of the price of shares he has been employed to sell,[170] but not to receive payment of the principal sum in a bond.[171]

3.31 Compensation—The right to compensate, or set off, one debt against another, with the result that each debt is pro tanto extinguished, is in Scotland referable to statute, namely, the Compensation Act 1592 (c.143). The terms of the Act exclude compensation after decree, and it has accordingly been decided that if A allows a decree (in foro or in absence) to pass against him he must pay his debt and recover any counterclaim by separate proceedings.[172] This rule probably holds only while both parties are solvent,[173] and does not apply unless there was an opportunity of pleading compensation against a claim for a sum decerned for as expenses.[174]

3.32 Liquid debts[175]—Compensation is pleadable only between liquid debts, with an exception, largely in the discretion of the court, in cases where an illiquid debt may be rendered liquid without delay.[176] So there is no right to compensate a debt instantly payable by a future or contingent debt,[177] or by a claim of damages arising on a separate ground. The right of retention when debts arise out of the same contract, or where bankruptcy has supervened, is considered further in a later chapter.[178] Compensation must be pleaded: cross-debts are not extinguished ipso facto.[179] So a debt may prescribe although, during the years of prescription, compensation might have been pleaded against it.[180] But if compensation is ultimately sustained, neither debt bears interest *ex lege* during the period of concourse.[181]

3.33 *Concursus debiti et crediti*—To admit of compensation there must be *concursus debiti et crediti*. The parties must be debtor and creditor not only at the same time but also in the same capacity. So an executor, when sued for his private debt, could not plead compensation in respect of a debt owed to him as executor.[182] A banker who has granted a deposit receipt payable to either of two persons, cannot

---

[167] *Wood v Clydesdale Bank*, 1914 S.C. 397.
[168] *International Sponge Importers v Watt*, 1911 S.C (HL) 57. Cf. *British Bata Shoe Co Ltd v Double M. Shah Ltd*, 1980 S.C. 311.
[169] *Smith v North British Ry* (1850) 12 D. 795.
[170] *Pearson v Scott* (1878) 9 Ch.D. 198.
[171] *Richardson v McGeoch's Trs* (1898) 1 F. 145.
[172] *Cunninghame v Wilson*, Jan. 17, 1809, FC.
[173] Bell, *Commentaries*, II, 121.
[174] *Fowler v Brown*, 1916 S.C. 597.
[175] See paras 3.11–3.12, above.
[176] See *Ross v Ross* (1895) 22 R. 461.
[177] *Paul & Thain v Royal Bank* (1869) 7 M. 361.
[178] See paras 10.14–10.17, below.
[179] Erskine, III, 4, 12; Bell, *Commentaries*, II, 124; *Cowan v Gowans* (1878) 5 R. 581; *National Westminster Bank v Halesowen Presswork* [1972] A.C. 785.
[180] *Carmichael v Carmichael* (1719) Mor. 2677.
[181] Bell, *Commentaries*, II, 124.
[182] *Stuart v Stuart* (1869) 7 M. 366.

plead compensation in respect of a debt due by one of them,[183] and the same rule holds in all cases where there are joint creditors.[184] The death of a debtor does not raise a separation of interests so as to preclude a plea of compensation against his executor. So where A died in debt to his law agent, and the latter was employed to ingather the estate, it was held that he was entitled to satisfy his claim against the deceased out of the executry funds which he had ingathered.[185] There is no *concursus debiti et crediti* between a debt due to a principal and a debt due by his agent.[186] But if the agency was not disclosed and the party with whom the agent dealt was not aware of it, he may plead compensation on a debt due by the agent provided that the right to compensate had accrued before he was informed of the principal's interest in the matter.[187] In proceedings against a government department, the Crown cannot, without leave of the court, avail itself of any set-off or counterclaim if the subject matter thereof does not relate to that department.[188]

Compensation in partnership—In partnership, a debtor to the firm cannot plead **3.34** compensation due to him by an individual partner. A partner, sued for his private debt, cannot plead compensation on a debt due to the firm, unless the firm, while still solvent, is dissolved, when the partner becomes the creditor in a pro rata share of the debts to the firm, and to that extent may plead compensation. A partner, suing for his private debt, may be met with a plea of compensation on a debt due by the firm. A firm may plead compensation on a debt due to an individual partner. The principle underlying these rules that a partner, so long as the firm remains undissolved, is not a creditor in debts due to the firm, whereas he is a debtor in debts due by the firm.[189]

Compensation in insolvency—The bankruptcy of one of the obligors so far **3.35** enlarges the right of compensation that by the exercise of the right of retention compensation may be pleaded on illiquid debts due by the bankrupt.[190] In other respects, the bankruptcy of one party effects a separation of interests, which precludes *concursus debiti et crediti*. So the debtor to a bankrupt estate cannot plead compensation on debts which he has acquired after the bankruptcy,[191] nor on debts subsequently incurred to him by the bankrupt.[192] If, however, A is a contingent creditor of B, and the contingency is purified after B's bankruptcy, A has the right to plead compensation, as in the case where a bill, accepted by the bankrupt, was at the date of bankruptcy held by a bank, and was subsequently paid by the drawer.[193] There is no compensation between a debt due by the bankrupt and a debt subsequently incurred to the trustee. So when a liquidator adopted and carried out a contract in which the company was engaged, it was held that his

---

[183] *Anderson v North of Scotland Bank* (1901) 4 F. 49.
[184] *Burrell v Burrell's Trs*, 1916 S.C. 729.
[185] *Mitchell v Mackersy* (1905) 8 F. 198, overruling *Gray's Trs v Royal Bank* (1895) 23 R. 199.
[186] *National Bank v Dickie's Tr.* (1895) 22 R. 740; *Matthews v Auld & Guild* (1874) 1 R. 1224.
[187] *Wester Moffat Colliery Co v Jeffrey*, 1911 S.C. 346; *Kaltenbach v Lewis* (1885) 10 A.C. 617; *Greer v Downs Supply Co* [1927] 2 K.B. 28.
[188] Crown Proceedings Act 1947 s.50; see *Atlantic Engine Co (1920) Ltd v Lord Advocate*, 1955 S.L.T. 17; *Laing v Lord Advocate*, 1973 S.L.T. (Notes) 81; *Smith v Lord Advocate (No.2)*, 1980 S.C. 227.
[189] See *Heggie v Heggie* (1858) 21 D. 31; *Mitchell v Canal Basin Co* (1869) 7 M. 480.
[190] See para.10.17, below.
[191] *Cauvin v Robertson* (1783) Mor. 2581.
[192] *Meldrum's Trs v Clark* (1826) 5 S. 122.
[193] *Hannay's Tr. v Armstrong Bros* (1875) 2 R. 399; affd. (1877) 4 R. (HL) 43.

action for payment could not be met by a plea of compensation or retention in respect of separate claims against the company.[194] And where a landlord took over a waygoing crop from the trustee in the tenant's sequestration it was held that there was no *concursus debiti et crediti* between the price and a claim for arrears of rent. The one was a debt due by the bankrupt, the other a debt subsequently incurred to the trustee.[195] A debt due by a company can be set off against a claim by the receiver of the whole property and undertaking of the company for a debt due to the company.[196]

3.36 Specific appropriation—Compensation cannot be pleaded if the plea is in conflict with the express or implied terms of a contract between the parties. So, if money is placed in A's hands for a specific purpose, and that purpose cannot be effected, A cannot refuse to return the money on the ground that the depositor was otherwise indebted to him.[197]

3.37 Novation—Where a new document of debt is accepted with the result of extinguishing all liability on the prior document, the case is said to be one of novation; when a new obligor is accepted, with the result of freeing the original debtor, the case is more strictly one of delegation. But the term novation is often used to cover both cases.[198] Either novation or delegation has the effect of releasing a cautioner for the original debt or for the original obligor.[199] But either requires the consent of the creditor and, although that consent may in certain circumstances be implied, there is a presumption against novation. A creditor who accepts a new voucher of his debt, or a new obligor, without any express discharge of the old, is presumed to have obtained an additional voucher or guarantor for his debt rather than to have surrendered the rights which he already held,[200] and it is only in exceptional cases, or on proof of a custom of trade,[201] that the original obligor, or a cautioner for him, can successfully maintain that he had been impliedly discharged. The classic case of pure novation is the renewal of a bill of exchange. When a new bill is accepted, and the old one given up, the inference is that all liability on the old bill is extinguished,[202] though in one very special case it was held that the renewal of a promissory note given for a loan, at a time when the original note was on the verge of prescription, did not exclude a claim for interest on the loan during the currency of the original note, in spite of the fact that the

---

[194] *Asphaltic Limestone Co v Corp of Glasgow*, 1907 S.C. 463. Cf. *Smith v Lord Advocate (No.1)*, 1978 S.C. 259, where both claims arose after liquidation.

[195] *Taylor's Tr. v Paul* (1888) 15 R. 313; *Sutherland v Urquhart* (1895) 23 R. 284.

[196] *McPhail v Cunninghame D.C.*, 1985 S.L.T. 149; cf. *McPhail v Lothian R.C.*, 1981 S.C. 119. In *Taylor v Scottish and Universal Newspapers Ltd*, 1981 S.C. 408, it was held that there need not be *concursus debiti et crediti* prior to the receiver's appointment, but this is not consistent with the reasoning of the Inner House in *Forth & Clyde Construction Co Ltd v Trinity Timber & Plywood Co Ltd*, 1984 S.C. 1. Note also *Myles J. Callaghan Ltd v City of Glasgow D.C.*, 1987 S.C. 171 (an illiquid claim).

[197] *Middlemas v Gibson*, 1910 S.C. 577; *Reid v Bell* (1884) 12 R. 178; *Mycroft, Petitioner*, 1983 S.L.T. 342.

[198] Bell, *Principles*, s.576.

[199] *Commercial Bank of Tasmania v Jones* [1893] A.C. 313. The assignation of a debt, and consequent introduction of a new creditor, does not amount to novation, so as to liberate a cautioner: *Bradford Old Bank v Sutcliffe* [1918] 2 K.B. 833.

[200] See opinion of Lord President Inglis, *McIntosh v Ainslie* (1872) 10 M. 344.

[201] *North v Basset* [1892] 1 Q.B. 333.

[202] *Stevenson v Lord Duncan*, 1805 Hume 245.

note had been given up to the debtor.[203] If the original bill or note is retained by the creditor there would seem to be no case for novation. So where the original bill was renewed for one of a smaller amount, and the balance was not paid, it was held that there was no objection to an action for that balance against a party who had signed the original bill as a cautioner.[204]

Delegation—The general presumption is also strongly against delegation.[205] **3.38**
Where a creditor accepted a promissory note from his debtor's factor the liability of the debtor was in no way affected.[206] A statutory provision under which the personal obligation in a bond and disposition in security may transmit against a purchaser of the lands was construed as giving the creditor an additional obligor, not, without his express consent, as depriving him of the obligation of his original debtor.[207] Where a partner in a firm retires and the firm continues without the introduction of any new partners, the mere fact that the creditor in an outstanding debt continues to accept interest, or ultimately ranks in the bankruptcy of a firm, does not amount to delegation so as to discharge the liability of the retiring partner.[208] But in such a case delegation may be inferred from the fact that a party from whom the firm as originally constituted had ordered goods supplied them after the change, and in full knowledge of the facts, entered the new firm as his debtor in his books.[209] Where new partners are introduced the acceptance of the obligation of the firm as newly constituted, with some change in the form of the obligation (as where a bill, or deposit receipt, is renewed) will amount to delegation in a question with a partner who has retired.[210] It is laid down in England that where two companies amalgamate, very clear evidence is required to prove that a creditor of one of the original companies has accepted the obligation of the amalgamation in substitution for that of his original debtors.[211]

Confusion—When the same person is creditor and debtor in an obligation, it may **3.39**
be extinguished confusione,[212] a doctrine which will not be extended to cases not covered by the prior authorities.[213] The obligation must be for the payment of money, and therefore a permanent right, such as that involved in a lease,[214] a superiority,[215] or a ground annual,[216] is not extinguishable confusione, though while the same person is debtor and creditor the annual prestations, such as rent or feu-duty, do not come into existence. The merger of the interests of debtor and creditor may arise either by succession, when the debtor succeeds as heir to his creditor, or vice versa; or by contract, when the creditor in a bond acquires the

---

[203] *Hope Johnstone v Cornwall* (1895) 22 R. 314.

[204] *Hay & Kyd v Powrie* (1886) 13 R. 777.

[205] Erskine, III, 4, 22; *W.J. Harte Construction Ltd v Scottish Homes*, 1992 S.C. 99.

[206] *McIntosh v Ainslie* (1872) 10 M. 304.

[207] *University of Glasgow v Yuill's Tr.* (1882) 9 R. 643.

[208] *Morton's Trs v Robertson's Judicial Factor* (1892) 20 R. 72; *Smith v Patrick* (1901) 3 F. (HL) 14; Partnership Act 1890 s.17(3).

[209] *Pearston v Wilson* (1856) 91 D. 197.

[210] *Buchanan v Somerville* (1779) Mor. 3402; *Bilborough v Holmes* (1876) 5 Ch.D. 255.

[211] *Re Family Endowment Society* (1870) L.R. 5 Ch. 118; *Halsbury's Laws of England* (4th edn, Reissue), Vol.9(1), para.1042, p.781.

[212] Stair, I, 8, 9; Erskine, III, 4, 23. The English term is "merger".

[213] *Craig v Mair's Trs*, 1914 S.C. 893, per Lord President and Lord Johnston.

[214] *Lord Blantyre v Dunn* (1858) 20 D. 1188.

[215] *Motherwell v Manwell* (1903) 5 F. 619. As to the effect of consolidation, see *Earl of Zetland v Glover Incorporation* (1870) 8 M. (HL) 144.

[216] *Craig v Mair's Trs*, 1914 S.C. 893.

subjects over which it is secured, under an arrangement by which the amount of the bond is deducted from the price, or where the owner of an estate acquires bonds which affect it. In such cases the confusion of interests is absolute and the debt is extinguished ipso facto, and, in the case of bonds, is not kept alive by the indication of intention involved in taking an assignation instead of a discharge. If for any reason it is desired that the bond shall still subsist, it must be assigned to a trustee.[217]

3.40　Confusion excluded by separation of interests—Confusion does not operate where there is any separation of interests, but only where the full and absolute right of the creditor and the full and absolute right of the debtor merge in one person. Thus, there is sufficient distinction between the position of a party deceased and his executor to preclude the extinction of a debt by confusion when a debtor confirms as executor to his creditor, or a creditor as executor to his debtor.[218] Bonds affecting an entailed estate are not extinguished when the creditor becomes heir in possession, because his right is a limited and not an absolute one.[219] The same rule holds when bonds are acquired by a fiar during the subsistence of a liferent.[220] Where a prior bondholder obtained, in security of a further advance, a disposition ex facie absolute of the subjects, it was held that the prior bond was not extinguished confusione[221]; and a similar decision was pronounced where, in course of the arrangements for the assignation of a prior bond, the right of creditor and debtor had temporarily been vested in the same party.[222] And no confusion takes place where a person only subsidiarily liable for the debt, such as a cautioner, acquires the right of the creditor. It may still be enforced against the principal debtor.[223]

3.41　Lapse of time: End of fixed period—The effect of lapse of time primarily depends upon whether the obligation or contract has been entered into for a definite period or not. When a contract is entered into for a definite period, as a general rule the lapse of that period extinguishes the obligation on either side. But this is subject, in contracts of lease, service and partnership, to the principle of tacit relocation, under which a new contract may be implied. There is no authority for extending the principle beyond these contracts.

3.42　Tacit relocation: Leases—A lease, if neither party gives due notice of his intention to end it at the expiry of its term, is continued by tacit relocation on the old terms, except in reference to duration. In that respect, if the lease was for less than a year, continuation for the same period is inferred; if for more than a year, continuation for a year is inferred.[224] The period of notice depends on the nature

---

[217] *Codrington v Johnston's Trs* (1824) 2 Sh.App. 118; *Balfour-Melville's Trs v Gowans* (1896) 4 S.L.T. 111.

[218] *Salaman v Sinclair's Tr.*, 1916 S.C. 698.

[219] *Colville's Trs v Marindin*, 1908 S.C. 911.

[220] *Fraser v Carruthers* (1875) 2 R. 595.

[221] *King v Johnston*, 1908 S.C. 684.

[222] *Whiteley v Delaney* (1914) A.C. 132.

[223] Stair, I, 18, 9.

[224] Stair, II, 9, 23; J. Rankine, *The Law of Leases in Scotland*, 3rd edn (Edinburgh: W. Green, 1916), p.598; Agricultural Holdings (Scotland) Act 1991 s.3. See especially *Douglas v Cassillis & Culzean Estates*, 1944 S.C. 355 at 361, where Lord Justice-Clerk Cooper points out that, in tacit relocation, while the contract may be new, the lease is not; *Smith v Grayton Estates*, 1960 S.C. 349 at 354, per Lord President Clyde.

of the subjects let.[225] The contract under tacit relocation is binding on both parties, whether the tenant continues in possession or not. Tacit relocation rests on implied contract, and is therefore excluded by an arrangement for a new lease, even though not in probative form.[226] And where the landlord intimated an increase of rent, and the tenant, though refusing to pay it, did not give notice to end the lease, and in fact stayed on after the term, it was held that tacit relocation was inapplicable, and that the tenant must be taken to have assented to the landlord's terms.[227] But where a house and shop were let together, it was held that notice to quit the shop only was ineffectual, and did not exclude tacit relocation of the whole subjects.[228] The question whether, in case of joint tenancy, all the tenants must concur in giving notice in order to avoid a renewal by tacit relocation has been considered but not decided.[229] If a landlord, after giving notice to quit, takes no further steps, and allows the tenant to remain in possession, he may be held to have passed from his notice, and a new lease by tacit relocation may be inferred.[230] If a tenant, after giving notice, refuses to leave, he is in the position of an intruder without a title, and liable for violent profits, i.e. for the largest sum for which the subjects could be let.[231] The inference of a new lease by tacit relocation has been held to be based on universal understanding, and is therefore probably not applicable to seasonal lets of grass parks, furnished houses, shootings or fishings. In these cases the obligations on either side terminate without notice.[232] And a party who occupies a house as part of his remuneration on a contract of service must remove when his contract comes to an end.[233]

Service—In certain contracts of service the law of tacit relocation applies, and if **3.43** neither party gives notice a reasonable time before the expiry of the term, a new contract is inferred either for the original period, or, at the longest, for a year, on the same terms. "The law of tacit relocation has reference only to specific classes of servants, agricultural, domestic, and the like."[234] So it was held not to be applicable to a contract between dressmakers and the manager of their fur department.[235] It does not apply to contracts of service on exceptional terms, such as an arrangement, made during a strike, under which a workman, usually engaged and paid by the week, was guaranteed employment for a year.[236] Nor does it apply to part-time employments, nor, probably, to any employment for a period exceeding a year.[237]

---

[225] See para.35.25, below.

[226] *Buchanan v Harris & Sheldon* (1900) 2 F. 935. For the modern law, see Requirements of Writing (Scotland) Act 1995.

[227] *McFarlane v Mitchell* (1900) 2 F. 901.

[228] *Gates v Blair*, 1923 S.C. 430.

[229] *Graham v Stirling*, 1922 S.C. 90.

[230] *Taylor v Earl of Moray* (1892) 19 R. 399.

[231] *Tod v Fraser* (1889) 17 R. 226. See para.35.13, below.

[232] *Macharg* (1805) Mor. App. Removing, 4.

[233] *Dunbar's Trs v Bruce* (1900) 3 F. 137; *Sinclair v Tod*, 1907 S.C. 1038; *Cairns v Innes*, 1942 S.C. 164.

[234] per Lord Justice-Clerk Moncreiff in *Lennox v Allan* (1880) 8 R. 38, approved by Lord President Dunedin in *Stanley v Hanway* (1911) 48 S.L.R. 757. But see *Stevenson v N.B. Ry* (1905) 7 F. 1106.

[235] *Stanley v Hanway* (1911) 48 S.L.R. 757.

[236] *Lennox v Allan* (1880) 8 R. 38.

[237] *Brenan v Campbell's Trs* (1898) 25 R. 423.

3.44 Partnership—In partnership for a fixed period no notice is required to terminate the contract at the expiry of the term.[238] But if the partnership business is continued a partnership at will is inferred, in which the rights and duties of the partners continue as they were, in so far as is consistent with a partnership at will.[239]

3.45 Outbreak of war[240]—The general rule is that the outbreak of war between this country and another puts an end to all executory contracts which for their further performance require commercial intercourse between a British subject and an enemy alien.[241] The rule rests on the principle that it is contrary to public policy that a relationship should continue which may strengthen the enemy or facilitate communication with him. But the principle is not carried to its logical conclusion and there is no general rule that a state of war avoids all contracts between subjects and alien enemies.[242] A debt due to an alien enemy, incurred before the declaration of war (including a debt arising from a contract which is itself abrogated) is not extinguished and at common law may be recovered after the war,[243] and property belonging to an enemy alien is not confiscated, though the existence of these rights may be an indirect source of strength to the enemy. But by statute enemy property, including debts, vests in the Custodian of Enemy Property and is dealt with by him on the restoration of peace.[244] In certain rare cases[245] such a contract has been held to have survived the outbreak of war, e.g. a lease,[246] a power of attorney[247] and a policy of life assurance.[248]

FURTHER READING

Bell, *Principles of the Law of Scotland*, 10th edn by W. Guthrie (1899), ss.5–85.
Brand, F. and Brodie, D. "Good Faith in Contract Law", in Zimmermann, R., Visser, D. and Reid, K.G.C. (eds), *Mixed Legal Systems in Comparative Perspective: Property and Obligations in Scotland and South Africa* (Oxford: Oxford University Press, 2004).
Erskine, *Institute*, Book III.
Forte, A.D.M. (ed.), *Good Faith in Contract and Property* (Oxford: Hart, 1999).
Gretton, G.L., "Constructive Trusts I and II" (1997) 1 Edin. L.R. 281, 408 (two parts).
Hogg, M., *Obligations*, 2nd edn (Edinburgh: Avizandum, 2006).
Hood, P., "What Is So Special About Being a Fiduciary?" (2000) 4 Edin. L.R. 308.

---

[238] *Wallace v Wallace's Trs* (1906) 8 F. 558; Partnership Act 1890 s.27.

[239] Partnership Act 1890 s.27. See *McGown v Henderson*, 1914 S.C. 839.

[240] See Lord McNair and A.D. Watts, *Legal Effects of War*, 4th edn (Cambridge: Cambridge University Press, 1966).

[241] As to meaning of "enemy alien" see para.44.03, below.

[242] See opinion of Lord Dunedin in *Ertel Bieber & Co v Rio Tinto Co Ltd* [1918] A.C. 260 at 267–9.

[243] *Ertel Bieber & Co* [1918] A.C. 260; *Schering Ltd v Stockholms Enskilda Bank Aktiebolag* [1946] A.C. 219 at 241; *Arab Bank v Barclays Bank* [1954] A.C. 495.

[244] Trading with the Enemy Act 1939, as amended by the Emergency Laws (Miscellaneous Provisions) Act 1953 and the Foreign Compensation Act 1969 s.1.

[245] McNair and Watts, *Legal Effects of War* (1966), p.134.

[246] *Halsey v Lowenfeld* [1916] 2 K.B. 707, a lease now being regarded as "a concomitant of a right of property", Lord Dunedin's phrase in *Ertel Bieber* [1918] A.C. 260 at 269.

[247] *Tingley v Muller* [1917] 2 Ch. 144, where the circumstances were very special.

[248] *Seligman v Eagle Insurance Co* [1917] 1 Ch. 519, a doubtful decision.

Hugo, C., "Payment", in MacQueen, H.L. and Zimmermann, R. (eds), *European Contract Law: Scots and South African Perspectives* (Edinburgh: W. Green, 2006).

Macgregor, L. and Whitty, N.R., "Payment of Another's Debt, Unjustified Enrichment and ad hoc Agency" (2011) 15 Edin. L.R. 57.

MacQueen, H.L., "Payment of Another's Debt", in Johnston, D. and Zimmermann, R. (eds), *Unjustified Enrichment: Key Issues in Comparative Perspective* (Cambridge: Cambridge University Press, 2002).

MacQueen, H.L., "Good Faith", in MacQueen, H. and Zimmermann, R. (eds), *European Contract Law: Scots and South African Perspectives* (Edinburgh: Edinburgh University Press, 2006).

McBryde, W.W., *The Law of Contract in Scotland*, 3rd edn (Edinburgh: W. Green, 2007), Chs 24, 25.

Reid, E.C. and Blackie, J.W.G., *Personal Bar* (Edinburgh: W. Green, 2006).

Stair, *Institutions of the Law of Scotland*, Book I.

Thomson, J., "Suspensive and Resolutive Conditions in the Scots Law of Contract", in Gamble, A.J. (ed.), *Obligations in Context: Essays in Honour of Professor D.M. Walker* (Edinburgh: W. Green, 1990).

CHAPTER 4

PRESCRIPTION OF OBLIGATIONS

Prescription and limitation—This chapter is concerned only with negative **4.01** prescription, i.e. the extinction of a right or obligation, through lapse of time. The law of positive prescription, i.e. the establishment or definition of a right or title through lapse of time, is dealt with in the section on Property law.[1] The law relating to limitation, which does not affect the subsistence of rights or obligations but merely renders them unenforceable by court action after a certain time, is to be found in the chapter on Reparation.[2]

Common law and the 1973 Act—It is doubtful whether lapse of time can at **4.02** common law fortify a right or extinguish an obligation. The effect of mere delay (mora) on obligations has already been considered.[3] There is limited and unsatisfactory evidence in favour of a 40-year acquisitive prescription of moveables.[4] There are no more than vague hints that if a particular exaction or usage has been submitted to for 40 years it may become exigible at common law, though the creditor may be unable to explain the basis or origin of his claim.[5] Almost all of the law relating to prescription is statutory. The Prescription and Limitation (Scotland) Act 1973[6] repeals much previous legislation and in Pt I[7] enacts a comprehensive new scheme of prescription, consisting of positive prescription, a 20-year negative prescription of obligations and rights relating to property, a five-year negative prescription of certain obligations, and a two-year prescription in the case of recovery between joint wrongdoers. The Consumer Protection Act 1987 inserted Pt IIA[8] in the 1973 Act, creating a 10-year prescription in respect of

---

[1] See paras 34.30–34.37.

[2] See paras 25.44–25.45, below. Where a right or obligation is affected by limitation rather than by prescription, alternative methods of enforcement such as security or lien, remain open to the creditor. Furthermore, if payment has been made, the fact that the debt was affected by limitation does not afford ground for a *conditio indebiti*. Some rights and obligations may be subject to both prescription and limitation: e.g. rights and obligations arising from damage caused by defective products: see the Prescription and Limitation (Scotland) Act 1973 (the "1973 Act") ss.22A–22D (as inserted by the Consumer Protection Act 1987 Sch.1); and see para.4.26, below.

[3] See paras 3.07–3.10, above.

[4] D.L. Carey Miller, *Corporeal Moveables in Scotland*, 2nd edn (Edinburgh: W. Green, 2005), paras 7.01–7.04; A.R.C. Simpson, "Positive Prescription of Moveables in Scots Law" (2009) 13 Edin. L.R. 445.

[5] *Kirk Session of South Leith v Scott* (1832) 11 S. 75; *Mann v Brodie* (1885) 12 R. (HL) 52 at 57.

[6] As amended principally by the Land Registration (Scotland) Act 1979 s.10, the Law Reform (Miscellaneous Provisions) (Scotland) Act 1980, the Prescription and Limitation (Scotland) Act 1984, the Bankruptcy (Scotland) Act 1985, the Law Reform (Miscellaneous Provisions) (Scotland) Act 1985, the Prescription (Scotland) Act 1987, the Consumer Protection Act 1987, and the Protection from Harassment Act 1997. All subsequent statutory references are to the 1973 Act as amended, unless otherwise indicated.

[7] 1973 Act ss.1–16, Pt I came into force on July 25, 1976: s.25(2)(b).

[8] 1973 Act ss.22A–22D.

rights and obligations arising out of damage caused by defective products.[9] Numerous statutes contain special provisions about periods of prescription (or limitation) specific to certain type of obligations or actions.[10]

4.03 Choice of law[11]—Where the substantive law of a country other than Scotland falls to be applied by a Scottish court as the law governing an obligation,[12] the court is to apply any relevant rules of law of that country relating to the extinction of the obligation to the exclusion of any corresponding rule of Scots law.[13] The foreign law is not to be applied, however, where: (a) it appears to the court that the application of the relevant foreign rule of law would be incompatible with the principles of public policy applied by the court[14]; or (b) the application of the corresponding rule of Scots law had extinguished the obligation prior to the coming into force of the Prescription and Limitation (Scotland) Act 1984.[15]

4.04 Negative prescription: Twenty year, five year, ten year and two year—Lapse of time in the negative prescription extinguishes rights and obligations relating to both heritable and moveable property. The creditor may be deemed by his non-enforcement thereof to have abandoned his claim.[16] Before the coming into force[17] of Pt I of the Prescription and Limitation (Scotland) Act 1973 there were several negative prescriptions of differing periods which fell into two groups: (a) prescriptions which extinguished rights and obligations after certain periods of time[18]; and (b) prescriptions which did not extinguish rights and obligations but which merely affected the onus and method of proof.[19] Part I of and Sch.5 to the 1973 Act as

---

[9] See para.4.26, below.

[10] For some examples, see D. Johnston, *Prescription and Limitation* (Edinburgh: W. Green, 1999), App.2; *Eunson v Braer Corp.* 1999 S.L.T. 1405; *Gray v Braer Corp.*, 1999 S.L.T. 1410; *Assuranceforeningen Skuld v International Oil Pollution Compensation Fund (No.2)*, 2000 S.L.T. 1348.

[11] 1973 Act s.23A inserted by Prescription and Limitation (Scotland) Act 1984 s.4, implementing the recommendations of the Scottish Law Commission in their Report No.74, Prescription and Limitation of Actions: Report on Personal Injuries Actions and Private International Law Questions (November 1982). The Law Commission envisaged that any relevant foreign rule of prescription or limitation should be applied, irrespective of its classification as substantive or procedural: see paras 1.3 and 1.4 of the Report.

[12] See generally, P. Beaumont and P. McEleavy, *Anton's Private International Law*, 3rd edn (Edinburgh: W. Green, 2011); *Cheshire, North and Fawcett: Private International Law*, 14th edn (Oxford: Oxford University Press, 2008); *Dicey, Morris and Collins on the Conflict of Laws*, 14th edn (London: Sweet and Maxwell, 2010).

[13] 1973 Act s.23A. See *Kleinwort Benson Ltd v Glasgow City Council (No.3)*, 2002 S.L.T. 1190.

[14] 1973 Act s.23A(2).

[15] 1973 Act s.23A(3), i.e. prior to September 26, 1984: see 1984 Act s.7(2). Note that s.23A does not affect any proceedings commenced before September 26, 1984: 1984 Act s.5(2). The Law Commission comment that the state of the law prior to September 26, 1984 might have influenced the choice of forum, and it would therefore be inappropriate to apply s.23A to proceedings already commenced.

[16] *Macdonald v North of Scotland Bank*, 1942 S.C. 369 at 373, per Lord Justice-Clerk Cooper.

[17] See fn.6.

[18] The septennial prescription of cautionary obligations (Cautioners Act 1695 (c.7)); the long negative prescription (Prescription Acts 1469 (c.4); 1474 (c.9); 1617 (c.12)), although quaere whether the last prescription was truly extinctive; see *Stirling's Trs v Legal and General Assurance Society*, 1957 S.L.T. 73; A.E. Anton and P.R. Beaumont, *Private International Law*, 2nd edn (Edinburgh: W. Green, 1990), p.302 (not in 3rd edn).

[19] The triennial prescription (Prescription Act 1579 (c.21)); the quinquennial prescription (Prescription Acts 1669 (c.14) and 1685 (c.14)); the sexennial prescription (Bills of Exchange (Scotland) Act 1772 (c.72)); and the vicennial prescription of holograph writings (Prescription Act 1699 (c.14)).

amended abolished these prescriptions and replaced them with two extinctive prescriptions, one of five years and one of 20 years. The Prescription and Limitation (Scotland) Act 1984 introduced a third extinctive prescription of two years relating to joint wrongdoers.[20] The Consumer Protection Act 1987 introduced a fourth extinctive prescription of 10 years relating to product liability.[21] It is impossible to contract out of the statutory provisions relating to negative prescription.[22]

Twenty-year negative prescription—If an obligation[23] becomes enforceable[24] **4.05** and thereafter subsists for a continuous period of 20 years[25] without any relevant claim being made in relation to the obligation and without the subsistence of the obligation being relevantly acknowledged, then as from the expiration of that period the obligation is extinguished.[26] The right may be extinguished even although the creditor may never have been aware of its existence.[27] Thus in *K v Gilmartin's Executrix*, where a victim of child abuse between 1955 and 1961 sought damages from the abuser's estate some 40 years later, the obligation of reparation was held to have prescribed at the end of 1981, the prescription also affecting a claim for psychiatric injury developed in 1995 on the victim's memories being triggered by a police investigation into the abuser, since the abuse gave rise to a single obligation to make reparation.[28] Similarly, if a right[29] relating to property (heritable or moveable) becomes exercisable or enforceable and thereafter subsists for a continuous period of 20 years without being exercised or enforced, and without any relevant claim being made in relation to the right, then as from the expiration of that period the right is extinguished.[30] It appears that the onus of establishing that an obligation has subsisted for the prescriptive period generally rests on the party pleading it, the defender.[31]

---

[20] See para.4.25, below. The two-year period relating to joint wrongdoers was previously a limitation, not a prescription: see 1973 Act s.20, repealed by the 1984 Act.

[21] See para.4.26 below.

[22] 1973 Act s.13: commented on in *McPhail v Cunninghame D.C.*, 1985 S.L.T. 149 at 153; *Ferguson v McIntyre*, 1993 S.L.T. 1269. The details are unclear. It may be arguable that, while one cannot by contract apply a longer prescriptive period, one might apply a shorter one.

[23] Any reference to an obligation includes a reference to the right correlative thereto: s.15(2).

[24] See 1973 Act s.11(4) for definition of "enforceable" in the context of obligations to make reparation whether arising from any enactment, rule of law, or by reason of breach of contract or promise. See also paras 4.08, 4.18 and 4.24, below.

[25] The period of the long negative prescription was originally 40 years: Prescription Acts 1469 (c.4); 1474 (c.9); 1617 (c.12). It was reduced (with the exception of servitudes, public rights of way and other public rights) to 20 years by the Conveyancing (Scotland) Act 1924 s.17, as amended by the Conveyancing Amendment (Scotland) Act 1938 s.4.

[26] 1973 Act s.7(1).

[27] See, e.g. *Beard v Beveridge Herd & Sandilands WS*, 1990 S.L.T. 609.

[28] *K v Gilmartin's Executrix*, 2002 S.C. 602, affd. 2004 S.C. 784. It was also held that s.7 could not be read in any other way under the Human Rights Act 1998 s.3 (see further above, para.1.41).

[29] Any reference to a right includes a reference to the obligation (if any) correlative thereto: s.15(2).

[30] 1973 Act s.8. This section applies to any right relating to property (heritable or moveable) not being a right designated as imprescriptible (see para.4.07, below) nor a right falling within s.6 or s.7 as being a right correlative to an obligation to which either of those sections applies: s.8(2). It is thought that s.8 was necessary, despite s.7 and the provision for correlative rights in s.15(2), for the reason that while every obligation must have a correlative right, a right need not have a correlative obligation.

[31] *Strathclyde R.C. v W.A. Fairhurst & Partners*, 1997 S.L.T. 658.

4.06 To what rights and obligations applicable—The 20-year negative prescription
applies to all rights and obligations which have become enforceable including
those obligations affected by the five-year prescription[32] but excluding obligations
arising from damage caused by defective products[33]; those rights and obligations
designated as imprescriptible[34] and any obligation to make reparation in respect of
personal injuries within the meaning of Pt II of the 1973 Act or in respect of the
death of any person as a result of such injuries.[35]

4.07 Imprescriptible rights and obligations: Schedule 3—The rights and obligations specified in Sch.3 can never prescribe.[36] These are any real right of ownership in land[37]; the right in land of the lessee under a recorded lease; any right to
recover property extra commercium; the obligation of a trustee[38] to account, make
reparation in respect of any fraudulent breach of trust, or make trust property
furthcoming[39]; any obligation of a mala fide recipient of trust property to make
it furthcoming; any right to recover stolen property from the thief or anyone
privy to the theft; any right to be served as heir to an ancestor or to take any steps
necessary for making up or completing title to any interest in land[40]; and any
right exercisable as a *res merae facultatis*, i.e. a right which the creditor may
assert or not as he pleases, without losing the right by failure to assert it for the
prescriptive period.[41]

---

[32] 1973 Act s.7(2). Because of the special rules applying to the five-year prescription (see para.4.18,
below) it is possible that an enforceable obligation might subsist for 20 years without being extinguished by five-year prescription. Hence the need for s.7(2).

[33] 1973 Act s.7(2) as amended by the Consumer Protection Act 1987; see para.4.26, below.

[34] See para.4.07, below.

[35] 1973 Act s.7(2) as amended by the Prescription and Limitation (Scotland) Act 1984 s.6(1), Sch.1
para.2, implementing the recommendation of the Scottish Law Commission in their Report,
*Prescription and Limitation of Actions: Report on Personal Injuries Actions and Private International
Law Questions* (HMSO, 1982), Scot. Law Com. No.74. Section 7(2) as amended affects any obliga-
tion which had not been extinguished by 20-year prescription before the coming into force of the 1984
Act, i.e. before September 26, 1984: 1984 Act s.5(3).

[36] 1973 Act ss.7(2), 8(2).

[37] On "real right", see *Macdonald v Scott*, 1981 S.C. 75, *Gibson v Hunter Home Designs*, 1976 S.C.
23; *Sharp v Thomson*, 1997 S.C. (HL) 66; *Burnett's Trustee v Grainger*, 2004 S.C. (HL) 19.

[38] "Trustee" is widely defined in s.15(1) and includes not only executors, tutors, curators, and judicial factors, but anyone who could be said to be holding property in a fiduciary capacity for another.
In *Sinclair v Sinclair* Unreported September 24, 1985 OH (Lord McCluskey) it was held that the duty
of an executor-nominate to account for the executry estate is imprescriptible; this would not apply if it
was regarded merely as a claim for payment. It has been said obiter that where trustees are acting in
the discharge of an ordinary obligation rather than a fiduciary duty the obligation is not imprescriptible: *Countess of Cawdor v Earl of Cawdor*, 2007 S.C. 285.

[39] *Hobday v Kirkpatrick's Trs*, 1985 S.L.T. 197.

[40] See, e.g. *Bain v Bain*, 1994 G.W.D. 7–410. A contractual right to demand delivery of a disposition
was held not to be an "interest in land" within Sch.3 para.(h): *Macdonald v Scott*, 1981 S.C. 75. Cf.
Stewart's Exrs v Stewart, 1993 S.L.T. 440, where it was held that an obligation to grant a disposition
was not imprescriptible within the meaning of Sch.3 para.(h). Note also *Porteous' Exrs v Ferguson*,
1995 S.L.T. 649, where the personal right of an uninfeft beneficiary was extinguished by the long
negative prescription before the Act of 1973 came into effect; and *Mason's Exrs. v Smith*, 2002 S.L.T.
1169.

[41] Rights exercisable as *res merae facultatis* include the right to exercise the ordinary incidents of
property: *Inglis v Clark* (1901) 4 F. 288; and the right to make certain other uses of property which can
be lost, if at all, only when by possession on a sufficient title another party acquires an adverse right
by positive prescription: see e.g. *Leck v Chalmers* (1859) 21 D. 408 at 417. A public means of access
to an ancient monument under a guardianship agreement between its proprietor and the state has been
held imprescriptible so long as the agreement was not terminated, even if the public did not use it:
Duffield Morgan Ltd v Lord Advocate, 2004 S.L.T. 413. A right of servitude is not exercisable as a *res*

Any right to challenge a deed on the ground that it is ex facie invalid or was forged is also imprescriptible.[42]

Computation of period—Where the prescriptive period commences at a time **4.08** other than at the beginning of the day, the period is deemed to have commenced at the beginning of the next following day.[43] If the prescriptive period ends on a holiday (as defined[44]) the period is extended to include the next succeeding day which is not a holiday.[45] Any time during which any person against whom prescription is pled was under legal disability[46] is to be reckoned as if the person were free from that disability.[47] In general, regard is to be had to the principles formerly applicable in computing the prescriptive periods for the purposes of the Prescription Act 1617.[48] Thus, the prescriptive period runs from the midnight after an obligation has become enforceable[49] (or a right exercisable or enforceable[50]). In the case of a debt, prescription runs from the midnight following upon the date when the debt became payable,[51] in the case of legitim and *jus relictae*, as a general rule, from the midnight following upon the date of death[52]; in the case of a positive servitude, from the midnight following upon the date of the last exercise of the servitude.

Effect—Twenty-year prescription extinguishes rights and obligations which have **4.09** not been enforced. When the prescriptive period expires, the right or obligation is gone. So, in the case of a debt, it is of no consequence that the debtor may admit that he never paid. Equally, a prescribed obligation cannot be set off against a

---

merae facultatis and may therefore prescribe: see *Bowers v Kennedy*, 2000 S.C. 555; likewise a right of access to land over another's land: see *Peart v Legge*, 2008 S.C. 93.

[42] 1973 Act s.12(2).

[43] 1973 Act s.14(1)(c).

[44] 1973 Act s.14(2). "Holiday" means a Saturday, a Sunday, and a Scottish bank holiday.

[45] 1973 Act s.14(1)(d).

[46] Legal disability is defined in s.15(1) as meaning legal disability by reason of nonage or unsoundness of mind. The Age of Legal Capacity (Scotland) Act 1991 s.1(2) (which came into force on September 25, 1991) provides that any reference to "legal disability by reason of nonage" is to be construed as a reference to a person under the age of 16 years. The former categories of pupillarity and minority (see, e.g. *Fyfe v Croudace Ltd*, 1986 S.C. 80; 1986 S.L.T. 528; and Chs 43, 44, below) are abolished. There are transitional provisions in s.8 of the 1991 Act to avoid prejudice to persons who were aged between 16 and 18 immediately before the commencement of the 1991 Act.

[47] 1973 Act s.14(1)(b) except in the circumstances in s.6(4) (including that subsection as applied by s.8A) which provides, inter alia, that "any period during which the original creditor (while he is the creditor) was under legal disability shall not be reckoned as, or as part of, the prescriptive period". As the Scottish Law Commission indicate in their Report, *Prescription and Limitation of Actions* (*Latent Damage and Other Related Issues*) (HMSO, 1989), Scot. Law Com. No.122, para.4.14: "The reference to the 'original creditor' indicates that the legal disability of an assignee of that creditor's rights would not postpone or suspend the prescriptive period." It is not clear to what extent the 1973 Act affects the equitable common law plea of *non valens agere cum effectu* (not able to act effectually). There may be grounds other than nonage or unsoundness of mind which could form the basis of the plea: cf. *Campbell's Trs v Campbell's Trs*, 1950 S.C. 48 at 57, per Lord President Cooper. However, it has been said that the plea should not be extended beyond the decided cases: *Pettigrew v Harton*, 1956 S.C. 67 at 73, per Lord Justice-Clerk Thomson. See also Johnston, *Prescription and Limitation* (1999), paras 7.18–7.25.

[48] 1973 Act s.14(1)(c).

[49] 1973 Act s.7(1); s.14(1)(c).

[50] 1973 Act s.8(1); s.14(1)(c).

[51] cf. Erskine, III, 7, 36.

[52] cf. *Sanderson v Lockhart-Mure*, 1946 S.C. 298; *Campbell's Trs v Campbell's Trs*, 1950 S.C. 48; but see *Mill's Trs v Mill's Exrs*, 1965 S.C. 384.

subsisting one; and any obligations which are accessory to a prescribed principal
obligation must be extinguished along with it.

4.10 Interruption: Obligations: Section 7—To interrupt the running of the long
negative prescription, a relevant claim in relation to the obligation must be made,[53]
or the subsistence of the obligation must be relevantly acknowledged.[54] However,
in the case of an obligation arising from a bill of exchange or a promissory note,
only a relevant claim will suffice to interrupt prescription.[55] If a relevant claim or
a relevant acknowledgment is made, it is thought that the prescriptive period starts
anew from the midnight following upon the date on which the interruption ends[56]:
the point has been discussed in several cases.[57]

4.11 Relevant claim: Obligations—A relevant claim in relation to s.7 is defined in
s.9(1) as a claim made by or on behalf of the creditor for implement or part-
implement of the obligation, being a claim made: (a) in appropriate proceedings[58];
or (b) by the presentation of, or concurring in, a petition for sequestration or by the
submission of a claim under s.22 or s.48 of the Bankruptcy (Scotland) Act 1985[59];
or (c) by a creditor to the trustee acting under a trust deed as defined in s.5(2)(c)
of the Bankruptcy (Scotland) Act 1985[60]; or (d) by the presentation of, or the
concurring in, a petition for the winding up of a company or by the submission of
a claim in a liquidation in accordance with rules made under s.411 of the
Insolvency Act 1986.[61] Prior to the 1973 Act it was held that a summons, although
not in proper form and therefore incompetent, could nevertheless interrupt

---

[53] 1973 Act s.7(1); and see paras 4.11 and 4.12, below. The claim must be made against the debtor
in the obligation: *Kirkcaldy D.C. v Household Manufacturing Ltd*, 1987 S.L.T. 617; but note *Bank of
Scotland v Laverock*, 1992 S.L.T. 73, where it was held that the claim may be made against the
debtor's judicial factor or executor.

[54] 1973 Act s.7(1).

[55] Proviso to s.7(1).

[56] Thus, e.g. a fresh prescriptive period would begin to run from the midnight following upon the
date of the final disposal of a relevant court action, including any appeal procedure. For further details,
Johnston, *Prescription and Limitation* (1999), paras 5.34 et seq.

[57] See *G.A. Estates Ltd v Caviapen Trs Ltd*, 1993 S.L.T. 1051, IH; 1993 S.L.T. 1045, OH; obiter
dicta in *British Railways Board v Strathclyde R.C.*, 1981 S.C. 90; *George A. Hood v Dumbarton D.C.*,
1983 S.L.T. 238; *R. Peter & Co Ltd v The Pancake Place Ltd*, 1993 S.L.T. 322; *Hogg v Prentice*,
1994 S.C.L.R. 426; and cf. recommendations by the Scottish Law Commission in their *Report
on Prescription and Limitation of Actions (Latent Damage and Other Related Issues)*, paras 4.41
et seq.

[58] See fn.53, above.

[59] s.22 relates to the submission of claims by creditors to the interim trustee for the purposes
of voting at the statutory meeting of creditors held within 28 days after the date of the award of
sequestration; s.48 relates to the submission of claims by creditors to the permanent trustee (with a
view to obtaining a dividend or voting at any other meetings). The Prescription (Scotland) Act 1987
deals with the effect of the presentation of a petition for liquidation or submission of a claim in a
liquidation.

[60] Sub-paras (b) and (c) were inserted by the Bankruptcy (Scotland) Act 1985 Sch.7 para.11,
brought into force on April 1, 1986 (s.78(2) of the 1985 Act and SI 1985/1924); and see s.78(4)
of the 1985 Act for transitional provisions. Note also the 1985 Act, ss.8(5), 22(8), 48(7), 73(5), Sch.5
para.3.

[61] Sub-para.(d) was inserted by the Prescription (Scotland) Act 1987, effective as regards any
claim (whenever submitted) in a liquidation in respect of which the winding up commenced on or
after December 29, 1986: 1987 Act s.1(3); and see the sequence of the legislation in 1986 S.L.T.
(News) 345.

prescription.[62] Where a claim is made in an arbitration, and the nature of the claim has been stated in a preliminary notice, the date of interruption is the date on which the preliminary notice is served.[63] If diligence is executed against a debtor in an attempt to enforce an obligation, the diligence is deemed to be a relevant claim.[64]

Relevant acknowledgment: Obligations—Relevant acknowledgment is defined **4.12** in s.10(1) as such performance by or on behalf of the debtor towards implement of the obligation as clearly indicates that the obligation still subsists,[65] or an unequivocal written admission by or on behalf of the debtor to the creditor or his agent clearly acknowledging that the obligation still subsists.[66] A very free approach as to what amounted to a clear and unequivocal written admission was taken in one case, in holding that even a letter written without prejudice to liability might, when viewed against the whole background and other communications between the parties, amount to a relevant acknowledgment.[67] If the nature of the obligation requires the debtor to refrain from doing something or to permit or suffer something to be done or maintained, he will be regarded as acknowledging the obligation if he so refrains, permits or suffers.[68] If an obligation is relevantly acknowledged by the performance of, or on behalf of, one joint obligant, the running of prescription is interrupted as respects each joint obligant.[69] If, on the other hand, a written admission is made by or on behalf of one joint obligant, the running of prescription is only interrupted as respects that joint obligant.[70] Where an obligation affects a trust estate, it matters not whether one trustee acknowledges by performance or by written admission: the running of prescription is interrupted as respects the liability of the trust estate and any liability of each of the trustees.[71]

---

[62] *Bank of Scotland v Fergusson* (1898) 1 F. 96. See too *British Railways Board v Strathclyde R.C.*, 1981 S.C. 90; *George A. Hood v Dumbarton D.C.*, 1983 S.L.T. 238; but it has been observed that an action which is fundamentally null would not constitute an interruption of the prescriptive period: *Shanks v Central R.C.*, 1987 S.L.T. 410, OH; 1988 S.L.T. 212, Ex Div; *Thomas Menzies (Builders) Ltd v Anderson*, 1998 S.L.T. 794. An action of declarator has been held not to constitute a relevant claim in respect of an obligation to indemnify: *Wylie v Avon Insurance Co Ltd*, 1988 S.C.L.R. 570.

[63] 1973 Act s.9(3),(4); s.4(4). See *Douglas Milne Ltd v Borders R.C.*, 1990 S.L.T. 558 in relation to the necessity for stating the nature of the claim, and having an appointed arbiter at the material time. See also *John O'Connor (Plant Hire) v Kier Construction*, 1990 S.C.L.R. 761; *R. Peter & Co Ltd v The Pancake Place Ltd*, 1993 S.L.T. 322. In another case where it was argued that there was no "dispute" to be referred to arbitration in that the claim had prescribed, it was held that the issue of prescription was a further matter of dispute between the parties and should be decided by the arbiter: *Albyn Housing Society v Taylor Woodrow Homes*, 1985 S.L.T. 309.

[64] 1973 Act s.9(1); *Hogg v Prentice*, 1994 S.C.L.R. 426.

[65] See, e.g. the payment of interest on a debt. Cf. *Kermack v Kermack* (1874) 2 R. 156. However, it has been held that the payment of interest under a principal bond does not interrupt the running of prescription against the obligation in a bond of corroboration: *Yuill's Trs v Maclachlan's Trs*, 1939 S.C. (HL) 40. In *Gibson v Carson*, 1980 S.C. 356, the fact that a landlord allowed a tenant to occupy a house for many years without payment of rent was held not to constitute a relevant acknowledgment by the landlord of an obligation on his part under an oral contract to grant a title to the tenant. In *Inverlochy Castle Ltd v Lochaber Power Co*, 1987 S.L.T. 466, the supplying of electricity constituted performance.

[66] See, e.g. *Fortunato's J.F. v Fortunato*, 1981 S.L.T. 277 (resolution of trustees recorded in minute and communicated to creditor's agents); and cases cited in fnn.133 and 134, below.

[67] *Richardson v Quercus Ltd*, 1999 S.C. 278; cf. *Wilkie v Direct Line Insurance Plc*, 2000 G.W.D. 30–1197. Note also *Wilkie v Direct Line Insurance Plc (No.2)*, 2002 S.L.T. 530.

[68] 1973 Act s.10(4).

[69] 1973 Act s.10(2)(a). See *Smithy's Place Ltd v Blackadder & McMonagle*, 1991 S.L.T. 790 at 793.

[70] 1973 Act s.10(2)(b).

[71] 1973 Act s.10(3).

4.13 Interruption: Rights: Section 8[72]—To interrupt the running of the 20-year prescription, the right must be exercised or enforced, or a relevant claim in relation to the right must be made.[73]

4.14 Relevant claim: Rights—A relevant claim in relation to s.8 is a claim made in appropriate proceedings[74] by or on behalf of the creditor to establish the right or to contest any claim to a right inconsistent therewith.[75]

Where a claim is made in an arbitration, and the nature of the claim has been stated in a preliminary notice, the date of interruption is the date on which the preliminary notice is served.[76]

4.15 The five year prescription—If after the "appropriate date"[77] an obligation[78] to which s.6 applies[79] subsists for a continuous period of five years without any relevant claim being made in relation to the obligation and without the subsistence of the obligation being relevantly acknowledged, then as from the expiration of that period the obligation is extinguished.[80] It appears that in general the onus of establishing that an obligation has prescribed rests on the party pleading that.[81]

4.16 To what obligations applicable: Schedule 1—Unlike the 20-year negative prescription, the five-year prescription applies only to a limited but important group of obligations,[82] namely any obligation: (a) to pay a sum of money due in respect of a particular period[83]; (b) based on redress of unjustified enrichment[84]; (c) arising from *negotiorum gestio*; (d) arising from liability to make reparation, other than reparation in respect of personal injuries or death[85]; (e) under a bill of

---

[72] For the ambit of s.8, see s.8(2) and fn.30, above.

[73] 1973 Act s.8(1).

[74] See fn.53, above.

[75] 1973 Act s.9(2) as amended by the 1984 Act Sch.1.

[76] 1973 Act s.9(3),(4); s.4(4).

[77] See para.4.18, below.

[78] See s.15(2): this includes a right correlative to the obligation.

[79] It has been held that the quinquennial prescription does not apply to breach of Convention rights: *Docherty v Scottish Ministers* [2011] CSIH 58; 2011 S.L.T. 1181.

[80] 1973 Act s.6(1). The five-year period need not necessarily commence immediately after the appropriate date: *R. Peter & Co Ltd v The Pancake Place Ltd*, 1993 S.L.T. 322. Note that s.6 may apply to public law obligations too: *Lord Advocate v Butt*, 1992 S.C. 140.

[81] *Dunlop v McGowans*, 1979 S.C. 22 at 27; *Strathclyde R.C. v W.A. Fairhurst & Partners*, 1997 S.L.T. 658.

[82] 1973 Act s.6(2); Sch.1 para.1.

[83] i.e. interest, an annuity instalment, rent or other periodical payment in respect of the occupancy or use of land or a periodical payment under a land obligation: Sch.1 para.1(a). A payment which becomes due only from time to time, such as a casualty payable when assignees take over a lease, is not a periodical payment: *MRS Hamilton v Arlott* (Unreported, 1995). It has been held that the five-year prescription does not apply to interest accruing on unpaid tax in terms of the Taxes Management Act 1970: *Lord Advocate v Butt*, 1992 S.C. 140. Cf. also *Flynn v UNUM*, 1996 S.L.T. 1067; *Zani v Martone*, 1997 S.L.T. 1269. A grassum under a lease is not a periodical payment but part of the reddendo for the landlord's grant of occupation and possession: *Glasgow City Council v Morrison Developments Ltd*, 2003 S.L.T. 263.

[84] *Devos Gebroeder N.V. v Sunderland Sportswear Ltd (No.2)*, 1990 S.C. 291; *McCafferty v McCafferty*, 2000 S.C.L.R. 256; *G.W. Tait & Sons v Taylor*, 2002 S.L.T. 1285; *Virdee v Stewart* [2011] CSOH 50; *Rowan Timber Supplies (Scotland) Ltd v Scottish Water Business Stream Ltd* [2011] CSIH 26.

[85] 1973 Act Sch.1 para.2(g); and see paras 4.22 et seq., below. Certain obligations have been held not to arise from liability to make reparation within Sch.1 para.1(d): see, e.g. *Holt v Dundee D.C.*, 1990 S.L.T. (Lands Tr.) 30 (a liability to pay statutory compensation under planning legislation); *Miller v Glasgow D.C.*, 1988 S.C. 440 (a claim for reinstatement of premises altered as a result of a local authority refurbishment scheme).

exchange or promissory note,[86] (f) of accounting[87]; and (g) arising from, or by reason of any breach of, a contract or promise.[88] Cautionary obligations are affected by the five-year prescription.[89]

To what obligations not applicable—The Act specifically provides[90] that the **4.17** five-year prescription is not to apply to: (a) any obligation to recognise or obtemper a court decree, arbitration award, or an order of any tribunal or authority exercising jurisdiction under any enactment[91]; (b) any obligation arising from the issue of a bank note; (c) any obligation under a contract of partnership or of agency, not being an obligation remaining or becoming prestable on or after the termination of the relationship between the parties under the contract[92]; (d) any obligation relating to land including an obligation to recognise a servitude[93]; (e) any obligation to satisfy any claim to terce, courtesy, legitim, jus relicti or jus relictae, or to any prior right of a surviving spouse under s.8 or s.9 of the Succession (Scotland) Act 1964; (f) any obligation to make reparation in respect of personal injuries[94] or in respect of the death of any person as a result of such injuries; (g) any obligation to make reparation or otherwise make good in respect of defamation within the meaning of s.18A of the 1973 Act[95]; (h) any obligation arising from liability under s.2 of the Consumer Protection Act 1987, to make reparation for damage caused wholly or partly by a defect in a product[96]; and (i) any obligation specified in Sch.3 as imprescriptible.[97] The previous exception from the five-year prescription of obligations constituted or evidenced by a

---

[86] Cheques are therefore affected by the five-year prescription: Bills of Exchange Act 1882 s.73. Bank notes are not: 1973 Act Sch.1 para.2(b).

[87] Other than accounting for trust funds, which is imprescriptible: Sch.3 para.(e). In *Lord Advocate v Hepburn*, 1990 S.L.T. 530, and *Lord Advocate v Butt*, 1992 S.C. 140, obligations in respect of unpaid tax and Class 4 contributions were held not to be obligations of accounting.

[88] See, e.g. *Bank of Scotland v Laverock*, 1992 S.L.T. 73 (sums outstanding in bank accounts); *Douglas Milne Ltd v Borders R.C.*, 1990 S.L.T. 558 (obligation in terms of cl.66 of I.C.E. Conditions of Contract to refer any difference or dispute to the contract engineer).

[89] 1973 Act Sch.1 paras 2(c) and 3. See *Royal Bank of Scotland v Brown*, 1982 S.C. 89; *Smithy's Place Ltd v Blackadder & McMonagle*, 1991 S.L.T. 790; 1991 S.C.L.R. 512; *Glasgow D.C. v Excess Insurance Co Ltd*, 1986 S.L.T. 585 (performance bond); *Glasgow D.C. v Excess Insurance Co Ltd (No.2)*, 1990 S.L.T. 225 (performance bond).

[90] 1973 Act Sch.1 para.2.

[91] "Enactment" is defined in s.15(1).

[92] Discussed in *Sinclair v Sinclair* Unreported September 24, 1985 OH (Lord McCluskey); see too *Coull v Maclean*, 1991 G.W.D. 21-1249.

[93] But excluding those obligations to make periodical payments in terms of Sch.1 para.1(a) to which the five-year prescription does apply. Certain obligations in missives may be "obligations relating to land": *Barratt Scotland Ltd v Keith*, 1994 S.L.T. 1343; *Wright v Frame*, 1992 G.W.D. 8–447; also building obligations in a lease: *Glasgow City Council v Morrison Developments*, 2003 S.L.T. 263; but not a letter of obligation (*Lieberman v G.W. Tait & Sons*, *S.S.C.*, 1987 S.L.T. 585), nor an obligation to make reparation for breach of an obligation to do something on land (*Lord Advocate v Shipbreaking Industries Ltd*, 1991 S.L.T. 838; *Clydeport Properties Ltd v Shell U.K. Ltd*, 2007 S.L.T. 547; *Warren James (Jewellers) Ltd v Overgate GP Ltd* [2010] CSOH 57), nor a unilateral written undertaking to enter an agreement to sell land (*Smith v Stuart* [2010] CSIH 29; 2010 S.C. 490).

[94] "Personal injuries" includes any disease and any impairment of a person's physical or mental condition: Sch.1 para.2(g) and s.22(1). See paras 4.22 et seq., below. Unless actions of harassment under the Protection from Harassment Act 1997 relate to "personal injuries", obligations to make reparation for harassment will prescribe under s.6 as well as s.7.

[95] 1973 Act Sch.1 para.2, as amended by the Law Reform (Miscellaneous Provisions) (Scotland) Act 1985 s.12(5).

[96] 1973 Act Sch.1 para.2, as amended by the Consumer Protection Act 1987 Sch.1.

[97] See para.4.07, above.

probative writ was repealed, so far as documents executed after August 1, 1995 are concerned, by the Requirements of Writing (Scotland) Act 1995.[98]

4.18 Computation of period—The rules set out in s.14 apply equally to the five-year prescription as they do to the 20-year negative prescription.[99] However, while the 20-year negative prescription invariably commences when the obligation has become enforceable,[100] the five-year prescription begins to run after "the appropriate date", which is usually but not always the date when the obligation became enforceable.[101] Thus, for example, the prescription begins to run from the midnight of the date of a bill of exchange or cheque payable on demand[102]; or from the midnight after the expiry of the period of notice, where payment is due only after a certain period after demand.[103] An obligation to repay an overdraft may arise only when a demand is made by raising an action.[104] An obligation to pay the price for heritage in terms of missives has been held to become enforceable only when a validly executed disposition was available for delivery.[105] Where a guarantee bound the guarantors to make payment of all sums due "on demand", the five-year prescription began to run on the date when the creditor wrote to each guarantor demanding payment of the balance still outstanding.[106] A principal debtor's obligation to repay the cautioner became enforceable on the date when payment was made to the creditor by the cautioner.[107] Where a performance bond became enforceable "on default by the contractor", the five-year prescription began to run on the date when a receiver was appointed to the contractor, that being a "default" in terms of the building contract.[108] Where in terms of the parties' contract, liability to pay could only be ascertained from an architect's certificate, the five-year prescription began to run from the date of issue of the certificate and not from an earlier date when a receiver was appointed to one of the parties.[109] Where cloth was supplied to manufacturers, an obligation to make recompense to the suppliers became enforceable when the manufacturers first became enriched by making up and selling the cloth, and the five-year prescription began to run from that date.[110] In reparation actions (other than actions for personal injuries or death, which are excluded from this prescription) the starting point is the date on which loss has flowed from the wrongful act or omission,

---

[98] Requirements of Writing (Scotland) Act 1995 s.14(2) and Sch.5, s.15(2).

[99] 1973 Act s.14.

[100] See para.4.08, above.

[101] 1973 Act s.6(3). The five-year period need not necessarily commence immediately after the appropriate date: *R. Peter & Co Ltd v The Pancake Place Ltd*, 1993 S.L.T. 322.

[102] cf. *Stephenson v Stephenson's Trs* (1807) Mor. App. Bill No.20; Bills of Exchange Act 1882 ss.3(1), 10(1), (2).

[103] cf. *Broddelius v Grischotti* (1887) 14 R. 536.

[104] *Royal Bank of Scotland Plc v Home*, 2001 S.C. 224.

[105] *Muir & Black v Nee*, 1981 S.L.T. (Sh. Ct) 89.

[106] *Royal Bank of Scotland v Brown*, 1982 S.C. 89; followed in a case of payment due under a supply of goods contract, *Johnson and Smart (Projects) Ltd v Sinclair* [2011] CSOH 166.

[107] *Smithy's Place Ltd v Blackadder & McMonagle*, 1991 S.L.T. 790; 1991 S.C.L.R. 512.

[108] *City of Glasgow D.C. v Excess Insurance Co Ltd*, 1986 S.L.T. 585; contrast with *City of Glasgow D.C. v Excess Insurance Co Ltd (No.2)*, 1990 S.L.T. 225 (contractor's liability could only be determined by an architect's certificate, and the date of issue of that certificate was held to be the starting point).

[109] *McPhail v Cunninghame DC*, 1983 S.C. 246; see also *Scottish Equitable Plc v Miller Construction Ltd*, 2002 S.C.L.R. 10.

[110] *Devos Gebroeder N.V. v Sunderland Sportswear Ltd (No.2)*, 1990 S.C. 291.

sometimes described as the concurrence of *injuria* and *damnum*.[111] This presents many problems in practice, some of which are discussed below.[112]

"The appropriate date" is defined for certain special purposes in Sch.2:

(a) Series of transactions: sale, hire or services rendered: where goods are supplied on sale[113] or hire, or where services are rendered, in the form of a series of transactions between the same parties charged on a continuing account, the appropriate date in respect of any obligation to pay for the goods or services is the date on which payment for the goods last supplied or the services last rendered became due.[114] Prescription cannot be elided by inserting a charge for keeping the account in question.[115] If an account has been definitely closed, the prescriptive period will begin to run on the appropriate date although trading between the parties may continue.[116] The death of the debtor is equivalent to the closing of the account.[117] "Services rendered" has been held not to apply to the case of employer and employee.[118]

(b) Money lent to or deposited with the debtor[119]: the appropriate date is the date stipulated in the contract as the repayment date; or if no such date is stipulated, the date when a written demand for payment is first made.[120]

(c) Termination of partnership or agency: where an obligation arises under a contract of partnership or of agency, being an obligation remaining or becoming presentable on or after the termination of the relationship between the parties under the contract, the appropriate date is the date stipulated in the contract as the date on or before which performance of the obligation is due, and if no such date is stipulated, the date when the relationship terminated.[121]

(d) Instalment of a sum of money or to execute an instalment of work, the appropriate date is the date on which the last of the instalments is due to be paid or executed.[122] This provision therefore appears to cover only cases where a total liability is fixed and is gradually discharged.

---

[111] As being "the date when the loss, injury or damage occurred": s.11(1) and see para.4.24, below, and cases therein cited.

[112] See para.4.24, below.

[113] Sale includes hire-purchase, credit-sale or conditional sale: Sch.2 para.1(2)(a).

[114] 1973 Act Sch.2 para.1. See, e.g. *H.G. Robertson v Murray International Metals Ltd*, 1988 S.L.T. 747; *R. Peter & Co Ltd v The Pancake Place Ltd*, 1993 S.L.T. 322; *Wilson v Chief Constable, Lothian and Borders Police* Unreported December 11, 1998 (Lord Hamilton). See also special provision for the termination of a series of transactions on the bankruptcy of a partnership or partner: para.1(3).

[115] 1973 Act Sch.2 para.1(2)(b).

[116] cf. *Christison v Knowles* (1901) 3 F. 480.

[117] cf. Bell, *Commentaries*, I, 349.

[118] *Reid v Beaton*, 1995 S.C.L.R. 382.

[119] Note that "debtor" does not include "guarantor": *Royal Bank of Scotland Ltd v Brown*, 1982 S.C. 89.

[120] 1973 Act Sch.2 para.2. As to what may constitute a "written demand for payment", see *Bank of Scotland v Laverock*, 1991 S.C. 117. The demand for payment may be made to the debtor's judicial factor or executor: *Bank of Scotland v Laverock*, 1991 S.C. 117. Note that in the context of banking the Scottish Law Commission recommended in their report on the *Reform of the Law Relating to Prescription and Limitation of Actions* (HMSO, 1970), Scot. Law Com. No.15, para.74 that five-year prescription should run from the date when the creditor demands repayment, but that 20-year prescription should run (as before) from the date of deposit in accounts where the bank is debtor, and from the date of advance in accounts where the bank is creditor: *Macdonald v North of Scotland Bank*, 1942 S.C. 369. This recommendation appears to have been implemented in the Act.

[121] 1973 Act Sch.2 para.3. See, e.g. *Coull v MacLean*, 1991 G.W.D. 21–1249 (de facto termination of partnership held relevant, rather than a date of dissolution deemed for accountancy purposes).

[122] 1973 Act Sch.2 para.4.

4.19 Effect of fraud, error or legal disability—In computing the five-year period, no
account is to be taken of time during which the creditor was induced to refrain
from making a relevant claim by reason of fraud on the part of the debtor or his
agent, or error on the creditor's part induced by the debtor or his agent.[123] However,
once the creditor could with reasonable diligence[124] have discovered the fraud or
error, any time elapsing thereafter is to be included in the prescriptive period.[125]
Any period during which the original creditor (while he is the creditor) was under
legal disability[126] is not to be reckoned as part of the prescriptive period.[127] The
fact that any time is to be discounted on the ground of fraud, error or disability is
not to be regarded as separating the periods before and after that time.[128]

4.20 Effect—Unlike most of the former short prescriptions, which did not extinguish
rights or obligations but merely affected the onus and method of proof, the five-
year prescription extinguishes obligations (and rights correlative thereto) which
have not been enforced. When the prescriptive period expires, the obligation
ceases to exist.[129]

4.21 Interruption—To interrupt the running of the five-year prescription, a relevant
claim in relation to the obligation must be made,[130] or the subsistence of the
obligation must be relevantly acknowledged.[131] However, in the case of an
obligation arising from a bill of exchange or a promissory note, only a relevant
claim will suffice to interrupt prescription.[132]

---

[123] 1973 Act s.6(4)(a); cf. *Caledonian Railway v Chisholm* (1886) 13 R. 773; *Inglis v Smith*, 1916
S.C. 581; *Fisher & Donaldson v Steven*, 1988 S.C.L.R. 337, Sh. Ct (fraud); *Greater Glasgow Health
Board v Baxter Clark & Paul*, 1990 S.C. 237 (error); *Safdar v Devlin*, 1995 S.L.T. 530 (error); *BP
Exploration Operating Co Ltd v Chevron Shipping Co*, 2001 S.C. (HL) 19 (error); *Rowan Timber
Supplies (Scotland) Ltd v Scottish Water Business Stream Ltd* [2011] CSIH 26 (error).
[124] cf. *Peco Arts v Hazlitt* [1983] 1 W.L.R. 1315; *Greater Glasgow Health Board v Baxter Clark &
Paul*, 1990 S.C. 237; *Southside Housing Association Ltd v Harvey Scott & Partners*, 1992 G.W.D.
27–1593; *Dumfries Labour and Social Club and Institute Ltd v Sutherland Dickie & Copland*, 1993
G.W.D. 21–1314; *Sinclair v MacDougall Estates Ltd*, 1994 S.L.T. 76; *Glasper v Rodger*, 1996 S.L.T. 44.
[125] Proviso to s.6(4).
[126] "Legal disability" is defined in s.15(1) as meaning legal disability by reason of nonage or
unsoundness of mind. Legal disability by reason of nonage is to be construed as a reference to a person
under the age of 16 years: see Age of Legal Capacity (Scotland) Act 1991.
[127] 1973 Act s.6(4)(b).
[128] 1973 Act s.6(5). Thus a creditor who, e.g. becomes temporarily insane two years after an obligation has become enforceable, will have a further three years after regaining his sanity within which to
claim.
[129] For some of the consequences, see para.4.09, above.
[130] 1973 Act s.6(1); s.9; and see para.4.11, above. The execution of diligence may constitute a relevant claim: s.9(1); *Hogg v Prentice*, 1994 S.C.L.R. 426. The claim must be made against the debtor in
the obligation: *Kirkcaldy D.C. v Household Manufacturing Ltd*, 1987 S.L.T. 617; but note *Bank of
Scotland v Laverock*, 1991 S.C. 117 (claim may be made against debtor's judicial factor or executor).
Where the interruption sought to be relied upon is a claim made in an arbitration, there must be an
arbitration in existence at the material time: *Douglas Milne Ltd v Borders R.C.*, 1990 S.L.T. 558; cf.
John O'Connor (Plant Hire) v Kier Construction, 1990 S.C.L.R. 761 (preliminary notice referring
dispute to arbitration, but no subsequent claim in arbitration proceedings); *R. Peter & Co Ltd v The
Pancake Place Ltd*, 1993 S.L.T. 322 (no concluded agreement to arbitrate). A complaint to an
ombudsman has been held not a reference to arbitration and so not a relevant claim interrupting the
prescriptive period: *Clark v Argyle Consulting Ltd* [2010] CSOH 154; 2011 S.L.T. 180.
[131] 1973 Act s.6(1); s.10; and para.4.12, above. See, e.g. *Fortunato's J.F. v Fortunato*, 1981 S.L.T.
277; *Greater Glasgow Health Board v Baxter Clark & Paul*, 1990 S.C. 237; *Lieberman v G.W. Tait &
Sons, S.S.C.*, 1987 S.C. 213; *Barratt Scotland Ltd v Keith*, 1994 S.L.T. 1343; *Steel v Dundaff Ltd*, 1995
G.W.D. 8–457, IH; *Wilkie v Direct Line Insurance plc (No.2)*, 2002 S.L.T. 530.
[132] Proviso to s.6(1).

A relevant claim may be constituted by a writ with unspecific averments,[133] ultimately requiring substantial amendment after the expiry of the five-year period.[134] But it has been held that no relevant claim was made on an obligation where a writ required amendment outwith the five-year period in order to substitute a new and distinct obligation in place of the original obligation, such as recompense for payment,[135] or contract for delict,[136] or a contract other than that originally founded upon[137]; or an entirely different breach of duty from that originally founded upon[138]; nor where amendment was required to add a conclusion for specific implement in a writ seeking declarator.[139]

If a relevant claim is made, the prescriptive period cannot run during the currency of the proceedings.[140] Similarly, the prescriptive period cannot run during the currency of a relevant acknowledgment.[141] It is thought that the prescriptive period starts anew from the midnight following upon the date on which the interruption ends: the point has been discussed in several cases.[142]

---

[133] *British Railways Board v Strathclyde R.C.*, 1981 S.C. 90; *George A. Hood v Dumbarton D.C.*, 1983 S.L.T. 238; *Kinnaird v Donaldson*, 1992 S.C.L.R. 694 (whole writ, including crave or conclusions, condescendence and pleas-in-law, to be taken into account); *Link Housing Association Ltd v PBL Construction Ltd* [2009] CSIH 54, 2009 S.C. 653; *Royal Insurance (UK) Ltd v Amec Construction (Scotland) Ltd* [2008] CSOH 107; 2008 S.L.T. 825. However, it has been observed that a fundamentally null action would not constitute an interruption of the prescriptive period: *Shanks v Central R.C.*, 1987 S.L.T. 410; 1988 S.L.T. 212; and an action of declarator has been held not to constitute a relevant claim in respect of an obligation to indemnify: *Wylie v Avon Insurance Co Ltd*, 1988 S.C.L.R. 570.

[134] *Macleod v Sinclair*, 1981 S.L.T. (Notes) 38; *Kinnaird v Donaldson*, 1992 S.C.L.R. 694; *Mackinnon v Avonside Homes Ltd*, 1993 S.C.L.R. 976; *Safdar v Devlin*, 1995 S.L.T. 530. In assessing whether an amendment has been made within the five-year period, the relevant point in time is the date when the minute of amendment was allowed to be received: *Boyle v Glasgow Corporation*, 1975 S.C. 238; *Stewart v Highlands & Islands Development Board*, 1991 S.L.T. 787. The lodging of the minute of amendment itself may amount to the making of a relevant claim, even though amendment was not allowed at the time: *Kinnaird v Donaldson*, 1992 S.C.L.R. 694.

[135] *N.V. Devos Gebroeder v Sunderland Sportswear Ltd*, 1990 S.C. 291, distinguished in *Ductform Ventilation (Fife) Ltd v Andrews-Weatherfoil Ltd*, 1995 S.L.T. 88, where a claim, initially for payment under a contract, was amended outwith the five-year period to a claim for damages for breach of that contract.

[136] *Middleton v Douglass*, 1991 S.L.T. 726.

[137] *Lawrence v J.D. McIntosh & Hamilton*, 1981 S.L.T. (Sh. Ct) 73; *Wright v Invergordon Distilleries Ltd*, 1993 G.W.D. 22–1393.

[138] *J.G. Martin Plant Hire v Bannatyne Kirkwood France & Co*, 1996 S.C. 105.

[139] *Wylie v Avon Insurance Co Ltd*, 1988 S.C.L.R. 570.

[140] *G.A. Estates Ltd v Caviapen Trs Ltd*, 1993 S.L.T. 1051, IH; 1993 S.L.T. 1045, OH; *British Railways Board v Strathclyde R.C.*, 1981 S.C. 90; *George A. Hood & Co v Dumbarton D.C.*, 1983 S.L.T. 238. Thus an action may constitute an interruption even although the action is subsequently abandoned. But where a relevant claim was constituted by the service and registration of letters of inhibition on the dependence of an action (which was not itself proceeded with until over five years later) the interruption was held to have begun and ended on the day of registration: *Hogg v Prentice*, 1994 S.C.L.R. 426.

[141] *Barratt Scotland Ltd v Keith*, 1994 S.L.T. 1343 (pursuer's unequivocal admission on record effective to prevent the running of the prescriptive period until minute of abandonment); cf. dicta in *G.A. Estates Ltd v Caviapen Trs Ltd*, 1993 S.L.T. 1051 at 1059G. Note that in order to defeat a plea of prescription, the relevant acknowledgment must have been made within the five years preceding the raising of the action: *R. Peter & Co Ltd v The Pancake Place Ltd*, 1993 S.L.T. 322.

[142] See *G.A. Estates Ltd v Caviapen Trs Ltd*, 1993 S.L.T. 1051; *British Railways Board v Strathclyde R.C.*, 1981 S.C. 90. Thus, e.g. a fresh prescriptive period would begin to run from the midnight following upon the date of the final disposal of a relevant court action, including any appeal procedure.

4.22 Reparation[143]—For the purposes of prescription, the 1973 Act in effect divides reparation into two categories: (a) reparation in respect of personal injuries or death[144]; and (b) reparation in respect of any other loss, injury or damage, arising from, for example, negligent acts in relation to property, or breach of contract or promise.[145] Rights and obligations arising from damage caused by defective products are the subject of special rules and are dealt with separately.[146]

4.23 Personal injuries or death—An obligation to make reparation in respect of personal injuries or death cannot be extinguished by five-year prescription,[147] nor by 20-year prescription.[148]

4.24 Other loss, injury or damage—Any other obligation to make reparation is extinguished by five-year prescription.[149] Thus it applies to a variety of claims, including claims for breach of contract, property damage, and professional negligence resulting in loss or damage other than personal injuries or death.[150] In computing the prescriptive period, the obligation is regarded as having become enforceable on the date when the loss, injury or damage occurred[151]; or in the case

---

[143] Reparation is not defined in the Act, but appears to have been used in its widest sense, namely, the making good of any civil wrong usually by an award of damages. See, e.g. the terms of s.11, *Miller v Glasgow D.C.*, 1988 S.C. 440. Note that special prescriptive rules apply to reparation arising from product liability: see para.4.26, below.

[144] "Personal injuries" includes any disease or any impairment of a person's physical or mental condition: s.22(1). A claim for damages for inconvenience caused by breach of contract is not a claim for personal injuries: *Mack v Glasgow City Council*, 2006 S.C. 543, over-ruling *Fleming v Strathclyde R.C.*, 1992 S.L.T. 161.

[145] For a case of breach of unilateral promise see *Smith v Stuart* [2010] CSIH 29; 2010 S.C. 490.

[146] See the 1973 Act Pt IIA (ss.22A–22D) (inserted by the Consumer Protection Act 1987) and para.4.26, below.

[147] 1973 Act Sch.1 para.2(g). However, limitation may prevent enforcement by court action after three years: see para.29.11. It is now clear that a trustee in sequestration can sist himself as pursuer in place of the bankrupt even in claims (such as one for solatium) which he would not himself have had title to raise: *Coutts' Tr. v Coutts*, 1998 S.C.L.R. 729; cf. also *Grindall v John Mitchell (Grangemouth) Ltd*, 1986 S.C. 121; 1987 S.L.T. 137; *Watson v Thompson*, 1990 S.C. 38.

[148] The 1973 Act s.7(2) as amended by the 1984 Act Sch.1. Such obligations could, however, be extinguished by 20-year prescription if they had subsisted without claim or acknowledgement for 20 years prior to September 26, 1984: see *Paterson v George Wimpey & Co Ltd*, 1999 S.L.T. 577.

[149] 1973 Act s.6(2); Sch.1 para.1(d).

[150] See, e.g. *Curran v Docherty*, 1994 G.W.D. 39–2321. In *Hobday v Kirkpatrick's Trs*, 1985 S.L.T. 197, beneficiaries under a trust disposition and settlement raised an action of count reckoning and payment against the trustees seeking restoration to the trust estate of the value of trust property wrongly parted with: the obligation resting on the trustees was held not to be one arising from liability to make "reparation" within para.1(d) of Sch.1.

[151] 1973 Act s.11(1); See *Dunlop v McGowans*, 1980 S.C. (HL) 73 (concurrence of *injuria* and *damnum*: here, the date on which the proprietor was deprived of the opportunity of obtaining vacant possession of subjects as a result of the defender's failure to serve a notice timeously); *Highland Engineering Ltd v Anderson*, 1979 S.L.T. 122 (in an action of negligence against an accountant and the partners of his firm, it was held that prescription in relation to partnership debts or obligations ran from the date on which the debt or obligation was constituted against the partnership by decree); *George Porteous (Arts) Ltd v Dollar Rae*, 1979 S.L.T. (Sh. Ct) 51 (date on which local authority served demolition enforcement notice on proprietor following upon defenders' failure to obtain planning permission); *Riddick v Shaughnessy Quigley & McColl*, 1981 S.L.T. (Notes) 89 (date on which pursuer was put out of premises); *British Railways Board v Strathclyde R.C.*, 1981 S.C. 90 (date on which tunnel collapsed); *Renfrew Golf Club v Ravenstone Securities Ltd*, 1984 S.C. 22 (where held that an underlying defect in a newly constructed golf course may not necessarily constitute damnum until some damage such as waterlogged greens occurred); *East Hook Purchasing Corp. Ltd v Ben Nevis Distillery (Fort William) Ltd*, 1985 S.L.T. 442 (date on which the depositary of whisky parted with possession of any quantity of the goods); *Scott Lithgow Ltd v Secretary of State for Defence*, 1989 S.C.

of loss, injury or damage arising as a result of a continuing act, neglect or default, on the date when the latter ceased[152]; or where the creditor is unaware of any damage, on the date when the creditor first became aware or could with reasonable diligence[153] have become aware that the loss, injury or damage had occurred.[154] Latent defects in buildings and other construction works have given rise to difficult questions of prescription.[155]

Two-year prescription: Contribution between wrongdoers—Where two or **4.25** more persons are found jointly and severally liable in delict the court can apportion the damages between or amongst them.[156] A joint defender who pays more than his fair share of damages has then a right of relief against another joint defender and can recover the appropriate sum apportioned to that defender.[157] However, a pursuer may have elected to sue one or some but not all of a number of joint wrongdoers. The court cannot order a person who has not been called as

---

(HL) 9 (date of discovery of defective submarine cables, being date when Secretary of State's contractual obligation to indemnify contractor arose); *Beard v Beveridge, Herd & Sandilands, W.S.*, 1990 S.L.T. 609 (date of execution of lease containing defective rent review clause); *Roulston v Boyds*, 1990 G.W.D. 12–633 (date of recording of challenged standard security); *Fergus v MacLennan*, 1991 S.L.T. 321 (date by which, as a result of positive prescription acting in favour of another, a beneficiary irretrievably lost her right to heritable property bequeathed to her but not conveyed to her despite her instructions to solicitors); *Sinclair v MacDougall Estates Ltd*, 1994 S.L.T. 76 (date when certain major building defects and damage were evident or discovered); *J.G. Martin Plant Hire v Bannatyne Kirkwood France & Co.*, 1996 S.C. 105 (date of raising of defective court action); *Strathclyde R.C. v Border Engineering Contractors Ltd*, 1997 S.C.L.R 100 (date of completion or purported completion of building contract); *Osborne & Hunter Ltd v Hardie Caldwell*, 1999 S.L.T. 153 (date of loan to suspect borrower); *G.W. Tait & Sons SSC v Taylor*, 2002 S.L.T. 1285 (breach of obligation to deliver a valid standard security); *Jackson v Clydesdale Bank*, 2003 S.L.T. 273 (date of receiver's contract to sell company in receivership at under-value); *AMN Group Ltd v Gilcomston North Ltd* [2008] CSOH 90; 2008 S.L.T. 835; *Monaghan v Buchanan* [2010] CSOH 69; *Pelagic Freezing Ltd v Lovie Construction Ltd* [2010] CSOH 145.

[152] 1973 Act s.11(1). *Fergus v MacLennan*, 1991 S.L.T. 321; *Smith v Gordon & Smyth* Unreported August 16, 2011 (Lady Paton).

[153] cf. *Peco Arts v Hazlitt* [1983] 1 W.L.R. 1315; *Greater Glasgow Health Board v Baxter Clark & Paul*, 1990 S.C. 237; *Southside Housing Association Ltd v Harvey Scott & Partners*, 1992 G.W.D. 27–1593; *Dumfries Labour and Social Club and Institute Ltd v Sutherland Dickie & Copland*, 1993 G.W.D. 21–1314, *Sinclair v MacDougall Estates Ltd*, 1994 S.L.T. 76; *Glasper v Rodger*, 1996 S.L.T. 44; *Beveridge & Kellas WS v Abercromby*, 1997 S.C. 88; *Milne v Moores Rowland* Unreported December 23, 1999 (Lord Macfadyen); *Graham v E.A. Bell & Co* Unreported March 24, 2000 (Lord Hardie); *Cole v Lonie*, 2001 S.C. 610; *Smith v Gordon & Smyth* Unreported August 16, 2001 (Lady Paton); *Britannia Building Society v Clarke*, 2001 S.L.T. 1355; *Adams v Thorntons W.S. (No.3)*, 2005 1 S.C. 30.

[154] 1973 Act s.11(3), i.e. loss, injury or damage giving rise to an obligation to make reparation: *Dunfermline D.C. v Blyth & Blyth Associates.*, 1985 S.L.T. 345; *Curran v Docherty*, 1994 G.W.D. 39-2321. In *Greater Glasgow Health Board v Baxter Clark & Paul*, 1990 S.C. 237; 1992 S.L.T. 35, and in *Kirk Care Housing Association Ltd v Crerar & Partners*, 1996 S.L.T 150, it was held that the pursuers' ignorance as to the identity of the person upon whom the obligation to make reparation lay did not defer the start of the prescriptive period: but see recommendations of the Scottish Law Commission in their *Report on Prescription and Limitation of Actions (Latent Damage and Other Related Issues)*, paras 2.37 et seq.

[155] Scottish Law Commission, *Report on Prescription and Limitation of Actions (Latent Damage and Other Related Issues)*; H. MacQueen, "Latent Defects Collateral Warranties and Time Bar", 1991 S.L.T. (News) 77, 91, 99; *Sinclair v MacDougall Estates Ltd*, 1994 S.L.T. 76; *Musselburgh and Fisherrow Cooperative Society Ltd v Mowlem Scotland Ltd*, 2004 S.C.L.R. 412.

[156] Law Reform (Miscellaneous Provisions) (Scotland) Act 1940 s.1(1).

[157] Thus, where a settlement has been reached between the pursuer and one joint defender, the court will be reluctant to assoilzie that defender pending the establishment of any right of relief against him in the course of action: *Magee & Co (Belfast) Ltd v Bracewell Harrison & Coton*, 1981 S.L.T. 107.

a defender to pay damages.[158] Nevertheless, there is a right of relief or contribution in terms of s.3(2) of the Law Reform (Miscellaneous Provisions) (Scotland) Act 1940, which provides that one joint wrongdoer who has paid damages or expenses in satisfaction of a decree against him is entitled to recover a proportion from any other person who, if he had been sued, might also have been held liable. This applies only where there has been a judicial determination of liability in Scottish proceedings (including cases where the court pronounces a decree giving effect to the terms of a settlement between the parties).[159] Section 8A[160] of the Prescription and Limitation (Scotland) Act 1973 provides that if the obligation to make a contribution by virtue of s.3(2) above has subsisted for a continuous period of two years after the date on which the right to recover the contribution became enforceable by the creditor in the obligation without any relevant claim[161] having been made in relation to the obligation, and without the subsistence of the obligation having been relevantly acknowledged,[162] then as from the expiration of that period the obligation is extinguished.[163] In computing the two-year period, no account is to be taken of time during which the creditor was induced to refrain from making a relevant claim by reason of fraud on the part of the debtor or his agent, or error on the creditor's part induced by the debtor or his agent.[164] Once the creditor could with reasonable diligence[165] have discovered the fraud or error, any time elapsing thereafter is included in the prescriptive period.[166] Any period during which the original creditor (while he is the creditor) is under legal disability[167] is not to be included in the computation. The fact that any time is to be discounted on the ground of fraud, error or disability is not to be regarded as separating the periods before and after the time.[168]

4.26 Product liability—Section 2 of the Consumer Protection Act 1987[169] imposed strict liability upon producers, importers and others in relation to damage caused by defective products.[170] The 1987 Act also amended the Prescription and

---

[158] See, e.g. *Findlay v N.C.B.*, 1965 S.L.T. 328. The Scottish Law Commission comment that damages cannot be awarded against a person not called as a defender even although called as a third party (Scot. Law Com. No.74 (1983)).

[159] See *Comex Houlder Diving Ltd v Colne Fishing Co Ltd*, 1987 S.C. (HL) 85; also *Singer v Gray Tool Co (Europe) Ltd*, 1984 S.L.T. 149; *Dormer v Melville Dundas & Whitson*, 1989 S.L.T. 310; 1990 S.L.T. 186; *Farstad Supply A/S v Enviroco Ltd* [2010] UKSC 18; 2010 S.C. (UKSC) 87.

[160] Inserted by the Prescription and Limitation (Scotland) Act 1984 s.1.

[161] See s.9 of the 1973 Act as amended and paras 4.11 and 4.14, above.

[162] See the 1973 Act s.10, as amended and para.4.12, above.

[163] Thus, the former two-year limitation under the Limitation Act 1963 s.10, and the 1973 Act s.20, is made an extinctive prescription, implementing the recommendations of the Scottish Law Commission in their report *Prescription and Limitation of Actions: Report on Personal Injuries Actions and Private International Law Questions* (HMSO, 1983), Scot. Law Com. No.74. S.20 is repealed by the 1984 Act Sch.1.

[164] 1973 Act s.8A(2); s.6(4); s.14(1)(b), as amended by the 1984 Act.

[165] cf. *Peco Arts v Hazlitt* [1983] 1 W.L.R. 1315; *Greater Glasgow Health Board v Baxter Clark & Paul*, 1990 S.C. 237; 1992 S.L.T. 35; *Dumfries Labour and Social Club and Institute Ltd v Sutherland Dickie & Copland*, 1993 G.W.D. 21–1314; *Sinclair v MacDougall Estates Ltd*, 1994 S.L.T. 76; *Glasper v Rodger*, 1996 S.L.T. 44.

[166] 1973 Act s.8A(2); proviso to s.6(4).

[167] See para.4.08, above.

[168] 1973 Act s.6(5).

[169] Consumer Protection Act 1987 s.2 came into force on March 1, 1988 (SI 1987/1680).

[170] See para.27.03, below.

Limitation (Scotland) Act 1973 by introducing a 10-year prescription of obligations arising from defective products,[171] and a three-year limitation of actions.[172]

Ten-year prescription: defective products—In terms of s.22A of the 1973 Act, **4.27** an obligation to make reparation for damage caused wholly or partly by a defect in a product is extinguished if a period of 10 years has expired from the relevant time,[173] unless a relevant claim[174] was made within that period and has not been finally disposed of.[175] If a claim is made during the 10-year period, it appears that prescription continues to run against the obligation even while the claim is in dependence. No product liability obligation can come into existence after the expiration of the 10-year period.[176]

The Crown—The Act binds the Crown.[177] Prescription may therefore be pleaded **4.28** against the Crown.[178]

FURTHER READING

Johnston, D., *Prescription and Limitation of Actions* (Edinburgh: W. Green, 1999; 2nd edn forthcoming 2012).

Millar, J.H., *A Handbook of Prescription According to the Law of Scotland* (Edinburgh: W. Green, 1893).

Napier, N., *Commentaries on the Law of Prescription in Scotland* (Edinburgh: T&T Clark, 1854).

Simpson, A.R.C., "Positive Prescription of Moveables in Scots Law" (2009) 13 Edin. L.R. 445.

Stair Memorial Encyclopaedia, Vol.16.

Walker, D.M., *The Law of Prescription and Limitation of Actions*, 5th edn (Edinburgh: W. Green, 1996).

---

[171] See the Consumer Protection Act 1987 Sch.1, which also came into force on March 1, 1988 (SI 1987/1680) and inserted Pt IIA (ss.22A–22D) in the 1973 Act.

[172] Limitation is outwith the scope of this chapter: see paras 25.44–25.45, below. For further details, see the 1973 Act ss.22B and 22C.

[173] Consumer Protection Act 1987 s.4(2): the time when the product was supplied (or last supplied) to the consumer.

[174] "Relevant claim" is defined in s.22A(3) as meaning a claim made by or on behalf of the creditor for implement or part implement of the obligation, being a claim made: (a) in appropriate proceedings within the meaning of the 1973 Act s.4(2) (see para.4.11, above); or (b) by the presentation of, or the concurring in, a petition for sequestration or by the submission of a claim under the Bankruptcy (Scotland) Act 1985 s.22 or s.48; or (c) by the presentation of, or the concurring in, a petition for the winding up of a company or by the submission of a claim in a liquidation in accordance with the rules made under the Insolvency Act 1986 s.411. Where a relevant claim is made in an arbitration, and the nature of the claim has been stated in a preliminary notice (within the meaning of the 1973 Act s.4(4)), the date of service of the notice is deemed to be the date of the making of the claim: s.22A(4); and cf. *Douglas Milne Ltd v Borders R.C.*, 1990 S.L.T. 558; and see generally para.4.11, fn.63, above.

[175] If a relevant claim has been made but has not been finally disposed of, the obligation is extinguished when the claim is finally disposed of: s.22A(2). For the definition of "finally disposed of", see s.22A(3).

[176] 1973 Act s.22A(1).

[177] 1973 Act s.24.

[178] cf. *Lord Advocate v Graham* (1844) 7 D. 183. See para.34.31(b), below.

SECTION A
CONTRACT

CHAPTER 5

FORMATION OF VOLUNTARY OBLIGATIONS: PROMISE
AND CONTRACT

Obligations from consent: Gratuitous promise—The law recognises as a **5.01**
general principle that an obligation may arise from mere consent: that if a person
undertakes to do or pay something, or to abstain from some course of action, he
has incurred an obligation which may be enforced against him by some form
of legal process. The undertaking may take the form of a promise, when the
resulting obligation is commonly termed unilateral, or of the acceptance of
an offer, when the result is usually a mutual contract. Differing in this respect
from the law of England, Scots law holds that consent will infer an obligation
although there may be no consideration. An obligation to give, or to do or abstain
from doing something, without asking for any return is, in so far as its enforceability by legal process is concerned, on a par with an obligation for which a
return or consideration is demanded and promised.[1] The distinction in this
respect between the laws of England and Scotland is most clearly brought out
in the case of an offer to sell, with an undertaking to keep the offer open for a
certain period. Assuming that nothing is paid for the engagement to keep the
offer open, it is an undertaking without consideration, and consequently, in
English law, is not binding unless made in a deed.[2] In Scotland, where consideration is not necessary, it is a binding obligation, and the offeree, if he accept
the offer within the time specified, and his acceptance be rejected, will be entitled
to damages.[3]

Effects of promise—The distinction between promise and an offer requiring the **5.02**
offeree's acceptance to become a binding contract is essentially one of the intention of the party making the statement in question.[4] It may be difficult to know
whether a statement is a promise subject to some condition of performance by the
promisee or an offer requiring the offeree's acceptance to become a contractual
obligation.[5] Promises do not require delivery to or acceptance by the promisee to

---

[1] *Morton's Trs v Aged Christian Friendly Society* (1899) 2 F. 82.

[2] *Dickinson v Dodds* (1876) 2 Ch.D. 463. On how to execute a deed in English law, see Law of
Property (Miscellaneous Provisions) Act 1989 s.1 (as amended by the Regulatory Reform (Execution
of Deeds and Documents) Order 2005 (SI 2005/1906)), and Companies Act 2006 ss.44, 46 (previously
Companies Act 1985 s.36A(4)).

[3] *Littlejohn v Hadwen* (1882) 20 S.L.R. 5; approved by Lord Dunedin in *Paterson v Highland Ry*,
1927 S.C. (HL) 32 at 38.

[4] See further below, para 5.11, and e.g. *Morrison v Leckie*, 2005 G.W.D. 40–734 (Paisley Sheriff
Court).

[5] On conditions see above, paras 3.11–3.12.

be binding,[6] and the promisee need not be in existence at the time the promise is made for it to be binding.[7] The presence or absence of communication to the other party may be an adminicle of evidence as to whether the statement amounts to a promise in law.[8] The promisee may reject the benefit of the promise, whereupon it will cease to be a binding obligation.[9]

5.03 Gratuitous, onerous—While the law of Scotland has rejected consideration as an essential element in the constitution of a voluntary obligation, and much that is said in the remainder of this Section is as applicable, mutatis mutandis, to gratuitous promises as to contracts, this does not mean that the question of consideration is in all cases irrelevant, or that a gratuitous promise and a mutual contract stand in all respects on the same footing.[10] Where a promise is made, other than one made in the course of business, writing is required for its constitution.[11] While in the case of an onerous contract the obligations are binding although one of the obligants may have entered into the contract by reason of some error or mistake on his own part, the person who has given a gratuitous promise, and can show that it was given under essential error, is entitled to resile, even though there is no averment or proof that the error was induced by misrepresentation.[12] A difference between onerous and gratuitous obligations is also recognised in the law of bankruptcy. Certain prior obligations of the bankrupt are reducible or unenforceable if they were entered into gratuitously, whereas onerous contracts in the same circumstances would be unaffected.[13]

5.04 Definitions of contract—No satisfactory or comprehensive definition of what constitutes a contract has yet been formulated. Sometimes contracts are defined in terms of promises,[14] but this does not seem helpful when the institutional writers view contract as an obligation distinguishable from other kinds of obligations including promises.[15] Modern works on our law of contract stress the consensual nature of the obligation, the requirement of patrimonial interest and an intention to be bound.[16]

5.05 Mutual contracts, agreements—A contract involves, and is dependent on, agreement. Agreement means generally that the minds of the parties are at one with regard to the point at issue. The First Division of the Court of Session has held that there may be agreement amounting to contract between parties still

---

[6] Stair, I, 10, 4. The extent to which under the principle of delivery of deeds a written promise can bind only if the writing is delivered has been little explored in modern writing; see W.W. McBryde, *The Law of Contract in Scotland*, 3rd edn (Edinburgh: W. Green, 2007), Ch.4; para.6.03, below.

[7] *Morton's Trs v Aged Christian Friend Society of Scotland* (1899) 2 F 82.

[8] *Countess of Cawdor v Earl of Cawdor*, 2007 S.C. 285 at [15], per Lord President Hamilton.

[9] *Stair Memorial Encyclopaedia*, Vol.15, para.613.

[10] See further, M. Hogg, *Obligations*, 2nd edn (Edinburgh: Avizandum, 2006), Ch.2.

[11] Requirements of Writing (Scotland) Act 1995 s.1(2)(a)(ii). To be formally valid, subscription by the promisor will be sufficient: s.2(1). See further below, para.6.04.

[12] *Hunter v Bradford Property Trust*, 1970 S.L.T. 173 (HL). See further below, para.7.27.

[13] See below, paras 49.22–49.23.

[14] See, e.g. Restatement (Second) of Contracts s.1; *Chitty on Contracts*, edited by H.G. Beale, 30th edn (London: Sweet and Maxwell, 2008), para.1.001; M. Hogg, *Promises and Contract Law: Comparative Perspectives* (Cambridge: Cambridge University Press, 2011).

[15] Stair, I, 10, 3; Erskine, III, 1, 2 et seq.; Bell, *Principles*, s.5; Bell, *Commentaries*, I, 312.

[16] McBryde, *The Law of Contract in Scotland* (2007), Ch.1; *Stair Memorial Encyclopaedia*, Vol.15, paras 611, 619, 655–658. See further H.L. MacQueen and J.M. Thomson, *Contract Law in Scotland*, 3rd edn (Edinburgh: Bloomsbury Professional, 2012), paras 1.9–1.10 and Ch.2.

negotiating on some other points of the bargain between them.[17] In most disputed cases, however, the question is to discover the parties' apparent, rather than their real, intentions. In matters of contract a party is generally entitled to act on the assumption that the other means what he says. The question whether the parties have agreed is to be decided not by proof of what each party really intended, but by considering what conclusion a reasonable person would draw from their words or acts. It is clear that if A uses words which have an ordinary meaning, and has no reason to suppose that B will interpret them otherwise, A cannot be heard to say that he attached a different meaning to his words, or spoke with a mental reservation.[18] Even if the parties are really at cross purposes, if one uses language which to a reasonable hearer would convey the impression that he meant to agree, he will be bound, unless the difference between their mental attitudes is so fundamental as to preclude any real consent.[19]

> "Commercial contracts cannot be arranged by what people think in their inmost minds. Commercial contracts are made according to what people say."[20]

Agreement may also be inferred from the parties' conduct[21] and conduct following verbal negotiations may be construed as concluding a contract on the basis of the verbal terms.[22] It is not necessary to analyse every agreement in terms of the rules on offer and acceptance described later in this chapter: for example, the parties' agreement may be embodied in a document signed by each of them after a process of negotiation.[23]

Essentials of the contract—*Consensus in idem* occurs when agreement has been **5.06** reached upon all the essentials of the contract; what the essentials are may vary according to the particular contract under consideration.[24] In contracts for the sale of heritable property, the subjects are regarded as an essential element of a contract for the sale of heritage,[25] but it now appears to be settled that agreement as to date of entry is not essential.[26] An offer which does not provide the means for determining the price of heritable property lacks an element essential for the conclusion of a contract[27]; but in a contract for the supply of goods, a reasonable price may be implied where it is clear that the parties have agreed there should be a price.[28] In *Avintair Ltd v Ryder Airline Services Ltd*,[29] it was held that where services were rendered under an agreement, but neither a price nor a method of

---

[17] *Avintair Ltd v Ryder Airline Services Ltd*, 1994 S.C. 270, commented upon by G.D.L. Cameron, "Consensus in dissensus", 1995 S.L.T. (News) 132.

[18] *Duran v Duran* (1904) 7 F. 87, a form of marriage, with a mental reservation by one party.

[19] See *Stuart v Kennedy* (1885) 13 R. 221, and below, paras 7.23 et seq.

[20] *Muirhead and Turnbull v Dickson* (1905) 7 F. 686, per Lord President Dunedin.

[21] *Morrison-Low v Paterson*, 1985 S.L.T. 255, per Lord Fraser following W.M. Gloag, *Law of Contract*, 2nd edn (Edinburgh: W. Green, 1929), pp.46–47.

[22] *Gordon Adams and Partners v Ralph Jessop*, 1987 S.C.L.R. 735.

[23] McBryde, *The Law of Contract in Scotland* (2007), para.6.05.

[24] See *Dempster v Motherwell Bridge & Engineering Co*, 1964 S.C. 308 at 329, per Lord President Clyde, Lord Guthrie at 332.

[25] *Grant v Gauld & Co*, 1985 S.C. 251.

[26] *Secretary of State for Scotland v Ravenstone Securities Ltd*, 1976 S.C. 171; *Gordon D.C. v Wimpey Homes Holdings Ltd*, 1988 S.L.T. 481; *Sloans Dairies Ltd v Glasgow Corp*, 1977 S.C. 223.

[27] *MacLeod's Exr v Barr's Trs*, 1989 S.L.T. 392.

[28] Sale of Goods Act 1979 s.8; *British Coal Corp v South of Scotland Electricity Board*, 1991 S.L.T. 302.

[29] *Avintair Ltd v Ryder Airline Services Ltd*, 1994 S.C. 270.

calculating price had been settled, there was an implied term that a reasonable price should be paid on the principle quantum meruit. It has been held that the period of a loan and the payment of interest are not essential terms of a loan contract because a loan can be repayable on demand and may be interest free.[30] Price is not an essential of a gratuitous obligation, even if it relates to land.[31]

5.07 Certainty—In order to be binding as a contract an agreement must be certain or definite, and the test of whether it is sufficiently definite is whether it would be possible to frame a decree of specific implement.[32] Agreement for all legal purposes may be reached when a party has undertaken some definite obligation, though he may not be aware of the interpretation which the law will put on his expressions or acts, or may think that the terms to which he has bound himself are other than they are ultimately determined to be. It is for the court, not for either party, to interpret a contract, and decide upon the conditions, express or implied. So when a party had agreed to sell an entailed estate "subject to the ratification of the Court" it did not affect the validity of the contract that he had formed an erroneous impression of the process involved in ratification by the court.[33]

5.08 Intention to create legal relations: Patrimonial interest—It is not every agreement of which the courts will take cognisance.[34] The agreement must be one concerned with legal relations. Social engagements cannot be enforced by legal process. There are cases, however, where the parties may have meant to incur obligations, but where the question between them is not one which lies within the province of the courts to decide. To justify judicial interference a patrimonial interest—some material gain or loss, or chance of material gain or loss—must be involved. Thus the question whether a member of a club, averring that he has been wrongfully expelled, can find a legal remedy, depends upon whether the club possesses property in which the members have an interest. If it has none, no patrimonial interest of the member expelled has been affected, and the court will not take account of the loss of opportunities of social intercourse.[35] A like principle applies to the case of a member of a voluntary church, alleging wrongful expulsion, in contrast with the case of a minister of a similar body, who, if expelled, loses a position which gives him a chance of employment and income, and may therefore obtain legal redress.[36] There is no presumption, however, that the relationship between a church and one of its ministers is not intended to create legal relations, and a contract of employment may therefore exist between the parties.[37] An agreement between friends to share any winnings of any one of them in a game of chance was held to be an enforceable contract.[38]

5.09 Intention to create legal relations: Absence of intention—An agreement, even a commercial one, will not be binding if it appears that the parties did not intend

---

[30] *Neilson v Stewart*, 1991 S.C. (HL) 22.
[31] *Miller Homes Ltd v Frame*, 2002 S.L.T. 459 (option to purchase).
[32] *McArthur v Lawson* (1877) 4 R. 1134; *Murray's Trs v St. Margaret's Convent Trs*, 1907 S.C. (HL) 8, and cases collected at p.12 of Gloag, *Law of Contract* (1929).
[33] *Stewart v Kennedy* (1890) 17 R. (HL) 25. See also *Laing v Provincial Homes Co*, 1909 S.C. 812; *Stobo Ltd v Morrisons (Gowns) Ltd*, 1949 S.C. 184.
[34] As to *pacta illicita* see below, Ch.9.
[35] *Anderson v Manson*, 1909 S.C. 838.
[36] *Skerret v Oliver* (1896) 23 R. 468.
[37] *Percy v Church of Scotland*, 2006 S.C. (HL) 1.
[38] *Robertson v Anderson*, 2003 S.L.T. 235.

that it should be legally enforceable. This may appear from the surrounding circumstances[39] or from the terms of the agreement.[40] In *Kleinwort Benson Ltd v Malaysia Mining Corporation Bhd*,[41] comfort letters were given to a bank by a parent company in respect of loans to its subsidiary. These were not held to have created a legally enforceable obligation. The letters simply stated that it was the defendants' "policy" to ensure the financial stability of their subsidiary. This clause was contrasted with another which stated that the defendants "confirmed" that they would not withdraw capital support for the subsidiary: this was viewed as creating an enforceable obligation. A "collective agreement" is conclusively presumed not to have been intended by the parties to be a legally enforceable contract unless it is in writing and contains a provision, however expressed, that the parties intended that the agreement would be legally enforceable; an agreement which satisfies these requirements is conclusively presumed to have been intended to be legally enforceable.[42] A "collective agreement" is an agreement made by a trade union and an employer or an employers' association and relating to terms and conditions of employment.[43]

Offer and acceptance—A contract may be considered as consisting of an **5.10** offer by one party and an acceptance by the other.[44] An offer is a proposal of sufficiently definite terms for a contract made to another person or persons with the intention to be legally bound should that other accept;[45] an acceptance is an unqualified assent to the proposal in the offer. The offer, or the acceptance, or both, may be in words, spoken or written, or may be inferred from the actions of the parties. So when newspapers are laid out on a bookstall and one is taken, a contract of sale is completed, though nothing may have been said. The keeper of the bookstall, by laying out the newspapers, offers to sell them, the party who takes one accepts the offer and agrees to pay the price. A contract has been held entered into by offer and acceptance made by email.[46] In sealed competitive bidding, a "referential bid", i.e. £100 in excess of any other offer", was held, in the circumstances, not to be a valid offer.[47]

Offer and intention—It may often be difficult, alike in the construction of **5.11** words and of conduct, to distinguish between a mere expression of readiness to do business in a particular line and an offer to enter into a contract. A person who indicates willingness to contract does not necessarily make an offer which can be turned into a contract by acceptance. The indication may only be of readiness

---

[39] *Ford Motor Co v Amalgamated Union of Engineering and Foundry Workers* [1969] 2 Q.B. 303. In England there is a presumption that an agreement between husband and wife is not intended to create a legal relationship: *Gould v Gould* [1970] 1 Q.B. 275. But there is no reason why spouses cannot conclude a binding contract with each other: *Raith v Raith* (1923) 39 Sh. Ct Rep. 133.

[40] *Rose and Frank Co v Crompton* [1925] A.C. 445; *Tannahill v Glasgow Corp*, 1935 S.C. (HL) 15.

[41] *Kleinwort Benson Ltd v Malaysia Mining Corporation Bhd* [1989] 1 W.L.R. 379, CA.

[42] Trade Union and Labour Relations (Consolidation) Act 1992 s.179.

[43] Trade Union and Labour Relations (Consolidation) Act 1992 s.178.

[44] There are types of contract which do not fit easily into the normal analysis of a contract as being constituted by offer and acceptance: *Gibson v Manchester City Council* [1979] 1 W.L.R. 294 at 297, per Lord Diplock.

[45] See e.g. *William Lippe Architects Ltd v Innes* [2006] CSOH 182, aff'd on this point [2007] CSIH 84 at [24]–[26].

[46] *Baillie Estates Ltd v Du Pont (UK) Ltd* [2009] CSIH 95; 2010 S.C.L.R. 192. A contract may also be formed through the interaction of an individual with an inter-active e-commerce website or automated vending machine.

[47] *Harvela Investments Ltd v Royal Trust Co of Canada (C.I.) Ltd* [1986] 1 A.C. 207.

to receive and to consider offers. The question whether a party has merely indicated an intention or has made an offer must depend on the circumstances of each case; words or acts which, if used in one connection, would amount to an offer, may, if used in another, merely indicate a readiness to chaffer or bargain. So a trader who quotes prices of the commodity in which it deals, either in response to a request or *ex proprio motu*, will, in general, be held to have made an offer to sell[48]: the statement of the lowest price which would be accepted for a particular estate, made in response to an inquiry as to the owner's readiness to sell, was read merely as an indication of willingness to consider an offer of that price.[49] A shopkeeper, by placing goods in the shop window, with or without prices annexed, only indicates readiness to trade,[50] but a party who is under a duty to exercise a vocation, such as a common carrier or innkeeper, makes a continuous offer, subject, no doubt, to implied conditions, but which will bind him to carry or entertain any applicant who complies with these conditions.[51] The display of goods for hire beside a notice stating the hire charge has been treated as an offer, as has a vending machine dispensing car-park tickets.[52]

5.12 Expression of intention not binding—It may probably be stated without qualification that if it is decided, on the particular facts, that a party has only indicated an intention, that person has incurred no liability.[53] Where railway companies intimated that a reduced rate would be charged for a certain period, it was held that they were not precluded from withdrawing the concession before the period had expired.[54] A company circular which "proposes" the issue of new shares does not commit the company to do this.[55] The announcement that I intend to do something does not bind me not to change my mind, and anyone who acts or incurs expense on the assumption that I will carry out my intention does so at his own risk. So when negotiations for a loan were broken off before any definite offer had been made, it was held that the party who had proposed to lend had no claim for the expenses he had incurred in investigating the other's title to subjects which were contemplated as security, nor to interest on the money which he had kept in hand in order to make the proposed advance.[56]

5.13 Liability after failure to conclude contract—In the case just cited (*Gilchrist v Whyte*), certain earlier cases,[57] quoted as authorities for the proposition that if A indicates an intention to contract, and knows that B is incurring expense in expectation of a contract, A, if he changes his mind, must meet the expenses B has incurred, were distinguished or overruled. But it was observed that to indicate an

---

[48] *Philp v Knoblauch*, 1907 S.C. 994; but see *Scancarriers A/S v Aotearoa International Ltd* [1985] 2 Lloyd's Rep. 419, PC, where quotation of freight rates by a carrier was held not to constitute an offer.

[49] *Harvey v Facey* [1893] A.C. 552.

[50] That at least is the law in England: *Pharmaceutical Society of Great Britain v Boots Cash Chemists (Southern) Ltd* [1953] 1 Q.B. 401; *Fisher v Bell* [1961] 1 Q.B. 394. But these cases leave unanswered the question of what constitutes acceptance of the customer's offer to purchase.

[51] *Campbell v Ker*, February 24, 1810, FC; *Rothfield v North British Ry*, 1920 S.C. 805.

[52] *Chapelton v Barry Urban D.C.* [1940] 1 K.B. 532; *Thornton v Shoe Lane Parking Ltd* [1971] 2 Q.B. 163. On internet websites, see MacQueen and Thomson, *Contract Law in Scotland* (2012), para.2.15.

[53] *Countess of Cawdor*, 2007 S.C. 285, citing Stair, I, 10, 2.

[54] *Paterson v Highland Ry*, 1927 S.C. (HL) 32.

[55] *Mason v Benhar Coal Co* (1882) 9 R. 883.

[56] *Gilchrist v Whyte*, 1907 S.C. 984. See also *Maddison v Alderson* (1883) 8 App. Cas. 467.

[57] *Walker v Milne* (1823) 2 S. 379; *Dobie v Lauder's Trs* (1873) 11 M. 749; *Hamilton v Lochrane* (1899) 1 F. 478.

intention to contract when no such intention had been formed, and thereby to lead another party to incur expense, would be an actionable wrong.[58] More recent cases leave open the possibility that a claim for reimbursement based on *Walker v Milne*,[59] if supported by averments of definite loss, and not merely of deprivation of problematical gain, is maintainable where expenditure by one party was occasioned by the representations of the other and the former acted in reliance on an implied assurance by the latter that there was a binding contract between them, when in fact there was no more than an agreement which fell short of being a binding contract; but these decisions have been questioned.[60] Where someone benefits from work done by another before there is a contract, an unjustified enrichment claim for recompense may be allowed: but what is done must benefit or enrich that party.[61] It may be that a party who invites the submission of tenders obliges himself to consider these.[62] The effect of a "letter of intent" may or may not be contractual; this depends on its terms and on the communings between the parties.[63]

Parties to whom offer is made—An offer may be made to a particular indi- **5.14** vidual, or to a specified class. Only the named offeree may accept such an offer.[64] An offer may also be made to the general public, as in the case of an offer of a reward for the recovery of lost property,[65] or of insurance in timetables or diaries.[66] In such cases it is not necessary that the party who claims fulfilment of the offer shall have given any express acceptance; acceptance is implied in doing the act called for, though it is probably necessary that the act shall have been done in the knowledge that the offer has been made. Where the proprietors of a preventive for influenza offered a payment to anyone who used it in accordance with their directions and yet caught the disease, it was held that they could not refuse payment on the ground that the claimant had not expressly indicated that she accepted the offer and proposed to try the preventive.[67] It has been argued that this and the cases cited in the two preceding notes are better analysed as conditional promises.[68]

---

[58] *Gilchrist v Whyte*, 1907 S.C. 984, per Lord Ardwall.

[59] *Walker v Milne* (1823) 2 S. 379. See further MacQueen and Thomson, *Contract Law in Scotland* (2000), paras 2.91–2.96.

[60] *Khaliq v Londis Holdings Ltd*, [2010] CSIH 13; 2010 S.C. 432, doubting *Dawson International Plc v Coats Paton Plc*, 1988 S.L.T. 854, affd 1989 S.L.T. 655. See MacQueen and Hogg, "Melville Monument liability: some doubtful dicta" (2010) 14 Edin. L.R. 451; also *Gray v Johnston's Exr*, 1928 S.C. 659; *Bank of Scotland v 3i Plc*, 1990 S.C. 215; and MacQueen and Thomson, *Contract Law in Scotland* (2012), paras 2.89–2.96.

[61] *Gilchrist v Whyte*, 1907 S.C. 984; *Microwave Systems (Scotland) Ltd v Electro-Physiological Instruments Ltd*, 1971 S.C. 140; *Site Preparations Ltd v Secretary of State for Scotland*, 1975 S.L.T. (Notes) 41.

[62] *Blackpool and Fylde Aero Club Ltd v Blackpool B.C.* [1990] 3 All E.R. 25. For public procurement controls under EU law, beyond the scope of the present work, see *Chitty on Contracts*(2008), paras 10.044–10.048.

[63] *Robertson Group (Construction) Ltd v Amey-Miller (Edinburgh) Joint Venture*, 2005 S.C.L.R. 854, affd 2006 S.C.L.R. 772; *Uniroyal Ltd v Miller & Co Ltd*, 1985 S.L.T. 101; *British Steel Corp v Cleveland Bridge and Engineering Co Ltd* [1984] 1 All E.R. 504.

[64] *Fleming Buildings Ltd v Forrest* [2010] CSIH 8. See also *City of Glasgow Council v Peart*, 1999 Hous. L.R. 117.

[65] *Petrie v Earl of Airlie* (1834) 13 S. 68.

[66] *Hunter v General Accident Co*, 1909 S.C. (HL) 30.

[67] *Carlill v Carbolic Smoke Ball Co* [1893] 1 Q.B. 256.

[68] See now Hogg, *Obligations* (2006), paras 2.77–2.83. For conditional promises, see above, para.5.02.

5.15 Express acceptance, when necessary—Apart from offers to the general public, it is a question of construction in each case whether express acceptance of an offer is necessary to complete a contract. The question to be solved is whether the offer calls for an act, or for a promise to undertake a reciprocal obligation. So an order for goods does not require express acceptance; it is accepted by sending the goods.[69] On the other hand, when the directors of a company sent a circular offering to cancel the allotment of shares it was held that this offer required express acceptance, and therefore, in the ensuing liquidation of the company, those shareholders who had accepted the offer were free from liability, while those who had done nothing were liable as contributors.[70]

5.16 Acts amounting to acceptance—When a party who has received an offer proceeds to act in a way which is justifiable only on the assumption that he has accepted it, his acts, if unequivocal,[71] infer acceptance. Action of this kind may be treated as equivalent to acceptance even if in words the offer has been refused. A ship had been stranded, and the owner offered to abandon her to the underwriters as a constructive total loss. The underwriters refused to accept the notice of abandonment, but proceeded in attempts to salve the ship in a manner which caused further damage. It was held that their actions, in spite of their formal refusal, amounted to acceptance of the notice of abandonment, or, on an alternative view, were such as to bar them from maintaining that they had not accepted.[72] Parties may agree that an offer is to be regarded as accepted if it is not refused within a specified time. And in ordinary business matters if a party receives an order for the goods in which he deals and does not promptly intimate his refusal he will be deemed to have accepted the order and will be liable in damages if he does not fulfil it.[73] In other cases a person is not entitled to force a contract into existence merely by intimating that the offer will be treated as accepted if it is not refused. Goods sent without an order, and without a previous course of dealing from which an order may be implied, may safely be rejected.[74] When A, writing to B in reference to a dispute, proposed a compromise, and added that he would assume that his proposal was accepted if he did not hear to the contrary within a certain number of days, it was held that B's failure to reply did not make the compromise binding on him.[75] Where an employee continued to work after receiving notice of the terms of employment and failed to sign a written acknowledgment thereof, it was held that he had accepted employment on those terms.[76]

5.17 No acceptance of offer garbled in transmission—Where an offer has been altered in a material respect in the course of transmission, the offeree's acceptance does not result in the conclusion of a contract. So where an offer sent by telegram was misread by the telegraph clerk and was transmitted in a form materially

---

[69] Bell, *Commentaries*, I, 343.

[70] *Edinburgh Employers Assurance Co v Griffiths* (1892) 19 R. 550.

[71] See *Oastler v Henderson* (1877) 2 Q.B.D. 575. For an implied rejection, see *Lawrence v Knight*, 1972 S.C. 26.

[72] *Robertson v Royal Exchange Assurance Corp*, 1925 S.C. 1.

[73] *Barry, Ostlere and Shepherd v Edinburgh Cork Importing Co*, 1909 S.C. 1113.

[74] *Jaffrey v Boag* (1824) 3 S. 375; *Gilbert v Dickson*, 1803 Hume 334. Note also the Consumer Protection (Distance Selling) Regulations 2000 (SI 2000/2334), discussed below, para.14.22.

[75] *Jaffrey v Boag* (1824) 3 S. 375.

[76] *SOS Bureau Ltd v Payne*, 1982 S.L.T. (Sh. Ct) 33.

different from its original terms, no contract resulted from the acceptance, because the circumstances precluded any real agreement.[77]

Withdrawal of offer—As a general rule, an offer may be withdrawn at any time **5.18** before acceptance. But a person may promise to enter into a contract if the party to whom the offer is made chooses to accept, and does so if it is stated that the offer is open for a certain time.[78] And while in the ordinary case an application for shares in a company may be withdrawn before it is accepted by allotment, an application expressly stated to be irrevocable binds the applicant to take the shares if they are allotted to him.[79] An offer is impliedly withdrawn by the death of either party or by the offerer's insanity, even although the insanity has not been made public by any legal process, and the party who has accepted the offer was not aware of it.[80] A formal written offer to purchase (or sell) heritable property may be withdrawn verbally so long as this is communicated to the offeree before he or she has accepted the offer.[81]

Conclusion of contract by acceptance: Time—An offer cannot be withdrawn **5.19** after acceptance. Where parties are in instantaneous communication with each other (across the table, or on the telephone, or by means of email or text message) the contract is concluded when the offerer actually becomes aware of the acceptance.[82] The rule is that acceptance takes effect when it is made in the manner indicated by the offer.[83] In offers made by post it will be assumed, in the absence of any provision to the contrary, that an acceptance by letter is indicated; if so, the acceptance takes effect, and the contract is complete and binding, when the letter of acceptance is posted.[84] A message of any kind withdrawing the offer is too late if it does not arrive until after the acceptance has been posted.[85] But this rule assumes that both parties are acting in matters of business in an ordinary business way; when an offer was withdrawn by telegram which would have reached the offeree in time had he been at his place of business, it was held that the offer was effectually withdrawn although the offeree, writing to accept from some other place, had posted his letter before he actually received the telegram.[86] If there is a time fixed for acceptance it is sufficient for the acceptor to show that he posted his letter in time, although, by a delay in the post, it arrived too late.[87] It has been held in England that proof that an acceptance has been posted is sufficient to complete

---

[77] *Verdin v Robertson* (1871) 10 M. 35; *Henkel v Pape* (1870) L.R. 6 Exch. 7.

[78] Above, para.5.01. There is, however, a distinction between stipulating a period during which the offer cannot be withdrawn and stipulating a period within which the offer must be accepted: *Effold Properties Ltd v Sprot*, 1979 S.L.T. (Notes) 84; *Heys v Kimball and Morton* (1890) 17 R. 381 at 385.

[79] *Premier Briquette Co v Gray*, 1922 S.C. 329.

[80] *Thomson v James* (1855) 18 D. 1 at 10; *City of Glasgow Council v Peart*, 1999 Hous. L.R. 117. Previous editions of this work state that the offerer's supervening bankruptcy has a similar effect, but the only authority to this effect is Bell, *Principles*, s.79. Cf. McBryde, *The Law of Contract in Scotland* (2007), para.26.21.

[81] *McMillan v Caldwell*, 1991 S.L.T. 325.

[82] *Brinkibon Ltd v Stahag Stahl und Stahlwaren GmbH* [1983] 2 A.C. 34; *Entores Ltd v Miles Far East Corp* [1955] 2 Q.B. 327. *Sed quaere* telephone answering machines, voice mail and email.

[83] *Holwell Securities Ltd v Hughes* [1974] 1 W.L.R. 155.

[84] *Thomson v James* (1855) 18 D. 1. Neither European Parliament and EC Council Directive 2000/31/E.C., arts 9–11, nor its UK implementation in the Electronic Commerce (EC Directive) Regulations 2002 (SI 2002/2013), regs 9, 11, 12, resolve the issue of whether the postal rule applies to email or other electronic communications. It is suggested not.

[85] *Thomson v James* (1855) 18 D. 1; *Henthorn v Fraser* [1892] 2 Ch. 27.

[86] *Burnley v Alford*, 1919 2 S.L.T. 123.

[87] *Jacobsen v Underwood* (1894) 21 R. 654.

the contract even though the letter never arrives,[88] but this has been doubted in Scotland,[89] and the question must be considered to be open.

5.20 Withdrawal of acceptance—From the theory that a contract is completed when a postal acceptance is dispatched it might be inferred that such an acceptance cannot be withdrawn. But in the only decision on the subject it was held that an acceptance was withdrawn effectually if the notice of withdrawal reached the offerer before, or together with, the letter of acceptance.[90] The decision has been regarded with reserve by academic writers on the grounds that it could be regarded as relating to withdrawal of an offer rather than an acceptance, and that it involved an element of agency[91]; a different result has been reached in other jurisdictions.[92] It may, however, be observed that under two international conventions relating to the sale of goods, revocation of acceptance is treated as being effective so long as this is communicated before, or together with, the acceptance.[93] In an era where there are many methods of communication of varying degrees of immediacy, the possibility of a postal acceptance being effectively overtaken by a faster method of communication—e.g. telephone call, email—may well be appropriate for recognition by the law.

5.21 Reasonable time—Acceptance must be within the time fixed by the offer, if any; if none, within a reasonable time. The question of what is a reasonable time may be solved by proof of a custom in the particular trade,[94] or may be decided on the whole circumstances of the case.[95] Business offers, to buy or sell commodities which fluctuate in value, are assumed to be open for acceptance only by return of post.[96] An acceptance too late is in effect a new offer, which the original offerer may ignore without incurring any liability.[97] If a person to whom an offer has been made admits that the offer was not accepted within the proper time, but alleges that in the course of negotiation the time was extended, it lies on that person to prove a definite agreement to that effect.[98]

5.22 Qualified acceptance—An acceptance must meet the offer.[99] If what bears to be an acceptance proposes new conditions it is in effect a new offer, which the other

---

[88] *Household Fire Insurance Co v Grant* (1879) 4 Ex. D. 216. Cf. *Holwell Securities Ltd v Hughes* [1974] 1 W.L.R. 155.

[89] *Mason v Benhar Coal Co* (1882) 9 R. 883. Note also *Higgins & Sons v Dunlop, Wilson & Co* (1847) 9 D. 1407 at 1414, per Lord Fullerton (1848) 6 Bell 195.

[90] *Countess of Dunmore v Alexander* (1830) 9 S. 190.

[91] P. Winfield, "Some Aspects of Offer and Acceptance" (1939) 55 L.Q.R. 499, 512; A. Hudson, "Retraction of Letters of Acceptance" (1966) 82 L.Q.R. 169; G.H. Treitel, *Law of Contract*, 13th edn (London: Sweet and Maxwell, 2011), p.30 note. See also Gloag, *Law of Contract* (1929), p.38; D.M. Walker, *The Law of Contract and Related Obligations in Scotland*, 3rd edn (Edinburgh: T & T Clark, 1995), p.132; McBryde, *The Law of Contract in Scotland* (2007), paras 6.06 and 6.53; MacQueen and Thomson, *Contract Law in Scotland* (2012), para.2.34.

[92] *Wenckheim v Arndt* (N.Z.) 1 J.R. 73 (1873); *Morrison v Thoelke*, 155 So. 2d. 889 (1963); *A to Z Bazaars (Pty) Ltd v Minister of Agriculture*, 1974 (4) S.A. 392(C).

[93] Uniform Law on the Formation of Contracts for the International Sale of Goods (1964) art.10: implemented in the United Kingdom by the Uniform Laws on International Sales Act 1967 s.2(1); United Nations Convention on Contracts for the International Sale of Goods (1980) art.22; the United Kingdom has not yet ratified this Convention.

[94] *Murray v Rennie* (1897) 24 R. 965.

[95] *Flaws v International Oil Pollution Compensation Fund*, 2001 S.L.T. 897.

[96] *Wylie & Lochhead v McElroy* (1873) 1 R. 41, per Lord President Inglis.

[97] *Wylie & Lochhead v McElroy* (1873) 1 R. 41.

[98] *Glasgow Steam Shipping Co v Watson* (1873) 1 R. 189.

[99] *Mathieson Gee (Ayrshire) Ltd v Quigley*, 1952 S.C. (HL) 38.

party may accept or not as he pleases. But if the acceptance contains a meaningless condition, that condition will be ignored and the contract, if otherwise good, held to be concluded.[100] A request for more information or for clarification is not a rejection which causes the offer to fall.[101] On the making of a qualified acceptance and counter-offer, the original offer falls and, if the counter-offer is refused, the party cannot fall back and accept the original offer.[102] Where the qualification in the acceptance is very limited, it may be read as otherwise incorporating the whole of the offer.[103] Where an exchange of missives reveals that there are two (counter-) offers in existence, one by the purchaser the other by the seller, it is open to either party to withdraw his offer and accept, without qualification, the remaining offer.[104] A party who accepts an offer may be bound, although in his acceptance he may propose conditions as to the method in which the contract may be carried into effect.[105] This question has arisen chiefly in cases where an offer, made verbally or by letter, is met by an acceptance "subject to contract", "subject to formal contract", or other equivalent terms. Is this merely a condition as to the method in which the contract which has been completed may be carried out, or does it postpone the mutual agreement until the formal contract has been drawn up and signed? In *Erskine v Glendinning*,[106] an offer to let was accepted with the qualification "subject to lease drawn out in due form". It was held that a contract was completed by this acceptance, and that the party who had accepted could not withdraw. But where an imperfectly authenticated acceptance contained the words "subject to contract" it was held, distinguishing *Erskine v Glendinning*, that the obligation was suspended.[107] Where parties to an action agree to a settlement of the litigation, though with a provision that its terms are to be embodied in a joint minute, the agreement is completely binding.[108]

"Battle of the forms"—Where the offer refers to one set of conditions and the **5.23** acceptance refers to a different set, there is the so-called "battle of the forms". The result depends on the content of the conditions: if the two sets are reconcilable, both may apply; if they conflict, the "acceptance" may be treated as a counter-offer and, if it is accepted, the conditions referred to therein may prevail.[109] If the offer contains an overriding clause, providing that the conditions referred to

---

[100] *Nicolene Ltd v Simmonds* [1953] 1 Q.B. 543. But if terms are so interrelated that the removal of one would affect the others, it will not be treated as *pro non scripto: MacLeod's Exr v Barr's Trs*, 1989 S.C. 72.

[101] *Stevenson v McLean* (1880) 5 Q.B.D. 346; *Gibson v Manchester City Council* [1979] 1 All E.R. 972.

[102] *Wolf and Wolf v Forfar Potato Co*, 1984 S.L.T. 100; *Rutterford Ltd v Allied Breweries Ltd*, 1990 S.L.T. 249 (where arguments that the terms of an offer may be classified as being either essential or inessential, and that qualification or variation of the latter should be treated as being a proposal for modification rather than as a rejection, were rejected); *Tenbey v Stolt Comex Seaway Ltd*, 2001 S.C. 638.

[103] *Howgate Shopping Centre Ltd v GLS 164 Ltd*, 2002 S.L.T. 820.

[104] *Findlater v Maan*, 1990 S.C. 150.

[105] See *Ingram-Johnson v Century Insurance Co*, 1909 S.C. 1032; *Thomson v James* (1855) 18 D. 1 at 14, 23.

[106] *Erskine v Glendinning* (1871) 9 M. 656.

[107] *Stobo Ltd v Morrisons (Gowns) Ltd*, 1949 S.C. 184.

[108] *Dewar v Ainslie* (1892) 20 R. 203; *Murphy v Smith*, 1920 S.C. 104.

[109] *Uniroyal Ltd v Miller & Co Ltd*, 1985 S.L.T. 101; *Butler Machine Tool Co Ltd v Ex-Cell-O Corp (England) Ltd* [1979] 1 All E.R. 965; *Tekdata Intercommunications v Ampenol Ltd* [2010] 2 All E.R. (Comm) 302 (C.A.). Cf. *Ferguson Shipbuilders Ltd v Voith Hydro GmbH & Co KG*, 2000 S.L.T. 229.

therein will apply unless a variation is confirmed in writing by the offerer, the offerer's terms may prevail.[110]

5.24 *Locus poenitentiae*—While the engagement is still incomplete, e.g. while the offer remains unaccepted, or the writing, where this is required by law or has been stipulated for,[111] has yet to be executed, parties have the right to withdraw from negotiations; this right is termed *locus poenitentiae*.[112] It may, in the case where an offer is met by a qualified acceptance, be lost if the party proposing to withdraw has allowed the other to act on the assumption that the contract is complete. Such actions by the other party are known as *rei interventus*.[113] The meaning of this term will be considered in dealing with verbal or informal agreements relating to heritage.[114] In cases where full agreement has never been reached but one or other of the parties has acted on the assumption that it has, it may be shown that they mistook each other's attitude so completely that the contract supposed to be accepted was a different one from that which was offered. In that event, despite any action that may have followed, the conclusion must be that since there was no agreement to any contract, matters must be restored as far as possible to their original position, and that neither party is under any obligation. This was the solution in a case where, owing to a misunderstanding, a tenant had made two offers for a farm, materially different in their conditions, and had entered into possession. It was held that there had been no agreement and that the tenant must remove.[115] In the more common case where substantial agreement has been reached, but minor details are still unsettled, it will be held that the offerer, if he knows that the other is proceeding to act in reliance on the contract, and does not interfere, has waived his objection to the terms proposed.[116] Where a person is barred by his actions from founding on the informality of contract, but it eventually proves that the other party cannot offer a valid title, he is entitled to repudiate.[117] A party may lose the right to resile by means of waiver, express or inferred.[118]

5.25 **Incorporation of terms**—An offer may be made conditionally: the conditions (or, more accurately, terms or stipulations) may be incorporated by express reference in the contract documents to the rules of an association,[119] or to printed conditions a copy of which is obtainable from the offerer,[120] or to articles of association of a company,[121] or to a foreign statute.[122] If the offer is met by general

---

[110] *Roofcare Ltd v Gillies*, 1984 S.L.T. (Sh. Ct) 8. This case is not easily reconciled with *Butler Machine Tool* [1979] 1 All E.R. 965.

[111] Below, para.6.04; see *Stobo Ltd*, 1949 S.C. 184, per Lord President Cooper at 192.

[112] Bell, *Principles*, s.25. See, e.g. *Karoulias S.A. (W.S.) v The Drambuie Liqueur Co Ltd*, 2005 S.L.T. 813, noted by G. Black, "W.S. Karoulias S.A. v The Drambuie Liqueur Co Ltd" (2006) 10 Edin. L.R. 132.

[113] Gloag, *Law of Contract* (1929), pp.46, 172.

[114] Below, para.6.05.

[115] *Buchanan v Duke of Hamilton* (1878) 5 R. (HL) 69.

[116] *Colquhoun v Wilson's Trs* (1860) 22 D. 1035; *Roberts & Cooper v Salvesen*, 1918 S.C. 794.

[117] *Kinnear v Young*, 1936 S.L.T. 574.

[118] *Armia Ltd v Daejan Developments Ltd*, 1979 S.C. (HL) 56; *Lousada & Co Ltd v J.E. Lesser (Properties) Ltd*, 1990 S.L.T. 823; *James Howden & Co Ltd v Taylor Woodrow Property Co Ltd*, 1998 S.C. 853. On waiver, see further above, para.3.09.

[119] *Stewart Brown & Co v Grime* (1897) 24 R. 414.

[120] *Smith v U.M.B. Chrysler (Scotland) and South Wales Switchgear Co*, 1978 S.C. (HL) 1.

[121] *Muirhead v Forth and North Sea Steamboat Mutual Insurance Association* (1893) 21 R. (HL) 1.

[122] *Standard Oil Co of New York v Clan Line Steamers Ltd*, 1924 S.C. (HL) 1.

acceptance, without any express reference to the conditions, in ordinary cases this will be read as an acceptance of the offer in the terms in which it was made; but if the conditions to which reference is made would effect a substantial modification of the rights of the parties, the offerer must take reasonable steps to bring them to the notice of the other party by supplying a copy of them or by other means.[123] Even if there is no express incorporation in the principal contract, terms set out elsewhere may be imported into the contract if reasonable steps have been taken to bring them to the notice of the other party—e.g. by a letter heading,[124] a placard,[125] a ticket, a "pull-down" menu on a website or computer screen display. Subject to what is said in the next two paragraphs, conditions cannot be incorporated into a contract if they are not brought to the notice of the other party before the contract is completed.[126]

Incorporation by course of dealing or custom of trade—If, however, there has **5.26** been a consistent course of dealing between the parties and in each of the previous transactions conditions have been sent, after the contract was completed, by one party to the other, who has raised no query or objection, it may be held that the conditions are incorporated in a subsequent contract if each party has led the other reasonably to believe that he intended that the rights and liabilities which would otherwise arise by implication of law from the nature of the contract should be modified in accordance with the conditions.[127] Where both parties are in the same trade and of equal bargaining power, the conditions habitually imposed in contracts of the particular type may be held to be incorporated on the basis of the common understanding of the parties that the usual conditions would apply.[128]

Ticket cases—"Ticket cases" are perhaps in a special category.[129] In certain well- **5.27** known types of case, in particular those relating to carriage and deposit, it is now settled that a reference to conditions, legibly printed on the face of the ticket, is sufficient notice of those conditions. The person who buys a railway ticket or a cloakroom ticket is doing a thing which is now recognised by the public in general as entering into a contract which may contain special conditions. This is a situation which is now regarded as notorious and customary.[130] Where a ticket is issued by a carrier, and conditions, limiting the carrier's liability for the safe carriage of the passenger or his luggage, are printed on or issued with it, such conditions may,

---

[123] *McConnell & Reid v Smith*, 1911 S.C. 635; *Grayston Plant Ltd v Plean Precast Ltd*, 1976 S.C. 206; *Continental Tyre & Rubber Co Ltd v Trunk Trailer Co Ltd*, 1985 S.C. 163; *Wm Teacher & Sons Ltd v Bell Lines Ltd*, 1991 S.L.T. 876; *Interfoto Picture Library Ltd v Stiletto Visual Programmes* [1989] Q.B. 433 (an example of a non-exclusionary term); *Montgomery Litho Ltd v Maxwell*, 2000 S.C. 56.

[124] *Oakbank Oil Co v Love & Stewart*, 1918 S.C. (HL) 54.

[125] *W.N. White & Co v Dougherty* (1891) 18 R. 972; *Wright v Howard Baker & Co* (1893) 21 R. 25; *Lewis v Laird Line*, 1925 S.L.T. 316. See also *Palmer v Inverness Hospitals Board*, 1963 S.C. 311 (circular).

[126] *McCutcheon v David MacBrayne*, 1964 S.C. (HL) 28; *Olley v Marlborough Court* [1949] 1 K.B. 532; *Thornton v Shoe Lane Parking* [1971] 2 Q.B. 163.

[127] *Henry Kendall & Sons v William Lillico & Sons* [1969] 2 A.C. 31; *Hollier v Rambler Motors (A.M.C.)* [1972] 2 Q.B. 71; *Grayston Plant v Plean Precast*, 1976 S.C. 206. See, as to the specification of prior dealings, *McCrone v Boots Farm Sales Ltd*, 1981 S.C. 68; *G.E.A. Airexchangers Ltd v James Howden & Co Ltd*, 1984 S.L.T. 264.

[128] *British Crane Hire Corp v Ipswich Plant Hire* [1975] 1 Q.B. 303.

[129] *McCutcheon v David MacBrayne Ltd*, 1964 S.C. (HL) 28 at 38, per Lord Guest and per Lord Pearce at 45.

[130] *Taylor v Glasgow Corp*, 1952 S.C. 440 at 444, per Lord Justice-Clerk Thomson.

if sufficient notice has been given to the ticket-holder, be taken as being part of the contract, and so binding upon him and his representatives.[131] The question whether they are imported into the contract depends partly on the character of the ticket, partly on the knowledge of the passenger who takes it. If the conditions are printed on the back of the ticket, and no indication of their existence is given on the front, the passenger, who can satisfy the court that he was not aware that there were any conditions, is not bound by them.[132] If he has actually read the conditions he is clearly bound by them. If he knew that there were conditions, but did not read them, he will be bound by them, provided that they are reasonable and of such a character as might be expected on a ticket of the particular class.[133] On the other hand, where the conditions are not issued with the ticket or otherwise expressly made part of the contract, they cannot be incorporated into it by knowledge on the part of the passenger that conditions were usually imposed without knowledge of what they were.[134] If the front of the ticket referred to conditions printed on the back, but the passenger did not notice the reference, and was in fact unaware that there were any conditions, the question depends on the adequacy of the means adopted to bring them to his notice. A reference to conditions on the back, printed on the front of a steamer ticket, was held ineffectual when it was printed in the smallest known type, and in such a way as to be easily overlooked by a passenger, even if he were exercising ordinary care.[135] But when a ticket for a transatlantic voyage was enclosed in an envelope, with a distinct reference thereon to conditions printed on the ticket, it was held that the passenger was bound by them, though his evidence was that he had not noticed the reference and was unaware that there were any conditions on the ticket.[136] The ordinary form of a railway ticket, in which reference is made on the front to conditions on the back, and the conditions there contain nothing but a further reference to the carrier's timetables and bills, has been approved as affording sufficient notice to the passenger.[137] These rules will not readily be extended beyond tickets issued in relation to contracts of carriage or deposit.[138]

FURTHER READING

Black, G., "Formation of Contract: The Role of Contractual Intention and Email Disclaimers", 2011 Jur. Rev. 97.

Hogg, M. and Lubbe, G., "Formation of Contract", in Zimmermann, R., Visser, D. and Reid, K.G.C., *Mixed Legal Systems in Comparative Perspective: Property and Obligations in Scotland and South Africa* (Oxford: Oxford University Press, 2005).

Hogg, M., *Obligations*, 2nd edn (Edinburgh: Avizandum, 2006), Ch.2.

Hogg, M., *Promises and Contract Law: Comparative Perspectives* (Cambridge: Cambridge University Press, 2011).

---

[131] e.g. *McKay v Scottish Airways*, 1948 S.C. 254.

[132] *Henderson v Stevenson* (1875) 2 R. (HL) 71; *McCafferty v Western S.M.T. Co*, 1962 S.L.T. (Sh. Ct) 39.

[133] *Lyons v Caledonian Ry*, 1909 S.C. 1185. Cf. *L'Estrange v Graucob* [1934] 2 K.B. 394.

[134] *McCutcheon v David MacBrayne*, 1964 S.C. (HL) 28.

[135] *Williamson v North of Scotland Navigation Co*, 1916 S.C. 554.

[136] *Hood v Anchor Line*, 1918 S.C. (HL) 143.

[137] *Gray v L. and N.E. Ry*, 1930 S.C. 989; *Penton v Southern Ry* [1931] 2 K.B. 103.

[138] *Taylor v Glasgow Corp*, 1952 S.C. 440.

Lubbe, G., "Formation of Contract"; Sellar, W.D.H., "Promise", both in Reid, K.G.C. and Zimmermann, R. (eds), *A History of Private Law in Scotland* (Oxford: Oxford University Press, 2000), Vol.2.

MacQueen, H.L. and Thomson, J.M., *Contract Law in Scotland*, 3rd edn (Bloomsbury Professional, 2012), Ch.2.

McBryde, W.W., *The Law of Contract in Scotland*, 3rd edn (Edinburgh: W. Green, 2007), Chs 5 and 6.

Quinot, G., "Offer, Acceptance, and the Moment of Contract Formation"; Forte, A.D.M., "The Battle of Forms", both in MacQueen, H.L. and Zimmermann, R., *European Contract Law: Scots and South African Perspectives* (Edinburgh: Edinburgh University Press, 2006).

Scottish Law Commission, *Formation of Contract* (The Stationery Office, 2012), Discussion Paper No.154.

Stair Memorial Encyclopaedia, Vol.15, paras 611–699.

CHAPTER 6

FORM, CONTENT, AND CONSTRUCTION OF CONTRACTS

This chapter surveys the law on requirements of form in contracts (in particular **6.01** writing and signature), the contents of a contract (including rectification of written documents), and the construction or interpretation of a contract. Though the law of evidence is beyond the scope of this work, the chapter will also consider some of its rules affecting contracts. In particular, Scots law has frequently tried to solve problems of interpretation by means of (often exclusionary) rules of evidence, and this approach continues to make the law more difficult than it needs to be. The law has been much altered by the reforms occasioned by the Law Reform (Miscellaneous Provisions) (Scotland) Act 1985, the Requirements of Writing (Scotland) Act 1995 (subsequently referred to as the "1995 Act") and the Contract (Scotland) Act 1997 (the "1997 Act"), but a truly modern approach would be simply to say that all relevant evidence is admissible and provide guidelines on the construction and interpretation of the contracts shown by that evidence to be in existence. This chapter seeks to follow that general approach so far as the current state of the law allows.

FORM

No general requirements of form—The general rule is that writing is unneces- **6.02** sary for the constitution of a contractual obligation.[1] A contract may be entered into orally, or in writing, or it may be inferred from the conduct of the parties. And the fact that an obligation has been undertaken may be proved *prout de jure*, that is, by the evidence of witnesses (parole evidence) and by the production of any writings that may be available. Parties are free to use formal writing, including self-proving documents, to constitute their contract.[2] Formerly, certain contracts which did not require to be constituted in writing nevertheless might only be proved by reference to the defender's writ or oath or by admission on record. Thus loans, obligations of relief and innominate and unusual contracts could only be proved by these restricted means. Proof by writ or oath has been abolished[3] and, consequently, such contracts may now be proved by any competent means.

Delivery of deeds—Writings embodying or constituting obligations in general **6.03** become effective upon delivery, that is, transfer of possession from granter to grantee. The underlying principle was classically stated by Erskine:

---

[1] Requirements of Writing (Scotland) Act 1995 (the "1995 Act") s.1(1).
[2] For self-proving documents see below, para.6.10.
[3] 1995 Act s.11(1).

"A writing, while it is in the granter's own custody, is not obligatory; for as long as it is in his own power, he cannot be said to have come to a final resolution of obliging himself by it."[4]

The principle, however, is confined by the important exception that it does not apply to mutual contracts, i.e. a document embodying a contract and subscribed by all its parties. Erskine once again provides the rationale:

"The bare subscription of the several parties proves the delivery of the deed by the other subscribers to him in whose hands it appears."[5]

The requirement thus has its greatest significance for documents embodying unilateral obligations and undertakings such as bonds, dispositions, assignations, declarations of trust and cautionary obligations. Delivery may be by post but that takes effect no earlier than the document's arrival at its destination.[6] There may also be delivery to or by authorised third parties such as solicitors.[7] Registration of the writing may suffice, or intimation of an assignation to the debtor.[8]

6.04 **Contracts requiring to be constituted in writing**—Under the 1995 Act contracts or unilateral obligations for the creation, variation or extinction of an interest in land require to be in writing subscribed by the granter(s) in order to be validly constituted. Gratuitous unilateral obligations (i.e. promises),[9] though not ones undertaken in the course of business, also require to be constituted in subscribed writing.[10] "Writing" means "typing, printing, lithography and other modes of representing or reproducing words in a visible form".[11] "Interest in land" is defined to mean

"any estate, interest or right in or over land, including any right to occupy or to use land or to restrict the occupation or use of land".[12]

However, a lease for less than one year or a right to occupy or use land for less than one year need not be constituted in writing.[13] A six-month option to terminate does not convert a licence to use land for 12 years into one for less than one year for these purposes.[14] Land does not include growing crops or moveable buildings

---

[4] Erskine, III, 2, 43. The classic illustration is *Stamfield's Creditors v Scot's Children* (1696) IV Bro Supp 344.
[5] Erskine, III, 2, 44. The other exceptions set out here by Erskine are discussed in detail in W.W. McBryde, *The Law of Contract in Scotland*, 3rd edn (Edinburgh: W. Green, 2007), Ch.4.
[6] McBryde, *The Law of Contract in Scotland* (2007), paras 4.19–4.20.
[7] McBryde, *The Law of Contract in Scotland* (2007), paras 4.15–4.18.
[8] McBryde, *The Law of Contract in Scotland* (2007), paras 4.21–4.30.
[9] See discussion of this phraseology in M. Hogg, *Obligations*, 2nd edn (Edinburgh: Avizandum, 2006), paras 2.06–2.11.
[10] 1995 Act s.1(2)(a)(i), (ii), and (b). For a unilateral gratuitous promise made in the course of business see *Morrison v Leckie*, 2005 G.W.D. 40–734 (Paisley Sheriff Court). Gratuitous cautionary obligations which are not undertaken in the course of a business must be constituted in writing and will need to be subscribed and attested in order to be self-proving.
[11] Interpretation Act 1978 Sch.1; Interpretation and Legislative Reform (Scotland) Act 2010 s.25 and Sch.1.
[12] 1995 Act s.1(7).
[13] 1995 Act s.1(7). Unless the tenancy or right is for recurring periods with a gap of more than a year between the start of the first period and the end of the last.
[14] *Caterleisure Ltd v Glasgow Prestwick International Airport*, 2006 S.C. 602.

or structures.[15] Missives for the sale and purchase of heritable property will therefore need to be in subscribed writing since they represent a contract for the "transfer of an interest in land". It has been held in the Outer House that a faxed missive of acceptance did not conclude a contract for the sale of land since the document in the hands of the offeror contained only a facsimile of the subscription of the acceptor.[16]

Personal bar—The 1995 Act retains the doctrine of *rei interventus* but in an **6.05** altered form from the previous common law (hence "statutory *rei interventus*").[17] Where a contract is required by the Act to be constituted in writing and this is not done, or is not done in the proper form, then, if one of the parties acts or refrains from acting in reliance on the contract with the knowledge and acquiescence of the other party, the latter is not entitled to resile from the contract and it will not be treated as being invalid,[18] provided that the first party's position has been affected to a material extent[19] and would be further adversely affected to a material extent if withdrawal were permitted.[20] Similar provision is made in relation to the variation of contracts and obligations.[21] Where writing is absent or not in the proper form required by the Act, there must still be evidence that the parties had reached consensus in idem.[22] The agreement must precede the actings alleged to constitute bar.[23] It will not, however, be the case that proof of the existence of agreement between the parties will be restricted to the defender's writ or oath.[24]

Facts amounting to personal bar—The new form of *rei interventus* may consist **6.06** in alterations in the property which is the subject of the contract,[25] in payment of the price or some substantial part of it,[26] or even, in the case of leases, in absten-

---

[15] 1995 Act s.1(8).

[16] *Park Petitioners* [2009] CSOH 122; 2009 S.L.T. 871, noted by R. Anderson, "Subscription and settlement by fax and email", 2010 S.L.T. (News) 67; G. Gretton, "Missives by fax or pdf?" (2010) 14 Edin. L.R. 280.

[17] Though it replaces both *rei interventus* and homologation in relation to contracts and obligations specified in s.1(2): see s.1(5). For how the legislation fits with the general principles of personal bar, see E.C. Reid and J.W.G. Blackie, *Personal Bar* (Edinburgh: W. Green, 2006), Ch.7.

[18] 1995 Act s.1(3).

[19] But not irretrievably so: see Bell, *Principles*, s.26 which, in this respect, appears to be reflected in the legislation.

[20] 1995 Act s.1(4). See *Caterleisure Ltd v Glasgow Prestwick International Airport*, 2006 S.C. 602.

[21] 1995 Act s.1(6).

[22] *Aisling Developments Ltd v Persimmon Homes Ltd* [2008] CSOH 140; 2009 S.L.T. 494. The agreement need no longer be proved by writ or oath, and may be constituted by words or actings. See *Advice Centre for Mortgages Ltd v McNicoll*, 2006 S.L.T. 591, per Lord Drummond Young at [31]. Pre-1995 Act cases may still be of use: e.g. *East Kilbride Development Corp v Pollok*, 1953 S.C. 370; *Colquhoun v Wilson's Trs* (1860) 22 D. 1035; *Wight v Newton*, 1911 S.C. 762. Note also W.M. Gloag, *Law of Contract*, 2nd edn (Edinburgh: W. Green, 1929), pp.46–47, quoted with approval in *Morrison-Low v Paterson*, 1985 S.C. (HL) 49.

[23] *Advice Centre for Mortgages Ltd v McNicoll*, 2006 S.L.T. 591 (noted by A. McAllister, "Leases and the requirement of writing", 2006 S.L.T. (News) 254 and E.C. Reid, "Personal bar: three cases" (2006) 10 Edin. L.R. 437); *Tom Super Printing and Supplies Ltd v South Lanarkshire Council*, 1999 G.W.D. 31–1496, 38–1854. See also R. Rennie, "Statutory personal bar" (2001) 6 S.L.P.Q. 197, but note that s.1(3) of the 1995 Act requires the agreement to be a "contract" (i.e. all that prevents the agreement being such is its informality).

[24] 1995 Act s.11(1); as discussed in *Advice Centre for Mortgages Ltd v McNicoll*, 2006 S.L.T. 591 at [26]–[31]. *Errol v Walker*, 1966 S.C. 93 is no longer good law although the same result would be reached on the facts under the 1995 Act.

[25] *Colquhoun v Wilson's Trs* (1860) 22 D. 1035.

[26] *Foggo v Hill* (1840) 2 D. 1322.

tion, on the landlord's part, from efforts to obtain another tenant,[27] or, on the tenant's part, from efforts to obtain other accommodation[28]; this is, however, not an exhaustive list.[29]

6.07 Completion of title—Where an action on an improperly constituted agreement has been successful on proof of *rei interventus*, the defender may be ordained to execute a formal contract (sale or lease, as the case may be) in accordance with the agreement established against him.[30] On his refusal a remit may be made to a conveyancer to draw up an appropriate instrument, and, on a continued refusal to sign, the Clerk of Court may be authorised to sign on the defender's behalf.[31]

6.08 Interests of third parties—Before any proceedings have been taken to establish the validity of an informal sale followed by *rei interventus*, the land in question may be resold to a third party. If he had no notice of the prior informal sale, his title is unchallengeable. If he had notice, he is bound to inquire and is not entitled to accept blindly the seller's statement that the prior negotiations had been broken off without reaching an agreement.[32] In the case of leases where the tenant has entered into possession, any lease which could in any way be enforced against the landlord may be enforced against his singular successor.[33]

6.09 Conveyance as superseding prior writs—As a general rule for contracts entered into before June 21, 1997, a disposition, even one which bears to be in execution of prior missives, supersedes the contract and becomes the sole measure of the rights and duties of the parties.[34] Under s.2 of the 1997 Act, however,

> "where a deed is executed in implement, or purportedly in implement, of a contract [entered into on or after June 21, 1997], an unimplemented, or otherwise unfulfilled, term of the contract shall not be superseded by virtue only of that execution or of the delivery and acceptance of the deed."

This provision is without prejudice to any agreement which the parties to the contract may reach (whether or not by an agreement incorporated into the contract) as to supersession of the contract.[35] Under the previous law, where the missives contained a collateral obligation distinct from the obligation to convey the heritage, e.g. an undertaking to restore central heating to working order, that remained enforceable.[36] Where the missives, or a separate document, or the

---

[27] *Sutherland v Hay* (1845) 8 D. 283, per Lord Medwyn; *Kinnear v Young*, 1936 S.L.T. 574.

[28] *Danish Dairy Co v Gillespie*, 1922 S.C. 656.

[29] See the broad terms of Bell, *Principles*, s.26, fn.19, above.

[30] *Stodart v Dalzell* (1876) 4 R. 236 (feu); *Wight v Newton*, 1911 S.C. 762 (lease).

[31] *Whyte v Whyte*, 1913 2 S.L.T. 85.

[32] *Petrie v Forsyth* (1874) 2 R. 214; *Stodart v Dalzell* (1876) 4 R. 236; *Rodger (Builders) v Fawdry*, 1950 S.C. 483.

[33] *Wilson v Mann* (1876) 3 R. 527.

[34] *Lee v Alexander* (1883) 10 R. (HL) 91. Note also, *A & J Inglis v Buttery & Co* (1878) 5 R. (HL) 87; *Edinburgh United Breweries Ltd v Molleson* (1894) 21 R. (HL) 10; *Korner v Shennan*, 1950 S.C. 285; *Winston v Patrick*, 1980 S.C. 246; *Pena v Ray*, 1987 S.L.T. 609; *Central Govan Housing Association Ltd v Maguire Cook & Co*, 1988 S.L.T. 386; *Taylor v McLeod*, 1990 S.L.T. 194; *Porch v MacLeod*, 1992 S.L.T. 661.

[35] Contract (Scotland) Act 1997 s.2(2).

[36] *Pena v Ray*, 1987 S.L.T. 609; *Central Govan Housing Association Ltd v Maguire Cook & Co*, 1988 S.L.T. 386; *Taylor v MacLeod; Winston v Patrick*, 1980 S.C. 246. *Jamieson v Welsh* (1900) 3 F. 176; *McKillop v Mutual Securities Ltd*, 1945 S.C. 166.

disposition provided for the continuance of some personal (non-collateral) obligation, that obligation remained enforceable.[37] Finally, where missives created obligations regarding moveable subjects, these remained enforceable because it was inappropriate to include these in the disposition.[38] Prior writings may also be referred to in a question as to the conditions on which a sale took place.[39] It may be proved that two conveyances, although executed without reference to each other, were really interdependent.[40] Where the terms of a written contract are ambiguous, it is probably legitimate to refer to writings of the parties (or their conduct) after the contract was concluded.[41]

Self-proving documents—When a document is subscribed by its granter or **6.10** granters, signed by one witness and contains a statement of the latter's name and address, the authenticity of the granter's signature is presumed.[42] In contrast, should the genuineness of a signature to a document that is not self-proving be challenged, this will have to be proved by the party founding on that signature.[43] A document must be self-proving to be registered in the Land Register or court books. Missives will not, however, require to be self-proving as they are not usually recorded or registered, although in practice they are usually witnessed as well as subscribed.[44] Only one witness is needed to sign a document to make it self-proving.[45] The witness must either see the granter subscribe or hear him acknowledge his signature.[46] If the witness does not see the granter subscribe his signature, or signs it before the granter does, or if he does not sign *unico contextu* with the granter's acknowledgement of his signature, the presumption that the document was subscribed by the granter is displaced.[47] This presumption will also be displaced where what purports to be the signature of the witness is not truly his signature, or where the witness is also the subscriber, or it can be established that at the time the witness signed he did not know the granter, or was under 16 years of age, or was mentally incapable of acting as a witness.[48] The name and address of the witness, which need not be written by the witness himself, may be added at any time before the document is founded on in any legal proceedings or is registered for preservation in the Books of Council and Session or in the sheriff court books.[49]

Party unable to write—A party who is blind or unable to write may subscribe by **6.11** initial or mark if this is how he usually signs.[50] This will also be permitted where

---

[37] *Winston v Patrick*, 1980 S.C. 246; *Taylor v MacLeod*, 1990 S.L.T. 194; *Porch v MacLeod*, 1992 S.L.T. 661.

[38] *Winston v Patrick*, 1980 S.C. 246; *Jamieson v Welsh*, (1900) 3 F. 176.

[39] *Young v McKellar*, 1909 S.C. 1340.

[40] *Claddagh Steamship Co v Steven*, 1919 S.C. (HL) 132.

[41] *Turner v MacMillan-Douglas*, 1989 S.L.T. 293.

[42] 1995 Act s.3(1).

[43] *McIntyre v National Bank of Scotland*, 1910 S.C. 150 (a case concerning a bill of exchange). The privilege of writs in re mercatoria was abolished by the 1995 Act s.11(3)(b)(ii).

[44] Note that the Automated Registration of Title to Land ("ARTL") system enabling the use of electronically transmitted documents to record titles in the Land Register does not apply to the preceding contracts of sale. See 1995 Act ss.1(2B), 2A–2C and 12(1); Automated Title to Land (Electronic Communications) (Scotland) Order 2006 (SI 2006/491).

[45] 1995 Act s.3(1)(b).

[46] 1995 Act s.3(7).

[47] 1995 Act s.3(4)(d), (e).

[48] 1995 Act s.3(4)(a)–(c).

[49] 1995 Act s.3(3).

[50] 1995 Act s.7(2)(c)(i).

the granter intends that his initial or mark should be treated as being his signature.[51] Where the granter of a deed is blind or unable to write and does not choose to sign by initial or mark, the document may be subscribed on his behalf and with his authorisation by a practising solicitor,[52] an advocate, a justice of the peace or a sheriff clerk.[53] A notary public need only be used "in relation to the execution of documents outwith Scotland".[54] The person signing on behalf of the granter must only do so after reading out the document to be signed to the granter, unless the latter expressly dispenses with the need to do so.[55] Subscription of a document in these circumstances must take place in the granter's presence.[56] Should such a document confer a right to either money or money's worth on the subscriber (or his spouse or children), that part of the document conferring the benefit will be invalid but the validity of the remainder of the document will not be affected. It is, therefore, no longer an objection to the validity of a document that it confers a benefit on the subscriber.[57]

6.12 Electronic signatures—Section 7 of the Electronic Communications Act 2000[58] defines an electronic signature as follows:

> ". . . so much of anything in electronic form as—
>
> (a) is incorporated into or otherwise logically associated with any electronic communication or electronic data; and
> (b) purports to be so incorporated or associated for the purpose of being used in establishing the authenticity of the communication or data, the integrity of the communication or data, or both."

This can include names typed into an email or word-processed document, or electronic facsimiles of a "wet ink" signature. The substantive effect of s.7 is to make an electronic signature admissible in evidence in any legal proceedings in relation to any question as to the authenticity or integrity of the communication or data into or with which it is either incorporated or logically associated. This is enabling rather than a direct statement that electronic signatures are capable of having binding effects in contracts expressed in electronic form. But it seems that an electronic signature can suffice if it is clear that by attaching it to an electronic version of a contract document a party intended to become bound by that contract.

Section 7(3) further provides:

> "For the purposes of this section an electronic signature incorporated into or associated with a particular electronic communication or particular electronic data is certified by any person if that person (whether before or after the making of the communication) has made a statement confirming that—

---

[51] 1995 Act s.7(2)(c)(ii).

[52] i.e. who holds a practising certificate as defined in s.4(c) of the Solicitors (Scotland) Act 1980.

[53] 1995 Act s.9(6).

[54] 1995 Act s.9(6).

[55] 1995 Act s.9(1).

[56] 1995 Act s.9(2).

[57] For the earlier law, see the 10th edn of this work, para.6.5.

[58] Implementing Directive 1999/93/EC of the European Parliament and of the Council of December 13, 1999 on a Community framework for electronic signatures.

(a) the signature,
(b) a means of producing, communicating or verifying the signature, or
(c) a procedure applied to the signature,

is (either alone or in combination with other factors) a valid means of establishing the authenticity of the communication or data, the integrity of the communication or data, or both."

Certification thus provides the electronic signature with an authenticating device in the same way as the signature of a witness in relation to self-proving documents.[59] Certification service providers have yet to emerge for common use by business and other users, but other systems, specifically tailored to the function or organisation they serve, have developed. An example is the system developed by the Keeper of the Registers of Scotland for electronic (or automated) registration of title to land.[60]

Formal electronic writing—As originally drafted, the 1995 Act does not recog- **6.13** nise electronic signatures as any form of authenticating subscription, nor does it seem possible to conclude a contract for which writing is required under the Act in purely electronic form. When the Land Registration etc (Scotland) Act 2012 comes into force, however, the 1995 Act will be significantly amended to deal with these matters.[61] It will then be possible to constitute any obligation requiring formal writing in purely electronic form, provided that the document is authenticated by electronic signatures of the parties meeting the requirements for such signatures to be set out in regulations made under the 2012 Act. The overall result will be two distinct methods of constituting obligations formally: (1) the "traditional" method, using paper and "wet ink" signatures; and (2) the "electronic", using only the digital medium and electronic signatures. The new law does not seem to permit the use of mixed media—for example, an emailed or faxed acceptance of a traditional or paper offer—and it will not remove the difficulty about whether a facsimile version of a person's subscription on an electronically transmitted copy of an original paper document has binding effect.[62] But an electronic document electronically signed in a manner meeting further requirements to be set out in regulations made under the 2012 Act will be capable of self-proving, or probative, status.[63] An electronic document will also be capable of being delivered electronically or by such other means as are reasonably practicable, so long as the document is in a form and the delivery by means that the intended recipient has agreed to accept and which it is reasonable in all the circumstances for the intended recipient to accept.[64]

---

[59] See above, para.6.09.
[60] Known commonly as ARTL: see above, para.6.10 fn.44.
[61] Pt 10 of the Land Registration etc (Scotland) Act 2012 inserts a new Pt 3 (ss.9A–9G) and Sch.3 into the 1995 Act.
[62] *Park Petitioners* [2009] CSOH 122; 2009 S.L.T. 871 (see above, para.6.04).
[63] 1995 Act ss.9C–9E, as inserted by Land Registration etc (Scotland) Act 2012 s.93(2). On self-proving status see above, para.6.10.
[64] 1995 Act s.9F as inserted by the Land Registration etc (Scotland) Act 2012 s.93(2). On delivery of deeds in general see above, para.6.03.

CONTENT

6.14 Terms of the contract—The terms of a contract consist first of those expressed by the parties' agreement, whether recorded in whole or in part in writing, or proved to have been agreed orally where a contract does not require to be in writing under the rules described in the previous section. Terms may also be implied into the contract so long as not inconsistent with the parties' express agreement. Such implied terms may arise from the law applying to a contract of the kind formed by the parties, or from the conduct of the parties, or in the facts and circumstances of the particular case.

6.15 Extrinsic evidence of additional terms in written contracts—Under s.1 of the Contract (Scotland) Act 1997 an apparently complete document will be presumed to contain all the terms of the contract, but contrary evidence may be led to show that there are additional terms, written or otherwise. If the document expressly states that it comprises the whole terms of the contract (an "entire agreement" clause), then that is conclusive, and no contrary evidence is allowed. An entire agreement clause does not prevent an action for rectification or claims for pre-contractual misrepresentation.[65]

6.16 Bills of exchange—Section 100 of the Bills of Exchange Act 1882 provides:

> "In any judicial proceedings in Scotland, any fact relating to a bill of exchange, bank cheque, or promissory note, which is relevant to any question of liability thereon, may be proved by parole evidence."

The generality of this enactment has been so far limited by decision that it has been held that parole evidence of payment is incompetent,[66] and that when the alleged liability is not rested exclusively on the bill, but on the bill as a method of carrying out a prior written contract, the section is not applicable.[67] So where a business carried on in leasehold premises was sold, and promissory notes given for the price, it was held that s.100 did not authorise parole evidence of the alleged verbal agreement that payment of the notes was not to be demanded until the lease had expired.[68] But it is competent to prove that the bill was granted for the accommodation of a particular party,[69] or that it had been agreed to renew it until the occurrence of a certain event.[70] The competency of proof that the holder had agreed that one of the parties to the bill should incur no liability is not settled.[71]

6.17 Implied terms—There are several types of implied term that may be included in contracts without the parties' express agreement or incorporation (although a term cannot be implied in a contract to contradict its expressed terms[72]). A term may be implied in a contract because the law infers the term as an incident of contracts of

---

[65] *Macdonald Estates Plc v Regenesis (2005) Dunfermline Ltd* [2007] CSOH 123; 2007 S.L.T. 791; *BSkyB Ltd v HP Enterprise Services UK Ltd* [2010] B.L.R. 267.
[66] *Robertson v Thomson* (1900) 3 F. 5; *Nicol's Trs v Sutherland*, 1951 S.C. (HL) 21.
[67] *Stagg & Robson v Stirling*, 1908 S.C. 675; *McAllister v McGallagley*, 1911 S.C. 112.
[68] *Stagg & Robson v Stirling*, 1908 S.C. 675.
[69] *Viani v Gunn* (1904) 6 F. 989.
[70] *Dryburgh v Roy* (1903) 5 F. 665. See also *Thompson v Jolly Carters Inn*, 1972 S.C. 215.
[71] *National Bank of Australasia v Turnbull* (1891) 18 R. 629.
[72] *Cummings v Charles Connell & Co (Shipbuilders)*, 1968 S.C. 305.

a particular class[73]; by custom of trade[74]; by a previous course of dealing[75]; or because in the circumstances of the particular contract it is necessary to give the contract business efficacy. As to the last of these cases:

"The Court will only hold a term or condition to be implied in a written contract if its nature is such that it must necessarily be implied to give the contract business efficacy".[76]

A term may also be implied on the basis that

"every reasonable man . . . would desire [it] for his own protection . . . and that no reasonable man . . . would refuse to accede to it".[77]

But implication of a term on the basis of such presumed intention may be rebutted on the particular facts of a case. So, where goods hired under an agreement were bought at the hirers' request, were inspected only by them, and were not even delivered by the other party to the agreement, it was held that it was not an implied term of the hire agreement that the goods were hire-worthy.[78] The courts have, however, been willing to imply an obligation upon contracting parties to co-operate and facilitate each other's performance in some cases.[79] It has been said in the Privy Council that a term should only be implied in fact when it is reasonably clear from the contract's express terms read against the background of relevant surrounding circumstances what that term should be.[80]

Usage of trade—The fact that a contract has been entered into in writing does not **6.18** exclude proof of usage of trade to introduce an implied term into the contract. Unless the contract is expressly made subject to the usage, the latter cannot rule if it contradicts the actual provisions of the writing. Thus, where a contractor accepted an offer for "the whole of the steel" required for a bridge "the estimated quantity to be 30,000 tons, more or less", it was held that the plain meaning of the words could not be qualified by proof of a usage in the steel trade that such an offer meant an offer to supply 30,000 tons only.[81] If the contract expressly refers

---

[73] Gloag, *Law of Contract* (1929), p.286; *Sterling Engineering Co v Patchett* [1955] A.C. 534 at 547, per Lord Reid; *Lister v Romford Ice and Cold Storage Co* [1957] A.C. 555, per Viscount Simonds at 579, Lord Tucker at 594; *Liverpool City Council v Irwin* [1977] A.C. 239, per Lord Wilberforce at 253, Lord Cross at 257; *Prestwick Circuits Ltd v McAndrew*, 1990 S.L.T. 654.

[74] Below, para.6.18.

[75] Above, para.5.26.

[76] *McWhirter v Longmuir*, 1948 S.C. 577 at 589, per Lord Jamieson. The well-known dictum of Bowen L.J. in *The Moorcock* (1889) 14 P.D. 64 at 68, has been criticised (Gloag, *Law of Contract* (1929), p.289). There is also the "officious bystander" test: *Shirlaw v Southern Foundries* [1939] 2 K.B. 206 at 227, per MacKinnon L.J.; see also *Microwave Systems (Scotland) v Electro-Physiological Instruments*, 1971 S.C. 140; *North American Continental Sales Inc. v Bepi (Electronics) Ltd*, 1982 S.L.T. 47; *Prestwick Circuits Ltd v McAndrew*, 1990 S.L.T. 654; *Crawford v Bruce*, 1992 S.L.T. 524; *J. & H. Ritchie Ltd v Lloyd Ltd* [2007] UKHL 9; 2007 S.C. (HL) 89.

[77] *Wm Morton & Co v Muir Bros & Co*, 1907 S.C. 1211 at 1224, per Lord McLaren.

[78] *G.M. Shepherd Ltd v North West Securities Ltd*, 1991 S.L.T. 499.

[79] *Scottish Power Plc v Kvaerner Construction Ltd*, 1999 S.L.T. 721; *E. & J. Glasgow Ltd v UGC Estates Ltd* [2005] CSOH 63. Cf. *Thomson v Thomas Muir (Waste Management) Ltd*, 1995 S.L.T. 403.

[80] *Attorney General of Belize v Belize Telecom Ltd* [2009] 1 W.L.R. 1988, P.C. (Lord Hoffmann), criticising undue reliance on *BP Refinery (Westernport) Pty Ltd v Hastings Shire Council* [1977] 180 C.L.R. 266, P.C.

[81] *Tancred, Arrol & Co v Steel Co of Scotland* (1887) 15 R. 215, affd (1890) 17 R. (HL) 31; *Affréteurs Réunis v Walford* [1919] A.C. 801; *Arthur Duthie & Co v Merson and Gerry*, 1947 S.C. 43; *Sworn Securities Ltd v Chilcott*, 1977 S.C. 53.

to a usage, as where in a charter-party the provisions for loading expressly refer to the custom of the port, it is immaterial that one or both parties may be unaware of what the actual custom is.[82] And where a person authorises another to deal for him on a particular exchange, he must be deemed to have consented to his contract being interpreted in accordance with the usages of that exchange.[83] In other cases, usage of trade will not affect a contract unless both parties were aware of it.[84] It has been held that while in a particular trade there may be a customary rate of wages which will be binding in the absence of express agreement, this will not prevail where, as between parties, there is a well-established practice of paying and receiving another rate.[85] A usage to be admissible must be reasonably fair,[86] and generally (though not necessarily universally) recognised in the trade.[87] It has been observed that a usage cannot be established by proof of a series of protests against it.[88]

6.19 Alteration of written contract—If a contract requires to be in formal writing under the 1995 Act, such writing is also required for variation.[89] Where parties have entered into a written contract where writing is not so required, a verbal agreement to alter its provisions is not binding, and, if no action has followed on it, either party may resile and insist on the performance of the contract in its original terms.[90] But if there has been an agreement to alter the terms of the contract, and one party, to the knowledge of and without objection from the other, has proceeded to act upon the contract as altered, such action may amount to *rei interventus* and bar the right to resile.[91] Mere acquiescence in acts which, assuming that the original terms of the contract remained in force, would be a breach thereof, can at the highest merely bar a claim of damages for what is past; it can confer no sanction for the future.[92] To establish an alteration in the terms of the contract for the future there must either be a writing to that effect or a verbal agreement on which action has followed.[93] And the action in question must be clearly inconsistent with the original terms of the contract. Thus, where A, who was liable under a decree, averred that his creditor had agreed to accept payment by weekly instalments, and that certain instalments had been paid, it was held that as the acceptance of instalments was not inconsistent with the right to demand immediate payment of the balance, there were no relevant averments of *rei interventus*, and the alleged verbal agreement could not be admitted to proof.[94]

---

[82] *Strathlorne S.S. Co v Baird*, 1915 S.C. 956, revd 1916 S.C. (HL) 134.

[83] *Forget v Baxter* [1900] A.C. 467. See *Robinson v Mollet* (1875) L.R. 7 H.L. 802.

[84] *Holman v Peruvian Nitrate Co* (1878) 5 R. 657.

[85] *Eunson v Johnson & Grieg*, 1940 S.C. 49.

[86] *Bruce v Smith* (1890) 17 R. 1000; *Devonald v Rosser* [1906] 2 K.B. 728.

[87] *Hogarth v Leith Cotton Seed Oil Co*, 1909 S.C. 955; *Dick v Cochrane & Fleming*, 1935 S.L.T. 432.

[88] *Strathlorne S.S. Co v Baird*, 1916 S.C. (HL) 134, per Lord Shaw.

[89] 1995 Act ss.1(6), 11(3)(a); see above, paras 6.04 et seq.

[90] See opinion of Lord President Inglis, *Kirkpatrick v Allanshaw Coal Co* (1880) 8 R. 327 at 332. But if the alteration consists of an addition to the written terms, then that may be proved parole and will be binding (Contract (Scotland) Act 1997 s.1).

[91] *Bargaddie Coal Co v Wark* (1856) 18 D. 772, revd (1859) 3 Macq. 467; *Kirkpatrick v Allanshaw Coal Co* (1880) 8 R. 327.

[92] *Carron Co v Henderson's Trs* (1896) 23 R. 1042.

[93] See *Earl of Ancaster v Doig*, 1960 S.C. 203 at 211, per Lord Justice-Clerk Thomson.

[94] *Lavan v Gavin Aird & Co*, 1919 S.C. 345.

Defective expression: Common law—Defective expression of a contract occurs   **6.20**
where parties, having reached an agreement in one form, further agree that the
agreement should be recorded in another form, and the agreement is not accurately expressed in that second form. The most common case arises when, after a
written contract is duly signed, it is discovered that owing to a mistake of an
amanuensis it does not represent the agreement which the parties had made. Thus,
where a clerk was told to draw up an agreement between a hotel-keeper and his
manager, and by an arithmetical mistake, which was not discovered until both
parties had signed the agreement, gave the manager a larger share of the profits
than had been agreed to, it was held that the mistake might be proved by witnesses
and corrected.[95] Where the parties entered into missives for the sale of a farm and
the subsequent disposition, owing to a mistake on the part of the solicitors
concerned, conveyed, not only the farm, but also an adjacent coal-mine, it was
held that the disposition could be reduced.[96] Accounts, docqueted as correct, may
be challenged on the ground of arithmetical errors.[97]

Defective expression: Statutory rectification—Where a document intended to   **6.21**
express or give effect to an agreement fails to express accurately the common
intention of the parties to the agreement at the date when it was made, the court
now has a statutory power to rectify the document in any manner that it may
specify in order to give effect to that intention.[98] In exercising this power the court
may have regard to all relevant evidence, whether written or oral.[99] Rectification
may be made of a contract drawn up with an entire agreement clause.[100] Any other
document intended to express or give effect to an agreement which is defectively
expressed by reason of the defect in the original document may also be rectified.[101] But where the parties' intentions differ as to the agreement reached, neither
missives nor disposition may be rectified.[102] A rectified document shall have
effect as if it had always been so rectified[103] and, where a document recorded
in the Register of Sasines is rectified and the rectification order is likewise
recorded, the document is to be treated as having been always recorded as
rectified.[104] The power to rectify cannot be used to change retrospectively the
character of a document to something other than was intended at the time of
execution.[105] A rectification order is not to be made if the rectification would
adversely affect, to a material extent, the interests of a person, other than a party
to the agreement, who has acted or refrained from acting in reliance on the terms
of the document or on the title sheet of an interest in land registered in the Land
Register of Scotland, being an interest to which the document relates.[106]

---

[95] *Krupp v Menzies*, 1907 S.C. 903.

[96] *Anderson v Lambie*, 1954 S.C. (HL) 43.

[97] *McLaren v Liddell's Trs* (1862) 24 D. 577.

[98] Law Reform (Miscellaneous Provisions) (Scotland) Act 1985 s.8. This does not affect the
common law rules discussed above; see, e.g. *Aberdeen Rubber Ltd v Knowles & Sons (Fruiterers) Ltd*,
1995 S.C. (HL) 8.

[99] Law Reform (Miscellaneous Provisions) (Scotland) Act 1985 s.8(2).

[100] *Macdonald Estates Plc v Regenesis (2005) Dunfermline Ltd* [2007] CSOH 123; 2007 S.L.T. 791;
for entire agreement clauses, see above, para.6.15. The position is the same in England: see *Surgicraft
Ltd v Paradigm Biodevices Inc* [2010] EWHC 1291 (Ch).

[101] Law Reform (Miscellaneous Provisions) (Scotland) Act 1985 s.8(3).

[102] *Angus v Bryden*, 1992 S.L.T. 884.

[103] Law Reform (Miscellaneous Provisions) (Scotland) Act 1985 s.8(4).

[104] Law Reform (Miscellaneous Provisions) (Scotland) Act 1985 s.8(5).

[105] *Bank of Scotland v Brunswick Developments (1987) Ltd (No.2)*, 1999 S.C. (HL) 53.

[106] Law Reform (Miscellaneous Provisions) (Scotland) Act 1985 s.9.

CONSTRUCTION OF CONTRACTS

6.22 Established approach—The established approach of the Scottish courts to the task of construing and interpreting contracts is an objective one. Parties should be able to assume that the words used have the usual or reasonable meaning, and those resolving disputes about the meaning of words need to adopt the position of a reasonable and disinterested third party.[107] The starting point is the words used by the parties, understood in the context of the contract as a whole.[108] The words are to be given their natural and ordinary meaning unless it is clear from the contract that some other meaning is intended.[109] A construction which enables the contract to take operative effect is to be preferred to one which does not (*ut res magis valeat quam pereat*),[110] as is one which gives effect to all rather than only some terms.[111] Where a word has more than one possible meaning it is permissible to look at admissible surrounding circumstances to determine which meaning should be chosen. Negotiations prior to the formation of the contract, and the conduct of the parties and other circumstances since the formation of the contract, are inadmissible for this purpose, however.[112] In modern practice the distinction between an ambiguity patent on the face of the contract and so to be resolved by construction of the terms alone, and latent ambiguity (when the meaning is only rendered doubtful by a knowledge of the surrounding circumstances, e.g. when property is conveyed by name, and it turns out that there are two properties to which that name would apply[113]), seems to be ignored, with extrinsic evidence being admitted to resolve a patent ambiguity in a number of cases.[114] Agreements may also be considered in the "matrix of fact" in which to the knowledge of both parties they were set at the time of formation, including the nature of the parties' business or the field of activity to which the contract relates, its commercial purpose, the history of previous dealings (rather than negotiations) between the parties, and the parties' conduct and statements at the time the contract was made.[115] The fact that a contract has been entered into in writing does not exclude proof of usage of trade to give to the words used a meaning which they would not ordinarily bear. There would seem to be no limit to the variation of meaning which may be given to any particular word on this basis: the word "thousand" has been held to mean "twelve hundred".[116]

---

[107] Gloag, *Law of Contract* (1929), pp.398–9; McBryde, *The Law of Contract in Scotland* (2007), paras 8.02–8.05.

[108] Gloag, *Law of Contract* (1929), p.399; McBryde, *The Law of Contract in Scotland* (2007), para.8.17.

[109] Gloag, *Law of Contract* (1929), p.399; McBryde, *The Law of Contract in Scotland* (2007), paras 8.10–8.11.

[110] Gloag, *Law of Contract* (1929), p.402; McBryde, *The Law of Contract in Scotland* (2007), para.8.16.

[111] Gloag, *Law of Contract* (1929), p.399.

[112] McBryde, *The Law of Contract in Scotland* (2007), paras 8.22–8.24, 8.28–8.33.

[113] *Raffles v Wichelhaus* (1864) 2 Hurl. & C. 906; *Houldsworth v Gordon-Cumming*, 1909 S.C. 1198, revd 1910 S.C. (HL) 49.

[114] See *Walker and Walker: The Law of Evidence in Scotland*, edited by M.L. Ross and J.P. Chalmers, 3rd edn (Tottel, 2009), paras 26.20.1–26.21.2.

[115] *Prenn v Simmonds* [1971] 1 W.L.R. 1381 at 1385, per Lord Wilberforce; McBryde, *The Law of Contract in Scotland* (2007), paras 8.22–8.23. See also *Jacobs v Scott* (1899) 2 F. (HL) 70; *Claddagh Steamship Co v Steven*, 1919 S.C. 184; 1919 S.C. (HL) 132; *Bovis v Whatlings*, 1995 S.L.T. 1339, HL.

[116] *Smith v Wilson* (1832) 3 B. & Ad. 728.

Development of established approach—In a number of English House of Lords' **6.23**
decisions the general approach described in the previous paragraph has been
significantly modified, to allow admissible surrounding circumstances always to
be considered in the process of construing a contract, without any prior need
for ambiguity in the text to be construed.[117] Lord Hoffmann has said that this
background may lead the judge to conclude that the contract has been drawn up in
the wrong or in mis-ordered words and to read it instead to give effect to what the
parties must have intended.[118] These decisions have been referred to in many
subsequent Scottish decisions, without it being clear that the English approach is
to be generally adopted.[119] The courts here in general favour "commercially
sensible" constructions and resist meanings seeming to give rise to absurd results,
preferring those giving the contract reasonable effect or fulfilling its perceived
commercial purpose.[120] While it has been said in the First Division that there is no
requirement of ambiguity before a court may consider admissible surrounding
circumstances, a subsequent Supreme Court judgment in a Scottish appeal referred
to such a requirement without comment.[121] There is judicial reluctance to
encourage extensive investigation into background circumstances and it is not
clear, for example, whether the courts would go as far as the House of Lords in
Bank of Commerce and Credit International v Ali, where a release clause in a
redundancy agreement, stated to be "in full and final settlement of all or any
claims of whatsoever nature that exist or may exist", was read not to prevent a
subsequent claim against the former employer of a kind only approved by the
House of Lords itself in another decision made after the redundancy agreement
was concluded.[122] It remains the law in both England and Scotland that in general
evidence from pre-contractual negotiations as to the meaning of a contract is inadmissible, as also in general evidence of the parties' conduct subsequent to the
contract.[123] But the Scottish courts may still, despite a contrary decision of the
House of Lords in an English appeal, admit evidence that in negotiations a party
used a word or phrase with a particular meaning to the knowledge of, and without

---

[117] *Charter Reinsurance v Fagan* [1997] A.C. 313; *Mannai Investments Co Ltd v Eagle Star Life
Insurance Co Ltd* [1997] A.C. 749; *Investors Compensation Scheme v West Bromwich Building
Society* [1998] 1 W.L.R. 896 (HL) (speech of Lord Hoffmann); *Chartbrook Ltd v Persimmon Homes
Ltd* [2009] UKHL 38; [2009] 1 A.C. 1101. See further McBryde, *The Law of Contract in Scotland*
(2007), paras 8.25–8.27.

[118] *Investors Compensation Scheme* [1998] 1 W.L.R. 896 (HL) at 912–13.

[119] See Scottish Law Commission, *Interpretation of Contract* (The Stationery Office, 2011), Scot.
Law Com. D.P. No.147, Ch.5, for an analysis of the relevant case law.

[120] See in particular the opinion of Lord President Rodger in *Bank of Scotland v Dunedin Property
Investment Co Ltd*, 1998 S.C. 657; *Multi-Link Leisure Developments Ltd v North Lanarkshire Council*
[2010] UKSC 47; 2011 S.C. (UKSC) 53; *Aberdeen City Council v Stewart Milne Ltd* [2011] UKSC
56; 2012 S.L.T. 205. Lord Clarke at [33] holds the latter case to be one of an implied term.

[121] *Luminar Lava Ignite Ltd v Mama Group Plc* [2010] CSIH 01; 2010 S.C. 310, per Lord Hodge at
[38]; cf. Lord Hope in *Multi-Link Leisure Developments Ltd v North Lanarkshire Council* [2010]
UKSC 47; 2011 S.C. (UKSC) 53 at [11]. In *Aberdeen City Council v Stewart Milne Ltd* [2011] UKSC
56; 2012 S.L.T. 205 Lord Clarke states (at [33]), that the commercial sense approach should only be
used when the words to be interpreted may reasonably bear more than one meaning, applying his
earlier judgment in *Rainy Sky SA v Kookmin Bank* [2011] UKSC 50; [2011] 1 W.L.R. 2900.

[122] *Bank of Commerce and Credit International v Ali* [2002] 1 A.C. 251 (note the dissenting speech
by Lord Hoffmann). Cf. in *Scotland Semple Cochrane Plc v Clark*, 2003 S.L.T. 532.

[123] *Bank of Scotland v Dunedin Property Investment Co Ltd*, 1998 S.C. 657; *Cameron (Scotland)
Ltd v Melville Dundas*, 2001 S.C.L.R. 691; *Chartbrook Ltd v Persimmon Homes Ltd* [2009] UKHL 38;
[2009] 1 A.C. 1101 (note references by Lord Hoffmann and Lord Rodger to Lord Gifford's dictum in
A & J Inglis v Buttery (1877) 5 R. 58 at 69–70, affd (1878) 5 R. (HL) 87 at 102); *Luminar Lava Ignite
Ltd v Mama Group Plc* [2010] CSIH 01; 2010 S.C. 310.

objection from, the other party in order to give that meaning to the word in the subsequent contract.[124] There also remains the unsatisfactory rule that evidence of the actions of the parties under a contract is competent, on the principle of *contemporanea expositio*, if it is of ancient date,[125] but not if it is *de recenti*.[126]

6.24 Other guidelines for construction—There are a number of other principles of interpretation to which the courts often make reference as useful guidance, without feeling the need to apply them rigidly or invariably. Where a contract is a mixture of negotiated and pre-printed standard terms, the former will be taken as the better indicator of the parties' actual intention.[127] Where the general common law imposes obligations upon a party, a contract will not be read as excluding them unless this was clearly the parties' intention.[128] Vague general terms are limited by more precise ones (*specialia generalibus derogant*),[129] while the scope of general words preceded by a list of specific things having some generic identity will, unless clearly intended to be absolutely general, be limited by that generic character (the *ejusdem generis* rule).[130] So where a charter-party made allowance for delay in loading a ship caused by

> "holidays, strikes, stoppage at the colliery at which the ship is booked to load first, detention by railway or cranes, stoppage of trains, accidents to machinery, or any other unavoidable cause"

it was held that the final words did not extend to delay caused by shipping congestion in the port, as that was not a breakdown of normal arrangements in the port such as mentioned in the specific list, but was rather caused by the port's limited capacity.[131] The expression of one specific thing may be taken as excluding another not mentioned or where there are no general words (*expressio unius est exclusio alterius*).[132] Where a contract document has been prepared by one of the parties rather than being the outcome of negotiations between them both, the court will in cases of ambiguity prefer the construction least favourable to the interests of the party who prepared the document (the *contra proferentem* rule).[133]

---

[124] *Houldsworth v Gordon-Cumming*, 1910 S.C. (HL) 49; not referred to in the English appeal of *Chartbrook* (see [43]–[47]). The approach in *Houldsworth* may also have been used in *Bank of Scotland v Dunedin Property Investment Co Ltd*, 1998 S.C. 65: see Scottish Law Commission, *Interpretation of Contract*, para.5.24.

[125] *North British Ry v Magistrates of Edinburgh*, 1920 S.C. 409.

[126] *Scott v Howard* (1881) 8 R. (HL) 59, opinion of Lord Watson. But in a case of contradictory statements in the contract as to the acreage and boundaries of the subjects conveyed, it was held that evidence of acting upon it was competent, although the contract was of recent date: *Watcham v Att Gen. of East Africa* [1919] A.C. 533.

[127] Gloag, *Law of Contract* (1929), p.399; *Barry D. Trentham Ltd v McNeil*, 1996 S.L.T. 202.

[128] *Mars Pension Trs Ltd v County Properties and Developments Ltd*, 1999 S.C. 267.

[129] See, e.g. *Kilwinning Parish Council v Cunninghame Combination Board*, 1909 S.C. 829.

[130] The *Admiralty v Burns*, 1910 S.C. 531; *Glasgow Corp v Glasgow Tramway and Omnibus Co Ltd* (1898) 25 R. (HL) 77.

[131] *Abchurch Steamship Co v Stinnes*, 1911 S.C. 1010.

[132] Gloag, *Law of Contract* (1929), pp.404–405.

[133] Gloag, *Law of Contract* (1929), p.400; McBryde, *The Law of Contract in Scotland* (2007), paras 8.38–8.43. For a statutory formulation, see Unfair Terms in Consumer Contracts Regulations (SI 1999/2083) reg.7 (below, para.9.25).

FURTHER READING

Cabrelli, D., *Commercial Agreements in Scotland: Law and Practice* (Edinburgh: W. Green, 2006).

Cabrelli, D., "Interpretation of Contracts, Objectivity and the Elision of the Significance of Consent Achieved through Concession and Compromise", 2011 Jur. Rev. 121.

Clive, E., "Interpretation" in Reid, K.G.C. and Zimmermann, R. (eds), *A History of Private Law in Scotland* (Oxford: Oxford University Press, 2000), Vol.2.

Gretton, G.L. and Reid, K.G.C, *Conveyancing*, 4th edn (Edinburgh: W. Green, 2011).

Lewison, K., *The Interpretation of Contracts*, 5th edn (London: Sweet and Maxwell, 2011).

Macgregor, L. and Lewis, C., "Interpretation of Contract", in Zimmermann, R., Visser, D. and Reid, K.G.C. (eds), *Mixed Legal Systems in Comparative Perspective: Scots and South African Law of Property and Obligations* (Oxford: Oxford University Press, 2004).

McBryde, W.W., *The Law of Contract in Scotland*, 3rd edn (Edinburgh: W. Green, 2007), Chs 5, 8.

McMeel, G., *The Construction of Contracts*, 2nd edn (Oxford: Oxford University Press, 2011).

MacQueen, H.L. and Thomson, J.M., *Contract Law in Scotland*, 3rd edn (Edinburgh: Bloomsbury Professional, 2012), Chs 2, 3.

Reid, D., "Rectification of Deeds", 2009 Prop. L.B. 103–1 and 104–1 (2 parts).

Reid, E.C. and Blackie, J.W.G., *Personal Bar* (Edinburgh: W. Green, 2006), Ch.7.

Scottish Law Commission, *Report on Requirements of Writing* (HMSO, 1988), Scot. Law Com. No.112.

Scottish Law Commission, *Report on Three Bad Rules in Contract Law* (HMSO, 1996), Scot. Law Com. No.152.

Scottish Law Commission, *Interpretation of Contract* (The Stationery Office, 2011), Scot. Law Com. D.P. No.147.

Stair Memorial Encyclopaedia, Vol.15, paras 753-62.

Walker and Walker: The Law of Evidence in Scotland, edited by Ross, M. and Chalmers, J., 3rd edn (Tottel, 2009), Chs 22–26.

Chapter 7

DEFECTIVE AGREEMENTS

No obligation despite consent—The statement that an obligation may result **7.01** from mere consent is to be taken as a general rule, subject to important qualifications. There are many cases where real or apparent consent may have been given and yet no obligation may arise. This may result: (1) from want of capacity in the party[1]; (2) from defect of form[2]; (3) from the nature of the means by which consent was obtained[3]; (4) from error precluding real consent[4]; or (5) from the illegality of the matter involved.[5] The first, second and fifth of these topics are dealt with elsewhere in this book as undernoted; this chapter considers the third and fourth, and also the closely related subject of misrepresentation. But it begins with discussion of the general concepts of voidness (nullity) and voidability (annullability) applicable in all five areas.

I. AGREEMENTS VOID OR VOIDABLE

Contracts void, voidable or unenforceable—These objections to the validity of **7.02** consent may, according to the circumstances, render the obligation void, voidable or unenforceable. If an agreement, or apparent agreement, is void, it is to be treated, for all legal purposes, as a mere nullity: no one can enforce it. If the contract obliges a party to convey property, any conveyance is also likely to be tainted with the same invalidity. In that case, no title to that property is given, even in a question with a third party, such as a sub-purchaser, who has no notice of the grounds of nullity.[6] An agreement which is not void but merely voidable is valid until it is set aside by the party entitled to avoid it, with the result that if property has passed on a contract merely voidable, and has been transferred for value to a party who has no notice of any invalidity, that party's title is not affected by the reduction of the original contract.[7] An agreement is termed unenforceable when, owing to some statutory or other rule, it cannot be enforced by action, but is not so forbidden as to render it void, or to exclude the creation of incidental rights.

---

[1] See Ch.43.
[2] See para.6.04, above.
[3] See paras 7.11–7.20, below.
[4] See paras 7.21–7.31, below.
[5] See Ch.9.
[6] D.L. Carey Miller, *Corporeal Moveables in Scotland*, 2nd edn (Edinburgh: W. Green, 2005), paras 8.06–8.10; K.G.C. Reid, *The Law of Property in Scotland* (Edinburgh: Butterworths, 1996), paras 606–617; W.W. McBryde, *The Law of Contract in Scotland*, 3rd edn (Edinburgh: W. Green, 2007), paras 13.01–13.11.
[7] See *Morrisson v Robertson*, 1908 S.C. 332; cf. *MacLeod v Kerr*, 1965 S.C. 253.

7.03 Conditions of avoidance—The fact that an obligation is voidable does not imply that in all circumstances it may be reduced. That is doubtless the general rule; in particular cases it may find exception on the grounds: (a) that restitutio in integrum is impossible; (b) that the interests of third parties are involved; (c) that the validity of the obligation has been recognised by homologation, in the case of voidable contracts, or by adoption, in the case of a void contract or an apparent contract; (d) that there has been undue delay.

7.04 Restitutio in integrum[8]—It is a general principle that where a party proposes to reduce a contract, he must be able to offer restitutio in integrum; in other words, must be able to restore the other party to the position in which he was before he entered into the contract. So if contractors have erected a building in pursuance of a contract which proves to be voidable, the reduction of the contract is precluded, whatever remedies may in the particular case be available, on the ground that the original position of matters cannot be restored.[9] When an unincorporated company was incorporated under statute, it was held that, as the original shares had been so altered that they could no longer be restored, a reduction of the contract to take shares was impossible.[10] When a particular thing has been sold, and resold by the purchaser, he cannot reduce the sale because he cannot restore the thing. His title to reduce the sale is not improved by re-acquiring the thing from the sub-purchaser.[11] But when the sub-sale was also reducible on the same ground (a misrepresentation as to the condition of the thing), and was on that ground reduced by the sub-purchaser, it was held that a reduction of the original sale was competent.[12] Restitutio in integrum may be given in cases where the question depends on the possibility of restoring a particular thing, although that thing may in the meantime have diminished in value. So a contract to take shares may be reduced so long as the company is a going concern, though the shares may have become valueless.[13] The interest in a partnership could be restored though the business was openly insolvent.[14] If a particular thing has been transferred under the contract and has been accidentally destroyed, it would appear that the contract cannot be reduced.[15] But if it has perished owing to the fault of the party proposing to maintain the contract, as when a horse, warranted sound in work, ran away and was killed, that party cannot found upon his own wrong or breach of contract, and so cannot resist the reduction of the contract (involving repayment of the price) on the plea that restitutio in integrum cannot be offered.[16] And when a person by fraud has been able to purchase something, he may not in bar of restitution rely upon dealings with the thing purchased which his fraud has enabled him to carry out.[17]

---

[8] See also R. Evans-Jones, *Unjustified Enrichment* (Edinburgh: W. Green, 2003), Vol.1, paras 9.125–9.134.

[9] *Boyd & Forrest v Glasgow and S.W. Ry*, 1915 S.C. (HL) 20. See also *Hay v Rafferty* (1899) 2 F. 302.

[10] *Western Bank v Addie* (1867) 5 M. (HL) 80.

[11] *Edinburgh United Breweries v Molleson* (1894) 21 R. (HL) 6.

[12] *Westville Shipping Co v Abram Shipping Co*, 1922 S.C. 571; affd 1923 S.C. (HL) 66.

[13] *Western Bank v Addie* (1867) 5 M. (HL) 80, opinion of Lord Cranworth; *Armstrong v Jackson* [1917] 2 K.B. 822.

[14] *Adam v Newbigging* (1888) 13 App. Cas. 308.

[15] See opinion of Lord Atkinson, *Boyd & Forrest v Glasgow and S.W. Ry*, 1915 S.C. (HL) 20 at 29.

[16] *Kinnear v Brodie* (1901) 3 F. 540; *Rowland v Divall* [1923] 2 K.B. 500.

[17] *Spence v Crawford*, 1939 S.C. (HL) 52.

Interests of third parties—The interests of third parties do not preclude the **7.05**
reduction of a contract in so far as that contract involves merely a personal obligation. So if a bond is granted under circumstances which render it voidable in a
question with the original creditor, it remains voidable in a question with anyone
to whom it may be assigned.[18] The obligation of an insurance company on a
policy of insurance, if voidable on the ground of misrepresentation by the insured,
may be reduced in a question with the assignee.[19] In cases of the assignation of a
debt or other personal obligation (not embodied in a negotiable instrument) the
maxim *assignatus utitur jure auctoris* (the assignee uses his author's right)
applies, and the assignee may be met by any defence which was available against
the cedent.[20] But if the result of the contract was not merely to create a personal
obligation but was to transfer a real right in some particular property—as where
land is conveyed or goods are sold on a contract induced by misrepresentation—
the original seller cannot reduce the contract so as to recover the property if it has
been transferred to a third party either by sale or in security. The original sale
carries a title to the property, and, though that title may be voidable, it is valid until
reduced, and third parties may acquire indefeasible rights under it. This rule,
recognised as a general principle in the earliest authorities,[21] may be stated in
the language of the Sale of Goods Act 1979 s.23: when the seller of goods has a
voidable title thereto, but his title has not been avoided at the time of the sale, the
buyer acquires a good title to the goods, provided he buys them in good faith
and without notice of the seller's defect in title.[22]

Interests of creditors—When third parties are interested in maintaining a **7.06**
contract, not as the holders of subordinate real rights, but merely as personal
creditors of the original party, it is a general rule that their interests do not preclude
the reduction of the contract. The distinction between the position of heritable
creditors, who obtain a real right to the lands, and adjudgers, who were only
personal creditors, was taken in an early and leading case.[23] And it is settled that
a trustee in a sequestration cannot take advantage of the bankrupt's fraud, and
therefore cannot maintain a right which the bankrupt has acquired by fraudulent
means.[24] The chief exception to this rule is the case where shares are taken in
reliance on misrepresentations in the prospectus. It is established law, proceeding
largely on inferences derived from the terms of the Companies Acts, that the
contract cannot be reduced after the company has gone into liquidation, on
the ground that the real interest is then in the creditors, or, where all creditors are
paid, in the other shareholders.[25] It has been observed that a partner, reducing the

---

[18] *Nisbet's Creditors v Robertson* (1791) Mor. 9554; *McDonells v Bell & Rennie* (1772) Mor. 4974.
[19] *Scottish Widows' Fund v Buist* (1876) 3 R. 1078; *Graham Joint Stock Shipping Co v Merchants Marine Insurance* [1924] A.C. 294.
[20] See opinion of Lord President Inglis, *Scottish Widows' Fund v Buist* (1876) 3 R. 1078.
[21] Stair, IV, 40, 21.
[22] For illustrative cases, see *Bryce v Ehrmann* (1905) 7 F. 5; *Morrisson v Robertson*, 1908 S.C. 332 (contrast between void and voidable contract); *Price & Pierce v Bank of Scotland*, 1910 S.C. 1095; affd 1912 S.C. (HL) 19.
[23] *Thomson v Douglas Heron & Co* (1786) Mor. 10229; 3 Ross' Leading Cases, 132. See also opinion of Lord Watson, *Heritable Reversionary Co v Millar* (1892) 19 R. (HL) 43.
[24] *Colquhoun's Tr. v Campbell's Trs* (1902) 4 F. 739; *A.W. Gamage v Charlesworth's Tr.*, 1910 S.C. 257.
[25] *Oakes v Turquand* (1867) L.R. 2 H.L. 325; *Tennent v City of Glasgow Bank* (1879) 6 R. (HL) 69; *Burgess' Case* (1880) 15 Ch. D. 507. Contrast the case where the contract to take shares is actually void, as where A, intending to apply for shares in one company, applied for shares in another: *Baillie's Case* [1898] 1 Ch. 16.

contract of partnership on the ground that he has been induced to enter into it by fraud, would remain liable to the creditors of the firm.[26]

7.07 Homologation—Homologation is implied by any acts whereby a party, in the knowledge that a particular obligation is voidable, recognises its validity.

> "The law of homologation proceeds on the principle of presumed consent by the party who does the acts to pass from grounds of challenge known to him, and sciens et prudens to adopt the challengeable deed as his own."[27]

Such acts as the payment or receipt of rent on a voidable lease,[28] payment of interest on a bond,[29] continuance of business with a banker on a system to which the customer might have objected,[30] amount to homologation and bar any subsequent challenge. Delivery of a deed lacking the required solemnities is not per se homologation.[31] As a rule, and in all cases of isolated acts, it is necessary to prove that the party alleged to have homologated was aware of all the material facts,[32] but in certain cases of long sustained relationship adequate means of knowledge have been held to be sufficient.[33] The effect of homologation is to validate the obligation from the date of its inception.

7.08 Adoption—Adoption applies to cases where there is nothing but the semblance of an obligation. By recognising its validity the party may render himself liable on a new contract to be inferred from his acts. The most important cases have related to forged bills. If a party whose signature is forged chooses to accept liability, he has adopted the bill, and he may act in such a way as to amount to adoption and consequent liability without any express recognition of his signature.[34] But this will not be easily inferred, and it is now established that mere silence, in the face of an intimation that the bill is due, does not amount to adoption and infers no liability.[35] Where a person discovers that his signature has been forged to a document, it is his duty to inform the creditor at once, but the creditor can recover against him only if he can establish that he has been prejudiced by any delay in informing him.[36] If the objection to the contract be that the body which entered into it was acting ultra vires, no acts approving of it can cure the invalidity, or have any legal effect, unless in the meantime the contractual powers of the body have been enlarged.[37]

7.09 Delay—In certain cases delay in taking action will preclude reduction of a contract.[38] This primarily depends on the nature of the defect which renders the

---

[26] Opinion of Lord Chancellor Cairns in *Tennent v City of Glasgow Bank* (1879) 6 R. (HL) 69.

[27] *Gardner v Gardner* (1830) 9 S. 136. Quoted and approved by Lord President Clyde, *Danish Dairy Co v Gillespie*, 1922 S.C. 656 at 664. For a discussion of the limits of homologation, see *Westville Shipping Co v Abram Shipping Co*, 1922 S.C. 571; affd 1923 S.C. (HL) 66.

[28] *Rigg v Durward* (1776) Mor. App. Fraud, No.2; *Lord Advocate v Wemyss* (1899) 2 F. (HL) 1.

[29] *McCalman v McArthur* (1864) 2 M. 676.

[30] *Crerar v Bank of Scotland*, 1921 S.C. 736; affd 1922 S.C. (HL) 137.

[31] *Clark's Exr v Cameron*, 1982 S.L.T. 66.

[32] *Danish Dairy Co v Gillespie*, 1922 S.C. 656.

[33] *Lord Advocate v Wemyss* (1899) 2 F. (HL) 1; *Crerar v Bank of Scotland*, 1921 S.C. 736.

[34] *Greenwood v Martins Bank* [1933] A.C. 51.

[35] *MacKenzie v British Linen Co* (1881) 8 R. (HL) 8; *British Linen Co v Cowan* (1906) 8 F. 704; *Muir's Exrs v Craig's Trs*, 1913 S.C. 349.

[36] *Muir's Exrs v Craig's Trs*, 1913 S.C. 349.

[37] *General Property Investment Co v Matheson's Trs* (1888) 16 R. 282; and see below, para.46.12.

[38] See also paras 3.07–3.10, above.

contract voidable. Some grounds of avoidance are not maintainable unless they are taken advantage of within a specified or a reasonable time. Thus a contract entered into by a person between the ages of 16 and 18 may be reduced if it is a prejudicial transaction, but only if he takes action before attaining the age of 21.[39] The right to reject goods, and treat the contract as repudiated in the case where the goods are disconform to contract, must be exercised within a reasonable time.[40] The right to reduce a contract to take shares, on the ground of misrepresentation in the prospectus, must certainly be exercised within a reasonable time,[41] and probably must be followed by steps for the rectification of the register.[42] In other cases, for instance in the case of contracts voidable on the ground of fraud or misrepresentation, in a question between the original parties any delay, short of the negative prescription of five or 20 years, is not a bar to reduction.[43] But, if in consequence of unnecessary delay evidence has been lost, any point which it might have elucidated will be presumed in the defender's favour.[44] As a general principle, the interests of third parties are not relevant in considering the consequences of delay.[45]

II. GROUNDS OF INVALIDITY

Means by which consent obtained—A contract may be rendered void or void- **7.10** able because the consent of one of the parties has been obtained by improper means, or given under error. Under this head may be considered the effect of: (1) extortion; (2) fraud; (3) facility and circumvention; (4) undue influence; (5) error. Non-fraudulent misrepresentation also requires separate consideration.

(1) EXTORTION[46]

Force or fear[47]—It is probably the law that a contract induced by violence, or by **7.11** threats sufficient to overcome the fortitude of a reasonable man, is void,[48] with an exception in the case of a bill of exchange, which is merely voidable, and may be enforced by a holder who can establish affirmatively that he gave value for the bill without notice of any objection.[49] Threats need not be of actual physical violence; an allegation by a workman of threatened loss of employment has been held

---

[39] para.43.02, below.
[40] Sale of Goods Act 1979 s.35(4).
[41] *Aaron's Reefs v Twiss* [1896] A.C. 273.
[42] *First National Re-Insurance Co v Greenfield* [1921] 2 K.B. 260.
[43] See, e.g. *Robinson v Robinson's Trs*, 1934 S.L.T. 183.
[44] *Bain v Assets Co* (1905) 7 F. (HL) 104.
[45] For discussion of general principle, and limited circumstances in which third party rights may be relevant (e.g. proceedings relating to insolvency), see E.C. Reid and J.W.G. Blackie, *Personal Bar* (Edinburgh: W. Green, 2006), paras 4.19–4.20.
[46] Since consent may be extorted in different ways, the generic term "extortion" is thought preferable: see *Priestnell v Hutchison* (1857) 19 D. 495 at 499, per Lord Deas; *Hislop v Dickson Motors (Forres)*, 1978 S.L.T. (Notes) 73. Note also Stair, I, 9, 6. See generally McBryde, *The Law of Contract in Scotland* (2007), Ch.17.
[47] Earlier editions of this work employed the heading "Force and Fear" following Morison's Dictionary, s.v. Vis et Metus. Stair I, 9, 8 refers to force or fear indicating the possibility of separate pleas. See generally J.E. Du Plessis, *Compulsion and Restitution* (Edinburgh: Stair Society, 2004), Vol.51, Chs 3 and 4.
[48] Stair, I, 9, 8; Erskine, III, I, 16. Cases in Morison, s.v. Vis et Metus.
[49] Bills of Exchange Act 1882 ss.29, 30, 36.

relevant.[50] But threats of steps which the party may lawfully and warrantably take, such as proceedings in bankruptcy, or under the former law, imprisonment for debt, do not invalidate a payment or security thereby induced,[51] though they fall under the general rule of force and fear if used to extort consent to some independent contract.[52] And an obligation granted by a party who had been imprisoned under irregular diligence was reduced.[53] When a payment or promissory note is given in order to avoid a prosecution, it is valid if it is given merely as repayment of what the giver has stolen.[54] The case of payment for the same purpose by a third party is more doubtful,[55] and it is probably settled that any payment or obligation extending beyond reimbursement of money stolen cannot be defended.[56] Threats of violence or injury to near relations have the same legal effect as threats to the party himself.[57] Threats by someone who is not a party to the contract may render the contract ineffectual in a question with a party to the contract who is not responsible for, and not aware of, the threats.[58] Obligations granted by a married woman for her husband's debt may be reduced if they were obtained by threats used by the other party or by the husband; it is not sufficient that they were granted out of affection for him, and in order to save him from proceedings in bankruptcy.[59]

7.12 Extortionate bargains[60]—Except in the case of loans of money, there is no authority at common law for holding it to be a relevant ground for the reduction of a contract that its terms are extortionate, even with the addition of averments that the defender had a great advantage over the pursuer in respect of education or business experience.[61] In the case of loans, until 1854, when they were finally repealed, the usury laws limited the rate of interest which might lawfully be charged. It has twice been held at common law that a loan by a moneylender might be challenged where the circumstances were exceptional and the borrower a person inexperienced in business.[62] The English law as to bargains with expectant heirs is not recognised in Scotland.[63] English law accepts that a contract may be avoided if entered into under "economic duress": mere commercial pressure will not suffice.[64] It may be that extortion, a concept which encompasses

---

[50] *Gow v Henry* (1899) 2 F. 46. See *Pao On v Lau Yiu Long* [1980] A.C. 614.

[51] *Ker v Edgar* (1698) Mor. 16503; *Rudman v Jay*, 1908 S.C. 552, opinion of Lord Ardwall; *Hunter v Bradford Property Trust*, 1977 S.L.T. (Notes) 33; *Hislop v Dickson Motors (Forres)*, 1978 S.L.T. (Notes) 73; *Euan Wallace & Partners v Westcot Homes Plc*, 2000 S.L.T. 327.

[52] *Nisbet v Stewart* (1708) Mor. 16512.

[53] *McIntosh v Chalmers* (1883) 11 R. 6.

[54] *Lamson Co v MacPhail*, 1914 S.C. 73.

[55] *Ferrier v Mackenzie* (1899) 1 F. 597.

[56] *Canison v Marshall* (1764) 6 Paton 759; *Kaufman v Gerson* [1904] 1 K.B. 591; opinion of Lord Salvesen in *Lamson Co v MacPhail*, 1914 S.C. 73.

[57] Bell, *Principles*, s.12.

[58] *Cassie v Fleming* (1632) Mor. 10279; *Trustee Savings Bank v Balloch*, 1983 S.L.T. 240; cf. *Stewart Brothers v Keddie* (1889) 7 S.L.T. 92 at 93, per Lord Trayner.

[59] *Priestnell v Hutchison* (1857) 19 D. 495.

[60] See generally, McBryde, *The Law of Contract in Scotland* (2007), paras 17.12–17.22.

[61] *Cal. Ry v N.B. Ry* (1881) 8 R. (HL) 23, opinion of Lord Blackburn, *Wood v N.B. Ry* (1891) 18 R. (HL) 27; *Mathieson v Hawthorne* (1899) 1 F. 466. The statutory provisions as to unfair credit bargains are treated below in para.15.32.

[62] *Young v Gordon* (1896) 23 R. 419; *Gordon v Stephens* (1902) 9 S.L.T. 397.

[63] *McKirdy v Anstruther* (1839) 1 D. 855.

[64] *North Shipping Co Ltd v Hyundai Construction Co Ltd* [1979] Q.B. 705; *Pao On v Lau Yiu Long* [1980] A.C. 614; *Universe Tankships Inc. of Monrovia v International Transport Worker's Federation* [1983] A.C. 366; *Alec Lobb (Garages) Ltd v Total Oil G.B. Ltd* [1985] 1 All E.R. 303; *Atlas Express Ltd v Kafco (Importers & Distributors) Ltd* [1989] Q.B. 833.

not only force and fear but also "pressure of a certain degree" could be applied to cover cases involving economic duress.[65]

(2) Fraud[66]

Definition and effects—Fraud is a machination or contrivance to deceive, by **7.13** words or acts.[67] Unless the result of the fraud is to exclude any real consent, a contract induced by fraudulent practices is not void, but only voidable.[68] To induce a party to contract by fraud is a civil wrong, and therefore the party defrauded may not only reduce the contract but also recover damages for any loss he may have suffered. If, for reasons already explained,[69] the contract cannot be reduced, a claim for damages remains competent.[70] Where a contract has been induced by fraudulent misrepresentation, damages may be recovered even though the pursuer does not offer to rescind.[71] It is impossible to enumerate the various words or acts which the law will regard as fraudulent, but some light may be thrown on the question from the negative side.

No legal fraud—There is no such thing as legal, apart from moral, fraud. **7.14** Conscious dishonesty must be proved. In the leading English case, *Derry v Peek*,[72] the directors of an insolvent tramway company were sued for damages on the ground that the plaintiff had been induced to take shares by misrepresentation in the prospectus. The misrepresentation in question was that the company had obtained authority from the Board of Trade to work the tramway by steam power. This was proved to be untrue, but it was also proved that the directors honestly believed it to be true, having misapprehended the result of their negotiations with the Board of Trade. It was held, even on the assumption that the defendants had not taken reasonable care to verify their statement, that they were not liable in damages for fraud because there was no dishonesty.[73] In *Manners v Whitehead*,[74] M had been induced to enter into a partnership with W by inaccurate statements contained in balance sheets of the business which W was carrying on. The business failed, and M sued for damages. He proved that the balance sheets were inaccurate; he did not succeed in proving fraud on the part of W. It was held that the action was not maintainable; a claim for damages in such circumstances, as the law then stood, had to rest on proof of conscious fraud. The general rule illustrated in these cases must be taken with the qualification that if a man does not know, or has forgotten, the truth on any particular question, he has no right to

---

[65] *Hislop v Dickson Motors (Forres)*, 1978 S.L.T. (Notes) 73 at 75, per Lord Maxwell. On the correct conceptual basis for the doctrine of economic duress in Scots law see Thompson, 1985 S.L.T. (News) 85 and, in response, McKendrick, 1985 S.L.T. (News) 277.

[66] See generally, McBryde, *The Law of Contract in Scotland* (2007), Ch.14; *Stair Memorial Encyclopaedia*, Vol.11, s.v. "Fraud".

[67] Bell, *Principles*, s.13.

[68] *Morrisson v Robertson*, 1908 S.C. 332; *MacLeod v Kerr*, 1965 S.C. 253, and see below, para.7.28.

[69] Above, paras 7.03 et seq.

[70] *Boyd & Forrest v Glasgow and S.W. Ry*, 1912 S.C. (HL) 93.

[71] *Bryson & Co Ltd v Bryson*, 1916 1 S.L.T. 361; *Smith v Sim*, 1954 S.C. 357, OH, an action founded on delict.

[72] *Derry v Peek* (1889) 14 App. Cas. 337. See also *Boyd & Forrest v Glasgow and S.W. Ry*, 1912 S.C. (HL) 93; *Lees v Tod* (1882) 9 R. 807.

[73] In England and Scotland a negligent statement may now give rise to a claim for damages. See below, para.7.35.

[74] *Manners v Whitehead* (1898) 1 F. 171.

make any positive assertion on the subject, and therefore that fraud may be established although there may be no proof that the speaker was aware that his statement was untrue. It is enough that the real state of his mind was that he did not know whether it was true or not. And the absence of any reasonable grounds for belief may be evidence, to be taken with the other evidence in the case, that no positive belief existed.[75]

7.15 Disclosure—Mere failure to disclose material facts does not amount to fraud; nor, except in certain special contracts or where the parties stand to each other in some confidential relationship, is it a ground for the reduction of a contract. So a bank, when offered a guarantee for a customer's account, is not bound to inform the guarantor of the state of that account.[76] When A knew that B's mine contained a valuable seam of coal, and also knew that B was unaware of the fact, it was held that a lease obtained by A was unchallengeable.[77] A settlement of an action for £20 was sustained, although obtained by the defender in a private interview with the pursuer by concealing the fact that he had already made a tender of £50.[78] And it is probably established that the seller of goods is under no obligation to reveal latent defects.[79]

But this rule does not hold in insurance,[80] nor in guarantees for the fidelity of an official[81]; nor, probably, in negotiations for entering into partnership.[82] In these contracts (known as contracts uberrimae fidei) each party is bound to reveal all facts known to him which it would be material for the other to know. A similar duty of disclosure may arise from the fact that the parties stand to each other in some relationship. Thus concealment of material facts will serve to avoid a contract between parent and child,[83] trustee and beneficiary,[84] partners,[85] agent and principal.[86] A solicitor contracting with his client is under a particularly stringent obligation; he must not only reveal all material facts but must also show that the contract is one which he, if consulted in a case where he was not personally interested, would have advised the client to make.[87] The general rule must now also be qualified at least in cases where one spouse grants a cautionary obligation in respect of the other spouse's indebtedness to a bank.[88] In such situations the bank is under an obligation of good faith towards the cautioner, breach of which may give rise to reduction of the cautionary obligation. If the bank has reason to

---

[75] See opinion of Lord President Inglis, *Lees v Tod* (1882) 9 R. 807; of Lord Herschell in *Derry v Peek* (1889) 14 App. Cas. 337.

[76] *Royal Bank of Scotland v Greenshields*, 1914 S.C. 259; but see now *Smith v Bank of Scotland*, 1997 S.C. (HL) 111, discussed below, and at paras 16.15–16.17.

[77] *Gillespie v Russell* (1856) 18 D. 677; (1857) 19 D. 897; (1859) 3 Macq. 757.

[78] *Welsh v Cousin* (1899) 2 F. 277.

[79] *Ward v Hobbs* (1878) 4 App. Cas. 13; *Philip's Trs v Reid* (1884) 21 S.L.R. 696.

[80] para.20.05, below.

[81] *Bank of Scotland v Morrison*, 1911 S.C. 593.

[82] See *Manners v Whitehead* (1898) 1 F. 171; *Ferguson v Mackay*, 1985 S.L.T. 94. There is no definite authority. A contract of employment is not uberrimae fidei: *Walker v Greenock and District Combination Hospital Board*, 1951 S.C. 464.

[83] *Smith Cunninghame v Anstruther's Trs* (1872) 10 M. (HL) 39.

[84] *Dougan v Macpherson* (1902) 4 F. (HL) 7.

[85] *Law v Law* [1905] 1 Ch. 140. See also *Cassels v Stewart* (1881) 8 R. (HL) 1.

[86] *McPherson's Trs v Watt* (1877) 5 R. (HL) 9.

[87] *Aitken v Campbell's Trs*, 1909 S.C. 1217; *Gillespie v Gardner*, 1909 S.C. 1053.

[88] For what follows, see in general *Smith v Bank of Scotland*, 1997 S.C. (HL) 111, speech of Lord Clyde, applying *Barclays Bank Plc v O'Brien* [1994] 1 A.C. 180 in Scotland. See further paras 16.15–16.17, below.

suspect that there may be factors arising from the spouses' relationship undermining the validity of the cautioner's consent, such as undue influence or misrepresentation, it must take certain steps to remain in good faith, for example by
warning the cautioner of the possible consequences and advising that independent
advice be taken.[89] There is no requirement that the bank investigate the parties'
relationship. Where a cautioner seeks reduction of its obligation on this ground,
however, the factor undermining its validity (the third party influence or misrepresentation) must be proved to have existed in fact.[90] The obligation of good faith
means, however, that where the cautioner took independent advice even although
not warned to do so the obligation does not fall to be reduced, at least where the
substance of the advice given has not been revealed to the court.[91]

Half-truths—The general rule that concealment does not affect the validity of a **7.16**
contract applies only to a case of mere non-disclosure, when no representation has
been made. It is fraudulent to tell a half-truth; that is, to make a statement true in
itself, and withhold some explanation which would alter its whole bearing. A
prospectus may satisfy the statutory conditions as to disclosure but, nevertheless,
by the concealment of facts which would alter the impression conveyed by the facts
disclosed, amount to fraud.[92] So if an agent for a bank makes any statement to a
party who offers to guarantee an account, he must reveal all the relevant facts.[93]
Again, if a statement made is honestly but mistakenly believed, the party who
makes it is bound to reveal the actual facts if they come to his knowledge. There is
the same duty of disclosure if by a change of circumstances the original statement
ceases to be true. So when A had honestly and truthfully stated that there was no
risk that a machine, which B proposed to buy, would be requisitioned by the
Government, it was held that A was bound to inform B of any change of attitude on
the part of the Government officials.[94] The rule that mere failure to disclose is not
fraudulent does not extend to the case of dealing with articles which ex facie
pretend to be what they are not, such as forged stamps or faked antiques. A purchaser
may reduce the contract to buy them, though the seller may have made no representation that the articles are genuine.[95] And it is fraudulent to exhibit unrepresentative
specimens in an auction room, though the conditions of the sale may be that
intending purchasers must satisfy themselves as to the condition of the goods in
bulk.[96] Any devices to conceal defects in an article are clearly fraudulent.

Verba jactantia—The general rule that statements known to be untrue are **7.17**
fraudulent has certain qualifications. It is not to be applied too rigorously to advertisements, though the line which separates mere extravagant recommendation
(*verba jactantia*) from fraudulent misstatements cannot be exactly drawn.[97] It has

---

[89] On independent advice, see *Forsyth v Royal Bank of Scotland Plc*, 2000 S.L.T. 1295; *Clydesdale Bank v Black*, 2002 S.C. 555.
[90] *Braithwaite v Bank of Scotland*, 1999 S.L.T. 25; *Royal Bank of Scotland v Wilson*, 2004 S.C. 153.
[91] *Clydesdale Bank v Black*, 2002 S.C. 555.
[92] *R. v Lord Kylsant* [1932] 1 K.B. 442.
[93] *Falconer v North of Scotland Bank* (1863) 1 M. 704; *Royal Bank of Scotland v Greenshields*, 1914 S.C. 259.
[94] *Shankland v Robinson*, 1919 S.C. 715; revd 1920 S.C. (HL) 103.
[95] *Patterson v Landsberg* (1905) 7 F. 675, opinion of Lord Kyllachy; *Gibson v National Cash Register Co*, 1925 S.C. 500.
[96] *White v Dougherty* (1891) 18 R. 972.
[97] Contrast *Bile Beans Co v Davidson* (1906) 8 F. 1181, and *Plotzker v Lucas* (1907) 15 S.L.T. 186. Note also *Paul & Co v Glasgow Corp* (1900) 3 F. 119.

been decided by the Judicial Committee that when the manager of a company was bound by his duty to his employers not to disclose the fact that a particular report had been received, and knew that a refusal to make any statement would give the inquirer the information he wanted, he was not liable in damages for fraud though he gave an answer which was wilfully false.[98] But a good motive is no excuse for a fraudulent act.[99]

7.18 Attempts to defraud—Attempts to defraud cause no injury, and therefore afford no remedy. Where a seller adopted fraudulent devices to conceal the defects in a gun, and the buyer bought it without making any examination, it was held that, as he had not been deceived, he could not reduce the contract on the ground of fraud.[100] An action to reduce a contract to take shares failed where the shareholder was forced to admit that the particular statements in the prospectus which he could prove to be untrue had not affected his mind.[101] But it is no answer to an action based on fraud that the party defrauded could have discovered the true facts if he had taken the trouble to investigate.[102]

(3) FACILITY AND CIRCUMVENTION[103]

7.19 Facility and circumvention—A contract (or disposition) may be avoided on the ground of facility and circumvention.[104] Three things must be proved: (a) facility; (b) lesion; and (c) circumvention.[105] These criteria need not be given equal weight; so where the facility is serious and the lesion considerable, circumvention may be little more than a matter of inference.[106] "Facility" means mental weakness (but not insanity) and may be attributable to age, grief or illness. Alcoholic overindulgence which stops short of inebriation might render one facile. "Lesion" simply means harm or loss. Circumvention is the most problematic aspect of the plea. In *Mackay v Campbell*,[107] it was indicated that deceit or dishonesty had to be shown, which suggests that proof of fraud is necessary. That case may be contrasted with *Gibson's Executor v Anderson*[108] in which the need to show fraud was rejected. It may be that the facts of the first case are special and that the general rule is that fraud need not be shown.[109]

---

[98] *Tackey v McBain* [1912] A.C. 186.

[99] *Menzies v Menzies* (1893) 20 R. (HL) 108, per Lord Ashbourne.

[100] *Horsfall v Thomas* (1862) 1 H. & C. 90.

[101] *Smith v Chadwick* (1884) 9 App. Cas. 187. Cf. *Ritchie v Glass*, 1936 S.L.T. 591, a case of innocent misrepresentation.

[102] *Redgrave v Hurd* (1881) 20 Ch. D. 1; *Gluckstein v Barnes* [1900] A.C. 240; *Strover v Harrington* [1988] Ch. 390.

[103] See generally, McBryde, *The Law of Contract in Scotland* (2007), paras 16.01–16.21. As to facility and circumvention in relation to wills, see below, para.39.02.

[104] *Gall v Bird* (1855) 17 D. 1027.

[105] *Mackay v Campbell*, 1967 S.C. (HL) 53; *Gibson's Exr v Anderson*, 1925 S.C. 774; *MacGilvary v Gilmartin*, 1986 S.L.T. 89; *Wheelans v Wheelans*, 1986 S.L.T. 164; *Anderson v The Beacon Fellowship*, 1992 S.L.T. 111.

[106] *Mackay v Campbell*, 1967 S.C. (HL) 53.

[107] *Mackay v Campbell*, 1967 S.C. (HL) 53.

[108] *Gibson's Executor v Anderson*, 1925 S.C. 774.

[109] McBryde, *The Law of Contract in Scotland* (2007), para.16.17.

(4) Undue Influence[110]

Definition and effects—So far as contracts are concerned,[111] undue influence **7.20** involves neither fraud nor deceit nor coercion. It is the abuse or exploitation of the confidence or trust reposed by one party in another.[112] At one time, the relationships to which the doctrine might be applied were restricted, but this is no longer the case.[113] The same facts may be capable of sustaining a plea of facility and circumvention as well as one of undue influence.[114] Undue influence renders a contract voidable.[115] There has been no case where a contract has been held to be voidable where the influence exercised was in genuine devotion to the interests of the person influenced and not in the interests of the other party to the agreement.[116]

(5) Error[117]

Error—One who contracts under an erroneous belief which is due to his own **7.21** misconception, is said to contract under error, or error in intention.[118] There is no doubt of the general rule that a party cannot reduce a contract on the ground that he has entered into it in error, if his contention is merely that he would not have contracted if he had known all the relevant facts. A plea to that effect has been judicially characterised as "so utterly preposterous as to be undeserving of any attention".[119] But the question is one of degree. Cases may arise where the error is so material as to preclude any real consent, and therefore to leave a contract, or apparent contract, without that basis of agreement on which all contractual obligation must rest. In such cases, the apparent contract is not voidable on the ground of error but void because there never was a contract at all. While the interpretation of contractual obligations must accept, as a fundamental rule, that a party must be taken to mean what he says, and is barred from asserting that his words or acts did not represent his intention,[120] that rule may come in conflict with one equally fundamental, namely, that the contractual obligations of the parties must rest on their consent. The attempt of the law to reconcile the conflict may be approached by considering the various forms of error by which a contract, or apparent contract, may be affected.

Categories of error—It is helpful to distinguish between errors in transaction **7.22** (sometimes known as error in expression) and errors in motive (sometimes known

---

[110] See generally, McBryde, *The Law of Contract in Scotland* (2007), paras 16.22–16.36.

[111] It may be otherwise with wills. See *Weir v Grace* (1899) 2 F. (HL) 80 and below, para.39.02.

[112] *Gray v Binny* (1879) 7 R. 332; *Forbes v Forbes' Trs (No.2)*, 1957 S.C. 325; *Honeyman's Exrs v Sharp*, 1978 S.C. 223.

[113] *Honeyman's Exrs v Sharp*, 1978 S.C. 223 (an art dealer and his client).

[114] *Honeyman's Exrs v Sharp*, 1978 S.C. 223; *Anderson v The Beacon Fellowship*, 1992 S.L.T. 111.

[115] *Logan's Trs v Wood* (1855) 12 R. 1094; *Gray v Binny* (1879) 7 R. 332.

[116] *Forbes v Forbes' Trs*, 1957 S.C. 325; but see *Allan v Allan*, 1961 S.C. 200.

[117] McBryde, *The Law of Contract in Scotland* (2007), Ch.15; *Stair Memorial Encyclopaedia*, Vol.15, paras 686–94; H.L. MacQueen and J.M. Thomson, *Contract Law in Scotland*, 3rd edn (Bloomsbury Professional, 2012), paras 4.36–4.66.

[118] The equivalent term in England is "mistake".

[119] *Forth Marine Insurance Co v Burnes* (1848) 10 D. 689, per Lord Fullerton.

[120] Above, para.5.04.

as error in intention).[121] An error in transaction is an error related in some way to an express or implied term of the purported contract, in particular misunderstandings of the term's meaning or effect. Such errors may be mutual, as when the parties attach different meanings to a term, or common, that is, shared by the parties. An error in transaction may also be unilateral, when one party has made an error about a term of the contract and this is known to the other party. In general, to make the contract void, an error in transaction must also relate to the substantials of the contract. An error in motive is an error of fact made by a party, causing that party to enter the contract. Before such an error can be used to challenge the contract, it must be shown to result from a misrepresentation by the other party. Where there is such a misrepresentation, the contract is voidable; otherwise the error is irrelevant.

7.23 Mutual error—If the terms of an offer are intrinsically ambiguous, and the parties reasonably attach different meanings to them, there is no contract when, even applying the usual objective criteria, the court cannot determine the correct meaning of the terms.[122] Where an order was given for stone coping at so much per "foot", a term equally applicable to a lineal and a superficial foot, it was held that the contract was not binding.[123] Where the parties were negotiating by telegram in code and the coded offer could reasonably be deciphered in a way different from that intended by the offerer and the offeree did read it in the alternative sense, it was held that there was no binding contract.[124] Similarly, there may be no contract where the ambiguity arises from extrinsic circumstances. If parties are contracting about a particular thing, and use language which is equally applicable to some other thing, then, assuming that they differ as to the meaning of the terms which they employ, they have reached no agreement and concluded no contract. This may happen in the case of the sale of an estate by its name if there is a reasonable difference of opinion as to the extent of the lands covered by that name.[125] The result was the same in the sale of the cargo from "the ship Peerless coming from Bombay" when there were two ships of that name coming from Bombay and the parties had different ships in mind.[126] If, in the course of negotiations, one party has indicated his interpretation of an ambiguous word and the other party has not contradicted him, the latter cannot subsequently advance an alternative meaning of the concluded contract.[127] It may be simpler in many cases to rely on the rules relating to contract formation instead of pleading mutual error.[128]

7.24 Shared error[129]—Where both parties contract under the same mistaken belief about a matter related to the contract, there is shared (or common) error and the contract is void.[130] In some cases, however, error need not be pleaded. Where, for

---

[121] cf. McBryde, *The Law of Contract in Scotland* (2007), para.15.21.

[122] For these usual criteria, see para.5.05, above, and paras 6.22–6.24, above.

[123] *Stuart v Kennedy* (1885) 13 R. 221.

[124] *Falck v Williams* [1900] A.C. 176.

[125] *Houldsworth v Gordon Cumming*, 1910 S.C. (HL) 49.

[126] *Raffles v Wichelhaus* (1864) 2 Hurl. & C. 906.

[127] *Sutton & Co v Ciceri & Co* (1890) 17 R. (HL) 40.

[128] *Came v City of Glasgow Friendly Society*, 1933 S.C. 69.

[129] In earlier editions of this work, the heading of this section was "Mutual Error". In the ninth edition this was changed to "Common Error", and in the tenth to "Shared Error". The latter is reintroduced in this edition in place of "Common or Shared Error".

[130] *Grieve v Wilson* (1828) 6 S. 454, affd (1838) 6 W. & S. 543; *Hamilton v Western Bank* (1861) 23 D. 1033.

example, specific goods have, unknown to the parties, perished at the time when a contract for their sale is made, then the contract is void by statute.[131] It may sometimes be difficult to distinguish the case where the continued existence of the thing was known to be doubtful, and each took the risk.[132] A mutual discharge of claims may be re-opened on proof of an error common to both, whether in fact or in law, which had induced the settlement.[133] And it would appear that, even in the case where a thing sold has been examined by the purchaser, the contract may be void if it proceeded on the assumption, common to both, that the thing had some specific and essential quality which it did not in fact possess.[134] But—though the point may not be settled beyond question—it is conceived that a sale will stand though the article turns out to have a value which neither seller nor purchaser suspected, as in the case of the sale of a book afterwards discovered to be valuable as a rarity.[135] It has been held that a contract, under which a director received compensation for loss of office, could not be reduced on the ground that it was entered into when both parties were in ignorance of the fact that the director had been guilty of conduct which would have justified his dismissal.[136] When a contract is affected by shared error, neither party is entitled to insist on a contract such as would probably have been made if the true facts had been known.[137]

Unilateral error—Another class of case is where one party has made an error **7.25** affecting a term of the contract, and the other party is aware of the error and takes advantage of it. In *Steuart's Trustees v Hart*,[138] reduction of a disposition of heritable subjects was permitted where the seller thought that the subjects were burdened with a cumulo feuduty of £9. 15s. but the buyer knew that this was only 3s. and that the seller had made a mistake in reading the contract which had the effect of lowering the sale price significantly. Gloag doubted the correctness of this decision[139] and, more recently, doubt has twice been cast upon it judicially.[140] This notwithstanding, the most recent Outer House decisions to consider the case follow it,[141] and it is supported by several other commentators.[142] It is submitted that *Steuart's Trustees* is a case of unilateral error in transaction, being related to

---

[131] Sale of Goods Act 1979 s.6. Note also *Couturier v Hastie* (1856) 5 H.L.C. 673 and *Associated Japanese Bank v Crédit du Nord S.A.* [1989] 1 W.L.R. 255.

[132] *Pender-Small v Kinloch's Trs*, 1917 S.C. 307.

[133] *Dickson v Halbert* (1854) 16 D. 586; *Ross v Mackenzie* (1842) 5 D. 151.

[134] *Edgar v Hector*, 1912 S.C. 346. The report does not bring out clearly that both parties were in error as to the nature of the chairs in question.

[135] *Dawson v Muir* (1851) 13 D. 843. Cf. *Scott v Coulson* [1903] 2 Ch. 249.

[136] *Bell v Lever Bros* [1932] A.C. 161. See also *Great Peace Shipping Ltd v Tsavliris Salvage (International) Ltd* [2003] Q.B. 679.

[137] *Pender-Small v Kinloch's Trs*, 1917 S.C. 307.

[138] *Steuart's Trustees v Hart* (1875) 3 R. 192.

[139] W.M. Gloag, *Law of Contract*, 2nd edn (Edinburgh: W. Green, 1929), p.438 points out: "When a book is exposed for sale in a bookstall it is generally supposed that a collector may buy it at the price asked, though he knows that it is rare and valuable, and must know that the bookseller is unaware of its value, and yet in all essential points such a case is on all fours with *Steuart's Trs v Hart*."

[140] *Brooker Simpson v Duncan Logan (Builders)*, 1969 S.L.T. 304; *Spook Erection (Northern) Ltd v Kaye*, 1990 S.L.T. 676. Note also *McLaughlin v New Housing Association Ltd*, 2008 S.L.T. (Sh. Ct) 137.

[141] *Angus v Bryden*, 1992 S.L.T. 884; noted by J.M. Thomson, "Error revised", 1992 S.L.T. (News) 215; *Parvaiz v Thresher Wines Acquisitions Ltd* [2008] CSOH 160; 2009 S.C. 151; noted by M. Hogg, "The continuing confused saga of contract and error" (2008) 14 Edin. L.R. 286.

[142] *Stair Memorial Encyclopaedia*, Vol.15, para.694; MacQueen and Thomson, *Contract Law in Scotland* (2012), para.4.55. See also McBryde, *The Law of Contract in Scotland* (2007), paras 15.30–15.33.

the terms of the contract, and is correctly decided, whereas those cases not following it were cases of error in motive, in which misrepresentation was necessary before any challenge to the contract was possible.[143] The matter will not be resolved, however, until fully considered by a court of authority. If a party does not know that the offer which he receives is in a form which was not intended by the offeror and accepts this in good faith, the contract is binding.[144]

7.26 **Error in substantials**—To render a contract void, an error in transaction, whether shared or unilateral in the senses discussed above, must be in the substantials of the contract.[145]

> "Error in substantials, whether in fact or in law, invalidates consent, or rather excludes real consent, where reliance is placed on the thing mistaken."[146]

The question in such a case is not whether a contract is reducible on the ground of error, but whether there is any contract to enforce. Such error in substantials may arise in relation to: (1) the nature of the contract itself; (2) the identity of the person with whom the contract is supposed to have been made; (3) the subject-matter of the contract; (4) in certain cases, the quality of the subject-matter; and (5) the price.[147] The question whether the error is such as to exclude consent is one of degree in each case. As has been stated, the normal effect of misrepresentation is to make the contract merely voidable, but where a misrepresentation induces an error in substantials, the contract is void[148]; it is therefore appropriate to consider here such cases as well as those of uninduced error in substantials.

7.27 **Error as to contract**—The predominant view is that where one party avers uninduced unilateral error as to the nature of the obligation undertaken, then where there is a written, signed, onerous contract the courts will not look behind the written document to see what was in the mind of the party averring error.[149] Other than in cases involving gratuitous contracts,[150] it is unlikely that the courts will permit reduction of an onerous, written, contract on the basis of uninduced unilateral error.[151] It is otherwise where a party, intending to bind himself to one contract, is fraudulently induced to sign a document binding him to another, as where a party signed a guarantee, being told and believing that he was signing a policy of insurance. It was held that the contract was not merely voidable on the ground of fraud, but void on the ground of the want of real consent, and that no

---

[143] On error in motive, see para.7.32, below. Gloag's example (fn.139, above) is also a case of error in motive.

[144] *Seaton Brick Co. v Mitchell* (1900) 2 F. 550; *Steel's Tr. v Bradley Homes (Scotland)*, 1972 S.C. 48.

[145] For a discussion of whether the contract might be rendered voidable rather than void, see T.B. Smith, *A Short Commentary on the Law of Scotland* (Edinburgh: W. Green, 1962), pp.810, 815.

[146] Bell, *Principles*, s.11, 10th edn; Stair, I, 10, 13; see opinion of Lord Watson in *Stewart v Kennedy* (1890) 17 R. (HL) 25 at 26.

[147] Gloag, *Law of Contract* (1929), pp.441–6.

[148] *Morrisson v Robertson*, 1908 S.C. 332.

[149] *Stewart v Kennedy* (1890) 17 R. (HL) 25; *Hunter v Bradford Property Trust Ltd*, 1970 S.L.T. 173; *Steel v Bradley Homes (Scotland) Ltd*, 1972 S.C. 48; *Royal Bank of Scotland v Purvis*, 1990 S.L.T. 262; *Spook Erection (Northern) Ltd v Kaye*, 1990 S.L.T. 676; *McCallum v Soudan*, 1989 S.L.T. 552.

[150] *Hunter v Bradford Property Trust Ltd*, 1970 S.L.T. 173; *Security Pacific Finance Ltd v T & I Filshie's Trustees*, 1994 S.C.L.R. 1100, affd 1995 S.C.L.R. 1171.

[151] cf. *Ellis v Lochgelly Iron Co*, 1909 S.C. 1278.

liability could be founded on the fact that, had he exercised reasonable care, the party would have discovered what he was signing.[152] In order to sustain the plea of *non est factum*—that the party had no intention to bind himself—there must have been a definite mistake, usually that the party thought he was entering into one contract while he was really entering into another. If obligatory documents are signed in reliance on an assurance that they are mere matters of form, the party who signs them will be liable.[153] If a draft contract has been revised, and the party signs the extended copy without noticing that it has been fraudulently altered, he will be bound, in a question with anyone not involved in the fraud, unless the alteration is so material as to make it a different contract.[154]

Error as to identity—If a party believes that he was contracting with A, and in **7.28** reality is contracting with B, he has given no consent and incurred no obligation, provided that, in the circumstances, the identity of the other party was material. So where A, pretending to be the son and agent of a well-known farmer, induced a dealer to sell him on credit and deliver two cows, and at once resold them, it was held that the dealer might recover them from the purchaser. He had not merely been induced to sell by A's fraud (which would only have rendered the sale void-able in a question with A); he had never intended to contract with A at all. The sale was not merely voidable, but void.[155] So, again, where a party obtained a consign-ment of goods by pretending in correspondence to be a well-known retail dealer, it was held that the contract was void and the rogue obtained no title, so that the firm which had sent the goods could recover them from parties to whom they had been resold.[156] The same conclusion has been reached by the House of Lords in a modern English case, recognising the importance of the matter in a world where "identity theft" is common in transactions conducted electronically.[157] However, where both parties to the purported agreement were present at its making, the courts have tended to hold that the contract was intended to be made with the person who was present and not with the person whose identity he had falsely assumed.[158] Error as to identity is not limited to the case where one person is mistaken for another.[159]

Error as to subject-matter—Where certain barrels, some containing tow, others **7.29** hemp, were put up for auction merely by their numbers, it was decided that a party who bid for a barrel of tow under the impression that it was a barrel of hemp had come under no obligation. His bid was read not as a bid for a particular barrel, but for a barrel of hemp; it was accepted as a bid for a barrel of tow.[160] But such cases

---

[152] *Carlisle Banking Co v Bragg* [1911] 1 K.B. 489; *Foster v Mackinnon* (1869) L.R. 4 C.P. 704; *Buchanan v Duke of Hamilton* (1878) 5 R. (HL) 69.

[153] *Howatson v Webb* [1908] 1 Ch. 1. And see opinion of Lord Sands in *Fletcher v Lord Advocate*, 1923 S.C. 27.

[154] *Selkirk v Ferguson*, 1908 S.C. 26; *Ellis v Lochgelly Iron Co*, 1909 S.C. 1278; *Hogg v Campbell* (1864) 2 M. 846.

[155] *Morrisson v Robertson*, 1908 S.C. 332. This decision is discussed in *MacLeod v Kerr*, 1965 S.C. 253; see also T.B. Smith, "Error and transfer of title" (1967) 12 J.L.S.S. 206, 346.

[156] *Cundy v Lindsay* (1878) 3 App. Cas. 459. On the property aspects of this case and those cited in the next note, the approach of Scots law is different: see paras 7.02 and 7.05, above.

[157] *Shogun v Hudson* [2004] 1 A.C. 919. See also *Lake v Simmons* [1927] A.C. 487 and *Ingram v Little* [1961] 1 Q.B. 31.

[158] *MacLeod v Kerr*, 1965 S.C. 253; *Phillips v Brooks* [1919] 2 K.B. 243; *Lewis v Averay (No.1)* [1972] 1 Q.B. 196.

[159] *Harrison v Butters*, 1969 S.L.T. 183.

[160] *Scriven v Hindley* [1913] 3 K.B. 564.

are very exceptional; as a general rule if a party offers to sell goods of a particular description, and does so in words which, reasonably construed, have only one meaning, he is bound to fulfil his contract, though he may have mistakenly thought that the goods which he tenders were of the description which he has undertaken to supply.[161]

7.30 Error as to price—The mere fact that the contract does not settle the consideration to be paid does not raise a case of error. If no acts have followed it would generally be regarded as a case where negotiations had not reached the stage of contract[162]; if it has been carried into effect the court will fix a reasonable consideration.[163] In *Sword v Sinclair*,[164] the seller's agent mistakenly offered to sell tea at 2s. 8d. per pound instead of 3s. 8d. per pound as his principal had instructed; it was held that the principal was not bound but no reason is given for the decision. Perusal of the Session Papers in the case suggests that the case was argued on the basis of error as to price and that, like *Steuart's Trustees v Hart*,[165] it was decided on the basis that the buyer knew and took advantage of the agent's error.[166] *Steuart's Trustees* itself was decided on the basis that there was an error as to price by the seller. The seller had sold to the buyer to hold a *me vel de me*, with a view to relieving himself of the burden of the feu duty which so long as the buyer held of the seller would be payable by the former to the latter. As Lord Shand remarked, in these circumstances, "feu duty is really price",[167] while Lord Deas said:

> "It is clear that that price was fixed upon the footing that the property was burdened with a feu duty of £9.15s. If that had not been so understood, the price would have been at least double."[168]

In *Wilson v Marquis of Breadalbane*,[169] although on the basis of what was said the parties appeared to have agreed on the price of stots, it was held in the Inner House that, as one believed that the price had been fixed and the other party thought that it was still to be fixed according to the quality of the cattle delivered, there was no consensus in idem and therefore no contract. This decision is difficult to reconcile with principle.[170] Where a contractor made an error in his private calculations and submitted a tender which was lower than it should have been he was held bound when the tender was accepted.[171] On the other hand, where the contract is to be by schedule rates and the miscalculation is obvious on the face of the offer, the parties will be taken to have contracted on the basis of the correctly calculated sum.[172]

---

[161] Sale of Goods Act 1979 s.13; *Wallis v Pratt* [1911] A.C. 394.

[162] *Macarthur v Lawson* (1877) 4 R. 1134; *Hillas v Arcos* (1931) 36 Com. Cas. 353; *Foley v Classique Coaches* [1934] 2 K.B. 1.

[163] Sale of Goods Act 1979 s.8(2). "Where the price is not determined . . . the buyer must pay a reasonable price": *Glen v Roy* (1882) 10 R. 239 (rent).

[164] *Sword v Sinclair* (1771) Mor. 14241.

[165] Above, para.7.25.

[166] See W.W. McBryde, "A Note on Sword v Sinclair and the Law of Error", 1997 Jur. Rev. 281.

[167] *Steuart's Trs v Hart* (1875) 3. R. 192 at 197.

[168] *Steuart's Trs v Hart* (1875) 3. R. 192, at 200. The mechanism of a transfer *a me vel de me* is explained in the opinion of Lord President Inglis at 199.

[169] *Wilson v Marquis of Breadalbane* (1859) 21 D. 957.

[170] W.A. Wilson, "The Importance of Analysis" in D. Carey Miller and D.W. Meyers (eds), *Comparative and Historical Essays in Scots Law* (Edinburgh: Butterworths, 1992), pp.163–164.

[171] *Seaton Brick Co v Mitchell* (1900) 2 F. 550. See also *Steel's Trs v Bradley Homes (Scotland) Ltd*, 1972 S.C. 48.

[172] *Jamieson v McInnes* (1887) 15 R. 17; *Wilkie v Hamilton Lodging House Co* (1902) 4 F. 951.

Error as to quality of subject-matter—In general, an error as to the qualities of the   **7.31**
contract's subject-matter does not affect the validity of the contract, and can only
give rise to liability if there is a warranty of the quality or it has been the subject of
a misrepresentation. But there may be extreme cases when, though parties are agreed
as to the particular subject-matter, the contract is void because one of the parties
supposed it to be possessed of qualities it in fact did not possess, provided that the
difference between the thing as the party supposed it to be and the thing as it actually
was amounted to a difference in kind.[173] An example may be *Earl of Wemyss v
Campbell*,[174] in which a lease of what was described as a deer forest was found void
because stags were never to be found there during the stalking season. But an error
about the value of land sold is not an essential error as to its quality.[175]

Error in motive—Certain forms of error only affect the motive of the party who   **7.32**
gives it, and clearly do not preclude consent. Such cases are referred to in Bell's
Principles as cases of error concomitans, as opposed to error in substantials.
Under this head fall errors as to extraneous facts and circumstances, which may
lead a party mistakenly to suppose a contract advantageous. Such errors generally
leave the contract unaffected and have no legal result, unless the error was induced
by misrepresentation[176] or the obligation was gratuitous,[177] in which case the
contract is voidable. So the guarantor of a bank account may be able to say that he
would not have given his guarantee had he known the true state of the account,
yet, in the absence of any misrepresentation by the bank, he will be liable.[178]
A case equally clear is an error as to the quality of the thing to which the contract
relates; there is no doubt that when a person buys or hires a specific thing, the
contract is not affected by that person's error as to its value or suitability. Again, a
contract is not rendered voidable by the fact that one of the parties mistook its
legal result, or the obligations which it imposed; as already explained, these are
matters for the court to determine.[179]

Induced error: Misrepresentation—A statement honestly believed may never-   **7.33**
theless, if untrue, mislead the party to whom it is made, and induce him to contract
under what is known as induced error.[180] This will render the contract voidable.[181]
Such errors are also sometimes known as essential errors following a dictum of
Lord Watson: "Error becomes essential whenever it is shown that but for it one of
the parties would have declined to contract."[182] This is probably a general rule,
though one case suggests that it is stated too broadly, and that there may be
misrepresentations regarding collateral matters which, though in fact they induced

---

[173] Gloag, *Law of Contract* (1929), p.447.
[174] *Wemyss v Campbell* (1858) 20 D. 1090.
[175] *Woods v Tulloch* (1893) 20 R. 477.
[176] para.7.33, below.
[177] *Hunter v Bradford Property Trust Ltd*, 1970 S.L.T. 173; *Security Pacific Finance Ltd v T & I Filshie's Trustee*, 1994 S.C.L.R. 1100, affd 1995 S.C.L.R. 1171.
[178] *Royal Bank of Scotland v Greenshields*, 1914 S.C. 259. See also *Welsh v Cousin* (1899) 2 F. 277; *Hogg v Campbell* (1864) 2 M. 848.
[179] para.7.03, above; *Stewart v Kennedy* (1890) 17 R. (HL) 25; see also *Manclark v Thomson's Trs*, 1958 S.C. 147.
[180] For a comment on the use of this terminology, see Smith, *A Short Commentary on the Law of Scotland* (1962), pp.809, 811.
[181] *Stewart v Kennedy* (1890) 17 R. (HL) 25. As to the conditions for avoidance, see above, paras 7.03 et seq.
[182] per Lord Watson, *Menzies v Menzies* (1893) 20 R. (HL) 108 at 142.

the contract, are not sufficiently material, in the absence of fraud, to render it voidable.[183] On this theory such misrepresentations are spoken of as inducing, not essential error, but error *dans causam contractui*. But other authorities hold that a contract is voidable if it has been induced by any misrepresentation, giving more weight to the consideration that a man has no right to profit by a misrepresentation he has made, no matter how innocently, and would do so if he were allowed to retain the contract thereby induced.[184]

7.34 Misrepresentations and expressions of opinion—A misrepresentation must relate to a matter of fact to be relevant. A statement may be construed neither as a representation nor as a warranty, but as an expression of the speaker's opinion or of his intentions for the future. While it is fraudulent to induce a contract by expressing an opinion or an intention which is not formed,[185] an honest statement of opinion, though unfounded, leaves the contract unaffected, and a person who states his intention does not represent that he will not change his mind.[186] While it must always be a question of construction whether a man has confined himself to stating his opinion, or has made a definite assertion, the former interpretation will generally be accepted in cases where in ordinary business the other party would make independent inquiries, e.g. a statement as to the capacity of a farm to carry a certain head of stock.[187] A statement made in the course of business and in a context in which it is reasonable to rely on it without seeking independent advice, may be treated as a misrepresentation.[188] Where an airline had a policy of overbooking flights and wrote to a customer "confirming" a reservation, this was treated as a statement of fact and not of intention.[189] While a misrepresentation as to the legal effect of a contract will render it voidable,[190] it is probable that a statement as to a general principle of law would be regarded merely as an expression of opinion.[191]

7.35 Liability for misrepresentation apart from fraud: Remedy for negligent misrepresentation—The misrepresentation inducing a contract may be made either by some third party who does not stand in a contractual relationship with the party deceived, or by one of the contracting parties. In the former case, a remedy in damages and based in delict lies against the third party.[192] But prior to the coming into force of the Law Reform (Miscellaneous Provisions) (Scotland) Act 1985, damages could not be claimed where the misrepresentor was the other party to the contract and the misrepresentation was negligent rather than fraudulent.[193] Such a claim is now competent under s.10(1) of the 1985 Act which states:

---

[183] *Woods v Tulloch* (1893) 20 R. 477; and see Erskine, III, 1, 16; *Edgar v Hector*, 1912 S.C. 348; and *Ritchie v Glass*, 1936 S.L.T. 591.

[184] *Stewart v Kennedy* (1890) 17 R. (HL) 25; *Mair v Rio Grande Rubber Co*, 1913 S.C. (HL) 74; *Westville Shipping Co v Abram S.S. Co*, 1922 S.C. 571, opinion of Lord President Clyde (affd 1923 S.C. (HL) 68).

[185] *Edgington v Fitzmaurice* (1885) 29 Ch.D. 459.

[186] Above, para.3.06(2).

[187] *Hamilton v Duke of Montrose* (1906) 8 F. 1026.

[188] *Esso Petroleum Co v Mardon* [1976] Q.B. 801.

[189] *British Airways Board v Taylor* [1976] 1 All E.R. 65, HL; the statement being false, there was a successful prosecution under the Trade Descriptions Act 1968.

[190] *Stewart v Kennedy* (1890) 17 R. (HL) 25.

[191] See *Brownlie v Miller* (1880) 7 R. (HL) 66.

[192] On the basis of *Hedley Byrne & Co v Heller & Partners* [1964] A.C. 465. The *Hedley Byrne* principle is endorsed in *Kenway Ltd v Orcantic Ltd*, 1979 S.C. 422. See para.26.08, below.

[193] *Manners v Whitehead* (1898) 1 F. 171 (followed in *Foster v Craigmillar Laundry Ltd*, 1980 S.L.T. (Sh. Ct) 100).

"A party to a contract who has been induced to enter into it by negligent misrepresentation made by or on behalf of another party to the contract shall not be disentitled, by reason only that the misrepresentation is not fraudulent, from recovering damages from the other party in respect of any loss or damage he has suffered as a result of the misrepresentation; and any rule of law that such damages cannot be recovered unless fraud is proved shall cease to have effect."

This provision merely alters the law as declared in *Manners v Whitehead*[194] and permits the courts to award damages in respect of negligent misrepresentation as has been possible in England since at least 1967.[195] The pursuer will still have to show that (a) the misrepresentor owed him a duty of care, and (b) that the misrepresentation caused him to contract.[196] It has been decided that, under English law, failure to take an opportunity to check up on a representation is no bar to a claim for damages provided that, in the circumstances, it was not reasonable to expect this.[197]

Representations and contractual terms—It may often be difficult to determine **7.36** whether a particular statement is to be regarded as a term of the contract, or merely as a representation. Thus the statement by a party selling an engine that it will develop a certain horse-power, may be regarded as a representation to that effect, or as a guarantee of the engine's power.[198] If it is read as a representation, the only legal result (apart from allegations of fraud or negligence) of its untruth is to render the contract voidable, and then only if the statement was material, so that the purchaser would not have given the price he did had he known the true facts. If, on the other hand, the statement is read as a guarantee, the party who gives it is liable in damages for breach of contract if it is not fulfilled, and the terms of the contract may be such as to render it voidable even if the point guaranteed was not material. The latter question has been illustrated chiefly in cases relating to policies of insurance. These are commonly preceded by a proposal form, in which certain questions are answered by the insured. If it is expressly agreed that the validity of the policy is conditional on the truth of the answers in the proposal form, the policy will be avoided even if it may appear that the particular answer proved to be untrue related to a point which was not material.[199] In a case where there was no express provision that the validity of the policy should depend upon the accuracy of the answers in the proposal form, but it was provided in the policy that the proposal form should be the "basis of the contract", the House of Lords, by a narrow majority, held that the insured warranted the statements in the proposal form, and therefore that the policy was avoided by the inaccuracy of a statement therein, even though it was not material and did not affect the amount of the premium charged.[200] Such a conclusion, however, will not be reached if there is any ambiguity in the terms of the policy.[201]

---

[194] Above, para.7.14.

[195] See *Howard Marine and Dredging Co Ltd v A. Ogden & Sons (Excavations) Ltd* [1978] Q.B. 574 and other decisions on the Misrepresentation Act 1967.

[196] See, e.g. *Hamilton v Allied Domecq Plc*, 2001 S.C. 829, criticised by J.M. Thomson, "Misrepresentation", 2001 S.L.T. (News) 279. For the final disposal of this case by the House of Lords, see *Hamilton v Allied Domecq Plc*, 2007 S.C. (HL) 142.

[197] *Smith v Eric S. Bush* [1990] 1 A.C. 831.

[198] *Robey v Stein* (1900) 3 F. 276.

[199] *Standard Life Assurance Co v Weems* (1884) 11 R. (HL) 46.

[200] *Dawsons Ltd v Bonnin*, 1922 S.C. (HL) 156; *McPhee v Royal Insurance Co Ltd*, 1979 S.C. 304.

[201] *Provincial Insurance Co v Morgan* [1933] A.C. 240.

7.37 Representation or warranty—There are no *voces signatae* by which to distinguish between a representation and a contractual warranty. The latter is clearly excluded by an express provision that the statement in question is not guaranteed. And statements which do not relate to the res about which the parties are contracting, but to collateral matters which may affect motive, are merely representations. In the case of statements which do relate to the res, it is always a question of intention whether they are to be regarded as representations or as contractual warranties.[202] It is merely an element in the question that one party had full means of information and the other had not.[203] The fact that the statement in question was made verbally in relation to a contract in writing does not necessarily preclude the conclusion that it was intended as a warranty. So a verbal assurance that the drains of a house were in good order, a point on which the lease was silent, was held to be a warranty, breach of which subjected the landlord to damages.[204]

7.38 Title to sue on misrepresentation—A misrepresentation, whether innocent, negligent or fraudulent, affords no right of action except to the person or persons to whom, expressly or impliedly, it was addressed. Thus when A fraudulently induced B to accept a transfer of shares in a company it was held that the liquidator of the company had no title to reduce the contract, in order to place A on the list of contributories.[205] If the seller of an article, by fraudulent devices, obtains more than the proper price, a sub-purchaser, though he may be the actual loser, has no title to reduce the sale.[206] Anyone who acquires securities, whether from the company or on the market, has a right to compensation from those responsible for the listing particulars or prospectus, should he suffer loss as a consequence of any untrue or misleading statement therein or omission therefrom.[207] Misleading or false statements in other documents, such as rights circulars, may ground an action at common law.[208] If the speaker, as a reasonable man, must be aware that others than the party he addresses will act on his statement, he will be liable to them. So a banker, answering queries from another banker as to a customer's financial standing, must be aware that customers of the latter bank may be interested and will be liable to them if his statements are fraudulent.[209]

FURTHER READING

McBryde, W.W., *The Law of Contract in Scotland*, 3rd edn (Edinburgh: W. Green, 2007), Chs 13–17.

McBryde, W.W., "Error", in Reid, K.G.C. and Zimmermann, R. (eds), *A History of Private Law in Scotland* (Oxford: Oxford University Press, 2000), Vol.2.

MacQueen, H.L. and Thomson, J.M., *Contract Law in Scotland*, 3rd edn (Edinburgh: Bloomsbury Professional, 2012), Ch.4.

---

[202] *Hyslop v Shirlaw* (1905) 7 F. 875 at 881.
[203] *Heilbutt v Buckleton* [1913] A.C. 30.
[204] *De Lassalle v Guildford* [1901] 2 K.B. 215. See also *Renison v Bryce* (1898) 25 R. 521.
[205] *McLintock v Campbell*, 1916 S.C. 966.
[206] *Edinburgh United Breweries Co v Molleson* (1894) 21 R. (HL) 6.
[207] Financial Services and Markets Act 2000 ss.86, 90.
[208] *Peek v Gurney* (1873) L.R. 6 H.L. 377; *Al Nakib Investments v Longcroft* [1990] 1 W.L.R. 1390.
[209] *Robinson v National Bank of Scotland*, 1916 S.C. (HL) 154. See also *Fortune v Young*, 1918 S.C. 1.

du Plessis, J.E., *Compulsion and Restitution* (Edinburgh: Stair Society, 2004), Vol.51.

du Plessis, J.E., "Threats and Excessive Benefits or Unfair Advantage" in MacQueen, H.L. and Zimmermann, R. (eds), *European Contract Law: Scots and South African Perspectives* (Edinburgh: Edinburgh University Press, 2006).

du Plessis, J.E. and McBryde, W.W., "Defects of Consent" in Zimmermann, R., Visser, D. and Reid, K.G.C. (eds), *Mixed Legal Systems in Comparative Perspective: Property and Obligations in Scotland and South Africa* (Oxford: Oxford University Press, 2004).

Scottish Law Commission, *Defective Consent and Consequential Matters* (1978), Memorandum No.42.

Scottish Law Commission, *Obligations: Report on Negligent Misrepresentation* (HMSO, 1985), Scot. Law Com. No.92.

Scottish Law Commission, *Obligations: Report on Rectification of Contractual and Other Documents* (HMSO, 1983), Scot. Law Com. No.79.

Stair Memorial Encyclopaedia, Vol.11 ("Fraud"); Vol.15, paras 670–95.

Walker, D.M., *The Law of Contracts and Related Obligations in Scotland*, 3rd edn (Edinburgh, 1995), Chs 14–15.

CHAPTER 8

THIRD PARTY RIGHTS

Third party rights—Scots law recognises the principle of privity of contract. In **8.01** the ordinary case the only persons whose rights and liabilities are affected by a contract are the contracting parties. Strangers to the contract have no right to sue upon it and incur no liabilities under it. But this statement is subject to very wide exceptions. There are cases where others than the contracting parties have a right to sue, and cases also where others may incur liabilities. One important case, contracts by agents, may be reserved for another chapter.[1] In the present chapter we proceed to consider: (1) the possible rights and liabilities of third parties at the time when the contract was made; (2) the cases in which rights or liabilities may subsequently be transmitted or assigned.

Contract imposes no liability on third parties—A contract cannot impose **8.02** any contractual liability on a third party. Contractual liability depends on consent, and the third party has given no consent. A and B, in contracting, cannot impose any liability on C, unless C has in some way authorised them to do so.[2] There is more complexity in the question whether a third party may acquire a title to sue.

Laws of *jus tertii* —The primary rule is that the contracting parties alone have a **8.03** title to enforce a contract and that the mere fact that a third party may have an interest does not give him a title. An obligation imposed by a contract is *jus tertii* to third parties, and they have no right to enforce it.

This has been illustrated in various circumstances. A creditor has no title to sue his debtor's debtor. A, incurring a debt to B, is under no liability to B's creditor, unless the debt has been assigned.[3] And the mere fact that A has undertaken to B to pay B's creditors will not give them any direct right of action against him. Thus, where a company took over a trader's business and agreed with him to pay all the outstanding debts, it was held that an individual creditor of the trader acquired no title to sue the company.[4] When a manufacturer attempted to recover charges made by a railway company on the ground that they exceeded the rates fixed in a contract between that railway and another, it was decided that because the contract was made between the two railways for their own purposes, it conferred no rights upon anyone else.[5] Where it was the rule of a police force that no constable should sue any member of the staff without the consent of the chief constable, it was held that the rule was *jus tertii* to a police surgeon, and that he could not plead it in bar

---

[1] Ch.18, below.
[2] See, e.g. *Osborne v BBC*, 2000 S.L.T. 150.
[3] *Henderson v Robb* (1889) 16 R. 341.
[4] *Henderson v Stubbs Ltd* (1894) 22 R. 51.
[5] *Finnie v Glasgow and S.W. Ry* (1857) 3 Macq. 75.

of an action by a constable.[6] The fact that a particular enterprise by a firm is prohibited by the terms of the partnership deed, or, in the case of a company, is ultra vires, gives no right of interdict to a third party whose interests may be affected.[7] The tenants of a vassal under a feu have, in the absence of a *jus quaesitum tertio* in their favour, no title to sue the vassal's superior for the determination or enforcement of the rights and conditions contained in the vassal's grant from the superior.[8] In certain circumstances a third party's title, initially good, may lapse during the continuance of an action, with the result that he is no longer entitled to the remedy which he seeks.[9]

8.04 *Jus quaesitum tertio*—The rule that the contracting parties alone have the right to enforce their contract suffers exception in cases where it is shown that their object or intention was to advance the interests of a third party. That may create a *jus quaesitum tertio*, which will give the third party, or tertius, a title to sue.[10] In order to make this possible the tertius, or a particular class of which he is a member, must be named or referred to in the contract. A contract intended to confer advantages on the general public would not confer a title on anyone who chose to sue upon it.[11]

8.05 Where express title given to tertius—Whether there is a *jus quaesitum tertio* or not is a question of the intention of the contracting parties, which means not only that the party creditor in the contract should have intended to confer a benefit on the tertius, but also that the debtor should have intended to subject himself to liability to him. That intention may be shown by an express provision in the contract that liability to a tertius is undertaken.[12] So, where money is lodged on deposit receipt, payable to a third party, that third party, though a stranger to the contract, may demand payment from the bank.[13] And there would seem to be no rule of law which would deny effect to a provision in any contract whereby it is provided that a third party may sue upon it, even in cases where that third party has no personal interest involved.[14]

8.06 Where sole interest in tertius—Without any express provision, a *jus quaesitum tertio* may be inferred in cases where the only party who has any substantial interest in the fulfilment of the contract is a tertius. Thus, a promise to give a subscription to a charitable society may be enforced by the society, though not made to the society itself nor to anyone acting as agent for it.[15] Where the rules of a trade union provided benefits to the dependants of a member who had become insane, it was held that a *jus quaesitum* was conferred.[16] But where one of the

---

[6] *A. v B.*, 1907 S.C. 1154.

[7] *D & J Nicol v Dundee Harbour Trs*, 1914 S.C. 374; 1915 S.C. (HL) 7.

[8] *Eagle Lodge v Keir & Cawdor Estates*, 1964 S.C. 13.

[9] See *Donaghy v Rollo*, 1964 S.C. 278.

[10] *Peddie v Brown* (1857) 3 Macq. 65; *Finnie v Glasgow and S.W. Ry* (1857) 3 Macq. 75.

[11] *Finnie v Glasgow and S.W. Ry* (1857) 3 Macq. 75, per Lords Cranworth and Wensleydale.

[12] *Braid Hills Hotel Co v Manuel*, 1909 S.C. 120; *Nicholson v Glasgow Blind Asylum*, 1911 S.C. 391 at 399, per Lord President Dunedin; *MacDonald v Douglas*, 1963 S.L.T. 191 at 200, per Lord Justice-Clerk Grant.

[13] *Dickson v National Bank*, 1917 S.C. (HL) 50, per Lord Dunedin.

[14] See *Pagan & Osborne v Haig*, 1910 S.C. 341.

[15] *Morton's Trs v Aged Christian Friendly Society* (1899) 2 F. 82. See also *Lamont v Burnett* (1901) 3 F. 797; *Cambuslang West Church v Bryce* (1897) 25 R. 322.

[16] *Love v Amalgamated Society of Printers*, 1912 S.C. 1078.

contracting parties has a substantial interest to enforce the contract, it is doubtful whether a *jus quaesitum tertio* can be inferred unless there is some indication, beyond the fact that the tertius has an interest, of an intention to confer a title to sue on him. His interest is otherwise only an incidental result of a contract between two parties for their own purposes, and is not enough to give him a title to sue.[17] Where, however, a bank agreed with a customer to transfer funds paid in by the customer to the customer's creditor, the bank's continuing interest, arising from the customer's general indebtedness to it, did not prevent the other creditor from having an enforceable right as a tertius against the bank.[18]

Actions of damages—There are several obiter dicta which indicate that although **8.07** a third party may sue for non-performance of the contract he cannot sue for damages for defective performance thereof.[19] There are, however, cases which suggest that a claim for damages may be competent[20] and the view has been judicially expressed that there is no reason in principle why a third party cannot sue for damages.[21] It is submitted that the better view is that damages for defective performance are competent.

***Jus quaesitum*, when irrevocable**—When A and B in contracting make C the **8.08** creditor in their contract, for instance in a bond or policy of insurance, it is clear that C has a title to sue, but it does not follow that he has a *jus quaesitum* in the money. In *Carmichael v Carmichael's Executrix*[22] it was held that where, by contract between A and B, A was taken bound to pay to C, the mere terms of the contract were not enough to vest any irrevocable right in C. If there was nothing beyond the terms of the contract, A and B were at liberty to alter their arrangement. On the other hand it was not absolutely necessary, in order to confer a jus quaesitum on C, that the document in which the contract was embodied should be delivered or formally intimated to him. It was a question of proof of the *animus donandi*, and of this the terms of the contract were important, though not conclusive, evidence. When the contract was expressed in C's favour, and he was made acquainted with the fact, the provision became irrevocable and he acquired a *jus quaesitum*.[23] This broad approach to when a contract in favour of a third party becomes irrevocable may also be seen in *Love v Amalgamated Society of Lithographic Printers*,[24] where the society operated a scheme providing benefits for the relatives of sick members but also for alteration of the rules of the scheme. When a particular relative claimed under the scheme, she was held to have a *jus*

---

[17] *Finnie v Glasgow and S.W. Ry* (1857) 3 Macq. 75.

[18] *Mercedes-Benz Finance Ltd v Clydesdale Bank Plc*, 1997 S.L.T. 905.

[19] *Robertson v Fleming* (1861) 4 Macq. 167; *Rae v Meek* (1888) 15 R. 1033; (1889) 16 R. (HL) 1; *Tully v Ingram* (1891) 19 R. 65; *Edgar v Lamont*, 1914 S.C. 277. To like effect are W.M. Gloag, *Law of Contract*, 2nd edn (Edinburgh: W. Green, 1929), p.239 and early editions of this work.

[20] *Cullen v James McMenamin Ltd*, 1928 S.L.T. (Sh. Ct) 2; *Blumer & Co v Scott & Sons* (1874) 1 R. 378.

[21] *Scott Lithgow Ltd v G.E.C. Electrical Projects Ltd*, 1989 S.C. 412. See also *Stair Memorial Encyclopaedia*, Vol.15, paras 837 and 838; W.W. McBryde, *The Law of Contract in Scotland*, 3rd edn (Edinburgh: W. Green, 2007), para.10.24.

[22] *Carmichael v Carmichael's Executrix*, 1919 S.C. 636; revd 1920 S.C. (HL) 195. See also *Drysdale's Trs v Drysdale*, 1922 S.C. 741.

[23] Gloag, *Law of Contract* (1929), p.230. See, however, *Allan's Trs v Lord Advocate*, 1971 S.C. (HL) 45, speech of Lord Reid at 54.

[24] *Love v Amalgamated Society of Lithographic Printers*, 1912 S.C. 1078.

quaesitum since the rules, although revocable, had not in fact been changed or revoked at the time the claim was made.

8.09 Title of transferees of property—In cases where no one but the parties was originally interested in the contract, third parties may acquire rights and liabilities as transferees of the subject or *res* to which the contract relates; as assignees of the contract; or as successors of the contracting parties. The law will be considered in this order.

8.10 Contracts running with lands—The cases where contractual rights and liabilities may be so attached to a particular subject that they pass with the ownership of that subject mainly relate to heritable property, and the law is commonly referred to as the law of contracts running with the lands. Much of the law on this subject was concerned with contracts between superiors and vassals, and may be regarded as obsolete since the Abolition of Feudal Tenure etc. (Scotland) Act 2000 came into force on November 28, 2004. When there is no continuing relationship such as that of superior and vassal, it is less easy to infer that contracts will run with the lands. A disponer of lands may create a servitude over other lands which he retains, and the right and burden thus created will run with the ownership of the dominant and the servient tenements.[25] But, with the doubtful exception of a clause of warrandice,[26] any personal obligation undertaken in a disposition of lands does not run with the lands so as to be enforceable by singular successors of the disponee, unless the right to enforce it is expressly assigned to them.[27] Nor will personal rights, which are valid against the disponer, be exercisable against his disponee, even if the disponee has prior knowledge of them.[28] The law on real burdens is now to be found in the Title Conditions (Scotland) Act 2003, and is considered elsewhere in this work.[29]

8.11 Landlord and tenant—Contractual rights and liabilities may run with the relationship of landlord and tenant. This will be considered in a later chapter.[30]

8.12 Contracts do not run with moveables—As a general rule, contracts do not run with moveables. The purchaser of an article acquires no title to sue on contracts which the seller may have made in relation to that article, nor is he bound by them. So the rights under a charter-party do not pass to a purchaser of the ship.[31] When a firm of engineers had failed to carry out a contract to fit engines in a ship it was held that a purchaser of the ship had no title to sue them for damages. He was not the party with whom they had contracted, and the mere purchase of the ship conferred no title to sue on contracts relating to it.[32] Similarly, a purchaser of

---

[25] See, as to servitudes, paras 34.39–34.50, below; D.J. Cusine and R.R.M. Paisley, *Servitudes and Rights of Way* (Edinburgh: W. Green, 1998).

[26] See *Christie v Cameron* (1898) 25 R. 824; but cf. K.G.C. Reid, *The Law of Property in Scotland* (Edinburgh: Butterworths, 1996), para.712.

[27] *Maitland v Horne* (1842) 1 Bell's App. 1; *Marquis of Breadalbane v Sinclair* (1846) 5 Bell's App. 353; *Speirs v Morgan* (1902) 4 F. 1068. This rule does not apply to a separate obligation expressed to be in favour of a party and his successors in a particular tenement: *Magistrates of Dunbar v Mackersy*, 1931 S.C. 180.

[28] *Morier v Brownlie & Watson* (1895) 23 R. 67; *Wallace v Simmers*, 1960 S.C. 255.

[29] paras 34.54–34.79, below.

[30] Ch.35, below.

[31] *Fratelli Sorrentino v Buerger* [1915] 3 K.B. 367.

[32] *Blumer v Scott* (1874) 1 R. 378; *Craig v Blackater*, 1923 S.C. 472.

moveables incurs no liabilities. If he is a sub-purchaser, he is not liable for the price to the original seller. At common law, if goods were sold under a condition (usually termed a price-maintenance agreement) as to the price at which they might be resold, that condition was binding only on the party who had agreed to it; it did not run with the goods so as to be binding on anyone who acquired them.[33] Whether a sub-purchaser who has notice of the price-maintenance agreement is bound by it is an unsettled question.[34]

Exceptions in shipping law—The general rule that contracts do not run with **8.13** moveables finds some exceptions in shipping law. The right to freight runs with the ownership of the ship.[35] Under the Carriage of Goods by Sea Act 1992, the lawful holder of a bill of lading, a consignee named in a sea waybill, and any person entitled to delivery of goods in terms of a ship's delivery order

> "shall . . . have transferred to and vested in him all rights of suit under the contract of carriage as if he had been a party to that contract".[36]

Title of assignees—When a contract is assigned the assignee acquires the right to **8.14** sue and in some cases may be saddled with the liabilities arising under it. An assignee may sue in his own name, or may sist himself as pursuer in an action commenced by his cedent.[37] The assignee is subject to the defences that could have been used by the debtor against the cedent[38]: but not, it seems, to the debtor's counterclaims.[39] In cases where both the contracting parties consent to the assignation there is no difficulty, but it is a question of some complexity how far one party to a contract can assign without the consent of the other.

Assignability: Where contract executed—It is an established rule that the **8.15** benefit arising under a contract is assignable, in the absence of any express provision to the contrary.[40] Therefore, if a contract is so far performed that nothing remains except to pay for what has been done, or to transfer a particular thing, the right to receive payment or the thing may be assigned. Such contracts are termed executed, as opposed to executory or executorial contracts. So a debt is assignable, if there be not provision to the contrary.[41] Where there was an agreement for

---

[33] See opinion of Lord Shaw, *National Phonograph Co v Menck* [1911] A.C. 336. In *British Motor Trade Association v Gray*, 1951 S.C. 586, the petition contained such phrases as "the vehicle concerned was subject to a covenant", but this was not the ground of the judgment. Minimum re-sale price conditions are now, in general, prohibited by virtue of the Competition Act 1998 s.2.

[34] As to the common law, see *McGruther v Pitcher* [1904] 2 Ch. 306; *Dunlop v Selfridge* [1915] A.C. 847; *McCosh v Crow* (1903) 5 F. 670; *Morton v Muir*, 1907 S.C. 1211; *Lord Strathcona Co v Dominion Coal Co* [1926] A.C. 108; *BMTA v Salvadori* [1949] Ch. 556 (liability in tort).

[35] *Stewart v Greenock Marine Insurance Co* (1848) 1 Macq. 328.

[36] Carriage of Goods by Sea Act 1992 s.2(1). This Act repeals in toto the Bills of Lading Act 1855.

[37] *Fraser v Duguid* (1838) 16 S. 1130.

[38] *Scottish Widows' Fund v Buist* (1876) 3 R. 1078; 5 R. (HL) 64.

[39] *Binstock Miller & Co v Coia & Co Ltd*, 1957 S.L.T. (Sh. Ct) 47; *Alex Lawrie Factors Ltd v Mitchell Engineering Ltd*, 2001 S.L.T. (Sh. Ct) 93 (report corrected at 2001 S.L.T. 110); *Stair Memorial Encyclopaedia*, Vol.15, para.864; McBryde, *The Law of Contract in Scotland* (2007), paras 12.71–12.73.

[40] *Aurdal v Estrella*, 1916 S.C. 882; *Whiteley v Hilt* [1918] 2 K.B. 808.

[41] Stair, III, 1, 3. As to when there is provision to the contrary, see *Linden Gardens Trust Ltd v Lenesta Sludge Disposals Ltd; St Martin's Property Corp Ltd v Sir Robert McAlpine & Sons Ltd* [1994] 1 A.C. 85, which it is thought would generally be followed in Scotland. See further, *James Scott Ltd v Apollo Engineering Ltd*, 2000 S.C. 228. On reasonableness of refusal of consent to

the sale of a ship, it was held that the party who had agreed to sell could not object to an assignation of the right to receive, although in the particular circumstances he had a defence in a question with the purchaser which was not pleadable against the assignee.[42]

8.16 *Delectus personae*—Contracts where something more than mere payment or delivery of a particular thing remains to be done are, as a general rule, not assignable if it is a matter of reasonable inference that one party entered into the contract in reliance on the qualities possessed by the other. The contract is then said to involve *delectus personae*. The most obvious case is where a party agrees to do something which involves personal skill. It is clear, as has been judicially remarked,[43] that a contract with an artist to paint a portrait cannot either be assigned as a contract, or carried out by the agency of anyone else. And the principle covers all cases of personal service.[44] The more difficult cases arise when the performance involved, such as the supply of goods by a broker, could be given by any person in the same line of business, or where the work required must necessarily be done through the instrumentality of hired labour and not by the obligant personally.[45]

It is not generally competent for a party to a contract, whatever its nature may be, to assign it so as to get rid of the liabilities he has undertaken. He may be entitled to tender performance by a third party, but will remain liable if that third party's performance be defective. So, when a page was hired in a serial circular issued by a wine-merchant, it was held that the contract could not be assigned to a company which took over the business of the wine-merchant, and which was prepared to continue the issue of the circular. The company's position was not merely that they were entitled to tender performance, but that they were entitled to come in the place of the wine-merchant so as to relieve him of all liability.[46] The general rule that the debtor under a contract cannot delegate his liabilities finds an exception in the case of contracts which run with lands, where the element of property bulks more largely than the element of contract.[47] And if the contract is of a duration so great that it cannot be supposed that continued personal performance was contemplated, it may be held that both parties must have intended to make it completely assignable. This was the conclusion arrived at in the case of a contract whereby a quarry master undertook to supply a company with all the chalk it might require. The contract was for 50 years, and it was held to be assignable to another company, although the assignee's requirements in chalk might be different from those of the cedent.[48]

---

assignation under provision requiring consent see *Ashworth Frazer Ltd v Gloucester City Council* [2001] 1 W.L.R. 2180 (HL, speech of Lord Rodger of Earlsferry) and *Burgerking Ltd v Rachel Charitable Trust*, 2006 S.L.T. 224. A requirement of reasonableness will not necessarily be implied: *Duke of Portland v Baird & Co* (1865) 4 M. 10; *Marquis of Breadalbane v Whitehead & Sons* (1893) 21 R. 138.

[42] *Aurdal v Estrella*, 1916 S.C. 882.
[43] See opinion of Lord President Dunedin, *Cole v Handasyde*, 1910 S.C. 68.
[44] *Hoey v MacEwan & Auld* (1867) 5 M. 814; *Berlitz Schools v Duchene* (1903) 6 F. 181.
[45] See, e.g. *Scottish Homes v Inverclyde D.C.*, 1997 S.L.T. 829.
[46] *Grierson, Oldham & Co v Forbes Maxwell & Co* (1895) 22 R. 812.
[47] para.8.11, above.
[48] *Tolhurst v Associated Portland Cement Co* [1903] A.C. 414. See, however, *Magistrates of Arbroath v Strachan's Trs* (1842) 4 D. 538.

Delegated performance—Though liability cannot be delegated a party may be **8.17** entitled to assign his rights under the contract, or to tender performance by a third party. There is not necessarily *delectus personae* in all contracts, merely because the particular party has been chosen for the contract. If the contract is one which involves no special skill, and does not call for performance by the obligant personally, he may get it performed by a third party, and there would then seem to be no objection to his assigning to that third party the right to sue for the price of his work. The right to delegate performance has been sustained in the case of an upholsterer employed to beat and relay a carpet[49]: of a paviour who had contracted to lay and upkeep a street[50]; and of a company which had undertaken to keep railway wagons in repair.[51] In none of these cases did it appear that the employer relied on any special skill in the party to whom he gave the order. This element was present in *Cole v Handasyde*,[52] where a broker was employed to supply black grease, and selected because he was an expert in that commodity. But it was also provided that the grease might be rejected if it failed to pass a specified test, and it was held that this provision excluded *delectus personae*, and that the contract could be enforced by a party to whom it had been assigned, although he was not possessed of the broker's expert knowledge. There is a presumption against delegation though this may be rebutted by clearly expressed language which discloses an intention to delegate.[53]

Contracts involving mutual obligations—In all these cases the contract was **8.18** reducible to an obligation to do a particular piece of work, or get it done, on the one side, and to pay for it on the other. If the contract is of a more complex character, involving further obligations on one party or other, it would seem that it is not assignable. So, where, in a contract of a year's duration for the supply of eggs, the purchaser undertook not to buy eggs from any other dealer, it was held that this provision introduced the element of *delectus personae* and that the contract could not be enforced by a successor of the purchaser in business, to whom it had been assigned.[54] And when A ordered a particular machine from B, undertaking to engage in a course of business which would involve ordering other machines, and B undertook to supply these machines at cost price, it was held that the contract, involving obligations on both sides other than supplying and paying for the initial machine, could not be enforced by a company to which B had assigned it.[55] *Delectus personae* may be involved in the fact that the party who orders goods or work is a creditor of the party to whom he gives the order, and would therefore be entitled to set off the price against his debt. The contract cannot then be assigned to a third party, so as to give him a right to fulfil the order and sue for the price.[56]

Title of representatives—On the death of one of the parties to a contract his **8.19** representatives in succession may acquire a title to sue, and, in so far as they benefit in the succession, may incur liability. Debts pass to the executor of the

---

[49] *Stevenson v Maule*, 1920 S.C. 335.
[50] *Asphaltic Limestone Concrete Co v Corp of Glasgow*, 1907 S.C. 463.
[51] *British Waggon Co v Lea* (1880) 5 Q.B.D. 148.
[52] *Cole v Handasyde*, 1910 S.C. 68.
[53] Erskine, III, 9, 22; *W.J. Harte Construction Ltd v Scottish Homes*, 1992 S.C. 98.
[54] *Kemp v Baerselman* [1906] 2 K.B. 604.
[55] *International Fibre Syndicate v Dawson* (1900) 2 F. 636; affd (1901) 3 F. (HL) 32.
[56] *Boulton v Jones* (1857) 2 H. & N. 564.

creditor, and, in the absence of any provision to the contrary, may be recovered from the whole estate of the debtor.[57] In the case of uncompleted contracts the title of representatives to sue may depend on whether the contract involved *delectus personae*. Thus, the death of either employer or employee dissolves the contract, and the relationship does not transmit to the representatives of either party.[58] But while, if it be clear that the personal qualities of an obligant are relied on, his death terminates the contract, there are cases where a contract may transmit to representatives though it would not be assignable inter vivos. Thus, the interest of a tenant in a lease passes to his heir, although from the nature or the express terms of the lease it may not be assignable without the landlord's consent.[59] And probably all commercial or engineering contracts, unless it be clear that the personal attention of the obligant was promised, pass to and are enforceable against the personal representatives of the contracting parties.[60] Thus, it was observed that, while a contract of service was ended by the death of the employer, a contract *operis faciendi*, such as a contract to build a house, would transmit to and be enforceable against the heir of the person who had ordered the work.[61]

8.20 Insolvency: Bankruptcy—A permanent trustee in sequestration may have the right to enforce contracts in which the bankrupt was engaged. He is never bound to carry out the bankrupt's contracts, and a decree *ad factum praestandum* will not be pronounced against him. He may adopt any contract made by the bankrupt before sequestration where he considers that its adoption would be beneficial to the administration of the bankrupt estate, except where adoption is precluded by the express or implied terms of the contract.[62] If he refuses to adopt a contract the remedy of the other party is to lodge a claim for damages in the sequestration.[63] The authorities are not clear on the question how far the element of *delectus personae* in a contract precludes its adoption by a trustee in sequestration, or by the liquidator of a company. The trustee cannot adopt a contract when the personal services of the bankrupt are engaged.[64] It has been decided that a contract to publish a book did not pass to the trustee in the publisher's bankruptcy.[65] On the other hand the bankrupt's interest in a lease, though it may not be assignable, will pass to his trustee in sequestration, unless there is an express provision to the contrary.[66] The case of ordinary commercial contracts was considered in *Anderson v Hamilton*.[67] The bankrupt had contracted to supply iron by instalments. The trustee intimated that he adopted the contract; the purchasers, that they regarded it as cancelled. The decision in the purchasers' favour was based on the ground that

---

[57] *Gardiner v Stewart's Trs*, 1908 S.C. 985.

[58] *Hoey v MacEwan & Auld* (1867) 5 M. 814.

[59] Bell, *Principles*, s.1219; J. Rankine, *The Law of Leases in Scotland*, 3rd edn (Edinburgh: 1916), p.157.

[60] See the distinction between assignability and transmissibility drawn by *Lord Lindley in Tolhurst v Associated Portland Cement Co* [1903] A.C. 414.

[61] per Lord President Inglis, *Hoey v MacEwan & Auld* (1867) 5 M. 814.

[62] Bankruptcy (Scotland) Act 1985 s.42(1).

[63] *Kirkland v Cadell* (1838) 16 S. 860; *Asphaltic Limestone Concrete Co v Corp of Glasgow*, 1907 S.C. 463.

[64] *Caldwell v Hamilton*, 1919 S.C. (HL) 100 at 104, per Viscount Cave.

[65] *Gibson v Carruthers* (1841) 8 M. & W. 321, opinion of Lord Abinger. See *Griffith v Tower Publishing Co* [1897] 1 Ch. 21.

[66] Stair, II, 9, 26; Bell, *Principles*, s.1216; *Dobie v Marquis of Lothian* (1864) 2 M. 788

[67] *Anderson v Hamilton* (1875) 2 R. 355.

the trustee, assuming that he had a right to adopt the contract, had not intimated his decision to do so within a reasonable time, but from the opinions given, and from a later case,[68] there can be little doubt that a contract under which the bankrupt has undertaken to deliver goods, or to execute some building or engineering work, can be adopted by the trustee in his sequestration, even although its terms might be such as to preclude voluntary assignation by the bankrupt.[69] The trustee must within 28 days of a written request from any party to a contract made by the bankrupt or within such longer period as the court may allow, adopt or refuse to adopt the contract; if he fails to reply in writing within the period allowed, he is deemed to have refused to adopt the contract.[70] Even where that procedure is not operated the trustee must intimate his intention to adopt the contract within a reasonable time or he will be taken to have abandoned it. In *Anderson v Hamilton*[71] it was held that in a contract relating to goods which fluctuate in value, each party was entitled to know at once whether the contract would be carried out, and that where the bankrupt failed on March 14, and the trustee did not intimate his decision to carry out the contract until April 8, his intimation was too late, and the other party was entitled to hold the contract as cancelled. A trustee in sequestration, if he decides to adopt a contract, cannot insist on fulfilment of the provisions in his favour unless he is prepared to implement the provisions incumbent on the bankrupt. So, where A had undertaken to erect various buildings on land feued from B, and B had agreed to allocate the feu-duty on a building which was in course of erection, it was held that A's trustee in sequestration could not require fulfilment of the obligation to allocate the feu-duty unless he was prepared to adopt and implement the contract for the erection of the other buildings.[72] But if the bankrupt has two separate contracts with the same party, the trustee is entitled to adopt one and refuse to carry out the other.[73] If a trustee adopts a contract in which the bankrupt was engaged, or continues the bankrupt's business, he incurs personal liability.[74] In the case of a lease, he renders himself personally liable for all the obligations incumbent on the tenant, including all arrears of rent.[75]

Insolvency: Liquidation—A liquidator is in the same position as a trustee in sequestration as to the adoption of contracts made by the company.[76] He must intimate his intention to adopt a contract within a reasonable time.[77] The court, on the application of any person who is entitled to the benefit or subject to the burden of a contract with the company, may make an order rescinding the contract in such terms as to payment by or to either party of damages for non-performance of the contract, or otherwise, as the court thinks just.[78] Any damages payable under the order to such a person can be proved in the liquidation.

8.21

---

[68] *Asphaltic Limestone Concrete Co v Corp of Glasgow*, 1907 S.C. 463.
[69] This is the law in England: see *Tolhurst v Associated Portland Cement Co* [1903] A.C. 414, opinion of Lord Lindley.
[70] Bankruptcy (Scotland) Act 1985 s.42(2), (3).
[71] *Anderson v Hamilton* (1875) 2 R. 355.
[72] *Mitchell's Tr. v Galloway's Trs* (1903) 5 F. 612.
[73] *Asphaltic Limestone Concrete Co v Corp of Glasgow*, 1907 S.C. 463.
[74] *Mackessack v Molleson* (1886) 13 R. 445; *Sturrock v Robertson's Trs*, 1913 S.C. 582.
[75] *Gibson v Kirkland* (1833) 6 W. & S. 340; Rankine, *The Law of Leases in Scotland* (1916), p.698.
[76] *Asphaltic Limestone Concrete Co v Glasgow Corp*, 1907 S.C. 463.
[77] *Crown Estate Commissioners v Liquidators of Highland Engineering Ltd*, 1975 S.L.T. 58.
[78] Insolvency Act 1986 (the "1986 Act") s.186. There is a doubt as to whether this section is intended to apply to Scotland.

8.22 Insolvency: Receivership—Where a receiver is appointed under a floating charge, a contract made by the company prior to his appointment continues in force (subject to its terms) but the receiver does not incur any personal liability on any such contract.[79] The receiver is personally liable on any contract entered into by him in the performance of his functions except in so far as the contract otherwise provides.[80] He is also personally liable on any contract of employment adopted by him in the carrying out of those functions, but he is not to be taken to have adopted a contract of employment by reason of anything done or omitted to be done within 14 days after his appointment.[81] Where a receiver is personally liable on a contract, he is entitled to be indemnified out of the property subject to the floating charge.[82] A contract made by a receiver continues in force even if his powers are suspended because of the appointment of a receiver under a prior floating charge.[83] The receiver is an agent of the company in relation to the property subject to the charge.[84]

An administrator appointed under Pt II of the Insolvency Act 1986 is an agent of the company.[85] The appointment does not affect prior contracts made by the company (subject to their terms). He does not incur personal liability on contracts entered into, or contracts of employment adopted, by him, but liabilities incurred under such contracts are a charge on the company's property in priority to any floating charge.[86] He is not to be taken to have adopted a contract of employment by reason of anything done, or omitted to be done, within 14 days after his appointment.[87]

FURTHER READING

Anderson, R.G., *Assignation* (Edinburgh: Avizandum, 2008).
Huntley, J. and Dedouli, A., "Third Party Rights, Promises and the Classification of Obligations", 2004 Jur. Rev. 303.
McBryde, W.W., *The Law of Contract in Scotland*, 3rd edn (Edinburgh: W. Green, 2007), Chs 10, 12.
MacQueen, H.L., "Third Party Rights in Contract: Jus Quaesitum Tertio" in Reid, K.G.C. and Zimmermann, R. (eds), *A History of Private Law in Scotland* (Oxford: Oxford University Press, 2000), Vol.2.
MacQueen, H.L. and Thomson, J.M., *Contract Law in Scotland*, 3rd edn (Bloomsbury Professional, 2012), Ch.2.
Scottish Law Commission, *Stipulations in Favour of Third Parties* (1977), Memorandum No.38.
Stair Memorial Encyclopaedia, Vol.15 (1996), paras 814–64.
Sutherland, P. and Johnston, D., "Contracts for the Benefit of Third Parties" in Zimmermann, R., Visser, D. and Reid, K.G.C. (eds), *Mixed Legal Systems in*

---

[79] 1986 Act s.57(4).
[80] 1986 Act s.57(2).
[81] 1986 Act s.57(5).
[82] 1986 Act s.57(3).
[83] 1986 Act s.57(7).
[84] 1986 Act s.57(1).
[85] 1986 Act Sch.B1 para.69 (as substituted by Enterprise Act 2002 s.248 and Sch.16).
[86] 1986 Act Sch.B1 para.99(4).
[87] 1986 Act Sch.B1 para.99(5)(a).

Comparative Perspective: Property and Obligations in South Africa (Oxford: Oxford University Press, 2004).

Sutherland, P., "Third-Party Contracts"; Lubbe, G., "Assignment" both in MacQueen, H.L. and Zimmermann, R. (eds), *European Contract Law: Scots and South African Perspectives* (Edinburgh: Edinburgh University Press, 2006).

CHAPTER 9

PACTA ILLICITA AND UNFAIR CONTRACT TERMS

Illegality—An agreement may fail in obligatory effect because it is illegal, or **9.01**
because its object was the furtherance of some illegal purpose. The main grounds
of illegality in contract may be divided into three classes: (1) when the object of
the parties was to secure a result which is either criminal or generally recognised
as immoral; (2) when the particular contract is forbidden by some positive rule,
either of common law or statute; and (3) when the particular method of contracting
is prohibited. Instances of the various forms of illegality will appear in the sequel;
for the present it may be enough to mention, in the first class, an agreement to
secure the commission of a crime[1]; in the second, an unqualified agreement not to
exercise a particular trade[2]; and in the third, a sale where the subjects sold are
estimated by other than weights and measures lawful for use for trade,[3] or a transaction requiring, yet lacking, a Government licence.[4]

Effects of illegality—To whichever class a particular contract may belong the **9.02**
contract is so far void that it cannot be directly enforced, nor can the party who
refuses to carry it out be subjected in damages. It is the duty of the court to take
notice of the illegality if it appears ex facie of the contract, although neither party
may plead it.[5]

Turpis causa—Further results depend upon the nature of the illegality. To cases **9.03**
of the first class the maxims *in turpi causa melior est conditio defendentis* (in a
claim arising out of an immoral consideration, the position of the defender is
stronger) and *ex turpi causa non oritur actio* (no right of action arises from an
immoral consideration) apply, with the result that even if the contract has been
carried out the court will take no cognisance of the relations of the parties. The
party who has happened to profit, though only by disregarding the terms to which
he has agreed, may keep what he has secured; the party on whom a loss has fallen
cannot enforce an agreement to share it. In a question between a thief and a
resetter, the law cannot interfere. So when a director and the manager of a company
entered into a contract, held to be a conspiracy to defraud the shareholders, by
which a certain sum should be voted to the manager and he should pay a bonus to
the director, the court declined to entertain an action for the bonus.[6] When a joint
adventure, definitely illegal under an Order in Council, had resulted in a loss, the

---

[1] Below, para.9.11.
[2] Below, para.9.13.
[3] *Cuthbertson v Lowes* (1870) 8 M. 1073.
[4] See *O'Toole v Whiterock Quarry Co*, 1937 S.L.T. 521.
[5] *Hamilton v McLauchlan* (1908) 16 S.L.T. 341. See *North-Western Salt Co v Electrolytic Alkali Co* [1914] A.C. 461; *Rawlings v General Trading Co* [1921] 1 K.B. 635.
[6] *Laughland v Millar* (1904) 6 F. 413; *Scott v Brown* [1892] 2 Q.B. 724.

party on whom the loss had happened to light had no right to insist that the other should pay his share.[7]

To the general rule that the court will not interfere in a case involving *turpis causa* there are certain exceptions.

9.04 Parties not *in pari delicto*—While it is no objection that the defender is pleading and taking advantage of his own illegal act, there are certain cases where the parties, though both involved in illegality, are not regarded as equally blameworthy—are not *in pari delicto*. If so, the one less blameworthy may enforce rights incidentally arising under the contract. This rule is illustrated in cases of collusive agreements in bankruptcy. While any secret payment by a bankrupt to an individual creditor is a *pactum illicitum*,[8] because the creditor who exacts and the bankrupt who may really be forced to accede are not *in pari delicto*, the trustee may recover what the bankrupt has paid, whereas the creditor cannot enforce an obligation to pay.[9]

9.05 Illegality in interests of special class—If it is held that the illegality of a contract is recognised or enacted for the benefit of a particular class, a member of that class may found upon it.[10] But this exception has very narrow limits; in general the illegality of a contract rests on the interests of the state, not of any particular class.[11]

9.06 Money demanded back before purpose effected—It has been decided in England that money paid in advance for an illegal purpose may be recovered if demanded before the illegal purpose has been carried out. So where money has been deposited with a stakeholder to await the result of an illegal bet, it may be recovered at any time before it has actually been paid to the winner.[12] On this rule there is no decision in Scotland; and the limits of the English decisions are ill-defined. It is hardly conceivable that the man who has paid in advance for the commission of a theft could in any circumstances maintain an action for the recovery of his payment.[13] In a Scottish case, A was held unable to recover from B, an official, a payment made to B to prevent withdrawal of the public-house licence of A's spouse, although the licence was nevertheless withdrawn.[14]

9.07 Illegal conditions separable—If a contract as a whole is lawful, the mere fact that one clause involves an illegality does not necessarily taint the other provisions so as to affect their enforceability. The general test is whether the pursuer can maintain his case without founding on the illegal provision.[15] Thus, while in a contract for the supply of goods a clause providing for the suspension of

---

[7] *Stewart v Gibson* (1840) 1 Robinson 260.

[8] *Farmers Mart v Milne*, 1914 S.C. (HL) 84; *Munro v Rothfield*, 1920 S.C. (HL) 165.

[9] *Macfarlane v Nicoll* (1864) 3 M. 237.

[10] *Phillips v Blackhurst*, 1912 2 S.L.T. 254.

[11] *Mahmoud v Ispahani* [1921] 2 K.B. 716.

[12] *Burge v Ashley* [1900] 1 Q.B. 744; *Hermann v Charlesworth* [1905] 2 K.B. 123.

[13] See *Berg v Sadler & Moore* [1937] 2 K.B. 158; *Bigos v Bousted* [1951] 1 All E.R. 92.

[14] *Barr v Crawford*, 1983 S.L.T. 481. See further, R. Evans-Jones, *Unjustified Enrichment* (Edinburgh: W. Green, 2003), Vol.I, Ch.5, and below, para.25.14.

[15] See opinion of Lord Dunedin, *Farmers Mart v Milne*, 1914 S.C. (HL) 84. Cf. *Fegan v Dept of Health*, 1935 S.C. 823, where, however, the dissenting judgment of Lord Fleming seems correct.

deliveries during war is contrary to public policy and illegal, the insertion of such a clause does not in any way affect the validity of the contract during peace.[16]

Contracts merely prohibited—Contracts where the illegality does not consist in **9.08** the object of the contract being to secure an illegal or immoral result, but merely in the fact that the particular contract, or method of contracting, is prohibited (i.e. cases falling within the second and third heads mentioned in para.9.01) are at one with contracts involving *turpis causa* in respect that they cannot be enforced, but differ in respect that the court will not refuse to give effect to the rights of the parties when the contract has been carried into effect. So, where there was a contract for the sale of potatoes calculated by a Scots measure (a method of contracting declared by statute to be "void and null"), and the potatoes were actually delivered, it was held that, although the contract could not be enforced in defiance of the statute, as there was "no turpitude in a man selling his potatoes by the Scots and not by the imperial acre", the buyer was bound to pay the market price[17]; but this does not hold where the contract is actually prohibited and illegal.[18] While an insurance by a party who has no insurable interest is by statute "null and void to all intents and purposes whatsoever", if the insurance company has chosen to pay, the court will decide questions between competing claimants for the money.[19]

Rights of third parties—As a general rule an illegal contract cannot be founded **9.09** on even by third parties who have no notice of the illegality. Thus, no one can acquire a title to stolen goods.[20] A bond for the price of goods which had been smuggled was held to be unenforceable even by a bona fide assignee.[21] There is statutory exception to this in the case of bills and notes granted for an illegal consideration.[22]

Statutory illegality—In endeavouring to indicate what contracts are illegal, a **9.10** distinction may be made between contracts rendered illegal by statute and contracts illegal at common law.[23] As a general rule, where a statute limits freedom of contract it does so either by declaring a particular contract or method of contracting to be void or unenforceable,[24] or by imposing a penalty on the persons who contract.[25] A contract declared by statute to be void can never be enforced, although, as has been explained, if the only objection is the statutory provision, the court will give effect to rights arising when the contract is performed.[26] If,

---

[16] *Zinc Corp v Hirsch* [1916] 1 K.B. 541. See also *Kearney v Whitehaven Colliery* [1893] 1 Q.B. 700.

[17] *Cuthbertson v Lowes* (1870) 8 M. 1073. For modern examples see *Dowling & Rutter v Abacus Frozen Foods Ltd*, 2002 S.L.T. 491, noted by J.M. Thomson, "Illegal Contracts in Scots Law", 2002 S.L.T. (News) 153; *Malik v Ali*, 2004 S.L.T. 1280.

[18] *Jamieson v Watt's Tr.*, 1950 S.C. 265. See further discussion in Evans-Jones, *Unjustified Enrichment* (2003), Ch.5, s.3.

[19] *Hadden v Bryden* (1899) 1 F. 710. The contrary has been decided in England: *Re London County Commercial Re-Insurance Co* [1922] 2 Ch. 67.

[20] Bell, *Principles*, s.527.

[21] *Nisbet's Creditors v Robertson* (1791) Mor. 9554.

[22] Bills of Exchange Act 1882 ss.30, 38.

[23] W.M. Gloag, *Law of Contract*, 2nd edn (Edinburgh: W. Green, 1929), p.549.

[24] e.g. Unfair Contract Terms Act 1977 ss.16, 19, 20, 21, 23. See also Financial Services and Markets Act 2000 ss.26–30; Equality Act 2010 Pt 10.

[25] e.g. Mock Auctions Act 1961.

[26] *Cuthbertson v Lowes* (1870) 8 M. 1073.

without declaring a contract to be void, a statute imposes a penalty on the persons who enter into it, it is always a question of the construction of the particular statute whether or not avoidance of the contract is implied.[27] It is a strong argument against avoidance in cases where the method of contracting, rather than the contract, is penalised, that the penalty may be incurred by mere inadvertence.[28] Where the penalty is imposed for failure to stamp a contract, the presumption is that the provision is merely for revenue purposes, and that the contract may be enforced.[29] Subject to these provisos, the general rule is that where a contract is subjected to a penalty, its illegality and consequent avoidance is implied,[30] except in cases where the penalty is the deprivation of an office.[31] A defender who pleads statutory illegality, e.g. in defence of an action of payment for work carried out, must, however, relevantly aver and prove that the work was done unlawfully.[32]

9.11 Illegal at common law—In contracts at common law there is a general, though not an exact, distinction between contracts objectionable on moral grounds and contracts contrary to public policy. In the former class are contracts for the commission of an act criminal at common law, involving a fraud on third parties,[33] or sexual immorality, with the exception of a provision made for a mistress after sexual intercourse has ceased.[34] The rule extends beyond contracts where the direct consideration is the commission of a criminal, fraudulent or immoral act, and reaches cases where the contract is, to the knowledge of the parties, intended to further criminality or immorality. So where a brougham was hired to a prostitute "as a part of her display, to attract men", the hire could not be recovered.[35] A similar decision was given with regard to the rent of a house occupied, to the landlord's knowledge, by persons living in immoral relations.[36] The doctrine of public policy, as a ground for the avoidance of contracts, was at one time very loosely and widely applied in the English courts, reaching perhaps its culminating point in *Egerton v Brownlow*,[37] where it was held that a bequest to a peer, dependent on his obtaining a higher rank, involved a condition contrary to public policy, as tending to induce him to misuse his position as a legislator in order to obtain the higher rank. Subsequently, on the principle that it is a cardinal object of public policy that contracts should be observed, opinions have been expressed that the objection is open only where there is a direct precedent or plain analogy.[38] The mere fact that a direct precedent is forthcoming is not conclusive. It is open to the answer that instructed opinion may have altered on the point.[39]

---

[27] *Whiteman v Sadler* [1910] A.C. 514, per Lord Dunedin.

[28] *Whiteman v Sadler* [1910] A.C. 514, per Lord Mersey.

[29] *Learoyd v Bracken* [1894] 1 Q.B. 114.

[30] *Jamieson v Watt's Tr.*, 1950 S.C. 265.

[31] *Drysdale v Nairne* (1835) 13 S. 348; *Aberdeen Ry v Blaikie* (1851) 14 D. 66, revd on other grounds (1854) 1 Macq. 461.

[32] *Designers & Decorators (Scotland) v Ellis*, 1957 S.C. (HL) 69.

[33] *Laughland v Millar* (1904) 6 F. 413.

[34] Bell, *Principles*, s.37; *Webster v Webster's Tr.* (1886) 14 R. 90.

[35] *Pearce v Brooks* (1886) L.R. 1 Ex. 213.

[36] *Upfill v Wright* [1911] I K.B. 506. But see *Heglibiston Establishments v Heyman* (1978) 36 P. & C.R. 351.

[37] *Egerton v Brownlow* (1853) 4 H.L. Cas. 1.

[38] per Lord Watson, *Nordenfelt v Maxim Nordenfelt Gun Co* [1894] A.C. 535; but see *McCaig's Trs v Kirk-Session of Lismore*, 1915 S.C. 426.

[39] *Bowman v Secular Society* [1917] A.C. 406. See further H.L. MacQueen and A. Cockrell, "Illegal Contracts", in R. Zimmermann, D. Visser and K.G.C. Reid (eds), *Mixed Legal Systems in Comparative Perspective: Property and Obligations in Scotland and South Africa* (Oxford: Oxford University Press, 2004), for comparison of Scots and South African approaches to public policy in contracts.

Illustrations of public policy—Among contracts which are illegal as contrary **9.12** to public policy are contracts interfering with the foreign policy of the state, such as a contract with an enemy state or with alien enemies.[40] On the same principle, it is clear law in England that contracts involving the violation of the laws of a friendly state are unenforceable.[41] Contracts for smuggling[42]; for interfering with the free exercise of his duties by the holder of a public office[43] or member of a representative body[44]; for the employment of private influence to secure advantages from the Government[45]; for the evasion of legislative provisions limiting or regulating the sale of certain commodities[46]; for suppression of information which might lead to a conviction of crime,[47] are all illegal as contrary to public policy.[48]

Restrictive covenants[49]—As a general rule, contracts which involve an undue **9.13** interference with personal liberty are void as being oppressive. But this rule is qualified to the extent that it may be lawful, if certain conditions are satisfied, to secure freedom from competition by contracts, usually termed restrictive covenants, by which a party undertakes not to carry on a particular trade or profession. The test which is applied to decide whether restrictive agreements of this nature can be enforced is whether the agreement is reasonable as between the parties,[50] and is consistent with the interests of the public.[51] The court has to ascertain what were the legitimate interests of the party in whose favour the restriction was imposed which he was entitled to protect and then to see whether the restriction was more than adequate for that purpose.[52] The practical effects of the restriction, rather than its form, are to be examined.[53] In all cases, it is probably necessary that there should be some limit, either in point of area or in point of time. Subject to this, where the seller of the goodwill of a business has agreed that in future he will

---

[40] See below, para.43.03.

[41] *Ralli v Compania Naviera* [1920] 2 K.B. 287; *Regazonni v K.C. Sethia (1944) Ltd* [1958] A.C. 301. On the other hand, income tax is payable on the fruits of such an adventure: see *Lindsay v Inland Revenue*, 1933 S.C. 33.

[42] Bell, *Principles*, s.42.

[43] *Henderson v Mackay* (1832) 11 S. 225.

[44] *Hoggan v Wardlaw* (1735) 1 Paton 148; *Amalgamated Society of Ry Servants v Osborne (No.1)* [1910] A.C. 87.

[45] *Stewart v Earl of Galloway* (1752) Mor. 9465; *Montefiore v Menday Motor Co* [1918] 2 K.B. 241.

[46] *Trevalion v Blanche*, 1919 S.C. 617; *Eisen v McCabe*, 1920 S.C. (HL) 146.

[47] *Howard v Odhams Press* [1938] 1 K.B. 1.

[48] See further W.W. McBryde, *The Law of Contract in Scotland*, 3rd edn (Edinburgh: W. Green, 2007), Ch.19.

[49] See generally, McBryde, *The Law of Contract in Scotland* (2007), paras 19.80–19.138.

[50] See *Nordenfelt v Maxim Nordenfelt Gun Co* [1894] A.C. 535; *Mason v Provident Clothing Co* [1913] A.C. 724; *Morris v Saxelby* [1916] 1 A.C. 688; *Fitch v Dewes* [1921] 2 A.C. 158; *Vancouver Malt and Sake Brewing Co v Vancouver Breweries Ltd* [1934] A.C. 181. See also Gloag, *Law of Contract* (1929), pp.569 et seq.

[51] *Vancouver Malt and Sake Brewing Co v Vancouver Breweries Ltd* [1934] A.C. 181 at 189, per Lord Macmillan; *George Walker & Co v Jann*, 1991 S.L.T. 771.

[52] *Bridge v Deacons* [1984] 1 A.C. 705. Cf. *Dallas McMillan & Sinclair v Simpson*, 1989 S.L.T. 454, where a 20-mile radius ban on a solicitor from acting for anyone, even persons who had never been clients of his old firm, was found to be unreasonable.

[53] *Stenhouse Australia v Phillips* [1974] A.C. 391. The cases indicate clearly that the courts do not adopt a literal approach to the interpretation of restraints. Faced with two interpretations, one extreme (and probably absurd given the context), the other normal (i.e. easily referable to the facts), the latter interpretation will be chosen: *Scottish Farmers' Dairy Co v McGhee*, 1933 S.C. 148; *Bluebell Apparel Ltd v Dickinson*, 1978 S.C. 16; *Home Counties Dairies Ltd v Skilton* [1970] 1 W.L.R. 526.

not carry on a similar business in competition with the buyer of the goodwill, the only tenable objection to the restriction is that it is wider than is required in the interests of the business it is designed to protect. Thus, while a world-wide restriction (limited as to time) was sustained in the case of a maker of cannon,[54] a restriction within the United Kingdom was held to be far too wide, and consequently unenforceable, in the case of the business of a local carrier.[55] Where the covenant is contained in a partnership agreement, the fact that it is binding on each of the partners is a factor to be taken into account in determining whether it is reasonable between the parties.[56] Where a servant or apprentice has agreed that after leaving his present employer he will not take up employment with a competitor or set up business on his own account, the limits of freedom of contract are much narrower. The result of the decisions in the House of Lords has been judicially summarised as follows:

> "While a purchaser of the goodwill of a business may properly protect himself by covenant from the competition of his vendor, it is not permissible for an employer to protect himself merely from the competition of his former servant after his service has terminated. It is permissible for the employer by covenant to protect his trade or professional secrets, and to protect himself also against his clients being enticed away by his former assistant; in other words to protect his connection."[57]

So restrictions designed to protect business contacts, where an employee acquires influence over customers (including former and possibly even future customers) have been sustained.[58] A world-wide restriction for a period of two years has been upheld.[59] Restrictions on disclosure of a secret manufacturing process, confidential information regarding customer lists, or business pricing policy may be permitted.[60] When it was proved that the object of a restriction, imposed on a film actor, was not to protect a business but to obtain a hold upon the actor by rendering it difficult for him to obtain other employment, it was held that he was entitled to disregard it.[61] A restraint which applies no matter how the contract is terminated, may be unreasonable because it applies even where the covenantee has wrongfully terminated the contract.[62]

The party who proposes to enforce a restrictive covenant must have an interest to enforce it, and cannot, therefore, do so if he has ceased to carry on, or has parted

---

[54] *Nordenfelt v Maxim Nordenfelt Gun Co* [1894] A.C. 535.

[55] *Dumbarton Steamboat Co v Macfarlane* (1899) 1 F. 993.

[56] *Bridge v Deacons* [1984] 1 A.C. 705. As to partnerships, see *Trego v Hunt* [1896] A.C. 7; *Whitehill v Bradford* [1952] 1 Ch. 236; *Anthony v Rennie*, 1981 S.L.T. (Notes) 11, OH; *Kerr v Morris* [1986] 3 All E.R. 217.

[57] *Fitch v Dewes* [1920] 2 Ch. 159, per Younger L.J. at 185; [1921] 2 A.C. 158.

[58] *Scottish Farmers' Dairy Co v McGhee*, 1933 S.C. 148; *Stenhouse Australia v Phillips* [1974] A.C. 391; *Rentokil v Kramer*, 1986 S.L.T. 114. As to former customers, see *G.W. Plowman & Son Ltd v Ash* [1964] 2 All E.R. 10. As to future customers with whom contact was established prior to departure, see *Gledhow Autoparts v Delaney* [1965] 3 All E.R. 288 and *Rentokil v Kramer*, 1986 S.L.T. 114.

[59] *Bluebell Apparel Ltd v Dickinson*, 1978 S.C. 16.

[60] *Commercial Plastics Ltd v Vincent* [1965] 1 Q.B. 623; *SOS Bureau Ltd v Payne*, 1982 S.L.T. (Sh. Ct) 33; *Faccenda Chicken Ltd v Fowler* [1987] Ch. 117. Restrictions on the disclosure of confidential information should identify what is confidential: *Malden Timber Ltd v Leitch*, 1992 S.L.T. 757.

[61] *Hepworth Manufacturing Co v Ryott* [1920] 1 Ch. 1.

[62] See, e.g. *Living Design (Home Improvements) Ltd v Davidson*, 1994 S.L.T. 753; but cf. *Rock Refrigeration Ltd v Jones* [1997] 1 All E.R. 1.

with, the business it was designed to protect.[63] He cannot enforce a restriction if he is himself in a material breach of contract, as where the servant restricted is unjustifiably dismissed.[64] A restriction imposed in a contract of service is not assignable.[65] If imposed on the seller of a business, it may be assigned with that business, unless it appears that the restriction was undertaken solely in favour of the purchaser.[66] It is not settled whether a third party has a title to maintain that a restrictive covenant is unenforceable.[67] If the restriction imposed is too wide, it falls; the court will not enforce it within narrower limits.[68] But where there are two restrictions, one reasonable, the other oppressive, the contract may be regarded as separable, and the reasonable restriction enforced.[69] The effect of a term of a contract stating that the parties agree that a restraint is reasonable is unclear. It may be that such a term should be disregarded as an attempt to oust the jurisdiction of the courts.[70] If a restraint is worded in a manner which prevents one party from setting up business on his own account, it will not apply to a rival company formed by that party and vice versa.[71]

Restraint of trade—Closely allied to the two kinds of restrictive covenant **9.14** discussed above are those agreements which restrict a person's free exercise of his trade or business. Such agreements arise where manufacturers or merchants combine to regulate their trade relations, for instance by agreeing to restrict their output or to fix the selling price of a certain commodity.[72] While it was once the rule that contracts of this nature were contrary to public policy and, therefore, *pacta illicita*,[73] they are now regarded as a necessary part of commercial life. Such agreements are, at common law, legal and enforceable unless they involve a restriction on liberty greater than is necessary for the interest they are designed to protect, or their object is to raise wages or prices.[74] Again, the test in deciding whether any particular agreement is to be upheld, is the double standard of whether the agreement is reasonable as between the parties, and whether it is

---

[63] *Berlitz Schools v Duchene* (1903) 6 F. 181.

[64] *General Billposting Co v Atkinson* [1909] A.C. 118. For doubt as to this doctrine in the light of modern developments in the law of repudiatory breach generally, see *Rock Refrigeration Ltd v Jones* [1997] 1 All E.R. 1.

[65] *Berlitz Schools v Duchene* (1903) 6 F. 181.

[66] *Rodger v Herbertson*, 1909 S.C. 256.

[67] *British Motor Trade Association v Gray*, 1951 S.C. 586.

[68] *Dumbarton Steamboat Co v Macfarlane* (1899) 1 F. 993.

[69] *Mulvein v Murray*, 1908 S.C. 528; *Attwood v Lamont* [1920] 3 K.B. 571. *Mulvein v Murray* may be contrasted with an Outer House decision, *Hinton & Higgs (U.K.) Ltd v Murphy*, 1989 S.L.T. 450. Here the contract provided that if the court considered the restrictions imposed to be unreasonable, but that they would be reasonable on deletion of some part or by reducing the period of the restraint, then the unreasonable part should be so deleted or amended. The Lord Ordinary described this as a contractual mechanism designed to operate on the occurrence of a particular event and declined to take the view that this was an attempt to have the contract rewritten by the court.

[70] *Hinton & Higgs (U.K.) Ltd v Murphy*, 1989 S.L.T. 450 at 452, per Lord Dervaird.

[71] *WAC Ltd v Whillock*, 1990 S.L.T. 213; *Taylor v Campbell*, 1926 S.L.T. 260.

[72] The categories of agreements in restraint of trade are not closed: see as to "solus agreements", *Petrofina (G.B.) v Martin* [1966] Ch. 146 at 169, per Lord Denning M.R. See also *MacIntyre v Cleveland Petroleum Co*, 1967 S.L.T. 95 (conditions contained in a back letter); *Esso Petroleum Co v Harper's Garage (Stourport)* [1968] A.C. 269; *A. Schroeder Music Publishing Co v Macaulay* [1974] 1 W.L.R. 1308 (exclusive services).

[73] *Barr v Carr* (1766) Mor. 9564; *Corp of Shoemakers v Marshall* (1798) Mor. 9573; *Hilton v Eckersley* (1855) 6 El. & Bl. 47; see dicta of Harman L.J. in *Petrofina (G.B.) v Martin* [1966] Ch. 146 at 175.

[74] *North-Western Salt Co v Electrolyte Alkali Co* [1914] A.C. 461; *English Hop Growers v Dering* [1928] 2 K.B. 174.

consistent with the public interest.[75] But in this case, where the parties themselves are regarded as being in an equal position of bargaining and the best judges of the fairness of the agreement, the court will not readily allow them to escape from their obligations by claiming that the agreement was unreasonable.[76] However, where a member of a co-operative union dedicated to a non-competitive system of trading was prohibited from trading in a certain area by a ruling of its union, it was held, on its resigning from the union, that the ruling ceased to be binding on it; it was unreasonable to suppose that on joining the union and agreeing to submit to its ruling, it intended to bind itself for all time, whether or not it continued to be a member.[77] The legality at common law of price maintenance agreements, i.e. agreements by which an agent or retailer undertakes not to sell goods below list prices, seems to be established.[78] The common law principles on this subject are now, however, relatively unimportant because of the far-reaching statutory provisions under the Competition Act 1998 and the Enterprise Act 2002. Further discussion of this complex topic is beyond the scope of this work, and guidance should be sought in more specialist texts.[79]

9.15　Gambling transactions—Until s.335 of the Gambling Act 2005 came into force on September 1, 2007, gaming contracts could not be enforced. The ground of the refusal of action was not that such contracts were illegal, but that they were *sponsiones ludicrae*, unworthy to occupy judicial time.[80] Accordingly, the courts would not sustain an action for a bet, allow proof as to the result of a race,[81] or allow an action for recovery of money paid for losses, even on averments that the play was unfair.[82] Section 335 of the Gambling Act 2005, however, provides that the fact that a contract relates to gambling shall not prevent its enforcement. This is without prejudice, however, to any rule of law preventing the enforcement of a contract on the grounds of unlawfulness (other than a rule relating specifically to gambling). Gambling continues to be unlawful in the United Kingdom unless permitted under the Act, or if it is pursuant to the Financial Services and Markets Act 2000.[83] But the policy of the 2005 Act is to liberalise the market for the provision of gambling services and facilities, subject to regulation by the Gambling Commission and a new licensing regime administered by either the Commission or by licensing authorities specified under the Act. The Gambling Act also repeals a number of Acts the effect of which was to invalidate gaming transactions: the only one of these possibly applicable in Scotland was the Gaming Act 1835.[84]

---

[75] *McEllistrim v Ballymacelligott Cooperative Agricultural & Dairy Society* [1919] A.C. 548 at 562, per Lord Chancellor Birkenhead.

[76] *English Hop Growers v Dering* [1928] 2 K.B. 174 at 180, per Scrutton L.J.

[77] *Bellshill & Mossend Cooperative Society v Dalziel Cooperative Society*, 1960 S.C. (HL) 64.

[78] *Dunlop Pneumatic Tyre Co v New Garage Co* [1915] A.C. 79; *Palmolive Co v Freedman* [1928] 1 Ch. 264.

[79] e.g. R. Whish, *Competition Law*, 6th edn (London: LexisNexis, 2008) (7th edn forthcoming 2012); *Stair Memorial Encyclopaedia*, Reissue, "Competition Law" and updates.

[80] *Wordsworth v Pettigrew* (1799) M. 9524; *Knight v Stott* (1892) 19 R. 959. The Betting, Gaming and Lotteries Act 1963 did not affect this principle: *Johnston v T.W. Archibald*, 1966 S.L.T. (Sh. Ct) 8.

[81] *O'Connell v Russell* (1864) 3 Mor. 89; *Kelly v Murphy*, 1940 S.C. 96 (football pool).

[82] *Paterson v Macqueen* (1866) 4 M. 602.

[83] Financial Services and Markets Act 2000 s.412. See *City Index Ltd v Leslie* [1991] 3 All E.R. 180.

[84] See previous editions of this work for the possible effect of the Act in Scotland; for doubt on the subject, see McBryde, *The Law of Contract in Scotland* (2007), para.19.60. The repeal is not retrospective in effect (s.334(2)).

Cases not covered by the *sponsiones ludicrae* doctrine—Even before the   **9.16**
Gambling Act 2005, the courts had come to treat the doctrine of *sponsiones ludi-crae* quite narrowly. If the result of a race or other contest was admitted, the stakeholder had to pay the winner,[85] and the court would entertain the question of who, according to the rules of the particular sport, is entitled to receive the prize.[86] A person employed to make bets, as he is not gambling but acting as an agent, might recover payments made on behalf of his principal.[87] The rights of parties under a joint adventure for gaming purposes could be judicially considered.[88] It was held in the Outer House that money lent to pay gambling losses could be recovered.[89]

Unfair terms[90]—The Unfair Contract Terms Act 1977 renders ineffectual some   **9.17**
types of contractual terms excluding or restricting liability for breach of contract; in some cases the Act makes the term void; in other cases, the term has no effect if it was not fair and reasonable to incorporate it in the contract. It is not possible to evade the effect of the Act by means of a secondary contract[91] or by a term applying, or purporting to apply, a foreign law to the contract.[92] The following are regarded as forms of exclusion or restriction[93]: (a) making the liability or its enforcement subject to any restrictive or onerous conditions; (b) excluding or restricting any right or remedy in respect of the liability, or subjecting a person to any prejudice in consequence of his pursuing any such right or remedy; (c) excluding or restricting any rule of evidence or procedure; (d) excluding or restricting an obligation or duty implied by law.[94] The Act has been extended to apply to non-contractual disclaimers.[95] An agreement to submit any question to arbitration is not an exclusion or restriction. The Act does not apply to international contracts for the supply of goods.[96] The Act does not affect a contractual provision which is authorised or required by the express terms or necessary implication of an enactment or which, being made with a view to compliance with an international agreement to which the United Kingdom is a party, does not operate more restrictively than is contemplated by the agreement.[97]

---

[85] *Calder v Stevens* (1871) 9 M. 1074. The promoter of a "football pool" is not a stakeholder: *Wilson v Murphy*, 1936 S.L.T. 564; *Kelly v Murphy*, 1940 S.C. 96; *Ferguson v Littlewoods Pools Ltd*, 1997 S.L.T. 309.

[86] *Graham v Pollok* (1848) 10 D. 646, 11 D. 343.

[87] *Levy v Jackson* (1903) 5 F. 1170.

[88] *Mollison v Noltie* (1889) 16 R. 350; *Forsyth v Czartowski*, 1961 S.L.T. (Sh. Ct) 22; *Robertson v Anderson*, 2003 S.L.T. 235.

[89] *Hopkins v Baird*, 1920 2 S.L.T. 94. Not, on English authority, if the particular form of gaming is a criminal offence: *Moulis v Owen* [1907] 1 K.B. 746. See, as to a cheque given in payment for chips in a gambling club, *Cumming v Mackie*, 1973 S.C. 278.

[90] McBryde, *The Law of Contract in Scotland* (2007), Ch.18.

[91] Unfair Contract Terms Act 1977 s.23. See *Chapman v Aberdeen Construction Group Ltd*, 1993 S.L.T. 1205, dealing with a term in a share option contract which purported to exclude rights under an employment contract.

[92] Unfair Contract Terms Act 1977 s.27(2).

[93] Unfair Contract Terms Act 1977 s.25(3).

[94] Unfair Contract Terms Act 1977 s.25(5).

[95] Law Reform (Miscellaneous Provisions) (Scotland) Act 1990 s.68, amending Unfair Contract Terms Act 1977 s.16(1). The amendment came into force on April 1, 1991: see Law Reform (Miscellaneous Provisions) (Scotland) Act 1990 (Commencement No.3) Order 1991 (SI 1991/330).

[96] Unfair Contract Terms Act 1977 s.26.

[97] Unfair Contract Terms Act 1977 s.29(1).

9.18 Contracts affected—The Act applies to any contract to the extent that it:

> (a) relates to the transfer of the ownership or possession of the goods from one person to another (with or without work having been done on them);
>
> (b) constitutes a contract of service or apprenticeship;
>
> (c) relates to services of whatever kind, including (without prejudice to the foregoing generality) carriage, deposit and pledge, care and custody, mandate, agency, loan and services relating to the use of land;
>
> (d) relates to the liability of an occupier of land to persons entering upon or using that land;
>
> (e) relates to a grant of any right or permission to enter upon or use land not amounting to an estate or interest in the land.[98]

Contracts of insurance and contracts relating to the formation, constitution or dissolution of any body corporate or unincorporated association or partnership are excepted.[99] The Act applies only to a limited extent to charter-parties, and contracts of salvage or towage.[100] It does not affect the validity of any discharge or indemnity given by a person in consideration of the receipt by him of compensation in settlement of any claim which he had.[101]

9.19 Breach of duty—"Breach of duty" is the breach of any obligation arising from the express or implied terms of a contract to take reasonable care or exercise reasonable skill in the performance of the contract, or the breach of any common law duty to take reasonable care or exercise reasonable skill, or the breach of the duty of reasonable care imposed by s.2(1) of the Occupiers' Liability (Scotland) Act 1960.[102] A term of a contract which purports to exclude or restrict liability for breach of duty arising in the course of any business or from the occupation of any premises used for business purposes of the occupier, is void in any case where such exclusion or restriction is in respect of death or personal injury; in any other case, the term has no effect if it was not fair and reasonable to incorporate the term in the contract.[103]

9.20 Unreasonable exemptions—The provision of the Act which has the widest effect applies to two types of terms in "consumer contracts" and "standard form contracts". Terms in such contracts have no effect for the purpose of enabling a party to the contract:

> (a) who is in breach of a contractual obligation, to exclude or restrict any liability of his to the consumer or customer in respect of the breach;
>
> (b) in respect of a contractual obligation, to render no performance, or to render a performance substantially different from that which the consumer or customer reasonably expected from the contract;

---

[98] Unfair Contract Terms Act 1977 s.15(2).
[99] Unfair Contract Terms Act 1977 s.15(3)(a).
[100] Unfair Contract Terms Act 1977 s.15(3)(b).
[101] Unfair Contract Terms Act 1977 s.15(1).
[102] Unfair Contract Terms Act 1977 s.25(1).
[103] Unfair Contract Terms Act 1977 s.16(1). The liability need not be that of a party to the contract; see *Melrose v Davidson & Robertson*, 1993 S.C. 288. See also *Langstane Housing Association Ltd v Riverside Construction (Aberdeen) Ltd* [2009] CSOH 52; 2009 S.C.L.R. 639 (clause excluding joint and several liability to the extent that it would make a party liable for more than its contribution to another's loss held not subject to s.16).

if it was not fair and reasonable to incorporate the term in the contract.[104] Where a term in a holiday booking form reserved the right to change the mode of transport, and where a coach without a toilet was substituted for one with, as promised in a holiday brochure, it was decided that the effect of this term would permit the tour operator to render performance substantially different from what a holidaymaker was reasonably entitled to expect.[105]

A "consumer contract" is a contract (not being a contract of sale by auction or competitive tender) in which (a) one party to the contract deals, and the other party to the contract ("the consumer") does not deal or hold himself out as dealing, in the course of a business, and (b) in the case of contracts relating to the transfer of the ownership or possession of goods from one person to another, the goods are of a type ordinarily supplied for private use or consumption. The onus of proving that a contract is not to be regarded as a consumer contract lies on the party so contending.[106]

"Standard form contract" is not defined[107] but light is thrown on its meaning by the definition of customer as

> "a party to a standard form contract who deals on the basis of written standard terms of business of the other party to the contract who himself deals in the course of a business."[108]

It includes any contract, whether wholly written or partly oral, which includes a set of fixed terms which the proponer applies, without material variation, to contracts of the kind in question.[109]

Unreasonable indemnity clauses—A term of a "consumer contract" has no **9.21** effect for the purpose of making the consumer indemnify another person (whether a party to the contract or not) in respect of "liability" which that other person may incur as a result of breach of duty or breach of contract, if it was not fair and reasonable to incorporate the term in the contract.[110] "Liability" means a liability arising in the course of any business or from the occupation of any premises used for business purposes of the occupier. The corresponding

---

[104] Unfair Contract Terms Act 1977 s.17(1). It would seem that the expectation can be based on something other than the terms of the contract.

[105] *Elliot v Sunshine Coast International Ltd*, 1989 G.W.D. 28–1252. See also *Macrae & Dick Ltd v Phillip*, 1982 S.L.T. (Sh. Ct) 5; *Johnstone v Bloomsbury Health Authority* [1992] Q.B. 333, and *The Zockoll Group Ltd v Mercury Communications Ltd* [1999] E.M.L.R. 385 (CA).

[106] Unfair Contract Terms Act 1977 s.25(1). A company may be a consumer under this definition: *R & B Customs Brokers Ltd v United Dominions Trust Ltd* [1988] 1 All E.R. 847. A director's employment contract has been regarded as a consumer contract: *Chapman v Aberdeen Construction Group Ltd*, 1993 S.L.T. 1205. Note also s.15(2)(b). Cf. in *England Keen v Commerzbank AG* [2007] I.R.L.R. 132 (CA) but note the slightly different statutory background in Pt I of the 1977 Act.

[107] See *McCrone v Boots Farm Sales Ltd*, 1981 S.C. 68; *Border Harvesters Ltd v Edwards Engineering (Perth) Ltd*, 1985 S.L.T. 128. Note also *Keen v Commerzbank AG* [2007] I.R.L.R. 132 (CA).

[108] Unfair Contract Terms Act 1977 s.17(2).

[109] *McCrone v Boots Farm Sales Ltd*, 1981 S.C. 68. It may be that a term should not be regarded as fixed unless it has been employed more than once: see D.J. Cusine, "What is a standard form contract?", 1981 S.L.T. (News) 241; *Border Harvesters Ltd v Edwards Engineering (Perth) Ltd*, 1985 S.L.T. 128. Standard terms drafted by a professional body for general use have been held not caught by s.17: *Langstane Housing Association Ltd v Riverside Construction (Aberdeen) Ltd* [2009] CSOH 52; 2009 S.C.L.R. 639.

[110] Unfair Contract Terms Act 1977 s.18.

English section[111] makes it clear that the liability may be to the person dealing as consumer.

9.22 Guarantees of consumer goods—A "guarantee" is a document containing or purporting to contain some promise or assurance (however worded or presented) that defects will be made good by complete or partial replacement, or by repair, monetary compensation or otherwise. Section 19 affects a guarantee which relates to goods of a type ordinarily supplied for private use or consumption and which is not given by one party to the other party to a contract under or in pursuance of which the ownership or possession of the goods to which the guarantee relates is transferred. A term of such a guarantee is void in so far as it purports to exclude or restrict liability for loss or damage (including death or personal injury) arising from the goods proving defective while in use otherwise than exclusively for the purposes of a business or in the possession of a person for such use, and resulting from the breach of duty of a person concerned in the manufacture or distribution of the goods.

9.23 Supply contracts—The Act limits the exclusion or restriction of liability for breach of the terms as to title, description and quality or fitness implied by law in contracts of sale and hire-purchase.[112] It makes a similar provision in respect of the corresponding terms in other contracts relating to the transfer of ownership or possession of goods from one person to another (with or without work being done on them), e.g. contracts of hire or for work and materials.[113]

9.24 The "reasonableness" test—The onus of proving that it was fair and reasonable to incorporate a term in a contract lies on the party so contending.[114] In applying the "reasonableness" test, regard is to be had only to the circumstances which were, or ought reasonably to have been, known to or in the contemplation of the parties to the contract at the time the contract was made.[115] Where a term in a contract purports to restrict liability to a specified sum of money, regard is to be had in particular to (a) the resources which the party seeking to rely on that term could expect to be available to him for the purpose of meeting the liability should it arise, and (b) how far it was open to that party to cover himself by insurance.[116] The "guidelines" for application of the "reasonableness" test provided in Sch.2 to the Act[117] relate only to contracts of sale and hire-purchase and other contracts for the supply of goods; but some of the "guidelines" may be found to be of use in

---

[111] Unfair Contract Terms Act 1977 s.4.

[112] Unfair Contract Terms Act 1977 s.20. As to sale, see *Knight Machinery (Holdings) Ltd v Rennie*, 1994 S.C. 338; *Denholm Fishselling Ltd v Christopher Anderson Ltd*, 1991 S.L.T. (Sh. Ct) 24. See further below, paras 12.28–12.34.

[113] Unfair Contract Terms Act 1977 s.21. As to hire, see *G.M. Shepherd Ltd v North West Securities Ltd*, 1991 S.L.T. 499.

[114] Unfair Contract Terms Act 1977 s.24(4); see *Landcatch Ltd v Marine Harvest Ltd*, 1985 S.L.T. 478 (a supply case); *George Mitchell (Chesterhall) Ltd v Finney Lock Seeds Ltd* [1983] 2 A.C. 803 (decided under Sale of Goods Act 1979 s.55); *Phillips Products Ltd v Hyland* [1987] 2 All E.R. 620; *Thompson v Lohan* [1987] 1 W.L.R. 649; *Continental Tyre & Rubber Co Ltd v Trunk Trailer Co Ltd*, 1987 S.L.T. 58. There is a requirement to aver that terms are reasonable or otherwise as the case may be, if one wishes to raise the issue: see *Landcatch Ltd v Marine Harvest Ltd* and *William Teacher & Sons Ltd v Bell Lines Ltd*, 1991 S.L.T. 876.

[115] Unfair Contract Terms Act 1977 s.24.

[116] Unfair Contract Terms Act 1977 s.24(3). See *Langstane Housing Association Ltd v Riverside Construction (Aberdeen) Ltd* [2009] CSOH 52; 2009 S.C.L.R. 639.

[117] See below, para.12.34.

applying the "reasonableness" test to other types of contract.[118] A term is to be taken to have been fair and reasonable to incorporate if it is incorporated or approved by, or incorporated pursuant to a decision or ruling of, a "competent authority" acting in the exercise of any statutory jurisdiction or function and is not a term in a contract to which the "competent authority" is itself a party.[119] A "competent authority" is any court, arbiter, government department or public authority.[120]

Unfair terms in consumer contracts—The EC Directive on Unfair Terms in Consumer Contracts[121] imposes controls over contract terms which are additional to those found in the Unfair Contract Terms Act 1977. Effect has been given to the Directive in the United Kingdom by the Unfair Terms in Consumer Contracts Regulations 1999, which replaced earlier Regulations promulgated in 1994.[122] As the title indicates, the Directive and also the Regulations apply only to consumer contracts and a "consumer" is a natural person who makes a contract "for purposes which are outside his trade, business or profession".[123] The contracts to which the Directive and Regulations apply are contracts for the sale of goods and contracts for the supply of goods and services. "Goods", however, includes land and interests in land for these purposes.[124] In each case, the seller or supplier must be acting "for purposes relating to his trade, business or profession".[125] The Regulations apply only to contract terms which have not been "individually negotiated" by the seller or supplier and the consumer[126]: thus, standard form contracts are squarely within the ambit of the Regulations unless they are exempted.[127] The Regulations do not apply to contract terms which have been incorporated in order to comply either with UK legislation or delegated legislation, or with the provisions or principles of international conventions to which

9.25

---

[118] See *Smith v Eric S. Bush* [1990] 1 A.C. 831 (surveyor's disclaimer unreasonable; cf. however *Bank of Scotland v Fuller Peiser*, 2002 S.L.T. 574, noted by J.M. Thomson, "A general duty to protect pure economic loss?", 2002 S.L.T. (News) 225); *Stewart Gill Ltd v Horatio Myer & Co Ltd* [1992] Q.B. 600 (restriction on customer's right of set-off unreasonable; cf. however *Schenkers Ltd v Overland Shoes Ltd* [1998] 1 Lloyd's Rep. 498); *St Albans City and District Council v International Computers Ltd* [1996] 4 All E.R. 481 (exclusion clause in software supply contract unreasonable; cf. however *Watford Electronics Ltd v Sanderson CFL Ltd* [2001] 1 All E.R. (Comm) 696 (CA)) and note further *Balmoral Group Ltd v Borealis (U.K.) Ltd* [2006] 2 Lloyd's Rep. 629. On "entire agreement" clauses as unfair terms, see A.J. Bowen, "Threshing through the undergrowth: entire agreement clauses and the Unfair Contract Terms Act 1977", 2004 S.L.T. (News) 37.

[119] Unfair Contract Terms Act 1977 s.29(2).

[120] Unfair Contract Terms Act 1977 s.29(3).

[121] Directive 93/13 [1993] OJ L95/29.

[122] SI 1999/2083, replacing SI 1994/3159. The current Regulations came into force on October 1, 1999.

[123] SI 1999/2083 reg.4(1). See *Cape SNC v Ideal Service Srl, Idealservice MN RE SAS v OMAI Srl* (Joined Cases C541/99 and C542/99) [2003] 1 C.M.L.R. 42 (company cannot be consumer); *Prostar Management Ltd v Twaddle*, 2003 S.L.T. (Sh. Ct) 11 (professional footballer not a consumer of his agent's services); *Standard Bank London Ltd v Apostolakis (No.1)* [2000] I.L.Pr. 766.

[124] *Khatun v London Borough of Newham* [2005] Q.B. 985; McBryde, *The Law of Contract in Scotland* (2007), para.18.44.

[125] SI 1999/2083 reg.3(1). A public authority may be a supplier for these purposes: *Khatun* [2005] Q.B. 985.

[126] SI 1999/2083 reg.5(1). Terms which have been drafted in advance of the conclusion of a contract and whose contents the consumer has been unable to influence are not to be regarded as having been individually negotiated: reg.5(2).

[127] If, looked at as a whole, a contract is a pre-formulated, standard form, agreement, the fact that one term has been individually negotiated does not prevent the Regulations being applied to the rest of the contract: SI 1999/2083, reg.5(3).

the EU or the Member States are party.[128] Also exempted are terms which define the "main subject matter" of the contract and those which concern the adequacy of the price or remuneration as against the goods or services sold or supplied.[129] It has been held in England that the Regulations do not apply to terms implied at common law.[130] The onus of showing that a term was individually negotiated rests with the seller or supplier.[131] A court may however raise the question of its own motion.[132] A contract term will be treated as unfair where, contrary to good faith, it causes a "significant imbalance" between the rights and obligations of the contracting parties. Such a term is declared to be "contrary to the requirement of good faith".[133] In assessing the fairness of the term, the nature of the goods or services supplied must be taken into account and fairness must be assessed taking into account all the circumstances at the time when the contract was concluded.[134] An indicative, but not exhaustive, list of terms which may be unfair is set out in Sch.2.[135] The list includes the following terms: terms excluding or limiting a seller's or supplier's liability for death or personal injury caused by act or omission on their part; terms imposing a "disproportionately" large sum by way of compensation; terms which permit a seller or supplier to vary, unilaterally, a contract's terms without having to specify a reason for doing so; and terms which oblige the consumer to perform his part of the bargain but which do not impose a similar obligation on the seller or supplier. Jurisdiction clauses have been treated as unfair.[136] If a contract term is found to be unfair, it is unenforceable against the consumer but the contract itself remains valid so long as it can exist without the inclusion of the unfair term.[137] The Regulations also impose on sellers and suppliers a duty to word their contracts in "plain, intelligible language" and, where there is doubt as to the meaning of the wording, it will be construed contra proferentem.[138] Opting out of the Regulations by means of a choice of law clause which declares the applicable law to be that of a non-Member State is struck at

---

[128] SI 1999/2083 reg.4(2).

[129] SI 1999/2083 reg.6(2). See further *Director General of Fair Trading v First National Bank Plc* [2002] 1 A.C. 481; *Abbey National v Office of Fair Trading* [2010] 1 A.C. 696. Core terms are, however, subject to the "intelligibility" requirement of reg.7 (below): *Bankers Insurance Co Ltd v South* [2003] EWHC 380; *Office of Fair Trading v Foxtons Ltd* [2009] EWHC 1681 (Ch).

[130] *Bagbut v Eccle Riggs Country Park Ltd, The Times*, November 13, 2006.

[131] SI 1999/2083 reg.5(4).

[132] *Caja de Ahorros y Monte de Piedad de Madrid v Asociación de Usuarios de Servicios Bancarios (Ausbanc)* (C-484/08) [2010] E.C.R. I- 4785; [2010] 3 C.M.L.R. 43.

[133] SI 1999/2083 reg.5(1). On good faith, see *Director General of Fair Trading v First National Bank Plc* [2002] 1 A.C. 481. Note also *Munkenbeck & Marshall v Harold* [2005] EWHC 336 (indemnity and interest clauses in architect's letter of appointment unfair as unusual (although in use industry-wide), onerous, to the consumer's detriment and not brought to consumer's notice at time of appointment).

[134] SI 1999/2083 reg.6(1).

[135] SI 1999/2083 reg.4(4).

[136] *Oceano Grupo Editorial SA v Rocio Murciano Quintero* (C-240/98) [2000] E.C.R. I-4941 (note, however, that in *Freiburger Kommunalbauten GmbH Baugesellschaft & Co KG v Hofstetter* (C-237/02) [2004] E.C.R. I-3403, the European Court of Justice held that it would not give rulings on the fairness of particular clauses). Further on jurisdiction clauses see *Standard Bank London Ltd v Apostolakis (No.2)* [2001] Lloyd's Rep. Bank 240; *Picardi v Cuniberti* [2002] B.L.R. 487; cf. *Lovell Projects Ltd v Legg* [2003] B.L.R. 452; *Westminster Building Co Ltd v Beckingham* [2004] B.L.R 265. Adjudication clauses in building contracts have been held to be fair: *Bryen & Langley Ltd v Boston* [2005] B.L.R. 508; *Allen Wilson Shopfitters v Buckingham* [2005] EWHC 1165.

[137] SI 1999/2083 reg.8.

[138] SI 1999/2083 reg.7. See *Bankers Insurance Co Ltd v South* [2003] EWHC 380; *Office of Fair Trading v Foxtons Ltd* [2009] EWHC 1681 (Ch).

where the contract has "a close connection with the territory of a Member State".[139] In order to prevent the continued use of unfair contract terms in consumer contracts, the Office of Fair Trading can act on any complaint made to it by seeking an interdict against its continued use.[140] Qualifying bodies specified in Sch.1 may also so act, but must notify the Office before doing so and have its consent before seeking an interdict.[141]

"Pay when paid" clauses in construction contracts—A provision in a construc- **9.26** tion contract making payment conditional on the payer receiving payment from a third party (a "pay when paid" clause) is ineffective unless the third person is insolvent.[142]

FURTHER READING

Cabrelli, D. and Zahn, R., "Challenging Unfair Terms: Some Recent Developments", 2010 Jur. Rev. 115.

Davidson, F.P., "Unfair Terms in Consumer Contracts" (1996) 1 S.L.P.Q. 93.

Davidson, F.P., "Unfair Terms in Consumer Contracts Revisited" (2001) 6 S.L.P.Q. 1.

Ervine, W.C.H., "The Unfair Contract Terms Regulations Mark II", 1999 S.L.T. (News) 253.

Ervine, W.C.H., "The Unfair Terms in Consumer Contracts Regulations in the Courts", 2004 S.L.T. (News) 127.

Evans-Jones, R., *Unjustified Enrichment Volume 1: Enrichment by Deliberate Conferral: Condictio* (Edinburgh: W. Green, 2003), Ch.5.

Law Commission and Scottish Law Commission, *Report on Unfair Terms in Contracts* (HMSO, 2005), Law Com. No.292, Scot. Law Com. No.199.

Law Commission and Scottish Law Commission, *Issues Paper on Unfair Terms in Consumer Contracts* (July 2012).

McBryde, W.W., *The Law of Contract in Scotland*, 3rd edn (Edinburgh: W. Green, 2007), Chs 13, 18, 19.

Macgregor, L., "Illegal Contracts and Unjustified Enrichment"' (2000) 4 Edin. L.R. 18.

Macgregor, L., "Pacta Illicita"; Thomson, J.M., "Judicial Control of Unfair Contract Terms"; Sutherland, P.J., "Contractual Restrictive Covenants", all in Reid, K.G.C. and Zimmermann, R. (eds), *A History of Private Law in Scotland* (Oxford: Oxford University Press, 2000), Vol.2.

MacQueen, H.L. and Cockrell, A., "Illegal Contracts", in Zimmermann, R., Visser, D. and Reid, K.G.C. (eds), *Mixed Legal Systems in Comparative Perspective: Property and Obligations in Scotland and South Africa* (Oxford: Oxford University Press, 2004).

---

[139] SI 1999/2083 reg.7.

[140] SI 1999/2083 reg.10. See further *Office of Fair Trading v Foxtons Ltd* [2009] EWCA Civ 288; [2010] 1 W.L.R. 663; and the Office of Fair Trading website on unfair contract terms, accessible at *http://www.oft.gov.uk/about-the-oft/legal-powers/legal/unfair-terms/* [Accessed July 5, 2012].

[141] SI 1999/2083 regs 10–12. See further, Unfair Terms in Consumer Contracts (Amendment) Regulations 2001 (SI 2001/1186).

[142] Housing Grants, Construction and Regeneration Act 1996 s.113 (as amended by the Enterprise Act 2002 (Insolvency) Order 2003 (SI 2003/2096)). For the definition of construction contract see McBryde, *The Law of Contract in Scotland* (2007), para.18.53 and provisions there referred to.

MacQueen, H.L. and Thomson, J.M., *Contract Law in Scotland*, 3rd edn (Bloomsbury Professional, 2012), Ch.7.

Office of Fair Trading website on Unfair Contract Terms (*http://www.oft.gov.uk/ about-the-oft/legal-powers/legal/unfair-terms/* [Accessed July 6, 2012]).

Smith, T.B., *Property Problems in Sale* (London: Sweet and Maxwell, 1978), Ch.IV.

Stair Memorial Encyclopaedia, Vol.15, paras 722–52, 763–79.

Stewart, W.J., "Ten Years of Fair Contracts in Scotland?", 1987 S.L.T. (News) 361.

Stewart, W.J., "Fifteen Years of Fair Contracts in Scotland?", 1993 S.L.T. (News) 15.

CHAPTER 10

BREACH OF CONTRACT

Introduction—A contract is said to be broken when a party fails to perform the   **10.01**
contract according to its terms. Such failure may be total or partial, or may consist
in defective or late performance of the party's obligations. Refusal to perform
may also amount to breach of contract. If a refusal to perform is made before the
obligation falls due, there is anticipatory breach.[1] The party not in breach has
available a number of remedies against the other party, which can be classified as
(1) judicial; or (2) self-help. Judicial remedies are those obtainable by way of
court action, and include specific implement, interdict, actions for payment and
damages. Self-help remedies may be exercised by a party without a prior court
order, although there is nothing to prevent such an order being obtained. The self-
help remedies include withholding one's own performance under the contract
(retention) and terminating the contract altogether (rescission). The risk in
proceeding without a court order is that the other party may challenge the use of
the remedy as unjustified and as itself a breach of contract by non-performance.
A party may exercise more than one of the remedies cumulatively in respect of
a breach of contract, provided that they are not inconsistent with each other
(e.g. rescission and specific implement).

JUDICIAL REMEDIES

Right to specific implement—When one party to a contract refuses, or fails, to   **10.02**
fulfil his obligations the other may generally insist on specific implement. If the
obligation in question is of a positive character, it may be enforced by a decree ad
factum praestandum, and if of a negative, by interdict.[2] A person who fails to
obtemper a decree *ad factum praestandum* may be imprisoned until he does, but
for not more than six months, and only if the court is satisfied that his refusal to
comply with the decree is wilful.[3] Breach of interdict is punishable by fine or
imprisonment. Legislation gives the court a wide discretion, based upon "justice
and equity", to make orders in lieu of imprisonment when enforcing decrees of
specific implement. Express mention is made of orders for the payment of money
and to have searches made for moveables. There could also perhaps be orders
for performance by third parties, to be paid for by the contract-breaker, or the
provision of further opportunity to perform. These additional powers of the
court have been particularly useful when the contract-breaker is a company or

---

[1] See further, para.10.24, below.
[2] See on this distinction *Church Commissioners for England v Abbey National Plc*, 1994 S.C. 651
(Court of Five Judges).
[3] Law Reform (Miscellaneous Provisions) (Scotland) Act 1940 (the "1940 Act") s.1; *Nelson v
Nelson*, 1988 S.C.L.R. 663.

other association where the sanction of imprisonment may be of little or no coercive value.[4]

10.03 Cases where specific implement refused—Subject to the discretion of the court to refuse decree when it would cause exceptional hardship,[5] the right to demand specific implement of a contract is, in Scots law, a general rule.[6] The following are the leading exceptions. (1) Where the obligation in question is the payment of money. As a rule the sole remedy of a creditor is to enforce payment by diligence; he is not entitled to a decree *ad factum praestandum*, which might result in the imprisonment of the debtor. Such a decree is by statute competent in the case of a contract to take up and pay for debentures of a company[7]; and may be granted in other cases where there is an order for consignation of money in court.[8] (2) Where the contract, if fulfilled, would involve an intimate relationship, where forced compliance would be worse than none. So specific implement will not be granted of a contract of service,[9] or of a contract to enter into partnership.[10] (3) Where compliance with the decree would be impossible. A decree *ad factum praestandum* will not be pronounced where the defender cannot possibly comply with it, even if the impossibility may be due to his own fault.[11] Thus, if a man undertakes to do something which he cannot lawfully do, e.g. to execute work on land to which he has no right of access, he may be liable in damages for failure, but specific implement is not an appropriate remedy.[12] (4) Where the court cannot enforce the decree. Where the defender is a foreigner, subject to the jurisdiction of the Scottish courts only on some exceptional ground, these courts, as they have no power to enforce a decree *ad factum praestandum* by his imprisonment, will not pronounce a decree which would be futile.[13] The remedy is competent against a company, however, since it can be enforced by way of the sanctions available under the Law

---

[4] See 1940 Act s.1(2); *Postel Properties Ltd v Miller & Stenhouse Plc*, 1993 S.L.T. 353, and *Grosvenor Developments (Scotland) Ltd v Argyll Stores Ltd*, 1987 S.L.T. 738, citing what is now W.W. McBryde, *The Law of Contract in Scotland*, 3rd edn (Edinburgh: W. Green, 2007), pp.703–704. See, as to the position of a receiver, *Macleod v Alexander Sutherland*, 1977 S.L.T. (Notes) 44; and, as to a defender outside the jurisdiction, *Ford v Bell Chandler*, 1977 S.L.T. (Sh. Ct) 90.

[5] *Grahame v Magistrates of Kirkcaldy* (1882) 9 R. (HL) 91.

[6] *Stewart v Kennedy* (1890) 17 R. (HL) 1; the English law is contrasted by Lord Watson, at 9. See further, *Retail Parks Investments Ltd v Royal Bank of Scotland Plc (No.2)*, 1996 S.C. 227, and *Highland and Universal Properties Ltd v Safeway Properties Ltd*, 2000 S.C. 297, and contrast in England, *Cooperative Insurance Society Ltd v Argyll Stores (Holdings) Ltd* [1998] A.C. 1. The court cannot, however, grant decree of specific implement against the Crown: Crown Proceedings Act 1947 s.21(1).

[7] Companies Act 2006 s.740.

[8] *Mackenzie v Balerno Paper Mill Co* (1883) 10 R. 1147.

[9] Trade Union and Labour Relations (Consolidation) Act 1992 s.236; *Skerret v Oliver* (1896) 23 R. 468 at 485. Cf. *Murray v Dumbarton C.C.*, 1935 S.L.T. 239; interdict against transfer of a teacher, so as, in effect, to enforce compliance, refused. See more recently *Anderson v Pringle of Scotland*, 1998 S.L.T. 754 and *Peace v Edinburgh City Council*, 1999 S.C.L.R. 593 (employer interdicted from using redundancy or disciplinary procedures other than those in contract of employment). An employment tribunal may make an order for reinstatement or re-engagement of an employee, failure to comply with which may result in an additional award of compensation: Employment Rights Act 1996 ss.113–117; see below, para.17.48.

[10] *Macarthur v Lawson* (1877) 4 R. 1134 at 1136; *Pert v Bruce*, 1937 S.L.T. 475.

[11] *Macarthur v Lawson* (1877) 4 R. 1134, per Lord President Inglis; *Rudman v Jay*, 1908 S.C. 552.

[12] *Sinclair v Caithness Flagstone Co* (1898) 25 R. 703.

[13] Note, however, *Ford v Bell Chandler*, 1977 S.L.T. (Sh. Ct) 90, where it was held that a decree is competent against a party outwith the jurisdiction because an order for payment can be substituted for the warrant for imprisonment: 1940 Act s.1(2).

Reform (Miscellaneous Provisions) Act 1940.[14] (5) Where there is no *pretium affectionis*. In the case of generic sales, i.e. sales of a certain quantity of a commodity which can be procured in the open market, it has been held that the purchaser's remedy is to supply himself at the seller's expense, and decree of specific implement against the seller is incompetent.[15] It is doubtful whether previous authority justified this conclusion, and it is also not compelled by the Sale of Goods Act.[16] Where an alternative source of supply is unavailable, or not readily available, specific implement may certainly be granted.[17]

Damages for breach of contract[18]—Where specific enforcement of a contract is either incompetent, or not demanded, the party aggrieved by a breach is always entitled to damages, nominal or substantial, where it causes him loss or, at least, inconvenience.[19] There is, however, no reason why there should not be a claim for damages in addition to one for specific implement if a loss has been caused by the defender's previous non-performance. In principle, however, where there is no loss or inconvenience, no damages (not even nominal damages) should be awarded.[20] Damages will also not be awarded where there is an enforceable conventional provision for the consequence of a breach of contract. Where the breach consists in failure to pay money at the appointed date, then, though interest may be due, no general damages can be demanded.[21] Damages are intended—and the rule holds in cases of wrongs as well as in cases of breach of contract[22]—as compensation to the injured party,[23] not as a punishment of the party in breach. It is, consequently, irrelevant to consider how far a party who has broken his contract has gained by doing so,[24] or the question whether he is rich or poor.[25] Neither point affects the loss which the pursuer has sustained, and for which he is to be compensated. **10.04**

---

[14] See cases cited above at fn.4.

[15] *Union Electric Co v Holman*, 1913 S.C. 954.

[16] A.D. Smith, "Specific Implement", in K.G.C. Reid and R. Zimmermann (eds), *History of Private Law in Scotland* (Oxford: Oxford University Press, 2000), Vol.2, pp.195 et seq; Sale of Goods Act 1979 s.52(4).

[17] *Sky Petroleum v V.I.P. Petroleum* [1974] 1 W.L.R. 576; cf. *Re London Wine Co (Shippers)* [1986] P.C.C. 121. Note also *Howard E. Perry & Co v British Railways Board* [1980] 1 W.L.R. 1375 which seems to justify the view in *Sky Petroleum Ltd* [1974] 1 W.L.R. 576.

[18] See D.M. Walker, *Law of Civil Remedies in Scotland* (Edinburgh: W. Green, 1974), Pt VIII.

[19] On causation see *A/B Karlshamns Oljefabriker v Monarch Steamship Co Ltd*, 1949 S.C. (HL) 1 ("but for" test); *John Doyle Construction Ltd v Laing Management (Scotland) Ltd*, 2004 S.C. 713 (global claim relevant for proof of links between breach and different elements of loss); *Douglas Shelf Seven Ltd v Cooperative Wholesale Society Ltd*, 2007 G.W.D. 9–167 (breach one of several factors). For examples of damages for inconvenience, see *Gunn v National Coal Board*, 1982 S.L.T. 526; *Mack v Glasgow City Council*, 2006 S.C. 543.

[20] *Wilkie v Brown*, 2003 S.C. 573 at 579C, per Lord Justice-Clerk Gill; disapproving contrary dictum of Lord President Inglis in *Webster v Cramond Iron Co* (1875) 2. R. 752 at 754. Doubt about this dictum had previously been expressed in *Aarons & Co v Fraser*, 1934 S.C. 125.

[21] Erskine, III, 3, 86; Bell, *Principles*, s.32.

[22] *Black v N.B. Ry*, 1908 S.C. 444.

[23] *Watson Laidlaw & Co v Pott, Cassels, & Williamson*, 1914 S.C. (HL) 18.

[24] *Teacher v Calder* (1899) 1 F. (HL) 39. But cf. in England *Att Gen v Blake* [2001] 1 A.C. 268 and subsequent developments discussed in *Chitty on Contracts*, edited by H.G. Beale, 30th edn (London: Sweet and Maxwell, 2008), paras 26.020–26.029 and H. McGregor, *McGregor on Damages*, 18th edn (London: Sweet and Maxwell, 2010), Ch.12; see also J.M. Thomson, "Restitutionary and Performance Damages", 2001 S.L.T. (News) 71; D. Campbell, "The Treatment of *Teacher v Calder in AG v Blake*" (2002) 65 M.L.R. 256; G. Black, "A New Experience in Contract Damages? Reflections on *Experience Hendrix v PPX Enterprises*", 2005 Jur. Rev. 31; H.L. MacQueen and J.M. Thomson, *Contract Law in Scotland,* 3rd edn (Bloomsbury Professional, 2012), para.6.17.

[25] *Black v N.B. Ry*, 1908 S.C. 444.

10.05 Loss—Loss is generally assessed as at the date of the breach but exceptionally account can be taken of events occurring after that date, such as a post-breach declaration of war frustrating the contract or entitling the other party to terminate it.[26] There may be included the expenses directly incurred by the party whose contract has been broken, if such expenses would have been incurred by a reasonable man[27]; the cost of litigation with third parties, if traceable to the breach of contract and if reasonably incurred[28]; and the loss of a sub-contract, in cases of failure to supply or carry goods, if that sub-contract contained no exceptional conditions.[29] In many cases a person who supplies an article impliedly warrants that it is fit for ordinary use, and any injury which may result from the fact that it is unsuitable or inadequate will form part of the damages.[30] Where the breach consists of a failure to take care where there was a duty of care, the loss is assessed by comparing the resultant position with that if the care required had been exercised.[31] Where a contract might have been performed in any one of a number of reasonable ways, the loss is measured by comparing the performance actually made with the one least unfavourable for the defender.[32] It was a general rule in cases of breach of contract that the law will consider material loss or inconvenience only, not injury to feelings arising from the breach or the circumstances in which it was made[33]; but in cases where one party was contracting on a non-commercial basis sums have been awarded in respect of mental distress, disappointment and frustration.[34] In employment contracts, where there is a relationship of mutual trust and confidence, an employee may recover "stigma" damages in respect of reputation lost as a result of the employer's breach of duty.[35] It is now established that, in accordance with the principle that compensation to the injured party should be limited to the true loss which he has suffered, consideration of his income tax liability is a necessary element in the calculation of the amount to be awarded as damages.[36]

---

[26] *Golden Strait Corp v Nippon Yusen Kubishka Kaisha* [2007] 2 A.C. 353 (by a 3:2 majority). See also, e.g. *Radford v De Froberville* [1977] 1 W.L.R. 1262 and *Dodd Properties (Kent) Ltd v Canterbury City Council* [1980] 1 W.L.R. 433. In *Douglas Shelf Seven Ltd v Co-operative Wholesale Society Ltd*, 2007 G.W.D. 9–167 (OH), where the breach was a continuing one over a 10-year period, held that damages were to be assessed at the most recent date practicable, not at the beginning of the period of breach.

[27] *Le Blanche v London & N.W. Ry* (1876) 1 C.P.D. 286; *Fielding v Newell*, 1987 S.L.T. 530. It has been held in England that such claims are limited by the profit (if any) that the party would have made from the contract's full performance: *C & P Haulage v Middleton* [1983] 1 W.L.R. 1461; and see also *CCC (London) Films Ltd v Imperial Quadrant Films* [1985] Q.B. 16; *Commonwealth of Australia v Amann Aviation Pty Ltd* (1991) 66 A.L.J.R. 123.

[28] *Munro v Bennett*, 1911 S.C. 337; *Buchanan & Carswell v Eugene*, 1936 S.C. 160.

[29] *Stroms Bruks AIB v Hutchison* (1905) 7 F. (HL) 131. Contrast *Horne v Midland Ry* (1872) L.R. 8 C.P. 131.

[30] *Dickie v Amicable Property Investment Co*, 1911 S.C. 1079.

[31] *South Australia Asset Management Corp v York Montague Ltd* [1997] A.C. 191.

[32] *Paula Lee Ltd v Robert Zehil & Co Ltd* [1983] 2 All E.R. 390; *Douglas Shelf Seven Ltd v Co-operative Wholesale Society Ltd*, 2007 G.W.D. 9–167.

[33] *Addis v Gramophone Co* [1909] A.C. 488; *Johnson v Gore Wood & Co* [2002] 2 A.C. 1; *Johnson v Unisys Ltd* [2003] 1 A.C. 518. Cf. *Eastwood v Magnox Electric; McCabe v Cornwell CC* [2005] 1 A.C. 503, where held that financial loss from psychiatric or other illness caused to a wrongfully dismissed employee by pre-dismissal unfair treatment is recoverable as damages for breach of contract. See below, para.17.43.

[34] *Diesen v Samson*, 1971 S.L.T. (Sh. Ct) 49; *Jarvis v Swans Tours* [1973] 1 Q.B. 233; *Jackson v Horizon Holidays* [1975] 1 W.L.R. 1468; *Ruxley Electronics & Construction v Forsyth* [1996] A.C. 344; *Farley v Skinner* [2002] 2 A.C. 732; *Hamilton Jones v David and Snape* [2004] 1 All E.R. 657. See further Bowen, 2003 S.L.T. (News) 1.

[35] *Malik v Bank of Commerce and Credit International* [1998] A.C. 20.

[36] *McDaid v Clyde Navigation Trs*, 1946 S.C. 462; *British Transport Commission v Gourley* [1956] A.C. 185. See also *Spencer v Macmillan's Trs*, 1958 S.C. 300; *Stewart v Glentaggart*, 1963 S.L.T. 119.

Loss suffered by third party—In several decisions of the House of Lords on **10.06** English appeals it has been held that a contracting party which has suffered no loss in its own right may nevertheless recover damages in respect of losses suffered by a third party as a result of the other contracting party's breach, so long as the third party is without a legal entitlement to make a claim in its own right.[37] In the last of these cases Lord Clyde suggested that the problem might be less acute in Scots law, since the third party could have a direct claim under the doctrine of *jus quaesitum tertio*[38]; and this approach has been deployed in a sheriff court decision.[39] A difficulty may be that the original contract is often not one intended for the benefit of any third party, and in this position it has been held in the Outer House that the loss involved is suffered by the first contracting party when the defective performance is completed and is therefore recoverable by that party even although it materialises later for the third party.[40] This is, however, difficult to reconcile with the basic distinction between *injuria* and *damnum* in Scots law, although it can be argued that for the party in breach the question of who actually suffers the loss resulting from that breach is *res inter alios acta*.[41]

Mitigation of loss—Where injury is inflicted, whether by breach of contract or by **10.07** a wrongful or negligent act, the damages that may be claimed are limited by the principle that the party who is aggrieved is bound to take all reasonable means to minimise his loss.[42] So a servant who has been wrongfully dismissed must endeavour to find other employment[43]; a buyer, if the seller has failed to supply the goods, must take measures to supply himself, if there is an available market in which the goods in question can be obtained.[44] Whether such efforts to minimise the loss have in fact been taken or not, the damages awarded will not exceed the loss which their adoption could not have prevented. Similarly, if reasonable care in the inspection of a defective article would have averted some item of loss, that loss will not be included in the damages recoverable from the party who supplied the article.[45] It has been laid down that

> "a contracting party is not entitled to proceed so as to cause unnecessary loss to the other party without any resulting benefit to himself."[46]

---

[37] *The Albazero* [1977] A.C. 774; *St Martins Property Corp Ltd v Sir Robert McAlpine & Sons Ltd* [1994] 1 A.C. 85; *Darlington Borough Council v Wiltshier Northern Ltd* [1995] 1 W.L.R. 68 (HL); *Alfred McAlpine Construction Ltd v Panatown Ltd* [2001] 1 A.C. 518. See also *GUS Property Management Ltd v Littlewoods Mail Order Stores*, 1982 S.C. (HL) 157 for the characterisation of the difficulty as the "black hole" problem.

[38] *Panatown* [2001] 1 A.C. 518 at 534–535. On the doctrine of *jus quaesitum tertio*, see paras 8.04 et seq., above. It is no objection to the claim of the tertius that the first contracting party retains an interest in the contract.

[39] *Clark Contracts Ltd v Burrell Co (Construction Management) Ltd*, 2003 S.L.T. (Sh. Ct) 73.

[40] *McLaren Murdoch & Hamilton Ltd v Abercromby Motor Group Ltd*, 2003 S.C.L.R. 323.

[41] See the speech of Lord Griffiths in *St Martins* [1994] 1 A.C. 85, and the dissents of Lords Goff and Millett in *Alfred McAlpine Construction Ltd v Panatown* [2001] 1 A.C. 518. Cf. J.M. Thomson, "Restitutionary and Performance Damages", 2001 S.L.T. (News) 71; G. Hawkes, "Emerging from a black hole", 2003 S.L.T. (News) 285.

[42] *The Admiralty v Aberdeen Steam Trawling Co*, 1910 S.C. 553.

[43] *Ross v Macfarlane* (1894) 21 R. 396.

[44] *Warin & Craven v Forrester* (1876) 4 R. 190; affd 4 R. (HL) 75; Sale of Goods Act 1979 s.50. It has been held in England that a disappointed buyer may even have to accept some offer by way of compromise made by the seller: see *Houndsditch Warehouse Co v Waltex* [1944] 1 K.B. 579.

[45] *Carter v Campbell* (1885) 12 R. 1075; *Wilson v Carmichael* (1894) 21 R. 732.

[46] *Dunford & Elliot v Macleod* (1902) 4 F. 912, per Lord McLaren.

Where, however, the pursuer can show that he has taken all reasonable means to minimise the loss, he has done enough; the defender cannot successfully avert a claim for damages by proof that some extraordinary or exceptional measures might have been adopted.[47] The pursuer's contributory negligence may only be pleaded in breach of contract cases when the breach itself consists in the defender's actionable negligence (whether in contract or delict).[48]

10.08 Remoteness of loss—The formula as to the measure of damages in the case of breach of contract is often referred to as the rule of *Hadley v Baxendale*,[49] but that case merely restated a principle of remoteness of loss which had long been recognised in Scotland.[50] The formula or rule is expressed in *Hadley v Baxendale* in the following terms:

> "Where two parties have made a contract which one of them has broken, the damages which the other party ought to receive in respect of such breach of contract should be such as may fairly and reasonably be considered either arising naturally, i.e. according to the usual course of things, from such breach of contract itself, or such as may reasonably be supposed to have been in the contemplation of both parties at the time they made the contract as the probable result of the breach of it."

The former alternative points to the general rule of what are known as ordinary damages: everyone, as a reasonable person, is taken to know the ordinary course of things and consequently what loss is liable to result from a breach of contract in that ordinary course.[51] The latter shows that to this knowledge, which a party in breach is assumed to possess whether he actually possesses it or not, there may have to be added in a particular case any knowledge which he does actually possess, through e.g. prior notice or special experience, of special circumstances which would be liable, in the event of a breach, to cause more loss.[52] The measure, in short, depends upon the knowledge, actual or imputed, of the party in breach:

> "a party who breaks his contract is liable for those consequences which a reasonable man, possessing the knowledge which the party had at the time of contracting, would have anticipated".[53]

---

[47] *Gunter & Co v Lauritzen* (1894) 31 S.L.R. 359; *Clippens Oil Co v Edinburgh Water Trustees*, 1907 S.C. (HL) 9.

[48] Law Reform (Contributory Negligence) Act 1945 ss.1, 4 and 5; *Lancashire Textiles (Jersey) Ltd v Thomson Shepherd & Co Ltd*, 1986 S.L.T. 41; *Concrete Products (Kirkcaldy) Ltd v Anderson and Menzies*, 1996 S.L.T. 587. See also the English cases *Forsikringsaktieselskapet Vesta v Butcher (No.1)* [1989] A.C. 852; *Barclays Bank Plc v Fairclough Building Ltd* [1995] Q.B. 214. Note that the Scottish provisions of the 1945 Act are slightly wider than their English equivalents, and see further MacQueen and Thomson, *Contract Law in Scotland* (2012), paras 6.42–6.45.

[49] *Hadley v Baxendale* (1854) 9 Ex. 341; Bell, *Principles*, s.33; *A/B Karlshamns Oljefabriker v Monarch S.S. Co.*, 1949 S.C. (HL) 1; *Victoria Laundry (Windsor) v Newman Industries* [1949] 2 K.B. 528.

[50] M.P. Brown, *A Treatise on the Law of Sale* (1821), p.214.

[51] See, e.g. *Waddington v Buchan Poultry Products*, 1963 S.L.T. 168.

[52] *Den of Ogil Co v Cal. Ry* (1902) 5 F. 99; *Victoria Laundry (Windsor)* [1949] 2 K.B. 528, in which see opinion of Asquith L.J. at 539; *Cosar Ltd v UPS Ltd*, 1999 S.L.T. 259.

[53] W.M. Gloag, *Law of Contract*, 2nd edn (Edinburgh: W. Green, 1929), p.697; *Koufos v C. Czarnikow* [1969] 1 A.C. 350; *Caledonian Property Group Ltd v Queensferry Property Group Ltd*, 1992 S.L.T. 738; *Balfour Beatty Construction (Scotland) Ltd v Scottish Power Plc*, 1994 S.C. (HL) 20.

The breach itself does not have to have been foreseeable,[54] nor does the amount of the loss so long as loss of the same kind was foreseeable.[55] The test is based on the reasonable contemplation of the parties at the formation of the contract, not at the time of breach.[56]

Consequential damages—So damages for injury resulting from some excep- **10.09** tional use of goods will be due only where the party supplying it had notice that such a use of it was contemplated.[57] Among the items of loss which would not fall under ordinary damages, but might be recovered as consequential damages, in cases where the party in breach had notice of the actual facts, are the loss incurred where goods are supplied or conveyed too late for a particular market[58]; or the loss involved by delay in the provision or carriage of an article from the want of which some larger enterprise is brought to a standstill.[59] In the latter case, e.g. where some necessary part of a mill or of a ship is delayed in transit, it is possibly the law that mere notice of the facts is not enough to render the carrier liable for the exceptional loss which his delay may cause; there must be something such as the payment of a special rate, indicating that he took the risk.[60]

Interest—As already noticed, mere failure to pay at the appointed time does **10.10** not give rise to any claim for damages for the loss which may have resulted. It may, however, render the party in delay liable for interest. This may be expressly provided, with or without a period of credit. Interest may also, but only in a limited class of cases, be due *ex lege*. It has been stated to be due when the pursuer

> "is deprived of an interest bearing security or a profit-producing chattel . . . or . . . by virtue of a principal sum having been wrongfully withheld and not paid on the day when it ought to be paid."[61]

It is due when possession is taken on the sale of land, even if the price is not settled or the title not complete.[62] It is due, after maturity, on a bill of exchange or promissory note.[63] It is also due on money lent,[64] unless the circumstances of the case were exceptional.[65] In the case of an IOU, interest, unless stipulated for, is

---

[54] *H. Parsons (Livestock) v Uttley Ingham & Co* [1978] Q.B. 791.

[55] *H. Parsons* [1978] Q.B. 791; *Brown v KMR Services Ltd* [1995] 4 All E.R. 598. *Balfour Beatty*, 1994 S.C. (HL) 20 may be difficult to reconcile with this approach.

[56] *Transfield Shipping Inc v Mercator Shipping Inc (The Achilleas)* [2009] 1 A.C. 61; *Jackson v Royal Bank of Scotland* [2005] 1 W.L.R. 377 (HL); *Douglas Shelf Seven Ltd v Cooperative Wholesale Society Ltd*, 2007 G.W.D. 9–167.

[57] *Cory v Thames Ironworks, etc. Co* (1868) L.R. 2 Q.B. 181.

[58] *Macdonald v Highland Ry* (1873) 11 M. 614; *Anderson v N.B. Ry* (1875) 2 R. 443.

[59] *Hadley v Baxendale* (1854) 9 Ex. 341; *Den of Ogil Co v Cal. Ry* (1902) 5 F. 99; *Hydraulic Engineering Co v McHaffie* (1878) 4 Q.B.D. 670.

[60] See *British Columbia Saw Mills Co v Nettleship* (1868) L.R. 2 C.P. 499; *Cosar Ltd v UPS Ltd*, 1999 S.L.T. 259.

[61] *Kolbin & Sons v Kinnear & Co*, 1931 S.C. (HL) 128 at 137, per Lord Atkin.

[62] *Greenock Harbour Trustees v Glasgow and S.W. Ry*, 1909 S.C. 1438, affd 1909 S.C. (HL) 49; *Prestwick Cinema Co v Gardiner*, 1951 S.C. 98.

[63] Bills of Exchange Act 1882 s.57.

[64] *Cunningham v Boswell* (1868) 6 M. 890.

[65] *Forbes v Forbes* (1869) 8 M. 85; *Smellie's Exrx v Smellie*, 1933 S.C. 725.

due only from the date of citation.[66] It may be recovered by a solicitor on his outlays, but not on his professional charges.[67] It is due on money paid under protest which ultimately turns out not to have been legally exigible.[68] It is not due on arrears of rent or feu-duties.[69] The general rule with regard to tradesmen's and professional accounts is that no interest is due unless there has been a judicial demand for payment, or an intimation that interest will be charged on the account if not paid on a specified date.[70] But under the Late Payment of Commercial Debts (Interest) Act 1998 there is an implied term giving businesses a claim to simple interest on late payments of debt by other businesses and the public sector, at rates fixed by order. Parties may contract out of this regime after the debt has been created, but any attempt to do so before the debt is created is void unless a substantial remedy is provided for late payment. Terms providing for postponement of payment must be reasonable. No interest is due on sums payable as demurrage.[71] Interest has been allowed on a salvage award.[72] Where interest is due under the contract, the decree should award interest at the contract rate until payment.[73] Where legal action is taken, and the debt arises directly from contract, interest will be due from the date of citation.[74] Where the action concludes for damages, either for breach of contract or on some other ground, the general rule is that no interest is due until the damages are awarded, and the decree has become enforceable.[75] The court has, however, a discretion to award interest on damages for the whole or any part of the period between the date when the right of action arose and the date of the decree.[76]

SELF-HELP REMEDIES

10.11 Mutuality of contract—There is a general presumption that a contract is to be regarded as a whole, that the stipulations on either side are the counterparts and consideration given for each other, and therefore that failure by one party will justify the other in breaking off contractual relations, or in withholding performance of the obligations incumbent on him, according to the degree of materiality of the breach in question.[77] A party who is in breach of contract is not entitled to claim performance of its counterparty's obligations under the contract, at least if

---

[66] *Winestone v Wolifson*, 1954 S.C. 77.

[67] *Blair's Trs v Payne* (1884) 12 R. 104. Cf. *Drummond v Law Society of Scotland*, 1980 S.C. 175 (counsel's fees).

[68] *Haddon's Exrx v Scottish Milk Marketing Board*, 1938 S.C. 168.

[69] *Marquis of Tweeddale's Trs v Earl of Haddington* (1880) 7 R. 620; J. Rankine, *The Law of Leases in Scotland*, 3rd edn (Edinburgh: 1916), p.460.

[70] *Somervell's Tr. v Edinburgh Life Assurance Co*, 1911 S.C. 1069.

[71] *Pollich v Heatley*, 1910 S.C. 469 at 478, per Lord President Dunedin.

[72] *The "Ben Gairn"*, 1979 S.C. 98.

[73] *Bank of Scotland v Davis*, 1982 S.L.T. 20.

[74] Erskine, III, 3, 10.

[75] *Roger v Cochrane*, 1910 S.C. 1; *McCormack v NCB*, 1957 S.C. 277.

[76] Interest on Damages (Scotland) Act 1958 s.1, as substituted by the Interest on Damages (Scotland) Act 1971 s.1. See *Macrae v Reed & Mallik*, 1961 S.C. 68; *R. & J. Dempster v Motherwell Bridge & Engineering Co*, 1964 S.C. 308; *Fraser v Morton Wilson (No.2)*, 1966 S.L.T. 22; *James Buchanan & Co v Stewart Cameron (Drymen)*, 1973 S.L.T. (Notes) 78.

[77] Stair, I, 10, 16; *Turnbull v McLean & Co* (1874) 1 R. 730; *Barclay v Anderston Foundry Co* (1856) 18 D. 1190; *Dingwall v Burnett*, 1912 S.C. 1097; *Graham & Co v United Turkey Red Co Ltd*, 1922 S.C. 533; *Laurie v British Steel Corp*, 1988 S.L.T. 17; *Hoult v Turpie*, 2004 S.L.T. 308; *Purac Ltd v Byzak Ltd*, 2005 S.L.T. 37.

the breach is sufficiently material.[78] It is also competent to prove that two contracts are so related to each other that their respective provisions are interdependent, meaning that when one is broken, self-help remedies may be exercised in relation to the other.[79] Thus, where a verbal contract for the sale of two ships was, for reasons of convenience, carried into effect by two separate bills of sale, it was held that there was really only one contract, and therefore that the seller, who was unable to supply one of the ships, could not insist on the purchaser taking the other.[80]

Presumption of interdependence may be overcome—There is only a presump- **10.12** tion that the provisions of a contract are dependent on each other. There is nothing to prevent two separate contracts, for instance a lease and an option to buy, being recorded in the same deed, and it is then a question of construction whether they are interdependent or not.[81] And even when there is clearly only one contract, some of its provisions may be independent covenants. As Stair notes, there must not be

> "wholly different matters, which are frequently accumulated in the same contracts, or the one is but the occasion and motive, and not the proper cause, of the other".[82]

The best illustration is *Pendreigh's Tr. v Dewar*.[83] There a tenant undertook to lay out £200 on repairs, to be repaid on the expiry of the lease; it was held that, although the tenant was in breach of his contract under the lease, the right to repayment of the sum which he had expended was an independent stipulation, which was not affected by the fact that the other provisions of the lease had not been implemented. In *Bank of East Asia Ltd v Scottish Enterprise* an instalment due under a building contract on a certain date could not be withheld in respect of a damages claim arising after that date: the House of Lords emphasised the need for the performances on either side to be the counterparts of each other ("contemporaneity") before they could be regarded as mutual or interdependent.[84] In *Macari v Celtic Football Club* it was held that a residence requirement in the club manager's contract was not counterpart to his employer's obligation of trust and confidence.[85]

Interdependence or independence of contract terms—Illustrations of the **10.13** presumption that the provisions of a contract are interdependent are found in the decisions that where a restrictive covenant is imposed on an employee the employer cannot enforce it if he has wrongfully dismissed the employee and is

---

[78] *Graham & Co v United Turkey Red Co Ltd*, 1922 S.C. 533; *Forster v Ferguson & Forster* [2010] CSIH 38; 2010 S.L.T. 867.

[79] *Inveresk Plc v Tullis Russell Papermakers Ltd* [2010] UKSC 19; 2010 S.C. (UKSC) 106.

[80] *Claddagh Steamship Co v Steven*, 1919 S.C. 184; 1919 S.C. (HL) 132.

[81] *Penman v Mackay*, 1922 S.C. 385.

[82] Stair, I, 10, 16.

[83] *Pendreigh's Tr. v Dewar* (1871) 9 M. 1037.

[84] *Bank of East Asia Ltd v Scottish Enterprise*, 1997 S.L.T. 1213 (HL). See also *Redpath Dorman Long Ltd v Cummins Engine Co Ltd*, 1981 S.C. 370; W.W. McBryde, "Mutuality Retained" (1996) 1 Edin. L.R. 135.

[85] *Macari v Celtic Football Club*, 1999 S.C. 628; J.M. Thomson, "An unsuitable case for suspension?" (1999) 3 Edin. L.R. 394.

therefore himself in breach of contract[86]; and that where a landlord undertook to take over a sheep stock on a farm at the tenant's waygoing, the tenant could not enforce the obligation when he was in breach of the material conditions of the lease.[87]

10.14 **Retention**—In cases where a contract has been so far performed that its rescission would confer no advantage, and also in certain cases where the breach is not so material as to justify rescission, the party aggrieved by a breach of contract may find his remedy in withholding performance of the obligation incumbent on him.[88] This right, when it takes the form of refusal to pay a debt, is always known as a right of retention; when it takes the form of a refusal to deliver a particular thing it is more commonly referred to as a lien. But in this connection the terms retention and lien are often used as synonymous.

10.15 **Retention not a general rule**—While on the principle of compensation debts which are liquid and payable may be set against each other and extinguished,[89] there is no general rule that a party who is debtor in a liquid debt has any right to refuse or delay payment in respect of any illiquid claim he may have against his creditor. His obligation is to pay the liquid debt at once; his only right is to receive payment when his illiquid claim is established. So a purchaser cannot refuse to pay for goods on the ground that he has a claim of damages for the defective quality of goods previously supplied by the seller[90] or for the fraud by which he was induced to buy.[91] When a company had two contracts with the town council for the paving of streets, and, through its liquidator, executed one contract, it was held that the town council could not refuse to pay for the work done on the plea that they had a claim of damages in respect of the company's failure to carry out the other contract.[92] The provisions of r.55 of the First Schedule to the Sheriff Courts (Scotland) Act 1907,[93] it has been held, made no alteration in the law.[94] But the general rule, that an action for a liquid debt cannot be met by a plea of retention based on an illiquid claim, must be stated with the qualification that it has been allowed in exceptional cases, either when the illiquid claim admitted of

---

[86] *General Billposting Co v Atkinson* [1909] A.C. 118; *Measure Bros v Measure* [1910] 2 Ch. 248; *Rock Refrigeration Ltd v Jones* [1997] 1 All E.R. 1.

[87] *Marquis of Breadalbane v Stewart* (1904) 6 F. (HL) 23.

[88] In a number of recent cases Lord Drummond Young has developed a theory that for a breach to justify retention by the other party it must be such as to threaten the future performance of the contract (*Hoult v Turpie*, 2004 S.L.T. 308; *Purac Ltd v Byzak Ltd*, 2005 S.L.T. 37; *Wyman-Gordon Ltd v Proclad International Ltd*, 2011 S.C 338); but it is thought that this over-states the position and that the breach does not need to be so material that it would justify rescission (McBryde, *The Law of Contract in Scotland* (2007), para.20.60). The position was left open in *Inveresk Plc v Tullis Russell Papermakers Ltd* [2010] UKSC 19; 2010 S.C. (UKSC) 106.

[89] As to compensation, see paras 3.31–3.36, above.

[90] *Mackie v Riddell* (1874) 2 R. 115.

[91] *Smart v Wilkinson*, 1928 S.C. 383.

[92] *Asphaltic Limestone Concrete Co v Corp of Glasgow*, 1907 S.C. 463.

[93] "Where a defender pleads a counterclaim it shall suffice that he state the same in his defences, and the sheriff may thereafter deal with it as if it had been stated in a substantive action, and may grant decree for it in whole or in part, or for the difference between it and the claim sued on." The rule is now r.19.4 (SI 1993/1956) and there are differences in wording, the sheriff being given power "to regulate procedure in relation to the counterclaim as he thinks fit." See also Rules of Court of Session (SI 1994/1443) Ch.25.

[94] *Christie v Birrell*, 1910 S.C. 986. But it is indisputable that this is not consistent with some of the reasoning in *Armour & Melvin v Mitchell*, 1934 S.C. 94; see also *Croall & Croall v Sharp*, 1954 S.L.T. (Sh. Ct) 35.

instant verification,[95] or where, in the opinion of the court, it would be inequitable to reject the plea.[96] The more definite exceptions to the rule arise: (1) when both claims arise under the same contract; (2) when the creditor in the liquid claim is bankrupt.

Retention where debts arise from the same contract—When two claims, one **10.16** liquid, the other in the nature of a claim for damages, arise from the same contract the creditor in the claim for damages may withhold payment of his debt until the amount due to him as damages is established. On this principle is based the rule, in leases, that if the landlord fails, to any material extent, to execute repairs or improvements which he has agreed to make, the tenant may withhold payment of his rent.[97] A carrier's demand for freight may be met by a claim for damages for injury done to the goods.[98] A purchaser of goods may retain the price, in respect of the seller's failure to deliver within a specified, or within a reasonable, time.[99] But if the price is payable by instalments, the buyer is not entitled to retain earlier instalments in security for damages so long as the amount of the unpaid instalments exceeds the amount of his claim.[100] A bondholder in possession under a decree of maills and duties may be met by a plea of retention based on judgments in the tenants' favour in actions previously brought to enforce their rights under their leases.[101] The contract may exclude the right of retention expressly or by necessary implication.[102] A party to a construction contract may not withhold payment after the final date for payment of a sum due under the contract unless he has given an effective notice of intention to withhold payment. To be effective such a notice must specify (a) the amount proposed to be withheld and the ground for withholding payment, or (b) if there is more than one ground, each ground and the amount attributable to it, and must be given not later than the prescribed period before the final date for payment.[103]

Retention in insolvency—In bankruptcy a party who is a debtor to the bankrupt **10.17** and has an illiquid claim against him is entitled to withhold payment until the amount of his illiquid claim is ascertained, and then to compensate the one debt with the other, even although the two debts do not arise out of the same contract.[104]

---

[95] *Ross v Ross* (1895) 22 R. 461.

[96] See discussion by Lord Rodger in *Inveresk Plc v Tullis Russell Papermakers Ltd* [2010] UKSC 19; 2010 S.C. (UKSC) 106.

[97] *McDonald v Kydd* (1901) 3 F. 923; *Earl of Galloway v McConnell*, 1911 S.C. 846; *Haig v Boswall-Preston*, 1915 S.C. 339. As to agreement not to withhold payment of rent, see *Skene v Cameron*, 1942 S.C. 393.

[98] *Taylor v Forbes* (1830) 9 S. 113. Cf. *Aries Tanker Corp v Total Transport* [1977] 1 W.L.R. 185.

[99] *British Motor Body Co v Shaw*, 1914 S.C. 922.

[100] *Dick & Stevenson v Woodside Iron & Steel Co* (1888) 16 R. 242.

[101] *Marshall's Trs v Banks*, 1934 S.C. 405.

[102] *Redpath Dorman Long Ltd v Cummins Engine Co Ltd*, 1981 S.C. 370. See further *Melville Dundas Ltd v Hotel Corp of Edinburgh Ltd*, 2007 S.C. 12.

[103] Housing Grants, Construction and Regeneration Act 1996 s.111. Parties are free to prescribe the period of notice, but otherwise the period is that provided for under the Scheme for Construction Contracts. See *Melville Dundas Ltd v George Wimpey (U.K.) Ltd*, 2007 S.C. (HL) 116; *SL Timber Systems Ltd v Carillion Construction Ltd*, 2002 S.L.T. 997; *Melville Dundas Ltd v Hotel Corp of Edinburgh Ltd*, 2007 S.C. 12. For "construction contracts" see provisions cited in McBryde, *The Law of Contract in Scotland* (2007), paras 18.53–18.54.

[104] Bell, *Commentaries*, II, 122.

The principle applies in liquidation and it is not necessary to aver that the company is insolvent.[105]

10.18 Lien: Special lien—In contracts of employment, if the party employed has been placed in possession of an article or property belonging to his employer he has the right to retain possession until his claim for payment for his work is satisfied. This right, known as a special lien, is based on the principle that one party to a contract may withhold performance of his obligation to return the article until performance of the counter obligation, namely, payment for the work, is made or tendered.[106] The substantial result is to create a right in security.[107]

10.19 Rescission—The party confronted with a material breach of contract may have the right to rescind the contract, that is, to break off all contractual relations, or, in the words of s.15B(1)(b) of the Sale of Goods Act 1979, to "treat the contract as repudiated".[108] If one party shows by words or conduct that he does not intend to perform his obligations, he is said to "repudiate" the contract and the other party can accept the repudiation and rescind the contract. If one party fails to perform a material obligation under the contract, that is deemed repudiation and the other party can treat the contract as repudiated and rescind the contract.[109] Where a material breach is remediable, the party in breach should probably be given a second chance to put things right.[110] Repudiation does not bring the contract to an end.[111] First, the innocent party may choose to affirm his rights by raising an action for specific implement against the party in material breach.[112] Secondly, if he elects to rescind, this relieves him of his obligation to perform further his part of the bargain,[113] but it does not absolve the party in breach from obligations already incurred under the contract.[114] Thirdly, some contract terms, such as arbitration or exclusion or liquidate damages clauses, are worded so

---

[105] *Liquidators of Highland Engineering Ltd v Thomson*, 1972 S.C. 87; *G. & A. (Hotels) Ltd v T.H.B. Marketing Services Ltd*, 1983 S.L.T. 497.

[106] Bell, *Principles*, ss.1411, 1419; *Robertson v Ross* (1887) 15 R. 67; *Paton's Trs v Finlayson*, 1923 S.C. 872.

[107] Rights in Security, Ch.36, below.

[108] As added by Sale and Supply of Goods Act 1994 s.5(1).

[109] *Blyth v Scottish Liberal Club*, 1982 S.C. 140 at 149, per Lord Dunpark; *Lloyds Bank Plc v Bamberger*, 1993 S.C. 570; *Wyman-Gordon Ltd v Proclad International Ltd (No. 3)* [2010] CSIH 99 (proposal to vary a contract not repudiation unless coupled with refusal to perform existing obligations).

[110] *Lindley Catering Investments v Hibernian Football Club*, 1975 S.L.T. (Notes) 56. There is a trace of approval of this approach in *Millars of Falkirk Ltd v Turpie*, 1976 S.L.T. (Notes) 66. See also *Strathclyde R.C. v Border Engineering Contractors Ltd*, 1998 S.L.T. 175; McBryde, *The Law of Contract in Scotland* (2007), paras 20.122–20.127.

[111] *Johannesburg Municipal Council v Stewart*, 1909 S.C. 860 at 878, per Lord President Dunedin: "That does not mean that the contract is gone forever; on the contrary, the contract remains and is only the measure of liability for damages." Note also, *Photo Production Ltd v Securicor Transport Ltd* [1980] A.C. 827 at 844, per Lord Diplock: "when in the context of a breach of contract one speaks of 'termination,' what is meant is no more than that the innocent party, or in some cases, both parties, are excused from further performance." Note also *Port Jackson Stevedoring Pty Ltd v Salmond & Spraggon (Australia) Pty Ltd* [1980] 3 All E.R. 257; *G.L. Group Plc v Ash Gupta Advertising Ltd*, 1987 S.C.L.R. 149.

[112] *Salaried Staff London Loan Co Ltd v Swears and Wells Ltd*, 1985 S.C. 189.

[113] *Heyman v Darwins Ltd* [1942] A.C. 356.

[114] *Photo Production Ltd v Securicor Transport Ltd* [1980] A.C. 827; *Lloyd's Bank Plc v Bamberger*, 1993 S.C. 570; *Fargnoli v GA Bonus Plc*, 1997 S.C.L.R. 12.

as to survive the breach of contract and govern its consequences.[115] Although rescission is thus basically prospective in effect, it may in at least some circumstances entail restitution of performances already rendered under the contract: as, for example, with the buyer's right of rejection and repetition of the price in sale of goods, or a party reclaiming an advance payment made in respect of a performance never received.[116] The advance payer's right to restitution cannot be exercised against the assignee of the original creditor of the advance, even where the payer has in fact made payment directly to the assignee. The latter is not subject to the cedent's liabilities; and if the contract between the assignor and the advance payer in fact dealt with the situation where advance payment was made but the assignor's performance was not completed, then in any event a claim in unjustified enrichment is excluded, even against one who was a third party to that contract.[117] But, it seems, a right to payment of interest for non-payment of the purchase price of heritable property will not be sustained if it is worded in a way which indicates that interest is due only where the contract is being performed.[118]

Material term or material breach—There is a source of confusion in that, in considering what justifies rescission, some authorities refer to "material terms" and others to "material breach". It seems that there are terms any breach of which is sufficient to justify rescission and others breach of which is not ground for rescission unless the consequences of the breach are sufficiently serious. The following cases have to be considered: (1) The question whether any particular provision in a contract is a material term of the contract[119] is one which the parties may settle for themselves. If they choose to provide that the whole contract shall be dependent on the fulfilment of one provision or condition, then, no matter how trivial it may appear to be, the court will give effect to the expressed intention of the parties.[120] An implied intention will also be given effect.[121] (2) There may be an implication of law that breach of a certain term will justify rescission. Thus the Sale of Goods Act 1979 provides that breach of a term as to the quality of the goods or their fitness for a purpose in a consumer contract of sale shall be deemed to be a material breach.[122] (3) A declaration by one party that he refuses to perform

10.20

---

[115] *Heyman v Darwins Ltd* [1942] A.C. 356; *Alexander Stephen (Forth) Ltd v J.J. Riley (U.K.) Ltd*, 1976 S.C. 151; *Sanderson & Son v Armour & Co*, 1922 S.C. (HL) 117; *Muir Construction Ltd v Hambly Ltd*, 1990 S.L.T. 830.

[116] Gloag, *Law of Contract* (1929), pp.59–60; H. MacQueen, "Unjustified Enrichment and Breach of Contract",1994 Jur. Rev. 137. Cf. McBryde, *The Law of Contract in Scotland* (2007), paras 20.132 et seq. The problem case is *Connelly v Simpson*, 1993 S.C. 391.

[117] *Compagnie Commerciale Andre SA v Artibell Shipping Co Ltd (No.2)*, 2001 S.C. 653; *Pan Ocean Shipping Co Ltd v Creditcorp Ltd (The Trident Beauty)* [1994] 1 W.L.R. 161 (HL).

[118] *Lloyds Bank plc v Bamberger*, 1993 S.C. 570. Although the decision is difficult to reconcile with the law on liquidated damages, it has been followed in a number of cases on interpretation of the relevant provisions in the contracts concerned: *Black v McGregor*, 2007 S.C. 69; *Wipfel Ltd v Auchlochan Developments Ltd* [2006] CSOH 183.

[119] The English term is "condition precedent". "Precedent" refers to materiality, not to time.

[120] *Standard Life Assurance Co v Weems* (1884) 11 R. (HL) 48; *Dawsons v Bonnin*, 1922 S.C. (HL) 156; *Provincial Insurance Co v Morgan* [1933] A.C. 240.

[121] *Bunge Corp v Tradax Export S.A.* [1981] 1 W.L.R. 711.

[122] Sale of Goods Act 1979 s.15B(2)(a); added by the Sale and Supply of Goods Act 1994 s.5(1). But see para.12.38, below.

his obligations under the contract entitles the other party to rescind.[123] Repudiation may be effected by conduct.

> "If the defender has behaved in such a way that a reasonable person would properly conclude that he does not intend to perform the obligations he has undertaken, that is sufficient."[124]

An unjustified rescission may be treated as a repudiation which entitles the other party to rescind and recover damages.[125] An unjustified rescission need not be regarded as a repudiation where done in the honest belief that it is justified and on the clear understanding that, should this belief be shown to be wrong, the contract will be performed according to its terms.[126] (4) The breach itself may make further performance of the contract impossible, e.g. where the contract was to install equipment in a factory and a defect in the equipment caused a fire which destroyed the factory,[127] the contract was rescinded and the innocent party had no option but to accept repudiation. (5) A total failure of performance is obviously material. (6) The terms of the contract may indicate that a stipulation is so material that breach of it per se justifies rescission. The term must be one which goes to the root and essence of the contract. Two cases may be narrated as illustrations. In *Wade v Waldon*,[128] a comedian undertook to perform in a theatre on a date subsequent to the contract. It was stipulated that he should give a fortnight's notice, with bill matter, before the date of appearance. He failed to comply with this stipulation, and the manager of the theatre in consequence refused to fulfil his engagement. It was held that the comedian was entitled to damages, on the ground that, although he was in breach of contract in failing to send the notice, the breach was not sufficiently material to justify the manager in breaking off the whole contract. In *Graham v United Turkey Red Co*[129] an agent for the sale of goods undertook not to sell the same goods supplied by others. He broke that condition. It was accepted that it was a material condition, and that the breach precluded the agent from suing for the commission to which he was entitled under the contract. Any claim he might have must rest on the ground, apart from the contract, that his employers had taken benefit from his service. (7) There are cases where rescission is justified by the nature of the breach. While it is a term of a contract of service that the employee will obey orders, whether disobedience justifies rescission in a particular instance is a question of facts and circumstances.[130] The breach "must fundamentally affect the fair carrying out of the bargain as a whole"[131]; it must have

---

[123] *Davie v Stark* (1876) 3 R. 1114; see para.10.24, below, as to anticipatory breach.

[124] *Forslind v Bechely-Crundall*, 1922 S.C. (HL) 173 at 179, per Viscount Haldane. See, e.g. *Edinburgh Grain Ltd (in liquidation) v Marshall Food Group Ltd*, 1999 S.L.T. 15.

[125] *Carswell v Collard* (1893) 20 R. (HL) 47; *Forbes v Campbell* (1885) 12 R. 1065; *Municipal Council of Johannesburg v Stewart*, 1909 S.C. 860 at 877, per Lord President Dunedin.

[126] *Woodar Investment Development Ltd v Wimpey Construction U.K. Ltd* [1980] 1 All E.R. 571 (HL). Cf. *Blyth v Scottish Liberal Club*, 1982 S.C. 140.

[127] *Harbutt's "Plasticine" Ltd v Wayne Tank and Pump Co Ltd* [1970] 1 Q.B. 447.

[128] *Wade v Waldon*, 1919 S.C. 571. The following passage in the opinion of Lord President Dunedin has been frequently referred to: "It is familiar law, and quite well settled by decision, that in any contract which contains multifarious stipulations there are some which go so to the root of the contract that a breach of those stipulations entitles the party pleading the breach to declare that the contract is at an end. There are others which do not go to the root of the contract, but which are part of the contract, and which would give rise, if broken, to an action of damages."

[129] *Graham v United Turkey Red Co*, 1922 S.C. 533.

[130] *Blyth v Scottish Liberal Club*, 1982 S.C. 140.

[131] *Forslind v Bechely-Crundall*, 1922 S.C. (HL) 173, per Lord Shaw at 190.

"the effect of depriving the other party of substantially the whole benefit which it was the intention of the parties that he should obtain from the contract".[132]

Building contracts—There is some difficulty in the law relating to building **10.21** contracts, mainly due to the fact that a failure by a builder to observe the building contract conditions may not materially affect the value of the building and yet may not be remediable without inordinate expense.[133] If the builder so far deviates from his contract as to produce a building substantially different from that ordered, the owner may reject it; if he prefers to keep it, he is not liable for the contract price, but only *quantum lucratus*—in so far as he is enriched by the building.[134] If the defects are of minor importance and admit of being remedied, the builder may recover the contract price under deduction of the sum necessary to bring the building into consonance with the plans.[135] If the deviation is irremediable without demolition, e.g. where the wrong kind of cement has been used, it was held in *Steel v Young*,[136] that even if the difference in value was inappreciable, the builder could not sue for the contract price, and that, if his action contained no conclusions for payment on the basis of *quantum lucratus*, it must be dismissed. But this decision has been doubted in *Forrest v Scottish County Investment Co*.[137] From the opinions there given, it would appear that if the contract had scheduled prices for each item (a measure and value, as distinguished from a lump-sum, contract) failure in one item would not preclude action for the amount due for the rest. The effect of an irremediable but immaterial failure in a lump-sum contract is doubtful[138]; in an English case, opinions were given to the effect that the builder might sue for the contract price under deduction of any damage which the owner might have suffered.[139]

Materiality of time of performance—The question whether time of performance is **10.22** material, or, as it is sometimes put, whether time is of the essence of the contract, depends upon the nature of the obligations undertaken. Time is clearly material, and failure will justify rescission, in contracts for the supply, or carriage, of goods which vary in price from day to day.[140] In other commercial contracts, where the element of fluctuation in price is absent, performance on the actual day is not generally material, but any lengthened delay will justify rescission.[141] In contracts for the construction of a particular article, delay is not generally sufficiently material to justify the rejection of the article when ultimately tendered.[142] Failure to tender a marketable title to heritage on the day fixed will not entitle a buyer to resile,[143] but will entitle him to intimate that he will resile if the title is not tendered at some definite date in the

---

[132] *Photo Production Ltd v Securicor Transport Ltd* [1980] A.C. 827, per Lord Diplock at 849.

[133] See discussion in MacQueen, "Unjustified Enrichment and Breach of Contract", 1994 Jur. Rev. 137, 149–66.

[134] *Ramsay v Brand* (1898) 25 R. 1212.

[135] *Speirs v Petersen*, 1924 S.C. 428.

[136] *Steel v Young*, 1907 S.C. 360.

[137] *Forrest v Scottish County Investment Co*, 1916 S.C. (HL) 28.

[138] See comments on *Forrest v Scottish County Investment Co* in *Graham v United Turkey Red Co*, 1922 S.C. 533.

[139] *H. Dakin & Co v Lee* [1916] 1 K.B. 566. See also *Eshelby v Federated European Bank* [1932] 1 K.B. 423.

[140] *Colvin v Short* (1857) 19 D. 890; *Nelson v Dundee East Coast Shipping Co*, 1907 S.C. 927.

[141] *Carswell v Collard* (1892) 19 R. 987, affd (1893) 20 R. (HL) 47.

[142] *Macbride v Hamilton* (1875) 2 R. 775.

[143] *Kelman v Barr's Tr.* (1878) 5 R. 816.

future.[144] It is clear that time of performance is not so material in a lease as to justify the tenant in throwing up the lease in the event of the landlord failing to execute improvements or repairs within the time stipulated.[145]

10.23 Degrees in materiality—There are degrees in materiality. A failure may not be sufficiently material to justify the rescission of the contract, yet may justify the party aggrieved in withholding performance of the obligations incumbent on him, i.e. in exercising the remedy of retention.[146] This has been illustrated chiefly in the case of leases. Failure by a landlord to place, or to uphold, the subject in the condition required by the contract may be so material as to justify the tenant in abandoning the subjects and claiming damages; or, where less material, may justify him in withholding payment of his rent; or may be in such a subordinate point that the tenant's only remedy is a claim for damages. The questions involved depend so much on the particular circumstance, and on the reasonableness, or otherwise, of the conduct of the parties, that it is not proposed to deal with the cases here.[147] Similar rules, equally insusceptible of precise definition, prevail in the case of a contract for the supply of goods by instalments.[148] It does not follow that because the loss caused by a breach is small, then the breach is trivial and not material.[149]

10.24 Anticipatory breach of contract—A definite refusal by one party to perform his obligations under a contract, even if made before the time for performance has arrived, may be treated by the other as an actual breach of contract which entitles him at once to the remedies which such a breach may entail.[150] He may accept the refusal as final; if he does so, any subsequent offer of performance comes too late.[151] He may decline to accept the refusal, and, when the time for performance arrives, sue for damages measured by the loss suffered at the date of failure, not at the date of the anticipatory refusal.[152] By adopting this attitude he puts it in the power of the other to reconsider his refusal, and also to take advantage of any intervening circumstance, such as a declaration of war, which, by rendering performance impossible or illegal, may offer a defence to a claim for damages.[153] In a case where he has the active duties under the contract, he has also the option, rather than accepting the refusal and claiming damages for breach of contract, of disregarding it so that the contract remains effectual. If he can carry out the contract without the co-operation, active or passive,[154] of the other party, he may proceed to do so and then claim for the full contract price.[155] It may be, however,

---

[144] *Stickney v Keeble* [1915] A.C. 386; see also *Rodger (Builders) v Fawdry*, 1950 S.C. 483 at 492, per Lord Sorn (OH).

[145] *McKimmie's Trs v Armour* (1899) 2 F. 156.

[146] See McBryde, *The Law of Contract in Scotland* (2007), paras 20.57–20.61, 20.88–20.131. On retention, see paras 10.14–10.18, above.

[147] See para.35.11, below; Rankine, *The Law of Leases in Scotland* (1916), pp.245, 326.

[148] para.12.45, below.

[149] *Devos Gebroeder N.V. v Sunderland Sportwear Ltd*, 1987 S.L.T. 331.

[150] *Hochster v De La Tour* (1853) 2 El. & Bl. 678, as explained by *Lords Haldane and Wrenbury in Bradley v Newsom* [1919] A.C. 16; *Monklands D.C. v Ravenstone Securities*, 1980 S.L.T. (Notes) 30; *Edinburgh Grain Ltd (in liquidation) v Marshall Food Group Ltd*, 1999 S.L.T. 15.

[151] *Gilfillan v Cadell & Grant* (1893) 21 R. 269.

[152] *Howie v Anderson* (1848) 10 D. 355; *Millet v Van Heek* [1921] 2 K.B. 369; *Tai Hing Cotton Mill v Kamsing Knitting Factory* [1979] A.C. 91.

[153] *Avery v Bowden* (1856) 6 El. & Bl. 953.

[154] *Hounslow L.B.C. v Twickenham Garden Developments Ltd* [1971] Ch. 233.

[155] *White & Carter (Councils) v McGregor*, 1962 S.C. (HL) 1, overruling *Langford & Co v Dutch*, 1952 S.C. 15. See *Finelli v Dee* (1968) 67 D.L.R. (2d) 393; *Decro-Wall International S.A. v*

that, if he has no legitimate interest to do so, he will not be allowed to saddle the other party with an additional burden which will involve no benefit to himself[156]; but it is for the other party to aver and prove the absence of legitimate interest.[157] Mere indications of doubt as to ability to perform cannot safely be regarded as an anticipatory breach[158]; but where A had attempted to evade his obligations, and had persistently failed to give any definite answer to demands for performance, it was held that his whole attitude amounted to a refusal to perform, which entitled B to treat the contract as repudiated by him.[159] If performance is due on demand, or on the occurrence of an uncertain event, any act by which the obligant puts it out of his power to perform, as when A transfers to B the article which he has agreed to sell to C, on demand or on the occurrence of some event, amounts to a repudiation of the contract.[160] C in such a case has bargained not merely for ultimate performance, but for the expectation of performance in the meantime, and to deprive him of that expectation is a material breach of the contract.[161] If, on the other hand, the date for performance is fixed, the obligant fulfils his contract if he is ready to perform when that date arrives, and it is doubtful whether any intervening act of his with regard to the subject to which the contract relates can be regarded as so irremediable as to amount to a refusal of ultimate performance.[162]

Provisions for breach of contract—The remedies for breach of contract considered in the preceding pages may in particular cases be supplemented by a provision for an irritancy or a penalty. The position with exclusion or limitation clauses is considered in a previous chapter.[163] **10.25**

Irritancies—An irritancy is a right to put an end to the contractual relation. When it is conditional on a breach of contract it is a general rule of construction that, no matter how it is expressed, it can be enforced only by the party aggrieved by the breach. It gives no right to the party in default. Thus a provision, in a contract between A and B, that the contract shall be void in the event of a specified breach by B, is read as rendering it voidable at A's option, not as giving B the opportunity of getting rid of his contract by committing a breach thereof.[164] **10.26**

Legal irritancies—Irritancies may be legal, imposed by law, or conventional, provided in the particular contract. The only legal irritancies known to the law relate to the non-payment of feu-duty or rent. Legal irritancies are purgeable, and **10.27**

Practitioners in Marketing Ltd [1971] 1 W.L.R. 361; *Attica Sea Carriers Corp v Ferrostaal Poseidon Bulk Reederei GmbH* [1976] 1 Lloyd's Rep. 250.

[156] per Lord Reid in *White & Carter (Councils)*, 1962 S.C. (HL) 1 at 14; *Gator Shipping Corp v Trans-Asiatic Oil Ltd S.A. and Occidental Shipping Establishment* [1978] 2 Lloyd's Rep. 357; *Clea Shipping Corp v Bulk Oil International Ltd* [1983] 2 Lloyd's Rep. 645.

[157] *Salaried Staff London Loan Co Ltd v Swears and Wells Ltd*, 1985 S.C. 189.

[158] *Johnstone v Milling* (1886) 16 Q.B.D. 460; *Thorneloe v McDonald* (1892) 29 S.L.R. 409.

[159] *Forslind v Bechely-Crundall*, 1922 S.C. (HL) 173.

[160] *Leith School Board v Rattray's Trs*, 1918 S.C. 94; *Synge v Synge* [1894] 1 Q.B. 466.

[161] See opinion of Lord President Clyde, *Sanderson v Armour*, 1921 S.C. 18, affd 1922 S.C. (HL) 117.

[162] *Harvey v Smith* (1904) 6 F. 511; *Smith v Butler* [1900] 1 Q.B. 694.

[163] Above, paras 9.17–9.25.

[164] *Bidoulac v Sinclair's Tr.* (1889) 17 R. 144; *New Zealand Shipping Co v Societé des Ateliers* [1919] A.C. 1.

an action to enforce them may be met by tender of payment at any time before decree is granted.[165]

10.28 Conventional irritancies—A conventional irritancy may be inserted in any contract, and is a matter which parties may arrange as they please. But what is in terms an irritancy may in substance amount to a penalty, and then cannot be enforced unless it can be regarded as a pre-estimate of damages.[166] So, where in a contract of sale with a price payable by instalments a provision is made for the irritancy of the contract (involving forfeiture of all that has been paid), this is in substance a penalty and one which the law will not enforce.[167] A conventional irritancy cannot be purged; considerations of hardship are out of place in a question of enforcing an unambiguous provision in a contract.[168] But conventional provisions in feus, and probably in leases if they merely express the irritancy which the law would infer, may be purged[169] and a statutory modification has been made in relation to certain types of lease.[170] And the court has an equitable jurisdiction to allow an irritancy to be purged when its exercise could be shown to be oppressive, as where it was enforced without giving adequate notice that the debt was due.[171]

10.29 Irritancy as precluding damages—The enforcement of an irritancy in a feu contract, by annulling the contract, not only precluded any claim for damages but barred any claim for arrears of feu-duties.[172] In leases, if the event for which the irritancy is provided is the bankruptcy of the tenant, its enforcement is a bar to any claim for damages.[173] But the charterer of a ship may take advantage of a cancelling clause in the charter-party, and also recover damages, if the non-arrival of the ship by the cancelling date is due to the fault of the shipowner.[174]

10.30 Penalty clauses—A provision in a contract for the incurring of a penalty in the event of a breach will not be enforced according to its terms unless it admits of being construed as a pre-estimate of damages.

> "If the penalty be truly a penalty–that is, a punishment–the Court will not allow that, because the law will not let people punish each other."[175]

---

[165] Erskine, I, 5, 27. See history of the law in *Duncanson v Giffen* (1878) 15 S.L.R. 356.

[166] See para.10.30, below.

[167] *Steedman v Drinkle* [1916] 1 A.C. 275.

[168] *Lyon v Irvine* (1874) 1 R. 512; *McDouall's Trs v MacLeod*, 1949 S.C. 593; *Anderson v Valentine*, 1957 S.L.T. 57; *Dorchester Studios (Glasgow) v Stone*, 1975 S.C. (HL) 56.

[169] *Duncanson v Giffen* (1878) 15 S.L.R. 356; see *Anderson*, 1957 S.L.T. 57.

[170] See Law Reform (Miscellaneous Provisions) (Scotland) Act 1985 ss.4–7 and para.35.26, below.

[171] *Stewart v Watson* (1864) 2 M. 1414; *McDouall's Trs*, 1949 S.C. 593; *Precision Relays Ltd v Beaton*, 1980 S.C. 220; *C.I.N. Properties Ltd v Dollar Land (Cumbernauld) Ltd*, 1992 S.C. (HL) 104; *Blythswood Investments (Scotland) Ltd v Clydesdale Electrical Stores Ltd (in receivership)*, 1995 S.L.T. 150; *Aubrey Investments Ltd v D.S.C. (Realisations) Ltd (in receivership)*, 1999 S.C. 21.

[172] *Magistrates of Edinburgh v Horsburgh* (1834) 12 S. 593; *Malcolm v Donald*, 1956 S.L.T. (Sh. Ct) 101.

[173] *Buttercase and Geddie's Tr. v Geddie* (1897) 24 R. 1128.

[174] *Nelson v Dundee East Shipping Co*, 1907 S.C. 927.

[175] *Robertson v Driver's Trs* (1881) 8 R. 555, per Lord Young. An interesting case on penalties, involving the Roman-Dutch law, is *Pearl Assurance Co v Union of South Africa* [1934] A.C. 570.

Where, however, a contract term provides for payment of a penalty on the occurrence of an event other than breach of contract, it will be enforced[176]; unless it occurs in a consumer contract in which case it may be invalid under the Unfair Terms in Consumer Contracts Regulations 1999.[177]

Penalty and liquidate damages—The rule is general, and applies to a clause of **10.31** irritancy if in substance it amounts to a penalty. It has been illustrated in cases where there is a provision for the payment of a specified sum in the event of a breach of the contract. This may be termed a penalty, or may be termed liquidate damages, but the result does not depend on the term used. It is regarded as a penalty unless it bears some intelligible relation to the loss which the breach will probably cause; as liquidate damages if it can be regarded as a fair, though not necessarily exact, pre-estimate of the amount of that loss. If the provision is sustained as liquidate damages, proof of the actual damage sustained is unnecessary,[178] and proof that damage has been sustained beyond the pre-estimate is inadmissible[179]; if regarded as a penalty, nothing can be recovered without proof of actual loss, and the amount fixed as a penalty is not a limit to the amount of damages that may be awarded.[180]

Penalties in bonds and leases—There are two cases where clauses providing for **10.32** a penalty or liquidate damages are inoperative. One is a clause in a bond, imposing a penalty on failure of punctual payment of interest. This is not enforceable according to its terms,[181] though there is no legal objection to the enforcement of a provision whereby, though interest at a lower rate than that fixed in the bond will be accepted, the full rate will be exacted on failure of punctual payment.[182] The other case is a provision in an agricultural lease for the payment of increased rent (usually termed "pactional rent") or other liquidated damages for breach of the terms of the lease. By statute such a provision is unenforceable.[183]

Liquidate damages—Apart from these two special cases the tendency of modern **10.33** decisions has been to sustain clauses providing for liquidate damages, unless the amount is plainly exorbitant, or where the same sum is fixed for any breach of a contract involving various obligations, some of trivial, and some of relatively great, importance. Such a provision indicates that no real pre-estimate of damages was aimed at, only a punishment of the defaulter.[184] Thus, where in a lease of an hotel various obligations were laid on each party, it was held that a general clause providing for a payment of £50 by either party in the event of any failure could not be regarded as a pre-estimate of damages, and, as a penalty, could not be enforced.[185]

---

[176] *Bell Bros (H.P.) Ltd v Aitken*, 1939 S.C. 77; *Granor Finance v Liquidator of Eastore*, 1974 S.L.T. 296; *E.F.T. Commercial Ltd v Security Change Ltd*, 1992 S.C. 414. Note also *Highland Leasing Ltd v Lyburn*, 1987 S.L.T. 92 and *City Inn Ltd v Shepherd Construction Ltd*, 2003 S.L.T. 885.

[177] See para.9.25, above.

[178] *Clydebank Engineering Co v Castaneda* (1904) 7 F. (HL) 77.

[179] *Diestal v Stevenson* [1906] 2 K.B. 345; *Cellulose Acetate Silk Co v Widnes Foundry* [1933] A.C. 20.

[180] *Dingwall v Burnett*, 1912 S.C. 1097.

[181] *Nasmyth v Samson* (1785) 3 Paton 9; Debts Securities (Scotland) Act 1856 s.7 (not applicable to a standard security: Conveyancing and Feudal Reform (Scotland) Act 1970 s.32, Sch.8 para.1).

[182] *Gatty v Maclaine*, 1921 S.C. (HL) 1.

[183] Agricultural Holdings (Scotland) Act 1991 s.48.

[184] See opinion of Lord Watson, *Lord Elphinstone v Monkland Iron Co* (1886) 13 R. (HL) 98. Such clauses, if exorbitant, are also struck at by the Unfair Terms in Consumer Contracts Regulations 1999 where they appear in a consumer contract: para.9.25, above.

[185] *Dingwall v Burnett*, 1912 S.C. 1097.

But it is not an objection that the same sum is fixed for a number of specified acts, if these acts are all of the same class, and if, from the nature of the case, the actual damage likely to result from each act is difficult or impossible to determine. So where agents for the sale of tyres agreed not to tamper with the tyre marks, to export without written consent, or to sell under list prices, a penalty of £5 per tyre was sustained.[186] In a leading case torpedo boats were ordered by the Spanish Government, with a penalty of £500 per week for late delivery. It was held that as it was impossible to prove the amount of loss which a nation might sustain owing to the want of torpedo boats any reasonable pre-estimate, whether termed a penalty or liquidate damages, would be sustained.[187] And it may perhaps be regarded as settled that in a contract for work to be done within a specified time, a penalty calculated at so much per day, week, or month will be sustained, unless plainly exorbitant.[188] In a hire-purchase case, where terms were agreed upon the basis of which the hirer had an option to return the hired article to the seller and he exercised that option, it was held that despite the use of the term "liquidate damages" as applying to the sum to be paid, the case was truly neither one of penalty nor of liquidate damages.[189] On the other hand, where a hire-purchase contract was terminated by the owner on the ground that the hirer was in breach, it was found necessary to consider whether a clause requiring the hirer to pay in that event the same amount as he would have had to pay had he exercised his option to terminate, was a penalty.[190]

10.34   **Deposits on sale**—In sale it is a common provision that the purchaser must deposit a portion of the price, to be forfeited if he fails to carry out his contract. This, though in substance a penalty, because it "creates by the fear of its forfeiture a motive in the payer to perform the rest of the contract",[191] is not so regarded, and the contract may be enforced according to its terms[192]; unless the sale is a consumer contract in which case such a term, if not individually negotiated, may be invalid under the Unfair Terms in Consumer Contracts Regulations 1999.[193]

10.35   **Penalty does not excuse performance**—It is a general rule that where the consequences of a breach of contract are provided for by a penalty or by liquidate damages, the provision is to be read as an addition to the remedies which the party aggrieved would otherwise possess, not as a licence to the other party to break his contract on payment of the penalty. So building restrictions, though fortified by a penalty, may be enforced by interdict,[194] and the same rule applies to the case where a party has agreed not to carry on a particular business.[195] Penalties are spoken of as "by and attour performance".

---

[186] *Dunlop Pneumatic Tyre Co v New Garage Co* [1915] A.C. 79, followed, *Imperial Tobacco Co v Parslay* [1936] 1 All E.R. 515.

[187] *Clydebank Engineering Co v Castaneda* (1904) 7 F. (HL) 77.

[188] *Cameron-Head v Cameron*, 1919 S.C. 627.

[189] *Bell Bros v Aitken*, 1939 S.C. 577. See also *Granor Finance v Liquidator of Eastore*, 1974 S.L.T. 296; *Euro London Appointments Ltd v Claessens International Ltd* [2006] EWCA Civ 385.

[190] *Bridge v Campbell Discount Co* [1962] A.C. 600.

[191] *Zemhunt (Holdings) Ltd v Control Securities Plc*, 1992 S.C. 58, per Lord Morison.

[192] *Commercial Bank v Beal* (1890) 18 R. 80; *Roberts & Cooper v Salvesen*, 1918 S.C. 794; *Zemhunt (Holdings) Ltd v Control Securities Plc*, 1992 S.C. 58. In the last two cases a deposit was treated as a pledge or guarantee of performance.

[193] Unfair Terms in Consumer Contracts Regulations 1999 reg.4(4) and Sch.3 para.1(d). For discussion of the regulations, see para.9.25, above.

[194] *Dalrymple v Herdman* (1878) 5 R. 847.

[195] *Curtis v Sandison* (1831) 10 S. 72.

Exclusion clauses—Apart from the provisions of the Unfair Contract Terms Act **10.36**
1977 and those of the Unfair Terms in Consumer Contracts Regulations 1999,[196]
it is open to the parties to a contract to provide by means of exclusion or exemption clauses that the failure by one of them in the performance of his obligations
under the contract will not entitle the other to recover damages or to rescind the
contract. It is now accepted that it is possible to frame a clause of this kind which
will exclude liability for even a "total" or "fundamental" breach.[197] But such
clauses are strictly construed, and it is a question of construction in each case
whether the clause is so clearly and unambiguously expressed as to be effectual
where there has been a fundamental breach of contract.[198] Clauses which merely
limit liability must equally be strictly construed and read contra proferentem but
they are to be judged by a less exacting standard.[199] In England it was at one time
held that if, on a fundamental breach, the innocent party rescinded the contract,
the other party could not then rely on a clause limiting liability because the
contract, including the exclusion clause, had ceased to exist; and the result was the
same where the fundamental breach itself brought the contract to an end.[200]
Although it has been held that that is not the law of Scotland,[201] the Unfair
Contract Terms Act 1977 s.22, provides "for the avoidance of doubt" that where
the Act requires that the incorporation of a term in a contract to which the Act
applies must be fair and reasonable for that term to have effect: (a) if that requirement is satisfied, the term may be given effect to notwithstanding that the contract
has been terminated in consequence of breach of that contract, (b) for the term to
be given effect to, that requirement must be satisfied even where a party who is
entitled to rescind the contract elects not to rescind it.

FURTHER READING

Clive, E. and Hutchison, D., "Breach of Contract"; Miller, S., "Unjustified
    Enrichment and Failed Contracts" both in Zimmermann, R., Visser, D. and
    Reid, K.G.C. (eds), *Mixed Legal Systems in Comparative Perspective:
    Property and Obligations in Scotland and South Africa* (Oxford: Oxford
    University Press, 2004).
Eiselen, S., "Specific Performance and Special Damages"; Naudé, T., "Termination
    for Breach of Contract" both in MacQueen, H.L. and Zimmermann, R. (eds),

---

[196] See paras 9.17–9.25, above.

[197] There is a problem of nomenclature. "Fundamental term" may refer to a term breach of which
justifies rescission: *Photo Production Ltd v Securicor Transport Ltd* [1980] A.C. 827 at 849, per Lord
Diplock; or to a term breach of which, it was thought, could not be covered by an exclusion clause:
Smeaton Hanscomb & Co Ltd v Sassoon 1. Setty Son & Co [1953] 1 W.L.R. 1468 at 1470, per Devlin
J. Similarly, "fundamental breach" is used to refer to a breach which justifies rescission: *Suisse
Atlantique Societe d'Armement Maritime S.A. v N.V. Rotterdamsche Kolen Centrale* [1967] 1 A.C. 361
at 397, per Lord Reid, or to a breach which, it was thought, could not be covered by an exclusion
clause: *Charterhouse Credit Co Ltd v Tolly* [1963] 2 Q.B. 683 at 704, per Donovan L.J.

[198] *Pollock v Macrae*, 1922 S.C. (HL) 192; *Mechans v Highland Marine Charters*, 1964 S.C. 48.
See, as to whether such a clause exempts a party from the consequences of his own negligence,
Canada Steamship Lines Ltd v The King [1952] A.C. 192; *Smith v U.M.B. Chrysler (Scotland) Ltd*,
1978 S.C. (HL) 1; *Evans v Glasgow District Council*, 1979 S.L.T. 270; *Verrico v Geo. Hughes & Son*,
1980 S.C. 179; *Golden Sea Produce Ltd v Scottish Nuclear Plc*, 1992 S.L.T. 942.

[199] *Ailsa Craig Fishing Co Ltd v Malvern Fishing Co Ltd*, 1982 S.C. (HL) 14.

[200] *Harbutt's "Plasticine" v Wayne Tank and Pump Co* [1970] 1 Q.B. 447.

[201] *Alexander Stephen (Forth) v J.J. Riley (U.K.)*, 1976 S.C. 151.

European Contract Law: Scots and South African Perspectives (Edinburgh: Edinburgh University Press, 2006).

Johnston, D., "Breach of Contract"; Smith, A.D., "Specific Implement" both in Reid, K.G.C. and Zimmermann, R. (eds), *A History of Private Law in Scotland* (Oxford: Oxford University Press, 2000), Vol.2.

McBryde, W.W., *The Law of Contract in Scotland*, 3rd edn (Edinburgh: W. Green, 2007), Chs 20, 22, 23.

McBryde, W.W., "A Mixed Legal System in Operation: the Scots Law of Breach of Contract" (2001) 6 Edin. L.R. 5.

Macgregor, L., "The Expectation, Reliance and Restitution Interests in Contract Damages", 1996 Jur. Rev. 227.

Macgregor, L., "Specific Implement in Scots Law", in Smits, J. (ed.), *Specific Performance in Contract Law: National and Other Perspectives* (Edinburgh: W. Green, 2008).

MacQueen, H.L. and Thomson, J.M., *Contract Law in Scotland*, 3rd edn (Bloomsbury Professional, 2012), Chs 5 and 6.

Scottish Law Commission, *Report on Penalty Clauses* (HMSO, 1999), Scot. Law Com. No.171.

Scottish Law Commission, *Report on Remedies for Breach of Contract* (HMSO, 1999), Scot. Law Com. No.174.

Stair Memorial Encyclopaedia, Vol.15, paras 779–813, 891–1000.

Steven, A.J.M., *Pledge and Lien* (Edinburgh: Edinburgh Legal Education Trust, 2008), Chs 9–17.

Stewart, W.J., "The Theory of the Scots Law of Contract", 1996 Jur. Rev. 403.

Walker, D.M., *The Law of Civil Remedies in Scotland* (Edinburgh: W. Green, 1974).

CHAPTER 11

IMPOSSIBILITY OF PERFORMANCE

Contracts to perform impossibility—It is generally supposed, though without **11.01**
any actual decision, that a contract to do something believed by all educated
persons to be physically impossible would be void, even although both parties
believed it to be possible.[1] But impossibility which is not obvious, but depends
upon intricate calculations, as in the case of a contract to build a ship on a certain
model and with a specified carrying capacity, leaves the contract unaffected.[2] The
plea of commercial impossibility, that is, that the value of a ship when repaired
would not cover the cost of repairs ordered, has been put forward, but unhesitat-
ingly rejected.[3] Contracts to do something legally impossible, i.e. to do an act for
which the law provides no facilities, as, for instance, to execute a valid entail after
the Register of Tailzies was closed by the Entail Act, are void.[4]

Supervening impossibility: Frustration—A contract may be dissolved by a **11.02**
change of circumstances, or of the law, which either renders performance impossible or illegal, or so alters the conditions that performance, if given, would in
substance be performance of a different contract from that to which the parties
agreed. To such cases the term frustration of the adventure has been applied.[5] It is
a general principle that the change in circumstances in question must have
occurred from some cause independent of the volition of the contracting parties.
So the statutory provision that on an agreement to sell specific goods the agreement is avoided if the goods perish before the risk passes to the buyer, is qualified
by the proviso that the goods shall have perished without any fault on the part of
the seller or buyer.[6] And where a ship hired under a time charter-party was detained
in a waterway when a war broke out, the contract was held to have been
frustrated.[7]

General result of impossibility—It is not an absolute rule that a contract is at an **11.03**
end because performance has become impossible. But the development of the
law, starting with the principle that if an unqualified obligation has been undertaken its supervening impossibility may be a ground for excusing actual performance but is no answer to a claim for damages, has been in the direction of holding

---

[1] Stair, I, 10, 13 ("contracts of impossibilities are void"). See Indian Contract Act 1872 s.56. The
illustration given is a contract to recover treasure by magic. See also Sale of Goods Act 1979 s.6.
[2] *Gillespie v Howden* (1885) 12 R. 800.
[3] *Hong-Kong, etc. Dock Co v Netherton Shipping Co*, 1909 S.C. 34.
[4] *Caledonian Insurance Co v Matheson's Trs* (1901) 3 F. 865; *George Packman & Sons v Dunbar's
Trs*, 1977 S.L.T. 140.
[5] See paras 11.14 and 11.15, below.
[6] Sale of Goods Act 1979 s.7. See *Mertens v Home Freeholds Co* [1921] 2 K.B. 526; and W.M.
Gloag, *Law of Contract*, 2nd edn (Edinburgh: W. Green, 1929), p.344.
[7] *The Evia (No.2)* [1983] 1 A.C. 736; *The Chrysalis* [1983] 1 Lloyd's Rep. 503.

that obligations are rarely intended to be unqualified, but are undertaken under the implied condition that performance shall continue to be possible.[8] The result is that there are now few cases where impossibility is not an effectual plea. Still, it is probably the law that an agreement to sell a certain quantity of a particular commodity is not affected by the fact that the commodity has become unprocurable[9] where the contract does not stipulate the source from which the order is to be satisfied. It is an established rule in shipping law that if a certain number of days (lay days) are provided in a charter-party for loading the ship, it is no answer to a claim for damages that owing to any circumstances, not expressly provided for and not due to the fault of the shipowner, it has proved to be impossible to load within the lay-days.[10] Even where there is no provision for lay-days, the charterer is absolutely bound to have the cargo ready on receiving reasonable notice of the arrival of the ship, and is liable in damages for her detention even although his failure was due to conditions over which he had no control.[11]

11.04 **Contract with time limits**—The strongest case for the enforcement of a contract according to its terms is where, as in the shipping cases above mentioned, there is an obligation to perform within a specified time, with a contractual provision for the consequences of failure. But even here it is not an absolute rule that impossibility of timely performance may not be a relevant defence. Thus, when a joiner undertook to finish his work on a house by a given date, with a penalty in the event of the time being exceeded, and met a demand for the penalty by the plea that his delay was due to the fact that observance of the time limit was impossible owing to the failure of other tradesmen employed on the house, the opinions of the majority of the court were in favour of the validity of his plea.[12]

11.05 *Rei interitus*—The clearest case for the dissolution of a contract on the ground of impossibility is where an obligation is undertaken which cannot be performed unless some specific thing continues to exist and to be available for the contractual purposes. Then the accidental destruction of that thing (*rei interitus*) or, without actual destruction, some event which precludes the performance of the contract through its means, will put an end to the contract.[13] Thus, if a specific thing sold has perished before the property has passed to the buyer[14]; if a subject has been accidentally destroyed,[15] or has been requisitioned by the Government,[16] or, in the case of a lease of salmon fishing, has been so affected by the action of a

---

[8] See the history of the law traced by McCardie J. in *Blackburn Bobbin Co v Allen* [1918] 1 K.B. 540, affd [1918] 2 K.B. 467.

[9] *Blackburn Bobbin Co* [1918] 1 K.B. 540. *Re Badische Co* [1921] 2 Ch. 331, does not controvert the view expressed in the text. One interpretation of this decision is that the contract was frustrated because both parties intended the subject-matter of the contract to come from Germany. Another is that the case concerns supervening illegality (i.e. the outbreak of the First World War) rather than supervening impossibility.

[10] *Hansa v Alexander*, 1919 S.C. (HL) 122.

[11] *Ardan S.S. Co v Weir* (1905) 7 F. (HL) 126.

[12] *T & R Duncanson v Scottish County Investment Society*, 1915 S.C. 1106. The decision turned on a specialty.

[13] Bell, *Principles*, s.29.

[14] Sale of Goods Act 1979 s.7; *Leitch v Edinburgh Ice, etc. Co* (1900) 2 F. 904.

[15] *Walker v Bayne* (1815) 6 Paton 217; *Allan v Robertson's Trs* (1891) 18 R. 932; *Cantors Properties (Scotland) Ltd v Swears & Wells Ltd*, 1978 S.C. 310.

[16] *Mackeson v Boyd*, 1942 S.C. 56.

Government department as to be incapable of possession as a fishing[17]; if a ship, though not actually lost, has been so injured as to become totally unfit for the purpose for which she was chartered[18]; if a music hall, hired for a particular day for the purpose of giving a concert, has been burned[19]; in all cases the contract is avoided or discharged, and no damages can be recovered from the party who has failed to fulfil his obligations. An analogous case is where a party has undertaken to perform some service, as, for example, to play at a concert, which is only possible if he remains in health. His illness amounts to *rei interitus*; he no longer exists as a concert-playing man, and the contract is dissolved.[20] It has been decided in Scotland that where the destruction or loss of a thing is due to the negligence of one of the contracting parties, this does not preclude a successful plea of frustration.[21] The position in England may be different and, in any event, is far less clearly stated.[22]

Building in course of erection—When a building in course of construction is **11.06** accidentally destroyed the question has been, not whether the contract is discharged (which would probably depend on the stage which the building had reached), but whether the builder has any claim for payment for his work or materials. In the cases in Scotland, the question has been treated on the basis of property. As the property in the unfinished building has passed to the owner of the ground, on the principle of accession[23] the general maxim *res perit domino* applies, the loss falls on him and the builder has a claim for his work and materials.[24]

Recovery of payments in advance—When payment in advance has been made **11.07** for a contract which is ultimately dissolved on the ground of impossibility, our law follows the *condictio causa data, causa non secuta* of the civil law, and holds that where money is paid in advance in consideration of some service to be rendered in future, it may be recovered if that service is not rendered, even though, as in the case of impossibility, no breach of contract may be involved. Thus, in a contract for the construction of a ship's engines for an Austrian firm an instalment of the price was paid on signing the contract. Before the construction of the engines had begun, war with Austria was declared. It was not in dispute that this put an end to the contract.[25] It was held on the conclusion of peace, that the Austrian firm might recover the deposit.[26]

---

[17] *Tay Salmon Fisheries Co v Speedie*, 1929 S.C. 593.
[18] *London and Edinburgh Shipping Co v The Admiralty*, 1920 S.C. 309.
[19] *Taylor v Caldwell* (1863) 3 B. & S. 826.
[20] *Robinson v Davidson* (1871) L.R. 6 Ex. 269.
[21] *London and Edinburgh Shipping Co v The Admiralty*, 1920 S.C. 309.
[22] *In The Super Servant Two* [1990] 1 Lloyd's Rep. 1, the Court of Appeal held that negligence did operate as a bar to frustration. This is contrary to obiter dicta in *Joseph Constantine S.S. Co v Imperial Smelting Corp Ltd* [1942] A.C. 154. Note also *The Hannah Blumenthal* [1983] 1 A.C. 854 and *Hare v Murphy Bros Ltd* [1974] 1 All E.R. 940.
[23] See para.31.06, below.
[24] *McIntyre v Clow* (1875) 2 R. 278; *Richardson v Dumfriesshire Road Trs* (1890) 17 R. 805.
[25] See para.3.45, above.
[26] *Cantiere San Rocco v Clyde Shipbuilding Co*, 1922 S.C. 723, revd 1923 S.C. (HL) 105. The law of England has since been brought into line with Scots law: *Fibrosa Spolka Akcyjna v Fairbairn & Co* [1943] A.C. 32; Law Reform (Frustrated Contracts) Act 1943, applied in *BP Exploration Co (Libya) Ltd (No.1) v Hunt* [1976] 1 W.L.R. 788, and *Gamerco SA v ICM Fair Warning (Agency) Ltd* [1995] 1 W.L.R. 1226.

11.08 Supervening events altering value of contract—Some early cases on leases extended the principle of *rei interitus* to the case where the subjects let failed to produce the expected return. The lease was not avoided, but no rent was due for the period of sterility.[27] But the authority of these cases was called into question in *Gowans v Christie*.[28] It was there held that a mineral lease was not avoided by the failure of the seam, and observed that in a lease for years the tenant expected to make his profit on a balance of good and bad years, and that there was no equity in refusing rent for a year which had proved unproductive. And generally, except in cases where the execution of the contract is interrupted and the plea of frustration of the adventure is available,[29] the fact that supervening events, or a change in the law, have made the contract more burdensome or less profitable is irrelevant.[30] Thus, no rise or fall of prices or wages has so far been held to avoid a contract for the supply of goods or labour.[31] Inflation per se does not constitute frustration.[32] It is for the legislature, by emergency legislation, to provide for exceptional cases where a change in conditions would make the performance of certain contracts ruinous. There is a general statutory provision under which, when a new duty is imposed, or an existing duty increased or diminished, on any article which is the subject of a sale or an agreement to sell, an increase or diminution of the price, as the case may be, may be claimed by the seller or purchaser.[33] At common law it was held that the loss due to an alteration in duties must fall where it might happen to light.[34] It may be regarded as an exception to the general rule that if a subject let is partially destroyed the tenant is entitled to an abatement of rent.[35]

11.09 Object of contract defeated—Events, without rendering literal performance of the contract impossible, may disappoint the object for which one of the parties contracted. If this object was known to him alone the contract is clearly unaffected; a seller is not concerned with the motives which induce the buyer to buy. Even if the object was known to both, its disappointment will not affect the contract unless the result would be to render it completely nugatory. So an agreement for the sale of jute remained binding, although the export of jute was subsequently forbidden, since the contract did not provide that the sale was for export.[36] But there may be exceptional cases where the disappointment of the only purpose which could have induced it, even although no mention may have been made of that purpose in the contract itself, will avoid the contract. A series of cases, usually referred to as the Coronation cases, arose out of the postponement of a procession which had been fixed for the coronation of Edward VII. Rooms had been hired on the route of the procession, without any express mention of it, but on terms which clearly indicated the object for which they were rented. On the postponement of

---

[27] *Foster v Adamson* (1762) Mor. 10131.

[28] *Gowans v Christie* (1873) 11 M. (HL) 1; W.M. Gordon, *Roman Law, Scots Law and Legal History* (Edinburgh: Edinburgh University Press, 2007), Ch.11.

[29] Below, para.11.14.

[30] *Holliday v Scott* (1830) 8 S. 831.

[31] *Wilson v Tennants* [1917] A.C. 495.

[32] *Wates Ltd v Greater London Council* (1983) 25 B.L.R. 1 (CA). Note also *British Movietonews Ltd v London and District Cinemas* [1952] A.C. 166 (currency depreciation) and *Multiservice Bookbinding Ltd v Marden* [1979] Ch. 84 (currency depreciation).

[33] Finance Act 1901 s.10(1); scope enlarged by Finance Act 1902 s.7.

[34] *Maclelland v Adam* (1795) Mor. 14247.

[35] *Muir v McIntyre* (1887) 14 R. 470; *Sharp v Thomson*, 1930 S.C. 1092.

[36] *McMaster & Co v Cox McEuen & Co*, 1920 S.C. 566, revd 1921 S.C. (HL) 24.

the procession it was held that the case could be treated as one where performance had been rendered impossible, and that the contracts were avoided.[37]

Violent acts by third parties—The effect of impossibility due to the violent or **11.10** unwarrantable acts of third parties is not free from doubt, but it would appear that it is not a ground for the dissolution of a contract. Thus, it has been held in England in cases which, though questioned, have not been overruled, that an obligation to load cargo at a particular port is not affected by the fact that civil disturbance or the unwarrantable acts of the port authorities have rendered it impossible.[38] In *Milligan v Ayr Harbour Trustees* it was decided that the obligation of a harbour trust to provide facilities for unloading a ship was not excused by reasonable apprehensions that the result would be a strike and, in the opinion of Lord Guthrie, would not have been excused even if it had been certain that compliance would have brought the business of the harbour to a standstill.[39] Where a tenant's crops were carried off by rebel forces this was held to be no ground for a refusal to pay rent.[40]

Change in law: Illegality—If a change in the law renders performance illegal the **11.11** contract is dissolved, on the theory that it is not to be presumed that a man bound himself to commit an illegal act. So, for example, a partnership is dissolved by the happening of any event which makes it unlawful for the business of the firm to be carried on, or for the members of the firm to carry it on in partnership.[41] The effect of a declaration of war as dissolving contracts with the enemy is considered above.[42] It is probably established that a contract which is to be performed in a foreign country is dissolved if a change in the law of that country renders performance illegal there.[43]

Change in law: Impossibility—If a change in the law renders performance **11.12** impossible, the result is to dissolve the contract. Thus, a contract for the export of goods is dissolved if their export is prohibited by statutory authority, so long as the prohibition is absolute and applies to the whole time available for performance.[44] Where A contracted to leave a particular piece of ground unbuilt upon, and a railway company, under statutory powers, acquired the ground and built a station on it, it was held that A was not liable in damages.[45] But if, in similar circumstance, it is within the obligant's power to secure a clause which would safeguard his obligation, he is bound to do so.[46]

---

[37] *Krell v Henry* [1903] 2 K.B. 740; *Chandler v Webster* [1904] 1 K.B. 493. Contrast *Herne Bay Steamboat Co v Hutton* [1903] 2 K.B. 683. It was further held in *Krell* and *Chandler* that the money paid in advance for the seats could not be recovered, but these decisions have been overruled on this point, para.11.07, above.

[38] *Jacobs v Credit Lyonnais* (1884) 12 Q.B.D. 589; *Ashmore v Cox* [1899] 1 Q.B. 436. See opinions in *Matthey v Curling* [1922] 2 A.C. 180.

[39] *Milligan v Ayr Harbour Trustees*, 1915 S.C. 937.

[40] *Strachan v Christie* (1751) Mor. 10129.

[41] Partnership Act 1890 s.34.

[42] See para.3.45, above.

[43] *Ralli Bros v Compania Naviera* [1920] 2 K.B. 287; *Trinidad Shipping Co v Alston* [1920] A.C. 888.

[44] *Re Anglo-Russian Merchant Traders & Batt* [1917] 2 K.B. 679, distinguished in *Ross T. Smyth & Co Ltd v W.N. Lindsay Ltd* [1953] 1 W.L.R. 1280.

[45] *Baily v De Crespigny* (1869) L.R. 4 Q.B. 180.

[46] *Leith School Board v Rattray's Trs*, 1918 S.C. 94.

11.13   Impossibility: When final—A party is not entitled to cancel his contract on the ground that events are looming in the future which will probably render performance impossible, and, if he takes that course, will be liable in damages even although his apprehensions may be justified by the event.[47] The question how far it may be assumed that an existing bar to performance will remain permanent is in some respects doubtful. It is an established rule that no court can predict how long a war may last and, therefore, that contracts affected by war are dissolved at once.[48] Probably, a statute which renders performance illegal or impossible may be regarded as conclusive. But this is not clear with regard to Orders in Council having statutory force, and in one case where the export of confectionery was prohibited by Order it was held that a party who had undertaken to export it was bound to wait to see whether the Order would remain in force, and was not justified in rescinding the contract at once.[49] Where administrative measures taken by a foreign government rendered performance impossible it was held that the question whether the contract could be cancelled at once depended on whether there was or was not a reasonable probability that the measures in question would be altered in time to admit of the performance.[50]

11.14   Frustration of the adventure—The object of the principle known as frustration is to find some satisfactory way whereby the court may allocate between the parties to a contract the risk of supervening events. The general idea behind it has been judicially explained as follows[51]:

> "When a lawful contract has been made and there is no default, a Court of law has no power to discharge either party from the performance of it unless either the rights of someone else or some Act of Parliament give the necessary jurisdiction. But a Court can and ought to examine the contract and the circumstances in which it was made, not of course to vary, but only to explain it, in order to see whether or not from the nature of it the parties must have made their bargain on the footing that a particular thing or state of things would continue to exist . . . no Court has an absolving power, but it can infer from the nature of the contract and the surrounding circumstances that a condition which is not expressed was a foundation on which the parties contracted."

While the principle was, in the early stages of its history, developed particularly with regard to the interruption of business activities by delay, it admits of almost indefinite application, as diverse as are the possibilities of a contract being interrupted by a vital change of circumstances. The application of the general principle must depend on the circumstances of each case; and it is for the court to decide, looking to what has actually happened and its effect on the possibility of performing the contract, what is the true position between the parties.[52] Where there is frustration, a dissolution of the contract occurs automatically, independent

---

[47] *Watts Watts & Co v Mitsui* [1917] A.C. 227.
[48] *Horlock v Beal* [1916] 1 A.C. 486; *Geipel v Smith* (1872) L.R. 7 Q.B. 404.
[49] *Andrew Millar & Co v Taylor* [1916] 1 K.B. 402.
[50] *Embiricos v Reid* [1914] 3 K.B. 45.
[51] By Lord Loreburn in *F.A. Tamplin Steamship Co v Anglo-Mexican Petroleum Co* [1916] 2 A.C. 397 at 403, quoted by Lord Radcliffe in *Davis Contractors Ltd v Fareham U.D.C.* [1956] A.C. 696 at 727.
[52] *James B. Fraser & Co v Denny Mott & Dickson*, 1944 S.C. (HL) 35 at 42–3, per Lord Wright.

of the choice or election of either party.[53] It is immaterial that the possibility of the frustrating event was within the contemplation of both parties; the only thing that is essential is that the parties should have made no provision for it in their contract.[54] Where a clause can be read as providing specifically for the event which occurred, the rule can have no application.[55]

Theory or principle of frustration—While the doctrine of frustration is itself **11.15** now well established, the search for a theoretical basis for it has continued. Dicta in the House of Lords have over the years favoured a variety of theories, and, while the results have in most cases been consistent, it may be a matter of significance which theory is applied.[56] According to what may be called the "implied term" theory, which has had wide support in past decisions of the House of Lords in English appeals, the principle upon which supervening impossibility was held to dissolve a contract was that it is an implied condition in the particular contract that performance is promised only if it remains possible and legal. The court, it was said, has no power to dissolve or vary a contract, but it has the power and duty to give effect to the intentions of the parties by interpreting the contract according to its conditions, implied as well as express.[57] The implied term theory was, however, not without its critics,[58] and seems now to have been rejected in favour of another which has had some currency in the past and seems more in line with the Scottish approach.[59] According to this view, which may be called the "material change" theory, as contractual obligation rests on consent, there can be no obligation to perform in circumstances so altered that performance, if given, would in substance be the performance not of the original contract, but of a different contract, and one to which the parties have not consented. Lord Radcliffe in *Davis Contractors Ltd v Fareham U.D.C.*[60] formulated the theory as follows:

"frustration occurs whenever the law recognises that without default of either party a contractual obligation has become incapable of being performed because the circumstances in which performance is called for would render

---

[53] *Hirji Mulji v Cheong Yue S.S. Co* [1926] A.C. 497 at 510.

[54] *Tamplin Co* [1916] 2 A.C. 397; *Ocean Tramp Tankers Corp v V/O Sovfracht (The Eugenia)* [1964] 2 Q.B. 226 at 240, per Lord Denning M.R.

[55] *Scott v Del Sel*, 1922 S.C. 592, affd 1923 S.C. (HL) 37; *The Evia (No.2)* [1983] A.C. 736.

[56] *Davis Contractors Ltd v Fareham U.D.C.* [1956] A.C. 696, per Lord Reid at 719, Lord Radcliffe at 728.

[57] See opinion of Earl Loreburn, *F.A. Tamplin Co v Anglo-Mexican Petroleum Co* [1916] 2 A.C. 397 at 405, of Lord Dundas, *McMaster v Cox, McEuen & Co*, 1920 S.C. 566, revd 1921 S.C. (HL) 24; of Lord Simon in *Joseph Constantine Steamship Line v Imperial Smelting Corp* [1942] A.C. 154 at 164; of Lord Simon and Lord Simonds in *British Movietonews v London and District Cinemas* [1952] A.C. 166 at 183, 187.

[58] See, e.g. Lord Wright in *James B. Fraser & Co*, 1944 S.C. (HL) 35 at 43; Lord Reid in *Davis Contractors Ltd* [1956] A.C. 696 at 720.

[59] See opinion of Lord Dunedin, *Metropolitan Water Board v Dick, Kerr & Co* [1918] A.C. 119. The Scottish approach has been that the court in the exercise of its equitable jurisdiction does, upon a proper construction of the contract, what seems just in the circumstances: see Lord Cooper, "Frustration of Contract in Scots Law" (1946) 28 J. Comp. Leg. 1, 5; W.W. McBryde, *The Law of Contract in Scotland*, 3rd edn (Edinburgh: W. Green, 2007), paras 21.05–21.12. An argument that the Scottish courts have a power of "equitable adjustment" in relation to contracts affected by change of circumstances was however rejected in *Lloyds TSB Foundation for Scotland v Lloyds Banking Group Plc* [2011] CSIH 87; 2012 S.C. 259 (under appeal to the UK Supreme Court).

[60] *Davis Contractors Ltd v Fareham U.D.C.* [1956] A.C. 696 at 729. See also *Tsakiroglou & Co Ltd v Noblee Thorl GmbH* [1962] A.C. 93; *The Eugenia* [1964] 2 Q.B. 226, per Lord Denning M.R. at 238–40; *Pioneer Shipping Ltd v B.T.P. Tioxide Ltd* [1982] A.C. 724 at 751.

it a thing radically different from that which was undertaken by the contract. *Non haec in foedera veni*. It was not this that I promised to do".

Lord Reid's opinion in the same case,[61] that frustration depends upon the true construction[62] of terms of the contract and of the relevant surrounding circumstances when the contract was made, is really another way of saying the same thing. As he puts it, the question in each case is whether the contract which the parties did make is, on its true construction, wide enough to apply to the new situation; if not, it is at an end.

11.16 Illustrations—The application of this rule will most easily be understood by examples. Where a servant is unable to attend to his duties through illness, this does not form a breach of contract on his part, but if the time for which he is absent is in the circumstances material, it does bring the case within the law of frustration of the adventure, and the employer is entitled to cancel the contract.[63] In what is usually regarded as the leading case, A undertook to send a ship to Cardiff to load a cargo for South America. His obligation was to arrive with all convenient speed, unless prevented by perils of the sea. By perils of the sea the ship was injured, with the result that her voyage to Cardiff took some five months more than the normal time. Though she had arrived in time according to the terms of the contract, it was held that the delay so altered the conditions as to entitle the charterer to declare it cancelled.[64] Where a house let furnished was requisitioned by the military authorities it was held that both landlord and tenant were liberated by "constructive total destruction" of the premises.[65] And where a vessel which had been chartered to carry a cargo was so damaged by a violent explosion that she was unable to perform the charter-party, it was held that the voyage had been frustrated and that the owners were not liable in damages for non-performance.[66]

11.17 Limits of principle of frustration—The principle does not apply to a change in economic conditions which may render the contract more onerous than had been contemplated; the fact that it had become more expensive or commercially less attractive for one party than he anticipated is not enough to bring about a frustration of the contract.[67] A policy of marine insurance is not affected by the declaration of war, however seriously that may affect the risk.[68] The principle of frustration of the adventure operates automatically for the good or ill of both

---

[61] *Davis Contractors Ltd* [1956] A.C. 696 at 720.

[62] For an earlier statement of the "true construction" approach, see Lord Simon in *British Movietonews* [1952] A.C. 166 at 185; Lord Wright in *James B. Fraser & Co* 1944 S.C. (HL) 35 at 42–43.

[63] *Manson v Dowie* (1885) 12 R. 1103; *Poussard v Speirs & Pond* (1876) 1 Q.B.D. 410; *Notcutt v Universal Equipment Co (London) Ltd* [1986] 1 W.L.R. 641. There is no need for the employer (in a proper case) to give notice of termination: *Westwood v Scottish Motor Traction Co*, 1938 S.N. 8.

[64] *Jackson v Union Marine Insurance Co* (1874) L.R. 10 C.P. 125. See also *Nelson v Dundee East Shipping Co*, 1907 S.C. 927.

[65] *Mackeson v Boyd*, 1942 S.C. 56; see also *Metropolitan Water Board v Dick, Kerr & Co* [1918] A.C. 119.

[66] *Joseph Constantine Steamship Line v Imperial Smelting Corp* [1942] A.C. 154.

[67] *Wilson v Tennants* [1917] A.C. 495; *Davis Contractors Ltd v Fareham U.D.C.* [1956] A.C. 696; *Tsakiroglou & Co* [1962] A.C. 93; *The Eugenia* [1964] 2 Q.B. 226, per Lord Denning M.R. at 239.

[68] *Brown v Maxwell* (1824) 2 Sh. App. 373.

...nd the person who relies upon it lies under no obligation to disprove fault ...is part in connection with the frustrating event.[69]

FURTHER READING

Evans-Jones, R., *Unjustified Enrichment Volume 1: Enrichment by Deliberate Conferral: Condictio* (Edinburgh: W. Green, 2003), Ch.4 (section 2).

Forte, A., "Economic Frustration of Commercial Contracts: A Comparative Analysis with Particular Reference to the United Kingdom", 1986 Jur. Rev. 1.

Gordon, W.M., *Roman Law, Scots Law and Legal History* (Edinburgh: Edinburgh University Press, 2007), Ch.11.

Hondius, E. and Grigoleit, H. (eds), *Unexpected Circumstances in European Contract Law* (Cambridge: Cambridge University Press, 2011).

McBryde, W.W., *The Law of Contract in Scotland*, 3rd edn (Edinburgh: W. Green, 2007), Ch.21.

Macgregor, L., "The Effect of Unexpected Circumstances on Contracts in Scots and Louisiana Law", in Palmer, V.V. and Reid, E.C. (eds), *Mixed Jurisdictions Compared: Private Law in Louisiana and Scotland* (Edinburgh: Edinburgh University Press, 2009), Ch.9.

MacQueen, H.L. and Thomson, J.M., *Contract Law in Scotland,* 3rd edn (Bloomsbury Professional, 2012), Ch.4.

Miller, S., "Unjustified Enrichment and Failed Contracts", in Zimmermann, R., Visser, D. and Reid, K.G.C. (eds), *Mixed Legal Systems in Comparative Perspective: Property and Obligations in Scotland and South Africa* (Oxford: Oxford University Press, 2004).

Stair Memorial Encyclopaedia, Vol.15, paras 880–9.

---

[69] *Joseph Constantine Steamship Line* [1942] A.C. 154. As to the effect on a contract of employment of the employee being given a custodial sentence, see *F.C. Shepherd & Co Ltd v Jerrom* [1986] 3 W.L.R. 801.

SECTION B:
PARTICULAR CONTRACTS

CHAPTER 12

SUPPLY OF GOODS

Sale of Goods Act—The law of sale of goods was first comprehensively regu- **12.01**
lated by the Sale of Goods Act 1893. That statute, in its main provisions applicable both to Scotland and England, was with regard to the law of England in
substance a codification of the pre-existing law; in regard to the law of Scotland
it made changes which may be called revolutionary. It was amended in important
respects by the Supply of Goods (Implied Terms) Act 1973 and the Consumer
Credit Act 1974. The law is now consolidated in the Sale of Goods Act 1979 (the
"1979 Act")[1] which has been amended by the Sale and Supply of Goods Act 1994
(hereinafter referred to as the "1994 Act"), the Sale of Goods (Amendment) Act
1995 (hereinafter referred to as the "1995 Act"),[2] and the Sale and Supply of
Goods Regulations 2002 (SI 2002/3045) (hereinafter referred to as the "2002
Regulations").[3]

Meaning of "goods"—Goods are defined as including, in Scotland, "all corpo- **12.02**
real movables except money". The term "includes emblements, industrial growing
crops and things attached to or forming part of the land which are agreed to be
severed before sale or under the contract of sale".[4] The provisions of the Act have
been held applicable to the sale of ships,[5] standing trees,[6] and growing crops,[7] but
not to a mineral lease.[8]

---

[1] The Act applies to contracts made on or after January 1, 1894 but Sch.1 modifies some sections
as they apply to contracts made before various dates. For the background, see A.F. Rodger, "The codification of commercial law in Victorian Britain" (1992) 108 L.Q.R. 570. The Act applies without
modification to contracts made on or after May 19, 1985 (SI 1983/1572).

[2] The Sale and Supply of Goods Act 1994 (the "1994 Act") came into force on January 3, 1995 and
applies to contracts of sale made on or after that date, s.8(3). The 1994 Act was based on the joint
report by the English and Scottish Law Commissions: *The Sale and Supply of Goods* (HMSO, 1987),
Law Com. No.160, Scot. Law Com. No.104, Cm.137. The Sale of Goods (Amendment) Act 1995 (the
"1995 Act") came into force on September 19, 1995 but has no retrospective effect. It implements
another joint report of the English and Scottish Law Commissions: *Sale of Goods Forming Part of a
Bulk* (HMSO, 1993), Law Com. No.215, Scot. Law Com. No.145, HC Paper No.807.

[3] The Regulation 2002/3045 on the sale and supply of goods to consumers [2002] came into force
on March 31, 2003 and implement Directive 1999/44/EC of the European Parliament and of the
Council of May 25, 1999 on certain aspects of the sale of consumer goods and associated guarantees
[1999] (O.J. No.L171, July 7, 1999, p.12).

[4] Sale of Goods Act 1979 (the "1979 Act") s.61(1).

[5] *Behnke v Bede Shipping Co* [1927] 1 K.B. 649.

[6] *Morison v Lockhart*, 1912 S.C. 1017; *Munro v Liquidator of Balnagown Estates Co*, 1949 S.C.
49. See fn.36, below.

[7] *Kennedy's Tr. v Hamilton* (1897) 25 R. 252; *Paton's Trs v Finlayson*, 1923 S.C. 872; *Allan v
Millar*, 1932 S.C. 620.

[8] *Morgan v Russell* [1909] 1 K.B. 357.

12.03 Sale as contract and as transfer of property—The effect of the alterations in the common law of Scotland introduced by the 1893 Act may be apprehended by considering that the law of sale has two main aspects.[9] It deals with sale as a contract, and indicates the contractual obligations on either side which will be implied in the absence of any express provision. In this aspect the alterations due to the Act are of minor importance, and may be indicated in summarising the statutory provisions. But it also deals with sale as a method of transferring the property (*jus in re*) of the thing sold, and in this aspect the law has been altered so fundamentally that it is desirable to insert a statement of the common law and of the modifications introduced by prior legislation.

12.04 Transfer of goods sold: Common law—By the common law of Scotland, a contract to sell goods has no effect on the property of the goods in question. The property, and the real right, *jus in re*, remained with the seller (whether the price had been paid or not) until the goods were delivered to the buyer. Until delivery a purchaser had no right higher than that of a creditor in a personal obligation to deliver the goods. Sale was an example of the general rule, expressed in the maxim *traditionibus, non nudis pactis, dominia rerum transferuntur* (rights of property are transferred by delivery and not by mere agreements), that a contract for the transfer of a thing merely created a *jus in personam*, or personal claim against the transferor. It did not carry the real right in the thing. This was a rule of law, independent of the volition of the parties. It was, it is true, open to the parties, by selling under a suspensive condition, to reserve to the seller the property in the thing even after it had been delivered[10]; it was not within their power to transfer the property before delivery.[11] But the risk of accidental destruction or damage passed to the buyer before delivery: in the sale of specific goods, when the contract was concluded; and in the sale of unascertained goods, when the seller appropriated particular goods to the contract for delivery to the buyer.[12]

12.05 Results of rules of common law—The most important practical results of the general rule that property in the goods sold could not pass until they were delivered were the following: (a) in the event of the sequestration of the seller before delivery the buyer, though he might have paid the price, could not obtain the article sold. It was still the property of the seller, and passed, with the rest of his property, to the trustee in his sequestration. The buyer had merely a claim for damages for the non-fulfilment of the contract, his right being to rank for a dividend on that claim with the other personal creditors of the seller.[13] (b) The seller, being still undivested owner, could, in a question with the purchaser or in his bankruptcy, retain the thing sold in security of any debt which might be due to him by the purchaser.[14] (c) The seller had a similar right in a question with a sub-purchaser. He was still the owner of the goods, the sub-purchaser had merely a personal right to delivery, and that personal right was postponed to the seller's right to retain his position as owner, and therefore to withhold delivery of the

---

[9] See also paras 12.09 and 12.11, below and para.1.09, above.
[10] *Macartney v Macredies's Creditors* (1799) Mor. App. Sale/1; *Murdoch v Greig* (1889) 16 R. 396.
[11] As to the common law see Bell, *Commentaries*, I, 181.
[12] See the discussion of the common law in *Widenmeyer v Burn Stewart & Co*, 1967 S.C. 85.
[13] *Mathison v Alison* (1854) 17 D. 274.
[14] *Wyper v Harveys* (1861) 23 D. 606.

...he had received payment, not only of the price,[15] but of any general ...which might be due to him by the original purchaser.[16]

Mercantile Law Amendment Act—The general principle that the property in **12.06** goods sold did not pass until delivery ruled until the Sale of Goods Act 1893 came into operation (1894), but certain of its practical results were affected by the Mercantile Law Amendment (Scotland) Act 1856 ss.1 to 5. As these sections were repealed by the Schedule to the Sale of Goods Act 1893, it is unnecessary to deal with their provisions in detail. Their general result was to entitle the purchaser of specific goods in a deliverable state to delivery in a question with the trustee in the sequestration of the seller,[17] and to abolish the right of an undivested seller to retain goods, in a question with a sub-purchaser, for any general balance due by the original purchaser.[18]

General effect of Sale of Goods Act—The provisions of the Sale of Goods Act **12.07** with regard to the passing of the property in goods sold are detailed later,[19] but it may be stated generally that the 1893 Act introduced the English law on the subject, under which the passing of the property does not depend upon the delivery of the goods but on the force of the contract. The property passes at the time when the parties intend it to pass, whether the goods are delivered or not.

Sale of Goods Act: Construction and scope—With these preliminary explana- **12.08** tions we pass to the consideration of the Act. It was laid down with reference to the 1893 Act as a general canon of construction that the fair meaning of the words used in the Act had to be taken, although that meaning might be inconsistent with the result of prior decisions and although there might be no apparent reason for supposing that a change in the law was intended.[20] The Sale of Goods Act 1979, like the 1893 Act, does not deal with such questions as the effects of error, misrepresentation or fraud, which fall to be decided according to the general law of contract. Section 62(2) provides that the rules of the common law, including the law merchant, save in so far as they are inconsistent with the express provisions of the Act, shall continue to apply to the contract of sale of goods. In the following pages the figures in square brackets refer to the sections of the Act as amended by the 1994 Act and the 2002 Regulations, which should in all cases be read.

Definition of contract of sale—The contract of sale is defined (s.2) as a contract **12.09** by which the seller transfers or agrees to transfer[21] the property in goods for a money consideration, called the price. Capacity to buy and sell is regulated by the general law as to capacity to contract, but where necessaries are sold and delivered to a person who, by reason of mental incapacity or drunkenness, is incompetent to contract, he must pay a reasonable price for them (s.3). The contract may be entered into orally, and proved by parole evidence. So an oral sale of a ship is

---

[15] *McEwan v Smith* (1849) 6 Bell's App. 340.
[16] *Melrose v Hastie* (1851) 13 D. 880.
[17] *McMeekin v Ross* (1876) 4 R. 154.
[18] See as to the result of the Mercantile Law Amendment Act, *Wyper v Harveys* (1861) 231 D. 606; *Distillers' Co v Russell's Tr.* (1889) 16 R. 479.
[19] See paras 12.14–12.17, below.
[20] *Bristol Tramways Carriage Co v Fiat Motors* [1910] 2 K.B. 831.
[21] These are the alternatives referred to in paras 12.03, above and 12.11, below.

binding.[22] Such subjects as growing crops or standing trees, though included in the definition of "goods", are heritable, and probably a contract for their sale would be required to be in writing.[23] It is not settled whether computer software is to be treated as goods.[24]

12.10 Sale and other contracts—The definition serves to distinguish sale from such contracts as pledge, where there is no agreement to transfer the property in goods; donation, where there is no price; and barter, where the consideration is not in money.[25] And where in a contract for building a ship, it was provided that the ship, as she was constructed, and all materials intended for her, should become the property of the purchasers, it was decided that there was only a contract for the sale of a complete ship, and that the provision as to the unfinished ship and the materials was not a sale but an attempt to create a right in security, which required delivery in order to make it effectual.[26]

12.11 Sale and agreement to sell—The Act draws a distinction between a sale and an agreement to sell. It depends on the transfer of the property in the goods. When the property is transferred under the contract it is a sale; where the transfer of the property is to take place at a future time or subject to some condition thereafter to be fulfilled, it is an agreement to sell. An agreement to sell becomes a sale when the time elapses or the conditions are fulfilled subject to which the property in the goods is to be transferred (s.2(6)).[27] A "sale", under the Act, is both a contract and a transference of the property in goods; an "agreement to sell" is merely a contract.

12.12 Sale and security—By s.62(4), it is provided that

> "the provisions of this Act about contracts of sale do not apply to a transaction in the form of a contract of sale which is intended to operate by way of mortgage, pledge, charge, or other security".

In the case of such transactions the common law as to passing of the property in goods is still applicable, and, therefore, the property in the goods which are nominally sold does not pass without delivery. The mere contract does not confer on the nominal purchaser any real right in the goods, and he has no claim to them which he can vindicate in the bankruptcy of the nominal seller. So where £40 was advanced to a dealer in bicycles, and he granted a promissory note for that amount, and also a document in the form of a receipt for certain bicycles sold to the lender, it was decided that the sale of the bicycles was a transaction intended to operate by way of security; that the provisions of the Sale of Goods Act did not apply; and that the nominal purchaser had no real right in the bicycles until they were

---

[22] *McConnachie v Geddes*, 1918 S.C. 391.

[23] *Morison v Lockhart*, 1912 S.C. 1017.

[24] See *Beta Computers (Europe) Ltd v Adobe Systems (Europe) Ltd*, 1996 S.L.T. 604; *St Albans City and D.C. v International Computers Ltd* [1996] 4 All E.R. 481, and discussion in P.S. Atiyah, J.N. Adams and H.L. MacQueen, *Sale of Goods*, 12th edn (Longman, 2010), pp.74–79.

[25] For a modern case on barter, see *Widenmeyer v Burn Stewart & Co*, 1967 S.C. 85. On "trading in" second-hand cars, *Sneddon v Durant*, 1983 S.L.T. (Sh. Ct) 38. See also para.12.56, below.

[26] *Reid v Macbeth & Gray* (1904) 6 F. (HL) 25.

[27] *A.K. Stoddart v Scott*, 1971 J.C. 18.

delivered.[28] The transaction was not really a sale, but an attempt to give a security in a method which the law of Scotland does not recognise. But it may be stipulated, without bringing the transaction within the purview of s.62(4), that the seller shall have a right to repurchase the goods at the same price,[29] or that the purchaser, if he makes any profit by a resale of the goods, shall be bound to account for that profit to the seller.[30] And probably if the legal relations of buyer and seller are created the transaction is to be regarded as a sale to which the Act will apply, although it may be proved that the object of the parties in entering into the transaction was to give security for money borrowed. It is inconsistent with the legal relationship of buyer and seller that the nominal seller should be bound by some obligation (e.g. a promissory note) to repay the price; it is not inconsistent with that relationship that the seller should have an option to repay, and a right, on repayment, to recover the goods.[31]

Price—The Act provides (s.8) that the price of goods sold may be fixed by the **12.13** contract, left to be fixed in some manner agreed to, or determined by the course of dealing between the parties. If not so determined, the buyer must pay a reasonable price.[32] If it is agreed that the price shall be fixed by a third party, and that third party cannot or does not act, an agreement to sell is avoided, but if any part of the goods has been delivered to and appropriated by the buyer he must pay a reasonable price therefor. If the third party is prevented from fixing the price by the fault of the buyer or seller, the party in fault is liable in damages (s.9). It is no objection to the validity of a contract of sale that the buyer is left to fix his own price.[33]

Transfer of property: Unascertained goods; bulk—In dealing with sale as a **12.14** method of transferring the property in goods it must be noted that the contract may either relate to particular and existing things, identified at the time the contract is made, and referred to in the Act as specific or ascertained goods (*venditio rei specificae*); or to future goods, goods to be manufactured or obtained by the seller after the contract is made; or to generic goods, so much of some particular commodity (*venditio generis*); or to an unsevered portion of some particular quantity of goods.[34] In the last three cases the goods are unascertained, and the property does not pass to the purchaser until they are ascertained (s.16). Unascertained goods also include "bulk" goods, a mass of goods of the same kind which is contained in a defined space or area and is such that any goods in the bulk are inter-changeable with any other goods therein of the same number or quantity (s.61(1)).[35] Property in an undivided share in the bulk will be transferred to the buyer, and the buyer also becomes owner in common of the whole bulk, if the contract is for the sale of a specified quantity of unascertained goods which is part of a bulk identified in the contract or by subsequent agreement, and if the buyer

---

[28] *Jones & Co's Tr. v Allan* (1901) 4 F. 374; see also *Robertson v Hall's Tr.* (1896) 24 R. 120; *Hepburn v Law*, 1914 S.C. 918; *Scottish Transit Trust v Scottish Land Cultivators*, 1955 S.C. 254; *G. & C. Finance Corp v Brown*, 1961 S.L.T. 408; *Ladbroke Leasing (South West) Ltd v Reekie Plant Ltd*, 1983 S.L.T. 155. As to an "all sums" retention of title clause, see para.12.17.

[29] *Gavin's Tr. v Fraser*, 1920 S.C. 674; *Newbigging v Ritchie's Trustee*, 1930 S.C. 273.

[30] *McBain v Wallace* (1881) 8 R. (HL) 106.

[31] *Gavin's Tr. v Fraser*, 1920 S.C. 674; see opinion of Lord President Clyde; *Newbigging v Ritchie's Trustee*, 1930 S.C. 273.

[32] *Glynwed Distribution Ltd v S. Koronka & Co*, 1977 S.C. 1.

[33] *Lavaggi v Pirie* (1872) 10 M. 312.

[34] See *Hayman v McLintock*, 1907 S.C. 936.

[35] Added by s.2 of the 1995 Act.

has paid the price for some or all of the goods. The buyer's individual bulk at any time is such share as the quantity of goods paid for and d. buyer out of the bulk bears to the quantity of goods in the bulk at that time. the aggregate of the undivided shares of buyers in a bulk determined in this exceeds the whole of the bulk at any time, each buyer's individual share is reduce proportionately so that the aggregate of the undivided shares is equal to the whole bulk. If a buyer has paid the price for only some of the goods due to him out of a bulk, any delivery to him out of the bulk is ascribed in the first place to the goods in respect of which payment has been made; payment of part of the price for any goods is treated as payment for a corresponding part of the goods. (See for the foregoing s.20A.) For these purposes, delivery includes such appropriation of the goods to the contract as results in property in the goods being transferred to the buyer (s.61(1)). A person who has become an owner in common of a bulk is deemed to have consented to any delivery of goods out of the bulk to any other owner in common of the bulk, being goods due to him under his contract; and to any dealing with, or removal, delivery or disposal of goods in the bulk by any other person who is an owner in common of the bulk in so far as the goods fall within that co-owner's individual share in the bulk at the time of the transaction in question (s.20B(1)). Delivery here has the same meaning as with regard to undivided shares (s.61(1)).

12.15 Ascertained goods—Goods become ascertained when goods of that description and in a deliverable state[36] are unconditionally appropriated to the contract either by the seller with the consent of the buyer or by the buyer with the consent of the seller (s.18, r.5(1)).[37] Notification of such appropriation is not essential if the necessary consent can be implied from the terms of the contract.[38] If the seller delivers the goods to a carrier for transmission to the buyer, and does not reserve the right of disposal, he is deemed to have unconditionally appropriated them to the contract (s.18, r.5(2)). Where there is a contract for the sale of a specified quantity of unascertained goods in a deliverable state forming part of a bulk which is identified either in the contract or by subsequent agreement between the parties and the bulk is reduced to (or less than) that quantity, then, if the buyer under that contract is the only buyer to whom goods are then due out of the bulk, the remaining goods shall be taken as appropriated to that contract at the time when the bulk is so reduced, and the property in those goods then passes to that buyer (s.18, r.5(3)). The same rule applies with the necessary modifications where a bulk is reduced to (or less than) the aggregate of the quantities due to a single buyer under separate contracts relating to that bulk and he is the only buyer to whom goods are then due out of that bulk (s.18, r.5(4)).[39]

12.16 Specific goods: General rules—The general rule as to the transfer of the property in specific goods is given in s.17:

"(1) Where there is a contract for the sale of specific or ascertained goods the property in them is transferred to the buyer at such time as the parties to the

---

[36] *Philip Head & Sons v Showfronts* (1970) 113 S.J. 978.

[37] The appropriation may be by a third party; *Wardar's (Import & Export) Co v W. Norwood & Sons* [1968] 2 Q.B. 663.

[38] See *Widenmeyer v Burn Stewart & Co Ltd*, 1967 S.C. 85 at 101, per Lord President Clyde.

[39] Rules 5(3) and (4) are added by s.1(2) of the 1995 Act. For an example of "ascertainment by exhaustion", see *A/B Karlshamns Oljefabriker v Eastport Navigation Corp* [1982] 1 All E.R. 208.

contract intend it to be transferred. (2) For the purpose of ascertaining the intention of the parties regard shall be had to the terms of the contract, the conduct of the parties, and the circumstances of the case".

In contrast with the common law, which demanded delivery in order to pass the property, this section places it in the power of the parties to the contract to decide when the property is to pass. It depends on their intention. In some cases that intention may be clear, either from the express terms of the contract or from the circumstances of the case. But in many cases the buyer and seller do not consider the question of the property in the goods, and have really no intention in the matter. It is a question which rises into importance if the creditors of the seller, or his trustee in sequestration, assert a right to the goods, or if the goods are accidentally injured or destroyed. Where no actual intention can be ascertained the presumed intention is to be gathered from rules given in s.18. It must be remembered that these rules are not applicable if there is proof of intention to the contrary.[40]

Rule 1—

"Where there is an unconditional contract for the sale of specific goods[41] in a deliverable state the property in the goods passes to the buyer when the contract is made, and it is immaterial whether the time of payment or the time of delivery, or both, be postponed."

It may be presumed that in this, the general rule for the ordinary case of sale of specific articles, the term "unconditional" means without any condition relating to the passing of the property, and that the property in an article which is sold in a deliverable state will pass at once to the purchaser, although the contract may involve conditions as to the quality of the article. Goods are in a deliverable state when they are in such a state that the buyer would, under the contract, be bound to take delivery of them (s.61(5)).

Rule 2—

"Where there is a contract for the sale of specific goods and the seller is bound to do something to the goods for the purpose of putting them into a deliverable state, the property does not pass until the thing is done and the buyer has notice that it has been done."[42]

From the opinions in an English case it would appear that the rule does not apply, and that the passing of the property is not postponed, merely because the seller has undertaken to pack the goods, or because, as in the case of a billiard-table, the article sold must be taken to pieces before it can be removed. But where the article sold was at the date of the contract affixed to a building the property did not pass until it was severed.[43] And there may be a narrow distinction between putting

---

[40] As examples see *Re Anchor Line* [1937] 1 Ch. 1; *Lacis v Cashmarts* [1969] 2 Q.B. 400; *Aluminium Industrie Vaassen B.V. v Romalpa Aluminium* [1976] 1 W.L.R. 676.

[41] Specific goods are "goods identified and agreed on at the time a contract of sale is made" (s.61). Standing trees sold for felling and removal cannot become the property of the buyer until they are severed from the ground; *Morison v Lockhart*, 1912 S.C. 1017; *Munro v Liquidator of Balnagown Estates Co*, 1949 S.C. 49.

[42] e.g. *Lombard North Central Ltd v Lord Advocate*, 1983 S.L.T. 361.

[43] *Underwood v Burgh Castle Syndicate* [1922] 1 K.B. 343.

goods into a deliverable state and initiating the process of delivery, *when* growing potatoes were sold, and the seller undertook to lift and put them *in pits at maturity,* and to cart them to the station, it was decided that the potatoes *had reached* a deliverable state, and that the property passed to the purchaser, *when* they were put into pits; the subsequent obligation of the seller, to *cart* the potatoes to the station, relating not to deliverable state but to actual *delivery.*[44]

Rule 3—

> "Where there is a contract for the sale of specific *goods* in a deliverable state but the seller is bound to weigh, measure, *test,* or do some other act or thing with reference to the goods for the *purpose* of ascertaining the price, the property does not pass until the act or *thing is* done, and the buyer has notice that it has been done."

This rule is applicable only where the seller *has* undertaken to weigh, measure or test the goods—not to the case where *there is* no agreement on the point, though the price cannot as a matter of fact *be* ascertained until such operation has been performed. So in the sale of "my crop *per* of hay" the property was held to pass at once, though the sale was at so much *per ton,* and the price consequently could not be ascertained until the hay was weighed.[45] Similarly, when it was agreed that the goods should be weighed at the station and the result accepted by both parties as determining the price, it was held that Rule 3 was inapplicable because there was no obligation on the seller to weigh the goods.[46]

(Rule 4, relating to the contract of sale and return, will be considered subsequently, para.12.55.)

12.17 Reservation of title—In recent years there has been much litigation as to the effect of clauses providing that property will not pass to the buyer until the price has been paid.[47] Such clauses may attempt to give the seller, if the goods have been re-sold, rights against the sub-purchaser or over the proceeds in the hands of the buyer; they may also purport to give the seller rights over products which have been manufactured from the goods by the buyer. It is clear that a simple provision that property in the goods sold will not pass until the price has been paid will be given effect and, in the event of the sequestration or liquidation of the buyer, the seller can recover the goods.[48] He is not obliged to account to the buyer for any part of the value of the goods but a partial payment may be repayable.[49] However, where an administration order is made in relation to the buyer under Pt II of the Insolvency Act 1986, the rights of a seller under a conditional sale agreement may be constrained. It has now been established that a reservation of title until the price and all other sums due to the seller or to members of its combine have been

---

[44] *Cockburn's Tr. v Bowe,* 1910 2 S.L.T. 17. See also *Woodburn v Motherwell,* 1917 S.C. 533; *Paton's Trs v Finlayson,* 1923 S.C. 872.

[45] *Kennedy's Tr. v Hamilton* (1897) 25 R. 252.

[46] *Woodburn v Motherwell,* 1917 S.C. 533.

[47] Such clauses are often called "Romalpa clauses": see *Aluminium Industrie Vaassen B.V. v Romalpa Aluminium* [1976] 1 W.L.R. 676. In statutory usage an instalment sale subject to such a clause is a "conditional sale": Hire Purchase Act 1964 s.29(1); Consumer Credit Act 1974 s.189(1).

[48] *Archivent Sales & Development Ltd v Strathclyde R.C.,* 1985 S.L.T. 154; *Zahnrad Fabrik Passau GmbH v Terex Ltd,* 1985 S.C. 364.

[49] *Armour v Thyssen Edelstahlwerke A.G.,* 1990 S.L.T. 891 at 895, per Lord Keith. For a discussion of the various problems which can arise, see *Clough Mill v Martin* [1985] 1 W.L.R. 111 and G. McCormack, "Mixture of Goods" (1990) 10 L.S. 293.

paid is effectual; it is not an attempt to create a security in the form of a sale.[50] It is not possible in a reservation of title clause to create an effectual trust over proceeds to be received by the buyer at some future time.[51] It is thought that a clause giving the seller rights over products manufactured from the goods and other materials which were never the seller's property would be ineffectual as an attempt to create a security without possession.[52]

Risk: Generic sales—The question of risk, i.e. the question on whom the loss is **12.18** to fall if goods sold are accidentally injured or destroyed, is, in general, raised only in the case of the sale of specific articles. If a man agrees to supply a certain quantity of a particular commodity there is nothing under the contract at risk. *Genus nunquam perit*, the particular commodity does not cease to exist, although the seller's whole stock may be accidentally destroyed. In all ordinary cases he remains liable under his contract.[53] Even if the particular commodity has ceased to exist, or has become unprocurable, the contract is not affected, if the buyer has no notice of the seller's sources of supply. So where A agreed to supply a certain quantity of Finnish birch, he was held liable in damages for failure to fulfil his contract, in spite of the fact that owing to war conditions it had become impossible to procure that particular commodity.[54] But where the subject of sale was a particular chemical, and both parties were aware that it was to be imported from Germany, and therefore during the war could not be obtained without trading with the enemy, it was held that the contract was avoided.[55]

Risk: Specific goods—Where the contract relates to specific goods, or to goods **12.19** which have been unconditionally appropriated to the contract by one party with the consent of the other, the result of their accidental destruction depends upon the date of that occurrence. If, without the knowledge of the seller, they have perished at the date when the contract was made, the contract is void (s.6). This has been held to apply to a case of partial destruction by theft.[56] Except in the case of consumer contracts, unless otherwise agreed, they are at the seller's risk until the property has passed to the buyer, thereafter at the buyer's risk whether they have been delivered or not (s.20).[57] If they are accidentally destroyed before the risk has passed to the buyer the contract is avoided, and neither party is under any

---

[50] *Armour v Thyssen Edelstahlwerke A.G.*, 1990 S.L.T. 891.

[51] *Clark Taylor & Co Ltd v Quality Site Development (Edinburgh) Ltd*, 1981 S.C. 111. Cf. *Tay Valley Joinery Ltd v C.F. Financial Services Ltd*, 1987 S.L.T. 207, and see K. Reid, "Trusts and floating charges", 1987 S.L.T. (News) 113.

[52] See *Re Bond Worth Ltd* [1980] Ch. 228; *Borden (UK) Ltd v Scottish Timber Products Ltd* [1981] Ch. 25; *Re Peachdart Ltd* [1984] Ch. 131. These cases were largely concerned with whether a charge had been created which required registration pursuant to Companies Act 1948 s.95 (now Companies Act 2006 ss.860–861), a question which was also discussed in *Clough Mill v Martin* [1985] 1 W.L.R. 111. In Scotland, a fixed security over corporeal movables other than ships or aircraft does not require to be registered: see Companies Act 2006 s.878. Other English cases are: *Hendy Lennox (Industrial Engines) Ltd v Grahame Puttick Ltd* [1984] 2 All E.R. 152; *Re Andrabell Ltd* [1984] 3 All E.R. 407 (proceeds in buyer's hands); *E. Pfeiffer GmbH v Arbuthnot Factors Ltd* [1988] 1 W.L.R. 150; *Tatung (UK) Ltd v Galex Telesure Ltd* (1989) 5 B.C.C. 325; *Re Weldtech Equipment Ltd* [1991] B.C.L.C. 393 (rights against sub-purchaser).

[53] *Anderson and Crompton v Walls* (1870) 9 M. 122.

[54] *Blackburn Bobbin Co v Allen* [1918] 2 K.B. 467.

[55] *Re Badische Co* [1921] 2 Ch. 331.

[56] *Barrow Lane & Ballard v Phillips* [1929] 1 K.B. 574.

[57] cf. the common law rule that risk passed when the contract was completed, not when property in the goods passed: see *Widenmeyer v Burn Stewart & Co Ltd*, 1967 S.C. 85.

liability (s.7). Otherwise the maxim *res perit domino* (a thing perishes to the disadvantage of its owner) applies, and if the risk has passed to the buyer he must pay the price.[58] It is, however, open to the parties to agree that the risk shall not pass with the property, and such agreement may be express or implied. If the seller has undertaken to deliver the goods the general rule is that both property and risk pass to the buyer when they are delivered to a carrier, and, by the transfer of the bill of lading or otherwise, they are placed at the buyer's disposal (s.18, r.5(2); s.32) but if the contract is read as an obligation to deliver the goods at a particular place the risk is with the seller until they arrive there.[59] It is possible that the risk may be divided; the risk of total destruction being on one party, the risk of deterioration on the other. So where herrings were sold, and, owing to delay on the voyage, arrived in a state unfit for consumption, it was held that the buyer might reject them, even on the assumption that the property in the herrings, and with it the risk of their accidental destruction, had passed to him.[60]

12.20 Where one party is at fault—In the case of specific goods, the risk may be affected by the fact that one or other party was at fault. If the destruction of the goods is due to the fault of one or other party, he will be liable in damages. If delivery be delayed through the fault of buyer or seller, the risk is on the party at fault as regards any loss which might not have occurred but for that fault (s.20). If goods are sent to the buyer by a route involving sea transit in circumstances where it is usual to insure, and the seller fails to give such notice to the buyer as may enable him to insure, the goods are at the seller's risk during the sea transit (s.32(3)).

12.21 Consumer contracts—In consumer contracts where the buyer is a consumer the normal rule is disapplied and the goods remain at the seller's risk until delivered to the consumer (s.20(4)). Similarly, where the seller is authorised or required to deliver the goods delivery to a carrier is not delivery to the consumer buyer (s.32(4)).

12.22 Title of buyer—As a general rule the purchaser of goods obtains no better title to them than the seller possessed.[61] So if the seller be a thief, or a person who has no right to be in possession of the goods or to dispose of them, the purchaser obtains no title in a question with the true owner. It is immaterial, in Scots law, that the sale may have taken place in a public market or market overt.[62] The general rule is qualified by the proviso to s.21(1)[63] and by other statutory provisions which give effect to the ostensible authority to dispose of goods which is involved in possession of the goods or of the documents of title to them. The proviso to s.21(1) that the owner may be precluded by his conduct from denying the seller's authority to sell does not apply where there has been only an agreement to sell.[64]

---

[58] *Woodburn v Andrew Motherwell*, 1917 S.C. 533; *Wardar's (Import & Export) Co v W. Norwood & Sons* [1968] 2 Q.B. 663.

[59] *Henckell Du Buisson v Swan* (1889) 17 R. 252.

[60] *Pommer v Mowat* (1906) 14 S.L.T. 373. In such cases the buyer takes the risk of deterioration necessarily incident to the transit (s.33). See also *Sterns v Vickers* [1923] 1 K.B. 78.

[61] Sale of Goods Act 1979 (the "1979 Act") s.21. As to the distinction between void and voidable agreements, see para.7.05, above.

[62] *Todd v Armour* (1882) 9 R. 901. The doctrine of market overt was abolished in England and Wales by the Sale of Goods (Amendment) Act 1994.

[63] *Central Newbury Car Auctions v Unity Finance* [1957] 1 Q.B. 371.

[64] *Shaw v Commissioner of Police* [1987] 1 W.L.R. 1332.

Sale under voidable title—When the seller of goods has a voidable title but his **12.23** title has not been avoided at the time of the sale, the buyer acquires a good title to the goods, provided he buys them in good faith and without notice of the seller's defect of title (s.23). To rescind the contract the seller must communicate with the other party.[65]

Part III of the Hire Purchase Act 1964—Under these provisions, a private **12.24** purchaser of a motor vehicle for value acting in good faith who obtains it from a person in possession under a hire-purchase or a conditional sale agreement obtains the title that the true owner had.[66] A "private purchaser" is any purchaser other than a trade or finance purchaser, i.e. one who carries on a business consisting wholly or partly of dealing in motor vehicles or providing finance by purchasing them for the purpose of hiring them under hire-purchase agreements or agreeing to sell them under conditional sale agreements.[67]

Sales by ostensible owner—By the Factors Act 1889 (extended to Scotland by **12.25** the Factors (Scotland) Act 1890) s.2, it is provided:

"Where a mercantile agent is, with the consent of the owner, in possession of goods or of the documents of title to goods, any sale, pledge, or other disposition of the goods, made by him when acting in the ordinary course of business of a mercantile agent, shall, subject to the provisions of this Act, be as valid as if he were expressly authorised by the owner of the goods to make the same; provided that the person taking under the disposition acts in good faith, and has not at the time of the disposition notice that the person making the disposition has not authority to make the same."

By the Sale of Goods Act 1979 ss.24 and 25 (re-enacting ss.8 and 9 of the Factors Act) similar provisions are made for the case of an unauthorised disposition of goods to a party who takes in good faith either: (a) by a person who has sold goods but continues in possession of the goods or of the documents of title to them; or (b) by a person who has bought or agreed to buy goods and has obtained, with the consent of the seller, possession of the goods or of the documents of title to them. Section 24 provides:

"Where a person having sold goods continues or is in possession of the goods, or of the documents of title to the goods, the delivery or transfer by that person, or by a mercantile agent acting for him, of the goods or documents of title under any sale, pledge, or other disposition thereof, to any person receiving the same in good faith and without notice of the previous

---

[65] *Macleod v Kerr*, 1965 S.C. 253.

[66] Hire-Purchase Act 1964 s.27. It seems likely that where the original hire-purchase agreement is vitiated by essential error no title can be obtained from the seller. Cf. the situation in England following *Shogun Finance Ltd v Hudson* [2004] 1 A.C. 919. It is doubtful whether, in Scotland, the person who let the vehicle on hire has any remedy against a trade purchaser, who, having acquired the vehicle in good faith from the hirer, resells it to a private purchaser, who thus may acquire a good title: *North-West Securities v Barrhead Coachworks*, 1976 S.C. 68. Cf. *F.C. Finance v Langtry Investment Co*, 1973 S.L.T. (Sh. Ct) 11, where the doctrine of specificatio was applied. For the English position, see *Moorgate Mercantile Co v Twitchings* [1977] A.C. 890.

[67] Hire-Purchase Act 1964 s.29(2); see *GE Capital Bank Ltd v Rushton* [2005] EWCA Civ 1556.

sale, has the same effect as if the person making the delivery or transfer were expressly authorised by the owner of the goods to make the same."

The test is continuity of possession regardless of any alteration of the legal title under which the possession is held.[68] "The owner of the goods" must be read as "the original buyer of the goods", so that if the seller (X) having stolen the goods from W, sold them to Y and then, while still in possession of them, delivered them under a sale to Z, that delivery would not be treated as if it had been expressly authorised by W.[69]

Section 25(1) provides:

"Where a person having bought or agreed to buy goods obtains, with the consent of the seller, possession of the goods or the documents of title to the goods, the delivery or transfer by that person, or by a mercantile agent acting for him, of the goods or documents of title, under any sale, pledge, or other disposition thereof, to any person receiving the same in good faith and without notice of any lien or other right of the original seller in respect of the goods, has the same effect as if the person making the delivery or transfer were a mercantile agent in possession of the goods or documents of title with the consent of the owner."

If the seller in fact consents it is immaterial that his consent has been obtained by fraud.[70] There must be a voluntary transfer of actual or constructive possession.[71] Delivery by the seller to the sub-purchaser satisfies the requirement of the section.[72] Section 9 of the Factors Act is wider in scope than s.25(1) of the Sale of Goods Act in that it extends to the buyer who has taken possession under any agreement for sale, pledge or other disposition. But this will not protect the sub-purchaser acquiring goods under a reservation of title clause from a buyer which itself has acquired under such a clause, unless and until the sub-purchaser has fulfilled the conditions for the passage of property from the buyer.[73] The buyer must be acting in the way in which a mercantile agent would normally be expected to act.[74] Once again the words "the owner" in the last phrase of the subsection cause difficulty and must be read as "the owner who entrusted them to him"; if a thief sells the goods to X who then sells them to Y, who takes in good faith, Y does not get a good title against the person from whom the goods were stolen. For purposes of s.9 of the Factors Act and s.25(1) of the Sale of Goods Act, a buyer under a conditional sale agreement is to be taken not to be a person who has bought or agreed to buy goods.[75] A private purchaser of a motor vehicle which is the subject of a prior conditional sale agreement may, however, acquire a good

---

[68] *Pacific Motor Auctions Pty v Motor Credits (Hire Finance)* [1965] A.C. 867; *Worcester Works Finance v Cooden* [1972] 1 Q.B. 210.

[69] *National Employers' Mutual General Insurance Association Ltd v Jones* [1990] A.C. 24.

[70] *Du Jardin v Beadman Bros Ltd* [1952] 2 Q.B. 712.

[71] *Ladbroke Leasing (South West) Ltd v Reekie Plant Ltd*, 1983 S.L.T. 155. See also *Forsythe International (UK) Ltd v Silver Shipping Co (The Saetta)* [1994] 1 W.L.R. 1334; *Michael Gerson (Leasing) Ltd v Wilkinson* [2001] 1 All E.R. 148.

[72] *Four Point Garage Ltd v Carter* [1985] 3 All E.R. 12; *Graham v Glenrothes Development Corp*, 1967 S.C. 284.

[73] *Re Highway Foods International Ltd* [1995] B.C.C. 271.

[74] *Newtons of Wembley v Williams* [1965] 1 Q.B. 560; *Archivent Sales and Development Ltd v Strathclyde R.C.*, 1985 S.L.T. 154.

[75] Factors Act 1889 s.9 (as amended by Consumer Credit Act 1974 Sch.4 para.2); 1979 Act s.25(2).

title to it if he purchases in good faith and without notice of the prior agreement.[76]

Meaning of good faith—A person who takes goods or documents of title in the **12.26** circumstances covered by these statutory provisions takes in good faith if he in fact takes honestly, whether he takes negligently or not (s.61(3)). But absence of inquiry, or an inadequate price, may be evidence of want of good faith.[77] Where bills of lading were taken by A in the ordinary course of business, in the knowledge that the person from whom he took them (B) was in financial difficulties and had not paid for the goods, but without any notice that B had obtained the bills of lading fraudulently, it was held that A's title was unchallengeable.[78]

Mere possession confers no power to dispose of goods—There may be excep- **12.27** tional cases in which a party who is in possession of goods or of documents to title, but who is neither a mercantile agent, nor a seller left in possession, nor a buyer entrusted with possession, is able to confer a good title by a fraudulent sale of the goods, on the ground that the party who allowed him to be in possession is personally barred from disputing his authority to sell.[79] But there is no general rule that mere possession of goods, as for instance by a hirer,[80] or a carrier or forwarding agent,[81] gives the possessor any ostensible right to dispose of them, or is any ground for a plea of personal bar put forward by a party who had bought the goods from the person in possession, and whose right is challenged by their true owner.[82]

Warranties—Warranties by a seller of goods may be express, imposed by statute, **12.28** implied, or annexed by custom of trade. The question whether a particular statement is to be read as a warranty, or merely as a representation, has been already considered.[83] An example of a warranty imposed by statute is the Agriculture Act 1970 s.72, by which, in a sale of any material for use as a feeding stuff for animals, there is implied a warranty by the seller that the material is suitable to be used as such. The term has effect notwithstanding any contract or notice to the contrary.

Implied terms—The terms implied in sale are dealt with by ss.12–15. An express **12.29** term does not negative an implied term unless inconsistent with it.[84] The Act formerly provided for implied warranties and conditions which reflected a well-established distinction in English law.[85] The 1994 Act removed this distinction in

---

[76] Hire Purchase Act 1964 ss.27–29, as substituted by Consumer Credit Act 1974 Sch.4 para.22.
[77] See *Jones v Gordon* (1877) 2 App. Cas. 616; *Hayman v American Cotton Oil Co* (1907) 45 S.L.R. 207; 15 S.L.T. 606.
[78] *Price & Pierce v Bank of Scotland*, 1910 S.C. 1095; 1912 S.C. (HL) 19.
[79] See *London Joint Stock Bank v Simmons* [1892] A.C. 201, opinion of Lord Herschell; *Commonwealth Trust v Akotey* [1926] A.C. 72, on which see opinion of Lord Sumner in *R.E. Jones v Waring & Gillow* [1926] A.C. 670.
[80] *Mitchell v Heys* (1894) 21 R. 600; *Lamonby v Foulds*, 1928 S.C. 89; *George Hopkinson Ltd v Napier & Son*, 1953 S.C. 139 (diligence).
[81] *Martinez y Gomez v Alison* (1890) 17 R. 332.
[82] *Mitchell v Heys* (1894) 21 R. 600; *Farquharson v King* [1902] A.C. 325.
[83] See para.7.37, above.
[84] 1979 Act s.55(2); *Douglas v Milne* (1895) 23 R. 163.
[85] See, as to conditions and warranties in English law, 1979 Act s.11; opinion of Fletcher Moulton L.J. in *Wallis v Pratt* [1910] 2 K.B. 1003; *Baldry v Marshall* [1925] 1 K.B. 260.

favour of the single concept of an implied term. Implied terms are of three classes: terms as to title, as to description, and as to quality.

12.30 **Implied terms of title**—There is (a) an implied term on the part of the seller that, in the case of a sale, he has the right to sell the goods, and that, in the case of an agreement to sell, he will have a right to sell the goods at the time when the property is to pass; and (b) an implied term that the goods are free, and will remain free until the time when the property is to pass, from any charge or encumbrance not disclosed or known to the buyer before the contract is made and that the buyer will enjoy quiet possession of the goods except in so far as it may be disturbed by the owner or other person entitled to the benefit of any charge or encumbrance so disclosed or known (s.12(1) and (2)).[86] These provisions do not apply in the case in which there appears from the contract or is to be inferred from the circumstances of the contract an intention that the seller should transfer only such title as he or a third person may have; in such a case there is: (a) an implied term that all charges or encumbrances known to the seller and not known to the buyer have been disclosed to the buyer before the contract is made; and (b) an implied term that neither: (i) the seller, nor (ii) in a case where the parties to the contract intend that the seller should transfer only such title as a third person may have, that person, nor (iii) anyone claiming through or under the seller or that third person otherwise than under a charge or encumbrance disclosed or known to the buyer before the contract is made, will disturb the buyer's quiet possession of the goods (s.12(3), (4) and (5)). Any term of a contract which purports to exclude or restrict liability for breach of the obligations arising from any of these implied undertakings as to title or to exclude or restrict the undertakings themselves is void.[87] With regard to these provisions it may be noted that if the buyer knows that the seller has only a limited right he cannot insist on an implied term of an absolute one.[88] It has been held that a seller did not fulfil the warranty of his right to sell when he supplied goods with a label which constituted an infringement of a third party's trade mark, and which the buyer could not deal with without risk of a law suit.[89] The buyer may recover the price paid as damages, but recovery should be based on the value of the goods at the date of eviction.[90] The implied term of "quiet possession" does not import a warranty against unfounded claims by third parties, and therefore the buyer cannot recover from the seller the expenses he has incurred in resisting these.[91]

12.31 **Implied terms of description**—

"Where there is a contract for the sale of goods by description, there is an implied term that the goods will correspond with the description" (s.13).

---

[86] For s.12(1) see *McDonald v Provan (of Scotland Street) Ltd*, 1960 S.L.T. 231 and for an example of a breach of s.12(2)(b) see *Rubicon Computer Systems Ltd v United Paints Ltd* (2000) 2 T.C.L.R. 453.

[87] Unfair Contract Terms Act 1977 ss.20(1)(a), 25(5).

[88] *Leith Heritages Co v Edinburgh Glass Co* (1876) 3 R. 789.

[89] *Niblett v Confectioners' Materials* [1921] 3 K.B. 387. See also *Microbeads AG v Vinhurst Road Markings* [1975] 1 W.L.R. 218.

[90] *Spink & Son v McColl*, 1992 S.L.T. 470.

[91] *Stephen v Lord Advocate* (1878) 6 R. 282; *Dougall v Magistrates of Dunfermline*, 1908 S.C. 151.

A sale of goods is not prevented from being a sale by description by reason only that, being exposed for sale or hire, the goods are selected by the buyer (s.13(3)). The word "description", which is not defined in the Act, may be synonymous with "kind".[92] Thus it has been observed:

> "If a man offer to buy peas of another, and he sends him beans, he does not perform his contract, but that is not a warranty, there is no warranty that he should sell him peas; the contract is to sell peas, and if he sends him anything else in their stead, it is a non-performance of it".[93]

In this meaning of the word "description", there is no difficulty in holding that the party who orders goods of a particular description, and gets either different goods or a consignment, in part of the goods ordered, and in part of goods of a different description, is entitled to reject them.[94] Statements as to the quality will not usually be treated as part of the description.[95] But the word "description" may refer to any statement as to the origin or history of the goods[96] as, for instance, that they form part of a particular stock,[97] that they have been shipped in a particular month,[98] that they have been carried,[99] or packed,[100] in a specified way. In such cases, failure to answer the description may make no difference to the value of the goods. If the seller is in breach of the implied term that the goods will correspond with the description, the buyer can claim damages[101] and he may also be entitled to reject the goods if the breach is material[102] or if the contract of sale is a consumer contract made on or after January 3, 1995.[103] Where the contract is a consumer contract the buyer may also invoke the additional remedies in Pt 5A of the Sale of Goods Act 1979.[104]

Implied terms as to quality—At common law, the rule was expressed in **12.32** the statement that a fair price demanded a fair article, and therefore it was held that, in the absence of any provision to the contrary, the seller undertook to supply goods of reasonably good quality.[105] The English law on the subject,

---

[92] *Rutherford & Son v Miln & Co*, 1941 S.C. 125 at 135. In *Christopher Hill Ltd v Ashington Piggeries Ltd* [1972] A.C. 441, it was said that description went to the identification of the goods. "One must look to the contract as a whole to identify the kind of goods that the seller was agreeing to sell and the buyer to buy": *Berger & Co Inc. v Gill & Duffus S.A.* [1984] A.C. 382 at 394, speech of Lord Diplock. See also *Harlingdon and Leinster Enterprises Ltd v Christopher Hull Fine Art Ltd* [1991] 1 Q.B. 564.

[93] *Chanter v Hopkins* (1838) 4 M. & W. 399, per Lord Abinger.

[94] *Jaffe v Ritchie* (1860) 23 D. 242; *Carter v Campbell* (1885) 12 R. 1075; *Rutherford & Son v Miln*, 1941 S.C. 125; see also *Christopher Hill v Ashington Piggeries* [1972] A.C. 441, and the opinions in *McCallum v Mason*, 1956 S.C. 50, as to the effects of mixed ingredients.

[95] See *Christopher Hill v Ashington Piggeries* [1972] A.C. 441, and *Border Harvesters Ltd v Edwards Engineering (Perth) Ltd*, 1985 S.L.T. 128.

[96] *Varley v Whipp* [1900] 1 Q.B. 513.

[97] *Thomson Bros v Thomson* (1885) 13 R. 88.

[98] *Bowes v Shand* (1877) 2 App.Cas. 455.

[99] *Meyer v Travaru* (1930) 46 T.L.R. 553; contrast *Meyer v Kivisto* (1929) 142 L.T. 480.

[100] *F.W. Moore & Co v Landauer* [1921] 2 K.B. 519.

[101] 1979 Act s.15B(1)(a); see below, para.12.40.

[102] 1979 Act s.15B(1)(b). In the case of consumer contracts such a breach is deemed to be material see s.15(2). See also s.11(5) of the Act which was repealed by Sch.3 to the 1994 Act.

[103] 1979 Act s.15B(2); as to the meaning of a consumer contract, see para.9.20, above.

[104] This part of the Act was inserted by 2002 Regulations implementing the Consumer Guarantees Directive.

[105] *Whealler v Methuen* (1843) 5 D. 402.

generally referred to by the phrase caveat emptor (let the buyer beware), was applied to Scotland by s.5 of the Mercantile Law Amendment Act Scotland 1856, but that section is now repealed. Prior to amendment by the 1994 Act, the Sale of Goods Act provided that in certain circumstances there could be an implied condition that the goods were of merchantable quality.[106] For contracts made on or after January 3, 1995, there are implied terms that the goods will be of satisfactory quality and, where the buyer makes known to the seller any particular purpose for which the goods are being bought, a further term that they will be fit for that purpose.[107] Section 14 (as amended) provides as follows:

"(1) Except as provided by this section and section 15 below and subject to any other enactment, there is no implied term about the quality or fitness for any particular purpose of goods supplied under a contract of sale.

(2) Where the seller sells goods in the course of a business, there is an implied term that the goods supplied under the contract are of satisfactory quality.

(2A) For the purposes of this Act, goods are of satisfactory quality if they meet the standard that a reasonable person would regard as satisfactory, taking account of any description of the goods; the price (if relevant) and all the other relevant circumstances.

(2B) For the purposes of this Act, the quality of goods includes their state and condition and the following (among others) are in appropriate cases aspects of the quality of goods—

(a) fitness for all the purposes for which goods of the kind in question are commonly supplied,
(b) appearance and finish,
(c) freedom from minor defects,
(d) safety, and
(e) durability.

(2C) The term implied by subsection (2) above does not extend to any matter making the quality of goods unsatisfactory—

(a) which is specifically drawn to the buyer's attention before the contract is made,
(b) where the buyer examines the goods before the contract is made, which that examination ought to reveal, or
(c) in the case of a contract for sale by sample, which would have been apparent on a reasonable examination of the sample.

(2D) If the buyer deals as consumer or, in Scotland, if a contract of sale is a consumer contract, the relevant circumstances mentioned in subsection (2A) above include any public statements on the specific characteristics of the goods made about them by the seller, the producer or his representative, particularly in advertising or on labelling.

(2E) A public statement is not by virtue of subsection (2D) above a relevant circumstance for the purposes of subsection (2A) above in the case of a contract of sale, if the seller shows that—

---

[106] See 1979 Act s.14(2) prior to amendment.
[107] See below, para.12.34.

(a) at the time the contract was made, he was not, and could not reasonably have been, aware of the statement,

(b) before the contract was made, the statement had been withdrawn in public or, to the extent that it contained anything which was incorrect or misleading, it had been corrected in public, or

(c) the decision to buy the goods could not have been influenced by the statement.

(2F) Subsections (2D) and (2E) above do not prevent any public statement from being a relevant circumstance for the purposes of subsection (2A) above (whether or not the buyer deals as consumer or, in Scotland, whether or not the contract of sale is a consumer contract) if the statement would have been such a circumstance apart from those subsections.

(3) Where the seller sells goods in the course of a business and the buyer, expressly or by implication, makes known—

(a) to the seller, or

(b) where the purchase price or part of it is payable by instalments and the goods were previously sold by a credit-broker to the seller, to that credit-broker,

any particular purpose for which the goods are being bought, there is an implied term that the goods supplied under the contract are reasonably fit for that purpose, whether or not that is a purpose for which such goods are commonly supplied, except where the circumstances show that the buyer does not rely, or that it is unreasonable for him to rely, on the skill or judgment of the seller or credit-broker.

(4) An implied term about quality or fitness for particular purpose may be annexed to a contract of sale by usage."

A "business" includes a profession and the activities of any government department (including a Northern Ireland department) or local or public authority (s.61(1)). The provisions apply to a sale by a person who in the course of a business is acting as agent for another as they apply to a sale by a principal in the course of a business, except where the other is not selling in the course of a business and either the buyer knows that fact or reasonable steps are taken to bring it to the notice of the buyer before the contract is made.[108] Habitual dealing in the type of goods sold is not required for a sale to be in the course of a business. A displenishing sale of a farm and the stock and plenishing thereof is a sale in the course of a business.[109] The term that the goods will be of satisfactory quality will not be implied into the contract if the seller specifically draws to the buyer's attention any matter which makes the quality of the goods unsatisfactory or if the buyer examines the goods prior to the contract and ought to have discovered the matter.[110]

---

[108] 1979 Act s.14(5). The provisions will apply even where the principal is undisclosed and is not selling in the course of a business, but employs an agent who is so selling. In these circumstances the buyer can elect to sue either the principal or the agent: *Boyter v Thomson*, 1995 S.C (HL) 15.

[109] *Buchanan-Jardine v Hamilink*, 1983 S.L.T. 149; *MacDonald v Pollock* [2012] CSIH 12; 2012 S.L.T. 462.

[110] 1979 Act s.14(2C) which largely follows the wording formerly found in s.14(2)(a) and (b); see also *Turnock v Fortune*, 1989 S.L.T. (Sh. Ct) 32. *MacDonald v Pollock* [2012] CSIH 12; 2012 S.L.T. 462 makes clear that it is the actual examination carried out by the buyer that is relevant.

A "credit-broker" is a person acting in the course of a business of credit brokerage carried on by him—that is, a business of effecting introductions of individuals desiring to obtain credit—

(i) to persons carrying on any business so far as it relates to the provision of credit, or

(ii) to other persons engaged in credit brokerage.[111]

12.33 Satisfactory quality—The definition of satisfactory quality is in two parts. A general definition relates it to what a reasonable person would consider satisfactory taking account of the price, any description and all other circumstances (s.14(2A)).[112] This is amplified in the following subsection which, after pointing out that the quality of goods includes their state and condition, adds that, in appropriate cases, a number of factors are also aspects of the quality of goods. This definition was introduced by the 1994 Act and replaced the previous standard of merchantable quality. It is not clear how far decisions on merchantable quality are relevant in construing satisfactory quality though sheriffs principal have observed that previous cases tend not to be of much assistance since cases tend to turn on their own facts.[113] The reasonable person is not an expert[114] or someone "equipped with the buyer's personal agenda"[115] but "a construct by whose standards the judge is required to evaluate the quality of the goods".[116] The definition is necessarily general in that it must cover a wide range of goods both new and second-hand. The Inner House has emphasised that a manufacturer's warranty is not relevant in determining whether a product is of satisfactory quality.[117] The description criterion points to this and it has been said that the buyer of a very expensive brand item is entitled to expect it to be ". . . perfect or nearly so"[118] while "ordinary commercial generators, obtained from stock"[119] would not be subject to such an exacting standard. Price is an ambiguous criterion but can be relevant.[120] "Other relevant circumstances" as a result of amendment made by the 2002 Regulations include in the case of consumer contracts public statements by the seller, the producer or his representative (s.14(2D–2F)). In addition they might include the place of sale[121] and the commercial context of the transaction.[122]

---

[111] 1979 Act s.61(1), added to s.14(3) of the Sale of Goods Act 1893 (the "1893 Act") by Consumer Credit Act 1974 Sch.4 para.3.

[112] See W.C.H. Ervine, "Satisfactory Quality: What Does it Mean?" [2004] J.B.L. 684.

[113] *Thain v Anniesland Trade Centre*, 1997 S.L.T. (Sh. Ct) 102 at 105; *Lamarra v Capital Bank Plc*, 2005 S.L.T. (Sh. Ct) 21 at [28]. The decision was approved by an Extra Division of the Inner House in *Lamarra v Capital Bank Plc* [2006] CSIH 49; 2007 S.C. 95. See also the views of Mustill L.J. in *Rogers v Parish (Scarborough) Ltd* [1987] Q.B. 933 at 942 and Lloyd L.J. in *M/S Aswan Engineering Establishment Co v Lupdine Ltd* [1987] 1 W.L.R. 1 at 7 on earlier changes to the definition.

[114] Hale L.J. in *Clegg v Andersson* [2003] EWCA Civ 320 at [73].

[115] Hale L.J. in *Clegg v Andersson* [2003] EWCA Civ 320 at [78].

[116] *Clegg v Andersson* [2003] EWCA Civ 320. See also *Lamarra v Capital Bank Plc*, 2007 S.C. 95 at [76] and [77].

[117] *Lamarra v Capital Bank Plc*, 2007 S.C. 95 at [62]–[68].

[118] See *Clegg v Andersson* [2003] EWCA Civ 320 at [73] which was applied in *Lamarra v Capital Bank Plc*, 2005 S.L.T. (Sh. Ct) 21.

[119] *Wartsila France SAS v Genergy Plc* [2003] All E.R. (D) 29 (QB) at [44].

[120] See *Thain v Anniesland Trade Centre*, 1997 S.L.T. (Sh. Ct) 102 and *Clegg v Andersson* [2003] EWCA Civ 320.

[121] See Sedley L.J. in *Jewson Ltd v Boyhan* [2003] EWCA Civ 1030.

[122] *Wartsila France SAS v Genergy Plc* [2003] All E.R. (D) 29; *Britvic Soft Drinks Ltd v Messer UK Ltd* [2002] EWCA Civ 548.

Section 14(2B) contains the other aspects of quality that may be taken into account. It is significant that fitness for purpose appears in this list having been demoted from the general definition of merchantable quality contained in 1979 Act prior to 1995. It will usually be of great importance but in the earlier version of the quality definition it may have led to usability being given too great importance at the expense of other factors.[123] Appearance and finish and freedom from minor defects are also to be taken into account though these are more likely to be relevant to new rather than used goods. The addition of these aspects of quality in effect overrules *Millars of Falkirk v Turpie*.[124] There has never been any doubt that unsafe goods were not of the quality demanded by law[125] and this is explicitly recognised in the definition. Durability is also and was the central issue in the first reported case on the new definition.[126]

Fitness for particular purpose—The general application of the implied stipula- **12.34** tion that the goods must be fit for a particular purpose may be illustrated by a case where hay was sold as "good, sound, timothy hay". The buyer's purpose, resale in a particular market, the conditions of which were known to the seller, was disclosed. The hay, though not of bad quality, did not satisfy the market conditions. It was held that the buyer was entitled to reject the hay, and recover damages, in respect that the seller had impliedly warranted that it was fit for the particular purpose for which, to his knowledge, the buyer required it. It was also decided that the circumstances involving the implied stipulation could be proved by parole evidence although the contract was in writing.[127] There is a strong body of authority to the effect that in the case of articles which are commonly used for one purpose only, e.g. milk,[128] articles of food,[129] a hot-water bottle,[130] coals,[131] the buyer's purpose is sufficiently made known to the seller merely by asking for the article, without any express statement as to the object for which he requires it. The stipulation can be implied in the sale of second-hand goods.[132] Where the buyer has a particular susceptibility this must be communicated to the seller if the term is to apply.[133]

---

[123] See the comments of the Law Commissions in *Sale and Supply of Goods*, para.3.31. This aspect is discussed in *Jewson Ltd v Boyhan* [2003] EWCA Civ 1030 and was important in *SW Tubes Ltd v Owen Stuart Ltd* [2002] EWCA Civ 854.

[124] *Millars of Falkirk v Turpie*, 1976 S.L.T. (Notes) 66. In *Lamarra v Capital Bank Plc*, 2007 S.C. 95, it was recognised that the decision in this case would probably be different under the current definition (see [28]). On appeal the Inner House did not find *Millers of Falkirk* helpful. See *Lamarra v Capital Bank Plc*, 2007 S.C. 95 at [68]

[125] See the pre-1995 cases of *Godley v Perry* [1960] 1 WL.R. 9 (QBD) and *Lambert v Lewis* [1982] A.C. 225 and the post-1995 decision in *Clegg v Andersson* [2003] EWCA Civ 320.

[126] *Thain v Anniesland Trade Centre*, 1997 S.L.T. (Sh. Ct) 102. For a comment see "Satisfactory Quality: *Thain v. Anniesland Trade Centre*", 1998 Jur. Rev. 379. See also *Crowther v Shannon Motor Co Ltd* [1975] 1 W.L.R. 30.

[127] *Jacobs v Scott* (1899) 2 F. (HL) 70. See also *Manchester Liners v Rea* [1922] 2 A.C. 74; *Buchanan & Carswell v Eugene*, 1936 S.C. 160; *Slater v Finning Ltd*, 1997 S.C. (HL) 8.

[128] *Frost v Aylesbury Dairy Co* [1905] 1 K.B. 608.

[129] *Wallis v Russell* [1902] 2 Ir. R. 585, "two nice fresh crabs for tea".

[130] *Preist v Last* [1903] 2 K.B. 148.

[131] *Duke v Jackson*, 1921 S.C. 362. Cf. on the result in this case *Wilson v Rickett Cockerell & Co Ltd* [1954] 1 Q.B. 598.

[132] *Bartlett v Sidney Marcus* [1965] 1 W.L.R. 1013; *Crowther v Shannon Motor Co* [1975] 1 W.L.R. 30. See also *Thain v Anniesland Trade Centre*, 1997 S.L.T. (Sh. Ct) 102.

[133] *Griffiths v Peter Conway* [1939] 1 All E.R. 685; *Slater v Finning Ltd* [1997] A.C. 473.

12.35 Sale by sample—In the case of a sale by sample there is an implied term (a) that the bulk will correspond with the sample in quality; (b) examination of the sample (ss.14(2C)(c) and 15).[134] If the sale is also by description the bulk must correspond not only with the sample but with the description (s.13(2)). A sale is a sale by sample when there is a term in the contract, express or implied, to that effect (s.15). So where the conditions of a sale by auction provided that intending purchasers must satisfy themselves of the condition of the goods in bulk, it was held that the sale was not by sample, in spite of the fact that a sample was open to inspection in the auction room.[135]

12.36 Exclusion of implied terms—A right, duty or obligation arising by implication under a contract of sale may be negatived or varied by express agreement, or by the course of dealing between the parties or by usage if the usage is such as to bind both parties to the contract,[136] but the extent to which this can be done in respect of the implied terms discussed in the five preceding paragraphs is severely limited by the provisions of the Unfair Contract Terms Act 1977.[137] In the case of other terms in consumer contracts it should be noted that these may be subject to the Unfair Terms in Consumer Contracts Regulations 1999 discussed in Ch.9.

Any term of a contract which purports to exclude or restrict[138] liability for breach of any obligation arising from the seller's implied undertakings as to description, quality, fitness for purpose or conformity with samples or to exclude or restrict the obligation itself,[139] is, in the case of a consumer contract, void against the consumer; in the case of other contracts, such a term has no effect if it was not fair and reasonable to incorporate the term in the contract.[140]

A consumer contract of sale is a contract of sale in which one party to the contract deals, and the other party to the contract (the consumer) does not deal, or hold himself out as dealing, in the course of a business,[141] and, where the buyer is not an individual, the goods are of a type ordinarily supplied for private use or consumption.[142] "Consumer contract" does not include a contract in which the buyer is an individual and the goods are second-hand goods sold by public auction at which individuals have the opportunity of attending in person or one where the buyer is not an individual and the goods are sold by auction or competitive tender.[143] The onus of proving that a contract is not to be regarded as a consumer contract lies on the party so contending.

In determining whether it was fair and reasonable to incorporate a term in a contract which is not a consumer contract, regard is to be had only to the circumstances which were, or ought reasonably to have been, known to or in the

---

[134] *Drummond v Van Ingen* (1887) 12 App. Cas. 284; *F.E. Hookway Co v Alfred Isaacs & Son* [1954] 1 Lloyd's Rep.491 at 511, per Devlin J.; *Godley v Perry* [1960] 1 W.L.R. 9.

[135] *White v Dougherty* (1891) 18 R. 972.

[136] 1979 Act s.55(1). Such terms are strictly construed: *Wallis v Pratt* [1911] A.C. 394; *Baldry v Marshall* [1925] 1 K.B. 260.

[137] See para.9.23, above. As to exclusion of the implied term of title, see para.12.28, above.

[138] Unfair Contract Terms Act 1977 (the "1977 Act") s.25(3). The references to sections in the succeeding part of this section are to sections of that Act. Other sections of the Act may also be used in sale of goods cases: see paras 9.17–9.23.

[139] 1979 Act s.25(5).

[140] 1977 Act s.20(2); see *George Mitchell (Chesterhall) Ltd v Finney Lock Seeds Ltd* [1983] 2 A.C. 803; *R. & B. Customs Brokers Co Ltd v United Dominions Trust Ltd* [1988] 1 W.L.R. 321; *St Albans City and D.C. v International Computers Ltd* [1995] F.S.R. 676, applied [1996] 4 All E.R. 481.

[141] See *R. & B. Customs Brokers Co Ltd v United Dominions Trust Ltd* [1988] 1 W.L.R. 321.

[142] 1979 Act s.25(1).

[143] 1979 Act s.25(1B).

contemplation of the parties to the contract at the time the contract was made.[144] Regard is to be had in particular to[145]:

(a) the strength of the bargaining positions of the parties relative to each other, taking into account (among other things) alternative means by which the consumer's requirements could have been met[146];

(b) whether the customer received an inducement to agree to the term, or in accepting it had an opportunity of entering into a similar contract with other persons, but without having to accept a similar term;

(c) whether the customer knew or ought reasonably to have known of the existence and extent of the term (having regard, among other things, to any custom of the trade and any previous course of dealing between the parties)[147];

(d) where the term excludes or restricts any relevant liability if some condition is not complied with, whether it was reasonable at the time of the contract to expect that compliance with that condition would be practicable[148];

(e) whether the goods were manufactured, processed or adapted to the special order of the customer.

Where the term purports to restrict liability to a specified sum of money regard should be had to: (a) the resources which the party seeking to rely on that term could expect to be available to him for the purpose of meeting the liability should it arise; (b) how far it was open to that party to cover himself by insurance.[149] The onus of proving that it was fair and reasonable to incorporate a term lies on the party so contending[150] and he must aver upon which of the above matters (a) to (e) he relies.[151]

Rules as to delivery—It is the obligation of the seller to deliver the goods, of the **12.37** buyer to accept and pay for them, in accordance with the terms of the contract (s.27). Unless otherwise agreed, delivery and payment of the price are concurrent conditions, so that the seller is not bound to deliver the goods unless the price is paid or tendered, while the buyer is not bound to pay the price unless the goods are delivered (s.28). The case of a sale on credit is an obvious example of an agreement to the contrary. But in the absence of any express provision on the subject, inference from a previous course of dealing between the parties, or proof of custom of trade, a sale is presumably for cash and the seller, if he chooses to stand on his strict rights, may refuse delivery unless the price is tendered.[152] Even where the sale is on credit, or a term is fixed for delivery before the term of payment, the seller is not bound to deliver the goods if the buyer is insolvent. He may retain them in the exercise of his right of lien, or, if they have been dispatched

---

[144] 1979 Act s.24(1).
[145] 1979 Act s.24(2), Sch.2. See *Rasbora v J.C.L. Marine* [1977] 1 Lloyd's Rep.645.
[146] See *Denholm Fishselling Ltd v Anderson*, 1991 S.L.T. (Sh. Ct) 24.
[147] See *Knight Machinery (Holdings) Ltd v Rennie*, 1995 S.L.T. 166.
[148] *Knight Machinery (Holdings) Ltd v Rennie*, 1995 S.L.T. 166.
[149] 1979 Act s.24(3).
[150] 1979 Act s.24(4).
[151] *Landcatch Ltd v Marine Harvest Ltd*, 1985 S.L.T. 478; *William Teacher & Sons Ltd v Bell Lines Ltd*, 1991 S.L.T. 876.
[152] *Hall v Scott* (1860) 22 D. 413.

and are in course of transit, recover them by the exercise of his right of stoppage in transit.[153]

The time for delivery may be fixed; if not, the law will infer a time reasonable in the whole circumstances of the case (s.29(3)). Late delivery will give the buyer the right to retain the price in security of his claim for damages.[154] Whether it will entitle him to rescind the contract, and refuse to accept the goods, depends upon whether, in the particular case, the delay amounts to a material failure on the part of the seller.[155]

Whether the seller is to send the goods to the purchaser, or the purchaser to send for them, depends upon the agreement, express or implied, in each case. If the seller is to send them by carrier he must make a reasonable contract of carriage.[156] In the absence of any agreement to the contrary the expense of putting the goods in a deliverable state falls on the seller (s.29(6)). Prima facie the place of delivery is the seller's place of business, if he has one; if not, his residence. But if the contract is for specific goods, which, to the knowledge of the parties when the contract is made, are in some other place, then that place is the place of delivery (s.29(2)).

12.38 Remedies of buyer: Failure to deliver—The remedies of the buyer depend on the nature of the seller's failure. If he fails to supply the goods, he is liable in damages. Where there is an available market for the goods,[157] the measure of damages is prima facie to be ascertained by the difference between the contract price and the market price at the time when they ought to have been delivered; if no time was fixed, then at the time of refusal to deliver (s.51). The buyer may also demand specific implement of the contract (s.52), but this remedy is available only when the sale is of some specific article, and the buyer can show a *pretium affectionis*, some reason for preferring the thing he contracted for to other things of the same kind; it is not competent when the sale is merely of a certain quantity of some particular commodity.[158] If the seller delivers less than he contracted to sell, the buyer may reject the goods if the shortfall is material, but if he accepts them he must pay for them at the contract rate. If the seller delivers goods in excess of what he contracted to sell and the excess is material, the buyer may accept the amount he contracted for and reject the rest, or he may reject the whole. If he accepts the whole of the goods delivered, he must pay for them at the contract rate (s.30). If the seller delivers the goods contracted for mixed with goods of a different description, the buyer may accept the goods which are in accordance with the contract, and reject the rest, or he may reject the whole (s.35A). For contracts made prior to January 3, 1995, the buyer only enjoys a right of partial rejection if some of the goods do not conform to the description.[159] There is no right of partial rejection if some of the goods, though of the same description, are of inferior quality.[160] For contracts made after January 3, 1995, the right of partial rejection applies when there has been a breach on the part of the seller which affects some or all of

---

[153] See below, paras 12.51, 12.52.

[154] *British Motor Body Co v Shaw*, 1914 S.C. 922. See para.10.16, above.

[155] See below, para.12.38.

[156] *Young v Hobson* (1949) 65 T.L.R. 365.

[157] *Marshall & Co v Nicoll & Son*, 1919 S.C. 244, affd 1919 S.C. (HL) 129, on meaning of "available market". See also *Thompson v Robinson* [1955] Ch. 177; *Charter v Sullivan* [1957] 2 Q.B. 117.

[158] *Union Electric Co v Holman*, 1913 S.C. 954 at 958.

[159] 1979 Act s.30(4), repealed by the 1994 Act s.3(3) and Sch.3.

[160] *Aitken, Campbell & Co v Boullen*, 1908 S.C. 490.

the goods. The right of partial rejection of the goods will not apply if a contrary intention appears in, or is to be implied from, the contract (s.35A).

Defective quality: Common law—The law as to the remedies of the buyer where **12.39** the goods delivered are not of the quality demanded by the contract, is a subject on which the 1893 Act made an important alteration in the law of Scotland. At common law the sole remedy of a buyer, if the goods tendered were disconform to contract, was to reject them, and, on doing so, to recover damages for breach of contract. If, however, he chose to accept the goods—and in certain cases the exigencies of his business might make acceptance unavoidable—then (except in the case of latent defects) he was held to have condoned their defects, and could not recover damages for their defective quality. The *actio quanti minoris*, which involves the right to retain goods and claim from the seller the difference between their value and the value they would have possessed had they fulfilled the contractual conditions, was not recognised by the law of Scotland.[161]

Remedies provided by Act—The remedies available to a buyer have been signif- **12.40** icantly altered by the 1994 Act and, in the case of consumer contracts, by the 2002 Regulations.[162] For contracts made prior to January 3, 1995, the buyer's remedies depend on s.11, which, it may be noted, has separate provisions for England and Scotland.

> "In Scotland, failure by the seller to perform any material part of a contract of sale is a breach of contract, which entitles the buyer either within a reasonable time after delivery to reject the goods and treat the contract as repudiated,[163] or to retain the goods and treat the failure to perform such material part as a breach which may give rise to a claim for compensation or damages."[164]

Under this provision, as interpreted by decisions, the buyer has alternative remedies, in the case where the seller's failure is material, i.e. (a) he may reject the goods, treat the contract as repudiated by the seller, and claim damages; (b) he may keep the goods and claim damages for their defective state, in substance the *actio quanti minoris* of the civil law.[165] For contracts made on or after January 3, 1995, the relevant provision of the Act is s.15B. If the seller is in breach of any term of the contract, the buyer can claim damages. In addition, if the breach is material, the buyer can reject any goods delivered and treat the contract as repu-

---

[161] *McCormick v Rittmeyer* (1869) 7 M. 854, opinion of Lord President Inglis.

[162] The 2002 Regulations added Pt 5A to the 1979 Act. It is discussed at para.12.46, below.

[163] As to the construction of clauses whereby the buyer undertakes not to reject goods tendered, with provision for arbitration as to their defects, see *Leary v Briggs* (1904) 6 F. 857; *Munro v Meyer* [1930] 2 K.B. 312.

[164] See ss.11(5), 53 and 58 of the 1979 Act, and *George Cohen, Sons & Co v Jamieson & Paterson*, 1963 S.C. 289.

[165] It is conceived that there is nothing in the Act to affect the common law distinction between the laws of England and Scotland, to the effect that, according to Scots law, any material failure in the quality of the goods will entitle the buyer to reject them, whilst according to English law, rejection is incompetent for a failure in quality not amounting to a difference in kind, unless there is an express provision for it. See opinion of Lord Chelmsford in *Cousten, Thomson & Co v Chapman* (1872) 10 M. (HL) 74 at 81; referred to, as applicable to the existing law, by Lord Dunedin, *Pollock v McCrae*, 1922 S.C. (HL) 192 at 202–3.

diated. If the contract of sale is a consumer contract,[166] a breach by the seller of
any of the terms relating to quality, fitness for purpose, description or conformity
with samples, is deemed to be a material breach of contract.[167]

12.41 Rejection excluded by acceptance—The right to reject is excluded if the buyer
has accepted the goods,[168] even though after acceptance the goods reveal latent
defects.[169] If he has not previously examined them, he is not deemed to have
accepted them unless and until he has had a reasonable opportunity of examining
them for the purpose of ascertaining whether they are in conformity with the
contract and, in the case of a contract for sale by sample, of comparing the bulk
with the sample (s.35(2)). He is deemed to have accepted them when he intimates
to the seller that he has accepted them[170] or when the goods have been delivered
to him and he does any act in relation to them which is inconsistent with the
ownership of the seller or when, after the lapse of a reasonable time, he retains the
goods without intimating to the seller that he has rejected them (s.35(2) and (4)).
Thus, where it was a condition of a contract for the supply of a boiler for a tank
which was being built for the Navy that it should have passed Admiralty tests, it
was held that the buyer, by fitting the boiler in the tank, had done an act inconsistent with the ownership of the seller, and could not reject it on the ground that
the tests had not been passed.[171] But the fact that the property of a thing in course
of construction may have passed to the buyer does not preclude his ultimate rejection of it. So where there was a contract to build a yacht, with provisions under
which the property passed to the buyer as the various instalments of the price were
paid, it was held that the buyer was still entitled to reject when, on completion, the
yacht proved disconform to contract.[172] What is a reasonable time is notoriously
difficult to assess as it depends on the facts of cases but is generally considered to
be fairly short, often a matter of days or weeks.[173] However, it has been held that
it is not necessarily too late to reject after the lapse of two years when the goods
had been stored and the defect was discovered only when they were taken out,[174]
after a delay of several months where the buyer was awaiting technical information from the seller which was necessary to make a decision on whether to
reject,[175] or over a year after the sale where the vehicle had been sold with the
intention it should be resold.[176] Where the defect is latent it has been held that time
should be calculated from the date of delivery of the goods.[177]

---

[166] 1979 Act ss.15B(2) and 61(1); for the definition of consumer contract see para.12.31, above.
[167] cf. *Millars of Falkirk v Turpie*, 1976 S.L.T. (Notes) 66.
[168] *Mechan v Bow, McLachlan & Co*, 1910 S.C. 758; *Woodburn v Motherwell*, 1917 S.C. 533;
Hardy v Hillerns [1923] 2 K.B. 490 (resale); W.M. Gloag, *Law of Contract*, 2nd edn (Edinburgh: W.
Green, 1929), p.611.
[169] *Morrison & Mason v Clarkson Bros* (1898) 25 R. 427; *Mechans v Highland Marine Charters*,
1964 S.C. 48.
[170] 1979 Act s.35(1)(a); see also *Mechans v Highland Marine Charters*, 1964 S.C. 48 (unqualified
acceptance).
[171] *Mechan v Bow, McLachlan & Co*, 1910 S.C. 758. See also *Morrison & Mason v Clarkson Bros*
(1898) 25 R. 427.
[172] *Nelson v Chalmers*, 1913 S.C. 441.
[173] The Law Commission and the Scottish Law Commission, *Consumer Remedies for Faulty Goods*
(HMSO, 2009), Law Com. No.317, Scot. Law Com. No.216, paras 2.17–2.20.
[174] *Burrell v Harding's Exrs*, 1931 S.L.T. 76 (a decision on relevancy).
[175] *Clegg v Andersson* [2003] EWCA Civ 320; *Fiat Auto Financial Services v Connelly*, 2007 S.L.T.
(Sh. Ct) 111 .
[176] *Truk (UK) Limited v Tokmakidis GmbH* [2000] 2 All E.R. (Comm) 594.
[177] *Douglas v Glenvarigill Co Ltd*, 2010 S.L.T. 634 (fifteen months was not a reasonable time).

For contracts made on or after January 3, 1995, the Act provides that the buyer under a consumer contract cannot lose his right to have a reasonable opportunity of examining the goods by agreement, waiver or otherwise (s.35(3)). In addition, the buyer is not deemed to have accepted the goods merely by asking for, or agreeing to, repair of the goods[178] or by delivering the goods to another under a sub-sale or other disposition (s.35(6)). If the buyer accepts any goods included in a commercial unit, he is deemed to have accepted all the goods making up the unit (s.35(7)).

Conditions of rejection—Rejection is inconsistent with any further use of the goods. So it is established that if the buyer merely intimates rejection and, on the seller refusing to take the goods back, continues to use them, he cannot insist on his right to reject.[179] In one case it was decided that in these circumstances the buyer, having by his notice of rejection elected one of two alternative remedies, was bound by the election, and could not fall back on the alternative of keeping the goods and claiming damages for their defective condition.[180] But this decision has been authoritatively disapproved.[181] Where the buyer has lost or foregone his right of rejection and is confined to a claim for damages, a clause which purports to exclude liability may not be operative if there has been a fundamental breach of contract on the part of the seller.[182] But it has been emphasised that the applicability of such an exceptions clause in that situation depends upon the true construction of the particular contract.[183] Continued use after intimation of rejection will still, it is conceived, bar rejection, but will not bar a claim for damages on the principle of the *actio quanti minoris*. **12.42**

Duty when goods rejected—When the buyer rejects the goods he has no right to retain them in security of his claim of damages.[184] In the absence of any express provision, he is not bound to return them to the seller (s.36). But where a horse was rejected as unsound, and the seller refused to take it back, opinions were expressed that it was the duty of the buyer either to have it placed in neutral custody or to obtain judicial authority for its resale.[185] If the goods rejected are perishable the buyer is entitled, and probably bound, to resell them at once.[186] **12.43**

Examination of goods—In a question of rejection, the buyer is bound to examine the goods within a reasonable time. What is a reasonable time is a question of the circumstances of each particular case.[187] But two general points are established. (a) When, as in the case of machinery, the defect is apparently remediable, and the seller, on being appealed to, attempts to remedy the defect, no lapse of time or continued use of the article while his attempts are still in progress will bar **12.44**

---

[178] *J&H Ritchie Ltd v Lloyd Ltd*, 2007 S.C. (HL) 89; see also *Munro & Co v Bennet & Son*, 1911 S.C. 337.
[179] *Electric Construction Co v Hurry & Young* (1897) 24 R. 312; *Croom & Arthur v Stewart* (1905) 7 F. 563. See also *MacDonald v Pollock* [2012] CSIH 12; 2012 S.L.T. 462
[180] *Electric Construction Co v Hurry & Young* (1897) 24 R. 312.
[181] *Pollock v McCrae*, 1922 S.C. (HL) 192.
[182] *Pollock v McCrae*, 1922 S.C. (HL) 192.
[183] *Suisse Atlantique v N.V. Rotterdamsche* [1967] 1 A.C. 361; *Alexander Stephen (Forth) Ltd v J.J. Riley (UK) Ltd*, 1976 S.C. 151; and see para.13.09, below.
[184] *Lupton v Schulze* (1900) 2 F. 1118.
[185] *Malcolm v Cross* (1898) 25 R. 1089.
[186] *Pommer v Mowat* (1906) 14 S.L.T. 373.
[187] See *Hyslop v Shirlaw* (1905) 7 F. 875.

ultimate rejection by the buyer.[188] (b) Where goods are ordered for export, the buyer, unless he can prove that the circumstances rendered it impossible, should examine the goods before forwarding them, and failure to do so may preclude rejection on the ground of any defect which a prompt examination would have revealed, on the principle that a seller is entitled to have an opportunity to remedy the goods.[189]

12.45 Failure in minor respects—The Act formerly contained no provision for the case of failure by the seller in some respect which was not material. The rule at common law is that the buyer is not then entitled to reject the goods, but may recover damages for the defect.[190] The Act, as amended by the 1994 Act, provides that a breach of any term of the contract which is not material entitles the buyer to claim damages (s.15B(1)(a)). What is a material failure is a question of the circumstances of each case, and of degree. Any serious defect in quality is undoubtedly material. Failure in respect of time of delivery is as a rule material in the case or mercantile contracts for the supply of goods where time is usually of the essence of the contract,[191] but not in the case of a contract for the supply of an article to be built or manufactured by the seller.[192] In consumer contracts made on or after January 3, 1995, the breach of any term relating to quality, fitness of purpose, description or conformity with samples, will be deemed to be a material breach (s.15B(2)).

12.46 Additional rights of consumer buyers—The 2002 Regulations inserted Pt 5A into the 1979 Act providing remedies for buyers who purchase by means of consumer contracts where the goods do not conform to the contract at the time of delivery.[193] Goods do not conform if there is a breach of an express term of the contract or a term implied by ss.13–15 of the 1979 Act (s.48F). Where goods do not conform to the contract at any time within six months of the date of delivery they are deemed not to have conformed at the date of delivery unless it is established that they did conform at that date or the application of this provision is incompatible with the nature of the goods or the lack of conformity (s.48A(3) and (4)). The buyer's primary remedy is to require the seller to repair or replace the goods which must be done within a reasonable time and without significant inconvenience to the buyer with the seller bearing any costs incurred including in particular the cost of any labour, materials or postage (s.48B(1) and (2)). If buyers request repair or replacement they must not invoke any other remedy until they have given the seller a reasonable time in which to comply (s.48D). These remedies do not apply where they are impossible, one is disproportionate in comparison to the other or they are disproportionate in comparison to a reduction in price or rescission of the contract. One remedy is disproportionate to another if the one imposes costs on the seller which, in comparison to those imposed on him by the other, are unreasonable taking into account the value which the goods would have

---

[188] 1979 Act s.35(6); and see *Munro & Co v Bennet & Son*, 1911 S.C. 337; *Aird & Coghill v Pullan* (1904) 7 F. 258.

[189] *Pini v Smith* (1895) 22 R. 699; *Magistrates of Glasgow v Ireland* (1895) 22 R. 818; *Dick v Cochrane & Fleming*, 1935 S.L.T. 432.

[190] *Webster v Cramond Iron Co* (1875) 2 R. 752; *Bradley v Dollar* (1886) 13 R. 893.

[191] *Shaw, Macfarlane & Co v Waddell* (1900) 2 F. 1070.

[192] *Macbride v Hamilton* (1875) 2 R. 775.

[193] The 2002 Regulations came into force on March 31, 2003 and implement Directive 1999/44/EC. See W.C.H. Ervine, "The Sale and Supply of Goods to Consumers Regulations 2002", 2003 S.L.T. (News) 67 and M. Hogg, "The consumer's right to rescind under the Sale of Goods Act: a tale of two remedies", 2003 S.L.T. (News) 277.

if they conformed to the contract, the significance of the lack of conformity and whether the other remedy could be effected without significant inconvenience to the buyer (s.48B(3) and (4)). If repair or replacement are not appropriate or have not been achieved within a reasonable time and without significant inconvenience to the buyer, he or she may require the seller to reduce the price by an appropriate amount or rescind the contract. Where the contract is rescinded any reimbursement may be reduced to take account of the use that the buyer has had of the goods since they were delivered (s.48C). Buyers may enforce the rights to repair or replacement by seeking an order of specific implement but a court may provide one of the other remedies (s.48E).[194]

Instalment contracts—Contracts for the supply of goods by instalments, with **12.47** provisions for intermediate payments, have raised the question whether the delivery of defective goods, or failure of delivery, in respect of one instalment, and, conversely, whether delay in payment of one instalment of the price, will justify the party aggrieved in rescinding the contract as repudiated by the other. Section 31 states that it depends on the terms of the contract and the circumstances of each case. The answer to that question would appear to depend on whether the conduct of the party in default is such as to justify the other in inferring that he does not intend to fulfil his contract, or is unable to do so. That inference may more easily be drawn in the case of a party's failure in the early instalments. The law has been judicially stated as follows:

> "If on one occasion the seller should tender goods inferior to contract quality, the purchaser would not in ordinary circumstances be justified in rescinding the whole contract, though he would be entitled to return the particular lot of goods which were objectionable. But if a seller systematically sends goods which are not conformable to contract, and the contract is for successive deliveries, I do not doubt that, where such conduct is persisted in, so as to make it evident that the seller does not intend to fulfil his contract, the purchaser may rescind the contract and refuse to take further deliveries".[195]

Only in exceptional circumstances would delay in payment justify the seller in rescinding the contract.[196]

Rights of seller: Refusal to accept—Questions as to the rights of the seller arise **12.48** where the buyer wrongfully refuses to accept the goods, or when he fails to pay the price. In the case of refusal to accept and pay for the goods the seller may maintain an action of damages for non-acceptance, the measure of damages being, if there is an available market for the goods,[197] the difference between the contract

---

[194] 1979 Act Pt 5A has been discussed in *Douglas v Glenvarigill Co Ltd*, 2010 S.L.T. 634 and *O'Farrell v Moroney*, 2008 G.W.D. 35–533 Sheriff Court (Lothian and Borders). In *Gebr Weber GmbH v Wittmer Putz v Medianess Electronics GmbH* (Joined cases C-65/09 and C-87/09) [2011] 3 C.M.L.R. 27 the European Court of Justice discussed the remedies of repair and replacement.

[195] *Govan Rope Co v Weir* (1897) 24 R. 368, per Lord McLaren. See *Dunford & Elliot v Macleod & Co* (1902) 4 F. 912; *Mersey Steel Co v Naylor Benzon & Co* (1884) 9 App. Cas. 434; *Maple Flock Co v Universal Furniture Products* [1934] 1 K.B. 148; *Regent ohG Aisestadt und Barig v Francesco of Jermyn Street Ltd* [1981] 3 All E.R. 327.

[196] 1979 Act s.10(1); *Barclay v Anderston Foundry Co* (1856) 18 D. 1190; *Linn v Shields* (1863) 2 M. 88.

[197] *Thompson v Robinson* [1955] Ch. 177 (where there was no available market); *Charter v Sullivan* [1957] 2 Q.B. 117. Cf. *Lazenby Garages v Wright* [1976] 1 W.L.R. 459.

price and the market price ruling at the date when the goods ought to have been accepted (s.50). He is also entitled to a reasonable charge for the care and custody of the goods (s.37). Refusal by the buyer, either to accept the goods or to pay the price, would seem to amount to a repudiation of the contract by him, which would justify the seller in an immediate resale, preferably under a warrant from the sheriff.[198]

12.49 Failure in payment—Where the buyer fails to pay the price we have to consider (a) the seller's right of action, and (b) his rights over the goods.

If the property in the goods has passed to the buyer, i.e. if the contract was a sale, as contrasted with an agreement to sell, the seller may maintain an action for the price (s.49(1)). He may also do so if the price was payable on a day certain,[199] irrespective of delivery, although the property in the goods has not passed, and the goods have not been appropriated to the contract (s.49(2)). In other cases, his action is for damages for non-acceptance (s.50). Mere failure to pay the price does not entitle the seller to rescind the contract and demand redelivery of the goods after the property has passed to the buyer.[200] But if the contract was induced by fraud, the seller may reduce it and recover the goods in a question either with the buyer himself or with the trustee in his sequestration, and it is sufficient proof of fraud if it be established that the buyer bought the goods without any intention to pay for them.[201]

12.50 Rights of unpaid seller over goods—The rights of a seller over the goods are dealt with in Pt V of the Act, under the heading "Rights of Unpaid Seller against the Goods".[202] A seller is deemed to be unpaid (a) when the whole of the price has not been paid or tendered, or (b) when a bill of exchange or other negotiable instrument has been received as conditional payment, and the condition on which it was received has not been fulfilled by reason of the dishonour of the instrument or otherwise (s.38).[203] The unpaid seller may have one or more of the following rights: lien; stoppage in transit; resale.

12.51 Lien—Lien is the right of the seller while still in possession of the goods (whether the property has passed or not) to retain them until payment or tender of the price, in the following cases: (a) where the goods have been sold without any stipulation as to credit; (b) where the goods have been sold on credit but the period of credit has expired; (c) where the buyer becomes insolvent (s.41). A buyer is deemed to be insolvent if he either has ceased to pay his debts in the ordinary course of business or cannot pay his debts as they become due (s.61(4)). A right of lien is lost: (a) when the seller delivers the goods to a carrier for the purpose of transmission to the buyer without reserving the right of disposal; (b) when the buyer or his agent lawfully obtains possession of the goods[204]; (c) by waiver (s.43). A right of

---

[198] Bell, *Principles*, s.128.
[199] On meaning of "a day certain", see *Henderson & Keay Ltd v A.M. Carmichael Ltd*, 1956 S.L.T. (Notes) 58.
[200] *Muirhead & Turnbull v Dickson* (1905) 7 F. 686.
[201] *Gamage v Charlesworth's Tr.*, 1910 S.C. 257.
[202] See J.J. Gow, *Mercantile and Industrial Law of Scotland* (Edinburgh: W. Green, 1964), pp.186–201.
[203] *McDowall & Neilson's Tr. v Snowball Co* (1904) 7 F. 35.
[204] But where a seller retakes possession from the buyer he does not necessarily regain his right of lien: *London Scottish Transport v Tyres (Scotland) Ltd*, 1957 S.L.T. (Sh. Ct) 48; *Hostess Mobile Catering v Archibald Scott Ltd*, 1981 S.C. 185.

lien is not affected by the fact that the buyer may have resold or pledged[205] the goods to a third party (s.47). But in a case before the 1893 Act it was held that where A had sold to B on a month's credit and B resold to C, who intimated the subsale to A within the month, A had waived his right of lien in a question with C and must deliver to him, although B was bankrupt and could not pay A.[206] And if the buyer had obtained a document of title to the goods, and that document had been transferred to a person who took it in good faith,[207] and for valuable consideration, then if that transfer was by way of sale the original seller's right of lien is defeated, while if it was by way of pledge, the right of lien can only be exercised subject to the rights of the pledgee (s.47). Delivery of part of the goods does not preclude the exercise of lien over the remainder (s.42).

Stoppage in transit—Stoppage in transit, formerly known as stoppage in tran- **12.52** situ, is a principle which was introduced into the law of Scotland by the decision of the House of Lords in *Jaffrey v Allan, Stewart & Co*,[208] in place of a doctrine, which was then disapproved, that if a buyer took delivery of goods within three days of stopping payment he was presumed to have taken them fraudulently, and the seller could recover them in a question with the trustee in his sequestration.

The right of stoppage in transit, as now regulated by the Act, is the right of an unpaid seller, in the case where the property has passed to the buyer, and the goods are in course of transit to him, to resume possession, and to retain the goods until payment or tender of the price (s.44). Where the property has not passed to the buyer the unpaid seller has a right of withholding delivery similar to and co-extensive with the right of stoppage in transit (s.39(2)). The right of stoppage can be exercised only when the buyer becomes insolvent.[209] If the seller stops the goods and is unable to prove that the buyer is insolvent he is liable in damages.

Stoppage in transit may be effected either by taking actual possession of the goods, or by giving notice to the carrier requiring him to redeliver the goods to the seller, at the latter's expense (s.46). Notice may be given either to the actual custodier, or to his principal, e.g. to the shipping company. In the latter case it must be given in time to allow of communication with the actual custodier (s.46(3)). Where the contract of carriage has been made by the buyer, the seller, by giving notice to stop, incurs personal liability for the freight.[210] If the carrier disregards the notice, and delivers the goods to the buyer, the stoppage is defeated, and the goods fall to be treated as part of the assets in the buyer's sequestration, but the carrier is liable in damages to the seller.[211]

Stoppage in transit is competent only while the goods are in transit. The Act deals with the duration of the transit in seven rules (s.45). These should be referred to, but it may be convenient to state the general law. The transit may end either at the actual place of delivery or when the buyer or his agent obtains possession at some intermediate place. Actual delivery is not necessary to end the transit, if the carrier acknowledges to the buyer that he holds the goods for him after their arrival at the place of destination. So where goods were sent by rail to a particular

---

[205] Since *ex hypothesi* the seller is still in possession and pledge requires delivery (para.37.13, below), the circumstances in which the buyer can pledge must be exceptional.

[206] *Fleming v Smith* (1881) 8 R. 548.

[207] As to the meaning of "good faith", see above, para.12.26.

[208] *Jaffrey v Allan, Stewart & Co* (1790) 3 Paton 191.

[209] As to the meaning of "insolvency", see above, para.12.51.

[210] *Booth Steamship Co v Cargo Fleet Iron Co* [1916] 2 K.B. 570.

[211] *Mechan v N.-E. Ry*, 1911 S.C. 1348.

station, and the consignee there signed a receipt for them but did not take them away, it was held that the transit had ended, and that a subsequent notice to stop came too late.[212] There is no room for stoppage in transit if the buyer sends for the goods. If he charters a ship the goods are in his custody, and cannot therefore be stopped, as soon as they are put on board.[213] But the duration of the transit is not affected by the fact that the contract of carriage with the shipowner is made by the buyer, if the ship is not chartered by him in such a way as to make the captain of the ship his servant.[214]

If part of the goods is delivered to the buyer, the remainder may be stopped, unless the part delivery has been made in such circumstances as to show an agreement to give up possession of the whole (s.45(7)). When two lifeboats arrived by rail at Sunderland station, and one of them was delivered to a carter who had general instructions to take all goods arriving for the consignee, and the other would have been delivered to the carter if he had had room for it, it was held that the circumstances did not show an agreement by the railway company to give up possession of the second boat, and that it might still be stopped in transit.[215] Rules, similar to those applicable to lien,[216] apply where a document of title has been transferred to a third party either as a sub-purchaser or as a pledgee.

12.53 Resale—The unpaid seller, if in possession of the goods, either under lien or after he has stopped them in transit, is entitled to resell them either, if they are perishable or if he has given notice to the buyer of his intention to resell, and the buyer does not within a reasonable time pay or tender the price. The contract of sale is not rescinded by the exercise of a right of lien or of stoppage in transit (s.48(1)) but, if the seller then resells, the contract is rescinded, whether the resale is of the goods or part of them, and the property in them reverts to the seller who may then recover from the original buyer damages for non-acceptance (s.48(3)).[217] If the seller expressly reserves the right of resale in case the buyer should make default, and, on the buyer making the whole of the goods or part of them, and the property in them reverts to the seller in case the buyer should make default, and, on the buyer making default, resells, the original contract of sale is rescinded, without prejudice to any claim the seller may have for damages (s.48(4)). In all cases of resale the buyer obtains a good title to the goods as against the original buyer (s.48(2)).

12.54 Auction sales—The law of sale by auction is regulated by s.57. Prima facie each lot is to be regarded as a separate contract of sale. So it was held that where wine was sold in lots the purchaser was entitled to reject lots which were defective and to keep the rest.[218]

A sale by auction is complete when the auctioneer announces its completion by the fall of the hammer. Until such announcement is made any bidder may retract his or her bid (s.57(2)). The common law, which will still rule in sales to which the Act does not apply, e.g. sales of heritage, was not settled, but probably was

---

[212] *Muir v Rankin* (1905) 13 S.L.T. 60.
[213] *Rosevear China Clay Co* (1879) L.R. 11 Ch.D. 560.
[214] *Booth Steamship Co Ltd v Cargo Fleet Iron Co* [1916] 2 K.B. 570.
[215] *Mechan v N.-E. Ry*, 1911 S.C. 1348.
[216] 1979 Act s.47, and see above, para.12.51.
[217] *Ward (R.V.) v Bignall* [1967] 1 Q.B. 534.
[218] *Couston, Thomson & Co v Chapman* (1872) 10 M. (HL) 74.

that a bid could not be retracted, unless it were refused, or a higher bid made.[219] It has been held to follow from the statutory provision that as each bidder may retract his bid, the exposer has a corresponding right to withdraw the article even after the bidding has commenced.[220]

A reserve price is lawful (s.57(3)) but, unless the right of the seller to bid is expressly reserved, it is unlawful and may be treated as fraudulent for him to bid or to employ anyone else, commonly spoken of as a white-bonnet, to bid for him (s.57(4), (5)). Should it transpire that fraudulent bids of this kind have been made, the highest bona fide bidder is entitled to the article at the last bid he made before the fraudulent bidding commenced.[221] If, however, the objection to the sale is merely that a person has made bids who was not entitled to do so, and there is no proof of fraud, the bidder to whom the article is ultimately adjudged must pay the full price he has offered.[222] But if the party disqualified proves to be the highest bidder the sale is open to reduction by other bidders or by anyone who can show an interest in obtaining the highest possible price.[223] It is a general rule that a party directly interested in the sale is not entitled to bid. So a beneficiary may not bid in a sale by a trustee,[224] and one of several part-owners is equally disqualified.[225] It is doubtful whether the creditor in a bond and disposition in security, exposing the subjects for sale under the powers in his bond, is entitled to bid; in any event the disqualification does not apply where there are several creditors, and bids are made by one.[226]

It has twice been held in Scotland that when an intending bidder bribed others not to compete with him his conduct amounted to fraud on the exposer, which entitled the latter to reduce the sale and recover the expenses of it from the party implicated.[227] It was decided in England that such an agreement was not a *pactum illicitum*, and that its conditions could be enforced by the parties to it inter se.[228] However, by the Auctions (Bidding Agreements) Act 1927, if any dealer[229] agrees to give, or gives, or offers to give, any gift or consideration to any other person as a reward for abstaining, or for having abstained, from bidding at a sale by auction, he and any person who agrees to accept, or accepts, or attempts to obtain, any such gift commits a criminal offence. Where goods are purchased at an auction by a person who has entered into an agreement with another or others that the other or others (or some of them) will abstain from bidding for the goods (not being an agreement to purchase the goods bona fide on joint account) and he or the other party, or one of the other parties, to the agreement is a dealer, the seller may avoid the contract under which the goods were purchased. If restitution of the goods is not made, the parties to the bidding agreement are jointly and severally

---

[219] *Cree v Durie* Unreported December 1, 1810 FC.

[220] *Fenwick v Macdonald, Fraser & Co* (1904) 6 F. 850.

[221] *Faulds v Corbet* (1859) 21 D. 587. See also *Barry v Heathcote Ball & Co (Commercial Auctions) Ltd* [2001] 1 All E.R. 944, CA where failure in an auction without reserve to accept the highest bid exposed the auctioneer to an action of damages for breach of contract.

[222] *Wishart v Howatson* (1897) 5 S.L.T. 84.

[223] *Shiell v Guthrie's Trs* (1874) 1 R. 1083.

[224] *Shiell v Guthrie's Trs* (1874) 1 R. 1083.

[225] *Monice v Craig* (1902) 39 S.L.R. 609.

[226] *Wright v Buchanan*, 1917 S.C. 73. As to a sale by a permanent trustee in a sequestration, see Bankruptcy (Scotland) Act 1985 s.39(8).

[227] *Murray v McWhan* (1783) Mor.9567; *Aitchison* (1783) Mor.9567.

[228] *Rawlings v General Trading Co* [1921] 1 K.B. 635.

[229] Defined as "a person who in the normal course of his business attends sales by auction for the purpose of purchasing goods with a view to reselling them".

liable to make good to the seller the loss (if any) he sustained by reason of the operation of the agreement.[230] Conduct which would formerly have infringed the Mock Auctions Act 1961 will now breach the Consumer Protection from Unfair Trading Regulations 2008 and thus be subject to administrative and criminal sanctions.[231]

12.55 Sale or return: Sale on approval—The contract of sale or return is usually entered into when goods are supplied by a wholesaler to a retail dealer on the condition, variously expressed, that the latter may sell them to his customers, but has the option to return them. A sale on approval implies that possession of an article is given, with an unqualified option to buy it or to return it within a specified period. When a horse was sold with a warranty, and delivered on a week's trial it was held that the contract was not a sale on approval. The buyer's option to return the horse within the week was not unqualified: he could do so only if it failed to fulfil the warranty.[232]

In the question of the passing of the property in the goods, the contracts of sale or return and sale on approval are dealt with in the same subsection of the Act (s.18, r.4):

> "When goods are delivered to the buyer on approval or on sale or return or other similar terms the property in the goods passes to the buyer: (a) when he signifies his approval or acceptance to the seller or does any other act adopting the transaction; (b) if he does not signify his approval or acceptance to the seller but retains the goods without giving notice of rejection; then, if a time has been fixed for the return of the goods, on the expiration of that time, and, if no time has been fixed, on the expiration of a reasonable time".[233]

In certain cases the retail dealer, having obtained goods on sale or return, has pawned them, and the question of the title of the pawnbroker in a question with the wholesale dealer has been raised. If the contract merely provides that the retail dealer may sell the goods or may return them it is probably established that by pawning them (although fraudulently) he does an act adopting the transaction, the property passes to him, and the pawnbroker obtains a good title.[234] The wholesale dealer may seek to protect himself by stipulating that, before disposing of any article, the retail dealer must have it invoiced by him. In *Bryce v Erhmann*[235] opinions were expressed that in spite of such a clause a pawnbroker would obtain a good title but, in view of a contrary English decision,[236] the law cannot be regarded as settled. Goods on sale or return do not pass to the trustee in the sequestration of the retail dealer,[237] nor, it is conceived, could they be attached by his

---

[230] Auctions (Bidding Agreements) Act 1969 s.3.

[231] The Mock Auctions Act 1961 was repealed by Consumer Protection from Unfair Trading Regulations 2008 (SI 2008/1277) Sch.4(1) para.1.

[232] *Cranston v Mallow*, 1912 S.C. 112.

[233] See *Poole v Smith's Car Sales* [1962] 1 W.L.R. 744. In *Atari Corp (UK) Ltd v Electronics Boutique Stores (UK) Ltd* [1998] Q.B. 539 the English Court of Appeal held that any intimation to the seller that the buyer did not wish to exercise the option to purchase was sufficient.

[234] *Bryce v Ehrmann* (1904) 7 F. 5; *Kirkham v Attenborough* [1897] 1 Q.B. 201.

[235] *Kirkham v Attenborough* [1897] 1 Q.B. 201.

[236] *Weiner v Gill* [1906] 2 K.B. 574.

[237] *Macdonald v Westren* (1888) 15 R. 988; *Ross & Co v Plano Manufacturing Co* (1903) 11 S.L.T. 7.

creditors by poinding. But as *invecta et illata* they are possibly covered by the landlord's hypothec, and could be attached by him by sequestration.[238]

Sale: f.o.b.; c.i.f.—In sale f.o.b. (free on board) or, in inland carriage, f.o.r. (free **12.56** on rail) the seller undertakes to ship the goods at the port of shipment, or to load them at the station named, the expense of the carriage, and of insurance, falling upon the buyer, on whom the risk falls. The property in the goods may not pass to the buyer on shipment if the seller has reserved a right of disposal by taking the bill of lading with the goods deliverable to the seller or his agent.[239] Any charge necessarily payable before the goods are put on board, such as an export duty newly imposed, falls upon the seller.[240]

A sale c.i.f. (cost, insurance, freight) imports that the price includes the freight of the goods to their destination, and their insurance during transit. If, as is usual, the arrangement with the shipowner is that the freight is to be paid by the buyer or consignee on delivery of the goods, the amount is deducted from the invoice price. The obligation of the seller, in a contract c.i.f., is to ship the goods and transmit to the buyer the shipping documents, these being an invoice, a bill of lading and a policy of insurance. When these are sent to the buyer the property and risk pass to him[241] unless a contrary intention appears from the conduct of the parties and the circumstances of the case.[242] On tender of the shipping documents the buyer is bound to pay the price, and is not entitled to withhold payment until the goods arrive and he has had an opportunity of examining them.[243] Refusal to pay on presentation of the documents is a fundamental breach of contract.[244] But payment of the price does not imply acceptance of the goods, and if they arrive and are disconform to contract, the buyer may still reject them, and recover the price or damages.[245] If the goods are lost in transit the buyer cannot recover the price; his remedy lies in the policy of insurance.[246] When timber in New Brunswick was sold "c.i.f. Glasgow" it was decided, in a question of stoppage *in transitu*, that it was in course of transit until it reached Glasgow, in spite of the fact that in the contract it was stated to be "deliverable" at a New Brunswick port.[247]

A development of the c.i.f. contract is that the buyer agrees to open in favour of the seller a confirmed banker's credit on which the seller may draw on presentation of the shipping documents, possibly with other documents.[248] The buyer is bound to keep the credit open during the whole period allowing for shipping.[249]

---

[238] See para.12.57, below.

[239] 1979 Act s.19; *Mitsui & Co Ltd v Flota Mercante Grancolombiana S.A.* [1988] 1 W.L.R. 1145, CA.

[240] *Bowhill Coal Co. v Tobias* (1902) 5 F. 262.

[241] *Delaurier v Wyllie* (1889) 17 R. 167.

[242] *The Albazero* [1977] A.C. 774.

[243] *Horst v Biddell* [1912] A.C. 18; *Ross T. Smyth & Co Ltd v T.D. Bailey Son & Co* [1940] 3 All E.R. 60.

[244] *Berger & Co Inc. v Gill & Duffus S.A.* [1984] A.C. 382.

[245] *Pommer v Mowat* (1906) 14 S.L.T. 373; *Harrower, Welsh & Co v McWilliam*, 1928 S.C. 326; *Kwei Tek Chao v British Traders and Shippers Ltd* [1954] 2 Q.B. 459.

[246] *Delaurier v Wyllie* (1889) 17 R. 167; *Manbre Saccharine Co v Corn Products Co* [1919] 1 K.B. 198.

[247] *Mcdowall & Neilson's Tr. v Snowball Co* (1904) 7 F. 35.

[248] *Pavia & Co, S.p.A. v Thurmann-Nielson* [1952] 2 Q.B. 84; *Trans Trust S.P.R.L. v Danubian Trading Co* [1952] 2 Q.B. 297; *United City Merchants (Investments) Ltd v Royal Bank of Canada* [1983] 1 A.C. 168, per Lord Diplock at 182–8. As to incorporation of the Uniform Customs and Practice for Documentary Credits, see *Forestal Minosa Ltd v Oriental Credit Ltd* [1986] 1 W.L.R. 631.

[249] *Pavia & Co, S.P.A. v Thurmann-Neilson* [1952] 2 Q.B. 84.

12.57 Hire-purchase—The term "hire-purchase" is commonly used to describe a variety of different types of agreement. Strictly, however, a contract of hire-purchase is one under which articles are taken on hire and the hirer is granted the option to purchase them on his fulfilling certain conditions of the contract.[250] This type of contract is to be contrasted with a contract of sale under which the buyer and seller are under binding obligations to each other respectively to buy and to sell.[251] Accordingly, if the terms of the hire-purchase agreement in any way bind the hirer to purchase the article hired, the contract is one of sale, not of hire-purchase.[252] This distinction is of importance in considering whether a hirer has conferred a good title upon an innocent third party to whom he has purported to sell the article hired. If the contract is only one of hire-purchase, the third party does not obtain a good title.[253] If on the other hand, it is one of sale, the hirer is a person who has bought or agreed to buy goods and is in possession of them with the consent of the owner; and under the provisions of s.25(1) of the Sale of Goods Act[254] he has the power to give a good title to the third party.[255] But where the contract is truly one of hire-purchase, the hirer has the right to acquire the article by completing the payments and this right he may assign to a third party. If he sells the article, at least if there is no proof that in doing so he acted fraudulently, it will be assumed that he transferred all the right he possessed, and the purchaser from him, though he will not get a complete title to the article, will be entitled to retain it and complete his right by payment of the remaining instalments of the hire-purchase, provided that there is no term in the agreement forbidding assignation.[256] Articles on hire-purchase do not pass to the trustee in the hirer's sequestration, but presumably he has the power to adopt the contract and acquire them by completing the payments.[257] They fall under the landlord's hypothec.[258]

The Supply of Goods (Implied Terms) Act 1973 (as amended by the 2002 Regulations) ss.8–11, imposes implied stipulations as to the title, description, quality and fitness of goods let on hire-purchase, corresponding to those implied in the sale of goods. Remedies for breach of these terms are set out in s.12A of the 1973 Act. Section 20 of the Unfair Contract Terms Act 1977 applies to these terms.[259]

12.58 Contracts for the transfer of goods—The Supply of Goods and Services Act 1982[260] provides for comparable terms to be implied into contracts for the transfer of goods. A contract is a contract for the transfer of goods if one person transfers

---

[250] Compare, however, the definition of "hire-purchase agreement" in the Consumer Credit Act 1974 s.189.

[251] *Murdoch v Greig* (1889) 16 R. 396, especially per Lord President Inglis at 400, and per Lord Shand at 402.

[252] The court will examine the substance of each agreement carefully to see whether it is one of hire-purchase or sale, whatever its terms: *Murdoch v Greig* (1889) 16 R. 396; *Scottish Transit Trust v Scottish Land Cultivators*, 1955 S.C. 254.

[253] *Helby v Matthews* [1895] A.C. 471. Motor vehicles are now a statutory exception where sold to a private purchaser by the hirer: Hire-Purchase Act 1964 Pt III; see above, para.12.24.

[254] See above, para.12.24.

[255] *Lee v Butler* [1893] 2 Q.B. 318. But see para.12.25, above as to conditional sales which are subject to the Consumer Credit Act 1974.

[256] *Whiteley v Hilt* [1918] 2 K.B. 808.

[257] Bankruptcy (Scotland) Act 1985 s.42.

[258] *Rudman v Jay*, 1908 S.C. 552.

[259] See para.12.36, above.

[260] Supply of Goods and Services Act 1982 (the "1982 Act") Pt 1A, introduced by the 1994 Act s.6 and Sch.1.

transfer ownership at the end of the contract,[19] and the hirer can terminate the contract "by returning the thing hired to its owner"[20] (subject to the provisions of the lease). Conversely, under a conditional sale agreement,[21] the party using and possessing the item which is the subject of the contract, has undertaken to purchase it,[22] i.e. there is "a legal obligation to buy".[23] Payments are made in instalments, and are subject to a "suspensive condition" that, although the purchaser possesses the thing, ownership in it does not pass until all the instalments are paid.[24] Therefore, up until the final payment is made, and the condition fulfilled, the purchaser has no title to the asset,[25] and so, in this regard, is in a similar position to a person who is hiring goods-use, but not ownership, for a payment. Under a hire-purchase agreement, the hirer pays a periodic rental, as in an ordinary hire contract, but, unlike a hire contract, the hirer, in a hire-purchase agreement, has an option to purchase the thing hired, at the end of the hire period, usually for a nominal sum, and so obtain title to it.[26] This differs from a conditional sale, as there is no requirement to purchase the item at the end of the contract[27] (i.e. it is not a deferred sale). It is when the option is exercised that the hire-purchase agreement changes character from being one of hire to one of sale.[28] Thus, what distinguishes the hire-purchase agreement from an ordinary hire agreement is the option to purchase the hired asset.[29]

Obligations of lessor—The lessor undertakes to supply either a specific thing, or a thing of a particular kind, according to the terms of the contract. He is bound to take care that the article he supplies is of satisfactory quality and also, where the purpose of the hire is known, either expressly or by implication, that the article is reasonably fit for that purpose, and he is liable for failure in either respect.[30] But if the lessor can demonstrate that the hirer did not rely on his skill or judgment, or that it was unreasonable for the hirer to do so, the implied term as to fitness is displaced.[31] Should the thing cause injury to the hirer the lessor is liable if he was aware of its dangerous character and failed to give warning.[32] A mere lender on **13.05**

---

[19] Although the hirer under a finance lease is treated as the owner for accounting purposes, see Statement of Standard Accounting Practice (SSAP 21), "Accounting for leases and hire purchase contracts".

[20] *Helby v Matthews* [1895] A.C. 471 at 479, per Lord Watson; see also *Murdoch & Co Ltd v Greig* (1889) 16 R. 396 at 400, per Lord President Inglis.

[21] For a discussion of a conditional sale agreement, see *Lee v Butler* [1893] 2 Q.B. 318; *Murdoch & Co Ltd v Greig* (1889) 16 R. 396; *McEntire v Crossley* [1895] A.C. 457 at 463, per Lord Herschell L.C.; *Helby v Matthews* [1895] A.C. 471; and *Forthright Finance Ltd v Carlyle* [1997] 4 All E.R. 90.

[22] *McEntire v Crossley* [1895] A.C. 457 at 463, per Lord Herschell L.C.; *Helby v Matthews* [1895] A.C. 471 at 475, per Lord Herschell L.C.; *Murdoch & Co Ltd v Greig* (1889) 16 R. 396.

[23] *Helby v Matthews* [1895] A.C. 471 at 475, per Lord Herschell L.C.

[24] See *Murdoch & Co Ltd v Greig* (1889) 16 R. 396 at 401 per Lord President Inglis, at 402 per Lord Shand, and at 403 per Lord Adam.

[25] *Murdoch & Co Ltd v Greig* (1889) 16 R. 396 at 401, per Lord President Inglis.

[26] *Helby v Matthews* [1895] A.C. 471 and *Entire v Crossley Bros* [1895] A.C. 457. See also the definition of "hire-purchase" in 1974 Act s.189(1) (as amended).

[27] See Lord Watson in *Helby v Matthews* [1895] A.C. 471 at 479.

[28] P.S. Atiyah, J.N. Adams and H.L. MacQueen, *Sale of Goods*, 12th edn (Longman, 2010), p.13.

[29] The taxation treatment in relation to capital allowances is also different, see the Capital Allowances Act 2001 and para.13.16, below.

[30] Supply of Goods and Services Act 1982 s.11J(2), (5) and (6) (added by the Sale and Supply of Goods Act 1994 s.6 and Sch.1). Implied terms as to the right to transfer possession and where hire is by description or by sample are found in ss.11H(1), 11I and 11K.

[31] Supply of Goods and Services Act 1982 s.11J(7).

[32] *Coughlin v Gillison* [1899] 1 Q.B. 145. See *Clarke v Army and Navy Cooperative Society Ltd* [1903] 1 K.B. 155.

gratuitous terms has no further duty, and is not liable merely because he has failed to examine the thing he lends.[33] Should the thing hired occasion some exceptional expense to the hirer, the lessor will be liable for the expense, provided that it was necessary and not due to any fault of the hirer, and that notice was given by the hirer to the lessor as soon as the circumstances permitted.[34] Where damage is caused by a defective product, the lessor may be liable.[35] The lessor may also be guilty of a criminal offence if he supplies[36] consumer goods which fail to comply with certain safety requirements.[37] Further, in terms of the Health and Safety at Work etc. Act 1974 (as amended), the lessor has a duty to ensure, so far as is reasonably practicable, that an article supplied for use at work is safe and without risks to health.[38]

13.06 Obligations of hirer—The obligations of a hirer are set out in the paragraphs which follow. However, the main obligation on the hirer is to pay the hire or rental agreed upon in the contract of hire or, in the absence of any express agreement, a reasonable hire. The accidental destruction of the thing terminates the contract, and with it the obligation to pay hire; an accidental injury gives the hirer the option of terminating the contract or claiming a proportionate reduction of the hire.[39]

13.07 Degrees of care—The hirer is bound to take reasonable care for the safety of the article hired. The care required is such as a diligent and prudent man takes of his own property. In estimating it, the value of the article is obviously a relevant consideration. The civilian distinction between *culpa lata, culpa levis* and *culpa levissima*, though possibly still recognised in the law of Scotland,[40] is difficult to apply in any concrete case. If the distinction is still maintainable at all, the liability of a hirer, as the contract of hire is one beneficial to both parties, is for *culpa levis*[41]: liability for *culpa levissima* would be appropriate, in commodate, where the contract is beneficial only to the party in fault, and liability for *culpa lata* would be applicable in contracts like gratuitous mandate or deposit where the party alleged to be in fault is acting solely in the interests of the other. It has been suggested, though not decided, that a party who hires an article, or undertakes the care of it for reward, is liable for loss or injury due to the fault of his employee,

---

[33] *Oliver v Saddler*, 1929 S.C. (HL) 94, per Lord Atkin at 101.

[34] Bell, *Commentaries*, I, 482; *Johnston v Rankin* (1687) Mor.10080.

[35] Consumer Protection Act 1987 (the "1987 Act") ss.2(3) and 46. Liability arises where the lessor fails to identify the manufacturer or trademark-owner or importer, despite being requested to do so: see s.2 and Ch.28, below. Note that in finance leasing, the dealer or retailer, rather than the finance company is liable: 1987 Act s.46(2). See also Health and Safety (Leasing Arrangements) Regulations 1992 (SI 1992/1524).

[36] In the course of his business: s.46(5) of the 1987 Act.

[37] The General Product Safety Regulations 2005 (SI 2005/1803) and the Consumer Protection Act 1987 (Pt II). A contravention of safety regulations made under the 1987 Act can give rise to a civil action: s.41. Note that in finance leasing the dealer or retailer rather than the finance company is liable: s.46(2).

[38] 1974 Act s.6(1), as amended by Consumer Protection Act 1987 s.3 and Sch.3.

[39] Bell, *Principles*, s.141; *Muir v McIntyre* (1887) 14 R. 470.

[40] *Wernham v McLean, Baird & Neilson*, 1925 S.C. 407. See, however, opinion of Lord Atkin, *Kolbin v Kinnear*, 1931 S.C. (HL) 128, at 139. In *Giblin v McMullen* (1868) L.R. 2 P.C. 317, Lord Chelmsford said: "though degrees of care are not definable, they are with some approach to certainty distinguishable".

[41] Bell, *Commentaries*, I, 483.

even though acting outwith the scope of his employment, whereas no such liability would rest on a gratuitous depositary.[42]

Facts indicating fault—Fault, or want of reasonable care, on the part of a hirer, **13.08** may consist in overloading or overworking the article hired,[43] or using it in some way involving an extra risk, which was not contemplated at the time of the contract.[44] Probably if the article is injured by use in the way contemplated by the contract, the onus of proof that he was not at fault, or failed to take reasonable care, lies on the hirer.[45] Fault, or a want of reasonable care, may also consist in the want of reasonable precautions against loss or theft, a question necessarily of circumstances[46]; or in failure to take the proper steps after an injury or loss has occurred, as where an agister of cattle failed to give notice, either to the owner or the police, that the cattle had been stolen, and was held to be liable unless he could prove that the notice would have been useless.[47] It is cogent evidence of negligence that the hirer took less care of the article hired than he did of his own property.[48] However, it is no defence that he treated his own property with the same lack of care.[49]

Exclusion clauses in hire contracts—Both the Unfair Contract Terms Act 1977[50] **13.09** and the Unfair Terms in Consumer Contracts Regulations 1999[51] apply to contracts of hire.[52] Under the Unfair Contract Terms Act 1977 (the "1977 Act"), contractual terms or a provision of a notice[53] purporting to restrict or exclude liability for breach of duty may be void in relation to death or personal injury,[54] as may terms purporting to exclude implied terms as to description, quality, fitness for purpose or title in consumer contracts.[55] In all other cases the test is one of what is "fair and reasonable".[56] The Act will apply to both "business-to-business" hire

---

[42] *Central Motors (Glasgow) Ltd v Cessnock Garage & Motor Co*, 1925 S.C. 796; *Coupe Co v Maddick* [1891] 2 Q.B. 413.

[43] *Pullars v Walker* (1858) 20 D. 1238.

[44] *Seton v Paterson* (1880) 8 R. 236; *Gardner v McDonald* (1792) Hume 299.

[45] *Hinshaw v Adam* (1870) 8 M. 933.

[46] See *Davidson* (1749) Mor.10081; *McLean v Warnock* (1883) 10 R. 1052; *Giblin v McMullen* (1868) L.R. 2 P.C. 317.

[47] *Coldman v Hill* [1919] 1 K.B. 443.

[48] *Campbell v Kennedy* (1828) 6 S. 806.

[49] *Re United Service Co, Johnston's Claim* (1871) L.R. 6 Ch.App. 212; *Raes v Meek* (1889) 16 R. (HL) 31 at 33 (trust).

[50] Unfair Contract Terms Act 1977 (the "1977 Act") s.15(2)(a). But rights, duties or liabilities arising under a contract for the hire of goods may be negatived or varied if not struck at by the 1977 Act: Supply of Goods and Services Act 1982 s.11L(1).

[51] Unfair Terms in Consumer Contracts Regulations 1999 (SI 1999/2083) (the "1999 Regulations") and the Office of Fair Trading Guidance issued in September 2008 available on *http://www.oft.gov.uk/shared_oft/reports/unfair_contract_terms/oft311.pdf* [Accessed July 14, 2012] with Annexes at *http://www.oft.gov.uk/shared_oft/reports/unfair_contract_terms/oft311annexea.pdf* [Accessed July 14, 2012].

[52] Both pieces of legislation are discussed above in Ch.9, "Pacta Illicita and Unfair Contract Terms".

[53] As defined in 1977 Act s.25(1), as amended by the Law Reform (Miscellaneous Provisions) (Scotland) Act 1990 s.68.

[54] 1977 Act s.16, as amended by the Law Reform (Miscellaneous Provisions) (Scotland) Act 1990 s.68.

[55] 1977 Act s.21; *G.M. Shepherd Ltd v North West Securities Ltd*, 1991 S.L.T. 499; *Stair Memorial Encyclopaedia*, "Leasing and Hire of Moveables" (Reissue), Vol. 5, para.53. A consumer contract is defined in 1977 Act s.25(1).

[56] 1977 Act ss.16 and 24.

agreements, e.g. finance leases, and "consumer hire agreements", e.g. operating leases.[57]

13.10 **Unfair terms**[58]—In contrast to the Unfair Contract Terms Act 1977, the Unfair Terms in Consumer Contracts Regulations 1999[59] cover only "unfair terms"[60] in consumer contracts[61] concerning the sale or supply of goods; they do not apply to so-called "business-to-business" contracts, or to the exceptions provided in the 1999 Regulations.[62] A "consumer" is defined to mean "any natural person who, in contracts covered by these Regulations, is acting for purposes which are outside his trade, business or profession".[63] This means that the 1999 Regulations will, normally, be applicable to operating leases[64] only, as finance leases[65] tend to be between commercial parties and do not involve consumers. Consequently, the 1999 Regulations will apply to a consumer hire contract where a term of that contract has not been "individually negotiated", so that, "contrary to . . . good faith", the term "causes a significant imbalance in the parties' rights and obligations arising under the contract, to the detriment of the consumer."[66] If this is so, the term does not bind the consumer.[67] A term's "unfairness" will be determined by considering "the nature of the goods or services for which the contract was concluded" plus "all the circumstances" concerning the contract's conclusion, as well as the other provisions of the hire contract or another contract it is dependent on.[68] There is also a requirement that contracts coming within the 1999 Regulations be "in plain, intelligible language",[69] with any ambiguity being decided in the consumer's favour.[70] In addition, the Office of Fair Trade has issued "Guidance" on Unfair Standard Terms.[71] This Guidance, whilst not legally binding, is important as the Office of Fair Trading ("OFT"), has a "duty" "to consider any complaint made to it that any contract drawn up for general use is unfair", unless the complaint is "frivolous or vexatious" or a "qualifying body"[72] tells the OFT that it "will consider the complaint".[73] "Indicative and non-exhaustive" examples of potentially unfair clauses in consumer contracts, are set out in Sch.2 to the 1999 Regulations.[74] Those which might be relevant to contracts of hire include (but are not limited to): (i) A clause which "inappropriately" excludes or limits a consumer's "legal rights" against "the seller or supplier or another party" where there is a

---

[57] Although an operating lease can also be a business to business lease.

[58] For a fuller general discussion, see para.9.25 above.

[59] 1999 Regulations. These replaced the Unfair Terms in Consumer Contract Regulations 1994 (SI 1994/3159), see reg.2 of the 1999 Regulations. All references are to the 1999 Regulations.

[60] reg.4(1) of the 1999 Regulations. "Unfair Terms" are defined and explained in reg.5.

[61] "Consumer" is defined in reg.3(1).

[62] reg.4(2) of the 1999 Regulations.

[63] reg.3(1) of the 1999 Regulations.

[64] See para.13.17, below.

[65] See para.13.13, below.

[66] reg.5(1) of the 1999 Regulations. As many consumer hire contracts are standard form printed contracts, the 1999 Regulations are likely to be applicable.

[67] reg.8 of the 1999 Regulations.

[68] reg.6(1) of the 1999 Regulations.

[69] regs 6(2) and 7 of the 1999 Regulations.

[70] reg.7(2) (which is subject to reg.12) of the 1999 Regulations.

[71] See fn.51, above.

[72] Defined in reg.3, with reference to Sch.1 to the 1999 Regulations. One of the bodies referred to in Sch.1 which is relevant is the Consumers Association.

[73] reg.10(1) of the 1999 Regulations. See also reg.12.

[74] Pursuant to reg.5(5).

"total or partial non-performance or inadequate performance by the seller or supplier of any of the contractual obligations", including setting off "a debt owed to the seller or supplier against a claim the consumer may have against" the same. This regulation may impact upon no set-off provisions in leases which seek to require rental payments regardless.[75] (ii) A term which requires a consumer who has not fulfilled "his obligations to pay a disproportionately high sum in compensation".[76] This prohibition would cover penalties, but it is not clear whether this would cover claims for future rentals where the breach is repudiatory. Such a clause might cover termination sums, although it is not clear how this differs from a penalty or whether it would also include termination sums not involving breaches of the lease. The OFT's Guidance, Unfair Standard Terms, suggests that not only penalties, but also other types of "[o]ver-severe sanctions . . . are . . . likely to be considered unfair".[77] Despite this, as the 1999 Regulations concern the non-fulfilment of contractual "obligations", it is unlikely that the payment of future rentals where the lease has been terminated due to a specified event in the lease or where the hirer has an option to terminate on terms would be challengeable.[78] (iii) A term irrevocably binding the consumer to terms "he had no real" chance to become "acquainted" with prior to concluding "the contract",[79] e.g. this might include a provision to the effect that the consumer acknowledges the equipment leased is in good order.[80] (iv) A provision requiring a "consumer to fulfil all his obligations" although "the seller or supplier does not" fulfil his obligations, e.g. this could apply to no set-off provisions in leases concerning the payment of rent.[81] The OFT has indicated that a provision stating that "In default of payment we [i.e. the supplier] may enter any premises at any time to repossess the goods" is unfair[82]; this may have potential implications for a lessor seeking to recover leased equipment upon default (e.g. non-payment of rentals) by the hirer. (v) A provision which excludes or hinders the right of a consumer (i.e. hirer) to bring legal proceedings "or exercise any other legal remedy".[83] Again, this could apply to no set-off clauses in leases. The OFT has indicated that this paragraph may apply where a clause requires a "consumer to bear inappropriate rights",[84] and lists as an example a provision that "The customer indemnifies the company against all third party claims".[85]

The above list is not definitive, and so care needs to be taken with standard form hire contracts in operating leases involving consumers.

Obligation to restore article: Unauthorised disposal—The hirer is bound to **13.11** restore the article on the expiry of the time agreed upon, or, if no time was fixed, on demand. Failure in this respect involves liability for accidental loss.[86]

---

[75] 1999 Regulations Sch.2 para.1(b).

[76] 1999 Regulations Sch.2 para.1(c).

[77] Office of Fair Trading Guidance, September 2008, p.40, fn.51, above.

[78] See Office of Fair Trading Guidance, September 2008, p.49, fn.51, above.

[79] 1999 Regulations Sch.2 para.1(i).

[80] Office of Fair Trading Guidance, September 2008, p.50, "Binding consumers to hidden terms" and "Consumer Declarations", at p.77.

[81] 1999 Regulations Sch.2 para1(O).

[82] Office of Fair Trading Guidance, September 2008, p.74.

[83] 1999 Regulations Sch.2 para.1(q).

[84] Office of Fair Trading Guidance, September 2008, p.72.

[85] For examples of terms considered unfair by the OFT see Annexe A to its Guidance published separately at *http://www.oft.gov.uk/shared_oft/reports/unfair_contract_terms/oft311annexea.pdf* [Accessed July 14, 2012].

[86] *Shaw v Symmons* [1917] 1 K.B. 799.

Otherwise, the hirer is not liable for deterioration by ordinary wear and tear, nor for the accidental destruction of the article. But it would appear, from analogous cases, that the onus of proof of accidental loss lies on the hirer.[87] A hirer has no ostensible authority to dispose of the article, nor to subject it to a lien, and third parties acquire no right against its owner.[88]

13.12 Claim by third party—Where an article hired is claimed by a third party, the hirer should have recourse to an action of multiple poinding. A refusal to return the article to the lessor, based merely on the ground of notice of an adverse claim, is a breach of contract, unless the hirer can prove that the adverse claim was well founded.[89]

13.13 What is a finance lease?—A finance lease is a long-term lease of corporeal moveable property during which the hirer "has substantially all the risks and rewards associated with ownership of the asset, other than the legal title"[90]; the legal title remains with the lessor, whose interest, in practical terms, is "a financial one".[91] In most cases, the period of hire will equate to the "useful economic life"[92] of the asset being leased, and there will, normally, be only one hirer.[93] For accounting purposes, a lease is a finance lease if the rentals "amount to substantially all (normally 90 per cent or more) of the fair value of the leased asset".[94] The rentals (which will, usually, be in excess of that 90 per cent figure), are calculated, amongst other things, to cover the cost of purchase of the equipment by the lessor as well as provide a return on his capital,[95] i.e. the cost of the purchase price of the equipment is amortised (or paid off/extinguished) over the period of hire with the surplus providing a profit.[96] Thus, this type of lease is often called "a 'full pay-out

---

[87] *Wilson v Orr* (1879) 7 R. 266; *Copland v Brogan*, 1916 S.C. 277. See also conflicting opinions in *Moes Moliere & Co v Leith, etc Shipping Co* (1867) 5 M. 988; *Mustard v Paterson*, 1923 S.C. 142.

[88] *Murdoch v Greig* (1889) 16 R. 396, and see, as to hire-purchase, para.12.55, below; *Mitchell v Heyes* (1894) 21 R. 600; *Lamonby v Foulds*, 1928 S.C. 89. See, however, *Albemarle Supply Co v Hind* [1928] 1 K.B. 307.

[89] *Ex p. Davies* (1881) L.R. 19 Ch. D. 86.

[90] Statement of Standard Accounting Practice 21 (SSAP 21), "Accounting for leases and hire purchase contracts", para.8; see also at paras 15 and 16. See too the definition of "finance lease" in Capital Allowances Act 2001 s.219.

[91] *On Demand Information Plc v Michael v Gerson (Finance) Plc* [2001] 1 W.L.R. 155 at 171H, per Robert Walker L.J. The decision of the Court of Appeal was reversed by the House of Lords, see [2003] 1 A.C. 368.

[92] Statement of Standard Accounting Practice 21 (SSAP 21), "Accounting for leases and hire purchase contracts", para.7.

[93] *Goode on Commercial Law*, p.768.

[94] Statement of Standard Accounting Practice 21 (SSAP 21), "Accounting for leases and hire purchase contracts", para.12.

[95] A similar view is taken in Statement of Standard Accounting Practice 21 (SSAP 21), "Accounting for leases and hire purchase contracts", para.8, and by *Goode on Commercial Law*, p.767–8. See also Nicholls L.J. in *Lombard North Central Plc v Butterworth* [1987] 1 Q.B. 527 at 543; Vinelott J. in *Orion Finance Ltd v Crown Financial Management Ltd* [1994] 2 B.C.L.C. 607 at 609g; and the summary of submissions of senior counsel for the defender in *Summit Lease Finance (No.2) Ltd v Lithoprint (Scotland) Ltd*, 1999 G.W.D. 27–1266 and Lexis, see p.2 of the transcript (July 16, 1999). If the rentals merely covered the cost of the purchase price, this would amount to an interest free loan to the hirer.

[96] See also *Goode on Commercial Law*, p.768. There are various other factors which are taken into account when calculating rentals, e.g. capital allowances (see para.13.16 below) and the rate of corporation taxation, see, e.g. cl.5 of the specimen finance lease in *Greens Practice Styles* (Edinburgh: W. Green), Vol.II, section J ("Moveables"), Style J01–01.

lease' ".[97] Owing to the length of time the hirer has the asset and the amount of rentals paid, a finance lease is treated as "substantially similar . . . to an outright purchase" and so the leased item is "capitalised" in the hirer's accounts.[98] In theory, it is the hirer's rights in the asset, plus the requirement to pay rentals, which are capitalised.[99] Finance leases—as the name indicates—are, thus, a form of financing, as the hirer has the use of an asset for most, or all, of that asset's "useful life", but can spread his payments over the rental period, and does not have to make a large up-front capital payment-the rentals loosely equating to a repayment schedule of principal and interest under a loan agreement.[100]

Structure of a finance lease—In a typical finance lease, the asset to be hired is, **13.14** normally, purchased from its original owner by a financier who (as lessor) then leases the asset to the hirer; it is the hirer who will, usually, have selected the asset beforehand, with the lessor providing the finance to purchase the asset from the original owner.[101] There are, thus, two discrete, but not unconnected, contracts: (i) the initial contract of sale; and (ii) a subsequent contract of hire by the purchaser under the first contract.[102] The lessee will, commonly, sign an "acceptance note"[103] indicating that the goods have been delivered to him in an appropriate condition, and the lessor, upon receiving confirmation or certification of this, will then sign the lease.[104] The initial hiring period, under the lease, is called the "primary period". It is during this period that the lessor recovers his capital outlay and makes a return on that outlay; thereafter, the hirer may have an option to hire the equipment, at lower rental, for a further period called the "secondary period"; this lower rental reflects the recovery of the purchase cost and profit made during

---

[97] See *Stair Memorial Encyclopaedia*, Vol.7 (Reissue "Leasing and Hire of Moveables"), para.5; and *Summit Lease Finance (No.2) Ltd v Lithoprint (Scotland) Ltd*, 1999 G.W.D. 27–1266.

[98] Statement of Standard Accounting Practice 21 (SSAP 21), "Accounting for leases and hire purchase contracts", para.10.

[99] Statement of Standard Accounting Practice 21 (SSAP 21), "Accounting for leases and hire purchase contracts", para.12.

[100] See too *Stair Memorial Encyclopaedia*, Vol.7 (Reissue "Leasing and Hire of Moveables"), para.5, which refers to the finance lease providing "not just the use of an asset for a period for a period, but also or principally the finance for the acquisition of that asset, so that its use can then be enjoyed by the lessee".

[101] The structure of a finance lease is well-documented in both the work of writers and case law, see *Stair Memorial Encyclopaedia*, Vol.7 (Reissue "Leasing and Hire of Moveables"), para.5; *Goode on Commercial Law*, pp.769–771; *Lombard North Central Plc v Butterworth* [1987] 1 Q.B. 527; *Orion Finance Ltd v Crown Financial Management Ltd* [1994] 2 B.C.L.C. 607; *Mercat Leasing Ltd v Woodchester Equipment Leasing Ltd*, 1996 G.W.D. 2–72; and *Summit Lease Finance (No.2) Ltd v Lithoprint (Scotland) Ltd*, 1999 G.W.D. 27–1266. For a specimen finance lease, see *Green's Practice Styles*, Vol.III, Style J01–01.

[102] See also *Goode on Commercial Law*, pp.771, who refers to the two contracts, but observes "there is no contractual nexus between" the original seller and the hirer. Nonetheless, it is suggested, both contracts have the common factor of the financier/lessor, and the first contract is necessary for the second to come into existence.

[103] As in *Orion Finance Ltd v Crown Financial Management* [1994] 2 B.C.L.C. 607 at 613. See also *Encyclopaedia of Forms and Precedents*, 5th edn (LexisNexis UK, 1999) Reissue, Vol.25(2), "Leasing of Equipment", para.6 [8011].

[104] See, e.g. *Orion Finance Ltd v Crown Financial Management* [1994] 2 B.C.L.C. 607; *Encyclopaedia of Forms and Precedents* (1999), Vol.25(2), para.6 [8011]; *Goode on Commercial Law*, pp.771. See *Stair Memorial Encyclopaedia*, Vol.7 (Reissue "Leasing and Hire of Moveables"), para.5 and paras 26–31 (where there is a contract to acquire the equipment, the lessee and the original owner (the seller) prior to the lessor's (financier's) involvement, there are three mechanisms used to bring the lessor into the contractual equation: "novation", "assignation" or "sale and leaseback").

the primary period. The lease may also allow for an upgrade of the item being leased-common examples of which include computers[105] or photocopiers.

13.15 Quality problems—A finance lease (and an operating lease[106]) will be subject to the Supply of Goods and Services Act 1982 (as amended),[107] as indicated in para.13.05, above. That Act, as indicated, implies, inter alia, a term concerning the quality[108] of the leased goods, subject to defences,[109] unless the implied terms are excluded, which is likely[110]; any exclusion is subject to the Unfair Contract Terms Act 1977.[111] If an exclusion of liability in the lease is valid, this creates the difficulty that if there is something wrong with the goods, and liability as to quality has been excluded, the hirer has no contractual recourse against the lessor (as the supplier under the lease), nor does the hirer have any recourse against the original owner (the seller), with whom he has no contract.[112] An assignation by the lessor, to the hirer, of the lessor's claim against the seller, under the sale contract, for the sale of goods of "unsatisfactory quality"[113] will be of limited value to the hirer, as there will, commonly, be a provision requiring payment of rentals by the hirer to be without set-off,[114] and so the lessor will not have lost anything because of the defect[115]; also, as the lessor will not be liable for the defect, the lessor cannot claim he has suffered damage due to the seller's breach.[116] Consequently, any damages for breach of the sale contract by the seller of the sale agreement will be nominal.[117] It is unlikely that a *jus quaesitum tertio* would arise in relation to the initial sale contract,[118] as the whole purpose, legally, is to keep the contract of sale and contract of lease separate.[119]

13.16 Capital allowances and post termination resale—It is beyond the scope of this work to go into detail about the taxation of finance leases. One area of importance is capital allowances, as either "first year allowances"[120] or "writing down

---

[105] As in *Re Atlantic Computer Systems Plc* [1992] Ch. 505 and *Orion Finance Ltd v Crown Financial Management* [1994] 2 B.C.L.C. 607.

[106] See para.13.17, below.

[107] The 1982 Act was amended, for Scotland, by the Sale and Supply of Goods Act 1994 s.6 and Sch.1 para.1.

[108] 1982 Act s.11J (as amended). This section also applies in the case of agency, see s.11J(9). There is also a provision concerning description (see s.11I) and hire by sample (see s.11K).

[109] Such as s.11J(4) of the 1982 Act (as amended).

[110] See, e.g. cl.7.1 the specimen finance lease in *Greens Practice Styles*, Vol.III, Style J01–01.

[111] See s.11L(1) of the 1982 Act (as amended). The applicable section of the 1977 Act is s.21. The 1999 Regulations are unlikely to be applicable, as finance leases are between commercial parties and do not involve consumers; see the discussion of the 1999 Regulations in para.24.10, below.

[112] *Goode on Commercial Law*, pp.774. See *Stair Memorial Encyclopaedia* (Reissue "Leasing and Hire of Moveables"), para. 91.

[113] "Unsatisfactory quality" for sale of goods is defined in s.14(2) of the Sale of Goods Act 1979 (as amended).

[114] See, e.g. cl.4.6 of the specimen finance lease in *Greens Practice Styles*, Vol.II, Style J01–01.

[115] *Goode on Commercial Law*, p.772.

[116] *Goode on Commercial Law*, p.772.

[117] *Goode on Commercial Law*, p.772.

[118] As to *jus quaesitum tertio*, see paras 8.04–8.09 hereof.

[119] *Stair Memorial Encyclopaedia* (Reissue "Leasing and Hire of Moveables"), para.94 notes that a *jus quaesitum tertio* would have to be expressly included in the sale contract. Such a provision is unlikely, it is suggested.

[120] See Capital Allowances Act 2001 ss.11(4), 15(1), 39, 44, 45, 52. The Capital Allowances Act 2001 which replaced the Capital Allowances Act 1990—for a discussion of the old law, see J. Tiley and D. Collison, *Butterworth's UK Tax Guide 1999/2000* (Butterworths, 1999), paras 8.31–8.41 (especially paras 8.31 and 8.39). Explanatory notes and links to a Table of Destinations and Table of Origins

allowances".[121] Under a finance lease, capital allowances can be claimed by the owner (the lessor) of the equipment leased out under a lease,[122] and are passed on to the hirer in the form of lower rentals. This is different from a hire-purchase agreement, where these allowances can be claimed by the hirer.[123] Hence, it is important that any agreement involving the sale of the assets after the end of the contract of hire is carefully structured so that it is not treated as a hire-purchase agreement with the result that the owner/lessor loses the capital allowances.[124] One common way is to appoint the hirer as the sales agent of the owner in relation to the sale of the thing, and let the hirer receive a large percentage of the sale price (usually between 95 and 99 per cent).[125]

Operating leases—In contrast to a finance lease, an operating lease is a lease **13.17** involving multiple short hirings of a thing by different parties at different times. Common examples include car hire or DIY equipment.[126] As with a finance lease, the lessor will own the asset, however, unlike a finance lease, it is the lessor who "retains most of the risks and rewards of ownership of" the thing hired.[127] The lessor, under an operating lease, will make his profit through the volume of hirings, rather than leasing the equipment to one party for the effective life of the asset,[128] i.e. the rentals reflect the equipment's "use-value".[129] As a consequence, operating leases are not capitalised in the hirer's accounts.[130] An operating lease may come within the definition of "Consumer hire agreement" under the Consumer Credit Act 1974 (as amended).[131]

"Big ticket" and "small ticket" leases—Certain terminology has grown up in **13.18** the leasing industry. Two common terms, are "big ticket" and "small ticket" leases. A "big ticket" lease is the lease of a large expensive item of equipment-a common example of which is an airplane. A "small ticket" lease, by contrast, is a lease of a smaller item with lower rentals, e.g. a photocopier.[132]

---

are available at: *http://www.opsi.gov.uk/acts/en2001/2001tb02.htm* [Accessed July 14, 2012]. The "Table of Destinations" was used in the production of this section.

[121] See Capital Allowances Act 2001 ss.11(4), 15(1), 55, 56, 59(3), 65, 102(4), 109(4).

[122] See fnn.19 and 20 above.

[123] See Capital Allowances Act 2001 ss.67, 68 and 229.

[124] For various ways of doing this, see *Stair Memorial Encyclopaedia* (Reissue "Leasing and Hire of Moveables"), para.67; and *Encyclopaedia of Forms and Precedents* (1999), Vol.25(2), para.10.6 [8033]; see also cl.14 of the specimen finance lease in *Green's Practice Styles*, Vol.III, Style J01-01.

[125] See, e.g. *Mercat Leasing Ltd v Woodchester Equipment Leasing Ltd*, 1996 G.W.D. 2–72 (where the rebate was 99%); *Summit Lease Finance (No.2) Ltd v Lithoprint (Scotland) Ltd*, 1999 G.W.D. 27–1266 (where the rebate was 99%); and *On Demand Information Plc v Michael Gerson (Financial) Plc* [2001] 1 W.L.R. 155 (giving a 95% rebate). The decision in this case was reversed on appeal, see [2003] 1 A.C. 368.

[126] See also *Encyclopaedia of Forms and Precedents* (1999), Vol.25(2), para.3 [8004].

[127] Statement of Standard Accounting Practice 21 (SSAP 21), "Accounting for leases and hire purchase contracts", para.7. See also *Stair Memorial Encyclopaedia* (Reissue "Leasing and Hire of Moveables"), para 12.

[128] See also *Encyclopaedia of Forms and Precedents* (1999), Vol.25(2), para.3 [8004], and *Goode on Commercial Law*, p.767.

[129] *Goode on Commercial Law*, p.767.

[130] Statement of Standard Accounting Practice 21 (SSAP 21), "Accounting for leases and hire purchase contracts", para.10.

[131] 1974 Act s.15 (as amended). For a fuller discussion of this, see *Stair Memorial Encyclopaedia* (Reissue "Leasing and Hire of Moveables"), para.51. As to the 1974 Act (as amended), see Ch.18 below.

[132] As, for example, in *Eurocopy Rentals Ltd v Tayside Health Board*, 1996 S.L.T. 224.

13.19 Insurance and indemnity—Under a finance lease (and often an operating lease), the hirer will be required to insure the leased equipment in relation to it: (i) becoming damaged, or a "total loss" or a "constructive total loss"; and (ii) causing injury or damage to third parties or other property.[133]

A lessor will also, normally, require an indemnity from the hirer in relation to any claims against the lessor by third parties.[134] The effect of such a provision is a matter of construction.[135]

13.20 Early termination of the lease: Recovery of future rentals and penalties— Subject to its terms, a finance (or operating) lease may be terminated early in three main ways—the first two by the lessor and the third by the hirer. First, where there has been a breach of the lease by the hirer, e.g. the non-payment of rentals (which is the most common ground), the lessor may bring the lease to an end.[136] Secondly, where it is stated in the lease that on the occurrence of a particular event, or particular events, the lessor has a right to terminate the lease, even though this event does not involve a breach of the lease.[137] In this second situation, the specified event will have a significant impact on the performance of the lease, and so is made an event of termination, and may well result in a breach of the lease, e.g. the insolvency of the hirer is likely to cause a breach of the payment covenant in the lease.[138] Thirdly, a lease may provide for early termination by the hirer, on terms, which, usually, involves the payment of monetary compensation to the lessor.[139] Of these three methods, the first two are the most important, and will be the focus of this section.

Where the lease is terminated for either or both of the first two reasons, the lessor will not only seek recovery of its asset (the leased equipment), but also recovery of any outstanding and future rentals. The combination of future and outstanding rentals, less a discount (usually 3–5 per cent) for having the money in advance,[140] is commonly called the "termination sum", and will, usually, be

---

[133] See, e.g. *Stair Memorial Encyclopaedia* (Reissue "Leasing and Hire of Moveables"), para.62; *Encyclopaedia of Forms and Precedents* (1999), Reissue, Vol.25(2), "Leasing of Equipment", para.35 [8192]; J. Adams, *Commercial Hiring and Leasing* (Butterworths, 1989), para.3.45; and cl.11 of the specimen finance lease in *Greens Practice Styles*, Vol.III, Style J01–01.

[134] See cl.8 of the specimen finance lease in *Green's Practice Styles*, Vol. III, Style J01–01; and cll. III and IV of the contract in *Stirling v Norwest Holst Ltd*, 1997 S.L.T. 973 at 974.

[135] *Stirling v Norwest Holst Ltd*, 1997 S.L.T. 973; *Cameron v McDermotts (Scotland) Ltd*, 1995 S.L.T. 542 (an exclusion clause case); *Lindsay Plant Ltd v Norwest Group Plc*, 2000 S.C. 93, and the cases referred to there, particularly, *Canada Steamship Lines Ltd v The King* [1952] A.C. 192; *Smith v UMB Chrysler (Scotland) Ltd*, 1978 S.C. (HL) 1.

[136] See, e.g. *Lombard North Central Plc v Butterworth* [1987] Q.B. 527; *Eurocopy Rentals Ltd v Tayside Health Board*, 1996 S.L.T. 224, which cited the former case with approval; both were cases of finance leases.

[137] See, e.g. *Granor Finance Ltd v Liquidator of Eastore Ltd*, 1974 S.L.T. 296; *EFT Commercial Ltd v Security Change Ltd (No.1)*, 1992 S.C. 414, both cases of finance leases.

[138] A similar view is expressed by Lord Caplan in *EFT Commercial Ltd v Security Change Ltd (No.1)*, 1992 S.C. 414 at 432.

[139] See, e.g. *Bell Brothers (H.P.) Ltd v Aitken*, 1939 S.C. 577, where the contract was one of hire-purchase, although this does not affect the point in issue. The compensation for early termination by the hirer involved payment of the future unpaid rentals under the agreement, less the leased good's value when returned, see pp.578–9. See also *Stair Memorial Encyclopaedia* (Reissue "Leasing and Hire of Moveables"), para 66.

[140] As to the importance of the discount and the calculation of it, see *Robophone Facilities Ltd v Blank* [1966] 1 W.L.R. 1428 at 1445, per Diplock L.J.; and Harman L.J. at 1440. See too *Interoffice Telephones v Robert Freeman Co Ltd* [1958] 1 Q.B. 190, which was cited with approval in the *Robophone* case.

specified in the lease.[141] The importance of the discount is that if it was not given, the lessor would receive more than he bargained for by receiving his money early,[142] i.e. the lessor would be unjustly enriched. Sometimes, the lessor may allow the hirer "credit" for payments received on the resale of the goods,[143] which, it is suggested, is an application of the rule about mitigating loss.[144] Where the lease is terminated by the hirer, rather than the lessor, there will also be a claim for future rentals by the lessor.[145] The position is most acute in finance leases terminated by the lessor, which are the main focus of this section.

The rationale for the lessor seeking future rentals, as well as the outstanding rentals, is that, as referred to in para.13.13 above, a finance lease, from the lessor's perspective, is predicated upon the lessor making a profit from leasing the equipment to the hirer for a certain period of time in exchange for a rental stream; when the lease is terminated early, this profit element is threatened, as is the possibility of recovering the equipment's purchase price. Therefore, the lessor will seek to recover all the rentals that would have been payable under the lease if it had run its full course.

Where the lessor claims the termination sum because of a breach of the lease by the hirer, such as non-payment of rentals, there is a risk that the provision will not be enforced, as it may constitute a penalty.[146] The position is otherwise where the termination sum is claimed by the lessor because of a specific event which brings the contract to an end, e.g. the hirer's insolvency, as the law of penalties applies where a breach of contract has occurred.[147] This distinction has been said to be anomalous.[148] Also, where the lease is terminated by the hirer, pursuant to a provision in it, and the lease provides for payment of a sum involving future rentals, this sum is not a penalty, but "the financial conditions which the hirer must observe in return for the advantage of terminating the contract at his own hand".[149]

The lessor can overcome the difficulty about claiming future rentals where there has been a breach of the lease per se, by making payment of the rentals a material term of the contract,[150] e.g. by stating "time is of the essence" in relation

---

[141] See, e.g. the definition of "termination payment" (concerning future rentals) in cl.1.1, as well as cll.12 and 13 of the specimen finance lease in *Green's Practice Styles*, Vol.III, Style J01–01. See also *Stair Memorial Encyclopaedia* (Reissue "Leasing and Hire of Moveables"), para.73.

[142] See too *Stair Memorial Encyclopaedia* (Reissue "Leasing and Hire of Moveables"), para.72.

[143] See, e.g. *Lombard North Central Plc v Butterworth* [1987] Q.B. 527 at 542, referring to *Capital Finance Co Ltd v Donati* (1977) 121 S.J. 270, Court of Appeal (Civil Division) Transcript No.132; there was no such provision in the lease in the *Lombard* case, see at 542.

[144] A similar view is expressed in *Stair Memorial Encyclopaedia* (Reissue "Leasing and Hire of Moveables"), para.72.

[145] See the terms of the hire-purchase agreement in the *Bell Brothers* case, 1939 S.C. 577, referred to in fn.4 above.

[146] See, e.g. *Lombard North Central Plc v Butterworth* [1987] Q.B. 527; *Eurocopy Rentals Ltd v Tayside Health Board*, 1996 S.L.T. 224.

[147] *Bell Brothers (H.P.) Ltd v Aitken*, 1939 S.C. 577; *Granor Finance Ltd v Liquidator of Eastmore Ltd*, 1974 S.L.T. 296; *EFT Commercial Ltd v Security Change Ltd (No.1)*, 1992 S.C. 414; *Summit Lease Finance (No.2) Ltd v Lithoprint (Scotland) Ltd*, 1999 G.W.D. 27–1266. This is also the view in England, see *Export Credits Guarantee Department v Universal Oil Products Co* [1983] 1 W.L.R. 399, cited with approval in *EFT Commercial Ltd v Security Change Ltd (No.1)*, 1992 S.C. 414.

[148] See *EFT Commercial Ltd v Security Change Ltd (No.1)*, 1992 S.C. 414 at 431, per Lord Weir; and, at 434, per Lord Caplan.

[149] *Bell Brothers (H.P.) Ltd v Aitken*, 1939 S.C. 577 at 588, per Lord President Normand; see also *Granor Finance Ltd v Liquidator of Eastore Ltd*, 1974 S.L.T. 296 at 298, per Lord Keith.

[150] *Lombard North Central Plc v Butterworth* [1987] Q.B. 527; *Eurocopy Rentals Ltd v Tayside Health Board*, 1996 S.L.T. 224.

to payment.[151] The effect of this is that the non-payment by the hirer constitutes a repudiatory breach of the contract, which, if accepted by the lessor (as it will be), allows the lessor to rescind the contract and sue for the loss of his bargain,[152] i.e. an "expectation loss".[153]

If payment of rentals is not made a material term, it is treated as a non-material term, which only allows a damages claim for the outstanding rentals, i.e. a "reliance loss".[154] Because the contract is still operative, an attempt to claim future rentals, in these circumstances, will be considered penal in nature because the term is considered "disproportionate"[155] to the actual loss suffered by the lessor.[156] The concern of the courts has been that a minor breach should not lead to the same results as a repudiatory breach.[157] However, where a clause is unenforceable as it is penal, that clause is not, in effect, deleted from the contract,[158] rather the lessor's claim is confined to the loss he has suffered.[159] The onus of proving a clause is penal rests on the hirer.[160]

13.21 Sub-leasing—Sub-leasing of the equipment will often be prohibited under a finance lease, as the lessor wants to retain a degree of control over "his" equipment. Where sub-leasing is permitted, there are two leases involving the equipment: (i) the original (or "head")-lease between the original lessor (known as the "head lessor") and the original hirer, and (ii) a sub-lease between the original hirer (now the "sub-lessor") and a sub-lessee (or "end-user"). It is common for a sub-lease to be nearly identical to the head-lease, except that the rental under the sub-lease will, normally, be higher than that under the lead-lease. The head lessor will, often, obtain an assignation from the sub-lessor of the rentals due from the end-user to it (the sub-lessor) under the sub-lease.[161] Thus, the head-lessor will receive the rentals under the sub-lease directly (with the sub-lessor subsequently receiving the difference between the two rentals). If (as is likely) the sub-lessor is a company, then the assignation of the rentals by the sub-lessor to the head lessor will require registration under s.878(7)(viii) of the Companies Act 2006, as it will be a security over the sub-lessor's "book debts".[162] If the head-lease is terminated,

---

[151] *Lombard North Central Plc v Butterworth* [1987] Q.B. 527, and cll.4.4 and 12.1 of the specimen finance lease in *Green's Practice Styles*, Vol.III, Style J01–01.

[152] *Lombard North Central Plc v Butterworth* [1987] Q.B. 527; *Eurocopy Rentals Ltd v Tayside Health Board*, 1996 S.L.T. 224. See also Lord President Normand in *Bell Brothers (H.P.) Ltd v Aitken*, 1939 S.C. 577 at 588.

[153] This is the classification used by L. Fuller and W. Purdue, "The Reliance Interest in Contract Damages" (1936) 46 Yale L.J. 53 and 373 (in two parts).

[154] L. Fuller and W. Purdue, "The Reliance Interest in Contract Damages" (1936) 46 Yale L.J. 53 and 373.

[155] *EFT Commercial Ltd v Security Change Ltd (No.1)*, 1992 S.C. 414 at 432, per Lord Caplan.

[156] See, e.g. *Lombard North Central Pc v Butterworth* [1987] Q.B. 527; *Eurocopy Rentals Ltd v Tayside Health Board*, 1996 S.L.T. 224.

[157] *Lombard North Central Plc v Butterworths* [1987] Q.B. 527 at 542; and *Eurocopy Rentals Ltd v Tayside Health Board*, 1996 S.L.T. 224 at 229.

[158] *Jobson v Johnson* [1989] 1 W.L.R. 1026 at 1040, per Nicholls L.J., cited by Lord Penrose in *Summit Lease Finance (No.2) v Lithoprint Scotland Ltd*, 1999 G.W.D. 27–1266.

[159] *EFT Commercial Ltd v Security Charge Ltd (No.1)*, 1992 S.C. 414 at 426–7, per Lord President Hope, and the cases cited there, and, at 433, per Lord Caplan; *Jobson v Johnson* [1989] 1 W.L.R. 1026 at 1040, cited with approval in *Summit Lease Finance (No.2) v Lithoprint Scotland Ltd*, 1999 G.W.D. 27–1266; *Philips Hong Kong Ltd v At Gen of Hong Kong* (1993) 61 B.L.R. 41 at 55, PC.

[160] *Robophone Facilities Ltd v Blank* [1966] 1 W.L.R. 1428 at 1447; *Philips Hong Kong Ltd v Att Gen of Hong Kong* (1993) 61 B.L.R. 41 at 60, citing the *Robophone* case with approval.

[161] An example of such a situation arose in the English cases of *Re Atlantic Computer Systems Plc* [1992] Ch. 505, and *Orion Finance Ltd v Crown Financial Management Ltd* [1994] 2 B.C.L.C. 607.

[162] See, e.g. *Orion Finance Ltd v Crown Financial Management Ltd* [1994] 2 B.C.L.C. 607.

e.g. because the sub-lessor becomes insolvent,[163] then, as with the sub-leases of heritable property,[164] the sub-lease of the thing terminates, permitting the lessor to recover its equipment from the end-user.[165] However, to avoid any difficulties, a provision can be inserted into the sub-lease stating that if the head-lease terminates, then the sub-lease also terminates.

Deposit—The contract of deposit, *locatio custodiae*, is, like hire, a form of location.[166] The obligations of a depositary are to provide a secure place of custody, and to exercise due care to prevent damage or loss in connection with the property.[167] A contractual term or a provision of a notice[168] purporting to exclude or restrict liability for breach of duty may be void or unenforceable.[169] The fact that the contract was gratuitous, might, in narrow and doubtful cases, be of weight in determining whether sufficient care had been taken to exclude liability for the loss of the article.[170] So the degree of care required from bankers taking articles for safe custody has been held to depend on whether they make any charge.[171] But where a carrier undertook, gratuitously, to carry a parcel, and lost it, it was held that he was liable for its value, unless he could explain the loss or prove that he had exercised reasonable care.[172] Where the deposit is for reward, the standard of care, unless the depositary is an innkeeper or livery stable keeper, is that required from a hirer.[173] If a person undertakes to repair, or do other work on, an article for the owner (*locatio operis faciendi*) and has the article in his possession for that purpose, the contract normally includes an element of *locatio custodiae*, with the consequent obligations.[174] **13.22**

---

[163] As in *Re Atlantic Computer Systems Plc* [1992] Ch. 505, and *Orion Finance Ltd v Crown Financial Management Ltd* [1994] 2 B.C.L.C. 607.

[164] See, e.g. *Middleton v Yorstoun* (1826) 5 S. 162, and *Middleton v Megget* (1828) 7 S. 76 (which contains the judges' reasons in the former case).

[165] *Stair Memorial Encyclopaedia* (1987), Vol.14, "Location" (as updated), para.1092. Cf. the position in England, see *Goode on Commercial Law*, pp.791–792, fn.40.

[166] See W.W. McBryde, *The Law of Contract in Scotland*, 3rd edn (Edinburgh: W. Green, 2007), para.9–52; *Stair Memorial Encyclopaedia*, Vol.8 ("Deposit"). As to deposit in the context of a money deposit in the purchase of property, see *Zemhunt (Holdings) Ltd v Control Securities*, 1992 S.C. 58; and article by W.J. Stewart, "Restitution", 1992 S.L.T. (News) 47.

[167] Bell, *Principles*, s.155, adopted in *Ballingall & Son Ltd v Dundee Ice, etc. Co*, 1924 S.C. 238. See as to motor parking place, *Ashby v Tolhurst* [1937] 2 K.B. 242; *Drynan v Scottish Ice Rink Co*, 1971 S.L.T. (Sh. Ct) 59; garage, *Tognini Bros v Dick Bros*, 1968 S.L.T. (Sh. Ct) 87; *B.G. Transport Services Ltd v Marston Motor Co* [1970] 1 Lloyd's Rep.371; *Verrico v Hughes*, 1980 S.C. 179; bonded warehouse, *Brooks Wharf v Goodman* [1937] 1 K.B. 534; restaurant, *Martin v Alongi*, 1987 G.W.D. 20–758; friend for safe-keeping, *Fisher v Donnelly*, 1990 G.W.D. 35–1984; warehouse at a wharf, *Castle Cement Ltd v Lagan Cement Ltd*, 1997 G.W.D. 16–714 (no liability on the facts). Many of these cases must be read in the light of the 1977 Act.

[168] As defined in s.25 as amended by the Law Reform (Miscellaneous Provisions) (Scotland) Act 1990 s.68.

[169] 1977 Act s.15(2)(c). See Ch.9. Alternatively, the terms of any notice may be insufficient to exclude negligence or breach of duty on the part of the depositary: *Verrico v Hughes*, 1980 S.C. 179. Additionally, a term may be invalid under the 1999 Regulations: para.9.25, above.

[170] Stair, I, 13, 2; *Cogs v Bernard* (1703) 1 Smith L.C., 13th edn, p.125; *Houghland v R.R. Low (Luxury Coaches)* [1962] 1 Q.B. 694; *Walker v Scottish & Newcastle Breweries*, 1970 S.L.T. (Sh. Ct) 21; *Verrico v Hughes*, 1980 S.C. 179.

[171] *Giblin v McMullen* (1868) L.R. 2 P.C. 317.

[172] *Copland v Brogan*, 1916 S.C. 277.

[173] *Central Motors (Glasgow) Ltd v Cessnock Garage & Motor Co*, 1925 S.C. 796; *Verrico v Hughes*, 1980 S.C. 179.

[174] *Sinclair v Juner*, 1952 S.C. 35; *Macrae v K. & I.*, 1962 S.L.T. (Notes) 90; *Forbes v Aberdeen Motors*, 1965 S.L.T. 333; *Miller v Howden*, 1968 S.L.T. (Sh. Ct) 82; *Uprichard v J. Dickson & Son Ltd*, 1981 S.L.T. (Sh. Ct) 5 (repair of gun: element of deposit).

13.23 **Innkeepers and livery stable keepers**—An innkeeper and a livery stable keeper may in certain cases incur a slightly higher degree of liability than other depositaries. They, like common carriers,[175] fall under the provisions of the Praetorian Edict.[176] Under the head of *stabularii* are included all livery stable keepers, whether attached to an inn or not,[177] but probably not the keeper of a motor garage.[178] In England, the exceptional liability of an innkeeper is held to depend on the custom of the realm and not on the Praetorian Edict.[179]

13.24 **Liability under edict**—An innkeeper or livery stable keeper is at common law liable for the loss of, or injury to, property brought to the inn or stable, unless he can prove that the loss or injury arose from the negligence of the owner,[180] or is attributable to the Queen's enemies or to an act of God.[181] This latter term excludes liability for fire caused by pure accident, but the onus is on the depositary to prove the cause of the fire, or at least to exclude his own negligence.[182] Act of God has been defined, generally, as an accident due to natural causes, directly and exclusively, without human intervention, which could not have been prevented by any amount of foresight and pains and care reasonably to be expected.[183] As it is clear that a depositary for reward is in any event liable for loss due to the negligence of his servants, and is probably also liable for any loss or injury from unexplained causes, the practical difference between one who is, and one who is not, subject to the edict, would seem to be that the former alone is liable for loss by theft or by the wrongful act of third parties.[184]

13.25 **Hotel proprietors act**—The liability of hotel proprietors is regulated by the Hotel Proprietors Act 1956, which repealed the Innkeepers' Liability Act 1863. An establishment, but only such an establishment, which is an hotel within the meaning of the Act,[185] is deemed to be an inn; and its proprietor, as an innkeeper, has the same duties, liabilities and rights which before the commencement of the Act attached to an innkeeper as such, in particular under the Edict. The proprietor's liability under the Edict extends to the making good to any guest of any damage to property brought to the hotel, as well as the loss of such property.[186] On the other hand, he is not subject to the liability of an innkeeper

---

[175] As to common carriers, see para.21.02, below.

[176] Dig., IV, 9, 1. *Nautae, caupones, stabularii, quod cujusque salvum fore receperint, nisi restituant, in eos judicium dabo*. This edict has been adopted into Scots law, "with certain modifications". See *Anderson v Jenkins Express Removals Ltd*, 1967 S.C. 231 at 233, per Lord Mackintosh referring to Bell's *Principles*, ss.235 and 239. This case was decided in 1967 and followed in *James Kemp (Leslie) Ltd v Robertson*, 1967 S.C. 215. See also *Mustard v Paterson*, 1923 S.C. 142.

[177] *Mustard v Paterson*, 1923 S.C. 142.

[178] *Central Motors (Glasgow) Ltd v Cessnock Garage & Motor Co*, 1925 S.C. 796; *Verrico v Hughes*, 1980 S.C. 179.

[179] *Calye's Case*, 1 Smith L.C., 13th edn, p.130.

[180] *Medawar v Grand Hotel Co* [1891] 2 Q.B. 11.

[181] Bell, *Principles*, s.237.

[182] *Sinclair v Juner*, 1952 S.C. 35; *Burns v Royal Hotel (St Andrews)*, 1958 S.C. 354.

[183] James L.J. in *Nugent v Smith* (1876) L.R. 1 C.P.D. 423; adopted by Lord Hunter in *Mustard v Paterson*, 1923 S.C. 142.

[184] *Mustard v Paterson*, 1923 S.C. 142; *Macpherson v Christie* (1841) 3 D. 930; *Whitehouse v Pickett*, 1908 S.C. (HL) 31; *Winkworth v Raven* [1931] I K.B. 652.

[185] "Hotel" is defined (s.1(3)) as "an establishment held out by the proprietor as offering food, drink and, if required, sleeping accommodation, without special contract, to any traveller presenting himself who appears able and willing to pay a reasonable sum for the services and facilities provided and who is in a fit state to be received."

[186] Hotel Proprietors Act 1956 s.1(2).

under the Edict, whatever may be his liability under contract or for negligence, in respect of any loss of or damage to any vehicle or property left therein, or any horse or other live animal or its harness or equipment, nor does his lien extend to these articles.[187]

Without prejudice to any other ground of liability, the proprietor is only liable as an innkeeper to make good loss or damage to the property of a traveller for whom at the time of the loss or damage sleeping accommodation had been engaged, and where the loss or damage occurred during the period commencing with the midnight immediately preceding, and ending with the midnight immediately following, a period for which the traveller was a guest at the hotel and entitled to use such accommodation.[188] The proprietor may also limit his liability as an innkeeper to £50 for any one article or £100 in the aggregate, provided that at the time when the property in question was brought to the hotel a notice in statutory form[189] was conspicuously displayed in a place where it could conveniently be read by guests at or near the reception desk or, if none, at or near the main entrance. But this limit will not apply where: (a) the property was stolen, lost or damaged through the default, neglect or wilful act of the proprietor or his employee[190]; (b) the property was deposited expressly for safe custody; or (c) if not so deposited, it had been offered for deposit and refused, or if not so offered, where the guest wishing to offer it for deposit was unable to do so through the default of the proprietor or his employee.[191] It has been held under the 1863 Act that, in order to satisfy the condition that the property has been "deposited expressly", the fact of the deposit must be definitely brought to the innkeeper's notice, and that where there is no such express deposit the onus of proof of fault or neglect on the part of the innkeeper lies on the guest.[192]

Liability of storekeepers—Storekeepers are under an implied duty, arising from the contract of storage to store goods received "in a proper manner", and an additional duty of reasonable inspection in order "to see that the goods were not being damaged".[193] These duties may be modified by trade custom or usage.[194] The onus of proof would appear to rest on the storekeeper to show that any damage to the goods in his possession was not due to his breach of duty, which is the same for a custodier of goods.[195] **13.26**

---

[187] Hotel Proprietors Act 1956 s.2(2).

[188] Hotel Proprietors Act 1956 s.2(1).

[189] See Hotel Proprietors Act 1956 Sch.

[190] *Kott & Kott v Gordon Hotels* [1968] 2 Lloyd's Rep. 228.

[191] Hotel Proprietors Act 1956 s.2(3).

[192] *Whitehouse v Pickett*, 1908 S.C. (HL) 31.

[193] *J. & R. Snodgrass v Ritchie & Lamberton* (1890) 17 R. 712 at 715, per Lord Rutherfurd Clark, cited with approval in *Alexander Inglis & Son Ltd v Forth Parts Ltd*, 2000 G.W.D. 27–1035. See also *Allan & Poynter v J.R. Williamson* (1870) 7 S.L.R. 214 and the cases cited in *Alexander Inglis & Son Ltd v Forth Parts Ltd*, 2000 G.W.D. 27–1035 at [35]–[37] of the transcript.

[194] *Gibson & Stewart v Brown & Co* (1876) 3 R. 328 at 330-1, per Lord President Inglis; *Alexander Inglis & Son Ltd v Forth Parts Ltd*, 2000 G.W.D. 27–1035.

[195] See the argument of counsel for the pursuers in *Alexander Inglis & Son Ltd Forth Parts Ltd*, 2000 G.W.D. 27–1035 at [35] of the transcript (which was not doubted) and the cases referred to there: *Wilson v Orr* (1879) 7 R. 266; *McLean v Warnock* (1883) 10 R. 1052; *Mustard v Paterson*, 1923 S.C. 142; and *Sinclair v Juner*, 1952 S.C. 35.

13.27 Donation—Donation is one method by which property can be acquired. There are two main forms of donation, donation inter vivos and donation *mortis causa*. Here only the former is discussed, the latter being dealt with in para.39.05. All forms of property can be the subject of inter vivos donation though corporeal movables, especially money, and heritable property tend to predominate in the cases.[196] To establish a donation it must be shown that the donor had a present intention to make a gift, the *animus donandi*, and that a form of delivery appropriate to the type of property forming the gift has occurred.[197]

13.28 Animus donandi—It must be shown that the transaction relied upon to indicate donation was entered into with a present intention to confer a gift.[198] An intention to give at some future time does not suffice.[199] All the circumstances surrounding the alleged donation will be considered and clear proof is required.[200] There is a presumption against donation[201] which "requires very strong and unimpeachable evidence to overcome it".[202] "Mere loose conversational expressions" are not sufficient to indicate an *animus donandi*.[203] It may be easier to overcome the presumption where the parties are related for example, when a parent is benefitting a child.[204] The presumption against donation is less strong between husband and wife while relations are harmonious.[205] Where the parties are creditor and debtor the presumption against donation will be buttressed by a further presumption that a debtor is not presumed to make a gift to his creditor (*debitor non praesumitur donare*).[206] The extent of the alleged donation may be relevant. The fact that it was one fifth of the donor's assets was relevant in deciding that there was a donation[207] whereas an alleged gift consisting of virtually all of a woman's assets indicated the opposite.[208]

13.29 Delivery—Proof of *animus donandi* is necessary but not sufficient to effect a valid donation. In addition, delivery or its equivalent is required to transfer ownership to the donee.[209]

---

[196] For discussion of the origins of donation in Roman Law and its history in Scots Law see W.M. Gordon, "Donation" in *Stair Memorial Encyclopedia of the Laws of Scotland* (Reissue) (Butterworths, 2011).

[197] See Lord Young in *Milne v Grant's Executors* (1884) 11 R. 887 at 890.

[198] *Brownlee's Executrix v Brownlee*, 1908 S.C. 232; 15 S.L.T. 635; *Grant's Trustees v M'Donald*, 1939 S.C. 448; 1939 S.L.T. 391; *Macaulay v Milliken*, 1967 S.L.T. (Notes) 30.

[199] *Wright's Trustees* (1870) 8 M. 708.

[200] Lord Fullerton in *British Linen Co v Martin* (1849) 11 D. 1004 at 1008 and *Heron v M'Geoch* (1851) 14 D. 25 at 30.

[201] Stair, I,8,2; *Sharp v Paton* (1883) 10 R. 1000.

[202] Lord President Inglis in *Sharp v Paton* (1883) 10 R. 1000 at 1006.

[203] *Little v Little* (1856) 18 D. 701 at 703.

[204] *Malcolm v Campbell* (1889) 17 R. 255.

[205] *Stair Memorial Encyclopaedia*, "Donation" (Reissue), Vol.6, para.26; *Edward v Cheyne* (1888) 15 R. (HL) 37.

[206] Stair, I, 8, 2; IV, 42, 21; IV, 45, 17 XV; *Johnstone v Haviland* [1896] A.C. 95 especially Lord Watson at 103 and Lord Herschell at 104.

[207] *Malcolm v Campbell* (1889) 17 R. 255.

[208] *Lord Advocate v M'Neill* (1866) 4 M. (HL) 20, especially Lord Chelmsford at 24. Cf. *Lord Advocate v M'Court* (1893) 20 R. 488 where a gift of a very substantial proportion of the donor's estate was upheld.

[209] *Brownlee's Executrix v Brownlee*, 1908 S.C. 232; 15 S.L.T. 635; *Hubbard v Dunlop's Trustees*, 1933 SN 62, HL; *Thompson v Aktien Gesellschaft für Glasindustrie*, 1917 2 S.L.T. 266, OH; *Gauld v Middleton*, 1959 S.L.T. (Sh. Ct) 61.

FURTHER READING

Adams, J.N., *Commercial Hiring and Leasing* (Butterworths, 1989).

Bell, *Principles*, s.133.

Encyclopaedia of Forms and Precedents, 5th edn (1999), Vol.25(2), "Leasing of Equipment".

Gordon, W.M., "Donation" in *Stair Memorial Encyclopedia of the Laws of Scotland* (Reissue) (Butterworths, 2011).

Gow, J.J., *Mercantile and Industrial Law of Scotland* (Edinburgh: W. Green, 1964), Ch.3.

Forte, A.D.M., "Finance Leases and Implied Terms of Quality and Fitness: A Retrospective and Prospective Review", 1995 Jur. Rev. 119.

Goode, R.M., *Goode on Commercial Law*, edited by McKendrick, E., 4th edn (2010), Chs 27 ("Conditional Sale and Hire Purchase"); and 28 ("The Finance Lease").

MacQueen, H.L. and Hogg, M., "Donation in Scots Law", 2012 Jur. Rev. 1.

Stair Memorial Encyclopaedia, Vol.14, "Location".

Chapter 14

CONSUMER PROTECTION

This chapter deals with the protection of private consumers of goods and services. **14.01**
It is a relatively new area of law which often draws on existing topics such as
contract and delict. The Unfair Contract Terms Act 1977 and the Unfair Terms in
Consumer Contracts Regulations 1999 are good examples and these will not be
discussed here as they are fully considered elsewhere. Similarly, there is special
protection for consumers in relation to the acquisition of goods and this is dealt
with in the chapter on Supply of Goods. One of the best known consumer protection cases is *Donoghue v Stevenson*[1] and it and the creation by Pt 1 of the Consumer
Protection Act 1987 of strict liability in delict for dangerous goods are discussed
elsewhere (Consumer Credit is discussed in Ch.16). This chapter refers to the
institutions created to protect consumers and deals mainly with the control of
business practices which might affect them, many of which are sanctioned by
criminal penalties. No attempt is made to deal with the Food Safety Act 1990 or
the Weights and Measures Acts.

Consumer protection is one of the areas reserved to the Westminster Parliament
by the Scotland Act 1998[2] though certain matters that are usually thought of as
coming under this heading are devolved. The Department for Business, Innovation
and Skills therefore has the major responsibility for consumer law and policy.
Much of the day-to-day enforcement of the law is the responsibility of district and
island councils. The Office of Fair Trading ("OFT") created by the Enterprise Act
2002 has an important role in consumer protection.[3] It has a general duty to obtain
and keep under review information needed to carry out its functions[4]; it advises
government on possible changes in the law[5]; and also promotes good consumer
practice which can include encouraging the development of codes of practice.[6] In
addition to these general duties, the OFT has important functions in protecting
consumers by administrative means. It regulates estate agency and, as noted in
Ch.16, it operates the credit licensing system, is one of the enforcers under the
Unfair Terms in Consumer Contracts Regulations 1999, and has powers to deal
with misleading advertising.[7] It may also entertain "super-complaints" from
certain consumer organisations.[8]

---

[1] *Donoghue v Stevenson* [1932] A.C. 562; 1932 S.C. (HL) 31.

[2] Scotland Act 1998 Sch.5 ss.C7–C9; *Imperial Tobacco Ltd, Petitioner* [2012] CSIH 9.

[3] The OFT is the successor to the Director General of Fair Trading, an office created by the Fair
Trading Act 1973.

[4] Enterprise Act 2002 (the "2002 Act") s.5.

[5] 2002 Act s.7.

[6] 2002 Act s.8.

[7] See the Control of Misleading Advertisements Regulations 1988 (SI 1988/915).

[8] 2002 Act s.11. The Enterprise and Regulatory Reform Bill before Parliament will abolish the
OFT and transfer most of its functions to a new Competition and Markets Authority.

14.02 Administrative control of trade practices: Enforcement orders—Part 8 of the
Enterprise Act 2002 enables various bodies known as "enforcers" to seek an
enforcement order by applying to the Court of Session or the sheriff.[9] This may be
done when the enforcer thinks that someone

> "(a) has engaged or is engaging in conduct which constitutes a domestic or a
> Community infringement, or (b) is likely to engage in conduct which consti-
> tutes a Community infringement".[10]

A domestic infringement is

> "an act or omission which (a) is done or made by a person in the course of a
> business, (b) falls within s.211(2), and (c) harms the collective interests of
> consumers in the United Kingdom".[11]

Subsection (2) sets out a number of kinds of conduct, which may be breaches of
civil or criminal law, that the Secretary of State can specify in more detail in a
statutory instrument.[12] The legal obligation breached does not have to be one
which applies specifically to consumers nor does specified legislation have to
contain any sanction for the benefit of consumers. It is not necessary for convictions to have been obtained where criminal offences are concerned or for legal
proceedings to have been taken in civil cases. The fact that a consumer has waived
his or her contractual rights does not prevent reliance being placed on the breach.[13]

A Community infringement is an act or omission which harms the collective
interests of consumers and which contravenes a listed Directive as given effect by
the laws, regulations or administrative provisions of an EEA state, or contravenes
such laws, regulations or administrative provisions which provide additional
permitted protections.[14] The laws, regulations or administrative provisions of an
EEA state which give effect to a listed Directive provide additional permitted
protections if they provide protection for consumers which is in addition to the
minimum protection required by the Directive concerned, and such additional
protection is permitted by that Directive.[15]

What is meant by "the collective interests of consumers", is not defined in the
Act or the Directive though recital 2 states that these interests "do not include the
cumulation of interests of individuals who have been harmed by an infringement".
In *Office of Fair Trading v MB Designs (Scotland) Ltd* reference was made to the

---

[9] 2002 Act s.215. Pt 8 implements European Parliament and Council Directive 98/27/EC on injunctions for the protection of consumers' interests ("the Injunctions Directive") (OJ L166, 11.06.98),
p.51. It replaces powers previously contained in the Fair Trading Act 1973 Pt III ss.34–42.

[10] 2002 Act s.215(1).

[11] 2002 Act s.211(1). A business includes a professional practice, any other undertaking carried on
for gain or reward and any undertaking in the course of which goods or services are supplied otherwise
than free of charge.

[12] The current statutory order, in force from June 20, 2003, is the Enterprise Act 2002 (Part 8
Domestic Infringements) Order 2003 (SI 2003/1593). It lists a large number of statutes including the
familiar consumer protection statutes such as the Sale of Goods Act 1979, the Consumer Protection
Act 1987 and the Consumer Credit Act 1974 as well as various "Rules of Law".

[13] 2002 Act s.211(4).

[14] 2002 Act s.212(1).

[15] 2002 Act s.212(2). The 2002 Act s.212(3) permits the Secretary of State by order to specify the
law in the United Kingdom which gives effect to the listed Directives or gives additional permitted
protections and this has been done by the Enterprise Act 2002 (Part 8 Community Infringements
Specified UK Laws) Order 2003 (SI 2003/1374) art.3, Sch. (amended by SI 2004/2095).

French version of this recital which could be translated as "interests which are not a mere accumulation of the interests of individuals".[16] It was pointed out that

> "'collective interests' is not something wholly separate from the interests of individual consumers who have been harmed by infringements ... but amount to something more than the mere aggregation of those interests".[17]

It is distinct from the rights that any particular consumer may have against his or her supplier, whether under the general law of contract or statute, and is designed to enforce trading standards.[18]

An examination of the list of Directives attached to the Injunctions Directive and the domestic legislation referred to in the Orders indicates that the Directive is intended to protect the safety, health and economic interests of consumers. The Audiovisual Media Services Directive[19] goes further by including references to ensuring that advertising does not offend human dignity and religious beliefs or involve discrimination.

There are three types of enforcers. "General enforcers", comprise the Office of Fair Trading, every local weights and measures authority in Great Britain (i.e. the trading standards officials of district and island councils) and the Department of Enterprise, Trade and Investment in Northern Ireland.[20] "Designated enforcers", are any persons or bodies (whether or not incorporated) which the Secretary of State thinks has as one of its purposes the protection of the collective interests of consumers and are designated by order.[21] The third type is "Community enforcers", that is a qualified entity for the purposes of the Injunctions Directive which is for the time being specified in the list published in the Official Journal of the European Communities, but which is not a general enforcer or a designated enforcer.[22]

The Enterprise Act 2002 defines the class of consumers who are to benefit from the protection provided for in Pt 8 of the Act. In relation to a domestic infringement, they are those to whom goods or services are or are sought to be supplied in the course of a business carried on by the person supplying or seeking to supply them. The individual receiving or seeking to receive the goods or services must do

---

[16] *Office of Fair Trading v MB Designs (Scotland) Ltd*, 2005 S.L.T. 691 at [13]. Emphasis in the original.

[17] *Office of Fair Trading v MB Designs (Scotland) Ltd*, 2005 S.L.T. 691.

[18] *Office of Fair Trading v MB Designs (Scotland) Ltd*, 2005 S.L.T. 691. Paras 13 and 14 of this judgment have a useful discussion of "collective interests".

[19] Directive 2010/13/EU on the coordination of certain provisions laid down by law, regulation or administrative action in Member States concerning the provision of audiovisual media services ("Audiovisual Media Services Directive") art.9.

[20] 2002 Act s.213(1).

[21] 2002 Act s.213(2)–(4). The Financial Services Authority is a designated enforcer in respect of all infringements: see the 2002 Act (Part 8) (Designation of the Financial Services Authority as a Designated Enforcer) Order 2004 (SI 2004/935). For designated public bodies, see the Enterprise Act 2002 (Part 8 Designated Enforcers: Criteria for Designation, Designation of Public Bodies as Designated Enforcers and Transitional Provisions) Order 2003 (SI 2003/1399) art.5, Sch. (amended by SI 2003/3182). The Secretary of State may designate a person or body which is not a public body only if the person or body satisfies such criteria as the Secretary of State specifies by order. These criteria for are set out in SI 2003/1399 arts 3 4. The Enterprise Act 2002 (Part 8) (Designation of the Consumers' Association) Order 2005 (SI 2005/917) art.2 designates the Consumers' Association (now known as *Which?*), a private charitable organisation, as the first and, so far, only body designated in this category.

[22] 2002 Act s.213(5).

so otherwise than in the course of a business carried on by him, or with a view to carrying on a business but not in the course of a business carried on by him. For the purposes of a domestic infringement it is immaterial whether a person supplying goods or services has a place of business in the United Kingdom.[23] In relation to a Community infringement, a consumer is a person who is a consumer for the purposes of the Injunctions Directive and the listed Directive concerned.[24]

Before applying for an enforcement order, an enforcer must normally engage in appropriate consultation with the person against whom the enforcement order would be made and the OFT. This does not apply if the OFT thinks that an application for an enforcement order should be made without delay.[25] It has been held that enforcement orders are not to be regarded as interdicts and that less precision is required on applications for them.[26]

14.03 **The Consumer Protection from Unfair Trading Regulations 2008**—With the enactment of the EU Directive on Unfair Commercial Practices[27] which has been implemented in the United Kingdom by the Consumer Protection from Unfair Practices Regulations 2008 ("the CPRs") there has been a major change in way in which unfair trade practices are regulated. Where the approach, in the main, had been to use the criminal law to ban specific practices a more general duty not to trade fairly has been introduced. Enforcement of the new regulations is primarily by civil sanctions though criminal sanctions are also available.

Implementation of the EU Directive required major changes in UK law because, with limited exceptions, it is a maximum directive: that is, its objectives had to be realised precisely, neither being exceeded nor underachieved. For this reason it is relevant to set out the scope of the directive.[28] Article 5 of the directive prohibits unfair commercial practices and art.3 deals with the scope of the directive. It makes clear that it applies only to unfair business-to-consumer commercial practices and is without prejudice to contract law and, in particular, to the rules on the validity, formation or effect of a contract as well as Community or national rules relating to the health and safety aspects of products. In the case of conflict between the provisions of the Directive and other Community rules regulating specific aspects of unfair commercial practices, the latter shall prevail and apply to those specific aspects. For six years from June 12, 2007, Member States will be able to continue to apply national provisions within the field approximated by this Directive which are more restrictive or prescriptive than this Directive and which implement directives containing minimum harmonisation clauses. Such measures must be essential to ensure that consumers are adequately protected against unfair commercial practices and must be proportionate to the attainment of this objective. The Directive is without prejudice to the rules determining the jurisdiction of the courts and codes of conduct or other specific rules governing regulated professions. In relation to financial services, as defined in Directive 2002/65/EC, and immovable property, Member States may impose requirements which are more restrictive or prescriptive than this Directive. It is also made clear that the Directive

---

[23] 2002 Act s.210(2)–(5).
[24] 2002 Act s.210(6).
[25] 2002 Act s.214.
[26] *Office of Fair Trading v MB Designs (Scotland) Ltd*, 2005 S.L.T. 691 at [17].
[27] European Parliament and Council Directive 2005/29/EC concerning unfair business-to-consumer commercial practices in the internal market (OJ L149, 11.6.2005), p.22.
[28] On this point see the judgment of the ECJ in *NV v Total Belgium NV and Galatea BVBA v Sanoma Magazines Belgium NV* (Joined cases C-261/07 and C-299/07) [2009] E.C.R. I-02949.

does not apply to the certification and indication of the standard of fineness of articles of precious metal.

This background explains why the CPRs amend or repeal so many pieces of legislation.[29] Amongst the better known casualties are the Trade Descriptions Act 1968, the Fair Trading Act Part III and its associated code of practice, the Consumer Transactions (Restrictions on Statements) Order 1976, the Business Advertisements (Disclosure) Order 1977 and the Control of Misleading Advertisements Regulations 1988.

The CPRs and unfair practices—Regulation 3 of the CPRs provides that "unfair **14.04** commercial practices are prohibited". A commercial practice

> "means any act, omission, course of conduct, representation or commercial communication (including advertising and marketing) by a trader, which is directly connected with the promotion, sale or supply of a product to or from a consumer, whether occurring before, during or after a commercial transaction in relation to a product".

"Product" in this context means any goods or service and includes immovable property, and "consumer" is defined as any individual who in relation to a commercial practice is acting for purposes which are outside his business. In one respect the definition of commercial practice goes further than the similar definition in the directive as it covers not only the sale or supply of a product *to* a consumer but also sale or supply by a consumer to a trader.[30]

Definitions: "Transactional decision" and "average consumer"—Before **14.05** considering what practices are regarded as unfair, it is necessary to deal with two terms which appear frequently in the definitions of those practices. These are the "average consumer" and "transactional decision". "Transactional decision" is defined as

> "any decision taken by a consumer whether to act or to refrain from acting concerning (a) whether, how and on what terms to purchase, make payment in whole or in part for, retain or dispose of a product; or (b) whether, how and on what terms to exercise a contractual right in relation to a product".

In *Office of Fair Trading v Purely Creative Ltd* it was held that

> "any decision with an economic consequence was a transactional decision, even if it was only a decision between doing nothing or responding to a promotion by posting a letter, making a premium rate telephone call or sending a text message."[31]

---

[29] See Consumer Protection from Unfair Trading Regulations 2008 (SI 2008/1227) ("the CPRs") reg.30 and Schs 2 and 4.

[30] This would catch the situation which arose in the Trade Descriptions Act 1968 case of *Fletcher v Budgen* [1974] 1 W.L.R. 1056, where a second hand car dealer made false statements about a car which was traded-in in order to offer a lower price for it. This is permissible in spite of the fact that the directive is largely a maximum one because it does not cover consumer to business transactions.

[31] *Office of Fair Trading v Purely Creative Ltd* [2011] EWHC 106 (Ch) at [68]. This point was not raised in the appeal to the Court of Appeal (see *Purely Creative Limited v The Office of Fair Trading* [2011] EWCA Civ 920) when other issues were referred to the European Court of Justice.

The "average consumer" is one whose material characteristics include being "reasonably well informed, reasonably observant and circumspect".[32] If the practice is directed at a "particular group of consumers", it will be the average member of that group that is relevant.[33] Such a group will be constituted by a clearly identifiable group of consumers

> ". . . who are particularly vulnerable to the commercial practice or to the underlying product because of their mental or physical infirmity, age or credulity in a way which the trader could reasonably be expected to foresee . . ."[34]

In deciding whether such a group has been affected one should ignore "the common and legitimate advertising practice of making exaggerated statements or statements which are not meant to be taken literally".[35] In applying the test generally, account may be taken of social, cultural and linguistic factors and the test is not a statistical one. National courts and authorities will have to exercise their own faculty of judgement, having regard to the case-law of the Court of Justice, to determine the typical reaction of the average consumer in a given case.[36]

14.06 Unfair practices—Regulation 3 paras (3) and (4) set out the circumstances when a commercial practice is unfair. These are where it contravenes the requirements of professional diligence and materially distorts or is likely to materially distort the economic behaviour of the average consumer (the general clause); it is a misleading action under the provisions of reg.5; it is a misleading omission under the provisions of reg.6; it is aggressive under the provisions of reg.7; or it is listed in Sch.1. The promotion of any unfair commercial practice by a code owner in a code of conduct is also prohibited.[37]

14.07 The general clause—Regulation 3(3) sets out a general prohibition on unfair business to consumer commercial practices which is designed to catch practices which do not fall within any other category.[38] To come within the general prohibition a practice must both contravene the requirements of professional diligence and materially distort the economic behaviour of the typical consumer with regard

---

[32] The CPRs reg.2(10) and (2). The test is taken from the case law of the European Court of Justice which has considered this matter in cases dealing with free movement of goods and the Misleading Advertising Directive. There is an extensive range of cases discussing the "average consumer" of which the most important are *Pall Corp. v Dahlhausen* (C-283/89) [1990] E.C.R. I-4827; *Verband Sozialer Wettbewerb e.V v Clinique Laboratoires SNC and Estée Lauder Cosmetics GmbH* (C-315/92) [1994] E.C.R. I-317; *Mars* (C-470/93) [1995] E.C.R. I923; *Commission v Germany "Sauce Hollandaise"* (C-51/94) [1995] E.C.R. I-3299; *Gut Springenheide* (C-210/96) [1998] E.C.R. I-4657; *Estée Lauder v Lancaster* (C-220/98) E.C.R. I-117.

[33] The CPRs reg.2(3)–(5).

[34] The CPRs reg.2(5).

[35] The CPRs reg.2(6).

[36] See European Parliament and Council Directive 2005/29/EC (OJ L149, 11.6.2005), p.22, Recital 18. For the application of the test in an English case see *Office of Fair Trading v Purely Creative Ltd* [2011] EWHC 106 (Ch) at [62]–[68].

[37] The CPRs reg.4.

[38] ". . . it serves as a safety net to catch any current or future practices that cannot be categorised as either misleading or aggressive. The primary motivation is to ensure that the Directive is future-proof." G. Abbamonte, "The Unfair Commercial Practices Directive and its General Prohibition", in S. Weatherill and U. Bernitz (eds), *The Regulation of Unfair Commercial Practices under EC Directive 2005/29* (Oxford and Portland Oregon: Hart Publishing, 2007), pp.20–21.

to the product or be likely to do so. The first test is concerned with the conduct itself, that is, the standards of the trader's practice. The second is concerned with the actual or likely effect the practice has on the typical consumer's economic behaviour. Professional diligence is defined as

> "the standard of special skill and care which a trader may reasonably be expected to exercise towards consumers which is commensurate with either (a) honest market practice in the trader's field of activity, or (b) the general principle of good faith in the trader's field of activity, or both."

In addition to failing to meet the standard of professional diligence, the practice must also materially distort or be likely to material distort the economic behaviour of the average consumer. This is defined as

> "appreciably to impair the average consumer's ability to make an informed decision thereby causing him to take a transactional decision that he would not have taken otherwise".[39]

Misleading actions (reg.5)—There are four ways according to reg.5 in which a **14.08** commercial practice can be unfair because it is a misleading action. It may contain false information generally about a range of matters[40]; although not false, its overall presentation may deceive; it may create confusion through the marketing of the product with a competitor's products; or it may concern the failure of a trader to honour firm commitments made in a code of conduct. In each case it must be shown that the misleading action would cause the average consumer

> "to take a transactional decision he would not have taken otherwise, taking account of its factual context and of all its features and circumstances".[41]

The first of these kinds of misleading actions is more fully spelt out in reg.5(2)(a) which provides that a practice can be misleading if it contains false information and is therefore untruthful in relation to any of the matters in para.(4) or if it or its overall presentation in any way deceives or is likely to deceive the typical consumer in relation to any of the matters in that paragraph, even if the information is factually correct.[42] The false information must relate to various things set out in reg.5(4) of which price and the main characteristics of the product will probably be the most important. Price is self explanatory and will cover a wide range of possible types of unfairness. The main characteristics comprise a long list set out in reg.5(5). These include the availability of the product, its benefits, risks, composition and accessories, fitness for purpose, quantity, origin, expected results from use and the results of tests carried out on it. These provisions would, for example, catch the common practice of turning back the mileage recorder on a car.

---

[39] The CPRs reg.2.
[40] These are set out in 2008 Regulations reg.5(4).
[41] The CPRs reg.5(2)(b) and 5(3). For examples of practices falling within 2008 Regulations reg.5 see *Office of Fair Trading v Ashbourne Management Services Ltd* [2011] EWHC 1237 (Ch).
[42] For an example from the Trade Descriptions Act 1968 (now repealed) see cf. *R v A & F Pears Ltd* (1982) 90 ITSA MR 142.

14.09 Misleading omissions—Practices may be misleading not only because they positively mislead by giving false information but also by failing to give consumers
the information they need to make an informed choice. Regulation 6 provides that
this occurs when practices omit or hide material information, provide it in an
unclear, unintelligible, ambiguous or untimely manner or fails to identify its
commercial intent, unless this is already apparent from the context. The practice
must also be shown to result in the average consumer taking, or being likely
to take, a different transactional decision.[43] The context is to be taken into
account and, in particular certain factors such as the features and circumstances
of the commercial practice, the limitations of the medium used to communicate
the commercial practice (including limitations of space or time), and where the
medium used to communicate the commercial practice imposes limitations of
space or time, any measures taken by the trader to make the information available
to consumers by other means.[44] The missing information must be "material"
which means information that the typical consumer needs, in the context, to make
informed decisions.[45] It includes any information required by European derived
(EC) law, such as the Package Travel, Package Holidays and Package Tours
Regulations[46] and the Consumer Protection (Distance Selling) Regulations.[47]
    Special provision is made for an "invitation to purchase" which is

> "a commercial communication which indicates characteristics of the product
> and the price in a way appropriate to the means of that commercial commu-
> nication and thereby enables the consumer to make a purchase".[48]

The information that is deemed to be material in invitations to purchase includes the
main characteristics of the product, the identity of the trader, the trader's address,
the price of the product (including taxes) or, where the price cannot be reasonably
calculated in advance, the way it will be calculated and any freight, delivery or
postal charges. Also required are any arrangements for payment, delivery, performance and complaint handling that differ from consumers' reasonable expectations.[49]
Where products involve a right of withdrawal or cancellation these must be
mentioned.[50] As reg.6(3) requires rights contained in existing directives such as the
Distance Selling and Doorstep Selling Directives[51] to be disclosed in all cases this
requirement will only apply to such rights contained in domestic legislation.

14.10 Aggressive practices—A commercial practice is aggressive if, in its factual
context, taking account of all of its features and circumstances it significantly
impairs or is likely significantly to impair the average consumer's freedom of
choice or conduct in relation to the product concerned through the use of harassment, coercion or undue influence.[52] In addition, it must cause or be likely to

---

[43] The CPRs reg.6(1)(a).
[44] The CPRs reg.6(2).
[45] The CPRs reg.6(3).
[46] Package Travel, Package Holidays and Package Tours Regulations 1992 (SI 1992/3288).
[47] Consumer Protection (Distance Selling) Regulations 2000 (SI 2000/2334).
[48] The CPRs reg.2(1). See *Konsumentombudsmannen v Ving Sverige AB* (C-122/10) [2011] W.L.R.
(D) 181.
[49] The CPRs reg.6(4).
[50] The CPRs reg.6(4)(g).
[51] Directive 97/7/EC and Directive 85/577/EC on distance selling and doorstep selling ("Distance
Selling and Doorstep Selling Directives").
[52] The CPRs reg.7(1)(a).

cause the consumer to take a transactional decision he or she would not have taken otherwise.[53] In determining whether a commercial practice uses harassment, coercion or undue influence account shall be taken of: its timing, location, nature or persistence; the use of threatening or abusive language or behaviour; the exploitation by the trader of any specific misfortune or circumstance of such gravity as to impair the consumer's judgment; any onerous or disproportionate non-contractual barrier imposed by the trader where a consumer wishes to exercise rights under the contract, including rights to terminate a contract or to switch to another product or another trader; and any threat to take any action which cannot legally be taken.[54] For the purposes of the definition "coercion" includes the use of physical force; and "undue influence" means exploiting a position of power in relation to the consumer so as to apply pressure, even without using or threatening to use physical force, in a way which significantly limits the consumer's ability to make an informed decision.[55]

Schedule 1 unfair practices—Schedule 1 to the Regulations sets out 31 practices **14.11** which are considered unfair in all circumstances. Unlike the other kinds of unfair practice there is no need to consider their effects on consumers. Included are four involving false claims about involvement in trade organisations or schemes, false claims that a product can legally be sold, that it will be available for only a limited time, that consumers' legal rights are a distinctive feature of an offer or that the trader is about to close down. Various marketing frauds are included such as pyramid schemes, bogus prize schemes, and "free" gifts which involve further payments beyond the cost of responding or collecting the product[56] as well as false claims that a product can facilitate winning at games of chance, cure illnesses, dysfunctions or malformations or that an after sales services is available outside the state in which it has been sold or will be available. Direct exhortations to children to buy advertised products or persuade their parents or other adults to do so are also banned as is creating the impression that the consumer cannot leave the premises until a contract is formed.

Enforcement—The Directive on which the Regulations are based provides that **14.12** "Member States shall ensure that adequate and effective means exist to combat unfair commercial practices". Article 13 adds that

> "Member States shall lay down penalties for infringements of national provisions adopted in application of this Directive and shall take all necessary measures to ensure that these are enforced".

---

[53] The CPRs reg.7(1)(b).

[54] The CPRs reg.7(2).

[55] The CPRs reg.7(3). For examples of unfair commercial practices falling under reg.7 see *Office of Fair Trading v Ashbourne Management Services Ltd* [2011] EWHC 1237 (Ch); [2011] All E.R. (D) 276.

[56] In *Office of Fair Trading v Purely Creative Ltd* [2011] EWHC 106, Briggs J. held in a case involving prize draws that the creation of a false impression was a critical requirement and that the layout and get up of the communication were relevant in addition to its wording when deciding whether such an impression had been created. Whether an impression that a prize or equivalent benefit had been won would be falsified by a requirement that the consumer make some payment or incur some cost in claiming it would depend upon the particular facts, both about the prize or benefit, and about the cost of claiming. Following an appeal to the Court of Appeal (see *Purely Creative Limited v Office of Fair Trading* [2011] EWCA Civ 920) these issues were referred to the European Court of Justice.

Such penalties "must be effective, proportionate and dissuasive" but it is clear from comparing the terms used in other languages that this does not mean that the penalties have to be criminal in nature.[57] The duty to enforce is placed on the OFT and local trading standards services.[58] There is no private right of action for breach of the regulations at present.[59]

Enforcers are to

> "have regard to the desirability of encouraging control of unfair commercial practices by such established means as it considers appropriate having regard to all the circumstances of the particular case".[60]

Examples might be the Advertising Standards Authority which deals with complaints about advertisements and PhonepayPlus the regulator or premium rate telecommunications. Enforcers may take civil enforcement action in respect of any breach of the CPRs as Community Infringements under Pt 8 of the Enterprise Act 2002.[61]

Breach of the CPRs in almost all cases will be criminal offences, one requiring proof of mens rea, and the others being strict liability offences. Regulation 8 is the mens rea offence making traders criminally liable for breach the general duty not to trade unfairly contained in reg.3. To prove this offence it must be shown that the trader "knowingly or recklessly" engaged in a commercial practice which contravenes the requirements of professional diligence; and

> "the practice materially distorts or is likely to materially distort the economic behaviour of the average consumer with regard to the product under regulation 3(3)(b)".

The first part of the test is in similar terms to that in the now repealed s.14 of the Trade Descriptions Act 1968. It should be noted that reg.8(2) adopts the meaning of "recklessly" advocated by Widgery L.C.J. in *MFI Warehouses Ltd v Nattrass*.[62]

The other offences are strict liability offences of the kind that have been common in consumer protection statutes and, like them have due diligence defences. Regulation 9 makes it an offence to engage in a commercial practice which is a misleading action under reg.5(1) except for breaches of commitments in codes of conduct referred to in reg.5(3)(b). Misleading omissions as defined by reg.6(1) are offences under reg.10, and reg.11 makes practices which reg.7 defines as aggressive criminal offences as well. Most of the commercial practices listed in Sch.1 are also criminal offences by virtue of reg.12. The exceptions are the offence in para.11 of the schedule of promoting a product in editorial content in the media without revealing that the material has been paid for and the offence

---

[57] European Parliament and Council Directive 2005/29/EC art.13.

[58] The CPRs regs 20 and 2 (defining "enforcement authority"). The OFT will soon cease to exist and its powers will move to some, as yet, unspecified body in relation to Scotland.

[59] The Law Commissions have recommended that there should be such a right; see The Law Commissions Report, *Consumer Redress for Misleading and Aggressive Practices* (HMSO, 2012) Law Com. No.332, Scot. Law Com. No.226.

[60] The CPRs reg.20(4).

[61] See para.14.02, above. The UCPD and the CPRs have been added to the list of specified laws in the Enterprise Act 2002 (Part 8 Community Infringements Specified Laws) Order 2003 (SI 2003/1374) by the CPRs reg.30(1) and Sch.2 para.100.

[62] *MFI Warehouses Ltd v Nattrass* [1973] 1 All E.R. 762 at 768.

in para.28 of including in an advertisement a direct exhortation to children to buy advertised products or persuade their parents or other adults to buy advertised products for them.

Defences—In any proceedings under the Act, it is a defence that the com- **14.13** mission of the offence was due to a mistake, or to reliance on information supplied, or to the act or default of another person, an accident or some other cause beyond the control of the person charged, and that he took all reasonable precautions and exercised all due diligence to avoid the commission of such an offence by himself or any person under his control.[63] The mistake must be that of the person charged.[64] The act or default relied on may be that of a manager or servant; but where the accused is a body corporate the other person cannot be a director, manager, secretary or similar officer.[65] Where the basis of the defence is that the offence occurred because of a third party's act or default, or because information given by the third party was relied on, notice has to be served seven days prior to the case being heard which identifies, or helps identify, the third party.[66] It is a defence to a charge of supplying or offering to supply goods to which a false trade description is applied that the person charged did not know, and could not with reasonable diligence have ascertained, that the goods did not conform to the description or that the description had been applied to the goods.[67]

Unsolicited goods and services—If the following conditions are satisfied: **14.14** (a) "unsolicited"[68] goods are sent to a person ("the recipient") with a view to his acquiring them; (b) the recipient has no reasonable cause to believe the goods were "sent"[69] with a view to their being acquired for the purposes of a business; and (c) the recipient has neither agreed to "acquire"[70] nor agreed to return them[71]; then the recipient may, as between himself and the "sender",[72] treat them as if they were an unconditional gift to him[73] with any right of the sender to the goods being

---

[63] As the wording is the same as that in other consumer protection statutes earlier case law especially that under the Trade Descriptions Act 1968 (the "1968 Act") will still be relevant. See e.g. the case law on the 1968 Act s.24(1); *Aitchison v Reith and Anderson (Dingwall and Tain) Ltd*, 1974 J.C. 12; *Costello v Lowe*, 1990 J.C. 231; *London Borough of Ealing Trading Standards Dept v Taylor* [1995] Crim. L.R. 166; *Carrick District Council v Taunton Vale Meat Trades Ltd*, *The Times*, February 15, 1994 (concerning the "due diligence defence" under the Food Safety Act 1990 where it was held the defence applied where "a meat trader" reasonably relied "on a meat inspection certificate"); see also *Popely v Scott* (2001) 165 J.P. 742 where the due diligence defence was made out under a similar provision in the Timeshare Act 1992 (c.35) in relation to relying on legal opinions beforehand.
[64] *Birkenhead and District Cooperative Society v Roberts* [1970] 1 W.L.R. 1497.
[65] *Tesco Supermarkets v Nattrass* [1972] A.C. 153; *Transco Plc v HM Advocate (No.1)*, 2004 J.C. 29.
[66] The CPRs reg.17(2) which is in the same terms as 1968 Act s.24(2); *Bilon v W.H. Smith Trading Ltd* [2001] EWHC Admin. 469.
[67] 1968 Act s.24(3). See *Barker v Hargreaves* [1981] R.T.R. 197; *Rotherham M.B.C. v Raysun (UK) Ltd* [1989] C.C.L.R. 1; *Hurley v Martinez & Co Ltd* [1991] C.C.L.R. 1.
[68] "Unsolicited goods" is defined in reg.24(6) of the Consumer Protection (Distance Selling) Regulations 2000 (SI 2000/2334) (the "2000 Regulations").
[69] "Send" is defined in the 2000 Regulations reg.24(6).
[70] "Acquire" is defined in the 2000 Regulations reg.24(6).
[71] The 2000 Regulations reg.24(1), which replaced, in part, s.1 of the Unsolicited Goods and Services Act 1971 (the "1971 Act") (s.1 was repealed by reg.22 of the 2000 Regulations).
[72] "Sender" is defined in the 2000 Regulations reg.24(6).
[73] 2000 Regulations reg.24(2), replacing, in part, s.1 of the 1971 Act.

extinguished.[74] The sending of unsolicited goods and unjustified demands for payment will constitute breaches of the Consumer Protection from Unfair Trading Regulations 2008 and attract the sanctions discussed above. A person is not liable to make payment for inclusion of an entry relating to him in a directory, unless an order or note satisfying specified requirements has been signed by him.[75] It is an offence to send or cause to be sent to another person, in the knowledge that it is unsolicited, a book, magazine or leaflet which describes or illustrates human sexual techniques or advertising material for such a publication.[76]

14.15 Price marking—Orders may require that the price or charge is indicated on or in relation to goods which a person indicates are or may be for sale by retail and for services which a person indicates may be provided except those provided only for purposes of businesses carried on by other persons.[77] Where goods are subject to value added tax, the order may make provision as to the indication to be given of the tax included in, or payable in addition to, the price.

14.16 Price Marking Order 2004 (the "2004 Order")—Under this Order,[78] a "trader"[79] is required to indicate the "selling price"[80] of any product which is, or might be, for sale to a "consumer"[81] pursuant to the Order,[82] except for "products sold from bulk"[83] or an "advertisement"[84] for a product[85] (other exceptions are products supplied when providing a service, and auction sales, art work or antiques which are not subject to the Order[86]). A trader is also required to indicate the "unit price" of a product that is, or might be, for sale to a consumer[87] where the product is sold from bulk, or required, pursuant to the Weights and Measures Act 1985,[88] to be marked with a quantity indication or made up in a quantity in accordance with that Act.[89] Exceptions exist for products listed in Sch.2 to the Order, such as products whose unit and selling price are the same, products which are pre-packaged in a constant quantity and sold by a "small shop",[90] or products sold by an itinerant trader or from a vending machine.[91] The Order also specifies how the selling and unit price are to be indicated,[92] including stating both prices in sterling[93] and

---

[74] 2000 Regulations reg.24(3), replacing, in part, s.1 of the 1971 Act.
[75] 1971 Act s.3. An attempt to recover payment is an offence.
[76] 1971 Act s.4; *Director of Public Prosecutions v Beate Uhse (UK)* [1974] Q.B. 158.
[77] Prices Act 1974 s.4 (as amended by Price Commission Act 1977); Price Marking Order (SI 2004/102) implementing Council Directive 79/581/EEC on consumer protection in the indication of the prices of foodstuffs [1979] (OJ L158); see also *Allen v Redbridge L.B.C.* [1994] 1 W.L.R. 139.
[78] SI 2004/102 (the "2004 Order") , replacing the Price Marking Order 1999.
[79] "Trader" is defined in 2004 Order reg.1(2).
[80] "Selling price" is defined in 2004 Order reg.1(2).
[81] "Consumer" is defined in 2004 Order reg.1(2).
[82] 2004 Order reg.4(1).
[83] "Products sold from bulk" is defined in 2004 Order reg.1(2).
[84] "Advertisement" is defined in 2004 Order reg.1(2).
[85] 2004 Order reg.4(2).
[86] 2004 Order reg.3.
[87] 2004 Order reg.5(1).
[88] Pt IV of the 1985 Act and the Weights and Measures (Packaged Goods) Regulations 2006.
[89] 2004 Order reg.5(2).
[90] "Small shops" is defined in 2004 Order reg.1(2).
[91] 2004 Order reg.5(3).
[92] 2004 Order regs 6, 7 and 8.
[93] 2004 Order reg.6(1).

making sure that prices are not ambiguous and are easily identifiable, legible and proximate to the product.[94] The Order is enforced under the Prices Act 1974.[95]

Property misdescriptions—It is an offence to make a false or misleading state- **14.17** ment about a prescribed matter in the course of an estate agency business or a property development business, other than in providing conveyancing services.[96] There are five elements to the offence: (1) the party complained of "made the statement alleged"; (2) the statement "was false and misleading"; (3) the statement related to the description of property; (4) it was in the course of property development business; and (5) the "statement was made by . . . [the party complained of] or one their employees".[97] Statements must be "of present fact" and not "mere promises for the future".[98] There is a due diligence defence.[99] The prescribed matters include: the location, physical characteristics, history and price of the subjects.[100]

Trading schemes and pyramid selling—Part XI of the Fair Trading Act 1973[101] **14.18** empowers the Secretary of State to make regulations in relation to "trading schemes".[102] The current regulations are the Trading Schemes Regulations 1997[103] and Trading Schemes (Exclusion) Regulations 1997.[104] The Trading Scheme Regulations[105] "disapply" previous regulations concerning the practice known as "pyramid selling",[106] as from February 6, 1997.

Safety: Part II of the Consumer Protection Act 1987—This part of the Act is **14.19** designed to prevent the supply of goods which are not safe by permitting regulations to be made to ensure the safety of goods. It no longer includes s.10 which contained a general duty not to supply unsafe goods such a duty now being contained in the General Product Safety Regulations 2005.[107] Safety regulations may be made contravention of which gives rise to criminal and civil liability.[108] The Secretary of State may serve on a person a "prohibition notice" prohibiting

---

[94] 2004 Order reg.7(1).

[95] Prices Act 1974 (c.24) Sch. para.6.

[96] Property Misdescriptions Act 1991 s.1; *R. v Bexley Justices, Ex p. Barratt Homes Ltd* Unreported March 9, 2000 Divisional Court; *Lewin v Barratt Homes Ltd* [2000] 3 E.G. 132.

[97] *R. v Bexley Justices, Ex p. Barratt Homes Ltd* Unreported, per Schiemann L.J. at [6].

[98] *Lewin v Barratt Homes Ltd* [2000] 3 E.G. 132, per Simon Brown L.J. at [79A].

[99] Property Misdescriptions Act 1991 s.2.

[100] Property Misdescriptions (Specified Matters) Order 1992 (SI 1992/2834).

[101] As amended by the Trading Schemes Act 1996 (c.32).

[102] "Trading Scheme" is defined in s.118(8) of the Fair Trading Act 1973 (the "1973 Act") (as amended).

[103] Fair Trading Act 1973, implemented pursuant to s.119 of the 1973 Act.

[104] Trading Schemes (Exclusion) Regulations 1997 (the "1997 Regulations") (SI 1997/31), implemented pursuant to s.118(6)(b) of the 1973 Act.

[105] 1997 Regulations reg.2.

[106] See the Pyramid Selling Schemes Regulations 1989 (SI 1989/2195), amended by Pyramid Selling Schemes (Amendment) Regulations 1990 (SI 1990/150).

[107] General Product Safety Regulations (SI 2005/1803) Pt 4 reg.46(2). This duty is discussed in the next section.

[108] Consumer Protection Act 1987 (the "1987 Act") ss.11(1), 12(1), 41; e.g. Toys (Safety) Regulations 1989 (SI 1989/1275) and many more covering a wide range of goods. *R. v Secretary of State for Health, Ex p. United States Tobacco International Inc* [1992] 1 Q.B. 353. For a discussion of the Toys (Safety) Regulations 1989 (SI 1989/1275) (the "1989 Regulations"), see *R. v Liverpool City Council* (2000) 2 L.G.L.R. 689 English Div. Court.

the person from supplying specified kinds of goods[109]; similarly, a "notice to warn" may require a person to publish at his own expense a warning about goods he has supplied.[110] Contravention of either type of notice is an offence.[111] An enforcement authority, if it has reasonable grounds for suspecting that a safety provision has been contravened, can serve a "suspension notice" prohibiting the person concerned from supplying the relevant goods for a period of not more than six months without the consent of the authority.[112] Contravention of a notice is an offence,[113] but compensation is payable if there has in fact been no contravention of a safety provision and there has been no neglect or default on the part of the supplier.[114] However, a local council cannot issue a "press release" stating that particular goods are "unsafe".[115] The sheriff may order forfeiture of goods for destruction in relation to which there has been a contravention of a safety provision.[116] There is a defence of due diligence to the various offences.[117] Consumer safety measures may also be made under the European Communities Act 1972 to implement Community obligations.

14.20 General Product Safety Regulations 2004 (the "2004 Regulations")—These Regulations[118] implement the European Parliament and Council Directive of December 3, 2001 on general product safety.[119] The products covered are those intended for consumers or likely, under reasonably foreseeable conditions, to be used by consumers even if not intended for them and which are supplied or made available, whether for consideration or not, in the course of a commercial activity. New, used or reconditioned products are included as well as those supplied or made available to consumers for their own use in the context of providing a service.[120] "Producer" means the manufacturer of a product, when he is established in a Member State and any other person presenting himself as the manufacturer by affixing to the product his name, trade mark or other distinctive mark, or the person who reconditions the product. When the manufacturer is not established in a Member State his representative established in a Member State,

---

[109] 1987 Act s.13(1)(a); "Goods" are defined in s.11(7). *R. v Liverpool City Council, Ex p. Baby Products Association* (2000) 2 L.G.L.R. 689 English Div. Court.

[110] 1987 Act s.13(1)(b); *R. v Liverpool City Council, Ex p. Baby Products Association* (2000) 2 L.G.L.R. 689 English Div. Court.

[111] 1987 Act s.13(4).

[112] 1987 Act s.14(1), (2); see *R. v Birmingham City Council, Ex p. Ferrero Ltd* [1993] 1 All E.R. 530, holding that consultation is not required before a suspension notice (or a prohibition notice) is issued; *R. v Liverpool City Council, Ex p. Baby Products Association* (2000) 2 L.G.L.R. 689 English Div. Court.

[113] 1987 Act s.14(6).

[114] 1987 Act s.14(7).

[115] *R. v Liverpool City Council, Ex p. Baby Products Association* (2000) 2 L.G.L.R. 689 English Div. Court.

[116] 1987 Act s.17.

[117] 1987 Act s.39; *P. & M. Supplies (Essex) Ltd v Devon C.C.* [1991] C.C.L.R. 71; *Tesco Stores Ltd v Donnelly*, 1994 G.W.D. 27–1609; *Balding v Lew-Ways Ltd* [1996] E.C.C. 417, holding that where there are relevant regulations (there the 1989 Regulations) the defence does not apply by showing that a "British standard", rather than the regulations, was satisfied.

[118] General Product Safety Regulations 2005 (SI 2005/1803).

[119] European Parliament and Council Directive 2001/95/EC on general product safety (OJ No.L11, 15/1/2002), p.4. This Directive superseded Council Directive 92/59/EEC (OJ No.L228, 11/8/1992), p.24 on general product safety which was implemented by the General Product Safety Regulations 1994 (SI 1994/2328). The 1994 Regulations are consequently revoked by reg.1(2) of these Regulations.

[120] 2004 Regulations reg.2. Regulation 4 excludes second-hand products which are expressly supplied for repair or reconditioning.

or the importer of the product will be deemed to be the producer.[121] Also included are other professionals in the supply chain, insofar as their activities may affect the safety properties of a product.[122] The Regulations apply except where there are no other specific safety provisions in rules of Community law other than the Directive.[123]

The principal obligation placed on producers is only to place safe products on the market.[124] Products which comply with certain safety standards are presumed to be safe unless there is evidence to the contrary.[125] Producers must inform customers about the risks of products and to monitor the risks their products pose.[126] Distributors must act with due care so as not to supply unsafe products and to co-operate in monitoring the safety of products[127] and both producers and distributors must notify an enforcement authority if a product placed on the market poses risks that are incompatible with the general product safety requirement.[128]

Regulation 10 imposes a duty on certain enforcement authorities to enforce the Regulations.[129] It requires all enforcement authorities to act in a proportionate manner, to take account of the precautionary principle and to encourage voluntary compliance with the Regulations except in cases of serious risk. Regulations 11–15 contain the enforcement powers which enforcement authorities may exercise in appropriated cases by issuing safety notices of various kinds. These are suspension notices to suspend the supply of a product[130]; requirements to mark which require warnings to be marked on a product[131]; requirements to warn those who have already been supplied with a product[132]; withdrawal notices requiring products not to be placed on the market or supplied[133]; and recall notices requiring the recall from consumers of products that have been supplied to them.[134] Breach of regs 5–8 can be sanctioned by criminal prosecutions[135] and a due diligence defence is available.[136]

Doorstep selling—The Cancellation of Contracts made in a Consumer's Home or Place of Work etc Regulations 2008[137] replace the Consumer Protection (Cancellation of Contracts Concluded away from Business Premises) Regulations **14.21**

---

[121] 2004 Regulations reg.2.
[122] 2004 Regulations reg.2.
[123] 2004 Regulations reg.3.
[124] For the meaning of "safe" see reg.2.
[125] 2004 Regulations reg.6.
[126] 2004 Regulations reg.7.
[127] 2004 Regulations reg.8.
[128] 2004 Regulations reg.9. This does not apply to antiques or products supplied for repair or reconditioning.
[129] "Enforcement authority" is defined in reg.2 as "the Secretary of State, any other Minister of the Crown in charge of a government department, any such department and any authority or council mentioned in regulation 10". In practice, it is the latter, the district and island councils, that do the day-to-day enforcement work.
[130] 2004 Regulations reg.11.
[131] 2004 Regulations reg.12.
[132] 2004 Regulations reg.14.
[133] 2004 Regulations reg.13.
[134] 2004 Regulations reg.14.
[135] 2004 Regulations reg.20.
[136] 2004 Regulations reg.29.
[137] Cancellation of Contracts made in a Consumer's Home or Place of Work etc Regulations 2008 (SI 2008/1816).

1987.[138] Both were enacted to implement an EC Directive.[139] They apply to contracts (including consumer credit agreements) between a consumer[140] and a trader[141] for the supply of goods or services to the consumer by a trader and which are made during a visit by the trader to the consumer's home or place of work, to the home of another individual, during an excursion organised by the trader away from his business premises, or after an offer made by the consumer during such a visit or excursion.[142] Excluded from the Regulations are contracts relating to immoveable property but not those for the repair of improvement of a building, the construction of extensions, patios, conservatories or driveways or the incorporation of goods in immoveable property. Also excluded are contracts for the supply of food, drink or other goods intended for current consumption by use in the household and supplied by regular roundsmen as well as those for the supply of goods or services contained in a trader's catalogue, contracts of insurance, and various credit contracts.[143]

Contracts to which the regulations apply are not enforceable unless the trader has given the consumer a prominent notice that the consumer has cancellation rights.[144] During the period of seven days from the making of the contract consumers may cancel contracts by giving written notice of cancellation which need be in no particular form as long as it indicates the intention to cancel the contract.[145] Where the right to cancel is exercised any money that has been paid becomes repayable and there is a lien for its repayment over any goods supplied under the contract which may be in the possession of a consumer.[146] Subject to this lien, consumers who are in possession of goods are under a duty to take reasonable care of them pending their return to the supplier. Although under no obligation to deliver the goods to the supplier other than at their own homes, consumers may choose to return them to the person on whom a cancellation notice could have been served. These duties to take reasonable care of the goods and to return them are statutory duties and are actionable as such.[147] There are detailed provisions in the regulations dealing with the return of goods given in part-exchange[148] and the repayment of credit.[149] It is not possible to contract out of the Regulations.[150]

---

[138] Consumer Protection (Cancellation of Contracts Concluded away from Business Premises) Regulations 1987 (SI 1987/2117) implementing Directive 85/577/EC, of December 20, 1985, to Protect the Consumer in Respect of Contracts Negotiated away from Business Premises [1985] OJ L372, p.31.

[139] Directive 85/577, p.31. The Consumer Rights Directive (Directive 2011/83/EU) repeals this directive. When it is implemented (as it must by December 13, 2013) these regulations will have to be replaced.

[140] Cancellation of Contracts Regulations 2008 (SI 2008/1816) reg.2.

[141] Cancellation of Contracts Regulations 2008 reg.2.

[142] Cancellation of Contracts Regulations 2008 regs 5 and 3. The Court of Justice of the European Community has ruled, in *Bayerische Hypotheken-und Wechselbank A.G. v Dietzinger* (Case C-45/96) [1998] All E.R. (EC) 332, that the directive does not apply to a contract of guarantee concluded by a natural person who was not acting in the course of his trade or profession where repayment of a debt contracted by another person who was acting in the course of his trade or profession was being guaranteed.

[143] Cancellation of Contracts Regulations 2008 Sch.3.

[144] Cancellation of Contracts Regulations 2008 reg.7 and Sch.4 Pt 1.

[145] Cancellation of Contracts Regulations 2008 reg.8.

[146] Cancellation of Contracts Regulations 2008 reg.10.

[147] Cancellation of Contracts Regulations 2008 reg.13.

[148] Cancellation of Contracts Regulations 2008 reg.14.

[149] Cancellation of Contracts Regulations 2008 reg.12.

[150] Cancellation of Contracts Regulations 2008 reg.15.

The Distance Selling Regulations—The Consumer Protection (Distance Selling) **14.22**
Regulations 2000[151] revoke the Mail Order Transactions (Information) Order
1976.[152] The Regulations apply to a "distance contract"[153] which is one for goods
or services where the "supplier"[154] exclusively uses at least one "means of distance
communication"[155] before and at the time of the conclusion of the contract with
the "consumer",[156] i.e. the parties are not physically present simultaneously.[157]
Examples of such communication methods, as set out in Sch.1, include: letters,
catalogue, and telephone.[158] The Regulations allow for full and partial exceptions.
In the first category are: (i) sale of land contracts; (ii) construction contracts;
(iii) financial services contracts[159]; (iv) contracts involving automated vending
machines or automated commercial premises; (v) contracts made with a telecommunications operator via a public pay-phone; and (vi) auctions.[160] In the second
category are: (i) timeshares[161]; (ii) contracts to regularly supply food, beverages
or other goods intended for everyday consumption at the consumer's abode
or place of work[162]; (iii) contracts concerning accommodation, transport,[163]
catering or leisure services on a particular day or during a particular period[164]; or
(iv) package holidays.[165]

The Regulations require certain pre-contractual information to be given to
the consumer: (i) the supplier's name, and, if payment is in advance, his address;
(ii) the major features of the goods or services; (iii) price; (iv) delivery costs;
(v) payment, delivery or performance arrangements; (vi) cancellation rights;
(vii) means of distance communications costs which do not accord with the
standard rate; (viii) how long an offer or price is valid; and (ix) a contract's
minimum duration where the supply of goods or services is permanent or recur-
rent.[166] Also, prior to the contract's conclusion, the consumer is to be advised if
substitute goods or services of equal standard and at the same price are to be
supplied in the event of unavailability,[167] and that the supplier will incur the cost
if the consumer returns the substitute goods.[168]

---

[151] Consumer Protection (Distance Selling) Regulations 2000 (SI 2000/2334) (the "2000
Regulations"), implementing Directive 97/7/EC [1997] OJ L144/19 (except art.10 thereof), under
s.2(2) of the European Communities Act 1972. The Consumer Rights Directive (Directive 2011/83/
EU) repeals this directive. When it is implemented (as it must by December 13, 2013) these Regulations
will have to be replaced.

[152] Mail Order Transactions (Information) Order 1976 (SI 1976/1812), which was revoked by reg.2
of the 2000 Regulations.

[153] "Distance contract" is defined in 2000 Regulations reg.3(1).

[154] "Supplier" is defined in 2000 Regulations reg.3(1).

[155] "Means of distance communication" is defined in 2000 Regulations reg.3(1).

[156] "Consumer" is defined in 2000 Regulations reg.3(1).

[157] See definition of "means of distance communication" in 2000 Regulations reg.3(1).

[158] See definition of "means of distance communication" in 2000 Regulations reg.3(1) and the
examples in Sch.1.

[159] See the inclusive list in 2000 Regulations Sch.2.

[160] 2000 Regulations reg.5(1).

[161] 2000 Regulations reg.6(1) disapplying regs 7–20.

[162] 2000 Regulations reg.6(2) disapplying regs 7–19(1).

[163] See *Easycar (United Kingdom) Ltd v Office of Fair Trading* (C336/03) [2005] W.L.R. (D) 23
ECJ.

[164] *Easycar (United Kingdom) Ltd v Office of Fair Trading* (C336/03) [2005] W.L.R. (D)
23 ECJ.

[165] 2000 Regulations reg.6(3) disapplying regs 19(2)–(8) and 20.

[166] 2000 Regulations reg.7(1)(a).

[167] 2000 Regulations reg.7(1)(b).

[168] 2000 Regulations reg.7(1)(c).

The above information is to be supplied clearly and comprehensibly in a way befitting the means of distance communication used, and having regard to the principles of good faith in commercial transactions and laws protecting persons, like minors, who cannot give consent.[169]

In addition to the above, information is required which includes, amongst other things, what is involved where a consumer decides to cancel the contract as permitted under the Regulations.[170] For instance, information is required as to: notice to the consumer where the consumer is to return the goods under the contract; notice about which party bears the cost when the goods are returned or recovered, if the contract is cancelled by the consumer; the supplier's business address; post-sales service; and the conditions concerning a cancellation right under the contract where the contract is open ended or is for greater than one year.[171] In the case of a contract for the supply of services the consumer is also to be informed how the right to cancel may be affected by the consumer agreeing to performance of the services beginning before the end of the cancellation period.[172]

Exceptions to this include "one-off" services where an invoice is provided by the "operator of the means of distance communication".[173] Notice or information provided under the Regulations is to be written or in another form that lasts and which the recipient has access to.[174]

A consumer can cancel a contract by a notice.[175] There are provisions for service of the notice.[176] The Regulations provide cancellation periods for goods and for services which start with the day on which the contract is concluded. In relation to goods this period ends in three circumstances: (i) seven working days from the day after receipt of goods, where the additional written information above has been received; (ii) where this information is supplied within three months of the day after receipt of the goods by the consumer, the period is seven working days from the day after receipt of the information; and (iii) where no information is supplied, the period is three months and seven working days from the day after receipt of the goods.[177] In the case of services cancellation is possible in three situations. Where the supplier has supplied the required information on or before the day on which the contract is concluded, the cancellation period ends on the expiry of the period of seven working days beginning with the day after the day on which the contract is concluded. If the supplier has not supplied the required information in good time but does so in writing or in another durable medium available and accessible to the consumer, within the period of three months beginning with the day after the day on which the contract is concluded, the cancellation period ends on the expiry of the period of seven working days beginning with the day after the day on which the consumer receives the information. Otherwise, the cancellation period ends on the expiry of the period of three months and seven working days beginning with the day after the day on which the contract is concluded. However, where performance of the contract has begun with the consumer's agreement within seven working days of the conclusion of

---

[169] 2000 Regulations reg.7(2).
[170] Cancellation is allowed under 2000 Regulations reg.10.
[171] 2000 Regulations reg.8(2)(a)–(e).
[172] 2000 Regulations reg.8(1)(iii).
[173] 2000 Regulations reg.9. "Operator of a means of communication" is defined in reg.3(1).
[174] 2000 Regulations regs 8, 10 and 11.
[175] 2000 Regulations reg.10(1), (2) and (3).
[176] 2000 Regulations reg.10(4), (5).
[177] 2000 Regulations reg.11(1)–(4).

the contract and the supplier has not supplied the required information before performance began, but provides it in good time during the performance of the contract, the cancellation period ends (a) on the expiry of the period of seven working days beginning with the day after the day on which the consumer receives the information; or (b) if the performance of the contract is completed before then on the day when the performance of the contract is completed.[178] To these rights of cancellation, there are six exceptions: (i) a contract of services in which performance has started with the consumer's consent prior to the cancellation period ending; (ii) contracts for goods or services where the price depends on financial market movements outwith the supplier's control; (iii) specifically made or personalised goods; (iv) videos, audio recordings or computer software; (v) newspapers and magazines; and (vi) gambling services.[179]

When the contract is cancelled, the consumer is to receive a refund within 30 days.[180] Where the consumer is required to return the goods under the contract, after exercising his cancellation rights, he may be charged the recovery costs if he does not return the goods.[181]

Provision is made for the situation where the goods or services contract is cancelled and there is a "related credit agreement".[182] Where a consumer has cancelled a contract, a duty is imposed on him prior to cancellation to keep goods in his possession and take reasonable care of those goods.[183] When the contract has been cancelled, there is an obligation of restoration on the consumer concerning the goods, with the above two duties applying in the interim.[184] No obligation is placed on the consumer concerning delivery of the goods, other than at his own premises pursuant to a written request from the supplier prior to or when there was collection of the goods from the premises.[185] The consumer's duty to keep the goods in his possession is discharged where the goods are delivered to a party entitled to a cancellation notice or are sent, at the consumer's cost, to that party.[186] The duty of care towards the goods ends where the goods are delivered either at the consumer's premises or another place, or are sent, although there is a duty to ensure the supplier receives the goods.[187] Where a request to deliver goods, made within 21 days of a contract being cancelled, is not complied with by the consumer, the obligations of retention and care in relation to the goods in the consumer's possession remain whilst the goods are not delivered or sent.[188] Where the contract expressly requires the goods be returned to the supplier and no issue of rejection arises, the 21-day period above instead becomes six months.[189] The supplier must return assets given as security before the obligation to return the goods can be enforced.[190] A consumer who breaches an obligation in relation to returning goods is liable for breach of statutory duty.[191]

---

[178] 2000 Regulations reg.12 as amended by the Consumer Protection (Distance Selling) (Amendment) Regulations 2005 (SI 2005/689) reg.2.
[179] 2000 Regulations reg.13(1).
[180] 2000 Regulations reg.14(1)–(3).
[181] 2000 Regulations reg.14(5).
[182] 2000 Regulations regs 15 and 16; see also reg.20.
[183] 2000 Regulations reg.17(2).
[184] 2000 Regulations reg.17(3).
[185] 2000 Regulations reg.17(4).
[186] 2000 Regulations reg.17(5).
[187] 2000 Regulations reg.17(6).
[188] 2000 Regulations reg.17(7).
[189] 2000 Regulations reg.17(8).
[190] 2000 Regulations reg.17(9).
[191] 2000 Regulations reg.17(10).

The Regulations provide for part exchanges.[192] Subject to a contrary intention, a contract is to be performed by a supplier no later than 30 days from the sending of the consumer's order.[193] Where the contract cannot be performed, due to the unavailability of goods or services, the consumer is to be informed, and a refund made no later than the 30 days after "the period of performance".[194] Where there is no contractual performance within "the period for performance", the contract is regarded as being void ab initio, except in relation to the consumer's remedies or rights due to non-performance.[195] Security for performance is to be refunded immediately where the supplier cannot perform.[196] Substitute goods are permitted where the contract clearly says so, and the consumer is advised of this pursuant to the Regulations.[197]

Where a third party fraudulently pays for goods or services using a consumer's card, the consumer can cancel the transaction and obtain a refund from the supplier.[198]

Contracting out of the Regulations is prohibited. Contractual terms not consistent with the Regulations are void, as are terms imposing obligations or liabilities in addition to those in the Regulations.[199] A very limited exception applies to a provision concerning returning goods where the contract has been cancelled.[200] Use of choice of law clauses to escape the Regulations is prohibited.[201]

An "enforcement authority" (which includes the Office of Fair Trading)[202] is to consider complaints.[203] The Office of Fair Trading (or other enforcement authority in certain circumstances) has power to apply for an interdict[204] to ensure the Regulations are complied with.[205] A party in breach may give an undertaking to such an authority.[206]

14.23 The Electronic Commerce Regulations—The E-Commerce Directive[207] is designed to encourage the development of trade within the EU by electronic means. Some of its provisions which have been implemented by the Electronic Commerce (EC Directive) Regulations 2002[208] provide protection for consumers which adds to that provided by the Distance Selling Regulations.[209] Those providing an information society service[210] must make available to the recipient of

---

[192] 2000 Regulations reg.18.

[193] 2000 Regulations reg.19(1).

[194] 2000 Regulations reg.19(2). See also reg.19(3), (4). "The period of performance" is defined in reg.19(2).

[195] 2000 Regulations reg.19(5).

[196] 2000 Regulations reg.19(6).

[197] 2000 Regulations reg.19(7). The relevant regulation is reg.7(1)(b), (c), and 7(2).

[198] 2000 Regulations reg.21(1), (2).

[199] 2000 Regulations reg.25(1), (2).

[200] 2000 Regulations reg.25(2)–(4).

[201] 2000 Regulations reg.25(5).

[202] Defined in the 2000 Regulations reg.3.

[203] 2000 Regulations reg.26.

[204] The 2000 Regulations refer to "injunction": see reg.27.

[205] 2000 Regulations reg.27(3).

[206] 2000 Regulations reg.26(4).

[207] Directive 2000/31/EC of the European Parliament and of the Council on certain legal aspects of information society services [2000] OJ L178/1.

[208] Electronic Commerce (EC Directive) Regulations 2002 (SI 2002/2013) (the "2002 Regulations").

[209] See previous section.

[210] 2002 Regulations reg.2 defines "information society services" as "any service normally provided for remuneration, at a distance, by means of electronic equipment for the processing (including digital

the service and any relevant enforcement authority, in a form and manner which is easily, directly and permanently accessible, certain information. This includes the full name of the business, its geographic address, contact details (including an email address, to enable rapid, direct and effective communication), details of any publicly accessible trade or similar register with which it is registered and, if the service is subject to an authorisation scheme, details of the relevant supervisory authority. In addition, if the provider is a member of a regulated profession, details of any professional body with which he or she is registered, any professional titles held, and the EU Member States in which the titles have been granted together with a reference to the professional rules and how they can be accessed must also be provided. If the service provider is subject to VAT the registration number must be included and where prices are referred to there must be a clear and unambiguous indication of those prices and whether they include taxes and delivery costs.[211]

The Regulations set out certain conditions for commercial communications by which is meant any form of communication designed to promote, directly or indirectly, the goods, services or image of a company, organisation or person who is carrying out a commercial, industrial or craft activity or regulated profession. It does not include independent reviews that have not been paid for, or communications that only give direct access to the activity of the trader such as a domain name or web address.[212] Such communications must be clearly identifiable as such, clearly identify the person whose behalf it is made as well as identifying promotional offers and competitions and ensuring that their entry conditions are easily accessible and clearly presented.[213]

Where contracts are concluded by electronic means (other than by exchange of emails or by equivalent individual communications), consumers must be informed in a clear, comprehensible and unambiguous manner before an order is placed about the different technical steps to follow to conclude the contract, whether or not the contract will be kept by the provider and be accessible by it. The languages in which the contract may be concluded and the technical means for identifying and correcting input errors prior to the placing of the order must be indicated and where there are terms and conditions applicable to the contract they must be available in a way that allows the consumer to store and reproduce them.[214] Where consumers place orders through technological means, they must receive acknowledgement of the receipt of the order electronically without delay, and be provided with effective and accessible technical means allowing them to identify and correct input errors before their order is placed.[215] Failure to comply with the latter requirement entitles a consumer to rescind the contract unless a court orders otherwise.[216]

Package holidays—The Package Travel, Package Holidays and Package Tours **14.24** Regulations 1992[217] "imposes stringent requirements on the descriptive matter

---

compression) and storage of data, and at the individual request of a recipient of a service". It includes, for example, any marketing or selling of services to consumers and businesses on the internet as well as the use of interactive TV or phone texting.

[211] 2002 Regulations reg.6.
[212] 2002 Regulations reg.2(1).
[213] 2002 Regulations reg.7.
[214] 2002 Regulations reg.9.
[215] 2002 Regulations reg.11.
[216] 2002 Regulations reg.15.
[217] Package Travel, Package Holidays and Package Tours Regulations 1992 (SI 1992/3288) (as amended) (the "1992 Regulations").

relating to package holidays".[218] In summary, the Regulations have been said to contain requirements as to "brochures"[219] about "packages"[220] made available to consumers (reg.5), as to information to be provided to an intended "consumer"[221] before a contract[222] is concluded (reg.7), and as to information to be provided in good time before the start of the journey (reg.8). All those requirements are backed by criminal penalties in the case of any breach. A number of other regulations within the 1992 Regulations imply terms into the contract between the "organiser"[223] and the consumer, including a term giving a right to compensation to the consumer in the event of non-performance of the contract (reg.12). The 1992 Regulations also seek to ensure that the consumer enjoys financial security in the event of the "other party to the contract"[224] becoming insolvent.[225] The first is reg.16(1), which requires "the other party" to have sufficient evidence always that it has security for refunds to, and repatriation of, consumers if insolvency occurs.[226] Subject to various exceptions, the other party is to have in force arrangements described in regs 17, 18, 19 or 20, or, if the other party is not acting in the course of business, arrangements as described in those regulations or in reg.21.[227] This requirement is backed by criminal sanctions—regs 17 and 18 refer to various forms of bonding; reg.19 to insurance under an appropriate policy, and reg.20 to holding the money paid by the consumer in trust. In the case of reg.17, the bond must be one under which an authorised institution binds itself to pay money to an approved body of which the other contracting party is a member in the event of that party's insolvency (see reg.17(1)). "Authorised institution" is clearly intended to refer to a financial institution.[228]

The regulations thus apply to all "packages"[229] sold or offered in the United Kingdom.[230] A party cannot obviate the implied terms imposed by the 1992 Regulations via a choice of law clause.[231] An "organiser"[232] or "retailer"[233] must

---

[218] *Spordur Ehf v Wilkinson* Unreported October 22, 1999 Court of Appeal, per Chadwick L.J. at p.4 of the transcript. See also the 1992 Regulations reg.4.

[219] "Brochure" is defined in the 1992 Regulations reg.2(1).

[220] "Package" is defined in the 1992 Regulations reg.2(1).

[221] "Consumer" is defined in the 1992 Regulations reg.2(2).

[222] "Contract" is defined in the 1992 Regulations reg.2(1).

[223] "Organiser" is defined in the 1992 Regulations reg.2(1).

[224] "The other party to the contract" is defined in the 1992 Regulations reg.2(1), and means the organiser and/or the retailer.

[225] *R. v Association of British Travel Agents, Ex p. Sunspell Ltd* [2000] All E.R. (D) 1368 at [9] (internal inverted commas added).

[226] See *Dillenkofer v Federal Republic of Germany* [1997] Q.B. 259 at 298, ECJ, where it is said, inter alia, "that the Directive does not require member states to adopt specific measures in relation article 7 [which corresponds to reg.16 of the 1992 Regulations] in order to protect package travellers against their own negligence"; *Verein für Konsumenteninformation v Österreichische Kreditverischerungs A.G.* (C-364/96) [1999] 1 C.M.L.R. 1430 at 1441, [18]–[22] (where consumers who had paid for a package holiday, including accommodation, were required to pay for their hotel by "the hotel owner" when the other party to the contract became insolvent).

[227] 1992 Regulations reg.16(2). See also reg.22.

[228] *R. v Association of British Travel Agents, Ex p. Sunspell Ltd* [2000] All E.R. (D) 1368 at [11].

[229] Packages is defined in 1992 Regulations reg.2(1). *Club-Tour Viagens e Turismo SA v Lobo Goncalves Garrido* (C-400/00) [2002] E.C.R. I-4051, EU; *R. v Civil Aviation Authority, Ex p. Association of British Travel Agents Ltd (ABTA)* [2006] EWCA Civ 1356.

[230] 1992 Regulations reg.3(1).

[231] 1992 Regulations reg.28.

[232] "Organiser" is defined in 1992 Regulations reg.2(1).

[233] "Retailer" is defined in 1992 Regulations reg.2(1).

not supply descriptive matter about a package which contains misleading information.[234] If he does, the consumer can seek compensation for loss.[235]

Package holiday brochure requirements—Under the 1992 Regulations, **14.25** "brochures"[236] must contain legible, comprehensible and accurate information about the price,[237] as well as: (i) the destination; (ii) the type of accommodation and its main features; (iii) the meals; (iv) the itinerary; (v) passports and visas; (vi) the sum to be paid on account; (vii) whether a minimum number of persons are required and any deadline; (viii) arrangements concerning delays; and (ix) arrangements concerning security of the money paid over by the consumer and repatriation of the consumer if insolvency occurs.[238] It is an offence for a retailer to make a brochure available to a potential consumer if the retailer knows, or has reasonable cause to believe, it is incompatible with the above.[239] There are three exceptions.[240]

Pre-contractual information—Prior to the conclusion of any contract, a **14.26** consumer must have information about: (i) passports and visas (including likely waiting times); (ii) health formalities for the journey and stay; (iii) arrangements for paying over money paid by the consumer; and (iv) the consumer's repatriation if "the other party to the contract"[241] becomes insolvent.[242] Failure to do so is an offence.[243] Information about: (i) intermediate stops and transfers; (ii) details of local representatives or agents; (iii) contacting a child under 16 who is travelling or staying abroad; and (iv) insurance information, except where the contract requires insurance, must be provided in good time prior to the journey's commencement by the other contractual party.[244] It is an offence to fail to do so.[245] The contract between the consumer and the other contractual party is to be a written one (or one in a form comprehensible and accessible to the consumer) with the consumer having notice of the terms prior to contracting, except where the time between contracting and departing makes this impracticable.[246] The consumer is to be supplied with a written copy of the contract's terms.[247] The contract is to contain information concerning: (i) the destination and period of stay, with dates; (ii) the means and types of transport, with dates, times and places of departure and return; (iii) the location of the accommodation, the tourist category and main features; (iv) meals; (v) whether a minimum number of persons is required and the deadline for acceptance; (vi) the itinerary, visits and excursions

---

[234] 1992 Regulations reg.4(1). Cf. reg.5 and *Inspirations East Ltd v Dudley Borough Council*, Case No.CO-30-97, Unreported November 11, 1997 Divisional Court, per Pill L.J. at p.5 of the transcript, that "Regulation 4 deals with misleading information in a way which Regulation 5 does not".

[235] 1992 Regulations reg.4(2).

[236] "Brochure" is defined in 1992 Regulations reg.2(1).

[237] 1992 Regulations reg.5(1).

[238] 1992 Regulations reg.5(1) applying Sch.1 which lists these factors. See *Inspirations East Ltd v Dudley B.C.*, Unreported November 11, 1997 Divisional Court at 6–7, per Pill L.J. and 7–8, per Garland J.

[239] 1992 Regulations reg.5(2), (3).

[240] 1992 Regulations reg.6.

[241] "Other party to the contract" is defined in 1992 Regulations reg.2(1).

[242] 1992 Regulations reg.7(1), (2).

[243] 1992 Regulations reg.7(3).

[244] 1992 Regulations reg.8(1), (2).

[245] 1992 Regulations reg.8(3).

[246] 1992 Regulations reg.9(2).

[247] 1992 Regulations reg.9(1)(c).

included; and (vii) name and address of the organiser, retailer and (where relevant) insurer.[248] A breach of these requirements is a material contractual breach permitting the contract to be rescinded.[249] It is an implied term in the contract that, upon giving reasonable notice, a consumer can transfer the booking to another person who complies with the package condition where the consumer is unable to proceed with the package, although the transferor and transferee are jointly and severally liable to the other party for the price of the package or additional costs due to the transfer.[250]

14.27 **Price alterations**—The 1992 Regulations provide that a provision in the contract revising prices is void and of no effect unless: (i) the contract provides for the revision up or down of prices; (ii) the basis of how the revision is calculated is stated; and (iii) the revision is due to transport costs (including fuel costs), dues, taxes, or fees for services, e.g. landing or disembarkation fees or the exchange rates applied to the package have changed.[251] Furthermore, price increases must be made at least 30 days prior to departure. For an individual customer, there cannot be a price increase in relation to variations which would produce an increase of less than two per cent, or such greater percentage as the contract may specify ("non-eligible variations"), and that these non-eligible variations are to be omitted from the calculations.[252]

14.28 **Changes to essential contractual terms**—It is an implied term that where it is necessary for the organiser, prior to departure, to significantly alter an essential contractual term (including price, so far as permitted), the organiser must notify the consumer as soon as possible, so that the consumer can make appropriate decisions, including withdrawing from the contract without penalty, or accepting an addendum to the contract stating the changes and their effect on the price.[253] The consumer is to advise the organiser or retailer as soon as possible as to what he decides.[254] If either an essential contractual term is altered leading to the consumer's withdrawal from that contract, or the package is cancelled by the organiser prior to leaving, without fault on the consumer's part, the consumer has three options: (i) take a substitute package of the same or better quality (if available); (ii) take a package of lower quality with a refund; or (iii) receive a refund.[255] Compensation is also payable for non-performance by the organiser, except if the minimum numbers requirement has not been met and the consumer is given written notice within the permitted time, or cancellation is due to unforeseen circumstances beyond the organiser's control which all due care would not have avoided.[256]

14.29 **Defective or non-performance by the organiser**—If, once the consumer has left, a significant proportion of the services cannot be provided by the organiser,

---

[248] 1992 Regulations reg.9(1)(a) applying Sch.2.
[249] 1992 Regulations reg.9(4).
[250] 1992 Regulations reg.10(1), (2).
[251] 1992 Regulations reg.11(1), (2).
[252] 1992 Regulations reg.11(3).
[253] 1992 Regulations reg.12(a).
[254] 1992 Regulations reg.12(b).
[255] 1992 Regulations reg.13(1), (2). These are implied terms.
[256] 1992 Regulations reg.13(3).

the organiser must[257]: (i) provide appropriate alternative arrangements, without charge, for the package to continue, and pay the consumer compensation (if appropriate) for any discrepancies concerning the services contracted for and the services provided[258]; or (ii) arrange commensurate return transportation, and pay compensation (if appropriate) where the alternatives cannot be made or the consumer does not accept them.[259]

Liability for proper performance of a contract lies with the other party, even where the contractual obligations are to be performed by third parties,[260] although this "regulation . . . says nothing about the content of . . . [the] performance".[261] Where the consumer suffers damage due to a performance failure or improper performance, the other party is liable to the consumer, except where the failure is due to: (a) the consumer's fault; (b) the fault of an unconnected third party which was not foreseeable or avoidable; or (c) (i) circumstances that are unusual or unforeseeable and outwith the control of the party relying on this exclusion and whose effects all due care could not have prevented, or (ii) an event not foreseeable or forestallable, even with all due care, by the other party to the contract or other service supplier.[262] In relation to (b) and (c), prompt assistance is to be provided by the other party to the contract concerning a consumer in difficulty.[263] It has been held that this regulation does not impose strict liability on the other party.[264] Regard has to be had to the contract's provisions, and

> "in the absence of the assumption of an absolute obligation, the implication will be that reasonable skill and care will be used in the rendering of the relevant service".[265]

Where there is a complaint about performance of a contract, the other party to the contract or his local representative should try to resolve this quickly.[266] Complaints are to be written and prompt.[267] Compensation for non or incomplete performance can be limited pursuant to a relevant international convention[268] or, except for personal injury, by a contractual provision, provided the limitation is not unreasonable.[269] However, liability cannot be excluded.[270]

---

[257] 1992 Regulations reg.14(1).

[258] 1992 Regulations reg.14(2).

[259] 1992 Regulations reg.14(3).

[260] 1992 Regulations reg.15(1). However, the other party's remedies against the suppliers of other services remain unaffected.

[261] *Hone v Going Places Leisure Travel Ltd* [2001] EWCA Civ 947 Unreported June 13, 2001 CA, per Longmore L.J. at [14].

[262] 1992 Regulations reg.15(2); *Hone v Going Places Leisure Travel Ltd* [2001] EWCA Civ 947, at [15] and [18]; *Williams v First Choice Holidays and Flights Ltd* [2001] C.L.Y. 4282; *Logue v Flying Colours Ltd* [2001] C.L.Y. 4281 (complying with "local standards").

[263] 1992 Regulations reg.15(7).

[264] *Hone v Going Places Leisure Travel Ltd* [2001] EWCA Civ 947; *McRae v Thomsons Holiday Ltd* [2001] C.L.Y. 4291.

[265] *Hone v Going Places Leisure Travel Ltd* [2001] EWCA Civ 947, per Longmore L.J. at [15]; see also at [16].

[266] 1992 Regulations reg.15(8).

[267] 1992 Regulations reg.15(9). Other suitable communication mediums are permitted.

[268] 1992 Regulations reg.15(3). *Norfolk v Mytravel Group Plc* [2004] 1 Lloyd's Rep.106.

[269] 1992 Regulations reg.15(4).

[270] 1992 Regulations reg.15(5); *Bensusan v Air Tours Holidays Ltd* [2001] C.L.Y. 4277.

14.30 Consumer security—Security and repatriation are dealt with in regs 16–21 of the 1992 Regulations (i.e. bonds, insurance or trust moneys), which have been outlined above. It is an offence for the other party to make a false statement concerning the release of trust moneys.[271]

14.31 Offences—It is an offence to breach "the relevant regulations",[272] with fines being imposed.[273]

14.32 Defences—There is a general defence of due diligence concerning breaches of the relevant regulations.[274] Leave of the court is needed where the defence concerns an allegation that the offence was due to either another's act or default, or reliance on information given by another, unless a notice is served seven days before the trial identifying or assisting to identify the other person who committed the act or default, or who gave the information.[275] Any such reliance on a third party's information has to be reasonable, which will include verification steps.[276]

14.33 Liability of other persons—Where the commission of an offence by a person is due to a third party's act or default, in the course of that third party's business, that third party is guilty of the offence and can be charged regardless of whether the first person is or not.[277] In the case of a body corporate, if the offence is due to the consent or connivance of an officer of the company or is attributable to any neglect on their part, they, as well as the body corporate, can be liable.[278] Where the body corporate is managed by members, the members can be liable.[279]

14.34 Time limits—No prosecution for an offence is to be brought: (a) three years after the commission of the offence; or (b) a year after the discovery of the offence by the prosecutor, whichever is the earlier.[280]

14.35 Time share—The Timeshare, Holiday Products, Resale and Exchange Contracts Regulations 2010[281] apply to certain holiday accommodation contracts. These are those that are to any extent governed by the law of: the United Kingdom, or a part of the United Kingdom; a third country if the accommodation which is the subject of the contract is immoveable property situated in an EEA state, and the parties to the contract are to any extent subject to the jurisdiction of a court in the United Kingdom in relation to the contract; or a non-EEA state and the contract is not directly related to immoveable property, the trader[282] party to the contract carries on or directs commercial or professional activities in the United Kingdom, and the contract falls within the scope of those activities.[283] For the purposes of the

---

[271] 1992 Regulations reg.22.
[272] These are defined in 1992 Regulations Sch.3 as regs 5, 7, 8, 16 and 22; see also reg.23.
[273] See 1992 Regulations regs 5, 7, 8, 16 and 22.
[274] 1992 Regulations reg.24(1).
[275] 1992 Regulations reg.24(2), (3).
[276] 1992 Regulations reg.23(2).
[277] 1992 Regulations reg.25(1).
[278] 1992 Regulations reg.25(2).
[279] 1992 Regulations reg.25(3).
[280] 1992 Regulations reg.26.
[281] Timeshare, Holiday Products, Resale and Exchange Contracts Regulations 2010 (SI 2010/2960) (the "2010 Regulations").
[282] For the definition of 'trader', see 2010 Regulations reg.11.
[283] 2010 Regulations reg.5.

regulations, a holiday accommodation contract means a timeshare contract, a long-term holiday product contract, a resale contract or an exchange contract.[284]

A trader must give a consumer[285] clear, comprehensible and accurate key information in relation to a holiday accommodation contract which is sufficient to enable the consumer to make an informed decision about whether or not to enter the contract.[286] This duty may not be limited or excluded by any contractual term or other means and failure to comply with it is actionable by civil proceedings.[287]

"Key information" means the information in the relevant standard information form required by Pts 1 and 3, and set out in Pt 2 of the regulations.[288] This includes the identity, place of residence and legal status of the trader; a description of the property or product which is the subject of the contract; the exact nature and content of the rights subject to the contract; the exact period or duration of the contract; the price; a summary of key services and any associated costs; a summary of facilities; rights of withdrawal; and termination arrangements. Specific provision is made for the language in which the information must be provided.[289] Failure to provide the key information in the standard information form in writing, free of charge and in a manner which is easily accessible to the consumer is an offence.[290]

Any advertising related to regulated contracts must indicate how the key information in relation to the contract can be obtained.[291] At a promotion or sales event, traders must not offer opportunities to enter into regulated contracts unless the invitation to the event clearly indicates the commercial purpose and nature of the event and the key information in relation to the proposed contract is made available to the consumer for the duration of the event.[292] It is also an offence for a trader to market or sell a proposed timeshare or long-term holiday product contract as an investment if the proposed contract would be a regulated contract.[293]

If a holiday accommodation contract is entered into by the parties, it must set out the required key information in relation to that contract with no changes other than permitted changes.[294] The contract must be in writing, must identify the parties and the date and place of conclusion of the contract, and must include the standard withdrawal form.[295] If a trader enters into a regulated contract that does not comply with these requirements, he commits an offence and the contract is unenforceable against the consumer.[296] Specific provision is made for the language in which the contract must be drawn up.[297]

Before entering the contract, the trader must draw the consumer's attention to the right of withdrawal under the contract, the length of the withdrawal period and

---

[284] 2010 Regulations reg.4(1). For the definitions of "timeshare contract", "long-term holiday product contract", "resale contract" and "exchange contract", see regs 7–10.
[285] For the definition of "consumer", see 2010 Regulations reg.11.
[286] 2010 Regulations reg.12(1), (4).
[287] 2010 Regulations reg.35(1), (4), (5).
[288] 2010 Regulations reg.12(3).
[289] See 2010 Regulations reg.12(6), (7).
[290] 2010 Regulations reg.12(5), (8).
[291] 2010 Regulations reg.14(1).
[292] 2010 Regulations reg.14(2).
[293] 2010 Regulations reg.14(3), (5).
[294] 2010 Regulations reg.15(3).
[295] 2010 Regulations reg.15(2), (7), Sch.5. Any contractual term is void to the extent that it purports to allow consumers to waive rights conferred on them by the Regulations: 2010 Regulations reg.19.
[296] 2010 Regulations reg.15(8).
[297] 2010 Regulations regs 17, 18.

the prohibition on advance payment or other consideration during the withdrawal period.[298] The trader must obtain the signature of the consumer in relation to each section of the contract dealing with the above matters and must provide the consumer with a copy of the contract at the time the contract is concluded.[299] Failure to comply with these requirements is an offence and the contract is unenforceable against the consumer.[300]

If consumers wish to exercise a right to withdraw from a contract, they must do so by giving the trader a written notice of withdrawal during the withdrawal period[301] though they do not have to give any reason for the withdrawal.[302] The withdrawal period runs for fourteen days following the start date, which is the later of the date of conclusion of the contract or the date on which the consumer receives a copy of the contract.[303] The obligations of the parties under the contract are terminated with effect from the date the consumer sends the notice of withdrawal[304] and the consumer is not liable for any related costs or charges. Any related credit agreement is automatically terminated at no cost to the consumer.[305]

In some cases a longer withdrawal period may apply. Where the standard withdrawal notice is not included in the contract, the withdrawal period ends one year and 14 days after the start date.[306] If the standard withdrawal form is provided within one year beginning on the start date, then the withdrawal period ends 14 days after the date on which the consumer receives the form.[307] Where the key information is not provided in accordance with the regulations, the withdrawal period ends three months and 14 days after the start date.[308] Similarly, if the key information is provided within three months of the start date, the withdrawal period ends 14 days after the date on which the consumer receives the information.[309]

FURTHER READING

Parry, D., Rowell, R. and Ervine, C., *Butterworths Trading and Consumer Law* (LexisNexis/Butterworths).

Ervine, W.C.H., *Consumer Law in Scotland*, 4th edn (Edinburgh: W. Green, 2008).

Woodroffe, G., *Encyclopaedia of Consumer Law* (London: Sweet & Maxwell).

Law Commissions, *Consumer Redress for Misleading and Aggressive Practices* (HMSO, 2012), Law Com. No.332, Scot. Law Com. No.226, Cm.8323.

---

[298] 2010 Regulations reg.16(1). It is an offence for payments or other consideration to be taken from a consumer before the end of the relevant withdrawal period: 2010 Regulations reg.25(7).

[299] 2010 Regulations reg.16(2), (3).

[300] 2010 Regulations reg.16(4).

[301] 2010 Regulations reg.20(1).

[302] 2010 Regulations reg.20(3).

[303] 2010 Regulations reg.21(1), (2).

[304] 2010 Regulations reg.22(2).

[305] 2010 Regulations regs 22(4), (5), 23.

[306] 2010 Regulations reg.21(3), (4)(a).

[307] 2010 Regulations reg.21(4)(b).

[308] 2010 Regulations reg.21(5), (6)(a).

[309] 2010 Regulations reg.21(6)(b).

CHAPTER 15

LOAN AND CONSUMER CREDIT TRANSACTIONS

Introduction—This chapter deals with both loan and consumer credit transac- **15.01**
tions. It begins with a general discussion of the contract of loan before dealing
with consumer credit transactions.

Loan—Loan[1] is a contract under which the owner of an asset gives, for the **15.02**
temporary accommodation of another, the use of the asset or services derivable
from it.[2] If the obligation is to return the particular thing, the contract is known as
commodate, or proper loan; if it is to return an equivalent amount, as in the case
of money, or goods which are consumed by use, it is known as mutuum, or
improper loan. In commodate, the property in the thing does not pass to the
borrower, and, on his bankruptcy, it may be recovered by the lender; in mutuum,
the property passes and the lender is merely a personal creditor.[3] In mutuum, the
borrower takes the risk of accidental destruction[4]; in commodate, while the
standard of care required is a high one, proof of accidental loss, or accidental
injury, the onus of proof being on the borrower, will excuse him. But the borrower
is bound not to put the article to a use other than that (if any) indicated, and will
be liable for any loss due to his failure in this respect.[5] Certain monetary loans to
individuals are governed by the Consumer Credit Act 1974 (as amended).[6]

Money loans and advances—As a general rule, a loan of money is characterised **15.03**
by an obligation, on the borrower, to repay, subsequently, the amount lent[7];
this distinguishes it from an advance which concerns a "pre-payment"[8] (i.e. "an

---

[1] See W.A. Wilson, *Scottish Law of Debt*, 2nd edn (Edinburgh: W. Green, 1991), para.4.1; J.J. Gow, *Mercantile and Industrial Law of Scotland* (Edinburgh: W. Green, 1964), p.261; *Stair Memorial Encyclopaedia*, Vol.13, "Loan"; as to proof of loan, see para.7.06, above.

[2] Bell, *Principles*, s.194. It is unnecessary to specify the time and manner of restoration or repayment: *Neilson v Stewart*, 1991 S.C. (HL) 22. However, this will normally be done, especially for money loans.

[3] Bell, *Principles*, s.1315. As to following trust money, see para.41.15, below.

[4] *Anderson & Crompton v Walls* (1870) 9 M. 122, opinion of Lord Neaves.

[5] *Bain v Strang* (1888) 16 R. 186.

[6] Inter alia, lenders require to be licensed. There are restrictions on advertising and canvassing. There are provisions for "cooling-off periods" and the supply of adequate information and documenta-tion to the borrower. Extortionate loan agreements may be reopened by the court.

[7] See the submissions of counsel for the respondent (which were not disputed) and the reasoning of the court in *Graham-Stewart v Feeney*, 1995 G.W.D. 35–2048 (available on Lexis) discussed in *Smith v Barclay* Unreported 2006 Dundee Sheriff Court (available on Lexis); and see *Pie in the Sky v McCafferty*, 1996 G.W.D. 34–2040 (Sh. Ct). See too Walton J. in *Champagne Perrier-Jouet v Finch Ltd* [1982] 1 W.L.R. 1359 at 1363, referring to the definition of "loan" in the *Shorter Oxford English Dictionary*, 3rd edn (1944).

[8] See the submissions of counsel for the respondent in *Graham-Stewart v Feeney*, 1995 G.W.D. 35–2048, which were not disputed.

advance" involves "future consideration"[9]). However, the Inner House has held that "payments . . . which are only made because of some possibility occurring in the future", may, nonetheless, constitute "a loan rather than an advance for future consideration".[10] It was acknowledged that "[t]he distinction . . . between a loan which is recognised as such by the parties concerned and which is only made because the lending party has an expectation as to some future event on the one hand, and on the other hand an advance which is made towards a future debt which the granter of the advance will require to meet in the future if certain eventualities occur" might "be a narrow one".[11]

Where a loan is made jointly and severally to two or more borrowers, and one borrower has repaid the whole debt, that borrower can obtain relief from his co-obligant or co-obligants, "based on the principle of recompense".[12]

15.04 Overdrafts and terms loans—Money loans fall into two basic categories: (i) term loans, and (ii) overdrafts. A term loan is a loan of money which is repayable over a period of time, e.g. five years. The debt is thus owing, but not due, in the absence of the lender being able to accelerate the loan owing to a default by the borrower (i.e. an event of default).[13] The borrower will, usually, make periodic payments of principal and interest over the duration of the loan, and so will amortise the debt by the last payment. If the loan is a "bullet" loan, the borrower merely makes interest payments during the life of the loan and repays the outstanding capital at the end of the loan. If the loan facility is a revolving one, the borrower may redraw amounts repaid during the life of the loan, but must repay the amount outstanding by the end of the loan. Term loans will, normally, be documented, either as a facility letter or a loan agreement, and can be either secured or unsecured.[14]

With an overdraft, the repayment of the loan is "on demand".[15] An overdraft may be converted into a term loan by the conduct of the lender.[16] This problem can be avoided by stating that whilst the overdraft facility may be reviewed after a certain period, e.g. "12 months",[17] it nonetheless remains payable "on demand".[18] Where a term loan is mistakenly called in early, the lender can be liable in damages for breach of contract.[19] Sometimes a term loan and an overdraft facility will co-exist—a term loan for a specific purpose, and an overdraft for general

---

[9] per Lord Sutherland, giving the reasons of the Inner House in *Graham-Stewart v Feeney*, 1995 G.W.D. 35–2048, from the Lexis transcript of the case.

[10] *Graham-Stewart v Feeney*, 1995 G.W.D. 35–2048, per Lord Sutherland.

[11] *Graham-Stewart v Feeney*, 1995 G.W.D. 35–2048.

[12] *Moss v Penman*, 1993 S.C. 300 at 304, per Lord President Hope.

[13] For examples of events of default, see cl.13 of the specimen facility letter in *Greens Practice Styles* (Edinburgh: W. Green), Vol.I, section B ("Banking"), Style B01.

[14] As to security for a loan, see Ch.36 on "Rights in Security", and Ch.16 on "Cautionary Obligations".

[15] *Williams & Glyn's Bank Ltd v Barnes* [1980] Com. L.R. 205, Vol.10 Legal Decisions Affecting Banks at 220; *Lloyds Bank Plc v Lampert* [1999] 1 All ER (Comm) 161; [1999] Lloyd's Rep Bank 138.

[16] *Williams & Glyn's Bank Ltd v Barnes* [1980] Com. L.R. 205. As to the meaning of "on demand", see the English case of *Sheppard & Cooper Ltd v TSB Bank Plc (No.2)* [1996] B.C.C. 965.

[17] See, e.g. "Part 1—Terms of facilities (2) Overdraft facilities—Availability" of the specimen facility letter in *Greens Practice Styles*, Vol.I, Style B01–01. See too *Societe General S.A. v Lloyds TSB Bank Plc* Unreported September 17, 1999, Second Division, available at *http://www.scotcourts. gov.uk/opinions/CA914(2)99.html* [Accessed July 14, 2012]; and *Royal Bank of Scotland v Home*, 2001 S.C. 224.

[18] This approach has been approved in England, see *Lloyds Bank Plc v Lampert* [1999] Lloyd's Rep. Bank 138 at 142.

[19] See, e.g. *Crimpfil v Barclays Bank Plc* Unreported April 20, 1994 decision of Judge Horden QC (sitting as a Deputy High Court Judge) noted [1994] *Journal of International Banking Law* N-151.

matters[20]; like term loans, overdrafts can be secured or unsecured. Sometimes, term loans may be pre-paid; such a pre-payment may be subject to terms and conditions,[21] when a loan is pre-paid early, there may be "breakage charges", under the loan agreement which the borrower will have to pay.[22] Where there are several lenders, the loan is said to be "syndicated".

Interest—Interest is the cost of borrowing money, i.e. it is a charge imposed, by **15.05** a lender, on a borrower for his utilisation of the lender's money.[23] It provides the lender with a profit on the financial service provided (i.e. lending money). Interest on money loans can be either at: (i) a fixed rate (e.g. some mortgage lending, usually for a limited period, or a loan between two private individuals); or (ii) a floating (or variable) rate; of these two, the more common, in bank and building society lending, is a floating rate. This section will concern itself with bank and building society lending.

The rate of interest on bank loans will either be charged in relation to: (i) the bank's base rate; or (ii) the London interbank offered rate ("LIBOR").[24] LIBOR is the rate at which banks can borrow funds in the London interbank market.[25] Funds borrowed by banks are lent out at a higher rate, which provides a return on the banks borrowing—the difference between the rate the bank borrows at and the rate it lends out at, is called the "margin". Base rates references will, usually, be for overdrafts,[26] domestic loans (e.g. house lending), or small commercial loans, and will be a percentage over base rate.[27] The base rate should be advertised,[28] and will, usually, be a variable rate.[29] With larger commercial loans, the LIBOR rate will be applied, and the borrower will be charged a certain number of basis points over LIBOR; a basis point is one one-hundredth of one per centum (0.01 per cent). Where a loan is in pounds sterling, the interest will be calculated using a 365-day calendar[30]; whereas for a non-sterling loan, e.g. United States dollars, the

---

[20] See, e.g. the specimen facility letter in *Greens Practice Styles*, Vol.I, Style B01–01.

[21] As per "Prepayment" in "(1) Term loan facilities' of Part 1–Terms of facilities" in the specimen facility letter in *Green's Practice Styles*, Vol. I, Style B01–01.

[22] *Bank of Scotland v Dunedin Property Investment Co Ltd*, 1998 S.C. 657 (this case involved a swap transaction).

[23] A similar view is expressed by R. Cranston, *Principles of Banking*, 2nd edn (Oxford: Oxford University Press, 2002), p.337.

[24] See the discussion of interest in Cranston, *Principles of Banking* (2002), p.337, and M. Hapgood, *Paget's Law of Banking*, 13th edn (Butterworths, 2006), Ch.13.

[25] For a discussion of LIBOR, see J.R. Lingard, *Tolley's Commercial Loan Agreements* (Tolley, 1990), paras 4.11–4.14. LIBOR is commonly defined in Loan agreement or facility letters, see, e.g. cl.6 "Interest" (in relation to "The Loan Facility") of the "Specimen Facility Letter" in App.2 of Lingard, *Tolley's Commercial Loan Agreements* (1990), p.112.

[26] See, e.g. "Interest Rate:" in cl.2 ("overdraft") of "Part 1–Terms of facilities" in the specimen facility letter in *Greens Practice Styles*, Vol.I, section B ("Banking"), Style B01–01. See too cl.2 of the "Specimen Facility Letter" in App.2 of Lingard, *Tolley's Commercial Loan Agreements* (1990), p.110.

[27] See, e.g. "Interest Rate" in cll.1 ("term loan") and 2 ("overdraft") of "Part 1–Terms of facilities" in the specimen facility letter in *Greens Practice Styles*, Vol.I, Style B01–01. For a discussion of "base rate", see P. Moles and N. Terry, *The Handbook of International Financial Terms* (Oxford: Oxford University Press, 1998).

[28] The Lending Code (March 2011), found at *http://www.lendingstandardsboard.org.uk/docs/lendingcode.pdf* [Accessed July 16, 2012], which replaces the Banking Code, refers to where information about interest rates can be found and informing the customer about changes at several points and especially in s.5.

[29] *Provincial North West Plc v Bennett, The Times*, February 28, 1999 CA (Civ Div), Lexis and Westlaw.

[30] See, e.g. "Interest Rate" in cl.1 ("term loan") and cl.2 ("overdraft") of "Part 1–Terms of Facilities" in the specimen facility letter in *Green's Practice Styles*, Vol.I, Style B01–01.

calculation is based on a 360-day calendar.[31] Banks will, normally, charge interest on a compound basis, rather than a simple basis,[32] i.e. interest will be charged on a combined figure of the outstanding principal and the outstanding interest.[33] Whilst interest will "accrue daily",[34] it will, usually, be calculated on a monthly,[35] quarterly[36] or half-yearly basis[37] and later debited to the borrower's account. Loan agreements or facility letters commonly define "interest periods". However, the matter will, ultimately, be a question of construction of the loan agreement or facility letter.[38]

If a borrower defaults in payment, the creditor will, pursuant to the loan document, commonly, charge "default interest" (i.e. a rate of interest in excess of the prescribed rate in the loan contract), until payment is made.[39] It has been held, in England, that where the rate of default interest is "modest" and it "applies from the date of default", then it will not be unenforceable "as a penalty".[40] The court also noted that "the increase" had to be "commercially justifiable" and not have the "dominant purpose" of deterring a breach by the borrower.[41]

A bank or building society is required under The Lending Code,[42] to give personal customers, small businesses and small charities information about interest rates and changes in interest rates.

15.06 Prohibited loans—In this regard, the two most common types of illegal loans[43] are: (i) loans in breach of s.678 of the Companies Act 2006, relating to a company giving "financial assistance" to a party for the purchase of that company's shares[44]; and (ii) loans, quasi-loans and credit transactions by a company to its directors,[45] subject to certain small exceptions.[46] With regard to "financial assistance", the

---

[31] For a discussion of interest calculations, see Hapgood, *Paget's Law of Banking* (2006), pp.234–5; and *Kitchen v HSBC Bank Plc* [2000] Lloyd's Law Rep. Bank 173 at 176.

[32] A banker's "implied" right to charge compound interest, based on "the usage of bankers", has been confirmed by the House of Lords in *National Bank of Greece S.A. v Pinios Shipping Co (No.1); The Maira (No.3)* [1990] 1 A.C. 637 at 684. See also *G. Dunlop & Sons JF v Armstrong (No.3)*, 1996 G.W.D. 30–1782 (involving evidence of banking practice about charging compound interest), and *Kitchen v HSBC Bank Plc* [2000] Lloyd's Law Rep. Bank 173 (on compound interest, and bank practice and the calculation of interest rates). Compounding interest is often referred to as capitalising interest, see e.g. *The Maira (No.3)* [1990] 1 A.C. 637.

[33] See, e.g. Lord Justice-Clerk Inglis in *Reddie v Williamson* (1863) 1 Macq. 228 at 236–7, cited with approval in *The Maira (No.3)* [1990] 1 A.C. 637 at 681; see too at 684.

[34] See, e.g. *Kitchen v HSBC Bank Plc* [2000] Lloyd's Law Rep. Bank 173 at 174 (referring to cl.5 of the loan agreement).

[35] As in "Interest Rate": in cll.1 ("term loan") and 2 ("overdraft") of "Part 1–Terms of facilities" in the specimen facility letter in *Green's Practice Styles*, Vol.I, Style B01–01.

[36] As in *Kitchen v HSBC Bank Plc* [2000] Lloyd's Law Rep. Bank 173 at 174–5; and *The Maira (No.3)* [1990] 1 A.C. 637.

[37] See, e.g. Lingard, *Tolley's Commercial Loan Agreements* (1990), p.31 at para.9.1, who also refers to two monthly interest periods; and Cranston, *Principles of Banking Law* (2002), p.310.

[38] As *Kitchen v HSBC Bank Plc* [2000] Lloyd's Law Rep. Bank 173, makes clear.

[39] See, e.g. cl.7 of the specimen facility letter in *Green's Practice Styles*, Vol.I, Style B01–01.

[40] *Lordsvale Finance Plc v The Bank of Zambia* [1996] Q.B. 752 at 767 (in that case, the default rate was one per centum above the rate in the loan agreements). As to penalties, see paras 10.30–10.36 above.

[41] *Lordsvale Finance Plc v The Bank of Zambia* [1996] Q.B. 752.

[42] See fn.28.

[43] See on illegality, Ch.9, "Pacta Illicita and Unfair Contract Terms".

[44] For a discussion of "financial assistance", see para.46.25 below.

[45] ss.197–203 of the Companies Act 2006. See also para.46.25 below for a fuller discussion.

[46] ss.204–209 of the Companies Act 2006.

contract is void,[47] unless severance is possible,[48] and there are criminal sanctions.[49] In relation to loans to directors by a company, the loan is voidable at the instance of the company, unless restitution is not possible, or the rights of a bona fide purchaser for value without notice are affected.[50] The director is required to account to the company for any gain he has made, and "indemnify the company for any loss or damage".[51] Other examples of prohibited or void loans are: (i) a loan by an insolvent company, which is "void"[52]; and (ii) a loan by a bankrupt, which is of "no effect".[53]

Consumer credit: Scope of the legislation—The Consumer Credit Act 1974 (the **15.07** "1974 Act")[54] establishes a system of licensing of persons concerned with the provision of credit and regulates consumer credit transactions of all kinds. It replaced the Pawnbrokers Acts, the Moneylenders Acts and the Hire-Purchase (Scotland) Act 1965. The mode of operation of ancillary credit business[55] and, in particular, of credit reference agencies,[56] is controlled. The Office of Fair Trading ("OFT") has the duty of generally superintending the working and enforcement of the 1974 Act, of administering the licensing system set up by the Act, and of exercising various adjudicatory functions under the Act.[57] With regard to the 1974 Act, it has been said that it

> "was plainly enacted to protect consumers, most of whom are likely to be individuals. The contract is likely to be in standard form and relatively complex with a number of detailed provisions".[58]
>
> It is, thus, "concerned with issues of social policy".[59]

The 1974 Act remains in force but has been amended by the Consumer Credit Act 2006 (the "2006 Act") to extend the range of credit agreements regulated by it, reform the licensing system, enable debtors to challenge unfair relationships with creditors and provide for an Ombudsman scheme to hear complaints in relation to businesses licensed under the 1974 Act.

---

[47] See *Heald v O'Connor* [1971] 1 W.L.R. 497 at 501–2, referring to s.54 of the Companies Act 1948 (as amended), the precursor to s.678 of the Companies Act 2006. The document here was a guarantee for a loan, but the principle is the same.

[48] *Carney v Herbert* [1985] A.C. 301; *Neilson v Stewart*, 1991 S.C. 22.

[49] s.680 of the Companies Act 2006.

[50] s.213(2) of the Companies Act 2006.

[51] s.213(3) and (4) of the Companies Act 2006.

[52] s.127 of the Insolvency Act 1986 (as amended).

[53] s.32(8) of the Bankruptcy (Scotland) Act 1985 (as amended).

[54] The provisions of the Act are not fully implemented. It is not proposed to make regulations under ss.53, 54, 55, 64(3), 112, 156 and 179: *Hansard*, HC Deb. Vol.28, col.103 (1982).

[55] Consumer Credit Act 1974 (the "1974 Act") Pt X.

[56] 1974 Act ss.157–160; Consumer Credit (Credit Reference Agency) Regulations 2000 (SI 2000/290), revoking Consumer Credit (Credit Reference Agency) Regulations 1977 (SI 1977/329); Consumer Credit (Conduct of Business) (Credit References) Regulations 1977 (SI 1977/330), as amended by Consumer Credit (Conduct of Business) (Credit References) (Amendment) Regulations 2000 (SI 2000/291).

[57] s.1 as amended by the Enterprise Act 2002 (c.40) Sch.25 para.6(2)(b)(ii). The Financial Services Bill before Parliament contains a clause permitting the Treasury to transfer these powers to the proposed Financial Conduct Authority.

[58] *Woodchester Lease Management Services Ltd v Swain & Co (a firm)* [1999] 1 W.L.R. 263 at 267E–F, per Kennedy L.J.

[59] *Wilson v First County Trust Ltd (No.2)* [2002] Q.B. 74 at 93, per Morritt V.C. a point emphasised at various points in the appeal to the House of Lords, see [2004] 1 A.C. 816.

15.08 Licensing—A licence is required to carry on a consumer credit or consumer hire business or an ancillary credit business.[60] A regulated agreement (other than a non-commercial agreement) made when the trader or credit-broker was unlicensed is enforceable against the debtor only where the OFT has made an order applying to the agreement.[61] A person is not to be treated as carrying on a particular type of business merely because occasionally he enters into transactions belonging to a business of that type.[62] A local authority and a body corporate empowered by a public general Act naming it to carry on a business do not need a licence.[63]

A "standard licence" is issued to a person, a partnership or an unincorporated body of persons. A standard licence is granted to a person who satisfies the OFT that he is a fit person to engage in activities covered by the licence and that the name under which he applies is not misleading or otherwise undesirable.[64] A "group licence" covers such persons and such activities as are described in the licence and may be issued only where it appears to the OFT that the public interest is better served by doing so than by obliging the persons concerned to apply separately for standard licences.[65] The OFT has powers to vary, suspend or revoke a licence.[66] In addition, it has power to fine those who breach the conditions of a licence.[67]

---

[60] 1974 Act ss.21, 145. Ancillary credit business is credit brokerage, debt-adjusting, debt counselling, debt-collecting, the operation of a credit reference agency, debt administration and credit information services (s.145). An advocate acting in that capacity and a solicitor engaging in business done in or for the purposes of proceedings before a court or an arbiter are not engaged in ancillary credit business–see s.146 which contains further limitations on the meaning of this term. As to credit brokerage, see *Hicks v Walker* [1984] C.C.L.R. 19; *Brookes v Retail Credit Cards Ltd* [1986] Fin. L.R. 86.

[61] 1974 Act ss.40, 149. See s.148 as to the agreement between the customer and the unlicensed person carrying on an ancillary credit business. In the case of a consumer credit EEA firm, an agreement will only be unenforceable if it was made contrary to a consumer credit prohibition issued under the Financial Services and Markets Act 2000 s.203, or a consumer credit restriction issued under the 2000 Act s.204.

[62] 1974 Act s.189(2); *R. v Marshall* [1989] C.C.L.R. 47; *Hare v Schurek* [1993] C.C.L.R. 47.

[63] 1974 Act s.21.

[64] 1974 Act ss.24A and 25. Prior to the implementation of the Consumer Credit Act 2006 (the "2006 Act") on April 6, 2008, licences were issued for five years. This basic period was preserved for the purposes of the new licensing regime by Consumer Credit (Information Requirements and Duration of Licences and Charges) Regulations (SI 2007/1167) reg.42. Under these regulations, the "prescribed period" is a period of five years though, in practice, licences are issued for indefinite periods. On the death, sequestration or incapacity of the licensee the business may be carried on under the licence by some other person: s.37; Consumer Credit (Termination of Licences) Regulations 1976 (SI 1976/1002), as amended by SI 1981/614 and the Consumer Credit Act 1974 (Electronic Communications) Order 2004 (SI 2004/3236). See, as to refusal of a licence, *North Wales Motor Auctions Ltd v Secretary of State for Trade* [1981] C.C.L.R. 1. New subss.(1A)–(1E) were inserted by the Consumer Credit Act 2006 s.34(2) and came into force (in so far as relating to subss.(1B), (1E) for certain purposes) on June 16, 2006: see Consumer Credit Act 2006 (Commencement No.1) Order 2006 (SI 2006/1508) art.3(1), Sch.1 and (for remaining purposes) on April 6, 2008, see Consumer Credit Act 2006 (Commencement No.3) Order 2007 (SI 2007/3300) art.3(2), Sch.2. Amendments to subs.(1) made by the Consumer Credit Act 2006 s.34(1) came into force on April 6, 2008, and a new subs.(5A) (inserted by the Consumer Credit Act 2006 s.33(2)) and subs.(9) and (10) were repealed by the Consumer Credit Act 2006 s.70 and Sch.4, with effect from the same date, see SI 2007/3300 art.3(2), Sch.2.

[65] 1974 Act s.22. A group licence issued to the Law Society of Scotland covers all solicitors holding practising certificates in respect of consumer credit, credit brokerage, debt adjusting, debt-counselling, debt-collecting, debt administration And the provision of credit information services (including credit repair) in activities arising in the course of practice as a solicitor: Office of Fair Trading, General Notice No.1145. A group licence has been issued to cover persons appointed to be a liquidator, receiver, executor, judicial factor, trustee in sequestration, curator bonis, or trustee under a deed of arrangement or trust deed: Office of Fair Trading, General Notice No.1005.

[66] 1974 Act ss.29–34 as amended by 2006 Act ss.38–42 with effect from April 6, 2008: see 2007 Order art.3(2), Sch.2.

[67] See 1974 Act ss.39A, 39B and 39C added by 2006 Act ss.52–54 with effect from April 6, 2008: see 2007 Order art.3(2), Sch.2.

Decisions on these matters are subject to a right of appeal to the First-tier Tribunal (Consumer Credit) against the decision of the OFT on the issue of a licence.[68]

Definitions—A "consumer credit agreement" is an agreement between an indi- **15.09** vidual ("the debtor") and any other person ("the creditor") by which the creditor provides the debtor with credit of any amount.[69] An "individual" includes a partnership consisting of two or three persons not all of whom are bodies corporate; and an unincorporated body of persons which does not consist entirely of bodies corporate and is not a partnership.[70] "Credit" includes a cash loan and any other form of financial accommodation.[71] An item entering into the total charge for credit is not treated as credit even though time is allowed for its payment.[72] It has been held that

> "[d]ebt is deferred and credit extended whenever the contract provides for the debtor to pay, or gives him the option to pay, later than the time at which payment would otherwise have been earned under the express or implied terms of the contract".[73]

A hire-purchase agreement is regarded as a provision of a fixed-sum credit to finance the transaction of an amount equal to the total price of the goods, less the aggregate of the deposit (if any) and the total charge for credit.[74] A hire-purchase agreement is an agreement, other than a conditional sale agreement, under which goods are hired in return for periodical payments, and the property will pass to the hirer if the terms of the agreement are complied with and the hirer exercises an

---

[68] 1974 Act s.41(1) (amended by the Enterprise Act 2002 (c.40) s.278(1), Sch.25 para.6(21), the 2006 Act s.56(1) and the Transfer of Functions of the Consumer Credit Appeals Tribunal Order 2009 (SI 2009/1836).

[69] 1974 Act s.8(1) amended by the 2006 Act s.2(1)(a) (with full effect from October 1, 2008). *Zoan v Rouamba* [2000] 1 W.L.R. 1509; *Dimond v Lovell* [2001] 2 W.L.R. 1121; *McMillan Williams v Range* [2004] EWCA Civ 294.

[70] 1974 Act s.189(1). As amended by 2006 Act s.1—see the Consumer Credit Act 2006 (Commencement No.2 and Transitional Provisions and Savings) Order 2007 (SI 2007/123) art.3(2) and Sch.2. With the exceptions set out in art.5 of the Order this amendment affects only agreements made before April 6, 2007.

[71] 1974 Act s.9(1).

[72] 1974 Act s.9(4); *Humberclyde Finance Ltd v Thompson (Trading as A.G. Thompson)* [1997] C.C.L.R. 23. Items included in the total charge for credit are specified in the Consumer Credit (Total Charge for Credit) Regulations 1980 (SI 1980/51), as amended by Consumer Credit (Total Charge for Credit) (Amendment) Regulations (SI 1985/1192), Consumer Credit (Total Charge for Credit and Rebate on Early Settlement) (Amendment) Regulations (SI 1989/596) and Consumer Credit (Total Charge for Credit, Agreements and Advertisements) (Amendment) Regulations (SI 1999/3177); *Huntpast Ltd v Leadbeater* [1993] C.C.L.R. 15; *National Westminster Bank Plc v Devon County Council* [1993] C.C.L.R. 69; *Humberclyde Finance Ltd v Thompson* [1997] C.C.L.R. 23; *Scarborough Building Society v Humberside Trading Standards Department* [1997] C.C.L.R. 47; *Watchtower Investments Ltd v Payne* [2001] EWCA Civ 1159; *Wilson v First County Trust Ltd (No.2)* [2003] UKHL 40; [2004] 1 A.C. 816; *Wilson v Robertsons (London) Ltd* [2005] EWHC 1425; [2000] 1 W.L.R. 1248; *Southern Pacific Securities 05–2 Plc v Walker* [2010] UKSC 32; [2010] 1 W.L.R. 1819.

[73] R.M. Goode, *Consumer Credit Legislation* (Butterworths, 1989), Vol.1, para.43, quoted with approval in the Court of Appeal in *Dimond v Lovell* [2000] 1 Q.B. 216 at 230, per Scott V.C., and without disapproval in the House of Lords: [2000] 2 W.L.R. 1121 at 1128, per Lord Hoffmann (who delivered the leading speech). Cf. Lord Hobhouse, above at 1138H who warned that this "test" is not a universal one, especially in relation to "commercial" matters.

[74] 1974 Act s.9(3).

option to purchase, or any party to the agreement does another specified act or another specified event occurs.[75]

A "consumer credit agreement" is an agreement between an individual ("the debtor") and any other person ("the creditor") by which the creditor provides the debtor with credit of any amount.[76] A consumer credit agreement is a "regulated agreement" if it is not an "exempt agreement".[77]

There is, however, another class of "regulated agreement"—a consumer hire agreement is a regulated agreement if it is not an exempt agreement.[78] A "consumer hire agreement" is an agreement for the hiring of goods to an individual, which is not a hire-purchase agreement, which is capable of subsisting for more than three months.[79]

A "running-account credit" is a facility under a consumer credit agreement whereby the debtor can receive cash, goods and services to a value such that, taking repayments by the debtor into account, the credit limit is not exceeded, the credit limit being in any period the maximum debit balance permissible in the period, disregarding any term of the agreement which allows the maximum to be exceeded merely temporarily.[80] A "fixed-sum credit" is any facility other than a running-account credit under a consumer credit agreement whereby the debtor is enabled to receive credit in one amount or by instalments.[81]

15.10 Exempt agreements—The following are "exempt agreements":

(1) certain debtor-creditor-supplier and debtor-creditor agreements[82] secured over land where the creditor is a local authority, a building society, a bank or a body specified in an order made by the Secretary of State[83];

(2) debtor-creditor-supplier agreements for a fixed-sum credit where the number of payments to be made by the debtor does not exceed four and those payments are to be made within a period not exceeding 12 months with the exception of: (a) agreements financing the purchase of land; (b) conditional sale agreements and hire-purchase agreements; and (c) agreements secured by a pledge (other than a pledge of documents of title or bearer bonds)[84];

(3) debtor-creditor-supplier agreements for running-account credit providing for payments by the debtor in relation to specified periods and requiring that the number of payments to be made in repayment of

---

[75] 1974 Act s.189(1).

[76] 1974 Act s.8(1) (amended by the 2006 Act s.2(1)(a) with full effect from October 1, 2008).

[77] 1974 Act s.8(3) as amended by the 2006 Act s.5(1) with effect from April 6, 2008.

[78] 1974 Act s.15(2). For the definition of "regulated agreement" see s.189(1).

[79] 1974 Act s.15(1); *Eurocopy (Scotland) Plc v Lothian Health Board*, 1995 S.C. 564; 1995 S.C.L.R. 862; 1995 S.L.T. 1356 approved by the House of Lords in *TRM Copy Centres (UK) Ltd v Lanwall Services Ltd* [2009] UKHL 35; [2009] 4 All E.R. 33.

[80] 1974 Act s.10(1), (2). A bank overdraft is a running-account credit (Sch.2, Exs 18, 23).

[81] 1974 Act s.10(1)(b); e.g. a loan granted in instalments or a hire-purchase agreement (Sch.2, Exs 9, 10).

[82] There is a circularity in the definitions: regulated agreements are consumer credit agreements which are not exempt agreements; exempt agreements include debtor-creditor-supplier and debtor-creditor agreements which are defined as including some regulated agreements.

[83] 1974 Act s.16(1); Consumer Credit (Exempt Agreements) Order 1989 (SI 1989/869), as amended (the "1989 Order").

[84] 1989 Order art.3(1)(a)(i) as amended by the Consumer Credit (EU Directive) Regulations 2010 (SI 2010/1010) reg.66; *Zoan v Rouamba* [2000] 1 W.L.R. 1509; *Murphy v Madden*, 2000 G.W.D. 13–460; *Dimond v Lovell* [2000] 2 W.L.R. 1121; *Ketley v Gilbert* [2001] 1 W.L.R. 986.

the whole amount of the credit provided in each such period shall not exceed one (there are the same exceptions as in (2))[85];

(4) debtor-creditor-supplier agreements financing the purchase of land where the number of payments to be made by the debtor does not exceed four[86];

(5) certain debtor-creditor-supplier agreements for fixed-sum credit financing insurance premiums[87];

(6) debtor-creditor agreements with a "credit union"[88] as a creditor and where the "total charge for credit"[89] does not exceed 26.9 per cent[90];

(7) debtor-creditor agreements of a kind not offered to the general public, but offered to a specific class, or particular class of individuals, where the only charge for credit is "interest"[91] which cannot at any time exceed the higher of the sum of one per cent plus the highest of certain "prescribed banks"[92] base rates 28 days before that time.[93] This is inapplicable to agreements where the total amount payable is varied pursuant to a formula set out in the agreements and having "effect by reference to movements in the level of any index or to any other factor"[94];

(8) debtor-creditor agreements of a kind not offered to the general public, but to a specific class, or particular classes, of individuals where the rate or amount of an item included in the total charge for credit (or which would be included but for reg.14 of the Total Charge for Credit Regulations 1980)[95] cannot be increased after the "relevant date",[96] and where the rate of the total cannot be greater than the sum of 1 per cent plus the highest of certain "prescribed banks" base rates 28 days before the making of the agreement.[97] The same qualification concerning the provision's applicability as in (7) above applies to (8)[98];

(9) agreements made in connection with trade in goods or services between the United Kingdom and other countries or within a country or between countries outside the United Kingdom, being agreements under which credit is provided to the debtor in the course of a business carried on by him[99];

---

[85] 1989 Order art.3(1)(a)(ii).

[86] 1989 Order art.3(1)(b).

[87] 1989 Order art.3(1)(c), (d).

[88] "Credit union" is defined in 1989 Order art.4(4) (as amended).

[89] "Total charge for credit" is defined in s.189(1) of the 1974 Act.

[90] 1989 Order art.4(1)(a) (as substituted by the Consumer Credit (Exempt Agreements) (Amendment) Order 1999 (SI 1999/1956) art.3) and amended by SI 2006/1273 arts 2, 3. The 1999 Order revoked the Consumer Credit (Exempt Agreements) (Amendment) Order 1998 (SI 1998/1944).

[91] "Interest" is defined in 1989 Order art.4(4) (as substituted by Consumer Credit (Exempt Agreements) (Amendment) Order 1999 (SI 1999/1956), which revoked Consumer Credit (Exempt Agreements) (Amendment) Order 1998 (SI 1998/1944)).

[92] 1989 Order. The prescribed banks are listed in art.4(3).

[93] 1989 Order art.4(1)(b).

[94] 1989 Order art.4(2).

[95] Total Charge for Credit Regulations 1980 (SI 1980/51), as amended by Consumer Credit (Total Charge for Credit) (Amendment) Regulations 1985 (SI 1985/1192) and Consumer Credit (Total Charge for Credit and Rebate on Early Settlement) (Amendment) Regulations 1989 (SI 1989/596).

[96] "Relevant date" is defined in art.4(4) of the 1989 Order and has the same meaning as in the Total Charge for Credit Regulations 1980 (SI 1980/51), as amended by SI 1985/1192 and SI 1989/596.

[97] 1989 Order art.4(1)(c).

[98] 1989 Order art.4(2).

[99] 1989 Order art.5(a). As to a further exemption where the creditor is listed and the debtor is connected with the US forces, see art.5(b).

(10) consumer hire agreements for meters or metering equipment owned by electricity, gas or water suppliers[100];

(11) consumer credit agreements where the creditor is a housing authority and the agreement is secured on a dwelling[101];

(12) consumer credit agreements or consumer hire agreements[102] where: (1) the debtor or hirer is a natural person; (2) in the case of a consumer credit agreement other than an agreement secured on land, the agreement is for credit which exceeds £60,260[103]; (3) the agreement includes a declaration made by him to the effect that he agrees to forgo the protection and remedies that would be available to him under the Act if the agreement were a regulated agreement[104]; (4) a statement of high net worth has been made to him[105]; (5) that statement was made during the period of one year ending with the day on which the agreement was made; and (6) a copy of it was provided to the creditor or owner before the agreement was made.[106] A statement of high net worth is a statement to the effect that, in the opinion of the person making it, the natural person in relation to whom it is made received during the previous financial year income of a specified description totalling not less than the specified amount, or had throughout that year net assets of a specified description with a total value of not less than the specified value[107];

(13) consumer credit and consumer hire agreements entered into by the debtor or hirer wholly or predominantly for the purposes of a business carried on, or intended to be carried on, by him where the credit provided or hire payments to be made exceed £25,000.[108] An agreement will be presumed to be wholly or predominantly for business purposes where it includes a declaration by the debtor or hirer to that effect,[109] unless at the time it was made, the creditor or owner, or any person who has acted on his behalf in connection with the entering into of the agreement, knows or has reasonable cause to suspect, that the declaration is not true[110];

(14) Credit agreements which are secured by a mortgage on land where less than 40 per cent of the land is used or intended to be used as a dwelling

---

[100] 1989 Order art.6.

[101] 1974 Act s.16(6A).

[102] Consumer Credit (Exempt Agreements) Order 2007 (SI 2007/1168) (in force with effect from April 6, 2008) (made under powers conferred in the 1974 Act s.16A(1)–(7) (added by the 2006 Act s.3)).

[103] Added to SI 2007/1168 reg.2 by the Consumer Credit (EU Directive) Regulations 2010 (SI 2010/1010) reg.92.

[104] SI 2007/1168 art.3, Sch.1. This does not affect the application of the provisions on unfair relationships contained in the 1974 Act ss.140A–140C; see the1974 Act s.16A(8) (added by the 2006 Act s.3) (with effect from April 6, 2008)

[105] SI 2007/1168 arts 4, 5, Sch.2.

[106] SI 2007/1168 art.2(a)–(e).

[107] 1974 Act s.16A(2) (added by the 2006 Act s.3). The specified amount of income is £150,000 and the specified value of net assets is £500,000: see SI 2007/1168 Sch.2 (in force with effect from April 6, 2008).

[108] 1974 Act s.16B(1) (added by the 2006 Act s.4) (with effect from April 6, 2008). The application of 1974 Act ss.140A–140C (added by the 2006 Act ss.19–21) relating to unfair relationships is not affected.

[109] 1974 Act s.16B(2) (with effect from April 6, 2008). For the form of the declaration, see SI 2007/1168 art.6, Sch.3 (in force with effect from April 6, 2008).

[110] 1974 Act s.16B(3) (with effect from April 6, 2008).

by the debtor or person connected with him (or as a beneficiary under a trust where the credit is provided to the trustee).[111]

Restricted-use agreements—A "restricted-use agreement" is a regulated **15.11** consumer credit agreement of one of three types: (a) financing a transaction between the debtor and the creditor; (b) financing a transaction between the debtor and someone other than the creditor (the "supplier") whose identity need not be known when the agreement is made; (c) refinancing any existing indebtedness to the creditor or another person.[112] It has been held, in relation to a restricted-use agreement, that there needs to be "an express or implied term that the loan shall be used for . . . [the] purpose" of financing a transaction or re-financing existing indebtedness.[113] It is important to note that an agreement is not a restricted-use one if credit is in fact provided in such a way as to leave the debtor free to use it as he chooses, even though certain uses would contravene that or any other agreement.[114] An "unrestricted-use agreement" is a regulated consumer credit agreement which is not a restricted-use one.[115]

Creditor-supplier "arrangements"—A consumer credit agreement is made **15.12** under pre-existing arrangements between a creditor and a supplier if it is entered into in accordance with, or in furtherance of, arrangements previously made between the creditor or his associate and the supplier or his associate.[116] "Associates" are, broadly, relatives, partners and controlled bodies corporate.[117] A consumer credit agreement is entered into in contemplation of future arrangements if it is entered into in the expectation that arrangements will subsequently be made between the creditor or his associate and the supplier or his associate for the supply of cash, goods or services to be financed by the agreement.[118] If the creditor is an associate of the supplier's, the agreement is treated as entered into under pre-existing arrangements unless the contrary is proved.[119] Arrangements are disregarded if they are merely arrangements for the making, in specified circumstances, of payments to the supplier by the creditor and the creditor holds himself out as willing to make, in such circumstances, payments of the kind to suppliers generally.[120] Arrangements are also disregarded if they are for the electronic transfer of funds from a current account at a bank.[121]

Debtor-creditor-supplier agreements—A "debtor-creditor-supplier agreement" **15.13** is a regulated consumer credit agreement being:

---

[111] 1974 Act s.16C(1)–(4) (added by the Legislative Reform (Consumer Credit) Order 2008 (SI 2008/2826) art.3) (with effect from October 31, 2008). Examples would be buy to let properties. Debtors under such agreements are able to take advantage of the unfair relationship provisions in the 1974 Act see s.16C(6).

[112] 1974 Act s.11(1). In relation to (b), see also s.11(4). *Office of Fair Trading v Lloyds TSB Bank Plc* [2006] EWCA Civ 268. Permission to appeal on this point to the House of Lords was refused.

[113] *Story v National Westminster Bank Plc* [1999] Lloyd's Rep. Bank 261 at 268, per Auld L.J.

[114] 1974 Act s.11(3).

[115] 1974 Act s.11(2).

[116] 1974 Act s.187(1). For discussion of the meaning of "arrangements" see *Office of Fair Trading v Lloyds TSB Bank Plc* [2006] EWCA Civ 268; [2006] 3 W.L.R. 452. An appeal on another point dismissed, see [2007] UKHL 48; [2008] 1 All E.R. 205.

[117] 1974 Act s.184.

[118] 1974 Act s.187(2). See case referred to at fn.63 above.

[119] 1974 Act s.187(5).

[120] 1974 Act s.187(3).

[121] 1974 Act s.187(3A), inserted by Banking Act 1987 s.89.

(a) one financing a transaction between the debtor and the creditor; or
(b) one financing a transaction between the debtor and the supplier with "arrangements", pre-existing or contemplated; or
(c) an unrestricted-use agreement with pre-existing "arrangements" and knowledge on the part of the creditor that the credit is to be used to finance a transaction between the debtor and the supplier.[122]

A "debtor-creditor agreement" is a regulated consumer credit agreement being:

(a) one financing a transaction between the debtor and the supplier without "arrangements"; or
(b) one refinancing any existing indebtedness to the creditor or another person; or
(c) an unrestricted-use agreement without "arrangements" and without knowledge on the part of the creditor that the credit is to be used to finance a transaction between the debtor and the supplier.[123]

15.14 Other definitions—A "multiple agreement" is an agreement part of which falls within one category of agreement and part in another or an agreement which, or part of which, falls within two or more categories of agreement mentioned in the Act.[124] A part of a multiple agreement is to be treated as a separate agreement.[125] Multiple agreements have as their primary rationale stopping the

> "frustration of the Act's protection to borrowers by the artificial combination of two or more agreements in one so as to take the total credit negotiated above the limit qualifying for protection".[126]

The provision in the Act dealing with such agreements has been the subject of academic and professional controversy for lacking clarity.[127] However, it has been held that a multiple agreement does not include an "accident car hire agreement",[128] which appears

> "to sever the provisions that create the debt (hiring the car) from the provisions that allow credit for payment of the debt. Whatever a multiple

---

[122] 1974 Act s.12; e.g. a bank credit-card agreement so far as it relates to goods (Sch.2, Ex.16). See case referred to at fn.63 above.

[123] 1974 Act s.13; e.g. an agreement for a bank overdraft (Sch.2, Ex.18).

[124] 1974 Act s.18(1).

[125] 1974 Act s.18(2).

[126] *Story v National Westminster Bank Plc* [1999] Lloyd's Rep. Bank 261, per Auld L.J. at 265.

[127] *Story v National Westminster Bank Plc* [1999] Lloyd's Rep. Bank 261. See also *Goshawk Dedicated (No.2) Ltd v Governor and Company of the Bank of Scotland* [2005] EWHC 2906 (Ch); [2006] 2 All E.R. 610; and *Heath v Southern Pacific Mortgage Ltd* [2009] EWHC 103 (Ch); [2009] All E.R. (D) 267.

[128] These agreements involve a party whose car has been damaged by another driver entering into a contract with an "accident car hire company" under which that company provides a substitute car to the victim, who assigns their claim against the other driver (the wrongdoer) to the "accident car hire company", see *Dimond v Lovell* [2000] 2 W.L.R. 1121 at 1124 and 1125–6. Other terms used to describe these contracts include: "replacement vehicle hire agreement", see *Zoan v Rouamba* [2000] 1 W.L.R. 1509 at 1514B, per Chadwick L.J.; and "accident hire agreement", see J.K. MacLeod, "Credit Hire in the House of Lords" [2001] J.B.L. 14 at 20. In *Dimond v Lovell* [2000] 2 W.L.R. 1121 at 1124, Lord Nicholls of Birkenhead refers to "accident car hire" companies; Lord Hoffmann refers, at 1126, to "accident hire company".

agreement may be, one cannot divide up a contract in that way. The creation of the debt and the terms on which it is payable must form parts of the same agreement. The . . . hiring agreement was a single contract".[129]

Furthermore, it has been said, obiter, that

"the word 'part' in . . . [the 'context' of multiple agreements] includes, but is not restricted to, a facility that is different as to some of its terms from another facility granted under the same agreement or one that can stand on its own as a separate contract bargain",[130]
i.e. it is to be interpreted broadly and
"include . . . a separate facility provided with others under an agreement where, even if the facility as a contractual entitlement does not stand on its own, the debtor's use, or non-use, of it does not affect the contractual nature of agreement as a whole, in particular, his entitlement to use those other facilities".[131]

By contrast, "category", in relation to "categories of agreement", should have a narrower interpretation, and be applicable only to the different categories within Pt II of the Act, rather than every type of agreement referred to in the Act.[132] A transaction, other than one for the provision of security, is a "linked transaction" in relation to an actual or prospective regulated agreement (the "principal agreement") if it is entered into by the debtor or his relative in compliance with a term of the principal agreement, or if it is financed by a principal debtor-creditor-supplier agreement, or if the other party to the transaction is a person of a specified class and the transaction is suggested by a person of a specified class and it is entered into to induce the creditor to enter into the principal agreement, or for another purpose related to the principal agreement, or, where the principal agreement is a restricted use credit agreement, for a purpose related to a transaction financed, or to be financed, by the principal agreement; the specified classes of persons are: the creditor, his associate, a person who knows that the principal agreement has been made or who contemplated that it might be made and a person who, in the negotiation of the transaction, is represented by a credit-broker who is also a negotiator in antecedent negotiations for the principal agreement.[133] A linked transaction entered into before the principal agreement has no effect until that agreement is made.[134]

A "small agreement" is: (a) a regulated consumer credit agreement for credit not exceeding £50 other than a hire-purchase or conditional sale agreement; or (b) a regulated consumer hire agreement which does not require the hirer to make payments exceeding £50, being, in either case, an agreement which is unsecured or secured only by a guarantee or indemnity.[135]

---

[129] *Dimond v Lovell* [2000] 2 W.L.R. 1121 at 1130, per Lord Hoffmann.
[130] *Story v National Westminster Bank Plc* [1999] Lloyd's Rep. Bank 261 at 266, per Auld L.J.
[131] *Story v National Westminster Bank Plc* [1999] Lloyd's Rep. Bank 261.
[132] This includes ss.11 and 18.
[133] 1974 Act s.19. The "negotiator" is defined by s.56(1).
[134] 1974 Act s.19(3). For exceptions see Consumer Credit (Linked Transactions) (Exemptions) Regulations 1983 (SI 1983/1560).
[135] 1974 Act s.17(1); Consumer Credit (Increase of Monetary Limits) Order 1983 (SI 1983/1878), as amended by SI 1998/996. There are provisions to prevent evasion by the splitting of an agreement into several small agreements: s.17(3), (4).

A "non-commercial agreement" is a consumer credit or hire agreement not made by the creditor or owner in the course of a business carried on by him.[136]

15.15 Regulated agreements—The provisions of the Act which affect regulated agreements generally are summarised in this section[137]; thereafter, provisions affecting special kinds of regulated agreement will be noticed.

In the antecedent negotiations, the negotiator is deemed to be the creditor's agent and he cannot validly be made the debtor's agent.[138] Regulated agreements must be in the prescribed form and have the prescribed content.[139] The document must be readily legible, must be signed by the debtor and the creditor and must embody all the terms of the agreement other than implied terms.[140] The debtor must be given a copy of the executed agreement and, if the agreement does not become executed when he signs it, a copy of the unexecuted agreement.[141] An agreement which does not conform to the foregoing requirements is "improperly-executed" and is enforceable, if at all, only on the order of the court.[142] It has been held by the House of Lords, in an English case, that an accident car hire agreement, on its wording, was a "regulated agreement".[143] "Unjust enrichment", in

---

[136] 1974 Act s.189(1). The following do not apply to a non-commercial agreement: ss.55, 57–73, 75, 77–80, 82, 83, 103, 107–10, 112 and 114–23.

[137] References to the "debtor" include references to the hirer. There are important exceptions to some of the following provisions. Part V (ss.55–74), dealing with entry into agreements, does not, except for s.56, apply to non-commercial agreements or to certain current account overdraft agreements or to certain debtor-creditor agreements to finance certain payments arising on death: s.74(1); Consumer Credit (Payments Arising on Death) Regulations 1983 (SI 1983/1554); and does not, except for s.56, apply to a small debtor-creditor-supplier agreement for restricted-use credit: s.74(2). There are exceptions to the exception where a term of the agreement is expressed in writing: s.74(4). The seeking of business is governed by ss.43–54; the Consumer Credit (Advertisements) Regulations 2004 (SI 2004/1484); Consumer Credit (Content of Quotations) and Consumer Credit (Advertisements) (Amendment) Regulations 1999 (SI 1999/2725), as amended. See *Jenkins v Lombard North Central Plc* [1984] 1 W.L.R. 307; *R. v Secretary of State for Trade and Industry, Ex p. First National Bank Plc* [1990] C.C.L.R. 105; *Metsoja v H. Norman Pitt & Co Ltd* [1990] C.C.L.R. 12; *Ford Credit Plc v Normand*, 1994 S.L.T. 318; *Clydesdale Group Plc v Normand*, 1994 S.L.T. 1302; *Carrington Carr Ltd v Leicestershire County Council* [1994] C.C.L.R. 14; *Rover Group Ltd v Sumner* [1995] C.C.L.R. 1; *R. v Mumford and Aherne* [1995] C.C.L.R. 16; (s.46); *Alliance & Leicester Building Society v Babbs* [1993] C.C.L.R. 77 at 80–81, per Wright J. Discrimination in providing credit facilities is unlawful: Equality Act 2010 ss.13 and 29(1).

[138] 1974 Act s.56. On s.56, see *UDT v Whitfield* [1987] C.C.L.R. 60; *Powell v Lloyd's Bowmaker Ltd*, 1995 S.L.T. (Sh. Ct) 117 (which did not apply to the *UDT* case); *Forthright Finance Ltd v Ingate* [1997] C.C.L.R. 95 (which approved the *UDT* case and disapproved the *Lloyds Bowmaker* case); *Lombard North Central Plc v Gate* [1998] C.C.L.R. 52 (s.56 does not refer to "sureties"). *Blackhorse Ltd v Langford* [2007] EWHC 907 (QB); [2007] RTR 38 demonstrates the limitations of s.56.

[139] 1974 Act s.60; Consumer Credit (Agreements) Regulations 1983 (SI 1983/1553), as amended. As to information about variation of the interest rate by the creditor, see *Lombard Tricity Finance Ltd v Paton* [1989] C.C.L.R. 21, but see *Paragon Finance Plc v Staunton* [2001] EWCA Civ 1466.

[140] 1974 Act s.61; *P.B. Leasing Ltd v Patel* [1995] C.C.L.R. 82; *Bhoyrub v Cadzow*, 1999 S.C.L.R. 539, Sh. Ct; *Dimond v Lovell* [2000] 2 W.L.R. 1121.

[141] 1974 Act ss.62, 63.

[142] 1974 Act s.65; *Bhoyrub v Cadzow*, 1999 S.C.L.R. 539, Sh. Ct; *Dimond v Lovell* [2000] 2 W.L.R. 1121. See also s.127(3) concerning enforcement orders in relation to s.65(1). Section 127(3) has been held to be compatible with the Human Rights Act 1998 (c.42), in England, see *Wilson v First County Trust Ltd (No.2)* [2003] UKHL 40; [2004] 1 A.C. 816. In relation to agreements entered into after April 6, 2007, s.127(3)–(5) which, in some circumstances, prevented an enforcement order being made ceased to have effect, by virtue of the Consumer Credit Act 2006 s.15 and the Consumer Credit Act 2006 (Commencement No.2 and Transitional Provisions and Savings) Order 2007 art.3(2) and Sch.2. Agreements made before that time are subject to those subsections by virtue of the Consumer Credit Act 2006 s.69(1) and Sch.3 para.11.

[143] *Dimond v Lovell* [2000] 2 W.L.R. 1121.

relation to this provision, has been rejected.[144] A debtor under a regulated consumer credit agreement, other than an excluded agreement, may within 14 days beginning with the day after the relevant day[145] withdraw from the agreement, without giving any reason.[146] An agreement may be cancelled by the debtor within a specified period if the antecedent negotiations included oral representation made by the negotiator in the presence of the debtor, unless the agreement is secured on land, or is for the purchase of land, or the debtor signed the agreement at the premises of the creditor or the negotiator or any party to a linked transaction.[147] Any linked transaction is also cancelled.[148] Notice of his cancellation rights must be given to the debtor.[149] There are provisions for the recovery of sums paid by the debtor,[150] the return of goods and the repayment of any credit extended on cancellation[151]; these provisions also operate, so far as applicable, where the debtor has withdrawn from a prospective regulated agreement.[152]

Restrictions are placed by s.76 of the 1974 Act on the creditor's liberty to do any of the following acts whether he is acting under the terms of the agreement, or by reason of a breach of the agreement by the debtor:

   (i) demanding earlier payment of any sum;
   (ii) recovering possession of any goods or land;
  (iii) treating any right of the debtor (other than a right to draw credit) as terminated, restricted or deferred;
  (iv) terminating the agreement; or
   (v) enforcing any security.

In general, he cannot do any of these acts without giving notice to the debtor[153] and the debtor, on receipt of the notice, can apply to the court for relief. The creditor cannot enforce a term of an agreement by doing any of (i), (ii) or (iii) during the specified period of duration of the agreement without giving not less than seven days' notice to the debtor, unless the right to enforce arises from the debtor's breach of the agreement.[154] Similarly, the creditor cannot terminate the agreement for reasons other than the debtor's breach during the specified period

---

[144] *Dimond v Lovell* [2000] 2 W.L.R. 1121, per Lord Hoffmann at 1131.

[145] For the "relevant day" see 1974 Act s.66A(3).

[146] 1974 Act s.66A inserted by the Consumer Credit (EU Directive) Regulations 2010 (SI 2010/1010) reg.13, as of February 1, 2011. It does not apply to certain types of agreement specified in s.74.

[147] 1974 Act ss.67–69. A statement of fact or opinion or a future undertaking capable of inducing a debtor to enter into a credit agreement amounts to a "representation" entitling the debtor, who signs the credit agreement at his premises, to be told of his right to cancellation under s.67, see *Moorgate Services Ltd v Kabir* [1995] C.C.L.R. 74.

[148] 1974 Act s.69(1)(i). For exceptions, see Consumer Credit (Linked Transactions) (Exemptions) Regulations 1983 (SI 1983/1560).

[149] 1974 Act s.64; Consumer Credit (Cancellation Notices and Copies of Documents) Regulations 1983 (1983/1557) as amended.

[150] 1974 Act s.70; *Colesworthy v Collmain Services Ltd* [1993] C.C.L.R. 4.

[151] 1974 Act ss.71–72; Consumer Credit (Repayment of Credit on Cancellation) Regulations 1983 (SI 1983/1559).

[152] 1974 Act s.57.

[153] Consumer Credit (Enforcement, Default and Termination Notices) Regulations 1983 (SI 1983/1561), as amended; *Woodchester Lease Management Services Ltd v Swain & Co (a firm)* [1999] 1 W.L.R. 263.

[154] 1974 Act s.76. A right of enforcement arising by reason of breach of the agreement is not affected: s.76(6); nor is the creditor's right to restrict or defer the drawing on any credit: s.76(4).

of duration of the agreement without giving not less than seven days' notice to the debtor.[155]

If, under a power contained in the agreement, the creditor varies the agreement, the variation does not take effect before notice of it is given to the debtor in the prescribed manner.[156] The creditor is obliged to give the debtor, on request and payment of a fee, information as to the state of the debt,[157] and the debtor is under a similar duty to inform the creditor as to the whereabouts of any goods to which the agreement relates and which are required by the agreement to be kept in the debtor's possession or control.[158] There are rules as to the appropriation of payments where there are two or more agreements.[159]

A credit-broker, a supplier or a negotiator is deemed to be the creditor's agent for the purpose of receiving any notice rescinding the agreement.[160]

It is an offence for a trader to fail to give a customer who serves an appropriate notice on him a counter-notice stating either that the customer's indebtedness is discharged or his grounds for alleging that the indebtedness is not discharged.[161]

15.16 Debtor's death—On the debtor's death, the creditor in an agreement which has a specified period of duration which has not ended cannot do any of the acts (i) to (v) specified in para.16.09, above, if at the death the agreement is fully secured.[162] If the agreement is only partly secured or is unsecured, he can do them only on an order of the court which will be made only if the creditor proves that he has been unable to satisfy himself that the debtor's present and future obligations under the agreement are likely to be discharged.[163]

15.17 Default—Where there is a breach of the agreement by the debtor the creditor cannot by reason of the breach do any of the acts (i) to (v) specified in para.16.09, above, unless he has served on the debtor a default notice in the prescribed form.[164] Such a notice cannot be served until the creditor, under a regulated running-account or fixed-sum agreement, (but not non-commercial agreements or small agreements) has provided the debtor with a notice regarding arrears.[165] The default notice must specify, inter alia, what action is required to remedy the breach, or, if the breach is not capable of remedy, the compensation required to be paid therefore[166] and include a copy of the current default information sheet prepared by the

---

[155] 1974 Act s.98.

[156] 1974 Act s.82; Consumer Credit (Notice of Variation of Agreements) Regulations 1977 (SI 1977/328), as amended by SI 1979/661 and 667 and the Consumer Credit (EU Directive) Regulations 2010 (SI 2010/1010).

[157] 1974 Act ss.77–79; Consumer Credit (Prescribed Periods for Giving Information) Regulations 1983 (SI 1983/1569); Consumer Credit (Running-Account Credit Information) Regulations 1983 (SI 1983/1570) as amended.

[158] 1974 Act s.80.

[159] 1974 Act s.81.

[160] 1974 Act s.102.

[161] 1974 Act s.103.

[162] 1974 Act s.86. The creditor may, however, restrict or defer the drawing on any credit: s.86(4); and the section does not affect the operation of an agreement that sums will be paid out of the proceeds of a policy of assurance on the debtor's life: s.86(5).

[163] 1974 Act s.128.

[164] 1974 Act s.87; *Lombard North Central Plc v Power-Hines* [1995] C.C.L.R. 24; *John Lewis Plc v Siwek*, 1998 S.C. 875; *Woodchester Lease Management Services Ltd v Swain & Co (a firm)* [1999] 1 W.L.R. 263. See also fn.89, above.

[165] 1974 Act ss.86A–86E inserted by inserted by the 2006 Act ss.8–12.

[166] 1974 Act s.88.

OFT under s.86A. If the action is taken or the compensation paid within a period of not less than 14 days specified in the notice, the breach shall be treated as not having occurred.[167] Summary diligence cannot be used to enforce payment of a debt due under a regulated agreement or under any security related thereto.[168]

Time orders—There are four ways in which the agreement can come before the   **15.18** court: (a) when the creditor applies for an enforcement order; (b) on an application by the debtor, after service of a default notice, a notice of termination, or a notice of intention to do the acts (i), (ii) or (iii) specified in para.16.09, above, under the agreement; (c) when the creditor brings an action to enforce the agreement or a security, or to recover possession of any goods or land; and (d) on an application by the debtor who has received a notice of sums in arrears under either a fix-sum or running-account credit agreement as required by ss.86B and 86C of the 1974 Act.[169]

In any of these circumstances, the court may make a "time order" providing for payment by instalments of any sum due under the agreement or for the remedying of any breach other than non-payment of money by the debtor within a specified time.[170] A time order cannot be made if a time to pay direction or order[171] has previously been made in relation to the debt.[172] Payment by instalments can be ordered only where it appears just to do so, and, in considering what is just, the creditor's position, as well as the debtor's, must be taken into account.[173] In any order made in relation to an agreement, the court may make the operation of a term conditional on the doing of certain acts by any party or may suspend the operation of any term.[174] The court may also include in the order such provision as it considers just for amending the agreement or security in consequence of a term of the order.[175] On the application of the creditor or owner, the court may make such order as it thinks just for the protection of his property or of property, subject to a security pending the determination of the proceedings.[176]

Enforcement orders—Where an application is made for an enforcement order,   **15.19** there are some situations in relation to agreements made before April 6, 2007 in which the court cannot make the order, e.g. where the agreement was a cancellable one and the debtor was not given a notice of his right to cancel. In relation to agreements made after April 6, 2007 these provisions will not apply.[177] In other situations, e.g. in the case of some improperly executed agreements, the court is to dismiss the application if it considers it just to do so having regard to the prejudice caused to any person by the contravention in question and the degree of

---

[167] 1974 Act s.89.

[168] 1974 Act s.93A, inserted by Debtors (Scotland) Act 1987 Sch.6 para.16.

[169] 1974 Act s.129(1)(ba) inserted into subs.(1), from October 1, 2008, by virtue of the 2006 Act s.16(1) and the 2007 Order art.3(3) and Sch.3.

[170] 1974 Act s.129; *Cedar Holdings Ltd v Thompson* [1993] C.C.L.R. 7; *Murie McDougall Ltd v Sinclair*, 1994 S.L.T. (Sh. Ct) 74; cf. *Southern and District Finance Plc v Barnes* [1995] C.C.L.R. 62, CA.

[171] See para.15.09, above.

[172] 1974 Act s.129(3), inserted by Debtors (Scotland) Act 1987 Sch.6 para.17.

[173] *First National Bank Plc v Syed* [1991] C.C.L.R. 37, CA.

[174] 1974 Act s.135.

[175] 1974 Act s.136; *Murie McDougall Ltd v Sinclair*, 1994 S.L.T. (Sh. Ct) 74; cf. *National Guardian Mortgage Corp v Wilkes* [1993] C.C.L.R. 1; *Cedar Holdings Ltd v Thompson* [1993] C.C.L.R. 7; *Southern and District Finance Plc v Barnes* [1995] C.C.L.R. 62 at 67–8, per Leggatt L.J.

[176] 1974 Act s.131.

[177] 1974 Act s.127(4). See fn.89, above.

culpability for it and having regard also to the court's powers, already mentioned, to make conditional or suspended orders or to vary the terms of the agreement.[178] In an enforcement order, the court may reduce or discharge any sum payable by the debtor or by a surety to compensate him for any loss suffered as a result of the contravention.[179] Where the agreement is not in the correct form but the debtor did sign a document containing all the prescribed terms, the order may direct that the agreement is to have effect as if it did not include a term omitted from that document.[180]

15.20 Securities—Documents embodying regulated agreements have to embody any security[181] provided in relation to the agreement by the debtor.[182] If the person by whom a security is provided (the "surety") is not the debtor, the security must be expressed in writing. The document containing all the terms of the security other than implied terms must be signed by or on behalf of the surety and a copy of the document and the principal agreement given to him.[183] If these requirements are not satisfied, the security is enforceable against the surety only on an order of the court. If an application for such an order is dismissed (except on technical grounds) the security is treated as never having effect; property lodged with the creditor for purposes of the security must be returned; any entry relating to the security in any register must be cancelled; and any amount received by the creditor on realisation of the security must be repaid to the surety.[184] There is a partial exemption for heritable securities.[185] The creditor is obliged to give the surety on request a copy of the principal agreement and of the security instrument and information about the present state of the debtor's indebtedness.[186]

A copy of any default notice served on the debtor must be served on the surety.[187] A security cannot be enforced so as to benefit the creditor to an extent greater than would be the case if there were no security and the obligations of the debtor were carried out to the extent (if any) to which they would be enforced under the Act.[188] Accordingly, if a regulated agreement is enforceable only on a court order, or on an order of the OFT, the security is enforceable only where an order has been made[189] and, generally, if the agreement is cancelled or becomes unenforceable, the security becomes ineffective.[190] The point is the

---

[178] 1974 Act s.127(1); *Wilson v First County Trust Ltd (No.2)* [2001] 3 W.L.R. 42 at 53–4; *Harrison v Link Financial Limited* [2011] EWHC 1653 (QB). On what amounts to enforcement see *McGuffick v Royal Bank of Scotland Plc* [2009] EWHC 2386 (Comm); [2010] 1 All E.R. 634.

[179] 1974 Act s.127(2); *National Guardian Mortgage Corp v Wilkes* [1993] C.C.L.R. 1; *Rank Xerox Finance Ltd v Hepple* [1994] C.C.L.R. 1, County Ct.

[180] 1974 Act s.127(5).

[181] A "security" means a mortgage (including a heritable security), charge, pledge, bond, debenture, indemnity, guarantee, bill, note or other right provided by the debtor or at his request to secure the carrying out of his obligations: s.189(1). Note, however, that a document "embodies" a provision if the provision is set out either in the document itself or in another document referred to in it: s.189(4).

[182] 1974 Act s.105(9); reg.2(8) of the Consumer Credit (Agreements) Regulations 1983 (SI 1983/1553), as amended.

[183] 1974 Act s.105. A guarantee or indemnity must be in the prescribed form: Consumer Credit (Guarantees and Indemnities) Regulations 1983 (SI 1983/1556) as amended by the Consumer Credit Act 1974 (Electronic Communications) Order 2004 (SI 2004/3236).

[184] 1974 Act s.106.

[185] 1974 Act s.177(5).

[186] 1974 Act ss.107–110.

[187] 1974 Act s.111.

[188] 1974 Act s.113(1).

[189] 1974 Act s.113(2).

[190] 1974 Act s.113(3).

same where security is given with regard to a linked transaction, either actual or prospective.[191]

Enterprise Act enforcement orders—The OFT and, in certain prescribed **15.21** circumstances, other enforcement agencies may seek enforcement orders under Pt 8 of the Enterprise Act 2002 to stop breaches of the 1974 Act.[192]

Pledges[193]—It is an offence to take an article "in pawn" from a minor.[194] It is also **15.22** an offence for the "pawnee" to fail to give the "pawnor" a copy of the agreement, notice of his cancellation rights and a pawn-receipt.[195] The pawn is redeemable during the "redemption period", i.e. six months after it was taken or the period fixed for the duration of the credit, if longer, or such longer period as the parties may agree; the pawn remains redeemable after the expiry of the redemption period until it is realised or the property in it passes to the pawnee.[196] No special charges or higher charges for safe-keeping of the pawn can be made on redemption after the expiry of the redemption period.[197]

The pawnee must deliver the pawn on surrender of the receipt and payment of the amount owing unless he knows or suspects that the bearer of the receipt is not the owner of the pawn.[198] If the owner claiming the pawn does not have the receipt he may make a statutory declaration (or, where the loan is not over £75,[199] a written statement in prescribed form) which is treated as the receipt.[200] It is an offence to fail without reasonable cause to allow redemption of a pawn.[201] Where a pawn is an article which has been stolen or obtained by fraud the court which has convicted a person of the offence may order delivery of the pawn to the owner subject to such conditions as to payment of the debt as it thinks fit.[202]

If the credit does not exceed £75, and the pawn has not been redeemed at the end of a redemption period of six months, the property in the pawn passes to the pawnee.[203] In other cases, the pawn becomes realisable if it has not been redeemed at the end of the redemption period.[204] The pawnor must be given notice of the pawnee's intention to sell and, after the sale, information as to the sale, its proceeds and expenses. If the net proceeds are not less than the debt, the debt is discharged and any surplus is payable to the pawnor; otherwise the debt is reduced pro tanto. On challenge, it is for the pawnee to prove that he used reasonable care to ensure

---

[191] 1974 Act s.113(8); *Citibank International Plc v Schleider, The Times*, March 26, 1999.

[192] These orders are discussed in Ch.14. See para.14.02.

[193] The provisions as to pledges do not apply to pledges of documents of title or of bearer bonds or to non-commercial agreements: 1974 Act s.114(3), as amended by Banking Act 1979 s.38(2).

[194] 1974 Act s.114(2).

[195] 1974 Act s.115. The form of receipt is prescribed by the Consumer Credit (Agreements) Regulations 1983 (SI 1983/1553) as amended, reg.4, Schs 1 and 2, where it is combined with the document embodying the agreement and otherwise by the Consumer Credit (Pawn Receipts) Regulations 1983 (SI 1983/1566) as amended.

[196] 1974 Act s.116. *Wilson v Robertsons (London) Ltd* [2005] EWHC 1425 (Ch); [2005] 3 All E.R. 873.

[197] 1974 Act s.116(4).

[198] 1974 Act s.117.

[199] Consumer Credit (Further Increase of Monetary Amounts) Order 1998 (SI 1998/997), revoking Consumer Credit (Increase of Monetary Amounts) Order 1983 (SI 1983/1571).

[200] 1974 Act s.118; Consumer Credit (Loss of Pawn-Receipt) Regulations 1983 (SI 1983/1567).

[201] 1974 Act s.119.

[202] 1974 Act s.122.

[203] 1974 Act s.120(1).

[204] 1974 Act s.120(2).

that the true market value was obtained and that the expenses of sale were reasonable.[205]

15.23 Negotiable instruments—Except in the case of a non-commercial agreement, a negotiable instrument cannot be taken as a security for discharge of a sum due under a regulated agreement and a negotiable instrument other than a bank note or cheque cannot be taken from a debtor or surety in discharge of a sum payable.[206] The person who takes the negotiable instrument is not a holder in due course and is not entitled to enforce it.[207] A cheque taken in discharge cannot be negotiated except to a banker[208] and negotiation to a non-banker is a defect in the negotiator's title.[209] Contravention of these provisions makes the agreement or security enforceable on order of the court only.[210] The rights of a holder in due course of a negotiable instrument are not affected but where the debtor or surety becomes liable to a holder in due course as a result of a contravention of these provisions the creditor must indemnify him.[211]

15.24 Consumer credit agreements—The debtor under a regulated consumer credit agreement is not liable to the creditor for any loss arising from use of the credit facility by another person not acting, or to be treated as acting, as the debtor's agent.[212] The debtor is entitled to discharge his indebtedness under the agreement at any time by notice to the creditor and payment of all amounts due to the creditor; the debtor may be entitled to a rebate for early payment.[213]

There is a restriction on the rate of interest which can be charged on sums which the debtor, in breach of the agreement, has not paid.[214]

15.25 Agreements about goods—The creditor under a regulated hire purchase, conditional sale or consumer hire agreement cannot enter premises to take possession of the goods except under an order of the court.[215] Contravention is actionable as a breach of statutory duty. Where, after the making of a time order in relation to

---

[205] 1974 Act s.121. Consumer Credit (Realisation of Pawn) Regulations 1983 (SI 1983/1568), as amended by Consumer Credit (Realisation of Pawn) (Amendment) Regulations (SI 1998/998); see also *Mathew v T.M. Sutton Ltd* [1994] C.C.L.R. 140.

[206] 1974 Act s.123; Consumer Credit (Negotiable Instruments) (Exemption) Order 1984 (SI 1984/435).

[207] 1974 Act s.125(1).

[208] 1974 Act s.123(2).

[209] 1974 Act s.125(2).

[210] 1974 Act s.124.

[211] 1974 Act s.125(3), (4).

[212] 1974 Act s.83. This does not apply to any loss arising from misuse of an instrument to which the Cheques Act 1957 s.4 as amended by the Cheques Act 1992 s.3, applies.

[213] 1974 Act ss.94–95 and 97; see the Consumer Credit (Rebate on Early Settlement) Regulations 1983 (SI 1983/1562) for occasions when a rebate must be allowed, and the methods of calculation. These regulations apply to regulated consumer credit agreements made before May 31, 2005 until May 31, 2007 for agreements for a term of 10 years or less and until May 31, 2010 for agreements for a term of more than 10 years. For agreements made from May 31, 2005 reference should be made to the Consumer Credit (Early Settlement) Regulations 2004 (SI 2004/1483). See *Forward Trust Ltd v Whymark* [1990] C.C.L.R. 1.

[214] 1974 Act s.93.

[215] 1974 Act s.92; *Ahmed v Toyota Finance*, 1996 G.W.D. 27–1566, Sh. Ct. It seems that in Scotland an owner is never entitled to retake goods at his own hand from a person who possesses them under a contract: J.J. Gow, *The Law of Hire-Purchase in Scotland*, 2nd edn (Edinburgh: W. Green, 1968), p.210. Section 134 dealing with "adverse possession" purports to apply to Scotland but is incomprehensible.

such an agreement, the debtor is in possession of the goods, he shall be treated as the custodier of the goods notwithstanding that the agreement has been terminated.[216]

Hire-purchase and conditional sale agreements[217]—If the debtor is in breach of **15.26** a hire-purchase or conditional sale agreement relating to goods but has paid one-third or more of the total price, the goods, even although they are the creditor's property, are "protected goods" and the creditor cannot recover possession of them without a court order.[218] If he does recover them without an order, the agreement is terminated and the debtor is released from all liability and can recover all that he has paid under the agreement.[219]

The debtor is entitled to terminate the agreement by giving notice at any time before the final payment.[220] He must, however, pay the creditor the amount (if any) by which one-half of the total price exceeds the aggregate of the sums paid and the sums due immediately before termination unless: (a) the agreement provides for a small payment or does not provide for any payment; or (b) the court makes an order for payment of a lesser sum which it is satisfied is equal to the loss sustained by the creditor in consequence of the termination of the agreement.[221] In addition, the debtor must recompense the creditor if he has contravened an obligation to take reasonable care of the goods.

Goods comprised in a hire-purchase or conditional sale agreement which have not become vested in the debtor are not subject to the landlord's hypothec in the period between service of a default notice and the date on which the notice expires or is earlier complied with, or, if the agreement is enforceable on an order of the court only, in the period between the commencement and the termination of the creditor's action.[222]

A time order, in relation to a hire-purchase or conditional sale agreement, may deal with sums which, although not payable at the time the order is made, would, if the agreement continued in force, become payable under it subsequently.[223]

In an application for an enforcement order, or a time order, in relation to a hire-purchase or conditional sale agreement, or in an action brought by the creditor to recover the goods, the court may make a "return order" or a "transfer order".[224] A "return order" is an order for return of the goods to the creditor[225]; a "transfer order" is an order for transfer to the debtor of the creditor's title to such of the goods as the court thinks just and the return to the creditor of the remainder of the goods.[226] A transfer order can be made only where the amount of the total price

---

[216] 1974 Act s.130(4).

[217] A conditional sale agreement is an agreement for the sale of goods or land under which the purchase price or part of it is payable by instalments and the property in the goods or land is to remain in the seller (notwithstanding that the buyer is to be in possession of the goods or land) until such conditions as to the payment of instalments or otherwise as may be specified in the agreement are fulfilled: s.189. The buyer under such an agreement which is a consumer credit agreement is deemed for purposes of s.25(1) of the Sale of Goods Act 1979 not to be a person who has bought or agreed to buy goods: Sale of Goods Act 1979 s.25(2). See para.12.23, above.

[218] 1974 Act s.90; *Kassam v Chartered Trust Plc* [1998] C.C.L.R. 54.

[219] 1974 Act s.91.

[220] 1974 Act s.99.

[221] 1974 Act s.100.

[222] 1974 Act s.104.

[223] 1974 Act s.130(2).

[224] 1974 Act s.133(1).

[225] 1974 Act s.133(1)(i).

[226] 1974 Act s.133(1)(ii).

which has been paid exceeds "the part of the total price referable"[227] to the transferred goods by at least one-third of the unpaid balance of the total price.[228]
Notwithstanding the making of a return order or a transfer order, the debtor may,
before the goods enter the creditor's possession, on payment of the balance of the
total price and on fulfilment of any other necessary conditions, "claim" the goods
ordered to be returned.[229] When, under that provision, or under a time order, the
total price is paid and any other necessary conditions are fulfilled, the creditor's
title to the goods vests in the debtor.[230] If goods are not returned under a return
order or transfer order the court may revoke so much of the order as relates to
those goods and order the debtor to pay the unpaid portion of so much of the total
price as is referable to those goods.[231]

15.27 **Conditional sale agreements relating to land**—When the debtor is in breach of
a conditional sale agreement relating to land, the creditor can recover possession
of the land on an order of the court only.[232] A conditional sale agreement relating
to land cannot be terminated after the title has passed to the debtor.[233]

15.28 **"Land mortgages"**—A "land mortgage" is any security charged on land, "land"
being defined to include heritable subjects of whatever description.[234]

Before sending to the debtor for signature an unexecuted agreement where the
prospective regulated agreement is to be secured on land, the creditor must give
the debtor a copy of the unexecuted agreement containing a notice indicating the
debtor's right to withdraw from the prospective agreement and how and when
the right is exercisable.[235] This does not apply to a restricted-use credit agreement
to finance the purchase of the land or to an agreement for a bridging loan in
connection with the purchase of the "mortgaged land" or other land.

A land mortgage is not properly executed unless in addition to the requirements
applying to regulated agreements generally: (a) the copy agreement and notice of
the withdrawal right are sent to the debtor; (b) the unexecuted agreement is sent
by post to the debtor for his signature not less than seven days after the copy was
given to him; (c) in the period between the giving of that copy and the expiry of
seven days after the sending of the unexecuted agreement for his signature (or its
return signed if earlier) the creditor refrained from approaching the debtor, in
person, by telephone or letter or otherwise, except in response to a specific request
made by the debtor; and (d) no notice of withdrawal by the debtor was received
by the creditor before the sending of the unexecuted agreement.[236]

A land mortgage securing a regulated agreement is enforceable (so far as
provided in relation to the agreement) on order of the court only.[237] Nothing in the

---

[227] 1974 Act s.133(7) defines "the part of the total price referable to any goods".
[228] 1974 Act s.133(3).
[229] 1974 Act s.133(4). The words ". . . may . . . claim . . ." are presumably used to mean "is entitled
to retain".
[230] 1974 Act s.133(5).
[231] 1974 Act s.133(6).
[232] 1974 Act s.92(2).
[233] 1974 Act s.99(3).
[234] 1974 Act s.189.
[235] 1974 Act s.58; Consumer Credit (Cancellation Notices and Copies of Documents) Regulations
1983 (SI 1983/1557) reg.4, as amended by the Consumer Credit (Amendment) Regulations 2010
(SI 2010/1969) reg.3(3).
[236] 1974 Act s.61.
[237] 1974 Act s.126.

Act is to affect the rights of a creditor in a heritable security, other than one carrying on the business of debt-collecting, who became the creditor for value and without notice of any defect in title arising by virtue of the other provisions of the Act or who derived title from such a creditor.[238]

Consumer hire agreements—The hirer is entitled to terminate a regulated **15.29** consumer hire agreement by giving to the person entitled to receive the sums payable thereunder notice which is not to expire earlier than 18 months after the making of the agreement.[239] A minimum period of notice is prescribed according to the intervals at which payment is made. This power to terminate is not available where the hire payments exceed £1,500 in any year or where the goods are hired for purposes of a business carried on by the hirer.

If the owner recovers possession of the goods otherwise than by action, the court, on the hirer's application, may, if it appears just to do so, having regard to the extent of the hirer's enjoyment of the goods, order that any sums already paid by the hirer shall be repaid and that the hirer's obligation to pay any sums owed to the owner shall cease.[240] Similar provisions may be made by the court in an order for delivery of the goods to the owner.

Connected lender liability—A substantial liability is imposed upon the creditor **15.30** in a debtor-creditor-supplier agreement in which there are "arrangements" between the creditor and the supplier.[241] If the debtor has, in relation to a transaction financed by such an agreement, any claim against the supplier in respect of a misrepresentation or breach of contract, he has a "like claim" against the creditor who is jointly and severally liable with the supplier, but has a right to be indemnified by the supplier[242]; moreover, the creditor can, pursuant to the relevant court rules, join the supplier as a party to any action by the debtor.[243] The provision does not apply to a non-commercial agreement, nor where the claim relates to any single item to which the supplier has attached a cash price not exceeding £100 or more than £30,000.[244] However, it is applicable where the debtor has exceeded his credit limit or has breached the agreement in another way.[245] The provision is particularly relevant where the supplier has become insolvent.[246] It has been held, in England, that the provision is applicable to an item purchased outwith the United Kingdom and to four party transactions, i.e. one where the card has been issued by an issuer other than the one with a direct link with the supplier and

---

[238] 1974 Act s.177.

[239] 1974 Act s.101. Subsection (8A), which was added by 2006 Act s.63(1), provides that where it appears to the OFT that it would be in the interests of hirers to do so, it may by general notice direct that this section shall not apply to a consumer hire agreement if the agreement falls within a specified description. No such notice has yet been made.

[240] 1974 Act s.132; *Automotive Financial Services Ltd v Henderson*, 1992 S.L.T. (Sh. Ct) 63.

[241] 1974 Act s.75. See Act of Sederunt (Consumer Credit Act 1974) 1985 (SI 1985/705), as amended. See further Office of Fair Trading Report, "Consumer Credit Act 1974 Section 75—Equal Liability", June 2000 (OFT 303).

[242] 1974 Act ss.75(1), (2); *Porter v General Guarantee Corp Ltd* [1982] R.T.R. 384, noted by H.L. MacQueen, "Hire purchase and connected lender liability" 1984 S.L.T. (News) 65; *Forthright Finance Ltd v Patel* Unreported April 3, 1995 CA, per Hutchison L.J.

[243] 1974 Act s.75(5).

[244] 1974 Act s.75(3) (as amended by Consumer Credit (Increase of Monetary Limits) Order 1983 (SI 1983/1878) arts 3, 4, Sch. Pts I and II).

[245] 1974 Act s.75(4).

[246] See, e.g. *Dalglish v National Westminster Bank Plc*, 2001 S.L.T. (Sh. Ct) 124.

consumer.[247] It has been held by the Inner House that the reference to a "like claim" does not normally mean that the credit agreement could be rescinded.[248]

Section 75A[249] complements s.75 and applies in circumstances where that section does not. If the debtor under a linked[250] credit agreement has a claim against the supplier in respect of a breach of contract he or she may pursue that claim against the creditor where any of the following conditions are met. These are: that the supplier cannot be traced; that the debtor has contacted the supplier but the supplier has not responded; that the supplier is insolvent; or that the debtor has taken reasonable steps to pursue his claim against the supplier but has not obtained satisfaction for his claim.[251] This section does not apply where the cash value of the goods or service is £30,000 or less, the linked credit agreement is for credit which exceeds £60,260, or the linked credit agreement is entered into by the debtor wholly or predominantly for the purposes of a business carried on, or intended to be carried on, by him.[252] The section does not apply to an agreement secured on land.[253]

15.31 Credit-token agreements—A credit-token is "a card, check, voucher, coupon, stamp, form, booklet or other document or thing" given to an individual by a person carrying on a consumer credit business who undertakes that he will supply, or reimburse a third party who supplies cash, goods and services on credit on production of the token. A credit-token agreement is a regulated agreement for the provision of credit in connection with the use of a credit-token.[254]

It is an offence to give a person a credit-token if he has not asked for it.[255] In the case of credit-token agreements, there are relaxations of the requirements to send the debtor a copy of the executed agreement and to send a notice of cancellation rights.[256] The debtor is not liable under a credit-token agreement for use made of the token by any person, unless the use constituted an acceptance of it by him or he had previously accepted it by signing it or a receipt for it on first using it.[257] The debtor may be liable to the extent of £50 (or the credit limit if lower) for loss to the creditor caused by use of the token when it is outwith the possession of the

---

[247] *Office of Fair Trading v Lloyds TSB Bank Plc* [2007] UKHL 48; [2008] 1 A.C. 316. See also *Jarrett v Barclays Bank Plc* [1999] Q.B. 1 (a time share in Spain).

[248] *Durkin v DSG Retail Ltd* [2010] CSIH 49; 2010 S.C. 662. This overrules the controversial decision in *United Dominions Trust v Taylor*, 1980 S.L.T. (Sh. Ct) 28, noted by F. Davidson, "The Missing Linked Transaction" (1980) 96 L.Q.R. 343–348, followed in *Renton v Henderson's Garage (Nairn) Ltd* [1994] C.C.L.R. 29 and *Forward Trust Ltd v Hornsby*, 1995 S.C.L.R. 574.

[249] Inserted by the Consumer Credit (EU Directive) Regulations 2010 (SI 2010/1010) reg.25, as of February 1, 2011.

[250] A "linked credit agreement" means a regulated consumer credit agreement which serves exclusively to finance an agreement for the supply of specific goods or the provision of a specific service and either the creditor uses the services of the supplier in connection with the preparation or making of the credit agreement, or the specific goods or provision of a specific service are explicitly specified in the credit agreement: s.75A(5).

[251] These steps need not include litigation, see s.75A(3). A debtor is to be deemed to have obtained satisfaction where he has accepted a replacement product or service or other compensation from the supplier in settlement of his claim, s.75A(4).

[252] 1974 Act s.75A(6).

[253] 1974 Act s.75A(8).

[254] 1974 Act s.14. Examples of credit-tokens are a bank credit-card (Sch.2, Ex.3) and a trading check (Ex.14); *Elliott v Director General of Fair Trading* [1980] 1 W.L.R. 977. As to credit card transactions, see *Richardson v Worrall* [1985] S.T.C. 693; *Re. Charge Card Services Ltd* [1989] Ch. 497.

[255] 1974 Act s.51.

[256] 1974 Act ss.63(4), 64(2).

[257] 1974 Act s.66.

debtor or of a person authorised by him to use it, the use being before the creditor has been given notice that the token is lost or stolen or for another reason liable to misuse.[258] The debtor may be liable to any extent for loss to the creditor from use (before similar notice) of the token by a person who got possession of it with the debtor's consent.[259] When, in connection with a credit-token agreement (other than a small agreement) a token (other than the first) is given to the debtor, the creditor must give him a copy of the executed agreement and of any other document referred to in it; if he fails to do this he cannot enforce the agreement and, if the default continues for one month, he commits an offence.[260]

The onus is on the creditor to prove that the token was lawfully supplied to the debtor and accepted by him. If the debtor alleges that any use of the token was not authorised by him, it is for the creditor to prove either that the use was so authorised, or that the use occurred before the creditor was given notice of the loss or theft of the token.[261]

When s.51A[262] comes into force it will be an offence for a person to provide credit card cheques[263] other than to a person who has asked for them.[264] They may be provided only on a single occasion in respect of each request that is made[265] and no more than three cheques may be provided in response to a request.[266] Where a single request is made for the provision of credit card cheques in connection with more than one credit-token agreement, the restrictions apply as if a separate request had been made in relation to each agreement.[267] These restrictions do not apply to credit card cheques provided to business customers.[268]

Unfair relationships—Sections 140A–140D will, after a transition period, **15.32** replace the extortionate credit provisions discussed in the previous section. Section 140A of the 1974 Act confers wide powers on the court to reopen agreements of any amount[269]

> "if it determines that the relationship between the creditor[270] and the debtor arising out of the agreement (or the agreement taken with any related agreement)[271] is unfair to the debtor"

---

[258] 1974 Act s.84, as amended by the Consumer Protection (Distance Selling) Regulations 2000 (SI 2000/2334) reg.21 inserting new subss.(3A) and (3B); Consumer Credit (Credit-Token Agreements) Regulations 1983 (SI 1983/1555).

[259] 1974 Act s.84(2).

[260] 1974 Act s.85.

[261] 1974 Act s.171(4).

[262] Added by Financial Services Act 2010 (c.28) s.15(2) but not yet in force.

[263] A "credit card cheque" means a cheque (whether or not drawn on a banker) which, whenever used, will result in the provision of credit under a credit-token agreement: 1974 Act s.51A(7).

[264] 1974 Act s.51A(1), (2).

[265] 1974 Act s.51A(3).

[266] 1974 Act s.51A(4).

[267] 1974 Act s.51A(5).

[268] 1974 Act s.51B added by Financial Services Act 2010 s.15(2). Not yet in force.

[269] 1974 Act s.140C(1) including those otherwise exempt by virtue of ss.16, 16A and 16B. Section 140D provides that advice and information published by the OFT under s.229 of the Enterprise Act 2002 shall indicate how the OFT expects ss.140A–140C to interact with Pt 8 of that Act. See "Unfair relationships–Enforcement action under Partt 8 of the Enterprise Act 2002" (May 2008, revised August 2011) available at *http://www.oft.gov.uk/shared_oft/business_leaflets/enterprise_act/oft854 Rev.pdf* [Accessed July 16, 2012].

[270] 1974 Act s.140C(2).

[271] The term "related agreement" used in ss.140A and 140B is defined by s.140C(4) as: "(a) a credit agreement consolidated by the main agreement; (b) a linked transaction in relation to the main

because of one of a number of factors. These are: any of the terms of the agreement or of any related agreement; the way in which the creditor has exercised or enforced any of his rights under the agreement or any related agreement; or any other thing done (or not done) by, or on behalf of, the creditor (either before or after the making of the agreement or any related agreement).[272] The court may have regard to "all matters it thinks relevant"[273] and the acts or omissions of any associate or former associate of the creditor which may be treated as the acts or omissions of the creditor himself.[274] These powers may be exercised even if the relationship of creditor and debtor has come to an end.[275]

Where a relationship is found to be unfair a court has the powers set out in s.140B(1) which are to:

(a) require repayment by the creditor and any associate or former associate of any payment made to anyone by the debtor or by a surety by virtue of the agreement or any related agreement;

(b) require the creditor and any associate or former associate to do or cease doing anything in connection with the agreement or any related agreement;

(c) reduce or discharge any sum payable by the debtor or a surety;

(d) direct the return to a surety of any property provided by way of security;

(e) set aside any obligation of the debtor or surety;

(f) alter the terms of the agreement or any related agreement;

(g) direct an accounting to be made between any persons.

The court may make an order even if it places on the creditor a burden "in respect of an advantage enjoyed by another person".[276] Where in any proceedings, the debtor or a surety alleges that the relationship between the creditor and the debtor is unfair to the debtor, the onus is on the creditor to prove the contrary.[277]

The powers can only be invoked by the debtor or a surety and where they initiate proceedings this must be done in the sheriff court for the district in which the debtor or surety resides or carries on business.[278] They may also invoke these powers in any proceedings in any court to which they are parties, being proceedings to enforce the agreement or any related agreement or where the amount paid or payable under the agreement or any related agreement is relevant.[279]

---

agreement or to a credit agreement within paragraph (a); (c) a security provided in relation to the main agreement, to a credit agreement within paragraph (a) or to a linked transaction within paragraph (b)."

[272] 1974 Act s.140A(1).

[273] 1974 Act s.140A(2). For cases discussing unfairness see *Patel v Patel* [2009] EWHC 3264 (QB); [2010] 1 All E.R. (Comm) 864; *Carey v HSBC Bank Plc* [2009] EWHC 3417; *Shaw v Nine Regions* [2009] EWHC 3514 (QB) and *Khodari v Al Tamimi* [2009] EWCA Civ 1109; *Maple Leaf Macro Volatility Master Fund v Rouvroy* [2009] EWHC 257 (Comm); [2009] 2 All E.R. (Comm) 287; [2009] 1 Lloyds Rep 475; *Harrison v Black Horse Limited* [2010] EWHC 3152 and *Barnes v Black Horse Ltd* [2011] EWHC 1416 (QB). Other cases are referred to on the OFT website at *http://www.oft.gov.uk/about-the-oft/legal-powers/legal/cca/CCA2006/unfair/unfair-rel-full/* [Accessed July 14, 2012].

[274] 1974 Act s.140A(3).

[275] 1974 Act s.140A(4). On the approach in England to the possibility of a claim being time-barred see *Patel v Patel* [2009] EWHC 3264 (QB); [2010] 1 All E.R. (Comm) 864.

[276] 1974 Act s.140B(3).

[277] 1974 Act s.140B(9).

[278] 1974 Act s.140B(2)(a) and (5).

[279] 1974 Act s.140B(2)(b) and (c).

The new powers are subject to transitional provisions[280] which provide for a "transitional period" of one year which started on April 6, 2007 the date on which the relevant provisions were brought into effect.[281] They apply to agreements made before that date (known as "existing agreements") in relation to applications made under s.140B(2)(a) only after the transitional period, and in relation to applications made under s.140B(2)(b) and (c) where proceedings were commenced after that date. However, if such an agreement became a "completed agreement" before that date or becomes so during the transition period an order cannot be made. An agreement becomes "completed" once no sum is, will or may be payable under it.[282]

Extortionate credit bargains—The provisions on unfair relationships discussed **15.33** above replace powers in ss.137–140 to reopen agreements on the grounds that they were extortionate. However, these provisions can still be relied upon in some cases.[283] As these will become increasingly rare reference should be made to the previous edition for discussion of them.

The repeal of ss.137–140, discussed in the previous section, will not affect the powers of the court to re-open an "existing agreement"[284] under those provisions and a completed agreement is also subject to them.[285]

Dispute resolution—The Consumer Credit Act 2006 provides for the extension **15.34** of the Financial Ombudsman Service to disputes relating to consumer credit[286] and this took effect from April 6, 2007.[287]

FURTHER READING

Chitty on Contract, edited by Beale, H.G., 30th edn (London: Sweet and Maxwell, 2010), Vol.2, "Specific Contracts", Ch.38.
Goode, R., *Consumer Credit Law and Practice* (Butterworths).
Lomnicka, E., *Encyclopaedia of Consumer Credit Law* (London: Sweet & Maxwell).
Hapgood, M., *Paget's Law of Banking*, 13th edn (Butterworths, 2006), Ch.3.
Stair Memorial Encyclopaedia, "Consumer Credit", 2010 Reissue.

---

[280] 1974 Act s.69, paras 14(4), 15(7) and (8).

[281] These provisions were inserted in the 1974 Act by ss.20 and 22(3) of the 2006 Act and brought into force by the Consumer Credit Act 2006 (Commencement No.2 and Transitional Provisions and Savings) Order 2007 art.3(2) and Sch.2.

[282] 2006 Act Sch.3 para.1(2).

[283] 2006 Act Sch.3 para.15.

[284] 2006 Act Sch.3 para.15(1) and (3).

[285] 2006 Act Sch.3 para.15(2).

[286] 2006 Act s.59.

[287] See 2006 Act ss.59–61, brought into force with effect from June 16, 2006 by the Consumer Credit Act 2006 (Commencement No.1) Order 2006 (SI 2006/1508).

CHAPTER 16

CAUTIONARY OBLIGATIONS

Nature of the contract—A cautionary obligation is an obligation which is acces- **16.01**
sory to a principal obligation, to answer for the payment of some debt or the
performance of some duty in the case of the failure of another person, who is
himself, in the first instance, liable to such payment or performance.[1] The person
undertaking the obligation is called, indifferently, cautioner, guarantor, or surety;
the party to whose debt or acts the obligation applies is known as the principal
debtor; the party entitled to exact performance is the creditor; and the debt owed
to the creditor by the principal debtor is called the principal debt. There may be
more than one cautioner.[2] If so, the respective cautioners are called co-cautioners
in relation to each other. An accessory (or, as it is sometimes called, secondary)
obligation

> "is not an independent obligation but is essentially conditional in nature,
> being properly exigible only on the failure of the principal debtor to pay at
> the maturity of his obligation",[3]

i.e. it is a contingent liability. By contrast, under an independent obligation, the
performance of the obligation in favour of the creditor is not dependent upon the
failure of another party to perform a prior obligation in favour of the creditor.
Whether an obligation should be held to be a cautionary or an independent obligation is a question of construction and often a difficult one.[4] The principal obligation may be for the payment of a debt already incurred; for debts to be incurred,
or furnishings to be supplied, in the future; for the faithful performance of an
office or contract of service; for the due execution of any contract[5]; for the
performance of obligations under a lease[6] or sub-lease[7]; or for the performance of
some particular act.

Cautionary: Proper and improper—In form, a cautionary obligation may be **16.02**
"proper" or "improper". It is "proper" when the fact that the parties are principal
debtor and cautioner appears in the instrument by which they are bound; it is

---

[1] W.M. Gloag and J.M. Irvine, *Law of Rights in Security* (Edinburgh: W. Green, 1897; reprinted in 1987), p.642 and fn.1 thereof.
[2] See paras 16.05, 16.13–16.14 and 16.26, below.
[3] Gloag and Irvine, *Rights in Security* (1897), p.644.
[4] See further below, para.16.09.
[5] *Moschi v Lep Air Services* [1973] A.C. 331 at 358, per Lord Kilbrandon; *Glasgow City Council v Excess Insurance*, 1986 S.L.T. 585 (a "performance bond" which on its construction, was cautionary in nature), but see fn.13 below concerning "on demand" performance bonds.
[6] *Waydale Ltd v DHL Holdings (UK) Ltd (No.2)*, 2001 S.L.T. 224.
[7] *Good Harvest Partnership LLP v Centaur Services Ltd* [2010] EWHC 330 (Ch); [2010] 2 W.L.R. 1312.

"improper", where, ex facie of the instrument, the parties appear as co-obligants, though inter se they are principal and cautioner. A contract of caution, whether proper or improper, implies several conditions, particularly in favour of the cautioner. However, the parties are free to conclude any lawful contract, and the cautioner may renounce any or all of the usual equities and privileges in his favour.[8] As a result, contracts are frequently encountered which are "analogous to but distinct from cautionry".[9]

16.03 Caution and security—As explained above, a cautionary obligation is one in which the cautioner undertakes a personal obligation to pay the principal debt to the creditor if the principal debtor defaults.[10] This personal obligation may be an unsecured guarantee or may be a secured guarantee (e.g. a personal guarantee secured by a standard security over the creditor's house).[11] As the obligation is personal, all the cautioner's assets are available to satisfy the debt. This is to be distinguished from an arrangement by which a party provides a security for another person's debt or other obligation without undertaking any personal liability towards the creditor. In such a case, if the security is insufficient to cover the principal debt, the creditor has no further recourse against the cautioner.[12] How far terms similar to those implied in a contract of caution can be implied in an analogous obligation is not clear and may depend on the particular terms and circumstances of the contract.[13]

16.04 Enforceability of the principal debt—If the apparent principal debt be unenforceable, as granted by a party with no power to contract, or in its nature a *pactum illicitum* (an unlawful agreement), the cautioner is not liable.[14] A guarantee, however, for some debt or other obligation to be contracted in the future is binding.[15] And there is some, though doubtful, authority to the effect that if the principal debtor, though a person unable to contract (e.g. a person under the age of 16), has actually entered into a morally binding engagement, the obligation of the

---

[8] *Aitken's Trs v Bank of Scotland*, 1944 S.C. 270 at 277.

[9] *Aitkens' Trs*, 1944 S.C. 270 at 277; see *AIB Group (UK) Plc v Martin* [2001] UKHL 63; [2002] 1 W.L.R. 94 and *Joint Liquidators of Simclar (Ayrshire) Ltd v Simclar Group Ltd* [2011] CSOH 54; as to the construction of contracts of caution, see para.16.10, below.

[10] *Braithwaite v Bank of Scotland*, 1999 S.L.T. 25; *Hewit v Williamson*, 1999 S.L.T. 313; 1998 S.C.L.R. 601; and the commentary on *Hewit v Williamson* by G.L. Gretton, "Commentary", 1998 S.C.L.R. at 616–618. See too *Wright v Cotias Investments Inc*, 2000 S.C.L.R. 324.

[11] *Braithwaite v Bank of Scotland*, 1999 S.L.T. 25; *Hewit v Williamson*, 1999 S.L.T. 313; and Gretton, "Commentary", 1998 S.C.L.R. at 616–618.

[12] *Braithwaite v Bank of Scotland*, 1999 S.L.T. 25; *Hewit v Williamson*, 1999 S.L.T. 313; and Gretton, "Commentary", 1998 S.C.L.R. at 616–618. This is an example of an arrangement which has some resemblance to cautionary obligations and it was suggested in the 11th edition of this work that it might be called "broad" caution as opposed to "narrow" caution, i.e. caution in the strict sense. However "broad caution" does not necessarily have the special implied incidents of cautionary obligations and is better classified as an obligation analogous to caution: see *Braithwaite v Bank of Scotland*, 1997 S.C. (HL) 111; 1999 S.L.T. 25 at 30; *Hewit v Williamson*, 1999 S.L.T. 313 at 316. As to the significance of *Smith v Bank of Scotland*, see below, para.16.17.

[13] See, e.g. *Cargill S.A. v Bangladesh Sugar Corp* [1998] 1 W.L.R. 461 (obligation to account). As to the nature of "on demand" performance bonds, see also *Attock Cement Co v Romanian Bank for Foreign Trade* [1989] 1 W.L.R. 1147.

[14] The cautioner may be liable if the illegality is merely technical, e.g. the inability of a company to purchase its own shares and the parties contracted on the assumption of legality; *Garrard v James* [1925] 1 Ch. 616.

[15] *Fortune v Young*, 1918 S.C. 1.

cautioner is enforceable.[16] If the party interposing as cautioner was aware that the principal obligation was invalid the doctrine of personal bar may be invoked so as to preclude the defence of invalidity.[17]

Cautioner's right to relief—A cautioner, on payment of the debt,[18] is entitled to **16.05** recover what he has paid from the principal debtor. The rationale for this rule lies in an implied mandate between the principal debtor and the cautioner[19]; an alternative basis of recovery could lie in the developing area of unjustified enrichment.[20] It is also a general rule, which will yield only to an express contract to the contrary, that where more than one cautioner is engaged, anyone who has paid more than his share may claim relief from the others.[21] On this principle, where A and B were cautioners for a contractor, and A, on the contractor's failure, carried out the contract at his own expense, he was held entitled to recover half his outlay from B.[22] In the case where all are ex facie co-obligants, parole evidence as to their real relationship is competent, because the written instrument by which the debt is constituted is intended to regulate the contract between the creditor and the obligants, not the rights of the obligants inter se.[23] In determining the amount of relief, those cautioners who are insolvent are not counted, e.g. if A, B and C are cautioners, and C is insolvent, A, who has paid the whole debt, is entitled to recover half of what he has paid from B.[24] Where each cautioner is liable for a specified sum, and the whole debt is exacted, no one has paid more than his share, and there can be no claim of relief. But if less than the whole debt is due, anyone who has paid more than his proportionate share may claim relief if the cautioners are bound in the same instrument; if, in separate contracts, each cautioner engages for a specific sum, there is no right of relief.[25]

Constitution of cautionary obligation—A cautionary obligation may arise from **16.06** an offer, addressed to a particular creditor, and offering to guarantee a particular debt or the conduct of a third party. It is then a question of construction, on which no definite rule can be given, whether an express acceptance is required, or whether the cautioner's liability is clinched when credit is given to the third party whose actings or dealings he has offered to guarantee.[26] A cautionary obligation may also arise from an undertaking to guarantee the debt or dealings of another, given to the party who is to be guaranteed, and not addressed to any particular

---

[16] See Bell, *Principles*, s.251.

[17] *Yorkshire Railway Waggon Co v McClure* (1881) 19 Ch.D. 478; *Stevenson v Adair* (1872) 10 M. 919. Whilst the principle in the text concerning caution and personal bar remains the same, the decisions themselves now need to be read in the light of the modern law of company capacity, see para.46.12, below.

[18] *Smithy's Place Ltd v Blackadder & McMonagle*, 1991 S.L.T. 790.

[19] Gloag and Irvine, *Rights in Security* (1897, reprinted 1987), p.797.

[20] A similar view has been taken in England by L.S. Sealy and R.J.A. Hooley, *Commercial Law: Text, Cases and Materials*, 4th edn (Oxford: Oxford University Press, 2009), p.1184. As to unjustified enrichment, see Ch.24, below.

[21] *Moss v Penman*, 1993 S.C. 300; *Primary Healthcare Centres (Broadford) Ltd v Humphrey* [2010] CSOH 129; 2010 G.W.D. 35–730; *Joint Liquidators of Simclar (Ayrshire) Ltd v Simclar Group Ltd* [2011] CSOH 54.

[22] *Marshall v Pennycook*, 1908 S.C. 276.

[23] *Hamilton v Freeth* (1889) 16 R. 1022; *Crosbie v Brown* (1900) 3 F. 83.

[24] *Buchanan v Main* (1900) 3 F. 215.

[25] *Morgan v Smart* (1872) 10 M. 610.

[26] See *Wallace v Gibson* (1895) 22 R. (HL) 56.

creditor.[27] In that case, anyone who has given credit on the faith of the guarantee is entitled to enforce it, unless, from its terms, it appears that it was limited to some particular class of prospective creditors.[28] However, a cautionary obligation will not arise where a party signs a document for a particular purpose in a representative capacity on behalf of another; such as a director signing on behalf of a company, and that document also contains a personal cautionary obligation on the part of the signatory which he was not aware of-for the cautionary obligation to be binding, the signatory must be made aware of its unusual terms.[29] The creditor is required to display perfect fairness of representation in entering into the contract,[30] but caution or suretyship is not a contract uberrimae fidei so that the requirements of disclosure which apply in insurance do not apply to caution. However, disclosure is necessary when there is "anything that might not naturally be expected to take place between the parties".[31]

16.07 **Writing**—By s.6 of the Mercantile Law Amendment Scotland Act 1856, it was provided that all guarantees, securities or cautionary obligations made or granted by any person for any other person should be in writing, and should be subscribed by the person undertaking the obligation, or by some person duly authorised by him, otherwise the same should have no effect. Section 6 also required writing in the case of "representations and assurances as to the character, conduct, credit, ability, trade or dealings of any person" made to enable that person to obtain credit or certain other financial advantages. These provisions were repealed by the Requirements of Writing (Scotland) Act with effect from August 1, 1995.[32] Such obligations do, however, still require to be constituted in writing if they are gratuitous unilateral obligations which have not been undertaken in the course of business.[33] In practice, in most cases, cautionary obligations will be written documents. In the case of consumers, if a cautionary obligation arises under a standard form written document, this may be subject to a test of "good faith" under the Unfair Terms in Consumer Contracts Regulations 1999.[34]

16.08 **Representations, letters of comfort and guarantees**—It is a question of construction whether a particular statement (i) amounts to a guarantee, or (ii) is merely a representation as to the character or credit of another,[35] or (iii) is a letter

---

[27] *Fortune v Young*, 1918 S.C. 1: but see Lord Guthrie at 8 "The defender knew it (the guarantee) was meant for the pursuer"; *Waydale Ltd v DHL Holdings (UK) Ltd (No.2)*, 2001 S.L.T. 224 at 231, [22] referring to a party in such circumstances, having the benefit of the guarantee if the "transactional scope is sufficiently defined".

[28] *Fortune v Young*, 1918 S.C. 1; *Waydale Ltd v DHL Holdings (UK) Ltd (No.2)*, 2001 S.L.T. 224.

[29] *Montgomery Litho Ltd v Maxwell*, 2000 S.C. 56.

[30] Gloag and Irvine, *Rights in Security* (1897), p.706.

[31] *Trade Indemnity Co v Workington Harbour and Dock Board*, 1937 A.C. 1, per Lord Atkin at 17: see further para.16.16, below. As to the requirements of good faith following on *Smith v Bank of Scotland*, see para.16.17, below.

[32] Mercantile Law Amendment Scotland Act 1856 s.14 and Sch.5. Transactions before the operative date are not affected: for the relevant law reference should be made to previous editions of this work.

[33] Requirements of Writing (Scotland) Act 1995 s.1(2)(ii). For a decision that cautionary obligations embodied in a standard security were not gratuitous for this purpose see *Royal Bank of Scotland v Wilson*, 2004 S.C. 153. For the significance of actings where the obligation has not been constituted in writing, see s.1(3) and (4).

[34] Unfair Terms in Consumer Contracts Regulations 1999 (SI 1999/2083). For example, see *Barclays Bank Plc v Kufner* [2008] EWHC 2319 (Comm); [2009] 1 All ER (Comm) 1 and para.9.25 on these Regulations.

[35] *Park v Gould* (1851) 13 D. 1049; *Fortune v Young*, 1918 S.C. 1.

of comfort.[36] If the statement, on its construction, amounts to a guarantee the writer is liable directly on his contractual obligation; but if the statement, on its construction, is only a representation, no contractual obligation has been undertaken; however, the statement may be a ground for the reduction of a contract or obligation induced by it and the writer may be liable in delict if his statement was fraudulent or negligent.[37] An honest, though mistaken opinion as to the credit of another infers no liability even if made negligently,[38] unless: (i) the relations of the writer and the person he addresses are of a fiduciary character, e.g. solicitor and client, and the inaccurate statement involves a breach of fiduciary duty, such as having a conflict of interests[39]; or (ii) where the relationship is contractual and the inaccurate statement involves a breach of contractual duty "to exercise due skill and care"[40]; or (iii) the person making the representation assumes responsibility for the accuracy of what he says and knows, or ought to know that what he says will be relied on by the party to whom it is made (i.e. reasonable reliance).[41] In such a case it has been held, in England, that as the ground of action is failure in the duty involved in the relationship, action may lie although the representation was verbal.[42] It has been held in England that where a parent company indicated to a creditor of a subsidiary that it was the parent's policy to ensure that the subsidiary was "in a position to meet its liabilities" to the creditor, the obligation should be construed as a "letter of comfort", and that the maker of the statement was not liable to the recipient of the statement (i.e. the creditor). This was because such a statement was not "a promise as to the future conduct of the" statement maker, but an assumption by him of "a moral responsibility only" and "not a legal liability".[43] The maker of the statement had not said that the policy would continue, and had not undertaken a joint and several obligation or given a guarantee.

Cautionary or independent obligation—There are many cases where it is **16.09** difficult to say whether an independent or a cautionary obligation has been undertaken.[44] If A orders goods to be supplied to B, and undertakes to be responsible for payment, this may, according to the circumstances, be either an independent obligation by A or a cautionary obligation for a debt primarily undertaken by B. It has been decided, in England, that agency del credere, when the agent guarantees the solvency of the party with whom he deals on his principal's behalf, is not to be regarded, in a question as to the necessity of writing, as a contract of guarantee.[45] Also a guarantee against loss from a contract, which

---

[36] *Kleinwort Benson Ltd v Malaysia Mining Corp Berhad* [1989] 1 W.L.R. 379.

[37] *Union Bank of Scotland v Taylor*, 1925 S.C. 835.

[38] *Robinson v National Bank of Scotland*, 1916 S.C. (HL) 154.

[39] *Nocton v Lord Ashburton* [1914] A.C. 932.

[40] *Nocton v Lord Ashburton* [1914] A.C. 932, at 958, per Viscount Haldane L.C.

[41] *Hedley Byrne & Co v Heller* [1964] A.C. 465; *Henderson v Merrett Syndicates Ltd* [1995] 2 A.C. 145; *White v Jones* [1995] 2 A.C. 207; *Williams v Natural Life Health Foods Ltd* [1998] 1 W.L.R. 830. For a discussion of pure economic loss and negligent misrepresentation, see paras 26.07 and 26.08.

[42] *Banbury v Bank of Montreal* [1918] A.C. 626; *Hedley Byrne & Co v Heller* [1964] A.C. 465. In Scotland, see *Andrew Oliver & Son Ltd v Douglas*, 1981 S.C. 192.

[43] *Kleinwort Benson Ltd v Malaysia Mining Corp* [1989] 1 W.L.R. 379 at 391, per Ralph Gibson L.J. The matter turns on the construction of the undertaking.

[44] For example, in *Barnicoat v Knight* [2004] 2 B.C.L.C. 464, where an obligation imposed on a purchaser in a share sale agreement to "procure the repayment" of loans by the company they acquired under the share sale agreement to the pre-sale directors of that company, this was held to have the same legal effect as a guarantee. For a further discussion of the differences between an obligation which is cautionary and one which is independent, see para.16.01 above.

[45] *Sutton v Grey* [1894] 1 Q.B. 285.

does not involve any obligation of performance by any principal debtor, e.g. an obligation to take over shares if they do not reach a certain price, is not a cautionary obligation.[46] However, a contract which does involve performance by a principal debtor, but is framed as a policy of insurance, may really be a cautionary obligation. So far as any rule can be stated in such cases, the incidents of the contract depend on the law of insurance if the guarantee is obtained by the creditor, on the law of cautionary obligations if it is obtained by the debtor.[47] It has been held in the Outer House that, on its wording, a "performance bond" was a cautionary obligation for the purposes of prescription,[48] but the Court of Appeal, in England, has held that an "on demand" performance bond is not a guarantee for purposes of determining its proper law.[49] The Court of Appeal, in England, has also ruled that a document which stated that it was a "guarantee" was in fact a performance bond imposing primary, rather than secondary liability, in terms of its wording.[50] Whether an obligation is cautionary or independent in nature will depend on the construction of the obligation.[51] Sometimes, the two are combined or a cautionary obligation is converted into an independent obligation in certain circumstances.[52]

16.10 Construction of cautionary obligations—At common law, the contract of cautionry in the strict sense was subject to a number of implied terms, for the protection of the cautioner. These included the benefits of discussion and division. There is also authority which suggests that the approach to construction also should be favourable to the cautioner.[53] On the other hand, as a contract, a cautionary obligation is subject to the normal rules of construction,[54] the purpose of which is to enable the court to ascertain the mutual intention of the parties objectively. In doing so, the court will be entitled to make use of the normal aids to construction such as reference to the factual background of the transaction and, where appropriate, rules such as the *contra proferentem* rule.[55] It has always

---

[46] *Milne v Kidd* (1869) 8 M. 250.

[47] *Laird v Securities Insurance Co* (1895) 22 R. 452; *Seaton v Burnand* [1899] 1 Q.B. 782 revd on other grounds [1900] A.C. 135; *Re Law Guarantee Trust and Accident Society* [1914] 2 Ch. 617. Again, however, the question is one of the actual terms of the contract and the particular circumstances.

[48] *Glasgow City Council v Excess Insurance*, 1986 S.L.T. 585; cited with approval in *Trafalgar House Construction (Regions) Ltd v Surety Guarantee Co Ltd* [1996] A.C. 199 at 206D, per Lord Jauncey of Tullichettle.

[49] *Attock Cement Co v Romanian Bank for Foreign Trade* [1989] 1 W.L.R. 1147; see also *Cargill S.A. v Bangladesh Sugar Corp* [1998] 1 W.L.R. 461.

[50] *Van der Merwes v IIG Capital LLC* [2007] EWCA Civ 542; [2008] 2 All E.R. (Comm) 1173. See also *Carey Value Added S.L. v Grupo Urvasco S.A.* [2010] EWHC 1905 (Comm).

[51] *Trafalgar House Construction (Regions) Ltd v Surety Guarantee Co Ltd* [1996] A.C. 199; *Trade Indemnity Co Ltd v Workington Harbour and Dock Board* [1937] A.C. 1 at 17, per Lord Atkin; *Aitken's Trs v Bank of Scotland*, 1944 S.C. 270 at 277, per Lord Justice Clerk Cooper; *Pitts v Jones* [2007] EWCA Civ 1301; [2008] Q.B. 706.

[52] For examples of this, see the guarantees in *Bank of Scotland v Macleod*, 1986 S.C. 165 and *Huewind Ltd v Clydesdale Bank Plc*, 1995 S.L.T. 392, affd on this point 1996 S.L.T. 369. See also *Aitken's Trs v Bank of Scotland*, 1944 S.C. 270 at 277, per Lord Justice Clerk Cooper.

[53] Gloag and Irvine, *Rights in Security* (1897), Ch.22.

[54] See paras 6.22–6.24 on the construction of contracts generally.

[55] There are conflicting decisions as to the application of the contra proferentem rule: see *Aitken's Trs v Bank of Scotland*, 1944 S.C. 270 at 277 per L.J.C. Cooper. Cf. *Royal Bank of Scotland v Brown*, 1982 S.C. 89 at 100, per L.J.C Wheatley (who did not appear to have the benefit of *Aitken's Trustees* being cited to him). In *Waydale Ltd v DHL Holdings (UK) Ltd (No.2)*, 2001 S.L.T. 224 at 232, [26], Lord Hamilton observed that the contra proferentem rule's application was not clear, and that the above two cases could not be reconciled.

been held to be possible to contract out of the usual incidents of cautionary obligation, at least where "clear and unambiguous language" is used,[56] and contracting
out has been common in practice in relation to matters such as giving time to the
principal debtor; binding co-cautioners; extinction of the principal debt; and the
release of securities.[57] In the context of the modern law of contract, it is not certain
how far caution can be regarded as subject to any special rules of construction. It
has been held in the Outer House that if, after applying the normal rules, there is
any "ambiguity or real doubt" about the meaning of a provision, this is to be
decided in the cautioner's favour,[58] but a difficulty in interpretation does not
constitute ambiguity.[59] Further, it has been stated, obiter, in the Outer House, that
it is doubtful whether it is relevant to look at "the fair bona fides of the transaction"[60]
in construing a guarantee.[61]

Use of English authority—It is well established that English cases on guarantees **16.11**
setting out general principles can be used in Scottish cases on cautionary obligations as they "are 'nearly the same'".[62] English cases have been variously
described as "persuasive authority",[63] and as being "entitled to be treated with
great respect".[64] Nonetheless, regard needs to be had to such differences as exist,
such as the use of good faith rather than constructive notice in relation to "spousal
guarantees",[65] and the place of equity in English law.[66]

Benefit of discussion—In proper cautionary, the cautioner had at common law, **16.12**
unless otherwise agreed, the benefit of discussion (*beneficium ordinis*). That is to
say, he was entitled to insist that before he was called upon, diligence should be
used against the principal debtor. No such right was implied in the case of improper
cautionary. The implied benefit of discussion was abolished by s.8 of the
Mercantile Law Amendment Act Scotland 1856, and, since that Act, requires
express stipulation. Without it there may be direct action against the cautioner,
and it is not necessary to establish the failure of the principal debtor before suing
the cautioner and using diligence against him on the dependence of the action.[67]

Benefit of division—The right of division (*beneficium divisionis*) also depends **16.13**
on the distinction between proper and improper cautionary. In proper cautionary,
where more than one cautioner is expressly bound as such for an obligation in its
nature divisible, such as a debt, none can be sued for more than his pro rata share,
unless the others are insolvent.[68] In improper cautionary, when all the obligants

---

[56] *Trafalgar House Construction (Regions) Ltd v Surety Guarantee Co Ltd* [1996] A.C. 199.
[57] See para.16.26 and the guarantees in *Bank of Scotland v Macleod*, 1986 S.C. 165 and *Huewind v Clydesdale Bank Plc*, 1995 S.L.T. 392; affd 1996 S.L.T. 369 on this point.
[58] *Waydale Ltd v DHL Holdings (UK) Ltd (No.2)*, 2001 S.L.T. 224; cf. *Baird v Corbett* (1835) 14 S. 41 at 47; *Tenant and Co v Bunten* (1859) 21 D. 631.
[59] *Waydale Ltd v DHL Holdings (UK) Ltd (No.2)*, 2001 S.L.T. 224 at 230, [19].
[60] *Watt v National Bank of Scotland* (1839) 1 D. 827 at 830, per Lord Gillies.
[61] *Waydale Ltd v DHL Holdings (UK) Ltd (No.2)*, 2001 S.L.T. 224 at 230, [19].
[62] L.J.C. Cooper in *Aitken's Trs v Bank of Scotland*, 1944 S.C. 270 at 279, citing Bell, *Commentaries*, I, 364.
[63] *Aitken's Trs v Bank of Scotland*, 1944 S.C. 270 at 279.
[64] *Royal Bank of Scotland v Brown*, 1982 S.C. 89 at 100, per L.J.C. Wheatley.
[65] *Smith v Bank of Scotland*, 1997 S.C. (HL) 111 at 118, per Lord Clyde.
[66] *Aitken's Trustees v Bank of Scotland*, 1944 S.C. 270 at 279.
[67] *Johannesburg Municipal Council v Stewart*, 1909 S.C. (HL) 53; *Scottish Metropolitan Property v Christie*, 1987 S.L.T. (Sh. Ct) 18.
[68] Bell, *Principles*, s.267.

are bound jointly and severally and ex facie as full debtors, anyone may be sued for the whole debt.[69]

16.14 Obligations by more than one cautioner—Where a cautionary obligation is to be undertaken by more than one cautioner it is as a general rule the duty of the creditor to secure that all become bound. Each cautioner who signs does so on the implied condition that the others are to be bound with him, and is not liable if this condition is not fulfilled.[70] This rule holds even though the form of the obligation is joint and several, provided that the creditor was aware that some of the obligants; were really cautioners. So where an insurance company agreed to lend money to A on condition that four other persons should become jointly and severally liable with him in a bond, and three of the four signed and A forged the signature of the fourth, it was held that the bond could not be enforced against any of the cautioners.[71] The general rule finds exception in judicial cautionary, where a bond is lodged in obedience to the orders of the court. No duty is then cast on the creditor to see that the signatures of all the obligants are obtained, and therefore an obligant who signed was held liable although the signature of the other obligant was forged.[72]

16.15 Effect of misrepresentation, undue influence, facility and circumvention or force and fear—A cautionary obligation is not challengeable because it was undertaken due to the debtor's misrepresentation; the position is also the same where the debtor's wrongdoing concerns undue influence, facility and circumvention or force and fear.[73] Two exceptions arise: (i) where the debtor is the creditor's agent; and (ii) where the creditor is regarded as having participated in the wrongdoing. Under the first exception, the debtor's agent's wrongdoing can be attributed to the creditor principal; and, under the second exception, the wrongdoing can be treated as being that of the creditor because of his participation.[74] Where the debtor's misrepresentation is fraudulent, for the cautionary obligation to be valid, the creditor must have no notice of the fraud and have given valuable consideration.[75]

16.16 Disclosure by the creditor to the cautioner—It is a general principle that a cautioner is to look after his own interests and make enquiry about the principal debtor,[76] but the rule is not absolute. The case law has identified the following exceptions, which require the creditor to "take steps in the interests of the cautioner", failing which, the cautionary obligation will be void.[77] First, where the cautioner and debtor are in a "personal relationship", and "the creditor should reasonably suspect" that there are factors which may bear upon the cautioner's

---

[69] *Richmond v Grahame* (1847) 9 D. 633.

[70] As to the discharge of co-cautioners, see para.16.26, below.

[71] *Scottish Provincial Assurance Co v Pringle* (1858) 20 D. 465. See also *Ellesmere Brewery Co v Cooper* [1986] 1 Q.B. 75.

[72] *Simpson v Fleming* (1860) 22 D. 679.

[73] *Smith v Bank of Scotland*, 1997 S.C. (HL) 111 at 116–17 and the cases cited there.

[74] *Smith v Bank of Scotland*, 1997 S.C. (HL) 111 at 117.

[75] *Smith v Bank of Scotland*, 1997 S.C. (HL) 111; *Clydesdale Banking Co v Paul* (1877) 4 R. 626 and *Universal Import Export GmbH v Bank of Scotland*, 1995 S.C. 73.

[76] *Smith v Bank of Scotland*, 1997 S.C. (HL) 111 at 117, per Lord Clyde; *Young v Clydesdale Bank* (1889) 17 R. 231; *Royal Bank of Scotland v Greenshields*, 1914 S.C. 259; *Hamilton v Watson* (1845) 4 Bell, App. 67 at 103; *Bank of Scotland Plc v Forbes* [2011] CSIH 23; 2011 G.W.D. 12–270.

[77] *Smith v Bank of Scotland*, 1997 S.C. (HL) 111 at 118.

independent consent, due to this relationship, the creditor may come under a duty of good faith which may require unusual steps to be taken, as discussed in the following paragraph. Secondly, where the cautionary obligation contains an unusual feature, which the cautioner would not normally expect.[78] Thirdly, where a reasonable man would suspect that fraud was used to obtain the consent of the cautioner.[79] Fourthly, where there is a representation by the creditor to the cautioner, it must be "full and fair", and not involve "withholding part of the truth".[80] Fifthly, where the cautioner makes a statement indicating to the creditor that the cautioner does not understand the principal debtor's position, the creditor must "give a true and accurate explanation".[81] The rationale for these situations is good faith.[82] An obligation of disclosure also arises in the case of guarantees for the fidelity of a servant or official: the employer is bound to disclose all prior irregularities or other facts calculated to influence the mind of the guarantor,[83] as the contract is, in substance, one of insurance, and falls within the rule that in insurance all material facts must be disclosed.[84]

Good faith in cautionary obligations: *Smith v Bank of Scotland*—In *Barclays* **16.17** *Bank Ltd v O'Brien*,[85] the House of Lords held that where there is a relationship between the principal debtor and the cautioner of a kind which might lead a reasonable person to suspect that the cautioner's agreement might not have been freely given, the creditor comes under duties to warn the cautioner about the risks of the transaction and suggest that independent advice be obtained. This decision was based on the doctrine of constructive notice and was explicitly said to be an extension of the law designed to protect vulnerable persons, and particularly wives involved in transactions with their husbands. In *Royal Bank of Scotland Plc v Etridge (No.2)*,[86] the House laid down detailed rules for deciding how the decision in *Barclays Bank v O'Brien* should be applied.[87] In *Smith v Bank of Scotland*,[88] a decision similar to *Barclays Bank v O'Brien* was reached in regard to Scotland, but based on the doctrine of good faith. There followed a series of Outer House decisions in which the effects of *Smith v Bank of Scotland* were explored. These were reviewed and the Scots law restated in *Royal Bank of Scotland v Wilson*.[89] It was made clear in that case that the rules laid down in *Etridge*, above, should not be treated as directly applicable to Scotland. It was also made clear that the foundation of the cautioner's right to challenge the validity of the obligation is misrepresentation or undue influence, which the cautioner must aver and if necessary prove, and that the creditor's duties only arise in a case where the cautionary obligation is gratuitous. The court, following *Smith v Bank*

---

[78] *Hamilton v Watson* (1845) 4 Bell, App. 67 at 103; *North Shore Ventures Ltd. v Anstead Holdings Inc* [2011] EWCA Civ 230; *Levett v Barclays Bank Plc* [1995] 1 W.L.R. 1260; and *Smith v Bank of Scotland*, 1997 S.C. (HL) 111 at 118.

[79] *Smith v Bank of Scotland*, 1997 S.C. (HL) 111 at 117.

[80] *Smith v Bank of Scotland*, 1997 S.C. (HL) 111; *Bank of Scotland Plc v Forbes* [2011] CSIH 23.

[81] *Smith v Bank of Scotland*, 1997 S.C. (HL) 111.

[82] *Smith v Bank of Scotland*, 1997 S.C. (HL) 111 at 118.

[83] *French v Cameron* (1893) 20 R. 966; *Bank of Scotland v Morrison*, 1911 S.C. 593.

[84] *Wallace's Factor v McKissock* (1898) 25 R. 642 at 653, per Lord McLaren.

[85] *Barclays Bank Ltd v O'Brien* [1994] 1 A.C. 180.

[86] *Royal Bank of Scotland Plc v Etridge (No.2)* [2002] 2 A.C. 773.

[87] Some commentators have treated these decisions as falling under the principle of unjust enrichment rather than contract: see e.g. P. Birks, *English Private Law* (Oxford: Oxford University Press, 2000).

[88] *Smith v Bank of Scotland*, 1997 S.C. (HL) 111.

[89] *Royal Bank of Scotland v Wilson*, 2004 S.C. 153.

of Scotland, above, declined to attempt to lay down precise rules as to what the creditor must do where a close personal relationship exists between creditor and cautioner. The governing principle is that the creditor should not take a security from the wife or other connected person where, on an objective judgment of the circumstances, he has reason to think that the wife's consent to grant it may have been vitiated by misrepresentation, undue influence or some other wrongful act committed by the creditor. It is important to note that it is only undue influence which may vitiate the transaction. It was further held, approving *Forsyth v Royal Bank of Scotland*,[90] that where the creditor knows that the cautioner has been advised by a solicitor, even where the solicitor is acting for both husband and wife, he is entitled to assume that the cautioner has been properly advised and that conflicts of interest have been properly taken into account, unless the circumstances indicate that that was not the case. The creditor cannot shelter behind these assumptions if there were circumstances which should have put him on enquiry.[91] *The Lending Code* also imposes obligations on banks in accepting securities and it would appear that these can be taken into account.[92] Questions of this kind commonly occur when a wife is consenting to the granting of a standard security over the matrimonial home for the debts of her husband or his business, and the transaction is, ex facie, not to the wife's advantage. The consent of the wife to giving a standard security over her share in the matrimonial home is required under the Matrimonial Homes (Family Protection) Act 1981. A failure by the creditor to act in good faith can result in the cautionary obligation being set aside against the creditor. It would seem, following English authority, that for a cautionary obligation to be set aside, restitutio in integrum by the cautioner must be possible.[93] The range of "close personal relationships"[94] giving rise to an obligation of good faith have not been definitively stated by the Scottish courts.[95] The obligation has been held to apply in the cases of: (i) husband and wife[96] (but not where there was a joint and several personal obligation by the husband and wife); and (ii) parent and child (where the parent was the cautioner).[97] It has been held not applicable where: (i) there was a joint loan to a husband and wife, who were joint owners of a house and who gave a joint and several secured personal obligation[98]; and (ii) a director/shareholder of a company who acted as cautioner for the company.[99] However, the use of a "close personal relationship" by an interested person, who is not a debtor, to prevail upon the cautioner to grant a cautionary obligation can impose an obligation of good faith where the creditor is aware of the relationship.[100] The similar rule applying in England, has been said to be applicable to: (i) co-habitants (whether heterosexual or homosexual)[101];

---

[90] *Forsyth v Royal Bank of Scotland*, 2000 S.L.T. 1295.

[91] *Thompson v Royal Bank of Scotland Plc (No.3)*, 2003 S.C.L.R. 964 (OH).

[92] March 2011 version (revised May 2012), paras 67–75, found at *http://www.lendingstandards-board.org.uk/docs/lendingcode.pdf* [Accessed August 3, 2012].

[93] *Dunbar Bank Plc v Nadeem* [1998] 3 All E.R. 876; see also the discussion of restitutio in integrum generally in para.7.04, above.

[94] *Wright v Cotias Investments Inc*, 2001 S.L.T. 353 at [19].

[95] *Smith v Bank of Scotland*, 1997 S.C. (HL) 111.

[96] *Smith v Bank of Scotland*, 1997 S.C. (HL) 111.

[97] *Wright v Cotias Investments Inc*, 2001 S.L.T. 353 at [20].

[98] *Ahmed v Clydesdale Bank Plc*, 2002 S.L.T. 423. This is the position in England, at present, see *CIBC Mortgages Plc v Pitt* [1994] 1 A.C. 200.

[99] *Wright v Cotias Investments Inc*, 2001 S.L.T. 353 at [21].

[100] *Wright v Cotias Investments Inc*, 2001 S.L.T. 353 at 335.

[101] *Barclays Bank Plc v O'Brien* [1994] 1 A.C. 180.

(ii) couples who, whilst not co-habitants have a long-standing "intimate relationship"[102]; and (iii) employer/employee (where the latter was the guarantor of the former's business).[103]

Extent of cautioner's liability—In a question with the creditor, the extent of the **16.18** cautioner's liability is wholly regulated by the terms of the guarantee which he has given.[104] The obligation undertaken by a cautioner may or may not be limited to a certain amount. If there is no limitation in amount, the cautioner is liable for all loss resulting from the failure in fulfilment of the obligation guaranteed, e.g. for interest, or for expenses reasonably incurred in attempting to enforce the debt against the principal debtor.[105] Normally, a guarantee will not be completely unlimited, i.e. "open-ended". Consequently, in determining the liability of a cautioner to a creditor, a distinction needs to be made between a cautioner undertaking to pay: (i) either an amount not exceeding a certain sum, or a certain amount (or part of it), on the one hand; and (ii) "all sums" owed to the creditor by the principal debtor (which, as indicated above, would include interest and expenses), subject to a limitation on the cautioner's liability up to a certain amount, on the other.[106] For example, in the first situation, if the debtor owes the creditor £1,500, but £1,000 has already been paid, the cautioner is only required to pay £500; once the cautioner has paid this sum to the creditor, the cautioner may then seek to recover it from the debtor or prove for it in the debtor's bankruptcy in competition with the creditor.[107] If the creditor advances sums in excess of the £1,500 to the debtor, the cautioner is not liable for those sums.[108] In the second situation, the cautioner is liable for advances by the creditor in excess of the £1,500, as the cautioner's obligation is for "all sums", subject to the limit the cautioner has placed on his own liability.[109] The effect of this is that, where there is a limit on the sum to be paid by the cautioner, and the cautioner has paid that sum, but part of the principal debt remains outstanding, the cautioner cannot seek to recover it from the principal debtor or prove in the principal debtor's bankruptcy until the whole of the principal debt has been paid off, even although the cautioner has fulfilled his obligations.[110] The cautioner's right to relief is, thus, postponed. Where an agreement provides that a cautioner guarantees the payment to the creditor of "all money now or at any time owing" by the debtor, it will be a matter of construction whether the cautioner's liability extends to all sums owed by the debtor to the creditor or is limited to sums owed by the debtor to the creditor under a factoring agreement entered into between the debtor and creditor contemporaneously with the guarantee.[111] A cautionary obligation may also be a

---

[102] *Massey v Midland Bank Plc* [1995] 1 All E.R. 929.

[103] *Credit Lyonnais Bank Nederland N.V. v Burch* [1997] 1 All E.R. 144.

[104] Gloag and Irvine, *Rights in Security* (1897), p.756.

[105] *Struthers v Dykes* (1847) 9 D. 1437; *Moschi v Lep Air Services* [1973] A.C. 331.

[106] *Veitch v National Bank of Scotland*, 1907 S.C. 554. Cf. paras 71–72 of *The Lending Code*, March 2011, which applies to individual customers, and states that a bank "should not take an unlimited guarantee from an individual". This will not apply in the case of a corporate cautioner.

[107] *Veitch v National Bank of Scotland*, 1907 S.C. 554. See too para.16.05 on the cautioner's right to relief.

[108] *Veitch v National Bank of Scotland*, 1907 S.C. 554.

[109] *Veitch v National Bank of Scotland*, 1907 S.C. 554, and *Bank of Scotland v Macleod*, 1986 S.C. 165.

[110] *Veitch v National Bank of Scotland*, 1907 S.C. 554. See also para.16.21, below.

[111] *Brady v Bibby Factors Scotland Ltd* [2005] CSIH 38. On the facts of this case, it was held that the cautioner's liability was limited to sums owed by the debtor to the creditor under the factoring agreement only.

"top slice guarantee" in which the cautioner is only liable for sums above a certain amount with a limit as to the amount the cautioner is to be liable for.[112] As cautionary is an accessory obligation, the cautioner's liability can never exceed that of the principal debtor. So where the creditor advanced the sum of £300 and the cautionary obligation took the form of a blank promissory note, which was later filled in for £2,000 by the principal debtor's agent, it was held, that in the cautioner's sequestration the creditor could not rank for a greater amount than he had advanced to the principal debtor in order to draw his actual advance of £300 as a dividend.[113] Where a cautionary obligation contains no limit of time, but does contain a limit of the amount for which the cautioner undertakes liability, it is a question of construction whether it is to be read as a continuing (or on-going) guarantee, such as for an overdraft facility with a bank, or as a guarantee which is ended when the limit of liability is reached.[114] In the former case, the cautioner is liable for the balance due when his obligation is ultimately enforced; in the latter, any payments made by the principal debtor, after the maximum of liability has been reached, go to diminish the amount for which the cautioner is responsible, and he is not liable for advances subsequently made.[115] Where the guarantor undertakes to make payment "on demand" his obligation is not enforceable until the creditor makes a demand.[116] However, a prior demand for payment is not required where the agreement in which the cautionary obligation is contained includes a 'consent to registration' clause.[117] Where the obligation is not incurred for any definite period, the cautioner may, subject to any contrary agreement, safeguard himself for any liability in the future by giving notice to the creditor that his guarantee is withdrawn. And a cautioner is entitled, on giving reasonable notice, to call upon the principal debtor to relieve him of all liabilities which he may have incurred. The principal debtor will be ordained to procure and deliver to the cautioner a discharge from the creditor.[118]

16.19 Cautioner's right to assignation of debt—On payment by a cautioner of the debt, the cautioner is entitled to demand from the creditor an assignation of the debt, any security held for it, and any diligence done upon it, so as to enable him to enforce his right of relief against the principal debtor, or against co-cautioners.[119] Where the debt and any security held for it by the creditor is assigned to the cautioner, the cautioner obtains a prior ranking over the principal debtor's other creditors.[120] Subject to the prohibition on double ranking, the cautioner, as assignee of the creditor, may rank in the principal debtor's sequestration.[121] It has been decided that no such right exists except upon full payment, so that where a

---

[112] *Huewind Ltd v Clydesdale Bank Plc*, 1996 S.LT. 369.

[113] *Jackson v McIver* (1875) 2 R. 882.

[114] *Bank of Scotland v Macleod*, 1986 S.C. 165; *Huewind Ltd v Clydesdale Bank Plc*, 1996 S.L.T. 369.

[115] *Scott v Mitchell* (1866) 4 M. 551.

[116] *Royal Bank of Scotland v Brown*, 1982 S.C. 89.

[117] *AIB Group (UK) Plc v Guarino*, 2006 S.L.T. (Sh. Ct) 138 at 140, per Sheriff Scott. A "consent to registration" clause is one in which the cautioner agrees that the document containing the cautionary obligation may be registered in the Books of Council and Session for preservation and/or execution. See further below, para.48.01(2).

[118] *Doig v Lawrie* (1903) 5 F. 295: the guarantee in this case expressly contemplated the possibility of withdrawal.

[119] Bell, *Principles*, ss.255 and 558; *Sligo v Menzies* (1840) 2 D. 1478; *Guthrie and McConnachy v Smith* (1880) 8 R. 106.

[120] *Joint Liquidators of Simclar (Ayrshire) Ltd v Simclar Group Ltd* [2011] CSOH 54.

[121] Bankruptcy (Scotland) Act 1985 s.60(3). See para.16.21, below.

cautioner was bankrupt, and a dividend was paid on the debt, his trustee could not demand an assignation.[122] In exceptional cases the creditor may refuse an assignation of the debt on the ground that to grant it would conflict with some legitimate interest of his own.[123] Where the demand is for the assignation of securities held for the debt, it cannot be refused on the ground that the creditor proposes to retain the securities to meet some other debt subsequently incurred.[124] It is a general principle that an assignation from the creditor, though it may afford a convenient means of enforcing a right of relief, does not in any way enlarge that right.[125] And it has been laid down that a cautioner with or without an assignation, can enforce only securities over the estate of the debtor, not securities granted by third parties.[126]

Right to share in securities—A cautioner is entitled to share in the benefit of any **16.20** securities which any of his co-cautioners may have obtained over the estate of the principal debtor.[127] The rule applies although the cautioner claiming the right to share had already engaged without any security.[128] But it yields to any express agreement which gives him the whole benefit; the fact that the other cautioners have agreed to this may be proved by parole evidence.[129] The theory underlying the rule is that the estate of the principal debtor is to be regarded as a fund in which all the cautioners have an equal right to share, and therefore it was held that it did not extend to the case where one cautioner had obtained a security from a third party.[130]

Ranking in bankruptcy—On the bankruptcy of the principal debtor, if the **16.21** creditor ranks for the debt, receives a dividend, and obtains payment of the balance from the cautioner, the latter is not entitled to a ranking for what he has paid, because to allow it would conflict with the principle that no debt can be ranked twice on a sequestrated estate.[131] Where the cautioner is liable for the whole debt, it is open to him to pay it, obtain an assignation and rank in place of the creditor. To this the creditor has no legitimate interest to object. If the cautioner's liability is limited to a fixed sum, and the principal debt exceeds this, the contract may be read as a guarantee of part of the debt. If so, the cautioner is entitled, on payment of the amount he has guaranteed, to rank in place of the creditor for that amount, or, if the creditor ranks, the cautioner's liability is limited to the balance of the guaranteed amount remaining after payment of the dividend.[132] On the other hand, if the bond is read as a guarantee of the whole debt, with a limit of the amount for which the cautioner is liable, the general construction of the obligation is that the creditor is entitled to rank for his whole debt to and recover from the cautioner any balance remaining, in so far as that balance does not exceed the limit for which the

---

[122] *Ewart v Latta* (1865) 3 M. (HL) 36.
[123] *Graham v Gordon* (1842) 4 D. 903.
[124] *Fleming v Burgess* (1867) 5 M. 856: in this case, however, the creditor acquired the security in question *pendente lite*.
[125] *Thow's Tr. v Young*, 1910 S.C. 588.
[126] *Thow's Tr. v Young*, 1910 S.C. 588 at 596, per Lord President Dunedin.
[127] Bell, *Commentaries*, I, 367.
[128] *Steel v Dixon* (1881) L.R. 17 Ch.D. 825.
[129] *Hamilton v Freeth* (1889) 16 R. 1022.
[130] *Scott v Young*, 1909 1 S.L.T. 47.
[131] *Anderson v Mackinnon* (1876) 3 R. 608; *Mackinnon v Monkhouse* (1881) 9 R. 393.
[132] *Veitch v National Bank of Scotland*, 1907 S.C. 554.

cautioner has engaged.[133] But if, before the sequestration of the principal debtor, the cautioner has paid any part of the debt, the creditor is bound to deduct what has been paid and rank for no more than the balance, whether the cautioner makes a claim for a ranking or not.[134]

16.22 Discharge of cautionary obligations—In addition to the methods applicable in general to the discharge of obligations the following require notice: (1) prescription; (2) extinction of the principal obligation; (3) death of the principal debtor, cautioner or creditor; (4) discharge of co-cautioner; (5) giving time to principal debtor; (6) release of securities; (7) alteration of the contract; (8) change in a partnership.

16.23 Prescription—By s.6 of the Prescription and Limitation (Scotland) Act 1973, the prescriptive period applicable to cautionary obligations is five years.[135] Thus, if a cautionary obligation, being an obligation arising from a contract, has subsisted for a continuous period of five years from the time when it became enforceable without any relevant claims having been made in relation to it and without the subsistence of the obligation having been relevantly acknowledged in terms of the Act, it will be extinguished.[136] Where the debtor fails to perform an obligation, the cautioner is immediately liable,[137] and the prescriptive period will start to run; but where the cautioner's obligation is to pay "on demand", the period does not begin until a demand is made.[138] Where there is no provision in the agreement between the cautioner and the creditor which clarifies the form the demand should take, correspondence passing between the creditor and cautioner which sets out the liability of the cautioner may inadvertently amount to a demand for payment from which the 5-year period of positive prescription runs.[139]

16.24 Extinction of principal obligation—As cautionary is an accessory obligation, payment of the debt or discharge of the principal debtor liberates the cautioner. Where the principal debt is paid but the payment is set aside, for example under bankruptcy law, the cautioner remains bound.[140] As regards discharge, the absolute discharge of the principal debtor implies the discharge of the cautioner, unless there is an express provision in the instrument of cautionry that, where the principal debtor has been discharged, but where the principal debt still subsists, the cautioner's obligation still remains, i.e. the cautioner's obligation becomes an independent (or primary) obligation.[141] There is a statutory exception to this in the

---

[133] *Harvie's Tr. v Bank of Scotland* (1885) 12 R. 1141; *Bank of Scotland v Macleod*, 1986 S.C. 165.

[134] *Mackinnon's Tr. v Bank of Scotland*, 1915 S.C. 411.

[135] Prescription and Limitation (Scotland) Act 1973 Sch.5. See Ch.4, above.

[136] Prescription and Limitation (Scotland) Act 1973 s.6(1)–(3) and Sch.1 paras 1(g) and 2(c); *Royal Bank of Scotland v Brown*, 1982 S.C. 89. Sch.2 para.2 does not apply to cautionary obligations. A cautionary obligation may also be affected by the long negative prescription of 20 years: see paras 4.05–4.06, above.

[137] *Moschi v Lep Air Services* [1973] A.C. 331 at 358, per Lord Kilbrandon; *Glasgow City Council v Excess Insurance*, 1986 S.L.T. 585, as read with *Glasgow D.C. v Excess Insurance (No.2)*, 1990 S.L.T. 225; *AIB Group (UK) Plc v Guarino*, 2006 S.L.T. (Sh. Ct) 138 at 140 per Sheriff Scott.

[138] *Royal Bank of Scotland v Brown*, 1982 S.C. 89.

[139] *Royal Bank of Scotland v Lyon* Unreported July 20, 2004 Inverness Sheriff Court, Sheriff Principal Sir Stephen S. T. Young QC.

[140] *Petty v Cook* [1871] L.R. 6 (QB) 790.

[141] As was the case in *Bank of Scotland v Macleod*, 1986 S.C. 165 and *Huewind v Clydesdale Bank Plc*, 1995 S.L.T. 392; affd on this point 1996 S.L.T. 369.

case of the discharge of the bankrupt in sequestration.[142] And a distinction is recognised between: (i) a discharge, which extinguishes the principal debt and also frees the cautioner; and (ii) a *pactum de non petendo*, whereby the creditor gives up his right to sue the principal debtor but reserves his claim against the cautioner. In the latter case, the cautioner is not discharged, and, on payment, may demand an assignation of the debt and sue the principal debtor thereon.[143] Apart from a discharge, the cautioner may be liberated by the extinction of the principal debt by other methods, as where it is allowed to prescribe.[144] Novation of the principal debt, in the case where the principal debt is discharged and a new one substituted, will liberate the cautioner.[145] The assignation of the debt, merely substituting a new creditor, has no such effect.[146] The fact that at some period in the history of the transaction compensation might have been pleaded in respect of a debt due by the creditor to the principal debtor does not extinguish the debt and therefore does not liberate the cautioner, but the latter is entitled, on a claim being made against him, to insist on any ground of compensation then available to the principal debtor.[147] The debt for which the cautioner is liable, and consequently his own liability, may be extinguished by the application of the rule that where indefinite payments are made, the earliest credit item goes to wipe out the earliest debit item.[148] This may happen if, when the cautioner's obligation for a continuous account, such as a cash credit with a bank, is in any way withdrawn or terminated, the account is continued with the principal debtor without any definite break. Then, though there may be a continuous adverse balance against the debtor, any payments made by him, if ascribed to meet the earliest debt in the account, will in time extinguish the balance due when the cautionary obligation was withdrawn, and, by thus extinguishing the principal debt, will liberate the cautioner.[149]

Death of one of the parties—The death of a cautioner has no effect on his existing **16.25** liability, which may be enforced against his representatives. And if the cautionary obligation is of the nature of a continuing guarantee—as in the case of a cash credit with a bank—the representatives of a deceased cautioner will remain liable for debts subsequently incurred, unless they intimate that the guarantee is withdrawn. It is immaterial that the cautioner's representatives were not aware of the obligation, and no duty is cast upon the creditor to intimate to them.[150] The death of the principal debtor will, as a general rule, exclude the liability of the cautioner for any debt not then due.[151] But where caution for expenses was the statutory condition of an appeal from the sheriff court, it was held that the cautioner was liable for expenses incurred after the death of the appellant, when his representatives were sisted as parties and carried on the appeal.[152] The death of the creditor does not

---

[142] Bankruptcy (Scotland) Act 1985 s.60(1). This does not cover private trust deeds for creditors.

[143] *Muir v Crawford* (1875) 2 R. (HL) 148.

[144] Erskine, III, 3, 66.

[145] *Commercial Bank of Tasmania v Jones* [1893] A.C. 313. See also *Hay & Kyd v Powrie* (1886) 13 R. 777; Gloag and Irvine, *Rights in Security* (1897), p.846; *De Montfort Insurance Co Plc v Lafferty*, 1998 S.L.T. 535 at 538F, per Lord Penrose.

[146] *Bradford Old Bank v Sutcliffe* [1918] 2 K.B. 833.

[147] *Bechervaise v Lewis* (1872) L.R. 7 C.P. 372.

[148] *Devaynes v Noble (Clayton's Case)* (1816) 1 Mer. 572. For the application of the rule, see *Hay & Co v Torbet*, 1908 S.C. 781 and para.3.27, above.

[149] *Royal Bank v Christie* (1841) 2 Rob. 118; *Cuthill v Strachan* (1894) 1 S.L.T. 527.

[150] *British Linen Co v Monteith* (1858) 20 D. 557.

[151] *Woodfield Finance Trust (Glasgow) v Morgan*, 1958 S.L.T. (Sh. Ct) 14.

[152] *Wilson v Ewing* (1836) 14 S. 262.

affect the liability of a cautioner for an existing debt. In guarantees for the fidelity of an employee, the death of the employer terminates the guarantee, even although the party employed is kept on by his representatives.[153]

16.26 Discharge of co-cautioners—Where there are several cautioners, the discharge of one without the consent of the others has, by statute, the effect of liberating them.[154] The section by which this rule is established expressly excepts the case of a cautioner's consent to the discharge of a co-cautioner who has become bankrupt.[155] It has been held, in England, that where the cautioner is released in such a way that the creditor expressly reserves his rights against a co-cautioner, the co-cautioner is not liberated.[156] And, by a decision in Scotland, the section applies only where the cautioners are bound jointly and severally for the whole debt, not to the case where each has engaged for a specific sum.[157]

16.27 Giving time—It is a general, and in some respects very technical, rule that a cautioner is liberated if the creditor has given time to the principal debtor.[158] It is possible for the cautioner and the creditor to disapply this common law rule, e.g. the inclusion of a "grant of indulgence in favour of the principal debtor" clause will empower the creditor to proceed directly against the cautioner without any prior enforcement of its rights against the debtor notwithstanding that the creditor has granted time to the debtor.[159] "Giving time" does not mean failure to press the principal debtor for payment or to rank in his bankruptcy. For such failure the cautioner has his remedy by paying the debt, obtaining an assignation of it and exercising the rights of the creditor.[160] By giving time is meant any act by which the creditor deprives himself of the right to sue for immediate payment, and thus alters the contract for which the cautioner undertook liability. This may be by an express agreement not to sue, or by taking a bill payable at some future date,[161] or by an arrangement for payment by instalments.[162] By such agreements the cautioner is, or may be, prejudiced since, as he can only stand in the place of the creditor, he loses the power to enforce immediate payment from the debtor. On this footing it is an established rule that he is liberated, and it is immaterial that he is unable to show that he has suffered any actual prejudice,[163] or that, before time was given, he had repudiated his liability on other grounds.[164] If the cautionary obligation is for a debt already incurred, the giving of time for any period, however short, precludes recourse against the cautioner; if the obligation is to guarantee

---

[153] *Stewart v Scot* (1834) 7 W. & S. 211.

[154] Mercantile Law Amendment Act Scotland 1856 s.9; *Royal Bank of Scotland v Welsh*, 1985 S.L.T. 439.

[155] It has been suggested (probably wrongly) that the Act used "cautioner" when "creditor" was intended: Gloag and Irvine, *Rights in Security*, p.912; Bell, *Principles*, s.261A, fn.(a). The scheme of the Bankruptcy (Scotland) Act 1985 means that the point may no longer be of great practical importance.

[156] *Thompson v Lack* (1846) 3 C.B. 540; cf. *James Graham & Co (Timber) Ltd v Southgate-Sands* [1986] Q.B. 80, where this was not the case.

[157] *Morgan v Smart* (1872) 10 M. 610.

[158] Bell, *Principles*, s.262.

[159] *Brady v Bibby Factors Scotland Ltd* [2005] CSIH 38.

[160] *Hay & Kyd v Powrie* (1886) 13 R. 777, per Lord Rutherfurd Clark; *Hamilton's Exr v Bank of Scotland*, 1913 S.C. 743, where the effect of a clause entitling the creditor to give time is considered.

[161] *Johnstone v Duthie* (1892) 19 R. 624; *Goldfarb v Bartlett* [1920] 1 K.B. 639.

[162] *Wilson v Lloyd* (1873) L.R. 16 Eq. 60.

[163] *Johnstone v Duthie* (1892) 19 R. 624; *Polak v Everett* (1876) L.R. 1 Q.B.D. 669.

[164] *Johnstone v Duthie* (1892) 19 R. 624.

payment of furnishings to be supplied in the future, the creditor is not held to have given time by allowing any ordinary period of credit, or taking a bill for the price. But the cautioner may have a valid defence if he can prove that the amount of credit given, or the currency of the bill, was unreasonably long; it is not sufficient to prove that the credit given was more than was usual in the particular trade.[165]

The rule that a cautioner is liberated if time be given to the principal debtor does not apply if in the contract by which time is given the rights of the cautioner against the principal debtor are expressly reserved.[166] The cautioner may then, by paying the debt and obtaining an assignation, enforce immediate payment and therefore, as he has suffered no injury, his liability is unaffected.[167] And if the creditor has obtained decree against the cautioner, the fact that he has subsequently given time to the principal debtor does not affect the cautioner's liability.[168]

Giving up securities—As a cautioner has the right, on payment of the debt, to an assignation of any security over the debtor's estate which the creditor may hold for it,[169] his position is prejudiced if, without his consent, any security is given up; and therefore the release of securities, if a voluntary act on the part of the creditor, will operate as a release to the cautioner.[170] Unless there is an express agreement that the creditor shall avail himself of a particular security before calling on the cautioner (when the release of that security operates as an absolute discharge),[171] the cautioner is released only in so far as he is prejudiced, i.e. to the extent of the value of the security which has been given up.[172] The same rules apply to the case where the creditor, without giving up a security, fails to take the steps necessary to make it effectual, as where the holder of a bond and disposition in security failed to complete his title, with the result that the trustee in the debtor's sequestration acquired a preferable right to the subjects.[173] It may be the law that a cautioner is released to the extent that he is prejudiced by the creditor's failure to take due care in realising the security.[174] **16.28**

Alteration of the contract-general—A cautioner is discharged if his position is adversely affected by a material alteration of the contract between the creditor and the principal debtor without the consent of the cautioner.[175] Where a clause in a contract between the cautioner and the creditor expressly provided that the cautioner agreed to the primary contract between the creditor and the principal debtor being varied without his consent, it was held in England that the court may nevertheless rule that the cautionary obligation had been discharged where the consent of the cautioner to the variation of the primary contract had not been obtained: this was on the ground that the effect of the purported "alteration" was **16.29**

---

[165] *Calder v Cruikshank's Tr.* (1889) 17 R. 74.

[166] As occurred in *Bank of Scotland v Macleod*, 1986 S.C. 165 and *Huewind v Clydesdale Bank Plc*, 1995 S.L.T. 392; affd on this point 1996 S.L.T. 369.

[167] *Muir v Crawford* (1875) 2 R. (HL) 148.

[168] *Aikman v Fisher* (1835) 14 S. 56.

[169] See above, para.16.19.

[170] *Sligo v Menzies* (1840) 2 D. 1478.

[171] *Drummond v Rannie* (1836) 14 S. 437.

[172] *Wright's Trs v Hamilton* (1835) 13 S. 380.

[173] *Fleming v Thomson* (1826) 2 W. & S. 277.

[174] *Lord Advocate v Maritime Fruit Carriers Co*, 1983 S.L.T. 357.

[175] See Bell, *Principles*, s.259; *N.G. Napier v Crosbie*, 1964 S.C. 129; *Hewit v Williamson*, 1999 S.L.T. 313; 1998 S.C.L.R. 601.

to constitute an agreement between the creditor and the principal debtor which was so different from the original agreement that the only possible construction was that a new agreement with new obligations had come into being.[176] The material alteration of the contract between the creditor and the principal debtor must take place after the cautioner has undertaken his obligation.[177] Thus where the creditors in a composition contract took a trust deed from the debtor, it was held that they had liberated the cautioner.[178] The mere fact that the creditor failed to disclose to the cautioner that he had grounds for suspecting forgery by the principal debtor was held to be no ground on which the cautioner could dispute his liability, though it was observed that the creditor, in the case of a cash credit bond, would not be justified in making further advances without disclosing to the cautioner any circumstances materially affecting the honesty of the debtor.[179] Where, however, a guarantee was limited to a certain sum irrespective of the sum due by the principal debtor and advances were made beyond the limit, it was held that the cautioner was not adversely affected and was not released.[180] The general rule about a material alteration applies only to cautionary obligations in the strict sense, subject always to the terms of particular contracts. Thus the rule does not apply in cases where a standard security is given in respect of an obligation of another person, without any personal obligation being undertaken. Even if the rule did apply to standard securities, it would not apply where the "cautioner" contemplates that the size of the principal debt might change, and the alteration falls within the "cautionary" obligation undertaken.[181] Otherwise, the application of the material alteration rule would render "all sums" standard securities ineffective where the standard security (cautionary obligation) covered not only a specific debt, but any other debt owed to the creditor by the principal debtor.[182]

16.30 Alteration of the contract-fidelity guarantees—In the case of fidelity guarantees, if in the original contract certain checks on the behaviour of the party guaranteed are provided for, the cautioner is discharged if they are not observed, and it is no defence to the creditor to prove that the checks would have been useless or that equivalent methods of supervision were instituted.[183] In the absence of any provision there is no implied obligation on the part of the creditor to exercise any special precautions, and therefore the cautioner will not escape liability by proof that more careful supervision would have precluded the failure in respect of which he is sued.[184] There is probably an exception to this in the case of a guarantee for the acts of a bank official, when the cautioner is entitled to rely on the checks, such as periodical audits, which are usual in banking business.[185] A change in the duties to be performed by the party guaranteed will release the cautioner if the terms of that party's appointment were made known to him at the time when he undertook the cautionary obligation, even when the change had no bearing on the

---

[176] *Triodos Bank NV v Dobbs* [2005] EWCA Civ 630; [2005] 2 Lloyd's Rep. 588.

[177] *Hewitt v Williamson*, 1999 S.L.T. 313 at 313; 1998 S.C.L.R. 601 at 607.

[178] *Allan, Allan & Milne v Pattison* (1893) 21 R. 195.

[179] *Bank of Scotland v Morrison*, 1911 S.C. 593; cf. *Smith v Bank of Scotland*, 1997 S.C. (HL) 111; see also para.16.16, above on disclosure.

[180] *Bank of Scotland v Macleod*, 1986 S.C. 165; *Huewind Ltd v Clydesdale Bank*, 1996 S.L.T. 369.

[181] *Hewit v Williamson*, 1999 S.L.T. 313 at 317 and 607 respectively.

[182] *Hewit v Williamson*, 1999 S.L.T. 313 at 317 and 607–8 respectively.

[183] *Haworth v Sickness, etc. Assurance Co* (1891) 18 R. 563; *Clydebank & District Water Trs v Fidelity & Deposit Co*, 1915 S.C. 69.

[184] *Mayor of Kingston v Harding* [1892] 2 Q.B. 494; *Mactaggart v Watson* (1835) I S. & McL. 553.

[185] *Falconer v Lothian* (1843) 5 D. 866 at 870.

loss for which the cautioner is sued.[186] This has been held even where the change in duties was due not to the act of the creditor but to the provisions of a statute.[187] The cautioner has engaged for a party performing particular duties, and he is not, without his consent, to be rendered liable for a party performing duties of a different kind. If, however, the particular nature of the duties to be performed was not known to the cautioner, and he gave a general guarantee, he will remain liable unless he can prove that the alteration in the contract of employment was material.[188] It has been held that if an employer discovers an act of dishonesty on the part of an official whose acts have been guaranteed, he is bound to give immediate notice to the cautioner, and failure to do so will justify the cautioner in repudiating his obligation even if he can offer no proof that the notice which was withheld would have been of any advantage to him.[189]

Change in a firm—It is provided by s.18 of the Partnership Act 1890, re-enacting **16.31** s.7 of the Mercantile Law Amendment Act Scotland 1856, and in substance reproducing the common law,[190] that a continuing guarantee or cautionary obligation given either to a firm or to a third person in respect of the transactions of a firm is, in the absence of agreement to the contrary, revoked as to future transactions by any change in the constitution of the firm to which, or of the firm in respect of the transactions of which, the guarantee or obligation was given. The change in the firm may be effected either by the admission of a new partner,[191] or by the retirement of an existing partner,[192] or, without any change in the persons composing the firm, by its registration as a company under the Companies Act 2006,[193] or, it would appear, conversion from a general partnership to a limited liability partnership under the Limited Liability Partnerships Act 2000.[194]

FURTHER READING

Bell, *Principles*, 10th edn (1899), Ch.8.

Crerar, L.D., *The Law of Banking in Scotland*, 2nd edn (Edinburgh: Tottel, 2007), Ch.11.

Davidson, F. and Macgregor, L., *Commercial Law in Scotland*, 2nd edn (Edinburgh: W. Green, 2008), Ch. 6.

Forte, A.D.M. (ed.), *Scots Commercial Law* (LexisNexis, 1997), Ch.6.

Gloag, W.M. and Irvine, J.M., *Rights in Security* (Edinburgh: W. Green, 1897; reprinted 1987), Chs 19–25.

Stair Memorial Encylopaedia, "Cautionary Obligations and Representations as to Credit", Vol.3.

Parsons, T.N., *Lingard's Bank Security Documents*, 4th edn (LexisNexis Butterworths, 2006).

---

[186] *Bonar v Macdonald* (1850) 7 Bell, App. 379; affirming (1847) 9 D. 1537.
[187] *Pybus v Gibb* (1856) 6 El. & Bl. 902.
[188] *Nicolson v Burt* (1882) 10 R. 121.
[189] *Snaddon v London, Edinburgh, etc. Assurance Co* (1902) 5 F. 182.
[190] *Royal Bank v Christie* (1841) 2 Rob. 118.
[191] *Spiers v Houston's Exrs* (1829) 3 W. & S. 392.
[192] *Royal Bank v Christie* (1841) 2 Rob. 118.
[193] *Hay & Co v Torbet*, 1908 S.C. 781.
[194] See s.1 of the Limited Liability Partnerships Act 2000 and the Explanatory Notes.

Gullifer, L., *Goode on Legal Problems of Credit and Security*, 4th edn (London: Sweet and Maxwell, 2008), Ch.VIII.

Goode, R., *Goode on Commercial Law*, 4th edn (Penguin, 2010), Ch.30.

Marks, D. and Moss, G., *Rowlatt on Principal and Surety*, 6th edn (London: Sweet and Maxwell, 2011).

Millett, R. and Andrews, G.M., *Law of Guarantees*, 5th edn (London: Sweet and Maxwell, 2008).

O'Donovan, J. and Phillips, J., *The Modern Contract of Guarantee*, 3rd edn (London: Sweet and Maxwell, 2003).

CHAPTER 17

EMPLOYMENT

Contract and regulation—In origin, employment, or as it used to be called, the **17.01** relationship of master and servant, is a contract. It is closely related to but in principle distinct from, a number of other types of contract which have similar economic purposes and effects: for example, agency, partnership and contracts to render services. In so far as the employment relationship is contractual, it was, and to an extent still is, subject to the jurisdiction of the ordinary courts and regulated by ordinary principles of contract. However, because of its economic importance and because of perceived opportunities for exploitation of the economically disadvantaged, a very extensive range of statutory regulations has been superimposed onto the "stem" of the basic contractual relationship.[1] Much of this regulation is designed to confer rights on employees to protect them against arbitrary or discriminatory action by their employers. Much ingenuity has been devoted to trying to minimise the effects of regulation, and of taxation, by devising arrangements which achieve effects equivalent to employment but fall outside the legal definitions of that relationship: examples are the treatment of workers as self-employed and the use of agency workers. Further, because of these arrangements and the uncertainty of the definition of employment itself, many of the statutory rights and protections have been extended beyond "employees" and apply to "workers", a term which is more broadly defined. The effect has been to create a number of detailed statutory codes dealing with matters such as minimum wages, working time, maternity and sick pay and time off work. Each of these codes contains its own definitions of the rights conferred and the conditions of eligibility and these are not always entirely consistent. The principal statute is the Employment Rights Act 1996 (hereafter referred to as "the ERA"). The law relating to labour relations has been consolidated in the Trade Union and Labour Relations (Consolidation) Act 1992 (the "1992 Act"), but some amendments and additions were made by the Employment Relations Act 1999 and the Employment Relations Act 2004: and significant provision in regard to giving information was added by regulations in 2004.[2] Employment rights and duties, and industrial relations are reserved matters under the Scotland Act 1998 Sch.5 Pt II Head H1. The European Union is a significant source of legislation relating to employment and frequent reference has to be made to decisions of the European Court of Justice/Court of Justice of the European Union. The European Convention on Human Rights and Fundamental Freedoms also plays an increasing role in employment litigation.[3]

---

[1] *Buckland v Bournemouth University Higher Education Corporation* [2010] EWCA Civ 121; [2010] 4 All E.R. 186 at 191f, per Sedley L.J.

[2] Information and Consultation of Employees Regulations 2004 (SI 2004/3246).

[3] Human Rights Act 1998; see *R. (on the application of G) v Governors of X School* [2011] UKSC 30; [2012] 1 A.C. 167; *Kulkarni v Milton Keynes Hospital NHS Trust* [2009] EWCA Civ 789; [2010] I.C.R. 101; [2009] I.R.L.R. 829 and *ASLEF v United Kingdom* [2007] I.R.L.R. 361. For an analysis of

17.02 Discrimination—In addition to the general regulation of employment rights, there has been statutory intervention to combat various forms of discrimination against particular classes of workers. Much of the impetus for this has come from EU Directives, and the UK law must be interpreted in the light of the terms of the relevant Directive. UK anti-discrimination law was consolidated by the Equality Act 2010 ("EqA").[4] The EqA provides protection to certain classes of workers on the basis of the "protected characteristics", namely age, disability, gender reassignment, marriage and civil partnership, pregnancy and maternity, race, religion or belief, sex and sexual orientation.[5] All these forms of protection should be seen in the context of the Equal Treatment Directives.[6] In all cases, the protection against discrimination includes discrimination in access to employment and so begins before the formation of an employment or other contractual relationship, and in certain cases discriminatory acts after the termination of employment may be actionable.[7] The differing strands of anti-discrimination law share many of the same concepts, such as direct and indirect discrimination, and decisions on provisions which apply to one strand can be referred to in relation to construction of another. There are, however, small but significant differences between the wording of the different provisions as they apply to particular protected characteristics which may lead to different results.[8] There can also be differences of approach, particularly in the context of disability and age discrimination.[9] Other Directives deal with the position of self-employed workers, fixed-term employees, agency workers and part-time workers.[10]

17.03 Scope and enforcement of rights—The statutory codes apply primarily to workers in the United Kingdom.[11] Any proceedings for the determination

---

the development of the "employment contract" against the backdrop of the emergence of the welfare state, see. S. Deakin and F. Wilkinson, *The Law of the Labour Market: Industrialization, Employment and Legal Evolution* (Oxford: Oxford University Press, 2005).

[4] In force from October 1, 2010. There is also protection for part-time workers, fixed-term employees, agency workers and other miscellaneous cases: see below para.17.35.

[5] Equality Act 2010 ("EqA") s.4.

[6] Directive 2006/54/EC of the European Parliament and of the Council of 5 July 2006 on the implementation of the principle of equal opportunities and equal treatment of men and women in matters of employment and occupation (recast) [2006] OJ L204/23 ("Recast Equality Directive"), Directive 2000/43/EC of the Council of 29 June 2000 implementing the principle of equal treatment between persons irrespective of racial or ethnic origin (the "Race Directive") and Directive 2000/78/EC of the Council of 27 November 2000 establishing a general framework for equal treatment in employment and occupation (the "Framework Directive"). See, para.17.22, below.

[7] EqA s.39.

[8] See, e.g. *Rowden v Dutton Gregory* [2002] I.C.R. 971; *Liversidge v Chief Constable of Bedfordshire* [2002] I.C.R. 1135.

[9] For example, the statutory concepts in ss.15 and 20–22 of the EqA apply to protect disabled employees only. Moreover, it is possible to justify direct age discrimination objectively in terms of s.13(2) EqA, which is not the position in the case of the other protected characteristics.

[10] Directive 86/613/EEC of the Council of 11 December 1986 on the application of the principle of equal treatment between men and women engaged in an activity, including agriculture, in a self-employed capacity, and on the protection of self-employed women during pregnancy and motherhood, Directive 97/81/EC of the Council of 15 December 1997 concerning the Framework Agreement on part-time work concluded by UNICE, CEEP and the ETUC, Directive 99/70/EC of the Council of 28 June 1999 concerning the Framework Agreement on fixed-term work and Directive 2008/104/EC of the Council of 19 November 2008 on temporary agency work.

[11] For the position of workers abroad, see *Lawson v Serco* [2006] UKHL 3; [2006] 1 All E.R. 823; *Duncombe v Secretary of State for Children, Schools and Families* [2011] UKSC 36; [2011] I.C.R. 1312 and *Ravat v Halliburton Manufacturing and Services Ltd*; [2012] UKSC 1; [2012] I.C.R. 389.

and enforcement of contractual claims can be brought in the ordinary courts. Generally speaking, proceedings to establish or enforce rights or claims under the statutory regulation of employment must be brought before an employment tribunal, which can make appropriate orders.[12] In many cases, a claimant must show that he has had a certain period of continuous employment to qualify him to claim a statutory right,[13] and most statutory claims are subject to relatively short time-limits.[14] Employment tribunals now also have jurisdiction in certain breach of contract cases.[15] Employment tribunals have jurisdiction to apply EU law in cases arising under UK legislation but do not have jurisdiction to deal with free-standing claims based on the Treaty on the Functioning of the European Union ("TFEU") or on a Directive.[16] A number of other statutory bodies including the Advisory Conciliation and Arbitration Service, and the Commission for Equality and Human Rights have important roles in relation to employment matters.[17]

Essentials of a contract of employment—A contract of employment is one by **17.04** which one person agrees to render services to another in return for some form of remuneration or advantage. Apprenticeship is a contract of employment in which the employer also undertakes to give instruction to the employee. In an onerous contract, at common law, the advantage accruing to the person employed need not take the form of wages; it may consist in an opportunity of earning, e.g. by tips, or by instruction in a trade or profession. The courts will look for the existence of certain minimum mutual obligations between the parties before deciding that a contract of employment exists, namely an obligation on the part of the purported employer to provide a minimum amount of work and pay for it on an ongoing basis and a corresponding obligation on the purported employee to perform work provided by the former on an ongoing basis.[18] There must be some element of mutuality and control, with an irreducible minimum of obligation to give personal service.[19] A person who attends in the hope of employment, even although he may receive payment for his attendance if no employment be available, is not an employee.[20] In previous editions it was said that there is no objection to a gratuitous obligation to work as an employee but any such arrangement must be affected by the minimum wage legislation.[21] In any event, such an obligation, if valid, may be better regarded as some arrangement other than employment. Where services are rendered without any express agreement, there is a general presumption (except possibly in cases of near relatives) in favour of an implied contract of service and consequent right to payment.[22] The

---

[12] In the rest of this chapter it has not been thought necessary to make repeated references to the fact that proceedings are brought before employment tribunals.

[13] Employment Rights Act 1996 ("ERA") ss.210–219.

[14] See G. Mansfield et al, *Blackstone's Employment Law Practice*, 6th edn (Oxford: Oxford University Press, 2011), Ch.3.

[15] Employment Tribunals (Extension of Jurisdiction) (Scotland) Order 1994 (SI 1994/1624).

[16] *Biggs v Somerset County Council* [1996] I.C.R. 364.

[17] The CEHR was set up under the Equality Act 2006 ("EqA 2006") with effect from October 1, 2007. See further, para.17.22, below.

[18] *Carmichael v National Power* [1999] I.C.R. 1226.

[19] *Montgomery v Johnson Underwood Ltd* [2001] I.C.R. 819; *MacFarlane v Glasgow City Council* [2001] I.R.L.R. 7.

[20] *Conlon v Glasgow Corp* (1899) 1 F. 869.

[21] National Minimum Wage Act 1998. See para.17.14, below.

[22] *Thomson v Thomson's Tr.* (1889) 16 R. 333.

presumption may be displaced by proof of a professional custom to render similar services gratuitously.[23] A belated claim, or one made by executors when no claim has been made by the deceased, is regarded unfavourably.[24] Where the parties are nearly related there may be a presumption in favour of the pursuer in the case of a claim by a son who has assisted his father in his work or business[25]; or in favour of the defender, in the case of a daughter or niece who claims payment for domestic services or for nursing.[26]

17.05 **Employees, workers and independent contractors**—The statutory definition of an employee is a person who works under a contract of employment, which means a contract of service or apprenticeship. The term "worker" is more widely defined, as a person who works under a contract of employment or any other contract whereby he undertakes to personally perform work or services for the other party whose status is not by virtue of the contract that of a client or a customer of any profession or business carried out by the worker.[27] For the purposes of many statutory employment rights, it is sufficient to have regard to the definition of "worker". However, it remains important, for some purposes, to distinguish between a contract of employment and some other form of contract, in particular a contract to render services as an independent or self-employed contractor. An employer is vicariously liable for acts of an employee, but not for those of an independent contractor or agent, although the rule is not absolute.[28] An employer has a duty of care for his employee, but not for an independent contractor, again subject to exceptions.[29] There are some statutory rights which apply only to employees. These include the right to a written statement of the terms of employment and an itemised pay statement; maternity, paternity and adoption rights; and rights in relation to unfair dismissal, redundancy and grievance and disciplinary proceedings. Other rights, such as the protection of wages, working time regulations and public interest disclosure protection apply to workers. The distinction between employment and other contracts is also important for tax, intellectual property ownership[30] and social security purposes.

At one time, it was thought that the overriding criterion was the degree of control exercised by the employer over the manner of doing the work.[31] Another suggestion was that the degree of integration of the worker with the business of the employer was the overriding factor.[32] These tests remain very important, but the modern view is that no single test or factor is conclusive in determining

---

[23] *Corbin v Stewart* (1911) 28 T.L.R. 99 (doctor attending widow of deceased colleague: but quaere if this is a case of employment at all).

[24] *Mackersy's Exrs v St Giles Managing Board* (1904) 12 S.L.T. 391; see *Mackison v Dundee B.C.*, 1910 S.C. (HL) 27.

[25] *Thomson v Thomson's Tr.* (1889) 16 R. 333; *Miller v Miller* (1898) 25 R. 995; *Urquhart v Urquhart's Tr.* (1905) 8 F. 42.

[26] *Russell v McClymont* (1906) 8 F. 821. In modern conditions, a right to remuneration may be more easily inferred.

[27] ERA s.230(3).

[28] See Ch.25, below.

[29] See Ch.25, below.

[30] Patents Act 1977 s.39 and Copyright, Designs, and Patents Act 1988 s.11.

[31] *Narich Pty Ltd v Payroll Tax Commissioner*, 1984 I.C.R. 286 PC.

[32] *Stevenson Jordan and Harrison Ltd v MacDonnell and Evans* [1952] 1 T.L.R. 101, per Denning L.J.

whether an individual who performs work or services for another is an employee or is self-employed.[33] The question has been expressed as:

> "Is the person who has engaged himself to perform these services performing them as a person in business on his own account?"[34]

There is no exhaustive list of factors to be considered, but relevant matters include, in addition to the mutuality of obligation, control and integration tests and the obligation of personal service, the actual terms of the contract, including holiday and sick pay arrangements; whether the person provides his own equipment; whether he hires his own helpers; whether he has the opportunity to work for other employers; what degree of financial risk he takes; and whether he has the opportunity of profiting from sound management in the performance of his task. Arrangements for tax and social security payments may also be relevant. The question whether the contract is one of employment or not is a question of mixed fact and law and the decision of a first instance tribunal properly directed in law will not normally be interfered with.[35]

Employment, agency and partnership—It may be difficult to distinguish **17.06** between employment on the one hand and partnership or agency on the other, particularly in examining the status of persons described as associates, consultants or salaried partners. The method of remuneration is often crucial to the distinction between a contract of employment and a joint adventure. Payment by salary is normally an indication of employment, but profit sharing is not by itself proof of partnership.[36] In England, it has been held that an equity partner and/or a partner entitled to a fixed share of the profits of a partnership or limited liability partnership cannot be an employee of his own firm, which can be contrasted with a "salaried partner", who will be an employee.[37] The distinction between agency and employment may be merely verbal, and the same person may act as an employee and as an agent. The term "agent" is, however, more properly applicable to the case where the duties of the person employed are to bring his employer into contractual relations with third parties.[38]

Temporary, part-time and agency workers—A person employed as a tempo- **17.07** rary worker who has the necessary length of service may acquire the rights given by the legislation, except in the case of a person employed to replace a woman on maternity or adoption leave.[39] Part time workers may also acquire statutory rights and, in addition, are entitled to be treated no less favourably than full-time

---

[33] *Ready Mixed Concrete (South East) Ltd v Minister of Pensions and National Insurance* [1968] 2 Q.B. 497.

[34] *Market Investigations Ltd v Minister of Social Security* [1969] 2 Q.B. 173 at 184, per Cooke J., appd in *Lee Ting Sang v Chung-Keung* [1990] 2 A.C. 374. See also *O'Kelly v Trusthouse Forte Plc* [1984] Q.B. 90; *Macfarlane v Glasgow City Council* [2001] I.R.L.R. 7.

[35] *O'Kelly v Trusthouse Forte* [1984] Q.B. 90; *Hall v Lorimer* [1994] I.C.R. 218; *Carmichael v National Power* [1999] I.C.R. 1226.

[36] See *Parker v Walker*, 1961 S.L.T. 252: Partnership Act 1890 s.2(3).

[37] *Tiffin v Lester Aldridge LLP* [2011] I.R.L.R. 105: cf. *Bates van Winkelhof Clyde & Co LLP* [2012] I.R.L.R. 548. For Scottish authority not considered in *Tiffin v Lester Aldridge LLP*, see *Fife County Council v Minister of National Insurance*, 1947 S.C. 629 at 636.

[38] See Ch.18, below.

[39] ERA s.106.

workers, except where a difference can be objectively justified.[40] Workers supplied to an employer by an agency and workers seconded by an employer to work in another business will normally continue to be employees of the agency or principal employer but in certain circumstances such workers may come to be regarded as employees of the business to which they are hired or seconded.[41] Since October 1, 2011, agency workers have the right not to be treated less favourably than the employees or workers of the hirer in respect of the pay-related terms and conditions of the agency worker's contract.[42] Where a person is employed by two or more companies which are associated, as defined in the ERA, he may be able to add together the periods of employment for the purpose of establishing entitlement to statutory rights.[43] But a series of limited period contracts with breaks between will not normally be held to give rise to an overarching or global contract,[44] unless the gaps between those contracts can be bridged on the ground that they amount to a temporary cessation of work.[45]

17.08 Company directors and other office holders—A director of a company may be an employee and the courts will determine whether the contract between the company and the director is a contract of employment or a contract for services in accordance with the usual tests[46] or whether it can be deemed to be a sham on the ground that it does not reflect the true agreement and relationship between the parties.[47] A company and a director may, subject to the requirements of the Companies Acts, competently enter into a contract of employment, which may be express or implied.[48] This is so even where the director is the controlling shareholder,[49] since it has been held in England that there is no reason in principle why someone whose shareholding in a company gives him partial or complete control of it cannot be an employee.[50] There are a number of cases of office holders, such as judges and magistrates, who are not classified as employees: and others, such as police officers, who have only limited rights. Traditionally, ministers of religion were not treated as employees, but following the decision in *Percy v Church of Scotland*[51] some at least may be employees. Owing to the fact that the relationship between a Roman Catholic parish priest and his diocesan bishop was sufficiently analogous to one of employment, it has been held in England that a

---

[40] Part-Time Workers (Prevention of Less Favourable Treatment) Regulations 2000: see para.17.35, below.

[41] *Motorola Ltd v Davidson* [2001] I.R.L.R. 4; *James v Greenwich Borough Council* [2007] I.R.L.R. 168.

[42] The Agency Workers' Regulations 2010 (SI 2010/93) reg.5.

[43] ERA s.231.

[44] *Hellyer Bros v McLeod* [1986] I.C.R. 122.

[45] ERA s.212(3)(b) and *Cornwall County Council v Prater* [2006] EWCA Civ 102; [2006] I.R.L.R. 362.

[46] See paras.17.04–17.05, above.

[47] *Autoclenz Ltd v Belcher* [2011] UKSC 41; [2011] ICR 1157; *Neufeld v Secretary of State for Business, Enterprise and Regulatory Reform* [2009] EWCA Civ 280; [2009] 3 All. E.R. 790 and *Firthglow Ltd (t/a Protectacoat) v Szilagi* [2009] EWCA Civ 98; [2009] I.C.R. 835.

[48] *Parsons v Albert J. Parsons and Sons Ltd* [1979] I.C.R. 271; *Folami v Nigerline (UK) Ltd* [1978] I.C.R. 277; see Companies Act 2006 s.227 and following.

[49] *Lee v Lee's Air Farming Ltd* [1961] A.C. 12; see Companies Act 2006 s.231.

[50] See *Neufeld v Secretary of State for Business, Enterprise and Regulatory Reform* [2009] EWCA Civ 280.

[51] *Percy v Church of Scotland*, 2006 S.C. (HL) 1; *Stewart v New Testament Church of God* [2007] EWCA Civ 1004; [2008] I.C.R. 282.

Roman Catholic diocese may be held vicariously liable for the torts of that priest, even though he was not an employee.[52]

Constitution of contract—A contract of employment may be entered into in the **17.09** same way as any other contract. The common law rule which required contracts of employment for more than one year to be constituted by writing has been abolished.[53] The ERA acknowledges that a contract under which an employee or worker is engaged may be oral or in writing, or may be implied.[54] But the employer must within two months after the beginning of an employee's period of employment give the employee a written statement identifying the parties, specifying the date when the employment began, and giving certain statutory particulars of the terms of employment.[55] Contractual conditions may be incorporated into individual employment contracts by reference to collective agreements[56] or works rulebooks.[57] Once made, the general rule is that a contract cannot be varied except by consent,[58] but where employment extends over periods of years, some development of the contract is inevitable and the courts may be prepared to hold that there has been an implied variation. In certain circumstances, refusal by an employee to agree to changes in working practices may be regarded as a special reason justifying dismissal.[59]

Obligations of employee—The varieties of types of employment preclude any **17.10** but a very general statement of the obligations of an employee. Modern authority has established that employers and employees owe to one another a duty to maintain trust and confidence.[60] In the case of the employee, that implies a duty of faithful service. He is bound to obey lawful and reasonable orders[61]; not to absent himself without leave during working hours; to refrain from such misconduct or immorality as may be incompatible with the reasonable performance of the particular service[62]; to do nothing to injure the employer's interests.[63] Refusal to obey orders may be justified if the demand, not excused by an emergency, is to do work other than that for which the employee was engaged[64]; if it is illegal[65]; or

---

[52] *E v English Province of Our Lady of Charity* [2012] EWCA Civ 938; [2012] I.R.L.R. 846.

[53] Requirements of Writing (Scotland) Act 1995 s.11(3).

[54] ERA s.230.

[55] ERA ss.1, 2 and 3; Merchant Seamen (s.199) and persons employed for less then one month (s.198) are excluded. It has been held that the corresponding Northern Ireland legislation cannot give rise to a claim for damages for breach of statutory duty: *Scally v Southern Health and Social Services Board* [1992] 1 A.C. 294.

[56] *Cadoux v Central RC*, 1986 S.L.T. 117; *Malone v British Airways Plc* [2011] I.R.L.R. 32.

[57] *Dryden v Greater Glasgow Health Board* [1992] I.R.L.R. 469.

[58] cf. *Bateman v Asda Stores* [2010] I.R.L.R. 370.

[59] See, e.g. *Grix v Munford Ltd* cited in N. Selwyn, *Selwyn's Law of Employment*, 16th edn (Oxford: Oxford University Press, 2010), p.118; for discussion of the application of the unfair contract terms legislation see D. Brodie, "The Employment Contract and Unfair Contracts Legislation" (2007) 27 *Legal Studies*, 95; Scottish Law Commission, *Unfair Terms in Contracts* (HMSO, 2005), Scot. Law Com. No.199, Pt 6.

[60] *Malik v BCCI* [1998] A.C. 20; *Imperial Group Pension Trust v Imperial Tobacco Ltd* [1991] I.C.R. 524; *Macari v Celtic Football and Athletic Co Ltd*, 2000 S.L.T. 80 (IH).

[61] *Blyth v Scottish Liberal Club*, 1983 S.L.T. 260.

[62] See P. Fraser, *Master and Servant* (Edinburgh: T.&T. Clark, 1882), p.84. And see, as to fiduciary position of an employee or agent, para.18.04, below.

[63] *Secretary of State for Employment v ASLEF (No.2)* [1972] 2 Q.B. 455.

[64] *Thomson v Douglas* (1807) Hume 392; *Moffat v Boothby* (1884) 11 R. 501.

[65] *Donovan v Invicta Airlines* [1970] 1 Lloyd's Rep 486; *Morrish v Henlys (Folkestone) Ltd* [1973] 2 All E.R. 137.

if compliance would expose the employee to some danger not contemplated at the time of engagement. The employee must not compete with his employer whilst the employment relationship subsists,[66] and this rule also applies where the employee works in his spare time for a competitor of the employer.[67] "Moonlighting" or engaging in other work during his employer's time is a breach of duty, as is taking a secret advantage. The employee is under a duty to preserve confidentiality in regard to his employer's affairs. Once the employment relationship has ended, the former employee will be under an implied obligation not to use or disclose trade secrets or highly confidential information.[68] He is, however, normally free to use knowledge and skills learnt or developed during his period of employment.[69] An employee's implied contractual duty of confidentiality may, in relation to certain types of information, be overridden in the public interest.[70] It has been held that an ordinary contract of employment does not involve any fiduciary relationship, and therefore that an employee is not bound to reveal the fact that he has been guilty of a breach of contract,[71] but an employee in a managerial position may have a duty to report the misconduct of subordinates even if that involves disclosure of his own breach.[72] An employee, if he does not hold himself out as belonging to any particular trade or profession, does enough if he performs his duties with reasonable care.[73] One engaged as a member of some trade or profession *spondet peritiam artis* (promises skill in the art) is liable in damages if he fails to exhibit the degree of skill reasonably to be expected from an ordinary member of his craft.[74]

17.11 **Remedies of employer**—The remedy of an employer for an employee's breach of contract is dismissal, and a claim for damages. If employees refuse to carry out the normal duties of their employment, the employer can suspend them and withhold pay for the period of suspension.[75] A decree *ad factum praestandum*, ordaining the employee to remain at his work, will not be pronounced.[76] A court cannot grant an order for specific implement or interdict which has the effect of compelling an employee to do any work or attend at any place for the doing of any work.[77] Where an employer is held vicariously liable for the fault or negligence of his employee, he is entitled to claim an indemnity from the employee for the

---

[66] *Thomas Marshall (Exports) Ltd v Guinle* [1979] I.C.R. 905.

[67] *Hivac v Park Royal Scientific Instruments* [1946] Ch 169; [1946] 1 All E.R. 350.

[68] *Lansing Linde v Kerr* [1991] I.C.R. 428; *Faccenda Chicken Ltd v Fowler* [1986] I.C.R. 297.

[69] *Printers and Finishers Ltd v Holloway* [1965] 1 W.L.R. 1.

[70] Public Interest Disclosure Act 1998; ERA Pt IVA. The employee is protected against victimisation while the employment continues and after it has terminated: *Woodward v Abbey National Plc* [2006] 4 All E.R. 1209.

[71] *Bell v Lever Bros* [1932] A.C. 161; but the recognition of the general duty of trust and confidence may affect this issue. See also *Nottingham University v Fishel* [2000] I.R.L.R. 471; *Item Software UK Ltd v Fassihi* [2004] EWCA Civ 1244; *Samsung Semiconductor Europe v Docherty* [2011] CSOH 32; 2011 G.W.D. 9–213; *Lonmar Global Risks v West* [2010] EWHC 2878 (QB); [2011] I.R.L.R. 138; *Customer Systems Plc v Ranson* [2012] EWCA Civ 841; [2012] I.R.L.R. 769.

[72] *Sybron Corp v Rochem Ltd* [1984] Ch. 112; cf. C. Wynn-Evans, "Self Incrimination in English Employment Law" (2005) 34 *Industrial Law Journal* 178.

[73] See *Gunn v Ramsay* (1801) Hume 384; *Lister v Romford Ice & Cold Storage Co* [1957] A.C. 555; *Janata Bank v Ahmed* [1981] I.C.R. 791.

[74] In the case of a doctor, see e.g. *Hunter v Hanley*, 1955 S.C. 200.

[75] *Laurie v British Steel Corp*, 1988 S.L.T. 17, appd *Miles v Wakefield M.D.C.* [1987] A.C. 539.

[76] Fraser, *Master and Servant* (1882), p.37; *Rose Street Foundry Co v John Lewis & Sons Ltd*, 1917 S.C. 341, per Lord Salvesen at 351.

[77] Trade Union and Labour Relations (Consolidation) Act 1992 s.236.

damages and expenses he has had to pay.[78] It is a wrong to induce an employee to break his contract.[79] An employee commits a criminal offence if he wilfully and maliciously breaks a contract of service in the knowledge that by the breach, whether done alone or in combination, serious injury to life or property will be entailed.[80] Seamen are subject to special civil and criminal liabilities in relation to their employment.[81]

Obligations of employer[82]—The obligations of an employer, like those of an **17.12** employee, can be indicated only in general terms. As noted above, there is an implied term that the employer will not without reasonable and proper cause do anything calculated to destroy or damage the relationship of confidence and trust between employer and employee.[83] The employer is thus bound to treat the employee with respect and may require to exercise any discretionary powers under the contract reasonably and with due regard to the interests of the employee.[84] He is also bound to respect the employee's privacy and confidentiality.[85] Breach of this term may entitle the employee to resign and claim that he has been constructively dismissed.[86] The employer has far-reaching duties, both common law and statutory, to protect the health and safety of employees: these now include protection against harassment.[87] The employer is bound to pay wages, bonuses and other payments due. Suspension without pay is, unless it can be justified in terms of the contract, a breach of contract for which damages may be recovered.[88] There is no general duty to provide work but in special circumstances, for example where remuneration is to be by piecework or the opportunity to do the work is important for the employee, work must be provided.[89] The employee is entitled to reimbursement of expenses reasonably incurred in performing the contract. The employer has a duty to insure against liability to third parties.[90] It is settled that an employer is not bound to give an employee a reference,[91] although a refusal to issue a reference for an ex-employee who had made a sex discrimination claim was held to amount to victimisation under the Sex Discrimination Act 1975.[92] In giving a reference an employer enjoys a qualified privilege, and averments of malice are necessary to the relevancy of an action of damages against him for

---

[78] *Lister v Romford Ice & Cold Storage Co* [1957] A.C. 555.
[79] *Lumley v Gye* (1853) 2 El. & Bl. 216; *Couper v Macfarlane* (1879) 6 R. 683. See para.25.10, below.
[80] Trade Union and Labour Relations (Consolidation) Act 1992 s.240.
[81] Merchant Shipping Act 1995 ss.58–60, 70–72.
[82] See also paras 17.49–17.53, below.
[83] *Malik v BCCI* [1998] A.C. 20; *Imperial Group Pension Trust v Imperial Tobacco Ltd* [1991] I.C.R. 524.
[84] *United Bank v Akhtar* [1989] I.R.L.R. 507; *Johnstone v Bloomsbury Health Authority* [1991] 2 All E.R. 293; [1991] I.R.L.R. 118; [1991] I.C.R. 269; *Land Securities Trillium Ltd v Thornley* [2005] I.R.L.R. 765.
[85] *Halford v United Kingdom* (1997) 24 E.H.R.R. 523.
[86] *Courtaulds Northern Textiles Ltd v Andrew* [1979] I.R.L.R. 84; *Woods v W.M.Car Services* [1981] I.C.R. 666.
[87] See paras 17.49–17.54 below and Protection from Harrassment Act 1997, para.17.28, below.
[88] *McArdle v Scotbeef Ltd*, 1974 S.L.T. (Notes) 78; cf. *Bird v British Celanese Ltd* [1945] K.B. 336.
[89] *Devonald v Rosser* [1906] 2 K.B. 728, *William Hill Organisation Ltd v Tucker* [1991] I.C.R. 291; cf. *Christie v Johnston Carmichael* [2010] I.R.L.R. 1016.
[90] Employers' Liability (Compulsory Insurance) Regulations 1998 (SI 1998/2573).
[91] *Fell v Lord Ashburton*, December 12, 1809, F.C.; Fraser, *Master and Servant* (1882), p.127; *Lawton v BOC Transhield Ltd* [1987] I.R.L.R. 404.
[92] *Coote v Granada Hospitality* [1999] I.C.R. 100.

defamation.[93] A character reference unduly laudatory may render him liable to a party who engages the employee in reliance on it and suffers loss.[94] There may be an implied obligation on the employer to take reasonable steps to publicise a term of the contract negotiated with a representative body which confers on the employee a valuable right contingent upon the employee's acting in a certain manner.[95] There may also be an implied term not to dismiss an employee while incapacitated if such action would deprive him of continued receipt of ill health benefits.[96] As from October 1, 2007, company directors are under a statutory obligation to consider the interests of their employees in deciding how to manage their operations.[97]

17.13 Remedies of employee—The remedy of an employee for an employer's breach of contract is damages. The employee may also be entitled to terminate the contract of employment depending on the nature of the employer's breach. For example, where an employer commits a repudiatory breach of an implied or express term of the contract of employment, the employee will have the option to affirm the contract, in which case, the contract of employment will continue to susbsist, or accept the employer's breach and rescind the contract of employment. An employer will be deemed to have committed a repudiatory breach where its actions evince an intention no longer to be bound by the contract of employment.[98] Where the employee chooses to accept the employer's breach and rescind the contract of employment, he/she will still be entitled to claim damages. Since a repudiatory breach on the part of an employer will not automatically terminate the contract of employment, it continues to subsist and so, it is possible for an employee to attain a decree of specific implement to enforce the contract or an interdict to restrain an employer from dismissing him/her.[99] At the time of writing, it is not wholly clear whether this is also the law in England.[100]

17.14 Wages: General and national minimum wage—In principle, the amount, frequency and method of payment of wages is a matter for agreement between the parties to the contract of employment. There is, however, a long history, going back to the Truck Act 1831, of legislative attempts to protect employees against underpayment of wages due, and also against the effects of lay-off because of fluctuations in the employer's business and of sickness. Workers also now have a right to paid holiday leave during their annual leave entitlement under the Working Time Regulations 1998.[101] A worker has an entitlement to be paid at a rate which is not less than the national minimum wage in terms of the National Minimum

---

[93] Bell, *Principles*, s.188; para.29.14, below. On the question of negligence, see *Spring v Guardian Assurance* [1994] 3 All E.R. 129.

[94] *Anderson v Wishart* (1818) 1 Murray 429.

[95] *Scally v Southern Health and Social Services Board* [1992] 1 A.C. 294; cf. *Crossley v Faithful and Gould Holdings Ltd* [2004] I.R.L.R. 377.

[96] *Aspden v Webbs Poultry and Meat Group (Holdings) Ltd* [1996] I.R.L.R. 521, *Villella v MFI Furniture Centre Ltd* [1999] I.R.L.R. 468; see also *Hill v General Accident Fire & Life Assurance Corp Plc*, 1999 S.L.T. 1157.

[97] Companies Act 2006 s.172.

[98] *General Billposting Co Ltd v Atkinson* [1909] AC 118 at 122, per Lord Collins.

[99] *Anderson v Pringle* [1998] I.R.L.R. 64; *Peace v City of Edinburgh Council*, 1999 S.L.T. 712.

[100] *Powell v LB of Brent* [1988] 1 Ch 176; *Robb v LB of Hammersmith* [1991] I.C.R. 514; *Alexander v Standard Telephones* [1990] I.C.R. 291; *Boyo v Lambeth London Borough Council* [1995] I.R.L.R. 50 (CA); *Gunton v Richmond-upon-Thames London Borough Council* [1980] I.R.L.R. 321 (CA); cf. *Société Générale, London Branch v Geys* [2011] I.R.L.R. 462 at 467, per Rimer L.J.

[101] See para.17.19, below.

Wage Act 1998. From October 2004, there are three rates of minimum wage: (i) the standard rate; (ii) a rate for persons aged between 18 and 22; and (iii) a rate for persons aged 16–17. Apprentices below the age of 18 and those over that age in the first 12 months of their apprenticeship are excluded along with some others working for the purpose of training or work experience.[102] Share fishermen, voluntary workers, prisoners, or members of the armed forces are also excluded.[103] Special provisions exist to bring agency workers and homeworkers within the national minimum wage regime.[104] An employee has a right not to suffer a detriment or be dismissed by reason of bringing proceedings relating to the enforcement of the national minimum wage.[105] The State also enforces the Act's provisions through officers who have power to inspect employers' wages records and to serve enforcement or penalty notices.[106]

Wages protection: Deductions—The Wages Act 1986 introduced a detailed **17.15** scheme dealing with the circumstances in which an employer could make deductions from wages. The provisions are now consolidated in the ERA. A complaint concerning an unauthorised deduction can be made to an employment tribunal, and this has had the, possibly unintended, effect of enabling tribunals to investigate the question of what wages are properly due under the contract.[107] An employer is prohibited from making any deduction from the wages of any worker employed by him or receiving any payment from such a worker unless: (a) the deduction or payment is authorised by statute[108] or by a relevant provision of the worker's contract; or (b) the worker has previously signified his agreement in writing.[109] Wages are very widely defined, including bonuses, tips, accrued holiday pay and benefits in kind, but not payments in lieu of notice, which are damages for breach of contract.[110] Moreover, the definition of wages covers a claim by an employer under the Working Time Regulations 1998[111] in respect of holiday pay accrued whilst he/she was absent from work due to illness, since it is a sum payable to a worker in connection with his employment otherwise than under his contract.[112] A relevant provision is a written term of the contract of which the employer has given the worker a copy prior to making the deduction or receiving the payment, or a term, which may be oral or implied, whose existence and effect have been notified to the worker. Neither a relevant provision varying the contract nor the worker's agreement can authorise any deduction or payment on account of any conduct of the worker or any event occurring before the variation took effect or the agreement was signified.[113] The prohibitions of the

---

[102] National Minimum Wage Act 1998 (the "1998 Act") s.1; National Minimum Wage Regulations 1999 (Amendment) Regulations 2010 (SI 2010/1901); the hourly rate from October 2012 is £6.19 for adults, £4.98 for those aged between 18 and 20, £3.68 for those aged 16–17 and £2.65 for apprentices. The Regulations contain detailed provisions for determining whether a worker is paid the minimum wage: see regs 30–37.

[103] See 1998 Act ss.37(1), 43, 44 and 45.

[104] 1998 Act ss.34 and 35.

[105] ERA s.104A.

[106] 1998 Act ss.11, 14 and 21.

[107] See, e.g. *New Century Cleaning Co v Church* [2000] I.R.L.R. 27 (CA).

[108] e.g. under an earnings arrestment: *Slater v Grampian RC*, 1991 S.L.T. (Sh. Ct) 72. Other examples are National Insurance, Income Tax and Child Support payments.

[109] ERA ss.13 and 15.

[110] *Delaney v Staples* [1992] 1 A.C. 687.

[111] Working Time Regulations 1998 (SI 1998/1833).

[112] *HM Revenue & Customs v Stringer* [2009] 4 All E.R. 1205.

[113] ERA s.13(2), (5) and (6).

Act do not, however, apply to: (a) reimbursement of overpayments of wages or expenses; (b) deductions or payments in consequence of disciplinary proceedings held by virtue of any statutory provision; (c) any deduction in pursuance of a statutory requirement imposed on the employer to deduct and pay over amounts determined by a public authority to be due to it from the worker; (d) any deduction in pursuance of arrangements established with the worker's written agreement under which the employer is to deduct and pay over to a third person amounts notified as being due to that person from the worker; (e) any deduction or payment on account of the worker having taken part in a strike or other industrial action; or (f) any deduction made with the worker's prior written agreement or any payment received by the employer towards the satisfaction of an order of a court or tribunal requiring payment by the worker to the employer.[114] Special provisions govern deductions made and payments received on account of cash shortages or stock deficiencies in retail employment.[115] Where an employee goes on strike, the employer is entitled to deduct 1/260th of his/her annual wage for every day of withdrawn labour.[116]

17.16 Wages protection: Lay-off, sickness and bankruptcy—The common law did qualify the employer's power to lay off, but only to a limited extent.[117] Statute now provides for guarantee payments to be made in respect of any whole day in which an employee, who has been continuously employed for at least one month, is not provided with work because of diminution in the requirements of the employer's business or other occurrence affecting its normal working.[118] The payment is not available in the event of a strike, lock-out or other industrial action involving employees of the employer or an associated employer or of unreasonable refusal by the employee of suitable alternative work[119] or of failure to comply with reasonable requirements imposed with a view to ensuring the availability of the employee's services. Payments are at a guaranteed hourly rate,[120] and cannot exceed five days in any period of three months.[121] Similar but more extensive protection applies where an employee is suspended because of a statutory or health and safety requirement imposed on the business: in this case, the employee is entitled to a week's pay during each week up to 26 weeks during which he is suspended.[122] Employees who are incapable of work because of illness or injury, who unreasonably refuse alternative work or who do not make themselves available for work, are excepted.[123] As regards sickness, the employer is liable to pay statutory sick pay to the employee for the first 28 weeks of incapacity.[124] An employer may recover an amount paid out as SSP if and only to the extent that it exceeds a percentage of his liability to pay national insurance contributions in the income tax month in question.[125] Sick pay is not payable for the first three days of

---

[114] ERA s.14.
[115] ERA ss.17–22.
[116] *Cooper v Isle of Wight College* [2008] I.R.L.R. 124.
[117] *Devonald v Rosser & Sons* [1906] 2 K.B. 729; cf. *Johnson v Cross* [1977] I.C.R. 872.
[118] ERA s.28(1)–(3).
[119] ERA s.29.
[120] Currently the maximum is £23.50 per day.
[121] ERA s.31; amended by SI 2011/3006.
[122] ERA s.64.
[123] ERA s.65.
[124] Social Security Contributions and Benefits Act 1992 ss.151, 155.
[125] Social Security Contributions and Benefits Act 1992 s.159A as amended by the Statutory Sick Pay Act 1994 s.1; Statutory Sick Pay Threshold Order 1995 (SI 1995/512).

a period of incapacity.[126] Payment is at a prescribed weekly rate related to normal weekly earnings[127] and the current weekly rate is £85.85.[128]

Unpaid wages up to a total of £800 owed by a bankrupt employer and accruing during the four months preceding bankruptcy constitute a preferential debt.[129] In addition, certain amounts owed by an insolvent employer may be recovered from the National Insurance Fund.[130] Payments in respect of arrears of pay are limited to eight weeks' pay and £400 in respect of any one week.[131] Every employee is now entitled to an itemised pay statement on each occasion that payment of wages or salary is made.[132]

Wages protection: Maternity pay—Subject to an important condition, an **17.17** employee who has been continuously employed for at least 26 weeks is entitled to statutory maternity pay from the employer for a period not exceeding 39 weeks during which she is absent from work because of pregnancy or confinement.[133] The condition is that she must give her employer 28 days' prior notice of the date from which she expects his liability to pay her statutory maternity pay to begin or, if that is not reasonably practicable, as soon as is reasonably practicable.[134] The first week of payment is normally the eleventh week before the expected week of confinement. Payment is at the higher rate equivalent to nine tenths of her normal weekly earnings for the first six weeks, and thereafter, it is the lower of £135.45 or the rate payable during the first weeks.[135] The employer may recover a proportion of the payments from the Department of Social Security.[136] An employee is also entitled to maternity leave and may be entitled to return to work after confinement.[137]

Pensions—Occupational pension schemes, like pension schemes generally, are **17.18** tightly controlled by statute, but for the most part these regulations belong to the law of trust and taxation.[138] From the point of view of employment law, only three points should be noted. First, a term of a contract of employment that the employee must be a member of an occupational pension scheme is void.[139] Secondly, as a consequence of the implied term of trust and confidence, employers are required to exercise their powers and duties under such schemes with proper regard to the interests of their employees[140] and to keep employees informed of advantageous

---

[126] Social Security Contributions and Benefits Act 1992 s.155.
[127] Social Security Contributions and Benefits Act 1992 s.157.
[128] Social Security Benefits Up-rating Order 2012 (SI 2012/780) art.9.
[129] Insolvency Act 1986 s.386, Sch.6 para.9; Insolvency Proceedings (Monetary Limits) Order 1986 (SI 1986/1996) art.4; Bankruptcy (Scotland) Act 1985 s.51, Sch.3 para.5(1); Bankruptcy (Scotland) Regulations 2008 (SSI 2008/82) reg.10.
[130] ERA ss.166–170 and 182–190.
[131] ERA ss.184(1) and 186(1); SI 2010/2926.
[132] ERA ss.8 and 9.
[133] Statutory Maternity Pay (General) Regulations 1986 (SI 1986/1960) reg.2(2) and Social Security Contributions and Benefits Act 1992 ss.164–165.
[134] Social Security Contributions and Benefits Act 1992 s.164(4).
[135] Statutory Maternity Pay (General) Regulations 1986 (SI 1986/1960) reg. 6 as amended by Social Security Benefits Up-rating Order 2012 (SI 2012/780) art.10 and Social Security Contributions and Benefits Act 1992 s.166.
[136] Social Security Contributions and Benefits Act 1992 ss.164–167.
[137] See para.17.21, below.
[138] See the Pension Schemes Act 1993 and the Pensions Act 1995.
[139] Pension Schemes Act 1993 s.160, some limited variation is permitted under s.64 of the 1995 Act.
[140] *Imperial Group Pension Trust v Imperial Tobacco Ltd* [1991] I.C.R. 524.

options open to them under the scheme.[141] Thirdly, occupational pension schemes must give equal treatment to men and women.[142]

17.19 Working time and holidays—The common law did not significantly restrict the freedom of employers and employees to agree working times and holiday periods, although it was held in *Johnstone v Bloomsbury Health Authority*[143] that the employer's duty to take reasonable care for the employee's health and safety might restrict his power to demand excessive hours of work, even if the contract appeared to entitle him to do so. There was some limited statutory restriction of shop hours[144] and some restriction of Sunday trading.[145] General regulation of hours of work was introduced by the Working Time Regulations 1998[146] which were made to implement the Working Time Directive[147] and the Young Workers Directive.[148] The Directives set out to establish a maximum of 48 hours in each week for most workers, but the regulations did not initially carry that intention into effect in two significant respects. First, the regulations imposed a qualifying period of 13 weeks' employment: this was held contrary to the Directive by the ECJ.[149] Secondly, the United Kingdom secured a derogation to permit the maximum to be exceeded with the worker's written consent[150]: this derogation remains controversial and no consensus could be reached at the EU level on a proposal to remove the opt-out in 2008/2009. Subject to this exception, the Regulations impose an upper limit of 48 hours on average in each working week and eight hours in each 48 hours for night workers.[151] The Regulations also provide for daily rest periods of at least 11 hours in each 24-hour period[152]; weekly rest periods of at least 24 hours in each seven-day period[153]; and rest breaks of at least 20 minutes after each six-hour period of work.[154] For young workers, that is those between 15 and 18, the limits are 40 hours per week or eight hours per day, and night work is effectively prohibited. Important categories of workers are excluded, including domestic servants, as are those whose working time is "unmeasured".[155] Regulations 13 and 13A entitle a worker to 5.6 weeks' annual holiday, with his normal pay, in each year.[156] The entitlement cannot be excluded or reduced by any provision in the contract of employment.[157] The practice of counting Bank Holidays as part of annual leave was brought to an end in April 2009. Detailed regulations provide for the calcula-

---

[141] *Scally v Southern Health and Social Services Board* [1991] I.C.R. 771, HL.

[142] EqA 2010 ss.61–63.

[143] *Johnstone v Bloomsbury Health Authority* [1991] I.C.R. 269: working hours of junior doctors.

[144] Shops Act 1950; repealed Deregulation and Contracting Out Act 1994.

[145] See now the Sunday Trading Act 1994.

[146] Working Time Regulations 1998 (SI 1998/1833); the Regulations came into force on October 1, 1998.

[147] Working Time Directive EC 93/04 [1993] OJ L307/18, now EC 2003/88 [2003] OJ L299/9.

[148] Young Workers Directive EC 94/33 [1994] OJ 216/12.

[149] *R. v Secretary of State for Trade and Industry, Ex p. Broadcasting Entertainment Cinematographic and Theatre Union* [2001] C.M.L.R. 7.

[150] Working Time Regulations 1998 regs 4 and 5; the worker is entitled to terminate the agreement on notice.

[151] Working Time Regulations 1998 regs 4 and 6. Detailed and complex provisions govern the calculation of the relevant periods.

[152] Working Time Regulations 1998 reg.10(1).

[153] Working Time Regulations 1998 reg.11.

[154] Working Time Regulations 1998 reg.12.

[155] Working Time Regulations 1998 regs 18–27A. There are also limited exclusions for agricultural workers; Sch.2.

[156] Normal pay is calculated in accordance with ss.221–224 of the ERA: see reg.16.

[157] Working Time Regulations 1998 reg.25.

tion of the worker's entitlement, including cases in which the worker has been employed for less than a full year. After some difference of judicial opinion in the United Kingdom, the ECJ held that the holiday pay entitlement must be paid at the time when the holiday is taken and cannot be rolled up as part of the normal weekly pay.[158] In another decision, the ECJ ruled that where a worker became ill during a period which had been allocated as annual leave, that worker was entitled to receive his or her annual leave at a time other than that which had originally been scheduled, i.e. compensatory holidays for the days in which he/she was ill during the original holidays.[159] It has also been held by the ECJ[160] that an employee who has been off sick for a long period is entitled to his annual leave and to be paid, even though any contractual or statutory sick pay has been exhausted, and even though he may be unfit for work during and after the leave period. This rule may provide an incentive to employers to dismiss the long-term sick instead of keeping them "on the books" as many choose to do. Dismissing such employees may be problematic because of the proscription of disability discrimination in the EqA, but the problem may be eased by the decision of the ECJ in *Chacon Navas v Eurest Collectividades SA*.[161] Where an employee works on an offshore installation on a two weeks on, two weeks off, working pattern, it has been held that the worker must have at least four remunerated weeks of the weekly cycle in which he is free from work commitments and so it is not open to an employer to stipulate that non-working days within the weekly working cycle (e.g. Saturdays and Sundays) must be treated as annual leave.[162]

Time off—An employer has a statutory obligation to permit employees in certain **17.20** categories to take time off during working hours. An official of an independent trade union recognised by the employer is entitled, subject to certain conditions, to paid time off—if the time off is taken for the purpose of enabling him to carry out his official duties and to undergo approved training in aspects of industrial relations relevant to the carrying out of these duties.[163] Similarly, a member of an independent trade union recognised by the employer in relation to employees of the same description as the member seeking time off is entitled to time off for activities as a representative of his trade union, excluding activities consisting of industrial action.[164] A Justice of the Peace or a member of certain public bodies is entitled to time off for the purpose of performing his public duties.[165] An employee who is given notice of dismissal by reason of redundancy and has been continuously employed for at least two years is entitled to paid time off to look for new employment or make arrangements for training for future employment.[166] An employee who is pregnant is entitled to paid time off to enable her to attend for the purpose of receiving ante-natal care.[167] Safety representatives and elected representatives are entitled to paid time off for the performance of their duties and

---

[158] *Robinson-Steele v RD Retail Services Ltd* [2006] 2 C.M.L.R. 34.

[159] *Pereda v Madrid Movilidad SA* [2010] 1 C.M.L.R. 103.

[160] *Stringer v HM Revenue and Customs* [2009] 2 C.M.L.R. 657.

[161] *Chacon Navas v Eurest Collectividades SA* [2006] 3 C.M.L.R. 40: holding that sickness was not a disability.

[162] *Russell v Transocean International Resources Ltd* [2012] 2 All E.R. 166.

[163] 1992 Act s.168.

[164] 1992 Act s.170.

[165] ERA s.50.

[166] ERA s.52.

[167] ERA s.55.

to undergo appropriate training.[168] An employee has the right to be permitted to take a reasonable amount of time off in order to take action which is necessary to care for ill or injured dependants, including making arrangements in consequence of the death of a dependant.[169] Employees who are trustees of an occupational pension scheme have a right to paid time off to perform their duties or to undergo appropriate training.[170] An employee who is an employee representative in relation to a redundancy situation or a transfer of undertaking has a right to reasonable time off to perform such duties or undergo appropriate training.[171] The employee is entitled to be paid for time taken off during working hours. An employee with more than one year's continuous service who has parental responsibility for a child may take unpaid parental leave in order to care for that child.[172] Such leave normally only applies to care for children under five years old although special provisions exist for disabled and adopted children. Parental leave is limited to 13 weeks in total[173] and must be taken in blocks of one week or more,[174] but no more than four weeks can be taken in respect of any one child in any one year.[175] In addition, a father is entitled to one or two weeks' paid leave on the birth or adoption of a child.[176] Certain employees aged 16 or 17 are entitled to paid time off for study or training.[177] The amount of time off which an employer is bound to permit to an employee in any of the above categories other than a pregnant employee and the conditions to which it may be subject are such as may be reasonable in all the circumstances. A pregnant employee has the right not to be unreasonably refused time off to enable her to keep an appointment for ante-natal care.[178]

17.21 Maternity leave and paternity leave—In addition to her rights to time off for ante-natal care and parental leave, an employee may be entitled to maternity leave.[179] There are three types of maternity leave. Compulsory maternity leave arises under s.72(1) of the 1996 Act which provides that an employer shall not permit a woman to work within two weeks of childbirth: this is really a health and welfare provision and criminal sanctions apply.[180] Ordinary maternity leave and additional maternity leave are options available to an employee (not to a "worker") who gives appropriate notice to her employer.[181] There is no continuous service requirement for ordinary maternity leave. Such leave will commence no earlier

---

[168] Safety Representatives and Safety Committee Regulations 1977 (SI 1977/500) and Health & Safety (Consultation with Employees) Regulations 1996 (SI 1996/1513).

[169] ERA s.57A. However, this section does not confer a right to bereavement leave: *Forster v Cartwright Black* [2004] I.C.R. 1728.

[170] ERA ss.58–60.

[171] ERA s.61.

[172] Maternity and Parental Leave Regulations 1999 (SI 1999/3312) reg.13 which implements EC Directive 96/34; see also *R. v Secretary of State for Trade and Industry, Ex p. TUC* [2000] I.R.L.R. 565.

[173] Maternity and Parental Leave Regulations 1999 reg.14: It is increased to 18 weeks where the child is entitled to a disability living allowance.

[174] *Rodway v South Central Trains Ltd* [2005] I.R.L.R. 583.

[175] Maternity and Parental Leave Regulations 1999 Sch.2.

[176] Paternity and Adoption Leave Regulations 2002 (SI 2002/2788): in certain circumstances, a woman may qualify for "paternity leave". See para.17.21, below for further details.

[177] ERA s.63A.

[178] ERA ss.55 and 56.

[179] ERA ss.71–75; Maternity and Parental Leave etc Regulations 1999 (SI 1999/3312).

[180] Maternity and Parental Leave etc Regulations 1999 (SI 1999/3312) reg.8. Other pregnancy-related health and safety regulations are found in Factories Act 1961 Sch.5 and Management of Health and Safety at Work Regulations 1999 (SI 1999/3242).

[181] ERA ss.71 and 73.

than the eleventh week before the expected week of childbirth and the leave lasts for 26 weeks.[182] An employee is entitled to return from ordinary maternity leave to the job in which she was employed before her absence. An employee who qualifies for ordinary maternity leave will also qualify for additional maternity leave.[183] Additional maternity leave commences on the last day of ordinary maternity leave[184] and can last for up to a further 26 weeks, unless the employee is dismissed prior to that date.[185] An employee on additional maternity leave is entitled to return from leave to the job in which she was employed before her absence, or if it is not reasonably practicable for her employer to permit her to return to that job, to another job which is both suitable for her and appropriate for her to do in the circumstances.[186] Notice provisions apply if an employee wishes to return early from ordinary or additional maternity leave.[187] The regulations make provision for the treatment of leave periods in regard to length of service, redundancy and other such matters. Dismissal of a woman who is employed under a contract of indefinite duration on the grounds of her pregnancy is direct sex discrimination under the Recast Equality Directive of 2006[188] (the "Recast Directive").[189] An employee may also be entitled to take paternity leave. An employee on paternity leave has the right to be absent from work for a period of one week's leave or two consecutive weeks' leave, with a further entitlement to take additional paternity leave for a period between two and 26 weeks for the purpose of caring for a child or supporting the child's mother.[190] However, the employee must satisfy certain conditions, namely the employee must show that he has been continuously employed for at least 26 weeks ending with the week immediately preceding the 14th week before the expected week of the child's birth, he must be the child's father or be the civil partner of the child's mother or married to the child's mother, he must have the main responsibility for the child's upbringing (apart from the mother's responsibility) and must also have provided the requisite statutory notice to the employer in advance.[191] The provisions relating to additional paternity leave apply only in relation to children whose expected week of birth was on or after April 3, 2011 and such leave may be taken by the employee at any time within the period which begins 20 weeks after the date on which the child is born and ending twelve months after that date.[192] Paternity leave may only be taken during the period which begins with the date on which the child is born and ends 56 days after that date or, where the child is born before the first day of the expected week of its birth, 56 days after that date.[193] Paternity leave and additional paternity leave can only be taken in blocks of one complete week or more and in the case of the latter, it must be taken in one continuous period.[194]

---

[182] Maternity and Parental Leave etc. Regulations 1999 (SI 1999/3312) reg.7.
[183] Maternity and Parental Leave etc. Regulations 1999 (SI 1999/3312) reg.4.
[184] Maternity and Parental Leave etc. Regulations 1999 (SI 1999/3312) reg.6(3).
[185] Maternity and Parental Leave etc. Regulations 1999 (SI 1999/3312) reg.7(4) and (5).
[186] Maternity and Parental Leave etc. Regulations 1999 (SI 1999/3312) reg.18(2).
[187] Maternity and Parental Leave etc. Regulations 1999 (SI 1999/3312) reg.11.
[188] Recast Equality Directive.
[189] As well as being automatically unfair under s.99 of the ERA.
[190] Paternity and Adoption Leave Regulations 2002 (SI 2002/2788) regs 4, 5 and 6 and Additional Paternity Leave Regulations 2010 (SI 2010/1055) regs 4, 5 and 6.
[191] Paternity and Adoption Leave Regulations 2002 (SI 2002/2788) regs 4 and 6 and Additional Paternity Leave Regulations 2010 (SI 2010/1055) regs 4 and 6.
[192] Additional Paternity Leave Regulations 2010 (SI 2010/1055) regs 3(1) & 5(1).
[193] Paternity and Adoption Leave Regulations 2002 (SI 2002/2788) reg.5(2).
[194] Paternity and Adoption Leave Regulations 2002 (SI 2002/2788) reg.5(1) and Additional Paternity Leave Regulations 2010 (SI 2010/1055) reg.5(3).

17.22 Equal treatment and discrimination—As mentioned above,[195] a series of legislative attempts have been made to end differential treatment in regard to employment as between different social groups. Much of the impetus for change in this field has come from developments in the European Union and there are a number of Directives which provide a framework for the interpretation and application of UK law. One of the earliest pieces of UK legislation was the Equal Pay Act 1970, which followed on from the Equal Pay Directive,[196] which in turn followed on from art.119 (now art.157 of the TFEU) of the then Treaty of Rome. The Equal Treatment Directive of 1976[197] enunciated the principle of equal treatment for men and women as regards access to employment and two further Equal Treatment Directives of 2000[198] extended the principle to differences of race, religion, disability, age or sexual orientation. The Equal Treatment Directive of 1976, the Burden of Proof Directive[199] and the Equal Treatment Directive of 2002[200] were repealed with effect from August 15, 2009 and consolidated into the Recast Directive.[201] The application of the principle of equality and non-discrimination in the United Kingdom was found first in the Sex Discrimination Act 1975 (the "1975 Act") which introduced the concepts of direct and indirect discrimination.[202] These concepts were used in the subsequent legislation, although with some modifications. The Race Relations Act 1976 was closely modelled on the 1975 Act, although the provisions were complicated by having two definitions of indirect discrimination. The Disability Discrimination Act 1995 was similar to the two previous Acts but contained no provision for indirect discrimination. Finally the Employment Equality (Religion or Belief) Regulations 2003[203] and the Employment Equality (Sexual Orientation) Regulations 2003[204] proscribed discrimination in the workplace on the grounds of religious belief and sexual orientation and the Employment Equality (Age) Regulations 2006[205] extended the prohibition of discrimination to any such conduct based on age. In 2010, all of the above UK legislation was repealed and the law was consolidated into one single piece of legislation: the EqA. Article 157 of the TFEU and some of the Directives made to give effect to it are directly applicable and can be founded on in proceedings in the United Kingdom.[206] The Commission for Equality and Human Rights[207] has been established with powers to investigate cases of possible

---

[195] See para.17.02, above.

[196] Directive 75/117/EEC of the Council of 10 February 1975 on the approximation of the laws of the Member States relating to the application of the principle of equal pay for men and women.

[197] Directive 76/207/EC of 9 February 1976 on the implementation of the principle of equal treatment for men and women as regards access to employment, vocational training and promotion, and working conditions [1976] OJ L39.

[198] The Framework Directive and the Race Directive.

[199] Directive 97/80/EC [1997] of the Council of 15 December 1997 on the burden of proof in cases of discrimination based on sex [1997] OJ L14/16.

[200] Directive 2002/73/EC of the European Parliament and the Council of 23 September 2002 amending Council Directive 76/207/EEC [2002] OJ L269/15.

[201] Recast Equality Directive.

[202] See para.17.27, below.

[203] Employment Equality (Religion or Belief) Regulations 2003 (SI 2003/1660).

[204] Employment Equality (Sexual Orientation) Regulations 2003 (SI 2003/1661).

[205] Employment Equality (Age) Regulations 2006 (SI 2006/1031).

[206] *Barber v Guardian Royal Exchange Assurance Group* [1990] E.C.R. I-1889; [1991] 1 Q.B. 344; *Coloroll Pension Trs Ltd v Russell* [1994] I.R.L.R. 586. However, differences between the domestic and the European laws arguably remain, on which, see the discussion in *North v Dumfries and Galloway Council* [2011] CSIH 2; 2011 S.L.T. 203.

[207] This body replaced the Equal Opportunities Commission, the Commission for Racial Equality and the Disability Rights Commission.

discrimination and take action to promote equality and enforce legislation.[208] Generally, persons who seek to assert rights under the anti-discrimination legislation are protected against victimisation.[209]

Equal pay—Under the EqA a sex equality clause is deemed to be included in **17.23** all personal work contracts in Great Britain.[210] The effect of a sex equality clause is that for men and women employed in the same employment on like work, or work rated as equivalent, or work of equal value, the terms and conditions of employment for one sex are not less favourable in any relevant respect than the terms and conditions applicable to the other sex,[211] but the clause does not apply if the employer proves that any variation is genuinely due to a material factor which is not the difference of sex and is a proportionate means of achieving a legitimate aim of the employer.[212] Market forces may be a relevant factor and a variation may be justified on the need to recruit, irrespective of sex, employees of a particular class.[213] In seeking to demonstrate that she is employed to do like work, work rated as equivalent or work of equal value in terms of s.65 of the EqA, a female employee must compare herself to an actual male comparator.[214] A man is a suitable comparator if he is employed by: (A) the same employer of the female claimant or an associate of the female claimant's employer at the same establishment as the female claimant; or (B) the same employer as the female claimant or an associate of the female claimant's employer at a different establishment to the female claimant and common terms and conditions are applied at both establishments (either generally or as between the man and the female claimant).[215] Like work means work of the same or a broadly similar nature in which any differences between the things done are not of practical importance in relation to terms and conditions of employment[216]: it is necessary to have regard to the frequency, nature and extent of any differences in those things done.[217] Differences in duties and responsibilities, if sufficiently significant, may be of practical importance[218] but in many cases they may appropriately be compensated, as may differences in hours and shifts, by the payment of a premium and so do not justify a difference in basic pay.[219] A sex equality clause does not preclude the payment of such a premium for additional or different work actually done.[220] By work "rated as equivalent" is meant a job which has been given an equal value to another job pursuant to a job evaluation study in terms of the demand made on a worker or which would have been given an equal value but for the evaluation being made on

---

[208] See Pt 1 of the EqA 2006.

[209] EqA s.27 and *St Helens Metropolitan Borough Council v Derbyshire* [2007] I.R.L.R. 540 (HL).

[210] EqA s.66(1).

[211] EqA s.66(2).

[212] EqA s.69(1).

[213] *Ratcliffe v North Yorkshire County Council* [1995] I.R.L.R. 439; *Glasgow City Council v Marshall*, 2000 S.L.T. 429; *Rainey v Greater Glasgow Health Board*, 1987 S.C. (HL) 1; see also *Enderby v Frenchay Health Authority* [1993] I.R.L.R. 591.

[214] EqA ss.64(1) and 79(1)–(4). Therefore, the EqA does not permit the use of hypothetical comparators.

[215] EqA s.79(1)–(4). See *British Coal Corp v Smith* [1996] I.C.R. 515; *Leverton v Clwyd County Council* [1989] A.C. 706.

[216] EqA s.65(2).

[217] EqA s.65(3).

[218] *Noble v David Gold and Son (Holdings)* [1980] I.R.L.R. 253.

[219] *Electrolux v Hutchinson* [1977] I.C.R. 252.

[220] *Dugdale v Kraft Foods Ltd* [1977] I.C.R. 48: but note *Kerr v Lister & Co Ltd* [1977] I.R.L.R. 259.

a system setting different values for men and women.[221] A job evaluation study is a study undertaken (usually at the behest of the employer) with a view to evaluating, in terms of the demands made on a person by reference to factors such as effort, skill and decision-making, the jobs to be done by some or all of the workers in the employer's undertaking or group of undertakings.[222] There is no legal obligation upon an employer to conduct a job evaluation study. If the employee is not engaged in like work, or work rated as equivalent to a comparator, she may claim that the demands of her job are such that the job is of equal value to that of the comparator's job.[223] A female claimant's work is of equal value to a male comparator if she is not engaged in like work or work rated as equivalent to that of the male comparator, but her work is nevertheless equal to the male's work in terms of the demands made on her by reference to factors such as effort, skill and decision-making.[224] On such a claim an employment tribunal has the power to order an evaluation by an independent expert in relation to the values of the two jobs in order to ascertain whether A's work is of equal value to a comparator B's work.[225] A final point to note is that a clause in a person's contract which purports to prevent or restrict them from disclosing any of their terms and conditions of employment (including remuneration details) is unenforceable against that person in so far as that person makes or seeks to make a relevant pay disclosure.[226] A disclosure is a relevant pay disclosure if it is made for the purpose of enabling that person or the person to whom it is made, to find out whether or to what extent there is a disparity in pay between that person and a member of the opposite sex engaged in like work, work rated as equivalent or work of equal value.[227]

17.24   Equal pay: Remedies—Any claim arising out of the operation of a sex equality clause may be presented to an employment tribunal.[228] The tribunal may determine the claim, including any question of arrears of remuneration or damages and it may make an order declaring the rights of parties in relation to the matters to which the proceedings relate.[229] A remedy for failure to comply with an equality clause may also be pursued as a breach of contract through the courts,[230] but the court has power to direct that the claim be referred to an employment tribunal.[231]

17.25   Equal pay: Exceptions—Equal pay claims must be made within a qualifying period of six months of the termination of the employment, except on a reference directed or made by a court.[232] Claims for arrears of pay are limited to a period of five years prior to the institution of proceedings, subject to an increase to a period of twenty years prior to that date if the case involves a relevant incapacity of the

---

[221] EqA s.65(4).
[222] EqA s.80(5).
[223] EqA s 65(1)(c) and (6); *Hayward v Cammell Laird Shipbuilders Ltd* [1988] A.C. 894.
[224] EqA s.65(6).
[225] EqA s.131.
[226] EqA s.77(1).
[227] EqA s.77(3).
[228] EqA ss.120 and 127.
[229] EqA s.132(2).
[230] EqA s.127(9).
[231] EqA s.128.
[232] EqA s.129(3).

employee or a relevant fraud or error.[233] The sex equality clause is excluded in so far as the terms and conditions of a woman's employment are affected by compliance with laws regulating the employment of women and any terms of work affording special treatment to women in connection with pregnancy or the birth of a child.[234] But equal access must be afforded to occupational pensions schemes[235] and any provision in contravention of art.157 of the TFEU (which requires equal pay for equal work) cannot receive effect.[236] The EqA also contains provisions for securing equality of treatment in relation to the pay of female employees on maternity leave and does so by inserting a maternity equality clause into their terms and conditions of employment.[237] The purpose of the maternity equality clause is to ensure that: (A) the increase in pay a woman receives (or would have received if she had not been on maternity leave) is taken into account in the calculation of her maternity-related pay where her terms do not already provide for this; (B) pay, including any bonus, is paid to the woman at the time she would have received it if she had not been on maternity leave; and (C) pay, on her return to work following maternity leave takes account of any pay increase which she would have received if she had not been on statutory maternity leave.[238]

The protected characteristics—The protections in the EqA are afforded to **17.26** employees, persons providing services on the basis of a contract of apprenticeship or a contract personally to do work[239] and the EqA makes use of the term "protected characteristics" which are listed as the following: age, disability, gender reassignment, marriage and civil partnership, pregnancy and maternity, race, religion or philosophical belief, sex and sexual orientation.[240] First, s.6 of the EqA directs that a person has a disability if he has a physical or mental impairment and the impairment has a substantial and long-term adverse effect on his ability to carry out normal day-to-day activities.[241] An impairment is long-term if it has lasted for at least 12 months, it is likely to last for at least 12 months or it is likely to last for the rest of the life of the person affected. In this context, "likely" means "could well happen" rather than "more probable than not."[242] Secondly, s.7 of the EqA provides that a person has the protected characteristic of "gender reassignment" if that person is proposing to undergo, is undergoing or has undergone a process (or part of a process) for the purpose of reassigning the person's sex by changing physiological or other attributes of sex.[243] Thirdly, the definition of "race" includes colour, nationality and ethnic or racial origin.[244] "Ethnic" is a wider term than "race" and connotes membership of a distinct community with, inter alia, a long shared history of which it is conscious and the memory of which it keeps alive as distinguishing it from other groups and with a distinct cultural tradition, social

---

[233] EqA s.132(5); *Preston v Wolverhampton Healthcare NHS Trust* [2000] I.R.L.R. 506 (ECJ); [2001] I.C.R. 217 (HL).
[234] EqA Sch.7 paras 1 and 2.
[235] EqA ss.61–63; para.17.18, above.
[236] *Worringham and Humphreys v Lloyds Bank* [1982] 1 W.L.R. 841.
[237] EqA s.73.
[238] EqA s.74(2), (3) and (4).
[239] EqA s.83(2).
[240] EqA s.4.
[241] EqA s.6.
[242] *SCA Packaging Ltd v Boyle* [2009] 4 All E.R. 1181; [2009] I.R.L.R. 746.
[243] EqA s.8.
[244] EqA s.9; *BBC v Souster*, 2001 S.L.T. 265, holding that Scots, English and Welsh are racial groups for the purposes of the Act.

customs and manners. Among the features relevant to whether a community is ethnic in character are common geographical or ancestral origins, common language, a common literature, a common religion distinct from the religion of neighbouring peoples, and the community's position as a minority or as an oppressed or dominant group within a larger community.[245] The Supreme Court has interpreted "ethnic origin" even more widely, holding that a person will have been subjected to unlawful discrimination on ethnic grounds if he is discriminated against on grounds of who he is descended from.[246] Fourthly, "religion" means any religion and a reference to religion includes a reference to a lack of religion, while "belief" means any religious or philosophical belief and a reference to belief includes a reference to a lack of belief. It has been held that a belief will be a "philosophical belief" if: (a) it is genuinely held; (b) it is a belief and not an opinion or viewpoint based on the present state of information available; (c) it is a belief as to a weighty and substantial aspect of human life and behaviour; (d) it has attained a certain level of cogency, seriousness, cohesion and importance; and (e) it is worthy of respect in a democratic society, not incompatible with human dignity and does not conflict with the fundamental rights of others.[247] Finally, sexual orientation means a person's sexual orientation towards persons of the same sex, persons of the opposite sex or persons of either sex.

17.27 Direct and indirect discrimination—The concepts of direct and indirect discrimination first appeared in the 1975 Act and recurred, with modifications, in later legislation. Direct discrimination occurs where, because of a protected characteristic, a person A treats another person B less favourably than A treats or would treat others.[248] The test for direct discrimination is objective: regard must be had to what was done, not to the motives for doing it.[249] However, where the factual criterion or criteria which influenced the employer to act in the way that it did are not inherently discriminatory or plain on their face, it is valid for the tribunal or court to explore the mental processes of the alleged discriminator, i.e. to examine the reason why the employer might have acted in the way that it did from an objective perspective.[250] The definition of direct discrimination in the EqA is sufficiently wide to outlaw less favourable treatment against a person because: (a) the employer thinks or perceives, incorrectly, that the person has a protected characteristic[251]; or (b) a person has an association with a third party who has a protected characteristic.[252] The formula for the establishment of direct discrimination requires an employee to show that he/she was treated less favourably than an actual or hypothetical comparator. Indirect discrimination arises where a person A applies to a person B a provision, criterion or practice ("PCP") which is discriminatory in relation to the relevant protected characteristic (in this case, age, disability, gender reassignment, marriage, civil partnership,

---

[245] *Mandla v Dowell Lee* [1983] 2 A.C. 548 (Sikhs); *Crown Suppliers (Property Services Agency) v Dawkins* [1991] I.C.R. 583 (Gypsies); *Seide v Gillette Industries Ltd* [1980] I.R.L.R. 427 (Jews).

[246] *R. v Governing Body of Jews Free School* [2009] UKSC 15; [2010] 2 A.C. 728.

[247] *Grainger Plc v Nicholson* [2010] I.R.L.R. 4.

[248] EqA s.13(1).

[249] *James v Eastleigh Borough Council* [1990] 2 A.C. 751.

[250] *R. v Governing Body of Jews Free School* [2009] UKSC 15; [2010] 2 A.C. 728.

[251] For example, where an employer treats an employee less favourably on the erroneous belief that he is homosexual.

[252] For example, the situation in *Coleman v Attridge Law* [2008] 3 C.M.L.R. 27 (ECJ) where an employee with a disabled child, for whom she was the principal carer, was treated less favourably because she was refused flexible working and insulted about her child's disabilities.

race, religion, belief, sex or sexual orientation) of B. The PCP is discriminatory in relation to a relevant protected characteristic of B's if: A applies, or would apply it to persons with whom B does not share the characteristic; it puts, or would put, persons with whom B shares the characteristic at a particular disadvantage when compared with persons with whom B does not share it; it puts, or would put, B at that disadvantage; and A cannot show it to be a proportionate means of achieving a legitimate aim.[253] There are a number of ways in which direct and indirect discrimination can be committed which may arise pre-employment,[254] during employment[255] and post-employment,[256] namely: by the arrangements the employer makes for the purpose of deciding to whom to offer employment; by the terms on which employment is offered; by refusal to offer employment; in regard to the employee's terms of employment; in regard to the way the employer accesses, or does not access, opportunities for promotion, transfer, training or other benefits; by dismissal or subjection to any other detriment; by acts or omissions arising out of and closely connected to a relationship which used to exist between the employer and the employee; in relation to conduct of a description constituting discrimination which would, if it occurred during the relationship between employer and employee, contravene the EqA.[257] Employers are liable not only for their own discriminatory acts but also (except for the purposes of criminal liability) for such acts done in the course of their employment by their employees,[258] even if done without the employer's knowledge or approval, unless the employer can prove that it took all reasonable steps[259] to prevent the employee from doing the act in question, or from doing acts of that description in the course of his employment.[260]

Harassment—Protection against harassment in employment was initially **17.28** approached as in part an application of an employer's responsibility for health and safety[261] and in part a development of the law of discrimination, particularly sex discrimination.[262] Although these approaches remain valid, recent developments have moved in the direction of treating harassment as a wrong in itself for which the employee has a remedy. The Protection from Harassment Act 1997 provides both criminal and civil remedies, and it has been held that an employer can be vicariously liable for harassment by employees in the course of their employment.[263] The EqA now provides that harassment occurs when a person A engages in unwanted conduct related to a relevant protected characteristic and that conduct has the purpose or effect of violating dignity or creating an intimidating, hostile, degrading, humiliating or offensive environment for a person B.[264] Unlike direct discrimination, this formula does not require the person B to draw comparisons

---

[253] EqA s.19.

[254] See EqA s.39(1).

[255] See EqA s.39(2).

[256] See EqA s.108(1).

[257] EqA ss.39(1) and (2) and 108(1).

[258] For the scope of "course of employment", see *Jones v Tower Boot Co* [1997] I.C.R. 254.

[259] For the scope of the words "took all reasonable steps to prevent", see *Croft v Royal Mail* [2003] I.C.R. 1425.

[260] EqA s.109.

[261] e.g. *W v Commissioner of Police of the Metropolis* [2000] I.R.L.R. 720.

[262] *Porcelli v Strathclyde RC* [1986] I.C.R. 564; but see *Stewart v Cleveland Guest (Engineering) Ltd* [1996] I.C.R. 535; *Pearce v Mayfield School* [2003] I.R.L.R. 512 (HL).

[263] *Majrowski v Guy's and St Thomas' NHS Trust* [2006] UKHL 34; [2006] 4 All E.R. 395.

[264] EqA s.26(1).

with the treatment of a person of the opposite sex.[265] A person A must not harass a person B who (i) is an employee of person A's or (ii) has applied to person A for employment[266] and it is now provided that an employer A will be liable for the harassment of employee B where B has been harassed by a third party C in the course of B's employment and A failed to take such steps as would have been reasonably practicable to prevent the third party from doing so.[267] The EqA also introduce a "free-standing" wrong of sexual harassment, which can be established without showing that men and women were treated differently, although it will remain necessary to show that the treatment was of a "sexual nature or . . . related to gender reassignment or sex".[268]

17.29 **Sex discrimination**—Sections 13 and 19 of the EqA prohibit direct and indirect discrimination because of sex or marital or civil partnership status, subject to considerations of health and to genuine occupational requirements that are a proportionate means of achieving a legitimate aim of the employer.[269] The protection of the EqA also extends to agency or contract workers.[270] Although the main impetus behind the prohibition of discrimination was to secure the protection of women, men are equally entitled to claim that they have suffered from sex discrimination. It is not unlawful to discriminate against women where it is necessary to do so to comply with certain statutory provisions designed to give protection against health risks specific to women.[271] Unlike the Sex Discrimination Act 1975, Sch.9 to the EqA does not provide concrete examples of genuine occupational requirements in the context of sex, but the exceptions specified in the former legislation are likely to be of continued relevance for the purposes of the latter. Therefore, provided that it is a proportionate means of achieving a legitimate aim of the employer, it is likely that a genuine occupational requirement in terms of the protected characteristic of sex will cover the following: (a) that the job calls for a person of one sex rather than the other for reasons of physiology (excluding: physical strength or stamina), or, in dramatic performances or other entertainment, for reasons of authenticity, so that the essential nature of the job would be materially different if carried out by a person of the other sex; or (b) that the job needs to be held by a person of one sex rather than the other to preserve decency or privacy or, where the job is likely to involve working or living in a private home, because objection might reasonably be taken to allowing a person of the other sex the degree of physical or social contact with the occupant of the home or the knowledge of intimate details of his life which is likely on account of the nature or circumstances of the job or the home; or (c) that it is impracticable for the employee to live elsewhere than in premises provided by the employer which are normally lived in by, and equipped with accommodation for, persons of one sex and it is not reasonable to expect the employer either to equip these premises with accommodation for the other sex or to provide other premises; or (d) that the premises within which the work is to be done are part of a hospital, prison or other establishment for persons requiring special care,

---

[265] That is the effect of the words "related to" in EqA s.26(1)(a).

[266] EqA s.40(1).

[267] EqA s.40(2). This statutory provision therefore means that the decision in *Pearce v Governing Body of Mayfield Secondary School* [2003] I.R.L.R. 512 is no longer good law.

[268] EqA s.40(3) and (4).

[269] See EqA Sch.9.

[270] EqA s.41.

[271] *Page v Freight Hire (Tank Haulage) Ltd* [1981] I.R.L.R. 13.

supervision or attention and these persons are all of one sex and it is reasonable, having regard to the essential character of the establishment, that the job should not be held by a person of the other sex; or (e) that the holder of the job provides individuals with personal services, promoting their welfare or education or the like, and these services can most effectively be provided by a person of one sex rather than the other; or (f) that the job needs to be held by a person of one sex rather than the other because it is likely to involve the performance of duties outside the United Kingdom in a country whose laws or customs are such that the duties could not effectively be performed by a person of the other sex; or (g) that the job is one of two to be held by a married couple. If a claimant establishes facts from which the court could decide, in the absence of any other explanation, that a person committed discriminatory conduct (i.e. a prima facie case of discrimination) the onus of showing that there was a non-gender-specific or non-discriminatory reason for what was done shifts to the employer.[272] Complaints of unlawful discrimination in employment are presented to an employment tribunal which has power to make orders declaring the rights of parties, to award compensation and . to make recommendations for specific action to obviate the effects of the discrimination, failure to comply with which may lead to an increase in compensation.[273] There is no statutory limit on the level of compensation available in cases of sex discrimination.[274]

Sex discrimination: Exclusions—Unlike the Sex Discrimination Act,[275] the EqA **17.30** is silent as to whether it only applies to employment at an establishment in Great Britain. Difficult questions may arise where a person is engaged in Great Britain but works entirely or predominantly overseas,[276] or the individual works partly in Great Britain.[277] The EqA does not apply to acts done under statutory authority,[278] or for the purpose of safeguarding national security.[279] Like the case law interpreting the Recast Directive,[280] the EqA permits "positive action" to promote the interests of under-represented or structurally disadvantaged groups in the workplace, i.e. where an employer reasonably thinks that: (a) persons sharing a protected characteristic suffer a disadvantage connected to that characteristic; (b) persons who share a protected characteristic have needs that are different from the needs of persons who do not share it; or (c) participation in an activity by persons who share a protected characteristic is disproportionately low, then provided that

---

[272] EqA s.136(1); *King v Great Britain-China Centre* [1992] I.C.R. 516; *Barton v Investec Henderson Crosthwaite Securities* [2003] I.C.R. 1205; *Wong v Igen Ltd* [2005] I.C.R. 931; *Madarassy v Nomura Plc* [2007] I.C.R. 867 (CA); *Hewage v Grampian Health Board* [2012] I.C.R. 1054.

[273] EqA ss.120 and 124.

[274] Employment Tribunals (Interest on Awards in Discrimination Cases) Regulations 1996 (SI 1996/2803).

[275] See Sex Discrimination Act 1975 ss.6(1) and 10; *Saggar v Ministry of Defence* [2005] I.R.L.R. 618; *Williams v University of Nottingham* [2007] I.R.L.R. 660 and *Tradition Securities and Futures SA v X* [2009] I.C.R. 88.

[276] See now *Lawson v Serco Ltd and Other Cases* [2006] UKHL 3; [2006] I.R.L.R. 289 and *Duncombe v Secretary of State for Children, Schools and Families* [2011] UKSC 36; T. Linden, "Employment Protection for Employees Working Abroad" (2006) 35 *Industrial Law Journal* 186.

[277] *British Airways Plc v Mak* [2011] I.C.R. 735.

[278] Sex Discrimination Act 1975 ss.51, 51A inserted by Employment Act 1989 s.3(3). See also 1989 Act ss.1, 4.

[279] EqA Sch.23 para.1 and s.192.

[280] *Kalanke v Freie Hansestadt Bremen* [1996] I.C.R. 314; *Re Badeck* [2000] All E.R. (EC) 289; *Marschall v Land Nordrhein Westfalen* [1998] IRLR 39; *EFTA Surveillance Authority v Kingdom of Norway* [2003] 1 C.M.L.R. 725.

it is a proportionate means of achieving a legitimate aim, the employer is not prohibited from taking action which: (i) enables or encourages persons who share the protected characteristic to overcome or minimise that disadvantage; (ii) meets those needs; or (iii) enables or encourages persons who share the protected characteristic to participate in that activity.[281] Positive action is also permitted in the context of recruitment and promotion, i.e. where an employer reasonably thinks that: (a) persons sharing a protected characteristic suffer a disadvantage connected to that characteristic; or (b) participation in an activity by persons who share a protected characteristic is disproportionately low, then the employer is not prohibited from taking action which treats a person A more favourably in connection with recruitment or promotion than another comparator person B because A has the protected characteristic but B does not, provided that such action is taken with the aim of enabling or encouraging persons who share the protected characteristic to: (i) overcome or minimise that disadvantage; or (ii) participate in that activity.[282] However, this is subject to three conditions, namely, that: (a) person A must be as qualified as the comparator person B to be recruited or promoted; (b) the employer does not have a policy of treating persons who share the protected characteristic more favourably in connection with recruitment or promotion than persons who do not share it; and (c) taking the action in question is a proportionate means of achieving the employer's legitimate aim.[283] As provisions for conferring benefits on persons of one sex only are lawful if contained in a charitable instrument,[284] discrimination between one sex and the other in a purely charitable provision for any class of employees is lawful. In employment, where the employer provides benefits, facilities, or services to the public and also furnishes those benefits, facilities and services to the public, any discriminatory acts suffered by an employee pursuant to the provision of those benefits, etc. will be lawful, provided that: (a) the benefit, etc. provided to the employee does not differ in a material respect from that provided to the public; (b) the provision of the benefit, etc. is not regulated by the terms of the employee's contract of employment or other terms on which the employee undertakes work for the employer; or (c) the benefit, etc. relates to training.[285]

17.31   Racial discrimination: General—Sections 13 and 19 of the EqA prohibit direct and indirect discrimination, because of race, colour, nationality, ethnic or national origins, in relation to all personal work contracts. The protection of the EqA also extends to agency or contract workers.[286] Direct discrimination arises if a person is treated less favourably on racial grounds, even though the treatment is not based on the race of the person so treated, i.e. discrimination by association is outlawed: for example where a white woman is refused a job on the ground that her husband is black or an employee is dismissed for refusal to obey a discriminatory order. To segregate a person from others on the basis of race is to treat him less favourably[287] but in general a difference of treatment is not discrimination if there is no detriment.[288] Subjecting an employee to a detriment because he

---

[281] EqA s.158(1) and (2).
[282] EqA s.159(1), (2) and (3).
[283] EqA s.159(4).
[284] EqA ss.193–194.
[285] EqA Sch.9 para.19.
[286] EqA s.41; cf. *Muschett v HM Prison Service* [2010] I.R.L.R. 451.
[287] EqA s.13(5).
[288] *Barclays Bank v Kapur* [1991] 2 A.C. 355.

brought proceedings under the EqA, made an allegation of contraventions of the EqA, or gave evidence or information in connection with proceedings under the EqA, is treated as victimisation.[289] Racial harassment is also prohibited.[290] The range of prohibited discriminatory acts is the same as that which applies in the case of sex discrimination, i.e. direct discrimination, indirect discrimination, victimisation and harassment, which are each of relevance pre-employment,[291] during employment[292] and post-employment.[293] The dismissal of an employee may constitute racial discrimination[294] and "dismissal" for this purpose includes constructive dismissal.[295] A racial insult may by itself amount to a detriment.[296]

Racial discrimination: Genuine occupational requirements—Unlike the **17.32** Race Relations Act 1976,[297] Sch.9 to the EqA does not provide concrete examples of genuine occupational requirements in the context of race, but the exceptions specified in the former legislation are likely to be of continued relevance for the purposes of the latter. Therefore, provided that it is a proportionate means of achieving a legitimate aim of the employer, it is likely that a genuine occupational requirement in terms of the protected characteristic of race will cover the following: (a) that the job calls for a person of one race rather than the other for reasons of authenticity in theatrical, dramatic or artistic works (e.g. plays or modelling) or in a specific setting such as an ethnic restaurant; or (b) where personal services are provided to members of a racial group and can best be provided by members of that group.[298] This exception applies across the whole range of racial discrimination as defined in the EqA. Moreover, Parliament or the Government are entitled to discriminate directly or indirectly against a person on the ground of race by applying to that person a provision, criterion or practice which relates to that person's place of ordinary residence or the length of time that that person has been present or resident in or outside the United Kingdom or an area within it.[299] As with sex discrimination, if an employee establishes facts from which the court could decide, in the absence of any other explanation, that a person committed discriminatory conduct, (i.e. a prima facie case of discrimination) the onus of showing that there was a non-gender-specific or non-discriminatory reason for what was done shifts to the employer.[300] However, the mere fact that an employer has treated

---

[289] EqA s.27(1) and (2). See *Kirby v Manpower Services Commission* [1980] I.R.L.R. 229; *Lindsay v Alliance & Leicester Plc* [2000] I.C.R. 1234.

[290] EqA s.26(1).

[291] See EqA s.39(1).

[292] See EqA s.39(2).

[293] See EqA s.108(1).

[294] EqA s.39(2).

[295] *Derby Specialist Fabrication Ltd v Burton*, 2001 I.R.L.R. 69. See para.17.43, below.

[296] *De Souza v Automobile Association* [1998] 2 C.M.L.R. 40.

[297] Race Relations Act 1976 s.5.

[298] See *London Borough of Lambeth v Commission for Racial Equality* [1990] I.C.R. 768.

[299] EqA Sch.23 para.1.

[300] EqA s.136(1); *King v Great Britain-China Centre* [1992] I.C.R. 516; *Barton v Investec Henderson Crosthwaite Securities* [2003] I.C.R. 1205; *Wong v Igen Ltd* [2005] I.C.R. 931; *Madarassy v Nomura Plc* [2007] I.C.R. 867 (CA); *Hewage v Grampian Health Board* [2012] I.C.R. 1054.

an employee unreasonably does not of itself give rise to an inference of discrimination.[301]

17.33 **Racial discrimination: Exceptions and remedies**—Unlike the Race Relations Act 1976,[302] the EqA is silent as to whether it only applies only to employment at an establishment in Great Britain. Difficult questions may arise where a person is engaged in Great Britain but works entirely or predominantly overseas[303] or the individual works partly in Great Britain.[304] There are exceptions for the provision of education or training for persons not ordinarily resident in Great Britain[305] and for the purpose of safeguarding national security.[306] As in the case of sex discrimination, conduct on the part of the employer which amounts to "positive action" and promotes the interests of under-represented or structurally disadvantaged groups in the workplace does not constitute unlawful racial discrimination.[307] A person aggrieved by racial discrimination in respect of employment may complain to an employment tribunal, which may make orders declaring the rights of the parties or for compensation for any damages sustained by the complainant, including injury to feelings.[308] There is no statutory limit on the level of compensation which can be awarded and the tribunal can also award interest on the compensation payment.[309] In addition, the tribunal may make a recommendation that the respondent take action to obviate or reduce the adverse effect on the complainant of any act of discrimination and in the case of failure, make an order for compensation or increase an amount of compensation already ordered.[310] In addition to the remedies available to the individual, compliance with the Act, in relation to employment as well as other matters, may be secured at the instance of the Commission for Equality and Human Rights by means of inquiries and investigations,[311] unlawful act notices,[312] binding agreements,[313] applications for an injunction or interdict,[314] judicial review and other legal proceedings[315] and providing legal assistance to employees.[316] The Commission for Equality and Human Rights has the right to use any of the aforementioned powers notwithstanding that it does not know or suspect that a person has been or may be affected by the unlawful act or application.[317]

---

[301] *Law Society v Bahl* [2003] I.R.L.R. 640. For an example of the application of the genuine occupational requirement in a religious belief case see *Glasgow City Council v McNab* [2007] I.R.L.R. 476.

[302] Race Relations Act 1976 ss.4(1) and (2) and 8; *Saggar v Ministry of Defence* [2005] I.R.L.R. 618; *Williams v University of Nottingham* [2007] I.R.L.R. 660 and *British Airways Plc v Mak* [2011] I.C.R. 735.

[303] See now *Lawson v Serco Ltd and Other Cases* [2006] UKHL 3; [2006] I.R.L.R. 289 and *Duncombe v Secretary of State for Children, Schools and Families* [2011] UKSC 36; Linden, "Employment Protection for Employees Working Abroad" (2006) 35 *Industrial Law Journal* 186.

[304] *British Airways Plc v Mak* [2011] I.C.R. 735.

[305] EqA Sch.23 para.4.

[306] EqA s.192.

[307] EqA ss.158 and 159.

[308] EqA ss.120 and 124. *Sharifi v Strathclyde RC* [1992] I.R.L.R. 259.

[309] Employment Tribunals (Interest on Awards in Discrimination Cases) Regulations 1996 (SI 1996/2803).

[310] EqA s.124(2)(c), (3) and (7).

[311] EqA 2006 ss.16 and 20.

[312] EqA 2006 ss.21–22.

[313] EqA 2006 s.23.

[314] EqA 2006 s.24.

[315] EqA 2006 s.30.

[316] EqA 2006 s.28.

[317] EqA 2006 s.24A.

Disability discrimination—The EqA provides that it is unlawful for an employer **17.34**
to discriminate against a disabled person in relation to employment. The protection of the EqA also extends to agency or contract workers.[318] The range of
discriminatory acts is the same as that which applies in the case of the other
protected characteristics.[319] There are four forms of disability discrimination,
namely (1) discrimination arising from disability,[320] (2) direct disability
discrimination,[321] (3) a failure to make reasonable adjustments[322] and (4) indirect
disability discrimination. The first occurs where the employer treats a disabled
employee unfavourably because of something arising in consequence of the
employee's disability and the employer cannot show that the unfavourable treatment is a proportionate means of achieving a legitimate aim. Therefore, if an
employee's arthritic condition is so serious that it amounts to a disability and
causes her to type slowly in the workplace, and the employer dismisses her on the
basis that she is typing too slowly (rather than on the grounds of her arthritic
condition), the employer will be liable on the grounds of "discrimination arising
from disability" if the employee can demonstrate that the dismissal amounted to
unfavourable treatment and the employer cannot show that the dismissal was a
proportionate means of achieving a legitimate objective. For the purposes of
demonstrating unfavourable treatment, one would expect the courts and employment tribunals to hold that the employee need only compare herself to an actual or
hypothetical employee who is not arthritic and disabled and who also types
slowly. In the example provided, if that comparator would not have been
dismissed, then it is likely that a court or employment tribunal would rule that
unfavourable treatment had been established. The second form of discrimination
occurs where, because of the disability of an employee (rather than a condition
associated with the disability), the employer treats that employee less favourably
than it treats or would treat others.[323] This is known as direct disability discrimination and the employee must invoke a comparator in seeking to demonstrate
less favourable treatment. That comparator can be real or hypothetical, but in all
cases, there must be no material difference between the circumstances relating to
the disabled employee's case and that of the comparator (except the employee's
disability).[324] The distinction between direct disability discrimination and
"discrimination arising from disability" is a fine one, and part of the role of the
former is to address stereotyping on the part of the employer about a particular
condition and the ability of an employee with such a disability to perform the
requirements of the job.[325] Thirdly, discrimination also occurs where the employer
fails to comply with its duty to make reasonable adjustments in terms of ss.20–22
of the EqA. The duty will arise where: (a) a provision, criterion or practice of
the employer's puts a disabled employee at a substantial disadvantage in relation
to a relevant matter in comparison with persons who are not disabled[326]; (b) a
physical feature of the employer's premises puts a disabled person at a substantial
disadvantage in relation to a relevant matter in comparison with persons who are

---

[318] EqA s.41.
[319] EqA ss.39(1) and (2) and 108(1).
[320] EqA s.15.
[321] EqA s.13.
[322] EqA ss.20–22 and Sch.8.
[323] EqA s.13(1).
[324] EqA s.23(1).
[325] *Aylott v Stockton-on-Tees BC* [2010] I.R.L.R. 994.
[326] EqA s.20(3).

not disabled[327]; or (c) a disabled person would, but for the provision of an auxiliary aid, be put at a substantial disadvantage in relation to a relevant matter in comparison with persons who are not disabled.[328] The employer's duty may include a duty to redeploy the employee, if it is reasonable to do so,[329] or even to create a new post for the disabled employee.[330] Therefore, the employer's duty to make reasonable adjustments involves a measure of positive discrimination in favour of disabled employees[331] and the employer's discretion in relation to the obligation is limited.[332] It has been held that the dismissal of a disabled employee can of itself, amount to a failure on the part of the employer to make a reasonable adjustment.[333] Finally, indirect disability discrimination will occur where the employer applies, or would apply, a provision, criterion or practice which puts, or would put, disabled persons who have the same kind of disability as the employee claimant[334] at a particular disadvantage when compared with non-disabled persons, it puts, or would put the disabled employee at that disadvantage and the employer cannot show it to be a proportionate means of achieving a legitimate aim.[335] An employer can seek to justify discriminatory treatment of the first and fourth kinds on the basis that what the employer did was a proportionate means of achieving a legitimate aim, but not the second or third. A statutory code of practice on employment has been published by the Equality and Human Rights Commission[336] and is extremely important in dealing with disability cases in practice. As with other forms of discrimination, harassment and victimisation are unlawful. Unlike the Disability Discrimination Act 1995,[337] the EqA is silent as to whether it only applies only to employment at an establishment in Great Britain. Difficult questions may arise where a disabled employee is engaged in Great Britain but works entirely or predominantly overseas.[338] There are exceptions for the provision of education or training for persons not ordinarily resident in Great Britain[339] and for the purpose of safeguarding national security.[340] As in the case of sex and racial discrimination, conduct on the part of the employer which amounts to "positive action" and promotes the interests of under-represented or structurally disadvantaged groups in the workplace does not constitute unlawful disability discrimination.[341] A person aggrieved by disability discrimination in respect of employment may complain to an employment tribunal, which may make orders declaring the rights of the parties or for compensation for any damages sustained by the complainant,

---

[327] EqA s.20(4).

[328] EqA s.20(5).

[329] *Archibald v Fife Council*, 2004 S.C. (HL) 117.

[330] *Chief Constable of South Yorkshire Police v Jelic* [2010] I.R.L.R. 744.

[331] *Archibald v Fife Council*, 2004 S.C. (HL) 117 at 128, [57], per Lady Hale.

[332] *Smith v Churchill's Stairlifts Plc* [2006] I.R.L.R. 41.

[333] *Fareham College v Walters* [2009] I.R.L.R. 991.

[334] EqA s.6(3)(b).

[335] EqA s.19.

[336] Available from *http://www.equalityhumanrights.com/uploaded_files/EqualityAct/employercode. pdf* [Accessed August 2, 2012].

[337] Disability Discrimination Act 1995 s.4(6).

[338] See now *Lawson v Serco Ltd and Other Cases* [2006] UKHL 3; [2006] I.R.L.R. 289 and *Duncombe v Secretary of State for Children, Schools and Families* [2011] UKSC 36; Linden, "Employment Protection for Employees Working Abroad" (2006) 35 *Industrial Law Journal* 186.

[339] EqA Sch.23 para.4.

[340] EqA s.192.

[341] EqA ss.158–159.

including injury to feelings.[342] There is no statutory limit on the level of compensation which can be awarded and the tribunal can also award interest on the compensation payment.[343] In addition, the tribunal may make a recommendation that the respondent take action to obviate or reduce the adverse effect on the complainant of any act of discrimination and in the case of failure, make an order for compensation or increase an amount of compensation already ordered.[344] The Commission for Equality and Human Rights has the power to call inquiries and investigations,[345] issue unlawful act notices[346] and binding agreements,[347] make applications for injunctions or interdicts,[348] institute judicial review and other legal proceedings[349] and provide legal assistance to employees.[350] The Commission may do so notwithstanding that it does not know or suspect that a person has been or may be affected by the unlawful act or application.[351]

Discrimination: Part-time workers—Tribunals and courts have frequently **17.35** found in the past that provisions, criteria or practices which result in less favourable treatment of part-time workers amounted to indirect sex discrimination contrary to the Sex Discrimination Act 1975.[352] Part-time workers can also look to the Part-Time Workers (Prevention of Less Favourable Treatment) Regulations 2000.[353] An employer may not treat a part-time worker less favourably than a comparable full-time worker as regards contractual terms or by subjecting the part-time worker to any other detriment.[354] The employer may attempt to justify the treatment on objective grounds. In considering whether there has been less favourable treatment in relation to pay and conditions, the part-time and full-time workers' pay are to be compared on a pro rata basis.[355] A part-time employee who considers that she has been discriminated against may apply for a written statement from her employer which gives reasons for the treatment.[356] If the principal reason for a part-time worker's dismissal relates to the worker's enforcement of rights under the Regulations, then the dismissal will be regarded as automatically unfair.[357]

Age discrimination—The EqA also prohibits an employer from discriminating **17.36** against a person because of his age. As with sex, racial and disability discrimination, the impetus for the legislation may have been to protect older workers, but younger workers are equally entitled to complain of differential treatment based

---

[342] EqA ss.120 and 124; *Sharifi v Strathclyde R.C.* [1992] I.R.L.R. 259.
[343] Employment Tribunals (Interest on Awards in Discrimination Cases) Regulations 1996 (SI 1996/2803).
[344] EqA s.124(2)(c), (3) and (7).
[345] EqA 2006 ss.16 and 20.
[346] EqA 2006 ss.21–22.
[347] EqA 2006 s.23.
[348] EqA 2006 s.24.
[349] EqA 2006 s.30.
[350] EqA 2006 s.28.
[351] EqA 2006 s.24A.
[352] See *R. v Secretary of State for Employment, Ex p. EOC* [1994] I.C.R. 317.
[353] Part-Time Workers (Prevention of Less Favourable Treatment) Regulations 2000 (SI 2000/1551) (the "2000 Regulations"), which implements EC Directive 97/81; see, e.g. *Matthews v Kent and Medway Towns Fire Authority* [2006] UKHL 8; 2 All E.R. 171.
[354] 2000 Regulations reg.5.
[355] 2000 Regulations regs 1 and 5(3).
[356] 2000 Regulations reg.6.
[357] 2000 Regulations reg.7.

on their relative youth.[358] The provisions in the EqA relating to age discrimination purport to give effect, in relation to age, to the Framework Directive.[359] As with other discrimination legislation, direct and indirect discrimination, harassment and victimisation are prohibited, and the range of discriminatory actions is also similar. Unusually, both direct and indirect discrimination can be justified if the employer can show that the treatment is a proportionate means of achieving a legitimate aim.[360] However, the nature of the justification defence differs depending on whether the claimant is seeking to prove direct or indirect discrimination and the range of aims which could justify indirect discrimination is wider than for direct discrimination.[361] For example, the Supreme Court has held that a distinction must be drawn between social policy objectives of a public interest nature (such as employment policy, the labour market or vocational training), which could justify direct age discrimination, and purely individual reasons particular to the employer's situation, which in general could not.[362] In the case of a direct discrimination claim, where an employer argues that the measures it adopted had the objectives of securing inter-generational fairness and preserving the dignity of older workers, it has been held that these were both capable of being legitimate aims, depending on the circumstances of the employment concerned and provided the means chosen were appropriate and necessary.[363] Meanwhile, it has been held that the requirement to have a law degree for career progression worked to the comparative disadvantage of an employee approaching compulsory retirement age and was indirectly discriminatory on grounds of age, unless the employer could show that such a requirement was a proportionate means of achieving a legitimate aim.[364] The extension of anti-discrimination into this field undoubtedly involves some differences of approach in the assessment of what is legitimate and proportionate and it may not necessarily be appropriate to rely on cases decided in relation to the other protected characteristics.[365] There are exceptions for genuine occupational requirements,[366] statutory authority,[367] the armed forces,[368] child care[369] and national security[370] and for some benefits based on length of service[371] and other similar matters.[372] As in the case of sex, racial and disability discrimination, there is also a potentially important exception under ss.158 or 159 of the EqA for positive action by way of affording to persons of a particular age group access to facilities or training or encouraging them to take advantage of opportunities to do particular work, if it is done to compensate for disadvantages suffered by that age group. Since April 6, 2011, the Coalition Government has been engaged in the process of gradually phasing out the default retirement age of 65. Therefore, when the default retirement age is finally

---

[358] See e.g. *Kücükdeveci v Swedex GmbH & Co KG* [2010] I.R.L.R. 346.
[359] Framework Directive 2000/78/EC.
[360] *Mangold v Rudiger Helm* [2005] E.C.R. I-9981.
[361] *Homer v Chief Constable of West Yorkshire* [2012] I.R.L.R. 601.
[362] *Seldon v Clarkson, Wright & Jakes* [2012] I.R.L.R. 590.
[363] *Seldon v Clarkson, Wright & Jakes* [2012] I.R.L.R. 590.
[364] *Homer v Chief Constable of West Yorkshire* [2012] I.R.L.R. 601.
[365] See J. Swift, "Justifying Age Discrimination" (2006) 35 *Industrial Law Journal* 228.
[366] EqA Sch.9 paras 10–16.
[367] EqA Sch.22 para.1.
[368] EqA Sch.9 para.4(3).
[369] EqA Sch.9 para.15.
[370] EqA s.192.
[371] EqA Sch.9 para.10.
[372] EqA Sch.9 paras 10–16.

abolished, if an employer automatically dismisses an employee on or after the age of 65 or the normal retirement age (if there is one), the employer will no longer be able to rely on the fact that it followed a prescribed statutory procedure as a defence and the dismissal will be unfair and/or discriminatory unless the employer can show that the dismissal was a proportionate means of achieving a legitimate aim.

Employment protection: Discipline and grievance—There were no mandatory **17.37** procedures for disciplinary and grievance matters until 2002. The Employment Act 2002 introduced statutory dismissal, disciplinary and grievance procedures which an employers and employees were bound to follow prior to dismissal (in the case of the employer) or the presentation of a complaint to an employment tribunal (in the case of the employee). However, in 2009, these statutory mandatory dismissal, disciplinary and grievance procedures introduced by the Employment Act 2002 were abolished on the grounds that they had become unworkable. Agreed procedures have formed part of many contracts of employment, particularly those incorporating a collective agreement, for many years, and there has also been an ACAS Code of Practice on Disciplinary and Grievance Procedures for some time.[373] Failure to observe contractual procedures may constitute a breach of contract for which contractual remedies will be available, including interdict to restrain action in breach of the procedure[374] and damages in respect of the employee's contractual notice period and also in respect of the period during which the employee would have remained employed while a disciplinary procedure which complied with the terms of his contract ran its course.[375] The ACAS Code is not mandatory but forms a very important source of guidance and will be taken into account by employment tribunals where relevant to the determination of any question which comes before them.[376] Where the employer fails to comply with the ACAS Code, the employment tribunal or court has the power to increase the compensatory award by up to 25 per cent.[377] Since 1999, a worker who is asked to attend a hearing which is disciplinary in substance has had a right to be accompanied by a companion, who has certain rights to speak at the hearing.[378] It is a general rule that this statutory right to be accompanied will not include a right to be legally represented, unless the outcome of the disciplinary hearing is likely to: (a) be determinative of; or (b) have a substantial influence or effect on, a subsequent hearing, inquiry or investigation whose purpose is to determine whether the employee's civil right to pursue a profession, trade or occupation should be restricted or prohibited.[379] The standard procedure for discipline and dismissal in the ACAS Code requires the employer to give the employee written notice of the matters in issue and invite him to a meeting. Until the meeting takes place, the employer cannot take any action except precautionary suspension. After the meeting, the employer must inform the employee of his decision, the reasons for the decision and tell him that he has a right of appeal; at that stage the employer is not barred from putting the disciplinary action into effect. If the

---

[373] The current Code of Practice is available from *http://www.acas.org.uk/CHttpHandler. ashx?id=1047&p=0* [Accessed August 2, 2012].

[374] *Peace v City of Edinburgh Council*, 1999 S.L.T. 712.

[375] *Gunton v Richmond-upon-Thames London Borough Council* [1980] I.R.L.R. 321 CA.

[376] *Lewis Shops Group v Wiggins* [1973] I.C.R. 335; *Lock v Cardiff Railway* [1998] I.R.L.R. 358.

[377] Trade Union and Labour Relations (Consolidation) Act 1992 s.207A and ERA s.124A.

[378] Employment Relations Act 1999 ss.10–15.

[379] *R. (on the application of G) v Governors of X School* [2011] UKSC 30; [2011] 3 W.L.R. 237.

employee decides to appeal, he must notify the employer who must invite him to a further meeting and inform the employee in writing of his final decision. The employer is not prevented from dismissing an employee summarily for gross misconduct. In such cases a fair disciplinary process should be followed, before dismissing for gross misconduct also involving written notice of the grounds of complaint and a meeting or meetings. There are parallel procedures for grievances by employees. Where an employer fails to follow fair and proper disciplinary procedures prior to the dismissal of an employee, the dismissal of the employee will be unfair and contrary to Pt X of the ERA notwithstanding the fact that the employer is able to show that if it had followed fair and proper procedures, it would have made no difference to its decision to dismiss.[380]

17.38 **Employment protection: Transfer of undertakings**—At common law, a contract of employment is a personal contract not capable of being assigned or transferred, without consent.[381] Accordingly, the transfer of a business to a new owner terminates the employment of the staff of the business. This situation has been altered by legislation originally stemming from the Acquired Rights Directive[382] and introduced to the United Kingdom in 1981.[383] The 1981 Regulations gave rise to a massive amount of litigation and were repeatedly amended.[384] They have now been replaced by the Transfer of Undertakings (Protection of Employment) Regulations 2006.[385] The regulations apply to a "transfer" which is defined as the transfer of an undertaking, business or part of a business situated immediately before the transfer in the United Kingdom to another person where there is a transfer of an economic entity which retains its identity; it is probably implied that the entity must be stable, that is, for example, not one for the performance of a single contract.[386] The requirement that there should be a transfer to another person excludes cases where ownership of a company changes by share transfer.[387] An extended definition of transfer applies to cases where there is a change in provision of services: simple examples are cases where there is a change in the contractor who provides cleaning or catering services. When one person ceases to provide services and another takes up the provision, there is a transfer if before the change there was an organised grouping of employees, the principal purpose of which was to carry out the activities in question on behalf of the client.[388] A single employee may constitute a "grouping".[389] There are exceptions for single event or short-term provision after

---

[380] *Polkey v AE Dayton* [1988] A.C. 344. However, in such circumstances, the tribunal has the power to reduce the amount of compensatory award to reflect that fact.

[381] *Nokes v Doncaster Amalgamated Collieries Ltd* [1940] A.C. 1014.

[382] Directive 77/187/EEC of 14 February 1977 on the approximation of the laws of the Member States relating to the safeguarding of employees' rights in the event of transfers of undertakings, businesses or parts of businesses [1977] OJ L61.

[383] Transfer of Undertakings (Protection of Employment) Regulations 1981 (SI 1981/1794).

[384] As was the Directive; see Directive 98/50 and Acquired Rights Directive 2001/23, which consolidated the European legislation. For the background see J. McMullen, "An Analysis of the Transfer of Undertakings (Protection of Employment) Regulations 2006" (2006) 35 *Industrial Law Journal* 113.

[385] New Transfer of Undertakings (Protection of Employment) Regulations (SI 2006/246) ("TUPE"), effective April 6, 2006.

[386] TUPE reg.3(1)(a); *Mackie v Aberdeen City Council* [2006] CSIH 36; [2006] All E.R. (D) 297 (Jun).

[387] *ECM (Vehicle Delivery Service) v Cox* [1999] 4 All E.R. 669.

[388] TUPE reg.3(1)(b): this provision goes further than the requirements of the Directive.

[389] TUPE reg.2(1).

the change and for activities consisting wholly or mainly in the supply of goods.[390] A transfer may be made by a series of transactions and there need not be any direct contract between transferor and transferee.[391] Where the Regulations apply, the transfer of an undertaking does not terminate the contracts of employment of employees of the transferor assigned to the undertaking or grouping transferred, but those contracts operate as if made with the transferee.[392] Liabilities in connection with the contracts of employment of the transferred employees pass to the transferee. The Regulations substantially restrict the freedom of the parties to the transfer to dismiss employees or vary their terms of employment. An employee cannot of course be compelled to work for the new employer: he is entitled to object to his contract passing to the transferee, but if he does so he cannot claim that he has been dismissed.[393] If an employee is dismissed and the sole or principal reason is the transfer or a reason connected with the transfer, the dismissal is treated as automatically unfair unless it is "an economic, technical or organizational reason entailing changes in the workforce". This expression has been given a limited meaning.[394] Redundancy may be such a reason, but it is still open to the employee to claim that his selection for redundancy is unfair. Variation of the contract terms is subject to similar limitations and the fact the employee may be willing to agree to the variation does not prevent it from being void under the Regulations if the reason is not an economic technical or organisational one, since an employee cannot waive the rights conferred by the Directive.[395] If the transfer would involve a substantial change in working conditions to the material detriment of the employee, he may treat the contract as terminated and claim constructive dismissal.[396] The obligations in relation to transfer of employment and the protection against dismissal do not apply if the transferor is subject to bankruptcy or analogous insolvency proceedings which have been instituted with a view to the liquidation of the assets of the transferor and are under the supervision of an insolvency practitioner: in such a case, there are potential limitations upon the liabilities which may pass to the transferee and some latitude is permitted in varying, in consultation with employee representatives, the contracts of transferred employees.[397] It has been held that the words "analogous insolvency proceedings" in the context of reg.8(7) do not include administration.[398] The Regulations also provide for consultation of employees in advance of a transfer, for giving certain other categories of information and in relation to trade union recognition and collective agreements.[399]

Employment protection: Trade union activities—It is unlawful to refuse a person employment because he is, or is not, a member of a trade union or because he is unwilling to take steps to become, or cease to be, or to remain or not to   **17.39**

---

[390] TUPE reg.3(3).

[391] TUPE reg.3(6).

[392] TUPE reg.4. Transfer is automatic, subject to the employee's right to refuse to work for the new employer: *Astley v Celtec Ltd* [2006] 4 All E.R. 27.

[393] TUPE reg.4(7) and (8).

[394] See, e.g. *Berriman v Delabole Slate Ltd* [1985] I.C.R. 546; *Hynd v Armstrong*, 2007 S.C. 409.

[395] *Foreningen af Arbejdslederei Danmark v Daddy's Dance Hall A/S* [1988] I.R.L.R. 315; *Wilson v St Helens Borough Council* [1998] I.C.R. 1141 (HL); *Credit Suisse First Boston (Europe) Ltd v Lister* [1998] I.R.L.R. 700.

[396] TUPE reg.4(9).

[397] TUPE regs 8 and 9.

[398] *Barke v OTG Ltd* [2011] I.R.L.R. 272.

[399] TUPE regs 11–16.

become, a member of a trade union or to make payments or suffer deductions in the event of his not being a member of a trade union. The sanction is that an employment tribunal may award compensation and may recommend that the person refusing employment take action to obviate or reduce the adverse effect arising from the refusal.[400] Dismissal on the ground of trade union membership or activities, or on the ground of membership of an independent trade union or non-membership of any trade union, is unfair in the statutory sense and gives rise to the remedies noticed below.[401] An employee is, however, also entitled to be protected against action by his employer, short of dismissal, taken for the purpose of: (1) preventing or deterring him from being, or seeking to become a member of an independent trade union, or from taking part in its activities at any appropriate time, or for making use of trade union services at an appropriate time; or (2) penalising him on these grounds; or (3) compelling him to become a member of a trade union.[402] In the event of infringement of any of these rights, a complaint may be made to an employment tribunal which, if it finds the complaint well founded, may make a declaration to that effect and award such compensation as it considers just and equitable, having regard to the infringement of the complainant's right and any loss sustained by him (including expenses reasonably incurred, and loss of any benefit which he might reasonably be expected to have had but for his employer's actions).[403] Individual workers also enjoy the right not to be excluded from a trade union and certain other rights in relation to membership, discipline and expulsion.[404] The general law governing the rights and liabilities of trade unions is beyond the scope of this chapter.

17.40 Employment protection: Redundancy—Part XI of the 1996 Act imposes upon employers the obligation to make a "redundancy payment" to any employee who, after continuous employment for two years,[405] is: (a) dismissed by reason of redundancy; or (b) laid off or kept on short time for specified periods, provided that in the latter event he gives written notice of his claim.[406] Dismissal has the same meaning as it has in relation to unfair dismissal claims, but with the addition that where an act on the part of the employer or an event affecting the employer operates to terminate the contract, the employee is taken to be dismissed: this covers situations such as the death or bankruptcy of the employer.[407] An employee is dismissed by reason of "redundancy" if his dismissal is due wholly or mainly to the cessation of the employer's business, or to the cessation or diminution of demands for work of a particular kind[408] or at a particular place.[409] Where there is a dismissal, it is presumed to be for reasons of redundancy unless the contrary is proved.[410] If the employee's contract is renewed or he is re-engaged on substantially the same terms within four weeks of the termination, no redundancy payment is due. The same is true if the employer makes an offer of suitable alternative

---

[400] 1992 Act ss.137–143.
[401] 1992 Act s.152; para.17.48, below.
[402] 1992 Act s.146.
[403] 1992 Act ss.147–150.
[404] 1992 Act ss.63–69 and 174–176.
[405] 1992 Act ss.135 and 155.
[406] 1992 Act s.148.
[407] ERA s.136.
[408] On the meaning of "work of a particular kind", see *Murray v Foyle Meats Ltd* [1999] I.R.L.R. 56.
[409] ERA s.139.
[410] ERA s.163(2).

employment and the employee unreasonably refuses it.[411] There are a number of statutory provisions which affect the process of selection for redundancy, including provisions for consultation. Moreover, the provisions of the EqA will have an impact on the employer's selection process,[412] as will the statutory provisions which protect employees on maternity leave.[413] The process must be fair, and unfair selection may give rise to a claim for unfair dismissal. There are a number of cases in which selection will be deemed unfair.[414]

Termination of employment—Like any other contract, employment may be **17.41** brought to an end by mutual consent, the expiry of a fixed term, frustration or repudiatory conduct by either party. At common law, employment is also brought to an end by the death of either party or by the bankruptcy of the employer. A contract of employment with a firm is dissolved by the death of a partner, but not by a change in the constitution of the firm.[415] Absence due to illness or accident is not a breach of contract on the employee's part. But where the accident was due to the employee's own fault it was held that the employer was justified in dismissal, and that no further wages were due.[416] Prolonged absence from illness, though no fault may be attributed to the employee, may justify the employer in treating the contract as frustrated, and therefore at an end.[417] Where an employee is sentenced to a term of imprisonment which makes it impossible for him to perform his part of the contract, his employment is automatically terminated at the date of the sentence.[418] Subject to the Transfer of Undertakings Regulations,[419] the sequestration or liquidation of an employer amounts to a breach of contract on his part. The employee is entitled to leave, and to claim the amount which he would have earned as wages. But his claim is for damages, not for wages, and is therefore not entitled to the preferential ranking accorded to wages.[420] The contract may also be brought to an end by notice given by either party to the other. It is an established rule at common law that an employer is entitled to dismiss an employee at any time on reasonable notice and paying wages, and that such dismissal does not involve a breach of contract.[421] There is no analogous rule in favour of the employee.[422] A right of appeal against dismissal may, however, be incorporated in a contract of employment in terms which constitute an appellate committee as a quasi-judicial tribunal. In that event any material departure in the appeal

---

[411] ERA ss.138 and 141.

[412] For example, any selection criterion chosen by the employer which has a direct or indirect negative impact on persons with one of the protected characteristics in the EqA s.4 will be unlawful.

[413] Maternity and Parental Leave etc. Regulations 1999 (SI 1999/3312) reg.10.

[414] See ERA s.105.

[415] Bell, *Principles*, s.179; *Hoey v MacEwan & Auld* (1867) 5 M. 814; but there may be an agreement that the firm should not be dissolved by the death of a partner: see Partnership Act 1890 s.33(1); *Hill v Wylie* (1865) 3 M. 541 and *W S Gordon & Co Ltd v Thomson Partnership*, 1985 S.L.T. 122.

[416] *McEwan v Malcolm* (1867) 5 S.L.R. 62; but the responsibility for an illness is irrelevant in the context of the unfair dismissal legislation, *London Fire & Civil Defence Authority v Betty* [1994] I.R.L.R. 384.

[417] *Manson v Dowie* (1885) 12 R. 1103; *Poussard v Speirs & Pond* (1876) L.R. 1 Q.B.D. 410; *Westwood v S.M.T. Co*, 1938 S.N. 8; *Egg Stores (Stamford Hill) Ltd v Leibovici* [1977] I.C.R. 260.

[418] *Hare v Murphy Bros* [1974] 3 All E.R. 940; *F.C. Shepherd & Co Ltd v Jerrom* [1985] I.R.L.R. 275.

[419] See para.17.38, above.

[420] *Day v Tait* (1900) 8 S.L.T. 40.

[421] *Graham v Thomson* (1822) 1 S. 309; *Mollison v Baillie* (1885) 22 S.L.R. 595.

[422] *Wallace v Wishart* (1800) Hume 383.

procedure from the principles of natural justice may nullify the dismissal.[423] The contract may be terminated without notice by the employer summarily dismissing the employee (e.g. for gross misconduct) or the employee abandoning the contract.

17.42 **Termination by notice**—The contract of employment will normally specify the notice required to be given by both employer and employee. Normal or conventional notice periods for certain occupations were prescribed at common law but these are now obsolete.[424] Part IX of the ERA prescribes minimum periods of notice which must be given by employers and employees.[425] With certain specified exceptions,[426] the Act applies to all contracts of employment in which the employee has been continuously employed for at least one month. The notice required to be given by an employer is one week for those who have been continuously employed for one month or more but less than two years; one week for each year of continuous employment for those employed for two years or more but less than 12 years; and 12 weeks for those employed for 12 years or more.[427] The period of notice to be given by an employee is at least one week.[428] These periods of notice are the minimum prescribed by statute. They cannot be reduced by conventional provisions, but either party can agree to waive his right to notice, or to accept payment in lieu of notice.[429] The Act preserves the contractual or common law right of an employee to receive longer notice than the statutory minimum, and retains the common law right of either party to treat the contract as terminable without notice by reason of such conduct as would have justified such termination before the Act.[430] The liability of an employer to an employee during a period of notice is set out in ss.87–91 of the Act. The principal effect is to entitle the employee to a normal week's pay and other benefits for each week of the period, but subject to exceptions, including any period in which the employee takes part in a strike. The employer may permit the employee not to attend for work during the notice period.[431] An employee who has been employed for more than one year prior to the effective date of termination has a right to request and obtain a written statement of reasons for dismissal.[432]

17.43 **Wrongful dismissal and constructive dismissal**—At common law, dismissal of an employee without the proper notice or payment in lieu is wrongful, unless the employer is justified in dismissing the employee summarily because of misconduct. Whether there has been misconduct sufficient to justify summary dismissal is a question of fact in each case.[433] There are, however, a number of

---

[423] *Palmer v Inverness Hospitals Board of Management*, 1963 S.C. 311; *Dietmann v Brent L.B.C.* [1988] I.C.R. 842; *Peace v City of Edinburgh Council*, 1999 S.L.T. 712; [1999] I.R.L.R. 417.

[424] See W.M. Gloag and R.C. Henderson, *Law of Scotland*, 10th edn (Edinburgh: W. Green, 1995), para.21.22, for these common law prescriptions.

[425] Similar provisions were first enacted in the Contracts of Employment Act 1963.

[426] ERA ss.86(5) and 199(1).

[427] ERA s.86(1). Continuous employment is calculated in accordance with ss.210–219 of the ERA.

[428] ERA s.86(2). See *Walmsley v C. & R. Ferguson Ltd*, 1989 S.L.T. 258.

[429] ERA ss.86(3) and 203. However, in Scots law, no implied right is conferred in favour of the employer to make a payment in lieu of notice where there is an express clause which provides for a specific notice period, on which, see *Morrish v NTL Group Limited*, 2007 S.C. 805.

[430] ERA s.86(6).

[431] For so-called "garden leave" clauses, see *William Hill Organisation Ltd v Tucker* [1999] I.C.R. 291, CA.

[432] ERA ss.92(1) and 93.

[433] For example, see *McCormack v Hamilton Academical Football Club Ltd* [2011] CSIH 68; [2012] I.R.L.R. 108.

well-recognised grounds, including gross misconduct, refusal to obey a lawful and reasonable order, and dishonesty. It has been said that the standards to be applied are those of the present day and that older decisions as to what may constitute misconduct cannot necessarily be relied on.[434] The employee's remedy for wrongful dismissal is an action of damages. He has no right to insist on remaining in a post from which he has been dismissed, even although the dismissal was not justified.[435] In special circumstances, however, the court may, where damages would not afford an adequate remedy, restrain the implementation of an invalid notice of dismissal.[436] The measure of damages in the case of wrongful dismissal is normally the amount which the employee would have earned (which may include discretionary bonuses and commission)[437] had the contract been duly fulfilled, not to be increased by proof that the dismissal had caused third parties to form unfavourable opinions of his character.[438] An employee cannot claim damages for hurt feelings or mental distress following a breach of contract by the employer.[439] But certain parties, e.g. an actor to whom publicity is of value, may recover damages for the loss of opportunity for gain through enhanced reputation arising from wrongful dismissal.[440] Moreover, an apprenticeship agreement is regarded as being of a special character and in the event of its wrongful termination by the employer damages may be awarded not only for loss of earnings during the remainder of the apprenticeship but for loss of training and loss of future prospects.[441] Where dismissal was justified, an action of damages by the employee is not rendered relevant by averments that the motives of the employer were malicious.[442] A dismissed employee is bound to minimise the loss by endeavouring to obtain other employment, and his claim for damages will be subject to deduction of what he has actually earned or with reasonable effort would have been able to earn.[443] If the employer is guilty of conduct amounting to a repudiation of the contract, the employee may be entitled to leave the employment and claim damages: this is often described as constructive dismissal. The question whether the employee is so entitled depends generally, as in other contracts, on the materiality of the breach in question.[444] Following his dismissal, the employee can bring an action seeking damages for breach of contract either in the civil courts or before an employment tribunal.[445] In certain cases, an employee

---

[434] *Wilson v Racher* [1974] I.C.R. 428, per Edmund Davies L.J.

[435] *First Edinburgh Building Society v Munro* (1884) 21 S.L.R. 291; *Chappell v Times Newspapers* [1975] 1 W.L.R. 482.

[436] *Hill v C.A. Parsons & Co* [1972] 1 Ch. 305; the law relating to the use of interdicts to prevent dismissals seems likely to require further consideration; *Anderson v Pringle of Scotland Ltd*, 1998 S.L.T. 754; *Peace v Edinburgh City Council*, 1999 S.L.T. 712.

[437] *Clark v Nomura International Plc* [2000] I.R.L.R. 766 and *Commerzbank AG v Keen* [2007] I.R.L.R. 132; cf. *Lavarack v Woods of Colchester Ltd* [1967] 1 Q.B. 278.

[438] *Addis v Gramophone Co* [1909] A.C. 488; *Cull v Oilfield Inspection Services Group Plc*, 1990 S.L.T. 205; *Johnson v Unisys Ltd* [2003] 1 A.C. 518; see also *Eastwood v Magnox Electric Plc* [2005] 1 A.C. 503: para.10.05, above.

[439] *French v Barclays Bank Plc* [1998] I.R.L.R. 646; *Johnson v Unisys Ltd* [2003] 1 A.C. 518 and *Eastwood v Magnox Electric Plc* [2005] 1 A.C. 503.

[440] *Clayton & Waller v Oliver* [1930] A.C. 209.

[441] *Dunk v Geo. Waller & Son* [1970] 2 Q.B. 163.

[442] *Brown v Edinburgh County Council*, 1907 S.C. 256.

[443] *Ross v Macfarlane* (1894) 21 R. 396.

[444] See, e.g. *Dignity Funerals Ltd v Bruce* [2005] I.R.L.R. 189; *Buckland v Bournemouth University Higher Education Corp* [2010] I.R.L.R. 445.

[445] Employment Tribunals Extension of Jurisdiction (Scotland) Order 1994 (SI 1994/1624), although there is a £25,000 limit on the amount of compensation which can be awarded by a tribunal under this jurisdiction.

may be entitled to claim damages for a breach of contract while remaining in the employment.[446]

17.44　Unfair dismissal—The employer's common law right to dismiss has been modified by statute. Under legislation originating in the Industrial Relations Act 1971 and now embodied in the ERA an employee, who has been continuously employed for a period of not less than two years,[447] has a right not to be unfairly dismissed.[448] There is a dismissal for the purposes of the Act in three situations: (1) if the contract is terminated by the employer with or without notice: what amounts to a dismissal is a question of facts and circumstances[449]; (2) where a fixed-term contract expires without renewal; and (3) where the employee terminates the contract[450] with or without notice in circumstances such that he is entitled to terminate it without notice by reason of the employer's conduct (i.e. constructive dismissal).[451] There is dismissal in the last of these senses only if the employer's conduct is a significant breach going to the root of the contract or shows that he no longer intends to be bound by one of its essential terms.[452] The imposition of significant changes in working practices may amount to constructive dismissal if there is a significant detriment to the employee, and may even amount to a direct dismissal.[453] There is no dismissal and so no infringement of the employee's rights where a contract of employment is frustrated, as may happen after a long period of absence through illness.[454] An employee taking part in unofficial industrial action has no right to complain of unfair dismissal.[455]

17.45　"Automatically unfair" dismissals—There are a number of situations in which dismissal will be regarded as automatically unfair. In most of these situations, the employee need not have the normal qualifying service.[456] A dismissal is to be regarded as unfair if it was by reason of trade union membership or activities or, with certain exceptions, by reason of non-membership of a trade union.[457] A dismissal by reason of redundancy is to be regarded as unfair if selection was by reason of trade union membership or activity or, was by reason of non-

---

[446] e.g. *Rigby v Ferodo Ltd* [1988] I.C.R. 29 (HL).

[447] ERA s.108, which applies in relation to dismissals after April 6, 2012. A qualifying period is not required for certain dismissals which are automatically unfair, see para.17.45, below.

[448] ERA s.94. There are some excluded categories of employees, including those whose work has no connection with Great Britain: see *Lawson v Serco Ltd* [2006] 1 All E.R. 823 (HL) and *Duncombe v Secretary of State for Children, Schools and Families* [2011] UKSC 36.

[449] See, e.g. *Robertson v Securicor Transport Ltd* [1972] I.R.L.R. 70; *Martin v Glynwed Distribution Ltd* [1983] I.C.R. 511; and compare and contrast *Futty v D. and D. Brekkes Ltd* [1974] I.R.L.R. 130 ("fuck off") with *King v Webb's Poultry Products (Bradford) Ltd* [1975] I.R.L.R. 135 ("fuck off and piss off").

[450] *Greater Glasgow Health Board v Mackay*, 1989 S.L.T. 729.

[451] ERA s.95.

[452] *Western Excavating (E.C.C.) v Sharp* [1978] Q.B. 761; *Buckland v Bournemouth University Higher Education Corp* [2010] I.R.L.R. 445; *Prestwick Circuits Ltd v McAndrew*, 1990 S.L.T. 654. As to the effect of rules made by the employer for the conduct of employees in the place of work within the scope of the contract, see *Dryden v Greater Glasgow Health Board* [1992] I.R.L.R. 469.

[453] *Alcan Extrusions v Yates* [1996] I.R.L.R. 327.

[454] *Jones v Wagon Repairs* [1968] I.T.R. 361; *Pritchard v Dinorwic Slate Quarries* [1971] I.T.R. 102; *Marshall v Harland & Wolff (No.2)* (1972) 7 I.T.R. 150; *Egg Stores (Stamford) v Leibovici* [1976] I.R.L.R. 376; cf. *Watts v Steeley* (1968) 3 I.T.R. 363; *Farmer v Willow Dye Works* [1972] I.T.R. 226; *Hebden v Forsey & Son* [1973] I.T.R. 656.

[455] 1992 Act s.237.

[456] ERA s.108(3).

[457] 1992 Act s.152.

membership of a trade union or was, without special reasons to justify it, in contravention of a customary arrangement or agreed procedure.[458] Dismissal connected with taking part in official industrial action[459] or seeking union recognition[460] is unfair. A dismissal is also to be regarded as unfair if the employee was dismissed for raising issues of health and safety at work.[461] Pregnancy, maternity and paternity leave dismissals are unfair.[462] Provisions for automatic unfair dismissal also apply in relation to pension scheme trustees[463]; employee representatives[464]; Sunday shop workers and betting shop workers[465]; and employees involved in a transfer of undertaking.[466] Persons who are dismissed for asserting rights under the National Minimum Wage Act[467]; Public Interest Disclosure Act[468]; part-time workers regulations[469]; fixed-term employees regulations[470]; Tax Credits Act 1999[471]; the Information and Consultation of Employees Regulations 2004[472]; the Transnational Information and Consultation of Employees Regulations 1999[473]; the Employment Relations Act 1999 (Blacklists) Regulations 2010[474]; and the Employment Relations Act 1999[475] have similar protection.

Unfair dismissal: Reasons—Unless one of the special rules discussed above **17.46** applies, the fairness or unfairness of a dismissal depends, first, on whether the reason for the dismissal was one capable of being fair and, secondly, on whether the employer acted reasonably in treating the reason as a sufficient reason for dismissal. The Act specifies five reasons which are capable of being fair, namely: (1) a reason relating to the employee's capability or qualifications for performing the work for which he was employed; (2) a reason related to the employee's conduct; (3) that the employee was redundant; (4) that his continued employment would involve contravention of a statutory obligation or restriction; or (5) some other substantial reason of a kind such as to justify dismissal.[476] It is for the employer to show the reason for dismissal (or, if there was more than one, the principal reason[477]) and that it falls within the ambit of those for which the Act provides. There is no such onus on him in relation to the reasonableness or unreasonableness of his actings.[478] There is not generally much difficulty in

---

[458] 1992 Act s.153.

[459] 1992 Act s.238A(2).

[460] 1992 Act Sch.A1 para.161.

[461] ERA s.100(1).

[462] ERA s.99; Maternity and Parental Leave Regulations 1999 (SI 1999/3312) reg.20.

[463] ERA s.102.

[464] ERA s.103.

[465] ERA s.101.

[466] Transfer of Undertakings (Protection of Employment) Regulations 2006 (SI 2006/246) reg.7. See para.17.38, above.

[467] ERA s.104A.

[468] ERA s.103A.

[469] SI 2000/1551 reg.7; see para.17.35, above.

[470] The Fixed-Term Employees (Prevention of Less Favourable Treatment) Regulations 2002 (SI 2002/2034) reg.6.

[471] ERA s.104B.

[472] Information and Consultation of Employees Regulations 2004 (SI 2004/3426) reg.30.

[473] Transnational Information and Consultation of Employees Regulations 1999 (SI 1999/3323) reg.28.

[474] Employment Relations Act 1999 (Blacklists) Regulations 2010 (SI 2010/493). See ERA s.104E.

[475] Employment Relations Act 1999 s.12(3).

[476] ERA s.98(1), (2) and (4).

[477] See *Smith v Glasgow D.C.*, 1987 S.L.T. 605.

[478] *Post Office (Counters) Ltd v Heavey* [1990] I.C.R. 1.

determining whether the reason shown by the employer is a qualifying reason; the difficult questions usually arise in relation to the question of reasonableness. It is worth noting, however, that long-term sickness may be a reason relating to capability and that the commercial interests of the employer may amount to some other substantial reason. If, on engaging an employee, an employer informs him in writing that his employment will be terminated on the resumption of work by an employee absent because of pregnancy or of suspension on medical grounds in accordance with a statutory requirement or recommendation, dismissal of that employee on the return of the employee whom he was replacing is to be regarded as having been for a substantial reason of a kind such as to justify dismissal.[479] That is, however, without prejudice to the question of the reasonableness of the dismissal.

17.47 Unfair dismissal: Reasonableness—The question whether the employer acted reasonably is to be decided in accordance with equity and the substantial merits of the case and among the circumstances to be taken into account are the size and administrative resources of the employer's undertaking.[480] The circumstances of cases differ so widely that only a few general observations can be made. The test is what a reasonable employer would have done, not what a tribunal thinks appropriate, and so if a decision to dismiss is within a band of decisions which an employer might take without forfeiting the title of reasonableness, the dismissal will not be unfair.[481] This test has been challenged but was reaffirmed by the Court of Appeal in *HSBC Plc v Madden*.[482] Similarly, if the employer genuinely believes that the facts on which the dismissal is based are correct, has reasonable grounds for that belief and has carried out reasonable investigations, his decision will not be interfered with.[483] Whether the employer has followed fair procedures will always be important. Nevertheless, a dismissal may be unfair even if fair procedures have been followed. If an employer fails to follow fair and proper disciplinary procedures prior to the dismissal of an employee, the dismissal of the employee will be unfair and contrary to Pt X of the ERA notwithstanding the fact that the employer is able to show that if it had followed fair and proper procedures, it would have made no difference to its decision to dismiss.[484]

It will also be significant if the employer has tried to find a way of dealing with the situation other than dismissal, e.g. by use of a final written warning or some other technique. The decision on questions of fairness is one of fact and the finding of an employment tribunal correctly directed in law should not be interfered with.[485]

---

[479] ERA s.106.

[480] ERA s.98(4); *P. v Nottinghamshire CC* [1992] I.R.L.R. 362, CA.

[481] *British Leyland (UK) v Swift* [1981] I.R.L.R. 91; *Iceland Frozen Foods Ltd v Jones* [1982] I.R.L.R. 439; *Dooley v Leyland Vehicles Ltd*, 1986 S.C. 272; *Foley v Post Office* [2000] I.R.L.R. 827. See also *Porter v Oakbank School*, 2004 S.C. 603, where the dismissal was held justified.

[482] *HSBC Plc v Madden* [2000] I.C.R. 1283, CA. The application of the "range of responses" test to constructive dismissal is not without problem, but the difficulties generated by the cases of *Abbey National v Fairbrother* [2007] I.R.L.R. 320, *GAB Robins (UK) Ltd v Triggs* [2007] I.R.L.R. 857 and *Claridge v Daler Rowney Ltd* [2008] I.R.L.R. 672 were resolved by the Court of Appeal in *Buckland v Bournemouth University Higher Education Corp* [2010] I.R.L.R. 445.

[483] *W. Devis & Sons v Atkins* [1977] A.C. 931; *British Home Stores v Burchell* [1978] I.R.L.R. 379; *West Midlands Cooperative Society v Tipton* [1986] I.C.R. 192; *A. Links & Co v Rose*, 1993 S.L.T. 209.

[484] *Polkey v AE Dayton* [1988] A.C. 344. However, in such circumstances, the tribunal has the power to reduce the amount of compensatory award to reflect that fact.

[485] *Kent County Council v Gilham* [1985] I.C.R. 227; *Porter v Oakbank School*, 2004 S.C. 603; but the temptation to meddle is hard to resist, see *Matthews v Kent & Medway Towns Fire Authority* [2006] 2 All E.R. 161 (HL) and *London Ambulance Service NHS Trust v Small* [2009] I.R.L.R. 563.

Unfair dismissal: Remedies—Where an employee is unfairly dismissed an **17.48** employment tribunal may, if the employee wishes it to do so, make an order for his reinstatement or re-engagement.[486] If reinstated, he is to be treated in all respects as if he had not been dismissed[487]; if the order is for re-engagement, its effect is that he is to be engaged in employment comparable to that from which he was dismissed, or other suitable employment, on terms specified in the order.[488] In exercising its discretion, the tribunal must first consider reinstatement, and take into account the dismissed employee's wishes, the practicability of reinstatement or re-engagement, and the justice of making an order where the employee caused or contributed to his dismissal. The fact that a permanent replacement has been engaged is to be left out of account in determining practicability unless the employer shows that it was not practicable to arrange for the dismissed employee's work to be done otherwise.[489] If the employee does not wish reinstatement or re-engagement, or if the tribunal does not make an order, or in the event of non-compliance by the employer with the order, the employee is entitled to an award of compensation consisting of a basic award calculated on the same basis as a redundancy payment, and a compensatory award of such an amount as is just and equitable having regard to the loss sustained in consequence of dismissal, in so far as that is attributable to the employer's action.[490] The loss so sustained is to be taken to include any expense reasonably incurred in consequence of dismissal and any benefit which the employee might reasonably be expected to have had but for dismissal,[491] but generally does not include non-patrimonial loss.[492] The employment tribunal is entitled to increase or reduce the compensatory award by up to 25 per cent if the employer or employee fails to comply with the ACAS Code of Practice[493] on Disciplinary and Grievance Procedures.[494] Where there has been non-compliance by the employer with an order for reinstatement or re-engagement, the employee is entitled to an additional compensatory award of 26–52 weeks' pay, unless the employer satisfies the tribunal that it was not practicable for him to comply with the order.[495] The basic award and the compensatory award may be reduced in respect of the employee's contribution to his dismissal,[496] and the basic award may be reduced in respect of unreasonable refusal of an offer of reinstatement.[497] A dismissed employee has a duty to mitigate his loss and failure to do so, including cases in which the employer has unreasonably prevented an order for reinstatement or re-engagement from being complied with, is to be taken into account in calculating his loss for the purposes of a

---

[486] ERA ss.113–116.

[487] ERA s.114(1).

[488] ERA s.115(1).

[489] ERA s.116(1). In relation to re-engagement the employee's contribution to his dismissal is a factor which bears on what the terms of any re-engagement order should be, as well as on whether such an order should be made.

[490] ERA ss.118, 119 and 123. The tribunal has powers to grant interim relief under ERA ss.128–132.

[491] ERA s.123(2). The compensatory award is subject to a limit of £72,300 for most cases (s.124(1) (b)). There is no maximum limit for some dismissals (ERA s.124(1A)).

[492] *Dunnachie v Kingston Upon Hull City Council* [2004] I.R.L.R. 727.

[493] Available from *http://www.acas.org.uk/CHttpHandler.ashx?id=1047&p=0* [Accessed August 2, 2012].

[494] ERA s.124A and the 1992 Act s.207A.

[495] ERA s.117.

[496] ERA ss.122(2) and 123(6); *Nairne v Highland and Islands Fire Brigade*, 1989 S.L.T. 754.

[497] ERA s.122(1).

compensatory award.[498] The existence of various deductions and statutory maximum has the consequence that the tribunal must adopt a particular order for calculating the final award.[499] A compromise agreement must fulfil certain conditions in order to effectively prevent an employee from bringing a claim.[500]

17.49 Health and safety at work—The employer is under a general duty at common law to take reasonable care for the health and safety of his employees. Although the relationship between an employer and his employee is regulated by contract, the liability of an employer to make reparation to an employee injured in the course of his employment is regarded as delictual.[501] The employer is vicariously liable where the negligence of one employee causes injury to another, the doctrine of common employment having been abolished.[502] The employer has a personal duty to take reasonable care for the safety of his employees.[503] In addition, very extensive statutory duties have been imposed on employers under the Health and Safety at Work etc. Act 1974 and later regulations and the employer may be liable to an employee in respect of injury caused by breach of statutory duty.[504]

17.50 Employer's personal duty—An employer at common law owes a duty to his employee to take reasonable care for his safety throughout the course of his employment. He has no duty to protect an employee from risks necessarily attaching to the job and against which no reasonable precautions can be taken, but he has a general duty not to expose an employee to unnecessary risks and that duty may, in some circumstances, involve withdrawing an employee from positions of danger created by a third party. But, where the third party is independent of the employer, that will be so only if the danger is very likely to occur.[505] The employer's duty may extend, where the employer has relevant and special knowledge, to advice calculated to minimise the consequences of injury sustained by an employee in the course of his employment, even if the injury was not attributable to the employer's fault. Thus, where an employer becomes aware of past circumstances connected with the employment which make it desirable for present employees to have a medical examination, he has a duty to advise them of that.[506] And there may be a duty to advise a prospective employee of risks inherent in the job which are, or ought to be, known to the employer and which are not common knowledge if such risks would be likely to affect the decision of a sensible level-headed person contemplating such employment.[507] An employer may be liable for psychiatric illness caused by work pressures.[508]

---

[498] ERA s.123(4). The basic award cannot be reduced on grounds of failure to mitigate loss, *Lock v Connell Estate Agents* [1994] I.R.L.R. 444.

[499] *Leonard v Strathclyde Buses*, 1998 S.L.T. 734; *Heggie v Uniroyal Englebert Tyres Ltd*, 2000 S.L.T. 227.

[500] ERA s.203; *Sutherland v Network Appliance Ltd* [2001] I.R.L.R. 12.

[501] *MacKinnon v Iberia Shipping Co*, 1955 S.C. 20.

[502] By the Law Reform (Personal Injuries) Act 1948 s.1(1). See *Lindsay v Connell*, 1951 S.C. 281.

[503] See para.17.50, below.

[504] See para.17.54, below.

[505] *Longworth v Coppas International (UK)*, 1985 S.L.T. 111.

[506] *Wright v Dunlop Rubber Co* (1971) 11 K.I.R. 311; cf. *Stokes v Guest, Keen & Nettlefold (Bolts and Nuts)* [1968] 1 W.L.R. 1776.

[507] *White v Holbrook Precision Castings* [1985] I.R.L.R. 215.

[508] *Walker v Northumberland County Council* [1995] I.R.L.R. 35; *Cross v Highlands & Islands Enterprise*, 2001 S.L.T. 1060; *Sutherland v Hatton* [2002] I.R.L.R. 263; *Barber v Somerset County Council* [2004] 2 All E.R. 385.

Whether or not an employer is in breach of duty depends upon the facts and circumstances of each case.[509] This duty is personal to the employer, and while he may delegate performance of the duty to a third party, he cannot escape liability in the event of negligent performance by that party.[510] However, the employer is not in the position of an insurer of the safety of his employee. Thus under a rule of the common law now abrogated by statute an employer was held not to be liable for an injury to an employee arising from a latent defect in a tool obtained from a reputable supplier.[511] The tendency of the courts to classify the nature of the employer's personal duty to exercise reasonable care for the safety of his employees into three categories of provision of competent staff, adequate plant and machinery, and a proper system of work,[512] serves to illustrate the scope of the duty, but the categories are neither conclusive nor exhaustive.[513]

Competent staff—The vicarious liability of an employer for the negligence of a **17.51** fellow employee[514] has largely overridden this aspect of the personal duty of the employer. However, the employer remains personally liable when it is shown that he has failed to exercise reasonable care to select competent staff for the task in question, as where a skilled employee lacks the necessary experience to meet a situation which the employer ought to have foreseen,[515] or where an employer fails to discharge an employee who has shown himself through his habitual conduct to be a source of danger to his fellow employees.[516]

Plant and machinery—The employer is bound to exercise reasonable care in the **17.52** provision and maintenance of adequate plant and materials for the job. Liability arises when the employer has not provided any plant,[517] or where the plant supplied is insufficient,[518] defective[519] or dangerous.[520] The extent of the duty is only to exercise reasonable care, and there is no liability for injury caused by a latent defect which reasonable inspection would not have revealed.[521] That formulation of the duty must now, however, be read subject to the statutory gloss that liability attaches to the employer where an employee suffers personal injury in the course of his employment in consequence of a defect in "equipment" provided by

---

[509] See Ch.26 (negligence); paras 25.34–25.37 (contributory negligence); paras 25.29 and 25.30 (exclusions of liability and volenti non fit injuria). As to the general nature of the employer's duty, see *English v Wilsons and Clyde Coal Co*, 1937 S.C. (HL) 46; *Paris v Stepney Borough Council* [1951] A.C. 367; *Lister v Romford Ice & Cold Storage Co.* [1957] A.C. 555; *Qualcast (Wolverhampton) Ltd v Haynes* [1959] A.C. 743; *Cavanagh v Ulster Weaving Co* [1960] A.C. 145, per Lord Keith at 164–6; and see *Smith v Austin Lifts* [1959] 1 W.L.R. 100 (HL), where employee working on the premises of a third party.

[510] *English v Wilsons and Clyde Coal Co*, 1937 S.C. (HL) 46, per Lord Thankerton at 57; per Lord Wright at 64; *Donnelly v Ronald Wilson (Plant Hire)*, 1986 S.L.T. 90.

[511] *Davie v New Merton Board Mills* [1959] A.C. 604.

[512] *English v Wilsons and Clyde Coal Co*, 1937 S.C. (HL) 46.

[513] Other examples are safe place of work and safe means of access.

[514] On which, see *Lister v Hesley Hall Ltd* [2001] UKHL 22; [2002] 1 A.C. 215, followed by the Outer House in *Sharp v Highlands and Islands Fire Board* [2005] S.C.L.R. 1049.

[515] *Black v Fife Coal Co*, 1912 S.C. (HL) 33.

[516] *Hudson v Ridge Manufacturing Co* [1957] 2 Q.B. 348.

[517] *Williams v Birmingham Battery & Metal Co* [1899] 2 Q.B. 338; *Lovell v Blundells & Crompton & Co* [1944] K.B. 502.

[518] *Machray v Stewarts & Lloyds* [1965] 1 W.L.R. 602.

[519] *Henderson v Carron Co* (1889) 16 R. 633.

[520] *Robertson v Thomas's* (1907) 15 S.L.T. 32 (vicious horse).

[521] *Gavin v Rogers* (1889) 17 R. 206; *Milne v Townsend* (1892) 19 R. 830; *McMillan v B.P. Refinery (Grangemouth)*, 1961 S.L.T. (Notes) 79.

his employer and the defect is attributable wholly or partly to the fault of a third party such as a manufacturer or supplier.[522] An employer may therefore be liable for a defect which is latent to him if it is attributable to the fault of someone else. "Equipment" is to be interpreted broadly and ranges from soap[523] to a ship of 91,000 tons gross.[524]

17.53 Proper system—The employer is bound to take reasonable care to institute and maintain a safe and proper system of work.[525] It is his duty to give such general safety instructions as a reasonably careful employer who has considered the problem presented by the work would give to his employees.[526] Each case, therefore, turns on its own facts and circumstances,[527] and even where facts closely correspond to a previous decision, no necessary inference as to the decision of the instant case arises.[528] Evidence of trade practice is not conclusive[529] but may be an indication of what reasonable care requires. If it is evident that a practice is dangerous, and a precaution which would avoid the risk could reasonably be adopted, it is no defence that accidents rarely occurred or that the practice was widespread.[530] Physical disability of the employee may render the performance of the duty by the employer more onerous, since the employer owes the duty to each of his employees as individuals.[531]

17.54 Statutory provisions—Many industries are closely regulated by statute.[532] This is an area where European Law has made significant inroads, in particular via the Health and Safety Framework Directive ("Framework Directive")[533] and the five daughter Directives promulgated under art.16(1) of the Framework Directive, namely the Workplace Directive,[534] the Work Equipment Directive,[535] the Personal Protective Equipment Directive,[536] the Manual Handling of Loads

---

[522] Employer's Liability (Defective Equipment) Act 1969 s.1; *Yuille v Daks Simpson*, 1984 S.L.T. 115; *Ralston v Greater Glasgow Health Board*, 1987 S.L.T. 386. But see now Provision and Use of Work Equipment Regulations 1998 (SI 1998/2306); *Robb v Salamis (M&I) Ltd*, 2007 S.L.T. 158 (HL) and *Reid v Sundolitt Ltd*, 2008 S.C. 49.

[523] *Ralston v Greater Glasgow Health Board*, 1987 S.L.T. 386.

[524] *Coltman v Bibby Tankers Ltd* [1988] A.C. 276.

[525] *English v Wilsons and Clyde Coal Co*, 1937 S.C. (HL) 46.

[526] *General Cleaning Contractors v Christmas* [1953] A.C. 180 at 189, per Lord Oaksey.

[527] *Grace v Alexander Stephen & Son*, 1952 S.C. 61.

[528] *Qualcast v Haynes* [1959] A.C. 743.

[529] *Morris v West Hartlepool Steam Navigation Co* [1956] A.C. 552; *Cavanagh v Ulster Weaving Co* [1900] A.C. 145, applying *Morton v William Dixon Ltd*, 1909 S.C. 807 at 809, per Lord Dunedin; *Brown v Rolls Royce*, 1960 S.C. (HL) 22; *Riddick v Weir Housing Corp*, 1970 S.L.T. (Notes) 71; *Macdonald v Scottish Stamping & Engineering Co*, 1972 S.L.T. (Notes) 73.

[530] *Brown v John Mills & Co (Llanidloes)* (1970) 8 K.I.R. 702.

[531] *Paris v Stepney Borough Council* [1951] A.C. 367.

[532] See M. Ford, J. Clarke and A. Smart, *Redgrave's Health and Safety*, 7th edn (LexisNexis Butterworths, 2010).

[533] Directive 89/391/EEC of the Council of 12 June 1989 on the introduction of measures to encourage improvements in the safety and health of workers at work [1989] OJ L183/1.

[534] Directive 89/654/EEC of the Council of 30 November 1989 concerning the minimum safety and health requirements for the workplace [1989] OJ L393/1.

[535] Directive 89/655/EEC of the Council of 30 November 1989 concerning the minimum safety and health requirements for the use of work equipment by workers at work [1989] OJ L393/13.

[536] Directive 89/656/EEC of the Council of 30 November 1989 on the minimum health and safety requirements for the use by workers of personal protective equipment at the workplace [1989] OJ L393/181.

Directive[537] and the Display Screen Equipment Directive.[538] Each of these Directives have been implemented in the United Kingdom, giving rise to the "six-pack" regulations, namely the Management of Health and Safety at Work Regulations 1999,[539] the Workplace (Health, Safety and Welfare) Regulations 1992,[540] the Provision and Use of Work Equipment Regulations 1998,[541] the Personal Protective Equipment at Work Regulations 1992,[542] the Manual Handling Operations Regulations 1992[543] and the Health and Safety (Display Screen Equipment) Regulations 1992.[544] In most cases the observance of the statutory regulations is protected by the sanction of a fine, but civil liability is inferred if the person injured by their non-observance was one whose interests the regulation was designed to protect.[545] The harm which the pursuer sustains must be harm of a type which the statute envisages,[546] although it is not generally essential that the harm must be sustained in a particular manner.[547] As with liability at common law the pursuer must establish on a balance of probabilities that a breach of the statutory provisions caused him injury.[548] It depends upon the facts in each case whether the breach leads to a legitimate inference that the injury resulted from it.[549] Thus an employer will escape liability if he can show that, even if he had provided the safety equipment enjoined by the statute, the injured workman would not have used it.[550] If the statutory duties are laid upon the employer, they involve liability for injury caused by failure to observe them, though the immediate cause of failure may have been the fault of a fellow employee or sub-contractor.[551] And it will not be easy for a defender to prove that statutory regulations supersede the common law duty of care.[552] If an absolute duty is placed upon an employer, his only defences in case of failure are such statutory defences as may be provided,[553] but this does not include defences provided against a criminal charge.[554] If they are laid upon a particular official, the employer is not necessarily liable for his negligence, but the onus of proof that the official was competent is laid upon

---

[537] Directive 90/269/EEC of the Council of 29 May 1990 on the minimum health and safety requirements for the manual handling of loads where there is a risk particularly of back injury to workers [1990] OJ L156/9.

[538] Directive 90/270/EEC of the Council of 29 May 1990 on the minimum safety and health requirements for work with display screen equipment [1991] OJ L156/14.

[539] Management of Health and Safety at Work Regulations 1999 (SI 1999/3242).

[540] Workplace (Health, Safety and Welfare) Regulations 1992 (SI 1992/3004).

[541] Provision and Use of Work Equipment Regulations 1998 (SI 1998/2306).

[542] Personal Protective Equipment at Work Regulations 1992 (SI 1992/2966).

[543] Manual Handling Operations Regulations 1992 (SI 1992/2793).

[544] Health and Safety (Display Screen Equipment) Regulations 1992 (SI 1992/2792).

[545] *Groves v Lord Wimborne* [1898] 2 Q.B. 402; *Bett v Dalmeny Oil Co* (1905) 7 F. 787; *McMullan v Lochgelly Iron, etc. Co*, 1933 S.C. (HL) 64; see also *Marshall & Son v Russian Oil Products*, 1938 S.C. 773.

[546] *Gorris v Scott* (1874) L.R. 9 Ex. 125.

[547] *Grant v N.C.B.*, 1956 S.C. (HL) 48.

[548] *Wardlaw v Bonnington Castings*, 1956 S.C. (HL) 26.

[549] *Gardiner v Motherwell Machinery and Scrap Co*, 1961 S.C. (HL) 1.

[550] *Qualcast v Haynes* [1959] A.C. 743; *McWilliams v Sir William Arrol & Co*, 1962 S.C. (HL) 70; *McKinlay v British Steel Corp*, 1988 S.L.T. 810; and see para.26.11, below.

[551] *Bett v Dalmeny Oil Co* (1905) 7 F. 787; *Rodger v Fife Coal Co*, 1923 S.C. 108; *Alford v National Coal Board*, 1952 S.C. (HL) 17.

[552] *Maruszczyk v National Coal Board*, 1953 S.C. 8; *Bux v Slough Metals* [1973] 1 W.L.R. 1358.

[553] *Bain v Fife Coal Co*, 1935 S.C. 681; *Reilly v William Beardmore & Co*, 1947 S.C. 275; *Millar v Galashiels Gas Co*, 1949 S.C. (HL) 31; *Taylor v National Coal Board*, 1953 S.C. 349.

[554] *Riddell v Reid*, 1942 S.C. (HL) 51.

him.[555] Contributory negligence may lead to apportionment of damages,[556] but the degree of care required of a man in a factory or mine may be lower than that required of an ordinary man not exposed to the noise, strains and risks of a factory or mine.[557] An employer who is in breach of statutory duty may avoid liability altogether if it is established that the conduct of the employee was the sole cause of the breach.[558]

FURTHER READING

Brodie, D., *The Contract of Employment* (Edinburgh: W. Green, 2008).

Connolly, M., *Discrimination Law*, 2nd edn (London: Sweet and Maxwell, 2011).

Deakin, S. and Morris, G.S., *Labour Law*, 6th edn (Hart Publishing, 2012).

Encyclopaedia of Labour Relations Law, edited by Blanpain, R. (Kluwer, continuously revised).

Ford, M., Clarke, J. and Smart, A., *Redgrave's Health and Safety*, 7th edn (LexisNexis Butterworths, 2010).

Harvey on Industrial Relations and Employment Law (LexisNexis, continuously revised).

Honeyball, S., *Honeyball & Bowers' Textbook on Labour Law*, 12th edn (Oxford University Press, 2012).

Middlemiss, S. and Downie, M., *Employment Law in Scotland* (Bloomsbury Professional, 2012).

Selwyn, N., *Selwyn's Law of Employment*, 17th edn (Oxford: Oxford University Press, 2012).

Smith, I. and Baker, A., *Smith & Wood's Employment Law*, 10th edn (Oxford: Oxford University Press, 2010).

---

[555] *Black v Fife Coal Co*, 1912 S.C. (HL) 33; *Connell v James Nimmo & Co Ltd*, 1924 S.C. (HL) 84.

[556] See paras 25.35–25.36, below.

[557] *Caswell v Powell Duffryn Associated Collieries Ltd* [1940] A.C. 152; *Hunter v Glenfield & Kennedy*, 1947 S.C. 536; *Barnes v Southhook Potteries*, 1946 S.L.T. 295; *John Summers & Sons Ltd v Frost* [1955] A.C. 740.

[558] See *Ross v Associated Portland Cement Manufacturers* [1964] 1 W.L.R. 768 and cases cited therein, where employee disobeyed instructions; also *Crowe v James Scott & Sons*, 1965 S.L.T. 54; *Lanigan v Derek Crouch Construction Ltd*, 1985 S.L.T. 346; and *Horne v Lec Refrigeration* [1965] 2 All E.R. 898; cf. *Quinn v J.W. Green (Painters)* [1966] 1 Q.B. 509.

CHAPTER 18

AGENCY

Meaning of agency—Agency has been defined as   **18.01**

> "the fiduciary relationship which exists between two persons, one of whom expressly or impliedly manifests assent that the other should act on his behalf so as to affect his relations with third parties, and the other of whom similarly manifests assent so to act or so acts pursuant to the manifestation. The one on whose behalf the act or acts are to be done is called the principal. The one who is to act is called the agent. Any person other than the principal and the agent may be referred to as a third party".[1]

Since agency is established by contract,[2] there can be many variations in the precise relationships of the parties: however, a case of agency in the full legal sense is one in which the agent has power, referred to as his "authority", to change the legal rights and obligations of the principal towards third parties. He may do this by subjecting his principal to binding obligations or by gaining rights for him by contract: and by acquiring or disposing of property for his principal. In the ordinary case, the agent himself does not acquire rights or incur obligations, but in exceptional circumstances he may do so.[3] The agent's authority may be actual, either express, that is, set out in the contract, or implied, by appointment to a position or in a capacity which normally carries such authority. If the principal represents to third parties that a person is his agent or allows him to act as if he were an agent, the principal may be bound by his actings: in that case the agent is said to have apparent or ostensible authority. Whether an employee has actual or ostensible authority depends on the nature of his employment.[4] Where the employment of an employee consists in bringing the employer into contractual relations with third parties, the law of agency applies in determining what rights and obligations are created between the principal and the third parties. There are many other cases where the principles of the law of agency apply but where the terms agent and principal may not commonly be used: directors are the agents of the company; a receiver is the agent of the company, though he recovers debts for behoof of the floating-charge holder[5]; and a partner, in dealing with partnership affairs, is the

---

[1] P. Watts, *Bowstead and Reynolds on Agency*, 19th edn (London: Sweet and Maxwell, 2010), para.1.001(1).

[2] On which, see *Graham & Co v United Turkey Red Co*, 1922 S.C. 533 at 546 and 549 (Lords Salvesen and Ormidale); *Lothian v Jenolite Ltd*, 1969 S.C. 111 at 120 (Lord Milligan); *Trans Barwil Agencies (UK) Ltd v John S. Braid & Co Ltd*, 1988 S.C. 222 at 230 (Lord McCluskey).

[3] For example, the agent may become bound where he acts for a non-existent principal, e.g. a club, congregation or unincorporated association: *McMeekin v Easton* (1889) 16 R 363.

[4] *Quinn v CC Automotive Group Ltd t/a Carcraft* [2010] EWCA Civ 1412; [2011] 2 All E.R. (Comm) 584.

[5] Insolvency Act 1986 s.57(1); *Forth & Clyde Construction Co v Trinity Timber & Plywood Co*, 1984 S.C. 1 at 11, per Lord President Emslie.

agent of the firm and of the other partners.[6] On the other hand, there are cases in which persons are employed as representatives and are referred to in common parlance as agents, but do not have the authority of an agent in the full sense. Persons employed as canvassers to introduce or attract business may be referred to as agents but may not have authority to conclude contracts. Estate agents normally introduce prospective buyers and sellers but do not conclude contracts. Other examples include distributors and franchise holders.[7] Aspects of the activities of certain agents have been subject to statutory regulation, e.g. directors by the Companies Acts, estate agents by the Estate Agents Act 1979, solicitors by the Solicitors (Scotland) Act 1980. A separate category of commercial agents has been created by the Commercial Agents (Council Directive) Regulations 1993.[8] These Regulations set out a regime governing the relationship in cases to which they apply, much of which is not subject to derogation, even if parties agree. They do permit parties to reach their own agreement, where the Regulations are silent, and in those cases the common law will still be relevant. However, because of the far-reaching effects of the Regulations, the regime which they establish requires separate consideration. This chapter deals first with the common law aspects of the relationship of principal and agent; then with the authority of an agent and the methods of contracting on behalf of a principal; and finally with commercial agency under the Regulations.

18.02 Mandate—If the contract is gratuitous, it is usually termed mandate instead of agency, and the terms mandant and mandatory are used instead of principal and agent.[9] If a mandate is given to do something in the mandatory's own interest, it is known as a procuratory in *rem suam* (or, in English law, as an authority coupled with an interest), and differs from other mandates in being irrevocable without the mandatory's consent.[10] So if an application for shares in a company is given to one who has an interest in the shares being allotted, the applicant is not entitled to withdraw his application.[11]

18.03 Constitution of the contract—The authority of an agent or mandatory may arise from an express contract,[12] which may be entered into orally[13] or may be inferred from the prior conduct of the parties.[14] The relationship of agency cannot be created after the death of the putative principal.[15] In a series of cases, it has been held that an agency relationship may be inferred on an ad hoc basis for the

---

[6] Partnership Act 1890 s.5; para.45.10, below.

[7] For further examples see *Chitty on Contracts*, edited by H.G. Beale, 30th edn (London: Sweet and Maxwell, 2008), Vol.II, 31.012 et seq.

[8] Commercial Agents (Council Directive) Regulations 1993 (SI 1993/3053) (as amended), implementing Council Directive 86/653/EEC of the Council of 18 December 1986 on the coordination of the laws of the Member States relating to self-employed commercial agents. See para.18.33, below.

[9] For the development of agency in Scots Law, see *Stair Memorial Encyclopaedia*, Vol.1, "Agency and Mandate" (Reissue), paras 7 et seq.

[10] Stair, *Institutions*, I, 12, 8; Bell, *Principles*, s.228.

[11] *Premier Briquette Co v Gray*, 1922 S.C. 329; *Carmichael's Case* [1896] 2 Ch. 643.

[12] *Barnetson v Petersen Bros* (1902) 5 F 86; *Bell v Ogilvie* (1863) 2 M 336 at 340 (Lord Justice Clerk Inglis).

[13] Requirements of Writing (Scotland) Act 1995 s.1.

[14] *Ben Cleuch Estates Ltd v Scottish Enterprise* [2006] CSOH 35 at [143] (Lord Reed). The principle of benevolent intervention (*negotorium gestio*) may operate to impose obligations on A where A acts on B's behalf without B's agreement, on which, see paras 24.24–24.28, below.

[15] *Lord Advocate v Chung*, 1995 S.L.T. 65 at 68.

purposes of a single transaction only,[16] but this line of authority would appear to conflict with the general rule that there must be clear evidence to support the inference of an agency relationship.[17]

Principal and agent inter se[18]—According to Bell: **18.04**

> "An agent is bound to show the most entire good faith and make the fullest disclosure of all facts and circumstances concerning the principal's business."[19]

This does not, however, imply that the agent is always subject to fiduciary duties similar to those incumbent on a trustee.[20] The circumstances of agency relationships vary very widely, and, in every case, the particular facts and circumstances must be examined to determine the scope of the agent's contractual and fiduciary duties and of the requirements of good faith arising from them,[21] as well as the degree of trust and confidence reposed by the principal in the agent.[22] Any fiduciary obligation will not extend beyond the agent's contractual sphere of responsibility,[23] but the fiduciary duties may continue notwithstanding the termination of the agency contract.[24] There is no implied condition of contract between agent and principal, at least where the contract is constituted in writing, that the agent shall not without the permission of his principal act, even in an outside matter, in such a way as to bring his interests into conflict with those of his principal.[25] In many respects, the rights and liabilities of principal and agent, in questions solely inter se and where no third party is affected, resemble those of master and servant. It has been said that the relationship of agent and principal, like that of master and servant, is not normally one in which the agent is under a duty to disclose his own wrongdoing.[26] The most common examples of the

---

[16] *Whitbread Group Plc v Goldapple Ltd*, 2005 S.L.T. 281; *Laurence McIntosh Ltd v Balfour Beatty Group Ltd and the Trustees of the National Library of Scotland* [2006] CSOH 1907; and *John Stirling t/a M & S Contracts v Westminster Properties Scotland Ltd* [2007] CSOH 117; [2007] B.L.R. 537.

[17] *Batt Cables Plc v Spencer Business Parks Ltd* [2010] S.L.T. 860 at 866 (Lord Hodge) and NB the requirement to establish a contract in *Rodewald v Taylor* [2011] CSOH 5; 2011 G.W.D 3–108. See also L. Macgregor and N. Whitty, "Payment of Another's Debt, Unjustified Enrichment and ad hoc Agency" (2011) 15 Edin. L.R. 57.

[18] In modern parlance, this is often called the "internal" aspect of the contract of agency, as against the "external" aspect of relationships with third parties.

[19] Bell, *Principles*, s.222; cf. W.M. Gloag, *Law of Contract*, 2nd edn (Edinburgh: W. Green, 1929), p.522. Discussion of this aspect of the law of agency often proceeds in terms of "fiduciary duties" possibly under the influence of English terminology, but it seems clear that in Scotland agency is fundamentally a relationship of good faith. This may be significant in view of the provisions of the Commercial Agents Regulations: see below, para.18.36.

[20] *Lothian v Jenolite Ltd*, 1969 S.C. 111, per Lord Stott (O) at 115, Lord Walker at 125.

[21] *Sao Paolo Alpargatus S.A. v Standard Chartered Bank*, 1985 S.L.T. 433, applying dicta of Lord Upjohn in *Boardman v Phipps* [1967] 2 A.C. 46 at 127; *Trans Barwil Agencies (UK) Ltd v John S. Braid & Co*, 1988 S.C. 222. For a discussion of fiduciaries, see Millett L.J. in *Bristol and West Building Society v Mothew* [1998] Ch. 1 at 16–22; *Kelly v Cooper* [1993] A.C. 205. Note particularly *Henderson v Merrett Syndicates Ltd* [1995] 2 A.C. 145 per Lord Brown-Wilkinson at 206.

[22] *York Building Co v Mackenzie* (1795) Paton's Appeal Cases 378; *Huntingdon Copper and Sulphur Company Ltd v Henderson* (1877) 4 R 294 at 299 (Lord Young).

[23] *Lothian v Jenolite Ltd*, 1969 S.C. 111.

[24] *Connolly v Brown*, 2007 S.L.T. 778 at 784, [49] (Lady Dorrian).

[25] *Lothian v Jenolite*, 1969 S.C. 111; cf. the recent English case of *Imageview Management Ltd v Jack* [2009] EWCA Civ 63; [2009] 2 All E.R. 666 at 669 (Jacob L.J.).

[26] *Healey v Francaise Rubastic SA* [1917] 1 K.B. 946; cf. *Bell v Lever Bros* [1932] A.C. 161 and *Commonwealth Oil & Gas Ltd v Baxter*, 2009 S.C. 156 at 162, [14] (Lord President Hamilton).

requirements of good faith arise in connection with the agent's duty to account, the rule against secret profits[27] and the obligation not to place himself in a position where his interests conflict with those of his principal.[28] It has been said, in England, that the principal is never under fiduciary duties towards the agent, but if the basis of the relationship is good faith, both parties must be subject to some such obligations.[29]

18.05 Agent to obey principal's instructions[30]—As an agent is acting on behalf of his principal, the agent is required to follow the instructions provided to him by that principal[31]; where there are no express instructions the agent is to

> "act pursuant to either the applicable trade usage, or, if there has been a course of dealing between the parties, in accordance with the custom that has prevailed formerly".

A failure to follow these instructions amounts to a breach of contract by the agent, who can be personally liable for any loss suffered by the principal as a result.[32] Where the principal has provided the agent with "an absolute discretion" in the performance of his duties, there is a possibility that the agent may be liable to the principal if the agent fails to exercise that discretion, or has "acted in a wholly unreasonable way".[33] The agent is under a duty not to disclose confidential information of the principal to third parties.[34]

18.06 Agent to act with reasonable care and skill—An agent undertaking an "obligation" for his principal is "bound to execute it with reasonable care".[35] In carrying out his duties with "reasonable care", the agent "must act with the care and diligence of a man of ordinary prudence in the line of employment".[36] The obligation to act with "reasonable care" is also applicable to a "gratuitous mandatory", who is required to exercise "such care as a man of common prudence generally exercises about his own property of like description".[37] Where the agent is a professional person, he "does not warrant that what he does will certainly have the effect which is expected from it"; he only warrants that, in performing the task given to him, he will exercise "the skill generally possessed by his brethren in the profession".[38]

---

[27] *Park's of Hamilton (Holdings) Ltd v Campbell* [2008] CSOH 177; 2009 G.W.D. 1–5.

[28] *Macpherson's Trs v Watt* (1877) 5 R (HL) 9 and see the recent English case of *Imageview Management Ltd v Jack* [2009] EWCA Civ 63; [2009] 2 All E.R. 666 at 669 (Lord Justice Jacob).

[29] Under the Commercial Agents Regulations, good faith is required of both parties: see para.18.36, below. For the effect of an agreement conferring "sole selling rights", see *G and S Properties v Francis*, 2001 S.L.T. 934.

[30] See also paras 18.30 and 18.33, below.

[31] Erskine, III, 3, 35; Bell, *Principles*, s.220.

[32] *Gilmour v Clark* (1853) 15 D. 478; *Wright v Baird* (1868) 6 S.L.R. 95.

[33] *Glasgow West Housing Association v Siddique*, 1998 S.L.T. 1081 at 1083–4.

[34] *Connolly v Brown*, 2007 S.L.T. 778.

[35] *Stiven v Watson* (1874) 1 R. 412 at 416, per Lord Justice-Clerk Moncrieff; *Stair Memorial Encyclopaedia*, "Agency and Mandate", para.87 (as updated).

[36] Bell, *Principles*, s.221; Bell, *Commentaries*, I, 516; Erskine, III, 3, 37.

[37] Bell, *Principles*, s.212, which was cited in *Copland v Brogan*, 1916 S.C. 277 at 282; *Trigon Tools Ltd v Andrew Wright (PVC) Ltd*, 2010 G.W.D. 30–612. Cf. *Chaudhry v Prabhakar* [1989] 1 W.L.R. 29, on the position in England concerning gratuitous agents.

[38] *Cooke v Falconer's Representatives* (1850) 13 D. 157 at 172, per Lord President Boyle; *Beattie v Furness-Houlder Insurance (Northern) Ltd*, 1976 S.L.T. (Notes) 60.

Obligation to account—The authorities establish that an agent is bound to **18.07** account to his principal for any incidental advantage which, without the knowledge and agreement of the principal, or due to an error by the principal,[39] the agent has obtained from his position as agent. So a director must account to the company for any benefit which he has received from a promoter, even although it cannot be shown that the company has suffered any loss.[40] Where an agent employed to sell a ship but unable to find a buyer on the cash terms the principal demanded, purchased it himself, having received an offer of a higher price although on less advantageous cash terms which he did not disclose to the principal, it was held that he must account to the principal for the profit he made on the transaction.[41] The rule so far rests on principles of trust that the agent's liability is measured by the gain he has made, and not by the loss, if any, which the principal has sustained[42]; but it has been held, in England, in the case of a secret commission, that the legal position of the principal was that of a creditor, and not that of a beneficiary. So in the bankruptcy of the agent the principal could rank only as a creditor, not as a beneficiary for whom the agent held money in trust.[43] An agent is under a general obligation to account.[44] This obligation does not depend on the honesty or dishonesty of the agent,[45] who bears the onus of showing that he has discharged his duty.[46] So where there was a shortfall in the stock of a shop which the agent had been appointed to manage, the agent was required to make up that shortfall, even though there was no issue as to the agent's honesty.[47] However, the obligation to account does not arise until the agent has received funds, or an asset or a benefit. Hence it was held that where a solicitor was acting for a seller of land, that solicitor was under no obligation to account for the proceeds of sale until he received them, and so these funds could not be arrested in the solicitor's hands until the proceeds of sale had been received, as it was not until then that a debt existed which was capable of being arrested.[48] It is unclear whether the agent's duty to account in Scots law can more naturally be considered to be an implied term of the contract existing between principal and agent, rather than a fiduciary duty imposed by law. If it is the latter, then the duty can continue notwithstanding the termination of the agency contract, as is the position in English law.[49]

Secret commissions—An agent employed to introduce business is not entitled, **18.08** without the knowledge and consent of his principal, to take any commission from the party with whom he deals. The principal will have knowledge of the agent's receipt of secret commission where the agent discloses that fact to the principal

---

[39] *Trans Barwil Agencies (UK) Ltd v John S. Braid & Co*, 1988 S.C. 222 and *Trans Barwil Agencies Ltd v John S. Braid & Co (No.2)*, 1990 S.L.T. 182 (liability for interest).

[40] *Henderson v Huntingdon Copper and Sulphur Co* (1877) 5 R. (HL) 1; *Boston Deep Fishing Co v Ansell* (1888) L.R. 39 Ch.D. 339; *Jubilee Cotton Mills v Lewis* [1924] A.C. 958.

[41] *De Bussche v Alt* (1878) L.R. 8 Ch.D. 286. See also *Graham v R & S Paton Ltd*, 1917 S.C. 203.

[42] *Ronaldson v Drummond and Reid* (1881) 8 R. 956.

[43] *Lister v Stubbs* (1890) L.R. 45 Ch.D. 1. But see now *Att Gen of Hong Kong v Reid* [1994] 1 A.C. 324, PC. As to agency and personal claims, see *Style Financial Services Ltd v Bank of Scotland*, 1996 S.L.T. 421, and *Style Financial Services Ltd v Bank of Scotland (No.2)*, 1998 S.L.T. 851.

[44] *Simpson v Duncan* (1849) 11 D. 1097; *Yasuda Fire & Marine Insurance Company of Europe Limited v Orion Marine Insurance Underwriting Agency Limited* [1995] 3 All E.R. 211.

[45] *Tyler v Logan* (1904) 7 F. 123.

[46] *Simpson v Duncan* (1849) 11 D. 1097 at 1100, per Lord President Boyle.

[47] *Tyler v Logan* (1904) 7 F. 123.

[48] *Royal Bank of Scotland Plc v Law*, 1996 S.L.T. 83 at 86E, per Lord Justice-Clerk Ross.

[49] *John Youngs Insurance Services Ltd v Aviva Insurance Service UK Ltd* [2011] EWHC 1515 (TCC) at 120 (Ramsey J.).

and the principal gives his informed consent.[50] The principal's consent may be presumed if the principal gave no payment, and if the agent's work was of a character not generally done gratuitously.[51] But a custom of trade, not known to the principal, is no defence for a secret commission.[52] Where an agent is proved to have received a secret commission, certain civil consequences ensue.[53] (1) The principal may dismiss the agent from his employment, and, as a creditor, recover the amount of the commission from him.[54] (2) He may also, whether he has settled with the agent or not, recover damages from the party who gave the secret commission, on the ground that such an act amounts to a civil wrong.[55] (3) The agent forfeits all claim to a commission (which the principal, if he has already paid it, may recover) for the particular transaction in question,[56] but not the right to his commission on other transactions which predate the breach and in respect of which he acted honestly[57] and the agent will be entitled to be paid sums in respect of services provided to the principal subsequent to the date of the breach to the extent that the principal has been *lucratus* by the provision of those services.[58] (4) The principal, on discovering that his agent has been bribed, may rescind or refuse to carry out the contract,[59] and if, in the case of sale, he has made a deposit, he may recover it.[60] As the agent and the party who offers a secret commission are engaged in an illegal transaction, the agent, whether the promise of the bribe has influenced his conduct or not, cannot recover it by action.[61]

18.09 **Sale or purchase between agent and principal**—An agent, employed to buy, is not entitled, without the principal's knowledge, to supply his own property.[62] A custom of a particular trade, not known to the principal, will afford no justification.[63] Thus, if an agent, employed by several persons to buy goods or shares, purchases a sufficient quantity to meet all his orders, and allocates to each principal the amount he has ordered at an average price, he is selling his own property instead of buying for his principal, and the latter is not bound by the contract.[64]

---

[50] *Commonwealth Oil & Gas Ltd v Baxter*, 2009 S.C. 156 at 161 (Lord President Hamilton). A principal may be deemed to have constructive knowledge of the secret profit where the agent makes disclosure to another agent of the principal: *Park's of Hamilton (Holdings) Ltd v Campbell* [2011] CSOH 38; 2011 G.W.D. 8–196.

[51] *Great Western Insurance Co v Cunliffe* (1874) L.R. 9 Ch. 525.

[52] *Ronaldson v Drummond & Reid* (1881) 8 R. 956; *Accidia Foundation v Simon C Dickinson Ltd* [2010] EWHC 3058 (Ch).

[53] For the criminal law consequences, see the Bribery Act 2010 s.2.

[54] *Ronaldson v Drummond & Reid* (1881) 8 R. 956. In *Powell v Evan Jones & Co* [1905] 1 K.B. 11, this was held to apply even to sub-agents.

[55] *Salford Corp v Lever* [1891] 1 Q.B. 168; *Mahesan v Malaysia Housing Society* [1979] A.C. 374.

[56] *Andrews v Ramsay* [1903] 2 K.B. 635; *Boston Sea Fishing v Ansell* (1888) 39 Ch. 339; *Rhodes v Macalister* (1923) 29 Com Cas 19.

[57] *Huntingdon Copper and Sulphur Co Ltd v Henderson* (1877) 4 R. 294 at 302–303, per Lord Young (Lord Ordinary). This was not disputed in the Inner House and the House of Lords ((1877) 5 R. (HL) 1); *Graham v United Turkey Red Co*, 1922 S.C. 533.

[58] *Graham v United Turkey Red Co*, 1922 S.C. 533.

[59] *Armagas Ltd v Mundogas S.A.* [1986] A.C. 717; *Logicrose Ltd v Southend United FC* [1988] 1 W.L.R. 1256.

[60] *Shipway v Broadwood* [1899] 1 Q.B. 369; *Alexander v Webber* [1922] 1 K.B. 642; see also *Daraydan Holdings Ltd v Solland International Ltd* [2005] 4 All E.R. 73.

[61] *Harrington v Victoria Graving Dock Co* (1878) L.R. 3 Q.B.D. 549.

[62] See, e.g. *Armstrong v Jackson* [1917] 2 K.B. 822.

[63] *Robinson v Mollett* (1874) L.R. 7 (HL) 802.

[64] *Maffett v Stewart* (1887) 14 R. 506.

Where an agent purchases property belonging to his principal without disclosing this fact, then even if a fair price is paid, the principal may reduce the sale.[65]

Delegation—It is a question depending on the nature of the employment in each **18.10** particular case whether an agent has any implied power to delegate his work.[66] The maxim *delegatus non potest delegare* (a person to whom a matter has been delegated cannot himself delegate it) is only a general presumption.[67] If the circumstances are such that delegation was permissible, the sub-agent and the principal may be brought into contractual relations, both in respect of the liability of the principal to pay for the services rendered, and in the application of the rule that no one in the position of an agent can obtain any secret advantage or commission.[68] Moreover, the sub-agent may owe fiduciary duties directly to the principal notwithstanding the absence of a contractual nexus between them.[69] Where, however, no privity exists between the principal and sub-agent, failure on the part of the sub-agent to carry out his duties in the proper way will infer the liability of the original agent.[70]

Relief—An agent is entitled to be relieved by the principal of all liabilities which **18.11** he may incur in the due performance of his contract as agent. Thus if, acting in accordance with his instructions, the agent so contracts as to render himself liable on the contract, the principal is bound to relieve him of his liability.[71] Where an agent was employed to make a report and a third party brought an unsuccessful action for damages for statements in the report which reflected on him, it was held that the principal was liable to the agent in the expenses—which the unsuccessful plaintiff was unable to pay—incurred in defending the action.[72]

Remuneration of agent—It is, generally, a question depending on circumstances **18.12** whether an agent, in the absence of any express provision on the point, is entitled to remuneration. Where the services rendered are of the nature of supplying an introduction, or introducing business, and the party who has rendered the service is a broker or commission agent, he will be entitled to payment, in cases where a private individual would have been assumed to have acted gratuitously,[73] if his claim can be shown to be sanctioned by a custom of trade.[74] Though the actual business done may not be directly due to the broker (or agent), he may be entitled to commission if he was the means of bringing the parties into relations with each

---

[65] *McPherson's Trs v Watt* (1877) 5 R. (HL) 9. The narrow view of this case, expressed in Gloag, *The Law of Contract in Scotland* (1929), pp.522–3, as applying only to a solicitor and client is questionable and difficult to reconcile with the decision of the House of Lords in *Aberdeen Railway Co v Blaikie Bros* (1854) 1 Macq. 461.

[66] Bell, *Commentaries*, I, 516–517.

[67] *Robertson v Beatson*, 1908 S.C. 921; *Black v Cornelius* (1879) 6 R. 581; *Knox & Robb v Scottish Garden Suburb Co*, 1913 S.C. 872.

[68] *De Bussche v Alt* (1878) L.R. 8 Ch.D. 286.

[69] *Liverpool Victoria Legal Friendly Society v Houston* (1900) 3 F. 42.

[70] *Mackersy v Ramsay, Bonar & Co* (1843) 2 Bell's App.30.

[71] *Robinson v Middleton* (1859) 21 D. 1089. See Lord McLaren's note to Bell, *Commentaries*, I, 534.

[72] *Re Famatina Development Corp* [1914] 2 Ch. 271; distinguished in *Tomlinson v Liquidators of Scottish Amalgamated Silks*, 1935 S.C. (HL) 1.

[73] See *White v Munro* (1876) 3 R. 1011 at 1028, per Lord Justice-Clerk Moncreiff (dissenting).

[74] *Walker, Donald & Co v Birrell* (1883) 11 R. 369; *Kennedy v Glass* (1890) 17 R. 1085; *Dawson v Fisher* (1900) 2 F. 941; *Howard Houlder & Partners Ltd v Manx Isles Steamship Co Ltd* [1923] 1 K.B. 110.

other[75]; not where the parties were already acquainted and the broker's claim is founded on a suggestion which was declined.[76] A term concerning introductions can be implied where it covers "an unanticipated eventuality not covered by an express term of the contract".[77] However, where an agent seeks (full) remuneration, alleging a breach of the agency agreement by its principal, that claim, which is one for damages, may be struck down as a penalty where it bears no correlation to the agent's loss because of the breach.[78] It is, however, a matter of construction of the contract.[79] The general principle that a mercantile agent is entitled to remuneration in some form may be excluded by proof of a custom in a particular trade known to both parties that agents rely exclusively on the proceeds of the sale of goods placed in their hands.[80] If the agent is to receive commission on completion of the contract, and he finds a customer willing to complete, he is entitled to damages if his principal refuses to complete.[81]

18.13 Obligation to furnish agent with work—Some difficult questions are raised when an agent is appointed for a definite period, and his remuneration is to be by commission. Does the appointment imply an obligation on the part of the principal to continue his business in order that the agent may have an opportunity of earning a commission? If the agency has been in any way paid for, as where the agent subscribes for shares in a company by which he is engaged, there is a strong though not conclusive presumption that an obligation not to discontinue business voluntarily is implied.[82] If no payment has been made for the agency the general rule of construction is that the agent takes his chance of getting employment, and cannot complain if his employer discontinues or transfers his business.[83] If, however, the contract contains an obligation to employ the agent,[84] or to execute any orders which he may be able to obtain,[85] an obligation not to discontinue the business voluntarily may be implied. An appointment as sole selling agent will generally prohibit the principal from appointing another agent to enter into a sale transaction on his behalf,[86] but does not preclude a sale by the principal himself, unless the terms of the contract provide to the contrary (which they often will).[87]

---

[75] *Walker, Donald & Co* (1883) 11 R. 369; *Walker, Fraser & Steele v Fraser's Trs*, 1910 S.C. 222; *Christie Owen and Davis Plc v King*, 1998 S.C.L.R. 786; cf. *Chris Hart (Business Sales) Ltd v Mitchell*, 1996 S.L.T. (Sh. Ct) 132 (use of particulars of an hotel by a former principal after the termination of the agency agreement did not establish a causal connection with the subsequent sale of the hotel by the former principal).

[76] *Van Laun v Neilson* (1904) 6 F. 644.

[77] *Robert Barry & Co v Doyle*, 1998 S.L.T. 1238 at 1243, per Lord Macfadyen.

[78] *Chris Hart (Business Sales) Ltd v Mitchell*, 1996 S.L.T. (Sh. Ct) 132 at 135–6.

[79] *Chris Hart (Business Sales) Ltd v Currie*, 1992 S.L.T. 544.

[80] *Dinesmann v Mair*, 1912 1 S.L.T. 217.

[81] *Dudley Bros v Barnet*, 1937 S.C. 632. The House of Lords in *Luxor (Eastbourne) v Cooper* [1941] A.C. 108 seems to have taken another view, but the Scottish decision seems preferable. See *Alpha Trading v Dunnshaw-Patten* [1981] Q.B. 290 for a discussion of Luxor.

[82] *Galbraith v Arethusa Ship Co* (1896) 23 R. 1011; *Ogdens Ltd v Nelson* [1905] A.C. 109.

[83] *Patmore v Cannon* (1892) 19 R. 1004; *State of California Co v Moore* (1895) 22 R. 562; *Rhodes v Forwood* (1876) L.R. 1 App. Cas. 256; *L French v Leeston Shipping Co* [1922] 1 A.C. 451; Gloag, *The Law of Contract in Scotland* (1929), p.294. Cf. *North American & Continental Sales Inc v Bepi (Electronics) Ltd*, 1982 S.L.T. 47 and *Alpha Trading v Dunnshaw-Patten* [1981] Q.B. 290.

[84] *Turner v Goldsmith* [1891] 1 Q.B. 544.

[85] *Reigate v Union Manufacturing Co* [1918] 1 K.B. 592.

[86] *Nicholas Prestige Homes v Neal* [2010] EWCA Civ 1552.

[87] *Bentall Horsely & Baldry v Vicary* [1931] 1 K.B. 253; *Lamb v Goring Brick Co* [1932] 1 K.B. 710; *Christie Owen and Davis Plc v King*, 1998 S.C.L.R. 786; *G. & S. Properties Ltd v Francis*, 2001 S.LT. 934.

Lien—In security of his wages or commission, or of any debt incurred by the **18.14** principal in the course of the agent's employment, an agent has a general lien over any property of the principal which has been placed in his hands.[88] It has been laid down that

> "every agent who is required to undertake liabilities or make payments for his principal, and who in the course of his employment comes into posses- sion of property belonging to his principal over which he has power of control and disposal, is entitled, in the first place, to be indemnified for the moneys he has expended or the loss he has incurred, and, in the second place, to retain such properties as come into his hands in his character of agent".[89]

Proof that a general lien is recognised in the particular branch of agency is not required.[90] But the factor on an estate has no general lien, unless he happens to be a solicitor,[91] and it is doubtful whether an accountant could assert anything more than a special lien on the plea that the particular work on which his claim was based was of the nature of agency.[92]

Termination of the contract—In most respects, the rules applicable to the termi- **18.15** nation of the contract of agency are the same as in other contracts of employ- ment.[93] Therefore, where an agent is abusive to the principal in an unprofessional manner, this will amount to an irremediable breach of the implied term of mutual trust and confidence of the agency contract, constituting a fundamental breach of contract which entitles the principal to terminate the agreement.[94] In the absence of express agreement to the contrary, the agent's duty to provide to the principal the records of transactions he has effected as agent, which duty is a legal conse- quence of the relationship of principal and agent, subsists notwithstanding termi- nation of the agent's authority.[95]

Relations with third parties[96]—It is now necessary to examine the relationships **18.16** which arise when an agent enters a legal relationship with a third party. The first question in many cases is whether the agent did deal with the third party as agent, or as principal or otherwise in such a way as to incur personal liability: this is a question of fact and of interpretation of the contract.[97] When an agent purports to enter into a contract with a third party, the rights and liabilities thence arising depend, first, on the nature and extent of his authority and, secondly, on the method by which the agent has contracted. He may contract: (1) as agent for a

---

[88] Bell, *Principles*, s.1445; and see, as to lien, para.36.15, below.

[89] *Glendinning v Hope*, 1911 S.C. (HL) 73 at 78, per Lord Kinnear.

[90] *Glendinning*, 1911 S.C. (HL) 73 (stockbroker).

[91] *Macrae v Leith*, 1913 S.C. 901. As to the lien of a solicitor, see para.36.23, below.

[92] See *Findlay v Waddell*, 1910 S.C. 670.

[93] See paras.17.41 and 17.42, above; but there is no statutory protection for agents, except, now, commercial agents. Death terminates the relationship, see *Lord Advocate v Chung*, 1995 S.L.T. 65 at 68.

[94] *Gledhill v Bentley Designs (UK) Ltd* [2010] EWHC 1965 (QB); [2011] 1 Lloyd's Rep. 270.

[95] *Yasuda Fire and Marine Insurance Co v Orion Marine Insurance Underwriting Agency Ltd* [1995] Q.B. 174.

[96] Often now referred to as the "external" aspect of the relationship.

[97] cf. *McCabe v Skipton Building Society*, 1994 S.L.T. 1272; *Rolls Royce Power Engineering Plc v Ricardo Consulting Engineers Ltd* [2004] 2 Comm. 129 (subsidiary contracting as principal or as agent for parent).

particular principal; (2) as an agent, but without disclosing for whom he is acting; or (3) ostensibly as a principal, without disclosing the fact of agency.

> "As a general rule, the position of the principal on the contract is not affected by the method in which the agent contracts: if he has given the agent authority, the principal is a party to the contract, has a title to sue on it and is liable on the obligations it entails, whether the fact of the agency was originally disclosed or not."[98]

18.17 ***Del credere* agency**—In the normal case, an agent in entering into a contract on behalf of his principal does not guarantee that the party with whom he contracts will fulfil his contract. If, by arrangement with his principal, he does so guarantee, he is said to act *del credere*.[99] An agent *del credere* is substantially a cautioner, though the former rule that cautionary obligations must be entered into in writing did not apply.[100] He is not, if he discloses the name of his principal, a party to the contract, and cannot be sued by the other party to it. Where goods are supplied for resale, it may often be a narrow question whether the contract is one of *del credere* agency or of sale and return.[101]

18.18 **Authority**—First, the agent may be acting with the express authority of his principal, either for a single transaction or for a series of transactions. In that case, the question whether the principal is bound depends on the facts and on the construction of the authority.[102] Secondly, the principal may have appointed the agent to a position such as manager, director or factor which, according to the terms of the appointment or the usual understanding in the trade or business, carries with it the power to make contracts for the principal. In that case, the agent may be said to have implied authority to enter into contracts within the scope of his appointment.[103] Thirdly, the principal may have represented to third parties, by words or conduct, that the agent has authority to act: in that case, the principal will be bound by actings of the agent within his apparent or ostensible authority. The distinction between implied and ostensible authority is not always clear cut, nor made clearly in the cases.

18.19 **Agent acting without authority**—If an agent enters into a contract without the authority of a principal, the latter is, generally, not bound, whether the contract is expressly made on his behalf or not.[104] The principal may become a party to the contract by ratifying the agent's unauthorised act.[105] Indeed if A, wholly unconnected with B, professes to contract on B's behalf, ratification of A's act is the only ground on which B can be held to be liable under the contract. Even if the agent's act was wholly without authority, actual or ostensible, the principal

---

[98] Gloag, *The Law of Contract in Scotland* (1929), p.127; see further, paras 18.31 and 18.32 below.

[99] Bell, *Commentaries*, I, 394; Bell, *Principles*, s.286.

[100] *Sutton v Grey* [1894] 1 Q.B. 285.

[101] *Michelin Tyre Co v Macfarlane*, 1917 2 S.L.T. 205 (HL).

[102] e.g. *Pharmed Medicare Private Ltd v Univar Ltd* [2003] 1 All E.R. Comm. 321 (CA); *Lorenz Consultancy Ltd v Fox-Davies Capital* [2011] EWHC 574 (Ch) and *Hexstone Holdings Ltd v AHC Westlink Ltd* [2010] EWHC 1280 (Ch).

[103] *Sinclair, Moorhead & Company v Wallace & Company* (1880) 7 R. 874.

[104] As to the agent's liability, see para.18.33, below.

[105] See para.18.25, below.

might nevertheless be liable to the third party on the principle of recompense, i.e. to the extent of the principal's enrichment.[106]

Authority exceeded—In the case of an agent who has some authority, but has **18.20** exceeded it, a distinction has been drawn between general and special agents. The former are persons who are employed either, as in the case of a factory and commission, to transact all the business of the principal, or, in the case of the master of a ship or a solicitor, to transact all the business of some particular kind. The latter are persons who are authorised for some special occasion or act. In the former case third parties are entitled to assume in the absence of notice to the contrary, that the agent possesses the powers which are usually conferred in agency of the particular kind[107] and general agents will possess a wide implied authority[108]; in the latter case there is no presumption of any authority beyond that which has been actually given.[109] But it may often be difficult to determine to which class a particular case belongs. The distinction is not clear-cut, and in every case it is necessary to ask what the agent's actual or ostensible authority was.[110] Where the third party knows that an agent has limited authority, ostensible general authority can never arise.[111] The law may be illustrated by reference to the ostensible authority of a solicitor, and of a mercantile agent.

Implied authority: Solicitors and counsel—A solicitor has implied authority to **18.21** receive payment of a sum decerned for in an action which he has been employed to conduct,[112] or to receive payments for shares which he has been employed to sell.[113] He has no such authority to receive payment of the principal sum due under a bond,[114] or to discharge a bond, or place it in the custody of the debtor.[115] There is no authority to bind the client to any contract, e.g. a lease,[116] or a bank overdraft.[117] The solicitor of a trust has no authority to have a trustee or executor registered as a shareholder in a company.[118] Employed to purchase lands or to arrange a heritable security, a solicitor has implied authority to authorise a search of the records for incumbrances, and has been held liable to his client for failure to do so.[119] In the conduct of litigation[120] counsel have a very wide authority to bind their client to any step in process,[121] and the solicitor has an implied authority

---

[106] *Commercial Bank of Scotland v Biggar*, 1958 S.L.T. (Notes) 46. See also Ch.24 on Unjustified Enrichment.

[107] In *United Bank of Kuwait v Hammoud* [1988] 1 W.L.R. 1051 at 1063, Staughton L.J. points out that the usual scope varies with changes in practice.

[108] *Burnett v Clark* (1771) M. 8491; *Batt Cables Plc v Spencer Business Parks Ltd*, 2010 S.L.T. 860.

[109] Bell, *Principles*, s.219.

[110] cf. Erskine, *Principles*, III, 3, 12: "The distinction is delusive since the extent of the authority in each case is matter of fact to be proved".

[111] *Russo-Chinese Bank v Li Yau Sam* [1910] A.C. 174; *Armagas Ltd* [1986] A.C. 717.

[112] *Smith v North British Ry* (1850) 12 D. 795.

[113] *Pearson v Scott* (1878) L.R. 9 Ch.D. 198.

[114] *Peden v Graham* (1907) 15 S.L.T. 143.

[115] *Bowie's Trs v Watson*, 1913 S.C. 326.

[116] *Danish Dairy Co v Gillespie*, 1922 S.C. 656; *Hopkinson v Williams*, 1993 S.L.T. 907; *Stewart's Exrs v Stewart*, 1993 S.L.T. 440.

[117] *Commercial Bank of Scotland v Biggar*, 1958 S.L.T. (Notes) 46.

[118] *Smith v City of Glasgow Bank* (1879) 6 R. 1017.

[119] *Fearn v Gordon & Craig* (1893) 20 R. 352.

[120] *Brodt v King*, 1991 S.L.T. 272.

[121] *Batchelor v Pattison & Mackersy* (1876) 3 R. 914; *Duncan v Salmond* (1874) 1 R. 329; *Zannetos v Glenford Investment Holdings Ltd*, 1982 S.L.T. 453; *Waugh v H.B. Clifford & Sons* [1982] Ch. 374,

to follow counsel's directions.[122] In limited circumstances, an advocate may be entitled to settle a case even without his client's approval.[123] Where counsel is not employed, a solicitor has ostensible authority to take any ordinary step in procedure, including marking an appeal to a higher court,[124] but not to grant delay in the execution of diligence,[125] nor to compromise an action.[126] In England, it has been held that a solicitor may owe a duty of care to a client as the latter's agent prior to the formation of a formal solicitor/client relationship, where the advice tendered to the client falls within the solicitor's implied authority, and that the solicitor will be liable, even though he/she would not consider the party in question necessarily to have the status of a client.[127]

18.22 Implied authority: Mercantile agency: Factors Acts—There is a general distinction between (i) a factor and (ii) a broker; the former being a party entrusted with the possession of goods or documents of title to goods, the latter being a mere intermediary, without possession.[128] The ostensible authority of a broker depends largely on the rules of the particular market or exchange in which he deals, though it would seem that no usage will justify a broker, employed to buy, in supplying commodities or shares belonging to himself.[129] The ostensible powers of a factor or mercantile agent are defined by the Factors Acts. By s.2 of the Factors Act 1889, extended to Scotland by the Factors (Scotland) Act 1890, a mercantile agent,[130] who is in possession of goods or of documents of title[131] with the consent of the owner, has ostensible authority to sell or pledge them, and any sale, pledge or other disposition made in the ordinary course of his business to anyone who takes in good faith and for value,[132] is as valid as if the mercantile agent had the express authority of his principal.[133] It has been held in England that in the case of a sale or pledge under these conditions the purchaser takes a statutory title, although there may be a custom in the particular trade that agents have no authority to sell or pledge.[134] A pledge of the documents of title to goods (e.g. a bill of lading, dock warrant or delivery order) is, if made by a mercantile agent, deemed to be a pledge of the goods, and, probably, gives an instant right which does not require completion by intimation to the custodier of the goods or any form of delivery.[135] In the case of property other than goods or documents of title, an agent in possession of negotiable securities has ostensible authority to pledge

---

which makes a clearer distinction between ostensible and implied authority than is found in the Scottish authorities.

[122] *Batchelor v Pattison & Mackersy* (1876) 3 R. 914; J.H. Begg, *A Treatise on the Law of Scotland Relating to Law Agents*, 2nd edn (Edinburgh: Bell & Bradfute, 1883), pp.88–95.

[123] *Brodt v King*, 1991 S.L.T. 272.

[124] *Riverford Finance Ltd v Kelly*, 1991 S.L.T. 300, distinguishing *Goodall v Bilsland*, 1909 S.C. 1152.

[125] *Cameron v Mortimer* (1872) 10 M. 817.

[126] *Cormie v Grigor* (1862) 24 D. 985; (1863) 1 M. 357; see also *Mowbray v Valentine*, 2004 S.L.T. 303.

[127] *Nayyar v Denton Wilde Sapte and Gauri Advani* [2009] EWHC 3218 (QB).

[128] See Bell, *Commentaries*, I, 505.

[129] *Robinson v Mollett* (1875) L.R. 7 H.L. 802; *Maffett v Stewart* (1887) 14 R. 506.

[130] Defined by Factors Act 1889 s.1(1).

[131] Defined by s.1(4).

[132] Factors Act 1889 s.5 and Factors (Scotland) Act 1890 s.1(2).

[133] This does not apply to a pledge in security of an antecedent debt of the mercantile agent: Factors Act 1889 s.4.

[134] *Oppenheimer v Attenborough* [1908] 1 K.B. 221.

[135] Factors Act 1889 s.3; *Inglis v Robertson & Baxter* (1898) 25 R. (HL) 70.

them. So a bank, taking securities from a stockbroker, is entitled to assume, in the absence of information to the contrary, that he has the authority of his clients to pledge them, though not that he has any authority to subject them to a lien for his own debit balance.[136] In the exceptional case of indicia of title other than documents of title to goods or negotiable instruments, it has been held in England that mere possession gives no ostensible title to dispose of them, but that if an agent has actual authority to pledge them the pledge is good though the authority be exceeded.[137]

Ostensible authority—A principal may also incur liability under a contract if the **18.23** agent's act in entering the contract was within his ostensible, though not within his actual, authority. Liability on the ground of ostensible authority cannot arise unless there was some prior contractual relationship between the agent and the party sued as principal, or in circumstances where it can be established that the principal held the agent out as possessing authority or made a representation as to his authority.[138] If A represents, manifests himself, behaves or allows B to behave such that the reasonable inference is that A has authorised B to act for him, and hence that B has any necessary actual authority, A may incur liability to anyone dealing with B, though in a question between A and B there may be no contract, or a contract of a different kind.[139] It is insufficient that a representation is made by the agent.[140] The basis of liability is personal bar.[141] Cases of ostensible authority to enter a particular transaction will rarely arise.[142] Occasionally, an agent may have apparent authority to communicate approval to third parties in relation to a transaction even though he has no authority on his own to enter into the transaction.[143]

The usual cases of ostensible authority arise: (1) where authority has been conferred, but has been withdrawn; or (2) where limited authority has been given and has been exceeded.

---

[136] *National Bank v Dickie's Tr* (1895) 22 R. 740; *London Joint Stock Bank v Simmons* [1892] A.C. 201.

[137] *Fry v Smellie* [1912] 3 K.B. 282 (share certificates with blank transfers).

[138] *First Energy (UK) Ltd v Hungarian International Bank* [1993] 2 Lloyd's Rep.194; *Armagas Ltd v Mundogas S.A.* [1986] A.C. 717; *Lovett v Carson Country Homes Ltd* [2009] EWHC 1143 (Ch); [2009] 2 B.C.L.C. 196.

[139] See *Hayman v American Cotton Oil Co* (1907) 45 S.L.R. 207; *Freeman & Lockyer v Buckhurst Park Properties (Mangal) Ltd* [1968] 2 Q.B. 480; *British Bata Shoe Co Ltd v D. M. Shah Ltd*, 1980 S.C. 311; *Armagas Ltd v Mundogas S.A.* [1986] A.C. 717; *Dornier GmbH v Cannon*, 1991 S.C. 310; *John Davidson (Pipes) Ltd v First Engineering Ltd*, 2001 S.C.L.R. 73; *Trigon Tools Ltd v Andrew Wright (PVC) Ltd,* 2010 G.W.D. 30–612. See generally L. Macgregor, "Unauthorised Agency in Scots Law" in D. Busch and L. Macgregor (eds), *The Unauthorised Agent: Perspectives from European and Comparative Law* (Cambridge: Cambridge University Press, 2009), pp.264–275.

[140] See *Stair Memorial Encyclopaedia*, Vol.1, "Agency and Mandate" (Reissue), paras 75–81 and *Batt Cables Plc v Spencer Business Parks Ltd* [2010] S.L.T. 860 at 866 (Lord Hodge).

[141] *Armagas Ltd* [1986] A.C. 717, per Lord Keith of Kinkel at 777 (estoppel); para.3.04, above. However, see the discussion in *Gregor Homes Ltd v Emlick*, 2011 G.W.D. 8–193 and L. Macgregor and D. Busch, "Apparent Authority in Scots Law: Some International Perspectives" (2007) 11 Edin. L.R. 349, 367–74.

[142] *Armagas Ltd* [1986] A.C. 717; and *Ferguson Shipbuilders Ltd v Voith*, 1999 G.W.D. 30–1500. In *re Selectmove Ltd* [1995] 1 W.L.R. 474 deals with the alleged ostensible authority of a collector of taxes to bind the Revenue to a particular arrangement for the recovery of arrears. In *Quinn v CC Automotive Group Ltd t/a Carcraft* [2010] EWCA Civ 1412; [2011] 2 All E.R. (Comm) 584, the issue was whether a car salesman employed by a car dealer had ostensible authority to enter into contracts to sell cars.

[143] *First Energy (UK) Ltd* [1993] 2 Lloyd's Rep.194, per Steyn L.J. at 203: *Skandinavska Enskilda Banken A.B. (Publ.) v Asia Pacific Breweries (Singpore) Pte Lt*d [2001] S.G.C.A 22.

18.24 Original authority withdrawn—Where a party has authorised another to act as his agent and has withdrawn his authority, that party is bound to give notice of the fact of withdrawal. If he fails to do so, he will be liable on contracts which the agent may make with parties who deal with him in the belief that the authority is still in force. Notice by advertisement is sufficient in a question with parties who had no prior dealings with the agent; with those who had, some specific notice is required.[144] The general rule is well established, and, in the case of a partner retiring from a firm, is statutory.[145] So where a gardener bought seeds over a four-month period and his employer paid for them, the employer was held liable for further large purchases by the gardener from the same supplier who had not been told that the gardener no longer had authority to buy from the supplier.[146]

18.25 Ratification—Where one party acts for another without any prior authority—express, inferred, or arising from necessity—the relationship of agent and principal may be constituted if the act of the ostensible agent is ratified or homologated by the party for whom he professed to act.[147] Where the agent lacks the authority to commit the principal to a contract with a third party, successful ratification means that the principal is treated as being bound by the contract from the moment at which the agent purported to conclude the contract on the principal's behalf. Ratification need not be in express words: it may be inferred from conduct.[148] All the material facts must be known, unless the words or conduct of the party ratifying can be construed as a ratification of whatever the agent may have done.[149] To admit of the ratification of a contract made without authority so as to make the ratifier a party to the contract as a principal, the agent must have contracted ostensibly as agent; if he contracted ostensibly as principal, though in the expectation that his contract would be ratified by another, that other cannot ratify so as to acquire the right to sue or subject himself to liability to be sued.[150] Where ratification takes effect, it relates back to the time when the agent purported to contract. So where an agent purports to make a contract without authority and the other party seeks to withdraw, subsequent ratification by the principal makes the withdrawal ineffective.[151] And to make ratification possible, the principal must have been in existence at the time when the agent acted; thus, a company cannot ratify contracts made ostensibly on its behalf before it came into existence.[152] If the acts of the agent could not competently have been performed by the principal, the principal cannot ratify these acts.[153] Ratification must be for the whole transaction, but if there are a number of separate transactions, a party may ratify some but not others.[154] Ratification may be impossible where a third party would be unfairly

[144] Bell, *Principles*, s.288; *North of Scotland Bank v Behn Moller & Co* (1881) 8 R. 423.

[145] Partnership Act 1890 s.36. See para.45.13, below.

[146] *Dewar v Nairne* (1804) Hume 340.

[147] See generally Macgregor, "Unauthorised Agency in Scots Law" in Busch and Macgregor (eds), *The Unauthorised Agent: Perspectives from European and Comparative Law* (2009), pp.275–91.

[148] *Ballantine v Stevenson* (1881) 8 R. 959; *Barnetson v Petersen* (1902) 5 F. 86; *AMB Generali Holding A.G. v SEB Trygg Liv Holding Aktisbolag* [2005] EWCA Civ 1237 (inaction).

[149] *Forman v The Liddesdale* [1900] A.C. 190.

[150] *Keighley, Maxsted & Co v Durant* [1901] A.C. 240.

[151] *Bolton Partners v Lambert* (1889) L.R. 41 Ch.D. 295; *Bedford Insurance Co v Instituto de Resseguros* [1985] Q.B. 966; *Presentaciones Musicales v Secunda* [1994] Ch. 271.

[152] *Tinnevelly Sugar Refining Co v Mirrlees* (1894) 21 R. 1009; *Kelner v Baxter* (1886) L.R. 2 C.P. 174; *Cumming v Quartzag Ltd*, 1980 S.C. 276. For the liability of the purported agent, see para.18.26, below. Companies Act 2006 s.51, on pre-incorporation contracts.

[153] *Boston Deep Sea Fishing Co v Farnham* [1957] 1 W.L.R. 1051.

[154] *Smith v Henniker-Major & Co* [2003] Ch. 182.

prejudiced.[155] Where the validity of an act depends on its being done within a certain time or before a certain event, and it is done timeously but without authority, subsequent ratification will not make the act valid.[156] It is an anomalous exception to this that in marine insurance a principal may ratify a contract of insurance made on his behalf and without his authority, even after he is aware of a loss.[157] And when ratification has to be inferred from conduct without any express statement, it has been held that that inference cannot be drawn unless the party ratifying had a choice in the matter. So where an agent had ordered repairs on a ship without authority, the shipowner did not ratify his act, and thereby incur liability to pay for the repairs, merely because he received and used the ship.[158]

Liability of agent exceeding his authority—Where a party contracts ostensibly **18.26** as agent, but in excess of his actual or ostensible authority, and with the result that no principal is bound by the contract, he will, as a rule, incur personal liability, but the nature and extent of that liability will depend on the circumstances of the case. If the contract is made professedly on behalf of a non-existent principal, the party who makes the contract is liable to carry it out and is treated as a party to it.[159] So where someone purports to contract or to undertake an obligation as agent for a company which has not yet been formed, subject to any agreement to the contrary he is personally liable on the contract or under the obligation.[160] The same rule holds where the nominal principal is a body unable to bind itself by contract, with the exception of the case of a contract on behalf of a government.[161] Where the principal, though in existence and able to give authority, has in fact not done so, the agent is not a party to the contract. If his conduct was fraudulent he will be liable in damages for fraud and where he owes a duty of care to the other party, he will be liable in damages for negligence,[162] but the principal will be unable to take advantage of the fraud of his agent and on that basis, any transactions purportedly entered into between the principal and a third party may be reduced.[163] If he honestly thought he had the principal's authority, as where an auctioneer, by mere mistake, sold a horse which was not for sale,[164] or solicitors believed that they were representing a trust when in fact there were no trustees,[165] the agent will incur liability on the theory that an agent impliedly warrants that he has the

---

[155] *The Borvigilant* [2003] EWCA Civ 935; [2003] 2 All E.R. (Comm) 736.

[156] *Goodall v Bilsland*, 1909 S.C. 1152; *Alexander Ward & Co v Samyang Navigation Co Ltd*, 1975 S.C. (HL) 26; *Presentaciones Musicales* [1994] Ch. 271.

[157] Marine Insurance Act 1906 s.86. This does not hold in fire insurance, see *Grover v Mathews* [1910] 2 K.B. 401.

[158] *Forman v The Liddesdale* [1900] A.C. 190. In Scots law the shipowner might be liable, on the principle of recompense, in so far as he was lucratus; see para.24.16, below and para.18.27, below.

[159] *McMeekin v Easton* (1889) 16 R 363: cf. *Halifax Life Ltd v DLA Piper Scotland Ltd*, 2009 G.W.D. 19–306 where it was held that in a normal commercial transaction, an agent will not be personally bound, unless this was the intention of the parties (which intention is to be ascertained in accordance with the ordinary rules of contractual interpretation).

[160] *Phonogram Ltd v Lane* [1982] Q.B. 938; Companies Act 2006 s.51; *Vic Spence Assocs v Balchin*, 1990 S.L.T. 10; and *Braymist Ltd v Wise Finance Co Ltd, The Times*, March 27, 2001.

[161] See para.18.28, below.

[162] Watts, *Bowstead and Reynolds on Agency* (2010), para.9.112 et seq.

[163] *Bird v Bank of Scotland* [2010] CSOH 162; 2011 G.W.D. 1–34. However, there are circumstances in which the principal may benefit from his agent's fraud, e.g. where the principal has given valuable consideration: *Traill v Smith's Trs* (1876) 3 R 770; *Clydesdale Bank v Paul* (1877) 4 R. 626 and *Rose v Spavens* (1880) 7 R 925.

[164] *Anderson v Croall* (1903) 6 F. 153.

[165] *Scott v J.B. Livingston & Nicol*, 1990 S.L.T. 305.

authority of the principal whom he names, and is liable in damages for breach of
that warranty if it turns out that he has no authority.[166] Thus, in order for an agent
to be liable for a breach of warranty of authority, the supposed agent, A, must
represent that he has authority to act for B in a particular transaction, with the
result that the third party, C, is induced to act on that representation: the representation must be made by A in relation to the person B for whom he purports to act,
not the capacity in which B will act, or as to the property they hold.[167] In England,
it has been held that an agent will not be in breach of warranty of authority where
he merely represents the fact of his agency, rather than the precise accuracy of the
name which he attributed to his principal.[168] The damages are measured by the
loss the other party has sustained in not having the obligation of the principal.
Thus, where an agent sells, without authority, he is liable for the difference
between the price paid and the actual value of the article.[169] But where a plumber
had done work on the instructions of an agent who, as it turned out, had no
authority, but the principal named was a company which was insolvent and had no
assets, it was held that as the obligation of the company was valueless, the plumber
had lost nothing by the want of it, and therefore could recover no damages from
the agent for breach of his implied warranty.[170] The rule as to the implied warranty
given by an agent does not apply where the question of the agent's authority is one
of law, and the other party has the means of judging for himself what that authority
is. So directors of a company which had no power to borrow were not liable on
debentures which they honestly but mistakenly issued, the question as to the
power to borrow being one of law.[171] But they did incur liability where the debentures were in excess of a borrowing limit, the question whether that limit had been
reached being one of fact.[172]

18.27 Contracts where identity of principal disclosed—Where the agent names his
principal, the general rule is that the principal alone is the contracting party, and
that the agent is under no liability and has no title to sue on the contract.[173] The
other party to the contract cannot, in respect of a debt arising out of it, plead
compensation on a debt due to him by the agent—a rule which holds even if the
name of the principal has not been disclosed,[174] but yields to proof of a custom of
trade known to all the parties.[175] Payment to the agent is valid if the agent had
authority to receive it, or if the nature of the agency was such as to involve ostensible authority to receive payment. Putting the matter broadly, it would appear that

---

[166] *Anderson v Croall* (1903) 6 F. 153; *Irving v Burns*, 1915 S.C. 260; *Royal Bank of Scotland v
Skinner*, 1931 S.L.T. 382. See also Macgregor, "Unauthorised Agency in Scots Law" in Busch and
Macgregor (eds), *The Unauthorised Agent: Perspectives from European and Comparative Law*
(2009), pp.291–96. In England, it has been held that there may be circumstances in which the warranty
is given to a person other than the one attempting to deal with the principal, see *Penn v Bristol and
West Building Society* [1997] 1 W.L.R. 1356.
[167] *Frank Houlgate Investment Company Ltd v Biggart Baillie*, 2010 S.L.T. 527 at 536 (Lord
Drummond Young).
[168] *Knight Frank LLP v Du Haney* [2011] EWCA Civ 404.
[169] *Anderson v Croall* (1903) 6 F. 153. See also *Salvesen v Rederi Nordstjernan* (1905) 7 F. (HL)
101.
[170] *Irving v Burns*, 1915 S.C. 260.
[171] *Beattie v Lord Ebury* (1874) L.R. 7 H.L. 102.
[172] *Firbank's Exrs v Humphreys* (1887) L.R. 18 Q.B.D. 54.
[173] See Bell, *Commentaries*, I, 540, Lord McLaren's note. See, as illustration, *McIvor v Roy*, 1970
S.L.T. (Sh. Ct) 58.
[174] *Matthews v Auld & Guild* (1874) 1 R. 1224.
[175] *Sweeting v Pearce* (1861) 9 C.B. (N.S.) 534.

if an agent is in possession of goods the buyer may assume that he has authority to receive payment of the price; if he is merely a broker or traveller employed to take orders, without possession of the goods, a payment to the agent, if misapplied by him, leaves the buyer liable to the principal.[176] Where, however, the agent is more than a mere instrument and has an interest in the transaction, the general rule does not apply. So, for example, an auctioneer acting for a disclosed principal may sue a bidder for the price of goods sold.[177] When bound by the agent to a contract with a third party, a principal has no entitlement to disclaim knowledge or understanding of his agent's actings and accounts.[178]

Personal liability of agent to third parties—While the general rule is that an **18.28** agent who is acting within his authority and who names his principal incurs no personal liability, there are exceptional cases in which that rule does not hold. The most common case will be where an agent in performing his agency puts himself in a position where he owes a duty of care to the person with whom he is dealing on behalf of his principal and will be liable to him if he makes a careless misrepresentation or does a careless act which causes loss, damage or injury to the third party.[179] Thus it has been said in England that, in principle, a professional agent of an employer could be liable to a contractor who was induced to tender because of negligent misrepresentations made by that agent.[180] If the contract is in writing, and the obligations under it are ex facie undertaken by the agent, he incurs personal liability even although the other party may have known that he was dealing with an agent, and may have known who the principal was.[181] So where a chartered accountant undertook to send a transfer of shares for signature it was held that it was incompetent to prove by parole evidence that he was merely an agent, and that this was known to the party with whom he dealt.[182] And where heritage was sold on behalf of a named client by a firm of solicitors who gave a letter of obligation to the purchaser's solicitors, undertaking to produce certain writs relating to the heritage within a specified period, the seller's solicitors were held personally liable when they failed to produce the writs.[183] Any qualification of the liability which the agent has apparently undertaken must appear from the terms of the writing.[184] Apart from cases of bills of exchange or promissory notes,[185] a signature "as agent" or "on behalf of" a principal, named or unnamed, will be sufficient to negative personal liability.[186] With the exception of the case where an agent acts on behalf of a British Government department,[187] or a foreign

---

[176] *International Sponge Importers v Andrew Watt & Sons*, 1911 S.C. (HL) 57.

[177] *MacKenzie v Cormack*, 1950 S.C. 183.

[178] *Seabourne Developments Ltd v Shiprow Development Company Ltd* [2007] CSIH 90.

[179] *McCullagh v Lane Fox & Partners* [1996] 1 E.G.L.R. 35 at 41, per Hobhouse L.J. See also para.26.08, below.

[180] *J. Jarvis & Sons Ltd v Castle Wharf Developments Ltd, The Times*, February 28, 2001.

[181] *Stewart v Shannessy* (1900) 2 F. 1288; *Lindsay v Craig*, 1919 S.C. 139; *Johnston v Little*, 1960 S.L.T. 129; *Muirhead v Gribben*, 1983 S.L.T. (Sh. Ct) 102; *Stirling Park & Co v Digby Brown & Co*, 1996 S.L.T. (Sh. Ct) 17.

[182] *Lindsay v Craig*, 1919 S.C. 139.

[183] *Johnston v Little*, 1960 S.L.T. 129.

[184] See *Armour v Duff*, 1912 S.C. 120.

[185] See para.19.08, below.

[186] *Universal Steam Navigation Co v McKelvie* [1923] A.C. 492; *Stone & Rolfe v Kimber Coal Co*, 1926 S.C. (HL) 45; *McLean v Stuart*, 1970 S.L.T. (Notes) 77; *Digby Brown & Co v Lyall*, 1995 S.L.T. 932.

[187] *Dunn v Macdonald* [1897] 1 Q.B. 555, discussed in Watt, *Bowstead and Reynolds on Agency* (2010), para.9.074.

Government[188] (where, though there may be no action against the principal, the agent is not personally liable), an agent incurs personal liability if the principal from whom he has received his authority, and on whose behalf he ostensibly contracts, is an unincorporated body which cannot be sued, such as a congregation,[189] or a club.[190]

18.29 Agent for foreign principal—Although historically, it may have been the case that if the agent named as his principal a person not subject to the jurisdiction of the British courts he could be held to have incurred personal liability, it is clear that this is no longer the case.[191] The rule, if indeed it was a rule at all,[192] was described as a presumption of fact only.[193] With improvements in communications, there is no reason to impose personal liability on an agent simply because he acts for a foreign principal.

18.30 Contracts as agent but identity of principal undisclosed—The legal results of a contract entered into as agent, but without disclosing the name of the principal, are a matter on which there is little authority in Scotland.[194] It may often be settled by a custom in a particular market or exchange that brokers deal with others as principals. Where there is no such custom in question, whether the agent is personally liable on the contract will depend on the circumstances and the intentions of both contracting parties as to whether the third party, who knows that he is dealing with an agent, is looking only to the credit of the agent, or is looking to the credit of the unnamed principal.[195] But it is settled that, where an agent signs a written contract buying or selling specific articles, he is personally liable.[196] On the other hand, an auctioneer who gives a warranty does not bind himself personally if he discloses the name of the exposer, and was authorised by him[197]; he incurs personal liability if the name of the exposer is not given.[198] In the case of goods in

---

[188] *Twycross v Dreyfus* (1877) L.R. 5 Ch.D. 605.

[189] *McMeekin v Easton* (1889) 16 R. 363. The recent case of *Halifax Life Ltd. v DLA Piper Scotland Ltd*, 2009 G.W.D 19–306 is an authority for the proposition that, outside these special cases, the issue should be determined by reference to the intention of the parties. In an ordinary commercial transaction, if there is no intention that the agent acting for a non-existent principal should be personally bound, then he will not be so bound.

[190] *Thomson v Victoria Eighty Club* (1905) 43 S.L.R. 628.

[191] *Millar v Mitchell* (1860) 22 D. 833 (opinion of majority of Whole Court).

[192] In *Millar v Mitchell* (1860) 22 D. 833, Lord Curriehill expressed the view that only two Scottish cases had been cited which purportedly could support such a rule, namely *Brown v McDougal*, November 30, 1802 and *Burgess v Bink and Co*, July 2, 1829. Only in the former case was the agent found liable. In the English case of *Teheran-Europe Co v S.T. Belton (Tractors)* [1968] 2 Q.B. 545, although *Elbinger Actiengesellschaft v Claye* (1873) L.R. 8 Q.B. 313 was identified as a case which potentially supported a rule of personal liability on the part of the agent acting for a foreign principal, each judge then confirmed that the rule does not represent the modern law, on which, see Denning L.J., Diplock L.J. and Sachs L.J. at 553, 552 and 558 respectively.

[193] *Millar v Mitchell* (1860) 22 D. 833.

[194] Gloag, *The Law of Contract in Scotland* (1929), p.138; Watt, *Bowstead and Reynolds on Agency* (2010), para.8.074. See further, *Boyter v Thomson*, 1995 S.C. (HL) 15; para.12.30, above.

[195] *N. & J. Vlassopulos Ltd v Ney Shipping Ltd* [1977] 1 Lloyd's Rep.478; *P. & M. Sinclair v Bamber Gray Partnership*, 1987 S.L.T. 674; *Ruddy v Marco*, 2008 S.C. 667.

[196] *H.O. Brandt & Co v H. N. Morris & Co* [1917] 2 K.B. 784; *Hichens, Harrison Woolston & Co v Jackson & Sons* [1943] A.C. 266.

[197] *Fenwick v Macdonald, Fraser & Co* (1904) 6 F. 850.

[198] *Ferrier v Dods* (1865) 3 M. 561.

the auction room, he impliedly undertakes to deliver them, but not that the purchaser will obtain a good title.[199]

Contracts ostensibly as principal—Where an agent contracts ostensibly as prin- **18.31** cipal, the agent will be bound in a contract with the third party. The principal can, however, at his option, intervene in the contract in order to enforce it against the third party. There are no limitations on the principal's rights in this respect and the principal's option to intervene is not limited to cases of the agent's insolvency. The third party, when he becomes aware of the existence of the principal, may opt to sue either the principal or the agent. The doctrine of the undisclosed principal is considered to be an anomaly, infringing settled principles of contracting. Where the principal acts in this way, the third party will find himself bound into a contract with a party who is a stranger to him. This is usually justified on the basis of commercial convenience.[200] The principal may, however, be prevented from suing where the third party has relied upon some personal quality of the agent.[201] It is no answer to an action or counterclaim by the agent for damages for breach of the contract that he personally has suffered no loss; he may sue on behalf of his principal.[202] Similarly, if the principal discloses himself and sues on the agent's contract he is subject to all the pleas which could have been maintained against the agent.[203] The other party to the contract may plead compensation based on a debt due by the agent, if that debt was incurred before he had notice of the existence of the principal.[204] And, on discovering the identity of the principal, he may sue him, and is not adequately met by the defence that the principal has already made payment to the agent.[205]

Election between agent and principal—The liability of principal or agent, in the **18.32** case where an agent has contracted ostensibly as principal, is alternative, and not joint and several.[206] The other party to the contract must at some time elect whether he will hold the principal or the agent as his debtor, and his election once made is final.[207] Election implies knowledge of the right to elect, and therefore nothing done before the existence of the principal is discovered can amount to election of the agent as debtor. It does not necessarily amount to election that the agent has been debited,[208] or even that an action for payment has been raised against him,[209] after the principal has been disclosed. But a decree against either party, even though it be a decree in absence and nothing may be recoverable under it, amounts to election and precludes a claim against the other.[210] The same rule

---

[199] *Benton v Campbell, Parker & Co* [1925] 2 K.B. 410.

[200] Bell, *Commentaries*, I, 540, Lord McLaren's note; *Siu Yin Kwan v Eastern Insurance Co Ltd* [1994] 2 A.C. 199.

[201] Gloag, *The Law of Contract in Scotland* (1929), pp.128–9, considered in *Tait v Brown & McRae*, 1997 S.L.T. (Sh. Ct) 63. See too the discussion in *Siu Yin Kwan* [1994] 2 A.C. 199 at 209 et seq.

[202] *Craig v Blackater*, 1923 S.C. 472; *James Laidlaw & Sons v Griffin*, 1968 S.L.T. 278.

[203] *Bennett v Inveresk Paper Co* (1891) 18 R. 975.

[204] *Wester Moffat Colliery Co v Jeffrey*, 1911 S.C. 346; *Greer v Downs Supply Co* [1927] 2 K.B. 28.

[205] *Irvine v Watson L.R.* (1880) 5 Q.B.D. 414.

[206] *David Logan & Son Ltd v Schuldt* (1903) 10 S.L.T. 598; *British Bata Shoe Co v D. M. Shah Ltd*, 1980 S.C. 311.

[207] *David Logan & Son Ltd v Schuldt* (1903) 10 S.L.T. 598.

[208] *Stevenson v Campbell* (1836) 14 S. 562.

[209] *Meier v KuchenmeisterFS* (1881) 8 R. 642; *Clarkson Booker v Andjel* [1964] 2 Q.B. 775.

[210] *Craig v Blackater*, 1923 S.C. 472; *Morel v Earl of Westmoreland* [1904] A.C. 11; *Moore v Flanagan* [1920] 1 K.B. 919.

holds in the case of a ranking in the bankruptcy of either principal or agent,[211] unless perhaps the claim against the other is expressly reserved. But it will probably not amount to election if only a claim in bankruptcy has been lodged.[212] Apart from any definite claim, a party's conduct under a contract may amount to election,[213] a question largely circumstantial. Where a horse was sold at auction, under circumstances which made both the auctioneer and the owner responsible for a warranty which had been given, it was held that the return of the horse to the owner was a conclusive election to treat him as the party responsible, and precluded a claim against the auctioneer for repetition of the price.[214]

18.33 **Commercial agents**[215]—Regulations introduced in 1993 have defined a class of commercial agents who are subject to special rules which materially differ from the ordinary law of agency in the United Kingdom. For the most part, these special rules affect the internal relationship of agent and principal, but they may also have consequences for relationships with third parties. Where the Regulations are silent, the common law continues in effect. Commercial agents had previously been recognised in Europe as a class of agents to whom special rules should apply. The purpose of the Directive was, as a matter of competition policy, to harmonise the laws of the Member States, and, also, as a matter of social policy, to set certain standards of protection for commercial agents. These purposes of the Directive should be recognised in interpreting the Regulations.[216] In order to understand these purposes, it is necessary to note some differences between the approach of European systems in dealing with agents of the class for whom protection has been thought necessary and the general law of agency in the United Kingdom. Commercial agents are employed, in broad terms, to promote and carry out sales of their principals' goods. In European systems, particularly in French and German law, the purpose of the relationship is taken to be that the agent and the principal are engaged in a joint exercise to build up a market, in which both will have an interest. The Directive and the Regulations are designed to apply where an agent builds up goodwill for his principal's business through his own efforts but cannot realise the share he has built up in that goodwill for his own benefit, with the result that his business activities are in a vulnerable position and require protection.[217] The agent is taken to have a share in the goodwill of the principal's business which he has helped to create and this share is an asset which the principal retains after the termination of the agency relationship and for which the agent is

---

[211] *Scarf v Jardine* (1882) L.R. 7 App. Cas. 345; *David Logan & Son Ltd v Schuldt* (1903) 10 S.L.T. 598; *British Bata Shoe Co v D. M. Shah Ltd*, 1980 S.C. 311. Contrast a case of joint and several liability, *Morton's Trs v Robertson's Judicial Factor* (1892) 20 R. 72.

[212] *Black v Girdwood* (1885) 13 R. 243.

[213] *Ferrier v Dods* (1865) 3 M. 561; *Lamont*, Nisbett & Co v Hamilton, 1907 S.C. 628.

[214] *Ferrier v Dods* (1865) 3 M. 561.

[215] See the Commercial Agents (Council Directive) Regulations 1993 (SI 1999/3053), introduced to implement the Council Directive relating to Self-Employed Commercial Agents 86/653/EEC. For a full analysis of the Regulations and the background see S. Saintier and J. Scholes, *Commercial Agents and the Law* (Informa Professional, 2005); F. Randolph and J. Davey, *Guide to the Commercial Agents Regulations*, 2nd edn (Hart Publishing, 2001).

[216] See, for examples of this approach, *Page v Combined Shipping and Trading Co Ltd* [1997] 3 All E.R. 656; *Moore v Piretta PTA Ltd* [1999] 1 All E.R. 174; *Roy v M. R. Pearlman*, 1999 S.C. 459; *King v T. Tunnock*, 2000 S.C. 424, IH, (but see *Lonsdale v Howard & Hallam Ltd* [2007] UKHL 32; [2007] 4 All E.R. 1).

[217] *McAdam v Boxpak Ltd*, 2006 S.L.T. 217 at 222 (Lord Abernethy); *Gailey v Environmental Waste Controls* [2004] Eu. L.R. 423; 2003 G.W.D. 40–1068 at [26] (Lord Drummond Young).

therefore entitled to compensation or indemnity.[218] The underlying principle governing the relationship is one of good faith.[219] The agent does not, in general, have any authority beyond that which is expressly given to him.[220] Consequently the principal is not exposed to the risk that he may become bound by actings of the agent beyond his actual authority. On the other hand, the agent is exposed to the risk that, after he has expended effort and incurred expense in building up a market, the principal may decide to deal direct with the customers and cut out the agent. The Directive set out to provide uniform protection against that risk by giving the agent a right to compensation or indemnity on the termination of the agency.[221] The Directive also gives protection against some other risks, including failure on the part of the principal to supply information to the agent.

Commercial agents: Definition—A "commercial agent" is defined as an inde- **18.34** pendent self-employed intermediary who has continuing authority either simply to negotiate or to negotiate and conclude the sale or purchase of goods on behalf of another person (the principal).[222] To enjoy the protection of the Regulations the agent must have been acting expressly as agent: consequently an agent acting for an undisclosed principal will not be protected. Likewise, an agent who has authority to contract in his own name as a principal will not enjoy the protections of the Regulations.[223] The requirement of independence distinguishes the status of agent from that of employee, so that the agent is free to act for other principals or for himself, so long as he does not compete with the principal.[224] The requirement that the agent be self-employed does not prevent a company from being an agent within the definition.[225] There is uncertainty about the meaning of continuing authority: for example, it is clear that an agent appointed for one transaction does not have such authority, but the position of one appointed for a large but finite number is uncertain, since the European Court of Justice has held that authority to negotiate or conclude a number of transactions is required and that there is no specific number of transactions which is determinative.[226] It is also uncertain whether an agent acting in pursuance of an implied, and still more an ostensible, authority will fall within the definition.[227] Negotiation involves some element of input of effort and skill by the agent, so that running a petrol station under an agreement with an oil company is not included.[228] However, it has been stressed that the courts should be slow to adopt a limited or restricted construction of the

---

[218] *Lonsdale v Howard & Hallam Ltd* [2007] UKHL 32; [2007] 4 All E.R. 1 at 6 (Lord Hoffmann).

[219] Commercial Agents (Council Directive) Regulations 1993 reg.4; *Page v Combined Shipping and Trading Co Ltd* [1997] 3 All E.R. 656 and *Cooper v Pure Fishing (UK) Ltd* [2004] 2 Lloyd's Rep. 518.

[220] Hence, in civil law countries, a tendency to divide agents into categories according to the powers generally given to them.

[221] Saintier and Scholes, *Commercial Agents and the Law* (2005). Before the Directive, German law gave a right to indemnity, and French law a right to compensation; see further, para.18.38, below.

[222] Commercial Agents (Council Directive) Regulations 1993 reg.2(1). The definition does not cover a person buying or selling a third party's goods as principal (*AMB Imballaggi Plastici Srl v Pacflex Ltd* [1999] 2 All E.R. (Comm) 249). It would appear that the agent and the principal must be in a contractual relationship (*Barnett Fashion Agency Ltd v Nigel Hall Menswear Ltd* [2011] EWHC 978 (QB).

[223] *Sagal (t/a Bunz UK) v Atelier Bunz GmbH* [2009] 4 All E.R. 1253.

[224] *Smith v Reliance Water Controls Ltd* [2003] EWCA Civ 1153; [2004] E.C.C. 38. Cf. *DeVere Group Plc v Pearce* [2011] EWHC 1240 (QB).

[225] *AMB Imballaggi Plastici Srl v Pacflex Ltd* [1999] 2 All E.R. (Comm) 249.

[226] *Poseidon Chartering BV v Marianne Zeeschip VOF* [2006] 2 Lloyd's Rep. 105.

[227] The position of sub-agents may also give rise to problems: *Light v Ty Europe Ltd* [2003] EWCA Civ 1238.

[228] *Parkes v Esso Petroleum* [2000] Eu. L.R. 25.

word "negotiate" which would exclude agents who are engaged to develop the principal's business and who have successfully generated goodwill for the principal.[229] Therefore, when an agent had the power to encourage or generate the interest of customers in a sale and suggest prices to those customers, it was held that he was covered by the protection of the Regulations.[230] In another decision, it was ruled that an agent who had continuing authority to negotiate and conclude sales on behalf of the principal continued to be a commercial agent when the authority to conclude sales on behalf of the principal was removed, but the authority to negotiate sales remained intact.[231] The agent must be employed in the sale or purchase of goods: an agent who is engaged in the provision of services is not included. Again, there may be difficulties in determining the position of an agent who deals in both goods and services. For example, it has been held that an agent who had authority to negotiate contracts *locatio operis faciendi* for the sale of conservatories or property extensions on behalf of a principal was not employed in the sale or purchase of goods and so, was not a commercial agent.[232] However, in another decision, a court ruled that the sale of software with ancillary hardware satisfied the condition that there must be a sale of "goods".[233]

18.35 Commercial agents: Exclusions—The Regulations specifically exclude from the definition officers of a company or association, partners and insolvency practitioners.[234] In addition, the Regulations do not apply to commercial agents whose activities are unpaid, to commercial agents operating in commodities or to the Crown Agents for Overseas Governments and Administrations.[235] Additional specific exclusions are made in the Schedule to the Regulations[236] which provides that mail order catalogue agents for consumer goods and consumer credit agents are presumed not to be covered. Further, by reg.2(3) and (4), which purport to give effect to provisions of the Directive, those whose acts as commercial agents are considered "secondary", as determined in accordance with the Schedule, are not covered.[237] The Schedule in effect describes commercial agency as an arrangement where the business of the principal is the sale or purchase of goods of a particular kind, such that the transactions are normally individually negotiated and concluded and the procuring of one transaction is likely to lead to others so that it is in the principal's interest to appoint a representative to develop the market.[238] It is provided that where it may reasonably be taken that the primary purpose of the arrangement is other than that, the activities of the agent are to be considered secondary. There then follow a number of factors which are to be taken as indications that an arrangement is one of commercial agency and a

[229] *P J Pipe & Valve* Co Ltd v *Audco India Ltd* [2005] EWHC 1904 (QB); [2006] Eu. L.R. 368.
[230] *Nigel Fryer Joinery Services Ltd v Ian Firth Hardware Ltd* [2008] 2 Lloyd's Rep. 108.
[231] *Claramoda Ltd v Zoomphase Ltd (t/a Jenny Packham)* [2010] 1 All E.R. (Comm) 830.
[232] *Marjandi v Bon Accord Glass Ltd*, 2007 G.W.D. 05–80.
[233] *Accentuate Ltd v Asigra Inc* [2010] 2 All E.R. (Comm) 738.
[234] Commercial Agents (Council Directive) Regulations 1993 reg.2(1).
[235] Commercial Agents (Council Directive) Regulations 1993 reg.2(2).
[236] Commercial Agents (Council Directive) Regulations 1993 Sch.1 para.5.
[237] See *Tamarind International Ltd v Eastern Natural Gas (Retail) Ltd* [2000] Eu. L.R. 708; *McAdam v Boxpak Ltd*, 2006 S.L.T. 217 and *Marjandi v Bon Accord Glass Ltd*, 2007 G.W.D. 05–80. See also *AMB Imballaggi Plastici Srl v Pacflex Ltd* [1999] 2 All E.R. (Comm) 249 where it is said obiter that reg.2(3) and (4) and the Schedule to the Regulations may be inconsistent with the Directive.
[238] The Schedule approaches the definition of commercial agency in a roundabout way: while the effect is as stated in the text, in any case of difficulty the precise terms of the Schedule have to be considered.

number which are indications that it is not. The positive indications may be said to concentrate on the identification of the principal with the goods and on the role of the agent as representative: the negative ones on the extent of direct relationship between the principal and the customer. The name given to the relationship by the parties is relevant but not conclusive. The method of remuneration for the agent is also relevant but although remuneration by commission may be normal, another method may be consistent with commercial agency.[239] These provisions of the Schedule have been described as "almost impenetrable".[240] The main difficulty is that the Directive appears to suggest that the exception applies where the agent's activities in relation to a particular principal are secondary in relation to the rest of the agent's business, but the terms of the Schedule suggest that what is required is an assessment of the agent's relationship with the principal.[241] This and other issues as to the meaning of "secondary" in the context have to be regarded as unresolved at present.

Relationship of agent and principal—Part II of the Regulations sets out the rights **18.36** and obligations arising between agent and principal, these being provisions from which no derogation is possible.[242] Each is to act dutifully and in good faith.[243] The agent is to make proper efforts to discharge his tasks, to communicate to his principal all the necessary information available to him and to comply with the principal's reasonable instructions.[244] The principal is to provide the agent with the necessary documentation relating to the goods concerned.[245] He is also to obtain for the agent the information necessary for the performance of the agency contract, and to tell the agent if there will be a significantly lower volume of transactions than that which the agent could normally have expected.[246] Additionally, the principal should inform the agent of the fate of any transaction negotiated by the agent.[247]

Commercial agents: Remuneration—Part III of the Regulations deals with the **18.37** question of remuneration. In the absence of agreement, a commercial agent is entitled to remuneration in accordance with local custom or, in the absence of such custom, to reasonable remuneration.[248] Where the agent is remunerated

---

[239] *Mercantile International Group Plc v Chuan Soon Huat International Group Ltd* [2002] EWCA Civ 288; [2002] 1 All E.R. (Comm) 788.

[240] *AMB Imballagi Plastici Srl* [1999] 2 All E.R. (Comm) 249, per Waller L.J.

[241] Watts, *Bowstead and Reynolds on Agency* (2010), para.11.022; see *Gailey v Environmental Waste Controls* [2004] Eu. L.R. 423; 2003 G.W.D. 40–1068, criticised in Saintier and Scholes, *Commercial Agents and the Law* (2005), p.49; *McAdam v Boxpak Ltd*, 2006 S.L.T. 217; *Edwards v International Connection (UK) Ltd*, April 27, 2006 (CA).

[242] Commercial Agents (Council Directive) Regulations 1993 reg.5. See further Watts, *Bowstead and Reynolds on Agency* (2010), paras 11.022 et seq.

[243] Commercial Agents (Council Directive) Regulations 1993 regs 3(1) and 4(1); see *Page v Combined Shipping and Trading Co Ltd* [1997] 3 All E.R. 656 (CA); *Parkes v Esso Petroleum* [2000] Eu. L.R. 25; *Bell Electric Ltd v Aweco Appliance Systems GmbH* [2002] EWHC 87; *Cooper v Pure Fishing (UK) Ltd* [2004] 2 Lloyd's Rep. 518.

[244] Commercial Agents (Council Directive) Regulations 1993 reg.3(2).

[245] Commercial Agents (Council Directive) Regulations 1993 reg.4(2)(a).

[246] Commercial Agents (Council Directive) Regulations 1993 reg.4(2)(b).

[247] Commercial Agents (Council Directive) Regulations 1993 reg.4(3).

[248] Commercial Agents (Council Directive) Regulations 1993 reg.6(1). Regulation 6 is concerned with "an agent's rate of remuneration" and not, in contradistinction to reg.7, transactions on which commission is payable; see *Kontogeorgas v Kartonpak A.E.* [1996] E.C.R. I-6643; [1997] 1 C.M.L.R. 1093 at 1108, para.18 (ECJ), referring to arts 6 and 7 of the Directive (i.e. regs 6 and 7 of the Regulations). The word "remuneration" does not contemplate a mark-up negotiated with end-users where the goods are resold by the agent who purchased them from his principal; see *AMB Imballaggi Plastici Srl v Pacflex Ltd* [1999] 2 All E.R. (Comm) 249.

wholly, or in part, by commission, regs 7–12 apply. "Commission" is defined in reg.2 as "any part of the remuneration of the [commercial agent] which varies with the number or value of business transactions". Therefore, a flat fee or retainer payment will not amount to "commission". Where a re-seller sold products and took a return by way of a mark-up above the price, the extent of the mark-up being not known to the original seller of the products (or under their control), it was held that this did not amount to "commission".[249] Regulation 7 sets out the preconditions for claiming commission during the period covered by the agency contract.[250] Regulation 8 makes provision for commission on transactions concluded after the agency contract has terminated. Apportionment of commission between new and previous commercial agents is dealt with in reg.9, and the crystallisation of the obligation to pay in reg.10. The right to commission can only be extinguished in very limited circumstances,[251] and the agent is entitled to regular statements of the commission due and to all the information necessary to check that amount.[252] Regulations 10–12 all prohibit agreements to derogate insofar as any such agreement is to the detriment of the agent.

18.38 **Creation and termination of agency: Compensation and indemnity**—Part IV of the Regulations deals with the constitution and termination of the agency contract. The principal and agent are each entitled to receive from the other on request a signed written document setting out the terms of their contract.[253] Continuing to perform an agency contract after the expiry of a period fixed in the contract is deemed to convert the arrangement into an agency contract for an indefinite period[254]; reg.15 then sets out the periods of notice to which the parties in a contract for an indefinite period are entitled. Immediate termination can take place in certain limited circumstances.[255] Article 17 deals with the alternative remedies of an indemnity[256] or compensation[257] to which the agent is entitled on termination of the agency contract. Unless specifically disapplied in the agency contract, the agent will be entitled to compensation.[258] A purposive interpretation may require that "termination" be held to include expiry of the agency agreement through the effluxion of time.[259] Where an agent has authority to negotiate sales and conclude sales for the principal and the principal removes the agent's right to

---

[249] *Mercantile International Group Plc v Chuan Soon Huat Industrial Group Plc* [2001] 2 All E.R. (Comm) 632 at [122]–[123] (Smith J.).

[250] See *Kontogeorgas v Kartonpak A.E.* [1996] E.C.R. I-6643; [1997] 1 C.M.L.R. 1093 at 1108, [16] dealing with art.7 of the Directive: cf. *Chevassus-Marche's Heirs v Groupe Danone* [2008] 2 All E.R. (Comm) 1093. Both cases provide guidance on the interpretation of art.7 of the Directive (reg.17 of the Regulations). See also *Moore v Piretta PTA Ltd* [1999] 1 All E.R. 174 at 177h–178b and *Tigana Ltd v Decoro Ltd* [2003] EWHC 23 (QB).

[251] Commercial Agents (Council Directive) Regulations 1993 reg.11.

[252] Commercial Agents (Council Directive) Regulations 1993 reg.12.

[253] Commercial Agents (Council Directive) Regulations 1993 reg.13.

[254] Commercial Agents (Council Directive) Regulations 1993 reg.14.

[255] Commercial Agents (Council Directive) Regulations 1993 reg.16.

[256] Commercial Agents (Council Directive) Regulations 1993 reg.7(3). The indemnity provisions have been drawn from German law, see *Moore v Piretta PTA Ltd* [1999] 1 All E.R. 174 at 180 and *King v T. Tunnock Ltd*, 2000 S.C. 424 at [35]. For a discussion of compensation under German law, see *Re Termination of an Agency Agreement* (Case VIII ZR 11/6/95) [1998] *European Commercial Cases* 248. In Germany, "compensation" is the equivalent of an "indemnity" under the British Regulations.

[257] Commercial Agents (Council Directive) Regulations 1993 reg.17(6) and (7).

[258] Commercial Agents (Council Directive) Regulations 1993 reg.17(2).

[259] *Frape v Emreco International Ltd*, 2002 S.L.T. 371; *Whitehead v Jenks & Cattell Engineering Ltd* [1999] Eu. L.R. 827; *Tigana Ltd v Decoro Ltd* [2003] EWHC 23 (QB).

conclude sales, but preserves the agent's right to negotiate, it was held that this did not amount to the termination of the agency contract.[260] The right to compensation or indemnity does not depend on the principal being in breach of contract and so, if the principal does not terminate the agency contract in response to an agent's material breach, but simply lets it expire at its termination date, the agent will nevertheless be entitled to compensation or indemnity.[261]

Before the Directive, the agent's remedy under French law was compensation, whereas German law provided for indemnity. The Directive left Member States free to decide whether the remedy should be compensation or indemnity, probably on the assumption that each state would opt for one or the other. However, the UK Regulations contain provisions for both, allowing the contracting parties to choose either compensation or indemnity. Initially, it was thought that compensation might be awarded on the model of the relevant French law.[262] The position has now been clarified by the decision of the House of Lords in *Lonsdale v Howard & Hallam Ltd*[263] where it was held that what the agent is entitled to receive is compensation for his loss as a result of the termination, which may be calculated by valuing the income shown which the agency would have generated by reference to what a hypothetical willing purchaser would be prepared to pay for the goodwill built up by the agent for the business of the principal. In making that valuation, it is necessary to assume that the agency would have continued and the hypothetical purchaser would have been able properly to perform the agency contract, but there was no reason to make any other assumptions contrary to what the position was in the real world at the date of termination.[264] If market conditions dictate that no hypothetical willing purchaser can be found at all, then this must be considered and could result in the award of no compensation.[265] A purposive interpretation of the Directive may require a Court considering the question of compensation to hold that the principal would not have been entitled to reduce his transactions to nil to minimise the commission payable to his agent.[266] The entitlement to seek compensation is lost if the agent does not give notice of his intention to seek such compensation within one year of the termination of the contract.[267]

The agent's right to be paid an indemnity is subject to a cap of one year's commission,[268] and is to be paid in order to reflect the fact that: (a) the agent has brought the principal new customers or significantly increased the principal's business with existing customers and substantial benefits continue to be derived by the principal from those customers; and (b) the payment of an indemnity is equitable in all the circumstances and in particular with regard to the commission lost by the agent on the principal's business with those customers.[269] Events which occur after termination of the agency are relevant in calculating the extent of the

---

[260] *Claramoda Ltd v Zoomphase Ltd (t/a Jenny Packham)* [2010] 1 All E.R. (Comm) 830.

[261] *Frape v Emreco International Ltd*, 2002 S.L.T. 371; *Cooper v Pure Fishing (UK) Ltd* [2004] 2 Lloyd's Rep. 518.

[262] See *King v T. Tunnock Ltd*, 2000 S.C. 424.

[263] *Lonsdale v Howard & Hallam Ltd* [2007] UKHL 32; [2007] 4 All E.R. 1.

[264] *Lonsdale v Howard & Hallam Ltd* [2007] UKHL 32; [2007] 4 All E.R. 1 at 7 (Lord Hoffmann).

[265] *Nigel Fryer Joinery Services Ltd v Ian Firth Hardware Ltd* [2008] 2 Lloyd's Rep. 108.

[266] *Page v Combined Shipping and Transport Co Ltd* [1997] 3 All E.R. 656.

[267] Commercial Agents (Council Directive) Regulations 1993 reg.17(9). The notice need not, however, satisfy any particular formalities: see *Hackett v Advanced Medical Computer Systems* [1999] C.L.C. 160.

[268] Commercial Agents (Council Directive) Regulations 1993 reg.17(4).

[269] Commercial Agents (Council Directive) Regulations 1993 reg.17(3).

indemnity payment. Therefore, if the principal becomes insolvent or suffers a downturn in trade after the date of termination, this will be taken into account and may operate to mitigate the indemnity payment to the agent.[270]

In reg.18, there are specified three situations in which indemnity or compensation shall not be payable and broadly, these are: (a) default by the agent leading to termination by the principal[271]; (b) termination by the agent; (c) or assignation by the agent in favour of a third party. Partial termination of the agency contract will not trigger the right to the payment of compensation or indemnity.[272] As in earlier provisions, no derogation from regs 17 and 18 to the detriment of the agent is permissible.[273] There are further provisions regarding restraint of trade clauses, a bar on disclosure of information if the disclosure would contravene public policy and the requirements for service of documents.[274]

18.39 Jurisdiction and choice of law—The European Court of Justice has held that the court which has jurisdiction over a commercial agency contract is the one within whose jurisdiction the place of the main provision of services by the agent was situated[275]: this could be provided for in the terms of the contract, or in absence of this, could be deduced from the actual place the performance was carried out, or if it could not be determined on that basis, then the place where the agent was domiciled. Choice of law clauses are provided for in the Regulations.[276] It is not, however, possible to use a choice of law clause to prevent the application of the Regulations to an agent carrying on his activities in a Member State, even where the principal is based in a non-Member State.[277]

FURTHER READING

Watts, P., *Bowstead and Reynolds on Agency*, 19th edn (London: Sweet and Maxwell, 2010).
Busch, D. and Macgregor, L. (eds), *The Unauthorised Agent: Perspectives from European and Comparative Law* (Cambridge: Cambridge University Press, 2009).
Chitty on Contract: Specific Contracts, edited by H.G. Beale, 30th edn (London: Sweet and Maxwell, 2008), Ch.31.
Davidson, F. and Macgregor, L., *Commercial Law in Scotland*, 2nd edn (Edinburgh: W. Green, 2008), Ch.2.
Forte, A.D.M. (ed.), *Scots Commercial Law* (LexisNexis UK, 1997), Ch.8.
Fridman, G.H.L., *The Law of Agency*, 7th edn (Butterworths, 1996).
Munday, R., *Agency: Law and Principles* (Oxford: Oxford University Press, 2010).

---

[270] *King v T. Tunnock*, 2000 S.C. 424. See *Semen v Deutsche Tamoil GmbH* [2009] 3 C.M.L.R. 12.

[271] In *Volvo Car Germany GmbH v Autohof Weidensdorf GmbH* [2011] 1 All E.R. (Comm) 906, the European Court of Justice decided that an agent will not be deprived of his right to compensation or an indemnity where the principal established a default by the agent which occurred after notice of the termination of the agency contract but before the contract expired, and which was of such a nature to justify the immediate termination of the contract.

[272] *Scottish Power Energy Retail Ltd v Taskforce Contracts Ltd*, 2009 S.C.L.R. 137.

[273] Commercial Agents (Council Directive) Regulations 1993 reg.19.

[274] Commercial Agents (Council Directive) Regulations 1993 regs 20, 21 and 22 respectively.

[275] *Wood Floor Solutions Andreas Domberger GmbH v Silva Trade SA* [2010] 1 W.L.R. 1900.

[276] By amendment contained in SI 1998/2868.

[277] *Ingmar G.B. Ltd v Eaton Leonard Technologies Inc* [2001] 1 All E.R. (Comm) 329.

Randolph, F. and Davey, J., *European Law of Commercial Agency*, 3rd edn (Hart Publishing, 2010).

Saintier, S. and Scholes, J., *Commercial Agents and the Law* (Informa Professional, 2005).

Sealy, L.S. and Hooley, R.J.A., *Commercial Law—Text, Cases and Materials*, 4th edn (Oxford: Oxford University Press, 2008), Chs 3, 4, 5 and 6.

Stair Memorial Encyclopaedia, Vol.1, "Agency and Mandate" (2002) (Reissue).

Story, J., *Commentaries on the Law of Agency*, 9th edn (1882).

CHAPTER 19

BILLS OF EXCHANGE

The law of bills of exchange, cheques and promissory notes was codified by the **19.01** Bills of Exchange Act 1882 ("the 1882 Act").[1] In its main provisions the Act applies both to Scotland and England.

Origin and use of bills[2]—In origin a bill of exchange was a method whereby a **19.02** merchant in one country might pay a debt due in another without the actual transmission of money. If A in London owed money to B in Paris, and was himself the creditor of C in Paris, a bill of exchange was the means by which the debt owed by C could be used to meet the debt due to B. A, known as the drawer, gave an order to C (the drawee) to pay to B (the payee). If C was willing to accede to this order he indicated the fact by signing his name on the bill, and thereby became the acceptor and incurred a direct liability to the payee. It was at an early period established that a bill of exchange in this, its ordinary form, was negotiable; that is to say, B, in the case supposed, by signing his name on the back of the bill (known as indorsement), could transfer his right as payee either to the bearer of the bill or to some named party.[3] And in the case of ordinary mercantile bills an indorsee, who paid for the bill and took it regularly and honestly, acquired, by law originally resting on the recognition of mercantile custom, an independent title, and was not affected by any imperfection or qualification of the title of the person from whom he took it. Such an indorsee is termed in the Act a holder in due course.[4] In modern banking practice, there are a number of other methods of payment, but bills remain important in commerce, particularly in international transactions, and the law relating to bills underlies that governing cheques.

Normal relations of parties—The following sketch of the main provisions of the **19.03** Bills of Exchange Act will be more easily understood if it is borne in mind that while the holder of a bill is entitled to demand payment from anyone whose name appears on it, drawer, acceptor or indorser, the relations of these parties inter se are regulated by the character in which they became parties to the bill. Before the bill is accepted, the principal debtor is the drawer, and any indorsers may recover from him and are liable among themselves in the order in which their names

---

[1] In this chapter references to sections without specifying any Act are references to sections of the Bills of Exchange Act 1882 (the "1882 Act"). For an account of the background to the codification see Appendix 3 to N. Elliott, *Byles on Bills of Exchange and Cheques*, 26th edn (London: Sweet and Maxwell, 1988); A.F. Rodger, "The codification of commercial law in Victorian Britain" (1992) 108 L.Q.R. 570. The operation of the Act was last reviewed in the Jack Report (Review Committee, *Banking Services: Law and Practice* (HMSO, 1989), Cm.622).

[2] See also J.M. Holden, *History of Negotiable Instruments in English Law* (London: The Athlone Press, 1955).

[3] There are other forms of instrument in use which claim, with greater or less justification, to be negotiable: see the Jack Report Appendix.

[4] 1882 Act s.29(1).

appear on the bill. After acceptance, the acceptor becomes the principal debtor; the drawer, and after him any indorsers in their order, are subsidiarily liable. In many respects the position of a person who becomes a party to a bill is that of a cautioner for those who are already parties to it, but, if forced to pay, he is entitled to recover the whole, and not merely a contribution, from anyone who, in the order of liability on the bill, ranks before him.

These rules as to the order of liability on a bill hold only in the absence of proof to the contrary. It is competent to prove in any particular case that the true relationship of the parties is not that which would appear on the face of the bill. It may be proved that the principal debtor is not the acceptor, but the drawer, or an indorser. Such cases generally arise when a bill is used, not for its original purpose of transferring a debt, but as a means whereby money is borrowed by one party, and a guarantee for its payment is given by another. Bills of this character are known as accommodation bills.[5]

In what follows it is proposed to deal first with the course of a normal bill of exchange, afterwards with exceptional cases, and finally with the law applicable to cheques and promissory notes.

19.04 Definitions—The following statutory definitions should be noted: A bill of exchange is an unconditional order in writing, addressed by one person to another, signed by the person giving it, requiring the person to whom it is addressed to pay on demand or at a fixed or determinable future time a sum certain in money to or to the order of a specified person, or to bearer.[6] "Holder" means the payee or indorsee of a bill who is in possession of it, or the bearer thereof.[7] This definition is extended to include a collecting bank which takes delivery from a customer of an unindorsed cheque.[8] As for the condition that the bill be in "writing", s.2 of the 1882 Act directs that "written" includes printed and "writing" includes print.[9] Indeed, it has been decided that a bill may be drawn up in pencil[10] and that the bill may take up more than one page, so long as it constitutes a single instrument.[11]

A holder in due course is a holder who has taken a bill, complete and regular on the face of it,[12] under the following conditions, namely: (a) that he became the holder of it before it was overdue, and without notice that it had been previously dishonoured, if such was the fact; (b) that he took the bill in good faith[13] and for value,[14] and that at the time the bill was negotiated to him he had no notice of any defect in the title of the person who negotiated it.[15]

---

[5] See *Macdonald v Whitfield* (1883) L.R. 8 App. Cas. 733, and para.19.32, below.

[6] 1882 Act s.3. See Cheques Act 1957 s.5. A building society withdrawal form is not a bill: *Weir v National Westminster Bank*, 1994 S.L.T. 1251. As to the meaning of an "unconditional" order, see *Guaranty Trust v Hannay* [1918] 2 K.B. 623 and *Hamilton v Spottiswoode* 154 E.R. 1182; (1849) 4 Ex. 200. The sum may be expressed, and judgment given, in foreign currency; ss.57(2) and 72(4) of the 1882 Act have ceased to have effect: Administration of Justice Act 1977 s.4.

[7] 1882 Act s.2.

[8] Cheques Act 1957 s.2; *Midland Bank v Harris* [1963] 1 W.L.R. 1021.

[9] See also *Arab Bank v Ross* [1952] 2 Q.B. 216.

[10] *Geary v Physic* (1826) 108 E.R. 87.

[11] *KHR Financings Ltd v Jackson*, 1977 S.L.T. (Sh. Ct) 6.

[12] See *Gerald McDonald & Co v Nash* [1924] A.C. 625; *Arab Bank v Ross* [1952] 2 Q.B. 216. As to cheques, see *Westminster Bank v Zang* [1966] A.C. 182.

[13] *B.C.C.I. v Dawson* [1987] Fin. L.R. 342. Cf. s.90.

[14] cf. *Clifford Chance v Silver*, 2 Bank. L.R. 11.

[15] 1882 Act s.29(1). A person who takes a negotiable instrument in contravention of s.123(1) or (3) of the Consumer Credit Act 1974 is not a holder in due course and cannot enforce the instrument: Consumer Credit Act 1974 s.125(1); see para.15.23, above.

In particular the title of a person who negotiates a bill is defective within the meaning of the Act when he obtained the bill, or the acceptance thereof, by fraud, duress, or force and fear, or other unlawful means, or for an illegal consideration, or when he negotiates it in breach of faith, or under such circumstances as amount to a fraud.[16]

A holder (whether for value or not), who derives his title to a bill through a holder in due course, and who is not himself a party to any fraud or illegality affecting it, has all the rights of that holder in due course as regards the acceptor and all parties to the bill prior to that holder.[17]

Stamp—Since a bill of exchange is negotiated rather than assigned pursuant to a sale, it does not require to be stamped.[18] A bill is not invalid by reason only that it is not stamped in accordance with the law of the place of issue.[19] **19.05**

Inland and foreign bills—A bill may be an inland or a foreign bill. It is an inland bill if it is or on the face of it purports to be (a) both drawn and payable within the British Islands, or (b) drawn within the British Islands on some person resident therein.[20] Unless the contrary appears on the face of the bill the holder may treat it as an inland bill.[21] The chief difference[22] between inland and foreign bills is that the latter, and not the former, when dishonoured by non-acceptance or non-payment, must be protested in order to preserve recourse against the drawer and indorsers.[23] **19.06**

Methods of signing bills—A person may become a party to a bill either when he signs it or when it is signed for him by a person to whom he has given authority. The latter case is termed a signature by procuration. A bill may be signed by initials or by a mark, and will then form a ground of action on proof that this was the party's usual method of signature.[24] The Act provides (s.23) that where a person signs a bill in a trade or assumed name he is liable thereon as if he had signed in his own name, and that the signature of the name of a firm is equivalent to the signature by the person so signing of the names of all the persons liable as partners of that firm. A bill of exchange is deemed to have been made, accepted or indorsed on behalf of a company if made, accepted or indorsed in the name of, or by or on behalf or on account of, the company by any person acting under its authority.[25] A **19.07**

---

[16] 1882 Act s.29(2). Where a person negotiates a cheque in contravention of s.123(2) of the Consumer Credit Act 1974, his doing so constitutes a defect in his title: Consumer Credit Act 1974 s.125(2); see para.15.23, above.

[17] 1882 Act s.29(3). The payee of a cheque is not, under any circumstances, a holder in due course: *Re Jones Ltd v Waring & Gillow* [1926] A.C. 670; applied in *Williams v Williams*, 1980 S.L.T. (Sh. Ct) 25 and *Abbey National Plc v JSF Finance & Currency Exchange Co Ltd* [2006] EWCA Civ 328. The drawer may become a holder in due course if the bill is renegotiated to him by a party who was a holder in due course: *Jade International Steel Stahl und Eisen GmbH & Co KG v Robert Nicholas (Steels)* [1978] Q.B. 917.

[18] Finance Act 1999 Sch.13 para.1.

[19] 1882 Act s.72(1).

[20] 1882 Act s.4(1).

[21] 1882 Act s.4(2).

[22] But see also 1882 Act s.72(2).

[23] 1882 Act s.51.

[24] Bell, *Principles*, s.323.

[25] Companies Act 2006 s.52; *Bondina Ltd v Rollaway Shower Blinds* [1986] 1 W.L.R. 517. For the position where the company name is not legible on the bill, see the Companies (Trading Disclosures) Regulations 2008 (SI 2008/495) regs 6(1)(b) and (c) and 10(1); *Scottish & Newcastle Breweries Ltd v Blair*, 1967 S.L.T. 72.

signature by procuration operates as notice that the party has but a limited authority to sign, and the principal is only bound by such signature if the agent in so signing was acting within the actual limits of his authority.[26] But if the agent has authority the principal will be liable though the agent has misused his authority for his own purposes.[27]

19.08 **Signature as agent**—Where a person signs a bill as drawer, indorser or acceptor and adds words to his signature, indicating that he signs for or on behalf of a principal, or in a representative capacity, he is not personally liable thereon; but the mere addition to his signature of words describing him as an agent, or as filling a representative character, does not exempt him from personal liability.[28] In determining whether a signature on a bill is that of the principal or that of the agent by whose hand it is written, the construction most favourable to the validity of the instrument must be adopted.[29] So if a bill is signed on behalf of an unincorporated body, such as a club or a congregation, which has no power to incur liability by bill, the persons who sign, although they may do so expressly on behalf of the body, incur personal liability.[30] But it is always open to any drawer or indorser to insert an express stipulation negativing or limiting his own liability to the holder.[31]

19.09 **Form of bill**[32]—A bill of exchange is usually expressed as an order by one person, known as the drawer, addressed to another, known as the drawee, requiring the drawee to pay a sum of money to the drawer himself, or to his order, or to a named payee, or to the bearer. But a man may draw a bill on himself; if so, any holder may, in his option, treat it as a bill or as a promissory note.[33] The same rule applies where the drawee is a fictitious person or a person who has no capacity to contract.[34] To form a bill of exchange the order must be solely for payment of money, and must be, on the face of it, unconditional: it is not unconditional if it is an order to pay out of some particular fund, but it may indicate the fund from which the drawee is to be indemnified, or the account which is to be debited.[35] An instrument which is expressed as a conditional order may, if transferred to a third party, be used by him as proof of a debt, but it is not a bill of exchange.[36]

19.10 **Liabilities of drawer**—The drawer of a bill incurs a conditional liability to subsequent holders. He is liable if the drawee refuses to accept the bill, or fails to pay it, provided that the requisite proceedings for notice on dishonour are duly taken.[37] He may exclude this liability by appropriate terms, the usual phrase being

---

[26] 1882 Act s.25; *Midland Bank v Reckitt* [1933] A.C. 1.
[27] *North of Scotland Bank v Behn* (1881) 8 R. 423; *Bryant Powis & Bryant Ltd v La Banque du Peuple* [1893] A.C. 170.
[28] 1882 Act s.26(1); *Brebner v Henderson*, 1925 S.C. 643.
[29] 1882 Act s.26(2).
[30] *McMeekin v Easton* (1889) 16 R. 363.
[31] 1882 Act s.16(1).
[32] For conflict of laws see s.72.
[33] However, an "IOU" is a promissory note, not a bill of exchange: *Muir v Muir*, 1912 1 S.L.T. 304.
[34] 1882 Act s.5(2). Cf. *Universal Import Export GmbH v Bank of Scotland*, 1995 S.C. 73. Where the payee is fictitious or non-existent, the bill may be treated as payable to bearer: *Bank of England v Vagliano Bros* [1891] A.C. 107; *Clutton v Attenborough* [1897] A.C. 90; *North and South Wales Bank v Macbeth* [1908] A.C. 137.
[35] 1882 Act s.3.
[36] See *Lawson's Exrs v Watson*, 1907 S.C. 1353.
[37] 1882 Act s.55(1)(a).

"without recourse".[38] He is precluded from denying to a holder in due course the existence of the payee and his then capacity to indorse.[39]

Negotiation of bill—Unless otherwise expressed a bill is negotiable, i.e. it is not **19.11** assigned and so, on negotiation, there is no requirement for intimation of the transfer of the debt to the drawer or drawee or a separate document of transfer.[40] If payable to bearer, it may be negotiated by mere delivery; if payable to a particular payee, it may be negotiated by that party indorsing the bill, i.e. writing his name on the back of it, followed by delivery.[41] If a bill contains words prohibiting transfer, or indicating an intention that it should not be transferred, it is valid as between the parties to it, but is not negotiable.[42]

Term of payment—A bill of exchange may be payable on demand, and is **19.12** assumed to be so if no term of payment is mentioned.[43] A bill may be payable on, or at a fixed period after, the occurrence of an event which is certain to happen, though the date of the occurrence is uncertain,[44] but a document payable on the occurrence of an event which may or may not happen is not in any event a bill of exchange.[45] Bills are usually made payable either after a certain period from the date at which they are drawn, or at a certain period after sight or presentation. The bill is due and payable on the last day of the time of payment as fixed by the bill or, if that is a non-business day, on the succeeding business day; there are now no days of grace.[46] Non-business days are Saturdays, Sundays, Good Friday, Christmas Day, bank holidays, days appointed by Royal proclamation as public fast or thanksgiving days, and days declared by order to be non-business days.[47]

Presentment for acceptance—If a bill is payable at a certain period after sight **19.13** or presentation, presentment for acceptance to the drawee is necessary in order to fix its maturity. In other cases presentment for acceptance is not necessary to render any party liable on the bill, unless it is expressly stated that it is required, or the bill is payable elsewhere than at the residence or place of business of the drawee.[48] The following rules as to presentment for acceptance are provided by s.41(1): (1) it must be made by or on behalf of the holder to the drawee or his agent at a reasonable hour on a business day and before the bill is overdue; (2) if there are two or more drawees, who are not partners, presentment must be made to all, unless one has authority to accept for the rest; (3) if the drawee is dead, presentment may be made to his personal representative; (4) if bankrupt, to him or to his trustee; (5) if authorised by agreement or usage, presentment may be made

---

[38] 1882 Act s.16(1).

[39] 1882 Act s.55(1)(b).

[40] *Connal & Co v Loder* (1868) 6 M. 1095 at 1102, per Lord Neaves.

[41] 1882 Act s.31(2) and (3); cf. s.21 and *Dextra Bank and Trust Co Ltd v Bank of Jamaica* [2001] UKPC 50.

[42] *Glen v Semple* (1901) 3 F. 1134.

[43] 1882 Act s.10(1)(b).

[44] For example, the death of an individual: *Roffey v Greenwell* (1839) 113 E.R. 86.

[45] 1882 Act s.11. A bill expressed to be payable "on or before" a certain date is not valid: *Williamson v Rider* [1963] 1 Q.B. 89; *Claydon v Bradley* [1987] 1 W.L.R. 521: see Elliott, *Byles on Bills of Exchange and Cheques* (1988), p.18.

[46] 1882 Act s.14(1) as substituted by the Banking and Financial Dealings Act 1971 s.3(2).

[47] 1882 Act s.92 as amended by the Banking and Financial Dealings Act 1971 ss.3(1), 4(4).

[48] 1882 Act s.39.

through the post office. The usual time allowed for acceptance is 24 hours, excluding non-business days.[49] If after the lapse of that period the bill is not accepted it must be treated as dishonoured by non-acceptance. Presentment is excused and the bill may be treated as dishonoured by non-acceptance where the drawee is dead or bankrupt, a fictitious person, or a person not having power to contract by bill, where it cannot be effected by reasonable diligence, or where, though the presentment has been irregular, acceptance is refused on some other ground. But reason to believe that the bill will be dishonoured is not an excuse for failure to present it.[50] Where presentment for acceptance is necessary the holder of the bill is bound to present or negotiate it within a reasonable time, and his failure discharges the drawer and all prior indorsers.[51]

19.14 Acceptance by other than drawee—No one but the drawee, or an agent authorised by him, can accept a bill, except in two cases. (1) Where the drawer or an indorser has inserted the name of a party ("the referee") to whom the holder may resort in case of need, that is if the bill is dishonoured by non-acceptance (or non-payment), it is in the option of the holder to resort to a referee.[52] (2) Where a bill has been protested for non-acceptance and is not overdue, any person, not already a party liable on it, may with the consent of the holder sign the bill in the capacity of an acceptor for honour. In the absence of any statement to the contrary, such a party is presumed to engage for the honour of the drawer.[53] He incurs liability to the holder and to all parties to the bill subsequent to the party for whose honour he has accepted.[54] Except in these cases any party who becomes a party to a bill, other than the drawer or acceptor, incurs the liabilities of an indorser to a holder in due course.[55]

19.15 Acceptance by drawee: Qualified acceptance—An acceptance must be in writing on the bill. The mere signature of the drawee is sufficient.[56] The acceptance may be general or qualified. It is qualified if it is: (a) conditional; (b) partial, for part only of the amount of the bill; (c) local, payable only at a particular place; (d) qualified as to time; (e) the acceptance of one or more drawees, but not of all.[57] It is in the option of the holder to take a qualified acceptance, or to treat the bill as dishonoured by non-acceptance.[58] If he takes it without the express or implied authority of the drawer or of a prior indorser, or their subsequent assent, their liability is discharged.[59] This rule does not apply to the case of a partial acceptance of which due notice has been given.[60]

---

[49] R. Thomson and J.D. Wilson, *A Treatise on the Law of Bills of Exchange*, 2nd edn (1865), p.213; *Bank of Van Diemen's Land v Bank of Victoria* (1871) L.R. 3 P.C. 526.

[50] 1882 Act s.41(2) and (3).

[51] 1882 Act s.40(1) and (2).

[52] 1882 Act s.15.

[53] 1882 Act s.65(1) and (4).

[54] 1882 Act s.66(2).

[55] 1882 Act s.56.

[56] 1882 Act s.17(2)(a). For conflict of laws, cf. s.72(1).

[57] 1882 Act s.19(2).

[58] 1882 Act s.44(1).

[59] 1882 Act s.44(2).

[60] 1882 Act s.44(2).

Liabilities of acceptor—An acceptor engages that he will pay the bill according **19.16** to the tenor of his acceptance.[61] He is precluded from denying to a holder in due course: (a) the existence of the drawer, the genuineness of his signature, and his capacity and authority to draw the bill; (b) if the bill is payable to the drawer's order, the then capacity of the drawer to indorse but not the genuineness or validity of his indorsement; (c) if payable to the order of a third party, the existence of the payee and his then capacity to indorse, but not the genuineness or validity of his indorsement.[62]

Indorsement[63]—The holder of a bill may at any stage transfer it by indorsement **19.17** and delivery. Where there are several indorsers their liability inter se is, in the absence of proof to the contrary, regulated by the order in which the indorsements appear on the bill since that is assumed to be the order in which they were made.[64] The indorser by indorsing a bill engages that it shall be accepted and paid according to its tenor, and that if it be dishonoured he will compensate the holder or a subsequent indorser who is compelled to pay it, provided that the requisite proceedings on dishonour are duly taken. He is precluded from denying to a holder in due course the genuineness and regularity of the drawer's signature and of all previous indorsements; and from denying to any subsequent indorsee, whether a holder in due course or not, that the bill was at the time of his indorsement a valid and subsisting bill, and that he had then a good title thereto.[65]

Holder in due course—Every holder of a bill is prima facie deemed to be a **19.18** holder in due course[66]; but if in an action on a bill it is admitted or proved that the acceptance, issue or subsequent negotiation of the bill is affected with fraud,[67] duress, force and fear, or illegality, the burden of proof is shifted, unless and until the holder proves that, subsequent to the alleged fraud or illegality, value has in good faith been given for the bill.[68]

Rights of holder—A holder in due course may sue on the bill in his own name. **19.19** He holds the bill free from any defect of title of prior parties, as well as from mere personal defences available to prior parties among themselves, and may enforce payment against all parties liable on the bill.[69] Thus a holder who takes under the conditions which make him a holder in due course gets a valid title to the bill although the person from whom he took it may be a thief, or may have obtained the bill by fraud.[70] But a party who has been fraudulently induced to sign a bill under the impression that it was a document of a different character is not liable

---

[61] 1882 Act s.54(1).

[62] 1882 Act s.54(2).

[63] For conflict of laws, cf. s.72(1).

[64] 1882 Act s.32(5).

[65] 1882 Act s.55(2).

[66] cf. s.29(1) and para.19.04, above.

[67] i.e. common-law fraud: *Osterreichische Länderbank v S'Elite Ltd* [1981] 1 Q.B. 565.

[68] 1882 Act s.30(2). For definition of holder in due course, see s.29(1) and para.19.04, above.

[69] 1882 Act s.38(1) and (2). Alteration of a bill makes it a nullity: *Smith v Lloyds TSB Group* [2001] Q.B. 541.

[70] Of course, where there has been no prior negotiation of the bill to the holder, the holder will not be a holder in due course in terms of s.29(1) and so will not be entitled to the protections in s.38(2), on which, see *Abbey National Plc v JSF Finance & Currency Exchange Co Ltd* [2006] EWCA Civ 328.

even to a holder in due course.[71] Even if his title is defective, a holder in due course who negotiates the bill to a holder in due course gives him a good title. A holder in due course with a defective title can give a valid discharge for a bill.[72]

A holder of a bill who is not a holder in due course, may sue on the bill in his own name,[73] but even although he has given value for the bill, he takes no higher right than that of the indorser, and is subject to all equities affecting him. Such is the case of a party who takes the bill when it is overdue or has been dishonoured[74]; or when it is not complete and regular on the face of it and with notice, or with good reason to suppose, that the title of the party from whom he takes is defective[75] or that it was delivered conditionally.[76]

19.20 Payee—A bill may be drawn payable to a named payee who must in that event be named with reasonable certainty[77]; or to two or more payees jointly; to the holder of an office[78]; or to order[79] or to bearer.[80] It becomes payable to bearer if indorsed by the payee in blank, that is, without specifying a particular indorsee.[81] When a bill has been indorsed in blank any holder may convert the blank indorsement into a special indorsement by writing above the indorser's signature a direction to pay the bill to, or to the order of, himself or some other person.[82] When the payee is a fictitious or non-existing person the bill may be treated as payable to bearer.[83] In the construction of this rule it has been held that it includes the case where the payee is actually non existent and also the case where the name of an existing party is inserted by the drawer without any intention that that party should receive the money or have any connection with the bill,[84] but not the case where the drawer intended the payee (an existing person) to receive the money, though he may have been induced to form that intention by fraud and the payee may be unaware that his name has been used.[85] These authorities show that if the bill may be treated as payable to bearer anyone who takes with the name of the payee indorsed upon it (though that indorsement be a forgery) may enforce it against prior parties, whereas, if the bill cannot be so treated, no one can acquire a valid title except on a genuine signature by the nominal payee.

19.21 Presentment for payment—A bill payable on demand must be presented for payment within a reasonable time after its issue, in a question as to the liability of the drawer, or within a reasonable time after indorsement, in a question as to the liability of the indorser.[86] But the drawer of a cheque is not discharged by delay in

---

[71] *Foster v Mackinnon* (1869) L.R. 4 C.P. 704; *Lewis v Clay* (1897) 67 L.J.Q.B. 224. As to forgery see para.19.34, below.

[72] 1882 Act s.38(3).

[73] 1882 Act s.38(1).

[74] *Semple v Kyle* (1902) 4 F. 421; cf. s.29(1).

[75] *Jones v Gordon* (1877) L.R. 2 App. Cas. 616.

[76] *Martini v Steel & Craig* (1878) 6 R. 342.

[77] 1882 Act s.7; *Adam Associates (Strathclyde) Ltd v CGU Insurance Plc*, 2001 S.L.T. (Sh. Ct) 18.

[78] 1882 Act s.7(2).

[79] 1882 Act ss.3(1) and 8(4).

[80] 1882 Act ss.3(1) and 7(3).

[81] 1882 Act s.34(1).

[82] 1882 Act s.34(4).

[83] 1882 Act s.7(3).

[84] *Bank of England v Vagliano* [1891] A.C. 107; *Clutton v Attenborough* [1897] A.C. 90.

[85] *North and South Wales Bank v Macbeth* [1908] A C. 137.

[86] 1882 Act s.45(2).

presentment except in so far as he has suffered damage thereby.[87] When a bill is payable at a fixed date it must be presented for payment at that date, failing which the drawer and indorsers are discharged.[88] Failure in presentment does not, however, affect the liability of the acceptor.[89]

Excuses for delay in presentment for payment—Delay in presentment is **19.22** excused where caused by circumstances beyond the control of the holder, and not attributable to any default, misconduct or negligence of his.[90] Presentment is dispensed with when it cannot be effected by the exercise of reasonable diligence, by waiver, express or implied, where the drawee is a fictitious party, but not merely because the holder has reason to believe that the bill if presented will be dishonoured.[91] The rules as to the method of presentment for payment are similar to those applicable to presentment for acceptance.[92]

Notice of dishonour—Where a bill has been dishonoured either by non- **19.23** acceptance or non-payment, notice of dishonour must be given to the drawer and each indorser, and any of these to whom notice is not given is discharged.[93] The notice must be given within a reasonable time, and as a general rule it is not given within a reasonable time unless, if the parties reside in the same place, it is dispatched in time to reach the party on the day after the bill was dishonoured, or unless, if the parties reside in different places, it is posted on that day.[94] It is sufficient if the holder can prove that he posted the notice in time though it may be delayed in transit, or may never arrive.[95] The notice is bad if it was received before the bill itself was dishonoured.[96] Notice may be oral or in writing, and no special form of notice is specified by the Act. The return of the dishonoured bill to the drawer or to an indorser is sufficient notice. Specific rules as to giving notice are set out in the Act (s.49).

Protest: When necessary—Besides giving notice the holder of a bill which on **19.24** the face of it bears to be a foreign bill must, in order to preserve recourse against the drawer or prior indorsers, protest it in the case of either non-acceptance or non-payment.[97] Protest is not necessary in the case of an inland bill merely to preserve recourse,[98] but is necessary if it is desired to enforce the bill by summary diligence.[99]

---

[87] 1882 Act s.74(1).

[88] 1882 Act s.45(1).

[89] 1882 Act s.52(1); *McNeill v Innes Chambers & Co*, 1917 S.C. 540 (summary diligence).

[90] 1882 Act s.46(1); *Bank of Scotland v Lamont* (1889) 16 R. 769; cf. *Fiorentin Com Giuseppe Srl. Farnesi* [2005] EWHC 160.

[91] 1882 Act s.46(2). As to circumstances amounting to waiver, see *McTavish's Judicial Factor v Michael's Trs*, 1912 S.C. 425.

[92] 1882 Act s.45(3)–(8) and see para.19.13, above. For the application of these rules to modern banking practice, see *Barclays Bank v Bank of England* [1985] 1 All E.R. 385; A.G. Guest, *Chalmers & Guest on Bills of Exchange*, 17th edn (London: Sweet and Maxwell, 2009), para.1138.

[93] 1882 Act s.48. See *Lombard Banking v Central Garage and Engineering Co* [1963] 1 Q.B. 220.

[94] 1882 Act s.49, r.12.

[95] 1882 Act s.49, r.15; *Dunlop v Higgins* (1848) 6 Bell's App.195.

[96] *Eaglehill v J. Needham* [1973] A.C. 992.

[97] 1882 Act s.51(2).

[98] 1882 Act s.51(1).

[99] See para.19.26, below.

19.25 **Form of protest: Noting**—For the purpose of protest the bill must be noted by a notary public not later than the succeeding business day after it has been dishonoured.[100] Noting is effected by the notary public marking on the bill the date of dishonour, his initials and the letters "N.P.".[101] The protest may be subsequently extended as of the date of the noting.[102] It must contain a copy of the bill, must be signed by the notary making it and must specify the person at whose request the bill is protested, the place and date of protest, the cause or reason for protesting, the demand made and the answer given, or the fact that the drawee or acceptor could not be found.[103] If the bill has been lost or destroyed, or is wrongly detained from the person entitled to hold it, protest may be made on a copy or written particular thereof.[104] In a question of recourse protest is dispensed with by any circumstances which would dispense with notice of dishonour.[105]

Where the services of a notary public cannot be obtained at the place where the bill was dishonoured, any householder or substantial resident of the place may, in the presence of two witnesses, give a certificate, signed by the witnesses, attesting the dishonour of the bill, and the certificate shall in all respects operate as if it were a formal protest of the bill.[106] It is doubtful whether a householder's certificate will form a warrant for summary diligence.[107]

19.26 **Summary diligence**—Summary diligence is the method by which payment of a bill or promissory note may be enforced without the necessity of an action to constitute the debt. It has been held in the Outer House that it is incompetent on a dishonoured cheque.[108] The Bills of Exchange Act provides (s.98) that nothing in the Act or in any repeal effected thereby shall extend or restrict or in any way alter or affect the law and practice in Scotland on the subject. The statutes in force are the Bills of Exchange Act 1681, the Inland Bills Act 1696, and the Bills of Exchange (Scotland) Act 1772 ss.42 and 43. Summary diligence is competent when a bill (or note) is dishonoured either by non-acceptance or non-payment. In the latter case it is competent against any party to the bill, including the acceptor; in the former against any actual party to the bill, but not against the drawee who has refused acceptance. For summary diligence a regular protest is required, and therefore while presentment for payment is not necessary to render the acceptor liable, it is necessary, and must be regularly made, in order to justify summary diligence against him.[109] But the practice under which a period of six months is allowed for presentment to the acceptor, without prejudice to summary diligence against him, has been sustained.[110] The protest of the bill or note must be registered not more than six months after dishonour (by non-acceptance or non-payment as the case may be) in the Books of Council and Session or the books of

---

[100] 1882 Act s.51(4).
[101] *Encyclopaedia of Scottish Legal Styles* (1935), Vol.1, p.415.
[102] 1882 Act s.51(4).
[103] 1882 Act s.51(7); *Encyclopaedia of Scottish Legal Styles* (1935), Vol.1, pp.416–20.
[104] 1882 Act s.51(8).
[105] 1882 Act s.51(9).
[106] 1882 Act s.94. See *Sommerville v Aaronson* (1898) 25 R. 524.
[107] *Sommerville v Aaronson* (1898) 25 R. 524 at 525, per Lord Kyllachy (Ordinary); *Mcrobert v Lindsay* (1898) 14 (Sh. Ct) Rep.89; (1898) 5 S.L.T. 317.
[108] *Glickman v Linda*, 1950 S.C. 18, where the Lord Ordinary examines the history of summary diligence.
[109] *Neill v Dobson* (1902) 4 F. 625.
[110] *McNeill v Innes Chambers & Co*, 1917 S.C. 540.

a sheriff court to whose jurisdiction the party is subject.[111] The process cannot be used against a party who is not subject to the jurisdiction of the Scottish courts, even although the bill may be payable in Scotland.[112] When registered, an extract may be obtained, which is a warrant for arrestment, or for a charge for payment to be followed by poinding or by a petition for sequestration. The induciae of the charge are six days.[113]

When summary diligence competent—Summary diligence is competent only **19.27** for the amount of the bill or note, with interest. Damages or expenses must be recovered by action.[114] It is generally competent only when the liability of the party appears on the face of the bill without extrinsic proof,[115] and hence is not competent against a party who has signed the bill merely by initials,[116] or against an acceptor who has accepted conditionally,[117] or on a bill which has been cancelled by mistake.[118] But it was held competent against a firm carrying on business under a descriptive name, in the case where the bill was signed by all the partners.[119]

Bill as assignation[120]—The Act provides (s.53(2)): **19.28**

> "In Scotland, where the drawee of a bill (other than a cheque) has in his hands funds available for the payment thereof, the bill operates as an assignment of the sum for which it is drawn in favour of the holder, from the time when the bill is presented to the drawee."[121]

This rule applies, in the case of bills, where the bill has been presented for acceptance, and acceptance has been refused. The holder acquires a completed right to any funds in the hands of the drawee which are available to meet the bill, in a question either with the drawee himself, or with other parties having competing assignations.[122] As the principle is that presentment operates as intimation of the assignation of the debt due by the drawee to the drawer, it is no objection that it may have been irregular in form.[123] In the case of cheques, presentment for payment, though payment may be refused on the ground of insufficient funds to meet the cheque, no longer operates as a completed assignation of any balance there may be to the drawer's credit.[124]

---

[111] Bills of Exchange Act 1681.

[112] *Charteris v Clydesdale Bank* (1882) 19 S.L.R. 602; *Davis v Cadman* (1897) 24 R. 297.

[113] Bills of Exchange Act 1681; Graham Stewart, *A Treatise on the Law of Diligence* (Edinburgh: W. Green, 1898), p.313.

[114] Erskine, III, 2, 36.

[115] *Summers v Marianski* (1843) 6 D. 286.

[116] *Munro v Munro* (1820) Hume 81.

[117] Thomson and Wilson, *A Treatise on the Law of Bills of Exchange* (1865), p.223.

[118] *Dominion Bank v Bank of Scotland* (1889) 16 R. 1081; affd (1891) 18 R. (HL) 21.

[119] *Rosslund Cycle Co v McCreadie*, 1907 S.C. 1208.

[120] See D. Cusine, "The Cheque as an Assignation", 1977 Jur. Rev. 98. In England, the drawee of a bill has no liability until acceptance.

[121] For the position in relation to a cheque, see para.19.37, below.

[122] *Watt's Trs v Pinkney* (1853) 16 D. 279.

[123] *Watt's Trs v Pinkney* (1853) 16 D. 279 at 287, opinion of Lord Ivory.

[124] 1882 Act s.53(2), as amended by the Banking Act 2009 s.254(4).

19.29 Discharge of bill—A bill is discharged by payment in due course, when made by or behalf of the drawee or acceptor.[125] Payment in due course means payment at or after the maturity of the bill to the holder thereof in good faith and without notice that his title is defective.[126] In the case of an accommodation bill payment in due course by the person accommodated discharges the bill.[127] Payment by the drawer or by an indorser does not discharge the bill; it remains available as a document of debt against the acceptor or other antecedent party.[128] When the acceptor of a bill is or becomes the holder of it at or after its maturity, in his own right, the bill is discharged.[129] On the other hand, the mere fact that a party liable in a bill is in possession of it raises a presumption of payment, but does not necessarily discharge the bill.[130] So where a promissory note was given up, and a new one granted, it was held that the fact that the debtor was in possession of the original note did not infer abandonment of any claim for interest on it.[131] A bill may also be discharged by a renunciation at or after its maturity by the holder of his rights against the acceptor, or any other party to the bill.[132] The renunciation, unless the bill is given up to the party discharged, must be in writing, and is not effectual in a question with a holder in due course without notice.[133] A bill is discharged by its cancellation by the holder or his agent,[134] and the liability of any party on the bill is discharged by the intentional cancellation of his signature by the holder or his agent, this carrying with it the discharge of any indorser who would have had a right of recourse against the party whose signature is cancelled.[135] Cancellation which is unintentional, without the authority of the holder, or done under a mistake, is inoperative, but the onus of proof is laid upon the party founding on the cancelled bill.[136]

19.30 Alteration of bill—Where a bill or acceptance is materially altered without the assent of all parties liable on it, the bill is avoided,[137] except as against a party who has himself made, authorised or assented to the alteration, and subsequent indorsers, unless the alteration is not apparent, and the bill is in the hands of a holder in due course who may enforce payment of the bill according to its original tenor.[138] It is immaterial that the party founding on the alteration as involving avoidance has suffered no prejudice.[139] The drawee of a bill of exchange owes no duty to those into whose hands the bill may come to exercise any care in accepting

---

[125] 1882 Act s.59(1); *Coats v Union Bank*, 1929 S.C. (HL) 114. It has been held that proof of payment must be by writ or oath: *Nicol's Trs v Sutherland*, 1951 S.C. (HL) 21; but see now M. Ross and J. Chalmers, *Walker and Walker: The Law of Evidence in Scotland*, 3rd edn (Tottel, 2009), para.24.7.1; *Stair Memorial Encyclopaedia*, Vol.2, "Banking, etc." (Reissue), para.264.

[126] 1882 Act s.59(1).

[127] 1882 Act s.59(3).

[128] 1882 Act s.59(2) stating also certain qualifications.

[129] 1882 Act s.61; and see *Nash v De Freville* [1900] 2 Q.B. 72.

[130] Erskine, III, 4, 5.

[131] *Hope Johnstone v Cornwall* (1895) 22 R. 314.

[132] 1882 Act s.62(1).

[133] 1882 Act s.62(2).

[134] 1882 Act s.63(1).

[135] 1882 Act s.63(2).

[136] 1882 Act s.63(3). See *Dominion Bank v Anderson* (1888) 15 R. 408.

[137] The result is that the bill is worthless and no action of damages can be brought by a party who would otherwise have had contractual rights to do so: *Smith v Lloyds TSB Group Plc* [2000] 3 W.L.R. 1725, CA.

[138] 1882 Act s.64(1); *Slingsby v District Bank* [1932] 1 K.B. 544.

[139] *Koch v Dicks* [1933] 1 K.B. 307.

it, and therefore where a bill was accepted with a blank space which rendered it possible to alter the amount, and the amount was altered, it was held that the acceptor was not liable to a holder in due course for any more than the original sum in the bill.[140] But this rule does not apply in a case between banker and customer.[141]

Inchoate bills—The Act provides (s.20):　　　　　　　　　　　　　　　　**19.31**

> "Where a simple signature on a blank paper is delivered by the signer in order that it may be converted into a bill, it operates as a prima facie authority to fill it up as a complete bill for any amount using the signature for that of the drawer, or the acceptor, or an indorser; and in like manner, when a bill is wanting in any material particular, the person in possession of it has a prima facie authority to fill up the omission in any way he thinks fit."

Once the bill has been filled up and transferred, complete and regular on the face of it, to a holder in due course, it may be enforced by him according to its tenor,[142] although it has not been filled up according to the authority given, as where a larger sum than that agreed upon was inserted,[143] or after material delay, as where a blank acceptance was kept and filled up after the giver had become bankrupt and obtained a discharge.[144] In a question between the original parties it must be filled up "within a reasonable time, and strictly in accordance with the authority given".[145] Thus the party receiving the blank acceptance, at least if, as is usual, it was given for his accommodation, cannot fill it up after the giver has been sequestrated.[146] The onus of proof that the bill has not been filled up in accordance with the authority given rests on the party who signed and delivered it.[147] In the absence of any contract to the contrary there is implied authority to fill in the name of a third party as drawer,[148] or, in the case of a bill payable to the drawer's order, to the drawer to insert his own name as payee.[149] Where an acceptance addressed to A was found after his death still uncompleted, it was doubted whether his executor had any right to complete it as a bill of exchange, but held that he might sue upon it as a document of debt, which laid on the party who signed the onus of proof that it was not delivered as an acknowledgment of debt, or that the debt had afterwards been paid.[150]

Accommodation bills—According to Scots law the fact that no consideration has **19.32** been given for a bill, as where it was, for instance, a donation, is no objection to its enforcement, either by the drawer in a question with the acceptor, or by any holder.[151] Every party whose signature appears on a bill is prima facie deemed to

---

[140] *Scholfield v Londesborough* [1896] A.C. 514.
[141] See para.19.38, below.
[142] 1882 Act s.20(2).
[143] *Lloyds Bank v Cooke* [1907] 1 K.B. 794.
[144] *McMeekin v Russell* (1881) 8 R. 587.
[145] 1882 Act s.20(2).
[146] *McMeekin v Russell* (1881) 8 R. 587.
[147] *Anderson v Somerville* (1898) 1 F. 90.
[148] *Russell v Banknock Coal Co* (1897) 24 R. 1009.
[149] *Gerald McDonald & Co v Nash* [1924] A.C. 625.
[150] *Lawson's Exrs v Watson*, 1907 S.C. 1353.
[151] *Law v Humphrey* (1876) 3 R. 1192.

have become a party thereto for value.[152] If, however, it is admitted or proved that the true relations of the parties are not as they appear on the face of the bill, and that one or more of the parties have received no value for the liability they have incurred, the bill may be regarded as an accommodation bill, and differs in certain of its incidents from a bill granted for value. The normal case of an accommodation bill is where, as between themselves, the drawer is the true debtor, and the acceptor a party who has interposed as cautioner for him. The Act provides (s.28):

> "An accommodation party to a bill is a person who has signed a bill as drawer, acceptor or indorser, without receiving value therefor, and for the purpose of lending his name to some other person."[153]

In a question with any holder who has given value for the bill, an accommodation party is liable, and it is immaterial whether the holder did or did not know that the bill was an accommodation bill.[154] "Holder" in this case includes a transferee of the bill, who has taken it for value, but without indorsement.[155] But in questions between the original parties their rights are regulated by the true relations between them which may be proved by parole evidence.[156] So where several directors had indorsed a promissory note it was held, on proof that they had done so as guarantors for the company, that the general rule that a prior indorser was liable to a later indorser was displaced, and that the director who had been compelled to pay could recover a proportionate share from each of the others.[157] The holder of an accommodation bill, when the acceptor is the person lending his name and the claim is made against the drawer as the person accommodated, is not barred by failure to present the bill for payment,[158] failure to give notice of dishonour,[159] or failure to protest the bill for non-acceptance or non-payment.[160]

19.33 Accommodation bills in bankruptcy[161]—Where an accommodation bill is discounted and the parties are sequestrated the bank as holder may rank on each estate for the whole amount of the bill. As no debt can be ranked twice on the same estate, the trustee on the estate of the party who has lent his name cannot rank on the estate of the party accommodated for the dividend paid by the estate under his charge on the bill. Nor can he secure the same result by claiming a right of retention over property in his hands belonging to the estate of the party accommodated, in the case where that property was not expressly pledged, to meet the liability arising on the bill.[162] If it was so pledged, the rule in Scotland is that it may be applied to relieve the estate of the party who has lent his name for any dividend paid on the bill, and that any surplus is an asset in the estate of the party accommodated; the English rule is that property so pledged may be taken by the

---

[152] 1882 Act s.30(1).
[153] "Value" is defined by s.27.
[154] 1882 Act s.28(2).
[155] *Hood v Stewart* (1890) 17 R. 749.
[156] 1882 Act s.100.
[157] *Macdonald v Whitfield* (1883) L.R. 8 App. Cas. 733.
[158] 1882 Act s.46(2)(c).
[159] 1882 Act s.50(2)(c). The same applies to an indorser: s.50(2)(d).
[160] 1882 Act s.51(9).
[161] H. Goudy, *The Law of Bankruptcy in Scotland*, 4th edn (Edinburgh, 1914), pp.571–6.
[162] *Anderson v Mackinnon* (1876) 3 R. 608. See also *Mackinnon v Monkhouse* (1881) 9 R. 393.

holder of the bill, who deducts its value from the sum due on the bill, and ranks on the estates of the parties to it only for the balance.[163]

Forged bills—As a general rule no liability is incurred by a person whose name **19.34** is forged as a party to a bill, or used without his authority.[164] He cannot ratify but may adopt the bill, and will then be liable upon it.[165] Short of adoption he may be personally barred from disputing the validity of his signature if his conduct has caused loss to the holder.[166] But such cases are very exceptional; and mere failure to repudiate the bill at once will not infer liability.[167]

The Act provides (s.24):

"Subject to the provisions of this Act, where a signature on a bill is forged or placed thereon without the authority of the person whose signature it purports to be, the forged or unauthorised signature is wholly inoperative, and no right to retain the bill or to give a discharge therefor, or to enforce payment thereof against any party thereto can be acquired through or under that signature, unless the party against whom it is sought to retain or enforce payment of the bill is precluded from setting up the forgery for want of authority."

The provisions of the Act forming exceptions to this rule are: (1) the safeguards for a banker who pays a cheque on a forged indorsement[168]; (2) the right to treat the bill as payable to bearer when the payee is a fictitious or non-existent person[169]; (3) the rule that, in a question with a holder in due course, the acceptor is precluded from denying the genuineness of the signature of the drawer[170]; and an indorser from denying both the genuineness of the signature of the drawer or of prior indorsers[171] and, in a question with his immediate or a subsequent indorsee, that the bill was at the time of his indorsement a valid and subsisting bill, and that he had then a good title thereto.[172] Thus the acceptor of a bill, who pays on a forged indorsement, cannot charge the drawer, and a bank which pays on behalf of the acceptor cannot charge its customer.[173] A person who has unwittingly paid on a bill vitiated by forgery or after a material and unauthorised alteration may recover from the holder, unless by delay he had prejudiced the holder's right of recourse against other parties to the bill.[174]

Prescription—The five-year negative prescription applies to bills of exchange **19.35** and promissory notes, but not to bank notes. Prescription can be interrupted only by a relevant claim.[175]

---

[163] *Royal Bank v Saunders' Trs* (1882) 9 R. (HL) 67.
[164] 1882 Act s.24. Cf. *Strathmore Group Ltd v Credit Lyonnais*, 1994 S.L.T. 1023.
[165] *Mackenzie v British Linen Co* (1881) 8 R. (HL) 8.
[166] *Mackenzie v British Linen Co* (1881) 8 R. (HL) 8; *Greenwood v Martins Bank* [1933] A.C. 51.
[167] *Mackenzie v British Linen Co* (1881) 8 R. (HL) 8; *British Linen Co v Cowan* (1906) 8 F. 704.
[168] See now Cheques Act 1957 s.1; para.19.39, below.
[169] 1882 Act s.7(3); para.19.20, above.
[170] 1882 Act s.54(2)(a).
[171] 1882 Act s.55(2)(b).
[172] 1882 Act s.55(2)(c).
[173] *Bank of England v Vagliano* [1891] A.C. 107 at 131, per Lord Watson. See also *Duncan v American Express Services Europe Ltd*, 2009 S.L.T. 112.
[174] *Imperial Bank of Canada v Bank of Hamilton* [1903] A.C. 49.
[175] Prescription and Limitation (Scotland) Act 1973 s.6(1) and Sch.1 paras 1(e) and 2(b).

19.36 Evidence—The construction of s.100, which allows parole evidence of any facts relevant to any question of liability on a bill, has been already considered.[176]

19.37 Cheques[177]—The statutory definition of a cheque is: "A bill of exchange drawn on a banker payable on demand".[178] It is enacted that except where otherwise provided in Pt III of the Act the statutory provisions applicable to a bill of exchange payable on demand apply to a cheque. So the holder of a cheque, if in circumstances which satisfy the provisions of s.29,[179] has all the rights of the holder in due course of a bill of exchange.[180] The chief difference is that delay in presentment of a cheque does not give the drawer any remedy except in so far as he has suffered prejudice, which he can only do in the event of the bankruptcy of the banker.[181] In Scotland, since April 2009, presentation of the cheque is no longer an assignation of funds if there are funds available.[182]

19.38 Banks: Contract between banker and customer[183]—A banker undertakes to pay cheques drawn by his customer so long as he has funds in his hands and to take reasonable care in doing so.[184] He may determine the contract at any time by giving notice, but, provided that he has funds to meet them, must pay cheques drawn before the notice was received.[185] He is under no obligation to allow an overdraft, and no such obligation can be inferred for the future merely from the fact that the customer has been allowed to overdraw in the past.[186] Even where a banker holds a cash credit bond there is no obligation, in the absence of express agreement, to allow the customer to overdraw to the extent of the cash credit, though a refusal to honour a cheque without prior notice to the customer would probably be wrongful.[187] Where a customer keeps several accounts, for example a current and loan account, with a banker, the latter is not entitled, without notice, to mass the accounts together and to refuse to honour a cheque in respect of a debit balance thence arising.[188] But it has been held that where a customer had current accounts with two branches of a bank, the bank was entitled, without notice, to refuse to honour a cheque on the ground that, taking the two accounts together, the customer was overdrawn.[189] A bank is not bound to pay at a branch other than that where the account is kept.[190] Dishonour of a cheque, without adequate grounds, is a breach of contract, and one for which the customer has been found entitled to damages; but damages will usually be nominal unless the

---

[176] See para.6.16, above.
[177] W.A. Wilson, *The Scottish Law of Debt*, 2nd edn (Edinburgh: W. Green, 1991), Ch.6; Guest, *Chalmers & Guest on Bills of Exchange* (2009), Pt III; *First Sport Ltd v Barclays Bank Plc* [1993] 1 W.L.R. 1229.
[178] 1882 Act s.73; see Guest, *Chalmers & Guest on Bills of Exchange* (2009), para.1858.
[179] See para.19.04, above.
[180] *McLean v Clydesdale Bank* (1883) 11 R. (HL) 1.
[181] 1882 Act s.74(1).
[182] 1882 Act s.53(2), as amended by the Banking Act 2009 s.254(4).
[183] See Guest, *Chalmers & Guest on Bills of Exchange* (2009), para.1918.
[184] *Selangor United Rubber Estates Ltd v Cradock (No.3)* [1968] 1 W.L.R. 1555; *Lipkin Gorman v Karpnale Ltd* [1991] 2 A.C. 548. The duty is contractual: *National Bank of Greece v Pinios Co (No.1)* [1990] 1 A.C. 637, CA.
[185] *King v British Linen Co* (1899) 1 F. 928.
[186] *Ritchie v Clydesdale Bank* (1886) 13 R. 866.
[187] *Johnston v Commercial Bank* (1858) 20 D. 790.
[188] *Kirkwood v Clydesdale Bank*, 1908 S.C. 20 at 25.
[189] *Garnet v McKewan* (1872) L.R. 8 Ex. 10.
[190] *Clare v Dresdner Bank* [1915] 2 K.B. 576; *Richardson v Richardson* [1927] P. 228.

customer is a trader, whose credit may be injured,[191] or can show that he has sustained actual loss.[192] Entries in a bank pass-book or counterfoil are prima facie evidence of the receipt of that amount of money against a bank which disputes their accuracy, and the onus of displacing the presumption of accuracy lies upon the bank.[193]

The customer's duties to his banker are strictly limited. He owes a duty to take reasonable care in drawing cheques and, if he draws them in a manner which facilitates alteration and the banker pays an altered cheque in good faith and without negligence, he may debit the customer with the full amount he has paid.[194] The customer is also under a duty to disclose forgeries when he becomes aware of them, and he will be barred from raising the matter at a later stage if he remains silent and allows the banker to pay.[195] It is a condition of the contract between the bank and its customer regulating the use of a cheque card that the customer who draws a cheque in conjunction with a card cannot countermand it. In addition, the bank gives its customer authority within specified limits, by using the card, to bind the bank to pay the cheque, irrespective of the state of the customer's account. The bank thereby comes under an obligation to the payee, through the agency of its customer, not to dishonour the cheque.[196] A bank which issues travellers' cheques may be under a duty to refund the value of lost or stolen cheques.[197]

While debit cards are not themselves negotiable instruments, it appears that the same principles as apply to a bank's obligation to honour the cheques of its customers apply to instructions by customers to the bank to make electronic transfers.[198]

Indorsement—The object of the Cheques Act 1957 was to restrict the circum- **19.39** stances in which indorsement of cheques is required. To that end it is provided that when a cheque drawn on a banker is paid by the banker in good faith and in the ordinary course of business, he is deemed to have paid the cheque in due course, although there is no indorsement or the indorsement of the name of the payee is irregular,[199] for example where the initials of the indorsement do not match those of the payee. He may therefore charge his customer with the amount so paid, and incurs no liability by reason only of the absence of, or irregularity in, indorsement. Consequently the banker may in practice ignore indorsements. But the protection thus given to a banker does not apply where the cheque, before

---

[191] *King v British Linen Co* (1899) 1 F. 928.

[192] *Gibbons v Westminster Bank* [1939] 2 K.B. 882. These rules relate to dealings with a customer's current account. They may not be applicable where the dealings are with the type of deposit account on which cheques cannot be drawn: *Gibb v Lombank Scotland (No.2)*, 1962 S.L.T. 288.

[193] *Couper's Trs v National Bank* (1889) 16 R. 412; *Docherty v Royal Bank of Scotland*, 1963 S.L.T. (Notes) 43.

[194] *London Joint Stock Bank v Macmillan* [1918] A.C. 777; *Slingsby v District Bank* [1932] 1 K.B. 544; *Tai Hing Cotton Mill Ltd v Liu Chong Hing Bank* [1986] A.C. 80.

[195] *Greenwood v Martins Bank* [1933] A.C. 51; *Price Meats Ltd v Barclays Bank Plc* [2000] 2 All E.R. (Comm) 346.

[196] *R. v Charles* [1977] A.C. 177 at 182, per Lord Diplock; *Re Charge Card Services* [1987] Ch. 150 at 166, per Millett J. (point left open by the Court of Appeal [1989] Ch. 497); Guest, *Chalmers & Guest on Bills of Exchange* (2009), para.1935. On the position where a forged cheque is presented with a cheque card, see *First Sport Ltd v Barclays Bank Plc* [1993] 1 W.L.R. 1229.

[197] *El Awadi v B.C.C.I.* [1990] 1 Q.B. 606; Guest, *Chalmers & Guest on Bills of Exchange* (2009), para.1880.

[198] On cheques: *Barclays Bank Plc v W.J. Simms Son & Cooke (Southern) Ltd* [1980] Q.B. 677 at 699–700; on electronic transfers: *Lloyds Bank Plc v Independent Insurance Co Ltd* [2000] Q.B. 110 at 118, CA.

[199] Cheques Act 1957 s.1.

payment, has obviously been altered in a material particular,[200] nor where the cheque is crossed and the banker pays in disregard of the crossing.[201] In such circumstances the banker pays the cheque at his own risk. And the section applies only to the banker on whom the cheque is drawn, and does not protect any third party who may pay on a forged indorsement.[202]

To allow the collecting banker to sue on a cheque which has not been indorsed, it is provided that a banker who gives value for, or has a lien on, a cheque payable to order which the holder delivers to him for collection without indorsing it, has such (if any) rights as he would have had if, upon delivery, the holder had indorsed it in blank.[203] This is so even where the holder lodges the cheque for collection for an account other than his own.[204]

An unindorsed cheque which appears to have been paid by the banker on whom it is drawn is evidence of the receipt by the payee of the sum payable by the cheque.[205] The practical effect is that the payee is not now required to indorse the cheque when he lodges it with his bank for collection. As a matter of banking practice, an indorsee is required to indorse the cheque when he lodges it for collection. It is still, of course, necessary for the payee to indorse the cheque if he is negotiating it to a third party.

19.40 Determination of authority to pay—The 1882 Act provides (s.75) that the duty and authority of a banker to pay a cheque drawn on him are determined by countermand of payment and notice of his customer's death. Since April 2009, on notice of the customer's death, it is no longer the case that the cheque (if duly presented) will operate as an assignation in favour of the payee of any funds in the banker's hands available to meet the cheque.[206] Countermand of payment does not affect the liability of the drawer to any indorsee of the cheque who is in the position of a holder in due course, for instance, to the bank to whom the payee may have paid the cheque.[207] The authority of a banker to pay a cheque is terminated by the vesting of the customer's estate in a permanent trustee in sequestration,[208] but if the banker proves that, when he paid the cheque in the ordinary course of business, he was unaware of the sequestration and had no reason to believe that the customer's estate had been sequestrated or was the subject of sequestration proceedings, the payment will be valid.[209] The banker's authority to pay is also determined by the liquidation of a customer company,[210] by the appointment of a curator bonis on a customer's estate,[211] or by arrestment.[212] A banker is under no obligation to inquire into the motives of the payee in taking payment.[213]

---

[200] *Slingsby v District Bank* [1932] 1 K.B. 544.

[201] *Smith v Union Bank* (1875) L.R. 1 Q.B.D. 31.

[202] *Ogden v Benas* (1874) L.R. 9 C.P. 513; but for statutory protection of collecting banker, see para.19.43, below.

[203] Cheques Act 1957 s.2; see *Midland Bank v R.V. Harris Ltd* [1963] 1 W.L.R. 1021.

[204] *Westminster Bank v Zang* [1966] A.C. 182.

[205] Cheques Act 1957 s.3, see as to the effect of this, *Westminster Bank v Zang* [1966] A.C. 182.

[206] 1882 Act s.53(2), as amended by the Banking Act 2009 s.254(4); and see para.19.28, above.

[207] *McLean v Clydesdale Bank* (1883) 11 R. (HL) 1.

[208] Bankruptcy (Scotland) Act 1985 s.32(8).

[209] Bankruptcy (Scotland) Act 1985 s.32(9).

[210] Insolvency Act 1986 s.127; cf. *Re Gray's Inn Construction Co Ltd* [1980] 1 W.L.R. 711 for validation.

[211] *Mitchell & Baxter v Cheyne* (1891) 19 R. 324.

[212] D.B. Caskie, *Wallace and McNeil's Banking Law*, 10th edn (Edinburgh: W. Green, 1991), pp.210–11.

[213] *Dickson v National Bank of Scotland*, 1917 S.C. (HL) 50.

Crossed cheques—A cheque is crossed generally when it bears across its face **19.41** two parallel lines, with or without the words "& Co", and with or without the words "not negotiable". It is crossed specially, and to the banker named, when it bears across its face the name of a banker, with or without the words "not negotiable".[214] A cheque may be crossed by the drawer, or by any holder. Where a cheque is crossed generally the holder may cross it specially, and may add the words "not negotiable". Where a cheque is crossed specially the banker to whom it is crossed may again cross it specially to another banker for collection. Where an uncrossed cheque, or a cheque crossed generally, is sent to a banker for collection, he may cross it specially to himself.[215] Except in these respects it is not lawful for any person to add to, or alter the crossing. The crossing is a material part of the cheque, and any unauthorised alteration avoids it.[216] But when the obliteration or alteration of the crossing is not apparent on the face of the cheque a banker who pays in good faith and without negligence may charge his customer with the amount so paid.[217]

Effect of crossing—The effect of a general crossing is that if the banker on whom **19.42** it is drawn pays to anyone except a banker he is liable to the customer for any loss sustained owing to the cheque being so paid; of a special crossing, that the same liability is incurred by payment to anyone except the banker to whom the cheque is crossed, or his agent for collection being a banker.[218] If it is paid in good faith and without negligence in accordance with the crossing, the banker is placed in the same position and has the same rights as if payment had been made to the true owner of the cheque, i.e. the banker may debit his customer although the cheque has been stolen or paid on a forged indorsement.[219]

Protection of collecting bank[220]—The obligation of a collecting bank, when a **19.43** cheque is lodged, is simply to present it for payment to the paying bank.[221] Section 4 of the Cheques Act 1957 extended to a banker collecting on uncrossed cheques and other instruments the protection which was formerly provided by s.82 of the 1882 Act to a banker collecting upon a crossed cheque. Where in good faith and without negligence he receives payment for a customer of a cheque,[222] bank draft, customer's payment order or certain other instruments[223] or, having credited a customer's account with the amount of such an instrument, receives payment thereof for himself, and the customer has no title or a defective title thereto, the banker will not incur any liability to the true owner by reason only of having received such payment.[224] To render a person a "customer" within the meaning of the section he must have had some form of account with the bank before the

---

[214] 1882 Act s.76(2).
[215] 1882 Act s.77(6).
[216] 1882 Act s.78, see as to alteration of a material part, para.19.30, above.
[217] 1882 Act s.79(2).
[218] 1882 Act s.79(2).
[219] 1882 Act s.80. The section does not apply to the case where a cheque has been materially altered (*Slingsby v District Bank* [1932] 1 K.B. 544) but does apply to a cheque which is not transferable under s.81A or otherwise: Cheques Act 1992 s.2.
[220] For a description of the process of collection and presentation of cheques, see *Barclay's Bank v Bank of England* [1985] 1 All E.R. 385. See also ss.74–74C of the Act.
[221] *McLaughlin v Allied Irish Bank Plc*, 2001 S.L.T. 403.
[222] Including a cheque which is not transferable under s.81A or otherwise: Cheques Act 1992 s.3.
[223] See Cheques Act 1957 s.4(2).
[224] Cheques Act 1957 s.4(1).

cheque in question was presented; it is not enough that the bank had on previous occasions cashed cheques for him.[225] A banker is not to be treated as having been negligent[226] for this purpose by reason only of his failure to concern himself with the absence of or irregularity in indorsement of the instrument[227]; but the onus is on the banker to show that he acted in good faith and without negligence.[228] In a decision of the Sheriff Court, it has been decided that s.4 of the Cheques Act is of no relevance to Scots law, since it is designed to provide collecting bankers with relief from liability in respect of the English law tort of conversion, which is a concept unknown to Scots law.[229]

19.44 **Cheques marked "not negotiable"**—When a cheque bears on it the words "not negotiable" it does not mean that the cheque cannot be transferred but that the transferee gets no better title than his author had, and no better title can be obtained by an indorsee from him.[230] It is probably the law that no other words on a cheque can make it not negotiable.[231]

19.45 **Non-transferable cheques**—Where a cheque is crossed "account payee" or "a/c payee", whether or not with the word "only", the cheque is not transferable, and is only valid as between the parties to it. The payee therefore remains the owner in spite of any attempt to transfer title to the cheque.[232] A banker is not negligent by reason only of failing to concern himself with a purported indorsement of a cheque which is non-transferable.[233] If satisfied that the indorsement is authentic, the bank can therefore act upon it.

19.46 **Certified cheques**—When a bank certifies a cheque it undertakes that the customer has funds to meet it, and therefore will be liable on his failure.[234] Where, after certification, the cheque was fraudulently altered in amount, and, as altered, was paid to the holder by the certifying bank, it was held that the bank was entitled to recover from the holder.[235]

19.47 **Cheque guarantee cards and debit cards**—Plastic cards of various descriptions have become a familiar means of performing financial transactions. There are many different varieties of card, most of which now perform more than one function. A full description of the range of available cards is beyond the scope of this chapter and reference should be made to works on banking practice and credit

---

[225] *Great Western Ry v London and County Bank* [1901] A.C. 414; *Taxation Commissioners v English, Scottish and Australian Bank* [1920] A.C. 683; *Woods v Martins Bank* [1959] 1 Q.B. 55.

[226] As to facts amounting to negligence, see *A Underwood Ltd v Bank of Liverpool* [1924] 1 K.B. 775; *Midland Bank v Reckitt* [1933] A.C. 1; *Marfani & Co v Midland Bank* [1968] 1 W.L.R. 956; *Lumsden & Co v London Trustee Savings Bank* [1971] 1 Lloyd's Rep.114. Negligence is not necessarily excluded by proof that an established banking practice has been followed: *Lloyds Bank v Savory* [1932] 2 K.B. 122, affd [1933] A.C. 201.

[227] 1882 Act s.4(3). For contributory negligence, see Banking Act 1979 s.47.

[228] *Lloyds Bank v Savory* [1933] A.C. 201 at 229, per Lord Wright; *Marfani & Co v Midland Bank* [1968] 1 W.L.R. 956.

[229] *Nimmo v Armour*, 2005 Scot (D) 18/4.

[230] 1882 Act s.81; *Ladup Ltd v Shaikh* [1983] Q.B. 225.

[231] *Glen v Semple* (1901) 3 F. 1134 (against cheque); *Importers Co v Westminster Bank* [1927] 2 K.B. 297.

[232] 1882 Act s.81A(1), inserted by the Cheques Act 1992 s.1.

[233] 1882 Act s.81A(2).

[234] *Gaden v Newfoundland Savings Bank* [1899] A.C. 281.

[235] *Imperial Bank of Canada v Bank of Hamilton* [1903] A.C. 49.

control. Two card functions are, however, directly relevant to bills and cheques. A cheque guarantee card issued by a bank or building society guarantees a payment by cheque up to the amount specified on the card. If used in accordance with the conditions of issue, the cheque will be honoured even if the account on which it is drawn has insufficient funds. The bank's obligation to pay comes into force when the card is used, so that the payment cannot be countermanded.[236] Debit cards function like cheques, although not subject to the Act, by debiting a bank account through the system known as electronic funds transfer at point of sale.

Promissory notes[237]—Promissory notes are dealt with by ss.83–89 of the Act. **19.48** The statutory definition is (s.83(1)):

> "A promissory note is an unconditional promise in writing made by one person to another signed by the maker, engaging to pay, on demand, or at a fixed or determinable future time, a sum certain in money to, or to the order of, a specified person or to bearer."

It is inchoate and incomplete until delivered to the payee or bearer.[238] The section provides that an instrument payable to maker's order is not a note within the section until it has been indorsed by the maker,[239] and that a note is not invalid merely because it contains a pledge of collateral security with a power to dispose thereof.[240] An instrument may be a promissory note though the words "agree to pay", and not "promise to pay", are used,[241] but not if it reserves an option to pay at an earlier date than the fixed date and so creates an uncertainty or contingency as to the time of payment.[242] A document which contained, in addition to a promise to pay, further and separate contractual stipulations was held not to be a promissory note.[243] In questions of stamp law it has been held that documents expressed as an obligation to pay a debt of unspecified amount,[244] or as a written obligation of indebtedness,[245] or as a mere receipt,[246] or as a promise to pay a certain sum with interest at an unspecified rate,[247] were not promissory notes. A mere obligation to pay, not addressed to anyone, and not bearing to be payable to bearer, was held not to be a promissory note, and to be invalid as a "blank bond" under the Blank Bonds and Trusts Act 1695.[248] It is no objection to the validity of a note that it contains provisions safeguarding the holder in the event of time being given to one or other of the joint makers.[249]

---

[236] *R. v Charles* [1977] A.C. 177; *First Sport Ltd v Barclays Bank Plc* [1993] 3 All E.R. 789; *R. v Lambie* [1982] A.C. 449. Cf. para.19.38, above.

[237] See J.J. Gow, *The Mercantile and Industrial Law of Scotland* (Edinburgh: W. Green, 1964), pp.455–6; Wilson, *The Scottish Law of Debt* (1991), pp.75–77.

[238] 1882 Act s.84.

[239] 1882 Act s.83(2).

[240] 1882 Act s.83(3).

[241] *Macfarlane v Johnston* (1864) 2 M. 1210; *Vallance v Forbes* (1879) 6 R. 1099; *McTaggart v MacEachern's J.F.,* 1949 S.C. 503.

[242] *Williamson v Rider* [1963] 1 Q.B. 89; *Claydon v Bradley* [1987] 1 W.L.R. 521.

[243] *Dickie v Singh*, 1974 S.L.T. 129.

[244] *Henderson v Dawson* (1895) 22 R. 895.

[245] *Todd v Wood* (1897) 24 R. 1104.

[246] *Welsh's Trs v Forbes* (1885) 12 R. 851.

[247] *Lamberton v Aiken* (1899) 2 F. 189.

[248] Blank Bonds and Trusts Act 1695 (c.25). See also *Duncan's Trs v Shand* (1872) 10 M. 984.

[249] *Kirkwood v Carroll* [1903] 1 K.B. 531.

The provisions of the Act as to bills apply also to promissory notes.[250] In applying them the maker of a note corresponds with the acceptor of a bill, the first indorser with the drawer of an accepted bill payable to drawer's order.[251] The provisions relating to: (a) presentment for acceptance; (b) acceptance; (c) acceptance supra protest; and (d) bills in a set do not apply to promissory notes.[252] A further difference is that where a foreign note is dishonoured protest is unnecessary.[253]

Presentment for payment is necessary in order to make an indorser liable,[254] but is not necessary in order to make the maker liable, unless it is in the body of it made payable at a particular place.[255] It must then be presented at that place, but not necessarily at the date of payment of the principal sum or of any instalment.[256] If a note payable on demand is not presented for payment within a reasonable time of indorsement the indorser is discharged.[257] But it is not deemed to be overdue, so as to affect a holder with defects of title of which he had no notice, because it appears that a reasonable time for presenting it for payment had elapsed.[258]

The maker of a note, by making and delivering it, engages that he will pay it according to its tenor, and is precluded from denying to a holder in due course the existence of the payee and his then capacity to indorse.[259]

FURTHER READING

Bell, *Commentaries*, I, 411.

Caskie, D.B., *Wallace and McNeil's Banking Law*, 10th edn (Edinburgh: W. Green, 1991).

Crerar, L.D., *The Law of Banking in Scotland*, 2nd edn (Edinburgh: Tottel, 2007).

Davidson, F. and Macgregor, L., *Commercial Law in Scotland*, 2nd edn (Edinburgh: W. Green, 2008), Ch.5.

Elliot, N., *Byles on Bills of Exchange and Cheques*, 26th edn (London: Sweet and Maxwell, 1988).

Goode, R., *Goode on Commercial Law*, 4th edn (Penguin, 2010), Ch.17.

Grier, N., *Banking Law in Scotland* (Edinburgh: W. Green, 2001).

Guest, A.G., *Chalmers and Guest on Bills of Exchange*, 17th edn (London: Sweet and Maxwell, 2009).

Hamilton, A.M., *A Commentary on the Bills of Exchange Act 1882* (1904).

Holden, J.M., *History of Negotiable Instruments in English Law* (London: The Athlone Press, 1955).

Maher, G. and Cusine, D., *The Law and Practice of Diligence* (Butterworths, 1990).

Stair Memorial Encyclopaedia, Vol.2, "Banking and Commercial Paper" (Reissue).

Wilson, W.A., *The Scottish Law of Debt*, 2nd edn (Edinburgh: W. Green, 1991), Ch.5.

---

[250] 1882 Act s.89(1).
[251] 1882 Act s.89(2).
[252] 1882 Act s.89(3).
[253] 1882 Act s.89(4).
[254] 1882 Act s.87(2).
[255] 1882 Act s.87(1).
[256] 1882 Act s.87(1); *Gordon v Kerr* (1898) 25 R. 570.
[257] 1882 Act s.86(1).
[258] 1882 Act s.86(3).
[259] 1882 Act s.88. As to delivery, see s.84.

CHAPTER 20

INSURANCE

Nature of contract—It is difficult to give a precise definition of a contract of **20.01** insurance: a useful practical statement is that it is a contract by which one party (the insurer, or in marine insurance the underwriter) undertakes in return for a money consideration (the premium) to pay the other party (the insured) a sum of money or provide a corresponding benefit on the occurrence of one or more specified events which are adverse to the insured and involve an element of uncertainty as to (a) whether they will happen or not or (b) the time at which they will happen.[1] It may therefore be a contract to indemnify against possible loss or to make payment on the occurrence of a certain event.[2] The contract need not necessarily provide for payment of a sum of money so long as it confers a benefit equivalent to payment, i.e. money's worth.[3] The continued existence or safety of anything, or the occurrence or non-occurrence of any event, may be made the subject of a policy of insurance, and there has been no case where, apart from questions of insurable interest, a policy has been held void as in substance a bet or *sponsio ludicra*.[4] The main distinction between contracts classed under the general name of insurance is between those cases where the contract is one of indemnity, under which the insured recovers and can only recover, the amount of his loss, except in the case of valued policy,[5] and those which are merely contracts to pay on a certain condition being fulfilled. In the former class are fire and marine and third party accident insurance, in the latter, whole-life and endowment insurance.[6] In the case of indemnity insurance, where the insurer is liable to indemnify the insured, the payment of the insured's claim made under the policy is classified as a contractual obligation to pay a sum of money equivalent to the insured's loss, rather than an obligation to pay damages for breach of contract or

---

[1] *Prudential Insurance Co v IRC* [1904] 2 K.B. 658, per Channell J.; *Department of Trade and Industry v St Christopher Motorists' Association* [1974] 1 W.L.R. 99; *Medical Defence Union Ltd v Department of Trade* [1980] Ch. 82.

[2] Insurance contracts are unaffected by the Unfair Contract Terms Act 1977: 1977 Act s.15(3)(a). However, contracts of insurance taken out by a consumer are subject to the Unfair Terms in Consumer Contracts Regulations 1999 (SI 1999/2083).

[3] *Department of Trade and Industry v St Christopher Motorists' Association* [1974] 1 W.L.R. 99; *Re Sentinel Securities Plc* [1996] 1 W.L.R. 316. Cf. *Medical Defence Union Ltd v Department of Trade* [1980] Ch. 82.

[4] See *Carlill v Carbolic Smoke Ball Co* [1893] 1 Q.B. 256; *Re London County, etc Re-insurance Co* [1922] 2 Ch. 67. However, public policy may render a contract unenforceable: *Gray v Barr* [1971] 2 Q.B. 554.

[5] See paras 20.25, 20.43, below.

[6] Almost any contingency can be insured against, and new forms of insurance, too many to describe in this chapter, are constantly being devised: for example, products liability, legal expenses and contractor's risk insurance: see N. Legh-Jones, J. Birds, D. Owen, *Macgillivray on Insurance Law*, 11th edn (London: Sweet and Maxwell, 2008), Chs 31 and 32. All are, however, subject to the same general principles.

otherwise.[7] Marine insurance law, which has many specialities, has been codified by the Marine Insurance Act 1906. Before dealing with particular forms it may be well to consider certain principles which are generally applicable.

20.02 Regulation of insurance companies—The right to act as insurer, in various forms of insurance, including life, fire and accident, motor vehicle, marine, aviation and transit, is limited by legislation. The relevant statutory provisions are now found in the Financial Services and Markets Act 2000 ("FSMA").[8] Regulation is under the control of the Financial Services Authority ("FSA"), which operates under the supervision of the Treasury. The statute prohibits the carrying on of insurance business without prior authorisation: for the purposes of the Act, insurance business is divided into a number of classes, and separate authorisation is required for each class.[9] Many of the detailed rules governing the conduct of insurance business are found in the FSA Handbook.[10] The handbook prescribes specific requirements as to the fitness of persons to conduct insurance business. These deal with honesty, integrity and reputation: competence; and financial soundness. There are also extensive requirements as to the conduct of insurance business. Many are directed to securing proper accounting, but they also include matters such as product disclosure and the role of intermediaries. The FSA has powers of investigation and intervention. In addition, an ombudsman scheme for handling complaints has been established under the 2000 Act.

20.03 Formation of contract—A policy of insurance need not be in writing[11] unless specifically required by statute,[12] but policies of insurance are almost invariably written documents. An indemnity policy is, however, often preceded by a temporary contract of insurance which may or may not be in writing. A written contract for a specified, limited period, during which the applicant is insured while the company decides whether it will take the risk, is called a "cover note". This forms a binding contract and the company will be liable even although the risk is ultimately declined.[13] In the ordinary practice of marine insurance the policy is preceded by a document known as a slip, by which the underwriters indicate that they accept the risk and settle the amount which each will contribute on a loss. At one time the view taken was that a marine slip was not a contract.[14] This may no longer be the case.[15] Where a formal policy is not required a slip can be converted into a policy by affixing a suitably worded "Slip Policy".

---

[7] *Scott Lithgow Ltd v Secretary of State for Defence*, 1989 S.C. (HL) 9; *Strachan v Scottish Boatowners' Mutual Insurance Association*, 2010 S.C. 367.

[8] Superseding the Insurance Companies Act 1982 and earlier legislation.

[9] Financial Services and Markets Act 2000 ("FSMA") s.19: for the effect of contracts with unauthorised persons, see ss.26–28.

[10] This is frequently amended: the most up-to-date version can be found at *http://www.fsa.gov.uk/pages/handbook* [Accessed August 3, 2012].

[11] Requirements of Writing (Scotland) Act 1995 ss.1 and 11(3).

[12] Marine Insurance Act 1906 (the "1906 Act") s.22.

[13] *Neil v S.E. Lancashire Insurance Co*, 1932 S.C. 35; *Cunningham v Anglian Insurance Co*, 1934 S.L.T. 273.

[14] *Clyde Marine Insurance Co v Renwick*, 1924 S.C. 113.

[15] *Bhugwandass v Netherlands India Sea & Fire Insurance Co of Batavia* (1889) L.R. 14 App. Cas. 83; Finance Act 1959 ss.30(6), 37(5). Note also *Home Marine Insurance Co v Smith* [1898] 2 Q.B. 351. G. Gilman, *Arnould's Law of Marine Insurance*, 17th edn (London: Sweet and Maxwell, 2010), para.48 concludes that a slip containing the "statutory particulars" is a marine policy under the Marine Insurance Act 1906.

Insurable interest generally[16]—Both at common law and by statute, such as the **20.04**
Life Assurance Act 1774 and the Marine Insurance Act 1906, possession of an
insurable interest is a prerequisite of a valid contract of insurance: a contract
without such an interest is void.[17] The question what amounts to an insurable
interest depends upon the particular form of insurance involved.[18] The Life
Assurance Act 1774 applies not only to life insurance but also to non-marine
indemnity contracts other than ones relating to "goods or merchandises".[19] In
England it was at one time held that the 1774 Act applied to buildings insurance or
liability insurance, but this view has been disapproved.[20] A person is presumed to
have an insurable interest in his own life[21] and spouses are presumed to have
insurable interests in each others' lives.[22] The same rule now seems to apply to
civil partners.[23] Apart from the case of husband and wife, family relationship does
not in itself constitute an insurable interest: there must be some element of financial interest, such as an obligation of support.[24] Beyond the family, a pecuniary
interest may support the existence of an insurable interest in the life of another
person. Thus, a creditor may have an insurable interest in the life of his debtor: a
cautioner in that of the principal debtor: and an employer in that of an employee.[25]
As regards property insurance, since the owner of heritable property manifestly
has an insurable interest therein, the applicability or otherwise of the Act is not
unduly problematic. Mere possession of property, heritable or moveable, probably
does not give rise to an insurable interest but where the possessor has a right to
enjoyment of the property in some way or may come under a liability or suffer a
loss if it is damaged, there is an insurable interest.[26] If an insurer honours a claim
under a policy, otherwise void for lack of interest, the court will entertain an action
to decide who is entitled to the proceeds.[27] A tenant has an insurable interest in the

---

[16] For a comprehensive overview of the law of insurable interest, including the law reforms
proposed by the Scottish Law Commission and the Law Commission, see Ch.3 of the Joint Consultation
Paper of the Law Commission and Scottish Law Commission, *Insurance Contract Law: Post Contract
Duties and Other Issues* (HMSO, 2012), Law Com. Consultation Paper No.201 and Scot. Law Com.
Discussion Paper No.152.

[17] Life Assurance Act 1774 s.1; Marine Insurance Act 1906 ss.4(2)(a) and 5(2); Bell, *Principles*,
ss.457, 520: for a discussion of the development of the rule requiring interest from rules against
wagering policies, see H. Bennet, *Marine Insurance*, 2nd edn (Oxford: Oxford University Press,
2006), para.3.20.

[18] *Glengate KG Properties v Norwich Union Fire Insurance Society Ltd* [1996] 1 Lloyd's Rep. 614;
Feasey v Sun Life Assurance of Canada [2003] 2 All E.R. (Comm) 587.

[19] Life Assurance Act 1774 s.4.

[20] *Mark Rowlands Ltd v Berni Inns Ltd* [1986] Q.B. 211; [1985] 3 All E.R. 473; disapproved in *Siu
Yin Kwan v Eastern Insurance Co Ltd* [1994] 2 A.C. 199, on which, see the discussion in J. Birds,
Birds' Modern Insurance Law, 8th edn (London: Sweet and Maxwell, 2010), para.3.9.1.

[21] In English law, *Wainewright v Bland* (1835) 1 Mood. & R. 481.

[22] *Wight v Brown* (1845) 11 D. 459; *Champion v Duncan* (1867) 6 M. 17.

[23] Civil Partnerships Act 2004 s.253; *Murphy v Murphy* [2004] Lloyd's Rep. I.R. 744 at 751.

[24] Legh-Jones, Birds and Owen, *MacGillivray on Insurance Law* (2008), paras 1–092ff; cf. Family
Law (Scotland) Act 1985 s.1(3).

[25] *Lindsay v Barmcotte* (1851) 13 D. 718; *Simcock v Scottish Imperial Insurance Co Ltd* (1902) 10
S.L.T. 286; *White v Cotton* (1846) 8 D. 872; *Turnbull & Co v Scottish Provident Institution* (1896) 34
S.L.R. 146; see also *Feasey v Sun Life Assurance Co of Canada* [2003] 2 All E.R. (Comm) 587.

[26] *Macaura v Northern Assurance Co Ltd* [1925] A.C. 619; *Aberdeen Harbour Board v Heating
Enterprises (Aberdeen) Ltd*, 1990 S.L.T. 416.

[27] *Hadden v Bryden* (1899) 1 F. 710; *Carmichael v Carmichael's Exrx*, 1919 S.C. 636. The position
under English law is less clear. *Gedge v Royal Exchange Insurance Corp* [1900] 2 Q.B. 214 indicates
that an insurer cannot ignore an illegality and waive the requirement of interest; cf. *Attorney General
v Murray* [1904] 1 K.B. 165.

subjects leased.[28] If the lease stipulates that the tenant is obliged either to insure the subjects against damage or destruction or to rebuild them if destroyed, he has an interest in their full value. If his obligation is merely to maintain and repair premises let, he does not have an insurable interest in their full value.[29] A tenant does not have an insurable interest in a part of a building not occupied by him under the lease.[30] A security holder has an interest at least to the extent of the debt secured.[31] Property owned by a company or partnership and held in its name does not confer an insurable interest on a shareholder or partner.[32] Creditors do not have an insurable interest in a debtor's property.[33] A carrier or custodier of goods, who will be liable for their loss or destruction, has an insurable interest.[34] A main contractor and sub-contractors may have insurable interests in the contract works.[35] If A, without B's authority, and with no insurable interest, insures B's property against fire, and the insurance company pay on a loss without objection, it would appear that B has no claim to the money.[36] The return of the premiums paid may be claimed if the insurance was induced by the fraudulent representations of the insurance agent,[37] but not merely because the insured was unaware of the law.[38]

20.05 Duty of disclosure[39]—All forms of insurance are uberrimae fidei, in which each party is bound to reveal all material facts known to him. Failure in this respect, a fortiori any misrepresentation in any material point, whether fraudulent or not, renders the policy voidable.[40] Though most cases have related to concealment by

---

[28] *Mark Rowlands Ltd v Berni Inns Ltd* [1986] Q.B. 211.

[29] *Fehilly v General Accident Fire and Life Assurance Corp*, 1982 S.C. 163.

[30] *Aberdeen Harbour Board v Heating Enterprises (Aberdeen) Ltd*, 1990 S.L.T. 416.

[31] *Westminster Fire Office v Glasgow Provident Investment Society* (1888) L.R. 13 App. Cas. 699.

[32] *Macaura v Northern Assurance Co* [1925] A.C. 619; *Arif v Excess Insurance Group Ltd*, 1987 S.L.T. 473; *Mitchell v Scottish Eagle Insurance Co Ltd*, 1997 S.L.T. 793; *Cowan v Jeffrey Associates*, 1998 S.C. 496.

[33] *Macaura v Northern Assurance Co* [1925] A.C. 619.

[34] *Dalgleish v John Buchanan & Co* (1854) 16 D. 332.

[35] *Petrofina (UK) Ltd v Magnaload Ltd* [1984] 1 Q.B. 127; *Deepak Fertilisers and Petrochemicals Ltd v Davy McKee (London) Ltd* [1999] 1 All E.R. (Comm) 69: but see also *Ramco v International Insurance Co of Hannover* [2004] 2 All E.R. (Comm) 847; Legh-Jones, Birds and Owen, *Macgillivray on Insurance Law* (2008), paras 1–161ff. For recovery of over-payments, see *Scottish Equitable Plc v Derby* [2001] EWCA 369; [2001] 3 All E.R. 818.

[36] *Ferguson v Aberdeen P.C.*, 1916 S.C. 715.

[37] *Hughes v Liverpool Victoria Legal Friendly Society* [1916] 2 K.B. 482. However, the insured may be able to recover under the law of unjustified enrichment the premiums paid under the void contract erroneously thought to be valid.

[38] *Harse v Pearl Life Co* [1904] 1 K.B. 558; see also *Re London, etc. Reinsurance Co* [1922] 2 Ch.67; *Came v City of Glasgow Friendly Society*, 1933 S.C. 69, a decision under the Industrial Assurance Act 1923, which provides expressly for repayment of premiums.

[39] See Chs 1 and 3 of the Joint Consultation Paper of the Law Commission and Scottish Law Commission, *Insurance Contract Law: The Business Insured's Duty of Disclosure and the Law of Warranties* (HMSO, 2012), Law Com. Consultation Paper No.204 and Scot. Law Com. Discussion Paper No.155 for a comprehensive overview of the law of disclosure, including the law reforms proposed by the Scottish Law Commission and the Law Commission. The duty of disclosure normally relates to the formation or renewal of the contract: as to whether there is any continuing duty of disclosure, see *Manifest Shipping Co Ltd v Uni-Polaris Shipping Co Ltd (The Star Sea)* [2001] UKHL 1; *K/S Merc-Scandia v Lloyds' Underwriters* [2001] Lloyd's Rep. I.R. 802; *Agapitos v Agnew* [2002] EWHC 1558; *Axa General Insurance Ltd v Gottlieb* [2005] 1 All E.R. (Comm) 445; *Eagle Star Insurance Co v Games Video Co* [2004] 1 All E.R. (Comm) 560.

[40] Bell, *Principles*, ss.474, 522; Bell, *Commentaries*, i, 665; *Craig v Imperial Union Accident Assurance Co* (1894) 1 S.L.T. 646; *Highlands Insurance Co v Continental Insurance Co* [1987] 1 Lloyd's Rep.109; *The Dora* [1989] 1 Lloyd's Rep.69. See P. Macdonald Eggers, S. Picken and P. Foss, *Good Faith and Insurance Contracts*, 3rd edn (Informa, 2010).

the insured, the same rules apply to the insurer.[41] The question has been raised whether the principle of good faith places any limit on the insurer's right to declare a policy void for non-disclosure: so far, the answer appears to be in the negative.[42] At present, under English law, the materiality of an undisclosed fact in both life and indemnity insurance is defined by reference to the reaction of a reasonable and prudent insurer to the non-disclosure.[43] It has been decided that the insurer must show that a prudent underwriter would have taken the fact into account when assessing the risk and that the actual underwriter was induced by the non-disclosure to enter into the contract.[44] In Scotland it has been held that in life[45] and health[46] insurance, the test is that of the reasonable insured. In indemnity contracts, it has been decided by a court of authority that the appropriate test is that of the reasonable insurer.[47] So, while the tests of materiality adopted by both jurisdictions coincide in relation to indemnity contracts, they diverge in relation to life contracts. The reasonable insurer test is applied to marine contracts made in England or Scotland.[48] Circumstances may make any fact material, so though the name of the party having interest in a ship is not usually material, when the party having the main interest was a Greek, and ships belonging to Greeks were at the time uninsurable, it was held that concealment of his identity was sufficient to render a policy voidable.[49] However, in any case in which the identity, race or other characteristics of a party might be treated as material, regard must now be had to the Equality Act 2010 which prohibits discrimination because of an insured's sex, sexual orientation, age, disability, gender reassignment, marital status, pregnancy/maternity, race, religion or belief.[50] Where the policy is preceded by a proposal form and one of the queries therein is left unanswered without objection, it will be assumed that the insurers accept the point as not material,[51] but the fact that the queries are all answered does not justify the concealment of a material point regarding which there is no query.[52] Where an insured is a consumer, a genuine and honest answer to a query will not usually amount to a

---

[41] The Marine Insurance Act 1906 stresses that a marine policy may be avoided if the utmost good faith "be not observed by either party". Note also *Life Association of Scotland v Foster* (1873) 11 M. 351. For examples in which non-disclosure by the insurer was an issue, see *Banque Financiere de la Cite S.A. v Westgate Insurance Co Ltd* [1990] 2 All E.R. 947 (HL); *Manifest Shipping v Uni-Polaris Insurance Co (The Star Sea)* [2001] UKHL 1; [2003] 1 A.C. 469.

[42] *Brotherton v Aseguradora Calsegura S.A.* [2003] 2 All E.R. (Comm) 298; *Drake Insurance Plc v Provident Insurance Plc* [2004] Q.B. 601.

[43] *Lambert v Cooperative Insurance Society* [1975] 2 Lloyd's Rep. 485; *Mutual Life Insurance Co of New York v Ontario Metal Products Co Ltd* [1925] A.C. 344; *Highlands Insurance Co v Continental Insurance Co* [1987] 1 Lloyd's Rep. 109.

[44] *St. Paul Fire & Marine Insurance Co (UK) Ltd v McConnell Dowell Construction Ltd* [1996] 1 All E.R. 96; *Pan-Atlantic Insurance Co Ltd v Pine Top Insurance Co Ltd* [1995] A.C. 501; *Assicurazioni Generali SpA v Arab Insurance Group (BSC)* [2002] EWCA Civ 1642; *Mitchell v Hiscox Underwriting Ltd* [2010] CSIH 18; 2010 G.W.D. 13–244. Cf. *Mutual Life Insurance v Ontario Metal Products* [1925] A.C. 344.

[45] *Life Association of Scotland v Foster* (1873) 11 M. 351: referred to with approval by the Second Division in *Hooper v Royal London General Insurance Co Ltd*, 1993 S.C. 242.

[46] *Cuthbertson v Friends' Provident Life Office*, 2006 S.L.T. 567 (OH).

[47] *Hooper v Royal London General Insurance Co Ltd*, 1993 S.C. 242.

[48] 1906 Act s.18(2). Under both of the former ABI Statements of Practice the test applied was a blend of the reasonable insured and the reasonable insurer tests: ABI members had agreed not to reject a claim for non-disclosure if the insured could not reasonably be expected to have disclosed a fact.

[49] *The Spathari*, 1925 S.C. (HL) 6.

[50] See Ch.17, above.

[51] *Joel v Law Union Co* [1908] 2 K.B. 863.

[52] *Life Association v Foster* (1873) 11 M. 351.

misrepresentation or a non-disclosure and so, there is no need to show that the insured had reasonable grounds for his answer.[53] This can be contrasted with commercial insurance, where the insured will be expected to have had reasonable grounds for his genuine and honest answer.[54] In the case of certain policies, amongst which are fire and accident policies, where the insurers may decline to renew the policy at the expiry of the original period, each renewal is made on the understanding that the original representations remain true and that no new fact has emerged which ought to be disclosed.[55] The points on which disclosure is not required are, in marine insurance and probably also in other forms, the following[56]: (a) any circumstance which diminishes the risk; (b) any circumstance which is known or presumed to be known to the insurer and the insurer is presumed to know matters of common notoriety or knowledge, and matters which an insurer in the ordinary course of his business, as such, ought to know[57]; (c) any circumstance as to which information is waived by the insurer[58]; (d) any circumstance which it is superfluous to disclose by reason of any express or implied warranty.[59] At the time of writing, the Consumer Insurance (Disclosure and Representations) Act 2012 ("Consumer Insurance Act") had been passed and given Royal Assent, but was not yet in force. Once in force, this piece of legislation will implement, with modifications, the majority of the recommendations set out in the Law Commission and the Scottish Law Commission's 2009 joint report, *Consumer Insurance Law: Pre-Contract Disclosure and Misrepresentation*.[60] The Consumer Insurance Act applies to a consumer insurance contract, that is to say, an insurance contract entered into between an individual who enters into the contract wholly or mainly for purposes unrelated to the individual's trade, business or profession (i.e. the consumer insured) and a person who carries on the business of insurance and who becomes a party to the contract by way of that business (i.e. the insurer).[61] Where the consumer insured and insurer enter into a consumer insurance contract, the common law duty of disclosure and duty not to misrepresent material facts and the equivalent statutory duties in the Marine Insurance Act 1906 are replaced by a single duty which obliges the consumer insured to take reasonable care not to make a misrepresentation before the contract is formed or varied.[62] Unlike the position under the common law,[63] the standard of care to be discharged by the consumer insured is that of the reasonable consumer, unless the insurer was, or ought to have been, aware of any particular characteristics or circumstances of

---

[53] *Economides v Commercial Union Assurance Co Plc* [1997] 3 All E.R. 636; *Zeller v British Caymanian Insurance Co Ltd* [2008] UKPC 4; [2008] Lloyd's Rep. IR 545.

[54] *M'Phee v Royal Insurance*, 1979 S.C. 304.

[55] *Law Accident Insurance Society v Boyd*, 1942 S.C. 384; *Lambert v Cooperative Insurance Society* [1975] 2 Lloyd's Rep. 485.

[56] 1906 Act s.18(3).

[57] See *London General Insurance Co v General Marine Underwriters Association Ltd Association* [1921] 1 K.B. 104.

[58] *Mann, Macneal & Steeves v Capital, etc. Insurance Co* [1921] 2 K.B. 300.

[59] See opinion of Lord President Dunedin, *Gunford Steamship Co v Thames, etc. Insurance Co*, 1910 S.C. 1072, revd 1911 S.C. (HL) 84.

[60] Law Commission and Scottish Law Commission, *Consumer Insurance Law: Pre-Contract Disclosure and Misrepresentation* (HMSO, 2009), Law Com No.319, Scot. Law Com. No. 219.

[61] Consumer Insurance (Disclosure and Representations) Act 2012 (the "Consumer Insurance Act") s.1.

[62] Consumer Insurance Act s.2(2).

[63] *St. Paul Fire & Marine Insurance Co (UK) Ltd v McConnell Dowell Construction Ltd* [1996] 1 All E.R. 96; *Pan-Atlantic Insurance Co Ltd v Pine Top Insurance Co Ltd* [1995] A.C. 501.

the actual consumer or the representation made by the consumer was dishonest.[64] The insurer will have a remedy where the consumer insured breaches the duty to take reasonable care not to make a misrepresentation and this misrepresentation has induced the insurer to enter into the contract.[65] If the consumer breaches the duty by making a deliberate or reckless misrepresentation, the insurer has the remedy of treating the contract as if it never existed i.e. the contract is voidable and the insurer has the right to refuse all claims and retain all of the premiums paid, except to the extent (if any) that it would be unfair to the consumer to retain them.[66] Meanwhile, if the consumer makes a careless misrepresentation, the nature of the insurer's remedy is dependent on whether the insurer would have entered into the contract on different terms.[67] If the insurer would not have entered into the contract, then it may avoid the contract, i.e. the contract is voidable, but it must return all of the premiums paid.[68] However, if it would have entered into the contract, but on different terms, then the contract is treated as if it includes those different terms and if it would have levied a higher premium, the insurer may reduce proportionately the amount to be paid to the consumer on a claim.[69] A misrepresentation by the consumer insured must be (i) deliberate or reckless or (ii) careless, and it will be deliberate or reckless if the consumer knew that (a) it was untrue or misleading or did not care whether or not it was untrue or misleading and (b) the matter to which the misrepresentation related was relevant to the insurer or the consumer did not care whether or not it was relevant to the insurer.[70] The burden of proving that the misrepresentation was deliberate or reckless lies with the insurer.[71]

Disclosure in questions with agents—Where insurance is effected through an **20.06** intermediary such as an insurance broker the legal effect of non-disclosure by the intermediary to the insurer of a material fact disclosed to him by the insured is dependent on whether the intermediary is the agent of the insurer or the insured.[72] This area is fraught with difficulty by virtue of the fact that it is often a challenge to determine for whom the intermediary is acting. Where, on the facts, the intermediary can be viewed as the insurer's agent, failure to pass on such information will not entitle the insurer to avoid the contract for non-disclosure.[73] An intermediary will be acting as an agent for the insurer where he is employed by or tied to the insurer and in that capacity, he initiates the relationship between the insurer and the insured.[74] Where the converse obtains and the intermediary is the insured's agent, the insurer is entitled to avoid the contract but the intermediary may be liable in damages to the insured.[75] The principles to be applied in such cases are

---

[64] Consumer Insurance Act s.3(3)(4) and (5).

[65] Consumer Insurance Act s.4.

[66] Consumer Insurance Act Sch.1(2).

[67] Consumer Insurance Act Sch.1(4).

[68] Consumer Insurance Act Sch.1(5).

[69] Consumer Insurance Act Sch.1(6), (7) and (8).

[70] Consumer Insurance Act s.5(2) and (3).

[71] Consumer Insurance Act s.5(4).

[72] *Life and Health Assurance Assoc. Ltd v Yule* (1904) 6 F. 437; *McMillan v Accident Insurance Co Ltd*, 1907 S.C. 484; *National Farmers Union Mutual Insurance Soc. Ltd v Tully*, 1935 S.L.T. 574.

[73] *Cruikshank v Northern Accident Insurance Co Ltd* (1895) 23 R. 147; *Stockton v Mason* [1978] 2 Lloyd's Rep. 430; *Woolcott v Excess Insurance Co Ltd (No.2)* [1979] 2 Lloyd's Rep. 210.

[74] *Winter v Irish Life Assurance Plc* [1995] 2 Lloyd's Rep. 274.

[75] *McNealy v Pennine Insurance Co Ltd* [1978] 2 Lloyd's Rep. 18; *Alfred James Dunbar v A. and B. Painters Ltd* [1986] 2 Lloyd's Rep. 38; *Roberts v Plaisted* [1989] 2 Lloyd's Rep. 341: for the extent of a broker's liability, see *Aneco Reinsurance Underwriters Ltd (in administration) v Johnson & Higgins Ltd* [2001] 2 All E.R. Comm. 929 (HL).

that what is known to the agent is deemed to be known to his principal[76] and that an agent to insure is assumed to know, and bound to disclose, every circumstance which in the ordinary course of business ought to be known by, or to have been communicated to, him, and every material circumstance which the insured is bound to disclose, unless it comes to his knowledge too late to be communicated to the agent.[77] Misrepresentation of facts not disclosed to the insured's agent may render him liable in damages to the insured should the insurer avoid the policy.[78] Non-disclosure or misrepresentation by an intermediary will not invalidate other policies on the same risk effected through other brokers.[79] Once in force, s.12(5) of the Consumer Insurance Act will operate to preserve the general common law position on the duties of agents of the insured and so the insured in a consumer insurance contract will continue to be responsible for the actions of his agent. Therefore, if the agent makes a deliberate or reckless misrepresentation, the insurer may have the right to avoid the insurance policy notwithstanding that the consumer insured had himself acted reasonably and honestly. In such circumstances, the insurer will have the same remedies that it would have had against a careless consumer which are set out in Sch.1 to the Consumer Insurance Act. A particular innovation in the Consumer Insurance Act is the provision of guidance as to when an insurance intermediary will be taken to be the agent of the insurer or a consumer insured in the context of a consumer insurance contract. It is stated that an intermediary will be the agent of the insurer when the former (i) does something in the agent's capacity as the appointed representative of the insurer for the purposes of s.39(3) of the Financial Services and Markets Act 2000,[80] (ii) collects information from the consumer insured and the insurer had given the former express authority to do so as the insurer's agent, (iii) enters into the consumer insurance contract as the insurer's agent and the insurer had given the agent express authority to do so.[81] It is then provided that in any other case, it is to be presumed that the intermediary is acting as the consumer's agent unless, in the light of all the relevant circumstances, it would appear that the intermediary is acting as the insurer's agent.[82] Relevant factors which may tend to confirm that the intermediary is acting for the consumer are that (i) the intermediary undertakes to give impartial advice to the consumer, (ii) the intermediary undertakes to conduct a fair analysis of the market and (iii) the consumer insured pays the intermediary a fee.[83] Meanwhile, the following matters may provide support for the argument that the intermediary is acting as the agent of the insurer, namely (i) the intermediary places insurance of the type in question with only one of the insurers who provide insurance of that type, (ii) the intermediary is under a contractual

---

[76] *Stockton v Mason* [1978] 2 Lloyd's Rep. 430; *Woolcott v Excess Insurance Co Ltd (No.2)* [1979] 2 Lloyd's Rep. 210.

[77] 1906 Act s.19. See *MacDuff Shellfish (Scotland) Ltd v Masson & Glennie* [2007] CSOH 155.

[78] *Warren v Henry Sutton & Co* [1976] 2 Lloyd's Rep. 276.

[79] *Blackburn v Haslam* (1888) L.R. 21 Q.B.D. 144. As to a broker's duties and liabilities generally, see the Insurance Conduct of Business Sourcebook drawn up by the Financial Services Authority at *http://fsahandbook.info/FSA/html/handbook/D136* [Accessed August 3, 2012]; *Claude R. Ogden & Co v Reliance Sprinkler Co* [1975] 1 Lloyd's Rep. 52; *Warren v Henry Sutton & Co* [1976] 2 Lloyd's Rep. 276, *Beattie v Furness-Houlder Insurance*, 1976 S.L.T. (Notes) 60; *Cherry v Allied Insurance Brokers* [1978] 1 Lloyd's Rep. 274.

[80] This provision directs that an insurer is directly liable for the actions and omissions of one of its agents.

[81] Consumer Insurance Act Sch.2(1) and (2).

[82] Consumer Insurance Act Sch.3(1).

[83] Consumer Insurance Act Sch.3(3).

obligation which has the effect of restricting the number of insurers with whom the intermediary places insurance of the type in question, (iii) the insurer provides insurance of the type in question through only a small proportion of agents who deal in that type of insurance, (iv) the insurer permits the intermediary to use the insurer's name in providing the agent's services, (v) the insurance in question is marketed under the name of the intermediary and (vi) the insurer asks the intermediary to solicit the custom of the consumer insured.[84]

Warranties[85]—Where reduction of a policy is attempted on the ground of failure **20.07** in disclosure, or of misrepresentation, the fact in question must be material to the risk. But certain facts may be warranted by the insured, either (in marine insurance) impliedly,[86] or expressly. If a particular fact or statement is warranted as true, the validity of the policy depends on the warranty being fulfilled, and it does not matter whether the fact or statement be material or not.[87] Thus if the policy is preceded by a proposal form, and is issued expressly on the condition that the answers to the queries in the proposal form are true, any untruth, even on a minor point will vitiate the policy. In such circumstances, the insurer will be automatically discharged from liability under the insurance policy from the moment of the breach of warranty.[88] The same rule is applied where it is provided that the proposal form "shall be the basis of the contract and be held as incorporated herein",[89] although once the Consumer Insurance Act comes into force, such "basis of the contract" clauses will no longer be of any effect in consumer insured contracts.[90] A misstatement as to the place where a motor car, which was the subject of the policy, was garaged, was held to render the policy voidable, though it was not material to the risk, and in spite of an express provision that only material misstatements should avoid the contract.[91] And in such cases where the accuracy of the answers in the proposal form is contractually the test of the validity of the policy, it is no answer to the company that the true facts were within the knowledge of their agent, or that the proposal form was actually filled up by him, and the inaccuracy due to his misunderstanding of the information furnished by the insured.[92] Nor will it necessarily save the policy that the statement was one (e.g. as to freedom from latent disease) of which the insured

---

[84] Consumer Insurance Act Sch.3(4).

[85] See Ch.2 of the Joint Consultation Paper of the Law Commission and Scottish Law Commission, *Insurance Contract Law: The Business Insured's Duty of Disclosure and the Law of Warranties* (for a comprehensive overview of the law of warranties, including the law reforms proposed by the Scottish Law Commission and the Law Commission).

[86] See below, para.20.32.

[87] *O'Connor v Bullimore Underwriting Agency Ltd*, 2004 S.C.L.R. 346 (OH). For the position in marine insurance, see *Bank of Nova Scotia v Hellenic Mutual War Risk Assurance (Bermuda) Ltd (The Good Luck) (No.2)* [1992] 1 A.C. 233.

[88] *Bank of Nova Scotia v Hellenic Mutual War Risk Assurance (Bermuda) Ltd (The Good Luck) (No.2)* [1992] 1 A.C. 233.

[89] *Standard Life Assurance Co v Weems* (1884) 11 R. (HL) 48; *Unipac (Scotland) Ltd v Aegon Insurance Co (UK) Ltd*, 1996 S.L.T. 1197. The former ABI Statement of General Insurance Practice exhorted insurers not to use a "basis of the contract" clause as a means of creating past and present (though not future) warranties: they were enjoined to create only specific, express, warranties.

[90] Consumer Insurance Act s.6.

[91] *Dawsons v Bonnin*, 1922 S.C. (HL) 156; cf. *Provincial Ins. Co v Morgan* [1932] 2 K.B. 70, affd [1933] A.C. 240, where answers in the proposal form were held to be merely descriptive of the risk and *Forfar Weavers Ltd v MSF Pritchard Syndicate*, 2006 S.L.T. (Sh. Ct) 19.

[92] *McMillan v Accident Insurance Co*, 1907 S.C. 484; *National Farmers, etc. Society v Tully*, 1935 S.L.T. 574.

could have no actual knowledge; although, in doubtful cases, such statements will be read as assertions of opinion and not of fact.[93] Where the answers to the questions asked by a proposal form are declared to be true to the best of the insured's knowledge and belief, he must have a reasonable basis for believing his opinions to be correct. It has been held that an inaccurate guess, where the facts were readily ascertainable, will justify the insurer's refusal to meet a claim.[94] The insurer may be held to have waived, by words or conduct, his right to avoid the policy, but the scope for an argument based on waiver is limited.[95] In some circumstances, however, it may be held that the insurer has restricted the ambit of required disclosure by express questions in the proposal form and in such a case an argument based on waiver may have greater force.[96]

20.08 Duty not to make fraudulent claims[97]—Owing to the fact that an insurance contract is a contract uberrimae fidei, an insured is under an obligation not to make a fraudulent claim under the policy.[98] Where an insured fraudulently exaggerates a claim, eg by claiming recovery of a fictitious asset, the common law prescribes that the whole claim is forfeited even though it may have been partly genuine.[99] Where the insured makes a fraudulent claim, the insurer's sole remedy in Scots law is forfeiture of that claim and the insurer is not entitled to avoid the insurance contract. Therefore, where an insured has made a prior claim and the insurer has indemnified the insured under the policy in respect of that claim, a subsequent fraudulent claim on the part of the insured does not operate retrospectively to forfeit, or enable the insurer to recover the insurance money paid out pursuant to, the prior claim.[100] However, in English law, the legal position on avoidance in this context is presently unclear.[101] A separate issue is whether a subsequent claim is effectively precluded on the basis that a prior claim was made fraudulently under the same insurance policy and here it has been suggested that the subsequent claim is valid since the fraudulent nature of the prior claim does not automatically terminate the contract.[102] It has also been suggested in England that damages are unavailable as a remedy against the insured where the latter has made a fraudulent claim,[103] although the insurer may be entitled to pursue damages for the tort of deceit in English law.[104]

---

[93] *Standard Life Assurance Co v Weems* (1884) 11 R. (HL) 48, opinion of Lord Blackburn.

[94] *McPhee v Royal Insurance Co Ltd*, 1979 S.C. 304. The former ABI Statement of General Insurance Practice suggested that proposal forms should declare that all answers are given on the basis that they are true to the best of the proposer's knowledge and belief.

[95] *WISE Underwriting Agency Ltd v Grupo Nacional Provincial S.A.* [2004] EWCA Civ 962; [2004] 2 All E.R. (Comm) 613.

[96] *Doheny v New India Assurance Co Ltd* [2004] EWCA Civ 1705; [2005] 1 All E.R. (Comm) 382, per Longmuir L.J.

[97] See Chs 2 and 5 of the Joint Consultation Paper of the Law Commission and Scottish Law Commission, *Insurance Contract Law: Post Contract Duties and Other Issues* for an exposition of the law on fraudulent claims.

[98] *Manifest Shipping Co Ltd v Uni-Polaris Insurance Co Ltd (The Star Sea)* [2001] UKLH 1; [2003] A.C. 469.

[99] *Galloway v Guardian Royal Exchange (UK) Ltd* [1999] Lloyds Rep. IR 209.

[100] *Fargnoli v GA Bonus Plc*, 1997 S.C.L.R. 12; [1997] C.L.C. 653; [1997] 6 Re. L.R. 374.

[101] *Manifest Shipping Co Ltd v Uni-Polaris Insurance Co Ltd (The Star Sea)* [2001] UKHL 1; [2003] 1 A.C. 469; *K/S Merc-Scandia XXXXII v Certain Lloyd's Underwriters (The Mercandian Continent)* [2001] EWCA Civ 1275; [2001] 2 Lloyd's Rep 563 and *Agapitos v Agnew (No.1) (The Aegeon)* [2002] EWCA Civ 247; [2003] Q.B. 556.

[102] *Fargnoli v GA Bonus Plc*, 1997 S.C.L.R. 12; [1997] C.L.C. 653; [1997] 6 Re. L.R. 374.

[103] *London Assurance v Clare* (1937) 57 Ll. L. Rep. 254.

[104] *Insurance Corporation of the Channel Islands Ltd v McHugh* [1997] 1 L.R.L.R. 94.

Liability of insurer to pay damages for late payment[105]—In Scots law, when an **20.09**
insured makes a valid claim for indemnity under the insurance policy, the obligation of the insurer is treated as a contractual duty to pay a sum of money equivalent to the insured's loss.[106] Therefore, the insured's right is not to a payment
which may be categorised as damages. Before the insurer pays out, it has the right
first to investigate a claim made by the insured in order to ascertain whether it is
genuine and valid. If the insurer wrongfully repudiates the insured's valid claim
or exercises unjustifiable delay in investigating the insured's claim and paying
out, it will be in breach of contractual duty. The basis for this liability is breach of
an implied term that the insurer will pay out the insurance money within a reasonable time and damages may be claimed by the insured for lost profits in such
circumstances.[107] The legal position in Scotland may be contrasted with English
law. It has been held in England that an insurer's primary obligation under an
insurance policy is not to pay valid claims but to hold the insured harmless from
loss. The upshot of this analysis is that a breach of contract on the part of the
insurer arises on the occurrence of the harm, rather than when the insured's claim
is made and the insurance payment is treated as damages for that breach. On that
basis, damages are not a remedy available for the insurer's failure to pay
damages.[108]

Assignation—A policy of insurance is assignable unless there is a provision to the **20.10**
contrary.[109] The transfer of the subject at risk does not amount to an assignation of
the policy.[110] The assignation of a policy does not require to be in writing[111] unless
it is an assignation of a life policy.[112] When the question is one of donation no
special words are necessary to constitute an assignation; in doubtful cases
the construction of the writing may be assisted by parole evidence of the
circumstances under which it was prepared, executed and delivered.[113] Where
the question is with the other creditors of the insured or with the trustee in his
sequestration, a mere assignation, with or without the transfer of the policy, is not
sufficient to give the assignee a real right in the policy or in its proceeds. The
assignation must be followed by intimation to the insurance company.[114] Both at
common law and by statute[115] an assignee of the policy may sue in his own name.
But he is subject to any defence which the insurer could state in a question with
the original insured.[116] Thus, in life insurance, the company may refuse payment

---

[105] Chs 1 and 5 of the Joint Consultation Paper of the Law Commission and Scottish Law
Commission, *Insurance Contract Law: Post Contract Duties and Other Issues* summarise the law on
damages for late payment and set out the proposals of the Law Commission and the Scottish Law
Commission for reform.

[106] *Carrick Furniture House Ltd v General Accident Fire and Life Assurance Corp Ltd*, 1977 S.C.
308; *Scott Lithgow Ltd v Secretary of State for Defence*, 1989 S.C. (HL) 9; *Anderson v Commercial
Union Assurance Co Plc*, 1998 S.L.T. 826; *Strachan v The Scottish Boatowners' Mutual Insurance
Association*, 2010 S.C. 367.

[107] *Alonvale Ltd v J M Ing*, 1993 G.W.D. 36–2345.

[108] *Sprung v Royal Insurance (UK) Ltd* [1999] 1 Lloyd's Rep IR 111.

[109] Bell, *Principles*, s.516; Marine Insurance Act 1906 s.50.

[110] *Rayner v Preston* (1881) L.R. 18 Ch.D. 1 (fire); Marine Insurance Act 1906 s.15.

[111] Requirements of Writing (Scotland) Act 1995; although most assignations are likely to be in
writing.

[112] Policies of Assurance Act 1867 s.5.

[113] *Carmichael v Carmichael's Ex.*, 1920 S.C. (HL) 195.

[114] *Strachan v McDougle* (1835) 13 S. 954; *Wylie's Ex. v McJannet* (1901) 4 F. 195.

[115] Policies of Assurance Act 1867 s.1.

[116] See para.20.11, below, as to statutory assignations.

to an assignee on the ground of misstatements by the insured in the proposal form. The brocard assignatus utitur jure auctoris applies.[117] In marine insurance, when a ship is lost by the fault of the owner, a claim by a mortgagee will fail if he is merely the assignee of the policy,[118] but may succeed if his interest, as well as that of the owner, was originally insured, and where therefore he has an independent and not merely a derivative right.[119] An endorsement of a heritable creditor's interest on a policy may also give an original interest in the policy rather than a derivative right.[120]

20.11 **Rights under policy in bankruptcy**—In the ordinary case, if the policy is not assigned, and is not made payable to any third party, any sum becoming due under it passes to the trustee in the sequestration of the insured.[121] At common law, there was no exception to this rule in the case of insurance against liability arising from injury to third parties.[122] Under the Third Parties (Rights against Insurers) Act 1930,[123] where "a person is insured against liabilities to third parties which he may incur", and is bankrupt, or has made a composition with his creditors (or, in the case of a company, in the event of a winding-up order, an administration order, a receivership, a voluntary arrangement in terms of the Insolvency Act 1986), his rights under the policy are transferred to, and vest in, the party to whom the liability has been incurred, whether the injury to him occurred before or after the bankruptcy.[124] The party to whom the claim under the policy is transferred takes no higher right in a question with the insurance company, than the insured possessed.[125] It is a prerequisite for a valid claim under the Act that liability of the insured be established and quantified.[126] It has been decided in England that, where the insolvent insured's liability is unascertained, the third party should obtain the court's leave to sue the insured and so fix his liability.[127] The insurer is not entitled to set off against the claim of a judgment creditor the amount of premiums due from a judgment debtor.[128] In cases involving compulsory employer's liability insurance, the insurer cannot rely on terms of the policy requiring notification of an accident to be made within a specific time, or making liability contingent on taking reasonable precautions, against an employee.[129] The 1930 Act is to be replaced by the Third Parties (Rights against Insurers) Act 2010 which has not yet come into force.[130] Once in force, it will apply where a person "incurs or . . . is subject to a liability to a third party against which that person is

---

[117] *Scottish Equitable v Buist* (1877) 4 R. 1076, affd (1878) 5 R. (HL) 64.

[118] *Graham Joint Stock Shipping Co v Merchants' Marine Insurance Co* [1924] A.C. 294.

[119] *P. Samuel & Co v Dumas* [1924] A.C. 431.

[120] *Bank of Scotland v Guardian Royal Exchange Plc*, 1995 S.L.T. 763.

[121] Bankruptcy (Scotland) Act 1985 s.31.

[122] *Hood's Trs v Southern Union Insurance Co* [1928] 1 Ch. 793.

[123] As amended by, inter alia, the Insolvency Act 1986 and the Bankruptcy (Scotland) Act 1985.

[124] As to the meaning of liability in this context, see *Re OT Computers (in administration)* [2004] EWCA Civ 653; [2004] Ch. 317.

[125] *Greenlees v Port of Manchester Insurance Co*, 1933 S.C. 383. But see para.20.14, below.

[126] *Post Office v Norwich Union Fire Insurance Society* [1967] 2 Q.B. 363; *Bradley v Eagle Star Insurance Co Ltd* [1989] A.C. 957; *Firma C-Trade S.A. v Newcastle Protection and Indemnity Association* [1991] 2 A.C. 1.

[127] *Post Office v Norwich Union Fire Insurance Society* [1967] 2 Q.B. 363.

[128] *Murray v Legal & General Assurance Society* [1970] 2 Q.B. 495.

[129] Employers' Liability (Compulsory Insurance) Act 1969 s.1(3)(a) and the Employers' Liability (Compulsory Insurance) Regulations 1998 (SI 1998/2573).

[130] The 2010 Act implements a Joint Report of the Law Commission and the Scottish Law Commission, *Third Parties—Rights Against Insurers* (HMSO, 2001) Scot. Law Com. Report No.184.

insured under a contract of insurance", and is bankrupt, or has entered into a protected trust deed or made a composition with his creditors (or, in the case of a company, in the event of a winding-up order, an administration order, a receivership, or a voluntary arrangement in terms of the Insolvency Act 1986).[131] In such a case, his rights under the policy are transferred to, and vest in, the party to whom the liability has been incurred, whether the injury to him occurred before or after the bankruptcy.[132] The Third Parties (Rights against Insurers) Act 2010 will change the law: in order for the third party to have a valid claim against the insurer, the third party will be entitled to initiate proceedings against the insurer without having first established the liability of the insured.[133] However, before the third party will have the right to enforce the rights transferred against the insurer, the third party must first establish the liability of the insured and this may be done in one set of proceedings, e.g. by obtaining a court declarator, judgment or decree or an arbitral award.[134] Subject to certain exceptions, the Third Parties (Rights against Insurers) Act 2010 continues the rule that the party to whom the claim under the policy is transferred takes no higher right in a question with the insurance company, than the insured possessed.[135] The Third Parties (Rights against Insurers) Act 2010 will also improve the third party's rights to information about the insurance policy. The third party will be permitted to access information at an early stage about the rights transferred to him in order to enable him to take an informed decision about whether or not to commence or continue litigation.[136] Another noteworthy point is that the insurer is given the right to set off the amount of the insured's liability against the amount of the insurer's own liability to the third party in relation to the transferred rights.[137] Therefore, if the insured had not paid all of the insurance premiums, the insurer will be entitled to deduct the amount of those unpaid premiums from the amount payable to the third party to whom the claim under the insurance policy has been transferred, to the extent to which it would have been permitted to do so had the claim been raised by the insured.

Protection for policyholders—Provision was first made for the protection of **20.12** policyholders whose insurance companies were unable to meet their liabilities by legislation in 1975.[138] Under that scheme, a body known as the Policyholders Protection Board acted as an industry-funded safety-net to indemnify or otherwise assist policyholders who had been prejudiced by an insurance company's inability to meet its liabilities. As from November 30, 2001, the responsibility for policyholders' protection was taken over by the Financial Services Compensation Scheme ("FSCS") under the FSMA.[139] The FSCS applies to insurance business

---

[131] Third Parties (Rights against Insurers) Act 2010 s.1.
[132] Third Parties (Rights against Insurers) Act 2010 s.1(1) and (2). As to the meaning of liability in this context, see *Re OT Computers (in administration)* [2004] EWCA Civ 653; [2004] Ch. 317.
[133] Third Parties (Rights against Insurers) Act 2010 s.1(3).
[134] Third Parties (Rights against Insurers) Act 2010 s.1(4).
[135] Third Parties (Rights against Insurers) Act 2010 s.9.
[136] Third Parties (Rights against Insurers) Act 2010 s.11.
[137] Third Parties (Rights against Insurers) Act 2010 s.10.
[138] Policyholders Protection Act 1975, as amended by the Insurance Companies Acts 1980, 1981, the 1982 consolidating Act, the Friendly Societies Act 1992, by statutory instruments, and Policyholders Protection Act 1997.
[139] See para.20.02, above: the scheme is accessible at *http://www.fscs.org.uk/* [Accessed August 3, 2012].

conducted by authorised insurers[140] and, from January 14, 2005, insurance broking. The scheme was set up mainly to assist private individuals, although smaller businesses are also covered. Larger businesses are generally excluded. There are limits to the compensation which may be paid. The scheme is financed by contributions from the insurance industry. The scheme also provides cover for some other financial services besides insurance.

20.13 **Motor vehicle insurance**—By the Road Traffic Act 1988,[141] it is provided that it is unlawful for any person to use,[142] or to cause or permit any other person to use,[143] a motor vehicle on a road unless there is in force in relation to the use of the vehicle by that person or that other person a policy of insurance covering third party risks which complies with the requirements of that Act.[144] This provision does not, however, render the owner of a motor vehicle personally liable in a case where he has permitted a third party, covered by his insurance, to drive it, and the third party's negligence has caused injury.[145] But the owner of a car who allows another person to use it, when there is no adequate policy in regard to third party risks, is liable for any loss caused by the fault of the driver which the driver cannot meet.[146]

An injured person who has obtained judgment against a wrongdoer, to whom a policy has been issued in accordance with the statutory requirements, may recover direct from the insurer such a sum as is payable under the policy.[147] This will not be the case, however, where the risk is not one covered by the policy.[148] The right of direct recovery avails even though the insurer is entitled to avoid the policy or has already done so.[149] Despite the presence of certain exceptions to liability in the policy, e.g. relating to the vehicle's condition or the number of occupants permitted, these are no defence to a claim by the third party.[150] These restrictions on the rights of insurers to avoid meeting liability are, however, subject to several exceptions.[151] For example, under s.152(2), insurers may obtain a declaration that the policy may be avoided for non-disclosure or misrepresentation of a material fact. To be effective, this declaration must be obtained no later than three months after judgment has been obtained against the actual insured. In these proceedings, the claimants or the insured are entitled to be

---

[140] i.e. authorised by the FSA. European insurers operating in the United Kingdom and authorised by the regulator of their home state are also covered.

[141] As amended by the Road Traffic Act 1991.

[142] The concept of "use" is very wide and goes much further than the physical act of driving, on which, see *Turnbull v MNT Transport (2006) Ltd* [2010] CSOH 163; 2011 S.L.T. 650 at 657 (Lord Emslie).

[143] Road Traffic Act 1988 s.143. See *Houston v Buchanan*, 1940 S.C. (HL) 17; also *Kelly v Cornhill Insurance Co*, 1964 S.C. (HL) 46.

[144] Road Traffic Act 1988 s.145 as amended by the Motor Vehicles (Compulsory Insurance) Regulations 1992 (SI 1992/3036). Provided that the insurer is a member of the Motor Insurers' Bureau, it is no longer a requirement that the insurer be authorised to carry on motor insurance business within the United Kingdom: s.145(5). Note also s.148.

[145] *Lindsay v Robertson*, 1933 S.C. 158. As to the liability of an employee under a contract of service, see *Lister v Romford Ice & Cold Storage Co* [1957] A.C. 555.

[146] *Houston v Buchanan,* 1940 S.C. (HL) 17; *Fleming v McGillivray*, 1946 S.C. 1.

[147] Road Traffic Act 1988 s.151.

[148] *Robb v McKechnie*, 1936 J.C. 25.

[149] Road Traffic Act 1988 ss.151(5), 152(2).

[150] Road Traffic Act 1988 s.148.

[151] Road Traffic Act 1988 s.152; the insurer must be given notice of the proceedings within seven days of commencement, see *Wake v Page, The Times*, February 9, 2001.

heard.[152] The third party's right, it should also be noted, was substantially under-written by an agreement made in June 1946 between the Minister of Transport and the Motor Insurers' Bureau and supplemented by numerous agreements between the latter and the Secretary of State for Transport.[153] Under each agreement the Bureau undertakes to satisfy any unsatisfied decree arising from any liability required by the Act[154] to be covered by a policy of insurance. There is an impor-tant exception for liability to a passenger in a vehicle who knew or ought to have known that there was no insurance in force in relation to the use.[155] It is a condi-tion for recovery from the Bureau of whole or part of the damages and expenses awarded against an uninsured person that notice of the action is given to the Bureau within seven days of its commencement. Where the Motor Insurers' Bureau is involved, it may not be possible to obtain an interim award of damages.[156] Where a car has been comprehensively insured, the insurers may be liable in damages if there has been undue delay in having the car repaired.[157]

FIRE INSURANCE

Nature of contract—Fire insurance is a contract of indemnity in which the **20.14** insured must prove the amount of his loss and can recover no more.[158] A policy under which the subjects insured are valued beforehand may nevertheless be valid, unless there appears to be fraudulent intent.[159] Unless the policy contains an average clause applicable where there has been under insurance,[160] the whole amount of the insurance may be recovered on a partial loss, provided that damage to that amount has been suffered. This contrasts with an average policy, usual in marine insurance, when the insured is entitled on a partial loss, to no more than a proportional part of the sum insured. The insured may be unable to recover this loss if he has failed to comply with specific conditions in the policy.[161] A funda-mental alteration in the risk may release the insurer from liability.[162]

---

[152] *Zurich, etc. Ins. Co v Livingston*, 1938 S.C. 582. For sequel, see *Zurich, etc. Insurance Co v Leven*, 1940 S.C. 406.

[153] Full texts of the agreements are to be found at *http://www.mib.org.uk/Downloadable+Documents/en/Agreements/Default.htm* [Accessed August 3, 2012]. The adequacy of the Untraced Drivers Agreement has been challenged by reference to EU Directive 84/5 in *Evans v Secretary of State for the Environment* [2001] P.I.Q.R. P3. See now *Tiffney v Flynn*, 2007 S.L.T. 929.

[154] See *Lees v Motor Insurers' Bureau* [1952] 2 All E.R. 511.

[155] *Pickett v Roberts* [2004] EWCA Civ 06; [2004] 1 W.L.R. 2450; *White v White* [2001] UKHL 9, discussing the background of the Second Council Directive, 84/5/EEC.

[156] *Martin v McKinsley*, 1980 S.L.T. (Notes) 15. Cf. *Cameron v Gellatly*, 2009 S.C. 639.

[157] *Davidson v Guardian Royal Exchange Assurance*, 1979 S.C. 192 (40 weeks for repair).

[158] Bell, *Principles*, s.511. The principles governing fire insurance apply generally to other forms of insurance against loss of or damage to property.

[159] Assessment of loss, e.g. the value of property destroyed or damaged, may not be easy: see *Carrick Furniture House Ltd v General Accident Fire & Life Assurance Corp Ltd*, 1977 S.C. 308 (market value or reinstatement value); *Keystone Properties Ltd v Sun Alliance & London Insurance*, 1993 S.C. 494; Legh-Jones, Birds and Owen, *MacGillivray on Insurance Law* (2008), paras 19–010ff; J.J. Gow, *Mercantile and Industrial Law of Scotland* (Edinburgh: W. Green, 1964), p.343. Overvaluation of the property may be evidence of fraud; cf. *Hercules Insurance v Hunter* (1835) 14 S. 1137.

[160] *Buchanan v Liverpool, London and Globe* (1884) 11 R. 1032. Average clauses are very common in practice.

[161] *Laidlaw v John M. Monteath & Co*, 1979 S.L.T. 78 (failure to have fire extinguishing appliances available at places where blow-torches were being used); *Currie v CK Heating*, 2008 G.W.D. 36–539.

[162] *Swiss Reinsurance Co v United India Insurance Co* [2005] EWHC 237 (Comm); [2005] 2 All E.R. (Comm) 367.

20.15 Insurable interest—Fire insurance is a form of indemnity insurance and probably not one of the forms of insurance to which the Life Assurance Act 1774 applies[163] and so, the insured must have an interest at the time when the insurance is effected and certainly at the time when the loss occurs. That interest may consist in the ownership of the subjects insured,[164] or in some subordinate right, such as that of a lessee or the holder of a security.[165] A mere expectancy, such as that of an heir, does not furnish an insurable interest.[166] A shareholder, even though he holds all the shares, has no insurable interest in the property of the company.[167] Neither has a creditor in the property of his debtor.[168] Where property which is insured is sold and the risk has passed to the purchaser before the price is paid the right under the policy does not pass to the purchaser unless the policy is assigned to him.[169] Should a fire then occur the seller has still an interest which will entitle him to recover from the insurance company, in respect that the buyer may fail to pay the price, but if the price is met, the company may recover when they have paid.[170] As an alternative to assignation of the seller's policy, the purchaser can effect his own insurance as soon as missives are concluded.[171]

20.16 Subrogation—From the principle that fire insurance is a contract of indemnity, in which the insured is not entitled to recover more than he has lost, spring the rights of subrogation and of contribution. The right of subrogation arises when some third party is liable for the loss covered by the policy, either by contract, or because the loss arose from his wrongful or negligent act.[172] The insurance company is not entitled to refuse payment of the sum due on the policy merely on the ground that a third party is liable for the loss,[173] nor, conversely, is that third party entitled to plead the insurance as a defence.[174] But the insurer, on payment, and without any assignation, is subrogated to the rights of the insured, and may recover from any third party who would have been liable in a question with the insured.[175] Another aspect of the principle of subrogation is that if the insured, after payment on the policy, recovers anything from a third party who is liable for the loss, he must account to the insurance company for what he has recovered.[176] If the insured

---

[163] See para 20.04, above.

[164] *Arif v Excess Insurance Group Ltd*, 1987 S.L.T. 473.

[165] Bell, *Principles*, s.509; *Fehilly v General Accident Fire and Life Assurance Corp*, 1983 S.L.T. 141; see also para.20.04, above.

[166] Bell, *Principles*, s.461; *Lucena v Craufurd* (1806) 2 Bos. & P. (N.R.) 325.

[167] *Macaura v Northern Assurance Co* [1925] A.C. 619; *Cowan v Jeffrey Associates*, 1998 S.C. 496; see too *Arif v Excess Insurance Group Ltd*, 1987 S.L.T. 473: no insurable interest where a hotel was a partnership asset but the policy was taken out in name of an individual; see also para.20.04, fn.30.

[168] *Macaura v Northern Assurance Co* [1925] A.C. 619.

[169] *Rayner v Preston* (1881) 18 Ch.D. 1.

[170] *Castellain v Preston* (1883) L.R. 11 Q.B.D. 380.

[171] Thus making provision for the situation which arose in *Sloan's Dairies Ltd v Glasgow Corp*, 1976 S.L.T. 147, affd 1977 S.C. 223 (subjects damaged by fire before disposition delivered). A further alternative is a provision in the missives that risk shall not pass to the purchaser until the price has been paid, the seller remaining responsible for adequate insurance until that date.

[172] *Caledonia North Sea Ltd v British Telecommunications Plc*, 2002 S.C. (HL) 117.

[173] *Castellain v Preston* (1883) L.R. 11 Q.B.D. 380; Marine Insurance Act 1906 s.14(3).

[174] *Port Glasgow Sailcloth Co v Cal. Ry* (1892) 19 R. 608.

[175] *Castellain v Preston* (1883) L.R. 11 Q.B.D. 380; *King v Victoria Insurance Co* [1896] A.C. 250; *Caledonia North Sea Ltd v London Bridge Engineering Ltd*, 2002 S.C. (HL) 117. As to interest on damages, see *H. Cousins & Co v D. & S. Carriers* [1971] 2 Q.B. 230.

[176] *Darrell v Tibbitts* (1880) L.R. 5 Q.B.D. 560; *Castellain v Preston* (1883) L.R. 11 Q.B.D. 380. Also the insurer must have indemnified the insured; cf. *Scottish Union National Insurance Co v Davis* [1970] 1 Lloyd's Rep. 1 (motor vehicle).

recovers more from the third party than he has received under the policy, subject to the wording of the policy, he is not obliged to account to the insurers for the excess.[177] The insured cannot, after a loss has occurred, defeat the insurer's right of subrogation by any gratuitous discharge of his claims against third parties. Should he do so he must give credit to the insurance company for the value of the claim which he has abandoned.[178] If the insured has waived liability to him by a third party, he has no rights to which his insurer can be subrogated.[179]

Contribution—The right of contribution arises where property is insured in more **20.17** than one office, and a fire causes loss less than the combined amount of the policies. Then prima facie the insured may recover from any one office the whole amount insured by it,[180] but there is usually a clause in the policy providing that each shall be liable to contribute rateably only.[181] Any company which has paid more than its rateable share of the total loss has, by implication of law and without any assignation from the insured, a right of contribution, i.e. a right to recover from the other companies their rateable shares.[182] To admit of the right of contribution the insurances must not only be over the same physical subject, but over the same interest in that subject. If parties having separate interests insure, there is no right of contribution. Thus where a wharfinger, who was liable for corn stored with him in the event of fire, insured it, and the owners also insured, it was held that the company with which the wharfinger had insured had no right of contribution against the company with which the owners had insured.[183] The same principle was applied, and the right of contribution was negatived, where separate policies were effected covering the interest of prior and of postponed bondholders over a building which was destroyed by fire.[184] If, as is usual in such cases, the policies are taken out by the debtor to cover his own interest and that of the respective bondholders, there is the apparent objection to the recovery on both policies that the owner, by the extinction or reduction of the sum due on the bonds, will gain more than he has lost by the fire. But this is met by holding that the company, paying on its policy to the postponed bondholder, is entitled to an assignation of the bond.[185]

Reinstatement—Fire policies invariably contain a provision entitling the **20.18** company, at their option, to reinstate or replace the property which has been injured, instead of paying the amount of the loss.[186] It would appear that, if the company indicate which course they propose to take, by entering into negotiations

---

[177] *L. Lucas Ltd v Export Credits Guarantee Department* [1974] 1 W.L.R. 909; *Yorkshire Insurance Co v Nisbet Shipping Co* [1962] 2 Q.B. 330.

[178] *West of England Fire Co v Isaacs* [1897] 1 Q.B. 226; *Phoenix Assurance Co v Spooner* [1905] 2 K.B. 753.

[179] *Mark Rowlands Ltd v Berni Inns Ltd* [1985] 3 W.L.R. 964.

[180] *Glasgow Provident Society v Westminster Fire Office* (1887) 14 R. 947, affd (1888) 15 R. (HL) 89, per consulted judges, 14 R. 965; Marine Insurance Act 1906 s.32.

[181] As to rateable proportion clauses, see *Commercial Union Assurance Co v Hayden* [1977] Q.B. 804. Where two insurance policies cover the same risk, and each contains a clause excluding liability in the event of the risk being covered by another policy, the general rule is that both companies are equally liable subject to any rateable proportion clause: *Steelclad Ltd v Iron Trades Mutual Insurance Co Ltd*, 1984 S.L.T. 304; *Turnbull v MNT Transport (2006) Ltd*, 2011 S.L.T. 650.

[182] *Sickness, etc. Association v General Accident Co* (1892) 19 R. 977.

[183] *North British and Mercantile Co v London Liverpool and Globe* (1876) 5 Ch.D. 569.

[184] *Scottish Amicable, etc. Association v Northern Assurance Co* (1883) 11 R. 287.

[185] *Glasgow Provident Society v Westminster Fire Office* (1887) 14 R. 947.

[186] See, e.g. *Carrick Furniture House v General Accident*, 1977 S.C. 308.

as to the amount of the damage, they have conclusively elected to pay and not to reinstate.[187]

20.19 Notice of loss—In fire, as also in accident insurance policies, there are generally provisions whereby the claim on the policy is made contingent on notice of a loss being given within a certain period. Such conditions are effectual, and failure to comply with them is not excused on the ground that it was due to circumstances beyond the insured's control.[188] But the company may be barred from taking the objection, as in a case where they had intimated rejection of the claim upon another and untenable ground.[189]

20.20 Indirect loss—In the absence of any special provision a fire policy covers only loss directly resulting from the destruction or injury of the subject insured, not indirect loss, such as injury to business or the loss of rent.[190]

LIFE INSURANCE

20.21 Nature of contract—Life insurance is a contingent contract, payment being made on the death of the insured, or in the case of an endowment policy, on attaining an agreed age.[191] The business of providing life assurance is regulated by the FSA under the FSMA.[192] Neither the indemnity principle nor the doctrine of subrogation applies to life insurance. As a non-renewable contract, there is no continuing duty of disclosure after the contract is concluded.[193]

20.22 Insurable interest—Under the Life Assurance Act 1774, the party who takes out a policy of life insurance must have an insurable interest[194] at the time the insurance is effected.[195] A man has always an interest in his own life. But if he merely takes the policy, and assigns it without paying any premium, it may be held void as an evasion of the Act.[196] In order to support a policy on the life of another the interest in the life must be of a pecuniary nature, not a mere relationship. The pecuniary interest may be contractual, or may consist in a right to aliment. On the former ground a creditor has an interest, limited to the amount of his debt in the life of his debtor[197]; a cautioner, in the life of the principal debtor[198]; an employee, if engaged for a specific term, in the life of his employer[199]; an employer

---

[187] *Scottish Amicable, etc. Association v Northern Assurance Co* (1883) 11 R. 287.

[188] *Worsley v Wood* (1796) 6 T.R. 710; *London Guarantie Co v Fearnley* (1880) L.R. 5 App. Cas. 911, per Lord Blackburn. See also *Friends Provident Life and Pensions Ltd v Sirius International Insurance* [2005] EWCA Civ 601; [2005] 2 All E.R. (Comm) 145 and *HLB Kidsons (A Firm) v Lloyd's Underwriters* [2008] EWCA Civ 1206; [2009] 2 All E.R. (Comm) 81.

[189] *Shiells v Scottish Assurance Corp* (1889) 16 R. 1014; *Donnison v Employers Accident Co* (1897) 24 R. 681.

[190] *Menzies v North British Insurance Co* (1847) 9 D. 694.

[191] See *Fuji Finance Inc v Aetna Life Insurance Co* [1996] 3 W.L.R. 871.

[192] See para.20.02, above.

[193] *Banque Financiere de la Cite S.A. v Westgate Insurance Co Ltd* [1990] 2 All E.R. 947.

[194] See para.20.04, above. Note also Bell, *Principles*, s.520.

[195] *Dalby v India & London Life Assurance Co* (1854) 15 C.B. 365.

[196] *Macdonald v National Mutual Life Association* (1906) 14 S.L.T. 173 at 249.

[197] *Lindsay v Barmcotte* (1851) 13 D. 718; *Simcock v Imperial Insurance Co* (1902) 10 S.L.T. 286.

[198] *Stevenson v Cotton* (1846) 8 D. 872.

[199] *Hebdon v West* (1863) 3 B. & S. 579.

in the life of an agent through whose endeavour he obtains business.[200] On the latter ground, an obligation to aliment, husband and wife have an interest in each other's lives.[201] A child under the age of 25[202] probably has an insurable interest in its parents' lives. Parents do not have an insurable interest in their children's lives on this basis[203] but they may enjoy it on some other basis.[204] Where a person maintains a foster-child for reward, he is deemed to have no insurable interest in the child's life.[205] If there was an insurable interest at the time when the policy was taken, it may be kept up after the interest has lapsed,[206] and assigned to an assignee who has no interest.[207]

No insurance until premium paid—Proposals for life insurance are commonly **20.23** accepted subject to the condition that there is no insurance until the premium is paid. The result of this condition is that the company may refuse to accept the premium, and to issue a policy, if there has been any intervening and material change, e.g. a change in the health of the applicant.[208]

MARINE INSURANCE[209]

Generally—The law of marine insurance,[210] which developed largely from **20.24** recognition of the customs of those engaged in the trade,[211] presents so many special features that only the leading points can be considered here. For other aspects of the law, in so far as not dealt with in the preceding pages, reference must be made to the Marine Insurance Act 1906 (the "1906 Act"), or to the leading textbooks.[212] The Act expressly bears to be a codifying statute, but in certain respects it has been held to alter the law.[213] By s.91 the rules of the common law, including the law merchant, save in so far as they are inconsistent with the express provisions of the Act, are preserved.

How far contract of indemnity—Marine insurance is described in the Act (s.1) **20.25** as a contract of indemnity. But it is a recognised and common practice that the

---

[200] *Turnbull v Scottish Provident* (1896) 34 S.L.R. 146; *Glenlight Shipping Ltd v Excess Insurance Company Ltd*, 1981 S.C. 267 (dispute as to whether employee's death "accidental").

[201] *Wight v Brown* (1849) 11 D. 459.

[202] See the Family Law (Scotland) Act 1985 s.1(1)(c), (5).

[203] Family Law (Scotland) Act 1985 s.1(1) does not include children in the list of those under an obligation of aliment.

[204] e.g. as a creditor or an employer.

[205] Foster Children (Scotland) Act 1984 s.18.

[206] *Turnbull v Scottish Provident* (1896) 34 S.L.R. 146.

[207] Bell, *Principles*, s.520. For example, see *Dalby v India & London Life Assurance Co* (1854) 15 C.B. 365.

[208] *Canning v Farquhar* (1886) L.R. 16 Q.B.D. 727; *Sickness, etc. Assurance v General Accident* (1892) 19 R. 977.

[209] See Chs 4 and 5 of the Joint Consultation Paper of the Law Commission and Scottish Law Commission, *Insurance Contract Law: Post Contract Duties and Other Issues* for a comprehensive overview of the law on policies and premiums in marine insurance, including the law reforms proposed by the Scottish Law Commission and the Law Commission.

[210] See Gow, *Mercantile and Industrial Law of Scotland* (1964), p.353. For maritime law generally, see para.22.01, below.

[211] *Moore v Evans* [1918] A.C. 185.

[212] R.J. Lambeth, *Templeman on Marine Insurance*, 6th edn (Financial Times Management, 1986); H. Bennett, *Law of Marine Insurance*, 2nd edn (Oxford: Oxford University Press, 2006).

[213] *Polurrian S.S. Co v Young* [1915] 1 K.B. 922.

value of the subject matter insured may be agreed on beforehand and specified in the policy, and that in such a policy, known as a valued policy, the amount agreed upon is, in the absence of averments of fraud, conclusive as between the parties, except for the purpose of ascertaining whether there has been a constructive total loss.[214] Thus where the rules of a mutual insurance society provide that a certain proportion of the ship must remain uninsured, it is a proportion of the agreed-on, and not the actual, value, that has to be considered.[215] There must be clear agreement between the parties of a specific value being allocated to the insured item for the policy to be a valued policy,[216] and a reference to a 'sum insured' in a policy is insufficient to render it a valued policy.[217]

20.26 Form of policy—The contract must be embodied in a policy of insurance which may be issued at the time the contract is concluded or afterwards.[218] The policy must specify the name of the assured, or of his agent, and must be signed by him or on his behalf.[219] The subject matter insured must be designated with reasonable certainty.[220]

20.27 Subjects of marine adventure—A policy of marine insurance must relate to a marine adventure: the risk must be "consequent upon or incidental to the navigation of the sea".[221] It may cover a ship in course of building, or being launched, or actually exposed to maritime perils. It may also cover goods so exposed, freight, profit, the security for any advance, loan or disbursements, or liability to third parties by reason of maritime perils.[222] But a time policy on specific goods is not a marine policy, or subject to the provisions of the Act, merely because the goods are sent to a destination involving sea transit.[223]

20.28 Floating policy—A floating policy is one effected by a merchant to cover goods which he intends to ship, usually specifying the particular kind of goods, the ports of loading and discharge, and a limit of time, but not the ship in which the goods are to be sent. It is expressed to be "by ship or ships to be declared".[224] The effect is that the policy vests at once, and the goods are covered as soon as they are shipped.[225] The insured is bound to declare each shipment (usually by

---

[214] 1906 Act s.27. Policies generally provide that the agreed-on value is to be conclusive in a question of a constructive total loss: J. Gilman, *Arnould's Law of Marine Insurance* (London: Sweet and Maxwell, 2010), pp.395, 423. As to the business reasons for valued policies, see *Gunford Ship Co v Thames, etc. Insurance Co*, 1911 S.C. (HL) 84.

[215] *Muirhead v Forth, etc. Association* (1894) 21 R. (HL) 1.

[216] *Kyzuna Investments Ltd v Ocean Marine Mutual Insurance Association* [2000] 1 All E.R. (Comm) 557.

[217] *Thor Navigation Inc v Ingosstrakh Insurance Co Ltd* [2005] EWHC 19 (Comm); [2005] 1 Lloyd's Rep. 547.

[218] 1906 Act s.22. As to a "slip", see above, para.20.03.

[219] 1906 Act ss.23(1), 24(1).

[220] 1906 Act s.26(1); see Gow, *Mercantile and Industrial Law of Scotland* (1964), pp.356–7.

[221] *Continental Illinois National Bank and Trading Co of Chicago v Bathhurst* [1985] 1 Lloyd's Rep. 625.

[222] 1906 Act ss.2, 3. As to the possible twofold insurance in the case of goods, namely in respect of the goods themselves and of the adventure, see *Rickards v Forestal Land, Timber and Ry* [1942] A.C. 50.

[223] *Moore v Evans* [1918] A.C. 185.

[224] 1906 Act s.29: for the requirements of disclosure in a floating or "open" policy, see *Glencore International AG v Alpina Insurance Co Ltd* [2003] EWHC 2792.

[225] Gilman, *Arnould's Law of Marine Insurance* (2010), p.271; *Stephens v Australasian Insurance Co* (1872) L.R. 8 C.P. 18 (customs of trade proved and accepted as law).

indorsement on the policy) as soon as he is aware of it. He is bound to declare all shipments falling within the terms of the policy in their order, and therefore is not entitled to leave some shipments uninsured, or insured with third parties.[226] If he fails to declare any shipment the underwriter may treat it as declared, and if in this way the sum fixed in the policy is exhausted, may refuse to pay for a loss on a subsequent shipment.[227] If by inadvertence a shipment is not declared, it is the duty of the insured to rectify the omission, and he may do so even after a loss has occurred.[228] But where the policy provided for a declaration within a time limit it was held that the declaration was a condition precedent to any claim, and therefore that the insured could not recover for a loss on a shipment which had been declared too late.[229] As the underwriter in a floating policy has undertaken liability for any shipments made he cannot refuse payment on the ground of failure in disclosure or innocent misrepresentation regarding the character of the ship actually selected. So where, on a particular shipment, a declaration on a floating policy was made, and also a new and independent policy was taken out, it was held that the latter, but not the former, was rendered voidable by a material but not fraudulent misstatement as to the age of the ship.[230]

Insurable interest—The insured must have an insurable interest at the time of a **20.29** loss under the policy; not necessarily at the time when the policy is effected.[231] He cannot acquire an interest after he is aware of a loss.[232] If, in the usual form, the subject matter is insured "lost or not lost", the insured may recover though he may not have acquired his interest until after the loss, unless at the time of effecting the contract the assured was aware of the loss, and the insurer was not.[233] The Act, reproducing earlier legislation, provides (s.4):

"(1) Every contract of marine insurance by way of gaming or wagering is void. (2) A contract of marine insurance is deemed to be a gaming or wagering contract—(a) Where the assured has not an insurable interest as defined by this Act, and the contract is entered into with no expectation of acquiring such an interest; or (b) Where the policy is made 'interest or no interest' or 'without further proof of interest than the policy itself' or 'without benefit of salvage to the insurer', or subject to any other like term; Provided that, where there is no possibility of salvage, a policy may be effected without benefit of salvage to the insurer."[234]

It has been held that where a policy is effected in such terms (usually known as p.p.i., policy proof of interest; or f.i.a., full interest admitted) it is void, even although the insured had in fact an insurable interest.[235] By the Marine Insurance (Gambling Policies) Act 1909, the issue of a marine policy without interest is a criminal offence on the part of the insurer, insured or broker. In spite

---

[226] 1906 Act s.29; *Stephens v Australasian Insurance Co* (1872) L.R. 8 C.P. 18.

[227] *Dunlop Bros v Townend* [1919] 2 K.B. 127.

[228] 1906 Act s.29(3).

[229] *Union Insurance Society of Canton v Wills* [1916] 1 A.C. 281.

[230] *Ionides v Pacific, etc. Co* (1871) L.R. 6 Q.B. 674.

[231] 1906 Act s.6(1).

[232] 1906 Act s.6(2).

[233] 1906 Act s.6(1) and Sch.I r.1: for modern forms of policy covering the "lost-not lost" situation, see Bennet, *Law of Marine Insurance* (2006), para.3.15.

[234] See *Re London County Re-insurance Co* [1922] 2 Ch. 67.

[235] *Cheshire v Vaughan* [1920] 3 K.B. 240.

of these statutory regulations, p.p.i. policies are still in common use and their existence is a material fact which the insured must disclose to subsequent underwriters.[236]

20.30 Nature of interest—Insurable interest is thus defined (s.5):

> "Subject to the provisions of this Act, every person has an insurable interest who is interested in a marine adventure. In particular a person is interested in a marine adventure where he stands in any legal or equitable relation to the adventure or to any insurable property at risk therein, in consequence of which he may benefit by the safety or due arrival of insurable property, or may be prejudiced by its loss, or by damage thereto, or by the detention thereof, or may incur liability in respect thereof." [237]

The interest may be defeasible, contingent or partial. The insurer has an interest to reinsure. A mortgagor or lender on bottomry, to the extent of the amount due, the master and seamen in respect of wages, a party who has paid freight in advance have all insurable interests.[238] The owner of property has an insurable interest in respect of the full value thereof though some third party may have agreed, or be liable to indemnify him in case of loss.[239]

20.31 Insurable value—Except in the case of a valued policy the insurable interest is limited to the insurable value of the subject matter at risk. Reference must be made to the Act for a definition of the insurable value of a ship, of freight and of goods.[240]

20.32 Warranties: Seaworthiness—The rules with regard to disclosure of material facts, innocent misrepresentation, and express warranties are in their main aspects the same as those applicable to other forms of insurance.[241] In marine insurance, however, breach of a warranty (defined as a condition which must be exactly complied with) discharges the insurer from liability with immediate and automatic effect, without requiring action by the insurer.[242] The warranties are set forth in the Act in ss.17–21 and 33–41. The principal implied warranty is that of seaworthiness. It is warranted, in the absence of any provision to the contrary, in a voyage policy, i.e. in a policy from one port to another, not in time policies, when the insurance is for a definite period of time. In the latter case if the ship is, with the privity of the insured, sent to sea in an unseaworthy state, the insurer is not liable for any loss attributable to unseaworthiness.[243] In voyage policies the

---

[236] *Gunford Ship Co v Thames, etc. Insurance Co*, 1911 S.C. (HL) 84.

[237] For comment see *O'Kane v Jones* [2005] Lloyd's Rep. I.R. 174.

[238] 1906 Act ss.7–14.

[239] 1906 Act s.14(3).

[240] 1906 Act s.16; *Williams v Atlantic Assurance Co* [1933] 1 K.B. 81; *Berger and Light Diffusers v Pollock* [1973] 2 Lloyd's Rep. 442.

[241] See above, paras 20.05–20.07.

[242] 1906 Act s.33(3): *Bank of Nova Scotia v Hellenic Mutual War Risk Assurance (Bermuda) Ltd (The Good Luck) (No.2)* [1992] 1 A.C. 233; para.20.07, above.

[243] 1906 Act s.39; *Compania Maritima v The Oceanus Mutual* [1977] Q.B. 49; *The Eurysthenes* [1976] C.L.Y. 2571; *Murray v Scottish Boatowners Mutual Insurance Association*, 1986 S.L.T. 329; *Stephen v Scottish Boatowners Mutual Insurance Association*, 1989 S.L.T. 283; *Manifest Shipping Co Ltd v Uni-Polaris Shipping Co Ltd* [2001] 2 W.L.R. 170. As to the meaning of seaworthiness, see para.22.05, below.

warranty is that the ship is seaworthy at the commencement of the voyage; in voyages performed in different stages, during which the ship requires different kinds of or further preparation of equipment, the warranty is that at the commencement of each stage the ship is seaworthy in respect of such preparation of equipment for the purposes of that stage.[244] There is no implied warranty, in a policy on goods, that they are seaworthy, but in a voyage policy on goods there is an implied warranty that at the commencement of the voyage the ship is not only seaworthy as a ship but also that she is reasonably fit to carry the goods to the destination contemplated by the policy.[245]

Deviation—An insurer may be discharged from liability by a change in the voyage, or by deviation. A change in the voyage occurs when the destination of the ship is voluntarily changed from the destination contemplated by the policy. In the absence of any provision to the contrary the insurer is discharged from the time when determination to change was manifested, although the loss may have occurred before the ship has actually left her course.[246] An insurer is also discharged from liability by deviation from the course contemplated by the policy. In general the rules as to deviation in questions of affreightment apply in questions of marine insurance,[247] but the provision, in the Carriage of Goods by Sea Act 1971 (the "1971 Act"), by which deviation in attempting to save property at sea, or any reasonable deviation, is excused,[248] is not applicable to policies of insurance. In the Marine Insurance Act the following excuses for deviation (also for delay) are enumerated: (a) when authorised by any special term in the policy; (b) where caused by circumstances beyond the control of the master and his employer; (c) where reasonably necessary in order to comply with an express or implied warranty; (d) where reasonably necessary for the safety of the ship or subject matter insured; (e) for the purpose of saving human life or aiding a ship in distress where human life may be in danger; (f) where reasonably necessary for the purpose of obtaining medical or surgical aid for any person on board the ship; (g) where caused by barratrous conduct of the master or crew, if barratry be one of the perils insured against.[249] There is often a clause in the policy authorising a change of voyage or deviation, at an increase of premium to be mutually agreed upon, provided that notice of the change be given.[250]

20.33

Perils insured against—The sum due under a policy becomes payable when there has been a loss, total or partial, of the subject matter of the insurance, and that loss has been occasioned by one of the perils insured against. What these perils are may depend on the terms of the particular policy; the following are enumerated in the statutory form[251]:

20.34

---

[244] 1906 Act s.39. So, in a voyage in stages, the ship must have sufficient fuel for each stage, not necessarily for the whole voyage: *Greenock Steamship Co v Maritime Insurance Co* [1903] 2 K.B. 657.

[245] 1906 Act s.40. See *Elder, Dempster & Co v Paterson* [1924] A.C. 522.

[246] 1906 Act s.45.

[247] See below, para.22.21.

[248] Carriage of Goods by Sea Act 1971 Sch. art.IV r.4.

[249] 1906 Act s.49.

[250] *Maritime Assurance Co v Stearns* [1901] 2 K.B. 912 at 917.

[251] 1906 Act Sch.I. In the rules given in the Schedule the meaning of the terms used in the policy is explained.

> "Touching the adventures and perils which we the assurers are contented to bear and do take upon us in this voyage: they are of the seas,[252] men of war, fire, enemies, pirates, rovers, thieves, jettisons, letters of mart and counter-mart, surprisals, takings at sea, arrests, restraints and detainments of all kings, princes, and people, of what nation, condition, or quality soever, barratry of the master and mariners, and of all other perils, losses and misfortunes, that have or shall come to the hurt, detriment or damage of the said goods and merchandises, and ship etc., or any part thereof."

The general words with which this enumeration ends include only perils similar in kind to the perils specifically mentioned,[253] and "perils" refers only to fortui-tous accidents or casualties of the seas, and does not include the ordinary action of the winds and waves.[254]

20.35 *Causa proxima*—The general rule has been long recognised that in considering whether a particular loss was due to one of the perils insured against the maxim *causa proxima non remota spectatur* applies. The rule is expressed in the Act as follows (s.55):

> "Subject to the provisions of this Act and unless the policy otherwise provides,[255] the insurer is liable for any loss proximately caused by a peril insured against, but, subject as aforesaid, he is not liable for any loss which is not proximately caused by a peril insured against."

In recent cases it has been explained that the term proximate cause does not neces-sarily mean the cause latest in time[256] and if there is more than one proximate cause, it is sufficient if one of them is caused by a peril insured against, so long as the other is not excluded.[257] In considering the question, not infrequently raised, whether a stranding or collision has been caused by a war-like operation or a marine risk, the House of Lords has reiterated the rule that the proximate cause of the loss of a ship is not necessarily that which operates last, but is the effective and predominant cause, selected from among co-operating causes.[258] Thus where a ship was torpedoed, and necessarily towed to a harbour where she was stranded and wrecked, it was held that the war risk involved in the torpedo, and not the subsequent stranding, was the cause of her loss. It was observed that the term *causa proxima* might be rendered "dominant cause" or "cause proximate in efficiency".[259] A distinction is recognised between loss due to a peril insured against and loss resulting from measures due to apprehension of that peril. Thus

---

[252] *Stephen v Scottish Boatowners Mutual Insurance Association*, 1989 S.L.T. 283 ("peril of the sea").

[253] 1906 Act Sch.I r.12.

[254] Sch.I r.7; *P. Samuel & Co v Dumas* [1924] A.C. 431; *Rhesa Shipping Co v Edmunds (The Popi M)* [1985] 2 All E.R. 712 (HL); *Kastor Navigation Co Ltd v AGF MAT (The Kastor Too)* [2004] EWCA Civ 277; [2005] 2 All E.R. (Comm) 720.

[255] *Oei v Foster* [1982] 2 Lloyd's Rep.170; *The Miss Jay Jay* [1987] 1 Lloyd's Rep. 32.

[256] See, e.g. *Wayne Tank and Pump Co v Employer's Liability Assurance Corp* [1974] Q.B. 57.

[257] *Seashore Marine S.A. v The Phoenix Assurance Plc* [2002] 1 All E.R. Comm 152.

[258] *Yorkshire Dale S.S. Co v Minister of War Transport* [1942] A.C. 691.

[259] *Leyland Shipping Co v Norwich Union* [1918] A.C. 350. See also *Britain S.S. Co v The King* [1921] 1 A.C. 99; *Canada Rice Mills v Union Marine & General Insurance Co* [1941] A.C. 55; *Wayne Tank and Pump Co v Employers' Liability Assurance Corp* [1974] Q.B. 57; *Soya GmbH v White* [1983] 1 Lloyd's Rep. 122 (HL); *Rhesa Shipping Co SA v Edmunds (The Popi M)* [1985] 1 W.L.R. 948.

where, in 1914, a German ship, not actually pursued by Allied ships, put into a neutral port, with resultant loss, it was held that the loss was not due to "restraint of princes" but to measures adopted to avoid that restraint.[260] But restraint of princes was held to apply where, on hearing of the declaration of war, and without any actual compulsion, a British ship abandoned a voyage to a German port.[261] Other questions have led to equally fine distinctions. Thus if a particular peril is encountered owing to negligent navigation, the peril in question, and not the preceding negligence, is the proximate cause of the loss,[262] whereas if the peril is incurred owing to an act deliberately wrongful, with the intent to wreck the ship, the wrongful act, and not the subsequent peril, is the proximate cause.[263] The distinction has been explained on the ground that in the former case, and not in the latter, there is the element of the fortuitous or unexpected in the mishap.[264] There can be more than one proximate cause of loss or damage.[265] If the policy covers loss or damage caused by one such cause and does not refer to the other, the insurer incurs liability.[266] But if one cause is covered and the other is specifically excluded the insurer does not incur liability.[267]

Total and partial loss—A loss may be total or partial. A partial loss may in certain **20.36** cases, and at the option of the insured, be treated as a constructive total loss. In the absence of any provision to the contrary an insurance against total loss includes a constructive, as well as an actual, total loss.[268] The Act provides that there is an actual total loss when the subject matter is destroyed, or so damaged as to cease to be a thing of the kind insured, or where the assured is irretrievably deprived thereof, or where a ship is missing, and after a reasonable time no news of her has been received.[269] Thus, for example, if goods insured arrive in an unmarketable state,[270] or if they are sold at an intermediate port on the ground that symptoms of decay show that they cannot be safely carried to their destination,[271] there is an actual total loss. Where a ship is sunk the question whether she is an actual total loss depends on the possibility of raising her.[272] Where a ship is abandoned by her crew and taken possession of by salvors, the loss is only partial, but if she is sold by a decree of a competent court at the instance of the salvors, there is an actual total loss.[273] There is no total loss of freight if, by the arrival of the cargo, it is earned, though it may never be paid, or though, owing to the abandonment of the ship to the underwriters, they, and not the insured, are entitled to payment.[274] But there is a total loss of freight where the cost of temporary repairs to a vessel would

---

[260] *Becker, Gray & Co v London Assurance* [1918] A.C. 101.

[261] *British and Foreign Marine Insurance Co v Sanday* [1916] 1 A.C. 650.

[262] 1906 Act s.55(2); *Trinder, Anderson & Co v Thames, etc. Assurance Co* [1898] 2 Q.B. 114.

[263] *P. Samuel & Co v Dumas* [1924] A.C. 431.

[264] *Trinder, Anderson & Co* [1898] 2 Q.B. 114.

[265] *The Miss Jay Jay* [1987] 1 Lloyd's Rep. 32.

[266] *The Miss Jay Jay* [1987] 1 Lloyd's Rep. 32.

[267] *Wayne Tank and Pump Co v Employers' Liability Assurance Corp* [1974] Q.B. 57.

[268] 1906 Act s.56(3).

[269] 1906 Act ss.57, 58.

[270] *Asfar v Blundell* [1896] 1 Q.B. 123.

[271] *Roux v Salvador* (1836) 2 Bing N.C. 266.

[272] *Blairmore Co v Macredie* (1898) 25 R. (HL) 57.

[273] *Cossman v West* (1888) L.R. 13 App. Cas. 160.

[274] *Scottish Marine Insurance Co v Turner* (1853) 1 Macq. 334.

exceed the repaired value.[275] In the event of an actual total loss the insured is entitled to recover under the policy without giving notice of abandonment.[276]

20.37 Constructive total loss—Where the loss is not an actual total loss, it may amount to a constructive total loss. In that event the insured may either treat the loss as a partial loss or abandon the subject matter insured to the insurer and treat the loss as if it were an actual total loss.[277] There is a constructive total loss where the subject matter insured is reasonably abandoned on account of an actual total loss appearing to be unavoidable, or because it could not be preserved from actual total loss without an expenditure which would exceed its value when the expenditure had been incurred.[278] In the case of loss of possession, e.g. by enemy capture, there is a constructive total loss if the cost of recovery would exceed the value when recovered, or if it is unlikely that the subject can be recovered.[279] Under this provision it is no longer, as it was before the Act, sufficient to prove that the recovery of a captured ship was uncertain; the proof must establish that it was unlikely.[280] Where a ship is damaged the Act provides that she is a constructive total loss if the cost of repairing her would exceed her value when repaired.[281] It is doubtful whether this provision, which leaves out of account the break-up value of the wreck, excludes the test established by the prior authorities, which was whether a prudent owner, if uninsured, would repair the ship or not.[282] In the case of damage to goods there is a constructive total loss when the cost of repairing the damage and forwarding the goods to their destination would exceed their value on arrival[283]; also if the voyage is frustrated, though the goods are not damaged, as where, on the declaration of war, it became illegal to proceed to the enemy port of destination and the goods were landed intact at a British port.[284] There may be a claim for constructive total loss by an insured peril even where there is a subsequent actual total loss which cannot be shown to be due to an insured peril.[285]

20.38 Notice of abandonment—Where the insured proposes to claim as on a constructive total loss he must give notice of abandonment to the underwriter,[286] unless there is nothing to abandon, and no possibility of benefit to the underwriter,[287] as in the case of a policy on freight when the ship is wrecked,[288] or a policy on a ship which is captured by an enemy,[289] or in circumstances where the insured only learns of a constructive total loss after the ship has also become an actual total

---

[275] *Kulukundis v Norwich Union* [1937] 1 K.B. 1.

[276] 1906 Act s.57(2).

[277] 1906 Act s.61.

[278] 1906 Act s.60. The definition in the section is exhaustive: *Irvin v Hine* [1950] 1 K.B. 555.

[279] 1906 Act s.60(2).

[280] *Polurrian S.S. Co v Young* [1915] 1 K.B. 922; as to barratry, see *Marstrand Fishing Co v Beer* (1936) 53 T.L.R. 287.

[281] 1906 Act s.60(2).

[282] See *Macbeth v Maritime Assurance Co* [1908] A.C. 144.

[283] 1906 Act s.60(2).

[284] *British and Foreign, etc. Co v Sanday* [1916] 1 A.C. 650.

[285] *Kastor Navigation Co Ltd* [2004] EWCA Civ 277; *Bank of America National Trust and Savings Association v Christmas (The Kyriaki)* [1993] 1 Lloyd's Rep. 137.

[286] 1906 Act s.62; *Watt's Tr v Scottish Boatowners Mutual Insurance Association*, 1968 S.L.T. (Sh. Ct) 79.

[287] 1906 Act s.62(7).

[288] *Potter v Rankine* (1873) L.R. 6 H.L. 83.

[289] *Roura, etc. v Townend* [1919] 1 K.B. 189; *Petros Nomikos v Robertson* [1938] 2 K.B. 603.

loss.[290] Notice may be given verbally or in writing.[291] It must be given with reasonable diligence after the receipt of reliable information of the loss.[292] On receiving notice the underwriter may accept it, expressly or by implication.[293] His mere silence is not acceptance.[294] If, without express acceptance, he takes measures for the safety or recovery of a wreck, it is a question of circumstances whether he thereby indicates acceptance of the notice, or whether he is acting as a salvor of property which has been abandoned and become res nullius.[295] It would appear that notice of abandonment or acceptance of notice given under a material mistake of fact is a nullity.[296]

Measure of indemnity—On an actual or constructive total loss, in a valued **20.39** policy, the sum fixed by the policy may be recovered; in an unvalued policy, the insurable value of the subject matter.[297] This is termed in the Act the measure of indemnity.[298]

Subrogation—On payment as for a total loss, actual or constructive, the insurer **20.40** is entitled, on the principle of subrogation, to exercise the rights of the insured in the subject matter of the policy.[299] He may recover the damages due from the third party from whose wrongful or negligent act the loss has resulted,[300] but where the insured himself recovers damages from the third party, the insurer may not recover from the insured a greater sum than he himself has already paid over to the insured.[301] If a ship has reached her port of destination, and earned freight, but has arrived so damaged as to be abandoned to the underwriters, they are entitled to the freight.[302] They are also entitled, where a ship has been abandoned as a constructive total loss, to a transfer which will enable them to be registered as her owners.[303] But the insurers, in virtue of their right of subrogation, stand in the same position as the insured, and may be met by any defence which would have been available against him. So where two ships belonging to the same owner came into collision, and the underwriters of the ship which was not in fault, and which was wrecked, paid the insurance, it was held that they had no right to a ranking on the amount paid into court to meet claims against the offending ship. They could make no claim which the insured could not have made, and he could not have claimed against himself.[304] It has been held that where a P. & I. club's rules contain a "pay to be paid" clause, a third party having a claim against a member of the club, who

---

[290] *Kastor Navigation Co Ltd* [2004] EWCA Civ 277.

[291] 1906 Act s.62.

[292] 1906 Act s.62(3). See *Fleming v Smith* (1848) 6 Bell's App.278; *Kaltenbach v Mackenzie* (1878) L.R. 3 C.P.D. 467.

[293] *Watt's Tr v Scottish Boatowners Mutual Insurance Association*, 1968 S.L.T. (Sh. Ct) 79.

[294] 1906 Act s.62(5).

[295] *Shepherd v Henderson* (1881) 9 R. (HL) 1; *Robertson v Royal Exchange Corp*, 1925 S.C. 1.

[296] *Norwich Union v Price* [1934] A.C. 455.

[297] 1906 Act s.68.

[298] 1906 Act s.67.

[299] 1906 Act s.79; see *Boag v Standard Marine Insurance Co* [1937] 2 K.B. 113; cf. para.20.16, above.

[300] *North of England Assurance Co v Armstrong* (1870) L.R. 5 Q.B. 244.

[301] *Yorkshire Insurance Co v Nisbet Shipping Co* [1962] 2 Q.B. 330.

[302] *Stewart v Greenock Insurance Co* (1848) 1 Macq. 328.

[303] *Whitworth v Shepherd* (1884) 12 R. 204.

[304] *Simpson v Thomson* (1877) 5 R. (HL) 40. See also *Societe du Gaz v Armateurs Francais*, 1925 S.C. 332.

has gone into liquidation, is bound by that rule.[305] These clauses do not contravene s.1(3) of the Third Parties (Rights Against Insurers) Act 1930 or s.17 of the Third Parties (Rights Against Insurers) Act 2010, since they attempt neither to avoid the contract of indemnity nor alter the parties' rights thereunder.

20.41 **Liabilities in case of abandonment**—Abandonment when accepted divests the insured of the property in the subject matter, and also frees him from any liabilities subsequently effeiring to it, such as the liability to meet the expenses of local authorities having statutory powers to remove wrecks.[306] It would seem to be a doubtful point whether the insurer, if on abandonment he merely pays for a total loss and takes no active steps to invest himself with the subject mater, comes under any liability.[307]

20.42 **Partial loss: Particular average**—Where damage occurs through a peril insured against which is not of sufficient gravity to amount to a constructive total loss, or which the insured does not choose to treat as such, there is a partial loss. The partial loss may result from a sacrifice which amounts to a general average act, and is then known as a general average loss.[308] Where there is not a general average loss, a partial loss is known as a particular average, or sometimes as an average, loss.[309] Where, in a policy covering ship and cargo, certain kinds of goods are "warranted free from average", the insurer is not liable for a partial loss of the goods in question, unless the contract be apportionable. The contract may be apportionable either expressly, e.g. by the insertion of such words as "to pay average on each package as if separately insured", or impliedly, e.g. where the insurance is general, but on separate articles wholly distinct in their nature.[310] In such cases the underwriter is liable for a total loss of any separate package or article. Where goods are warranted free from average under a certain percentage of their value, he is not liable unless the damage exceeds that percentage.[311] Such conditions are inserted in a clause, known as the memorandum, appended to the policy. In the statutory form of policy the words are "free from average, unless general, or the ship be stranded". Under a policy in these terms the insurer is liable if the ship be stranded, although the stranding may not be the cause of the injury to the goods.[312] To stranding is added, in some policies, sinking, burning and collision.[313]

20.43 **Measure of indemnity**—The amount which may be recovered as a partial loss, or the "measure of indemnity", is, in the case of injury to a ship which has been repaired, the reasonable cost of the repairs, "less the customary deductions, but not exceeding the sum insured in respect of any one casualty".[314] The principal customary deduction, recognised before the Act as a custom of trade, is a deduction of one-third of the cost of the repairs in respect of the advantage gained by the

---

[305] *Firma C-Trade S.A. v Newcastle Protection and Indemnity Association* [1991] 2 A.C. 1.
[306] *Barraclough v Brown* [1897] A.C. 615.
[307] Lambeth, *Templeman on Marine Insurance* (1986), Ch.7.
[308] As to general average, see paras 22.34–22.42, below.
[309] 1906 Act s.64.
[310] See generally Lambeth, *Templeman on Marine Insurance* (1986), Ch.8.
[311] 1906 Act s.76.
[312] *The Alsace Lorraine* [1893] P. 209.
[313] *The Glenlivet* [1894] P. 48 (burning).
[314] 1906 Act s.69(1).

insured in having new material instead of old.[315] If the ship is partially repaired the insured is entitled to the cost of repairs, under like deduction, and also to the depreciation resulting from the unrepaired damage. When the ship has not been repaired, and has not been sold in her damaged state during the risk, the insured is entitled to the depreciation in value, provided that does not exceed the reasonable cost of repair.[316] If she is sold unrepaired, the measure of indemnity is the difference between her value, if undamaged, at the place of sale, and the actual price obtained.[317] When there is a partial loss of freight the measure of indemnity is such proportion of the sum fixed by the policy, in the case of a valued policy, or of the insurable value in the case of an unvalued policy, as the proportion of freight lost by the assured bears to the whole freight at the risk of the assured under the policy.[318] For the complicated rules with regard to the measure of indemnity in the case of a partial loss of goods reference must be made to the Act, and to the exposition in Templeman on Marine Insurance.[319]

Successive losses—Unless the policy otherwise provides the insurer is liable for successive losses, even although the total amount of such losses may exceed the sum insured.[320] But when a partial loss has not been repaired and is followed by a total loss, whether from a peril insured against or not, the underwriter is not liable for the partial loss, and it is immaterial that under another policy by which the cause of the total loss is covered a deduction may be made for the loss in value caused by the partial loss.[321] **20.44**

Suing and labouring clause—In certain cases, under a clause in the policy known as the suing and labouring clause, a sum in excess of that fixed in the policy may be recovered. This clause, in its usual form, provides that in case of any loss or misfortune, it shall be lawful to the assured "to sue, labour and travel for in and about the defence safeguard and recovery" of the ship or goods, and that the insurers will contribute to the charges thereof.[322] This clause is read as supplementary to the contract of insurance, and entitles the insured to recover from the underwriters any sums reasonably expended in endeavour to prevent or minimise a loss, provided that it was a loss insured against under the policy.[323] A claim of this nature may be made although the underwriters have paid for a total loss,[324] or, in the case of a partial loss, though the policy was free of particular average.[325] The clause does not cover anything paid for salvage, although services of a similar kind, if rendered under contract and not as salvage, fall within it.[326] Nor does it include general average losses and contribution.[327] The Act provides that: **20.45**

---

[315] *Aitchison v Lohre* (1879) L.R. 4 App. Cas. 755.

[316] 1906 Act ss.69(2), (3); *Irvin v Hine* [1950] 1 K.B. 555.

[317] *Pitman v Universal Marine Insurance Co* (1882) L.R. 9 Q.B.D. 192.

[318] 1906 Act s.70.

[319] 1906 Act s.71; Lambeth, *Templeman on Marine Insurance* (1986), p.273.

[320] 1906 Act s.77; this section only applies to successive repaired losses, *Kusel v Atkin* [1997] 2 Lloyd's Rep. 749.

[321] *British and Foreign Insurance Co v Wilson Shipping Co* [1921] 1 A.C. 188.

[322] Lambeth, *Templeman on Marine Insurance* (1986), Ch.12.

[323] 1906 Act s.78(3); *Kidston v Empire Marine Insurance Co* (1867) L.R. 2 C.P. 357; *Wilson Bros Bobbin Co v Green* [1917] 1 K.B. 860; *Nishina Trading Co v Chiyoda Fire and Marine Insurance Co* [1969] 2 Q.B. 449.

[324] 1906 Act s.78(1); *Aitchison v Lohre* (1879) 4 App. Cas. 755.

[325] 1906 Act s.78(1); *Kidston* (1867) L.R. 2 C.P. 357.

[326] *Aitchison v Lohre* (1879) L.R. 4 App. Cas. 755.

[327] 1906 Act s.78(2).

"[I]t is the duty of the assured and his agent, in all cases, to take such measures as may be reasonable for the purpose of averting or minimising a loss."[328]

This has been interpreted as requiring the insured to act as any reasonable person would to safeguard his property and unusual expenditure may be recovered if it can be shown that a prudent insured would have incurred it.[329]

20.46 **Marine insurance policies and arrestment of ships**—An action to enforce a contract of marine insurance has been held not to provide a proper basis for the arrestment of a ship in terms of s.47 of the Administration of Justice Act 1956.[330]

FURTHER READING

Bennet, H., *Law of Marine Insurance*, 2nd edn (Oxford: Oxford University Press, 2006).

Clarke, M.A., *The Law of Insurance Contracts* (Informa Professional, 2002).

Gilman, G., *Arnould's Law of Marine Insurance*, 17th edn (London: Sweet and Maxwell, 2010).

Gow, J.J., *The Mercantile and Industrial Law of Scotland* (Edinburgh: W. Green,1964).

Ivamy, E.R.H., *Fire and Motor Insurance* (LexisNexis Butterworths, 2001).

Ivamy, E.R.H., *Marine Insurance*, 4th edn (LexisNexis Butterworths, 1985).

Ivamy, E.R.H., *Personal, Accident, Life and Other Insurance*, 2nd edn (LexisNexis Butterworths, 1980).

Ivamy, E.R.H., *General Principles of Insurance Law*, 6th edn (LexisNexis Butterworths, 1993).

McGee, A., *Modern Law of Insurance*, 3rd edn (LexisNexis Butterworths, 2011).

Lambeth, R.J., *Templeman on Marine Insurance*, 6th edn (Financial Times Management, 1986).

Legh-Jones, N., Birds, J. and Owen, D., *Macgillivray on Insurance Law*, 11th edn (London: Sweet and Maxwell, 2008) with supplement (2011).

Joint Consultation Paper of the Law Commission and Scottish Law Commission, *Insurance Contract Law: Post Contract Duties and Other Issues* (HMSO, 2012), Law Com. Consultation Paper No.201 and Scot. Law Com. Discussion Paper No.152.

Joint Consultation Paper of the Law Commission and Scottish Law Commission, *Insurance Contract Law: The Business Insured's Duty of Disclosure and the Law of Warranties* (HMSO, 2012), Law Com. Consultation Paper No.204 and Scot. Law Com. Discussion Paper No.155.

---

[328] 1906 Act s.78(4).

[329] *Integrated Container Service Inc v British Traders Insurance Co* [1984] 1 Lloyd's Rep. 154, CA.

[330] *West of England Ship Owners v Aifanourios Shipping S.A., The Aifanourios*, 1980 S.C. 346; *Gatoil International Inc v Arkwright-Boston Manufacturers Mutual Insurance Co*, 1985 S.L.T. 68.

CHAPTER 21

CARRIAGE BY LAND

In Scots law, carriage is a species of contract for work and services.[1] It is a contract **21.01** for the carriage of passengers or goods in a vehicle provided and operated by the carrier or someone on his behalf. It does not include, for example, the service provided by a supplier delivering goods in his own vehicle nor a contract to hire a vehicle to be driven by the hirer or an employee.[2] A carrier of goods or passengers comes under duties both in contract and delict. In addition, Scots law has applied principles of strict liability derived from Roman law to those carriers who fall into the limited class of common carriers.[3] Carriers of goods and passengers by road and rail are subject to strict statutory controls. Operators of vehicles for the carriage of goods for hire or reward or in connection with a trade or business require to be licensed[4] and there are extensive controls on the carriage of various types of goods, particularly dangerous goods.[5] Licensing requirements also apply in relation to the carriage of passengers by road.[6] Taxi services are also subject to licensing and control. The organisation and regulation of railway services has been repeatedly changed and may be subject to further change.[7] Carriage of passengers and goods within the EU and between Member States of the EU is subject to more and more regulation by the European Union, and provisions are also increasingly concerning purely domestic services.[8] Carriage by rail and road is a reserved matter under the Scotland Act 1998.[9]

---

[1] *Locatio operis faciendi*: contrast English law, in which it is a form of bailment: see *Chitty on Contracts*, edited by H.G. Beale, 30th edn (London: Sweet and Maxwell, 2008), para.36–001.

[2] Note, however, that the statutory licensing regulations may apply: see below.

[3] See next paragraph.

[4] Goods Vehicles (Licensing of Operators) Act 1995, as amended and EC Reg 1072/2009 (common rules for access to the international road haulage market): see *Wilkinson's Road Traffic Offences*, edited by K. McCormac et al, 25th edn (London: Sweet and Maxwell, 2011), paras 13.29–13.72; A. Brown, *Wheatley's Road Traffic Law in Scotland*, 4th edn (Edinburgh: Bloomsbury Professional, 2007).

[5] e.g. Carriage of Dangerous Goods and Use of Transportable Pressure Equipment Regulations 2009 (SI 2009/1348).

[6] Public Passenger Vehicles Act 1981, Transport Act 1985, Transport (Scotland) Act 2001; *Wilkinson's Road Traffic Offences*, (2011), paras 13.112 et seq. and Regulation (EC) No 1073/2009 of the European Parliament and of the Council of 21 October 2009 on common rules for access to the international market for coach and bus services (OJ L130, 14.11.2009, p.88).

[7] See currently, Railways Act 2005, Transport (Scotland) Act 2005: up-to-date information can be found at Office of Rail Regulation at *http://www.rail-reg.gov.uk* [Accessed July 6, 2012]: see generally *Stair Memorial Encyclopaedia*, Vol.3, "Carriage" (Reissue).

[8] See paras 21.13 and 21.15 below.

[9] See Sch.5, Heads E1–E5 of the Scotland Act 1998, as amended by inserting a few additions to the exceptions.

21.02 Common carriers—A carrier may or may not be a common carrier. A common carrier is one who undertakes for hire[10] to transport the goods of all who choose to employ him in the business which he professes to ply. He may be a common carrier though he limits the class of goods which he is willing to carry, or though he indicates that certain goods will be carried only on special conditions, but it is essential that he should profess to be willing to carry for all those who choose to employ him.[11] If he makes no such profession he is a private carrier. There are significant differences between common and private carriers in two main respects: (1) in the obligation to accept employment; (2) in the degree of liability for loss or injury to goods.[12] In modern conditions, the common carrier is an endangered, if not quite extinct, species.[13] By statute, no person is to be regarded as a common carrier by railway.[14] The National Rail Conditions of Carriage apply to all rail tickets in the United Kingdom.[15] Any person providing a "universal postal service" under the Postal Services Act 2000 is not to be regarded as a common carrier.[16] Although under the Carriers Act 1830 a common carrier cannot limit his liability simply by notice, he may do so by contract,[17] and most, if not all, contracts for carriage are subject to standard terms which are likely to contain limitations of liability. The courts have at times shown some reluctance to hold that a carrier is a common carrier.[18] Taxi and public service vehicle operators may, however, still fall to be treated as common carriers, and there are some other such cases.[19] The distinction also remains significant because many of the decided cases on the liability of carriers turn on or refer to it.

21.03 Obligation to carry—A private carrier may accept any offer of employment or refuse it. A common carrier makes a continuous offer to carry[20] provided, in the case of goods, that they are of the class he professes to carry, that they are not dangerous or insufficiently packed; that they arrive in time; that he has room in his conveyance; that his charges are paid or tendered; in the case of passengers also that they are in a reasonably fit state to be carried.[21] An unjustifiable refusal is a ground for an action for damages.[22] A common carrier is bound by a list of fares publicly advertised,[23] and in any case is not entitled to charge more than a reasonable fare.[24]

---

[10] See *Barr v Caledonian Ry* (1890) 18 R. 139.

[11] *Great Northern Ry v L.E.P.* [1922] 2 K.B. 742.

[12] A common carrier has no higher liability for injury to passengers than does a private carrier.

[13] cf. *Chitty on Contracts* (2008), para.36–010.

[14] Railways Act 1993 s.123: similar provision has been made for the operators of the Channel Tunnel and for London Transport.

[15] See *http://www.nationalrail.co.uk* [Accessed July 6, 2012].

[16] Postal Services Act 2000 s.99.

[17] See s.6: this, of course, is subject to the Unfair Contract Terms Act 1977.

[18] See *Belfast Ropeworks v Bushell* [1918] 1 K.B. 210, but see next note.

[19] See, e.g. *A. Siohn & Co and Academy Garments (Wigan) v R.H. Hagland & Son (Transport)* [1976] 2 Lloyd's Rep. 428.

[20] *A. Siohn & Co and Academy Garments (Wigan) v R.H. Hagland & Son (Transport)* [1976] 2 Lloyd's Rep. 428.

[21] Bell, *Principles*, s.159; *Clarke v West Ham Corp* [1909] 2 K.B. 858. Note the analogous obligation of an innkeeper: *Rothfield v N.B.R.*, 1920 S.C. 805.

[22] Bell, *Principles*, s.159.

[23] *Campbell v Ker* Unreported February 24, 1810 FC.

[24] *Great Western Ry v Sutton* (1868) L.R. 4 (HL) 226 at 237.

Strict liability of common carrier[25]—The exceptional liability for the loss of **21.04** goods which rests on a common carrier is in Scotland based on the Praetorian Edict; in England, on the custom of the realm.[26] The common carrier is in the position of an insurer, and is liable for loss of or damage to goods without affirmative proof of negligence. Proof that the goods were stolen is no defence.[27] For loss by accidental fire, which was an exception to the carrier's liability at common law,[28] a common carrier by land, though not by sea, is liable by statute.[29] It is a valid defence to the carrier that the goods have been lost by the fault of the sender, as where they are insufficiently addressed[30]; by act of God; by the Queen's enemies, including the case of a rebellion, not of a mere riot[31]; or by their inherent vice, as where a horse struggled through an opening left as a feeding window.[32] These defences are available only if the carrier has not deviated from the route agreed upon, or can show that the particular event would have happened even if he had not deviated.[33] In addition, he must show that neither he nor his servants contributed to the casualty through their negligence.[34] In the absence of express agreement to the contrary, a carrier who issues a ticket or consignment note is responsible for the whole journey, though it is known that he carries only for part of it.[35]

Passengers—Any person who holds himself out as willing to carry members of **21.05** the public is a common carrier of passengers inasmuch as he is bound to carry persons willing to pay the fare unless there is some good reason for not doing so.[36] However, there is no edictal liability imposed for the safety of the passengers carried.[37]

Passenger's luggage—A common carrier is liable for the loss of a passenger's **21.06** luggage.[38] The relevant rules were largely formulated in cases relating to luggage accompanying rail passengers. The National Rail conditions of carriage will now

---

[25] A private carrier is liable only for fault or negligence: Stair, I, 13, 3; Bell, *Principles*, s.235; *Copland v Brogan*, 1916 S.C. 277 (gratuitous carriage).

[26] Dig., IV, 9, 1; Stair, I, 13, 3; Bell, *Principles*, s.235; and see above, para.15.07; and *Burns v Royal Hotel (St Andrews)*, 1958 S.C. 354. The question of how the edict *nautae, caupones, stabularii* ("carriers by sea, innkeepers, stablers") came to apply to carriers by land is considered in A. Rodger, "The Praetor's Edict and Carriage of Goods by Land in Scots Law" (1968) 3 Ir. Jur. (N.S.) 175.

[27] Bell, *Principles*, s.238.

[28] See above, para.13.08 and *Burns v Royal Hotel (St Andrews)*, 1958 S.C. 354, as to onus of proof.

[29] Mercantile Law Amendment (Scotland) Act 1856 s.17. A private carrier is also liable under s.17: *James Kemp (Leslie) v Robertson*, 1967 S.L.T. 213; *Graham v The Shore Porters Society*, 1979 S.L.T. 119; *Boomsma v Clark & Rose*, 1983 S.L.T. (Sh. Ct) 67. It may be possible to contract out of the statutory liability under s.17: *Graham v The Shore Porters Society*, 1979 S.L.T. 119; *Boomsma v Clark & Rose*, 1983 S.L.T. (Sh. Ct) 67. The loss must have occurred in Scotland: *Atlantic Computing Services (UK) Ltd v Burns Express Freight Ltd*, 2004 S.C. 365.

[30] *Caledonian Ry v Hunter* (1858) 20 D. 1097.

[31] See *Curtis v Mathews* [1919] 1 K.B. 425.

[32] *Ralston v Caledonian Ry* (1878) 5 R. 671.

[33] *Morrison v Shaw Savill, etc. Co* [1916] 2 K.B. 783.

[34] *Burns v Royal Hotel (St Andrews)*, 1958 S.C. 354.

[35] *Logan v Highland Ry* (1899) 2 F. 292, referred to in *Aberdeen Grit Co v Ellerman's Wilson Line*, 1933 S.C. 9.

[36] *Clarke v West Ham Corp* [1909] 2 K.B. 858.

[37] As to liability for negligence, see para.21.10, below; but note the increasing reach of European Regulations on domestic carriage, see para.21.13.

[38] *Parker v L.M.S. Ry*, 1930 S.C. 822; *Campbell v Cal. Ry Co* (1852) 14 D. 806; but again note the increasing reach of European Regulations on domestic carriage, see para.21.13.

govern the position in relation to luggage carried by rail. The older rules are, however, probably still applicable to operators of public service vehicles.[39] There is liability for loss even if the luggage is inside the vehicle with the passenger unless the carrier can show that its loss was due to lack of reasonable care on the part of the passenger.[40] The liability ends when the luggage is delivered at the end of the journey, though it may then be left with the carrier as a depositary or custodier,[41] in which case he is only liable for negligence.[42] A carrier is not bound to carry, as passenger's luggage, anything the passenger may choose to bring with him. The following general definition of passenger's luggage has been given:

> "Whatever the passenger takes with him for his personal use or convenience, according to the habits or wants of the particular class to which he belongs, either with reference to the immediate necessities or to the ultimate purpose of the journey."[43]

The carrier is also entitled to refuse to carry, without additional charge, articles requiring special care in carriage, such as a bicycle, gun or fishing-rod, not so packed as to be readily carried without special precautions.[44] Where, without notice to the carrier, articles are taken which are not properly passenger's luggage he is not liable for their loss.[45]

21.07 Delay in transit—The obligation of a common carrier does not amount to insurance against loss or injury caused by delay in transit. It is an obligation to carry within a time reasonable in the circumstances. So where goods were damaged by delay due to a general strike of railwaymen,[46] or to a block on the line caused by an accident not due to the company's negligence,[47] it was held that there was no liability. The carrier, if aware of circumstances likely to cause delay, is bound to warn the passenger or sender of goods.[48] Should delay threaten damage to perishable goods the carrier, as an agent by necessity, is entitled to sell them, but before doing so is bound to communicate with the owner, if reasonably practicable.[49] An obligation to carry within a particular time may be expressly undertaken, or may be inferred from advertisement, as where a railway advertises trains to meet a particular market.[50] Proof that a railway company regularly gave preference in transit to goods marked perishable was held to render them liable for injury on an occasion when they had failed to do so.[51]

---

[39] See para.21.15, below.
[40] *Jenkyns v Southampton Steam Packet Co* [1919] 2 K.B. 135; *Vosper v G.W. Ry* [1928] 1 K.B. 340; *Parker v L.M.S. Ry*, 1930 S.C. 822.
[41] *Parker v L.M.S. Ry*, 1930 S.C. 822.
[42] *Lyons v Caledonian Ry*, 1909 S.C. 1185.
[43] *Jenkyns v Southampton Steam Packet Co* [1919] 2 K.B. 135; *Buckland v The King* [1933] 1 K.B. 329.
[44] *Britten v Great Northern Ry* [1899] 1 Q.B. 243.
[45] *Macrow v Great Western Ry* (1871) L.R. 6 Q.B. 612.
[46] *Sims v Midland Ry* [1913] 1 K.B. 103.
[47] *Anderson v N.B.R.* (1875) 2 R. 443.
[48] *McConnachie v Great North of Scotland Ry* (1875) 3 R. 79; *Jarvie v Cal. Ry* (1875) 2 R. 623.
[49] *Springer v Great Western Ry* [1921] 1 K.B. 257.
[50] *Finlay v N.B.R.* (1870) 8 M. 959.
[51] *Macdonald v Highland Ry* (1873) 11 M. 614.

Delay in carriage of passengers—With regard to passengers, the general obliga- **21.08** tion is merely to carry within a time reasonable in all the circumstances of the case. The publication of a timetable indicating times of departure and connections does not amount to an undertaking that these times will be observed, but it may amount to an undertaking that the trains indicated will be run.[52] It has been held that where a connection was missed, owing to want of reasonable care on the part of the company, the question whether the passenger could recover, as damages, the expense of a special train which he had ordered depended upon whether he would probably have done the same if he had had no recourse.[53] As has been seen, liability in connection with rail travel will now only arise from breach of the terms of the contract of carriage, but these rules still apply in substance to the liability of a common carrier who has not made special contractual arrangements with his customer.[54]

Statutory limitation of liability—Section 1 of the Carriers Act 1830, provides **21.09** that the liability of a common carrier by land for loss or injury to goods (including passengers' luggage[55]) is excluded, in the case of certain specified goods, unless their nature and value have been declared when they are placed in the carrier's hands, and an increased charge, if demanded, has been paid. Thirty-six classes of goods are specified, having the common characteristic of great value relative to their bulk, and including the precious metals, bank notes or securities, jewellery, pictures, furs and lace. Such goods must be declared if their value exceeds £10. If an increased charge is to be made it must be posted in the office or receiving-house of the carrier, but failure in this respect does not deprive the carrier of the statutory immunity.[56] The nature and value of the goods must be declared; it is not sufficient to make a general statement that they are valuable.[57] The Act does not protect the carrier from loss due to any theft, embezzlement or forgery of his servants, but the sender of the goods must prove circumstances, beyond the mere fact of opportunity, which render it more likely that the goods have been stolen by the carrier's servants than by some other thief.[58]

Liability for negligence—Quite apart from the strict liability of common carriers, **21.10** all carriers, whether common or private, are subject to the ordinary principles of the law of reparation.[59] Thus a carrier is liable for his own or his servants' negligence, whether it constitutes a breach of the implied conditions of the contract or a breach of the carrier's duty to take reasonable care for the safety of persons or property lawfully placed in his charge.[60] Negligence involves failure in a duty, and therefore in cases where the responsibility of a common carrier does not attach, there is no liability for injury by pure accident, by the criminal or wrongful

---

[52] *Denton v Great Northern Ry* (1856) 5 El. & Bl. 800.

[53] *Le Blanche v L. and N.-W. Ry* (1876) L.R. 1 C.P.D. 286.

[54] Note also the increasing reach of European Regulations on domestic carriage, see para.21.13.

[55] *Casswell v Cheshire Lines Committee* [1907] 2 K.B. 499.

[56] *Rusk v N.B.R.*, 1920 2 S.L.T. 139.

[57] *Rusk*, 1920 2 S.L.T. 139.

[58] Carriers Act 1830 (the "1830 Act") s.8, as amended by the Criminal Law Act 1967; *Campbell v N.B.R.* (1875) 2 R. 433.

[59] See Chs 25–28. Note also the increasing reach of European Regulations on domestic carriage, including their provisions on the obligations of carriers and the rights of passengers, see para.21.13.

[60] *Meux v Great Eastern Ry* [1895] 2 Q.B. 387; *Boomsma v Clark & Rose*, 1983 S.L.T. (Sh. Ct) 67.

acts of parties, such as fellow passengers, for whom the carrier is not responsible,[61] or from a breakdown in the carriage which could not have been prevented by a reasonable system of inspection.[62] If goods are delivered to a private carrier in good condition, and tendered by him in a damaged state, that is prima facie evidence of fault.[63] Similarly, anything in the nature of a railway accident is prima facie evidence of negligence, and it rests with the railway company to prove that the accident was due to some cause, for example a latent and undiscoverable flaw, for which they were not responsible.[64] It would appear that the carrier's duty of care does not extend to persons who travel surreptitiously, or in violation of the carrier's regulations.[65] But his responsibility does extend to persons carried gratuitously.[66]

21.11 Exclusion of or limitation of liability by contract—The Carriers Act 1830 prevents a common carrier from limiting his liability by public notice or declaration but leaves it open to him to make special arrangements with individuals excluding or restricting liability for loss of or damage to goods,[67] and private carriers were always free to contract on their own terms.[68] However, the Unfair Contract Terms Act 1977 applies to all contracts of carriage.[69] A contractual term or a provision of a notice[70] purporting to exclude or restrict liability for breach of duty[71] arising in the course of the carrier's business or from the occupation of the carrier's business premises is void if it excludes or restricts liability in respect of death or personal injury, and may be unenforceable if it was not fair and reasonable to incorporate the term in the contract or to allow reliance on the provision of the notice.[72] The fact that a passenger agreed to, or was aware of, the term or provision is not in itself sufficient evidence that he knowingly and voluntarily assumed the risk.[73] "Breach of duty" does not extend to duties higher than the duty to use reasonable care and skill,[74] and thus the Act does not cover any clause avoiding the strict liability of the common carrier. But neither a private nor a common carrier may exclude liability for death or injury

---

[61] *East Indian Ry v Mukerjee* [1901] A.C. 396.

[62] *Readhead v Midland Ry* (1869) L.R. 4 Q.B. 379; *Reynolds v Lanarkshire Tramways Co* (1908) 16 S.L.T. 230.

[63] *Sutton & Co v Ciceri & Co* (1890) 17 R. (HL) 40.

[64] *Ballard v N.B.R.*, 1923 S.C. (HL) 43.

[65] *Thompson v N.B.R.* (1882) 9 R. 1101; *Grand Trunk Ry v Barnett* [1911] A.C. 361.

[66] *Austin v Great Western Ry* (1867) L.R. 2 Q.B. 442.

[67] 1830 Act s.6.

[68] A clause seeking to exclude liability for negligence or breach of contract will be construed contra proferentem: *Graham v The Shore Porters Society*, 1979 S.L.T. 119; *Boomsma v Clark & Rose*, 1983 S.L.T. (Sh. Ct) 67.

[69] Unfair Contract Terms Act 1977 (the "1977 Act") s.15(2)(c); *Boomsma v Clark & Rose*, 1983 S.L.T. (Sh. Ct) 67.

[70] ss.15 and 16 of the 1977 Act as amended by the Law Reform (Miscellaneous Provisions) (Scotland) Act 1990 s.68. "Notice" includes an announcement whether or not in writing and any other communication or pretended communication: s.25(1) as amended by the 1990 Act.

[71] "Breach of duty" is defined in s.25(1).

[72] 1977 Act s.16(1) as amended; *Boomsma v Clark & Rose*, 1983 S.L.T. (Sh. Ct) 67. As to reasonableness, see para.9.24, above. See also *Granville Oil and Chemicals Ltd v Davis Turner & Co Ltd* [2003] EWCA Civ 570; [2003] 1 All E.R. (Comm) 819 (time-bar clause). Note also the increasing reach of European Regulations on domestic carriage, which provide mandatory minimum levels of compensation, see para.21.13.

[73] 1977 Act s.16(3), as amended.

[74] 1977 Act s.25(1).

caused by their negligence.[75] A clause purporting to exclude or restrict liability for breach of contract or for unsatisfactory performance may be unenforceable if the contract of carriage is either a consumer contract[76] or a standard form contract.[77] Any valid exclusion or restriction clause must be shown to have been incorporated in the contract.[78] It has been held that if a carrier deviates from the agreed route, he loses the benefit of any valid conditions in his favour, and is liable for damages however caused.[79] The right of the carrier to found on a valid limitation clause may be lost by actings which amount to repudiation of the contract.[80]

Ejection from conveyance—There is some authority for the view that any carrier **21.12** has at common law the right to eject from his conveyance a passenger who refuses to pay the fare.[81] The Railways Board had express statutory power to arrest and detain any person who travelled, or attempted to travel, without paying his fare, and with the intent to avoid payment[82]; and this was held to justify summary expulsion of a passenger who had a ticket which was not available on a particular day, though there was no averment that he had any intention to travel without paying his fare.[83] Any unnecessary violence in ejecting a passenger will found an action for damages.[84]

Changes to passenger rights on certain domestic services (EC and EU **21.13** **Regulations)**—For rail carriage of passengers by undertakings licensed in accordance with the Railway Undertakings Licensing Directive[85]—even for purely domestic services—the EC Regulation on rail passengers' rights and obligations[86]

---

[75] 1977 Act s.16. See too the Public Passenger Vehicles Act 1981 s.29, in relation to operators of public service vehicles.

[76] "Consumer contract" is defined in s.25(1).

[77] 1977 Act ss.15(2)(c), 17, 25(1). As to purported indemnity clauses in consumer contracts, see s.18. See generally Ch.9, above.

[78] See para.5.25, above; cf. *McCutcheon v MacBrayne*, 1964 S.C. (HL) 28; *William Teacher & Sons Ltd v Bell Lines Ltd*, 1991 S.L.T. 876. As to provisions of notices, see s.16(1A) of the 1977 Act, as amended.

[79] *Lord Polwarth v N.B.R.*, 1908 S.C. 1275: but the carrier did not lose the benefit of a statutory limitation of liability; *L. and N. W. Ry v Neilson* [1922] 2 A.C. 263; *Hain S.S. Co v Tate & Lyle* [1936] 2 All E.R. 597. See also para.22.21, below, for deviation in sea carriage.

[80] *John Carter (Fine Worsteds) v Hanson Haulage (Leeds) Ltd* [1965] 2 Q.B. 495. Contrast with actings amounting to material breach entitling the other party to rescind: see 1977 Act s.22, and Ch.9, above.

[81] *North-Eastern Ry v Mathews* (1866) 5 Irvine 237; but see opinions in *Harris v N.B.R.* (1891) 18 R. 1009.

[82] Railways Clauses Consolidation (Scotland) Act 1845 ss.96, 97; *Gerber v British Railways Board*, 1969 S.C. 7.

[83] *Highland Ry v Menzies* (1878) 5 R. 887.

[84] *Maxwell v Cal. Ry* (1898) 25 R. 550.

[85] Council Directive 95/18/EC of 19 June 1995 on the licensing of railway undertakings. OJ L 143, 27.6.1995, p.70.

[86] Regulation (EC) No 1371/2007 of the European Parliament and of the Council of 23 October 2007 on rail passengers' rights and obligations, OJ L315, 3.12.2007, p.14. The EC Regulation harmonises the laws across the EU Member States, for international and domestic services alike; it is embedded into the legal framework within the United Kingdom by the Rail Passenger's Rights and Obligations Regulation 2010 (SI 2010/1504) and the Rail Passenger's Rights and Obligations (Exemptions) Regulation 2009 (SI 2009/2970). The latter exempts domestic services (defined in EC Regulation 1371/2007 art.3(11) as rail passenger services "which do not cross a border of a Member State") until December 4, 2014 (unless renewed beyond that date, see EC Regulation 1371/2007 art.2(4)) from the requirements of additional Regulation provisions which are in force for inter-European travel; insofar see para.21.22.

imposes mandatory rules[87] relating to availability of tickets,[88] liability for passengers and their luggage,[89] mandatory insurance of the railway undertaking,[90] the right to transport for and information on the accessibility of railway services by disabled persons and persons with reduced mobility ("DPRMs"),[91] and on ensuring passenger's personal security.[92] These rules came into force on December 4, 2009, overriding the old law. The designated enforcement body is the Office of Rail Regulation while the Rail Passengers' Council or the London Transport Users' Committee, as the case may be, are the complaints handling bodies.[93]

From March 1, 2013, by virtue of the EU Regulation on passenger rights in bus and coach transport,[94] mandatory rules[95] apply for certain regular passenger services by bus or coach,[96] also covering domestic services. Even if the exemption[97] is used by the United Kingdom, rules on non-discriminatory contract conditions,[98] rights to transport for DPRMs within boundaries of safety and feasibility,[99] disability training for personnel of carriers,[100] compensation levels in respect of wheelchairs and other mobility equipment,[101] minimum information to be provided to passengers and on handling of complaints[102] and general rules on enforcement[103] cannot be excluded. Further provisions, subject to potential exemption, concern rules on tickets,[104] compensation and assistance to passengers in the event of accidents resulting in death or personal injury or loss of or damage to luggage,[105] non-discrimination and mandatory assistance for DPRMs[106] and rights of passengers in the event of cancellation or delay.[107]

---

[87] EC Regulation 1371/2007 art.6; however, conditions more favourable to the passenger can be applied.

[88] EC Regulation 1371/2007 art.9.

[89] EC Regulation 1371/2007 art.11, referring largely to the provisions as set out in the Convention concerning the International Carriage by Rail of 9 May 1980 as amended by the Protocol of 3 June 1999 for the Modification of the Convention concerning International Carriage by Rail (COTIF) of 9 May 1980 (Protocol 1999), Appendix A, "Uniform Rules concerning the Contract of International Carriage of Passengers by Rail (CIV)", as set out in more detail in para.21.21.

[90] EC Regulation 1371/2007 art.12.

[91] EC Regulation 1371/2007 arts 19, 20(1).

[92] EC Regulation 1371/2007 art.26.

[93] The Rail Passenger's Rights and Obligations Regulation 2010 (SI 2010/1504) Pt 3.

[94] Regulation (EU) No 181/2011 of the European Parliament and of the Council of 16 February 2011 concerning the rights of passengers in bus and coach transport; OJ L55, 28.2.2011, p.1.

[95] EU Regulation 181/2011 art.6; however, conditions more favourable to the passenger can be applied.

[96] Carriage has to be from or to a Member State and differences in provisions apply whether the service is for a scheduled distance of more that 250km or less and whether the services occasional or mostly operated outside the EU (see EU Regulation 181/2011 art.2(1–5)). Member States can make exemptions for certain domestic services or services largely performed outside the EU for a period of up to four years, renewable once (see EU Regulation 181/2011 art.2(4 and 5)).

[97] See EU Regulation 181/2011 art.2 (4 and 5) and art.16(2); taking into account the corresponding SI for rail services, it seems likely that the United Kingdom will use the power to exempt relevant services before the date of entry into force of the Regulation.

[98] EU Regulation 181/2011 art.4(2).

[99] EU Regulation 181/2011 arts 9 and 10(1).

[100] EU Regulation 181/2011 art.16(1b) and (2).

[101] EU Regulation 181/2011 art.17(1–2).

[102] EU Regulation 181/2011 arts 24–27.

[103] EU Regulation 181/2011 art.28.

[104] EU Regulation 181/2011 art.4(1).

[105] EU Regulation 181/2011 arts 7–8.

[106] EU Regulation 181/2011 arts 9–18.

[107] EU Regulation 181/2011 arts 19–23.

Lien of carrier—A carrier has at common law a special lien over goods for **21.14** his charges for their carriage, but no lien for a general balance.[108] He is not entitled to detain a passenger, or any part of his clothing, for the fare.[109] A contract between a carrier and a trader whereby the former obtains a general lien is effectual in a question with the trustee in the sequestration of the trader.[110] A provision in a contract whereby goods were carried at owner's risk, under which the goods were subjected to a general lien for all charges due by the "owners", was held not to preclude the senders of the goods, as unpaid sellers, from exercising their right of stoppage *in transitu*, and thereby acquiring a right to delivery preferable to a claim by the railway company for a general balance due by the consignee.[111]

Road haulage—With certain exceptions[112] no haulier may use a goods vehicle **21.15** for the carriage of goods for hire or reward or in connection with his trade or business without an operator's licence.[113] An operator's licence may be standard or restricted, national or international.[114] Community authorisation is required for the international carriage of goods by road for hire or reward within the EC.[115] All hauliers are subject to the common law, as modified by the Carriers Act 1830,[116] and any conditions contained in licences. A road haulier may, and usually does, limit his liability by special conditions.[117] The modern practice is for road hauliers to limit their profession to that of private carriers.

Public service vehicles[118]—Any motor vehicle is a public service vehicle if it is **21.16** adapted to carry more than eight passengers and is used for carrying passengers for hire or reward, or is not so adapted but is used for carrying passengers for hire or reward at separate fares in the course of a business of carrying passengers.[119] Tramcars are excluded.[120] All operators of public service vehicles require to be

---

[108] *Peebles v Cal. Ry* (1875) 2 R. 346.

[109] *Wolf v Summers* (1811) 2 Camp.631.

[110] *Great Eastern Ry v Lord's Tr* [1909] A.C. 109.

[111] *US Steel Products Co v G.W. Ry* [1916] 1 A.C. 189.

[112] See, e.g. the Goods Vehicles (Licensing of Operators) Regulations 1995 (SI 1995/2869), as amended, and the Goods Vehicles (Licensing of Operators) (Temporary Use in Great Britain) Regulations 1996.

[113] Goods Vehicles (Licensing of Operators) Act 1995 as amended.

[114] See the Goods Vehicles (Licensing of Operators) Regulations 1995 as amended. See too, the International Road Haulage Permits Act 1975.

[115] Goods Vehicles (Community Authorisation) Regulations 1992 (SI 1992/3077) and Regulation (EC) No 1072/2009 of the European Parliament and of the Council of 21 October 2009 on common rules for access to the international road haulage market, but see also Regulation (EC) No 1071/2009 of the European Parliament and of the Council of 21 October 2009 establishing common rules concerning the conditions to be complied with to pursue the occupation of road transport operator.

[116] 1830 Act s.6.

[117] See para.21.11, above; e.g. the Conditions issued by the Road Haulage Association. For an example of effective limitation under these conditions see *Cert Plc v George Hammond Plc* [1999] 2 All E.R. (Comm) 976.

[118] See generally, *Wilkinson's Road Traffic Offences*, Ch.13.

[119] Transport Act 1985 (the "1985 Act") s.137(2); Public Passenger Vehicles Act 1981 (the "1981 Act") s.1(1). Re "hire or reward", see 1981 Act s.1(5) and 1985 Act s.137(3); *Wilkinson's Road Traffic Offences*, paras 13.53, 13.130 and 13.131–13.134.

[120] 1981 Act s.1(1). A "stretch limousine" was held not to be a PSV even though nine passengers could be accommodated because it was not adapted for such carriage: *Vehicle & Operators' Service Agency v Johnson* [2003] EWHC 2104.

licensed and all drivers must hold a passenger carrying vehicle licence.[121] The Transport Act 1985 largely dismantled the pre-existing controls by way of licensing on the provision of services but some controls remain in regard to local services, that is, services operating over distances of less than 15 miles.[122] International passenger services are also subject to regulation.[123] The liabilities of the owner of a public service vehicle in respect of injury to passengers or their luggage are those of a common carrier,[124] although in most cases his liability is modified or restricted by contract.[125]

21.17 International carriage—International carriage by land has been the subject of several international conventions and European Regulations.[126] The Unfair Contract Terms Act 1977 does not strike at any restriction or exclusion clause authorised by such conventions if the United Kingdom is a party thereto.[127]

21.18 International carriage by road: Goods ("CMR")—The CMR, as implemented by the Carriage of Goods by Road Act 1965,[128] applies to every contract for the carriage of goods by road[129] in vehicles[130] for reward, when the place of taking over of the goods and the place designated for delivery, as specified in the contract, are situated in two different countries, at least one being a contracting country.[131] The residence or nationality of the contracting parties is irrelevant.[132] It does not, however, apply to carriage between the United Kingdom and the Republic of Ireland.[133] With certain limited exceptions, it is impossible to contract out of the

---

[121] 1981 Act s.12; *Wilkinson's Road Traffic Offences*, paras 13–01 et seq.

[122] "Local services" are defined in the 1985 Act s.2; see *Wilkinson's Road Traffic Offences*, para.13–121.

[123] See Road Transport (International Passenger Services) Regulations 1984 (SI 1984/748) as amended; EC Regulation 1073/2009 (common rules for access to the international market for coach and bus services) and the Interbus Agreement; *Wilkinson's Road Traffic Offences*, para.13–191.

[124] See para.21.02.

[125] The courts are reluctant to hold that a carrier is a common carrier: see *Belfast Ropeworks v Bushell* [1918] 1 K.B. 210. In relation to modification or restriction by contract, see para.21.11, above.

[126] See below. The texts of the conventions and EC/EU Regulations are detailed, and should be referred to in any particular case.

[127] 1977 Act s.29.

[128] The provisions of the Geneva Convention on the Contract for the International Carriage of Goods by Road 1956 ("CMR"), as amended by the 1978 SDR Protocol (introducing Special Drawing Rights as units of account), are set out in the Sch. to the 1965 Act. The Protocol amendments had been added by the Carriage by Air and Road Act 1979 s.4(2).

[129] As to carriage partly by road and partly by other modes of transport, see CMR art.2, and see *Thermo Engineers v Ferrymasters* [1981] 1 All E.R. 1142 (goods damaged on board ship while being loaded by stevedores) and *Quantum Corp Inc v Plane Trucking Ltd* [2002] EWCA Civ 350; [2002] 1 W.L.R. 2678 (carriage by air and road, based on actual performance of contract, fell within CMR art.1(1)) and *Datec Electronic Holdings Ltd v United Parcels Service Ltd* [2007] UKHL 23; [2007] 1 W.L.R. 1325 (contract for carriage within the meaning of art.1 of the CMR, despite non-conformity of goods with standard terms, as carriage was in fact performed).

[130] "Vehicles" are defined in art.1(2) of the CMR.

[131] CMR art.1(1). See, e.g. the Carriage of Goods by Road (Parties to Convention) Order (SI 1967/1683), as amended by SI 1980/697. The CMR does not apply to carriage performed under the terms of any international postal convention; to funeral consignments; or to furniture removals: art.1(4). The CMR does apply to carriage by states and governmental institutions: art.1(3). Note that for the purposes of the CMR Convention, Jersey is not a different country from the United Kingdom: *Chloride Industrial Batteries v F. & W. Freight* [1989] 1 W.L.R. 823, CA.

[132] Carriage of Goods by Road Act 1965 ("1965 Act") Sch. (thereafter "CMR") art.41.

[133] CMR Protocol of Signature.

statutory provisions.[134] Carriage should be effected under a consignment note, containing certain particulars.[135] The requirement of a consignment note does not preclude the application of the Convention between the parties to the contract, where a consignment note cannot be completed contemporaneously with the conclusion of the contract, as in long-term contracts for unascertained goods.[136] However, a claim under the Convention against a continuing carrier failed, where the latter had not accepted the consignment note.[137] The note is prima facie evidence of the contract, and gives rise to certain presumptions.[138] The sender's rights and obligations are set out in detail, as are the carrier's.[139] The carrier is liable for loss of or damage to goods, and for delay in delivery[140] but not for remote consequential loss.[141] In certain circumstances,[142] his liability is excluded and, if not excluded, is limited,[143] but he cannot benefit from the Act's protection where he has been guilty of wilful misconduct or default.[144] Where several carriers are liable, damages will be apportioned.[145] Any action under the 1965 Act must be

---

[134] CMR arts 40, 41.

[135] CMR arts 4–6.

[136] *Gefco UK Ltd v Mason (No.1)* [1998] 2 Lloyd's Rep. 585 and CMR art.4.

[137] *Parr v Clark & Rose Ltd*, 2002 S.C.L.R. 222.

[138] CMR arts 4–9; *SGS-Ates Componenti Elettronici S.p.A. v Grappo* [1977] R.T.R. 442 (acceptance of consignment note by successive carrier).

[139] CMR arts 7–16. The sender may, inter alia, stop the goods in transit, or change the consignee. The carrier may, inter alia, sell perishable goods. The carrier has a lien over the goods for carriage charges shown to be due in the consignment note; the CMR (arts 13(2) with 41) creates a self-contained code so that contractual lien clauses going beyond the scope provided by the CMR are null and void: *T Comedy (UK) Ltd v Easy Managed Transport Ltd* [2007] EWHC 611 (Comm); [2007] 2 Lloyd's Rep. 397.

[140] CMR art.17.

[141] *Sandeman Coprimar S.A. v Transitos y Transportes Integrales SL* [2003] Q.B. 1270.

[142] CMR arts 17–18; e.g. where the loss or damage was caused by the claimant's wrongful act; or by the claimant's instructions; or by inevitable accident; or by inherent vice. The following cases illustrate unsuccessful attempts by carriers to rely on arts 17–18: *Ulster Swift Ltd v Taunton Meat Haulage* [1975] 2 Lloyd's Rep. 502 (heating of carcasses not "inherent vice"); *Michael Galley Footwear v Iaboni* [1982] 2 All E.R. 200 (theft); *Centrocoop Export-Import S.A. v Brit. European Transport* [1984] 2 Lloyd's Rep. 618 (freezing of meat not unavoidable circumstances); *W. Donald & Son (Wholesale Meat Contractors) Ltd v Continental Freeze Ltd*, 1984 S.L.T. 182 (freezing of meat not decay); *JJ Silber v Islander Trucking* [1985] 2 Lloyd's Rep. 243 (robbery not unavoidable circumstances); cf. *GL Cicatiello S.R.L. v Anglo European Shipping Services Ltd* [1994] 1 Lloyd's Rep. 678 (robbery unavoidable).

[143] CMR arts 23–26; *William Tatton & Co v Ferrymasters* [1974] 1 Lloyd's Rep. 203 (compensation payable for damaged machine) and see *Thermo Engineers v Ferrymasters* [1981] 1 All E.R. 1142 (obiter: return freight recoverable); *James Buchanan & Co v Babco Forwarding & Shipping (UK)* [1978] A.C. 141 (art.23(4) recoverable "other charges" include excise duty on stolen whiskey).

[144] CMR art.29. See consideration of "wilful misconduct" in *National Semiconductors (UK) Ltd v U.P.S. Ltd* [1996] 2 Lloyd's Rep. 212 (theft of vehicle); *Micro Anvika Ltd v TNT Express Worldwide (Euro Hub) NV* [2006] EWHC 230 (Comm); 2006 WL 502983 ("round the corner theft"); *TNT Global SpA v Denfleet International Ltd* [2007] EWCA Civ 405; [2007] 2 Lloyd's Rep. 504 (driver falling asleep) and *Datec Electronic Holdings Ltd v United Parcels Service Ltd* [2005] EWCA Civ 1418; [2005] 2 C.L.C. 1025, affirmed by [2007] UKHL 23; [2007] 1 W.L.R. 1325 (employee theft, shown on strong balance of probability).

[145] CMR arts 34–39, which by virtue of s.5 of the 1965 Act prevail to the exclusion of other statutory remedies for contribution or remedies; see *Rosewood Trucking Ltd v Balaam* [2005] EWCA Civ 1461; [2006] 1 Lloyd's Rep. 429, and *Cummins Engine Co v Davis Freight Forwarding (Hull)* [1981] 1 W.L.R. 1363 (CA). But see art.40. One carrier may seek contribution or indemnity under the CMR from another carrier by way of third party proceedings: *ITT Schaub Lorenz v Birkart Johann Internationale Spedition* [1988] 1 Lloyd's Rep. 487 (CA).

raised within certain time limits.[146] Where a right of action is time-barred, it may not be exercised by way of set off.[147]

21.19 International and European carriage by road: Passengers and luggage—The Carriage of Passengers by Road Act 1974, which would have implemented the Geneva Convention on the Contract for the International Carriage of Passengers and Luggage by Road of 1973 ("CVR"),[148] was never brought into force and eventually repealed by the Statute Law (Repeals) Act 2004.[149]

However, from March 1, 2013, the EU Regulation on passenger rights in bus and coach transport[150] will apply and regulate domestic and international carriage for certain regular passenger services by bus or coach; although Member States have the option to delay full application of the Regulation to certain domestic services and services largely performed outside the EU.[151]

21.20 International carriage by rail ("COTIF")—One convention, including several Uniform Rules, governs the international carriage by rail of goods, passengers and luggage.[152] The COTIF convention established the permanent intergovernmental organisation for international carriage by rail, OTIF, with headquarters in Berne.[153] Disputes arising from the convention may be referred to arbitration.[154] With effect from July 1, 2011, the EU[155] acceded COTIF.[156] Article 2 of the Accession Agreement provides for the relationship between EU law and COTIF

---

[146] CMR art.32, generally one year and three years in cases of wilful misconduct; *Muller Batavier v Laurent Transport Co* [1977] R.T.R. 499 (art.32(1): when time starts running between successive carriers); *I.C.I. Plc v Mat Transport Ltd* [1987] 1 Lloyd's Rep. 354 (art.32(1)(b) total loss means only actual total loss, but note art.20: delay can amount to loss); *Poclain S.A. v S.C.A.C. S.A.* [1986] 1 Lloyd's Rep. 404 (CA) (art.32(2): suspension of limitation period and authority to receive claim); *Microfine Minerals & Chemicals Ltd v Transferry Shipping Co Ltd* [1991] 2 Lloyd's Rep. 630 (art.32(2): suspension of limitation period and rejection of claim).

[147] CMR art.32(4).

[148] The CVR entered into force on April 12, 1994; the United Kingdom has, as of July 2011, not become party to the Convention and is unlikely to join. The CVR regulates every contract for the carriage of passengers and their luggage in vehicles (for definitions see art.1(2)) by road (or mixed modes, see arts 2 and 3) when the contract provides that the carriage shall take place in the territory of more than one state, and that either or both the place of departure or place of destination is situated in a contracting state's territory (art.1(1). It is impossible to contract out of the CVR (art.23).

[149] Statute Law (Repeals) Act 2004 s.1(1) and Sch.1 Pt 14.

[150] EU Regulation 181/2011, p.1.

[151] EU Regulation 181/2011 art.2(4 and 5) and art.16(2); for details of the provisions see above para.21.13.

[152] Convention concerning International Carriage by Rail of 9 May, 1980 in the version of the Protocol of Modification of Vilnius of June 3, 1999 (or Convention relative aux Transports Internationaux Ferroviaires—COTIF) brought into force in the United Kingdom on July 1, 2006, by the Railways (Convention on International Carriage by Rail) Regulations 2005 r.3(1) (SI 2005/2092), also repealing the implementation of the previous 1980 version of COTIF. COTIF 1980, together with its Appendices only remains relevant for contracts made before July 1, 2006. Any modification to COTIF 1999, which may be made from time to time by certain OTIF Committees, shall automatically have the force of law (r.2(2) of the 2005 Regulations). The initial text of the Convention in the version of the 1999 Protocol can be found in Command Paper Cm.4873, or—including potential amendments—on the website of OTIF at *http://www.otif.org* [Accessed July 6, 2012].

[153] COTIF arts 1– 4, 13–21.

[154] COTIF arts 28–32.

[155] As regional economic integration organisation, see COTIF art.38.

[156] Accession Agreement of 23 June, 2011: Agreement between the European Union and the Intergovernmental Organisation for International Carriage by Rail on the Accession of the European Union to the Convention concerning International Carriage by Rail (COTIF) of 9 May, 1980, as amended by the Vilnius Protocol of 3 June, 1999.

rules. Insofar as the matter has been regulated on EU level, the EU rules take precedence between EU Member States, but COTIF Rules apply otherwise and in relation with other non- EU state parties.

International carriage by rail: Passengers and luggage (COTIF Appendix A: **21.21** **CIV)**—The Uniform Rules in COTIF Appendix A[157] regulate: (a) any carriage of passengers by rail where place of departure and place of destination are situated in two different Member States,[158] and in case of a single contract also including ancillary internal road or inland waterway carriage or, on registered services also supplementary sea or transfrontier inland waterway carriage; and (b) persons accompanying consignments effected in accordance with the Convention relating to carriage of goods by rail ("CIM").[159] Whilst the contract must be confirmed by one or more tickets issued to the passenger and the ticket has evidential value, its absence, irregularity or loss does not affect the existence or validity of the contract, nor the application of the Uniform Rules.[160] The rules are mandatory[161] and regulate, inter alia, liability for death or personal injury; failure to keep to the timetable, loss of or damage to luggage and vehicles; and delay in delivery.[162] Claims may become time barred, and rights of action may in certain circumstances be extinguished.[163]

The carrier is liable for death or personal injury to a passenger caused by an accident arising out of the operation of the railway and happening while the passenger was in, entering or alighting from railway vehicles,[164] as well as to resulting loss or damage to hand luggage.[165] The carrier is relieved of liability in certain circumstances,[166] and its liability in respect of certain heads of claim is limited[167] although the limits do not apply at all where the carrier's misconduct caused the loss.[168] The Uniform Rules are mandatory and unless otherwise provided in the Rules, it is impossible to contract out.[169]

---

[157] Hereafter referred to CIV; replacing the previous version, CIV 1980.

[158] The identity of Member States and any modifications to the Convention shall be published by the Secretary of State in the manner he thinks fit: r.4 of the 2005 Regulations. Status information can also be found directly on the depository's, that is OTIF's, website.

[159] CIV art.1 (1–4).

[160] CIV art.6(2) and (3).

[161] CIV art.5.

[162] CIV, arts 26–47.

[163] CIV arts 54–60. For example, art.58: right of action for death or personal injury extinguished (with certain exceptions) if "notice of the accident" is not given within 12 months of becoming aware of the loss or damage; art.59: acceptance of registered luggage may (with certain exceptions) extinguish a claim; art.60(1): period of limitation for actions of damages for death or personal injury: three years from the day after the accident (or three years from the day after the death of the passenger, subject to a maximum of five years from the day after the accident); art.60(2): period of limitation for other actions: one year (two years where damage was caused with intent or recklessly with the knowledge that such loss or damage would probably result). A claim presented under art.55 may suspend the running of the limitation period: art.60(4).

[164] CIV art.26.

[165] CIV art.33, but not otherwise to hand luggage in the responsibility of the passenger, unless loss or damage was caused by the fault of the carrier.

[166] CIV art.26: e.g. passenger's own fault; third-party's behaviour; circumstances unconnected with the operation of the railway.

[167] See, e.g. CIV arts 30 (death and personal injury) and 34 (hand luggage and animals).

[168] CIV art.48.

[169] CIV art.5.

The carrier is also liable for delay in delivery of, and loss[170] of or damage to, registered luggage, i.e. luggage, other than hand luggage, registered for carriage under a luggage registration voucher,[171] and vehicles. There are detailed provisions relating to the damages recoverable.[172] In certain circumstances, the carrier may be relieved of liability,[173] or liability may be limited.[174]

21.22 **European carriage by rail: Passengers and luggage EU**—The EC Regulation on rail passengers' rights and obligations[175] applies to rail journeys and services throughout the Community provided by undertakings licensed in accordance with the Railways Undertakings Licensing Directive.[176] It imposes mandatory rules,[177] largely, subject to the Regulation provisions,[178] implementing the CIV provisions on liability for death of and personal injury to passengers, loss or damage to or delay of luggage and for failure to keep to the timetable.[179] However, it also provides further rules on the transport contract, information to be supplied to the passenger and on the availability of tickets,[180] on mandatory insurance of the railway undertaking,[181] for further duties and liabilities on the occasion of delays, missed connections and cancellations above those provided for in CIV.[182] It also stipulates detailed rules on the right to transport, access and support for disabled persons and persons with reduced mobility ("DPRMs"),[183] and on ensuring passenger's personal security,[184] as well as rules on complaints procedures, quality standards and the providing of information on rights and enforcement of these rights to passengers.[185]

---

[170] For presumption of loss on non-delivery within 14 days of a request for delivery, see CIV art.40.

[171] CIV arts 16–22.

[172] CIV arts 36–43 (registered luggage) and arts 44–47 (vehicles and other articles).

[173] CIV art.36(2): passenger's own fault; passenger's order; inherent vice; unavoidable circumstances or consequences. Article 36(3): "special risks" such as inadequate packing; special nature of luggage; despatch of unacceptable articles.

[174] To a certain number of units of account per kilogramme or per item: CIV arts 41 and 43 (registered luggage), 44 and 45 (vehicles) and 46 (other articles).

[175] EC Regulation 1371/2007, p.14. The EC Regulation, in force since December 4, 2009, is embedded into the legal framework within the United Kingdom by the Rail Passenger's Rights and Obligations Regulation 2010 (SI 2010/1504) and the Rail Passenger's Rights and Obligations (Exemptions) Regulation 2009 (SI 2009/2970), which exempts purely domestic services until December 4, 2014 from certain provisions. Domestic services however remain bound to some core provisions of the EC Regulation; insofar see above para.21.13.

[176] Council Directive 95/18/EC, p.70.

[177] EC Regulation 1371/2007 art.6; however, conditions more favourable to the passenger can be applied.

[178] Conflicts between the COTIF Regulations and the COTIF Convention and the Rail Passenger's Rights and Obligations Regulation 2010 (SI 2010/1504), the latter will prevail (reg.4 of the 2010 Regulations).

[179] EC Reg 1371/2007 arts 11 and 15 referring to the relevant provisions of CIV; for a discussion of the CIV provisions see above, para 21.21.

[180] EC Regulation 1371/2007 arts 4–10.

[181] EC Regulation 1371/2007 art.12.

[182] EC Regulation 1371/2007 arts 15–18.

[183] EC Regulation 1371/2007 arts 20(2)–25.

[184] EC Regulation 1371/2007 art.26.

[185] EC Regulation 1371/2007 arts 27–31. Part 3 of the Rail Passenger's Rights and Obligations Regulation 2010 (SI 2010/1504) has designated the Office of Rail as the enforcement body and the Rail Passengers' Council or the London Transport Users' Committee, as the case may be, as complaints handling body.

International carriage by rail: Goods (COTIF Appendix B: CIM)—The **21.23**
Uniform Rules[186] in COTIF Appendix B regulate every contract for the carriage
of goods by rail for reward where place of taking over the goods and the place
designated for delivery are situated in two different Member States, also covering,
in case of a single contract ancillary internal road or inland waterway traffic or, on
registered services, any supplementary sea or trans-frontier inland waterway
carriage.[187] The parties to a contract may agree on the application of CIM, where
only one of the two different States is a Member State.[188] Whilst the contract shall
be confirmed by a consignment note, this has only evidential value and is no
longer a requirement for application of the Uniform Rules.[189] Unless otherwise
provided, the Rules are mandatory and the carrier cannot derogate from them, but
may increase his liability and obligations.[190] The rules regulate liability for loss of
or damage to goods, and delay in transit. Claims may become time-barred, and
rights of action may in certain circumstances be extinguished.[191] The carrier is
liable for loss[192] of or damage to the goods between the time of acceptance for
carriage and the time of delivery, and for loss or damage resulting from the transit
period being exceeded.[193] There are detailed provisions relating to the damages
recoverable.[194] The carrier is relieved of liability in certain circumstances,[195] and
its liability in respect of certain heads of claim is limited,[196] although liability is
unlimited where the carrier caused the loss or damage with intent or recklessly
and with knowledge that such loss or damage would probably result.[197]

FURTHER READING

Brown, A., *Wheatley's Road Traffic Law in Scotland*, 4th edn (Edinburgh:
Bloomsbury Professional, 2007).
Bugden, P. and Lamont-Black, S., *Goods in Transit*, 2nd edn (London: Sweet and
Maxwell, 2010).
Chitty on Contracts, edited by H.G. Beale, 30th edn (London: Sweet and Maxwell,
2008), Vol.2.

---

[186] Hereafter referred to CIM; replacing the previous version, CIM 1980.

[187] CIM art.1(1), (2) and (3).

[188] CIM art.1(2).

[189] CIM art.6(2).

[190] CIM art.5.

[191] CIM arts 43–48. For example, art.47: acceptance of goods may (with certain exceptions) extinguish a claim; art.48: period of limitation for actions arising from contract-one year (two years in certain circumstances including wilful misconduct and fraud). The dates of commencement of the relevant periods are set out in art.48(2). A claim presented under art.43 may suspend the running of the limitation period: art.48(3).

[192] For presumption of loss on non-delivery within 30 days after the expiry of the transit period, see CIM art.29.

[193] CIM art.23.

[194] CIM arts 30–38.

[195] CIM art.26(2): if the loss, etc. was caused by the fault or order of the "person entitled"; inherent vice; unavoidable circumstances and consequences. Art.26(3): "special risks", including carriage by open wagon, poor packing, and breakable or perishable goods.

[196] For example, CIM art.30(2): compensation for loss of goods limited to 17 units of account per kilogramme of gross mass short; art.31: percentage allowance for goods subject to wastage; art.33(1): where transit period exceeded, compensation limit of three times carriage charges.

[197] CIM art.36.

Clarke, M.A., *International Carriage of Goods by Road: CMR*, 3rd edn (London: Sweet and Maxwell, 1997).

Clarke, M.A. and Yates, D., *Contracts of Carriage by Land and Air*, 2nd edn (London: LLP Professional Publishing, 2008).

Harris, B., *Ridley's Law of the Carriage of Goods by Land, Sea and Air*, 8th edn (London: Sweet and Maxwell, 2010).

Kahn Freund, O.S., *The Law of Inland Transport*, 4th edn (London: Stevens, 1965).

Stair Memorial Encyclopaedia, Vol.3 ("Carriage"), Reissue.

Wilkinson's Road Traffic Offences, edited by McCormac, K., 25th edn (London: Sweet and Maxwell, 2011).

CHAPTER 22

MARITIME LAW: CARRIAGE BY SEA WITH GENERAL AVERAGE AND SALVAGE

Maritime law is an extensive and complex subject which may be said to include **22.01** all matters relating to shipping and navigation. Broadly speaking, navigation is the activity of traversing navigable waters, which for most purposes are the open sea and tidal waters, rather than inland or enclosed waters, and a ship is a structure which can be navigated upon those waters. Most of maritime law is concerned with navigation; for commercial purposes rather than, for example, pleasure sailing, but there are exceptions. In consequence, maritime law encompasses the definition of a ship, for various purposes; questions of nationality, ownership and registration of ships; the employment of masters and crew; carriage by sea; safety in navigation; collisions at sea and wreck; and general average and salvage.[1] Maritime law is derived from a wide range of sources, including common law (much of which is very similar between the main trading nations), national legislation and international conventions, which have become a major source.[2] Maritime law is a reserved matter under the Scotland Act 1998.[3] The treatment in this work is restricted to those areas of maritime law which are most likely to be of importance to traders and others who are not primarily engaged in navigation and which are most likely to be encountered outwith a specialised maritime law practice. These are the law of carriage by sea, general average and salvage and marine insurance, all of which affect importers and exporters of goods.[4]

Carriage by sea: Constitution of the contract[5]—There are two principal **22.02** methods by which a person may arrange for the carriage of goods by sea. The first is to hire, or charter, a ship or part thereof to be employed as the charterer directs. The second is to arrange for the goods to be carried in a ship controlled by another person[6] usually along with goods belonging to other shippers. The typical form of contract used in the first case is referred to as a charterparty; in the second case, the typical form of contract is a bill of lading or sea waybill. In either case the consideration for the carriage is referred to as freight.[7] In some cases, there may

---

[1] *Stair Memorial Encyclopaedia*, "Shipping and Navigation" (Reissue).

[2] *Stair Memorial Encyclopaedia*, "Shipping and Navigation" (Reissue), para.2.

[3] Scotland Act 1998 s.30, Sch.5 Pt II, Head E3: see Ch.1, para.27. See also *Stair Memorial Encyclopaedia*, "Carriage" (Reissue), para.146.

[4] For marine insurance, see Ch.20.

[5] Contracts for carriage by sea are frequently complex and are bedevilled by problems arising from the use of lengthy standard forms often completed inaccurately and inconsistently. The subject is also given to the use of shorthand or jargon terminology, not always clear or accurately employed. This chapter attempts to give an account of the main features of the most common forms of contract but it must be understood that in practice variations and hybrid forms of contract are frequently encountered.

[6] Often called a "general ship"; see *Stair Memorial Encyclopaedia*, "Carriage" (Reissue), para.148 for further information on general ships.

[7] Unless there is a time or bareboat charterparty (see para.22.03, below), where the charterer pays hire.

be both a charterparty and a bill of lading, which may give rise to difficult questions of interpretation.[8] There may also be complications arising from the relationship between the shipping (carriage) contract and a (sale) contract or contracts between the seller or shipper of the goods and the customer to whom they are ultimately to be delivered.[9] Again there are two common forms of such sale contracts. The first, and probably commonest, is a "cost, insurance, freight" ("CIF") contract: in that form, the price usually includes the cost of shipping and insuring the goods and the seller performs the contract by shipping the goods on a vessel for the specified destination and tendering to the buyer the documents, usually a bill of lading or equivalent, an insurance policy and an invoice. The other form is a "free on board" ("FOB") contract under which the seller puts the goods on board the vessel and pays the expense of doing so and the goods are at the buyer's risk when on board.[10]

A contract for the carriage of goods by sea, or affreightment,[11] may be entered into verbally,[12] and its terms are then to be gathered from proof of the words or actions of the parties, from advertisements, or from their prior business relations.[13] More commonly the contract of affreightment is entered into in writing. Then the relationship of the parties may depend upon a charterparty; on the combined effect of a charterparty and a bill of lading or on a bill of lading alone. The incidents of a bill of lading as a contract are largely governed by rules known as The Hague or, later, Hague-Visby rules and the (less popular) Hamburg rules.[14] In addition, there are a number of other documents in use which may contain or evidence the contract including a document known as a receipt[15]; a sea waybill; or a ship's

---

[8] Depending on the parties to each of the contracts and whether the bill of lading incorporates terms of the charterparty.

[9] See *Stora Enso Oyj v Port of Dundee* [2006] CSOH 40; [2006] 1 C.L.C. 453 (title to sue for loss of goods warehoused in transit; whether property and risk was still with the sellers: intention demonstrated was to contract "free on motor" and subject to the general trade rules; the use of the sale term "CIP", for lack of a more appropriate Incoterm, did not alter this position).

[10] S. Baughen, *Shipping Law*, 5th edn (Routledge-Cavendish, 2012), p.4; see also Y. Baatz et al, *Maritime Law*, 2nd edn (London: Sweet and Maxwell, 2011), Ch.3 or D.M. Sassoon, *C.I.F. and F.O.B. Contracts*, 4th edn (London: Sweet and Maxwell, 1995), paras 2 et seq. and paras 437 et seq.

[11] See B. Eder et al, *Scrutton on Charterparties and Bills of Lading*, 22nd edn (London: Sweet and Maxwell, 2011), para.1–001. The term "affreightment" can also be used for contracts (not being a charterparty) extending over a substantial period of time and more than one voyage; see further *Stair Memorial Encyclopaedia*, "Carriage" (Reissue), para.144, fn.2.

[12] *Nordstjernan v Salvesen* (1903) 6 F. 64 at 75; Bell, *Commentaries*, I, 586.

[13] *Hill v Scott* [1895] 2 Q.B. 371 at 713.

[14] The United Nations Convention on the Carriage of Goods by Sea, Hamburg, 1978 ("Hamburg Rules"), in force since 1992. It has 34 parties, although only few seafaring nations; information on contracting states can be found on the UN Treaty site via: *http://treaties.un.org/* [Accessed July 16, 2012]. In December 2008 another set of carriage Rules were adopted, named the Rotterdam Rules, although as of 2012 they have not yet come into force; see further fn.77.

[15] The receipt was introduced by the Carriage of Goods by Sea Act 1924. See now the Carriage of Goods by Sea Act 1971 (SI 1977/981) (the "1971 Act") Sch. art.VI; and para.22.18, below. The 1971 Act came into force on June 23, 1977 when it repealed the 1924 Act. The Hague Rules (the International Convention for the Unification of Certain Rules of Law relating to Bills of Lading, signed at Brussels on August 25, 1924) were set out in the 1924 Act; the Rules as amended by the 1968 Brussels Protocol (of February 23, 1968) are known as the Hague-Visby Rules and are set out in the Schedule to the 1971 Act (as further amended by the Protocol of December 21, 1979 introducing Special Drawing Rights as a method of computation of compensation). The unamended rules still govern the position in a number of jurisdictions and questions of their interpretation may continue to arise, e.g. *The River Gurara v Nigerian National Shipping Line Ltd* [1998] Q.B. 610 (CA). For information on contracting states to the Rules see Treaty information pages of the Belgian Government at *http://diplomatie.belgium.be/en/treaties/* [Accessed July 16, 2012].

delivery order.[16] Strict liability under the edict *nautae, caupones, stabularii* probably applied to all carriers by sea, not merely to common carriers[17] but the edict has largely been superseded by legislation[18] and in any event all carriers by sea carry under special contracts or under rules such as the Hague-Visby Rules.[19]

Charterparty—Charterparties may be classified in two ways, by the method of **22.03** definition of the contract period and by the extent of the rights conferred on the charterer. First, the contract may be either for a definite time (demise or time charter) or for a particular voyage or voyages (voyage charter). Secondly, it may either take the form of the hire of the ship or merely of the accommodation in the ship.[20] In the first form, in the case of hire under a demise of the ship or bareboat charter, the charterer takes for the time being the position of an owner. The master and crew are employed by the charterer, and the responsibility to third parties, for example in the case of a collision, rests solely with him.[21] The master of the ship, in signing a bill of lading, binds the charterer, and not the owner.[22] Where merely the accommodation in the ship is hired these responsibilities remain with the owner. Where not only the ship but its master and crew are hired, the contract will not be read as a demise of the ship merely because it is stated that the crew are to be in the service of the charterer, unless the power of appointment and dismissal is also vested in him.[23] In the second form, under a time charter, the use of the ship and its accommodation are hired to the charterer, who has certain powers to direct the operation of the ship, in return for the payment of hire. Navigation of the ship remains the responsibility of the master (working for the owner) but in the absence of some overriding factor, choice of route is a matter of the employment of the vessel and, therefore, for the charterers to decide.[24] Equally, navigation remains with the owner under a voyage charterparty where, in return for the payment of freight, the whole or a substantial part of the vessel is used by the charterer to perform a particular journey or several voyages.[25] In modern practice, particularly in connection with container traffic, part of the space in a ship may be contracted for under an agreement known as a "slot" charter.[26]

---

[16] See Carriage of Goods by Sea Act 1992 (the "1992 Act") implementing the recommendations of the Law Commissions in their report *Rights of Suit in Respect of Carriage of Goods by Sea* (HMSO, 1991) Scot. Law Com. No.130. The 1992 Act repealed the Bills of Lading Act 1855. Other possible forms of document are listed in Eder, *Scrutton on Charterparties and Bills of Lading* (2011), para.1–001.

[17] See *Stair Memorial Encyclopaedia*, "Carriage" (Reissue), para.166.

[18] e.g. the Merchant Shipping Act 1995, the Carriage of Goods by Sea Act 1971, and the Carriage of Goods by Sea Act 1992. The Carriers Act 1830 does not apply to carriage by sea.

[19] See fn.15, above and para.22.15, below.

[20] The latter is perhaps better seen as a contract for services rather than as a hire of the vessel: see A. Burrows (ed.), *English Private Law*, 2nd edn (Oxford: Oxford University Press, 2007), para.11.16.

[21] *Clarke v Scott* (1896) 23 R. 442; *The Briton* [1975] 1 Lloyd's Rep. 319; *Attica Sea Carriers Corp v Ferrostaal Poseidon Bulk Reederei GmbH* [1976] 1 Lloyd's Rep. 250. For discussion of the circumstances in which bareboat charters are likely to be used, see S.D. Girvin, *Carriage of Goods by Sea*, 2nd edn (Oxford: Oxford University Press, 2011) para.1.51.

[22] *Baumwoll Manufactur v Furness* [1893] A.C. 8.

[23] *Manchester Trust v Furness* [1895] 2 Q.B. 539. See also *Wills v Burrell* (1894) 21 R. 527.

[24] *Whistler International Ltd v Kawasaki Kisen Kaisha Ltd (The Hill Harmony)* [2001] 1 A.C. 638.

[25] Baughen, *Shipping Law* (2012), p.9.

[26] Girvin, *Carriage of Goods by Sea* (2011), para.1.50.

22.04 Normal form of charterparty—A charterparty, a term derived from the ancient custom of executing the document in duplicate and cutting it across, is a contract usually entered into by a printed form, with or without additional clauses, typed or in manuscript. In its normal form, in voyage charters, it describes the ship and the voyage proposed, and contains an undertaking to deliver the cargo to the charterer or his assignee on payment of freight. Provisions as to time for loading or unloading are added, and responsibility for loss occasioned by certain specified causes excluded.[27]

22.05 Seaworthiness—In a charterparty it is open to the contracting parties to exclude the liability of the shipowner for any cause of loss to the cargo.[28] But in the absence of any express stipulation to the contrary the law implies a warranty of seaworthiness, which is not excluded by any general exception of loss due to the negligence of the officers or crew, and is a guarantee that the ship is seaworthy, not merely that the owner has taken all reasonable steps to make her so.[29] Seaworthiness has been defined as

> "that degree of fitness which an ordinary careful and prudent owner would require his vessel to have at the commencement of her voyage, having regard to all the probable circumstances of it".[30]

The warranty is that the ship is fit to encounter the normal dangers of the voyage and to carry the cargo contracted for, that her refrigerating machinery, for instance, is in good order.[31] There is, however, a distinction between unseaworthiness due to unfitness to carry the cargo and bad stowage.[32] Seaworthiness involves the provision of a qualified master and competent crew.[33] It is a warranty that the ship is ready to receive the cargo at the time of loading, for example that a cattle ship has been properly disinfected,[34] and is fit to sail at the time of sailing. But for defects occurring during the voyage, and not due to initial unseaworthiness, the shipowner's obligation is only to execute and pay for repairs, not a

---

[27] But see para.22.18, below; Unfair Contract Terms Act 1977. A clause in a charterparty excluding liability for loss or damage arising out of "errors of navigation" has been held in England not to provide exemption in respect of negligent navigation: *Seven Seas Transportation v Pacifico Union Marina Corp* [1983] 1 All E.R. 672; [1984] 2 All E.R. 140; *Industrie Chimiche Italia Centrale v NEA Ninemia Shipping Co S.A.* [1983] 1 All E.R. 686.

[28] See previous note.

[29] *Steel & Craig v State Line Steamship Co* (1877) L.R. 4 R. (HL) 103; *A/B Karlshamns Oljefabriker v Monarch S.S. Co*, 1949 S.C. (HL) 1. See also *Onego Shipping & Chartering BV v JSC Arcadia* [2010] EWHC 777 (Comm); [2010] 2 Lloyd's Rep. 221 referring to *Canada Steamship Lines Ltd v King* [1952] A.C. 192 (P.C. (Canada): clauses excluding negligence and seaworthiness duty must be worded clearly).

[30] G.H. Treitel, *Carver on Bills of Lading*, 2nd edn (London: Sweet and Maxwell, 2005), para.9–014 following *McFadden v Blue Star Line* [1905] 1 K.B. 697. See also *Eridania SpA v Oetker* [2000] 2 Lloyd's Rep. 191.

[31] *Maori King v Hughes* [1895] 2 Q.B. 550.

[32] *The Thorsa* [1916] P. 257 (cargo of chocolate stowed beside gorgonzola cheese); *Elder Dempster v Paterson* [1924] A.C. 522 (cargo of palm oil in casks crushed by bags of palm kernels) and *Actis Co v Sanko S.S. Co* [1982] 1 All E.R. 390 (ship overloaded).

[33] *Gunford Ship Co v Thames, etc. Insurance Co*, 1911 S.C. (HL) 84; *Standard Oil Co of New York v Clan Line*, 1924 S.C. (HL) 1; *Hong Kong Fir Shipping Co v Kawasaki Kisen Kaisha* [1962] 2 Q.B. 26. As a result of these decisions there would not appear to be any disagreement between English and Scots law as to the effect of a breach of this warranty on the charterparty as a whole. Cf. *Universal Cargo Carriers Corp v Citati* [1957] 2 Q.B. 401 for a breach by the charterers.

[34] *Tattersall v National S.S. Co* (1884) L.R. 12 Q.B.D. 297.

warranty that repairs will not be necessary, and therefore he is not liable for delay due to a breakdown of machinery.[35] The question whether a temporary defect, for example a porthole left open or failure to case a pipe, is unseaworthiness, or a defect attributable to the negligence of the crew, depends upon whether, in the particular circumstances, it could be remedied during the voyage.[36] The onus of proving unseaworthiness primarily rests with the charterer who asserts it, but is displaced by proof that the ship broke down in the initial stage of her voyage.[37]

Laytime and demurrage—It is a common though not an invariable provision in **22.06** charterparties that a certain number of days, known as lay days, are allowed for loading and unloading, with a further provision for the payment of a fixed sum for a certain number of days after the lay days have expired. The fixed sum is known as demurrage. Should the period of demurrage be exceeded damages for detention are due by the charterer, but where demurrage is not restricted to a certain fixed period of time any damages claimed by the shipowners for delay owing to the detention of the vessel in circumstances where the demurrage provisions apply must be restricted to the sum fixed by those provisions.[38] A provision for loading or unloading at a fixed rate per day is equivalent to a provision for lay-days, and has the same legal results.[39] Where the provision is for "days" or "running days" the period is calculated without considering whether the days are working days or not; the term "working days" excludes Sundays and holidays at the port.[40] The obligation to load or unload the ship within the lay-days is an absolute one, and demurrage will be due although the delay is due to causes beyond the control of the charterer. His only relevant defences are either that the delay was occasioned by the fault of the shipowner, or that it was due to some cause excepted in the charterparty.[41] But there can be no claim where the ship is totally destroyed.[42] It has been held in England that the charterer is in breach of contract if he fails to load within the lay-days,[43] disapproving the suggestion of Lord Trayner that days on demurrage are really lay-days which have to be paid for.[44] The lay-days do not begin to run until the ship has arrived, has given a valid notice of readiness and is

---

[35] *Giertsen v Turnbull*, 1908 S.C. 1101.

[36] *Steel & Craig v State Line Co* (1877) L.R. 4 R. (HL) 103; *Gilroy v Price* (1892) 20 R. (HL) 1.

[37] *Klein v Lindsay*, 1911 S.C. (HL) 9.

[38] *Suisse Atlantique Societe d'Armement Maritime S.A. v N.V. Rotterdamsche Kolen Centrale* [1967] 1 A.C. 361, where the House of Lords regarded the demurrage clause as an agreed damages clause.

[39] *Hansa v Alexander*, 1919 S.C. (HL) 122.

[40] *Holman v Peruvian Nitrate Co* (1878) 5 R. 657.

[41] *Hansa v Alexander*, 1919 S.C. (HL) 122; *Reardon Smith Line v Ministry of Agriculture, Food and Fisheries* [1963] A.C. 691, where the whole question is extensively reviewed; *Tramp Shipping Corp v Greenwich Marine Inc* [1975] 1 W.L.R. 1042; *Armada Lines v Naviera Murueta S.A. (The Elexalde)* [1985] 2 Lloyd's Rep. 485 (strike). See also *Cero Navigation Corp v Jean Lion & Cie.* [2000] 1 All E.R. (Comm) 214 (clause excepting strikes did not extend laytime). The principle of "once on demurrage, always on demurrage" applies: a contractual provision that time spent treating the ship's holds shall not count cannot be relied upon where such treatment takes place after the permitted lay-days: *Dias Compania Naviera S.A. v Louis Dreyfus Corp (The Dias)* [1978] 1 W.L.R. 261 (HL).

[42] *A/S Gulnes v I.C.I.* [1938] 1 All E.R. 24.

[43] *Aktieselskabet Reidar v Arcos* [1927] 1 K.B. 352.

[44] *Lilly v Stevenson* (1895) 22 R. 278. As to the nature of demurrage in relation to a sale contract see *Fal Oil Ltd v Petronas Trading Corp SDN BDA* [2004] EWCA Civ 822; [2004] 2 All E.R. (Comm) 537; *Kronos Worldwide Ltd v Sempra Oil Trading SARL* [2004] EWCA Civ 3; [2004] 1 All E.R. (Comm) 915.

ready to load or discharge, as the case may be.[45] Where the charterparty contains no provisions for lay-days and demurrage the obligation of the charterer is merely to load within a time reasonable in the circumstances and in determining this any special causes of delay, such as a shortage of labour at the port, are to be taken into account.[46] He is, however, bound to have the cargo ready, and, in the absence of any express provisions in the charterparty, will be liable in damages for failure to do so, even although caused by circumstances beyond his control.[47]

22.07   **Obligations of shipowner**—The obligation of the shipowner is to have the ship ready to load at the time fixed by the charterparty or, if no time be fixed, within a reasonable time, unless prevented by causes specified in the contract. If delay is caused by an excepted cause, as for example by the perils of the sea, the ship-owner has not committed a breach of contract, yet the delay may be so great as to amount to frustration of the adventure, and to entitle the charterer to declare the contract at an end.[48] As this is a question of degree it is common to provide a clause, known as a cancelling clause, giving the charterer the option to declare the contract at an end if the ship is not ready to load by a certain date.[49] If the failure of the ship to arrive is due to the fault of the shipowner he is liable in damages.[50]

22.08   **Dead freight**—A charterer is usually bound to provide a full and complete cargo. Failure to do so, or in any case to provide the amount and kind[51] of cargo agreed upon, involves liability for dead freight,[52] which is a payment in compensation for the stow-room left empty. If not fixed in amount by the charterparty it is, in the case where the whole cargo is loaded by one charterer, the difference between the freight actually earned and the freight that would have been earned had the whole cargo been provided; in a general ship it has to be calculated under deduction of

---

[45] For decisions as to when a ship has arrived, see Eder, *Scrutton on Charterparties and Bills of Lading* (2011), paras 9–044—9–058; *E.L. Oldendorff & Co GmbH v Tradax Export S.A. (The Johanna Oldendorff)* [1974] A.C. 479 (whether ship in waiting area is arrived ship); *Federal Commerce and Navigation Co Ltd v Tradax Export S.A. (The Maratha Envoy)* [1978] A.C. 1 (ship not arrived waiting outside the limits of the port); *Micosta S.A. v Shetland Islands Council*, 1986 S.L.T. 193; [1984] 2 Lloyd's Rep. 525 (reparation; vessel made to wait outside port). See *Bulk Transport Group Shipping Co Ltd v Seacrystal Shipping Ltd (The Kyzikos)* [1989] A.C. 1264 ("Wibon" clause: whether ship arrived and notice of readiness valid where berth is available but not reachable) and *Suek AG v Glencore International AG* [2011] EWHC 1361 (Comm); [2011] 2 Lloyd's Rep. 278 (on effect of Wibon and Wipon clause in combination with tidal conditions preventing access); see also *Glencore Grain Ltd v Flacker Shipping Ltd (The Happy Day)* [2002] EWCA Civ 1068; [2002] 2 Lloyd's Rep. 487 (notice of readiness to discharge tendered from outwith port did not commence laytime, but started with subsequent discharge of cargo; charterers were deemed to have waived the requirement of a valid notice of readiness) and *Ocean Pride Maritime Ltd Partnership v Qingdao Ocean Shipping Co (The Northgate)* [2007] EWHC 2796 (Comm); [2008] 1 Lloyd's Rep. 511 (waiver of invalid notice of readiness). As to the effect of the charterer's consent to early commencement of laytime on loading, see *Tidebrook Maritime Corp v Vitol S.A. (The Front Commander)* [2006] EWCA Civ 944.

[46] *Rickinson v Scottish Cooperative Society*, 1918 S.C. 440.

[47] *Ardan S.S. Co v Weir* (1905) 7 F. (HL) 126.

[48] *Jackson v Union Marine Insurance Co* (1874) L.R. 10 C.P. 125.

[49] See, e.g. *The Mihalis Angelos* [1971] 1 Q.B. 164; *The North Sea* [1999] 1 Lloyd's Rep. 21.

[50] *Nelson v Dundee East Coast Shipping Co*, 1907 S.C. 927; *Monroe Bros v Ryan* [1935] 2 K.B. 28.

[51] *Angfartygs A/B v Price & Pierce* [1939] 3 All E.R. 672.

[52] *Aktieselskabet Reidar v Acros Ltd* [1927] 1 K.B 352 (CA); *Pentonville Shipping Ltd v Transfield Shipping Inc (The Jonny K)* [2006] EWHC 134 (Comm); [2006] 1 Lloyd's Rep. 666 (ship ordered to leave before completion of full loading to use high tide); *AIC Ltd v Marine Pilot Ltd (The Archimidis)* [2008] EWCA Civ 175; [2008] 1 Lloyd's Rep. 597 (vessel not allowed to load full contractual cargo at berth due to level of available water in dredged channel).

any expense saved to the shipowner, and of any sums he has received, or might have received, from carrying the goods of third parties.[53]

Cesser clause—A clause, known as the cesser clause, is commonly inserted in charterparties, whereby the charterer's liability under the contract ceases when the goods are put on board, and the shipowner's lien over the goods, which at common law only covers the freight, is extended to cover claims for dead freight and demurrage. This clause, unless expressed so as plainly to cover all grounds of liability, will not exempt the charterer from claims where his exemption would leave the shipowner without any remedy.[54] **22.09**

Freight *pro rata itineris*—As a general rule no freight is due unless and until the goods arrive at their destination. But if the voyage be interrupted by causes beyond the control of the shipowner, and the party entitled to the goods chooses to take delivery at some intermediate place, having the option to have the goods forwarded to their destination, he comes under an implied obligation to make a payment, estimated as a proportionate part of the freight and known as freight *pro rata itineris*.[55] To found a claim of this character there must be circumstances from which it may be inferred that the cargo owner dispenses with further carriage; the mere fact that he has accepted the goods at an intermediate port, when he had no option in the matter, is not enough to infer any liability.[56] **22.10**

Advance freight—It is sometimes provided in a charterparty that the freight, or an instalment thereof, shall be paid in advance. The Scottish courts, disagreeing with the English rule, held that if the voyage cannot be accomplished the amount paid as advance freight may be recovered.[57] **22.11**

Charterparty followed by bill of lading—A contract of charterparty may be, and usually is, followed by a bill of lading when the goods are put on board. If there is any discrepancy between the terms of the charterparty and the bill of lading, and the question raised is between shipowner and charterer, the charterparty is the ruling instrument and the bill of lading is regarded as a mere receipt.[58] Thus where the charterparty contained a provision exempting the shipowner from loss resulting from the negligence of master or crew, and no such provision **22.12**

---

[53] *McLean & Hope v Fleming* (1871) 9 M. (HL) 38; *Henderson v Turnbull*, 1909 S.C. 510.

[54] *Kish v Cory* (1874–75) L.R. 10 Q.B. 553; *Gardiner v Macfarlane* (1889) 16 R. 658 (no exception under cesser clause where lien clause only covered demurrage, but not the further detention incurred at load port); *Salvesen v Guy* (1885) 13 R. 85; and see *Hill S.S. Co v Hugo Stinnes*, 1941 S.C. 324 (charterparty with cesser clause; charterer named as shipper in bill of lading); *Overseas Transportation Co v Mineralimportexport (The Sinoe)* [1972] 1 Lloyd's Rep. 201 (CA: cesser clause ineffective insofar as lien clause did not extend to claims for demurrage at load port).

[55] Bell, *Principles*, s.425; *The Soblomsten* (1866) L.R. 1 A. & E. 293.

[56] *The Iolo* [1916] P. 206.

[57] *Watson v Shankland* (1871) 10 M. 142; affd (1873) 11 M. (HL) 51. See also *Cantiere San Rocco v Clyde Shipbuilding Co*, 1923 S.C. (HL) 105.

[58] Even where the charterer becomes indorsee of the bill of lading: *President of India v Metcalfe Shipping Co (The Dunelmia)* [1970] 1 Q.B. 289 (CA), a rule thought not to have been altered by the Carriage of Goods by Sea Act 1992: see Eder, *Scrutton on Charterparties and Bills of Lading* (2011), para.6–002; J. Cooper, *Current Law Statutes Commentary* (1992), pp.50–5. As to the operation of a cesser clause between the owner and the charterer, qua shipper, it was held that the bill of lading (held not to incorporate the cesser clause) ruled, thus holding the charterer liable for demurrage: *Hill S.S. Co v Hugo Stinnes*, 1941 S.C. 324. A bill of lading may incorporate terms from a charterparty: *Skips A/S Nordheim v Syrian Petroleum Co (The Varenna)* [1984] Q.B. 599.

appeared in the bill of lading, it was held that the shipowner was entitled to found on the negligence clause in a question with the charterer or with a party for whom he was acting as agent.[59] But this, which is the general rule, will yield to proof (which may be by parole evidence) that the parties intended to vary their contract by the bill of lading.[60] From the definition of "contract of carriage" in the Carriage of Goods by Sea Act 1971,[61] it would appear that the rules relating to bills of lading and contracts thereunder which are provided by that Act do not apply to cases where the charterparty is the ruling contract, but the charterparty may contain a clause paramount embodying these rules.[62] Where the bill of lading has been indorsed and the question is between the shipowner and the indorsee, the contract is that contained in the bill of lading and not that contained in the charter-party.[63] And a mere reference to the charterparty, for example "freight and other conditions as per charter", is construed as importing only conditions affecting the consignee at the port of discharge, not as introducing into the bill of lading an exemption from the consequences of negligence which is to be found in the char-terparty.[64] It lies on the charterer to see that bills of lading are not signed in terms inconsistent with the charterparty, and he will be liable to relieve the shipowner should the latter in consequence incur liability to an indorsee.[65]

22.13 Bill of lading—A bill of lading has been defined as a document which evidences a contract of carriage by sea and the taking over and loading of the goods by the carrier, and by which the carrier undertakes to deliver the goods against surrender of the document.[66] It is the normal document under which goods are carried in a general ship. It is considered here in its aspects as a receipt for the goods and as a contract of carriage.[67]

22.14 Bill of lading as receipt—In its ordinary form a bill of lading is signed by the master of a ship, acknowledges receipt of the goods, and contains an undertaking to deliver them to the shipper, or his assigns by indorsement. The Carriage of Goods by Sea Act 1971 provides that the carrier[68] must, on the demand of the shipper, furnish a bill of lading stating: (a) the leading marks for identification of the goods; (b) either the number of packages, or the quantity, or weight, as

---

[59] *Delaurier v Wyllie* (1889) 17 R. 167; *Rodocanachi v Milburn* (1887) L.R. 18 Q.B.D. 67. See discussion in Eder, *Scrutton on Charterparties and Bills of Lading* (2011), para.6–003, fn.11 (at least insofar as charterer was acting as agent for the principal in both, the charterparty and bill of lading).

[60] *Davidson v Bisset* (1878) 5 R. 706.

[61] See para.22.15, below.

[62] *Adamastos Shipping Co v Anglo-Saxon Petroleum Co* [1959] A.C. 133; and *Petroleum Oil & Gas Corp of South Africa (Pty) Ltd v FR8 Singapore PTE Ltd (The Eternity)* [2008] EWHC 2480 (Comm); [2009] 1 Lloyd's Rep. 107 (charterparty clauses incorporating parts of the Hague-Visby Rules).

[63] But see *President of India v Metcalfe Shipping Co* [1970] 1 Q.B. 289 (CA).

[64] *Delaurier v Wyllie* (1889) 17 R. 167; cf. *The Annefield* [1971] P. 168 (even though bill of lading provided "all the terms conditions and exceptions" of the charterparty "including the negligence clause, are incorporated herewith" did not incorporate arbitration clause: clauses not germane to bill of lading contracts to be incorporated only by express words). Further on charterparty incorporation clauses see Girvin, *Carriage of Goods by Sea* (2011) paras 12.20 et seq.

[65] *Kruger & Co Ltd v Moel Tryvan Ship Co* [1907] A.C. 272.

[66] Hamburg Rules art.1.7; see further Baughen, *Shipping Law* (2012), pp.6–9.

[67] Other aspects of bills of lading are dealt with in para.22.22, below. Note however that a "straight" bill of lading is a bill of lading within the Hague-Visby Rules, not a mere receipt: *J.I. MacWilliam Co Ltd v Mediterranean Shipping Co S.A. (The Rafaela S)* [2005] UKHL 11; [2005] 2 A.C. 423; although it is categorised as a sea waybill under the Carriage of Goods by Sea Act 1992 s.1(2)(a), (3).

[68] "Carrier" is defined in art.I(a) of the Schedule as including the owner or the charterer who enters into a contract of carriage with the shipper.

furnished in writing by the shipper; (c) the apparent order and condition of the goods, with the proviso that there is no obligation to state any marks, number, quantity or weight which the master has reasonable ground for suspecting not to be accurate, or which he has no reasonable means of checking.[69] The shipper is deemed to have guaranteed the accuracy of the information furnished by him, and is bound to indemnify the carrier for any loss, damages or expenses resulting from its inaccuracy.[70] The bill of lading is prima facie evidence of the receipt by the carrier of the goods as therein described[71] but, if the bill is transferred to a third party acting in good faith, proof to the contrary is not admissible.[72] Section 4 of the Carriage of Goods by Sea Act 1992 further provides that a bill of lading[73] signed by the master of the vessel[74] is conclusive evidence in favour of the lawful holder[75] of the bill against the carrier that the goods have been shipped or received.[76]

Bill of lading as contract—The incidents of a bill of lading as a contract of carriage are now largely regulated by the provisions of the Carriage of Goods by Sea Acts 1971 and 1992 and by rules known as the Hague-Visby Rules set out in the Schedule to the 1971 Act and declared to have the force of law.[77] These rules, **22.15**

---

[69] 1971 Act Sch. (thereafter also Hague-Visby Rules ("HVR")) art.III r.3.

[70] 1971 Act Sch. art.III r.5.

[71] *Att Gen of Ceylon v Scindia Steam Navigation Co, P.C.* [1962] A.C. 60. A bill of lading which described cargo as "11,000 tonnes" but which later stated "weight unknown" was held not to amount to evidence of the weight shipped: *Agrosin Pty Ltd v Highway Shipping Co Ltd (The Mata K)* [1998] 2 Lloyd's Rep. 614 (although this may be an issue in the light of HVR art.III.8).

[72] 1971 Act Sch. art.III r.4.

[73] i.e. a transferable bill of lading (such as "to X or order") and not a non-transferable or "straight" bill of lading ("to X") nor a sea waybill, which is in effect a non-transferable bill of lading. While s.4 of the 1992 Act applies to both "shipped" and "received for shipment" bills of lading, it does not apply to non-transferable bills of lading: see s.1(2) and Scottish Law Commission, *Rights of Suit in Respect of Carriage of Goods by Sea*, paras 2.48, 2.50. *Stair Memorial Encyclopaedia*, "Carriage" (Reissue), para.188.

[74] Or by the carrier's agent: 1992 Act s.4.

[75] As defined in the 1992 Act s.5(2). The holder must be in good faith.

[76] 1992 Act s.4 (replacing the Bills of Lading Act 1855 s.3 which made the bill of lading conclusive evidence against the signatory of the bill rather than against the carrier: see Cooper, *Current Law Statutes Commentary* (1992)), countering the effects of *Grant v Norway* (1951) 10 C.B. 665, but for transferable bills of lading only, not for waybills or straight bills.

[77] These rules were the product of lengthy international negotiations aimed at reconciling the often conflicting interests of shipowners and cargo owners: see *Stair Memorial Encyclopaedia*, "Carriage" (Reissue), para.212. A more "cargo friendly" set of rules, the Hamburg Rules, is sometimes met with but has not been adopted by any major trading nation: see Baughen, *Shipping Law* (2012), Ch.6. In an attempt to unify the, by now, somewhat diverse carriage regimes, a new carriage convention was negotiated, the United Nations Convention on contracts for the international carriage of goods wholly or partly by sea, 2008. This convention, termed the Rotterdam Rules, needs 20 ratifications to enter into force. As of April 2012 the Rules had 24 signatories, but only one ratification. The convention regulates the international carriage of goods, irrespective of the use of a particular type of transport document, although it does not apply to charterparties (art.6). It also extends to any carriage prior and/ or subsequent to sea carriage (art.5), although there is a limited possibility of agreeing the period of responsibility of the carrier (art.12). The liability regime is similar to the Hague-Visby rules. Most notably the seaworthiness obligation is continuous throughout the journey, the fire exclusion is narrower, the nautical fault exclusion is missing altogether and detailed rules as to burden of proof are provided (art.17). Liability is limited to 875 units of account per package or 3 units per kilogram (art.59) and to two and one-half times the freight for delay (art.60); suit must be made within two years, but set-off is possible even thereafter (art.62). Provisions for the liability of maritime performing parties are provided (arts 19–20). The convention encourages the use of electronic transport documents by including detailed provisions dedicated to them (Ch.3 and throughout). The transfer of rights of suit and of liabilities is regulated, but for negotiable transport documents only (arts 57–58). There

are to have effect in relation to and in connection with the carriage of goods[78] by sea in ships where the port of shipment is a port in the United Kingdom,[79] or where the goods are carried between ports in two different states and either the bill of lading is issued in a contracting state, or the carriage is from a port in a contracting state, or the bill of lading provides that the rules or legislation of any state giving effect to them are to govern the contract.[80] A "contract of carriage" is defined as applying only

> "to contracts of carriage covered by a bill of lading or any similar document of title, in so far as such document relates to the carriage of goods by sea, including any bill of lading or any similar document as aforesaid issued under or pursuant to a charterparty from the moment at which such bill of lading or similar document of title regulates the relations between a carrier and a holder of the same".[81]

In a contract of carriage, as thus defined, there is no warranty that the ship is seaworthy, though the carrier is bound to exercise due diligence: (a) to make the ship seaworthy; (b) properly to man, equip and supply the ship; (c) to make the holds, refrigerating and cool chambers, and all other parts in which goods are carried fit and safe.[82] When loss or damage has resulted from unseaworthiness the burden of proving the exercise of due diligence lies on the carrier.[83] The carrier does not discharge this obligation merely by showing that he exercised reasonable care in the selection of an independent contractor to render the ship seaworthy.[84]

The Carriage of Goods by Sea Act 1992 provides that the lawful holder[85] of a bill of lading, whether or not he owns the property in the goods, has vested in him all rights of suit under the contract of carriage as if he had been a party to that contract.[86] A person who acquires the bill of lading after delivery of

---

is very limited potential to alter the regime and attempts in favour or against the carrier's or the shipper/holder's position will be null and void (art.79). Arbitration and jurisdiction provisions are available for contracting states on an opt-in basis (see Chs 14 and 15). For more details see Baughen, *Shipping Law* (2012), p.137 et seq. or the several books written on the Rotterdam Rules as per the bibliography below.

[78] As defined in 1971 Act Sch. art.I(c); the period of carriage of goods is defined in Sch. art.I(e).

[79] 1971 Act s.1(3).

[80] 1971 Act Sch. art.I(6)(a); Sch. art.X.

[81] 1971 Act Sch. art.I(b); *Harland & Wolff v Burns and Laird Lines*, 1931 S.C. 722.

[82] Carriage of Goods by Sea Act 1971 s.3, Sch. art.III; cf. *Riverstone Meat Co Pty v Lancashire Shipping Co (The Muncaster Castle)* [1961] A.C. 807; *Northern Shipping Co v Deutsche Seereederei GmbH (The Kapitan Sakharov)* [2000] 2 Lloyd's Rep. 255 (CA).

[83] Carriage of Goods by Sea Act 1971 Sch. art.IV; *Northern Shipping Co* [2000] 2 Lloyd's Rep. 255 (CA).

[84] *Riverstone Meat* [1961] A.C. 807.

[85] Defined in 1992 Act s.5(2); considered in *Aegean Sea Traders Corp v Repsol Petroleo S.A. (The Aegean Sea)* [1998] 2 Lloyd's Rep. 39 and *Primetrade AG v Ythan Ltd (The Ythan)* [2005] EWHC 2399 (Comm); [2006] 1 Lloyd's Rep. 457.

[86] 1992 Act s.2, enacting one of the important changes brought about by this Act, namely that transfer of ownership of the goods concurrent with the bill is no longer a necessary prerequisite to the acquisition of the contractual rights of suit. A consignee of a sea waybill or a ship's delivery order ("the person to whom delivery . . . is to be made") is similarly able to assert contractual rights against the carrier and, in these particular cases, even without possession of the relevant document: s.2(1). Note also s.2(3), which provides for the vesting of contractual rights in sub-buyers with ship's delivery orders each relating to part of a larger bulk. In the context of sea waybills and ship's delivery orders (but not bills of lading) the original shipper and other intermediate holders retain their title to sue: s.2(5).

the goods may sue on the bill provided he obtained it under arrangements made before the delivery.[87] A person with rights of suit may exercise them on behalf of another who has suffered the loss or damage.[88] The person who asserts the contractual rights against the carrier becomes subject to the liabilities under the contract.[89]

Electronic data interchange—Section 1(5) and (6) of the Carriage of Goods by **22.16** Sea Act 1992 permit regulations to be made so as to apply the provisions of the 1992 Act to paperless transactions conducted by means of a telecommunication system or any other information technology.[90]

Claims for injury to goods—The 1971 Act makes provision as to the effect **22.17** of the receipt and removal of the goods. Unless notice in writing of loss or damage is given by the person entitled to receive the goods at the port of discharge prior to their removal, or, if the damage be not apparent, within three days, their removal is prima facie evidence of their delivery in the state described in the bill of lading.[91] Such notice need not be given if the state of the goods has been at the time of their receipt the subject of joint survey or inspection. In any event the carrier is discharged from all liability in respect of loss or damage unless suit is brought within one year after delivery of the goods or the date when the goods should have been delivered.[92] To commence an action, service of a summons is required: arrestment *ad fundandam* or on the dependence is not sufficient.[93] However, the parties may agree to extend the period after the cause of action has arisen. An action for indemnity against a third person may be brought even after the expiry of the year, provided that the action is not time-barred by the *lex fori*.[94]

---

[87] 1992 Act s.2(2). Similarly, a person who acquires the bill after the goods have been destroyed may sue on the bill, provided he obtained the bill under arrangements made before the destruction of the goods: s.2(2). In each case, the bill of lading ceased to be a transferable document of title before coming into the hands of the holder. One purpose of s.2(2) is to prevent the indorsement of exhausted bills of lading to those who have no interest in the goods but simply wish to buy a cause of action against the carrier: see Scottish Law Commission, *Rights of Suit in Respect of Carriage of Goods by Sea*, paras 2.43–2.44, and draft bill, p.49; and Cooper, *Current Law Statutes Commentary* (1992).

[88] 1992 Act s.2(4).

[89] 1992 Act s.3, and see para.22.24, below. Allowing a vessel to berth and sampling the cargo does not amount to a demand asserting a right to delivery: *Borealis AB v Stargas Ltd (The Berge Sisar)* [2001] UKHL 17; [2002] 2 A.C. 205; see also *The Ythan* [2005] EWHC 2399 (Comm).

[90] Including "any computer or other technology, by means of which information or other matter may be recorded or communicated without being reduced to documentary form": s.5(1). The Scottish Law Commission, *Rights of Suit in Respect of Carriage of Goods by Sea*, p.39, comment: "E.D.I. may eventually render otiose the concept of negotiability. A single paper transfer will be replaced by a series of teletransmitted undertakings by the carrier to successive transferees, the communication of each undertaking giving constructive delivery to the person receiving the communication." While no such regulations have yet been made, the Rotterdam Rules allow for electronic documents and their transfer and thus, if entering into force, may enable the further development and use of electronic transport documents.

[91] 1971 Act Sch. art.III r.6.

[92] 1971 Act Sch. art.III r.6. See *Aries Tanker Corp v Total Transport (The Aries)* [1977] 1 W.L.R. 185 (HL: application of r.6; after limitation no defence or set-off) and *Finagra (UK) Ltd v O.T. Africa Line Ltd* [1998] 2 Lloyd's Rep. 622 (conflict between r.6 and time bar clause in bill).

[93] *R.M. Supplies (Inverkeithing) Ltd v EMS Trans Schiffahrisges mbH & Co*, 2003 S.L.T. 133.

[94] 1971 Act Sch. art.III r.6 bis. The time allowed is at least three months from the date when the pursuer settled the claim or was served with process in the action against him.

22.18 **Exemption from and exclusion of liability**—Where carriage is effected under a bill of lading,[95] the Carriage of Goods by Sea Act 1971 provides that neither the carrier[96] nor the ship shall be liable for injury resulting from the undernoted causes,[97] nor in certain circumstances for loss of or damage to goods which were dangerous.[98] The carrier cannot, however, invoke the exception relating to dangerous goods if he has, himself, breached the obligation[99] to make the vessel seaworthy.[100] Nor is the carrier liable for loss of or damage to goods if the shipper knowingly misstated the nature or value of the goods in the bill of lading.[101] Other exemptions from liability under the 1971 Act have already been mentioned.[102] Section 186 of the Merchant Shipping Act 1995 provides that an owner of a United Kingdom ship[103] is not liable for any loss or damage caused by fire on board ship, or by theft of gold, silver, watches, jewels, or precious stones, unless the owner or shipper has, at the time of shipment, declared their nature and value

---

[95] Or possibly a receipt: 1971 Act s.1(6)(b).

[96] As to his servants or agents, see 1971 Act Sch. art.IV bis.

[97] 1971 Act Sch. art.IV r.2:

> "(a) Act, neglect or default of the master, mariner, pilot or the servants of the carrier in the navigation or in the management of the ship. (b) Fire, unless caused by the actual fault or privity of the carrier. (c) Perils, dangers and accidents of the sea or other navigable waters. (d) Act of God. (e) Act of war. (f) Act of public enemies. (g) Arrest or restraint of princes, rulers or people, or seizure under legal process. (h) Quarantine restrictions. (i) Act or omission of the shipper or owner of the goods, his agent or representative. (j) Strikes or lock-outs or stoppage or restraint of labour from whatever cause, whether partial or general. (k) Riots and civil commotions. (l) Saving or attempting to save life or property at sea. (m) Wastage in bulk or weight or any other loss or damage arising from inherent defect, quality or vice of the goods. (n) Insufficiency of packing. (o) Insufficiency or inadequacy of marks. (p) Latent defects not discoverable by due diligence. (q) Any other cause arising without the actual fault or privity of the carrier, or without the fault or neglect of the agents or servants of the carrier, but the burden of proof shall be on the person claiming the benefit of this exception to show that neither the actual fault or privity of the carrier nor the fault or neglect of the agents or servants of the carrier contributed to the loss or damage."

The term "in the navigation or in the management of the ship" in (a) above has been construed in England as limited to navigation, as distinguished from care of the cargo. Thus it does not cover negligently left open hatch covers or defective stowage: *Gosse Millard v Canadian Government Merchant Marine (The Canadian Highlander)* [1929] A.C. 223; *The Washington* [1976] 2 Lloyd's Rep. 453; but see *Ismail v Polish Ocean Lines (The Ciechocinek)* [1976] Q.B. 893 (defective stowing, but estoppel where master followed charterer's instructions); nor failure in refrigerating machinery, *Foreman & Ellams v Federal Steam Navigation Co* [1928] 2 K.B. 424. See *Albacora S.R.L. v Westcott and Laurence Line*, 1966 S.C. (HL) 19 (cargo care, salted fish, inherent vice, art. IV r.2(m); note the doubt cast upon *Gosse Millard* [1929] A.C. 223, on the need to prove that servants were not negligent in order to found on r.2 of art. IV) and further on the inherent vice exception, although in a marine insurance case: *Global Process Systems Inc v Syarikat Takaful Malaysia Bhd (The Cendor Mopu)* [2011] UKSC 5; [2011] 1 Lloyd's Rep. 560. See also *Leesh River Tea Co v British India Steam Navigation Co* [1967] 2 Q.B. 250 (CA: storm valves stolen during journey, art.IV r.2(q)); and further on exceptions see Eder, *Scrutton on Charterparties and Bills of Lading* (2011), Ch.11.

[98] 1971 Act Sch. art.IV r.6. "Dangerous" should be interpreted broadly: *Effort Shipping Co Ltd v Linden Management S.A. (The Giannis NK)* [1998] A.C. 605 (cargo infested with Khapra beetles).

[99] Under 1971 Act Sch. art.III r.1.

[100] *Mediterranean Freight Services Ltd v BP Oil International Ltd (The Fiona)* [1994] 2 Lloyd's Rep. 506 (CA), but see *Compania Sud Americana de Vapores SA v Sinochem Tianjin Import & Export Corp (The Aconcagua)* [2009] EWHC 1880 (Comm); [2010] 1 Lloyd's Rep. 1 where abnormal characteristics of the chemical caused the loss rather than the unseaworthy stowage.

[101] 1971 Act Sch. art.III r.5(h).

[102] See fn.97, above.

[103] Or part owner, charterer, manager, operator of the ship: Merchant Shipping Act 1995 (the "1995 Act") s.186(1) and (5). Also any master, member of the crew or servant: s.186(2).

in the bill of lading or otherwise in writing.[104] Liability is not excluded where it is proved that the loss resulted from personal act or omission, committed with intent to cause such loss, or recklessly and with knowledge that such loss would probably result.[105]

A clause in a bill of lading excluding liability in any manner other than that permitted by the Carriage of Goods by Sea Act 1971 is void.[106] Where carriage is effected under a receipt,[107] the parties may agree on any terms which are not contrary to public policy.[108] A clause in a charterparty, or a clause in a contract for the carriage of goods by ship, or a provision of a notice,[109] may be void if it excludes liability for death or personal injury, or may be unenforceable if one contracting party is a consumer and it was unfair and unreasonable to incorporate the clause in the contract or to allow reliance on the provision of a notice.[110] In a contract for the carriage by sea of passengers, a carrier cannot exclude liability for death or personal injury or loss of or damage to passengers' luggage occurring during the course of sea carriage and due to his own or his servants' or agents' fault or neglect.[111]

---

[104] 1995 Act s.186(1).

[105] s.186(3), referring to the 1995 Act Sch.7 Pt I art.4.

[106] 1971 Act Sch. art.III r.8. See *Unicoopjapan and Marubeni-Iida Co v Ion Shipping Co (The Ion)* [1971] 1 Lloyd's Rep. 541(on too short time for suit) or *Svenska Traktor AB v Maritime Agencies (Southampton)* [1953] 2 Q.B. 295 (part of deck stowage clause abrogating all liability was null and void); but see *Jindal Iron & Steel Co Ltd v Islamic Solidarity Shipping Co Jordan Inc* [2004] UKHL 49; [2005] 1 Lloyd's Rep. 57 (clause putting onus of loading and stowing on charterer does not breach art.III r.8). However, the carrier may validly contract to surrender his own rights and immunities under the 1971 Act: Sch. art.V.

[107] A non-negotiable instrument, marked as such, used in cases where shipments are not of an ordinary commercial character made in the ordinary course of trade: 1971 Act Sch. art.VI. Distinguish the receipt under s.6(b) of the Act, the latter providing for contractual incorporation of the Hague-Visby Rules into the receipt; note, that ordinary commercial shipments are often made under receipts, such as a sea waybill, where there is no need to sell or pledge the goods in transit.

[108] 1971 Act Sch. art.VI; subject, however, to the Unfair Contract Terms Act 1977. See now *Tiffney v Flynn*, 2007 S.L.T. 929.

[109] "Notice" includes an announcement, whether or not in writing, and any other communication or pretended communication: Unfair Contract Terms Act 1977 s.25, as amended.

[110] Unfair Contract Terms Act 1977 ss.15(3), 16, 25, as amended.

[111] art.3 of the Athens Convention relating to the Carriage of Passengers and their Luggage by Sea, 1974 (as amended by the 1976 Protocol), implemented into the law in the United Kingdom by s.183 and Sch.6 of the Merchant Shipping Act 1995 and, as of December 31, 2012, art.3 Athens Convention 2002, implemented into EU law by virtue of EU Regulation 392/2009 of the European Parliament and of the Council of April 23, 2009 on the liability of carriers of passengers by sea in the event of accidents (OJ L131, 28.5.2009, p.24); the latter providing for strict liability for shipping incidents and fault based for other risks. Note that carriage of passengers and their luggage by sea was only briefly and temporarily covered by the Unfair Contract Terms Act 1977 s.28, which applied the rules of the Athens Convention prior to the Convention's coming into force as a matter of international law. The provisions were applied to passenger carriage with a UK connection via s.28. Section 28 was redundant for contracts made after the coming into force of the Carriage of Passengers and their Luggage by Sea (Interim Provisions) Order 1980 (SI 1980/1092), which also covered domestic carriage. Both regimes were superseded by the coming into force in April 1987 of the Athens Convention for international carriage and, for intra UK carriage, of the Carriage of Passengers and their Luggage by Sea (Domestic Carriage) Order 1987 (made under the 1979 Merchant Shipping Act, which originally implemented the Athens Convention into the law of the United Kingdom). From December 31, 2012, the Athens Convention of 1974 as amended by the 2002 Protocol (Athens 2002) applies to international and national carriage within the European Union by virtue of EU Regulation 392/2009. Further on carriage of passengers see para.22.28 and *Stair Memorial Encyclopaedia*, "Carriage" (Reissue), paras 350 et seq.

Non-contracting parties, such as stevedores, may benefit from a valid exclusion clause.[112]

22.19 Limitation of liability—Where a carrier is neither exempted nor excluded from liability, his liability may nevertheless be limited. The Carriage of Goods by Sea Act 1971 provides that, in the case of loss of, or damage to, goods carried under a bill of lading,[113] a carrier[114] shall not be liable beyond 666.67 units of account[115] per package or unit,[116] or two units of account per kilogramme of gross weight, whichever is the higher, unless the nature and value of the goods were declared by the shipper before shipment, and were inserted in the bill of lading.[117] A higher limit may be fixed by agreement.[118] Where a carrier and his servants or agents are sued, the aggregate amount recoverable cannot exceed the specified limits.[119] However, the carrier cannot benefit from the limitation provisions where it is proved that the loss or damage resulted from an act or omission of the carrier, done with intent to cause damage, or recklessly with knowledge that damage would probably result.[120] Passenger claims are also subject to specific levels of limitation.[121]

22.20 Global limitation—In addition to the specific "package" limitation per cargo claim or the specific limits applicable to each passenger claim,[122] the shipowner[123]

---

[112] *New Zealand Shipping Company v A.M. Satterthwaite & Co (The Eurymedon)* [1975] A.C. 154 (PC).

[113] Or possibly a receipt: 1971 Act s.1(6)(b), for example a sea waybill or consignment note; see above fn.107 in fine and see *Browner International Ltd v Monarch Shipping Co Ltd (The European Enterprise)* [1989] 2 Lloyd's Rep. 185 (contractual incorporation and alteration of Rules).

[114] As to his servants or agents, see 1971 Act Sch. art.IV bis.

[115] A unit of account is a special drawing right ("SDR") as defined by the International Monetary Fund. The amount is converted into sterling on the basis of the value of sterling on the date of decree or judgment: 1971 Act Sch. art.IV r.5(d), as amended, implementing the SDR Protocol to the Hague-Visby Rules of 1979 (see fn.15, above). The total amount recoverable is calculated by reference to the value of the goods at the place and time where in terms of the contract the goods were or should have been discharged: 1971 Act Sch. art.IV r.5(b). For this see *El Greco (Australia) Pty v Mediterranean Shipping Co SA, Federal Court of Australia* [2004] FCAFC 202; [2004] 2 Lloyd's Rep. 537, but also note the less restrictive interpretation in *Laiterie Dupont Morin Flechard v Anangel Endeavour Cia Nav* Unreported March 17, 1989; extracts in J. Cooke et al, *Voyage Charters*, 3rd edn (LLP Professional Publishing, 2007), para.85.382.

[116] If the number of packages or units packed in a container, pallet or similar article is stated in the bill of lading, that number is deemed the number of packages or units for purposes of limitation; otherwise the article of transport is considered the package or unit: art.IV r.5(c); and not the individual items: see *El Greco* [2004] FCAFC 202. In a case under the Hague Rules it was similarly decided that, where proven, the number of packages counted rather than the number of containers: *Owners of Cargo Lately Laden on Board the River Gurara v Nigerian National Shipping Line Ltd (River Gurara)* [1998] Q.B. 610; [1998] 1 Lloyd's Rep. 225.

[117] 1971 Act Sch. art.IV r.5(a). For the effect of an alteration to the limitation clause under the contractually incorporated Hague Rules, see *Dairy Containers Ltd v Tasman Orient Line CV (The Tasman Discoverer)* [2004] UKPC 22; [2004] 1 W.L.R. 215.

[118] 1971 Act Sch. art.IV r.5(g). But any restriction clause not permitted by the Act is void: art.III r.8.

[119] 1971 Act Sch. art.IV bis, r.3.

[120] 1971 Act Sch. art.IV r.5(e); similarly for his servants or agents: Sch. art.IV bis, r.4.

[121] See below, para.22.28.

[122] See below, para.22.28.

[123] Which includes the owner, charterer, manager or operator of a seagoing ship: see Merchant Shipping Act 1995 Sch.7 Pt I art.1(2); and see *Aegean Sea Traders Corp v Repsol Petroleo SA (The Aegean Sea)* [1998] 2 Lloyd's Rep. 39 (charterer cannot limit in respect of claims brought by shipowner under charterparty); *CMA CGM SA v Classica Shipping Co Ltd (The CMA Djakarta)* [2004] EWCA Civ 114; [2004] 1 Lloyd's Rep. 460 (charterer does not need to undertake activities related to ownership) and *The MSC Napoli* [2008] EWHC 3002 (Admlty); [2009] 1 Lloyd's Rep. 246 (slot charterer was able to limit).

can invoke a global limitation against all relevant actions by virtue of s.185 of the Merchant Shipping Act 1995, implementing the Convention on Limitation of Liability for Maritime Claims 1976 and its 1996 Protocol,[124] whether the ship is seagoing or not.[125] This right to limit is available in respect of certain claims, including loss of life or personal injury and damage to property occurring on board or in direct connection with the operation of the ship.[126] There can be no limitation if it is proved that the loss resulted from personal act or omission, committed with the intent to cause such loss or recklessly and with knowledge that such loss would probably result.[127] Nor is there any limitation in respect of a claim by a person on board the ship or employed in connection with that ship under a United Kingdom contract of employment.[128] The limits of liability are calculated by units of account[129] related to the ship's tonnage.[130] Priority is given to claims for death and personal injury.[131] If legal proceedings are instituted, a shipowner may constitute a limitation fund with the court.[132]

Deviation—At common law a contract of carriage by sea implied a warranty that   **22.21** the carrier would not deviate from the prescribed course, or, where no course was prescribed, from that usual and customary.[133] Deviation was excused in order to

---

[124] Sch.7 to the 1995 Act; see *CMA CGM SA v Classica Shipping Co Ltd (The CMA Djakarta)* [2004] EWCA Civ 114; [2004] 1 Lloyd's Rep. 460 (Convention to be construed as it stands without English law preconceptions). The amount of the limitation fund has been increased with effect from May 2004. For more information on global limitation see Baughen, *Shipping Law* (2012), Ch.20 or Baatz et al, *Maritime Law* (2011), pp.308 et seq.

[125] See Sch.7 Pt II para.2 of the 1995 Act.

[126] A list of claims subject to limitation is set out in art.2(1) of the convention, Sch.7 Pt I to the 1995 Act. Certain types of claim are specifically excluded, see the 1995 Act s.185(4), as well as Sch.7 Pt I art.3 and Pt II para.4(1), in most cases because they are subject to a different regime altogether, for example claims in respect of oil pollution and nuclear damage.

[127] 1995 Act Sch.7 Pt I art.4; *M.S.C. Mediterranean Shipping Co S.A. v Delumar B.V.B.A.* [2000] 2 All E.R. (Comm) 458. Contrast with the wording of the Merchant Shipping Act 1894 (the "1894 Act") s.503, where limitation could be claimed where the loss, injury or damage occurred without the owner's "actual fault or privity": *Dreyfus v Tempus Shipping Co* [1931] A.C. 726. For cases under 1976 Convention see also *The Bowbelle* [1990] 3 All E.R. 746; *The Leerort and The Zion Paraens* [2001] EWCA Civ 1055; [2001] 2 Lloyd's Rep. 291; *Margolle v Delta Marine Co Ltd* [2002] EWHC 2452 (Admin); [2003] 1 Lloyd's Rep. 203.

[128] 1995 Act s.185(4); e.g. a seaman, master, pilot, caterer, or servant of the shipowner: Sch.7 Pt I art.3(e).

[129] Each unit being a special drawing right as defined by the International Monetary Fund: 1995 Act Sch.7 Pt I art.8. See Sch.7 Pt II para.7.

[130] 1995 Act Sch.7 Pt I arts 6 and 9. And see Sch.7 Pt II para.5 and the Merchant Shipping (Tonnage) Regulations 1997 (SI 1997/1510).

[131] 1995 Act art.6(2) of Sch.7 Pt I. If the limitation fund constituted in respect of personal injury claims is insufficient, the personal injury claimants can rank rateably in respect of the unpaid balance upon the limitation fund constituted by reference to the property claims.

[132] 1995 Act art.11 of Sch.7 Pt I. Note that in a decision under the 1894 Act s.503, it was held that interest runs *ex lege* on the limitation fund: see *The Devotion II*, 1979 S.C. 80, where the defenders' tender (of the amount of the limitation fund and expenses) made no explicit reference to interest. For jurisdictional issues on establishing the fund and bar to other actions see *Seismic Shipping Inc v Total E&P UK Plc (The Western Regent)* [2005] EWCA Civ 985; [2005] 2 Lloyd's Rep. 359 and *ICL Shipping Ltd v Chin Tai Steel Enterprise Co Ltd (The ICL Vikraman)* [2003] EWHC 2320 (Comm); [2004] 1 Lloyd's Rep. 21 (jurisdictional issues) and further Baughen, *Shipping Law* (2012), Ch.20. See also *Blue Nile Shipping Co Ltd v Iguana Shipping & Finance Inc (The Happy Fellow)* [1998] 1 Lloyd's Rep. 13 (limitation proceedings; stay of proceedings to avoid irreconcilable judgments) and *Maersk Olie & Gas A/S v Firma M de Haan en W de Boer* (Case C-39/02) [2005] 1 Lloyd's Rep. 210 (*lis pendens*; enforcement of limitation fund).

[133] Bell, *Principles*, s.408; Eder, *Scrutton on Charterparties and Bills of Lading* (2011), p.256.

save life, not in order to save property.[134] It was also excused if necessary for the repair of ship or cargo,[135] or if due to the unseaworthiness of the ship,[136] or to credible information of some imminent danger on the proper course.[137] The result of deviation if not so justified, was to displace the contract, and, consequently, to render the shipowner liable for any injury to the cargo, though arising from a cause excepted in the charterparty, and although the loss occurred after the proper course had been resumed.[138] The shipowner could plead in defence, when the loss occurred from the act of God, of the Queen's enemies, or from the inherent vice of the goods carried, that the loss would have occurred even if no deviation had taken place.[139] The law is so far modified by the Carriage of Goods by Sea Act 1971,[140] that, in cases to which the rules under that Act apply, deviation in saving or attempting to save property at sea, or any reasonable deviation,[141] shall not be deemed an infringement of those rules or of the contract of carriage, and the carrier shall not be liable for any loss or damage resulting therefrom. In circumstances where the contract of carriage has been held to be displaced by the deviation of the ship, the question arises of the freight that may be claimed by the shipowner on completion of the voyage, when no damage has been caused to the cargo. A claim for freight on the principle of quantum meruit appears possible.[142] There is however a question whether the fundamental breach doctrine, otherwise abolished by *Suisse Atlantique*[143] and *Photo Production Ltd v Securicor*,[144] still lives on in the cases of deviation or whether the applicability of contractual exceptions clauses is a matter of construction.[145]

22.22 Delivery of goods—At the conclusion of the voyage the carrier is bound to deliver the goods to the holder of the bill of lading. In the absence of any provision to the contrary the actual work of unloading falls to be done by the carrier or at his expense.[146] In any question as to injury to the goods they are to be regarded as delivered as soon as they pass over the ship's side and are received by porters employed by the consignee.[147] As bills of lading are commonly made out in sets of three, with a provision that on one being accomplished the others are to stand void, it is possible for the shipper fraudulently to indorse copies of the bill of lading to different indorsees, and thus to raise competing rights. The shipmaster,

---

[134] *Scaramanga v Stamp* (1880) L.R. 5 C.P.D. 295 (CA).

[135] *Phelps v Hill* [1891] 1 Q.B. 605 (CA).

[136] *Kish v Taylor* [1912] A.C. 604.

[137] *The Teutonia* (1872) L.R. 4 C.P. 171 (PC). As to the master's discretion in planning the voyage, see *The Hill Harmony* [2001] 1 A.C. 638.

[138] *Joseph Thorley Ltd v Orchis Co* [1907] 1 K.B. 660 (CA); *Hain S.S. Co v Tate & Lyle* (1936) 41 Com. Cas. 350 (HL). See *Lord Polwarth v North British Railway Co*, 1908 S.C. 1275 (land carriage).

[139] *Morrison v Shaw Savill, etc. Co* [1916] 2 K.B. 783 (CA).

[140] 1971 Act Sch. art.IV r.4.

[141] *Stag Line v Foscolo Mango & Co* [1932] A.C. 328; *Lyric Shipping Inc v Intermetals (The Al Taha)* [1990] 2 Lloyd's Rep. 117.

[142] See *Hain S.S. Co Lyle* (1936) 41 Com. Cas. 350 (HL).

[143] *Suisse Atlantique Societe d'Armement SA v NV Rotterdamsche Kolen Centrale* [1967] 1 A.C. 361; [1966] 1 Lloyd's Rep. 529.

[144] *Photo Production Ltd v Securicor Transport Ltd* [1980] A.C. 827; [1980] 1 Lloyd's Rep. 545.

[145] See Eder, *Scrutton on Charterparties and Bills of Lading* (2011), paras 12–013 et seq and discussion of this point in *Kenya Railways v Antares Co Pte. Ltd (The Antares)* [1987] 1 Lloyd's Rep. 424 at 430; *State Trading Corp of India Ltd v M. Golodetz Ltd* [1989] 2 Lloyd's Rep. 277 at 289; *Daewoo v Klipriver (The Kapitan Petko Voivoda)* [2003] EWCA Civ 451; [2003] 2 Lloyd's Rep. 1 at 13, [14].

[146] *Ballantyne v Paton*, 1912 S.C. 246.

[147] *Knight S.S. Co v Fleming Douglas & Co* (1898) 25 R. 1070.

if he has no notice of any competing right, is entitled to deliver the goods to the first party presenting a bill of lading; if he has notice, he must select the true claimant at his peril, or refuse delivery.[148] Delivery in these circumstances does not affect the ownership of the goods.[149] Should a party alleging right to the goods be unable to produce the bill of lading, as in cases where it has been lost or has not reached the consignee at the time when the ship arrives, the master's duty is either to deliver the goods at the carrier's risk[150] on receiving a guarantee or letter of indemnity against any possible liability,[151] or else to unload them and place them in a warehouse. Delivery without the production of a bill of lading may render the carrier liable to the consignor.[152]

Should he unreasonably refuse to take either course nothing can be recovered for the consequent detention of the ship.[153]

Warehousing—If the goods are not claimed on arrival, or if the holder of the **22.23** bill of lading fails to pay the freight, the shipmaster is at common law entitled, after waiting for a reasonable time, to warehouse the goods under reservation of his lien for freight.[154] This right is commonly expressly conferred in the bill of lading. Statutory provisions preserving a lien for freight after unloading no longer apply[155] and an extension of the common law possessory lien must be made by contract. A common law lien may allow the goods to be sold if they deteriorate otherwise.[156]

Liability for freight—A charterer, or the shipper of goods under a bill of lading, **22.24** is liable for the freight, unless his liability is excluded by a cesser clause. Should

---

[148] *Glyn Mills & Co v East & West India Dock Co* (1882) L.R. 7 App. Cas. 591; delivery will not decide ownership: *Pirie v Warden* (1871) 9 M. 523.

[149] *Meyerstein v Barber* (1870) L.R. 4 H.L. 317; *Pirie v Warden* (1871) 9 M. 523; note, the Carriage of Goods by Sea Act 1992 s.2 only deals with transfer of rights of suit, irrespective of who property is vested in.

[150] The carrier is liable for misdelivery where he delivers to the wrong person: *The Stettin* (1889) 14 P.D. 142; *Sze Hai Tong Bank v Rambler Cycle Co* [1959] A.C. 576 at 586 (PC); *MB Pyramid Sound NV v Briese-Shiffarts GmbH & Co KG (The Ines)* [1995] 2 Lloyd's Rep. 144; see also *Motis Exports Ltd v Dampskibsselskabet AF 1912 A/S (No.1)* [1999] 1 Lloyd's Rep. 837; affirmed by CA [2000] 1 Lloyd's Rep. 211 (delivery against forged bill of lading) and *Trafigura Beheer BV v Mediterranean Shipping Co SA (The MSC Amsterdam)* [2007] EWCA Civ 794; [2007] 2 Lloyd's Rep. 622; see further Girvin, *Carriage of Goods by Sea* (2011), Ch.10.

[151] In modern transactions, frequent use is made of letters of indemnity in lieu of a bill of lading. Delivery is made by the carrier against a letter of indemnity given by the seller to cover the carrier against any loss caused by delivering against a document other than a bill of lading: see *Stair Memorial Encyclopaedia*, "Carriage" (Reissue), para.260; W. Tetley, *Marine Cargo Claims*, 4th edn (Canada: Thompson Carswell, 2008), Vol.2, Ch.38, pp.2042 et seq., Scottish Law Commission, *Rights of Suit in Respect of Carriage of Goods by Sea*, p.7, fn.18.

[152] *East West Corp v DKBS 1912 A/S* [2002] EWHC 83 (Comm.); [2002] 1 All E.R. (Comm) 676, affirmed on partly differing grounds in *East West Corp v DKBS 1912 A/S, Utaniko Ltd v P & O Nedlloyd BV* [2003] EWCA Civ 83; [2003] 1 Lloyd's Rep. 239 (CA: bailment).

[153] *Carlberg v Wemyss Co*, 1915 S.C. 616; although it may not be unreasonable to withhold delivery where the master does not have the option to discharge the goods ashore and remain in control pending the production of the bill: see Eder, *Scrutton on Charterparties and Bills of Lading* (2011), para.13–010.

[154] Bell, *Commentaries*, I, 605.

[155] The provisions of the Merchant Shipping Act 1894 ss.492–501 were repealed by the Statute Law (Repeals) Act 1993 (c.50) s.1, Sch.1 Pt XV without being replaced; see *Stair Memorial Encyclopaedia*, "Carriage" (Reissue), para.261.

[156] See Eder, *Scrutton on Charterparties and Bills of Lading* (2011), para.18–009; more generally on lien see para.22.25, below.

the full cargo, as stated in the bill of lading, not be forthcoming at the port of discharge, the shipowner is entitled to freight only for what he has actually carried, but if the full freight has been paid he may set off a claim for dead freight in an action for repetition of the balance.[157] Liability for freight has been extended by statute to any lawful holder of a bill of lading[158] who demands delivery of the goods from the carrier, or who takes delivery, or who makes a claim against the carrier.[159]

22.25 Lien—At common law a shipowner has a lien over the goods for freight,[160] unless this is excluded by the terms of the contract, as where the freight was payable at a certain time after delivery,[161] or bills given for it were still current at the time when delivery was demanded.[162] Apart from express contract there is no lien for dead freight or demurrage.[163] Nor is there any lien for a general balance due to the shipowner on another account.[164] Release of the cargo under reservation of the right of lien can give rise to difficulties.[165]

22.26 Arrestment of ship, cargo—A ship may be arrested on the dependence of an action arising out of, inter alia, any agreement relating to the carriage of goods in any ship, whether by charterparty or otherwise.[166] At common law, cargo may be arrested on the dependence of such an action.[167] If a ship is to be sold under a warrant sale, the cargo owner may be directed to discharge the cargo.[168] Arrestment

---

[157] *Henderson v Turnbull*, 1909 S.C. 510, and note *Aries Tanker Corp v Total Transport* [1977] 1 W.L.R. 185 (HL); *The Alfa Nord* [1977] 2 Lloyd's Rep. 434 (CA).

[158] As "the person in whom rights are vested" by virtue of s.2(1) of the Carriage of Goods by Sea Act 1992, which includes persons holding the bill as a security: see Scottish Law Commission, *Rights of Suit in Respect of Carriage of Goods by Sea*, paras 2.30 et seq. (and contrast with the previous law, *Sewell v Burdick (The Zoe)* (1884) L.R. 10 App. Cas. 74). For persons demanding delivery, etc. prior to receiving the bill of lading, see s.3(1)(c). For provisions relating to sea waybills and ship's delivery orders, see the 1992 Act ss.1–3.

[159] 1992 Act ss.3 and 2(1). Section 3 provides that upon demanding delivery, etc. the lawful holder becomes "subject to the same liabilities under [the contract of carriage] as if he had been a party to that contract". In such circumstances, the shipper also remains liable for the freight and other obligations as an original party to the contract of carriage: s.3(3).

[160] For further information on lien see Ch.36, below. See also Eder, *Scrutton on Charterparties and Bills of Lading* (2011), Ch.18 or Baughen, *Shipping Law* (2012), p.214 et seq. and on maritime lien, p.353 et seq. or D.C. Jackson, *Enforcement of Maritime Claims*, 4th edn (LLP Professional, 2005), pp.459–604. See also A.J.M. Steven, *Pledge and Lien* (Edinburgh Legal Education Trust, 2008).

[161] *Foster v Colby* (1858) 3 H. & N. 705.

[162] *Tamvaco v Simpson* (1866) L.R. 1 C.P. 363.

[163] *McLean & Hope v Fleming* (1871) 9 M. (HL) 38.

[164] *Stevenson v Likly* (1824) 3 S. 291.

[165] *Georgia Pacific Corp v Evalend Shipping Co S.A.*, 1988 S.L.T. 683.

[166] Administration of Justice Act 1956 s.47(2)(e): see *The Aifanourios*, 1980 S.C. 346; *The Grey Dolphin*, 1982 S.C. 5; *Gatoil International Inc v Arkwright-Boston Manufacturers Mutual Insurance Co (The Sandrina)*, 1985 S.L.T. 68 (HL); *Nederlandse Scheepshypotheck Bank N.V. v Cam Standby Ltd*, 1994 S.C.L.R. 956; and arrestment in Scotland in support of substantive proceedings abroad by virtue of the Civil Jurisdiction and Judgments Act 1982 s.27: see *Clipper Shipping Co v San Vincente Partners*, 1989 S.L.T. 204 (substantive court proceedings commenced in Denmark; damages claim for causing third party to breach charterparty); *Oceaneering International AG, Petitioners* [2010] CSOH 161; 2011 S.L.T. 667 (substantive proceedings in England; Administration of Justice Act 1956 s.47(2) (k), (l)); *Fish & Fish Ltd v Sea Shepherd UK* [2011] CSOH 122 (substantive proceedings in England; Administration of Justice Act 1956 s.47(2)(a)).

[167] cf. *Svenska Petroleum AB v HOR Ltd*, 1982 S.L.T. 343; see *Hawkes (Western) Ltd v Szipt Ltd* [2007] CSOH 57 (arrestment of cargo in Scotland, substantive proceedings in France for freight) and see Administration of Justice Act 1956 ss.47C and 47D regarding arrestment of cargo.

[168] *Banque Indo Suez v Maritime Co Overseas Inc*, 1985 S.L.T. 117.

of the vessel or cargo in rem may be advantageous also in order to found jurisdiction on the merits.[169]

Cargoes of oil—Ships are subject to special legislation for carrying cargoes of oil **22.27** in bulk, as well as the ship's bunkers.[170]

Carriage by sea: Passengers and luggage—Liability for negligence during the **22.28** carriage of passengers and luggage by sea is regulated by the Merchant Shipping Act 1995.[171] The 1995 Act applies only to liability for negligence. Other aspects of carriage by sea of passengers and their luggage, such as delay or deviation not arising from negligence, or the provision of reasonable accommodation, continue to be governed by the common law and the Unfair Contract Terms Act 1977.

---

[169] It is submitted that the pre-existing law of Scotland that arrestment *ad fundandam jurisdictionem* provides a basis for jurisdiction still prevails for admiralty actions and is not negatively affected, but rather supported, by the International Convention for the Unification of Certain Rules relating to the Arrest of Sea-Going Ships 1952 art.7; with the latter referring back to the court's jurisdiction under domestic law. The claim must however relate to a matter set out in s.47(2) of the Administration of Justice Act 1956 (as per s.47(1) of the Act; see *The Sandrina*, 1985 S.L.T. 68 (HL)). This jurisdiction supported by the Arrest Convention is thus "specialised", having priority before the general rules of jurisdiction under the Brussels and Lugano Regime on the recognition and recognition and enforcement of judgments in civil and commercial matters (see art.57 of the Brussels Convention 1968, art.67 of the Lugano Convention 2007 and art.71 of the Brussels Regulation (EC Regulation 44/2001)). On the question of arrestment founding jurisdiction see *Ladgroup Ltd v Euroeast Lines SA*, 1997 S.L.T. 916 and *Marodi Service de D Mialich v Mikkal Myklebusthaug Rederi A/S*, 2002 S.L.T. 1013 and see *Owners of Cargo Lately Laden on Board the Tatry v Owners of the Maciej Rataj (The Tatry)* (C-406/92) [1999] Q.B. 515; [1995] 1 Lloyd's Rep. 302 (action in rem and in personam "same cause of action"; the provisions for *lis pendens* of the Brussels Convention 1968 are applicable despite jurisdiction being derived from the Arrest Convention 1952).

[170] Merchant Shipping Act 1995 Pt VI, as amended inter alia by the Merchant Shipping and Maritime Security Act 1997, the Merchant Shipping (Oil Pollution Compensation Limits) Order 2003 (SI 2003/2559), the Merchant Shipping (Oil Pollution) (Bunkers Convention) Regulations 2006 (SI 2006/1244), the Merchant Shipping Pollution Act 2006, the Merchant Shipping (Oil Pollution) (Supplementary Fund Protocol) Order 2006 (SI 2006/1265) and the Merchant Shipping (Implementation of Ship-Source Pollution Directive) Regulations 2009 (SI 2009/1210) implementing and providing for the many international and European developments in this area following major disasters. The grounding of the oil tanker "The Braer" in Shetland on January 5, 1993 gave rise to claims for compensation under the previous, similar, statutory provisions (principally the Merchant Shipping (Oil Pollution) Act 1971 and the Merchant Shipping Act 1974). Legal issues arose in connection with, inter alia, the ambit of the statutory scheme (*Shetland Seafarms Ltd v The Braer Corp*, 1999 S.L.T. 1189; *Skerries Salmon Ltd v The Braer Corp*, 1999 S.L.T. 1196; *Landcatch Ltd v The Braer Corp*, 1999 S.L.T. 1208; and *Black v The Braer Corp*, 1999 S.L.T. 1401 and see also *Alegrete Shipping Co Inc v International Oil Pollution Compensation Fund 1971 (The Sea Empress)* [2003] EWCA Civ 65; [2003] 1 Lloyd's Rep. 327 (endorsing the *Landcatch* decision)); the construction of the statute (*Skerries Salmon*, 1999 S.L.T. 1196; *Landcatch*, 1999 S.L.T. 1208 and *Eunson v The Braer Corp*, 1999 S.L.T. 1405) and the statutory time limits for claiming (*Eunson*, 1999 S.L.T. 1405; *Gray v The Braer Corp*, 1999 S.L.T. 1410). See also *Esso Petroleum Co Ltd v Hall Russell & Co Ltd*, 1988 S.L.T. 33, affd in part [1989] A.C. 643. See also the Merchant Shipping (Prevention of Oil Pollution) Regulations 1996 (SI 1996/2154) as amended, the Merchant Shipping (Dangerous or Noxious Liquid Substances in Bulk) Regulations 1996 (SI 1996//3010) as amended and the Environmental Damage (Prevention and Remediation) Regulations 2009/153 (although only with very limited application on marine pollution). For an overview see Baughen, *Shipping Law* (2012), Ch.17 or Baatz et al, *Maritime Law* (2011), Ch.10.

[171] 1995 Act ss.183–184 and Sch.6, implementing the Athens Convention relating to the Carriage of Passengers and their Luggage by Sea of 1974 and the Protocol of 1976 (hereafter Athens 1976), and operative as respects international and domestic carriage from April 30, 1987 (SI 1987/635; SI 1989/1880; made under the Merchant Shipping Act 1979, under which the Athens Convention was first implemented). An inflatable banana, used to carry passengers round a bay, is not a "ship" for the purposes of the Athens Convention: *McEwan v Bingham* [2000] C.L.Y. 4691.

However, from December 31, 2012, by virtue of an EU Regulation on the liability of carriers of passengers by sea in the event of accidents,[172] the Athens Convention 2002[173] applies to international and national[174] carriage within the European Union. The 2002 Athens Convention implements a mixture of fault based and strict liability, depending on level and type of damage. It also imposes compulsory insurance with direct action.[175]

The carrier is liable for the death of or injury to a passenger, and for loss of or damage to luggage,[176] if caused by the fault or neglect of the carrier or his servants or agents.[177] However, under Athens 2002, a strict liability regime applies for loss or damage resulting from death or personal injury caused by shipping incidents[178] up to a limit of 250,000 SDR, with the possibility of a further fault-based liability up to 400,000 SDR[179] which can be avoided if the carrier proves that the loss was caused without his fault or neglect.[180] His liability may be limited.[181] However, he

---

[172] EC Regulation 392/2009. The provisions of the Merchant Shipping Act 1995 will therefore need amending for carriage from December 31, 2012.

[173] The Athens Convention of 1974 as amended by the 2002 Protocol (hereafter "Athens 2002") (note: art.17(5) of the 2002 Protocol, requiring denunciation of the previous versions of the Athens Convention on ratification). The 2002 Convention has, as of April 2012, not yet achieved the required numbers of ratifications and it remains to see when it will come into force as a matter of international law. For its ratification status see the website of the depository, the International Maritime Organisation ("IMO") at *http://www.imo.org/About/Conventions/StatusOfConventions/Pages/Default.aspx* [Accessed July 16, 2012]. However, any delay in the coming into force of the Convention will not impact on the application within the EU as a matter of EU law as of December 31, 2012 (EC Regulation 392/2009 art.12).

[174] Application to domestic carriage within a single Member State is phased and includes an option for Member States to defer the implementation for up to 4–6 years; see arts 1(2),(3), 2 and 11 of EC Regulation 392/2009. Note: Directive 98/18/EC as referred to in the Regulation has been replaced by Directive 2009/45/EC (as amended by Directive 2010/36/EU).

[175] EC Regulation 392/2009 art.3 with Athens 2002, art.4 bis; note also the IMO Guidelines, as referred to as binding in arts 1(2) and 3(2) and set out in Annex II to the Regulation. The compulsory insurance for death and personal injury must be for no less than 250,000 SDR; up to this financial limit the convention provides for direct action against the insurer; against those claims, the issuers can only use the defences of wilful misconduct of the assured and bankruptcy or winding up of the carrier (art.4 bis (1), (10)).

[176] Excluding live animals: Athens 1976 (Merchant Shipping Act 1995 Sch.6) art.1 para.5(b); Athens 2002 (EU Regulation 392/2009 Annex I) art.1(5b).

[177] art.3(1) of the 1976 Athens Convention (Sch.6). In certain circumstances (shipwreck, collision, stranding, explosion or fire, or defect in the ship) fault on the part of the carrier is presumed, and the onus of proof lies with the carrier: art.3(3). Similarly, where luggage other than cabin luggage is lost or damaged, fault is presumed and the onus lies with the carrier: art.3(3).

[178] See Athens Convention 2002 art.3(5); liability for other incidents including so-called "hotel risks" remains negligence based (art.3(2)–(4)).

[179] See Athens 2002 art.7; note that it is possible for a State Party to impose higher limits or unlimited liability by national law (art.7(2)).

[180] Athens 2002 art.3(1), although the carrier can escape liability if he can prove that the incident resulted from: (a) an act of war, hostilities, civil war, insurrection or a natural phenomenon of an exceptional, inevitable and irresistible character; or (b) was wholly caused by an act or omission done by a third party with the intent to case the incident. For loss suffered as a result of death or personal injury caused by incidents other than shipping incidents, the carrier is only liable for fault or neglect, which has to be proven by the claimant (art.3(2)). Insofar as cabin luggage is lost or damaged the carrier's liability is fault-based, but, in case of shipping incidents, presumed (art.3(3)). For loss or damage to luggage other than cabin luggage it is upon the carrier to disprove his fault (art.3(4)).

[181] Athens 1976 arts 7, 8, 9, 10, 12, 13; note: from January 1, 1999 the Carriage of Passengers and their Luggage by Sea (United Kingdom Carriers) Order 1998 (SI 1998/2917) increased the Athens 1976 liability limits in case of death and personal injury from 46,666 SDR to 300,000 SDR for carriers with place of business in the United Kingdom. For Athens 2002, see arts 3(1), 7, 8, 9, 10, 12, 13 and note the revision clause in art.23, setting out an adjustment procedure for the limits of limitation in Athens 2002. Note that passenger claims are also subject to global limitation as per the Convention of Limitation of Liability for Maritime Claims 1976 (as amended), implemented by the Merchant Shipping Act 1995 s.185; see above, para.22.20.

cannot benefit from limitation where there was intent to damage, or reckless behaviour.[182] There are detailed provisions relating to performing carriers, valuables, contributory fault, time-limits in respect of giving notice to the carrier of damaged or lost luggage, a two-year time-bar for reparation actions, rules on jurisdiction, and nuclear damage.[183] It is impossible to contract out of the statutory provisions.[184] The EU Regulation on liability of carriers of passengers further contains rules on compensation in respect of mobility or other specific equipment,[185] global limitation of liability,[186] advance payment to cover immediate economic needs resulting from death or personal injury caused by a shipping incident[187] and information to be given to passengers regarding their rights.[188]

From December 18, 2012 the EU Regulation concerning the rights of passengers when travelling by sea and inland waterway[189] applies to carriers offering passenger services from a port of embarkation within a European Union Member State, or failing that, to cases where the carrier is a Union carrier[190] and the port of disembarkation is a port within the territory of a Member State or, with limited reach, also for cruises where the port of embarkation is within the territory of an EU Member State.[191] The Regulation imposes mandatory rules[192] relating to non-discrimination between passengers with regard to transport conditions offered by carriers,[193] non-discrimination and assistance for disabled persons and persons with reduced mobility ("DPRMs"),[194] on rights of passengers in cases of cancellation or delay,[195] on minimum information to be provided to passengers and on handling complaints[196] and general rules of enforcement.[197] Member States are due to inform the Commission of the rules and measure adopted relating to penalties by December 18, 2012.[198]

---

[182] art.13 of Athens 1976 and 2002.

[183] Athens 1976 arts 4–6, 15–17 and 20 and Athens 2002 arts 4, 5–6, 15–17 and 20, but note that the Convention's rules on jurisdiction as well as on recognition and enforcement (arts 17 and 17 bis) are not included in the application as a matter of EU law via EC Regulation 392/2009, since, within the EU, the latter questions are determined by EC Regulation 44/2001 on jurisdiction and the recognition and enforcement in civil and commercial matters (OJ L12, 16.1.2001, p.1), as amended. Also see art.5 of EC Regulation 392/2009 (applied within the EU instead of, although similar to Athens 2002 art.19) on primacy of global limitation of liability by virtue of the International Convention on Limitation of Liability for Maritime Claims 1976 (as amended by the Protocol of 1996), insofar as implemented by national law (the latter is implemented into United Kingdom law by s.185 of the Merchant Shipping Act 1995—see above, para.22.20).

[184] art.18 of Athens 1976 and 2002.

[185] EC Regulation 392/2009 art.4.

[186] EC Regulation 392/2009 art.5 and above fn.181 in fine.

[187] EC Regulation 392/2009 art.6; payment shall not constitute recognition of liability and may be offset against subsequent sums to be paid, but is generally non-refundable (art.6(2)).

[188] EC Regulation 392/2009 art.7.

[189] EU Regulation 1177/2010 of 24 November 2010 concerning the rights of passengers when travelling by sea and inland waterway and amending Regulation (EC) No.2006/2004 (OJ L334, 17.12.2010, p.1).

[190] Which under EU Regulation 1177/2010 art.3(e) is defined as a carrier established within the territory of a Member State or offering transport by passenger services operated to or from the territory of a Member State.

[191] EU Regulation 1177/2010 art.2(1); note the excluded vessels or services under paras 2–4 of art.2.

[192] EU Regulation 1177/2010 art.6.

[193] EU Regulation 1177/2010 art.4.

[194] EU Regulation 1177/2010 arts 7–15.

[195] EU Regulation 1177/2010 arts 16–21.

[196] EU Regulation 1177/2010 arts 22–24.

[197] EU Regulation 1177/2010 arts 25–28.

[198] EU Regulation 1177/2010 art.28; thus UK Regulations designating the enforcement body, rules and penalties are expected by that time.

Part 3 (services and public functions) of the Equality Act 2010 only applies to transportation by, or services provided on a ship or hovercraft in the way set out in regulations made by a Minister of the Crown.[199]

22.29 Dangerous vessels—A harbour master may direct a shipowner or master or other person in possession of a ship not to enter a harbour, or to remove a vessel therefrom, if the vessel presents a grave and imminent danger or risk.[200]

22.30 Safety at sea—The Merchant Shipping Act 1995 makes provision for health and safety regulations on board ship.[201] Improvement notices and prohibition notices may be served upon persons contravening statutory regulations.[202] Deaths on board a UK registered ship must be the subject of an inquiry,[203] and accidents involving ships the subject of investigation.[204] The master and owner may be guilty of an offence if a ship is dangerously unsafe,[205] and the master or seamen may be guilty of an offence where they endanger the safety of their ship.[206] A shipowner must take all reasonable steps to ensure that the ship is operated in a safe manner.[207]

22.31 Limitation/prescription in marine claims—Any action to enforce any claim or lien against a vessel or her owners in respect of any damage or loss to another vessel, her cargo or freight, or any property on board her, or damages for loss of life or personal injuries suffered by any person on board her, caused by the fault of the former vessel, must be commenced[208] within two years from the date when the damage or loss or injury was caused.[209] A court

---

[199] Equality Act 2010 s.30 (in force, except so far as they apply to the protected characteristic of age (SI 2010/2317, art.2(3a)); see Equality Act 2010 (Work on Ships and Hovercraft) Regulations 2011 (SI 2011/1771), in force since August 1, 2011.

[200] Dangerous Vessels Act 1985 s.1. The harbour master is himself subject to directions from the Secretary of State: s.3.

[201] 1995 Act ss.85–108A, as amended by the Merchant Shipping and Maritime Security Act 1997 and the Marine Safety Act 2003. Regulations are to be found in statutory instruments, implementing inter alia the many European rules on safety standards. As to limitation and exclusion of liability for personal injury, etc. see paras 22.18 and 22.28, above. Note also that EC Regulation 1406/2002 of 27 June 2002 establishing a European Maritime Safety Agency (OJ L208, 5.8.2002, p.1) as amended by EC Regulation 1644/2003, EC Regulation 724/2004 and EC Regulation 1891/2006 established a European Maritime Safety Agency with the purpose of ensuring a high, uniform and effective level of maritime safety, maritime security within certain limits, prevention of oil pollution and response to pollution by ships within the Union. Its objectives are to give technical and scientific assistance to the Member States and the Commission (art.1). For more detail on maritime safety rules and developments on international and EU level see Baatz et al, *Maritime Law* (2011), Ch.9 or A. Mandaraka-Sheppard, *Modern Maritime Law and Risk Management*, 2nd edn (Routledge-Cavendish, 2007), Ch.20.

[202] 1995 Act ss.261–262. Notices are served by Department of Trade inspectors: s.256.

[203] 1995 Act s.271.

[204] 1995 Act s.267.

[205] 1995 Act s.98. In certain circumstances, charterers and ship managers could be prosecuted.

[206] 1995 Act s.58.

[207] 1995 Act s.100. Failure in this duty is an offence: *Seaboard Offshore Ltd v Secretary of State for Transport* [1994] 1 W.L.R. 541 (HL). Demise charterers and ship managers may also be guilty in terms of s.100.

[208] The commencement of an action has been defined as the date of citation: *Miller v National Coal Board*, 1960 S.C. 376 at 383, per Lord President Clyde; *Barclay v Chief Constable, Northern Constabulary*, 1986 S.L.T. 562.

[209] 1995 Act s.190. For actions against the carrier of cargo, contrast the shorter one year time period for cargo claims under the Hague Rules art.3 r.6 or Hague-Visby Rules art.III r.6 (see above para.22.17) or, where not impeded by mandatory application of liability regimes, the often even shorter time frames as per contract (typically nine months).

may extend the two-year period to such extent and on such conditions as it thinks fit.[210]

Terrorism and carriage by sea—The Aviation and Maritime Security Act 1990 **22.32** is concerned with protection against terrorism. Part II[211] gives effect to the Rome Convention 1988,[212] and makes it an offence, inter alia, to hijack a ship; to damage a ship; to act violently on board ship so as to endanger safety; and to place devices such as bombs on board ship. The Secretary of State may give directions to harbour authorities, shipowners and charterers prohibiting a ship from going to sea, or persons or property from being taken on board.[213] Powers of inspection and search are also provided for.[214]

Hovercraft—A hovercraft is a vehicle which is designed to be supported when **22.33** in motion wholly or partly by air expelled from the vehicle to form a cushion of which the boundaries include the ground, water or other surface beneath the vehicle.[215] Many principles of maritime law have been made applicable to hovercraft.[216]

GENERAL AVERAGE

Particular and general average—Average is the term used in shipping law for **22.34** any loss or injury to ship or cargo during a voyage. Such a loss may be a particular or a general average loss. Under the head of particular average falls any loss which is not due to a voluntary act, as, for instance, injury to a ship by striking a rock, or cargo being washed overboard. It also includes losses which, though they are voluntarily incurred, do not satisfy the conditions of general average. In relation to marine insurance it is enacted that

> "a particular average loss is a partial loss of the subject-matter insured, caused by a peril insured against, and which is not a general average loss".[217]

A particular average loss must be borne by the party whose property is injured.[218]

---

[210] 1995 Act s.190(5). See *Taft v Clyde Marine Motoring Co Ltd*, 1990 S.L.T. 170 (decided under the previous provision).

[211] Aviation and Maritime Security Act 1990 ss.9–17.

[212] Convention for the Suppression of Unlawful Acts Against the Safety of Maritime Navigation of March 10, 1988 and the Protocol for the Suppression of Unlawful Acts against the Safety of Fixed Platforms Located on the Continental Shelf of March 10, 1988.

[213] Aviation and Maritime Security Act 1990 Pt III (ss.18–46) as amended by the Merchant Shipping and Maritime Security Act 1997.

[214] Aviation and Maritime Security Act 1990 Pt III (ss.18–46) as amended by the Merchant Shipping and Maritime Security Act 1997.

[215] Hovercraft Act 1968 s.4(1).

[216] Generally under the Hovercraft Act1968 s.1(1)(h). The 1995 Act and any instrument made thereunder may, by Order in Council under s.1(1)(h), be made applicable to hovercraft (1995 Act s.310).

[217] Marine Insurance Act 1906 s.64. See para.22.41, below.

[218] See Bell, *Principles*, s.437; Bell, *Commentaries*, I, 630.

22.35 History of general average—The law of general average was recognised in civil law as derived from the maritime law of Rhodes, the *lex Rhodia de jactu*,[219] and has been adopted, though with differences in detail, in all mercantile countries. In Scotland the law of England on the subject has been recognised. As the result of international conferences, rules known as the York-Antwerp Rules have been drawn up on the subject, and were more recently revised in 1974, 1994 and 2004.[220] They have no statutory authority, but are commonly incorporated in bills of lading. They differ, in certain minor respects, from the common law, which holds where the Rules have not been expressly incorporated.

22.36 Nature of general average act—The theory of general average is that when one of the three main interests at stake during a voyage, the ship, the cargo and the freight, is voluntarily sacrificed for the safety of all, the loss must be borne rateably by all interested. Such a voluntary sacrifice, known as a general average act, has been defined as follows:

> "There is a general average act when, and only when, any extraordinary sacrifice or expenditure is intentionally and reasonably made or incurred for the common safety for the purpose of preserving from peril the property involved in a common maritime adventure."[221]

22.37 Instances of general average—A general average act may cause loss to the cargo, to the ship, or to the freight. There is a general average loss to the cargo; when it is jettisoned for the safety of the ship; when, with the same object, it is landed at some place other than its destination[222]; or when, though the cargo may not be actually touched, its value is affected by measures, other than mere delay, taken for the common safety.[223] There is a general average loss to the ship when some portion, e.g. the mast or sails, is sacrificed, or where, without any actual sacrifice, the appurtenants of the ship are used in some abnormal way, with consequent injury, as where the engines were used to move a ship which had been stranded, and were damaged in the process.[224] Voluntary stranding to avoid a threatened wreck is probably general average at common law, and is recognised with a modification in r.V of the York-Antwerp Rules.[225] Where a ship, to avoid being wrecked or stranded, entered a harbour, knowing that in entering she would probably strike the pier, it was held that both the injury to the ship and the damages fixed for injury to the pier were general average.[226] The freight is affected when

---

[219] Digest 14.2.1, Paul 2 sententiarum: "Lege Rhodia cavetur ut, si levandae navis gratia iactus mercium factus est, omnium contributione sarciatur quod pro omnibus datum est." For relevant texts see R. Lowndes and G.R. Rudolf, *The Law of General Average and the York-Antwerp Rules*, 13th edn (London: Sweet and Maxwell, 2008), App.1; W. Buckland, *A Textbook of Roman Law*, 3rd edn (Cambridge, 1963), p.506. See also *Goulandris v Goldman* [1958] 1 Q.B. 74 at 93.

[220] See Lowndes and Rudolf, *The Law of General Average and York-Antwerp Rules* (2008), Section 3. For interpretation, see Lowndes and Rudolf, Section 4, "Rule of Interpretation", PRE.02–PRE 13 (pp.69–74).

[221] York-Antwerp Rules 1974, 1994 and 2004 r.A; Lowndes and Rudolf, *The Law of General Average and York-Antwerp Rules* (2008), p.79. For a statutory definition, see Marine Insurance Act 1906 s.66; *Athel Line Ltd v Liverpool & London War Risks Association Ltd* [1994] KB 87 at 94.

[222] *Royal Mail Steam Packet Co v English Bank of Rio de Janeiro* (1887) L.R. 19 Q.B.D. 362.

[223] *Anglo-Argentine Live Stock Co v Temperley Shipping Co* [1899] 2 Q.B. 403.

[224] *The Bona* [1895] P. 125.

[225] York-Antwerp Rules 1974, 1994 and 2004 r.V; see *The Seapool* [1934] P. 53.

[226] *Austin Friars Co v Spillers & Bakers* [1915] 3 K.B. 586 (CA).

cargo is sacrificed, and the freight for it consequently lost.[227] Mere delay, resulting in a loss of market for the cargo, or a partial loss of freight in a time charter, is not a general average loss.[228] A payment made under an indemnity in a towage contract may be a general average loss.[229] Once a vessel reaches her final berth, the voyage is complete and expenses incurred during cargo discharge cannot be the subject of a general average claim.[230]

Contribution—Those who have to contribute to meet a general average loss **22.38** are the owners of the ship, the various owners of the cargo, and the parties entitled to the freight. Although the aim of the York-Antwerp Rules is to keep matters of alleged fault separate from the average adjustment,[231] the claim to contribution in general of the party whose fault gave rise to the peril in question can be resisted.[232] The owner of the property sacrificed contributes rateably according to its value.[233] There is no claim on passenger's luggage or their effects carried without a bill of lading.[234] The owner of deck cargo, unless it is carried under a custom of trade or with the consent of the other cargo owners, has no claim if his property is jettisoned,[235] but is bound to contribute to another general average loss.[236] The party in right of the respective interest at the completion of the voyage, not the party in such right at the time when the sacrifice was made, is liable.[237]

Lien—The owner of cargo which has been jettisoned has a lien over the rest of the **22.39** cargo for a general average contribution. The captain is impliedly his agent in this respect, and is entitled to enforce the lien, and liable in damages if, when called upon, he refuses or fails to do so.[238]

Conditions of right to contribution—The right to a general average contribution **22.40** depends upon an act which has caused loss and which has been done for the safety of all. So a claim was rejected for damage caused by turning on steam into the hold under the mistaken impression that the ship was on fire.[239] It is a question in the circumstances of each case whether a general average act was done

---

[227] *Iredale v China Traders' Insurance Co* [1900] 2 Q.B. 515.

[228] *The Leitrim* [1902] P. 256.

[229] *Australian Coastal Shipping Commission v Green* [1971] 1 Q.B. 456.

[230] *The Trade Green* [2000] 2 Lloyd's Rep. 451.

[231] York-Antwerp Rules, 1974, 1994 and 2004 r.D.

[232] *Goulandris v Goldman* [1958] 1 Q.B. 74; *Diestelkamp v Baynes (Reading) (The Aga)* [1968] 1 Lloyd's Rep. 431; *EB Aaby's Rederi A/S v Union of India (The Evje) (No.2)*, affd. [1978] 1 Lloyd's Rep. 351; *The Hellenic Glory* [1979] 1 Lloyd's Rep. 424; *Guinomar of Conakry v Samsung Fire & Marine Insurance Co Ltd (The Kamsar Voyager)* [2002] 2 Lloyd's Rep. 57; York-Antwerp Rules, 1974, 1994 and 2004 r.D; see also Lowndes and Rudolf, *The Law of General Average and York-Antwerp Rules* (2008), D.26.

[233] *Strang, Steel & Co v Scott* (1889) L.R. 14 App. Cas. 601.

[234] Bell, *Commentaries*, I, 636; York-Antwerp Rules, 1974 r.XVII, although the 1994 and 2004 Rules have amended this slightly, excluding "mails, passenger luggage, personal effects and accompanied private motor vehicles" from contribution (York-Antwerp Rules 1994 r.XVII, and York-Antwerp Rules 2004 r.XVII(e)); Lowndes and Rudolf, *The Law of General Average and York-Antwerp Rules* (2008), paras 17.08, 17.10, 17.11, 17.72–17.87.

[235] *Strang, Steel & Co v Scott* (1889) 14 App. Cas. 601.

[236] Bell, *Commentaries*, I, 636.

[237] *Ranking v Tod* (1870) 8 M. 914.

[238] *Strang, Steel & Co v Scott* (1889) 14 App. Cas. 601.

[239] *Watson (Joseph) & Son Ltd v Firemen's Fund Insurance Co of San Francisco* [1922] 2 K.B. 355.

reasonably. Only those whose interests were actually in peril can be called upon to contribute. Thus, where gold was landed to ensure its safety, and not for the purpose of lightening the ship, its owner, as his property was not in peril, was not liable to contribute in respect of cargo that was afterwards jettisoned.[240] The party to whose fault the peril is due, e.g. the shipowner, when the peril is due to the negligence of the captain, has no claim to a general average contribution,[241] with an exception in the case of fire.[242]

22.41 General average expenditure—Certain expenditure by the shipowner, known as general average expenditure, may be the subject of contribution if it was incurred for the safety of all.[243] As a shipowner is bound under his contract to take measures for the safety of the ship he has no claim to an average contribution unless the circumstances were exceptional or abnormal.[244] So, on the ground that risk from submarines was a normal incident during war and there was no proof that the ship had been in actual peril, the owner of a sailing ship was refused contribution for the expenses of a tug hired to speed up the voyage and so to lessen the risk.[245] When a ship is forced to put in to a port of refuge, the expense of unloading the cargo with a view to repairs[246] is in all cases allowed as a general average charge; but the expense of reloading, though allowed by the York-Antwerp Rules,[247] is at common law admissible only if the reason why the port of refuge was necessary was a general average act, e.g. the deliberate sacrifice of some part of the ship's equipment as contrasted with accidentally springing a leak.[248]

22.42 General average in marine insurance[249]—In questions of insurance, an underwriter, in the absence of any provision to the contrary, is liable to the assured for any general average contribution which may be payable in respect of his interest covered by the policy.[250] He is liable for the whole amount if the interest in question is insured to its full contributory value; to a proportional amount if the

---

[240] *Royal Mail Steam Packet Co v English Bank of Rio de Janeiro* (1887) L.R. 19 Q.B.D. 362.

[241] *Strang, Steel & Co v Scott* (1889) 14 App. Cas. 601; cf. *Diestelkamp v Baynes (Reading) (The Aga)* [1968] 1 Lloyd's Rep. 431; *EB Aaby's Rederi AIS v Union of India, (The Evje) (No.2)* [1976] 2 Lloyd's Rep. 714, affd. [1978] 1 Lloyd's Rep. 351.

[242] Merchant Shipping Act 1995 s.186(1); *Dreyfus v Tempus Shipping Co* [1931] A.C. 726, decided on the construction of s.502 of the Merchant Shipping Act 1894 (now repealed).

[243] York-Antwerp Rules 1974, 1994 and 2004 r.A; *Australian Coastal Shipping Commission v Green* [1971] 1 Q.B. 456; *The Trade Green* [2000] 2 Lloyd's Rep. 451.

[244] *Ocean Steamship Co v Anderson Tritton & Co* (1883) L.R. 13 Q.B.D. 651; (1884) 10 App. Cas. 107.

[245] *Societe Nouvelle d'Armement v Spillers & Bakers* [1917] 1 K.B. 865.

[246] The cost of temporary repairs qualifies as general average expenditure if they effect a saving in expense which would have been incurred and allowed in general average if such repairs had not been effected: *The Bijela* [1994] 1 W.L.R. 615.

[247] York-Antwerp Rules 1974 and 1994 r.X (a) and (c); York-Antwerp Rules 2004 r.X(a)(i) and (c); Lowndes and Rudolf, *The Law of General Average and York-Antwerp Rules* (2008), paras 10.30–10.37 and paras 10.55–10.71.

[248] *Atwood v Sellar* (1880) L.R. 5 Q.B.D. 286; *Svendson v Wallace* (1885) 10 App. Cas. 404; Lowndes and Rudolf, *The Law of General Average and York-Antwerp Rules* (2008), paras 10.08–10.20.

[249] J. Gilman et al, *Arnould's Law on Marine Insurance and Average*, 17th edn (London: Sweet and Maxwell, 2008), paras 26–01, 26–87 et seq: for an example of the complex interrelation between general average and shipping and insurance contracts, see *Comatra Ltd v Lloyds Underwriters* [2001] 2 All E.R. (Comm) 609.

[250] Marine Insurance Act 1906 s.66(5).

insurance was only partial.[251] The assured may recover from the underwriters the proportion of any general average expenditure which falls upon him, and in the case of a general average sacrifice, the whole loss, without having enforced his right of contribution from the other parties liable to contribute.[252] Though all the interest in the ship, the cargo and the freight may be vested in one person, the insurer of any one of these interests is liable in a general average contribution in the same way as if they had been vested in different persons.[253]

SALVAGE

Nature of salvage—A claim for salvage rests not on any contract but on an **22.43** obligation implied by maritime law.[254] At common law, salvage was defined as

> "a reward or recompense given to those by means of whose labour, intrepidity or perseverance a ship, or goods, have been saved from shipwreck, fire or capture"[255]

but the law is now substantially to be found in the terms of the Merchant Shipping Act 1995 giving the force of law to the International Convention on Salvage 1989.[256] Article 1 of the Convention defines a salvage operation as

> "any act or activity undertaken to assist a vessel or any other property in danger in navigable waters or in any other waters whatsoever"

but in our law the Convention provisions do not apply if the salvage operation takes place in inland waters[257] of the United Kingdom and all the vessels involved are of inland navigation, or if the salvage operation takes place in inland waters of the United Kingdom and no vessel is involved.[258] So a person who saves the property of others on land has no claim,[259] nor, for example, has a person who saves another's lorry from an inland loch by using a crane operating from the bank. Salvage is applicable to the rescue of any ship[260] or craft or any structure capable of navigation,[261] but not to the rescue of fixed or floating platforms or mobile offshore drilling units when they are on location engaged in exploration, exploitation or production of sea-bed mineral resources.[262] However, an oil rig

---

[251] Marine Insurance Act 1906 s.73.

[252] Marine Insurance Act 1906 s.66(4).

[253] Marine Insurance Act 1906 s.66(7); *Montgomery & Co v Indemnity Mutula Marine Insurance Co* [1902] 1 K.B. 734.

[254] *Stair Memorial Encyclopaedia*, "Shipping and Navigation" (Reissue), s.295: J. Reeder, *Brice on Maritime Law of Salvage*, 5th edn (London: Sweet and Maxwell, 2011), para.1–07: see speech of Lord Mustill in *The Nagasaki Spirit* [1997] A.C. 455.

[255] Bell, *Principles*, s.443; *Commentaries*, I, 638.

[256] The Convention is in Sch.11 Pt I.

[257] Not including waters within the ebb and flow of the tide at ordinary spring tides or the waters of certain docks connected with such waters: 1995 Act Sch.11 Pt II para.2(2). See also *The Goring* [1988] A.C. 831. See *Stair Memorial Encyclopaedia*, "Shipping and Navigation" (Reissue), para.304.

[258] 1995 Act Sch.11 Pt II para.2(1).

[259] cf. *Falcke v Scottish Imperial Assurance Co* (1887) L.R. 34 Ch. D. 234.

[260] For state-owned vessels see Salvage Convention 1989 (Merchant Shipping Act Sch.11 Pt I) art.4.

[261] Salvage Convention 1989 art.1(b); excluding recreational craft such as jet skis, see *R. v Goodwin* [2006] 1 Lloyd's Rep. 432; Mandaraka-Sheppard, *Modern Maritime Law and Risk Management* (2007), pp.643–645.

[262] Salvage Convention 1989 art.3.

being towed from one location to another may be a subject of salvage.[263] Salvage is also applicable to the rescue of all kinds of property not permanently and intentionally attached to the shoreline, including cargo, stores, equipment, passengers' effects and freight at risk.[264] By convention, aircraft and hovercraft if in or on the sea or tidal water may be the subject of salvage.[265] No remuneration is due from a person whose life has been saved,[266] but if the person who saved the life took part in the services rendered on the occasion of the accident giving rise to salvage, then he is entitled to a fair share of the payment awarded to the salvor for salving the vessel or other property or for preventing or minimising damage to the environment.[267] To justify a claim for salvage, the subjects salved must have been in a position of danger, or at least believed by those in charge of them to be so.[268] Assistance to a ship which is disabled, but in no danger, is merely towage, a service which founds a claim for payment, but not for payment at salvage rates.[269] When a vessel is injured on going to the rescue of a ship run down by a third, she is not exposed to the plea that she assumed the risk. She goes in pursuance of a duty.[270]

22.44 Parties entitled to salvage—The persons entitled to salvage are those who perform salvage operations[271] and so may include the owners of the ship or ships which have rendered assistance, their masters and crew.[272] Since no payment is due unless the services rendered exceed what can be reasonably considered as due performance of any contract entered into before the danger arose,[273] the claimant must be a person who was not under any obligation to render the services prior to the emergency which rendered them necessary.[274] This excludes any claim by the master and crew of the ship salved; they are bound by their contract to do everything in their power for the safety of the ship.[275] Where the rules of a mutual assurance society provided that each assured should render assistance to every other, it was held that because such assistance was given under a contractual obligation, it afforded no ground for salvage.[276] Towage has to be distinguished from salvage, but a tug engaged to tow a vessel may be entitled to salvage if

---

[263] *The Key Singapore* [2005] 1 All E.R. (Comm) 99.

[264] Salvage Convention 1989 art.1(c).

[265] Reeder, *Brice on Maritime Law of Salvage* (2011), para.1–53.

[266] Salvage Convention 1989 art.16.1.

[267] Salvage Convention 1989 art.16.2. For environmental damage see para.22.47, below.

[268] *The Charlotte* (1848) 3 W. Rob. 68; *The Phantom* (1866) L.R. 1 A. & E. 58; Reeder, *Brice on Maritime Law of Salvage* (2011), paras 1–08 et seq and especially paras 1–142 et seq.

[269] *Robinson v Thoms* (1851) 13 D. 592; *Lawson v Grangemouth Dockyard Co* (1888) 15 R. 753; *The Kangaroo* [1918] P. 327; *The Troilus* [1951] A.C. 820; *Aberdeen Harbour Board v Marz H/F*, 1971 S.L.T. (Notes) 34; *The Texaco Southampton* [1983] 1 Lloyd's Rep. 94.

[270] *The Gusty v The Daniel* [1940] P. 159.

[271] Salvage Convention 1989 art.1(a).

[272] See *Bennet v Henderson* (1887) 24 S.L.R. 625; *The Golden Falcon* [1990] 2 Lloyd's Rep. 366; *The Sava Star* [1995] 2 Lloyd's Rep. 134. Agreements by which seamen give up their claim to salvage are, in general, void: Merchant Shipping Act 1995 s.39; *Nicholson v Leith Salvage, etc. Co*, 1923 S.C. 409.

[273] Salvage Convention 1989 art.17.

[274] cf. *The Gregerso* [1973] Q.B. 274. However, a salvage contract may be, and with professional salvors usually is, entered into after the emergency has arisen. Lloyd's has a standard form of salvage agreement. The Unfair Contract Terms Act 1977 applies to salvage contracts, to a limited extent: 1977 Act s.15(3)(b); see Ch.9, above. For a discussion of the circumstances in which a master may bind the cargo owners by such an agreement, see *The Choko Star* [1990] 1 Lloyd's Rep. 516.

[275] Bell, *Principles*, s.444. See *The Albionic* [1942] P. 81.

[276] *Clan Steam Trawling Co v Aberdeen Trawling Co*, 1908 S.C. 651.

unexpected circumstances create a danger and require exceptional services from the tug.[277] An agent for the shipowner may recover salvage, but any bargain which he may make will be unfavourably regarded and such claims are rare.[278] Cargo owners can claim salvage from shipowners in an appropriate case, provided that they do not do so as a result of a duty owed to the shipowners, nor from what is ordinarily required of a cargo owner, such as provision of information about the cargo to the shipowner.[279] Passengers, though not contractually bound, are under an obligation to assist in their own rescue and that of others, and a claim by them is not maintainable except in the case where, having an opportunity of leaving the ship, they voluntarily remained and assisted in saving her.[280] A ship which has been injured by a collision, though under a statutory obligation to render assistance to the other ship involved,[281] is, if not in fault, entitled to salvage,[282] and possibly even if she was in fault.[283] When salvage services are rendered by one of Her Majesty's ships, any claim by the officers and crew requires the consent of the Secretary of State for Defence.[284] It has been said that such a claim must be supported by proof of services of an exceptional kind,[285] but statute provides that the position of the Crown in relation to salvage claims by or against the Crown is the same as that of any other ship owner.[286] Where a public body, such as the Coast Guard, the police or the fire service provides assistance, they may do so in fulfilment of a statutory duty and if so, on general principles, no claim for salvage will be available; but if the public body merely has a power to provide the service or it goes beyond the requirements of any statutory duty, then, depending on the terms of any relevant legislation, a claim for salvage may be brought.[287] A salvor may require a licence if carrying out operations at or near a wreck of historical, archaeological or artistic importance.[288] A salvor may be directed by a harbour master not to enter a harbour, or to remove a vessel therefrom, if the vessel presents a danger or risk.[289] Note also the pending Pt IXA of the Merchant

---

[277] See Reeder, *Brice on Maritime Law of Salvage* (2011), paras 1–321 et seq. See generally A. Parks and E. Cattell, *Tug, Tow and Pilotage*, 3rd edn (London: Sweet and Maxwell, 1994), see esp. Ch.XII—"Salvage".

[278] *The Crusader* [1907] P. 196; Reeder, *Brice on Maritime Law of Salvage* (2011), p.91, paras 1–316—1–317.

[279] *The Sava Star* [1995] 2 Lloyd's Rep. 134 at 144.

[280] Kennedy and Rose, *The Law of Salvage*, 7th edn (London: Sweet and Maxwell, 2010), p.324 et seq. (paras 8.126–8.130); *Newman v Walters* (1804) 3 B. & P. 612; *The Sava Star* [1995] 2 Lloyd's Rep. 134.

[281] Merchant Shipping Act 1995 s.92(1).

[282] *Melanie (Owners) v San Onofre (Owners)* [1925] A.C. 246.

[283] *The Beaverford (Owners) v The Kafiristan (Owners)* [1938] A.C. 136.

[284] Merchant Shipping Act 1995 s.230(3). If consent has not been given, the claim is dismissed: s.230(5).

[285] *The Ulysses* (1888) L.R. 13 P.D. 205; *Swanney v Rederi Aktiebolag*, 1925 S.L.T. 491; *The Valverda* [1938] A.C. 173.

[286] Merchant Shipping Act 1995 s.230.

[287] See the discussion in Reeder, *Brice on Maritime Law of Salvage* (2011), paras 1–218—1–220, 1–228—1–235, and 1–238—1–263; *The Mars*, (1948) 81 Ll. L Rep. 452.

[288] Protection of Wrecks Act 1973 s.1 (amendment pending: in force at time of writing (April 2012), but due to be repealed by Marine (Scotland) Act 2010 Sch.4(2) para.4 (latter to come into force at such date as appointed)). See also the Merchant Shipping and Maritime Security Act 1997.

[289] Dangerous Vessels Act 1985 s.1: a grave and imminent danger to persons or property, or a grave and imminent risk that the vessel might founder and prejudice the use of the harbour. The harbour master is himself subject to directions from the Secretary of State: s.3.

Shipping Act, to give the force of law to the 2007 Nairobi International Convention on the Removal of Wrecks.[290]

22.45 Conditions of salvage claim—The essential elements of a salvage claim are danger and success. Danger means a risk of loss or damage to the ship or lives or property aboard, not necessarily a risk of total loss.[291]

Except in cases where an express bargain to pay for attempts to salve is proved[292] or the salvor has prevented or minimised damage to the environment,[293] success is a condition of a claim for salvage.[294] The efforts of a voluntary salvor, if unsuccessful, go unrewarded.[295] If nothing is saved, nothing is due.[296] If the ship is ultimately saved, those who were invited to assist her, though their efforts proved unsuccessful, have a claim.[297] Where a salvor removed the ship from a position of danger but left her in a position no more favourable, although the ship was ultimately saved, it was held that no salvage was due because the efforts to salve had met with no success.[298] Misconduct on the part of salvors, for instance fraud or other dishonest conduct such as looting, may deprive those implicated of the whole or part of the payment otherwise due.[299] A successful salvor may be liable for negligence on his part,[300] subject to the benefit of limitation of liability in terms of the Merchant Shipping Act 1995.[301]

22.46 Parties liable—The parties liable for salvage are all those who have a beneficial interest in the vessel and other property which is saved, generally the owners of

---

[290] The Convention is not yet in force, as also Pt IXA added by the Wreck Removal Convention Act 2011. The Convention had, as of April 2012, 5 of the 10 contracting states required for its entry into force. For the Convention's ratification status see the website of the depository, the International Maritime Organisation ("IMO") at *http://www.imo.org/About/Conventions/StatusOfConventions/Pages/Default.aspx* [Accessed July 16, 2012].

[291] Kennedy, *The Law of Salvage* (2010), Ch. 5—"Danger & Salvage Services"; esp. 5.005 (p.182) Degree of Danger.

[292] cf. *The Valverda* [1938] A.C. 173, holding that such a bargain is a true salvage agreement.

[293] Salvage Convention 1989 art.14.

[294] Salvage Convention 1989 art.12.1 and 12.2; note the particular form contracts based on the "no cure no pay" principle, the Lloyd's Open Form ("LOF"), which are regularly updated, e.g. LOF 1980, 1990, 2000 and 2011, and with the possibility of including the SCOPIC (Special Compensation Protection & Indemnity Club) clause for an alternative basis and calculation of remuneration to that of art.14.

[295] *Steel & Bennie v Hutchison* (1909) 2 S.L.T. 110.

[296] See Mandaraka-Sheppard, *Modern Maritime Law and Risk Management* (2007), p.665; Eder, *Scrutton on Charterparties and Bills of Lading* (2011), para.12–070. Since the traditional rule discourages attempts at salvage, and may in turn create environmental hazard, the International Convention on Salvage 1989, given effect by the Merchant Shipping Act 1995 s.224(1), Sch.11 Pt I art.14, provides for compensation equivalent to expenses for an unsuccessful salvor in cases where damage to the environment was threatened. See *Semco Salvage and Marine Pte Ltd v Lancer Navigation Co Ltd (The Nagasaki Spirit)* [1997] A.C. 455, particularly the speech of Lord Mustill. If environmental damage is prevented or minimised, the compensation may be increased by up to double.

[297] *Ross & Marshall v Owners and Master of S.S. "Davaar"* (1907) 15 S.L.T. 29.

[298] *Melanie (Owners) v San Onofre (Owners)* [1925] A.C. 246.

[299] Salvage Convention 1989 art.18. Cf. *The Clan Sutherland* [1918] P. 332.

[300] *The Tojo Maru* [1972] A.C. 242; obiter dicta in *The St Blane* [1974] 1 Lloyd's Rep. 557. The ordinary rules of contributory negligence apply: *The Key Singapore* [2005] 1 All E.R. (Comm) 99. Such a claim might be made by way of a counter-claim.

[301] 1995 Act s.185 and Sch.7. Note that in terms of s.185(4) there is no limitation of liability where loss of life or personal injury or loss of or damage to property has been sustained by a person who is on board the ship or employed in connection with that ship or with the salvage operations under a UK contract of employment.

the ship and cargo, and the persons entitled to the freight.[302] They may be sued personally[303] and are liable pro rata for the proportion which the value of their interest bears to the total value of all the property salved.[304] As a general rule, all those who are liable to contribute must be called as defenders, but where the peril of the ship was due to the fault of the shipowner, and he, had she been lost, would have been liable to the owners of the cargo, it was held that an action against him alone was competent; and opinions were expressed that in the case of a general ship, where the owners of the cargo are numerous, the action may be directed against the shipowner.[305] A claim for salvage may also be enforced by the retention of the property salved, if in the salvor's possession, or in that of the Receiver of Wreck for the district.[306] And the salvor has a maritime lien or hypothec, in virtue of which the ship may be arrested.[307] The salvor's lien, which cannot be enforced if he has been given satisfactory security for his claim,[308] takes priority over all other maritime liens.[309]

Amount of salvage award—The amount payable as salvage may be settled **22.47** by agreement between the parties. But such an agreement may be reduced or modified if it was entered into under undue influence or the influence of danger and its terms are inequitable, or if the payment due under the contract is in an excessive degree too large or too small for the services actually rendered.[310] Where there has been no agreement, and the amount has to be settled by the court, the reward should be fixed with a view to encouraging salvage operations.[311] The assessment by a court of first instance will hardly ever be disturbed.[312] The criteria to be taken into account in assessing or apportioning[313] a reward are: the salved value of the vessel and other property; the skill and efforts of the salvors in preventing or minimising damage to the environment; the measure of success obtained by the salvor; the nature and degree of the danger; the skill and efforts of the salvors in salving the vessel, other property and life; the time used and expenses and losses incurred by the salvors; the risk of liability and other risks run by the salvors or their equipment; the promptness of the services rendered; the availability and use of vessels or other equipment intended for salvage operations and the state of readiness and efficiency of the salvor's equipment and the value thereof.[314] The salved value of the vessel and property is a controlling element since the reward, exclusive of interest and recoverable legal costs, cannot exceed that value[315] and in no modern case has the award of salvage exceeded half

---

[302] Salvage Convention 1989 art.13.2. For freight, see Reeder, *Brice on Maritime Law of Salvage* (2011), paras 3–33 et seq.; para.22.38 above.

[303] *Peter Milne Duncan v The Dundee, Perth, and London Shipping Co* (1878) 5 R. 742.

[304] Salvage Convention 1989 art.13.2. Cf. *The M. Vatan* [1990] 1 Lloyd's Rep. 336.

[305] *Peter Milne Duncan v Dundee, Perth, and London Shipping Co* (1878) 5 R. 742.

[306] Merchant Shipping Act 1995 s.226; *Walker Steam Trawl Fishing Company Limited v Mitre Shipping Company Limited*, 1913 1 S.L.T. 67.

[307] *Hatton v Durban Hansen*, 1919 S.C. 154; *The Lyrma (No.2)* [1978] 2 Lloyd's Rep. 30.

[308] Salvage Convention 1989 art.20.2.

[309] *The Lyrma (No.2)* [1978] 2 Lloyd's Rep. 30.

[310] Salvage Convention 1989 art.7. As previously indicated, the Unfair Contract Terms Act 1977 applies in a modified way to salvage contracts: s.15(3)(b).

[311] Salvage Convention 1989 art.13.1; *The Amerique* (1874–75) L.R. 6 P.C. 468.

[312] But see *The Evaine* [1966] 2 Lloyd's Rep. 413; *The Nagasaki Spirit* [1997] A.C. 455; cf. Kennedy and Rose, *Law of Salvage* (2010), paras 14.106–14.108.

[313] Salvage Convention 1989 art.15.1.

[314] Salvage Convention 1989 art.13.1.

[315] Salvage Convention 1989 art.13.3.

the value of the property saved, except in the case of a derelict, where there is no claim put forward by the owners.[316] In addition, if a vessel by itself or its cargo threatened damage to the environment, then a salvor is entitled to special compensation to cover his expenses even though the salvage operations failed.[317] If those operations actually prevented or minimised damage to the environment, the court may increase the special compensation up to a maximum of 30 per cent of the salvor's expenses and, if it deems it fair and just to do so, and bearing in mind the criteria mentioned above, the court may increase it further up to a maximum of 100 per cent of the expenses.[318] The total special compensation is to be paid only if and to the extent that it is greater than the ordinary salvage reward, but the court is not obliged to maximise that reward before assessing special compensation.[319] In salvage actions the court has an equitable power to award interest.[320]

22.48 **Procedure**—With the repeal of s.547 of the Merchant Shipping Act 1894 the special rules on jurisdiction cease and the general provisions regulating the jurisdiction of the Sheriff Court and the Court of Session apply.[321] Proceedings must, however, be commenced within two years of the rendering of salvage services.[322] The period may only be extended by the potential defender making a declaration to the claimant during the two-year period.[323]

FURTHER READING

Aikens, L.J. and Bools, M., *Bills of Lading* (London: Informa Professional, 2006).
Baatz, Y., Debbattista, C., Lorenzon, F., Serdy, A., Staniland, H. and Tsimplis, M., *The Rotterdam Rules: A practical annotation* (London: Informa Law, 2009).
Baatz, Y. et al (eds), *Maritime Law,* 2nd edn (London: Sweet and Maxwell, 2011).
Baughen, S., *Shipping Law*, 5th edn (Routledge-Cavendish, 2012).
Berlingieri, F., *Berlingieri on the Arrest of Ships*, 5th edn (London: Informa Professional, 2011).
Branch, A.E., *Elements of Shipping*, 8th edn (Routledge, 2007).
Reeder, J., *Brice on Maritime Law of Salvage*, 5th edn (London: Sweet and Maxwell, 2011).
Bugden, P. and Lamont-Black, S., *Goods in Transit*, 2nd edn (London: Sweet and Maxwell, 2010).
Cooke, J., *Voyage Charters*, 3rd edn (London: Informa Professional, 2007).
Colinvaux, R., *Carver's Carriage by Sea*, 13th edn (London: Stevens, 1982).
Gilman, J., *Arnould's Law of Maritime Insurance and Average*, 17th edn (London: Sweet and Maxwell, 2008).

---

[316] See Kennedy and Rose, *Law of Salvage* (2010), Ch.15—"Salved Values".
[317] Salvage Convention 1989 art.14.1 and 14.3. Such compensation may be lost or reduced if the salvor's negligence resulted in him failing to prevent or to minimise damage to the environment: art.14.5.
[318] Salvage Convention 1989 art.14.2.
[319] Salvage Convention 1989 art.14.4 and 1995 Act Sch.11 Pt II para.4.
[320] *The Ben Gairn*, 1979 S.C. 98; Salvage Convention 1989 art.24.
[321] 1894 Act s.547 was repealed by s.8(4) and Sch.5 Pt II of the Merchant Shipping (Registration etc.) Act 1993, commenced with effect from May 1, 1994 by SI 1993/3137.
[322] Salvage Convention 1989 art.23.1.
[323] Salvage Convention 1989 art.23.2.

Girvin, S.D., *Carriage of Goods by Sea*, 2nd edn (Oxford: Oxford University Press, 2011).

Griggs, P., Williams R. and Farr, J., *Limitation of Liability for Maritime Claims*, 4th edn (London: Lloyd's of London Press, 2005).

Gűner-Özbek, M.D., *The United Nations Convention on Contracts for the International Carriage of Goods Wholly or Partly by Sea: an appraisal of the "Rotterdam Rules"* (Springer, 2011).

Jackson, D.C., *Enforcement of Maritime Claims*, 4th edn (LLP Publishing Professional, 2005).

Kennedy and Rose, *The Law of Salvage*, 7th edn (London: Sweet and Maxwell, 2010).

Lowndes. R., and Rudolf, G.R., *The Law of General Average and the York-Antwerp Rules*, 13th edn (London: Sweet and Maxwell, 2008).

Mandaraka-Sheppard, A., *Modern Maritime Law and Risk Management*, 2nd edn (Routledge-Cavendish, 2007).

Sassoon, D.M., *C.I.F. and F.O.B. Contracts*, 4th edn (London: Sweet and Maxwell, 1995) (5th edn expected in 2012).

Scrutton on Charterparties and Bills of Lading, edited by Eder, B. et al, 22nd edn (London: Sweet and Maxwell, 2011).

Stair Memorial Encyclopaedia, "Carriage" (Reissue); "Shipping and Navigation" (Reissue).

Sturley, M., Fujita, T., and van der Ziel, G., *The Rotterdam Rules: the UN Convention on Contracts for the International Carriage of Goods Wholly or Partly by Sea* (London: Sweet and Maxwell, 2010).

Tetley, W., *Marine Cargo Claims*, 4th edn (Canada: Thompson Carswell, 2008).

Thomas, D.R., *A New Convention of the Carriage of Goods by Sea—The Rotterdam Rules* (Lawtext Publishing, 2009).

Treitel, G.H., *Carver on Bills of Lading*, 2nd edn (London: Sweet and Maxwell, 2005).

Wilson, J.F., *Carriage of Goods by Sea*, 7th edn (Pearson Education, 2010).

CHAPTER 23

CARRIAGE BY AIR

General—As will be seen in the chapter on Landownership, property in land **23.01**
extends *a coelo usque ad centrum*, so that in strictness the passage of aircraft
over a person's land is a trespass. Since, however, the maintenance of such a
rule would largely defeat travel by air, the owner's rights have been restricted
by a statutory provision to the effect that no action shall lie in respect of
trespass or nuisance by reason only of the flight of aircraft at a reasonable
height above the ground, provided that the statutory requirements have been
complied with.[1]

The law relating to the use of the air has developed rapidly.[2] It is almost entirely
statutory, and depends on international conventions which leave very little room
for the common law. On occasion, however, ordinary principles of reparation
have been resorted to.[3] In theory, an air carrier might in some circumstances be
held to be a common carrier, but the possibility seems remote from reality.[4] This
chapter outlines some of the more important rules specifically relating to carriage
by air.

The aircraft and the outsider—The concession already noted as having been **23.02**
made by s.76(1) of the Civil Aviation Act 1982 is in respect of the bare fact of
flight over another's property and that only at a reasonable height. But where
material loss or damage is caused to any person or property on land or water by an
aircraft,[5] the owner is liable without proof of fault except in the case of contributory negligence.[6] In certain circumstances the owner may have a right to be
indemnified by a third party against a claim for loss or damage.[7] Where the aircraft
has been bona fide let or hired out for a period exceeding 14 days, and no pilot,
commander or other operative is employed by the owner, the hirer is liable.[8]
Dangerous flying is discouraged by heavy penalties.[9] A helicopter flight over a

---

[1] Civil Aviation Act 1982 (the "1982 Act") s.76(1). For current statutory requirements see Air
Navigation Order 2009 (SI 2009/3015) and any regulations made under it. See *Cubitt v Gower* (1933)
47 Ll. L. Rep. 65; *Lord Bernstein v Skyviews & General* [1978] Q.B. 479; *Steel-Maitland v British
Airways Board*, 1981 S.L.T. 110.

[2] *Shawcross and Beaumont: Air Law*, 4th edn (Butterworths), provides a useful noter-up.

[3] See, e.g. *Fosbroke-Hobbes v Airwork* [1937] 1 All E.R. 108, where the doctrine of res ipsa
loquitur was applied to the negligent handling of an aeroplane; *Shawcross and Beaumont: Air Law*,
Vol.1 Pt VII, Ch.22, paras 1–79; especially para.37 (negligence) and para.50 (res ipsa loquitur).

[4] *Aslan v Imperial Airways* (1933) 49 T.L.R. 415; *Shawcross and Beaumont:Air Law*, Vol.1 Pt VII,
Ch.22, paras 4 and 5 et seq.; A.D. McNair, *Law of the Air*, 3rd edn (London: Stevens and Sons, 1964),
pp.138–44.

[5] Or by a person in the aircraft, or an article, animal or person falling from the aircraft.

[6] 1982 Act s.76(2).

[7] 1982 Act s.76(3).

[8] 1982 Act s.76(4).

[9] 1982 Act s.81; the Air Navigation Order 2009 (SI 2009/3015) as amended (see particularly Pt 19
and Pt 31).

congested city area without written permission from the Civil Aviation Authority has been held to constitute an offence.[10] The potential of injury to others posed by aircraft is obviously great and the legislature has made provisions for lessening it. Thus, for example, an aircraft is bound to be registered, to bear the proper marks, to hold a certificate of "airworthiness", to have a certified and licensed crew, and to carry certain papers.[11] Similarly, an air transport licence is required where an aircraft is used for the carriage for reward of passengers or cargo.[12] Air carriers and aircraft operators are under statutory obligation to take out insurance meeting minimum levels of cover in respect of liability for passengers, baggage, cargo and third parties.[13] Noise, vibration, and other pollution from aircraft is regulated by statute.[14]

The analogy of the law of sea-transport has been and will probably continue to be influential in the development of the law of the air. Examples are the law relating to wreck, the saving of life or salvage of property, and in particular allowing to the owner of aircraft a reasonable reward for salvage services.[15] The common law rule allowing arrestment of a ship does not, however, extend to aircraft.[16]

The 1982 Act gives power to make regulations for the prevention of collisions at sea involving seaplanes on the surface of the water.[17] The general regulations applying to lights, signals and the rules of the air are found in Sch.1 to the Rules of the Air Regulations 2007.[18]

23.03 Aircraft as carrier—The common law in regard to the liability of carriers by air has been superseded[19] in both international and non-international carriage by the

---

[10] *Cameron v Smith*, 1982 S.L.T. 398.

[11] Air Navigation Order 2009 (SI 2009/3015) as amended and Air Navigation (General) Regulations 2006 (SI 2006/601) for nationally regulated aircraft; see EC Regulations 216/2008 (on common rules in the field of civil aviation and establishing a European Aviation Safety Agency), 1702/2003 (laying down implementing rules for the airworthiness and environmental certification of aircraft and related products, parts and appliances, as well as for the certification of design and production organizations) and 2042/2003 (on the continuing airworthiness of aircraft and aeronautical products, parts and appliances, and on the approval of organisations and personnel involved in these tasks) for EASA (European Aviation Safety Agency) regulated aircraft; see also fn.75 to para.23.06, below. On State recognition in the context of aviation permits see *R. (on the application of Kibris Turk Hava Yollari) v Secretary of State for Transport* [2010] EWCA Civ 1093; [2011] 1 Lloyd's Rep. 274.

[12] Civil Aviation Act 1982 s.64 et seq. See too Civil Aviation Authority Regulations 1991 (SI 1991/1672) as amended and EC Regulation 1008/2008 on common rules for the operation of air services in the Community (Recast) on licencing of Community Air Carriers together with the Operation of Air Services in the Community Regulations 2009 (SI 2009/41) providing the national framework; *Corner v Clayton* [1976] 1 W.L.R. 800; *Air Ecosse v Civil Aviation Authority*, 1987 S.L.T. 751.

[13] EC Regulation 785/2004 on insurance requirements for air carriers and aircraft operators (as amended by EC Regulation 1137/2008 and EU Regulation 285/2010), together with the Civil Aviation (Insurance) Regulations 2005 (SI 2005/1089) providing the national framework.

[14] See, e.g. the Civil Aviation Act 1982 ss.5, 6, 78, 81 and 82.

[15] Civil Aviation Act 1982 s.87.

[16] *Emerald Airways Ltd v Nordic Oil Services Ltd*, 1996 S.L.T. 403.

[17] Civil Aviation Act 1982 s.97.

[18] Rules of the Air Regulations 2007 (SI 2007/734), as amended; cf. *Dickson v Miln*, 1969 J.C. 75, although the latter has been decided under the then Rules of the Air and Air Traffic Control Regulations 1966 (SI 1966/1257).

[19] In matters covered by the Convention, there can be no resort to the provisions of domestic law: *Abnett v British Airways Plc*, 1997 S.C. (HL) 26 (limitation period under the Warsaw-Hague Convention). See also *Hook v British Airways Plc* [2011] EWHC 379; [2011] 1 All E.R. (Comm) 1128 (Montreal Convention via EC Regulation 2027/2002, no damages for hurt feelings for not meeting seating needs of disabled person) and *Cowden v British Airways Plc* [2009] 2 Lloyd's Rep 653 (Montreal Convention, no damages for distress for delay of baggage), both citing *Abnett v British Airways Plc*.

provisions of the amended Warsaw[20] and Montreal Conventions[21] (as applied by the Carriage by Air Act 1961),[22] the Carriage by Air (Supplementary Provisions) Act 1962,[23] the Carriage by Air Acts (Application of Provisions) Order 2004,[24] and the Civil Aviation Act 1982.[25]

The above Acts and Statutory Instruments incorporate the following air convention regimes into the law of the United Kingdom: (1) the Carriage by Air Act 1961 implements the Warsaw-Hague (Sch.1), Warsaw-Hague-MP4 (Sch.1A) and Montreal Conventions (Sch.1B) and works together with (2) the Carriage by Air (Supplementary Provisions) Act 1962, implementing the Guadalajara Convention. The latter is necessary under the Warsaw Conventions to extend the protective provisions in favour of the contractual carrier also to the actual carrier. (3) The Carriage by Air Acts (Application of Provisions) Order 2004[26] incorporates the 1929 Warsaw and Warsaw-MP1 Conventions[27] together with the Guadalajara Convention and also provides for the application of a modified version of the Montreal Convention as a matter of domestic law to non convention carriage. (4) In addition, in case of carriage of passengers and their luggage by Community Air carriers, the liability regime of the Montreal Convention is always applicable by means of art.3(1) of the amended EC Regulation on air carrier liability in respect of the carriage of passengers and their baggage by air[28] with s.1(2) of the Carriage by Air Act 1961 and s.3(2) of the Carriage by Air Acts (Application of Provisions) Order 2004[29]; and there are several European Regulations regarding air passengers, concerning their rights and treatment.[30]

---

[20] The Convention for the Unification of Certain Rules Relating to International Carriage by Air signed at Warsaw in 1929, with subsequent amendments. The Warsaw Convention of 1929 was substantially amended by the Hague Protocol of 1955, in a version generally referred to as the Warsaw-Hague Convention. In 1975 the Montreal Additional Protocols Nos 1–4 (MP1–4) were introduced to allow for various amendments to the Warsaw regime. Protocol No.3 never came into force; Protocols Nos 1 and 2 brought in the concept of Special Drawing Rights to calculate the limits of liability for the Warsaw and Warsaw-Hague Conventions respectively; No.2 being mostly superseded by the subsequent coming into force of Protocol No.4 which, in addition, includes further alterations to Warsaw-Hague (the so amended regime thus being known as "Warsaw-Hague-MP4" Convention). Since the contracting States to the Warsaw Convention have not all ratified the same or all subsequent amendments, a number of convention regimes exist and must be applied depending on the common ratification denominator between the States of departure and destination (see art.1 of the various conventions on their range of application).

[21] The Convention for the Unification of Certain Rules for International Carriage by Air done at Montreal on May 28, 1999 has been given the force of law in the United Kingdom as of June 28, 2004 by the Carriage by Air Act 1961 (the "1961 Act"), as amended by the Carriage by Air Acts (Implementation of the Montreal Convention 1999) Order 2002. As per its art.55, the Montreal Convention, where applicable, prevails over all other air carriage convention regimes.

[22] As amended.

[23] As amended, implementing the Guadalajara Convention (Convention Supplementary to the Warsaw Convention for the Unification of Certain Rules relating to International Carriage by Air performed by a Person other than the Contracting Carrier, signed in Guadalajara on September 18, 1961).

[24] Carriage by Air Acts (Application of Provisions) Order 2004 (SI 2004/1899); see para.23.05, below.

[25] Air Navigation Orders regulate air navigation including air traffic control: Civil Aviation Act 1982 s.60; and see *Stair Memorial Encyclopaedia*, "Aviation", (Reissue), paras 321 et seq.

[26] The Carriage by Air Acts (Application of Provisions) Order 2004 (SI 2004/1899).

[27] Although by s.5 and Sch.2 of the Order, the United Kingdom is applying modified Warsaw–Hague provisions to the States only party to the 1929 Warsaw Convention.

[28] EC Regulation 2027/97 of October 9, 1997 on air carrier liability in respect of the carriage of passengers and their baggage by air, as amended by EC Regulation No 889/2002; see also Air Carrier Liability Regulations 2004 (SI 2004/1418), as amended, providing sanctions for breach of arts 3a and 6 of the amended EC Regulation.

[29] Carriage by Air Acts (Application of Provisions) Order 2004 (SI 2004/1899).

[30] See below, para.23.07.

Moreover, each airline has detailed conditions of contract.[31]

23.04 International carriage—The Montreal and Warsaw Conventions[32] apply only to "international carriage", which is defined as

> "any carriage in which, according to the agreement between the parties, the place of departure and the place of destination . . . are situated either within the territories of two State Parties or within the territory of a single State Party, if there is an agreed stopping place within the territory of another state,[33] even if that state is not a State Party".[34]

Carriage between two points within the territory of a single State Party without an agreed stopping place in another state is not international carriage. A hot air balloon designated for the carriage of passengers had been taken to qualify as an aircraft.[35] The carrier must hand over the appropriate document, i.e. passenger ticket, baggage check or air waybill, containing certain specified information and including notice of limitation of liability. If he fails to do so he cannot rely on the provisions which exclude or limit his liability under most Warsaw Conventions, although he is able to limit under Montreal.[36] He is liable in damages for death of

---

[31] See, e.g. the passenger ticket conditions and the air waybills conditions to be used by airlines who are members of the International Air Transport Association ("IATA"): *Shawcross and Beaumont: Air Law*, Vol.1 Pt VII, Ch.22, para.71 et seq (Contractual terms) and Ch.29, para.996 et seq (Air Waybill conditions of contract).

[32] See para.23.03, above. (Note that the text in square brackets in Sch.1 to the 1961 Act never came into force; it includes the amendments, which would have been due, had both Montreal Protocols Nos 3 and 4 come into force; however MP3 failed to take effect). The text of the amended Warsaw Conventions is given in both English (as Part I) and French (Part II) in the Schs 1 and 1A to the 1961 Act, with the French text prevailing (s.1(8)), which can give rise to difficulties: *Rothmans Ltd v Saudi Airlines* [1981] Q.B. 368 (jurisdiction).

[33] art.1 Montreal and art.1 Warsaw Conventions; *Grein v Imperial Airways Ltd* [1937] 1 K.B. 50. The Conventions as implemented by the 1961 Act do not apply where the places of departure and destination and any agreed stopping places are all within the territory of a single foreign state: *Holmes v Bangladesh Biman Corp* [1989] A.C. 1112.

[34] art.1 Montreal and art.1 Warsaw Conventions; for a list of the State Parties, see the Carriage by Air (Parties to Convention) Order 1999 (SI 1999/1313). Those who are parties to the Convention as further amended by Montreal Protocol No.4 are certified in Carriage by Air (Parties to Protocol No.4 of Montreal, 1975) Order (SI 2000/3061). An up-to-date list of Convention Parties can be found on the Treaty collection website of the International Civil Aviation Authority ("ICAO") at *http://www.icao. int/* [Accessed July 18, 2012] ("Treaty Collection" tab). ICAO is depository for several of the air Treaties and is notified of any changes by other depositories.

[35] In the context of the predecessor of the Carriage by Air Acts (Application of Provisions) Order 2004 (SI 2004/1899), applying the convention regime to domestic carriage: *Laroche v Spirit of Adventure (UK) Ltd* [2009] EWCA Civ 12; [2009] 1 Lloyd's Rep. 316.

[36] arts 3–16 Montreal and Warsaw Conventions; See *Lisi v Alitalia-Linee Aeree Italiane SpA* [1967] 1 Lloyd's Rep. 140; 370 F 2d 508 (US Court of Appeals 2nd Circ) (affirmed [1968] 1 Lloyd's Rep. 505; 390 US 455 (1968)) (Warsaw); *Corocraft v Pan American Airways* [1969] 1 Q.B. 616, CA (Warsaw); *Ludecke v Canadian Pacific Airlines* [1975] 2 Lloyd's Rep. 87; [1979] 2 Lloyd's Rep. 260, Supreme Ct Canada (Warsaw); *Canadian Pacific Airlines v Montreal Trust Co* [1977] 2 Lloyd's Rep. 80, Supreme Ct Canada (as to the requirement of "notice" on ticket; Warsaw-Hague) and see *Fujitsu Computer Products Corp v Bax Global Inc* [2005] EWHC 2289 (Comm); [2006] 1 Lloyd's Rep. 367 (Warsaw; "notice" requirement on air waybill); but see *Collins v British Airways Board* [1982] Q.B. 734, CA (Warsaw-Hague; limitation allowed despite failure to complete baggage check details). Note: arts 3(2) (passengers) and 9 (cargo) of the Warsaw and Warsaw-Hague Conventions have different wording and requirements, but both disallow limitation if their documentary requirements are not met; whereas arts 3(5) and 9 of Montreal and art.9 (cargo only) of Warsaw-Hague-MP4 clarify that documentary insufficiencies do not affect the application of the Convention including their limitation provisions.

or injury[37] to a passenger[38] by accident[39] on board or in embarking or disembarking,[40] for loss of or damage[41] to registered baggage or cargo while in his charge on board or in an airport,[42] and for any delay in the carriage of passengers, baggage or cargo.[43] Title to sue in relation to cargo need not be restricted to those named in the air waybill; it may include persons having title under domestic law, provided the Convention does not actually bar suit at their instance.[44] Under the Warsaw Conventions, in the case of passengers and baggage, and damage occasioned by delay in the carriage of cargo, however, the carrier avoids liability if he proves that he and his agents or employees have taken all "necessary measures"[45] to avoid the damage or that it was impossible for him or them to take such measures.[46] Apart from delay claims, this ground for exclusion of liability is not available under the Montreal Convention where liability is strict,[47] although both sets of Conventions contain provisions relating to contributory negligence.[48] Unless by special contract a higher sum is agreed, liability under the Warsaw Conventions as amended by the Montreal Protocols for injury to a passenger is limited to 16,600 Special Drawing Rights ("SDR"), for registered baggage and cargo to 17 SDR per kilogramme and for hand luggage to 332 Special Drawing Rights per

---

[37] The expression "bodily injury" used in the Convention and its delineation from psychiatric harm and mental illness has been authoritatively construed in: *King v Bristow Helicopters Ltd*, 2002 S.C. (HL) 59.

[38] A police officer on board an aircraft chartered for surveillance work has been held to be a passenger: *Herd v Clyde Helicopters Ltd*, 1997 S.C. (HL) 86.

[39] See *Deep Vein Thrombosis and Air Travel Group Litigation, Re* [2005] UKHL 72; [2006] 1 A.C. 495 and *Barclay v British Airways Plc* [2008] EWCA Civ 1419; [2009] 1 Lloyd's Rep. 297.

[40] art.17 Montreal and Warsaw Conventions; 1961 Act s.3; *Adatia v Air Canada* [1992] P.I.Q.R. P238, CA: for location of "accident" with reference to disembarkation see also *Macdonald v Air Canada*, 439F. 2d 1402 (US Court of Appeals 1st Circ).

[41] The notion of damages in the Montreal Convention includes material and non-material damages: all are thus subject to the convention system, including its time limitation: *Axel Walz v Clickair SA* (C-63/09) [2011] All E.R. (EC) 326 (loss of baggage).

[42] arts 17(2) & 18 Montreal Convention and art.18 Warsaw Conventions; *Fothergill v Monarch Airlines* [1981] A.C. 251.

[43] art.19 Montreal Convention and Warsaw Conventions. See, e.g. *Panalpina International Transport Ltd v Densil Underwear Ltd* [1981] 1 Lloyd's Rep. 187 (delay of cargo intended for Christmas Market); see also *O'Carroll v Ryanair*, 2009 S.C.L.R. 125 (Aberdeen Sheriff Court: damages for delay of baggage included elements of expenses as well as inconvenience and stress), but see *Cowden v British Airways Plc* [2009] 2 Lloyd's Rep. 653 (County Ct: no damages for distress due to delay of baggage).

[44] *Western Digital Corp v British Airways Plc* [2001] Q.B. 733 (CA: cargo owner; but note the requirement of giving timely notice of damage).

[45] This must mean "proper" or "reasonable". If he took all necessary measures, there would be no damage.

[46] art.20 of the Warsaw Conventions.

[47] arts 16–19 Montreal Convention; although the carrier is only liable for hand luggage if the damage was caused by his acts or that of his servants or agents, and there are exclusion provisions for inherent defect, quality or vice of checked baggage (art.17(2)) or of cargo, and equally for loss of or damage to cargo due to defective packing, acts of armed conflict or of public authorities (art.18(2)). Please note also, that in case of death or injury of passengers, in order to avail himself of the limitation of liability set out in the convention, the carrier has to prove that the damage was not due to his negligence, other wrongful act or omission or that of his servants or agents, or that the damage was solely due to the negligence of a third party, art.21 Montreal Convention.

[48] art.20 Montreal Convention and art.21 of the Warsaw Conventions.

passenger.[49] Under the Montreal Convention the amended[50] limits are 113,100 SDR in case of injury to or death of passengers and 4,694 SDR for delay in the carriage of passengers, 1,131 SDR for loss of, damage to or delay of baggage (whether checked or unchecked)[51] and 19 SDR where cargo is concerned.[52] Any condition relieving the carrier of liability or fixing a lower limit is null and void.[53] Where a machine was transported in several packages, one of which was damaged, it was held that the limits of liability were to be calculated by reference to the weight of all the packages.[54] The carrier cannot rely on provisions excluding or limiting his liability[55] if the damage is caused by his own act or omission[56] or that of his servants or agents acting within the scope of their employment, done with intent to cause damage or recklessly and with knowledge that damage would probably result.[57] However, the limitation for cargo damage cannot be broken for any such reason under the Warsaw-Hague-MP4 and the Montreal Conventions.[58] "Knowledge" means actual appreciation or awareness that the conduct concerned

---

[49] art.22 of Warsaw-MP1 and Warsaw-Hague-MP4; note the differing limits under the unamended Warsaw and Warsaw-Hague Convention, still calculated by reference to the French Gold Franc. Cases illustrating limitation of liability include *Samuel Montagu & Co v Swiss Air Transport Co* [1966] 2 Q.B. 306 (CA); *Bland v British Airways Board* [1981] 1 Lloyd's Rep. 289 (CA); and *Data Card Corp v Air Express International Corp* [1983] 2 All E.R. 639; [1984] 1 W.L.R. 198. Note that it has been held in England that the limits under art.22(4) of Warsaw-Hague are comprehensive of everything (see art.24(1)) except expenses, and may not be exceeded by an award of interest upon damages: *Swiss Bank Corp v Brink's-MAT Ltd* [1986] Q.B. 853 (contrast with the Scottish decision in carriage by sea under a rather different framework: *The Devotion II*, 1979 S.C. 80); but note that Montreal, art.22(6), now specifically provides for interest, as litigation expenses.

[50] See the escalator clause in art.24(1) Montreal Convention, permitting review at five-year intervals. Changes to the initial Montreal limits were effective as of December 30, 2009 based on the first review of limits of liability conducted by the International Civil Aviation Organisation ICAO, as data suggested a 13.1% increase of inflation during the five-year period. These changes are added to the depository information available at the Treaty Collection of ICAO and are implemented into UK law by the Carriage by Air (Revision of Limits of Liability under the Montreal Convention) Order 2009 (SI 2009/3018).

[51] See art.17(4) Montreal Convention.

[52] arts 21 and 22 Montreal Convention; the former Montreal limits between June 28, 2004 and December 29, 2009 were at 100,000 SDR (passenger injury), 4,150 SDR (passenger delay), 1,000 SDR (baggage) and 17 SDR (cargo).

[53] art.26 Montreal Convention and art.23 Warsaw Conventions; see also art.25 Montreal Convention clarifying that parties can agree on higher limits or no limits, and art.27 Montreal Convention that the carrier's defences can be waived and conditions of carriage agreed, insofar as this is not in conflict with the Convention's provisions.

[54] Applied *Implants Technology Ltd v Lufthansa Cargo A.G.* [2000] 2 Lloyd's Rep. 46, applying the "affected value" provision of art.22(2)(b) of Warsaw-Hague; a principle also enshrined in art.22(4) Montreal Convention; however the position is different under the unamended 1929 Warsaw Convention where only the "damaged value" may be taken into account: *Data Card Corp v Air Express International Corp* [1983] 2 Lloyd's Rep. 81.

[55] A special declaration of interest under art.22 is such a provision limiting liability: *Antwerp United Diamond BVBA v Air Europe* [1996] Q.B. 317 (CA: where the declared value was only a fraction of the true value).

[56] Replacing the phrase "wilful misconduct" contained in art.25 of the 1929 Warsaw Convention. Insofar see *Rustenburg Platinum Mines v Pan American World Airways* [1979] 1 Lloyd's Rep. 19 (CA: wilful misconduct of airline's loaders while acting within the scope of their employment, art.25 Warsaw Convention) and, although a rail carriage case, *Bastable v North British Railway Co*, 1912 S.C. 555 (wilful misconduct due to overloaded wagons).

[57] arts 22(5) and 30(3) Montreal and arts 25 and 25A(3) Warsaw-Hague Conventions; see also the different wording in the unamended Warsaw Convention art.25; *Goldman v Thai Airways International Ltd* [1983] 1 W.L.R. 1186 (CA); *SS Pharmaceutical Co Ltd v Qantas Airways Ltd* [1989] 1 Lloyd's Rep. 319 (SC NSW); *Rolls Royce Plc v Heavylift-Volga DNEPR Ltd* [2000] 1 All E.R. (Comm) 796.

[58] See arts 22(5) and 30(3) Montreal Convention and arts 25 and 25A(3) Warsaw-Hague-MP4.

would probably result in the type of damage caused.[59] The Unfair Contract Terms Act 1977, while applying to contracts of carriage by air,[60] does not affect exclusion or limitation clauses authorised by an enactment such as the Carriage by Air Act 1961.[61] Complaint of damage to baggage must be made within seven days of delivery, of damage to cargo within 14 days and of delay within 21 days of receipt by the carrier.[62] Such complaint must be made by "the person entitled to delivery", who cannot be the carrier, actual or contracting.[63] Any right to damages is lost if the action is not brought within two years.[64] Where carriage is performed by various successive carriers, each is subject to the Convention.[65] Where a carrier delegates performance of a contract to another[66] both are subject to the Convention, the former for the whole of the carriage contemplated in the agreement, the latter solely for the carriage which he performs.[67] The delegating carrier is vicariously liable for the acts and omissions of the actual carrier and of his servants and agents acting within the scope of their employment.[68]

Non-international carriage—The Warsaw and Montreal Conventions do not **23.05** extend to carriage by air not falling within the definition of "international carriage".[69] However, the Montreal Convention has been applied with modifications[70] to "non-international" carriage, by the Carriage by Air Acts (Application of Provisions) Order 2004.[71] Thus the two-year time-bar applies.[72]

Safety of aircraft—Air Navigation Orders regulate the carriage of dangerous **23.06** goods[73] and prohibit reckless or negligent behaviour likely to endanger aircraft, person or property.[74] Several European Regulations are founded on the aim of

---

[59] *Nugent v Michael Goss Aviation Ltd* [2000] 2 Lloyd's Rep. 222 (CA).

[60] Unfair Contract Terms Act 1977 s.15(2)(c).

[61] Unfair Contract Terms Act 1977 s.29.

[62] art.31(2) Montreal Convention and art.26 of the Warsaw-Hague Conventions; however note that Warsaw and Warsaw-MP1 Convention time limits differ at 3 days (luggage), 7 days (cargo) and 14 days (delay). See also *Fothergill v Monarch Airlines* [1981] A.C. 251; *Western Digital Corp v British Airways Plc* [2001] Q.B. 733 (CA).

[63] *Compaq Computer Manufacturing Ltd v Circle International Ltd*, 2001 S.L.T. 368.

[64] art.35 Montreal Convention and art.29 Warsaw Conventions.

[65] art.36 Montreal Convention and art.30 Warsaw Conventions.

[66] The "actual carrier".

[67] art.1(4) and art.40 Montreal Convention; as well as Carriage by Air (Supplementary Provisions) Act 1962 Sch., the latter implementing the 1961 Guadalajara Convention, in relation to carriage under the several Warsaw Conventions.

[68] art.41 Montreal Convention; as well as Carriage by Air (Supplementary Provisions) Act 1962 Sch., (Guadalajara Convention) in relation to carriage under the Warsaw Conventions.

[69] See para.23.04, above.

[70] e.g. arts 3–16 (Ch.II) of the Convention, safe for art.3(3) and (5), do not apply to non-international carriage. Also liability for injury to a passenger is limited to 100,000 special drawing rights ("SDR"): art.21, and for cargo to 17 SDR: art.22(3) as in the original version of the Montreal Convention; the escalator clause of art.24 does not apply.

[71] Carriage by Air Acts (Application of Provisions) Order 2004 (SI 2004/1899) art.4 with Sch.1; note that the 2004 Order also incorporates the Warsaw and Warsaw-MP1 Conventions together with Guadalajara for the relevant international carriage which does not already fall within the Montreal, Warsaw-Hague and Warsaw-Hague-MP4 regimes (as implemented by the 1961 Act).

[72] art.35 of Sch.1 to the 2004 Order. See also, e.g. *Hardy v British Airways Board*, 1983 S.L.T. 45, a case at a time where the modified Warsaw Convention applied for domestic carriage, by virtue of, the then in force, Carriage by Air Acts (Application of Provisions) Order 1967.

[73] The Air Navigation (Dangerous Goods) Regulations 2002 (SI 2002/2786) and the Air Navigation Order 2009 (SI 2009/3015) art.132.

[74] Air Navigation Order 2009 (SI 2009/3015) Pt 19 "Prohibited Behaviour".

establishing and maintaining high uniform levels of civil aviation safety in Europe and environmental compatibility.[75]

23.07 **Protection for air passengers**—Air travel organisers (i.e. persons who make available or who hold themselves out as persons who may make available accommodation for the carriage of persons on aircraft) must be licensed[76] and must contribute to an Air Travel Trust.[77] The Air Travel Trust was established to meet customers' losses when air travel organisers could not meet their financial commitments.

Irrespective of the applicable convention regime,[78] in case of the carriage of passengers and their luggage, by EC Regulation,[79] Community Air Carriers are always subjected to the liability provisions of the Montreal Convention,[80] and are required to set out liability notices for passengers,[81] to make advance payments of compensation in order to meet immediate economic needs,[82] and to apply a tariff for extra charges on the occasion of a declared special value of a passenger's luggage.[83]

In addition, EC Regulations require air carriers who fly from an airport located in the territory of an EU Member State to compensate and assist passengers in case of denied boarding, cancellation or long delay of their flight[84] and those

---

[75] See, e.g. EC Regulation 216/2008 regulating inter alia airworthiness, essential requirements for environmental protection, on pilot licensing and on air operations and establishes a European Aviation Safety Agency, charged inter alia with issuing certificates, conducting inspections and investigations, with issuing opinions and assisting the Commission in certain tasks; EC Regulation 2042/2003, as amended, on the continuing airworthiness of aircraft and aeronautical products, parts and appliances, and on the approval of organisations and personnel involved in these tasks; EC Regulation 1702/2003 laying down implementing rules for the airworthiness and environmental certification of aircraft and related products, parts and appliances, as well as for the certification of design and production organisations; EEC Regulation 3922/91, as amended, on the harmonization of technical requirements and administrative procedures in the field of civil aviation; and EU Regulation 805/2011 laying down detailed rules for air traffic controllers' licences and certain certificates pursuant to EC Regulation 216/2008.

[76] 1982 Act s.71; Civil Aviation (Air Travel Organisers' Licensing) Regulations 2012 (SI 2012/1017), in force as of April 30, 2012 and, as of this date, revoking and replacing the 1995 Regulations; *Jet Travel v Slade Travel Agency* [1983] C.L.Y. 179; [1983] Com. L.R. 244; *Stair Memorial Encyclopaedia*, "Aviation", (Reissue), para.112.

[77] 1982 Act s.71A; Civil Aviation (Contributions to the Air Travel Trust) Regulations 2007 (SI 2007/2999), as amended.

[78] As set out above at para.23.04.

[79] EC Regulation 2027/97 on air carrier liability in respect of the carriage of passengers and their baggage by air (as amended by EC Regulation No 889/2002) with s.1(2) of the Carriage by Air Act 1961 and s.3(2) of the Carriage by Air Acts (Application of Provisions) Order 2004 (SI 2004/1899); see also Air Carrier Liability Regulations 2004 (SI 2004/1418), as amended, providing sanctions for breach of arts 3a and 6 of the amended EC Regulation).

[80] art.3 EC Regulation 2027/97.

[81] art.6 EC Regulation 2027/97.

[82] art.5 EC Regulation 2027/97.

[83] art.3a EC Regulation 2027/97.

[84] EC Regulation 261/2004 establishing common rules on compensation and assistance to passengers in the event of denied boarding and of cancellation or long delay of flights and Civil Aviation (Denied Boarding, Compensation and Assistance) Regulations 2005 (SI 2005/975), designating the Civil Aviation Authority as enforcement body. On delay claims under the EC Regulation see *Sturgeon v Condor Flugdienst GmbH* (C-402/07) [2009] E.C.R. I-10923; [2010] 1 Lloyd's Rep. 522 and for interpretation of "extraordinary circumstances" in case of cancellation (art.5(3) of the EC Regulation) see *Wallentin-Hermann v Allitalia-Linee Aeree Italienne SpA* (C-549/07) [2008] E.C.R. I-11061; [2009] 1 Lloyd's Rep. 406 and *Eglitis v Latvijas Republikas Ekonomikas Ministrija* (C-294/10) [2011] 2 Lloyd's Rep. 123 and on the interpretation of "cancellation", where a flight had to return after take-off, and "further compensation" under art.12 of the EC Regulation see *Sousa Rodríguez et al v Air*

flying from or to or transiting through an airport in the territory of an EU Member State to give assistance to disabled persons and to compensate for loss of or damage to wheelchairs or other mobility equipment.[85]

This additional layer of European Regulations on top of the Convention regimes creates problems of delineation between the systems. Where the Montreal Convention applies per se, it prevails over EC Regulations, as the European Union is a high contracting party to the Montreal Convention and as such bound to comply with its provisions.[86] However, where there is conflict with other Conventions ratified only by the Member States the situation is not as clear cut.[87]

The Civil Aviation Authority—The Civil Aviation Authority[88] is responsible **23.08** for the licensing of air transport.[89] It has other important functions, including the registration of aircraft, air safety, the control of air traffic[90] the certification of aircraft operators and the licensing of air crews and aerodromes.[91] The Authority's objectives are to provide a safe but economic air transport service, to promote the UK air industry, and to further the reasonable interests of users of air transport services.[92] The Secretary of State may in certain circumstances give the Authority directions[93] although the Authority is neither a servant nor agent of

---

France (C-83/10) [2012] 1 C.M.L.R. 40. See also *Rehder v Air Baltic Corp* (C-204/08) [2009] E.C.R. I-6073; [2010] Bus. L.R. 549 (jurisdiction for a compensation claim due to cancellation of a flight arising out of the EC Regulation 261/2004 and the respective meaning of place of performance of the obligation under art.5(1)(b) EC Regulation 44/2001) and *Niven v Ryanair Ltd*, 2008 G.W.D. 13–232 (Aberdeen Sheriff Court: art.33(1) Montreal Convention not applicable when determining jurisdiction for a compensation claim for cancellation under EC Regulation 261/2004).

[85] EC Regulation 1107/2006 concerning rights of disabled persons and persons with reduced mobility when travelling by air, together with the Civil Aviation (Access to Air Travel for Disabled Persons and Persons of Reduced Mobility) Regulations 2007 (SI 2007/1895), providing offences and fines for failure to comply with the EC Regulations and designating the Civil Aviation authority as enforcement body. However, these Regulations do not establish rights under the Regulation for individuals to claim for damages against air carriers outside the convention regimes: *Hook v British Airways Plc* [2011] EWHC 379; [2011] 1 All E.R. (Comm) 1128.

[86] See *Wallentin-Hermann v Allitalia–Linee Aeree Italiane SpA* (C-549/07) [2008] E.C.R. I-11061; [2009] 1 Lloyd's Rep. 406 at [28] (art.5(3) of Regulation 261/2004 must be interpreted in the light of and in compliance with the Montreal Convention provisions) and *Emirates Airlines Direktion für Deutschland v Schenkel* (C-173/07) [2008] E.C.R. I-5237; [2009] 1 Lloyd's Rep. 1 at [43] (primacy of the Montreal Convention before Secondary Community legislation).

[87] Whilst European Union law has supremacy over national laws, there is also an obligation under international law on States contracting in to international Treaties to comply with the Treaty obligations (see art.26 and 27 Vienna Convention on the Law of Treaties, 1969). See also *Bogiatzi (or Ventouras) v Deutscher Luftpool* (C-301/08) [2009] E.C.R. I-10185; [2010] 1 All E.R. (Comm) 555 on limitation period of the Warsaw Convention being applicable and not precluded by EC Regulation 2027/97; and *R. (on the application of International Air Transport Association (IATA)) v Department of Transport* (C-344/04) [2006] E.C.R. I-403; [2006] 2 C.M.L.R. 20 on questions of validity of EC Regulation 261/2004 and its consistency with the Montreal Convention.

[88] The Authority consists of 6–16 persons appointed by the Secretary of State for Transport: 1982 Act s.2 as amended by the Airports Act 1986 s.72; and the Transfer of Functions (Trade and Industry) Order 1983 (SI 1983/1127).

[89] 1982 Act s.3; *R. v Secretary of State for Transport, Ex p. Pegasus Holdings (London) Ltd* [1988] 1 W.L.R. 990 (Romanian-licensed pilots failing British CAA examinations).

[90] Extensive reform of air traffic control is contained in the Transport Act 2000.

[91] 1982 Act s.3.

[92] 1982 Act s.4; *Laker Airways v Department of Trade* [1977] Q.B. 643.

[93] 1982 Act s.6 (as amended by Sch.8 para.17 to the Transport Act 2000). See *Laker Airways* [1977] Q.B. 643.

the Crown.[94] The Secretary of State is required in certain circumstances to consult the Authority.[95]

23.09 Contract conditions—As international carriage is regulated by the Warsaw and Montreal Conventions, as well as European passenger carriage by European Passenger Regulations, little freedom of contract is conferred upon the airlines. Only when the statutory provisions are silent does the question of individual conditions arise, and even then the conditions may have been drafted to comply with standards, recommended practices, or standard conditions laid down by the International Civil Aviation Organisation ("ICAO")[96] or the International Air Transport Association ("IATA")[97].[98]

23.10 Prevention of crime and terrorism—Legislation has been passed to combat crime and terrorism relating to aircraft.[99]

23.11 Air accidents—An accident involving aircraft may be the subject of an inspector's investigation[100] or a fatal accident inquiry.[101]

23.12 Hovercraft—A hovercraft is part aircraft, part ship.[102] Its hybrid nature is reflected in the relevant subordinate legislation.[103] The Unfair Contract Terms Act 1977 applies to hovercraft, to a limited extent.[104]

---

[94] 1982 Act s.2(4).

[95] e.g. before giving the CCA directions in the national interest: 1982 Act s.6; before issuing regulations relating to air traffic distribution: s.31(4) of the Airports Act 1986: *Air 2000 Ltd v Secretary of State for Transport (No.2)*, 1990 S.L.T. 335; see too *Air 2000 Ltd v Secretary of State for Transport (No.1)*, 1989 S.L.T. 698 (title and interest to sue); *Stair Memorial Encyclopaedia*, "Aviation", (Reissue), para.46 and following.

[96] Further information on ICAO its work can be found on its website at *http://www.icao.int/* [Accessed July 18, 2012]. ICAO maintains a Treaty collection, available via its website, giving status information, including the state parties to the many air treaties.

[97] See *http://www.iata.org/* [Accessed July 18, 2012] for further information on IATA and its work; see, e.g. IATA Resolution 600b: air waybill—conditions of contract, incorporating the increased Montreal limits to all international carriage, irrespective of the prevailing convention.

[98] See *Shawcross and Beaumont: Air Law*, Vol.1, Pt VII, Ch.29, para.996 et seq (Air Waybill conditions of contract) and Vol.2, App. E, Ch.3 (IATA Recommended Conditions).

[99] 1982 Act and Aviation Security Act 1982, both as amended by the Anti-terrorism, Crime and Security Act 2001 Pt 9; Aviation Security Regulations 2010 (SI 2010/902) giving effect to EC Regulation 300/2008 on common rules in the field of civil aviation security (the Framework Regulation), together with the supplementing EC Regulation 272/2009, as amended, and EU Regulations 1254/2009 & 18/2010 as well as the implementing EU Regulations 72/2010 & 185/2010, as amended; Aviation and Maritime Security Act 1990 and Merchant Shipping and Maritime Security Act 1997 s.26 and Sch.5 (on piracy).

[100] The Civil Aviation (Investigation of Air Accidents and Incidents) Regulations 1996 (SI 1996/2798); *Stair Memorial Encyclopaedia*, "Aviation", (Reissue), paras 572–588. EC Regulation 996/2010 on the investigation and prevention of accidents and incidents in civil aviation. The EC Regulation takes into account the Convention on International Civil Aviation signed in Chicago on December 7, 1944 and implements the latest provisions set in ICAO Annex 13 laying down international standards and recommended practices for aircraft accident and incident investigation.

[101] Fatal Accidents and Sudden Deaths Inquiry (Scotland) Act 1976 s.1; "FAIs—after Lockerbie", 1991 S.L.T. (News) 225.

[102] Hovercraft Act 1968 as amended; and see the 1982 Act s.100.

[103] Hovercraft (Civil Liability) Order 1986 (SI 1986/1305); Hovercraft (General) Order 1972 (SI 1972/674) as amended; Hovercraft (Application of Enactments) Order 1972 (SI 1972/971) as amended, the latest amendment being SI 1998/1256, and Hovercraft (Application of Enactments) Order 1989 (SI 1989/1350), as amended.

[104] Unfair Contract Terms Act 1977 s.15(3), (4).

FURTHER READING

Blackshaw, C., *Aviation Law and Regulation* (Financial Times Prentice Hall, 1992).

Clarke, M.A. and Yates, D., *Contracts of Carriage by Land and Air*, 2nd edn (London: LLP Professional Publishing, 2008).

Harris, B., *Ridley's Law of the Carriage of Goods by Land, Sea and Air*, 8th edn (London: Sweet and Maxwell, 2010).

McNair, A.D., *Law of the Air*, 3rd edn (London: Stevens and Sons, 1964).

McClean, J.D., *Shawcross and Beaumont: Air Law*, 4th edn (Butterworths: looseleaf with updates).

Stair Memorial Encyclopaedia, (Reissue), "Aviation" and "Carriage".

SECTION C:
UNJUSTIFIED ENRICHMENT AND
NEGOTORIUM GESTIO

CHAPTER 24

UNJUSTIFIED ENRICHMENT AND NEGOTIORUM GESTIO

UNJUSTIFIED ENRICHMENT

The concept of unjustified enrichment—A person may be said to be unjustifi- **24.01**
ably enriched at another's expense when he has become owner of the other's
money or property or has used that property or otherwise benefited from his
actings or expenditure in circumstances which the law regards as actionably
unjust, and so as requiring the enrichment to be reversed.[1] The obligation does not
depend on agreement but is obediential, arising by operation of law.[2] Formerly, as
a general rule Scots law treated cases involving recovery of money under the
heading of repetition, and those involving recovery of moveable property under
the heading of restitution, while cases in which the defender benefited unjustifiably from expenditure or actings of the pursuer or from the use of his property,
were dealt with under the heading of recompense.[3] This structure was followed in
previous editions of this book. Now, thanks to decisions of the First Division of
the Court of Session and of the House of Lords between 1995 and 1998, Scots law
has moved to a position where, in principle, an enrichment at another's expense is
unjustified and should be reversed if its retention is supported by no legal ground.[4]
The underlying principles are the same in the various spheres,[5] with repetition,

---

[1] See R. Evans-Jones, *Unjustified Enrichment* (Edinburgh: W. Green, 2003), Vol.1, pp.1 et seq. For
negotiorum gestio see paras 24.24 et seq., below.

[2] Stair, I, 7, 1; Erskine, III, 1, 9 and 10.

[3] cf. *Morgan Guaranty Trust Co of New York v Lothian RC*, 1995 S.C. 151 at 155, per Lord
President Hope. For a historical analysis, see H.L. MacQueen and W.D.H. Sellar, "Unjust Enrichment
in Scots Law", in E.J.H. Schrage (ed.), *Unjust Enrichment* (Berlin: Duncker and Humblot, 1995),
p.289.

[4] See *Morgan Guaranty Trust Co of New York v Lothian RC*, 1995 S.C. 151; *Shilliday v Smith*, 1998
S.C. 725; and *Dollar Land (Cumbernauld) Ltd v C.I.N. Properties Ltd*, 1998 S.C. (HL) 90.

[5] In *Royal Bank of Scotland v Watt*, 1991 S.C. 48, there are remarks which suggest that enrichment
or benefit to the defender may not be necessary in an action of repetition of money. But, as the judges
recognised, a defender who becomes the creditor or owner of a sum of money, for however short a
period, is thereby prima facie enriched. The question then is whether in the circumstances of the case
it would be equitable to make him repay the money. See, however, para.24.21 below. "The fact of the
payment of money is itself prima facie proof of enrichment, but not conclusive proof. In assessing
whether defendant has been enriched by the payment, account must be taken of any performance
rendered by defendant which was juridically connected with his receipt of the money": *Govender v
Standard Bank of South Africa Ltd*, 1984 (4) S.A. 392(C) at 404, per Rose-Innes J. On that decision
see *First National Bank of Southern Africa Ltd v B. & H. Engineering*, 1995 (2) S.A. 279 (A). See
further Scottish Law Commission, *Recovery of Benefits Conferred under Error of Law* (HMSO,
1993), Scot. Law Com. Discussion Paper No.95, Vol.2, pp.96 et seq.

restitution and recompense being only the remedies with which an enrichment, once found to be unjustified, may be reversed. The remedies may be combined to achieve this end.[6] In *Dollar Land (Cumbernauld) Ltd v CIN Properties Ltd*[7] Lord Hope observed

> "that the pursuers must show that the defenders have been enriched at their expense, that there is no legal justification for the enrichment and that it would be equitable to compel the defenders to redress the enrichment".

This authoritative formulation identifies three elements in the cause of action in unjustified enrichment, namely: (1) the enrichment of the defender; (2) at the pursuer's expense; and (3) no legal justification for the enrichment. (4) The fourth matter mentioned (the equity of the court compelling redress) is not an element in the cause of action (that is, a requirement which has to be proved affirmatively by the pursuer); rather demonstration of inequity is a defence.[8] Recent judicial dicta which (following earlier authority[9]) continue to found on recompense as if it were still a cause of action with distinct requirements of liability[10] are inconsistent with this new approach and must to that extent be treated as per incuriam.

24.02 **Enrichment**[11]—Enrichment is the receipt or acquisition of a benefit of economic worth, leading either to an increase in the person's wealth or to the avoidance of loss of wealth. This can arise from: (1) addition of a new asset to a person's wealth; (2) adding value to a person's already existing asset; (3) preserving another's asset which would otherwise have been lost or reduced in value, saving that other the expense involved; or (4) performing an obligation lying upon another, saving that other the expense of performance. Enrichment may arise through its receipt from another person (the impoverished) or through the act of the person enriched or of a third party.[12] In cases of enrichment through the act of the impoverished, two situations fall to be distinguished: (a) the enrichment is brought about by a transfer or conferral of the benefit to the enriched with the recipient's consent, as for example in the case of the mistaken payment[13]; (b) the enrichment is imposed upon the enriched without that person's consent or authority, albeit that the latter thereafter seeks to retain the benefit thus received; an example is improvement of another's property.[14] Enrichment through the act of the person enriched occurs when that person acquires the benefit by interference with the impoverished person's rights, as for example by unauthorised use of another's

---

[6] See opinion of Lord President Rodger in *Shilliday v Smith*, 1998 S.C. 725.

[7] *Dollar Land (Cumbernauld) Ltd v CIN Properties Ltd*, 1999 S.C. (HL) 90 at 98H–I.

[8] *Compagnie Commerciale Andre SA v Artibell Shipping Co Ltd (No.2)*, 2001 S.C. 653 (OH) at 668I–669A citing *Morgan Guaranty Trust Co of New York v Lothian RC*, 1995 S.C. 151.

[9] *Varney (Scotland) Ltd v Lanark Burgh Council*, 1974 S.C. 245.

[10] *Property Selection & Investment Trust Ltd v United Friendly Insurance Plc*, 1999 S.L.T. 975 at 978, 981 and 985; *Transco Plc v Glasgow City Council*, 2005 S.L.T. 958 at [13]; *Satchwell v McIntosh*, 2006 S.L.T. (Sh. Ct) 117. Cf. *Mactaggart & Mickel Homes Ltd v Hunters* [2010] CSOH 130 at [97]–[99].

[11] See generally Evans-Jones, *Unjustified Enrichment* (2003), pp.1–5 and Ch.7.

[12] See N.R. Whitty and D. Visser, "Unjustified Enrichment"; also J. Blackie and I. Farlam, "Enrichment by Act of the Party Enriched", both in R. Zimmermann, D. Visser and K. Reid (eds), *Mixed Legal Systems in Comparative Perspective: Property and Obligations in Scotland and South Africa* (Oxford: Oxford University Press, 2004).

[13] See, e.g. *Morgan Guaranty Trust Co of New York v Lothian RC*, 1995 S.C. 151.

[14] See, e.g. *Newton v Newton*, 1925 S.C. 715.

property or funds.[15] Such cases also typify enrichment by way of avoidance of loss, or a saving, inasmuch as the enriched did not initially have to pay for the use made of the impoverished person's asset. The descriptions just given of the ways in which enrichment may come about are important because the reasons for regarding the enrichment as unjustified differ according to the category in which cases fall, as do the rules for determining at whose expense the enriched person retains the enrichment.[16] But the significance of the general principle against unjustified enrichment is that claims are not necessarily confined to the established categories, and there are cases where the courts have allowed recovery although neither transfer, imposition, nor interference could be readily identified on the facts.[17]

Enrichment at another's expense (causation)—The pursuer making an **24.03** enrichment claim must generally have suffered loss.[18] The role of the loss is primarily to help in identifying those cases where there is a right to recover at all, and who has that right. Thereafter the focus is on the enrichment: the law is concerned to reverse enrichments rather than to compensate for loss, and it is strictly irrelevant if for other reasons the loss no longer exists at the time the claim is made.[19] In transfer cases, this is usually a relatively straightforward matter, because the transferee's gain has a mirror image in the transferor's loss of the amount transferred. In cases of imposition such as improvements to another's property or payment of another's debt, loss can be readily identified in the cost of carrying out the improvements or making the payment.[20] Where enrichment arises from interference, the loss can usually be seen as the inability of the impoverished person to make, or bargain for the, use of its own property or rights, or the diminution in value of the property following its unauthorised use. The position where the interference enhances the value of property which would otherwise have deteriorated as a result of the owner's neglect is undecided in Scots law.[21]

Expenditure leading incidentally to another's enrichment—A person who has **24.04** expended money for a particular purpose which has been attained cannot appeal to the enrichment principle in support of a claim for payment from a party who has incidentally gained by the expenditure in question. If somebody does something for his own benefit which also incidentally confers a benefit on another, the former probably suffers no relevant loss; the latter's benefit did not cause him any extra expenditure.[22] In the leading case, the defender had leased advertising rights

---

[15] See, e.g. *Bennett v Carse*, 1990 S.L.T. 454.

[16] See below, paras 24.03, 24.07–24.20.

[17] See, e.g. *M. & I. Instrument Engineers Ltd v Varsada*, 1991 S.L.T. 106; *Mercedes-Benz Finance Ltd v Clydesdale Bank Plc*, 1997 S.L.T. 905, discussed further below, para.24.06.

[18] *Buchanan v Stewart* (1874) 2 R. 78 at 87, per Lord Neaves; *Exchange Telegraph Co v Giulianotti*, 1959 S.C. 19. See further Evans-Jones, *Unjustified Enrichment* (2003), Vol.1, Ch.8.

[19] It is suggested that *Smiths Gore v Reilly*, 2003 S.L.T. (Sh. Ct) 15 is wrongly decided on this point.

[20] See, e.g. *Garriock v Walker* (1873) 1 R. 100; *North British Railway Co Ltd v Tod* (1893) 9 Sh. Ct Rep. 326; *Brown v Meek's Trs* (1896) 4 S.L.T. 46; *Edinburgh Life Assurance v Balderston* (1909) 2 S.L.T. 323. See also *Wylie's Exx v McJannet* (1901) 4 F. 195 (solicitor pays from own funds premiums of client's insurance policy). Note *Graham's Exrs v Fletcher's Exrs* (1870) 9 M. 298.

[21] Note the example given in *Watson, Laidlaw & Co Ltd v Pott, Cassels and Williamson*, 1914 S.C. (HL) 18 at 31, per Lord Shaw of Dunfermline. There may be a claim for the intervener in *negotiorum gestio* if the owner's neglect is due to absence, ignorance or incapacity (para.24.25, below).

[22] See *Exchange Telegraph Co v Giulianotti*, 1959 S.C. 19; *Microwave Systems (Scotland) v Electro-Physiological Instruments*, 1971 S.C. 140.

on a company's tramcars and had agreed to supply boards on which to place his advertisements. In order to satisfy government regulations the company constructed new tramcars with boards in a roughly similar position. When the defender placed his advertisements on these boards, the company claimed a sum for the use of the boards on the ground that the lessee was saved the expense of erecting boards for himself. The claim was rejected; although the defender was a gainer by the company's expenditure, his gain was merely the incidental result of an expenditure which had secured its purpose.[23] It is sometimes said that the impoverished person must not have incurred the loss for his own benefit (*in suo*).[24] However, the mere fact that the pursuer carried out expenditure with a view only of his own interests does not always preclude recovery altogether. Thus, for example, an improver of land who does so in the honest but mistaken belief of owning the land in question is acting for his own benefit, but is not prevented from recovering for the enrichment of the true owner.[25] Similarly, recovery has been allowed in cases of mixed motives, where the pursuer acted partly in her own interest, partly in that of the defender.[26] The purpose of the expenditure must therefore be seen as merely a factor which can—but need not—be relevant in considering whether or not resultant enrichment is at the expense of the pursuer. After all, if the expenditure was intended to benefit the pursuer, that may point as much to donation as to unjustified enrichment. As the cases of imposed enrichment show, a more important factor than purpose is likely to be the directness with which the enrichment is created for the defender by the pursuer's activities. This also holds good for the interference cases, where the defender is enriched by use of the pursuer's property specifically.[27]

24.05 Indirect enrichment—There may be cases of indirect enrichment where A is enriched directly by B (whether by transfer, imposition or interference) but this arises indirectly from the actions of a third party C. Policy considerations against C being able to claim for A's enrichment include the prevention of double liability of A or double recovery by C, and A's loss of defences good against B, as well as the preservation of the parity of the general creditors of B in his bankruptcy and the rule against suing one's debtor's debtor.[28] So, where C performs work or service under a contract, "his intention is to further his own interests by performance of his contract"[29] with the other party B and, where no guarantor is involved, C will usually rely on the faith or credit of B.[30] Where B does not pay, C's loss is due to B's breach of contract[31] and, if A has the benefit of C's work, C cannot claim compensation from A.[32] While the underlying principles are not worked out fully in the judgments of the courts, it is clear that there is no doctrine in the law of Scotland that every person who

---

[23] *Edinburgh District Tramways Co v Courtenay*, 1909 S.C. 99.

[24] *Buchanan v Stewart* (1874) 2 R. 78 at 82, per Lord Neaves; *Exchange Telegraph Co v Giulianotti*, 1959 S.C. 19; *Microwave Systems (Scotland) v Electro-Physiological Instruments*, 1971 S.C. 140; *Varney (Scotland) Ltd v Lanark Burgh Council*, 1974 S.C. 245.

[25] See, e.g. *Newton v Newton*, 1925 S.C. 715.

[26] See, e.g. *Fernie v Robertson* (1871) 9 M. 437; *Shilliday v Smith*, 1998 S.C. 725.

[27] See the cases cited below, para.24.20.

[28] See Evans-Jones, *Unjustified Enrichment* (2003), Vol.1, Ch.8; N. Whitty, "Indirect enrichment in Scots law", 1994 Jur. Rev. 200, 239 (2 parts); para.8.03, above.

[29] *Gouws v Jester Pools (Pty) Ltd*, 1968 (3) S.A. 563 at 571, per Jansen J.

[30] cf. *Fernie v Robertson* (1871) 9 M. 437.

[31] See de Vos, 1960 Jur. Rev. 142 and 226 at 244 et seq.; *Gouws*, 1968 (3) S.A. 563 at 574.

[32] cf. W.M. Gloag, *Law of Contract*, 2nd edn (Edinburgh: W. Green, 1929), p.330.

has profited by work done under a contract is to be liable for that work.[33] So where a garage carried out repairs under a contract with an insurance company which went into liquidation, the owner of the car was not liable to pay the garage the amount by which he had benefited from the repairs.[34] Similarly, in a case where the plaintiffs constructed a swimming pool on land which they believed belonged to the other contracting party and he subsequently disappeared without paying, it was held that the plaintiffs could not recover from the true owner of the land any sum representing its increase in value.[35] Again, a person is not enriched merely because a debtor has paid a debt which was owed to him.[36] Therefore, in a bankruptcy a creditor has no preference on the ground that work which he has done under contract to the bankrupt has increased the value of the bankrupt's estate. The other creditors are not enriched merely because the dividend on their debts is larger.[37] Likewise, a party is not enriched by the acquisition of a thing for which he has paid, or which some party other than the pursuer in the enrichment action is bound to provide. Therefore, where an accountant undertook to carry out the amalgamation of two companies for a contract price, it was held that those who employed him, and who had paid the contract price were under no liability to a law agent who, on the accountant's instructions, had drawn up a necessary agreement.[38]

Cases of recovery of indirect enrichment—There is, however, no absolute bar **24.06** on recovery in cases of indirect enrichment. When tradesmen did work on the house of an incapacitated old lady under a contract with her daughter whom they regarded as acting for the old lady, the tradesmen were entitled to recover in recompense from the old lady's estate, since they had had in view the responsibility of both the old lady and her daughter.[39] Where a rogue defrauded a company of a large sum of money which he then used to purchase a house in the name of his mistress, it was held that the latter was obliged to repay the company on the ground that no-one is entitled to profit from another's fraud.[40] Recovery was also allowed at the instance of a company's creditor against a third party bank, although with hesitation, where the bank held funds paid in by the company for onward transfer to the creditor but did not make the transfer because the company was otherwise indebted to it. This was because the bank knew the purpose of its client's payments and that they would not have been made but for the bank's agreement that the funds would be applied for the creditor's benefit.[41] In general,

---

[33] *Cran v Dodson* (1893) 1 S.L.T. 354, per Lord Kyllachy.

[34] *Express Coach Finishers v Caulfield*, 1968 S.L.T. (Sh. Ct) 511; *Kirklands Garage (Kinross) Ltd v Clark*, 1967 S.L.T. (Sh. Ct) 60. Cf. *McCarthy Retail Ltd v Shortdistance Carriers CC*, 2001(3) S.A. 482 (S.C.A.).

[35] *Gouws v Jester Pools*, 1968 (3) S.A. 563. See further *ABSA Bank v Stander*, 1998(1) S.A. 939(C.) and also *Renfrewshire Council v McGinlay*, 2001 S.L.T. (Sh. Ct) 79, criticised by Evans-Jones, *Unjustified Enrichment* (2003), Vol.1, paras 8.117–8.118; *G.W. Tait & Sons v Taylor*, 2002 S.L.T. 1285.

[36] Kames, *Principles of Equity*, 5th edn (Bell and Bradfute, 1825), p.99; Gloag, *Law of Contract* (2009), p.331; *Universal Import Export GmbH v Bank of Scotland*, 1995 S.C. 73, per Lord Caplan.

[37] *Burns v McLellan's Creditors* (1735) Mor.13402; *Mess v Sime's Tr.* (1898) 1 F. (HL) 22.

[38] *J.M. & J.H. Robertson v Beatson, McLeod & Co*, 1908 S.C. 921; *Thomson, Jackson, Gourlay & Taylor v Lochhead* (1889) 16 R. 374 at 377, per L.J.-C. Macdonald.

[39] *Fernie v Robertson* (1871) 9 M. 437 at 442, per Lord Benholme.

[40] *M. & I. Instrument Engineers Ltd v Varsada*, 1991 S.L.T. 106.

[41] *Mercedes-Benz Finance Ltd v Clydesdale Bank Plc*, 1997 S.L.T. 905. The decision was also supported by application of the doctrine of *jus quaesitum tertio*: see above, para.8.06.

recovery appears to be allowed where the policy factors favouring that result, such as the prevention of fraud, outweigh those against it described in the previous paragraph.[42]

24.07 **Unjustified enrichment**—Enrichments fall to be reversed only if they are unjustified. The general approach is to say that an enrichment is unjustified when its retention can be supported by no legal ground.[43] Examples of legal grounds justifying the retention of an enrichment are those which arise under a valid and subsisting contract, or under an unconditional gift or donation, or a benefit conferred under a trust or legacy, or a payment received as the result of an order made by a court or following a lawful taxation demand. But the absence of a legal ground for retention of the enrichment is only a necessary, and not always a sufficient, basis for a successful enrichment claim. Otherwise it would be difficult to prevent claims in cases of incidental enrichment,[44] or to limit them in cases of imposed enrichment.[45] The distinctions in the ways in which enrichment comes about—transfer, imposition and interference[46]—are also useful in identifying the additional elements over and above absence of legal ground that will make an enrichment unjustified and a cause of action for the impoverished person.

(1) TRANSFER

24.08 In *Shilliday v Smith* it was held that the cases in which enrichment by transfer are reversed may be grouped under headings which reflect the Roman law origins of some of the principles involved and the terminology used in some of the cases: the *condictio indebiti*; the *condictio causa data causa non secuta*; the *condictio ob turpem vel injustam causam* and the *condictio sine causa* (a term not much used in Scottish writings).[47] These terms are not straitjackets and should be understood in their modern or Scots law rather than their Roman guise; they merely serve to distinguish various situations in which an enrichment remedy may be available, and it may be that some cases could be classified under more than one heading.

24.09 *Condictio indebiti* (**claim for recovery of a payment which is not due**)[48]— Money paid by the pursuer under the erroneous belief that it was due to be paid under a legal obligation to the recipient can be recovered in a personal action

---

[42] See for another example of recovery of indirect enrichment: *Extruded Welding Wire (Sales) Ltd v McLachlan & Brown*, 1986 S.L.T. 314 (where the defender was found to be in mala fide).

[43] *Dollar Land (Cumbernauld) Ltd v C.I.N. Properties Ltd*, 1998 S.C. (HL) 90 at 98, per Lord Hope of Craighead.

[44] para.24.04, above.

[45] para.24.16, below.

[46] para.24.02, above.

[47] *Shilliday v Smith*, 1998 S.C. 725 at 727–8, per Lord President Rodger. The *condictio furtiva* of Roman law has not been received into Scots law, but there are early references to the *condictio ob causam finitam* (Craig, *Jus Feudale*, III, v, 23; Stair, I, 7, 7), albeit these have not yet been taken up in the modern law. The latter *condictio* applies where an existing state of affairs provides the reason for the transfer but subsequently comes to an end. See further Evans-Jones, *Unjustified Enrichment* (2003), Vol.1, paras 6.06–6.11.

[48] Evans-Jones, *Unjustified Enrichment* (2003), Vol.1, Ch.3.

against the recipient,[49] unless the defender establishes factors which would make retention of the money equitable.[50] The pursuer's error may be as to the facts or as to the law relating to the transaction.[51] Doubt is not the same as error.[52] So the pursuer may have been mistaken as to facts which indicated that the sum was due, e.g. he paid a debt, being unaware that it had already been paid, or paid more than was due.[53] Thus where a feuar, on making use of a mutual gable, paid half the cost of erecting it, he was entitled to recover what he had paid on discovering that it had already been paid by his superior.[54] So, also, where as a result of common error a purchaser bought land with buildings and houses, but in fact most of the buildings were on a neighbouring feu, the contract of sale was reduced and the purchaser was entitled to recover the purchase price.[55] Likewise, averments that, due to a representation by the contractors which the pursuer had been unable to check, the purchaser had overpaid a contractors' account were held relevant in a claim to recover the excess payment.[56] Similarly, where a local authority entered into a currency exchange agreement with a merchant bank which both wrongly believed to be valid but which was in fact invalid because it was ultra vires the local authority, it was held that the merchant bank was entitled to recover the balance paid to the local authority, even though its belief that the sum was due had

---

[49] D.12.6; Voet 12.6; Stair, I, 7, 9; Erskine, III, 3, 54; Bell, *Principles*, s.531; Hume, *Lectures*, III, 172. See, as to exceptions, *Bell v Thomson* (1867) 6 M. 64. For the scope of the *condictio indebiti* see *Govender v Standard Bank of South Africa*, 1984 (4) S.A. 392 at 396 et seq., per Rose-Innes J. The theory of *promutuum* adopted by Stair, Erskine and Bell from Cujas (Paratitla on D.12.6 and Observationes 8.33) has not taken root in Scots law. See generally, Scottish Law Commission, *Recovery of Benefits Conferred under Error of Law* (HMSO, 1993), Scot. Law Com. Discussion Paper No.95, Vol.2. In *Castle Inns (Stirling) Ltd v Clark Contracts Ltd*, 2006 S.C.L.R. 663 at [25], Lord Drummond Young states obiter that the error may be that of a third party; but it is suggested that this would be a case of the *condictio sine causa* (for which see para.24.15, below).

[50] *Morgan Guaranty Trust Co of New York v Lothian RC*, 1995 S.C. 151, per Lord President Hope at 166; Erskine, III, 3, 54; Gloag, *Law of Contract* (1929), p.61; *Bell v Thomson* (1867) 6 M. 64, especially per L.J.-C. Patton at 69, apparently citing R.J. Pothier, *Traité du Contrat de Prêt de Consomption*, nn.140–1; *Credit Lyonnais v George Stevenson & Co Ltd* (1901) 9 S.L.T. 93, per Lord Kyllachy at 95; *Haggarty v Scottish Transport and General Workers Union*, 1955 S.C. 109; *Royal Bank of Scotland v Watt*, 1991 S.C. 48. A proof will therefore usually be necessary to explore the equities: *Haggarty*, 1955 S.C. 109. Interest is generally payable from the date of the erroneous payment either on the principle of restitution (*Gwydyr v Lord Advocate* (1894) 2 S.L.T. 280) or on the analogy of loan interest (*Duncan, Galloway & Co v Duncan Falconer & Co*, 1913 S.C. 265). But cf. *Sprot's Trs v Lord Advocate* (1903) 10 S.L.T. 452 (interest from date of payer's formal demand for repayment).

[51] *Morgan Guaranty*, 1995 S.C. 151, overruling *Glasgow Corp v Lord Advocate*, 1959 S.C. 203 and *Taylor v Wilson's Trs*, 1975 S.C. 146. In England, see now *Kleinwort Benson Ltd v Lincoln City Council* [1999] 2 A.C. 349 and *Deutsche Morgan Grenfell Group Plc v I.R.C.* [2007] 1 A.C. 558. These two cases illustrate the potential conundrum arising where the error of law is the result of a judicial decision post-dating the payment in question. If the decision is merely declaratory so that previous understandings of the law were wrong (the view of the majority in *Kleinwort*), then the payment was indeed made under mistake; but if the decision changes the law (the minority view), then there was no mistake at the time of payment, but only a misprediction as to the law. This debate may suggest that mistake is not the best way of approaching the problem; a better analysis may be through the absence of a legal ground for retaining the payment, subject to a defence that the payer knew that it was not liable to pay (see Meier and Zimmermann (1999) 115 L.Q.R. 556). However, a requirement of mistake may help to avoid prescription and limitation problems. See also from a Scottish point of view the speeches of Lord Hope of Craighead in the *Kleinwort* [1999] 2 A.C. 349 and *Deutsche Morgan* [2007] 1 A.C. 558 cases.

[52] cf. the English decision *Nurdin & Peacock Plc v Ramsden & Co Ltd* [1999] 1 W.L.R. 1249.

[53] Gloag, *Law of Contract* (1929), pp.60 et seq.; *Strathaird Farms Ltd v G.A. Chattaway & Co*, 1993 S.L.T. (Sh. Ct) 36.

[54] *Robertson v Scott* (1886) 13 R. 1127.

[55] *Hamilton v Western Bank* (1861) 23 D. 1033; above, para.7.24.

[56] *Balfour v Smith* (1877) 4 R. 454.

been based on an error of law.[57] Earlier cases involving error of law require to be read in the light of this decision of an enlarged court of five judges. Where, in any case the error was avoidable and the pursuer could have discovered the true facts, these factors will be relevant to any decision as to whether to grant the pursuer's claim on the grounds of equity.[58] Where, however, the pursuer waived any objection to payment, recovery will be denied.[59]

24.10 *Condictio indebiti* **(property other than money)**—Just as a person who pays money in error may be entitled to recover it,[60] so also a person who delivers property to another in the erroneous belief that he is under an obligation to do so may be entitled to recover it.[61] Though there is little Scottish authority on the point,[62] the same general principles should apply, since in each case the payment or transfer is made where it is not due.[63] So, for instance, just as a sum of money paid by an executor to a person not entitled to it can be recovered,[64] so also, it is thought, can a corporeal or incorporeal moveable which the executor has transferred to the wrong person. If the recipient of the property which has been transferred by error is in good faith, his obligation is to restore the property in the state in which it is at the time when the demand for restitution is made.[65]

24.11 **Excluded cases**—Repetition is not allowed in the case of money paid as a compromise, even one offered due to an error in fact,[66] since the compromise itself forms a fresh obligation to pay.[67] The *condictio indebiti* has also been held not to lie in the case of money paid as a charity,[68] because there can have been no erroneous belief that the payment was legally due, but only as to the circumstances which made it expedient or desirable. Money paid under a decree cannot be recovered merely because facts have come to light which would have formed a complete defence to the action, e.g. a receipt for the debt for which decree has been granted.[69]

---

[57] *Morgan Guaranty Trust Co of New York v Lothian RC*, 1995 S.C. 151.

[58] *Morgan Guaranty*, 1995 S.C. 151 at 166, per Lord President Hope; at 173, per Lord Clyde and at 175, per Lord Cullen. On "equity" in enrichment law, see Evans-Jones, *Unjustified Enrichment* (2003), Vol.1, paras 2.20–2.39.

[59] *Dalmellington Iron Co v Glasgow & S.W. Railway Co* (1889) 16 R. 523.

[60] See para.24.09, above.

[61] Stair, I, 7, 9; Bell, *Principles*, s.531; Voet 12.6.1; *Morgan Guaranty Trust Co of New York v Lothian RC*, 1995 S.C. 151 at 155, per Lord President Hope; *Govender v Standard Bank of South Africa*, 1984 (4) S.A. 392 at 396, per Rose-Innes J.

[62] cf. however, *Pride v St Anne's Bleaching Co* (1838) 16 S. 1376 (on which see W.J. Stewart, *The Law of Restitution in Scotland* (Edinburgh: W. Green, 1992), para.7.6); *Caledonian Ry v Harrison & Co* (1879) 7 R. 151.

[63] Pothier, *Traité du Contrat de Prêt de Consomption*, fnn.140 et seq. and fnn.165 et seq.; Voet 12.6.1.

[64] *Armour v Glasgow Royal Infirmary*, 1909 S.C. 916. *Anderson v Lambie*, 1954 S.C. (HL) 43 may be based, though not explicitly, on a similar kind of principle applied to heritable property.

[65] Pothier, *Traité du Contrat de Prêt de Consomption*, fn.166, but see Bell, *Principles*, s.537.

[66] Erskine, III, 3, 54; Bell, *Principles*, s.535.

[67] Erskine, III, 3, 54; Bell, *Principles*, s.535.

[68] *Masters and Seamen of Dundee v Cockerill* (1869) 8 M. 278, but see *Re Glubb* [1900] 1 Ch. 354 and para.24.15, fn.104, below. For further discussion of failed gifts and unjustified enrichment, arguing that Scots law recognises a *condictio donandi causa* and criticising the *Cockerill* case for relying on the *condictio indebiti*, see Evans-Jones, *Unjustified Enrichment* (2003), Vol.1, paras 6.82–6.96.

[69] *Marriot v Hampton* (1797) 7 T.R. 269; 2 Smith, L.C. 13th edn, 286.

***Condictio causa data causa non secuta* (claim for something transferred for a** **24.12**
future lawful purpose that failed)[70]—In these cases the pursuer seeks recovery
of money paid in advance for an anticipated return which has not been received,
or the failure of the purpose for which the money was transferred.[71] Although the
name used in Justinian's Digest is preserved, the doctrine has a rather different
scope in Scots law.[72] Many of the cases involve contracts, but the anticipated
return or purpose need not be a matter of contract or agreement between the
parties; it is enough that the recipient was aware of the transferor's purpose.[73] The
same principles apply where property other than money is transferred for a
purpose.[74] The defender must repay the amount by which he has been enriched, or
return the property transferred.[75]

Instances of the *condictio causa data causa non secuta*—It is possible to **24.13**
identify five main types of case from the Scottish authorities:

(1) Performance of a contract is frustrated and the defender is released from
his obligation to supply the consideration. Thus in a contract for the
construction of ship's engines for an Austrian firm, an instalment of
the price was paid on signing the contract. Before the construction of the
engines had begun, war with Austria was declared and this put an end to
the contract. It was held, on the conclusion of peace, that the Italian
successors of the Austrian firm might recover the deposit.[76] Similarly,
where the price was put on deposit receipt pending settlement of the sale

---

[70] On the translation see Evans-Jones, *Unjustified Enrichment* (2003), Vol.1, paras 4.06 et seq.

[71] D.12.4, Voet, *Commentarius ad Pandectas* (1698, 1704), 12.4; Stair, I, 7, 7; Erskine, III, i, 10; *Watson v Shankland* (1871) 10 M. 142, per Lord President Inglis at 152; *Haggarty v Scottish Transport and General Workers Union*, 1955 S.C. 109, per Lord Sorn at 114; *Connelly v Simpson*, 1993 S.C. 391; *Shilliday v Smith*, 1998 S.C. 725. Along with this *condictio*, Stair, I, 7, 7 discusses the *condictio ob non causam* (or *ob causam finitam*) covering cases where the initial legal cause for the payment later ceases.

[72] For the difference and the development from Roman law, see R. Zimmermann, *The Law of Obligations* (Cape Town: Juta and Co, 1990), pp.843–4, 857–62; W.W. Buckland, "Casus and Frustration in Roman and Common Law" (1933) 46 Harv. L.R. 1281; Evans-Jones, "Unjust enrichment, contract and the third reception of Roman law in Scotland" (1993) 109 L.Q.R. 663; G. MacCormack, "The condictio causa data causa non secuta", in R. Evans-Jones (ed.), *The Civil Law Tradition in Scotland* (Edinburgh: Stair Society, 1995); R. Evans-Jones, "The claim to recover what was transferred for a lawful purpose outwith contract (*condictio causa data causa non secuta*)" 1997 Acta Juridica 139.

[73] *Shilliday v Smith*, 1998 S.C. 725, disapproving of contrary language ("mutually agreed understanding") in *Grieve v Morrison*, 1993 S.L.T. 852.

[74] Stair, I, 7, 7; Erskine, III, 1, 10; Bankton, I, viii, 21. Cf. *Savage v McAlister* (1952) 68 Sh. Ct Rep. 11; *Nicolson v Schaw* (1711) Mor.9166 and *Grieve v Morrison*, 1993 S.L.T. 852.

[75] *Ogilvy v Hume* (1683) 2 Br. Supp.34, approved by Lord Shaw of Dunfermline in *Cantiere San Rocco v Clyde Shipbuilding Co*, 1923 S.C. (HL) 105 at 119–20; *Cutler v Littleton* (1711) Mor.583. See also *Mactaggart & Mickel Homes Ltd v Hunters* [2010] CSOH 130 at [102]–[104].

[76] *Cantiere San Rocco v Clyde Shipbuilding Co.*, 1923 S.C. (HL) 105. Lord Shaw of Dunfermline (at 119) purports to explain the reference to D.12.4.5.4, Ulpian 2 disputationem, in Erskine, III, 1, 10, but misunderstands the Digest text to which Erskine refers. See W.W. Buckland, *A Textbook of Roman Law*, 3rd edn (Cambridge: Cambridge University Press, 1963), pp.545–6; Buckland, "Casus and Frustration in Roman and Common Law" (1933) 46 Harv. L.R. 1281, especially at 1284; Zimmermann, *The Law of Obligations* (1990), pp.858–9. Lord Shaw's reference (at 117) to H.J. Roby, *Roman Private Law in the times of Cicero and of the Antonines* (University Press, 1902), Vol.2, p.78 should be read against this background (see also A. Rodger, "The Use of the Civil Law in the Scottish Courts" in D.L. Carey Miller and R. Zimmermann (eds), *The Civilian Tradition and Scots Law* (Berlin: Duncker and Humblot, 1997), p.228. The passage still causes difficulties: *Connelly v Simpson*, 1991 S.C.L.R. 295 at 297–8 (OH reversed on appeal, 1993 S.C. 391); see further Evans-Jones, *Unjustified Enrichment* (2003), Vol.1, paras 4.37–4.44. It has been suggested that the *Cantiere* case is truly an instance of the *condictio ob causam finitam*.

of subjects which were destroyed by fire before settlement, the purchaser was entitled to recover the price.[77]

(2) The defender, in breach of contract, fails to supply the consideration and the pursuer terminates the contract. Here the position is less clear. In the leading case[78] the pursuer agreed to pay for shares in a private company and paid in two stages. No shares were ever issued to him because, the pursuer not having wanted them until his divorce was over, the defender eventually put the company into members' voluntary liquidation, thereby rendering performance of the contract impossible. By a majority, the Extra Division refused to allow the pursuer to recover the price. Lord McCluskey based his decision on the broad ground that the *condictio* is not available, and the only remedy is damages, where a defender is in wilful breach of contract.[79] Lord Sutherland, on the other hand, held that the payments were not recoverable because, on a proper construction of the contract, they constituted payments of the price then due and payable[80]; if they had been advances towards a price not due and payable until delivery of the shares, they would, in principle, have been recoverable.[81]

(3) Where the pursuer, having paid a sum in advance, thereafter repudiates a contract before the defender performs his obligations, the pursuer can recover the advance, subject to any counterclaim by the defender for loss suffered due to the pursuer's breach of contract.[82] But if the sum is paid in advance as a deposit in security of the pursuer's performing the contract and he repudiates it, the pursuer cannot recover the deposit.[83]

(4) Where the contract is subject to a suspensive condition which does not materialise, and as a result the defender comes under no obligation to supply the consideration, the pursuer can recover any prepayment.[84]

(5) Transfers made between parties in contemplation of their marriage may be reversed where the marriage does not take place.[85] The classic case referred to by the institutional writers is that of things given to each other by betrothed parties (e.g. engagement rings), which must be returned if the engagement is broken off.[86] But modern cases have extended the scope of the *condictio* to the situation where transfers took place between

---

[77] *Singh v Cross Entertainments Ltd*, 1990 S.L.T. 77.

[78] *Connelly v Simpson*, 1993 S.C. 391. Lord Brand dissented. See MacQueen, "Unjustified enrichment and breach of contract" 1994 Jur. Rev. 137; R. Evans-Jones and J.A. Dieckmann, "The dark side of Connelly v Simpson", 1995 Jur. Rev. 90.

[79] *Connelly v Simpson*, 1993 S.C. 391.

[80] *Connelly v Simpson*, 1993 S.C. 391 at 414. As in *Leitch v Wilson* (1868) 7 M. 150.

[81] *Watson v Shankland* (1871) 10 M. 142, esp. at 152 et seq. The House of Lords deleted a passage related to certain aspects of the Lord President's remarks from the Court of Session interlocutor: (1873) 11 M. (HL) 51. Lord Sutherland in *Connelley v Simpson* (1993 S.C. 391 at 414) treats *Cantiere San Rocco v Clyde Shipbuilding Co*, 1923 S.C. (HL) 105 as ample authority for recovery of advances where the future event is not performed "for whatever reason". On Lord McCluskey's approach *Crofts v Stewart's Trs*, 1927 S.C. (HL) 65 may be regarded as a case of non-wilful breach.

[82] *Zemhunt (Holdings) Ltd v Control Securities*, 1992 S.C. 58 at 155, per Lord Morison.

[83] *Roberts and Cooper Ltd v Christian Salvesen and Co Ltd*, 1918 S.C. 794; *Zemhunt (Holdings) Ltd v Control Securities*, 1992 S.C. 58.

[84] Voet 12.6.3. See *Brown v Nielson* (1825) 4 S. 271. It is not clear whether this case should be classified under this heading or elsewhere, e.g. under *condictio indebiti*. See *Simon v Arnold*, 727 So 2d 699 (Louisiana 1999); D. Visser, *Unjustified Enrichment* (Cape Town: Juta and Co, 2008), pp.287, 536–8.

[85] *Shilliday v Smith*, 1998 S.C. 725. Cf. *Grieve v Morrison*, 1993 S.L.T. 852.

[86] Stair, I, 7, 7; Bankton, I, 8, 21; Erskine, III, 1, 9–10.

cohabiting parties not necessarily contemplating marriage but rather continuing to live together under the same roof and caring for each other.[87] The *condictio* has also been applied to allow recovery of a share of the purchase price of a property to be jointly owned and lived in by the parties, but where the defender neither contributed to the price nor cohabited there with the pursuer[88]; and, in another case, recovery of a contribution to the costs of building an extension to the defender's house in which the pursuer was to live but this was prevented by the defender's sale of the whole property after the extension was completed.[89]

***Condictio ob turpem vel injustam causam* (claim for recovery of money or property transferred for an immoral or illegal purpose)**[90]—Money paid under   **24.14** an unwarranted threat by the recipient can be recovered. So where someone pays money to avert a crime such as a threatened assault on himself or a near relation, or to prevent someone giving false testimony,[91] it may be recovered, whether or not the threat is carried out.[92] Payments made under economic duress can be recovered,[93] even if the duress was lawful in the country where it was applied.[94] On the other hand, money paid merely because the creditor threatens to take legal proceedings cannot be recovered,[95] and a mere protest will not justify recovery of money really paid to avoid the expense and inconvenience of a law suit.[96] But if a sum has been paid under protest to avoid some immediate inconvenience, such as seizure of goods for failure to pay market dues or threatened ejection from a vehicle in which the payer was travelling, it may be recovered on its being established that the demand in question was unwarrantable, even if through an action raised by a third party.[97] The same principles are applicable where property other than money has been transferred.[98] Recovery is not allowed if the parties to the transfer are equally responsible for the illegality (*in pari delicto potior est conditio possidentis*),[99] but the question of whether a transfer of value is illegal is distinct from the one whether any underlying contract is void or unenforceable as a result

---

[87] *Satchwell v McIntosh*, 2006 S.L.T. (Sh. Ct) 117 (criticised by Evans-Jones, "Causes of action and remedies in justified enrichment: Satchwell v McIntosh" (2007) 11 Edin. L.R. 105). The case may be better seen as one of the *condictio ob causam finitam*. See also *Moggach v Milne*, 2005 G.W.D. 8–107 (Sheriff Principal Sir Stephen Young QC, Elgin).

[88] *McKenzie v Nutter*, 2007 S.L.T. (Sh. Ct) 17.

[89] *Smith v Barclay* Unreported August 29, 2006, Dundee Sheriff Court (which refers also to *White v Docherty* Unreported January 8, 2002 and March 4, 2003, Arbroath Sheriff Court and Sheriff Principal R.A. Dunlop QC).

[90] D.12.5; Voet 12.5; Stair, I, 7, 8; Bankton, I, 8, 22; Erskine, III, 1, 10; Evans-Jones, *Unjustified Enrichment* (2003), Vol.1, Ch.5; J.E. Du Plessis, *Compulsion and Restitution* (Edinburgh: Stair Society, 2004), pp.175–7.

[91] Erskine, III, i, 10; Kames, *Principles of Equity* (1825), p.53.

[92] cf. D.12.5.1.2, Paul 10 ad Sabinum; 12.5.5, Julian 3 ad Urseium Ferocem.

[93] *Universe Tankships Inc. of Monrovia v I.T.F.* [1983] A.C. 366. For coercion affecting a bargain, cf. *Sutherland v Montrose Fishing Co Ltd* (1921) 37 Sh. Ct Rep. 239.

[94] *Dimskal Shipping Co S.A. v I.T.F.* [1992] 2 A.C. 152.

[95] See para.7.11, above.

[96] For payment without prejudice, see *British Railways Board v Glasgow Corp*, 1976 S.C. 224.

[97] *Maskell v Horner* [1915] 3 K.B. 106; *Brocklebank v The King* [1925] 1 K.B. 52.

[98] *Nisbet's Creditors' Tr. v Robertson* (1791) Mor.9554; *Bell's Octavo Cases* 349; *A v B.*, May 21, 1816 FC, not argued on this point in the House of Lords: *Duke of Hamilton v Esten* (1820) 2 Bligh 196.

[99] See above, para 9.04.

of the illegality.[100] But, as noted elsewhere in this book, contemporary decisions tend to see the presence of illegality as an absolute bar to recovery.[101]

24.15 *Condictio sine causa* **(claim for something retained without legal justification)**[102]—Although this heading is (or was) not often used,[103] it denotes an essential residual category covering a number of cases where Scots law recognises a right to repayment in situations which do not fit conveniently under any of the previous headings. They are cases where, without legal justification, the defender has been paid a sum of money to which the pursuer is entitled but there has been no liability error on the part of the pursuer. If the *condictio indebiti* was not confined to liability errors, many of the cases to be discussed in this paragraph could be treated simply as instances of undue transfers.[104] Thus, for example, where a transfer is made as a result of unlawful compulsion rather than liability error, recovery may be under the *condictio sine causa*.[105] In *Morgan Guaranty Trust Co of New York v Lothian Regional Council*,[106] the court left open the question whether the claim could have been based simply on the fact that payment had been made in respect of a contract which was subsequently held to be void by statute, rather than on the payer's error in law.[107] Recent authority also indicates that where a public body makes a demand for payment of taxes or other levies under an ultra vires enactment, prima facie an action of repetition may lie even though the pursuer did not labour under any mistake about this liability when he paid the sum demanded.[108] Again, if, for instance, A makes a gift of money to B, using C's money without his knowledge, it is thought that C is prima facie entitled

---

[100] See *Cuthbertson v Lowes* (1870) 8 M. 1073; *Dowling & Rutter v Abacus Frozen Foods Ltd*, 2002 S.L.T. 491 (noted by J. Thomson, "Illegal contracts in Scots law", 2002 S.L.T. (News) 153); *Malik v Ali*, 2004 S.L.T. 1280.

[101] See *Jamieson v Watt's Trustee*, 1950 S.C. 265; *Barr v Crawford*, 1983 S.L.T. 481; above, paras 9.01–9.12.

[102] Sometimes referred to as the *condictio sine causa specialis*. See Zimmermann, *The Law of Obligations* (1990), pp.856 et seq. and pp.871 et seq. Cf. Voet 12.7.1 and H. Grotius, *Inleiding tot de Hollandsche Rechts-geleertheyd* (1631) 3.30.18 (translated by R.W. Lee, *Introduction to the Jurisprudence of Holland* (corrected edition, London: Clarendon Press, 1953), Vol.1, pp.454–455).

[103] See, however, *Morgan Guaranty Trust Co of New York v Lothian RC*, 1995 S.C. 151 at 155, per Lord President Hope, and at 174, per Lord Cullen; *Shilliday v Smith*, 1998 S.C. 725 at 727E, per Lord President Rodger; Evans-Jones, *Unjustified Enrichment* (2003), Vol.1, Ch.6.

[104] The opinion of Rose-Innes J. in *Govender v Standard Bank of South Africa Ltd*, 1984 (4) S.A. 392 (C) at 396 et seq. contains an invaluable analysis. See further *First National Bank of Southern Africa Ltd v B. & H. Engineering*, 1995 (2) S.A. 279 (A) and *Commissioner of Customs & Excise v Bank of Lisbon International*, 1994 (1) S.A. 205 (N). Cf. also *G.M. Scott (Willowbank Cooperage) Ltd v York Trailer Co Ltd*, 1969 S.L.T. 87; 1970 S.L.T. 15, per Lord President Clyde at 1969 S.L.T. 87 at 88. It may be that in *Masters and Seamen of Dundee v Cockerill* (1869) 8 M. 278 the additional sum, which could not be recovered under the *condictio indebiti*, would have been held recoverable if this wider aspect of repetition had been considered. See the criticism of P. Birks, "Six questions in search of a subject: unjust enrichment in a crisis of identity", 1985 Jur. Rev. 227 at 240, and above, fn.68.

[105] Or the *condictio ob turpem vel injustam causam* (above, para.24.14). See, e.g. *British Oxygen Co v South of Scotland Electricity Board*, 1959 S.C. (HL) 17 and further Du Plessis, *Compulsion and Restitution* (2004), Vol.51.

[106] *Morgan Guaranty Trust Co of New York v Lothian Regional Council*, 1995 S.C. 151.

[107] See, further, A.F. Rodger, "Recovering payments under void contracts in Scots law", in W.J. Swadling and G. Jones (eds), *The Search for Principle: Essays in Honour of Lord Goff of Chieveley* (Oxford: Oxford University Press, 2000).

[108] *Woolwich Building Society v I.R.C.* [1993] A.C. 70; discussed in *Deutsche Morgan Grenfell v I.R.C.* [2007] 1 A.C. 558. See further *British Oxygen Co Ltd v South West Scotland Electricity Board*, 1959 S.C. (HL) 17; *British Railways Board v Glasgow Corp*, 1976 S.C. 224; *Amministrazione delle Finanze dello Stato v San Giorgio SpA* (C-199/82) [1983] E.C.R. 3595.

to recover the money from B, even though he did not make the transfer himself.[109] Where a stockbroker's clerk forged a cheque in favour of his employer and the cheque bore to be drawn on, and was ultimately paid by, the Clydesdale Bank, the bank was entitled to recover the sum from the stockbroker whose debt had been discharged by the clerk using the funds obtained from the bank.[110] In such circumstances the bank was entitled to recover, not because it could ever have thought that it was indebted to the stockbroker payee,[111] but because as a result of the clerk's forgery the bank believed that it was under a duty to its own customer to make the payment and the payee gave no valuable consideration.[112] But where the defender has given value for the payment and neither knew, nor ought to have inquired about, the source of the payment, the pursuer will not be entitled to recover his money which was wrongfully used to make the payment. So, where a debtor to a bank by fraudulent misrepresentations induced the pursuer to purchase certain shares and used the price to pay off his debt to the bank, the pursuer was not entitled to recover the price from the bank which had given value by pro tanto discharging the fraudster's debt and releasing its security.[113] Similarly, where trustees instructed a broker to sell shares and he used the price to reduce his personal overdraft with a bank, the bank was not liable to repay the trustees since there was nothing unusual in brokers making such payments into their private accounts and the bank neither knew about, nor had any reason to inquire into, the fraudulent misapplication of the trustees' funds.[114] Once again, the same principles are as applicable to transfers of property as to transfers of money.

(2) IMPOSITION

Two major examples of enrichment by imposition are found in the Scottish **24.16** authorities: (a) unauthorised improvements of another's property; and (b) unauthorised performance of another's obligation so as to discharge that other's liability under the obligation. It is necessary for the law to formulate limits on the ability of the unauthorised intervener in another's affairs to impose enrichment liability upon that other. The *condictiones* referred to in the discussion of enrichment by transfer are of limited utility in this regard, although an improvement

---

[109] cf. Grotius, *Inleiding tot de Hollandsche Rechts-geleertheyd* (1631), 3.30.18.

[110] *Clydesdale Bank v Paul* (1877) 4 R. 626. It makes no difference that the money is in cash or negotiable instruments: *M. & I. Instrument Engineers Ltd v Varsada*, 1991 S.L.T. 106.

[111] *Govender v Standard Bank of South Africa*, 1984 (4) S.A. 392 (C). In *Royal Bank v Watt*, 1991 S.C. 48, the alteration of the cheque by the rogue meant that the pursuers thought that they were under an obligation to their customers, Messrs W. & J. Burness, to honour their cheque by crediting the defender's account with the increased sum. But, as drawee bankers, they could not have believed that they were under a legal obligation to the defender who was simply the customer of another bank who had presented the cheque for payment. Hence, despite the terminology used, the head of repetition was not properly classified as the *condictio indebiti*. See, however, Scottish Law Commission, *Recovery of Benefits Conferred under Error of Law*, Vol.2, para.2.10.

[112] *Clydesdale Bank* (1877) 4 R. 626 at 629, per Lord Shand.

[113] *Gibbs v British Linen Co* (1875) 4 R. 630.

[114] *Thomson v Clydesdale Bank* (1893) 20 R. (HL) 50; *Style Financial Services Ltd v Bank of Scotland (No.1)*, 1996 S.L.T. 421; *(No.2)*, 1998 S.L.T. 851; *Eagle Trust v S.B.C. Securities* [1992] 4 All E.R. 488; *Cowan de Groot Properties Ltd v Eagle Trust* [1992] 4 All E.R. 700. *Thomson* is analysed in detail in *Westpac Banking v Savin* [1985] 2 N.Z.L.R. 41 at 61–3 and 70, per Sir Clifford Richmond. See P. Birks, "Misdirected funds: restitution from the recipient" [1989] Lloyd's M.C.L.Q. 296.

might be an undue transfer when made under a void contract,[115] or one that falls to be reversed because made for a purpose which fails.[116] Such approaches cannot be convincingly adopted in cases of performance of another's obligation, however, and are too limited to delimit when there can be recovery in such cases and in those of improvements. It should be noted that in cases where the imposition occurs as a result of the temporary or permanent absence, ignorance or disability of the owner of the property or the debtor in the obligation, as the case may be, there may be a claim in *negotiorum gestio* (benevolent intervention).[117] The differences between an enrichment claim and one in benevolent intervention are that the latter is dependent upon the pre-conditions mentioned in the previous sentence and is in general a claim for expenditure made rather than the other party's enrichment, although in some circumstances that enrichment may provide a cap to the amount of expenses that can be claimed.[118]

24.17 **(a) Improvements to another's property**[119]—In improvement cases outside benevolent intervention, the major control factor has been a requirement of the improver's error.[120] Where a party has expended money on property in the bona fide but erroneous belief that it is his own and is compelled to give it up to the true owner, he has a claim for his expenditure in so far as it has proved beneficial and the true owner consequently is enriched.[121] He has no such claim if his possession was not bona fide.[122] An improver who wrongly but in good faith believed that his possession would be followed by his gaining a title to the property improved was successful in a claim for recompense for his meliorations, although he knew the title would be open to challenge.[123] There are also cases of successful claims where the pursuer's error is that a third party whom he wishes to benefit is, or will become, the owner of, or entitled to, the property.[124] Where a person holding property on a limited title (as in the case of a liferenter) expends money on improvements, it will generally be assumed that he did so with a view to his own advantage,

---

[115] *Rutherglen Magistrates v Cullen* (1773) 2 Pat. 305; *Middleton v Newton Display Group Ltd*, 1990 G.W.D. 40–2305 (Glasgow Sheriff Court).

[116] *Shilliday v Smith*, 1998 S.C. 725.

[117] See para.24.25, below. *Fernie v Robertson* (1871) 9 M. 437 is a case where the improver who recovered the enrichment of the owner was a tradesman employed by an intervener managing the affairs of the owner of the property improved. *Paterson v Greig* (1862) 24 D. 1370 can be seen as an example of enrichment recovery by an improving an intervener who managed only in her own interest (Bankton, I, 9, 28; Erskine, III, 3, 53); but see *Stair Memorial Encyclopaedia*, Vol.15, para.132, fn.12.

[118] See further para.24.27, below.

[119] See J. Wolffe, "Enrichment by Improvements in Scots Law", in D. Johnston and R. Zimmermann (eds), *Unjustified Enrichment: Key Issues in Comparative Perspective* (Cambridge: Cambridge University Press, 2002); R. Evans-Jones, "Searching for 'Imposed' Enrichment in Improvements—Classifications and General Enrichment Actions in Mixed Systems: Scotland and South Africa" [2008] 16 Restitution L.R. 18.

[120] On benevolent intervention (negotiorum gestio), see below, paras 24.24 et seq.

[121] Erskine, III, 1, 11; W.M. Gordon, *Scottish Land Law*, 2nd edn (Edinburgh: W. Green, 1999), paras 14–52 et seq.; *Magistrates of Selkirk v Clapperton* (1830) 9 S. 9; *Newton v Newton*, 1925 S.C. 715 (criticised by R. Evans-Jones, "The distorting images of *Newton v Newton* and its lessons for the law of property and unjustified enrichment in Scotland" (2005) 9 Edin. L.R. 449). An improver has no right of retention against a purchaser who pays for the improved subjects, and the latter is also probably not liable to the improver: *Beattie v Lord Napier* (1831) 9 S. 639.

[122] *Barbour v Halliday* (1840) 2 D. 1279; *Trade Development Bank v Warriner Mason (Scotland) Ltd*, 1980 S.C. 74. There may perhaps be recovery for necessary repairs and maintenance: Bell, *Principles*, s.538 n.(g).

[123] *Yellowlees v Alexander* (1882) 9 R. 765. Gloag, *The Law of Contract* (1929), p.324 describes the case as "very special".

[124] *Duff, Ross & Co v Kippen* (1871) 8 S.L.R. 299; *McDowel v McDowel* (1906) 14 S.L.T. 125.

and his representatives will have no claim against the fiar for the amount by which the improvements have enriched him.[125] Such a claim, however, may be established on proof that the liferenter acted on a reasonable expectation that his expenditure would be repaid.[126] And there is early authority for the statement that if a house is destroyed by fire, and rebuilt by a liferenter, his representatives have a claim against the fiar.[127] It would appear to be the law that a heritable creditor in possession and expending money on the subjects has a claim against the debtor in so far as the subjects are increased in value.[128] Any claim by a tenant for improvements must rest on express contract or statutory provision.[129]

(b) Performance of another's obligation[130]—Where a party (P) pays or **24.18** performs to a creditor (C) the debt or obligation owed to C by a debtor (D), without P having the authority of D to do so, then if D's obligation to C is discharged by P's action, D is enriched by the saving in no longer having to pay or perform to C. This enrichment is at P's expense: P thus has an enrichment claim against D. While Scots law is not completely settled on when third party performance discharges a debt or obligation, the authorities seem to favour that result in cases of money debt,[131] leaving open the possibility of an enrichment claim by P against the discharged debtor D. In such money debt cases, error seems unimportant: P can still recover from D even though he paid C deliberately and with full knowledge of all the relevant facts.[132] What matters is whether or not the debt is discharged; and if C treats the payment as doing so, as he generally will, then D is liable. D would have had to pay anyway, under the now discharged obligation; the fact that he is having to pay someone else under a new enrichment obligation makes little or no difference to his basic position. So there is no real need in that case to add in protections for D against unwanted intervention in his affairs, especially if he can take against P those defences which he would have had against C, such as a right of retention in respect of breach of contract by the creditor.[133] There is also little distinction from the claim in benevolent intervention cases, since the amount of P's expenditure is generally the same as D's enrichment. Only if D is not absent, ignorant or incapacitated, or if P is acting in its own interests, must the claim be made under enrichment law.[134]

Non-money obligations—The position with non-money obligations may be **24.19** different, if only because D may have an interest in rendering the performance in

---

[125] *Wallace v Braid* (1900) 2 F. 754 at 760, per Lord Trayner; *Reedie v Yeaman* (1875) 12 S.L. Rep. 625; *Rankin v Wither* (1886) 13 R 903. The latter two cases involve husbands who improved their wives' property on the basis of becoming owner on the death of their spouses. Evans-Jones, *Unjustified Enrichment* (2003), Vol.1, para.4.24, suggests that these are cases for the application of the *condictio causa data causa non secuta* (for which see para.24.12, above).

[126] *Morgan v Morgan's Judicial Factor*, 1922 S.L.T. 247.

[127] *Halliday v Garden* (1706) Mor.13419.

[128] *Nelson v Gordon* (1874) 1 R. 1093. See Gloag, *The Law of Contract* (1929), p.326.

[129] *Thomson v Fowler* (1859) 21 D. 453; *Walker v McKnight* (1886) 13 R. 599.

[130] H.L. MacQueen, "Payment of Another's Debt", in Johnston and Zimmermann (eds), *Unjustified Enrichment: Key Issues in Comparative Perspective* (2002).

[131] Above, para.3.22.

[132] *Reid v Lord Ruthven* (1918) 55 S.L.R. 616; *Duncan v Motherwell Bridge & Engineering Co Ltd*, 1952 S.C. 131. But note that P's knowledge that he does not owe C means that, if the payment fails to discharge D's debt, P will not be able to use the condictio indebiti to recover the money from C (see para.24.09, above).

[133] cf. the position if P had been C's assignee: above, para.8.15.

[134] See further para.24.25, below.

order to earn a profit, or because C may have specific reasons for wishing to receive performance from D rather than P. Where these elements have not been present, P's enrichment claim against D has been successful. So when a contractor who had built houses also constructed sewers connecting them to the existing system of public sewers, the local authority whose statutory duty it was to have the sewers constructed was found liable in recompense to the contractor. The authority was not a profit-earning organisation, while the creditors in its obligation were the members of the public paying local taxes to the authority, who had no special interest in who performed the obligation.[135] But there have been different results in very similar cases. So where a local authority refused to comply with their statutory duty to construct sewers, and contractors constructed the sewers themselves, the contractors were not entitled to recover their costs because they could have brought proceedings to enforce the local authority's statutory duty.[136] Similarly, where a utility company carried out remedial works on a bridge which a local authority had a statutory obligation to maintain, the purpose of the works being to prevent damage to the utility's pipelines carried by the bridge, it was held that the utility company had no enrichment claim but should have sought to enforce the authority's statutory duty.[137] In yet another case where the person who was bound to repair a road under a contract with commissioners failed to do so and the commissioners did the work themselves instead of taking action to enforce their contract, it was held that they were not entitled to recover the cost of the work.[138] The outcome of these decisions appears to be that enrichment liability in cases of performance of another's obligation is controlled by a concept of subsidiarity, i.e. that there must be no other way of compelling the debtor to fulfil its obligation.[139] There is a conflict of views as to whether a requirement of error may be a further element to control liability in such cases,[140] but this seems an un-necessary elaboration of the law.

(3) INTERFERENCE

24.20 The liability for enrichment gained through interference with another's rights is usually explained on the basis that it supports property rights.[141] Where the defender uses the pursuer's property in the knowledge that the pursuer does not intend to give him the use gratuitously, the defender is liable to pay a reasonable

---

[135] _Lawrence Building Co v Lanarkshire County Council_, 1978 S.C. 30.

[136] _Varney (Scotland) Ltd v Burgh of Lanark_, 1974 S.C. 245 (criticised by Sellar, _Stair Memorial Encyclopaedia_, Vol.15, para.68).

[137] _Transco Plc v Glasgow City Council_, 2005 S.L.T. 958 (noted by N. Whitty, "Transco Plc v Glasgow City Council: developing enrichment law after Shilliday" (2006) 10 Edin. L.R. 113).

[138] _Northern Lighthouse Commissioners v Edmonston_ (1908) 16 S.L.T. 439.

[139] For an argument that subsidiarity is not, or should not be, a general concept running through the whole of enrichment law, see Whitty, "Transco Plc v Glasgow City Council" (2006) 10 Edin. L.R. 113; see also Evans-Jones, _Unjustified Enrichment_ (2003), Vol.1, paras 1.88–1.101, and H. MacQueen, "Unjustified enrichment in mixed legal systems" [2005] R.L.R. 21.

[140] See _Rankin v Wither_ (1886) 13 R. 903; _Gray v Johnston_, 1928 S.C. 659; _Varney (Scotland) Ltd v Burgh of Lanark_, 1974 S.C. 245.

[141] Scottish Law Commission, _Recovery of Benefits Conferred under Error of Law_, Vol.2, para.3.115. See also J. Blackie and I. Farlam, "Enrichment by Act of the Party Enriched", in R. Zimmermann, D. Visser and K. Reid (eds), _Mixed Legal Systems in Comparative Perspective: Property and Obligations in Scotland and South Africa_ (Oxford: Oxford University Press, 2004), especially at pp.490 et seq; M. Hogg, _Obligations_, 2nd edn (Edinburgh: Avizandum, 2006), Ch.6.

sum for it.[142] So where the defender had possession of shootings under a lease which was held to be invalid, he was liable to pay a "just and reasonable consideration",[143] and where a person hired the pursuer's sacks from a railway company, but kept them beyond the hire period, he was liable to pay the pursuer's charges.[144] The principle applies to the use of incorporeal property also, so that where the pursuer's employers used an invention which he had patented, without agreeing any payments to him and after he had demanded a royalty, it was held that they were bound to pay him a reasonable sum by way of royalty.[145] Even though a bona fide possessor who has ceased to possess another's property is not liable in restitution for the value of the property,[146] he is liable for any profit which he has made[147] but not for any fruits which he has consumed in good faith.[148] This applies when the bona fide possessor parts with possession to another from whom the owner can recover his property.[149] But the view has been expressed that, where a bona fide possessor destroys another's property, he is liable to make restitution of its value.[150] Thus where oil merchants mixed the pursuers' oil with other substances to make lard which belonged to the merchants by virtue of the doctrine of specification, the merchants were liable to the pursuers for the value of the oil which had ceased to exist.[151] A person who in bad faith[152] parts with or puts an end to the possession of another's property is liable in the value of the property[153] and of any fruits consumed in bad faith.[154] In principle, the interference need not necessarily be by the party enriched but by a third party, as where in an industrial accession case T puts P's goods as an accessory into D's principal property.[155]

Defences[156]—A number of possible defences to enrichment claims have been **24.21** noticed in the course of the preceding text of this chapter. Here some of these are

---

[142] Gloag, *The Law of Contract* (1929), pp.40 and 329–30; Wark, "Recompense", *Encyclopaedia of the Laws of Scotland*, Vol.12 (Edinburgh: W. Green, 1931), para.728; A.J.M. Steven, "Recompense for Interference in Scots Law", 1996 Jur. Rev. 51; K. Zweigert and H. Kotz, *An Introduction to Comparative Law*, 3rd edn (Oxford: Clarendon Press, 1998), pp.544 et seq.

[143] *Earl of Fife v Wilson* (1864) 3 M. 323. See also *H.M.V. Fields Properties Ltd v Skirt 'n' Slack Centre*, 1986 S.C. 114; *Shetland Islands Council v B.P. Petroleum Development Ltd*, 1990 S.L.T. 82.

[144] *Chisholm v Alexander & Son* (1882) 19 S.L.R. 835.

[145] *Mellor v William Beardmore*, 1927 S.C. 597, criticised by Gloag, *The Law of Contract* (1929), p.291, fn.11.

[146] Erskine, III, 1, 10.

[147] Stair, I, 7, 11; Erskine, III, 1, 10; Hume, *Lectures*, III, 234; *Scot v Low* (1704) Mor.9123; *Faulds v Townsend* (1861) 23 D. 437 at 439, per Lord Ordinary (Ardmillan) obiter; *Jarvis v Manson*, 1954 S.L.T. (Sh. Ct) 93. If the bona fide possessor has acted carelessly he may be liable for the whole value of the object: *Faulds* (1861) 23 D. 437; *Oliver & Boyd v Marr Typefounding Co* (1901) 9 S.L.T. 170.

[148] Stair, I, 7, 11; II, 1, 23; Erskine, II, 1, 25; Hume, *Lectures*, III, 240 et seq.; *Houldsworth v Brand's Trs* (1876) 3 R. 304; D.L. Carey Miller, *Corporeal Moveables*, 2nd edn (Edinburgh: W. Green, 2005), paras 6.04 et seq.; W.M. Gordon and S. Wortley, *Scottish Land Law*, 3rd edn (Edinburgh: W. Green, 2009), paras 14.48–14.59.

[149] *Faulds v Townsend* (1861) 23 D. 437; *International Banking Corp v Ferguson, Shaw & Sons*, 1910 S.C. 182 at 191–2, per Lord Low; *Harper Collins Publishers Ltd v Young* [2007] CSOH 65.

[150] *International Banking Corp*, 1910 S.C. 182, per Lord Low at 192. Lord Ardwall disagreed (at 193) and his view was adopted by Lord McDonald in *North West Securities v Barrhead Coachworks Ltd*, 1976 S.C. 68.

[151] *International Banking Corp*, 1910 S.C. 182.

[152] Serious fault may be treated as equivalent to fraud: *Faulds v Townsend* (1861) 23 D. 437.

[153] Stair, I, 7, 13; *Faulds v Townsend* (1861) 23 D. 437.

[154] Stair I, 7, 13; Erskine, II, 1, 26; Hume, *Lectures*, III, 240.

[155] See Steven, "Recompense for Interference in Scots Law", 1996 Jur. Rev. 51, 61–62.

[156] For the defence of prescription, see Ch.4. See generally Evans-Jones, *Unjustified Enrichment* (2003), Vol.1, Ch.10 (note that change of position is discussed at paras 9.56 et seq.); Scottish Law Commission, *Recovery of Benefits Conferred under Error of Law*, Vol.2, pp.63 et seq.

further elaborated while others are noted for the first time. (1) In *conditio indebiti* cases where money which was not due has been paid in error[157] it is reclaimable unless it is inequitable in the circumstances that the defender should be obliged to pay back the sum of money[158] or the residue which the defender retains.[159] Often such a defence will involve some kind of change of position (or loss of enrichment) on the part of the defender. So where the pursuer, wrongly believing himself to be the debtor, pays money to the defender who receives it in good faith and therefore surrenders his rights against the true debtor,[160] or fails to sue him before his bankruptcy,[161] or within the prescriptive period, repetition may be refused on equitable grounds. On the other hand, if the recipient has spent the money on an asset[162] or has changed his position in bad faith or has acted wrongfully[163] or unreasonably,[164] he will be obliged to repay. But an agent or intermediary, who receives payment in that capacity and pays it over to his principal in discharge of his obligation to the principal, is not liable in repetition, and the person seeking repetition must look to the principal.[165] Where, on the other hand, the nature of the alleged relationship with the principal should have put the defender on inquiry and the pursuers were not told of it, the defender was held liable in repetition even though most of the money had been paid to the alleged principal.[166] (2) There is a conflict of Outer House authority as to whether an equitable defence of change of position or loss of enrichment applies to payments made for a purpose which does not materialise.[167] Difficulty is caused by an obiter dictum of Lord President Inglis suggesting that in cases of *conditio causa data causa non secuta* the pursuer is always entitled to restoration of the whole amount transferred, "however great [the defender's] expenditure and consequent loss may have been".[168] The better view is that change of position is a defence applying across the whole of unjustified enrichment.[169] (3) It has been said obiter that an innocent donee of a thief who gives the money to charity may have a defence.[170] (4) Similarly, it has been indicated that equitable considerations would not be allowed to defeat a

---

[157] *Credit Lyonnais v George Stevenson & Co* (1901) 9 S.L.T. 93.

[158] *Royal Bank of Scotland v Watt*, 1991 S.C. 48, discussed in Evans-Jones, *Unjustified Enrichment* (2003), paras 9.69 et seq. See generally Zimmermann, *The Law of Obligations* (1990), pp.895 et seq.

[159] cf. *Lipkin Gorman v Karpnale Ltd* [1991] 2 A.C. 548 at 580, per Lord Goff (plaintiff's money paid by thief to innocent donee); *Mackay's Stores Ltd v Topward Ltd* [2008] CSOH 51, commented upon in Evans-Jones, "Equity and the condictio indebiti" (2008) 12 Edin. L.R. 429.

[160] Bell, *Principles*, s.536; *Wallet v Ramsay* (1904) 12 S.L.T. 111.

[161] *Ker v Rutherford* (1684) Mor.2928; *Duke of Argyle v Lord Halcraig's Representatives* (1723) Mor.2928; Kames, *Principles of Equity* (1825), p.200; Bell, *Principles*, s.536.

[162] *Armour v Glasgow Royal Infirmary*, 1909 S.C. 916.

[163] *Lipkin Gorman* [1991] 2 A.C. 548 at 580, per Lord Goff.

[164] *Royal Bank of Scotland v Watt*, 1991 S.C. 48 (treated by the court as a *conditio indebiti*).

[165] *Continental Caoutchouc Co v Kleinwort* (1904) 9 Com. Cas. 240; *Royal Bank of Scotland v Watt*, 1991 S.C. 48; *A.N.Z. Banking Group v Westpac Banking Corp* (1988) 164 C.L.R. 662.

[166] *Royal Bank of Scotland v Watt*, 1991 S.C. 48.

[167] *Grieve v Morrison*, 1993 S.L.T. 852 (no such defence) which was not cited in the Outer House decision in *Connelly v Simpson*, 1991 S.C.L.R. 295 where the defence was recognised so long as the defender was not at fault. That decision was reversed in the Inner House (1993 S.C. 391) but on another point. See also the sheriff court cases of *McQuarrie v Crawford*, 1951 S.L.T. (Sh. Ct) 84 and *Kirkpatrick v Kirkpatrick*, 1983 S.L.T. (Sh. Ct) 3, both seeming to recognise the defence.

[168] *Watson v Shankland* (1871) 10 M. 142 at 152. Note that the Lord President would have made an allowance to the extent that the pursuer was enriched by the defender's actings with the enrichment.

[169] See authorities cited in paras 24.12–24.13, above; also Evans-Jones, *Unjustified Enrichment* (2003), Vol.1, paras 9.56–9.94.

[170] *Lipkin Gorman* [1991] 2 A.C. 548 at 579.

claim for repetition of payments made under improper compulsion.[171] (5) Personal bar is a defence to a *condictio indebiti*[172] but, unlike the general equitable defence of change of position, it requires that the detrimental change in the defender's position flow from his reliance on an express or implied representation by the pursuer.[173] (6) There are conflicting authorities on whether the defence of bona fide consumption[174] applies to interest on a principal sum recoverable by a *condictio indebiti*[175] and on whether it applies to the principal sum itself rather than merely to interest on that sum.[176] (7) While *restitutio in integrum* is not a requirement of a *condictio indebiti*,[177] the pursuer may be required, as a condition of repetition, to restore benefits received from the defender[178] on the ground that "they who ask equity must be prepared to give it".[179]

Remedies[180]—The different kinds of enrichment explain why different remedies **24.22** may be necessary in enrichment law. In some cases restoration of the specific thing will be appropriate: money, for example (although, since money is fungible, the money repaid need not be exactly the same notes and coins that were originally received), or goods. Repetition (for money) and restitution (for property) are the appropriate remedies in such cases. Restitution is also to describe the payment of value which must sometimes be made in interference cases where the pursuer's property has been consumed, destroyed or sold on in bad faith or with fault. But improvements, services, and good faith use of property can never be restored; instead they will have to be valued and paid for. Similarly, a debt or obligation paid or performed by a third party also cannot be returned as such, although at least the amount of the money debt discharged can be precisely fixed. The remedy in all these cases is recompense. In Scots law the term "restitution" is used rather confusingly to describe two distinct remedies: (1) the claim of an owner to have something which remains his property restored to him (better referred to as "vindication"); (2) the claim of the pursuer that the defender has been unjustly enriched at his expense and should accordingly transfer ownership of some thing to the pursuer or compensate him for the defender's enjoyment of the thing.[181] The former claim is based on the pursuer's real right in the property, while the second is based on a personal right of the pursuer against the defender. Only the second

---

[171] *Unigate Foods Ltd v Scottish Milk Marketing Board*, 1975 S.C. (HL) 75 at 90, per Lord President Emslie.

[172] *Dixon v Monkland Canal Co* (1831) 5 W. & S. 447 (acquiescence).

[173] *Allied Times (Theatres) Ltd v Anderson*, 1958 S.L.T. (Sh. Ct) 29. See further E.C. Reid and J.W.G. Blackie, *Personal Bar* (Edinburgh: W. Green, 2006), paras 12.13–12.21.

[174] See para.34.13.

[175] For: Erskine, II, 1, 26; *Ferguson v Lord Advocate* (1906) 14 S.L.T. 52. Against: *Haldane v Ogilvy* (1871) 10 M. 62.

[176] See *Hunter's Trs v Hunter* (1894) 21 R. 949 at 953, per Lord Young (defence applicable to principal). Contrast *Darling's Trs v Darling's Trs*, 1909 S.C. 445, especially at 451, per Lord President Dunedin; approved by Lord Skerrington (dissenting) in *Morrison v School Board of St Andrews*, 1918 S.C. 51 at 64. Opinions reserved in *Rowan's Trs v Rowan*, 1939 S.C. 30 at 39, per Lord President Normand and at 48, per Lord Moncrieff.

[177] cf. *General Property Investment Co v Matheson's Trs* (1888) 16 R. 282.

[178] *North British and Mercantile Insurance Co v Stewart* (1871) 9 M. 534.

[179] *North British and Mercantile Insurance Co v Stewart*, (1871) 9 M. 534 at 537, per Lord Ormidale.

[180] See Evans-Jones, *Unjustified Enrichment* (2003), Vol.1, Ch.9.

[181] Birks, "Six questions in search of a subject: unjust enrichment in a crisis of identity", 1985 Jur. Rev. 227 at 233 et seq.; Carey Miller, *Corporeal Moveables in Scots Law* (2005), paras 10.02 et seq.; Scottish Law Commission, *Recovery of Benefits Conferred under Error of Law*, Vol.2, pp.108 et seq.; K. Reid, "Unjustified enrichment and property law", 1994 Jur. Rev. 167; Evans-Jones, *Unjustified Enrichment* (2003), Vol.1, paras 1.88–1.96.

kind of restitution falls to be considered in the context of the present chapter. In general, enrichment remedies are personal in effect and create no proprietary rights; unjustified enrichment by itself is not a ground for the creation of a constructive trust or any other proprietary right for the pursuer.

24.23 **Unjustified enrichment and contract**[182]—The cause of action for unjustified enrichment is properly applicable either to cases where there is no contract between the parties, or to cases where work has been done under a contract in circumstances which preclude any direct contractual claim. It is not a plea which is open to someone who has done work under a contract and has the right to sue the other party for the contract price.[183] So a contractor cannot claim recompense on the ground that the work he has done has enriched the employer to an amount greater than the price.[184] And a claim for payment for extra work done under a contract must, it is conceived, be founded on an express or implied agreement to pay, not on the principle of unjustified enrichment.[185] When work has been done under a contract which makes no express provision for payment, a claim for payment, though sometimes referred to as a claim for unjustified enrichment,[186] is more properly a claim under an implied contract for payment, measured, on the principle of *quantum meruit*, by the market value of the services rendered, and maintainable whether they have proved beneficial or not, in contrast to a claim *quantum lucratus*, measured and limited by the advantage which the services have produced to the recipient.[187] In such cases, however, assuming that the work has proved beneficial, a claim based either on unjustified enrichment or on implied contract may be open.[188] Typical cases for an enrichment action (usually for recompense) where work has been done under a contract but a direct contractual claim is precluded would appear to be two in number: (1) Where a party has done work or supplied goods[189] under a contract, but has so far departed from the contractual terms that a claim for the contract price is excluded. Thus, if a builder produces a building materially different from that ordered, he may have no claim directly under his contract, but if the employer does not choose to reject the building he is at least liable *quantum lucratus*.[190] And where a commission agent had broken a term in his contract under which he was precluded from acting for

---

[182] See Evans-Jones, *Unjustified Enrichment* (2003), Vol.1, paras 1.99–1.100, 6.97–6.123; S. Miller, "Unjustified Enrichment and Failed Contracts" in Zimmermann, Visser and Reid (eds), *Mixed Legal Systems in Comparative Perspective: Property and Obligations in Scotland and South Africa* (2004); Hogg, *Obligations* (2006), Ch.4, Pt II.

[183] See *Dollar Land (Cumbernauld) Ltd v C.I.N. Properties Ltd*, 1998 S.C. (HL) 90; followed in *Castle Inns (Stirling) Ltd v Clark Contracts Ltd*, 2006 S.C.L.R. 663. See also *Compagnie Commerciale Andre SA v Artibell Shipping Co Ltd (No.2)*, 2001 S.C. 653; *Wiltshier Construction (Scotland) Ltd v Drumchapel Housing Cooperative Ltd*, 2003 S.L.T. 443; *Hanover (Scotland) Housing Association Ltd v Reid*, 2006 S.L.T. 518 (deed of conditions); and *Duncan v American Express*, 2009 S.L.T. 112.

[184] *Boyd & Forrest v G. and S. W. Ry*, 1915 S.C. (HL) 20 at 22–3, per Earl Loreburn.

[185] *Wilson v Wallace* (1859) 21 D. 507; *Tharsis Co v McElroy* (1875) 5 R. (HL) 171.

[186] As in Bell, *Principles*, s.539.

[187] See *Landless v Wilson* (1880) 8 R. 289; *Avintair Ltd v Ryder Airline Services Ltd*, 1994 S.C. 270 (criticised by G.D.L. Cameron, "Consensus in dissensus", 1995 S.L.T. (News) 132); *E.R.D.C. Construction Ltd v H.M. Love & Co*, 1994 S.C. 620.

[188] *Anderson v Anderson* (1869) 8 M. 157; *Mellor v Beardmore*, 1927 S.C. 597. Query whether *Shilliday v Smith*, 1998 S.C. 725 was not also a case of implied contract (see W.D.H. Sellar, "Shilliday v Smith: unjust enrichment through the looking glass?" (2001) 5 Edin. L.R. 80).

[189] *Devos Gebroeder N.V. v Sunderland Sportswear*, 1990 S.C. 291.

[190] *Ramsay v Brand* (1898) 25 R. 1212; (1898) 35 S.L.R. 927; *Forrest v Scottish County Investment Co*, 1916 S.C. (HL) 28.

rival traders, it was held that he could not recover commission for the period in which he was thus in breach of his contract but observed that he might have a claim for unjustified enrichment on proof that his employers had benefited by the business he introduced.[191] (2) Where goods have been supplied or work done in circumstances where a direct contractual claim for the price must fail, either because the defender could plead his lack of contractual power[192] or because the contract is one which has been declared by statute to be void,[193] a claim for the value of the goods or work is generally relevant.

BENEVOLENT INTERVENTION (NEGOTIORUM GESTIO)

Benevolent intervention in another's affairs—Where one person acts on **24.24** another's behalf without his agreement, there is no contract between the parties, but in certain circumstances a regime of reciprocal rights and obligations may arise. These are dealt with here under the heading of benevolent intervention in another's affairs (traditionally known as *negotiorum gestio*, that is, literally, management of affairs).[194] The law of agency deals with cases where one person acts on behalf of another by agreement.[195] The principal elements of benevolent intervention are: (1) unauthorised administration by a person (the intervener) of another's affairs; (2) that other being absent, unaware of the administration, or incapable; (3) the intervener acting for the good of the other person but with the intention of recovering the expenses of the administration from that person; and (4) the administration was useful when first carried out.[196]

Unauthorised administration of another's affairs—A benevolent intervener is **24.25** then a person who, without any regular authority, intervenes to manage the affairs of another who, temporarily or permanently, is unable to manage them himself by reason of absence, ignorance or incapacity such as mental disability.[197] If the person whose affairs are managed is aware of the situation with which the manager is trying to deal and has never the less chosen not to act, the intervener has no claim under the principles of benevolent intervention and must make any claim under enrichment law.[198] The intervener's intervention must be of at least initial utility to the person whose affairs are managed (the principal control on becoming liable to officious intermeddlers with other people's business).[199] In earlier

---

[191] *Graham v United Turkey Red Co*, 1922 S.C. 533; *Abrahams v Campbell*, 1911 S.C. 353. On the cases cited in this and the preceding note, see H. MacQueen, "Contract, unjustified enrichment and concurrent liability: a Scots perspective" Acta Juridica (1997), at pp.190–2.

[192] See Sale of Goods Act 1979 s.3; *Sinclair v Brougham* [1914] A.C. 398, per Lord Dunedin at 434–5; *Stonehaven Burgh Council v Kincardineshire CC*, 1939 S.C. 760.

[193] *Cuthbertson v Lowes* (1870) 8 M. 1073, distinguished in *Jamieson v Watt's Tr*, 1950 S.C. 265, where the contract was illegal. See also *Duncan v Motherwell Bridge and Engineering Co*, 1952 S.C. 131.

[194] The terminology used here is drawn from C. von Bar, *Principles of European Law: Benevolent Intervention in Another's Affairs* (Sellier European Law Publishers, 2006).

[195] See Ch.18, above.

[196] See *Stair Memorial Encyclopaedia*, Vol.15, para.95.

[197] Stair, I, 8, 3; Erskine, III, 3, 52–3; Pothier, *Traité du contrat de mandat* (appendix); Kames, *Principles of Equity* (1825), i, 179 et seq.; Bell, *Principles*, s.540; Zimmermann, *The Law of Obligations* (1990), Ch.14 and pp.875 et seq.

[198] *Garriock v Walker* (1873) 1 R. 100; *North British Railway Co Ltd v Tod* (1893) 9 Sh. Ct Rep. 326. See, e.g. paras 24.03, 24.16–24.19, above.

[199] *Stair Memorial Encyclopaedia*, Vol.15, paras 117–22.

editions of this book it was said that the situation had to be one where it is reasonable to assume that authority would have been given had the circumstances rendered it possible to apply for it but this view has been persuasively challenged.[200] The administration can range from the preservation of property, such as putting a lost or abandoned car in a garage,[201] or putting goods in danger in a war-zone into a place of safety,[202] or repairing or improving a house,[203] to the payment of the debts of the person whose affairs are being managed[204]; but the concept has yet to be applied to the preservation of the life, health or well-being of the administration beneficiary. Such claims are admitted in other jurisdictions[205] and there would seem no reason in principle why it could not be so. The position is held by a salvor[206] and by one who acts on behalf of an absentee[207] or of a person who has become insane.[208]

24.26 Intervener's expenses claim—The intervener is entitled to be reimbursed for any initially useful expenditure incurred by him in the proper course of administration, even although it has not ultimately proved beneficial,[209] and to be relieved of all liabilities. On the other hand, an intervener is never entitled to recover more than his expenses and outlays.[210]

24.27 Intervener's extended expenses claim restricted to enrichment—In some cases (sometimes called impure gestio in the older authorities) in which the normal requirements of a benevolent intervention are not all met, an intervener has a claim to recover his expenses not exceeding any enrichment which may have accrued to the other party as a result of the intervention. There is institutional authority for the proposition that a party who manages another's affairs with a view only of his own interests has such a claim.[211] A similar claim for expenses capped by the other party's enrichment may be available to an intervener: (1) whose continued activity has been forbidden by the person whose affairs have been managed, although such a claim may be only for gains made through pre-prohibition expenditure[212]; (2) who has managed another's affairs in the good faith belief that they are his own[213]; or (3) who is managing the affairs of another not of full age.[214]

---

[200] See *Stair Memorial Encyclopaedia*, Vol.15, para.122.

[201] *S.M.T. Sales & Services Co v Motor & General Finance Co*, 1954 S.L.T. (Sh. Ct) 107.

[202] *Kolbin & Son v United Shipping Co*, 1931 S.C. (HL) 128.

[203] *Paterson v Greig* (1862) 24 D. 1370; *Fernie v Robertson* (1871) 9 M. 437.

[204] *Reid v Lord Ruthven* (1918) 55 S.L.R. 616.

[205] *Stair Memorial Encyclopaedia*, Vol.15, para.102. The rules on benevolent intervention might thus usefully supplement the protective provisions of the Adults with Incapacity (Scotland) Act 2000 as amended: see below, para.44.07.

[206] See paras 22.43–22.48.

[207] *Bannatine's Trs v Cunninghame* (1872) 10 M. 319, see *S.M.T. Sales & Services Co v Motor & General Finance Co*, 1954 S.L.T. (Sh. Ct) 107.

[208] *Dunbar v Wilson & Dunlop's Tr* (1887) 15 R. 210.

[209] Stair, I, 8, 3.

[210] *Stair Memorial Encyclopaedia*, Vol.15, paras 125–8.

[211] Bankton, I, 9, 27; Erskine, III, 3, 53; and see *Stair Memorial Encyclopaedia*, Vol.15, para.138.

[212] See *Stair Memorial Encyclopaedia*, Vol.15, para.139.

[213] The only authority for this proposition in Scots as distinct from Roman law is Hume, *Lectures*, Vol.3, pp.176–7. See discussion in *Stair Memorial Encyclopaedia*, Vol.15, para.140.

[214] *Stair Memorial Encyclopaedia*, Vol.15, para.141; see e.g. *Paterson v Greig* (1862) 24 D. 1370.

Liability of intervener—The intervener must account for his intromissions, and **24.28** is liable for any loss caused by his failure to exercise the care and diligence which a prudent man would have shown in relation to his own property.[215] If the intervener is enriched by his intervention, he is liable for that gain to the person whose affairs are managed.[216] A person reasonably and properly employed by an intervener, as, for example, a solicitor, has a direct right of action for his account against the party whose affairs have been managed.[217]

FURTHER READING

Blackie, J.W.G. and Farlam, I., "Enrichment by Act of the Party Enriched"; Miller, S., "Unjustified Enrichment and Failed Contracts"; Whitty, N.R. and Visser, D., "Unjustified Enrichment"; and Whitty, N.R. and van Zyl, D., "Unauthorized Management of Affairs (Negotiorum Gestio)", all in Zimmermann, R., Visser, D. and Reid, K.G.C. (eds), *Mixed Legal Systems in Comparative Perspective: Property and Obligations in Scotland and South Africa* (Oxford: Oxford University Press: 2004).

du Plessis, J.E., *Compulsion and Restitution* (Edinburgh: Stair Society, 2004), Vol.51.

du Plessis, J.E. "Towards a Rational Structure of Liability for Unjustified Enrichment: Thoughts from Two Mixed Jurisdictions" (2005) 122 S.A.L.J. 142.

Evans-Jones, R., *Unjustified Enrichment Volume 1: Enrichment by Deliberate Conferral: Condictio* (Edinburgh: W. Green, 2003).

Evans-Jones, R., "Searching for 'Imposed' Enrichment in Improvements— Classifications and General Enrichment Actions in Mixed Systems: Scotland and South Africa" [2008] 16 Restitution L.R. 18.

Hogg, M., *Obligations*, 2nd edn (Edinburgh: Avizandum, 2006), Chs 4 and 6.

Reid, K.G.C., "Unjustified Enrichment and Property Law", 1994 Jur. Rev. 167.

Lord Rodger, "Recovering Payments Under Void Contracts in Scots Law"', in Swadling, W. and Jones, G. (eds), *The Search for Principle: Essays in Honour of Lord Goff of Chieveley* (Oxford: Oxford University Press, 2000).

Scottish Law Commission, *Recovery of Benefits Conferred under Error of Law* (HMSO, 1993), Scot. Law Com. Discussion Paper No.95.

Visser, D., *Unjustified Enrichment* (Cape Town: Juta and Co, 2008).

Whitty, N.R., "Indirect Enrichment in Scots Law", 1994 Jur. Rev. 200 and 239 (two parts).

Whitty, N.R., "Negotiorum Gestio", *Stair Memorial Encyclopaedia*, Vol.15 (1996), paras 87–143.

Wolffe, J., "Enrichment by Improvements in Scots Law"; and MacQueen, H.L., "Payment of Another's Debt", both in Zimmermann, R. and Johnston, D. (eds), *The Comparative Law of Unjustified Enrichment* (Cambridge: Cambridge University Press, 2002).

---

[215] *Kolbin & Son v United Shipping Co*, 1931 S.C. (HL) 128 at 139, per Lord Atkin.
[216] *Stair Memorial Encyclopaedia*, Vol.1, para.133.
[217] *Fernie v Robertson* (1871) 9 M. 437; *Dunbar v Wilson & Dunlop's Tr.* (1887) 15 R. 210.

SECTION D
DELICT

CHAPTER 25

REPARATION: GENERAL PRINCIPLES

Terminology—Reparation is the term used in Scots law for the obligation **25.01**
arising from wrongful conduct. Reparation refers specifically to the obligation
to repair the damage done. Damages, however, is not always the remedy sought
and is not the primary remedy for a number of specific wrongs.[1] The modern
tendency is to refer to this area of law as delict. The term delict refers to the
wrong rather than the remedy so the modern preference may indicate the shift
that is said to have taken place from a response based classification to one
based on events.[2] Bell drew a distinction between delicts associated with
intentional conduct, and quasi-delict, which he associated with negligence.[3]
Quasi-delict had been a classification under which Justinian had placed four
praetorian actions so Bell's use of the term was novel in Scotland.[4] While the
presence or otherwise of the Roman quasi-delicts in Scots law remains a matter of
controversy, reference to quasi-delict as a category of Scots law is now seldom if
ever made. Bell's division, between delicts of intention and negligence, stands
however when the structure of delict is discussed; negligence, it is said, has its
own niche.[5]

Damnum injuria datum—It has been argued[6] that delictual liability in Scots law **25.02**
may be subsumed under the single general principle, *damnum injuria datum*, that
is, loss caused without legal justification, unlawfully or wrongfully. The principle
has also been expressed *damnum culpa datum*,[7] loss caused culpably, that is by
fault, fault being another way in which *injuria* is manifested. All three elements—
loss, wrongfulness, and causation—must be present before liability in reparation

---

[1] See D. Visser and N. Whitty, "The Structure of the Law of Delict" in K. Reid and R. Zimmermann
(eds), *A History of Private Law in Scotland, Vol.II: Obligations* (Oxford University Press, 2000),
pp.470–472 on the growth of interdict.

[2] See Visser and Whitty, "The Structure of the Law of Delict" in Reid and Zimmermann (eds),
A History of Private Law in Scotland, Vol.II: Obligations (2000), pp.439–445.

[3] Bell, *Principles*, s.525. See Visser and Whitty, "The Structure of the Law of Delict" in Reid and
Zimmermann (eds), *A History of Private Law in Scotland, Vol.II: Obligations* (2000), pp.451–452.

[4] Visser and Whitty, "The Structure of the Law of Delict" in Reid and Zimmermann (eds),
A History of Private Law in Scotland, Vol.II: Obligations (2000), p.451.

[5] Visser and Whitty, "The Structure of the Law of Delict" in Reid and Zimmermann (eds),
A History of Private Law in Scotland, Vol.II: Obligations (2000), p.452.

[6] See Visser and Whitty, "The Structure of the Law of Delict" in Reid and Zimmermann (eds), *A
History of Private Law in Scotland, Vol.II: Obligations* (2000), pp.437, 456–461; H. MacQueen and
W.D.H. Sellar, "Negligence", in Reid and Zimmermann (eds), *A History of Private Law in Scotland,
Vol.II: Obligations* (2000), pp.517–519, 521–526.

[7] H. McKechnie, "Reparation" in Lord Dunedin (ed.), *The Encyclopaedia of the Laws of Scotland*
(Edinburgh: W. Green & Son, 1930), Vol.12, para.1061.

arises. There can be no delictual liability for *damnum absque injuria* (*damnum sine injuria*), that is, loss caused without wrongful conduct.[8]

25.03 Wrongs—Stair provided for the general action for damage and interest.[9] At the time Stair wrote, assythment was the only action appropriate to personal injury and liability in negligence was yet to be developed. It has been argued that, in positing a general action in respect of loss wrongfully caused, Stair was ahead of his time, but he created space for future development as reparation for injury or loss caused negligently came to be sought through the general action.[10] As noted, negligence is generally accorded its own niche within the structure of delict and is considered separately from intentional delicts. It is doubtful, however, whether negligence in Scots law is accurately described as a delict.[11] Negligence is not a specific wrong; in a system where the right to reparation for harm wrongfully caused is said to be general, negligence may be seen as one way of acting culpably or wrongfully so as to give rise to liability. In addition to innominate wrongs that could be brought under the general action, Stair also noted delicts "of a special name and nature". It has been argued that it was Stair's view that liability in respect of these nominate delicts of intention could also be brought within the general principle.[12] Thus, while specific delicts provide a ground of action, and some have features, requirements for establishment or defences peculiar to themselves, an action may be grounded generally on wrongful conduct. Delictual liability is not dependent upon bringing "the facts of the claim within the boundaries of an existing claim".[13] There is no exhaustive list of nominate delicts.[14]

25.04 Interests—The wrong, nominate or innominate, gives rise to the obligation to make reparation, but for liability the loss must also be present and so delict may be presented according to the types of loss or interests recognised by law as reparable and thus protected against wrongful invasion.[15] There is no single accepted way of ordering reparable or protected interests, but the list is not fluid in the same sense as the list of wrongs. The law is flexible so that unprecedented wrongs may be reparable, but an interest will remain unprotected until, as a matter of policy, the decision is made to protect it.[16] The presentation of delict according to protected interests suggests groupings of nominate delicts along with relevant statutory regimes that are applicable to distinct interests. This approach also allows intentional and negligent invasions of specific interests to be contrasted, but the general tendency as noted is to present negligence separately. Protected

---

[8] Bell, *Principles*, s.553; also see Visser and Whitty, "The Structure of the Law of Delict" in Reid and Zimmermann (eds), *A History of Private Law in Scotland, Vol.II: Obligations* (2000), p.458.

[9] Stair, I, 9, 5.

[10] MacQueen and Sellar, "Negligence" in Reid and Zimmermann (eds), *A History of Private Law in Scotland, Vol.II: Obligations* (2000), pp.517–519, 521–526.

[11] MacQueen and Sellar, "Negligence" in Reid and Zimmermann (eds), *A History of Private Law in Scotland, Vol.II: Obligations* (2000), p.518.

[12] MacQueen and Sellar, "Negligence" in Reid and Zimmermann (eds), *A History of Private Law in Scotland, Vol.II: Obligations* (2000), pp.523–524; Visser and Whitty, "The Structure of the Law of Delict" in Reid and Zimmermann (eds), *A History of Private Law in Scotland, Vol.II: Obligations* (2000), pp.436–438.

[13] K. Norrie, "Intentional Delicts" in Reid and Zimmermann (eds), *A History of Private Law in Scotland, Vol.II: Obligations* (2000), p.479. See also, e.g. *Henderson v Chief Constable of Fife Police*, 1988 S.L.T. 361, discussed at para.29.31, below.

[14] *Micosta v Shetland Islands Council*, 1986 S.L.T. 193 at 198.

[15] See Stair, I, 4, 4.

[16] *Micosta v Shetland Islands Council*, 1986 S.L.T. 193 at 198.

interests may be brought under four broad headings: protection of the person, protection of liberty, protection of reputation and protection of interests in property. These headings may be further sub divided, either according to specific interests, e.g. the right to exclusive possession of heritable property; or according to specific wrongs, like trespass.[17]

Culpa—Culpa is understood as a generic term for fault.[18] This is in contrast to **25.05** common usage during the nineteenth and earlier twentieth centuries when it was often used as a synonym for negligence. Bell's twofold division between intentional and negligent conduct has become the classic way in which fault is presented in Scots law. Negligence may be understood broadly as failure to take sufficient care in circumstances where the law recognises a duty to take care. The description of intention, on the other hand, poses some difficulty. There are two principal views of intention.[19] First it can be said to be indicated by the deliberate performance of an act which has, as its normal and natural consequence, harm to others; thus, in the majority of instances in which the motive of the defender is irrelevant, the lack of any intention to cause harm will not afford a defence. Secondly, intention may refer to the specific aim of causing injury or loss to others, that is, *animus iniurandi*. It has been suggested that affront-based delicts require intention to injure while all other delicts may be committed intentionally, recklessly or negligently.[20] The present text has always dealt with this issue by separating intention from motive. Motive is generally irrelevant to delictual liability, but there are exceptions, notably in conspiracy, inducing breach of contract and in use of land in *aemulationem vicini*.[21] The concept of culpa has been judicially considered in *Kennedy v Glenbelle*.[22]

Culpa in specific contexts—It has been said that: **25.06**

> "the law of delict would be greatly improved if it could be determined what exactly the concept of fault entails and how it plays a role in the various categories of delict".[23]

Without denying the scope for useful debate and clarification, some observations may be made on the way in which culpa, or more broadly the requirement of *injuria*, may be met in specific contexts. It will be seen that it is necessary to employ the various nuances of *injuria*. Negligence as a form of fault is well

---

[17] See Visser and Whitty, "The Structure of the Law of Delict" in Reid and Zimmermann (eds), *A History of Private Law in Scotland, Vol.II: Obligations* (2000), pp.464–476 for discussion on the systematisation of delict in general.

[18] Affirmed in *Kennedy v Glenbelle*, 1996 S.C. 95; 1996 S.L.T. 1186.

[19] See Norrie, "Intentional Delicts" in Reid and Zimmermann (eds), *A History of Private Law in Scotland, Vol.II: Obligations* (2000), pp.478–480.

[20] Norrie, "Intentional Delicts" in Reid and Zimmermann (eds), *A History of Private Law in Scotland, Vol.II: Obligations* (2000), p.480.

[21] Visser and Whitty, "The Structure of the Law of Delict" in Reid and Zimmermann (eds), *A History of Private Law in Scotland, Vol.II: Obligations* (2000), p.468 suggest *aemulatio vicini* might form the basis for a wider doctrine of abuse of rights, but cf. E. Reid, "Strange Gods in the Twenty First Century: The Doctrine of Aemulatio Vicini" in E. Reid and D.L. Carey Millar (eds), *A Mixed Legal System in Transition* (Edinburgh: Edinburgh University Press, 2005); E. Reid, "Abuse of Rights in Scots Law" (2008) 2 Edin. L.R. 129–157.

[22] *Kennedy v Glenbelle*, 1996 S.C. 95; 1996 S.L.T. 1186.

[23] Visser and Whitty, "The Structure of the Law of Delict" in Reid and Zimmermann (eds), *A History of Private Law in Scotland, Vol.II: Obligations* (2000), p.486.

understood as failure to observe the standard of care required in the circumstances, that is, breach of the duty of care. Liability in defamation is founded on malice, but malice is presumed from the defamatory capacity of the statement complained of and need only be proved where the statement attracts qualified privilege.[24] Malice is also the basis for liability in verbal injury, but there is no equivalent presumption.[25] Proof of malice in defamation may be achieved by one of two methods. Either specific intent to harm must be shown or express malice will be inferred where the statement was made without honest belief in its truth or in reckless disregard of the truth.[26] Malice in the sense of spite or intent to harm must be proved in an action grounded on *aemulatio vicini*.[27] Liability in assault is based on intention, either in the sense that harm is intended or in the sense that the act is done deliberately knowing that harm is likely to occur or recklessly in disregard of the consequences.[28] Causing loss by unlawful means requires unlawful behaviour whereas liability for conspiracy may arise through the employment of lawful or unlawful means, but the concern is with the predominant joint motive to harm. Knowingly inducing a breach of contract is wrongful.[29] Fraud is constituted by intention to deceive.[30] It has been suggested that the right correlating to the wrong of fraud is a right not to be deceived,[31] but the interests damaged by fraud are normally property or economic interests, either directly or indirectly though inducement to contract. Fraud is also the basis for liability in the older nominate delict of seduction.[32] Occupation of property without right is the basis of intrusion and encroachment whereas unlawful deprivation of possession is the basis in ejection[33] and spuilzie with reference to heritable and moveable property respectively.[34] Liability for damages for trespass poses some difficulty; in contrast to England no damages are available in respect of a bare trespass, and it is necessary to show consequential loss, usually damage to property. Where property has been damaged the usual cause has been straying animals and so cases have been determined on rules specific to animals.[35] Liability in damages in an action grounded on nuisance requires intention, in the sense of a deliberate act done in the knowledge that harm will result or recklessly in disregard of the likely

---

[24] See para.29.02, below.

[25] See para.29.22, below.

[26] See para.29.12, below.

[27] *Dewar v Fraser* (1767) Mor. 12803; *Campbell v Muir*, 1908 S.C. 387; *More v Boyle*, 1967 S.L.T. (Sh. Ct) 38. See further, N. Whitty, "Nuisance", *Stair Memorial Encyclopedia* (Reissue) (2001), paras 33–36.

[28] See E. Reid, *Personality, Confidentiality and Privacy in Scots Law* (Edinburgh: W. Green, 2010), para.2.10. See also *Reid v Mitchell* (1885) 12 R. 1129.

[29] See G. Gordon, "The Economic Delicts" in J.M. Thomson (ed.), *Delict* (Edinburgh: W. Green), Ch.15.

[30] Erskine, III, I, 16.

[31] *Gloag and Henderson: The Law of Scotland*, 12th edn, edited by Lord Coulsfield and H.L. MacQueen (Edinburgh: W. Green, 2007), para.26–02.

[32] See Norrie, "Intentional Delicts" in Reid and Zimmermann (eds), *A History of Private Law in Scotland, Vol.II: Obligations* (2000), pp.512–513.

[33] See Norrie, "Intentional Delicts" in Reid and Zimmermann (eds), *A History of Private Law in Scotland, Vol.II: Obligations* (2000), pp.491–493; G. Cameron, "Trespass" in Thomson (ed.), *Delict*, para.14.116.

[34] Norrie, "Intentional Delicts" in Reid and Zimmermann (eds), *A History of Private Law in Scotland, Vol.II: Obligations* (2000), pp.488–491; D.L. Carey Millar with D. Irvine, *Corporeal Moveables in Scots Law*, 2nd edn (Edinburgh: W. Green, 2005), Ch.10.

[35] Cameron, "Trespass" in Thomson (ed.), *Delict*, paras 14.131–14.133; K. Reid, *The Law of Property in Scotland* (Edinburgh: LexisNexis, 1996), paras 186–190.

consequences.[36] It is doubtful whether liability in respect of nuisance can arise through negligence; indeed it has been argued strongly that negligent nuisance is an incoherent concept.[37] It must be noted that the requirement of culpa in particular refers to liability in reparation. Where other remedies are sought, different principles may operate. It must also be noted that statutory regimes may impose their own requirements.[38]

Judicial consideration of culpa in *Kennedy v Glenbelle*—Lord President Hope **25.07** approved a model of culpa used by Whitty for his treatment of nuisance in the *Stair Memorial Encyclopaedia*.[39] Lord Hope listed the categories of culpa as: malice, intention, recklessness, negligence and conduct causing a special risk of abnormal damage.[40] Lord Hope did not expand on the meaning of malice, but he characterised intention as "deliberate in the knowledge that his action would result in harm to the other party", and recklessness as action of a kind likely to cause harm carried out with "no regard to the question whether. . . it would have that result".[41] The theory underlying this model of culpa is a continuum in which the form of culpa changes as harm to the other party moves from being the object of action (malice) through being substantially certain (intention) to being highly likely (recklessness) to being a risk that can be avoided with sufficient care (negligence).[42] It can be seen that malice and intention in this model correspond to the two principal meanings of intention described above.[43] Lord Hope considered that "conduct giving rise to a special risk of abnormal damage" might be "just another example of recklessness".[44] When culpa takes this form "it may not be necessary to prove a specific fault as fault is necessarily implied in the result".[45] If culpa is to be viewed in terms of a continuum then it follows that the lines of demarcation between the various categories may not always be clearly drawn. Negligence will shade towards intention somewhere in the region of recklessness. There is, however, judicial guidance on the difference between intention and negligence in dicta considered by Lord Hope. So, for example, in *Edinburgh Railway Access and Property Co v John Ritchie & Co*[46] Lord Low stated:

> "If the necessary or natural result of the blasting was to cause structural damage to the pursuers' property, although there was no want of care and skill in the conduct of the operations, then the defenders were not, in my judgment, entitled to carry on the operations at all, because no man is entitled to cause an explosion in his property, the necessary or natural result of which is to blow down or injure his neighbour's house. On the other hand, if injury to the pursuers' buildings was not a necessary or natural result of the blasting,

---

[36] *Kennedy v Glenbelle*, 1996 S.C. 95; 1996 S.L.T. 1186.

[37] Visser and Whitty, "The Structure of the Law of Delict" in Reid and Zimmermann (eds), *A History of Private Law in Scotland, Vol.II: Obligations* (2000), paras 17, 77, 89, 104–106.

[38] See Ch.29, below.

[39] at 1188L; Whitty, "Nuisance", *Stair Memorial Encyclopaedia* (1988), paras 2087, 2089; see paras 87, 89 in 2001 edition. The origin of the model is the Second Restatement of the Law of Torts, American Law Institute 1979.

[40] *Kennedy v Glenbelle*, 1996 S.C. 95; 1996 S.L.T. 1186 at 1188L.

[41] *Kennedy v Glenbelle*, 1996 S.C. 95; 1996 S.L.T. 1186 at 1189L.

[42] Whitty, "Nuisance", *Stair Memorial Encyclopaedia* (2001), para.89.

[43] See para.25.05 above.

[44] *Kennedy v Glenbelle*, 1996 S.C. 95; 1996 S.L.T. 1186 at 1189L.

[45] *Kennedy v Glenbelle*, 1996 S.C. 95; 1996 S.L.T. 1186, per Lord President Hope at 1188L.

[46] *Edinburgh Railway Access and Property Co v John Ritchie & Co* (1903) 5 F 299.

but injury in fact resulted, the inference is that the operation was negligently or unskilfully conducted."[47]

The same distinction may be found in a dictum of Lord Justice Clerk Moncreiff:

"A good deal has been said as to the necessity of proving culpa. I think that culpa does lie at the root of the matter. If a man puts upon his land a new combination of materials, which he knows, or ought to know, are of a dangerous nature, then either due care will prevent injury, in which case he is liable if injury occurs for not taking that due care, or else no precautions will prevent injury, in which case he is liable for his original act in placing the materials upon the ground."[48]

25.08 Strict liability at common law—There is long standing authority to the effect that a delictual action for reparation at common law can only be sustained on the basis of averments of either negligence or some other form of culpa.[49] Possible exceptions have included liability for damage caused by *animals ferae naturae*, but this is now put on a statutory footing and the old rules abrogated.[50] In Roman law liability under the *actio de positis vel suspensis*, that is for things hung or suspended and under the *actio de effusis veldeiectis*, that is for things poured or thrown, was strict.[51] While it has been contended from time to time that these actions have passed into Scots law, there is no case in which there has been liability without culpa.[52] A recent attempt to revive the strict liability that attached to *nautae, caupones et stabularii* failed.[53] The English law rule in *Rylands v Fletcher*[54] was at first perceived in Scotland in terms of inferred fault.[55] When its true nature, as re-stating a medieval rule that a man acts at his peril, was revealed in *Read v Lyons*,[56] the Scottish reaction was swift.[57] By this time, however, the idea that liability in nuisance might be strict had to some extent taken hold, assisted by the ambivalent Scottish case of *Kerr v Earl of Orkney*.[58] The issue was

---

[47] *Edinburgh Railway Access and Property Co v John Ritchie & Co* (1903) 5 F 299, per Lord Low at 302, cited in *Kennedy v Glenbelle*, 1996 S.C. 95; 1996 S.L.T. 1186 at 1189C.

[48] *Chalmers v Dixon* (1876) 3 R. 461 at 464, cited in *Kennedy v Glenbelle*, 1996 S.C. 95; 1996 S.L.T. 1186 at 1189A. See also *Hester v MacDonald*, 1961 S.L.T. 414 at 424, per Lord Guthrie, cited in *Kennedy v Glenbelle*, 1996 S.C. 95; 1996 S.L.T. 1186 at 1189E; *Noble's Trustees v Economic Forestry (Scotland) Ltd*, 1988 S.L.T. 662 at 664 A–B, per Lord Jauncey, cited in *Kennedy v Glenbelle*, 1996 S.C. 95; 1996 S.L.T. 1186 at 1189F–G.

[49] e.g. *Campbell v Kennedy* (1864) 3 M. 121, per L.P. McNeill at 126, cited in *Kennedy v Glenbelle*, 1996 S.C. 95; 1996 S.L.T. 1186 at 1189A.

[50] Animals (Scotland) Act 1987 s.1(8).

[51] See Justinian, *Institutes*, 4.5.

[52] See e.g. *Gray v Dunlop* (1954) 70 Sh. Ct Rep. 270; 1954 S.L.T. (Sh. Ct) 75; *McDyer v Celtic Football and Athletic Co Ltd*, 2000 S.L.T. 736. For detailed consideration see W.M. Gordon, "Roman Quasi-delicts and Scots law" in W.M. Gordon (ed.) *Roman Law, Scots Law, and Legal History: Selected Essays* (Edinburgh: Edinburgh University Press, 2007), Ch.13.

[53] Shipowners, innkeepers and stablekeepers; *Drake v Dow*, 2006 G.W.D. 21–461. For analysis see P. DuPlessis, "Innkeeper's Liability for Loss Suffered by Guests: Drake v. Dow" (2007) 11 Edin. L.R. 89–94.

[54] *Rylands v Fletcher* (1868) L.R. 3 HL 330.

[55] Specifically, negligence. Bell, *Principles*, s.970.

[56] *Read v Lyons* [1947] A.C. 156.

[57] *McLauchlan v Craig*, 1948 S.L.T. 483, per Lord President Cooper at 490–491.

[58] *Kerr v Earl of Orkney* (1857) 20 D. 298. For literature supporting the idea of liability without fault see e.g. W.A. Elliott, "What is Culpa?", 1954 J.R. 6; K.W.B. Middleton, "Liability Without Fault", 1960 J.R. 72; G. MacCormack, "Culpa in the Scots Law of Reparation", 1974 J.R. 13; D.M. Walker, *Law of Delict in Scotland*, 2nd edn (Edinburgh: W. Green, 1981), pp.285–295; D.M. Walker, "Strict Liability in Scotland" (1954) 66 J.R. 231.

only resolved finally in *RHM Bakeries v Strathclyde Regional Council*[59] in which Lord Fraser extirpated *Rylands* from the law of Scotland and authoritatively interpreted older Scots authorities in terms of culpa.[60]

Lord Fraser did however suggest, with reference to *Caledonian Railway Co v Greenock Corporation*,[61] that there might be an exception in the case of harm resulting from the alteration of the course of a natural stream.[62] The possibility of this exception has been noted subsequently, in *GA Estates Ltd v Caviapen Trustees Ltd (No.1)*[63] and in *Kennedy v Glenbelle*,[64] though in neither case did the decision proceed on that basis. Strict liability was pled, though not relevantly, in *Viewpoint Housing Association Ltd v The City of Edinburgh Council*.[65] In brief, the view that liability in *Caledonian Railway Co v Greenock Corporation* was determined without proof of fault is misconceived and derives partly from the way in which the case was reported.[66] Only in the Appeal Cases report[67] are the speeches delivered in the House of Lords rendered in full while the opinions of the Lord Ordinary and of the bench of the Inner House are unreported. It is made clear in the opinion of the Lord Ordinary, Lord Dewar, that the pursuers undertook to prove negligence and did so to the satisfaction of his Lordship.[68] The speeches in the House of Lords are chiefly significant for imposing on persons making alterations to natural watercourses such as diverting, culverting or damming, a standard of sufficient provision to cope with extraordinary levels of rainfall.[69] It was held that the appellants' provision was insufficient to cope with foreseeable levels of rainfall let alone the extraordinary[70]; moreover they appeared to have neglected to consult available rainfall data for the district.[71] To the extent that the culvert built by Greenock Corporation had not been constructed to the standard imposed by law, and foreseeable damage to property resulted from this, negligence is clear. The view that there was liability without fault is difficult to sustain.[72] Lord Shaw, however, went beyond negligence quoting from the opinion of Lord Dewar:

---

[59] *RHM Bakeries v Strathclyde Regional Council*, 1985 S.C. (HL) 17; 1985 S.L.T. 214.

[60] *RHM Bakeries v Strathclyde Regional Council*, 1985 S.C. (HL) 17; 1985 S.L.T. 214 at 217.

[61] *Caledonian Railway Co v Greenock Corporation*, 1917 2 S.L.T. 67; 1917 S.C. (HL) 56.

[62] *RHM Bakeries v Strathclyde Regional Council*, 1985 S.C. (HL) 17; 1985 S.L.T. 214 at 217, 218.

[63] *GA Estates Ltd v Caviapen Trustees Ltd (No.1)*, 1993 S.L.T. 1037.

[64] *Kennedy v Glenbelle*, 1996 S.C. 95; 1996 S.L.T. 1186 at 1188I.

[65] *Viewpoint Housing Association Ltd v The City of Edinburgh Council*, 2007 S.L.T. 772.

[66] This argument is developed in G. Cameron, "Strict Liability and the Rule in Caledonian Railway v Greenock Corporation" (2000) 5 *Scottish Law and Practice Quarterly*, 356 – 375.

[67] *Caledonian Railway Co v Greenock Corporation* [1917] A.C. 556.

[68] Unreported opinion of the Lord Ordinary (Dewar), HL Appeal Cases 1917 Vol.656, 108 A–B. See also 101–102, 110D–111A.

[69] *Caledonian Railway Co v Greenock Corporation*, 1917 S.C. (HL) 56, per Lord Chancellor Findlay at 61–62, per Lord Shaw at 65–66, per Lord Wrenbury at 67, settling an issue left open in *Fletcher v Smith* [1877] 2 App Cas 781, per Lord Penzance at 787 and affirming dicta in *Tennant v Earl of Glasgow* (1864) 2 M. (HL) 23, per Lord Chancellor Westbury at 26. See also, *Samuel v Edinburgh & Glasgow Railway Co* (1850) 13 D. 312, per Lord Cockburn at 314; *Kerr v Earl of Orkney*, 1857 20 D. 298, per Lord Ardmillan at 300; *Pirie v Aberdeen Magistrates* (1871) 9 M. 412, per Lord Gifford at 417.

[70] *Caledonian Railway Co v Greenock Corporation*, 1917 S.C. (HL) 56, per Lord Dunedin at 65. See also [1917] A.C. 556, per Lord Shaw at 578 (unreported in S.C. and S.L.T.).

[71] Unreported opinion of the Lord Ordinary, 101–102.

[72] Culpability is further supported by the fact that there had been a previous instance of damage through flooding attributable to the corporation's works in response to which no remedial measures had been implemented. Unreported opinion of the Lord Ordinary, 110D–111A.

"I think it is out of the question for them [Greenock Corporation] to argue that they were entitled to bury the burn, which from time immemorial had carried flood water safely to the sea, and to alter the levels so that the public highway, leading on a descending gradient into the town, became the only means by which the flood water could escape."[73]

In short, the flooding was the natural and inevitable consequence of the appellants' deliberately conducted operation corresponding with the aspect of culpa discussed above.[74]

VICARIOUS LIABILITY

25.09　Vicarious liability[75]—A person may involve himself as a joint delinquent in a wrong which he did not personally commit by expressly authorising or subsequently ratifying the wrongful act, but his liability is then direct, not vicarious. In certain cases, however, the maxim *qui facit per alium facit per se*[76] is applied to produce vicarious liability for the act of another. It applies only to certain contractual relationships, namely those of partnership, principal and agent, employer and employee, and exceptionally to employer and independent contractor.[77] On principles of agency, vicarious liability for the negligence of the driver of a vehicle may attach to the owner of the vehicle if the driver was using it for the owner's purposes under delegation of a task or duty, but, where a car is owned by one spouse, vicarious liability for the negligent driving of the other spouse or someone driving on his behalf does not attach to the owner on the ground merely that the car is treated as a family car.[78] If the owner spouse is to be vicariously liable the car must have been used for his purposes under delegation of some task or duty. It is not sufficient that it was being used for the general purposes of the household.[79] A parent who, for the purpose of his child being conveyed as a passenger, lends his car to another may be liable for the driver's negligence if the proposal for use of the car originated from the parent but not if it originated from the child.[80] A club or other unincorporated association will not be vicariously liable to one of its members for injury to that member caused by the fault of another member or a servant of the club.[81] It has been suggested, obiter, that the vicarious liability of a principal for an agent may be less extensive than that of an employer for an employee in that

"it has never been laid down as a general proposition that all principals (as distinguished from employers) are liable for the negligence of their agents (as distinguished from servants) in the execution of their mandate".[82]

---

[73] Unreported opinion of the Lord Ordinary, 107B, quoted by Lord Shaw, [1917] A.C. 556 at 578–579. See also Lord Wrenbury, 1917 S.C. (HL) 56, 67 and 1917 A.C. 582–583.

[74] See para.25.07, above.

[75] See A. O'Donnell, "Liability for Delictual Actions" in Thomson (ed.), *Delict*, paras 4.23–4.75.

[76] "He who does something through the actions of another is treated as having done it himself".

[77] See para.25.15, below.

[78] *Morgans v Launchbury* [1973] A.C. 127; *Nottingham v Aldridge* [1971] 2 Q.B. 739.

[79] *Norwood v Nevan* [1981] R.T.R. 457.

[80] *Carberry v Davies* [1968] 1 W.L.R. 1103.

[81] *Harrison v West of Scotland Kart Club*, 2004 S.C. 615; *M v Hendron*, 2007 S.L.T. 467.

[82] *Mair v Wood*, 1948 S.C. 83 at 87, per Lord President Cooper.

It is thought, however, that the only material distinction between the two is that the right of an employer at all times to direct his employee how his work is to be done may extend the net of his vicarious liability wider than that of a principal for an agent, who is normally free of his principal's control as regards the manner in which he executes his mandate. As the same principles apply to vicarious liability both in agency and *locatio operarum*, it is proposed to treat both under the general head of employer and employee. The law in cases of partnership will be considered later.[83]

Vicarious liability: Employer and employee—It has long been established law **25.10** that an employer is vicariously liable for the wrongful or negligent acts of his employee committed within the general scope of his employment.[84] Without attempting to lay down an exhaustive definition of the phrase, "scope of employment" limits liability to those acts which the employee is required or entitled to do under his contract of service and to acts incidental thereto[85]—in other words, to acts related to the employer's business which he can only perform through an agent.[86] Where the phrase "course of employment" is used, it must be construed in this context in the same sense as "scope of employment", because the emphasis is upon the scope of the authority expressly or impliedly delegated to the servant or other agent by his employer. A principal is liable in damages to third parties

"for the frauds, deceits, concealments, misrepresentations, torts, negligences, and other malfeasances, or misfeasances, and omissions of duty, of his agent, in the course of his employment, although the principal did not authorise, or justify, or participate in, or indeed know of such misconduct, or even if he forbade the acts, or disapproved of them".[87]

"But although the principal is thus liable for the torts and negligences of his agent, yet we are to understand the doctrine with its just limitations, that the tort or negligence occurs in the course of the agency, for the principal is not liable for the torts or negligences of his agent beyond the scope of his agency, unless he has expressly authorised them to be done, or he has subsequently adopted them for his own use and benefit."[88]

Whether the agent is acting within the scope of his authority,[89] or the employee acting within the scope of his employment, is largely a question of fact.[90] An employer who entrusts the general management of his business to an employee is liable for the fraud of his employee on a client, although the employer obtained no benefit from it.[91] Conversely, benefit to the employer from the fraud of his employee will not render the employer liable if the employee had no authority to perform honestly the act which he performed

---

[83] See para.45.12, below.

[84] Bell, *Principles*, s.547.

[85] See *Bell v Blackwood Morton & Sons*, 1960 S.C. 11 at 26, per Lord Sorn.

[86] See *Neville v C. & A. Modes*, 1945 S.C. 175.

[87] J. Story, *Commentaries on the Law of Agency,* 9th edition (Boston: Little and Brown, 1882), s.452.

[88] *Story, Commentaries on the Law of Agency* (1882), s.456, quoted by Viscount Haldane in *Percy v Glasgow Corp*, 1922 S.C. (HL) 144 at 151, as applicable to a master and servant relationship.

[89] See *Laing v Provincial Homes Investment Co*, 1909 S.C. 812.

[90] *Kirby v N.C.B.*, 1958 S.C. 514 at 532, per Lord President Clyde; *Bell v Blackwood Morton & Sons*, 1960 S.C. 11.

[91] *Lloyd v Grace, Smith & Co* [1912] A.C. 716.

dishonestly.[92] Although the particular act which gives the cause of action may not be authorised, still if the act is done in the course of employment which is authorised, then the employer is liable for the act of the employee.[93]

The general rule, which is often difficult to apply, is that an employer is liable for authorised acts done in an unauthorised way but not for acts of a kind altogether unauthorised.[94] Thus, a general mandate of management involves the employer in liability for all acts, including criminal acts, of his manager done in that capacity.[95] But in more restricted fields of employment, the employer is not liable for acts which the employee was not employed to do.[96]

> "The criterion is whether the act which is unauthorised is so connected with acts which have been authorised that it may be regarded as a mode—although an improper mode—of doing the authorised act, as distinct from constituting an independent act for which the employer would not be liable."[97]

Examples of the former are as follows: smoking while working with inflammable materials[98]; use by employee of own uninsured motor car on employer's business[99]; garage attendant driving a car when instructed to move cars by hand[100]; blacksmith's apprentice without a driving licence voluntarily driving a car which was impeding his work[101]; and a substantial deviation from the direct route by a driver implementing his employer's contract to convey passengers from A to B.[102] An independent journey, undertaken for the employee's private purposes, is not

---

[92] *Sinclair Moorhead & Co v Wallace & Co* (1880) 7 R. 874 (borrowing money); *Armagas Ltd v Mundogas S.A.* [1986] A.C. 717; *Taylor v Glasgow DC*, 1997 S.C. 183.

[93] *Citizen's Life Assurance Co v Brown* [1904] A.C. 423 at 427–428, per Lord Lindley; quoted by Lord Justice Clerk Macdonald in *Mackenzie v Cluny Hill Hydropathic*, 1908 S.C. 200 at 205. See also *Lister v Hesley Hall Ltd* [2002] 1 A.C. 215 (acts of sexual abuse by warden of a residential home sufficiently closely connected with his duty to care for the children as to lead to vicarious liability of warden's employers). *Lister* was followed in *Mattis v Pollock* [2003] 1 W.L.R. 2158 (stabbing by nightclub bouncer). Compare also *AG of British Virgin Islands v Hartwell* [2004] 1 W.L.R. 1273 (no vicarious liability for police officer shooting civilian in course of personal vendetta) with *Bernard v AG of Jamaica* [2005] I.R.L.R. 398 (vicarious liability for unlawful shooting by off-duty police constable).

[94] *Kirby v N.C.B.*, 1958 S.C. 514.

[95] *Lloyd v Grace Smith & Co* [1912] A.C. 716; *Central Motors (Glasgow) v Cessnock Garage, etc., Co*, 1925 S.C. 796 (garage night watchman borrowing car); *Mackenzie v Cluny Hill Hydropathic*, 1908 S.C. 200.

[96] *Martin v Wards* (1887) 14 R. 814; *Beard v London General Omnibus Co* [1900] 2 Q.B. 530 (conductor driving bus); cf. *Ricketts v Tilling* [1915] 1 K.B. 644 (where driver negligent in permitting conductor to drive); *O'Brien v Arbib*, 1907 S.C. 975; and see A.T. Glegg, *The Law of Reparation in Scotland*, 3rd edn (Edinburgh: W. Green, 1939), pp.421–425.

[97] *Kirby v N.C.B.*, 1958 S.C. 514 at 533, per Lord President Clyde. Another test suggested is "whether the activity was reasonably incidental to the performance of his duties": see Lord Pearce in *Williams v A. & W. Hemphill*, 1966 S.C. (HL) 31 at 44.

[98] *Jefferson v Derbyshire Farmers Ltd* [1921] 2 K.B. 281; *Century Insurance Co v N.I.R.T.B.* [1942] A.C. 509.

[99] *Canadian Pacific Railway Co v Lockhart* [1942] A.C. 591.

[100] *London CC v Cattermoles (Garages) Ltd* [1953] 1 W.L.R. 997.

[101] *Mulholland v Reid & Leys*, 1958 S.C. 290.

[102] *Williams v A. & W. Hemphill*, 1966 S.C. (HL) 31. "It is a question of fact and degree in each case whether the deviation is sufficiently detached from the master's business to constitute a frolic of the servant unconnected with the enterprise for which he was employed": per Lord Pearce at 45. Cf. *Angus v Glasgow Corp*, 1977 S.L.T. 206 (deviating driver is outside the scope of his employment only when he departs altogether from his employer's business) and *R.J. McLeod (Contractors) v South of Scotland Electricity Board*, 1982 S.L.T. 274 (employer vicariously liable where, despite unauthorised diversion, original purpose of driver's journey had not been completely superseded).

within the scope of his employment.[103] But an act may fall within the scope of employment although prohibited.[104] The relevant connection of service between employer and employee commences, in the ordinary case, when the employee enters his employer's premises for the purpose of going to work[105] and continues while the employee is leaving a factory by an inside stairway after finishing work[106]; but an employee who goes to an unauthorised place for the sole purpose of performing a prohibited act, namely smoking during a work break, has temporarily broken that connection.[107] Exceptionally, the connection may commence when the employee begins his journey to work, if he is sent by his employer to work temporarily at a different location. This is so even if he departs from home to travel to the different location, or is returning directly to his home after finishing the work.[108] It is not enough to create vicarious liability that the act is done for the benefit of or at the request of the employer if it is outwith the scope of employment and is not part of a delegated task or duty.[109] Firemen called out by their employer are, however, acting within the scope of their employment while travelling to work,[110] although it has been held that firemen travelling deliberately slowly to a fire as part of a programme of industrial action are acting outwith the scope of their employment.[111]

Scope of employer's vicarious liability—An employer is not liable for the act of **25.11** an employee which the employer himself had no power to do,[112] but he is liable for the use of excessive force or wrongous detention by an employee to whom he has delegated, expressly or impliedly, the power to use force against persons or to detain them,[113] unless the employee was actuated by personal motives, such as hatred or spite.[114] Employers are vicariously liable for breaches of statutory duty by their employees, unless the statute expressly or impliedly excludes such liability.[115] Vicarious liability for defamation rests upon the same principles as other wrongs.[116] The only specialty arises when the employer is entitled to plead

---

[103] See cases in Glegg, *The Law of Reparation in Scotland* (1939), pp.422–423; cf. *Central Motors v Cessnock Garage Co*, 1925 S.C. 796, where delegation to a servant of the care of customers' cars brought "a frolic" of the servant within the scope of employment.

[104] *Canadian Pacific Railway Co v Lockhart* [1942] A.C. 591; *London CC v Cattermoles (Garages) Ltd* [1953] 1 W.L.R. 997; *Limpus v London General Omnibus Co* (1862) 1 Hurl. & C. 526 (bus driver racing another bus driver). For examples of prohibited acts which the servant was not employed to do, see *Alford v N.C.B.*, 1951 S.C. 248 (shot-firing); *Twine v Bean's Express* (1946) 62 T.L.R. 458, CA, and *Conway v George Wimpey & Co (No.2)* [1951] 2 K.B. 266 (drivers giving prohibited lifts); see also *Roberts v Logan*, 1966 S.L.T. 77, OH; *Rose v Plenty* [1976] 1 W.L.R. 141.

[105] *Compton v McClure* [1975] I.C.R. 378.

[106] *Bell v Blackwood Morton & Sons Ltd*, 1960 S.C. 11.

[107] *Kirby v N.C.B.*, 1958 S.C. 514.

[108] *Thomson v British Steel Corp*, 1977 S.L.T. 26; *Smith v Stages* [1989] A.C. 928.

[109] *Nottingham v Aldridge* [1971] 2 Q.B. 739.

[110] *Stitt v Woolley* (1971) 115 S.J. 708.

[111] *General Engineering Services Ltd v Kingston & St Andrews Corp* [1989] 1 W.L.R. 69.

[112] *Poulton v L. & S.W. Ry Co* (1867) L.R. 2 Q.B. 534 (wrongous detention).

[113] See cases in Glegg, *The Law of Reparation in Scotland* (1939), pp.426–429; *Percy v Glasgow Corp*, 1922 S.C. (HL) 144; *Mattis v Pollock* [2003] 1 W.L.R. 2158.

[114] See *Power v Central S.M.T. Co*, 1949 S.C. 376.

[115] *Majrowski v Guy's & St Thomas' NHS Trust* [2007] 1 A.C. 224, relating to the Protection from Harassment Act 1997.

[116] See *Ellis v National Free Labour Association* (1905) 7 F. 629; *Finburgh v Moss Empires*, 1908 S.C. 928; *Neville v C. & A. Modes*, 1945 S.C. 175; and cf. *Riddell v Glasgow Corp*, 1911 S.C. (HL) 35 (where the House of Lords held that the servant had no authority to make any statement on the point); *Eprile v Caledonian Ry* (1898) 6 S.L.T. 65, OH; and *Mandelston v N.B. Ry Co*, 1917 S.C. 442.

qualified privilege. In that event, express malice may be inferred from the reckless and extreme nature of charges made by the employee within the scope of his employment and the employer will be liable[117]; but the personal malice of the employee due to ill will and in no way connected with the employer's business excludes his liability.[118]

25.12 Vicarious liability for services—A distinction was formerly drawn between employees engaged to exercise professional skill and others, but this distinction is no longer valid and an employer is now vicariously liable for the negligence of full-time salaried employees in the exercise of their professions.[119] The existence of a contract of service is not, however, the factor which determines vicarious liability. There may be vicarious liability even in the case of a joint adventure if the person against whom vicarious liability is pleaded exercised superintendence and control of the work.[120] And A may have a contract of service with B and yet be acting as agent or servant *pro hac vice* of C. Thus if C borrows a car and appoints A to drive it on C's business, C will be liable for A's negligent driving jointly with A.[121] But difficulty may arise when the employee of A is lent or hired to B and the question is whether A or B is vicariously liable for the employee's act.[122] There is on the injured party a heavy onus of proving that the employee was transferred *pro hac vice* to the service of B.[123] In the case of a negligent act, regard must be had to all the circumstances of the case to determine whether A or B had the right to control the way in which that act was done.[124] Where a ship is let out on hire with its master to a charterer, or a vehicle let out with a driver,[125] or plant with an operator, the owner remains vicariously liable for the negligent control of the operator unless he has divested himself of all possession and control of his property in favour of another.

> "The reason is that he has delegated to the driver the task of driving his vehicle and he must be responsible for the way in which his delegate does his work."[126]

---

[117] *Finburgh v Moss Empires* (1908) S.C. 928: see Lord Ardwall's opinion at 940.

[118] *Aiken v Caledonian Ry Co*, 1913 S.C. 66.

[119] *Macdonald v Glasgow Western Hospitals*, 1954 S.C. 453 (resident physicians and surgeons); *Fox v Glasgow & South Western Hospitals*, 1955 S.L.T. 337 (nurse). A regional health board is not, however, liable for the negligence of a general practitioner within its area (*Bonthrone v Secretary of State for Scotland*, 1987 S.L.T. 34).

[120] *Bruce v Clapham*, 1982 S.L.T. 386.

[121] *Elliot v Beattie*, 1926 S.L.T. 588, OH; and see *Smith v Moss* [1940] 1 K.B. 424 (son driving mother's car on mother's business); cf. *Hewitt v Bonvin* [1940] 1 K.B. 188 (son driving father's car on son's business).

[122] It has been held in England that it is possible for A and B to be liable, under a principle of dual vicarious liability: *Viasystems (Tyneside) Ltd v Thermal Transfer (Northern) Ltd* [2006] Q.B. 510.

[123] *Malley v L.M.S. Ry*, 1944 S.C. 129 at 136–138, per Lord Justice Clerk Cooper; *Mersey Docks & Harbour Board v Coggins& Griffith Ltd* [1947] A.C. 1 at 10, per Viscount Simon; *McGregor v J.S. Duthie & Sons*, 1966 S.L.T. 133 (where the onus was held to be discharged, but the driver was driving a vehicle belonging to the temporary employer on that employer's business at the material time); *Moir v Wide Arc Services Ltd*, 1987 S.L.T. 495.

[124] See *Malley v L.M.S. Ry*, 1944 S.C. 129 and *Mersey Docks & Harbour Board v Coggins & Griffith Ltd* [1947] A.C. 1.

[125] See *Anderson v Glasgow Tramways Co* (1893) 21 R. 318.

[126] *John Young & Co Ltd v O'Donnell*, 1958 S.L.T. (Notes) 46, per Lord Denning. Note that a term in such a hiring contract that the driver or operator is to be the servant of the hirer will not exclude the owner's liability for injury to a third party: see *Mersey Docks & Harbour Board v Coggins & Griffith Ltd* [1947] A.C. 1 at 2 and 10. An indemnity clause provides the only effective protection.

The case of the owner of a vehicle hiring the employee of another to drive the hirer's vehicle presents no difficulty because the real interest in the method of driving is in the owner and the car is being driven on his business.[127]

Authorised pilots: The Crown: Fire authorities—The position of authorised 25.13 pilots is different; the general rule is that the employer of a duly authorised and licensed pilot is not vicariously responsible for damage caused by his negligence during pilotage, because when navigating the pilot is acting as an independent professional.[128] In general the owners of the vessel are liable for such fault.[129] There may, however, be situations where a harbour authority, which is actually the employer of an authorised pilot, will be vicariously liable for his negligence.[130] Mere authorisation of a pilot does not, however, make a harbour authority vicariously liable for his negligence.[131] The Crown is vicariously liable for delicts committed by its servants or agents, including independent contractors,[132] and firemen are the servants of the statutory fire authorities set up under the Fire Services Act 1947.[133]

Culpa tenet suos auctores—The vicarious liability of an employer does not affect 25.14 the employee's personal liability, as everyone is responsible for the consequences of his own wrongful or negligent acts. It is no defence that he was acting in accordance with instructions from a party whom he was contractually bound to obey,[134] or even, as in the case of a soldier obeying an unjustifiable order to fire, one to whom his obedience was due by statute.[135] An independent contractor is personally liable for his own acts or omissions (and for acts of his servants within the scope of their employment), whether or not his employer is also liable to the injured party.[136]

Liability of employer of independent contractor—In *Stephen v Thurso Police* 25.15 *Commissioners*[137] Lord Justice-Clerk Inglis said:

"The law is well established. In the first place, a master is liable for the injurious act of his servant. In the second place, if the wrongdoer be a contractor who is subject to the control of his employer, the latter is responsible; and, in the third place, if the contractor be independent, and may do as he pleases as regards the execution of the work, he is to be viewed as the principal, and alone is liable."

There are no exceptions to the first two propositions. Although the contract in the first is a *locatio operarum* (a letting of his services by the servant) and in the

---

[127] *Bowie v Shenkin*, 1934 S.C. 459.

[128] *Esso Petroleum Co Ltd v Hall Russell & Co Ltd*, 1988 S.L.T. 874 at 886–891.

[129] *Esso Petroleum Co Ltd v Hall Russell & Co Ltd*, 1988 S.L.T. 874; *Thom v J. & P. Hutchison*, 1925 S.C. 386; Pilotage Act 1987 s.16.

[130] *Esso Petroleum Co Ltd v Hall Russell & Co Ltd*, 1988 S.L.T. 874 at 891F; s.22 of the Pilotage Act 1987, by imposing a financial ceiling on the amount of damages payable, appears to contemplate such liability.

[131] Pilotage Act 1987 s.22(8).

[132] Crown Proceedings Act 1947 ss.2 and 38(2). Note that s.2(6) excludes, inter alia, police; vicarious liability was imposed on chief constables: Police (Scotland) Act 1967 s.39.

[133] *Kilboy v S.E. Fire Area Joint Committee*, 1952 S.C. 280.

[134] *Miller v Renton* (1885) 13 R. 309.

[135] *Rogers v Rajendro Dutt* (1860) 13 Moore P.C. 209.

[136] *Grieve v Brown*, 1926 S.C. 787.

[137] *Stephen v Thurso Police Commissioners* (1876) 3 R. 535 at 540.

second a *locatio operis faciendi* (a letting out of a job or piece of work to be done by a contractor), the maxims *qui facit per alium facit per se* and *respondeat superior* apply to both. If the employer of an independent contractor retains control of the work, he has the right to direct the contractor and his employees as to how the work is to be done, with the result that the contractor and his employees are deemed to be the employees *pro hac vice* of the employer.[138] The third proposition, above, lays down the general rule that the contractor alone is liable, and this is true provided that the employer is not personally at fault. Thus, when normal building operations were being carried out on private land, neither the owner nor the principal contractor was liable to a third party injured by colliding with a heap of lime left on the public street by servants of the plastering subcontractor.[139] But an employer may himself be negligent, for example by ordering dangerous work,[140] or by failing to take steps to remove or guard an obstacle placed on the highway by the contractor's men if the employer knew or ought to have known it was there,[141] in which case he will be liable for damage caused by his own negligence, whether or not the contractor has been negligent. The employer may also be negligent in selecting an incompetent contractor. It has been held that the duty to select a competent contractor does not, in general, include checking that the contractor has adequate insurance cover.[142] Certain other duties have been held to be personal to the employer so that, if they are not performed, he is liable, however careful he may have been in the selection of a competent contractor to perform them on his behalf.

25.16 Exceptions to general rule—The exceptions now recognised to the general rule that an employer is not liable for damage caused by work done by an independent contractor are as follows.

(1) When the employer has no legal right to do the work ordered by him, he will be liable not only for the infringement of the rights of others caused by the work per se but also for any other injuries which third parties may suffer as a result of negligence of the contractor or his servants. For example, a gas company, which had no authority to make excavations in the street but employed a contractor for that purpose, was held liable for injury to a member of the public caused by a heap of stones negligently left on the roadway by the contractor's servants.[143] The same principle would apply to the case of an employer instructing or authorising a contractor to execute lawful work in an unlawful manner to the injury of neighbouring proprietors.[144]

(2) Certain duties are personal to the employer, so that he cannot escape liability for breach by delegating the performance to competent parties

---

[138] *Nisbett v Dixon & Co* (1852) 14 D. 973; *Stephen v Thurso Police Commissioners* (1876) 3 R. 535; *Gregory v Hill* (1869) 8 M. 282; *Marshall v William Sharp & Sons Ltd*, 1991 S.L.T. 114, although this case may be an exception to the third proposition in *Stephen*, rather than an example of the second.

[139] *MacLean v Russell* (1850) 12 D. 887; *Blake v Woolf* [1898] 2 Q.B. 426 (owner not liable for overflow from cistern after repair by competent plumber).

[140] *Boyle v Glasgow Corp*, 1949 S.C. 254.

[141] See *Stephen v Thurso Police Commissioners* (1876) 3 R. 535 at 538, per Lord Justice Clerk Inglis; and *Burgess v Gray* (1845) 1 C.B. 578.

[142] *Payling v Naylor* [2004] P.I.Q.R. P36, followed in *Honeybourne v Burgess*, 2006 S.L.T. 585.

[143] *Ellis v Sheffield Gas Co* (1853) 2 El. & Bl. 767.

[144] See *Cameron v Fraser* (1881) 9 R. 26 and *Miller v Renton* (1885) 13 R. 309, although no question of incidental negligence arose in these cases.

or by any other means.[145] An employer's duty of care to his employee is non-delegable in the sense that he is personally liable for its performance. If therefore the duty is delegated by the employer and not properly performed, the employer remains liable to the employee.[146] Merely because a third party is involved in the provision of equipment[147] or the organisation of work for an employee[148] does not, however, make him an agent or delegate of the employer. There are many statutory duties which are personal to the employer, chiefly in the fields of local government[149] and health and safety at work.[150]

(3) In certain cases, where damage is the natural and probable consequence of negligent execution of the work, the employer has the personal obligation of seeing that the work is carefully and properly done. These cases fall broadly into two classes. The first covers excavations and other hazardous work on public roads and streets[151]; the second relates to hazardous work on private property, such as building operations which expose adjacent property to risk of damage,[152] work involving the risk of fire spreading to adjacent property[153] or injuring persons present[154] or any work involving an obvious inherent risk of serious injury.[155] The case of *Tarry v Ashton*[156] may be fitted under this head, where a lamp projecting over a public street was an obvious danger to the public if not secure. The owner was held liable to a passer-by, upon whom it fell, for the negligent execution of repair work by an independent contractor shortly before the accident. The perplexing case of *Cleghorn v Taylor*,[157] where a chimney-can fell and damaged adjacent property shortly after its repair by a master slater, could also have been decided under this head, although it is not the stated *ratio decidendi*.

---

[145] See *Stewart v Malik*, 2009 S.C. 265.

[146] *McDermid v Nash Dredging* [1987] A.C. 906.

[147] *Davie v New Merton Board Mills* [1959] A.C. 604—note that the provision of equipment is now regulated by the Employers' Liability (Defective Equipment) Act 1969, which makes the employer liable for defective equipment even though the defect is attributable to the fault of a third party.

[148] *Marshall v William Sharp & Sons Ltd*, 1991 S.L.T. 114.

[149] See *Stephen v Thurso Police Commissioners* (1876) 3 R. 535.

[150] See, e.g. Provision and Use of Work Equipment Regulations 1998 (SI 1998/2306) reg.5(1): "Every employer shall ensure that work equipment is maintained in an efficient state, in efficient working order and in good repair".

[151] *Gray v Pullen* (1864) 5 B. & S. 970 (subsidence of pavement after construction of drain); *Hardaker v Idle DC* [1896] 1 Q.B. 335 (gas main broken during construction of sewer); *Penny v Wimbledon U.D.C.* [1899] 2 Q.B. 72 (heap of soil on road after dark); *Holliday v National Telephone Co* [1899] 2 Q.B. 392 (risk of explosion during work on highway).

[152] *Bower v Peate* (1876) L.R. 1 Q.B.D. 321 (excavation of foundations); *Dalton v Henry Angus & Co* (1881) L.R. 6 App. Cas. 740 (interference with right of support); *Hughes v Percival* (1883) 8 App. Cas. 443; and see *Cameron v Fraser* (1881) 9 R. 26 at 29, per Lord Young (truly a nuisance case); *Borders RC v Roxburgh DC*, 1989 S.L.T. 837; and *G.A. Estates Ltd v Caviapen Trs Ltd (No.1)*, 1993 S.L.T. 1037.

[153] *Black v Christchurch Finance Co* [1894] A.C. 48; *Balfour v Barty King* [1956] 1 W.L.R. 779; *H & N Emanuel v Greater London Council* [1971] 2 All E.R. 835.

[154] *Honeywill & Stein v Larkin Bros* [1934] 1 K.B. 191, in which the words "absolute obligation" were used in lieu of "strict liability": see *Pass of Ballater* [1942] P. 112 at 115–116, per Langton J.

[155] *Stewart v Adams*, 1920 S.C. 129 (contract for removal of poisonous paint scrapings on pasture land: employer liable for death of cow).

[156] *Tarry v Ashton* (1876) 1 Q.B.D. 314.

[157] *Cleghorn v Taylor* (1856) 18 D. 664. See comment of Lord Justice Clerk Inglis in *Campbell v Kennedy* (1864) 3 M. 121 at 126; and J. Rankine, *The Law of Land-Ownership in Scotland*, 4th edn (Edinburgh: W. Green, 1909), p.375.

There is therefore no general rule that an employer is not liable for breach of his personal duties to an employee injured through the negligent work of an independent contractor employed by the employer, nor is there any general rule that an occupier of premises is not liable for damage to persons or property on the premises caused by such faulty work. The question of whether or not the employer has discharged his duty of taking reasonable care for the safety of his employee, or an occupier for the person who or whose property is injured on the premises, by selecting a skilled contractor of established reputation to carry out any work on plant or premises, including the inspection thereof, is a question of fact and degree in all the circumstances of the particular case and every decision on this subject should be treated as turning on its own facts.[158]

RECOVERY OF DAMAGES

25.17 **Title to sue**—The title to sue for damages in respect of a wrongful or negligent act rests with the party injured. Insurance against the particular injury is no objection to title.[159] If death has resulted from the injury, certain near relatives have a title to sue, but third parties, who may have suffered loss from the want of the injured person's services, have no such title.[160] And a relative cannot claim damages in respect of the loss of services previously rendered to him by a person who has been injured.[161] The injured person himself may, however, now include in his claim a reasonable sum by way of damages for his inability to render to a relative personal services which he might have been expected to render gratuitously and which, if rendered by a person other than a relative, would ordinarily be obtainable on payment.[162] He may also include in his claim a sum representing reasonable remuneration and repayment of reasonable expenses in respect of necessary services rendered by a relative to him in respect of his injuries.[163] The relative has no direct claim in respect of those matters but the injured person has an obligation to account to him. Necessary services may include management of the household and housekeeping,[164] but not the provision of organs for transplant.[165] A claim for necessary services rendered by the defender is unsustainable.[166]

---

[158] See opinions in *Davie v New Merton Board Mills* [1959] A.C. 604; *Sumner v William Henderson & Sons* [1964] 1 Q.B. 450; [1963] 2 W.L.R. 330, where Phillimore J. purported to lay down a general rule and was reversed by the Court of Appeal [1963] 1 W.L.R. 823. For property cases, see *Macdonald v Reid's Trs*, 1947 S.C. 726, OH, and cases cited therein; also *Green v Fibreglass* [1958] 2 Q.B. 245 at 253, per Salmon J. (and note the English Occupiers' Liability Act 1957 s.2(4)(b), the terms of which are implied in the Occupiers' Liability (Scotland) Act 1960 s.2(1)).

[159] *Port Glasgow Sailcloth Co v Caledonian Ry* (1892) 19 R. 608.

[160] *Reavis v Clan Line Steamers*, 1925 S.C. 725; *Gibson v Glasgow Corp*, 1963 S.L.T. (Notes) 16.

[161] Administration of Justice Act 1982 s.9(4). Where the injured party has died, the Damages (Scotland) Act 2011 s.6 provides that the relative may claim a reasonable sum for loss of services. This will form a specific head of damages in the relative's general patrimonial claim under s.4(3)(a).

[162] Administration of Justice Act 1982 s.9.

[163] Administration of Justice Act 1982 s.8. In *Forsyth's C.B. v Govan Shipbuilders Ltd*, 1989 S.L.T. 91, it was held that the claim extended only to expenses prior to the proof; the right to claim damages for services to be rendered in the future was, however, expressly conferred by the Law Reform (Miscellaneous Provisions) (Scotland) Act 1990 s.69.

[164] *Denheen v British Railways Board*, 1986 S.L.T. 249.

[165] *Duffy v Lanarkshire Health Board*, 1999 S.L.T. 906.

[166] *Hunt v Severs* [1994] 2 A.C. 350 at 363; see acknowledgement of this view in *Kozikowska v Kozikowski*, 1996 S.L.T. 386.

Title of spouses—The law formerly refused an action of reparation by one spouse **25.18** against another on the ground of the intimate relationship obtaining between them.[167] Since the Law Reform (Husband and Wife) Act 1962, however, each spouse has had the right to bring an action against the other in respect of a wrongful or negligent act or omission,[168] but the court has power to dismiss proceedings if it appears that no substantial benefit would accrue to either party from the continuation of the action.[169] An action of reparation has always been competent at the instance of a child against his parent,[170] and at the instance of a parent against his child.[171]

Title to sue: Claims by executors and trustees in sequestration—If the injury **25.19** causes patrimonial loss, the right to sue therefor passes, on the death of the injured party, to his executor[172]; on his bankruptcy, to his trustee.[173] Should the injured party be an undischarged bankrupt at the time of his accident his claim for patrimonial loss will vest in his trustee in sequestration.[174] The right to sue may be assigned, but does not pass, without express assignation, with the transfer of a damaged thing.[175]

Executors—The position in relation to actions by an executor is regulated by the **25.20** Damages (Scotland) Act 2011 (the "2011 Act"). The rights to damages in respect of personal injuries sustained by a deceased person which transmit to his executor are the like rights as were vested in the deceased immediately before his death, including the right to solatium, but damages by way of solatium or by way of compensation for patrimonial loss attributable to any period after the deceased's death are excluded.[176] The effect is that the executor's rights are restricted to recovery of solatium and patrimonial loss attributable to the period before death and compensation for services rendered by a relative to the deceased before his death.[177] Where, during his lifetime, the deceased had taken steps to reduce the liability of his estate to Inheritance Tax, which were negated by his premature death caused by the defender, it was not possible for his executors to recover the increased tax payable as damages.[178] An executor may pursue his recoverable losses by action whether or not the deceased had raised an action in his lifetime.[179]

Trustee in sequestration—If an action of damages is raised by an injured **25.21** party and he thereafter becomes bankrupt, his trustee in sequestration may sist

---

[167] *Harper v Harper*, 1929 S.C. 220; and see *Cameron v Glasgow Corp*, 1936 S.C. (HL) 26.

[168] Law Reform (Husband and Wife) Act 1962 s.2(1). Section 2 applies to Scotland only.

[169] Law Reform (Husband and Wife) Act 1962 s.2(2).

[170] *Young v Rankin*, 1934 S.C. 499.

[171] *Wood v Wood*, 1935 S.L.T. 431. Capacity to raise and defend proceedings is regulated by the Age of Legal Capacity (Scotland) Act 1991.

[172] Damages (Scotland) Act 2011 s.2.

[173] *Muir's Tr. v Braidwood*, 1958 S.C. 169 at 173; *Smith v Duncan Stewart & Co (No.2)*, 1961 S.C. 91; *Russell's Executrix v B.R.B.*, 1965 S.L.T. 413.

[174] *Grindall v John Mitchell Grangemouth Ltd*, 1987 S.L.T. 137.

[175] *Symington v Campbell* (1894) 21 R. 434.

[176] 2011 Act s.2(2). Awards for suffering lasting only minutes will be modest: *Beggs v Motherwell Bridge Fabricators*, 1998 S.L.T. 1215.

[177] See the Administration of Justice Act 1982 ss.7 and 8.

[178] *Mackintosh v Morrice's Exrs* [2006] CSIH 43; 2007 S.C. 6; 2006 S.L.T. 853.

[179] 2011 Act s.2, although unless a claim has been raised by the victim the executor will not be able to claim solatium in respect of defamation or verbal injury, see s.2(3).

himself as pursuer in lieu of the bankrupt and recover damages for solatium and patrimonial loss.[180] The trustee in sequestration cannot, however, initiate an action claiming solatium on behalf of the bankrupt, even if he has intimated a claim before sequestration.[181] If no action has been raised before sequestration, the title of the trustee is restricted to suing for patrimonial loss to the estate, unless the right to claim solatium has been assigned to him by the injured party.[182] If, however, a bankrupt raises an action of damages for personal injuries after sequestration, the trustee may be sisted as pursuer in the claim in respect of conclusions relating to both solatium and patrimonial loss.[183]

25.22 **Claims by relatives of deceased persons**—The right of a relative to damages for an injury resulting in death is regulated by the 2011 Act which governs the right of relatives of a deceased person to recover damages attributable to his death where that has been caused by the wrongful act of another.[184] Any member of the deceased's immediate family[185] may sue for damages for distress endured in contemplation of the suffering of the deceased before his death, grief caused by the death and loss of the society of the deceased.[186] The claim of a parent of a child who dies as a result of injuries sustained in utero was held not to be excluded under the previous legislation.[187] Patrimonial claims in respect of loss of support are available to immediate family plus any other relative actually supported by the deceased.[188] The total sum available to settle claims for loss of support is calculated by taking 75 per cent of the victim's net income to which the court may apply a multiplier in respect of future loss of support.[189] The court may vary the 75 per cent rule to avoid over or under compensation.[190] Funeral expenses, if incurred, may also be claimed[191] as may loss of personal services which had been rendered to the relative by the deceased.[192] In assessing loss of support, the court will take into account any part of a provisional award of damages relating to future patrimonial loss which was intended to compensate the deceased for a period beyond the date on which he died.[193] In assessing damages payable to a widow in respect of the death of her husband, whether for loss of support or loss of society, no account is taken of her remarriage or prospects of remarriage.[194] There are conflicting decisions on the relevance of a widow's cohabitation with another man after her husband's death.[195] A claim by the executor is not barred by

---

[180] *Thom v Bridges* (1857) 19 D. 721.

[181] *Smith v Duncan Stewart & Co (No.1)*, 1960 S.C. 329; *Muir's Tr. v Braidwood*, 1958 S.C. 169.

[182] *Traill v Dalbeattie* (1904) 6 F. 798; *Cole-Hamilton v Boyd*, 1963 S.C. (HL) 1; cf. *Muir's Tr. v Braidwood*, 1958 S.C. 169.

[183] *Watson v Thompson*, 1991 S.L.T. 683.

[184] 2011 Act s.3.

[185] Defined by the 2011 Act s.14(1)(a)–(d) that is, spouses or civil partners or cohabitants living as such, parents or children, siblings, grandparents or grandchildren.

[186] 2011 Act s.4(1)(3)(b).

[187] Damages (Scotland) Act 1976 s.1(1); *Hamilton v Fife Health Board*, 1993 S.L.T. 624.

[188] 2011 Act ss.4(1)(b), 4(3)(a), 14.

[189] 2011 Act s.7.

[190] 2011 Act s.7(2).

[191] 2011 Act s.4(3)(a). In England, recovery of £50,702 has been allowed for the cost of a funeral in accordance with a particular religious tradition—*St George v Turner* [2003] C.L.Y. 936. In Scotland reasonable funeral expenses are allowed.

[192] 2011 Act s.6.

[193] 2011 Act s.8(3).

[194] Law Reform (Miscellaneous Provisions) Act 1971 s.4.

[195] *Donnelly v Glasgow Corp*, 1949 S.L.T. 362; cf. *Morris v Drysdale*, 1992 S.L.T. 186.

the making of a claim by a relative nor is a relative's claim barred by a claim by the executor.[196] Action at the instance of the relatives is barred if liability has been excluded or discharged by the deceased during his lifetime,[197] unless the death was due to mesothelioma.[198]

Damages and title to sue: Quantification of damages—A wrongdoer is liable **25.23** to make good all loss caused naturally and directly by his wrongful act. An award of damages should, as nearly as possible, amount to the sum of money which will put the injured party in the position which he would have occupied if he had not sustained the wrong.[199] Damages are normally assessed on a once and for all basis but in personal injury cases where there is a risk that the injured person will develop a serious disease or suffer a serious deterioration in his condition, the court may award provisional damages.[200] Thus, the damages are assessed on the basis that the disease or deterioration will not occur but, if it does, the injured person can return to court to claim further damages.[201] Awards of provisional damages are only available against defenders who are either public authorities or public corporations or insured or otherwise indemnified.[202] It is also possible in appropriate cases to obtain an award of interim damages.[203] A person who is injured through the breach of duty of another is entitled to claim solatium as pecuniary reparation for pain and suffering inflicted upon him.[204] The effects of injury which are thereby compensated are (1) pain and suffering, (2) loss of faculties and amenities,[205] and (3) shortened life expectancy.[206]

Losses recoverable—Damages will also include wages[207] and pension rights, lost **25.24** by the injured party[208]; all medical expenses reasonably incurred[209] and other outlays; repair of a damaged article plus the cost of hiring a replacement pending repair and, in the case of destruction, the market value of that article less its scrap value plus the cost of hire for a reasonable period pending the acquisition of a replacement.[210] If there is no market for the article destroyed, the actual cost of replacement may be allowed.[211] Future loss of income, and damages for the future cost of caring for an injured party, are normally calculated by computing an annual loss (the multiplicand) to which is applied a multiplier appropriate to the age of

---

[196] Over-compensation is avoided by the restrictions on the executor's claim under s.2(2) of the 2011 Act.

[197] 2011 Act s.4(2).

[198] 2011 Act s.5. The exception only applies to relatives' claims for solatium under s.4(3)(b).

[199] *Livingstone v Rawyards Coal Co* (1880) L.R. 5 App. Cas.25, per Lord Blackburn at 39.

[200] Administration of Justice Act 1982 s.12.

[201] *McEwan and Paton on Damages for Personal Injuries in Scotland* (Edinburgh: W. Green), Ch.2.

[202] Administration of Justice Act 1982 s.12(1)(b).

[203] *McEwan and Paton on Damages*, Ch.1.

[204] See Bell, *Principles*, s.2032; *Traynor's Exrx v Bairds & Scottish Steel*, 1957 S.C. 311 at 314, OH, per Lord Guthrie. The victim must be aware of pain and suffering: *Dalgliesh v Glasgow Corporation*, 1976 S.C. 32.

[205] Available irrespective of awareness: *Lim Poh v Islington Area Health Authority* [1980] A.C. 174.

[206] 2011 Act s.1. This claim requires awareness: s.1(2).

[207] *Doonan v S.M.T.*, 1950 S.C. 136.

[208] See consideration of the quantification of such a loss in *Mitchell v Glenrothes Development Corp*, 1991 S.L.T. 284.

[209] *Rubens v Walker*, 1946 S.C. 215; and see the Law Reform (Personal Injuries) Act 1948 s.2(4).

[210] *Pomphrey v James A Cuthbertson (No.2)*, 1951 S.C. 147.

[211] *Clyde Navigation Trs v Bowring S.S. Co*, 1929 S.C. 715.

the party and other relevant circumstances.[212] This produces a lump sum which, when invested, should provide an annual income equivalent to the loss. Actuarial tables should be the starting point in selecting a multiplier.[213] Where the pursuer's expectation of life has, as a result of personal injuries to him, been reduced, he will be compensated in respect of loss of expected earnings or benefits during the "lost period", that is the difference between his notional date of death and expected date of death.[214] A deduction of 25 per cent is made from expected earnings during this period to reflect cover, notionally the purser's necessary living expenses during the lost period.[215] The court may vary the percentage deducted to avoid over or under compensation.[216] Damages may also be awarded for the loss of a chance, which may be either the loss of a chance which is itself a matter of legal right, such as a chance to bring an action or an appeal, or a chance of achieving some other benefit.[217] In the latter case, the chance of success may be too speculative to be taken into account.[218] In cases involving the failure of a sterilisation operation, and consequent pregnancy of the pursuer, damages awarded can include pain and suffering associated with pregnancy and birth, together with wage loss but not the cost of rearing the child.[219] Where negligence has damaged a woman's ability to have children, it may be possible to recover the cost of in vitro fertilisation treatment.[220] When heritable property is totally destroyed, reinstatement value will only be allowed in exceptional cases.[221] Interest may be awarded from the date when the right of action arose, or when the damage suffered became capable of ascertainment.[222] Where damages are awarded for personal injuries, unless there are special circumstances in a particular case, the court must award interest on these damages.[223] It is competent to award damages in foreign currency.[224]

25.25 Measuring damages—In awarding damages the court should take into account the decline in the value of money,[225] and must deduct the appropriate income

---

[212] For discussion of what is reasonable where a claimant is catastrophically injured and requires 24-hour care, see *Sowden v Lodge* [2005] 1 W.L.R. 2129, noting that the legislative background in Scotland derives from the Social Work (Scotland) Act 1968.

[213] The assumed rate of return was initially 3% in both England and Scotland: see *Wells v Wells* [1999] 1 A.C. 345, adopted in Scotland in *McNulty v Marshall's Food Group*, 1999 S.C. 195. The rate of return is now 2.5% (Damages (Personal Injury) (Scotland) Order 2002 (SSI 2002/46)), mirroring the change in England).

[214] 2011 Act s.1(5).

[215] 2011 Act s.1(6).

[216] 2011 Act s.1(7).

[217] *Kyle v P. & J. Stormonth Darling*, 1992 S.C. 533, following *Yeoman's Ex v Ferries*, 1967 S.L.T. 332; *Paul v Ogilvy*, 2001 S.L.T. 171. A claim based on diminution in the chances of recovery from illness attributed to late diagnosis has been rejected by the House of Lords: *Gregg v Scott* [2005] 2 A.C. 176.

[218] *Neill v Scottish Omnibuses Ltd*, 1961 S.L.T. (Notes) 42.

[219] *McFarlane v Tayside Health Board*, 2000 S.C. (HL) 1, affd by the House in *Rees v Darlington Memorial Hospital NHS Trust* [2004] 1 A.C. 309.

[220] See *Briody v St Helen's & Knowlsey A.H.A.* [2002] Q.B. 856 and cases referred to therein.

[221] *Hutchison v Davidson*, 1945 S.C. 395; *Fraser v Morton Wilson (No.1)*, 1965 S.L.T. (Notes) 81, OH. The Lord Ordinary also allowed interest from the date of citation: 1965 S.L.T. (Notes) 85.

[222] Interest on Damages (Scotland) Act 1958 s.1; see *Macrae v Reed & Malik*, 1961 S.C. 68; *Killah v Aberdeen Milk Marketing Board*, 1961 S.L.T. 232, OH; *R. & J. Dempster v Motherwell Bridge, etc. Co*, 1964 S.C. 308 at 333–334, per Lord President Clyde; *Boots the Chemist Ltd v G.A. Estates Ltd*, 1993 S.L.T. 136.

[223] Interest on Damages (Scotland) Act 1958 s.1A, inserted by the Interest on Damages (Scotland) Act 1971. See also *Orr v Metcalfe*, 1973 S.C. 57.

[224] *Fullemann v McInnes's Exrs*, 1993 S.L.T. 259.

[225] *Kelly v Glasgow City Council*, 1951 S.C. (HL) 15.

tax[226] and National Insurance contributions[227] and pension contributions[228] from a sum given for loss of earnings. Social security benefits must also be considered.[229] Where a compensation payment is made in consequence of any accident, injury or disease, and any listed benefits have been or are likely to be paid to the injured person during the relevant period, benefits must be deducted and repaid to the Department of Social Security.[230] The "relevant period" is five years following the accident or the first claim for benefit in connection with a disease.[231] Where the compensation payment is made before the expiry of five years, the relevant period ends on the day of payment.[232] The amount of benefit to be repaid will be specified by the Department of Work and Pensions in a certificate to be applied for by the person making the payment.[233] It will normally be the amount of benefit received by the injured person during the relevant period.[234] Difficulty has arisen in applying the wording of the Act where a court pronounces decree for payment.[235] It is now settled that interest on damages must be calculated on the gross sum before deduction of benefits.[236] In England, it has also been held that benefits repaid may be offset against interest as well as against the principal sum.[237] It has also been decided that the terms of the Act do not bar a claim for damages comprising social security benefits lost as a result of an accident.[238] Similar provisions have recently been introduced to allow recoupment of prescribed amounts as National Health Service charges following an accident.[239] These cover provision of an ambulance, and hospital treatment, but not care by a general practitioner.

Other deductions from damages—There are additional provisions governing **25.26** deductions from damages in the Administration of Justice Act 1982. By s.10, any benefit payable from public funds and designed to secure a minimum level of subsistence is to be taken into account so far as payable in respect of any period before the award of damages but not if payable in respect of a later period. Any remuneration or earnings from employment, unemployment benefit and any benevolent payment made by the person responsible for the damages, where made directly and not through a trust or other fund, are to be taken into account so as to reduce damages but not any contractual pension or benefit,[240] any pension or retirement benefit from public funds (other than those noticed above), any

---

[226] *British Transport Commission v Gourley* [1956] A.C. 185; *Stewart v Glentaggart*, 1963 S.C. 300; see also *Cockburn & Co v Scottish Motor Omnibus Co*, 1964 S.L.T. (Notes) 7.

[227] *Gibney v Eric Johnson Stubbs*, 1987 S.L.T. 132.

[228] *Dews v N.C.B.* [1988] A.C. 1.

[229] For consideration of the benefits position in a wrongful life case, see *Rand v East Dorset H.A. (No.2)* [2000] 2 Lloyd's Rep. Med. 377.

[230] Social Security (Recovery of Benefits) Act 1997. The list of benefits is in Sch.2.

[231] Social Security (Recovery of Benefits) Act 1997 s.3(2) and (3).

[232] Social Security (Recovery of Benefits) Act 1997 s.3(4).

[233] Social Security (Recovery of Benefits) Act 1997 s.4.

[234] Social Security (Recovery of Benefits) Act 1997 s.5.

[235] See *Mitchell v Laing*, 1998 S.L.T. 203.

[236] *Wisely v John Fulton (Plumbers) Ltd (No.2)*, 2000 S.C. (HL) 95.

[237] *Griffiths v B.C.C.* [2001] 1 W.L.R. 1493.

[238] *McKenna v Chief Constable Strathclyde Police*, 1998 S.L.T. 1161.

[239] Health and Social Care (Community Health and Standards) Act 2003 Pt 3, and the Personal Injuries (NHS Charges) (Amounts) (Scotland) Regulations 2006 (SI 2006/588). The new scheme is summarised in F. Maguire, "NHS recovery of charges", 2007 S.L.T. (News) 5.

[240] *Lewicki v Brown & Root Wimpey Highland Fabricators Ltd*, 1996 S.C. 200; *Cantwell v Criminal Injuries Compensation Board*, 2001 S.L.T. 966.

statutory redundancy payment, or its equivalent,[241] any payment made by an employer subject to an obligation of reimbursement in the event of an award of damages and any benevolent payment (other than that noticed above).[242] Any saving which is attributable to the maintenance of the injured person at public expense in a hospital or other institution is to be set off against any income lost by him.[243] Proceeds of insurance policies are normally to be regarded as collateral and non-deductible but in some circumstances a discretionary payment made by an employer to an employee in respect of an accident may be deductible.[244] In an action in respect of a person's death no account is to be taken of any gain or advantage accruing by way of succession or settlement, or any insurance money, benefit under the Social Security Act 1975, any payment by a friendly society or trade union for the relief or maintenance of a member's dependants, or any pension or gratuity payable as a result of the deceased's death.[245] A widow's private means are not a relevant factor.[246]

DEFENCES AND IMMUNITIES

25.27 In some cases, the pursuer in an action of reparation is unable to recover damages because a complete defence is available to the defender. In other cases, no duty of care arises because of the context in which the harmful event occurred. The identity of the proposed defender may also be relevant to the question of whether or not damages can be recovered; certain individuals and bodies are immune from liability to make reparation. Finally, the question of what damages can be recovered may be affected by the identity of the pursuer.

25.28 **Exclusion of liability: Contractual terms: Notice**—Under the Unfair Contract Terms Act 1977 (the "1977 Act"), a term of a contract which purports to exclude or restrict liability for breach of duty arising in the course of any business, or from the occupation of any premises used for business purposes, is void where the exclusion or restriction is in respect of personal injury or death and in any other case is of no effect if it is not fair and reasonable[247] or if it is not fair and reasonable to allow reliance on the provision.[248] Where the Act does not apply, delictual liability may generally be excluded by a contractual term to that effect agreed between the wrongdoer and the person injured. Formerly, the Scottish provisions of the Act did not apply to non-contractual disclaimers but the Act was amended by s.68 of the Law Reform (Miscellaneous Provisions) (Scotland) Act 1990, to include attempts to exclude or restrict liability by notice.[249]

---

[241] Which does not include severance pay received on redundancy: *Duncan v Glacier Metal Co Ltd*, 1988 S.L.T. 479.

[242] Administration of Justice Act 1982 s.10; *McEwan and Paton on Damages*, Ch.5.

[243] Administration of Justice Act 1982 s.11.

[244] *Wilson v National Coal Board*, 1978 S.L.T. 129.

[245] Damages (Scotland) Act 1976 s.1(5).

[246] *Cruickshank v Shiels*, 1953 S.C. (HL) 1.

[247] 1977 Act s.16(1).

[248] 1977 Act s.16.

[249] The effect of the 1977 Act on disclaimers of liability in reports prepared by surveyors was considered by the House of Lords in *Smith v Eric S. Bush* [1990] 1 A.C. 831.

Volenti non fit injuria—The phrase volenti non fit injuria means that in certain **25.29**
circumstances a pursuer will be held to have accepted the risk of the injury which
has befallen him, and on that ground to be precluded from claiming damages from
the party who has caused the injury.[250] It is to be observed that *injuria* means an
unlawful act, not an injury. Where a term of a contract is void or of no effect under
the Unfair Contract Terms Act 1977, agreement to or knowledge of that term is
not of itself sufficient evidence that a risk was knowingly and voluntarily assumed
so as to found a plea of volenti non fit injuria.[251]

> "The question raised by a plea of *volenti non fit injuria* is not whether the
> injured party consented to run the risk of being hurt, but whether the injured
> party consented to run that risk at his own expense so that he and not the
> party alleged to be negligent should bear the loss in the event of injury. In
> other words, the consent that is relevant is not consent to the risk of injury
> but consent to the lack of reasonable care that may produce that risk."[252]

The acceptance of risk must occur before, or contemporaneously with, the act or
omission constituting the negligence.[253] The consent must be free and voluntary
and so the plea may not be open to a defender in a question with an employee of
a third party who incurred the risk in the course of his employment.[254] Where,
however, the risk has been accepted, it is immaterial that it was done on a false
premise.[255] The principle applies to injuries sustained in any lawful game or sport,
provided the rules are observed. But where the rules are breached or risks otherwise incurred to which consent is not to be implied, a participant in sport owes a
duty of care to other participants for neglect of which he will be liable.[256] The
referee may also be liable if he has failed to uphold the rules.[257] The principle of
assumption of risk has also been applied to spectators at games and sports who
take the risk of physical damage caused to them by any act of a participant of
adequate skill and competence, unless the participant's conduct is such as to
evince a reckless disregard of the spectator's safety.[258] But the maxim is only
required if harm has been caused by a wrongful act or omission; if there is no legal
wrong, there is no need for this defence.[259] The plea is excluded by statute where
a passenger in a motor vehicle sues the driver on the ground of the latter's
negligence.[260] It has been applied to a passenger agreeing to ride in a plane flown
by a drunken pilot.[261]

---

[250] On defences generally see B. Rodger, "Defences to Delictual Liability" in Thomson (ed.),
Delict, Ch.8.

[251] 1977 Act s.16(3).

[252] *McCaig v Langan*, 1964 S.L.T. 121 at 124, per Lord Kilbrandon; cf. *Bankhead v McCarthy*, 1963
S.C. 263 at 265, per Lord Walker; T.B. Smith, *A Short Commentary on the Law of Scotland* (Edinburgh:
W. Green, 1962), p.704.

[253] *Sabri-Tabrizi v Lothian Health Board*, 1998 S.C. 373.

[254] *Burnett v British Waterways Board* [1973] 1 W.L.R. 700.

[255] *Bennett v Tugwell* [1971] 2 Q.B. 267.

[256] *Condon v Basi* [1985] 1 W.L.R. 866; *Lewis v Buckpool Golf Club*, 1993 S.L.T. (Sh. Ct) 43; *Sharp
v Highland and Islands Fire Board*, 2005 S.L.T. 855.

[257] *Smoldon v Whitworth & Nolan* [1997] P.I.Q.R. P133; *Vowles v Evans* [2003] 1 W.L.R. 1607.

[258] *Wooldridge v Sumner* [1963] 2 Q.B. 43; *Hall v Brooklands Auto Racing Co* [1933] 1 K.B. 205.

[259] See *Blake v Galloway* [2004] 1 W.L.R. 2844: injury during horseplay; claim based on negligence
and assault. No negligence, but successful defence of consent to assault.

[260] Road Traffic Act 1988 s.149; *Winnik v Dick*, 1984 S.L.T. 185.

[261] *Morris v Murray* [1991] 2 Q.B. 6.

25.30 Employment cases—In cases between employer and employee, when the ground of the action is an injury sustained through faulty organisation, the plea of volenti non fit injuria cannot be sustained merely by showing that the employee knew of the risk and continued to work in spite of it. The word in the maxim is *volenti,* not *scienti.*[262] Accordingly, the defence of *volenti* is rarely applicable in industrial injury cases,[263] and, since the abolition of contributory negligence as a complete defence, there has been increasing reluctance to find *volenti* as a defence.[264] It has been held in England that *volenti* is not a defence to a breach of the employer's own statutory duty,[265] but it does afford a complete defence to the employer's vicarious liability for the acts of a fellow-servant when the pursuer invited or freely aided and abetted his fellow-servant's disobedience of an order.[266]

25.31 Occupiers' liability cases—The plea is open to an occupier of property who is sued for damages by a person injured thereon.[267] Where let property is concerned, the maxim could apply, but probably only where the landlord could demonstrate clear acceptance of specific known risks.[268] Any acquiescence by the tenant cannot detract from the landlord's liability to other persons injured on the premises.[269] A person struck by a train while crossing a railway line is taken voluntarily to have accepted that risk.[270]

25.32 Rescue cases—The plea of *volenti* will not avail a person whose fault creates a situation of peril which he ought reasonably to have foreseen would invite rescue by another person who voluntarily exposes himself to danger in attempting rescue.[271] And the right of a servant to interfere in circumstances of danger for the safeguarding of an employer's property is also recognised.[272]

25.33 Participation in criminal enterprise—A pursuer's claim may be barred where the injury of which he complains was sustained in the course of a criminal enterprise in which he participated jointly with the defender. This rule has been applied when the pursuer was injured as a result of the defender's negligent driving of a car in which the pursuer was a passenger and in the theft of which he had been involved along with the defender,[273] and where the pursuer knew that the defender was under age for driving and was driving without the consent of the owner of the car.[274] It may also apply where, to the pursuer's knowledge, the defender is

---

[262] *Smith v Charles Baker & Sons* [1891] A.C. 325; *Wallace v Culter Paper Co* (1892) 19 R. 915.

[263] But see *Keenan v City Line*, 1953 S.L.T. 128.

[264] *ICI v Shatwell* [1965] A.C. 656 at 686, per Lord Pearce.

[265] *Wheeler v New Merton Board Mills* [1933] 2 K.B. 669.

[266] *ICI v Shatwell* [1965] A.C. 656; *Hugh v National Coal Board*, 1972 S.C. 252.

[267] See Occupiers' Liability (Scotland) Act 1960 s.2(3); and para.27.04, below.

[268] Occupiers' Liability (Scotland) Act 1960 s.3; Walker, *The Law of Delict in Scotland* (1981), p.348. The law before the 1960 Act, and the effects of the Act, are reviewed in *Hughes' Tutrix v Glasgow DC*, 1982 S.L.T. (Sh. Ct) 70.

[269] *Hughes' Tutrix v Glasgow DC*, 1982 S.L.T. (Sh. Ct) 70. There are certain statutory restrictions of a landlord's ability to contract out of statutory repairing obligations. See the Housing (Scotland) Act 2006 s.17.

[270] *Titchener v British Railways Board*, 1984 S.C. (HL) 34; 1984 S.L.T. 192.

[271] *Haynes v Harwood* [1935] 1 K.B. 146; *Baker v Hopkins* [1959] 3 All E.R. 225, CA; *Videan v B.T.C.* [1963] 2 Q.B. 650 at 669, per Lord Denning M.R.

[272] *Steel v Glasgow Iron & Steel Co,* 1944 S.C. 237.

[273] *Lindsay v Poole*, 1984 S.L.T. 269; *Sloan v Triplett*, 1985 S.L.T. 294.

[274] *Wilson v Price*, 1989 S.L.T. 484.

guilty of breaches of the Road Traffic Act, such as driving while intoxicated.[275] The rule is not, however, an absolute one and its application will sometimes only be capable of ascertainment after proof of the particular facts of the case.[276] It has been held in England that damages cannot be awarded for loss of an opportunity where the exercise of that opportunity would have involved the commission of an illegal act.[277] Further, no damages can be awarded to a claimant who seeks to rely on his own commission of a crime to establish a cause of action.[278] Illegality which is central to a particular head of loss will bar recovery of damages for that head.[279]

Contributory negligence—Although the fault of the pursuer is not now a **25.34** complete defence, the fact that the pursuer was contributorily negligent can be invoked by the defender to justify a reduction in the damages which he is found liable to pay. "The technical meaning of 'contributory negligence' is negligence on the part of the pursuer which is itself jointly causative of the accident along with the negligence of the defender,"[280] but in ordinary usage it means fault on the part of a pursuer either wholly causing or materially contributing to his injury. In this context "fault" connotes breach of a legal duty only in the sense that the law requires a man in his own interest to take reasonable care of himself.[281] The burden of proving that the pursuer's fault was at least one of the effective causes of his injury is on the defender.[282] Until the Law Reform (Contributory Negligence) Act 1945 (the "1945 Act"), if the pursuer was held to any extent to blame for his injury, his claim failed and he could recover nothing. To mitigate the harshness of this doctrine the courts developed the so-called "last opportunity" rule,[283] under which he who had the last opportunity of avoiding the accident was held liable. The fault of the first party was regarded as a *causa sine qua non*; that of the second and later party was regarded as the *causa causans* of the accident. This "was a fallacious test because the efficiency of the causes did not depend on their proximity in point of time".[284]

Contributory negligence under the 1945 Act—The 1945 Act provides[285] **25.35**

> "where any person suffers damage as the result partly of his own fault and partly of the fault of any other person or persons, a claim in respect of that damage shall not be defeated by reason of the fault of the person suffering

---

[275] See dicta of Lord Hunter in *Winnik v Dick*, 1984 S.L.T. 185 at 189; *Pitts v Hunt* [1991] 1 Q.B. 24.

[276] As in *Taylor v Leslie*, 1998 S.L.T. 1248. See observation of Stuart-Smith L.J. in *Vellino v Chief Constable of Greater Manchester Police* [2002] 1 W.L.R. 218 at [70] that maxim should apply where crime is punishable by imprisonment.

[277] *Rance v Mid Downs Health Authority* [1991] 1 Q.B. 587.

[278] *Clunis v Camden & Islington H.A.* [1998] Q.B. 978.

[279] *Hewison v Meridian Shipping Services Pte Ltd* [2003] I.C.R. 766.

[280] *Robinson v Hamilton (Motors)*, 1923 S.C. 838 at 841, per Lord President Clyde.

[281] *Nance v British Columbia Electric Ry Co* [1951] A.C. 601 at 611, per Viscount Simon; *Davies v Swan Motor Co* [1949] 2 K.B. 291 at 308, per Bucknill L.J., at 324, per Denning L.J.

[282] See para.26.11, below.

[283] *Davies v Mann* (1842) 10 M. & W. 546; *Carse v North British Steam Packet Co* (1895) 22 R. 475; *British Columbia Electric Co v Loach* [1916] 1 A.C. 719; *Ward v Revie*, 1944 S.C. 325 at 335, per Lord Moncrieff.

[284] *Davies v Swan Motor Co* [1949] 2 K.B. 291 at 321, per Denning L.J.; and see *Boy Andrew v St Rognvald*, 1947 S.C. (HL) 70; para.26.11, below.

[285] 1945 Act s.1(1).

the damage, but the damages recoverable in respect thereof shall be reduced to such extent as the court thinks just and equitable having regard to the claimant's share in the responsibility for the damage."

This provision is not to operate to defeat any defence arising under a contract.[286] The judge or jury must determine the total damages recoverable by the claimant had he not been at fault.[287] The jury can also determine the extent to which damages are to be reduced[288] in the same way as the court under s.1(1). Where any person dies as the result partly of his own fault and partly of the fault of any other person, the damages recoverable by any dependant of the deceased may be reduced according to the share of the deceased in the responsibility for his death.[289]

25.36 Measuring contributory negligence—Under the Act the court assesses the measure of contribution made by the pursuer to the end result and apportions liability accordingly.[290] Where more than one defender is found liable, the correct approach is to assess the pursuer's contribution as compared with the totality of the contribution made by the defenders. Thus, where the plaintiff and each of two defendants were all found to blame for an accident, contributory negligence was assessed at 50 per cent, before any question of contribution between the defendants *inter se* was dealt with.[291] Regard must be had both to the relative importance of the pursuer's act in causing the damage and also to his relative blameworthiness.[292] Given the destructive potency of a car, it is rare for a pedestrian to be found more responsible than a driver.[293] Consideration is not restricted to causation of the accident in a narrow sense, but extends to all the factors in respect of which fault can be imputed, contributing to the damage.[294] The section is applicable in cases of economic loss, when imprudence by a lender can be contributory negligence in an action alleging negligence by a valuer.[295]

25.37 Pursuer's standard of care—The standard of care required of a pursuer is such care for his own safety as is reasonable in the circumstances. He will be guilty of contributory negligence if he ought reasonably to have foreseen that, if he did not act as a reasonable, prudent man, he might hurt himself, and he ought to take into account the possibility of others being careless.[296] What amounts to reasonable care depends upon the circumstances of each case.[297] Allowance must be made for inadvertence due to necessary haste, fatigue or familiarity,[298] and also for

---

[286] 1945 Act s.1(1)(a).

[287] 1945 Act s.1(2) and (6).

[288] 1945 Act s.1(6).

[289] 1945 Act s.1(4), and see e.g. *Kelly v Glasgow Corp*, 1951 S.C. (HL) 15.

[290] See *Davies v Swan Motor Co* [1949] 2 K.B. 291 at 322, per Denning L.J.

[291] *Fitzgerald v Lane* [1989] A.C. 328.

[292] *Stapley v Gypsum Mines* [1953] A.C. 663 at 682, per Lord Reid; *Kilgower v N.C.B.*, 1958 S.L.T. (Notes) 48.

[293] *Eagle v Chambers* [2004] R.T.R. 9.

[294] *Davies v Swan Motor Co* [1949] 2 K.B. 291; *Froom v Butcher* [1976] Q.B. 286. The onus is, however, on the defender to show that the injuries sustained were, in part at least, caused by failure to adopt the precaution desired (e.g. wearing a seat-belt) (*Barker v Murdoch*, 1977 S.L.T. 75).

[295] *Platform Home Loans Ltd v Oyston Shipways Ltd* [2000] 2 A.C 190.

[296] *Jones v Livox Quarries* [1952] 2 Q.B. 608 at 615, per Denning L.J.

[297] See *Caswell v Powell Duffryn Association Collieries* [1940] A.C. 152 at 176, per Lord Wright.

[298] *Caswell v Powell Duffryn Association Collieries* [1940] A.C. 152 at 178–179; and see *John Summers & Sons v Frost* [1955] A.C. 740.

emergency action necessitated by the negligence of the defender.[299] Where the negligence consists of failure to safeguard a prisoner, the prisoner's suicide can amount to contributory negligence.[300] In the case of children it is always a question of circumstances whether they are guilty of contributory negligence. Relevant factors are their age and whether or not they appreciated or should have appreciated the danger.[301] A child should only be found guilty of contributory negligence if he or she is of such an age as to be expected to take precautions for his or her own safety; even then the child is only to be found guilty if blame should be attached.[302] It is contributory negligence to fail to wear a seat-belt,[303] or to allow oneself to be driven in a car in the knowledge that the driver is so drunk[304] or tired[305] as to be unable to drive safely. In England, a deduction has been made from damages awarded for asbestos-related lung cancer to reflect the deceased's smoking.[306] A servant or employee may be held to be negligent although his claim is based upon breach of statutory duty on the part of his master or employer[307]; but his erroneous assumption that the duty has been performed may not amount to negligence.[308]

Self-defence—Self-defence, or defence of those whom one has a duty to **25.38** protect, is an excuse for injury inflicted on the aggressor, unless the injury was unreasonably greater than the occasion warranted.[309] Even if it was, the attack or provocation may be proved in mitigation of damages.[310] Because it is a matter that depends essentially on the circumstances of each case, limits of the right to defend property, or to resort to self-help, cannot be clearly defined. Probably a thief could not claim damages for injury inflicted in an attempt to recover the stolen property. And a mere squatter, or a person whose title to possess has expired, and who refuses to remove, may be removed by force, without any liability except on the ground that the measures taken involved more injury than was reasonably necessary.[311] But if a title to possess can be shown, even though that title may be voidable, measures of self-help are not justifiable, and will found an action for damages for any injury that may have resulted.[312] A carrier has a very wide discretion in the use of force to remove passengers who refuse to pay the fare or to submit to reasonable regulations.[313] A similar discretion is accorded to the managers of a

---

[299] *Laird Line v US Shipping Board*, 1924 S.C. (HL) 37.

[300] *Reeves v Metropolitan Cmmissioner of Police* [2000] 1 A.C. 360.

[301] *Fraser v Edinburgh Tramways Co* (1882) 10 R. 264; *Yachuk v Oliver Blais & Co* [1949] A.C. 386; see also *Hughes v Lord Advocate*, 1961 S.C. 310 at 323, per Lord Wheatley.

[302] *Gough v Thorne* [1966] 1 W.L.R. 1387 at 1390, per Lord Denning M.R. But cf. *Barnes v Flucker*, 1985 S.L.T. 142.

[303] *Hill v Chivers*, 1987 S.L.T. 323. The wearing of seatbelts on coaches is considered in *Welsh v Messenger* [2006] C.L.Y. 296.

[304] *Hill v Chivers*, 1987 S.L.T. 323; *Winnik v Dick*, 1984 S.L.T. 185.

[305] *Smith v Stages* [1989] A.C. 928.

[306] *Badger v Ministry of Defence* [2006] 3 All E.R. 173.

[307] *Caswell v Powell Duffryn Association Collieries* [1940] A.C. 152; *Cakebread v Hopping Bros Ltd* [1947] K.B. 641.

[308] *Grant v Sun Shipping Co Ltd*, 1948 S.C. (HL) 73 at 97, per Lord du Parcq.

[309] Glegg, *The Law of Reparation in Scotland* (1939), p.131. Evidence of a harder than average blow will not, of itself, prevent the defence from succeeding: *Cross v Kirby* [2000] T.L.R. 268.

[310] *Falconer v Cochran* (1837) 15 S. 891. For a recent example, see *Ashmore v Rock Steady Security Ltd*, 2006 S.L.T. 207.

[311] *Macdonald v Watson* (1883) 10 R. 1079; *Sinclair v Tod*, 1907 S.C. 1038; *Hemmings v Stoke Poges Golf Club* [1920] 1 K.B. 720.

[312] *Brash v Munro* (1903) 5 F. 1102.

[313] *Highland Ry v Menzies* (1878) 5 R. 887; *Whittaker v London CC* [1915] 2 K.B. 676.

place of entertainment or of a public meeting.[314] The limits of the right to use force against trespassers have never been definitely settled.[315]

25.39 Statutory authority—What would otherwise amount to a wrong may be excused if it is done under the authority of a statute.

> "No action can be maintained for anything which is done under the authority of the legislature, though the act is one which, if unauthorised by the legislature, would be injurious and actionable."[316]

Any right to compensation must be founded on some provision in the statute in question.[317] But the defence of statutory authority is available only where the statutory operation is carried out without negligence, and negligence may consist either in carrying out work without reasonable care, or in neglecting precautions to avoid injury to third parties where such precautions are within the statutory powers.[318] It has been held that if work authorised by statute can be done in two ways, one injurious to a third party, the other innocuous, the body exercising the statutory powers is bound to choose the latter method, even though it be the more expensive.[319] In private Acts the plea of statutory authority is often in substance denuded by a clause providing that nothing in the Act shall excuse those acting under it from liability for the commission of a nuisance.[320]

When the legislature authorises a particular thing to be done, it impliedly legalises all results which necessarily flow from its being done. So, as railway companies ran their trains under statutory powers, it was held that their duty was merely to use the best type of spark arrester, and that they were not liable for fires caused by sparks which the spark arrester failed to prevent.[321]

25.40 State immunity[322]—Under the State Immunity Act 1978, a state is immune from the jurisdiction of the courts of the United Kingdom, subject only to certain statutory exceptions. These provisions cannot be circumvented by suing the responsible servants or agents of the state.[323] The European Court of Human Rights has found that this immunity does not breach art.6 of the Convention.[324]

---

[314] *Wallace v Mooney* (1885) 12 R. 710; *Doyle v Falconer* (1866) L.R. 1 P.C. 328.

[315] See *Wood v N.B. Ry* (1899) 2 F. 1.

[316] *Caledonian Ry v Walker's Trs* (1882) 9 R. (HL) 19 at 32, per Lord Blackburn.

[317] As to the construction of the phrase "injuriously affected" in private Acts incorporating the Companies Clauses or Railway Clauses Acts, see *Caledonian Ry v Walker's Trs* (1882) 9 R. (HL) 19.

[318] *Edinburgh Water Trs v Somerville* (1906) 8 F. (HL) 25; *Farnworth v Lord Mayor of Manchester* [1930] A.C. 171.

[319] *West v Bristol Tramways* [1908] 2 K.B. 14; see also *Metropolitan Asylums District Board v Hill* (1881) 6 App. Cas. 193.

[320] *Farnworth v Lord Mayor of Manchester* [1930] A.C. 171.

[321] *Port Glasgow, etc. Sailcloth Co v Caledonian Ry* (1893) 20 R. (HL) 35.

[322] On immunities generally see O'Donnell, "Liability for Delictual Actions" in Thomson (ed.), *Delict*, paras 4.93–4.106.

[323] *Jones v Saudi Arabia* [2007] 1 A.C. 270.

[324] *Al-Adsani v United Kingdom* (2002) 34 E.H.R.R. 11, although it is debatable whether art.6 was truly engaged: see observations in *Jones v Saudi Arabia* [2007] 1 A.C. 270.

Proceedings against the Crown[325]—Before 1947 the Crown, in modern times at **25.41** least,[326] was not vicariously liable for the wrongful acts of its servants or agents.[327] The effect of the Crown Proceedings Act 1947, however, was to render the Crown liable for wrongs committed by its servants or agents, provided that, apart from the provisions of the Act, the act or omission complained of would have rendered the servant or agent liable.[328] The Crown is also made liable in respect of any breach of those duties which a person owes to his servants and agents as their employer, and in respect of any breach of the duties attaching at common law to the ownership, occupation, possession or control of property.[329] Where the Crown is bound, whether expressly or by necessary implication, by a statutory duty which is binding also upon persons other than the Crown and its officers, it is liable for breach of such a duty in the same way as if it were a private person.[330] No proceedings, however, will lie against the Crown in respect of acts or omissions by judicial persons[331] or by public servants, such as policemen,[332] not directly or indirectly appointed by the Crown and paid out of the Consolidated Fund or certain other national sources.[333] Interdict, or interim interdict, or an order for specific performance, cannot be pronounced against the Crown in private law proceedings.[334] Such orders can, however, be made where the supervisory jurisdiction of the Court of Session is invoked against the Crown.[335] The Post Office is no longer regarded as an agent of the Crown or as enjoying Crown immunity.[336] The generality of the Crown's liability is further limited by s.11 of the Act, which specifically preserves all powers and authorities of a prerogative nature or conferred on the Crown by any statute, particularly those connected with defence. Section 10, which formerly protected the Crown from suit at the instance of injured members of the armed forces, was repealed with effect from May 15, 1987.[337] Its application to prevent claims which result from pre-1987 wrongs is not a breach of art.6 of the European Convention.[338] In battle conditions, one soldier does not owe a duty of care to another and the Crown does not owe a duty

---

[325] See generally J.D.B. Mitchell, *Constitutional Law*, 2nd edn (Edinburgh: W. Green, 1968), pp.304–312.

[326] At one stage it seems that an action of reparation against the Crown was competent; see Mitchell, *Constitutional Law* (1968), p.304.

[327] *Macgregor v Lord Advocate*, 1921 S.C. 847.

[328] Crown Proceedings Act 1947 s.2(1)(a). This proviso prevents the Crown from being sued where the defence of act of state would protect the individual. "Agent" is defined as including an independent contractor employed by the Crown (s.38).

[329] Crown Proceedings Act 1947 s.2(1)(b) and (c). The Occupiers' Liability (Scotland) Act 1960 s.4, binds the Crown.

[330] Crown Proceedings Act 1947 s.2(2).

[331] Crown Proceedings Act 1947 s.2(5), which has been held to cover sheriff clerks: *Wood v Lord Advocate*, 1996 S.C.L.R. 278, followed in *Quinland v Governor of Swaleside Prison* [2003] Q.B. 306.

[332] But see Police (Scotland) Act 1967 s.39.

[333] Crown Proceedings Act 1947 s.2(6).

[334] Crown Proceedings Act 1947 s.21(1), as interpreted by the House of Lords in *Davidson v Scottish Ministers*, 2006 S.C. (HL) 41.

[335] Crown Proceedings Act 1947 s.21(1), as interpreted by the House of Lords in *Davidson v Scottish Ministers*, 2006 S.C. (HL) 41.

[336] Post Office Act 1969 s.6(5).

[337] Crown Proceedings (Armed Forces) Act 1987; the subsection can, however, be revived if justified by national emergency.

[338] *Matthews v Ministry of Defence* [2003] 1 A.C. 1163.

to maintain a safe system of work.[339] An executive officer of the Crown may incur personal liability in respect of his own wrongful or negligent act.[340]

The sheriff court has jurisdiction in actions against the Crown, subject to the power of the Lord Advocate to have cases which are important remitted to the Court of Session.[341] In Scotland, actions against the Crown or any public department may be raised against the appropriate Law Officer who, before representing the Crown or the public department, must have their authority to do so.[342]

25.42 Judicial immunity—Judges of the Court of Session, the High Court of Justiciary and probably the sheriff court[343] enjoy absolute immunity at common law from civil action for anything done by them in their judicial capacity.[344] At common law, judges of an inferior court, such as magistrates or justices of the peace, probably could be sued for damages in respect of acts done in excess of their jurisdiction apart altogether from malice,[345] but their position is now regulated by statute. Under the Criminal Procedure (Scotland) Act 1995[346] no judge, clerk of court or prosecutor in the public interest may be found liable in damages in respect of any proceedings taken, act done or judgment, decree or sentence pronounced under that Act unless: (1) the person claiming damages was imprisoned in consequence thereof; (2) the proceeding complained of has been quashed; (3) malice and want of probable cause are specifically averred and proved; and (4) the action is begun within two months of the proceeding complained of. Where a judge acts in an administrative capacity,[347] he will be liable only on averment and proof that he acted maliciously and without probable cause.[348]

25.43 Criminal proceedings—The Lord Advocate is protected by absolute privilege in respect of matters in connection with criminal proceedings on indictment.[349] Since all prosecutions on indictment must have the authority of the Lord Advocate either in person or through his deputes,[350] that privilege extends to procurators fiscal and depute procurators fiscal acting on his authority and instructions.[351] In summary proceedings, procurators fiscal are protected by the Criminal Procedure (Scotland) Act 1995.[352] Those conducting a criminal defence in Scotland, whether solicitors or advocates, are immune from suit at the instance of the accused

---

[339] *Mulcahy v Ministry of Defence* [1996] Q.B. 732.

[340] *Macgregor v Lord Advocate*, 1921 S.C. 847; *Bainbridge v Postmaster General* [1906] 1 K.B. 178. For the defence of Act of State, see *Poll v Lord Advocate* (1899) 1 F. 823; *Johnstone v Pedlar* [1921] 2 A.C. 262; and Mitchell, *Constitutional Law* (1968), p.180.

[341] Crown Proceedings Act 1947 s.44.

[342] Crown Suits (Scotland) Act 1857, as amended by the Scotland Act 1998.

[343] *Harvey v Dyce* (1876) 4 R. 265, as applied in *Russell v Dickson*, 1998 S.L.T. 96. Doubts regarding the extent of a Sheriff's immunity in relation to his actings in a criminal case are expressed in Mitchell, *Constitutional Law* (1968), p.262.

[344] *Haggart'sTrs v Hope* (1824) 2 Shaw's App.125; *McCreadie v Thomson*, 1907 S.C. 1176 at 1182, per Lord Justice Clerk Macdonald.

[345] *McPhee v Macfarlane's Exr*, 1933 S.C. 163 at 169, per Lord President Clyde.

[346] Criminal Procedure (Scotland) Act 1995 s.170.

[347] On the distinction between "administrative" and "judicial" acts, see Walker, *Law of Delict in Scotland* (1981), pp.105–106.

[348] *Beaton v Ivory* (1887) 14 R. 1057; *McPherson v McLennan* (1887) 14 R. 1063.

[349] *Henderson v Robertson* (1853) 15 D. 292; *Hester v Macdonald*, 1961 S.C. 370.

[350] See Criminal Procedure (Scotland) Act 1995 s.64

[351] *Hester v Macdonald*, 1961 S.C. 370.

[352] Criminal Procedure (Scotland) Act 1995 s.170.

person.[353] Witnesses in a criminal case also enjoy immunity from suit, except in a subsequent action for malicious prosecution.[354]

Prescription and limitation—Positive prescription relates purely to real rights. **25.44** Negative prescription is to be distinguished from limitation of actions. By negative prescription an obligation and its correlative right are extinguished. By limitation it is merely the right to sue that is cut off; substantive rights and obligations, although no longer directly enforceable, remain in force and may be pleaded by way of exception. Prescription is therefore substantive while limitation is procedural.[355] While all obligations are subject to prescription[356] limitation applied only to actions in respect of personal injuries. The governing legislation has since been amended so that actions for defamation,[357] actions of harassment[358] and actions brought under Part 1 of the Consumer Protection Act[359] are all subject to limitation.

The law as to limitation of actions is contained in the Prescription and Limitation (Scotland) Act 1973 which provides that no action of damages, where the damages claimed consist of or include damages or solatium in respect of personal injuries, shall be brought unless commenced[360] within three years of the date when the injuries were sustained or, where there has been a continuing act or omission, within three years of the date on which the act or omission ceased, whichever is the later.[361] Where, however, the pursuer was not at that date aware that the injuries were sufficiently serious to justify his bringing an action of damages, or that they were attributable to an act or omission or that the defender was a person to whose act or omission they were attributable, the three-year period runs from the date on which he became aware, or on which, in the opinion of the court, it would have been reasonably practicable for him to become aware, of all those facts.[362] The test to be applied in deciding whether the pursuer should have been aware that the injuries were sufficiently serious to justify his bringing an action of damages is essentially an objective one, but takes into account the particular characteristics of the pursuer and the injury; and where a claim is time-barred as respects injuries caused initially, it is also time-barred as respects injuries subsequently emerging even if these may be described as being of a distinct nature.[363] A three-year limitation period applies on similar principles, but running from the date of death, to actions in which, following the death of any person from personal

---

[353] *Wright v Paton Farrell*, 2006 S.C. 404.

[354] *McKie v Strathclyde Joint Police Board*, 2004 S.L.T. 982.

[355] See Ch.4, above, on negative prescription and paras 34.30–34.37, below, on positive prescription.

[356] The prescriptive periods are either five years under Prescription and Limitation (Scotland) Act 1973 s.6 or 20 years under s.7. Schedule 1 specifies those obligations which fall under s.6. This includes the obligation to make reparation. See also s.11.

[357] Prescription and Limitation (Scotland) Act 1973 s.18A inserted by the Law Reform (Miscellaneous Provisions) (Scotland) Act s.12(2).

[358] Prescription and Limitation (Scotland) Act 1973 s.18B inserted by the Protection from Harassment Act 1997 s.10(1).

[359] Prescription and Limitation (Scotland) Act 1973 s.22B inserted by the Consumer Protection Act 1987 s.6, Sch.1 para.10.

[360] As to the meaning of "commenced", see *McGraddie v Clark*, 1966 S.L.T. (Sh. Ct) 36; see also *Miller v N.C.B.*, 1960 S.C. 376 at 382, per Lord President Clyde.

[361] Prescription and Limitation (Scotland) Act 1973 s.17(1) and (2).

[362] Prescription and Limitation (Scotland) Act 1973 s.17(2)(b).

[363] *Aitchison v Glasgow City Council* [2010] CSIH 9; 2010 S.C. 411 over-ruling in part *Carnegie v Lord Advocate (No 3)*, 2001 S.C. 802. See also *S v Poor Sisters of Nazareth* [2007] CSIH 39; 2007 S.C. 688.

injuries, damages are claimed in respect of the injuries or death.[364] But no such action can be brought if the person who sustained the injuries allowed the limitation period applicable to an action by him to elapse without taking proceedings.[365] If the pursuer is the person injured or, in an action following the death of the person injured, is a relative of that person, any time is to be disregarded, in computation of the limitation period, during which the pursuer was under legal disability by reason of nonage[366] or of unsoundness of mind.[367] It is not necessary for there to be a causal connection between the legal disability and the delay.[368]

25.45 Discretion to extend limitation period—In any case where proceedings are barred by the expiry of the limitation period, the court may, nonetheless, allow the action to be brought if it seems to it equitable to do so.[369] The discretion thus given to the court is unfettered and is to be exercised according to the circumstances of the case. All the relevant equitable considerations are to be balanced and a decision reached on the basis of the side on which the balance of equity falls. The prejudice to which either party may be subject and the availability to the pursuer of an alternative remedy are relevant factors.[370] The fact that for part of the time since an accident the triennium has not been running because the pursuer has been under a legal disability should not, however, be viewed as creating unfairness to the defender.[371] The court will not in general allow a pursuer by amendment to change the basis of his case or cure a radical incompetence in his action,[372] to substitute or call in another defender[373] or to amend his conclusion so as to enable the court to grant decree against a third party,[374] if he seeks to make such amendments outwith the period of the statutory limitation; but an amendment may be allowed if it would be equitable to override the time bar.[375]

25.46 Liability of joint wrongdoers *inter se*—Joint wrongdoers, while each is jointly and severally liable to the person wronged by them, are entitled to relief *inter se* in such proportions as seem just to the court, whether both have been sued in one action or

---

[364] Prescription and Limitation (Scotland) Act 1973 s.18.

[365] Prescription and Limitation (Scotland) Act 1973 s.18(4).

[366] i.e. 16: Age of Legal Capacity (Scotland) Act 1991 s.1(2).

[367] Prescription and Limitation (Scotland) Act 1973 ss.17(3) and 18(3).

[368] *Paton v Loffland Brothers North Sea Inc.*, 1994 S.L.T. 784; cf. *Bogan's C.B. v Graham*, 1992 S.C.L.R. 920.

[369] Prescription and Limitation (Scotland) Act 1973 s.19A. See, e.g. *M v Hendron*, 2005 S.L.T. 1122. For a contrary example in which the limitation period was not extended see *AS or B v Murray*, 2008 S.C.L.R. 19.

[370] *Donald v Rutherford*, 1984 S.L.T. 70; *Forsyth v A.F. Stoddard and Co*, 1985 S.L.T. 51; *Anderson v Glasgow DC*, 1987 S.L.T. 279; *Elliot v J. & C. Finney (No.1)*, 1989 S.L.T. 605; *McLaren v Harland & Wolff Ltd*, 1991 S.L.T. 85; *S v Poor Sisters of Nazareth* [2007] CSIH 39; 2007 S.C. 688.

[371] *McCabe v McLellan*, 1994 S.L.T. 346.

[372] See *Pompa's Trs v Edinburgh BC*, 1942 S.C. 119 at 125, per Lord Justice Clerk Cooper; *Dryburgh v N.C.B.*, 1962 S.C. 485; *O'Hare's Executrix v Western Heritable Investment Co Ltd*, 1965 S.L.T. 182. For cases in which amendments have been allowed on the view that they did not alter the basis of the pursuer's case, see *Emslie v Tognarelli's Exrs (No.2)*, 1969 S.L.T. 20; *Mazs v The Dairy Supply Co*, 1978 S.L.T. 208 and *Meek v Milne*, 1985 S.L.T. 318.

[373] *Miller v N.C.B.*, 1960 S.C. 376; *MacLean v B.R.B.*, 1966 S.L.T. 39 (an attempt to include further pursuers); *Marshall v Black*, 1981 S.L.T. 228; *Boslem v Paterson*, 1982 S.L.T. 216; but see *Pompa's Trs v Edinburgh BC*, 1942 S.C. 119; and *Dailly v Wilson*, 1990 S.L.T. 106.

[374] *Aitken v Norrie*, 1967 S.L.T. 4; *Travers v Neilson*, 1967 S.L.T. 64.

[375] *McCullough v Norwest Socea*, 1981 S.L.T. 201; *Carson v Howard Doris*, 1981 S.C. 278; *Webb v B.P. Petroleum Development Ltd*, 1988 S.L.T. 775.

not.[376] A decree of a Scottish court,[377] or some equivalent instrument constituting the debt, is an essential prerequisite to an action of relief by one wrongdoer against another; an extra-judicial settlement by one wrongdoer acting on his own which is not embodied in a decree[378] will not suffice for this purpose.[379] Relief is available against any person who if sued to judgment might also have been found liable.[380] The fact that such liability would have arisen for breach of contract, rather than in delict, does not prevent relief from being obtained.[381] Absolvitor or dismissal obtained as a result of a settlement with the injured party[382] or as a result of successfully founding on a plea of limitation[383] does not protect the person in whose favour it is granted from claims for a contribution in relief at the instance of others.

Abuse of process—The court has an inherent power to dismiss a claim where the party pursuing it has been guilty of an abuse of process. Abuse of process can take a number of forms.[384] In a case involving dishonesty, the exercise of the power will depend on whether the dishonesty has made a fair trial of the issue impossible.[385] **25.47**

Criminal charge[386]—To give information to the police or criminal authorities, to institute a prosecution, or in the case of a party entitled to arrest, to arrest on suspicion of a crime, are acts which are not actionable merely on the ground that they were founded on a mistake but only on averments and proof of malice and want of probable cause.[387] Facts and circumstances from which malice may be inferred must be stated. **25.48**

"A man has probable cause if, in giving information, he is acting in a way in which a reasonable man, swayed by no illegitimate motives, would act."[388]

A conviction on the charge made is fatal to the action, since it proves that probable cause existed[389]; an acquittal standing by itself is not enough to establish that there was no probable cause.[390] The exercise of powers of search and its abuse are subject to similar principles.

Position of prosecutors—Procurators fiscal and deputes acting on the authority of the Lord Advocate enjoy the same absolute privilege as the Lord Advocate in relation to prosecutions on indictment.[391] Quoad summary proceedings there is at common law no distinction in the law applicable in an action directed against a **25.49**

---

[376] Law Reform (Miscellaneous Provisions) (Scotland) Act 1940 s.3; *Central S.M.T. Co v Lanarkshire County Council*, 1949 S.C. 450.

[377] *Comex Houlder Diving Ltd v Colne Fishing Co Ltd*, 1987 S.L.T. 443.

[378] *Comex Houlder Diving Ltd v Colne Fishing Co Ltd*, 1987 S.L.T. 443.

[379] *N.C.B. v Thomson*, 1959 S.C. 353.

[380] See *ComexHoulder Diving Ltd v Colne Fishing Co Ltd*, 1987 S.L.T. 443.

[381] *Engdiv Ltd v G. Percy Trentham Ltd*, 1990 S.L.T. 617.

[382] *Singer v Gray Tool Co (Europe)*, 1984 S.L.T. 149.

[383] *Dormer v Melville Dundas & Whitson Ltd*, 1990 S.L.T. 186.

[384] Bad faith, dishonesty or improper ulterior motive are instanced in *Shetland Sea Farms Ltd v Assuranceforeningen Skuld*, 2004 S.L.T. 30 at [143].

[385] *Shetland Sea Farms Ltd v Assuranceforeningen Skuld*, 2004 S.L.T. 30 at [146].

[386] See Walker, *Law of Delict in Scotland* (1981), pp.870–876.

[387] *Hill v Campbell* (1905) 8 F. 220; *Mills v Kelvin & White*, 1913 S.C. 521; *Notman v Commercial Bank of Scotland*, 1938 S.C. 522.

[388] *Mills v Kelvin & White*, 1913 S.C. 521 at 528, per Lord President Dunedin.

[389] *Hill v Campbell* (1905) 8 F. 220.

[390] *Chalmers v Barclay, Perkins & Co*, 1912 S.C. 521.

[391] *Hester v Macdonald*, 1961 S.C. 370.

public or a private prosecutor.[392] By statute, however, actions against the former arising out of proceedings under provisions of the Criminal Procedure (Scotland) Act 1995 are subject to a time limit,[393] and are competent only where the pursuer has suffered imprisonment, the proceedings have been quashed, and the pursuer avers that the actings were malicious and without reasonable cause.[394] Express provision is, moreover, made that it is a defence to such an action that the pursuer was guilty of the offence in question and had undergone no greater punishment than was assigned by law.[395] A letter, intimating the charge, and followed by a prosecution, is to be taken as part of the prosecution, and its actionability to be judged by the same standards.[396]

25.50 **Unfounded litigation**[397]—No damages can be claimed for bringing a civil action, even if it proves to be unfounded. It would seem a doubtful point whether averments that the action in question was brought maliciously would make a claim for damages relevant.[398] It is not wrong to take a decree irregularly, as where a decree in absence was obtained when the defender had not been properly cited, provided that no diligence has followed on the decree. Repeated raising of proceedings which are unfounded can result in an application to have the pursuer declared a vexatious litigant under the Vexatious Actions (Scotland) Act 1898.[399]

25.51 **Wrongful diligence: Wrongful interdict**—If a party is using a legal right or remedy to which he is absolutely entitled, and which he can use without applying to a court for a special warrant, he is not liable in damages unless either: (1) there is an inherent vice in the form or regularity of the writ itself or the manner in which it is used; or (2) it can be shown that he acted maliciously and without probable cause.[400] Irregular diligence of any kind is a wrong that is in no way privileged. It may be irregular either because it proceeds on an insufficient warrant,[401] or because the statutory forms have not been observed. In either case the creditor who sets the diligence in motion is personally liable, though the actual fault or mistake may be on the part of the solicitor,[402] messenger-at-arms, or sheriff officer.[403] Probably the solicitor is only liable for his own act or omission,[404] not for a mistake on the part of the officials he employs.[405] A messenger-at-arms or sheriff officer is not liable unless he knew, or should have known, that the diligence was irregular.[406] As well as in the instances of irregularity in form or

---

[392] *Chalmers v Barclay, Perkins & Co*, 1912 S.C. 521.

[393] Two months: Criminal Procedure (Scotland) Act 1995 s.456(3).

[394] Criminal Procedure (Scotland) Act 1995 s.170(1); *Robertson v Keith*, 1936 S.C. 29; *Hester v Macdonald*, 1961 S.C. 370; *Bell v McGlennan*, 1992 S.L.T. 237.

[395] Criminal Procedure (Scotland) Act 1995 s.170(2).

[396] *Chalmers v Barclay, Perkins & Co*, 1912 S.C. 521.

[397] See Walker, *Law of Delict in Scotland* (1981), pp.848–859.

[398] See *Hallam v Gye* (1835) 14 S. 199.

[399] As in *HM Advocate v Bell*, 2002 S.L.T. 527 and *HM Advocate v Frost* [2006] CSIH 56.

[400] Bell, *Principles*, s.553(4).

[401] *Wilson v Mackie* (1875) 3 R. 18; *Emerald Airways Ltd v Nordic Oil Services Ltd*, 1996 S.L.T. 403. See *McGregor v McLaughlin* (1905) 8 F. 70 concerning the distinction between taking a decree irregularly and using diligence upon it.

[402] *Smith v Taylor* (1882) 10 R. 291; *Clark v Beattie*, 1909 S.C. 299 at 303–4, per Lord President Dunedin.

[403] *Le Conte v Douglas* (1880) 8 R. 175.

[404] *McRobbie v McLellan's Trs* (1891) 18 R. 470.

[405] *Henderson v Rollo* (1871) 10 M. 104; J. Graham Stewart, *A Treatise on the Law of Diligence* (Edinburgh: W. Green, 1898), p.799.

[406] *Clark v Beattie*, 1909 S.C. 299.

execution, diligence will be wrongful if it is unjustifiable.[407] It may be unjustifiable if the debt has been paid or discharged or tendered.[408] Further, where the party against whom diligence is used is not at that time subject to the jurisdiction of the court, owing to a failure to arrest to found jurisdiction, the diligence is unjustifiable, or subject to an inherent vice in the manner in which the warrant has been used.[409] Certain forms of diligence, including landlord's sequestration[410] and certain statutory warrants for arrestment,[411] are granted, as is interim interdict,[412] only on an ex parte statement of facts which render them necessary. Such forms are granted at the risk of the person who applies (*periculo petentis*), and he is responsible for the truth of the statement he makes, and will be liable in damages if that statement proves to be untrue and loss has been suffered. No privilege is involved, and therefore there is no necessity for averments of malice or of want of probable cause.[413] Abandonment of an action in which interim interdict has been granted necessarily means that the interdict was wrongly obtained, but it is necessary to plead and prove patrimonial loss stemming from obedience to the interdict before damages can be awarded.[414]

FURTHER READING

Bennett, S.A., *Personal Injury Damages in Scotland*, 5th edn (Barnstoneworth Press) (looseleaf).

Clerk & Lindsell on Torts, edited by Jones, M.A. et al, 20th edn (London: Sweet and Maxwell, 2010) (1st Supp. (2011)).

Johnston, D., *Prescription and Limitation of Actions* (Edinburgh: W. Green, 1999).

Kemp & Kemp: Quantum of Damages, edited by Norris, W. et al (London: Sweet and Maxwell) (looseleaf).

McEwan & Paton on Damages for Personal Injuries in Scotland, edited by Paton, Lady et al (Edinburgh: W. Green) (looseleaf).

McGregor, H., *McGregor on Damages*, 18th edn (London: Sweet and Maxwell, 2009).

Reid, K. and Zimmermann, R. (eds), *A History of Private Law in Scotland, Vol.II: Obligations* (Oxford University Press, 2000).

Scottish Law Commission, *Report on Damages for Wrongful Death* (HMSO, 2008), Scot. Law Com. No. 213.

Smith, T.B., *A Short Commentary on the Law of Scotland* (Edinburgh: W. Green, 1962).

Thomson, J.M. (ed.), *Delict* (Edinburgh: SULI /W. Green) (looseleaf continuing).

Thomson, J.M., *Delictual Liability*, 4th edn (Bloomsbury Professional, 2009).

Walker, D.M., *Law of Delict in Scotland*, 2nd edn (Edinburgh: W. Green, 1981).

---

[407] Graham Stewart, *A Treatise on the Law of Diligence* (1898), p.769.

[408] Graham Stewart, *A Treatise on the Law of Diligence* (1898), p.769.

[409] *Dramgate Ltd v Tyne Dock Engineering Ltd*, 2000 S.C. 43.

[410] *Gray v Weir* (1891) 19 R. 25; *Shearer v Nicoll*, 1935 S.L.T. 313.

[411] *Grant v Magistrates of Airdrie*, 1939 S.C. 738.

[412] *Kennedy v Fort-William Commissioners* (1877) 5 R. 302; *Glasgow District Ry v Glasgow Coal Exchange* (1885) 12 R. 1287; *Clippens Oil Co v Edinburgh Water Trustees*, 1907 S.C. (HL) 9 (measure of damages).

[413] *Wolthekker v Northern Agricultural Co* (1862) 1 M. 211; *Grant v Magistrates of Airdrie*, 1939 S.C. 738.

[414] *Wilson v Scottish Enterprise* Unreported March 28, 2003, Lord Eassie.

CHAPTER 26

NEGLIGENCE

In this chapter, the term "negligence" is used in the sense of harm caused uninten- **26.01** tionally as a consequence of failure to exercise such care as is reasonable in all the circumstances to avoid damage to others and to their property. Liability for negligence depends upon proof of three things, namely: (1) that the defender owed to the pursuer a duty of care; (2) that the defender was in breach of that duty; and (3) that the breach caused the damage complained of.[1] Negligence is not, therefore, synonymous with carelessness.[2] It involves a failure to exercise the duty of care, and the existence of this duty depends upon injury to the pursuer's person or property being a reasonably foreseeable consequence of that failure.

Duty of care: Development—The best known formulation of the duty to take **26.02** care is to be found in the case of *Donoghue v Stevenson*.[3] In holding that the manufacturer of a bottle of ginger beer owed to the ultimate consumer a duty of care regarding the contents of the bottle, Lord Atkin stated[4]:

> "You must take reasonable care to avoid acts or omissions which you can reasonably foresee would be likely to injure your neighbour. Who then in law is my neighbour? The answer seems to be—persons who are so closely and directly affected by my act that I ought reasonably to have them in contemplation as being so affected when I am directing my mind to the acts or omissions which are called in question."

As the law of negligence has evolved, however, it has become apparent that this formulation of the duty is not conclusive; while foreseeability of injury between the parties is necessary before a duty can arise, not every situation falling within Lord Atkin's definition of neighbourhood will give rise to liability when loss is sustained. In order to limit the scope of potential liability it has proved necessary to develop additional factors that may be drawn upon to determine the existence or otherwise of duties of care. The additional elements have been stated to be incapable of further definition,[5] but have often been described as "proximity"[6] and whether it is just and reasonable that a duty of care should exist.[7] Although the

---

[1] Note that a defender is not necessarily liable for all the consequences of his negligence, those heads of loss which are "too remote" from the negligence being excluded: see para.26.12, below.

[2] See *Donoghue v Stevenson*, 1932 S.C. (HL) 31 at 70, per Lord Macmillan.

[3] *Donoghue v Stevenson*, 1932 S.C. (HL) 31.

[4] *Donoghue v Stevenson*, 1932 S.C. (HL) 31 at 44.

[5] *Caparo Industries Plc v Dickman* [1990] 2 A.C. 605 at 618 and 633.

[6] See the comments of Lord Nicholls of Birkenhead on the limitations of this concept in his dissenting speech in *Stovin v Wise* [1996] A.C. 923 at 932.

[7] *Governors of the Peabody Donation Fund v Sir Lindsay Parkinson & Co* [1985] A.C. 210 at 240–241, per Lord Keith; *Caparo Industries Plc v Dickman* [1990] 2 A.C. 605 at 618 and 633. The

requirement of justice and reasonableness is expressed as a separate consideration, it has on some occasions been relied on by the courts as an additional factor
demonstrating that the requisite degree of proximity is either present in or absent
from a particular relationship.

There have been several attempts by the courts to formulate a test applicable to
every situation. In *Home Office v Dorset Yacht Company*,[8] a case where liability
was held to attach to prison officers who had been negligent in their supervision
of Borstal boys in their charge, allowing the boys to damage property nearby,
Lord Reid expressed the view that the Atkin dictum ought to apply as a test of
liability unless there were some justification for its exclusion. In *Anns v London
Borough of Merton*,[9] Lord Wilberforce formulated a two-stage test of liability: a
prima facie duty of care arose if there was sufficient proximity or neighbourhood
between the parties to lead to foreseeability by one party that his carelessness
would injure the other, this prima facie duty then being negatived by particular
considerations appropriate to individual situations. Between 1985 and 1990, in a
succession of cases mainly dealing with economic loss rather than physical injury
or damage to property, the House of Lords expressed reservations about the width
of the test propounded by Lord Wilberforce. Finally in *Murphy v Brentwood DC*[10]
the House of Lords departed from *Anns*. In three English House of Lords cases
involving the provision of professional or quasi-professional services by the
defendant, the test for the existence of a duty of care was stated to be whether or
not the defendant assumed responsibility to the plaintiff for the provision of such
services, on which the plaintiff relied.[11] In summary, it is now clear that there is
no longer a single test for the existence of a duty of care.[12] Different tests may be
used in different circumstances.[13]

In circumstances in which duties of care are well established by precedent,
liability proceeds on *Donoghue* principles. Particular relationships such as
employer and employee or fellow road users and pedestrians in the vicinity are
well recognised as giving rise to a duty of care, in so far as personal injury or
damage to property is concerned. It has been observed that

> "rarely, if ever, does the law absolve from any obligation of care a person
> whose acts or omissions are manifestly capable of causing physical harm to
> others in a structured relationship into which they have entered".[14]

"tripartite" approach was explicitly followed by the majority of the Second Division in *BT Plc
v James Thomson & Sons Ltd*, 1997 S.C. 57, and in the House of Lords (1999 S.C. (HL) 9).

[8] *Home Office v Dorset Yacht Company* [1970] A.C. 1004.

[9] *Anns v London Borough of Merton* [1978] A.C. 728.

[10] *Murphy v Brentwood DC* [1991] 1 A.C. 398.

[11] The speech of Lord Goff in *Spring v Guardian Assurance Plc* [1995] 2 A.C. 296; *Henderson
v Merrett Syndicates Ltd* [1995] 2 A.C. 145; and *White v Jones* [1995] 2 A.C. 207. For an example of
the "assumption of responsibility" test being followed in a case involving physical injury, see *Costello
v Chief Constable of Northumbria* [1999] 1 All E.R. 550.

[12] In *Merrett v Babb* [2001] Q.B. 1174 at [41], May L.J. characterised as "reaching for the moon" the
search for "a single short abstract formulation". In *Williams v Natural Life Health Foods Ltd* [1998] 1
W.L.R. 830 at 837, Lord Steyn commented that "coherence must sometimes yield to practical justice".

[13] In *Parkinson v St James and Seacroft University Hospital NHS Trust* [2002] Q.B. 266 at [17]–
[27], Brooke L.J. summarises the various different approaches to have emerged from the House of
Lords, later describing these as a "battery of tests" (at [50]).

[14] *Vowles v Evans* [2003] 1 W.L.R. 1607 at [25], per Lord Phillips of Worth Matravers (rugby
referee). Other cases involving dangerous sports where the courts have recognised that there can be
liability on those with control of the sport include *Watson v British Boxing Board of Control Ltd* [2001]
Q.B. 1134 and *Harrison v West of Scotland Kart Club*, 2004 S.C. 615.

In novel circumstances, where the relationship of the parties is not well established as giving rise to a duty of care in respect of the kind of loss sustained, the current approach is to apply the tripartite test laid down in *Caparo Industries Plc v Dickman*.[15] Harm to the pursuer must be reasonably foreseeable, there must be a close relationship of proximity between the parties, and it must be fair, just and reasonable for the courts to recognise a duty. While this test was formulated in the context of pure economic loss it is now applied in all novel circumstances regardless of the form taken by the loss.[16] All elements of the test are accorded equal weight and the fair, just and reasonable requirement allows an explicit role for considerations of policy. The attempt to lay down general principles to determine the existence of duties of care has been abandoned in favour of a more pragmatic approach. The tripartite test requires the consideration of proximity factors that have proved significant in determining previous cases and promotes an incremental development of duties of care by analogy with established categories where duties have been recognised.[17]

Duty of care: Foreseeability—The duty to take care is not owed to the world at large, but to those to whom injury may reasonably and probably be anticipated if the duty is not observed.[18] It is not sufficient to say that the defender ought to have contemplated injury to somebody, proximity demands that the pursuer is a person or within a reasonably well defined class of persons who ought to have been within the contemplation of the defender before a duty of care will be recognised.[19] There may be liability to parties who are injured in preventing or attempting to prevent injury to other persons[20] or damage to property[21] imperilled by the defender's acts. For example, a person who negligently starts a fire can be liable to a fireman injured while fighting the fire.[22] There is, however, no duty owed by an occupier of premises to firemen to provide means of access and egress which will remain safe during the fire, even if a duty to provide similar precautions might be owed to employees.[23] It has been held in England that the duty is owed to a child in utero at the time of an accident in respect of injuries attributable to that accident which persist after birth.[24] The test of "reasonable foreseeability" of injury along with the requirement of proximity can thus be seen as defining the class of persons to whom the duty of care is owed, but foreseeability may also be used to determine whether or not the defender is liable in damages for the

26.03

---

[15] *Caparo Industries Plc v Dickman* [1990] 2 A.C. 605.

[16] See for example: *Gibson v Chief Constable of Strathclyde*, 1999 S.C. 420; *Mitchell v Glasgow City Council*, 2009 S.L.T. 247 (personal injury); *Marc Rich & Co A.G. v Bishop Rock Marine Co Ltd* [1996] A.C. 211 (property damage); *McFarlane v Tayside Health Board*, 2000 S.C. (HL) 1; 2000 S.L.T. 154 (wrongful conception).

[17] The general approach follows Brennan J. in *Sutherland Shire Council v Heyman* (1985) 60 A.L.R. 1 at 43–44, cited with approval by Lord Bridge in *Caparo Industries* [1990] 2 A.C. 605 at 618.

[18] *Bourhill v Young*, 1942 S.C. (HL) 78 at 88, per Lord Macmillan.

[19] *Hill v Chief Constable of West Yorkshire* [1989] A.C. 53; cf. *Gibson v Chief Constable of Strathclyde*, 1999 S.C. 420.

[20] *Haynes v Harwood* [1935] 1 K.B. 146; *Baker v Hopkins* [1959] 1 W.L.R. 966; *Videan v British Transport Commission* [1963] 2 Q.B. 650; see also *Carmarthenshire CC v Lewis* [1955] A.C. 549.

[21] *Steel v Glasgow Iron & Steel Co*, 1944 S.C. 237. But note that the deceased had responsibilities for the safety of his employer's property: see per Lord Justice-Clerk Cooper at 250.

[22] *Ogwo v Taylor* [1988] A.C. 431. For duties owed by members of the emergency services, see paras 26.06–26.09, below.

[23] *Bermingham v Sher Bros*, 1980 S.C. (HL) 67.

[24] *B. v Islington Health Authority* [1993] 3 Q.B. 204, following *Watt v Rama* [1972] V.R. 353. In *Cohen v Shaw*, 1992 S.L.T. 1022, Lord Cullen declined to express a view on whether or not the same approach as in *B. v Islington* would be adopted in Scotland.

consequences of his acts or omissions.[25] "Legal liability is limited to those consequences of our acts which a reasonable man of ordinary intelligence and experience so acting would have in contemplation."[26] The question that may be asked is whether the harm sustained is within the scope of the duty. To attract liability it is necessary that the kind of injury sustained[27] and the manner in which it was sustained[28] should be reasonably foreseeable but the precise chain of events leading up to the particular accident need not be foreseeable.[29] Thus, an employer's liability for psychiatric injury consequent on physical injury may extend to include damages for the eventual suicide of the employee.[30]

26.04 Duty of Care: Nervous shock and psychiatric injury—"The outdated (yet persistent) expression 'nervous shock' is not synonymous with psychiatric injury. Nervous shock is a type of psychiatric injury, but it is not the only type."[31] The term "nervous shock" has traditionally been used to describe the psychological effects of a sudden and traumatic event. Before damages can be awarded for nervous shock, the pursuer must have sustained more than mere fright or distress of mind; such an emotional reaction must have been followed by some physical, mental or nervous injury.[32] If the pursuer is within the area of potential danger (i.e. of reasonably foreseeable physical injury) created by a careless act, the duty of care exists and the defender will be liable to make reparation for nervous shock caused by fear of bodily harm, although the pursuer may escape physical injury.[33] It may also be sufficient that the pursuer reasonably thought he was in physical danger or, although originally outwith the area of physical danger, he later came within it as a rescuer.[34] Whether there is liability for nervous shock sustained by a person outwith the area of potential physical danger as a result only of seeing or hearing an accident to a third party or of becoming aware of its consequences, has given rise to much difficulty. In *Bourhill v Young*,[35] a motorcyclist negligently collided with a car and was killed. The pursuer, a fishwife unloading her creel from a tramway car nearby, did not see the collision but heard the noise. She suffered nervous shock, and a miscarriage which she alleged was caused by the nervous shock. It was held that the motorcyclist owed no duty to the pursuer, injury to a person in her position not being reasonably foreseeable. Where,

---

[25] Note that this is a different question from that of the defender's liability for all the consequences of his negligence: see para.26.12, below; and *McKillen v Barclay Curle*, 1967 S.L.T. 41.

[26] *Muir v Glasgow Corp*, 1943 S.C. (HL) 3 at 10, per Lord Macmillan.

[27] *Hughes v Lord Advocate*, 1963 S.C. (HL) 31; *Blaikie v British Transport Commission*, 1961 S.C. 44.

[28] *Hughes v Lord Advocate*, 1963 S.C. (HL) 31; *Malcolm v Dickson*, 1951 S.C. 542; see also *Doughty v Turner Mfg Co* [1964] 1 Q.B. 518 and *Bell v Scottish Special Housing Association*, 1987 S.L.T. 320.

[29] *Harvey v Singer Mfg Co*, 1960 S.C. 155; *Carmarthenshire CC v Lewis* [1955] A.C. 549 at 564, per Lord Reid; *Jolley v Sutton LBC* [2000] 1 W.L.R. 1082 and *Jebson v Ministry of Defence* [2001] 1 W.L.R. 2055.

[30] *Corr v IBC Vehicles Ltd* [2008] 1 A.C. 884. On an employer's liability to its employees, see generally paras 17.49–17.54.

[31] *Cross v Highlands & Islands Enterprise*, 2001 S.L.T. 1060 at [61], per Lord Macfadyen.

[32] *Simpson v ICI*, 1983 S.L.T. 601. The relevant injury in this case was post traumatic stress disorder.

[33] *Brown v Glasgow Corp*, 1922 S.C. 527; and *Page v Smith* [1996] A.C. 155, where the House of Lords distinguished between primary and secondary victims, the plaintiff in that case being at risk of injury and therefore a primary victim. The classification of a victim as primary or secondary is not always clear: see *W. v Essex CC* [2001] 2 A.C. 592. See also *Salter v UB Frozen and Chilled Foods Ltd*, 2003 S.L.T. 1011; *Anderson v Christian Salvesen Plc*, 2006 S.L.T. 815.

[34] *McFarlane v E.E. Caledonia Ltd* [1994] 2 All E.R. 1; *Campbell v North Lanarkshire CC*, 2000 S.C.L.R. 373.

[35] *Bourhill v Young*, 1942 S.C. (HL) 78.

however, the plaintiff was informed that her husband and three children had been involved in a road accident two hours earlier and taken to hospital where she saw her family and learned that her youngest daughter had been killed, it was held that she was entitled to recover damages for nervous shock.[36] In such cases, it is necessary to show that the pursuer is within the class of persons in whom nervous shock was foreseeable, that there is the required degree of proximity between the pursuer and the accident and that the shock was directly caused.[37] The first limb of this test can be presumed to be satisfied where the relationship between the pursuer and the injured person is a close family one; the question of proximity, however, connotes both closeness to the accident in time and space and direct perception of it. Thus, a claim may fail where the pursuer has only learned of an accident by watching television.[38] A fellow employee is not within the class of persons who can recover damages for nervous shock.[39] Further, the employer/employee relationship does not in itself facilitate the recovery of damages for nervous shock.[40]

Conceptually distinct from nervous shock cases are those where psychological harm is directly caused without a particular traumatic event. Again, it is necessary that psychiatric illness be suffered; stress alone is not sufficient. Damages for psychiatric injury may be recovered by an employee from his employer where the injury was reasonably foreseeable by the employer and the employer has failed to take steps to prevent it. In such cases, the pursuer may be categorised as a primary victim.[41] In both Scotland and England, reliance has been placed on the decision of the Court of Appeal in *Hatton v Sutherland*,[42] in which Lady Hale set out 16 propositions clarifying the law in this area.[43] Foreseeability will generally require an awareness by the employer, before the onset of psychiatric illness, that the employee is suffering stress or other psychological difficulties at work.[44] Other relationships may give rise to a duty to avoid causing psychiatric injury. Such a duty may be owed to a vulnerable prisoner by the police[45] or prison authorities.[46] A duty to avoid causing psychiatric injury may also be owed by solicitors towards a client facing a criminal trial.[47] A parent suffering psychiatric injury on learning that the organs of her deceased child were retained after a post-mortem examination is a primary victim.[48] In Scotland, unauthorised removal and retention of organs is an independent legal wrong, as is an unauthorised post-mortem, if the purpose of the

---

[36] *McLoughlin v O'Brian* [1983] 1 A.C. 410. See also *Galli-Atkinson v Seghal* [2003] Lloyd's Rep. Med. 285.

[37] *Alcock v Chief Constable of South Yorkshire Police* [1992] 1 A.C. 310; *McFarlane v E.E. Caledonia Ltd* [1994] 2 All E.R. 1.

[38] *Alcock v Chief Constable of South Yorkshire Police* [1992] 1 A.C. 310.

[39] *Robertson v Forth Road Bridge Joint Board*, 1995 S.C. 364; cf. *Salter v UB Frozen Foods*, 2003 S.L.T. 1011.

[40] *Frost v Chief Constable of South Yorkshire Police* [1999] 2 A.C. 455; applied in *Keen v Tayside Contracts*, 2003 S.L.T. 500.

[41] *Fraser v State Hospitals Board for Scotland*, 2001 S.L.T. 1051 at [128].

[42] *Hatton v Sutherland* [2002] I.C.R. 613.

[43] *Hatton v Sutherland* [2002] I.C.R. 613 at [43]. These propositions were referred to but not directly endorsed, other than in the dissenting speech of Lord Scott, when one of the cases heard with *Hatton* came before the House of Lords: *Barber v Somerset CC* [2004] 1 W.L.R. 1089.

[44] But not invariably—the duties the employee is required to perform may be a foreseeable cause of psychiatric illness for any employee, as in *Melville v Home Office* [2005] I.C.R. 782.

[45] *Reeves v Commissioner of Police of the Metropolis* [2000] 1 A.C. 360.

[46] *Butchart v Home Office* [2006] 1 W.L.R. 1155.

[47] *McLoughlin v Jones* [2002] Q.B. 1312. A more straightforward approach in this case would have been to characterise the damnum as loss of liberty, with the psychiatric illness consequent on that (see Lady Hale at [57]).

[48] In *Re Organ Retention Group Litigation* [2005] 2 W.L.R. 358.

post-mortem was non-diagnostic or the diagnostic purpose had been fulfilled.[49] It
is therefore possible that damages could be recovered for injury falling short of
psychiatric illness.[50] It has been held in England that a mother developing psychiatric illness as a consequence of birth injury to her child can recover damages, it
being possible to classify her as either a primary or secondary victim.[51] In *Rothwell
v Chemical and Insulating Co*[52] the House of Lords refused to award damages in
respect of clinical depression consequent on the discovery of pleural plaques in
the lungs of one of the appellants. Pleural plaques are indicative of exposure to
asbestos, but they are not of themselves harmful, nor are they indicative of future
development of mesothelioma. The view taken was that the appellant had suffered
no material harm, but his depression was attributable to apprehension of a condition, mesothelioma, which had not, and might well not materialise. Scottish courts
have in the past made awards of provisional damages in such circumstances and,
following *Rothwell*, the Damages (Asbestos-Related Conditions) (Scotland) Act
2009 has been enacted to allow this process to continue.

26.05 **Duty of care: Actions of third parties**—A pursuer suffering loss or injury caused
directly by the actions of a third party may seek damages from a defender on the
basis that but for the alleged negligence of the defender, the third party would not
have been able to cause the damage. Typically, this occurs where the third party
causing the damage is unidentified or has no assets with which to satisfy an award
of damages. The third party may have acted negligently or deliberately and his
actions may amount to a crime.[53] In such cases, the courts are concerned to impose
some limit or control mechanism to prevent liability attaching simply for omitting
to prevent the infliction of harm, rather than for active conduct. The circumstances
in which liability will attach to a defender for damage which is directly caused by
a third party were reviewed by the House of Lords in *Maloco v Littlewoods
Organisation Ltd*.[54] There, vandals entered a disused cinema belonging to the
defenders and started a fire which spread to a neighbouring cafe and church,
belonging to the pursuers. It was held that the defenders were not liable to the
pursuers. Lord Mackay saw the question as one of foreseeability, to be answered
by examining from the standpoint of the defenders the level of likelihood of the
conduct of the third party causing the damage. Lord Goff, however, considered
that the case could not be resolved solely by assessing foreseeability but necessitated a consideration of the circumstances in which it would be appropriate to
impose on a defender a duty to prevent the infliction of damage on others by a
third party. In *Mitchell v Glasgow City Council*[55] the House of Lords determined
that the defenders owed no duty of care to warn Mitchell in advance that they
were to hold a meeting with a violent neighbour. Following the meeting, at which
he was threatened with eviction, the neighbour killed Mitchell. Lord Hope made
the following three related points. First, foreseeability of harm is an insufficient
basis upon which to base a duty; secondly, the law does not normally impose a
positive duty on a person to protect others; thirdly, the law does not impose a duty

---

[49] *Stevens v Yorkhill Hospital NHS Trust*, 2006 S.L.T. 889.
[50] *Stevens v Yorkhill Hospital NHS Trust*, 2006 S.L.T. 889 at [63].
[51] *Farrell v Merton, Sutton & Wandsworth HA* (2001) 57 B.M.L.R. 158.
[52] *Rothwell v Chemical and Insulating Co* [2008] 1 A.C. 281.
[53] e.g. *McLean v University of St Andrews*, 2004 Rep. L.R. 54: university not liable to student raped
while on placement in Odessa.
[54] *Maloco v Littlewoods Organisation Ltd*, 1987 S.C. (HL) 37; 1987 S.L.T. 425.
[55] *Mitchell v Glasgow City Council*, 2009 S.L.T. 247.

to prevent a person being harmed by the criminal act of a third party based simply on foreseeability.[56] It is clear from the speeches of Lords Hope, Scott and Brown that liability for negligence for the criminal acts of a third party will arise only in the following circumstances: (1) where there is vicarious liability[57]; (2) where there is an obligation to supervise the third party[58]; (3) where the defender creates the risk of danger; and (4) where there is an assumption of responsibility. It is therefore clear that liability will not be imposed simply because the defender has created the opportunity for a third party to act in a way which could have been anticipated.[59]

Duty of care: Public bodies—Although a pursuer has suffered injury, or loss of or **26.06** damage to property, as a result of the actings of a public body exercising its powers or implementing its duties, he may be unable to recover damages because no common law duty of care was owed. A distinction has been recognised between the actings of a public body falling within the ambit of the exercise of discretion and actions in implementation of discretionary decisions. If the public body is acting within the ambit of its discretion it will not be liable in damages unless bad faith is present. Thus, where children have allegedly sustained injury as a result of an adverse reaction to vaccination it has been held that, in the absence of allegations of bad faith, no liability attaches to the Secretary of State, who has the responsibility of promoting the vaccination of children, for the content of information made available to the public about risks.[60] In the field of financial regulation, the courts have been similarly unwilling to recognise a duty of care. In *Yuen Kun Yeu v Attorney General of Hong Kong*[61] it was held that the Commissioner of Deposit Taking Companies in Hong Kong did not owe a duty of care to individual depositors, who were thus unable to sue him for alleged failures to discover irregularities in the conduct of the affairs of a finance company which later collapsed. When exercising his discretion whether or not to register a company, the Commissioner had no special relationship either with the company or with potential depositors.[62] Once a public body moves into what is termed the operational area of its activities, a duty of care towards individuals may arise, although there can be difficulty in distinguishing discretionary and operational decisions.[63] In addition, such a distinction is only of use in identifying decisions which do not give rise to a duty of care; merely because a public body is within the operational area of its activities does not necessarily mean that a duty of care is owed to individuals.[64]

The question of the existence of such a duty will depend on a number of factors, including what is perceived to be the purpose for which the body is endowed with the powers concerned. Attempts have been made in a number of cases to argue

---

[56] Citing with approval Lord Keith in *Yuen Kun Yeu v Attorney General of Hong Kong* [1988] A.C. 175 at 192 and Lord Goff in *Maloco v Littlewoods Organisation Ltd*, 1987 S.C. (HL) 37; 1987 S.L.T. 425 at [77]–[83].

[57] As, e.g. in *Lister v Hesley Hall Ltd* [2001] UKHL 22; [2002] 1 A.C. 215.

[58] As, e.g. in *Home Office v Dorset Yacht Company* [1970] A.C. 1004.

[59] See also *P. Perl (Exporters) v Camden London BC* [1984] Q.B. 342; *Topp v London Country Bus (South West) Ltd* [1993] 1 W.L.R. 976.

[60] *Bonthrone v Secretary of State for Scotland*, 1987 S.L.T 34; *Ross v Secretary of State for Scotland*, 1990 S.L.T. 13; see also *Johnstone v Traffic Commissioner*, 1990 S.L.T. 409.

[61] *Yuen Kun Yeu v Attorney General of Hong Kong* [1988] A.C. 175.

[62] See also *Davis v Radcliffe* [1990] 1 W.L.R. 821; cf. *Lonrho Plc v Tebbit* [1992] 4 All E.R. 280; and *Deloitte Haskins & Sells v National Mutual Life Nominees Ltd* [1993] A.C. 774.

[63] *Rowling v Takaro Properties Ltd* [1988] A.C. 473.

[64] *Rowling v Takaro Properties Ltd* [1988] A.C. 473.

that a local authority responsible for monitoring the construction of buildings owes a duty to the owner of the building to take reasonable care that the building is constructed properly. It has been held, however, that no such duty exists in relation to financial loss sustained as a result of the defective construction of the building,[65] or physical injury due to its non-compliance with building regulations.[66] Section 51 of the Building (Scotland) Act 2003 now provides for civil liability for failure to comply with building regulations. In itself, the fact that statutory powers or duties are conferred for the safety of the public, such as the duties of highway authorities to maintain roads, will not be sufficient to create a common law duty of care to prevent injury.[67] Similar issues have arisen in litigation against local authorities for their actings in connection with the protection of children from abuse. Initially, the House of Lords held that the principles set out in *Caparo*,[68] particularly the requirement that imposition of a duty of care should be just and reasonable, led to there being no common law duty of care on a local authority when it was deciding whether or not to take a child into care.[69] On a subsequent complaint to the European Court of Human Rights, however, the plaintiffs in *X v Bedfordshire CC* were found to have suffered a breach of their rights under art.3 of the Convention.[70] The European Court has also held that art.13 requires domestic law to provide an appropriate means of determining allegations of breach of art.3 by local authorities in such circumstances.[71] Article 6 secures the right to have a claim relating to a party's civil rights brought before a domestic court, but it has been affirmed that the content of such rights is to be determined by domestic law.[72] It has now been acknowledged in the House of Lords that the proposition in *X v Bedfordshire CC* was stated too broadly and that local authorities or medical personnel performing child protection duties may owe common law duties to the children.[73] But health professionals do not ordinarily owe a parent under suspicion a duty not to cause harm in making their diagnosis of child abuse.[74] This identifies the potential conflict of interest that could occur by having to take the rights of parents into account in circumstances where the welfare of the child is paramount. Similar reasoning has been applied in respect that no duty was owed to the operators of a nursing home when statutory powers were exercised to close the home for the protection of the elderly residents.[75] In relation to the education of children with special needs, local authorities may be

---

[65] *Governors of the Peabody Donation Fund v Sir Lindsay Parkinson & Co* [1985] A.C. 210 at 241. See the further discussion of cases concerning defective buildings in para.26.07, below.

[66] *Forbes v Dundee DC*, 1997 S.L.T. 1330.

[67] *Stovin v Wise* [1996] A.C. 923. This 3:2 decision of the House of Lords illustrates the difficulties in this area. The two speeches delivered reach opposite conclusions on whether a roads authority could be liable at common law for failing to use its statutory powers to improve a junction. *Stovin* was further examined by the House of Lords in *Gorringe v Calderdale MBC* [2004] 1 W.L.R. 1057, where Lord Rodger observes (at [24]) that "the common law of Scotland is somewhat more generous to those injured due to the failure to maintain the roads than was English common law". Compare *McKnight v Clydeside Buses Ltd*, 1999 S.L.T. 1167 (roads authority had duty to provide signs warning of hazard) and *Bennett v J. Lamont & Sons*, 2000 S.L.T. 17 (no duty to fence road).

[68] *Caparo Industries Plc v Dickman* [1990] 2 A.C. 605. See para.26.02, above.

[69] *X v Bedfordshire CC* [1995] 2 A.C. 633.

[70] *Z v United Kingdom* [2001] 2 F.C.R. 246.

[71] *DP v United Kingdom* [2003] 1 F.L.R. 50.

[72] *Roche v United Kingdom* (2006) 42 E.H.R.R. 30.

[73] *D v East Berkshire Community Health NHS Trust* [2005] 2 A.C. 373.

[74] *D v East Berkshire Community Health NHS Trust* [2005] 2 A.C. 373. See also *Fairlie v Perth & Kinross NHS Trust*, 2004 S.L.T. 1200; *Lawrence v Pembrokeshire CC* [2007] EWCA Civ 446.

[75] *Jain v Trent Strategic Health Authority* [2009] UKHL 23.

vicariously liable for the professional negligence of educational psychologists and other employees in dealing with individual children.[76] In cases involving the possible existence of a common law duty of care in the context of actings by public bodies in exercise of statutory powers, it is relevant to consider whether the imposition of a common law duty would be inconsistent with, or discourage the due performance of, statutory duties.[77] A further factor which is likely to militate against the imposition of a duty of care is the availability in public law of a means of challenging the decision complained of, such as judicial review or a statutory appeal procedure.[78]

Whether or not the police owe a duty of care in respect of their actions will also depend on the circumstances in individual cases.[79] No specialty arises in situations which are well recognised as giving rise to a duty of care, for example individual police officers on the public road owe duties of care to other road users. The police can also owe a duty of care to a drunk[80] or suicidal[81] man in their custody. An informer may also be owed a duty of care, on the basis of an assumption of responsibility by the police to preserve confidentiality.[82] But no duty is owed by police officers to prevent an arrested person being injured whilst trying to escape from their custody.[83]

In relation to the duties of police officers in connection with the maintenance of public safety and the investigation of crime, the position is less clear. In a case concerning crowd control at a football match, the court proceeded on the basis that the police were protected from actions of damages unless their actings were malicious and without probable cause.[84] In *Hill v Chief Constable of West Yorkshire*,[85] a case relating to the apprehension of a criminal, the House of Lords held that the necessary degree of proximity was lacking between police officers charged with the investigation of past crimes and the potential future victims of the criminal. Thus, no duty of care was capable of arising. In addition, to impose such a duty would be contrary to public policy.[86] Cases involving alleged failures by the police and other emergency services to respond adequately to urgent requests for assistance have also arisen. In England, it has been held that receipt

---

[76] *Phelps v Hillingdon LBC* [2001] 2 A.C. 619. See para.26.10 below, regarding professional negligence.

[77] See *Harris v Evans* [1998] 1 W.L.R. 1285 (unsuccessful attempt to impose common law duties on an Inspector of the Health and Safety Executive) and *Mitchell v Glasgow City Council*, 2009 S.L.T. 247.

[78] See *Jones v Department of Employment* [1989] Q.B. 1; *Johnstone v Traffic Commissioner*, 1990 S.L.T. 409; *Clunis v Camden & Islington HA* [1998] Q.B. 978.

[79] The delictual liability of Chief Constables is discussed in J.M. Thomson, "Delictual Liability of Chief Constables", 2000 S.L.T. (News) 281.

[80] *Wilson v Chief Constable, Lothian and Borders Police*, 1989 S.L.T. 97.

[81] *Kirkham v Chief Constable of Greater Manchester Police* [1990] 2 Q.B. 283. The deceased's suicide will not be a *novus actus interveniens*; it may, however, be contributory negligence: *Reeves v Metropolitan Commissioner of Police* [2000] 1 A.C. 360. See para.25.37, above.

[82] *Swinney v Chief Constable of Northumbria* [1997] Q.B. 464.

[83] *Vellino v Chief Constable, Greater Manchester Police* [2002] 1 W.L.R. 218.

[84] *Ward v Chief Constable, Strathclyde Police*, 1991 S.L.T. 292: duty of care by the police was not discussed. See also *Ancell v McDermott* [1993] 4 All E.R. 355: no duty of care to protect road users from hazards on the highway; cf. *Gibson v Orr*, 1999 S.C. 420: duty of care once police had taken control of the hazard.

[85] *Hill v Chief Constable of West Yorkshire* [1989] A.C. 53.

[86] *Hill v Chief Constable of West Yorkshire* [1989] A.C. 53. Adverse comment on this decision in the European Court of Human Rights appears itself to have been largely retracted. Compare *Osman v United Kingdom* (1998) 29 E.H.R.R. 245 with *Z v United Kingdom* [2001] 2 F.C.R. 246.

by the police[87] or the fire brigade[88] of an emergency call does not create a duty of care either to attend or, when in attendance, to prevent harm, save for the obligation not to take steps that worsen the situation.[89] But in *Burnett v Grampian Fire and Rescue Services*, the view was taken that firemen can owe a duty, when dealing with a fire, to take reasonable care to ensure that it has been extinguished and will not reignite.[90] The position of the ambulance service may be more straightforward, with a duty of care to a victim arising when an emergency call is accepted.[91] This is due to there being greater similarity between ambulancemen and other professionals working in the NHS than between the ambulance service and other emergency services.[92] In summary, cases alleging negligence on the part of a public body discharging its statutory function present particular difficulty. The incorporation into domestic law of the European Convention on Human Rights may provide remedies for those who would not succeed with a claim in delict or tort. Whether this will, in itself, effect a change in the substantive law of reparation remains to be seen.[93]

26.07 **Duty of care: Pure economic loss**—Where the loss sustained by a pursuer is purely economic, as distinct from injury to his person or damage to his property, it is generally more difficult to recover damages.[94] This is not so much because of the character of the loss in itself as because the scope of a duty of care may not be wide enough to include those whose loss is purely economic. Thus, in claims for alleged negligence in connection with sterilisation operations, parents cannot claim as damages the cost of raising a child born after the operation,[95] although solatium has been awarded in respect of pain, suffering and inconvenience associated with pregnancy and childbirth where parents were negligently and wrongly informed that a vasectomy had been successful.[96] There is, in general, no duty to take care to avoid causing financial loss to individuals who suffer such loss as a direct result of negligence which kills or injures other persons with whom they had some form of relationship by contract or otherwise. Thus, an employer cannot claim reparation for the loss caused to him by the death or injury of an employee through the fault of a third party, even if the employer has been injured in the same

---

[87] *Alexandrou v Oxford* [1993] 4 All E.R. 328.

[88] *Capital & Counties Plc v Hampshire CC* [1997] Q.B. 1004—a decision which has also been applied to the coastguard service; *OLL Ltd v Secretary of State for Transport* [1997] 3 All E.R. 897.

[89] *Capital & Counties Plc v Hampshire CC* [1997] Q.B. 1004 at 1031E.

[90] *Burnett v Grampian Fire and Rescue Services*, 2007 S.L.T. 61.

[91] *Kent v Griffiths* [2001] Q.B. 36.

[92] *Kent v Griffiths* [2001] Q.B. 36 at [45].

[93] That this is a developing area of the law was acknowledged in *W v Metropolitan Commissioner of Police* [2000] 1 W.L.R. 1607 at 1613, per Lord Slynn.

[94] *Caparo Industries Plc v Dickman* [1990] 2 A.C. 605 at 618–619; *Weir v National Westminster Bank Plc*, 1994 S.L.T. 1251.

[95] *McFarlane v Tayside Health Board*, 2000 S.C. (HL) 1, affd in *Rees v Darlington Memorial Hospital NHS Trust* [2004] 1 A.C. 309. Where the negligence consists of failing to offer parents antenatal testing to ascertain if their child is handicapped, the additional costs generated by that handicap were recovered but not the ordinary costs of raising the child (*McLelland v Greater Glasgow Health Board*, 2001 S.L.T. 446). See also *Parkinson v St James & Seacroft University Hospital NHS Trust* [2002] Q.B. 266 (failed sterilisation followed by birth of disabled child). In *Rees v Darlington Memorial Hospital NHS Trust* [2004] 1 A.C. 309 (failed sterilisation where mother disabled but child healthy) the House of Lords by a majority reversed the decision of the Court of Appeal in which the visually impaired mother had been awarded extra costs consequent on her own impairment and awarded instead, in addition to damages for pregnancy and childbirth, a "conventional sum" of £15,000.

[96] *McFarlane v Tayside Health Board*, 2000 S.C. (HL) 1.

accident.[97] Nor, cases of death apart, is any duty owed to relatives in respect of the loss of the support or services of an injured person on which they relied.[98] Similarly, there is, in general, no duty owed to individuals who sustain financial loss when deprived of services through damage, negligently caused, to the property of another. Thus when, on the pursuers' averments, contractors negligently damaged an electricity supply cable belonging to the electricity board so that the supply of electricity to the pursuer's factory was cut off and loss of production with consequent financial loss ensued, the action was dismissed.[99] It does not assist the pursuer in such a claim to show that physical damage to his property has also been sustained.[100] Similarly, where contractors were laying a pipe belonging to the Gas Board and were responsible for any damage to the pipe during laying, they were unable to recover damages from a third party who damaged the pipe.[101] If, however, the pursuer can demonstrate that he has rights in connection with the property which, though falling short of ownership, amount to a substantial interest, he may be able to recover damages.[102]

Where the owner of property discovers a defect in the property which is due to allegedly negligent construction, his claim for the cost of rectifying the defect or replacing the property, or for loss sustained on resale of the property, is a claim for pure economic loss. The House of Lords has held that damages are not recoverable for such loss. This exclusion has been applied to a claim by developers in respect of a failure by a local authority to prevent the developers from departing from approved plans, resulting in a defective building[103] and where plans which did not comply with building regulations were prepared by experts employed by the developers, approved by the local authority and utilised to the financial loss of the developers.[104] It has also been applied where defects in construction have emerged during the ownership of, or occupation by, a subsequent acquirer of the building who has attempted to claim damages from the builder[105] or from the local

---

[97] *Reavis v Clan Line Steamers*, 1925 S.C. 725.

[98] *Robertson v Turnbull*, 1982 S.C. (HL) 1. The injured person can seek damages for inability to render services or for services which require to be rendered to him. See Administration of Justice Act 1982 and para.25.17, above.

[99] *Dynamco v Holland and Hannen and Cubitts (Scotland)*, 1972 S.L.T. 38; cf. *S.C.M. (United Kingdom) v W.G. Whittall and Sons* [1971] 1 Q.B. 137; *Spartan Steel Alloys v Martins and Co (Contractors)* [1973] Q.B. 27. See also *East Lothian Angling Association v Haddington Town Council*, 1980 S.L.T. 213; *Candlewood Navigation Corp v Mitsui Osk Lines* [1986] A.C. 1; *Scott Lithgow v G.E.C. Electrical Projects Ltd*, 1992 S.L.T. 244. Such claims can now be excluded by a term in the contract of supply: Electricity Act 1989 s.21, considered in *A.E. Beckett & Sons (Lyndons) Ltd v Midland Electricity Plc* [2001] 1 W.L.R. 281.

[100] *Coleridge v Miller Construction Ltd*, 1997 S.L.T. 485.

[101] *Nacap v Moffat Plant*, 1987 S.L.T. 221.

[102] *North Scottish Helicopters Ltd v United Technologies Corp Inc.*, 1988 S.L.T. 77. Scots law has found difficulty in determining a threshold for title to sue in respect of damage to property that is not owned by the pursuer. *North Scottish Helicopters* is said to represent a qualitative approach based on possession akin to ownership which is inherently vague. An alternative approach based on a real right in the subjects may lead to harsh results. See e.g. *TCS Holdings Ltd v Ashstead Plant Hire*, 2003 S.L.T. 117. There may be an alternative approach based on the nature of the pursuer's interest in the subjects. See e.g. *Blackburn v Sinclair*, 1984 S.L.T. 368 at 369, per Lord Allanbridge; *Mull Shellfish Ltd v Golden Sea Produce Ltd*, 1992 S.L.T. 703. For discussion see G. Cameron, "Capacity and parties" in J.M. Thomson, *Delict* (Edinburgh: W. Green), paras 3.11–3.29.

[103] *Governors of the Peabody Donation Fund v Sir Lindsay Parkinson & Co* [1985] A.C. 210.

[104] *Investors in Industry Commercial Properties Ltd v South Bedfordshire DC* [1986] Q.B. 1034, CA.

[105] *D. & F. Estates Ltd v Church Commissioners for England* [1989] 1 A.C. 177; *Department of the Environment v Thomas Bates & Son Ltd* [1991] 1 A.C. 499.

authority which passed the plans.[106] Dicta in some of the earlier cases suggested that damages were recoverable where the defect, when discovered, posed a risk to health or safety, but it is now established that even such a risk does not make the economic loss recoverable.[107] It was suggested that claims which at first sight appear to be pure economic loss claims might in fact be cases in which the pursuer has suffered damage to other property which he owns. Thus, in a complex structure such as a building, a defect in one part may cause damage to another part of the structure.[108] The difficulties incurred in attempting to formulate and apply such a test have, however, been acknowledged.[109] It has been stated that in Scots law there is no automatic exclusion of claims in delict for the diminution in value of property resulting from negligent work on that property.[110]

There are some cases where the pursuer has suffered pure economic loss but the relationship between the parties is of such a character that damages are recoverable. A category of case in which it has been recognised that pure economic loss may be recoverable is that of negligent misrepresentation, which is discussed in the next paragraph. In two English appeals, the House of Lords has held that the principles underlying recovery of loss in cases of negligent misrepresentation can be extended to other situations in which the defendant provides professional or quasi-professional services to the plaintiff. In both *Henderson v Merrett Syndicates Ltd*[111] and *White v Jones*[112] the House of Lords held that the relationship between the parties disclosed an assumption of responsibility by the defendant to the plaintiff and a concomitant reliance by the plaintiff on the quality of the services provided, leading to liability when the services fell below the requisite standard.[113] *Henderson v Merrett* is now regarded as the leading case in economic loss. Under *Henderson* rules the recognition of a duty of care depends upon a voluntary assumption of responsibility[114] for the economic interests of the pursuer with concomitant reliance by the pursuer of the defender's skill and expertise. This reliance must be known to the defender. A disclaimer of responsibility will prevent a duty from arising since it negates any assumption of responsibility, but will be subject to the fair and reasonableness test in the Unfair Contract Terms Act 1977.[115] *White* concerned failures by solicitors in the preparation of a will, leading to loss to potential beneficiaries. In a nineteenth century Scottish appeal to the House of Lords, it was stated that there could be no liability in such a situation,[116] but this authority is no longer regarded as binding in Scotland.[117] Furthermore,

---

[106] *Murphy v Brentwood DC* [1991] A.C. 398, departing from *Anns v Merton London BC* [1978] A.C. 728.

[107] *Murphy v Brentwood DC* [1991] A.C. 398.

[108] *D. & F. Estates Ltd v Church Commissioners for England* [1989] 1 A.C. 177 at 206–207, per Lord Bridge.

[109] *Murphy v Brentwood DC* [1991] A.C. 398 at 476–479, per Lord Bridge.

[110] *Parkhead Housing Association Ltd v Phoenix Preservation Ltd*, 1990 S.L.T. 812 at 816.

[111] *Henderson v Merrett Syndicates Ltd* [1995] 2 A.C. 145.

[112] *White v Jones* [1995] 2 A.C. 207.

[113] Assumption of responsibility is perhaps best seen as a sufficient but not necessary test for liability in economic loss cases: *Commissioners of Customs and Excise v Barclays Bank Ltd* [2007] 1 A.C. 181.

[114] Which may be inferred, *Royal Bank of Scotland v Bannerman, Johnstone, Maclay*, 2005 1 S.C. 437.

[115] s.16(1)(b). Note that the test applies not only to attempts to evade or restrict liability in respect of breach, but also in respect of terms which are intended to prevent a duty from arising, s.25(5). See, e.g. *Bank of Scotland v Fuller-Peiser*, 2002 S.L.T. 574.

[116] *Robertson v Fleming* (1861) 4 Macq. 167.

[117] *Robertson v Watt & Co* Unreported July 4, 1995 2nd Div.; *Holmes v Bank of Scotland*, 2002 S.L.T. 544.

it appears that the principle enunciated by the majority in *White v Jones* would be followed in Scotland.[118] In an English case concerning negligence in administering an estate, it has been observed that solicitors should not escape liability because of a dichotomy between the person entitled to claim against them for a breach of duty and the person suffering loss.[119]

Some guidance on the tests to be applied in determining a duty of care in respect of economic loss was provided by the House of Lords in *Customs and Excise Commissioners v Barclays Bank*.[120] Faced with a case of pure economic loss in novel circumstances, *Henderson* rules will apply where there is a voluntary assumption of responsibility. In such cases there is no requirement to consider policy issues. Absence of a voluntary assumption of responsibility will not end matters. The *Caparo* test may then be applied as it falls to be applied in any novel circumstance. The class of cases not involving negligent misrepresentation or any assumption of responsibility, but in which the relationship of the parties is sufficiently close for a duty of care to exist in respect of pure economic loss must be seen as very limited. It does not include the relationship between the architects of a building and its future tenants.[121] In other cases, such factors as nomination by the pursuers of the defenders as subcontractors and whether or not the pursuers can be said to have relied on the defenders will be important.[122] Where reliance is a central feature, it is not necessary for the pursuers to demonstrate that the defenders intended such reliance to occur.[123] The significance in a delictual claim of a contractual relationship between the parties has not always been clear.[124] It has now been stated by the House of Lords in *Henderson* that the correct approach is to consider whether the plaintiff is precluded by his contract from suing in tort; if not, he may choose to sue in either.[125]

Duty of care: Negligent misrepresentation—When the alleged negligence **26.08** relates to statements, verbal or written, and not to deeds, it has long been recognised that a duty to take reasonable care that such statements are accurate may arise from special relationships in special circumstances.[126] In *Hedley Byrne & Co v Heller and Partners* the House of Lords considered the circumstances in which a party sustaining financial loss as a direct result of acting upon an incorrect statement, given by another with whom there was no contractual relationship, might sue for damages on the ground of negligence.[127] The "special relationships" contemplated by the House of Lords were independent of contract and extended beyond fiduciary relationships. Lord Reid could see

---

[118] *Holmes v Bank of Scotland*, 2002 S.L.T. 544, though subsequent cases suggest that *White* may be given a restrictive interpretation. See *Fraser v McArthur Stewart*, 2009 S.L.T. 31; *Matthews v Hunter and Robertson*, 2008 S.L.T. 634.

[119] *Chappell v Somers & Blake* [2004] Ch. 19 at [16].

[120] *Customs and Excise Commissioners v Barclays Bank* [2007] 1 A.C. 181.

[121] *Strathford East Kilbride Ltd v HLM Design Ltd*, 1999 S.L.T. 121.

[122] *Junior Books v The Veitchi Co Ltd*, 1982 S.L.T. 492; *Scott Lithgow Ltd v G.E.C. Electrical Projects Ltd*, 1992 S.L.T. 244.

[123] *Royal Bank of Scotland v Bannerman Johnstone Maclay*, 2005 S.C. 437.

[124] Contrast, e.g. *Middleton v Douglass*, 1991 S.L.T. 726 and *Comex Houlder Diving Ltd v Colne Fishing Co Ltd (No.2)*, 1992 S.L.T. 89.

[125] *Henderson v Merrett Syndicates Ltd* [1995] 2 A.C. 145 at 194. Whether the correct approach involves one or two stages has been described as "only a terminological debate" (Longmore L.J. in *Riyad Bank v Ahli United Bank Plc* [2006] 2 Lloyd's Rep. 292 at [21]).

[126] *Robinson v National Bank of Scotland*, 1916 S.C. 154.

[127] *Hedley Byrne & Co v Heller and Partners* [1964] A.C. 465. See *John Kenway v Orcantic*, 1979 S.C. 422, acknowledging the existence of this principle in Scots law.

"no logical stopping place short of all those relationships where it is plain that the party seeking information or advice was trusting the other to exercise such a degree of care as the circumstances required, where it was reasonable for him to do that, and where the other gave the information or advice when he knew or ought to have known that the inquirer was relying on him."[128]

The principle established in *Hedley Byrne* was applied in a subsequent case where a local authority clerk failed to disclose to a third party the recording in a land register of a charge in favour of the plaintiffs, thus rendering the charge unenforceable against the third party, to the loss of the plaintiffs.[129] Where a surveyor is instructed by a lender to value property but knows that his report will be communicated to and probably relied upon by the borrower, the surveyor may owe a duty of care to the borrower,[130] although this is less likely if the borrower is a property developer.[131] Similarly, surveyors instructed by a borrower can owe a duty of care to a lender.[132] A surveyor instructed by a potential purchaser, A, can owe a duty to another person, B, who joins A in the purchase of the property but whose existence as a potential purchaser is not known to the surveyor.[133] In all cases involving the negligent valuation of property, however, the valuer will not be liable for loss truly attributable to a decline in the property market, even if the transaction would not have been undertaken but for his valuation.[134] A solicitor acting for a client can owe a duty of care to a third party who is relying on advice or information given to him by the solicitor, provided the necessary degree of proximity is present.[135] Under the "single survey" system introduced by the Housing (Scotland) Act 2006 surveyors will be liable to a purchaser suffering loss where the report is not based on an inspection of the house, or has not been prepared in a fair and unbiased way, or has not been prepared with reasonable skill.[136]

As already noted, the circumstances in which liability will attach for the making of a negligent statement, written or verbal, were reviewed by the House of Lords in *Caparo Industries Plc v James Dickman*.[137] The decision has become central to the analysis of duty of care since 1990, in cases concerning physical injury and property damage as well as cases involving alleged misrepresentation.[138] In *Caparo*, the plaintiffs had begun to purchase shares in a company a few days before the annual accounts were published to shareholders. In reliance on those accounts, they purchased further shares and took over the company. They alleged that they had since discovered that the accounts presented a falsely optimistic picture of the company and that if they had known the true picture they would not have taken over the company at all, or at any rate not at the price paid. The House of Lords considered whether or not the auditor of the accounts could be held to have owed a duty of care to the plaintiffs, either as existing shareholders or as potential future investors. It was held that no such duty was owed. As in many

---

[128] *Hedley Byrne & Co v Heller and Partners* [1964] A.C. 465 at 486.
[129] *Ministry of Housing v Sharp* [1970] 2 Q.B. 223.
[130] *Martin v Bell-Ingram*, 1986 S.L.T. 575; *Smith v Eric S. Bush* [1990] 1 A.C. 831.
[131] *Wilson v DM Hall & Sons* [2005] P.N.L.R. 22.
[132] *U.C.B. Bank Plc v Dundas & Wilson C.S.*, 1989 S.L.T. 243.
[133] *Smith v Carter*, 1995 S.L.T. 295.
[134] *Banque Bruxelles Lambert S.A. v Eagle Star Ins. Co* [1995] Q.B. 375.
[135] *Midland Bank Plc v Cameron, Thom, Peterkin & Duncans*, 1988 S.L.T. 611.
[136] Housing (Scotland) Act 2006 (Consequential Provisions) Order 2008 (SI 2008/1889).
[137] *Caparo Industries Plc v Dickman* [1990] 2 A.C. 605.
[138] See para 26.02 above.

such cases, the judges were reluctant to hold that such a duty existed in respect of representations which could potentially be relied upon by many different people in different situations and for many purposes.[139] Lord Bridge saw the limiting or control mechanism as being knowledge by the defendant that his statement would be communicated to the plaintiff, specifically in connection with a particular transaction, and that the plaintiff would be very likely to rely on it for the purpose of reaching a decision regarding that transaction.[140] The dissenting judgment of Lord Denning in *Candler v Crane Christmas & Co*,[141] a case overruled by the House of Lords in *Hedley Byrne*, was again approved by the House. The criteria set out in *Caparo* have since been applied by the Court of Appeal in England in other cases concerning failures by accountants in the preparation or auditing of accounts or other financial statements. In *James McNaughton Paper Group Ltd v Hicks Anderson & Co*[142] it was held that no duty was owed because of the particular circumstances surrounding the preparation of the accounts and the unlikelihood of reliance; whereas in *Morgan Crucible Co Plc v Hill Samuel & Co Ltd*[143] it was held that a duty could be owed not to mislead.[144] Auditors appointed to a local authority under statute owe a statutory duty and may also owe a common law duty of care to the local authority as the body whose accounts are being audited.[145] Auditors of a company's accounts may owe duties to third parties such as shareholders, creditors and potential investors if they act beyond their statutory role under the Companies Act 2006.[146] Where financial advice is imparted by a company, an individual director of that company will only be liable for loss caused by following the advice if he has personally assumed responsibility for it.[147]

Liability for negligent misrepresentation can also be established where an employer issues an inaccurate reference concerning a former employee to a potential employer of that employee, causing the loss of an opportunity of employment.[148] The duty may be excluded, in circumstances in which it would otherwise arise, by an express disclaimer of responsibility.[149] Negligent misstatements can afford a ground of action as representations inducing a contract that has resulted in loss.[150] Formerly fraudulent misrepresentation had to be proved.[151]

---

[139] *Caparo Industries Plc v Dickman* [1990] 2 A.C. 605 at 621, where Lord Bridge of Harwich quotes the familiar caveat of Cardozo C.J. that there could ensue "liability in an indeterminate amount for an indeterminate time to an indeterminate class": *Ultramares Corp v Touche* (1931) 174 N.E. 441 at 444.

[140] *Caparo Industries Plc v Dickman* [1990] 2 A.C. 605 at 621.

[141] *Candler v Crane Christmas & Co* [1951] 2 K.B. 164.

[142] *James McNaughton Paper Group Ltd v Hicks Anderson & Co* [1991] 2 Q.B. 113.

[143] *Morgan Crucible Co Plc v Hill Samuel & Co Ltd* [1991] Ch. 295.

[144] See also *Galoo Ltd v Bright Grahame Murray* [1994] 1 W.L.R. 1360.

[145] *West Wiltshire DC v Garland* [1995] Ch. 297. See also *Law Society v KPMG Peat Marwick* [2000] 1 W.L.R. 1921 (accountants reporting on solicitors' firm owe a duty to Law Society as trustee of compensation fund) and *Andrew v Kounnis Freeman* [1999] 2 B.C.L.C. 641 (company's auditors owed duty to Civil Aviation Authority, which relied on company's accounts in deciding to renew air transport operator's licence).

[146] *Royal Bank of Scotland v Bannerman Johnstone Maclay*, 2005 S.C. 437 with reference to the 1985 Act.

[147] *Williams v Natural Life Health Foods Ltd* [1998] 1 W.L.R. 830.

[148] *Spring v Guardian Assurance Plc* [1995] 2 A.C. 296. See also *Johnstone v Traffic Commissioner*, 1990 S.L.T. 409; cf. *Kapfunde v Abbey National Plc* [1999] I.C.R. 1.

[149] *Hedley Byrne & Co v Heller and Partners* [1964] A.C. 465; *Commercial Financial Services Ltd v McBeth & Co*, 1988 S.L.T. 528.

[150] See Law Reform (Miscellaneous Provisions) (Scotland) Act 1985 s.10.

[151] See para.7.35, above.

26.09 Negligence: Standard of care—The standard of care applied to determine whether or not the defender was negligent is that of a reasonable man of ordinary intelligence and experience.[152]

> "The reasonable man is presumed to be free both from over-apprehension and from over-confidence but there is a sense in which the standard of care of the reasonable man involves in its application a subjective element. It is still left to the judge to decide what in the circumstances of the particular case the reasonable man would have had in contemplation and what accordingly the party sought to be made liable ought to have foreseen."[153]

It is a question not only of what the reasonable man would have foreseen but also of the risks against which he would have taken precautions, although this latter point may also be addressed by considering what harm is within the scope of the duty. The degree of care varies directly with the risk involved. Thus a higher degree of care is required in activities which are obviously highly dangerous.[154] At the other end of the scale the risk may be so small that a reasonable man would feel justified in disregarding it.[155] The appropriate degree of care is not determined by reference solely to the actual knowledge of the defender but also to the sources of knowledge open to him and to the actual knowledge of kindred persons.[156] Where the pursuer alleges that a system of work was unsafe, evidence that that system is standard practice in the industry is not conclusive in favour of the defenders.[157] Conversely, a departure from standard practice is not conclusive in favour of the pursuer.[158] The pursuer's own knowledge and experience are also relevant to the question of what precautions were reasonable in the circumstances.[159] A greater degree of care is due to parties with abnormal susceptibilities or infirmities.[160] The magnitude of the risk must be weighed against the difficulty and expense of taking precautions and the importance of the particular operation.[161] Thus, where a member of the emergency services is injured in the course of his work, assessment of whether reasonable care was taken by his employer may have to be made in the light of the service's duty to the public and the resources available to it.[162] An emergency may justify the taking of a risk that

---

[152] *Muir v Glasgow Corp*, 1943 S.C. (HL) 3.

[153] *Muir v Glasgow Corp*, 1943 S.C. (HL) 3 at 10, per Lord Macmillan.

[154] *Dominion Natural Gas Co v Collins* [1909] A.C. 640 at 646, per Lord Dunedin; *Read v Lyons & Co* [1947] A.C. 156 at 171, per Lord Macmillan: "an exacting standard of care is incumbent on manufacturers of explosive shells". A high standard of care is also required of one who entrusts another with a gun: *Attorney General of British Virgin Islands v Hartwell* [2004] 1 W.L.R. 1273.

[155] See *Carmarthenshire CC v Lewis* [1955] A.C. 549 at 565, per Lord Reid; also *Overseas Tankship (UK) v Miller Steamship Co* [1967] 1 A.C. 617 at 641–644, PC, and *Bolton v Stone* [1951] A.C. 850.

[156] See *Balfour v William Beardmore & Co*, 1956 S.L.T. 205; cf. *Quinn v Cameron & Roberton*, 1956 S.C. 224 at 232, per Lord President Clyde (reversed on another ground, 1957 S.C. (HL) 22); *Cramb v Caledonian Ry* (1892) 19 R. 1054; *Roe v Ministry of Health* [1954] 2 Q.B. 66.

[157] *Cavanagh v Ulster Weaving Co* [1960] A.C. 145.

[158] *Brown v Rolls Royce Ltd*, 1960 S.L.T. 119.

[159] *Qualcast v Haynes* [1959] A.C. 743 at 754, per Lord Radcliffe; *Ross v Associated Portland Cement* [1964] 1 W.L.R. 768, HL.

[160] *McKibbin v Glasgow Corp*, 1920 S.C. 590, and *Haley v London Electricity Board* [1965] A.C. 778 (blind persons); *Paris v Stepney BC* [1951] A.C. 367 (man known to have only one eye); as to children, see *Taylor v Glasgow Corp*, 1922 S.C. (HL) 1; *Miller v S.S.E.B.*, 1958 S.C. (HL) 20; *Hughes v Lord Advocate*, 1963 S.C. (HL) 31.

[161] *Morris v West Hartlepool Steam Navigation Co* [1956] A.C. 552 at 574, per Lord Reid, and at 579, per Lord Cohen.

[162] *King v Sussex Ambulance Trust* [2002] I.C.R. 1413.

in other circumstances might be negligent.[163] The standard of care required of a police driver responding to a call is not necessarily the same as that required of an ordinary driver on a private occasion.[164]

Standard of care: Professional negligence—Where a person professes to have a **26.10** particular skill, in carrying out the work with which he is thereby entrusted he must display the same standard of care as other members of the profession, whether or not he possesses the same qualifications.[165] The standard of care against which the actions of a professional are measured depends on the state of scientific and technical knowledge prevailing at the time.[166] A professional person will not be held to have been negligent in the exercise of his judgment unless he has followed a course which no ordinarily competent member of his profession would have adopted if acting with ordinary care.[167] A court faced with conflicting testimony of experts as to the course which should have been adopted is not entitled simply to prefer one body of opinion over another.[168] If, however, one of the competing bodies of evidence is found not to be credible and reliable, the opposing testimony may be preferred.[169] The standard of reasonably competent members of the profession covers the giving of advice as well as the carrying out of work; thus, a doctor in omitting to warn a patient of the risk inherent in a particular form of treatment will not be faulted if he has followed an accepted practice, albeit that other doctors might have alerted the patient to the risk.[170] In issuing advice, a professional should take into account the nature, experience and understanding of the client concerned.[171] In an English appeal, the House of Lords has ruled that a barrister no longer enjoys immunity from suit, even in relation to his conduct of a litigation or criminal trial.[172] The position in Scotland was not argued,[173] but it has since been held that those conducting a criminal defence in Scotland, whether solicitors or advocates, are immune from suit at the instance of the accused person.[174]

Negligence: Causation—Once negligence is established, liability depends upon **26.11** proof that it caused the damage in issue. Where the alleged negligence was failure to provide a workman with a safety belt, it was suggested that there were four steps of causation: (1) a duty to supply a safety belt; (2) a breach; (3) that, if

---

[163] See, e.g. *Watt v Hertfordshire CC* [1954] 1 W.L.R. 835; also *Latimer v A.E.C. Ltd* [1953] A.C. 643, where it was held that failure to close a factory to prevent employees slipping on a flooded floor was not negligent.

[164] *Gilfillan v Barbour*, 2003 S.L.T. 1127.

[165] *Dickson v Hygienic Institute*, 1910 S.C. 352; cf. *Kirkcaldy DC v Household Manufacturing Ltd*, 1987 S.L.T. 617 (defenders not members of profession). See also *Ahmed v Glasgow City Council*, 2000 S.L.T. (Sh. Ct) 152 (whether acts of professional were within area of his professional judgement).

[166] *Roe v Ministry of Health* [1954] 2 Q.B. 66.

[167] *Hunter v Hanley*, 1955 S.C. 200.

[168] *Maynard v West Midlands R.H.A.* [1984] 1 W.L.R. 634; *Gordon v Wilson*, 1992 S.L.T. 849.

[169] *Peach v Ian G. Chalmers & Co*, 1992 S.C.L.R. 423; *Bolitho v City & Hackney H.A.* [1998] A.C. 232.

[170] *Sidaway v Bethlem Royal Hospital Governors* [1985] A.C. 871; *Moyes v Lothian Health Board*, 1990 S.L.T. 444.

[171] *Stewart v McLean, Baird & Neilson*, 1915 S.C. 13; *County Personnel (Employment Agency) Ltd v Alan R. Pulver & Co* [1987] 1 All E.R. 289.

[172] *Arthur J.S. Hall v Simons* [2002] 1 A.C. 615.

[173] *Arthur J.S. Hall v Simons* [2002] 1 A.C. 615, per Lord Steyn. The comments of Lord Hope of Craighead (at 714) while obiter, indicate his view that an advocate may be subject to claims of professional negligence in relation to his conduct of a litigation in court.

[174] *Wright v Paton Farrell*, 2006 S.C. 404.

there had been a safety belt, the workman would have used it; and (4) that, if the workman had been using a safety belt, he would not have been killed, and the failure to prove the third step rendered the first two steps inoperative.[175] The first two steps, however, are not truly links in the chain of causation, the tracing of which does not begin until the question is posed: "Did the proven breach of duty cause this event?"[176] Generally, the pursuer's claim will fail if it can be demonstrated as a matter of fact that the event would have occurred even if the breach of duty had not taken place.[177] A question may arise in a medical or other professional negligence case as to what, as a matter of fact, would have happened had a negligent omission not occurred. If the case concerns failure to warn a patient about a risk inherent in particular surgery, the patient may recover damages if the risk eventuates, despite being unable to prove that she would have avoided the operation had she known of the risk.[178] If the question of what would have occurred depends on whether a professional person would have taken further steps necessary to prevent the harm, the pursuer will have to show either that the particular professional concerned would have taken those steps or that failure to do so would itself have been professional negligence.[179] Where a number of factors contribute to an event, any one of which makes a material contribution thereto will be treated as a cause for the purpose of establishing liability.[180] If the defender's conduct in exposing the pursuer to a harmful agent materially increased the risk of harm occurring, it will be treated as having made a material contribution.[181] In *Fairchild v Glenhaven Funeral Services*,[182] different defenders had exposed the pursuer to a harmful agent at different times. The House of Lords treated each exposure as a material contribution and held the defenders jointly and severally liable. This was departed from in *Barker v Corus*[183] where the liability of each defender was held to be proportionate to the magnitude of risk of injury to which the claimant had been exposed. The claimant himself was responsible for exposure during a period of self employment. The position regarding recovery of damages for mesothelioma where there is more than one period of exposure to asbestos is now dealt with by statutory provision which has the effect of reinstating the rule in *Fairchild*.[184] Where harm is not mesothelioma, *Barker v Corus* remains the governing authority. Where there are a number of possible causes of a disease or disability, only one of which is the negligence of the defender, the onus remains on the pursuer to show that the negligence made at least a material contribution.[185] In a medical negligence case where the evidence demonstrated that on the balance of probabilities the disability was not caused by the negligence, it was held by the House of Lords that there was no scope for an award of damages to compensate for the loss of a chance of a better medical

[175] *McWilliams v Wm Arrol & Co*, 1962 S.C. (HL) 70 at 77, per Lord Chancellor Kilmuir. See also for failure to wear safety glasses, *McKinlay v British Steel Corp*, 1988 S.L.T. 810.

[176] See para.26.01, above.

[177] *Kay's Tutor v Ayrshire & Arran Health Board*, 1987 S.L.T. 577.

[178] *Chester v Afshar* [2005] 1 A.C. 134.

[179] *Bolitho v City & Hackney H.A.* [1998] A.C. 232.

[180] *Wardlaw v Bonnington Castings*, 1956 S.C. (HL) 26.

[181] *McGhee v National Coal Board*, 1973 S.C. (HL) 37.

[182] *Fairchild v Glenhaven Funeral Services Ltd* [2003] 1 A.C. 32.

[183] *Barker v Corus* [2006] 2 A.C. 572.

[184] Compensation Act 2006 s.3, imposing full liability on any defender responsible for exposure, and joint and several liability among defenders.

[185] *Wilsher v Essex Area Health Authority* [1988] A.C. 1074; *Cross v Highlands & Islands Enterprise*, 2001 S.L.T. 1060.

result.[186] By parity of reasoning, the House of Lords has also held that, where a claimant's prospects of surviving cancer were already below 50 per cent, worsening those prospects does not generate an award of damages.[187]

Once it has been established that the defender's conduct was a cause of the harm suffered by the pursuer, it is necessary to decide whether or not it was a cause of sufficient importance to lead to liability. Such a cause has been variously described as the real or efficient cause, or as the *causa causans*. The assessment of causation is "dealt with broadly, and upon common sense principles as a jury would probably deal with it".[188] Two or more causes may combine concurrently to cause an accident, with each being regarded as a *causa causans*.[189] Difficulty may arise when a number of factors operate consecutively to produce a result.[190] The mere fact that a subsequent act of negligence has been the immediate cause of the disaster does not exonerate the original wrongdoer if there is no sufficient separation of time, place and circumstances to justify the exclusion of the original negligence as an efficient cause.[191] This principle applies even if the final act of negligence is that of the pursuer himself[192] unless the final act is held to be the sole efficient cause of the accident.[193] But the chain of causation between the original negligent act and the ultimate consequences may be broken by "a new cause which disturbs the sequence of events, something which can be described as either unreasonable or extraneous or extrinsic, outside the exigencies of the emergency".[194] That new cause may be some act by the injured party himself or by a third party. If it is held to break the chain of causation, it is known as a *novus actus interveniens*; and, in determining whether or not such an act is sufficient to break the chain, the test of reasonable foreseeability may be applied.

The pursuer's own act will break the chain of causation if the effect of it is to render useless the precaution which he claimed ought to have been taken,[195] or if he has acted in wilful defiance of orders,[196] but probably not if he has merely been careless (which results in apportionment of blame), and certainly not if he has acted reasonably in the circumstances.[197] Where the breach of duty consists of

---

[186] *Hotson v East Berkshire Area Health Authority* [1987] A.C. 750.

[187] *Gregg v Scott* [2005] 2 A.C. 176.

[188] *Admiralty Commissioners v Owners of the SS Volute* [1922] A.C. 129 at 136, per Lord Chancellor Birkenhead.

[189] *Boy Andrew v St Rognvald*, 1947 S.C. (HL) 70.

[190] See discussion of causation of economic loss in *Banque Bruxelles Lambert S.A. v Eagle Star Ins. Co* [1995] Q.B. 375.

[191] *Admiralty Commissioners v Owners of the SS Volute* [1922] A.C. 129 at 144–5, per Lord Chancellor Birkenhead; see also *Grant v Sun Shipping Co*, 1948 S.C. (HL) 73 at 94, per Lord du Parcq; *Stapley v Gypsum Mines* [1953] A.C. 663 at 681–682, per Lord Reid; and *Drew v Western S.M.T.*, 1947 S.C. 222; *Rouse v Squires* [1973] 1 Q.B. 889; *Wright v Lodge* [1993] 4 All E.R. 299.

[192] Blame is then apportioned under the Law Reform (Contributory Negligence) Act 1945; and see *Ross v Associated Portland Cement* [1964] 1 W.L.R. 768, HL.

[193] See cases of deliberate disobedience of instructions referred to by Lord Reid in *Ross v Associated Portland Cement* [1964] 1 W.L.R. 768 at 776–7.

[194] *The Oropesa* [1943] P. 32 at 39, per Lord Wright.

[195] e.g. by refusing to wear a safety belt: see *McWilliams v Wm Arrol & Co*, 1962 S.C. (HL) 70.

[196] See *Stapley v Gypsum Mines Ltd* [1953] A.C. 663; *Ginty v Belmont Building Supplies* [1959] 1 All E.R. 414; *Horne v Lec Refrigeration* [1965] 2 All E.R. 898; also *Crowe v James Scott & Sons*, 1965 S.L.T. 54.

[197] *Steel v Glasgow Iron & Steel Co*, 1944 S.C. 237, in particular, Lord Jamieson at 268; cf. *Malcolm v Dickson*, 1951 S.C. 542; *Macdonald v David MacBrayne Ltd*, 1915 S.C. 716. See also *McFarlane v Tayside Health Board*, 2000 S.C. (HL) 1 (reasonable not to have an abortion after a failed sterilisation operation) and *Sabri-Tabrizi v Lothian Health Board*, 1998 S.L.T. 607 (*novus actus* to have sexual intercourse in knowledge that sterilisation had failed).

failure to prevent an event, the occurrence of that event cannot be regarded as a *novus actus interveniens*.[198] An error of judgment made by the pursuer when acting in an emergency created by the defender's negligence will not break the chain.[199] While the deliberate unwarranted intervention of a third party will break the chain if it is thought to be the proximate cause or not reasonably foreseeable,[200] an act which is reasonable in the circumstances will not. So a man who threw a lighted squib into a crowded market place was found liable in damages to the person injured when it exploded, notwithstanding the fact that it had only reached the injured party through the intervention of two other people who, acting in the interests of their own safety, had picked it up and thrown it onwards.[201] There is liability for all the natural and probable consequences of the negligent act[202]; and the fact that the last link in the chain is a wrongful[203] or negligent[204] or voluntary act[205] of a third party will not exclude liability if that act is a reasonably foreseeable consequence of the defender's original negligence. Negligent conduct is more likely to break the chain of causation than non-negligent conduct and positive acts are more likely to do so than inaction.[206]

26.12 Negligence: Remoteness of damage—

> "A wrongdoer is not held responsible for all the results which flow from his negligent act. Practical considerations dictate, and the law accepts, that there comes a point in the sequence of events when liability can no longer be enforced."[207]

Liability for injury to a person or damage to property through negligence extends to all the natural and direct consequences of that injury or damage.[208] There must be an unbroken causal connection between the original damage and every item of loss claimed to flow therefrom.[209]

> "The grand rule on the subject of damages is that none can be claimed except such as naturally and directly arise out of the wrong done, and such, therefore, as may reasonably be supposed to have been in the view of the wrongdoer."[210]

---

[198] *Reeves v Metropolitan Commissioner of Police* [2000] 1 A.C. 360.

[199] See *S.S. Baron Vernon v S.S. Metagama*, 1928 S.C. (HL) 21 at 26–27, per Viscount Dunedin.

[200] See *Weld-Blundell v Stephens* [1920] A.C. 956; cf. *Marshall v Caledonian Ry* (1899) 1 F. 1060. See para.26.05, above, for discussion of the separate but allied question of whether a defender not otherwise negligent is liable where the actions of a third party were the direct cause of loss.

[201] *Scott v Shepherd* (1773) 2 W. Bl. 892; see also *Clark v Chambers* (1878) 3 Q.B.D. 327; *The Oropesa* [1943] P. 32; and *Haynes v Harwood* [1935] 1 K.B. 146.

[202] *Scott's Trs v Moss* (1887) 17 R. 32; *Miller v S.S.E.B.*, 1958 S.C. (HL) 20; *Steel v Glasgow Iron & Steel Co*, 1944 S.C. 237 at 268, per Lord Jamieson.

[203] *Marshall v Caledonian Ry* (1899) 1 F. 1060.

[204] *Miller v S.S.E.B.*, 1958 S.C. (HL) 20; cf. *S.S. Singleton Abbey v S.S. Paludina* [1927] A.C. 16.

[205] See *Haynes v Harwood* [1935] 1 K.B. 146 (where boys caused horses to bolt); *Baker v Hopkins* [1959] 1 W.L.R. 966; and *Hosie v Arbroath Football Club*, 1978 S.L.T. 122.

[206] *Knightley v Johns* [1982] 1 W.L.R. 349.

[207] *Malcolm v Dickson*, 1951 S.C. 542 at 547, per Lord Justice-Clerk Thomson.

[208] See *Adm. Commrs v S.S. Susquehanna* [1926] A.C. 655 at 661, per Lord Dunedin; approved in *Hutchison v Davidson*, 1945 S.C. 395 at 404, by Lord Russell, and by Lord Moncrieff at 410; and by Lords Mackay and Patrick in *Pomphrey v James A Cuthbertson (No.2)*, 1951 S.C. 147 at 157 and 162.

[209] See *The Vitruvia*, 1925 S.C. (HL) 1; *The Cameronia v The Hauk*, 1928 S.L.T. 71; and *Carslogie S.S. Co v Royal Norwegian Government* [1952] A.C. 292.

[210] *Allan v Barclay* (1864) 2 M. 873 at 874, per Lord Kinloch.

Although this statement was made obiter by Lord Kinloch, it is an accurate statement of the rule in Scotland governing liability for both the immediate and subsequent consequences of negligence. It is, however, open to construction. "Naturally" means "according to the ordinary, usual or normal course of things" and this includes reasonable human conduct.[211] "Directly" means "without any break in the chain of causation".[212] Everything which arises in the ordinary course of things from the negligence without the intervention of any extraneous act or factor is in law deemed to have been in the view of the wrongdoer.[213] Damage which flows directly and naturally (i.e. in the ordinary course of things) from the wrongful act cannot be regarded as too remote.[214] While the foreseeability test may be of assistance in certain cases in determining whether the loss claimed has arisen from the negligent act "in the ordinary course of things" and is, therefore, a natural, ordinary or normal result as opposed to an unnatural, extraordinary and abnormal result,[215] our law does not permit that test to be pressed to the length of excluding liability for any item of loss which has arisen naturally and directly (in the sense before mentioned) from the negligence. For example, there is liability for all medical expenses reasonably incurred as a natural and direct consequence of physical injury and this liability extends to the expense of unnecessary treatment wrongly, but not negligently, prescribed by doctors.[216] The foreseeability test cannot be applied first and in isolation exclude liability for such expenses.[217] A more recent formulation of the test for remoteness[218] holds that the defender: cannot be liable for consequences that are not reasonably foreseeable; will not be liable for foreseeable consequences that result from a *novus actus interveniens*; will be liable for harm of a kind greater in extent than was foreseeable or was caused in a way that could not have been foreseen, providing it is of the same nature as that which was foreseeable[219]; takes his victim as he finds him; and is liable for psychiatric injury where he is in breach of a duty to avoid causing personal injury.[220] On this view the governing criteria for remoteness is foreseeability. Clearly remoteness does not operate in isolation from the other elements of liability. Ultimately, remoteness is a concept employed by courts which require

---

[211] See *S.S. Baron Vernon v S.S. Metagama*, 1928 S.C. (HL) 21 at 25, per Lord Haldane; *The Oropesa* [1943] P. 32 at 37–38, per Lord Wright; *Steel v Glasgow Iron & Steel Co*, 1944 S.C. 237 at 248 and 268; and *The Sivand* [1998] 2 Lloyd's Rep. 97. In *McKew v Holland & Hannen & Cubitts (Scotland) Ltd*, 1970 S.C. (HL) 20, the pursuer was held to have acted unreasonably.

[212] See para.26.11, above.

[213] Note: If "naturally" is construed in the broader sense above mentioned instead of the narrow sense of "in the ordinary course of nature", the difficulties created in England by the *Polemis* case ([1921] 3 K.B. 560) do not arise in respect that liability for the fire damage in both the *Polemis* case and *The Wagon Mound* ([1961] A.C. 388) must be excluded as being an unnatural (i.e. extraordinary or abnormal) consequence and such, therefore, as cannot reasonably be supposed to have been in the view of the wrongdoer.

[214] See *Clyde Navigation Trs v Bowring S.S. Co*, 1929 S.C. 715 at 723, per Lord Hunter, quoting Lord Herschell.

[215] See *Steel v Glasgow Iron & Steel Co*, 1944 S.C. 237 at 248, per Lord Justice-Clerk Cooper, and 268, per Lord Jamieson.

[216] *Rubens v Walker*, 1946 S.C. 215. If the treatment had been negligently prescribed, that negligence might be held on the facts to be a *novus actus interveniens* excluding the defender's liability for such expenses but exposing the doctors to a claim against them.

[217] See also *H.M.S. London* [1914] P. 72, where a claim for loss of use of a vessel in dock for collision repairs was allowed to cover the period of a shipyard strike as natural and direct loss.

[218] *Simmons v British Steel Plc*, 2004 S.L.T. 595, per Lord Rodger.

[219] Following *Hughes v Lord Advocate*, 1963 S.C. (HL) 31.

[220] Following *Page v Smith* [1996] A.C. 155.

to draw a line between losses that the defender must in justice meet and those that must be borne by the pursuer.

The negligent party "must take his victim as he finds him" and is liable for all the natural and direct effects of the original injury on the particular pursuer.[221] These include the consequences of inappropriate medical treatment if that was not negligent.[222] Death by suicide may not be too remote from a serious physical injury leading to depression.[223] Similar rules regarding remoteness of damage apply to patrimonial loss. Where a house is damaged with the result that it is left unoccupied, the person liable for that damage is not liable for further damage caused by squatters who enter the empty property.[224] Probable loss due to prospects of promotion being prejudiced is relevant, but the loss of hypothetical gain is too remote.[225] Where the pursuer's injuries adversely affect the business of a company in which he is the principal director and shareholder, no claim is maintainable for the company's loss of income, but the pursuer may claim damages for any corresponding loss of salary or dividend to him.[226] Lastly, in assessing the measure of damages applicable to the loss of working plant through negligence, extraordinary or abnormal loss, sustained by the owners as a result of their inability through impecuniosity to purchase a replacement, may be too remote, the financial embarrassment of the owners being an extrinsic and unusual factor which was the effective cause of that loss.[227] It has, however, been held that it was reasonable for a plaintiff to defer incurring expenditure on repairs, even though the deferral led to an increase in the cost of such repairs.[228] Unless the particular circumstances of the pursuer were or ought to have been known to the defender, the cost of obtaining loans will not be recoverable, it not being inevitable that the infliction of financial loss will lead to the need to borrow money.[229]

26.13 **Proof of negligence:** *Res ipsa loquitur*—The burden of proving negligence generally rests upon the pursuer and it must be established on "the balance of probabilities".[230] Thus the decision may ultimately turn upon the question of whether or not the pursuer has discharged the burden of proving negligence.[231] In some cases the pursuer may establish a prima facie case of negligence which transfers to the defender a tactical burden of proving that he was not negligent.[232] The pursuer may be assisted in establishing a prima facie case by proving that the defender was convicted of an offence in connection with the circumstances of the

---

[221] *McKillen v Barclay Curle & Co*, 1967 S.L.T. 41; *Cross v Highlands & Islands Enterprise*, 2001 S.L.T. 1060. This also appears to be the law of England: see *Smith v Leech Brain & Co* [1962] 2 Q.B. 405.

[222] cf. *Robinson v Post Office* [1974] 1 W.L.R. 1176, where although there was negligence in the medical treatment that negligence was not a cause of the condition which resulted from the treatment and so did not constitute a *novus actus interveniens*.

[223] *Corr v IBC Vehicles Ltd* [2008] 1 A.C. 884. Cf. *Cowan v N.C.B.*, 1958 S.L.T. (Notes) 19.

[224] *Lamb v Camden London BC* [1981] Q.B. 625.

[225] See *McCall v Foulis*, 1966 S.L.T. 47, and cases cited therein.

[226] *Anthony v Brabbs*, 1998 S.C. 894.

[227] See *Liesbosch v S.S. Edison* [1933] A.C. 449, in particular Lord Wright at 460 and 465–466.

[228] *Dodd Properties (Kent) Ltd v Canterbury City Council* [1980] 1 W.L.R. 433; *Alcoa Minerals of Jamaica Inc v Broderick* [2000] 3 W.L.R. 23.

[229] *Margrie Holdings Ltd v Edinburgh DC*, 1994 S.L.T. 971.

[230] *Hendry v Clan Line Steamers*, 1949 S.C. 320.

[231] *Hendry v Clan Line Steamers*, 1949 S.C. 320 at 322, per Lord Justice-Clerk Thomson; see also *Brown v Rolls Royce Ltd*, 1960 S.C. (HL) 22, per Lord Denning, as to the difference between the legal and provisional burden of proof.

[232] See, e.g. *Gunn v McAdam*, 1949 S.C. 31.

accident.[233] In other cases the admitted or proved fact that an accident occurred may per se yield an inference of negligence which must be negatived by the defender.[234] It is to the latter type of case

> "where the thing is shown to be under the management of the defendant or his servants, and the accident is such as in the ordinary case does not happen if those who have the management use proper care",[235]

that the maxim *res ipsa loquitur* ("the thing itself speaks") applies. It is a presumption of law to which effect must be given if the conditions for its operation are satisfied.[236] In this as in other similar cases

> "it is the policy of the law that intervenes to relax the logical stringency of proof and so invert the normal onus in order to avoid denial of justice to those whose rights depend on facts incapable of proof by them, and often exclusively within the knowledge and control of their opponent".[237]

Thus where shop owners were sued as a result of an accident due to spillage on the floor of the shop it was held that there was an onus on them to show that the accident did not occur through want of care on their part.[238] Once the onus is inverted, the defender can only exclude liability by proof that he was not negligent. It has been said, however, that it is essential to the application of *res ipsa loquitur* that the pursuer cannot reasonably be expected to know the exact cause of the accident and that, if he does, he must aver the cause and prove negligence. If the *res* does not per se exclude the possibility of the event having been caused by the pursuer or a third party for whom the defender is not responsible,[239] the pursuer, in order to establish a prima facie case, must adduce evidence which, if accepted, excludes interference by the pursuer and third parties.[240] If the pursuer fails to establish a prima facie case by his evidence, the legal burden of proving negligence remains on the pursuer throughout.[241]

If the cause of an accident is averred by the pursuer to have been a defect in the defender's plant, the onus of proving that the defect was patent (i.e. discoverable by reasonable inspection) and that the defender was at fault in failing to discover it is on the pursuer.[242] If the pursuer does not aver the exact nature of the defect and cannot reasonably be expected to do so, proof by the pursuer that the plant collapsed brings the maxim *res ipsa loquitur* into play so that the defender must

---

[233] Law Reform (Miscellaneous Provisions) (Scotland) Act 1968 s.10.

[234] See, e.g. *Ballard v N.B. Ry Co*, 1923 S.C. (HL) 43; *McDyer v Celtic Football & Athletic Co Ltd*, 2000 S.C. 379; and *Widdowson v Newgate Meat Corp.* [1998] P.I.Q.R. P138.

[235] *Scott v London, etc. Docks Co* (1865) 3 H. & C. 596, per Erle C.J., adopted by the House of Lords in *Ballard v N.B. Ry Co*, 1923 S.C. (HL) 43.

[236] *Henderson v Henry E. Jenkins and Sons* [1970] A.C. 282.

[237] *Elliot v Young's Bus Service*, 1945 S.C. 445 at 456, per Lord Justice Clerk Cooper; see also at 454, where the Lord Justice Clerk points out that it is "unsafe to generalise upon the question of who must prove what without due regard to the precise legal relationship between the parties".

[238] *Ward v Tesco Stores* [1976] 1 W.L.R. 810.

[239] See *Macfarlane v Thompson* (1884) 12 R. 232.

[240] *Inglis v L.M.S. Ry Co*, 1941 S.C. 551; cf. *Easson v L. & N.E.R.* [1944] K.B. 421; *Lloyde v West Midlands Gas Board* [1971] 1 W.L.R. 749.

[241] *Connelly v L.M.S. Ry Co*, 1940 S.C. 477; see also *Moore v R. Fox & Sons* [1956] 1 Q.B. 596 (alternative ground).

[242] *Gavin v Rogers* (1889) 17 R. 206; *Milne v Townsend* (1892) 19 R. 830.

exculpate himself.[243] If the defender pleads that the defect was latent and, there-fore, not ascertainable by reasonable examination, the defender must prove that defence.[244] But the defender will not exculpate himself by proving only that the defect was latent if it is a reasonable inference from the whole evidence that careless handling of the plant was an effective cause of the breakage.[245] If the exact cause of the accident is unknown to either party, proof or admission of the accident throws upon the defender the burden of proving that it happened without negligence on his part (i.e. that he had taken reasonable care in the circumstances of the case).[246] In the case of defective plant the defender may achieve this by proving that the plant was regularly and properly inspected and no defect found.[247]

Where the accident is of a kind which may occur without fault on the part of the person having control of the object causing the accident (for example a vehicle) *res ipsa non loquitur*. In such cases the pursuer must first establish a prima facie case of negligence by proving that the vehicle stopped or swerved suddenly for no apparent reason; thereafter, the defender can only exculpate himself by proving a reason for the driver's emergency action which negatives negligence on his part.[248] If, however, the pursuer avers that the sudden stop or swerve was made in order to avoid a collision with some person or thing on the roadway, the onus of proving negligence remains on the pursuer throughout.[249]

In Scotland, therefore, once the pursuer has established a prima facie case, or has led sufficient evidence to invoke the maxim *res ipsa loquitur*, the court will find for the pursuer unless the defender has cleared himself of negligence by "full legal proof".[250] But the pursuer is tied to his pleadings. Where the case established in evidence differs from that made out by the pursuer in his pleadings, he will not succeed on a case which is "new, separate and distinct" but will be successful if the case made out in evidence is only a variation, modification or development of the case in his pleadings.[251]

FURTHER READING

Booth, C. and Squires, D., *The Negligence Liability of Public Authorities* (Oxford University Press, 2006).

---

[243] *Macaulay v Buist & Co* (1846) 9 D. 245; *Fraser v Fraser* (1882) 9 R. 896; *Walker v Olsen* (1882) 9 R. 946.

[244] *Elliot v Young's Bus Service*, 1945 S.C. 445 at 456, per Lord Justice-Clerk Cooper; *Gibson v Concrete*, 1954 S.L.T. (Notes) 7; see also *Moore v R. Fox & Sons* [1956] 1 Q.B. 596 at 611–12, per Evershed M.R.

[245] *Ballard v N.B. Ry Co*, 1923 S.C. (HL) 43.

[246] *Elliot v Young's Bus Service*, 1945 S.C. 445; *Marshall & Son v Russian Oil Products*, 1938 S.C. 773 at 791, per Lord Justice Clerk Aitchison; *Devine v Colvilles*, 1969 S.C. (HL) 67. See also *Woods v Duncan (The Thetis)* [1946] A.C. 401.

[247] *Devine v Colvilles*, 1969 S.C. (HL) 67; *Elliot v Young's Bus Service*, 1945 S.C. 445 at 454–455, per Lord Justice Clerk Cooper.

[248] *Mars v Glasgow Corp*, 1940 S.C. 202; *O'Hara v Central S.M.T. Co*, 1941 S.C. 363; *Doonan v S.M.T.*, 1950 S.C. 136. See also *Roberts v Matthew Logan*, 1966 S.L.T. 77; *Ludgate v Lovett* [1969] 1 W.L.R. 1016.

[249] *Ballingall v Glasgow Corp*, 1948 S.C. 160; see also *McGregor v Dundee Corp*, 1962 S.C. 15, where the court inferred that a skid was caused by excessive speed.

[250] *O'Hara v Central S.M.T. Co*, 1941 S.C. 363.

[251] *Burns v Dixon's Iron Works Ltd*, 1961 S.C. 102; *McCusker v Saveheat Cavity Wall Insulation Ltd*, 1987 S.L.T. 24; cf. *Connelly v L.M.S. Ry Co*, 1940 S.C. 477.

Charlesworth and Percy on Negligence, edited by Walton, C.,12th edn with supplement (London: Sweet and Maxwell, 2011).

Jackson and Powell on Professional Liability, edited by Powell, J. et al, 7th edn (London: Sweet and Maxwell, 2011).

Thomson, J.M. (ed), *Delict* (Edinburgh: SULI / W. Green).

Thomson, J.M., *Delictual Liability*, 4th edn (Bloomsbury Professional, 2009).

CHAPTER 27

BREACH OF STATUTORY DUTY

Civil liability for breach of statutory duty[1]—Where loss is attributable to **27.01** breach of a duty imposed by statute, different possibilities arise, depending on the statutory provisions. First, where the statute provides expressly for civil liability in the event of breach, an action may be grounded on the statute.[2] This will not normally preclude a common law action from being brought in the alternative.[3] While they may do so, either expressly or impliedly, statutes do not generally extinguish common law rights and duties.[4] The existence of a statutory duty does not, on the other hand, create a common law duty that would not otherwise have existed.[5] There are statutes, moreover, in which common law duties are expressly superseded.[6] In such circumstances, actions may only be founded on the statute. There are other statutes in which civil liability under the statute is expressly excluded.[7] In such cases, notwithstanding the breach of statutory duty, actions for damages may only be brought at common law. Where statutory and common law actions are pled in the alternative it is possible for the statutory claim to succeed while the claim at common law fails[8] and vice versa.[9] Breach of statutory duty by an employee will normally give rise to vicarious liability on the part of the employer unless the statute expressly or impliedly indicates otherwise.[10]

Whether a right to civil action arises on breach is a matter of construction where the statute is silent on civil liability. The whole statute must be construed to determine whether Parliament intended a civil action to lie.[11] There is a clear role for policy in such determinations and while it has been observed that there is a clear

---

[1] Civil liability for harm or breach of human rights arising from the exercise of statutory powers is considered separately at para.26.06.

[2] See, for example: Animals (Scotland) Act 1987, see below para.27.02; Consumer Protection Act 1987, see below para.27.03; Occupiers' Liability (Scotland) Act 1960, see below para.27.04. For further examples see E. Russell, "Breach of Statutory Duty", in J.M. Thomson (ed.), *Delict* (Edinburgh: W. Green), para.6.08.

[3] While the action grounded on the statute is a common law action, the remedy sought, damages, being a common law remedy, such an action is distinguishable from an action grounded on negligence which may be available in the alternative. See *London Passenger Transport Board v Upson* [1949] A.C. 155, per Lord Wright at 168. See further, Russell, "Breach of Statutory Duty", in Thomson (ed.), *Delict*, para.6.02. In England, breach of statutory duty is regarded as a tort in its own right.

[4] *Matuszcyk v NCB*, 1953 S.C. 8, per Lord Keith at 15; *X (Minors) v Bedfordshire CC* [1995] 2 A.C. 633, per Lord Browne-Wilkinson at 765. See further, Russell, "Breach of Statutory Duty", in Thomson (ed.), *Delict*, para.6.01.

[5] *Gorringe v Calderdale MBC* [2004] 1 W.L.R. 1057, per Lord Scott at [71].

[6] e.g. Nuclear Installations Act 1965 s.12(1). For discussion of what constitutes "injury" and "damage to property" from radioactive particles, see *Magnohard v UKAEA*, 2003 S.L.T. 1083.

[7] e.g. Health and Safety at Work Act 1974 s.47(1); Patient Rights (Scotland) Act 2011 s.20(3).

[8] Where the standard of the statutory duty is set higher, e.g. *Millar v Galashiels Gas Co Ltd*, 1949 S.C. (HL) 3; *Matthews v Glasgow CC*, 2006 S.C. 349.

[9] e.g. *Bux v Slough Metals Ltd* [1973] 1 W.L.R. 1358.

[10] *Majrowski v Guy's and St Thomas' NHS Trust* [2007] 1 A.C. 224.

[11] *Cutler v Wandsworth Stadium* [1948] 1 K.B. 295, per Singleton J. at 312.

tendency to favour liability where industrial safety legislation is concerned, policy considerations may work against liability in other contexts.[12] While civil action on the statute is specifically excluded by the Health and Safety at Work Act 1974, regulations made under the Act do give rise to civil liability for breach of duty[13] and the tendency to find liability for breach is reinforced by the need to give a purposive interpretation to regulations implementing EU Directives. Such measures, notably the range of instruments known as the "Six Pack Regulations",[14] are given an interpretation compatible, where possible, with the underlying EU Framework Decisions.[15] In all cases of liability for breach of statutory duty it must be clear that the duty was imposed on the defender and applied to the circumstances that have arisen. The duty must have been mandatory, not merely permissive. The duty, moreover, must have been intended to protect the pursuer and so a bookmaker, for whom space was not made available at a dog track, failed in a claim for damages for breach of a duty which, on construction, was held to have been made for the good ordering of facilities at sporting venues in general and not for the benefit of bookmakers in particular.[16] The loss alleged must be of the type which Parliament had in contemplation, so when sheep were swept overboard during a storm at sea, the owner was not able to found on a breach of provisions requiring livestock to be penned, since this requirement was intended to prevent contagion of disease.[17]

Where Acts are silent on the question of civil liability for breach, there are three presumptions which may be brought to bear in the process of construction.[18] The first presumption is that where the statute provides a specific mode of enforcement, or criminal sanction for breach, no civil action lies in addition.[19] While the provision of criminal sanctions remains indicative that Parliament did not intend the availability of a civil action,[20] this is not of itself conclusive. There is a recognised exception to this presumption and an action may lie where the duty breached has been imposed for the benefit of a class of persons of which the pursuer is a member.[21] Typically, industrial safety provisions fall within this exception.[22] It has been argued that the possibility of judicial review will not trigger the first presumption.[23] The second presumption is that a right of civil action will lie where

---

[12] e.g. *R. v Deputy Governor of Pankhurst Prison, Ex p. Hague* [1992] 1 A.C. 58. See further Russell, "Breach of Statutory Duty", in Thomson (ed.), *Delict*, para.6.11.

[13] Health and Safety at Work Act 1974 s.47(2).

[14] Workplace (Health Safety and Welfare) Regulations (SI 1992/3004); Provision and Use of Work Equipment Regulations (SI 1998/2306); Personal Protective Equipment at Work Regulations (SI 1992/2966); Health and Safety (Display Screen Equipment) Regulations (SI 1992/2792); Manual Handling Operations Regulations (SI 1992/2793); Management of Health and Safety at Work Regulations (SI 1999/3242). See also para.17.54, above.

[15] See further Russell, "Breach of Statutory Duty", in Thomson (ed.), *Delict*, para.6.08; above, para.17.54.

[16] *Cutler v Wandsworth Stadium* [1948] 1 K.B. 295.

[17] *Gorris v Scott* (1873–4) L.R. 9 Ex 125.

[18] See further Russell, "Breach of Statutory Duty", in Thomson (ed.), *Delict,* paras 6.31–6.62.

[19] The origin of this presumption is *Doe dem; Murray, Lord Bishop of Rochester v Bridges* (1831) 1 B & Ad 847, per Lord Tenterden C.J. at 859.

[20] *X (Minors) v Bedfordshire CC* [1995] 2 A.C. 633, per Lord Browne-Wilkinson at 731.

[21] See *Lonrho v Shell Petroleum Co Ltd* [1982] A.C. 173, per Lord Diplock at 185. Lord Diplock also suggested there might be a second exception where the statute creates a public right and the pursuer is able to show special damage. This exception has not been developed by the courts.

[22] See e.g. *Black v Fife Coal Co Ltd*, 1912 S.C. (HL) 33.

[23] J.M. Thomson, *Delictual Liability*, 4th edn (Bloomsbury Professional, 2009), para.11.2; *Cullen v Chief Constable of the Royal Ulster Constabulary* [2003] 1 W.L.R. 1763. See Russell, "Breach of Statutory Duty", in Thomson (ed.), *Delict*, paras 6.63–6.71.

no provision is made in the statute for enforcement.[24] This presumption is necessary to give effective force to the provision which would otherwise be lacking.[25]
The third presumption is that the statute will create no additional right of action
where an existing private law remedy is available.[26]

Breach of a duty recognised by the common law gives rise to civil liability for
resultant harm only on proof by the pursuer of culpa on the part of defender.[27]
Duties imposed by Parliament may stipulate a standard of reasonable care,[28]
equally, a different standard may be set. Non-compliance is evidence of breach
where duties are stated in absolute terms.[29] There is little scope for defending an
action where such a provision is breached.[30] Liability may be strict, in which case
there is no onus on the pursuer to show fault, but statutorily prescribed defences
may be available.[31] Where duties are expressed in terms such as "so far as reasonably practicable" or "to the extent that is reasonably practicable", or "to the extent
that it is practicable" the duty may be described as "qualified". The onus of
showing that particular steps were not reasonably practicable falls on the defender.[32]
The onus is discharged where it can be shown that the sacrifice to be made in
implementing measures necessary to obviate the risk would be in gross dispropor-
tion to the magnitude of the risk itself.[33] The onus of proving causation lies on the
pursuer who must show, on a balance of probabilities, in statutory duty claims
alike with other actions for damages, that the breach either caused or at least materially contributed to the harm complained of.[34] Contributory negligence is generally available as a defence. There are statutes which make express provision for
volenti non fit injuria,[35] but it is not generally available in statutory duty cases.[36]

Liability for animals[37]—Liability for animals is mainly regulated by the provi- **27.02**
sions of the Animals (Scotland) Act 1987. The Act provides that if an animal
belongs to a species whose members generally are by virtue of their physical
attributes or habits likely (unless controlled or restrained) to injure severely or kill
persons or animals, or damage property to a material extent, the keeper of the
animal is liable for any injury or damage caused by the animal and directly referable to such physical attributes or habits.[38] The Act therefore imposes strict
liability on the keepers of dangerous animals causing injury or death and foraging
animals causing property harm. The keeper is any person who owns the animal or

---

[24] The second presumption is also attributed to *Doe dem; Murray, Lord Bishop of Rochester v
Bridges* (1831) 1 B & Ad 847.
[25] See *Cutler v Wandsworth Stadium* [1948] 1 K.B. 295, per Lord Simonds at 407; *X (Minors) v
Bedfordshire CC* [1995] 2 A.C. 633 at 731.
[26] See e.g. *Bollinger v Costa Brava Wine Co Ltd* [1960] Ch. 262; *WL Tinney & Co Ltd v John C
Dougall Ltd*, 1977 S.L.T. (Notes) 58.
[27] See paras 25.05–25.06, above.
[28] e.g. Occupiers' Liability (Scotland) Act 1960 s.2(1). See below, para.27.04.
[29] See *Black v Fife Coal Co Ltd*, 1912 S.C. (HL) 33, per Lord Kinnear at 41; *Nimmo v Alexander
Cowan & Sons Ltd*, 1967 S.C. (HL) 79, per Lord Reid at 95–96. On breach of statutory duty in general
see Russell, "Breach of Statutory Duty", in Thomson (ed.), *Delict*, paras 6.81–6.97.
[30] Except on grounds of contributory negligence.
[31] e.g. Animals (Scotland) Act 1987. See below, para.27.02.
[32] *Nimmo v Alexander Cowan & Sons Ltd*, 1967 S.C. (HL) 79.
[33] See *Edwards v NCB* [1949] 1 K.B. 704, per Asquith L.J. at 712.
[34] See *Wardlaw v Bonnington Castings Ltd*, 1956 S.C. (HL) 26, per Lord Reid at 31.
[35] e.g. Occupiers Liability (Scotland) Act 1960 s.2(3).
[36] Exceptionally, the defence succeeded in *ICI v Shatwell* [1965] A.C. 656.
[37] See further, K. Norrie, "Liability for Animals", in Thomson (ed.), *Delict*, Ch.21.
[38] Animals (Scotland) Act 1987 s.1(1).

has possession of it at the time or who has actual care and control of a child under 16 who owns the animal or has possession of it.[39] Dogs and dangerous wild animals within the meaning of s.7(4) of the Dangerous Wild Animals Act 1976[40] are deemed to be likely to injure severely or kill by biting, savaging, attacking or harrying; and cattle, horses, asses, mules, hinnies, sheep, pigs, goats and deer are deemed to be likely to damage to a material extent land and the produce of land whether harvested or not.[41] A person who was knocked down by a frisky dog was unable to recover damages under the Act, because the dog had not bitten, attacked or harried her.[42] In a subsequent case on similar facts the pursuer was allowed to lead evidence to establish that black labradors are, by virtue of their physical attributes or habits, likely to injure severely or kill persons or animals unless controlled or restrained.[43] In this way it was sought to establish strict liability under s.1(1)(b) in isolation from s.1(3), which specifies dogs as covered by the Act and contains the elaboration on injury and killing that it should be by biting, attacking or harrying. The pursuer failed to prove her case and so no liability under the Act arose. It may be thought that the earlier case represents better the intention of Parliament. The later case, *Welsh v Brady* may serve to identify a point of difficulty. The issue is whether strict liability for injury or killing by dogs and dangerous wild animals is qualified by the requirement that the harm is caused by biting, attacking or harrying. If not, this raises the prospect of strict liability for accidents caused by boisterous animals for which an action grounded on negligence is both competent and perhaps appropriate.

There is no liability under the Act where the injury consists of disease transmitted by means which are unlikely to cause severe injury other than disease,[44] or where injury or damage is caused by the animal's mere presence on a road or in any other place[45] or is caused to persons or animals present on land without authority or entitlement.[46] In the last case, however, there is no exemption from liability if the animal causing the damage was kept for the purpose of protecting persons or property unless the keeping of it there and the use made of it was reasonable and, in the case of a guard dog, there was compliance with s.1 of the Guard Dogs Act 1975.[47] This provision requires guard dogs to be under the control of a handler or otherwise restrained. Defences of the pursuer's sole fault, of contributory negligence and of volenti non fit injuria are competent.[48]

The Act also provides a defence to a common law action for killing an animal. This defence is available where an animal has been killed by a person acting in

---

[39] Animals (Scotland) Act 1987 s.5(1).

[40] That is, those animals listed in the Schedule to the Act.

[41] Animals (Scotland) Act 1987 s.1(3). This deeming provision does not prevent a pursuer from seeking to establish that an animal not mentioned is a member of a species "likely . . . to injure severely": *Foskett v McClymont*, 1998 S.L.T. 892 (concerning a bull).

[42] *Fairlie v Carruthers*, 1996 S.L.T. (Sh. Ct) 56.

[43] *Welsh v Brady*, 2009 S.L.T. 747. It may be observed that black labradors are a breed, not a species. Black labradors belong to the same species as all other domestic dogs, *canis familiaris*. Taken logically, to argue that a black labrador is of a species likely. . . to injure severely is to argue that all domestic dogs are likely. . . to injure severely. Other species belonging to the family *canidae* may be found listed in the Schedule to the Dangerous Wild Animals Act 1976. Not all *canidae* are included: foxes, for example, are excluded. Parliament seems not to have taken for granted a grasp of basic taxonomy by excluding from the coverage of the Act: viruses, bacteria, algae, fungi and protozoa, s.7.

[44] Animals (Scotland) Act 1987 s.1(4).

[45] Animals (Scotland) Act 1987 s.1(5).

[46] Animals (Scotland) Act 1987 s.2(1)(c).

[47] Animals (Scotland) Act 1987 s.2(2).

[48] Animals (Scotland) Act 1987 ss.1(6) and 2(1)(a) and (b).

self defence, in defence of another person or animal, or for the protection of livestock.[49] In all cases the defender must have had reasonable grounds for belief that there was no other practicable means of ending the attack or harrying[50] and the police must have been informed of the killing within 48 hours.[51] The defence is also available and subject to equivalent qualifications in respect of an anticipated attack or harrying.[52] In the case of killing to protect livestock, the defence is available only to those persons specified in s.4(3). That is: the keeper of the livestock, the owner or occupier of the land, or a person authorised by either of the foregoing to protect the livestock. The defence is not available where the animal is killed by a person who is present at the locus for a criminal purpose and who is engaging in that purpose.[53]

Liability for negligence is unaffected by the provisions of the Act. In situations not provided for, the rules of the common law are, therefore, relevant though the old rules imposing strict liability for harm done by animals *ferae naturae* are expressly replaced.[54] At common law, it is the duty of the owner or custodier of all animals to take reasonable care to prevent them from injuring third parties or their property[55] and there will be liability for accidents caused by negligently allowing animals to stray on to the highway, even sheep and cattle, if injury to a road user is a natural and probable consequence of their presence at the locus.[56]

Defective products[57]—Part I of the Consumer Protection Act 1987 implements **27.03** EC Directive 85/374, which imposes strict liability for defects in products.[58] The Act supplements, but does not replace, the common law.[59] The Act applies where any damage is caused wholly or partly by a defect in a product. "Product" is defined as any goods or electricity and includes a product comprised in another product.[60] "Goods" are widely defined, to include any natural or artificial substance, growing crops and things comprised in land, and any ship, aircraft or vehicle.[61] Blood used in medical transfusions has been held to be a product.[62] By s.2(2) of the Act, liability is imposed on the producer[63] of the product, on any person who, by putting his name or other mark on the product, has held himself

---

[49] Animals (Scotland) Act 1987 s.4(1).

[50] Animals (Scotland) Act 1987 s.4(4)(a).

[51] Animals (Scotland) Act 1987 s.4(1)(b).

[52] Animals (Scotland) Act 1987 s.4(4)(b).

[53] Animals (Scotland) Act 1987 s.4(2).

[54] Animals (Scotland) Act 1987 s.1(8). For an interesting discussion on the law prior to the 1987 Act, see Norrie, "Liability for Animals", in Thomson (ed.), *Delict*, paras 21.01–21.07.

[55] See *Henderson v John Stuart (Farms)*, 1963 S.C. 245, where Lord Hunter reviews the authorities.

[56] *Gardiner v Miller*, 1967 S.L.T. 29, OH. Note Lord Thomson's reference to the probable difference of the law of England on this point. For illustrations of liability for damage done by animals on the basis of negligence, see D.M. Walker, *The Law of Delict in Scotland*, 2nd edn (Edinburgh: W. Green, 1981), pp.621–3 and 634. A more recent case in which there was no liability, either at common law or under statute is *Bennett v Lamont & Sons*, 2000 S.L.T. 17.

[57] See further, F. McManus, "Product Liability and Consumer Protection" in Thomson (ed.), *Delict*, Ch.16.

[58] The first draft Directive was published in 1974, and the Law Commission and the Scottish Law Commission reported jointly in 1977: *Liability for Defective Products* (HMSO, 1977), Law Com. No.82, Scot. Law Com. No.45.

[59] Consumer Protection Act 1987 s.2(6).

[60] Consumer Protection Act 1987 s.1(2).

[61] Consumer Protection Act 1987 s.45.

[62] *A v National Blood Authority (No. 1)* [2001] 3 All E.R. 289.

[63] As defined by the Consumer Protection Act 1987 s.1(2).

out as the producer,[64] and on any person who has imported the product from outwith the Member States into a Member State. Liability may also be incurred by any person who has ever supplied the product if a person who has suffered damage caused by a product requests the supplier to identify one or more of the people referred to in s.2(2), the request is made within a reasonable time after the damage occurs and at a time when such identification is not reasonably practicable for the maker of the request, and the supplier fails either to comply with the request or to identify the person who supplied the product to him.[65]

The test for whether or not a product is defective depends on the expectation of the consumer; a product is defective if it is not as safe as persons generally are entitled to expect.[66] Relevant to this test are such factors as the marketing of the product, its presentation, any instructions or warnings and the use which might be expected to be made of the product.[67] Section 3(2)(c) also makes provision for account to be taken of the time when the product is supplied. A product is not rendered defective merely because the safety of a product subsequently supplied is greater.

A number of defences are set out in s.4 of the Act. Defects caused by compliance with any enactment or with any Community obligation do not incur liability.[68] The defender may also evade liability by showing that he did not at any time supply the product.[69] Any person who supplies a product outwith the course of business and either does not fall within s.2(2) at all, or does so only in relation to non-profit-making activities, is exempt from liability.[70] A defender may also establish that at the relevant time the defect did not exist in the product,[71] or that the state of scientific and technical knowledge at the relevant time was not such as to give rise to an expectation that a producer of such products would discover the defect.[72] It is also a defence to show that a defect was attributable to a subsequent product in which the product concerned was comprised.[73] In an appropriate case, a defender may plead that the pursuer was contributorily negligent.[74]

Death and personal injury fall within the definition of damage for which liability is imposed by the Act. Because the statute is designed to protect consumers, property damage may only be compensated if the property was of a type ordinarily intended for private use, occupation or consumption and was in

---

[64] This would include those companies who sell goods manufactured by others as their "own brand", although affixing a name or mark, e.g. as a sponsor or promoter, would not per se amount to "holding out". Even labelling narrating that the goods have been "produced for" a seller might be sufficient to evade this provision.

[65] Consumer Protection Act 1987 s.2(3).

[66] Consumer Protection Act 1987 s.3(1). See further, *A v National Blood Authority (No. 1)* [2001] 3 All E.R. 289.

[67] Consumer Protection Act 1987 s.3(2)(a) and (b).

[68] Consumer Protection Act 1987 s.4(1)(a).

[69] Consumer Protection Act 1987 s.4(1)(b).

[70] Consumer Protection Act 1987 s.4(1)(c). See Law Commission and Scottish Law Commission, *Liability for Defective Products*, para.43, pointing out the unreasonableness of imposing liability on a housewife who makes jam for a local church or a man who sells apples to a neighbour over a garden fence.

[71] Consumer Protection Act 1987 s.4(1)(d).

[72] Consumer Protection Act 1987 s.4(1)(e). See further, *A v National Blood Authority (No. 1)* [2001] 3 All E.R. 289.

[73] Consumer Protection Act 1987 s.4(1)(f).

[74] Consumer Protection Act 1987 s.6(4).

fact so intended by the person suffering the damage.[75] Property damage for which the amount awarded would be £275 or less is not covered by the Act.[76]

Occupiers' Liability (Scotland) Act 1960[77]—The effect of this Act was to **27.04** abolish the categories of invitee, licensee and trespasser which were introduced to the law of Scotland in 1929 by the House of Lords' decision in *Dumbreck v Addie & Sons*.[78] Section 2 of the Act provides:

> "The care which an occupier of premises is required, by reason of his occupation or control of the premises, to show towards a person entering thereon in respect of dangers which are due to the state of the premises or to anything done or omitted to be done on them and for which the occupier is in law responsible shall, except in so far as he is entitled to and does extend, restrict, modify or exclude by agreement his obligations towards that person, be such care as in all the circumstances of the case is reasonable to see that that person will not suffer injury or damage by reason of any such danger."

"Occupier of premises" is defined in s.1(1) as "a person occupying or having control of land or other premises." This includes "any fixed or moveable structure, including any vessel, vehicle or aircraft" and the duty extends towards all persons and property on such premises.[79] The Act substantially restores the pre–1929 common law relating to the duties of occupiers of land[80] and the "category" decisions between 1929 and 1959 are no longer relevant except on the question of "control".

The statutory concept of occupation or control is the same as the common law basis of liability, namely, possession and control.[81] The duty of care rests upon the person who has the right and means in the circumstances of taking effective steps to protect the visitor from the particular danger whether by removal, notice, fencing or forbidding entry to the premises.[82] Thus physical occupation per se will not impose the duty on a resident. The duty is owed by the occupier only if he is in control of the premises; if he is not, the obligation rests upon the party in control,[83] who may be the owner or tenant or a contractor conducting operations on the premises.[84]

The Act does not differentiate between public and private property, and the degree of care required from any occupier to any individual is deducible from and

---

[75] Consumer Protection Act 1987 s.5(3).

[76] Consumer Protection Act 1987 s.5(4).

[77] See further, A. McAllister, "Occupiers' Liability" in Thomson (ed.), *Delict*, Ch.17. Statutory provision in England is similar but not identical: Occupiers' Liability Acts 1957 and 1984.

[78] *Dumbreck v Addie & Sons*, 1929 S.C. (HL) 51; now disapproved even as a statement of the duty owed to a trespasser (*British Railways Board v Herrington* [1972] A.C. 877).

[79] Occupiers' Liability (Scotland) Act 1960 s.1(3). See *A.M.F. International v Magnet Bowling* [1968] 1 W.L.R. 1028.

[80] See *Shillinglaw v Turner*, 1925 S.C. 807 at 816, per Lord President Clyde; at 820, per Lord Sands.

[81] See *Laurie v Mags of Aberdeen*, 1911 S.C. 1226; and *Laing v Paull and Williamsons*, 1912 S.C. 196; *Kennedy v Shotts Iron Co Ltd*, 1913 S.C. 1143; *McIlwaine v Stewart's Trs*, 1914 S.C. 934.

[82] *Murdoch v A. & R. Scott*, 1956 S.C. 309; *Devlin v Jeffray's Trs* (1902) 5 F. 130, where owner had no right of entry.

[83] *Kennedy v Shotts Iron Co Ltd*, 1913 S.C. 1143; *McPhail v Lanarkshire CC*, 1951 S.C. 301; *Wheat v E Lacon & Co* [1966] A.C. 552, where the House of Lords held that the owners were occupiers of premises although their manager resided there under a service agreement.

[84] See *Murdoch v A. & R. Scott*, 1956 S.C. 309; also *Hartwell v Grayson, etc. Docks* [1947] K.B. 901; *Telfer v Glasgow Corp*, 1974 S.L.T. (Notes) 51.

referable to the particular facts of the case.[85] Accordingly, there is no general rule as to the liability of an occupier for damage caused by the faulty work of an independent contractor employed by him. The proposition that an occupier has a discrete duty to ascertain that an independent contractor has insurance cover has also been rejected.[86] The dangers which s.2 of the Act requires the occupier to guard against are those which are: (a) due to the state of the premises; (b) due to anything done on the premises; and (c) due to anything omitted to be done on the premises. "The state of the premises" certainly covers all dangers due to structural defects[87] and poisonous shrubs,[88] and probably also to unfenced shafts or excavations,[89] although the latter may be alternatively classified as a danger due to omission (i.e. to fence). Machinery which is not in use, such as an unlocked turntable upon which children were known to play,[90] must also come under this head. "Anything done on the premises" covers all dangers created by operations thereon[91] and is probably wide enough to cover keeping a vicious dog[92] and placing a savage horse in a field used by the public.[93] While the failure to fence or light holes and keep doors leading to cellars locked[94] may be classified under "state" or "omission", some dangers created by operations carried on may be due to omissions, e.g. the failure of a railway company's employees to close carriage doors before a train started.[95]

While the standard of care required of the occupier is that of the reasonable, prudent man, the degree of care required is "such care as in all the circumstances of the case is reasonable".

> "It will be extremely rare for an occupier of land to be under a duty to prevent people from taking risks which are inherent in the activities they freely choose to undertake upon the land".[96]

The antiquity of a building may be a circumstance to be taken into account.[97] The type of person likely to be present will also affect the range of care, which will vary from the maximum, in the case of a very young child on the premises for the first time by invitation of the occupier and known to him to be unaccompanied by an adult, to the minimum in the case of a trespasser whose presence is unknown to the occupier.

---

[85] See *McKinlay v Darngarvil Coal Co*, 1923 S.C. (HL) 34 at 37, per Lord Dunedin; cf. *McMurray v Glasgow School Board*, 1916 S.C. 9, where there was no averment that the occupiers knew that a gate was being used as a swing.

[86] *Honeybourne v Burgess*, 2006 S.L.T. 585.

[87] See A.T. Glegg, *The Law of Reparation in Scotland*, 3rd edition (Edinburgh: W. Green, 1939), pp.295–307.

[88] See *Taylor v Glasgow Corp*, 1922 S.C. (HL) 1.

[89] See Glegg, *The Law of Reparation in Scotland* (1939), pp.274–279, 281–272.

[90] *Cooke v M.G.W. Ry of Ireland* [1909] A.C. 229.

[91] e.g. *Messer v Cranston* (1897) 25 R. 7 (defective stow); *Rose v McCallum's Trs*, 1922 S.C. 322 (petrol in water pail); *Excelsior Wire Rope Co v Callan* [1930] A.C. 404; and *Murdoch v A. & R. Scott*, 1956 S.C. 309 (moving machinery).

[92] *Smillies v Boyd* (1886) 14 R. 150; *Hill v Lovett*, 1992 S.L.T. 994.

[93] *Lowery v Walker* [1911] A.C. 10.

[94] *Cairns v Boyd* (1879) 6 R. 1004.

[95] *Tough v N.B. Ry Co*, 1914 S.C. 291. For additional examples of dangers on land and premises, see cases cited in Glegg, *The Law of Reparation in Scotland* (1939), pp.60–72, and in Walker, *The Law of Delict in Scotland* (1981), p.591.

[96] *Tomlinson v Congleton B.C.* [2004] 1 A.C. 46, per Lord Hoffmann.

[97] *Hogg v Historic Building & Monuments Commission for England* [1989] C.L.Y. 2573.

"The section applies both to trespassers and to persons entering property by invitation or licence express or implied. But that does not mean that the occupier must always show equal care for the safety of all such persons. . . In deciding what degree of care is required,. . . regard must be had both to the position of the occupier and to the position of the person entering his premises and it may often be reasonable to hold that an occupier must do more to protect a person whom he permits to be on his property than he need do to protect a person who enters the property without permission."[98]

An occupier may not be required to fence a quarry or other dangerous place which is so far from a public road that it is not reasonably foreseeable that members of the public will come near it,[99] but secure fencing will be necessary if injury to the particular victim is reasonably foreseeable through proximity of the danger to a public road[100] or otherwise.[101] While the pre-1929 law relating to trespassers was far from clear,[102] the Act now imposes upon an occupier the duty of taking such care as is reasonable in the circumstances to protect from reasonably foreseeable injury a trespasser whose presence is reasonably foreseeable. In the case of a boy injured while climbing an electric transformer, that duty was held to be discharged by the erection of a barrier which could only be overcome by a deliberate act intended to defeat its obvious function.[103] In a roughly similar, but much later case, liability was established, but there was a reduction in damages for contributory negligence.[104] The age and capacity of persons entering premises are relevant considerations along with the likelihood of their being there.

"A measure of care appropriate to the inability or disability of those who are immature or feeble in mind or body is due from others who know of, or ought to anticipate, the presence of such persons within the scope and hazard of their own operations."[105]

The Act does not alter the law that the owner of a public park is not required to fence obvious dangers, such as a pond[106] or a river bank,[107] against which it is the duty of parents to protect their children; but parents are entitled to rely on such proprietors taking reasonable care to protect their children from injury from

---

[98] *McGlone v B.R.B.*, 1966 S.L.T. 2 at 9, per Lord Reid, HL.

[99] *Prentices v Assets Co* (1890) 17 R. 484; *Holland v Lanarkshire CC*, 1909 S.C. 1142 at 1149, per Lord President Dunedin; *Melville v Renfrewshire CC*, 1920 S.C. 61.

[100] *Black v Cadell* (1804) Mor.13905; *Gibson v Glasgow Police Commissioners* (1893) 20 R. 466 (a public highway case, but the ratio is relevant to s.2 of the Act).

[101] *Hislop v Durham* (1842) 4 D. 1168; *McFeat v Rankin's Trs* (1879) 6 R. 1043; *British Railways Board v Herrington* [1972] A.C. 877.

[102] See *McGlone v B.R.B.*, 1966 S.L.T. 2 at 9, per Lord Reid.

[103] *McGlone v B.R.B.*, 1966 S.L.T. 2. "The liability of an occupier cannot fairly be made to depend on the outcome of a conflict between his precautions to exclude entry and the ingenuity and agility of a youthful and determined trespasser": at 8, per Lord Guthrie.

[104] *McLeod v British Railways Board*, 2001 S.L.T. 238.

[105] *Taylor v Glasgow Corp*, 1922 S.C. (HL) 1 at 15, per Lord Sumner; see also *Johnstone v Lochgelly Magistrates*, 1913 S.C. 1078 at 1089, per Lord Kinnear; *Cooke v M.G.W. Ry of Ireland* [1909] A.C. 229 at 238, per Lord Atkinson: "The duty . . . must . . . be measured by his [the occupier's] knowledge, actual or imputed, of the habits, capacities and propensities of those persons"; and *Southern Portland Cement v Cooper* [1974] A.C. 623.

[106] *Fegan v Highland RC* [2007] CSIH 44; 2007 S.C. 723; 2007 S.L.T. 651; *Hastie v Edinburgh City Council*, 1907 S.C. 1102.

[107] *Stevenson v Glasgow Corp*, 1908 S.C. 1034.

anything in the nature of a hidden danger or trap, whether natural or artificial.[108] And a very high degree of care is incumbent upon local authorities who provide children's playgrounds and thus invite parents to send their children there unaccompanied.[109]

27.05 Exclusion of occupier's liability—Section 2(1) of the Act permits an occupier, in so far as he is entitled to do so,[110] to extend, restrict, modify or exclude his obligations to any person by agreement, i.e. by contract, written or verbal.[111] The English Act[112] adds "or otherwise" which seems to permit this to be done by the mere posting of a restricting or exempting notice,[113] whereas the Scottish Act does not. But the existence of such a notice in relation to a particular danger would be a relevant factor in determining whether or not the injured party had agreed to run the risk of injury through the occupier's lack of care, since the defence of volenti non fit injuria is expressly retained by the Act.[114] Where the premises are used for the business purposes of the occupier these rules on exclusion of liability have now to be read subject to the provisions of the Unfair Contract Terms Act 1977.[115]

27.06 Landlord's liability—Where premises are occupied or used by virtue of a tenancy or sub-tenancy under which the landlord is responsible for maintenance or repair of the premises, s.3 of the Act imposes on the landlord the same duty of care towards persons or property as s.2(1) imposes on the occupier, but only in respect of dangers arising from faulty maintenance or repair. "Tenancy" includes a statutory tenancy which does not in law amount to a tenancy[116] and also includes any contract conferring a right of occupation.[117] This section alters the law laid down in *Cameron v Young*,[118] and anyone in the house, be he tenant, member of the tenant's family, lodger or visitor, has a title to sue the landlord for injury caused through breach of his duty. Section 3 is silent as to the right of a landlord to vary his statutory liability by agreement. It seems that he retains the right, in appropriate circumstances, to plead volenti non fit injuria.[119] The Act applies to the Crown.[120] The Housing (Scotland) Act 2006[121] imposes obligations regarding maintenance on the landlords of let properties.[122]

---

[108] *Taylor v Glasgow Corp*, 1922 S.C. (HL) 1 (poisonous berries); and see at 10–12, per Lord Shaw. *Hastie, Stevenson* and *Taylor* are all discussed by Lord Hutton in *Tomlinson v Congleton BC* [2004] 1 A.C. 46.

[109] *Plank v Stirling Magistrates*, 1956 S.C. 92.

[110] e.g. the operator of a public service vehicle is not entitled to do so: see Public Passenger Vehicles Act 1981 s.29.

[111] e.g. by notice on ticket of such conditions: see para.5.27, above (ticket cases).

[112] Occupiers' Liability Act 1957 s.2(1).

[113] See *Ashdown v Williams* [1957] 1 Q.B. 409, decided before the English Act was passed.

[114] Occupiers' Liability (Scotland) Act 1960 s.2(3). See *McGlone v B.R.B.*, 1966 S.L.T. 2 at 12, per Lord Pearce.

[115] Unfair Contract Terms Act 1977 s.16.

[116] See Ch.35, below.

[117] e.g. under a service agreement.

[118] *Cameron v Young*, 1908 S.C. (HL) 7.

[119] See para.35.08, below.

[120] See the Occupiers' Liability (Scotland) Act 1960 s.4.

[121] Housing (Scotland) Act 2006 s.14.

[122] See para.35.08, below.

Public roads and streets[123]—The Occupiers' Liability Act does not apply to **27.07** public roads, streets or footpaths which at common law or by public or private Acts are the responsibility of public bodies. Public authorities responsible for the management and maintenance of public roads, streets and footpaths are bound to take reasonable care to maintain them in a condition safe for use by all members of the public.[124] They are liable to individuals injured by any type of danger of which they knew or ought to have known if regular inspections had been made. A local authority is not liable, however, for a defect in a footpath of such a nature as to be obvious to a pedestrian exercising reasonable care for his own safety.[125] There is a common law duty on a roads authority to adopt measures to counter risks posed by ice and snow but there is no claim for breach of statutory duty under the Roads (Scotland) Act 1984 if they do not do so.[126] As the basis of liability is "possession and control", the owner of the *solum* of a footpath is not liable for defects therein unless he also has control of it[127]; but he may be jointly liable with the local authority for failure to fence off a dangerous subsidence.[128] And a local authority may assume by private Act a joint responsibility with the owner for the safety of a private footpath.[129] Works on roads and streets by the providers of public services are controlled by a code laid down in the New Roads and Street Works Act 1991. In England it was held that the previous Act[130] did not confer upon an individual the right to bring an action for breach of statutory duty.[131] In Scotland, when the Gas Board were sued under the previous Act, they did not challenge the allegations of breach of statutory duty and it was held that the Act did not diminish the responsibility of a local authority.[132]

FURTHER READING

Miller, C.J. and Goldberg, R.S., *Product Liability*, 2nd edn (Oxford: Oxford University Press, 2004).

Munkman on Employer's Liability, edited by Cotter, B. and Bennett, D., 14th edn (London: LexisNexis, 2006).

Redgrave's Health and Safety, edited by Ford, M. and Clarke, J., 7th edn (London: Lexis Nexis, 2010).

Stanton, K., Skidmore, P., Harris, M. and Wright, J., *Statutory Torts* (London: Sweet and Maxwell, 2003).

Thomson, J.M. (ed.), *Delict* (Edinburgh: SULI /W. Green) (looseleaf).

Thomson, J.M., *Delictual Liability*, 4th edn (Bloomsbury Professional, 2009).

---

[123] See Glegg, *The Law of Reparation in Scotland* (1939), pp.104–105, 301–303; and Walker, *The Law of Delict in Scotland*, pp.599–608.

[124] Including blind persons, see *McKibbin v Glasgow Corp*, 1920 S.C. 590; *Haley v L.E.B.* [1965] A.C. 778, and see para.26.09, above.

[125] *McClafferty v British Telecommunications Plc*, 1987 S.L.T. 327.

[126] *Syme v Scottish Borders Council*, 2003 S.L.T. 601.

[127] *Laing v Paull& Williamsons*, 1912 S.C. 196.

[128] *Laurie v Mags of Aberdeen*, 1911 S.C. 1226.

[129] *Rush v Glasgow Corp*, 1947 S.C. 580; *Kinnell v Glasgow Corp*, 1950 S.C. 573; *Black v Glasgow Corp (No.1)*, 1958 S.C. 260.

[130] Public Utilities Street Works Act 1950.

[131] *Keating v Elvan Reinforced Concrete* [1968] 2 All E.R. 139.

[132] *McNair v Dunfermline Corp*, 1953 S.C. 183.

CHAPTER 28

ECONOMIC AND LAND INTERESTS

THE ECONOMIC DELICTS

Introduction—In a market economy individuals are free to cause economic loss **28.01** to others by lawful means, for example by undercutting prices, even though moti- vated by malice.[1] Liability may arise, however, where different parties combine to cause loss or where the means employed are unlawful. The economic delicts set out the parameters under which damages for economic loss caused intentionally may be recovered. Recovery of damages for economic loss caused negligently is a separate matter, as is fraud.[2] The economic delicts are largely a development of English law, albeit a Scots appeal to the House of Lords remains the leading case in lawful means conspiracy.[3] Economic delicts may most usefully be presented as separate wrongs, each with its own requirements for liability. In *OBG v Allan*[4] the House of Lords clarified the categories. The economic delicts may now be seen to consist of: inducing breach of contract; causing loss by unlawful means; and conspiracy (which is in turn sub-divided into conspiracy by unlawful or lawful means). Intimidation may now be seen as an unlawful means by which loss may be caused rather than as a separate delict.[5]

Inducing breach of contract—Liability for inducing breach of contract arises **28.02** when A induces B to breach B's contract with C and C suffers economic loss as a consequence. In such circumstances, B will be liable to C in contract for breach. A will be liable to C in delict for inducing the breach. A's liability in delict is accessory to B's liability in contract. The view that A's liability is accessory fits uneasily within Scots law, but is attributable to *OBG v Allan*.[6] The requirements for liability have been explained in *Global Resources Group v Mackay*.[7] First, there must have been a breach of contract; secondly, A must have known of the contract; thirdly, A must have had the intention to induce the breach; fourthly, A must in fact have induced the breach; finally, if the breach by B is justified then this affords a defence to A.[8] On the issue of knowledge, the evidential bar appears

---

[1] *Allen v Flood* [1898] A.C. 1 HL.
[2] See paras 7.13 (fraud) and 26.07 (economic loss).
[3] See para.28.04 below.
[4] [2007] UKHL 21; [2008] 1 A.C. 1.
[5] *OBG v Allan* [2007] UKHL 21; [2008] 1 A.C. 1 at [7], per Lord Hoffmann. For discussion see J.M. Thomson, "Redrawing the Landscape of the Economic Wrongs" (2008) 12 Edin. L.R. 267.
[6] For discussion see G. Gordon, "The Economic Delicts", in J.M. Thomson (ed.), *Delict* (Edinburgh: W. Green), para.15.26.
[7] *Global Resources Group v Mackay*, 2008 S.L.T. 104 at 106–107, per Lord Hodge.
[8] On justification see *Meretz Investments NV v ACP Ltd* [2007] EWCA Civ 1303; *Global Resources Group v Mackay*, 2008 S.L.T. 104 at [14], per Lord Hodge.

to have been set high by Lord Hoffmann who required actual knowledge that conduct would breach a contract for liability to arise.[9] While this does not sit well with English authority to the effect that liability might arise where the defender has turned a blind eye to the possibility of a breach of contract,[10] it is thought that sufficient knowledge may be constituted where a conscious decision not to enquire into the possibility of contractual terms or their breach has been made.[11] In *Mainstream Properties Ltd v Young*[12] a financier was exonerated. He had made positive enquiries into the possibility of breach and had received assurances that there was no breach from the parties who actually were in breach. For liability, breach of contract must have been intended, either as a means to an end or as an end in itself.[13] It is not sufficient for liability that breach was a foreseeable consequence of A's conduct. There must have been some positive act to induce the breach, but it is not necessary that unlawful means, such as intimidation, were used.

28.03 **Causing loss by unlawful means**—Causing loss by unlawful means arises when A uses unlawful means against B to cause economic loss to C. A will become liable to C in damages.[14] Unlawful means in this context is conduct which would give rise to civil liability on A's part and which inhibits B's freedom to deal with C.[15] So, for example, if A was to breach his contract with B in order to harm C in circumstances where B became unable, because of the breach, to perform his contract with C, this would be unlawful means, the breach rendering A civilly liable to B. Time will tell whether this view of what constitutes unlawful means will prevail though it does, at present, represent the law.[16] A different view of unlawful means is taken in unlawful means conspiracy.[17] To become liable to C in delict, loss to C must be intended by A, either as a means to an end or an end in itself, but there will be no liability if harm is a mere consequence of A's conduct.[18] As in inducing beach of contract, A's motive is irrelevant.

28.04 **Conspiracy by lawful means**—Conspiracy can operate so as to create liability where parties act in combination in circumstances where the act of a single party would give rise to no liability. Acting in combination means parties acting together

---

[9] *OBG v Allan* [2007] UKHL 21 at [39].

[10] *Emerald Construction Co Ltd v Lowthian* [1966] 1 W.L.R. 691 at 700f, per Lord Denning, approved by Lord Hoffmann in *OBG v Allan* [2007] UKHL 21 at [40] and [41].

[11] This is the position reached in *Rossleigh Ltd v Leader Cars Ltd*, 1987 S.L.T. 355. See also *BMTA v Gray*, 1951 S.C. 586; *Global Resources Group v Mackay*, 2008 S.L.T. 104 and for discussion: Gordon, "The Economic Delicts" in Thomson (ed.), *Delict*, paras 15.19–15.21.

[12] Conjoined appeal with *OBG v Allan* [2007] UKHL 21; [2008] 1 A.C. 1.

[13] *OBG v Allan* [2007] UKHL 21 at [8], per Lord Hoffmann. For discussion see Gordon, "The Economic Delicts" in Thomson (ed.), *Delict*, paras 15.22–15.23.

[14] The wrong is not restricted to interference with trade or business; defrauding the public revenue can also justify a claim for damages: *Commissioners of Customs and Excise v Total Network SL* [2008] A.C. 1174.

[15] *OBG v Allan* [2007] UKHL 21 at [45], per Lord Hoffmann. Baroness Hale and Lord Brown of Eaton-under-Heywood concurred at [302] and [319] respectively, but cf. Lord Nicholls at [162] and Lord Walker at [270].

[16] For discussion see Gordon, "The Economic Delicts" in Thomson (ed.), *Delict*, paras 15.38–15.42, 15.65 and 15.66.

[17] See para.28.05 below.

[18] See e.g. *Barretts v Baird (Wholesale) Ltd v Institution of Professional Civil Servants* [1987] I.R.L.R. 3.

towards a common purpose.[19] Where lawful means, that is actions giving rise in themselves to no civil liability, are employed to inflict economic loss on C, the motive of the defender is irrelevant unless acting in combination.[20] Economic loss caused by lawful means to C by A and B acting in combination will however incur liability provided that the predominant intention of A and B is economic loss to C. The leading case in lawful means conspiracy remains *Crofter Hand Woven Harris Tweed Co Ltd v Veitch*.[21] The harm to the pursuers in this case was incidental and so liability did not arise, the predominant intention having been the promotion of the interests of the TGWU.[22] The onus of proving predominant motive falls on the pursuer who must also establish economic loss.[23]

Conspiracy by unlawful means—The requirements of combination and action **28.05** in pursuit of a common goal found in lawful means conspiracy apply equally to conspiracy by unlawful means, as does the requirement that the pursuer has suffered economic loss. Conspiracy by unlawful means may be presented in two forms. Where the unlawful means employed would give rise to civil liability if conducted by a single actor, then conspiracy adds nothing and the victim will normally sue on the substantive delict or breach of contract according to the circumstances.[24] In the second form, conspiracy has the effect of broadening the meaning of "unlawful means" beyond activities giving rise to civil liability to embrace also those that incur criminal sanction or breach of statutory provisions.[25] There is, moreover, no requirement for a predominant intention to cause economic loss.[26] It is sufficient if causing economic loss is an intention of the parties; it need not be the predominant intention.[27]

NUISANCE

Definition—The only institutional description is found in Bell: **28.06**

> "Whatever obstructs the public means of commerce and intercourse whether in highways or navigable rivers; whatever is noxious, or unsafe, or renders life uncomfortable to the public generally or to the neighbourhood; whatever is intolerably offensive to individuals in their dwelling-houses, or inconsistent with the comfort of life, whether by stench . . . by noise . . . or by indecency . . . is a nuisance".[28]

---

[19] See e.g. *CBS Songs Ltd v Amstrad Consumer Electronics Plc* [1988] A.C. 1013. Some action by both parties is necessary—there is no liability where one party merely looks on with approval. See *Credit Lyonnais Nederland NV v Export Credits Guarantee Department* [1998] 1 Lloyd's Rep 19.

[20] *Allen v Flood* [1898] A.C. 1.

[21] *Crofter Hand Woven Harris Tweed Co Ltd v Veitch*, 1942 S.C. (HL) 1.

[22] Gordon, "The Economic Delicts" in Thomson (ed.), *Delict*, para.15.56 states that: "the predominant purpose requirement has the effect of excluding the possibility of liability in the great majority of cases which arise out of normal commercial trading or legitimate trade union type activity." He gives as an example of a successful action the case of *Huntley v Thomson* [1957] 1 All E.R. 234.

[23] *Lonrho v Fayed (No 5)* [1993] 1 W.L.R. 1489.

[24] J.M. Thomson, *Delictual Liability*, 4th edn (Bloomsbury Professional, 2009), para.2.8.

[25] *Customs and Excise Commissioners v Total Network SL* [2008] 1 A.C. 1174.

[26] *Lonrho v Fayed* [1991] 3 All E.R. 303.

[27] *Lonrho v Fayed* [1991] 3 All E.R. 303, per Lord Bridge at 307. This clarifies the position following *Lonrho v Shell Petroleum Co Ltd* [1981] 2 All E.R. 456.

[28] Bell, *Principles*, s.974.

This description is of limited assistance for modern purposes representing, as it does, nuisance at a particular stage in historical development when the focus of concern was on the nature of the source of harm, whereas the modern focus is firmly on the interest invaded.[29] No distinction is drawn in Scots law equivalent to the English distinction between public and private nuisance. It is apparent from Bell that Scots nuisance was never purely concerned with private interests, however,[30] and it has been suggested that nuisance protects not one, but two distinct interests: the first being an interest in the use of private land and the second being an interest in the use or enjoyment of public places.[31] The concern in the present text is with the former.[32]

28.07 **Protected interest**—The interest protected by nuisance is the comfortable enjoyment of property, free from serious disturbance, substantial inconvenience or material harm.[33] In contrast with English private nuisance there do not appear to be strict restrictions on title to sue[34]; title extends to those in possession and occupation where comfortable enjoyment is disturbed and to owner-occupiers or landlords in respect of damage to the physical integrity of the building or diminution in letting value.[35] Damages are available in respect of diminution in the value of property, or where harm is complete or abatement impossible, but the primary remedy is interdict. Interdict may be sought to end a continuing state of affairs or to prevent a prospective invasion.[36] Actions for damages in respect of nuisance were relatively rare before the twentieth century, but by the last quarter of that century they had come to outnumber actions for interdict.[37] This change in proportions may be a reflection of the availability of alternative administrative remedies in respect of intangible disturbances, at first under the municipal improvement and public health legislation of the nineteenth century, presently under the

---

[29] See N. Whitty, "Nuisance" in *Stair Memorial Encyclopaedia* (2001) Reissue, paras 2, 5. The shift in perception is significant in terms of the boundaries of nuisance. For further discussion see G. Cameron, "Making Sense of Nuisance in Scots Law" [2005] 56 NILQ 236, 250.

[30] This is also apparent from early case law in which petitions were presented in terms of nuisance to the neighbourhood generally. See e.g. *Kinloch v Robertson* (1756) Mor 13163; *Carrubers' Close Proprietors v Reoch; Wood v Sandeman* (1762) Mor 13175; *Vary v Thomson*, July 2, 1805, FC, Mor "Public Police" App No. 4. See also *Robertson v Thomas* (1877) 14 R. 822.

[31] Whitty, "Nuisance" in *Stair Memorial Encyclopaedia* (2001), para.2.

[32] See further, Whitty, "Nuisance" in *Stair Memorial Encyclopedia* (2001), paras 159–168. It is arguable that the association of nuisance with obstructions or interferences with enjoyment of public places is an accident of terminology and that this wrong is more properly termed purpresture. See *Slater v MacLellan*, 1924 S.C. 854, per Lord President Clyde at 858.

[33] *Watt v Jamieson*, 1954 S.C. 56, per Lord President Cooper at 58.

[34] In *Khorasandjian v Bush* [1993] Q.B. 727 the Court of Appeal by a majority granted a *quia timet* injunction to a young woman who had no legal interest in the property in which she was being subjected to nuisance phone calls. *Khorasandjian* was however overruled in *Hunter v Canary Wharf* [1997] A.C. 655 in which the House of Lords returned English rules on title in private nuisance to their twelfth century state, title being reserved to freeholders. In Scotland by contrast, a wife successfully sued for interdict and damages though she had no title in her husband's property in which she was subject to disturbance: *Shanlin v Collins*, 1973 S.L.T. (Sh. Ct) 21. Title, however, was not challenged. Title was challenged in *Hand v NSWA*, 2002 S.L.T. 798, but the pursuer, who held a registered lease in the relevant property, had sufficient interest for title to be recognised. See further Whitty, "Nuisance" in *Stair Memorial Encyclopedia* (2001), paras 133–134.

[35] e.g. *Fleming v Ure* (1750) Mor 13159 the first action in Scots law to be described in terms of nuisance.

[36] e.g. *Fleming v Hislop* (1886) 13 R. (HL) 43.

[37] Research in reported cases reveals 14 reparation actions and 7 for interdict between 1976 and 2000. See further, Cameron, "Making Sense of Nuisance in Scots Law" [2005] 56 NILQ 236, 258–259.

Environmental Protection Act 1990.[38] Moreover, the modern focus on the interest invaded, coupled with Lord Cooper's formulation in *Watt v Jamieson*[39] seems to have had the effect that proportionately more actions have been brought in respect of tangible physical harm; the scope of nuisance has expanded to include in particular, property harm caused by flooding[40] and by withdrawal of support.[41]

When nuisance actionable—Invasions amounting to nuisance are seldom **28.08** unlawful in themselves, but become actionable only because of their effect on the complainer's interest.[42] Actionable nuisance then, will always depend upon circumstances. A distinctive test has been developed in Scots law for determining the point at which conduct, an event or a state of affairs becomes sufficiently grave that it is actionable on grounds of nuisance. This is the *plus quam tolerabile* test established by Lord President Cooper in *Watt v Jamieson*[43]:

> "I deduce that the proper angle of approach to a case of alleged nuisance is rather from the standpoint of the victim of the loss or inconvenience than from the standpoint of the alleged offender; and that if any person so uses his property as to occasion serious disturbance or substantial inconvenience to his neighbour or material damage to his neighbour's property, it is in the general case irrelevant to plead merely that he was making a normal and familiar use of his own property. The balance in all such cases has to be held between the freedom of a proprietor to use his property as he pleases and the duty on a proprietor not to inflict material loss or inconvenience of adjoining property; and in every case the answer depends on considerations of fact and degree . . . The critical question is whether what he was exposed to was plus quam tolerabile when due weight has been given to all the surrounding circumstances of the offensive conduct and its effects."[44]

---

[38] s.79.

[39] *Watt v Jamieson*, 1954 S.C. 56, per Lord President Cooper at 58.

[40] Since 1951 a majority of reported reparation cases grounded in nuisance have involved flooding. See *Gourock Rope Works v Greenock Corporation*, 1966 S.L.T. 125; *RHM Bakeries (Scotland) Ltd v Strathclyde Regional Council*, 1985 S.L.T. 214; *Plean Precast v NCB*, 1986 S.L.T. 78; *Argyll and Clyde Health Board v Strathclyde Regional Council*, 1988 S.L.T. 381; *Logan v Wang (UK) Ltd*, 1991 S.L.T. 580; *GA Estates v Caviapen Trustees Ltd No 1*, 1993 S.L.T. 1037; *Dewar v Lothian*, 1996 G.W.D. 26–1538; *Anderson v White*, 2000 S.L.T. 78; *Hand v NSWA*, 2002 S.L.T. 798; *Viewpoint Housing Association Ltd v Edinburgh City Council*, 2007 S.L.T. 772. Earlier reparation actions for property harm caused by flooding were not grounded on nuisance.

[41] Actions for damages for withdrawal of support grounded in nuisance, sometimes with alternative pleas in negligence are: *McNab v McDevitt*, 1971 S.L.T. (Notes) 41; *Duncan's Hotel (Glasgow) Ltd v J&A Ferguson Ltd*, 1974 S.C. 191; *Lord Advocate v Reo Stakis Organisation Ltd*, 1984 S.L.T. 140; *Borders Regional Council v Roxburgh DC*, 1989 S.L.T. 1989; *Kennedy v Glenbelle*, 1996 S.C. 95; 1996 S.L.T. 1186; *Hamilton & Hamilton v Wahla*, 1999 Rep. L.R. 118. See further Whitty, "Nuisance" in *Stair Memorial Encyclopedia* (2001), para.29.

[42] "[E]very case depends on its own circumstances, and that is a nuisance which a jury of intelligent gentlemen think so in the circumstances of each case": *Arrott v Whyte* (1826) 4 Murr 149, per Lord Gillies at 158. See also H. Burn-Murdoch, *Interdict in the Law of Scotland* (Edinburgh/Glasgow: Wm Hodge & Co Ltd, 1933), p.209.

[43] The test has been affirmed subsequently, notably by Lord President Hope, in *Kennedy v Glenbelle*, 1996 S.C. 95; 1996 S.L.T. 1186 at 1188J: "A claim for damages for nuisance is a delictual claim, as it does not depend for its existence on any contract. It arises where there is an invasion of the pursuer's interest in land to an extent which exceeds what is reasonably tolerable."

[44] *Watt v Jamieson*, 1954 S.C. 56, per Lord President Cooper at 58.

Nuisance, then, will be established if the invasion complained of can be shown to be more than the reasonable proprietor ought to be expected to tolerate, taking into account the circumstances of both parties.

28.09 Relevant factors of circumstance and conduct—A balancing of the interests of the parties is strongly implicit in Lord Cooper's formulation.[45] Parties may lead evidence to prove factors that will tend either to affirm or negate the view that the harm complained of is more than ought reasonably to be tolerated in the circumstances. Relevant factors in evaluating the complainer's circumstances are: (1) the type of harm; (2) the extent, degree and duration of the harm; (3) the social value of the type of use or enjoyment invaded; (4) the suitability of the type of use or enjoyment invaded to the character of the locality; (5) the sensitivity to harm of the persons or property affected; and (6) the burden on the complainer of taking protective measures.[46] Relevant factors in evaluating the defender's conduct are: (1) the primary purpose of the conduct causing the invasion; (2) the suitability of the conduct to the character of the locality; and (3) the practicability of remedial measures.[47] Not all factors will be relevant in every case, indeed, the extent to which a balancing exercise takes place will depend upon what is pleaded. It will, however, always be relevant to establish that the harm, whether incurred or anticipated, is material. Materiality depends on the degree of harm, its duration and, depending on circumstances, the time at which it occurs.[48]

28.10 Burden of proof—An approach based on balancing interests has implications for the burden of proof. Whitty has suggested the following:

> "Proof that the harm is plus quam tolerabile depends on proof of a number of subsidiary averments of fact amounting to factors within the plus quam tolerabile test tending to favour liability and averred by the pursuer. The legal burden of proving those facts will rest on the pursuer throughout the proof. The ultimate burden of proving that the harm is plus quam tolerabile rests initially with the pursuer, and by proving facts favouring liability he may make a prima facie case. The legal burden of proving facts tending to negate liability averred by the defender will rest on the defender throughout. The ultimate burden, which rests on the pursuer initially, may shift in the course of the proof. For example, if the defender meets the pursuer's prima facie case by proving that the pursuer's property is ultra-sensitive to harm, the pursuer will normally fail unless he can prove malice on the defender's part. There is a difference between a defence properly so called and a 'factor' tending to negate liability as respects onus of proof. If such a factor is proved, the ultimate burden may shift back to the pursuer, whereas if the defence is established the pursuer fails."[49]

---

[45] For discussion see Whitty, "Nuisance" in *Stair Memorial Encyclopedia* (2001), para.40.

[46] Whitty, "Nuisance" in *Stair Memorial Encyclopedia* (2001), para.43. For discussion on each factor see paras 44–66.

[47] Whitty, "Nuisance" in *Stair Memorial Encyclopedia* (2001), para.62. For discussion on each factor see paras 68–77.

[48] Whitty, "Nuisance" in *Stair Memorial Encyclopedia* (2001), paras 50–54.

[49] Whitty, "Nuisance" in *Stair Memorial Encyclopedia* (2001), para.107.

Remedies—Interdict is available on establishing nuisance. Where nuisance is **28.11** established, interdict is available as of right and Scottish courts have no power to refuse interdict and make an award of damages instead.[50] It is not necessary to prove culpa in an action for interdict.[51] However, there must be grounds to anticipate future occurrence or re-occurrence of nuisance and no interdict will be awarded where its terms will be impossible to obey or enforce.[52] The terms of any interdict should be drawn as narrowly as possible so as to obviate the mischief without necessarily requiring the cessation of the activity or operation complained of.[53] Where the terms of interdict have required positive steps to avoid causing nuisance, an objection has been raised against the competence of interdict with the appropriate remedy argued to be an order *ad factum praestandum*.[54] This argument was rejected in *Anderson v White*. Although positive steps may be required to fulfill the terms of an interdict, the obligation being enforced, to refrain from causing a wrong, is essentially negative and so interdict is competent.[55] Decrees *ad factum praestandum* may also be appropriate though there is a minor controversy concerning their competence in nuisance.[56] There is certainly a body of authority in support of the view that positive action to abate nuisance may be required by order of the courts.[57] Awards of interim interdict are available at the discretion of the courts. Interim interdicts may be postponed to allow for the submission of proposals for remedial measures to be taken by respondents who will normally be responsible for the expense of proving the effectiveness of the measures.[58] Perpetual interdict also may be postponed at the discretion of the court where immediate implementation would either be contrary to the public interest or where the injury to the respondents would be greater than the wrong complained of.[59] This discretion can only be exercised where there has first been a finding on the facts.[60] Damages may also be recoverable in respect of harm to health or economic harm incidental to property disturbance; so in *Chalmers v Wm Dixon Ltd*[61] the pursuer sought damages in respect of injury to the health of

---

[50] See Whitty, "Nuisance" in *Stair Memorial Encyclopedia* (2001), para.146 and cases cited therein at fn.3.

[51] *Duke of Buccleuch v Cowan* (1866) 4 M. 475; *Logan v Wang (UK) Ltd*, 1991 S.L.T. 580. See further Whitty, "Nuisance" in *Stair Memorial Encyclopedia* (2001), para.144.

[52] See *Caledonian Railway v Baird and Co* (1876) 3 R. 898; *Barony Parochial Board v Cadder Parochial Board* (1883) 10 R. 510.

[53] Burn-Murdoch, *Interdict in the Law of Scotland* (1933), p.209; Whitty, "Nuisance" in *Stair Memorial Encyclopedia* (2001), para.146.

[54] The general rule is that interdict is incompetent to enforce a positive obligation, see *Grosvenor Developments (Scotland) Plc v Argyll Stores Ltd*, 1997 S.L.T. 738; *Church Commissioners for England v Abbey National Plc*, 1994 S.L.T. 954.

[55] *Anderson v White*, 2000 S.L.T. 37, per Lord Philip at 39F–G. It should be noted that this is an Outer House case.

[56] This derives from the Outer House case *Rae v Musselburgh Town Council*, 1974 S.L.T. 29, described by Whitty as a ruling made *per incuriam*: Whitty, "Nuisance" in *Stair Memorial Encyclopedia* (2001), para.157.

[57] Including: *Laing v Muirhead* (1822) 2 S. 73; *Mackay v Greenhill* (1858) 20 D. 1251; *Frame v Cameron* (1864) 3 M. 290; *Adam v Alloa Police Commissioners* (1874) 2 R. 143; *Wilsons v Brydone* (1877) 14 S.L.R. 667; all cited in Whitty, "Nuisance" in *Stair Memorial Encyclopedia* (2001), para.157.

[58] *Gavin v Ayrshire CC*, 1950 S.C. 197.

[59] *Clippens Oil Co v Edinburgh and District Water Trustees* (1897) 25 R. 370, per Lord McLaren at 383. See also *Ben Nevis Distillery v North British Aluminium Co Ltd*, 1948 S.C. 592; *Webster v Lord Advocate*, 1985 S.L.T. 361.

[60] *Ben Nevis Distillery v North British Aluminium*, 1948 S.C. 592.

[61] *Chalmers v Wm Dixon Ltd* (1876) 3 R. 461.

himself and his family as well as harm to crops when a neighbouring bing was fired, while in *Shanlin v Collins*[62] damages were awarded in respect of nervous debility consequent on a neighbour's dogs barking. In *The Globe (Aberdeen) Ltd v NSWA*[63] pub owners had a relevant claim for loss of takings when their trade suffered as a result of muddy pavements and inconvenience generated by road works. An award of damages requires a finding of nuisance and proof of culpa in addition.[64] A declaratory finding of nuisance may be useful in circumstances where title is disputed or where it is anticipated that defences of prescription or acquiescence may be pled.[65] Removal orders may be available under the Court of Session Act 1988.[66]

28.12 **Damages and culpa**—An award of damages requires proof of culpa.[67] In *Kennedy v Glenbelle*, Lord President Hope explicitly sought to differentiate pleadings of culpa that would support a case in negligence from those that would support a case in nuisance.[68] Accepting the pursuer's argument that the averments of fault regarding nuisance were based on intention, Lord Hope determined that averments of a deliberate act done in the knowledge that harm would be the likely outcome were relevant to support an action grounded on nuisance.[69] Subsequently, it has been held that this knowledge may be constructive.[70] In *Kennedy* the pursuer pled an alternative case based on negligence, but the averments of culpa on this ground alleged failure to take care in the proceedings and supervise the work, so the pleadings in negligence were clearly differentiated from the averments of intentional culpa in nuisance. It is clear from Lord Hope's opinion that relevant pleadings of culpa in nuisance may be based on intention or on conduct causing a special risk of abnormal damage.[71] He also stated that where culpa is established by demonstrating negligence "the ordinary principles of negligence will provide an equivalent remedy."[72] Taken at face value, and in the context of physical harm to property,[73] the suggestion seems to be that the question, whether to ground actions on nuisance or negligence, is to be determined by the form taken by culpa, so, where harm is caused intentionally or recklessly, a ground of nuisance with the *plus quam tolerabile* requirement is appropriate whereas in cases of unintentional harm, actions should proceed according to the ordinary rules of negligence with the usual averments of duty and breach, but no *plus quam tolerabile* test. This would accord with arguments concerning the inapplicability of the *plus quam tolerabile* test where harm is caused negligently and, by extension, to the effect that negligent nuisance is an incoherent concept.[74] The point may, however, benefit from clarification.[75] Finally, allowing a state of affairs to continue in the

---

[62] *Shanlin v Collins*, 1973 S.L.T. (Sh. Ct) 21.
[63] *The Globe (Aberdeen) Ltd v NSWA*, 2000 S.L.T. 674.
[64] *RHM Bakeries (Scotland) Ltd v Strathclyde Regional Council*, 1985 S.L.T. 214.
[65] See Whitty, "Nuisance" in *Stair Memorial Encyclopedia* (2001), para.149.
[66] ss.46 and 47. See, e.g. *Canmore Housing Association Ltd v Bairnsfather*, 2004 S.L.T. 673.
[67] *RHM Bakeries (Scotland) Ltd v Strathclyde Regional Council*, 1985 S.L.T. 214.
[68] *Kennedy v Glenbelle*, 1996 S.C. 95; 1996 S.L.T. 1186 at 1188 H–L.
[69] See also *Anderson v White*, 2000 S.L.T. 37.
[70] *Anderson v White*, 2000 S.L.T. 37, per Lord Philip at 40 I–J.
[71] See further para.25.07, above.
[72] *Kennedy v Glenbelle*, 1996 S.L.T. 1186 at 1189K.
[73] There is no role for negligence in cases of disturbance or inconvenience in the absence of tangible physical harm.
[74] Whitty, "Nuisance" in *Stair Memorial Encyclopedia* (2001), paras 17, 77, 89, 104, 105, 106.
[75] The sheriff clearly viewed negligence as a relevant form of culpa in nuisance in *British Waterways Board v Moore & Mulheron Contracts Ltd*, 1998 G.W.D. 11–569; the pursuers' pleadings in *The Globe*

knowledge, actual or constructive, that harm is being caused also amounts to intentional culpa and averments to this effect will be relevant in an action grounded on nuisance.[76] It will, however, be necessary to establish that the defenders were in a position to exercise control at the relevant time.[77]

Defences—The operative defences in nuisance are prescription, acquiescence and **28.13** statutory authority. The rule, that it is no defence that the complainer came to the nuisance,[78] is thought to preclude any role for *volenti non fit injuria*.[79] Equally, contributory fault is not thought to be a defence, the possibility of obviating harm being a relevant factor in evaluating the pursuer's circumstances in the *plus quam tolerabile* test.[80] No provision is made in the Prescription and Limitation (Scotland) Act 1973 for positive prescription and so it is not possible to acquire a prescriptive right to create a nuisance. The right to object to nuisance may be lost by negative prescription.[81] It is not entirely clear whether prescription of the obligation of reparation is the long negative prescription of 20 years under s.7 of the 1973 Act or the short negative prescription of five years under s.6. Obligations relating to land are disapplied from s.6,[82] but it is argued that the obligation arises not from land, but from fault.[83] Acquiescence plays a role equivalent to *volenti*. The right to object to nuisance may be lost if it can be shown that the pursuer had full knowledge, not only of the conduct or operation, but also of the harm, actual or potential. Proof of objections made within a reasonable time of the pursuer becoming aware of the harm will defeat a plea of acquiescence.[84] Statutory authority only affords a complete defence where nuisance is the inevitable outcome of the activity authorised, irrespective of care and diligence applied in execution.[85] No immunity is conferred where powers or discretion have been exercised under permissive provisions. It is presumed that Parliament did not intent to derogate from private rights and the burden of proving otherwise lies with defenders.[86]

FURTHER READING

Thomson, J.M. (ed.), *Delict* (Edinburgh: W. Green) (looseleaf).
Whitty, N.R., "Nuisance" in *Stair Memorial Encyclopaedia* (2001) (Reissue).

(Aberdeen) Ltd v NSWA, 2000 S.L.T. 674 were drafted in terms much more like negligence than intention; and in *Viewpoint Housing Association Ltd v The City of Edinburgh*, 2007 S.L.T. 772 alternative pleas of nuisance and negligence were based on the same averments of culpa.

[76] See the case against the second and third defenders in *Anderson v White*, 2000 S.L.T. 37; *Powrie Castle Properties Ltd v Dundee City Council*, 2001 S.C.L.R. 146.

[77] *Gourock Ropework Co Ltd v Greenock Corporation*, 1966 S.L.T. 125.

[78] *Fleming v Hislop* (1886) 13 R. (HL) 43.

[79] See Whitty, "Nuisance" in *Stair Memorial Encyclopedia* (2001), para.127.

[80] See Whitty, "Nuisance" in *Stair Memorial Encyclopedia* (2001), para.130.

[81] See further above, Ch. 4.

[82] Prescription and Limitation (Scotland) Act 1973 Sch.1 para.2(e).

[83] See further, Johnston, *Prescription and Limitation*, paras 6.62, 6.63; Whitty, "Nuisance" in *Stair Memorial Encyclopedia* (2001), para.123.

[84] See further Whitty, "Nuisance" in *Stair Memorial Encyclopedia* (2001), para.128.

[85] See *Geddes v Ban Reservoir Proprietors* (1873) 3 App Cas 430 and other cases cited in Whitty, "Nuisance" in *Stair Memorial Encyclopedia* (2001), paras 110–122.

[86] See *Metropolitan Asylum District Managers v Hill* (1881) 6 App Cas 193; *Hanley v Edinburgh Magistrates*, 1913 S.C. (HL) 27.

CHAPTER 29

DEFAMATION; BREACH OF CONFIDENCE; PRIVACY

Defamation—Defamation is a civil wrong, which grounds an action for damages, **29.01** or an interdict against publication or repetition. The principal function of the law of defamation is to protect reputation. Defamation therefore concerns injuries to character. Lord Cooper defined defamation in these terms:

> "the wrong or delict which is committed when a person makes an injurious and false imputation, conveyed by words or signs, against the character or reputation of another. Character or reputation must be here understood in the widest sense to include moral and social reputation and financial credit."[1]

Lord Atkin's test: "Would the words tend to lower the plaintiff in the estimation of rightthinking members of society generally?"[2] has been accepted as representing the law of Scotland.[3] However, while a useful formulation for gauging allegations of moral or social impropriety, it does not serve so well in the context of financial solvency.[4] The courts have drawn a distinction between defamation, which has been confined to derogatory or demeaning imputations against character, credit or reputation, and other types of verbal injury, for example: false statements affecting business interests; false statements with the intention of exposing the pursuer to public hatred, contempt or ridicule; and slander against a third party.[5]

Requisites of defamation—Defamation consists of the communication of a false **29.02** statement or idea, which is defamatory of the pursuer.[6] If the statement is untrue and defamatory, the defender's intention is irrelevant. Malice is presumed unless privilege is pleaded.[7] The statement may be oral, in writing or, in exceptional cases, inferred from the use of images, as where the waxwork figure of the

---

[1] F.T. Cooper, *The Law of Defamation and Verbal Injury*, 2nd edn (Edinburgh: W. Green, 1906), p.1. Clause 1 of the Defamation Bill 2012-13 before Parliament at the time of writing (HC Bill 51) requires serious harm to the reputation of the claimant. This clause is not presently intended to extend to Scotland.

[2] *Sim v Stretch* [1936] 2 All E.R. 1237 at 1240.

[3] *Steele v Scottish Daily Record and Sunday Mail*, 1970 S.L.T. 53; *Thomson v News Group Newspapers*, 1992 G.W.D. 14–825. See K. Norrie, *Defamation and Related Actions in Scots Law* (Butterworths Law, 1995), pp.8–11 for discussion on the nature of defamation. Norrie suggests Lord Atkin's test is based on the earlier treatment of defamation by Sheriff Guthrie Smith.

[4] It may also be thought that the test is problematic in a pluralistic society. See E. Reid, *Personality, Confidentiality and Privacy in Scots Law* (Edinburgh: W. Green, 2010), para.10.17.

[5] See paras 29.22–29.24, below.

[6] See paras 29.05 and 29.06, below.

[7] *Morrison v Ritchie* (1902) S.C. 4 F. 645, per Lord Moncreiff at 650. The *Reynolds* defence will also overcome the presumption of malice. See para.29.19, below.

plaintiff was placed in the department of an exhibition devoted to the effigies of notorious criminals.[8] Technically, written defamation is known as libel, oral as slander,[9] but the distinction is not of importance in the law of Scotland.

29.03 Statement must be untrue: *Veritas*[10]—To be actionable in defamation the statement must be untrue, as is indicated in the maxim *veritas convicii excusat*[11] (the truth of an insult excuses). Wrongful disclosure of truthful private information may be actionable as breach of confidence and may also be in breach of art.8 of the European Convention of Human Rights.[12] In the case of statements which are defamatory there is a presumption of their untruth, and the defender, if he relies on *veritas*, must affirm the truth of his statement in his defences and, where trial is by jury, table a definite counterissue. Without such a counterissue, evidence of the truth of the statement is not admissible.[13] Where there are two separate charges, it is competent to take a counterissue with regard to one of them,[14] but it has been held in England that the defendant cannot lead evidence of the truth of one defamatory charge in an article when the plaintiff is suing only in relation to another.[15] Although the defender need not prove the truth of everything complained of, he must establish the accuracy of the sting in the publication.[16] By the Defamation Act 1952,[17] where a statement sued on contains two or more charges against a pursuer, a defence of *veritas* is not to fail by reason only that the truth of every charge is not proved, provided that the words not proved to be true do not materially injure the pursuer's reputation in view of the proven truth of the remaining charges. A defamatory allegation that a person has been charged with, prosecuted or convicted for a criminal offence can be defended with *veritas* even though the conviction is spent under the Rehabilitation of Offenders Act 1974.[18] In these circumstances the defence will be lost if malice can be proved.[19]

29.04 Publication—In Scotland it is not necessary that the statement be communicated to a third party. It is sufficient if it was made or sent to the injured party because

---

[8] *Monson v Tussauds* [1894] 1 Q.B. 671; *Adamson v Martin*, 1916 S.C. 319; *Dwek v Associated Newspapers Ltd* [2000] E.M.L.R. 284. For defamation arising from unauthorised use of images in product endorsement see: *Tolley v Fry* [1931] A.C. 333; *Bradley v Menley & James Ltd*, 1913 S.C. 923.

[9] A representation in words and pictures in a film is libel not slander: *Youssoupoff v M.G.M.* (1934) 50 T.L.R. 581.

[10] See Norrie, *Defamation and Related Actions in Scots Law* (1995), Ch.9; Reid, *Personality, Confidentiality and Privacy in Scots Law* (2010), paras 11.02–11.07.

[11] *McKellar v Duke of Sutherland* (1859) 21 D. 222.

[12] See paras 29.30 and 29.31, below. See Reid, *Personality, Confidentiality and Privacy in Scots Law* (2010), paras 8.01–8.15 for discussion on truth in defamation and consideration of whether true statements may be actionable in verbal injury.

[13] *Craig v JexBlake* (1871) 9 M. 973; *Browne v Macfarlane* (1889) 16 R. 368.

[14] *O'Callaghan v Thomson & Co*, 1928 S.C. 532.

[15] *Cruise v Express Newspapers* [1999] Q.B. 931.

[16] *Sarwar v News Group Newspapers Ltd*, 1999 S.L.T. 327.

[17] Defamation Act 1952 s.5; *Polly Peck (Holdings) v Trelford* [1986] Q.B. 1000. Equivalent provisions are in the process of enactment in the Defamation Bill cl.2 which abolishes the common law defence of justification in England and also repeals s.5 of the 1952 Act. Clause 2 is not presently intended to extend to Scotland.

[18] Rehabilitation of Offenders Act 1974 s.8(3).

[19] Rehabilitation of Offenders Act 1974 s.8(5). The requirements for proving malice are the same as in the defence of qualified privilege: *Herbage v Pressdram* [1984] 1 W.L.R. 1160.

damages are recoverable for injured feelings.[20] The dictation of a defamatory letter to a clerk is not publication and no action would lie if the letter was not despatched.[21] In England, an action may be struck out if publication has been only minimal,[22] and the mere fact that the defamatory material was published on the internet does not imply that there has been publication of the extent required to justify proceedings.[23] But it has been held in England that each occasion on which a defamatory article in a defendants' internet archive is accessed constitutes a separate defamation.[24] Internet service providers ("ISPs") are given some protection against claims for damages or criminal penalties, but not interdict, under the Electronic Commerce (EC Directive) Regulations 2002[25] where the ISP has merely provided a conduit for transmission of defamatory material,[26] or where it has either cached or hosted the material, but removed it expeditiously on discovering its nature.[27]An ISP hosting a site on which defamatory material has been published may be able to avail itself of the defence in s.1 of the Defamation Act 1996, but the criteria for the defence will not be met in the event that the material is not removed on discovering its nature.[28]

What amounts to defamation—Whether or not the words complained of are **29.05** reasonably capable of bearing a defamatory meaning, either per se or by innuendo,[29] is a question of law for the court.[30] In determining this question the whole statement must be read.[31] Thus, the contents of a newspaper report, when read together with the heading, may negative the defamatory meaning of the heading alone.[32] But mere inclusion of the claimant's denial of allegations is very unlikely to neutralise the sting of a defamatory article[33]although it will be a relevant factor where the *Reynolds* defence of responsible journalism is considered.[34] If the court holds that the language may be construed in a defamatory sense, it is then a question for the jury to decide whether or not the proper construction in all the circumstances of the case is defamatory or innocent. Evidence may be led of the sense in which the words used were understood by those who read or heard them.[35] Words which are prima facie defamatory may be held to have been used

---

[20] *Mackay v McCankie* (1883) 10 R. 537; *Ramsay v Maclay* (1890) 18 R. 130. There have been no cases brought where imputations have been directed to the pursuer alone over the past hundred years. For discussion see Reid, *Personality, Confidentiality and Privacy in Scots Law* (2010), paras 10.35–10.36. The words "publish" and "statement" are given statutory definition in the Defamation Bill cl.14. This provision is intended to extend to Scotland.

[21] See *Evans v Stein* (1904) 7 F. 65.

[22] *Jameel v Dow Jones* [2005] Q.B. 946.

[23] *AlAmoudi v Brisard* [2007] 1 W.L.R. 113.

[24] *Loutchansky v Times Newspapers Ltd (Nos 25)* [2002] Q.B. 783.

[25] Electronic Commerce (EC Directive) Regulations 2002 (SI 2002/2003) implementing Directive 2000/31/EC.

[26] Electronic Commerce (EC Directive) Regulations 2002 reg.17.

[27] Electronic Commerce (EC Directive) Regulations 2002 regs 18 and 19. Clause 5 of the Defamation Bill provides a defence to website operators where the operator did not post the material complained of. The defence will be lost where the operator fails to respond to a complaint that the material is defamatory. Clause 5 is not presently intended to extend to Scotland.

[28] *Godfrey v Demon Internet* [2001] Q.B. 201.

[29] See para.29.06, below.

[30] *Russell v Stubbs*, 1913 S.C. (HL) 14 at 20, per Lord Kinnear; *Fraser v Mirza*, 1993 S.C. (HL) 27.

[31] *Campbell v Ritchie & Co*, 1907 S.C. 1097.

[32] *Leon v Edinburgh Evening News*, 1909 S.C. 1014.

[33] *Mark v Associated Newspapers Ltd (No.1)* [2002] E.M.L.R. 38.

[34] See para.29.19, below.

[35] *Muirhead v George Outram & Co*, 1983 S.L.T. 201.

in their slang sense[36] or in the heat of a quarrel (*in rixa*)[37] as words of mere abuse, but not if a definite charge is made.[38] It is not a complete answer that a defamatory statement was meant as a joke.[39]

29.06 Innuendo[40]—In some cases it may be necessary to explain technical, ironical or ambiguous language or to supply a stigma which may, but does not necessarily, lurk in the words used. This is done by setting forth on record and putting in issue an innuendo, i.e. the precise defamatory meaning which the pursuer attaches to the words.[41] The language itself may support the innuendo, but the pursuer may also aver facts extrinsic to the libel which tend to show that the language may reasonably be construed in the sense of the innuendo.[42] It is for the court to determine whether the innuendo is one which the words actually used may reasonably bear and for the jury to decide as matter of fact whether the language ought to be construed in the sense of the innuendo.[43]

> "The innuendo must represent what is a reasonable, natural, or necessary inference from the words used, regard being had to the occasion and the circumstances of their publication."[44]

The words must be judged not in isolation but in the context of the publication as a whole.[45] If the innuendo consists of a special meaning dependent on knowledge of specific facts, publication to persons aware of those facts at that time must be proved.[46] When the slander is in a foreign language, the English equivalent must be set forth in the same way as an innuendo.[47] An innuendo may also be used to extract the substance of the charge from a series of letters or articles, and to gather together the expressions therein which are defamatory.[48]

29.07 Types of defamatory imputation—Imputations against a man's moral character are defamatory.[49] Allegations of certain sexual conduct may be, for example, that

---

[36] *Murdison v Scottish Football Union* (1896) 23 R. 449; *Agnew v British Legal Assurance Co* (1906) 8 F. 422.

[37] *Watson v Duncan* (1890) 17 R. 404.

[38] *Christie v Robertson* (1899) 1 F. 1155 at 1157, per Lord McLaren.

[39] *Prophit v BBC*, 1997 S.L.T. 745.

[40] See Norrie, *Defamation and Related Actions in Scots Law* (1995), pp.13–17; Reid, *Personality, Confidentiality and Privacy in Scots Law* (2010), paras 10.08–10.13.

[41] *Murdison v S.F.U.* (1896) 23 R. 449 at 463, per Lord Kinnear; *James v Baird*, 1915 S.C. 23; *Fraser v Mirza*, 1993 S.C. (HL) 27.

[42] *James v Baird*, 1916 S.C. (HL) 158 at 165, per Lord Kinnear; *Smith v Walker*, 1912 S.C. 224; *Gordon v Leng*, 1919 S.C. 415; *Gollan v Thompson Wyles*, 1930 S.C. 599 at 603–604, per Lord President Clyde; *Lewis v Daily Telegraph* [1964] A.C. 234.

[43] *Langlands v Leng*, 1916 S.C. (HL) 102; *Ritchie & Co v Sexton* (1891) 18 R. (HL) 20, affirming (1890) 17 R. 680; *Slim v Daily Telegraph* [1968] 2 Q.B. 157; *Mitchell v Faber & Faber Ltd* [1998] E.M.L.R. 807.

[44] *Russell v Stubbs*, 1913 S.C. (HL) 14 at 24, per Lord Shaw; *Lord Hamilton v Glasgow Dairy Co*, 1931 S.C. (HL) 67. See *Fullam v Newcastle Chronicle and Journal* [1977] 1 W.L.R. 651, on requirements of pleading where innuendo would be drawn only by those with special knowledge.

[45] *Chalmers v Payne* (1835) 2 Cr. M. & R. 67; *Charleston v News Group Newspapers* [1995] 2 A.C. 65.

[46] *Grappelli v Derek Block (Holdings)* [1981] 1 W.L.R. 822; cf. *Hayward v Thompson* [1982] Q.B. 47.

[47] *Bernhardt v Abrahams*, 1912 S.C. 748.

[48] *Neilson v Johnston* (1890) 17 R. 442.

[49] *Brownlie v Thomson* (1859) 21 D. 480 at 485, per Lord Justice Clerk Inglis. See Cooper, *The Law of Defamation and Verbal Injury* (1906); Norrie, *Defamation and Related Actions in Scots Law* (1995), pp.17–27; Reid, *Personality, Confidentiality and Privacy in Scots Law* (2010), paras 10.25–10.34, for examples of defamatory imputations.

a man has associated with a known prostitute,[50] but an allegation of homosexuality is probably not now defamatory.[51] Imputations of guilt of crime or of attempt to commit a crime or of criminal intent are clearly defamatory, as are allegations of dishonesty, immorality and drunkenness, if seriously made. While the law affords no remedy for a reflection on manners, a definite charge of conduct usually regarded as dishonourable, either in general society,[52] or in a particular class to which the pursuer belongs,[53] is actionable. To say of a man that he is an informer may be actionable.[54]

Any imputation on solvency is actionable.[55] In the case of "black lists", i.e. lists of persons against whom decrees in absence have been pronounced, the publication of such a list, compiled from official sources, and accurate, cannot be made the subject of an action on the ground merely that it may be read as an imputation on the solvency of the parties whose names are included.[56] But it becomes actionable if prefaced by a caution against giving credit,[57] or if it is averred that the publication is generally read as inferring insolvency.[58] A party whose name is entered by mistake may claim damages. A prefatory statement, to the effect that the publication of a name does not import any inability to pay, will preclude an innuendo, by a party whose name has been inserted by mistake, that the insertion involves a charge of insolvency,[59] but not an innuendo that it involves a statement that he is a party to whom credit should not be given.[60]

False statements which disparage a man's professional or business capacity or fitness for his office or vocation may be defamatory,[61] but they must be distinguished from those which, while injurious, do not impugn his character or business reputation. The latter are not defamatory. Slander of title, slander of property and falsehoods causing business loss may be actionable under verbal injury.[62] There is also a material distinction between private individuals and public figures, critics of the latter being allowed a wide latitude in the public interest[63]; a person's status as a public figure is not, however, a defence to an allegation of defamation[64]and the impact on the pursuer's professional, as well as personal standing may be taken into account in assessing solatium.[65] It is defamatory of the holder of a public office to make criticisms from which it can reasonably be

---

[50] *Dwek v Macmillan Publishers Ltd* [2000] E.M.L.R. 284.

[51] *Quilty v Windsor*, 1999 S.L.T. 346.

[52] *Menzies v Goodlet* (1835) 13 S. 1136 (anonymous letter).

[53] *Griffin v Divers*, 1922 S.C. 605; *Tolley v Fry* [1931] A.C. 333; *Cuthbert v Linklater*, 1935 S.L.T. 94; *Lloyd v Hickley*, 1967 S.L.T. 225.

[54] *Winn v Quillan* (1899) 37 S.L.R. 38. Aliter in England and Ireland: see *Byrne v Deane* [1937] 1 K.B. 818; *Maure v Pigott* (1869) I.R. 4 C.L. 54; *Berry v Irish Times* [1973] I.R. 368.

[55] *A.B. v C.D.* (1904) 7 F. 22.

[56] *Taylor v Rutherford* (1888) 15 R. 608; *McLintock v Stubbs* (1902) 5 F. 1.

[57] *Andrews v Drummond* (1887) 14 R. 568.

[58] *Barr v Musselburgh Merchants*, 1912 S.C. 174.

[59] *Russell v Stubbs*, 1913 S.C. (HL) 14.

[60] *Mazure v Stubbs*, 1919 S.C. (HL) 112.

[61] See cases cited in Cooper, *The Law of Defamation and Verbal Injury* (1906), pp.61–75; and Norrie, *Defamation and Related Actions in Scots Law* (1995), pp.22–24; *Muirhead v George Outram & Co*, 1983 S.L.T. 201. Charitable intention has been held to afford qualified privilege to a statement regarding the treatment of pauper patients by a doctor: *James v Baird*, 1916 S.C. (HL) 158.

[62] See para.29.23, below.

[63] See para.29.14, below.

[64] *Bennett v Guardian Newspapers Ltd* [1995] T.L.R. 719.

[65] *Wray v Associated Newspapers*, 2000 S.L.T. 869.

inferred that he is dishonest or guilty of dishonourable behaviour or that his public conduct is combined with base and indirect motives.[66]

29.08 Defences—The following defences are open in an action for defamation:

(1) that the words founded on were not used by the defender;
(2) that the statement did not refer to the pursuer and could not reasonably be construed as referring to him[67];
(3) that the words used were not reasonably capable of bearing the alleged defamatory meaning ascribed to them[68];
(4) that the defender was involved only in innocent dissemination of the defamatory statement[69];
(5) that the pursuer has accepted an offer to make amends[70];
(6) that the defamation was unintentional, and that an offer of amends has been made[71];
(7) that the pursuer expressly or impliedly assented to the statement being made[72];
(8) that the statement was true (*veritas*)[73];
(9) absolute privilege[74];
(10) qualified privilege[75];
(11) fair retort[76];
(12) fair comment[77]; and
(13) *Reynolds* defence of responsible journalism.[78]

29.09 Unintentional slander—The pursuer in an action of defamation does not require to prove that the defender intended to disparage him or that he even knew of his existence. His obligation is to satisfy the court, as a matter of relevancy, that the words used might reasonably be read as referring to him, and to satisfy the jury that they were in fact so read. In *Jones v Hulton*[79] a novel, serialised in a newspaper referred to "Artemus Jones," a fictitious churchwarden from Peckham who absconded to France with a lady who was not his wife. The real Artemus Jones used his skills as a barrister to prove that the article had been read as referring to him and was found entitled to a substantial sum in damages from the publishers. Where publication is in a national newspaper with a very wide circulation it may

---

[66] *Mutch v Robertson*, 1981 S.L.T. 217; cf. *Fairbairn v Scottish National Party*, 1979 S.C. 393.
[67] See para.29.09, below.
[68] See para.29.05, above.
[69] Defamation Act 1996 s.1. See para.29.10, below.
[70] Defamation Act 1996 ss.2 and 3. See para.29.10, below
[71] Defamation Act s.4. See para.29.10, below.
[72] e.g. an employee who accepts as part of his contract of employment a disciplinary code which necessarily involves republication of an allegation about him as part of disciplinary proceedings: *Friend v C.A.A.* [1998] I.R.L.R. 253.
[73] See para.29.03, above. If the truth of the statement is evident from the pursuer's pleadings, the action is irrelevant: *Carson v White*, 1919 2 S.L.T. 215. The English equivalent common law defence of justification is to be abolished and placed on a statutory footing: Defamation Bill cl.2.
[74] See para.29.11, below.
[75] See para.29.12, below.
[76] See para.29.18, below.
[77] See paras 29.20 and 29.21, below. The common law defence of fair comment is to be abolished in England and placed on a statutory footing: Defamation Bill cl.3.
[78] See para.29.19, below. This common law defence is to be abolished in England and placed on a statutory footing: Defamation Bill cl.4.
[79] *Jones v Hulton* [1910] A.C. 20, followed in *Wragg v Thomson*, 1909 2 S.L.T. 409.

be possible to infer that some readers of the newspaper must have identified the claimant.[80] An action of damages lies for publication of a statement which is ex facie innocent but which is reasonably read in a sense defamatory of the pursuer by persons with knowledge of facts unknown to the defender.[81] So, in the case of a newspaper notice inserted by an unknown party, it has been held that malice may be inferred from the failure of the publishers to make sufficient inquiry into the genuineness of the notice and that the circumstances surrounding the publication of the notice are relevant only to quantum of damages.[82] These observations now have to be read in the light of the defence afforded by s.1 of the Defamation Act 1996.

Defamation Act 1996—Statutory defences to an action for defamation are set out **29.10** in the Defamation Act 1996. First, there is a defence available to an individual who can show that he was not the author, editor or publisher of the statement complained of. The defence will only be available if he can show that reasonable care was taken in relation to publication, and that he did not know and had no reason to believe that he was responsible for the publication of a defamatory statement.[83] Interpretations of author, editor and publisher are provided in s.1(2) and (3). Notably, the originator of a statement is not the author if they did not intend it to be published. Those without responsibility for publishing, such as production staff and newspaper vendors are protected by this defence.

Secondly, ss.2 to 4 of the Act set out a scheme for making amends. A person who has published an allegedly defamatory statement may offer to make amends. An offer to make amends will consist of an offer of (i) correction of the statement and an apology, (ii) publication of the correction and apology, and (iii) payment of compensation.[84] The offer cannot be made after an action by the aggrieved party has been defended,[85] although it can be accepted after proceedings have been raised.[86] If the offer is accepted, no proceedings for defamation may be brought or continued,[87] although proceedings to enforce the offer may be taken.[88] Such proceedings may include determination of the amount of compensation by the court.[89] If the offer is not accepted, the fact that one has been tendered may be relied on as a defence to the exclusion of other defences.[90] The defence that an offer was made is available where the defender neither knew nor had reason to believe that the statement referred to the aggrieved party and was false and defamatory of him, the defender however, has the considerable benefit of a presumption to this effect.[91]

---

[80] *Dwek v Macmillan Publishers Ltd* [2000] E.M.L.R. 284.

[81] *Morrison v Ritchie* (1902) 4 F. 645; *Cassidy v Daily Mirror* [1929] 2 K.B. 331.

[82] *Morrison v Ritchie* (1902) 4 F. 645; but note opinions of Lords Salvesen and Kinnear in *Wood v Edinburgh Evening News*, 1910 S.C. 895. See D.M. Walker, *The Law of Delict in Scotland*, 2nd edn (Edinburgh: W. Green, 1981), pp.783–4.

[83] Defamation Act 1996 s.1. The Defamation Bill cl.10 limits the jurisdiction of the court to hear actions brought against persons who are not the author, editor or publisher. This clause is not presently intended to extend to Scotland.

[84] Defamation Act 1996 s.2(4).

[85] Defamation Act 1996 s.2(5).

[86] *Moore v Scottish Daily Record & Sunday Mail Ltd*, 2007 S.L.T. 217.

[87] Defamation Act 1996 s.3(2).

[88] Defamation Act 1996 s.3(2).

[89] Defamation Act 1996 s.3(5). Any mitigatory effect of the amends procedure should be taken into account in assessing quantum—*Nail v News Group Newspapers Ltd* [2005] 1 All E.R. 1040. See also para.29.28, below.

[90] Defamation Act 1996 s.4(4).

[91] Defamation Act 1996 s.4(3). See *Milne v Express Newspapers Ltd (No 1)* [2005] 1 W.L.R. 772.

29.11 Absolute privilege—There are circumstances in which the interest in freedom of speech outweighs the right of any individual to their reputation. Where privilege is absolute no action can be based on defamatory words. Absolute privilege arises in relation to Parliamentary and judicial proceedings.

Parliamentary proceedings—Statements made in either House of the UK Parliament, whether on the floor, or in committees, or in other parliamentary proceedings over which either House has control are absolutely privileged. The same protection is extended to the Scottish Parliament and proceedings therein.[92] Repetition of a statement outside Parliament is not protected.[93] Absolute privilege does however attach to official reports, records and papers ordered to be published by Parliament[94] whereas fair and accurate reports of proceedings in a legislature anywhere in the world enjoy qualified privilege.[95] Aside from the overriding interest in free speech the courts lack constitutional authority over parliamentary proceedings.[96] Privilege may be waived in order to allow a court to consider evidence or submissions of statements made in Parliament, for example where an action is raised by a Member of Parliament.[97] Parliamentary privilege has survived a challenge in the European Court of Human Rights in which the claimant argued her art.6(1) right to a fair and public hearing was breached since statements made about her in the House of Commons could not be considered in court.[98] Statements made in petitions addressed to Parliament enjoy absolute privilege, letters to MPs do not.[99]

Judicial proceedings—Most statements made during judicial proceedings in courts of justice are covered by absolute privilege. Absolute privilege extends also to tribunals exercising judicial, but not administrative functions. Since there is no definitive list designating tribunals to either category it may prove necessary to consider the characteristics of a given tribunal to determine the point.[100] Absolute privilege does not therefore extend to correspondence seeking a contribution from parents to costs of local authority foster care of their child,[101] nor to local authority statements about a person in order to list him as a person unsuitable to work with children.[102] In England, the suggestion that comments to the Parole Board should be protected by absolute privilege has been rejected; such comments are, however, probably protected by qualified privilege.[103] Submission to an agreed industrial conciliation procedure does not imply acceptance of absolute privilege for what is said in the course of the proceedings,[104] indeed, the position of arbitration proceedings remains

---

[92] Scotland Act 1998 s.41(1)(a).

[93] *Buchanan v Jennings* [2005] 1 A.C. 115.

[94] Parliamentary Papers Act 1840 s.1; Scotland Act 1998 s.41(1)(b). Absolute privilege applies to official reports to any department of State or to a colonial government: *Dawkins v Lord Paulet* (1869) L.R. 5 Q.B. 94; *M Isaacs v Cook* [1925] K.B. 391 and to the memoranda of an acting ambassador to his home government: *AlFayed v AlTajir* [1988] Q.B. 712.

[95] Defamation Act 1996 s.15(1), Sch.1 Pt 1.

[96] Bill of Rights Act 1689; cf. Claim of Right 1689.

[97] Defamation Act 1996 s.13, considered in *Hamilton v AlFayed (No.1)* [2001] 1 A.C. 395.

[98] *A v United Kingdom* (2002) E.H.R.R. 51 (App No. 35373/97).

[99] *Rivlin v Bilainkin* [1953] All E.R. 534.

[100] *Trapp v Mackie*, 1979 S.C. (HL) 38. See Reid, *Personality, Confidentiality and Privacy in Scots Law* (2010), para.11.11.

[101] *Waple v Surrey CC* [1998] 1 W.L.R. 860.

[102] *S. v Newham LBC* [1998] 1 F.L.R. 1061.

[103] *Daniels v Griffiths* [1998] E.M.L.R. 489.

[104] *Tadd v Eastwood and Daily Telegraph* [1985] I.C.R. 132.

unclear.[105] There are older Scots authorities supportive of absolute privilege,[106] but in England the arbitrator enjoys only qualified privilege.[107]

Absolute privilege applies to any statement by a judge, of any court, while acting in his judicial capacity[108]; any statement by an advocate (i.e. by any person professionally addressing a court)[109] or by a witness whether made in court, on precognition,[110] or by way of some less formal interview.[111] But the privilege of a litigant, in statements made on record, or in statements which he instructs his counsel or solicitor to make in court, is qualified, not absolute.[112]

A fair and accurate report of proceedings in public before a UK court is protected by absolute privilege; the protection also extends to proceedings before the European Court of Justice, the European Court of Human Rights and any international criminal tribunal established by the United Nations or by an international agreement to which the United Kingdom is a party.[113] The report need not be verbatim, and it is for the jury to decide whether any omission deprives it of the character of a fair report.[114] The fact that the report was in breach of the provisions of the Judicial Proceedings (Regulation of Reports) Act 1926 does not exclude the defence of privilege.[115] The privilege covers the publication of any decree, or official record.[116] While it is doubtful whether privilege covers a report of statements made in the closed record of an action, it is clear that it does not extend to statements before the record is closed.[117] The publication of such statements amounts to contempt of court, and may be visited by penalties.[118]

Qualified privilege: Averments of malice—Qualified privilege does not relate **29.12** to persons or to the nature of statements but to occasions, and it is for the court to decide whether or not the occasion is privileged, although it may not be possible to do so until the relevant facts have been ascertained.[119]

---

[105] See Reid, *Personality, Confidentiality and Privacy in Scots Law* (2010), para.11.16.

[106] *Neil v Henderson* (1901) 3 F. 387; *Slack v Barr* (1918) 1 S.L.T. 133.

[107] Arbitration Act 1996 s.29.

[108] Considerable latitude is given to acting within judicial capacity. See *Primrose v Waterston* (1902) 4 F. 783.

[109] *Williamson v Umphray* (1890) 17 R. 905; *Rome v Watson* (1898) 25 R. 733.

[110] *Watson v McEwan* (1905) 7 F. (HL) 109.

[111] *B. v Burns*, 1994 S.L.T. 250.

[112] *Williamson v Umphray* (1890) 17 R. 905; *McLean v Hart*, 1908 S.C. 1130. See also *Bayne v Macgregor* (1862) 24 D. 1126, where the solicitor was sued on the ground that he had maliciously instructed counsel to make the statement. A litigant's statements will not be privileged at all unless they are pertinent to the questions at issue. See *Mackellar v Duke of Sutherland* (1859) 21 D. 1126; *Scott v Turnbull* (1884) 11 R. 1131.

[113] Defamation Act 1996 s.14. The report must be contemporaneous. S.14(3) is subject to amendment by cl.7(1) of the Defamation Bill. This amendment is not presently intended to extend to Scotland.

[114] *Wright & Greig v Outram* (1890) 17 R. 596; *Duncan v Associated Scottish Newspapers*, 1929 S.C. 14; *Harper v Provincial Newspapers*, 1937 S.L.T. 462; see Walker, *The Law of Delict in Scotland* (1981), pp.884–885.

[115] *Nicol v Caledonian Newspapers Ltd*, 2002 S.C. 493; the privilege involved would now be absolute, not qualified.

[116] *Buchan v N.B. Ry* (1894) 21 R. 379.

[117] *Macleod v J.P. of Lewis* (1892) 20 R. 218. Qualified privilege attaches to reports relating to documents founded on in a court hearing although not read out: *Cunningham v Scotsman Publications Ltd*, 1987 S.C. 107.

[118] *Young v Armour*, 1921 1 S.L.T. 211.

[119] *Adam v Ward* [1917] A.C. 309; *Minter v Priest* [1930] A.C. 558 at 571–572, per Viscount Dunedin.

"The proper meaning of a privileged communication is only this: that the occasion on which the communication was made rebuts the inference [of malice] prima facie arising from a statement prejudicial to the character of the plaintiff, and puts it upon him to prove that there was malice in fact—that the defendant was actuated by motives of personal spite or ill will, independent of the occasion on which the communication was made."[120]

Exceptionally, however, a statement may be so violent as to afford evidence that it could not have been fairly and honestly made.[121] As misuse of the occasion is the essence of the matter,[122] it may be sufficient to prove that the statement was actuated by malice even if the pursuer was not the object of that malice.[123] Facts and circumstances from which malice may be inferred must be set forth. Averments of a prior quarrel or ill feeling may be sufficient.[124] Absence of belief in the truth of a defamatory allegation actually or intended to be conveyed is usually conclusive evidence of an improper motive amounting to malice,[125] though it is not sufficient to aver that a charge was made without due enquiry,[126] or, short of recklessness, that it was the result of unreasonable prejudice[127] or that the defender refused to listen to the pursuer's explanation of his conduct,[128] or refused to withdraw the charge after it had been held unfounded in an official inquiry.[129] In a rare type of case it has been held competent to aver and prove malice on the part of the defender in order, not to defeat a plea of privilege, but to strengthen an inference that the defender was the author of a particular libel, namely, an anonymous letter.[130]

29.13 Statements in discharge of duty—Qualified privilege exists where the statement is

"fairly made by a person in the discharge of some public or private duty, whether legal or moral, or in the conduct of his own affairs, in matters where his interest is concerned".[131]

---

[120] *Wright v Woodgate* (1835) 2 C.M. & R. 573 at 577, per Parke B., quoted by Lord Hunter in *Cochrane v Young*, 1922 S.C. 696 at 701–702. See also *Watson v Burnet* (1864) 24 D. 494, per Lord Deas at 497.

[121] *Lyal v Henderson*, 1916 S.C. (HL) 167; *Anderson v Palombo*, 1986 S.L.T. 46.

[122] *Horrocks v Lowe* [1975] A.C. 135 at 149–150, per Lord Diplock; *Fraser v Mirza*, 1993 S.C. (HL) 27 at 33, per Lord Keith of Kinkel. Note that whether an occasion is privileged is a question of law for the judge, whether the occasion has been abused is a question of fact for the jury. See dicta of Lord Hope in *Reynolds v Times Newspapers Ltd* [2001] 2 A.C. 127 at 231ff.

[123] *Anderson v Palombo*, 1984 S.L.T. 332 at 334. Quaere, however, if this view wholly consists with the explanation that the occasion, in the absence of proof of malice, rebuts the inference of malice (against the pursuer).

[124] *Dinnie v Hengler*, 1910 S.C. 4.

[125] *Fraser v Mirza*, 1993 S.C. (HL) 27.

[126] *AB v XY*, 1917 S.C. 15; *Hayford v ForresterPaton*, 1927 S.C. 740.

[127] *Horrocks v Lowe* [1975] A.C. 135 (privileged if there was honest and positive belief coupled with absence of abuse of privileged position).

[128] *AB v XY*, 1917 S.C. 15.

[129] *Couper v Lord Balfour*, 1913 S.C. 492.

[130] *MacTaggart v MacKillop*, 1938 S.C. 847; and see *Swan v Bowie*, 1948 S.C. 46.

[131] *Toogood v Spyring* (1834) 1 C.M. & R. 181, per Parke B. at 193, adopted in *Macintosh v Dun* [1908] A.C. 390; *AB v XY*, 1917 S.C. 15; *Hines v Davidson*, 1935 S.C. 30 at 38, per Lord Anderson.

As is added later in the same judgment, the communication must be to some person legitimately interested in the matter[132] but the privilege is not lost merely because someone else happens to be present.[133] This protection exonerated solicitors who had instructed the insertion in a published apology of a particular passage to which an individual with the same name as their client took exception, but it did not avail the newspaper publishing the passage.[134] Publication in a specialist journal of matters of concern to the readership may fall within the necessary reciprocity of interest.[135] But a publisher attempting to set up a defence of qualified privilege cannot found on facts not known to him at the time of publication.[136]

Criticism in employment context—A well-recognised instance for the invocation of privilege is criticism by an employer of his employee,[137] either to the employee himself, or in speaking to some party who has an interest to inquire, but not in repeating his criticism unnecessarily to third parties.[138] Conversely, employee criticism of management directed to the appropriate professional body is also privileged.[139] Where a dismissed employee wrote to a television company complaining about his former employers and the television company communicated with the employers, their reply giving the reasons for his dismissal was held to be privileged.[140] A letter to a senior officer of the Prison Service alleging that a prison officer is unfit for office attracts qualified privilege.[141] A Member of Parliament has qualified privilege in passing on to the appropriate body a complaint received from a constituent about the conduct of a professional person.[142] There is older authority to suggest that an elector has qualified privilege in speaking of a candidate in his own constituency,[143] not in another.[144] A defamatory statement published by or for a candidate at a local or Parliamentary election is not privileged on the ground that it is material to a question at issue in the election.[145] The members of a public body or board are privileged in discussing any matter pertinent to the business.[146] Section 1(5) of the Public Bodies (Admission to Meetings) Act 1960, confers qualified privilege on the agenda of any meeting required by the Act to be open to the public, a copy of which is supplied to a

29.14

---

[132] The point is perhaps most concisely made by Lord Atkinson in *Adam v Ward* [1917] 2 A.C. 309 at 334: "A privileged occasion is . . . an occasion where the person who makes a communication has an interest or a duty, legal, social or moral, to make it to the person to whom it is made, and the person to whom it is so made has a corresponding interest or duty to receive it. This reciprocity is essential."

[133] See *Watt v Longsdon* [1930] 1 K.B. 130.

[134] *Watts v Times Newspapers* [1997] Q.B. 650.

[135] *Star Gems v Ford* [1980] C.L.Y. 1671. The Defamation Bill cl.6 extends qualified privilege to refereed scientific and academic journals. This provision is intended to apply in Scotland.

[136] *Loutchansky v Times Newspapers Ltd (No.1)* [2002] Q.B. 321.

[137] e.g. *McKay v Scottish Hydro Electric Plc*, 2000 S.C. 87. A comparable case is chairman and employee of a company: see *McGillivray v Davidson*, 1934 S.L.T. 45.

[138] *Bryant v Edgar*, 1909 S.C. 1080.

[139] *Pearson v Educational Institute for Scotland*, 1997 S.C. 245.

[140] *Sutherland v British Telecommunications*, 1989 S.L.T. 531.

[141] *Quilty v Windsor*, 1999 S.L.T. 346.

[142] *Beach v Freeson* [1972] 1 Q.B. 14.

[143] *Bruce v Leisk* (1892) 19 R. 482.

[144] *Anderson v Hunter* (1891) 18 R. 467.

[145] Defamation Act 1952 s.10, interpreted by the High Court in *Culnane v Morris* [2006] 1 W.L.R. 2880; and see *Plummer v Charman (No.1)* [1962] 1 W.L.R. 1469; *Fairbairn v Scottish National Party*, 1979 S.C. 393. The House of Lords has rejected a suggestion that publication of all political information should attract qualified privilege: *Reynolds v Times Newspapers Ltd* [2001] 2 A.C. 127.

[146] *Shaw v Morgan* (1888) 15 R. 865; *Griffin v Divers*, 1922 S.C. 605; *Mutch v Robertson*, 1981 S.L.T. 217.

member of the public attending the meeting or supplied for the benefit of a newspaper.

29.15 No probable cause—Want of probable cause, as well as malice, must be averred and proved where the statement complained of is made in reporting an alleged crime to the criminal authorities,[147] and where it is made by a public officer in the discharge of his duty. Such statements receive the additional protection on the ground of public interest.[148] In an ordinary action of defamation the words "without probable cause" have no place at all.[149]

29.16 Solicitor-client communications—The question of whether communications passing between solicitor and client on a subject upon which the client has retained the solicitor are protected by absolute or qualified privilege has not been decided in Scotland.[150] While it is thought that qualified, not absolute, privilege applies to all statements made by solicitors to third parties in their clients' interests,[151] it may be impossible to decide as a matter of relevancy whether or not the particular statement has gone beyond what is necessary to protect the client's interest. In such a case the whole circumstances in which it was made must be ascertained before the judge can decide that the occasion is privileged and direct the jury to decide whether or not malice is proved.[152] If the statement made by the solicitor is expressed in terms which may reasonably be read as an expression of his own opinion and not that of his client, malice must be proved.[153] A solicitor who publishes defamatory matter which is prima facie in his client's interests, upon his client's instructions, is entitled to plead at least qualified privilege in his own right whether or not the occasion is privileged quoad his client.[154]

29.17 Privilege under Defamation Act 1996—The Defamation Act 1996[155] confers privilege in a number of cases. Thus the publication in a newspaper or in a broadcast of a "fair and accurate" report of the following matters is privileged unless proved to be made maliciously: (1) public proceedings of a legislature anywhere in the world; (2) public proceedings before a court anywhere in the

---

[147] See para.29.28, below.

[148] *Macdonald v Martin*, 1935 S.C. 621; *Notman v Commercial Bank of Scotland*, 1938 S.C. 522.

[149] *Webster v Paterson & Sons*, 1910 S.C. 459 at 468, per Lord Dunedin; *Notman v Commercial Bank of Scotland*, 1938 S.C. 522.

[150] The answer may differ according to circumstances, but it is thought that the English decision of *More v Weaver* [1928] 2 K.B. 520 is consistent on its facts with public policy in respect that the communications seem to have been made in confidential circumstances in which it was not reasonably foreseeable that they would be disclosed by the solicitor to any third party; but see *Minter v Priest* [1930] A.C. 558, where opinions on this point were reserved.

[151] *Baker v Carrick* [1894] 1 Q.B. 838; cf. opinions in *Crawford v Adams* (1900) 2 F. 987; *Regan v Taylor* [2000] T.L.R. 188.

[152] See opinions in *Adam v Ward* [1917] A.C. 309 and *Wilson v Purvis* (1890) 18 R. 72. *Ramsay v Nairne* (1833) 11 S. 1033 should be treated as a case in which the judge left it to the jury to decide whether or not malice was proved.

[153] *Crawford v Adams* (1900) 2 F. 987.

[154] But see opinions of Lords Young, Trayner and Moncrieff in *Crawford v Adams* (1900) 2 F. 987, which suggest that statements made by a solicitor to third parties in strict accordance with his client's instructions are absolutely privileged.

[155] Defamation Act 1996 s.15 and Sch.1. A number of amendments are to be made on enactment of the Defamation Bill cl.7. Only cl.7(9) is presently intended to extend to Scotland. Clause 7(9) concerns qualified privilege of scientific and academic journals. See fn.135, above.

world[156]; (3) public proceedings of a person appointed to hold a public inquiry by a government or legislature anywhere in the world[157]; (4) public proceedings of an international organisation or conference. Similarly privileged are a fair and accurate copy or extract from a public register and a notice or advertisement published by or on the authority of a court anywhere in the world, as well as a fair and accurate copy of or extract from matter published by a government, legislature, international organisation or international conference. Then s.15(2) confers a conditional privilege in other cases, involving specified legislative, governmental and judicial functions, public meetings and the proceedings of public companies and associations. The condition is that the defender must publish, in a suitable manner, at the request of the pursuer a reasonable explanation or contradiction. The latitude thus given to newspapers is not, however, to protect the publication of any matter which is not of public concern and the publication of which is not for the public benefit[158] or any matter whose publication is prohibited by law.[159]

Fair retort—While sometimes listed separately, fair retort may be classified as a **29.18** species of qualified privilege inasmuch as a claim without averments of malice will be irrelevant where the statement complained of was made in response to an earlier attack on the author's reputation.[160] The fact that a party has been slandered however, is no justification for a slander by him.[161] But in repelling a charge made publicly, as by publication in a newspaper, the party who has been attacked is entitled to privilege, to the extent that his repudiation of the charge is not actionable on the ground that it involves, or states, an imputation against the party by whom the charge was made.[162]

> "If A should charge B with theft, a denial by B of the charge would not warrant an action of damages by A however vigorous or gross the language might be in which B's denial was couched. But if B should go on to charge A with theft, that would be actionable, and would not be protected or privileged to any extent on account of A's previous attack."[163]

The principle of fair retort can extend to refuting an attack on a deceased friend.[164] Statements by a party, verbal or written, in answer to a threat of legal action also attract privilege,[165] as does a statement by an agent to rebut criticism made of a client. [166]

---

[156] See para.29.11, above, on absolute privilege of courts in the United Kingdom and certain other international courts.

[157] Such a report need not be contemporaneous: *Tsikata v Newspaper Publishing Plc* [1997] 1 All E.R. 655, decided under the previous provisions contained in the 1952 Act.

[158] Defamation Act 1996 s.15(3).

[159] Defamation Act 1996 s.15(4).

[160] See Reid, *Personality, Confidentiality and Privacy in Scots Law* (2010), para.11.43.

[161] *Milne v Walker* (1893) 21 R. 155.

[162] *Gray v Society for Prevention of Cruelty to Animals* (1890) 17 R. 1185.

[163] *Milne v Walker* (1893) 21 R. 155 at 157, per Lord Kincairney, Lord Ordinary.

[164] *Vassiliev v Frank Cass & Co Ltd* [2003] E.M.L.R. 33.

[165] *Campbell v Cochrane* (1905) 8 F. 205.

[166] *Watts v Times Newspapers Ltd* [1997] Q.B. 650.

29.19 *Reynolds* defence of responsible journalism[167]—No special privilege is enjoyed at common law by a newspaper[168] or broadcaster,[169] but the reporting of a matter in the public interest will be protected if standards of responsible journalism are met.[170] This has become known as the *Reynolds* defence from its origin in *Reynolds v Times Newspapers Limited*.[171] The *Reynolds* defence protects freedom of speech by upholding the media's duty to inform and the public interest in being informed in circumstances where the publication has been made with due propriety. These essential elements of duty and interest mark the *Reynolds* defence as a species of qualified privilege yet it has been described as "a different jurisprudential creature from the traditional form of privilege from which it sprang."[172] It differs from ordinary qualified privilege in that the privilege attaches to the material rather than to the occasion of publication.[173] The conditions that have to be met for the defence to apply are such, moreover, as to establish the propriety of the defender's behaviour. Where the defence applies then, it is not open to the pursuer to offer to prove malice.[174] The two critical issues are whether the defender has acted responsibly and whether the information published is in the public interest. Public interest, as opposed to what is interesting to the public, is notoriously difficult to define.[175] There is judicial guidance given in *Reynolds* on factors to be taken into account in determining whether or not journalism is responsible. A 10 point, nonexhaustive list is given in the speech of Lord Nichols.[176] In *Jameel v Wall Street Journal*[177] it was established that Lord Nichol's points were not to be treated as strict tests, but were factors indicating the ingredients of responsible journalism which should be considered according to the particular circumstances of the case. Lord Hoffmann refined these factors down to three issues: (1) whether the subject matter of the article was a matter of public interest; (2) whether the inclusion of the defamatory statement was justifiable; and (3) whether the steps taken to gather and publish the material were responsible and fair.[178] It is possible for *Reynolds* privilege to attach to the original publication of an article in a newspaper but not to republication of the same article on the newspaper's website.[179]

---

[167] See Reid, *Personality, Confidentiality and Privacy in Scots Law* (2010), paras 11.23–11.38. The Defamation Bill cl.4 abolishes this common law defence in England and places it on a statutory footing. This provision is not presently intended to extend to Scotland.

[168] *Wright & Greig v Outram* (1890) 17 R. 596; *Langlands v Leng*, 1916 S.C. (HL) 102 at 110, per Lord Shaw.

[169] *Baigent v McCulloch*, 1998 S.L.T. 780.

[170] Assessment of a journalist's conduct can take into account that the article could be read in a non-defamatory way: *Bonnick v Morris* [2003] 1 A.C. 300.

[171] *Reynolds v Times Newspapers Ltd* [2001] 2 A.C. 127. *Reynolds* privilege is applicable in Scotland: *Adams v Guardian Newspapers Ltd*, 2003 S.C. 425.

[172] *Loutchansky v Times Newspapers* [2002] Q.B. 783 at [35].

[173] Noted by Lord Phillips in *Loutchansky v Times Newspapers* [2002] Q.B. 783 at [36].

[174] *Jameel v Wall Street Journal Europe Sprl* [2007] 1 A.C. 359.

[175] See discussion in Reid, *Personality, Confidentiality and Privacy in Scots Law* (2010), para.11.34. Reid suggests reference may usefully be made to general guidance by Walker, *The Law of Delict in Scotland* (1981), pp.842–847 in which is included "matters of state and government, administration of justice, the affairs of the Church, the conduct of persons in offices of public responsibility or trust, management of public institutions, local government and administration, and matters affecting the performance or management of arts and culture."

[176] *Reynolds v Times Newspapers Ltd* [2001] 2 A.C. 127 at 205.

[177] *Jameel v Wall Street Journal Europe Sprl* [2007] 1 A.C. 359.

[178] *Jameel v Wall Street Journal Europe Sprl* [2007] 1 A.C. 359 at [48]–[58]. The summary of Lord Hoffmann's dictum here is taken from Reid, *Personality, Confidentiality and Privacy in Scots Law* (2010), para.11.33.

[179] *Loutchansky v Times Newspapers Ltd (Nos 2–5)* [2002] Q.B. 783.

Fair comment[180]—*Veritas* serves to protect factual allegations. Fair comment, by **29.20** contrast, protects comments based on facts, so that statements presented as "deduction, inference, conclusion, criticism, remark, [or] observation" are not actionable.[181] Anyone is entitled to comment on matters of public interest, such as the policy and administration of a government department or local authority, the administration of justice, the conduct of the holder of any public office or aspirant thereto, literary or artistic productions, public exhibitions and entertainments, and indeed any published matter which invites comment from the general public. This liberty is the basis of the defence of fair comment.

Requisites of fair comment—(1) The first requisite of a plea of fair comment is **29.21** that the words complained of should be comment.[182] A comment is a statement of opinion or inference drawn from facts.[183] "The comment must explicitly or implicitly indicate, at least in general terms, the facts upon which it is based."[184] If the court holds that a sufficient substratum of fact cannot reasonably be implied from the words published, they must be construed as an allegation of fact, thus excluding the defence of fair comment, but unpublished facts cannot be used for the purpose of turning what on the face of it is a statement of fact into a comment.[185] Fact and comment may be so bound up together that it is difficult to distinguish the one from the other. In that situation both pleas may be taken and the jury has to decide into which category, fact or comment, the statements respectively fall, under direction from the judge as to the legal effect of their classification.[186] It is for the court to decide as a matter of law whether the statements founded on by the defender as comment may reasonably be classified in their context as such.[187] If comment is so much mixed up with fact that they cannot reasonably be separated, the whole publication may have to be treated as containing allegations of fact only. The plea of fair comment would then fall to be repelled.[188] If the defender establishes the substantial truth of the imputation, whether arising from fact or comment or both, the plea of *veritas* will be sustained, thereby rendering redundant a plea of fair comment.[189]

---

[180] See Norrie, *Defamation and Related Actions in Scots Law* (1995), Ch.10; Reid, *Personality, Confidentiality and Privacy in Scots Law* (2010), paras 11.44–11.59. The Defamation Bill cl.3 abolishes the common law defence of fair comment in England and places it on a statutory footing. This provision is not presently intended to extend to Scotland.

[181] See Reid, *Personality, Confidentiality and Privacy in Scots Law* (2010), para.11.49 quoting Cussen J. in *Clark v Norton* [1910] V.L.R. 494 at 499.

[182] "Fair comment is a defence to comment only and not to defamatory statements of fact": see *Broadway Approvals v Odhams Press* [1964] 2 Q.B. 683, and [1965] 1 W.L.R. 805 at 818, CA.

[183] See *Cooper v Lawson* (1838) 8 A. & E. 746 at 752, per Patterson J.: "He has murdered his father, and therefore is a disgrace to human nature", quoted by Lord Shaw of Dunfermline in *Sutherland v Stopes* [1925] A.C. 47 at 83. "Comment . . . is often to be recognized and distinguished from allegations of fact by the use of metaphor": *Grech v Odhams Press* [1957] 3 All E.R. 556 at 558, per Donovan J., approved [1958] 2 Q.B. 275 at 282, CA.

[184] *Spiller v Joseph* [2010] UKSC 53, per Lord Phillips at [105]. See also *Kemsley v Foot* [1952] A.C. 345.

[185] *Telnikoff v Matusevitch* [1992] 2 A.C. 343.

[186] *Hunt v Star Newspaper* [1908] 2 K.B. 309; *Aga Khan v Times Publishing Co* [1924] 1 K.B. 675 at 680–1, per Bankes L.J.; *Jones v Skelton* [1963] 1 W.L.R. 1362 at 1379–1380, PC. See also *London Artists v Littler* [1969] 2 Q.B. 375, where it was held that the defence of fair comment could not apply to an allegation of a plot as that was an allegation of fact.

[187] *Aga Khan v Times Publishing Co* [1924] 1 K.B. 675; *Jones v Skelton* [1963] 1 W.L.R. 1362.

[188] *Hunt v Star Newspaper* [1908] 2 K.B. 309 at 319–20, per Fletcher Moulton L.J.; approved by Lord Anderson in *Wheatley v Anderson*, 1927 S.C. 133 at 147.

[189] See *Sutherland v Stopes* [1925] A.C. 47 at 55, per Viscount Cave L.C.; also Defamation Act 1952 s.5.

(2) The second requisite is that the facts must be truly stated, that is either proved or admitted to be true, and the defender may in his defences expand and elucidate facts which the libel clearly adumbrates.[190] It is no longer necessary to prove the truth of every such fact provided that sufficient material is proved to found the comment.[191] Where the defence is based on unproven statements made on a privileged occasion, the defender must show that he has given a fair and accurate report of the occasion.[192]

(3) The third requisite of the defence of fair comment is that the comment must be upon a matter of public interest. This covers a wide field.[193] It is in the public interest that the conduct of public officials should be open to criticism,[194] but the right does not extend to criticism of their character or private conduct[195] unless their fitness for office is being questioned.

(4) The fourth requisite is that the comment on or criticism of these facts must be fair, though it has been suggested that since fairness is implicit in all the criteria and since the defence exists to preserve the freedom to express opinions, where the basic criteria are met, the scope for finding a comment is unfair is limited.[196] Normally it is for the jury to decide whether the comment was fairly and honestly made. Comments need not be reasonable, they may be couched in "vituperative or contumelious language"[197] and every latitude must be given to opinion and to prejudice.[198] The test for a theatrical review has been stated to be:

"Would any fair man, however prejudiced he may be, however exaggerated or obstinate his views, have said that which this criticism has said of the work which is criticised?"[199]

It is not for the defender to establish that the comment is an honest expression of his views,[200] rather it is for the pursuer to lead evidence to show an absence of genuine belief in the comment. This, as has been observed, is "a formidable burden for the claimant to discharge".[201] While criticism cannot be used as a cloak for mere invective or for personal imputations not arising out of the subject matter,[202] it appears that the defence will not necessarily fail on proof of malice.

---

[190] *Wheatley v Anderson*, 1927 S.C. 133 at 143, per Lord Justice Clerk Alness, and per Lord Anderson at 147–148: "The jury are entitled to know what was in a defender's mind at the time he made the comment."

[191] See Defamation Act 1952 s.6. This section does not apply if any of the allegations of fact is defamatory: *Broadway Approvals v Odhams Press* [1964] 2 Q.B. 683, and [1965] 1 W.L.R. 805 at 818, CA.

[192] *Brent Walker Group v Time Out* [1991] 2 Q.B. 33.

[193] See Walker, *The Law of Delict in Scotland* (1981), pp.846–850.

[194] *Langlands v Leng*, 1916 S.C. (HL) 102 at 106–107, per Viscount Haldane.

[195] *Gray v S.P.C.A.* (1890) 17 R. 1185 at 1200, per Lord McLaren.

[196] Reid, *Personality, Confidentiality and Privacy in Scots Law* (2010), para.11.57.

[197] *Archer v Ritchie* (1891) 18 R 719 at 727, per Lord McLaren.

[198] *Merivale v Carson* (1887) 20 Q.B.D. 275 at 280, per Lord Esher M.R. "The basis of our public life is that the crank, the enthusiast, may say what he honestly thinks just as much as the reasonable man or woman who sits on a jury": per Diplock J. in *Silkin v Beaverbrook Newspapers* [1958] 1 W.L.R. 743 at 747.

[199] *Merivale v Carson* (1887) 20 Q.B.D. 275 at 281, per Lord Esher M.R.; and see *Crotty v Macfarlane* Unreported January 27, 1891 OH (Lord Stormonth-Darling).

[200] *Telnikoff v Matusevitch* [1992] 2 A.C. 343.

[201] *Branson v Bower No. 2* [2002] QB 737 at [55], per Eady J.

[202] *McQuire v Western Morning News* [1903] 2 K.B. 100 at 109, per Collins M.R.

The position is not entirely clear in Scots law, but in England there has been subsequent approval of the following dictum of Lord Nicholls:

"Honesty of belief is the touchstone. Actuation by spite, animosity, intent to injure, intent to arouse controversy or other motivation, whatever it may be, even if it is the dominant or sole motive, does not of itself defeat the defence. However, proof of such motivation may be evidence, sometimes compelling evidence, from which lack of genuine belief in the view expressed may be inferred."[203]

Verbal injury—The courts have drawn a basic distinction between statements **29.22** which are per se or by innuendo defamatory and other false injurious statements which, while not being defamatory, are nevertheless actionable. Historically, there has been some uncertainty on the categories and precise scope of verbal injury,[204] but the only distinction with legal consequences is that between defamation and verbal injury.[205] The pursuer in verbal injury enjoys none of the presumptions operative in a defamation case. Accordingly, falsity, intent to injure and resultant injury all require to be proved.[206] It is therefore to the advantage of the pursuer if the words complained of can be construed as defamatory, but it may be open to the defender to attack relevancy if the words are not defamatory and a claim grounded on defamation ought to have been raised in verbal injury.[207] Following the more recent academic commentaries,[208] verbal injury may be considered under three headings: verbal injury affecting business; false statements with the intention of exposing the pursuer to pubic hatred, contempt and ridicule; and slander on a third party. The last category concerns injury caused by words directed at a third party. *North of Scotland Banking Co v Duncan*[209] provides authority that injury caused in this way is actionable, but there has been no Scots case in which damages have been recovered and subsequent authorities suggest that such a claim will only be admitted in narrow circumstances.[210]

Verbal injury in business context—Verbal injury affecting business may be **29.23** subdivided into: slander of title and slander of property; and falsehood about the

---

[203] *Tse Wai Chun Paul v Albert Cheng* [2001] E.M.L.R. 31 at [79].

[204] Walker, *The Law of Delict in Scotland* (1981), pp.730–740, divided verbal injury into three categories, namely, defamation, *convicium* and malicious falsehood. This may be contrasted with the treatment in T.B. Smith, *A Short Commentary on the Law of Scotland* (Edinburgh: W. Green, 1962), pp.724–732. For detailed consideration of *convicium* see Norrie, *Defamation and Related Actions in Scots Law* (1995), pp.35–38 and Reid, *Personality, Confidentiality and Privacy in Scots Law* (2010), paras 8.08–8.14.

[205] Norrie, *Defamation and Related Actions in Scots Law* (1995), p.34.

[206] *Paterson v Welch* (1893) 20 R. 744 at 749, per Lord President Robertson; *Argyllshire Weavers Ltd v A Macauley (Tweeds) Ltd*, 1965 S.L.T. 21; *Steele v Scottish Daily Record*, 1970 S.L.T. 53. The Defamation Act 1952 s.14(b) provides that in any action for verbal injury it shall not be necessary for the pursuer to aver or prove special damage if the words on which the action is founded are calculated to cause pecuniary damage to the pursuer.

[207] See R.T. Whelan's analysis in "Slander of Property: Continental Tyre Group Ltd v Robertson" (2011) 15 Edin. L.R. 437–442 of the sheriff court case *Continental Tyre Group Ltd v Robertson*, 2011 G.W.D. 14–331.

[208] Norrie, *Defamation and Related Actions in Scots Law* (1995), Ch.3; Reid, *Personality, Confidentiality and Privacy in Scots Law* (2010), Chs 6–9. See also K. Norrie, "Actions for verbal injury" (2000) 4 Edin. L.R. 390.

[209] *North of Scotland Banking Co v Duncan* (1857) 19 D. 881.

[210] *Broom v Ritchie* (1904) 6 F. 942; *Finburgh v Moss'Empires Ltd*, 1908 S.C. 928. See further Reid, *Personality, Confidentiality and Privacy in Scots Law* (2010), Ch.9.

pursuer causing business loss.[211] To cast doubt on the pursuer's right to sell goods whether on grounds of lack of ownership[212] or infringement of patent[213] is slander of title. While actions have failed because intent to injure has not been established,[214] the chief difficulty facing the pursuer is proof of specific sales opportunities lost.[215] To disparage the quality of the pursuer's property or goods is slander of property. On this basis an issue was allowed on an allegation that a row of houses was built on an insecure foundation,[216] and that typhoid fever had broken out in a dairy.[217] While damages were awarded to a merchant whose goods were described by the defender, a competitor, as "rotten and mildewed trash,"[218] it will not necessarily amount to verbal injury for a dealer to state that his article is better than that of his rival, and to give reasons for his statement, even though his reasons involve disparagement of the rival commodity.[219] Slander of title and slander of property are not exhaustive of actionable verbal injuries against businesses. Reid uses "falsehood about the pursuer causing business loss" as the residual category.[220] The leading modern case is *Steele v Scottish Daily Record and Sunday Mail Ltd*[221] in which a car dealer was accused of sharp business practices. While the court accepted both falsity and general intent to injure, the pursuer was not awarded damages for business losses, because his pleadings did not specify intent to injure his business. The case is also notable for the ruling on the pursuer's claim for solatium which he was not awarded either.

29.24 **Public hatred, contempt and ridicule**—Claims for solatium are of course more likely to arise in the final category of verbal injury, that is: false statements with the intention of exposing the pursuer to public hatred, contempt and ridicule. The formulation is taken from English law[222] and arose from attacks in the press on public figures. In the early Scots cases, *Sheriff v Wilson*[223] and *Cunningham v Phillips*,[224] it is evident that the persistence of the attacks was an important factor in the award of damages.[225] This category was brought within the general requirements for liability for verbal injury in *Paterson v Welch*[226] in which the expression of an unpopular opinion was ascribed to the pursuer resulting in an upsurge of local feeling against him and the loss of his seat at the following election. Mere ridicule, where the element of public hatred is absent, is not actionable.[227] While the ruling in *Sheriff v Wilson*, that solatium is available for verbal injury was

---

[211] See Reid, *Personality, Confidentiality and Privacy in Scots Law* (2010), Ch.7.

[212] *Philp v Morton* (1816) Hume 865.

[213] *Harpers v Greenwood & Batley* (1866) 4 S.L.T. 116; *Kennedy v Aldington* [2005] CSOH 58. There is a statutory remedy for statements threatening infringement proceedings (Patents Act 1949 s.65; Patents Act 1977 s.70, as amended by the Patents Act 2004 s.12). See *Speedcranes Ltd v Thomson*, 1972 S.C. 324.

[214] e.g. *Yeo v Wallace* (1867) 5 S.L.R. 253.

[215] See cases cited at fn.213, above both of which failed on this basis.

[216] *Bruce v Smith* (1898) 1 F. 327.

[217] *McLean v Adam* (1888) 16 R. 175. This action for damages failed for lack of intent to injure.

[218] *Hamilton v Arbuthnott* (1750) Mor 7682.

[219] *White v Mellin* [1895] A.C. 154; *Hubbuck v Wilkinson* [1899] 1 Q.B. 86.

[220] Reid, *Personality, Confidentiality and Privacy in Scots Law* (2010), paras 7.09–7.12.

[221] *Steele v Scottish Daily Record and Sunday Mail Ltd*, 1970 S.L.T. 53.

[222] See Reid, *Personality, Confidentiality and Privacy in Scots Law* (2010), para.8.17.

[223] *Sheriff v Wilson* (1855) 17 D. 528.

[224] *Cunningham v Phillips* (1868) 6 M. 926.

[225] See Reid, *Personality, Confidentiality and Privacy in Scots Law* (2010), paras 8.17–8.18.

[226] *Paterson v Welch* (1893) 20 R. 744 followed in *Waddell v Roxburgh* (1894) 21 R. 883.

[227] *McLaughlin v Orr* (1894) 22 R. 38.

affirmed in *Steele v Scottish Daily Record and Sunday Mail Ltd*, it was also held for such an award that evidence must be led to show that the public have been induced to think of the pursuer with hatred and contempt. This sets the bar for an award of solatium rather high although the pursuer in *Paterson v Welch* would presumably qualify since his effigy was burned outside his house. Finally, there have been cases of falsehood causing business loss where the courts have refused to hold employers vicariously liable for slander by employees on the basis that statements were made outwith the scope of employment.[228] It has been suggested that the reformulation of the test for vicarious liability in *Lister v Hesley Hall Ltd*[229] may make findings of vicarious liability in verbal injury more likely.[230]

Title to sue—Anyone who is defamed has title to sue, although the statement **29.25** complained of must be reasonably capable of being taken to refer to the pursuer.[231] When the injurious statement is made of a class of persons, it is a question of degree whether that class is sufficiently limited in numbers to make an imputation on the individual.[232] A defamatory statement about a deceased person does not afford any action to his representatives, unless, possibly, it can be read as amounting to a reflection on them.[233] Claims raised before death will, however, pass to the executor. [234] In England it has been held that a tort can be committed only on a body with legal personality,[235] but the rule is otherwise in Scotland where the title of voluntary associations[236] and charities[237] has been recognised. A member of an association cannot sue if the statements are comments upon the society and not upon individual action.[238] While a company or partnership can sue to protect good-will or corporate reputation,[239] it would be contrary to the public interest for organs of central or local government to have the right to sue for defamation.[240] Similarly, a political party cannot be permitted to maintain an action for defamation.[241] The position regarding trade unions is not settled.[242] Two or more persons may sue together in one action in respect of one defamatory statement alleged to refer to one or other or all of them provided that each concludes separately for damages.[243]

---

[228] *Craig v Inveresk Paper Merchants Ltd*, 1970 S.L.T. (Notes) 50; *Cameron v Young's Express Deliveries Ltd*, 1950 S.L.T. (Sh. Ct) 40.

[229] *Lister v Hesley Hall Ltd* [2002] 1 A.C. 215.

[230] Reid, *Personality, Confidentiality and Privacy in Scots Law* (2010), para.7.12.

[231] See cases discussed in Reid, *Personality, Confidentiality and Privacy in Scots Law* (2010), para.10.54.

[232] *Campbell v Ritchie*, 1907 S.C. 1097; *Browne v Thomson*, 1912 S.C. 359; *Knupffer v London Express Newspaper* [1944] A.C. 116; and see Walker, *The Law of Delict in Scotland* (1981), pp.745–748.

[233] *Broom v Ritchie* (1904) 6 F. 942; and see Walker, *The Law of Delict in Scotland* (1981), pp.750–752.

[234] Damages (Scotland) Act 2011 s.2(1)(b).

[235] *Electrical, Electronic, Telecommunication and Plumbing Union v Times Newspapers* [1980] Q.B. 585. But see Walker, *The Law of Delict in Scotland* (1981), p.749.

[236] *Highland Dancing Board v Alloa Publishing Co*, 1971 S.L.T. (Sh. Ct) 50.

[237] *Woodland Trust Ltd v Angus Macmillan* Unreported August 16, 2002 CSOH, Lord Eassie.

[238] *Campbell v Wilson*, 1934 S.L.T. 249.

[239] *Jameel v Wall St Journal Europe Sprl* [2007] 1 A.C. 359; *North of Scotland Bank v Duncan* (1857) 19 D. 881; and see cases in Reid, *Personality, Confidentiality and Privacy in Scots Law* (2010), para.10.55.

[240] *Derbyshire CC v Times Newspapers Ltd* [1993] A.C. 534.

[241] *Goldsmith v Bhoyrul* [1997] E.M.L.R. 407.

[242] See Reid, *Personality, Confidentiality and Privacy in Scots Law* (2010), para.10.57.

[243] *Mitchell v Grierson* (1894) 21 R. 367. Compare *Golden v Jeffers*, 1936 S.L.T. 388 (truly a case of a conspiracy to slander) with *Turnbull v Frame*, 1966 S.L.T. 24.

29.26 Parties liable[244]—At common law, the person who originates,[245] and the person who repeats, a defamatory statement, are equally liable in damages. In the past printers, publishers,[246] booksellers,[247] librarians[248] or broadcasters responsible for the dissemination or circulation of defamatory material have been sued, but most of these cases would now fall to be defended under s.1 of the Defamation Act 1996.[249] There is a statutory defence available to certain individuals who have innocently disseminated defamatory material.[250] The liability of an agent who publishes defamatory matter on the instructions of his principal follows that of his principal unless the agent is entitled to plead privilege in his own right.[251] The principles of vicarious liability for slander by an agent are the same as for employer and employee.[252] It is incompetent to conclude for damages jointly and severally against two or more defenders in respect of separate slanders without averments of conspiracy.[253]

29.27 Interdict—It may be possible to restrain publication of allegedly defamatory material by interdict. But it is now necessary for a court considering whether or not to grant an interim interdict to have regard to the importance of the Convention right to freedom of expression, and to whether any journalistic, literary or artistic material involved is already available to the public.[254] The court must also consider whether it would be in the public interest for any such material to be published.[255] An interim interdict cannot be granted unless the court is satisfied that the applicant is likely to succeed at proof in showing that the material should not be published.[256]

29.28 Damages[257]—A pursuer who proves that he has been defamed is *eo ipso* entitled to an award of damages, which may be nominal.[258] In addition he may recover special damages on proof that he has suffered or is likely to suffer financial loss. Patrimonial losses must be specified and quantified in the claim.[259] Where the damage stems from repetition by a third party, difficult issues of causation may

---

[244] As to the legality of an indemnity, see Defamation Act 1952 s.11. The Defamation Bill cl.9 limits the jurisdiction of courts in England and Wales to hear actions brought against persons not resident in the United Kingdom or in a Member State. This provision is not presently intended to extend to Scotland.

[245] For liability for unauthorised repetitions see *Slipper v BBC* [1991] 1 Q.B. 283.

[246] *A.B. v Blackwood* (1902) 5 F. 25.

[247] e.g. *Weldon v Times Book Co Ltd* (1911) 28 T.L.R. 143.

[248] e.g. *Vizetelly v Mudies's Select Library Ltd* [1900] 2 Q.B. 170.

[249] See para.29.10, above.

[250] Defamation Act 1996 s.1. See para.29.10, above.

[251] *Adam v Ward* [1917] A.C. 309 at 320, per Lord Finlay; and para.29.16, above, re solicitors.

[252] See para.25.10, above; note also comment on vicarious liability in verbal injury, para.29.24, above.

[253] *Hook v McCallum* (1905) 7 F. 528; *Golden v Jeffers*, 1936 S.L.T. 388; *Turnbull v Frame*, 1966 S.L.T. 24.

[254] Human Rights Act 1998 s.12(4).

[255] Human Rights Act 1998 s.12(4).

[256] Human Rights Act 1998 s.12(3). The test for likelihood of success was considered by the House of Lords in *Cream Holdings Ltd v Banerjee* [2005] 1 A.C. 253, followed in *X v BBC*, 2005 S.L.T. 796.

[257] See Reid, *Personality, Confidentiality and Privacy in Scots Law* (2010), paras 10.62–10.64.

[258] *Bradley v Menley and James*, 1913 S.C. 923 at 926, per Lord Justice Clerk Macdonald.

[259] *Hay v Institute of Chartered Accountants in Scotland*, 2003 S.L.T. 612. See Reid, *Personality, Confidentiality and Privacy in Scots Law* (2010), para.10.62; see also *Steele v Scottish Daily Record and Sunday Mail*, 1970 S.L.T. 53, para.29.23, above.

arise in relation to the liability of the original wrongdoer.[260] The quantum of solatium will vary with the circumstances and degree of affront.[261] Evidence of the circumstances of publication may aggravate the damages, for example proof of deliberate intention, recklessness or persistent repetition.[262] The failure of a plea of *veritas* may result in aggravated damages; this does not entitle the pursuer to make averments of aggravation simply on the basis of the pleaded defence.[263] Ground for mitigation, on the other hand, has been found in the fact that there was provocation to make the statement, that there was probable cause for making it, that it was common talk and that the pursuer had a bad character.[264] By the Defamation Act 1952[265] it is competent to mitigate by proving that damages have been recovered or action has been brought in respect of publication of words similar to those on which the action is based, or that the pursuer has settled or agreed to settle in respect of such a publication. Where an offer of amends has been accepted but the parties cannot agree on the amount of damages, damages will be assessed by the court on the same principles as in defamation proceedings.[266] In such assessment, the court may take into account evidence concerning the directly relevant background context of the allegations.[267] The assessment will also reflect the mitigating effect which the offer of amends and apology has already had.[268]

Expenses—Where a tender is lodged, and the damages ultimately awarded are **29.29** less than the amount tendered, the tender does not have its normal effect of entitling the defender to expenses after its date unless it is accompanied by a retraction and apology.[269] But it is sufficient to offer an apology without any admission that the statement complained of was made.[270]

Breach of confidence[271]—The publication of true information may be actionable **29.30** as a breach of confidence. An obligation of confidentiality may derive from the relationship between the parties, such as husband and wife[272] or doctor and patient,[273] or from a contract between them.[274] In such situations, disclosure of confidential information can be characterised as wrongful, and damages awarded for injury to feelings or for patrimonial loss. Where there is no such relationship,

---

[260] *McManus v Beckham* [2002] 1 W.L.R. 2982.

[261] See cases cited in Reid, *Personality, Confidentiality and Privacy in Scots Law* (2010), para.10.62.

[262] See Cooper, *The Law of Defamation and Verbal Injury* (1906), p.250; *Cunningham v Duncan* (1889) 16 R. 383.

[263] *Sarwar v News Group Newspapers Ltd*, 1999 S.L.T. 327.

[264] Cooper, *The Law of Defamation and Verbal Injury* (1906), p.254; *Corrigan v Monaghan*, 1923 S.C. 1; *Bryson v Inglis* (1844) 6 D. 363; *Hobbs v Tinling* [1929] 2 K.B. 1; *Burstein v Times Newspapers Ltd* [2001] 1 W.L.R. 579.

[265] Defamation Act 1952 s.12.

[266] Defamation Act 1996 s.3(5).

[267] *Turner v News Group Newspapers Ltd* [2006] 1 W.L.R. 3469.

[268] *Nail v News Group Newspapers Ltd* [2005] 1 All E.R. 1040. See also *Veliu v Mazrekaj* [2007] 1 W.L.R. 495: assessment of damages where one defendant had used amends procedure but other had not.

[269] *Faulks v Park* (1854) 17 D. 247. See Lord Davidson and Lord Carloway, *Green's Litigation Styles* (Edinburgh: W. Green), para.E0350.

[270] *Malcolm v Moore* (1901) 4 F. 23.

[271] For an extensive treatment see Reid, *Personality, Confidentiality and Privacy in Scots Law* (2010), Chs 12–19.

[272] *Duchess of Argyll v Duke of Argyll* [1967] Ch. 302.

[273] e.g. *Cornelius v De Taranto* [2002] E.M.L.R. 6: Doctor disclosing medical report on patient without her consent.

[274] e.g. disclosure of trade secrets by a former employee.

the question of whether the disclosure of confidential information is actionable has posed greater difficulty. Formerly, it was considered that it was necessary for the recipient of information to know that it was originally communicated in confidence before he could be liable for breach of confidence in disclosing it.[275] The existence of a prior relationship of confidentiality is no longer necessary.[276] The test for the existence of a duty of confidentiality is now that the person receiving the information knows or ought to know that the information is fairly and reasonably to be regarded as confidential.[277] Information may be regarded as confidential if the pursuer had a reasonable expectation of privacy in the circumstances.[278] It has been held in England that a claimant may fail to satisfy this test if the information is "shocking and immoral".[279] Breach of confidence has been relied on in England by celebrities wishing to prevent a magazine from publishing illicit photographs of their wedding.[280] In that case, damages were also awarded for the harm caused to the claimants' interests by being prevented from exploiting for commercial gain information about the wedding. On appeal by a rival publisher, which had contracted with the couple for the exclusive right to publish photos of the wedding, the House of Lords held that the publisher was also entitled to damages for breach of an obligation of confidentiality.[281]

29.31 Protection of privacy—Questions have also arisen as to whether there is in domestic law a broader right to claim damages for invasion of privacy. Protection of privacy is required under art.8 of the European Convention on Human Rights and the developments that have taken place in breach of confidence have served largely to protect informational privacy. Informational privacy is only one aspect of the far broader concept of privacy enshrined in art.8.[282] English law has set itself firmly against a broad tort of invasion of breach of privacy.[283] The underlying structural considerations for this approach do not apply in Scotland and it has been argued that Scots law is well equipped to develop the law in this area independently.[284] The historical influence of the *actio injuriarum* has provided the basis for actions for solatium arising from affront. One consequence of this influence is the recognition in Scots law of infringements of dignity as giving rise to remedies. This is seen clearly in the case law on assault.[285] The contrast with English law can perhaps be seen most readily by comparing *Wainwright v Home Office*,[286]an

---

[275] Lord Justice Clerk Ross in *Lord Advocate v The Scotsman Publications Ltd*, 1989 S.C. (HL) 122 at 141.

[276] *Campbell v Mirror Group Newspapers Ltd* [2004] 2 A.C. 457.

[277] *Campbell v Mirror Group Newspapers Ltd* [2004] 2 A.C. 457. See also *A. v B. Plc* [2003] Q.B. 195.

[278] See e.g. *Murray v Express Group Newspapers Plc* [2008] EWCA Civ 446; *Mosely v News Group Newspapers Ltd* [2008] EWHC 1777.

[279] *Maccaba v Lichtenstein* [2005] E.M.L.R. 6. The extent to which this proposition holds good may be questionable in the light of *Mosely v News Group Newspapers Ltd* [2008] EWHC 1777.

[280] *Douglas v Hello! Ltd (No.6)* [2006] Q.B. 125.

[281] *Douglas v Hello! Ltd (No.7)* [2007] 2 W.L.R. 920.

[282] For discussion see Reid, *Personality, Confidentiality and Privacy in Scots Law* (2010), paras 17.01–17.09.

[283] *Campbell v Mirror Group Newspapers* [2004] 2 A.C. 457, per Lord Nicholls at [11].

[284] See Reid, *Personality, Confidentiality and Privacy in Scots Law* (2010), paras 17.15–17.17; N.R. Whitty, "Rights of Personality, Property Rights and the Human Body in Scots Law" (2005) 9 Edin. L.R. 194; N. Whitty and R. Zimmermann (eds), *Rights of Personality in Scots Law: A Comparative Perspective* (Dundee: Dundee University Press, 2009).

[285] e.g. *Beaton v Drysdale* (1818) 2 Mur 151; *Tullis v Glenday* (1834) 13 S. 698; *Ewing v Earl of Mar* (1851) 14 D. 314.

[286] *Wainwright v Home Office* [2004] A.C. 406.

English appeal concerning the strip searching of visitors to prison, in which the House of Lords confirmed that no actionable wrong had taken place, with *Henderson v Chief Constable of Fife Police*[287] in which damages were awarded for an unjustified infringement of the pursuer's liberty when police officers removed the brassiere of a striking laboratory worker taken into police custody. The crucial difference between the jurisdictions is that the English approach requires recognition of a new tort and this is believed to be beyond judicial competence.[288] Remedies in Scotland have never depended upon causes of action and expansion of the ambit of civil liability requires no more than judicial recognition of invasion of privacy as a wrong.[289] Protection of privacy is, arguably, an aspect of protection of dignity[290] and so no quantum leap would be required to secure protection against infringements of privacy within the broader field of recognised personality rights. There is debate about the way in which the law should be developed.[291] It has been suggested that the *actio iniuriarum* serves as an available model for development,[292] and certainly it continues to be invoked in legal argument,[293] but this view has been countered on a number of grounds.[294] Whereas liability under the *actio injuriarum* depends on *animus injuriandi* it has been suggested that adequate protection of privacy in modern circumstances may require a balancing of lawful, but conflicting, interests and, moreover, that liability for negligent infringements should also be contemplated.[295]

FURTHER READING

Collins, M., *The Law of Defamation and the Internet*, 3rd edn (Oxford: Oxford University Press, 2010).

Cooper, F.T., *The Law of Defamation and Verbal Injury*, 2nd edn (Edinburgh: W. Green, 1906).

Milmo, P. et al, *Gatley on Libel and Slander*, 11th edn (London: Sweet and Maxwell, 2010).

Norrie, K., *Defamation and Related Actions in Scots Law* (Butterworths Law, 1995).

Reid, E., *Personality, Confidentiality and Privacy in Scots Law* (Edinburgh: W. Green, 2010).

Walker, D.M., *The Law of Delict in Scotland*, 2nd edn (Edinburgh: W. Green, 1981), Chs 23 and 24, and pp.902–7.

Whitty, N. and Zimmermann, R. (eds), *Rights of Personality in Scots Law: A Comparative Perspective* (Dundee: Dundee University Press, 2009).

---

[287] *Henderson v Chief Constable of Fife Police*, 1988 S.L.T. 361.

[288] See Reid, *Personality, Confidentiality and Privacy in Scots Law* (2010), para.17.15.

[289] See paras 25.03–25.04, above.

[290] See Reid, *Personality, Confidentiality and Privacy in Scots Law* (2010), para.17.05.

[291] See generally, Whitty and Zimmermann (eds), *Rights of Personality in Scots Law: A Comparative Perspective* (2009).

[292] Notably by Whitty, "Rights of Personality, Property Rights and the Human Body in Scots Law" (2005) 9 Edin. L.R. 194.

[293] e.g. *Ward v Scotrail Railways Ltd*, 1999 S.C. 255; *Martin v McGuiness*, 2003 S.L.T. 1424; *Hardey v Russel and Aitken*, 2003 G.W.D. 2–50; *Stevens v Yorkhill NHS Trust*, 2006 S.L.T. 889.

[294] See Reid, *Personality, Confidentiality and Privacy in Scots Law* (2010), para.17.12.

[295] See Reid, *Personality, Confidentiality and Privacy in Scots Law* (2010), paras 17.13–17.14.

PART III

PROPERTY

SECTION A
REAL RIGHTS

CHAPTER 30

PROPERTY: GENERAL MATTERS

Property and ownership—The law of property is concerned with proprietary **30.01** rights, a class of right denoting some form of overriding entitlement relationship—ownership being the primary form—with anything classed as property.[1] The label "real rights" is applied to this wide and diverse class of rights in different forms of property.[2] A real right, having a proprietary character, is different in kind from a personal right, characterised by a relationship factor. In *Burnett's Trustee v Grainger* Lord Rodger of Earlsferry refers to an "unbridgeable division".[3] The distinction is sometimes made by saying that a real right is available against the whole world whereas a personal right is available only against the party concerned. However, this difference follows from the fundamental difference between, on the one hand, a right in and to a thing and, on the other, a right against only a particular person.[4] In simplest terms the difference is that between property and a claim. Ownership is the ultimate real right in the sense of being the most comprehensive right. However, the exclusivity aspect—rather than comprehensiveness—protected by legal remedy makes ownership a real right, in common with other more limited, or more specific, real rights—e.g. a real right of security or one of servitude or lease.[5]

An important difference between real and personal rights, going to the essence of property, is that the former is an established category to which new forms can be added only through recognition by the law. To this extent, the civilian closed list label (*numerus clausus*) is apposite but should not obscure the truth that the category does change—demonstrated in recent identification of a class of "personal real burdens".[6] The category of personal rights, on the other hand, is open ended at least in the sense that persons have wide freedom to determine the form of their contractual relationships within the controlling position of the law. On the basis of this difference it has been observed that "[f]reedom of contract is not matched by freedom of property".[7]

---

[1] See para.30.02, below.

[2] See para.1.09, above.

[3] *Burnett's Trustee v Grainger*, 2004 S.C. (HL) 19 at [87]; Lord Rodger adopted this label from a modern classic of Roman Law (B. Nicholas, *An Introduction to Roman Law* (Oxford: Oxford University Press, 1996), p.100).

[4] See para.1.09, above.

[5] K.G.C. Reid, *The Law of Property in Scotland* (Edinburgh: Butterworths, 1996), para.5 lists the main real rights.

[6] See R. Paisley, "Personal Real Burdens", 2005 Jur. Rev. 377.

[7] K.G.C. Reid and C.G. van der Merwe, "Property Law: Some Themes and Some Variations" in R. Zimmermann, D. Visser and K.G.C. Reid, *Mixed Legal Systems in Comparative Perspective: Property and Obligations in Scotland and South Africa* (Oxford: Oxford University Press, 2005), p.654.

Rational analysis, recognised in civil law and accepted by Scottish writers, characterises ownership in terms of constituent rights of use (*usus*), fruits (*fructus*) and consumption or disposal (*abusus*). Erskine speaks of "the right of using and disposing of a thing as our own".[8] The scope of the totality of rights of an owner lends itself to the possibility of lesser rights, nonetheless real, being hived off but leaving the core right of ownership intact. A common example of this, frequently applied to facilitate acquisition of heritable (or "immoveable") property, is the granting by an owner of a standard security giving a creditor party a real right in the property concerned functioning to secure, as a matter of priority, the creditor's interest. The right of disposal—seen as the essential core of ownership[9]—is not, in principle, curtailed but while the standard security subsists, disposition can only be subject to it. In practice, this means that disposition is usually not possible until the debtor landowner has obtained from the creditor a termination of the standard security.

The comprehensiveness of the right of ownership means that it is open to extensive fragmentation. It is generally true, especially regarding land, that property is owned subject to the application and exercise of many and various forms of right reflecting the complexities of social need. Accordingly, a given property may be subject to a range of real rights held by persons other than the owner. In addition to the familiar established forms of real right such as liferent, security and servitude, the law, for policy reasons, from time to time, creates new forms of fragmentation by the recognition of rights which have the character of real rights in terms of their implications for the relevant core right of ownership. An important example is occupancy rights in a matrimonial home.[10] Recent examples of policy-based revision of aspects of ownership rights can be found in the according of general public rights of access to land[11] and in the radical community right to buy legislation in terms of the Land Reform (Scotland) Act 2003.[12]

Ownership and possession of property is frequently subject to controlling limitations and restrictions. It is trite that rights only exist in a legal context which controls the scope. In general the limits and restrictions applying to property rights exist as a "given" in the sense that a particular right—e.g. ownership of a motor vehicle—is necessarily subject to whatever controls and limits the law applies and, of course, this is open to revision.

As indicated, the constituent rights of ownership may be accorded to different parties on the basis of the breakdown recognised by law. The classic position is, on the one hand, ownership (*dominium*); on the other hand, real rights held by others (*jurae in re aliena*) in the property concerned.[13] For example: A is owner of

---

[8] Erskine, II, 2, 1; see *Anstruther v Anstruther* (1836) 14 S. 272 at 286.

[9] See Stair, II, 1, Pr: the "power of disposal of things in their substance, fruits or use." Bankton, II, 1, 6 notes that while the notion of a thing being "one's own" is "inherent in" the power of disposal the exercise of this power may be curtailed because of disability. Bell, *Commentaries*, I, 177 links exclusivity and power of disposal: "Correctly speaking, property imports dominium—the entire and exclusive dominion over the thing spoken of—the proprietor being the dominus and having the sole disposal of it."

[10] See s.1 of the Matrimonial Homes (Family Protection) (Scotland) Act 1981 and para.44.17, below. Parallel provision for same-sex couples is made under the Civil Partnerships Act 2004 s.101.

[11] See Pt 1 ("Access Rights"; ss.1–32) of the Land Reform (Scotland) Act 2003. In *Tuley v Highland Council*, 2009 S.C. 456; 2009 S.L.T. 616 at [17] the Court of Session analysed the core "responsible exercise" aspect of the access right.

[12] See Pt 2 ("The Community Right to Buy"; ss.33–67) of the Land Reform (Scotland) Act 2003. See M.M. Combe, "Parts 2 and 3 of the Land Reform (Scotland) Act 2003: a definitive answer to the Scottish land question?", 2006 Jur. Rev. 195.

[13] See Reid, *The Law of Property in Scotland* (1996), para.6.

Northbrae; B, as owner of adjacent Southbrae, has a real right of servitude giving access to the public road; the C bank's capital loan to A is secured by a real right of standard security over Northbrae. This sort of division on the basis of recognised constituent rights is commonplace. In a different sense, the right of ownership itself is indivisible in that there is only one concept of ownership. This position was confirmed in the House of Lords decision in *Burnett's Trustee v Grainger*[14] which proceeded on the basis of the Court of Session decision in *Sharp v Thomson*[15] in which the Lord President (Hope) adopted Professor Reid's statement that:

> "Scots law, following Roman law, is unititular, which means that only one title of ownership is recognised in any one thing at any one time."

The significance of the unititular character of ownership is that Scots law does not recognise any concept of beneficial or equitable ownership as a real right.[16]

While ownership, as a concept, is indivisible, the right may, of course, be held by more than one person at the same time. But "[t]wo different persons cannot have each of them the full property of the same thing at the same time".[17] As shown, however, lesser real rights in a given entity of property necessarily involve a co-existence with the parent right of property held by one person and the lesser, derived right, by another.

Trust law, it may be noted, has particular specialised implications for ownership. In the civilian property model, as represented by Scots law, the trust concept is accommodated by compromise because it does not readily fit into the essential position of rights as either real or personal; rather, the trust has its fundamental roots in English legal development in which "in-between" rights with proprietary quality are recognised. The 2009 Draft Common Frame of Reference ("DCFR")[18] model[19] has been a focus of the trust debate[20] in Scots law and other systems which know only one form of ownership.

The right of a trust beneficiary resembles a real right[21] and, of course, this is significant for the ownership of the trustee. Strictly, however, in terms of the unitary ownership of Scots law, the beneficiary's right can only be personal.[22] As Lord Coulsfield observed in the First Division decision in *Sharp v Thomson*[23]

> "it has always been evident that there is some difficulty in reconciling the concept of a trust with the principle of the unity of ownership".

---

[14] *Burnett's Trustee v Grainger*, 2004 S.C. (HL) 19.

[15] *Sharp v Thomson*, 1995 S.C. 455 at 469.

[16] Except, anomalously, in the context of a floating charge to the extent that the specific decision in *Sharp v Thomson*, 1997 S.C. (HL) 66 was not overruled by *Burnett's Tr. v Grainger*, 2004 S.C. (HL) 19. The judges in *Burnett's Tr.* reached their conclusion by distinguishing *Sharp v Thomson*, thereby erecting a cordon sanitaire around that case.

[17] Erskine, II, 1.

[18] See below, para.30.07.

[19] DCFR, X.

[20] See S. Swann, K.G.C. Reid, B. McFarlane, A. Braun and S. Van Erp, "Symposium" (2011) 15 Edin. L.R. 462–482.

[21] Reid, *The Law of Property in Scotland* (1996), para.10.

[22] See para.1.12, above and generally, G.L. Gretton, "Trusts" in K.G.C. Reid and R. Zimmermann, *A History of Private Law in Scotland* (Oxford: Oxford University Press, 2000), I, 480 at pp.482–484. See further below, Ch.41(I), "Trusts".

[23] *Sharp v Thomson*, 1995 S.C. 455 at 502.

The position appears to reflect a particular development of trust law rather than an application of the general law of property as in English law. Because the trust dispensation is, in effect, a ring-fenced position, trusts must be specifically created and there is no scope for the open-ended concept of constructive trust of English law.[24] In terms of the structure of the law it is appropriate to think of the trust as a facilitation device functioning alongside the system of property law rather than within it.

It is worth noting that property law very much reflects the historical continuity of the law of Scotland as a whole with centuries of native growth of roots deep in European legal development. Aspects of the system may have been subject to major change or adjustment to meet new policy priorities but the essential functioning features of the system largely remain in place. Lord Rodger's reference to a classic modern textbook of Roman law (noted above[25]) to explain how "Scots law distinguishes between real rights, rights in rem, and personal rights, rights in personam"[26] illustrates the point.

30.02 Classification of property—Property law operates at different levels of relevance. It exists, first, as a body of principle generally applicable to different forms of property. Secondly, property law is concerned with the controlling legal position relevant to particular categories of property; an obvious example is the law specific to "conveyancing" —the transfer of real rights in heritable property. Both at its general and particular levels property law may have a distinct role within a particular legal context—succession and insolvency are obvious examples of this contextual function.

Certain aspects of law have implications for property but are not part of property in the central sense of property law. The law of contract and that of property frequently come together in the context of derivative acquisition but even where the entire process is dealt with in a consolidated code there has to be a distinction between the two aspects because in the context of a controlling distinction between personal and real rights it must be possible to determine the point in time at which property passes.[27]

"Property" for the purposes of the law includes entities which have no physical existence but are identifiable as property in the sense of being definable units involving some interest open to ownership and disposal. From the point of view of coming into the scope of property law, the criterion of being open to disposal applies equally to items without a physical existence.

In the classification of property—or "the classification of things"[28]—there are two primary bases of distinction: corporeal/incorporeal and heritable/moveable. The former is the natural distinction, recognised by the law, between things with a physical existence and entities with no physical existence; the latter is a legal distinction based on the obvious natural difference between immoveable land— with its central role and significance to any nation state—and moveable things. These two distinct bases of differentiation give the four discreet categories of corporeal heritage; corporal moveable; incorporeal heritage; and incorporeal

---

[24] *Sharp v Thomson*, 1995 S.C. 455 at 512.

[25] See fn.3.

[26] *Burnett's Trustee v Grainger*, 2004 S.C. (HL) 19 at [87].

[27] This dichotomy is present in the Sale of Goods Act 1979; even though the transaction is consolidated in the sense that a "sale" is a contract under which property in goods is transferred from seller to buyer (s.2(4)) there is detailed provision in ss.17 and 18 to determine when property passes.

[28] See para.1.11, above.

moveable. These branches are fundamental to the structure of property law but, of course, may be significant for the substance of particular areas of law—including property law itself. Differences may be because of inherent factors, as in criminal law where, for example, the unlawful taking of incorporeal property is necessarily subject to different provision from that applying to corporeal moveable property. Differences may also derive from policy, as in property law where, for example, distinct policy considerations justify different forms of transmission of property rights, as in the difference between the formal process applicable to heritable property and the much simpler type of system applicable to corporeal moveables.

This work's general coverage aims to give a succinct account of the law applying to the usual forms of property: land and other forms of heritable property; corporeal moveables and the main forms of incorporeal property. There are also chapters on the real rights of lease and security.

Heritable/moveable distinction—The universally recognised distinction between **30.03** immoveable and moveable property, based on the natural difference between land and moveable things, has not been directly represented in the development of Scots law in which the relevant distinction has been between heritable and moveable property. What historically passed to an heir was the defining factor in terminology, of reduced relevance in modern law[29] and sometimes seen as anomalous.[30] Stair[31] explains the basis of the technical distinction in succession but at the same time identifies the fundamental basis of the immoveable/moveable division.

While the heritable/moveable terminology may seem dated it reflects the pervasive historical continuity factor of Scots law. The distinction's primary general significance lies in differences which may be applicable depending upon whether property is heritable or moveable and it remains a factor in succession, conveyancing, diligence, bankruptcy and questions of jurisdiction.[32] It may be relevant to what the law prescribes or requires in particular contexts; less frequently, the distinction determines the legal outcome in a particular context. An example of the former is that a real right in heritable property can only be transmitted by registration whereas property in a moveable can be transferred without formality, An example of the latter is that the "legal rights" of succession to which spouses and children are entitled apply only to a deceased's moveable estate.[33]

Bell[34] noted three bases relevant to identifying items of property as heritable or moveable: nature, connection and destination. On the basis of the primary, and usually straightforward, nature factor, a farm or a tenement flat is heritable property whereas a necklace or a horse is moveable. The criterion of connection is applicable where the issue is whether entities are separate or attached so that the lesser accedes to the greater on the basis of the principle of accession. The most common incidence of this classification issue arises in the context of whether the separate identity of a moveable thing has been subsumed in accession to a building

---

[29] See Reid, *The Law of Property in Scotland* (1996), para.13: "little now turns on the distinction".

[30] W.M. Gordon and S. Wortley, *Scottish Land Law*, 3rd edn (Edinburgh: W. Green, 2009), Ch.1 ("Heritable and Immoveable Property") provides a comprehensive examination of this issue; para.1–01 points out while the distinction may seem unsatisfactory—heritable being a matter of law, moveable of nature—the problem is essentially one of nomenclature.

[31] Stair, II, 1, 2.

[32] See Gordon and Wortley, *Scottish Land Law* (2009), paras 1–25—1–54.

[33] See below, para.38.08.

[34] Bell, *Principles*, s.1470.

to which it is attached. The frequently occurring question of fixtures will be dealt with in Ch.31. The factor of destination is conceptually associated with accession but involves an association of things, such as the door-keys to a house or flat, rather than a physical joining. Destination in this simple sense of a moveable which belongs with heritable property is unexceptional. A more problematic application, which will not be pursued here, is in the context of succession. The concept applies on the basis of a deceased, by so intending, being taken to have caused moveable things to be converted to and so pass with heritable assets.[35]

30.04 Allodial/feudal distinction—This distinction is concerned with the concept of ownership as, on the one hand, a right in principle absolute (allodial) and, on the other hand, a right held in principle subject to the ultimate right of a superior (feudal). This "double system of jurisprudence"[36] prevailed for much of the development of the law. Until the twenty-first century feudal reform legislation[37] the distinction between allodial and feudal tenure was largely synonymous with the moveable/heritable distinction.[38] The demise of the feudal system made allodial tenure the predominant form and resulted in "an enormous simplification of the structure of Scottish land law."[39]

A residual instance of the feudal factor remains in the principle that moveable things once but no longer owned vest in the Crown.[40]

30.05 Corporeal/incorporeal distinction—Elaborating on the above introduction to this distinction, things with a physical existence, open to physical possession, whether heritable or moveable, are designated "corporeal" because they have body (*corpus*) in the sense of physical existence. As Lord Kinnear noted in an early twentieth-century case:

> "*Res corporales* are . . . physical things which can be touched; and *res incorporales* are things which do not admit of being handled, but consist *in jure*, and so are more property rights than subjects".[41]

Entities which in their essence[42] do not have a physical existence character but are nonetheless items of property in the sense of being definable units open to disposition and protection as property are "incorporeal" for the purposes of this distinction.

While the basic distinction is straightforward the matter becomes more complex concerning whether incorporeal property is heritable or moveable. As with the

---

[35] See Reid, *The Law of Property in Scotland* (1996), para.15.

[36] Bell, *Principles*, s.636.

[37] The Abolition of Feudal Tenure (Scotland) Act 2000 came into effect on November 28, 2004. See, generally, K.G.C. Reid, *The Abolition of Feudal Tenure in Scotland* (LexisNexis UK, 2003).

[38] See the dictum of Lord Rodger, quoting Craig (*Jus Feudale*, 1.9.25), in *Burnett's Trustee v Grainger*, 2004 S.C. (HL) 19 at [86].

[39] Gordon and Wortley, *Scottish Land Law* (2009), para.2–02.

[40] See below, para.31.04.

[41] *Burghead Harbour Co Ltd v George* (1906) 8 F. 982 at 996. This dictum alludes to a longstanding debate deriving from the unnecessary difficulty of distinguishing a proprietary interest, whether in a physical or non-physical thing, which may be owned and disposed of, and a mere derived right, naturally incorporeal, which may exist in either form of property.

[42] The law requires incorporeal heritable rights and certain incorporeal moveable rights to be constituted by written deed—a right of standard security and an endowment insurance policy are respective examples—but the essence of such entities is not the deed or document but the incorporeal right or entitlement.

distinction applied to corporeal property, some consideration, whether to do with entitlement or process, may turn on this issue.

A certain limited group of rights are heritable on the basis of their connection with land and all others are moveable. The general rule is that rights are heritable or moveable according to the nature of the subject matter. As stated, the most important general category of heritable incorporeals is that of rights connected with or affecting land—servitudes, the right of standard security, leases and other real rights in land.[43] A right of freshwater fishing is heritable.[44] A second general class of heritable incorporeals comprises those rights which are unconnected with land but yield a periodic benefit or interest. This somewhat anomalous classification, identified by Erskine as having "a degree of resemblance to feudal rights"[45] includes pension and annuity rights and personal bonds. In post-feudal law the rational basis can only be the character of a fund producing annual or periodic profits or benefits as somehow analogous to profits which may arise from heritable property.[46] An intrinsically logical form of heritable incorporeal property is goodwill associated with business premises rather than the trader's reputation, it being a question of circumstances whether the goodwill of a business is so connected with the premises in which it is carried on as to be heritable or otherwise.[47]

Incorporeal property which is not heritable must be moveable; this extensive and diverse category includes rights and interests which arise from debt, contract or delict, aliment, insurance, shares, copyright and so on.[48] Even claims for indemnification against the loss of, or damage to, heritable property are moveable.[49] Shares in companies[50] and the interest of a partner in a firm and its property, are moveable, although the property may include heritable subjects.[51]

But the extensive scope of the general notion of incorporeal property only underlines the importance of the distinction between real rights and claims.[52]

Cultural property—The identification of property as "cultural" does not reflect **30.06** a traditional classification but it is one of increasing prominence. This is acknowledged in a 2010 Scottish Law Commission Discussion Paper which considers whether the law of prescription should provide specially for cultural property.[53]

---

[43] See Reid, *The Law of Property in Scotland* (1996), para.14.

[44] See the Salmon and Freshwater Fisheries (Consolidation) (Scotland) Act 2003 s.66: "Notwithstanding any rule of law to the contrary, any contract entered into in writing for a consideration and for a period of not less than a year whereby an owner of land to which a right of fishing for freshwater fish in any inland waters pertains or the occupier of such a right authorises another person to so fish shall be deemed to be a lease to which the Leases Act 1449 (c.6) applies, and the right of fishing so authorised shall, for the purposes of succession to that right, be deemed to be heritable property."

[45] Erskine, II, 1, 6.

[46] See Reid, *The Law of Property in Scotland* (1996), paras 13 and 14.

[47] *Muirhead's Trs v Muirhead* (1905) 7 F. 496; see para.32.11, below.

[48] See, generally, Ch.32, below.

[49] *Heron v Espie* (1856) 18 D. 917 at 951; *Caledonian Ry v Watt* (1875) 2 R. 917; *Kelvinside Estate Co v Donaldson's Trs* (1879) 6 R. 995.

[50] Companies Act 2006 s.541; *Hog v Hog* (1791) Mor.5479.

[51] Partnership Act 1890 s.22; *Lord Advocate v Macfarlane's Trs* (1893) 31 S.L.R. 357; *Murray v Murray* (1805) Mor., "Heritable and Moveable", App. No.4; *Minto v Kirkpatrick* (1833) 11 S. 632; see also *Irvine v Irvine* (1851) 13 D. 1267.

[52] See Reid, *The Law of Property in Scotland* (1996), para.11: ". . . a more fruitful subdivision of incorporeal property is often into real rights and personal rights."

[53] Scottish Law Commission, *Prescription and Title to Moveable Property* (HMSO, 2010), Scot. Law Com. No.144, para.4.1. See also now Scottish Law Commission, *Report on Prescription and Title to Moveable Property* (HMSO, 2012), Scot. Law Com. No.228, paras 3.12–3.20.

The label is a problematic one in certain respects. A general notion of cultural property does not fit the structure of the law because it applies to both moveable and heritable property. More significantly, the identification of property as cultural is meaningless unless that factor brings with it special legal provision.[54] The general private law, the primary focus of this work, deals with what might be identified as "cultural property"—works of art, antiquities—on the basis of the law applicable to corporeal moveable property in general. Finds of treasure[55] may well be cultural property. The common law which vests property in finds in the Crown happens to be appropriate to the protection of cultural property for the benefit of the public; but its feudal basis is an accident of history not reflecting cultural property policy.

Heritable property may be "cultural" and this is seen in controls and limitations to which ownership is subject, as in the case of listed buildings.[56] But, of course, instances of this represent only another possible domestic policy reason for controlling rights in land and, to this extent, the label is of limited significance. The position in respect of "cultural objects" is different. Because these can be taken from one jurisdiction to another, possibly arising from or part of an illegal act, a body of trans-national law and convention provision has built up with potential implications for domestic law. A factor promoting the difficult process of development of international norms is the *lex situs* rule which most private international law systems apply to the classification of property and the transfer of corporeal movables.[57] Jurisdictions which favour the title position of a good faith purchaser may give scope to "title laundering" in respect of things wrongfully removed from another jurisdiction.[58] Generally recognised norms in respect of objects of cultural significance tend to promote domestic law reform, as we see, at least in embryonic form, in the SLC Discussion Paper referred to. Anti-seizure legislation confers protection from seizure and forfeiture on certain cultural objects brought into the United Kingdom from overseas for public display.[59] These factors justify the "cultural property" or "cultural objects" label.

Perhaps most significant in respect of cultural objects is the factor of EU law and international convention provisions. The former is represented by a Directive on the return of Cultural Objects Removed from the Territory of a Member State.[60] The Directive is given effect to in UK law by the Return of Cultural Objects Regulations 1994.[61] Only a bare outline can be given here.[62] A "cultural object" is something classified as a national treasure of artistic, historic or archaeological value provided that it belongs to a category listed in the annex to the directive or is part of a public collection listed in the inventory of a museum, archive, library or ecclesiastical institution. The relevant annex covers an extensive and diverse

---

[54] See J.M. Carruthers, *The Transfer of Property in the Conflict of Laws* (Oxford: Oxford University Press, 2005), para.5.42: "... items of cultural property effectively lose their privileged status when they enter private law commercial channels."

[55] See para.31.05, below.

[56] See, e.g., the Planning (Listed Buildings and Conservation Areas) (Scotland) Act 1997.

[57] See Carruthers, *The Transfer of Property in the Conflict of Laws* (2005), paras 5.34 and 5.48.

[58] See, e.g. the English case of *Winkworth v Christie Mason and Woods Ltd* [1980] Ch. 496.

[59] Tribunals, Courts and Enforcement Act 2007 Pt 6.

[60] Directive 93/7/EEC of the Council on the return of cultural objects unlawfully removed from the territory of a Member State (1993) OJ L074, as amended by Directives 96/100/EC and 2001/38/EC.

[61] Return of Cultural Objects Regulations 1994 (SI 1994/501) as amended by the Return of Cultural Objects (Amendment) Regulations (SI 1997/1719) and the Return of Cultural Objects (Amendment) Regulations (SI 2001/3972).

[62] See Carruthers, *The Transfer of Property in the Conflict of Laws* (2005), paras 5.31, 32.

range of objects. Without displacing a possible legal remedy the directive provides for restoration to the state from which the thing was unlawfully removed regardless of the legal position and subject only to a deprived bona fide possessor having a right to compensation.

In 2002 the United Kingdom acceded to the UNESCO Convention on the Means of Prohibiting and Preventing the Illicit Import, Export and Transfer of Ownership of Cultural Property 1970. The Convention model, while different in details of scope and application, provides for an essentially similar approach to the subsequent EU Directive but, of course, on an international basis. UK accession was subject to a declaration specifically retaining the application of existing limitation rules. This leaves the Scottish position uncertain and that situation will prevail until the Convention is incorporated into municipal law.[63]

In this context it is important to mention the DCFR[64] which makes special provision for the positive prescription of cultural property as defined in the EU Directive. Extended periods of 30 years, presupposing good faith, and, otherwise, 50 years are provided for.[65]

Sources and integrity—Scots property law is mixed in terms of its external **30.07** sources; on the one hand, feudal law and, on the other, civil law—in the varied forms of its protracted European development—are the most significant sources of influence.[66] But the external sources are no more than ingredients in an extended continuity of domestic development.[67]

The feudal and civilian elements were prominent in the respective development of land law and moveable property. As a consequence of the Abolition of Feudal Tenure etc (Scotland) Act 2000, which came into effect on November 28, 2004, the formal vestiges of a feudal form of land tenure were finally excised. With origins in Anglo-Norman law a distinctive feudal model of landholding developed in Scotland and prevailed in pervasive form until the nineteenth century.[68] Both the development and decline of the feudal factor, in its long evolution until recent times, is a history of more or less continuous change.[69] But despite the prominence of feudalism, in the development of the law Romanist thinking and concepts were influential to the extent that in significant respects the law came to be unmistakably civilian.[70] The most recent major adjustment in the long and active development of land law has removed all residual aspects of the feudal structure leaving a modern civilian derived property law. The straightforward position, in the very much less active development of corporeal moveable property, is one of predominant Romanist models and thinking applied in a development which retains

---

[63] See Scottish Law Commission, *Prescription and Title to Moveable Property*, paras 4.15 and 4.16.

[64] See paras 30.01, above and 30.07, below.

[65] DCFR VIII.-4:101–102.

[66] See generally K.G.C. Reid, "Property Law: Sources and Development" in Reid and Zimmermann, *A History of Private Law in Scotland* (2000), I, 185.

[67] See Reid, "Property Law: Sources and Development", para.196: "It should not be supposed that the law of property in Scotland was simply an amalgam of the laws of other countries. On the contrary, there was much that was home-made, and even foreign importations had a tendency to acquire native features."

[68] Reid, "Property Law: Sources and Development", para.188.

[69] For the best modern account see G.L. Gretton, "Trusts" in Reid, *The Law of Property in Scotland* (1996), paras 41–113.

[70] The process of transfer of ownership being an important example; see D.L. Carey Miller, "Transfer of Ownership" in Reid and Zimmermann, *A History of Private Law in Scotland* (2000), I, 269.

certain distinctive Scottish features. The decline of a feudal factor and the concomitant ascendancy of a civilian model in land law has given scope, or greater scope, for an assimilation, not, of course, in the necessarily different details of particular provision but in terms of the broad controlling principles of the heritable and moveable sides of the subject.

In an age of European legal harmonisation projects the civilian orientation of Scottish property has been noted. The Scottish reporter team in a recent publication project commented that while the private law of Scotland was generally "mixed", for the most part the property law is "resolutely civilian and shares far more in common with the legal systems of continental Europe than with England."[71] One consequences of this affinity is that sources developed with a view to possible future European harmonisation may have particular potential in the development of the law of Scotland. The 2009 DCFR,[72] cited in the previous section, is the most significant example.

30.08 Co-ownership—While ownership is indivisible in the sense of there being only one model and no possibility of differing forms, the right itself, or one or more of its possible constituent rights, may, of course, be held by more than one party at the same time. Put another way, any number of parties may hold a given entity of property, or be entitled to a given proprietary right, in undivided shares—pro-indiviso. It is aptly said that:

"[t]he defining characteristic of pro-indiviso ownership is that a single thing is held by two or more people as an undivided whole, and without particular parts of the thing being individually attributed."[73]

Of course co-ownership could not be ownership if it did not allow a right of disposal. This is implicit in Bell's[74] description of co-ownership as a general concept:

"Common property is a right of ownership vested pro indiviso in two or more persons . . . Although the whole cannot be disposed of otherwise than by mutual consent, each joint owner may sell his own pro indiviso right."[75]

On the basis of ownership being a unitary concept the law does not recognise, in any general sense, the possibility of any alternative form of "ownership" with features departing from the norm.[76] As distinct—on a correct analysis —from

---

[71] See D.L. Carey Miller, M.M. Combe, A. Steven and S. Wortley, "National Report on the Transfer of Movables in Scotland" in W. Faber and B. Lurger (eds), *National Reports on the Transfer of Movables in Europe II* (Sellier European Law Publishers, 2009), p.312.

[72] *Principles, Definitions and Model Rules of European Private Law: Draft Common Frame of Reference*, prepared by the Study Group on a European Civil Code and the Research Group on EC Private Law (Acquis Group) and edited by C. Von Bar, E. Clive and H. Schulte-Nölke; published by Sellier in 2009 in six volumes (the DCFR text and full comparative commentary) and an outline volume with the DCFR text alone. For an overview see W. Faber, "Book VIII of the DCFR: overview of content and methodology" (2010) 14 Edin. L.R. 498.

[73] Reid, *The Law of Property in Scotland* (1996), para.17.

[74] Bell, *Principles*, s.1072.

[75] DCFR VIII–1:203 provides for co-ownership in which "two or more co-owners own undivided shares in the whole goods and each co-owner can dispose of that co-owner's share by acting alone unless otherwise provided by the parties."

[76] Since *Burnett's Trustee*, 2004 S.C. (HL) 19 this cannot be in doubt.

ownership in common (true co-ownership) the law recognises the different concept of joint property. Unfortunately a mid-twentieth century decision applied the terminology of English law[77] implying assimilation with that system of co-ownership and joint ownership as alternative forms of common ownership. In fact joint ownership is a specialised concept of limited application. In particular contexts it provides for the joint holding of a proprietary unit without power of disposal by the joint holders. The situation of trustees holding trust property—which is retained intact regardless of changes in the group of persons holding—is the classic instance of joint ownership. In the joint ownership form an "owner's" position and interest is a specialised one not reflecting the normal and general position of ownership as represented in ownership in common which, on any proper analysis, is the only true form of co-ownership.[78]

Possession—Possession, like ownership, is a general concept but one with partic- **30.09** ular implications in the different forms of property. While the essence of ownership is the abstract factor of "title"—i.e. a state of having the requisite legally recognised entitlement, associated with some process of acquisition—the essential feature of possession is the physical holding or control of a thing for some intended purpose. Hence Stair's wide definition: "holding or detaining of any thing by ourselves, or others for our use".[79]

The fact of possession (as opposed to the right of possession) of a corporeal thing, whether heritable or moveable, involves occupation or physical holding on the basis of an intention to hold or control the thing. These are the respective *corpus* and *animus* elements. Both are required because the essential physical holding or control[80] aspect cannot be a bare or colourless state of detention but must have some basis. The *animus* aspect is wide and open because it reflects any of the whole range of bases, lawful or otherwise, under which a thing may be held. Frequently *animus* can be inferred from the circumstances under which the thing is held. In the case of a hired car one would assume possession by the hirer for the limited purpose of the contract. In the case of an old chair left by the previous owner of a house and used as furniture by the new owner one would assume possession involving the assertion of a right of ownership.

Possession may be seen as a wide concept covering a range of situations from detention for some limited purpose to holding on the basis of a justifiable assertion of ownership. Scots law follows Roman law in recognising the distinctive character of the latter—as the strongest form of possession—because holding in terms of an assertion of ownership may be in competition with the title of another. In the application of the law, recognition of the differences inherent in the many possible variations, in the chemistry between physical holding and associated state of mind, is of greater importance than any quest for a definition of a "true" notion of possession.

The right of ownership encompasses a right to possession and it is frequently the case that the two rights are concurrent. However, an owner may dispose of the right to possession or simply part with it on a contractual basis. A disposal of the real right to possession occurs in the context of an owner's giving a liferent to or

---

[77] See *Banff Burgh Council v Ruthin Castle Ltd*, 1944 S.C. 36 at 68, per Lord Justice Clerk Cooper.
[78] On the difference see Reid, *The Law of Property in Scotland* (1996), para.20.
[79] Stair, II, 1, 18.
[80] In the DCFR (VIII–1:205) the control factor is central to possession of goods: "[p]ossession, in relation to goods, means having direct physical control or indirect physical control over the goods." "Indirect physical control" is control exercised through another person.

a lease of the property concerned.[81] The right may be parted with by hire, loan or in terms of any other contract under which the owner parts with possession. This exemplifies the "right to possession" aspect as a real right retained where another party has the thing, or access to it, under a contact.

Possession and its concomitant right may be acquired on a derivative or original basis. The right may have a valid legal basis or no legal basis. The possession of heritable property by a squatter lacks a supporting legal basis but it is nonetheless possession and is protected as such.[82] The position of one asserting a right of possession over another's land is not in principle strengthened by the statutory right of public access to private land because that right would be forfeited by any assertion of a right to possession.[83] Possession of corporeal moveable property gives rise to a presumption of ownership, a concept which is considered in the next chapter.[84]

Because there can be no physical holding of incorporeal property, possession in the simple sense applied to corporeal things has no application to incorporeals. At the same time, "possession" of an incorporeal is obviously competent in the sense of the de facto exercise and control of a right not deriving from any basis of title to it. The difference between "possession" of a right of servitude in the sense of the assertion of a certain right over another's land and the legal holding of such a right illustrates the possible "possession" of an incorporeal.[85] The possibility of the "possession" of incorporeal property in this sense means that the exercise or assertion of rights may be hived off from the title. The composer/owner of a musical composition may, without parting with title, accord to another party, on a temporary basis, the right to perform the composition.

Possession may be natural or civil. Natural possession is the simple situation of actual possession by physical detention of the thing. This may be by the party who holds the right to possession or by one with only a limited right or, indeed, no right at all. But even the de facto position of natural possession has its limits. One who absent-mindedly gets into the driver's seat of another's car thinking it is his does not become natural possessor of the vehicle. Arguably, access to the keys is a prerequisite to possession of a car but, in this case, the primary failing is that there is not any intention element because the absent-minded driver thinks he is getting into his own car. Civil possession, on the other hand, is possession "through the physical detention of another".[86] Possession in the strong sense of holding the thing on the basis of a right of ownership is consistent with a retention of control where physical detention is passed to another party. In this situation the civil possessor has parted with physical control but retains ultimate control over the thing detained by another.

The most important feature of the concept of possession is its open character accommodating a wide range of forms involving the three factors of physical holding or control, state of mind, and right or entitlement.

---

[81] Reid, *The Law of Property in Scotland* (1996), para.127.

[82] Reid, *The Law of Property in Scotland* (1996), para.5 notes that the squatter's possession is a real right because "the bare fact of possession of property confers the right not to be dispossessed except by consent or by order of a court".

[83] See fn.11; *Tuley v Highland Council*, 2009 S.C. 456; 2009 S.L.T. 616 at [17].

[84] See para.31.02, below.

[85] As Reid, *The Law of Property in Scotland* (1996), para.120 shows the special "possession" of incorporeal property features in various statutory contexts.

[86] Reid, *The Law of Property in Scotland* (1996), para.121.

Proprietary remedies—The real right of property is protected by legal action avail- **30.10** able against any transgressor. A real right is "available against the whole world" on the basis of the holder's entitlement in the subject whether this is a right of ownership or a lesser real right. The remedy derives from the interest in the entity of property, corporeal or incorporeal, and is accordingly distinguishable from a personal action deriving from a relationship between parties, e.g. a contract relating to a thing.

The essence of a real right in property lies in qualities of universal applicability and priority, depending upon the nature of the right. The universality aspect is borne out in the recovery of property or assertion of a proprietary interest; in proprietary claims of this sort the identity of the defender is only relevant to the extent that the party concerned can establish a relevant right to the thing deriving from the claimant. The priority factor applies in the assertion of a real security interest in according to the holder priority over all lesser rights. A chapter of relatively recent case law[87] demonstrates the significance of the distinction between a real right of property and a personal claim relating to property. This fundamental distinction is only important because real rights are more extensively protected than personal rights. The technical legal means by which proprietary interests are protected differs between the different forms of property and will be dealt with in context in the following chapters.

In principle the status quo of possession is protected against unsanctioned interference. A natural possessor subject to unauthorised dispossessed is, in principle, entitled, against the dispossessor, to restoration of the status quo ante as a preliminary to any adjudication as to the merits.[88] In the circumstances of the wide range of forms which possession may take, protection limited to restoring the status quo position of natural possession is the only option in terms of a general remedy. There may well be an issue of entitlement behind the possession position protected on the basis of the right concerned. Even though possession is protected by a remedy of limited scope, the significance of possession—especially of corporeal moveable property—means that the remedy is an important one.

Original and derivative acquisition—As a matter of general proposition property **30.11** rights may be acquired on either an original or a derivative basis. Acquisition is "original" in those situations in which a right comes into being as a consequence of an act or occurrence giving a new proprietary position. An everyday incidence of this is the accession of building materials and fixtures and fittings to land in any permanent building project. The process of "derivative" acquisition involves transmission of a right in property from the holder to an acquiring party. Clearly, the transmission of proprietary rights pursuant to sale is the most common form of derivative acquisition and an everyday occurrence in respect of corporeal moveables.

An important difference between the two forms is that original acquisition is unitary in the sense that a self-standing act or position leads to acquisition whereas derivative acquisition occurs as the culmination of a process. It is true that in the process of derivative acquisition the defining aspect of acquisition is a separate act transferring the property or, at very least, the recognition of the point in time at which property passed. On this basis it seems that while the different forms of original acquisition are unitary, derivative acquisition is a process at least in the sense that the critical aspect occurs in a context.

---

[87] See *Sharp v Thomson*, 1997 S.C. (HL) 66 and *Burnett's Tr. v Grainger*, 2004 S.C. (HL) 19. *Sharp v Thomson* was originally decided in the Outer House by Lord Penrose on May 11, 1994 (1994 S.L.T. 1068). The judgment of the House of Lords in *Burnett's Tr. v Grainger* was issued on March 4, 2004.
[88] See Reid, *The Law of Property in Scotland* (1996), para.166.

Original acquisition has its primary application in the context of corporeal moveable property in the sense that most instances involve the acquisition of corporeal moveables. That said, a major application of accession is in fixtures—the process by which the property in corporeal moveable things is subsumed into heritage.[89]

Derivative acquisition in the context of heritable property involves the process of conveyancing. Within this process original acquisition by prescription plays a part, although, in modern law, to a less significant extent than formerly. The development in this regard is considered in Ch.35(V).

The range of forms of acquisition will be dealt with in the following chapter.

30.12 Conveyancing—While the transfer and control of rights in heritable property by conveyancing remains a specialist matter it can now be properly seen as part of a unified law of property.[90] It has been observed that "conveyancing is part of the law of property, and not the other way about".[91]

Conveyancing is concerned with the process of transmission of real rights in heritable property. In the very common case of derivative acquisition pursuant to sale the process has distinct stages. First, there is a contractual stage, in which the parties to a transaction enter into a contractual arrangement for the sale and purchase of heritable property. The contract normally takes the form of "missives"; that is, a collection of written communications beginning with an offer and ending with an acceptance, and, in between, documenting a process of adjustments in which the terms of the contract are fine-tuned. Strictly speaking, this process of negotiation takes the form of refusal and counter-offer rather than offer and qualified acceptance. Most significantly, the conclusion of this stage only creates a personal right.[92] A person who enters into a contract to purchase land has a right against the seller to have that bargain implemented, and may sue the seller for damages in the event of his default. The buyer equally is bound to the seller.

The conclusion of missives will normally be followed by the payment of the price to the seller and the delivery of the title documents—the disposition—to the purchaser, following which the purchaser will generally take entry. None of this is sufficient to divest the seller of his ownership of the property.[93] It is only upon registration in the Land Register that property and therefore ownership passes, and a real right is created.[94]

Conveyancing is a specialist subject involving a complex and constantly developing body of law.[95] Any detailed consideration is outwith the scope of this work.[96]

---

[89] See below, paras.31.08–31.11.

[90] The adoption of the position contended for in Reid, *The Law of Property in Scotland* (1996), paras 1–3 by the Court of Session has been endorsed by the House of Lords; see the dicta of Lord President Hope, as he then was, in *Sharp v Thompson*, 1995 S.C. 455 at 463 and Lord Rodger of Earlsferry in *Burnett's Tr. v Grainger*, 2004 S.C. (HL) 19 at [87].

[91] Reid, *The Law of Property in Scotland* (1996), para.1, fn.12.

[92] As evidenced by *Burnett's Tr. v Grainger*, 2004 S.C. (HL) 19.

[93] As was found by the purchaser in *Burnett's Tr. v Grainger*, 2004 S.C. (HL) 19.

[94] For confirmation that ownership passes on registration, see Abolition of Feudal Tenure (Scotland) Act 2000 s.4.

[95] Since 1999 Professors Kenneth G.C. Reid and George L. Gretton have published annual reviews of the subject; see, at the time of writing, their most recent *Conveyancing 2010* (Edinburgh: Avizandum, 2011).

[96] For further information, see George L. Gretton and Kenneth G.C. Reid, *Conveyancing*, 4th edn (Edinburgh: W. Green, 2011), and David A. Brand, Andrew J.M. Steven and Scott Wortley, *Professor McDonald's Conveyancing Manual*, 7th edn (LexisNexis UK, 2004).

Constitutional protection of property—Regarding the protection of property **30.13**
under the ECHR,[97] the relevant art.1, Protocol 1 provides:

> "Every natural or legal person is entitled to the peaceful enjoyments of his
> possessions. No one shall be deprived of his possessions except in the public
> interest and subject to the conditions provided for by law and by the general
> principles of international law. The preceding provisions shall not, however,
> in any way impair the right of the State to enforce such laws as it deems
> necessary to control the use of property in accordance with the general interest
> or to secure the payment of taxes or other contributions or penalties."

The accepted interpretation of this provision[98] involves three distinct but related
aspects: (1) that persons are entitled to the peaceful enjoyment of their posses-
sions; (2) that no one shall be deprived of property unless this is in the public
interest and carried out in conformity with domestic and international law; (3) that
this protection shall not limit the state's right to enforce laws considered necessary
to control the use of property according to the general interest, or to secure
payment of taxes or other contributions or penalties. Applying these considerations to any particular case, the initial question "whether there has been an
interference"[99] is determined. In the event of an affirmative answer, the issue
becomes one of justification[100] or possible compensation, on the basis of the
principle that an interference should be compensated.[101]

The case of *Karl Construction Ltd v Palisade Properties Plc*[102] is an example
of the application of art.1, Protocol 1. In this matter Lord Drummond Young
found Scots law's exceptional position in allowing the inhibition of property on an
open-ended basis in favour of the claimant pending the outcome of civil litigation
to be contrary to ECHR protection. It is important to note that litigation arising
from the Damages (Asbestos-related Conditions) (Scotland) Act 2009 has
produced much judicial comment on art.1, Protocol 1.[103]

Article 8 which provides for a right to respect for private and family life and the
home also has property implications.[104]

Relevant ECHR issues are noted in the context of the following chapters in
respect of particular forms of property.

FURTHER READING

Bell, *Principles*, ss.1470–1505.
Carey Miller, D.L., Combe, M.M., Steven, A. and Wortley, S., "National Report
on the Transfer of Movables in Scotland" in Faber, W. and Lurger, B. (eds),

---

[97] See above, para.1.22.
[98] *Sporrong & Lonnroth v Sweden* [1982] 5 E.H.R.R. 35.
[99] See R. Reed and J. Murdoch, *Human Rights Law in Scotland*, 3rd edn (Tottel, 2011), para.8.05.
[100] See Reed and Murdoch, *Human Rights Law in Scotland* (2011), paras 8.26–8.27 and 8.35
regarding the criteria applicable to a justified interference.
[101] See Reed and Murdoch, *Human Rights Law in Scotland* (2011), para.8.39.
[102] *Karl Construction Ltd v Palisade Properties Plc*, 2002 S.L.T. 312; see A. Steven, "The Progress
of Article 1 Protocol 1 in Scotland" (2002) 6 Edin. L.R. 396.
[103] See *Axa General Insurance Ltd v Lord Advocate*, 2010 S.L.T. 179 at [180]–[226]; 2011 S.L.T.
439 at [99]–[149]; 2011 UKSC 46 at [20]–[28], [73]–[83], [86]–[96] and [109]–[134].
[104] See Reed and Murdoch, *Human Rights Law in Scotland* (2011), para.6.24.

National Reports on the Transfer of Movables in Europe II (Sellier European Law Publishers, 2009).

Erskine, *Institutes*, II.

Gordon, W.M. and Wortley, S., *Scottish Land Law*, 3rd edn (Edinburgh: W. Green, 2009).

Reid, K.G.C., *The Law of Property in Scotland* (Butterworths, 1996).

Reed, R. and Murdoch, J., *A Guide to Human Rights Law in Scotland*, 3rd edn (Edinburgh: Tottel, 2011), Ch.8.

CHAPTER 31

MOVEABLE PROPERTY: CORPOREAL

Introduction—This chapter aims to give a succinct general account of the subset **31.01**
of property law applicable to corporeal moveables. The focus is restricted to
concepts of property law and the treatment does not seek to cover aspects of other
areas of law with implications for moveables, for example succession.[1] Security
relevant to moveable property is dealt with in Ch.36.[2]

Distinct relevance of possession—The clear position of the law in distinguishing **31.02**
ownership and possession holds good in the context of corporeal moveable property but, at the same time, possession does have special significance. Ownership
may be acquired in the range of ways considered below. Nonetheless, as a consequence of the nature of corporeal moveables, a default position is provided by the
recognition that, unless the circumstances indicate the contrary, the possession of
a moveable gives rise to a presumption of ownership.

The application of the presumption is, of course, limited to circumstances
otherwise consistent with the possessor being owner or, put another way, being in
a position to aver an independent title. It will not come into play where the
possessor holds on a subordinate basis, for example, under a contract of hire or
loan acknowledging the ownership of another.[3] Where the possessor holds in
assertion of a right of ownership the presumption requires a challenger claiming
possession to establish: (1) a right of ownership; and (2) that his or her possession
was lost or parted with in circumstances not consistent with the transfer of
that right.[4] In the circumstances of moveable property, establishing the right of
ownership requires no more than proof of purchase or some other possible
basis of acquisition, e.g. by gift or succession. The second requirement will
commonly be met by proof of loss by theft. In the common scenario of the innocent purchase of stolen property the owner will, in principle, be able to recover
from the possessor by proof of the two elements. Although the presumption has
no application where moveables are possessed on a basis incompatible with a
claim to ownership, where it applies it gives a "considerable advantage"[5] to the
possessor. Probably in view of its operation as a presumption its significance
is not uniformly acknowledged in the case law[6] but its role is nonetheless a

---

[1] See Chs 38 and 39, below.
[2] See below paras 36.12–36.27.
[3] K.G.C. Reid, *The Law of Property in Scotland* (Edinburgh: Butterworths, 1996), para.150.
[4] Stair, IV, 21, 5; see also II, 1, 42: "he must instruct the manner how his possession ceased, as
being either taken from him by violence, or by stealth, or having strayed, and being lost or the like".
See also Hume, IV, 510.
[5] Reid, *The Law of Property in Scotland* (1996), para.150.
[6] See, e.g. *Anderson v Buchanan* (1848) 11 D. 270 at 284, per Lord Cockburn.

structural one in the context of moveable property and its position and function can hardly be in doubt.[7]

An associated doctrine of "reputed ownership" which applies

> "where the true owner allows another to assume publicly the appearance of ownership . . . to deceive and mislead creditors by raising a false ground of credit"[8]

is of limited significance in modern law.[9]

Natural possession, without regard for its basis, is protected to the extent that the remedy of spuilzie is available to obtain restoration from an immediate dispossessor[10] but recourse to this once important remedy[11] is largely unknown in modern law,[12] though occasional, infrequent, instances do arise.[13] The better view is that the remedy of spuilzie is a limited one concerned with restoration of the status quo in the circumstances of an interference with natural possession. This follows from the key feature—and controlling limit—of the remedy requiring only proof of an unauthorised interference with possession without entering into any question of title or right. The wider protection of rights to and interests in possession necessarily involve proof going beyond the simple position of an interference with natural possession.[14]

The defence of possession against interference with the right (i.e. "intrusion"), rather than dispossession, is only applicable to a limited range of moveables (e.g. ships).[15] In principle remedies against intrusion applicable to land should be potentially applicable to moveables.[16] The possessor/occupier of a moveable caravan should in principle have access to spuilzie to protect against another's unauthorised intrusion.

31.03 Modes of acquisition—Ownership in corporeal moveable property may be acquired on an original or a derivative basis.[17] Original acquisition involves the acquiring of a right in property not by transmission from a predecessor but on the basis of an event or through circumstances. Such a basis in principle includes

---

[7] See Hume, IV, 510: "a notorious and well established article of our common law"; note application in *Chief Constable, Strathclyde Police v Sharp*, 2002 S.L.T. (Sh. Ct) 95. See, generally, D. Carey Miller with D. Irvine, *Corporeal Moveables in Scots Law* (Edinburgh: W. Green, 2005), para.1.19.

[8] *Marston v Kerr's Tr.* (1879) 9 R. 898 at 901, per Lord Gifford; see also *George Hopkinson Ltd v Napier & Son*, 1953 S.C. 139 at 147, per Lord President Cooper.

[9] Reid, *The Law of Property in Scotland* (1996), para.532 (Gordon); see also Carey Miller with Irvine, *Corporeal Moveables in Scots Law* (2005), para.1.19.

[10] Reid, *The Law of Property in Scotland* (1996), para.161.

[11] J.W. Cairns, "Historical Introduction", in K.G.C. Reid and R. Zimmermann, *A History of Private Law in Scotland* (Oxford: Oxford University Press, 2000), I, p.73: "Perhaps the most common action in fifteenth-century Scotland".

[12] K.G.C. Reid, "Property Law: Sources and Doctrine", in Reid and Zimmerman, *A History of Private Law in Scotland*, I, pp.212–214.

[13] See *Mackinnon v Avonside Homes Ltd*, 1993 S.C.L.R. 976 for an interesting application of the remedy. *Gemmell v Bank of Scotland*, 1998 S.C.L.R. 144, points to the scope for spuilzie in cases involving repossession and eviction (including unlawful eviction).

[14] See D.L. Carey Miller, "Delictual Protection of Possessory Interests in Corporeal Moveable Property" in J. Thomson (ed), *Delict* (Edinburgh: W. Green), para.13.64.

[15] Reid, *The Law of Property in Scotland* (1996), para.191.

[16] *Leitch & Co v Leydon*, 1931 S.C. (HL) 1; *Wilson v Shepherd*, 1913 S.C. 300; Reid, *The Law of Property in Scotland* (1996), para.192.

[17] See para.30.11.

acquisition by occupation, accession, specification, confusion and prescription. Derivative acquisition, on the other hand, involves transmission by a party disposing of the thing to one acquiring it. Distinct forms of the process of transmission apply, depending upon whether the common law or the Sale of Goods Act applies. The forms will be considered in the following sections.

Occupation—Acquisition by occupation occurs on the taking possession **31.04** of a thing open to acquisition in an act of assertion of a right of ownership. Stair[18] notes the universality of this doctrine of natural law acknowledged in the maxim: *quod nullius est, fit primi occupantis* (unowned property goes to the first taker).

The prerequisite condition of the availability of an unowned thing for acquisition by occupation is curtailed by common law and statute. The maxim *quod nullius est fit domini regis* (that which belongs to no one is the Crown's[19]) limits scope for acquisition of previously owned property which would otherwise have come to be unowned—typically by being abandoned. This principle is retained in the feudal reform legislation which does not affect powers exercisable by the sovereign under the Royal prerogative.[20] The relevant text includes: "prerogative rights as respects ownerless or unclaimed property".[21] Consistent with the bar to acquisition of previously owned property, both abandoned property and an owner's interest in lost property are protected in comprehensive legislative provisions.[22] It may be noted that the possible reform of aspects of this area of law is mooted in a Scottish Law Commission Report.[23]

Property in things which have never had an owner may be acquired by occupation. Without specific appropriation a wild animal, even though protected and preserved on private property, is *res nullius*—a thing not belonging to anyone.[24] Accordingly, it will become the property of the taker, including the person who kills it, in principle even if the party concerned is a trespasser or one acting in contravention of the law.[25] Acquisition by a poacher on the basis of the common law is, of course, subject to the possibility of denial of acquisition or forfeiture provided for by statute.[26] In principle, a wild creature, once appropriated, remains owned property provided possession is retained; as such, it is not capable of being acquired by another by occupation. But if it escapes and regains its natural liberty, the right of property "is lost so soon as the owner ceaseth to pursue for possession".[27] The *quod nullius* rule vesting ownership in the Crown, does not apply to wild animals which, on regaining a natural state of freedom, become unowned; but the fixed category of "tame" animals (e.g. cats and dogs) vest in the

---

[18] Stair, II, 1, 33.

[19] See Reid, *The Law of Property in Scotland* (1996), para.540 (Gordon).

[20] Abolition of Feudal Tenure etc (Scotland) Act 2000 s.58(1).

[21] Abolition of Feudal Tenure etc (Scotland) Act 2000 s.58(2)(b)(i).

[22] Civic Government (Scotland) Act 1982 Pt VI. See, generally, Reid, *The Law of Property in Scotland* (1996), paras 547–52 (Gordon); Carey Miller with Irvine, *Corporeal Moveables in Scots Law* (2005), para.2.08.

[23] Scottish Law Commission, *Report on Prescription and Title to Moveable Property* (HMSO, 2012), Scot. Law Com. No.228.

[24] *Wilson v Dykes* (1872) 10 M. 444, per Lord Justice Clerk Moncreiff at 445.

[25] Erskine, II, 1, 10; see also *Valentine v Kennedy*, 1985 S.C.C.R. 89 at 90.

[26] *Scot v Everit* (1853) 15 D. 288; see also *Leith v Leith* (1862) 24 D. 1059 at 1062 and 1077; *Livingstone v Breadalbane* (1791) 3 Pat. App.221.

[27] Stair, II, i, 33. A subset of special rules applicable to whalefishing developed; see *Sutter v Aberdeen Arctic Co* (1862) 4 Macq. 355; Bell, *Principles*, para.1289.

Crown on becoming unowned.[28] Domesticated animals, or creatures that have a homing instinct (pigeons, bees), or those that carry a mark indicating private property, are not acquired by one who seizes and detains them even though this may prevent their return to the owner.[29]

31.05 Treasure—A find of buried or concealed treasure, being previously owned property, vests in the Crown in terms of the *quod nullius fit domini regis rule*.[30] In the leading modern case the basis of the rule was held to be royal prerogative rather than the sovereign's position as universal landlord in the then prevailing feudal land tenure structure. On this basis, the rule was held to apply to a find in the udal (rather than feudal) context of Shetland.[31] Accordingly, in terms of legal entitlement, a find of treasure is not differentiated from the category of lost or abandoned property in that there is no notion of "finder's rights". Rather, a finder is under a duty to report possession of the find.[32] The Scottish Archaeological Finds Allocation Panel[33] advises as to the destiny of finds and determines the amount of any ex gratia payment to be made to the finder.[34]

31.06 Accession—By an important mode of original acquisition a person becomes owner of something of an accessory nature by reason of his ownership of another, the principal, subject.[35] As the maxim *accessorium sequitur principale* states the accessory follows the principal. The owner of an animal becomes owner of its offspring[36]; things affixed to heritable property vest in the owner of the heritage as part of that property.[37] Also on this basis the interest produced by a fund and not otherwise disposed of has been held to belong to the owner of the fund.[38] Accession occurs either in respect of things which belong together (e.g. young and parent animal) or things which are brought together (e.g. paint applied to a house). Either way, acquisition through accession is original rather than derivative because it takes place on the basis of a happening rather than an act of will.

In the corporeal moveable context—which gives greatest scope for accession—the better view is that the process involves three elements[39]: sufficient physical

---

[28] See Lord Rodger, "Stealing Fish" in R.F. Hunter (ed.), *Justice and Crime: Essays in Honour of The Right Honourable The Lord Emslie* (Edinburgh: Butterworths, 1993), p.5. See also C.G. Van der Merwe and D. Bain, "The Fish that Got Away: Some Reflections on Valentine v Kennedy" (2008) 12 Edin. L.R. 418.

[29] Erskine, II, 1, 10; Bell, *Principles*, para.1290. See also *Valentine v Kennedy*, 1985 S.C.C.R. 89, commented on in Reid, *The Law of Property in Scotland* (1996), para.542, fn.9 (Gordon).

[30] Stair, II, 1, 5; Erskine, II, 1, 12; *Cleghorn & Bryce v Baird* (1696) Mor.13522.

[31] *Lord Advocate v University of Aberdeen*, 1963 S.C. 533. For a discussion of this notable litigation see D.L. Carey Miller, "St Ninian's Isle Treasure, Lord Advocate v University of Aberdeen and Budge" in J. Grant and E. Sutherland (eds) *Scots Law Tales* (Dundee: Dundee University Press, 2010), p.111.

[32] Civic Government (Scotland) Act 1982 s.67(6). See also "Treasure Trove in Scotland: A Code of Practice" (The Scottish Government, 2008), 2.5(ii), see *http://www.scotland.gov.uk/Publications/2008/12/04114930/0* [Accessed July 25, 2012].

[33] "Treasure Trove in Scotland: A Code of Practice" (2008), 3.2.

[34] "Treasure Trove in Scotland: A Code of Practice" (2008), 7; see also Carey Miller with Irvine, *Corporeal Moveables in Scots Law* (2005), para.2.06.

[35] Erskine, II, 1, 14–15. See *Zahnrad Fabrik Passau GmbH v Terex Ltd*, 1986 S.L.T. 84.

[36] *Lamb v Grant* (1874) 11 S.L.R. 672.

[37] See below, para.31.08.

[38] *Gillespies v Marshall* (1802) Mor., App. I, "Accessorium" No.2; cf. *Stewart v Stewart* (1669) Mor.50. See J. M'Laren, *The Law of Wills and Succession*, 3rd edn (1894), Vol.1, p.329.

[39] Particularly relevant as the criteria applicable to fixtures; see below, para.31.08.

attachment, subordination and permanency.[40] A moveable thing may accede to another moveable—in an obvious example, a quantity of paint accedes to the bicycle to which it is applied. A gearbox becomes part of the vehicle to which it is fitted; the essential point here being "functional subordination".[41] In these examples principal and accessory are readily identifiable and the subordination aspect is clear. Sometimes, however, the subordination aspect is more difficult because principal and accessory are not readily distinguishable. Does the valuable diamond accede to the less valuable ring to which it is fixed on the basis of functionality or does the ring accede to the diamond on the basis of the value factor? According to Stair[42] the former answer applies because the functionally dominant proprietary entity should be regarded as principal.[43]

Accession occurs as a consequence of physical factors, in principle regardless of circumstances and without reference to any intention factor.[44] The point is illustrated by noting that in principle the physical change which accession involves is not open to control or limitation by contract.[45] In contrast, the essence of derivative acquisition is intention which may, in principle, be effective without any associated physical act.[46] Arguably, there may be room for party control where the primary basis of accession is functionality. In principle a hired mechanical component functioning within the context of a principal mechanism would not accede if it could be readily removed at the end of the hire period.

By far the most important incidence of accession applies to the context of corporeal moveables which accede to land and, on this basis, are acquired by the landowner. This self-contained subject of "fixtures" is dealt with in a number of later paragraphs.[47] Accession may also take place by natural processes which may be brought together as "accession by fruits".

Accession by fruits—As a matter of obvious consequence animals *in utero* **31.07** accede to their mother; equally the natural produce of animals, until separated, accedes to the relevant animal and vests in its owner.[48] In principle, all things which grow in the soil are accessory to the land; as *"partes soli"* they "belong to the owner of the field which produced them".[49]

An important policy-based exception applies to cultivated annual crops which are deemed to be moveable "even before they are separated or ripe".[50] The interpretation that this exception applied only for the benefit of a tenant[51] was not followed in a decision which recognised the right of a seller to harvest a crop after acquisition of the land by the buyer.[52]

---

[40] See Reid, *The Law of Property in Scotland* (1996), para.571.

[41] Reid, *The Law of Property in Scotland* (1996), para.571.

[42] Stair, II, 1, 39.

[43] See, generally, Carey Miller with Irvine, *Corporeal Moveables in Scots Law* (2005), paras 3.19–3.20.

[44] Reid, *The Law of Property in Scotland* (1996), para.572.

[45] See *Shetland Islands Council v BP Petroleum Development*, 1990 S.L.T. 82 at 94, per Lord Cullen.

[46] See Stair, III, 2, 4.

[47] See paras 31.08–31.11, below.

[48] Reid, *The Law of Property in Scotland* (1996), para.595.

[49] Erskine, II, I, 14.

[50] Stair, II, I, 34; W.M. Gordon and S. Wortley, *Scottish Land Law* (Edinburgh: W. Green, 2009), para.4.39.

[51] *Chalmers' Tr. v Dick's Tr.*, 1909 S.C. 761.

[52] *Boskabelle Ltd v Donald Black Laird*, 2006 S.L.T. 1079; see comment in D.L. Carey Miller, "Right to Annual Crops" (2007) 11 Edin. L.R. 274.

Fruits separated from their principal "parent" entity are open to acquisition. In principle separated natural and industrial fruits (e.g. rent; interest on capital)[53] continue to vest in the owner of the principal thing but not to the exclusion of a liferenter, or the possible entitlement of a bona fide possessor, of the principal subject.[54]

31.08 Fixtures: General issues—When a moveable thing is brought into connection with heritage, the question may arise in a variety of circumstances as to the effect of this linkage upon the moveable. Whether property remains moveable or becomes heritable has—for differing reasons in different eras[55]—been a significant issue in the development of the law. Litigation in the not uncommon borderline situations has led to a considerable body of decisions, but juristic analysis has assisted in clarifying the case law.[56]

The word "fixture" has been authoritatively defined as meaning anything annexed to heritable property, that is, fastened to or connected with it, and not in mere juxtaposition,[57] and it is in this wide sense that the term is used here. The annexation may be either to the soil directly or to something, typically a building, which itself has become annexed to the soil. The latter form of "fixtures" may be contrasted with "fittings" which do not necessarily accede.[58] The general point that a thing attached to a building attaches to the relevant unit of land on which the building stands is simply an application of the principle that attachment is to the relevant proprietary entity which is principal. This is also illustrated by the fact that an internal attachment to a tenement flat becomes part only of the flat concerned because, in the tenement context, the relevant proprietary entity is the flat.[59]

Stair refers to the rule *inaedificatum solo, solo cedit*[60] as authority for the position that all buildings and things annexed to the soil "are accounted as parts of the ground".[61] In the landmark decision of *Brand's Trs v Brand's Trs*[62]—tending to the assimilation of Scots and English law[63]—Lord Cairns, noted that there is no general exception to this basic rule. Effective annexure to land has three consequences[64]: (i) the accessory loses its separate existence in becoming part of the land; (ii) the fixed accessory loses its moveable character and becomes heritable;

---

[53] Carey Miller with Irvine, *Corporeal Moveables in Scots Law* (2005), para.6.03.

[54] Reid, *The Law of Property in Scotland* (1996), para.596.

[55] Reid, *The Law of Property in Scotland* (1996), para.578; see also K.G.C. Reid, "The Lord Chancellor's Fixtures: Brand's Trs v Brand's Trs Re-examined" (1983) 28 J.L.S.S. 49.

[56] See J. Rankine, *The Law of Landownership in Scotland*, 4th edn (Edinburgh: W. Green, 1909), pp.116–133; Gordon and Wortley, *Scottish Land Law* (2009), paras 4.03–4.37; Reid, *The Law of Property in Scotland* (1996), paras 578–591; Carey Miller with Irvine, *Corporeal Moveables in Scots Law* (2005), paras 3.09–3.16. See also C.G. van der Merwe, "Accession by Building" in Reid and Zimmerman, *A History of Private Law in Scotland* (2000), I, p.245.

[57] *Brand's Trs v Brand's Trs* (1876) 3 R. (HL) 16 at 23, per Lord Chelmsford. On the term "fixture" see Gordon and Wortley, *Scottish Land Law* (2009), para.4.01.

[58] Reid, *The Law of Property in Scotland* (1996), para.578.

[59] Reid, *The Law of Property in Scotland* (1996), para.585.

[60] "What is built upon the ground accrues to it."

[61] Stair, II, 1, 40.

[62] *Brand's Trs v Brand's Trs* (1876) 3 R. (HL) 16; followed in *Miller v Muirhead* (1894) 21 R. 658, and *Howie's Trs v McLay* (1902) 5 F. 214. See also *Dowall v Miln* (1874) 1 R. 1180, at 1182–1183 where Lord Justice Clerk Moncreiff discusses the law of fixtures.

[63] Demonstrated by Reid, "The Lord Chancellor's Fixtures: Brand's Trs v Brand's Trs Re-examined" (1983) 28 J.L.L.S. 49; see also Reid, *The Law of Property in Scotland* (1996), para.578; C.G. van der Merwe, "Accession by Building" in Reid and Zimmerman, *A History of Private Law in Scotland* (2000), I, p.245.

[64] See Reid, *The Law of Property in Scotland* (1996), para.574; R.R.M. Paisley, *Land Law* (Edinburgh: W. Green, 2000), pp.83–84.

(iii) independent title to the fixed accessory is extinguished. As an illustration of the finality aspect, it has been held impossible, apart from statutory exception, to sever property in land from property in pipes and drains traversing the land.[65] *Brand's Trs.* adopted the basic unitary position that, in principle, what has once become part of the heritage cannot lawfully be severed and removed by one with a limited right.[66] It may be noted that a certain anomaly exists in valuation cases tending to be decided as a special subset[67] but the better view is that the modern law is unitary.[68] Following this position, two questions usually arise. First, has the thing been so affixed to the heritage as to become part of it? Secondly, insofar as this is so, is the annexed element, in a question with the owner of the heritage, open to any exceptional right of removal? The second issue is dealt with below.[69] It is important to note that the consequence of accession may, of course, be excluded by statute.[70]

Fixtures: Criteria—In the circumstances of a wide range of physical factors **31.09** being potentially relevant, whether an article has become a fixture is a question of fact to be decided in the circumstances of each case.[71] While writers are in agreement as to the essential criteria, analysis and presentation varies.[72] Professor Gloag[73] considered that the following might be taken into account, but his list is not exhaustive; nor does it reflect any position of priorities:

(1) the degree of attachment to the land, a factor which may be conclusive;
(2) whether the attachment is of a permanent or quasi-permanent character;
(3) whether the attachment can be removed without damage to itself or to the principal entity;
(4) whether the attachment is specially adapted to the principal entity;
(5) whether the principal entity is specially adapted to the attachment;
(6) whether installation of the attachment was a substantial, costly or time-consuming operation;
(7) the apparent intention of the party making the attachment determined objectively—not from extrinsic evidence, but from the nature of the article and the building and the manner of attachment.

---

[65] *Crichton v Turnbull*, 1946 S.C. 52.

[66] The decision in *Miller v Muirhead* (1894) 21 R. 658 reflects full understanding of *Brand's Trs*, setting it apart from the large number of cases where that position has been ignored or misinterpreted; see van der Merwe, "Accession by Building" in Reid and Zimmerman, *A History of Private Law in Scotland* (2000), pp.260–4.

[67] See, e.g. *Assessor for Lothian Region v Blue Circle Industries Plc*, 1986 S.L.T. 537.

[68] See Reid, *The Law of Property in Scotland* (1996), para.578.

[69] See para.31.10.

[70] See Gordon and Wortley, *Scottish Land Law* (2009), para.4.16 referring to the Agricultural Holdings (Scotland) Act 1991 s.18(1); the Water (Scotland) Act 1980 s.35(2) and the Planning (Listed Buildings and Conservation Areas) (Scotland) Act 1997 s.1. See also Paisley, *Land Law* (2000), p.83 noting that under the Sewerage (Scotland) Act 1968 ss.16, 18 public sewers do not accede to the landowner but remain the property of the sewerage authority.

[71] *Howie's Trs v McLay* (1902) 5 F. 214 at 216, per Lord President Kinross; *Assessor for Lothian Region v Blue Circle Industries Plc*, 1986 S.L.T. 537.

[72] See Reid, *The Law of Property in Scotland* (1996), p.579; Gordon and Wortley, *Scottish Land Law* (2009), para.4.05.

[73] Lord Dunedin and J. Wark (eds), *Green's Encyclopaedia of the Laws of Scotland*, Vol.VII, paras 362–363, approved in *Scottish Discount Co Ltd v Blin*, 1986 S.L.T. 123.

Probably the most appropriate analysis, already mentioned,[74] identifies the applicable necessary conditions for accession as: (1) physical attachment; (2) functional subordination; and (3) permanence.[75] Other, more general, approaches identify potentially relevant factors rather than prerequisites.[76]

The primary requirement of physical attachment may, in a given case, be met in such a way that functional subordination and permanence are necessarily concomitant. Fitted kitchen cupboards and worktops clearly fall into this category as do many other fixed elements that go to make up the standard dwelling as a permanent integrity to which the various fixed elements are functionally subordinate. On this basis the physical attachment or annexation factor may be conclusive.[77] Similar reasoning is applicable in a wide range of different building or construction contexts.

In applying criteria to particular circumstances it is important to bear in mind that accession occurs as a consequence of physical circumstances. While the outcome may be an intended one, it follows as a result of what happens between the elements of property concerned. Parties cannot will a consequence of annexation between items of property as a matter of derivative acquisition. The other, more practically important, side of this coin means that in principle parties cannot contract out of the consequences of accession.[78] On this basis, the decision of the First Division taking account of the hire-purchase factor in the context of the attachment of heavy machinery,[79] as indicating a relevant intention against accession, is open to criticism.[80] Parties to a land transaction cannot contract to designate as moveable items which are in fact fixtures with a view to reducing stamp duty land tax on the basis of the exemption of moveables.[81] All this said, reference to intention as a matter of confirmation of what the objective factors point to can hardly be open to objection.[82]

31.10 Fixtures: Relationship factor; severance—Historically, relationship factors were potentially relevant to the question of whether accession occurred.[83] Since *Brand's Trs*[84] this has no longer been the case and in modern law any relationship factor between the parties is primarily relevant in regard to a possible right of severance on termination of the relationship. In certain circumstances one with a limited right to the principal can sever and remove what he or she has annexed.[85]

---

[74] See above, para.31.06.

[75] Reid, *The Law of Property in Scotland* (1996), paras 579–582; Paisley, *Land Law* (2000), pp.84–85.

[76] Gordon and Wortley, *Scottish Land Law* (2009), paras 4.05–4.15; Carey Miller with Irvine, *Corporeal Moveables in Scots Law* (2005), paras 3.12–3.15.

[77] See *Christie v Smith*, 1949 S.C. 572 at 578.

[78] See the dictum of Lord Justice Clerk Cullen, as he then was, in *Shetland Islands Council v B.P. Petroleum Development Ltd*, 1990 S.L.T. 82 at 94.

[79] *Scottish Discount Co Ltd v Blin*, 1985 S.C. 216.

[80] See Reid, *The Law of Property in Scotland* (1996), para.583; Paisley, *Land Law* (2000), pp.85–86; as the latter learned writer points out, however, the approach in the *Scottish Discount* case has been followed in the subsequent decision in *Taylor Woodrow Property Co Ltd v S.R.C.*, 1996 G.W.D. 7–397.

[81] See Gordon and Wortley, *Scottish Land Law* (2009), para.4.12 where the learned authors refer to the Stamp Duty Land Tax manual available at *http://www.hmce.eu/manuals/sdltmanual/sdltm04010. htm* [Accessed July 25, 2012].

[82] Carey Miller with Irvine, *Corporeal Moveables in Scots Law* (2005), para.3.15.

[83] The pre-1964 position of a distinction between moveable and heritable property for purposes of the application of intestate succession caused the accession issue to be litigated not infrequently.

[84] *Brand's Trs* (1876) 3 R. (HL) 16.

[85] See Reid, *The Law of Property in Scotland* (1996), para.586.

In principle, of course, the owner of heritage has the right to disannex elements unless this has implications for another's real right in the principal entity. In *Glasgow City Council v Cannell*[86] the Council obtained an interdict to restrain an owner from disposing of stained glass panels in a listed building on the basis that they were fixtures. Here the question of ease of removal is irrelevant but the issue would be whether removal had implications for the building.

As between seller and buyer, there is, in principle, no need to make any reference to fixtures which are part of the unit of heritable property concerned. Independent moveables must, of course, be separately contracted for. In practice, missives are normally drafted to err on the side of avoiding any possible doubt.

Where a right of severance exists, its exercise has the effect of reinvesting ownership in the holder of the right.[87] It is settled that a tenant may remove fixtures attached by him for the purposes of his trade.[88] This right may be exercised at any time during the currency of the lease or within a short period of its termination.[89] A life-renter probably has a similar right but there is a lack of authority as to scope.[90] Regarding agricultural fixtures, s.18 of the Agricultural Holdings (Scotland) Act 1991[91] provides that, subject to certain conditions, any engine, machinery, fencing or other fixture affixed by a tenant, and any building erected by him remain the property of the tenant and removable by him up to six months from the expiry of the lease.[92]

As between the relevant parties, the right to remove a fixture may be modified by agreement. The person affixing the article may do so on the basis that he or she is entitled to remove it but, of course, an agreement to this effect will be binding as a personal right only between the parties.[93]

Fixtures: By destination; constructive—Unannexed corporeal moveables may, **31.11** by destination, become part of heritable subjects for purposes of succession on the basis of the deceased's unequivocal manifestation of intention to unite them to the heritage.[94] Building components and materials collected on the ground for use in a building in the course of erection by a deceased person[95] and the funds required to complete the work[96] have been held to be heritable for succession purposes. In a question as to the succession to a tenant of a farm, dung made on the farm was held to belong to the heir, as the tenant was under an obligation to apply it to the land, and it was to be presumed that his intention was to fulfil that obligation.[97]

---

[86] *Glasgow City Council v Cannell*, 2000 S.L.T. 1023.

[87] Reid, *The Law of Property in Scotland* (1996), para.586 suggests that reacquisition is derivative because the existence of the condition justifies an inference of consent to divesting on the part of the owner of the principal.

[88] *Brand's Trs v Brand's Trs* (1876) 3 R. (HL) 16; *Ferguson v Paul* (1885) 12 R. 1222.

[89] *Cliffplant Ltd v Kinnaird*, 1982 S.L.T. 2, 6; *David Boswell Ltd v William Cook Engineering Ltd*, 1989 S.L.T. (Sh. Ct) 61.

[90] See Gordon and Wortley, *Scottish Land Law* (2009), para.4.24.

[91] See below, para.35.29.

[92] See Lord Gill, *The Law of Agricultural Holdings in Scotland*, 3rd edn (Edinburgh: W. Green, 1997), Ch.26 regarding the complex statutory provisions concerning fixtures in the agricultural context.

[93] *Shetland Islands Council v B.P. Petroleum Development Ltd*, 1990 S.L.T. 82 at 94.

[94] See Gordon and Wortley, *Scottish Land Law* (2009), para.1.34.

[95] Erskine, II, 2, 14; *Johnston v Dobie* (1783) Mor.5443; *Gordon v Gordon* (1806) Hume 188; cf. *Stewart v Watson's Hospital* (1862) 24 D. 256.

[96] *Bank of Scotland v White's Trs* (1891) 28 S.L.R. 891; *Malloch v McLean* (1867) 5 M. 335; see *Fairlie's Trs v Fairlie's Curator Bonis*, 1932 S.C. 216, per Lord President Clyde.

[97] *Reid's Exrs v Reid* (1890) 17 R. 519; see Gordon and Wortley, *Scottish Land Law* (2009), para.1.34.

Constructive annexation applies to things which are moveable but manifestly belong to heritable subjects in terms of purpose. An appropriate criterion is to think in terms of the completeness or essential functioning of the heritable subject concerned. On this basis a moveable fire grate or a drain manhole cover are heritable whereas a reading lamp is not. In certain circumstances functional subordination alone may be sufficient for the purposes of constructive annexation. In one case the issue was whether an oil painting which concealed an unfinished area of wall could be taken to go with the house.[98] The better view is that this is not a case of constructive accession because the relationship between the items of property is not a matter of objective proprietary fact but exists only on the subjective basis of the intention of the person who hung the picture.

31.12 Specification—Subject to certain important limitations one who makes a new entity of property from another's materials acquires it by specification. This is original acquisition because the new thing has not had a prior owner. The primary limitation is that the making is not by arrangement with the owner of the materials[99]—a wedding dress made to order from the customer's silk is not acquired by the seamstress although it is clearly a "new thing". A policy limitation inherent to the act of making may require that it be in good faith.[100] The law could hardly allow acquisition by a thief when he or she had made a new thing from stolen property.[101] A statement by Bell,[102] accepted in the case law,[103] may be taken to encompass the exclusion of making for another in the requirement that the act be bona fide. Accordingly, specification occurs where a new thing is made from materials which the maker believes he or she is free to process for his or her own benefit. It may be noted that the provisions of the DCFR's counterpart concept of "production" apply similar limits in its systematic and comprehensive form. First, "production" can only take place "without the consent of the owner of the materials" or in the absence a "party agreement as to proprietary consequences".[104] Secondly, there can be no acquisition by production where "the labour contribution is of minor importance" or where the producer knows the material is owned by another who does not consent "unless the value of the labour is much higher than the value of the material."[105]

The coming into being of a new thing means a "new species or subject"[106] not merely a different or changed thing as in the "dying of cloth, or the like, which

---

[98] *Cochrane v Stevenson* (1891) 18 R. 1208 (see Reid, *The Law of Property in Scotland* (1996), para.581).

[99] *Wylie & Lochhead v Mitchell* (1870) 8 M. 552.

[100] The justification for this position is much debated; see Carey Miller with Irvine, *Corporeal Moveables in Scots Law* (2005), para.4.06.

[101] *McDonald v Provan*, 1960 S.L.T. 231.

[102] s.1298: "If the materials, as a separate existence, be destroyed in bona fide, the property is with the workman; the owner of the materials having a personal claim for a like quantity and quality, or for the price of the materials; if still capable of restoration to their original shape, the property is held to be with the owner of the materials; a claim against him for work and indemnity, in quantum lucratus, being competent to the workman".

[103] *International Banking Corp v Ferguson, Shaw & Sons*, 1910 S.C. 182; see Reid, *The Law of Property in Scotland* (1996), para.562 (Gordon).

[104] DCFR VIII.–5:101 (1).

[105] DCFR VIII.–5:201 (2).

[106] Erskine, II, 1, 16.

change not the species".[107] In an unreported Outer House decision[108] it was held that the development of adult salmon from smolt did not involve the coming into being of a new thing. There may be a tendency to give specification wider scope than is justified. The question whether a contractual relationship precludes specification did not need to be answered in this case. Arguably, as a default concept, specification does not apply where agreement is controlling. Accordingly, it has no application where materials are supplied, under a credit contract, for processing into new forms of property.[109] The DCFR provisions referred to appear to be consistent with this analysis.

Confusion of liquids and commixtion of solids—A reallocation of rights is   **31.13** necessary when a single proprietary entity is brought into being by the merging of separate elements or entities belonging to different parties.[110] The relevant rules apply where neither accession nor specification is applicable. Confusion refers to a merger of substances which is absolutely irreducible (e.g. the mixing of separate quantities of oil); commixtion refers to a mixing not absolutely irreducible but not reducible in practice (e.g. the mixing of quantities of the same grain). In either case, common ownership results.[111] A reallocation of rights occurs and is given effect to by "the extrication of the rights of parties by applying [a] rule of distribution amongst co-owners".[112] Ownership of the single resulting entity is determined by reference to the proportions involved; if the values of constitutent parts differ this should be factored in.

Where two or more persons have agreed to the mixing the resulting entity will belong to them as common property in shares as agreed or, failing agreement, in shares corresponding to the value of their respective contributions.[113] The bad faith factor is not an issue because the concept does not involve any possible loss of property. As Stair notes, "neither is there any difference, whether the confusion be made by the consent of the parties, by accident, or by mistake, or fault".[114]

Prescription—Positive prescription, as a process of original acquisition by   **31.14** possession subject to certain controlling requirements, has had a major role in the context of land law[115] but a limited one applied to moveable property.[116] The practical significance of a possible 40-year period of possession, as referred to by

---

[107] Stair, II, 1, 41.

[108] *Kinloch Damph Ltd v Nordvik Salmon Farms Ltd* (*http://www.scotcourts.gov.uk/opinions/ ca291499.html* [Accessed July 25, 2012]); see E. Metzger, "Acquisition of living things by specification" (2004) 8 Edin. L.R. 115.

[109] See *Armour v Thyssen Edelstahlwerke A.G.* [1991] 2 A.C. 339; see Reid, *The Law of Property in Scotland* (1996), para.562 (Gordon).

[110] Carey Miller with Irvine, *Corporeal Moveables in Scots Law* (2005), paras 5.06–5.05.

[111] See Reid, *The Law of Property in Scotland* (1996), para.564 (Gordon).

[112] *Tyzack & Branfoot Steamship Co Ltd v Sandeman & Sons*, 1913 S.C. (HL) 84 at 91, per Lord Shaw.

[113] *Wylie & Lochhead v Mitchell* (1870) 8 M. 552.

[114] Stair, II 1, 36.

[115] See below, paras 34.30–34.37.

[116] D. Johnston, *Prescription and Limitation of Actions* (Edinburgh: W. Green, 1999), para.18.01 states that it is "uncertain whether there exists a regime of acquisitive prescription of moveable property in Scotland." See also Reid, *The Law of Property in Scotland* (1996), para.565 (Gordon): "Prescription is scarcely necessary as a basis of acquisition of corporeal moveables in Scots law because, at least as a general rule, possession in itself presumes ownership."

Stair,[117] is clearly limited in the context of corporeal moveable property and early case law is inconclusive.[118]

Negative prescription is provided for in s.8 of the Prescription and Limitation (Scotland) Act 1973 by a bar to the right to recover moveable property unexercised for 20 years. The right to recover stolen property "from the person by whom it was stolen or from any person privy to the stealing thereof"[119] is preserved. However, a subsequent good faith acquirer of stolen property may benefit from the provision and, to this extent, the legislation is an exception to the common law *vitium reale* principle in terms of which an owner's right to recover stolen property is never lost.[120]

The Scottish Law Commission in a Report has mooted possible reform by the introduction of positive prescription.[121] The case for reform is partly, if not primarily, to obtain clarification of a possessor's title which is left uncertain where s 8 bars recovery by a claimant owner. The possessor in this situation is protected by the presumption of ownership[122] but the SLC view is that the property is technically un-owned and title accordingly vests in the Crown. An alternative view is that the presumption functions in this situation to protect the possessor as if he or she were owner.[123]

31.15 **Voluntary transference of property**—Derivative acquisition by voluntary transmission from disponer to acquirer is by far the most prevalent—and, accordingly, important—mode of acquisition of moveable property. As Stair[124] notes it achieves "the transmission or conveyance of real rights from the disponer to his singular successor". In terms of the common law the voluntary transmission of property in corporeal moveables involves and requires both the agreement of the parties to the transmission and a legal act of delivery of the subject in pursuance of that intention.[125] A contract to transmit the property is in itself ineffectual for that purpose; it creates nothing more than a set of rights and obligations which only bind the parties. In the common context of sale, rights and obligations relating to the key aspects of delivery and payment are correlative although, of course, delivery frequently proceeds on the basis of a credit arrangement. The centrality of the point that the law requires an act of transfer to pass property is underlined in a famous dictum of Lord President Inglis: "[a] mere assignation of corporeal moveables *retenta possessione* is nothing whatever but a personal obligation".[126] By mere agreement without delivery, the property or real right in the subject does not pass: *traditionibus non nudis pactis transferuntur rerum dominia*. It is important to note that the correct interpretation of this dictum in modern law is not that some

---

[117] Stair II, 7, 11.

[118] See *Parishioners of Aberscherder v Parish of Gemrie* (1633) Mor.10972; *Ramsay v Wilson* (1666) Mor.9113. See A.R.C. Simpson, "Positive Prescription of Moveables in Scots Law" (2009) 13 Edin. L.R. 445 and Carey Miller with Irvine, *Corporeal Moveables in Scots Law* (2005), paras 7.01–7.03.

[119] Prescription and Limitation (Scotland) Act 1973 Sch.3(g).

[120] See Carey Miller with Irvine, *Corporeal Moveables in Scots Law* (2005), para.7.05.

[121] Scottish Law Commission, *Report on Prescription and Title to Moveable Property*.

[122] See above, para.31.02.

[123] See D.L. Carey Miller, "Positive prescription of corporeal moveables?" (2011) 15 Edin. L.R. 452.

[124] Stair, III, 2, 5.

[125] Erskine, II, 2, 18; Stair, III, 2, 5; Bell, *Commentaries*, II, 11.

[126] *Clark v West Calder Oil Co* (1882) 9 R. 1017 at 1024.

form of delivery is necessarily required but, rather, that there is some separately identifiable legal act on the basis of which property passes.

In view of the controlling position that a right is either personal or real—with no in-between hybrid category[127]—it follows that two identifiable stages are involved in the transmission of a real right. In the classic derivative situation there is, in the first place, an agreement between the parties establishing the essential details of their transaction and creating reciprocal personal rights and obligations, and, in the second place, a subsequent act by which the relevant real right is actually transmitted.[128] In principle, the subsequent act is controlling to the extent that property may pass on the basis of a good act of transfer despite a defective contractual stage.[129] But, as shown in the "abstract/causal" distinction mentioned below, different models are possible. Largely driven by commercial needs, on the basis of an essentially Romanist model, a sophisticated range of modes of delivery was developed as the required legal act to transfer property. The primary categories of delivery are actual, constructive and symbolic.[130] In the development two aspects were fundamental: the agreement of seller and buyer that property would pass and some act or event which identified the relevant point in time of transmission of the real right.

The critical role of the parties' agreement that property should pass is illustrated in the difference between a void transfer and one that is merely voidable in the sense that the transfer of property is achieved but only on a defective basis which is open to challenge. In *Morrisson v Robertson*[131] property did not pass because the seller intended to transfer the livestock to a party known to him—but not involved in the transaction—who the fraudulent buyer was pretending to represent. In these circumstances the purported transfer by delivery to the rogue was void. In *MacLeod v Kerr*[132] the person offering a car for sale was taken in by a fraudulent party. The seller intended to transfer ownership of the car to the fraudster in exchange for the stolen cheque and property accordingly passed but, because of the fraud, the title obtained was defective and open to challenge—i.e. voidable. The important difference between the void and voidable positions is with regards to any possible subsequent transfer. A possessor holding on the basis of a void transfer has no title to pass to any subsequent party. On the other hand, one who holds on a title which is merely voidable can transfer that title until it is avoided; moreover, in principle, a subsequent party who acquires in good faith—innocent as to the defect—will obtain a title unaffected by the defect.[133]

The relevant common law principles are applicable to the transfer of property on the basis of donation[134]; an intention to gift (*animus donandi*) and delivery of the thing is required for the donor to "divest himself of, and invest the donee with,

---

[127] See the "unbridgeable gap" dictum of Lord Rodger referred to in para.30.01, above.

[128] Stair, III, 2, 3 analyses the process in terms of a preliminary "resolution to dispone", a subsequent "paction, contract or obligation" to dispone, and the final act of "present will or consent that that which is the disponer's be the acquirer's". While the first and second elements may be coalesced, the second and third must necessarily be separate.

[129] See Reid, *The Law of Property in Scotland* (1996), para.608.

[130] Reid, *The Law of Property in Scotland* (1996), paras 619–623 (Gordon); Carey Miller with Irvine, *Corporeal Moveables in Scots Law* (2005), paras 8.12–8.27. Regarding forms applicable to real security rights, see below at para.36.12.

[131] *Morrisson v Robertson*, 1908 S.C. 332. See above, para.7.28.

[132] *MacLeod v Kerr*, 1965 S.C. 253.

[133] See Reid, *The Law of Property in Scotland* (1996), para.692.

[134] See para.13.29, above.

the subject of the gift".[135] A presumption against donation[136] is relevant to the level of proof.[137]

The common law position as to the transmission of property is properly analysed as "abstract" rather than "causal". This is because by a requisite act of delivery property may pass on the basis of the parties' agreement to that effect without necessary reference to the underlying cause of a valid contract. Hence, in principle, property passes on delivery where A contemplates sale at market price while B believes that a gift is intended. The better view is that the critical aspect of a requisite act of delivery on the basis of the mutual intention that property will pass achieves this.[138]

A significant departure from the common law came in the Sale of Goods Act in 1893 (now 1979) which abandoned the requirement of a prescribed act of delivery.[139] The uniform position introduced made the transmission of property a matter for the intentions of the parties. It nonetheless remains that under the system of the Act the essential prerequisites must be agreed before any, conceptually distinct, agreed position as to the passing of property can be given effect to. It remains the case that the passing of property from A to B will occur at an identifiable point in time at which the real right in the subject of the sale transmits to the buyer.[140] The process of transmission under the sale Act is distinguishable because the unitary form means that a failure of contract leaves no scope for a nonetheless good transmission of property.

As derivative acquisition is a process of transmission of real rights, contracts regarding moveables do not run with the moveables concerned.[141] This is demonstrated in the double sale situation where, in principle, transfer of property in a thing to a second buyer trumps the unfulfilled personal right position of a first buyer. The "offside goals" rule[142] is not an exception to this; the first buyer in a double sale situation can reduce the transfer to a second buyer with knowledge of the first's personal right but that is only because the second buyer's acquisition is defective by reason of his or her bad faith. As Lord Rodger of Earlsferry noted in *Burnett's Trustee v Grainger*[143] a defective title results from the bad faith of one who obtains title aware of another's prior right to acquire the property concerned.

31.16 Property in ships—Ships are moveable property, but are subject to special rules which require separate notice.[144] Considerations of national policy led the English Parliament, in the seventeenth century, to legislate in regard to shipping, and this

---

[135] *McNicol v McDougall* (1889) 17 R. 25, per Lord Young.

[136] *Brownlee's Exrx v Brownlee*, 1908 S.C. 232; *Milne v Grant* (1884) 11 R. 887; *Thompson v Dunlop* (1884) 11 R. 453; *Grant's Trs v McDonald*, 1939 S.C. 448. See *Newton v Newton*, 1923 S.C. 15.

[137] See W.M. Gordon, "Donation" in *Stair Memorial Encyclopedia*, (Reissue) (2011), paras 19–27.

[138] See Erskine, II, 1, 18 and III, 3, 90. See also Reid, *The Law of Property in Scotland* (1996), paras 608, 609.

[139] Sale of Goods Act 1979 s.17(1): "Where there is a contract for the sale of specific or ascertained goods the property in them is transferred to the buyer at such time as the parties to the contract intend it to be transferred"; see above paras 12.07 and 12.14–12.16. See also now DCFR VIII.– 2:101.

[140] See Reid, *The Law of Property in Scotland* (1996), para.628 (Gamble); see also Carey Miller with Irvine, *Corporeal Moveables in Scots Law* (2005), para.9.01.

[141] See above, para.8.13.

[142] *Rodger (Builders) Ltd v Fawdry*, 1950 S.C. 483; Reid, *The Law of Property in Scotland* (1996), para.690; S. Wortley, "Double sales and the offside trap: some thoughts on the rule penalising private knowledge of a prior right", 2002 Jur. Rev. 291.

[143] *Burnett's Trustee v Grainger*, 2004 S.C. (HL) 19 at [67]. See also the relevant dicta of Lord Eassie in *Alex Brewster and Sons v Caughey*, 2002 G.W.D. 10–318.

[144] See A.R.M. Fogarty, *Merchant Shipping Legislation* (Informa Professional, 2004). See also *Stair Memorial Encyclopaedia*, "Shipping and Navigation" (Reissue).

legislation was copied in Scotland after the Restoration. The regulation of shipping thus introduced has been continued in modern times. The leading statute now in force is the Merchant Shipping Act 1995.

Registration and transfer of ships—The term "ship" includes every description **31.17** of vessel used in navigation not propelled by oars. The former registration of British ships in three registers is now replaced by a single register.[145] The new register must contain a separate part for the registration of fishing vessels and may be divided into other parts "so as to distinguish between classes or descriptions of ships".[146] A ship is a British ship if, inter alia, it is registered in the United Kingdom under the Merchant Shipping Act1995[147] and ships on bareboat charter to a person qualified to own British ships may also be entered in the register even though registered in another country.[148] Registration regulations will determine what persons are qualified to own British ships and the extent of the ownership qualification.[149] The registered owner of a ship or a share therein has a power of disposal thereof.[150] Transfer of a ship or a share therein is effected by a bill of sale unless this will result in the vessel ceasing to have a British connection.[151] The registration regulations will prescribe the form of the bill of sale and the information and evidence needed to accompany an application to the registrar,[152] as well as the manner in which the bill of sale is to be registered.[153] While the provisions of the 1995 Act relate to the mode of transfer of the property in a ship or shares therein, a contract for the sale of these is valid though made without writing.[154]

Protection of corporeal moveable property—The protection of the status quo **31.18** of possession by the remedy of spuilzie has already been referred to.[155]

In terms of proprietary remedies the primary protection is by assertion of a real right of property—whether ownership or a lesser real right. Only the protection of ownership model will be considered here. The protection of property in the present context does not, of course, extend to claims giving effect to obligations. That distinction is important because the better view is that the concept of restitution, properly understood, encompasses the proprietary remedy of vindication and a possible claim for compensation which is a matter for the law of obligations.[156] In principle property may be recovered on the basis of proof of the right of ownership. A possessor defending against such an asserting of title, typically a good

---

[145] Merchant Shipping Act 1995 ss.8–23.

[146] Merchant Shipping Act 1995 s.8(5).

[147] Merchant Shipping Act 1995 s.1.

[148] Merchant Shipping Act 1995 s.17. The registrar may, however, refuse registration where this would be inappropriate: s.9(3).

[149] Merchant Shipping Act 1995 ss.9(1), (2) and 10 and Merchant Shipping (Registration of Ships) Regulations (SI 1993/3138).

[150] Merchant Shipping Act 1995 s.16, Sch.1 para.1(1).

[151] Merchant Shipping Act 1995 s.16, Sch.1 para.2(1).

[152] Merchant Shipping Act 1995 s.10(6), Sch.1 para.2(1); s.10(2)(b). Section 10 should be consulted for the other prerequisites prior to registration which will be prescribed by the registration regulations. The registration requirements are principally found in SI 1993/3138 as amended.

[153] Merchant Shipping Act 1995 s.16, Sch.1 para.2(3).

[154] *McConnachie v Geddes*, 1918 S.C. 391; Requirements of Writing (Scotland) Act 1995.

[155] See above, para.31.02.

[156] See Carey Miller with Irvine, *Corporeal Moveables in Scots Law* (2005), para.10.07. On relevant aspects of enrichment see paras 24.10, 24.12, 24.14 and 24.15, above.

faith purchaser, is protected by the presumption that the possessor is owner.[157] This requires that the claimant establish not only a right of ownership but, also, that possession was parted with or lost in circumstances not consistent with transfer. The second leg of the presumption proceeds on the basis that an owner's intention to transfer property may be inferred. This position is recognised in the range of exceptions to the basic principle that a transfer of possession will only pass property when driven by the owner's active intention.[158] In the distinguishable situation in which the defender asserts a right to possession deriving from the claimant the issue will only be the continuing existence of that right.[159]

FURTHER READING

Carey Miller, D. (with Irvine, D.), *Corporeal Moveables in Scots Law*, 2nd edn (Edinburgh: W. Green, 2005).

Carey Miller, D., Combe, M., Steven, A., and Wortley, S., "National Report on the Transfer of Movables in Scotland" in Faber, W. and Lurger, B. (eds), *National Reports on the Transfer of Movables in Europe II* (Sellier European Law Publishers, 2009).

Fogarty, A.R.M., *Merchant Shipping Legislation*, 2nd edn (Informa Professional, 2004).

Gill, Lord, *The Law of Agricultural Holdings in Scotland*, 3rd edn (Edinburgh: W. Green, 1997).

Gordon, W.M. and Wortley, S., *Scottish Land Law*, 3rd edn (Edinburgh: W. Green, 2009).

Reid, K.G.C. (with Gretton, G.L., Duncan, A.G.M., Gordon, W.M. and Gamble, A.J.), *The Law of Property in Scotland* (Edinburgh: Butterworths, 1996).

Reid, K.G.C., "Property Law: Sources and Doctrine", in Reid, K.G.C. and Zimmermann, R., *A History of Private Law in Scotland* (Oxford: Oxford University Press, 2000), I, p.185.

Scottish Law Commission, *Report on Prescription and Title to Moveable Property* (HMSO, 2012), Scot. Law Com. No.228.

Stair Memorial Encyclopaedia, "Shipping and Navigation" (Reissue).

---

[157] See above, para.31.02.
[158] See Carey Miller with Irvine, *Corporeal Moveables in Scots Law* (2005), paras 10.15 et seq.
[159] See Reid, *The Law of Property in Scotland* (1996), para.150.

CHAPTER 32

MOVEABLE PROPERTY: INCORPOREAL*

Within the category of incorporeal moveable property are included subjects as **32.01** diverse as rights to debts (*nomina debitorum*) or obligations, claims *ex contractu* and *ex delicto*, rights to shares in companies, goodwill, and various intellectual property rights. Some of these are dealt with in other parts of this book; some intellectual property rights, namely trade marks, copyright, design rights, and patents, are dealt with in Ch.33. The main topic for consideration here is the mode and effect in transferring incorporeal moveable property.

Assignations—Incorporeal property cannot be transferred by delivery or posses- **32.02** sion. However, the transfer of the right in the property from one owner to another may be evidenced by deed. Such deed is known as an assignation. This term is applied to deeds conveying either such moveable rights or rights in heritage which are either incapable of infeftment or on which infeftment has not followed. If the subject is heritage, and the deed is granted by one who is infeft in that heritage, it is styled a disposition.[1] The grantor of an assignation is known as the cedent; the grantee as the assignee or (less commonly) cessionary. It is a general rule that unilateral deeds are not effective unless they are delivered.[2]

As a general rule anyone in right of a subject may at pleasure convey it to another. The exceptions to this are few. An alimentary provision and rights which are personal to the creditor from the *delectus personae* or choice made of him by the grantor of the right cannot be assigned.[3] Strictly speaking, a proper liferent is not assignable, but its profits may be assigned.[4] A conditional obligation, or *spes successionis*, may be assigned, and the assignation will become effectual if the condition is purified or the *spes* comes to be vested in the cedent.[5]

Form of assignation—It was once considered that a creditor could not substitute **32.03** another as creditor in his place without the consent of the debtor. As a result, a direct assignation of a debt was impossible. It has since become possible to make the assignee the mandatory of the cedent for the purpose of exacting and discharging the debt but without any obligation to account to the cedent. The older bonds were in the form of mandates, but in the course of time deeds of direct conveyance came into use and have long been sanctioned. The Transmission of

---

* This chapter captures the law and other substantive reference materials as at December 16, 2011.
  [1] Stair, III, 1, 1 and 16; Erskine, II, 7, 2, and III, 5, 1. Erskine's view that a particular moveable subject is transmitted by assignation and not by disposition is controverted by Ross (Lects, i, 189).
  [2] *Connell's Trs v Connell's Tr.*, 1955 S.L.T. 125 and para.41.40, below.
  [3] Erskine, III, 5, 2; see para.8.17, above and para 41.40, below.
  [4] See para.41.41, below.
  [5] *Bedwells & Yates v Tod*, 2 Dec. 1819, FC; *Kirkland v Kirkland's Tr.* (1886) 13 R. 798 at 805; *Buchanan v Alba Diagnostics Limited* [2001] R.P.C. 851; [2004] S.L.T. 255.

Moveable Property (Scotland) Act 1862, without prohibiting the use of the forms then in existence, provides short forms of assignation.[6]

In general, an assignation of incorporeal moveable property need not be in writing.[7]

> "If anything is settled in the law of Scotland it is that no words directly importing conveyance are necessary to constitute an assignation but that any words giving authority or directions, which if fairly carried out will operate a transference, are sufficient to make an assignation".[8]

The phrase "do hereby assign" is considered unambiguous and appears favoured by drafters.[9] Thus a bill of exchange drawn by a beneficiary for whom trustees held funds on these trustees in favour of another was treated as constituting an assignation in his favour,[10] and a writing containing the words "I hand over my life policy to my daughter" was held to be a valid assignation of the grantor's right in the policy.[11] While a document that is overtly an assignation is effective assignation without consideration, a mandate may, depending on circumstances, operate as an assignation.[12]

32.04 Obligations of cedent—In assignations the law implies that the cedent confers on his assignee everything which is necessary to make the assignation effectual.[13] It is also implied that the cedent warrants that the debt is subsisting: that the bond, decree or other deed assigned is such as can never be reduced, and that the cedent has undoubted right to the debt.[14] However, there is no implied warranty of the solvency of the debtor.[15]

32.05 Intimation—As between the cedent (or his executor) and the assignee, the execution and delivery of the assignation are sufficient to give the latter a valid right.[16] But for the purpose of giving the assignee a right effectual as against all parties, intimation of the assignation to the debtor or holder of the fund is necessary. The assignation is thereby brought to the knowledge of the debtor or holder so as to interpel him from paying the debt or making over the fund to the original creditor or to any other assignee. If thereafter he chooses to do so, this will afford him no defence to the claim by the assignee who gave him intimation.[17]

---

[6] Transmission of Moveable Property (Scotland) Act 1862 Schs A–C, as amended by the Requirements of Writing (Scotland) Act 1995 s.14(1), Sch.4 paras 14–15.

[7] Requirements of Writing (Scotland) Act 1995 ss.1 and 11(3)(a); some statutes prescribe particular forms to be adopted, i.e. Policies of Assurance Act 1867. See also Scottish Law Commission, *Discussion Paper on Moveable Transactions* (HMSO, 2011), Scot. Law Com. Discussion Paper No.151, paras 4.29–4.31.

[8] *Carter v McIntosh* (1862) 24 D. 925 at 933, per Lord Justice-Clerk Inglis; see also *Gallemos Ltd v Barratt Falkirk Ltd*, 1989 S.C. 239; *Christie, Owen and Davies Plc v Campbell*, 2009 S.C. 436.

[9] Scottish Law Commission, *Discussion Paper on Moveable Transactions*, para.4.32.

[10] *Carter v McIntosh* (1862) 24 D. 925.

[11] *Brownlee v Robb*, 1907 S.C. 1302.

[12] *National Commercial Bank v Millar's Tr.*, 1964 S.L.T. (Notes) 57 at 59.

[13] *Miller v Muirhead* (1894) 21 R. 658.

[14] *Barclay v Liddel* (1671) Mor.16591; *Reid v Barclay* (1879) 6 R. 1007.

[15] Erskine, II, 3, 25.

[16] *Thome v Thome* (1683) 2 Brown's Sup. 49; Stair, III, 1, 15.

[17] See *McGill v Laureston* (1558) Mor.843; *McDowal v Fullerton* (1714) Mor.576 at 840.

It has long been settled that intimation is necessary to complete the assignee's right: "The assignation itself is not a complete valid right till it be orderly intimated to the debtor."[18] It is the point from which the passing of the right is dated and also the criterion by which the right of the assignee is determined in a question with other assignees or claimants to the fund or debt. If A, having assigned a debt due to him to B, subsequently assigns it to C, the assignation to C, although later in date, will if it is first intimated, carry the debt. So also an arrestment prior in date to the intimation, though subsequent to the assignation itself, will prevail over the assignation. But if it is later in date than the intimation, the assignation will be preferred.[19] Further, the intimation of the assignation of a debt will prevent the debtor X from pleading compensation against the assignee B, in respect of a debt due by the cedent A, which X has acquired after the date of the intimation; the right to the debt having passed from A with the intimation, there is no proper concourse of credit and debt between the same persons.[20] But if prior to the intimation the right to compensate was vested in the debtor X, then it will be available to him against the assignee B.[21] The intimation also has the effect of making it incompetent to prove any exception against the debt, whether of payment or otherwise, by the oath of the cedent unless the subject has been rendered litigious before intimation or the assignee admits on reference to his oath that the assignation is gratuitous or in trust for the cedent.[22]

Forms of intimation—The old, and still competent, form of regular intimation is **32.06** for a procurator for the assignee to deliver to the debtor, in the presence of a notary and witnesses, a copy of the assignation and to take the instruments in the notary's hands.[23] But by the Transmission of Moveable Property (Scotland) Act 1862 alternative forms are introduced. These are: (a) delivery by a notary of a certified copy of the assignation, or (b) transmission by the holder of the assignation or his agent of a certified copy by post, the first being vouched by the notary's certificate of intimation, the second by the debtor's written acknowledgment. Of a complex deed only a copy of the part containing the assignation need be sent.[24] Where there are several obligants, as in the case of trustees, or joint debtors, intimation should be made to all unless some one or more of them take the whole management; for otherwise, while intimation to one would complete the assignation, it would not interpel the others from paying the cedent.[25] The Partnership Act 1890 provides that notice to any partner who habitually acts in the partnership business of any matter relating to partnership affairs operates as notice to the firm.[26] The Companies Act 2006 also provides for the service of document on a company

---

[18] Stair, III, 1, 6; Erskine, III, 5, 3; Bell, *Commentaries*, II, 16; *Liquidator of Union Club v Edinburgh Life Assurance Co* (1906) 8 F. 1143 at 1146, per Lord McLaren.

[19] Stair, III, 1, 43 and 44; Erskine, III, 6, 19; *Liquidator of Union Club v Edinburgh Life Assurance Co* (1906) 8 F. 1143; see also Scottish Law Commission, *Discussion Paper on Moveable Transactions*, paras 4.36–4.38, 14.29–14.32.

[20] See para.3.33, above; *Macpherson's J.F. v Mackay*, 1915 S.C. 1011; *Wallace v Edgar* (1663) Mor.837; *Chambers' J.F. v Vertue* (1893) 20 R. 257.

[21] *Shiells v Ferguson, Davidson & Co* (1876) 4 R. 250.

[22] *Lang v Hislop* (1854) 16 D. 908.

[23] For details see A.M. Bell, *Lectures on Conveyancing*, 3rd edn (1882), I, 311; W.W. McBryde, *The Law of Contract in Scotland*, 3rd edn (Edinburgh: W. Green, 2007), para.12–96.

[24] See also Scottish Law Commission, *Discussion Paper on Moveable Transactions*, para.4.41–43.

[25] Erskine, III, 5, 5; *Jameson v Sharp* (1887) 14 R. 643. See *Browne's Tr. v Anderson* (1901) 4 F. 305.

[26] Partnership Act 1890 s.16.

registered under the Act to be effective by leaving it at, or sending it by post to the company's registered office.[27]

32.07 Equivalents of intimation[28]—The law admits equivalents of intimation where the notice of the assignation given to the debtor is equally strong.[29] Thus, diligence or a suit against the debtor founded on the assignation at the instance of the assignee, or a claim in a multiplepoinding to which the debtor is a party supplies the want of intimation, as these are judicial and public acts which bring the assignation to the eyes of the public and of the debtor.[30] The assignee's possession of the right by entering into enjoyment of the rents or interest is also equal to an intimation, for it imports not only notice to, but actual compliance by, the debtor.[31] An assignation of a lease, or of the rents and profits of land, is perfected by intimation to the landlord and the assignee's possessing the ground or levying the rents. Assignations of heritable bonds, real burdens, registered leases and securities over these are completed by registration in the Register of Sasines or the Land Register[32]; but the registration of assignations of personal rights as bonds, contracts, etc. in the Books of Council and Session or of the sheriff courts does not suffice, as these are merely for preservation and diligence and not for publication.[33] Notice to the common debtor's factor in entire control of the estate, followed by entry thereof in his books,[34] and an assignee's attending and voting at the meeting of a company in virtue of the share assigned to him[35] have also been held sufficient proof of intimation.

In a competition between an unintimated assignation and other claims, the defect in the assignee's title due to the absence of intimation will not be cured by the fact that the debtor was aware of the assignation.[36] But the following have been held to be equivalents of intimation: a written promise by the debtor to pay the debt to the assignee[37]; payment by him of part of the capital or the interest of the debt[38]; the participation by him as a party[39] (not as a witness[40]) to the assignation.

---

[27] Companies Act 2006 s.1139.

[28] See also Scottish Law Commission, *Discussion Paper on Moveable Transactions*, paras 14.5–14.81.

[29] See also fn.8, above.

[30] *Whyte v Neish* (1622) Mor.854; *Dougall v Gordon* (1795) Mor.851.

[31] Erskine, *Principles*, III, 5, 3.

[32] *Edmond v Mags of Aberdeen* (1858) 3 Macq. 116. It should be noted that, in the case of a "long lease", registration in the Land Register is the only means of obtaining a real right in an area in respect of which the Land Registration etc. (Scotland) Act 2012 will come into operation. See para.35.05, below.

[33] *Tod's Trs v Wilson* (1869) 7 Mor.1100; see *Cameron's Trs v Cameron*, 1907 S.C. 407. Cf. *Carmichael v Carmichael's Executrix*, 1920 S.C. (HL) 195, per Lord Dunedin.

[34] *Earl of Aberdeen v Earl of March* (1730) 1 Pat. 44.

[35] *Hill v Lindsay* (1847) 10 D. 78.

[36] *Lord Rollo v Laird of Niddrie* (1665) 1 Brown Sup.510. It would seem (although the point is not altogether clear) that, according to the decisions, even where there is no such competition, the debtor's knowledge of the assignation will not render him liable to the assignee if he pays the debt to the cedent while no intimation has been given. See Stair, II, 1, 24 and More's Note cclxxxi; Bell, *Commentaries*, II, 18; *Dickson v Troner* (1776) Mor.873, Hailes 675; *Faculty of Advocates v Dickson* (1718) Mor.866; *L. Westraw v Williamson & Carmichael* (1626) Mor.859; *Adamson v McMitchell* (1624) Mor.859; and cf. *Leith v Garden* (1703) Mor.865, and Erskine, III, 5, 5.

[37] *Home v Murray* (1674) Mor.863.

[38] *Livingston v Lindsay* (1626) Mor.860.

[39] *Turnbull v Stewart* (1751) Mor.868.

[40] *Murray v Durham* (1622) Mor.855.

If the assignation is granted to the debtor in the obligation, or to or by the person to whom intimation would in the ordinary course fall to be made, intimation is unnecessary. Thus, where the beneficiary under a trust was also the sole trustee, it was held that intimation of an assignation by him was not required, seeing that he intimated it to himself as trustee when he granted the deed.[41]

Effect of assignation—The effect of an assignation is to place the assignee in the **32.08** shoes of the cedent. He may sue and do diligence to enforce the right which has been assigned to him. But that right is vested in him subject to all the contingencies which affected the author. *Assignatus utitur jure auctoris.*

No higher right can be conferred by the cedent than that which he himself possesses. *Nemo plus juris ad alium transferre potest quam ipse habet.*[42] Thus a person who has a temporary right, or one which is liable to be withdrawn or defeated, cannot give to his assignee a permanent or absolute right; if the right comes to an end or is withdrawn or defeated, the assignee's right falls.[43] In *Johnstone-Beattie v Dalzell*[44] a sum was settled by a father in his daughter's marriage-contract in trust to pay a sum on his death to the husband. The husband assigned this sum in security to creditors. Subsequently he was divorced and thereby forfeited his right to the sum, and it was held that the right of his assignees was resolved by this forfeiture. So also, if trustees have a discretionary power to withdraw or reduce the interest of a beneficiary the exercise of that power will be effectual in a question with one to whom the beneficiary has assigned his interest.[45]

Moreover, the right passes to the assignee subject to all the pleas and exceptions pleadable by the debtor against the cedent. As against the assignee, the debtor may avail himself of every defence which would have been competent to him against the cedent; and it matters not that the assignee is a bona fide purchaser.[46] Thus, if a person who takes out an insurance on his life is guilty of misrepresentations which render the policy reducible in a question with him, this is pleadable by the insurance company against an onerous assignee of the insurer.[47] And if one party to a contract assigns it, the other may maintain against the assignee the claims arising out of the contract or in respect of its breach which would have been available against the cedent.[48] Thus, in *Arnott's Trs v Forbes*,[49] a vassal was held entitled to retain his feu-duty in respect of a breach of contract by his superior in a question with a heritable creditor to whom the superiority had been disponed in security.

This rule is without exception in the sphere in which it is applicable—the assignation of personal obligations. It does not apply to the transmission of heritable estate

---

[41] *Browne's Trs v Anderson* (1901) 4 F. 305; *Russell v Breadalbane* (1831) 5 W. & S. 256.

[42] Dig., 50, 17, 54.

[43] *Resoluto jure dantis, resolvitur jus accipientis.*

[44] (1868) 6 M. 333.

[45] *Chamber's Trs v Smiths* (1878) 5 R. (HL) 151; *Train v Clapperton*, 1907 S.C. 517, affd 1908 S.C. (HL) 26.

[46] Stair, I, 10, 16; III, 1, 20; and IV, 40, 21; Erskine, III, 5, 10; *McDonells v Bell & Rennie* (1772) Mor.4974.

[47] *Scottish Widows' Fund v Buist* (1876) 3 R. 1078; 5 R. (HL) 64; *Shiells v Ferguson, Davidson & Co* (1876) 4 R. 250.

[48] Elchies' Annotations, 62.

[49] (1881) 9 R. 89; see also *Duncan v Brooks* (1894) 21 R. 760.

"for there the disponee rests upon the faith of the records and so may disregard all rights granted by his author upon which an infeftment has not been taken before that which proceeded on his own disposition";

or to the sale of corporeal moveables, or to negotiable instruments, because "a free course of commerce" must be secured.[50]

But a person may waive his rights under the law, and so the debtor in an obligation may undertake in express terms that the pleas and counterclaims between the original parties shall not be pleadable in a question with assignees.[51] This undertaking will receive effect; and, according to a series of cases in England concerned with such documents as debentures and letters of credit, even without express stipulation the same result will follow when it appears from the nature or terms of the contract that it must have been intended to be assignable free from and unaffected by such pleas and counterclaims.[52] Moreover, the debtor may by his behaviour towards the assignee be precluded from urging pleas which otherwise would have been open to him. Thus, if an insurance company, in the knowledge that there were clear objections to the validity of an insurance policy, continued to receive the premiums from an assignee of the policy, this may deprive them of the right to challenge the policy.[53]

32.09 Latent trusts and claims—The general rule that an assignee takes subject to all the pleas which would have been available against the cedent must not be understood as meaning that he is necessarily exposed to all the latent claims to which the cedent is open. This is brought out in the case of *Redfearn v Somervail*.[54] There, one who appeared to the world as owner of a share in a private company, but in reality had acquired it as trustee for a firm of which he was a partner, assigned it to a creditor in security of a private loan. The assignation was taken by the creditor in the honest belief that the cedent was the absolute owner of the share and it was duly intimated. A competition then ensued between the firm claiming the share as partnership property and the creditor as assignee, in which it was held that the latter's claim must prevail. The ground on which this decision proceeded was that the question was not amongst the debtor in the obligation, the company, and the assignee "but between the assignee and a person setting up a collateral claim in the nature of that of a *cestui que trust*".[55] Under the rule *assignatus utitur jure auctoris*, the assignee was exposed to all the pleas which would have been available to the company against the cedent; but that rule had no application to the case of another party intervening to set up a right to the subjects as beneficiary under a latent trust.

The principle established in this decision is that if an assignation is onerous and is taken in good faith, the assignee takes the subject free from all latent trusts or equities affecting the cedent's right. It is otherwise if the assignee is aware of the

---

[50] Erskine, III, 5, 10; *Scottish Widows' Fund v Buist* (1876) 3 R. 1078, per Lord President Inglis; see para.32.10, below.

[51] See *Bovill v Dixon* (1854) 16 D. 619, per Lord Rutherford, affd 3 Macq. 1.

[52] F. Pollock, *Principles of Contract*, 13th edn (London: Stevens and Sons, 1950), pp.180–182; McBryde, *The Law of Contract in Scotland* (2007), paras 12–68—12–78. See also Scottish Law Commission, *Discussion Paper on Moveable Transactions*, para.4.21.

[53] *Scottish Equitable Life Assurance Society v Buist* (1877) 4 R. 1076, per Lord President Inglis; *Bovill v Dixon* (1854) 16 D. 619.

[54] *Redfearn v Somervail* (1813) 1 Dow 50; see also *Burns v Laurie's Trs* (1840) 2 D. 1348. Cf. *Scottish Equitable Life Assurance Society v Buist* (1877) 4 R. 1076; 5 R. (HL) 64.

[55] *Redfearn v Somervail* (1813) 1 Dow 50 at 71; the English term for a beneficiary under a trust.

equity, or does not take the assignation in the honest belief that the cedent is entitled lawfully to enter into the transaction; or, if the assignee, although taking in good faith, does not give any valuable consideration for the assignation. Gratuitous assignees are not protected. Nor does the principle of *Redfearn v Somervail* apply to the case of a general body of creditors under a sequestration who take the rights of the bankrupt *tantum et tale* as they stand in his person.[56] Thus, where a bankrupt appeared on the Register of Sasines as owner of heritable property, but had executed an unregistered declaration that he held this property as trustee for a company, it was held that the property did not pass to the trustee in his sequestration, for the trustee merely represented creditors who had no dealings with the bankrupt in relation to that property and who had given no value for the interest in it which he claimed. The trustee was not therefore in a position to found on the principle which protects onerous bona fide alienees.[57] Now, by statute, property held by the bankrupt in trust for any other person does not vest in the trustee in the sequestration.[58] Where the purchaser of a heritable property has paid the purchase price, received the relevant disposition and taken possession of the property, but not registered the disposition as required, and where the vendor is sequestrated, the right to the property and the purchase price transfer to the trustee. Ownership is determined by the status at the registry. Delivery of the disposition does not transfer any real right in the property.[59]

Negotiable instruments—Any person obtaining money in good faith and for **32.10** valuable consideration is entitled to retain it notwithstanding that it has been lost or stolen from a former owner.[60] A different rule, as has been shown, prevails in regard to the assignation of rights and claims: the holder of the assignation is affected by infirmities in the title of his author. But there is a class of documents which the law, following mercantile usage, assimilates to money and treats as in effect part of the currency. The documents belonging to this class are known as negotiable instruments.[61]

A negotiable instrument is a document containing an obligation to pay money and possessing two distinguishing characteristics. The document must be such that (1) delivery of it will transfer to the transferee the right to the obligation contained in it, and (2) a bona fide holder for value will acquire a title valid against all the world notwithstanding any defect in the title of the transferor or prior holders.

Both of these characteristics must be present, otherwise the document is not a negotiable instrument.[62] In the first place the document must be such that when transferred it will pass in its own corpus the thing it represents without intimation.[63] If, for this purpose, a deed of transfer and not simple delivery of the

---

[56] *Gordon v Cheyne* (1824) 2 S. 675.

[57] *Heritable Reversionary Co v Millar* (1892) 19 R. (HL) 43. In his speech Lord Watson refers to "the well-known principle that a true owner who chooses to conceal his right from the public, and to clothe his trustee with all the indicia of ownership, is thereby barred from challenging rights acquired by innocent third parties for onerous consideration under contracts with his fraudulent trustee". See also *Bank of Scotland v Liquidators of Hutchison, Main & Co*, 1914 S.C. (HL) 1.

[58] Bankruptcy (Scotland) Act 1985 s.33(1)(b).

[59] *Burnett's Tr. v Grainger*, 2004 S.L.T. 513. See also, para.30.12.

[60] Bell, *Principles*, s.528.

[61] See generally E.A. Marshall, *Scots Mercantile Law*, 3rd edn (Edinburgh: W. Green, 1997), Ch.6.

[62] *London Joint Stock Bank v Simmons* [1892] A.C. 201. See W.M. Gloag and J.M. Irvine, *Law of Rights in Security* (Edinburgh: W. Green, 1987), p.548; Marshall, *Scots Mercantile Law* (1997), p. 384.

[63] *Connal & Co v Loder* (1868) 6 M. 1095 at 1102, per Lord Neaves.

document is required, the document is not a negotiable instrument.[64] Even in the case of documents which transfer the right by mere delivery they must, to be negotiable, be in a state in which this can be accomplished. Thus if a bill of exchange or cheque is so drawn as to require indorsement for its transference, it is not negotiable until it has been indorsed.

The second characteristic is the more important. If a document is negotiable a valid title may be acquired to it, even though it was stolen from, or passed out of the possession of, the owner or was delivered to the holder without the owner's consent:

> "The general rule of the law is, that where a person has obtained the property of another from one who is dealing with it without the authority of the true owner, no title is acquired as against that owner, even though full value be given, and the property be taken in the belief that an unquestionable title is being obtained, unless the person taking it can show that the true owner has so acted as to mislead him into the belief that the person dealing with the property had authority to do so. If this can be shown, a good title is acquired by personal bar[65] against the true owner. There is an exception to the general rule, however, in the case of negotiable instruments. Any person in possession of these may convey a good title to them, even when he is acting in fraud of the true owner, and although such owner has done nothing tending to mislead the person taking them."[66]

This protection is given only to one who has taken the bill for value and in good faith.[67] A bona fide holder is one who takes the instrument honestly and without knowledge of any defect in the title of the transferor. Negligence or foolishness in not suspecting that there is something wrong in that title when there are circumstances which might lead to that suspicion is not inconsistent with good faith; but if suspicion or doubt is in fact created and the bill is taken without any inquiry, or if on inquiry the suspicion or doubt is not removed, the holder would not be in good faith.[68]

Documents may be made negotiable either by statute or by mercantile usage recognised by the law. But it is not within the power of private persons to give by stipulation this privilege to a document. Such a stipulation may be good as between the immediate parties, but it cannot affect the rights of subsequent holders so as to place these at the mercy of any thief who can find a bona fide purchaser or to give them a right to sue on the document.[69]

> "Independently of the law merchant and of positive statute . . . the law does not either in Scotland or in England enable any man by a written engagement to give a floating right of action at the suit of anyone into whose hands the writing may come, and who may thus acquire a right of action better than the right of him under whom he derives title."[70]

---

[64] *London & County Banking Co v London & River Plate Bank* (1888) L.R. 20 Q.B.D. 232; 21 Q.B.D. 535.

[65] E.C. Reid and J.W.G. Blackie, *Personal Bar* (Edinburgh: W. Green, 2006), Ch. 17.

[66] *London Joint Stock Bank v Simmons* [1892] A.C. 201 at 215, per Lord Herschell; *Walker & Watson v Sturrock* (1897) 35 S.L.R. 26.

[67] *Banque Belge v Hambrouck* [1921] 1 K.B. 321.

[68] *Jones v Gordon* (1877) L.R. 2 App. Cas. 616, per Lord Blackburn; *London Joint Stock Bank v Simmons* [1892] A.C. 201, per Lord Herschell.

[69] *Crouch v Credit Foncier of England* (1873) L.R. 8 Q.B. 374, per Lord Blackburn.

[70] *Bovill v Dixon* (1856) 3 Macq. 1 at 16, per Lord Cranworth L.C.

Among the class of British negotiable instruments are bills of exchange, cheques and promissory notes[71] (except in so far as they are restrictively indorsed or have lost the character of negotiability through being overdue or otherwise), banknotes, exchequer bills and bonds (unless registered), treasury bills, dividend warrants, debenture bonds of a British company payable to bearer, scrip certificates to bearer for shares, and share warrants to bearer. The class is not, however, stereotyped. If the court is satisfied that other documents have, by general usage of traders and merchants, come to be treated as negotiable instruments, it will recognise and give effect to this usage.[72] Post Office money orders and postal orders are not negotiable instruments.[73] A bill of lading is not strictly a negotiable instrument, as the transferee does not get a better title than the transferor[74]; nor are documents of title under the Factors Act and deposit receipts.[75]

Goodwill— The goodwill of a business was said by Lord Eldon to be "nothing **32.11** more than the probability that the old customers will resort to the old place".[76] This is an important element in goodwill, but as a definition the statement is too narrow.[77] The goodwill of a business is the whole advantage, whatever it may be, of the reputation and connection of the firm:

> "It is the connection thus formed, together with the circumstances, whether of habit or otherwise, which tend to make it permanent, that constitutes the goodwill of a business. It is this which constitutes the difference between a business just started, which has no goodwill attached to it, and one which has acquired a goodwill. The former trader has to seek out his customers from among the community as best he can. The latter has a custom ready made. He knows what members of the community are purchasers of the articles in which he deals, and are not attached by custom to any other establishment."[78]

Goodwill may be sold, and the vendor thereby bars himself from representing that he is continuing the old business; he therefore cannot use the firm name[79] or trade mark, nor can he solicit the customers of that business to transfer their custom to him.[80] The vendor may, however, set up for himself in the old trade under his own name, and even in close proximity to the premises in which the business he has sold is carried on; and he may deal with customers of the old business who come to him of their own accord without solicitation.[81] The executor carrying through a contract for the sale of a business concluded by the deceased was held not entitled to solicit the customers of that business.[82] Where a sale of the debtor's business is

---

[71] See para.19.48, above, also Bills of Exchange Act 1882.
[72] *Goodwin v Robarts* (1875) L.R. 10 Exch. 337; 1 App. Cas. 476; *Bechaunaland Exploration Co v London Trading Bank* [1898] 2 Q.B. 658.
[73] *Fine Art Society v Union Bank of London* (1886) L.R. 17 Q.B.D. 705.
[74] See also Scottish Law Commission, *Discussion Paper on Moveable Transactions*, paras 15.3–15.7.
[75] *Barstow v Inglis* (1857) 20 D. 230; *Wood v Clydesdale Bank*, 1914 S.C. 397. As to the nature of a deposit receipt, see *Dickson v National Bank of Scotland*, 1917 S.C. (HL) 50.
[76] *Cruttwell v Lye* (1810) 17 Ves 335 at 346.
[77] *Trego v Hunt* [1896] A.C. 7.
[78] *Trego v Hunt* [1896] A.C. 7 at 17–18, per Lord Herschell; *Inland Revenue Comrs v Muller & Co's Margarine* [1901] A.C. 217 at 223, per Lord Macnaghten.
[79] *Smith v McBride & Smith* (1888) 16 R. 36.
[80] *Dumbarton Steamboat Co v Macfarlane* (1899) 1 F. 993; *Curl Bros v Webster* [1904] 1 Ch. 685.
[81] *Re David & Matthews* [1899] 1 Ch. 378; but see para.33.02, below (passing off).
[82] *Boorne v Wicker* [1927] 1 Ch. 667.

effected by the trustee in his sequestration or by a trustee for creditors, it has been held that the debtor cannot be prevented from soliciting the customers of that business.[83]

The Partnership Act 1890[84] provides that the mere receipt of part of the profits of a business by a person, in respect of the sale by him of the goodwill, does not make him a partner. If the matter is not dealt with in the contract of copartnery, the goodwill of the business is part of the assets of the firm, and on its dissolution, any partner or the representative of a deceased partner can insist on its being sold.[85] A provision in a contract of copartnery whereby one partner undertakes not to carry on the same business after the dissolution of the firm is not a mere personal contract between the partners, but passes with the goodwill, and may be enforced by a purchaser thereof.[86]

In the case of a professional business depending on the personal qualities of the practitioner, the goodwill of the practice may not be considered to have the value which belongs to the goodwill of a commercial business.[87]

Goodwill may be moveable or heritable. This is a question of fact depending on whether the goodwill is associated with the premises in which the business has been carried on or with the reputation of the trader.[88] In some cases both of these elements may be present, and if so, the goodwill is treated as partly heritable and partly moveable.[89]

FURTHER READING

Anderson, R.G., *Assignation* (Edinburgh: Avizandum, 2008).

Halliday, J.M., *Conveyancing Law and Practice in Scotland*, 2nd edn (Edinbugh: W. Green, 1997).

Marshall, E., *Scots Mercantile Law*, 3rd edn (Edinburgh: W. Green, 1997).

McBryde, W.W., *The Law of Contract in Scotland*, 3rd edn (Edinburgh: W. Green, 2007).

Scottish Law Commission, *Discussion Paper on Moveable Transactions* (HMSO, 2011), Scot. Law Com. Discussion Paper No.151, Chs 4, 14, and 15.

Steven, A.J.M., *Pledge and Lien* (Edinburgh: Edinburgh Legal Educational Trust, 2008).

---

[83] *Walker v Mottram* (1881) L.R. 19 Ch.D. 355; *Farey v Cooper* [1927] 2 K.B. 384; *Melrose Drover v Heddle* (1902) 4 F. 1120.

[84] Partnership Act 1890 s.2(3)(e). See also s.3 in respect of the purchaser of goodwill in consideration of a share of the profits of the business.

[85] Bell, *Principles*, s.379; *Re David & Matthews* [1899] 1 Ch. 378.

[86] *Townsend v Jarman* [1900] 2 Ch. 698.

[87] *Bain v Munro* (1878) 5 R. 416; *Rodger v Herbertson*, 1909 S.C. 256; *Thatcher v Thatcher* (1904) 11 S.L.T. 605; see *May v Thomson* (1882) L.R. 20 Ch.D. 705 at 718, per Jessel M.R.

[88] *Muirhead's Trs v Muirhead* (1905) 7 F. 496; *Graham v Graham's Trs* (1904) 6 F. 1015; *Hughes v Assessor for Stirling* (1892) 19 R. 840.

[89] *Murray's Tr. v McIntyre* (1904) 6 F. 588; *Assessor for Edinburgh v Caira & Crolla*, 1928 S.C. 398.

CHAPTER 33

INTELLECTUAL PROPERTY*

Introduction—Space allows only a brief treatment of this complex and multi- **33.01** faceted subject. The focus of the treatment here is the UK legislation on the subject, although given that much of this now flows from or is influenced by European directives, regulations and conventions and that European intellectual property law regimes operate within the United Kingdom as part of the European Community, due regard must be had to the decisions of the various European institutions active in the field. It is not possible here to deal with, for example, the impact upon the intellectual property of such Community law principles as those promoting the free movement of goods and services ("exhaustion of rights"), or competition. Guidance on these should be sought in more specialised works.[1]

I. TRADE NAMES AND MARKS

Passing off—Apart from statute there can be no right of property in a name or **33.02** mark[2]; but the common law recognises the right of a trader to prevent other parties from using the trader's name or mark, or a similar name or mark, in such a way as is likely to mislead the public into thinking that the business carried on, or the goods or services sold, under these parties' name or mark are those of the trader.[3]

> "[N]o man is entitled to represent his goods as being the goods of another man, and no man is permitted to use any mark, sign or symbol, device or other means whereby, without making a direct false representation himself to a purchaser who purchases from him, he enables such purchaser to tell a lie, or to make a false representation, to somebody else who is the ultimate customer."[4]

The use of a "get-up" of goods may constitute passing off.[5] In an action by a trader seeking to prevent other's use of a name or device in connection with goods or

---

* This chapter captures the law and other substantive reference materials as at December 16, 2011.

[1] See, e.g. C. Stothers, *Parallel Trade in Europe: Intellectual Property, Competition and Regulatory Law* (Oxford: Hart Publishing, 2007).

[2] *Charles P. Kinnell & Co v Ballantine & Sons*, 1910 S.C. 246, per Lord President Dunedin and Lord Skerrington.

[3] *Williamson v Miekle*, 1909 S.C. 1272 at 1278, per Lord Skerrington.

[4] *Singer Co v Loog* (1880) Ch.D. 395 at 412; *Cellular Clothing Co v Maxton & Murray* (1899) 1 F. 29; *Wise Property Care Ltd v White Thomson Preservation Ltd* [2008] CSIH 44 at [36]: "no man is entitled to carry on his business in such a way or by such a name as to lead to the belief that he is carrying on the business of another man or to lead to the belief that the business which he is carrying on has any connection with the business carried on by the other man . . ." citing Romer L.J. in *Clock Ltd v Clockhouse Hotel Ltd* (1936) R.P.C. 269 at 275.

[5] *John Haig & Co v Forth Blending Co*, 1954 S.C. 35 (dimple bottle); *Reckitt & Colman Products Ltd v Borden Inc (No.3)* [1990] 1 W.L.R. 491 (lemon shaped container).

services, it is incumbent on the trader pursuer to prove that that name or device has become so associated with his goods or services as to denote in the market that they are his.[6] If the name is an invented or fancy word, this proof is much easier than in the case of an ordinary word descriptive of the quality or place of manufacture of the article. However, even a descriptive word may acquire a secondary significance as denoting and distinguishing the goods or services of a particular trader so as to make its use without qualification by a rival trader misleading.[7] Traders may also share a name or mark which distinguishes their goods collectively; those traders may seek to protect the goodwill so acquired.[8] It is not necessary to prove fraud on the part of the defender[9] or that any member of the public has been actually deceived[10]; but it must be shown that the defender's use of the name or device is likely to deceive the public.[11] An individual cannot be restrained from carrying on business or selling his goods under his own name unless it appears from his conduct that he is seeking to take advantage of the similarity of his name with that of another trader for the purpose of passing off his own goods as those of the other trader[12] or as associated with that other trader.[13] However, a newly formed limited company may be prohibited from using a name which is liable to be confused with that of another established business in the same or related line of trade, although the name selected is, or incorporates, the personal name of one of the directors or shareholders.[14] Where a trader makes false representations as to his goods amounting to a fraud on the public, he is thereby disentitled to protection for the name used by him in regard to these goods.[15] A professional designation such as CA or WS may be protected from use by unqualified persons.[16] A person who provides others with the means of deceiving the public may be liable for passing off.[17]

33.03 **Registration of trade marks**—While the right to protect a trade name is left to depend on the common law, trade marks have since 1875[18] been afforded further protection by a series of statutes. The present statutory provisions are contained in

---

[6] *Charles P. Kinnell & Co v Ballantine & Sons*, 1910 S.C. 246.

[7] *Reddaway v Banham* [1896] A.C. 199; *Cellular Clothing Co v Maxton & Murray* (1899) 1 F. 29.

[8] *Bollinger (J.) v Costa Brava Wine Co (No.3)* [1960] Ch. 262 (champagne); *Vine Products v Mackenzie & Co* [1969] R.P.C. 1 (sherry); *Walker (John) & Sons v Henry Ost & Co* [1970] 1 W.L.R. 917 (whisky); *Erven Warnink Besloten Vennootschap v J. Townend & Sons (Hull) Ltd* [1979] A.C. 731 (advocaat); *John Walker & Sons Ltd v Douglas Laing & Co Ltd*, 1993 S.L.T. 156 (whisky); *Taittinger S.A. v Allbev Ltd* [1994] 4 All E.R. 75 (champagne); *Chocosuisse Union des Fabricants de Chocolat v Cadbury Ltd* [1999] R.P.C. 826 (Swiss chocolate); *Diageo North America Inc v Intercontinental Brands (ICB) Ltd* [2010] EWCA Civ 920; [2011] 1 All E.R. 242 (vodka).

[9] *The "Singer" Machine Manufacturers v Wilson* (1877) L.R. 3 App. Cas. 376 at 391, per Lord Cairns L.C.

[10] *Charles P. Kinnell & Co v Ballantine & Sons*, 1910 S.C. 246.

[11] *Dunlop Pneumatic Tyre Co v Dunlop Motor Co*, 1907 S.C. 15.

[12] *Dunlop Pneumatic Tyre Co v Dunlop Motor Co* (1906) 8 F. 1146, per Lord Kyllachy; *Reddaway v Banham* [1896] A.C. 199, per Lord Herschell; *WH Dorman & Co v Henry Meadows* [1922] 2 Ch. 332; *Jaeger v Jaeger Co* (1927) 44 R.P.C. 437.

[13] *Wise Property Care Ltd v White Thomson Preservation Ltd* [2008] CSIH 44 at [45].

[14] *John Haig & Co v John D.D. Haig*, 1957 S.L.T. (Notes) 36; *Kingston, Miller & Co v Thomas Kingston & Co* [1912] 1 Ch. 575; see also para.32.11, above (goodwill).

[15] *Bile Bean Manufacturing Co v Davidson* (1906) 8 F. 1181.

[16] *Society of Accountants in Edinburgh v Corp of Accountants* (1893) 20 R. 750.

[17] *Farina v Silverlock* (1855) 1 K & J 509; *British Telecommunications Plc v One in a Million* [1999] 1 W.L.R. 903.

[18] Trade Marks Registration Act 1875.

the Trade Marks Act 1994 ("TMA").[19] But these in no way affect the common law rights and remedies against anyone for passing off.[20] Under the Act,[21] a trade mark is defined as,

> "any sign capable of being represented graphically which is capable of distinguishing goods or services of one undertaking from those of other undertakings".

And it may "consist of words (including personal names), designs, letters, numerals or the shape of goods or their packaging". Signs (such as sounds or scents) which are not perceptible visually can be trade marks if they are capable of being represented graphically in a clear, precise, self-contained, easily accessible, intelligible, durable and objective manner.[22] The Act makes provision for the registration of trade marks in a register kept at the UK Intellectual Property Office. By registration of his mark, the proprietor obtains a property right, entitling him to the rights and remedies under the Act, and is relieved of the burden, which rested on him under the common law, of establishing his title to the mark by proof of user.[23] The registration is for a period of 10 years, but may be renewed for a period of 10 years at a time.[24] A mark must be registered for specified services or goods, or classes of goods.[25] In a change from the 1938 Act, under the 1994 Act, the register is no longer divided into two parts, but is now a single register into which trade marks will be entered in the prescribed manner.[26] Provision is made for preventing the registration of marks on either: (a) absolute grounds,[27] which relate to the nature of the trade mark; or (b) relative grounds,[28] which are concerned with the trade mark's relationship with an earlier mark. Registration will be refused on absolute grounds on the basis that the mark lacks a distinctive character,[29] merely indicates the purpose, value, origin, time of production of goods or rendering of services and such like,[30] or consists exclusively of signs or indications which have become customary in the current language or practices of the trade.[31] However, these absolute grounds may be overcome if before the date

---

[19] This Act repeals the Trade Marks Act 1938, and implements the First Trade Marks Council Directive 89/104/EEC of 21 December 1988 to approximate the laws of the Member States relating to trade marks which is now codified as Directive 2008/95/EC of the European Parliament and Council of 22 October 2008 to approximate the laws of the Member States relating to trade marks. The Community law origins of much of the Act make the Court of Justice of the European Union an important source of guidance on the relevant law. As to the 1938 Act, see T.A. Blanco White et al, *Kerly's Law of Trade Marks and Trade Names*, 12th edn (London: Sweet and Maxwell, 1986).

[20] Trade Marks Act 1994 ("TMA") s.2.

[21] TMA s.1(1). See *British Sugar Plc v James Robertson and Sons Ltd* [1996] R.P.C. 281.

[22] *Sieckmann v Deutsches Patent- und Markenamt* (Case C-273/00) [2003] E.C.R. I-11737; *Shield Mark BV v Joost Kist* (Case C-283/01) [2003] E.C.R. I-14313.

[23] TMA s.2(1). See *Boord & Son v Thom & Cameron*, 1907 S.C. 1326 at 1342.

[24] TMA ss.42, 43.

[25] TMA s.34; see also Trade Mark Rules 2008 (SI 2008/1797) rr.7–9.

[26] TMA s.63.

[27] TMA s.3. See also *Phones 4U Ltd v Phone4U.co.uk Internet Ltd* [2006] EWCA Civ 244; [2007] R.P.C. 5.

[28] TMA s.5.

[29] TMA s.3(1)(b). See *British Sugar Plc v James Robertson and Son Ltd* [1996] R.P.C. 281. See also *Audi AG v Office for Harmonisation in the Internal Market ("OHIM")* (C-398/08 P) [2010] E.T.M.R. 18.

[30] TMA s.3(1)(c). See *Windsurfing Chiemsee v Huber* (Joined Cases C-108/97 and C-109/97) [2000] Ch. 523.

[31] TMA s.3(1)(d). See *Merz & Krell GmbH & Co* (C-517/99) [2002] E.C.R. I-6959.

of application for registration, the mark has acquired a distinctive character from its use. Registration will also be refused on absolute grounds on the basis that the mark is contrary to public policy or accepted morality, or is likely to deceive the public.[32] Also, a sign is not registrable if it does not qualify as a trade mark as defined above,[33] or if it consists of a shape which results from the nature of the goods, or which is necessary to obtain a technical result, or which gives substantial value to the goods.[34] And to the extent that a trade mark application is made in bad faith, the registration will be refused.[35] Refusal to register a trade mark under the relative grounds will arise, inter alia, where: (i) a trade mark is identical to an earlier trade mark[36] and the later trade mark relates to identical goods or services protected under the earlier trade mark[37]; (ii) a later trade mark is identical to the earlier trade mark and relates to goods or services similar to those protected under the earlier trade mark, or the later trade mark is similar to the earlier trade mark and relates to goods or services identical or similar to those protected under the earlier trade mark, and in either event is likely to lead to public confusion with the earlier mark[38]; or (iii) a later trade mark is identical or similar to an earlier trade mark, regardless of the goods or services underlying the marks, if the earlier trade mark has a reputation in the United Kingdom[39] and the use of the later trade mark without due cause would take unfair advantage of, or be detrimental to, the distinctive character or the repute of the earlier trade mark.[40] However, if the proprietor of the earlier trade mark or earlier rights consents to the registration of the later trade mark, registration may not be refused on relative grounds.[41]

33.04 Applications for registration—These are made to the registrar on the basis that the trade mark is being used or the applicant has bona fide intention to use it.[42] The mark under question is then examined to ensure there are no absolute grounds for refusal to register. The examiners also note if there are relative grounds for refusal to register. However it is up to the owners of potentially conflicting marks to oppose the application on relative grounds within three months once the application is advertised.[43] Within those three months, notice of opposition may be given by any person,[44] and any person may make written observation as to a trade mark's registrability.[45] Once an application has been accepted without any

[32] TMA s.3(3).

[33] TMA s.3(1)(a).

[34] TMA s.3(2). See *Lego Juris A/S v OHIM* (C-48/09 P) [2010] E.T.M.R. 63.

[35] TMA s.3(6); see also s.3(5) regarding the circumstances concerning the non-registration of specially protected emblems such as Royal Arms under s.4, and s.3(4) regarding illegality under UK or Community law.

[36] As defined in TMA s.6.

[37] TMA s.5(1). See *Reed Executive Plc v Reed Business Information Ltd* [2004] EWCA Civ 159; [2004] R.P.C. 40.

[38] TMA s.5(2). See *Sabel BV v Puma AG* (C-251/95) [1997] E.C.R. I-6191; *Lloyd Schuhfabrik GmbH v Klijsen BV* (C-342/97) [1999] E.C.R. I-3819; *Medion AG v Thomson Multimedia Sales Germany & Austria GmbH* (C-120/04) [2005] E.C.R. I-8551; *esure Insurance Ltd v Direct Line Insurance Plc* [2008] EWCA Civ 842; [2009] Bus. L.R. 438.

[39] Or the European Community if it is a Community trademark or international trade mark (EC).

[40] TMA s.5(3). See *Intel Corp Inc v CPM United Kingdom Ltd* (C-252/07) [2008] E.C.R. I-8823. See also TMA s.5(4) concerning unregistered trade marks and earlier rights.

[41] TMA s.5(5).

[42] TMA s.32.

[43] TMA s.38; s.81—publication is in the Trade Marks Journal.

[44] TMA s.38(2).

[45] TMA s.38(3).

successful opposition and upon timely payment of any prescribed fee for registration, the registrar must register the trade mark unless it has come to his notice since the application that the registration requirements other than those set out in s.5(1), (2), or (3) were not met at that time.[46] The trade mark when registered will be registered as of the date of filing of the application for registration; and that date will be deemed the date of registration. There is an appeal process to an appointed person[47] or the court from any decision of the registrar, save as otherwise set out by rules.[48] A registration must be taken as valid after five years' of continuous use, unless the application for registration was in bad faith.[49]

Transactions affecting registered mark—A registered mark can be assigned[50] **33.05** or licensed[51] either with limitation(s) on the manner or locality of use or the registered goods or services for which the trade mark may be used, or without limitation.[52] However, such a transaction must be in writing and signed or sealed by the assignor or the licensor, as the case may be, or his agent.[53] This applies also to an assignation by way of security.[54] A registered trade mark can be the subject of a security "in the same way as other personal or moveable property".[55] The assignation of and the grant of licence or security interest over a registered trademark, inter alia, are "registrable transactions".[56] There are also provisions with respect to the rectification of and the removal of marks from the register.[57] It is an offence punishable by fine for anyone who makes false representations that a mark is a registered trade mark or as to the goods or services for which a trade mark is registered while knowing or having reason to believe that the representation is false.[58]

Infringement—A registered trade mark is infringed by the use in the course of **33.06** trade and without the trade mark owner's consent[59] of: (1) a sign identical with the registered trade mark and in relation to goods or services identical with those for which the mark is registered[60]; (2) a sign identical with the registered trade mark in relation to goods or services similar to those for which the mark is registered, or a sign similar to the registered trade mark in relation to goods or services identical or similar to those for which the mark is registered, in either case there must be a likelihood of public confusion (which includes the likelihood

---

[46] TMA s.40.

[47] As defined in TMA s.77.

[48] TMA s.76 defines "decision" to include "any act of the registrar in the exercise of a discretion vested in him by or under" the Act. Nevertheless, under TMA s.34(2), the registrar's decision is final on questions of classification of goods and services.

[49] TMA s.48.

[50] TMA s.24.

[51] TMA ss.28–31.

[52] TMA s.24(2) in respect of assignation; TMA s.28(1) in respect of licensing.

[53] TMA s.24(3) in respect of assignation; TMA s.28(2) in respect of licensing. As to the execution of the assignation by the assignor, see s.48 of the Companies Act 2006 which refers to the Requirements of Writing (Scotland) Act 1995 (c. 7).

[54] TMA s.24(4).

[55] TMA s.24(5).

[56] TMA s.25(2).

[57] TMA ss.64 and 46–47.

[58] TMA s.95.

[59] TMA ss.9 and 10.

[60] TMA s.10(1). See also *Google France Sarl v Louis Vuitton Malletier SA* (C-236/08, C-237/08, C-238/08) [2011] All E.R. (EC) 411.

of public association)[61]; (3) a sign identical with or similar to the registered
trade mark, where the trade mark has a reputation in the United Kingdom and
the use, being without due cause, takes unfair advantage of or is detrimental to the
distinctive character or repute of the trade mark.[62] The use of a sign includes
affixing it to goods or their packaging, dealing in goods or services under the
sign, and use on business paper or in advertising.[63] Any person may use a registered trade mark to identify goods or services as those of the proprietor, but use
otherwise than in accordance with honest practices in industrial or commercial
matters is infringement if, without due cause, it takes unfair advantage of or is
detrimental to the distinctive character or repute of the mark.[64] The statute sets
out various defences to claims of infringement, in particular use by a person of
his own name or address, and the use of indications concerning characteristics
of goods or services.[65]

II. COPYRIGHT

33.07 The copyright regime is heavily influenced by European directives[66] and has
received considerable attention for reform under recent UK government
initiatives.[67]

Under the Copyright, Designs and Patents Act 1988 ("CDPA"), the owner of
the copyright has certain exclusive economic rights in relation to a copyright
work.[68] These economic rights are generally referred to here as "copyright".
Nevertheless the creator of the work retains "moral rights"[69] in specified works.

Under Pt I of the CDPA,[70] copyright is a property right which subsists in (1)
original literary, dramatic, musical or artistic works; (2) sound recordings, films

---

[61] TMA s.10(2). See also *British Sugar Plc v James Robertson and Sons Ltd* [1996] R.P.C. 281;
Sabel BV v Puma AG (C-251/95) [1997] E.C.R. I-6191; *Canon Kabushiki Kaisha v MGM Inc*
(C-39/97) [1998] E.C.R. I-5507.

[62] TMA s.10(3). See also *Interflora Inc v Marks & Spencer Plc* (C-323/09) [2012] E.T.M.R. 1. On
"reputation" see *General Motors v Yplon* [1999] E.C.R. I-5421.

[63] TMA s.10(4).

[64] TMA s.10(6). On "honest practices" see *Barclays Bank Plc v R.B.S. Advanta* [1996] R.P.C. 307;
Wolters Kluwer (UK) Ltd v Reed Elsevier (UK) Ltd [2005] EWHC 2053; [2006] F.S.R. 28. See also
L'Oreal SA v Bellure NV (No.2) [2010] EWCA Civ 535; [2010] Bus. L.R. 1579.

[65] TMA s.11. See also *Adidas AG v Marca Mode CV* (C-102/07) [2008] E.C.R. I-2439; *Hotel
Cipriani Srl v Cipriani (Grosvenor Street) Ltd* [2010] EWCA 110; [2010] Bus. L.R. 1465.

[66] e.g. The Duration of Copyright and Rights in Performances Regulations (SI 1995/3297) implements EEC Council Directive 93/98/EEC. The Copyright and Related Rights Regulations 1996 (SI
1996/2967) implement Council Directive 92/100/EEC (rental right and lending right) and Council
Directive 93/83/EEC (satellite broadcasting and cable retransmission), inter alia. The Copyright and
Rights in Databases Regulations 1997 (SI 1997/3032) implement Council Directive 96/9/EC (databases). The Copyright and Related Rights Regulations 2003 (SI 2003/2498) implement Council
Directive 01/29/EC (information society).

[67] See The Gowers Review of Intellectual Property (December 2006) available at *http://www.
official-documents.gov.uk/document/other/0118404830/0118404830.pdf* [Accessed July 18, 2012];
I. Hargreaves, "Digital Opportunity—a review of intellectual property and growth" (May 2011)
available at: *http://www.ipo.gov.uk/ipreview-finalreport.pdf* [Accessed July 18, 2012], and the UK
Government responses thereto.

[68] Copyright, Designs and Patents Act 1988 ("CDPA") s.2(1).

[69] CDPA ss.2(2), 205C–205N; Artist's Resale Right Regulations 2006 (SI 2006/346). See para.33.14,
below.

[70] This Part of the CDPA restates and amends provisions of the Copyright Act 1956 as amended. See
CDPA s.172 regarding the construction of the current legislation vis-à-vis the prior legislation.

or broadcasts, and (3) the typographical arrangement of published editions.[71] Part II of the CDPA confers rights on performers in respect of certain performances, and on recorders of these performances by requiring the performers' consent to the exploitation of the performances.[72] Under both Parts, for copyright to subsist, the author of the work must be a qualifying person, that is, connected by citizenship, domicile, residence or incorporation within the copyright area[73] (the United Kingdom and other countries to which the Act has been extended)[74] or the work must have been first published in or broadcast from the copyright area.[75]

Definition—Under Pt I of the CDPA, "copyright works" are: (a) original literary, **33.08** dramatic, musical or artistic works, (b) sound recordings, films or broadcasts, and (c) the typographical arrangement of published editions.[76] "Original" in this connection refers to the form or expression of thought and not to the thought expressed.[77] The material on which the author has worked may not be new, but the result of his skill and labour as applied to that material must be to produce an original work.[78] Nor need the expression be in a novel form so long as it is not copied from another work but originates from the author.[79] A "literary work" is any work, other than a dramatic or musical work, which is written, spoken or sung and includes a table or compilation other than a database, a computer program and a database.[80] A "dramatic work" can include a film or cinematography.[81] A "musical work" is a work consisting of music, exclusive of any words or action intended to be sung, spoken or performed with the music.[82] There is no copyright in a literary, dramatic or musical work until it is recorded in writing or otherwise.[83] An "artistic work" is: (a) a graphic work (including any painting, drawing, diagram, map, chart or plan and any engraving or similar work), photograph,

---

[71] CDPA s.1. See para.33.08, below.

[72] CDPA ss.180–205A. See also para.33.10, below.

[73] Part I: CDPA s.154; Pt II: CDPA ss.181 and 206–210.

[74] Copyright and Performances (Application to other Countries) Order 2009 (SI 2009/2745).

[75] CDPA ss.155, 156.

[76] CDPA s.1(1), (2).

[77] *Harpers v Barry, Henry & Co* (1892) 20 R. 133; *Baigent v Random House Group Ltd* [2007] EWCA Civ 247; [2008] E.M.L.R. 7; *Nova Productions Ltd v Mazooma Games* [2007] EWCA Civ 219; [2007] Bus. L.R. 1032.

[78] e.g. *Joy Music v Sunday Pictorial* [1960] 2 Q.B. 60; *Sawkins v Hyperion Records Ltd* [2005] EWCA Civ 565; [2005] 1 W.L.R. 3281.

[79] *Macmillan & Co v Cooper* (1924) 40 T.L.R. 186, approving the judgment of Peterson J. in *University of London Press v University Tutorial Press* [1916] 2 Ch. 601, and Lord Kinloch's opinion in *Black v Murray*, 1870 S.L.T. 261 at 264; *Leslie v Young & Sons* (1894) 21 R. 57; *G.A. Cramp & Sons v Frank Smythson* [1944] A.C. 329.

[80] CDPA s.3(1). For the definition of database, see CDPA s.3A(1). Copyright subsists in a database if it is original, i.e. if, and only if, by reason of the selection or arrangement of the contents of the database it constitutes the author's own intellectual creation (CDPA s.3A(2)). To attract protection, a database may be original in this sense but may also involve in its making substantial investment in obtaining, verifying or presenting its contents, for which see the Copyright and Rights in Databases Regulations 1997 (SI 1997/3032); *British Horseracing Board Ltd v William Hill Organisation Ltd* [2005] EWCA Civ 863; [2006] E.C.C. 16 applying *British Horseracing Board Ltd v William Hill Organisation Ltd* (C-203/02) [2004] E.C.R. I-10415; also *Football Dataco Ltd v Sportradar GmbH* [2011] EWCA Civ 330; [2011] 1 W.L.R. 3044 referring the matter to the Court of Justice of the European Union. As to "original literary work", see *Exxon Corp v Exxon Insurance Consultants International Ltd* [1982] Ch. 119; *Newspaper Licensing Agency Ltd v Meltwater Holding BV* [2011] EWCA Civ 890; [2012] Bus. L.R. 53.

[81] *Norowzian v Arks Ltd (No.2)* [1998] EWHC 315; [1999] F.S.R. 79.

[82] CDPA s.3(1).

[83] CDPA s.3(2).

sculpture or collage, irrespective of artistic quality; (b) a work of architecture being a building or a model for a building; or (c) a work of artistic craftsmanship.[84] The "author" of a work is the person who creates it.[85]

Under Pt II of the CDPA, a "performance" is a dramatic performance (including dance and mime), a musical performance, a reading or recitation of a literary work, or a performance of a variety act or a similar presentation, which is, or so far as it is, performed live by one or more individuals. A "recording" in relation to a performance is a film or sound recording made directly from the live performance, from the broadcast of the performance or from another recording of the performance.[86]

33.09   **Ownership and licensing**—Under Pt I of the CDPA, the author is the first owner of the copyright unless a literary, dramatic, musical or artistic work has been made by the author in the course of his employment, in which case the employer is the owner of the copyright subject to any agreement to the contrary.[87] The copyright is transmissible by assignation, by testamentary disposition or by operation of law as moveable property.[88] A bequest of a document recording or embodying an unpublished work includes the copyright unless a contrary intention is indicated.[89] A licence granted by the owner is binding on his successors in title, except a purchaser in good faith for valuable consideration and without notice, actual or constructive, of the licence or a person deriving title from such a purchaser.[90] A "licensing body" is an organisation which has as one of its main objects the negotiation or granting of copyright licences as owner or his agent, and whose objects include the granting of licences covering the works of more than one author.[91] The terms of a licensing scheme proposed to be operated by a licensing body may be referred to the Copyright Tribunal.[92]

Under Pt II of the CDPA, a "performer's property rights" include the reproduction right, distribution right, rental and lending rights, and making available right.[93] These rights are transmissible by assignment, by testamentary disposition or by operation of law as personal or moveable property.[94] Rights to a future recording of a performance may also be assigned or licensed.[95] Where under a bequest a person is entitled to any material thing containing an original recording of a performance which was not published before the death of the testator, the bequest shall be construed as including any performer's rights in relation to the recording, unless the testator's will indicates a contrary intention.[96] In default of agreement as to the amount of equitable remuneration payable, the person by or to whom it is payable may apply to the Copyright Tribunal to determine the

---

[84] CDPA s.4. As to "graphic work": *Nova Productions Ltd v Mazooma Games* [2007] EWCA Civ 219; [2007] Bus. L.R. 1032. As to "sculpture": *Lucasfilm Ltd v Ainsworth* [2011] UKSC 39; [2012] 1 A.C. 208. As to "artistic craftsmanship": *George Hensher v Restawile Upholstery (Lancs)* [1976] A.C. 64.

[85] CDPA s.9(1).

[86] CDPA s.180.

[87] CDPA s.11. See *Stevenson Jordan & Harrison v McDonnell & Evans* [1952] 1 T.L.R. 101.

[88] CDPA s.90(1).

[89] CDPA s.93.

[90] CDPA s.90(4).

[91] CDPA s.116(2).

[92] CDPA s.118. See also CDPA ss.116–152; Copyright Tribunal Rules 2010 (SI 2010/791).

[93] CDPA s.191A(1), referring to CDPA s.182A–C.

[94] CDPA s.191B.

[95] CDPA s.191C.

[96] CDPA s.191D.

amount.[97] By contrast, certain rights conferred on a performer against the restricted acts set out below[98] are not assignable or transmissible except to a limited extent. These rights are referred to as "performer's non-property rights".[99]

Economic rights—The restricted acts as relate to the copyright works under Pt I **33.10** of the CDPA include: (a) copying the work which, in the case of a literary, dramatic, musical or artistic work, includes reproducing the work in any material form and storing it in any medium by electronic means, in the case of an artistic work, includes making a copy in three dimensions of a two-dimensional work and making a copy in two dimensions of a three dimensional work, and in the case of a film or broadcast, includes making a photograph of the whole or any substantial part of any image forming part of the film or broadcast[100]; (b) issuing copies of the work to the public by putting into circulation copies not previously put into circulation in the EEA by or with the consent of the copyright owner, or by putting into circulation outside the EEA copies not previously put into circulation in the EEA or elsewhere[101]; (c) renting or lending of copies of literary, dramatic, musical and most artistic works, as well as films and sound recordings[102]; (d) performing in public a literary, dramatic or musical work which includes the delivery of lectures, addresses, speeches and sermons, or to play or show a sound recording, film or broadcast in public[103]; (e) transmitting or making available electronically a literary, dramatic, musical or artistic work, a sound recording or film, or a broadcast[104]; (f) adapting a literary dramatic or musical work, or doing any of the aforementioned acts in relation to such an adaptation; an adaptation includes a translation of a literary work, a conversion of a dramatic work to a non-dramatic work and vice versa, and an arrangement or transcription of a musical work.[105] Copyright in a work is infringed by doing these acts, or authorising another to do them, without the licence of the owner of the copyright in the work.[106]

Additionally, there is secondary infringement where, without the licence of the copyright owner, a person knowingly imports infringing copies of the work into the United Kingdom otherwise than for private and domestic use, or a person knowingly possesses in the course of business, sells, lets for hire or offers or exposes for sale or hire what he knows or has reason to believe are infringing copies, inter alia.[107]

Under Pt II of the CDPA, a performer's rights are infringed where without the performer's consent (a) by making a recording of the whole or a substantial part of a qualifying performance directly from the live performance, broadcasting live the whole or a substantial part of a qualifying performance, or making a recording of the

---

[97] CDPA s.191H.

[98] See para.33.10, below.

[99] CDPA ss.192A, 192B, 193.

[100] CDPA s.17. The taking must be at least of a substantial part: see CDPA s.16(3)(a); *Ladbroke (Football) Ltd v William Hill (Football) Ltd* [1964] 1 W.L.R. 273 at 276, per Lord Reid; *Cantor Fitzgerald International v Tradition (UK) Ltd* [2000] R.P.C. 95; *Designers Guild Ltd v Russell Williams (Textiles) Ltd* [2000] UKHL 58; [2000] 1 W.L.R. 2416; *Nova Productions Ltd v Mazooma Games* [2007] EWCA Civ 219; [2007] Bus. L.R. 1032; *Newspaper Licensing Agency Ltd v Meltwater Holding BV* [2011] EWCA Civ 890; [2012] Bus. L.R. 53.

[101] CDPA s.18.

[102] CDPA s.18A. The excluded artistic works are works of architecture in the form of a building or a model for a building, and works of applied art.

[103] CDPA s.19.

[104] CDPA s.20. See *Shetland Times v Wills*, 1997 S.C. 316.

[105] CDPA s.21.

[106] CDPA s.16(2).

[107] See CDPA ss.22–27 for a fuller coverage of secondary infringements.

broadcast of the whole or a substantial part of a qualifying performance from a broadcast of the live performance[108]; (b) by making a copy of a recording of the whole or a substantial part of a qualifying performance[109]; (c) by issuing to the public copies of a recording of the whole or a substantial part of a qualifying performance by putting into circulation in the EEC copies not previously put into circulation in the EEA by or with the performer's consent, or putting into circulation outside the EEA copies not previous put into circulation in the EEA or elsewhere[110]; (d) by renting or lending to the public copies of a recording of the whole or a substantial part of a qualifying performance[111]; (e) by electronically making available for public access a recording of the whole or a substantial part of a qualifying performance[112]; (f) by showing or playing in public, or communicating to the public the whole or a substantial part of a qualifying performance by means of a recording which was and which the person showing, playing or communicating it has reason to believe was made without the performer's consent[113]; and (g) by importing into the United Kingdom otherwise than for own private and domestic use, or by possessing, selling or letting for hire, or offering or exposing for sale or hire, or distributing in the course of a business a recording of a qualifying performance which is, and which the person importing, possessing, selling, or letting for hire or offering or exposing for sale or hire, or distributing knows or has reason to believe is an illicit recording.

The rights of person having recording rights for a performance is infringed (a) by making a recording of the whole or a substantial part of the performance without that person's consent[114]; (b) by showing, playing in public, or communicating to the public without the consent of the performer or the person having recording rights the whole or a substantial part of the performance by means of a recording which that person knows or has reason to believe was made without appropriate consent[115]; (c) by importing into the United Kingdom otherwise than for own private and domestic use, or selling, letting for hire, offering or exposing for sale or hire, or distributing in the course of a business a recording of the performance which is, and which the person importing, possessing, selling, or letting for hire or offering or exposing for sale or hire, or distributing knows or has reason to believe is an illicit recording.[116]

33.11 Permitted acts—There are, however, many types of act which do not infringe copyright.[117] Fair dealing is allowed for the purposes of private study and research,

---

[108] CDPA s.182.
[109] CDPA s.182A regarding "reproduction right".
[110] CDPA s.182B regarding "distribution right".
[111] CDPA s.182C regarding "rental right" and "lending right".
[112] CDPA s.182CA regarding "making available right".
[113] CDPA s.183.
[114] CDPA s.186.
[115] CDPA s.187.
[116] CDPA s.188.
[117] CDPA ss.28–76. It is not possible to deal with this matter in detail. Relevant statutory instruments include: Copyright (Recording for Archives of Designated Class of Broadcasts and Cable Programmes) (Designated Bodies) Order 1993 (SI 1993/74); Copyright (Recordings of Folksongs for Archives) (Designated Bodies) Order 1989 (SI 1989/1012); Copyright (Sub-Titling of Broadcasts and Cable Programmes) (Designated Body) Order 1989 (SI 1989/1013); Copyright (Material Open to Public Inspection) (International Organisations) Order 1989 (SI 1989/1098); Copyright (Material Open to Public Inspection) (Marking of Copies of Maps) Order 1989 (SI 1989/1099); Copyright (Computer Programs) Regulations 1992 (SI 1992/3233); Copyright (Visually Impaired Persons) Act 2002 (c.33); Legal Deposit Libraries Act 2003 (c.28); Copyright and Related Rights Regulations 2003 (SI 2003/2498).

criticism, review and news reporting.[118] Some incidental inclusion in another work is allowed.[119] Copying and other acts are allowed for certain educational purposes.[120] Copyright is not infringed by anything done for the purposes of parliamentary or judicial proceedings.[121] Public reading or recitation of a reasonable extract from a published literary or dramatic work does not infringe if it is accompanied by sufficient acknowledgement.[122] There are special provisions as to libraries and archives[123] and for the visually impaired.[124]

The provisions for permitted acts for Pt II of the CDPA in respect of rights in performances are set out in CDPA Sch.2.[125]

Remedies— An infringement of copyright is actionable by the owner and he may **33.12** obtain relief by way of damages, interdict and count, reckoning and payment.[126] Additional damages may be awarded having regard to the flagrancy of the infringement and any benefit accruing to the defender by reason of the infringement.[127] Damages are not recoverable if the defender did not know, and had no reason to believe, that copyright subsisted in the work.[128] However, where a service provider has actual knowledge of another person using the service to infringe copyright, the Court of Session has the power to grant an injunction against that service provider.[129] An owner may obtain an order for delivery up of infringing copies and articles specifically designed or adapted for making copies of a particular copyright work[130]; the order may be that the copies or article shall be forfeited to the copyright owner or destroyed.[131] Where infringing copies are found exposed or otherwise immediately available for sale or hire, the copyright owner may seize and detain them if he has given prior notice to the local police station; the right is subject to the qualification that there may not be seized anything in the possession, custody or control of a person at a permanent or regular place of business of his, and force may not be used.[132] The owner of copyright in a published literary, dramatic or musical work, or in a sound recording or film, may, by giving notice to the Commissioners of Customs and Excise, have the infringing copies treated as prohibited goods.[133] An exclusive licensee has

---

[118] CDPA ss.29–30. On criticism and review, see *Pro Sieben Media A.G. v Carlton UK Television Ltd* [1999] 1 W.L.R. 605; on news reporting, *British Broadcasting Corp v British Satellite Broadcasting Ltd* [1992] Ch. 141; *Hyde Park Residence Ltd v Yelland* [2000] EWCA Civ 37; [2001] Ch. 143. It seems that these statutory exceptions are to be read in the light of the Human Rights Act 1998: *Ashdown v Telegraph Group Ltd* [2001] EWCA Civ 1142; [2002] Ch. 149.

[119] CDPA s.31.

[120] CDPA ss.32–36.

[121] CDPA s.45.

[122] CDPA s.59.

[123] CDPA ss.37–44A.

[124] CDPA s.31A–E.

[125] CDPA s.189.

[126] CDPA s.96.

[127] CDPA s.97(2). See *Redrow Homes Ltd v Bett Brothers Plc* [1998] UKHL 2; [1999] 1 A.C. 197.

[128] CDPA s.97(1).

[129] CDPA s.97A.

[130] CDPA s.99.

[131] CDPA s.114; and Copyright, etc. and Trade Marks (Offences and Enforcement) Act 2002.

[132] CDPA s.100; Copyright and Rights in Performances (Notice of Seizure) Order 1989 (SI 1989/1006).

[133] CDPA s.111; Copyright (Customs) Regulations 1989 (SI 1989/1178).

rights and remedies concurrent with those of the copyright owner.[134] Various dealings with infringing copies are criminal offences.[135]

Part II of the CDPA provides similar remedies in respect of an infringement of a performer's property right[136] and in respect of illicit recordings.[137]

33.13   **Duration**—Copyright in a literary, dramatic, musical or artistic work expires at the end of 70 years from the end of the calendar year in which the author dies.[138] Copyright in a sound recording authored by a national of an EEA state[139] expires at the end of 50 years from the end of the calendar year in which it was made, or, if it was published or made available to the public before the end of that period, 50 years from the end of the calendar year in which it was published or made publicly available[140]; in the case of a broadcast authored by a national of an EEA state, it expires at the end of 50 years from the end of the calendar year in which the broadcast was made.[141] Copyright in a film expires at the end of 70 years from the end of the calendar year in which the death occurs of the last to die of the principal director, the screenplay author, the dialogue author, or the composer of music specially created for and used in the film.[142] Copyright subsists in the typographical arrangement of a published edition of the whole or any part of one or more literary, dramatic or musical works, but not to the extent that it reproduces the typographical arrangement of a previous edition[143]; such copyright expires at the end of 25 years from the end of the calendar year in which the edition was first published.[144]

The economic rights for a performer (who is an EEA state national) to his performance expire at the end of 50 years from the end of the calendar year in which the performance takes place, or 50 years from the end of the calendar year in which the recording of the performance is released if it is released during the first 50 years after the performance.[145]

33.14   **Creator's rights**—To protect the creators of copyright works, "moral rights" in these works remain with their creators even when the creators no longer own the copyright or the copyright works. The CDPA recognises moral rights for performers of qualified performances under Pt II, namely: the right to be identified as the performer and the right to object to derogatory treatment.[146]

The CDPA recognises the moral rights in respect of other copyright works under Pt I: the first is the right to be identified as the author or director in specified circumstances of a copyright literary, dramatic, musical or artistic work, and of a work of architecture in the form of a building, and the director of a copyright

---

[134] CDPA ss.92, 101.

[135] CDPA ss.107–110. See also the Copyright, etc. and Trade Marks (Offences and Enforcement) Act 2002.

[136] CDPA ss.191I–191M

[137] CDPA ss.194–204B.

[138] CDPA s.12; Duration of Copyright and Rights in Performances Regulations 1995.

[139] CDPA s.172A.

[140] CDPA s.13A.

[141] CDPA s.14.

[142] CDPA s.13(B).

[143] CDPA ss.1(1)(c), 8. See *Newspaper Licensing Agency Ltd v Marks and Spencer Plc* [2001] UKHL 38; [2003] 1 A.C. 551.

[144] CDPA s.15.

[145] CDPA s.191.

[146] CDPA ss.205C–N.

film.[147] For example, the author of a literary work (other than words intended to be sung or spoken with music) or a dramatic work has the right to be identified whenever the work is published commercially, or performed in public.[148] However, this right is not infringed unless it has been asserted in accordance with the CDPA.[149] The second moral right is that the author of a copyright literary, dramatic, musical or artistic work or the director of a copyright film has the right, in specified circumstances, not to have his work subjected to derogatory treatment, that is, treatment which amounts to a distortion or mutilation of the work or which is otherwise prejudicial to the honour or reputation of the author or director.[150] For example, in the case of a literary, dramatic or musical work, the right is infringed by a person who publishes commercially, performs in public or communicates to the public a derogatory treatment of the work.[151] The third moral right is that a person has a right not to have a literary, dramatic, musical or artistic work falsely attributed to him as author, and not to have a film falsely attributed to him as director.[152] For example, this right applies where contrary to the fact, a literary, dramatic or musical work is falsely represented as being an adaptation of the work of a person.[153] The fourth moral right is that a person who commissions the taking a photograph or the making of a film for private and domestic purposes has the right not to have the work issued or communicated to the public or exhibited in public.[154] Finally, the author of a copyright work of graphic or plastic art, such as a painting or a sculpture, has a right to a royalty on certain sale of a work subsequent to the first transfer of ownership by the author.[155] This right as well as the above-mentioned rights as to identification, derogatory treatment and privacy subsist so long as copyright subsists in the work[156]; the right against false attribution continues for 20 years after the author's or director's death[157]; the moral rights in performances subsist so long as the economic rights in those performances subsist.[158]

The rights here are not assignable[159] but do transmit in limited circumstances.[160] Other than resale right, they may be waived.[161] An infringement of these rights, other than resale right, is actionable as a breach of statutory duty,[162] but in the case of the right as to derogatory treatment the court may, if it thinks it is an adequate

---

[147] CDPA s.77. There are exceptions: CDPA s.79.

[148] CDPA s.77(2).

[149] CDPA s.78.

[150] CDPA s.80. There are exceptions: CDPA ss.81–82. See *Morrison Leahy Music Ltd v Lightbond Ltd* [1993] E.M.L.R. 144 and *Tidy v Natural History Museum* (1995) 39 I.P.R. 501.

[151] CDPA s.80(3).

[152] CDPA s.84. See *Clark v Associated Newspapers Ltd* [1998] EWHC Patents 345; [1998] 1 W.L.R. 1558.

[153] CDPA s.84(8).

[154] CDPA s.85. There are exceptions: CDPA s.85(2).

[155] The Artist's Resale Right Regulations 2006 (SI 2006/346) regs 3(1), 4.

[156] CDPA s.86(1), in respect of resale right: the Artist's Resale Right Regulations 2006 (SI 2006/346) reg.3(2).

[157] CDPA s.86(2).

[158] CDPA s.205I.

[159] CDPA s.94, in respect of performances: CDPA s.205L; in respect of resale right: the Artist's Resale Right Regulations 2006 (SI 2006/346) reg.7(1).

[160] CDPA s.95, in respect of performances: CDPA s.205M; in respect of resale right: the Artist's Resale Right Regulations 2006 (SI 2006/346) regs 7(3), 9, 16.

[161] In respect of resale right: the Artist's Resale Right Regulations 2006 (SI 2006/346) reg.8(1), CDPA s.87; in respect of performances: CDPA s.205J.

[162] CDPA s.103(1), in respect of performances: CDPA s.205N.

remedy, grant an interdict prohibiting the doing of the act unless a disclaimer is made dissociating the author from the treatment of the work.[163]

III. DESIGNS

33.15 Design right—Certain original designs are protected automatically under Pt III of the Copyright, Designs and Patents Act 1988.[164] Some designs may also attract protection under the Registered Designs Act 1949 ("RDA"). Additionally, designs may attract protection at the Community level under its registered and unregistered right regimes.[165] The focus here is on domestic legislation. Under Pt III of the CDPA, a "design" means the design of any aspect of the shape or configuration (internal or external) of the whole or part of an article.[166] A design is not original and cannot attract design right protection if it is commonplace in the design field in question at the time of its creation.[167] The right does not subsist, however, in: (a) a method or principle of construction; (b) features of shape or configuration of an article which—(i) enable the article to be connected to, or placed in, around or against, another article so that either article may perform its function ("must fit"), or, (ii) are dependent upon the appearance of another article of which the article is intended by the designer to form an integral part ("must match"); or (c) surface decoration.[168] Although a design need not be registered to attract protection, rights in relation to it under the CDPA do not subsist until an article has been made to the design or the design has been recorded in a "design document", i.e. any record of the design.[169] The design must also qualify for protection by reference to the designer or person by whom the design was commissioned or the designer employed or the person by whom and country in which articles made to the design were first marketed, inter alia.[170] The designer is the person who created the design.[171]

33.16 Design right: Ownership—The designer is the first owner of the design right unless either the design was created in pursuance of a commission, in which case the person who commissioned it is the owner, or the design was created by an employee in the course of his employment, in which case the employer is the first

---

[163] CDPA s.103(2).

[164] CDPA s.213(1).

[165] Council Regulation (EC) No 6/2002 of 12 December 2001 on Community designs, art.1.

[166] CDPA s.213(2). On configuration, see *Mackie Designs Inc v Behringer Specialised Studio Equipment (UK) Ltd* [1999] EWHC Ch 252; [1998–99] Info. T.L.R. 125; *Lambretta Clothing Co Ltd v Teddy Smith (UK) Ltd* [2004] EWCA Civ 886; [2005] R.P.C. 6. On the whole or part of an article, see *A. Fulton Co Ltd v Totes Isotoner (UK) Ltd* [2003] EWCA Civ 1514; [2004] R.P.C. 16.

[167] CDPA s.213(4); see also *C & H Engineering v F. Klucznik & Sons Ltd* [1992] F.S.R. 421 at 428, per Aldous J.; *Ocular Sciences v Aspect Vision Care (No.2)* [1997] R.P.C. 289; *Farmers Build Ltd v Cariers Bulk Materials Handling Ltd* [1999] R.P.C. 461; *Lambretta Clothing Co Ltd v Teddy Smith (UK) Ltd* [2004] EWCA Civ 886; [2005] R.P.C. 6; *Dyson Ltd v Qualtex (UK) Ltd* [2006] EWCA Civ 166; [2006] R.P.C. 31.

[168] CDPA s.213(3). In relation to "must fit", see *Ocular Sciences v Aspect Vision Care (No.2)* [1996] EWHC Patents 1; [1997] R.P.C. 289; *Ultraframe (UK) Ltd v Eurocell Building Plastics Ltd* [2005] EWCA Civ 761; [2005] R.P.C. 36. In relation to "must fit" and "must match", see *Dyson Ltd v Qualtex (UK) Ltd* [2006] EWCA Civ 166; [2006] R.P.C. 31.

[169] CDPA ss.213(6), 263(1).

[170] CDPA ss.213(5), 217–220.

[171] CDPA s.214. As to joint designs, see CDPA s.259.

owner of the right.[172] Where a design does not qualify for protection by reference to its designer, commissioner or employer, it may qualify if the first marketing of articles made to the design is by a qualifying person who is exclusively authorised to market them in the United Kingdom and it takes place there, elsewhere in the European Community or in another state to which the provision extends by order; that person is then the first owner of the right.[173] The design right is transmissible by assignation in writing, by testamentary disposition, or by operation of law as personal or moveable property.[174]

Design right: Exercise—The owner has the exclusive right to reproduce the **33.17** design for commercial purposes by making articles to the design or by making a design document recording the design for the purpose of enabling such articles to be made.[175] Reproduction means copying the design so as to produce articles exactly or substantially to that design, and it may be direct or indirect.[176] The test as to whether an allegedly infringing article is made substantially to the pursuer's design is an objective one, "to be decided through the eyes of the person to whom the design is directed".[177] It is a primary infringement of the design right to, without the licence of the owner, do or authorise another person to do, anything which is the exclusive right of the owner.[178] It is a secondary infringement to knowingly and without the licence of the owner import into the United Kingdom or possess for commercial purposes or sell or let for hire in the course of business, articles made in infringement of the design right.[179] There are exceptions to the rights of the design owner where the act concerned is an infringement of copyright,[180] where a licence of right has been obtained[181] or where the design is used for the services of the Crown.[182] The remedies for infringement include: damages (which may be increased because of the flagrancy of the infringement or the benefit to the defender), interdict[183] and count, reckoning and payment of profits.[184] Damages are not to be awarded where the primary infringement was innocent in that the defender did not know, and had no reason to believe, that design right subsisted in the design.[185] A person aggrieved by groundless threats of infringement proceedings may obtain a declaration that the threats are unjustifiable, an interdict against their continuance, and damages in respect of loss sustained by the threats.[186] In the last five years of the design right term, any person is entitled to a licence as of right.[187] The design right part of the CDPA may be extended to the Channel Islands, the Isle of Man or any colony and a

---

[172] CDPA s.215.
[173] CDPA s.220.
[174] CDPA s.222.
[175] CDPA s.226(1).
[176] CDPA s.226(2), (4); see also *C & H Engineering v F. Klucznik & Sons Ltd* [1992] F.S.R. 421 at 428.
[177] *C & H Engineering v F. Klucznik & Sons Ltd* [1992] F.S.R. 421.
[178] CDPA s.226(3).
[179] CDPA ss.227, 228.
[180] CDPA s.236.
[181] CDPA ss.237–239.
[182] CDPA ss.240–244.
[183] *Squirewood Ltd v H. Morris & Co Ltd*, 1993 G.W.D. 20–1239 as noted by H.L. MacQueen, "A Scottish case on unregistered designs" [1994] E.I.P.R. 86.
[184] CDPA ss.229–233.
[185] CDPA s.233.
[186] CDPA s.253(1).
[187] CDPA s.237.

country may be designated by order as one enjoying reciprocal protection under this Part.[188]

33.18 Design right: Duration—Design right expires 15 years from the end of the calendar year in which the design was first recorded or an article was first made to the design, whichever first occurred, or, if articles made to the design are made available for sale or hire within five years from the end of that calendar year, 10 years from the end of the calendar year in which that first occurred.[189]

33.19 Copyright and design right—It is not an infringement of design right to do anything which is an infringement of the copyright in the same work.[190] It is not an infringement of any copyright in a design document or a model recording or embodying a design for anything other than an artistic work or a typeface, to make an article to the design or to copy an article made to the design.[191] Where an artistic work is involved, and it has been exploited by making by an industrial process copies of the work and marketing them, copyright in the work is not infringed if after 25 years from the end of the calendar year in which the articles were first marketed the work is copied by making articles of any description, or doing anything for the purpose of making articles of any description. "Making by an industrial process" is defined by subordinate legislation which excludes from this provision, inter alia, certain articles which are primarily of a literary or artistic character.[192] Copyright in an artistic work is not infringed by anything done in good faith by an assignee or licensee of the registered proprietor of a corresponding design, in reliance on the registration and without notice of any proceedings for cancellation, invalidation or rectification of the registration.[193] In relation to an artistic work, copying includes making a copy in three dimensions of a two-dimensional work and the making of a copy in two dimensions of a three-dimensional work.[194]

33.20 Registered designs—Under the current EC harmonised[195] Registered Designs Act 1949[196] "design" means

"the appearance of the whole or a part of a product resulting from the features of, in particular, the lines, contours, colours, shape, texture or materials of the product or its ornamentation".

---

[188] CDPA ss.255–256.

[189] CDPA s.216.

[190] CDPA s.236.

[191] CDPA s.51(1). See *Mackie Designs Inc v Behringer Specialised Studio Equipment (UK) Ltd* [1999] EWHC Ch. 252; [1998–99] Info. T.L.R. 125; *Lambretta Clothing Co Ltd v Teddy Smith (UK) Ltd* [2004] EWCA Civ 886; [2005] R.P.C. 6; *Lucasfilm Ltd v Ainsworth* [2011] UKSC 39; [2012] 1 A.C. 208.

[192] CDPA s.52(2)–(3); Copyright (Industrial Process and Excluded Articles) (No.2) Order 1989 (SI 1989/1070).

[193] CDPA s.53.

[194] CDPA s.17(3).

[195] European Designs Directive (Directive 98/71/EC of the European Parliament and of the Council 13 October 1998).

[196] The legislation has been amended substantially since its enactment. Earlier versions of the legislation continue in effect for registered designs applied for before August 1, 1989 and December 9, 2001.

"Product" means any industrial or handicraft item other than a computer program, and includes packaging, get-up, graphic symbols, and parts intended to be assembled into a complex product.[197]

The person claiming to be the proprietor of such a design which is new and has individual character may apply for the registration of the design at the UK Intellectual Property Office.[198] Such registration gives the proprietor the exclusive right to use the design and any design which does not produce on the informed user a different overall impression.[199] The proprietor thereby enjoys the exclusive right in the United Kingdom of making, offering, putting on the market, importing, exporting, and using the product bearing the registered design, or stocking the product for these purposes.[200] However, right in a registered design does not subsist in those features of appearance (i) which are solely dictated by the product's technical function,[201] (ii) which must necessarily be reproduced in their exact form and dimensions to permit the product to be mechanically connected to, or placed in, around or against another product so that either product may perform its function unless the design serves to allow multiple assembly or connection of mutually interchangeable products within a modular system,[202] or (iii) which are contrary to public policy or accepted principles of morality.[203] On registration the proprietor obtains a right in the design for five years, which may be extended for four further periods of five years.[204]

IV. PATENTS

Patents—Patents are granted by the Sovereign in the exercise of the royal prerog- **33.21** ative. The right which the patentee acquires by the grant is one of monopoly in an invention, enabling him to exclude others from manufacturing in a particular way, and using, that invention.[205] The statutory foundation of the law can be traced to the English Statute of Monopolies 1623[206]—extended to Scotland at the Union[207]—by which monopolies were declared to be illegal, but exception was made of

> "letters-patent and grants of privilege for the term of fourteen years or under, hereafter to be made, of the sole working or making of any manner of new manufactures within this realm to the true and first inventor or inventors of such manufactures which others at the time of making such letters-patent and grants shall not use so as also they be not contrary to the law nor mischievous

---

[197] Registered Designs Act 1949 ("RDA") s.1.

[198] RDA ss.1B, 3.

[199] RDA s.7(1). *Procter & Gamble Co v Reckitt Benckiser (UK) Ltd* [2007] EWCA Civ 936; [2008] Bus. L.R. 801; *Dyson Ltd v Vax Ltd* [2011] EWCA Civ 1206; [2012] F.S.R. 4.

[200] RDA s.7(2). See also RDA s.7A for exceptions.

[201] RDA s.1C(1).

[202] RDA s.1C(2), (3). See *AMP Inc v Utilux Pty* [1972] R.P.C. 103; *Interlego Inc v Tyco* [1989] 1 A.C. 217 (PC).

[203] RDA s.1D. See *Masterman's Design* [1991] R.P.C. 89.

[204] RDA s.8(1), (2).

[205] Bell, *Principles*, s.1349; *Steers v Rogers* (1893) 10 R.P.C. 245; *Edwards & Co v Picard* [1909] 2 K.B. 903.

[206] 21 Jac. 1, c.3.

[207] *Neilson v Househill Coal and Iron Co* (1842) 4 D. 470 at 475, per Lord Cunningham's note; Bell, *Commentaries*, IV, 105.

to the state by raising prices of commodities at home, or hurt of trade, or generally inconvenient".[208]

The law is primarily contained in the Patents Act 1977 ("PA") which incorporates the United Kingdom obligations under the Patent Co-operation Treaty ("PCT") and the European Patent Convention ("EPC"—not an EU instrument), and which has been updated by the Patents Act 2004.[209] In addition to establishing a new "domestic" patent system, the Act provides for the treatment of European patent (UK) applications and international applications for a patent (UK) under the PCT as domestic applications.[210] It has therefore departed from much of the earlier authority, and the prior law and decisions on the prior statutes must be used with caution.[211] Judicial notice now has to be taken of any decision of, or expression of opinion by, a court established under the EPC and the PCT among others on any question arising under or in connection with the relevant convention.[212] However, national courts may reach different conclusions in evaluating the evidence in the light of the relevant principles which are intended to be shared among these courts.[213] In Scotland, proceedings relating primarily to patents are competent in the Court of Session only; the sheriff court has patent jurisdiction only in relation to incidental questions.[214]

As at the time of writing, proposals for a "Regulation of the European Parliament and of the Council implementing enhanced cooperation in the area of the creation of unitary patent protection" and for a Unified Patent Court are under consideration.

33.22 Subject matter of the patent—Patents are granted for inventions. The first requirement is that the applicant has made an "invention", a term which is not defined.[215] The invention must be new, involve an inventive step, and be capable of industrial application.[216] An invention is new if it does not form part of the state of the art; the state of the art being all matter which has at any time before the date of application for the patent been made available to the public in the United Kingdom or elsewhere by written or oral description, by use or in any other way.[217] An invention involves an inventive step if it is not obvious to a

---

[208] English Statute of Monopolies 1623, 21 Jac. 1, c.3, s.6.

[209] The Patents Act 2004 was driven largely by the implementation of EPC 2000 which came into force December 2007. See, e.g. clarification in EPC 2000 of the scope of protection for the specific, new and inventive use of a patented product in a method of therapy: *Actavis UK Ltd v Merck & Co Inc* [2008] EWCA Civ 444; [2009] 1 W.L.R. 1186; *Abbott Respiratory/Dosage regime* [2010] E.P.O.R 26.

[210] See the Patents Act 1977 ("PA") Pt II ss.77–95.

[211] *Dr Reddy's Laboratories (UK) Ltd v Eli Lilly and Co* [2009] EWCA 1362; [2010] R.P.C. 9.

[212] PA s.91(1)(c); *Genentech Inc's Patent* [1989] R.P.C. 147; *Actavis UK Ltd v Merck & Co Inc* [2008] EWCA Civ 444; [2009] 1 W.L.R. 1186; *Generics (UK) Ltd v H Lundbeck A/S* [2009] UKHL 12; [2009] 2 All E.R. 955; *Grimme Landmaschinenfabrik GmbH & Co KG v Scott* [2010] EWCA Civ 1110; [2011] F.S.R. 7, [79]–[81].

[213] *Eli Lilly & Co v Human Genome Science Inc* [2011] UKSC 51; [2012] 1 All E.R. 1154, per Lord Neuberger at [85], citing Lord Walker in *Generics (UK) Ltd v H Lundbeck A/S* [2009] UKHL 12; [2009] 2 All E.R. 955, see also [86] and [87].

[214] PA s.98(1).

[215] *Biogen Inc v Medeva Plc* [1996] UKHL 18; [1997] R.P.C. 1 at 31, per Lord Mustill and at 41, per Lord Hoffmann; *Generics (UK) Ltd v H Lundbeck A/S* [2009] UKHL 12; [2009] 2 All E.R. 955. See also *Essentially Biological Processes* [2011] E.P.O.R. 27 at [128].

[216] PA ss.1(1), 130(7).

[217] PA s.2; *SmithKline Beecham Plc's (Paroxetine Methanesulfonate) Patent (No.2)* [2005] UKHL 59; [2006] 1 All E.R. 685; *Arrow Generics Ltd v Akzo NV* [2008] CSIH 31; 2008 S.C. 518.

person skilled in the art.[218] An invention is capable of industrial application if it can be made or used in any kind of industry, including agriculture, but methods of treatment or diagnosis practised on the human or animal body cannot attract patent protection.[219] The following are not inventions for purposes of the Act only to the extent that a patent or patent application relates to them as such: a discovery,[220] scientific theory or mathematical method; literary, dramatic, musical or artistic work or any other aesthetic creation; schemes, rules or methods for performing a mental act, playing a game or doing business, or a program for a computer; the presentation of information.[221] A patent will not be granted for an invention the commercial exploitation of which would be contrary to public policy or morality.[222] Exploitation is not regarded as contrary to public policy or morality only because it is prohibited by law in force in the United Kingdom.[223] Biotechnological inventions, that is inventions concerning a product consisting of or containing biological material or a process by means of which biological material is produced, processed or used, are patentable[224]; but the following are not patentable inventions: the human body; a gene sequence; human cloning processes; industrial and commercial uses of human embryos; processes for modifying the genetic identity of animals likely to cause them suffering without any substantial medical benefit to man or animal; animals resulting from such processes; and any variety of animal or plant, or any essentially biological process for the production of animals or plants, not being a micro-biological or other technical process or the product of such a process.

Grant of patent—An application for a patent may be made, by any person **33.23** who claims to be the actual deviser of an invention, to the comptroller of the UK Intellectual Property Office.[225] The application must contain a request for the grant of a patent, an abstract, and a specification describing the invention in a manner clear enough and complete enough for the invention to be performed by a person skilled in the art. The specification must also contain a claim or claims which define the matter for which the applicant seeks

---

[218] PA s.3; *Windsurfing International Inc v Tabur Marine (Great Britain) Ltd* [1985] R.P.C. 59; *Hallen Co v Brabantia (UK) Ltd (No.1)* [1991] R.P.C. 195; *Molnlycke AB v Procter & Gamble Ltd (No.5)* [1992] F.S.R. 549 at 577–579; *Biogen Inc v Medeva Plc* [1996] UKHL 18; [1997] R.P.C. 1; *Pozzoli SpA v BDMO SA* [2007] EWCA Civ 588; [2007] F.S.R. 37; *Arrow Generics Ltd v Akzo NV* [2008] CSIH 31; 2008 S.C. 518; *Generics (UK) Ltd v H Lundbeck A/S* [2009] UKHL 12; [2009] 2 All E.R. 955. See also *Generics (UK) Ltd v Daiichi Pharmaceutical Co Ltd* [2009] EWCA Civ 646; [2009] R.P.C. 23; *Actavis UK Limited v Novartis AG* [2010] EWCA Civ 82; [2010] F.S.R. 18; *Schlumberger Holdings Ltd v Electromagnetic Geoservices AS* [2010] EWCA Civ 819; [2010] R.P.C. 33.

[219] PA ss.4, 4A; *Eli Lilly & Co v Human Genome Science Inc* [2011] UKSC 51; [2012] 1 All E.R. 1154—regarding art.57 of the EPC.

[220] See *Genentech Inc's Application* [1989] R.P.C. 147.

[221] PA s.1(2). See *Aerotel Ltd v Telco Holdings Ltd; Macrossan's Patent Application* [2006] EWCA Civ 1371; [2007] 1 All E.R. 225. See also E.P.O. Guidelines (2010), C, IV, 2; (2012), G, II, 3 (in force June 20, 2012).

[222] PA s.1(3).

[223] PA s.1(4).

[224] PA s.76A and Sch.A2, which gives effect to European Parliament and Council Directive 98/44/EC arts 1–11. For background and authority on the provisions, see *Ciba Geigy* [1984] O.J.E.P.O. 112; *Lubrizol* [1990] O.J.E.P.O. 71; *Harvard/Oncomouse* [1990] O.J.E.P.O. 589; *Plant Genetic Systems* [1995] E.P.O.R. 357; *Howard-Florey/Relaxin* [1995] E.P.O.R. 541; *Novartis* [2000] O.J.E.P.O. 111; *Harvard/Transgenic animal* [2005] E.P.O.R. 31; *Essentially Biological Processes* [2011] E.P.O.R. 27.

[225] PA s.7. *Yeda Research and Development Co Ltd v Rhone-Poulenc Rorer International Holdings Inc* [2007] UKHL 43; [2008] 1 All E.R. 425.

protection.[226] After publication in the journal published by the comptroller,[227] the application is referred by the comptroller to an examiner who, where and to the extent appropriate, makes first a preliminary examination and search to determine whether the invention is new and involves an inventive step.[228] Subsequently, on a request by the applicant, the examiner makes a substantive examination and reports whether the application complies with the requirements of the Acts.[229] Any person may make observations in writing to the comptroller on the question of whether the invention is patentable and the comptroller shall consider the observations in accordance with rules.[230] If the examiner reports that the application complies with the requirements of the Acts, the comptroller may, on payment of the prescribed fee, grant the patent.[231] Upon the grant of a patent, notice of the grant is published in the journal, as is the specification, among other information required by the Patent Rules and information deemed appropriate to the comptroller.[232]

33.24 Infringement—A person infringes a patent if without the consent of the proprietor and where the invention is a product, he makes, disposes of, offers to dispose of, uses or imports the product or keeps it, whether for disposal or otherwise; or, where the invention is a process, and he knows or it is obvious to a reasonable person that the use would be an infringement, he uses the process or offers it for use in the United Kingdom, or he disposes of, offers to dispose of, uses, imports, or keeps any product obtained directly by the process or keeps any such product whether for disposal or otherwise.[233] It is also an infringement where without the consent of the patent proprietor a person supplies or offers to supply in the United Kingdom anyone not entitled to work the invention with any means (other than a staple commercial product that is not supplied for inducing an infringement) relating to an essential element of the invention to work the invention when he knows or when it is obvious to a reasonable person in the circumstances that those means are suitable for and are intended for putting the invention into effect in the United Kingdom.[234]

33.25 Duration and ownership—The term during which the monopoly in the patent is secured to the inventor is 20 years.[235] A patent is incorporeal moveable property[236] and may pass to the proprietor's representatives on his death or on his

---

[226] PA s.14. See *Biogen Inc v Medeva Plc* [1996] UKHL 18; [1997] R.P.C. 1, distinguished in *Generics (UK) Ltd v H Lundbeck A/S* [2009] UKHL 12; [2009] 2 All E.R. 955.

[227] PA s.16.

[228] PA s.17.

[229] PA s.18.

[230] PA s.21.

[231] PA s.18(4).

[232] PA s.24, subject to security and safety concerns: s.22.

[233] PA s.60.

[234] *Grimme Landmaschinenfabrik GmbH & Co KG v Scott* [2010] EWCA Civ 1110; [2011] F.S.R. 7.

[235] PA s.25. In the case of medicinal products, see Regulations (EC) Nos 469/2009 (of 6th May 2009, concerning the supplementary protection certificate for medicinal products) and 1901/2006 (of 12th December 2006, on medicinal products for paediatric use) of the European Parliament and of the Council. In the case of plant protection products, see Regulation (EC) No.1610/96 of 23rd July 1996, concerning the creation of a supplementary protection certificate for plant protection products.

[236] PA s.31(2). See *Conor Medsystems Inc v Angiotech Pharmaceuticals Inc* [2008] UKHL 49; [2008] 4 All E.R. 621 where the parties have settled the matter of revocation in dispute, Lord Hoffmann noted (at [2]): "But a patent confers proprietary rights *in rem* and the validity of a patent cannot be established simply by a judgement in default of opposition."

sequestration. The person becoming entitled to a patent is required to register his title in the register of patents.[237] The patent may be assigned and a security can be granted over it.[238] A licence may be granted under a patent for working the invention.[239] If a proprietor desires to make his patent available, as a matter of right, to any person seeking a licence and that on such terms as may be settled by agreement or, in default of agreement, by the Comptroller, he may apply to the Comptroller for an entry to be made in the register to the effect that licences are to be available as of right and the Comptroller shall make that entry if satisfied that the patent proprietor is not prevented from granting such license by contract.[240] In certain circumstances compulsory licences may be granted.[241]

Remedies—Infringement of the patent entitles the proprietor to, inter alia, inter- **33.26** dict against the infringer, and also to damages or an account of profits (but not both)[242] unless the infringer proves that at the date of the infringement he was not aware, and had not reasonable grounds for supposing, that the patent existed.[243] Where the infringement is widespread, the proprietor has been held entitled to damages on a royalty basis.[244] The defender may not only deny the infringement, but may also counterclaim for revocation of the patent.[245]

Revocation of patent—The court or the comptroller may, on the application of **33.27** any person,[246] revoke a patent on any of the following grounds: that the invention was not patentable; that the patent was granted to a person not entitled to be granted that patent; that the specification does not disclose the invention clearly and completely enough for it to be performed by a person skilled in the art; that the matter disclosed in the specification extends beyond that disclosed in the application; or that the protection conferred by the patent has been extended by an inadmissible amendment.[247] The grounds are also available as defences to an action for infringement.[248] In patent disputes, the nature of the invention for which the patent was granted must be ascertained from the specification, which falls to be construed by the court.[249]

---

[237] PA s.32. As to evidence, see PA s.32(9) and (10).
[238] PA s.31(3). See *Buchanan v Alba Diagnostics Ltd* [2004] UKHL 5; 2004 S.C. 9.
[239] PA s.31(4).
[240] PA s.46.
[241] PA s.48.
[242] PA s.61. As to damages, see *United Horse Shoe Co v Stewart & Co* (1888) 15 R. 45.
[243] PA s.62(1).
[244] *British Thomson-Houston Co v Charlesworth, Peebles & Co*, 1923 S.C. 599.
[245] PA s.74(1).
[246] See *Conor Medsystems Inc v Angiotech Pharmaceuticals Inc* [2008] UKHL 49; [2008] 4 All E.R. 621.
[247] PA s.72(1); *Conoco Speciality Products (Inc) v Merpro Montassa Ltd (No.3)*, 1992 S.L.T. 444; *Biogen Inc v Medeva Plc* [1996] UKHL 18; [1997] R.P.C. 1; *Generics (UK) Ltd v H Lundbeck A/S* [2009] UKHL 12; [2009] 2 All E.R. 955.
[248] PA s.74(1).
[249] See as to the method of construction, European Patent Convention art.69, Protocol; *Catnic Components Ltd v Hill & Smith Ltd* [1982] R.P.C. 237; *Improver Corp v Remington Consumer Products Ltd* [1990] F.S.R. 181; *Union Carbide v B.P. Chemicals* [1999] R.P.C. 409; *Kirin-Amgen Inc v Hoechst Marion Roussel Ltd* [2004] UKHL 46; [2005] 1 All E.R. 667; *Arrow Generics Ltd v Akzo NV* [2008] CSIH 31; 2008 S.C. 518; *Virgin Atlantic Airways v Premium Aircraft Interiors UK Ltd* [2009] EWCA Civ 1062; [2010] R.P.C. 8.

FURTHER READING

Bainbridge, D., *Intellectual Property*, 8th edn (Harlow: Pearson Higher Education, 2010).

Bently, L. and Sherman, B., *Intellectual Property Law*, 3rd edn (Oxford: Oxford University Press, 2009).

Copinger and Skone James on Copyright, edited by K. Garnett, 16th edn (London: Sweet and Maxwell, 2011).

Colston, C. and Galloway, J., *Modern Intellectual Property*, 3rd edn (London: Routledge, 2010).

Cornish, W., Llewelyn, D. and Aplin, T., *Intellectual Property*, 7th edn (London: Sweet and Maxwell, 2010).

Howe, M., *Russell-Clarke and Howe on Industrial Designs*, 8th edn (London: Sweet and Maxwell, 2010).

Kerly's Law of Trade Marks and Trade Names – electronic resource.

Vitoria, M. et al, *Laddie, Prescott and Vitoria: The Modern Law of Copyright*, 4th edn (London: LexisNexis, 2011).

MacQueen, H., Waelde, C., Laurie, G. and Brown, A., *Contemporary Intellectual Property Law and Policy*, 2nd edn (Oxford: Oxford University Press, 2010).

Miller, R., *Terrell on The Law of Patents*, 17th edn (London: Sweet and Maxwell, 2011).

Stair Memorial Encyclopaedia, Vol.18 (1993), "Intellectual Property".

Torremans, P., *Holyoak and Torreman's Intellectual Property Law*, 6th edn (Oxford: Oxford University Press, 2010).

Wadlow, C., *The Law of Passing Off: Unfair Competition by Misrepresentation*, 4th edn (London: Sweet and Maxwell, 2010).

CHAPTER 34

LAND OWNERSHIP

Introductory—Ownership of land is governed not only by the general principles **34.01**
of common law and by various statutes but is also largely bound up with questions
of conveyancing and planning law. Neither of these is within the scope of this
chapter, but it is important to appreciate that what a landowner is entitled to do on
his own land is greatly affected by both. Building on his land will often involve
him in requiring the consent of the planning authorities.[1] Equally, the nature and
extent of his rights will depend on a number of issues conventionally discussed
under the heading "conveyancing".[2] For example, the validity of his title to the
land will depend on the formal validity of the deed transferring the title to him.[3]
The geographical extent of his title will depend on the proper interpretation of the
description of the land given in that deed. And the landowner may be subject to
certain title conditions with respect to what he and others are permitted to do on
or in relation to the land. Real burdens and servitudes are the main examples of
title conditions.[4] The validity of these title conditions and their enforceability or
eventual discharge are matters for the law of conveyancing. In short, apart from
the general law discussed in this chapter, it will always be important to have
regard to the particular law which applies because of the contents of the title
deeds, as well as to the constraints of planning legislation.

Some knowledge of the elementary principles of land tenure and property law
is necessary in order to provide the background to the issues discussed in this
chapter.[5]

The cardinal feature of Scots conveyancing is the system of registration of titles
to land or "heritage".[6] In 1617 there was instituted the Register of Sasines.[7] This is
a register of deeds constituting or transferring rights in land. It is open to the public;
and for the purpose of ascertaining the ownership of land and the burdens which

---

[1] Town and Country Planning (Scotland) Act 1997. See also the Planning etc. (Scotland) Act 2006
and the Building (Scotland) Act 2003.

[2] See G.L. Gretton and K.G.C. Reid, *Conveyancing*, 4th edn (Edinburgh: W. Green, 2011);
J.M. Halliday, *Conveyancing Law and Practice*, 2nd edn (Edinburgh: W. Green, 1997); D. Brand et al,
Professor McDonald's Conveyancing Manual, 7th edn (LexisNexis, 2004). The Land Registration etc.
(Scotland) Act 2012 brings into effect proposals for the reform of the system for land registration in
Scotland and associated matters made in the Scottish Law Commission Report, *Report on Land
Registration* (HMSO, 2010), Scot. Law Com. No.222.

[3] See Brand et al, *Professor McDonald's Conveyancing Manual* (2004), para.29.13.

[4] Title Conditions (Scotland) Act 2003; Robert Rennie, "Pre-2004 real burdens—the end game",
2011 S.L.T. 23, 163–168, anticipates the 10-year anniversary of the new regime in 2014.

[5] See Ch.30, above for further information on the law in respect of heritable property in Scotland.

[6] See the Land Registration etc. (Scotland) Act 2012, which brings into effect the proposals in
the Scottish Law Commission, *Report on Land Registration* respecting the review and reform of
the system of land registration in Scotland.

[7] Registration Act 1617. For a comprehensive historical treatment of sasines, see D.L. Carey
Miller, "Transfer of Ownership" in K.G.C. Reid and R. Zimmermann (eds), *A History of Private Law
in Scotland* (Oxford: Oxford University Press, 2000), Vol.1, pp.282–9.

have been imposed on it recourse must be had to this register. The Land Registration (Scotland) Act 1979 introduced a system of registration of interests in land[8] in a Land Register of Scotland which was intended to supersede the recording of deeds in the Register of Sasines, through a process of phasing-in on a county by county basis.[9] The phasing-in process commenced with Renfrewshire on April 6, 1981, and was completed on April 1, 2003, by which date the system had been extended to all areas of Scotland.[10] The Land Register's fourth decade in operation in Scotland was preceded by the publication, on February 26, 2010, of a Report by the Scottish Law Commission making recommendations for the reform of the system of land registration in Scotland.[11] The report was given effect by the Land Registration etc. (Scotland) Bill, which completed its Scottish Parliamentary passage on May 31, 2012 and received Royal Assent on July 10, 2012. The Act will have a significant impact upon various rights in land, particularly in relation to prescription, and the form of disposition known as *a non domino*.

A person who enters into a contract to purchase land has a right as against the seller to have the bargain implemented and may sue him for damages if he fails to implement it. But he does not have a real right against all and sundry: he is not in fact the owner until the conveyance to him has been placed on the register.[12] Similarly, for a burden to form a charge on the land, no matter what changes occur in ownership, it must appear on the register. The current form of security over land is the standard security which has superseded the bond and disposition in security.[13] The owner of land who has borrowed money binds himself to repay the loan and grants a standard security over the land, so that the lender may not only sue the borrower but may have recourse against the land for payment of his debt.[14] But unless the standard security appears on the register it would not form an effectual charge on the land as against a purchaser. On the other hand, if the standard security is registered, it will affect the lands, whoever may be the owner and whatever the title by which he has acquired it.

A person who appears on the register as the owner of land is said to be infeft. In the earliest times, in conformity with the principle that delivery was the sole means of transmitting property, the transference of heritage was effected by the only possible form of delivery, namely, symbolical delivery. If heritable subjects were

---

[8] "Interest in land" is defined in s.28 of the Act, as amended by the Abolition of Feudal Tenure etc. (Scotland) Act 2000 Sch.12 para.39, so as to refer to rights in or over land (including heritable securities and servitudes but excluding leases other than long leases); the amended statute also indicates that the land itself, where the context admits, may be covered by the term "interest in land".

[9] The progress of the phasing-in process is charted in Gretton and Reid, *Conveyancing* (2011), para.8–02.

[10] 1997 S.L.T. (News) 218.

[11] See fn.6, above.

[12] This principle is confirmed by the Abolition of Feudal Tenure etc. (Scotland) Act 2000 s.4. See also *Burnett's Trustee v Grainger*, 2004 S.L.T. 513.

[13] Conveyancing and Feudal Reform (Scotland) Act 1970. See D.J. Cusine and R. Rennie, *Standard Securities*, 2nd edn (LexisNexis, 2002) for a detailed consideration of the form.

[14] e.g. a statutory standard condition normally incorporated in the standard security empowers the creditor, upon the debtor's default, to sell the land in satisfaction of the debt, although this option is now closed off in relation to residential accommodation in consequence of provisions in the Home Owner and Debtor Protection (Scotland) Act 2010, making it impossible for a creditor to rely upon the standard condition alone in order to effect sale. See also *Royal Bank of Scotland Plc v Wilson (John)* [2010] UKSC 50; 2011 S.C. (UKSC) 66. Furthermore, the creditor must exercise his rights *civiliter* and with proper regard to the interests of the debtor: *Armstrong*, 1988 S.L.T. 255; see also *Dick v Clydesdale Bank Plc*, 1991 S.C. 365. For a more recent case in the Outer House, see *Wilson v Dunbar Bank Plc*, 2006 S.L.T. 775.

sold, appropriate symbols such as earth and stone for land, a clap and happer for a mill and a net for a salmon fishing, were handed over by the seller to the purchaser in the presence of witnesses. This constituted sasine. The transaction was then recorded in a deed known as an instrument of sasine which described the subjects and detailed the ceremony; and this instrument was registered in the Register of Sasines, thereby enabling the public to learn of the change in the ownership of the land. By this means the buyer became infeft, or, in other words, obtained a real right to the subjects. In course of time it was recognised that the important feature was the appearance of the transaction on the register. The cumbrous proceeding of delivering symbols dropped out.[15] It came to suffice that the record (the instrument of sasine), although what was recorded in it had not actually taken place, should be entered in the register; and finally the record has disappeared and all that is necessary is that the deed of conveyance itself should be registered. Infeftment now depends on the registration of the deed transferring the land or registration of an interest in land. The purchaser of land is infeft when, and only when, his title is recorded or his interest registered; and the owner of a security over land, by registering the deed showing the existence of the security in the register, acquires a charge on the land effectual against all who may have rights of property in it.[16]

There are, however, some complexities. A floating charge, when it attaches to heritable property, operates as a prior fixed security over the company's property in favour of the holder. But the House of Lords has held that in this specific context "property" does not include land for which the seller company has received payment and of which it has delivered a disposition to the buyer, although the buyer has not yet registered his title.[17] This is because the seller is regarded as retaining no beneficial interest in the land. Subsequently, the notion of beneficial interest as a form of generally applicable intermediate real right received a setback in the House of Lords,[18] and the general rule that ownership follows upon registration endures.

The feudal system and its abolition—The historic system of land tenure in Scotland was until recently feudal: under which there was a hierarchy of interests in the same land, the greatest of which was that of the Crown.[19] For a given piece of land, beneath the Crown there might be several persons, each holding the land under his feudal superior and obliged to observe the feuing conditions imposed on him by his superior. This system is now abolished. Section 1 of the Abolition of Feudal Tenure etc. (Scotland) Act 2000 (the "2000 Act") provides: **34.02**

> "The feudal system of land tenure, that is to say the entire system whereby land is held by a vassal on perpetual tenure from a superior is, on the appointed day, abolished."

---

[15] See "Infeftment: As it was" (1980) 25 J.L.S.S. 90 for an example of the old style of conveyancing practice.

[16] See generally, K.G.C. Reid, *The Law of Property in Scotland* (Edinburgh: Butterworths, 1996).

[17] *Sharp v Thomson*, 1997 S.C. (HL) 66. Otherwise the floating charge would cover not just the price already received for the land but also the land sold in exchange for it.

[18] *Burnett's Tr. v Grainger*, 2004 S.C. (HL) 19. In this case, the House of Lords distinguished *Sharp v Thomson*, 1997 S.C. (HL) 66, rather than overruling it. The effect is to erect a *cordon sanitaire* around the issue of beneficial interest. *Sharp v Thomson* is now considered as being restricted to floating charges. See further paras 30.01 and 36.33.

[19] For a basic summary of the system of feudal law in Scotland, see G.L. Gretton and A. Steven, *Property, Trusts and Succession* (Sussex: Tottel, 2009), pp.457–464.

From the appointed day, dominium utile (the lowest form of feudal estate) ceased to exist and became ownership of the land, and every feudal estate above it followed it into oblivion.[20] The principal result of this abolition was that superiors ceased to be able to enforce feuing conditions or real burdens which they previously were able to enforce solely by virtue of superior status.[21] The Act provided for the payment to them of compensation in limited circumstances,[22] as well as for a statutory scheme for the enforcement of conditions which are important for reasons of conservation. These "conservation burdens" may be enforced at the instance of a designated conservation body or the Scottish Ministers.[23] The "appointed day" upon which the principal provisions of the Act came into force was November 28, 2004.[24]

This chapter deals with the rights of the Crown, the regalia; the effects of possession of heritable property; the incidents of ownership, including such matters as the law of minerals, game, natural rights and servitudes; common property and common interest; and time-shares.

I. REGALIA

34.03 **Introductory**—The Abolition of Feudal Tenure etc. (Scotland) Act 2000 binds the Crown.[25] Accordingly, with effect from the appointed day the Crown's ultimate feudal superiority ceased to exist, as did the superiority of the Prince and Steward of Scotland. The Act, however, expressly preserves "any power exercisable by Her Majesty by virtue of Her prerogative".[26] Her Majesty's prerogative includes the prerogative of honour, and "any power exercisable" includes prerogative rights as respects ownerless or unclaimed property,[27] and the regalia majora.[28]

34.04 **Regalia: Majora and minora**—The rights of the Crown in heritable property fall into two classes. The first consists of those rights which the Crown holds in trust for the public and which cannot be alienated; the second, of proprietary rights which belong to the Crown without restriction either as to their exercise or as to their alienation.

> "These two ideas [of sovereignty and of property in the Crown] are perfectly separate and distinct . . . The Crown, if it has not granted it out, has a right of

---

[20] Abolition of Feudal Tenure etc. (Scotland) Act 2000 (the "2000 Act") s.2; this also applies to the Crown's ultimate superiority: s.58. For recent cases generally illustrative of the impact of the Act, see *Sheltered Housing Management Ltd v Bon Accord Bonding Co Ltd*, 2010 S.C. 516 and *Greenbelt Property Ltd v Riggens*, 2010 G.W.D. 28–586.

[21] 2000 Act s.17.

[22] 2000 Act ss.33–40.

[23] 2000 Act ss.27–28. See also Pt 3 of the Title Conditions (Scotland) Act 2003.

[24] Abolition of Feudal Tenure etc. (Scotland) Act 2000 (Commencement No.2) (Appointed Day) Order 2003 (SSI 2003/456). The apparent delay in the coming into force of the provisions is explained by the fact that Pt IV of the Act allowed superiors to register notices to preserve certain real burdens. This Part could not come into force until the enactment of the Title Conditions (Scotland) Act 2003. Thereafter, it was necessary to allow superiors a reasonable time to register notices before appointing a day for the principal provisions of the Act to come into force.

[25] 2000 Act ss.2(2), 58(1).

[26] 2000 Act s.58(1).

[27] As illustrated in *Lord Advocate v University of Aberdeen and Budge*, 1963 S.C. 533.

[28] 2000 Act s.58(2).

property in the foreshore which may be alienated, and also a right of sovereignty as guardian of the public interests for navigation, fishing, and other public uses which cannot be alienated."[29]

The inalienable rights are called regalia majora[30]; the others are the regalia minora. They are indeed distinct, but there are cases, for example the foreshore, in which, as the above quotation shows, they are both found existing in regard to the same object.

The sea—The sea below the foreshore and within the 12-mile limit (nautical **34.05** miles) belongs to the Crown in trust for the public rights of navigation and white fishing.[31] The Crown appears to be able to alienate the seabed,[32] but no right in it which, if exercised by the grantee, would interfere with the rights of the public can be granted without the sanction of Parliament.[33]

Maritime burdens, being real burdens over the sea bed or foreshore in favour of the Crown, have survived feudal abolition, and continue to be enforceable by the Crown. The effect of s.60 in the Abolition of Feudal Tenure etc. (Scotland) Act 2000 was to convert feudal maritime burdens into personal real burdens.

The foreshore—The foreshore is the shore between the high—and low—water **34.06** marks of ordinary spring tides.[34] In the foreshore the Crown has, as already noticed, a double right—a right of sovereignty and a right of property. In virtue of the former right the foreshore is vested in the Crown for the benefit of the public.[35] More than one public right is included. Of these, the two most important are the right of navigation and the right of white fishing. The former includes the right to anchor, to load and discharge goods, to embark and disembark, and to take in ballast.[36] The latter includes the right to dry nets and (with the exception of oysters and mussels which belong to the Crown[37]) to take shellfish.[38] Both these rights are inalienable by the Crown.[39] In addition, the public probably has a right to go on

---

[29] *Smith v Lerwick Harbour Commrs* (1903) 5 F. 680 at 691.

[30] No title, deed, or document is required to establish the existence of these fundamental inalienable rights: cf. Land Registration (Scotland) Act 1979 s.28(1)(g); also the Land Registration etc. (Scotland) Act 2012.

[31] *Gibson v Lord Advocate*, 1975 S.C. 136; *Crown Estate Commissioners v Fairlie Yacht Slip*, 1979 S.C. 156; *Walford v Crown Estates Commissioners*, 1988 S.L.T. 377; *Walford v David*, 1989 S.L.T. 876. For the extension of the limit from three miles to 12 miles see the Territorial Sea Act 1987 s.1. In *Crown Estate Commissioners, Petitioners*, 2010 S.L.T. 741, the Lord Ordinary (Uist), rejected a suggestion that the sea might be conveyed in property, and that that would carry with it the sea bed on the *a caelo usque ad infernos* principle (for which see further below, para.34.15).

[32] *Shetland Salmon Farmers v Crown Estate Commissioners*, 1991 S.L.T. 166. See, however, Lord Murray's reservations at 183; and see generally *Stair Memorial Encyclopaedia*, Reissue ("Sea and Continental Shelf").

[33] *Lord Advocate v Wemyss* (1899) 2 F. (HL) 1, per Lord Watson at 8 and 9. Also *Agnew v Lord Advocate* (1873) 11 M. 309.

[34] *Agnew v Lord Advocate* (1873) 11 M. 309; *Fisherrow Harbour Comrs v Musselburgh Real Estate Co* (1903) 5 F. 387, per Lord Low at 393–394; and see generally Reid, *The Law of Property in Scotland* (1996), paras 313 et seq, and Stair, II, I, 5.

[35] See *Burnet v Barclay*, 1955 J.C. 34; T.B. Smith, *A Short Commentary on the Law of Scotland* (Edinburgh: W. Green, 1962), p.64.

[36] *Crown Estate Commissioners v Fairlie Yacht Slip*, 1979 S.C. 156.

[37] *Parker v Lord Advocate* (1904) 6 F. (HL) 37.

[38] Balfour's *Practicks*, 626; *Hall v Whillis* (1852) 14 D. 324.

[39] *McDouall v Lord Advocate* (1875) 2 R. (HL) 49. The Crown may from time to time confer upon persons rights in relation to shellfish and shellfish fisheries, see the Sea Fisheries (Shellfish) Act 1967, but such rights are time-limited and remain particular to the recipients. For a recent example, see the Loch Crinan Scallops Several Fishery Order 2005 (SSI 2005/304).

the foreshore for recreation,[40] and, indeed, s.5(4) of the Land Reform (Scotland) Act 2003 states that the existence or exercise of access rights under the Act does not diminish or displace and public rights under the guardianship of the Crown in relation to the foreshore.[41] Accordingly, the public now enjoy statutory access rights and common law rights over the foreshore.

The foreshore itself, however, may be alienated, and an adjacent proprietor is held to own it if he has from the Crown either a specific grant of it, or a title habile to include it which has been followed by possession for the prescriptive period. Against the Crown the prescriptive period is 20 years.[42] Such possession need not be, and indeed cannot be, such as to exclude the public entirely, for the rights of the public cannot be impaired.[43] An application to register an interest in land including foreshore may result in indemnity being excluded by the Keeper of the Registers[44] and notification of the application therefore having to be made to the Crown Estates Commissioners.[45] The owner has the exclusive use of taking sea-ware[46] and other materials from the foreshore, provided he does nothing to hinder the public in the exercise of its rights.

34.07 Navigable rivers—Rivers which are tidal and navigable are regarded as part of, and subject to the same rule as, the sea. The solum belongs to the Crown, subject to the public rights of navigation and fishing.[47]

On the other hand, if the river is navigable but non-tidal, the solum belongs not to the Crown but to the riparian proprietors.[48] The public have a right of navigation,[49] but no other rights in regard to the river. The banks are private property and cannot be used by the public except for purposes incidental to navigation.[50] The right of public navigation is not a servitude and cannot be lost through disuse.[51] It follows, from the right of navigation, that a member of the public can prevent any interference with the bed of the river which affects that

---

[40] *Hope v Bennewith* (1904) 6 F. 1004; *Mather v Alexander*, 1926 S.C. 139 (erecting hut on foreshore); *Burnet v Barclay*, 1955 J.C. 34. But see *Alfred F. Beckett v Lyons* [1967] Ch. 449. For the powers of local authorities in regard to the seashore, see the Civic Government (Scotland) Act 1982 ss.120–123; cf. *Magistrates of Buckhaven & Methil v Wemyss Coal Co*, 1932 S.C. 201.

[41] Land Reform (Scotland) Act 2003 s.5(4). The access rights are stated in s.1 of the Act.

[42] Prescription and Limitation (Scotland) Act 1973 s.1(1) and (4) as amended by the Land Registration (Scotland) Act 1979 s.10. See *Luss Estates Co v BP Oil Refinery Ltd*, 1981 S.L.T. 97; 1982 S.L.T. 457; 1987 S.L.T. 201.

[43] *Marquis of Bute v McKirdy & McMillan*, 1937 S.C. 93. See also Land Reform (Scotland) Act 2003 Pt I, "Access Rights".

[44] A key feature of the system of registration of title is that a title which has been registered is guaranteed by an indemnity from the Keeper, unless this has been excluded. This feature continues under the Land Registration etc. (Scotland) Act 2012.

[45] The notification provision was formerly in s.14 of the Land Registration (Scotland) Act 1979, the object being to alert the Crown Commissioners to any title which has not yet been fortified by prescriptive possession. This provision is repealed by the Land Registration etc. (Scotland) Act 2012, but a new provision in s.45 of that Act introduces a substitute requirement of notification of more widespread application; extending to proprietors generally and to others where there is the potential for them to be able to take steps to complete title, and to the Crown.

[46] *Paterson v Marquis of Ailsa* (1846) 8 D. 752.

[47] *Orr Ewing v Colquhoun's Trs* (1877) 4 R. (HL) 116; and see generally *Stair Memorial Encyclopaedia*, Vol.25, "Water and Water Rights: Rivers".

[48] See, e.g. *Stirling v Bartlett*, 1992 S.C. 523; 1993 S.L.T. 763.

[49] *Wills' Trs v Cairngorm Canoeing and Sailing School*, 1976 S.C. (HL) 30; *Scammell v Scottish Sports Council*, 1983 S.L.T. 462; *Burton's Trs v Scottish Sports Council*, 1983 S.L.T. 418; Reid, *The Law of Property in Scotland* (1996).

[50] *Leith-Buchanan v Hogg*, 1931 S.C. 204.

[51] *Wills' Trs v Cairngorm Canoeing and Sailing School*, 1976 S.C. (HL) 30.

right; but he has no title to object to any structure being put in the river unless it obstructs navigation. His right is one of passage,[52] and there may be many operations in a river to which an opposite heritor would have a title to object, but which are quite lawful in a question with the public.[53] The prevention of pollution in rivers is principally governed by the Water Environment (Controlled Activities) (Scotland) Regulations 2011.[54]

Ferry: Port and harbour—These rights are classed as regalia, though in certain **34.08** respects they differ from the other regalia. They are rights belonging to the Crown, which may be acquired from it by grant or prescription.[55]

A right of ferry is an incorporeal heritable right.[56] It is the right to carry persons by water across a narrow sea, river or loch, from one definite place to another. The place is not necessarily confined to a particular spot, but may be a stretch of shore. It involves the right to charge a fee for services and to exclude others from carrying passengers within the limits of the ferry, and the duty of receiving any person for carriage at reasonable times. Neighbouring proprietors may keep boats for the ferrying of their own families and servants, but may not, by carrying strangers for hire, interfere with the right of ferry.[57] Ferries are the responsibility of local authorities.[58] A council may acquire, maintain and operate ferries; lease or hire ferries; make arrangements for their operation; fix fares and charges; and subsidise ferries from the local rates.

Harbours[59] are either private or public. The former belong to individuals and are used for their own purposes, and the public have no right to resort to them, except with the permission of the proprietor.[60] Public harbours are those which anyone may use on payment of the proper dues.[61] The right of port and harbour may be granted by the Crown to an individual[62] or a harbour trust[63] or a corporation,[64] and confers the right to exact dues.[65] The corresponding duty of the grantee of the right is to maintain the harbour so far as the dues received are

---

[52] *Scammell v Scottish Sports Council*, 1983 S.L.T. 462; *Burton's Trs v Scottish Sports Council*, 1983 S.L.T. 418.

[53] *Orr Ewing v Colquhoun's Trs* (1877) 4 R. (HL) 116; *Campbell's Trs v Sweeney*, 1911 S.C. 1319.

[54] Water Environment (Controlled Activities) (Scotland) Regulations 2011 (SSI 2011/209), made under the Water Environment and Water Services (Scotland) Act 2003. See para.34.27, below.

[55] See *L.M. & S. Ry v McDonald*, 1924 S.C. 835.

[56] *Baillie v Hay* (1866) 4 M. 625; *Duke of Montrose v Macintyre* (1848) 10 D. 896; and see, generally, W.M. Gordon and S. Wortley, *Scottish Land Law*, 3rd edn (Edinburgh: W. Green, 2009), Vol.1, para.7–25; Reid, *The Law of Property in Scotland* (1996).

[57] *Weir v Aiton* (1858) 20 D. 968.

[58] Local Government (Scotland) Act 1973 s.153 as amended.

[59] See generally *Stair Memorial Encyclopaedia*, Vol.11, "Harbours"; Gordon and Wortley, *Scottish Land Law* (2009), Vol.1, paras 7–04—7–22.

[60] *Colquhoun v Paton* (1859) 21 D. 996.

[61] But see the difficulties experienced by a member of the public in *Coutts v J.M. Piggins Ltd*, 1982 S.L.T. 213; 1983 S.L.T. 320.

[62] As in *Crown Estate Commissioners v Fairlie Yacht Slip Ltd*, 1979 S.C. 156.

[63] See Harbours (Scotland) Act 1982. In relation to the privatisation of the ports industry, the Ports Act 1991 provides for the transfer of ports and harbours to companies rather than trustees.

[64] *Earl of Stair v Austin* (1880) 8 R. 183; *Macpherson v Mackenzie* (1881) 8 R. 706; *Crown Estate Commissioners v Fairlie Yacht Slip Ltd*, 1979 S.C. 156.

[65] See, e.g. *Aberdeen Harbour Board v Irvin & Sons Ltd*, 1980 S.L.T. (Sh. Ct) 89. In *Crown Estate Commissioners, Petitioners*, 2010 S.L.T. 741 it was held that the grant of free port and harbour carried with it a right of unimpeded access to the port or harbour, and not a right of gratuitous use thereof.

sufficient for that purpose.[66] The Scottish Ministers have the power[67] to develop, maintain and manage harbours made by or maintained by them by virtue of an Act or order.[68] They may make loans to harbour authorities.[69] Local authorities have general responsibility for harbours.[70] They may acquire compulsorily any harbour in a poor state of repair, or a harbour whose maintenance is to be discontinued by its owner. The harbour trustees may remove unserviceable vessels from the harbour.[71]

34.09 Precious metals: Forestry: Highways—These subjects are pure regalia minora. They are part of the patrimony of the Crown, but they may be alienated, and the public has no rights in any of them. Precious metals are dealt with elsewhere.[72]

The chief privilege flowing from a right of forestry was that one-third of the value of cattle forfeited for straying into the forest went to the forester, the other two-thirds going to the Crown. The right is of no practical importance in modern times.[73]

Highways are included in the regalia.[74] They belong to the Sovereign. The solum of a highway belongs, unless it has been acquired from him, to the proprietor of the lands, the highway being merely a right of passage over the soil.[75]

34.10 Salmon fishings—Salmon fishing was until recently a separate feudal right, which was vested in the Crown. This was changed with the coming into force of the Abolition of Feudal Tenure etc. (Scotland) Act 2000, which binds the Crown.[76] Salmon fishing is a species of separate tenement, and, accordingly, the 2000 Act treats it in exactly the same way as other land. Accordingly, a person holding dominium utile of salmon fishings became on the appointed day of November 28, 2004 its outright owner.[77] The Act, however, expressly preserves "any power exercisable by Her Majesty by virtue of Her prerogative".[78]

Salmon fishing is among the regalia minora,[79] and the right of salmon fishing may, therefore, be granted by the Crown to a subject. With effect from the appointed day of November 28, 2004, all superiority interests were extinguished. Regalian rights which were at that date unfeued, and accordingly still held by the

---

[66] *Firth Shipping Co v Earl of Morton's Trs*, 1938 S.C. 177.

[67] These functions, which were previously held by the Secretary of State, were transferred to the Scottish Ministers by virtue of s.53 of the Scotland Act 1998. Other functions in respect of harbours are conferred upon the Scottish Ministers by the Transport and Works (Scotland) Act 2007.

[68] Harbours Development (Scotland) Act 1972.

[69] Harbours (Loans) Act 1972, as amended by the Transport Act 1981 Sch.12.

[70] Local Government (Scotland) Act 1973 s.154.

[71] *Peterhead Harbours Trs v Chalmers*, 1984 S.L.T. 130.

[72] See para.34.16, below.

[73] For a review of the law relating to forestry management, see *Stair Memorial Encyclopaedia*, Vol.11, "Forestry".

[74] Bankton, I, 3, 4; II, 1, 5; Erskine, II, 6, 17. There has been extensive legislation in relation to highways: see generally *Stair Memorial Encyclopaedia*, Reissue, "Roads".

[75] *Galbreath v Armour* (1845) 4 Bell's Apps 374; *Waddell v Earl of Buchan* (1868) 6 M. 690. See also Lord Marnoch in *Moncrieff v Jamieson*, 2005 S.L.T. 225 at 229.

[76] 2000 Act s.58(1).

[77] 2000 Act s.2(1).

[78] 2000 Act s.58(1).

[79] Except in Orkney and Shetland (*Lord Advocate v Balfour*, 1907 S.C. 1360). See Gordon and Wortley, *Scottish Land Law* (2009), para.8–41.

Crown, remain alienable. A Crown grant of salmon fishing can still be made, but only by disposition,[80] whereas, formerly, the title might result from an express grant of the salmon fishings[81] or else a barony title[82] or charter with fishings (*cum piscationibus*) coupled with possession for the prescriptive period.[83] It was formerly thought that possession must, as a rule, be by fishing by net and coble. It seems, however, that fishing by rod or by any other legal method ought to be sufficient for purposes of prescription, provided it is such as to amount to an assertion of right.[84] Where a grant or lease of salmon fishing is made by the Crown, it carries with it, unless it is specifically limited, the exclusive right to fish by all lawful and legitimate means.[85]

If the owner of the salmon fishings owns the land on both banks he has the whole fishings. But if the banks are owned by different proprietors, the fishing rights depend on the terms of the titles. If each proprietor has a right of salmon fishing along the extent (*ex adverso*) of his lands, the general rule is that each may fish from any point up to the mid-point (*medium filum*) of the river; if the parties are in dispute, the court will make the necessary arrangement.[86] These rules apply only if neither of the parties has established a higher right by immemorial possession or by prescriptive possession upon a sufficient title.[87] Where the owner of a salmon fishings is not a riparian proprietor, the presumption is that he has a right to the whole fishings unless one of the riparian proprietors has an adverse right.[88] He has a right of access to the river and a right to moor boats, dry nets, fix posts, and do anything necessary for the exercise of his right, provided he pays due regard to the rights of the owner of the bank.[89]

Many statutes from the fourteenth century onwards have been passed to regulate salmon fishing. The statutory provisions were consolidated by the Scottish Parliament in 2003 in the Salmon and Freshwater Fisheries (Consolidation) (Scotland) Act 2003.[90] Part 1 of the Act deals chiefly with four subjects: (1) weekly close time for salmon, and the protection of young salmon; (2) prohibition

---

[80] 2000 Act s.59.

[81] The conveyancing phrase "parts and pertinents" generally does not include salmon fishings: *McKendrick v Wilson*, 1970 S.L.T. (Sh. Ct) 39; for discussion, Gordon and Wortley, *Scottish Land Law* (2009), paras 8–57—8–61.

[82] Land is held on a barony title when it is held direct from the Crown and has been erected by the grant in *liberam baroniam*, i.e. into a freehold barony. A grant of barony carries with it various special rights and advantages: *Lord Advocate v Cathcart* (1871) 9 M. 744.

[83] Prescription and Limitation (Scotland) Act 1973 s.1(1) and (4) as amended by the Land Registration (Scotland) Act 1979 s.10. (Note that the prescriptive period is usually 10 years, but 20 years when prescription is pled against the Crown); cf. *Maxwell v Lamont* (1903) 6 F. 245; *Fothringham v Passmore*, 1984 S.C. (HL) 96; J.H. Tait, *Game and Fishing Laws of Scotland*, 2nd edn (Edinburgh: W. Green, 1928), p.122; Reid, *The Law of Property in Scotland* (1996).

[84] *Sinclair v Threipland* (1890) 17 R. 507; *Warrand's Trs v Mackintosh* (1890) 17 R. (HL) 13 at 23; *Ogston v Stewart* (1896) 23 R. (HL) 16 at 19; *Maxwell v Lamont* (1903) 6 F. 245 at 259.

[85] *Joseph Johnston & Son v Morrison*, 1962 S.L.T. 322; *Walford v Crown Estates Commissioners*, 1988 S.L.T. 377. In *Tummel Valley Lesiure Ltd v Sudjic*, 2010 S.L.T. (Sh. Ct) 170 it was held by the Sheriff Principal that the erection of decking over part of river bank preventing fly fishing, but not spinning, constituted interference with right to fish.

[86] *Fothringham v Passmore*, 1984 S.C. (HL) 96. For the earlier law, *Gay v Malloch*, 1959 S.C. 110.

[87] *Earl of Zetland v Tennent's Trs* (1873) 11 M. 469; *Campbell v Muir*, 1908 S.C. 387; *Fothringham v Passmore*, 1984 S.C. (HL) 96.

[88] *Lord Monimusk v Forbes* (1623) Mor.14264.

[89] *Berry v Wilson* (1841) 4 D. 139; *Middletweed Ltd v Murray*, 1989 S.L.T. 11 (right of access held not to include vehicular access).

[90] Note, however, that the Aquaculture and Fisheries (Scotland) Act 2007 has commenced the process of amending the consolidation Act.

of fixed engines and certain other methods of fishing[91]; (3) offences related to fishing for salmon and freshwater fish; and (4) restrictions on the erection of obstructions to the free passage of the fish up and down the river. The Scottish Ministers have general superintendence of salmon fisheries except in the Tweed. The fisheries and the adjoining sea have been divided into districts, each district being under the charge of a district board elected by the fishery proprietors of the district.[92] Protection orders in relation to catchment areas of rivers may be made, and wardens appointed to secure compliance with the orders.[93]

Under the Act the annual close time for each district is a continuous period of not less than 168 days.[94] No person may fish or take salmon during Sunday, and the weekly close time, except for rod and line, is from 18.00 on Friday to 06.00 on Monday.[95] The Scottish Ministers may vary the annual close time for any district on the application of the district board, or of two salmon fisheries proprietors.[96]

Salmon fishing by cruives is lawful in rivers above the highest point at which the ebb and flow of the tide is perceptible, where the right is derived from an express grant of cruives by the Crown or from possession for the prescriptive period proceeding on a habile title from the Crown.[97] Apart from rod fishing, the only other lawful method of fishing for salmon in inland waters, other than the tributaries of the Solway, is by net and coble.[98] Cruives have now practically disappeared.[99] The tests of the legality of the method of fishing by net and coble are these: (1) that when the net is in the water it is constantly in motion; (2) that one end never leaves the hand of the fisherman; and (3) that the fish are surrounded by the whole net and drawn ashore with it.[100]

Obstructions remain subject to regulation by by-laws made under earlier statutes, now repealed, which provide, inter alia, that no mill dam shall be so altered as to create a greater obstruction to the passage of fish than already existing, and that every dam, weir or cauld shall be provided with a salmon ladder.[101] However, the 2003 Act includes provisions to the effect that (1) any person who does any act for the purpose of preventing salmon from passing through any fish pass, or taking any salmon in its passage through the same, shall be guilty of an offence,[102] and (2) any person who places any device or engine for the purpose of obstructing the passage of any smolt, parr, salmon fry or alevin shall be guilty of an offence, and any person

---

[91] *Lockhart v Cowan*, 1980 S.L.T. (Sh. Ct) 91; *Salar Properties (UK) v Annandale & Eskdale DC*, 1992 G.W.D. 7–381.

[92] Salmon and Freshwater Fisheries (Consolidation) (Scotland) Act 2003 s.34. See also *Cormack v Crown Estates Commissioners*, 1985 S.C. (HL) 80; 1985 S.L.T. 426. Proprietors of salmon fishings may present a petition to have constituted a district fishery board: *Fraser, Petitioner*, 1980 S.L.T. (Sh. Ct) 70.

[93] Salmon and Freshwater Fisheries (Consolidation) (Scotland) Act 2003 ss.48 and 49.

[94] Salmon and Freshwater Fisheries (Consolidation) (Scotland) Act 2003 s.37(1).

[95] Salmon and Freshwater Fisheries (Consolidation) (Scotland) Act 2003 s.13.

[96] Salmon and Freshwater Fisheries (Consolidation) (Scotland) Act 2003 s.37(4), Sch.1.

[97] See generally Gordon and Wortley, *Scottish Land Law* (2009), Vol.1, paras 8–99—8–100.

[98] Salmon and Freshwater Fisheries (Consolidation) (Scotland) Act 2003 s.1(1).

[99] Notwithstanding which, see the very limited exception for cruives in the Salmon and Freshwater Fisheries (Consolidation) (Scotland) Act 2003 s.1(1)(c)(i).

[100] Tait, *Game and Fishing Laws of Scotland* (1928), p.179; *Stair Memorial Encyclopaedia*, Vol.11, "Fisheries", para.11; Gordon and Wortley, *Scottish Land Law* (2009), paras 8–93 et seq.; Scott Robinson, *The Law of Game, Salmon and Freshwater Fishing in Scotland* (Butterworths, 1990); *Hay v Magistrates of Perth* (1863) 1 M. (HL) 41.

[101] Gordon and Wortley, *Scottish Land Law* (2009), Vol.1, paras 8–98 and 8–101. See also *Stair Memorial Encyclopaedia*, Vol.11, "Fisheries", para.19.

[102] Salmon and Freshwater Fisheries (Consolidation) (Scotland) Act 2003 s.10.

who during the annual close time obstructs or impedes salmon in their passage to any spawning bed or any bank or shallow in which the spawn of salmon may be shall be guilty of an offence.[103] The 2003 Act also includes provision to the effect that the Scottish Ministers shall have the power to make regulations with respect to salmon fishing, including, inter alia, the construction and alteration of dams, lades or water wheels so as to afford a reasonable means for the passage of salmon.[104] Any such regulations might supersede any bylaws made under the earlier legislation.[105]

Salmon fishing in the Tweed is regulated by special statutes.[106] The Upper Esk remains[107] regulated by the Salmon and Fresh Water Fisheries Act 1975.[108] The Solway Firth, previously the subject of some special legislation,[109] is now regulated under the 2003 Act, insofar as it lies within Scotland.

The right of salmon fishing in the sea is obtained in the same way as the right of fishing in rivers, i.e. by Crown grant, express or implied.[110] The prohibition of fishing by fixed instruments does not extend to the seashore.[111] Stake nets, for example, are therefore legal.[112] Fishing for salmon at sea is, however, now regulated by statute.[113] The import of live fish of the salmon family was formerly prohibited under the Diseases of Fish Act 1937,[114] but this Act has now been repealed, and replaced by a new statutory regime in the form of Regulations,[115] made under the European Communities Act 1972, implementing the Council of the European Union Directive 2006/88/EC of October 24, 2006 on animal health requirements for aquaculture animals and products thereof, and on the prevention and control of certain diseases in aquatic animals.

The Scottish Ministers may forbid the import of live fish which might compete with, displace, prey on or harm the habitat of any freshwater fish, shellfish or salmon in Scotland.[116] Measures for the control of disease prohibit the introduction of live fish or live spawn of any fish into inland waters.[117]

---

[103] Salmon and Freshwater Fisheries (Consolidation) (Scotland) Act 2003 s.23.

[104] Salmon and Freshwater Fisheries (Consolidation) (Scotland) Act 2003 ss.31–33.

[105] Gordon and Wortley, *Scottish Land Law* (2009), Vol.1, paras 8–98 and 8–101.

[106] Scotland Act 1998 (River Tweed) Order 2006 (SI 2006/2913). Also Tweed Regulation Order 2007 (SSI 2007/19). See Gordon and Wortley, *Scottish Land Law* (2009), paras 8–121 et seq.

[107] Salmon and Freshwater Fisheries (Consolidation) (Scotland) Act 2003 s.70(2).

[108] Salmon and Freshwater Fisheries (Consolidation) (Scotland) Act 2003 s.39, as amended by the Salmon Act 1986 s.26; Water Act 1989 Schs 17 and 27; and Water Consolidation (Consequential Provisions) Act 1991 Sch.1. See *Haddon v Craig*, 1967 S.L.T. (Sh. Ct) 25; *Stair Memorial Encyclopaedia*, Vol.11, "Fisheries", para.46; see, too, Water Act 1989 s.141(4)(b) (National Rivers Authority's duties), the Scotland Act 1998 (Border Rivers) Order 1999 (SI 1999/1746), and the Scotland Act 1998 (River Tweed) Order 2006 (SI 2006/2913).

[109] e.g. Solway Fisheries Act 1804, Solway Salmon Fisheries Commissioners (Scotland) Act 1877; both now repealed.

[110] *McDouall v Lord Advocate* (1875) 2 R. (HL) 49.

[111] Tait, *Game and Fishing Laws of Scotland* (1928), p.162; Gordon and Wortley, *Scottish Land Law* (2009), para.8–103.

[112] See the Salmon and Freshwater Fisheries (Consolidation) (Scotland) Act 2003 s.1(2)(c).

[113] Sea Fish (Conservation) Act 1967 as amended; Salmon and Migratory Trout (Prohibition of Fishing) (No.2) Order 1972 (SI 1973/207). See, too, the Inshore Fishing (Scotland) Act 1984, as amended by the Inshore Fishing (Scotland) Act 1994; the Sea Fisheries (Wildlife Conservation) Act 1992; and the Aquaculture and Fisheries (Scotland) Act 2007; *Wither v Cowie*, 1994 S.L.T. 363; 1990 S.C.C.R. 741; and *Stair Memorial Encyclopaedia*, Vol.11, "Fisheries"', paras 148 seriatim.

[114] Diseases of Fish Act 1937 s.1 as amended by the Diseases of Fish Act 1983 s.1; both repealed by the Aquatic Animal Health (Scotland) Regulations 2009 (SSI 2009/85).

[115] Aquatic Animal Health (Scotland) Regulations 2009 (SSI 2009/85).

[116] Import of Live Fish (Scotland) Act 1978. See also the Aquaculture and Fisheries (Scotland) Act 2007.

[117] Aquaculture and Fisheries (Scotland) Act 2007 s.35.

II. POSSESSION OF HERITAGE

34.11 Possession and possessory remedies—In the law of heritable property possession has three practical effects. First, a possessor has the right to maintain or
recover possession by availing himself of the possessory remedies. Secondly,
possession in good faith, even by one who has no valid title, gives the possessor
certain advantages. Thirdly, possession is an essential factor in positive
prescription.

Possessory remedies are of two kinds, according as they are designed to repel
encroachment and retain possession or to recover possession which has been
lost.[118]

Prior to 1907 the sheriff courts had only a limited jurisdiction in heritage, and
prior to 1877 none at all, with the Court of Session having exclusive jurisdiction
in disputes over heritable rights. The sheriff courts were, however, able to determine matters in respect of rights of possession of heritage.[119] Actions in the sheriff
court based upon a prima facie title and seven years' possession had an obvious
appeal over actions in the Court of Session requiring a complete proof of sasine
title, with a positive prescriptive period of, until 1874, 40 years,[120] and until 1970,
20 years.

This situation was changed in 1907. Section 5(4) of the Sheriff Courts (Scotland)
Act 1907 confers on the sheriff court a broad jurisdiction in matters of heritable
right, viz.

"Actions relating to questions of heritable right or title (except actions of
adjudication save in so far as now competent and actions of reduction)
including all actions of declarator of irritancy and removing, whether at the
instance of a superior against a vassal or of a landlord against a tenant."[121]

Historically, the list of nominate possessory remedies was comprised of: (a)
removing; (b) ejection; (c) intrusion; (d) maills and duties; (e) molestation; and (f)
succeeding in the vice. Of this list, molestation and succeeding in the vice are now
regarded as being virtually obsolete. The diligence of maills and duties is due to
be abolished.[122]

Removing, along with ejection and intrusion, are the remedies available for
recovering possession which has been lost. In all cases some prima facie title is
required.[123] Infeftment is obviously the best of all titles, but a lease is sufficient,[124]
or a title which, though not expressly including the subject, is prima facie

---

[118] A.J.G. Mackay, *Manual of Practice in the Court of Session* (Edinburgh: W. Green, 1893), p.176;
H. Burn-Murdoch, *Interdict in the Law of Scotland* (Caledonian Books, 1986), p.75.

[119] See Burn-Murdoch, *Interdict in the Law of Scotland* (1986), p.76.

[120] The period was reduced to 10 years by the Conveyancing and Feudal Reform (Scotland) Act
1970 s.8 (since repealed), subsequently the Prescription and Limitation (Scotland) Act 1973 s.1. The
earlier statutes are the Prescription Act 1617 (c.12) and the Conveyancing (Scotland) Acts 1874 and
1924.

[121] Sheriff Courts (Scotland) Act 1907 (7 Edw. 7, c.51). The reference to superior and vassal is now
superseded. Provisions in the Bankruptcy and Diligence etc. (Scotland) Act 2007 at ss.79 and 80 will,
once commenced, abolish adjudication for debt. See paras 48.01 and 48.33.

[122] The abolition provisions are in the Bankruptcy and Diligence etc. (Scotland) Act 2007 s.207, and
are subject to commencement. See paras 48.01 and 48.33.

[123] *Carson v Miller* (1863) 1 M. 604 at 611, per Lord Justice-Clerk Inglis; cf. Stair, IV, 3, 47; *Watson
v Shields*, 1994 S.C.L.R. 819 (Sh. Ct); 1996 S.C.L.R. 81, IH.

[124] *Galloway v Cowden* (1884) 12 R. 578.

applicable thereto. Interdict has on occasion been granted even to a party who could not show a title,[125] but a good deal seems to turn on what kind of title, if any, the other party is able to show.[126]

The possession required must be for not less than seven years,[127] which may include the possession of persons from whom the possessor obtained title, and it must be open, peaceful and exercised as a matter of right. Thus if the assertion of a right is constantly challenged and active steps are taken to prevent its exercise (as, for example, where fences are erected by the owner of property across a foot-path over it which another or the public claim a right to use), the possession is not of the peaceful kind required.[128] Or if a person holds a subject under contract his possession will probably be ascribed rather to his right under the contract than to an independent right of possession.[129]

A judgment in a possessory action does not settle any question of heritable right. It decides merely that the existing state of possession is not to be inverted. The parties to the possessory action may have no title to raise questions of heritable right, and if they have a title and wish to have such questions settled, the appropriate process is an action of declarator or of reduction. But, standing a possessory judgment in his favour, the holder has the rights of a bona fide possessor,[130] and is entitled to retain possession until he is ousted by an action challenging his title on its merits.

In addition, interdict provides a general possessory remedy. The remedy of interdict is designed to maintain the existing state of possession and to prevent any threatened or attempted disturbance of that possession. The question of seven years' possession is immaterial for interdict.[131]

It has been suggested that because of the extension of sheriff court jurisdiction possessory actions or judgments based upon prima facie title and seven years' possession are now obsolescent.[132] Modern Scots law gives the option of an action for the recovery of possession of heritable property under the Summary Cause Rules,[133] to which may be added other statutory provisions particular to the various tenancy regimes.[134] The surviving earlier forms of action however remain competent[135] and have not fallen wholly into desuetude, being possessed of some utility as a means of buying time.[136]

---

[125] *Irvine v Robertson* (1872) 11 M. 298. See also Gordon and Wortley, *Scottish Land Law* (2009), Vol.1, para.14–32.

[126] *Cruickshank v Irving* (1854) 17 D. 286.

[127] *Colquhoun v Paton* (1859) 21 D. 996.

[128] *McKerron v Gordon* (1876) 3 R. 429.

[129] *Calder v Adam* (1870) 8 M. 645.

[130] See para.34.12, below.

[131] See Burn-Murdoch, *Interdict in the Law of Scotland* (1986), p.80.

[132] Burn Murdoch, *Interdict in the Law of Scotland* (1986), pp.76–7.

[133] Sheriff Courts (Scotland) Act 1971 s.35(1); Act of Sederunt (Summary Cause Rules) 2002 (SI 2002/132) Ch.30.

[134] For example proceedings by a landlord under the Housing (Scotland) Act 1988 for the recovery of possession of a house let under an assured or a short assured tenancy. See para.35.74, below.

[135] Gordon and Wortley, *Scottish Land Law* (2009), Vol.1, para.14–11. For a full treatment of possessory actions and judgments, including interdict, see Gordon and Wortley, *Scottish Land Law* (2009), paras 14–11—14–39.

[136] See the report on *Little v Irving and Dalgliesh* Unreported January 25, 2000 Dumfries Sheriff Court in R. Paisley and D.J. Cusine, *Unreported Property Cases from the Sheriff Courts* (Edinburgh: W. Green, 2000), p.120.

34.12 Bona fide possession—A bona fide possessor is one who, though not in fact proprietor, believes himself proprietor on probable grounds and with a good conscience.[137] It is necessary that the possession should have been on a colourable title and in bona fide.[138] An obvious case of a colourable title is one *ex facie* regular but which is subsequently reduced because granted *a non domino*. Of bona fides there is an excellent instance in the undernoted case,[139] where the holder took the advice of counsel as to his rights, and in accordance with the opinion continued to exercise the rights of a proprietor.

A bona fide possessor, however, is put in mala fide when the true owner vindicates his right. This may happen if the true owner produces clear and irrefutable evidence of his right. Otherwise, the possessor is put in mala fide only by the decree of a court. It depends on circumstances whether the judgment of a Lord Ordinary will have this effect. In a case of great difficulty the possessor may be protected until judgment in the Inner House, or even in some exceptional cases in the House of Lords.[140]

34.13 Effects of bona fide possession—The effect of bona fides is threefold. In the first place it affords the possessor a defence to a demand by the true owner of the subject for restoration of the fruits drawn (that is, separated from it). Under the strict rule of law one who has, without a valid title, been in possession and drawn the fruits of a subject might be required by the true owner to restore both the subject and these fruits. But where the possession has been held by a bona fide possessor he is allowed the benefit of an equitable plea in defence to the claim for restoration, the effect of which is that he is permitted to retain the fruits drawn from it.[141] Of this plea Stair observes that as it: "is in favour of the innocent possessor, so it is in hatred of the other party not pursuing his right".[142]

Fruits while still growing belong to the owner of the soil, but when severed they become moveable and the property of the bona fide possessor.[143] In terms this applies to natural fruits, but the rule extends to industrial fruits, and to civil fruits, such as rents. Everything severed while the possessor is in bona fide belongs to him.

The second advantage which accrues to a bona fide possessor is that he is entitled to recompense for improvements made by him on the subject possessed in the belief that he was enhancing the value of his own property. The true owner must repay him the amount of his expenditure, in so far as, and to the extent to which, it has benefited the subjects.[144] But, if a life-renter executes improvements on the life-rented property he has no such claim, as presumably he was led to do so for his own benefit while his right subsisted.[145]

Lastly there is no liability for violent profits. A possessor in bad faith is responsible for violent profits. "Violent profits are profits acquired by violence by an intruder without colour of law who must account on the strictest footing."[146] They include not only all the profits which the owner could have made if he had been

---

[137] Erskine, II, 1, 25.
[138] Gordon and Wortley, *Scottish Land Law* (2009), Vol.1, para.14–43.
[139] *Huntly's Trs v Hallyburton's Trs* (1880) 8 R. 50; see also *Menzies v Menzies* (1863) 1 M. 1025.
[140] Gordon and Wortley, *Scottish Land Law* (2009), Vol.1, para.14–45.
[141] *Menzies v Menzies* (1863) 1 M. 1025, per Lord Ardmillan.
[142] Stair, II, 1, 23.
[143] *Duke of Roxburghe v Wauchope* (1825) 1 W. & S. 41.
[144] See further above, para.24.17.
[145] *Wallace v Braid* (1900) 2 F. 754.
[146] *Houldsworth v Brand's Trs* (1876) 3 R. 304, per Lord Justice-Clerk Moncreiff.

in possession, but also all damage which the subject may receive at the hands of the possessor.[147] Violent profits in the case of houses and other urban subjects in burghs were customarily double the rent.[148]

III. INCIDENTS OF OWNERSHIP

Right to use property—The right of property in land entitles the proprietor to **34.14** make what use of it he pleases, subject only to such restrictions as may be imposed by the common law or by statute or by the necessity for observing the rights of his neighbours or of the public generally. In addition to such general restrictions he may also be limited in his right of use by the conditions of his title or by rights which have been created in favour of other persons.

Of the common law restrictions that which has probably most engaged the attention of the courts is the restraint laid upon a proprietor by the law of neighbourhood. The law acknowledges

> "the undoubted right of the proprietor to the free and absolute use of his own property, but there is this restraint or limitation imposed for the protection of his neighbour, that he is not so to use his property as to create that discomfort or annoyance to his neighbour which interferes with his legitimate enjoyment".[149]

It is laid down by the institutional writers that a proprietor may be restrained from operations on his property, otherwise lawful, if these are in *aemulationem vicini*, i.e. for the sole purpose of inconveniencing or injuring his neighbour.[150] The presumption is that the proprietor is not acting emulously[151]; and, if the operations have been undertaken by him with a view to his own convenience or benefit, however inconsiderable, they cannot be restrained.[152] There is a frequent reference to "this valuable rule of our law"[153] in the older cases.[154] *Bradford Corporation v Pickles*[155] indicates that English law is different. But in Scotland the doctrine has since been affirmed,[156] and continues to be applied in the courts.[157]

---

[147] *Gardner v Beresford's Trs* (1877) 4 R. 1091, per Lord President Inglis; see *Inglis' Trs v Macpherson*, 1910 S.C. 46.

[148] Erskine, II, 6, 54; Bell, *Principles*, s.1268(c); *Jute Industries v Wilson & Graham*, 1955 S.L.T. (Sh. Ct) 46.

[149] *Fleming v Hislop* (1886) 13 R. (HL) 43, per Lord Fitzgerald.

[150] Erskine, II, 1, 2; Bankton, IV, 45, 112; Bell, *Principles*, s.964. Cf. the German Civil Code, 226 "The exercise of a right which can have no purpose except the infliction of injury on another is unlawful"; Smith, *A Short Commentary on the Law of Scotland* (1962), p.530; *More v Boyle*, 1967 S.L.T. (Sh. Ct) 38.

[151] Bankton, IV, 45, 112.

[152] *Dunlop v Robertson* (1803) Hume's Decs. 575; *Somerville v Somerville* (1613) Mor.12769. The doctrine applies only to active operations: *Graham v Greig* (1838) 1 D. 171.

[153] *Ritchie v Purdie* (1833) 11 S. 771, per Lord Gillies.

[154] These are collected in J. Rankine, *The Law of Landownership in Scotland*, 4th edn (Edinburgh: W. Green, 1909), p.381, and *Encyclopaedia of Scots Law* (1931), Vol.XII, p.497; *Weir v Aiton* (1858) 20 D. 968.

[155] *Bradford Corporation v Pickles* [1895] A.C. 587 at 597, per Lord Watson. But cf. *Young & Co v Bankier Distillery Co* (1893) 20 R. (HL) 76 at 77.

[156] *Campbell v Muir*, 1908 S.C. 387, especially per Lord President Dunedin at 393.

[157] See, e.g. *Canmore Housing Association Ltd v Bairnsfather*, 2004 S.L.T. 673, OH, and *More, Mclelland and Campbell v Boyle (Nos 1 and 2)* Unreported October 3, 1966 Kilmarnock Sheriff Court in Paisley and Cusine, *Unreported Property Cases From the Sheriff Courts* (2000), p.299. See also *Stair Memorial Encyclopaedia*, Reissue, "Nuisance", paras 33–36.

34.15 Right to exclusive possession—The right of property in land extends, subject to what is said in the next paragraph, *a caelo usque ad centrum*, i.e. from the heavens to the centre of the earth. There are at common law no limits in the vertical direction except such as physical conditions impose.[158] A conveyance of land, therefore, in unqualified terms will give the disponee not merely a right to the surface but also to everything beneath the surface.[159] It follows from the exclusive nature of the right of property[160] that a proprietor is entitled to prohibit encroachment into or trespass on his lands. The legal remedy available to the proprietor against trespass is interdict,[161] which will not, however, be granted in the absence of any actual trespass or of an explicit threat of trespass, or if there is no reasonable probability of a trespass being repeated.[162] But "the exclusive right of a landowner yields wherever public interest or necessity requires that it should yield".[163] Thus property may be entered for the purpose of extinguishing a fire, in pursuit of a criminal, or by a constable for the purpose of ascertaining whether a crime or offence is being committed,[164] and a right to enter premises without the proprietor's permission may be conferred by statute.[165]

As the proprietor may prevent trespass on the surface of his lands, so may he prevent any encroachment below[166] or above the surface. Thus he has been held entitled to insist on the removal of a cornice on his neighbour's house which projected a few inches beyond the boundary[167]; he is not bound to submit to the branches of his neighbour's trees overhanging his ground, and may remove such branches[168]; he may prevent the jib of a crane passing over his property.[169] The court has an equitable power in exceptional circumstances to refuse to enforce a proprietor's right in a question of encroachment by a neighbouring proprietor.[170]

---

[158] *Glasgow City and District Ry v MacBrayne* (1883) 10 R. 894 at 899, per Lord McLaren.

[159] See *Campbell v McCutcheon*, 1963 S.C. 505. There are peculiarities in relation to what was formerly known in common law as "the law of tenements". The law of tenements is considered at paras 34.85–34.88, below. It should be noted that the "law of tenements" has now been replaced by statutory provision, in the form of the Tenements (Scotland) Act 2004 (asp 11). The Act provides a default, providing rules where none have otherwise been agreed preserves the *a caelo usque ad centrum* rule, conferring the right upon the owner of the solum.

[160] See para.30.01, above.

[161] Where the nuisance has come and gone, damages can be sought. See *McMillan v Ghaly*, 2002 G.W.D. 30–1046 (a sheriff court case) for an illustration.

[162] Bell, *Principles*, s.961; Rankine, *The Law of Landownership in Scotland* (1909), p.140; see also *Inverurie Town Council v Sorrie*, 1956 S.C. 175.

[163] Bell, *Principles*, s.956.

[164] *Shepherd v Menzies* (1900) 2 F. 443; *Southern Bowling Club v Ross* (1902) 4 F. 405.

[165] Thus the Health and Safety at Work, etc. Act 1974 s.20, authorises inspectors to enter upon premises without the permission of the owner; cf. *Skinner v John G. McGregor (Contractors)*, 1977 S.L.T. (Sh. Ct) 83; *Tudhope v Laws*, 1982 S.L.T. (Sh. Ct) 85; *Laws v Keane*, 1983 S.L.T. 40; and see Gordon and Wortley, *Scottish Land Law* (2009), Vol.1, para.13–14. Part 9 of the Housing (Scotland) Act 2006 (asp 1) is a more recent example of a statutory right of access to premises, in relation to issues of housing maintenance and disrepair, housing renewal area status and housing in multiple occupation ("HMO") licensing. Breach of the access provisions in the act may result, on summary conviction, in a fine not exceeding level 3 on the standard scale.

[166] *Davey v Harrow Corp* [1958] 1 Q.B. 60; *Property Selection and Investment Trust Ltd v United Friendly Insurance plc*, 1999 S.L.T. 975.

[167] *Milne v Mudie* (1828) 6 S. 967; *Hazle v Turner* (1840) 2 D. 886.

[168] *Halkerson v Wedderburn* (1781) Mor.10495; *Lemmon v Webb* [1895] A.C. 1.

[169] *Brown v Lee Constructions*, 1977 S.L.T. (Notes) 61.

[170] *Sanderson v Geddes* (1874) 1 R. 1198; *Begg v Jack* (1875) 3 R. 35; *Grahame v Magistrates of Kirkcaldy* (1882) 9 R. (HL) 91; *Wilson v Pottinger*, 1908 S.C. 580; (1908) 15 S.L.T. 941, *Anderson v Brattisanni's*, 1978 S.L.T. (Notes) 42; *Strathclyde RC v Persimmon Homes (Scotland) Ltd*, 1996 S.L.T. 176, reserving until after proof the question whether to order removal (of a road) or damages.

Technological advances such as the development of aviation and the use of space have perhaps rendered the presumption of the unlimited upward extent of ownership debatable. This notwithstanding, the sale or lease of airspace is a clear matter of commercial utility, and if there is no authority confirming the position there equally is none against the conveyance of airspace, and it is not contrary to principle. The Leases Act 1449 certainly appears broad enough to accommodate a lease of airspace, and constitute it as a real right. The flight of aircraft is exempted from liability in trespass or nuisance, but the owner is strictly liable for damage caused by anything falling from the aircraft.[171]

Minerals[172]—Mines of gold and silver, and mines of lead of such fineness that **34.16** three halfpennies of silver may be got out of the pound of lead, belong to the Crown.[173]

The Crown, however, is not merely entitled, but is bound, when required, to make a grant of these precious minerals to the proprietor of the lands in which they are found in consideration of payment of a royalty.[174] Coal is vested in the Coal Authority.[175] So far as petroleum is concerned, the Crown has the exclusive right of searching and boring for and getting petroleum in strata in Great Britain and beneath the territorial sea adjacent to the United Kingdom.[176] All other minerals belong to the owner of the land in which they are found. A lease of minerals differs from the ordinary lease of urban or agricultural subjects.

> "The true nature of a mineral lease seems to be rather a grant of a temporary privilege—a privilege during a period of removing and appropriating so much of the substance of the minerals within a certain area as the grantee may be able or may choose to excavate, and that for a consideration or price calculated according either to the duration of the privilege or the amount appropriated."[177]

What is called a mineral lease is really, when properly considered, an out-and-out sale of a portion of the land.[178] The consideration under the lease is either rent or royalties (i.e. a payment on the amount of minerals won by the lessee) or it may be both. But the term "rent" is figurative, as the payment is not for the use of the soil but for the consumption or taking away of part of it.[179] Agreement as to duration is an essential prerequisite of a valid lease of minerals.[180] Rights to minerals can be enjoyed under a life-rent, subject to specialities.[181]

---

[171] Civil Aviation Act 1982 s.76.

[172] There has been much controversy as to whether particular substances such as freestone, whinstone, clay, oil-shale, are or are not minerals; for the details see Gordon and Wortley, *Scottish Land Law* (2009), Vol.1, para.5–55.

[173] Royal Mines Act 1424.

[174] Mines and Metals Act 1592; *Earl of Hopetown v Officers of State* (1750) Mor.13527; *Earl of Breadalbane v Jamieson* (1875) 2 R. 826.

[175] Coal Industry Act 1994 s.7(3). Working of the coal will normally be granted out to licensed operators. For the previous regimes (National Coal Board and British Coal Corp), see Coal Industry Nationalisation Act 1946 s.5; Coal Industry Acts 1987 and 1990.

[176] Petroleum Act 1998 s.2.

[177] *Fleeming v Baird* (1871) 9 M. 730, per Lord Justice-Clerk Moncreiff.

[178] *Gowans v Christie* (1873) 11 M. (HL) 1 at 12.

[179] *Nugent v Nugent's Trs* (1899) 2 F. (HL) 21 at 22.

[180] *Cumming v Quartzag*, 1980 S.C. 276.

[181] See Gordon and Wortley, *Scottish Land Law* (2009), Vol.1, paras 17–40—17–41.

34.17 **Minerals under railways, the foreshore, the sea or highways**—Special provisions apply to these minerals. Under the Railway Clauses Consolidation (Scotland) Act 1845, as amended by ss.15–17 of the Mines (Working Facilities and Support) Act 1923,[182] minerals under land purchased for construction of railways are not included in the sale of the land, except insofar as they are expressly purchased or must be dug out, carried away or used in the construction. More important nowadays is that, if the party in right of the minerals lying under the "area of protection" desires to work them, he must give notice to the railway and to the royalty owner (if any). The railway then has the right to prevent the working of the minerals on paying compensation to the mine owner and the royalty owner. The "area of protection" is the area comprising any railway or works and extending from it on all or both sides at each point along the railway to one-half the depth of the seam at that point, or 40 yards, whichever is greater.[183]

Minerals under the foreshore belong to the Crown as owner of the foreshore, but may be alienated in favour of a subject, provided the rights of the public are not interfered with.[184] The excavation of minerals on or under the seashore (other than minerals more than 50 feet below the surface) is prohibited, except with the consent of the Scottish Ministers.[185]

Minerals under the sea within the 12-mile limit also belong to the Crown. The opinion has been expressed that, in so far as they are capable of being worked without causing disturbance, they may be alienated in favour of a subject.[186]

Minerals under roads may be excavated by the owner. Road trustees and other authorities have no right to them, but may prevent workings which endanger the road.[187]

34.18 **Game**[188]—Game falls within the class of animals which are not the subject of property until appropriated.[189] From an early date, statutes were promulgated for the regulation of the exercise of the taking of game,[190] and until recently, much of the body of legislation known as the "Game Laws" came out of the nineteenth century, with the earliest statute not in desuetude being the Game (Scotland) Act 1772. That Act, and many of its nineteenth and twentieth century successors, were repealed by the Wildlife and Natural Environment (Scotland) Act 2011.[191] The 2011 Act amends the Wildlife and Countryside Act 1981, and these two Acts must now be regarded as comprising the main body of the Game Laws. Historically, the various Game Acts contained no general definition of "game", but hares, pheasants, partridges and grouse were included in all the Acts. These species are all preserved in the modern statutory regime. The definition of game birds in the

---

[182] For details see *Stair Memorial Encyclopaedia*, Vol.14, "Mines and Quarries", paras 1690 et seq.

[183] See Gordon and Wortley, *Scottish Land Law* (2009), Vol.1, paras 5–96—5–99. For a recent English case, see *National Grid Gas Plc v Lafarge Aggregates Ltd* [2006] EWHC 2559 (Ch).

[184] See para.34.06, above.

[185] Coast Protection Act 1949 s.18; see *British Dredging (Services) v Secretary of State for Wales and Monmouthshire* [1975] 1 W.L.R. 687.

[186] *Lord Advocate v Wemyss* (1899) 2 F. (HL) 1, per Lord Watson.

[187] *Waddell v Earl of Buchan* (1868) 6 M. 690.

[188] Tait, *Game and Fishing Laws of Scotland* (1928); *Stair Memorial Encyclopaedia*, Vol.11, "Game"; Gordon and Wortley, *Scottish Land Law* (2009), Vol.1, Ch.9; Scott Robinson, *The Law of Game, Salmon and Freshwater Fishing in Scotland* (1990).

[189] See para.31.04, above.

[190] For example, the Wild Birds Act 1427 (c.12) and the Wild Birds Act 1457 (c.51), both now repealed.

[191] Wildlife and Natural Environment (Scotland) Act 2011 (asp 6).

1981 Act is repealed by the 2011 Act,[192] and instead game birds are incorporated into the 1981 Act provisions covering wild birds generally. Rabbits are also accorded protection, as are hares, and new provisions create an offence of taking and killing hares during the close season, with separate close seasons being set for brown and for common hares.[193] The right to kill game is an incident of the right of landed property; a privilege *sui generis*, which has nothing to do with the ordinary use of land.[194] A tenant as such has no right to take the game, since it is a right belonging to the proprietor alone. The Wildlife and Countryside Act 1981[195] protects black grouse from December 11–August 19, ptarmigan and red grouse from December 11–August 11, partridges from February 2–August 31, and pheasants from February 2–September 30.

Fishing[196]—Fish belong to no one while they are in their natural state, but if **34.19** enclosed in a fish-pond they become the property of the person having right to, and enclosing them in, the pond.[197] The right of angling for trout in private streams is an accessory to the right of property in the adjoining lands,[198] and there is no common right of fishing for trout belonging to the public at large or to such members of the community as may have access to the water by virtue of a right of passage along the banks,[199] or in exercise of statutory rights of access. The same rule applies to lochs[200] and to rivers which are navigable but not tidal.[201] With regard to the rights of opposite proprietors, each has a right to fish up to the middle of the stream, and, at least in small rivers, each has a common interest in that part of the river which he does not own.[202] Difficulties may arise where a river changes its course.[203]

IV. NATURAL RIGHTS OF PROPERTY

Natural rights and servitudes—Ownership of property carries with it certain **34.20** rights against, and obligations towards, owners and occupiers of neighbouring property. Some of these rights arise by law from the relative situations of the properties: these may be called natural rights. Other rights, which are created by prescription or agreement, express or implied, being servitudes or real burdens,

---

[192] Wildlife and Natural Environment (Scotland) Act 2011 s.2.

[193] Wildlife and Natural Environment (Scotland) Act 2011 s.2.

[194] *Welwood v Husband* (1874) 1 R. 507.

[195] As amended by the Wildlife and Natural Environment (Scotland) Act 2011.

[196] Tait, *Game and Fishing Laws of Scotland* (1928); Gordon and Wortley, *Scottish Land Law* (2009), Vol.1, Ch.8. For salmon fishing, see para.34.10, above.

[197] *Copland v Maxwell* (1871) 9 M. (HL) 1. The Salmon and Freshwater Fisheries (Consolidation) (Scotland) Act 2003 s.11, provides that whosoever, without permission, takes fishes "in a proper stank or lochs" shall be liable to a fine. The taking of fish from a stank is theft: *Pollok v McCabe*, 1910 S.C. (J.) 23.

[198] See, e.g. *East Lothian Angling Association v Haddington Town Council*, 1980 S.L.T. 213, where an angling association with licences to fish granted by riparian proprietors, but with no real right or interest in the fishing as such, could not recover damages for injury to the fishing.

[199] *Fergusson v Shirreff* (1844) 6 D. 1363.

[200] *Montgomery v Watson* (1861) 23 D. 635.

[201] *Grant v Henry* (1894) 21 R. 358.

[202] *Arthur v Aird*, 1907 S.C. 1170. But cf. para.34.10, above. For salmon fishing, the House of Lords in *Fothringham v Passmore*, 1984 S.C. (HL) 96 took a broader view.

[203] *Annandale & Eskdale DC v N.W. Water Authority*, 1978 S.C. 187 (where the river was also part of the boundary between England and Scotland).

and are dealt with later.[204] The former are necessary for the comfortable enjoy-ment of property, and are real rights of the same nature as ownership itself. They are incidents of the title to the property. They may be modified by the operation of contract, express or implied, for example by a servitude; but they cannot properly be said to be discharged or extinguished by contract, seeing that, if the contractual superimposed right comes to an end, the original natural right revives in full force.[205] Certain of these rights are sometimes described as natural servitudes, but it seems better to reserve the term servitude to denote rights which do not arise by law, but from grant or prescription. It has been held, in the context of landlocked land (meaning a parcel of land entirely surrounded by other land through which there is no servitude or other right of access), that a right of access, being *res merae facultatis*, is an inherent and imprescriptible incident of ownership.[206]

Natural rights of property may be considered with reference to (a) the right of support to land, and (b) rights in water incidental to property in land.

34.21 Right of support—Land in general requires support both from below and from the surrounding land; if the necessary subjacent or adjacent support is withdrawn, it subsides with or without surface cracking. Here it is necessary to distinguish between land in its natural state and land carrying buildings. Obviously land carrying buildings requires greater support than it would if in its natural state, and a neighbouring owner may be bound to afford sufficient support for the land itself, but not bound to support the additional burden of the buildings.

An owner of land has an unqualified right to such support as is necessary to uphold the land in its natural state.[207] Questions regarding support generally arise where underlying supporting strata have been removed by mining.[208]

> "If A conveys minerals to B reserving the property of the surface, or if A conveys the surface to B reserving the property of the minerals below it, A in the one case retains, and B in the other gets, a right to have the surface supported unless the contrary shall be expressly provided or shall appear by plain implication from the terms of the conveyance."[209]

---

[204] See Pts V and VI, below.

[205] Rankine, *The Law of Landownership in Scotland* (1909), p.385.

[206] *Bowers v Kennedy*, 2000 S.C. 555. See also *Inverness Seafield Development Ltd v Mackintosh*, 2000 S.L.T. 118 and R. Paisley, "Bower of Bliss" (2002) 6 Edin. L.R. 101. The recent case of *Peart v Legge*, 2008 S.C. 93 considered whether a right of access constituted in a disposition was imprescrip-tible on the basis that it was *res merae facultatis* (see further above, para 4.07). The case was debated in the Edinburgh Law Review; see R. Paisley, "Right to make roads and *res merae facultatis*" (2007) 11 Edin. L.R. 95 (commenting upon the judgment on the sheriff court) and D.L. Carey Miller, "*Res merae facultatis*: mysterious or misunderstood?" (2008) 12 Edin. L.R. 455 (following the decision of the Inner House).

[207] *Dalton v Angus* (1881) L.R. 6 App. Cas. 740; *Bank of Scotland v Stewart* (1891) 18 R. 957; Reid, *The Law of Property in Scotland* (1996), paras 252–272.

[208] For the right of support for pipes laid under statutory authority, see *Edinburgh and District Water Trs v Clippens Oil Co* (1900) 3 F. 156, and *Midlothian County Council v N.C.B.*, 1960 S.C. 308. For liability of the Coal Authority for damage caused by subsidence, see the Coal Mining Subsidence Act 1991 as amended by the Coal Industry Act 1994; for an example of a recent (unsuccessful) claim, see *Marquis of Lothian v Coal Authority* [1996] R.V.R. 252. See also *Brady v National Coal Board*, 1999 G.W.D. 22–1070, 2nd Div., for a claim under the previous legislation, the Coal Mining Subsidence Act 1957.

[209] *White v Wm Dixon* (1883) 10 R. (HL) 45, per Lord Watson; *Caledonian Ry v Sprot* (1856) 2 Macq. 449; *Butterknowle Colliery Co v Bishop Auckland Industrial Cooperative Co* [1906] A.C. 305. The principles governing the decisions are applicable in both England and Scotland; *Caledonian Ry v Sprot* (1856) 2 Macq. 449 at 461; *Buchanan v Andrew* (1873) 11 M. (HL) 13 at 16.

Where the right of support is not displaced by provision or implication, and a subsidence occurs, it is an actionable wrong, involving liability in damages independent of negligence; but this liability is owed only to the landowner as an incident of ownership in respect of damage to his property, and not to other parties for personal injury.[210] Each fresh subsidence is a new wrong allowing of a further action of damages, even though no further mining has taken place between the earlier and the later subsidence.[211] This right to bring more than one action of damages is not an exception to the general rule that the whole damages resulting from one wrong must be sued for in one action, for the ground of action in this case is not the mining but the subsidence, and each fresh subsidence is a new and independent infringement of the surface owner's rights. But a successor in title is not liable for the acts of a predecessor in title where subsidence resulting from that predecessor's acts occurs during the successor's tenure of the land.[212]

Somewhat similar questions may arise between adjacent owners. Where there is rock close to the surface, little adjacent support may be necessary, but where the ground is friable considerable subsidence might be caused by a neighbour digging or quarrying right up to the edge of his property: in such a case the neighbour is bound to stop excavating at such a distance from his boundary as will leave sufficient support for the neighbouring land.

Where buildings are placed on the lands there can be no natural right of support for the surface thus altered. In England the right of support of buildings is regarded as of the nature of a servitude.[213] In Scotland the law is not so clearly developed. The right of support for buildings may be acquired in various ways. Thus it may be obtained by express grant, but it more usually arises from implied grant.[214] Where the ownership of the minerals is severed from that of the surface after buildings have been erected, it will be held that the mineral owner is bound to afford sufficient support for the enjoyment of the surface with buildings as they exist when the severance takes place, for parties cannot be held to have contemplated that existing buildings were not to be supported. On the other hand, it cannot be implied that the mineral owner has undertaken to support and to be liable for damage to all buildings, however extensive, which may afterwards be erected, for this might subject him to heavy claims for damages in respect of property which the parties never had in contemplation.[215] But if, at the time of the severance of the ownership of the minerals from that of the land, the land was conveyed expressly with a view to the erection of buildings or to any other use which might render increased support necessary, there is an implied right to such support as the contemplated use of such land requires.[216]

---

[210] *Angus v N.C.B.*, 1955 S.C. 175.

[211] *Darley Main Colliery Co v Mitchell* (1886) L.R. 11 App. Cas. 127.

[212] *Angus v N.C.B.*, 1955 S.C. 175. See also Gordon and Wortley, *Scottish Land Law* (2009), Vol.1, para.5–113; Rankine, *The Law of Landownership in Scotland* (1909), p.495.

[213] See Tang Hang Wu, "The right of lateral support of buildings from the adjoining land", *Conveyancer and Property Lawyer*, Conv. 2002, May/Jun, 237–260. The issue of easements and covenants was the subject of a Law Commission project, the aim of which is to produce a more coherent scheme of easements and covenants which is compatible with both the commonhold system and the system of registration introduced in England and Wales by the Land Registration Act 2002. The Report covering the Law Commission's recommendations was published on June 8, 2011, and is available at *http://lawcommission.justice.gov.uk/areas/easements.htm* [Accessed August 15, 2012].

[214] *Dalton v Angus* (1881) L.R. 6 App. Cas. 740 at 792, 803. See also Gordon and Wortley, *Scottish Land Law* (2009), Vol.1, paras 5–90—5–105.

[215] *Hamilton v Turner* (1867) 5 M. 1086 at 1095, 1099, 1100.

[216] *Caledonian Ry v Sprot* (1856) 2 Macq. 449; *North British Ry v Turners* (1904) 6 F. 900; *Dalton v Angus* (1881) L.R. 6 App. Cas. 740 at 792.

The right of the surface owner to support may also be acquired by agreement or by grant under the Mines (Working Facilities and Support) Act 1966.[217] The extent of the right may be modified by the terms of the title or by agreement, entitling the mineral owner to bring down the surface on payment of damages[218] or even without paying damages.[219] Conversely, the 1966 Act gives the Court of Session power to grant a person having the right to work minerals various ancillary rights provided these are required for the proper and convenient working of the minerals. These ancillary rights include a right to let down the surface on payment of compensation.[220]

The support due by the owner of a building to a contiguous building or to the upper storey of the same building is noticed under the heading of Common Interest.[221] The law in respect of support and shelter in tenements has been reviewed by the Scottish Parliament, and the modern statutory provisions are contained in the Tenements (Scotland) Act 2004.

34.22 Rights in water—Historically, the common law pertaining to the extent of property rights in water on or underneath the land in Scotland has caused difficulties.[222] In relation to the ownership of water, Scots law has in general followed the Roman law approach of distinguishing between standing (and percolating) water and running water. Running waters are common to all, whereas standing water may be appropriated.[223] However, a right to the exploitation of water may be enjoyed without the need for any assertion of ownership of that water. Therefore, in practical terms, it is the extent to which the law allows private individuals the right to exploit a water resource that is the most important issue, and not that of the extent to which water is susceptible to private ownership.

This section deals with the rights of landowners in respect of the water that is upon or below or flows through their land. The common law in this area has been affected by recent statutory reforms, driven by the need to comply with the European Water Framework Directive.[224] Paragraph 1 of the Directive states: "Water is not a commercial product like any other but, rather, a heritage which must be protected, defended and treated as such." The Directive has been given effect to by the Scottish Parliament by the Water Environment and Water Services (Scotland) Act 2003, and further developed by the Water Environment (Controlled Activities) (Scotland) Regulations 2011.[225] These

---

[217] As amended by the Mines (Working Facilities and Support) Act 1974, the Ancient Monuments and Archaeological Areas Act 1979, the Town and Country Planning (Minerals) Act 1981, and the Coal Industry Acts 1987 and 1990.

[218] *Anderson v McCracken Brothers* (1900) 2 F. 780.

[219] *Buchanan v Andrew* (1873) 11 M. (HL) 13; *Bank of Scotland v Stewart* (1891) 18 R. 957; *Pringle v Carron Co* (1905) 7 F. 820.

[220] Mines (Working Facilities and Support) Act 1966 ss.1, 2 and 8.

[221] See para.34.84, below; and see *Lord Advocate v Reo Stakis Organisation Ltd*, 1982 S.L.T. 140.

[222] See J. Ferguson, *Law of Water and Water Rights of Scotland* (1907); Reid, *The Law of Property in Scotland* (1996), paras 273–308; *Stair Memorial Encyclopaedia*, Vol.25 ("Water and Water Rights"). For a historical treatment of water law regimes in Scotland, see Reid and Zimmermann, *A History of Private Law in Scotland* (2000), Vol.1, pp.421–479.

[223] See Stair, II, 1, 5. Also Erskine, II, 1, 5 and Bankton, I, 3, 2.

[224] Directive 2000/60/EC of the European Parliament and of the Council of October 23, 2000, establishing a framework for Community action in the field of water, OJ L321, December 22, 2000.

[225] Water Environment (Controlled Activities) (Scotland) Regulations 2011 (SSI 2011/209), replacing the Water Environment (Controlled Activities) (Scotland) Regulations 2005. See B. Clark, "Water Law in Scotland, The Water Environment and Water Services (Scotland) Act 2003 and the European Convention on Human Rights" (2006) 10 Edin. L.R. 60 and B. Clark, "Water Use Reform in Scotland: A Critical Analysis" (2006) 18 J. Env L. 375.

provisions introduced a statutory scheme for the abstraction and impoundment of water in Scotland, including provisions on registration and licensing, to operate alongside the existing common law rights.

The effects of these provisions will be considered below,[226] at the conclusion of the following analysis of the common law situation. It should be noted that whilst the common law as stated in paras 34.23 and 34.24 below, remains, in principle, valid, individual attempts to implement particular common law rights falling within the ambit of the new regulatory regime may be prohibited under that regime.[227]

Water not in a definite channel—Surface water, or water percolating through **34.23** the ground, may be appropriated by the owner of the land where it is found. It cannot be conveyed as property separately from the land itself.[228] A neighbouring proprietor may have a right to object to the appropriation of water from a definite stream or watercourse, but until water has reached such a stream it is entirely at the disposal of the person in whose land it is found.[229] So an owner may appropriate underground percolating water by sinking a well, notwithstanding that this may cause his neighbour's well to dry up; his neighbour has no right to object, even if he enjoyed for the prescriptive period the well now rendered useless.[230] But, in the general case, an owner desires not to appropriate but to get rid of surface water. Such water may drain directly into a stream, and in that case no difficulty arises. On the other hand, it may drain naturally on to lower land owned by a different proprietor, and in that case, the owner of the lower land is bound to receive it.[231] But the owner of the higher ground is not entitled to increase this burden on his neighbour by draining in such a way as to send down to the neighbouring land water which would not naturally run that way, or by sending down water artificially brought to the surface by pumping operations or conveyed from a distant stream.[232] It is otherwise in the case of ordinary agricultural drainage. This may alter the natural run-off of surface water, and may thereby considerably increase the burden on the adjacent owner. Nevertheless the latter is bound to receive it. It might be thought that the inferior owner should not be bound to suffer any increase of the natural burden, but it has long been settled that, as agricultural drainage is a necessary operation, the adjacent owner has no right to object to it and is bound to submit to the consequent alteration of the natural flow of water on to his land.[233] Provision for regulating such drainage on application to, and under the authority of, the sheriff is made by the Land Drainage (Scotland) Act 1930. The Scottish Ministers also have power to make schemes for the drainage of agricultural land.[234] The obligation of an inferior owner to receive the natural run-off

---

[226] See paras 34.26–34.29, below.

[227] See Clark, "Water Use Reform in Scotland: A Critical Analysis" (2006) 18 J. Env L. 375.

[228] *Crichton v Turnbull*, 1946 S.C. 52.

[229] *Milton v Glen-Moray Glenlivet Distillery Co Ltd* (1898) 1 F. 135; (1898) 6 S.L.T. 206.

[230] *Chasemore v Richards* (1859) 7 H.L. Cas. 349; *Bradford Corporation v Pickles* [1895] A.C. 587; *Milton v Glen-Moray Glenlivet Distillery Co* (1898) 1 F. 135; *Bradford Corp v Ferrand* [1902] 2 Ch. 655; *Langbrook Properties v Surrey County Council* [1970] I W.L.R. 161.

[231] *Campbell v Bryson* (1864) 3 M. 254; *Logan v Wang (UK) Ltd*, 1991 S.L.T. 580.

[232] *Young v Bankier Distillery* (1893) 20 R. (HL) 76; cf. *Anderson v Robertson*, 1958 S.C. 367. Different considerations arise where an artificial embankment has been constructed to protect land from the sea: *McLaren v British Railways Board*, 1971 S.C. 182.

[233] *Campbell v Bryson* (1864) 3 M. 254.

[234] Land Drainage (Scotland) Act 1958, as amended by the Local Government (Scotland) Act 1994. For non-agricultural land it is the Flood Risk Management (Scotland) Act 2009 that applies.

may also arise in connection with mining. A mineowner is entitled to work his minerals right up to his boundary, although this may cause water to drain into adjacent workings. The neighbouring mineowner has no right to object to this; if he requires protection he must protect himself by leaving an adequate barrier of his own minerals.[235]

34.24 Streams[236]—Once water has reached a watercourse, however small it may be[237] and whether it be above or below the surface, very different principles apply. Such water is no longer subject to the sole control of the owner on whose land it happens to be. All the riparian proprietors, from the source to the mouth of the stream, have a common interest in it, and are entitled to object if their particular interests are infringed. Members of the public have no right to interfere in any case except where a stream is navigable.[238]

The bed or alveus of a non-tidal stream belongs to the proprietor of the land through which it flows, and if the stream separates the lands of two proprietors, each is prima facie owner of the soil of the bed up to the *medium filum*, or middle line, of the stream.[239] It is stated in Gordon and Wortley, *Scottish Land Law*, on the authority of *North British Railway v Magistrates of Hawick*,[240] that

> "where property is bounded by a river (other than a tidal navigable river, in which the bed belongs to the Crown), the presumption is that the boundary is the *medium filum* of the river. But the presumption can be displaced and where the river is not given as the boundary the bed may not be claimed as a pertinent, merely because the land lies on the river bank."[241]

But although the bed of the stream may belong to a proprietor, he has no right to interfere with it in any way which may result in injury to the interest of any other riparian proprietor.[242] A proprietor may, however, acquire, by the operation of prescription, certain rights which prejudice other riparian proprietors.[243]

Apart from fishing questions, an upper heritor is not concerned with the operations of a lower heritor except in so far as these cause, or are likely to cause, the water to regurgitate and prevent it from flowing freely away from the upper-heritor's land.[244] But the position of the lower heritor exposes him to greater risk that his rights in the water may be prejudiced by the interference of the upper heritor with the quantity or quality of flow of the stream.

A riparian proprietor has a right to take water from the stream for what are known as the primary uses, i.e. drink for man and beast and ordinary domestic

---

[235] *Durham v Hood* (1871) 9 M. 474.

[236] For a discussion of the definition of "stream", see Gordon and Wortley, *Scottish Land Law* (2009), Vol.1, paras 6–25—6–26.

[237] *Cruikshanks & Bell v Henderson*, 1791 Hume 506.

[238] See para.34.07, above.

[239] *Menzies v Marquess of Breadalbane* (1901) 4 F. 55; cf. *Stirling v Bartlett*, 1992 S.C. 523; 1993 S.L.T. 763.

[240] *North British Railway v Magistrates of Hawick* (1862) 1 M. 200.

[241] Gordon and Wortley, *Scottish Land Law* (2009), Vol.1, para.3–34. The rebuttability of the presumption is considered in *MacDonald (or Dalton) v Turcan Connell (Trustees) Ltd*, 2005 S.C.L.R. 159 (Notes).

[242] *Morris v Bicket* (1866) 4 M. (HL) 44; *Plean Precast Ltd v National Coal Board*, 1985 S.C. 77; *G.A. Estates Ltd v Caviapen Trs Ltd (No.1)*, 1993 S.L.T. 1037.

[243] For example, mooring a houseboat, or building a crossing.

[244] *Hope v Heriot's Hospital* (1878) 15 S.L.R. 400.

purposes, even though the result should be to exhaust the water altogether. He may be entitled to draw off water for other purposes, for example irrigation or manufacturing operations, but he can do so only if no other riparian proprietor's interest is thereby infringed.[245]

"A riparian proprietor is entitled to have the water of the stream on the banks of which his property lies flow down as it has been accustomed to flow down to his property, subject to the ordinary use of the flowing water by upper proprietors, and such further use, if any, on their part, in connection with their property as may be reasonable under the circumstances. Every riparian proprietor is thus entitled to the water of his stream in its natural flow without sensible diminution or increase, and without sensible alteration in its character or quality. Any invasion of this right causing actual damage, or calculated to found a claim which may ripen into an adverse right, entitles the party injured to the intervention of the Court."[246]

If the natural speed or direction of flow of the stream as it comes down to the lower proprietor's land is altered, this may injure him by requiring him to strengthen the banks of the stream in his property, or it may have the effect of altering the channel of the stream when it reaches him. So also if the natural flow of the stream is altered (e.g. if it is stored up and released at intervals), the inferior heritor who is injured by the resulting intermittent flow of the stream, may object.[247] But a lower heritor has in general no interest to object to an upper heritor diverting a part or even the whole of the stream, provided that the water is returned to the stream without sensible diminution in quantity or deterioration in quality before the stream reaches the property of the lower heritor.[248] Whilst obviously the natural overflow of a stream involves nobody in liability, an overflow of one which has been converted to use as a public sewer by, for example, a local authority, may render the authority liable.[249]

A riparian proprietor has also an interest to prevent any interference with the stream by the proprietor of the land on the opposite side. No riparian proprietor is, even on his own portion of the alveus, entitled to do anything which prejudicially affects the common interest in the flowing water or from which such a result may reasonably be apprehended: any such operation may be prevented unless the court is satisfied that there is not, and will not at any future time be, any injury resulting from it.[250] A heritor is entitled to put an embankment on his own lands, if this is necessary to prevent their being flooded, although it has the effect of increasing the flood on the lands of the opposite heritor[251]; but he has no right to obstruct the regular channels through which the river flows in time of flood, even if these are dry at other times.[252] In a question with an opposite heritor an owner is not entitled

---

[245] *McCartney v Londonderry & Lough Swilly Ry* [1904] A.C. 301; *Young v Bankier Distillery Co* (1893) 20 R. (HL) 76, per Lord Macnaghten; *Rugby Joint Water Board v Walters* [1967] Ch. 397.

[246] *Young v Bankier Distillery Co* (1893) 20 R. (HL) 76, per Lord Macnaghten.

[247] *Hunter & Aitkenhead v Aiken* (1880) 7 R. 510.

[248] *Orr Ewing v Colquhoun's Trs* (1877) 4 R. (HL) 116 at 127, per Lord Blackburn.

[249] See *Greyhound Racing Trust v Edinburgh Corp*, 1952 S.L.T. 35. See too the Control of Pollution Act 1974 and the Water Environment and Water Services (Scotland) Act 2003.

[250] *Morris v Bicket* (1866) 4 M. (HL) 44; *Orr Ewing v Colquhoun's Trs* (1877) 4 R. (HL) 116, per Lord Blackburn; *McGavin v McIntyre Brothers* (1890) 17 R. 818, per Lord Trayner; *Kensit v Great Eastern Ry* (1884) L.R. 27 Ch.D. 122, per Cotton L.J.

[251] *Farquharson v Farquharson* (1741) Mor.12779; *Gerrard v Crowe* [1921] A.C. 395.

[252] *Menzies v E. Breadalbane* (1828) 3 W. & S. 235.

to divert water for any purpose even though he returns it before the stream leaves his property, for any such diversion must diminish the stream flowing past the opposite heritor's property.[253]

A heritor may also prevent any operations that cause appreciable change in the quality of the water flowing past his property. Discharge of sewage or other matter into a stream is not prohibited at common law so long as no appreciable pollution results. Perhaps the most frequently adopted criterion of pollution is whether or not the addition of the material objected to makes the water of the stream unfit for use for any of the primary purposes, but this is not in all cases the proper test. An upper heritor's operations may leave the water fit to drink but unfit for some special use to which the lower heritor has been putting it, for example distilling: in such a case the lower heritor is entitled to object.[254] The fact that a certain amount of pollution may have already existed apart from the operations complained of does not entitle any heritor to increase the amount of pollution if such increased pollution causes any damage to lower heritors.[255] Some degree of pollution may have become legalised by continuing for the prescriptive period, and in that case the heritor causing the pollution is entitled to continue his operations, but not to increase the amount of noxious matter which he discharges into the stream. The common law has, however, been substantially replaced on the question of river pollution by statutory provisions. These were formerly contained in Pt II of the Control of Pollution Act 1974,[256] key parts of which were subsequently repealed.[257] The new relevant provisions are contained in the Water Environment (Controlled Activities) (Scotland) Regulations 2011, made under the Water Environment and Water Services (Scotland) Act 2003, which made provisions for the transfer of authorisations under the Control of Pollution Act 1974 to the new regime under the 2003 Act and for the interaction of the various pollution control regimes so as to bring about an integrated approach to the control of water pollution at source.[258]

34.25 Lochs—Lochs fall into two classes. First, there are those which are entirely surrounded by the lands of one proprietor. In that case the whole loch (water and solum) belongs to the owner of the surrounding land and is under his sole control. If a stream runs out of it, however, he is limited in his use of the loch by the necessity for respecting the rights of the riparian owners in the stream. Secondly, the loch may be one on which the lands of several owners abut. In this case there is a presumption that each has a separate right of property. The titles or the titles coupled with the state of possession may, however, be such as to give one owner the exclusive right.[259] When there are separate rights each proprietor has an exclusive right to the solum from his own shore up to the middle of the loch.[260] But he must not interfere with the enjoyment by the other owners

---

[253] *White & Sons v White* (1906) 8 F. (HL) 41.

[254] *Young v Bankier Distillery* (1893) 20 R. (HL) 76.

[255] *McIntyre Brothers v McGavin* (1893) 20 R. (HL) 49.

[256] As amended by the Water Act 1989 s.169 and Sch.23 and the Environment Act 1995 s.106 and Sch.16.

[257] It should be noted that the 1974 Act has not been wholly repealed.

[258] Water Environment (Controlled Activities) (Scotland) Regulations 2011 (SSI 2011/209). Water Environment and Water Services (Scotland) Act 2003. SEPA (the Scottish Environment Protection Agency) is the public body responsible for environmental protection in Scotland. SEPA is responsible to the Scottish Parliament through Ministers. SEPA has both regulatory and advisory functions.

[259] *Scott v Lord Napier* (1869) 7 M. (HL) 35.

[260] *Cochrane v Earl of Minto* (1815) 6 Pat. 139.

of their right to the water, which is common to all.[261] All proprietors have the right to sail and fish upon the loch, but the court may restrict or regulate the number of boats each proprietor may put on it.[262] The common law rights of owners of lands surrounding an artificial loch or reservoir are not clearly settled.[263] There are statutory provisions concerning pollution and damage arising from certain operations.[264]

The European Water Framework Directive—The law in relation to Scotland's **34.26** water environment has been affected by recent statutory reforms, driven by the need to comply with the European Water Framework Directive.[265] The Directive has been given effect to by the Scottish Parliament by the Water Environment and Water Services (Scotland) Act 2003, as developed by the Water Environment (Controlled Activities) (Scotland) Regulations 2011 (hereinafter "the Regulations").[266].

The 2003 Act defines "water environment" very broadly,[267] so as to include all surface water, groundwater and wetlands, and includes all standing or flowing water on the surface of the land other than transitional water (water in the vicinity of river mouths which is partly saline in character as a result of its proximity to coastal water but which is substantially influenced by freshwater flows) within the landward limits of coastal water. It therefore encompasses water (other than groundwater) within the area extending landward from the 3-mile limit up to the limit of the highest tide or, where appropriate, the seaward limits of any bodies of transitional water. It is sufficient for the purposes of this chapter to accept the Act as including all wetlands, rivers, lochs, transitional waters (estuaries), coastal waters and groundwater.

Environment (Controlled Activities) (Scotland) Regulations 2011—The **34.27** Regulations control a wide range of activities, including: abstractions from surface and groundwater; impoundments of rivers, lochs, wetlands and transitional waters; groundwater recharge; engineering in rivers, lochs and wetlands; engineering activities in the vicinity of rivers, lochs and wetland which are likely to have a significant adverse impact upon the water environment; activities liable to cause pollution; direct or indirect discharge of various substances to groundwater; and any other activities which directly or indirectly is liable to cause a significant adverse impact upon the water environment.[268]

Under the new statutory regime, since April 1, 2006, all existing and any new abstraction or impoundment activities require an authorisation. An abstraction is

---

[261] *Menzies v Macdonald* (1854) 16 D. 827; affd 2 Macq. 463.

[262] *Menzies v Wentworth* (1901) 3 F. 941.

[263] *Kilsyth Fish Protection Association v McFarlane*, 1937 S.C. 757.

[264] See, e.g. the Pt II of the Control of Pollution Act 1974 ss.30A–42, subject to various repeals; Water Environment and Water Services (Scotland) Act 2003; Water Environment (Controlled Activities) (Scotland) Regulations 2011 (SSI 2011/209).

[265] Directive 2000/60/EC of the European Parliament and of the Council of October 23, 2000, establishing a framework for Community action in the field of water, OJ L3211, December 22, 2000.

[266] The Water Environment (Controlled Activities) (Scotland) Regulations 2011 superseded the Water Environment (Controlled Activities) (Scotland) Regulations 2005. The 2011 Regulations consolidated a number of water environment and water services amending instruments, and introduced additional amendments. It is stated in the Executive Note attached to the 2011 Regulations that "this is likely to be the last major suite of policy amendments for the foreseeable future; thus it is considered a suitable time to produce a consolidated version of The Regulations."

[267] Water Environment and Water Services (Scotland) Act 2003 s.3.

[268] Water Environment (Controlled Activities) (Scotland) Regulations 2011 reg.3.

the removal of water from the water environment by mechanical means, by pipe or by any engineering structure or works, irrespective of whether the water is removed or diverted permanently or temporarily and including removal of water for the purposes of transferring it to another part of the water environment.[269]

An impoundment is any dam, weir, or other works by which surface water may be impounded, or any works diverting surface waters in connection with the construction or alteration of any dam, weir or other works.[270] The artificially increased level of an existing natural loch might therefore, depending upon the particular circumstances, be considered to be an impoundment.

Also from April 1, 2006 the provisions formerly contained in the Control of Pollution Act 1974 regarding the discharge of pollutants to rivers, lochs, coastal waters and groundwaters were replaced with new provisions contained in the Regulations, broadly similar in extent to those in the 1974 Act and the Groundwater Regulations 1998 (which were also replaced), though different in form. The new regime concerns itself with point source discharges of pollution. Point source pollution is pollution from a single source such as a pipe. Diffuse source pollution is to be subject to a separate regulatory regime.

34.28 Levels of authorisation—The Regulations provide for a three-tier system of three levels of authorisation: (i) General Binding Rules, (ii) Registration, and (iii) Licence.

(i) General Binding Rules represent the basic level of control. They form part of the Regulations and cover listed low risk activities. Where such activities are taking place in compliance with the rules, they remove the need for an application for authorisation from the Scottish Environment Protection Agency (SEPA), as compliance with a General Binding Rules is considered as authorisation. An undertaker of a listed activity is not therefore required to contact SEPA before proceeding with that activity; therefore the issue of charging does not arise. The General Binding Rules activities are identified at Sch.3 of the Regulations, and include, inter alia: discharges of surface water run-off; discharges into a surface water drainage system; construction of boreholes for small-scale abstraction or for the purpose of dewatering an excavation; small-scale abstraction from boreholes where this is for the purpose of testing or sampling; temporary abstraction of groundwater for the purpose of dewatering at construction sites (during and after development) and its subsequent discharge; abstraction and discharge of groundwater which has been abstracted for the purpose of providing geothermal energy; existing passive weirs which result in less than 1 metre change in water level; abstractions of less than 10 cubic metres per day; dredging of rivers less than 1 metre wide that have been previously straightened or canalised; construction of minor and temporary bridges; laying of pipeline or cable; control of bank erosion covering less than 10 metres; operating plant or machinery in, or in the vicinity of, water, whilst carrying out another activity covered by the General Binding Rules; sediment removal in the area of impounded water upstream of a weir; sediment management within 10 metres of a closed culvert; boulder placement. Each activity is

---

[269] Water Environment and Water Services Act 2003 s.20(6).
[270] Water Environment and Water Services Act 2003 s.20(6).

associated with one or more binding rules. Failure to comply with or contravention of a General Binding Rule is an offence.[271]

(ii) Registrations[272] allow for the authorisation of small-scale activities which individually pose a small environmental risk but, cumulatively, might result in harm to the water environment. Operators must apply to SEPA to register these activities. A registration will include details of the scale of the activity and its location, and will be valid so long as the activity is carried out in accordance with the terms of the application. There is an application fee for registrations. It should be noted that SEPA is the public body responsible for environmental protection in Scotland. A proportion of SEPA's funding comes from the Scottish Government, with the balance coming from charges made to operators that SEPA regulate, under the polluter-pays principle. Application fees are therefore an important source of revenue for SEPA.[273]

(iii) Licences allow for site-specific conditions to be set to protect the water environment. Licences are also able to cover linked activities on a number of sites over a wide area, as well as multiple activities on a single site. Application fees apply to all licences and annual subsistence charges may apply. SEPA has divided licence activities into simple licence and complex licence activities dependent on risk.[274]

Applications for authorisation to carry out one or more controlled activities, for example where the activities in question exceed bounds of the General Binding Rules regime, are subject to an application procedure. The Generally Binding Rules have a source in statute.[275] The distinction between Registration and Licensing, and, in the latter case, between a simple licence and a complex licence, is dependent upon the nature and extent of the activities in question, and SEPA have issued illustrative guidelines on the level of authorisation applicable for controlled activities.[276] SEPA's authority to do so is founded upon the Water Environment (Controlled Activities) (Scotland) Amendment Regulations 2011 regs 7(1), 8(1) and 15(5).

Applications for authorisation—Authorisation is subject to an application **34.29** procedure.[277] There is a time-limit for the determination of applications and failure to determine within the period provided is deemed as being refusal.[278] The Scottish Ministers have the power to require SEPA to refer individual applications, and such general classes and descriptions of applications as may be specified, to them for determination.[279] Authorisations may be subject to conditions,[280] and, once granted, may be subject to review, modification or termination.[281]

---

[271] The list derives from the table of General Binding Rules in the Water Environment (Controlled Activities) (Scotland) Regulations 2011 Sch.3.

[272] Water Environment (Controlled Activities) (Scotland) Regulations 2011 reg.7.

[273] See the Scottish Environment Protection Agency website: *http://www.sepa.org.uk* [Accessed August 15, 2012].

[274] See the SEPA website: *http://www.sepa.org.uk* [Accessed August 15, 2012].

[275] Water Environment (Controlled Activities) (Scotland) Regulations 2011 Sch.3.

[276] SEPA has a website and network of local offices throughout Scotland from which up-to-date information can be obtained.

[277] Water Environment (Controlled Activities) (Scotland) Regulations 2011 Pt III.

[278] Water Environment (Controlled Activities) (Scotland) Regulations 2011 reg.17.

[279] Water Environment (Controlled Activities) (Scotland) Regulations 2011 reg.20.

[280] Water Environment (Controlled Activities) (Scotland) Regulations 2011 regs 7 and 8.

[281] Water Environment (Controlled Activities) (Scotland) Regulations 2011 Pt IV.

Appeals may be made to the Scottish Ministers.[282] Regulations confer enforcement powers on SEPA.[283] Regulations also specify a wide range of offences under the regulatory regime, punishable, on summary conviction, to a fine not exceeding £40,000 or to imprisonment for a term not exceeding six months, or to both; and in the continuing offence, to a further fine not exceeding £250 for every day that the offence is continued after conviction. Where conviction is on indictment, the level of the fine is unlimited and the term of imprisonment is increased to five years. The daily penalty for continuing offences is increased to £1,000. Provision is made for offences by bodies corporate. Defences of unforeseeability of accident, natural causes or force majeure are available.[284] There is a protocol between SEPA and the Crown Office and Procurator Fiscal Services ("COPFS") to set out the framework for effective liaison, communication and co-operation in the investigation and prosecution of environmental crime.[285]

Statute requires that the Scottish Ministers and SEPA must exercise their functions under the relevant enactments and responsible authorities must exercise their designated functions so as to secure compliance with the requirements of the Directive.[286] Under Regulations, before determining an application, SEPA must amongst other things assess the risk to the water environment posed by carrying out the proposed activity, and assess what steps may be taken to ensure efficient and sustainable water use.[287] Regulations specify that it shall be a duty of any person carrying out a controlled activity to take all steps to secure sustainable and suitable water use.[288] As a result, statute will cut across much of the common law considered above. With a statutory regulatory regime operating alongside common law rights, as now exists in Scotland, it seems inevitable that there must emerge issues and possible disputes relating to the interaction between the two, and in particular the question of what legal issues and remedies might result when a licensed abstraction impacts or might impact upon the common law rights of other users.[289]

V. POSITIVE PRESCRIPTION

34.30 Positive prescription—The main purposes of positive prescription are to render defective titles unchallengeable and to fix the extent of titles where the deed in question leaves the boundaries uncertain.[290] Positive prescription depends on

---

[282] Water Environment (Controlled Activities) (Scotland) Regulations 2011 Pt VIII.

[283] Water Environment (Controlled Activities) (Scotland) Regulations 2011 Pt V.

[284] Water Environment (Controlled Activities) (Scotland) Regulations 2011 reg.48.

[285] Accessible through the SEPA website.

[286] Water Environment and Water Services (Scotland) Act 2003 s.2.

[287] Water Environment (Controlled Activities) (Scotland) Regulations 2011 reg.15.

[288] Water Environment (Controlled Activities) (Scotland) Regulations 2011 reg.5.

[289] It should be noted that where SEPA receives an application it may, where it considers that the controlled activity has or is likely to have a significant adverse impact on the water environment, require the application to be advertised in accordance with this regulation. Regard must be had to written representations made within 28 days of the date of that advertisement: Water Environment (Controlled Activities) (Scotland) Regulations 2011 reg.13.

[290] The Land Registration etc (Scotland) Act 2012 gives effect to proposals made in the Scottish Law Commission, *Report on Land Registration*. The statute introduces changes in respect of the operation of prescription in relation to land in Scotland, as part of an overall updating of the system for land registration. Schedule 5 of the 2012 Act amends various provisions in the Prescription and Limitation (Scotland) Act 1973.

continued possession in relation to: (a) title to a real right in land,[291] and (b) servitudes and public rights of way.[292] "Land" includes heritable property of any description, therefore including buildings and minerals.[293] The title to a real right in land is normally, although not invariably, recorded in the General Register of Sasines or registered in the Land Register of Scotland.[294] Special provisions exist for those cases where title has not been recorded, for example in the case of unrecorded leases.[295] The abolition of feudal tenure, effected by means of the Abolition of Feudal Tenure (Scotland) Act 2000, has had a considerable impact upon the law in relation to prescription, not least reflected in the fact that this section no longer requires to consider such matters as superiority titles, the *dominium utile* of a vassal and interest in allodial land.[296]

The rules in respect of the prescriptive ownership of land and of the form of conveyance known as the *a nondomino* disposition are amended by the Land Registration etc. (Scotland) Act 2012. The Act revised and updates the Scots law in respect of land registration. The Act preserves the Land Register of Scotland, and to this end it largely repeals and replaces the Land Registration (Scotland) Act 1979. The 2012 Act also hastens the eventual demise of the General Register of Sasines by increasing the number of events that will trigger first registration in the Land Register, including conferring upon the Keeper of the Registers the power to register a title without application. Many of the provisions in the 1979 Act are preserved, albeit in amended form, in the 2012 Act, including the Keeper's warranty and rectification of the register. Detailed consideration of the 2012 Act is outwith the bounds of this Chapter. The policy background to the Act is to be found in the 2010 Scottish Law Commission *Report on Land Registration*. The law stated in this Part of the Chapter is the law as it applied as at Summer 2012, following the passage of the 2012 Act but prior to its full commencement.

Period   **34.31**

    (a) 10 years: Where possession of an interest in land is founded upon a recorded title or registered interest, the period of the positive prescription is 10 years.[297] If the foundation writ is a decree of adjudication for debt, the prescriptive period does not begin to run until after the expiry of a 10-year period known as "the legal".[298]

---

[291] Prescription and Limitation (Scotland) Act 1973 s.1(1).

[292] Prescription and Limitation (Scotland) Act 1973 s.3. See also para.34.48, below.

[293] Prescription and Limitation (Scotland) Act 1973 s.15(1).

[294] Prescription and Limitation (Scotland) Act 1973.

[295] Prescription and Limitation (Scotland) Act 1973 s.2.

[296] All land in Scotland is now non-feudal land, i.e. allodial land; see Gordon and Wortley, *Scottish Land Law* (2009), Vol.1, para.2–01.

[297] Prescription and Limitation (Scotland) Act 1973 s.1, as amended by the Land Registration (Scotland) Act 1979 s.10. The period of positive prescription was originally 40 years: Prescription Act 1617. It was reduced (with the exception of servitudes, public rights of way and other public rights) to 20 years by the Conveyancing (Scotland) Act 1874 s.34, as restated by the Conveyancing (Scotland) Act 1924 s.16. It was further reduced (with the exception of servitudes, public rights of way, other public rights; and foreshores and salmon fishings in any question with the Crown) to 10 years by the Conveyancing and Feudal Reform (Scotland) Act 1970 s.8.

[298] Prescription and Limitation (Scotland) Act 1973 s.1(4). The debtor can redeem his land during the legal. He may also redeem his land after the expiry of the legal unless the adjudger obtains a decree of declarator of expiry of the legal without payment. The diligence of adjudication is however to be abolished—see fn.121, above.

(b) 20 years: In certain less common cases the period of positive prescription is 20 years. Possession for 20 years is required in order to establish or define a title to an interest in foreshores and salmon fishings in any question with the Crown.[299] A period of 20 years is also necessary in certain special cases where the foundation writ does not require to be, and has not in fact been, recorded. Thus where prescriptive possession is founded upon an unrecorded lease or sub-lease or upon an unrecorded title or where prescriptive possession is relied upon in any other case where by virtue of pre-1973 law the foundation writ need not be recorded, a period of 20 years is required.[300] Finally, a period of 20 years is required where prescription is relied upon as establishing or fortifying a servitude[301] or public right of way.[302]

34.32 Requisites: Real right in land—If a real right in particular land has been possessed by any person[303] for a continuous period of 10 years openly, peaceably and without any judicial interruption, and if the possession was founded on and followed (i) the recording in the General Register of Sasines of a deed[304] which is sufficient in respect of its terms to constitute in favour of that person a title to that interest in the particular land,[305] or (ii) registration of that interest in favour of that person in the Land Register of Scotland subject to an exclusion of indemnity under s.12(2) of the Land Registration (Scotland) Act 1979,[306] the validity of the title so far as relating to the interest in land is rendered unchallengeable, except on the ground that the recorded deed is *ex facie* invalid or was forged or that registration proceeded upon a forged deed and the person in whose favour the registration was made was aware of the forgery at the time of registration.[307] A title subject to exclusion of indemnity was formerly thought to be the only case under a registration of title system which might require the benefit of the positive prescription in rendering a title unchallengeable. Provisions in Sch.5 of the Land Registration etc. (Scotland) Act 2012 will however give effect to the proposal in the Scottish

---

[299] Prescription and Limitation (Scotland) Act 1973 s.1(5). Ten years suffices where a claim is made against someone other than the Crown. Possession in relation to a foreshore was discussed in *Luss Estates Co v BP Oil Grangemouth Refinery Ltd*, 1981 S.L.T. 97; affd 1982 S.L.T. 457; 1987 S.L.T. 201; and briefly in *Hamilton v McIntosh Donald Ltd*, 1994 S.L.T. 793; and possession in relation to salmon fishings in *Fothringham v Passmore*, 1984 S.C. (HL) 96. See too *Crown Estate Commissioners, Petitioners*, 2010 S.L.T. 741 for a recent foreshore case; and R. Rennie, "Possession: Nine Tenths of the Law", 1994 S.L.T. (News) 261. Note the special provisions in the Land Registration (Scotland) Act 1979 s.14, for notice to be given to the Crown where a person claims prescriptive possession of and title to the foreshore.

[300] Prescription and Limitation (Scotland) Act 1973 ss.2, 15(1). See, e.g. *Wallace v University of St Andrews* (1904) 6 F. 1093.

[301] Prescription and Limitation (Scotland) Act 1973 s.3(1), (2).

[302] Prescription and Limitation (Scotland) Act 1973 s.3(3); *Richardson v Cromarty Petroleum Co Ltd*, 1982 S.L.T. 237; *Strathclyde (Hyndland) Housing Society Ltd v Cowie*, 1983 S.L.T. (Sh. Ct) 61; *Cumbernauld and Kilsyth DC v Dollar Land (Cumbernauld) Ltd*, 1993 S.C. (HL) 44; *Hamilton v Dumfries and Galloway Council*, 2009 S.C. 277.

[303] Or by any person and his successors: Prescription and Limitation (Scotland) Act 1973 s.1(1).

[304] "Deed" includes a judicial decree, and any instrument of sasine, notarial instrument or notice of title which narrates or declares that a person has a title to an interest in land: s.5(1), including *a non domino* disposition: *Hamilton v McIntosh Donald Ltd*, 1994 S.L.T. 793.

[305] Or in land of a description habile to include the particular land: s.1(1)(a)(ii). See, e.g. *Lock v Taylor*, 1976 S.L.T. 238; *Suttie v Baird*, 1992 S.L.T. 133.

[306] cf. dicta in *Short's Tr. v Keeper of the Registers of Scotland*, 1994 S.L.T. 65; 1996 S.C. (HL) 14.

[307] Prescription and Limitation (Scotland) Act 1973 s.1(1A), as amended by the Land Registration (Scotland) Act 1979 s.10.

Law Commission Report on Land Registration that positive prescription should apply to all titles registered on the Land Register.

As regards those real rights requiring the recording of a deed in the Sasine Register, it should be noted that where there is no foundation writ, that no length of possession will suffice so as to create a real right in property.[308] One consequence of the coming into force of the Land Registration etc. (Scotland) Act 2012 will be to close off and ultimately to wholly supersede the Sasine Register. A general tightening up of practice on the part of the Keeper of the Registers in relation to the registration on the basis of an *a non domino* disposition, or where there is a title sheet which points to the ownership of the subjects by another person, was followed by a number of important decisions between 2005 and 2007.[309] These developments, and, in particular, the progress of the English case of *J.A. Pye (Oxford) Ltd* through the domestic courts and up to the European Court of Human Rights Grand Chamber during that same period, raised questions as to the survival of the doctrine of positive prescription in Scots law.[310] The view of the Scottish Law Commission was that on the basis of the majority opinion of the Grand Chamber in the case of *Pye*, the Scottish system was compatible with art.1 of the First Protocol to the European Convention of Human Rights, but there was no room for complacency on the point. As a result, proposals were made in the Scottish Law Commission *Report on Land Registration* of 2010, as part of an overall reform of the law of land registration in Scotland, so as to preserve and, in short, render "Convention-proof" the principle of positive prescription in respect of heritable property in Scotland.[311] These proposals are given effect to by provisions in the land Registration etc. (Scotland) Act 2012.

Recorded deed or registered interest—Where a deed forms the basis of prescription, the deed must be *ex facie* valid.[312] Intrinsic defects, such as the lack of the proper statutory solemnities of execution, are struck at, but not extrinsic defects such as fraud or duress.[313] Under current law *ex facie* invalidity arises only if the deed is not subscribed by its granter.[314] The foundation deed must also be recorded in the General Register of Sasines or registered in the Land Register of Scotland,[315]

34.33

---

[308] See *British Railway Board v Ogilvie-Grant Sykes*, in Paisley and Cusine, *Unreported Property Law Cases from the Sheriff Courts* (2000), p.463.

[309] See *Board of Management of Aberdeen College v Youngson*, 2005 S.L.T. 371; *J.A. Pye (Oxford) Ltd v United Kingdom* (2008) 46 E.H.R.R. 45; and *Beaulane Properties Ltd v Palmer* [2005] 3 W.L.R. 554.

[310] See K.G.C. Reid and G.L. Gretton, *Conveyancing* (2005), pp.62–72; (2007), pp.150–153. See also K. Swinton, "Prescription, Human Rights and the Land Register: Pye v UK" (2005) 73 *Scottish Law Gazette* 179; D. Johnston, "J.A. Pye (Oxford) Limited v United Kingdom: Deprivation of Property Rights and Prescription" (2006) 10 Edin. L.R. 277; G.L. Gretton, "Pye: A Scottish View" (2007) 15 E.R.P.L. 281.

[311] Scottish Law Commission, *Report on Land Registration*, Vol.1, p.364, para.35.34.

[312] Prescription and Limitation (Scotland) Act 1973 s.1(2), as amended by the Land Registration (Scotland) Act 1979 s.10. See, e.g. *Scammell v Scottish Sports Council*, 1983 S.L.T. 462. The deed may be an *a non domino* disposition: *Hamilton v McIntosh Donald Ltd*, 1994 S.L.T. 793. The mode of *a non domino* disposition known as an A-to-A disposition, whereby a person dispones to himself in the same status or capacity (as opposed to where the capacities are different, for example where a person dispones land to a trust of which he is a trustee) was considered by the Lord Ordinary in the case of *Board of Management of Aberdeen College v Youngson*, 2005 S.L.T. 371, and deemed to be ineffective in terms of constituting a foundation writ. This case has been commented on in Reid and Gretton, *Conveyancing 2005* (2006), pp.62–72.

[313] cf. Bell, *Principles*, s.610; *Cooper Scott v Gill Scott*, 1924 S.C. 309; *Abbey v Atholl Properties*, 1936 S.N. 97; dicta in *Short's Tr. v Keeper of the Registers of Scotland*, 1994 S.L.T. 65.

[314] Requirements of Writing (Scotland) Act 1995 ss.1(2), 2.

[315] Prescription and Limitation (Scotland) Act 1973 ss.1(1)(b), 15(1).

except, as has been indicated, in certain special cases,[316] and in such cases possession for 20 years is required.[317]

It is no objection to the plea of prescription that the title proceeds from a party who had no title to the lands in question or no right to dispose of them.[318] This is indeed the very objection which it is the object of prescription to exclude: good titles stand in no need of prescription.[319] Nor is bona fides necessary: the plea of prescription may be taken by a party who has been in possession in the knowledge that his title was defective.[320]

34.34 Possession—Possession is a question of fact,[321] and may be actual or civil. A clear case is the civil possession of a landlord exercised through the actual possession of tenants.[322] Possession must be continuous, and must not be possession by force (*vi*), by stealth (*clam*), or by leave (*precario*) rather than as a matter of right.

Possession must be referable to the title,[323] and not proceed on some other basis which might not be adequate for prescription. So, for instance, where possession can as readily be ascribed to a lease or a servitude, it does not amount to possession relevant to an assertion of ownership.[324] The requisite possession may fortify a title although the adverse right was a grant by the possessor himself, or his predecessor in title.[325]

There must be a sufficient degree of possession in order for prescription to take effect. Very occasional acts of possession, such as clearing rubbish, trimming hedges and cutting grass may not suffice. Possession should be sufficient to signal to a reasonably observant competitor in title that a rival party was occupying the subjects.[326]

34.35 Computation of period—The Act provides certain rules for computation.[327] Thus positive prescriptions will in most cases run from the midnight following upon the recording of the deed[328] or the registration of the interest in land, or from

---

[316] Namely, the interest in land of the lessee under a lease or sub-lease; any other interest in land the title to which could in terms of pre-1973 law be established without the necessity of recording the foundation writ: s.2. Cf. para.34.30, above.

[317] Prescription and Limitation (Scotland) Act 1973 s.2(1)(a). If the deed has in fact been recorded, or an interest registered, 10 years' possession suffices: Prescription and Limitation (Scotland) Act 1973 s.2(3).

[318] Erskine, III, 7, 4; *Fraser v Lord Lovat* (1898) 25 R. 603.

[319] *Cooper Scott v Gill Scott*, 1924 S.C. 309 at 315 and 326; *Hamilton v McIntosh Donald Ltd*, 1994 S.L.T. 793 (*a non domino* disposition); and see Rennie, "Possession: Nine Tenths of the Law", 1994 S.L.T. (News) 261. See also Gordon and Wortley, *Scottish Land Law* (2009), Vol.1, para.12–39.

[320] *Duke of Buccleuch v Cunynghame* (1826) 5 S. 57; contrary to Bell, *Principles*, s.2004.

[321] See, e.g. *Bain v Carrick*, 1983 S.L.T. 675; *Hamilton v McIntosh Donald Ltd*, 1994 S.L.T. 793; *First National Bank of South Africa Ltd v McStay* Unreported June 16, 2000, temporary judge T.G. Coutts QC. Possession has been considered more recently, in the context of judicial rectification, in *Safeway Stores Plc v Tesco StoresPplc*, 2003 G.W.D. 20–610, IH.

[322] At least in one instance a landlord has been allowed to rely even on possessory acts of third parties: *Hamilton v McIntosh Donald*, 1994 S.L.T. 793.

[323] Possession in relation to a barony title was discussed in *Luss Estates Co v BP Oil Grangemouth Refinery Ltd*, 1981 S.L.T. 97; affd 1982 S.L.T. 457; 1987 S.L.T. 201.

[324] *Houstoun v Barr Ltd*, 1911 S.C. 134 at 143; *Fothringham v Passmore*, 1984 S.C. (HL) 96 at 99; *BG Hamilton v Ready Mixed Concrete (Scotland) Ltd*, 1999 S.L.T. 524.

[325] *Wallace v University of St Andrews* (1904) 6 F. 1093.

[326] See *Hamilton v McIntosh Donald Ltd*, 1994 S.L.T. 212. See also *Stevenson-Hamilton's Exrs v McStay (No.2)*, 2000 G.W.D. 22–872 (OH).

[327] Prescription and Limitation (Scotland) Act 1973 s.14.

[328] Prescription and Limitation (Scotland) Act 1973 ss.1(1), 14(1)(c); and cf. *Simpson v Marshall* (1900) 2 F. 447.

the midnight following upon possession if possession is subsequent to recording or if recording is unnecessary. At common law, the appropriate period runs until the midnight on the same-numbered day in the same-numbered month.[329]

Effect—Positive prescription excludes all inquiry into the previous titles and **34.36** rights to the lands.[330] It may also define the extent of an interest in land, positive servitude or public right of way either where there is no foundation writ or where the extent of the right is not precisely set forth in the title.[331] Where, however, the boundaries of a title are delimited (e.g. by reference to measurements, a plan or a clear description), it is not possible to rely on possession for prescription of land lying beyond the boundaries.

Interruption—Only interruption of possession or "judicial" interruption will **34.37** stop the running of the positive prescription.[332] Judicial interruption is defined[333] as the making in appropriate proceedings[334] by any person having a proper interest to do so of a claim[335] which challenges[336] the possession in question. It has been observed that any form of claim, brought in an appropriate forum by a person with proper interest to bring it, which competently puts in issue the validity of the defender's possession of the interest in land is apt to constitute judicial interruption.[337] The date of interruption is normally the date when the claim was made.[338] In arbitration proceedings where the nature of the claim has been stated in a preliminary notice the date of interruption is the date on which the preliminary notice is served by one party on the other requiring him to appoint an arbiter or

---

[329] *Simpson v Marshall* (1900) 2 F. 447; *Cavers Parish Council v Smailholm Parish Council*, 1909 S.C. 195.

[330] Prescription and Limitation (Scotland) Act 1973 s.1(l); and cf. *Fraser v Lord Lovat* (1898) 25 R. 603.

[331] See, e.g. Prescription and Limitation (Scotland) Act 1973 s.3(3), (4), and long title to the Act. Cf. *Lord Advocate v Cathcart* (1871) 9 M. 744; *Auld v Hay* (1880) 7 R. 663 at 681, per Lord President Inglis; dicta in *Hamilton v McIntosh Donald Ltd*, 1994 S.L.T. 793 at 797.

[332] Prescription and Limitation (Scotland) Act 1973 s.1(1); *British Railways Board v Strathclyde RC*, 1981 S.C. 90; *George A. Hood & Co v Dumbarton DC*, 1983 S.L.T. 238; *G.A. Estates Ltd v Caviapen Trs Ltd (No.2)*, 1993 S.L.T. 1051, IH; 1993 S.L.T. 1045, OH.

[333] Prescription and Limitation (Scotland) Act 1973 s.4.

[334] "Appropriate proceedings" are any proceedings in a court of competent jurisdiction and any arbitration proceedings provided that the arbitration award would be enforceable in Scotland: Prescription and Limitation (Scotland) Act 1973 s.4(2). No claim is made in an arbitration if no arbiter has been appointed at the material time; *Douglas Milne Ltd v Borders RC*, 1990 S.L.T. 558; *John O'Connor (Plant Hire) v Kier Construction*, 1990 S.C.L.R. 761; *R. Peter & Co Ltd v The Pancake Place Ltd*, 1993 S.L.T. 322. The definition does not include proceedings initiated in the Court of Session by a summons which is not subsequently called: Prescription and Limitation (Scotland) Act 1973 s.4(2)(a). Cf. *Barclay v Chief Constable of the Northern Constabulary*, 1986 S.L.T. 562, where it was held obiter that the starting point was the citation of the defender, and that the calling of the summons might occur outwith the five-year period, provided it was called within a year and a day of citation or such lesser period as was fixed by protestation under Rule of Court 80 (now Rules of the Court of Session (SI 1994/1443) r.13.14).

[335] Which may be an initial writ grossly lacking in specification: *British Railways Board v Strathclyde RC*, 1981 S.C. 90, or a writ ultimately requiring substantial amendment (see para.4.21), but probably not a writ giving rise to a fundamentally null action: *Shanks v Central RC*, 1987 S.L.T. 410, OH; 1988 S.L.T. 212, Ex Div. Cf. *Thomas Menzies (Builders) Ltd v Anderson*, 1998 S.L.T. 794.

[336] See dicta in *Scammell v Scottish Sports Council*, 1983 S.L.T. 462 at 467.

[337] *MRS Hamilton Ltd v Baxter*, 1998 S.L.T. 1075.

[338] Prescription and Limitation (Scotland) Act 1973 s.4(3)(b). The commencement of an action has been defined as the date of citation: *Miller v N.C.B.*, 1960 S.C. 376 at 383, per Lord President; *Barclay v Chief Constable, Northern Constabulary*, 1986 S.L.T. 562 (cf. authorities cited in D.M. Walker, *The Law of Prescription and Limitation of Actions in Scotland*, 4th edn (Edinburgh: W. Green, 1990), p.97).

to agree to the appointment of an arbiter or to submit the dispute to the arbiter previously designated.[339] Interruption may take place on the last day of the prescriptive period.[340] If a relevant claim is made, it is thought that the prescriptive period starts anew from the midnight following upon the date on which the interruption ends[341]: the point has been discussed in several cases.[342]

VI. TITLE CONDITIONS

34.38 Introductory—The term "title condition" is taken to represent rights benefiting land and obligations encumbering land. These rights exist to regulate land use on a continuing basis; that is to say the right runs with the land, rather than with a particular landowner. Title conditions are held by a landowner in their capacity as proprietor of that property, and are enforceable in relation to another piece of heritable property. They can be divided into a number of categories,[343] the most common of these being the categories of "servitude"[344] and "real burden".[345] Prior to feudal abolition an element of overlap between these categories existed, though this has now been clarified by the Title Conditions (Scotland) Act 2003.[346] Servitudes and real burdens represent the same species of right, both of a related character but serving a distinct function. Servitudes generally impose an obligation allowing a landowner to make some use of a neighbouring piece of land, whilst real burdens impose obligations requiring a landowner to take particular action, or to refrain from particular action, which can be imposed by the owner of the neighbouring piece of land. Powers lie with the Lands Tribunal to vary or discharge title conditions under statute.[347] It should be noted that provisions in the Land Registration etc (Scotland) Act 2012 (asp 5) will, when commenced, have an effect upon the rules in respect of the registration of title conditions. In this respect, the changes introduced under the 2012 Act may be characterised as fine tuning of the existing system as considered below.

SERVITUDES

34.39 Definition[348]—The term "servitude" has occasionally been used in a wide sense to denote a multiplicity of burdens affecting land such as subsidiary real rights,[349]

---

[339] Prescription and Limitation (Scotland) Act 1973 s.4(3)(a) and (4); in relation to stating the nature of the claim, see *Douglas Milne Ltd v Borders RC*, 1990 S.L.T. 558. The 1973 Act is amended by provisions in the Arbitration (Scotland) Act 2010 s.23, but these provisions are subject to commencement.

[340] *Simpson v Marshall* (1900) 2 F. 447.

[341] Thus, e.g. a fresh prescriptive period would begin to run from the midnight following upon the date of the final disposal of a relevant court action, including any appeal procedure.

[342] See *G.A. Estates Ltd v Caviapen Trs Ltd*, 1993 S.L.T. 1051; 1993 S.L.T. 1045, OH, obiter dicta in *British Railways Board v Strathclyde*, 1981 S.C. 90 at 99, 102, 104; *George A. Hood v Dumbarton DC*, 1983 S.L.T. 238; *R. Peter & Co Ltd v The Pancake Place Ltd*, 1993 S.L.T. 322; *Hogg v Prentice*, 1994 S.C.L.R. 426.

[343] Title Conditions (Scotland) Act 2003 s.122(1).

[344] See para.34.39, below.

[345] See para.34.54, below.

[346] Title Conditions (Scotland) Act 2003 ss.80–81.

[347] Title Conditions (Scotland) Act 2003 Pt 9.

[348] See in general, D.J. Cusine and R. Paisley, *Servitudes and Rights of Way* (Edinburgh: W Green, 1998).

[349] Such as leases: Stair, II, 9, 2.

public rights and even statutory regulation and impositions.[350] A narrower, and more useful, meaning limits the term "servitude" to a particular kind of real right. It is to the real right denoted by this narrower meaning that these paragraphs shall confine their attention. The institutional writers distinguish "personal" and "praedial" servitudes, the former benefiting a person and the latter benefiting a person owning a dominant tenement. The only "personal" servitude was proper liferent[351] and, as this classification has now been largely abandoned, one may conclude that the servitudes known to Scots law are all praedial.

A "servitude" is a real right held by the owner of one piece of land (traditionally referred to as "the dominant tenement" and also known as "the benefited property")[352] to carry out activity within a neighbouring piece of land (traditionally known as "the servient tenement" and also known as "the burdened property"). From the point of view of the dominant tenement a servitude is a right, whereas, as regards the servient tenement, it is a burden or encumbrance. As it permits the carrying out of activity within the land of another person a servitude may be regarded as a *ius in re aliena*. As a real right it is enforceable against the world and not just the owner of the servient tenement.

Prior to November 28, 2004, servitudes were distinguished into "positive" and "negative".[353] The effect of a negative servitude was to require the burdened proprietor to submit to a restriction on the use of his land such as a prohibition on building. On November 28, 2004 all existing negative servitudes were automatically converted into negative real burdens[354] and since that date no new negative servitudes can be created.[355] Consequently, all servitudes are now "positive" servitudes in that they require the burdened proprietor to submit to certain uses of his land by the owner of the benefited property. Following the Civilian tradition,[356] the institutional writers distinguish servitudes as urban and rural. Urban are such as relate to buildings (whether in the town or the country); rural to lands. Albeit this distinction carried significant consequences in Roman law[357] it is of no relevance to Scots law.[358] It is a redundant classification that should be dispensed with.

Essentials of servitudes—The essentials of servitudes are as follows: **34.40**

(a) A servitude exists for the benefit of the dominant tenement and a prerequisite of a servitude is utility to the particular dominant tenement. This is known as the requirement of *utilitas*. It continues to benefit all parts of the dominant tenement after the same has been split into parts.[359] It cannot be extended to benefit other land outside the dominant tenement.[360] Except insofar as the right has been extended to them by

[350] Stair, II, 6, 20.
[351] See para.41.31, below.
[352] This updated terminology is sanctioned by the Title Conditions (Scotland) Act 2003 Pt 7.
[353] Stair, II, 7, 5; Bell, *Principles*, s.979; Bankton, II, 7, 5 (Stair Society Reprint, Vol.41, p.675); Reid, *The Law of Property in Scotland* (1996), para.441.
[354] Title Conditions (Scotland) Act 2003 s.80.
[355] Title Conditions (Scotland) Act 2003 s.79.
[356] Justinian, *Inst.*, 2, 2, 3.
[357] See W.W. Buckland, *A Textbook of Roman Law: From Augustus to Justinian*, edited by P. Stein, 3rd edn (Cambridge: Cambridge University Press, 1963), p.262.
[358] Rankine, *The Law of Landownership in Scotland* (1909), p.446.
[359] *Alba Homes Ltd v Duell*, 1993 S.L.T. (Sh. Ct) 49.
[360] *Scott v Bogle*, July 6, 1809, FC; *Irvine Knitters Ltd v North Ayrshire Cooperative Society Ltd*, 1978 S.C. 109.

statutory provision,[361] no one can enforce a servitude except as proprietor of the tenement. A servitude is inseparable from the dominant tenement, and the dominant proprietor cannot convey or assign it to anyone not connected with that tenement or set up a right to it independently of the right to the benefited tenement.

(b) The two tenements must be in separate ownership because a proprietor cannot hold a servitude burdening his own land: *res sua nemini servit*. No servitude can be created by express reservation where the granter remains the owner of the alleged servient tenement.[362] However, this does not preclude the registration of a deed of conditions when the proposed dominant and servient tenement are in single ownership in terms of which servitudes are created to become real when the intended burdened and benefited lands are split up into separate ownership.[363]

(c) The tenements must be sufficiently closely located for the dominant proprietor to have a praedial interest to enforce the servitude.[364] This is known as the requirement of *vicinitas*.

(d) A servitude benefits the proprietor of the dominant tenement and his singular successors and burdens the owner of the servient tenement and his singular successors.

(e) A servitude may burden and benefit only heritable property.

(f) The burden imposed on the owner of the servient tenement is not to do anything active (*in faciendo*) but merely to suffer the restraint of his rights involved in the proper exercise of the servitude (*in patiendo*).[365] Consequently, in the case of a servitude of way the owner of the servient tenement is under no obligation to repair the way.[366] If the servient proprietor is to be obliged in this regard parties must have resort to the device of real burden.

(g) The rights afforded to the dominant proprietor must not be so extensive or invasive as to be repugnant with the right of property in the servient tenement.[367]

34.41 Inessentials—The following are not essential to servitude rights:

(a) A servitude does not require to have perpetual endurance. Perpetual servitudes are the most commonly encountered type of servitude but a maximum duration may be expressly imposed by means of express servitude condition. So too may servitudes impose forfeiture or irritancy clauses or conditions in terms of which a servitude will expire upon the happening of a particular event which may or may not be certain to happen.

(b) It is not necessary that the dominant proprietor is able to exercise the facility of the servitude free from a requirement to make a continuing or

---

[361] Such an extension might possibly be afforded by the Matrimonial Homes (Family Protection) (Scotland) Act 1981 s.2(1)(c) but the section is general in its terms and the matter untested.

[362] *Hamilton v Elder*, 1968 S.L.T. (Sh. Ct) 53.

[363] Title Conditions (Scotland) Act 2003 s.75(2); *Candleberry Ltd v West End Homeowners Association*, 2006 S.C. 638.

[364] Erskine, II, 9, 33.

[365] *Tailors of Aberdeen v Coutts* (1840) 1 Robin. App.296 at 310, per Lord Corehouse.

[366] *Allan v MacLachlan* (1900) 2 F. 699.

[367] *Dyce v Hay* (1849) 11 D. 1266, 1 Macq. 312; *Moncrieff v Jamieson* [2007] UKHL 42; *Holms v Ashford Estates Limited*, 2009 S.L.T. 389; Title Conditions (Scotland) Act 2003 (asp 9) s.76(2).

occasional return to the burdened proprietor. A dominant proprietor is normally free to enjoy the servitude without payment of "rent" or other payment to the servient proprietor but a requirement to make such a payment may be imposed by servitude condition.[368]

(c) The tenements need not be corporeal plots of land. For example, the dominant tenement in a servitude of access may be an incorporeal tenement of salmon fishing.[369]

(d) It is not essential that the servitude is capable of exercise throughout its endurance at any time chosen by the dominant proprietor. A deed of servitude may expressly impose limitations on the times at which a servitude may be exercised or may require the dominant proprietor to give notice prior to exercise.

(e) Not all of the entitlements of a servitude require to be written out at length in a deed even where the servitude is created by express grant or reservation. In appropriate cases servitudes comprise ancillary rights that will be granted or reserved even if the deed is silent. This may be illustrated by reference to a servitude of way which includes the right to repair the roadway.[370] In particular circumstances this may extend to a right to upgrade a road by tarring the surface,[371] or to park on adjacent land.[372]

Particular servitudes—The servitudes recognised by Scots common law are way, **34.42** *aquaehaustus* (the abstraction of water), *aqueductus* (the conveyance of water), pasturage, fuel, feal and divot, support and stillicide. The common law list has been retrospectively extended to include a servitude right "to lead a pipe, cable, wire or other such enclosed unit over or under land for any purpose"[373] but it is arguable that this statutory provision is no more than declaratory of the common law. Albeit the limitations of this *numerus clausus* have been abolished as regards servitudes expressly created by a deed executed after November 28, 2004, duly registered as regards both the dominant and servient tenement,[374] the closed list remains relevant to servitudes created by other means such as prescriptive exercise. It has been stated that class of servitudes recognised at common law is not rigid,[375] but it is fair to say that there was no great development of the closed list at common law. In this regard one may have regard to the recognition of servitudes for septic tanks[376] (albeit this is perhaps a mere development of a servitude of sinks and cess pool[377]) and access by flanged wheeled vehicles moving on tracks laid on the ground[378] which is a development of a servitude of way. There was initially less judicial enthusiasm for the recognition at common law of servitudes of vehicle

---

[368] e.g. *Stewart v Steuart* (1877) 4 R. 981 at 984, per Lord President Inglis.
[369] *Middletweed Ltd v Murray*, 1989 S.L.T. 11.
[370] *Lord Burton v Mackay*, 1995 S.L.T. 507.
[371] *Wimpey Homes Holdings Ltd v Collins*, 1999 S.L.T. (Sh. Ct) 16.
[372] *Moncrieff v Jamieson* [2007] UKHL 42.
[373] Title Conditions (Scotland) Act 2003 s.77(1) and (2).
[374] Title Conditions (Scotland) Act 2003 s.76(1).
[375] *Patrick v Napier* (1867) 5 M. 683, per Lord Ardmillan; *Dyce v Hay* (1849) 11 D. 1266, 1 Macq. 312, per Lord St Leonards; *Harvey v Lindsay* (1853) 15 D. 768, per Lord Ivory; Rankine, *The Law of Landownership in Scotland* (1909), p.419.
[376] See, e.g. *McLellan v Hunter*, 1987 G.W.D. 21–799; *Todd v Scoular*, 1988 G.W.D. 24–1041.
[377] e.g. *Ewart v Cochrane* (1861) 23 D. (HL) 3; 4 Macq. 117.
[378] *North British Railway Co v Park Yard Co Ltd* (1898) 25 R. (HL) 47.

parking albeit it was not entirely ruled out[379] and most recently the House of Lords has appeared to be receptive to the idea.[380] A more conservative approach however was evident in the refusal to recognise a servitude to lead cables for a private electricity supply.[381] Similarly, extension of the closed list was ruled out in relation to a proposed servitude of shop signage,[382] although recognition of a servitude of *projiciendi* (overhang) has proved more successful.[383]

The types of servitudes recognised at common law clearly remain capable of creation after November 28, 2004 and are as follows:

(1) Way. A servitude of way comprises a right of passage to and from the dominant tenement through the servient tenement and onward usually to a public road or other lands owned by the dominant proprietor. The way may be a footpath, a horse road or a carriage road, and the terms of the grant or the extent of possession during the prescriptive period will determine the character of the passage to which the dominant proprietor is entitled.[384] As regards servitudes constituted by prescriptive exercise, a vehicular servitude will include a right to pedestrian traffic. This is not necessarily the case with servitudes created by express grant or reservation because the terms of the relevant grant or reservation may expressly permit vehicles but expressly exclude pedestrian traffic.[385] There is some old authority suggesting that the destination of the road may impose a limitation on its use by confining it to traffic for certain purposes, as in the case of a church road or a road to a market.[386] However, the application of such authority in modern conditions is highly controversial and if a special limitation is sought as regards the method by which a servitude of access may be imposed this is best done by the imposition of servitude conditions. The better view is that if a servitude of way is acquired by prescription, there is no restraint on its use by the dominant tenement by reference to the purpose of the traffic passing over it: the road may be used generally by the dominant owner for all purposes to which the dominant tenement may be put irrespective of whether the traffic during the prescriptive period was for agricultural or building or any other particular purpose.[387] As already mentioned, the owner of the servient tenement is not bound to repair the road, and he may erect on it gates so long as these do not cause a material obstruction to the proper enjoyment of the servitude.[388] A servitude of way may also include express or

---

[379] See *Moncrieff v Jamieson*, 2005 S.L.T. 225; *Nationwide Building Society v Walter D. Allan Ltd* Unreported August 4, 2004, Lady Smith, available on the Scottish Courts' website (*http://www.scotcourts.gov.uk* [Accessed August 15, 2012]).

[380] *Moncrieff v Jamieson* [2007] UKHL 42; 2008 S.C. (HL) 1.

[381] *Neill v Scobie*, 1993 G.W.D. 13–887. That authority, however, is not beyond criticism as being overly conservative: *Tod v Scoular*, 1988 G.W.D. 24–1041; Cusine and Paisley, *Servitudes and Rights of Way* (1998), paras 1.03, 1.06 and 3.44. English law has recognised an easement relative to a private electricity supply: *Harrison v Dace* [1998] EWCA Civ 1524 (October 13, 1998).

[382] *Romano v Standard Commercial Property Securities Ltd*, 2008 S.L.T 859.

[383] *Compugraphics International Ltd v Nikolic* [2011] CSIH 34; 2011 S.C. 744.

[384] Prescription and Limitation (Scotland) Act 1973 s.3(2); *Carstairs v Spence*, 1924 S.C. 380; *Malcolm v Lloyd* (1886) 13 R. 512.

[385] *Crawford v Lumsden*, 1951 S.L.T. 64; 1951 S.L.T. (Notes) 62 discussed in Cusine and Paisley, *Servitudes and Rights of Way* (1998), para.12.194.

[386] See the discussion in *Carstairs v Spence*, 1924 S.C. 380.

[387] *Carstairs v Spence*, 1924 S.C. 380, per Lord President Clyde.

[388] *Wood v Robertson*, March 9, 1809, FC; *Drury v McGarvie*, 1993 S.C. 95.

implied ancillary rights. There is no closed list of such ancillary rights but they cannot impose a positive obligation on the servient proprietor or be repugnant with his right of ownership. Express ancillary rights depend on the terms of the constitutive deed and are commonly illustrated by a right on the part of the dominant proprietor to maintain a servitude road. The implication of ancillary rights will depend on the reasonable necessity of these rights to the use and enjoyment of the servitude, and whether these rights were reasonably foreseeable at the time when the servitude was created.[389] They could include an implied ancillary right to park if the circumstances are so unusual as to result in such necessity.[390] However, an ancillary right to construct a flight of steps in order to comply with statutory health and safety requirements has not been recognised as implied into a servitude of way where these requirements emerged long after the creation of the servitude.[391]

(2) *Aquaehaustus* gives the right to take water from or to water cattle at a well or stream in the servient tenement. It includes as an implied ancillary right a right of access by the dominant owner (together with his cattle) and a right to clean out or repair the well.[392]

(3) *Aqueductus* is the right to convey water by pipes or canals through the servient tenement.[393] The duty of maintaining the aqueduct in proper condition is on the dominant owner, and he is entitled to access to it for this purpose.[394] Similar to this servitude is that of a dam or damhead by which one acquires a right of gathering water on his neighbour's land and of building banks or dykes for containing the water.[395] Frequently the ancillary rights such as access to the dam or the right to take stone and other materials to repair it are spelled out expressly in the constitutive deed. It may be possible that the right to construct a small dam or settling tank could be implied as an ancillary right where it is essential to make this servitude effective.[396]

(4) Pasturage is the right to feed cattle or sheep on another's ground or on a common.[397] It is usually found as a right enjoyed in common with others. If the extent of the right is not expressly defined, it is the amount of stock the servient tenement can winter.[398] The servient owner is entitled to use

---

[389] *Moncrieff v Jamieson* [2007] UKHL 42; 2008 S.C. (HL) 1.

[390] *Moncrieff v Jamieson* [2007] UKHL 42; 2008 S.C. (HL) 1. The English courts have emphasised the point that the facts would have to be "quite exceptional": *Waterman v Boyle* [2009] EWCA Civ 115 (circumstances in which held that no ancillary right to park was implied).

[391] *SP Distribution Ltd v Rafique*, 2009 S.C.L.R. 891.

[392] Stair, II, 7, 11; Bankton, II, 7, 28; Erskine, II, 9, 13; Bell, *Principles*, ss.987 and 1011; Rankine, *The Law of Landownership in Scotland* (1909), pp.571 et seq.

[393] Stair, II, 7, 12; Bankton, II, 7, 28 and 30; Erskine, II, 9, 13; Bell, *Principles*, s.1012. See e.g. *More v Boyle*, 1967 S.L.T. (Sh. Ct) 38.

[394] The owner of the servient tenement has a duty not to obstruct the enjoyment of the dominant owner of his rights, and not to interfere with or render more expensive the rights of the dominant owner to access to the water: *Central RC v Ferns*, 1979 S.C. 136.

[395] *Scottish Highland Distillery Co v Reid* (1877) 4 R. 1118.

[396] *Chalmers Property Investment Company Ltd v Robson*, 2008 S.L.T. 1069, HL.

[397] Craig, *Ius Feudale* 2, 8, 35; Stair, II, 7, 14; Erskine, II, 9, 14; Bell, *Principles*, s.1013; Rankine, *The Law of Landownership in Scotland* (1909), p.454; *Fraser v Secretary of State for Scotland*, 1959 S.L.T. (Notes) 36; *Fearnan Partnership v Grindlay*, 1992 S.L.T. 460, HL (circumstances in which held that no servitude had been constituted).

[398] *L. Breadalbane v Menzies* (1741) 5 Br. Supp.710; but see *Ferguson v Tennant*, 1978 S.C. (HL) 19; 1978 S.L.T. 165.

the surplus pasturage. The dominant owner may interdict the servient owner from carrying out operations that might damage the pasture or detract from the value of the servitude even where the dominant owner is not in fact exercising the right of pasturage.[399]

(5) Fuel, feal and divot is a servitude which gives the right to cut and remove peat for fuel and turf for fences.[400]

(6) Support includes the servitudes known in the civil law as *tigni immit-tendi* and *oneris ferendi*. The former is the right to let a beam or other structural part of the dominant building into the wall of the servient tene-ment and to keep it there; the second is the right to have a building supported.[401] These servitudes are noticed by the institutional writers, but there is little to be found in the reported decisions regarding them.[402] There is one recent decision of note,[403] which discusses the *oneris ferendi* combined with the servitude from the civil law known as *jus projiciendi*. The latter, a right of overhang, has been otherwise unknown in Scots law[404] though this decision confirms the possibility of its existence.

(7) Stillicide. No proprietor can build so as to throw the rainwater falling from his own house immediately upon his neighbour's ground; but this servitude of stillicide or eavesdrop entitles him to do so.[405]

Other servitudes which have been recognised at common law are the right to use ground for the purpose of bleaching clothes,[406] and of taking stone from the servient for the use of the dominant tenement.[407] These are rarely of importance today because the practice of bleaching has virtually disappeared whilst the extraction of stone in the land of another is usually authorised by means of a lease.

34.43 Manner of exercise of servitudes—All servitudes are subject to a number of legally implied servitude conditions. The legally implied servitude conditions are frequently supplemented by expressly constituted servitude conditions the content of which is usually agreed initially by the parties to the grant. The legally implied servitude conditions are as follows:

(a) A servitude is for the use and benefit of the dominant tenement and not for purposes unconnected with that tenement. Hence a servitude of way in favour of one estate cannot be used for the benefit of

---

[399] *Ferguson v Tennant*, 1978 S.C. (HL) 19.

[400] Stair, II, 7, 13; Bell, *Principles*, s.1014; Rankine, *The Law of Landownership in Scotland* (1909), p.456.

[401] Erskine, II, 9, 7; Bell, *Principles*, s.1003; Rankine, *The Law of Landownership in Scotland* (1909), p.656.

[402] *Murray v Brownhill* (1715) Mor.14521; *Troup v Aberdeen Heritable Securities Co*, 1916 S.C. 918; *Dalton v Angus* (1881) L.R. 6 App. Cas. 740. See also *Rogano Ltd v British Railways Board*, 1979 S.C. 297.

[403] *Compugraphics International Limited v Nikolic* [2011] CSIH 34; 2011 S.C. 744.

[404] It is noted, however, that in some circumstances it may simply be manifest in another form as a right ancillary to a servitude permitting the installation and use of service media: Title Conditions (Scotland) Act 2003 s.77.

[405] Stair, II, 7, 7; Erskine, II, 9, 9; Bell, *Principles*, ss.941 and 1004.

[406] *Home v Young* (1846) 9 D. 286.

[407] *Murray v Magistrates of Peebles*, December 8, 1808, FC.

another.[408] Similarly, a servitude of digging for slates and stones does not entitle the dominant owner to use his right for the purpose of selling the slates and stones to third parties who have no connection with the tenement.[409]

(b) The servitude must be exercised *civiliter*, that is to say, reasonably.

(c) The servitude may not be exercised in a manner that increases the burden on the burdened property beyond that which is permitted in terms of the particular right. This is sometimes more generally, albeit less accurately, stated to the effect that, consistently with its proper enjoyment, the servitude is to be exercised in the manner least burdensome to the servient tenement.[410] In all cases one must determine what is the maximum acceptable burden on the burdened tenement and keep within those limits.

In addition to this, no servitude may be exercised in a manner that creates a nuisance.[411]

Rights of the servient proprietor—The owner of the burdened tenement **34.44** remains owner of that tenement. He may make use of his property as he pleases provided he respects the servitude right and causes no material interference with, or material obstruction to, its proper exercise.[412] Hence, the owner of a moor, over which there exists a servitude of digging and winning peat, is free to plough the moor so long as he leaves what is sufficient for the servitude unploughed.[413] The proprietor of a stream subject to a servitude of watering cattle may cover over the stream if he leaves open so much as is required for the use of the cattle.[414] The proprietor of land over which is a servitude of footpath may erect swing gates across the path.[415]

The servient owner has, in the case of a way acquired by prescription, been allowed to alter its line where the new line would be equally convenient to the dominant owner, but this is excluded at common law where the servitude has been constituted by a grant or reservation in which the line of road has been laid down.[416] The common law rights of the servient proprietor to vary the route of a servitude are coexistent with, but have largely been replaced in practice by, the powers of the Lands Tribunal to vary and discharge "title conditions".[417] In the exercise of its power the Lands Tribunal has varied of the route of a servitude of way provided the servient proprietor is willing to provide a substitute route.[418]

---

[408] *Scott v Bogle*, July 6, 1809, FC.; *Irvine Knitters Ltd v North Ayrshire Cooperative Society Ltd*, 1978 S.C. 109.

[409] *Murray v Magistrates of Peebles*, December 8, 1808, FC.

[410] *Alvis v Harrison*, 1991 S.L.T. 64, HL; *Stansfield v Findlay*, 1998 S.L.T. 784.

[411] *Cloy v T M Adams & Sons,* 2000 S.L.T. (Sh. Ct) 39.

[412] Erskine, II, 9, 34; *Fraser v Secretary of State for Scotland*, 1959 S.L.T. (Notes) 36; *Ferguson v Tennant*, 1978 S.C. (HL) 19.

[413] *Watson v Dunkennar Feuars* (1667) Mor.14529.

[414] *Beveridge v Marshall*, November 18, 1808, FC.

[415] *Sutherland v Thornson* (1876) 3 R. 485; *Orr Ewing v Colquhoun's Trs* (1877) 4 R. (HL) 116 at 121, 137; *Drury v McGarvie*, 1993 S.L.T. 987.

[416] *Hill v Maclaren* (1879) 6 R. 1363; *Moyes v Macdiarmid* (1900) 2 F. 918; Bell, *Principles*, s.1010.

[417] Title Conditions (Scotland) Act 2003 Pt 9.

[418] E.g. *George Wimpey East Scotland Ltd v Fleming*, 2006 S.L.T. (Lands Tr.) 2 and 59.

34.45 Methods of creating servitudes—There are various methods of creating servitudes. The method of creation will determine the means whereby one may determine the extent of the right. Where a servitude is created by express grant or reservation, the terms of the grant and not the actual possession following thereon determine the extent of the servitude right. Where a servitude is acquired by prescriptive exercise the possession affords the measure of the right acquired: *tantum praescriptum quantum possessum*[419] (there is only prescription in so far as there has been possession). According to Erskine, however, a servitude by prescription may sometimes justly be extended beyond former usage, but the extension would apparently be admitted only where it was such a development of the use as might be held to be involved in the possession.[420]

The principal methods for the creation of servitudes are as follows.

34.46 Express grant or reservation—Until the advent of Land Registration, this was the most common method of the creation of servitudes. The method is recognised at common law[421] and is now, to some extent, varied and regulated by statutory provision.[422] The grant must be contained in writing[423] and should be in favour of the owner of the dominant tenement.[424] It is not necessary to use the words "servitude" in the grant or reservation albeit this is desirable for clarity.[425] The granter of the servitude requires to hold sufficient title to enable him to make the grant. Consequently, the grant must be made by one who either is at the time or subsequently becomes owner of the servient tenement.[426] A *pro indiviso* proprietor cannot grant a servitude over property owned commonly owned with others without the express consent of those others.[427] If, however, a grant is made *a non domino*, it may be perfected by positive prescription. If there is possession for a continuous period of 20 years openly, peaceably and without any judicial interruption, and the possession was founded on and followed the execution of a deed which is sufficient in respect of its terms expressly to constitute the servitude, the validity of the servitude as so constituted becomes unchallengeable.[428]

A deed of servitude represents a contract between the parties once it is delivered.[429] The rights conferred become real only when a further public stage is completed. At common law that stage involved several alternatives. At common law the deed might appear in the titles of the tenements or may be contained in a separate deed. At common law it it is not essential that it should appear in the Register of Sasines or the Land Register of Scotland but if it does not enter the Register, the grant of a positive servitude at common law is not effectual against

---

[419] *Kerr v Brown*, 1939 S.C. 140.

[420] Erskine, II, 9, 4; Rankine, *The Law of Landownership in Scotland* (1909), p.50.

[421] Erskine, II, 9, 35; *Inglis v Clark* (1901) 4 F. 288; *Metcalfe v Purdon* (1902) 4 F. 507; *Ferguson v Tennant*, 1978 S.C. (HL) 19.

[422] Title Conditions (Scotland) Act 2003 s.75.

[423] Requirements of Writing (Scotland) Act 1995 s.1(2).

[424] *Safeway Food Stores v Wellington Motor Company (Ayr)*, 1976 S.L.T. 53.

[425] *Moss Bros Group Plc v Scottish Mutual Assurance Plc*, 2001 S.L.T. 641.

[426] *Stephen v Brown's Trs*, 1922 S.C. 136 (operation of accretion). A grant by a person who is not yet owner does not take effect as a real right until he becomes owner.

[427] *Fearnan Partnership v Grindlay*, 1990 S.L.T. 704. (The question of *pro indiviso* proprietorship was not discussed in the House of Lords: 1992 S.C. (HL) 38.

[428] Prescription and Limitation (Scotland) Act 1973 s.3(1).

[429] Stair, II, 7, 1; Erskine, II, 9, 3; Bankton, II, 7, 1.

singular successors unless it is followed by possession. As regards deeds of servitude granted after November 28, 2004, the common law has been varied but not wholly abrogated. The common law position remains applicable to service media servitudes relating to enclosed units but, as regards other positive servitudes, a deed is not effective to create a positive servitude by express provision unless it is registered against both the benefited property and the burdened property.[430] This is known as "dual" registration.

Implied grant or reservation—Albeit there is a considerable body of cases on **34.47** implied grant or reservation, it should not be suggested that creation by such means is as common or as commercially important as creation by express grant or reservation. The constitution of a servitude by implication may occur when the owner of a plot of land severs it into two or more parts and alienates one or more of these parts. A, the proprietor of an estate, for example, dispones a portion to B and retains the other portion. B claims that, although there are no words in the disposition creating a servitude over the portion retained by A, such a servitude has been created by implication from the circumstances surrounding the conveyance. This is a claim to a servitude constituted by implied grant. On the other hand, the proprietor A may claim that the retained portion has by implication a servitude over the portion granted to B. This is a claim to a servitude constituted by implied reservation. Traditionally these two cases are regarded as distinct and as ruled by different considerations but this is inaccurate. It is simply the case that some of the factors favourable or adverse to the creation of a servitude exist in greater measure or have greater force in particular circumstances. It remains true to say that it is more difficult to establish that a servitude has been impliedly reserved. The authorities indicate that there are a number of conditions for the creation of a servitude by grant or reservation from the facts and circumstances surrounding a conveyance of land are as follows:

(a) The servitude must be reasonably necessary for the comfortable enjoyment of the benefited tenement.[431] Absolute necessity in the form of landlocking of enclaved land is not required.[432]

(b) The two tenements must have been owned at the same time by the same party in the same capacity.

(c) The servitude must generally have been foreshadowed prior to the severance by some exercise of the activity which is now claimed to be justified by the servitude.[433]

(d) Claims to an implied reservation of a servitude over lands conveyed in favour of lands retained are regarded with less favour than claims to an implied grant of a servitude over retained lands in favour of lands conveyed. Adverse to a claim of an implied reservation is the principle that a granter should not derogate from his grant. However, such reservations have been recognised where other factors have been regarded as sufficient.[434]

---

[430] Title Conditions (Scotland) Act 2003 ss.75 and 77.

[431] *Ewart v Cochrane* (1861) 23 D. (HL) 3; (1861) 4 Macq. 427.

[432] For access to such land the enclaved proprietor may have recourse to the separate doctrine of an inherent right of access: *Bowers v Kennedy*, 2000 S.C. 555.

[433] *Louttit's Trs v Highland Railway* (1892) 19 R. 791.

[434] *Inverness Seafield Development Ltd v Mackintosh*, 2000 S.L.T. 118; *Union Heritable Securities Co Ltd v Mathie* (1886) 13 R. 670; *Fergusson v Campbell*, 1913 1 S.L.T. 241.

(e) The terms of the deed effecting the severance will require to be examined to ensure they do not exclude implied grant or reservation.[435]

(f) The common author requires to have both title and capacity to create a servitude as at the date of the implied grant or reservation.

34.48 Positive prescription—A servitude may be constituted by positive prescription, or the grant of a servitude may be fortified by positive prescription. In either case the servitude must have been possessed for a continuous period of 20 years openly, peaceably and without judicial interruption. The effect is that the existence of the servitude as so possessed becomes unchallengeable.[436] In the case of fortification of a grant, it is the validity of the servitude as conferred in the grant which is fortified by prescription.[437] For the purposes of positive prescription the acts of possession may be carried out by anyone in possession of the dominant tenement.[438] The acts of possession must be overt in the sense that they must in themselves be of such character or be done in such circumstances as to indicate unequivocally to the proprietor of the servient tenement the fact that a right[439] is asserted and the nature of that right; and it must be shown that they either were known or ought to have been known, to the owner of the servient tenement or to the persons to whom he entrusted the charge of his property.[440]

34.49 Statute—A statute may create a servitude right either expressly or by implication.[441] Servitudes are created by force of statute when registered in the Land Register of Scotland.[442] The Keeper will usually require the application for registration to be accompanied by a deed in which the servitude is constituted by express grant or reservation. However, once registration is complete, the servitude flows from the register and not the prior deed.

34.50 Extinction of servitudes—A servitude may be extinguished in various ways. They include the following:

(1) It may be renounced expressly or impliedly by the proprietor of the dominant tenement.

(2) It may be extinguished through the operation of the negative prescription. A positive servitude will be lost by non-exercise for 20 years.[443] This period will run from the midnight following upon the last occasion on which the dominant owner exercised his right.[444] The operation of

---

[435] *McEachen v Lister*, 1976 S.L.T. (Sh. Ct) 38.

[436] Prescription and Limitation (Scotland) Act 1973 s.3(2).

[437] Prescription and Limitation (Scotland) Act 1973 s.3(1).

[438] Prescription and Limitation (Scotland) Act 1973 s.3(4).

[439] *Aberdeen City Council v Wanchoo*, 2008 S.L.T. 106; *Neumann v Hutchison*, 2008 G.W.D. 16–297; *Nationwide Building Society v Walter D. Allan Ltd* Unreported August 4, 2004, Lady Smith, available on the Scottish Courts' website (*http://www.scotcourts.gov.uk* [Accessed August 15. 2012]).

[440] *McInroy v Duke of Atholl* (1891) 18 R. (HL) 46, per Lord Watson; *McGregor v Crieff Cooperative Society*, 1915 S.C. (HL) 93.

[441] *Central RC v Ferns*, 1979 S.C. 136 (Water (Scotland) Act 1946).

[442] Land Registration (Scotland) Act 1979 s.3(1)(a); *Orkney Housing Association Ltd v Atkinson*, 2011 G.W.D. 30–652.

[443] Prescription and Limitation (Scotland) Act 1973 s.8. Although s.3(5) implies that the draftsman thought servitudes might prescribe under s.7, the better view is that they do so under s.8. See, e.g. D. Johnston, *Prescription and Limitation* (Edinburgh: W. Green, 1999), paras 7.14 and 17.05 with further references.

[444] Prescription and Limitation (Scotland) Act 1973 s.14.

negative prescription will not be averted by the fact that the servitude appears in the title of the servient tenement.[445] However, there is a small class of servitude rights exempted from the operation of negative prescription by virtue of their classification as *res merae facultatis*.[446] This categorization is controversial and appears to be limited to rights to make a road through the servient tenement under certain limited conditions.

(3) A servitude may be discharged by the Lands Tribunal upon application by anyone against whom the servitude is enforceable[447] if the Lands Tribunal is satisfied, having regard to a list of statutory factors, that it is "reasonable" to do so.[448]

(4) If the servient tenement is acquired under compulsory powers, it is taken free of all servitudes unless the compulsory purchase order or the conveyance provides otherwise.[449]

(5) If either the dominant or the servient tenement is destroyed, the servitude is extinguished, for in that case nothing remains to be the subject of a servitude. But if the dominant is only temporarily rendered unfit for the servitude, the servitude is suspended for the time but is not extinguished.[450]

(6) It may be extinguished *confusione*, i.e. by both tenements passing into the ownership of the same person.[451] If the tenements thereafter come to belong to different persons, the servitude does not thereupon revive, but requires to be constituted anew.[452]

(7) A servitude may also be abandoned if there is conduct on the part of the dominant owner showing an intention to relinquish it coupled with non-use.[453]

Public right of way—Traditionally servitudes of way and public rights of way **34.51** have been treated together because they both may afford passage over land not owned by the individual wishing to take passage. However, they are very different legal creatures. The differences between a public right of way and a servitude of way may be summarised thus:

---

[445] *Graham v Douglas* (1735) Mor.10745. A real right of ownership in land is imprescriptible: Prescription and Limitation (Scotland) Act 1973 Sch.3 para.(a) and so is the inherent right of access: *Bowers v Kennedy*, 2000 S.C. 555.

[446] *Smith v Stewart* (1884) 11 R. 921; (1884) 21 S.L.R. 623; *Peart v Legge*, April 5, 2006 and November 8, 2006 and reversed by Extra Division at [2007] CSIH 70; 2008 S.C. 93.

[447] Title Conditions (Scotland) Act 2003 s.90(1)(a).

[448] Title Conditions (Scotland) Act 2003 Pt 9 s.98. The statutory factors are set out in s.100. Most cases involve diversion of servitudes of access e.g. *Colecliffe v Thompson*, 2009 G.W.D. 23–375; *Gibb v Kerr*, 2009 G.W.D. 38–646; *Jensen v Tyler*, 2008 S.L.T. (Lands Tr.) 39; 2008 G.W.D. 25–393; *Graham v Parker*, 2007 G.W.D. 30–524 but other servitudes, e.g. the drying of clothes, may be discharged: *McKenzie v Scott*, 19 May 2009, Lands Tribunal, LTS/TC/2008/12.

[449] Title Conditions (Scotland) Act 2003 ss.106 and 107.

[450] Erskine, II, 9, 37; Bell, *Principles*, ss.995–996.

[451] *Baird v Fortune* (1861) 4 Macq. 127, per Lord Cranworth; *Donaldson's Trs v Forbes* (1839) 1 D. 449; *Ord v Mashford,* 2006 S.L.T. (Lands Tr.) 15.

[452] Erskine, II, 9, 37; *Union Bank v Daily Record* (1902) 10 S.L.T. 71; *Ord v Mashford*, 2006 S.L.T. (Lands Tr.) 15.

[453] *Magistrates of Rutherglen v Bainbridge* (1886) 13 R. 745; *Hogg v Campbell*, April 2, 1993, OH, Lord Clyde, available on *http://www.lexis.com* [Accessed August 15, 2012]; *Pullar v Gauldie* Unreported August 25, 2004, Arbroath Sheriff Court, noted in K.G.C. Reid and G.L. Gretton, *Conveyancing 2010* (Edinburgh: Avizandum, 2011), pp.15 and 179–180.

(a) A public right of way is a public right and not a private right. Consequently, it exists for the benefit of the public and may be vindicated by members of the public even if they own no land. A servitude of way, on the other hand, is for the use and benefit of the dominant tenement alone, and it is only the proprietor of that tenement who has a title to sue in regard to it.[454]

(b) As a public right, a public right of way does not form part of the assets or estate of any person. In this regard it differs from a servitude. A public right of way cannot be conveyed from one person to another. It cannot be subjected to derivative real rights such as leases or securities. It does not form part of the estate of an individual upon death or insolvency.

(c) It is likely that a public right of way may be created only by prescriptive exercise[455] or by statutory provision and it cannot be created by express or implied grant or reservation.

34.52 The essentials for a public right of way—A public right of way is a right in the public to pass from one public place to another public place.[456] The road must follow a definite route.[457] Like a servitude of way, it may be a footpath, a horse road or a carriage road,[458] or indeed a motor road.[459] The use must be by the public, and not such as can be reasonably ascribed to a private servitude; it must be of such a character as to indicate that a right to use the track is asserted, for a use which is due to the permission or tolerance of the proprietor will not suffice; and it must be continuous, open and peaceable and without any judicial interruption. The amount of unrestricted public use which must be proved varies with circumstances; in a thinly populated district use by a small number of persons may be sufficient.[460] If the right of way is established, the use is not limited to passage from one end to the other; a member of the public is entitled to use it for part of its course, as for example for the purpose of reaching his own property.[461] As in the case of a servitude road, the proprietor of the lands over which the way runs is not debarred from dealing with his property in any lawful manner which does not interfere with the right of the public.[462] A member of the public cannot carry out any activity other than passage on a public right of way. For example, he or she cannot camp, hunt, shoot or fish or camp on a public right of way or to use the public right of way for purposes other than passage.[463]

---

[454] *Thomson v Murdoch* (1862) 24 D. 975, per Lord Deas; *Jenkins v Murray* (1866) 4 M. 1046, per Lord Curriehill.

[455] Prescription and Limitation (Scotland) Act 1973 s.3(3).

[456] *Campbell v Lang* (1853) 1 Macq. 451; *Young v Cuthbertson* (1854) 1 Macq. 455; *Rhins District Committee of Wigtownshire CC v Cuninghame*, 1917 2 S.L.T. 169 (a useful summary of the requirements); *Marquis of Bute v McKirdy & McMillan*, 1937 S.C. 93 (foreshore); *Love-Lee v Cameron*, 1991 S.C.L.R. 61.

[457] *Mackintosh v Moir* (1871) 9 M. 574; (1872) 10 M. 517.

[458] *Mackenzie v Bankes* (1868) 6 M. 936. A footpath apparently extends to bicycle use too: *Aberdeenshire CC v Lord Glentanar*, 1999 S.L.T. 1456 (Note) (decided in 1930).

[459] *Smith v Sexton*, 1927 S.N. 92.

[460] *Macpherson v Scottish Rights of Way Society* (1888) 15 R. (HL) 68; *Richardson v Cromarty Petroleum Co Ltd*, 1982 S.L.T. 237. For a decision involving an urban area, see *Strathclyde (Hyndland) Housing Society Ltd v Cowie*, 1983 S.L.T. (Sh. Ct) 61.

[461] *McRobert v Reid*, 1914 S.C. 633; *Lord Burton v Mackay*, 1995 S.L.T. 507.

[462] *Reilly v Greenfield Coal and Brick Co*, 1909 S.C. 1328 at 1338, per Lord President Dunedin; *Midlothian DC v McKenzie*, 1985 S.L.T. 36 (a landowner has to justify anything that restricts the unobstructed use of a public right of way).

[463] *Sutherland v Thornson* (1876) 3 R. 485.

A right of way constituted by use will be lost by disuse for the prescriptive period.[464] It seems that a right of way may also be lost by its physical or legal destruction or by loss of the public character of one or both of the termini.[465]

An action for vindication of a right of way may be brought by any member of the public,[466] or by a local authority.[467] When the question of the existence of a particular right of way has been properly raised and decided, the decision is res judicata in any subsequent action even when raised by a different party.[468] So also an action of declarator that there is no right of way may be defended by any member of the public or by the local authority,[469] and here also a judgment will be res judicata. The same result follows if the action is raised or defended by a society formed to defend rights of way.[470] The owner of land traversed by a public right of way has been held to owe a duty of care to the users thereof.[471]

Statutory public rights—The statutory rights created by the Land Reform (Scotland) Act 2003 (asp 2) are wider than mere passage. They are (a) the right to be on land for certain specified purposes, and (b) the right to cross that land.[472] The purposes specified in the 2003 Act are recreational purposes, educational activity purposes and commercial or profit-making activities which the person could carry on otherwise than commercially or for profit.[473] Educational activity is defined in the 2003 Act as an activity which is carried on by a person for the purposes of furthering that person's understanding of natural or cultural heritage or for the purposes of enabling or assisting another person to further their understanding of natural or cultural heritage.[474] By contrast, there is no statutory definition of recreational activity nor of commercial or for profit activity. The 2003 Act provides that commercial activity must be activity which is capable of being carried on a non-profit basis. This would include a guide leading tours of mountains because he or she could work commercially or for no financial reward. However, where a commercial activity cannot be carried on for no financial reward it will be excluded. An excluded commercial activity would be sale of goods because this, by definition, requires payment. So the setting up of an ice cream stall on Ben Nevis would be excluded. **34.53**

The 2003 Act provides that a person only has these access rights if they are exercised responsibly,[475] before specifically elaborating certain activities that are not to be taken as exercising access rights responsibly.[476] These are as follows:

(a) being on or crossing land in breach of an interdict or other order of a court;

---

[464] Prescription and Limitation (Scotland) Act 1973 s.8.

[465] *Lord Burton v Mackay*, 1995 S.L.T. 507.

[466] *Potter v Hamilton* (1870) 8 M. 1064.

[467] Local Government (Scotland) Act 1973 ss.189 and 235 as amended by the Local Government etc. (Scotland) Act 1994.

[468] This is because the action is raised by a member of the public for the interest of the public as a whole: *Thomson v Murdoch* (1862) 24 D. 975 at 982.

[469] cf. *Alston v Ross* (1895) 23 R. 273; *Alexander v Picken*, 1946 S.L.T. 91.

[470] *Macfie v Scottish Rights of Way Society* (1884) 11 R. 1094.

[471] *Johnstone v Sweeney*, 1985 S.L.T. (Sh. Ct) 2.

[472] Land Reform (Scotland) Act 2003 s.1(2).

[473] Land Reform (Scotland) Act 2003 s.1(3).

[474] Land Reform (Scotland) Act 2003 s.1(5).

[475] Land Reform (Scotland) Act 2003 s.2(1). See *Tuley v Highland Council*, 2009 S.C. 456 (IH (Ex Div)), considered in M.M. Combe, "Access to land and to landownership" (2010) 14 Edin. L.R 106.

[476] Land Reform (Scotland) Act 2003 s.9.

  (b) being on or crossing land for the purposes of doing anything which is an offence or a breach of an interdict or order of a court;
  (c) hunting, shooting or fishing;
  (d) being on or crossing land while responsible for a dog or other animal which is not under proper control;
  (e) being on or crossing land for the purpose of taking away, for commercial purposes or for profit, anything in or on the land;
  (f) being on or crossing land in or with a motorised vehicle or vessel (other than a vehicle or vessel which has been constructed or adapted for use by a person who has a disability and which is being used by such a person);
  (g) being, for any of the purposes set out in s.1(3) of the 2003 Act, on land which is a golf course. This means that no member of the public can claim an entitlement to be on a golf course for recreational purposes, educational activity purposes or commercial or profit-making activities which the person could carry on otherwise than commercially or for profit. The crossing of land which forms part of a golf course is not excluded.

The statutory rights of access created in the Land Reform (Scotland) Act 2003 are exercisable above and below and on the surface of "land".[477] They therefore include activities such as potholing and paragliding. Land is defined in the statute[478] as including bridges and other structures built on or over land, inland waters, canals and the foreshore which extends between the high and low water marks of the ordinary spring tides. This statutory definition comprises most rural areas and could extend to some suburban areas. There is, however, a statutory list of specific types of land over which access rights are stated not to be exercisable.[479] Ministers may modify the exclusion provisions.[480] These exclusions are presently as follows[481]:

  (a) Land on which there is erected a building or other structure or works, plant or fixed machinery.
  (b) Land on which there is erected a caravan, tent or other place affording a person privacy or shelter.
  (c) Land which forms the curtilage of a building which is not a house or of a group of buildings none of which is a house.
  (d) Land which forms a compound or other enclosure containing any such structure, works, plant or fixed machinery as is referred to in (a) above.
  (e) Land which is contiguous to and used for the purposes of a school.
  (f) Land which comprises in relation to a house or any of the places mentioned in (c) above sufficient adjacent land to enable persons living there to have a reasonable measure of privacy in that house or place and to ensure that their enjoyment is not unreasonably disturbed. The location and other characteristics of the house or other place are factors to be taken into account in determining the amount of excluded land

---

[477] Land Reform (Scotland) Act 2003 s.1(6).
[478] Land Reform (Scotland) Act 2003 s.32.
[479] Land Reform (Scotland) Act 2003 s.6.
[480] Land Reform (Scotland) Act 2003 s.8.
[481] Land Reform (Scotland) Act 2003 s.6.

to go with that house.[482] Presumably a larger house may require a larger garden.

(g) Land which is owned in common and used by two or more persons as a private garden. Thus, the ornamental squares in Edinburgh are excluded where they are owned in common.

(h) Land to which public access is prohibited, excluded or restricted under an enactment. Thus, public rights of access do not permit the public to walk along railway lines.

(i) Land which has been developed or set out as a sports or playing field or for a particular recreation purpose.

(j) Land to which for not fewer than 90 days in the year ending on January 31, 2001 members of the public were permitted only on payment and after that date for not fewer than 90 days in each year beginning on February 1, 2001 members of the public are or are to be so admitted.

(k) Land on which building, civil engineering or demolition works or other works are being carried out.

(l) Land on which works are being carried out by a statutory undertaker for the purposes of the undertaking.

(m) Land which is used for the working of minerals by surface workings including quarrying.

(n) Land on which crops have been sown or are growing.

(o) Land which has been specified in an order under s.11 of the Reform Act 2003 (exemption of land from access rights) or bye-laws under s.12 as land in respect of which access rights are not exercisable.

REAL BURDENS

Definition—"Real burdens"[483] form a class of obligations and rights otherwise **34.54** known as "real conditions". They are real rights which burden land, and bind successors in title. They are similar in nature to servitudes; however, unlike servitudes they do not derive from the Civilian tradition. Their development comes from early urbanisation and related conveyancing practice. Two categories of real burdens existed at common law, with a third class introduced through statutory creation. The first of these, feudal real burdens, are burdens created by feudal superiors over the *dominium utile* of land, enforceable by the feudal superior against the vassal. On November 28, 2004, feudal real burdens were abolished unless preserved in a different form.[484] The second classification is that most commonly encountered, which can be considered under the term "praedial" real burden. A praedial real burden is an encumbrance on land ("the burdened property") in favour of the owner of another piece of land ("the benefited property") in their capacity as owner of that land.[485] The last class is that denoted by the term "personal" real burden.[486] It is also an encumbrance on land, but is distinguished

---

[482] Land Reform (Scotland) Act 2003 s.7(5). See *Gloag v Perth and Kinross Council*, 2007 S.C.L.R. 530; *Snowie v Stirling Council*, 2008 S.L.T. (Sh. Ct) 61; *Forbes v Fife Council*, 2009 S.L.T. (Sh. Ct) 71; *Creelman v Argyll and Bute Council*, 2009 S.L.T. (Sh. Ct) 165; M.M. Combe, "No place like home: access rights over 'gardens'" (2008) 12 Edin. L.R. 463.

[483] This is the terminology adopted in statute; Title Conditions (Scotland) Act 2003 s.1.

[484] Abolition of Feudal Tenure etc (Scotland) Act 2000 s.17.

[485] Title Conditions (Scotland) Act 2003 s.1(1)–(2).

[486] Title Conditions (Scotland) Act 2003 s.1(3).

by the nature of the right to enforce. A personal real burden is held in favour of a person, natural or juristic, other than by reference to that person's capacity as owner of any land. Simply there is a "burdened property" but no "benefited property." The person with right to enforce this type of real burden is commonly a local authority or other body specifically entitled by statute.

Furthermore, in addition to these classifications it is also possible to classify real burdens based on the type of obligations imposed, be that "positive" or "negative". Positive real burdens (or "affirmative real burdens")[487] create an obligation on the burdened owner to do something,[488] and negative real burdens create an obligation to refrain from doing something.[489] They do not create an obligation allowing use of, or entry to, the burdened property, and any real burdens "allowing use" have been converted into positive servitudes.[490] It is possible, however, that a real burden may be coupled with an obligation allowing the benefitted proprietor to access the burdened property for the purpose of the real burden. This is known as an "ancillary burden".[491]

34.55 Praedial real burdens—As noted above, praedial real burdens are the class of burden enforceable by the proprietor of one plot of land in respect of another plot of land. They commonly occur on the first subdivision of land or in flat and housing scheme building developments. The burdens imposed in the first of these examples are often referred to as "neighbour burdens", in that the benefit and burden are found in neighbouring plots. Here a single house plot is split off from a larger estate, neighbour burdens are commonly imposed so that they will be enforceable only against the burdened property, with no reciprocal rights of enforcement. However, where a number of houses or units are developed and disponed to purchasers, the burdens imposed are generally reciprocal. The title of all units may include the same restrictions, and the restrictions may be declared to be enforceable by the proprietors of all units *inter se*. These burdens are known as "community burdens".[492] Community burdens are subject to particular rules regarding enforcement, variation and discharge.[493]

34.56 General requirements as to content—Proprietors are given a large measure of freedom as to the content of real burdens with the result that they are highly flexible and used in a widespread manner. In contrast to the categories of servitudes recognised at common law,[494] there are no fixed types of obligation which can be created as a real burden. That is not to say that there are no rules as to content of a real burden: not every obligation can be constituted as a real burden. What can be said, however, is that the rules of requisite content are much more flexible in relation to real conditions as compared to servitudes. Two general rules may be noted:

> (a) There must be a praedial burden. The real burden must relate in some way to the burdened property,[495] be it through a direct or indirect rela-

---

[487] This is the terminology adopted in statute; Title Conditions (Scotland) Act 2003 s.2(2)(a).
[488] Title Conditions (Scotland) Act 2003 s.2(1)(a).
[489] Title Conditions (Scotland) Act 2003 s.2(1)(b).
[490] Title Conditions (Scotland) Act 2003 s.81.
[491] Title Conditions (Scotland) Act 2003 s.2(3).
[492] Title Conditions (Scotland) Act 2003 s.25.
[493] Title Conditions (Scotland) Act 2003 Pt 2.
[494] See para.34.42, above.
[495] Title Conditions (Scotland) Act s.3(1).

tionship, but not merely through the circumstances that the obligated person is the owner of the burdened property.[496] The obligation sought to be imposed must relate to land or the buildings and other fixtures thereon or the use of land or buildings and fixtures. It should not relate to the landowners or occupiers of that land.

(b) There must be a praedial benefit. The real burden must be for the utility of the benefitted property and not the mere benefit of an individual.[497] This is known as *utilitas*. An exception is in relation to community burdens, which may be for the benefit of the community to which it relates or of some part of the community, rather than for the benefit of the property itself.[498] This statutory provision regarding community benefit removes some of the rigidity of the common law, particularly in relation to the protection of businesses and the benefit to commerce.[499] The requirement of praedial benefit makes it difficult to use real burdens as a device to require clawback payments[500] unless, of course, this is expressly permitted in relation to particular types of real burdens such as economic development burdens[501] and healthcare burdens.[502]

Particular requirements as to content—More detailed restrictions on the **34.57** permissible content of real conditions were identified by Lord Corehouse giving the opinion of the Court in *Incorporation of Tailors of Aberdeen v Coutts*.[503] In this judgement it was confirmed that a real burden must comply with the following requirements:

(a) It must not be contrary to law.[504] A real burden cannot require a proprietor to do something which is illegal. A landowner cannot be required to carry out activities which would amount to a criminal offence or breach of any statutory code. Statutory reform of the law of title conditions has not altered this aspect of the requirement, but the content of this aspect could alter from time to time as the more general statutory law renders certain matters now legal to be illegal or declares certain activities which are presently illegal to be legal.

(b) It must not be contrary to public policy.[505] At common law certain restrictions which purport to create trade monopolies, thus impeding the commerce of land, have been regarded as contrary to public policy.[506] It is difficult to say with certainty exactly what this means. The rule does not preclude simple restrictions which prevent the use of property where such restrictions are imposed to protect the amenity of surrounding subjects. It may, however, render invalid a restriction against the use of a plot of ground for particular commercial use where the purpose of

---

[496] Title Conditions (Scotland) Act s.3(2).

[497] Title Conditions (Scotland) Act s.3(3). See *Halladale (Shaftesbury) Ltd v Applicants*, June 20, 2005, Lands Tribunal noted in Reid and Gretton, *Conveyancing 2006* (Edinburgh: Avizandum, 2007), p.16.

[498] Title Conditions (Scotland) Act s.3(4).

[499] *Aberdeen Varieties Ltd v James F Donald (Aberdeen Cinemas) Ltd*, 1940 S.C. (HL) 52.

[500] *I & H Brown Ltd, Applicants*, April 28, 2010, Lands Tribunal, LTS/TC/2009/46.

[501] Title Conditions (Scotland) Act 2003 s.45(3).

[502] Title Conditions (Scotland) Act 2003 s.46(3).

[503] *Incorporation of Tailors of Aberdeen v Coutts* (1840) 1 Rob. App. 296.

[504] Also now found in statute: Title Conditions (Scotland) Act 2003 s.3(6).

[505] Title Conditions (Scotland) Act 2003 s.3(6).

[506] *Aberdeen Varieties Ltd v James F Donald (Aberdeen Cinemas) Ltd*, 1940 S.C. (HL) 52.

the restriction is not to enhance amenity, but merely to protect the trade of another neighbouring commercial property. Statutory reform reflects commercial reality and permits restraints of trade to a greater extent. The statutory restatement merely requires that a real burden must not be contrary to public policy as, for example, by creating an unreasonable restraint of trade.[507] Clearly reasonable restraints of trade are possible. In addition, the position regarding monopolies has been clarified in statute.[508] In general, a real burden must not create a monopoly through the appointment of managers or other service providers, subject to specific exceptions within the Act.[509]

(c) It must not be "vexatious" or "useless".[510] In one sense all restrictions on land are vexatious but this is not what this requirement means. Generally, an obligation which is imposed for no real benefit and is simply imposed to make life miserable for the owner will not be enforced. The recent statutory reform has not altered or restated this requirement and it can probably be regarded as an aspect of the requirement of praedial utility or *utilitas* in any event. Further, it is clear from the statute that in order to enforce a real burden a person requires not only title but interest.[511] Given the definition of interest to enforce[512]—largely related to a material diminution in the value of the dominant tenement or the amenity thereof—it is hard to see how anyone could have any legitimate interest to enforce a vexatious or useless burden.[513]

(d) It must not be inconsistent with the nature of the species of property. Otherwise stated, it must not be repugnant with ownership.[514] This phrase has two broad elements:

(i) First, it requires that a real burden must not purport to remove from the burdened proprietor the right to use and possess his property to an undue extent.

(ii) Second, a real burden must not preclude the exercise of juristic acts.

34.58 Use and possession—The broad principle regarding use and possession is that a person cannot be made a proprietor, but also be prohibited from exercising his ownership through the vehicle of real burdens.[515] The extent of this element is rather vague because all real burdens do deprive the burdened proprietor of his rights freely to use his property to some extent. Extensive restrictions are sometimes acceptable. For example, an obligation not to use the property except for an ice rink has been regarded as valid.[516] So too has a burden prohibiting use of residential subjects for a trade, business or profession[517] and a provision restricting to a specific

---

[507] Title Conditions (Scotland) Act 2003 s.3(6).
[508] Title Conditions (Scotland) Act 2003 s.3(7).
[509] Notably, the exceptions in relation to manager burdens (a subset of personal real burdens) under Title Conditions (Scotland) Act 2003 ss.63–67.
[510] *Aberdeen Varieties Ltd v James F Donald (Aberdeen Cinemas) Ltd*, 1940 S.C. (HL) 52.
[511] Title Conditions (Scotland) Act 2003 s.8(1).
[512] Title Conditions (Scotland) Act 2003 s.8(3).
[513] The matter of enforcement is dealt with at para.34.64, below.
[514] Title Conditions (Scotland) Act 2003 s.3(6).
[515] *Moir's Trustees v McEwan* (1880) 7 R. 1141, per Lord Young at 1145.
[516] *Cumbernauld Development Corp v County Properties and Developments Ltd*, 1996 S.L.T. 1106.
[517] *Snowie v Museum Hall LLP*, 2010 S.L.T. 971.

use the manager's office and guest room in a sheltered housing development.[518] Nevertheless it is more likely that a real burden will be inconsistent with the use and possession of property where it allows the benefitted proprietor to carry out activity within the burdened property. Where real conditions purport to arrogate to the benefitted proprietor the exclusive right to use the burdened property for shooting[519] or social occasions[520] they have been regarded as invalid at common law. Rights to enter or otherwise make use of the burdened property, unless they are servitudes, could now exist only as ancillary burdens.[521] The dividing line between what is acceptable and what is too invasive is not easy to draw. The impact of this restriction on the content of real conditions is likely to be reduced considerably given that the right to carry out activity on the burdened property has been reclassified as a servitude in terms of statutory reform.[522]

Juristic acts—As regards the second element concerning juristic acts, a real **34.59** burden cannot absolutely remove the right of a proprietor to sell land, lease it[523] or grant securities over it. In respect of co-owned property, a real burden cannot prevent the co-owner's entitlement to raise an action of division and sale.[524] Nevertheless, it is possible to limit (rather than remove totally) the exercise of these rights by means of real burden. Thus rights known as rights of pre-emption are competent, subject to statutory limitations.[525]

Pre-emption—Pre-emption rights constituted as real burdens allow the owner of **34.60** a benefitted property to have the right to purchase the burdened property if the burdened proprietor sells that property. The right usually allows the benefitted proprietor to purchase the property at the like price[526] to that which is offered by a third party prospective purchaser. Another common variant is that the offer made by the seller will be also made on the same terms and conditions as that which is offered by the prospective purchaser. Pre-emptions are strictly construed at common law[527] and albeit this canon of construction has been relaxed by statutory provision,[528] the courts are still likely to seek to afford the burdened proprietor freedom to carry out juristic acts when they are not clearly restricted. The disponee in the deed is precluded from carrying out the juristic act of sale to a third party only to the extent that the real burden—the pre-emption in question—expressly states. Statutory limitations impose a time limit upon the acceptance of any offer to sell made in terms of a pre-emption.[529] This period is 21 days or such shorter date as is specified in the deed creating the right. After November 28, 2004

---

[518] *Sheltered Housing Management Ltd v Jack*, January 5, 2007, Lands Tribunal, LTS/TC/2006/01 available on the website of the Lands Tribunal for Scotland.

[519] *Beckett v Bissett*, 1921 2 S.L.T. 33. Cf. *Harper v Flaws*, 1940 S.L.T. 150.

[520] *Kirkintilloch Kirk Session v Kirkintilloch School Board*, 1911 S.C. 1127; *Scott v Howard* (1881) 8 R. (HL) 59.

[521] Title Conditions (Scotland) Act 2003 s.2(3) and (4).

[522] Title Conditions (Scotland) Act 2003 s.81.

[523] *Moir's Trustees v McEwan* (1880) 7 R. 1141.

[524] *Grant v Heriot's Trust* (1906) 8 F. 647.

[525] Title Conditions (Scotland) Act 2003 Pt 8.

[526] In this context, the like price plainly means the same price offered by another party: *Grampian Joint Police Board v Pearson*, 2000 S.L.T. 90 per Lord Kingarth, affd 2001 S.C. 772.

[527] *Roebuck v Edmonds*, 1992 S.L.T. 1055 at 1056J; *Grampian Joint Police Board v Pearson*, 2001 S.C. 772.

[528] Title Conditions (Scotland) Act 2003 s.14.

[529] *Christie v Jackson*, 1898 S.L.T. 245; *Mathieson v Tinney*, 1989 S.L.T. 535; *Grampian Joint Police Board v Pearson*, 2001 S.C. 772.

it is only competent to create a pre-emption right as a real burden, but it is not competent to create a real burden which consists of a right of redemption (to buy back at a time dictated by the entitled party) or any other type of option to acquire the burdened property.[530]

34.61 Creation—Real burdens may be distinguished from servitudes in the manner of their creation. Positive servitudes may be created by prescriptive exercise for 20 years.[531] Real burdens cannot arise by use alone even if that use continues for the prescriptive period of 20 years, nor can they arise by virtue of grant or reservation implied from the circumstances surrounding a conveyance. Prior to November 28, 2004 all real burdens required to be created in a conveyance of the burdened property or in a deed of declaration of conditions which forms part of the title of the burdened land. After this date, the position is simply that real burdens must be created in a deed (of any type)[532] which must be registered against both the titles of the benefitted and burdened properties.[533] This is referred to in statute as the "constitutive deed".[534] The burden is not effective as a burden until this deed is dual registered.

34.62 Particular requirements as to creation—To create a real burden it is essential to use words which are clear, unambiguous and precise. A number of subsidiary rules in this regard may be identified:

(a) At common law no special technical words (*voces signatae*) were required to create a real burden but it had to be clearly shown that the obligation was intended to affect the property and the successive owners of the property and not just the original grantee and his heirs. It is more likely that the parties to a deed intended that the obligation imposed should be a real burden if the deed expressly states that the obligation concerned is a "real burden" or a "real condition" and uses those exact words. If those words are not used or if such a declaration is not inserted in the deed the courts will look at the nature of the obligation for guidance. If the obligation is capable of performance by a single act (such as an obligation to erect a fence or a house) there is a presumption—but only a presumption—that it is not as a real burden but simply a contractual obligation affecting the original grantee.[535] Conversely, obligations to maintain a fence or to keep in good repair the walls of a house are obligations which require repeated acts or a series of acts over a period time and these are likely to be regarded as real burdens. This common law rule has been altered in terms of statute. From November 29, 2004 onwards it has been necessary to use the word "real burden" in any deed which creates a real burden, or to refer to a specific type of real burden.[536] If there is no express reference, then no real burden is created.

(b) The full text of the real burden must be included in the deed which is registered or recorded.[537] Extrinsic evidence is not generally admissible

---

[530] Title Conditions (Scotland) Act 2003 s.3(5).

[531] Prescription and Limitation (Scotland) Act 1973 s.3(2).

[532] The possibility of use of a minute of waiver to create the burden is therefore now competent.

[533] Title Conditions (Scotland) Act 2003 ss.4(1), 6.

[534] Title Conditions (Scotland) Act 2003 ss.4–5, 122.

[535] *Edinburgh Mags v Begg* (1883) 11 R. 352.

[536] Title Conditions (Scotland) Act 2003 s.4(2)(a), (3).

[537] *Aberdeen Varieties Ltd v James F. Donald (Aberdeen Cinemas) Ltd*, 1940 S.C. (HL) 52.

and it is not competent to refer to an unrecorded deed for greater detail. If the full text of the restriction is not set out within the "four corners" of the deed the purported real condition will be invalid as such, but may survive as a contract between the original parties. Thus an obligation to comply with a statute or Act of Parliament cannot be created as a real burden if all the draftsman does is to refer to the legislation. This is altered to a limited extent by statute in that reference to a public register or roll is permitted where this is referred to in a deed in order to determine a method of ascertaining a cost payable by an owner.[538] For example, it is permissible to refer to the valuation roll to determine the level of maintenance charges payable by a proprietor. This removes some of the prior difficulties under the common law which provided that the deed must specify the payment of a sum of money as a definite amount.

(c) At common law there were particular requirements regarding identification of the property subject to the real burden. For burdens created prior to November 28, 2004, there is a requirement that the burdened property must be precisely defined.[539] This requirement has been extended by statute for real burdens created after the appointed date, in that both the burdened and benefitted properties must now be identified in the deed.[540] In the case of community burdens where there is no benefitted property, the affected community must be identified.[541] Such identification should be done by reference to a plan or title number.

(d) The deed need not specify the duration of the real burden, but in the instance that no specification is made the real burden will be treated as perpetual[542] and will endure for so long as the property right endures, subject to specific rules regarding termination.[543] The parties may, however, restrict the endurance of a real burden by express clause to a limited period of time or to termination upon the happening of a future event.

Interpretation of real burdens—The Title Conditions (Scotland) Act 2003 **34.63** provides that provisions imposing real burdens will be interpreted in the same manner as other provisions in deeds relating to land and intended for registration.[544] The provision is retrospective in effect. In addition to this a number of general common law principles of interpretation continue to apply. These principles are based on the presumption in Scots law that land should be free from restrictions. Primary amongst these is the principle that real burdens will be interpreted *contra proferentem*. Words will also be given their normal, objective meaning and will not be overly-extended or given an interpretation based on the subjective intentions of the parties.

Enforcement—A person wishing to enforce a real burden must have both title to **34.64** enforce and an interest to enforce.[545]

---

[538] Title Conditions (Scotland) Act 2003 s 5.
[539] *Anderson v Dickie*, 1914 S.C. 706.
[540] Title Conditions (Scotland) Act 2003 s.4(2)(c).
[541] Title Conditions (Scotland) Act 2003 s.4(4).
[542] Title Conditions (Scotland) Act 2003 s.7.
[543] See para.34.68, below.
[544] Title Conditions (Scotland) Act 2003 s.14.
[545] Title Conditions (Scotland) Act 2003 s.8(1).

34.65 Title to enforce—The owner of the benefitted property has title to enforce a real burden.[546] This means that the original creator of the burden and his successors in title as owner will have title to enforce. Title to enforce has also been extended by statute to include tenants holding a real right under a lease, proper liferenters and those who have occupancy rights in the benefited property.[547]

Prior to November 28, 2004 difficulty often arose in relation to identification of the benefitted property, particularly given that deeds did not have to include express nomination of that property. Without sufficient nomination, it is unclear who holds title to enforce. The position has been clarified under statute for all real burdens created after November 28, 2004, in that they must be registered against both the burdened and benefitted properties.[548] In respect of deeds created before the appointed date a number of rules apply:

(a) At common law the doctrine of *ius quaesitum tertio* continues to have relevance. This permits the express nomination of the benefitted property or properties, allowing rights of enforcement to lie with these proprietors despite the creation of these rights in deeds to which they were not a party. This is common in deeds of conditions.

(b) In the situation where no express identification of the benefitted property is made, the Title Conditions (Scotland) Act 2003 provides a set of rules in order to imply rights of enforcement.[549] These rules abolish any rules of implied enforcement found under the common law.[550] They provide as follows:

(i) Real burdens found in the titles of "related properties"[551] in a common scheme[552] where the deed in question was registered before November 28, 2004 are mutually enforceable by the properties in that common scheme.[553]

(ii) Real burdens found in the title of a property in a common scheme where the deed was registered prior to November 28, 2004 are mutually enforceable by the properties in that common scheme.[554] There is no need that the properties be "related" but there must be notice that the common scheme exists in the deed creating the burdens for that property[555] and the deed must contain nothing that excludes mutual enforceability.[556]

(iii) Real burdens imposed in a deed registered prior to November 28, 2004 regulating the maintenance, management, reinstatement or

---

[546] Title Conditions (Scotland) Act 2003 s.8(2).

[547] Title Conditions (Scotland) Act 2003 s.8(2)(b).

[548] Title Conditions (Scotland) Act 2003 s.4(5).

[549] Title Conditions (Scotland) Act 2003 ss.52–57.

[550] Title Conditions (Scotland) Act 2003 s.49. Although it is noted that some of the provisions replicate the earlier law.

[551] This term is undefined in the 2003 Act, but illustrative circumstances from which an inference that the properties are "related" may arise are set out in s.53(2). See *Brown v Richardson*, 2007 G.W.D. 28–490, Lands Tribunal, LTS/TC/2006/41.

[552] This term is undefined in the 2003 Act, but can be taken to cover the situation where same, or similar, burdens are imposed on a group of properties by the same person.

[553] Title Conditions (Scotland) Act 2003 s.53.

[554] Title Conditions (Scotland) Act 2003 s.52. This is a restatement of the common law principle of implied *ius quaesitum tertio* found in *Hislop v MacRitchie's Trustees* (1881) 8 R. (HL) 95.

[555] Title Conditions (Scotland) Act 2003 s.52(1).

[556] Title Conditions (Scotland) Act 2003 s.52(2).

use of facility are enforceable by all properties to which the facility is of benefit.[557]

(iv) Real burdens imposed in a deed registered prior to November 28, 2004 regulating the provision of a service are all enforceable by all properties to which the service is to be provided.[558]

(v) Real burdens created without an expressly nominated dominant tenement in "non feudal deeds"[559] registered prior to November 28, 2004 remain enforceable by the proprietor of the benefitted property implied by common law rules (usually the land retained by the granter at the time of creation) for a period of ten years following November 28, 2004.[560] The owner of the benefitted property in these circumstances may enable continued enforceability if he registers the requisite notice of preservation before November 28, 2014.[561]

(vi) Feudal real burdens created prior to November 28, 2004 and preserved by notice registered before that date are enforceable by the benefitted property identified in that notice.[562]

Interest to enforce—A party wishing to enforce a real burden must show that he **34.66** has an interest to enforce it at the time he wishes to enforce. Such interest is also needed at the time of creation for the burden to be validly created. This interest (or *utilitas*) must relate to the land and not merely to the personal circumstances of the owner for the time being. Under statute, a person has such interest if breach of the real burden results in, or will result in, material detriment to the value or enjoyment of the person's right in the benefitted property.[563] In the determination of this interest a major factor will be the distance between the burdened and benefitted properties. There is no fixed rule as to a maximum distance beyond which no interest will be deemed to exist and the distance will certainly vary according to the nature of the particular obligation, its purpose and the nature of the burdened and benefitted properties. The nature and extent of the breach will also have relevance. The material detriment test may impose a higher threshold for enforcement than that found under the test employed in the previous common law.[564]

Special rules exist relating to interest to enforce an affirmative burden which requires payment of a cost. The person who seeks payment of this obligation (and has grounds to seek that payment) is regarded as having interest to enforce.[565]

---

[557] Title Conditions (Scotland) Act 2003 s.56(1)(a). See *Greenbelt Properties Ltd v Riggens*, 2010 G.W.D. 28–586.

[558] Title Conditions (Scotland) Act 2003 s.56(1)(b).

[559] Any non-feudal deeds—such as dispositions—creating burdens prior to November 28, 2004.

[560] Title Conditions (Scotland) Act 2003 s.49(2). This rule is based on the common law principle of implied enforcement rights in subdivision cases found in *JA MacTaggart & Co v Harrower* (1906) 8 F. 1101. For a recent discussion of the issue see *Barr v Macrae*, November 30, 2010, Lands Tribunal, reference LTS/TC/2009/37, 38 and 39.

[561] Title Conditions (Scotland) Act 2003 s.50.

[562] Abolition of Feudal Tenure (Scotland) Act s.18.

[563] Title Conditions (Scotland) Act 2003 s.8(3)(a).

[564] It has been argued that "material" detriment equates with "substantial" detriment; *Barker v Lewis*, 2007 S.L.T. (Sh. Ct) 48. The case was upheld by the Sheriff Principal, although it was noted that the threshold of enforcement is not as high as that originally suggested; *Barker v Lewis*, 2008 S.L.T. (Sh. Ct) 17. See also *Kettlewell v Turning Point Scotland*, 2011 S.L.T. (Sh. Ct) 143.

[565] Title Conditions (Scotland) Act 2003 s.8(3)(b).

34.67 Remedies for breach—The remedies available to a party wishing to enforce a real burden or condition include a personal action against the burdened proprietor for specific implement, interdict or damages. Under the common law the possibility of an 'irritancy' clause existed, which permitted the burdened proprietor's title to be extinguished if a real burden was breached. The abolition of irritancy in respect of real burdens is now found in statute. It discharges all rights of irritancy in respect of the breach of a real burden and precludes the future creation of such remedies.[566]

34.68 Extinction—Real burdens may be extinguished in various ways which include the following:

> (a) express discharge;
> (b) implied discharge;
> (c) loss of interest to enforce;
> (d) negative prescription;
> (e) compulsory purchase;
> (f) failure to appear in the Land Register;
> (g) variation and discharge by the Lands Tribunal.

If, however, there is no express time limitation and no inference to that effect which readily arises from the deed, the presumption in favour of freedom may not be used to terminate the real condition ahead of perpetuity. This results in many titles being burdened by real burdens which are manifestly out of date. The problem of obsolete real burdens has therefore been provided for in the Title Conditions (Scotland) Act 2003 which provides mechanisms for terminating the endurance of real burdens after a set period of time with limited provisions for extension. This involves a "sunset" rule whereby a burdened proprietor may trigger the application of rules to terminate the burden by service of notice on the benefited proprietor.[567] The sunset rule provides that the burdened owner may discharge real burdens which are more than 100 years old by drawing up a notice of termination,[568] and sending it to those benefited properties within 4 metres distance of the burdened property.[569] Notices must also be placed on lampposts in the vicinity and at the burdened property itself.[570] Benefitted owners then have eight weeks to apply to the Lands Tribunal for renewal of the burden.[571] If no application is made, the notice of termination may be registered[572] and the burden extinguished.[573]

34.69 Express discharge—The benefitted proprietor has a right to grant a discharge of the real burden.[574] The deed effecting the discharge is known as a minute of

---

[566] Abolition of Feudal Tenure (Scotland) Act 2000 s.53 in respect of feudal burdens; and Title Conditions (Scotland) Act 2003 s.67 in respect of non feudal burdens.

[567] Title Conditions (Scotland) Act 2003 ss.20–24.

[568] Title Conditions (Scotland) Act 2003 s.21, Schs 2 and 3.

[569] Title Conditions (Scotland) Act 2003 s.21(2)(a) and (3)(b).

[570] Title Conditions (Scotland) Act 2003 s.21(2)(b).

[571] Title Conditions (Scotland) Act 2003 ss.20(5) and 90(1)(b)(i). See *Council for Music in Hospitals v Trustees for Richard Gerard Associates*, 2008 S.L.T. (Lands Tr.) 17 and 44; *Brown v Richardson*, 2007 G.W.D. 28–490; 2007 G.W.D. 38–666.

[572] Title Conditions (Scotland) Act 2003 s.23.

[573] Title Conditions (Scotland) Act 2003 s.24.

[574] Title Conditions (Scotland) Act 2003 s.15.

waiver. Usually a sum of money is expected in exchange for an express discharge although the introduction of the Lands Tribunal jurisdiction (introduced in 1970) has tended to keep the amount within reasonable bounds, especially as the Tribunal may be willing to award expenses against a benefitted proprietor who has acted particularly unreasonably.[575] Once the deed of discharge is granted it should be registered in the General Register of Sasines or the Land Register of Scotland and it then becomes binding upon the granter of the discharge and his successors in title in the dominant tenement.[576]

In the case of community burdens it is possible for a deed of discharge to be signed by a simple majority of owners in the community,[577] or by all benefitted proprietors in "adjacent units",[578] rather than by every benefitted proprietor. In a similar manner to the "sunset" rule, the deed must then be served on all non-signatories, allowing them eight weeks to apply to the Lands Tribunal to preserve the burden,[579] after which time the deed may be registered and the burden discharged.

Implied discharge—In some situations a dominant proprietor will be deemed to have granted a discharge not by granting a deed but by his actions or inaction. If the benefitted proprietor knows of a breach of a real burden and does nothing in relation to that breach, and the burdened proprietor has relied on that inaction the rule of acquiescence does not allow that obligation to be enforced at a later date. The most obvious case is where a house has been built in contravention of a real burden without protest. Acquiescence is a feature of the common law, but the rule has also now been restated in statutory form in relation to real burdens.[580] Under the statutory rule, the following matters must be satisfied: **34.70**

(a) the real burden is breached;
(b) material expenditure has been incurred by the burdened proprietor in respect of that breach;
(c) the benefit of that expenditure would be the lost if the burden were to be enforced;
(d) the owner of the benefitted property consented to the work, or all those who hold enforcement rights in relation to the burden either consented or failed to object within 12 weeks of substantial completion of the work;
(e) the work is sufficiently obvious, so that those with enforcement rights either knew or ought to have known about it.

Under this statutory rule, the burden will be extinguished to the extent of the breach if all the aforementioned criteria are satisfied. The position is, therefore, that discharge with be implied once the 12 week period has expired with no raised objections.

Loss of interest to enforce—Loss of interest to enforce a real burden[581] may occur where such a change of circumstances has occurred that there is no point in enforcing the burden. The consequence of this is that loss of interest may occur **34.71**

---

[575] *Harris v Dunglass*, 1993 S.L.T. (Lands Tr.) 56.
[576] Land Registration (Scotland) Act 1979 s.18.
[577] Title Conditions (Scotland) Act 2003 s.33.
[578] Title Conditions (Scotland) Act 2003 s.35.
[579] Title Conditions (Scotland) Act 2003 Sch.4.
[580] Title Conditions (Scotland) Act 2003 s.16.
[581] Title Conditions (Scotland) Act 2003 s.17.

without any act on the part of the dominant proprietor—it may simply result from events. It would seem, however, there is no single reported case in which the principle has been applied to extinguish a burden.[582] As a result this doctrine is not of much use to a burdened proprietor seeking freedom from a burden and it has largely been superseded by the operation of the powers of the Lands Tribunal.

34.72 **Negative prescription**—A failure to enforce a real burden in the face of a contravention for a period of twenty years will render the land obligation unenforceable under the common law. The position has been improved by statute which provides that where a real burden is breached to any extent and during a period of five years beginning with the breach neither a relevant claim nor a relevant acknowledgement is made, then the burden shall be extinguished on the expiry of that five year period to the extent of the breach.[583]

34.73 **Compulsory purchase**—Real burdens affecting a plot of ground may be extinguished when the plot of ground which they affect is compulsorily purchased.[584] Under the common law there has always been doubt as to whether the extinction was limited to those real burdens which were inconsistent with the purposes for which the purchase was made. Statute clarifies this obscurity by providing that real burdens will be extinguished in all time coming on the acquisition of land following upon from a confirmed compulsory purchase order.[585]

34.74 **Failure to appear in the land register**—The mere fact that a real burden appears in the Land Register is not a guarantee of its enforceability. By contrast, where a real burden fails to be entered or summarised on the Title Sheet of a registered interest in land it will be extinguished.[586] In some cases the Keeper may be willing to take a view with little prompting that a burden is no longer subsisting and he will delete it. In other cases he may require the party seeking deletion to obtain declarator that the burden is unenforceable whereupon he will remove the burden as part of the process of rectification.[587]

34.75 **Variation and discharge by the lands tribunal**—The Title Conditions (Scotland) Act 2003 Pt 9 confers power on the Lands Tribunal to vary "title conditions" as defined in that Act. The definition is wide and includes real burdens; servitudes; affirmative obligations in servitudes where these fall on the benefitted proprietor, such as obligations on the benefitted proprietor to maintain a servitude road over which a servitude of access is granted; and conditions relating to land in registerable leases.[588] The standard conditions in a standard security cannot be varied by the Lands Tribunal as they are not included in the definition of "title condition". Nor can the Lands Tribunal vary servitude conditions that impose negative restraints on the exercise of a servitude or limit the purpose for which the

---

[582] The high standard of the law was exemplified in *Howard de Walden Estates Ltd v Bowmaker Ltd*, 1965 S.C. 163.

[583] Title Conditions (Scotland) Act 2003 s.18. There are special rules for pre-emptions, redemptions or reversions in s.18(2).

[584] *Town Council of Oban v Callander and Oban Railway* (1892) 19 R. 912.

[585] Title Conditions (Scotland) Act 2003 ss.106–107.

[586] Land Registration (Scotland) Act 1979 s.3(1)(a).

[587] *Brookefield Developments Ltd v Keeper of the Registers of Scotland*, 1989 S.C.L.R. 435.

[588] Title Conditions (Scotland) Act 2003 s.122(1).

servitude may be exercised. So too the Lands Tribunal cannot alter the fractions of the various co-owners who hold *pro indiviso* shares in common property.[589]

In terms of the 2003 Act the Lands Tribunal for Scotland has power on application by the burdened proprietor to grant an order varying or discharging a title condition.[590] The terms "discharge" and "variation" are not defined, but the former is taken to means that the obligation is removed in full whilst the latter means that only part of the obligation is removed or that the obligation is altered in some way. The order of the Tribunal is binding on all parties having interest when an extract thereof is registered in the General Register of Sasines (or the Land Register of Scotland as the case may be).[591] The Lands Tribunal now also has power to issue a declarator of enforceability of a real burden.[592]

There are special provisions for variation and discharge of community burdens which may be made by the owners of at least one quarter of the units in a community.[593]

Excluded title conditions—The Lands Tribunal can vary or discharge most title **34.76** conditions but there are certain excluded title conditions which cannot be varied or discharged. These include[594]:

    (a) obligations relating to the right to work minerals;
    (b) obligations imposed on behalf of the Crown for the purposes of naval, military or air force purposes;
    (c) obligations imposed on behalf of the Crown or an international airport authority for civil aviation purposes or in connection with the use of land as an aerodrome; and
    (d) obligations imposed in any agricultural tenancy or croft.

Title conditions cannot be varied within five years of their creation if the deed in which the burden was created provides expressly that this is the case. If the deed is silent the real burden is capable of variation and discharge from the first day of creation.[595] The Tribunal may exercise its power to vary or discharge only where it is satisfied in all the circumstances that it is "reasonable"[596] having taken into account a statutory list of various different factors into consideration in reaching its view.[597]

Payment of compensation—A benefitted proprietor is not guaranteed a payment **34.77** of compensation for the variation or discharge of a title condition but the requirement to pay compensation is again a matter for the discretion of the Tribunal. In exchange for the Lands Tribunal granting a variation or discharge, the burdened proprietor may be directed to pay to the benefitted proprietor compensation. This

---

[589] *Dalby v Bracken*, June 13, 2008, Lands Tribunal, LTS/TC/2007/51.
[590] There is now a considerable volume of case law but the leading case remains *Ord v Mashford*, 2006 S.L.T. (Lands Tr.) 15. There is a sequel to that case in *Lawrie and Ronald v Mashford*, 2008 G.W.D. 7–129; Lands Tribunal, LTS/TC/2007/28.
[591] Title Conditions (Scotland) Act 2003 s.104.
[592] Title Conditions (Scotland) Act 2003 s.90(1)(a)(ii).
[593] Title Conditions (Scotland) Act 2003 s.91. See *Fenwick v National Trust for Scotland*, 2009 G.W.D. 32–538, Lands Tribunal.
[594] Title Conditions (Scotland) Act 2003 s.90(3) and Sch.11.
[595] Title Conditions (Scotland) Act 2003 s.92.
[596] Title Conditions (Scotland) Act 2003 s.98.
[597] Title Conditions (Scotland) Act 2003 s.100.

compensation may be paid only under one of two alternative heads of claim.[598]
These are either:

> (a) a sum to compensate for any substantial loss or disadvantage resulting
> from the order. The loss or disadvantage must be substantial but there
> is no minimum sum for compensation. It is possible that even in these
> circumstances no compensation whatsoever may be awarded. It is
> possible, however, that where there is a very substantial loss or disadvan-
> tage this might be a reason for refusing a variation or discharge.
>
> (b) a sum to make up for any substantial loss or disadvantage resulting from
> the order or a sum to make up for any effect which the title condition
> produced, at the time when it was first imposed, in reducing the consid-
> eration paid for the burdened tenement. A common situation is where
> land is sold off by a proprietor to a local authority on the basis that it will
> be permanently used for public purposes.[599] This obligation is inserted in
> the titles by means of a real burden. The price for the land is substantially
> less than would have been obtained if the land were sold on the open
> market. Years later the public use ceases and the purchaser wishes to
> develop the land for a retail use. The party entitled to enforce the real
> burden is unwilling to discharge the land obligation without payment of
> a sum of money in exchange. That party is entitled to receive some
> compensation given the original reduced consideration for the plot.
> However, the Lands Tribunal cannot adjust the sum awarded to take
> account of inflation or award any interest.[600]

There is no ground upon which the person entitled to enforce the title condition is
entitled to what is known as "a cut of the action"—a share of the development
value of land. So if a party entitled to enforce a real burden wishes to grant a
minute of waiver only in exchange for a share of the increased development value
of the land his claim for compensation will be rejected by the Lands Tribunal.

34.78 Substitute provisions—The Lands Tribunal has a power to impose substitute
title conditions as appear to the Lands Tribunal to be reasonable as a result of the
variation or discharge of the original burden provided these are accepted by the
burdened proprietor.[601] As a result, the burdened proprietor may veto the use of
this power but if he does so the variation or discharge for which he has applied
may not be granted. This power has been used in a number of cases to allow variations which might otherwise not have been granted, for example, by permitting
building subject to conditions such as the installation of sound insulation to
prevent the drifting of music, the operation of fans to remove smells of food of the
planting of screening by trees to protect privacy.[602] Whilst there is little authority
on the matter it is submitted that the obligations which can be so imposed must
comply with the rules of content relative to real conditions or servitudes as the
case may be.

---

[598] Title Conditions (Scotland) Act 2003 s.90(6)–(7).

[599] *Gorrie & Banks Ltd v Musselburgh Town Council*, 1974 S.L.T. (Lands Tr.) 5.

[600] *Watt v Garden*, 2011 Hous. L.R. 79, Lands Tr.

[601] Title Conditions (Scotland) Act 2003 s.90(8) and (11).

[602] e.g. *Jarron v Stuart*, March 23 and May 5, 2011, Lands Tribunal, LTS/TC/2010/18. See also a
case under earlier legislation: *Crombie v George Heriot's Trust*, 1972 S.L.T. (Lands Tr.) 40.

Personal real burdens—Scottish common law does not generally recognise real **34.79**
burdens which are enforceable by a person or a legal entity who does not own a
separate tenement. A functional exception to this was in relation to feudal real
burdens, which allowed enforcement by the superior despite the fact that no separate benefitted property was held—however, in this context the rule was complied
with as the *dominium directum* was a real right albeit in the same item of property.
However, true personal real burdens did exist in a ragbag of statutory provisions
generally conferring powers on authorities to control land.[603] The most significant
of these remains obligations in agreements regulating the development and use of
land entered into in terms of the Town and Country Planning (Scotland) Act 1997
s.75. Following feudal abolition, the concept of personal enforcement has been
expanded into a separate family of legal devices by virtue of the Title Conditions
(Scotland) Act 2003 under the collective name of "personal real burden".[604] These
types of burdens include:

(a) *Conservation burdens.*[605] These are burdens for protecting architectural
or historical characteristics of land, and other special characteristics
including nature conservation. They can only be held by Scottish
Ministers or bodies prescribed by Scottish Ministers as a conservation
body.[606]

(b) *Rural housing burdens.*[607] Held by designated "rural housing bodies"[608]
these burdens are limited in content to pre-emption rights regarding
housing offered at a reduced rate. A rural housing burden enables the
rural housing body a pre-emption right to buy back the land on subsequent re-sales.[609]

(c) *Maritime burdens.*[610] On behalf of the public, the Crown has power to
impose real burdens on the sea bed or foreshore within territorial
waters.[611]

(d) *Economic development burdens.*[612] This type of burden must be in favour
of a local authority or the Scottish Ministers and promote economic
development, such as through the disposal of land which must be used
for a particular type of industry.

(e) *Health care burdens.*[613] This type of burden must be in favour of the
Scottish Ministers and promote the provision of healthcare facilities, and
is similar in nature to the economic development burden.

(f) *Climate change burdens.*[614] This enables the creation of a personal real
burden in obligation in favour of a public body or trust, or the Scottish
Ministers for the purpose of reducing greenhouse gas emissions.

---

[603] R.R.M. Paisley, "Personal Real Burdens", 2005 Jur. Rev. 377–422.
[604] Title Conditions (Scotland) Act 2003 s.1(3).
[605] Title Conditions (Scotland) Act 2003 s.38.
[606] Title Conditions (Scotland) Act 2003 s.38(4).
[607] Title Conditions (Scotland) Act 2003 s.43.
[608] Title Conditions (Scotland) Act 2003 s.43(1) and (5).
[609] Title Conditions (Scotland) Act 2003 s.84(1) proviso.
[610] Title Conditions (Scotland) Act 2003 s.44.
[611] Title Conditions (Scotland) Act 2003 s.44(1) and (3).
[612] Title Conditions (Scotland) Act 2003 s.45. See *Teague Developments Ltd v City of Edinburgh Council*, February 27, 2008, Lands Tribunal, LTS/AFT44/2007/02.
[613] Title Conditions (Scotland) Act 2003 s.46.
[614] Title Conditions (Scotland) Act 2003 s.46A.

    (g) *Manager burdens.*[615] This type of burden permits a developer to appoint a manager for a development,[616] to allow the developer to keep an element of control in relation to incomplete developments.

    (h) *Personal pre-emption burdens.* This type of burden is a former feudal burden which conferred a right of pre-emption, which has been converted and preserved under Abolition of Feudal Tenure (Scotland) Act 2000 s.18A.

    (i) *Personal redemption burdens.* Similar to personal pre-emption burdens, person redemption burdens preserve feudal burdens which conferred rights of redemption.[617]

As there is no benefitted tenement such obligations cannot be varied or discharged by the Lands Tribunal in terms of the Title Conditions (Scotland) Act 2003 Pt 9 unless there is an express statutory exception. Further, in respect of personal real burdens, interest to enforce is presumed.[618]

VII. COMMON PROPERTY AND INTEREST

34.80 Nature of right—Property may be vested in two or more persons either jointly or in common. Where property is held jointly the owners have no separate estates but only one estate vested in them *pro indiviso*, not merely in respect of possession but also in respect of the right of property. The right of a joint owner accresces on his death to the others and cannot be alienated or disposed of either *inter vivos* or *mortis causa*. Instances of this mode of holding are found in the ownership of trustees, the rights of members in the property of a club, and joint liferents.

    In the case of property held in common each proprietor has a title to his own share which he may alienate or burden[619] by his separate act. On the death of one of the common owners his share will pass under his will or transmit to his heirs.[620] Examples of this holding include that of heirs-portioners under the former law of intestate succession, and disponees in a disposition granting property to "A and B".[621]

34.81 Management of common property—All the proprietors are entitled to a voice in the management of the property, and no one of them has a right to a greater measure of control than another. Any one of them may, therefore, prevent any alteration of the condition of the property or any "extraordinary use" of the

---

[615] Title Conditions (Scotland) Act 2003 s.63.

[616] Title Conditions (Scotland) Act 2003 s.63(1), (2) and (4).

[617] Abolition of Feudal Tenure (Scotland) Act 2000 s.18A.

[618] Title Conditions (Scotland) Act 2003 s.47. This statutory presumption is irrebuttable: *Teague Developments Limited v City of Edinburgh Council*, February 27, 2008, Lands Tribunal.

[619] *McLeod v Cedar Holdings Ltd*, 1989 S.L.T. 620.

[620] *Cargill v Muir* (1837) 15 S. 408, per Lord Moncreiff; *Johnston v Craufurd* (1855) 17 D. 1023, per Lord Curriehill; *Schaw v Black* (1889) 16 R. 336, per Lord Shand. On the distinction between common property and joint property see *Banff Burgh Council v Ruthin Castle Ltd*, 1944 S.C. 36 at 64; *Munro v Munro*, 1972 S.L.T. (Sh. Ct) 6; Smith, *Short Commentary on the Law of Scotland* (1962), p.479; Gordon and Wortley, *Scottish Land Law* (2009), Vol.1, paras 15–09 et seq.; K.G.C. Reid, "Common Property: Clarification and Confusion", 1985 S.L.T. (News) 57; Reid, *The Law of Property in Scotland* (1996), paras 17 et seq.

[621] See Gordon and Wortley, *Scottish Land Law* (2009), Vol.1, paras 15–11 et seq.; *Steele v Caldwell*, 1979 S.L.T. 228; *Smith v Mackintosh*, 1988 S.C. 453; 1989 S.L.T. 148; Reid, *The Law of Property in Scotland* (1996), paras 17 et seq.

subject,[622] and the purported creation of a right of servitude over the property at the instance of one owner will be null if the others do not consent.[623] The rule is *in re communi melior est conditio prohibentis* (in common property the objector is in the better position). An exception to this rule is admitted in regard to necessary operations in rebuilding and repairing; these are not to be stopped by the opposition of any of the owners.[624]

It is also a general, although not a universal, rule that all the proprietors must concur in actions against other parties relative to the common property.[625] One proprietor alone has no title to bring a declarator of property in regard to the subjects, for a decree in the action would not be *res judicata* as against the other common proprietors[626]; nor can one prosecute an action of removing against a tenant possessing under a lease granted by all.[627] But any one of the proprietors may take proceedings for the purpose of protecting the subject from encroachment or trespass.[628]

Where one common owner without the agreement of the others enjoys sole occupation of the subjects, recompense is not an appropriate remedy in a dispute between them.[629] Agreement to such occupation does not constitute a lease.[630] Where common property is a matrimonial home,[631] either spouse may seek the court's authority to carry out non-essential repairs or improvements appropriate for the reasonable enjoyment of the spouse's occupancy rights.[632] The court may apportion any expenditure incurred between the spouses.[633] The court may also

---

[622] Bell, *Principles*, s.1075; cf. *Bailey's Exrs v Upper Crathes Fishing Ltd*, 1987 S.L.T. 405. The question of "what is ordinary use" was considered in the sheriff court in the case of *Apps v Sinclair* Unreported February 23, 2006, Sheriff Principal R.A. Dunlop QC, Sheriffdom of Tayside Central and Fife, A1173/04, in which it was held by the Sheriff Principal that "in the absence of agreement to the contrary, the ordinary use of common property ought primarily to be judged by reference to the nature of that property". See also *Mason v Jones*, 2009 G.W.D. 9–152; *Rafique v Amin*, 1997 S.L.T. 1385; *Carmichael v Simpson*, 1932 S.L.T. (Sh. Ct) 16. The matter is discussed in Reid and Gretton, *Conveyancing 2006*, pp.10–11 and *Conveyancing 2009*, pp.106–107.

[623] *W.V.S. Office Premises v Currie*, 1969 S.C. 170; *Fearnan Partnership v Grindlay*, 1992 S.C. (HL) 38; 1992 S.L.T. 460.

[624] Bell, *Principles*, s.1075; *Deans v Woolfson*, 1922 S.C. 221, a case now disapproved insofar as it held that the rights of common owners in relation to control and management of property were governed by equitable considerations: *Rafique v Amin*, 1997 S.L.T. 1385.

[625] *Lade v Largs Bakery Co* (1863) 2 M. 17, per Lord Deas; cf. *Michael v Carruthers*, 1998 S.L.T. 1179.

[626] *Millar v Cathcart* (1861) 23 D. 743.

[627] Erskine, II, 6, 53; *Aberdeen Station Committee v N.B. Ry* (1890) 17 R. 975 at 984.

[628] *Warrand v Watson* (1905) 8 F. 253; *Aberdeen Station Committee v N.B. Ry* (1890) 17 R. 975 at 981 and 984.

[629] *Denholm's Trs v Denholm*, 1984 S.L.T. 319; Gordon and Wortley, *Scottish Land Law* (2009), Vol.1, para.15–32.

[630] It has been held by the House of Lords that co-owners cannot grant a lease in favour of one of their number: *Clydesdale Bank Plc v Davidson*, 1998 S.C. (HL) 51. Davidson could not acquire a real right such as to enable him to resist the Bank. The House of Lords held that he occupied as a co-proprietor, and not as a tenant. See Gordon and Wortley, *Scottish Land Law* (2009), Vol.1, para.15–19.

[631] Matrimonial Homes (Family Protection) (Scotland) Act 1981 s.22, as amended by the Law Reform (Miscellaneous Provisions) (Scotland) Act 1985 s.13. See also the Civil Partnership Act 2004 s.135(1).

[632] Matrimonial Homes (Family Protection) (Scotland) Act 1981 s.2(4)(a); and see Ch.44, below. See also the Civil Partnership Act 2004 s.102(4)(a). It should be noted that the treatment of matrimonial homes and civil partnership family homes in this paragraph is predicated upon the model of common ownership, where spouses or civil partners both have entitled status in terms of the statutes. The rights of non-entitled spouses and civil partners, and of co-habitees, are more properly the subject of Ch.44, below.

[633] Matrimonial Homes (Family Protection) (Scotland) Act 1981 s.2(4)(b). See also the Civil Partnership Act 2004 s.102(4)(b).

pronounce an exclusion order against one spouse,[634] or otherwise regulate their rights of occupancy.[635]

An important innovation was made under the Civil Partnership Act 2004. A civil partnership is a relationship between two people of the same sex which is formed when they register as civil partners of each other.[636] The Act uses the term family home rather than matrimonial home, but, nevertheless, contains management of common property provisions which are parallel to those for matrimonial homes. It should be noted that in an action for divorce either party to the marriage, and in an action for dissolution of a civil partnership either civil partner, may apply to the court for, amongst other remedies, an order for the transfer of property to him by the other party to the action.[637]

34.82 Division of the property—No one is bound to remain indefinitely associated with another or others in the ownership of common property. Any one of the proprietors may, even against the wish of the others, insist on a division of the property.[638] This right to have the property divided is a necessary incident of common property, and it is in law impossible to create common property and at the same time to exclude this right.[639] But the right must be exercised with due regard to the interests of all the proprietors. While the right of the proprietor who wishes to terminate the community is to have the subject divided,[640] where division is impracticable or would entail a sacrifice to an appreciable extent of the interests of the parties (as was formerly found in the case of a feuing estate), a sale of the whole and division of the price will be ordered.[641] An action of ejection by one common owner against another is probably incompetent[642] except where associated with division and sale.[643]

In an action at the instance of one spouse for the division and sale of a matrimonial home owned by the spouses in common decree may, in the discretion of the court, be refused or postponed for such period as the court may consider reasonable or granted subject to such conditions as it may prescribe.[644] In

---

[634] Matrimonial Homes (Family Protection) (Scotland) Act 1981 s.4, as amended. See also the Civil Partnership Act 2004 s.104.

[635] Matrimonial Homes (Family Protection) (Scotland) Act 1981 s.3. See also the Civil Partnership Act 2004 s.103.

[636] Civil Partnership Act 2004 s.1. See further below, Ch.44.

[637] Family Law (Scotland) Act 1985 s.8(1)(aa), as amended by the Family Law (Scotland) Act 2006 s.20(3).

[638] *Brock v Hamilton* (1857) 19 D. 701; *Anderson v Anderson* (1857) 19 D. 700; *Upper Crathes Fishings Ltd v Bailey's Exrs*, 1991 S.C. 30; 1991 S.L.T. 747; *Farquharson v Farquharson*, 1991 G.W.D. 5–271; in proceedings for division a counterclaim for the defender's expenditure has been held competent: *Johnston v Robson*, 1995 S.L.T. (Sh. Ct) 26. In general, see Gordon and Wortley, *Scottish Land Law* (2009), Vol.1, para.15–29 seriatim; Reid, *The Law of Property in Scotland* (1996), para.32.

[639] *Grant v George Heriot's Trust* (1906) 8 F. 647 at 658.

[640] *Morrison v Kirk*, 1912 S.C. 44; *Williams v Cleveland and Highland Holdings Ltd*, 1993 S.L.T. 398.

[641] *Brock v Hamilton* (1857) 19 D. 701; *Thom v Macbeth* (1875) 3 R. 161; *Campbell v Murray*, 1972 S.L.T. 249 (sale by private bargain competent); *Scrimgeour v Scrimgeour*, 1988 S.L.T. 590 (competent to grant warrant to a wife to purchase her husband's one-half share at the open market price fixed by a reporter); *Berry v Berry (No.2)*, 1989 S.L.T. 292; *Miller Group Ltd v Tasker*, 1993 S.L.T. 207; *Grieve v Morrison*, 1993 S.L.T. 852. The division need not necessarily be an equal one: see e.g. *Ralston v Jackson*, 1994 S.L.T. 771.

[642] *Price v Watson*, 1951 S.C. 359. See also *Langstane (SP) Housing Association Ltd v Davie*, 1994 S.C.L.R. 158 (an action for recovery of possession held incompetent).

[643] *Barclay v Penman*, 1984 S.L.T. 376; *Stewart's Trustee v Stewart*, 2011 G.W.D. 31–671.

[644] Matrimonial Homes (Family Protection) (Scotland) Act 1981 s.19; *Hall v Hall*, 1987 S.L.T. (Sh. Ct) 15; *Berry v Berry (No.1)*, 1988 S.L.T. 650. The Matrimonial Homes (Family Protection) (Scotland)

exercising that discretion the court is to have regard to all the circumstances of the case and, in particular, to the conduct of the spouses, their needs and resources, the needs of any child of the family, any business use of the home and whether the spouse seeking decree has offered suitable alternative accommodation to the other spouse.[645] As these provisions apply only to an action between spouses they cannot be invoked after the dissolution of the marriage, but there is no limitation on the length of any period of postponement.[646] Similar provisions also apply in the case of family homes owned in common by civil partners.[647]

An action of division and sale may also be sisted pending the outcome of an application by one spouse for an order for the transfer of the property of the matrimonial home.[648]

Commonty: Runrig—Commonty[649] is a species of common property,[650] once **34.83** highly important, but now almost extinct, held as an accessory of the private estates of the commoners. Originally it was regarded as of value only for pasturage and other uses of the surface, but it has been held to carry right to the minerals. Difficulty has been experienced in distinguishing this right from a servitude of pasturage. In questions as to the uses to which a commonty may be put, the rule *melior est conditio prohibentis* applies, and nothing which is not sanctioned by usage may be done without the consent of all the commoners.[651] No action of division of commonty lands was competent until the Division of Commonties Act 1695 (c.38), whereby it is enacted:

> "that all commonties, except the commonties belonging to the King and royal burghs may be divided at the instance of any having interest by summons raised against all concerned before the Lords of Session who are hereby empowered . . . to value and divide the same according to the value of the rights and interests of the several parties concerned."

Under the statute where the commonty is divided among the common proprietors each receives a share of the commonty next to, and corresponding to the value of, his lands.[652] Where the value of the subjects in dispute is small, the action may be brought in the sheriff court.[653]

Act 1981 Act ss.7 and 9(2), do not apply to actions of division and sale: *Dunsmore v Dunsmore*, 1986 S.L.T. (Sh. Ct) 9. Cf. *Burrows v Burrows*, 1986 S.L.T. 1313; *Bush v Bush*, 2000 S.L.T. (Sh. Ct) 22. See also the Civil Partnership Act 2004 s.110.

[645] For a decision in the sheriff court (Lothian and Borders) at Edinburgh see *B v B*, 2010 G.W.D. 24-454. This case has been the subject of a number of commentaries, including Reid and Gretton, *Conveyancing 2010* (2011), pp.9-10; S. Lilley, "A burden discharged" (2010) J.L.S.S. 49 (August), and "Division and sale—matrimonial home", Fam. L.B. 2010, 107-7 (September).

[646] *Crow v Crow*, 1986 S.L.T. 270.

[647] Civil Partnership Act 2004 s.110. The wording of s.110 is based upon that in the Matrimonial Homes (Family Protection) (Scotland) Act 1981 s.19. The two Acts mirror each other in respect of many provisions. It is therefore possible that the courts may have regard to matrimonial homes case law in determining civil partnership disputes.

[648] *Rae v Rae*, 1991 S.L.T. 454 (contrast with the previous law: *Dickson v Dickson*, 1982 S.L.T. 270).

[649] See Gordon and Wortley, *Scottish Land Law* (2009), Vol.1, paras 15-179—15-188.

[650] See, however, Lord Justice Clerk Ross, obiter, in *Johnston v MacFarlane's Trustees*, 1987 S.L.T. 593 at 597, citing Bell, *Principles*, s.1087.

[651] *Campbell v Campbell* Unreported January 24, 1809, FC; *Innes v Hepburn* (1859) 21 D. 832.

[652] See *Macandrew v Crerar*, 1929 S.C. 699.

[653] Sheriff Courts (Scotland) Act 1907 s.5.

Runrig lands are those which are in alternate or intermixed patches and belong to different proprietors. The Runrig Lands Act 1695 (c.23) authorises the division of such lands.[654]

The Crofting Reform (Scotland) Act 2010[655] specifies that the Keeper of the Registers of Scotland must establish and maintain a public register of crofts, common grazings and land held runrig.

34.84　Common interest—In a passage[656] which has been accepted as an authoritative exposition of the meaning of this term,[657] Bell says that:

> "[A] species of right differing from common property takes place among the owners of subjects possessed in separate portions but still united by their common interest. It is recognised in law as 'common interest'. It accompanies and is incorporated with the several rights of individual property. In such a case a sale or division cannot resolve the difficulties which may arise in management, but the exercise and effect of the common interest must, when dissensions arise, be regulated by law or equity."

Riparian proprietors have a common interest in the water of the stream.[658] Where a square is laid out in a town with a central garden for the use of the owners of the houses forming the square, these, in the general case, have a common interest in the garden, although they may have no right of property in it.[659] Neighbouring owners may have a common interest in a passage giving a common access or in a boundary wall or in an area reserved for light or common use.[660] Interdict will normally be the most appropriate remedy in cases involving acts contrary to the common interest.[661]

But it was historically most commonly in the case of flatted houses that the most frequent illustration of this interest could be found. The Tenements (Scotland) Act 2004 (asp 11) has abolished the common law rules of common interest in respect of tenements, except for questions affecting both a tenement and some other land or building, or where an issue relates to a tenement and any land not pertaining to the tenement.[662] Whilst the Tenements (Scotland) Act has regulated and clarified many of the opacities in the common law of tenement, it operates by substantially enacting the common law of tenement as a default law, taking effect where the title deeds have not dealt with a particular issue regulated under the

---

[654] For fuller particulars as to commonty and runrig see Rankine, *The Law of Landownership in Scotland* (1909), pp.598 et seq.; Bell, *Principles*, ss.1087–1099.

[655] Crofting Reform (Scotland) Act 2010 (asp 14). Subject to commencement.

[656] Bell, *Principles*, s.1086.

[657] See *Grant v George Heriot's Trust* (1906) 8 F. 647 at 658; *Giuliani v Smith*, 1925 S.C. (HL) 45 at 57; *Fearnan Partnership v Grindlay*, 1992 S.C. (HL) 38; 1992 S.L.T. 460; Gordon and Wortley, *Scottish Land Law* (2009), Vol.1, paras 15–37 et seq.

[658] See para.34.24, above.

[659] *George Watson's Hospital v Cormack* (1883) 11 R. 320; *Grant v George Heriot's Trust* (1906) 8 F. 647.

[660] *Mackenzie v Carrick* (1869) 7 M. 419; *Grant v George Heriot's Trust* (1906) 8 F. 647; *Thom v Hetherington*, 1987 S.C. 185; 1988 S.L.T. 724 (a decision which provoked a Scottish Law Commission Consultation Paper, *Mutual Boundary Walls*: see 1992 S.L.T. (News) 199). As to the common interest of the inhabitants of a burgh in a street and the space above it, see *Donald & Sons v Esslemont & Macintosh*, 1923 S.C. 122.

[661] See, e.g. *Donald & Sons v Esslemont & Macintosh*, 1923 S.C. 122.

[662] Tenements (Scotland) Act 2004 s.7.

Act.[663] The doctrine of common interest still pertains in relation to such matters as non-tidal waters, and gables, and boundary walls and fences.[664]

Flatted houses—Historically, where different floors or storeys of the same **34.85** house belonged to different persons, there was no common property among the proprietors of the several floors or storeys, but the respective rights of property in them were qualified by the common interest of all. As already noted, the Tenements (Scotland) Act 2004 has, subject to two qualifications,[665] abolished the common law rules of common interest in respect of tenements.[666] As was formerly the case, the titles may contain express provision as to the rights and obligations of the proprietors, in which case the provisions in the title would apply, but, in the absence of such provision, what was known as the "law of the tenement" came into effect. The law of the tenement is now superseded by provisions in the Tenements (Scotland) Act 2004. This Act operates by substantially enacting the common law of tenement as a default law, taking effect where the title deeds have not dealt with a particular issue regulated under the Act. It is accordingly still important to have an awareness of the old common law provisions. At the very least, cases decided under the common law may still help inform the interpretation of the new statutory provisions. Furthermore, an understanding of the former law of the tenement may assist in the interpretation of opt-out provisions in old titles.

Common law of the tenement—Briefly stated, the law of the tenement was as **34.86** follows[667]: the owners of the lower storeys must uphold them for the support of the upper; and the owner of the highest storey must uphold it as a cover for the lower. But there is no absolute duty of support or protection, and to establish liability to make reparation the relevant proprietor must be shown to have been negligent.[668] The obligation to repair falls on the proprietor of the part requiring repair, while the common interest of the other proprietors entitles them to insist

---

[663] For analyses of the Act, see Reid and Gretton, *Conveyancing* (2004), pp.121–50 and C.G. Van der Merwe, "The Tenements (Scotland) Act 2004: A Brief Evaluation", 2004 S.L.T. (News) 211–13.

[664] In *Willemse v French* [2011] CSOH 51, the Lord Ordinary (Tyre) considered whether a claimed right in relation to a private road might constitute common property, common interest or servitude. It was held, in the particular circumstances, that the words "a right in common . . . to the access" created a servitude and not common property. The case is discussed in Reid and Gretton, *Conveyancing* (2011), pp.102–103.

[665] Tenements (Scotland) Act 2004 s.7(a) and (b). The two exceptions relate to questions affecting both the tenement and some other building or former building, and questions affecting both the tenement and any land not pertaining to the tenement.

[666] See para.34.84, above.

[667] *Giuliani v Smith*, 1925 S.C. (HL) 45; and see *Wells v New House Purchasers*, 1964 S.L.T. (Sh. Ct) 2; Gordon and Wortley, *Scottish Land Law* (2009), Vol.1, paras 15–46 et seq; Reid, *The Law of Property in Scotland* (1996), paras 227 et seq.

[668] *Thomson v St Cuthbert's Cooperative Association*, 1958 S.C. 380; *Kerr v McGreevy*, 1970 S.L.T. (Sh. Ct) 7; *Doran v Smith*, 1971 S.L.T. (Sh. Ct) 46. In *Stewart v Malik*, 2009 S.C. 265 and *Crolla v Hussain*, 2008 S.L.T. (Sh. Ct) 145 the Inner House and the Sheriff Principal, Lothian and Borders, allowed proofs in similar cases in which proprietors had instructed works by independent contractors which had resulted in the loss of support. These cases were decided under the old law of the tenement and do not refer to the 2004 Act. In the former case, it was held by Lord President Hamilton that "in Scotland the law of the tenement . . . casts on the 'servient' proprietor a positive duty in carrying out works which may affect support to avoid endangering the 'dominant' property. That duty, which is personal to him, cannot, in my view, be elided by the instruction of an independent contractor to execute the works." See also the Lord Ordinary (Emslie) in *Morris Amusements Ltd v Glasgow City Council*, 2009 S.L.T. 697 at [43].

that the repairs be carried out.[669] The roof belongs to the owner of the highest storey, but he may be compelled to keep it in repair and to refrain from injuring it. If that storey is divided among several proprietors, each must uphold that portion of the roof which covers his property.[670] A garret may not without consent be converted into an attic storey.[671] The solum on which the flatted house is erected, the area in front, and the back ground are presumed to belong to the owner of the lowest floor, or to the owners thereof severally, subject to the common interest of the other proprietors to prevent injury to their flats, especially by depriving them of light.[672] The external walls belong to each owner in so far as they enclose his flat[673]; but the other owners can prevent operations on them which would endanger the security of the tenement. The gables are common to the owner of each flat, so far as they bound his property, and to the owner of the adjoining house, but he and the other owners in the tenement have cross-rights of common interest to prevent injury to the stability of the building.[674] The floor and ceiling of each flat are divided in ownership by an imaginary line drawn through the middle of the joists; they may be used for the ordinary purposes, but may not be weakened or exposed to unusual risk from fire.[675] The common passages and stairs are the common property of all to whose premises they form an access, and the walls which bound them are the common property of these persons and the owners on their further side.[676]

Under the provisions in the Tenements (Scotland) Act 2004, the former common law doctrine of common interest is abolished for tenements, subject to the two exclusions identified above. The doctrine also still lives on in relation to such matters as non-tidal waters and boundary walls and fences. In relation to tenements the former common law of common interest has been restated in statutory form. Section 8 of the Act introduces a duty to maintain so as to provide support and shelter etc., while s.9 specifies a prohibition on interference with support or shelter etc.

34.87 **The Tenements (Scotland) Act 2004**—The Tenements (Scotland) Act 2004 (hereinafter the "2004 Act") came into force on November 28, 2004. The Act had its origins in the Scottish Law Commission's Report on the Law of the Tenement, which was published in 1998.

As already noted, the 2004 Act provided default rules in relation to ownership of parts in tenemented properties and in relation to the maintenance and management of such properties that would apply where the titles deed did not provide otherwise. The main elements of the reform was that parts of a tenement building would belong to those whose flats they serve, in equal shares; that decisions on repairs would be taken by majority[677]; and liability for them would in general be equal.

---

[669] *Duncan Smith & McLaren v Heatly*, 1952 J.C. 61; see also *Musselburgh Town Council v Jameson*, 1957 S.L.T. (Sh. Ct) 35.

[670] *Sanderson's Trs v Yule* (1897) 25 R. 211.

[671] *Sharp v Robertson* (1800) Mor. "Property" App. No.3; *Watt v Burgess' Trust* (1891) 18 R. 766.

[672] *Boswell v Magistrates of Edinburgh* (1881) 8 R. 986.

[673] See, e.g. *Anderson v Brattisanni's*, 1978 S.L.T. (Notes) 42.

[674] *Gellatly v Arrol* (1863) 1 M. 592. See *Todd v Wilson* (1894) 22 R. 172.

[675] *McArly v French's Trs* (1883) 10 R. 574.

[676] Rankine, *The Law of Landownership in Scotland* (1909), p.677.

[677] The question of what constitutes a "majority" was considered in the Outer House in *PS Properties (2) Ltd v Calloway Homes Ltd*, 2007 G.W.D. 31–526. Lady Dorrian's judgment is discussed in a note in Reid and Gretton, *Conveyancing 2007* (2008) at pp.139–141.

The 2004 Act defines a "tenement" as meaning a building or part of a building comprising two or related flats; which are, or which are designed to be, in separate ownership; and are divided from each other horizontally. Therefore, as a bare minimum, a tenement must be on two floors and must compromise of two flats which are, or which are designed to be, in separate ownership. "Tenement" also encompasses (except where the context otherwise requires) the solum and any other land pertaining to that building, or, as the case may be, part of the building.[678] "Flat" includes any premises whether or not used or intended to be used for residential purposes, or on the one floor or otherwise.[679] The statute therefore encompasses residential accommodation, including maisonettes, and office suites, i.e. residential and commercial accommodation and any combination thereof in a building,[680] making a tenement somewhat more than "a series of houses which, by some mischance, happen to have been built one on top of the other".[681]

The 2004 Act breaks tenements up into constituent sectors. A "sector" means a flat, any close or lift, or any other three-dimensional space not comprehended by a flat, close or lift, and the tenement building shall be taken to be entirely divided into sectors.[682]

The 2004 Act begins by codifying the common law in relation to the boundaries and pertinents within a tenement, apportioning ownership on the same basis as under the common law. Therefore, the bottom flat takes the solum, and, with the solum, the airspace above it,[683] subject only to the statutory innovation that where the roof of the tenement building slopes, a sector which includes the roof (or any part of it) shall also include the airspace above the slope of the roof (or part) up to the level of the highest point of the roof.[684] The effect of this new provision is to allow the owners of the owner of a top flat, and accordingly of the roof,[685] to construct dormer windows. The issue of "pertinents" is dealt with in s.3 of the Act. The Act lists as pertinents a close and a lift by means of which access can be obtained to more than one of the flats.[686] Other possible pertinents include a path, outside stair, fire escape, rhone, flue, conduit, cable, tank or chimney stack.[687] Where the titles are silent on the ownership of these parts, the Act provides that each flat served will have a right of common property in any close or lift by means

---

[678] Tenements (Scotland) Act 2004 (the "2004 Act") s.26(1).

[679] 2004 Act s.29(1).

[680] See *PS Properties (2) Ltd v Calloway Homes Ltd*, 2007 G.W.D. 31–526.

[681] See Reid and Gretton, *Conveyancing* (2004), p.123. See also Van der Merwe, "The Tenements (Scotland) Act 2004: A Brief Evaluation", 2004 S.L.T. (News) 211–13.

[682] 2004 Act s.29(1). In *Hunter v Tindale*, 2010 G.W.D. 38–776; 2011 S.L.T. (Sh. Ct) 11, it was held that a pend was not part of a tenement, but the circumstances in the case were somewhat unusual. The cause was raised under the Small Claims Rules, and the parties were party litigants. The decision was discussed in a note in Reid and Gretton, *Conveyancing 2010* at pp 96–97, in which it was suggested that the pend qualified as "scheme property", but that no liability could be attached to the owner of the pend as he did not own a flat in the tenement, only the pend. See also Lu Xu, "Law of the tenement: misunderstood and individualistic as ever", 2011 S.L.T. 3, 17–18. The case subsequently went to appeal, with the Sheriff Principal reversing the sheriff's judgment; see *Hunter v Tindale*, 2012 S.L.T. (Sh. Ct) 2. The Sheriff Principal held that the pend did form part of the tenement, being a "sector", and that the owner of the pend was liable for a share of the costs. The Sheriff Principal's decision was discussed in a note in Reid and Gretton, *Conveyancing 2011* at pp.129–132. See also D. Bain and C. Bury, "*Hunter v Tindale*: Tenement disrepair?", 2012 Jur. Rev. 251.

[683] 2004 Act s.2(4) and (6).

[684] 2004 Act s.2(7).

[685] 2004 Act s.2(3).

[686] 2004 Act s.3(1).

[687] 2004 Act s.3(4). See the judgments in *Hunter v Tindale* (fn.682, above) for judicial consideration in relation to closes.

of which access is afforded to more than one flat. No right of common property attaches where a flat is not so benefited.[688] The right of common property is in the whole thing, and not simply in the thing to the extent to which an individual property is served by it. Therefore, for example, a right of common ownership in the whole of a close will attach as a pertinent to the owner of a flat on the ground floor of a tenement, irrespective of the fact that only a very small part of the close may serve his property.[689]

Section 4 of the 2004 Act introduces the Tenement Management Scheme, which will apply to all tenements, except for those governed by a Development Management Scheme under Pt 6 of the Title Conditions (Scotland) Act 2003, which is an alternative statutory scheme for the management of tenements available to developers and forecast as being of limited and particular application due to the complexities inherent in the Development Management Scheme; for example, where the scale of a development is extensive.

The Tenement Management Scheme sets out a number of default rules which will apply in relation to the management and maintenance of the scheme property of a tenement in the absence of any provision in the title deeds.

"Scheme property" includes any part of a tenement that is the common property of two or more of the owners, and also certain parts of the tenement that may be in the exclusive ownership of one owner, for example the ground on which the tenement is built, the foundations, a load-bearing wall in a flat, or the tenement roof. The ownership of these parts will remain with individual owners, but the Tenement Management Scheme makes them the subject of a management regime under which the other owners in the tenement will have a say in their maintenance and management, on a majority basis except in the case of necessary work in relation to the duty to provide support and shelter,[690] and emergency work.[691] The scheme, where it applies, will have the effect of preventing one owner from having a veto over the execution of necessary works in a tenement. An owner who is unhappy with a scheme decision has the right to apply within 21 days of that decision to a sheriff to have it annulled.[692] The Tenement Management Scheme is set out in Sch.1 to the 2004 Act. Rule 7 of Sch.1 allows for emergency work to be instructed or carried. "Emergency work" means work which, before a scheme decision can be obtained, requires to be carried out to scheme property to prevent damage to any part of the tenement, or in the interests of health or safety. The owners in the tenement are liable for the cost of any emergency work instructed or carried out as if the cost of that work were normal scheme costs.

The liability and apportionment of scheme costs is governed under r.4 of Sch.1 to the 2004 Act. The phrase "scheme costs" is defined in some detail, but can be briefly summarised as meaning the costs arising from scheme decisions and from emergency work.

The general rule is for apportionment in equal shares amongst all of the owners of flats in the tenement, subject to the qualification that repairs to the common property of two or more owners are shared equally between those common owners. Notwithstanding this, the costs relating to the roof in a tenement, which will be commonly owned by the owners of the top flats, but which might include

---

[688] 2004 Act s.3(2).
[689] See Van der Merwe, "The Tenements (Scotland) Act 2004: A Brief Evaluation", 2004 S.L.T. (News) 211–213.
[690] 2004 Act ss.8(3) and 10.
[691] Tenement Management Scheme r.7.
[692] 2004 Act s.5.

a part over a commonly owned close, where some ownership may lie with lower floor owners, are apportioned between all of the flats in the tenement under the normal default rules. Provision is made in the Tenement Management Scheme for a means for apportioning costs based upon floor space, where the floor area of the largest (or larger) flat is more than one-and-a-half times that of the smallest (or smaller) flat. In such circumstances each owner is liable to contribute towards those costs in the proportion which the floor area of that owner's flat bears to the total floor area of all (or both) the flats.[693]

The 2004 Act also makes provisions in relation to access for repairs, a compulsory obligation upon owners to insure their flats and pertinents, the installation of service pipes etc. and matters relating to the demolition and abandonment of tenement buildings.

Under the Pt VIII of the Civic Government (Scotland) Act 1982, Pt 4 of the Building (Scotland) Act 2003 and Pts 1 and 2 of the Housing (Scotland) Act 2006, local authorities have statutory powers to require repairs to be carried out in the interests of health and safety or of preventing damage, and to effect such repairs, and recover the expense of doing so.[694]

The 2004 Act deals in large part with tenement repairs: the word used in the Act is "maintenance", and maintenance is defined as including "repairs and replacement, the installation of insulation, cleaning, painting and other routine works, gardening, the day to day running of a tenement and the reinstatement of a part (but not most) of the tenement building, but does not include demolition, alteration or improvement unless reasonably incidental to the maintenance."[695] The Act accordingly does not cover such improvement works as are not reasonably incidental to repairs etc. In respect of maintenance under the provisions in the Act, the general rule, as has already been noted, is one of majority rule, but where proposed improvements do not fall within the ambit of the statutory definition, the normal rule in respect of common property would require the agreement of all of the co-proprietors.[696] A statutory exception to this limitation is now available under s.37 of the Equality Act 2010; a UK statute, which empowers the Scottish Ministers to make regulations to provide that a disabled person is entitled to make relevant adjustments to common parts in relation to premises in Scotland. s.37 came in to force on July 11, 2011.[697]

Part 9 of the Title Conditions (Scotland) Act 2003 confers upon the Lands Tribunal extensive powers in relation to the variation of title conditions. As the 2004 Act establishes a set of default rules which come into effect in the absence of express provisions in the title deeds in a tenement or where such provisions are in some way defective, the question is posed as to what the effect would be where a proprietor in a tenement were to apply to the Lands Tribunal for a variation or discharge of a title condition. The law in respect of this matter is not yet settled.[698]

---

[693] Tenements (Scotland) Act 2004 Sch.1 r.4.

[694] Civic Government (Scotland) Act 1982 ss.87–109; Building (Scotland) Act 2003 ss.28–30; *Purves v Edinburgh D.C.*, 1987 S.L.T. 366. See also Gordon and Wortley, *Scottish Land Law* (2009), Vol.1, paras 15–147–15–178.

[695] Tenements (Scotland) Act 2004 Sch.1 r.1.5, as amended by the Climate Change (Scotland) Act 2009 s.69.

[696] Bell, *Principles*, s.1075.

[697] Equality Act 2010 (Commencement No 7) Order 2011 (SI 2011/1636). See Reid and Gretton, *Conveyancing* (2010), p.102 for a brief note on the new provisions.

[698] A note in Reid and Gretton, *Conveyancing* (2010) at pp.97–102 considers two such cases; *Kennedy v Abbey Lane Properties*, March 29, 2010, Lands Tribunal, where the application was refused; and *Patterson v Drouet*, January 20, 2011, Lands Tribunal, where the application was

**34.88	Common gables**—For the purpose of saving space a gable may be built or may come to stand on a boundary. It may be, or may be held to have been, erected one-half on each side of the boundary so as to accommodate houses erected or to be erected on each side. The right to encroach beyond the boundary is founded on the custom of burghs and of other populous places where houses are erected street-wise. Much discussion has arisen with regard to the right of the first builder and his successors in the ownership to recover one-half of the cost from the owner of the adjoining stance. It seems to be settled that, in the absence of stipulation to the contrary, this right cannot be enforced until the adjacent owner for the time being actually begins to make use of the wall.[699] The better view is that each party has a right of property in his own share and a common interest in the whole.[700] The customary uses to which the gable may be put are mainly the insertion of joists, dooks, fireplaces and chimneys, and the binding into it of front and back walls.[701] A fence or division wall cannot, without agreement, be converted into a house gable.[702] Neighbouring tenements may share a gable wall. As already noted, common gables are owned *ad medium filum* by the respective owners on either side. This meant that the proprietor of each flat owned to the mid-point the common gable bounding his property, and had a right of common interest in the remainder. Whilst the Tenement (Scotland) Act 2004 abolished the common law rules of common interest in respect of tenements, the concept of common interest was retained for questions affecting both a tenement and some other land or building.[703] Gable walls bounding tenements, or a tenement and another building, continue to be subject to the common interest doctrine.

Tenements can often be constructed in terraces, sometimes posing the problem of determining where one building ends and another begins. This might result in difficulties where, for example, one side of a gable wall there is a tenement and on the other a semi-detached dwellinghouse.[704] The Tenements (Scotland) Act 2004 allows recourse to the titles in situations when the true extent of a particular tenement is not immediately apparent, so as to ensure a clear answer.[705]

**34.89	March-fences and division walls**—Under the March Dykes Act 1661 (c.41),[706] a proprietor of lands is enabled to compel the owner of conterminous lands to bear half the expense of erecting, repairing, or where necessary re-building[707] the march dyke or fence between their lands. The Act applies only to lands exceeding

---

continued to consider the question of competency. It was argued in *Patterson* that allowing the variation would have the effect of bringing the Tenement Management Scheme into operation.

[699] *Law v Monteith* (1855) 18 D. 125; Gordon and Wortley, *Scottish Land Law* (2009), Vol.1, paras 3–37—3–39.

[700] *Jack v Begg* (1875) 3 R. 35; *Glasgow Royal Infirmary v Wylie* (1877) 4 R. 894; *Berkeley v Baird* (1895) 22 R. 372; *Robertson v Scott* (1886) 13 R. 1127; *Baird v Alexander* (1898) 25 R. (HL) 35; *Wilson v Pottinger*, 1908 S.C. 580; *Trades House of Glasgow v Ferguson*, 1979 S.L.T. 187; and see Gordon and Wortley, *Scottish Land Law* (2009), Vol.1, para.3–37; Law Commission Consultation Paper, *Mutual Boundary Walls*, 1992 S.L.T. (News) 199; Reid, *The Law of Property in Scotland* (1996), para.218.

[701] *Lamont v Cumming* (1875) 2 R. 784.

[702] *Grahame v Magistrates of Kirkcaldy* (1882) 9 R. (HL) 91.

[703] Tenements (Scotland) Act 2004 s.7.

[704] See Reid and Gretton, *Conveyancing* (2004), p.123.

[705] Tenements (Scotland) Act 2004 s.26.

[706] Stair, II, 3, 75; Erskine, II, 6, 4; Bankton, I, 10, 153–154; Rankine, *The Law of Landownership in Scotland* (1909), pp.613 et seq; Gordon and Wortley, *Scottish Land Law* (2009), Vol.1, paras 3–46 et seq.; Reid, *The Law of Property in Scotland* (1996), paras 216 et seq.

[707] *Paterson v MacDonald* (1880) 7 R. 958.

five or six acres.[708] The fence must be advantageous to both proprietors, but the advantage need not be equal.[709] The Act has been supplemented by the March Dykes Act 1669 (c.17), dealing with straightening of the marches. As in the case of applications under the earlier Act, the court will refuse an application which would result in oppression or unfairness. These Acts are rarely invoked in modern practice.

Without having recourse to these statutes, adjoining heritors may agree to erect a fence at common expense; or it may be that, without express agreement, a fence has been recognised and treated as a march-fence; and in such cases there is a common obligation on the part of the heritors to maintain and repair it.[710] In the case of such fences, and also of mutual division walls, questions may arise whether the wall or fence is common property or is owned by each proprietor, usually up to the mid-point (*ad medium filum*), in so far as built on his ground. The latter appears to be the better view where there are no special considerations pointing to the contrary.[711] The property in the fence or wall is then subject to a right of common interest but each proprietor has a right to build or otherwise carry out operations *in suo* on or against his part of the wall provided there is no significant harm to the structure of the wall or other infringement of the common interest.[712] If, on the other hand, the wall is regarded as common property, the right of division and sale normally incident to such property is excluded.[713]

VIII. TIME-SHARES

Time-shares—Heritable property may be vested in one owner, who sells rights of **34.90** occupancy for certain periods to other individuals.[714] Such arrangements are known as time-shares. The nature and effect of the rights granted depend upon the terms of the particular contract. Generally, the holder of a time-share may sell it to another, or gift or bequeath or otherwise dispose of it, as incorporeal property.[715] A time-share could take the form of a lease, but it can often be the case that an arrangement is intended to last in perpetuity, meaning that other legal devices will also have to be used.[716] Mechanisms based in common ownership would,

---

[708] *Penman v Douglas* (1739) Mor.10481; *Secker v Cameron*, 1914 S.C. 354.

[709] *Blackburn v Head* (1903) 11 S.L.T. 521, per Lord Kyllachy.

[710] *Strang v Steuart* (1864) 2 M. 1015.

[711] Rankine, *The Law of Landownership in Scotland* (1909), pp.620–621 and 636–637; *Thom v Hetherington*, 1987 S.C. 185; 1988 S.L.T. 724. A fence or wall constructed wholly on the land of one of them would, however, belong to him.

[712] *Gray v MacLeod*, 1979 S.L.T. (Sh. Ct) 17; *Gill v Mitchell*, 1980 S.L.T. (Sh. Ct) 48; *Thom v Hetherington*, 1987 S.C. 185.

[713] Rankine, *The Law of Landownership in Scotland* (1909), pp.620–621 and 636–637.

[714] Gordon and Wortley, *Scottish Land Law* (2009), Vol.1, paras 15–10, 18–16.

[715] The contract may impose certain restrictions on disposal.

[716] Case law involving time-shares in Scotland tends to dwell on matters other than the legal vehicles used to bring them into existence: *Forest Hills Trossachs Club v Assessor for Central Region*, 1991 S.L.T. (Lands Tr.) 42 concerns rateable occupation. *Barratt International Resorts Ltd v Barratt Owners' Group*, A2387/99, December 20, 2002, concerns damages for defamation in a dispute between a management company and a number of aggrieved timeshare owners. *Christlieb v The Melfort Club* [2006] CSOH 69 is an offshoot of earlier litigation involving a right of way, but the judgement considers the management structure of the timeshare. *Abbott v Forest Hills Trossachs Club*, 2001 S.L.T. (Sh. Ct) 155 concerns title and interest to sue, and of necessity considers the management structure in the time-share arrangement. *Trustees for Coylumbridge Highland Lodges Club v Assessor for Highland and Western Isles Valuation Joint Board*, Case Ref: LTS/VA/2009/01–61 Lands Tr., February 11, 2010, a recent rating case, includes a useful summary of the operation of one such scheme at paras 12–24.

however, be problematic. There are difficulties associated with the possibility of a co-owner having exclusive occupation of the commonly owned property for a period of time, even as limited as one week in the year.[717] Furthermore, agreement to such occupation does not constitute a lease.

A time-share could be effected through the vehicle of a trust, whereby the real right of property in the subjects of the times-share, most commonly land or salmon fishings, is held by a trustee for the benefit of the beneficiaries of the trust, being the time-share purchasers. Alternatively, the real right of property could be held by a limited company in which the timeshare owners make up the body of shareholders.[718]

It has been held in one particular case[719] that the court could intervene in the actings of a time-share association or club where they affected the patrimonial interests or civil rights of its members. The particular circumstances in the case were that the pursuers were seeking to vindicate their personal rights as against the defenders. Under the management agreement the time-share association or club had delegated its responsibilities to a management company, which accordingly stood in the association's shoes in relation to those functions, and its actions were accordingly considered no less actionable than if carried out by the association. In the judgment of the Sheriff Principal, the rule in *Foss v Harbottle*[720] was distinguished. The effect of the management contract had been to delegate some of the timeshare club's functions to the management company, allowing the pursuers to sue the agent as well as the principal.

Legislation offers protection to persons entering into time-share agreements.[721]

FURTHER READING

Cusine, D.J. and Paisley, R., *Servitudes and Rights of Way* (Edinburgh: W. Green, 1998).

Cusine, D.J. and Rennie, *Standard Securities*, 2nd edn (Bloomsbury Professional, 2002).

Gordon, W.M. and Wortley, S., *Scottish Land Law*, 3rd edn (Edinburgh: W. Green, 2009), Vol.1.

Gretton, G.L. and Reid, K.G.C., *Conveyancing*, 4th edn (Edinburgh: W. Green, 2011).

Gretton, G.L. and Steven, A., *Property, Trusts and Succession* (Sussex: Tottel, 2009).

---

[717] See paras 30.09 and 34.80–34.82, above.

[718] See Paisley, "Real Rights: Practical Problems and Dogmatic Rigidity" (2005) 9 Edin. L.R. 267. See also R.R.M. Paisley, *Land Law* (Edinburgh: W. Green, 2000), p.167.

[719] *Abbott v Forest Hills Trossachs Club*, 2001 S.L.T. (Sh. Ct) 155.

[720] *Foss v Harbottle* (1843) 2 Hare 461. Sheriff Principal R.A. Dunlop QC quotes the rule in *Foss v Harbottle* by reference to another judgment as being that "the proper plaintiff in an action in respect of a wrong alleged to be done to a company or association of persons is prima facie the company or the association of persons itself. Secondly, where the alleged wrong is a transaction which might be made binding on the company or association and on all its members by a simple majority of the members, no individual member of the company is allowed to maintain an action in respect of that matter."

[721] The Timeshare, Holiday Products, Resale and Exchange Contracts Regulations 2010 (SI 2010/2960) came into force on February 23, 2011 and repealed and replaced the previous statutory regime, contained in the Timeshares Act 1992 (c.35).

Talman, I.J.S., *Halliday's Conveyancing Law and Practice in Scotland* (Edinburgh: W. Green,1984).

Jauncey, Lord, *Fishing in Scotland: Law for the Angler*, 2nd edn (Edinburgh: W. Green, 1984).

Lands Tribunal for Scotland, *http://www.lands-tribunal-scotland.org.uk/title.html* [Accessed August 15, 2012] (where decisions of the Lands Tribunal on title conditions cases may be accessed).

Paisley, R., *Land Law* (Edinburgh: W. Green, 2000).

Paisley, R., *Review of Access Rights and Rights of Way: A Guide to the Law in Scotland* (The Scottish Rights of Way and Access Society, 2006).

Rankine, J., *The Law of Landownership in Scotland*, 4th edn (Edinburgh: W. Green, 1909).

Reid, K.G.C., *The Law of Property in Scotland* (Edinburgh: Butterworths, 1996).[722]

Reid, K.G.C. and Gretton, G.L., *Conveyancing* (Edinburgh: Avizandum, annual review since 1999).

Reid, K.G.C. and Zimmermann, R., *A History of Private Law in Scotland,* 2 Vols (Oxford: Oxford University Press, 2000).

Robinson, S.S., *The Law of Game, Salmon and Freshwater Fishing in Scotland* (Butterworths, 1990).

Stair Memorial Encyclopaedia, Vol.11 ("Fisheries", "Forestry", "Harbours"); Vol.14 ("Mines and Quarries"); Vol.18 ("Property: Landownership"); Reissue ("Roads"); Reissue ("Sea and Continental Shelf"); Vol.25 ("Water and Water Rights").

Scottish Law Commission, *Report on Land Registration* (HMSO, 2010), Scot. Law Com. No.222.

Tait, J.H., *A Treatise on the Law of Scotland as applied to Game Laws and Trout and Salmon Fishing*, 2nd edn (Edinburgh: W. Green, 1928).

---

[722] In essence, a reprint of *Stair Memorial Encyclopaedia*, Vol.18, "Property: Landownership" but omitting the section on intellectual property. It is the practice in this part to cite to Reid, *The Law of Property in Scotland* (1996), rather than to *Stair Memorial Encyclopaedia*, Vol.18.

CHAPTER 35

LEASES

The common law of leases, for social and economic reasons, has for many years **35.01**
been substantially eclipsed by statute, especially with regard to the security of the
tenant's tenure and the amount of rent which he can be required to pay. Few
lettings in town or country are now unaffected by statutory codes and those of
residential property and agricultural land are particularly closely controlled. The
common law is still, nevertheless, of importance, and it and those statutory
provisions of general application are dealt with first in this chapter. Thereafter the
codes dealing with agricultural holdings, agricultural tenancies, landholders,
crofters, and dwelling-houses and shops will be summarised.

It should be noted that the Scottish Parliament has been particularly active in
relation to the law of landlord and tenant. In addition to various statutes considered below concerning tenancy rights, the statutory regulation of house-letting,
landlord regulation, disrepair, antisocial conduct other matters, two new Acts
were passed in Parliament in the summer of 2012, as the text of this chapter was
being finalised. These Acts are the Long Leases (Scotland) Act 2012 and the Land
Registration etc. (Scotland) Act 2012. Both statutes give effect to recommendations from the Scottish Law Commission.

I. GENERAL LAW

Nature of contract—The contract of lease is one whereby an owner or occupier **35.02**
of land grants exclusive possession of it to a tenant in return for rent, in money or
goods. The analogous contract in the case of moveables is hire.[1] Although a
mineral lease involves a conveyance of part of the subjects and not merely their
fruits, and so may be regarded as a sale, it has been treated under the law of
leases.[2] A right to the use of a heritable subject, where no possession of any
specific part is given, for example a right to exhibit advertisements on the walls of
a building, is a contract which does not fall under the law of leases.[3] The right to
possession conferred by the contract must be exclusive.[4] However, a limited
reservation in favour of a landowner or a limitation in the nature of the use to

---

[1] See Ch.13.

[2] See G. Paton and J. Cameron, *The Law of Landlord and Tenant in Scotland* (Edinburgh:
W. Green, 1967), p.65.

[3] *UK Advertising Co v Glasgow Bag-Wash Co*, 1926 S.C. 303; but see *Brador Properties Ltd v
British Telecommunications Plc*, 1992 S.L.T. 490; 1992 S.C.L.R. 119. The question whether a bargain
about the use of land is a lease or not has been discussed in land valuation cases: e.g. *Perth Burgh
Council v Assessor for Perth*, 1937 S.C. 549; *LNER Ry v Assessor for Glasgow*, 1937 S.C. 309. See
Paton and Cameron, *Landlord and Tenant* (1967), pp.12–15.

[4] *Chaplin v Assessor for Perth*, 1947 S.C. 373; *Conway v City of Glasgow Council*, 1999 Hous.
L.R. 20.

which the occupier can use the land is not necessarily inconsistent with the existence of a landlord and tenant relationship.[5] Where an employee is given the occupancy of a house, the contract may be regarded as a contract of service and not as a lease,[6] and the employee a "service occupier" and not a tenant. For this to be so the employee's residence in the house must be ancillary and necessary to the performance of his duties.[7] This is a matter of interpretation of the contract in all the circumstances.[8] Where a person is permitted to occupy premises as an act of grace or friendship, and the intention to create a tenancy is not present, the right conferred on him may be construed as a mere licence to occupy, and not a lease.[9] This depends on considering the whole circumstances of the case, rather than merely the word the parties have chosen to describe their arrangement. There are four cardinal elements in a lease, the parties,[10] the subjects, the rent and the duration; in the absence of *consensus in idem* as to these elements, or at least the first three, there will be no lease.[11] The occupant of a house or other subject belonging to another is, however, presumed to occupy as tenant and though no direct obligation to pay rent is proved is bound to pay the annual value of the subject to the proprietor.[12] Until recently it could be assumed that there was no limit on the time for which subjects could be let, and that if no term was expressed the contract

---

[5] *South Lanarkshire Council v Taylor*, 2005 S.C. 182; *Possfund Custodian Trustee Ltd v Kwik-Fit Properties Ltd*, 2009 S.L.T. 133.

[6] See *Dunbar's Trs v Bruce* (1900) 3 F. 137; *Sinclair v Tod*, 1907 S.C. 1038; *Carron Co v Francis*, 1915 S.C. 872. As a service occupier he is not entitled to security of tenure or rent protection under the Rent Acts: see *Marquis of Bute v Prenderleith*, 1921 S.C. 281.

[7] *Cairns v Innes*, 1942 S.C. 164; *McGregor v Dunnett*, 1949 S.C. 510 at 514, per Lord President Cooper; *Cargill v Phillips*, 1951 S.C. 67.

[8] W.M. Gordon and S. Wortley, *Scottish Land Law*, 3rd edn (Edinburgh: W. Green, 2009), para.18–10; Paton and Cameron, *Landlord and Tenant* (1967), pp.9–11.

[9] *Commissioners of HM Works v Hutchison*, 1922 S.L.T. (Sh Ct) 127; *Scottish Residential Estates Development Co Ltd v Henderson*, 1991 S.L.T. 490; but see too *Brador Properties Ltd v British Telecommunications Plc*, 1992 S.C. 12; 1992 S.L.T. 490; *Morrison v Murdoch*, 1997 S.L.T. 381; Paton and Cameron, *Landlord and Tenant* (1967), pp.12–15; cf. *Heslop v Burns* [1974] 1 W.L.R. 1241. See also *Stirrat v Whyte*, 1967 S.C. 265, where fields were let for a rotation of cropping on condition that the let should terminate in the event of the sale of the farm at any time. S.3 of the Agricultural Holdings (Scotland) Act 2003 (the "2003 Act") puts agreements for grazing or mowing of land for up to 364 days on a statutory footing: *Scottish Youth Hostels Association v Paterson*, 2007 S.L.C.R. 1.

[10] See *I. & H. Brown (Kirkton) Ltd v Hutton*, 2005 S.L.T. 885 for the position in relation to tenants in common and how such tenancies are distinguished from joint tenancies. A landlord may enter into an agreement with a group of persons including himself qua tenant: *Pinkerton v Pinkerton*, 1986 S.L.T. 672. But this is not a lease: e.g. *pro indiviso* proprietors cannot competently grant a lease to one of their number: *Bell's Exrs v Inland Revenue*, 1986 S.C. 252; 1987 S.L.T. 625; *Clydesdale Bank Plc v Davidson*, 1998 S.C. (HL) 51; Gordon and Wortley, *Scottish Land Law* (2009), paras 15–19, 18–12 and 18–13. A landlord may grant a lease to a partnership of which he is one of the partners, subject to the controls contained in Pt 6 of the 2003 Act: *MacFarlane v Falfield Investments Ltd*, 1998 S.L.T. 145. Note too the decision in *Kildrummy (Jersey) Ltd v Inland Revenue Commissioners*, 1991 S.C. 1; 1992 S.L.T. 787, where a lease granted by a married couple to a company (which had undertaken by deed of trust to hold the subjects as nominee in trust for the couple) was held a nullity as being an attempt by the couple to enter into a contract with themselves for their own benefit. A single lease may exist over an area of land subdivided between different owners: *Crewpace Ltd v French*, 2012 S.L.T. 126.

[11] *Gray v Edinburgh University*, 1962 S.C. 157; *Erskine v Glendinning* (1871) 9 M. 656; *Trade Development Bank v David W. Haig (Bellshill)*, 1983 S.L.T. 510 at 514, per Lord President Emslie; *Shetland Islands Council v BP Petroleum Development Ltd*, 1990 S.L.T. 82; 1989 S.C.L.R. 48; *Scottish Residential Estates Development Co Ltd v Henderson*, 1991 S.L.T. 490; Gordon and Wortley, *Scottish Land Law* (2009), para.18–05.

[12] *Glen v Roy* (1882) 10 R. 239. If need be, a claim for recompense can be pursued: *Rochester Poster Services Ltd v A.G. Barr Plc*, 1994 S.L.T. (Sh. Ct) 2; *GTW Holdings Ltd v Toet*, 1994 S.L.T. (Sh. Ct) 16; cf. *Shetland Islands Council v BP Petroleum Development Ltd*, 1990 S.L.T. 82.

would be treated as a lease for a year only, and not in perpetuity.[13] However, there is now statutory provision for a maximum period of let of 175 years,[14] and new legislation which will have the effect of converting qualifying long leases into ownership.[15] Leases for not more than one year do not require to be constituted by writing,[16] nor is writing necessary in order to prove that there is a lease.[17] Writing is necessary in the case of leases for more than a year[18] and, if they are to be registered or recorded, the writing has to be signed by the granter and attested by one witness.[19]

Lease as a real right—At common law a lease was merely a personal contract, **35.03** binding on the lessor and his representatives, not upon his singular successors as purchasers or creditors; the tenant thus had no security of tenure against the lessor's singular successor, who could repudiate the lease. This was altered by the Leases Act 1449: if its provisions are complied with, the tenant obtains a real right in the subjects let. The Act is applicable to leases of lands, houses, mines, and salmon fishing, but not to leases of shootings, which are not capable of being created separate tenements, and so cannot bind a singular successor.[20] By statute a tenant under a written lease of freshwater fishings for not less than a year obtains a real right.[21] The conditions required to bring a lease within the purview of the Leases Act, and so make it binding on singular successors, are: (1) that the lease (if for more than a year) must be in writing and signed by the parties[22]; (2) that there must be a specific continuing rent[23]; (3) that there must be an ish, or term of expiry; and (4) that the tenant must have entered into possession.[24] There

---

[13] *Dunlop v Steel Co of Scotland* (1879) 7 R. 283; *Gray v Edinburgh University*, 1962 S.C. 157; *Tom Dickson Cameras (Glasgow) Ltd v Scotfilm Laboratories Ltd*, 1987 G.W.D. 31–1152.

[14] Abolition of Feudal Tenure etc (Scotland) Act 2000 s.67, applicable to all leases executed after June 9, 2000, except for those implementing pre-existing obligations, and sub-leases associated with leases executed before that date.

[15] The Long Leases (Scotland) Bill completed its Scottish Parliamentary passage on June 28, 2012.

[16] Requirements of Writing (Scotland) Act 1995 s.1(7).

[17] *Morrison-Low v Paterson (No.1)*, 1985 S.C. (HL) 49; 1985 S.L.T. 255, per Lord Keith of Kinkel; distinguished in *Strachan v Robertson-Coupar*, 1989 S.C. 130.

[18] For recent discussions on this matter see *Serup v McCormack* Edinburgh April 18, 2012, SLC/73/10, and *Nelson v Kinnaird* Sheriffdom of Tayside Central and Fife at Perth (Case ref. A198/08) October 11, 2011, available at *http://www.scotcourts.gov.uk/opinions/A198_08.html* [Accessed July 25, 2012]. The latter case is discussed in C. Bury and D. Bain, "*Nelson v Kinnaird*: Vigilantibus et non dormientibus jura subveniunt down on the farm", 2012 *Scottish Law Gazette* Vol.80 No.1 (March) 16.

[19] Requirements of Writing (Scotland) Act 1995 s.1(2)(b); cf. para.6.04, above. Any variation of a lease entered into for a period of more than one year must be made in writing, unless s.1(3) and (4) of the 1995 Act applies: *Keenan v Whitehead*, 2003 G.W.D. 10–289; *Coatbridge Retail No.1 Ltd v Oliver*, 2010 G.W.D. 19–374 (Sh. Ct). The exception for leases of a year might, in the context of certain statutory regimes, need to be considered carefully, as demonstrated by *Serup v McCormack* Edinburgh April 18, 2012, SLC/73/10, which added twenty years onto what was initially a one year unwritten lease by virtue of an upgrade to a short limited duration tenancy of five years then a further upgrade to a limited duration tenancy of a further 15 years, under ss.4 then 5 of the 2003 Act.

[20] *Birkbeck v Ross* (1865) 4 M. 272. A lease of e.g. a deer forest, where the tenant has the exclusive occupation of the lands themselves is not a lease of shootings: *Farquharson* (1870) 9 M. 66. See Gordon and Wortley, *Scottish Land Law* (2009), para.18–138 and the cases cited thereunder.

[21] Salmon and Freshwater Fisheries (Consolidation) (Scotland) Act 2003 s.66.

[22] *The Advice Centre for Mortgages v McNicoll*, 2006 S.L.T. 591.

[23] *Mann v Houston*, 1957 S.L.T. 89.

[24] Bell, *Principles*, s.1190. An incoming tenant who in advance of the term is allowed to perform certain acts on the ground may not have possession for the purpose of the Act: *Millar v McRobbie*, 1949 S.C. 1.

is a limit to the number of years for which a lease, valid against singular successors, may be granted. The statutory maximum period is 175 years.[25] However, where the lease is for a definite period, with a continual option to the tenant to demand a new lease on the expiry of the old, the arrangement is binding on a singular successor only for the period current at the commencement of his interest.[26] The rent must not be illusory, a term never exactly interpreted, but it is no objection, providing there is a continuing rent, that a capital sum, known as a grassum, has been taken at the beginning of the lease.[27]

35.04   **Real and personal conditions**—When a lease falls within the provisions of the Leases Act 1449, all its ordinary conditions are binding on singular successors. But there may be conditions which are not *inter naturalia* of the lease, that is, provisions which have reference to the private relations of the contracting parties, and not to their general relations as landlord and tenant. By such provisions a singular successor of the landlord is not bound. Examples are a provision under which rent is to be ascribed to payment of a prior debt,[28] or a provision that a deduction from the rent is to be made for services to be rendered by the tenant,[29] or a provision in a back letter to a lease conferring rights of exclusivity upon a tenant,[30] or a provision, in a lease for 999 years, under which the landlord undertook to grant a feu on demand,[31] or a provision in a lease conferring an option in favour of the tenant to purchase the leased subjects,[32] or a personal arrangement permitting a change of use.[33] But an obligation to pay for improvements executed by the tenant,[34] or to take over sheep stock at valuation,[35] transmits against singular successors.[36] *Richardson's Trustees v The Ballachulish Slate Quarries*

---

[25] Abolition of Feudal Tenure etc. (Scotland) Act 2000 s.67. The statutory ceiling for residential leases is 20 years, per s.8 of the Land Tenure Reform (Scotland) Act 1974 (the "1974 Act"), subject to relaxations introduced in s.36 of the Private Rented Housing (Scotland) Act 2011. Older leases for more than 175 years may be affected by provisions in the Long Leases (Scotland) Act 2012. With the coming into force of the Land Registration etc. (Scotland) Act 2012, long leases— leases of 20 years or more—will be subject to new provisions in respect of statutory registration, and the Leases Act 1449 will cease to have application where registration is required (see para.35.05, below).

[26] See *Bisset v Magistrates of Aberdeen* (1898) 1 F. 87. See also K.G.C. Reid and G.L. Gretton, *Conveyancing* (Edinburgh: Avizandum, 2006), pp.102–109.

[27] Bell, *Principles*, s.1201; See *Mann v Houston*, 1957 S.L.T. 89.

[28] Bell, *Principles*, s.1202.

[29] *Ross v Duchess of Sutherland* (1838) 16 S. 1179. See also *Montgomery v Carrick* (1848) 10 D. 1387.

[30] *Optical Express (Gyle) Ltd v Marks & Spencer Plc*, 2000 S.L.T. 644.

[31] *Bisset v Magistrates of Aberdeen* (1898) 1 F. 87. The example fails to stand up to contemporary scrutiny on the basis of the length of the lease and the ability to demand a feu, but the principle stands. In modern Scots law a lease of 999 years would not be competent. The modern Scots law in respect of long leases will be reformed with the coming into force of the Land Registration etc. (Scotland) Act 2012. Under the Long Leases (Scotland) Act 2012, qualifying long leases will be converted into ownership.

[32] *The Advice Centre for Mortgages v McNicoll*, 2006 S.L.T. 591. See Reid and Gretton, *Conveyancing* (2006). In *Multi-link Leisure Developments Ltd v North Lanarkshire Council* [2010] UKSC 47; 2011 S.C. (UKSC) 53 the Supreme Court considered the question of options clauses in the context of valuation of the subjects for the purpose of the purchase.

[33] *BP Oil Ltd v Caledonian Heritable Estates Ltd*, 1990 S.L.T. 114.

[34] *Stewart v McRae* (1834) 13 S. 4.

[35] *Panton v Mackintosh* (1903) 10 S.L.T. 763.

[36] Whether a right in favour of a landlord transmits in favour of singular successors is a matter of construction of the contractual documentation, e.g. in *Waydale Ltd v DHL Holdings (UK) Ltd (No.3)*, 2000 S.L.T. 224, it was held that a cautionary obligation granted by a third party in favour of a landlord which guaranteed the obligations of a tenant under a lease transmitted in favour of a singular successor of that landlord.

Ltd suggests a tenant's right to sever fixtures enforceable against the original landlord may be enforceable against his successors and against heritable creditors.[37]

Long leases—Historically, the Leases Act 1449 has been the main statutory **35.05** provision by means of which a lease might come to have real effect; i.e. to have effect as a real as opposed to a personal right. In the case of leases of lands and heritage in Scotland for a period exceeding 20 years—i.e. long leases—it was necessary for the law to be extended so as to provide for an alternative (and an equivalent) to the 1449 Act as a means of obtaining a real right. This extension was effected by means of the Registration of Leases (Scotland) Act 1857 and, later, provisions in the Land Registration (Scotland) Act 1979. The coming into force of provisions in the Land Registration etc (Scotland) Act 2012 has the effect of amending the 1857 Act and largely superseding the 1979 Act; and of disapplying the 1449 Act in cases where the 2012 Act has effect.

For information in respect of the law as it formerly was, readers are advised to consult the previous (12th) edition of this work.

Under the Land Registration etc (Scotland) Act 2012, long leases are registrable deeds. Transactions terminating, extending the duration of, or otherwise altering the terms of such leases are also registrable. Existing recorded long leases will be suffered to remain in the General Register of Sasines, but their termination, extension or other variation will be registrable.

Prior to the amendments made by the Land Tenure Reform (Scotland) Act 1974 the period of a long lease required to be at least 31 years, and the subjects let, except in the case of a lease of mines and minerals, required not to exceed 50 acres in extent. On the other hand, no rent is necessary, and no definite ish is required. The period must exceed 20 years. The particular value of the Acts is that they enable the lessee of a registered lease to borrow on the security of the lease by conferring an effectual real right on his assignee in security without relinquishing possession to him. Such leases may be assigned absolutely or in security. The Registration of Leases (Scotland) Act 1857 provides forms of deeds for executing the assignation of such recorded leases, but the grant of a right under a lease by way of a heritable security requires now to take the form of a standard security.[38] The 2012 Act has amended the Registration of Leases (Scotland) Act 1857 by making allowances for electronic assignations and renunciations of leases; the Requirements of Writing (Scotland) Act 1995 is also amended so as to facilitate this innovation. Real conditions may be created when such leases are assigned to the same effect as if the assignee had been a grantee of the lease.[39] Title conditions created in registered leases may be varied or discharged by the Lands Tribunal under Pt 9 of the Title Conditions (Scotland) Act 2003.[40] The sheriff has power to grant a renewal of a long lease where the landlord has failed to renew it in implement of an obligation to do so.[41] This power is available in cases where the

---

[37] *Richardson's Trustees v The Ballachulish Slate Quarries Ltd* (1918) 1 S.L.T. 413.

[38] Conveyancing and Feudal Reform (Scotland) Act 1970 ss.9(3), 32, Sch.8.

[39] The Registration of Leases (Scotland) Act 1857 s.3(2), (2A), (2B) and (2C), as amended by the Law Reform (Miscellaneous Provisions) (Scotland) Act 1985 s.3, Pt 1 of Sch.15 to the Title Conditions (Scotland) Act 2003, and the Land Registration etc (Scotland) Act 2012.

[40] Title Conditions (Scotland) Act 2003 ss.90–104; *McQuiban v Eagle Star Insurance Company*, 1972 S.L.T. (Lands Tr.) 39. See also *Co-operative Group Ltd v Propinvest Paisley LP*, 2011 S.L.T. 987, where the jurisdiction of the Lands Tribunal is considered. See fn.159, below.

[41] Law Reform (Miscellaneous Provisions) (Scotland) Act 1985 s.2 (inserting s.22A into the Land Registration (Scotland) Act 1979).

landlord has failed to renew the lease having been given written notice by the tenant that he requires the landlord to do so, and in cases where the landlord is unknown or cannot be found.[42] Prior to September 1, 1974 it was permissible to provide in leases of long duration for the payment of a casualty on events such as the assignation of the lease to a singular successor,[43] but the Leasehold Casualties (Scotland) Act 2001 abolished all leasehold casualties.[44] It remains permissible, however, to stipulate for review of rent or a periodical variation of rent on terms prescribed in the lease.

35.06 **Limitation on residential use of property let under long leases**—The Land Tenure Reform (Scotland) Act 1974[45] prohibited the imposition in deeds executed after the commencement of that Act of any feuduty, ground annual or other periodical payment. It also provided for the right to redeem, and in certain circumstances, redemption by law of such payments in deeds executed before that date. The majority of Pt 1 of the Land Tenure Reform (Scotland) Act 1974[46] has now been repealed by the Abolition of Feudal Tenure etc (Scotland) Act 2000 and feuduties were extinguished on the appointed day.[47] The reforms introduced by Pt 1 of the Land Tenure Reform (Scotland) Act 1974 were thought likely to result in more extensive use of long leases. In order to protect residential tenants (e.g. from retention by the landlord of buildings or other improvements made by tenants at their own expense), it is a condition of every long lease executed after September 1, 1974 that no part of the property which is subject to the lease shall be used as or as part of a private dwelling-house.[48] An exception is made in the case of use as a private dwelling-house which is ancillary to the use of the remainder of the subjects let for other purposes, where it would be detrimental to the efficient use of the remainder of the subjects if the ancillary use did not occur on that property.[49] A further exception is made in the case of a long lease executed after the commencement of the Housing (Scotland) Act 2010[50] where at the time the lease is executed the lessee is a social landlord, a body connected to a social landlord, a rural housing body or a body prescribed or of a type prescribed by the Scottish Ministers by order made by statutory instrument.[51] Caravan sites, agricultural holdings, short limited duration tenancies and limited duration tenancies under the Agricultural Holdings (Scotland) Act 2003, small landholdings and crofts are also exempted from the prohibition.[52] "Long lease" for this purpose is defined as meaning any grant of a lease or a liferent or other right of occupancy

---

[42] Land Registration (Scotland) Act 1979 s.22A(7).

[43] e.g. *Crawford v Campbell*, 1937 S.C. 596.

[44] Leasehold Casualties (Scotland) Act 2001 s.1.

[45] 1974 Act Pt 1.

[46] Only s.2 of the 1974 Act survives. The "appointed day" was November 28, 2004 (the Abolition of Feudal Tenure etc (Scotland) Act 2000 (Commencement No.2) (Appointed Day) Order 2003 (SSI 2003/456)).

[47] Abolition of Feudal Tenure etc (Scotland) Act 2000 s.76(2) and Pt 1 of Sch.13.

[48] 1974 Act s.8, as amended by Law Reform (Miscellaneous Provisions) (Scotland) Act 1985 s.1; see, as to the meaning of this expression, *Brown v Crum Ewing Trs*, 1918 1 S.L.T. 340; *Assessor for Lothian Region v Viewpoint Housing Association*, 1983 S.L.T. 479.

[49] 1974 Act s.8(3).

[50] Housing (Scotland) Act 2010 (asp 17) (the "2010 Act"). Commencement was on March 1, 2011 per the Housing (Scotland) Act 2010 (Commencement No. 2, Transitional, Transitory and Saving Provisions) Order (SSI 2011/96) Sch.1 para.1.

[51] 1974 Act s.8 as amended by the 2010 Act s.138 and the Private Rented Housing (Scotland) Act 2011 s.36.

[52] 1974 Act s.8(5).

granted for payment subject to a duration which could extend for more than 20 years, or if there is to be liability to make some payment or perform some other obligation if renewal so as to extend the period for more than 20 years is not effected.[53] If a breach of the statutory prohibition occurs, the lessor may give notice to the lessee to terminate the use that constitutes the breach within 28 days.[54] If the lessee does not do so within that period the lessor may raise an action of removing to terminate the lease, but the lessee may avoid the consequences by ceasing the use at any time before decree is extracted.[55] If it is proved that the lessor has either expressly or by his actings approved of the use which contravenes the statutory prohibition, the lessee is not subject to immediate removal, but the remaining duration of the lease is restricted so as not to continue for more than 20 years.[56] This defence is available only to a lessee who is actually occupying the subjects, but provision is made to enable a sub-lessee to be sisted in the action and to plead the defence if the use has been approved by the lessor in his sub-lease.[57] Provision is also made for the intimation of the action to heritable creditors, who may seek to be sisted in the action and plead any defence which could be pleaded by the defender.[58]

Tenants-at-will—A tenancy-at-will is an anomalous type of holding which has **35.07** become established by custom and usage in certain parts of Scotland, particularly in fishing and rural villages of the north-east coast, in Highland villages and a mining village in Lanarkshire.[59] Tenancies-at-will which have been recognised by the Lands Tribunal in the past tend to have been established in places where there has been a pressing social need for housing adjacent to a place of work (such as fishing or mining), where the residents have required security of tenure for themselves and their families but have been unable to afford the expense of formal conveyancing, and where landlords have been trusted to provide security of tenure in accordance with informal, but well-recognised, conventions.[60] The system is that the tenant rents land from the landowner for building a house, but obtains no formal title to the land. A ground rent is paid in respect of the land, and the right to occupy the land and the building or buildings which have been placed on it changes hands by means of a simple receipt for the price and intimation of the change of tenant to the landlord or the factor of the estate. If the tenant fails to pay the rent the house reverts to the landlord, who sells it in order to recover the arrears of rent. The informality of this kind of holding carries with it certain disadvantages, particularly due to the fact that the tenant-at-will, not having a recorded title, cannot normally borrow on the security of his house and has no contractual right to demand a formal title. His position has, however, been recognised by statute and improved upon in two important respects. He is treated as if he were the owner of the house for the purpose of obtaining an improvement grant from the local authority.[61] And he is

---

[53] 1974 Act s.8(4).

[54] 1974 Act s.9(1).

[55] 1974 Act s.9(3), (6).

[56] 1974 Act s.9(4).

[57] 1974 Act s.10(3), (5).

[58] 1974 Act s.10(2).

[59] Paton and Cameron, *Landlord and Tenant* (1967), pp.68–69. See *Allen v MacTaggart* [2007] CSIH 24 for an excellent discussion of the history of these tenancies, how they operate in practice and on whether a person is a tenant-at-will. See also *Wright v Shoreline Management Ltd*, 2009 S.L.T. (Sh. Ct) 83 and D. Cabrelli, "Tenancies-at-will: Allen v McTaggart" (2007) 11 Edin. L.R. 436.

[60] *Allen v MacTaggart* [2007] CSIH 24, per Lord Nimmo Smith.

[61] See definition of "owner" in the Housing (Scotland) Act 1987 (the "1987 Act") ss.246, 338.

entitled to acquire his landlord's interest in the land which is subject to the tenancy-at-will and to obtain a conveyance of it upon payment to him of compensation of an amount fixed, failing agreement, by reference to a statutory formula together with the expenses reasonably and properly incurred by the landlord in conveying his interest.[62] Disputes as to whether a person is a tenant-at will,[63] the extent or boundaries of the land,[64] the value of any tenancy land, expenses and what are the appropriate terms and conditions subject to which the landlord's interest in the tenancy land is to be conveyed are determined by the Lands Tribunal, which also has powers to deal with the case where the landlord is unknown or cannot be found.[65] An appeal from the Lands Tribunal to the Inner House of the Court of Session is available.[66] If the landlord fails to convey his interest or is unknown or cannot be found a conveyance may be obtained by application to the sheriff.[67] Provision is also made with reference to heritable securities over tenancy land, whereby the heritable creditor is entitled to be a party to an application to the Lands Tribunal for the determination of disputes, and the tenancy land may be disburdened of the security if the heritable creditor fails to do so or is unknown and cannot be found.[68]

35.08 Rights of tenant—The tenant's principal right is to be placed in full possession of the subjects let,[69] and to be allowed to remain there for the duration of the lease. In agricultural and urban leases alike, although not in the case of leases of minerals, there is an implied warranty that the subjects are reasonably fit for the purpose for which they are let.[70] There is, however, no general implication of fitness for any particular business which the tenant may desire to carry on there, the presumption being that the tenant has satisfied himself of the suitability of the subjects for his own purposes.[71] In agricultural leases the landlord is under an implied obligation to put the houses, offices and fences into "tenantable repair", in other words into such a condition that they will last, with reasonable care, for the period of the lease.[72] During the lease the obligation lies on the tenant to keep up and repair

---

[62] Land Registration (Scotland) Act 1979 s.20: see generally Gordon and Wortley, *Scottish Land Law* (2009), para.18–122.

[63] *Ferguson v Gibbs*, 1987 S.L.T. (Lands Tr.) 32; *MacLean's Exr v Kershaw*, 1993 S.L.C.R. 145; *Allen v MacTaggart* [2007] CSIH 24 (the ground rent must be payable in respect of the land, rather than any buildings on it, the ground rent must not have been increased at any time during the period of the tenancy, the right of occupancy of the land must be without ish and there must be evidence that the land is located in one of those few places in Scotland where tenancies-at-will have "by custom and usage" been recognised to exist.)

[64] cf. *Duthie v Watson*, 1997 Hous. L.R. 129.

[65] Land Registration (Scotland) Act 1979 s.21(1), (2).

[66] Tribunals and Inquiries Act 1992 s.11(1) and (7).

[67] Land Registration (Scotland) Act 1979 s.21(3), (4).

[68] Land Registration (Scotland) Act 1979 s.22.

[69] In *Possfund Custodian Trustee Ltd v Kwik-Fit Properties Ltd* [2008] CSIH 65 the court took the view that, as a lease is in essence a grant of possession of subjects, the landlord should be excluded from taking any action which materially encroaches upon the tenant's possession of those subjects, unless the lease specifies otherwise.

[70] Erskine, II, 6, 39; J. Rankine, *The Law of Leases in Scotland*, 3rd edn (Edinburgh: 1916), pp.240–1, 249; Gordon and Wortley, *Scottish Land Law* (2009), para.18–149; *Todd v Clapperton*, 2009 S.L.T. 837; A. Stalker, "Todd v Clapperton: The evolving law on repairing obligations and claims against landlords of residential property", 2010 S.L.T. (News) 31.

[71] *Glebe Sugar Refining Co v Paterson* (1900) 2 F. 615; *Paton v MacDonald*, 1973 S.L.T. (Sh. Ct) 85.

[72] *Davidson v Logan (No.2)*, 1908 S.C. 350; *Christie v Wilson*, 1915 S.C. 645 (water supply). As to houses, see *Reid v Baird* (1876) 4 R. 234; *Wolfson v Forrester*, 1910 S.C. 675; *Mearns v Glasgow City Council*, 2000 S.L.T. (Sh. Ct) 49.

the buildings and fences on the farm so that they are in the same tenantable condition at the ish; but he is not liable for extraordinary repairs rendered necessary by *damnum fatale* or natural wear and tear.[73] The common law regime is essentially restated by s.5 of the Agricultural Holdings (Scotland) Act 1991 and was essentially restated by s.16 of the Agricultural Holdings (Scotland) Act 2003 in the case of agricultural holdings, short limited duration tenancies and limited duration tenancies, but note s.16 has now been amended for limited duration tenancies and short limited duration tenancies. A landlord must within 6 months of the commencement of the tenancy (if practicable) provide such fixed equipment as will enable the tenant to maintain efficient production of the subjects for the specified use and put the fixed equipment so provided into the condition specified in a schedule (which must be provided under s.16(2) of the Agricultural Holdings (Scotland) Act 2003), and thereafter effect such renewal or replacement of the fixed equipment so provided as may be rendered necessary by natural decay or by fair wear and tear.

In the case of urban subjects, however, the obligation to repair lies at common law, in default of stipulations to the contrary,[74] upon the landlord.[75] The obligation is to uphold the subjects during the currency of the lease in a tenantable or habitable condition, and wind and watertight so that they will be proof against the ordinary attacks of the elements,[76] but he is not liable for defects due to *damnum fatale*[77] or which arise out of failures by third parties to perform their obligations. The landlord's common law obligation is not a warranty to the tenant that no disrepair will occur, nor is there an absolute duty to keep the subjects free from defects; it amounts to an undertaking to put matters right on receiving notice of their existence, and there is no breach until a particular defect is brought to his notice and he fails to remedy it.[78] Landlords have accordingly been held not to be liable in damages under the common law for injury sustained by the tenant owing to a chance defect arising during the currency of the lease.[79] The obligation is confined to the maintenance of the subjects let, and the landlord is not in breach of it if damage occurs within them caused by defects in property which lies beyond

---

[73] *Johnstone v Hughan* (1894) 21 R. 777; *McCall's Entertainments (Ayr) Ltd v S. Ayrshire CC (No.2)*, 1998 S.L.T. 1421. In default of stipulations to the contrary, neither is the landlord, see e.g. *Little Cumbrae Estate Ltd v Island of Little Cumbrae Ltd*, 2007 S.L.T. 631 and *Bayne v Walker* (1815) 3 Dow 233.

[74] Stipulations to the contrary are extremely common in urban commercial leases, see e.g. *West Castle Properties Ltd v Scottish Ministers*, 2004 S.C.L.R. 899; *Dean (t/a Abbey Mill Business Centre) v Freeman (No.2)*, 2006 G.W.D. 22–492; *Westbury Estates Ltd v The Royal Bank of Scotland Plc*, 2006 S.L.T. 1143; *Abacus Estates Ltd v Bell Street Estates Ltd*, 2007 G.W.D. 2–31; *Co-operative Insurance Society Ltd v Fife Council*, 2011 G.W.D. 19–458.

[75] Rankine, *The Law of Leases in Scotland* (1916), p.241; Erskine, II, 6, 43.

[76] *Wolfson v Forrester*, 1910 S.C. 675 at 680, per Lord President Dunedin. See also *Reid v Baird* (1876) 4 R. 234; *McGonigal v Pickard*, 1954 S.L.T. (Notes) 62; *Gunn v N.C.B.*, 1982 S.L.T. 526 (dampness); *McLaughlin v Inverclyde DC*, 1986 G.W.D. 2–34 (Sh. Ct) (alleged water penetration); *McArdle v Glasgow DC*, 1989 S.C.L.R. 19 (Sh. Ct) (dampness); *Morrison v Stirling DC*, 1991 G.W.D. 12–714 (dampness); *Mearns v Glasgow City Council*, 2002 S.L.T. (Sh. Ct) 49 (burst pipe); *Mack v Glasgow City Council*, 2006 S.C. 543 (water penetration, dampness and stench); *Campbell v Aberdeen City Council*, 2007 G.W.D. 9–168 (dampness and minor water penetration).

[77] In default of stipulations to the contrary, neither is the tenant, see, e.g. *Little Cumbrae Estate Ltd v Island of Little Cumbrae Ltd*, 2007 S.L.T. 631 and *Bayne v Walker* (1815) 3 Dow 233.

[78] *Evans v Glasgow DC*, 1978 S.L.T. 17; 1979 S.L.T. 270; *John Menzies Plc v Ravenseft Properties Ltd*, 1987 S.L.T. 64 (notice); *Fry's Metals Ltd v Durastic Ltd*, 1991 S.L.T. 689 (acts of third parties); cf. *Neilson v Scottish Homes*, 1999 S.L.T. (Sh. Ct) 2.

[79] *Hampton v Galloway* (1899) 1 F. 501; *Dickie v Amicable Property Investment Co*, 1911 S.C. 1079; *North British Storage Co v Steele's Trs*, 1920 S.C. 194.

the curtilage of the subjects.[80] All of these obligations may be displaced by agreement to the contrary in the lease, except where statute imposes obligations from which the parties may not contract out.[81]

The Housing (Scotland) Act 2006 (the "2006 Act") displaces the mixture of common law, statutory standards and statutory implied terms which apply to the landlord's repairing obligation in the context of private residential tenancies.[82] The 2006 Act applies to private residential tenancies of houses let for human habitation which are not Scottish secure tenancies, short Scottish secure tenancies, houses occupied by tenants of tenancies under the Agricultural Holdings (Scotland) Act 1991 and Agricultural Holdings (Scotland) Act 2003, crofts or small landholdings.[83] Section 13 of the 2006 Act sets out the relevant repairing standard. A private dwelling-house meets the repairing standard if (i) the house is wind and water tight and in all other respects reasonably fit for human habitation,[84] (ii) the structure of the exterior of the house (including drains, gutters and external pipes) are in a reasonable state of repair and in proper working order, (iii) the installations in the house for the supply of water, gas and electricity and for sanitation, space heating and heating water are in a reasonable state of repair and in proper working order, (iv) any fixtures, fittings and appliances provided by the landlord under the tenancy are in a reasonable state of repair and in proper working order, (v) any furnishings provided by the landlord under the tenancy are capable of being used safely for the purpose for which they are designed, and (vi) the house has satisfactory provision for detecting fires and for giving warning in the event of fire or suspected fire.[85] Subject to certain exceptions,[86] the landlord is under a duty to ensure that the house let for human habitation in the case of a private residential tenancy meets the repairing standard in s.13, (a) at the start of the tenancy and (b) at all times during the tenancy, but the duty in relation to (b) is only applicable where the tenant notifies the landlord of the work which requires to be carried out or the landlord otherwise becomes aware of such required work.[87] The landlord's duty to repair and maintain includes a duty to make good any damage caused by carrying out any work for the purposes of complying with the repairing standard in s.13.[88] The landlord discharges his duty to ensure that the house meets the repairing standard at all times during the tenancy if he undertakes any requisite work within a reasonable time of being notified by the tenant, or otherwise becoming aware, that the work is required.[89] It is only

---

[80] *Golden Casket (Greenock) v B.R.S. (Pickfords)*, 1972 S.L.T. 146.

[81] *Evans v Glasgow DC*, 1978 S.L.T. 17; *Mars Pension Trs Ltd v County Properties and Developments Ltd*, 1999 S.C. 10 and 267; *William Collins & Sons Ltd v CGU Insurance Plc*, 2006 S.C. 674.

[82] The relevant sections of the Housing (Scotland) Act 2006 (the "2006 Act") are ss.12–29, which came into force on September 3, 2007 by virtue of the Housing (Scotland) Act 2006 (Commencement No.5, Savings and Transitional Provisions) Order 2007 (SSI 2007/270).

[83] 2006 Act s.12.

[84] The meaning of this phrase under the now repealed Sch.10 to the 1987 Act was considered in *Gunn v Glasgow DC*, 1997 Hous. L.R. 3; *Kearney v Monklands DC*, 1997 Hous. L.R. 39. The new statutory scheme was considered in *Todd v Clapperton*, 2009 S.L.T. 837. This judgment is discussed in Stalker, "Todd v Clapperton: The evolving law on repairing obligations and claims against landlords of residential property", 2010 S.L.T. (News) 31.

[85] 2006 Act s.13.

[86] The exceptions are contained in s.16(1). The most important exception is contained in s.16(1)(a) which empowers a landlord and tenant to agree that a tenant is under the obligation to carry out repair and maintenance in the case of a tenancy for a period of not less than three years.

[87] 2006 Act s.14(1) and (3).

[88] 2006 Act s.14(2).

[89] 2006 Act s.14(4).

possible for a landlord and tenant to contract out of the provisions of s.14 of the 2006 Act with the consent of a sheriff.[90] Where a landlord fails to meet the repairing standard, the tenant may make an application to the private rented housing panel seeking a repairing standard enforcement order from the private rented housing committee.[91] Failure to comply with such a repairing standard enforcement order is a criminal offence. A landlord may apply to the panel for assistance in accessing property in order to view the state and condition, and in order to comply with the landlord's repairing obligations.[92]

The landlord's obligations, conventional, statutory or at common law, carry with them a liability to any persons who or whose property may be on the premises for any injury or damage arising to them as a result of any failure on his part to perform them.[93] The obligation of upkeep is subject to the law of *rei interitus*, and therefore the accidental destruction of a house puts an end to the obligation on either side.[94] Total destruction of the subjects of lease, without fault, has the effect of putting an end to the contract and liberating both landlord and tenant from its obligations.[95] In the case of partial injury it is a question of degree whether the tenant is entitled to abandon the lease.[96] If not, or if he does not choose to do so, he is entitled to claim a proportionate deduction, or abatement, from the rent.[97] A landlord is under no implied obligation to abstain from using other property in competition with the business carried on by the tenant.[98] If by alterations or repairs on other property he interferes with the tenant's interests, he will be liable, even though there is no proof that the work in question was not carried out with reasonable care, for any structural damage, and for injury to the tenant's effects or interference with his business, but not for injury resulting merely from noise, vibration or temporary interference with access.[99] A tenant, as the occupier, normally pays the rates, but in the case of a furnished letting, in a question between himself and the landlord, the landlord is by custom bound to relieve the tenant of this liability in the absence of express stipulation to the contrary,[100] but note that in respect of residential accommodation, dwellings are subject to Council Tax.[101]

---

[90] 2006 Act ss.17 and 18.

[91] 2006 Act ss.21–28. This part of the 2006 Act has been amended by provisions in the Private Rented Housing (Scotland) Act 2011 (asp 14).

[92] 2006 Act s.28A–C.

[93] Occupier's Liability (Scotland) Act 1960 s.3; see also *Haggarty v Glasgow Corp*, 1964 S.L.T. (Notes) 54; *Lamb v Glasgow DC*, 1978 S.L.T. (Notes) 64; *Morrison v Stirling DC*, 1991 G.W.D. 12–714; *Todd v Clapperton*, 2009 S.L.T. 837; Stalker, "Todd v Clapperton: The evolving law on repairing obligations and claims against landlords of residential property", 2010 S.L.T. (News) 31.

[94] *Cameron v Young*, 1908 S.C. (HL) 7; *Tay Salmon Fisheries v Speedie*, 1929 S.C. 593; *Mackeson v Boyd*, 1942 S.C. 56. See, too, para.11.05, above. As to the case where a house is rendered unfit to live in by reason of war damage, see the War Damage to Land (Scotland) Act 1941. The law of *rei interitus* may be displaced by agreement in the lease, see, e.g. *Little Cumbrae Estate Ltd v Island of Little Cumbrae Ltd*, 2007 S.C. 525; 2007 S.L.T. 631.

[95] Stair, I, 15, 2; *Duff v Fleming* (1870) 8 M. 769; *Cantors Properties (Scotland) v Swears & Wells*, 1978 S.C. 310.

[96] *Allan v Markland* (1882) 10 R. 383.

[97] *Muir v McIntyre* (1887) 14 R. 470; *Sharp v Thomson*, 1930 S.C. 1092.

[98] *Craig v Millar* (1888) 15 R. 1005.

[99] *Huber v Ross*, 1912 S.C. 898; and cf. *Chevron Petroleum (UK) Ltd v Post Office*, 1986 S.C. 291; 1987 S.L.T. 588; 1987 S.C.L.R. 97 (whether derogation of grant by landlord). But see *Central Car Auctions Ltd v Sher*, 2006 G.W.D. 29–645, where it was held that a tenant was not entitled to rescind a lease by notice where the interference with the tenant's quiet possession was not material.

[100] *Macome v Dickson* (1868) 6 M. 898; *Sturrock v Murray*, 1952 S.C. 454.

[101] See Local Government Finance Act 1992 (c.14) Pt II. The persons liable to pay Council Tax are specified at s.75.

35.09 Rights of public sector tenants: Scottish secure tenancies and the right to purchase—The Housing (Scotland) Act 2001[102] and the Housing (Scotland) Act 1987[103] provide tenants of dwelling-houses in the public sector with a series of important rights. In terms of overall impact, the most important of these rights has been the right of the tenant of a dwelling-house let under a Scottish secure tenancy[104] to purchase the dwelling-house in terms of Pt III of the Housing (Scotland) Act 1987.[105] This right was generally available to the tenant once he had been in continuous occupation for not less than five years,[106] the landlord being a local authority, a registered social landlord[107] or a water or sewerage authority.[108] This right has in recent years become subject to a number of limitations, including, in various circumstances, its complete exclusion. Radical reform of the right to buy was effected by Pt 14 of the Housing (Scotland) Act 2010.[109] Subject to protection in the case of persons being re-accommodated by a landlord,[110] the tenants of properties let after March 1, 2011[111] who are new to the social rented sector or who are returning to it after a break, shall not have the right to purchase.[112] Furthermore, even where the right to purchase is preserved, it may be suspended for up to 10 years in relation to particular areas or particular house types in a local authority area where that authority determines that particular area or house type to be "pressured."[113] New supply social housing is also excluded from the right to purchase. New supply social housing is housing let under a Scottish secure tenancy on or after March 1, 2011 where the property was not let under a Scottish secure tenancy on or before June 25, 2008 or was acquired by the landlord on or after the same date.[114] The right is, however, preserved in specified circumstances.

---

[102] Housing (Scotland) Act 2001 (the "2001 Act") (asp 10).

[103] 1987 Act Pt III, consolidating and amending, inter alia, the Tenant's Rights etc (Scotland) Act 1980 which introduced secure tenancies and the right to purchase. The 1987 Act was itself further amended by the Housing (Scotland) Act 1988, the 2001 Act, the 2010 Act, the Leasehold Reform, Housing and Urban Development Act 1993, and the Local Government etc (Scotland) Act 1994. See, generally, commentary by P. Watchman, *The Housing (Scotland) Act 1987* (Edinburgh: W. Green, 1991); C. Himsworth, *Housing Law in Scotland*, 4th edn (Butterworths, 1994); Gordon and Wortley, *Scottish Land Law* (2009), para.18–87.

[104] For the meaning of "Scottish secure tenancy", see the 2001 Act s.11, Sch.1 (which specifies the excepted categories); *Nisala v Glasgow City Council*, 2006 G.W.D. 34–703.

[105] A tenant required in terms of his contract of employment to occupy the house for the better performance of his duties may not be eligible to purchase: *Campbell v Edinburgh DC*, 1986 S.C. 153; 1987 S.L.T. 51; *Forbes v Glasgow DC*, 1988 G.W.D. 31–1330 (parks department employees); *McKay v Livingston Development Corp*, 1990 S.L.T. (Lands Tr.) 54 (security duties); *De Fontenay v Strathclyde RC*, 1990 S.L.T. 605; *Little v Borders RC*, 1990 S.L.T. (Lands Tr.) 2; *McTurk v Fife RC*, 1990 S.L.T. (Lands Tr.) 49 (school janitor); *Jack v Strathclyde RC*, 1992 S.L.T. (Lands Tr.) 29. Note also that a right of pre-emption contained in the title deeds may not restrict the secure tenant's right to purchase: *Ross and Cromarty DC v Patience*, 1997 S.C. (HL) 46. Disputes in respect of tenants' rights to buy fall under the jurisdiction of the Lands Tribunal for Scotland, see *http://www.lands-tribunal-scotland.org.uk/* [Accessed July 25, 2012].

[106] 1987 Act s.61(2)(c), as amended by 2001 Act s.42(1)(b); for the meaning of "continuous occupation", see s.61(10)(a), as amended by the 2001 Act s.42(2); *McLoughlin's C.B. v Motherwell DC*, 1994 S.L.T. (Lands Tr.) 31; *Beggs v Kilmarnock and Loudoun DC*, 1996 S.L.T. 461.

[107] Under the pre-2001 Act legislation, tenancies between tenants and registered social landlords had been treated as private sector lets.

[108] 1987 Act s.61(2), as amended by the 2001 Act Sch.10.

[109] The "2010 Act".

[110] 2010 Act s.140.

[111] The commencement date, per SSI 2011/96 Sch.1 para.1.

[112] 2010 Act s.141.

[113] 2010 Act s. 142.

[114] 2010 Act s.143.

Where the right is preserved, detailed statutory provisions are made for the procedure to be adopted by purchasing tenants and their landlords, for the conditions to be attached to the sale,[115] for limitations on the tenant's right to buy[116] and for the price to be paid[117] which includes the right to obtain discounts from the purchase price by reference to the length of time for which the tenant or his spouse has been in occupation of housing in the public sector.[118] The statutory right to buy cannot be excluded by contract,[119] nor can the landlord impose financial penalties or other conditions which might discourage a tenant from buying.[120] Where a tenant dies after concluding missives, but before delivery of the disposition, his executors may enforce the missives.[121] The Housing (Scotland) Act 2001 provides public sector tenants with security of tenure by restricting the circumstances in which a Scottish secure tenancy may be brought to an end. A Scottish secure tenancy may not be brought to an end except where the tenant consents to this either by written agreement with the landlord[122] or by giving four weeks' notice to the landlord,[123] or where he dies leaving no qualified person to succeed him,[124] or where, if there is a qualified person, that person declines the tenancy or subsequently dies,[125] or where the dwelling-house has ceased to be occupied,[126] or by conversion of the Scottish secure tenancy to a short Scottish secure tenancy,[127]

---

[115] See, e.g. *Forsyth v Scottish Homes*, 1990 S.L.T. (Lands Tr.) 37 (deletion of conditions relating to repair work); *MacDonald v Strathclyde RC*, 1990 S.L.T. (Lands Tr.) 10 (insertion of conditions relating to emergency egress); *McLuskey v Scottish Homes*, 1993 S.L.T. (Lands Tr.) 17 (liability for maintenance of common parts); *Glasgow DC v Doyle*, 1993 S.L.T. 604 (possible condition that the subjects to be conveyed would be less than the subjects let); *East of Scotland Water Authority v Livingstone*, 1999 S.C. 65 (landlord obliged to sell if he serves his notice refusing to sell late).

[116] 1987 Act ss.61A–66E, introduced by the 2001 Act ss.44–47, and the further amendments introduced by the 2010 Act Pt 14 already outlined (above).

[117] 1987 Act s.62.

[118] 1987 Act ss.61 et seq. These provisions do not apply e.g. to houses with special facilities for the elderly or disabled: *Kennedy v Hamilton DC*, 1996 S.L.T. 1276. Note that in the event of resale within three years, repayment of the discount may be necessary: ss.72, 73; *Clydebank DC v Keeper of the Registers of Scotland*, 1994 S.L.T. (Lands Tr.) 2. See generally *Keay v Renfrew DC*, 1982 S.L.T. (Lands Tr.) 33; *Motherwell DC v Gliori*, 1986 S.C. 189; 1986 S.L.T. 445; *McGroarty v Stirling DC*, 1987 S.L.T. 85; *Edinburgh City Council v Davis*, 1987 S.L.T. (Sh. Ct) 33. As to "occupation" for the purposes of calculating the discount, see *Drummond v Dundee DC*, 1993 G.W.D. 26–1637; *Kelly v Dundee DC*, 1994 S.L.T. 1268; *McLean v Cunnighame DC*, 1996 S.L.T. (Lands Tr.) 2; *Hamilton v Glasgow DC*, 1996 S.L.T. (Lands Tr.) 14; 1996 S.C. 460; *McKay v Dundee DC*, 1996 S.L.T. (Lands Tr.) 9. A further right to abatement of the price on the ground of the landlord's default was introduced by the Leasehold Reform, Housing and Urban Development Act 1993 ss.144 and 145.

[119] 1987 Act s.61(1).

[120] 1987 Act s.75. *Lord Advocate v Glasgow DC*, 1990 S.L.T. 721; *Brookbanks v Motherwell DC*, 1988 S.L.T. (Lands Tr.) 72; *Wingate v Clydebank DC*, 1990 S.L.T. (Lands Tr.) 71.

[121] *Cooper's Exrs v Edinburgh DC*, 1990 S.L.T. 621; 1991 S.L.T. 518, HL; *Jack's Exrx v Falkirk DC*, 1992 S.L.T. 5.

[122] 2001 Act s.12(1)(e).

[123] 2001 Act s.12(1)(f) and s.13 in the case of a joint tenant.

[124] 2001 Act s.22(3), for the meaning of "qualified person", see Sch.3; *Edinburgh City Council v Johnston*, 2005 G.W.D. 26–513; *Cooper's Exrs v Edinburgh DC*, 1991 S.C. (HL) 5; 1991 S.L.T. 518 (missives concluded prior to the death of qualified person enforceable by deceased's executors); *Hamilton DC v Lennon*, 1990 S.C. 230; 1990 S.L.T. 533 (nephew caring for relative not a joint tenant); *Roxburgh DC v Collins*, 1991 S.L.T. (Sh. Ct) 49; 1991 S.C.L.R. 575 (Sh. Ct) (son living and working elsewhere); and see Gordon and Wortley, *Scottish Land Law* (2009), para.18–54.

[125] 2001 Act s.22(2) and (4).

[126] 2001 Act s.18; see too abandonment by tenant: ss.17 and 20.

[127] 2001 Act s.35.

or by an order for possession granted by the court.[128] In the case of rent arrears, amendments under the Housing (Scotland) Act 2010 will have the effect of introducing pre-action requirements so as to give additional protection to tenants.[129] Scottish secure tenants are also given the right to a written lease which embodies the terms of the tenancy,[130] the right to information regarding their right to buy[131] and other information,[132] the right to assign or sub-let with the landlord's consent which shall not be unreasonably refused[133] and, also with consent (not to be unreasonably withheld), to carry out alterations and improvements to the house.[134] In certain circumstances, an approved private sector landlord may acquire, from a public sector landlord, houses occupied by Scottish secure tenants.[135] Tenants retain their right to buy, but have the lesser security of tenure available under the assured tenancy regime.[136]

35.10 Protection against harassment and eviction—The tenant, as a residential occupier, is protected by the Rent (Scotland) Act 1984[137] and the Housing (Scotland) Act 1988[138] against harassment by any person, including the landlord, which is intended to induce him to give up the occupation of the premises or any part of them, or to refrain from exercising any right or pursuing any remedy to which he is entitled in respect of the premises. Where the tenancy has come to an end and the occupier continues to reside in the premises he has the right not to be ejected without a court order[139]; the landlord's proper course is to apply to the court for a warrant for his ejection, and if he attempts to eject the occupier at his own hand he may be liable in damages for wrongous ejection[140] as well as to the criminal penalty provided by the 1984 Act.[141]

---

[128] 2001 Act s.16(2). For the grounds on which such an order may be made see s.14(2) and (4) and Sch.2 paras 1–15; *Edinburgh City Council v T*, 2003 G.W.D. 29–821; *Langstane H.A. v Morrow*, 2005 G.W.D. 34–647; *City of Edinburgh Council v Dougan*, 2006 G.W.D. 28–629. For cases under the 1987 Act related to secure tenancies, see *Scottish Special Housing Association v Lumsden*, 1984 S.L.T. (Sh. Ct) 71; *Charing Cross & Kelvingrove Housing Association v Kraska*, 1986 S.L.T. (Sh. Ct) 42; *Monklands DC v Johnstone*, 1987 S.C.L.R. 480; *Glasgow DC v Brown (No.2)*, 1988 S.C.L.R. 679 (Sh. Ct); *Midlothian DC v Brown*, 1991 S.L.T. (Sh. Ct) 80; 1990 S.C.L.R. 765 (Sh. Ct); *Midlothian DC v Drummond*, 1991 S.L.T. (Sh. Ct) 67; *Renfrew DC v Inglis*, 1991 S.L.T. (Sh. Ct) 83; 1992 S.C.L.R. 30 (Sh. Ct); *Glasgow DC v Erhaigonoma*, 1993 S.C.L.R. 592.
[129] 2010 Act s.155.
[130] 2001 Act s.23(1).
[131] 2001 Act s.23(4).
[132] 2001 Act s.23(6).
[133] 2001 Act s.32.
[134] 2001 Act ss.27–31, although the primary responsibility for repairs rests upon the landlord, e.g. s.27 and Sch.4.
[135] Housing (Scotland) Act 1988 (c.43) (the "1988 Act") Pt III, as amended by the 2001 Act; and see e.g. *Waverley Housing Trust v Roxburgh DC*, 1995 S.L.T. (Lands Tr.) 2.
[136] See the annotations to the Housing (Scotland) Act 1988 by P. Robson, *Scottish Current Law Statutes 1988*, Vol.4.
[137] Rent (Scotland) Act 1984 (the "1984 Act") s.22(2) and (2A).
[138] 1988 Act ss.36–38.
[139] 1984 Act ss.22, 23, and s.23A (inserted by the 1988 Act s.40); cf. *N.C.B. v McInnes*, 1968 S.C. 321.
[140] See Rankine, *The Law of Leases in Scotland* (1916), p.592; *Cairns v Innes*, 1942 S.C. 164; 1988 Act s.36; *Anderson v Cluny Investment Service Ltd*, 2004 S.L.T. (Sh. Ct) 37; *City of Edinburgh Council v Burnett*, 2012 G.W.D. 13–257.
[141] 1984 Act s.22, as amended by the 1988 Act s.38.

The Equality Act 2010[142] makes discrimination on specified grounds unlawful in the letting of premises, in affording access to facilities in premises let, and in evicting tenants.

Tenant's remedies—If the subjects are at the outset to a material extent unfit for **35.11** their purpose, the tenant may refuse to enter into possession and claim damages.[143] He has the same remedy where the subjects are advertised as possessing certain qualities or advantages which they do not possess.[144] If during the currency of the lease the landlord fails to execute repairs, with the result that the subjects become unfit for their purpose, the tenant may abandon the lease. If he proposes also to claim damages he is probably bound to give immediate notice; if not, and the landlord accepts his renunciation, a compromise between the parties, involving an abandonment of the tenant's claim for damages, will be inferred.[145] The question whether a tenant may abandon the lease depends upon the materiality of the defects, which admits of no rule more definite than that both parties must behave reasonably in the matter.[146] Short of abandoning the lease, the tenant may find a remedy in damages,[147] or in the retention of his rent. This right has been rested on the principle that payment of rent, and furnishing a subject in the condition agreed upon, expressly or impliedly, are the correlative obligations in a mutual contract, and therefore that any material failure on the part of the landlord justifies the tenant in the exercise of a right of retention.[148] In an agricultural holding, a landlord will be in material breach where he fails to implement his statutory obligation to put the fixed equipment on the holding into a thorough state of repair, thus entitling the tenant to withhold rent.[149] A defect will more readily be held to be material, especially in the case of failure to carry out improvements, in the later than in the earlier years of the lease.[150] An offer to consign the rent is an element in favour of the tenant's case, but is not per se a good answer to a demand for payment.[151] The fact that the tenant has paid certain instalments of the rent while the defects of which he complains were obvious does not bar an ultimate plea of

---

[142] Equality Act 2010 (c.15). The law had formerly been contained in the Sex Discrimination Act 1975, the Race Relations Act 1976, the Disability Discrimination Act 1995, Equality Act 2006 and the Equality Act (Sexual Orientation) Regulations 2007. The Equality Act 2010 supersedes these earlier statutes.

[143] *Critchley v Campbell* (1884) 11 R. 475.

[144] *Brodie v McLachlan* (1900) 8 S.L.T. 145.

[145] *Lyons v Anderson* (1886) 13 R. 1020; Rankine, *The Law of Leases in Scotland* (1916), pp.244–5.

[146] *McKimmie's Trs v Armour* (1899) 2 F. 156 (house had become insanitary). Note that destruction of the subjects, such as by accidental fire, puts an end to the lease altogether: see paras 35.08, above and 35.26, below.

[147] See, e.g. *Morrison v Stirling DC*, 1991 G.W.D. 12–714. Continued occupation in the knowledge that a house is in a dangerous state may, on the principle of *volenti non fit injuria*, bar a claim for damages: *Dickie v Amicable Property Investment Co*, 1911 S.C. 1079; *Mullen v CC of Dunbarton*, 1933 S.L.T. 185; *Proctor v Cowlairs Cooperative Society*, 1961 S.L.T. 434.

[148] *Christie v Birrell*, 1910 S.C. 986; *Earl of Galloway v McConnell*, 1911 S.C. 846; *Haig v Boswall-Preston*, 1915 S.C. 339; *Fingland & Mitchell v Howie*, 1926 S.C. 319; *Renfrew DC v Gray*, 1987 S.L.T. (Sh. Ct) 70. For a discussion of the principle of mutuality in relation to lease, see Paton and Cameron, *Landlord and Tenant* (1967), p.90; *Edmonstone v Lamont*, 1975 S.L.T. (Sh. Ct) 57. See also above, paras 10.14–10.17.

[149] See *Alexander v Royal Hotel (Caithness) Ltd*, 2001 S.L.T. 17, considering the Agricultural Holdings (Scotland) Act 1991 (the "1991 Act") s.5(2)(a).

[150] *Bowie v Duncan* (1807) Hume 839.

[151] *Earl of Galloway v McConnell*, 1911 S.C. 846. See also *City of Edinburgh District Council v Robbin*, 1994 S.L.T. (Sh. Ct) 51.

retention.[152] It is a question of circumstances whether the payment of rent without objection will bar an ultimate claim for damages for defects existing during the period for which rent was paid.[153] It is open to the parties to agree that the tenant shall not withhold payment of the rent.[154]

35.12 Obligations of tenant—A tenant is bound to enter into possession, to occupy and use the subjects. The tenant of a hotel, who had shut it up in the interests of a rival house of which he had obtained a lease, was found liable in damages for breach of a material condition.[155] A landlord was held entitled to terminate a lease on the same ground when the tenant who had undertaken to reside on the farm leased was sent to prison for a substantial period.[156] More recently, the question has arisen particularly in connection with clauses in commercial leases obliging the tenant to continue to trade from the premises ("keep open" clauses). Material breach of such a clause entitles a landlord to obtain damages,[157] although the lease does not continue where the tenant is in material breach of a term but has validly served notice of termination upon the landlord.[158] Provided such a clause is sufficiently precise, a landlord is entitled to decree of specific implement to compel the tenant to comply with the clause or to interdict the tenant from ceasing to trade from the premises.[159] The law in England is different.[160] In his occupation and use the tenant is bound to exercise reasonable care. Thus damages were held to be due for injury caused by burst pipes, in a case where a tenant had left the house in winter without turning off the water or giving notice to the landlord.[161] In the cases where the landlord has a right of hypothec the tenant is bound to plenish or stock the subjects, and the obligation may be enforced by a replenishing order in the sheriff court.[162] The tenant may not invert the possession, by utilising the subjects for some purpose other than that for which they were let. So the tenant of

---

[152] *Haig v Boswall-Preston*, 1915 S.C. 339.

[153] *Ramsay v Howison*, 1908 S.C. 697. Opinion of Lord Salvesen in *Haig v Boswall-Preston*, 1915 S.C. 339.

[154] *Skene v Cameron*, 1942 S.C. 393.

[155] *Graham v Stevenson* (1792) Hume 781. See *Smith v Henderson* (1897) 24 R. 1102.

[156] *Blair Trust Co v Gilbert*, 1940 S.L.T. 322, affd 1941 S.N. 2. For a recent discussion on the termination of a lease by a landlord where there is averred to be a material breach on the part of the tenant see *Crieff Highland Gathering Ltd v Perth and Kinross Council*, 2011 S.L.T. 992, Lord Pentland (Ordinary) at [54].

[157] *Douglas Shelf Seven Ltd v Cooperative Wholesale Society Ltd*, 2007 G.W.D. 9–167.

[158] See *Allied Dunbar Assurance Plc v Superglass Sections Ltd*, 2003 S.L.T. 1420, in which the court was of the view that where a break option has been exercised, the lease comes to an end at the thereby accelerated ish irrespective of whether the tenant is in breach.

[159] *Church Commissioners for England v Abbey National Plc*, 1994 S.L.T. 959; *Retail Parks Investments Ltd v The Royal Bank of Scotland Plc*, 1996 S.C. 227; *Highland and Universal Properties Ltd v Safeway Properties Ltd*, 1996 S.L.T. 559; 2000 S.L.T. 414; *Cooperative Wholesale Society Ltd v Saxone Ltd*, 1997 S.L.T. 1052; *Cooperative Insurance Society Ltd v Halfords (No.2)*, 1998 S.C. 212; *Britel Fund Trs Ltd v Scottish and Southern Energy Plc*, 2002 S.L.T. 223; *Oak Mall Greenock Ltd v McDonald's Restaurants Ltd*, 2003 G.W.D. 17–540; *Cooperative Wholesale Society Ltd v Ravenseft Properties Ltd (No.3)*, 2003 S.C.L.R. 509; 2003 G.W.D. 11–324; *Allied Dunbar Assurance Plc v Superglass Sections Ltd*, 2003 S.L.T. 1420; *Douglas Shelf Seven Ltd v Cooperative Wholesale Society Ltd*, 2007 G.W.D. 9–167. The Lands Tribunal's jurisdiction to vary such a clause in a long lease (under the Title Conditions (Scotland) Act 2003 s.90(1)(a)) was questioned in the case of *Propinvest Paisley LP v Co-operative Group Ltd*, 2012 S.C. 51, in which the Inner House recalled a decision of the Tribunal and allowed proof before answer.

[160] *Cooperative Insurance Society Ltd v Argyll Stores (Holdings) Ltd* [1998] A.C. 1.

[161] *Mickel v McCoard*, 1913 S.C. 1036.

[162] *Whitelaw v Fulton* (1871) 10 M. 27; *Wright v Wightman* (1875) 3 R. 68. See para.36.14, below.

a farm is not entitled to use it as a posting station[163]; a priest may not erect, in premises let as his residence, wooden huts for the accommodation of evicted tenants.[164] On the other hand the tenant of a furnished house may alter the position of the furniture or pictures[165]; the tenant of a shop may sell his stock by auction.[166] There are special provisions for diversification of agricultural lets.[167] The tenant is also bound to pay rent when it becomes due. A tenant may have certain duties of care on the expiry of a lease.[168]

Rent: Rent reviews—It is common in the case of leases of longer duration and **35.13** more or less universal practice in commercial leases for the lease to contain a clause providing for the review of rent at regular intervals, such as every five years. A time limit may be set by the clause as to when an application for review of the rent may be made, if it is to be made at all, but as a general rule time will not be treated as of the essence so to bar a late application for review unless there is some special reason for doing so such as an express statement to this effect in the clause or a provision for fixing the rent if no review takes place.[169] Acceptance of rent without qualification or explanation may be sufficient, however, to imply that the landlord has abandoned and thus waived his right to seek a review.[170] Owing to the serious financial consequences for the parties of whether it is the original or an increased rent under the lease which is to be payable, there has been a good deal of litigation on the question of rent review.[171] A statutory rent review procedure is contained in the Agricultural Holdings (Scotland) Act 2003 in relation to limited duration tenancies, which procedure will be amended to outlaw landlord initiated only or upwards only reviews by the Agricultural Holdings (Amendment) (Scotland) Act 2012.[172]

Landlord's hypothec—A landlord has the ordinary remedies of a creditor for the **35.14** recovery of his rent. He may raise an action for payment of the rent even if the tenant has purported to renounce the lease and is no longer in possession of the

---

[163] *Baillie v Mackay* (1842) 4 D. 1520.

[164] *Kehoe v Marquess of Lansdowne* [1893] A.C. 451.

[165] *Miller v Stewart* (1899) 2 F. 309.

[166] *Keith v Reid* (1870) 8 M. (HL) 110; *Morrison v Forsyth*, 1909 S.C. 329 (clearance sale).

[167] 2003 Act s.39. See para.35.48, below.

[168] See, e.g. *Fry's Metals Ltd v Durastic Ltd*, 1991 S.L.T. 689.

[169] *United Scientific Holdings v Burnley BC* [1978] A.C. 904; *Scottish Development Agency v Morrisons Holdings Ltd*, 1986 S.L.T. 59; *Yates, Petitioner*, 1987 S.L.T. 86; *Leeds Permanent Pension Scheme Trs v William Timpson*, 1987 S.C.L.R. 571; *Legal and Commercial Properties Ltd v Lothian RC*, 1988 S.L.T. 463; 1988 S.C.L.R. 201; *Visionhire Ltd v Britel Fund Trs Ltd*, 1991 S.L.T. 883, IH; 1992 S.C.L.R. 236, IH; *EAE (RT) Ltd v EAE Property Ltd*, 1994 S.L.T. 627; *Scottish Life Assurance Co Ltd v Agfa-Gevaert Ltd*, 1998 S.C. 171; *Charterhouse Square Finance Co Ltd v A. & J. Menswear*, 1998 S.L.T. 720; *Bradford and Bingley Building Society v Thorntons Plc* Unreported November 26, 1998 Lord Hamilton; *City Wall Properties (Scotland) Ltd v Pearl Assurance Plc (No.1)*, 2004 S.C. 214; *Howgate Shopping Centre Ltd v Catercraft Services Ltd*, 2004 S.L.T. 231; *City Wall Properties (Scotland) Ltd v Pearl Assurance Plc (No.2)*, 2005 G.W.D. 35–666; *Prow v Argyll and Bute Council* [2012] CSOH 77.

[170] *Banks v Mecca Bookmakers (Scotland)*, 1982 S.C. 7; 1982 S.L.T. 150.

[171] See the cases cited in fn.169; in addition, on the question whether the clause is sufficiently certain, *Crawford v Bruce*, 1992 S.L.T. 524; *Aberdeen City Council v Clark*, 1999 S.L.T. 613; in general, M.J. Ross and D.J. McKichan, *Drafting and Negotiating Commercial Leases in Scotland*, 2nd edn (Butterworths, 1993), Ch.6. On review by the court of the rent fixed by an expert, *AGE Ltd v Kwik Save Stores Ltd*, 2001 S.L.T. 841; *Homebase Ltd v Scottish Provident Institution*, 2004 S.L.T. 296; *East Renfrewshire Council v J.H. Lygate and Partners* [2005] CSIH 27.

[172] Agricultural Holdings (Amendment) (Scotland) Act 2012 s.9.

subjects, so that by suing for the outstanding rent he is seeking implement of only one of the tenant's obligations under the lease.[173] In certain subjects he has, in addition, a right in security known as hypothec, which the landlord could formerly seek to enforce by means of the process known as landlord's sequestration. However, the diligence of sequestration for rent was abolished with the coming into force of the provisions of the Bankruptcy and Diligence etc (Scotland) Act 2007.[174]

At common law the landlord's hypothec was a general incident of the contract of lease, but it was abolished in 1880 for all subjects let for agriculture or pasture and exceeding two acres in extent,[175] and it was recently considerably further restricted by the 2007 Act.

In cases where hypothec still exists, mainly in leases of commercial premises, shops, mines and market gardens, the hypothec covers the ordinary equipment, the stock-in-trade in a shop. The subjects covered are known as the *invecta et illata*.[176] At common law, certain items were exempt.[177] The categories of exempt items by statute are now listed in the Debt Arrangement and Attachment (Scotland) Act 2002[178] and the Bankruptcy and Diligence etc (Scotland) Act 2007.[179] Property (i) kept in a dwelling-house, (ii) kept on agricultural land, (iii) kept on a croft, (iv) owned by a person other than the tenant, and (v) acquired by a third party in good faith from the tenant, are all exempt under the Bankruptcy and Diligence etc (Scotland) Act 2007.[180] Importantly, the effect of s.208(4) of the Bankruptcy and Diligence etc (Scotland) Act 2007 is that the hypothec no longer covers goods brought to the premises, though they do not belong to the tenant, as in the case of hired furniture.[181] It has been held that the hypothec applies whether the whole of the tenant's plenishing, or merely a single article,[182] is obtained on hire or hire-purchase, though not where the subjects are let furnished and an additional article is obtained on hire.[183] As hypothec continues to survive, albeit subject to considerable restriction, much of the case law continues to be of relevance, subject also to restriction; but the effect of the recent reforms has been to obscure rather than clarify the law,[184] and clarification is needed.

---

[173] *Salaried Staff London Loan Co v Swears & Wells*, 1985 S.C. 189; 1985 S.L.T. 326.

[174] Bankruptcy and Diligence etc (Scotland) Act 2007 (the "2007 Act") s.208, with commencement on April 1, 2008 by means of Bankruptcy and Diligence etc (Scotland) Act 2007 (Commencement No.3, Savings and Transitionals) Order 2008 (SSI 2008/115) art.3(1)(f). See A. McAllister, "The Landlord's Hypothec: Down But Is It Out?", 2010 Jur. Rev. 65; S. Skea and A. Steven, "The Landlord's Hypothec: Difficulties in Practice", 2010 S.L.T. (News) 120. It is suggested by Skea and Steven that the enforcement procedure to be used may now be attachment under the Debt Arrangement and Attachment (Scotland) Act 2002. This repeats an observation made in A. Steven, "Goodbye to Sequestration of Rent", 2006 S.L.T. (News) 17.

[175] Hypothec Abolition (Scotland) Act 1880. See Rankine, *The Law of Leases in Scotland* (1916), pp.371–2.

[176] Gordon and Wortley, *Scottish Land Law* (2009), para.18–191.

[177] For example, money, bonds, bills and tenant's clothes (Bell, *Principles*, s.1276); the tenant's tools of trade, by analogy with the law relating to other forms of diligence (*Macpherson v Macpherson's Tr.* (1905) 8 F. 191); Rankine, *The Law of Leases in Scotland* (1916), p.374.

[178] Debt Arrangement and Attachment (Scotland) Act 2002 (asp 17) ss.11(1) and 60(2).

[179] 2007 Act s.208.

[180] 2007 Act s.208(3)–(9).

[181] See the cases of *McIntosh v Potts* (1905) 7 F. 765; *Nelmes v Ewing* (1883) 11 R. 193; *Novacold v Fridge Freight (Fyvie) Ltd*, 1999 S.C.L.R. 409.

[182] *Dundee Corp v Marr*, 1971 S.C. 96.

[183] *Edinburgh Albert Building Co v General Guarantee Corp*, 1917 S.C. 239.

[184] See *Stair Memorial Encyclopaedia*, "Bankruptcy" (Reissue), pp.423.

Hypothec: Rents covered—Following the coming into force of s.208 of the **35.15**
Bankruptcy and Diligence etc (Scotland) Act 2007, hypothec is now security for
rent due and unpaid only; and subsists for so long as that rent remains unpaid.
There is no requirement that action must be taken to enforce the hypothec within
the current rental year, and it would appear that the normal rules on negative
prescription would apply, giving a landlord a five-year window within which
rights may be enforced.[185] This considerably expands upon the former position in
which hypothec secured one year's rent already due or else rent falling due,[186] and
fell if not put in force by sequestration within three months of the last term of
payment.

Sequestration—Hypothec was formerly enforced by means of the action of **35.16**
sequestration for rent, but the diligence of sequestration for rent was abolished
when s.208(1) of the Bankruptcy and Diligence etc (Scotland) Act 2007 came into
force on April 1, 2008.[187] Sequestration for rent was exclusively a sheriff court
process.[188] The ordinary course of procedure was that a warrant to sequestrate was
granted on an ex parte statement, the goods were inventoried and valued by a
sheriff officer, and ultimately sold, under a separate warrant from the sheriff, by
auction. After being inventoried the goods were in the custody of the court, and
anyone who removed them, be he the tenant, a purchaser, or another creditor, had,
if in good faith, to account for their value, and, if in bad faith, was liable for the
rent.[189] It has been suggested that hypothec may be enforced during the currency
of a lease by attachment, but the law is far from clear and has been the subject of
comment and calls for clarification.[190]

Right of retention under hypothec—A landlord may interdict the removal of the **35.17**
invecta et illata,[191] and, if they have been removed, may obtain a warrant to have
them brought back. It has been held that such a warrant should not be pronounced
without intimation to the tenant, except for some exceptional reason specified in
the judgment.[192] Interdict and recovery of goods constitute exceptional remedies,
and the landlord will be liable in damages, either if the statement on which he
obtains authority proves untrue,[193] or if there is a genuine dispute as to the rent and
the circumstances render extreme measures unnecessary.[194] Where a tenant transfers property in breach of an interdict, and a third party acquires that property in
good and for value, the property ceases to be subject to the hypothec upon
acquisition.[195]

---

[185] *Stair Memorial Encyclopaedia*, "Bankruptcy" (Reissue), p.425.
[186] *Young v Welsh* (1833) 12 S. 233.
[187] Bankruptcy and Diligence etc. (Scotland) Act 2007 (Commencement No. 3, Savings and
Transitionals) Order 2008 (SSI 2008/115).
[188] *Duncan v Lodijensky* (1904) 6 F. 408.
[189] Bell, *Principles*, s.1244.
[190] *Stair Memorial Encyclopaedia*, "Bankruptcy" (Reissue), p.425; Skea and Steven, "The landlord's Hypothec: Difficulties in Practice", 2010 S.L.T. (News) 120; McAllister, "The Landlord's
Hypothec: Down but is it Out?", 2010 Jur. Rev. 65.
[191] 2007 Act s.208(5).
[192] *Johnston v Young* (1890) 18 R. (J.) 6; *Jack v Black*, 1911 S.C. 691.
[193] *Jack v Black*, 1911 S.C. 691; *Shearer v Nicoll*, 1935 S.L.T. 313.
[194] *Gray v Weir* (1891) 19 R. 25.
[195] 2007 Act s.208(5).

35.18 Rent: Legal and conventional terms—The terms of payment of rent are usually expressly agreed as between landlord and tenant in the lease. But in a question in the succession of the landlord or, if the landlord sells the subjects let, between him and the purchaser, the allocation of the rents may depend, in agricultural or pastoral leases,[196] on the legal and not on the conventional terms. The legal terms, in farms primarily arable, and where the tenant's entry is at Martinmas, are the Whitsunday and Martinmas[197] following the term of entry. In a pastoral farm, with entry at Whitsunday, the first half-year's rent is legally due at entry, the second at the following Martinmas.[198] The underlying theory is that rent is not due legally (though it may be conventionally) until the tenant has had the benefit of the crop. Rents conventionally payable before the legal term are known as "forehand"; payable later, as "backhand". The legal terms rule in allocating rents between the heir of a landlord and his executor, and also between a fiar and the representatives of the life-renter, except when the rent is forehand, when the conventional terms rule. The executor is entitled to all backhand rents which were legally due for the term preceding the landlord's death, and also, under the Apportionment Act 1870, to a share of the next term's rent corresponding to the number of days by which the deceased survived that term.[199] In the case of a sale, in the absence of any express provision, the purchaser is entitled to the rents to become due for the possession following his term of entry, according to the legal and not the conventional terms, except in the case of forehand rents, in which case he is entitled to the rents payable at the conventional terms following the term of entry.[200]

35.19 Assignability: Sub-letting—A lease may or may not be assignable.[201] Where there is no express provision in the lease an exclusion of the power to assign or sublet will be implied at common law in accordance with the principle of *delectus personae*, subject to certain exceptions. Judicial or legal assignees are not excluded. Leases of unfurnished urban subjects, in town or country, may be assigned, for here the element of *delectus personae* is less strong.[202] Leases of rural subjects may also be assigned where they are for an extraordinary duration, on the basis that such a lease amounts in effect to a right of property.[203] Rural leases of ordinary duration, however, i.e. farm leases whether arable or pastoral, leases of shootings and fishings, are according to the general rule, not assignable.[204] Sub-letting follows the same rules.[205] A provision (once common in mining leases) that the tenant shall not assign without the landlord's consent gives the

---

[196] These rules do not apply to the rents of residential property, which accrue from day to day: *Butter v Foster*, 1912 S.C. 1218.

[197] In terms of the Term and Quarter Days (Scotland) Act 1990, Whitsunday and Martinmas signify May 28 and November 28 respectively, unless otherwise defined in the lease: see *Provincial Insurance Plc v Valtos Ltd*, 1992 S.C.L.R. 203 (Sh. Ct).

[198] See opinion of Lord Johnstone in *Butter*, 1912 S.C. 1218 at 1224; *Baillie v Fletcher*, 1915 S.C. 677.

[199] *Campbell v Campbell* (1849) 11 D. 1426; *Balfour-Kinnear v Inland Revenue*, 1909 S.C. 619.

[200] Titles to Land Consolidation Act 1868 s.8, as amended by the Abolition of Feudal Tenure etc (Scotland) Act 2000 Sch.13(1) para.1; *Baillie v Fletcher*, 1915 S.C. 677.

[201] Gordon and Wortley, *Scottish Land Law* (2009), paras 18–28—18–39.

[202] *Robb v Brearton* (1895) 22 R. 885; Rankine, *The Law of Leases in Scotland* (1916), pp.174–5.

[203] Rankine, *The Law of Leases in Scotland* (1916), p.173; *Bain v Mackenzie* (1896) 23 R. 528 at 532, per Lord Kinnear. The necessary duration appears to be more than 21 years; *Scottish Ministers v Trs of the Drummond Trust*, 2001 S.L.T. 665 (99-year lease).

[204] Bell, *Principles*, s.1214; *Mackintosh v May* (1895) 22 R. 345; *Moray Estates Development Co v Butler*, 1999 S.L.T. 1338.

[205] Bell, *Principles*, s.1216; Gordon and Wortley, *Scottish Land Law* (2009), para.18–35.

landlord an absolute right to refuse, or to impose conditions.[206] A clause frequently used provides that the landlord's consent to assignation should not be unreasonably withheld.[207] Prior to the Land Tenure Reform (Scotland) Act 1974, a proprietor who had granted a lease to a tenant could not interpose another party as tenant so as to degrade the first lessee into the position of a sub-tenant.[208] It is, however, now competent.[209] In the cases of agricultural holdings, short limited duration tenancies and limited duration tenancies, the common law rules on assignation and sub-letting are supplemented by special statutory provisions.[210] For example, there is a statutory prohibition on the assignation or sub-letting of a short limited duration tenancy.[211]

Effects of assignation—The assignation of a lease is completed, in questions **35.20** between the landlord, the tenant and the assignee, by intimation to the landlord.[212] While a sub-lease involves no change of tenant so far as the landlord is concerned and the original tenant continues bound to implement the obligations of the lease, an assignation involves the substitution of the assignee as the sole tenant. The result is that the cedent disappears and has no further rights or obligations after the date of entry, while the assignee incurs liability to the landlord for all future rents, and also probably (together with the cedent) for arrears.[213] There is no rule to preclude the assignation of an unprofitable lease, if assignable, to a person of no means. A sub-let, on the other hand, neither brings the sub-tenant into any contractual relations with the landlord, nor does it involve him in any liability to the landlord for rent, nor does it affect the liability of the tenant.[214] Against competing assignees or other third parties, the assignee's right is completed only by actual possession,[215] unless the lease is registered in the appropriate form under the Registration of Leases (Scotland) Act 1857[216] or the Land Registration etc (Scotland) Act 2012.[217]

---

[206] *Marquis of Breadalbane v Whitehead* (1893) 21 R. 138; *Lousada & Co Ltd v J.E. Lesser (Properties) Ltd*, 1990 S.C. 178; 1990 S.L.T. 823 (suspensive condition). See, however, as to discrimination by withholding consent, the Equality Act 2010.

[207] See, e.g. *Renfrew DC v A.B. Leisure (Renfrew) Ltd*, 1988 S.L.T. 635; 1988 S.L.C.R. 512; sequel in 1990 S.C.L.R. 375; *Brador Properties Ltd v British Telecommunications Plc*, 1992 S.C. 12; *Scotmore Developments Ltd v Anderton*, 1996 S.C. 368; *Scottish Tourist Board v Deanpark Ltd*, 1998 S.L.T. 1121; *Sears Properties Netherlands BV v Coal Pension Properties Ltd*, 2001 S.L.T. 761; *Legal and General Assurance Society Ltd v Tesco Stores Ltd*, 2001 G.W.D. 18–707; *Ashworth Frazer Ltd v Gloucester City Council* [2002] 1 All E.R. 377; *Scottish Property Investment Ltd v Scottish Provident Ltd*, 2004 G.W.D. 6–120; *Burgerking Ltd v Rachel Charitable Trust*, 2006 S.L.T. 224; Gordon and Wortley, *Scottish Land Law* (2009), para.18–30.

[208] *Wilson v Wilson* (1859) 21 D. 309 at 312, per Lord Justice-Clerk Inglis.

[209] 1974 Act s.17; *Kildrummy (Jersey) Ltd v Calder (No.2)*, 1997 S.L.T. 186. Validity in a crofting context was confirmed in *Scottish Ministers v Pairc Trust Ltd*, 2007 S.L.C.R. 166.

[210] 1991 Act s.10A and the 2003 Act ss.6 and 7.

[211] 2003 Act s.6(1).

[212] *Inglis v Paul* (1829) 7 S. 469; and see *Smith v Place D'Or 101 Ltd*, 1988 S.L.T. (Sh. Ct) 5 (circumstances in which held that delivery of a formal deed of assignation was not necessary in addition to intimation to render the assignation effective).

[213] *Skene v Greenhill* (1825) 4 S. 25; *Burns v Martin* (1887) 14 R. (HL) 20, opinion of Lord Watson; *Primary Health Care Centres (Broadford) Ltd v Ravangave* [2008] CSOH 14; 2008 Hous. L.R. 24.

[214] Bell, *Principles*, s.1252. As to possible endurance of sub-lessee's right of possession beyond termination of head lease, see Gordon and Wortley, *Scottish Land Law* (2009), para.18–37.

[215] *Ramsay v Commercial Bank* (1842) 4 D. 405.

[216] Registration of Leases (Scotland) Act 1857 ss.2, 16, as amended by the Land Registration etc (Scotland) Act 2012; see para.35.05, above.

[217] Superseding the former provisions in the Land Registration (Scotland) Act 1979 s.3(3).

35.21 Transfer of tenancy of matrimonial home and family home—Prior to 1981 a lease of premises occupied by a husband and wife as their matrimonial home which had been granted in favour of one spouse gave no right of occupation to the other spouse. The Matrimonial Homes (Family Protection) (Scotland) Act 1981,[218] however, introduced an important change in the law as to the rights of occupancy of spouses[219] in the matrimonial home. The Civil Partnership Act 2004 introduced corresponding provisions which provide protection to civil partners[220] in the family home.[221] A spouse who is neither the owner nor the tenant of it now has the right, if in occupation, to continue to occupy the matrimonial home and, if not in occupation, to enter into and take occupation of it.[222] The Civil Partnership Act 2004 has the same effect in the case of a civil partner and the family home.[223] In addition, the Matrimonial Homes (Family Protection) (Scotland) Act 1981 and the Civil Partnership Act 2004 contain provisions which enable the court to make an order transferring the tenancy of the matrimonial home or family home from one spouse or civil partner to the other.[224] The effect of such an order is to vest the tenancy in the other spouse or civil partner without intimation to the landlord, subject to all the liabilities under the lease other than for any arrears of rent for the period prior to the making of the order which remain the liability of the spouse or civil partner who was originally entitled to the house.[225] Where both spouses or civil partners are joint or common tenants of the matrimonial home the court may, on the application of one of them, make an order vesting the tenancy in that spouse or civil partner solely, subject to the payment by the applicant to the other spouse or civil partner of such compensation as seems just and reasonable.[226] Some protection for the interests of the landlord is afforded by the fact that the court is required to have regard to the suitability of the applicant to become the tenant or sole tenant of the house and to his or her capacity to perform the obligations under the lease.[227] A copy of the application must also be served on the landlord and the court must give him an opportunity of being heard before making an order trans-

---

[218] As amended by the Law Reform (Miscelleneous Provisions) (Scotland) Act 1985 s.13, the Civil Partnership Act 2004 and the Family Law (Scotland) Act 2006 s.31(3). See further below, Ch.44 (Family Law).

[219] As to cohabiting couples, see the Matrimonial Homes (Family Protection) (Scotland) Act 1981 s.18.

[220] Civil Partnership Act 2004 ss.101–116.

[221] The "family home" is defined in similar terms to a "matrimonial home" under s.18A(3) of the Matrimonial Homes (Family Protection) (Scotland) Act 1981.

[222] Matrimonial Homes (Family Protection) (Scotland) Act 1981 s.1. The spouse's rights to continue occupying or to enter and occupy include the right to do so together with any child of the family: s.1(1A).

[223] Civil Partnership Act 2004 s.101.

[224] s.13 of the Matrimonial Homes (Family Protection) (Scotland) Act 1981, as amended by the Family Law (Scotland) Act 1985 Sch.1 and the Agricultural Holdings (Scotland) Act 2002 Sch.1 para.5(b); and s.112 of the Civil Partnership Act 2004.

[225] s.13(5) of the Matrimonial Homes (Family Protection) (Scotland) Act 1981; s.112(5) of the Civil Partnership Act 2004.

[226] s.13(9) of the Matrimonial Homes (Family Protection) (Scotland) Act 1981; see *McGowan v McGowan*, 1986 S.L.T. 112; also Housing (Scotland) Act 1986 s.11 and Housing (Scotland) Act 1987 Sch.3 para.16. In the case of civil partners, see s.112(10) of the Civil Partnership Act 2004. In *Souter v McAuley*, 2010 S.L.T. (Sh. Ct) 121 the court considered the transfer of a tenancy where two same-sex partners, whose relationship had broken down, were in competition for the tenancy of the local authority property which they had formerly shared as joint tenants.

[227] s.13(3) of the Matrimonial Homes (Family Protection) (Scotland) Act 1981; s.112(3) of the Civil Partnership Act 2004.

ferring the lease.[228] Certain types of lease are excluded from this procedure altogether.[229] It is not competent for an application to be made where the matrimonial home or family home is or is part of an agricultural holding or is let under a long lease. Nor is it competent where the premises are let to the spouse by his or her employer as an incident of employment and the lease is subject to a requirement that the spouse must reside therein, or if the spouses are joint or common tenants that they must both reside there. There are exceptions also in the case of premises which are on or pertain to a croft or the subject of a cottar or the holding of a landholder or statutory small tenant or are part of the tenancy land of a tenant-at-will, but these do not apply where both spouses are joint or common tenants of the matrimonial home or family home. Other methods whereby a tenancy may be transferred from one spouse or civil partner to another remain competent, but the advantage of the statutory procedure is that an order for transfer may be obtained irrespective of whether the other spouse, civil partner or the landlord is willing to consent to it.

Sale by landlord—When lands subject to a lease are sold, the original landlord, **35.22** and his executors after his death, remain liable on all obligations which do not transmit against the purchaser.[230] Whether he remains liable on obligations which do transmit is not fully settled, but the law probably is that he remains liable on all obligations to pay money, such as an obligation to pay for improvements executed by the tenant, but that the purchaser alone is liable for upkeep and repairs.[231]

Bankruptcy of tenant—Except under an express provision, bankruptcy of the **35.23** tenant does not put an end to the lease.[232]

Whether a lease is assignable voluntarily or not it will pass, in the absence of an express provision to the contrary, to the trustee in sequestration of the tenant.[233] However, certain tenancies such as assured tenancies, protected tenancies and Scottish secure tenancies do not pass to the trustee in sequestration unless the trustee serves notice on the bankrupt tenant that such tenancies now form part of his estate and are vest in the permanent trustee.[234] The trustee is never bound to adopt the lease. If he does, he incurs personal liability not only for the rent, but for arrears.[235] He is entitled to a reasonable time to consider the question, and temporary intromissions with the subjects, for the purpose of realising the bankrupt's effects, will not readily be construed as precluding ultimate rejection.[236] A conventional exclusion of the right of a trustee in sequestration is construed as giving the landlord an option to refuse, and cannot be founded on by the bankrupt.[237]

---

[228] s.13(4) of the Matrimonial Homes (Family Protection) (Scotland) Act 1981; s.112(4) of the Civil Partnership Act 2004.

[229] See s.13(7) and (10) of the Matrimonial Homes (Family Protection) (Scotland) Act 1981; s.112(8) and (11) of the Civil Partnership Act 2004.

[230] *Gardiner v Murray Stewart's Trs*, 1908 S.C. 985; *Riddell's Exrs v Milligan's Exrs*, 1909 S.C. 1137. As to sales by public sector landlords, see the Housing (Scotland) Act 1988 Pt III, as amended by the Housing (Scotland) Act 2001 Sch.10 para.14.

[231] *Walker v Masson* (1857) 19 D. 1099.

[232] *Dobie v Marquis of Lothian* (1864) 2 M. 788; Rankine, *The Law of Leases in Scotland* (1916), pp.693–694.

[233] Bell, *Principles*, s.1216. As to the trustee's right to dispose of growing crops, see *McKinley v Hutchison's Tr.*, 1935 S.L.T. 62.

[234] Bankruptcy (Scotland) Act 1985 s.31(9).

[235] *Dundas v Morison* (1857) 20 D. 225.

[236] *McGavin v Sturrock's Tr.* (1891) 18 R. 576.

[237] *Dobie v Marquis of Lothian* (1864) 2 M. 788.

35.24 Succession to tenant—Prior to the assimilation of heritable and moveable succession by the Succession (Scotland) Act 1964,[238] a lease was heritable in the succession to a deceased tenant, and vested on his intestacy in his heir-at-law. It now vests in the tenant's executor by virtue of the confirmation,[239] and the right to succeed, unless carried by a destination in the lease[240] or by a valid testamentary bequest,[241] passes to his heirs in intestacy. To avoid cases where, because the deceased tenant has made no valid bequest of the lease or it has not been accepted by the legatee, a lease might otherwise require to be divided among several of the heirs in intestacy, the Act extended to the executor a limited power to assign the lease; this power may be exercised notwithstanding a prohibition of assignation in the lease, whether this be express or implied.[242] He may transfer the lease under this statutory power to any one of the deceased's heirs in intestacy,[243] or in or towards the satisfaction of a claim by a person entitled to legal or prior rights out of the deceased's estate; but, where he has to rely on this power, he may not transfer the lease to anyone else without the consent of the landlord. The power must be exercised within a period of one year, or such longer period as may be fixed by agreement or failing agreement by the sheriff on summary application by the executor.[244] Failure to obtain confirmation to the deceased tenant's interest and to transfer it within that period will result in termination of the lease.[245] As a gratuitous trustee the executor is subject to the common law prohibition against acting as *auctor in rem suam*, and if he transfers the lease to himself he will be liable to the consequences in law of breach of that prohibition.[246]

Unless the lease could be assigned inter vivos the tenant had no power at common law to bequeath his lease so as to compel the landlord to accept his legatee,[247] although if the landlord accepts the legatee as tenant the bequest will be effective.[248] The 1964 Act, however, conferred on the tenant a limited right of bequest in cases where a prohibition of assignation was merely implied. Provided there is no express prohibition, the tenant may validly bequeath the lease to any one of the persons who would have been entitled to succeed to it as his intestate heirs.[249] A slightly wider right of bequest was afforded by the Agricultural Holdings and Crofters Acts, which is unaffected by this provision of the 1964

---

[238] Succession (Scotland) Act 1964 (the "1964 Act") s.1.

[239] 1964 Act ss.14, 36(2); see *Cormack v McIldowie's Exrs*, 1975 S.C. 161; 1975 S.L.T. 214.

[240] See Gordon and Wortley, *Scottish Land Law* (2009), para.18–41.

[241] Although the case of *Gardner v Curran*, 2008 S.L.T. (Sh. Ct) 105 related to succession to a croft, it can be taken as wider authority for the proposition that a bequest of the residue of the estate is enough to carry the tenancy without any specific reference to it, although there may be situations where an element of *delectus personae* will prevent assignation to certain persons are therefore also succession. See H. Hiram, "Bequests of Residue and Crofting Tenancies: *Gardner v Curran*" (2009) 13 Edin. L.R.143.

[242] 1964 Act s.16(1)(2); cf. *Sproat v South West Services (Galloway) Ltd*, 2000 G.W.D. 37–1416, Temp. Judge T.G. Coutts QC.

[243] *MacLean v MacLean*, 1988 S.L.T. 626.

[244] 1964 Act s.16(3).

[245] *Rotherwick's Trs v Hope*, 1975 S.L.T. 187; *Morrison-Low v Paterson*, 1985 S.C. (HL) 49; 1985 S.L.T. 255, per Lord Keith of Kinkel; cf. *Paul v Ogilvy*, 2001 S.L.T. 171 (mainly concerned with damages for professional negligence in this context).

[246] *Inglis v Inglis*, 1983 S.C. 8; 1983 S.L.T. 437; cf. para.41.13, below. Cf. also *Sarris v Clark*, 1995 S.L.T. 44.

[247] See R. Hunter, *A Treatise on the Law of Landlord and Tenant*, 4th edn (Edinburgh Bell and Bradfute, 1876) i, pp.225 and 237; *Bain v Mackenzie* (1896) 23 R. 528; *Reid's Trs v Macpherson*, 1975 S.L.T. 101.

[248] *Kennedy v Johnstone*, 1956 S.C. 39 at 47, per Lord Sorn.

[249] 1964 Act s.29(1).

Act.[250] In the case of dwelling-houses which are subject to the Rent Acts certain persons are entitled to succeed to the lease to the extent of remaining in the house by virtue of the Acts on the death of the tenant, independently of any rights at common law. One transmission of the right to remain in occupation may occur; thereafter, in the case of a contractual tenancy, the normal law of succession will operate.[251] The Housing (Scotland) Act 1988 and the Housing (Scotland) Act 2001 make provisions for succession to assured tenancies[252] and Scottish secure tenancies[253] respectively.

Termination: Notice—A lease comes to an end if either party gives notice within a certain period before the term fixed for its expiry. The effect of the service of notice by a party is the unilateral termination of the lease and it is unsound in law for a landlord to contend that the service of notice by a tenant is of no legal effect on the basis that the tenant has materially breached a term of the lease.[254] Such notice to terminate is necessary because in its absence, and in the absence of circumstances showing that the parties regard the lease as at an end, the relationship of landlord and tenant is continued by tacit relocation.[255] The lease is then renewed, on the same terms and conditions as the original lease, and for the same term as the original lease, if that term was for less than a year, failing which for a year.[256] The legal effect of tacit relocation is that all the stipulations and conditions of the original contract remain in force, so far as these are consistent with a lease from year to year or such lesser period as pertains; an option to renew a lease for a longer period will not be exercisable during tacit relocation.[257] In the case of an urban lease, verbal notice within the necessary period by either party of intention to terminate the contract is sufficient to prevent the setting in of tacit relocation.[258] Where there are joint tenants, to exclude tacit relocation, a notice of removal by one of them will be enough.[259] If, having served notice to quit, the landlord continues regularly and without reservation to accept rent from the tenant he may be held to have departed from the notice or to be barred from

35.25

---

[250] 1964 Act s.29(2); see, generally, Gordon and Wortley, *Scottish Land Law* (2009), para.18–43.

[251] See para.35.68, below.

[252] Housing (Scotland) Act 1988 s.31. A short assured tenancy being a species of assured tenancy, s.31 applies equally to such tenancies. Assured tenancies may devolve upon the will or intestacy of the former tenant. In such circumstances Schedule 5 ground 7 offers a mandatory ground for possession, subject to due process and a time limit, and subject also to the statutory rights of spouses and civil partners under s.31. See para.35.76, below. See also Gordon and Wortley, *Scottish Land Law* (2009), para.18–53.

[253] 2001 Act s.22. There is no statutory succession to a short Scottish secure tenancy, s.34(6). See para.35.09, above.

[254] *Allied Dunbar Assurance Plc v Superglass Sections Ltd*, 2003 S.L.T. 1420.

[255] See *Signet Group Plc v C. & J. Clark Retail Properties Ltd*, 1996 S.C. 444; also para.3.42, above; unless the lease expressly excludes tacit relocation; *MacDougall v Guidi*, 1992 S.C.L.R. 167 (Sh. Ct). Note also A.G.M. Duncan, "Tacit Relocation in Leases", 1978 S.L.T. (News) 157.

[256] Gordon and Wortley, *Scottish Land Law* (2009), para.18–25; Paton and Cameron, *Landlord and Tenant* (1967), p.221; Rankine, *The Law of Leases in Scotland* (1916), p.602.

[257] *Commercial Union Assurance Co v Watt & Cumine*, 1964 S.C. 84; 1964 S.L.T. 62; *Sea Breeze Properties Ltd v Bio-Medical Systems Ltd*, 1998 S.L.T. 319.

[258] See Rankine, *The Law of Leases in Scotland* (1916), p.597; *Craighall Cast Stone Co v Wood Bros*, 1931 S.C. 66. See *Marley Waterproofing Ltd v J.H. Lightbody & Son Ltd*, 2006 G.W.D. 6–113 where a sub-tenant vacated the leased premises before the expiry of the one-year period of tacit relocation.

[259] *Smith v Grayton Estates*, 1960 S.C. 349; *Stair Memorial Encyclopaedia*, "Landlord and Tenant", para.368; Paton and Cameron, *Landlord and Tenant (1967)*, pp.225–226; Gordon and Wortley, *Scottish Land Law* (2009), para.18–26.

insisting on it, so that a new lease will arise by tacit relocation.[260] If on the expiry of the contractual term the tenant remains in possession after notice to quit, he is in the position of an intruder without title, and may be liable for violent profits.[261] The landlord's remedy in order to recover possession from the tenant is to raise an action of removing against him.[262] In order to be effective, the landlord's notice to quit, or the tenant's notice of removal, must be served so as to give due notice to the other party.[263] The period of notice required is laid down by statute and varies according to the type of lease. The leading provisions may be summarised as follows[264]:

(a) In the case of lands exceeding two acres in extent where the lease is not a short limited duration tenancy or limited duration tenancy within the meaning of the Agricultural Holdings (Scotland) Act 2003,[265] written notice must be given, failing an agreement to the contrary, not less than one or more than two years before the ish[266]; where the lease is from year to year, however, or for any other period less than three years, the minimum period is six months.[267] Where the lease is one of agricultural or pastoral land and falls within the Agricultural Holdings Act 1991, the period of notice, of not less than one or more than two years, is fixed by law and cannot be varied by agreement; this period applies in all cases, including leases from year to year, except where the lease is for a period of less than year to year.[268] Where the lease is an agricultural holding to which the 1991 Act applies, the tenant is a limited partnership and the

---

[260] See W.M. Gloag, *Law of Contract*, 2nd edn (Edinburgh: W. Green, 1929), p.735; *Milner's C.B. v Mason*, 1965 S.L.T. (Sh. Ct) 56; *Stair Memorial Encyclopaedia*, "Landlord and Tenant", para.371.

[261] See para.3.42, above. For an example of an ejection and caution for violent profits, see *Middleton v Booth*, 1986 S.L.T. 450; and for an action of removing and caution for violent profits, see *Imperial Hotel (Glasgow) Ltd v Brown*, 1990 S.C.L.R. 86 (Sh. Ct). See also *Ashford & Thistle Securities LLP v Kerr*, 2006 S.L.T. (Sh. Ct) 37.

[262] For procedure in actions of removing, see Sheriff Courts (Scotland) Act 1907 Sch.1 (as amended) rr.34.5–34.10 (formerly rr.103–107); such actions are subject to the summary cause procedure: Sheriff Courts (Scotland) Act 1971 s.35, as amended by the Law Reform (Miscellaneous Provisions) (Scotland) Act 1985 s.18 and Sch.2; see Housing (Scotland) Act 2001 s.14(1) which states that proceedings for recovery of possession in respect of Scottish secure tenancies are by summary cause. Note the special provisions for the protection of agricultural employees and their families occupying tied houses in Rent (Scotland) Act 1984 s.24.

[263] On service of notices in general: *Muir Construction Ltd v Hambly Ltd*, 1990 S.L.T. 830; *Prudential Assurance Co Ltd v Smith Foods*, 1995 S.L.T. 369 at 370, per Lord Morton; *Charisma Properties Ltd v Grayling (1994) Ltd*, 1996 S.C. 556; *Mannai Investment Co Ltd v Eagle Star Life Assurance Co Ltd* [1997] A.C. 749 at 776, per Lord Hoffmann; *Chaplin v Caledonian Land Properties Ltd*, 1997 S.L.T. 384; *Esson Properties Ltd v Dresser UK Ltd*, 1997 S.L.T. 949; *Capital Land Holdings Ltd v Secretary of State for the Environment*, 1997 S.C. 109; *Grovebury Management Ltd v McLaren*, 1997 S.L.T. 1083; *McGhie v Dunedin Property Investment Co Ltd* Unreported November 5, 1998 Lord Johnston; *Scottish Life Assurance Co v Agfa-Gevaert Ltd*, 1998 S.C.L.R. 238 at 242–243, per Lord Caplan; *Christie Owen & Davis Plc v Alan King*, 1998 S.C.L.R. 786; *Perth City Wall Ltd v Smart Events Ltd*, 2001 S.C. (D) 2/7 at [8], per Temporary Judge T.G. Coutts QC; *Ben Cleuch Estates Ltd v Scottish Enterprise* Unreported March 1, 2006 Outer House, Lord Reed (2006 S.C. (D) 23/3); and D.A. Cabrelli, *Commercial Agreements in Scotland: Law & Practice* (Edinburgh: W. Green, 2006), paras 10.26–10.28.

[264] See, for a full statement, Paton and Cameron, *Landlord and Tenant* (1967), p.262. See also A. Stalker, *Evictions in Scotland* (Edinburgh: Avizandum, 2007), Ch.3.

[265] Sheriff Courts (Scotland) Act 1907 s.37A.

[266] Sheriff Courts (Scotland) Act 1907 s.34(a).

[267] Sheriff Courts (Scotland) Act 1907 s.34(b).

[268] 1991 Act s.21; see *Kildrummy (Jersey) Ltd v Calder (No.1)* 1994 S.L.T. 888; and also para.35.30, below. See also *Edinburgh City Council v Little*, 2008 S.L.C.R. 18, on the effectiveness of a renunciation without reference to s.21.

lease has been continued in accordance with the procedure contained in s.73 of the Agricultural Holdings (Scotland) Act 2003, the landlord must follow a "double notice" (i.e. intimation plus notice to quit) procedure if he wishes to terminate the tenancy before the expiry of its term. First, intimation of the landlord's intention to terminate the tenancy must be given to the tenant not less than two years nor more than three years before the expiry of the stipulated endurance of the lease; and second, the actual notice to quit must state that the tenant shall quit the land on the expiry of the stipulated endurance of the lease constituting the tenancy and must be given not less than one year nor more than two years before the expiry of the stipulated endurance of the lease, provided that not less than 90 days have elapsed from the date on which the intimation of the intention to terminate was given.[269] The validity of this section was called into question in *Salvesen v Riddell*.[270] That case related to the transition regime that existed between September 16, 2002 and July 1, 2003, whereby the dissolution of a limited partnership by a (landowner) limited partner could be countered by a summary notice of the (farmer) general partner to the effect that the general partner was now an outright 1991 Act tenant (per s.72(6) of the Agricultural Holdings (Scotland) Act 2003). Such a tenant could not be removed by the "double notice" procedure of s.73 of the Agricultural applicable from July, 2003, but the Inner House characterised this statutory upgrade without compensation to the landowner as non-compliant with the landowner's art.1 Protocol 1 of the Convention right to peaceful enjoyment of property. In so doing, s.72 as a whole was declared to be "not law" (in accordance with s.29(1) and s.102 of the Scotland Act 1998). An appeal to the Supreme Court has been made. In the case of short limited duration tenancies constituted under s.4 of the Agricultural Holdings (Scotland) Act 2003, termination can only be made by agreement between the parties provided the tenancy makes provision as to compensation by the landlord or the tenant to the other.[271] In the case of the limited duration tenancy created under s.5 of the Agricultural Holdings (Scotland) Act 2003 (including converted short limited duration tenancies),[272] termination may occur by agreement in the same manner as the short limited duration tenancy and the landlord may terminate by complying with a "double notice" (i.e. intimation plus notice to quit) procedure in s.8 of the said Act. In this case, first, intimation of the landlord's intention to terminate the limited duration tenancy must be given to the tenant not less than two years nor more than three years before the expiry of the term of the tenancy; and secondly, the actual notice to quit must state that the tenant shall quit the land on the expiry of the term of the limited duration tenancy and must be given not less than one year nor more than two years before the expiry of the term of the tenancy, provided that not less than 90 days have elapsed from the date on which the intimation of the intention to terminate was given.[273] If the tenant wishes to terminate the

---

[269] 2003 Act s.73(4) and (5).
[270] *Salvesen v Riddell*, 2012 S.L.T. 633.
[271] 2003 Act s.8(1).
[272] 2003 Act s.5(2), as amended by the Public Services Reform (Agricultural Holdings) (Scotland) Order 2011 (SSI 2011/232). See *Serup v Reid*, SLC/73/10.
[273] 2003 Act s.8(4) and (5).

limited duration tenancy by notice, the procedure is much simpler. The crucial difference is that the tenant can only terminate by notice at or after the expiry of the term of the tenancy by serving notice upon the landlord.[274] If the tenant wishes to terminate prior to the date of expiry of the tenancy, it must seek agreement under s.8(1) of the said Act or seek an assignation or sub-let of the lease.

(b) In the case of houses or land not exceeding two acres in extent, fishings and shootings, the period of notice prescribed, unless otherwise agreed, is a minimum of 40 days before May 15 or November 11[275] according to the term at which the tenancy is to end[276]; where the subjects are let for a period not exceeding four months the period of notice must be one-third of the full duration of the lease.[277] These requirements are reinforced by a general provision with regard to dwelling-houses now contained in the Rent (Scotland) Act 1984,[278] which cannot be varied by agreement, that a minimum of four weeks' notice must be given in all cases where a notice to quit is required. The notice must be given four weeks before the date when it is to take effect, which means that the period of notice should be calculated with reference to the date of the ish.[279]

In the case of leased premises in respect of which a closing order or the like has been made, either the landlord or the tenant may apply to the sheriff for an order determining the lease.[280] If an executor, to whom a lease has devolved in intestacy, is satisfied that he cannot dispose of the lease (not being a short limited duration tenancy or a limited duration tenancy to which the Agricultural Holdings (Scotland) Act 2003 applies) according to law or has in fact not done so within a period of one year from the date of the deceased tenant's death, or such longer period as may be fixed by agreement or failing agreement by the sheriff on summary application by the executor, he or the landlord may, by giving due notice, terminate the lease altogether.[281] An application by executors for an extension of the one year period was held to be incompetent when it was not made until after one year after the deceased tenant's death, notice of termination of the lease having been given in the meantime by the landlord.[282] In the case of a short limited duration tenancy or limited duration tenancy constituted under the Agricultural Holdings (Scotland) Act 2003 which has devolved upon an executor in intestacy, the rules are slightly different. In such circumstances, if the executor is satisfied that he cannot dispose of the tenancy according to the law and notifies the landlord to that effect, he may terminate the tenancy if termination is in the best

---

[274] 2003 Act s.8(13) and (14).

[275] Quaere whether the Term and Quarter Days (Scotland) Act 1990 s.1(2)(a) affects the Sheriff Courts (Scotland) Act 1907 s.37.

[276] Sheriff Courts (Scotland) Act 1907 s.37, but see *MacDougall v Guidi*, 1992 S.C.L.R. 167 (Sh. Ct), where 40 days' notice held unnecessary in a lease which expressly excluded tacit relocation; note that, under s.38, notice to quit is obligatory, where the lease is for a period of less than one year, only in the absence of express stipulation. See also Removal Terms (Scotland) Act 1886 s.4, and note the effect of the Term and Quarter Days (Scotland) Act 1990, particularly s.1(2)(a).

[277] Sheriff Courts (Scotland) Act 1907 s.38 and Removal Terms (Scotland) Act 1886 s.5, both as amended by Rent (Scotland) Act 1971 Sch.18 Pt II.

[278] Rent (Scotland) Act 1984 s.112; see *Schnabel v Allard* [1967] 1 Q.B. 627.

[279] *Hamilton DC v Maguire*, 1983 S.L.T. (Sh. Ct) 76.

[280] 1987 Act s.322.

[281] 1964 Act s.16(3), (4).

[282] *Gifford v Buchanan*, 1983 S.L.T. 613.

interests of the deceased's estate, although, in effecting such termination, it is not clear from the Succession (Scotland) Act 1964 whether the executor must serve notice of such termination on the landlord.[283] Furthermore, if the executor has not in fact disposed of the tenancy within a period of one year from the date of death of the deceased, the tenancy automatically terminates at the expiry of such one-year period notwithstanding any provision in the lease or any rule of law to the contrary.[284] The said one-year period may be extended by agreement or, failing agreement, by the Land Court on the application of the executor.[285]

Termination: Irritancies—Although a lease is normally terminated by a notice **35.26** to quit or of removal, it may also be brought to an end before the date of its natural expiration by the destruction of the subjects,[286] or their acquisition in whole or part by a third party acting under compulsory powers,[287] or because there is no one left who can claim to be a tenant, as where a lease was granted in favour of a partnership and the partnership has been dissolved by death.[288] However, where the landlord ceases to exist by dissolution, a lease is not automatically terminated by operation of law since the landlord's title vests in some other party, e.g. the Queen's and Lord Treasurer's Remembrancer.[289] The lease itself may contain provisions for its premature termination, known as breaks, in favour of either party or both, that in the option of the tenant being a power to renounce and that in favour of the landlord being a power to resume.[290] A power in favour of the landlord to resume for planting woodlands is common in agricultural leases.[291] The landlord may also consent to a renunciation of the subjects by the tenant before the ish. Where a tenant allows another party to occupy the leased premises, this does not necessarily create any legal relationship between the licensee and the landlord and the fact that a landlord tolerates this state of affairs does not mean that the landlord has renounced the lease in favour of the tenant far less that the landlord has granted a new lease in favour of the licensee.[292]

---

[283] 1964 Act s.16(4C)(a) and (4E)(b).

[284] 1964 Act s.16(4A), (4B), (4C) and (4D).

[285] 1964 Act s.16(4D)(a).

[286] *Duff v Fleming* (1870) 8 M. 769; *Cantors Properties (Scotland) v Swears & Wells*, 1978 S.C. 310.

[287] *Mackeson v Boyd*, 1942 S.C. 56.

[288] *Inland Revenue v Graham's Trs*, 1971 S.C. (HL) 1; *Jardine-Paterson v Fraser*, 1974 S.L.T. 93.

[289] *Urquhart v Sweeney*, 2005 S.C. 591 at 601, per Lord Justice Clerk Gill.

[290] Rankine, *The Law of Leases in Scotland* (1916), p.527; Paton and Cameron, *Landlord and Tenant* (1967), p.242; Gordon and Wortley, *Scottish Land Law* (2009), para.18–55. See on notice of renunciation, *Trade Development Bank v Warriner & Mason (Scotland) Ltd*, 1980 S.L.T. 223; *Capital Land Holdings Ltd v Secretary of State for the Environment*, 1996 S.C. 109; *P & O Property Holdings Ltd v Glasgow City Council*, 2000 S.L.T. 444 (tenant still liable to pay rates since there had been neither irritancy nor acceptance by the landlord of repudiation); *Ben Cleuch Estates Ltd v Scottish Enterprise*, 2008 S.C. 252 and *Batt Cables Plc v Spencer Business Parks Ltd*, 2010 S.L.T. 860 (effect of tenant serving notice of break option on wrong legal person); *Allan v Armstrong*, 2004 G.W.D. 37–768 (whether a break option is enforceable by a tenant against singular successors of the landlord is often a matter of the singular successor's knowledge of the term and thus personal bar); *Wishaw & District Housing Association v Neary*, 2004 S.C. 463 (the existence of a break option in a short assured tenancy agreement did not mean that the duration of the tenancy was less than six months, cf. *Caterleisure Ltd v Glasgow Prestwick International Airport Ltd*, 2005 S.C. 602); *Littman v Aspen Oil (Broking) Ltd* [2005] EWCA Civ 1579; [2006] 2 P & CR 35; *Fitzroy House Epworth Street (No.1) v The Financial Times Ltd* [2006] 1 W.L.R. 2207.

[291] *Sykes and Edgar*, 1974 S.L.T. (Land Ct) 4; *Fothringham v Fothringham*, 1987 S.L.T. (Land Ct) 10; *Thomson v Murray*, 1990 S.L.T. (Land Ct) 45; and see para.35.30, below.

[292] *Kingston Communications (Hull) Plc v Stargas Nominees Ltd*, 2005 S.C. 139.

A lease may also be terminated before the date of its natural expiration by the enforcement of an irritancy,[293] legal or conventional, in which case the tenant's right to occupy the subjects will be forfeited or annulled.[294] The legal irritancies relate solely to non-payment of rent. An irritancy is recognised at common law, and enforceable only by an extraordinary action of removing in the Court of Session, in all cases where two years' rent is unpaid.[295] There is no other legal irritancy in urban subjects. In subjects falling under the Agricultural Holdings Act 1991, where six months' rent is due and unpaid, the landlord may raise an action in the sheriff court concluding for the removal of the tenant at the next term of Whitsunday or Martinmas.[296] In the case of short limited duration tenancies and limited duration tenancies constituted under the Agricultural Holdings (Scotland) Act 2003, irritancies are conventional rather than legal, although it is specified that a landlord must give the tenant notice in writing of its intention to remove the tenant not less than two months before the date on which the tenant is to be removed.[297] Conventional irritancies[298] are unlimited in number and may be used to underwrite a variety of obligations; usually they cover non-payment of rent, the various forms of insolvency and material breaches of the lease. A landlord who enforces an irritancy cannot also claim damages for the premature determination of the lease.[299] Whatever may be the terms in which a conventional irritancy is expressed, it is construed as giving the landlord an option to avoid the lease, not as giving the defaulting tenant a right to abandon it.[300]

Legal irritancies may be purged at any time before decree is pronounced. The common law rule was that conventional irritancies could not be purged unless they merely expressed the irritancy which the law would infer. Once incurred they were strictly enforced,[301] and while power was reserved to the court to prevent oppressive

---

[293] The word "irritancy" has been said to mean forfeiture: see *Dorchester Studios (Glasgow) v Stone*, 1975 S.C. (HL) 56 at 74, per Lord Fraser of Tullybelton. It may be thought, however, that it simply means that the lease is void. As to procedure and content of notice of irritancy and the methods by which a tenant can lawfully resist the enforcement of an irritancy by making payment of rent, see *C.I.N. Properties Ltd v Dollar Land (Cumbernauld) Ltd*, 1992 S.C. (HL) 104; 1992 S.L.T. 669; *Whitbread Group Plc v Goldapple Ltd (No.2)*, 2005 S.L.T. 281; *Ethel Austin Properties Holdings Ltd v D. & A. Factors (Dundee) Ltd* Unreported June 21, 2005 Kirkcaldy Sheriff Court, Sheriff P. Arthurson (2005 S.C. (D) 23/6); *Ashford and Thistle Securities LLP v Kerr*, 2007 S.L.T. (Sh. Ct) 60. Note that where one landlord has disponed the property to another, assignation of the notice of irritancy may be required: *Life Association of Scotland v Blacks Leisure Group*, 1989 S.L.T. 674.

[294] Where a tenant remains in bona fide possession after the irritancy, he may be liable to pay a reasonable rent: *H.M.V. Fields Properties Ltd v Skirt n' Slack Centre of London Ltd*, 1986 S.C. 114; 1987 S.L.T. 2. If payment is offered after the irritancy, a landlord should take care to avoid acts amounting to either waiver of the notice of irritancy, or oppression: *H.M.V. Fields Properties Ltd v Bracken Self Selection Fabrics Ltd*, 1991 S.L.T. 31; 1990 S.C.L.R. 677; *C.I.N. Properties Ltd v Dollar Land (Cumbernauld) Ltd*, 1992 S.L.T. 211, IH; *MacDonald's Trs v Cunningham*, 1997 S.C.L.R. 986; *Wolanski & Co Trustees Ltd v First Quench Retailing Ltd*, 2004 G.W.D. 33–678; *Whitbread Group Plc v Goldapple Ltd (No.2)*, 2005 S.L.T. 281; *Dean (t/a Abbey Mill Business Centre) v Freeman*, 2005 G.W.D. 9–137.

[295] Erskine, II, 6, 44. As to the construction of irritancies, see para.10.28, above.

[296] 1991 Act s.20: in terms of the Term and Quarter Days (Scotland) Act 1990, Whitsunday and Martinmas signify May 28 and November 28 respectively, unless the lease provides otherwise; see *Provincial Insurance Plc v Valtos Ltd*, 1992 S.C.L.R. 203 (Sh. Ct).

[297] 2003 Act s.18(1) and (7). See para.35.4 below.

[298] As to their scope, see *Auditglen Ltd v Scotec Industries Ltd*, 1996 S.L.T. 493; on purging of conventional irritancies, see *McDouall's Trs v MacLeod*, 1949 S.C. 593.

[299] *Buttercase v Geddie* (1897) 24 R. 1128; *H.M.V. Fields Properties Ltd v Skirt n' Slack Centre of London Ltd*, 1986 S.C. 114; 1987 S.L.T. 2.

[300] *Bidoulac v Sinclair's Tr.* (1889) 17 R. 144.

[301] Note, however, the limited protection where the lease is vested in an executor: 1964 Act s.16(7).

use or abuse of the irritancy[302] the circumstances in which this could be exercised were so closely defined as to provide the tenant with no relief if it was his own inadvertence which led to the irritancy being incurred.[303] The position as regards conventional irritancies has now been modified by the Law Reform (Miscellaneous Provisions) (Scotland) Act 1985.[304] A distinction is drawn for this purpose between pecuniary obligations on the one hand and non-pecuniary obligations and changes in the tenant's circumstances on the other. The landlord is not entitled to rely on a provision for irritancy in the event of the tenant's failure to pay rent or make any other payment on or before the due date or within a stipulated period unless he has served a notice on the tenant after the date when the payment became due, specifying the period from which the rent arrears arise[305] and requiring him to make payment of the sum which he has failed to pay together with interest within the period—being not less than 14 days—which is specified in the notice and stating that if he does not do so the lease may be terminated.[306] If the tenant fails to make payment within the specified time limit the irritancy is no longer purgeable and the strict rules of the common law apply.[307] So far as the non-pecuniary obligations and changes in the tenants' circumstances such as liquidation or insolvency are concerned, the landlord is not entitled to rely on a provision for irritancy in that event if in all the circumstances of the case a fair and reasonable landlord would not seek to do so, regard being had to whether a reasonable opportunity has been afforded to the tenant to remedy the breach if it was capable of being remedied within reasonable time.[308] Once an irritancy has been enforced, a tenant is unlikely to have a claim in relation to the landlord's unjustified enrichment.[309]

---

[302] See *Lucas's Exrs v Demarco*, 1968 S.L.T. 89; *C.I.N. Properties Ltd v Dollar Land (Cumbernauld) Ltd*, 1992 S.C. (HL) 104; 1992 S.L.T. 669; *Whitbread Group Plc v Goldapple Ltd*, 2005 S.L.T. 281.

[303] *Dorchester Studios (Glasgow) v Stone*, 1975 S.C. (HL) 56; *H.M.V. Fields Properties v Skirt n' Slack Centre of London*, 1982 S.L.T. 477; 1987 S.L.T. 2; *H.M.V. Fields Properties v Tandem Shoes*, 1983 S.L.T. 114.

[304] Law Reform (Miscellaneous Provisions) (Scotland) Act 1985 ss.4–7. The 1985 Act came into force on October 30, 1985, and applies to all leases, whether entered into before or after the Act, except leases of land used wholly or mainly for residential purposes; agricultural holdings; and holdings of crofter, cottars, small landholders or statutory small tenants, in which cases there is other protection for tenants. It is impossible to contract out of the 1985 Act: s.6(1). It has been noted, however, that the irritancy provisions in s.4 do not operate in such a way as to disadvantage the recipient when set against his contractual rights: *Edinburgh Tours Ltd v Singh*, 2012 G.W.D. 4–75.

[305] *Scott v Muir*, 2012 G.W.D. 5–94.

[306] Law Reform (Miscellaneous Provisions) (Scotland) Act 1985 s.4. See the circumstances by which a tenant will be held to have validly made payment of the rent due subsequent to the service of such notice: *Whitbread Group Plc v Goldapple Ltd*, 2005 S.L.T. 281; *Mount Stuart Trust v McCulloch*, 2010 S.C. 404.

[307] *C.I.N. Properties Ltd v Dollar Land (Cumbernauld) Ltd*, 1992 S.C. (HL) 104; 1992 S.L.T. 669.

[308] Law Reform (Miscellaneous Provisions) (Scotland) Act 1985 s.5, and see dicta of Lord Justice-Clerk Ross in the Inner House in *C.I.N. Properties Ltd v Dollar Land (Cumbernauld) Ltd*, 1992 S.L.T. 211, and in the House of Lords, Lord Jauncey (common law rules and oppression); see also *Blythswood Investments (Scotland) Ltd v Clydesdale Electrical Stores Ltd (in receivership)*, 1995 S.L.T. 150 ("fair and reasonable landlord"); *Scottish Exhibition Centre Ltd v Mirestop Ltd (No.2)*, 1996 S.L.T. 8; *Aubrey Investments Ltd v DSC (Realisations) Ltd*, 1999 S.C. 21; *Maris v Bachory Squash Racquets Club Ltd*, 2007 S.L.T. 477 (the phrase "all the circumstances of the case" did not render it appropriate to take into account repairs effected by the tenant after the service of notice or the raising of an action against the tenant by the landlord). In *Dean (t/a Abbey Mill Business Centre) v Freeman*, 2005 G.W.D. 9–137, it was held that a landlord is not entitled to take advantage of an uninduced error in his own notice of irritancy. In *Dean*, the landlord had referred to the insolvency event as "receivership" when in fact the tenant had entered into liquidation.

[309] *Dollar Land (Cumbernauld) Ltd v C.I.N. Properties Ltd*, 1998 S.C. (HL) 90; this turns, however, on the terms of the particular contract.

II. AGRICULTURAL TENANCIES[310]

35.27 **Agricultural Holdings Acts**—At common law a tenant who made improvements on the subjects let had no claim for compensation against the landlord, the legal presumption being that he made the improvements in the hope of recouping himself during the remaining years of the lease.[311] While this remains the law in urban leases, a series of statutes have introduced a right to compensation in the case of agricultural holdings with the object of encouraging the tenant to farm well and to make the necessary improvements to his holding. The rules of good husbandry and good estate management are still to be found in the Agriculture (Scotland) Act 1948. The code relating to agricultural holdings is contained principally in the Agricultural Holdings (Scotland) Act 1991.[312] However, the 1991 Act has now been varied extensively by the Agricultural Holdings (Scotland) Act 2003. The 2003 Act introduces a new regime for agricultural leases with effect from November 27, 2003 which supersedes the 1991 Act regime. However, the regime of agricultural holdings under the 1991 Act remains important for the reason that there will continue to be leases regulated by the 1991 Act for some time. Such 1991 Act tenancies are preserved by virtue of s.1(4) of the 2003 Act and are called "1991 Act tenancies".[313] Accordingly, the 1991 Act will be considered alongside the 2003 Act in this section. Note that contract farming, that is a scheme whereby the landowner contracts directly with another party to farm the land without any kind of tenancy, is not governed by these detailed statutory regimes.

The 1991 Act was a consolidating measure, and decisions under earlier enactments[314] remain of importance. Besides conferring on the tenant important compensation rights, the 1991 Act has afforded him substantial security of tenure and regulates closely the rights and obligations of each party under the lease. The 1991 Act recognises only one type of tenant, that is, the tenant entitled to claim the benefit of the statutory provisions in favour of agricultural tenants[315]; and contracting out of the statutory provisions is widely prohibited.[316] The 2003 Act allows for further 1991 Act tenancies,[317] but in practice it is very unlikely that parties will agree to enter into an agricultural lease regulated by the 1991 Act. The only tenancies which are available under the 2003 Act are short limited duration tenancies and limited duration tenancies. It is also possible for the parties under a 1991 Act tenancy to choose to convert the tenancy into a limited duration tenancy in terms of the procedure under s.2 of the 2003 Act.[318] However, in such cases, the tenancy must convert into a limited duration tenancy of no less than 25 years.

---

[310] See B. Gill, *Law of Agricultural Holdings in Scotland*, 3rd edn (Edinburgh: W. Green, 1997); annotations to the 1991 Act by A.G.M. Duncan in *Scottish Current Law Statutes* (1991), Vol.3; and article by A.G.M. Duncan, "The Agricultural Holdings (Scotland) Act 1991", 1992 S.L.T. (News) 1.

[311] *Walker v McKnight* (1886) 13 R. 599.

[312] The Act came into force on September 25, 1991.

[313] 2003 Act s.1(4).

[314] Especially Agricultural Holdings (Scotland) Act 1923; Small Landholders and Agricultural Holdings (Scotland) Act 1931; Agriculture (Scotland) Act 1948; Agricultural Holdings (Scotland) Act 1949, as amended by the Agriculture Act 1958, the Agriculture (Miscellaneous Provisions) Acts 1968 and 1976, and the Agricultural Holdings (Amendment) (Scotland) Act 1983.

[315] cf. *Dalgety's Trs v Drummond*, 1938 S.C. 709.

[316] e.g. 1991 Act ss.3, 48 and 53.

[317] 2003 Act s.1(2).

[318] For an unsuccessful attempt to use s.2 for conversion from a 1991 Act tenancy to a 25 year limited duration tenancy after (and notwithstanding) the parties had agreed a renunciation of that tenancy, see *Edinburgh City Council v Little*, 2008 S.L.C.R. The (former) tenant's argument that the notice to quit procedure in s.21 of the 1991 Act was mandatory, and therefore a standalone renunciation was not effective, was not accepted by the Land Court.

A. 1991 ACT—AGRICULTURAL HOLDINGS

Agricultural holding: Meaning—The 1991 Act defines the term "agricultural **35.28** holding" as:

"the aggregate of the agricultural land comprised in a lease, not being a lease under which the land is let to the tenant during his continuance in any office, appointment or employment held under the landlord".[319]

"Agricultural land" is itself defined[320] as meaning "land used for agriculture for the purposes of a trade or business" including any other land which may be designated as agricultural land by the Secretary of State under the 1948 Act.[321] The definition of the word "agriculture" in the 1991 Act is comprehensive and covers every kind of horticultural and farming activity.[322] "Lease" is defined as meaning "a letting of land for a term of years, or for lives, or for lives and years, or from year to year".[323]

Incidents of lease: Minimum term—Subject to certain exceptions,[324] s.2 of the **35.29** 1991 Act contained a general restriction on letting agricultural land for less than from year to year. This restriction is now repealed by virtue of s.1(3) of the 2003 Act. When the ish of a 1991 Act tenancy is reached the lease is held to be continued in force from year to year by tacit relocation until notice to terminate is given by either party.[325]

Written lease—Where there is no written lease[326] embodying the terms of a tenancy, either party may require the other to enter into a written agreement for this purpose.[327] Where a written lease has been entered into but it does not contain any one or more of the matters specified in Sch.1[328] to the 1991 Act or is inconsistent with it or with the provisions of s.5 as to the liability for the maintenance

---

[319] 1991 Act s.1(1).

[320] 1991 Act s.1(2). Consider *O'Donnell v McDonald*, 2006 S.L.T. (Sh. Ct) 107, reversed in part *O'Donnell v McDonald*, 2007 S.L.T. 1227. Sheriff Principal Lockhart held that the substantial purpose of the lease as a riding school was not an agricultural purpose. Accordingly, it could not be an agricultural tenancy. The Inner House agreed with this approach.

[321] Under Agriculture (Scotland) Act 1948 s.86(1).

[322] 1991 Act s.85(1).

[323] 1991 Act s.85(1); see *Stirrat v Whyte*, 1967 S.C. 265, for an example of a let which was held not to be a lease within the meaning of this definition. See also *Morrison-Low v Paterson (No.1)*, 1985 S.C. (HL) 49, in which it was held that evidence of actings was sufficient to justify the inference that a lease had been granted for not more than a year and thus from year to year for the purposes of the Act and *Bell v Inkersall Investments Ltd*, 2006 S.C. 507; *Pickard v Ritchie*, 1986 S.L.T. 466 (averments of actings insufficient to support inference of a lease); *Strachan v Robertson-Coupar*, 1989 S.L.T. 488 (an arrangement not amounting to a lease); *Dickson v MacGregor*, 1992 S.L.T. (Land Ct) 83 (complications arising from formation of a limited partnership); *Commercial Components (Int) Ltd v Young*, 1993 S.L.T. (Sh. Ct) 15 (facts and circumstances not capable of supporting inference of lease).

[324] Which were contained in 1991 Act s.2(1).

[325] 1991 Act s.3; see *Smith v Grayton Estates*, 1960 S.C. 349; *Morrison v Rendall*, 1986 S.C. 69 dicta at 73 (also sub nom. *Morrison's Exrs v Rendall*, 1986 S.L.T. 227 dicta at 230G–H).

[326] As to meaning of "lease in writing", see *Grieve v Barr*, 1954 S.C. 414.

[327] 1991 Act s.4(1)(a).

[328] These matters are: (i) the names of the parties, (ii) particulars of the holding, with reference to a map or plan, (iii) the term of the lease, (iv) the rent and the dates on which payable, (v) certain undertakings by the parties relating to damage to buildings and the destruction of harvested crops.

of fixed equipment, a similar request may be made.[329] If parties are unable to agree the matter may be referred to the Land Court for determination.[330]

Liability for maintenance—The 1991 Act deems[331] the incorporation in every lease of an undertaking by the landlord to put the fixed equipment on the holding into a thorough state of repair, and to provide the necessary buildings and other equipment. The landlord is also bound to make such replacement or renewal as may be rendered necessary by natural decay or by fair wear and tear. The tenant's liability is limited to an undertaking to maintain the equipment in a state of good repair, fair wear and tear excepted.[332]

Variation of rent—The 1991 Act enables either party to seek a variation of the contractual rent; either party may have the issue determined by the Land Court.[333] The rent properly payable in respect of the holding for this purpose is normally the rent at which, having regard to the terms of the lease (other than those relating to rent) but not to the personal circumstances of the tenant[334] or any distortion in rent due to a scarcity of lets,[335] the holding might reasonably be expected to be let in the open market.[336] But the Land Court must take account of certain other factors in arriving at the appropriate rent; first, information about rents of other agricultural holdings (including when fixed) and any factors affecting those rents (or any of them) except any distortion due to a scarcity of lets must be taken into account[337]; secondly, the current economic conditions in the relevant sector of agriculture must be considered.[338] In *Morrison-Low v Paterson's Executors* the Inner House ruled that farming subsidies, in the form of single farm payment, could be taken into account by the Land Court.[339] A review of the rent by this process may be obtained at intervals of not less than three years.[340] Certain legal acts are not counted as variations in that period, such as rent varied for another reason under the 1991 Act or a change to the VAT treatment.[341] The landlord, where he has carried out certain specific improvements, has an absolute right to increase the rent by an amount equal to the increase in the rental value of the holding attributable to the carrying out of the improvements[342]; the increase operates from the date of completion and the landlord must serve notice in writing on the tenant.

Pactional rent—A provision in a lease for penal or pactional rent, i.e. for payment of a fixed sum as damages for any breach of its conditions, is not binding.

---

[329] 1991 Act s.4(1)(b).

[330] 1991 Act s.4(1)(b), as amended by the Schedule to the 2003 Act.

[331] 1991 Act s.5(2)(a).

[332] 1991 Act s.5(2)(b).

[333] 1991 Act s.13(1), as amended by the Schedule to the 2003 Act. Parties cannot contract out of that section: cf. *Moll v Macgregor*, 1990 S.L.T. (Land Ct.) 59; 1991 S.L.C.R. 1 at 173 (a decision relating to earlier legislation: Agricultural Holdings (Scotland) Act 1949 s.7). For a consideration of the effect of break clauses in an agricultural lease on the rent review provisions in s.13, see *Firm of AC Stoddart & Sons, Colstoun (1995) v Balfour Thomson CA*, 2007 S.L.T. 593.

[334] The decision in *Guthe v Broatch*, 1956 S.C. 132, is thus superseded.

[335] 1991 Act s.13(3), as amended by s.63(b) of the 2003 Act.

[336] 1991 Act s.13(3); certain other factors relating to improvements and dilapidations are also to be disregarded: s.13(5) and (7); *Broadland Properties Estates Ltd v Mann*, 1994 S.L.T. (Land Ct) 7 (allocated milk quota not an improvement); *Grant v Broadland Properties Estates Ltd*, 1997 S.L.T. 1030.

[337] 1991 Act s.13(4), as amended by s.63(c) of the 2003 Act.

[338] 1991 Act s.13(4); *Aberdeen Endowments Trust v Will*, 1985 S.L.T. (Land Ct) 23.

[339] *Morrison-Low v Paterson's Executors* [2012] CSIH 10; 2012 G.W.D. 8–158

[340] 1991 Act s.13(8).

[341] The Value Added Tax relaxation was introduced by the Agricultural Holdings Amendment (Scotland) Act 2012.

[342] 1991 Act s.15.

The landlord, in spite of the existence of such a clause in the lease, must prove the actual damage which he has sustained in consequence of the tenant's breach of the conditions of the lease.[343]

Withholding of rent—The tenant may obtain a Land Court order which enables him to withhold rent in relation to the failure of the landlord to comply with a Land Court order the subject-matter of which relates to a failure on his part to fulfil any obligation he owes towards the tenant in respect of fixed equipment.[344] The landlord's failure must be material.[345]

Freedom of cropping—A tenant may practise any system of cropping arable lands, and may dispose of the produce of the farm other than manure produced on it as he pleases, notwithstanding any provision of the lease or local custom which may bind him to some particular method of cultivation.[346] This provision does not apply to the last year of the lease, nor, in leases from year to year, to the year before the tenant leaves; and it does not apply to land in grass which is to be retained in that condition throughout the tenancy.[347] Failure to cultivate in accordance with good practice may affect the tenant's right to compensation as well as his security of tenure.[348] The tenant must make provision against the deterioration of the holding; and, in the case of crops sold contrary to the provisions of the lease or to local custom, must return to the holding the full equivalent manurial value thereof. The landlord is entitled to obtain an interdict from the Land Court to restrain the exercise of the tenant's freedom of cropping if he allows the holding to deteriorate, and to damages from the Land Court for his failure in these duties.[349] After notice to terminate has been given, the tenant may not remove any manure or compost unless and until he has given the landlord or the incoming tenant a reasonable opportunity to purchase it at its fair market value.[350]

Fixtures—It is provided that any engine, machinery, fencing or other fixture affixed to a holding by a tenant, and any building erected by him for which he is not entitled to compensation, and which is not affixed or erected in pursuance of some obligation, or in substitution for some fixture or building belonging to the landlord, shall be the property of the tenant and removable by him before, or within six months after, the termination of the lease. The right of removal is conditional on the tenant having paid all rent owing by him and satisfied his other obligations in respect of the holding. In removal no avoidable damage to other buildings must be done, and all damage done must be made good. The tenant must give one month's notice in writing of his intention to remove a fixture or building, and the landlord may elect to purchase it at a price which is the equivalent of the fair value to an incoming tenant.[351]

Record of holding—Either landlord or tenant may at any time require the making of a record of the condition of the fixed equipment on and of the cultivation of the holding[352]; the tenant may also require the making of a record of the existing improvements carried out by him for which he, with the consent in

---

[343] 1991 Act s.48.
[344] 1991 Act s.15A(1).
[345] 1991 Act s.15A(2).
[346] 1991 Act s.7(1).
[347] 1991 Act s.7(5).
[348] 1991 Act ss.26, 45.
[349] 1991 Act s.7(3), (3A) and (4).
[350] 1991 Act s.17.
[351] 1991 Act s.18.
[352] 1991 Act s.8.

writing of his landlord, has paid compensation to an outgoing tenant, and of any fixtures or buildings which he is entitled to remove. Such record will be made by a person to be appointed by agreement between the parties, but in the absence of such agreement, the Scottish Ministers shall on the application of either party appoint a person to make a record.[353] The cost of such an appointment by the Scottish Ministers shall be charged in accordance with what they consider to be reasonable.[354] In leases entered into after the Act of 1949, however, a record of the condition of the fixed equipment must be made forthwith.[355] The existence of such a record is a prerequisite to any claim by the tenant for compensation for continuous good farming, and to any claim by the landlord for compensation for deterioration.[356]

35.30 Notice to quit and removal—Where a tenant is six months in arrears with his rent, the landlord may raise an action in the sheriff court for his removal at the next term of Martinmas or Whitsunday.[357] Timeous notice must be given to the tenant.[358] Decree of removal and ejection of the tenant may follow, unless the tenant pays the arrears due by him or finds caution for them to the sheriff's satisfaction. A lease terminated in this way is treated[359] as if it had expired naturally at that term, and the tenant will be entitled to the usual away-going rights.[360]

Where a tenancy is to be terminated otherwise than of consent at the expiry of the stipulated period for the endurance of the lease, notice to quit or of removal must be given.[361] In order to be effective, such notice[362] must be given not less than one or more than two years before the expiry of the lease, notwithstanding any contractual provision to the contrary[363]; failing such notice, the lease is renewed by tacit relocation from year to year. Where there are two possible anniversary dates of a lease, the landlord is entitled to serve notices against both

---

[353] 1991 Act s.8(3), as amended by s.61(a) of the 2003 Act.

[354] 1991 Act s.8(3A), as amended by s.61(a) of the 2003 Act.

[355] 1991 Act s.5.

[356] 1991 Act ss.44–47.

[357] 1991 Act s.20(1). Note that a liferent beneficiary under a trust does not fall within the statutory definition of landlord in s.85(1): *Fforde v McKinnon*, 1998 S.L.T. 902. Under the Term and Quarter Days (Scotland) Act 1990 s.1(1)(a) and (2)(a), the terms Whitsunday and Martinmas signify May 28 and November 28 respectively; see also *Austin v Gibson*, 1979 S.L.T. (Land Ct) 12; *Provincial Insurance Plc v Valtos Ltd*, 1992 S.C.L.R. 203.

[358] *Downie v Trustees of the Earl of Stair's 1970 Trust*, 2007 S.L.T. 827.

[359] 1991 Act s.20(2).

[360] Quaere whether the tenant would be entitled to compensation for disturbance and reorganisation: see *Scottish Current Law Statutes*, Vol.3, annotations to 1991 Act, and A.G.M. Duncan, "The Agricultural Holdings (Scotland) Act 1991", 1992 S.L.T. (News) 1 at 2.

[361] 1991 Act s.21(1); *Morrison v Rendall*, 1986 S.C. 69, sub nom. *Morrison's Exrs v Rendall*, 1986 S.L.T. 227 (precursor of s.21(1)). The tenant's unilateral renunciation of the lease may be effective: Gill, *Law of Agricultural Holdings in Scotland* (1997), para.14.03. The landlord's right to remove a tenant whose estate has been sequestrated, or who has incurred an irritancy under the lease, remains unaffected: s.21(6). On establishing that there has been renunciation, see *Knapdale (Nominees) Ltd v Donald*, 2001 S.L.T. 617.

[362] See Removal Terms (Scotland) Act 1886 s.6; Sheriff Courts (Scotland) Act 1907 ss.36, 37 and Form H2 (formerly Form L); Term and Quarter Days (Scotland) Act 1990. As to the effect of deviation from the requirements of the prescribed Form, see *Rae v Davidson*, 1954 S.C. 361; *Callander v Watherston*, 1970 S.L.T. (Land Ct) 13; *Mackie v Gardner*, 1973 S.L.T. (Land Ct) 11; *Gemmell v Andrew*, 1975 S.L.T. (Land Ct) 5; *Taylor v Brick*, 1982 S.L.T. 25; *Morrison's Exrs v Rendall*, 1989 S.L.T. (Land Ct) 89. As to the need for writing, see s.21(3)(a) and *Morrison v Rendall*, 1986 S.C. 69 (sub nom. *Morrison's Exrs v Rendall*, 1986 S.L.T. 227).

[363] 1991 Act s.21(3); *Duguid v Muirhead*, 1926 S.C. 1078.

dates, each notice being without prejudice to the other. But at the stage where the landlord, in judicial proceedings, asserts his right to remove the tenant, he must specify on which notice he founds.[364] Where notice is served on the tenant, he may within one month serve a counter-notice on the landlord.[365] This has the effect of restricting the operation of the notice to quit to cases where the landlord can obtain the consent of the Land Court, except in certain special circumstances,[366] for example where the notice is given by reason of the tenant's apparent insolvency,[367] or on the issue within the last nine months by the Land Court of a certificate of bad husbandry,[368] or because the tenant has failed to comply with a demand in writing to remedy a breach of any term or condition of his tenancy,[369] or where the tenant has acquired right to the lease by succession or as a legatee,[370] and in each case it is stated in the notice to quit that it is given by reason of these circumstances.

The Land Court may only give their consent, where it is required, to the operation of a notice to quit if they are satisfied as to one or more of the following reasons, which the landlord must specify in his application[371]:

   (a) that the carrying out of the purpose for which the landlord proposes to terminate the tenancy is desirable in the interests of good husbandry;

   (b) that its carrying out is desirable in the interests of sound management of the estates of which it forms part[372];

   (c) that its carrying out is desirable for the purposes of agricultural research, experiments, etc;

---

[364] *Steven v Innes Ker*, 2007 S.L.T. 625 at 630, [37], per Lord Justice Clerk Gill. Whether this obiter statement applies to all leases (i.e. not merely agricultural holdings) is unclear.

[365] Under the 1991 Act s.22.

[366] 1991 Act s.22(2); the tenant may refer any question arising under this subsection to the Land Court for determination by written notice to the landlord: s.23(2); *Fane v Murray*, 1995 S.L.T. 567.

[367] 1991 Act s.22(2)(f). In *West Errol Trust's Trustees v Lawrie*, 2000 S.L.T. 911, it was held that a landlord had not waived its entitlement to enforce a notice to quit served upon a tenant who had entered into sequestration where the landlord had stated in the covering letter to the notice that it might not enforce the notice to quit if the sequestration was recalled within a year and it subsequently reached agreement with the tenant regarding an increase in the level of the rent for the coming years.

[368] 1991 Act ss.22(2)(c) and 26. For the rules of good husbandry, see s.85(2), (2A) and (2B) of the 1991 Act, referring to the Agriculture (Scotland) Act 1948 Sch.6; *Austin v Gibson*, 1979 S.L.T. (Land Ct) 12; *Luss Estates Co v Firkin Farm Co*, 1985 S.L.T. (Land Ct) 17; *Cambusmore Estate Trs v Little*, 1991 S.L.T. (Land Ct) 33.

[369] 1991 Act s.22(2)(d), subject, however, in the case of a breach relating to fixed equipment to the special provisions of ss.32, 66 and *Alexander v Royal Hotel (Caithness) Ltd*, 2001 S.L.T. 17 which held that s.22(2)(d) is not engaged where a landlord has materially breached their statutory obligation in s.5(2)(a) of the 1991 Act to put the fixed equipment into a proper state of repair and the tenant has retained rent in response to that material breach. In such cases, there is no rent due and accordingly s.22(2)(d) is not applicable. Note that the rights afforded by sub-heads (c) and (d) (formerly sub-heads (d) and (e)) are mutually exclusive: *MacNabb v A & J Anderson*, 1955 S.C. 38.

[370] 1991 Act s.22(2)(g), read with s.25. Note that special provisions apply in the case of tenancies acquired by succession or as legatees by near relatives, for the termination of which the consent of the Land Court is required: see para.35.35, below.

[371] 1991 Act s.24(1) and see s.24(2), as amended by s.67(2)(b) of the 2003 Act: consent to be withheld if a "fair and reasonable landlord" would not insist on possession. See, too, *Altyre Estate Trs v McLay*, 1975 S.L.T. (Land Ct) 12.

[372] See *Gemmell v Andrew*, 1975 S.L.T. (Land Ct) 5; *Prior v J. & A. Henderson*, 1984 S.L.T. (Land Ct) 51; the reference is to the landlord's own estate, not land which has passed into other hands: *Smoor v MacPherson*, 1981 S.L.T. (Land Ct) 25.

(d) that greater hardship would be caused by withholding than by giving consent to the operation of the notice[373]; or

(e) that the landlord's purpose is to employ the land for use other than for agriculture.

Further protection is afforded to the tenant by s.24(2) which provides that the Land Court may withhold their consent in all the circumstances, if it appears to them that (a) a fair and reasonable landlord would not insist on possession, or (b) where the notice is to quit the whole of the holding, that use of the land for the purpose for which the landlord proposes to terminate the tenancy would not create greater economic and social benefits to the community than would exist were the tenancy not terminated.[374] An application to the Land Court for the granting of consent is competent in cases where the notice to quit has been served without prejudice to other proceedings in the Land Court, such as proceedings for a declaration that the lease has expired. This is so, since the Land Court now has jurisdiction to adjudicate on questions as to whether or not an agricultural holding exists or has been terminated.[375] A landlord may have a power of resumption for building, planting or other non-agricultural purposes. When exercising such a power, the normal rules relating to notices to quit do not apply.[376]

35.31 Compensation to tenant for improvements: Land court—A tenant is entitled on quitting the holding, to compensation for certain improvements.[377] The rules relating to the improvements for which compensation may be claimed are set out in ss.33–39 of the 1991 Act and Schedules of some complexity. Schedules 3–6, to which reference must be made, enumerate the improvements and they are classified (a) according to the dates when they were begun, and (b) according as they call or do not call for the consent of or notice to the landlord. It should be noted that a landlord, if the holding has deteriorated through the failure of the tenant to cultivate according to the rules of good husbandry, may claim compensation in his turn.[378] In the cases of leases entered into after certain dates, no claim is good unless a record of the condition of the holding has been made. The amount of compensation will be ascertained, in default of agreement, by the Land Court.[379] In fixing compensation for improvements the Land Court is to give such sum as fairly represents the value of the improvement to an incoming tenant[380] and is bound in certain cases to take into account any benefit which the landlord has given or allowed in consideration of the tenant executing the improvement.[381] It was held[382] that no compensation was due if the tenant was expressly bound to

---

[373] As to the evidence required to show greater hardship, see *Somerville v Watson*, 1980 S.L.T. (Land Ct) 14; *Hutchison v Buchanan*, 1980 S.L.T. (Land Ct) 17; *Clamp v Sharp*, 1986 S.L.T. (Land Ct) 2.

[374] 1991 Act ss.24(1) and (2), as amended by s.67(2)(b) of the 2003 Act; *Altyre Estate Trs v McLay*, 1975 S.L.T. (Land Ct) 12; *North Berwick Trust v Miller*, 2009 S.C. 305.

[375] 2003 Act s.75, introducing the 1991 Act s.60.

[376] 1991 Act s.21(7). The word "feuing" appears in the statute notwithstanding the Abolition of Feudal Tenure etc (Scotland) Act 2000. See, generally, Gordon and Wortley, *Scottish Land Law* (2009), para.18–57.

[377] 1991 Act ss.33–39.

[378] 1991 Act ss.45–48. For a case which dealt with the equivalent provisions in the Agricultural Holdings (Scotland) Act 1923 s.9, see *Palmer's Executors v Shaw*, 2004 S.L.T. 261.

[379] 1991 Act s.36.

[380] 1991 Act s.36(1).

[381] See the 1991 Act s.36(2).

[382] *Earl of Galloway v McClelland*, 1915 S.C. 1062.

execute the improvement in question, but this is no longer the law except as to leases before January 1, 1921.[383] In general, contracting out of the compensation provisions of the Act is not allowed.[384]

Determination by the Land Court is the method by which all claims of whatever nature by the tenant or the landlord[385] arising under the 1991 Act or on or out of the termination of the holding are to be settled.[386] For example, either party may obtain a review of the rent by referring the question of what rent should properly be payable in respect of the holding to the Land Court for determination.[387] A general reference to the Land Court, as to "any question or difference between the landlord and the tenant", is made by the 1991 Act to cover cases for which no express provision is made.[388] Prior to the introduction of s.75 of the Agricultural Holdings (Scotland) Act 2003, it was clear that the jurisdiction of the Land Court in this context was not wide enough to encompass a dispute as to whether a relationship of landlord or tenant of an agricultural holding subsisted between the parties. In such a case it was clear that only the courts had jurisdiction.[389] This is no longer the case. Section 75 of the Agricultural Holdings (Scotland) Act 2003 introduces a new s.60 into the Agricultural Holdings (Scotland) Act 1991 which gives the Land Court the express power to determine whether the tenancy of an agricultural holding exists. Where the question or difference relates to a demand in writing served on the tenant by the landlord requiring the tenant to remedy a breach of any term or condition of the tenancy by the doing of any work of provision, repair, maintenance or replacement of fixed equipment, the Land Court has power to modify that demand.[390]

Compensation to tenant for disturbance—When a landlord gives notice to quit **35.32** (or the tenant gives a counter-notice under s.22) and the tenant leaves the holding, he is entitled to compensation for disturbance,[391] unless s.43(2) applies. The minimum amount is one year's rent[392] and the tenant may claim a greater amount where he has given the landlord not less than one month's notice of the sale of certain goods, implements, fixtures, produce or stock.[393] Written notice of an

---

[383] 1991 Act s.34(2).

[384] 1991 Act s.53(1); *Young v Oswald*, 1949 S.C. 412 was decided on the very different wording of the Act of 1923 and is of doubtful application. However, see *Palmer's Executors v Shaw*, 2004 S.L.T. 261 where it was held that an irritancy clause in an agricultural lease governed by the Agricultural Holdings (Scotland) Act 1923 which entitled the landlord to irritate the lease without notice in the case of non-payment of rent by the tenant for three months did not deprive the tenant of his right to give notice to the landlord of his intention to claim compensation under s.9 of the Agricultural Holdings (Scotland) Act 1923 (now s.44 of the 1991 Act) in contravention of s.45 of the Agricultural Holdings (Scotland) Act 1923 (now s.53 of the 1991 Act). See also *Downie v Trs of the Earl of Stair's 1970 Trust*, 2007 S.L.T. 827, where the court held that an irritancy clause (which enabled the landlord to irritate the lease by notice where one half year's rent had remained unpaid for one month after the due date for payment) was not rendered void ab initio by s.53 of the 1991 Act.

[385] As to the meaning of landlord, see s.85(1) and Gill, *Law of Agricultural Holdings in Scotland* (1997), paras 35.01–35.02. See also *Crewpace Ltd v French*, 2012 S.L.T. 126.

[386] 1991 Act ss.60–61. Note that, if both parties agree, recourse may be made to arbitration instead of the Land Court: s.61(1).

[387] 1991 Act s.13(1); see para.35.29, above.

[388] 1991 Act s.60(1).

[389] cf. *Brodie v Ker*, 1952 S.C. 216; *Cormack v McIldowie's Exrs*, 1974 S.L.T. 178 (reported further 1975 S.C. 161); *Craig, Applicant*, 1981 S.L.T. (Land Ct) 12; *Hiskett v Wilson (No.1)*, 2003 S.L.T. 58.

[390] 1991 Act s.66.

[391] 1991 Act s.43(1).

[392] 1991 Act s.43(4)(a).

[393] 1991 Act s.43(4)(b).

intention to make a claim must be given to the landlord within two months of the termination of the tenancy even where the claim is restricted to the minimum.[394] The notice of intention to claim must specify the nature of the claim. There is sufficient specification if the notice refers to the statutory provision, custom or term of an agreement under which the claim is made.[395]

Where he is entitled to compensation for disturbance, the tenant is in certain cases entitled under ss.54–55 of the 1991 Act to payment in addition of a sum to assist in the reorganisation of his affairs, being a sum equal to four times the annual rent or an appropriate proportion in the case of part of a holding.[396] No such sum is payable, however, if the tenancy is terminated by virtue of a notice to quit which contains a statement,[397] and, if an application is made to the Land Court for consent to the operation of the notice, the court is satisfied that the carrying out of the purpose for which the landlord proposes to terminate the tenancy is desirable on one or other of a number of grounds set out in s.24 of the Act. These grounds relate to good husbandry, sound management of the estate of which the holding forms part, agricultural research, and to the fact that the landlord will suffer hardship unless the notice to quit has effect.[398] The right to an additional payment is also excluded in cases where the tenancy is terminated by notice to quit served on a tenant who has acquired right to the lease by succession or as a legatee.[399]

35.33 Compensation for damage by game and other damage—A tenant is entitled to compensation for damage by game (i.e. deer, pheasants, partridges, grouse, black game) provided that the amount of damage done exceeds 12 pence per hectare of the area affected, and that the tenant has no permission in writing to kill the game in question.[400] Provision is made for timely notice to the landlord of a claim under this head.[401] A shooting tenant is bound to indemnify the landlord against claims for such compensation.[402] It has been held to be no objection to a claim that the damage was done by black game coming from another property and at a season of the year when it was unlawful to kill them.[403] When a tenant has permission from the landlord to kill any of the enumerated kinds of game, no claim for compensation in respect of damage by game of that kind is competent.[404]

35.34 Ground game—An agricultural tenant, if there is no stipulation to the contrary in his lease, may kill rabbits, and may authorise anyone else to do so.[405] Under the

---

[394] 1991 Act s.62.

[395] 1991 Act s.62(3); Gill, *Law of Agricultural Holdings in Scotland* (1997), para.22.02. For an examination of what is meant by "special circumstances" in s.62(5) of the 1991 Act and the discretion these words afford the Secretary of State, see *Southesk Trust Co Ltd v Secretary of State for Scotland*, 2000 S.L.T. 680.

[396] This is a fixed payment, regardless of actual loss: *Copeland v McQuaker*, 1973 S.L.T. 186.

[397] As to this requirement, see s.55, and *Barns-Graham v Lamont*, 1971 S.C. 170; *Copeland v McQuaker*, 1973 S.L.T. 186.

[398] 1991 Act ss.24(1), 55(1). Note, however, that s.55(1) does not apply if the reasons given by the Land Court for consent to the operation of the notice include or would have included the reason that the landlord's purpose is to employ the land for use other than agriculture: see s.55(2).

[399] 1991 Act s.55(2)(b).

[400] 1991 Act s.52.

[401] 1991 Act s.52(2), as amended by s.50(2) of the 2003 Act; and cf. *Earl of Morton's Trs v Macdougall*, 1944 S.C. 410.

[402] 1991 Act s.52(4).

[403] *Thomson v Earl of Galloway*, 1919 S.C. 911; 1991 Act s.52(1).

[404] *Ross v Watson*, 1943 S.C. 406.

[405] *Crawshay v Duncan*, 1915 S.C. (J.C.) 64. The lease may exclude this right, but the tenant's statutory right would be unaffected by that exclusion.

Ground Game Act 1880, an occupier of land has the right, declared to be "incident to and inseparable from his occupation of the land", and of which he cannot deprive himself by any contract,[406] to kill hares and rabbits. This right may be exercised by the occupier himself, or, with his authority in writing, by members of his household resident on the land, persons in his ordinary employment, and one other person bona fide employed for reward[407]; the occupier and the owner or any other person having the right to kill or take game on the land may make an agreement for the joint execution, or the execution for their joint benefit, of that right otherwise than by the use of firearms.[408] Only the occupier and one other person authorised in writing may use firearms,[409] except where authorisation of additional persons is sanctioned by the Scottish Ministers.[410] There are limitations as to the period of the year during which the occupier's right to kill ground game with firearms may be exercised.[411]

Bequest of lease: Succession—The tenant of a holding may, unless his power to do   **35.35**
so is expressly excluded by the lease,[412] bequeath his lease, under s.11 of the 1991 Act, to his son-in-law or daughter-in-law or to any one of the persons who would be, or would in any circumstances have been, entitled to succeed to the estate on his intestacy.[413] Where a joint tenant dies bequeathing her interest in an agricultural tenancy to the remaining joint tenant, the deceased's interest in the lease vests in her executors who have the power to transfer that interest to the remaining joint tenant, at which point there is no longer a joint tenancy, just one single tenant, who is the only person who could consent to the continuance of the lease.[414] The legatee must intimate the bequest to the landlord within 21 days of the tenant's death or, if he is prevented by some unavoidable cause from giving such notice within that period, as soon as practicable thereafter. By doing so he accepts the lease, which then becomes binding upon both as from the date of the deceased's death unless the landlord, within one month of intimation being made, gives a counter-notice to the legatee that he objects to receiving him as tenant. If such objection is made, the legatee may apply to the Land Court for an order declaring him to be tenant under the lease, which the Land Court must grant unless a reasonable ground of objection is established by the landlord.[415] If the legatee refuses the bequest or is rejected, the right to the lease will be treated as intestate estate of the deceased tenant, and will pass accordingly.[416] A legatee who accepts the bequest but fails to give timeous notification of his acceptance has no right to possess, nor does any other person who claims right to the lease by transfer of the tenant's interest to him.[417] The acquirer of such a lease, that is to say any person to whom the lease is transferred under s.16 of the

---

[406] Ground Game Act 1880 s.3; *Sherrard v Gascoigne* [1900] 2 Q.B. 279.

[407] Ground Game Act 1880 s.1; *Stuart v Murray* (1884) 12 R. (J.C.) 9; *Niven v Renton* (1888) 15 R. (J.C.) 42.

[408] Agriculture (Scotland) Act 1948 s.48(4).

[409] Ground Game Act 1880 s.1(1)(a).

[410] See Agriculture (Scotland) Act 1948 s.48(2); Pests Act 1954.

[411] Ground Game Act 1880 s.1(3), as amended by Agriculture (Scotland) Act 1948 s.48(1).

[412] *Kennedy v Johnstone*, 1956 S.C. 39.

[413] 1991 Act s.11(1); Gordon and Wortley, *Scottish Land Law* (2009), para.18–41.

[414] *Stephen v Innes Ker*, 2007 S.L.T. 625 at 629, [29], per Lord Justice Clerk Gill.

[415] 1991 Act s.11(6). Such a ground must be personal to the heir; e.g. *Reid v Duffus Estate*, 1955 S.L.C.R. 13; *Reid's Trs v Macpherson*, 1975 S.L.T. 101; *Harvey v Mactaggart & Mickel Ltd*, 1998 S.L.T. (Land Ct) 20.

[416] 1991 Act s.11(8).

[417] *Coats v Logan*, 1985 S.L.T. 221.

Succession (Scotland) Act 1964,[418] must also within 21 days notify the landlord, who may again give a counter-notice, remitting the matter to the Land Court.[419] As in the case of a bequest, time is of the essence and an acquirer who fails to give notice within 21 days will have no right to possess under the lease.[420] A person who is a near relative of the deceased tenant and has acquired right to the lease of an agricultural holding under s.16 of the 1964 Act or as a legatee under s.11 of the 1991 Act is subject to the special provisions which the 1991 Act provides for the termination of tenancies acquired by succession.[421]

35.36 Termination of tenancies acquired by succession—A near relative of the deceased tenant who has acquired right to the lease of the holding under s.16 of the 1964 Act or as a legatee under s.11 of the 1991 Act is in a privileged position as regards termination of the lease on its expiry as compared with other such successors.[422] In the case of other successors the landlord is able to terminate the tenancy on the expiry of the lease by notice to quit without the consent of the Land Court.[423] But a landlord cannot avail himself of this notice to quit procedure in respect of a partial interest in a tenancy.[424] In the case of near relatives, however, a category which is confined to the deceased tenant's spouse, civil partner, child or grandchild,[425] the consent of the Land Court is required to the operation of the notice to quit and the grounds on which it is given must be specified in the notice.[426] The grounds for consent differ from those which apply in other cases where the Land Court's consent to the operation of a notice to quit is required,[427] and different grounds apply depending upon whether the tenancy was let before January 1, 1984 or on or after that date.[428] Where the holding was let before January 1, 1984 consent must be given if the Land Court are satisfied: (1) that the tenant has neither sufficient training in agriculture nor sufficient experience in the farming of land to enable him to farm the holding with reasonable efficiency; (2) that the holding is not a viable unit and the landlord proposes to amalgamate it with other land[429]; or (3) that the tenant is the occupier of other agricultural land which he has occupied since before the deceased tenant's death and which is a viable unit.[430] A "viable unit" is an agri-

---

[418] See para.35.24, above.

[419] 1991 Act s.12; as to the notice to be given by the acquirer to the landlord, see *Garvie's Trs v Garvie's Tutors*, 1975 S.L.T. 94; *Knapdale (Nominees) Ltd v Robert Donald*, 2001 S.L.T. 617.

[420] *Coats v Logan*, 1985 S.L.T. 221.

[421] 1991 Act s.25.

[422] Where a joint tenant dies bequeathing her interest in an agricultural tenancy to the remaining joint tenant, the deceased's interest in the lease vests in her executors who have the power to transfer that interest to the remaining joint tenant, at which point there is no longer a joint tenancy, just one single tenant. In such circumstances, s.25 is not applicable, since it is designed to cover the position where a stranger to the lease acquires an interest in it by succession and accordingly these statutory provisions are not appropriate or necessary where the survivor of a joint tenancy becomes a sole tenant: *Stephen v Innes Ker*, 2007 S.L.T. 625.

[423] 1991 Act s.22(2)(g). See *Steven v Innes Ker*, 2007 S.L.T. 625 at 629, per Lord Justice Clerk Gill.

[424] *Steven v Innes Ker*, 2007 S.L.T. 625 at 629, [30]–[33], per Lord Justice Clerk Gill.

[425] 1991 Act s.25(2), read with s.25(5) and Sch.2 Pt III, as amended by the Agricultural Holdings (Amendment) Scotland Act 2012. A previous specific reference to adopted children was rendered otiose by the Adoption and Children (Scotland) Act 2007.

[426] 1991 Act s.25; and see the article by R.D. Sutherland, "Unforeseen Consequences of the Agricultural Holdings (Scotland) Act 1991", 1993 S.L.T. (News) 351.

[427] See para.35.30, above.

[428] 1991 Act Sch.2 Pts I and II.

[429] As to the meaning of "amalgamation", see *Mackenzie v Lyon*, 1984 S.L.T. (Land Ct) 30.

[430] "Occupier" in this context means occupier as an individual and not as a partner in a firm which is the owner or tenant of other land: *Haddo House Estate Trs v Davidson*, 1984 S.L.T. (Land Ct) 14.

cultural unit capable of providing an individual occupying it with full-time employment and the means to provide for both the rent payable in respect of the unit and adequate maintenance of the unit.[431] Where the holding was let on or after that date, there is a further ground, namely that the tenant does not have sufficient financial resources to enable him to farm the holding with reasonable efficiency, and the ground about insufficient training and experience is modified to enable account to be taken of the fact that the tenant is already engaged on a suitable course of training in agriculture. There is one other important difference, namely, that, except in the case of the ground involving amalgamation of holdings, the onus is on the successor tenant to satisfy the Land Court that the circumstances are not as specified in the landlord's notice to quit.[432] The general rule which applies in all other cases where the Land Court's consent is required is that the onus is on the landlord to satisfy the Land Court as to the grounds of his application.[433] The effect of these differences is that it is likely to be easier for a landlord to obtain consent and thus terminate the tenancy where the holding was let on or after January 1, 1984.

Tenant's right to buy—The tenant of a 1991 Act tenancy has the right under 35.37 Pt 2 of the 2003 Act to make a pre-emptive compulsory purchase of the agricultural land from the landlord.[434] The "right to buy" is engaged where the landlord or the landlord's heritable creditor proposes to sell the agricultural land to a third party. The scheme envisaged under the 2003 Act enables a 1991 Act tenant to register a notice of interest with the Register of Community Interests in Land maintained by the Keeper of the Registers of Scotland.[435] Where the landlord or the landlord's heritable creditor gives notice to the 1991 Act tenant of a proposal to transfer the agricultural land or any part of it to a third party or the landlord or the heritable creditor takes any action with a view to the transfer of the agricultural land to a third party, the 1991 Act tenant is given a right of pre-emption in respect of the purchase of such land.[436] The purchase price is to be set by the agreement of the parties or by valuation provisions contained in the 2003 Act.[437] Certain transfers do not give rise to any right on the part of the 1991 Act tenant to effect a purchase. For example, where the transfer is otherwise than for value, or is between companies in the same corporate group, or is a transfer implementing missives or options to purchase which existed before a notice of interest was registered with the Keeper, the 1991 Act tenant will enjoy no right of pre-emption. There are many other exceptions.[438]

B. 2003 ACT—AGRICULTURAL TENANCIES

Introduction to the Agricultural Holdings (Scotland) Act 2003—Prior to the 35.38 enactment of the 2003 Act, all leases of agricultural holdings had been subject to statutory indefinite security of tenure. Thus, subject to certain exceptions,

---

[431] The concept of "viable unit" was introduced by the Public Services Reform (Agricultural Holdings) (Scotland) Order 2011 (SSI 2011/232). Prior to that reform, the test related to a two-man unit, i.e. capable of providing employment to the occupier and at least one other man.

[432] 1991 Act s.25(3)(b).

[433] *McLaren v Lawrie*, 1964 S.L.T. (Land Ct) 10.

[434] 1991 Act ss.24–38.

[435] 1991 Act ss.24–25.

[436] 1991 Act ss.28–29.

[437] 1991 Act s.32.

[438] 1991 Act s.27.

landlords had no power to terminate agricultural leases under the 1991 Act or its predecessors where the duration of the lease had expired. This was the position even where the parties had entered into an agreement which enabled such termination at the ish. In response to this, a practice evolved whereby landlords would not enter into agricultural leases with tenants as natural persons. Instead, agricultural leases were granted to limited partnerships constituted under the Limited Partnerships Act 1907. The flexibility of the limited partnership structure enabled the landlord to circumvent the statutory indefinite security of tenure which pertained under the 1991 Act. This was achieved by the landlord agreeing to become the limited partner in the limited partnership.[439] The tenant would become the general partner in the limited partnership. When the limited partnership was dissolved in accordance with the limited partnership agreement or some other agreement, the statutorily secure agricultural lease would automatically terminate on the basis that the tenant had ceased to exist. Hence, the landlord was able to ensure that statutory security of tenure was not conceded. It was felt by the agricultural sector and the Scottish Government that such limited partnership arrangements were largely artificial and that a change in the regime for the letting of agricultural tenancies was necessary. The mischief behind the 2003 Act is to balance the need for a degree of security of tenure on the part of agricultural tenants against the landlord's need to recover vacant possession of agricultural land at the expiry of the fixed term of the lease. In order to achieve this, the 2003 act introduced two fixed-term tenancies, namely the "short limited duration tenancy" and the "limited duration tenancy". In addition, it is no longer competent to enter into 1991 Act tenancies except by express agreement. There is also a procedure whereby 1991 Act tenancies can be converted into short limited duration tenancies or limited duration tenancies. A provision is contained in the 2003 Act which enables the general partner of a tenant which is a limited partnership to continue the 1991 Act tenancy where the landlord as limited partner purports to dissolve the limited partnership and thus terminate the 1991 Act tenancy.[440]

35.39 **Short limited duration tenancy and limited duration tenancy: Meaning**—The 2003 Act defines a short limited duration tenancy as a lease of agricultural land for a term of not more than five years, which is not a 1991 Act tenancy or a grazing or mowing lease[441] and where the agricultural land comprised in the lease is not let to the tenant during the tenant's continuation in any office, appointment or employment held under the landlord.[442] A limited duration tenancy is defined in similar terms, the principal difference being that the duration must be not less than 10 years.[443] At any time during the term of a limited duration tenancy, the landlord and the tenant may extend the term by written agreement.[444] "Agricultural land" is defined[445] as meaning "land used for

---

[439] *MacFarlane v Falfield Investments Ltd*, 1998 S.L.T. 145

[440] This provision has been called into question, in the Inner House case of *Salvesen v Riddell*, 2012 S.L.T. 633.

[441] On the difference between a 1991 Act tenancy and a grazing or mowing let (governed originally by s.2 of the 1991 Act and now by s.3 of the 2003 Act), see *Nelson v Kinnaird*, 2012 G.W.D. 4–57 and *Scottish Youth Hostels Association v Paterson* (RN SLC/16/07 August 21, 2007).

[442] 1991 Act s.4(1).

[443] 1991 Act s.5(1), as amended by the Public Services Reform (Agricultural Holdings) (Scotland) Order 2011. The original term was 15 years.

[444] 1991 Act s.8(15).

[445] 1991 Act s.93.

agriculture for the purposes of a trade or business" and the word "agriculture" is to be interpreted in accordance with the 1991 Act.[446] The effect of the 2003 Act is that it is difficult, albeit not impossible, to create a lease which endures for a period between five and ten years.[447] Whether a short limited duration tenancy or limited duration tenancy exists is a matter within the jurisdiction of the Land Court.[448] An appeal may be made to the Court of Session against the determination of the Land Court on a question of law within 28 days of the determination.[449]

Incidents of lease: Written lease—Where in respect of a short limited duration **35.40** tenancy or limited duration tenancy there is not in force a lease in writing embodying the terms of a tenancy, either party may require the other to enter into a written agreement for this purpose.[450] Where a written lease has been entered into but it does not contain any one or more of the matters specified in Sch.1[451] to the 1991 Act or is inconsistent with it or with the provisions of s.16 relating to fixed equipment, a similar request may be made.[452] If parties are unable to agree the matter may be determined by the Land Court.[453]

Liability for maintenance—When a lease constituting a short limited duration tenancy or a limited duration tenancy is entered into, any fixed equipment provided to enable the tenant to maintain efficient production as respects the use of the land as specified in the lease must be documented in writing by the parties in the form of a schedule of fixed equipment. This schedule specifies the relevant fixed equipment and its condition and, on being agreed by the parties or as determined by the Land Court, is deemed to form part of the lease.[454] The Act deems[455] the incorporation in every lease constituting a short limited duration tenancy or limited duration tenancy of an undertaking by the landlord to put the fixed equipment on the land into a thorough state of repair, and to provide the necessary buildings and other equipment. The landlord is also bound to make such replacement or renewal as may be rendered necessary by natural decay or by fair wear and tear.[456] The tenant's liability is limited to an undertaking to maintain the equipment in a state of good repair, fair wear and tear excepted.[457]

Variation of rent—The 2003 Act enables either party to seek a statutory review of the contractual rent triennially in the case of a limited duration tenancy[458]; either party may serve a written notice on the other party not less than one year or

---

[446] See para.35.28, above.

[447] See A. Fox, "Breaking Down a Brick Wall?", 2007 JLSS (March) 42, written from the perspective of the original fifteen-year regime for limited duration tenancies.

[448] 2003 Act s.77(2)(a).

[449] 2003 Act s.88(1).

[450] 2003 Act s.13(1)(a).

[451] These matters are: (i) the names of the parties, (ii) particulars of the holding, with reference to a map or plan, (iii) the term of the lease, (iv) the rent and the dates on which payable, (v) certain undertakings by the parties relating to damage to buildings and the destruction of harvested crops.

[452] 2003 Act s.13(1)(b).

[453] 2003 Act s.13(3).

[454] 2003 Act s.16(2).

[455] 2003 Act s.16(1)(a).

[456] 2003 Act s.16(1)(a).

[457] 2003 Act s.16(4).

[458] 2003 Act s.9. The parties may include their own rent review procedure by agreement, but such procedure will be void if it provides for upwards only variation or for initiation by the landlord only, per the amendments introduced by the Agricultural Holdings Amendment (Scotland) Act 2012.

more than two years before the rent review date.[459] If the landlord wishes to review the rent in the case of a short limited duration tenancy, such provisions for review will require to be agreed contractually and be compliant with law. The rent properly payable in respect of the holding for this purpose is normally the rent at which, having regard to the terms of the lease but not to the personal circumstances of the tenant,[460] the holding might reasonably be expected to be let in the open market on a willing landlord and willing tenant basis.[461] The Land Court has jurisdiction to ascertain the level at which the reviewed rent should be fixed.[462] The Land Court is directed to take account of certain other factors in arriving at the appropriate rent: the terms of the tenancy[463]; information about rents for other agricultural tenancies and any factors affecting those rents except any distortion due to a scarcity of lets[464]; the current economic conditions in the relevant agricultural sector[465]; and any increase in the rental value of the land resulting from the use of the land for a purpose that is not an agricultural purpose.[466] The landlord, where he has carried out certain specific improvements, has an absolute right to increase the rent by an amount equal to the increase in the rental value of the land resulting from the carrying out of the improvements[467]; the increase operates from the date of completion and the landlord must serve notice in writing on the tenant.[468] The Land Court also has an incidental power to vary rent when determining the conditions of a lease or matters relating to fixed equipment.[469]

Pactional rent—A provision in a lease for penal or pactional rent, i.e. for payment of a fixed sum as damages for any breach of its conditions, is not binding where the fixed sum is in excess of the damage actually suffered by the landlord in consequence of the breach or non-fulfillment.[470]

Withholding of rent—In the case of both short limited duration tenancies and limited duration tenancies, the tenant may obtain a Land Court order which enables him to withhold rent in relation to the failure of the landlord to comply with a Land Court order the subject-matter of which relates to a failure on his part to fulfil any obligation he owes towards the tenant in respect of fixed equipment.[471] The landlord's failure must be material.[472]

Freedom of cropping—A tenant may practise any system of cropping arable lands, and may dispose of the produce of the farm other than manure produced on it as he pleases, notwithstanding any provision of the lease or local custom which

---

[459] 2003 Act s.9(2).

[460] 2003 Act s.9(3)(a)(i). The decision in *Guthe v Broatch*, 1956 S.C. 132, is thus superseded.

[461] 2003 Act s.9(3)(a); certain other factors relating to improvements, distortions in rents due to a scarcity of lets and dilapidations are also to be disregarded: s.9(3)(a)(ii), (5) and (7); *Broadland Properties Estates Ltd v Mann*, 1994 S.L.T. (Land Ct) 7 (allocated milk quota not an improvement); *Grant v Broadland Properties Estates Ltd*, 1997 S.L.T. 1030. For the meaning of "improvements", see s.9(6)(a) and Sch.5 to the 1991 Act. See also *Morrison-Low v Paterson's Executors*, 2012 S.L.T. 648 where farming subsidies were allowed to be factored into the calculation.

[462] 2003 Act s.77(2)(a). Note that the matter may be determined instead by the Land Court at first instance if the parties so agree: s.78.

[463] 2003 Act s.9(3)(b)(i).

[464] 2003 Act s.9(3)(b)(ii).

[465] 2003 Act s.9(3)(b)(iii).

[466] 2003 Act s.9(4).

[467] 2003 Act s.10.

[468] 2003 Act s.10(2).

[469] 2003 Act ss.11 and 13.

[470] 2003 Act s.56.

[471] 2003 Act s.12(1).

[472] 2003 Act s.12(2).

may bind him to some particular method of cultivation.[473] This provision neither applies as respects the year before the expiry of the lease nor to land in grass which is to be retained in that condition throughout the tenancy.[474] The landlord is entitled to obtain an interdict from the Land Court to restrain the exercise of the tenant's freedom of cropping if he allows the holding to deteriorate, and to damages from the Land Court for the tenant's failure in these duties.[475]

Specification of fixed equipment—Either landlord or tenant may at any time after the commencement of the lease add to, or vary, the specification of fixed equipment outlined in the lease.[476] The existence of such a specification of fixed equipment is a prerequisite to any claim by the tenant for compensation for continuous good farming.[477] There is no similar provision for the specification of improvements in the 2003 Act.[478]

Premature termination by agreement—The landlord and tenant may terminate **35.41** a short limited duration tenancy by agreement.[479] A limited duration tenancy may also be terminated by agreement, provided that the agreement is entered into in writing, subsequent to the commencement of the tenancy and provides for compensation from one of the parties to the other.[480] If a limited duration tenancy is not terminated by agreement at its expiry, tacit relocation operates to continue the tenancy. The limited duration tenancy continues in a number of cycles: first, it continues for three years; secondly, it continues for a second cycle of three years; and thirdly, by a long cycle of 10 years. The first and second cycles are termed "short continuations" and the 10-year cycle is called a "long continuation".[481]

Termination by the landlord at the ish—The landlord may seek to terminate a **35.42** limited duration tenancy at the ish by following the dual notice procedures in the 2003 Act. First, the landlord must serve written notice upon the tenant of their intention to terminate the tenancy not less than two years or more than three years before the expiry of the term of the tenancy.[482] This may be termed a "notice of intention to terminate". Once the notice of intention to terminate has been served upon the tenant properly, the landlord may subsequently terminate the tenancy at the ish. This is achieved by the landlord serving written notice upon the tenant which states that the tenant shall quit the land on the expiry of the term of the tenancy not less than one year or more than two years before the expiry of the term of the tenancy, provided that not less than 90 days have elapsed from the date on which the notice of intention to terminate was served.[483]

Irritancy—Where a short limited duration tenancy or limited duration tenancy is **35.43** to be terminated otherwise than of consent at the expiry of the stipulated period for the endurance of the lease, the landlord must demonstrate that a ground of

---

[473] 2003 Act s.14.
[474] 2003 Act s.14(c) and (d), incorporating s.7 of the 1991 Act.
[475] 2003 Act s.14 and the 1991 Act, s.7(3), (3A) and (4).
[476] 2003 Act s.16(3).
[477] ss.53 and 44 of the 1991 Act.
[478] cf. the 1991 Act s.8(2).
[479] 2003 Act s.6(2).
[480] 2003 Act s.8(1).
[481] 2003 Act s.8(6), as amended by the Public Services Reform (Agricultural Holdings) (Scotland) Order 2011 (which reduced the long continuation from 15 years to 10 years).
[482] 2003 Act s.8(5).
[483] 2003 Act s.8(3), (4) and (5).

irritancy in the lease has been invoked.[484] It is not possible to include a provision in a short limited duration tenancy or limited duration tenancy which provides for the lease to be irritated solely on the grounds that the tenant is not or has not been resident on the land.[485] The landlord must give the tenant notice in writing of any intention of the landlord so to remove the tenant pursuant to a ground of irritancy not less than two months before the date on which the tenant is to be removed.[486] A lease which provides for irritancy on the ground that the tenant has not used the land in accordance with the rules of good husbandry is common in practice. What is meant by the words "good husbandry" is governed by Sch.6 to the Agriculture (Scotland) Act 1948.[487] Certain conservation activities are treated as being in accordance with the rules of good husbandry.[488] Any disputes regarding the termination of a short limited duration tenancy or limited duration tenancy are to be determined by the Land Court, subject to appeal to the Court of Session.[489] In comparison with the provisions of the 1991 Act, it is abundantly clear that it is much simpler to terminate a short limited duration tenancy or limited duration tenancy constituted under the 2003 Act prematurely or at the ish.

35.44 Resumption—A landlord is entitled to resume land or any part of the land comprised in a lease under a short limited duration tenancy or limited duration tenancy. In order to do so, the landlord must comply with the written notice procedure contained in the 2003 Act where the resumption is for a non-agricultural purpose in respect of which permission requires to be obtained, and has been obtained, under the enactments relating to town and country planning by any person (including the tenant) in the case of a short limited duration tenancy, or any person with the exception of the tenant in the case of a limited duration tenancy.[490] The lease must not expressly prohibit resumption for that purpose.[491] The written notice of resumption must be given not less than one year before the date on which the resumption is to take place and must specify the date of resumption.[492] Within 28 days of receipt of the landlord's written notice or the determination of any matter arising from the notice, the tenant may respond by terminating the tenancy with written notice.[493] In such an event, the termination takes effect on the date of resumption narrated in the landlord's written notice of resumption.[494]

35.45 Compensation to tenant for improvements: Land court—Subject to certain conditions, a tenant under a short limited duration tenancy or limited duration tenancy is entitled on quitting the land, to compensation for certain improvements.[495] The most important condition is that the landlord must have consented in writing to the improvement before it was carried out.[496] The rules relating to the improvements for which compensation may be claimed are set out in ss.45–48 of

---

[484] 2003 Act s.18(1).
[485] 2003 Act s.18(2).
[486] 2003 Act s.18(7).
[487] 2003 Act s.18(3).
[488] 2003 Act s.18(4).
[489] 2003 Act ss.77(2) and 88.
[490] 2003 Act s.17(1).
[491] 2003 Act s.17(1)(b).
[492] 2003 Act s.17(2).
[493] 2003 Act s.17(3).
[494] 2003 Act s.17(3).
[495] 2003 Act s.45(1).
[496] 2003 Act s.48.

the 2003 Act and Sch.5 to the 1991 Act. Schedule 5 to the 1991 Act, to which reference must be made, enumerates the improvements and they are classified as (a) the laying down of permanent pasture, (b) the making of water-meadows or works of irrigation, (c) the making of gardens, (d) the planting of orchards or fruit bushes, among many other things. The level of compensation will be such sum as fairly represents the value of the improvement to an incoming tenant.[497] In ascertaining the amount of compensation, account is to be taken of any benefit which the landlord has agreed in writing to give the tenant in consideration of the tenant carrying out the improvement[498] and there are special rules where a grant was awarded to the tenant in connection with the improvements.[499] The amount of compensation is to be ascertained, in default of agreement, by the Land Court.[500] The Land Court has jurisdiction to determine disputes in connection with any matter arising out of the termination of a short limited duration tenancy or limited duration tenancy.

Compensation to tenant for disturbance—When a landlord resumes land or **35.46** part of the land comprised in the lease under a tenancy or the tenant responds to the landlord's notice of resumption by terminating the tenancy, the landlord is bound to pay compensation to the tenant for disturbance.[501] The compensation payable is equal to the amount of the loss or expense directly attributable to the quitting of the tenancy which is unavoidably incurred by the tenant upon or in connection with the sale or removal of his household goods, implements of husbandry, fixtures, farm produce or farm stock on or used in connection with the tenancy, including any expenses reasonably incurred by the tenant in the preparation of his claim for compensation.[502] The compensation shall be an amount equal to one year's rent of the tenancy at the rate at which rent was payable immediately before the termination of the tenancy without proof by the tenant of any such loss or expense.[503] Additional compensation is payable by the landlord to the tenant of an amount equal to the additional benefit (if any) which would have accrued to the tenant if the land (instead of being resumed on the date of resumption) had been resumed on the expiry of the period of 12 months from the end of the year of tenancy current at the date two months before the date of resumption.[504]

Compensation for other damage—A tenant is also entitled to compensation **35.47** where the value of a short limited duration tenancy or limited duration tenancy is increased during the tenancy by the continuous adoption of a standard of farming or a system of farming which was more beneficial to the tenancy than the standard or system of farming required by the lease or the system of farming normally practised on comparable tenancies in the district.[505] In such cases, the level of compensation will be commensurate to the value to an incoming tenant of the adoption of that more beneficial standard or system.[506] Compensation may also be

---

[497] 2003 Act s.47(1).
[498] 2003 Act s.47(2)(a).
[499] 2003 Act s.47(2)(b).
[500] 2003 Act s.77(2)(b) and (c).
[501] 2003 Act s.52(1).
[502] 2003 Act s.52(2) and 1991 Act s.43(3).
[503] 2003 Act s.52(2) and 1991 Act s.43(4)(a).
[504] 2003 Act s.52(5).
[505] 2003 Act s.53(1) and s.44(1) of the 1991 Act.
[506] 2003 Act s.53(1) and s.44(1) of the 1991 Act.

claimed by a tenant for damage by game (i.e. deer, pheasants, partridges, grouse, black game) in exactly the same manner as applies to agricultural holdings.[507]

35.48 Diversification—Compensation for a landlord might be relevant where a tenant has engaged in diversification under the 2003 Act,[508] that is the conversion of the use of the land or part of the land from agricultural to non-agricultural purposes pursuant to a notice procedure.[509] Diversification is governed by Pt 3 of the 2003 Act. Prior to its enactment, tenant diversification ran the risk of being classified as inversion.[510] Although the 2003 Act allows for a degree of tenant empowerment, there is no need for a landowner to actively facilitate a tenant's diversification scheme beyond the terms of the legislation.[511]

35.49 Bequest of lease: Succession—The tenant of a short limited duration tenancy or limited duration tenancy may, unless his power to do so is expressly excluded by the lease,[512] bequeath his lease, under s.21 of the 2003 Act, to his son-in-law or daughter-in-law or to any one of the persons who would be, or would in any circumstances have been, entitled to succeed to the estate on his intestacy.[513] The legatee must intimate the bequest to the landlord within 21 days of the tenant's death or, if he is prevented by some unavoidable cause from giving such notice within that period, as soon as practicable thereafter. By doing so he accepts the lease, which then becomes binding upon both as from the date of the deceased's death unless the landlord, within one month of intimation being made, gives a counter-notice to the legatee that he objects to receiving him as tenant. If such objection is made, the legatee may apply to the Land Court for an order declaring him to be tenant under the lease, which the Land Court must grant unless a reasonable ground of objection is established by the landlord.[514] If the legatee refuses the bequest or is rejected, the right to the lease will be treated as intestate estate of the deceased tenant, and will pass accordingly.[515]

35.50 Intestate succession—In the case of both a short limited duration tenancy and a limited duration tenancy, an executor may transfer an interest in the lease to anyone entitled to the deceased's estate, or to claim certain rights in it, or to any other person.[516] A legatee who accepts the bequest but fails to give timeous notification of his acceptance has no right to possess, nor does any other person who claims right to the lease by transfer of the tenant's interest to him.[517] The transferee of such a lease, that is to say any person to whom the short limited duration tenancy or limited duration tenancy is transferred under s.16 of the Succession (Scotland) Act 1964,[518] must also within 21 days notify the landlord, who may

---

[507] 2003 Act s.53(3) and s.52 of the 1991 Act. See para.35.33, above.

[508] 2003 Act s.45A, read with s.53(2) for limited duration tenancies.

[509] 2003 Act ss.39–42.

[510] See para.35.11. See also *Cayzer v Hamilton (No 2)*, 1996 S.L.T. (Land Ct) 21.

[511] *Grant v Glengarry Estate Trust*, 2008 S.L.C.R 63 (no obligation for a landlord to grant a wayleave over its land to a third party even if that might render a tenant's diversification not viable).

[512] *Kennedy v Johnstone*, 1956 S.C. 39.

[513] 2003 Act s.21(1).

[514] 2003 Act s.21(1) and s.11(6) of the 1991 Act.

[515] 2003 Act s.21(3).

[516] 2003 Act s.20 and s.16(4A), (4B), (4C), (4D) and (4E) of the 1964 Act.

[517] *Coats v Logan*, 1985 S.L.T. 221.

[518] See para.35.24, above.

again give a counter-notice, remitting the matter to the Land Court.[519] As in the case of a bequest, time is of the essence and any transferee who fails to give notice within 21 days will have no right to possess under the lease.[520] A landlord can acquire a lease from a transferee by notice on terms not less favourable to the transferee.[521] The executor also has the option of terminating the lease. If the executor is satisfied that he cannot dispose of the tenancy according to the law and notifies the landlord to that effect, he may terminate the tenancy if termination is in the best interests of the deceased's estate, although, in effecting such termination, it is not clear from the Succession (Scotland) Act 1964 whether the executor must serve notice of such termination on the landlord.[522] Furthermore, if the executor has not in fact disposed of the tenancy within a period of one year from the date of death of the deceased, the tenancy automatically terminates at the expiry of such one-year period notwithstanding any provision in the lease or any rule of law to the contrary.[523] The said one-year period may be extended by agreement or, failing agreement, by the Land Court on the application of the executor.[524] Termination in these circumstances is to be treated as termination at the expiry of the term of the tenancy for the purposes of any compensation payable under the 2003 Act.[525]

III. LANDHOLDERS AND CROFTERS

Small Landholders Acts—A substantial proportion of agricultural and pastoral **35.51** land in Scotland does not fall under the Agricultural Holdings Acts, but is dealt with, as landholders' holdings or as crofts, by separate statutory provisions. These holdings are lettings of agricultural land which do not exceed 20 hectares whatever the rent, or do not exceed £50 yearly in rent, whatever the area; in the case of crofts the maximum area, whatever the rent, is 30 hectares. These lettings were originally brought under statutory control by the Crofters Holdings (Scotland) Act 1886, which applied only in the crofting counties.[526] That Act was amended by the Small Landholders (Scotland) Act 1911, which extended the statutory protection to similar holdings throughout the country; the 1911 Act was itself amended by the Land Settlement (Scotland) Act 1919, and the Small Landholders and Agricultural Holdings (Scotland) Act 1931. In 1955 the separate category of crofters was reinstituted in the crofting counties only by the Crofters (Scotland) Act 1955.[527]

The 1911 Act established the Scottish Land Court,[528] which superseded the Crofters Commission operating under the 1886 Act. A new Crofters Commission was set up by the 1955 Act for administrative purposes, but the Land Court continues to have jurisdiction over crofters as well as landholders in judicial

---

[519] 2003 Act s.22(2) and s.12 of the 1991 Act.

[520] *Coats v Logan*, 1985 S.L.T. 221.

[521] 2003 Act s.22(3).

[522] 1964 Act s.16(4C)(a) and (4E)(b).

[523] 1964 Act s.16(4A), (4B), (4C) and (4D).

[524] 1964 Act s.16(4D)(a). See para.35.23, above.

[525] 2003 Act s.23.

[526] The former counties of Argyll, Caithness, Inverness, Orkney, Ross and Cromarty, Sutherland and Zetland: see now the Crofters (Scotland) Act 1993 s.61(1).

[527] See para 35.56, below.

[528] Small Landholders (Scotland) Act 1911 (the "1911 Act") s.24; see now the Scottish Land Court Act 1993, as amended by the Crofting Reform etc Act 2007 s.34; and see para.2.15, above.

matters, and it has many important functions with regard to agricultural holdings.[529] The Land Court is final on all questions of fact, but may *ex proprio motu*, and must, on the application of either party, state a case on a question of law to either Division of the Court of Session. There is no appeal to the Supreme Court.[530] The powers and jurisdiction of the Land Court lie solely within the limits which statute has laid down, and questions which it has no jurisdiction to decide require to be determined in the ordinary courts.[531] An order or determination of the Land Court may be enforced as if it were a decree of the sheriff having jurisdiction in the area in which the order or determination is to be enforced.[532]

35.52 Landholders: Meaning—The Small Landholders Acts apply to agricultural holdings,[533] other than market gardens,[534] outside the crofting counties,[535] which are holdings under the 1911 Act, that is holdings which were, in April 1912, let at a rent not exceeding £50 unless such land, exclusive of common grazings, did not exceed 20 hectares in extent.[536]

The provisions of the 1911 Act extended to existing holdings held under the 1886 Act, new holdings registered under the 1911 Act,[537] and holdings held by tenants under an existing lease from year to year.[538] The tenants in the last category, existing yearly tenants, are required, in order to qualify under the Act, to reside on or within three kilometres of the holding, and to cultivate the holding themselves or with members of their family, with or without hired labour.[539] It is also necessary, in order to qualify as a "landholder" and so benefit fully under the Act, that the tenant or his predecessor in the same family should have provided or paid for the whole or greater part of the buildings and permanent improvements without receiving payment for them from the landlord or his predecessor in title[540]; if the existing yearly tenant did not fulfil this latter requirement, he became a "statutory small tenant".[541] Tenants under an existing lease for more than a year who qualified under the 1911 Act became landholders or statutory small tenants on the expiry of the period of the contractual lease.[542]

Grass parks, let for the purposes of a business not primarily agricultural, are excluded[543]; so are subjects let: "to any innkeeper or tradesman placed in the

---

[529] See paras 35.27–35.50, above.

[530] Scottish Land Court Act 1993 s.1. As to members' tenure of office, see *Mackay v HM Advocate*, 1937 S.C. 860.

[531] *Garvie's Trs v Still*, 1972 S.L.T. 29; *Eagle Star Insurance Co Ltd v Simpson*, 1984 S.L.T. (Land Ct) 37.

[532] Scottish Land Court Act 1993 Sch.1 para.16.

[533] See para.35.28, above.

[534] See *Grewar v Moncur's C.B.*, 1916 S.C. 764.

[535] Holdings in these counties (see fn.526, above) are regulated by the Crofters (Scotland) Act 1993; see para.35.56, below.

[536] 1911 Act s.26, as amended by Agriculture (Adaptation of Enactments) (Scotland) Regulations 1977 (SI 1977/2007). See *Malcolm v McDougall*, 1916 S.C. 283.

[537] 1911 Act s.7, as amended by Land Settlement (Scotland) Act 1919 s.9, and SI 1977/2007.

[538] 1911 Act s.2(1).

[539] 1911 Act s.2(1)(ii), as amended by Agriculture (Adaption of Enactments) (Scotland) Regulations 1977.

[540] 1911 Act s.2(1)(iii), proviso (a).

[541] See para.35.55, below.

[542] 1911 Act s.2(1)(iii).

[543] 1911 Act s.26(3)(g).

district by the landlord for the benefit of the neighbourhood".[544] It has been held where the subjects would have been a holding under the Acts but for the existence of a second house, which was not used for the purpose of the holding but for letting in summer, that this house might be excised and the statutory provisions applied to the rest of the holding.[545] Occupants of land for less than a year, and persons who did not satisfy the conditions as to residence and cultivation, are not within the Act. If, however, a tenant became either a landholder or a statutory small tenant on the 1911 Act coming into operation, he does not lose his rights as such by a subsequent agreement with the landlord under which he accepts a lease for less than a year.[546]

Tenure of landholder—The following are the main provisions regulating the **35.53** tenure of a landholder, and these are not affected by any agreement to the contrary.

Fair rent—While the Acts fixed the rent at its existing level, parties were left free to negotiate a new rent by agreement. Failing agreement, application may be made by either party to the Land Court to fix a fair rent. The Land Court may cancel arrears of rent, in whole or part, where it considers it reasonable to do so. Once the rent has been fixed it cannot be altered, except by agreement, for the next seven years. The Land Court is directed, in fixing a fair rent, to consider all the circumstances of the case, holding and district.[547] It has been held that they should take into consideration any special circumstances affecting the holding, for example on the one hand, its suitability for summer letting,[548] on the other, its liability to damage from game or deer.[549] But they may not take into consideration the fact that the tenant has incurred the burden of a loan from his landlord to enable him to build a house on the holding.[550]

Security of tenure—The landholder cannot be removed from his tenancy except on certain clear grounds specified in the Acts, termed statutory conditions. These include non-payment of rent for a year or more; failure to cultivate the holding; execution of a deed purporting to assign the holding; sub-letting; apparent insolvency or execution of a trust deed for the benefit of his creditors; opening a public-house without the landlord's consent.[551]

Resumption by landlord: Renunciation—The landlord has the right, on making application to the Land Court, and on making such compensation as that court may determine, to resume possession of the holding: "for some reasonable purpose, having relation to the good of the holding or of the estate."[552] Building, letting, and planting are among the grounds expressly specified. The landlord's intention to reside on the holding is not a ground of resumption of possession.[553]

---

[544] Crofters Holdings (Scotland) Act 1886 s.33. See *Stormonth-Darling v Young*, 1915 S.C. 44; *Taylor v Fordyce*, 1918 S.C. 824. Section 33 was repealed so far as applying to the crofting counties by the Crofters (Scotland) Act 1993 Sch.7.

[545] *McNeill v Duke of Hamilton's Trs*, 1918 S.C. 221.

[546] *Clelland v Baird*, 1923 S.C. 370.

[547] Crofters Holdings (Scotland) Act 1886 s.6.

[548] *McNeill v Duke of Hamilton's Trs*, 1918 S.C. 221.

[549] *McKelvie v Duke of Hamilton's Trs*, 1918 S.C. 301.

[550] *Department of Agriculture v Burnett*, 1937 S.L.T. 292.

[551] Crofters Holdings (Scotland) Act 1886 ss.1 and 3; 1911 Act s.10.

[552] Crofters Holdings (Scotland) Act 1886 s.2; 1911 Act s.19, and, as to statutory small tenant, s.32(15); Gordon and Wortley, *Scottish Land Law* (2009), para.18–60. See *Whyte v Stewart*, 1914 S.C. 675.

[553] Small Landholders and Agricultural Holdings (Scotland) Act 1931 s.8.

A landholder may renounce his holding on giving one year's notice to the landlord.[554]

Compensation for improvements—On renunciation, or on being removed from the holding, the tenant is entitled, in addition to his rights under the Agricultural Holdings Acts,[555] to compensation for any permanent improvements, if suitable to the holding, executed or paid for by himself or a predecessor in the same family, and not made in obedience to a specific obligation in writing.[556] The compensation is fixed, failing agreement, by the Land Court; this forms an important part of the court's work.

Assignation: Sub-letting—A landholder has in general no power to assign his holding. But if he is unable to work the holding through age or infirmity, he may apply to the Land Court for power to assign it to his son-in-law or to any person who would succeed him on intestacy.[557] He has no power, without the landlord's consent, to subdivide the holding or to sub-let it, except to "holiday visitors"[558] or, probably, for a period less than a year.[559] Unless he is a new holder established by the Scottish Ministers, he is not entitled to erect a new house on his holding, except in substitution for one already existing; a new holder may do so with the consent of the landlord and the Scottish Ministers.[560]

Succession—The landholder may bequeath his holding to his son-in-law or to any one of the persons who would be, or would in any circumstances have been, entitled to succeed to his estate on his intestacy; otherwise a holding passes to the tenant's executor on his death according to the law of intestate succession.[561]

Provisions are made for the compulsory enlargement of holdings,[562] for the rights of a landlord in the event of a vacancy in a holding,[563] for the regulation of common grazing,[564] and for a record, by the Land Court, as to the state of the holding.[565]

35.54 Right to convert to crofts—With effect from June 25, 2007, a small landholder has had the right to apply to the Crofters Commission, now known as the Crofting Commission, to have their tenanted holding converted into a croft.[566] In order for the Commission to constitute the tenanted holding as a croft, certain conditions must be satisfied.[567]

---

[554] Crofters Holdings (Scotland) Act 1886 s.7; 1911 Act s.18; Gordon and Wortley, *Scottish Land Law* (2009), para.18–61.

[555] See para.35.27, above.

[556] Crofters Holdings (Scotland) Act 1886 s.8.

[557] 1911 Act s.21, as amended by the 1964 Act Sch.2 para.15.

[558] Crofters Holdings (Scotland) Act 1886 s.1(4); 1911 Act s.10.

[559] *McNeill v Duke of Hamilton's Trs*, 1918 S.C. 221.

[560] Crofters Holdings (Scotland) Act 1886 s.1(4); 1911 Act s.10(2).

[561] Crofters Holdings (Scotland) Act 1886 s.16(h) and 1911 Act s.21, as amended by 1964 Act Sch.2 paras 9 and 15.

[562] Crofters Holdings (Scotland) Act 1886 s.11; 1911 Act s.16, as amended by Land Settlement (Scotland) Act 1919 s.11, Small Landholders and Agricultural Holdings (Scotland) Act 1931 s.7, and SI 1977/2007.

[563] 1911 Act s.17.

[564] 1911 Act s.24.

[565] Small Landholders and Agricultural Holdings (Scotland) Act 1931 s.10.

[566] Crofting Reform etc Act 2007 (asp.7) s.6, Crofters (Scotland) Act 1993 (the "1993 Act") ss.3A, 3B and 3C, and Crofting Reform etc Act 2007 (Commencement No.1) Order 2007 (SSI 2007/269).

[567] See para.35.56, below.

Statutory small tenants—A statutory small tenant is a person who would have **35.55**
been a landholder but for the fact that the whole or greater part of the buildings
and permanent improvements were not provided by him nor by any predecessor
in the same family.[568] Save as provided by s.32 of the 1911 Act, the provisions of
the Acts do not apply to him. Under that section he is entitled, notwithstanding
any agreement to the contrary,[569] to obtain, on application to the Land Court, a
renewal of his tenancy at the expiry of the lease, unless the landlord can satisfy the
court that there is a reasonable objection to him.[570] Either he or the landlord may
apply to the court to fix an "equitable" rent. An equitable rent is one which would
be equitable as between a willing lessor and a willing lessee, but allowing no rent
in respect of improvements made by the tenant or his predecessors in title and for
which no payment has been received. Unless the lease permits, he has no power
to assign his lease.[571] The landlord has power to resume the subjects under the
same conditions as those specified for resumption in the case of a landholder,[572]
and the statutory small tenant is entitled in the event of a resumption to the like
compensation as would be payable under the Agricultural Holdings Acts to a
tenant on whom a notice to quit has been served.[573] The 1931 Act gave the statutory small tenant the option, on giving notice to the landlord, of converting his
tenure into that of a landholder, and becoming entitled to all the consequent rights
and privileges.[574]

The Crofters Acts—The category of crofters, and with it the Crofters Commission, **35.56**
were reintroduced to the crofting counties by the Crofters (Scotland) Act 1955.[575]
The effect of the Act was to substitute in these counties a fresh code of law for that
which had applied to landholders and statutory small tenants; the distinction
between landholders and statutory small tenants was abolished. The statutory
rights to a fair rent, security of tenure and compensation for permanent improvements, first introduced by the Crofters Holdings (Scotland) Act 1886, remain the
basis of crofting tenure. The Crofters (Scotland) Act 1993 consolidated and to
some extent amended the legislation relating to crofting.[576] The largely consolidating Crofters (Scotland) Act 1993 has now been amended by the Crofting
Reform etc. Act 2007 and the Crofting Reform (Scotland) Act 2010.[577] The 2007
Act is now fully in force, whereas the 2010 Act is largely in force, including the
provisions which reorganise and rename the Crofters Commission as the Crofting

---

[568] See 1911 Act s.2(1)(iii), proviso (b).
[569] See *Clelland v Baird*, 1923 S.C. 370.
[570] 1911 Act s.32(4).
[571] 1911 Act s.32(1). As to succession, see Gordon and Wortley, *Scottish Land Law* (2009),
paras.18–50.
[572] 1911 Act s.32(15).
[573] 1911 Act s.13; 1991 Act ss.54 and 59.
[574] Small Landholders and Agricultural Holdings (Scotland) Act 1931 s.14; see also 1911 Act
s.32(11).
[575] Amended by the Crofters (Scotland) Act 1961, Crofting Reform (Scotland) Act 1976, and
Crofter Forestry (Scotland) Act 1991. See now the consolidating Crofters (Scotland) Act 1993 and the
Crofting Reform etc. Act 2007. The crofting counties are the former counties of Argyll, Caithness,
Inverness, Orkney, Ross and Cromarty, Sutherland and Zetland: see s.61(1) and fn.526, above.
[576] 1993 Act came into force (with the exception of s.28) on January 5, 1994. There are transitional
provisions in Sch.6. The Act implemented most of the recommendations of the Scottish Law
Commission, *Report on the Consolidation of Certain Enactments Relating to Crofting* (HMSO, 1993),
Scot. Law Com. No.141, Cm.2187. Contracting out of the Act is limited: s.5(3). Subsequent statutory
references are to the 1993 Act, unless otherwise indicated.
[577] Crofting Reform (Scotland) Act 2010 (asp 14).

Commission (referred to in the statute and herein by the neutral term "the Commission").[578] The reforms that are not in force as at April 1, 2012 will not be taken into account. That means the innovation of a map based register of crofts, common grazings and lands held runrig, to be known as the Crofting Register and established and maintained by the Keeper of the Registers of Scotland in accordance with Pt 2 of the 2010 Act, will not be considered.

A crofter is defined as the tenant of a croft.[579] The definition of a croft is complex. A croft is defined by s.3 (read with ss.3A–3C) of the 1993 Act[580] as: a holding in the crofting counties which was a landholder's (whether occupied or not) holding immediately before the 1955 Act came into operation[581]; a holding in the crofting counties which was a statutory small tenant's holding immediately before the 1955 Act came into operation[582]; every holding in the crofting counties which was constituted a croft by the registration of the tenant thereof as a crofter in the Crofters Holdings Book under s.4 of the 1955 Act; as from June 25, 2007, every holding which had been entered in the Register of Crofts on June 25, 2007 for a continuous period of at least 20 years ending with that date and in respect of which no application or reference seeking a declaration or order that the holding was not a croft was on June 25, 2007 pending before any court[583]; as from the date 20 years after registration, every holding entered in the Register of Crofts for a continuous period of 20 years ending after June 25, 2007 and in respect of which no application or reference seeking a declaration or order that the holding is not a croft is at the end of that period pending before any court[584]; or a holding entered in the Register of Crofts by the Commission in accordance with their decision under s.15(4) of the 1955 Act where neither landlord nor tenant, having been notified of the decision, successfully challenged it.[585] A croft may be enlarged by the addition of non-crofting land by agreement of the owner and the crofter so long as the enlarged area, exclusive of any common pasture or grazing land held therewith, does not exceed 30 hectares.[586] The Commission may in certain circumstances authorise the enlargement of a holding which exceeds these limits.[587]

The Crofting Reform etc. Act 2007 also provides for the establishment of new crofts.[588] Such new crofts may be applied for by the owner of any land situated in the crofting counties or areas lying outwith the crofting counties which are

---

[578] Crofting Reform (Scotland) Act 2010 s.1. The Crofting Reform (Scotland) Act 2010 (Commencement, Saving and Transitory Provisions) Order 2010 (SSI 2010/437) and the Crofting Reform (Scotland) Act 2010 (Commencement No. 2, Transitory, Transitional and Saving Provisions) Order 2011 (SSI 2011/334).

[579] 1993 Act s.3(3).

[580] 1993 Act ss.3, 3A, 3B and 3C; as to whether rights in pasture or grazing land held by the tenant form part of the croft, see s.3(4) and (5). See also *Ross v Graesser*, 1962 S.C. 66; *Stornoway Trust v Mackay*, 1989 S.L.T. (Land Ct) 36. For the definition of "croft land", see s.12(3) and *Crofters Commission v Scottish Ministers*, 2002 S.L.T. (Land Ct) 19.

[581] 1993 Act s.3(1)(a).

[582] 1993 Act s.3(1)(b).

[583] 1993 Act s.3(1)(f), as introduced by the Crofting Reform etc Act 2007 s.21(a)(iii).

[584] 1993 Act s.3(1)(g), as introduced by the Crofting Reform etc Act 2007 s.21(a)(iii).

[585] 1993 Act s.3(1)(e). A holding, unless qualifying in terms of s.3, may lack the necessary legal attributes to be a croft despite an existing entry in the Register of Crofts: *Palmer's Trs v Crofters Commission*, 1990 S.L.T. (Land Ct) 21. There are further statutory provisions, for example to relating to the return of land to crofting status after a temporary resumption: s.3(1)(cd).

[586] 1993 Act s.4(1), as amended by the Crofting Reform etc Act 2007 Sch.1 para.2 and Sch.2. A further amendment of this section, relative to the Crofting Register, will be introduced when the relevant part of the 2010 Act is implemented.

[587] 1993 Act s.4(1) and (2), as amended by the Crofting Reform etc Act 2007 Sch.1 para.2 and Sch.2.

[588] Crofting Reform etc Act 2007 s.6, introducing ss.3A, 3B and 3C into the 1993 Act.

duly designated for these purposes by the Scottish Ministers.[589] Where such an application is made to the Commission, they have the power to constitute the land as a croft by entering it as such in the Register of Crofts in accordance with the provisions of the 1993 Act.[590] Moreover, a separate application procedure exists in the case of small landholders or statutory small tenants holding land in areas outwith the crofting counties which are designated by the Scottish Ministers.[591] Small landholders or statutory small tenants have the right to apply to the Commission to constitute the land (of which they are a tenant) as a croft. Provided such small landholders or statutory small tenants are able to obtain a certificate from the Land Court confirming their existing status as a small landholding or a statutory small tenancy under the Small Landholders legislation, that no part of their holding is leased other than as such a tenancy and certain conditions are met,[592] the Commission has the power to constitute the land as a croft by entering it as such in the Register of Crofts. The conditions are that: (i) the landholding is not comprised within a larger agricultural unit, the landholding and that larger unit being, or having been, worked, managed or let as a single unit; (ii) the tenant is a natural person; and (iii) such fixed equipment on the landholding as is necessary to enable the tenant to cultivate is not provided by the landlord. An important point to make is that the Commission may not constitute a holding as a croft in response to the application of the small landholder or statutory small tenant until they are satisfied that the owner of the land has had an opportunity to appeal the application and the tenant has paid the owner any compensation agreed or found to be due[593] for the impact of the change.[594] Essentially, these provisions operate as a means of enabling a small landholder or statutory small tenant to convert their holding to a croft.

The four general functions of the Commission are regulating, reorganising and promoting the interests of crofting, whilst keeping under review matters relating to crofting.[595] In exercising those functions, the Commission must have regard to the desirability of supporting population retention in the traditional crofting counties and any new crofting areas, and the impact of changes to the overall area of land held in crofting tenure on the sustainability of crofting. The Commission's sphere of action is primarily administrative, and jurisdiction over legal matters, which may be referred to them by the parties themselves or by the Commission, remains with the Land Court.[596] For example, should the crofting tenancy come to an end, a crofter (or his representatives) may be eligible for compensation for any permanent improvements to the land, but conversely they may be liable to the

---

[589] 1993 Act s.3A(1)(a) and (b) and (13). Arran, the Cumbraes, Bute and Moray have been so designated: the Crofting (Designation of Areas) (Scotland) Order 2010 (SSI 2010/29).

[590] 1993 Act s.3A(1)(a) and (b) and (13).

[591] 1993 Act s.3A(2).

[592] 1993 Act s.3A(2), (3) and (12).

[593] s.3B of the 1993 Act makes provision for ascertaining the level of compensation to be paid by the tenant to the landlord where an application has been made by a tenant in terms of the procedure contained in s.3A(2). The amount of the compensation is to be fixed by a valuer to be appointed by agreement between the applicant and the owner and will be the difference in the value of the small landholding or statutory small tenancy under the existing tenure arrangements and its value as a croft. Both the applicant or the owner may appeal the valuer's assessment of compensation to the Lands Tribunal for Scotland within 21 days of the valuer's notice of the level of compensation: see ss.3B and 3C of the 1993 Act.

[594] 1993 Act s.3A(4).

[595] 1993 Act s.1, as amended by s.3 of the Crofting Reform (Scotland) Act 2010. In contrast to its predecessor Crofters Commission, the Crofting Commission has less statutory focus on the promotion of the interests of crofters.

[596] 1993 Act ss.2, 52A and 53, as amended by the Crofting Reform etc. Act 2007 s.33(2).

landlord for any deterioration or damage to the croft, which would be within the remit of the Land Court with little or no recourse to the Commission.[597]

35.57 Crofting tenure—Every tenancy of a croft is subject to the statutory conditions set out in Sch.2[598] to the Crofters (Scotland) Act 1993, which include timeous payment of rent, cultivation and maintenance of the croft, and allowing the landlord to take minerals,[599] water, timber and peats, and to exercise certain other rights. Since October 1, 2011, a crofter has also been subject to certain duties, namely a duty to reside on, or within 32 kilometres of, that crofter's croft,[600] a duty not to misuse or neglect the croft[601] and the (effectively mirror) duty to cultivate the croft or put it to another purposeful use.[602] Applications for the fixing of a fair rent for the croft are made to the Land Court, and the fair rent is determined on a consideration of all the circumstances including the croft, the district, and any permanent or unexhausted improvements on the croft executed or paid for by the crofter or his predecessors.[603] Further provisions regulate the resumption of a croft by the landlord[604] and the reversion of the resumed land to a croft,[605] the renunciation of the tenancy by the crofter,[606] and the compensation payable in either event.[607] The crofter has security of tenure, but he may be removed by the Land Court on the landlord's application where one year's rent remains unpaid, one of the statutory conditions of tenure[608] has been broken or one of his statutory duties relating to residence, misuse or cultivation.[609] The crofter may also be ultimately removed by the Land Court[610] on the application of any member of the crofting community in the locality of the croft to the Commission that the crofter is in breach of one of the statutory conditions.[611] The crofter may sub-let his croft for a period not exceeding 10 years without the consent of the landlord of his croft, but may not sub-let his croft without the Commission's consent except to

---

[597] 1993 Act ss.30 and 34.

[598] As amended by the Crofting Reform etc. Act 2007 s.7(2)(e), (f), (g) and (h).

[599] *Strathern v MacColl*, 1992 S.C. 339.

[600] 1993 Act s.5AA, introduced by the Crofting Reform (Scotland) Act 2010 s.33 and made operational by the Crofting Reform (Scotland) Act 2010 (Commencement No. 2, Transitory, Transitional and Saving Provisions) Order 2011.

[601] 1993 Act s.5B.

[602] 1993 Act s.5C.

[603] 1993 Act s.6; *Sutherland Estates v Sutherland*, 1998 S.L.T. (Land Ct) 37.

[604] ss.20 and 21 of the 1993 Act, as amended by the Crofting Reform etc. Act 2007 s.22; see also s.21(1), (1A)–(1C) (decrofting in the event of resumption), Gordon and Wortley, *Scottish Land Law* (2009), para.18–60; *Portman Trs v Macrae*, 1971 S.L.T. (Land Ct) 6; *Wester Ross Salmon Ltd v MacLean*, 1986 S.L.T. (Land Ct) 11. Resumptions will normally be authorised only where the purpose for which this is sought is likely to be put into effect in the near future: *Cameron v Corpach Common Graziers*, 1984 S.L.T. (Land Ct) 41.

[605] 1993 Act s.21A.

[606] 1993 Act s.7.

[607] 1993 Act ss.30–35: compensation to the crofter in respect of permanent improvements, and compensation to the landlord in respect of deterioration or damage: *Fennell v Paterson*, 1990 S.L.C.R. 42; *Cameron v MacKinnon*, 1996 S.L.T. (Land Ct) 5. Interest on compensation may be awarded. In addition to compensation, a crofter may be entitled to a share in the value of the land where the land has been resumed: 1993 Act s.21; *MacKenzie v Barr's Trs*, 1993 S.L.T. 1228.

[608] See list in the 1993 Act Sch.2.

[609] 1993 Act ss.5, 26; see e.g. *Burton Property Trust v MacRae*, 1989 S.L.C.R. 34; *Cheyne v Hunter*, 1989 S.C.L.R. 38. Under s.26A, the Commission must investigate any apparent breach of duty advertised to it by certain interested parties (including local crofting community members).

[610] The Land Court may make another order, e.g. an order that the breach be remedied.

[611] s.5A of the 1993 Act, as introduced by s.8 of the Crofting Reform etc Act 2007. See also s.26H, introduced by s.37 of the Crofting Reform (Scotland) Act 2010.

holiday visitors,[612] nor may he assign it to a member of his family unless the landlord, whom failing the Commission, has given written consent,[613] nor may he divide it without the consent of the Commission and the landlord.[614] The crofter may bequeath the croft to any member (and, from October 1, 2011, members) of his family.[615] A bequest is rendered "null and void" unless the landlord and the Commission are notified within 12 months, but there is no longer any need to obtain the Commission's approval.[616] In a case of intestacy, or the failure of a bequest, the right to the croft is treated as intestate estate of the deceased crofter in accordance with Pt I of the Succession (Scotland) Act 1964.[617] If the executor fails within 24 months to furnish to the landlord particulars of the transferee under s.16(2) of the 1964 Act, the Commission shall give notice to the landlord, any confirmed executor or (if no executor is confirmed) any person who may be entitled to claim the croft tenancy in out of the intestate estate that they intend to terminate the tenancy and declare the croft vacant, inviting requiring them to intimate to the Commission within a one month of the notice.[618] When a croft becomes vacant, the landlord may apply for a decrofting direction,[619] subject to the regime contained in s.24 including the constraints introduced by the 2010 Act in the amended s.24(3A) (which allows the Commission to not consider a landlord's application where they have asked him for proposals to re-let the croft) and s.25. This allows the Commission, during the course of establishing whether a decrofting application is for a reasonable purpose, to consider the sustainability of crofting in the locality of the croft or such other area in which crofting is carried on, the crofting community in that locality or the communities in such an area, the landscape of that locality or such an area, the environment of that locality or such an area and the social and cultural benefits associated with crofting. Similar provisions exist in relation to resumption.[620] If a proposed decrofting (or resumption) is in respect of a development for which planning permission exists, the Commission may also take into account the effect the proposed decrofting will have on the croft, the estate and the crofting community in the locality of the croft.[621]

Cottars—A cottar is defined as being the occupier of a dwelling-house situated in **35.58** the crofting counties with or without land who pays no rent, or the tenant from year to year of a dwelling-house situated in those counties who resides therein and pays an annual rent not exceeding £6 whether with or without garden ground but

---

[612] 1993 Act s.27, as amended by s.11 of the Crofting Reform etc Act 2007; s.29 and Sch.2 para.6.

[613] 1993 Act s.8 and Sch.2 para.2. Assignation to a person other than a member of the family is possible only with the Commission's written consent.

[614] 1993 Act s.9 and Sch.2 para.7.

[615] 1993 Act s.10(1), as amended by s.49 of the Crofters (Scotland) Act 2010. "Family" is now defined very widely to include a crofter's wife, spouse, civil partner, sibling (and such sibling's spouse or civil partner), father, mother, son, daughter, grandchild, aunt and uncle, among others. See s.61(2), as amended by s.36 of the 2007 Act.

[616] 1993 Act s.10(1).

[617] 1993 Act ss.10(5) and 11.

[618] 1993 Act s.11(4) and (5).

[619] *Mackay v Crofters Commission*, 1997 S.L.T. (Land Ct) 4; *Chandler v Crofters Commission*, 1998 S.L.T. (Land Ct) 27; *Gammie v Crofters Commission*, 1999 S.L.C.R. 49. Cf. also *MacIntyre v Crofters Commission*, 2001 S.L.T. 929.

[620] 1993 Act s.25(1A)(a), read with s.25(1B).

[621] 1993 Act s.25(1A)(b).

without arable or pasture land.[622] Under the 1993 Act a cottar who, if not paying rent, is removed from his dwelling and any land or buildings occupied by him in connection therewith, or, if paying rent, renounces his tenancy or is removed, is entitled to compensation for permanent improvements.[623] Failing agreement the amount of compensation payable is fixed by the Land Court in the same manner as for crofters.[624]

35.59 **Rights of acquisition**—The Crofting Reform (Scotland) Act 1976 introduced important new rights in favour of crofters and cottars. A crofter now has the right, failing agreement with the landlord, to apply to the Land Court to acquire croft land tenanted by him.[625] It is worth emphasising that there is no requirement for the crofter to register any notice with the Commission before he acquires a right to acquire the croft house. He has an absolute right, subject to such terms and conditions as the Land Court may determine, to a conveyance of the site of the dwelling-house on or pertaining to his croft including the building thereon and garden ground, and a cottar has the same right to a conveyance of the site of the dwelling-house occupied by him.[626] It is in the discretion of the Land Court whether or not to make an order authorising the crofter to acquire croft land, but they are directed not to make such an order where they are satisfied that to do so would cause a substantial degree of hardship to the landlord or that the acquisition would be substantially detrimental to the sound management of the estate.[627] Failing agreement, the consideration payable in respect of the acquisition of croft land and the conveyance of the site of the dwelling-house, and the terms and conditions to be imposed, are to be determined by the Land Court.[628] Provision is made for the repayment to the landlord or his representative of part of the consideration if the former crofter or a member of his family disposes of the croft land or any part of it other than by lease for crofting or agricultural purposes at any time within ten years.[629] A crofter who has purchased his landlord's interest (or a successor to him) is now recognised as an "owner-occupier crofter".[630] Owner-occupier crofters are subject to duties similar to tenant crofters,[631] and special

[622] 1993 Act s.12(5), as to the difference between a non-rent paying cottar and a squatter, see *Duke of Argyll's Trs v MacNeill*, 1983 S.L.T. (Land Ct) 35; and see also *Philips v MacPhail*, 1994 S.L.T. (Land Ct) 27.

[623] 1993 Act s.36(1).

[624] 1993 Act s.36(2).

[625] 1993 Act ss.12(1) and 25(4), as amended by s.23(b)(vi) of the Crofting Reform etc. Act 2007. The sale should be effected by a disposition: *Fulton v Noble*, 1983 S.L.T. (Land Ct) 40. As to the meaning of "croft land", see s.12(3); *MacMillan v MacKenzie*, 1995 S.L.T. (Land Ct) 7; *MacKenzie v Barr's Trs*, 1993 S.L.T. 1228 at 1237; *Bowman v Guthrie*, 1998 S.L.T. (Land Ct) 2.

[626] 1993 Act ss.12(2), (4) and 16; see *Campbell v Duke of Argyll's Trs*, 1977 S.L.T. (Land Ct) 22; *MacIntyre v Crofters Commission*, 2001 S.L.T. 929.

[627] 1993 Act s.13; see *Geddes v Gilbertson*, 1984 S.L.T. (Land Ct) 55; *Fraser v MacKintosh*, 1995 S.L.T. (Land Ct) 45; *Mackenzie v Hardy*, 1999 S.L.C.R. 63 ("emotional" hardship not relevant).

[628] 1993 Act ss.14, 15; *Ferguson v Ross Estates*, 1977 S.L.T. (Land Ct) 19; *Cameron v Duke of Argyll's Trs*, 1981 S.L.T. (Land Ct) 2; *MacLeod's Exr v Barr's Trs*, 1989 S.C. 72; *Anderson v Williamson*, 1997 S.L.T. (Land Ct) 46.

[629] 1993 Act s.14(3), as amended by s.41 of the Crofting Reform (Scotland) Act 2010. The 2010 Act introduced another important reform that narrowed the classification of nominees a crofter could select for a back-to-back sub-sale, providing that a nominee could only be a family member of the crofter exercising the right to buy. These two reforms mitigate the effect of the decision in *Whitbread v Macdonald*, 1992 S.C. 479. See further M.M. Combe, "Crofting, nominee sales and the separation of powers" (2010) 14 Edin. L.R. 458.

[630] 1993 Act s.19B, as introduced by Crofting Reform (Scotland) Act 2010 s.34.

[631] 1993 Act s.19C.

rules exist where an owner-occupier crofter wishes to let his land.[632] Finally a crofter now has, in addition to his right to any compensation, the right to a share in the value of any part of his croft which is resumed by the landlord or is acquired by an authority possessing compulsory powers.[633] On the application of the Commission or the landlord, provided certain conditions are met, the Land Court now has the power to make an order that resumed land shall revert to being a croft.[634]

In addition to these individual rights of acquisition, provision has been made for crofting property held by the Scottish Ministers to be disposed of by them to crofters' representatives, such as crofters' trusts.[635] Part 3 of the Land Reform (Scotland) Act 2003 offers another route for a crofting community to acquire their (mutual) landlord's interest, by allowing crofting communities to associate together as a company limited by guarantee.[636] Absent any voluntary agreement, and assuming compliance with the process prescribed in the legislation to the Scottish Ministers' satisfaction,[637] the crofting landlord is compelled to convey his land to the crofting community on payment of an independently set price.[638]

Administration of crofting—The Commission is given wide powers to enable **35.60** it to perform its function of promoting the welfare and development of the crofting communities. It has the duty of compiling a Register of Crofts,[639] and of exercising a general supervision over common grazings.[640] Where a croft becomes vacant, the landlord must give notice of the fact to the Commission, may only re-let it with the Commission's consent and must proactively submit proposals for re-letting a vacant croft to the Commission.[641] The consent granted by the Commission may be challenged by raising an ordinary action of reduction in the Court of Session, rather than by way of a petition for judicial review.[642] If the landlord fails to take steps to re-let it, the Commission must step in and re-let it themselves on his behalf[643]; in certain cases where the croft has become vacant the Commission has power to direct that it cease to be a croft,[644] but any pre-2010 Act case law must be measured against the factors which the Commission must keep in mind when exercising its functions, including "the impact of changes to the overall area of land held in crofting tenure on the sustainability of crofting".[645] The Commission has power to prepare reorganisation schemes, re-allocating land in a manner conducive to its proper and efficient use; a crofter may exercise a right of appeal to the Land Court by way of stated case in respect

---

[632] 1993 Act s.26J. On the previous regime, see *Sutherland v Sutherland*, 1986 S.L.T. (Land Ct) 22.

[633] 1993 Act ss.21, 37; *Macrae v Secretary of State*, 1981 S.L.T. (Land Ct) 18.

[634] 1993 Act s.21A, introduced by s.22(3) of Crofting Reform etc. Act 2007.

[635] Transfer of Crofting Estates (Scotland) Act 1997.

[636] See further M.M. Combe, "Parts 2 and 3 of the Land Reform (Scotland) Act 2003: A Definitive Answer to the Scottish Land Question?", 2006 Jur. Rev. 195.

[637] As set out in Ch.2 of Pt 3 of the Land Reform (Scotland) Act 2003.

[638] Land Reform (Scotland) Act 2003 s.88.

[639] 1993 Act s.41.

[640] 1993 Act ss.47–52.

[641] 1993 Act s.23, as amended by the Crofting Reform (Scotland) Act 2010 s.44.

[642] *MacColl v Crofters Commission*, 2007 G.W.D. 27–481.

[643] 1993 Act s.23(5ZC), as inserted by the Crofting Reform (Scotland) Act 2010 s.44.

[644] 1993 Act ss.24(2) and (3), and 22(11) (decrofting applicable to part of a croft); see also *Gray v Crofters Commission*, 1980 S.L.T. (Land Ct) 2; *MacColl v Crofters Commission*, 1986 S.L.T. (Land Ct) 4.

[645] 1993 Act s.1(2A)(b).

of the Commission's re-organisation scheme.[646] If no appeal is made, or the re-organisation scheme is modified by the Land Court, it is then for the Commission to put the scheme into effect.[647]

IV. DWELLING-HOUSES AND SHOPS

35.61 General—The statutory code relating to tenancies of dwelling-houses is now contained in the Housing (Scotland) Act 2006, the Housing (Scotland) Act 1988 and the Rent (Scotland) Act 1984. The 1988 Act is intended gradually to supersede previous legislation,[648] and in particular the 1984 Act. The provisions of the 2006 Act which relate to private sector tenancies set out a statutory code of the landlord's repairing and maintenance obligations have been considered elsewhere in this chapter and so are not considered in this section.[649] The main purposes of the Acts have always been to provide for the security of tenure of tenants of certain dwelling-houses by restricting the landlord's right to remove them at the end of the lease, and to control or regulate the amount of rent which the tenant can be required to pay. The 1988 Act weakens security of tenure and restricts the circumstances in which rent may be regulated. The Acts also contain provisions prohibiting the charging of premiums by a landlord, and giving power to the court in certain cases to mitigate hardship to a landlord who is the debtor in a heritable security.

The legislation is notoriously complicated, and has been said to bristle with difficulties.[650] For political and economic reasons the extent and pattern of control have fluctuated considerably since legislation on this subject was first introduced. The Act of 1920 consolidated a series of earlier Acts which had been passed between 1915 and 1919. It provided for a system of control of rents, security of tenure and control of heritable securities, and it applied to the majority of dwelling-houses which were let unfurnished to tenants. The 1923, 1933 and 1938 Acts, while taking many of the more valuable dwelling-houses out of control, extended and amended the provisions of the 1920 Act relating to security of tenure. The 1939 Act reimposed control over a wide range of dwelling-houses let unfurnished, and introduced, in relation to those houses which had been newly controlled by it, a separate system to be applied in order to assess the limit of recoverable rent. The 1957 Act decontrolled many dwelling-houses which were at the time subject to control, but the situation was again reversed by the 1965 Act which not only brought into protection most of the houses which had been decontrolled by the 1957 Act but also introduced a new form of rent regulation and made a number of amendments to the system of security of tenure.

---

[646] 1993 Act ss.38, 38A and 39, as amended by s.20 of the 2007 Act.

[647] 1993 Act s.39(1A), as amended by s.20 of the 2007 Act.

[648] The principal Acts were the Rent (Scotland) Act 1920, the Rent Restriction Act 1923, the Rent Restriction Act 1933, the Increase of Rent and Mortgage Interest (Restrictions) Act 1938, the Rent Restriction Act 1939, the Housing (Repairs and Rents) (Scotland) Act 1954, the Rent Act 1957, the Rent Act 1965, the Rent (Scotland) Act 1971, the Rent Act 1974, and the Tenants' Rights, etc (Scotland) Act 1980. The principal Acts relating to furnished lettings were the Rent of Furnished Houses (Scotland) Act 1943 and the Landlord and Tenant (Rent Control) Act 1949.

[649] ss.12–29 of the Housing (Scotland) Act 2006, which came into force on September 3, 2007 by virtue of the Housing (Scotland) Act 2006 (Commencement No.5, Savings and Transitional Provisions) Order 2007 (SSI 2007/270), see para.35.08, above.

[650] See the collection of epithets in the preface to R. Megarry, *The Rent Acts*, 10th edn (London, 1967) and 11th edn (London, 1988).

The protection of tenants of dwelling-houses let furnished originated from the 1943 Act, which introduced a system whereby reasonable rents for the dwelling-houses might be assessed by a Rent Tribunal and registered. The 1949 Act introduced a measure of security of tenure to tenants who chose to take advantage of the provisions of the 1943 Act as to rent. The 1971 Act preserved the distinction which then existed between dwelling-houses let unfurnished on the one hand and those let furnished on the other, but this distinction was removed by the 1974 Act. The 1980 Act removed the distinction which had existed since 1965 between controlled tenancies on the one hand, being those tenancies which were still covered by the system of rent control contained in the Acts prior to that date, and regulated tenancies on the other by providing for all remaining controlled tenancies to be converted to regulated tenancies. It also introduced a new category known as the short tenancy, under which, on compliance with certain conditions, the landlord can be assured of recovering possession on the expiry of the stipulated period of the lease.

The provisions of the Housing (Scotland) Act 1988 and the Rent (Scotland) Act 1984 are too complicated to state here in detail, and reference must be made to the specialist textbooks and to the relevant legislation.[651] What follows is merely a statement in outline of the main features of the current legislation. The main essential is to understand which tenancies are and which are not assured or protected, and the categories into which these tenancies have been divided. Chronologically, the key dividing line falls on January 2, 1989, the date on which the Housing (Scotland) Act 1988 came into force. Before that date, the law is mainly to be found in the 1984 Act and the important concepts are those of the regulated tenancy and its subcategories of protected and statutory tenancy. After that date, it is the 1988 Act that applies, and the relevant categories are the assured and short assured tenancy. In this chapter the provisions are discussed separately, beginning with those of the 1984 Act.

Landlord regulation—Following the reconvening of the Scottish Parliament in 1999 there have been enacted a number of statutes dealing with residential properties. In addition to dealing with such matters as repairing and maintenance obligations and tenancy rights, a number of statutes have introduced and expanded regulatory systems in respect of residential accommodation. In the private rented sector this has taken the form of landlord registration. Social landlords—registered social landlords, local authority landlords and local authorities providing housing services[652]—are subject to regulation and the superintendence of the Scottish Housing Regulator.[653] Statute also requires for the licensing of houses in multiple occupation ("HMOs"). **35.62**

---

[651] Especially *Stair Memorial Encyclopaedia*, Vol.13, paras 590 et seq.; Megarry, *The Rent Acts* (1988); D.G. Fraser, *The Rent and House-letting Acts in Scotland*, 2nd edn (Edinburgh: W. Green, 1952) is now substantially out of date. For a convenient statement of the current legislation and references to the relevant statutory instruments, see *Parliament House Book*, Division L; see also the annotations to the Housing (Scotland) Act 1988 in *Scottish Current Law Statutes 1988*, Vol.4 and the annotations to the Housing (Scotland) Act 2006, in *Scottish Current Law Statutes 2006* (Service File), where a more complete review of the legislation and case law is to be found.

[652] 2010 Act s.165.

[653] 2010 Act s.1. The new Scottish Housing Regulator is independent from ministers, per s.7 of the Act. It replaces the former Scottish Housing Regulator, which was an executive agency of the Scottish Government. This, in turn, had taken over the work of Communities Scotland Regulation and Inspection division in 2008. Communities Scotland was an executive agency of the Scottish Government from 2001–2008, which superseded Scottish Homes, which in turn superseded the

The earliest of the post-1999 reforms was the licensing of HMOs, which was effected by means of the exercise of powers under the Civic Government (Scotland) Act 1982 s.44, to designate activities which may be made subject to licensing.[654] The licensing regime is now located in Pt 5 of the Housing (Scotland) Act 2006. The licensing regime requires that the owner of a HMO must have a local authority license before giving permission for its occupation. It is the property that is licensed.[655] HMOs are shared accommodation—living accommodation occupied by three or more persons who are not all members of the same family or of one or other of two families.[656] Living accommodation encompasses a house, or a part of a premises or group of premises, owned by the same person where the one or more basic amenities are shared (toilet; personal washing facilities; facilities for the preparation of cooked food).[657] Certain classes of accommodation are exempted from the licensing regime,[658] but there is no general exemption for local authorities and social rented landlords.[659] Before a licence will be granted, a local authority must be satisfied that the landlord is a fit and proper person to hold a license,[660] and that the property meets certain standards.[661] Statute provides for enforcement by local authorities[662] and specifies offences relating to HMOs,[663] with a right of appeal by summary application to the sheriff.[664]

Whereas HMO licensing licenses particular properties, including those owned by social landlords, with the landlord being subject to a "fit and proper person" test, landlord registration applies directly to private landlords, and does not include social landlords.[665] Private landlord registration was introduced by means of the Antisocial Behaviour etc (Scotland) Act 2004 Pt 8, as amended by the Housing (Scotland) Act 2006 and the Private Rented Housing (Scotland) Act 2011. Applications for registration must be made by a relevant person.[666] A relevant person is a person who owns a house which is subject to a lease or an occupancy arrangement by virtue of which an unconnected person may use a house as a dwelling.[667] "Relevant person" means a person who is not a local authority, a registered social landlord or Scottish Homes.[668] "Unconnected person" means a person who is not a member of the family of the relevant person. Family membership is construed in accordance with provisions in the Housing (Scotland) Act 2001.[669]

Scottish Special Housing Association. The process of change was commenced by the Housing (Scotland) Act 1988.

[654] By way of the Civic Government (Scotland) Act 1982 (Licensing of Houses in Multiple Occupation) Order 2000 (SSI 2000/177).

[655] 2006 Act s.124.

[656] 2006 Act s.125(1).

[657] 2006 Act s.125(2)–(3).

[658] 2006 Act s.126.

[659] Thus, in Aberdeen in 2010 the local authority embarked upon and then abandoned a challenge of its own refusal of an HMO license; see *http://committees.aberdeencity.gov.uk/mgAi.aspx?ID=5692* [Accessed July 26, 2012] and "Hostel plans scrapped as council abandons court battle", *Aberdeen Press and Journal*, July 29, 2010.

[660] 2006 Act s.130. See *Thomson v Aberdeen City Council*, 2011 S.L.T. (Sh. Ct) 218.

[661] 2006 Act s.131.

[662] 2006 Act ss.144–153.

[663] 2006 Act ss.154–157.

[664] 2006 Act ss.158–159.

[665] Antisocial Behaviour etc. (Scotland) Act 2004 (the "2004 Act") s.83.

[666] 2004 Act s.83(1).

[667] 2004 Act s.83(1).

[668] 2004 Act s.83(1). Scottish Homes, formerly a non-departmental public body, no longer exists, but remains in the statute.

[669] 2004 Act ss.83(8) and 101(3); 2001 Act s.108(1) and (2).

As with HMO licensing, there is a "fit and proper person"[670] test, and certain classes of accommodation are excluded from the regulatory regime.[671] A landlord may be refused registration,[672] or, if registered, may be removed from the register.[673] In either case, there is a right of appeal.[674] Any person may apply for information from a local authority in respect of the registered status of owners, or persons acting for owners, or properties, including whether a person is listed in the register or has been refused entry in the register or removed from the register.[675] An owner leasing or entering into an occupancy agreement where registration is required, but that person is not registered, shall be guilty of an offence[676] and may become subject to disqualification.[677] A local authority may serve a notice to the effect that no rent is payable in respect of a house which is subject to a lease or occupancy agreement but in respect of which no relevant person has been registered,[678] such notice does not affect the validity of any lease or occupancy arrangement.[679] Any such notice may be subject to appeal.[680] Registration is for a three-year period.[681]

Certain classes of residential property are excluded from the registration regime. These are listed at s.83(6) of the 2004 Act. Illustrative examples of exempted properties include lets to family members, houses used for holiday purposes, houses occupied by virtue of a liferent, and dwellings where there is a resident landlord. Other classes of exempted properties are listed in the statute, and the list has been and may continue to be varied from time to time by means of Scottish Statutory Instrument.

1984 Act Tenancies[682]—This legislation is relevant to tenancies which came into being before the 1988 Act. The definition of the expression "protected tenancy" in the 1984 Act[683] takes the form of providing that every tenancy under which a dwelling-house is let as a separate dwelling is a protected tenancy, and then   **35.63**

---

[670] 2004 Act ss.84–85A. HMO licensing predates landlord registration and incorporates an assessment of whether an owner is a fit and proper person. The view of the Scottish Government has been that HMO licensing is the stricter regime as HMO licensing considers the suitability of the landlord and the condition of the property. Therefore, a licensed HMO landlord may be passported automatically into the landlord register. See Scottish Government, *General guidance for Local Authorities to administer and manage the Private Landlord Registration Scheme* (October 2009) available at *http:// www.scotland.gov.uk/Resource/Doc/287769/0087783.pdf* [Accessed July 26, 2012].

[671] 2004 Act s.83.

[672] 2004 Act s.84(2)(b).

[673] 2004 Act s.89.

[674] 2004 Act s.92.

[675] 2004 Act s.88A.

[676] 2004 Act s.93.

[677] 2004 Act s.93A.

[678] 2004 Act s.94.

[679] 2004 Act s.94(8).

[680] 2004 Act s.97.

[681] 2004 Act s.86(4).

[682] See generally A.G.M. Duncan and J.A.D. Hope, *The Rent (Scotland) Act 1984* (Edinburgh: W. Green, 1986). Following upon the Housing (Scotland) Act 1988, there will be no new protected tenancies, except in special transitional cases (1988 Act s.42), and in the case of short tenancies (s.42(2), and para.35.64, below). Pre-existing protected tenancies continue: 1988 Act Sch.4 para.13. At one time most private residential leases in Scotland would have fallen under the Rent Acts regime but with the passing of time tenancies under the 1988 Act are becoming fewer. This edition however conforms to the established model of considering regulated tenancies before tenancies under the 1988 Act; therefore matters common to both tenancy regimes will receive primary treatment in the context of the 1984 Act.

[683] 1984 Act s.1(1).

excepting certain specific tenancies from this description. For details of the exceptions reference must be made to the Act. Among them are lets which include payments in respect of board or attendance; lets by educational institutions to students pursuing courses there; holiday lets; and lets where the landlord is resident in the same building.[684]

The full protection of the Rent Acts was extended to furnished tenancies (which were previously not covered by the Rent Acts) by the Rent Act 1974,[685] and they now fall within the definition of protected tenancy unless excluded from it by one or other of the exceptions. The expression "tenancy" is defined[686] as including a sub-tenancy, but the right to possession conferred upon the tenant must be exclusive and a right which amounts merely to a licence to occupy will be excluded from protection under the Acts.[687] Similarly a service occupier, whose occupancy of the dwelling-house is attributable not to a lease but to his contract of service, is not protected.[688] The term "dwelling-house" for this purpose covers, as well as self-contained dwelling-houses, part of a house if let as a separate dwelling, even if it amounts only to a single room[689]; but it does not cover the lease of a house which contains a number of units of habitation within it.[690] Premises do not lose their character as a dwelling-house merely because part of the house is used for business purposes, provided that the main use can be said to be residential occupation.[691] The premises must, however, be such as would within accepted principles be held to be a dwelling-house for the purposes of the Acts.[692] Where any retail trade or business is carried on from the house so as to bring the premises within the definition of "shop" for the purposes of the Tenancy of Shops (Scotland) Act 1949, the tenancy will not be a regulated tenancy.[693] Unless he retains possession of the dwelling-house as his residence the tenant will not be entitled to the protection of the Acts.[694] Since the whole policy of the Acts is to protect the home, a tenant who ceases to reside in the premises to any substantial extent loses protection even though he may continue to use the premises for other purposes.[695] Where the tenant is a company, which by its nature is incapable of being in physical occupation of a dwelling-house, it is entitled to the benefit of the Acts so far as regards the rent but cannot obtain security of tenure as a statutory tenant when the contractual tenancy comes to an end.[696]

---

[684] See 1984 Act ss.1, 2, 6 and 10. Note that larger houses (whose rateable value exceeded £200 on March 23, 1965 or, if first entered on the valuation roll after April 11, 1985, £1,600) are excluded from the provisions of the Act: ss.1(1)(a), 7; SI 1985/314.

[685] Rent Act 1974 s.1.

[686] Rent Act 1974 s.115(1).

[687] *Commissioners of HM Works v Hutchison*, 1922 S.L.T. (Sh. Ct) 127; *Heslop v Burns* [1974] 1 W.L.R. 1241; *Marchant v Charters* [1977] 1 W.L.R. 1181; cf. *Street v Mountford* [1985] A.C. 809.

[688] *Cairns v Innes*, 1942 S.C. 164; *MacGregor v Dunnett*, 1949 S.C. 510; *Cargill v Phillips*, 1951 S.C. 67.

[689] 1984 Act s.1(1); *Neale v Del Soto* [1945] K.B. 144; *Cole v Harris* [1945] K.B. 474.

[690] *Horford Investments v Lambert* [1976] Ch. 39; *St Catherine's College v Dorling* [1980] 1 W.L.R. 66. For the notion of "separate dwelling" in relation to shared accommodation, see *Street v Mountford* [1985] A.C. 809; *AG Securities v Vaughan* [1990] 1 A.C. 417.

[691] *Cargill v Phillips*, 1951 S.C. 67; *Cowan & Sons v Acton*, 1952 S.C. 73.

[692] *Maunsell v Olins* [1975] A.C. 373; *Horford Investments v Lambert* [1976] Ch. 39.

[693] 1984 Act s.10(2); see para.35.77, below.

[694] 1984 Act s.3(1); *Menzies v Mackay*, 1938 S.C. 74; *Cowan & Sons v Acton*, 1952 S.C. 73; *Langford Property Co v Tureman* [1949] 1 K.B. 29.

[695] *Stewart v Mackay*, 1947 S.C. 287 at 293, per Lord President Cooper.

[696] *Hiller v United Dairies (London)* [1934] 1 K.B. 57; *Ronson Nominees v Mitchell*, 1982 S.L.T. (Sh. Ct) 18.

Regulated, statutory and short tenancies—(a) Regulated tenancies—Until **35.64**
1980 it was necessary to distinguish between the categories of controlled and
regulated tenancies. This distinction is now of historical interest only, because the
Tenants' Rights, etc (Scotland) Act 1980 provided that all remaining controlled
tenancies should cease to be controlled tenancies and become regulated tenancies.[697] For the purposes of the 1984 Act, a tenancy is a regulated tenancy if it is a
protected or statutory tenancy.[698]

(b) Statutory tenancies—The Act draws a distinction between the tenant who
occupies under a contract or a relocated contract and the tenant who remains in
occupation after the expiry of the lease by virtue of the Rent Acts. The tenant in
the former case is called a protected tenant, and his tenancy is a protected tenancy
for so long as he is entitled to retain possession of the dwelling-house under a
contractual tenancy.[699] After the protected tenancy has come to an end the person
who immediately before that termination was the protected tenant of the dwelling-
house is, for so long as he retains possession of it, the statutory tenant of the
dwelling-house and his tenancy is called a statutory tenancy.[700] The transition
from a protected tenancy to a statutory tenancy takes place where the tenant has
invoked the protection of the Acts in answer to a notice to quit and his contractual
right to occupancy has otherwise ceased. If no notice to quit is served the tenant
will continue in occupation as a protected tenant under tacit relocation.

(c) Short tenancies—In order to encourage landlords to make accommodation
available for letting, the 1980 Act introduced a new category of tenancy, known
as the short tenancy, as to which the landlord is assured of recovery of possession
when the lease comes to an end. A tenancy falls within this category if: (a) the
tenant was not already a protected or statutory tenant of the dwelling-house before
its creation; (b) it is for a specified period of not less than one nor more than five
years; (c) it does not contain any provision whereby the landlord may terminate
the tenancy before the expiry of that period other than for non-payment of rent or
for breach of any other obligation of the tenancy; (d) before its creation the landlord has served on the tenant a notice in writing informing him that the tenancy
will be a short tenancy; and (e) a fair rent has already been registered for the
dwelling-house or an application for its registration is made within 14 days after
the commencement of the tenancy.[701]

Recoverable rent—The rent that can be recovered from the tenant during contrac- **35.65**
tual periods is limited by what is called the contractual rent limit.[702] The amount
of any excess over that limit is irrecoverable from the tenant, notwithstanding
anything in any agreement.[703] Where a rent for the dwelling-house has been registered, the rent so registered is the contractual rent limit[704]; until registration has
taken place the only limit on the rent which can be recovered during contractual
periods is that upon which the parties have agreed. The limit on the rent which is

---

[697] Tenants' Rights, etc (Scotland) Act 1980 s.46.
[698] 1984 Act s.8. Where rent is payable weekly, the tenant is entitled to a rent book: s.113.
[699] 1984 Act s.1(1).
[700] 1984 Act s.3(1); see also *Jessamine Investment Co v Schwartz* [1978] Q.B. 264.
[701] Tenants' Rights, etc (Scotland) Act 1980 s.9(1). It is still possible to grant new short tenan-
cies:1988 Act s.42(2).
[702] 1984 Act s.28.
[703] 1984 Act s.28(1); *North v Allan Properties (Edinburgh) Ltd*, 1987 S.L.T. (Sh. Ct) 141; 1987
S.C.L.R. 644 (Sh. Ct).
[704] 1984 Act s.28(2).

recoverable during statutory periods is set by the registered rent or, if registration has not yet taken place, by the amount of rent which was recoverable for the last contractual period, subject to certain adjustments which are permitted with respect to charges for the provision of services or the use of furniture.[705] Where the rent is payable weekly, the landlord is required to provide a rent book.[706]

35.66 **Registration of rent**—The 1965 Act introduced machinery for the determination of fair rents for tenancies by local rent officers and Private Rented Housing Committees, and for their registration.[707] Either party or both may apply to the rent officer to fix a fair rent for the dwelling-house. When fixed, the fair rent forms the basis for the figure which is registered by the rent officer for the house; the registered rent becomes the rent limit, an amount in excess of which will be irrecoverable from the tenant.[708] The term "fair rent" is not defined, but certain guidelines are set,[709] for instance: (1) that regard should be had to all the circumstances other than circumstances personal to the parties themselves; (2) that the rent officer or Private Rented Housing Committee as the case may be should apply their knowledge and experience of current rents of comparable property in the area; (3) that it should be assumed that there is no substantial shortage of accommodation for letting in the locality; and (4) that improvements carried out by the tenant should be disregarded.[710] Regard must be had therefore to current market rents, making such adjustment as may be necessary to take account of scarcity.[711] Since a fair rent should be fair to the landlord as well as to the tenant, a fair return to the landlord on the capital value of the property is also a relevant and necessary consideration to be taken into account.[712] In considering the capital value of the house the fact that there is a sitting tenant with a right to possess the house is a personal circumstance to which regard must not be had.[713] Subject to these considerations the appropriate method or methods of valuation will depend on the circumstances.[714]

---

[705] 1984 Act ss.29 and 31.

[706] 1984 Act s.113.

[707] See now 1984 Act Pt V ss.43–54. Pt V was amended by the Deregulation and Contracting Out Act 1994 Sch.16 and the Housing (Scotland) Act 2006 Sch.6 para.7. See also *Western Heritable Investment Co Ltd v Inglis*, 1978 S.C. 304.

[708] 1984 Act ss.28, 29, 49.

[709] See the 1984 Act s.48; *Western Heritable Investment Co Ltd v Johnston*, 1997 S.L.T. 74; *Western Heritable Investment Co Ltd v Hunter*, 2004 S.C. 635 ((1) in a determination of fair rent for a dwelling house, the rent actually passing for other dwelling houses of a comparable nature is a relevant factor and the fact that a rent for a dwelling house of that nature had been registered under the Act could not of itself render it irrelevant, and "fair" rent could not, as a matter of statutory construction, mean market rent in the restricted sense of excluding registered rents, less scarcity and disregards; (2) the question whether market rents for truly comparable properties might constitute not only relevant but highly persuasive evidence for the purposes of the determination of a fair rent was a matter of judgment, not of law. No method, as a matter of law, was "primary", but the evidence available might suggest that a particular class of evidence was, as a matter of judgment, of primary importance).

[710] See *Stewart's J.F. v Gallagher*, 1967 S.C. 59.

[711] *Learmonth Property Investment Co v Aitken*, 1970 S.C. 223; *Western Heritable Investment Co v Husband*, 1983 S.C. (HL) 60; 1983 S.L.T. 578.

[712] *Learmonth Property Investment Co v Aitken*, 1970 S.C. 223; *Skilling v Arcari's Exrx*, 1974 S.C. (HL) 42.

[713] *Skilling v Arcari's Exrx*, 1974 S.C. (HL) 42.

[714] *Albyn Properties v Knox*, 1977 S.C. 108; 1977 S.L.T. 41.

The fair rent may be agreed between the parties themselves, and a joint application made on that basis to the rent officer.[715] Alternatively, applications for registration may be made by one party only, and the other may or may not lodge objections. In either case the rent officer has an overriding discretion as to the amount which is fair in the circumstances; he may himself determine the appropriate figure after consultation with the parties. Either party has the right to appeal against his decision to the Private Rented Housing Committee, whose decisions are final in fact but not on points of law. The Committee is bound to observe the rules of natural justice[716] and to give reasons for its decision.[717] A certificate of fair rent may be sought in advance by a person intending to let a house which is not subject to a regulated tenancy at the time.[718] The certificate, obtainable on application to the rent officer, specifies the rent which would in the rent officer's opinion be a fair rent under a regulated tenancy of the dwelling-house and so provides an indication of the return which the prospective landlord can expect on his expenditure.

Entries may be made in the register which will enable the landlord to vary the rent in respect of naturally fluctuating expenditure incurred by him in connection with the tenancy, such as in relation to the use of furniture or the provision of services, without further recourse to the rent officer.[719] Otherwise the registered rent remains fixed for three years. Any application for variation of the figure by either party within that period will only be entertained on the ground that owing to some change of circumstance the registered rent no longer represents a fair rent for the dwelling house,[720] except that a landlord alone may make an application within the last three months of the three-year period. After three years an application for variation can be made by either party alone for a new consideration of the fair rent, when once again the whole circumstances, including any improvements made in the mean time, will be taken into account.

Security of tenure—While the contract of tenancy exists and the tenant continues **35.67** to occupy the premises as a contractual tenant he has security of tenure under his contract; he cannot be ejected by his landlord except for a breach of the conditions of the lease, and he does not need the protection of the Acts. But, when the contractual tenancy is terminated, the Rent Acts will enable the tenant to retain possession of the dwelling-house, whatever contractual undertaking he may have made to remove as a statutory tenant, provided he continues personally to occupy the house as his residence. Unless he voluntarily gives up possession of the house, he may only be removed by decree of removal granted by the court. The court[721] may not make an order for possession of a house which is let on a protected tenancy or is subject to a statutory tenancy except on certain conditions.[722] These are (1) that it considers it reasonable to make such an order,[723] and (2) either that

---

[715] For procedure in applications to rent officers, see s.46 and Sch.5; see also Gordon and Wortley, *Scottish Land Law* (2009), para.18–161.

[716] *Learmonth Property Investment Co v Aitken*, 1970 S.C. 223.

[717] *Albyn Properties v Knox*, 1977 S.C. 108.

[718] 1984 Act s.47 and Sch.6.

[719] 1984 Act s.49. (Note that subss.(4) and (5) were repealed by the Housing (Scotland) Act 1988 s.72 and Sch.10.)

[720] 1984 Act s.46(3); see *London Housing and Commercial Properties v Cowan* [1977] Q.B. 148.

[721] Normally the sheriff: see 1984 Act s.102.

[722] 1984 Act s.11(1).

[723] See *Smith v Poulter* [1947] K.B. 339; *Barclay v Hannah*, 1947 S.C. 245.

suitable alternative accommodation[724] is available for the tenant or will be available for him when the order in question takes effect, or that the landlord can establish that his application falls within any of the Cases set out in Pt I of Sch.2 to the 1984 Act. There are a number of additional Cases, set out in Pt II of Sch.2, in which if the landlord can establish his right to possession at common law the court must order possession.[725]

The Cases listed in Pt I of the Schedule, being the grounds on which the court has a discretion whether or not to make an order for possession, are in summary as follows: (a) non-payment of rent, or breach of an obligation of the tenancy; (b) conduct on the part of the occupiers of the dwelling-house which is a nuisance to adjoining occupiers, or its use for an illegal or immoral purpose; (c) deterioration of the condition of the dwelling-house owing to neglect or default on the part of the tenant, any person residing with him or his sub-tenant; (d) deterioration of the condition of any furniture provided for use under the tenancy owing to ill treatment by the tenant, any person residing with him or his sub-tenant; (e) steps taken by the landlord in consequence of a notice to quit given by the tenant; (f) unauthorised assignation or sub-letting by the tenant; (g) requirement of the dwelling-house by the landlord for occupation as a residence for his employee; (h) requirement[726] of the dwelling-house by the landlord for occupation as a residence for himself or certain members of his family, provided the landlord did not become landlord of the dwelling-house by purchase after certain dates[727]; (i) rent charged by the tenant for sub-letting of any part of the dwelling-house in excess of the rent recoverable under the Act; (j) overcrowding, where the tenant has failed to take reasonable steps to alleviate the situation. The court has a general discretion to adjourn the application, sist the action, suspend execution of the order for possession or postpone the date of for such periods and on such terms as it thinks fit.[728]

The Cases listed in Pt II of the Schedule are those in which the court is directed to make an order for possession if the circumstances of the Case are established.[729] They are in summary as follows: (i) requirement of the dwelling-house by the owner for occupation as a residence for himself on retirement[730]; (ii) requirement of the dwelling-house for occupation by a member of the family of the owner on the death of the latter; (iii) where the dwelling-house had been the subject of a holiday letting and is let out of season for a specified period not exceeding eight months; (iv) where the dwelling-house has been the subject of a student letting and is let out on another tenancy between student lettings for a specific period not exceeding 12 months; (v) where the dwelling-house was let on a short tenancy,[731] on the termination of that tenancy; (vi) requirement of the dwelling-house for occupation by a minister or full-time lay missionary; (vii) requirement of the dwelling-house by the landlord for occupation by a person employed by him in agriculture; (viii) as Case (vii), where an amalgamation has been carried out under

---

[724] *Turner v Keiller*, 1950 S.C. 43; see also Sch.2 Pt IV; *Hill v Rochard* [1983] 1 W.L.R. 478.

[725] 1984 Act s.11(2).

[726] As to requirement, see *Kennealy v Dunne* [1977] Q.B. 837.

[727] Note, however, that the court is directed not to make the order if greater hardship would be caused by granting it than by refusing to do so: 1984 Act s.11(3) and Sch.2 Pt III; see also *Kerr v Gordon*, 1977 S.L.T. (Sh. Ct) 53.

[728] 1984 Act s.12.

[729] 1984 Act ss.11(2), 12(5).

[730] See *Tilling v Whiteman* [1980] A.C. 1; *Kennealy v Dunne* [1977] Q.B. 837.

[731] For definition of "short tenancy", see s.9(1) of the 1984 Act.

the provisions of the Agriculture Act 1967; (ix) requirement of the dwelling-house by the landlord for occupation by a person responsible for the control of the farming of any part of the land or by a person employed by him in agriculture, in certain situations where neither Case (vii) nor Case (viii) would apply; (x) where the dwelling-house has been designed or adapted for use by a person with special needs, is no longer occupied by such a person and the landlord requires it for occupation by a person who has such special needs; and (xi) where the dwelling-house was occupied by a person who at the time when he acquired it was a member of the regular armed forces of the Crown, and he requires it for his residence. In all of these Cases the tenant must be warned in writing at the outset that the relevant provisions of the 1984 Act may be invoked by the landlord, although in some of them the court has a discretion to dispense with this requirement if it is of the opinion that it is just and equitable to make an order for possession.[732]

Transmission on death—The persons who are protected by the Rent Acts are **35.68** spoken of in the Acts as tenants. The expression "tenant" is defined[733] as including a statutory tenant, and this expression in turn includes statutory tenants by succession.[734] If the dwelling-house was the only or principal home of the original tenant's spouse or civil partner at the time of the tenant's death, that spouse or civil partner is the statutory tenant by succession so long as he or she retains possession of the dwelling-house without being entitled to do so under a contractual tenancy.[735] If the tenant leaves no such spouse or civil partner, the statutory tenant by succession will be such member of the tenant's family as may be decided by agreement between the parties, or in default of agreement by the sheriff,[736] provided that member was residing with the tenant for not less than six months immediately before his death. The effect of these provisions is to confer a right on the tenant's successor to remain in occupation of the dwelling-house after the tenant's death; this is the case whether the deceased was a contractual or a statutory tenant,[737] and no formal claim is required. Prior to the 1965 Act it was the rule that only one statutory transmission could take place,[738] and then only in favour of one person.[739] The 1965 Act and subsequent legislation provided for a further transmission to a second successor, similarly qualified, who is entitled to remain in occupation on the first successor's death.[740] The Housing (Scotland) Act 1988[741] reverted to one statutory successor: only a spouse or civil partner may be statutory tenant by succession as "first successor" although other members of the family[742] may acquire a statutory assured tenancy. There is no second

---

[732] Cases 11, 12.

[733] 1984 Act s.115(1).

[734] 1984 Act s.3(1)(b); Sch.1.

[735] 1984 Act Sch.1 para.2.

[736] 1984 Act Sch.1 para.3; see *Williams v Williams* [1970] 1 W.L.R. 1530. As to the expression "family", see *Dyson Holdings v Fox* [1976] Q.B. 503; *Joram Developments v Sharratt* [1979] 1 W.L.R. 928, HL.

[737] 1984 Act s.3(1)(b); *Moodie v Hosegood* [1952] A.C. 61; *Walker v McArdle*, 1952 S.L.T. (Sh. Ct) 60.

[738] *Joint Properties v Williamson*, 1945 S.C. 68; *Campbell v Wright*, 1952 S.C. 240.

[739] *Dealex Properties v Brooks* [1966] 1 Q.B. 542.

[740] 1984 Act Sch.1 paras 5–7.

[741] See the 1984 Act s.3 and Sch.1, as amended by the Housing (Scotland) Act 1988 s.46 and Sch.6; and see Gordon and Wortley, *Scottish Land Law* (2009), para.18–54.

[742] If resident with the original tenant: 1984 Act Sch.1A para.3.

succession on the death of the first successor, but there may be a statutory assured tenancy.[743]

A statutory tenancy is regarded as a purely personal right, which cannot be assigned; a statutory tenant cannot bequeath his right to occupancy by will, nor will it transmit on his intestacy to his executor.[744] Where the contractual tenancy still subsists at the tenant's death, however, the right to occupy the house under the lease may pass under the deceased's will or to his executor; in such a case, in view of the provisions for statutory transmission, complicated situations can arise. Where the heir and the person who would be entitled to occupy the house as a successor are one and the same person, he will be presumed to occupy the house as a successor and not as a contractual tenant, unless he intimates to the landlord the fact that he has inherited the lease.[745] The mere payment and acceptance of rent from a contractual tenant's widow will not of itself constitute a fresh contractual tenancy in her favour where her occupancy can be attributed to a succession under the Acts.[746] If the person to whom the lease would pass by testate or intestate succession is not the same as the successor, the heir's rights and obligations are suspended while the successor continues to occupy the house.[747] While the contractual tenancy is suspended, however, the landlord still has the right to terminate the lease at the ish, and it is recommended that this be done to prevent an eventual succession by the deceased tenant's heir.[748]

35.69 Termination of statutory tenancy: Release from rent regulation—Generally speaking, so long as the statutory tenant continues to occupy the dwelling-house he will continue to be protected by the Acts. He will, however, lose the right to protection if he voluntarily surrenders possession of the house,[749] or fails to use the house as his residence, or if the house ceases to exist. His tenancy will come to an end if he accepts a new contractual tenancy from the landlord, or, it is thought, agrees to a rent which is less than two-thirds of the relevant rateable value of the house. It will also be terminated where decree of removal is granted by the sheriff,[750] or where, by reason of a change in the law or the scope of the Acts, the statutory protection ceases to apply to the dwelling-house. Under current legislation, the 1984 Act provides[751] for the release from rent regulation of houses of any class or description on the making of an order to that effect by the Secretary of State. Where such an order is made, transitional provisions may be included to avoid or mitigate hardship to existing tenants.[752]

35.70 Part VII contracts—Protection was given to tenants of furnished houses by the Rent of Furnished Houses Control (Scotland) Act 1943, the Landlord and Tenant (Rent Control) Act 1949, and the Rent Act 1965. All of these were consolidated in

---

[743] See the 1984 Act Sch.1A paras 5 and 6; and s.3A(2) and Sch.1B. As to assured tenancies, see para.35.76, below.

[744] *John Lovibond & Sons v Vincent* [1929] 1 K.B. 687.

[745] *Grant's Trs v Arrol*, 1954 S.C. 306.

[746] *Campbell v Wright*, 1952 S.C. 240.

[747] *Moodie v Hosegood* [1952] A.C. 61.

[748] See Fraser, *The Rent Acts in Scotland* (1952), pp.8–9.

[749] Note, however, protection against harassment, 1984 Act s.22(2)(a).

[750] See para.35.67, above.

[751] 1984 Act s.95, as amended by the Housing (Scotland) Act 1988 Sch.10; cf. re Pt VII contracts, s.64(3).

[752] 1984 Act s.95(2); cf. Rent Act 1957 Sch.4, for transitional provisions applicable to de-control under that Act.

the Rent (Scotland) Act 1971 and then in Pt VII of the Rent (Scotland) Act 1984. As a result of the Housing (Scotland) Act 1988, no new Pt VII contracts can be entered into, and where the rent under a Pt VII contract is varied after the commencement date of the 1988 Act, it ceases to be a Pt VII contract.[753] The security of tenure under these contracts is much less than under a protected tenancy.

Part VII contracts are contracts whereby one person grants to another the right to occupy as a residence a house or part of a house in consideration of a rent which includes payment for the use of furniture or for services.[754] Where, however, the house is subject to a regulated tenancy, Pt VII of the Act is expressly excluded.[755] There are certain other express exclusions: a letting is not subject to Pt VII if the contractual rent includes a substantial element attributable to board[756] or if the interest of the lessor belongs to a government department[757]; a right to occupy a house or part of a house for a holiday is not to be treated as a right to occupy it as a residence[758]; and an owner-occupier who grants to another person a right to occupy his house which is a Pt VII contract and gives the requisite written notice to that person may recover possession when he requires the house again as his residence without the intervention of the Private Rented Housing Committee.[759] Part VII of the 1984 Act applies within the same limits of rateable value as are set for protected tenancies.[760]

Since furnished tenancies have now been brought within the full protection of the Rent Acts and where appropriate fall within the definition of regulated tenancy,[761] they usually no longer fall within Pt VII of the 1984 Act except where there is a resident landlord.[762] On the other hand, a tenancy which is precluded from being a protected tenancy by virtue only of the fact that there is a resident landlord is treated as a Pt VII contract even although the rent may not include payment for the use of furniture or for services.[763] Resident landlord lettings have therefore replaced furnished lettings as the main concern of this part of the legislation. It also extends to other cases where protection is not available, for example where the tenant shares accommodation with his landlord[764]; where the right to occupy in consideration of a rent which includes payment for the use of furniture is a licence and not a tenancy[765]; where there is substantial attendance[766]; where the rent includes any payment in respect of board[767]; where there is a furnished tenancy but at a rent too low for it to be a protected tenancy[768]; or where there is a student letting which includes payment for furniture or services.[769] There must,

---

[753] Housing (Scotland) Act 1988 s.44, subject to certain exceptions for transitional cases.

[754] 1984 Act s.63(1). Where the rent is payable weekly, a tenant is entitled to a rentbook and written conditions: s.79.

[755] 1984 Act s.63(3)(d).

[756] 1984 Act s.63(3)(c).

[757] 1984 Act s.63(3)(a); *McLaughlin v Greater Glasgow Health Board*, 1989 S.L.T. 793.

[758] 1984 Act s.63(6).

[759] 1984 Act s.73.

[760] 1984 Act ss.1(1), 64(1); see para.35.63, above.

[761] See para.35.61, above.

[762] 1984 Act s.6.

[763] 1984 Act s.98.

[764] 1984 Act s.96.

[765] cf. *Luganda v Services Hotels* [1969] 2 Ch. 209.

[766] 1984 Act s.2(1)(b)(4).

[767] 1984 Act s.2(1)(b).

[768] 1984 Act s.2(1)(a).

[769] 1984 Act s.2(1)(c).

however, be a subsisting contract as at the date of reference to the Private Rented Housing Committee.[770]

Rent control is effected by a reference of the contract by either party to the Private Rented Housing Committee. In this context the Committee acts as a tribunal of first instance, as distinct from the appellate role which it has with regard to the determination of rents for regulated tenancies. The Committee may, on consideration of the case, approve the rent payable under the contract, or reduce it to such sum as they may in all the circumstances think reasonable, or dismiss the application.[771] Once fixed, the rent is entered on a register kept by the Committee, and becomes the limit beyond which any payment in excess is irrecoverable[772]; it may be varied on the application of either party on proof of change of circumstances.[773] The rent fixed by the Committee must not be lower than any amount which has been registered for the house as the rent recoverable under a regulated tenancy under Pt V of the 1984 Act.[774]

Security of tenure of a temporary nature is available to the lessee under a Pt VII contract on the service on him of a notice to quit.[775] In this case a distinction is drawn between Pt VII contracts which were entered into before December 1, 1980 and those entered into on or after that date. In the former case the system which was originally set up to deal with furnished lettings applies, whereby if an application has already been made to the Committee to fix or reconsider the rent, a subsequent notice to quit will not have effect before the expiry of six months after the Committee's decision, unless the Committee sees fit in the circumstances to substitute a shorter period; an application made after the service of the notice will also entitle the lessee to this extension of notice.[776] Thereafter, unless the Committee has substituted a shorter period, further extensions of not more than six months at a time may be granted.[777] In the case of Pt VII contracts entered into on or after December 1, 1980, the power to grant a postponement of the operation of a notice to quit is vested in the sheriff and the period of postponement is limited to three months.[778] Because this mechanism for protecting the lessee in occupation after the expiry of the lease operates only by means of extensions of periods of notice on a reference to the Committee, it has been held not to apply where the contract is terminated by the expiration of a fixed period.[779] Owner-occupiers who have previously occupied the dwelling-house as a residence are able to exclude these provisions for security of tenure in advance when granting the right to occupy under a Pt VII contract to another person, with the result that they will be able to obtain vacant possession at once upon the expiration of the period stated in the notice to quit.[780] The passage of time makes it highly improbable that any significant number of Pt VII contracts are still in existence.

---

[770] *R. v City of London Rent Tribunal, Ex p. Honig* [1951] 1 K.B. 641.

[771] 1984 Act s.65 (as amended by the 1988 Act s.68), s.66.

[772] 1984 Act ss.67, 69.

[773] 1984 Act s.66(4).

[774] 1984 Act s.66(2).

[775] 1984 Act ss.71–74.

[776] 1984 Act s.71(1).

[777] 1984 Act s.72.

[778] 1984 Act s.76.

[779] *Langford Property Co v Goodman* (1954) 163 E.G. 324, QB; see also *Schnabel v Allard* [1967] 1 Q.B. 627 at 631–632, per Lord Denning M.R. Note, however, that under the Sheriff Courts (Scotland) Act 1907 ss.37 and 38, a notice to quit is mandatory where a house is let for a period of a year or more.

[780] 1984 Act s.73.

Tenancies under shared ownership agreements—Tenancies under shared **35.71** ownership agreements[781] are excluded from regulation under the Rent (Scotland) Act 1984; nor do they qualify as assured tenancies.[782]

1988 Act tenancies—Assured tenancies[783] were introduced by the Housing **35.72** (Scotland) Act 1988,[784] and are available only to persons becoming tenants after the Act came into force. From that date there will be no new protected or statutory tenancies, but existing protected tenancies continue as such, with all the rights attaching thereto.[785] The consequence is that there can be no new tenancies under which tenants have full security of tenure as well as the right to have a fair rent fixed. There are two types of assured tenancy: (a) the "assured tenancy" which provides some security of tenure but no recourse to the rent registration service[786]; and (b) the fixed term "short assured tenancy", where there is no security of tenure, but there may be a right to have the rent reduced.

Assured tenancies—An assured tenancy is a tenancy[787] under which a house is **35.73** let as a separate dwelling[788] where the tenant[789] is an individual[790] and the house is his only or principal home.[791] Assured tenancies (and short assured tenancies) are not covered by the fair rent system applicable to tenancies governed by the 1984 Act. A landlord may serve on the tenant a notice of increase of rent[792]; the rent stated in it applies unless the parties agree otherwise or the tenant refers it to the Private Rented Housing Committee. On a referral, the Committee determines the rent it considers the house might reasonably be expected to fetch in the open market, let by a willing landlord under an assured tenancy beginning on the date stated in the notice, on the same terms and subject to the same notices as were given to the tenant.[793] No account is taken of the fact that there is a sitting tenant or of voluntary improvements to the house or of any breach of the lease by the tenant.[794] The rent as assessed becomes the rent due from the date in the notice,

---

[781] Such as contracts with non-profit housing associations, whereby the occupier buys a percentage of the equity in his home and pays rent for the remainder: cf. *Link Housing Association v McCandless*, 1990 G.W.D. 39–2270.

[782] 1988 Act s.47.

[783] See, generally, Gordon and Wortley, *Scottish Land Law* (2009), para.18–79; annotations by P. Robson to the 1988 Act in *Scottish Current Law Statutes 1988*, Vol.4; and article by T. Mullen, "The Housing (Scotland) Act 1988: Private Sector Rented Accommodation", 1989 S.L.T. (News) 245.

[784] As amended by the Housing Act 1988. Pt II of the Act came into force on January 2, 1989.

[785] 1988 Act Sch.4 para.13. For transitional exceptions see s.42. For protected tenancies (private sector) see para.35.61, above. For secure tenancies (public sector) see para.35.09, above.

[786] As to rent registration, see para.35.66, above.

[787] Other than an excluded tenancy: see the 1988 Act s.12(2), Sch.4. Examples of excluded tenancies are: tenancies at low rents; tenancies of shops and agricultural land; lettings to students; and holiday lettings.

[788] Note special provisions relating to shared living accommodation occupied along with separate accommodation: 1988 Act ss.14, 21; sub-let accommodation: ss.15, 28; and houses let together with other land: s.13.

[789] Or at least one of the joint tenants: 1988 Act s.12(1)(b).

[790] See difficulties arising in *Ronson Nominees v Mitchell*, 1982 S.L.T. (Sh. Ct) 18; *Hilton v Plustitle* [1989] 1 W.L.R. 149; [1988] 3 All E.R. 1051.

[791] 1988 s.12(1)(b); *Barns-Graham v Ballance*, 2000 Hous. L.R. 11.

[792] Assured Tenancies (Forms) (Scotland) Regulations 1988 (SI 1988/2109), as amended by the Assured Tenancies (Forms) (Scotland) Amendment Regulations 1993 (SI 1993/648).

[793] 1988 Act s.25(1).

[794] 1988 Act s.25(2).

unless on grounds of hardship the Committee postpones the date.[795] There is security of tenure, discussed below.[796] Existing rights of protection against unlawful eviction and harassment[797] are augmented by the 1988 Act.[798] It is also an offence to require premiums or advance payment of rent in respect of an assured tenancy.[799]

When the contractual tenancy terminates and the tenant remains in possession, a statutory assured tenancy comes into being.[800] The statutory assured tenancy comprises all the rights and obligations of the original agreement.[801] The terms of the statutory assured tenancy may subsequently be adjusted,[802] and the rent may be increased.[803]

35.74 **Security of tenure**—The landlord cannot bring the contractual or the statutory tenancy to an end unless he establishes one or more of the grounds in Sch.5, and obtains an order from a sheriff in terms of Pt II of the 1988 Act.[804] When certain grounds are established, the sheriff must make an order for possession in favour of the landlord.[805] These grounds are listed in Pt I of Sch.5, in short that: (1) the landlord requires the house as a home for himself or his spouse or civil partner; (2) a prior heritable creditor requires the house to sell with vacant possession[806]; (3) the let was of a holiday house for not more than eight months; (4) the let was for a specified period of not more than 12 months; (5) the let was for occupation by a minister or full-time missionary; (6) the landlord needs possession in order to carry out works of development or reconstruction or other substantial works; (7) the tenancy devolved on the death of the tenant and the landlord began proceedings within 12 months of the death or of knowing of the death; (8) at the date of serving notice on the tenant and at the date of the hearing before the sheriff, the rent was at least three months in arrears. In the case of grounds (1) to

---

[795] 1988 Act s.25(6). Note that by agreement the landlord and tenant may vary any terms of the lease: s.25(8).

[796] Note that the landlord has a duty to provide the tenant with a written tenancy document and a rent book: s.30.

[797] 1984 Act ss.22–23.

[798] 1988 Act ss.36–38. Sections 36 and 37 deal with unlawful eviction. Section 38 inserts s.22(2A) in the 1984 Act (offence if the landlord does acts calculated to interfere with the peace or comfort of the tenant, or if he withdraws services reasonably required for the occupation of the tenant).

[799] 1988 Act s.27. Section 89A of the Housing (Scotland) Act 1984, inserted by means of s.32 of the Private Rented Housing (Scotland) Act 2011, provides that the Scottish Ministers may by regulations make provision about sums which may be charged in connection with the grant, renewal or continuance of a protected tenancy. Section 27 of the 1988 Act has the effect of extending this provision to assured tenancies.

[800] 1988 Act s.16.

[801] Except for rights and obligations relating to termination by the landlord or the tenant; and certain provisions for increases in rent: s.16(1), and unless the terms of the original tenancy either specifically permitted or prohibited assignation or sub-letting, there is an implied term in the statutory assured tenancy that assignation or sub-letting would require the landlord's consent: s.23.

[802] 1988 Act s.17 (which specifically excludes adjustment of the amount of the rent).

[803] 1988 Act ss.24 and 25. It is the landlord who initiates proceedings: the tenant can only respond to the landlord's initiatives, e.g. by referring the proposed increase to a Private Rented Housing Committee. See Gordon and Wortley, *Scottish Land Law* (2009), para.18–171.

[804] 1988 Act ss.16(2), 18, 19 and 20. A tenant may be entitled to removal expenses, but only where ground (6) or (9) applies: s.22.

[805] 1988 Act s.18(3). In each case the landlord must have served notice on the tenant specifying the grounds on which he relies for removal: s.19(1)–(3); the sheriff may dispense with this, except in the case of ground (8): s.19(5).

[806] *Tamroui v Clydesdale Bank Plc*, 1997 S.L.T. (Sh. Ct) 20. Section 152 of the Housing (Scotland) Act 2010 puts the protection recognised by the court in *Tamroui* onto a statutory basis.

(5), the tenant must have been given notice at the time of entering into the lease that the landlord might rely on one of these grounds for removing him.[807]

For the remaining grounds, the sheriff must be satisfied not only that the ground has been established, but also that it is reasonable to make an order for possession.[808] These grounds are listed in Pt II of Sch.5, namely that: (a) suitable alternative accommodation is or will be available for the tenant; (b) the tenant has given notice to quit and is still in occupation without a new tenancy; (c) the tenant has persistently delayed in paying the rent when due; (d) there were arrears of rent when notice was served on the tenant (or notice was dispensed with); (e) the tenant is in breach of an obligation under the lease other than making payment; (f) the tenant is responsible for deterioration of the house or any of its common parts; (g) the tenant or another resident or visitor has caused nuisance or annoyance to neighbours or been convicted of using the house for immoral or illegal purposes; (h) the tenant is responsible for deterioration of furniture provided; (i) the let is to an employee whose employment has ceased. In Pt II cases the sheriff has power to suspend the execution of the order or the date for taking possession.[809]

Short assured tenancies—A short assured tenancy is an assured tenancy for a **35.75** minimum term of six months,[810] in respect of which a notice in the prescribed form has been served.[811] The tenant may apply to the Private Rented Housing Committee for a determination of the rent: this will apply from the date directed by the committee, and no further increase may be made until a year later.[812] The landlord has an automatic right to recover possession at the end of the term of the tenancy, provided that he has given at least two months' notice that he requires possession of the house.[813] The sheriff has no discretion to refuse to grant recovery of possession, or to suspend execution of the order granting possession.[814] In addition, the landlord can regain possession by establishing any of the assured tenancy repossession grounds.[815] Where a short assured tenancy comes to an end, and there is tacit relocation or a new contractual tenancy of the same or substantially the same premises, then such a tenancy is also a short assured tenancy.[816]

Transmission on death—The 1988 Act provides for one statutory transmission **35.76** only. Where a tenant under an assured tenancy dies, his spouse or cohabitee

---

[807] For grounds (1) and (2) the sheriff may dispense with this requirement.

[808] 1988 Act s.18(4). Even if the action is undefended, the landlord must satisfy the sheriff as to reasonableness: see e.g. *Midlothian DC v Drummond*, 1991 S.L.T. (Sh. Ct) 67; *Gordon DC v Acutt*, 1991 S.L.T. (Sh. Ct) 78; *Midlothian DC v Brown*, 1991 S.L.T. (Sh. Ct) 80; *Renfrew DC v Inglis*, 1991 S.L.T. (Sh. Ct) 83; *Grampian Housing Association v Pyper*, 2004 Hous. L.R. 22.

[809] 1988 Act s.20.

[810] On the facts of *Wishaw & District Housing Association v Neary*, 2004 S.C. 463, it was held that the existence of a break option in the short assured tenancy agreement did not mean that the duration of the tenancy was less than six months.

[811] 1988 Act s.32: i.e. a notice to the effect that the tenancy is a short assured tenancy: cf. Assured Tenancies (Forms) (Scotland) Regulations 1988 (SI 1988/2109), as amended by the Assured Tenancies (Forms) (Scotland) Regulations 1988 (SI 1993/648). The actual length of the tenancy need not in fact be "short".

[812] 1988 Act s.34(4)(a); see too s.32(5); Gordon and Wortley, *Scottish Land Law* (2099), para.18–173.

[813] 1988 Act s.33.

[814] 1988 Act s.20(6).

[815] 1988 Act s.33(1), Sch.5.

[816] 1988 Act s.32(3): whether or not it is a tenancy for at least six months, and whether or not a notice has been served.

becomes entitled to a statutory assured tenancy.[817] Ground 7 of Sch.5[818] does not apply where a spouse or cohabitee succeeds under s.31 or under the will or intestacy of a tenant.

35.77 Tenancy of shops—Security of tenure for the tenant of a shop is afforded by the Tenancy of Shops (Scotland) Acts 1949 and 1964. The expression "shop" is defined in the 1949 Act as including any shop within the meaning of the Shops Acts,[819] that is, any premises where any retail trade or business is carried on.[820] The Act has been held not to apply to sub-tenants of a shop[821]; and a tenant who occupies premises which fall within the 1949 Act cannot claim the protection of the Rent Acts as the tenant of a regulated tenancy.[822] Where the tenant has been given notice of the termination of his tenancy and he is unable to obtain a renewal of it on terms which are satisfactory to him, he may apply to the sheriff for a renewal of the tenancy, provided that he does so within 21 days after the service of the notice and before it takes effect.[823] Where such an application is made, the sheriff may grant a renewal for such period not exceeding one year, at such rent and on such conditions as he thinks reasonable.[824] Thereafter a new lease is deemed to take effect, and the landlord's notice to quit is treated as having lapsed.[825] The tenant may apply for further renewals, having the same right to do so as if the tenancy had been renewed by agreement between the parties.[826] Applications are conducted and disposed of under the summary cause procedure, and the sheriff's decision is final.[827]

Where he thinks it reasonable to do so, the sheriff has power to dismiss the tenant's application. He may in any event not renew the tenancy if he is satisfied as to certain grounds for a termination specified in the Act.[828] For instance, a tenant will not be able to obtain a renewal where he is in breach of a material condition of the lease; where he has refused an offer by the landlord of reasonable alternative accommodation on terms and conditions which the sheriff thinks reasonable; or if it can be shown by the landlord that greater hardship would be caused by renewing the tenancy than by refusing to do so.[829]

---

[817] 1988 Act s.31. The house must have been the spouse/civil partner's principal home immediately before the tenant's death. The right of succession does not apply where the deceased tenant had himself acquired the tenancy by succession.

[818] Permitting repossession by the landlord within 12 months where the tenancy devolves under the will or intestacy of the former tenant.

[819] 1988 Act s.3(2).

[820] See *Golder v Thos. Johnston"s (Bakers)*, 1950 S.L.T. (Sh. Ct) 50; *Thom v British Transport Commission*, 1954 S.L.T. (Sh. Ct) 21; *Wright v St Mungo Property Co* (1955) 71 Sh. Ct Rep. 152; *King v Cross Fisher Properties*, 1956 S.L.T. (Sh. Ct) 79.

[821] *Ashley Wallpaper Co v Morrisons Associated Cos*, 1952 S.L.T. (Sh. Ct) 25; G. Junor, "Can We Keep the Shop? Invoking the Tenancy of Shops (Scotland) Act 1949", 2009 Prop. L.B. 98–5.

[822] 1984 Act s.10(2).

[823] Tenancy of Shops (Scotland) Act 1949 s.1(1); *Superdrug Stores Plc v Network Rail Infrastructure Ltd*, 2006 S.C. 365.

[824] Tenancy of Shops (Scotland) Act 1949 s.1(2); *McMahon v Associated Rentals Ltd*, 1987 S.L.T. (Sh. Ct) 94; *Robertson v Bass Holdings Ltd*, 1993 S.L.T. (Sh. Ct) 55.

[825] *Scottish Gas Board v Kerr's Trs*, 1956 S.L.T. (Sh. Ct) 69.

[826] Tenancy of Shops (Scotland) Act 1949 s.1(4).

[827] Tenancy of Shops (Scotland) Act 1949 s.1(7), as amended by Sheriff Courts (Scotland) Act 1971 Sch.1.

[828] *Kennealy v Dunne* [1977] Q.B. 837; Tenancy of Shops (Scotland) Act 1949 s.1(3).

[829] See *Craig v Saunders & Connor*, 1962 S.L.T. (Sh. Ct) 85; *Jalota v Salvation Army Tr. Co*, 1994 G.W.D. 12–770.

FURTHER READING

Duncan, A.G.M., *The Agricultural Holdings (Scotland) Act 1991* (Edinburgh: W. Green, 1991).

Fraser, D.G., *Rent and House-letting Acts in Scotland*, 2nd edn (Edinburgh: W. Green, 1952).

Gill, Lord, *Law of Agricultural Holdings in Scotland*, 3rd edn (Edinburgh: W. Green, 1997).

Gordon, W.M. and Wortley, S., *Scottish Land Law*, 3rd edn (Edinburgh: W. Green, 2009).

Graham, K.H.R., *Scottish Land Court, Practice and Procedure* (Edinburgh: Butterworths, 1993).

Himsworth, C., *Housing Law in Scotland*, 4th edn (Butterworths, 1994).

Hunter, R., *Landlord and Tenant*, 4th edn (Edinburgh, 1876).

McAllister, A., *Scottish Law of Leases*, 3rd edn (Edinburgh: Bloomsbury Professional, 2002).

MacCuish, D. and Flyn, D., *Crofting Law* (Butterworths, 1990).

Megarry, R., *Rent Acts*, 11th edn (London, 1988).

Paton, G.C.H. and Cameron, J.G.S., *The Law of Landlord and Tenant in Scotland* (Edinburgh: W. Green, 1967).

Rankine, J., *The Law of Leases in Scotland*, 3rd edn (Edinburgh, 1916).

Robson, P. and Vennard, A., *Residential Tenancies*, 3rd edn (Edinburgh: W. Green, 2011).

Ross, D.J. and McKichan, A.H., *Drafting and Negotiating Commercial Leases in Scotland*, 2nd edn (Bloomsbury Professional, 1993).

Ross and Watchman, P., *The Housing (Scotland) Act 1987* (Edinburgh: W. Green, 1991).

Scott, J., *Law of Smallholdings* (Edinburgh: W. Green, 1933).

Stair Memorial Encyclopaedia, Vol.1, "Agriculture: Crofting and Smallholdings"; Vol.13, "Landlord and Tenant".

Stalker, A., *Evictions in Scotland* (Avizandum, 2007).

CHAPTER 36

RIGHTS IN SECURITY

I. GENERAL CONSIDERATIONS

Nature of rights in security—The term "right in security" has been defined as   **36.01**

> "any right which a creditor may hold for ensuring the payment or satisfaction of his debt distinct from, and in addition to, his right of action and execution against the debtor under the latter's personal obligation".[1]

In this broad sense, the term includes both rights in relation to property and also rights against persons other than the debtor.[2] In a narrower and technical sense, a right in security is a subordinate real right[3] in property belonging to someone other than the creditor which secures the performance of some obligation owed to the creditor. The property over which the security is granted need not belong to the debtor: a third party may be prepared to burden his property in security of the debtor's obligation.[4] The creditor may normally, by virtue of his right in security, have the property in question realised for the purpose of satisfying his rights against the debtor. The key feature of a right in security in this sense is that, as a real right, it is, in general, good against other creditors of the owner (and in particular against subsequent diligences) and against purchasers from him. Provided a right in security has been effectually constituted it survives the sequestration or liquidation of the owner of the property and is good against the trustee in sequestration or liquidator.

Constitution of rights in security—A right in security may be constituted by   **36.02** express grant, by operation of law or by diligence.[5] The available mode or modes

---

[1] W.M. Gloag and J.M. Irvine, *Law of Rights in Security* (Edinburgh: W. Green, 1897), pp.1–2.

[2] The latter are considered elsewhere.

[3] i.e. a real right subordinate to and existing alongside the owner's real right of ownership.

[4] There are two possibilities. The third party may grant a cautionary obligation to the creditor and also a right in security over some property of his securing his own personal obligation, or he may simply grant a right in security over some property of his securing the debtor's obligation to the creditor (e.g. as in *Braithwaite v Bank of Scotland*, 1999 S.L.T. 25). In the latter case the owner incurs no personal liability to the creditor but the creditor has all the rights against the security subjects which are incidental to the right in security granted. In either situation, the creditor may not be entitled to enforce his apparent rights under the security if the circumstances of its creation were such as to put him on inquiry in relation to some vitiating factor (such as fraud, misrepresentation or undue influence on the part of the debtor) and he did not take reasonable steps to ensure that he remained in good faith: *Smith v Bank of Scotland*, 1997 S.C. (HL) 111. See further Ch.16; S. Eden, "Cautionary Tales—The Continued Development of Smith v Bank of Scotland" (2003) 7 Edin. L.R. 107; and S. Eden, "More Cautionary Tales" (2004) 8 Edin. L.R. 276.

[5] As to diligence, see Ch.48.

by which a right in security may be constituted depend on the nature of the security subjects, the nature of the debtor[6] and the nature of the obligation secured.[7] In the case of securities constituted by express grant, the mere undertaking of an obligation to transfer some specific thing to the creditor in security[8] or to set aside some particular fund in order to meet the debt[9] is not enough. In order to create a real right in security some further step, the nature of which depends on the nature of the property and the security right in question, is normally required. For example, delivery is required to constitute a pledge over corporeal moveable property. Where the security right is created in writing, three stages in the transaction may be identified: (1) agreement to grant the security; (2) delivery of the security documents to the creditor; and (3) completion of the security by the mode appropriate to the property in question.[10] As a matter of property law a real right in security is constituted only at the last stage.[11] The detailed rules for the constitution of particular rights in security are dealt with below.

36.03 **Functional securities**—A creditor may obtain some or all of the practical benefits given by a right in security by employing other legal mechanisms. Although these are not rights in security in the strict sense they may in a functional sense be regarded as providing security.[12]

(1) A creditor may take ownership of certain property subject to a personal obligation to reconvey it upon discharge of the obligation secured.[13] The property is not available to the subsequent diligence of the debtor's creditors and the "secured" creditor's position is not prejudiced by the debtor's sequestration or liquidation[14] or by any subsequent transaction by the debtor.[15] This mechanism may no longer effectively be used for the purpose of securing any debt by way of a heritable security.[16] In relation to corporeal moveables, its practical utility is affected by the combined effects of (a) s.62(4) of the Sale of Goods Act 1979, which states that the provisions of the Act do not apply to a transaction in the form of a contract of sale which is intended to operate by way of security,

---

[6] Notably only companies and several other commercial entities may create a floating charge: see paras 36.05, 36.33–36.34.

[7] e.g. obligations to pay seamen's wages, the master's remuneration and disbursements and reparation in respect of damage caused by the ship are secured by maritime hypothecs.

[8] *Bank of Scotland v Hutchison, Main & Co*, 1914 S.C. (HL) 1.

[9] *Graham v Raeburn & Verel* (1893) 23 R. 84; *Brown v Port-Seton Harbour Commissioners* (1898) 1 F. 373.

[10] e.g. registration in the appropriate register in the case of a standard security over heritable property, a ship mortgage or a share transfer, or intimation of the assignation in the case of most incorporeal assets.

[11] Until then the creditor merely holds a personal right; see *Burnett's Tr. v Grainger*, 2004 S.C. (HL) 19, per Lord Hope at [19] and [20] and Lord Rodger at [87].

[12] See G. Gretton, "The Concept of Security" in *A Scots Conveyancing Miscellany: Essays in Honour of Professor J.M. Halliday*, edited by D.J. Cusine, (Edinburgh: W. Green, 1987), p.126.

[13] This is not a right in security in the strict sense because the creditor becomes owner of the property and does not acquire a subordinate real right in security in the property of someone else. Some of the differences between this type of transaction and a right in security in the strict sense are mentioned in para.36.04.

[14] Assuming it is not challengeable as an unfair preference or a gratuitous alienation.

[15] Such events may, however, affect the scope of the creditor's security: *Union Bank of Scotland Ltd v National Bank of Scotland Ltd* (1886) 14 R. (HL) 1; *Campbell's J.F. v National Bank of Scotland Ltd*, 1944 S.C. 495.

[16] Conveyancing and Feudal Reform (Scotland) Act 1970 (the "1970 Act") s.9(3), (4).

and (b) the common law requirement of delivery to effect a transfer of ownership of corporeal moveables.

(2) A seller of goods may retain title in the goods until the buyer has paid the purchase price or indeed other obligations owed by him to the seller.[17] While such a device protects the seller in the buyer's insolvency and against the subsequent diligences of the buyer's creditors,[18] the seller remains vulnerable to a voluntary transfer by the buyer to a third party who is in good faith.[19]

(3) A seller may likewise achieve the effect of a security for payment of the purchase price by way of a contract of hire purchase.[20] Not only is the seller protected on the buyer's insolvency and against the diligence of his creditors[21] but, normally, except in the case of motor cars,[22] the hirer will be unable to give good title to a third party.[23]

(4) If property is held by the debtor in a properly constituted trust[24] (of which the creditor is the beneficiary) it is not attachable by subsequent diligence of the debtor's creditors and is not available to the debtor's trustee in sequestration[25] or liquidator.[26] But the creditor's interest in the property could be defeated if the trustee were to transfer the property for value to a good faith third party.[27]

---

[17] *Armour v Thyssen Edelstahlwerke AG*, 1990 S.L.T. 891; *Kinloch Damph Ltd v Nordvik Salmon Farms Ltd* Unreported June 30, 1999, Lord Macfadyen.

[18] Previously goods delivered to a lessee subject to a clause of retention of title and on the lease subjects could fall within the landlord's hypothec and be attached and sold by the process of sequestration for rent: *Lawsons Ltd v Avon India-Rubber Co Ltd*, 1915 2 S.L.T. 327. Section 208(4) of the Bankruptcy and Diligence etc. (Scotland) Act 2007 changed the position so that the landlord's hypothec no longer arises in relation to property which is owned by a person other than the tenant. Note also that by s.208(1) the diligence of sequestration for rent has been abolished; see A. McAllister, "The Landlord's Hypothec: Down but is it Out?", 2010 Jur. Rev. 65 and S. Skea and A.J.M. Steven, "The Landlord's Hypothec: Difficulties in Practice", 2010 S.L.T. (News) 120.

[19] Sale of Goods Act 1979 s.25(1); *Archivent Sales and Development Ltd v Strathclyde RC*, 1985 S.L.T. 154; for a failed attempt to obtain a priority over the proceeds by way of a trust see *Clark Taylor & Co Ltd v Quality Site Development (Edinburgh) Ltd*, 1981 S.C. 111. Section 25 does not apply if the sale was a conditional sale agreement as defined in s.25(2).

[20] See para.12.55, above.

[21] Previously goods possessed by a lessee under a hire or hire purchase contract and on the leased premises could fall within the landlord's hypothec and be attached and sold by the process of sequestration for rent: *Dundee Corp v Marr*, 1971 S.C. 96; *Rudman v Jay & Co*, 1908 S.C. 552. The position changed when s.208 of the Bankruptcy and Diligence etc. (Scotland) Act 2007 came into force; see above, fn.18.

[22] Hire Purchase Act 1964 Pt III.

[23] But see *Brechin Auction Co v Reid* (1895) 22 R. 711.

[24] For the use of trusts in commercial contexts see *Export Credits Guarantee Department v Turner*, 1979 S.C. 286; *Clark Taylor & Co Ltd v Quality Site Development (Edinburgh) Ltd*, 1981 S.C. 111; *Tay Valley Joinery Ltd v C.F. Financial Services Ltd*, 1987 S.L.T. 207; *Mercedes-Benz Finance Ltd v Clydesdale Bank Plc*, 1997 S.L.T. 905; *Balfour Beatty Ltd v Britannia Life Ltd*, 1997 S.L.T. 10; *Style Financial Services Ltd v Bank of Scotland (No.2)*, 1998 S.L.T. 851.

[25] Bankruptcy (Scotland) Act 1985 s.31; *Heritable Reversionary Co v Miller* (1892) 19 R. (HL) 43; for discussion see K.G.C. Reid, "Constitution of Trust" 1986 S.L.T. (News) 177; K.J.M. Young, "Intimation—The Equivalent to Delivery of What?", 1996 S.L.T. (News) 373; D. Cabrelli, "Can Scots Lawyers Trust Don King? Trusts in the Commercial Context" (2001) 6 S.L.P.Q. 103; R.G. Anderson, "Fraud on Transfer and on Insolvency: ta . . . ta . . . tantum et tale?" (2007) 11 Edin. L.R. 187.

[26] Or, it would appear, to a receiver: *Tay Valley Joinery Ltd v C.F. Financial Services Ltd*, 1987 S.L.T. 207; *Sharp v Thomson*, 1997 S.C. (HL) 66; but see Reid, "Trust and Floating Charges", 1987 S.L.T. (News) 113.

[27] *Redfearn v Somervail* (1813) 1 Dow 58, 1 Pat. App.707; *McGowan v Robb* (1864) 2 M. 943; *Thomson v Clydesdale Bank* (1893) 20 R. (HL) 50. See also Trusts (Scotland) Act 1961 s.2 and *Brodie v Secretary of State for Scotland*, 2002 G.W.D. 20–698.

(5) A debtor may assign to his creditor rights to receive payment from a third party. Such an assignation must be intimated to the third party. Some cases refer to the mandate in rem suam[28]—being a mandate which allows the mandatory to do something which is in his own interest, such as enforcing the rights of the mandant by bringing proceedings in the mandant's name but keeping any sums which are recovered—but there are serious difficulties with these cases. It is, in particular, doubtful whether a mandate in rem suam would protect the mandatory on the mandant's insolvency.[29]

36.04 General features of rights in security

(1) Accessory. A right in security is an accessory right.[30] Its purpose is to secure the performance of an obligation of the debtor. It follows that a security for a fixed amount is extinguished upon discharge (by performance or otherwise) of the debt secured.[31] The creditor is obliged to return the security subjects to their owner[32] or (if appropriate) to grant any formal discharge which may be required for evidential purposes.[33] If the creditor has taken an ex facie absolute title, he is bound to reconvey the subjects upon satisfaction of the debt.[34]

(2) Redemption. A right in security is by its nature a redeemable right.[35] A clause limiting the debtor's right to redeem will not be enforced literally. A declaratory action is required and may be met at any time by an offer to discharge the obligation secured. If a conveyance of property is truly in security, even if it is expressed as an ex facie absolute conveyance, a provision that the right of redemption will expire after a certain period will not receive effect according to its strict terms. A declarator of the extinction of the former proprietor's right is necessary and may at any time be met by an offer to discharge the obligation secured.[36]

(3) Scope of security. At common law, where a subject has been transferred expressly in security, it secures only the obligation for which it was

---

[28] J. Graham Stewart, *A Treatise on the Law of Diligence* (Edinburgh: W. Green, 1898), p.144; *Carter v McIntosh* (1862) 24 D. 925; *British Linen Bank v Carruthers & Ferguson* (1883) 10 R. 923. Indeed, this device was the forerunner of assignation properly so called: *Caledonia North Sea Ltd v London Bridge Engineering Ltd*, 2000 S.L.T. 1123 at 1139–40, per Lord President Rodger.

[29] See R.G. Anderson, *Assignation* (Edinburgh: Avizandum, 2008), paras 2.25 et seq and 5.13 et seq.

[30] See, e.g. *Trotter v Trotter*, 2001 S.L.T. (Sh. Ct) 42. See also A.J.M. Steven, "Accessoriness and Security Over Land" (2009) 13 Edin. L.R. 387.

[31] Gloag and Irvine, *Rights in Security* (1897), p.2. On securities for a fluctuating amount see Gretton, "The Concept of Security" in *A Scots Conveyancing Miscellany: Essays in Honour of Professor J.M. Halliday* (1987), p.128.

[32] *Mackirdy v Webster's Tr.* (1895) 22 R. 340; *Crerar v Bank of Scotland*, 1921 S.C. 736; 1922 S.C. (HL) 137; for pledges securing regulated agreements under the Consumer Credit Act 1974 (the "1974 Act") see ss.117, 119, 122 of that Act.

[33] e.g. *G. Dunlop & Son's JF v Armstrong (No.1)*, 1994 S.L.T. 199. Section 18(2), (3) of the Conveyancing and Feudal Reform (Scotland) Act 1970 provides a means of clearing the register where the debtor in a standard security is unable to obtain a discharge.

[34] *Heritable Reversionary Co v Millar* (1892) 19 R. (HL) 43; *Forbes' Trs v Macleod* (1898) 25 R. 1012.

[35] For standard securities, see Conveyancing and Feudal Reform (Scotland) Act 1970 ss.11, 18, 23(3); *G. Dunlop & Son's J.F. v Armstrong*, 1994 S.L.T. 199; for pledges securing regulated agreements under the 1974 Act, see s.116 of that Act.

[36] W.M. Gloag, *Law of Contract*, 2nd edn (Edinburgh: W. Green, 1929), pp.669–71; *Smith v Smith* (1879) 6 R. 794.

granted,[37] and gives the holder no preferential right in the sequestration of the debtor for any obligation subsequently contracted.[38] By contrast, if the title of the creditor is in form absolute, his security, unless limited by some express contract,[39] involves a right of retention, which will secure future advances.[40] At common law, notice to the creditor that the reversionary right, or right to demand a reconveyance, has been transferred to a third party, deprives the creditor of his preference in respect of further advances or of interest falling due after intimation.[41] This rule has been modified in relation to heritable securities[42] and special provision has been made for floating charges.[43]

(4) Power to realise. At common law, where a subject has been transferred expressly in security, a secured creditor has no implied power to sell the security subjects. By contrast, where the creditor has taken ownership, qualified by a personal obligation to reconvey, he has power to sell the subjects without notice to the debtor.[44] If he should sell in breach of an unrecorded agreement between the parties he may be liable in damages but the purchaser's title is unaffected.[45] Where the creditor's right is a right in security in the strict sense, then if he has not been granted an express power of sale[46] he may apply to the court for such a power.[47] The common law position has been modified in certain cases by statute. A creditor with a standard security over heritage may without application to the court take possession of the subjects and sell them if the debtor has failed to comply with a calling-up notice.[48] In relation to pledges subject to the Consumer Credit Act 1974, the pledgee may sell the pledge on the expiry of the redemption period without application to the court.[49] An innkeeper has a statutory power to sell goods left with him by someone who is indebted to him for board or lodging.[50] In exercising a power of sale, at common law, the creditor should have regard to the interests of the owner and other secured creditors, and is subject to control by the court.[51] The creditor (or, in the case of a floating charge, the receiver or administrator[52]) has an

---

[37] Which may, it should be noted, be expressed to cover all sums due and to become due.

[38] *National Bank v Forbes* (1858) 21 D. 791; *Colquhoun's Tr. v Diack* (1901) 4 F. 358.

[39] *Anderson's Tr. v Somerville* (1899) 36 S.L.R. 833.

[40] *Hamilton v Western Bank* (1856) 19 D. 152; *National Bank of Scotland v Union Bank of Scotland* (1886) 14 R. (HL) 1.

[41] *Callum v Goldie* (1885) 12 R. 1137; *Union Bank of Scotland v National Bank of Scotland* (1886) 14 R. (HL) 1; *Campbell's J.F. v National Bank of Scotland Ltd*, 1944 S.C. 495.

[42] Conveyancing and Feudal Reform (Scotland) Act 1970 ss.13, 42.

[43] Companies Act 1985 s.464(5). This provision is due to be repealed and replaced by ss.40(5), (6) and 46(1) of the Bankruptcy and Diligence etc. (Scotland) Act 2007, although no date has yet been set for the commencement of these provisions of the 2007 Act.

[44] *Baillie v Drew* (1884) 12 R. 199; *Aberdeen Trades Council v Shipconstructors etc. Association*, 1949 S.C. (HL) 45.

[45] *Duncan v Mitchell* (1893) 21 R. 37; *Aberdeen Trades Council v Shipconstructors etc. Association*, 1949 S.C. (HL) 45.

[46] Bell, *Commentaries*, II, 269–75.

[47] Bell, *Principles*, s.207; for liens see *Gibson & Stewart v Brown & Co* (1876) 3 R. 328; *Parker v Andrew Brown & Co* (1878) 5 R. 979.

[48] Conveyancing and Feudal Reform (Scotland) Act 1970 s.20, but the enforcement procedures in relation to residential properties should be noted; see further para.36.09.

[49] 1974 Act ss.120 and 121.

[50] Innkeepers Act 1878 s.1.

[51] Bell, *Commentaries*, II, 271; *Beveridge v Wilson* (1829) 7 S. 279.

[52] On floating charges, receivers and administrators generally, see below, paras 36.33 et seq.

implied obligation to take reasonable care to obtain the best price reasonably obtainable in the circumstances.[53] A creditor is not entitled to purchase subjects which he is himself selling pursuant to a power of sale[54] except under particular provisions applicable only to heritable securities.[55] But a creditor may purchase at a sale by another secured creditor[56] or at a sale under a security in which he is one of a number of creditors,[57] or (subject to the provisions of s.39(8) of the Bankruptcy (Scotland) Act 1985) at a sale by the owner's trustee in sequestration.[58] Failure by a creditor to comply with the terms of the power of sale may entitle a purchaser to rescind[59] and the owner to interdict the sale.[60]

(5) Application of the proceeds of realisation. In general, a creditor who has realised the security subjects is obliged to account to the owner for the proceeds to the extent that the proceeds exceed the amount necessary to satisfy the obligation secured.[61]

(6) Ranking. Since a right in security is a subordinate real right in property, it follows that, except where the nature of the asset and the type of security available preclude this, more than one creditor may have a security right over the same item of property. The ranking between security rights is, in the absence of agreement, fixed by law. Ranking in relation to particular types of security is mentioned below.

(7) Catholic and Secondary Securities. When creditor A has a security over two subjects belonging to the debtor and creditor B has a postponed security over only one of those subjects, A is termed the catholic and B the secondary creditor. If in those circumstances, A chooses to realise the subject over which B also has a security, and thereby obtains payment of his debts, he is bound to convey his security over the other subjects to B.[62] If both subjects are realised and the debtor is bankrupt, it will be assumed that the catholic creditor exhausted first the estate over which the secondary security did not extend, and therefore that the secondary creditor has a preferable right to the balance of the sum realised from both subjects in a question with the general creditors of the debtor represented by his trustee in sequestration.[63] But the secondary creditor

---

[53] *Davidson v Scott*, 1915 S.C. 924; *Forth & Clyde Construction Co Ltd v Trinity Timber & Plywood Co Ltd*, 1984 S.C. 1 at 11, per Lord President Emslie; *Clydesdale Bank Plc v Spencer*, 2001 G.W.D. 17–667; for standard securities see Conveyancing and Feudal Reform (Scotland) Act 1970 s.25; for pledges subject to the 1974 Act, see 1974 Act s.121(6), (7).

[54] *Taylor v Watson* (1846) 8 D. 400; see generally *Shiell v Guthrie's Trs* (1878) 1 R. 1083; ownership of pledged property regulated by the 1974 Act and securing credit limited to £75 passes automatically to the creditor if the pledge is not redeemed; s.120 of the Act.

[55] Conveyancing and Feudal Reform (Scotland) Act 1970 s.28; Abolition of Feudal Tenure etc. (Scotland) Act 2000 s.69.

[56] e.g. *Begbie v Boyle* (1837) 16 S. 232.

[57] *Wright v Buchanan*, 1917 S.C. 73.

[58] *Cruickshank v Williams* (1849) 11 D. 614.

[59] *Ferguson v Rodger* (1895) 22 R. 643.

[60] *Kerr v McArthur's Trs* (1848) 11 D. 301; but see in relation to standard securities *Associated Displays Ltd v Turnbeam Ltd*, 1988 S.C.L.R. 220; *Gordivoran Ltd v Clydesdale Bank Plc*, 1994 S.C.L.R. 248.

[61] *Armour v Thyssen Edelstahlwerke AG*, 1990 S.L.T. 891 at 895, per Lord Keith of Kinkel; for standard securities see the 1970 Act s.27; for pledges subject to the 1974 Act, see 1974 Act s.121(3).

[62] Bell, *Commentaries*, II, 417–419.

[63] *Littlejohn v Black* (1855) 18 D. 207; *Nicol's Tr. v Hill* (1889) 16 R. 416.

is not in general entitled to object to a discharge of the security over the subjects not covered by his own security.[64] The catholic creditor may disregard the interests of the secondary creditor in pursuance of any legitimate interest of his own. So if he holds a security for another debt over the subjects not secured to the secondary creditor, he is entitled, in realising, to exhaust first the subjects covered by the secondary security, so as to leave the largest possible surplus to meet his own postponed security.[65] If there are secondary securities on each estate, the burden of the catholic security is, in a question between the secondary creditors, to be apportioned rateably, according to the value of each estate, and irrespective of which secondary security was prior in date.[66] It has been said that a receiver's freedom to choose which parts of the property attached upon the crystallisation of a floating charge[67] to realise is not subject to the constraints imposed by the common law upon the actings of a catholic creditor in the interests of a secondary creditor.[68]

Fixed and floating charges—A fixed security is a subordinate real right in security over some specific property. As such, it is unaffected by the sale of the property to a third party and prevails over the later diligence of other creditors. By contrast, a floating charge does not affect any of the debtor's assets unless and until the occurrence of some statutory event, in which event the charge "crystallises" as if it were a fixed charge over the property then owned by the debtor and covered by the charge. Prior to the enactment of the Companies (Floating Charges) (Scotland) Act 1961,[69] it was (with one minor exception) not competent in Scots law to grant a floating charge.[70] To be effective any security required to be a fixed security by which a real right in the property was constituted in favour of the creditor. Under the 1961 Act it became competent for a company incorporated under the Companies Acts to secure any existing or future debts, including any balance on cash account, by creating in favour of a creditor a floating charge[71] over the whole or any part of the property, heritable or moveable, which might from time to time be comprised in its property and undertaking.[72] At present, the **36.05**

---

[64] *Morton (Liddell's Curator)* (1871) 10 M. 292.

[65] *Preston v Erskine* (1715) M. 3376.

[66] *Ferrier v Cowan* (1896) 23 R. 703; see also *Earl of Moray v Mansfield* (1836) 14 S. 886.

[67] See para.36.33, below.

[68] *Forth & Clyde Construction Co Ltd v Trinity Timber & Plywood Co Ltd*, 1984 S.C. 1 at 11, per Lord President Emslie.

[69] 9 & 10 Eliz II, c. 46.

[70] *Carse v Coppen*, 1951 S.C. 233; see also *Ballachulish Slate Quarries v Menzies* (1908) 45 S.L.R. 667. The exception was the agricultural charge: Agricultural Credits (Scotland) Act 1929 ss.5–8; see also Agricultural Marketing Act 1958 s.15.

[71] The floating charge has had a controversial history in Scots law; see D. Cabrelli, "The Case against the Floating Charge in Scotland" (2005) 9 Edin. L.R. 407 and the further references cited therein.

[72] This phrase has been said to refer to property available for the use of the company, in which it has a beneficial interest, rather than to strict notions of property law. Thus, once the company has delivered a disposition of heritable property to a purchaser, the property ceases to be comprised in the company's "property and undertaking" and is not attached if a floating charge granted by the company crystallises before the disposition is recorded in the appropriate property register: *Sharp v Thomson*, 1997 S.C. (HL) 66. It should be stressed that the scope of the *Sharp* decision remains unclear and it could be the case that an asset leaves the "property and undertaking" of the company at an earlier stage, for example on the conclusion of missives. It has however been clarified by the House of Lords that the decision in *Sharp* is restricted to the technical construction of that phrase where used in statutory provisions concerning floating charges (such as ss.462 and 463 of the Companies Act 1985) and does not have wider implications for the general body of Scots property law; see *Burnett's Tr. v Grainger*, 2004 S.C.

relevant provisions in relation to incorporated companies are principally to be found in Pt XVIII of the Companies Act 1985, Pt II and Ch.II of Pt III of the Insolvency Act 1986 and Pt 25 of the Companies Act 2006.[73] Part XVIII of the 1985 Act is, however, due to be repealed by the Bankruptcy and Diligence etc. (Scotland) Act 2007.[74] When the relevant provisions of the 2007 Act come into force, they will restate, with some significant amendments, the law relating to floating charges.[75] The details of the current rules, and of the impending restatement and amendments, are discussed in detail below. Limited liability partnerships, European Economic Interest Groupings and Industrial and Provident Societies may also grant floating charges.[76]

36.06 **Registration of charges created by companies**[77]—Section 878 of the Companies Act 2006 provides that every charge created by a company registered in Scotland[78] to which the section applies is void against the liquidator or administrator and any creditor of the company unless the prescribed particulars of the charge together with a certified copy of the instrument by which the charge is created or evidenced, are delivered to or received by the Registrar of Companies within 21 days of the creation of the charge.[79] The section applies to charges on land (wherever

---

(HL) 19 at [83] and [84], per Lord Rodger; D. McKenzie-Skene, "The Shock of the Old: Burnett's Tr v Grainger", 2004 S.L.T. (News) 65; G. Gretton, "Ownership and Insolvency: Burnett's Trustee v Grainger" (2004) 8 Edin. L.R. 389; and Scottish Law Commission, *Report on Sharp v Thomson* (HMSO, 2007), Scot. Law Com. No.208.

[73] On the approach to be taken to construction of these provisions see *Forth & Clyde Construction Co Ltd v Trinity Timber & Plywood Co Ltd*, 1984 S.C. 1 at 11 per Lord President Emslie; *Sharp v Thomson*, 1997 S.C. (HL) 66; *Lindop v Stuart Noble & Sons Ltd* [1999] B.C.C. 616 at 632–3, per Lord Macfadyen; 1999 S.C.L.R. 889.

[74] Bankruptcy and Diligence etc. (Scotland) Act 2007 s.46(1).

[75] The saving and transitional arrangements in s.46 of the 2007 Act should be noted.

[76] Limited Liability Partnerships (Scotland) Regulations 2001 (SSI 2001/128) reg.3 and Sch.1; the European Economic Interest Grouping Regulations 1989 (SI 1989/638) reg.18 and Sch.4; and the Industrial and Provident Societies Act 1967 s.3, as substituted by s.26 of the Companies Consolidation (Consequential Provisions) Act 1985.

[77] Note that the regime as outlined here is due to change. The Department for Business, Innovation and Skills launched a consultation in March 2010 (*Registration of Charges Created by Companies and Limited Liability Partnerships*) on proposed amendments to the charges registration regime. This has been supplemented by several further rounds of consultation and regulations are now expected in the course of 2012.

[78] Charges created by companies registered in England and Wales are provided for in the Companies Act 2006 (the "2006 Act") ss.860–877. Charges created by an "overseas company" (i.e. a company incorporated outside of the United Kingdom; 2006 Act s.1044) which has registered particulars of a United Kingdom establishment with the Registrar of Companies are subject to their own regime; with effect from October 1, 2011 such charges do not require to be registered with the Registrar of Companies and instead such companies are required to maintain an in-house register of charges; see the Overseas Companies (Execution of Documents and Registration of Charges) Regulations 2009 (SI 2009/1917) as amended by the Overseas Companies (Execution of Documents and Registration of Charges) (Amendment) Regulations 2011 (SI 2011/2194).

[79] 2006 Act s.889; see *Bank of Scotland v T.A. Neilson & Co*, 1990 S.C. 284. Section 886 of the 2006 Act has clarified that the period allowed for registration is 21 days beginning with the day after the day on which the security was created. For charges created outside of the United Kingdom the 21-day period begins on the day after the day on which a copy of the instrument by which the security is created or evidenced could, in due course of post (and if despatched with due diligence) have been received in the United Kingdom; s.886(1)(b). Special provision is made for charges associated with debentures: 2006 Act esp. ss.738, 879(2), 882, 883 and 886(3). The court has power to extend the time for registering in certain circumstances: 2006 Act s.888; see further *Prior, Petitioner*, 1989 S.L.T. 840 and *Salvesen, Petitioner*, 2010 S.L.T. 342 (both of which were decided under s.420 of the Companies Act 1985, the predecessor to s.888 of the 2006 Act).

situated[80]), securities over goodwill and over certain intellectual property rights, over the book debts of the company,[81] over the uncalled share capital of the company, securities over a shop or aircraft or any share in a ship and floating charges.[82]

Under current law, the date of creation of the charge is, in the case of a floating charge, the date on which the instrument creating the charge was executed by the company, and, in any other case, the date on which the creditor's right was constituted as a real right.[83] The Bankruptcy and Diligence etc. (Scotland) Act 2007, once the relevant provisions are in force, will change the position in respect of floating charges.[84] The Act provides that the Keeper of the Registers of Scotland must establish and maintain a Register of Floating Charges.[85] A floating charge will cease to be created merely upon execution by the company; consistent with general principle, the date of creation will be the date of registration[86] in the Register of Floating Charges.[87]

It is to be noted that, under current law, a security granted by a company is very often subject to a dual registration requirement. For example, a standard security granted by a company must be registered in the Land or Sasine Register in order for the real right to be created. The security must also be registered in the

---

[80] 2006 Act s.879(3). See also *Amalgamated Securities Ltd, Petitioners*, 1967 S.C. 56.

[81] This does not include the giving of a negotiable instrument to secure the payment of any book debts of the company: 2006 Act s.879(4).

[82] 2006 Act s.878(7). The relevance of the Financial Collateral Directive (2002/47/EC) should be noted. The Directive obliges Member States to, amongst other things, ensure that the creation, validity, perfection and enforceability of "financial collateral arrangements" are not dependent upon any "formal acts". The Directive has been transposed by the United Kingdom by the Financial Collateral Arrangements (No.2) Regulations 2003 (SI 2003/3226) (as amended by inter alia the Financial Markets and Insolvency (Settlement Finality and Financial Collateral Arrangements) (Amendment) Regulations 2010/2993). In general terms, the 2003 Regulations give effect to the Directive by disapplying various provisions of domestic company and insolvency law which would otherwise apply to financial collateral arrangements. In this context, it should be noted that reg.5 provides that the registration requirements of s.878 of the 2006 Act do not apply in relation to "financial collateral arrangements" or any charge created or otherwise arising under a financial collateral arrangement. Likewise, s.252 of the Banking Act 2009 provides that the provisions of the Companies Act 2006 concerned with the registration of charges do not apply to a charge if the person interested in that charge is the Bank of England, the central bank of a country or territory outside the United Kingdom or the European Central Bank.

[83] 2006 Act s.879(5); *AIB Finance Ltd v Bank of Scotland*, 1993 S.C. 588. There is special provision for charges over property outside the United Kingdom: 2006 Act s.884.

[84] The provisions of the 2007 Act regarding floating charges were based on the recommendations of the Scottish Law Commission; see their *Report on Registration of Rights in Security by Companies* (HMSO, 2004), Scot. Law Com. No.197. The Commission recommended that the changes they proposed regarding floating charges should be extended to limited liability partnerships, European Economic Interest Groupings and Industrial and Provident Societies (see para.2.27 of the report). It is expected that the changes regarding limited liability partnerships and European Economic Interest Groupings will be made by statutory instrument. Provision is made for Industrial and Provident Societies in s.49 of the 2007 Act.

[85] Bankruptcy and Diligence etc. (Scotland) Act 2007 s.37. It is not clear when, or if, the provisions of the 2007 Act relating to the Register of Floating Charges will be brought into force. A Technical Working Group, led by Registers of Scotland, reported to the Scottish Government in August 2011 on legal and administrative aspects of the proposed Register. At the time of writing, the response of the Scottish Government is awaited.

[86] Bankruptcy and Diligence etc. (Scotland) Act 2007 s.39 will permit, in a situation where a company proposes to grant a floating charge, the company and the person in whose favour the charge is to be granted to register a joint notice of the proposed charge in the Register of Floating Charges. Provided the floating charge is registered within 21 days of the registration of the advance notice, the charge will be treated as having been created when the advance notice was registered; s.39(3).

[87] Bankruptcy and Diligence etc. (Scotland) Act 2007 s.38(3).

Companies Register within 21 days of creation in terms of s.878 of the Companies Act 2006. The 2006 Act contains provisions to enable this double registration requirement to be brought to an end. Section 893 provides that if a security is registered in a "special register" then there is not a need for a second registration in the Companies Register. It will be the job of the keeper of the "special register" to pass on the relevant information about the security to the Registrar of Companies. At the time of writing no orders have been made under s.893, but it is anticipated that the Land Register, the Sasine Register and the Register of Floating Charges will all be designated as "special registers".[88]

Where a company acquires property which is subject to a charge which would, if granted by the company, require to be registered under s.878, the company is under a duty to register the charge with the Registrar of Companies within 21 days after the date on which the transaction was settled,[89] but the statute does not provide that the charge is void if this duty is not complied with.

The Registrar of Companies is obliged to issue a certificate of registration of registered charges. The certificate is conclusive evidence that the requirements of the Companies Act as to registration have been complied with.[90] The Registrar of Companies is empowered to enter on the register a memorandum of satisfaction on application being made to him in the prescribed form and on receipt of a statement verifying that the debt for which a registered charge was given has been paid or satisfied in whole or in part or that part of the property charged has been released from the charge or has ceased to form part of the company's property.[91] If a charge does not fall within the list of charges in s.878, registration with the Registrar of Companies is not required,[92] but every company must keep at its registered office a register of all fixed and floating charges granted by it.[93]

The Secretary of State has the power to amend, by regulation, the provisions of the Act regarding registration of charges.[94]

36.07 Securities subject to the Consumer Credit Act 1974—A security[95] granted by the debtor securing a regulated agreement[96] under the Consumer Credit Act must

---

[88] See the Department for Business, Innovation & Skills, *Government Response: Consultation on Registration of Charges created by Companies and Limited Liability Partnerships* (December 2010).

[89] 2006 Act ss.880 and 886(2). If the property is situated and the charge was created outside the United Kingdom, the 21-day period begins from the day after the day on which a copy of the instrument by which the charge was created or evidenced could, in due course of post (and if despatched with due diligence) have been received in the United Kingdom; s.886(2)(b).

[90] 2006 Act s.885.

[91] 2006 Act s.887. Under s.1112 of the 2006 Act it is an offence for a person to knowingly or recklessly make a statement to the Registrar that is misleading, false or deceptive in a material particular. A failure to record such a memorandum does not mean that a release cannot have effect: *Scottish & Newcastle Plc v Ascot Inns Ltd*, 1994 S.L.T. 1140.

[92] *Scottish Homes Investment Co, Petitioners*, 1968 S.C. 244.

[93] 2006 Act s.891.

[94] 2006 Act s.894. See above, fn.77, regarding the current consultation on proposed amendments to the charges registration regime which are intended to be introduced by regulations under s.894.

[95] 1974 Act s.189.

[96] Previously the 1974 Act only applied to agreements where the credit provided or the hire payments to be made did not exceed £25,000. This limit was removed by s.2 of the Consumer Credit Act 2006 so that all consumer credit agreements and consumer hire agreements are regulated by the 1974 Act unless exempted (see ss.8 and 15 of the 1974 Act, as amended). Consumer credit agreements entered into by building societies, banks and certain other bodies are exempt: s.16 of the 1974 Act. See also ss.16A, 16B and 16C of the 1974 Act, providing for exemptions in relation to high net worth debtors, certain agreements entered into for business purposes and certain agreements secured on land. It is to be noted that the requirements of the 1974 Act and ancillary subordinate legislation do not apply

be embodied in the agreement,[97] i.e. set out in the agreement itself or in another document referred to in the agreement.[98] Copies of the documentation must be provided to the debtor in accordance with ss.61A–63 of the Act and the Consumer Credit (Cancellation Notices and Copies of Documents) Regulations 1983.[99] In the event of non-compliance with the statutory requirements, the regulated agreement is enforceable only by order of the court[100] and the security may only be enforced if such an order has been made.[101] A security[102] granted to secure the creditor's rights under a regulated agreement must be expressed in writing.[103] If it is not, the security is enforceable against the surety[104] only on an order of the court.[105] Service of a default notice on the debtor or hirer and on any third party security provider is required before the creditor may enforce any security regulated by the Act.[106] A security over land to which the Act applies is enforceable only on an order of the court.[107] Where an application to the court for an enforcement order is dismissed other than on technical grounds and in various other prescribed circumstances the security is treated as never having had effect.[108] The Act contains special provisions relating to pledges.[109] A creditor or owner is prohibited from taking a negotiable instrument as security for the discharge of any sum payable by the debtor or hirer under a regulated agreement or by any surety in relation to such an agreement.[110]

---

in a uniform manner across all regulated consumer credit agreements. The implementation into domestic law of the Consumer Credit Directive (2008/48/EC) (by way of statutory instruments and amendment to the 1974 Act and effective in full from February 1, 2011) has introduced a further layer of complexity into the regime; see further Ch.14.

[97] Consumer Credit (Agreements) Regulations 1983 (SI 1983/1553) regs 2(10), 3(7) and Consumer Credit (Agreements) Regulations 2010 (SI 2010/1014) reg.3(5).

[98] 1974 Act s.189(1), (4).

[99] Consumer Credit (Cancellation Notices and Copies of Documents) Regulations 1983 (SI 1983/1557). The creditor or owner is also obliged to provide certain specified information to the debtor or hirer in advance of the regulated agreement being executed; see 1974 Act s.55, the Consumer Credit (Disclosure of Information) Regulations 2004 (SI 2004/1481) and the Consumer Credit (Disclosure of Information) Regulations 2010 (SI 2010/1013). Note also the requirements in ss.55A–55C of the 1974 Act relating to the provision of pre-contractual information to the debtor, the assessment of the debtor's creditworthiness and the provision of a draft copy of the prospective consumer credit agreement to the debtor. Special provision is made for securities over land: Consumer Credit Act 1974 ss.58, 61.

[100] 1974 Act ss.61–65; for enforcement orders see s.127.

[101] 1974 Act s.113(2).

[102] See the definition of "security" in 1974 Act s.189(1).

[103] 1974 Act s.105(1). No regulations have been made prescribing the form of the documentation for real rights in security: the Consumer Credit (Guarantees and Indemnities) Regulations 1983 (SI 1983/1556) apply only to guarantees and indemnities: reg.2.

[104] "Surety" means the party providing the security (whether that is the debtor or hirer (as applicable) or a third party); see s.189(1).

[105] 1974 Act s.105(7); see s.127.

[106] 1974 Act ss.87, 111. Sections 86B–86E of the 1974 Act impose an obligation on the creditor or owner to serve notices in certain circumstances in respect of arrears and default sums; failure to comply with these requirements renders the agreement unenforceable during the period of non-compliance.

[107] 1974 Act s.126.

[108] 1974 Act ss.105(8), 106. There is a limited exception in favour of purchasers from heritable creditors who have the protection of s.41 of the Conveyancing (Scotland) Act 1924 and s.32 of the Conveyancing and Feudal Reform (Scotland) Act 1970: s.177.

[109] 1974 Act ss.114–122; see further below.

[110] 1974 Act s.123. There is an exception for consumer hire agreements made in connection with international or foreign trade where the hirer hires the goods in the course of business: Consumer Credit (Negotiable Instruments) (Exemption) Order 1984 (SI 1984/435).

II. HERITABLE SECURITIES[111]

36.08 **The standard security**[112]—Before 1970, rights in security in heritable property were created by means of a bond and disposition in security, a cash credit bond and disposition in security or an ex facie absolute disposition with back bond or letter.[113] While pre-1970 securities may continue to affect property,[114] since the coming into force of Pt II of the Conveyancing and Feudal Reform (Scotland) Act 1970 a grant of any right over land or a real right in land[115] for the purpose of securing any debt by way of a heritable security has only been capable of being effected by way of a standard security.[116] A standard security in one or other of the two prescribed forms[117] operates, upon recording in the General Register of Sasines or registration in the Land Register, to vest in the grantee a real right in security for performance of the contract to which the security relates.[118] Standard securities are regulated by the standard conditions set out in Sch.3 to the Conveyancing and Feudal Reform (Scotland) Act 1970 except insofar as those conditions have been competently varied.[119] The standard conditions, inter alia, oblige the debtor to maintain and repair the security subjects,[120] to comply with conditions and obligations imposed upon him in relation to the security subjects by virtue of his title thereto or under any enactment,[121] and to insure the security

---

[111] See generally J.M. Halliday, *Conveyancing Law and Practice*, edited by I.J.S Talman, 2nd edn (Edinburgh: W. Green, 1997), Vol.2, Pt VII; *Stair Memorial Encyclopaedia*, Vol.20, paras 108–272.

[112] See generally D.J. Cusine and R. Rennie, *Standard Securities*, 2nd edn (Bloomsbury Professional, 2002).

[113] On these forms of security see Halliday, *Conveyancing Law and Practice* (1997), Vol.2, Chs 47–49.

[114] Note that by s.69 of the Abolition of Feudal Tenure etc. (Scotland) Act 2000 the rules contained in ss.14–30 of the Conveyancing and Feudal Reform (Scotland) Act 1970—which relate to matters such as the assignation, variation, discharge and calling-up of standard securities—now apply to heritable securities granted before November 29, 1970.

[115] As originally enacted, s.9(3) referred to the grant of a right over "an interest in land". The change to the current wording was effected by the Abolition of Feudal Tenure etc. (Scotland) Act 2000 Sch.12 para.30. A standard security may be granted in respect of a pro indiviso right of ownership: *McLeod v Cedar Holdings Ltd*, 1989 S.L.T. 620.

[116] 1970 Act s.9(3), (4); but see para.36.10 for other forms of security over heritable property. It should be noted that by s.9(2B) of the 1970 Act, inserted by the Title Conditions (Scotland) Act 2003 s.128(1) and Sch.14 para.4(2)(a), it is not competent to grant a standard security over a personal pre-emption burden or a personal redemption burden.

[117] 1970 Act s.9(2), Sch.2. For the effect of certain clauses in the forms see s.10. The subjects require to be described sufficiently to identify them: Sch.2 note 1 (as amended by para.30(23)(a) of Sch.12 to the Abolition of Feudal Tenure etc. (Scotland) Act 2000). The note is deemed to have been originally enacted as amended: Abolition of Feudal Tenure etc. (Scotland) Act 2000 s.77(3), retrospectively over-ruling *Beneficial Bank Plc v McConnachie*, 1996 S.C. 119. If the security secures a regulated agreement under the Consumer Credit Act 1974, the requirements of that Act as to the form of documentation and procedure must also be complied with: see especially s.58.

[118] 1970 Act ss.9(2), 11(1); Land Registration (Scotland) Act 1979 s.2(3)(i). The creditor does not obtain a real right unless and until the standard security is registered or recorded; any doubt about this proposition created by *Sharp v Thomson*, 1997 S.C. (H.L.) 66 has been removed by *Burnett's Tr. v Grainger*, 2004 S.C. (HL) 19. A standard security granted by a company should also be registered in the register of charges kept by the Registrar of Companies, although this double registration requirement is likely to be removed by the making of an order under s.893 of the 2006 Act: see further above, para.36.06.

[119] 1970 Act s.11, Sch.3. The conditions providing for procedure on redemption and relating to the powers of sale and foreclosure and to the exercise of those powers may not be varied: s.11(3), (4).

[120] Standard Condition 1.

[121] Standard Conditions 3 and 4.

subjects.[122] They prohibit the debtor from altering any buildings which form part of the security subjects[123] and from letting the subjects[124] without the creditor's consent. The legislation provides for the assignation,[125] restriction,[126] variation[127] and discharge[128] of standard securities. The debtor or, where the debtor is not proprietor of the security subjects, the proprietor is entitled to redeem the security on giving two months' notice of his intention to do so.[129]

Creditors' remedies[130]—The Conveyancing and Feudal Reform (Scotland) Act 1970 makes three procedures available to heritable creditors.[131] **36.09**

(1) Calling-up. Where a creditor in a standard security intends to require discharge of the debt secured and, failing discharge, to exercise any power conferred by the security to sell the subjects or any other power which he may appropriately exercise on the failure of the debtor to comply with a calling-up notice, the creditor shall[132] serve a calling-up

---

[122] Standard Condition 5.

[123] Standard Condition 2.

[124] Standard Condition 6. A lease granted in breach of this condition may be reducible at the instance of the heritable creditor: *Trade Development Bank v Warriner & Mason (Scotland) Ltd*, 1980 S.C. 74; *Trade Development Bank v David W. Haig (Bellshill) Ltd*, 1983 S.L.T. 510; see K.G.C. Reid, "Real Conditions in Standard Securities", 1983 S.L.T. (News) 169, 189. This is subject, in the case of assured tenancies, to s.18 of the Housing (Scotland) Act 1988: *Tamroui v Clydesdale Bank Plc*, 1996 S.C.L.R. 732; *Cameron v Abbey National Plc* [1999] Hous. L.R. 19. See now s.152 of the Housing (Scotland) Act 2010 which puts the *Tamroui* case on a statutory footing by inter alia inserting s.24(10) into the Conveyancing and Feudal Reform (Scotland) Act 1970.

[125] 1970 Act s.14; *Sanderson's Trs v Ambion Scotland Ltd*, 1994 S.L.T. 645; Gretton, "Assignation of All Sums Standard Securities", 1994 S.L.T. (News) 207; *Watson v Bogue (No.1)*, 2000 S.L.T. (Sh. Ct) 125.

[126] 1970 Act s.15.

[127] 1970 Act s.16; *Sanderson's Trs v Ambion Scotland Ltd*, 1994 S.L.T. 645.

[128] 1970 Act s.17.

[129] 1970 Act s.18(1). The Act also provides specifically that the debtor may (subject to any agreement to the contrary) redeem without notice at any time after the expiry of any period stated in a notice of default but before conclusion by the heritable creditor of an enforceable contract for sale of the subjects: s.23(3).

[130] See generally M. Higgins, *The Enforcement of Heritable Securities* (Edinburgh: W. Green, 2010), although it is to be noted that this was published before the Supreme Court decision in *Royal Bank of Scotland Plc v Wilson* [2010] UKSC 50; 2011 S.C. (UKSC) 66 on which see below, fn.132.

[131] It would appear to be open to the parties to supplement these provisions by agreement: Halliday, *Conveyancing Law and Practice* (1997), paras 54–55; *David Watson Property Management v Woolwich Equitable Building Society*, 1990 S.L.T. 764 at 767, per Lord President Hope, affd 1992 S.C. (HL) 21; see e.g. *Clydesdale Bank Plc v A.G. Davidson*, 1993 S.C.L.R. 984. The heritable creditor may also proceed to enforce the personal obligation in the ordinary way. If the security secures a regulated agreement under the 1974 Act, it is enforceable only by order of the court: s.126 of the Act. For an attempt to prevent the creditor from exercising its powers see *Grantly Developments Ltd v Clydesdale Bank Plc*, 2000 G.W.D. 6–213.

[132] *Royal Bank of Scotland Plc v Wilson* [2010] UKSC 50; 2011 S.C. (UKSC) 66; prior to this decision it was thought that a creditor who was seeking the discharge and payment of the debt secured by a standard security had a free choice between which of the three enforcement routes (i.e. calling-up notice, notice of default or application to court) it preferred, but the Supreme Court in *Wilson* held that in such cases the creditor must proceed by way of a calling-up notice. The overall effect of *Wilson* is that, in practice, notices of default and s.24 court applications—which post-*Wilson* are only relevant in cases of non-monetary breach—are now of much less relevance to heritable creditors. However, in the case of standard securities over land used for residential purposes, the s.24 court application procedure is given an important role by the Home Owner and Debtor Protection (Scotland) Act 2010; see further below.

notice.[133] The form of notice requires full payment of the outstanding principal sum, interest and expenses within two months.[134] Where the calling-up notice indicates that any sum and any interest thereon due may be subject to adjustment in amount, the creditor is obliged to furnish the debtor, if requested to do so, with a statement of the amount as finally determined within a month from the service of the calling-up notice.[135] If the debtor fails to comply with the calling-up notice, thereby putting himself in default in terms of Standard Condition 9 (1)(a), the creditor is entitled to exercise such of his rights under the security as he may consider appropriate, including the right to sell the subjects.[136] The creditor's rights specified in Standard Condition 10 include: (1) the right to sell the subjects; (2) the right to enter into possession of the subjects; (3) the right to enter upon the subjects to effect repairs, make good defects and carry out such other works as would be expected of a prudent proprietor to maintain the market value of the subjects; and (4) the right to apply to the court for a decree of foreclosure. A calling-up notice ceases to have effect five years after its date or, where the subjects have been offered or exposed for sale, the date of the last offer or exposure.[137]

(2) Notice of default. Where the debtor is in default within the meaning of Standard Condition 9(1)(b)—namely that the debtor has failed to comply with any "other"[138] requirement arising out of the security—and the default is remediable the creditor may serve a notice calling on the debtor and on the proprietor of the subjects (if he is not the debtor) to purge the default.[139] The form of notice requires the default to be remedied within one month.[140] The person upon whom such a notice has been served may

---

[133] 1970 Act s.19(1). Provision is made for service in s.19(2)–(8); see also *Santander UK Plc v Gallagher*, 2011 S.L.T. (Sh. Ct) 203. As to whether the debt has to be due and resting owing before it may be called-up see *AIB Group (UK) Plc v Guarino*, 2006 S.L.T. (Sh. Ct) 138 and K.G.C. Reid and G.L. Gretton, *Conveyancing*, 3rd edn (2006), pp.114–16. Where the standard security is over land or a real right over land used to any extent for residential purposes the creditor must also serve a notice on the occupier in terms of s.19A of the 1970 Act (inserted by s.4(1) of the Mortgage Rights (Scotland) Act 2001). Failure to comply with this requirement results in the calling-up notice being of no effect: s.19A(3). See also the requirement to provide notice to the relevant local authority; s.19B of the 1970 Act (inserted by s.11(2) and Sch.1 para.1 of the Homelessness etc. (Scotland) Act 2003). If the security secures a regulated agreement under the 1974 Act, a default notice under that Act must be served: ss.87, 111. See also above, fn.106.
[134] 1970 Act Sch.6 Form A.
[135] 1970 Act s.19(9); *Bank of Scotland v Flett*, 1995 S.C.L.R. 591.
[136] 1970 Act s.20(1), (2). Where the standard security is over land or a real right in land used to any extent for residential purposes, the creditor is entitled to exercise those rights only where the conditions in s.20(2A) (as inserted into the 1970 Act by the Home Owner and Debtor Protection (Scotland) Act 2010 s.1(1)) are satisfied; see further below. It should also be noted that it is open for the debtor to challenge the calling-up notice itself: see *Gardiner v Jacques Vert Plc*, 2002 S.L.T. 928.
[137] 1970 Act s.19(11); *Bank of Scotland v Tait*, 2007 S.C. 731. See also s.19(12) of the 1970 Act, inserted by the Home Owner and Debtor Protection (Scotland) Act 2010 s.8(1)(c).
[138] The meaning of "other" is not clear from the terms of the 1970 Act itself but, following the Supreme Court decision in *Royal Bank of Scotland Plc v Wilson* [2010] UKSC 50; 2011 S.C. (UKSC) 66, it is to be understood as referring to non-monetary breaches; see above, fn.132.
[139] 1970 Act s.21(1). If the security secures a regulated agreement under the 1974 Act, a default notice under that Act must be served: ss.87, 111. See above, fn.106. A creditor who serves a notice of default under a standard security over land or a real right over land used to any extent for residential purposes is required to serve a notice on the occupier and the relevant local authority in terms of s.21(2A) of the 1970 Act (as inserted by s.4 of the Mortgage Rights (Scotland) Act 2001 and amended by s.11(2) and Sch.1 para.3 of the Homelessness etc. (Scotland) Act 2003).
[140] 1970 Act Sch.6 Form B.

object to the notice by application to the court.[141] If no objection is made or the notice has been upheld or varied by the court the person upon whom the notice has been served is under a duty to comply with any requirement in the notice.[142] If he does not do so the creditor may enter upon the subjects to effect repairs, make good defects and carry out such other works as would be expected of a prudent proprietor to maintain the market value of the subjects, and may proceed to sell the subjects and apply for a decree of foreclosure.[143]

(3) Application to the court. Where the debtor is in default within the meaning of Standard Condition 9(1)(b)—namely that the debtor has failed to comply with any "other"[144] requirement arising out of the security—or Standard Condition 9(1)(c)—namely that the proprietor of the subjects has become insolvent[145]—the creditor may apply to the court for warrant to exercise any of the remedies which he would be entitled to exercise on failure to comply with a calling-up notice.[146] The court has no discretion to refuse such a warrant once it is satisfied that the creditor is entitled to the remedy.[147]

The enforcement of standard securities granted over land or a real right in land which is used to any extent for residential purposes is now controlled by the provisions of the Home Owner and Debtor Protection (Scotland) Act 2010, which operates to introduce important amendments to the 1970 Act. Controls on a creditor's right to enforce a standard security over property used for residential purposes were previously introduced by the Mortgage Rights (Scotland) Act 2001. The approach of the 2001 Act was, in broad terms, to give the proprietor (and other specified parties) a right to apply to court to suspend the enforcement of the standard security by the creditor. The 2010 Act has revised the approach—and much of the 2001 Act has therefore been repealed[148]—by giving proprietors

---

[141] 1970 Act s.22.

[142] 1970 Act s.23(1).

[143] 1970 Act s.23(2), Standard Conditions 10(2), (6) and (7). Where the standard security is over land or a real right in land used to any extent for residential purposes, the creditor is entitled to exercise the right to sell the property only where the conditions in s.23(4) (as inserted into the 1970 Act by the Home Owner and Debtor Protection (Scotland) Act 2010 s.1(2)) are satisfied; see further below.

[144] See above, fn.138.

[145] *United Dominions Trust Ltd v Site Preparations Ltd (No.1)*, 1978 S.L.T. (Sh. Ct) 14; *United Dominions Trust Ltd v Site Preparations Ltd (No.2)*, 1978 S.L.T. (Sh. Ct) 21.

[146] 1970 Act s.24(1). This does not apply to a creditor in a standard security over land or a real right in land used to any extent for residential purposes; s.24(1A). Such a creditor may, where the debtor is in default within the meaning of paragraph (a), (b) or (c) of Standard Condition 9(1), apply to the court by summary application for warrant to exercise any of the remedies which he would be entitled to exercise on a default within the meaning of Standard Condition 9(1)(a) but only where the creditor has first complied with the pre-action requirements imposed by s.24A of the 1970 Act; see s.24(1B)–(1D) as inserted by the Home Owner and Debtor Protection (Scotland) Act 2010 s.2(2). Where a creditor makes such an application to the court in respect of a standard security over residential property, he must serve notice of the application on various parties in accordance with s.24(3) of the 1970 Act (as amended).

If the security secures a regulated agreement under the 1974 Act, a default notice under that Act must be served: ss.87, 111; see also above fn.106; for the procedure when the debtor has been sequestrated see *Abbey National Plc v Arthur (No.2)*, 2000 S.L.T. 103.

[147] *Halifax Building Society v Gupta*, 1994 S.C. 13; for discussion see T. Guthrie, "Controlling Creditors' Rights under Standard Securities", 1994 S.L.T. (News) 93.

[148] Although most of the notice requirements set out in s.4 of the Mortgage Rights (Scotland) Act 2001 remain (as amended by s.8(4)(b) of the 2010 Act)—see above fnn.133 and 139.

an automatic layer of protection by obliging creditors to take the matter to court for shrieval scrutiny. Previously, it was possible for the creditor to avoid going to court by choosing to enforce by way of the calling-up notice or notice of default procedure. This has been changed by the 2010 Act so that in all such cases enforcement must—with one exception[149]—proceed by way of an application to the court under section 24.[150] Prior to making an application under s.24, a heritable creditor is required to comply with certain pre-action requirements.[151] Calling-up notices are not, however, redundant. The combined effect of the amendments to the 1970 Act effected by the 2010 Act and the decision in *Royal Bank of Scotland Plc v Wilson*[152] is that in the majority of cases where a standard security over residential property is being enforced, the heritable creditor must both serve a calling up notice (as required by *Wilson*) and apply to the court (as required by those amendments).

Through complying with the relevant rules and procedures of the 1970 Act, a creditor may become entitled to take possession of the subjects secured by the standard security held by him. However, if the proprietor of the subjects refuses to leave the subjects, the creditor will need to obtain a warrant to eject. To obtain that warrant to eject, it is not enough for a creditor to show that he has complied with the 1970 Act rules and procedures; he must also comply with the requirements of s.5 of the Heritable Securities (Scotland) Act 1894 which provides that a creditor may only take proceedings to eject the proprietor where the proprietor has made default in the punctual payment of the interest due under the security or in due payment of the principal after formal requisition.[153]

If the creditor enters into possession of the subjects, all rights and obligations of the proprietor relating to leases or other rights of occupancy, and the management and maintenance of the subjects are deemed to be assigned to the creditor.[154] The creditor is entitled to receive the rents.[155] He is empowered to let the subjects.[156] Once one heritable creditor has entered into possession it would be a wrong for another heritable creditor to attempt to do so.[157] A creditor who has the right to sell the subjects may exercise that right by private bargain or by exposure to sale,[158] but in either event it is the creditor's duty to advertise the sale and to take all reasonable steps to ensure that the price is the best that can be reasonably

---

[149] The exception is where the security subjects are unoccupied and voluntarily surrendered; see ss.20(2A)(a), 23(4)(a)(i) and 23A of the 1970 Act.

[150] See ss.20(2A)(b), 23(4)(b) and 24(1A) and (1B) of the 1970 Act.

[151] See ss.24(1C) and 24A of the 1970 Act and the Applications by Creditors (Pre-Action Requirements) (Scotland) Order 2010 (SSI 2010/317).

[152] *Royal Bank of Scotland Plc v Wilson* [2010] UKSC 50; 2011 S.C. (UKSC) 66; see above, fn.132 and G. Gretton, "Upsetting the Apple-Cart: Standard Securities before the Supreme Court" (2011) 15 Edin. L.R. 251.

[153] *Royal Bank of Scotland Plc v Wilson* [2010] UKSC 50; 2011 S.C. (UKSC) 66. It is to be noted however that the serving of a calling-up notice—which, following *Wilson*, will in practice be the applicable procedure in the majority of cases (see above, fn.132)—suffices as a "formal requisition"; see *Royal Bank of Scotland Plc v Wilson* [2010] UKSC 50, per Lord Hope at [59].

[154] 1970 Act s.20(5), Standard Condition 10(5); *David Watson Property Management v Woolwich Equitable Building Society*, 1992 S.C. (HL) 21; *U.C.B. Bank Plc v Hire Foulis Ltd (in liquidation)*, 1999 S.C. 250.

[155] Standard Condition 10(3); *U.C.B. Bank Plc v Hire Foulis Ltd (in liquidation)*, 1999 S.C. 250.

[156] Standard Condition 10(4). Any lease of more than seven years' duration must be authorised by the court: 1970 Act s.20(3), (4).

[157] *Skipton Building Society v Wain*, 1986 S.L.T. 96.

[158] Subject to ss.37(5)(e) and 40(1) of the Land Reform (Scotland) Act 2003, which prohibit the transfer of land registered under that Act except in accordance with its provisions.

obtained.[159] The debtor or the proprietor of the security subjects is entitled to redeem the security at any time prior to the conclusion by the creditor of an enforceable contract to sell the subjects.[160] The proceeds of sale are held by the creditor in trust to be applied by him, after payment of his expenses,[161] to payment of the amounts due under any prior security, in payment of the amount due under his own security and any security ranking pari passu with his own security, and in payment of any amounts due under postponed securities.[162] Any residue falls to be paid to the person entitled to the security subjects at the time of sale or to any person authorised to give receipts for the proceeds of sale.[163] Where the heritable creditor has exposed the subjects to sale[164] at a price not exceeding the amount due under the security and any prior or pari passu ranking security, and has failed to find a purchaser, or where, having so failed, he has succeeded in selling only a part of the subjects at a price less than the amount so due, he may apply to the court for decree of foreclosure.[165] Decree of foreclosure declares that the creditor has right to the subjects or any unsold part thereof at the price at which they were last exposed to sale under deduction of the price received for any part sold.[166] On recording of an extract of the decree of foreclosure any right to redeem the security is extinguished, the creditor is vested in the subjects as if he had received a disposition from the owner and the subjects are disburdened of the standard security.[167] The personal obligation of the debtor remains in effect except to the extent that it is reduced by the price at which the creditor has acquired the subjects and the price for which any part of the subjects has been sold.[168]

It has been said that the heritable creditor should exercise his powers civiliter and with proper regard to the interests of the debtor,[169] although it appears that it would only be in unusual cases that the court would intervene to control the creditor's exercise of those powers.[170]

---

[159] 1970 Act s.25; see *Dick v Clydesdale Bank Plc*, 1991 S.C. 365; *Bisset v Standard Property Investment* Unreported July 8, 1999, Lord Hamilton; *Davidson v Clydesdale Bank Plc*, 2002 S.L.T. 1088; *Kensington Mortgage Co v Robertson*, 2004 S.C.L.R. 312 (Notes); *Wilson v Dunbar Bank Plc*, 2006 S.L.T. 775. On the quantification of damages for breach of this duty and the interest thereon see *Wilson v Dunbar Bank Plc*, 2008 S.C. 457. It has been held that it is incompetent for the debtor to interdict the creditor from concluding or implementing missives which are alleged to breach the creditor's obligations under s.25: *Associated Displays Ltd v Turnbeam Ltd*, 1988 S.C.L.R. 220; *Gordivoran Ltd v Clydesdale Bank Plc*, 1994 S.C.L.R. 248; but see *Kerr v McArthur's Trs* (1848) 11 D. 301.

[160] 1970 Act ss.18, 23(3); *G. Dunlop & Sons' JF v Armstrong*, 1994 S.L.T. 199.

[161] The expenses must be "properly incurred" by the creditor; see s.27(1)(a) and *Royal Bank of Scotland Plc v Kinnear*, 2005 Hous. L.R. 2 (Sh. Ct).

[162] It has been held that "securities" in this context includes inhibitions: *Halifax Building Society v Smith*, 1985 S.L.T. (Sh. Ct) 25; but see for the contrary view *Alliance & Leicester Building Society v Hecht*, 1991 S.C.L.R. 562; G.L. Gretton, *The Law of Inhibition and Adjudication*, 2nd edn (Edinburgh: LexisNexis, 1996), pp.140–150.

[163] 1970 Act s.27.

[164] On the meaning of this phrase see D. Cusine, "The Creditor's Remedies Under a Standard Security" (1998) 3 S.L.P.Q. 79, 84.

[165] 1970 Act s.28.

[166] 1970 Act s.28(5).

[167] 1970 Act s.28(6).

[168] 1970 Act s.28(7).

[169] *Armstrong v G Dunlop & Son's J.F.*, 1988 S.L.T. 255.

[170] *Halifax Building Society v Gupta*, 1994 S.C. 13.

36.10 Other forms of security over heritable property—A company[171] may grant a floating charge over, inter alia, its heritable property.[172] Such a charge need not be registered in the property registers.[173] The provisions of the Insolvency Act 1986 in relation to winding up have effect as if the floating charge were a fixed security over the property to which it has attached.[174] Local authorities have power to create charges over heritable property in their own favour in respect of expenses incurred by them under certain statutory provisions.[175]

36.11 Ranking

(1) Standard securities *inter se*. Subject to any express agreement as to ranking,[176] standard securities rank inter se according to the date of recording or registration.[177]

(2) Standard securities and floating charges. In the absence of an express ranking agreement or a provision in the floating charge prohibiting or restricting the creation of any fixed security having priority over or ranking pari passu with the floating charge,[178] a standard security which has been constituted as a real right by recording or registration before crystallisation of a floating charge ranks ahead of the floating charge irrespective of the respective dates of the floating charge and the standard security.[179] The position is to change under the Bankruptcy and Diligence etc. (Scotland) Act 2007.[180] Section 40, which is not in force at the time of writing, provides that floating charges are to rank with other securities, whether fixed[181] or floating, by date of creation.[182] Section 41 will permit security holders to depart from these default rules and agree how the securities are to rank. A receiver has power to sell the property subject to the security with the consent of the heritable creditor or warrant of the court.[183]

(3) Statutory charges. Statutory charges over land rank in accordance with any provisions in the relevant statute.[184]

(4) Standard securities and adjudications. The general rule is that adjudgers and heritable creditors rank according to the respective dates of recording

---

[171] And certain other commercial entities; see above, para.36.05.

[172] Companies Act 1985 s.462: see paras 36.05, 36.33–36.34. This provision is to be repealed by the Bankruptcy and Diligence etc. (Scotland) Act 2007; for the equivalent provision under the 2007 Act see s.38 (not in force at the time of writing).

[173] Companies Act 1985 s.462(5). See above, para.36.06, regarding the new Register of Floating Charges to be established under the Bankruptcy and Diligence etc. (Scotland) Act 2007.

[174] Companies Act 1985 s.463(2). The equivalent provision in the Bankruptcy and Diligence etc. (Scotland) Act 2007, not in force at the time of writing, is s.45(5).

[175] Civic Government (Scotland) Act 1982 s.108; Housing (Scotland) Act 1987 s.131(2), Sch.9.

[176] e.g. *Alloa Brewery Co Ltd v Investors in Industry Plc*, 1992 S.L.T. 121.

[177] Stair IV, 35, 8; Land Registration (Scotland) Act 1979 s.7.

[178] Companies Act 1985 s.464(1), (1A). In practice, such a provision is known as a "negative pledge"; see further D. Cabrelli, "Negative Pledges and Ranking Reconsidered" (2002) 7 S.L.P.Q. 18, 18.

[179] Companies Act 1985 s.464(4).

[180] The 2007 Act creates a default law which is in line with current standard practice on ranking provisions.

[181] Standard securities being a fixed security; see above, para.36.05.

[182] The date of creation of a fixed security is the date on which the right to the security is constituted as a real right (see s.40(3)(a) of the 2007 Act). For the current rule as to the date of creation of a floating charge, and the change to be effected by the 2007 Act, see above, para.36.06.

[183] Insolvency Act 1986 (the "1986 Act") s.61. An administrator has a similar power; see below, para.36.36.

[184] *Sowman v City of Glasgow DC*, 1985 S.L.T. 65.

in the property registers.[185] However, a security granted after the adjudging creditor has recorded a notice of litigiosity in the Register of Inhibitions and Adjudications[186] cannot prejudice the adjudging creditor's preference provided there is no undue delay in completion of the diligence.[187]

(5) Standard securities and inhibitions.[188] A standard security voluntarily granted after an inhibition takes effect[189] is reducible at the instance of the inhibiting creditor.[190] A security granted before (or pursuant to an obligation incurred before) the inhibition is unaffected by it, except perhaps in relation to future advances.[191] The extent to which a post-security inhibition could have a preference in the proceeds of sale of the security subjects was the subject of conflicting authority.[192] The position is now controlled by s.154 of the Bankruptcy and Diligence etc. (Scotland) Act 2007 which provides that an inhibition does not confer any preference in any sequestration, insolvency proceeding[193] or any other process in which there is ranking. This includes the process, under s.27(1) of the 1970 Act, of applying the proceeds of sale where a creditor in a standard security has effected a sale of the security subjects.[194] This rule does not affect any process where the inhibition has taken effect before the date on which s.154 came into force, being April 22, 2009.[195]

(6) Standard securities and insolvency regimes. Sequestration and liquidation do not affect a standard security which has been constituted as a real right. The trustee in sequestration or liquidator is entitled to sell property subject to a standard security, but may do so only with the consent of the heritable creditor unless he achieves a price sufficient to discharge every

---

[185] Stair, IV, 35, 8.

[186] Titles to Land Consolidation (Scotland) Act 1868 s.159 (as amended by s.164(1) of the Bankruptcy and Diligence etc. (Scotland) Act 2007) and Sch.(RR).

[187] Stair, IV, 35, 8. Under the Bankruptcy and Diligence etc. (Scotland) Act 2007, the relevant provisions of which are not yet in force, adjudication will be abolished and replaced by a new diligence to be known as land attachment. On creation, the land attachment will confer a subordinate real right on the creditor (s.81(5)). As to the ranking of a land attachment with a standard security, see the new s.13A to the 1970 Act to be inserted by s.85 of the 2007 Act. The Register of Inhibitions and Adjudications shall also be renamed the Register of Inhibitions; s.80 of the 2007 Act.

[188] See Gretton, *The Law of Inhibition and Adjudication* (1996), Ch.9.

[189] An inhibition generally takes effect from the beginning of the day on which it is registered in the Register of Inhibitions and Adjudications (to be renamed the Register of Inhibitions when s.80 of the Bankruptcy and Diligence etc. (Scotland) Act 2007 comes into force); s.155(1) of the Titles to Land Consolidation (Scotland) Act 1868 as substituted by s.149 of the 2007 Act. In circumstances where a notice of inhibition is registered, the schedule of inhibition is served on the debtor after the notice of inhibition is registered and the inhibition is registered within 21 days of the registration of that notice, the inhibition takes effect from the beginning of the day on which the schedule of inhibition is served; s.155(2), (3) of the Titles to Land Consolidation (Scotland) Act 1868 as substituted by s.149 of the 2007 Act.

[190] Stair, IV, 50, 11, 18–19 and Bankruptcy and Diligence etc. (Scotland) Act 2007 s.160.

[191] See Gretton, *The Law of Inhibition and Adjudication* (1996), pp.150–4.

[192] See Gretton, *The Law of Inhibition and Adjudication* (1996), pp.141–50.

[193] "Insolvency proceedings" is defined as meaning (a) winding up, (b) receivership, (c) administration and (d) proceedings in relation to a company voluntary arrangement within the meaning of the 1986 Act; s.154(4) of the 2007 Act.

[194] Bankruptcy and Diligence etc. (Scotland) Act 2007 s.154(3).

[195] Bankruptcy and Diligence etc. (Scotland) Act 2007 s.154(2) and the Bankruptcy and Diligence etc. (Scotland) Act 2007 (Commencement No. 4, Savings and Transitionals) Order 2009 (SSI 2009/67).

heritable security.[196] During the period a company is in administration, no steps may be taken by the heritable creditor to enforce the standard security except with consent of the administrator or leave of the court.[197] The administrator may be empowered by the court to dispose of property subject to a standard security.[198]

(7) Notice of subsequent security or transfer. Where the creditor in a prior standard security receives notice[199] of the creation of a subsequent security over the same subjects or the subsequent transfer of the subjects, the creditor's preference in ranking is (subject to any ranking agreement) restricted to security for his present advances and any future advances which he may be required to make under the contract to which the security relates together with interest and expenses.[200]

III. SECURITIES OVER CORPOREAL MOVEABLE PROPERTY

36.12 General[201]—Securities over corporeal moveable property may be granted expressly (conventional securities) or arise by operation of law (legal or tacit securities). They may be dependent for their constitution and existence on the goods being in the possession of the creditor (possessory securities) or may be capable of arising while the goods are in the possession of their owner, the debtor or some third party (hypothecs). The ordinary conventional security over corporeal moveables at common law is pledge. Pledge is a possessory security.[202] The common law also recognises that a legal possessory security or lien may arise in certain recognised circumstances.[203] The only conventional hypothecs over corporeal moveable property recognised at common law are bonds of bottomry and respondentia,[204] but statute has created additional non-possessory securities, notably the floating charge[205] and ship[206] and aircraft[207] mortgages. A small number of legal hypothecs are accepted in Scots law. The landlord of certain types of subjects[208] has a hypothec which arises by operation of law to secure

---

[196] Bankruptcy (Scotland) Act 1985 s.39; 1986 Act s.169(2) and r.4.22(5) of the Insolvency (Scotland) Rules 1986 (SI 1986/1915).

[197] 1986 Act Sch.B1 para.43(2). See s.11(3) of the 1986 Act for the equivalent provision for administrations under the pre-Enterprise Act 2002 procedure. Generally on the 2002 Act, see below, para.36.34.

[198] 1986 Act Sch.B1 para.71. See s.15(2), (5), (6) of the 1986 Act for the equivalent provision for administrations under the pre-Enterprise Act 2002 procedure. Generally on the 2002 Act, see below, para.36.34.

[199] As to which see the 1970 Act s.13(2).

[200] the 1970 Act s.13; see generally Halliday, *Conveyancing Law and Practice* (1997), Vol.2, para. 51–20.

[201] Note that the Scottish Law Commission is currently engaged in a review of this area; see *Discussion Paper on Moveable Transactions* (HMSO, 2011), Scot. Law Com. DP No.151.

[202] See paras 36.13–36.14. See generally, A.J.M. Steven, *Pledge and Lien* (Edinburgh: Edinburgh Legal Educational Trust, 2008).

[203] See paras 36.15–36.26.

[204] See para.36.27, below.

[205] See paras 36.05, 36.33–36.34 below; the agricultural charge is also a conventional hypothec.

[206] See para.36.27, below.

[207] Civil Aviation Act 1982 s.86; Mortgaging of Aircraft Order 1972 (SI 1972/1268).

[208] The restriction on the applicability of the landlord's hypothec provided for in the Hypothec Abolition (Scotland) Act 1880 has now been repealed; s.226 and Sch.6 of the Bankruptcy and Diligence etc. (Scotland) Act 2007. The position is now controlled by s.208(3) of the Bankruptcy and Diligence etc. (Scotland) Act 2007 (which came into force on April 1, 2008) which provides that the

payment of all rent due and unpaid[209] over moveable items brought onto the subjects.[210] The landlord's hypothec was previously enforced by the process of sequestration for rent, but sequestration for rent was abolished by the Bankruptcy and Diligence etc. (Scotland) Act 2007[211] and the correct procedure for enforcing the landlord's hypothec is now uncertain.[212] There are a number of recognised maritime hypothecs.[213] The court may grant a solicitor a charge (which is of the nature of a hypothec) to secure payment of his expenses over corporeal moveables which he has recovered or preserved for his client.[214] The superior's hypothec in respect of feuduty was abolished along with the feudal system.[215]

Pledge—The constitution of a pledge in general requires the conjunction of: (1) an intention on the part of the owner[216] of the goods pledged to grant the pledge; and (2) delivery of the goods pledged to the creditor.[217] Delivery may be actual, constructive or symbolic. **36.13**

(1) Actual delivery. In general, where the debtor himself has possession of the goods, they must be actually delivered to the creditor or his agent or to a carrier or custodier holding the goods for and subject to the order of the creditor. But where barrels in the yard of a company were enclosed by a fence and the key of its gate was given to the creditor, it was held that the security had been completed by delivery.[218]

(2) Constructive delivery. If the goods are in the custody of a third party (such as a warehouse-keeper) who holds them for or to the order of the owner, the owner can effect constructive delivery by instructing the third party to hold them for or to the order of the creditor.[219] The following conditions must be met for a real right to be created by this method. (1) Intimation of the instruction must be made to the third party. Thus, the

---

landlord's hypothec does not arise in relation to property which is kept in a dwellinghouse, on agricultural land or on a croft.

[209] s.208(8) of the Bankruptcy and Diligence etc. (Scotland) Act 2007. This replaces the common law position which was that the landlord's hypothec secured one year's rent, including future rent. The 2007 Act removes the future rent element but does extend the scope of the security to cover all arrears and not just one year's rent.

[210] s.208(4) of the Bankruptcy and Diligence etc. (Scotland) Act 2007 changed the previous common law position so that the landlord's hypothec no longer arises in relation to property which is owned by a person other than the tenant.

[211] Bankruptcy and Diligence etc. (Scotland) Act 2007 s.208(1).

[212] See McAllister, "The Landlord's Hypothec: Down but is it Out?", 2010 Jur. Rev. 65 and Skea and Steven, "The Landlord's Hypothec: Difficulties in Practice", 2010 S.L.T. (News) 120.

[213] See para.36.27, below.

[214] Solicitors (Scotland) Act 1980 s.62.

[215] Abolition of Feudal Tenure etc. (Scotland) Act 2000 s.13(3).

[216] A pledge granted by a mercantile agent who is, with the consent of the owner, in possession of goods or the documents of title to goods, and who acts in the ordinary course of business of a mercantile agent, to a pledgee who takes the goods in good faith is as valid as if the agent had been expressly authorised by the owner to grant the pledge: Factors Act 1889 s.2; Factors (Scotland) Act 1890. Likewise a pledge by the seller of goods or his mercantile agent, who remains in possession of the goods or the documents of title to them after the sale, or by the buyer of goods or his mercantile agent where he has obtained, with the consent of the seller, possession of the goods or of the documents of title to them to a bona fide pledgee is effective: Sale of Goods Act 1979 ss.24, 25; Factors Act 1889 ss.8, 9.

[217] *Moore v Gledden* (1869) 7 M. 1016. It has been suggested that if the goods are so situated that any form of delivery is impossible, as in the case of pipes sunk into the ground, an assignation in writing would be effectual in the event of the borrower's bankruptcy: *Darling v Wilson's Tr.* (1887) 15 R. 180.

[218] *West Lothian Oil Co Liquidator v Mair* (1892) 20 R. 64; *Pattison's Trs v Liston* (1893) 20 R. 806.

[219] *Pochin & Co v Robinow* (1869) 7 M. 622.

indorsation and delivery to the creditor of a warrant granted by a warehouse-keeper that he holds the goods to the order of the debtor and his assignees does not give the creditor a real right in security unless and until intimation is made to the warehouse-keeper.[220] The theory of the law is that the warehouse-keeper, upon intimation, ceases to hold the goods as custodier for the grantor, and holds them subsequently as custodier for the grantee. (2) Intimation must be made to the actual custodier, the keeper of the store where the goods are. It is not sufficient to intimate to a party, for instance, an excise officer in a bonded store, who may have control of the goods but is not the keeper of the store.[221] (3) The custodier must be an independent third party, not the servant of the owner of the goods.[222] The law does not recognise constructive delivery by means of orders addressed by the owner of goods to the keeper of his own store.[223] (4) The goods must be ascertained, so that those referred to in the delivery order may be distinguished from the general bulk of goods kept by the transferor in the particular store. So, where there were a number of bags of flour in a store, with no marks whereby one bag could be distinguished from another, a delivery order for a certain number of bags, though intimated to the storekeeper and entered by him in the store books, did not effect constructive delivery, because there was no means of determining which bags were transferred and which were not.[224] In such a case, however, if the goods are subsequently ascertained by being physically separated from the general mass, they are constructively delivered at the date when they are so ascertained.[225]

(3) Symbolic delivery. A bill of lading is a symbol of the goods and its transfer, in pursuance either of a sale or of a pledge of the goods to which it refers, has the same effect as delivery of the goods themselves.[226]

It has been said, on the authority of *Hamilton v Western Bank of Scotland*,[227] that the constitution of a pledge requires actual possession and custody of goods to be given to the creditor.[228] In *Hamilton*, it was held that intimation of a delivery order transferred ownership in the goods rather than a mere right in security. But the proposition has been controverted[229] and appears to be inconsistent with later House of Lords authority.[230]

---

[220] *Inglis v Robertson & Baxter* (1898) 25 R. (HL) 70.

[221] *Rhind's Tr. v Robertson & Baxter* (1891) 18 R. 623; see also *Dobell v Neilson* (1904) 7 F. 281.

[222] *Anderson v McCall* (1866) 4 M. 765.

[223] *Anderson v McCall* (1866) 4 M. 765; *Pochin & Co v Robinow* (1869) 7 M. 622.

[224] *Hayman v McLintock*, 1907 S.C. 936; contrast *Price & Pierce v Bank of Scotland*, 1910 S.C. 1095; 1912 S.C. (HL) 19.

[225] *Black v Incorporation of Bakers* (1867) 6 M. 136; *Pochin & Co v Robinow* (1869) 7 M. 622.

[226] Gloag and Irvine, *Rights in Security* (1897), pp.274–5; *North-Western Bank Ltd v Poynter, Son and MacDonalds* (1894) 22 R. (HL) 1.

[227] *Hamilton v Western Bank of Scotland* (1856) 19 D. 152; see also *Mackinnon v Max Nanson & Co* (1868) 6 M. 974; *Hayman v McLintock*, 1907 S.C. 936.

[228] *Stair Memorial Encyclopaedia*, Vol.20, para.18.

[229] Bell, *Commentaries*, II, 21 (note by McLaren). Gloag and. Irvine, *Rights in Security* (1897), pp.256–7; consider also Factors Act 1889 s.3 and *Inglis v Robertson & Baxter* (1898) 25 R. (HL) 70.

[230] *North-Western Bank Ltd v Poynter, Son and MacDonalds* (1894) 21 R. 513; see A. Rodger, "Pledge of Bills of Lading", 1971 Jur. Rev. 193; G. Gretton, "Pledge, Bills of Lading, Trusts and Property Law", 1990 Jur. Rev. 23; and D.L. Carey Miller with D. Irvine, *Corporeal Moveables in Scots Law*, 2nd edn (Edinburgh: W. Green, 2005), para.11.07. The reasoning in *Moore v Gledden* (1869) 7 M. 1016 would also appear to be at odds with the general proposition referred to.

Various attempts to avoid the practical inconvenience of the delivery requirement have failed. When it was attempted to complete a right in security over the moveable machinery in a mill by stopping the mill and going through a form of taking sasine of both the mill and the machinery, it was held that delivery of the machinery had not been effected.[231] The placing of labels bearing the name of the lender on machinery has been said not of itself to be enough.[232] A sale of standing trees was followed by cutting and removing a few of them with a written minute declaring that the purchaser had thereby "entered into his bargain". It was held that the trees were not delivered, and passed to the trustee in the seller's sequestration.[233] The provisions of the Sale of Goods Act 1979 (which allow ownership of goods to be transferred pursuant to a contract of sale without delivery) do not apply to a transaction in the form of a contract of sale which is intended to operate by way of security.[234] But a transaction which is in fact a sale may not be objectionable merely because it may have the practical effect (or indeed ulterior motive) of security.[235] Proposals for reform of the law, which would allow a fixed security to be obtained over corporeal moveables without transfer of possession, have not been implemented.[236]

In the absence of agreement to the contrary, at common law the pledgee has in general no right to use the pledge[237] or to sell it without the authority of the court.[238] The pledge is extinguished if the pledgee gives up or loses possession of the goods. But this does not prevent him from leaving or placing the goods in the custody of some other person, through whom the pledgee remains in civil possession. There is authority to the effect that the real right of pledge cannot be held by the pledgee by mere civil possession through the owner.[239] But goods (such as tools and building materials) brought onto a building site by the contractor may be held to be pledged to the owner of the site in terms of a provision in the building contract, even though the goods remain in the custody of their owner, the contractor, the owner of the site having possession of goods brought onto his land pursuant to such a contract.[240] And a bill of lading which has been pledged may be returned to the pledgor so that the latter may sell the goods as the pledgee's agent.[241]

---

[231] *Stiven v Cowan* (1878) 15 S.L.R. 422.

[232] *Orr's Trs v Tullis* (1870) 8 M. 936.

[233] *Paul v Cuthbertson* (1840) 2 D. 1286.

[234] Sale of Goods Act 1979 s.62(4); see e.g. *Robertson v Hall's Tr.* (1896) 24 R. 120; *Gavin's Tr. v Fraser*, 1920 S.C. 674; *Scottish Transit Trust v Scottish Land Cultivators*, 1955 S.C. 254; S.C. Styles, "Debtor to Creditor Sales and the Sale of Goods Act 1979", 1995 Jur. Rev. 365.

[235] *Gavin's Tr. v Fraser*, 1920 S.C. 674. See also *Union Bank v Mackenzie* (1865) 3 M. 765; *Duncanson v Jefferis* (1881) 8 R. 563; *Orr's Tr. v Tullis* (1870) 8 M. 936.

[236] A.L. Diamond, *A Review of Security Interests in Property* (Department of Trade and Industry, 1989). See also Department of Trade and Industry, *Security over Moveable Property in Scotland: A Consultation Paper* (1994). Research has raised doubts about whether legislative reform in this area is required; see Scottish Executive Central Research Unit, *Business Finance and Security Over Moveable Property* (2002), especially para.4.10. See further Carey Miller with Irvine, *Corporeal Moveables in Scots Law* (2005), para.11.18. See now the Scottish Law Commission's *Discussion Paper on Moveable Transactions*, especially Ch.10.

[237] Bell, *Principles*, s.1364; *Wolifson v Harrison*, 1977 S.C. 384; for an example of a pledge with an express power to use the subjects see *Moore v Gledden* (1869) 7 M. 1016.

[238] Bell, *Principles*, s.1364; for pledges governed by the 1974 Act, see para.36.14, below.

[239] Bell, *Principles*, s.1364; Bell, *Commentaries*, II, 22.

[240] *Moore v Gledden* (1870) 8 M. 1016.

[241] *North-Western Bank v Poynter, Son & MacDonalds* (1894) 22 R. (HL) 1.

36.14 Pledges governed by the Consumer Credit Act 1974—The Consumer Credit Act 1974 contains provisions[242] applicable to pledges ("pawns") under a regulated agreement.[243] The provisions only apply to agreements made by the creditor in the course of a business carried on by him,[244] to pledges of documents of title[245] or of bearer bonds.[246] At the time when he receives the pawn the creditor is obliged to give the pawnor a receipt in a prescribed form (a "pawn receipt").[247] The pawn receipt may be incorporated in the regulated agreement itself[248] or may be issued separately.[249] The pawn is redeemable until the latest of (a) six months after the pawn was taken, (b) the period agreed by the parties for the duration of the credit, or such longer period as they may agree, and (c) the realisation of the pawn by the pawnee under s.121 of the 1974 Act or the passing of the property to the pawnee under s.120(1)(a).[250] On surrender of the pawn receipt and payment of the amount owing, the pawnee must deliver the pawn to the bearer of the pawn-receipt unless he knows or should suspect that the bearer is neither the owner nor authorised by the owner to redeem the pledge.[251] Provision is made for loss of the pawn receipt.[252] If at the end of the redemption period the pawn has not been redeemed, the pawn becomes realisable by the pawnee or (if the redemption period is six months, the pawn is security for not more than £75 credit and the pawn was not immediately before the making of the regulated consumer credit agreement a pawn under another regulated consumer credit agreement in respect of which the debtor has discharged his indebtedness in part under s.94(3) of the 1974 Act) property in the pawn passes to the pawnee.[253]

36.15 Lien[254]—A lien is a right to retain property until some debt or other obligation is satisfied. If constituted by express contract it is a pledge under another name, and it is only liens implied by law that need be considered here.

"Lien" and "right of retention" are sometimes used as synonymous terms, but, more strictly, a lien is a subordinate real right founded on mere possession, retention a right founded on ownership. A lien is a right to remain in possession of a subject until the owner of the subject fulfils the obligation or obligations he owes to the party in possession; a right of retention is the right of a person, who has ownership of property subject to an obligation to convey, to refuse to implement his obligation until some counter-obligation due by the party entitled to demand conveyance has been fulfilled. In what follows lien is taken in its more restricted sense as a right founded on possession of property belonging to another.

---

[242] 1974 Act ss.114–122.
[243] 1974 Act Sch.3 para.39, as amended by Consumer Credit Act 1974 (Commencement No.8) Order 1983 (SI 1983/1551) reg.3(a)(ii).
[244] 1974 Act ss.114(3)(b), 189(1).
[245] 1974 Act s.114(3)(a).
[246] 1974 Act s.114(3)(a).
[247] 1974 Act s.114(1). Failure to do so is an offence: s.115.
[248] In which case it must comply with the Consumer Credit (Agreement) Regulations 1983 (SI 1983/1553) (as amended) and the Consumer Credit (Agreements) Regulations 2010 (SI 2010/1014) regs 2 and 6.
[249] In which case it must comply with the Consumer Credit (Pawn-Receipts) Regulations 1983 (SI 1983/1566) (as amended).
[250] 1974 Act s.116.
[251] 1974 Act s.117.
[252] 1974 Act s.118.
[253] See s.120 (as amended most recently by the Consumer Credit (EU Directive) Regulations 2010 (SI 2010/1010) Pt 2 reg.35) and s.121.
[254] See generally, Steven, *Pledge and Lien* (2008).

Special and general liens—Liens are classed as special and general. A special **36.16** lien is a right implied by law to retain an article until some specific debt is paid. A general lien is a right to retain until some general balance, arising between the parties to certain types of contract, has been discharged. The law of Scotland does not recognise as a general corollary from mere possession, as distinguished from ownership, any right in the possessor to continue in possession until all debts due to him by the owner are paid.[255] Instances of special lien arise in sale and in contracts for services. The lien of an unpaid seller has been already considered.[256]

Special lien: Contracts for services—In contracts for services it is a general **36.17** rule, based on principles of the mutuality of contract,[257] that if the party engaged to provide services has been placed in possession of an article belonging to the other party to the contract[258] he has a right to retain it until he is paid for his work under that contract. The mutual obligations of the parties are on the one hand to pay for the work done and on the other to return the article, and the party engaged to provide services is not bound to fulfil his obligation until the obligation due to him, and arising out of the same contract, is fulfilled.[259] On this footing the assertion of a special lien does not require proof of custom of trade; it is an implied condition in all contracts for services.[260] So it is immaterial that no work has actually been done on the article over which the lien is claimed, and an accountant, who had been placed in possession of business books in order to collect debts, was held to be entitled to a lien over the books, and the defence that he had done no work on the books themselves was rejected.[261] But to found a special lien the party employed must be placed in possession of the article; an employee, who has merely the custody, and not the possession, of his employer's property, has no lien.[262] Where a hire purchase contract forbids the creation of any lien by the hirer, a repairer who carries out repairs on the article on behalf of the hirer does not acquire a lien.[263]

General lien—A general lien is recognised by the custom of certain professions **36.18** and trades.[264] Its range depends on the usage of the particular trade, and varies from a right covering all debts arising from prior employment, as in the case of a

---

[255] *Harper v Faulds* (1791) Bell's 8vo Cases, 440, 2 Ross. L.C. 708, January 27, 1791, FC; *Anderson's Tr. v Fleming* (1871) 9 M. 718.

[256] See para.12.49, above.

[257] *National Homecare Ltd v Belling & Co Ltd*, 1994 S.L.T. 50.

[258] Thus the party delivering the article must either be the owner or an agent of the owner; *Air and General Finance Ltd v RYB Marine Ltd* [2007] CSOH 177 (OH) discussed in A.J.M. Steven, "Missing the Boat: Lien for Damages" (2008) 12 Edin. L.R. 270.

[259] The party engaged to provide services is also entitled to retain the article until any damages due as a result of breach of the services contract are paid; *Moore's Universal Carving-Machine Company, Limited v Austin* (1896) 4 S.L.T. 38 and Steven, *Pledge and Lien* (2008), paras 16.20–16.23.

[260] Bell, *Commentaries*, II, 92; *Miller v Hutcheson* (1881) 8 R. 489; *Robertson v Ross* (1887) 15 R. 67.

[261] *Meikle & Wilson v Pollard* (1880) 8 R. 69; *National Homecare Ltd*, 1994 S.L.T. 50.

[262] *Barnton Hotel Co v Cook* (1899) 1 F. 1190; contrast *Findlay v Waddell*, 1910 S.C. 670. See also *Wilmington Trust Co v Rolls Royce Plc* [2011] CSOH 151.

[263] *Lamonby v Foulds*, 1928 S.C. 89. See J.J. Gow, *Law of Hire-Purchase in Scotland*, 2nd edn (Edinburgh: W. Green, 1968), p.164; W.A. Wilson, *The Scottish Law of Debt*, 2nd edn (Edinburgh: W. Green, 1991), p.95.

[264] A general lien may also be created by express contract: *Anderson's Tr. v Fleming* (1871) 9 M. 718.

solicitor,[265] to a right covering merely the balance due on the working of a particular year, as in the case of a bleacher.[266] In a case not covered by decision the question whether a general lien exists is to be determined on the evidence of parties engaged in the trade that their dealings were on the footing of a lien. The fact that a general lien is recognised in a particular trade in England is evidence, though not necessarily conclusive evidence, that it is also recognised in that trade in Scotland.[267]

Among cases of general lien particular notice may be taken of the lien of (a) a factor, (b) a banker, (c) a solicitor, and (d) an innkeeper.

36.19 **(a) Lien of factor**—A factor or mercantile agent has a general lien over all goods, bills, money or documents belonging to his principal which have come into his possession in the course of his employment.[268] It covers all advances made to the principal, the factor's salary or commission, and any liabilities incurred on the principal's behalf.[269] It entitles the factor to retain possession of the factor or an agent for him,[270] and also gives the factor a preference over the price of goods payable to the factor.[271] A mercantile agent is defined, for the purposes of the Factors Act 1889, as a mercantile agent

> "having in the customary course of his business as such agent authority either to sell goods, or to consign goods for the purpose of sale, or to buy goods, or to raise money on the security of goods".[272]

In questions of lien the term is used somewhat more widely, and the factor's or mercantile agent's lien has been held to belong to an auctioneer,[273] and to a stockbroker.[274]

36.20 **(b) Lien of banker**—A banker has a general lien over all bills, notes and negotiable securities. It covers any balance due by the customer.[275] There is no case in Scotland extending the lien to any instrument not negotiable, for instance, to share certificates. In order that negotiable securities may be subject to the lien they must have been lodged with the banker in his capacity as monetary agent, not merely for safe keeping. Thus when exchequer bills were sent to a bank in a locked box, of which the bank had no key, it was held that there was no lien over them, although the bills were periodically taken from the box and given to the banker in order that he might collect the interest.[276] But the terms of a receipt given by the bank and indicating that the documents were held for safe keeping does not necessarily exclude a lien, in a case where there is proof that the bank, relying on lien, had made advances to the customer.[277] Where negotiable securities are lodged

---

[265] See paras 36.21–36.23, below.
[266] *Anderson's Tr. v Fleming* (1871) 9 M. 718.
[267] *Strong v Philips* (1878) 5 R. 770 (packer).
[268] Bell, *Principles*, s.1445.
[269] *Sibbald v Gibson* (1852) 15 D. 217; *Glendinning v Hope*, 1911 S.C. (HL) 73.
[270] *Gairdner v Alexander Milne* (1858) 20 D. 565.
[271] Bell, *Commentaries*, II, 2, 3; *Miller v McNair* (1852) 14 D. 955.
[272] Factors Act 1889 s.1(1).
[273] *Miller v Hutcheson* (1881) 8 R. 489.
[274] *Glendinning v Hope*, 1911 S.C. (HL) 73.
[275] Bell, *Principles*, s.1451.
[276] *Brandao v Barnett* (1846) 12 Cl. & F. 787.
[277] *Robertson's Tr. v Royal Bank* (1890) 18 R. 12.

with a banker by a stockbroker, the banker, in the absence of notice to the contrary, may be entitled to assume that they are the stockbroker's own property, and claim a lien over them in the stockbroker's bankruptcy, in a question with the clients to whom they really belong. But where the banker has notice, either express, or from his knowledge of the usual course of business, that the securities are the property of the stockbroker's clients, there is a difference between a right founded on express pledge and one founded on the lien implied by law. Where securities are expressly pledged for a specific advance, the banker is entitled to assume that the stockbroker has the authority of his clients so to pledge them, and may, therefore, on the stockbroker's failure, retain them to meet the amount advanced. But a claim to retain them to meet the general balance due by the stockbroker, founded on lien and not on any specific pledge, is in a different position, because the banker has no right to assume that the stockbroker has any authority to subject his client's securities to a lien for his own general balance.[278] It would appear that a banker's right in the exercise of lien is merely to retain the securities, not to realise them.[279]

(c) Lien of solicitor—A solicitor has a general lien over all papers placed in his **36.21** hands by his client. It extends over title deeds of any description, and miscellaneous documents, such as the client's will.[280] It does not entitle the solicitor to obstruct the course of justice by refusing to produce papers entrusted to him for the purposes of an action,[281] but it does entitle him to refuse production of papers required for a professional negligence case against him.[282] Nor can the lien be exercised over the register of shareholders of a company, which, because of the statutory right of the public to consult it,[283] cannot be subjected to any form of security.[284] The lien covers the solicitor's business accounts, and advances usually made in the ordinary course of business, such as to counsel or witnesses.[285] It does not cover cash advances to the client,[286] nor, it would appear, the account of an Edinburgh solicitor in Court of Session proceedings, if paid by the country solicitor[287]; nor the account of an English solicitor, unless a Scottish solicitor has paid it, or is liable for it.[288] The solicitor's lien, so far as it is a general lien, rests on professional usage, and is not enjoyed by persons similarly employed who are not solicitors. Thus an accountant has a lien over papers entrusted to him only for his charge for work done in connection with those papers, not a general lien for his whole professional account,[289] and the scope of the lien of the factor or land agent on an estate has been held to depend upon whether he is a qualified solicitor.[290]

Solicitor's lien in questions with third parties—The lien of a solicitor may be **36.22** exercised against the client, and also, in certain cases, against parties deriving

---

[278] *National Bank v Dickie's Tr.* (1895) 22 R. 740.
[279] *Robertson's Tr. v Royal Bank* (1890) 18 R. 12.
[280] *Paul v Meikle* (1868) 7 M. 235. See also *McIntosh v Chalmers* (1883) 11 R. 6.
[281] *Callman v Bell* (1793) Mor.6255.
[282] *Yau v Ogilvie & Co*, 1985 S.L.T. 91.
[283] Companies Act 2006 s.116.
[284] *Garpel Haematite Co v Andrew* (1866) 4 M. 617.
[285] *Richardson v Merry* (1863) 1 M. 940 at 946.
[286] *Christie v Ruxton* (1862) 24 D. 1182; *Wylie's Exrx v McJannet* (1901) 4 F. 195.
[287] *Largue v Urquhart* (1883) 10 R. 1229.
[288] *Liquidator of Grand Empire Theatre v Snodgrass*, 1932 S.C. (HL) 73.
[289] *Findlay v Waddell*, 1910 S.C. 670; *Morrison v Fulwell's Tr.* (1901) 9 S.L.T. 34.
[290] *Macrae v Leith*, 1913 S.C. 901.

right from him. Thus the solicitor of a seller may retain title deeds against the purchaser, the solicitor of a borrower against the lender on heritable security. In neither case can he exercise this right if he acts for both parties (i.e. for seller and purchaser, or for borrower and lender) unless he has intimated to the purchaser or lender that he holds the title deeds and proposes to claim a lien over them.[291] In any event a solicitor cannot acquire a lien, in a question with a heritable creditor, after the date of recording or registering the security.[292] Where the lien is exercised, the solicitor's right cannot be evaded by raising an action, obtaining a diligence for the recovery of documents, and calling on the solicitor to produce the title deeds as a haver.[293]

36.23 Solicitor's lien in sequestration—A trustee in sequestration,[294] or the liquidator of a company,[295] is entitled to insist on the production of all papers relating to the estate under his charge. The solicitor, who must give them up, does so under implied reservation of his lien: express reservation is unnecessary.[296] The result is not to give him any claim against the trustee or liquidator,[297] but to entitle him to be ranked for his account as a preferred creditor.[298] It is not decided how he ranks in competition with other preferred creditors, but he is postponed to the expenses of the liquidation or sequestration.[299]

The solicitor's lien does not give him the right to dispose of the papers, only to retain them.[300] Accordingly, his lien is worthless in a case where there is nothing in the bankrupt's estate over which he can be given a preference. In that case he ranks as an ordinary creditor.[301]

36.24 (d) Lien of innkeeper—An innkeeper has a lien over his guest's luggage for the amount of his bill.[302] He cannot detain the guest or the clothes he is wearing.[303] The lien covers articles not of the nature of ordinary luggage, such as a solicitor's letter book.[304] It does not cover articles not brought as luggage, but hired by the guest during his stay at the inn,[305] or articles, not luggage, handed to the innkeeper as security for the bill,[306] or delivered by a third party for the use of guests.[307] By statute it also does not cover "any vehicle or any property left therein, or any horse

---

[291] *Gray v Graham* (1855) 2 Macq. 435; *Drummond v Muirhead & Guthrie Smith* (1900) 2 F. 585.

[292] Conveyancing (Scotland) Act 1924 s.27; Land Registration (Scotland) Act 1979 s.29(2).

[293] *Dalrymple v Earl of Selkirk* (1751) 2 Elchies 198.

[294] Bankruptcy (Scotland) Act 1985 s.38(4); *Garden, Haig-Scott & Wallace v Stevenson's Tr.*, 1962 S.C. 51.

[295] 1986 Act s.144; *Train & McIntyre v Forbes*, 1925 S.L.T. 286 (accountants), applying *Renny & Webster v Myles* (1847) 9 D. 619.

[296] *Adam & Winchester v White's Tr.* (1884) 11 R. 863, per Lord President Inglis at 865; *Garden, Haig-Scott & Wallace v Stevenson's Tr.*, 1962 S.C. 51.

[297] *Adam & Winchester v White's Tr.* (1884) 11 R. 863; *Lochee Sawmill Co v Stevenson*, 1908 S.C. 559.

[298] *Skinner v Henderson* (1865) 3 M. 867.

[299] *Miln's J.F. v Spence's Trs*, 1927 S.L.T. 425.

[300] *Ferguson v Grant* (1856) 18 D. 536 at 538.

[301] *Garden, Haig-Scott & Wallace v Stevenson's Tr.*, 1962 S.C. 51.

[302] Bell, *Principles*, s.1428. This lien can be regarded as a special lien: see Gloag and Irvine, *Rights in Security* (1897), p.397.

[303] *Sunbolf v Alford* (1838) 3 M. & W. 248.

[304] *Snead v Watkins* (1856) 1 C.B. (N.S.) 267.

[305] *Broadwood v Granara* (1854) 10 Ex. 417.

[306] *Marsh v Commissioner of Police* (1943) 60 T.L.R. 96.

[307] *Bermans and Nathans Ltd v Weibye*, 1983 S.C. 67.

or other live animal or its harness or other equipment".[308] It may be exercised even if the articles brought as luggage do not belong to the guest, and the innkeeper is aware of the fact.[309] Under the Innkeepers Act 1878,[310] an innkeeper is entitled, after advertisement, to sell by auction goods brought to or left in his inn, provided that a debt for board and lodging, or for the keep of any horse, shall have been six weeks outstanding. He must account to the guest for any surplus.

Limit of rights under liens—It has been laid down that lien is a right over which **36.25** the court may exercise an equitable control and, therefore, in particular circumstances a ship might be released from a lien for repairs on terms to be fixed by the court.[311] And no lien founded on possession can be asserted if it would conflict with the express or implied terms of the contract under which possession was obtained. Thus if a bill is sent to a banker for discount, and he refuses to discount it, he cannot retain it under lien.[312] Where money was deposited with a solicitor in order to effect a composition with the depositor's creditors, and this proved impracticable, it was held that the solicitor could not retain the money to meet a general balance on his business account in a question with the trustee in the depositor's sequestration.[313] And it is a general principle that when a security is constituted by express pledge it cannot be extended, on the plea of lien, to cover other debts or a general balance. The primary purpose of a lien is to constitute a security for payment of charges incurred in connection with the object over which the lien exists.[314] But this is a right of limited value unless, where the debtor proves recalcitrant, the object in question can be sold.[315]

Extinction of lien—As a lien is founded on possession it is lost if possession is **36.26** relinquished,[316] but it is possible to give up physical custody of goods while retaining possession of them for the purposes of maintaining a lien.[317] Some of the articles held under lien may be restored without affecting the lien over the rest.[318] Where a bill is taken for the debt, and subsequently dishonoured, the presumption is that the bill has been taken as an additional security, and the lien is not affected, unless the currency of the bill is unusually long, when the lien will be held to have been relinquished unless it was expressly reserved.[319]

---

[308] Hotel Proprietors Act 1956 s.2(2).

[309] *Bermans and Nathans Ltd v Weibye*, 1983 S.C. 67. It has been suggested that this rule is incompatible with art.1 of Protocol 1 of the European Convention on Human Rights; see Steven, *Pledge and Lien* (2008), para.16.83.

[310] Innkeepers Act 1878 s.1.

[311] *Garscadden v Ardrossan Dry Dock Co*, 1910 S.C. 178. See also *Onyvax Ltd v Endpoint Research (UK) Ltd* [2007] CSOH 211.

[312] *Borthwick v Bremner* (1833) 12 S. 121.

[313] *Middlemas v Gibson*, 1910 S.C. 577.

[314] But in the case of a depositary to whom goods have been handed over for repairs, etc. the depositary cannot exercise his lien over the goods to secure payment of garaging or other storage costs unless that is a matter of separate agreement with the depositor: *Stephen v Swayne* (1861) 24 D. 158; *Carntyne Motors v Curran*, 1958 S.L.T. (Sh. Ct) 6.

[315] *Gibson & Stewart v Brown & Co* (1876) 3 R. 328; *Parker v Andrew Brown & Co* (1878) 5 R. 979.

[316] *Miller v McNair* (1852) 14 D. 955 at 959, per L.J.-C. Hope; Bell, *Commentaries*, II, 89. For a possible qualification see *Hostess Mobile Catering v Archibald Scott Ltd*, 1981 S.C. 185 and *Goudie v Mulholland*, 2000 S.C. 61.

[317] e.g. *Renny v Rutherford* (1840) 2 D. 676; *Renny v Kemp* (1841) 3 D. 1134; *North-Western Bank Ltd v Poynter, Son & MacDonalds* (1894) 22 R. (HL) 1.

[318] *Gray v Graham* (1855) 2 Macq. 435.

[319] *Palmer v Lee* (1880) 7 R. 651; approving Bell, *Commentaries*, II, 109.

36.27 Maritime securities—Special rules apply to ships and their cargo[320] because of the nature of ships as valuable corporeal moveable property, not typically located in one place, in relation to which extensive liabilities may arise.

(1) Ship Mortgages. The Merchant Shipping Act 1995 provides for the registration, discharge and transfer of mortgages over a British ship or shares therein.[321] If an instrument in the appropriate form is produced to the registrar, he is directed to enter it in the register.[322] Every registered mortgagee has power, if the mortgage money or any part of it is due, to sell the security subjects.[323] The mortgage may provide for the power of sale to arise also in other circumstances.[324] The power of sale implies the power to take possession of the ship.[325] Otherwise, the mortgagee's rights depend on the terms of the contract between him and mortgagor. Subject to the terms of the particular contract, the owner is probably obliged to keep the ship in repair.[326] The mortgagee may be entitled to interdict the vessel setting to sea where the mortgagor has failed to comply with its obligations under the mortgage and as a result setting to sea would materially prejudice the security.[327] The general rule is that ship mortgages rank inter se according to the order in which the mortgages were registered.[328] However, an intending mortgagee may register a priority notice which will give his security (provided it is registered within the prescribed period of time) priority over a mortgage registered after the priority notice.[329] A subsequent mortgagee may not sell the security subjects without approval of the court or the consent of every prior mortgagee.[330]

(2) Bonds of Bottomry and Respondentia. At common law the owner or master of a ship may create a conventional hypothec over it by granting a bond of bottomry. The master has implied power to grant a bond of bottomry when the ship is in a foreign port, unable to proceed with the

---

[320] For securities in relation to oil platforms see *Stair Memorial Encyclopaedia*, Vol.20, paras 266–272.

[321] Merchant Shipping Act 1995 s.16, Sch.1; the Merchant Shipping (Registration of Ships) Regulations 1993 (SI 1993/3138), regs 57–63. At common law, a bill of sale or other conveyance in writing, followed by actual possession or by possession inferred from the receipt of the earnings of the ship, may create a security over a ship effectual in the bankruptcy of the owner: *Watson v Duncan* (1879) 6 R. 1247.

[322] Merchant Shipping Act 1995 Sch.1 para.7(2), (3). If the charge is created by a company it should also be entered in the register of charges kept by the Registrar of Companies: para.36.06, above. For circumstances in which a mortgage, its entry in the register and the certificate of registry were reduced see *Lombard North Central Ltd v Lord Advocate*, 1983 S.L.T. 361, discussed in K.G.C. Reid, "Unintimated Assignations", 1989 S.L.T. (News) 267.

[323] Merchant Shipping Act 1995 Sch.1 para.9(1); e.g. *Banque Indo Suez v Maritime Co Overseas Inc*, 1984 S.C. 120. As to exercise of the mortgagee's power of sale where the ship has been arrested on the dependence of a personal action against the owner see *Clydesdale Bank Ltd v Walker & Bain*, 1926 S.C. 72.

[324] *The Maule* [1997] 1 W.L.R. 528.

[325] Bell, *Principles*, s.1382n; on the position of a mortgagee in possession see *Havilland Routh & Co v Thomson* (1864) 3 M. 313.

[326] *Tyne Dock Engineering Co Ltd v Royal Bank of Scotland Ltd*, 1974 S.L.T. 57.

[327] *Laming & Co v Seater* (1889) 16 R. 828.

[328] Merchant Shipping Act 1995 Sch.1 para.8(1).

[329] Merchant Shipping Act 1995 Sch.1 para.8(2); Merchant Shipping (Registration of Ships) Regulations 1993 (SI 1993/3138) reg.59.

[330] Merchant Shipping Act 1995 Sch.1 para.9(2).

voyage without an advance of money and no money is procurable on the personal credit of the owner.[331] The master must, if practicable, communicate with the owner before granting the bond.[332] The lender cannot enforce the security unless the ship arrives safely at its destination. Bonds of bottomry rank *inter se* in reverse order of date, so that the bond last granted ranks first. The master likewise may grant a hypothec over the ship's cargo by way of a bond of respondentia, if there is no other means of raising money necessary for the prosecution of the voyage, provided he has communicated (if communication is practicable) with the cargo-owner.[333] The bond is effectual if the cargo arrives at the port of destination even if the ship does not.[334] If the cargo is attached and sold under a bond of respondentia, the shipowner is liable to the cargo-owner for its value.[335]

(3) Possessory Liens. A ship-repairer has a lien, dependent on possession, of a ship entrusted to him for the purposes of repair until his account for that repair has been paid.[336] A salvor has a right to retain the salved ship and cargo in security of his salvage claim.[337] The salvor's right is qualified, in relation to wrecks, by his statutory obligation to give notice to the receiver of wreck, and to hold the wreck to the receiver's order to deliver it to the receiver.[338] A common law possessory lien for towage has been suggested.[339] Detention (by virtue of ss.44 or 74 of the Harbour, Docks and Piers Clauses Act 1847 or similar statutory powers) by a harbour authority to enforce a claim to harbour dues or to reparation for damage to the harbour by the ship gives the authority a possessory lien.[340]

(4) Maritime Hypothecs. The law recognises hypothecs (habitually but confusingly called maritime liens[341]) over ships[342] to secure the rights of a salvor to payment of salvage,[343] of a seaman to his wages,[344] of the

---

[331] Bell, *Principles*, s.452.

[332] *Kleinwort, Cohen & Co v Cassa Marritima* (1877) L.R. 2 App. Cas. 156.

[333] *Dymond v Scott* (1877) 5 R. 196.

[334] Bell, *Commentaries*, I, 584.

[335] *Anderston Foundry Co v Law* (1869) 7 M. 836.

[336] *Barr & Shearer v Cooper* (1875) 2 R. (HL) 14; *Ross & Duncan v Baxter & Co* (1885) 13 R. 185. The lien prevails over a ship mortgage: *Tyne Dock Engineering Company Ltd v Royal Bank of Scotland Ltd*, 1974 S.L.T. 57.

[337] *Mackenzie v Steam Herring Fleet Ltd* (1903) 10 S.L.T. 734. His possessory lien is additional to the maritime hypothec in his favour.

[338] Merchant Shipping Act 1995 s.236.

[339] A.R.G. McMillan, *Scottish Maritime Practice* (William Hodge, 1926), pp.249–50; but see *Stair Memorial Encyclopaedia*, Vol.20, para.303. A possessory lien is often expressly provided for in towage contracts: see *Lukoil-Kalingradmorneft Plc v Tata Ltd (No.2)* [1999] 2 Lloyd's Rep. 129.

[340] *Mersey Docks and Harbour Board v Hay* [1923] A.C. 490.

[341] See now s.48(2) of the Administration of Justice Act 1956 (inserted by the Bankruptcy and Diligence etc. (Scotland) Act 2007 s.213, Sch.4 para.1(c)) which provides that, under the 1956 Act and in any other enactment (including an Act of the Scottish Parliament and any enactment comprised in subordinate legislation under such an Act), the term "maritime lien" shall mean a hypothec over a ship, cargo or other maritime property.

[342] The hypothec also attaches to freight being earned and due when the hypothec is created, to cargo (but only in respect of claims based on bottomry, respondentia and salvage) and to flotsam, jetsam, lagan, derelict and wreck (but only in respect of claims for salvage).

[343] Bell, *Principles*, s.1397.

[344] Bell, *Principles*, s.1398. A seaman may not contract out of this right: Merchant Shipping Act 1995 s.39(1). As to whether someone who pays seamen's wages is entitled to the preference accorded to seamen, see *Clark v Bowring*, 1908 S.C. 1168 and *Clydesdale Bank Ltd v Walker & Bain*, 1926 S.C. 72.

master to remuneration and to payment for disbursements,[345] of a property owner or (arguably) an injured person to reparation for damage caused by the negligent navigation of the ship,[346] of the receiver of wrecks to his expenses,[347] of the coastguard service for remuneration for services rendered in watching or protecting ship-wrecked property,[348] (possibly) of a harbour authority to reparation without proof of fault (by virtue of s.74 of the Harbours, Docks and Piers Clauses Act 1847 or similar legislation) for damage caused by the ship to the authority's property,[349] and (possibly) of an owner or occupier of land to compensation for damage caused in rendering assistance to shipwrecked persons or property.[350] Whether there is a maritime hypothec for pilotage has been left open.[351] There is no hypothec in respect of a claim for necessaries provided to a ship in a home port.[352] It has been said that the scope of the maritime hypothecs is the same in Scots and English law.[353] As a right in security, a maritime hypothec survives sale of the vessel to a third party.[354] Maritime hypothecs prevail over mortgages.[355] Maritime hypothecs are enforced by admiralty action in rem, an essential feature of which is an arrestment of the ship in rem.[356]

(5) Statutory Arrestments in rem. By statute, warrant may be granted for an arrestment in rem of a ship in proceedings concerning a dispute as to the right to ownership or possession of the ship; the mortgage, hypothecation of or existence of any other charge on the ship; any forfeiture or condemnation of the ship or its cargo; or between co-owners as to ownership, possession, employment or earnings of the ship.[357]

IV. SECURITIES OVER INCORPOREAL PROPERTY

36.28 General[358]—Many valuable assets are incorporeal. A right to payment from a third party is perhaps the paradigm example. And rights may, subject to any

---

[345] Merchant Shipping Act 1995 s.41.

[346] *The Bold Buccleuch* (1852) 7 Moo. P.C. 267; *Currie v McKnight* (1896) 24 R. (HL) 1; *The Rama* [1996] 2 Lloyd's Rep. 281. The lien is well established in respect of property damage. On the question of its application to personal injury see D.R. Thomas, *Maritime Liens* (London: Stevens and Sons, 1980), pp.132–3; D.C. Jackson, *Enforcement of Maritime Claims*, 4th edn (Informa Professional, 2005), pp.39–40.

[347] Merchant Shipping Act 1995 s.249(3).

[348] Merchant Shipping Act 1995 s.250(3).

[349] *The Merle* (1874) 2 Asp. M.L.C. 402; but see Jackson, *Enforcement of Maritime Claims* (2005), pp.50–51.

[350] Merchant Shipping Act 1995 s.234(6); see Thomas, *Maritime Liens* (1980), p.20; cf. Jackson, *Enforcement of Maritime Claims* (2005), p.49.

[351] *The Ambatielos, The Cephalonia* [1923] P. 68.

[352] *Clydesdale Bank Ltd v Walker & Bain*, 1926 S.C. 72.

[353] *Currie v McKnight* (1896) 24 R. (HL) 1.

[354] *Bankers Trust Ltd v Todd Shipyards* [1981] A.C. 221.

[355] *The Ripon City* [1897] P. 226; *The Athena* (1923) 14 Ll.L. Rep. 515; *Bankers Trust Ltd v Todd Shipyards* [1981] A.C. 221.

[356] Act of Sederunt (Rules of the Court of Session 1994) 1994 ("RCS") rr.46.2, 46.3; *Mill v Fildes*, 1982 S.L.T. 147.

[357] Administration of Justice Act 1956 s.47(3) (as amended by the Bankruptcy and Diligence etc. (Scotland) Act 2007 s.213 and Sch.4).

[358] Note that the Scottish Law Commission is currently engaged in a review of this area; see *Discussion Paper on Moveable Transactions*.

express[359] or implied[360] restriction on assignation and subject to any particular rules applicable to particular types of incorporeal property,[361] in general be transferred in security by an assignation followed by intimation to the debtor.[362] Scots law does not recognise any security by the mere deposit of title deeds.[363] Mere delivery of the voucher of a debt (unless it is a negotiable instrument[364]) or a mere assignation not followed by intimation to the debtor,[365] are each ineffectual. It has been held that no preferential right is created by the transfer of a policy of insurance without intimation to the insurance company.[366] The same principles were applied to an assignation of the uncalled capital of a company, which was held to be ineffectual as a security unless it was completed by intimation to each shareholder.[367]

Securities over shares in a company—Shares in a company may be used as a security by transferring them to the creditor, subject to an obligation by him to retransfer. In order to complete the security the transferee's name should be entered in the register of shareholders.[368] There is a practice of depositing with a creditor the share certificate with a blank transfer (i.e. a transfer executed by the transferor, but without the name of the transferee). Delivery of these documents does not create any right in security over the shares to which they relate, although it enables the creditor to have the transfer registered without any further procedure. The transferee will therefore be unprotected if the transferor becomes insolvent. **36.29**

Securities over intellectual property rights[369]—A security over a patent may be constituted by an assignation (ex facie absolute or expressly in security) registered in the Register of Patents.[370] Copyrights and unregistered design rights may be assigned in security although (unless the copyright has been licensed to a **36.30**

---

[359] e.g. *Linden Gardens Trust Ltd v Lenesta Sludge Disposals Ltd* [1994] 1 A.C. 85; *James Scott Ltd v Apollo Engineering Ltd*, 2000 S.C. 228.

[360] Rights in respect of which there is delectus personae are not assignable. A right to an alimentary payment is, in general, not assignable. No person can assign his liabilities without the creditor's consent. See generally Anderson, *Assignation* (2008), para.1.04 and *Stair Memorial Encyclopaedia*, Vol.15, para.859.

[361] See further below.

[362] As to assignation and intimation, see below.

[363] *Havilland, Routh & Co v Thomson* (1864) 3 M. 313.

[364] On securities over negotiable instruments see *Stair Memorial Encyclopaedia*, Vol.20, paras 56–60.

[365] *Gallemos Ltd (in receivership) v Barratt Falkirk Ltd*, 1990 S.L.T. 98.

[366] *Strachan v McDougle* (1835) 13 S. 954; *Wylie's Exrs v McJannet* (1901) 4 F. 195.

[367] *Liquidator of the Union Club v Edinburgh Life Assurance Co* (1906) 8 F. 1143.

[368] e.g. *Waddell v Hutton*, 1911 S.C. 575; *Crerar v Bank of Scotland*, 1921 S.C. 736; 1922 S.C. (HL) 137. See most recently *Enviroco Ltd v Farstad Supply A/S* [2011] UKSC 16; see also R.G. Anderson, "Scottish Share Pledges in the Supreme Court" (2012) 16 Edin. L.R. 99. This proposition appears to hold true even in cases where the shares are "financial collateral" in terms of the Financial Collateral Directive (2002/47/EC); see G. Gretton, "Financial Collateral and the Fundamentals of Secured Transactions" (2006) 10 Edin. L.R. 209, especially 224–225 and 233–236.

[369] See generally, J. Macfarlane and S. Macpherson, "Securities over Intellectual Property in Scotland" (March 1993) *The In-House Lawyer* 18. A charge granted by a company over most types of intellectual property rights should be registered with the Registrar of Companies: see para.36.06, above.

[370] Patents Act 1977 ss.31–33; see D.P. Sellar, "Rights in Security over Scottish Patents" (1996) 1 S.L.P.Q. 137; for patents under the European Patent Convention see J.A. McLean, "Security Over Intellectual Property–A Scottish Perspective" [1988] 4 E.I.P.R. 115, 116–17; T. Guthrie and A. Orr, "Fixed Security Rights over Intellectual Property Rights in Scotland" (1996) 18 E.I.P.R. 597. See also *Buchanan v Alba Diagnostics Ltd*, 2004 S.C. (HL) 9 and R.G. Anderson, "Buchanan v Alba Diagnostics: Accretion of Title and Assignation of Future Patents" (2005) 9 Edin. L.R. 457.

licensee) there is no-one to whom intimation may be made and no register in which the assignation may be entered.[371] A security over a registered design may be constituted by an assignation registered in the Register of Designs.[372] A security over a trade mark may be constituted by an assignation registered in the Register of Trade Marks.[373] Plant breeders' rights are assignable,[374] and could no doubt be assigned in security. If the owner of an intellectual property right receives royalties under a licence it may be necessary to intimate any assignation to the licensee in order to secure the creditor's right to payment of the royalties.[375] Despite the competency of taking an assignation in security of intellectual property rights, they are uncommon: the effect of such an assignation is to transfer the intellectual property right to the creditor. And if the granter does not own the intellectual property right he cannot enforce it.[376] This incident of the assignation in security is usually prohibitive. Enforcement of the intellectual property right will be essential for most businesses. A floating charge will, however, cover intellectual property rights and allow the company to enforce its intellectual property rights. Alternatively, an assignation can be combined with a licence in favour of the debtor.

36.31 Securities over leases—At common law an effectual real right in security over the tenant's interest in a lease may be obtained (provided that assignation is not prohibited in terms of the lease) only by assignation followed by possession under the lease.[377] Following upon the Registration of Leases (Scotland) Act 1857,[378] a security could be taken over a registered lease without possession by recording or registering an assignation. Since 1970 the only competent method of constituting a right in security over a registered lease has been by way of a standard security.[379]

36.32 Solicitor's hypothec—A solicitor who has defrayed the costs of an action has at common law a right in the nature of an implied assignation in respect of any expenses to which his client may be found entitled.[380] This he may make effectual by moving for decree in his own name as agent-disburser[381] or indeed, in certain

---

[371] Copyright Designs and Patents Act 1988 ss.90, 222, 262. The same rules may apply to the design right in semiconductor topographies: see *Stair Memorial Encyclopaedia*, Vol.18, para.1248. While the assignation of copyright itself does not require intimation, this should be distinguished from an assignation of a right to claim an assignation of copyright; in such cases the normal intimation requirement stands; see R.G. Anderson, "Case Comment: Tayplan Ltd v D A Contracts", 2005 S.L.T. (News) 119.

[372] Registered Designs Act 1949 ss.15B, 19.

[373] Trade Marks Act 1994 s.24.

[374] Plant Varieties Act 1997 s.12.

[375] For patents, see Sellar, "Rights in Security over Scottish Patents" (1996) 1 S.L.P.Q. 137.

[376] See, e.g. Patents Act 1977 s.68 which provides that only the "registered proprietor" can sue for damages for infringement. See also Registered Designs Act 1949 s.7 where the rights accorded thereunder are to the "registered proprietor".

[377] Bell, *Principles*, s.1212; *Clark v West Calder Oil Co* (1882) 9 R. 1017; *Mess v Hay* (1898) 1 F. (HL) 22.

[378] Registration of Leases (Scotland) Act 1857 (c.26); see also Conveyancing (Scotland) Act 1924 s.24.

[379] Conveyancing and Feudal Reform (Scotland) Act 1970 s.30. It is also to be noted that it is common in practice for a landlord to give security to a creditor by assigning to his creditor his right to receive rental income from his tenant. This must be intimated to the tenant in order to complete the transfer; see above, para.36.28.

[380] *Gordon v Davidson* (1865) 3 M. 938. It will be apparent that, although commonly called the solicitor's hypothec, this is not a right in security over corporeal moveable property, but rather over the client's right to payment of expenses.

[381] J.A. Maclaren, *Court of Session Practice* (Edinburgh: W. Green, 1916), p.27; Sheriff Courts (Scotland) Act 1907 Sch.1 r.32.2. See Anderson, *Assignation* (2008), para.8.58.

situations, by sisting himself as a party.[382] The party liable in expenses is not, in general, entitled to resist decree in favour of the solicitor merely on the ground that he has a claim against the client on which he could plead compensation.[383] But if cross awards of expenses are made in the course of an action or in two actions arising out of the same matter the other party is entitled to set off the expenses to which he has been found entitled against the expenses for which he is liable.[384] This does not hold if the decree in the first action has been extracted before the second action comes into court[385] and is an exception to the solicitor's right which will not be extended.[386] If decree for expenses is granted in favour of the client, the solicitor may still, by giving notice of his claim to the person liable in the expenses, obtain a right to the expenses which will prevail over a trustee in sequestration,[387] though not over a prior arrestment[388] or intimated assignation.[389] By statute, where a solicitor has been employed by a client to pursue or defend any action, the court may declare the solicitor entitled in respect of the taxed expenses of the action, to a charge upon and a right to payment out of any property (of any kind) which has been recovered or preserved on behalf of the client by the solicitor in the action.[390] Any act done or deed granted by the client after the date of such a declaration (unless in favour of a bona fide purchaser or lender) is void.[391] A declaration is precluded by the client's sequestration[392] but not by a prior arrestment.[393] The court has a discretion to grant or refuse a declaration[394] but any charge will be restricted to the sum left after deduction of the other party's claim for expenses.[395]

V. FLOATING CHARGES, RECEIVERS AND ADMINISTRATORS

Floating charges: General—The essence of a floating charge is that it gives the creditor of a company[396] security[397] over the property (excluding, possibly, reserve capital)[398] which is subject to the charge, without the need for delivery, intimation   **36.33**

---

[382] *Ammon v Tod*, 1912 S.C. 306; *Peek v Peek*, 1926 S.C. 565.

[383] Bell, *Principles*, s.1390; cf. Anderson, *Assignation* (2008), para.8.58.

[384] *Lochgelly Iron Co v Sinclair*, 1907 S.C. 442; *Fine v Edinburgh Life Assurance Co*, 1909 S.C. 636; *Byrne v Baird*, 1929 S.C. 624.

[385] *William Baird & Co Ltd v Campbell*, 1928 S.C. 487.

[386] *Jack v Laing*, 1929 S.C. 426.

[387] *McTavish v Peddie* (1828) 6 S. 593.

[388] *Stephen v Smith* (1830) 8 S. 847.

[389] *Fleeming v Love* (1839) 1 D. 1097.

[390] Solicitors (Scotland) Act 1980 s.62(1). A declaration in favour of a country solicitor in Court of Session proceedings is competent: *Bannatyne, Kirkwood, France & Co, Noters*, 1907 S.C. 705.

[391] Solicitors (Scotland) Act 1980 s.62(2).

[392] *Tait v Wallace* (1894) 2 S.L.T. 252; but see *Philip v Willson*, 1911 S.C. 1203 (liquidation).

[393] *Automobile Gas Producer Syndicate v Caledonian Railway Co*, 1909 1 S.L.T. 499.

[394] *Carruthers' Tr. v Finlay & Watson* (1897) 24 R. 363.

[395] *O'Keefe v Grieve's Trs*, 1917 1 S.L.T. 305.

[396] Note that some commercial entities other than a company may also grant a floating charge; see above, para.36.05.

[397] See para.36.05, above.

[398] At least this has been held to be the case in England: *Re Mayfair Property Co* [1898] 2 Ch. 28. Property held in trust has been held to be unaffected by the crystallisation of a floating charge on the appointment of a receiver: *Tay Valley Joinery Ltd v C.F. Financial Services Ltd*, 1987 S.L.T. 207. The crystallisation of a floating charge does not affect heritable property of the company once a disposition has been delivered to a purchaser even if the disposition has not been recorded in the property registers: *Sharp v Thomson*, 1997 S.C. (HL) 66; see above, fn.72.

or, in the case of heritage, registration in the Register of Sasines or the Land Register.[399] The charge lies dormant until the company is wound up or a receiver is appointed,[400] leaving the company free in the meantime (subject to any restrictions in the agreement constituting the debt) to dispose of the property over which it extends; if it acquires new property that also may become subject to the charge. When a company goes into liquidation,[401] however, or on the appointment of a receiver, the charge crystallises or attaches to the property then comprised in the company's property and undertaking or such part of it as is subject to the charge.[402] Property which comes into the company's hands after crystallisation may also be attached by it if the terms of the charge admit of this interpretation.[403] The charge attaches as if it were a fixed security over the property to which it has attached.[404] Attachment consequent upon the company going into liquidation is subject to the rights of any person who has effectually executed diligence[405] on the property or any part of it, or who holds a fixed security or another floating charge over the property or any part of it which has priority of ranking.[406] Consignment

---

[399] Companies Act 1985 s.462: this does not define a floating charge. Section 462 is due to be repealed and replaced, subject to saving and transitional arrangements, by the Bankruptcy and Diligence etc. (Scotland) Act 2007; see ss.38 and 46.

[400] It should be noted that, subject to some exceptions, the holders of floating charges created on or after September 15, 2003 do not have the right to appoint an administrative receiver; see s.72A(2) of the 1986 Act, inserted by s.250 of the Enterprise Act 2002. In these cases the remedy for the holder of a floating charge is the appointment of an administrator; a floating charge will crystallise in these cases where the administrator files a notice with the Registrar of Companies under para.115 of Sch.B1 to the 1986 Act. For more details on these various points, see below, paras 36.34–36.36.

[401] i.e. the company passes a resolution for voluntary winding up or an order for its winding up is made: 1986 Act s.247(2). See also s.45(7) of the Bankruptcy and Diligence etc. (Scotland) Act 2007 which, once it comes into force, will expand the definition of "liquidation" in this context to cover the opening of insolvency proceedings in a court of a Member State of the European Union (other than the United Kingdom) which has jurisdiction as respects the company which granted the floating charge under the EC Regulation on Insolvency Proceedings (EC/1346/2000). Note, however, that by s.45(2) the floating charge will not attach in such a case until such time as a notice of attachment is registered in the Register of Floating Charges. On "winding-up" see paras 46.50–46.57, below.

[402] Companies Act 1985 s.463(1) (this provision is due to be repealed and replaced, subject to saving and transitional arrangements, by the Bankruptcy and Diligence etc. (Scotland) Act 2007; see ss.45 and 46); 1986 Act ss.53(7), 54(6); see *Independent Pension Tr. Ltd v LAW Construction Ltd*, 1997 S.L.T. 1105; *Sharp v Thomson*, 1997 S.C. (HL) 66 (see above, fn.72). A floating charge also crystallises when an administrator files a notice with the Registrar of Companies under para.115 of Sch.B1 to the 1986 Act.

[403] *Ross v Taylor*, 1985 S.C. 156; the charge extended to the whole of the property "which is or may be from time to time" comprised in the property and undertaking of the company. Note also *Scottish & Newcastle Plc v Ascot Inns Ltd (in receivership)*, 1994 S.L.T. 1140.

[404] Companies Act 1985 ss.463(2), 486(1); 1986 Act ss.53(7), 54(6), 70(1). The 1985 Act provisions are due to be replaced by ss.45(5) and 47 of the Bankruptcy and Diligence etc. (Scotland) Act 2007. See also *National Commercial Bank of Scotland v Liqrs of Telford Grier Mackay & Co*, 1969 S.C. 181 at 194, per Lord President Clyde. The appointment of a receiver of an English company has the same effect with regard to its property situated in Scotland: *Gordon Anderson (Plant) v Campsie Construction*, 1977 S.L.T. 7. See 1986 Act s.72.

[405] As to the meaning of "effectually executed diligence," see *Lord Advocate v Royal Bank of Scotland*, 1977 S.C. 155 (arrestment); *Armour & Mycroft, Petitioners*, 1983 S.L.T. 453 (inhibition); *Taymech Ltd v Rush & Tompkins Ltd*, 1990 S.L.T. 681 (inhibition); *Iona Hotels Ltd v Craig*, 1990 S.C. 330; *Commissioners of Customs and Excise v John D. Reid Joinery Ltd*, 2001 S.L.T. 588. See also S. Wortley, "Squaring the Circle: Revisiting the Receiver and 'Effectually Executed Diligence'", 2000 Jur. Rev. 325.

[406] Companies Act 1985 s.463(1); this is due to be replaced by s.45(3) of the Bankruptcy and Diligence etc. (Scotland) Act 2007. Compare the provisions relating to the powers of a receiver in the 1986 Act s.55(3).

of funds into court, in order to recall an arrestment and inhibition on the dependence, has the effect of removing them from the company's property to which a
floating charge may attach after consignment has taken place.[407] In the case
of book debts the attachment has effect as if an assignation of the debt to the
holder of the floating charge was duly intimated to the third party on the date of
the receiver's appointment, with the result that the debt is no longer capable of
arrestment after that date.[408] A debtor will be able to set off debts due to him
by the company which were due before the appointment, but not any debts which
he may have acquired by assignation after that date.[409] A floating charge is capable
of being assigned.[410] A floating charge granted in favour of a person connected
with the company within the period of two years ending with the "onset of
insolvency" of the company is restricted as to its validity.[411] A floating charge
granted to a person other than a person connected with the company within
the period of 12 months ending with the "onset of insolvency" is likewise
restricted as to its validity.[412] The "onset of insolvency" is, in the case of
liquidation, the date of the commencement of the winding up.[413] In the case
of administration, the date varies according to the method by which the administrator has come to be appointed.[414] Any floating charge affected by these rules
is invalid, except to the extent of so much of the consideration for the charge
as consists of money, goods or services or of the discharge or reduction of
debt given at the same time as, or after, the creation of the charge, together with
any interest payable on those amounts.[415] A charge which is created either at a
time between the presentation of a petition for an administration order and the
granting of the administration order or at a time between the lodging by the
company or its directors of a notice of intention to appoint an administrator and
the appointment is also invalid to the same extent, irrespective of whether or not
it is in favour of a person connected with the company.[416] The 1985 Act provides
for the alteration of a floating charge by execution of an instrument of alteration,[417]

---

[407] *Hawking v Hafton House Ltd*, 1990 S.C. 198. The case, however, arose from the appointment of
a receiver and the effect of the difference in wording between s.463(1) of the 1985 Act and ss.53(7)
and 54(6) of the 1986 Act.

[408] *Forth & Clyde Construction Co v Trinity Timber & Plywood Co*, 1984 S.C. 1.

[409] *Forth & Clyde Construction Co v Trinity Timber & Plywood Co*, 1984 S.C. 1.

[410] *Libertas-Kommerz v Johnson*, 1977 S.C. 191. Section 42 of the Bankruptcy and Diligence etc.
(Scotland) Act 2007, once in force, will provide statutory confirmation of the assignability of floating
charges. Registration of the assignation in the new Register of Floating Charges will be required to
complete the transfer; s.42(1). See above, para.36.06, regarding the new register.

[411] 1986 Act s.245(3)(a). This does not apply to any charge created or otherwise arising under a
security financial collateral arrangement; see the Financial Collateral Arrangements (No.2) Regulations
2003 (SI 2003/3226) reg.10(5).

[412] 1986 Act s.245(3)(b). However, such a charge is not affected unless the company was at the time
of the creation of the charge unable to pay its debts or became unable to pay its debts in consequence
of the transaction under which the charge was created: s.245(4).

[413] 1986 Act s.245(5)(d).

[414] See 1986 Act s.245(5)(a)–(c).

[415] 1986 Act s.245(2).

[416] 1986 Act s.245(3)(c) and (d), as substituted by the Enterprise Act 2002 s.248, Sch.17 para.31(4).

[417] Companies Act 1985 s.466. Section 466 is to be repealed by the Bankruptcy and Diligence etc.
(Scotland) Act 2007 s.46(1). Alterations to floating charges will be provided for in s.43 of the 2007
Act; any alteration to a document granting a floating charge which concerns the ranking of the charge
with any other floating charge or fixed security, the specification of the property subject to the charge,
or the obligations secured by the charge will not be valid unless registered in the Register of Floating
Charges (s.43(2), (3)).

but property may be released from a floating charge without such an instrument.[418]

As regards ranking, a fixed security arising by operation of law, such as a repairer's lien, ranks in priority over a floating charge.[419] Subject to that rule, the instrument creating the floating charge or any instrument of alteration may contain provisions restricting or prohibiting the creation of fixed or floating charges ranking prior to or pari passu with the charge,[420] or (with the consent of the holder of any subsisting floating charge and fixed security which would be adversely affected) regulating the order in which the floating charge shall rank with any other subsisting or future fixed and floating charges.[421] If no such provisions are contained in the instrument, a fixed security, the right to which has been constituted as a real right before the crystallisation of a floating charge, has priority over the floating charge, while floating charges rank inter se according to the time of registration with the Registrar of Companies, charges received by the same postal delivery ranking equally.[422] The default position is to change when s.40 of the Bankruptcy and Diligence etc. (Scotland) Act 2007 comes into force. A floating charge created thereafter will rank with other floating charges and fixed securities according to the date of creation.[423] Thus, whereas under the 1985 Act—in the absence of agreement to the contrary—a fixed security constituted in the time period between the creation and crystallisation of a floating charge ranks ahead of

---

[418] *Scottish & Newcastle Plc v Ascot Inns Ltd*, 1994 S.L.T. 1140. The position is to change under the Bankruptcy and Diligence etc. (Scotland) Act 2007. Section 43(5) will provide that the granting by the holder of a floating charge of consent to the release from the scope of the charge of any particular property, or class of property, which is subject to the charge is to be treated as constituting an alteration to the charge which requires registration in the Register of Floating Charges for it to be effective.

[419] Companies Act 1985 s.464(2). This rule is replicated in s.40(4) of the Bankruptcy and Diligence etc. (Scotland) Act 2007 (not yet in force); see also s.41(2)(b). Note also *Grampian Regional Council v Drill Stem (Inspection Services) Ltd*, 1994 S.C.L.R. 36 (Sh. Ct). However a "market charge" which is a floating charge has priority over an "unpaid vendor's lien" unless the chargee knows of the lien's existence when the property became subject to the charge: Companies Act 1989 s.179. "Market charge" is defined by s.173(1) of the 1989 Act.

[420] Companies Act 1985 s.464(1); for the effect of such a provision see s.464(1A); *AIB Finance Ltd v Bank of Scotland*, 1993 S.C. 588; *Griffith & Powdrill, Petitioners*, 1998 G.W.D. 40–2037; *Bank of Ireland v Bass Brewers Ltd (No.1)*, 2000 G.W.D. 20–786; *Bank of Ireland v Bass Brewers Ltd (No.2)*, 2000 G.W.D. 28–1077; D. Cabrelli, "Negative Pledges and Ranking Reconsidered" (2002) 7 S.L.P.Q. 18.

[421] Companies Act 1985 s.464(1).

[422] Companies Act 1985 s.464(3), (4).

[423] Bankruptcy and Diligence etc. (Scotland) Act 2007 s.40(2). Consistent with current law, the date of creation of a fixed security will be the date on which the right to the security is constituted as a real right; s.40(3)(a). The date of creation of a floating charge created before the coming into force of the 2007 Act will be the date when the charge was executed by the company granting the charge; s.40(3) (b). The date of creation of a floating charge granted after the coming into force of the 2007 Act will be the date the charge is registered in the newly created Register of Floating Charge: s.38(3). Section 39 of the 2007 Act will permit, in a situation where a company proposes to grant a floating charge, the company and the person in whose favour the charge is to be granted to have a joint notice of the proposed charge registered in the Register of Floating Charges. Provided the floating charge is registered within 21 days of the registration of the advance notice, the charge will be treated as having been created when the advance notice was registered: s.39(3). On the introduction of the Register of Floating Charges, see para.36.06. When the relevant provisions of the 2007 Act come into force, modified rules (covering inter alia the date of creation, assignation and alteration of floating charges) will apply in respect of floating charges granted in favour of a "central institution" (which means the Bank of England, the central bank of a country or territory outside the United Kingdom or the European Central Bank); see ss.38, 39, 42, 43 and 47 of the 2007 Act as amended by s.253 of the Banking Act 2009. Likewise, modified rules will apply in relation to floating charges which are created by or otherwise arise under a financial collateral arrangement; see the Financial Markets and Insolvency (Settlement Finality and Financial Collateral Arrangements) (Amendment) Regulations 2010 (SI 2010/2993) reg.5.

that charge, under the 2007 Act the floating charge, in these circumstances, will rank ahead of a subsequent fixed security.[424] The holder of a floating charge having a postponed ranking may restrict the preference of a floating charge which has priority of ranking by giving written intimation of the registration of his charge.[425] In the event of a winding up, the provisions of the Insolvency Act 1986 relating to winding up have effect as if the floating charge were a fixed security in respect of the principal of the debt or obligation to which it relates and any interest due or to become due thereon.[426] In the event of a receivership, special provisions apply in order to regulate the distribution of monies ingathered by the receiver.[427] In the event of administration, there are special provisions regarding the disposal of assets by the administrator which are subject to other floating charges, fixed securities or hire-purchase agreements.[428]

Floating charges: the Enterprise Act 2002—The law of corporate insolvency **36.34** was fundamentally reshaped by the Enterprise Act 2002. In an attempt to encourage a culture of corporate rescue, and to create an insolvency procedure in which the interests of all creditors, secured and unsecured, are taken into account,[429] the 2002 Act abolished administrative receivership and replaced it with an amended administration procedure.[430] From the point of view of floating charges, the amendments have resulted in two separate enforcement regimes, one which is applicable to floating charges created prior to September 15, 2003[431] and one which is applicable to floating charges created on or after this date.[432] With some exceptions,[433] the holder of a "qualifying floating charge"[434] created on or after September 15, 2003 may not appoint an administrative receiver.[435] Instead,

---

[424] The ability to alter these default rules by agreement will continue; see s.41 of the 2007 Act.

[425] Companies Act 1985 s.464(5). This provision is due to be repealed and replaced, subject to saving and transitional arrangements, by the Bankruptcy and Diligence etc. (Scotland) Act 2007; see ss.40(5), (6) and 46.

[426] Companies Act 1985 s.463(2); *National Commercial Bank of Scotland v Liqrs of Telford Grier Mackay & Co*, 1969 S.C. 181; *Site Preparations v Buchan Development Co*, 1983 S.L.T. 317. Section 463(2) is due to be repealed and replaced by the Bankruptcy and Diligence etc. (Scotland) Act 2007 ss.45(5) and 46.

[427] 1986 Act s.60(1).

[428] 1986 Act Sch.B1 paras.70, 71 and 72. See further below, para.36.36.

[429] See the Government White Paper, *Productivity and Enterprise: Insolvency–A Second Chance* (Cmnd. 5234, July 2001). Receivership was considered to operate too much in the favour of secured creditors to the undue detriment of unsecured creditors and the company itself.

[430] The change was effected by the insertion of a new Sch.B1 into the 1986 Act to replace the provisions of Pt II of the Act; see the Enterprise Act 2002 s.248 and Sch.16. On administration generally, see J.B. St Clair and the Hon. Lord Drummond Young, *The Law of Corporate Insolvency in Scotland*, 4th edn (Edinburgh: W. Green, 2011), Ch.5.

[431] Which is the date on which the amendments took effect; see the Enterprise Act 2002 (Commencement No.4 and Transitional Provisions and Savings) Order 2003 (SI 2003/2093).

[432] The position is now the same for limited liability partnerships; see the Limited Liability Partnerships Regulations 2001 (SI 2001/1090) (as amended).

[433] There are eight categories of floating charges which are exempt, namely: (a) capital market charges; (b) public-private partnership charges; (c) utilities charges; (d) urban regeneration project charges; (e) project finance charges; (f) financial market charges; (g) registered social landlord charges; and (h) certain water, rail and air traffic charges. See 1986 Act ss.72B–72H. In these cases, the law of receivership continues to apply.

[434] As to the meaning of this term, see below, para.36.36.

[435] 1986 Act s.72A as inserted by the Enterprise Act 2002 s.250(1). The restriction is on the appointment of an "administrative receiver". An "administrative receiver" is a receiver appointed in a case where the whole (or substantially the whole) of the company's property is attached by the floating charge; see ss.72A(1), (2) and 251 of the 1986 Act. The effect of this is that it is competent, even where

the holder of a qualifying floating charge is given the right to appoint an administrator under the revised administration procedure.[436] The ability of a holder of a floating charge to appoint an administrative receiver is preserved in respect of floating charges created prior to September 15, 2003. It is therefore necessary to consider the law relating to both receivers[437] and to administrators.[438]

36.35 **Receivers**[439]—The holder of a floating charge granted by a Scottish company has the ordinary remedies available to a creditor. He may raise an action for payment of his debt or petition for the winding up of the company. An additional ground of winding up is available in cases where a floating charge subsists over property comprised in the property and undertaking of a company which the Court of Session has jurisdiction to wind up, namely that the security of the creditor entitled to the benefit of the floating charge is in jeopardy.[440]

Subject to the comments made in the preceding paragraph, the holder of a floating charge has the power to appoint or to apply to the court for the appointment of a receiver.[441] This remedy is available to the holders of all floating charges created before September 15, 2003,[442] including those of subsisting floating charges created under the 1961 Act, and it need not be provided for in the instrument creating the charge. It remains competent for a holder of a floating charge who has secured the appointment of a receiver to apply for an order for a winding up. A receiver may be appointed on the occurrence of any event which is provided for in the instrument creating the charge as entitling the holder to make the appointment; and, in so far as the instrument does not otherwise provide, on the expiry of a period of 21 days after the making of a demand for payment of the whole or any part of the principal sum secured by the charge without payment being made, on the expiry of a period of two months during the whole of which interest due and payable under the charge has been in arrears, on the making of an order or the passing of a resolution for the winding up of the company, or on

---

the floating charge was created post-September 15, 2003, to appoint a receiver in a case where the floating charge will attach to less than substantially the whole of the company's assets. Note also the comment below (fn.441) in relation to foreign-based companies and the possibility of appointing a receiver under s.51 of the 1986 Act in certain circumstances despite the floating charge being of an "all assets" nature.

[436] The pre-2002 Act administration regime has been preserved for a small number of cases; see s.249 of the 2002 Act. Further, para.9 of Sch.B1 to the 1986 Act disapplies the new administration regime in cases involving certain insurance companies and banks, for which separate administration procedures exist; see further, St Clair and the Hon. Lord Drummond Young, *The Law of Corporate Insolvency in Scotland* (2011), Ch.5.

[437] See below, para.36.35.

[438] See below, para.36.36.

[439] This paragraph should be read subject to para.36.34, above.

[440] 1986 Act s.122(2).

[441] 1986 Act s.51(1), (2) as amended most recently by the Insolvency Act 1986 Amendment (Appointment of Receivers) (Scotland) Regulations (SSI 2011/140). See also Insolvency (Scotland) Rules 1986 (SI 1986/1915) Pt 3. Note that in cases where s.51(1)(b) is applicable (i.e. where the right to appoint a receiver derives from a court of a member state other than the United Kingdom having jurisdiction under Council Regulation (EC) No.1346/2000 on insolvency proceedings) there is now the possibility, even where the floating charge is an "all assets" charge, that a receiver may be appointed in respect of the company's Scottish assets; see s.51(2ZA) and H. Patrick, "Receivership of Foreign Based Companies: Scottish Government Acts", 2011 S.L.T. (News) 213. For the position regarding the receivership of limited liability partnerships see the Limited Liability Partnerships (Scotland) Regulations 2001 (SSI 2001/128) reg.4 and Sch 2.

[442] It should be noted that it remains possible for the holder of a floating charge created post-September 15, 2003 to appoint a receiver in a case where the floating charge will attach to less than substantially the whole of the company's assets; see above, fn.435.

the appointment of a receiver by virtue of any other floating charge created by the company.[443] The receiver may be appointed either by an instrument in writing executed by or on behalf of the holder of the charge,[444] or by the court to which the holder requires to apply by petition served on the company.[445] Where the appointment is by the charge holder, the appointment is of no effect unless it is accepted by the person appointed before the end of the business day next following receipt by him of the instrument of appointment.[446] The appointment of a receiver requires to be intimated to the Registrar of Companies.[447] On his appointment, the floating charge attaches to the property then subject to the charge as if it were a fixed security,[448] in the same way as on the commencement of a winding up. The receiver is required, within three months after his appointment or such longer time as the court may allow, to send a report to the Registrar and to the holder of the floating charge on matters relating to the receivership. This report is also to be sent to the secured creditors (if their addresses are known) and to their trustees, if any, and also sent or supplied to the unsecured creditors free of charge and laid before a meeting of these creditors unless the court otherwise directs.[449] A committee of creditors may be appointed to exercise the same functions as a committee of creditors in a winding up.[450]

The powers which the receiver is to have in relation to the property attached by the floating charge may be defined in the instrument creating the charge, but he has a wide range of statutory powers for ingathering the property and doing other acts, which may be exercised so far as not inconsistent with any provision contained in that instrument.[451] While a receiver may sue in his own name to ingather the company's property, he may only sue in the name and on behalf of the company in respect of debts owed to it.[452] In the exercise of these powers he is not subject to the control of the directors of the company. The board has, during the currency of the receivership, in general no power over assets in the possession or control of the receivers.[453] But the directors do not lose office by virtue of the appointment of the receivers and retain power to act in relation to assets which are not in the receiver's possession and control,[454] and there may be circumstances in which the board is entitled to exercise rights and powers of the company, e.g. where the receiver is disabled from exercising these powers.[455] The receiver's

---

[443] 1986 Act s.52.

[444] 1986 Act s.53.

[445] 1986 Act s.54; RCS rr.74.16–74.18; Sheriff Court Company Insolvency Rules 1986 (SI 1986/2297) rr.15, 16.

[446] 1986 Act s.53(6)(a).

[447] 1986 Act ss.53(1), 54(3). The receiver's appointment takes effect from the time he receives the instrument of appointment; and a docquet acknowledging receipt of the instrument, signed by him or on his behalf is conclusive evidence of receipt and also fixes the date of his appointment: *Secretary of State for Trade and Industry v Houston*, 1994 S.L.T. 775; s.53(6).

[448] 1986 Act ss.53(7), 54(6); see *Ross v Taylor*, 1985 S.C. 156.

[449] 1986 Act s.67(1), (2).

[450] 1986 Act s.68.

[451] 1986 Act s.55, Sch.2.

[452] *Taylor v Scottish & Universal Newspapers Ltd*, 1982 S.L.T. 172; *Myles J. Callaghan Ltd v City of Glasgow DC*, 1988 S.L.T. 227; for a style of instance see *Ritchie v EFT Industrial Ltd*, 1998 S.L.T. (Sh. Ct) 11.

[453] *Imperial Hotel (Aberdeen) v Vaux Breweries*, 1978 S.C. 86; *Independent Pension Trustee Ltd v LAW Construction Ltd*, 1997 S.L.T. 1105.

[454] *Independent Pension Trustee Ltd v LAW Construction Ltd*, 1997 S.L.T. 1105.

[455] *Newhart Developments Ltd v Co-operative Commercial Bank Ltd* [1978] Q.B. 814; *Shanks v Central RC*, 1987 S.L.T. 410; explained in *Independent Pension Trustee Ltd v LAW Construction Ltd*, 1997 S.L.T. 1105, see also *Toynar Ltd v Whitbread & Co Plc*, 1988 S.L.T. 433.

powers are, however, subject to the rights of every person who has effectually executed diligence on all or any part of the property prior to his appointment, and to the rights of the holder of a charge ranking prior to or pari passu with the floating charge by virtue of which he was appointed.[456] In deciding which property of the company to ingather or realise in the interest of the holder of the floating charge he is governed only by the code which the Act provides, which is complete in itself.[457] He is deemed to be the agent of the company in relation to its property and also in relation to contracts of employment adopted by him.[458] He is personally liable on any contracts entered into by him in the performance of his functions (unless the contract states otherwise) and to the extent of any qualifying liability on any contract of employment adopted by him.[459] A qualifying liability for these purposes is a liability to pay wages, salary or contributions to an occupational pension scheme incurred while the receiver is in office and in respect of services rendered wholly or partly after the adoption of the contract.[460] A receiver may be regarded as the occupier of company premises jointly with the company for the purposes of enforcing a statutory duty imposed on occupiers[461] but he is not personally liable for rates.[462] With regard to contracts of employment adopted by him, a receiver is not liable for the payment of wages, salaries, or pension contributions prior to adoption.[463] If the company is not at the time being wound up, he must pay out of any assets in his hands, in priority to the claims of the holder of the floating charge, claims which would have ranked as preferential debts in a winding up, provided they came to his notice by the end of a period of six months after he has advertised for claims.[464] If the company is in the course of being wound up, the receiver is entitled to take control of the property which is subject to the floating charge whether he was appointed before or after the commencement of the liquidation. If he does so he is primarily liable for the payment of the secured and preferential debts of the company.[465] In the distribution of moneys received by him, he is required to give preference to the holders of fixed securities which rank prior to or pari passu with the floating charge, persons who have effectually executed diligence over the property, and to creditors in respect of liabilities incurred by him.[466] Thereafter, subject to his own remuneration and expenses, all moneys received by him are to be paid to the

---

[456] 1986 Act s.55(3); see above as to the meaning of "effectually executed diligence".

[457] *Forth & Clyde Construction Co Ltd v Trinity Timber & Plywood Co Ltd*, 1984 S.C. 1 at 11, per Lord President Emslie.

[458] 1986 Act s.57(1), (1A), added by the Insolvency Act 1994 s.3(2). The 1994 Act was passed as a result of the decision of the Court of Appeal in *Paramount Airways Ltd (No.3)* [1994] B.C.C. 172. The presumption is rebuttable: *Inverness DC v Highland Universal Fabrications Ltd*, 1986 S.L.T. 556.

[459] 1986 Act s.57(2); see *Lindop v Stuart Noble & Sons Ltd*, 1999 S.C.L.R. 889.

[460] 1986 Act s.57(2A).

[461] *Lord Advocate v Aero Technologies Ltd (in receivership)*, 1991 S.L.T. 134.

[462] *McKillop Petitioner*, 1995 S.L.T. 216.

[463] 1986 Act s.57(2) and (2A) added by the 1994 Act s.3(3), (4).

[464] 1986 Act s.59. For the definition of "preferential debts" see s.386(1) of and Sch.6 to the 1986 Act as amended by the Enterprise Act 2002 s.251. The 2002 Act amended the categories of preferential debts by abolishing the preferential status of Crown debts. The benefit to the holder of a floating charge of the abolition of the Crown's status as preferential creditor is offset by s.176A of the 1986 Act, inserted by s.252 of the Enterprise Act 2002, which creates a "prescribed part" which must be kept in reserve for unsecured creditors; see the Insolvency Act 1986 (Prescribed Part) Order 2003 (SI 2003/2097). Note that the "prescribed part" only applies in cases where the floating charge was created on or after September 15, 2003; see 1986 Act s.176A(9).

[465] *Manley, Petitioner*, 1985 S.L.T. 42.

[466] As to which see *Lindop v Stuart Noble & Sons Ltd*, 1999 S.C.L.R. 889.

holder on account of the debt secured.[467] Any surplus is to be paid in accordance with their respective rights and interests to any other receiver, holder of a fixed security or the company or its liquidator.[468] The Act contains detailed provisions as to the provision of information to the receiver and the provision of information by him to the Registrar of Companies and other interested parties.[469] On an application by the floating charge holder or by the receiver the court may give the receiver directions in respect of any matter arising in connection with the performance of his functions.[470]

Administrators[471]—The Enterprise Act 2002 abolished the ability of holders of **36.36** floating charges created on or after September 15, 2003 to appoint an administrative receiver. As a replacement for receivership, the 2002 Act introduced a revised administration procedure.[472] Prior to the 2002 Act, an administrator could only be appointed by way of court order. The Act preserved, with some modifications, this court route into administration.[473] However, the 2002 Act expanded the availability of the administration process by creating an out-of-court means by which the holder of a "qualifying floating charge" can appoint an administrator.[474] A floating charge is a "qualifying floating charge" if it is created in an instrument which states that para.14 of Sch.B1 to the Insolvency Act 1986 applies to the charge; or it purports to empower the holder[475] of the floating charge to appoint an administrator of the company; or it purports to empower the holder to appoint an administrative receiver.[476] A qualifying floating charge must be enforceable before the holder may appoint an administrator.[477] However, an administrator may not be appointed if the company is in liquidation by virtue of a resolution for voluntary winding-up or a winding-up order.[478] Further, the holder of a qualifying floating charge may not appoint an administrator if a provisional liquidator of the company has been appointed or an administrative receiver of the company is in office.[479]

---

[467] 1986 Act s.60(1).

[468] 1986 Act s.60(2).

[469] 1986 Act ss.65, 66.

[470] 1986 Act s.63; RCS r.74.19; Sheriff Court Company Insolvency Rules 1986 (SI 1986/2297) r.17; *Jamieson, Petitioners*, 1997 S.C. 195.

[471] This account of administration is given largely from the perspective of the holder of a floating charge. For a more general account, see St Clair and the Hon. Lord Drummond Young, *The Law of Corporate Insolvency in Scotland* (2011), Ch.5.

[472] The availability of administration is not limited to companies incorporated in Scotland; see paras 111(1A), (1B) and 111A of Sch.B1 to the 1986 Act. The administration regime also applies to limited liability partnerships; see the Limited Liability Partnerships Regulations 2001 (SI 2001/1090) (as amended).

[473] See the 1986 Act Sch.B1 paras 10–13. Paragraph 12 specifies who may appoint an administrator through this court route.

[474] 1986 Act Sch.B1 para.14. See also para.22 which permits the company or the directors of the company to appoint an administrator by the out-of-court method. Note also that the court-based appointment route remains open to the holder of a qualifying floating charge; para.12(1)(c).

[475] As to the meaning of "holder" see Sch.B1 para.14(3).

[476] 1986 Act Sch.B1 para.14(2); see *Stephen, Petitioner* [2011] CSOH 119. The last of these possibilities is designed to permit the holder of a pre-September 15, 2003 floating charge to appoint an administrator rather than a receiver if it wishes to do so.

[477] 1986 Act Sch.B1 paras 16 and 18(2)(b). Note also the notice requirements in Sch.B1 para.15.

[478] 1986 Act Sch.B1 para.8(1). This is subject to paras 37 and 38. Paragraph 37 allows the holder of a qualifying floating charge who would be entitled to appoint an administrator but for the existence of a winding-up order to apply to the court for an administration order. Under paras 37 and 38 a liquidator may apply to the court for an administration order where the company is in liquidation.

[479] 1986 Act Sch.B1 para.17.

In contrast to the appointment of a receiver by the holder of a floating charge, the appointment of an administrator does not result in the crystallisation of the floating charge.[480] Instead, the appointment triggers a period of protection for the company by the imposition of a statutory moratorium on any insolvency proceedings[481] or other legal process.[482] Once the administrator is appointed by the holder of a qualifying floating charge any petition for the winding up of the company is suspended.[483] If there is already a receiver of part of the company's property in place, the receiver shall vacate office if required to do so by the administrator.[484] The aim is to give the company breathing space and to allow the administrator time to fulfil his functions. The job of an administrator is to manage the affairs, business and property of a company in financial difficulties.[485] Under para.3 of Sch.B1 to the Insolvency Act 1986, the administrator must perform his functions in the following order of priority with the objective of: (a) rescuing the company as a going concern; (b) achieving a better result for the creditors as a whole than would be likely if the company were wound up (without first being in administration); or (c) realising property in order to make a distribution to one or more secured or preferential creditors.

The administrator must publicise his appointment.[486] He must also obtain statements regarding the company's affairs[487] to enable him to prepare a statement setting out his proposals for achieving the purpose of the administration.[488] Detailed provision is made for the holding of creditors' meetings to approve and revise the administrator's proposals.[489]

The administrator acts as an agent of the company[490] and is given extensive powers to manage the affairs, business and property of the company.[491] In

---

[480] See D. Cabrelli, "The Curious Case of the 'Unreal' Floating Charge", 2005 S.L.T. (News) 127. Note, however, that a floating charge will crystallise upon the filing with the Registrar of Companies of a notice by an administrator confirming that the administrator believes the company has insufficient property to enable a distribution to be made to unsecured creditors (other than the "prescribed part", for which see fn.503 below); see Sch.B1 para.115(3).

[481] Meaning that no resolution may be passed, and no order may be made, for the winding up of the company; Sch.B1 para.42(2), (3). Note the exceptions contained in para.42(4).

[482] 1986 Act Sch.B1 para.43. This includes a prohibition on taking any steps to enforce a security; para.43(2). Paragraph 44 provides for an interim moratorium on insolvency proceedings and on other legal process. It should be noted that these, and various other provisions of the 1986 Act, do not apply to "financial collateral arrangements"; see the Financial Collateral Arrangements (No.2) Regulations 2003 (SI 2003/3226) reg.8 as amended by the Financial Markets and Insolvency (Settlement Finality and Financial Collateral Arrangements) (Amendment) Regulations 2010 (SI 2010/2993). Generally on financial collateral arrangements, see above, fn.82.

[483] 1986 Act Sch.B1 para.40(1). Note the exceptions contained in para.40(2).

[484] 1986 Act Sch.B1 para.41(2). Paragraph 41(1) provides that an administrative receiver must vacate office whenever an administration order by the court takes effect. This is not extended to the situation where the administrator is appointed by the holder of a qualifying floating charge by means of the out-of-court procedure because, as noted above (fn.479), an administrator cannot be appointed by the holder of a qualifying floating charge under para.14(1) if an administrative receiver is in office; see para.17(b). The same is true in a situation where the out-of-court appointment is by the company or the company's directors under para.22; see para.25(c).

[485] 1986 Act Sch.B1 para.1.

[486] 1986 Act Sch.B1 para.46.

[487] 1986 Act Sch.B1 paras 47 and 48.

[488] 1986 Act Sch.B1 para.49.

[489] 1986 Act Sch.B1 paras 50–8.

[490] 1986 Act Sch.B1 para.69. An administrator is also an officer of the court, whether or not he is appointed by the court; Sch.B1 para.5.

[491] 1986 Act Sch.B1 paras 59–64. By para.60, the powers of the administrator includes the powers specified in Sch.1 to the 1986 Act.

exercising his powers the administrator is obliged to act in accordance with the proposals agreed with creditors[492] and must perform his functions in the interests of the company's creditors as a whole.[493] An administrator must also comply with any directions of the court.[494]

The powers of the administrator include the power to dispose of any property which is subject to a floating charge, as if that property were not subject to the charge.[495] However, in order to protect the floating charge holder's position, the holder is accorded the same priority in respect of the acquired property as he had in respect of the property disposed of.[496] Property which is subject to a security other than a floating charge may also be disposed of by the administrator as if it were not subject to the security, but this is only possible by order of the court. The court will only make such an order if it considers that the disposal would promote the purpose of the administration.[497]

An administrator's statement of proposals may not include any action which would affect the rights of a secured creditor of the company to enforce his security.[498] A creditor who considers that the administrator is acting or proposing to act in an unfairly harmful way, or that the administrator is not performing his functions as quickly or as efficiently as is reasonably practicable, may apply to court for relief.[499] The administrator is entitled to make distributions to a creditor of the company.[500] This is subject to the provisions of s.175 of the Insolvency Act 1986 which provides that the company's preferential debts are to be paid in priority to all other debts.[501] The Crown's status as preferred creditor has been abolished.[502] From the perspective of the holder of a qualifying floating charge, this has reduced the number of claims having priority over it. However, this is offset by s.176A of the 1986 Act, inserted by s.252 of the Enterprise Act 2002, which creates a "prescribed part" which the administrator must keep in reserve and pay to unsecured creditors before the holder of a qualifying floating charge can start to receive what he is due.[503]

---

[492] 1986 Act Sch.B1 para.68(1). He must also perform his functions as quickly and efficiently as is reasonably practicable; Sch.B1 para.4.

[493] 1986 Act Sch.B1 para.3(2).

[494] 1986 Act Sch.B1 para.68(2), (3).

[495] 1986 Act Sch.B1 para.70(1).

[496] 1986 Act Sch.B1 para.70(2).

[497] 1986 Act Sch.B1 para.71. Where property in Scotland is disposed of under paras 70 or 71 the administrator must grant to the disponee an appropriate document of transfer or conveyance of the property. That document or the recording, intimation or registration of that document (where recording, intimation or registration of the document is a legal requirement for completion of title to the property) has the effect of disencumbering or freeing the property from the security; see para.113.

[498] 1986 Act Sch.B1 para.73(1)(a).

[499] 1986 Act Sch.B1 para.74; see for example *BLV Realty Organization Ltd v Batten* [2009] EWHC 2994 (Ch).

[500] 1986 Act Sch.B1 para.65(1). Note, however, that a distribution to a creditor who is neither secured nor preferential may not be made unless the court gives permission; para.65(3).

[501] 1986 Act Sch.B1 para.65(2).

[502] See 1986 Act s.386 as amended by the Enterprise Act 2002 s.251.

[503] See the Insolvency Act 1986 (Prescribed Part) Order 2003 (SI 2003/2097) for details. Where there is a shortfall under the floating charge the floating charge holder is not to be treated as an unsecured creditor for that shortfall for the purposes of claiming on the prescribed part, but a floating charge holder which has surrendered its security interest in full may be so treated; *Permacell Finesse Ltd (In Liquidation), Re* [2007] EWHC 3233 (Ch) and *Kelly v Inflexion Fund 2 Ltd* [2010] EWHC 2850 (Ch). For exceptions to the requirement to keep aside a prescribed part see s.176A(3)–(5) and *QMD Hotels Limited Administrators, Noters* [2010] CSOH 168.

In addition, the remuneration and expenses of an administrator whose appointment has ceased is charged on and payable out of property of which he had custody or control immediately before cessation, and is payable in priority to the floating charge security.[504]

The administration process may come to an end in a variety of ways. Unless an extension is obtained, administration automatically comes to an end after one year.[505] The administrator may apply to the court to bring his appointment to an end.[506] If the administrator was appointed by the out-of-court route, he may bring his appointment to an end where he considers that the purpose of the administration has been sufficiently achieved.[507] A creditor may apply to the court for the termination of the administrator's appointment on the basis of an alleged improper motive on the part of the person who instigated the administration.[508] Administration will also be terminated where a winding-up order is made for the winding up of the company in administration on a petition presented under s.124A or s.124B of the 1986 Act or s.367 of the Financial Services and Markets Act 2000.[509] A company may exit administration into a voluntary winding up.[510] Finally, if the administrator thinks that the company has no property which might permit a distribution to creditors, he may take the necessary steps to dissolve the company.[511]

FURTHER READING

Anderson, R.G., *Assignation* (Edinburgh: Avizandum, 2008).

Carey Miller, D.L. with Irvine, D., *Corporeal Moveables in Scots Law*, 2nd edn (Edinburgh: W. Green, 2005), Ch.11.

Cusine, D.J. and Rennie, R., *Standard Securities*, 2nd edn (Bloomsbury Professional, 2002).

Gloag, W.M. and Irvine, J.M., *Law of Rights in Security* (Edinburgh: W. Green, 1897).

Gretton, G.L., "The Concept of Security" in *A Scots Conveyancing Miscellany: Essays in Honour of Professor J.M. Halliday*, edited by Cusine, D.J. (Edinburgh: W. Green, 1987).

Gretton, G.L., "Financial Collateral and the Fundamentals of Secured Transactions" (2006) 10 Edin. L.R. 209.

Halliday's Conveyancing Law and Practice in Scotland, edited by Talman, I.J.S., 2nd edn (Edinburgh: W. Green, 1997), Vol.2, Chs 47–57.

Higgins, M., *The Enforcement of Heritable Securities* (Edinburgh: W. Green, 2010).

Pienaar, G. and Steven, A., "Rights in Security" in *Mixed Legal Systems in Comparative Perspective: Property and Obligations in Scotland and South*

---

[504] 1986 Act Sch.B1 para.99(3); for a controversial decision as to the interpretation of what constitutes administration expenses see *Bloom v Pensions Regulator* [2011] EWCA Civ 1124.

[505] 1986 Act Sch.B1 paras 76–8.

[506] 1986 Act Sch.B1 para.79.

[507] 1986 Act Sch.B1 para.80.

[508] 1986 Act Sch.B1 para.81.

[509] 1986 Act Sch.B1 para.82.

[510] 1986 Act Sch.B1 para.83.

[511] 1986 Act Sch.B1 para.84. See also paras 90–95 which apply where an administrator dies, resigns (para.87), is removed from office under para.88 or vacates office as a result of ceasing to be qualified to act as an insolvency practitioner in relation to the company (para.89).

Africa, edited by Zimmermann, R., Visser, D. and Reid, K.G.C. (Oxford: Oxford University Press, 2004).

Rodger, A., "Pledge of Bills of Lading", 1971 Jur. Rev. 193.

Scottish Law Commission, *Report on Sharp v Thomson* (HMSO, 2007), Scot. Law Com. No.208.

Scottish Law Commission, *Discussion Paper on Moveable Transactions* (HMSO, 2011), Scot. Law Com. Discussion Paper No.151.

St Clair, J. and the Hon. Lord Drummond Young, *The Law of Corporate Insolvency in Scotland*, 4th edn (Edinburgh: W. Green, 2011).

Stair Memorial Encyclopaedia, Vol.20 (1992).

Steven, A.J.M. "Rights in Security Over Moveables" in *A History of Private Law in Scotland*, edited by Reid, K.G.C. and Zimmermann, R. (Oxford: Oxford University Press, 2000).

Steven, A.J.M., *Pledge and Lien* (Edinburgh: Edinburgh Legal Educational Trust, 2008).

SECTION B:
TRANSMISSION OF PROPERTY ON DEATH

CHAPTER 37

GENERAL ISSUES

Introduction—The following two chapters deal with the law of succession, intes- **37.01**
tate and testate. This chapter is concerned with the general issues that are common
to both branches. The legal rights of surviving spouses and issue of the deceased
are dealt with primarily in the intestacy chapter, but the rules of interaction
between legal rights and testamentary provisions are discussed in the testacy
chapter.

Civil partners enjoy the same rights in the field of succession as spouses.[1] Any
reference in Chs 37–41 to a surviving spouse, marriage or divorce should therefore be read as including a civil partner, a registered civil partnership and its dissolution respectively.

Death—Succession concerns the distribution of the estate of a deceased person. **37.02**
The fact of death therefore has to be established. At common law a person was, in
the absence of proof of death, presumed to continue in life for a reasonable time.[2]
Both the common law and the previous statutory provisions have now been
replaced by the Presumption of Death (Scotland) Act 1977 (the "1977 Act") which
provides for the granting of declarator of death if the court is satisfied on a balance
of probabilities that a person who is missing:

(1) has died; or
(2) has not been known to be alive for a period of at least seven years.[3]

The court in granting declarator must find the date and time of death. If that is
uncertain it will be taken to be the end of the period to which the uncertainty
relates or, where the missing person has not been known to be alive for a period
of seven years or more, the end of the day occurring seven years after the date on
which he was last known to be alive.[4]

The court may also determine the domicile of the missing person at his death
and any question relating to an interest in property arising as a consequence of his
death, and may appoint a judicial factor on his estate.[5] At the expiry of the time for
appeal or, if an appeal is made, on the refusal or withdrawal of the appeal, the
decree of declarator is conclusive of all the matters contained in it and effective

---

[1] Civil Partnership Act 2004 s.131 and Sch.28 Pt 1 brought into force on December 5, 2005.
[2] *Greig v Edinburgh City Merchants Co*, 1921 S.C. 76. Stair suggests 80–100 years, IV, 14, 17.
[3] 1977 Act s.1.
[4] 1977 Act s.2(1).
[5] 1977 Act s.2(2).

against any person and for all purposes including the acquisition of rights to or in property belonging to any person.[6]

The decree may, nonetheless, be afterwards varied or recalled[7] (e.g. where the missing person reappears or fresh evidence pointing to a different date of death comes to light) but such variation or recall affects property rights only if the application for variation or recall is made within five years of the date of decree.[8] If the application is within that time, the court may make such order in relation to property rights as it considers fair and reasonable in all the circumstances of the case. The order does not, however, affect income accruing between the date of decree and the date of variation or recall, nor does it affect rights acquired by third parties in good faith and for value. If no order is made, property rights remain unaffected by the recall or variation of the decree. In considering what order should be made the court must, so far as practicable in the circumstances, have regard to restricting any rights which, as a result of the order, emerge under a trust, to rights in undistributed property plus the value, as at the date of distribution, of rights in property which has been distributed. The court must also have regard, if the facts in respect of which the decree was varied or recalled justify such a course, to the repayment to an insurer of any capital sum paid as a result of the decree. Trustees are required, on the granting of decree of declarator, to effect insurance against any claims which may arise if the decree is varied or recalled and insurers may, before paying any capital sum as a result of a decree of declarator, require the payee to effect insurance against any claim which the insurer may have in the event of variation or recall.

37.03 Survivance—In order to succeed a person must be shown to have survived the deceased and, where appropriate, any later date of vesting.[9] The standard of proof is on a balance of probabilities and the burden lies on those averring survivance.[10] The merest instant suffices unless the will provides for a longer period.[11] Prior to the Succession (Scotland) Act 1964 (the "1964 Act") there were no rules or presumptions as to whether one person survived another in the absence of evidence as to the order of death.[12] Section 31 of the 1964 Act introduced statutory provisions for the purposes of succession for situations where two persons died in circumstances indicating that they died simultaneously or rendering it uncertain which of them survived the other. It adopts the formula "it shall be presumed" for each provision. But these "presumptions" cannot be rebutted because they apply in terms only where there is no evidence as to the order of death. They are best thought of as rules of law. Although the rules are usually invoked where two or more people die in a common calamity, they are not limited to such situations.

The general rule which was introduced by the 1964 Act is that the younger person survives the elder[13]; but this rule is subject to two exceptions. Where the two persons were husband and wife, neither is deemed to have survived the

---

[6] 1977 Act s.3.

[7] 1977 Act s.4.

[8] 1977 Act s.5.

[9] e.g. surviving a liferenter or attaining a specified age.

[10] *Lamb v Lord Advocate*, 1976 S.C. 110.

[11] A period of about 30 days is often chosen for wills in which couples provide for each other; A.R. Barr et al, *Drafting Wills in Scotland*, 2nd edn (Butterworths, 2005), para.5.15.

[12] *Drummond's J.F. v HM Advocate*, 1944 S.C. 298; applied in *Ross's J.F. v Martin*, 1955 S.C. (HL) 56.

[13] 1964 Act s.31(1)(b).

other.[14] The result is that the husband, having failed to survive, fails to qualify as a beneficiary in the division of the wife's estate, and vice versa. This exception is intended to avoid situations in which the estate of the elder spouse would pass to the younger and then to the younger spouse's relatives to the exclusion of those of the elder, which might be contrary to the wishes of the elder spouse. This rule causes problems if a testamentary provision is left to one spouse and, in the event of that spouse predeceasing the testator, to a third party. Neither the spouse nor the third party takes because the spouse neither survives nor predeceases. The other exception to the general rule arises where the elder person has left a testamentary provision which contains a provision in favour of the younger, whom failing in favour of a third person. In this situation if the younger person has died intestate the elder person is deemed, for the purposes of that provision only, to have survived the younger.[15] This preserves the effect of the survivorship clause so as to prevent the legacy passing to the younger person's intestate heirs against the declared wishes of the elder.

Posthumous children—A child who was conceived but not born at the date of **37.04** death of the father will be treated as a child of that father if subsequently born alive and if it is to the advantage of the child to be so regarded.[16] Thus a man was held not to have died survived by issue where his only child was born posthumously because there was no benefit to the posthumous child in holding that he had so died.[17] A child born as a result of conception by artificial methods using stored genetic material from a man by then dead is not in law his child except for the purposes of birth registration.[18]

Forfeiture and relief from forfeiture—The Parricide Act 1594 prevents a person **37.05** who is convicted of killing their parent or grandparent from succeeding to the victim's estate. It is thought that the bar applies only to heritage.[19] The killer's issue are also debarred.[20]

There is also a common law rule that no one can succeed to a person whom he or she had unlawfully killed.[21] It is an aspect of a wider public policy based rule that perpetrators of crimes should not profit from their criminality. Unlawful killing includes murder and culpable homicide but probably does not include situations where the death was caused by mere negligence. Those who merely assist the killer afterwards to avoid detection, having played no part in the killing itself may not incur forfeiture.[22] But not every kind of culpable homicide necessarily results in an absolute bar to succession.[23] A criminal conviction is not necessary

---

[14] 1964 Act s.31(1)(a). For inheritance tax purposes where the order of death of any two persons is unknown neither is deemed to have survived the other, see Inheritance Act 1984 s.4(2).

[15] 1964 Act s.31(2). "Intestate" means leaving the whole or any part of the estate undisposed of by testamentary disposition, s.36(1).

[16] *Cox's Trs v Cox*, 1950 S.C. 117, based on the maxim *nasciturus pro jam nato habetur quando agitur de ejus commodo*.

[17] *Elliot v Lord Joicey*, 1935 S.C. (HL) 57.

[18] Human Fertilisation and Embyology Act 1990 s.29(3B).

[19] Bankton, *Institutes*, II, 301, 30.

[20] This effect may have been repealed by s.15(1) of the Criminal Justice (Scotland) Act 1949, conviction not to involve corruption of the blood.

[21] *Smith, Petitioner*, 1979 S.L.T. (Sh. Ct) 35; *Burns v Secretary of State for Social Services*, 1985 S.L.T. 351.

[22] *Tannock v Tannock*, 2011 G.W.D. 33–692.

[23] *Burns v Secretary of State of Social Services*, 1985 S.L.T. 351, per L.P. Emslie at 353.

to bar the killer succeeding; facts amounting to murder or culpable homicide could be established in civil proceedings[24] by the executors for forfeiture or more likely as a defence by the executors in the killer's action for payment. Civil proceedings may have to be resorted to if criminal proceedings cannot or will not be brought.

The effect of the common law rule is to debar the killer from any rights of succession in the victim's estate, such as testamentary provisions, donations *mortis causa*, legal rights, prior rights and rights to the free estate on intestacy. It does not extend beyond that necessary to achieve the public policy objective. Thus a husband who was convicted of murdering his wife was not regarded as having predeceased her for the purposes of a provision in her will in favour of her relatives should he fail to survive her.[25]

The Forfeiture Act 1982 empowers the court to modify the effect of the above common law rule where it is satisfied that the justice of the case so requires, having regard to the conduct of the killer and the victim and other material circumstances.[26] No modification is allowed if the killer murdered the victim.[27] The court may not grant total relief from forfeiture.[28] The killer's application to the civil court for relief from forfeiture has to be made within three months of conviction.[29]

37.06 Titles, honours etc.—Titles, coats of arms, honours and similar dignities have their own special rules of devolution on the holder's death. The way in which they are to devolve is often specified in the original grant and generally the rules of primogeniture and preference for males apply. The provisions removing distinctions between natural and adopted children and between children whose parents were married to each other and those born to unmarried parents do not apply in this area.[30] The husband or partner of the mother of a child born as a result of donor insemination and similar techniques is not the father for the purposes of titles etc.[31]

37.07 Aliment *ex jure representationis*—The deceased's widow and children who were owed an obligation of aliment by the deceased are entitled to aliment from the estate or those succeeding to it if otherwise left unprovided for. Such an alimentary claim is thought not to be available where the child is over 25 or over 18 and not undergoing further education or training.[32] It is thought that widowers, surviving civil partners and persons accepted by the deceased as members of his or her family can claim too.[33] Claims are rare in modern practice but one could be

---

[24] Hume, *Commentary on the Law of Scotland Respecting Crimes* (1819), Vol.II, 70–1.

[25] *Hunter's Exs, Petitioners*, 1992 S.L.T. 1141.

[26] Forfeiture Act 1982 s.2(2); *Paterson, Petitioners*, 1986 S.L.T. 121; *Cross, Petitioner*, 1987 S.L.T. 384; *Gilchrist, Petitioner*, 1990 S.L.T. 494.

[27] Forfeiture Act 1982 s.5.

[28] *Cross, Petitioner*, 1987 S.L.T. 384. Relief was given in respect of all the heritable estate and 99% of the moveable estate.

[29] Forfeiture Act 1982 s.2(3).

[30] Succession (Scotland) Act 1964 s.37(1); Law Reform (Parent and Child) (Scotland) Act 1986 s.9(1)(c). Parental orders under s.30 of the Human Fertilisation and Embryology Act 1990 have the same effect as adoption in this area.

[31] Human Fertilisation and Embryology Act 1990 s.29(5).

[32] A.B. Wilkinson and K. Norrie, *The Law Relating to Parent and Child in Scotland*, 2nd edn (Edinburgh: W. Green, 1999), pp.417–18.

[33] Lord Ivory's note to the 3rd edn of Erskine, I, 6, 58 states that aliment *ex jure representationis* is available where the deceased when alive owed an obligation of aliment to the claimant; approved in *Anderson v Grant* (1899) 1 F. 484, per the Lord Ordinary.

made by a needy widow or child where a sizeable estate was almost entirely heritable so that legal rights were worth very little.[34]

Renunciation—Rights of succession in another's estate may be renounced in **37.08** advance of their death. It is usual for separating couples to enter into a minute of agreement whereby each renounces such rights in the other's estate, but care has to be taken to renounce all such rights.[35] Renunciations may also occur in antenuptial agreements and cohabitation agreements. A renunciation of rights in intestacy may result in the Crown succeeding.

International aspects—The Scottish rules of succession apply to the moveable **37.09** estate of a person who dies domiciled in Scotland, and to the devolution of immoveable property situated in Scotland whatever the domicile of the deceased. The position of prior and legal rights is discussed in the next chapter.

FURTHER READING

Clive, E.M., *The Law of Husband and Wife in Scotland*, 4th edn (Edinburgh: W. Green, 1997).
Hiram, H., *The Scots Law of Succession*, 2nd edn (Edinburgh: Tottel, 2007).
Macdonald, D.R., *Succession*, 3rd edn (Edinburgh: W. Green, 2001).
McLaren, J., *The Law of Wills and Succession*, 3rd edn (Bell and Bradfute, 1894) and Dykes' supplement (Edinburgh: W. Green, 1934).
Meston, M.C., *Succession (Scotland) Act 1964*, 5th edn (Edinburgh: W. Green, 2002).
Stair Memorial Encyclopaedia, Vol.25.

---

[34] *Greig v Greig's Exs*, 1990 G.W.D. 15–834.
[35] *Price v Baxter*, 2009 G.W.D. 18–299.

CHAPTER 38

INTESTATE SUCCESSION

Introduction—This chapter sets out the rules for the devolution of intestate **38.01**
estate defined as so much of the deceased's estate as is not disposed of by testamentary disposition.[1] A testamentary disposition includes any deed taking effect
on the deceased's death which disposes of any part of the estate or under which
a succession thereto arises.[2] Wills, destinations in titles to property, marriage
contracts, nominations and donations *mortis causa* are examples of testamentary
dispositions. A testamentary disposition becomes ineffective if all the purposes
fail, as for example if the sole legatee renounces, and the estate falls into
intestacy.[3]

The law of intestate succession in Scotland was extensively altered by the
Succession (Scotland) 1964 Act with respect to deaths on or after September 10,
1964.[4] The most fundamental change was the assimilation, after the satisfaction
of prior and legal rights, of the deceased's heritable and moveable estate for the
purposes of succession. The rules which now fall to be applied without distinction
as between heritage and moveables are similar to those which regulated the
division of moveables under the previous law, but with wider possibilities
of representation; thus all the persons in the class nearest in degree to the deceased,
or their representatives per stirpes, share equally in the whole free estate.
Significant improvements were made in the position of the surviving spouse, both
as regards prior rights and in the succession to the free estate in which previously
the spouse took no part. In the line of ascent and the collateral line the rights of
the mother and her relations were equated with those of the father, and of the
collaterals of the half-blood uterine (i.e. where the common parent is the mother)
with those of the half-blood consanguinean (i.e. where the common parent is
the father).

Now under the 1964 Act there are three sets of rules of division, which require
to be considered in turn. First, after the debts and other liabilities of the estate have
been met, the prior rights of a surviving spouse, if any, must be satisfied.[5] There
then fall to be deducted from any moveable estate which remains such legal rights
as may be due to the surviving spouse or to issue.[6] The final division of the balance
of the deceased's moveable and heritable estate is made according to the rules of
intestate succession applicable to the free estate. The extent of the free estate will
thus vary from case to case. Where the intestate died survived by neither spouse
nor issue no prior or legal rights will arise so that the free estate rules will apply

---

[1] Succession (Scotland) Act 1964 (the "1964 Act") s.36(1).
[2] 1964 Act s.36(1).
[3] *Kerr, Petitioner*, 1968 S.L.T. (Sh. Ct) 61; see para.39.11 below.
[4] See M.C. Meston, *Succession (Scotland) Act 1964*, 5th edn (Edinburgh: W. Green, 2002), pp.7–9.
For an account of the prior law, see the 9th edition of this work, para.42.3.
[5] See paras 38.04–38.07, below.
[6] See paras 38.08–38.15, below.

to the whole of the estate after payment of debts. But often where the deceased is survived by a spouse the prior rights of the surviving spouse exhaust the whole estate, leaving nothing for legal rights or free estate. A surviving cohabitant may have a claim.[7]

With one minor exception[8] the division of the intestate part of an estate is unaffected by any testamentary disposition made by the deceased in relation to the rest of the estate.

A decree of judicial separation obtained by a wife used to have the effect of extinguishing all the rights of the husband in her intestate estate.[9] A decree of judicial separation now has no effect in succession in respect of estates of persons dying on or after May 4, 2006.[10]

38.02 Children—Under the common law only those of legitimate relationship were entitled to succeed on intestacy. The Succession (Scotland) Act 1964 contained limited exceptions. Radical changes were made by the Law Reform (Miscellaneous Provisions) (Scotland) Act 1968 which, so far as succession to, and legal rights in, their parents' estate and succession by parents to the estates of their children were concerned, equiparated children of unmarried parents with children of married parents.[11] Beyond that there was no succession through a relationship involving children of unmarried parents. Thus children of unmarried parents were excluded from succession by representation to their grandparents' estates, and children of unmarried parents could not succeed as siblings to each others' estates.[12] For the purposes of succession to the estate of a child of unmarried parents, the child was presumed not to be survived by his or her father unless the contrary was shown.[13] The Law Reform (Parent and Child) (Scotland) Act 1986, which supersedes the 1968 Act, now provides that the fact that a person's parents are not or have not been married to one another shall be left out of account in establishing the legal relationship between that person and any other person and that any such relationship shall have effect as if the parents were or had been married to one another.[14] As regards succession to the estate of anyone who died on or after December 8, 1986,[15] any distinction for the purposes of succession is abolished between a child of unmarried parents and a child of married parents and between ascendants, collaterals and issue who trace their relationship to the deceased through such parent-child links. Certain rules for the presumption of paternity are laid down[16] but there is no longer any presumption that a child of unmarried parents is not survived by the father.

The 1964 Act provides that, in relation to the succession to any person who died on or after September 10, 1964, an adopted person is to be treated for all purposes of succession as a child of the adopter, and not as the child of any

---

[7] See para.38.17 below.

[8] See para.38.07 below.

[9] Conjugal Rights (Scotland) Amendment Act 1861.

[10] Family Law (Scotland) Act 2006 Sch.3 repealing the 1861 Act; Family Law (Scotland) Act 2006 (Commencement, Transitional Provisions and Savings) Order 2006 (SSI 2006/212).

[11] Law Reform (Miscellaneous Provisions) (Scotland) Act 1968 ss.1, 2 and 3 and Sch.1.

[12] 1964 Act s.4(4) as amended by 1968 Act s.1.

[13] 1964 Act s.4(3).

[14] 1986 Act s.1(1).

[15] Law Reform (Parent and Child) (Scotland) Act 1986 (Commencement) Order 1986 (SI 1986/1983).

[16] 1986 Act s.5.

other person.[17] The only circumstance in which an adopted person is entitled to succeed to the estate of a natural parent, or to claim *legitim* in that estate, is when (a) that parent died on or after September 10, 1964, and (b) the adoptive parent or parents died before that date.[18] In relation to collaterals an adopted person adopted by two spouses jointly is treated as a brother or sister of the full blood of any other child or adopted child of both spouses. In any other situation where the relationship between an adopted child and another child or adopted child of the adopter is in issue the children are treated as brothers or sisters of the half blood only.[19]

A stepchild of the deceased, even if accepted by the deceased as a child of his or her family, has no rights of succession in the deceased's intestate estate.[20]

Incidence of liabilities—The whole of the deceased's estate is liable for the **38.03** deceased's debts, even before the deduction of legal rights[21] and prior rights. Formerly a creditor could sue either the heir-at-law or the executor,[22] but as between the heir and the executor the rule was that the former was liable for debts which were heritable or secured over heritage, and the latter for those that were moveable.[23] Hence, an heir who was required to pay a moveable debt had a right of relief against the executor, and the executor paying a heritable debt was entitled to relief from the heir.[24] Although the heir-at-law and the distinction between heritable and moveable for the purposes of succession to the free estate have disappeared, the 1964 Act expressly preserved[25] the existing law whereby particular debts fall to be paid out of a particular part of the estate. The incidence of liabilities remains of significance in computing the moveable estate for the purposes of legal rights.

Where the deceased concluded a contract for the purchase of heritable property but died before obtaining a disposition, then the deceased's personal right to the property is a heritable asset of the estate, but the price is payable out of moveables.[26] On the other hand, if the deceased sold heritable property but died before granting a disposition, the property is balanced by the heritable liability to convey it and the price receivable is to be added to the moveable estate.[27] Liability attaches to heritage where the estate is liable under a heritable security, for such securities remain heritable regarding the debtor's succession,[28] and also for annuities granted by the deceased as these are heritable rights.[29] Where a debt is secured over both a heritable and a moveable asset (a house and a life policy for example) the debt has to be apportioned between the assets according to their respective values.[30] A "mortgage protection" life policy designed to provide funds to pay off the loan

---

[17] 1964 Act s.23(1).

[18] Law Reform (Miscellaneous Provisions) (Scotland) Act 1966 s.5.

[19] 1964 Act s.24.

[20] There might be a claim for aliment *ex jure representationis*, see para 37.07 above.

[21] See *Naismith v Boyes* (1899) 1 F. (HL) 79 at 82, per Lord Watson.

[22] *British Linen Co v Lord Reay* (1850) 12 D. 949; *Carnousie v Meldrum* (1630) Mor.5204.

[23] Erskine, III, 9, 48; *Duncan v Duncan* (1882) 10 R. 1042.

[24] Erskine, III, 9, 48.

[25] 1964 Act s.14(3).

[26] *Ramsay v Ramsay* (1887) 15 R. 25; *Fairlie's Trs v Fairlie's Curator Bonis*, 1932 S.C. 216 at 220, per Lord President Clyde.

[27] *Chiesley* (1704) Mor.5531; *Heron v Espie* (1856) 18 D. 917; *McArthur's Exrs v Guild*, 1908 S.C. 743.

[28] *Bell's Trs v Bell* (1884) 12 R. 85.

[29] *Marquis of Breadalbane's Trs v Jamieson* (1873) 11 M. 912.

[30] *Graham v Graham* (1898) 5 S.L.T. 319. This has implications for prior and legal rights.

secured over property, usually the dwelling-house, does not reduce the secured debt for prior rights purposes. The policy proceeds go instead to increase the moveable estate.

SURVIVING SPOUSE'S PRIOR RIGHTS

38.04 Introduction—Where the deceased died intestate, but only then, the surviving spouse has certain rights in the deceased's estate, known as prior rights. As far as these rights are concerned the surviving spouse ranks next after the creditors of the deceased, and the rights must be satisfied before the estate becomes available to those entitled to legal rights and to the intestate heirs.[31] In a case of partial intestacy the surviving spouse is entitled to receive prior rights only out of the intestate part of the estate. There are three separate rights; under s.8 of the 1964 Act to the dwelling-house and to furniture and plenishings, and under s.9 to a financial provision out of the remainder of the intestate estate. Unlike the other rights of intestate succession the dwelling-house right (subject to certain exceptions) and the furniture and plenishings right are rights to specific items of property which the spouse is entitled to demand from the executor. It is competent for a surviving spouse to discharge or renounce one or more of the prior rights and this might be done in order to increase the children's share. The sums of money in the prior rights rules are changed from time to time by statutory instrument.[32]

38.05 Dwelling-house—As far as the dwelling house is concerned, the surviving spouse is entitled to receive the deceased's interest in the house, including any garden or other ground attached, provided the surviving spouse was ordinarily resident there at the date of the deceased's death, up to a value of £473,000.[33] It is not a requirement that the deceased should have been ordinarily resident in the house at that date. The interests available to the surviving spouse under this right are those of ownership or of tenancy under a lease, subject in either case to any heritable debts secured over the interest.[34] Tenancies of dwelling-houses under the Rent Acts are expressly excluded[35] as are secure tenancies under the Housing (Scotland) Act 2001.[36] The statutory scheme of succession by a surviving spouse to an assured tenancy impliedly excludes prior rights.[37] If the surviving spouse was ordinarily resident in more than one house an interest in which is included in the deceased's intestate estate, he or she has the right to elect within six months of the intestate's death which one to take under this section.[38] If the value of the interest in the house exceeds £473,000, the surviving spouse is entitled instead to a payment of £473,000 in cash. If the value is less than £473,000 the entitlement is to the interest in the house itself, with two exceptions where the entitlement is to

---

[31] See 1964 Act ss.1(2), 10(2).

[32] 1964 Act s.9A added by Law Reform (Miscellaneous Provisions) (Scotland) Act 1980 s.4. The latest instrument is the Prior Rights of Surviving Spouse and Civil Partner (Scotland) Order 2011 (SSI 2011/436) for deaths occurring after January 31, 2012.

[33] 1964 Act s.8(4) and (1), as amended by Prior Rights of Surviving Spouse and Civil Partner (Scotland) Order 2011 (SSI 2011/436).

[34] 1964 Act s.8(6)(d), and see para.38.03 above.

[35] 1964 Act s.8(6)(d).

[36] 1964 Act s.8(6)(d), as read with s.17(2) of the Interpretation Act 1978.

[37] Housing (Scotland) Act 1988 s.31.

[38] Proviso to 1964 Act s.8(1).

the value of the interest only. The first exception is where the house forms only part of the subjects comprised in one tenancy of which the deceased was the tenant. The second exception occurs where the house forms the whole or part of subjects falling into the intestate estate used by the deceased for carrying on a trade, profession or occupation and the likelihood is that the value of the estate as a whole would be substantially diminished if the house were to be disposed of otherwise than with the assets of that trade, profession or occupation.[39]

The dwelling house prior right is available only if the house is situated in Scotland, but it is available to the surviving spouse of a person dying domiciled furth of Scotland, provided the surviving spouse was ordinarily resident there at the date of the deceased's death. It appears to be accepted that this is still the position even where the spouse is entitled to a sum of money because the deceased's interest in the house is worth more than £473,000 or one of the other exceptions applies.[40]

Furniture and plenishings—The second right under s.8 is to furniture and **38.06** plenishings in the deceased's intestate estate, up to a maximum of £29,000.[41] The furniture and plenishings have to be situated in a dwelling house in which the surviving spouse was ordinarily resident at the date of the deceased's death,[42] but it is an entirely independent right, which exists even if the dwelling house in which they are contained does not fall within the deceased's intestate estate.[43] It is expressly provided[44] that the term "furniture and plenishings" does not include any article or animal used at the date of the intestate's death for business purposes, or money or securities for money, or any heirloom. Where the intestate estate comprises the furniture and plenishings of two or more dwelling-houses in each of which the surviving spouse was ordinarily resident he or she is limited to the furniture and plenishings of any one of them. The right to elect must be exercised within six months and is in no way dependent on the right to elect between the dwelling-houses themselves.

This being a right in relation to moveables it is available only if the deceased died domiciled in Scotland. The furniture and plenishings may, however, be situated in a house furth of Scotland.[45]

Financial provision—The right to a financial provision under s.9 is exigible out **38.07** of the balance of the estate only after any claims under s.8 have been satisfied. If the intestate was survived by issue in whatever degree, the right is to the sum of £50,000 out of the remainder of the intestate estate; if no issue survive the intestate the sum is £89,000.[46] Interest is due in each case at the rate of seven per cent per annum running from the date of death.[47] If the surviving spouse is entitled to receive any payment or benefit, other than a bequest of any house or furniture, by

---

[39] 1964 Act s.8(2).

[40] Meston, *Succession (Scotland) Act 1964* (2002), pp.133–4; P.R. Beaumont and P. E. McEleavy, *Anton's Private International Law*, 3rd edn (Edinburgh: W. Green, 2011), para.24–27

[41] 1964 Act s.8(3), amended as set out in fn.31, above.

[42] 1964 Act s.8(4).

[43] 1964 Act s.8(3).

[44] 1964 Act s.8(6)(b).

[45] Meston, *Succession (Scotland) Act 1964* (2002), p.134, but see R.D. Leslie, "Prior rights in succession: the international dimension", 1988 S.L.T. (News) 105.

[46] 1964 Act s.9(1) as amended by Prior Rights of Surviving Spouse and Civil Partner (Scotland) Order 2011 (SSI 2011/436).

[47] 1964 Act s.9(1), as amended by SI 1981/805.

virtue of a testamentary disposition out of the deceased's estate, the amount or value of the legacy must be deducted from the appropriate figure due under s.9. If the intestate estate is less than the amount which the surviving spouse is entitled to receive, the right is to a transfer of the whole of that estate. In many cases the whole of the balance of the intestate estate may pass to the surviving spouse under this right, leaving nothing upon which the legal rights of issue or the rules of succession to the free estate can operate. If the estate exceeds the entitlement, there is a division of the financial provision entitlement among the heritage and moveable property respectively left after the other prior rights in proportion to the respective amounts of those parts. This ensures that a proper balance is preserved for the calculation of legal rights which are exigible only from moveables.[48]

The financial provision entitlement is due out of moveables wherever situated and heritable property in Scotland where the deceased died domiciled in Scotland. But where the deceased died domiciled furth of Scotland it is available only out of any heritable property situated in Scotland.[49]

LEGAL RIGHTS OF SPOUSE AND ISSUE

38.08 Introduction—The legal rights available to the surviving spouse and issue of a deceased person are exigible only out of the net moveable estate. They are termed *jus relictae*[50] and *jus relicti*,[51] in the case of the widow and widower respectively, and *legitim* for issue. The legal right is a right to a sum of money representing the value of a part of such estate rather than to a part of the property itself.[52] The Succession (Scotland) Act 1964 abolished the previous legal rights of life-rent available to a widow and widower in the heritable estate of the deceased spouse, called "terce" and "courtesy" respectively. The 1964 Act also extended the right to claim *legitim* to the issue of predeceasing children.[53]

Legal rights are available only if the deceased died domiciled in Scotland but are then available out of moveables wherever situated. Immoveable property that is situated abroad is not regarded as moveable for Scottish legal rights even if the *lex situs* treats immoveables and moveables alike for its own internal rules of succession.[54]

38.09 Moveable estate—The moveable estate[55] is valued as at the date of death,[56] but if there has been realisation of the estate in ordinary course, it is the actual realised value and not the estimate as at the date of death which determines the amount of the estate for the purpose of calculating the legal rights.[57] It is the free moveable estate actually left by the deceased which is valued for this purpose and so where a partner's contingent right to the goodwill of a partnership was, in terms of the partnership agreement, extinguished on the partner's death, it was held that the

---

[48] 1964 Act s.9(3).
[49] Meston, *Succession (Scotland) Act 1964* (2002), pp.134–5.
[50] This rests on the common law.
[51] Married Women's Property (Scotland) Act 1881 s.6 gave a widower the like right as a widow.
[52] *Cameron's Trs v Mclean*, 1917 S.C. 416.
[53] 1964 Act s.11.
[54] *Macdonald v Macdonald*, 1932 S.C. (HL) 79.
[55] See paras 30.03 and 30.05 for what counts as moveable property.
[56] *Gilchrist v Gilchrist's Trs* (1889) 16 R. 1118; *Russel v Att Gen*, 1917 S.C. 28; see also *Milne v Milne's Trs*, 1931 S.L.T. 336.
[57] *Alexander v Alexander's Trs*, 1954 S.C. 436.

value of the goodwill did not require to be taken into account in determining the fund available for payment of legal rights.[58] It has been decided, however, that a discretionary death gratuity paid after death to the deceased's executors must be brought into account in the computation of legal rights,[59] but that income falling into intestacy through the operation of the legislation against accumulations is excluded.[60] Sums lent on heritable security, although moveable in the general succession of the creditor, are heritable for the purposes of legal rights.[61] Personal bonds are moveable, both as regards the general succession and legal rights, with the possible exception of those purporting to exclude executors or containing an obligation to grant the creditor a standard security on demand.[62]

Whether the interest of a beneficiary of a trust is heritable or moveable will depend upon the nature of the subject held in trust, for the *jus crediti* partakes of the nature and quality of that subject. However, if the truster has directed the trustees to sell the heritable property which is the subject of the trust and to make over the proceeds to the beneficiaries, then the beneficiaries' interest is regarded as moveable, even before the sale takes place. But if the trustees have merely a power to sell, then the interest remains heritable until that power is exercised.[63] The sale of heritage authorised by the court on the ground of expediency will not affect conversion if this was not the truster's intention.[64]

Deductible debts—Legal rights are claims in the nature of debts due from the deceased's estate. The claimants cannot, however, compete with creditors of the deceased; their claims attach to the free moveable estate remaining after these debts have been met,[65] and if there is a surviving spouse after satisfaction of his or her prior rights.[66] The deductible debts are funeral charges, the expense of confirming to and realising the estate,[67] inheritance tax in so far as it is due by the moveable estate, and ante-nuptial marriage contract provisions.[68] **38.10**

Avoidance of legal rights—Potential legal rights claims cannot be defeated by will but can be minimised or defeated by lifetime acts. The deceased may therefore diminish or defeat legal rights by converting the moveable estate in whole or in part into heritage or by giving away property. If a deed of alienation, although appearing ex facie to divest the owner of property while alive, in fact left it under his or her command, or, if there was any trust or understanding whereby the benefit of the property was retained by the owner or he or she was entitled to call **38.11**

---

[58] *Ventisei v Ventisei's Exrs*, 1966 S.C. 21.

[59] *Beveridge v Beveridge's Exrx*, 1938 S.C. 160.

[60] *Lindsay's Trs v Lindsay*, 1931 S.C. 586.

[61] Titles to Land Consolidation (Scotland) Act 1868 s.117, as amended by the Succession (Scotland) Act 1964 s.34 and Sch.3.

[62] Bonds Act 1661 and see Meston, *Succession (Scotland) Act 1964* (2002), p.60. Before the Bonds Act 1661 a personal bond bearing interest was heritable.

[63] *Buchanan v Angus* (1862) 4 Macq. 374; *Sheppard's Trs v Sheppard* (1885) 12 R. 1193; see also *Taylor's Trs v Tailyour*, 1927 S.C. 288.

[64] *Taylor's Trs v Tailyour*, 1927 S.C. 288.

[65] *Naismith v Boyes* (1899) 1 F. (HL) 79 at 81, 82, per Lord Watson, applied in *Petrie's Trs v Manders's Trs*, 1954 S.C. 430; *Russel v Att Gen*, 1917 S.C. 28; *Cameron's Trs v Maclean*, 1917 S.C. 416.

[66] 1964 Act s.10(2); see paras 38.04–38.07, above.

[67] *Russel v Att Gen*, 1917 S.C. 28. As to mournings and aliment to the widow, see *Baroness de Blonay v Oswald's Reps* (1863) 1 M. 1147; *McIntyre v McIntyre's Trs* (1865) 3 M. 1074; *Griffiths' Trs v Griffiths*, 1912 S.C. 626.

[68] *Bell v Bell* (1897) 25 R. 310.

for its re-conveyance, it will not be effectual to exclude the claims of the spouse and issue.[69] This is so, for example, if the fruits or income of the property were to be paid to, or applied for the benefit of, the owner. However, legal rights can be defeated by a disposition of the property to the desired legatee coupled with a reservation of a life-rent to the former owner, or by the creation of a trust to the same effect.[70] The mere circumstance that the deed was executed for the express purpose of shutting out the legal claims will not render it ineffectual[71]; and the fact that the beneficial right might in certain circumstances revert to the grantor of the deed does not make the deed revocable so long as the circumstances did not arise.[72] Another simple device to avoid *legitim* claims against a surviving spouse in a modest estate is to make a will leaving everything to the spouse without any destination-over. If *legitim* is claimed the surviving spouse renounces the bequest and the whole estate becomes intestate.[73] The surviving spouse's prior rights then exhaust the estate leaving nothing out of which legal rights can be claimed.

38.12 Amount and division of legal rights—Where the deceased is survived by a spouse and issue, the spouse and the issue as a class are each entitled to a sum of money representing one-third of the value of the net moveable estate. The remaining third (the dead's part) falls into the free estate. If the deceased is survived by a spouse and not by issue or by issue only, the spouse or the issue, as the case may be, get a sum of money representing one-half of the value of the net moveable estate. The other half (the dead's part) falls into the free estate. If the deceased is survived by neither spouse nor issue there are then no legal rights[74] so that the whole net estate, heritable and moveable, is dealt with as free estate.

Before the Succession (Scotland) Act 1964 the right to *legitim* was limited to the surviving children of the deceased. The 1964 Act introduced the principle of representation in *legitim*.[75] Accordingly, where a person dies predeceased by a child who has left issue, however remote, who survive the deceased, and the child would, if he or she had survived the deceased, have been entitled to *legitim*, such issue have the like right to *legitim* as the child would have had on surviving the deceased. Division among such issue, if more than one, is per stirpes at the level of the class nearest in degree to the deceased of which there are surviving members.[76]

Interest running from the date of death is payable on legal rights. The rate of interest will be fixed by the court (unless the parties agree a rate) looking at the actual yield of the estate and prevailing rates.[77]

38.13 Collation *inter liberos*—This doctrine is designed to preserve equality among the claimants on the legitim fund. "Collation" is in Scots law a technical term meaning

---

[69] Lord Fraser, *Husband and Wife* (Edinburgh: T&T Clark, 1876), ii, 1000; Bell, *Principles*, ss.1584, 1585; *Lashley v Hog* (1804) 4 Pat. 581; *Nicolson's Assignee v Hunter* Unreported March 3, 1841 FC; *Buchanan v Buchanan* (1876) 3 R. 556; *Drysdale's Trs v Drysdale*, 1940 S.C. 85.

[70] *Collie v Pirie's Trs* (1851) 13 D. 506.

[71] *Boustead v Cardner* (1879) 7 R. 139; *Skinner v Beveridge* (1872) 10 S.L.R. 12; *Scott v Scott*, 1930 S.C. 903; *Campbell v Campbell's Trs*, 1967 S.L.T. (Notes) 30.

[72] See *Scott v Scott*, 1930 S.C. 903, per Lord President Clyde at 915–916; also *Campbell v Campbell's Trs*, 1967 S.L.T. (Notes) 30.

[73] *Kerr, Petitioner*, 1968 S.L.T. (Sh. Ct) 61.

[74] There are no prior rights either.

[75] Succession (Scotland) Act 1964 s.11(1), as amended by Law Reform (Parent and Child) (Scotland) Act 1986.

[76] 1964 Act s.11(2) as amended.

[77] *Kearon v Thomson's Trs*, 1949 S.C. 287.

"the right which belongs to persons interested in a succession to have the particular part of the estate in which one of them has acquired a separate right thrown into the common fund in order to provide an equal division of the whole".[78]

If a child entitled to *legitim* has received gifts (somewhat misleadingly called "advances") from the parent in his or her lifetime, these may have to be collated by that child when the fund comes to be distributed among the issue. The effect of this is that the gifts are brought in to augment the total amount of the *legitim* fund and are then, in its division, set against the share of the fund falling to that child. This principle now applies to *legitim* claims made not only by children but also by remoter issue representing deceased children. Such issue must collate any gifts made to them by the person whose estate is being distributed, and also the appropriate proportion of any gifts made to the person whom they represent.[79]

Whether a gift does or does not fall to be collated depends on its nature and the circumstances in which it is made.[80] "Advances made for the purpose of setting the child up in trade or for a settlement in the world or for a marriage portion" must be collated.[81] On the other hand, sums lent to the descendant are not the subject of collation, as these are, like other debts, due to the whole estate (and not merely to the *legitim* fund) and recoverable for its behoof[82]; nor are payments by way of remuneration for services rendered by the descendant,[83] or made by the ancestor in discharge of his natural duty to maintain and educate the descendant.[84] There is no ground for requiring the collation of a gift of heritage[85] or of a legacy to the descendant, as these do not affect the *legitim* fund,[86] heritable subjects not being included in that fund and legacies being due only from the dead's part after that fund has been fixed. It has been held that a provision for a child in a marriage contract which contains no reference to discharge of legal rights must be collated if that child is to participate in the *legitim* fund.[87] Although a gift is of such a nature that it would fall to be collated, collation is excluded if it appears that it was the deceased's intention that the descendant should have the gift in addition to a share of the *legitim*.[88] Conversely, the deceased may stipulate that an otherwise non-collatable gift is to be taken as a payment to account of that child's share of *legitim*.[89]

Collation *inter liberos* arises only between children or issue of predeceasing children claiming *legitim*. There is no place for collation in a question between issue and the surviving spouse.[90] If there is only one claimant for *legitim*, neither the other descendants of the deceased nor the deceased's executors have any title

---

[78] *Young v Young's Trs*, 1910 S.C. 275 at 288, per Lord Kinnear.

[79] See 1964 Act s.11(3). It is not clear what the appropriate proportion is, see Meston, *Succession (Scotland) Act 1964* (2002), p.63.

[80] Stair, III, 8, 45; Erskine, III, 9, 24; *Duncan v Crichton's Trs*, 1917 S.C. 728.

[81] Bell, *Principles*, s.1588.

[82] *Webster v Rettie* (1859) 21 D. 915.

[83] *Minto v Kirkpatrick* (1833) 11 S. 632.

[84] Erskine, III, 9, 24.

[85] Erskine, III, 9, 25.

[86] Erskine, III, 9, 25. In a testate estate the child will have to choose between taking the legacy or claiming *legitim*, see para.39.34 below.

[87] *Elliot's Exrx v Elliot*, 1953 S.C. 43. Note that *legitim* may no longer be discharged by an ante-nuptial marriage contract: Succession (Scotland) Act 1964 s.12; para.38.14 below.

[88] Erskine, III, 9, 24; *Douglas v Douglas* (1876) 4 R. 105.

[89] *Young v Young's Trs*, 1910 S.C. 275; see also *Gilmour's Trs v Gilmour*, 1922 S.C. 753.

[90] Erskine, III, 9, 25.

to insist that that claimant shall collate gifts; nor, on the other hand, can that claimant require the other descendants, who are not claiming *legitim*, to collate gifts received by them.[91] In the division of an intestate estate it may be advantageous for a child who has received large collatable gifts to renounce the right to *legitim* so as to avoid having to collate them with his or her siblings.

38.14 **Prior discharge of legal rights**—Legal rights may be discharged during the lifetime of the ancestor or spouse by the person prospectively entitled thereto, but this intention has to be made clear in the deed; ambiguous expressions will not be construed as having this effect. When spouses separate and execute a minute of agreement regulating their financial affairs it will often contain a clause whereby each spouse discharges their prior, legal and all other rights of succession in the other's estate.[92] An ante-nuptial contract may contain a renunciation of *jus relictae* and *jus relicti*. This is usually done by express words of discharge,[93] but, even without such words, a settlement in the contract of the whole estate which may belong to one spouse at the date of death on the other spouse, being inconsistent with the assertion of such a claim, will exclude it.[94] Acceptance of a life-rent provided in a post-nuptial contract or other inter vivos deed will exclude a legal rights claim out of the fund burdened with the liferent as being inconsistent with a claim to part of the fee.[95] In the case of children it was possible, prior to the 1964 Act, for intending spouses to discharge prospectively the right of any child of the marriage to claim *legitim*, even if the provision in favour of children in the ante-nuptial marriage contract was made in such a way that some of them would take no benefit from it.[96] Where the trust constituted under such an ante-nuptial contract was brought to an end during the lifetime of the parties it was held that the termination of the trust did not by operation of law revive legal rights.[97] Now the right of a child or remoter issue to *legitim* cannot be discharged without that person's consent; nothing contained in an ante-nuptial marriage contract executed on or after September 10, 1964 will operate so as to exclude that right.[98]

The effect of a discharge of legal rights made while the deceased was alive is that the grantor of the discharge is treated as dead. Thus if a spouse has renounced his or her legal rights the *legitim* fund (if there are issue entitled to *legitim*) amounts to half the net moveable estate.[99] In the case of *legitim*, if one child has discharged his right, the entire fund is divisible among the other children just as if that child had predeceased the parent,[100] and if all the children have discharged their rights, the legal rights of any surviving spouse amount to half the net moveable estate.

---

[91] *Coats' Trs v Coats*, 1914 S.C. 744, *Gilmour's Trs v Gilmour*, 1922 S.C. 753.

[92] *Price v Baxter*, Sheriff McCartney at Hamilton, March 1, 2009.

[93] *Maitland v Maitland* (1843) 6 D. 244.

[94] McLaren, *Wills and Succession*, i, 136; *Home v Watson* (1757) 5 Brown's Supp., 330; *Fisher's Trs v Fisher* (1844) 7 D. 129.

[95] *Riddel v Dalton* (1781) Mor.6457; *Edward v Cheyne* (1888) 15 R. (HL) 33; *Smart v Smart*, 1926 S.C. 392.

[96] e.g. *Galloway's Trs v Galloway*, 1943 S.C. 339.

[97] *Callander v Callander's Executor*, 1972 S.C. (HL) 70. There might, however, be revival of legal rights if the deed terminating the trust showed an intention to that effect.

[98] 1964 Act s.12.

[99] Erskine, III, 9, 20.

[100] The child's issue, however, cannot claim by representation.

Post-death discharge of legal rights—It would be unusual for a person entitled **38.15** to legal rights out of an intestate estate to discharge or renounce his or her entitlement after the death of the deceased, except perhaps to avoid collation. The effect of such a renunciation is that the renounced portion falls into the free estate. It does not increase the share of others entitled to legal rights.[101]

THE FREE ESTATE

The free estate is that part of the intestate estate which remains after the deduction **38.16** of prior and legal rights. The order of succession to this part is set out in s.2 of the 1964 Act, by means of a statutory list. Broadly speaking, those nearer in relationship to the deceased are higher on the list and so are preferred to and exclude those lower down.

Separate sections[102] deal with representation, and the division of the intestate estate among those entitled to it. Representation is applied throughout the succession, except in relation to a parent or spouse of the intestate. The division is equally per capita among those who are in the same degree of relationship to the deceased starting at the level where there is at least one living member with the representatives of predeceasing members at that level taking per stirpes. So, for example, if the deceased is survived by one child, two grandchildren by a predeceasing son and three grandchildren by a predeceasing daughter, the child takes one-third, the son's two children share another third between them as do the daughter's three children. However, if the child had also predeceased without issue the free estate would be divided amongst the grandchildren equally, each taking one-fifth.

In the first instance the succession descends to the surviving children of the deceased, including adopted children, and the issue of predeceasing children. Failing children and their issue the succession opens to parents and siblings (brothers or sisters) or their issue.[103] If the deceased is survived by one or both parents but not by any siblings or issue of predeceasing siblings the free estate is divided equally between the parents or goes wholly to the sole surviving parent. If the deceased is survived by siblings or issue of predeceasing siblings but not by any parent, the former group share the whole estate which is divided amongst them according to the rules that apply for issue. Siblings of the half blood succeed only if there are none of the full blood.[104] If the deceased is survived by both parents and siblings (or issue of predeceasing siblings) each group takes half the estate which half is further divided as described above. In the absence of any issue, siblings (or issue of predeceasing siblings) or parents, the succession passes to the surviving spouse. Indeed, in such a situation as there are no issue to take *legitim*, the surviving spouse would be entitled to the entire intestate estate after payment of the deceased's debts. Failing a surviving spouse, the succession opens to ascendants, the relatives of the deceased's mother being placed on an equal footing with those of the father. The succession passes first to uncles or aunts of the deceased, then to grandparents, then to collaterals of grandparents, then to

---

[101] *Fisher v Dixon* (1840) 2 D. 1121, affd (1843) 2 Bell's App 63 (renunciation by issue); *Campbell's Trs v Campbell* (1862) 24 D. 1321 (renunciation by spouse).

[102] 1964 Act ss.5, 6.

[103] 1964 Act s.2(1)(b)–(d).

[104] And no surviving issue of predeceasers, 1964 Act ss.3 and 5.

great grandparents, then to their collaterals and so on to remoter ancestors of whatever degree. Collaterals of the half blood are postponed to those of the full blood.[105] If no heir, however remote, can be found the estate will fall to the Crown as *ultimus haeres*.[106]

COHABITANTS

38.17 A surviving cohabitant of the deceased, unlike a spouse or civil partner, is not entitled to prior[107] or legal rights, nor does he or she succeed to any part of the free estate.[108] However, under s.29 of the Family Law (Scotland) Act 2006, a surviving cohabitant may apply to the Court of Session or a sheriff court[109] for a discretionary award out of any net intestate estate.[110] The surviving cohabitant may discharge his or her right to apply under s.29, either before or after the deceased's death. Cohabitants are those living together as if they were husband and wife or civil partners so the definition covers both opposite-sex and same-sex relationships.[111] Various specified factors are to be taken into account in deciding whether or not two people were cohabitants.[112]

An application to the court by the surviving cohabitant is competent only if: (a) the deceased died wholly or partially intestate[113]; (b) the deceased died domiciled in Scotland[114]; (c) the surviving cohabitant and the deceased were cohabiting immediately before the latter's death[115]; and (d) the application is made within six months of the death.[116] The net intestate estate from which an award may be made is the intestate estate less inheritance tax, other liabilities having priority over prior and legal rights and where the deceased also left a spouse or civil partner their prior and legal rights.[117] The net intestate estate does not include immoveables situated outwith Scotland.

In deciding what award, if any, to make the court is directed to have regard to: (a) the size and nature of the net intestate estate; (b) any benefit received by the applicant as a result of the deceased's death; (c) other claims on, and liabilities of,

---

[105] 1964 Act s.3.

[106] 1964 Act s.7.

[107] But see 1964 Act s.8(2A), (2B) added by s.14 of the Crofting Reform etc. Act 2007 which gives a cohabitant prior rights to the dwelling house on a croft.

[108] The couple's household goods are presumed to be co-owned by both cohabitants so unless this presumption is rebutted the survivor is entitled to a half share of their value, Family Law (Scotland) Act 2006 s.26.

[109] The appropriate sheriff court is one in the sheriffdom where the deceased was habitually resident at death or if this is uncertain, Edinburgh Sheriff Court: s.29(5).

[110] In relation to deaths on or after May 4, 2006, Family Law (Scotland) Act 2006 (Commencement, Transitional Provisions and Savings) Order 2006 (SSI 2006/212).

[111] Family Law (Scotland) Act 2006 (the "2006 Act") s.25(1).

[112] 2006 Act s.25(2), see para.44.36 below; cohabitation doubted in *Harley v Robertson* Unreported December 9, 2011 Falkirk Sheriff Court, Sheriff Caldwell (a separation case).

[113] 2006 Act s.29(1)(a), "intestate" being construed in accordance with s.36(1) of the Succession (Scotland) Act 1964.

[114] 2006 Act s.29(1)(b)(i); *Chebotareva v King's Executor* Unreported March 28, 2008 Stirling Sheriff Court, Sheriff Ward.

[115] 2006 Act s.29(1)(b)(ii); *Carrigan v McClung's Executor* Unreported November 19, 2010 Edinburgh Sheriff Court, Sheriff Scott.

[116] 2006 Act s.29(6).

[117] 2006 Act s.29(10). In a partial intestacy only appropriate portions of the tax and other liabilities are deducted.

the estate; and (d) any other appropriate matters.[118] In *Savage v Purches (Voysey's Executor)* it was held that (d) enabled the court to look at the nature and quality of the relationship and gifts made by the deceased while alive to the applicant.[119] The court cannot however award more than the applicant would have been entitled to as a surviving spouse or civil partner.[120] The award may take the form of a capital sum and/or a transfer of property. The capital sum can be made payable at some specified future date or by instalments. Neither the amount of the capital sum nor the property to be transferred can be altered later, but the date or method of payment of the capital sum can be varied.[121] The court also has power to make an interim order pending determination of the application.[122]

VESTING

Vesting and prescription of rights on intestacy—The whole of the deceased's **38.18** estate, whether he or she died testate or intestate, vests in the executors by virtue of the confirmation.[123] But the vesting of a relative's rights of succession in relation to the intestate estate occurs earlier. Prior rights of the surviving spouse arise by virtue of his or her survivance and vest in the spouse on the death of the deceased. The right to *jus relictae, jus relicti* or *legitim* vests, and always has vested, on the death of the spouse or ancestor.[124] Since 1874 a personal right to the heritable portion of the free estate has vested in the heir on survivance[125] and the same has been true for moveables since 1823.[126]

The fact that rights of succession vest on the deceased's death means that the entitlement of a representative to participate must be determined at the date of death of the deceased; there is no provision by which a person dying during the administration of the deceased's estate can be represented by issue.[127] The rights of succession are personal rights as against the executors until payment is made or property transferred in satisfaction of them. These personal rights form part of the patrimony of the surviving spouse, issue or heir as the case may be and therefore are assignable, pass to their successors on their death and are available to their creditors. It is thought that a surviving cohabitant's right to claim under s.29 also vests on the deceased's death and forms part of his or her patrimony

Claims to prior rights, *jus relictae, jus relicti* or *legitim* are extinguished by the long negative prescription (20 years).[128] This prescriptive period also applies to the heirs' rights to the free estate.[129] Time runs from the date when the obligation

---

[118] 2006 Act s.29(3).

[119] *Savage v Purches (Voysey's Executor)*, 2009 S.L.T. (Sh. Ct) 36.

[120] 2006 Act s.29(4). In *Windram v Giacopazzi's Executor* Unreported October 21, 2009 Jedburgh Sheriff Court, Sheriff Scott, around 90% was awarded to the survivor of a long cohabitation with two school-age children.

[121] 2006 Act s.29(2), (7), (8) and (9).

[122] 2006 Act s.29(2)(b).

[123] Note, however, the exceptions in s.37(1).

[124] Stair, III, 8, 50; *Macdougal v Wilson* (1858) 20 D. 658 (*legitim*).

[125] Conveyancing (Scotland) Act 1874 s.9.

[126] Confirmation of Executors (Scotland) Act 1823 s.1; *Webster v Shiress* (1876) 6 R. 102.

[127] *MacLean v MacLean*, 1988 S.L.T. 626.

[128] Prescription and Limitation (Scotland) Act 1973 s.7. These rights are expressly excluded from the short five year prescription, Sch.1 para.2(f).

[129] Prescription and Limitation (Scotland) Act 1973 s.7 and not imprescriptible under Sch.3.

became enforceable and continues to run irrespective of the claimant's non-age or incapacity or lack of knowledge of the existence of the claim. Similarly, being led to refrain from claiming due to error or fraud does not stop time running.[130] The opinion has been expressed that in other exceptional circumstances where the claimant was unable to pursue the claim the common law plea of *non valens agere* formerly competent[131] may still be available.[132]

FURTHER READING

Hiram, H., *The Scots Law of Succession*, 2nd edn (Edinburgh: Tottel, 2007).

Macdonald, D.R., *Succession*, 3rd edn (Edinburgh: W. Green, 2001).

McLaren, J., *The Law of Wills and Succession*, 3rd edn (Edinburgh: Bell and Bradfute, 1894) and Dykes' supplement (Edinburgh: W. Green, 1934).

Meston, M.C., *Succession (Scotland) Act 1964*, 5th edn (Edinburgh: W. Green, 2002).

Reid, D., "From the cradle to the grave: politics, families and inheritance law" (2008) 12 Edin. L.R. 391.

Reid, K.G.C, de Waal, M. and Zimmermann, R. (eds), *Exploring the Law of Succession: Studies National, Historical and Comparative* (Edinburgh: Edinburgh University Press, 2007).

Stair Memorial Encyclopaedia, Vol.25.

Scottish Law Commission, *Report on Succession* (HMSO, 2009), Scot. Law Com. No.215 (Session 2008–2009).

---

[130] Prescription and Limitation (Scotland) Act 1973 s.14(1)(b).

[131] *Campbell's Trs v Campbell's Trs*, 1950 S.C. 48; *Pettigrew v Harton*, 1956 S.C. 67; cf. *Mill's Trs v Mill's Exrs*, 1965 S.L.T. 375, a case of intestacy supervening.

[132] D. Johnston, *Prescription and Limitation of Actions* (Edinburgh: W. Green, 1999), paras 7.18–7.25, 83.

CHAPTER 39

TESTATE SUCCESSION

Introduction—A will or testament is a declaration of what a person wishes to **39.01** be done with his or her estate after death.[1] In order that the declaration may be effectual it must be expressed in writing.[2] A certain degree of restriction is imposed by the existence of the legal rights of spouses and issue[3] and there are purposes to which, on grounds of public policy, the law will not permit property to be devoted by testamentary deed.[4] It is essential to the validity of a will that the testator had sufficient capacity to test, and that it satisfies the requirements of the law in point of form.

WILLS AND OTHER TESTAMENTARY DEVICES: ESSENTIAL VALIDITY

Capacity to test: Reduction of will—Children under 12 have no capacity to test. **39.02** A person aged 12 or over has testamentary capacity, which includes the capacity to exercise by testamentary writing any power of appointment.[5]

A testament executed by a person who at the time lacked mental capacity is ineffectual. It is necessary to the exercise of the power of testing that the testator should be capable of comprehending the nature and effect of the testamentary act.[6] If a person who lacks capacity has a lucid interval, a will made in that interval may be sustained.[7] Where there is no general incapacity on the part of the testator but merely delusions, it must appear that these delusions influenced the dispositions made in the will in order to deprive them of effect.[8]

The law also recognises the existence of a state known as facility, in which, while there is no incapacity to test, there is such weakness or pliability as exposes the testator to improper practices and solicitations by interested parties.[9] This facility may be due to natural disposition, or to old age, or to ill-health. It is not in

---

[1] Erskine, III, 9, 5.

[2] K.G.C. Reid, "Testamentary formalities in Scotland", in K.G.C. Reid, M. De Waal and R. Zimmermann (eds), *Comparative Succession Law Vol 1: Testamentary Formalities* (Oxford: Oxford University Press, 2011).

[3] See paras 39.33–39.37 below. A surviving spouse's prior rights emerge only in a case of intestacy: para.38.04, above.

[4] See para.39.31, below.

[5] Age of Legal Capacity (Scotland) Act 1991 s.2(2).

[6] *Boyle v Boyle's Exr*, 1999 S. C. 479.

[7] *Nisbet's Trs v Nisbet* (1871) 9 M. 937; cf. *Muirden v Garden's Exrs*, 1981 S.L.T. (Notes) 9.

[8] *Sivewright v Sivewright's Trs*, 1920 S.C. (HL) 63; *Ballantyne v Evans* (1886) 13 R. 652; *Smith v Smith's Trs*, 1972 S.L.T. (Notes) 80.

[9] *Morrison v Maclean's Trs* (1862) 24 D. 625.

itself fatal to the will; but, if, in addition, either fraud or circumvention has been used to impetrate the will, it will be reduced.[10]

Apart from cases of mental weakness, a will may be set aside on the ground that it was executed under error induced by misrepresentation,[11] or was obtained by undue influence (that is, an influence exercised by fraud, coercion[12] or a dominant person in whom the testator trusted).[13] A will in favour of the solicitor who prepared it is regarded with grave suspicion. The solicitor must clear himself or herself from the suspicion that it was obtained by deception or undue influence or that the testator lacked the necessary insight when making the will.[14] Preparation of a will by a prospective beneficiary who is not a law agent is less objectionable, being at most a suspicious circumstance.[15]

39.03 Intention to test—The law does not require that a will shall be in any particular form or that it shall be expressed in technical language. However imperfect the language, a document will receive effect as a will if it can fairly be construed as meaning that the author intended thereby to bequeath his estate in whole or in part.[16] A letter to the intended beneficiary may have this effect.[17] On the other hand, a mere list of names and sums of money is not sufficient for this purpose.[18]

If on the face of a writing there be something which raises a doubt whether it was meant to be a testament or, on the other hand, merely a memorandum or note of instructions for the preparation of a formal deed, evidence will be admitted for the purpose of determining the character of the writing. Thus, in *Munro v Coutts*[19] a testator, who had executed a formal settlement, sent to his agent a letter containing a holograph signed document beginning "I wish a codicil to be made to my last will and settlement in the following manner", and containing a number of bequests. There being doubt regarding this document, extrinsic evidence was admitted; and, on considering the terms of the correspondence between the testator and his agent and the other facts proved, the House of Lords came to the conclusion that the document, although not defective in form, was intended to be no more than instructions to the agent and not a final testamentary writing. The same conclusion has been reached in cases where the doubt as to the effect of the document was created by the language of a letter with which the document was forwarded to the writer's law agent.[20] The effect of a title or heading placed on a deed may be such as to cast doubt on the deed, and to allow of evidence as to the circumstances attending its execution. The fact that a writing, which was in other

---

[10] *McDougal v McDougal's Trs*, 1931 S.C. 102; cf. *West's Trs. v West*, 1980 S.L.T. 6; as to fraud and circumvention in the law of contract, see *Mackay v Campbell*, 1966 S.L.T. 329; 1967 S.L.T. 337, HL, applied in the context of reduction of a will in *Pascoe-Watson v Brock's Exr*, 1998 S.L.T. 40 and *Horne v Whyte* [2005] CSOH 115.

[11] *Munro v Strain* (1874) 1 R. 522.

[12] *Weir v Grace* (1899) 2 F. (HL) 30 at 31, per Lord Halsbury; *Forrest v Low's Trs*, 1907 S.C. 1240 at 1256, per Lord Kinnear; 1909 S.C. (HL) 16; *Williams v Philip* (1907) 15 S.L.T. 396; see also *McKechnie v McKechnie's Trs*, 1908 S.C. 93; *Gray v Binny* (1879) 7 R. 332; *Ross v Gosselin's Exrs*, 1926 S.C. 325; *Horne v Whyte* [2005] CSOH 115.

[13] *Gray v Binny* (1879) 7 R. 332; *Honeyman's Exs v Sharp*, 1978 S.C. 223.

[14] *Stewart v Mclaren*, 1920 S.C. (HL) 148; *Forrest v Low's Trs*, 1907 S.C. 1240; *Weir v Grace* (1899) 2 F. (HL) 30.

[15] *Tiarks v Paterson*, 1992 G.W.D. 23–1328.

[16] *Colvin v Hutchison* (1885) 12 R. 947; *Draper v Thomason*, 1954 S.C. 136.

[17] *Rhodes v Peterson*, 1971 S. C. 56.

[18] *Waddell's Trs v Waddell* (1896) 24 R. 189; *Cameron's Trs v Mackenzie*, 1915 S.C. 313.

[19] *Munro v Coutts* (1813) 1 Dow 437.

[20] *Young's Trs v Henderson*, 1925 S.C. 749; *MacLaren's Trs v Mitchell & Brattan*, 1959 S.C. 183.

respects a perfect will, was headed "Notes of Intended Settlement", was held, where the evidence was inconclusive, not sufficient to deprive the writing of effect.[21] But deeds entitled "Drafts" have been rejected.[22] The document must evince a present concluded testamentary intention.[23]

Limits to delegation of testing—Making a will is by definition[24] a personal act **39.04** which cannot be delegated so that a direction to trustees to dispose of the testator's estate as they think proper is ineffectual.[25] However, a testator may confer on trustees, or on a selected individual, power to choose the beneficiaries from among a class of persons or objects and, provided this class is sufficiently definite, the bequest will be sustained.[26] If the class is not a definite one,[27] or if the testator omits to appoint someone to make the choices,[28] the testator's directions will fail on the ground of uncertainty. The Adults with Incapacity (Scotland) Act 2000 has been used to authorise the alteration of an incapable adult's existing will and might be extended to making an original will for such an adult.[29]

Will substitutes—Besides deeds which are in their nature *mortis causa*, other **39.05** deeds may contain provisions which are regarded as testamentary. A special destination in the title to heritage will carry the property on the death of the proprietor to the person named in the destination.[30] If a party acquiring property in his own right chooses to take the title in such terms as to himself and A or the survivor of them, this will operate as a nomination of A as successor to that party in the right to the property.[31] Although such destinations may have certain testamentary effects they are not, however, strictly writings of a testamentary character.[32] A person acquiring property by virtue of a special destination takes it subject to any security or debt of the deceased. Thus, a bankrupt's share of heritable property held by him and his widow equally between them and the survivor of them passed to his widow on his death but she was found liable for his debts up to the value of his share.[33] Special destinations occurring in documents of title, such as bonds, debentures, certificates of debt, and stock or share certificates of public companies also have testamentary effect.[34] On the other hand, no such effect is given to

---

[21] *Hamilton v White* (1882) 9 R. (HL) 53.

[22] *Sprot's Trs v Sprot*, 1909 S.C. 272; *Forsyth's Trs v Forsyth* (1872) 10 M. 616.

[23] *Jamieson's Exrs, Petitioner*, 1982 S.C. 1; *Barker's Exrs and the Scottish Rights of Way Soc. Ltd*, 1996 S.C. 396.

[24] Erskine, III, 9, 5; D.R. Macdonald, *Succession*, 3rd edn (Edinburgh: W. Green, 2001) para.6.01.

[25] *Bannerman's Trs v Bannerman*, 1915 S.C. 398, per Lord Skerrington; *Anderson v Smoke* (1898) 25 R. 493; *Wood v Wood's Exrx*, 1995 S.L.T. 563.

[26] See *Crichton v Grierson* (1828) 3 W. & S. 329, and *Hill v Burns* (1826) 2 W. & S. 80, and cases there cited. Many discretionary trusts fall into this category.

[27] As in *Blair v Duncan* (1901) 4 F. (HL) 1; *Turnbull's Trs v Lord Advocate*, 1918 S.C. (HL) 88. The cases are discussed in *Reid's Trs v Cattanach's Trs*, 1929 S.C. 727. As to the effect of a bequest for "charitable" purposes see para.41.23, below.

[28] *Angus's Exrx v Batchan's Trs*, 1949 S.C. 335.

[29] *T, Applicant*, 2005 S.L.T. (Sh. Ct) 97. See also *J.G.*, 2009 S.L.T. (Sh. Ct) 122.

[30] H. Hiram, *The Scots Law of Succession*, 2nd edn (Tottel, 2007); see para.39.13 below for the effect of divorce.

[31] *Dennis v Aitchison*, 1923 S.C. 819 at 824, per Lord President Clyde; 1924 S.C. (HL) 122.

[32] *Hay's Tr. v Hay's Trs*, 1951 S.C. 329 at 333, per Lord President Cooper. See also *Gordon-Rogers v Thomson's Exrs*, 1988 S.C. 145.

[33] *Fleming's Tr. v Fleming*, 2000 S.L.T. 406; overruling *Barclays Bank v McGreish*, 1983 S.L.T. 344.

[34] *Connell's Trs v Connell's Trs* (1886) 13 R. 1175; *Dennis v Aitchison*, 1924 S.C. (HL) 122; *Drysdale's Trs v Drysdale*, 1922 S.C. 741; *Duff's Trs v Phillipps*, 1921 S.C. 287.

the terms of deposit-receipts; a deposit-receipt cannot operate as a will[35] and instructions attached to or written on a deposit-receipt do not receive testamentary effect unless they are indicative of an intention to bequeath.[36] Provisions in marriage contracts conceived in favour of parties who are to take on the death or failure of the spouses and issue of the marriage are generally treated as testamentary and, therefore, revocable.[37]

A donation *mortis causa* is an inter vivos gift made by an individual made in contemplation of death, but the individual need not be under immediate apprehension of death.[38] Delivery of the subject gifted is not essential as some equivalent may show an intention to gift.[39] The donee becomes the owner of the subject gifted but the law implies from the circumstances of the gift that it will revert to the donor if he or she revokes the gift during life or by will,[40] or if the donee predeceases the donor.[41] If the donor dies without having revoked the gift the donee acquires an effective right to it; however the gift is treated as part of the deceased's estate for the purposes of legal rights and the claims of creditors. Donations *mortis causa* are now almost unknown in practice.

A person who has an account with certain institutions, such as a friendly society[42] or a trade union, may be able to nominate to whom the money shall pass on his or her death. The nomination has to be made in accordance with the rules of the institution and can in general be cancelled by an express revocation in a later will.[43]

WILLS: FORMAL VALIDITY

39.06 Execution of wills after August 1, 1995—The rules set out in this paragraph apply to a will, testamentary trust disposition and settlement or codicil ("a will") executed in Scotland on or after August 1, 1995 when the Requirements of Writing (Scotland) Act 1995 came into force.[44] The formal validity of wills executed furth of Scotland is governed by the Wills Act 1963. The minimum requirement for formal validity is that the will must be in writing subscribed by the testator. What constitutes subscription is set out in s.7. The testator has to sign his or her full name as in the will or surname plus at least one forename or initial.[45] Another form of signature, such as a mark or "mum", may be valid if it is established that it was a usual method of signing such documents and it was intended to be a signature. The signature has to come at the end of the last page[46]; a signature

---

[35] *Dinwoodie's Exr v Carruthers' Exr* (1895) 23 R. 234. An "either or survivor" bank account also does not have testamentary effect.

[36] *Gray's Trs v Murray*, 1970 S.L.T. 105.

[37] See *Lord Advocate v Stewart* (1906) 8 F. 579 at 589; *Barclay's Trs v Watson* (1903) 5 F. 926; and *Law, Petitioners*, 1962 S.C. 500.

[38] *Morris v Riddick* (1867) 5 M. 1036; *Blyth v Curle* (1885) 12 R. 674.

[39] *Crosbie's Trs v Wright* (1880) 7 R. 823; *Graham's Trs v Gillies*, 1956 S.C. 437; *Forrest-Hamilton's Tr v Forrest-Hamilton*, 1970 S.L.T. 338; *Gray's Trs v Murray*, 1970 S.L.T. 105.

[40] The will must refer to the donation expressly, *Scott's Trs v Macmillan* (1905) 8 F. 214.

[41] *Morris v Riddick* (1867) 5 M. 1036; *Lord Advocate v Galloway* (1884) 11 R. 541.

[42] Friendly Societies Act 1974 s.66.

[43] *Ford's Trs v Ford*, 1940 S.C. 426; *Clark's Exs v Macaulay*, 1961 S.L.T. 109.

[44] Requirements of Writing (Scotland) Act 1995 (the "1995 Act") s.15(2), the Act being passed on May 1.

[45] Peers, wives of peers and the eldest sons of peers may continue to subscribe by their titles, 1995 Act s.7(6).

[46] 1995 Act s.7(1).

elsewhere such as on the back or in the middle is ineffective.[47] Wills that are simply subscribed have to be "set-up" as they are not self-proving and cannot found an application for confirmation.[48] Setting-up normally requires a summary application to the appropriate sheriff court with evidence that the will was indeed subscribed by the testator, but it can also be done in the course of other proceedings where the validity of the will is in issue.[49]

To be self-proving a will must bear to have been subscribed by the testator. If the will consists of more than one sheet, the last sheet must be signed at the end and each sheet apart from the last must be signed.[50] It must also bear to have been signed by a witness and the witness's name and address must appear in the body of the will or in the testing clause. The witness has to have had credible information at the time of signing as to the testator's identity and must see the testator sign or hear the testator acknowledge his or her subscription and then sign as witness.[51] A will that is holograph or adopted as holograph has no greater legal effect than one simply signed by the testator.

Where the testator is blind or cannot write, a will may be subscribed on his or her behalf by a relevant person being: a solicitor with a current practising certificate, an advocate, a justice of the peace or a sheriff clerk.[52] Blind people may sign their own wills instead of having them signed by a relevant person, but the will could be challenged on the ground that the testator was unaware of its terms.[53]

Execution of wills prior to August 1, 1995—The rules set out in this paragraph **39.07** apply to wills executed in Scotland before August 1, 1995. A will must be in writing, and the writing must be (1) a deed; subscribed[54] and attested in accordance with the rules as to the execution of deeds; or (2) a holograph writing, i.e. a document in the handwriting of, and signed by, the testator; or (3) a document to which the testator has appended in his own handwriting[55] the words "adopted as holograph" or similar words. Where the testator is blind or cannot write, the deed may be executed on his behalf by a notary, law agent, justice of the peace or parish minister (or his assistant or successor) acting within his own parish.[56] It is not essential to the validity of the will that this procedure be followed; a blind person may sign a will himself. Provided it is ex facie valid, the onus will be on any party challenging the deed to show that the testator did not comprehend its terms.[57]

In holograph documents of a testamentary character, subscription by the granter is essential to satisfy the requirements of a completed testamentary act.[58] Subscription by initials or by Christian name alone or by a familiar or pet name has been held to be sufficient if that was the writer's ordinary method of signing

---

[47] *Robbie v Carr*, 1959 S.L.T. (Notes) 16; *Boyd v Buchanan*, 1964 S.L.T. (Notes) 108.

[48] They can, however, be registered in the Books of Council and Session or sheriff court books, s.6(3).

[49] 1995 Act s.4.

[50] 1995 Act s.3(2).

[51] 1995 Act s.3(4), (5) and (7).

[52] See 1995 Act s.9 for the detailed provisions.

[53] *Duff v Earl of Fife* (1823) 1 Shaw's App. 498.

[54] See *Baird's Trs v Baird*, 1955 S.C. 286; *Ferguson, Petitioner*, 1959 S.C. 56.

[55] But see *McBeath's Trs v McBeath*, 1935 S.C. 471.

[56] Conveyancing (Scotland) Act 1924 s.18. See *Finlay v Finlay's Trs*, 1948 S.C. 16; *Hynd's Tr. v Hynd's Trs*, 1954 S.C. 112; 1955 S.C. (HL) 1; *McIldowie v Muller*, 1979 S.C. 271.

[57] *Duff v Earl of Fife* (1823) 1 Shaw's App.498.

[58] *Taylor's Executrices v Thom*, 1914 S.C. 79; *McLay v Farrell*, 1950 S.C. 149; *Lorimer's Exrs v Hird*, 1959 S.L.T. (Notes) 8.

comparable communications or can on other grounds be taken as indicating that what is written above the subscription is the concluded expression of the writer's intention.[59] If a number of writings can be read together as one document they are sufficiently authenticated by subscription of the last of them.[60] There must, however, be subscription, and it will not do to sign the deed in the middle,[61] in the margin[62] or on the back.[63] It is enough for the validity of the deed that the essential parts should be holograph; if a portion only of the document is written by the testator, as where a printed form of will is filled up, that portion will be allowed effect provided that it is in itself and apart from the other parts of the document sufficient to constitute a testamentary disposition.[64] A testamentary writing has been held to be holograph when it was typed by the granter, that being his method of writing,[65] but the document must *in gremio* state that it was typed by the granter.[66]

A statement in the writing that it is holograph of the granter has no evidential value unless the subscription is admitted or proved to be genuine[67]; and proof of genuineness is a prerequisite for confirmation of executors nominate under a holograph will.[68]

39.08 Validation of writings—Writings which are not in themselves capable of effect may be validated by adoption. Thus if the testator appended prior to August 1, 1995 to an informal document a signed note in his own handwriting adopting the document as holograph, it was thus made effectual.[69] This is the case also if the testator in a properly executed deed refers to, and adopts, prior informal writings; and it will be sufficient for this purpose if the later deed, without expressly adopting the earlier writings, recognises them and demonstrates that the testator intended that they should form part of his will.[70] Moreover, a testator may by anticipation provide in his settlement that future writings, although neither tested nor holograph, or even, it may be, unsigned,[71] shall be received as valid, and a direction of this kind imparts to writings which come within the description given in the settlement the same efficacy as if they actually formed part of that deed.[72] But if the testator has directed that the future writings are to be "under my hand", a writing to be effective must be subscribed, unless he has made it plain that it

---

[59] *Speirs v Home Speirs* (1879) 6 R. 1359; *Draper v Thomason*, 1954 S.C. 136; *Rhodes v Peterson*, 1971 S.C. 56; cf. *Jamieson's Exrs*, 1982 S.C. 1.

[60] *Lowrie's J.F. v McMillan's Executrix*, 1972 S.L.T. 159.

[61] *McLay v Farrell*, 1950 S.C. 149.

[62] *Robbie v Carr*, 1959 S.L.T. (Notes) 16.

[63] *Boyd v Buchanan*, 1964 S.L.T. (Notes) 108.

[64] *Bridgeford's Exr v Bridgeford*, 1948 S.C. 416; *Tucker v Canch's Tr.*, 1953 S.C. 270; *Gillies v Glasgow Royal Infirmary*, 1960 S.C. 438. See also *Ayrshire Hospice, Petitioners*, 1993 S.L.T. (Sh. Ct) 75.

[65] *McBeath's Trs v McBeath*, 1935 S.C. 471.

[66] *Chisholm v Chisholm*, 1949 S.C. 434.

[67] *Harper v Green*, 1938 S.C. 198.

[68] See 1964 Act s.21; an affidavit by each of two persons that the writing and signature are in the testator's handwriting is sufficient.

[69] *Gavine's Tr. v Lee* (1883) 10 R. 448; *Macphail's Trs v Macphail*, 1940 S.C. 560; *Hogg's Exr v Butcher*, 1947 S.N. 141 at 190. *Davidson v Convy*, 2003 S.C. 420, unsealed envelope with "my will" and signature held to adopt unsigned holograph document inside.

[70] *Callander v Callander's Trs* (1863) 2 M. 291; *Cross's Trs v Cross*, 1921 1 S.L.T. 244.

[71] As in *Crosbie v Wilson* (1865) 3 M. 870; *Taylor's Executrices v Thom*, 1914 S.C. 79, per Lord Skerrington.

[72] *Lowson v Ford* (1866) 4 M. 631, per Lord Cowan.

need not be so.[73] The reduction of the minimal formal requirements in post August 1, 1995 documents to mere subscription will lessen the need to rely on their adoption by more formal deeds.

Alterations—The Requirements of Writing (Scotland) Act 1995 contains detailed **39.09** provisions on the validity of alterations. An alteration is presumed to have been made before subscription if the will is self-proving and it contains a statement that the alteration was so made.[74] In other cases the court may certify that the addition was made before subscription on being satisfied by written or oral evidence that that was the situation.[75] In either case the alteration is treated as part of the will. Post-execution alterations require to be authenticated in the same way as a will; signature[76] for formal validity, subscription plus witnessing for self-proving status. Again a court can "set-up" an alteration that is merely signed. The pre-1995 rules for revocation of a testamentary provision by deletion or erasure are preserved.[77]

Unauthenticated alterations to a will executed before August 1, 1995 are generally inoperative but it has been observed that there may be circumstances in which they can receive effect if they are shown to have been made before execution.[78]

REVOCATION OF WILLS ETC.

Revocability of will—A will is in its nature revocable at any time by the testator. **39.10** The testator must have the requisite mental capacity; facility and circumvention or undue influence are also grounds for reduction of the revocation.[79] It matters not that the will has been delivered; and a statement in a testamentary deed that it is irrevocable is of no effect. A person may, however, agree or promise to leave his or her estate by will to another; and in that case a will made in contravention of the contract or promise may be reduced.[80]

A mutual will is a deed in which two or more parties give directions as to the disposal of their estates after their deaths. The entitlement of the survivor(s) to revoke the will after the death of one of the parties depends on the terms of the will and the circumstances of the parties.[81] Because of these difficulties, mutual wills are virtually unknown in modern practice.

Revocation of will—A will may be revoked in whole or in part in various ways. **39.11** Thus the testator may destroy, or tear up, the deed or may obliterate or cancel the writing. The rules relating to revocation of wills by deletion or erasure without

---

[73] *Waterson's Trs v St Giles Boys' Club*, 1943 S.C. 369, overruling *Ronalds' Trustees v Lyle*, 1929 S.C. 104. See too *Russell's Exr v Duke*, 1946 S.L.T. 242 (list of bequests on one side of used envelope and signature on other held a valid will).
[74] 1995 Act s.5(5).
[75] 1995 Act s.5(6).
[76] Signature need not be the full name, see para.39.06 above.
[77] 1995 Act s.5(2)(a), see para.39.11 below.
[78] *Syme's Exrs v Cherrie*, 1986 S.L.T. 161.
[79] See para.39.02, above.
[80] *Curdy v Boyd* (1775) M. 15946; *Paterson v Paterson* (1893) 20 R. 484; *Smith v Oliver (No.2)*, 1911 S.C. 103 at 111, per Lord President Dunedin. The promise can now be proved by any evidence, Requirements of Writing (Scotland) Act 1995 s.11(1).
[81] *Crawfords Trs v United Free Church of Scotland*, 1909 S.C. 25; *Duthie v Keir's Exr*, 1930 S.C. 645; *Saxby v Saxby's Exrs*, 1952 S.C. 352.

authentication have been expressly preserved by the Requirement of Writing (Scotland) Act 1995.[82] If a testator had custody of the duly executed will but it cannot be found after death, the presumption will be that the testator destroyed it *animo revocandi*.[83] But, if it be shown that the destruction or obliteration occurred without *animus revocandi* on the part of the testator, as, e.g. if it were accidental or were due to insanity, or were done without his consent, the will would not be revoked.[84] But the authenticated cancellation of a residue clause has been held to be valid, notwithstanding the apparent misapprehension of the testator that there would be no residue.[85] Where a second will was executed by a testatrix and an earlier one destroyed in accordance with professional practice by her solicitor, and later it was found that the second was invalid, it was held that the earlier will had not been revoked by its destruction, but that its effective revocation was conditional upon the valid execution of a later will.[86]

The testator may revoke the will by a subsequent testamentary writing. This may be express, the testator declaring that earlier wills are revoked; but even an express general revocation of prior wills does not necessarily revoke a bequest of a specific subject, at least if it is contained in a separate writing delivered to the beneficiary.[87] Revocation may be implied from the circumstance that the two deeds are inconsistent, in which case the later deed will prevail. A universal settlement of the testator's estate effected by the later deed will have that result.[88] A will which has other characteristics of a universal settlement may not be so regarded if it lacks a residue clause.[89] It is only in so far as the two deeds are inconsistent that the earlier one is revoked by implication; and if the two are only partially inconsistent, there is revocation only to the extent of that inconsistency. In so far as the deeds can be brought into harmony, they will be read as together forming the testator's will.[90] Where a testamentary writing has been revoked by a subsequent testamentary writing which is itself cancelled by the testator, the general rule is that the earlier will revive and receive effect as if it had never been revoked; but it has been suggested that this rule may, in certain circumstances, suffer exception.[91]

39.12 ***Conditio si testator sine liberis decesserit***—A settlement which makes no provision for children *nascituri* is presumed to be revoked by the subsequent birth of a child to the testator.[92] This presumption rests upon the supposition that in the altered circumstances the testator would not have desired that the will should remain in force; and the presumption may be rebutted by circumstances showing

---

[82] 1995 Act s.5(2)(a).

[83] *Bonthrone v Ireland* (1883) 10 R. 779 at 790, per Lord Young; *Clyde v Clyde*, 1958 S.C. 343.

[84] Bell, *Principles*, s.1866; McLaren, *Wills and Succession*, i, 409; *Fotheringham's Trs v Reid*, 1936 S.C. 831. See also *Lauder v Briggs*, 1999 S.C. 453 and *McLernan v Ash*, 2001 G.W.D. 10–374.

[85] *Thomson's Trs v Bowhill Baptist Church*, 1956 S.C. 217.

[86] *Cullen's Exr v Elphinstone*, 1948 S.C. 662.

[87] *Clark's Exr v Clark*, 1943 S.C. 216.

[88] *Macrorie's Exrs v McLaren*, 1984 S.L.T. 271; *Dick's Trs v Dick*, 1907 S.C. 953; *Bertram's Trs v Matheson's Trs* (1888) 15 R. 572.

[89] *Duthie's Exr v Taylor*, 1986 S.L.T. 142.

[90] *Stoddart v Grant* (1852) 1 Macq. 163; *Scott v Sceales* (1864) 2 M. 613; *Gordon's Exr v Macqueen*, 1907 S.C. 373; *Mitchell's Administratrix v Edinburgh Royal Infirmary*, 1928 S.C. 47; *Morton's Exr, Petitioner*, 1985 S.L.T. 14.

[91] See *Bruce's J.F. v Lord Advocate*, 1964 S.L.T. 316; 1968 S.L.T. 242; 1969 S.L.T. 337; 1969 S.C. 296; cf. *Scott's J.F. v Johnson*, 1971 S.L.T. (Notes) 41.

[92] The birth of a child to unmarried parents does not have this effect in the case of a deed executed before November 25, 1968, Law Reform (Miscellaneous Provisions) (Scotland) Act 1968 s.6(2) and (3) and now Law Reform (Parent and Child) (Scotland) Act 1986 s.1.

an intention that the will should stand notwithstanding the birth of the child.[93] The strongest case for the application of this rule is that of a testator who was childless when the will was made and died without having a reasonable opportunity of altering it. But it is not enough to displace the presumption that there were children in life at the date of the will[94] or that the testator survived the birth of the child for a considerable period without revising the will.[95] If the will is revoked, it is revoked in toto, but earlier wills expressly revoked by it are not revived.[96] If, however, the revocation of the earlier will was merely by implication, as in the case of a universal settlement, the earlier will becomes operative on the revocation of the later will by a subsequent birth.[97] The right to found on the *conditio* is personal to the after-born child, and no other party can challenge the will on this ground.[98]

Revocation of special destinations—As has been pointed out above,[99] a special **39.13** destination may have testamentary effect. There are cases in which such a destination is contractual as between the parties who have created it, so as to exclude the possibility of testamentary revocation except with the consent of all of them.[100] Thus where both A and B have contributed to the purchase of property of which the title is taken in name of A and B and the survivor, A and B are each free to deal with their respective shares by inter vivos deed,[101] but not by testamentary deed.[102] If one of the parties has paid the whole purchase price he may be entitled to revoke the special destination quoad his own share but the other party cannot revoke.[103] If, however, the disposition narrates that the purchase price was paid in equal shares, extrinsic evidence to show that it was in fact paid by one party is inadmissible,[104] unless both parties agree that the narrative is inaccurate.[105] Where there is no contractual element in a special destination, it may be revoked by testamentary deed but the deed has to contain a specific reference to the destination and a declared intention on the part of the testator to evacuate it.[106] A special destination involving spouses or civil partners is automatically revoked by their divorce, dissolution or annulment granted on or after May 4, 2006, unless the destination provides otherwise.[107]

---

[93] *Elder's Trs v Elder* (1895) 21 R. 704, 22 R. 505; *Millar's Trs v Millar* (1893) 20 R. 1040; *Stuart Gordon v Stuart Gordon* (1899) 1 F. 1005; *Greenan v Courtney*, 2007 S.LT. 355.

[94] *Knox's Trs v Knox*, 1907 S.C. 1123.

[95] *Nicolson v Nicolson's Tutrix*, 1922 S.C. 649; *Rankin v Rankin's Tutor* (1902) 4 F. 979.

[96] *Crown v Cathro* (1903) 5 F. 950; *Elder's Trs v Elder* (1895) 22 R. 505.

[97] *Nicolson v Nicolson's Tutrix*, 1922 S.C. 649; J. McLaren, *The Law of Wills and Succession*, Dykes' supplement (Edinburgh: W. Green, 1934), p.106.

[98] *Stevenson's Trs v Stevenson*, 1932 S.C. 657.

[99] See para.39.05, above.

[100] *Renouf's Trs v Haining*, 1919 S.C. 497.

[101] *Steele v Caldwell*, 1979 S.L.T. 228, followed in *Smith v Mackintosh*, 1989 S.L.T. 148.

[102] *Perrett's Tr. v Perrett*, 1909 S.C. 522; *Chalmers's Trs v Thomson's Exrx*, 1923 S.C. 271; and see *Shand's Trs v Shand's Trs*, 1966 S.L.T. 306; *Marshall v Marshall's Exr*, 1987 S.L.T. 49.

[103] *Brown's Trs v Brown*, 1943 S.C. 488; *Hay's Tr. v Hay's Trs*, 1951 S.C. 329.

[104] *Gordon-Rogers v Thomson's Exrs*, 1988 S.L.T. 618.

[105] As in *Hay's Tr.*, 1951 S.C. 329.

[106] Succession (Scotland) Act 1964 s.30; *Stirling's Trs*, 1977 S.L.T. 229; *Marshall v Marshall's Exr*, 1987 S.L.T. 49.

[107] Family Law (Scotland) Act 2006 s.19, Civil Partnership Act 2004 s.124A and the Family Law (Scotland) Act 2006 (Commencement, Transitional Provisions and Savings) Order 2006 (SSI 2006/212).

INTERPRETATION OF WILLS

39.14 Extrinsic evidence[108]—In construing a testamentary deed it is the object of the court to ascertain and give effect to the intention of the testator. That intention is to be collected from the language of the deed read in the light of those circumstances (such as the state of the testator's family and property) known to the testator and with reference to which the will was written[109]; and it is not permissible to search for the testator's intention apart from the terms of the will. Evidence of the testator's own opinion of the effect of the will is incompetent,[110] and it is doubtful whether revoked writings can be used as an aid to construction.[111] An interpretation which does not produce intestacy will be favoured over one that does.[112]

The cases in which extrinsic evidence in aid of the interpretation of a will is admitted are all of an exceptional nature. The rules on this point may be summarised thus.[113] (a) A testator is always presumed to use words in their strict and primary sense, unless it appears from the context that they were used in a different sense.[114] (b) In the absence of such a context, the words must have their strict and primary sense if, so interpreted, they are sensible with reference to extrinsic circumstances; if not so sensible, extrinsic evidence is admitted. (c) If the characters in which a will is written need deciphering, or the language requires to be translated, evidence is admitted to declare what the characters are or to inform the court of the meaning of the language. (d) For the purpose of determining the object of the testator's bounty or the subject of disposition or the quantity of interest given, the court may inquire into all the material facts as to the person or property or the circumstances of the testator and his or her family and affairs. In accordance with the maxim, *falsa demonstratio non nocet dummodo constet de persona (re)*, a mistake in the description of the subject or object is not fatal to the bequest, and extrinsic evidence is admissible in order to determine the person or thing intended. Thus, where a legacy was bequeathed to "William Keiller, confectioner, Dundee", and there was no such person, the court allowed evidence in order to determine whether the legatee was William Keiller, a confectioner in Montrose, or James Keiller, a confectioner in Dundee.[115] Where, however, there is no ambiguity, parole evidence of the testator's intention will not be admitted to give an enlarged meaning to a description which is capable of application in its terms.[116] Moreover, the accurate naming of a person or thing raises a very strong presumption that that was what the testator intended, rather than one that does not quite fit the name, but it is not an absolute rule.[117] If, after all competent evidence has been received, the subject or object of the legacy is uncertain it will fail on the ground of uncertainty.

---

[108] See M. Ross and J. Chalmers, *Walker and Walker: The Law of Evidence in Scotland*, 3rd edn (Tottel, 2009), Ch.26.

[109] *Trs of the Free Church of Scotland v Maitland* (1887) 14 R. 333; *Hannay's Trs v Keith*, 1913 S.C. 482; *Dunsmure v Dunsmure* (1879) 7 R. 261, per Lord Gifford.

[110] *Devlin's Trs v Breen*, 1945 S.C. (HL) 27.

[111] *Devlin's Trs*, 1945 S.C. (HL) 27 at 32.

[112] *Forsyth v National Kidney Research Fund*, 2006 G.W.D. 21–466 (IH).

[113] McLaren, *Wills and Succession*, i, 374.

[114] *Yule's Trs Petrs*, 1981 S.L.T. 250 ("child" interpreted as meaning "grandchild").

[115] *Keiller v Thomson's Trs* (1826) 4 S. 724; *Macfarlane's Trs v Henderson* (1878) 6 R. 288; *Johnstone's Exrs v Johnstone* (1902) 10 S.L.T. 42; *Cathcart's Trs v Bruce*, 1923 S.L.T. 722. Cf. also *Henderson's J.F. v Henderson*, 1930 S.L.T. 743.

[116] *Fortunato's J.F. v Fortunato*, 1981 S.L.T. 277.

[117] *Nasmyth's Trs v National Society for the Prevention of Cruelty to Children*, 1914 S.C. (HL) 76.

Where two clauses of a settlement are contradictory and cannot be reconciled, then, in the absence of any reason for preferring the one to the other, the later will receive effect as presumably embodying the latest expression of the testator's intention.[118]

Terms descriptive of legatee—The meaning of such terms depends in each case **39.15** on the context in which they appear,[119] but some of the more frequent of them have acquired a recognised prima facie meaning in legal interpretation. Thus the word "issue" includes all direct descendants,[120] unless the context demands a more restricted meaning[121]; and "children" does not normally include grandchildren.[122] In the case of a gift to a class of relatives followed by a provision that in the event of the predecease of any of such relatives the issue is to take, the issue of one who predeceases the making of the will does not take.[123]

In the absence of clear indication to the contrary, a reference in a private deed to the "heir" or "heirs" of a person dying on or after September 10, 1964, is considered to be a reference to those entitled to succeed on intestacy under the 1964 Act[124]; prima facie such a bequest must be construed as a reference to those who have rights of succession in that person's estate, and the heirs of that person cannot be ascertained until he or she dies.[125] Where the bequest is made to a person's "heirs and executors" this expression is held to mean heirs in intestacy, and executors-nominate are not included.[126]

"Next-of-kin" means the heirs apart from those who come in by representation.[127] The term "blood relations" covers all those who can show a traceable relationship by blood, and is not restricted to next-of-kin.[128] A bequest to "dependants" has been held to be void from uncertainty.[129] "Assignees" in a destination-over means those to whom the legatee may have assigned the subject, provided the legatee acquires a vested right, but not otherwise.[130] When a testator makes a bequest in favour of his or her own heirs or next-of-kin, these are normally ascertained at the date of the testator's death.[131]

When in any deed executed or provision made on or after November 25, 1968 terms of relationship are used to point out the legatee, the fact that any link in the

---

[118] McLaren, *Wills and Succession*, i, 354.

[119] See, e.g. *McGinn's Exrx v McGinn*, 1993 S.C. 137 where the vague word "family" was given meaning by the other provisions of the will.

[120] *Stewart's Trs v Whitelaw*, 1926 S.C. 701; *Murray's Trs v Mackie*, 1959 S.L.T. 129.

[121] See *Stirling's Trs v Legal and General Assurance Soc.*, 1957 S.L.T. 73, and cases cited therein.

[122] *Adam's Exrx v Maxwell*, 1921 S.C. 418; cf. *Lindsay's Trs*, 1954 S.L.T. (Notes) 51.

[123] *McKinnon's Trs v Brownlie*, 1947 S.C. (HL) 27.

[124] Succession (Scotland) Act 1964 s.1(1), but note exceptions in s.37(1). Sch.2 paras 1 and 2, expressly provide that references in any *enactment* to the heir-at-law or heirs of a deceased person are to be construed as references to the persons who are entitled by virtue of that Act to succeed on intestacy to that person's estate.

[125] See *Black v Mason* (1881) 8 R. 497 at 500, per Lord President Inglis; McLaren, *Wills and Succession*, ii, 757, 762.

[126] *Lady Kinnaird's Trs v Ogilvy*, 1911 S.C. 1136, but see also *Scott's Exrs v Methven's Exrs* (1890) 17 R. 389, and *Montgomery's Trs v Montgomery* (1895) 22 R. 824.

[127] *Gregory's Trs v Alison* (1889) 16 R. (HL) 10; *Steedman's Trs v Steedman*, 1916 S.C. 857; *Borthwick's Trs v Borthwick*, 1955 S.C. 227. See para.38.16, above.

[128] *Cuninghame v Cuninghame's Trs*, 1961 S.C. 32.

[129] *Robertson's J.F. v Robertson*, 1968 S.L.T. 32.

[130] *Bell v Cheape* (1845) 7 D. 614.

[131] *Anderson's Trs v Forrest*, 1917 S.C. 321; *Grant's Trs v Crawford's Tr.*, 1949 S.L.T. 374; but see R.C. Henderson, *The Principles of Vesting in the Law of Succession*, 2nd edn (Edinburgh: W. Green, 1938), pp.228–229, and at pp.92–97, for bequests to heirs of legatees.

relationship involves a person born to unmarried parents is immaterial, unless the contrary intention appears.[132] In earlier deeds and provisions only legitimate relations take and the descriptive terms "child", "children" and "issue" are not usually interpreted so as to include those born to unmarried parents.[133] But children could be legitimised by the subsequent marriage of their parents under the common law or the Legitimation (Scotland) Act 1968,[134] but cannot succeed if the estate had vested prior to their legitimation[135] or the law changed after the testator's death.[136]

For all purposes relating to the succession to a deceased person, an adopted person is to be treated as the child of the adopter[137]; this provision extends to deeds executed before as well as after the making of an adoption order.[138] It is also provided that in a deed executed after the making of an adoption order and on or after September 10, 1964, any reference to the child or children of the adopter is, unless the contrary intention appears, to be construed as including a reference to the adopted person and similarly any reference to a person related to the adopted person is to be construed as if the latter were a child of the adopter.[139] It has been held that the latter provision is designed only to apply where a deed has been executed by a granter in knowledge both of the statutory equality of adopted children and of the existence of an adoption order.[140]

A provision to a named person with a descriptive relationship added, e.g. to AB my wife, does not normally imply a condition that the person has to fulfil that relationship at the date of the testator's death.[141] However, a testamentary provision may be construed as made in favour of a wife in that capacity, in which case divorce subsequent to the date of the will disqualifies her from taking it.[142] There is no presumption in Scotland, where the word "wife" is used in a testamentary family provision, in favour of the wife who existed at the date of the will over the wife at the date of death.[143]

39.16 Cumulative and substitutional legacies—Testamentary writings may contain more than one legacy to the same legatee, so that a doubt arises whether the legatee is entitled to one only or to both. The testator's intention on this point may be made clear by an express provision; and in all cases the court will examine the deed or deeds for the purpose of discovering indications of what was intended. It may be said that differences in the bequests will be favourable to the claim that both are due as, for example, where a motive is stated for the one bequest which is not stated as to the other.[144] Assuming, however, that the testator's intention

---

[132] Law Reform (Miscellaneous Provisions) (Scotland) Act 1968 ss.5 and 22(5) and now Law Reform (Parent and Child) (Scotland) Act 1986 s.1(2), as amended by the Family Law (Scotland) Act 2006 s.21.

[133] *Scott's Trs v Smart*, 1954 S.C. 12.

[134] *Russell v Wood's Trs*, 1987 S.L.T. 503.

[135] *Dunbar of Kilconzie v Lord Advocate*, 1986 S.C. (HL) 1.

[136] *Wright's Trs v Callender*, 1993 S.L.T. 556.

[137] Succession (Scotland) Act 1964 s.23(1). Note that where the adopter died before September 10, 1964, and the natural parent died on or after that date, the adopted child retains rights of succession to the estate of the natural parent; Law Reform (Miscellaneous Provisions) (Scotland) Act 1966 s.5.

[138] *Salvesen's Trs, Petitioner*, 1992 S.C.L.R. 729.

[139] 1964 Act s.23(2); *mortis causa* deeds are deemed for the purposes of this provision to have been executed on the adopter's death.

[140] *Salvesen's Trs*, 1992 S.C.L.R. 729.

[141] *Henderson's J.F. v Henderson*, 1930 S.L.T. 743 (wife); *Couper's J.F. v Valentine*, 1976 S.L.T. 83 (wife); *Ormiston's Exr v Laws*, 1966 S.L.T. 110 (fiancée)

[142] *Pirie's Trs v Pirie*, 1962 S.C. 43.

[143] *Burn's Trs, Petitioner*, 1961 S.C. 17.

[144] *Horsburgh v Horsburgh* (1848) 10 D. 824.

cannot be ascertained, there are certain well-settled rules or presumptions which will be applied. A distinction is taken between legacies to the same legatee left in the same deed and legacies left in separate deeds. In the first case, i.e. where the legacies are contained in the same writing, when exactly the same amount is given twice, the presumption is that this is a mere repetition arising from some mistake or forgetfulness.[145] On the other hand, where the legacies are not of the same amount, they are presumed to be cumulative. Where the same amount is bequeathed to the same legatee in two distinct testamentary writings, both legacies are presumed to be due,[146] and a fortiori this is also so where the legacies are of different amounts.[147] These rules proceed on the assumption that both writings are operative and that the second does not revoke or supplant the earlier.[148]

Division amongst legatees—Where a bequest is made to a number of individuals, **39.17** although there are no words indicating the share to be taken by each, there is no room for doubt as to the mode of division: each will take an equal share. But if the legatees are called under a term or terms descriptive of a group, there may be doubt as to whether the fund is to be divided among all the beneficiaries as individuals (per capita) or according to the group or groups (per stirpes). It is clear that under a gift of residue to the children of A and the children of B either the family division may be disregarded so that each child of the two families receives an equal share, or the residue may be divided into halves and one-half distributed among the members of each family. It is within the power of the testator to use expressions which will remove all doubt on this point. The general presumption is in favour of per capita distribution, unless the language of the will or the frame of the bequest indicates the other mode of division.[149] There is, however, a presumption that where a bequest is given severally to parties in liferent and their issue in fee, the connection between the liferent and the fee implies stirpital division of the fee.[150]

A direction that residue shall "be equally divided between my nephews and nieces and their children" may mean either that nephews and nieces and their children are to take equal shares or that each nephew and niece is to take an equal share, the children of any predeceaser taking their parent's share. In *Clow's Trustees v Bethune*,[151] after considerable diversity of judicial opinion, the decision was for the latter construction, and the case illustrates the relevant considerations.

Accretion—Another question which may arise in regard to a legacy in favour **39.18** of a number of legatees is whether the legacy is joint or several. If the legacy be given to the legatees jointly or without words importing that they are to take separate shares then, if any of these die without acquiring a vested right, the survivors will be entitled to the whole of the fund or subject bequeathed. A legacy to A and B simply will, if A predecease the testator, give B right to the whole of that

---

[145] But see *Gillies v Glasgow Royal Infirmary*, 1960 S.C. 438, where legatee appeared twice in residue clause.

[146] *McLachlan v Seton's Trs*, 1937 S.C. 206.

[147] *Royal Infirmary of Edinburgh v Muir's Trs* (1881) 9 R. 352; *Fraser v Forbes' Trs* (1899) 1 F. 513.

[148] *Beattie v Thomson* (1861) 23 D. 1163.

[149] McLaren, *Wills and Succession*, ii, 780; *Cunningham's Trs v Blackwell*, 1909 S.C. 219; *Cobban's Exs v Cobban*, 1915 S.C. 82; *Robertson's Trs v Horne*, 1921 S.C. 817; *Campbell's Tr. v Welsh*, 1952 S.C. 343; cf. *Boyd's Tr. v Shaw*, 1958 S.C. 115; *Bailey's Trs v Bailey*, 1954 S.L.T. 282.

[150] *Home's Trs v Ramsay* (1886) 12 R. 314; *Bailey's Trs v Bailey*, 1954 S.L.T. 282; *Primrose's Trs v Gardiner*, 1973 S.L.T. 238.

[151] *Clow's Trustees v Bethune*, 1935 S.C. 754, and see *Boyd's Trs v Shaw*, 1958 S.C. 115, where a destination-over to issue of a named beneficiary "equally amongst them" was similarly construed.

sum.[152] But if words of severance, such as "equally" or "share and share alike", are used, accretion is excluded, and the share of a predeceaser will, in the case of a legacy, fall into residue (if there be a residuary bequest), or in the case of residue, lapse into intestacy. The rule has been authoritatively stated in these terms:

> "When a legacy is given to a plurality of persons named or sufficiently described for identification 'equally among them', or 'in equal shares', or 'share and share alike', or in any other language of the same import, each is entitled to his own share and no more, and there is no room for accretion in the event of the predecease of one or more of the legatees. The rule is applicable whether the gift is in liferent or in fee to the whole equally, and whether the subject of the bequest be residue or a sum of fixed amount or corporeal moveables. The application of this rule may, of course, be controlled or avoided by the use of other expressions by the testator importing that there shall be accretion in the event of the predecease of one of more of the legatees."[153]

The most important exception to this rule occurs in bequests to a class, where notwithstanding the use of such terms as "equally", "share and share alike", the share of a predeceaser accresces to the survivors.[154]

If it is intended that accrescing shares shall be subject to the same conditions as the original share, as e.g. where the original shares are settled on the beneficiaries in liferent, this should be made clear in the settlement, as there is no implication that the conditions apply to more than the original gift. Where the issue of the predeceaser take by virtue of the *conditio si institutus sine liberis decesserit* or a clause calling issue, it is only the parent's original share and not what would have accresced on survivance that can, as a general rule, be claimed by the issue, unless the will provides otherwise,[155] or adherence to the rule would result in intestacy.[156] In respect of provisions made on or after November 25, 1968 accretion operates for the benefit of a child of unmarried parents or of a person whose right is traceable through such a child, unless the contrary intention appears.[157]

TYPES OF LEGACIES

39.19 Classification of legacies—Legacies may be classified as general or special.[158] A general legacy is one in which the subject given is "bequeathed indefinitely without any character distinguishing it from others of the same kind belonging to the deceased",[159] as e.g. a sum of money or a certain quantity or amount of things falling under some generic description. In this case the legatee has no more than a

---

[152] Stair, III, 8, 27; *Andrew's Exrs v Andrew's Trs*, 1925 S.C. 844.

[153] *Paxton's Trs v Cowie* (1886) 13 R. 1191; applied in *Cochrane's Trs v Cochrane*, 1914 S.C. 403; *White's Tr., Petrs*, 1957 S.C. 322; *Fraser's Trs v Fraser*, 1980 (S.L.T.) 211; but see *Young's Trs v Young*, 1927 S.C. (HL) 6 and *Mitchell's Trs v Aspin*, 1971 S.L.T. 166.

[154] *Muir's Trs v Muir* (1889) 16 R. 954; *Roberts' Trs v Roberts* (1903) 5 F. 541.

[155] *Henderson v Henderson* (1890) 17 R. 293; *Young v Robertson* (1862) 4 Macq. 337; *Crosbie's Trs v Crosbie*, 1927 S.C. 159; *Miller's Trs v Brown*, 1933 S.C. 669.

[156] *Beveridge's Trs v Beveridge*, 1930 S.C. 578.

[157] Formerly Law Reform (Miscellaneous Provisions) (Scotland) Act 1968 ss.6(1)(b), (3) and 22(5) and now Law Reform (Parent and Child) (Scotland) Act 1986 s.1(2).

[158] Erskine, III, 9, 11; Bell, *Principles*, ss.1876, 1877; McLaren, *Wills and Succession*, i, 575.

[159] Erskine, III, 9, 13.

right of personal action against the executor or trustee for implementation of the legacy. A special legacy, on the other hand, is the bequest of a determinate subject such as a certain horse, some particular investment or a debt due to the testator by a particular person.[160] Demonstrative legacies are those in which the testator indicates the source from which the legacy is to be provided.[161] Where the legacy takes this form, the question may arise whether it is dependent on the existence or sufficiency of the funds denoted as the source of payment,[162] or whether the legatee has, in the event of these funds disappearing or proving insufficient, a claim against the general estate of the testator. Thus in *Douglas's Exrs*[163] the testator bequeathed sums of money "to be paid out of the arrears of income due to me from the Monteath trust estate", and, these arrears being insufficient, it was held that the balance must be made up out of the residue of the estate.

On the income front, legatees may be given a liferent interest in specified property or an annuity. The law does not recognise an interest intermediate between fee and liferent.[164]

Residue—In well-drawn testaments the bequest of legacies is usually followed **39.20** by a clause disposing of the residue of the testator's estate. Residue comprises the whole of the testator's estate, capital and income, not required for the antecedent purposes of the testamentary deed or deeds.[165] The residuary legatee is regarded by the law as taking the estate subject to the burden of the prior purposes of the will[166]; and if, and to the extent to which, a legacy fails, the subject of the legacy enures to residue. If the residue is given at the testator's death, it matters not that the failure of the legacy is not ascertained until a later date, the subject will fall to the residuary legatee. When a testator makes a bequest of the "free residue" of the estate, and legal rights are claimed, these as well as debts and legacies are prima facie to be deducted before the "free residue" is ascertained.[167]

The right of the heirs in intestacy is displaced only in so far as the estate is effectually disposed of in favour of others. If, therefore, there be no residuary bequest, the subject of any testamentary disposition which fails of effect will fall into intestacy; and similarly, if the residuary bequest fails, the residue to the extent of that failure will devolve on the heirs in intestacy. These heirs are ascertained at the date of the testator's death and acquire right then to any portion of the estate which may be found not to have been disposed of.[168]

Legatum rei alienae—This is the bequest of a subject which did not belong to the **39.21** testator at the date of the will. If the testator believed that he or she owned the subject (which is presumed to be the case until the contrary is proved), then the legacy fails; for it is assumed that the bequest would not have been made had the testator been aware that the subject did not belong to him or her.[169] However, if the testator knew that the subject did not belong to him or her then, as

---

[160] Stair, III, 8, 38.

[161] McLaren, *Wills and Succession*, i, 575.

[162] As in *Ballantyne's Trs v Ballantyne's Trs*, 1941 S.C. 35.

[163] *Douglas's Exrs* (1869) 7 M. 504.

[164] *Cochrane's Exrx v Cochrane*, 1947 S.C. 134, overruling *Heavyside v Smith*, 1929 S.C. 68. Followed in *Innes' Trs v Innes*, 1948 S.C. 406.

[165] *Sturgis v Campbell* (1865) 3 M. (HL) 70, per Lord Westbury.

[166] *Storie's Trs v Gray* (1874) 1 R. 953.

[167] *Samson v Raynor*, 1928 S.C. 899.

[168] *Lord v Colvin* (1865) 3 M. 1083.

[169] Erskine, III, 9, 10; *Meeres v Dowell's Exr*, 1923 S.L.T. 184.

it is not to be supposed that the testator intended a derisory bequest, effect is given to the legacy by requiring the executor to purchase the subject for the legatee or, if it cannot be purchased, to pay its value.[170]

39.22 Destinations-over—Destinations-over are frequently attached to bequests, e.g. to A, whom failing B. Here A is called the institute and B may be either a conditional institute or a substitute.[171] Should A predecease the testator (or the date of vesting) then B will take the bequest whatever its nature[172]; substitution and conditional institution here lead to the same result. Where A and B both survive the testator or the date of vesting A will take and if B is a conditional institute B has no further right, but if B is a substitute the subject of the bequest will pass to B unless A had disposed of it.[173] A is free so to dispose during life but the position with regard to *mortis causa* disposal is less clear.[174] There is a presumption for substitution where the bequest is of heritage[175] and for conditional institution where the bequest is of moveables[176] or mixed heritage and moveables.[177] The terms of the testator's will may, however, displace these presumptions.[178]

39.23 Powers of appointment—A power or faculty is an authority reserved by or conferred upon a person to dispose, either wholly or partially, of property either for his or her own benefit or for that of others.[179] Such powers may be general, by which is meant a power to dispose of the property at pleasure, or special, by which is meant a more limited power. The typical instance of a special power is that of appointing a fund among members of a specified class. The person from whom the power issues is known as the donor of the power and the recipient as the donee of the power.

Where a person settles his property, or takes a disposition, in favour of himself in liferent and at the same time reserves to himself a general power of disposing of the property, this is equivalent to a fee. He has right to the property independently of the settlement or disposition, and if he reserves to himself the enjoyment of the fruits of the property and the power to dispose of the property at pleasure, he remains substantially the proprietor.[180] In that situation, he is both donor and donee of the power and is outwith the ambit of the ordinary rule that the donee of a power cannot delegate the exercise thereof.[181]

---

[170] If the value cannot be ascertained the legacy falls, *Macfarlane's Trs v Macfarlane*, 1910 S.C. 325.

[171] J. McLaren, *The Law of Wills and Succession*, 3rd edn (Bell and Bradfute, 1894), p.623; *Cochrane's Exrx v Cochrane*, 1947 S.C. 134.

[172] But A's issue may take under the *conditio si institutus*, see para.39.30.

[173] The testator's executors should grant a disposition of the subject to "A whom failing B".

[174] Hiram, *The Scots Law of Succession* (2007), para.9.15 states that disposal *mortis causa* is effective. But in gifts with a destination to A and B and the survivor, as in *Brown's Trs v Brown*, 1943 S.C. 488, (which is two back-to-back destinations-over of half shares) neither A nor B can evacuate the destination *mortis causa*.

[175] *Watson v Giffen* (1884) 11 R. 444.

[176] *Crumpton's J.F. v Barnardo's Homes*, 1917 S.C. 713, per Lord President Strathclyde; *Greig v Johnstone* (1833) 6 W. & S. 406.

[177] *Allan v Fleming* (1845) 7D. 908.

[178] *Dyer v Carruthers* (1874) 1 R. 943 is a case of substitution in moveables.

[179] McLaren, *The Law of Wills and Succession* (1894), Ch.LX.

[180] *Morris v Tennant* (1855) 27 Sc. Jur.546; 30 Sc. Jur.943; *Baillie v Clark*, Feb. 23, 1809, FC.

[181] *Cuninghame v Cuninghame's Trs*, 1961 S.L.T. 194 at 197, per Lord Ordinary (Mackintosh), and Lord President Clyde at 201; *Monies v Monies*, 1939 S.C. 344.

If the donor confers on the donee a liferent with a power of disposal, both in unqualified terms, that is a gift of the fee,[182] and the donee may demand immediate payment or conveyance thereof. But if the liferent is declared to be alimentary, whatever may be the extent of the power,[183] or, although the liferent be unqualified, if the power is to be exercised in a particular manner, as by will or *mortis causa* deed only, or otherwise falls short of a general power, in either case the donee of the power is not in right of the fee of the property.[184]

The power must be exercised in accordance with the terms on which it is given. If the deed which confers it prescribes that it shall be exercised by will, it cannot be exercised by an inter vivos deed; but a power to appoint by "any writing under her hand" has been held wide enough to include inter vivos as well as testamentary deeds.[185] A mere reference in the power to the death of the donee of it, e.g. the postponement of payment to the fiars until the expiry of the donee's liferent, does not restrict him to choosing persons who survive him as the objects of the power, or suspend the vesting of indefeasible interests in the person chosen until the death.[186] In that event the power may be validly exercised by inter vivos deed. In interpreting a power there is no presumption that the objects should be the persons who would take failing its exercise.[187] It is not necessary to support a deed as an exercise of a power that it should make reference to the power; if there is no such reference, it becomes a question on the terms of the deed whether the donee intended to exercise the power.[188] It has long been recognised that words of general conveyance in a settlement are, unless a contrary intention appears, to be construed as including any estate which the testator had power to dispose of in any manner he might deem proper.[189] Thus, in *Hyslop v Maxwell's Trs*,[190] a power given by a testator to his niece, who enjoyed the liferent of a sum under his will, to dispose of that sum by will or deed after her death as she might think fit, was held to be exercised by her general settlement although it made no reference to the power and was executed before the death of the testator. As the power in this case was a general one, it fell under the rule. It is not yet finally settled whether a special power is to be held to be exercised by a general settlement which does not notice the power or purport to include property subject to disposal by the testator,[191] but the prevailing opinion is that it is.[192] The law to be applied to determine whether or not a power has been validly exercised by a testamentary writing is that of the domicile of the donee at the date of his death.[193]

The exercise of a power is open to objection if it amounts to what is termed a fraud on the power[194] or is ultra vires. The term "fraud" in this connection does not denote dishonest or immoral conduct on the part of the appointer; it means

---

[182] *Rattray's Trs v Rattray* (1899) 1 F. 510; *Mackenzie's Trs v Kilmarnock's Trs*, 1909 S.C. 472; *Baird v Baird's Tr.*, 1956 S.C. (HL) 93.

[183] *Ewing's Trs v Ewing*, 1909 S.C. 409.

[184] *Alves v Alves* (1861) 23 D. 712; *Howe's Trs v Howe's J.F.* (1903) 5 F. 1099.

[185] *Stirling's Trs v Legal & General Assurance Soc.*, 1957 S.L.T. 73.

[186] *Stainton v Forteviot Trust*, 1948 S.C. (HL) 115; *Neame v Neame's Trs*, 1956 S.L.T. 57.

[187] *Stainton v Forteviot Trust*, 1948 S.C. (HL) 115.

[188] *Smart v Smart*, 1926 S.C. 392.

[189] *Bray v Bruce's Exrs* (1906) 8 F. 1078.

[190] *Hyslop v Maxwell's Trs* (1834) 12 S. 413.

[191] *Alexander's Trs v Alexander's Trs*, 1917 S.C. 654; but see *Tarratt's Trs v Hastings* (1904) 6 F. 968.

[192] *Burns' Trs v Burns' Trs*, 1935 S.C. 905; *Gemmell's Trs v Shields*, 1936 S.C. 717.

[193] *Durie's Trs v Osborne*, 1960 S.C. 444.

[194] McLaren, *Wills and Succession*, ii, 1107.

that the power has been exercised for a purpose, or with an intention, beyond the scope of, or not justified by, the deed creating the power. Thus, it is a fraudulent exercise if the donee of a special power makes an appointment with the intention of benefiting himself or some other person not an object of the power[195]; or if the fund subject to the special power is appointed wholly to one object of the power in consequence of a bribe.[196] So also a parent cannot, in exercising a power of appointing a fund among his children, bargain with them for the purchase by him of other interests belonging to them.[197] But where the donee's purpose and intention in making the appointment was to benefit the objects of the power, the mere presence of an incidental benefit to himself, e.g. under an arrangement for the variation of trust purposes, will not be sufficient to constitute a fraud on the power.[198] Appointments in fraud of the power are voidable at the instance of an interested object of the power but challenge may be barred by homologation.[199]

The rule as to an ultra vires exercise has been thus stated:

> "If you cannot disconnect that which is imposed by way of condition or mode of enjoyment from the gift, the gift itself may be found to be involved in conditions so much beyond the power that it becomes void. But where that is not so, where you have a gift to an object of the power, and where you have nothing alleged to invalidate the gift but conditions which are attempted to be imposed as to the mode in which that object of the power is to enjoy what is given to him, then the gift may be valid and take effect without reference to those conditions".[200]

In the case of a power to apportion a fund among a class, it is, since the Powers of Appointment Act 1874 (which alters the former law), no longer an objection to the exercise that certain members of the class are omitted or receive only illusory shares; the whole of the fund may validly be appointed to one of the class. But in so far as the exercise purports to give any share of the fund to one who is not a member of the class it is bad.[201]

A power to apportion under restrictions and conditions is validly exercised by a gift of liferent of a share with an unqualified power of testamentary disposal, or by a gift of a share to one member of the class in liferent and to another in fee.[202] If the deed should appoint the fund to the children on condition that they forgive a certain debt or pay a certain sum, the condition could be severed from the substance of the appointment with the result that the deed would be good as an

---

[195] *Stein v Stein* (1826) 5 S. 101; *Craig v Craig's Trs* (1904) 12 S.L.T. 136, 620; *Dick's Trs v Cameron*, 1907 S.C. 1018.

[196] *Re Wright* [1920] 1 Ch. 108.

[197] *Smith Cunninghame v Anstruther's Trs* (1872) 10 M. (HL) 39.

[198] *Pelham Burn, Petitioner*, 1964 S.C. 3.

[199] *Callander v Callander's Exr*, 1976 S.L.T. 10; *Colquhoun's Trs v Marchioness of Lorne's Trs*, 1990 S.L.T. 34.

[200] *McDonald v McDonald's Trs* (1875) 2 R. (HL) 125, per Earl Cairns L.C.; *Dalziel v Dalziel's Trs* (1905) 7 F. 545, per Lord Dunedin; *Re Holland* [1914] 2 Ch. 595.

[201] See, e.g. *Moubray's Trs v Moubray*, 1929 S.C. 254, where the earlier cases are reviewed, and *Colquhoun's Trs*, 1990 S.L.T. 34. Children of unmarried parents are taken to be proper objects of a special power of appointment created by deed executed on or after November 25, 1968 unless the contrary appears (formerly Law Reform (Miscellaneous Provisions) (Scotland) Act 1968 ss.5(3) and 22(5) and now Law Reform (Parent and Child) (Scotland) Act 1986 s.1(2)); *Stein v Stein* (1826) 5 S. 101; *Craig v Craig's Trs* (1904) 12 S.L.T. 136; *Dick's Trs v Cameron*, 1907 S.C. 1018.

[202] *Moubray's Trs v Moubray*, 1929 S.C. 254; *Gemmell's Trs v Shields*, 1936 S.C. 717; *Angus's Trs v Monies*, 1939 S.C. 509.

appointment to the children, and the condition would be treated as void. Partial invalidity in the exercise of a power is not necessarily fatal to the whole exercise. The question is whether the appointer, if aware of the partial invalidity, would have left the rest of the appointment as it stands.[203]

The existence of a power of appointment over a fund bequeathed to a class does not suspend vesting in the members of the class; they take a right to an equal share of the fund, which may be defeated in whole or in part by an exercise of the power.[204] If the power is not exercised, or if the exercise is wholly invalid, the members of the class remain vested in equal shares of the fund.[205] The donee of a power may validly bind himself that he will not exercise the power so as to exclude or reduce below a certain amount the share of an object of the power. A liferent and power of disposal may be renounced, whereupon the fee vests in the objects in terms of the deed creating the power.[206]

VESTING

Vesting of legacies—A legacy is said to vest in a legatee when he acquires right **39.24** to it. The legatee's personal right against the executors or trustees becomes part of his patrimony; he may dispose of it by inter vivos or *mortis causa* deed; it may be made available to meet his debts; and on his death intestate it will transmit as part of his estate. It is not necessary that the legatee should be entitled to payment or possession of the legacy, for vesting may, and often does, take place although the legatee has no right to possession. Nor are the circumstances that the bequest is made through a trust, or that it is subject to a liferent or annuity, inconsistent with immediate vesting in the fiar.[207] Thus, if trustees are directed to hold a fund for A in liferent and, on his death, to hold it for or pay it to B, B will acquire a vested interest on the death of the testator.[208] Nor will a power in the trustees to encroach on capital operate so as to postpone vesting of the capital in the legatees.[209]

The date of vesting is to be determined in accordance with the testator's intention as disclosed in his testament. This is the governing principle, and the further rules which have been developed in the course of the decisions are all subject to this qualification, that they must yield to clear expressions of the testator's intention.[210] There is sometimes inserted in a testament an explicit declaration as to the time at which a legacy is to vest, and this usually settles the question, but not invariably, for such a declaration has been disregarded where it was irreconcilable with the terms of the bequest[211] and indeed it has been observed that the courts

---

[203] *Coat's Trs v Tillinghast*, 1944 S.C. 466; *Monies v Monies*, 1939 S.C. 344; *Middleton's Trs v Borwick*, 1947 S.C. 517; *Torrance's Trs v Weddel*, 1947 S.C. 91; *Cathcart's J.F. v Stewart*, 1948 S.C. 456; *MacLaren's Trs v Wilkie*, 1948 S.C. 652; *Wight's Trs v Milliken*, 1960 S.C. 137; *Ford's Trs v Calthorpe*, 1971 S.C. 115.

[204] *Sivright v Dallas* (1824) 2 S. 643; *Watson v Majoribanks* (1837) 15 S. 586; *Romanes v Riddell* (1865) 3 M. 348.

[205] *Wemyss's Trs v Wemyss*, 1994 G.W.D. 11–702.

[206] *Lawson v Cormack's Trs*, 1940 S.C. 210.

[207] *Carleton v Thomson* (1867) 5 M. (HL) 151; *Wemyss's Trs v Wemyss*, 1994 G.W.D. 11–702.

[208] Henderson, *The Principles of Vesting in the Law of Succession* (1938), p.24; *Whitelaw's Trs v Whitelaw's Trs*, 1981 S.L.T. 94.

[209] *MacGregor's Trs v MacGregor*, 1958 S.C. 326.

[210] *Carleton v Thomson* (1867) 5 M. (HL) 151; *Bowman v Bowman* (1899) 1 F. (HL) 69, per Lord Halsbury L.C.; *Barclay's Tr. v Inland Revenue*, 1975 S.C. (HL) 1.

[211] See *Croom's Trs v Adams* (1859) 22 D. 45.

have in general shown little enthusiasm for artificial vesting dates.[212] There are also two general considerations which influence the court. In the first place, there is a presumption in favour of early vesting; that is to say, in a case of doubt the court is favourable to that construction which will give the legatee a vested interest at the earliest date. As a will cannot come into effect until the testator's death, there can be no vesting prior to that time; and the presumption is, therefore, for vesting a *morte testatoris*.[213] Secondly, where a testator purports to dispose of his whole estate, the court is disinclined to adopt a construction which will involve total or partial intestacy, although it may be compelled to do so.[214]

The question must always depend mainly on the terms in which the particular bequest is made. If it be given to the legatee unconditionally, vesting will take place immediately. A legacy which is payable on a *dies certus*, i.e. a time or event which must arrive sooner or later (as e.g. the death of a liferenter or other person), is regarded as an unconditional legacy.[215] On the other hand, if it is uncertain whether the event contemplated will ever happen, it cannot be known in the meantime whether the legacy will ever become due, and, in accordance with the maxim *dies incertus pro conditione habetur* (an uncertain day is regarded as a condition), the legacy is regarded as conditional.[216]

39.25 Vesting of conditional bequests—In the case of conditional legacies, a distinction is drawn between suspensive (precedent) and resolutive (subsequent) conditions. The former operate to prevent vesting until the fulfilment of the condition, the latter do not prevent vesting, but render it liable to be defeated if the event occur— that is, there is vesting subject to defeasance. There is little trace of the doctrine of vesting subject to defeasance in regard to legacies prior to the decision of the House of Lords in *Taylor v Gilbert's Trs*,[217] but since then the doctrine has been considerably developed. As a general rule, conditions which are personal to the legatee have the effect of suspending vesting *pendente conditione*. The more usual of such conditions are those relating to the age of the legatee, or to his survivance of some time or event. If a testator leaves a bequest, or directs his trustees to pay a legacy, to A in the event of his attaining majority, there is no vesting in A while he is under 18. In this case, the condition as to age is adjected to the substance of the gift: A becomes the object of the testator's bounty only when he reaches the age of 18. But if a bequest takes the form of a bequest to A with a provision that it is to be paid to him when he attains majority the bequest will vest in A at once although he is not major. The gift here is made without qualification, and the provision as to majority refers to payment, and was presumably introduced only for the protection of A while he is under age.[218]

Where the qualification of the legacy consists of words of survivorship (to A, B and C and the survivors or survivor of them), the vesting of the legacy will depend

---

[212] See *Carruther's Trs v Carruthers' Trs*, 1949 S.C. 530 at 545, per Lord President Cooper. This case is concerned with an attempt, by the application of the maxim *quod fieri debet infectum valet* (what ought to be done avails although not done) to frustrate a testator's express direction as to vesting.

[213] *Carleton v Thomson* (1867) 5 M. (HL) 151; *Taylor v Gilbert's Trs* (1878) 5 R. (HL) 217, per Lord Blackburn.

[214] See *Cummings v Gillespie's Exrs*, 1994 G.W.D. 36–2158.

[215] See, e.g. *Mowbray's Trs v Mowbray*, 1931 S.C. 595; *Fraser's Trs v Cunninghame*, 1928 S.L.T. 425.

[216] McLaren, *Wills and Suucession*, ii, 783, 796; see Lord Skerrington's opinion in *Wylie's Trs v Bruce*, 1919 S.C. 211 at 240.

[217] *Taylor v Gilbert's Trs* (1878) 5 R. (HL) 217.

[218] *Alves' Trs v Grant* (1874) 1 R. 969; *Wemyss's Trs v Wemyss*, 1994 G.W.D. 11–702.

on the determination of the time to which these words refer. The testator may point out the time or event which the legatee must survive in order to acquire right to the legacy. Where he fails to do so, the rule laid down in the leading case of *Young v Robertson*[219] is as follows: The words of survivorship are to be referred to the period appointed by the settlement for payment or distribution of the subject matter of the gift. If a testator gives a sum of money or the residue of his estate to be paid or distributed among a number of persons and refers to the contingency of any one or more of them dying, and then gives the estate or the money to the survivor in that simple form of gift which is to take effect immediately on the death of the testator, the period of distribution is the period of death, and accordingly the contingency of death is to be referred to the interval of time between the date of the will and the death of the testator. Vesting in this case will take place a *morte testatoris*. On the other hand, if the testator gives a liferent in a sum of money or in the residue of his estate, and at the expiration of that liferent directs the money to be paid or the residue to be divided among a number of objects, and then refers to the possibility of some one or more of those persons dying, without specifying the time, and directs in that event the payment or distribution to be made among the survivors, it is understood by the law that he means the contingency to extend over the whole period of time that must elapse before the payment or distribution takes place. The result, accordingly, is that in such a case the survivors are to be ascertained in like manner by a reference to the period of distribution, namely the expiration of the liferent; and vesting is, therefore, suspended until that event.[220] A survivorship clause may, however, be so worded, notwithstanding the subsistence of a liferenter, as to import only survivorship of the legatees inter se; in that event vesting is suspended until only the survivor is left, and the right then vests in him whether or not he survives the liferenter.[221] But this doctrine of "intermediate" vesting cannot, it is thought, be extended to a case where the fee is destined to more than two persons and the words "survivors or survivor" are used.[222]

A similar rule holds in regard to destinations-over (to A, whom failing to B). When trustees are directed to pay a legacy to a beneficiary on the occurrence of an event and, failing him, to another or to other persons, then, if he does not survive that event, he takes no right under the settlement.[223] In the case of a simple bequest without postponement of payment, the destination-over is read as providing for the contingency of the legatee's predeceasing the testator, and as the destination-over ceases to be operative on the testator's death, the legacy vests at that date; but if the legacy is to be paid at a subsequent date, there is no vesting until that date. A destination-over to another person *nominatim* may take the form of a bequest to "A whom failing B", or to "A or B". At one time it was thought that the general rule did not apply where the persons called under the destination-over were described as the heirs of the institute, but it is now settled that under a destination-over to heirs vesting is suspended. Hence, if a legacy is bequeathed on the expiry or termination of a liferent to A or his heirs, it vests in A only at the

---

[219] *Young v Robertson* (1862) 4 Macq. 314.

[220] *Laing's Trs v Horsburgh*, 1965 S.L.T. 215; cf. *Stirling's Trs v Stirling*, 1977 S.L.T. 229. Forfeiture of the liferent on the liferenter's election to claim legal rights does not accelerate vesting (*Muirhead v Muirhead* (1890) 17 R. (HL) 45; *Munro's Trs Petrs*, 1971 S.C. 280).

[221] *Lindsay's Trs v Sinclair* (1885) 12 R. 964; *Macfarlane's Trs v Macfarlane's Curator Bonis*, 1934 S.C. 476.

[222] *Playfair's Trs v Stewart's Trs*, 1960 S.L.T. 351.

[223] *Bryson's Trs v Clark* (1880) 8 R. 142.

death of the liferenter[224]; vesting will not be accelerated by a renunciation of the liferent by the liferenter before that date[225] and, unless provision has been made for its disposal, income in the intervening period will fall into intestacy.[226] But such a renunciation, coupled with the valid exercise by the liferenter of a power to appoint the fee by inter vivos deed, will enable immediate payment of the capital to be made to the appointee.[227]

The rule as to the effect of words of survivorship or a destination-over on vesting in the legatee called in the first place is well settled. Somewhat different considerations affect the vesting in the person or persons called on that legatee's failure. If a testator directs his trustees to hold his estate for a person in liferent and, on his death, to divide it among such of certain persons as may then be alive, the issue of any of these who may predecease being entitled to their parent's share, do the issue of one who predeceases the liferenter take a vested right on their parent's death or is vesting in them suspended (as in the case of their parent) until the death of the liferenter? Or, if the bequest on the termination of the liferent be to A, whom failing to B, and A predeceases the liferenter, does B acquire a vested interest on A's death although he (B) may subsequently also predecease the liferenter? In a well-drawn settlement this should be made clear; but in the absence of express provision the question will depend on whether the conditions which affect the institute are by implication to be held to affect also the conditional institute. As a rule, if the gift-over to the issue of the legatee is substitutional, the condition of survivance of the termination of the liferent expressed with reference to the parent is held to apply to the issue also,[228] but if the gift to the issue is an original one, they may acquire a vested right notwithstanding that they predecease the liferenter.[229]

39.26 **Vesting subject to defeasance**[230]—There are three types of cases in which the application of this doctrine is now definitely recognised, and beyond which it will not readily be extended.[231]

> (1) "For A in liferent and his issue in fee, whom failing to B"—If trustees are directed to hold a fund for A in liferent and for his or her issue in fee, and failing issue of A, then for B in fee, B will, if there are no such issue in existence at the testator's death, take a vested right subject to defeasance if A subsequently has issue.[232] Should A never have issue, B's right is treated as having been from the first absolute, and it matters not that B predeceases the liferenter. On the other hand, if the bequest to A's issue comes into effect, B's right is wholly defeated. It is a condition of

---

[224] *Wylie's Trs v Bruce*, 1919 S.C. 211; *Mackenzie's Trs v Georgeson*, 1923 S.C. 517.

[225] *Middleton's Trs v Middleton*, 1955 S.C. 51; *Chrystal's Trs v Haldane*, 1960 S.C. 127. But see *Hurll's Trs v Hurll*, 1964 S.C. 12 (forfeiture).

[226] *Buyers Trustees and Nunan*, 1981 S.C. 313, overruling on this point *Middleton's Trs v Middleton*, 1955 S.C. 51.

[227] *Stainton v Forteviot Trust*, 1948 S.C. (HL) 115; *Neame v Neame's Trs*, 1956 S.L.T. 57.

[228] *Todd's Trs v Todd's Exrx*, 1922 S.C. 1; *Banks' Trs v Banks' Trs*, 1907 S.C. 125.

[229] *Campbell's Tr. v Dick*, 1915 S.C. 100, but see *Robertson's Trs v Mitchell*, 1930 S.C. 970 at 976, per Lord President Clyde.

[230] See Henderson, *The Principles of Vesting in the Law of Succession* (1938) and T.B. Smith, *A Short Commentary on the Law of Scotland* (Edinburgh: W. Green, 1962), pp.436 et seq.

[231] Approved per Lord Reid in *Barclay's Tr. v Inland Revenue*, 1975 S.C. (H.L.) 1 at 14. The word "readily" is to be stressed.

[232] *Taylor v Gilbert's Trs* (1878) 5 R. (HL) 217.

immediate vesting in B that his or her right can only be defeated by A having a child.[233] If the destination-over to B is framed so as to take effect on the death of A without leaving issue, the fee remains vested in B unless A is survived by issue.[234] If, however, the gift to B is qualified by conditions which in themselves suspend vesting, as, for example, by a destination-over to B's heirs or to another person *nominatim* (e.g. to A in liferent and his issue in fee, whom failing to B, whom failing to C), or by words which show that B's survivance of the expiry of the liferent is required, there is no room for vesting prior to that event, because the gift to B is not solely dependent upon A having no issue; in other words, it is subject to a double contingency.[235] But a contingency that issue may emerge to several liferenters (e.g. to A in liferent and his issue in fee, whom failing to B in liferent and his issue in fee, whom failing to C) is not such a double contingency as will suspend vesting in the ultimate beneficiary, C.[236]

(2) "For A in fee, with a direction to hold for A in liferent and his issue in fee"—If a bequest be made to A with a further direction that the trustees shall hold for him in liferent and for his issue in fee, it has been held in a series of cases that the fee will remain with A if he has no issue.[237] The ground for this construction is that the testator, having made a gift to A, is not to be taken to have intended by the further direction to revoke that gift, but rather to subordinate it to the bequest to the issue. In the event of there being issue, A's right is reduced to a liferent out of favour to the issue who are to have the fee; but if there are no issue, then A is to remain in enjoyment of the fee. It is essential in this case that there should be language sufficient to confer a right of fee upon A, for if, on the construction of the deed, it appears that nothing more than a liferent was in any circumstances given to him, the doctrine is inapplicable.[238]

(3) "For A in liferent and B in fee, whom failing to B's issue"—If trustees are directed to hold a fund for behoof of a legatee with a provision that, if he predeceases the expiry of a liferent or other event leaving issue, such issue shall take their parent's share, the legatee will take a vested right subject to defeasance if he predecease the event and leave issue. If he does not so predecease (whether he has issue or not), or if he predecease but does not leave issue, his right is not defeated. The only event on which divestiture of his right takes place is if he does predecease and is survived by issue.[239]

---

[233] *Steel's Trs v Steel* (1888) 16 R. 204.

[234] *Gregory's Trs v Alison* (1889) 16 R. (HL) 10. Note that in *Taylor v Gilbert's Trs* (1878) 5 R. (HL) 217, vesting in A's issue was dependent upon one or more of them (a) surviving A and (b) attaining majority. See also *Munro's Tr. v Monson*, 1962 S.C. 414.

[235] *Lees' Trs v Lees*, 1927 S.C. 886; *Nicolson's Trs v Nicolson*, 1960 S.C. 186.

[236] *Taylor v Gilbert's Trs* (1878) 5 R. (HL) 217; *G.'s Trs v G.*, 1937 S.C. 141; *Moss's Tr. v Moss's Trs*, 1958 S.C. 501.

[237] *Tweeddale's Trs v Tweeddale* (1905) 8 F. 264; *Donaldson's Trs v Donaldson*, 1916 S.C. (HL) 55; *Aitken's Trs v Aitken*, 1921 S.C. 807; *Livingston's Trs v Livingston's Trs*, 1939 S.C. (HL) 17. Distinguished in *Riddoch's Trs v Calder's Tr.*, 1947 S.C. 281, where there was held to be initial gift of fee; cf. *Scott's Trs v De Moyse-Bucknall's Trs*, 1978 S.C. 62.

[238] *Muir's Trs v Muir's Trs* (1895) 22 R. 553; *Nicol's Trs v Farquhar*, 1918 S.C. 358; *Smith's Trs v Clark*, 1920 S.C. 161.

[239] *Allan's Trs v Allan*, 1918 S.C. 164; *Gibson's Trs v Gibson*, 1925 S.C. 477; and see *Coulston's Trs v Coulston's Trs*, 1911 S.C. 881, where two contingencies were held to be alternative and not cumulative so as to suspend vesting.

In all these cases there is this common feature, that the legatee's interest is liable to be defeated only by the contingency that there may be issue born to the liferenter or legatee. There are, however, other cases of rather exceptional nature and not capable of classification, in which vesting subject to defeasance has been held to take place.[240]

39.27 **Vesting of class gifts**—The general rule is that (unless the will provides otherwise) those members only who are in existence when the time appointed for payment of the bequest arrives are entitled to participate in it. Hence, under a simple bequest to the children of A, where there is nothing to postpone payment beyond the testator's death, the children then alive take the bequest to the exclusion of children born later.[241] A child in utero is treated as if already born.[242]

But if the time of payment is postponed as, for example, if the gift be to A in liferent and to his children in fee, all the children who are born prior to the death of the liferenter are included.[243] In this case the gift vests in the children alive at the testator's death, or if there are none, in the child first born, subject to partial defeasance to the extent necessary to allow of children born later receiving equal shares.[244] The fact that the class is liable to be enlarged does not suspend the vesting. Where the bequest is to children, as and when they respectively attain majority and the shares are then to be paid over, it has been held that the bequest is limited to the children alive when the eldest child reaches majority and so becomes entitled to demand payment of his share, as otherwise the share to be paid to the eldest child could not be fixed.[245]

In the case of *Hickling's Trs v Garland's Trs*[246] the testator directed his trustees to hold a sum for a daughter in liferent, and on her death leaving issue to divide it among her issue. On the daughter's death two children were alive and two had predeceased her. It was held that the sum had vested in all four children. The bequest was dependent on the contingency of the daughter leaving, that is being survived by, children; but that contingency was not imported into the description of the class so as to confine the gift to those children who survived their mother. If, through the survivance of certain members of the class the bequest came into effect, it operated in favour of all the members of the class. It is otherwise if the bequest is so framed as to show that only those children who survive the contingency are meant to share in the fund, or if there is a destination-over in the case of the liferenter dying without leaving issue.[247]

---

[240] See, e.g. *Yule's Trs v Deans*, 1919 S.C. 570, per Lord Skerrington; *McCall's Trs v McCall*, 1957 S.L.T. (Notes) 16; *Martin's Trs v Milliken* (1864) 3 M. 326; *Bruce's Trs v Bruce's Trs* (1898) 25 R. 796.

[241] *Stopford Blair's Exrs v Heron Maxwell's Trs* (1872) 10 M. 760; *Hayward's Exrs v Young* (1895) 22 R. 757; *Wood v Wood* (1861) 23 D. 338, per Lord Cowan. Where the bequest is to children, children of unmarried parents are included in the class unless the contrary intention appears (Law Reform (Miscellaneous Provisions) (Scotland) Act 1968 s.5—applicable only to deeds executed on or after November 25, 1968—and see now Law Reform (Parent and Child) (Scotland) Act 1986 s.1).

[242] *Cox's Trs v Cox*, 1950 S.C. 117.

[243] *Hickling's Trs v Garland's Trs* (1898) 1 F. (HL) 7, per Lord Davey; *Christie v Wisely* (1874) 1 R. 436; *Ross v Dunlop* (1878) 5 R. 833; *Potter's Trs v Allan*, 1918 S.C. 173; *Murray's Tr. v Murray*, 1919 S.C. 552.

[244] *Douglas v Douglas* (1864) 2 M. 1008; *Carleton v Thomson* (1867) 5 M. (HL) 151.

[245] *Scott's Trs v Scott*, 1909 S.C. 773.

[246] *Hickling's Trs v Garland's Trs* (1898) 1 F. (HL) 7; cf. *Primrose's Trs v Gardiner*, 1973 S.L.T. 238.

[247] *Graham's Trs v Lang's Trs*, 1916 S.C. 723; *Craik's Trs v Anderson*, 1932 S.C. 61.

MISCELLANEOUS

Ademption of special legacies—Where the subject of a special legacy has ceased **39.28** to form part of the testator's estate at death, the legacy is adeemed and nothing is due to the legatee. The intention of the testator is not considered in this matter. The only inquiries necessary are (a) whether the legacy is a special one and, if so, (b) whether the thing bequeathed does or does not remain part of the testator's estate.[248] Thus, if the testator had alienated the thing bequeathed, or if it had perished, or if a debt due to the testator and bequeathed by him or her had been paid off,[249] or if an investment bequeathed had been realised and the money reinvested,[250] or if money in a particular bank was bequeathed and the account had been transferred to another bank,[251] or if the heritage bequeathed had been taken under compulsory powers,[252] in all these cases the legacy is adeemed. But it is not adeemed where the testator has transferred the subject of the legacy but at the testator's death something remains to be done to perfect the transferee's title.[253] Where the subject of bequest is shares in a company, and these shares are subdivided or converted into stock or otherwise altered by the act of the company, it seems that there is no ademption if the change is in name or form only.[254] The test is whether the subject of the testator's bequest has remained substantially the same thing at his death; if it has, there is no ademption.[255] A sale by a guardian or judicial factor will not result in ademption unless the sale was a necessary and unavoidable act[256]; this has been extended to sales by continuing attorneys.[257]

Abatement of legacies—If the testator's net estate should prove insufficient to **39.29** satisfy in full all the bequests, the classification of these is of importance, because on this depends the order in which they shall abate. A testator may provide for this contingency in the will, but in the absence of such a provision, the following order applies. Residual legacies abate first, these legatees having no right to receive anything until the prior legacies are paid in full. General legacies come next and finally special legacies.[258] Within each class the legacies abate rateably.[259] The order or numbering of the legacies does not give an earlier legacy priority over a later.[260]

Conditio si institutus sine liberis decesserit[261]—In certain cases, this condition is **39.30** read into a bequest, including a bequest of revenue.[262] The effect is that, if the

---

[248] *McArthur's Exrs v Guild*, 1908 S.C. 743, per Lord Kinnear.

[249] *Cobban's Exrs v Cobban*, 1915 S.C. 82; *Pagan v Pagan* (1838) 16 S. 383.

[250] *Anderson v Thomson* (1877) 4 R. 1101; *Maclean v Maclean's Exrx*, 1908 S.C. 838. See also *Thomsons' Trs v Lockhart*, 1930 S.C. 674.

[251] *Ballantyne's Trs v Ballantyne's Trs*, 1941 S.C. 35, distinguished in *Re Dorman (Deceased)* [1994] 1 W.L.R. 282.

[252] *Chalmers v Chalmers* (1851) 14 D. 57.

[253] *Tennant's Trs v Tennant*, 1946 S.C. 420.

[254] *Macfarlane's Trs v Macfarlane*, 1910 S.C. 325; see *Whittome v Whittome (No.1)*, 1994 S.L.T. 114 for a similar case in the area of family law.

[255] *Ogilvie-Forbes' Trs v Ogilvie-Forbes*, 1955 S.C. 405 at 411, per Lord President Clyde.

[256] *Macfarlane's Trs v Macfarlane*, 1910 S.C. 325.

[257] *Turner v Turner* [2012] CSOH 41.

[258] *Tennant's Trs v Tennant*, 1946 S.C. 420.

[259] Erskine, III, 9, 12 (general legacies); *Stair Memorial Encyclopedia*, Vol.25, para.856.

[260] *McConnel v McConnel's Trs*, 1931 S.N. 31.

[261] McLaren, *Wills and Succession*, i, Ch.XL; Henderson, *The Principles of Vesting in the Law of Succession* (1938), Ch.XVII.

[262] *Pattinson's Trs v Motion*, 1941 S.C. 290.

legatee dies without acquiring a vested interest leaving issue,[263] the issue (although they are not mentioned in the will) have right to the legacy in preference (as the case may be) to the conditional institute, or the residuary legatee, or the heirs *ab intestato* of the testator. In the case of a bequest of income, it applies so as to enable the payment of income to the issue of a beneficiary who before death had entered into and enjoyed the bequest.[264] It is applicable only to bequests by a testator to his or her own descendants or nephews and nieces,[265] including those related by an unmarried parent-child link,[266] but not to a step-child.[267] Where the legatees are nephews or nieces it is necessary that the testator should by the terms of the will have placed himself or herself in *loco parentis* to them, which means that the testator should have made a settlement in their favour similar to that which a parent might be supposed to make.[268] In such circumstances the presumption is that the *conditio* applies, in the absence of a contrary intention expressed or clearly implied in the deed itself or in other operative testamentary writings.[269] But it prevails over a destination-over, a survivorship clause or accretion in the will.[270] These limits to its application are now settled; but within these limits it is always a question of construction whether in any particular case the *conditio* is to be admitted.[271] It is favourable to its admission that the settlement is a universal one, that the beneficiaries are a class, and that the provision is of the nature of a family settlement.[272] On the other hand, the *conditio* does not apply if the bequest proceeds purely from *delectus personae* apart from the fact of relationship[273]; and, as its justification is the presumption that the failure to mention issue was due to the testator having overlooked the contingency of the legatee's predecease leaving issue, it does not apply if the terms of the will afford evidence that this is not so; and such evidence is found where the testator in other legacies has made express provision for the issue of predeceasing legatees.[274] It applies although the parent was called as a conditional institute,[275] but it cannot apply if the legatee was dead when the will was executed.[276] It admits the issue of a legatee who has either predeceased the testator or died after the testator without having acquired a vested

---

[263] Including, in provisions made on or after November 25, 1968, issue whose parents are unmarried (Law Reform (Miscellaneous Provisions) (Scotland) Act 1968 ss.6(1)(a), (3) and 22(5); Law Reform (Parent and Child) (Scotland) Act 1986 s.1).

[264] *Reid's Trs v Reid*, 1969 S.L.T. (Notes) 4.

[265] *Hall v Hall* (1891) 18 R. 690.

[266] Except in provisions made before November 25, 1968. See para.39.15, above.

[267] *Sinclair's Trs v Sinclair*, 1942 S.C. 362.

[268] *Bogie's Trs v Christie* (1882) 9 R. 453. See *Waddell's Trs v Waddell* (1896) 24 R. 189 and *Alexander's Trs v Paterson*, 1928 S.C. 371.

[269] *Knox's Exr v Knox*, 1941 S.C. 532; *Devlin's Trs v Breen*, 1945 S.C. (HL) 27 at 35, per Lord Thankerton; *Reid's Trs v Reid*, 1969 S.L.T. (Notes) 4.

[270] *Dixon v Dixon* (1841) 11 Rob App 1; *Devlin's Trs v Breen*, 1945 S.C. (HL) 27.

[271] *Devlin's Trs*, 1945 S.C. (HL) 27 at 32.

[272] *Blair's Exrs v Taylor* (1876) 3 R. 362; *Devlin's Trs*, 1945 S.C. (HL) 27.

[273] *Keith's Trs v Keith* (1908) 16 S.L.T. 390.

[274] *Greig v Malcolm* (1835) 13 S. 607; *McNab v Brown's Trs*, 1926 S.C. 387, approved in *Paterson v Paterson*, 1935 S.C. (HL) 7. See *Alexander's Trs v Paterson*, 1928 S.C. 371, and *Reid's Trs v Reid*, 1969 S.L.T. (Notes) 4.

[275] *Greig's Trs v Simpson*, 1918 S.C. 321.

[276] *Rhind's Trs v Leith* (1866) 5 M. 104; *Low's Trs v Whitworth* (1892) 19 R. 431; but see *Miller's Trs v Miller*, 1958 S.C. 125 (*conditio* applied where the bequest was confirmed by a codicil executed after the institute's death).

right.[277] It applies in marriage contracts as well as in testamentary deeds,[278] but not in the case of any other inter vivos deed.[279] As already mentioned, the issue take only the parent's original share.[280]

Ineffectual conditions and directions: Repugnancy—If a bequest is made subject **39.31** to a condition which is in its nature impossible, uncertain,[281] illegal, or *contra bonos mores*, the condition is held *pro non scripto*, and the bequest is effectual.[282] Thus, a legacy given *ob turpem causam*,[283] or subject to a condition amounting to an absolute and general restraint of marriage by the legatee[284] or to a wife on condition that she ceases to live with her husband,[285] or to a young child on condition that he shall not reside with his parents (of unobjectionable character),[286] receives effect as an unconditional legacy as these conditions are not sanctioned by the law; and testamentary directions requiring that the testator's estate should be disposed of in an unreasonable manner which conferred no benefit on any person or on the public have been refused effect as involving an abuse of the power of testation.[287] A legacy to an enemy alien remains legally incapable of payment during the war.[288]

Further, on the ground

> "that an act which, if done, can be at once undone by the person having an interest, will not be directed by the Court to be done",

it has been held in a series of cases that if trustees are directed to purchase an annuity payable to a person, that person (seeing that the annuity could be sold once purchased) may claim the purchase price of the annuity in lieu of it.[289] And where a vested, unqualified, and indefeasible right of fee in a bequest is given in a trust disposition and settlement to a beneficiary of full age, that beneficiary is entitled to payment of the bequest notwithstanding any direction to the trustees to retain the capital and to pay over the income to him or to apply the capital or income in some way for the beneficiary's behoof.[290] Such a direction is

---

[277] *Young v Robertson* (1862) 4 Macq. 337 at 340, per Lord Chancellor (Westbury); *Grant v Brooke* (1882) 10 R. 92; *Alexander's Trs v Paterson*, 1928 S.C. 371; cf. *Mitchell's Exrs v Gordon's J.F.*, 1953 S.C. 176, where Lord President Cooper suggested, obiter, that its applicability was dependent upon the institute predeceasing the testator; *sed contra: MacGregor's Trs v Gray*, 1969 S.L.T. 355.

[278] *Hughes v Edwardes* (1892) 19 R. (HL) 33.

[279] *Halliday* (1869) 8 M. 112; *Crichton's Tr. v Howat's Tutor* (1890) 18 R. 260; *Trs of Gwendolen Beatrice Thomson's Trust*, 1963 S.C. 141.

[280] See para.39.18, above.

[281] In *Veitch's Exr v Veitch*, 1947 S.L.T. 17, a condition that the legatee "occupy" a house was held not to be uncertain. See also *Hood v Macdonald's Trs*, 1949 S.C. 24.

[282] Bell, *Principles*, s.1785; McLaren, *Wills and Succession*, i, 600.

[283] For an immoral consideration: *Johnston v McKenzie's Exrs* (1835) 14 S. 106; *Young v Johnston & Wright* (1880) 7 R. 760.

[284] *Sturrock v Rankin's Trs* (1875) 2 R. 850; *Aird's Exrs v Aird*, 1949 S.C. 154.

[285] *Wilkinson v Wilkinson* (1871) L.R. 12 Eq. 604.

[286] *Grant's Trs v Grant* (1898) 25 R. 929; *Fraser v Rose* (1849) 11 D. 1466.

[287] *Aitken's Trs v Aitken*, 1927 S.C. 374; *Lindsay's Exr v Forsyth*, 1940 S.C. 568; *McCaig v The University of Glasgow*, 1907 S.C. 231; *McCaig's Trs v Kirk Session of United Free Church of Lismore*, 1915 S.C. 426; *Sutherland's Trs v Verschoyle*, 1968 S.L.T. 43.

[288] *Weber's Trs v Riemer*, 1947 S.L.T. 295.

[289] *Dow v Kilgour's Trs* (1877) 4 R. 403; *Dempster's Trs v Dempster*, 1921 S.C. 332; contrast *Branford's Trs v Powell*, 1924 S.C. 439.

[290] *Yuill's Trs v Thomson* (1902) 4 F. 815; *Miller's Trs v Miller* (1890) 18 R. 301; *Dowden's Trs v Governors of Merchiston Castle School*, 1965 S.C. 56; *Smith's Tr. v Michael*, 1972 S.L.T. 89; *Graham v Graham's Trs*, 1927 S.C. 388; contrast *Ford's Trs v Ford*, 1940 S.C. 426, where the later direction disposed of the fee.

considered to be repugnant to the right of fee vested in the beneficiary and, therefore, nugatory. But it is otherwise if there are other trust purposes which require that the subject of the bequest shall be retained by the trustees, or if the trustees are not merely directed to retain the bequest but are given a discretionary power to convert the beneficiary's fee into a liferent and to settle the fee on others.[291] In such circumstances the beneficiary cannot put an end to the trust management.

39.32 **Approbate and reprobate or election**—The doctrine of approbate and reprobate or election prevents a person from accepting certain provisions of a document and rejecting others in the same document. In a leading case,[292] children taking provisions made by a testatrix out of her own estate claimed also to be entitled to challenge her appointment of a fund made in the same deed and to take that fund as in default of valid appointment; but the court, applying the doctrine, held that acceptance of one part of the deed was inconsistent with rejection of another part. Lord President Inglis stated, in *Douglas's Trs v Douglas*,[293]

> "that, to make a proper case of election, the facts of the case must be such as to satisfy three conditions. In the first place, I think the party who is put to his election must have a free choice, and that whichever alternative he chooses, he shall have a right absolutely to that which he has chosen, without the possibility of his right being interfered with or frustrated by the intervention of any third party. In the second place, the necessity of making the election must arise from the will, express or implied, of someone who has the power to bind the person put to his election. And, in the third place, the result of the election of one or other of the alternatives must be to give legal effect and operation[294] to the will so expressed or implied".

In making an election, a person should have information as to the alternative rights available; and there are numerous cases in which an election made in ignorance or in circumstances which show that it does not represent a free and deliberate choice, has been held not to be binding.[295] It would be prudent to advise the person to seek independent legal advice.

The doctrine is most commonly found in cases where a bequest is made to a spouse or descendant who has legal rights in the estate of the testator.[296] A choice has to be made between the bequest and the legal rights.

LEGAL RIGHTS

39.33 **Legal rights**—The legal rights of the testator's surviving spouse and children[297] vest in them automatically at the date of the testator's death. The rules for quantifying legal rights in testate estates are the same as those applicable to intestate

---

[291] *Chamber's Trs v Smiths* (1878) 5 R. (HL) 151.

[292] *Crum Ewing's Trs v Bayly's Trs*, 1911 S.C. (HL) 18.

[293] *Douglas's Trs v Douglas* (1862) 24 D. 1191 at 1208.

[294] e.g. *Brown's Trs v Gregson*, 1920 S.C. (HL) 87 where the chosen legacy turned out to be invalid.

[295] See *Inglis v Breen* (1890) 17 R. (HL) 76; *Stewart v Bruce's Trs* (1898) 25 R. 965; *Dawson's Trs v Dawson* (1896) 23 R. 1006; *Walker v Orr's Trs (No.2)*, 1958 S.L.T. 220.

[296] See para.39.34, below.

[297] The issue of a pre-deceasing child are entitled to that child's share of *legitim*, Succession (Scotland) Act 1964 s.11.

estates set out in Ch.38 above, except that there are no prior rights to be deducted before ascertaining the net moveable estate from which legal rights are exigible. Legal rights cannot be defeated by will and so can be seen as a way of protecting close family from disinheritance or receiving inadequate provisions. They may be discharged by a person entitled to them either while the testator is alive or after the testator's death.[298] An express discharge prevents legal rights being claimed out of both the testate and intestate estate,[299] unless there is a reservation of the right to claim them out of estate that is intestate or which may subsequently fall into intestacy.[300]

Where a person entitled to legal rights has not been left any provision in the testator's will the position is relatively simple as there is no question of having to elect between legal rights and the testamentary provisions or deciding what happens to the forfeited provisions. The legal rights are paid out of the net estate and the legacies to the other beneficiaries abate in the normal order: residue, general legacies, demonstrative legacies, special legacies; unless the will provides for another scheme of abatement.[301]

Election between legal rights and testamentary provisions—A surviving **39.34** spouse or descendant will have to elect between the testamentary provisions and legal rights, unless (which is very uncommon) the will makes it clear that both can be taken. This rests on the doctrine of approbate and reprobate. Choosing the testamentary provisions contained in a will executed on or after September 10, 1964[302] involves forfeiture of legal rights as the will is presumed to contain a declaration that the testamentary provisions are in full and final satisfaction of legal rights.[303]

Likewise, choosing to take legal rights results in the forfeiture of the claimant's testamentary provisions. But a simple full and final satisfaction declaration, whether presumed or express, results in the forfeiture of legal rights only in so far as they conflict with the will. The surviving spouse or descendant may take the testamentary provisions and remain entitled to legal rights out of estate that is intestate or which may subsequently fall into intestacy.[304] An express declaration may, however, be framed in wider terms that prevent legal rights being claimed out of any intestate estate.

Effect on other beneficiaries of taking legal rights—In pre-1964 wills, in the **39.35** absence of a full and final satisfaction clause, the doctrine of equitable compensation meant that forfeiture of the testamentary provisions on taking legal rights occurred only to the extent necessary to indemnify those who had been prejudiced

---

[298] See paras 38.14 and 38.15 above as to the different effects of a pre-death and a post-death discharge.

[299] *Melville's Trs v Melville's Trs*, 1964 S. C. 105.

[300] *Petrie's Trs v Mander's Tr*, 1954 S.C. 430.

[301] *Tait's Trs v Lees* (1886) 13 R. 1104.

[302] In pre-September 10, 1964 wills claiming legal rights did not necessarily involve a complete forfeiture of the testamentary provisions in the absence of an express satisfaction clause; *White v Findlay* (1861) 24 D. 38; McLaren, *Wills and Succession*, i, 140 and *Macfarlane's Trs v Oliver* (1882) 9 R. 1138.

[303] Succession (Scotland) Act 1964 s.13, as amended by the Law Reform (Parent and Child) (Scotland) Act 1986 Sch.2 (formerly Law Reform (Miscellaneous Provisions) (Scotland) Act 1968 s.3 and Sch.1 para.6). A will could contain a clause disapplying this presumption.

[304] *Naismith v Boyes* (1899) 1 F. (HL) 79; but not illegal accumulations of income, *Lindsay's Trs*, 1931 S.C. 586.

by the taking of legal rights. Thus, in *Macfarlane's Trs v Oliver*,[305] a testator directed his trustees to hold his whole estate for behoof of his son and daughter equally in liferent and for their issue respectively in fee. The daughter having claimed her *legitim*, the trustees accumulated the share of income which would have been payable to her as liferentrix until it reached a sum which enabled them to make good to her brother and to the grandchildren the loss occasioned to them by her claim of *legitim*. It was held that, compensation having thus been made, the daughter was entitled to the future income of the share bequeathed to her and her children. But if a testamentary provision is made for a spouse or child on the express condition that it is to be taken in satisfaction of her or his legal rights, the assertion of these rights normally involves total forfeiture of the provision. In testamentary settlements executed on or after September 10, 1964, a clause of satisfaction is now implied[306]; accordingly, a claim for legal rights will result in forfeiture of all provisions made for the claimant in such a deed unless the will contains a statement to the contrary. Equitable compensation, however, still has a role in evaluating the rights of other beneficiaries when one beneficiary elects to take legal rights.[307]

As mentioned above, a simple full and final satisfaction declaration, whether implied or express, now results in the complete forfeiture of testamentary provisions on the beneficiary taking legal rights. A special or general legacy falls into residue and a gift of residue or a share of residue lapses into intestacy.[308] Where the testamentary provision takes the form of a liferent of a fund of which the fee is unvested the trustees continue to hold the fund and the income falls into residue after accumulations cease to be lawful or they have compensated those prejudiced by the taking of legal rights, whichever occurs first. Likewise, the income of a forfeited liferent of residue falls into intestacy. But in both cases the vesting of the fee may, under the terms of the will, be accelerated by the forfeiture of the liferent which then ceases and the capital is distributed. Acceleration is not the normal result,[309] but in *Hurll's Trs v Hurll*[310] the "termination" of the liferent was held to include its forfeiture by taking legal rights.

39.36 Forfeiture by issue—A child may be left a liferent with the fee going to his or her issue or a destination-over of the liferent to the child's spouse. Where the clause of satisfaction includes also a provision for forfeiture, it may expressly declare the forfeiture of their rights as well as those of the child taking *legitim* and this will be given effect to. Even in the absence of an express forfeiture by issue or spouse if, on a construction of the deed, it appears that the right of the issue or spouse is dependent on the liferent taking effect, their right is forfeited by the child's election to take *legitim*.[311] Their right is not forfeited if there is a separate

---

[305] *Macfarlane's Trs v Oliver* (1882) 9 R. 1138. And see *Thomson's Trs v Thomson*, 1946 S.C. 399.
[306] Succession (Scotland) Act 1964 s.13, as amended by the Law Reform (Parent and Child) (Scotland) Act 1986 Sch.2. See formerly, Law Reform (Miscellaneous Provisions) (Scotland) Act 1968 s.3 and Sch.1 para.6; *Munro's Trs, Petitioner*, 1971 S.L.T. 313; 1971 S.C. 280.
[307] *Munro's Trs*, 1971 S.C. 280.
[308] *Samson v Raynor*, 1928 S.C. 899; *Tindall's Trs v Tindall*, 1933 S.C. 419.
[309] *Taylor's Executrices v Thom*, 1914 S.C. 79; *McLay v Farrell*, 1950 S.C. 149; *Lorimer's Exrs v Hird*, 1959 S.L.T. (Notes) 8.
[310] *Hurll's Trs v Hurll*, 1964 S.C. 12.
[311] *Campbell's Trs v Campbell* (1889) 16 R. 1007; *McCaull's Trs v McCaull* (1900) 3 F. 222; *Ballantyne's Trs v Ballantyne*, 1952 S.C. 458; *McCartney's Trs v McCartney's Exrs*, 1951 S.C. 504.

and independent gift to them,[312] and the issue get the benefit of any doubt.[313] The two cases of *Ballantyne's Trs*, where there was an express forfeiture clause only for a child should he claim *legitim*, are good illustrations. In the first case[314] the issue forfeited the fee of the share liferented by a son taking *legitim*. In terms of the forfeiture clause half of that fee passed to the testator's daughter. When she died many years later without issue part of her share was to pass to the son's issue. They were held in the second case[315] not to have forfeited this as it was a separate and independent gift to them, they being institutes of the daughter not the son. Where the clause of satisfaction does not contain an express forfeiture, it is doubtful whether forfeiture of the conventional provision by any person other than the one taking legal rights will be inferred.[316] If, however, a forfeiture clause for child and issue is combined with a destination-over in the event of forfeiture and the destination-over fails, e.g. because there is no one to take under it, the child who takes *legitim* forfeits any testamentary provisions but the forfeiture for the issue does not take effect.[317] If the issue are not then vested the trustees continue to hold the fund for them until the date of vesting arrives.

FURTHER READING

Henderson, R.C., *The Principles of Vesting in the Law of Succession*, 2nd edn (Edinburgh: W. Green, 1938).

Hiram, H., *The Scots Law of Succession*, 2nd edn (Edinburgh: Tottel, 2007).

Macdonald, D.R., *Succession*, 3rd edn (Edinburgh: W. Green, 2001).

McLaren, J., *The Law of Wills and Succession*, 3rd edn (Edinburgh: Bell and Bradfute, 1894) and Dykes' supplement (Edinburgh: W. Green, 1934).

Meston, M., *Succession (Scotland) Act 1964*, 5th edn (Edinburgh: W. Green, 2002).

Reid, K.G.C., "Testamentary formalities in Scotland", in Reid, K.G.C., De Waal, M. and Zimmermann, R. (eds), *Comparative Succession Law Vol 1: Testamentary Formalities* (Oxford: Oxford University Press, 2011).

Reid, K.G.C, de Waal, M. and Zimmermann, R. (eds), *Exploring the Law of Succession: Studies National, Historical and Comparative* (Edinburgh: Edinburgh University Press, 2007).

Stair Memorial Encyclopaedia, Vol.25.

---

[312] *Fisher v Dixon* (1831) 10 S. 55; affd 6 W. & S. 431; *Jack v Marshall* (1879) 6 R. 543; *Brown's Trs v Gregson*, 1916 S.C. 97; *Hurll's Trs v Hurll*, 1964 S.C. 12; *Munro's Trs*, 1971 S.C. 280. See also *Ballantyne's Trs v Ballantyne*, 1992 S.C.L.R. 889, where forfeiture of the rights of issue did not prevent their succession as conditional institutes under another provision of the will.

[313] *Ballantyne's Trs v Ballantyne*, 1952 S.C. 458 at 465, per Lord President Cooper.

[314] *Ballantyne's Trs v Ballantyne*, 1952 S.C. 458.

[315] *Ballantyne's Trs v Ballantyne*, 1992 S.C.L.R. 889.

[316] See *Nicolson's Trs v Nicolson*, 1960 S.C. 186 at 193, per Lord President Clyde; *Hurll's Trs*, 1964 S.C. 12 at 19, per Lord Justice-Clerk Grant.

[317] *Hannah's Trs v Hannah*, 1924 S.C. 494; *MacNaughton v MacNaughton's Trs*, 1954 S.C. 312.

CHAPTER 40

EXECUTORS

Appointment of executor—The title to ingather and distribute the estate, both **40.01** heritable and moveable,[1] of a deceased person belongs to the executor nominated by the deceased or appointed by the court, and in either case authorised to do so by confirmation by the court. Where the estate falls to the Crown as *ultimus haeres* those in possession have to hand it over to the Queen's and Lord Treasurer's Remembrancer who does not have to be confirmed. An executor is appointed (a) either expressly or impliedly by the deceased (executor-nominate), or (b) by the court (executor-dative). With regard to (a), the persons who may be executors are, in order: (i) the executor nominated[2] by the deceased; or failing such an appointment, (ii) the testamentary trustees; or failing them, (iii) any general disponee or universal legatory or residuary legatee.[3]

Where the deceased dies intestate or there is no executor-nominate, the executor is appointed by the decerniture of the sheriff on an application for this purpose. The court in which the application should be made is that of the sheriffdom in which the deceased was domiciled, or, if the deceased had no domicile in Scotland or was domiciled in Scotland but not in any particular sheriffdom, in the Sheriff Court of Edinburgh. The order of preference[4] observed in making the appointment is: (1) general disponees, universal legatories or residuary legatees[5]; (2) the next-of-kin and, if these do not claim, the representatives of next-of-kin who have died after the deceased but before the confirmation is expede; (3) creditors; (4) special legatees; and (5) the procurator fiscal. Where the father or mother of the deceased have right to a share of the estate, they rank pari passu with the next-of-kin in competition for the office.[6] The husband, if he is entitled to *jus relicti*, has right to the office, but not in competition with his wife's next-of-kin.[7] Where the deceased has died intestate but is survived by a spouse, and the intestate estate is less than the amount which the surviving spouse is entitled to receive under prior rights, the surviving spouse has the right to be appointed executor[8]; otherwise the preference of the surviving spouse's right to the office will depend

---

[1] Succession (Scotland) Act 1964 (the "1964 Act") s.14.

[2] *Tod* (1890) 18 R. 152.

[3] Executors (Scotland) Act 1900 s.3.

[4] See E.M. Scobbie, *Currie on Confirmation of Executors*, 9th edn (Edinburgh: W. Green, 2011), paras 6.02–6.06 and 6.14–6.96.

[5] General disponees, universal legatories and residuary legatees can be decerned executor-nominate under the Executors (Scotland) Act 1900 s.3, but all those entitled have to be confirmed. Where this is inconvenient a dative appointment is preferable, see Scobbie, *Currie on Confirmation of Executors* (2011), para.6.15.

[6] *Webster v Shiress* (1878) 6 R. 102; *Muir* (1876) 4 R. 74.

[7] *Campbell v Falconer* (1892) 19 R. 563.

[8] 1964 Act s.9(4), but perhaps not an exclusive right, see Scobbie, *Currie on Confirmation of Executors* (2011), paras 6.28–6.43 and *Murray, Petitioner*, Sheriff McCulloch at Kirkcaldy, March 15, 2012.

on the extent to which the deceased's estate exceeds the value of these rights.[9] All applicants having an equal right in the estate are entitled to be conjoined in the office, but it is competent for one or more of them to decline appointment. As the appointment of an executor is an administrative rather than a judicial function, the court has no discretion to choose between applicants of equal rank.[10]

40.02 Confirmation of executors—The appointment of a person as executor does not in itself confer authority to intromit with the estate of the deceased. In order to obtain such authority, the executor must expede confirmation, that is, he or she must apply for, and obtain from the sheriff, a decree authorising him or her to "uplift, receive, administer and dispose of" the estate and to act in the office of executor. An executor who intromits with the estate without confirmation is a vitious intromitter.[11] The office of executor is purely administrative.[12]

As a condition of confirmation, an executor-dative must find caution to make the estate forthcoming to parties interested, but this is not required in the case of an executor-nominate or a spouse[13] who has right to the whole intestate estate and is executor-dative.[14] All executors must give up on oath a full and true inventory of the whole estate, heritable and moveable, known to have belonged to the deceased, including property outwith Scotland.[15] Where the deceased died domiciled in Scotland and the confirmation includes any estate, real or personal, of the deceased in England and Wales or Northern Ireland,[16] the confirmation is treated as equivalent to a grant of probate or letters of administration so that the executors can ingather and deal with such estate without further procedure.[17] Confirmation to part only of the estate known to exist is prohibited by statute (except in the case of an executor-creditor[18]) and is of no effect.[19] If any part of the estate has been omitted, wrongly described so that it cannot be ingathered[20] or undervalued, the executor may by an eik have the same confirmed in addition to the estate originally confirmed; and it is also open to a creditor or other party interested to apply for confirmation *ad omissa vel male appretiata* (to items omitted or undervalued).[21] On such an application, if there has been no fraud on the part of the original executor, the sheriff will ordain the omitted subjects or the difference in value to be added to the original confirmation, or, if there be fraud, will grant a confirmation of the subjects to the exclusion of the original executor.

There are statutory provisions permitting payments of certain kinds under £5,000 without the exhibition of confirmation.[22] Property held by the deceased

---

[9] Scobbie, *Currie on Confirmation of Executors* (2011), paras 6.42–43.

[10] *Russo v Russo*, 1998 S.L.T. (Sh. Ct) 32.

[11] *Cunningham & Bell v McKirdy* (1827) 5 S. 315, see para.40.05 below.

[12] *Smart v Smart*, 1926 S.C. 392.

[13] A surviving civil partner must find caution.

[14] Confirmation of Executors (Scotland) Act 1823 s.2 (amended by the Law Reform (Miscellaneous Provisions) (Scotland) Act 1980 s.5); 1964 Act s.20, proviso. See *Harrison v Butters*, 1969 S.L.T. 183.

[15] Probate and Legacy Duties Act 1808 s.38 (as amended by the Law Reform (Miscellaneous Provisions) (Scotland) Act 1990). Immoveable property outwith the United Kingdom is noted in the inventory but is not confirmed to.

[16] Administration of Estates Act 1971 s.6.

[17] Administration of Estates Act 1971 ss.1 and 2.

[18] This is a diligence whereby a creditor can ingather and sell assets sufficient to satisfy the debt: see W.A. Wilson and A.G.M. Duncan, *Trusts, Trustees and Executors*, 2nd edn (Edinburgh: W. Green, 1995).

[19] Confirmation of Executors (Scotland) Act 1823 s.3; *Elder v Watson* (1859) 21 D. 1122.

[20] Scobbie, *Currie on Confirmation of Executors* (2011), para.17.02.

[21] Scobbie, *Currie on Confirmation of Executors* (2011), Ch.17.

[22] Administration of Estates (Small Payments) Act 1965 Sch.1; Administration of Estates (Small Payments) (Increase of Limit) Order 1984 (SI 1984/539).

and others on a title containing an unrevoked survivorship destination passes without confirmation, but the deceased's share has to be included in another section of the inventory.[23]

Confirmation in small estates—There is a simple method of obtaining confir- **40.03** mation in small estates. Where the gross value of the whole estate of the deceased does not exceed £36,000, an application may be made to the sheriff clerk, who fills up an inventory, takes the applicant's oath thereto, gets caution, if necessary, and expedes confirmation for a small fee. This procedure applies to both testate and intestate estates; and for the latter no separate petition for appointement of executors-dative is necessary.[24] But no help is given with the executors' subsequent functions in ingathering and distributing the estate.

Effect of confirmation—Every part of the deceased's estate, heritable and move- **40.04** able, falling to be administered under the law of Scotland, to which confirmation has been obtained, vests for the purposes of administration in the executor by virtue of the confirmation[25]; the confirmation confers full power to ingather, administer and dispose of the estate contained in the inventory. Before confirmation, an executor may indeed sue for a debt due to the deceased[26]; but without it cannot obtain an extract of decree for, or enforce, payment or grant an effectual discharge of, the debt. A debtor of the deceased is not bound to pay the debt to anyone except an executor who has confirmed to it.[27] If payment is made to anyone else, this does not discharge the debtor in a question with the executor who has confirmed. The executor alone has a title to sue those indebted to the deceased. Except in very special circumstances, an heir or residuary legatee has no such title[28]; but, if the executor is unwilling to raise an action against a debtor, the legatee may require the executor to lend his or her name as pursuer on condition of relieving the executor of liability for any expenses of the action.

The confirmation itself confers a personal right on the executor to the heritage contained in it.[29] The executor may then transfer this personal right to the beneficiary entitled thereto by means of a statutory form of docket which is endorsed on the confirmation.[30] The executor may also transfer it to a beneficiary or a purchaser by disposition. It is good practice for an executor who is also a beneficiary to transfer title from himself or herself as an executor to himself or herself as an individual.[31] A person who in good faith and for value subsequently acquires title

---

[23] Scobbie, *Currie on Confirmation of Executors* (2011), para.10.85 (for IHT purposes).

[24] Intestates' Widows and Children (Scotland) Act 1875; Small Testate Estates (Scotland) Act 1876, as amended by Confirmation to Small Estates (Scotland) Act 1979 s.1 and Law Reform (Miscellaneous Provisions) (Scotland) Act 1990 s.74(1) and (2) and Sch.8; Confirmation to Small Estates (Scotland) Order 2011 (SSI 2011/435); Scobbie, *Currie on Confirmation of Executors* (2011), Ch.11.

[25] 1964 Act s.14(1).

[26] *Chalmers' Trs v Watson* (1860) 22 D. 1060; *Bones v Morrison* (1866) 5 M. 240; *Mackay v Mackay*, 1914 S.C. 200.

[27] *Fraser v Gibb* (1784) Mor.3921; *Buchanan v Royal Bank of Scotland* (1843) 5 D. 211.

[28] *Morrison v Morrison's Ex*, 1912 S.C. 892.

[29] 1964 Act s.15(1). The inventory to the confirmation must contain such a description of the heritage as will be sufficient to identify the property or interest therein as a separate item in the estate: Act of Sederunt (Confirmation of Executors Amendment) Order 1966 (SI 1966/593). If registered in the Land Register, the title number should be given.

[30] 1964 Act s.15(2), Sch.1. The beneficiary acquires a real right by registration in the Land Register. The docket may be used as a link in title if the beneficiary sells without first registering his or her own title.

[31] This is not struck at by *Board of Management of Aberdeen College v Youngson*, 2005 S.C. 335, because the grantor and grantee, although the same person, are acting in different capacities.

to any interest in the heritage which was vested in the executor directly or indirectly, whether from the executor or from a person deriving title from the executor, is protected under the Succession (Scotland) Act 1964, in that no challenge may be made to that title on the ground that the confirmation was reducible or has been reduced, or that the title should not have been transferred to the person deriving title from the executor.[32] Similar protection is given to a person buying goods from the executor.[33]

40.05 **Vitious intromission**—An unauthorised intromitter may incur liability for the whole debts of the deceased, even if there was no fraudulent intention.[34] But the court has regard to the character and circumstances of the intromission and may relieve the vitious intromitter of the penal consequences. Thus, if the intromitter had a probable title for intromitting, e.g. as general disponee of the deceased (although this is not a competent title to intermeddle with the estate without confirmation), or acted in good faith, the intromitter may escape universal liability.[35] Intromission either necessary or *custodiae causa* (for the sake of custody) by the wife and children of the deceased holding possession for the purpose of preserving the estate for the benefit of all concerned, does not infer liability; and there is clearly no place for it if the goods intermeddled with did not belong to the deceased.[36]

This rule was introduced for the benefit of creditors of the deceased and it is not available as a ground of action to heirs or legatees.[37] It cannot be pleaded against the heirs of a deceased vitious intromitter, the heir being liable only in so far as lucratus through succession to the intromitter. Where several are concerned in the intromission, each is liable *in solidum* and may be sued without calling the others; but the intromitter who pays the debt has relief against the other intromitters. An intromitter who confirms before action is brought against him or her, or within a year and day afterwards, thereby becoming liable to account, purges the vitiosity of prior intromissions; but confirmation merely as executor-creditor[38] does not suffice for this purpose.[39]

40.06 **Duties of the executor**—The executor is not, in a question with creditors, to be regarded as a trustee for their behoof, but as proprietor of the executry burdened with the debts chargeable against it. As the deceased was debtor to his or her creditors, so is the executor who comes in the deceased's place, with this limitation, that the executor's liability does not extend beyond the estate confirmed to.[40] The executor is *eadem persona cum defuncto* (the same person as the deceased).[41]

---

[32] 1964 Act s.17.

[33] Sale of Goods Act 1979 s.23. There is no such protection for incorporeal moveables.

[34] *Forbes v Forbes* (1823) 2 S. 395; *Wilson v Taylor* (1865) 3 M. 1060.

[35] *Adam v Campbell* (1854) 16 D. 964; *Simpson v Barr* (1854) 17 D. 33; *Greig v Christie*, 1908 S.C. 370.

[36] *Greig v Christie*, 1908 S.C. 370.

[37] Erskine, III, 9, 54.

[38] Confirmation as executor-creditor is a diligence attaching only the property confirmed to.

[39] Erskine, III, 9, 52.

[40] Executors may become personally liable beyond this if they undertake obligations, for example in running the deceased's business.

[41] *Globe Insurance Co v Scott's Trs* (1849) 7 Bell's App.296; *Stewart's Trs v Stewart's Exr* (1896) 23 R. 739; *Mitchell v Mackersy* (1905) 8 F. 198; *Tait's Exrx v Arden Coal Co*, 1947 S.C. 100; *Murray's J.F. v Thomas Murray & Sons (Ice Merchants) Ltd*, 1992 S.L.T. 824.

All creditors using legal diligence by citation of the executors or by obtaining themselves confirmed executors-creditors, or citing other executors-creditors, within six months after their debtor's death, come in pari passu with those who have used more timely diligence.[42] Hence, an executor cannot be compelled to pay away any part of the estate until after the expiry of the six months, nor (unless the solvency of the estate is assured) can the executor safely do so, seeing that until that period has elapsed it cannot be known for certain how many creditors may have claims on the estate. There is an exception in the case of privileged debts, i.e. debts which have preference over all other debts and must in any case be paid, under which term are included deathbed and funeral expenses, mourning for the widow and family, the expenses of administering the deceased's estate and, probably, debts which would be preferred in sequestration.[43]

After the expiry of the six months, the executor may proceed to pay *primo venienti* (to the first who comes along) and is not answerable for so doing to creditors who appear afterwards. This rule protects executors acting fairly in the discharge of their duties; but there may be circumstances, e.g. if it became plain that the estate was insolvent, in which it would not be proper for the executor to pay off certain debts without regard to the claims of other creditors.[44] Even after the period of six months has expired, a creditor citing the executor who still has funds is entitled to participate in the division of these funds.[45] Where the validity of a creditor's claim is doubtful, the executor may require the creditor to constitute it by decree.[46]

After the claims of creditors have been met, it is the executor's duty (unless the sole beneficiary) to account for and distribute what remains of the estate to those who have right to it. These parties are not entitled to receive any benefit from the estate until the claims of creditors have been satisfied; and, if, in the knowledge that there are outstanding debts, the executor chooses to distribute the whole estate to the beneficiaries, he or she may be made personally liable to an unsatisfied creditor, unless the latter has consented to the payment or has so acted as to be personally barred from objecting to the executor's conduct.[47]

The Succession (Scotland) Act 1964 provides that an adopted person is to be treated for the purposes of succession as the child of the adopter; but an executor is not obliged, before distributing the estate, to check whether an adoption order has been made which would entitle a person to an interest in the estate.[48] Similarly, the executor is not obliged to ascertain whether a person born of unmarried parents exists, or has existed, the fact of whose existence is relevant to the distribution of the estate or whether any paternal relative of such a person exists who may have an interest in the estate.[49] Where an interest in a lease forms part of the deceased's estate and the deceased had not made a valid bequest or had made a bequest which has failed, the executor is entitled to transfer it, without the consent of the

---

[42] Act of Sederunt February 28, 1662; "Act anent executors-creditors".

[43] Erskine, III, 9, 43; *Barlass's Trs*, 1916 S.C. 741; Bankruptcy (Scotland) Act 1985 s.51, Sch.3.

[44] *Taylor & Ferguson v Glass Trs*, 1912 S.C. 165, per Lord Dunedin; *Stewart's Trs v Evans* (1871) 9 M. 810.

[45] *Russel v Simes* (1790) Bell's Oct. Cases 217.

[46] *McGaan v McGaan's Trs* (1883) 11 R. 249, per Lord President Inglis.

[47] *Lamond's Trs v Croom* (1871) 9 M. 662; *Heritable Securities Investment Association v Miller's Trs* (1893) 20 R. 675; *Campbell v Lord Borthwick's Trs*, 1930 S.N. 156.

[48] See 1964 Act s.24(2).

[49] Law Reform (Miscellaneous Provisions) (Scotland) Act 1968 s.7 (as amended by Law Reform (Parent and Child) (Scotland) Act 1986 Sch.1).

landlord, to any of the persons having rights of succession on intestacy in or towards the satisfaction of that person's claim.[50]

Although the office of the executor is distinct from that of trustee, both are governed by the general principles which apply to the administration of an estate by one person for behoof of others. In formal testamentary deeds trustees are usually also nominated executors, and in this case it is not easy to mark the point of differentiation between the respective duties of the two offices. Executors-nominate, as defined in the Executors (Scotland) Act 1900, are included in the definition of trustee for the purposes of the Trusts (Scotland) Acts 1921[51] and 1961,[52] and this definition was extended by the Succession (Scotland) Act 1964[53] so as to include executors-dative. Thus, executors have the same powers, privileges and immunities and are subject to the same obligations, limitations and restrictions as gratuitous trustees under those Acts,[54] except that an executor-dative does not have power to resign or to assume new trustees.

Removal of an executor from office for failure to co-operate with another executor in the administration, whilst a great rarity, is illustrated in at least two reported cases.[55]

40.07 Failure of executors by death: Confirmation *ad non executa*—Executry is an office and does not descend to heirs. Where there are two or more executors, the office accrues to the survivor(s), but if there is only one it ceases with that executor's death. The Executors (Scotland) Act 1900 contains provisions for the cases: (a) where any sole or last surviving trustee or executor has died with any property (heritable or moveable) in Scotland vested in him or her as trustee or executor; and (b) where a confirmation has become inoperative by the death or incapacity of all the executors in whose favour it has been granted. In the first case, the executor of the sole or last surviving trustee or executor may confirm, and this will enable that executor to recover and transfer the property[56]; in the second case, no title to intromit with the estate confirmed transmits to representatives of the executors, but confirmation *ad non executa* (to matters in respect of which an executry has not been completed) may be granted to those parties to whom confirmations *ad omissa* are granted and is a sufficient title to continue and complete the administration of the estate.[57]

Executors are not usually granted a formal discharge when their administration of the estate has been completed. In law the executor's office terminates then,[58] but it is good practice for the executor to have the executry accounts approved by the residuary beneficiaries.

---

[50] 1964 Act s.16. The deceased tenant's interest under a lease must have been confirmed to before the deed of transfer is executed, *McGrath v Nelson*, 2010 CSOH 149. The landlord may be entitled later to object to the transferee becoming a tenant, see para.35.50 above.

[51] Trusts (Scotland) Acts 1921 s.2.

[52] Trusts (Scotland) Acts 1961 s.6.

[53] 1964 Act s.20.

[54] See in particular 1921 Act ss.4 and 5; 1961 Act ss.2 and 4.

[55] *Wilson v Gibson*, 1948 S.C. 52; *Reid v McCabe's Executor*, 1998 S.L.T. 531.

[56] Executors (Scotland) Act 1900 s.6. If a note of property in England and Wales or Northern Ireland held in trust by a deceased person dying domiciled in Scotland is set forth in the inventory and is contained in, or appended to, the confirmation of Scottish estate which notes the domicile, the confirmation has the effect of a grant of representation in those countries in relation to the property specified in the note: Administration of Estates Act 1971 s.5.

[57] Executors (Scotland) Act 1900 s.7.

[58] Erskine, III, 9, 47; *Johnston's Executor v Dobie*, 1907 S.C. 31.

FURTHER READING

Scobbie, E.M., *Currie on Confirmation of Executors*, 9th edn (Edinburgh: W. Green, 2011).
Wilson, W.A. and Duncan, A.G.M., *Trusts, Trustees and Executors*, 2nd edn (Edinburgh: W. Green, 1995).

SECTION C: TRUSTS

CHAPTER 41

TRUSTS, LIFERENT AND FEE

I. TRUSTS

General—A trust has been described as   **41.01**

> "a legal relationship in which property is vested in one person, the trustee, who is under a fiduciary obligation to apply the property to some extent for the benefit of another person, the beneficiary".[1]

But the beneficiaries may be the general public, a specified sub-section of the public or the trust may be constituted for a specified public purpose.[2] Trusts have been part of Scots law for many centuries,[3] but most of the detailed rules were laid down by the courts in the eighteenth to early twentieth centuries. In general there has been limited statutory intervention in the common law relating to trusts, the main ones being: the Trusts (Scotland) Act 1921 (which was partly a consolidation of earlier legislation), the Trusts (Scotland) Act 1961 and the Charities and Trustee Investment (Scotland) Act 2005 which governs the investment powers of trustees and regulates charities (whether or not they are constituted as trusts). Trusts such as pension trusts and unit trusts are also subject to extensive statutory regulation.

Trustees for the purposes of the above Acts include executors and judicial factors, but exclude tutors, curators and guardians.[4] Trusts constituted by public general statutes are also outwith their scope.[5]

Types of trusts and terminology—A trust may be created: by persons, natural or   **41.02**
juristic; by inter vivos or *mortis causa* deed; orally or in writing; by enactment (primary or subordinate legislation)[6]; or by operation of law in certain circumstances independently of the will of the persons involved. The person who sets up

---

[1] W.A. Wilson and A.G.M. Duncan, *Trusts, Trustees and Executors*, 2nd edn (Edinburgh: W. Green, 1995), para.1.63.

[2] e.g. the maintenance of a bridge, *Templeton v Ayr Burgh Council*, 1910 2 S.L.T. 12.

[3] G.L. Gretton, "Trusts" in K.G.C. Reid and R. Zimmermann (eds), *A History of Private Law in Scotland*, Vol.1 (Oxford: Oxford University Press, 2000).

[4] Trusts (Scotland) Act 1921 (the "1921 Act") s.2, as amended by Succession (Scotland) Act 1964 (the "1964 Act") s.20; Age of Legal Capacity (Scotland) Act 1991 Sch.1; Children (Scotland) Act 1995 Sch.4 and the Adults with Incapacity (Scotland) Act 2000 Sch.6.

[5] 1921 Act s.2 and *Edinburgh Royal Infirmary, Petitioner*, 1959 S.C. 393.

[6] e.g. the sequestrated estate of a debtor is administered by a trustee under the Bankruptcy (Scotland) Act 1985 and a policy of assurance in favour of the life assured's spouse, civil partner or children is deemed to be held in trust for them in terms of the Married Women's (Policies of Assurance) (Scotland) Acts 1880 and 1980.

a trust is known as the truster, the person holding the trust property is known as the trustee and the person for whom the trust property is held is called the beneficiary. The same person may be involved in more than one capacity, such as both truster and trustee or as trustee and beneficiary, but the same person cannot be the sole beneficiary and the sole trustee.

Trusts can be either private trusts, where the beneficiaries are selected natural or juristic persons, or public trusts, where the benefit is to the public or a section of the public. Private trusts are enforced by the beneficiaries. Public trusts can be enforced at common law by the Lord Advocate or any member of the public who might benefit from the trust in question.[7] Such actions are rare but if a public trust is registered as a charity with the Office of the Scottish Charity Regulator ("OSCR") under the Charities and Trustee Investment (Scotland) Act 2005 it will be subject to regulation by OSCR. Different types of private or public trusts may be treated in different ways for tax purposes. Trusts may either confer vested or contingently vested rights to either income or capital on the beneficiaries or give the trustees a wide discretion as to the disposal of the trust property within a specified class of persons. These so-called discretionary trusts are the norm for public trusts and are now commonly used in the private trust field too.

41.03   The trustee—A trustee can be a specified natural or juristic person or the holder from time to time of a specified office (an ex officio trustee).[8] No one can be compelled to accept office as a trustee. Acceptance is a question of fact. It may be proved in any form—by written or verbal acceptance—or inferred from the fact that the person has acted as trustee.[9]

The trustee is the owner of the property subject to the trust:

> "The property of the thing intrusted, be it in land or in moveables, is in the person of the intrusted, else it is not proper trust".[10]

However, the property is owned by the trustee under the fiduciary obligation to use it for the behoof of the beneficiaries. Such property can be regarded as being in a patrimony separate from the trustee's private patrimony.[11] Where the trustee sells property in the trust patrimony the proceeds of sale and any property bought with such proceeds are part of that patrimony. This is the principle of real subrogation.[12] The fruits of property in the trust patrimony likewise fall into that patrimony, and so, are trust property. Property in the trust patrimony is not attachable by any diligence of the trustee's personal creditors,[13] nor does it form part of the trustee's sequestrated estate.[14] But such property is attachable for debts incurred by the trustee on trust business and may be sequestrated.[15]

---

[7] *Mitchell v Burness* (1878) 5 R 954; *Andrews v Ewart's Trs* (1886) 13 R. (HL) 69.

[8] e.g. the Lord Provost of Edinburgh; *University of Edinburgh v The Torrie Trs*, 1997 S.L.T. 1009.

[9] *Ker v City of Glasgow Bank* (1879) 6 R. (HL) 52.

[10] Stair, I, 13, 7. See also *Inland Revenue v Clark's Trs*, 1939 S.C. 11; *Parker v Lord Advocate*, 1960 S.C. (HL) 29; *Johnston v MacFarlane*, 1985 S.L.T. 339.

[11] K.G.C. Reid, "Patrimony not Equity: the Trust in Scotland" (2000) 8 *European Review of Private Law* 427; G.L. Gretton, "Trusts without Equity" (2000) 49 I.C.L.Q. 599.

[12] *Stair Memorial Encyclopaedia*, Vol.24, para.7.

[13] *Gordon v Cheyne*, 1824 2 S. 675; *Heritable Reversionary Co v Millar* (1892) 19 R. (HL) 43. The personal creditors must look to the trustee's private patrimony.

[14] Bankruptcy (Scotland) Act 1985 s.33(1)(b).

[15] Bankruptcy (Scotland) Act 1985 s.6(1)(a).

Where there are two or more trustees they own the trust property jointly. Thus if one trustee ceases to hold office the remaining trustees become the new joint owners.

The beneficiary—The beneficiary can be a specified natural or juristic person, or **41.04** a member of the public, or a specified sub-section of the public. The beneficiary of a trust has no right of ownership of the trust property. Instead he or she has a *jus crediti*—a bundle of personal rights against the trustees designed to compel them to administer the trust purposes in accordance with the trust provisions.[16] These personal rights include: a claim against the trustees for breach of trust or breach of fiduciary duty; an action of count, reckoning and payment[17]; recovery of trust property, either via the trustees or directly[18]; interdict or order *ad factum praestandum*[19]; declarator that the trustees' action are unlawful,[20] dealing with disputes about the trust provisions by means of a petition for directions,[21] or a special case[22]; and the removal of the trustees[23] or putting them under the supervision of the Accountant of Court.[24] A beneficiary's interest under a private trust forms part of his or her patrimony and (subject to any provisions in the trust deed) may be assigned by the beneficiary or attached by the beneficiary's personal creditors and forms part of the beneficiary's estate on death.

Constitution of express trusts—A trust other than one arising by operation of **41.05** law requires certain juridical acts for its constitution. The acts required depend on the type of trust. An inter vivos trust where the truster and trustee are different persons (a standard trust) may be constituted by a declaration of trust by the truster, which is almost always in writing when it is called the trust deed.[25] But oral trusts are competent.[26] No technical language is required for the declaration of trust; the word "trust" need not be used.[27] The phrases "for the behoof of" and "for the benefit of" are recognised equivalents.[28] The second step in a standard trust is the delivery or communication of the declaration to the trustees who accept office. The final step is the transfer of the trust property to the trustees.[29] One view is that all the steps are required so that a trust does not come into existence until the property is transferred to the trustees.[30] The alternative approach is that the

---

[16] *Inland Revenue v Clark's Trs*, 1939 S.C. 11; *Parker v Lord Advocate*, 1960 S.C. (HL) 29; *Sharp v Thompson*, 1995 S.C 455 at 475; 1995 S.L.T 837 at 851.

[17] *Cunningham-Jardine v Cunningham-Jardine's Trs*, 1979 S.L.T. 298.

[18] *Armour v Glasgow Royal Infirmary*, 1909 S.C. 916; *Johnston v MacFarlane*, 1987 S.L.T. 593.

[19] *Brown v Elder* (1906) 13 S.L.T. 391; *China National Star Petroleum Co v Tor Drilling (UK) Ltd*, 2002 S.L.T. 1339.

[20] *Martin v Edinburgh DC*, 1988 S.L.T. 329.

[21] *Taylor, Petitioner*, 2000 S.L.T. 1223.

[22] Court of Session Act 1988 s.27; *Turner's Trs v Turner*, 1943 S.C. 389.

[23] Trusts (Scotland) Act 1921 s.23; *Shariff v Hamid*, 2000 S.L.T. 294.

[24] 1921 Act s.17.

[25] 1921 Act s.2.

[26] In *McHugh v McHugh*, 2001 G.W.D. 1–56 an oral trust was established. Even trusts of heritage do not require writing for their constitution, although the transfer of the heritage to the trustees does, *Accountant in Bankruptcy v Mackay*, 2004 S.L.T. 777.

[27] *Gillespie v City of Glasgow Bank* (1878) 6 R. (HL) 104 at 107, per Earl Cairns L.C.; *Leitch v Leitch*, 1927 S.C. 823.

[28] *Gilpin v Martin* (1869) 7 M. 807; *Michie's Exs v Michie* (1905) 7 F. 509.

[29] The declaration of trust may be made in the deed of transfer of the property to the trustees.

[30] Wilson and Duncan, *Trusts, Trustees and Executors* (1995), paras 3.01 et seq.; *Stair Memorial Encylopaedia*, Vol.24, para.12. This will always be the case where the trust is created by the trustee's acknowledgment that the transferred property is held in trust.

trust comes into existence as between truster, trustees and beneficiaries once the declaration of trust is delivered or communicated to the trustees who accept office, but that property becomes immune from the truster's personal creditors only after its transfer to the trustees has been completed.[31]

For a *mortis causa* trust the truster's will or other testamentary writing sets out the terms of the trust. A written document complying with ss.1 and 2 of the Requirements of Writing (Scotland) Act 1995 is necessary as oral wills are ineffective. The truster's death creates the trust set out in the will or other writing. The testamentary trustees are not required to make up title to the estate to constitute the trust, nor does their making up title defeat the claims of the deceased's creditors. A bequest to a person followed by words expressive of the testator's wish or recommendation or confidence that the legatee will apply the subject bequeathed for behoof of other persons may be regarded as imposing a so-called precatory trust for this purpose on the legatee.[32]

In a truster-as-trustee trust the truster becomes the sole trustee of specified property owned by the truster. In this type of trust there is a single legal person who acts in two different capacities.[33] The first step in constituting such a trust is a trust declaration which must in general be in writing.[34] The owner of the property/ truster must then do something equivalent to delivery or transfer of the trust fund. Intimation of the declaration to one of several beneficiaries[35] or someone who is regarded as acting on behalf of the beneficiaries will suffice.[36] It has been held that property must be in existence at the time of intimation in order to be included in the trust patrimony.[37] On these steps being carried out, the specified property is deemed to have been transferred from the truster's private patrimony to the trust patrimony and so it is no longer attachable by the truster's personal creditors.

41.06 Constructive trusts—In certain circumstances the law imposes on a person the duties and liabilities which attach to a trustee expressly appointed and the person is treated as holding the property on a trust, known as a "constructive" trust, The circumstances are: where a person owing fiduciary duties gains a personal advantage from his or her position,[38] and where a third party acquires property (otherwise than as a beneficiary or for value[39]) that can be identified as having been, or having been derived from, trust property.[40] If the property is regarded as

---

[31] K.G.C. Reid., "Constitution of Trust", 1986 S.L.T. (News) 177; Scottish Law Commission, *Discussion Paper on the Nature and Constitution of Trusts* (HSMO, 1996), Scot. Law Com. No.133 (Session 2005–2006), Pt 3.

[32] McLaren, *Wills and Succession*, i, 345; *Garden's Exr v More*, 1913 S.C. 285; Wilson and Duncan, *Trusts, Trustees and Executors* (1995), paras 2.13–2.15.

[33] *Royal Insurance (UK) Ltd v Amec Construction Scotland Ltd*, 2008 S.L.T. 427

[34] Requirements of Writing (Scotland) Act 1995 s.1(2)(a)(iii), unless exceptionally s.1(3), (4) apply, see *McHugh*, 2001 G.W.D. 1–56.

[35] *Allan's Trs v Lord Advocate*, 1971 S.C. (HL) 45.

[36] *Clark's Trs v Inland Revenue*, 1972 S.C. 177.

[37] *Export Credits Guarantee Department v Turner*, 1979 S.C. 286; *Clark Taylor & Co Ltd v Quality Site Development (Edinburgh) Ltd*, 1981 S.C. 111; *Tay Valley Joinery Ltd v C.F. Financial Services Ltd*, 1987 S.L.T. 207; *Balfour Beatty Ltd v Britannia Life Ltd*, 1997 S.L.T. 10. Cf. K.G.C. Reid, "Constitution of trust", 1986 S.L.T. (News) 177.

[38] See *Jopp v Johnston's Tr.* (1904) 6 F. 1028; *Inglis v Inglis*, 1983 S.C. 8; *Sutman International Inc v Herbage*, 1991 G.W.D. 30–1772; *Southern Cross Commodities Property Ltd v Martin*, 1991 S.L.T. 83. See below, para.41.15.

[39] Purchasers are protected under s.2 of the Trusts (Scotland) Act 1961.

[40] *Stair Memorial Encyclopaedia*, Vol.24, para.30; *Huisman v Soepboer*, 1994 S.L.T. 682; *Mortgage Corp Ltd v Mitchells Robertson*, 1997 S.L.T. 1305.

being held to be in a constructive trust, the beneficiaries obtain a priority over ordinary unsecured creditors should the person holding the property be insolvent. Claims based on the alternative remedies of unjustified enrichment, delict or breach of trust are personal in nature and do not confer such priority.

If a trustee mixes trust funds with personal funds, the whole mixed fund is treated as trust funds except in so far as the trustee's own funds can be distinguished. Where the trustee thereafter draws cheques on the account for personal purposes, the rule of *Clayton's Case*[41] does not apply in a question between the trustee and the beneficiary. Although the trust funds may have been paid in first, it is assumed that the trustee meant to act honestly and is taken to have drawn out personal funds rather than those belonging to the trust,[42] unless the circumstances exclude this assumption, as in the case where, after the trust funds are paid into a bank, all the money in the bank account was drawn out before further money is paid in.[43] If property is acquired by the trustee from the mixed fund the beneficiaries can elect to have that property regarded as trust property, at least up to the value of the original trust funds contributed, unless the trustee can show that only personal funds were used.[44] This principle has been applied to those in a fiduciary position, although not trustees in the ordinary sense. Thus, where a law agent, who had, without the knowledge of his client, sold shares which she had entrusted to him and lodged the price in his bank account, subsequently became bankrupt, a sum equivalent to the price of the shares was, by order of the court, taken out of the sequestration and restored to the client.[45]

ADMINISTRATION OF THE TRUST

Assumption and appointment of trustees—The initial trustees will have been **41.07** appointed by the truster. Trustees have a statutory power to assume new trustees unless the trust deed provides otherwise.[46] It is thought that ex officio trustees can also assume new trustees.[47] The trust deed may confer power on the truster or others to appoint new trustees or replace the trustees. In the absence of any express power the truster in a private trust can appoint new trustees if there are none left in office.[48] A statutory form of assumption which may be used for the assumption of new trustees is given in the 1921 Act.[49]

Older trust deeds sometimes provide that the heir of the last surviving trustee is entitled to become the trustee.[50] The heir has to apply to the Sheriff in Chancery

---

[41] See para.3.27 above.

[42] *Jopp v Johnston's Tr.* (1904) 6 F. 1028.

[43] *Hofford v Gowans*, 1909 1 S.L.T. 153; *Style Financial Services Ltd v Bank of Scotland (No.1)*, 1996 S.L.T. 421. Where a mala fides fiduciary's bank account is overdrawn the misappropriated trust money cannot be traced as there is no fund to trace.

[44] *Southern Cross Commodities Property Ltd v Martin*, 1991 S.L.T. 83.

[45] *Jopp v Johnston's Tr.* (1904) 6 F. 1028; *Macadam v Martin's Tr.* (1872) 11 M. 33; see also *Southern Cross Commodities Property Ltd v Martin*, 1991 S.L.T. 83, per Lord Milligan especially at 85A–D; *Att Gen of Hong Kong v Reid* [1994] 1 A.C. 324, PC.

[46] Trusts (Scotland) Act 1921 s.3(b).

[47] *Winning, Petitioner*, 1999 S.C. 51.

[48] *Lord Glentanar v Scottish Industrial Musical Association Ltd*, 1925 S.C. 226.

[49] Trusts (Scotland) Act 1921 s.21 and Sch.B. It contains the necessary conveyance of the trust property and papers to the new trustees.

[50] *Glasgow Western Infirmary v Cairns*, 1944 S.C. 488.

for a declarator of status as heir.[51] More common nowadays is the use of s.6 of the Executors (Scotland) Act 1900, whereby the executors of the last surviving trustee can confirm to the trust property and so obtain limited powers to deal with it.

New trustees may be appointed by the Court of Session or sheriff court under s.22 of the Trusts (Scotland) Act 1921. The commonest case of such appointment is the lapsed trust where there are no trustees left and none can be appointed under the trust deed. But the statutory power can also be used where the sole trustee has become incapable or has been absent from the United Kingdom or has disappeared for six months. In addition, the Court of Session has power under the *nobile officium* to appoint new trustees which can be used if no other method exists, e.g. to resolve a deadlock[52] or where all the offices of the *ex officiis* trustees have been abolished.[53]

41.08 **Resignation and removal of trustees**—A trustee may in general resign; the power to do so is implied in every trust deed.[54] But a sole trustee is not entitled to resign unless he or she has assumed new trustees who have accepted office,[55] or new trustees or a judicial factor have been appointed by the court. Moreover, trustees who have accepted a legacy for acting as a trustee or who are appointed on a remunerated basis, may not resign unless it is otherwise provided in the trust deed; but such trustees may apply to the court for authority to resign.[56] The resigning trustee is divested of the trust estate, which accrues to the remaining trustees without the necessity for any conveyance.[57] If the trustee who resigns, or the representatives of a deceased trustee, cannot obtain a discharge from the remaining trustees and the beneficiaries refuse, or are unable, to grant a discharge, a petition may be presented to the court for a judicial discharge.[58]

Resignation may be effected by a minute in the trust sederunt book signed by all of the trustees or by a minute in the form of Sch.A signed by the resigning trustee and intimated to the others.[59] Other methods may be competent as long as the fact of resignation is brought to the attention of all the other trustees.[60] Taking no part in the affairs of the trust will not by itself constitute resignation.[61]

The trust deed may provide for the removal of a trustee by the truster, the beneficiaries, the other trustees[62] or some other person. In the absence of such power a trustee can be removed by the court. On application by a co-trustee, a beneficiary or anyone else interested in the trust property, the Court of Session or the sheriff court must remove a trustee who is either insane or incapable of acting by reason of mental or physical disability, and has a discretion to remove one who has been absent from the United Kingdom continuously or has disappeared for a

---

[51] Titles to Land Consolidation (Scotland) Act 1868 s.26B added by the Abolition of Feudal Tenure etc. (Scotland) Act 2000 s.68.

[52] *Taylor, Petitioners*, 1932 S.C. 1. There were two trustees who could not agree; the court appointed a third trustee.

[53] *Coal Industry Social Welfare Organisation, Petitioner*, 1959 S.L.T. (Notes) 3.

[54] 1921 Act s.3(a), see also s.19. At common law, trustees had no power to resign.

[55] It seems competent to appoint a single new trustee, *Kennedy Petitioner*, 1983 S.L.T. (Sh. Ct) 10 but this is not good practice.

[56] *Johnston, Petitioner*, 1932 S.L.T. 261.

[57] 1921 Act s.3(a); see also s.20.

[58] 1921 Act s.18.

[59] 1921 Act s.19(1).

[60] *McKenna v Rafique*, 2008 G.W.D. 13–250. Something in writing is probably required.

[61] *Ker v City of Glasgow Bank* (1879) 6 R. (HL) 52.

[62] *Gibb v Stanners*, 1975 S.L.T. (Notes) 30.

period of at least six months.[63] The Court of Session has also a common law power to remove trustees, but is reluctant to exercise this power unless the trustee has been guilty of malversation of office or is unfit to discharge the duties.[64] Mere disagreement between the trustees, or the commission of some irregularity or breach of trust by a trustee in good faith have not been deemed enough to warrant removal.[65]

Powers and duties of trustees—The trustees must administer the trust in accord- **41.09** ance with the directions given by the truster. They must do what they are enjoined to do so far as it is lawful and possible. They may do what they are authorised by the truster to do but must refrain from doing what the truster has forbidden them to do. Trustees have administrative powers and duties implied by common law; including ingathering trust property, managing it, paying debts and distributing the property in accordance with the trust deed.

If there are two trustees both must agree to any act. With three or more trustees decisions may be made by a quorum—a majority of the then acting trustees—unless the trust deed provides otherwise.[66] Occasionally a trustee is appointed by the truster on a sine quo non basis and then no decision can be reached without that trustee's agreement.[67] Although a quorum may decide a matter, every effort has to be made to inform all the trustees of the matters to be discussed in good time and to give them all an opportunity to put forward their views by attending any meeting or otherwise.[68]

Section 4 of the Trusts (Scotland) Act 1921[69] confers other powers on trustees which may be exercised so long as such acts are "not at variance with the terms or purposes of the trust".[70] They include: selling trust property[71]; excambing or granting leases of any duration of the heritable estate; borrowing money on the security of the trust estate; making investments; and acquiring with the trust funds any heritable property, whether or not for investment.[72] Where the trustees enter into a transaction in the purported exercise of certain of these powers, in particular with regard to heritage, the validity of the transaction and of any title acquired by the second party (other than a co-trustee or a beneficiary) under it cannot be challenged by the second party or any other person on the ground that the act in question was in fact at variance with the terms or purposes of the trust.[73] Thus a purchaser of heritage or other property from trustees is completely protected by this provision and need not look behind the purported exercise of the power under s.4. But this provision affords only a limited protection to the trustees themselves, for it leaves open any question of liability between them and co-trustees or the

---

[63] 1921 Act s.23.

[64] *Cherry v Patrick*, 1910 S.C. 32; *Stewart v Chalmers* (1904) 7 F. 163; *MacGilchrist v MacGilchrist's Trs*, 1930 S.C. 635; *Shariff v Hamid*, 2000 S.L.T. 294.

[65] *Gilchrist's Trs v Dick* (1883) 11 R. 22; *Hope v Hope* (1884) 12 R. 27; *Earl of Cawdor, Petitioner* [2006] CSOH 141.

[66] Trusts (Scotland) Act 1921 s.3(c).

[67] Wilson and Duncan, *Trusts, Trustees and Executors* (1995), para.23–18.

[68] *Wyse v Abbot* (1881) 8 R. 983; cf. *Malcolm v Goldie* (1895) 22 R. 968 where prior notification to one trustee was impracticable.

[69] As amended by the Trusts (Scotland) Act 1961 (the "1961 Act") s.4.

[70] See, as to the meaning of this expression, *Marquis of Lothian's C.B.*, 1927 S.C. 579 at 585; *Leslie's J.F.*, 1925 S.C. 464; *Cunningham's Tutrix*, 1949 S.C. 275; *Christie's Trs*, 1946 S.L.T. 309; *Bristow*, 1965 S.L.T. 225.

[71] See, e.g. *Mauchline, Petitioner*, 1992 S.L.T. 421 at 424, per Lord Prosser.

[72] 1921 Act s.4(1), (ea), (eb) added by the Charities and Trustee Investment (Scotland) Act 2005 s.93.

[73] 1961 Act s.2(1). The transactions are those listed in s.4(1)(a)–(eb) of the 1921 Act.

beneficiaries.[74] Where the trustees wish to exercise any of the powers listed in s.4 but the act in question would or might be at variance with the terms or purposes of the trust, they may present an application to the court under s.5. Under that section, the court is empowered to grant authority to the trustees to do any of these acts notwithstanding that such act is at variance with the terms or purposes of the trust, on being satisfied that such act is, in all the circumstances, expedient for the execution of the trust.[75] The court may, in exceptional cases, grant authority to carry out an act before it has been determined whether the trust is a private or public one.[76] It is also provided that the court may, under certain circumstances, authorise an advance of part of the capital of a fund destined either absolutely or contingently to beneficiaries who are not of full age.[77]

Trustees who desire to exercise powers which neither the trust deed[78] nor the statute provides may apply for authority to the court in the exercise of the *nobile officium*, as, for example, for authority to make advances to major beneficiaries.[79] Cases of this kind are exceptional and cannot be classified; but the *nobile officium* has been exercised to supply the deficiency "where something administrative or executive is wanting in the constituting document to enable the trust purposes to be effectually carried out",[80] or where there was an obvious *casus improvisus* (unforeseen situation) under the scheme of the trust or to relieve the trust of conditions which made it unworkable or tended to defeat its purpose,[81] or, in the case of trusts subject to the jurisdiction of a foreign court, to facilitate by means of an auxiliary jurisdiction the carrying out of an order of the foreign court.[82] While the court may give retrospective sanction to ultra vires acts of administration by trustees, this will be done only in exceptional circumstances and for compelling reasons[83]; and, where the trustees have acted contrary to the express terms of the trust or an interlocutor of the court, retrospective approval will usually be refused.[84]

The Court of Session can place a trust under the administration of the Accountant of Court, on an application by the trustees or any one of them.[85] The superintendence of the Accountant is limited, however, to the administration of the trust in so far as it relates to the investment of the trust patrimony and its distribution among the creditors and beneficiaries.[86]

Trustees under a trust deed (as defined by the Trusts (Scotland) Act 1921[87]) may obtain from the court directions on questions relating to the investment,

---

[74] 1921 Act s.2(2) (as substituted by Law Reform (Miscellaneous Provisions) (Scotland) Act 1980 s.8); see *Barclay, Petitioner*, 1962 S.C. 594.

[75] This section does not apply to trusts constituted by private or local Acts of Parliament; see *Church of Scotland General Trs*, 1931 S.C. 704.

[76] *Tod's Trs, Petitioners*, 1999 S.L.T. 308.

[77] 1921 Act s.16; *Macfarlane v Macfarlane's Trs*, 1931 S.C. 95; *Craig's Trs*, 1934 S.C. 34; *Anderson's Trs, Petitioners*, 1957 S.L.T. (Notes) 5.

[78] *Moss's Trs v King*, 1952 S.C. 523.

[79] *Frew's Trs*, 1932 S.C. 501; *Craig's Trs*, 1934 S.C. 34.

[80] *Anderson's Trs*, 1932 S.C. 226.

[81] *Hall's Trs v McArthur*, 1918 S.C. 646; see also observations in *Gibson's Trs*, 1933 S.C. 190.

[82] *Lipton's Trs*, 1943 S.C. 521; *Campbell-Wyndham-Long's Trs*, 1951 S.C. 685.

[83] *Gilray* (1876) 3 R. 619 (a judicial factor case where application granted); *Horne's Trs*, 1952 S.C. 70 (application refused).

[84] But see *Campbell-Wyndham-Long's Trs*, 1962 S.C. 132.

[85] 1921 Act s.17.

[86] *Coulson v Murison's Trs*, 1920 S.C. 322 (the law as to the competency of an application by one trustee is now altered); *Liddell's Trs v Liddell*, 1929 S.L.T. 169; *Donaldson's Trs*, 1932 S.L.T. 463.

[87] In *Leven Penny Savings Bank, Petitioners*, 1948 S.C. 147, the petitioning trustees failed to bring their trust within the definition.

distribution, management or administration of the trust estate, or as to the exercise of any power vested in, or as to the performance of any duty imposed on, them.[88] In seeking directions from the court, the trustees must not purport to surrender their discretion to the court.[89]

Where discretionary powers are conferred on trustees the court will not review an exercise of the powers unless the trustees considered the wrong question, did not apply their minds, perversely shut their eyes to facts, did not act honestly,[90] or the decision was so irrational that no sensible trustees could have made it.[91] The question whether the discretionary powers are given only to the original trustees or, on the other hand, can be exercised by assumed trustees, depends on the terms of the deed, but generally they may be so exercised unless they are given in terms which clearly disclose a *delectus personae*.[92] Where a power of selection amongst charities is not expressly or impliedly given to named trustees personally, it may probably be exercised by assumed trustees, but not by a judicial factor since such a court appointee has no connection with the testator.[93]

Investment powers—One of the usual duties of trustees is to find suitable invest- **41.10** ments for the trust. Trustees who fail to invest may be liable.[94] For trusts other than pension trusts, authorised unit trusts and trusts where the investment powers are regulated by an enactment, the trustees have statutory power to make any kind of investment.[95] Thus they may invest in land, wherever situated, securities of any kind and even fine art and wine. These powers apply to trusts whenever created, but any restriction on investment powers in a trust deed executed on or after August 3, 1961 remain valid, unless this is done by reference to the Trustee Investments Act 1961.[96] Restrictions in deeds executed before August 3, 1961 are to be ignored.[97] A trust deed could confer wider investment powers on the trustees but given the width of the statutory investment powers this seems unlikely. An application to the court under s.5 of the Trusts (Scotland) Act 1921 may be made where the trustees wish to invest in a manner prohibited by the trust deed. Another method of obtaining greater powers is an application under s.1 of the Trusts (Scotland) Act 1961,[98] but this requires the agreement of all the capable beneficiaries.

Trustees must confine themselves to investments they are authorised to make; to make investments outwith that class is an ultra vires breach of trust, for which liability is almost strict.[99] Investments must be chosen carefully and hazardous ones avoided.[100] In the exercise of their statutory powers of investment the trustees must have regard to the suitability to the trust of the proposed investments

---

[88] Court of Session Act 1988 s.6(vi); Act of Sederunt (Rule of the Court of Session 1994) 1994 (SI 1994/1443) ("RCS") rr.63.4–63.6; *Peel's Tr. v Drummond*, 1936 S.C. 786.

[89] *Joy Manufacturing Holdings Ltd*, 2000 S.L.T. 843.

[90] *Dundee General Hospitals Board of Management v Bell's Trs*, 1952 S.C. (HL) 78. The possible significance of this case is discussed in Derek Francis, "*Hastings-Bass* and his Scottish friends", 2008 S.L.T. (News) 161.

[91] *Associated Provincial Picture Houses Ltd v Wednesbury Corp* [1948] 1 K.B. 223.

[92] *Angus's Exrx v Batchan's Trs*, 1949 S.C. 335; but see *Leith's J.F. v Leith*, 1957 S.C. 307.

[93] *Angus's Exrx v Batchan's Trs*, 1949 S.C. 335; but see *Leith's J.F. v Leith*, 1957 S.C. 307.

[94] *Melville v Noble's Trs* (1896) 24 R. 243.

[95] 1921 Act s.4(1)(ea) added by the Charities and Trustee Investment (Scotland) Act 2005 s.93(2).

[96] 1921 Act s.4(1D).

[97] 1921 Act s.4(1C).

[98] *Henderson, Petitioner*, 1981 S.L.T. (Notes) 40.

[99] *Warren's J.F. v Warren's Ex* (1903) 5 F. 890.

[100] *Brownlie v Brownlie's Trs* (1879) 6 R. 1233, per Lord President Inglis at 1236.

and to the need for an appropriate diversification of investments.[101] Trustees must obtain and consider proper advice on proposed investments, unless they reasonably consider that it is not necessary to do so.[102] Even if the truster directs the trustees to retain investments made over to them, it is the trustees' duty to review them and, if necessary for the safety of the trust, to sell them.[103] Sections 29 and 30 of the Trusts (Scotland) Act 1921 contain provisions dealing with trustees lending money on the security of heritable property.

Trustees may authorise an agent to carry out their investment management functions, even on a discretionary basis, and have the trust investments held by a nominee on their behalf.[104] The duty of care obliges trustees to review the trust's investments from time to time[105] and the performance of any investment manager. Trustees must also keep a nominee service under review.[106]

41.11 Trustees' liability to creditors—Trustees are not liable for debts incurred by the truster beyond the value of the trust patrimony. But if the trustees contract debts or incur liabilities in the course of their administration (such as running the truster's or another business[107]), they are personally liable for these in a question with the creditors, unless the creditors transacted with them on the terms that the trust patrimony alone was to be responsible. When the trustees are personally liable, they are entitled to pay the amount due from the trust patrimony first,[108] unless they were in breach of trust in undertaking the liability.[109]

In entering into a contract it is open to the trustees in general to stipulate that the trust patrimony alone shall be liable, and this stipulation may be effectual. Thus where trustees borrowed money on a heritable bond in which they bound themselves "as trustees" it was held that they were not personally liable and that their liability was limited to the value of the trust patrimony.[110] The nature of the transaction may, however, be such as to prevent any effective limitation of their liability, as where the trustees were registered as the proprietors of shares of a bank that was incorporated with unlimited liability. As shareholders, the trustees were personally liable, for it was not within the power of the bank to differentiate between shareholders who were trustees and those who were not, to the effect of enabling the former to hold on any other terms than would apply if the holders were individuals holding for themselves.[111] On the other hand, the whole circumstances may show that the obligation was undertaken in the capacity of trustee even if no express stipulation to that effect was made.[112] However, trustee shareholders in companies incorporated under the Companies Acts will hardly ever incur personal liability; at worst the shares become valueless.[113] Trusts may

---

[101] 1921 Act s.4A(1).
[102] 1921 Act s.4A(3), (4).
[103] *Thomson's Trs v Davidson*, 1947 S.C. 654.
[104] 1921 Act ss.4B and 4C.
[105] *Clarke v Clarke's Trs*, 1925 S.C. 693 at 711.
[106] 1921 Act s.4B(6)
[107] *Ford & Sons v Stephenson* (1888) 16 R. 24.
[108] *Buchan v City of Glasgow Bank* (1879) 6 R. (HL) 44; *Cuningham v Montgomerie* (1879) 6 R. 1333, so personal liability arises only if the trust patrimony is insufficient.
[109] *City of Glasgow Bank v Parkhurst* (1880) 7 R. 749.
[110] *Gordon v Campbell* (1842) 1 Bell's App.428; see *Brown v Sutherland* (1875) 2 R. 615.
[111] *Lumsden v Buchanan* (1865) 3 M. (HL) 89; *Muir v City of Glasgow Bank* (1879) 6 R. (HL) 21.
[112] *Brown v Rysaffe Trustee Co Ltd* [2011] CSOH 26.
[113] Liability could arise from partly paid-up shares, but these are very uncommon nowadays.

be noticed in the register of a Scottish company.[114] Executors may transfer shares belonging to the deceased without being registered as the holders of the shares.[115]

If trustees conduct an unsuccessful litigation their liability in expenses to the successful litigant depends on the form of the decree for expenses. Where expenses are awarded against X and Y as trustees then only the trust patrimony is liable[116]; if against X and Y personally then the trustees have to pay out of their own patrimonies without any recourse against the trust patrimony[117]; and if against X and Y without qualification the trustees are personally liable but may be able to pay the amount from the trust patrimony.[118]

Accumulation—The Trusts (Scotland) Act 1961[119] prohibits accumulation of **41.12** income beyond one or other of four periods. Two further periods were added by the Law Reform (Miscellaneous Provisions) (Scotland) Act 1966[120] bringing the total number of periods now available to six. These are: (1) the life of the grantor of the deed; (2) a term of 21 years from the death of the grantor[121]; (3) a term of 21 years from the date of the deed[122]; (4) the duration of the minority[123] or respective minorities of any person or persons living or in utero at the date of the deed; (5) the duration of the minority or respective minorities of any person or persons living or in utero at the death of the grantor; and (6) the duration of the minority or respective minorities of any person or persons who, under the terms of the deed directing accumulation, would for the time being, if of full age, be entitled to the rents or income directed to be accumulated.

Period (1) can, by definition, apply only in the case of inter vivos deeds under which accumulation is directed during the grantor's lifetime,[124] but that period will not operate so as to prevent accumulation under periods (3), (4) or (6) continuing beyond the date of the grantor's death.[125] With this exception, however, the periods are alternative, not cumulative, and it is not permissible to add one period to another.[126] Period (6) is available in a case where an accumulation is directed from a period subsequent to the date of the grantor's death,[127] it not being required that the minor should be in life at that date.[128] But where the direction is to accumulate income from the date of the grantor's death, the restriction under

---

[114] This is not permitted in the case of companies registered in England and Wales: Companies Act 2006 s.126.

[115] Companies Act 2006 s.773.

[116] *Dyer v Craiglaw Developments Ltd*, 1999 S.L.T. 1228.

[117] *Law v Humphrey* (1876) 3 R. 1192.

[118] *Gibson v Caddell's Trs* (1895) 22 R. 889, per Lord McLaren at 893; *Anderson v Anderson's Tr.* (1901) 4 F. 96.

[119] 1961 Act s.5. This section replaced the Accumulations Act 1800.

[120] Law Reform (Miscellaneous Provisions) (Scotland) Act 1966 s.6.

[121] This period was added by the Law Reform (Miscellaneous Provisions) (Scotland) Act 1966.

[122] As to whether an arrangement under the 1961 Act may amount to a new settlement so as to introduce a new *terminus a quo*, see *Aikman, Petitioner*, 1968 S.L.T. 137.

[123] i.e. the period during which a person is under the age of 18: Age of Majority (Scotland) Act 1969 s.1(1) and (2).

[124] *Stewart's Trs v Stewart*, 1927 S.C. 350; *Union Bank of Scotland v Campbell*, 1929 S.C. 143.

[125] 1961 Act s.5(4); 1966 Act s.6(1) proviso. It is, however, essential that, where under an inter vivos deed an accumulation period has begun during the life of the granter any additional period beyond the granter's death should be a period "directed" by the granter (*McIver's Trs v Inland Revenue*, 1974 S.L.T. 202).

[126] *Union Bank of Scotland v Campbell*, 1929 S.C. 143.

[127] See *Carey's Trs v Rose*, 1957 S.C. 252.

[128] *Re Cattell* [1914] 1 Ch. 177.

periods (2) or (5) will apply, whether or not accumulation has in fact taken place during that period.[129]

The statutory restrictions are not confined to cases in which accumulation of income is expressly directed. If a trust deed is so framed that accumulation of income beyond the permitted period necessarily results, the Act will apply. Thus, where trustees were directed to convey the residue of the testator's estate to the children of M, and at the expiry of 21 years from the testator's death M was alive but had no children, it was held that, while it was the duty of the trustees within that period to accumulate the income for behoof of the residuary legatees, the income thereafter accruing could not be accumulated.[130] The statutory restrictions apply also in a case where the power to accumulate is merely discretionary, and there is no duty to exercise it.[131]

While the statutes put an end to accumulation after the prescribed periods, they do not otherwise affect the dispositions of the deed.[132] The deed is to be read as if it had expressly declared that the accumulation directed should then end, and for the rest it receives effect exactly as it stands.

The 1961 Act provides that the income directed to be accumulated contrary to its provisions shall

> "go to, and be received by, the person or persons who would have been entitled thereto if such accumulation had not been directed".[133]

Accordingly, if there is a present gift of the income-bearing subject and the direction for accumulation is merely a burden on that gift, so that apart from it the legatee would have taken the income, the income released by the statute will go to the legatee.[134] On the other hand, if the gift is a future one, the statute does not operate to accelerate or enlarge the right of the legatee.[135] Thus, if the gift is to be made over to the legatee at the termination of an annuity, any income accruing during the annuitant's lifetime, but after the period of 21 years from the testator's death, will not go to the legatee.[136] If the subject of the gift were residue, the income in that case would fall into intestacy.[137] Renunciation of a liferent would have the same effect. Where the income is that accruing on a legacy, the result of the statute is that the income will fall into residue if there be a residuary bequest which by means of present gift gives to the residuary legatee everything not otherwise disposed of (and its terms allow of the income being paid away, for the retention of the income for behoof of residuary legatees would be equivalent

---

[129] *Campbell's Trs v Campbell* (1891) 18 R. 992; *Carey's Trs v Rose*, 1957 S.C. 252.

[130] *Lord v Colvin* (1860) 23 D. 111; *Barbour v Budge*, 1947 S.N. 100. See also *Gibson's Trs*, 1963 S.C. 350.

[131] 1966 Act s.6(2).

[132] *Elder's Trs v Treasurer of the Free Church of Scotland* (1892) 20 R. 2, per Lord Kyllachy; *Maxwell's Trs v Maxwell* (1877) 5 R. 248, per Lord Justice-Clerk Moncreiff; *Landale's Trs v Overseas Missionary Fellowship*, 1982 S.L.T. 158.

[133] 1961 Act s.5(3).

[134] *Maxwell's Trs v Maxwell* (1877) 5 R. 248; *Mackenzie v Mackenzie's Trs* (1877) 4 R. 962; *Stewart's Trs v Whitelaw*, 1926 S.C. 701; McLaren, *Wills and Succession*, i, 313.

[135] *Russell's Trs v Russell*, 1959 S.C. 148; cf. *Young's Trs v Chapelle*, 1971 S.L.T. 147.

[136] *Smith v Glasgow Royal Infirmary*, 1909 S.C. 1231; *Wilson's Trs v Glasgow Royal Infirmary*, 1917 S.C. 527; *Pyper's Trs v Leighton*, 1946 S.L.T. 255; cf. *Dowden's Trs v Governors of Merchiston Castle School*, 1965 S.C. 56.

[137] *Elder's Trs, and Wilson's Trs* (1892) 20 R. 2; *Carey's Trs v Carey*, 1957 S.C. 252. Legal rights are not claimable out of the income thus brought into intestacy: *Lindsay's Trs v Lindsay*, 1931 S.C. 586.

to accumulation) or, otherwise, into intestacy.[138] A person in whom a fund has vested subject to defeasance is not entitled to the income under the statutory provision as the right of fee is not absolute.[139]

The Accumulations Act 1892 severely restricts the accumulation of income for the purchase of land.[140]

BREACH OF TRUST

General—Trustees may commit a breach of trust in the administration of the trust **41.13** by acting outwith their powers (ultra vires), as *auctor in rem suam*, or negligently. Trustees who have committed a breach of trust may be required to make good all the loss thereby occasioned to the estate. Section 3 of the Trusts (Scotland) Act 1921 provides that all trusts, unless the contrary be expressed, shall be held to include a provision that each trustee shall be liable only for his own acts and intromissions and shall not be liable for the acts and intromissions of co-trustees and shall not be liable for omissions. However, this will not protect a trustee who fails to monitor the other trustees or who authorises or acquiesces in breaches of trust committed by them. In general, therefore, the trustees will be jointly and severally liable, and one or more of them may be sued without calling all of them.[141]

Ultra vires breach—Trustees commit an ultra vires breach of trust when they act **41.14** outwith their powers. Liability for any loss suffered thereby is almost strict. If there are doubts about their powers or who the correct beneficiaries are the trustees should seek clarification from the court, but trustees may be exonerated if they have taken expert legal advice[142] or taken all possible steps to discover the true position.[143] Trustees may also escape liability if they have been misled by the true beneficiary.[144] There are statutory provisions protecting trustees who distribute trust property in ignorance of certain relationships.[145] Where the breach consists of an unauthorised investment of trust funds, the beneficiaries may either adopt the investment or repudiate it and have the trustees restore the sum invested to the trust with interest.[146]

Auctor in rem suam—It has long been established that trustees must not be *auctor* **41.15** *in rem suam*; that is to say, they must not place themselves in a situation in which their interest as individuals may conflict with their duty as trustees.[147] This rule applies to all persons having fiduciary duties to discharge such as an executor,

---

[138] *Smith v Glasgow Royal Infirmary*, 1909 S.C. 1231, per Lord President Dunedin at 1236; *Cathcart's Trs v Foresterhill Hospital*, 1977 S.L.T. 114.

[139] *Russell's Trs v Russell*, 1959 S.C. 148, per Lord President Clyde and Lord Russell (obiter).

[140] *Robertson's Trs v Robertson's Trs*, 1933 S.C. 639.

[141] *Allen v McCombie's Trs*, 1909 S.C. 710.

[142] *Warren's J.F. v Warren's Ex* (1903) 5 F. 890.

[143] *Lamond's Trs v Croom* (1871) 9 M. 662.

[144] *Buttercase & Geddie's Tr v Geddie* (1897) 24 R. 1128.

[145] Sussession (Scotland) Act 1964 s.24(2)—ignorance of adoption order; Law Reform (Miscellaneous Provisions) (Scotland) Act 1968 s.7—ignorance of persons born outwith marriage or their paternal relatives.

[146] *Beveridge's Trs v Beveridge*, 1908 S.C.791.

[147] *Aberdeen Railway v Blaikie Brothers* (1854) 1 Macq. 461. See also *The York Buildings Co v Mackenzie* (1795) 3 Pat. 378; *Hamilton v Wright* (1842) 1 Bell's App.574; *Huntington v Henderson* (1877) 4 R. 295, per Lord Young; *Sarris v Clark*, 1995 S.L.T. 44. The principle applies to an executor-dative by virtue of Succession (Scotland) Act 1964 s.20: *Inglis v Inglis*, 1983 S.C. 8.

guardian, judicial factor, agent, promoter or director of a company as well as a trustee in the strict sense. The fairness or unfairness of the transaction is immaterial and it is not necessary to prove that the trustee obtained some advantage in the transaction.[148] The trust deed or the beneficiaries may, however, authorise acts in breach of the *auctor in rem suam* rule.

Hence, under this rule, a sale of trust property by trustees to, or a loan by them to, one of their number (however fair the terms of the transaction may have been) are all open to challenge,[149] as is a transaction with a relative or business associate of a trustee.[150] The transaction is not void, but is voidable at the instance of the beneficiaries.[151] The rule is not, however, extended to the case of a trustee buying from a beneficiary his or her interest in the trust property. A trustee is not forbidden from doing this, but the trustee must show that full value was given and that all necessary information was afforded to the beneficiary at the time of the sale.[152]

It is also settled that a trustee may not make profit out of the office, unless this is authorised (either expressly or impliedly) by the truster or agreed to by all the beneficiaries.[153] If a trustee, for example, acts as solicitor or factor for the trust, or manages a business on its behalf, he or she is not entitled to any remuneration for such services unless such authority or consent is given.[154] Nor are trustees permitted to make a profit for themselves by means of their office. Whenever a person holding a fiduciary position gains, by reason of that position, any advantage it is held for behoof of the beneficiaries.[155] Thus in *Wilsons v Wilson*[156] a tutor who renounced the lease of a farm held for behoof of the pupils, and obtained a lease in his own name was held bound to account to the pupils for all the profits which he had obtained from the farm under the lease in his own favour. In *Magistrates of Aberdeen v University of Aberdeen*,[157] the town council purchased from themselves certain lands which they held as trustees. Afterwards they applied to the Crown for a grant of the salmon fishing opposite these lands on the representation that they were the owners of these lands, and obtained the grant. It was decided that the town council still held the lands in trust, and that moreover, as they had obtained the grant of the fishing in virtue of their possession of these lands, they were bound to hold the fishing as trustees for the benefit of the trust.

So also, if trustees in breach of duty employ funds belonging to the trust in trade, although any loss thereby incurred must be made good to the estate, any profit earned may be claimed by the beneficiaries.[158]

---

[148] *Aberdeen Railway v Blaikie Brothers* (1854) 1 Macq. 461 at 471, per Lord Cranworth L.C.

[149] *Ritchies v Ritchies' Trs* (1888) 15 R. 1086; *Croskery v Gilmour's Trs* (1890) 17 R. 697; *Johnston v MacFarlane*, 1987 S.L.T. 593; *Clark v Clark's Exrs*, 1989 S.L.T. 665. A creditor of the beneficiary is also entitled to challenge the transaction: *Meff v Smith's Trs*, 1930 S.N. 162.

[150] *Barr v Gilchrist*, 2011 CSOH 72.

[151] *Fraser v Hankey & Co* (1847) 9 D. 415.

[152] *Dougan v Macpherson* (1902) 4 F. (HL) 7.

[153] *Sleigh v Sleigh's J.F.*, 1908 S.C. 1112; *A.B.'s Curator Bonis*, 1927 S.C. 902; but in *Sarris v Clark*, 1995 S.L.T. 44, it was held that the doctrine did not apply where the truster, having foreseen a possible conflict, still appointed a person a trustee.

[154] *Mackie v Mackie's Trs* (1875) 2 R. 312; *Mills v Brown's Trs* (1901) 3 F. 1012. If a truster empowers his trustees to appoint one of their number as law agent, this implies that he may be remunerated by the trust; *Lewis' Trs v Pirie*, 1912 S.C. 574.

[155] Either because it is held in a constructive trust, see para.41.06 above, or because it regarded as part of the trust patrimony.

[156] *Wilsons v Wilson* (1789) Mor.16376. See also *McNiven v Peffers* (1868) 7 M. 181.

[157] *Magistrates of Aberdeen v University of Aberdeen* (1877) 4 R. (HL) 48.

[158] *Cochrane v Black* (1855) 17 D. 321; *Laird v Laird* (1855) 17 D. 984; (1858) 20 D. 972. The court may, at the option of the beneficiaries, alternatively award interest on the capital wrongly used.

Negligent administration—Trustees must administer the trust with due care; **41.16**
they are bound to exercise that degree of diligence which a person of ordinary
prudence would exercise in the management of his or her own private affairs.[159] It
is not clear whether the standard of care required of a professional trustee is higher
than that for a gratuitous trustee.[160] If trustees fail to administer the estate with the
required degree of care they may be liable for losses that can be shown to have
been caused by their negligence.

Immunity clauses and other protection for trustees—Trust deeds often contain **41.17**
a clause designed to alleviate the responsibility of the trustees in the administration of the estate. Thus, in the case of *Knox v Mackinnon*[161] the trust deed provided
that the trustees

> "should not be liable for omissions, errors or neglect of management, nor
> singuli in solidum, but each shall be liable for his own actual intromissions
> only".

It was held that clauses of this kind do not protect against gross negligence, a positive breach of duty or acting in bad faith. Lord Watson observed:

> "I see no reason to doubt that a clause conceived in these or similar terms
> will afford a considerable measure of protection to trustees who have bona
> fide abstained from closely superintending the administration of the trust or
> who have committed mere errors of judgment while acting with a single eye
> to the benefit of the trust and of the persons whom it concerns; but it is settled
> in the law of Scotland that such a clause is ineffectual to protect a trustee
> against the consequences of culpa lata, or of gross negligence on his part, or
> of any conduct which is inconsistent with bona fides. I think it is equally
> clear that the clause will afford no protection to trustees who, from motives
> however laudable in themselves, act in plain violation of the duty which
> they owe to the individuals beneficially interested in the funds which
> they administer."

Where a trustee has committed a breach of trust at the instigation or request or
with the consent in writing of a beneficiary, the court may, if it thinks fit, order
that all or any part of the interest of that beneficiary shall be applied in indemni-
fying the trustee.[162] The beneficiary must have known the facts which made what
was done a breach of trust and his or her concurrence must have been "clear
and direct".[163]

If the court considers that a trustee who has committed a breach of trust has
acted honestly and reasonably and ought fairly to be excused, then it may relieve
the trustee from personal liability.[164] Negligent trustees cannot take advantage of

---

[159] *Raes v Meek* (1889) 16 R. (HL) 31; *Knox v Mackinnon* (1888) 15 R. (HL). 83; *Tibbert v McColl*,
1994 S.L.T. 1227. A different standard applies to trustees of trusts registered as charities, see
para.41.22, below.

[160] In *Lutea Trs Ltd v Orbis Trs Guernsey Ltd*, 1998 S.L.T. 471 the court reserved its opinion.

[161] *Knox v Mackinnon* (1888) 15 R. (HL) 83; *Ferguson v Paterson* (1900) 2 F. (HL) 37; see also
Inglis, 1965 S.L.T. 326; *Lutea Trs Ltd v Orbis Trustees Guernsey Ltd*, 1998 S.L.T. 471.

[162] 1921 Act s.31.

[163] *Henderson v Henderson's Trs* (1900) 2 F. 1295.

[164] 1921 Act s.32; *Clarke v Clarke's Trs*, 1925 S.C. 693; *Re Evans* [1999] 2 All E.R. 777.

this provision. Finally a trustee is not liable for breach of trust merely by continuing to hold an investment which has ceased to be an authorised investment.[165]

41.18 Prescription—The following obligations of a trustee are imprescriptible: (a) the obligation to produce accounts of his intromissions with any of the trust property; (b) the obligation to make reparation or restitution in respect of any fraudulent breach of trust to which the trustee was party or was privy; (c) the obligation to make furthcoming to any person entitled thereto any trust property, or the proceeds of any such property, in the possession of the trustee, or to make good the value of any such property previously received by the trustee and appropriated to his own use.[166] The obligation of a third party to make furthcoming to any party entitled thereto any trust property received by the third party otherwise than in good faith and in his possession is also imprescriptible. It would seem that a trustee's obligation to make reparation for an ultra vires or negligent breach of trust is subject to the quinquennial prescription.[167]

REVOCABILITY, VARIATION ETC.

41.19 Revocability of trust—An inter vivos trust that a person set up merely for the administration of his or her own property is revocable by the truster as the sole beneficiary. Similarly, an inter vivos trust may be revocable if the beneficiaries (other than the truster) are not in existence or ascertainable,[168] or if all the purposes in favour of these other beneficiaries are of a testamentary nature and are to take effect only on the truster's death.[169] The right to revoke can be attached and exercised by the truster's personal creditors.[170] On the other hand, if the deed confers rights (and not mere *spes successionis* (hopes of succession)) on other parties, although these rights may not be vested but may be subject to contingencies, it is generally regarded as irrevocable.[171] The question depends, however, on the terms and purposes of the trust deed, and *in dubio* a declaration that it is irrevocable will probably be decisive.[172] A marriage contract may contain testamentary provisions which are always revocable, notwithstanding that the deed is declared to be irrevocable.[173]

41.20 Fulfilment of trust purposes—Where the purposes of a private trust[174] fail, either in whole or in part, or if the purposes do not exhaust the trust patrimony, then the property in that patrimony, or so much of it as is not required for the trust purposes, reverts to the truster or if dead to his or her representatives. Thus, if in a marriage contract or other trust deed, funds are settled on the truster's issue, and

---

[165] 1921 Act s.33.

[166] Prescription and Limitation (Scotland) Act 1973 Sch.3.

[167] Prescription and Limitation (Scotland) Act 1973 Sch.1 para.1(d). See *Hobday v Kirkpatrick's Trs*, 1985 S.L.T. 197.

[168] See, e.g. *Bertram's Trs v Bertram*, 1909 S.C. 1238.

[169] *Bulkeley-Gavin's Trs v Bulkeley-Gavins's Trs*, 1971 S.C. 209.

[170] *Byre's Trs v Gemmell* (1895) 23R. 332; *Scott v Scott*, 1930 S.C. 903.

[171] *Walker v Amey* (1906) 8 F. 376; *Scott v Scott*, 1930 S.C. 903; *Ross v Ross's Trs*, 1967 S.L.T. 12, OH; *Campbell v Campbell's Trs*, 1967 S.L.T. (Notes) 30; *Bulkeley-Gavin's Trs v Bulkeley-Gavins's Trs*, 1971 S.C. 209; *Lawrence v Lawrence's Trs*, 1974 S.L.T. 174; *Milligan v Ross*, 1994 S.C.L.R. 430.

[172] *Scott v Scott*, 1930 S.C. 903.

[173] *Barclays' Trs v Watson* (1903) 5 F. 926; *Law, Petitioners*, 1962 S.C. 500.

[174] See paras 41.26–41.29, below as to public trusts.

there are no issue, then, in the absence of any further trust purpose, the funds revert to the truster.[175] In the case of a *mortis causa* trust, the truster being dead, the property not required for the purposes of the trust will fall to be disposed of as part of the deceased's estate.[176] So, for example, if a woman by her trust-disposition and settlement conveys her estate to trustees with directions to settle the estate on her children and dies without leaving issue, the trustees would hand over the estate to her heirs in intestacy.

Variation of private trusts—At common law the powers of varying the purposes **41.21** of a private trust once it had taken effect are very limited.[177] Where all the beneficiaries interested in the trust agree that the trust should be varied or brought to an end, and if they are all legally capable of agreeing, the trustees are bound to comply on being exonerated and discharged.[178] But where by reason of nonage or otherwise one or more of the beneficiaries is incapable of agreeing, or where there is a contingent right in unborn issue, the concurrence of all those interested in the trust estate cannot be obtained. Furthermore, where one of the interests is an alimentary right properly constituted,[179] and accepted,[180] it cannot at common law be renounced by the beneficiary as part of such an arrangement. The Trusts (Scotland) Act 1961 allows these common law obstacles to be surmounted.

Section 1 of the 1961 Act empowers the court to approve a variation or termination of trust purposes on behalf of beneficiaries[181] who, owing to nonage[182] or other incapacity,[183] are incapable of assenting thereto, and may also authorise the variation or revocation of alimentary provisions. All the other beneficiaries capable of agreeing must still do so. To obtain approval the trustees or any of the beneficiaries present a petition to the Inner House of the Court of Session.[184] A declaration of irrevocability in an inter vivos trust deed does not preclude variation of its terms under this section.[185] Subsection (1) enables the court to grant approval of an arrangement varying or revoking all or any of the trust purposes, or enlarging the powers of the trustees of managing or administering the estate,[186]

---

[175] *Smith v Stuart* (1894) 22 R. 130; *Montgomery's Trs v Montgomery* (1895) 22 R. 824; *Higginbotham's Trs v Higginbotham* (1886) 13 R. 1016.

[176] This simply follows the normal rules for lapse of legacies.

[177] It was possible for the trustees to obtain extra administrative powers under the *nobile officium* or s.5 of the Trusts (Scotland) Act 1921.

[178] *Yuill's Trs v Thomson* (1902) 4 F. 815; *Earl of Lindsay v Shaw*, 1959 S.L.T. (Notes) 13, per Lord Justice-Clerk Thomson. As to rectification of an inter vivos trust deed which does not accurately express the intention of the grantor, see Law Reform (Miscellaneous Provisions) (Scotland) Act 1985 s.8.

[179] See para.41.40, below.

[180] A renunciation before entering into enjoyment of the alimentary liferent is effective: *Ford v Ford's Trs*, 1961 S.L.T. 128

[181] See 1961 Act s.1(6); *Countess of Lauderdale*, 1962 S.C. 302. The powers of the court under the Act are exercisable in relation to any trust under the Married Women's Policies of Assurance (Scotland) Act 1880: Married Women's Policies of Assurance (Scotland) (Amendment) Act 1980 s.4.

[182] For purposes of the 1961 Act a person who is of, or over, the age of 16 years, but has not attained the age of 18 years, is deemed to be incapable of assenting: s.1(2) (as amended by Age of Legal Capacity (Scotland) Act 1991 Sch.1 para.27).

[183] A guardian or other person appointed under the Adults with Incapacity (Scotland) Act 2000 with appropriate powers could agree on behalf of an incapable adult.

[184] See the following cases for judicial observations on this procedure: *Colville*, 1962 S.C. 185; *Robertson*, 1962 S.C. 196; *Gibson's Tr.*, 1962 S.C. 204; *Findlay*, 1962 S.C. 210; *Tulloch's Trs*, 1962 S.C. 245; also *Clarke's Trs*, 1966 S.L.T. 249, re jurisdiction.

[185] *Ommaney*, 1966 S.L.T. (Notes) 13.

[186] *Henderson, Petitioner*, 1981 S.L.T. (Notes) 40.

on behalf of: (a) any of the beneficiaries who by reason of nonage or other incapacity cannot assent; or (b) any person who may become a beneficiary at a future date[187]; or (c) any person as yet unborn. It is a condition of its granting approval that the court should be of the opinion that the carrying out of the arrangement would not be prejudicial to the persons on behalf of whom its approval is sought.[188] The interests of such persons are now protected by setting aside an actuarially calculated fund as insurance is no longer available. This may not be necessary if the liferenter has a power to appoint the fee which includes power to fix the date of vesting of the appointed shares,[189] or to protect remote beneficiaries whose interests are of negligible value.[190]

Under subs.(4), the court may authorise an arrangement whereby alimentary provisions are varied or revoked and may replace them by other provisions which may dispose of the whole or part of the capital of the trust estate. Such authorisation will, however, be granted only if the arrangement is approved either by the alimentary beneficiary or by the court on his or her behalf under subs.(1) and the court is satisfied that the carrying out of the arrangement would be reasonable, having regard to the whole income of the alimentary beneficiary and any other material factors.[191] Applications under subs.(4) have been refused as unnecessary on the following grounds: (a) that a liferenter was entitled to renounce a contingent alimentary liferent[192]; (b) that the liferent had ceased to be alimentary[193]; and (c) that the liferent created by a wife in favour of herself by a post-nuptial marriage contract was not a valid alimentary liferent.[194] The court will approve and authorise an arrangement under this section, which is only made possible by the exercise of a power of appointment, so long as the donee does not obtain any exclusive advantage thereby.[195]

PUBLIC TRUSTS

41.22 General—Public trusts are trusts that exist for the benefit of the public or a specified section of it, rather than for private persons selected by the truster. The distinction between a public and a private trust is not always easy to draw.[196] The magistrates and council are sometimes regarded as holding the common good in trust, but they are not trustees of a public trust.[197] Public trusts may be registered as charities with the OSCR if they meet the charity test or may fall within

---

[187] See *Buchan, Petitioner*, 1964 S.L.T. 51; *Allan, Petitioners*, 1991 S.L.T. 202.

[188] The introduction of additional beneficiaries in a discretionary trust is prejudicial to the existing beneficiaries, *Pollok-Morris*, 1969 S.L.T. (Notes) 60. As to prejudice to the beneficiaries, see also *Aikman, Petitioner*, 1968 S.L.T. 137.

[189] See *Colville*, 1962 S.C. 185, and *Dick*, 1963 S.C. 598.

[190] *Phillips*, 1964 S.C. 141. The trustees remain liable if the remote interest emerges later.

[191] *Gibson's Tr.*, 1962 S.C. 204; *Dick*, 1963 S.C. 598 at 602 per Lord President Clyde; cf. *Bergius's Trs, Petitioners*, 1963 S.C. 194, where liferent was contingent and application refused.

[192] *Findlay*, 1962 S.C. 210; *Smillie*, 1966 S.L.T. 41.

[193] *Strange*, 1966 S.L.T. 59; *Pearson*, 1968 S.C. 8; see also *Law, Petitioner*, 1962 S.C. 500, where the liferent had ceased to be alimentary on the death of the husband and the other provisions of an ante-nuptial marriage contract for which approval of variation was sought were testamentary and revocable by the wife. Cf. *Sutherland, Petitioner*, 1968 S.C. 200.

[194] *Cargill, Petitioners*, 1965 S.C. 122.

[195] *Pelham Burn, Petitioners*, 1964 S.C. 3.

[196] *University of Edinburgh v The Torrie Trs*, 1997 S.L.T. 1009.

[197] *Banff Burgh Council v Ruthin Castle Ltd*, 1944 S.C. 36; *Wilson v Inverclyde Council*, 2004 S.L.T. 265.

the definition of an "endowment" (educational or non-educational) under the Education (Scotland) Act 1980.[198] Some charities are not public trusts; they may be companies limited by guarantee or incorporated bodies.[199]

The general principles of trust administration[200] are as applicable to public as to private trusts, and public trusts are within the scope of the Trusts (Scotland) Act 1921. The main differences between public and private trusts are: (a) public trusts are enforceable in the Court of Session by the Lord Advocate[201] as well as by the actual or potential beneficiaries, and may be registered as charities and hence subject to regulation by OSCR; (b) the special procedures for varying or reorganising public trusts[202]; (c) the truster in a public trust cannot appoint new trustees unless such a power is conferred in the trust deed[203]; (d) the standard of care of trustees of a trust registered as a charity is based on that of a person managing the affairs of others,[204] but previous cases indicate that the courts are more lenient with trustees of public trusts who act honestly and in good faith but nevertheless err in their management of the trust[205]; and (e) the court is said to adopt a "benignant" approach in construing a deed which bears to constitute a public trust.[206]

Gifts to charity—If a testator leaves property to trustees in trust to divide it **41.23** among such "charitable" purposes as they may think proper, the descriptive word "charitable" is, out of favour for charities,[207] held by itself to denote a sufficiently definite class of beneficiaries, and the gift is sustained. On the other hand, if the purposes are described merely as "public", this description is held to be so vague as to invalidate the bequest. Instructions to trustees to divide the estate among "charitable or public",[208] "charitable or religious"[209] and "charitable or social"[210] objects have been held void from uncertainty in respect that two classes of beneficiaries were favoured, and that the words "public", "religious" and "social" used without further detail to describe the second class were too vague a direction to receive effect. But a conjunction of the words "charitable" and "benevolent" does not impair the peculiar virtues of "charitable".[211] If the trust purposes are in themselves uncertain, the fact that the benefit of the trust is confined to a particular locality will not save the trust.[212] And a gift to "charities" generally will

---

[198] Education (Scotland) Act 1980 s.122.

[199] Scottish Charitable Incorporated Organisations ("SCIOs") have been introduced by the Charities and Trustee Investment (Scotland) Act 2005.

[200] See paras 41.07–41.12, above.

[201] *Mitchell v Burness* (1878) 5 R. 954, per Lord Deas at 959.

[202] See paras 41.26–41.30.

[203] *Lord Glentanar v Scottish Industrial Musical Association*, 1925 S.C. 226. The Court of Session can appoint new trustees for trusts registered as charities, Charities and Trustee Investment (Scotland) Act 2005 s.34(5)d).

[204] Not their own affairs, see para.41.16, above.

[205] *Andrews v Ewart's Trs* (1886) 13 R. (HL) 69.

[206] K. McK. Norrie and E.M. Scobbie, *Trusts* (Edinburgh: W. Green, 1991), p.20.

[207] *Magistrates of Dundee v Morris* (1858) 3 Macq. 134.

[208] *Blair v Duncan* (1901) 4 F. (HL) 1; *Turnbull's Trs v Lord Advocate*, 1918 S.C. (HL) 88; *Campbell's Trs v Campbell*, 1921 S.C. (HL) 12; *Reid's Trs v Cattanach's Trs*, 1929 S.C. 727. There are numerous decisions as to the effect of various forms of bequest.

[209] *Macintyre v Grimond's Trs* (1905) 7 F. (HL) 90; but see *Brough v Brough's Trs*, 1950 S.L.T. 117.

[210] *Rintoul's Trs v Rintoul*, 1949 S.C. 297; contrast *Milne's Trs v Davidson*, 1956 S.C. 81.

[211] *Wink's Exrs v Tallent*, 1947 S.C. 470 at 484, per Lord Keith treats the words as synonymous. See also *Pomphrey's Trs v Royal Naval Benevolent Trust*, 1967 S.L.T. 61 at 63, per Lord Fraser.

[212] *Turnbull's Trs v Lord Advocate*, 1918 S.C. (HL) 88; *Harper's Trs v Jacobs*, 1929 S.C. 345.

fail if the testator does not appoint a particular person as trustee or executor to make a choice.[213]

41.24 Tax relief—For tax purposes the English law of charities is part of the law of Scotland and not foreign law.[214] Accordingly, the term "charitable purpose" in ss.2 and 3 of the Charities Act 2006 governs whether a Scottish public trust or other body qualifies for relief under UK tax statutes.[215] The definition in ss.2 and 3 is similar, but not identical, to the test in ss.7–9 of the Charities and Trustee Investment (Scotland) Act 2005 for a body to be registered as a charity by OSCR. Application for UK tax relief has to be made to HM Revenue and Customs.

Non-domestic rates relief is available in relation to premises in Scotland occupied by a charity and used wholly or mainly for charitable purposes. There is mandatory relief for 80 per cent of the amount of the rates and the local authority have a discretion to remit the remaining 20 per cent.[216] To qualify, a body must be entered on the Scottish Charity Register and therefore must have met the charity test under the 2005 Act.[217]

41.25 Registered charities—Bodies (whether constituted as public trusts or otherwise) have to apply to be registered as charities on the Scottish Charity Register, but only registered bodies can describe themselves in Scotland as charities[218] and are entitled to rating relief. Unregistered bodies can be interdicted from calling themselves charities.[219] OSCR is charged with deciding whether the applicant body meets the charity test set out in ss.7–9 of the 2005 Act. OSCR's refusal to register is appealable to the Scottish Charity Appeals Panel[220] and from there to the Court of Session.[221] There are procedures for removing from the register bodies that no longer meet the test.[222] Each entry contains information about the charity and its activities and the register is open to public inspection.[223] A registered charity is bound to produce properly audited accounts and an annual report and submit both to OSCR.[224] If no accounts are produced OSCR can appoint a person to draw them up at the charity managers' expense on the basis of information obtained from the charity.[225]

OSCR acts as the supervisor of registered charities. It may demand information about the charity and its activities and can intervene in the administration of the charity and protect its property.[226] OSCR may apply to the Court of Session for wider or permanent orders, including the appointment of a judicial factor or new

---

[213] *Angus's Exrx v Batchan's Trs*, 1949 S.C. 335. Cf. *Guild v Balden*, 1987 S.C.L.R. 221.

[214] *Inland Revenue v Glasgow Police Athletic Association*, 1953 S.C. (HL) 13; see also *Russell's Ex. v Inland Revenue*, 1992 S.L.T. 438.

[215] Income and Corporation Taxes Act 1988 s.505.

[216] See Local Government (Financial Provisions, etc.) (Scotland) Act 1962 s.4. Non-domestic water and sewerage charges still apply.

[217] Local Government (Financial Provisions, etc.) (Scotland) Act 1962 s.4(10), as amended by the Charities and Trustee Investment (Scotland) Act 2005 (the "2005 Act") Sch.4 para.1.

[218] Non-Scottish charities need not register if they do not have land or business premises in Scotland, 2005 Act s.14.

[219] 2005 Act ss.31(5) and 34(5).

[220] 2005 Act ss.71 and 76.

[221] 2005 Act s.78.

[222] 2005 Act s.18.

[223] 2005 Act s.21.

[224] 2005 Act s.44.

[225] 2005 Act s.45.

[226] 2005 Act ss.28 and 31.

trustees to run the charity.[227] An undischarged bankrupt or a person convicted of an offence involving dishonesty is disqualified from being a trustee.[228]

REORGANISATION OF PUBLIC TRUSTS

General—There are three main statutory procedures for reorganising public trusts that have come into existence: for trusts that are registered as charities, ss.39–42 of the Charities and Trustee Investment (Scotland) Act 2005[229]; for non-charity trusts, ss.9–11 of Law Reform (Miscellaneous Provisions) (Scotland) Act 1990; for endowments (whether or not educational) provided the body holding the endowment is not a charity, Pt VI of the Education (Scotland) Act 1980. These procedures do not preclude the Court of Session's cy près jurisdiction which has to be resorted to where the circumstances do not fit the statutory criteria[230] or in cases of initial failure.[231] **41.26**

Registered charities—A charity (whether or not a public trust) may apply to OSCR for approval of a reorganisation scheme.[232] The scheme may alter the constitution or purposes of the charity, amalgamate the charity with another charity or transfer its property to another charity.[233] OSCR has to be satisfied that one or more of the re-organisation conditions set out in s.42(2) apply.[234] These are: (a) that the purposes of the charity have been fulfilled or are otherwise adequately provided for, or have ceased to be charitable, or have ceased to be a suitable use of the property; (b) that the purposes of the charity provide a use for only part of its property; (c) that a provision of the charity's constitution (other than a provision setting out the charity's purposes) can no longer be given effect to or is otherwise no longer desirable; and (d) that it is desirable to introduce a provision (other than one setting out a new purpose) to the constitution. OSCR also has to be satisfied that for a condition falling within (a) or (b) that the scheme will enable the charity's resources to be put to better effect consistently with the spirit of its constitution, having regard to the changes in social and economic conditions, and for (d) that the change is consistent with the spirit.[235] The Court of Session may also approve a scheme on the same terms; the charity itself has no direct right to apply as only OSCR can apply either of its own accord or at the request of the charity.[236] **41.27**

Non-charity public trusts—Under the Law Reform (Miscellaneous Provisions) (Scotland) Act 1990 the Court of Session (or if the Scottish Ministers so order, the sheriff court where the annual trust income does not exceed a specified sum)[237] **41.28**

---

[227] 2005 Act s.34.

[228] 2005 Act s.69.

[229] As amended by the Public Services Reform (Scotland) Act 2010 s.124.

[230] See, e.g. *Mining Institute of Scotland Benevolent Fund Trs, Petitioners*, 1994 S.L.T. 785.

[231] See para.41.30, below.

[232] The application procedure is set out in the Charities Reorganisation (Scotland) Regulations 2007 (SSI 2007/204).

[233] 2005 Act s.42(3).

[234] As amended by the Public Services Reform (Scotland) Act 2010 s.124.

[235] 2005 Act s.39(1)(b).

[236] 2005 Act s.40.

[237] Law Reform (Miscellaneous Provisions) (Scotland) Act 1990 (the "1990 Act") s.9(5). No order has yet been made.

may, on the application of the trustees, approve a scheme for the variation or reorganisation of the trust purposes if it is satisfied that certain conditions are met. These are very similar to the reorganisation conditions for charities under the 2005 Act.[238] They are: (a) that the trust purposes, whether in whole or in part, have been fulfilled as far as it is possible to do so or can no longer be given effect to, whether in accordance with the directions or spirit of the trust deed or other document constituting the trust or otherwise; or (b) that the trust purposes provide a use for only part of the property available under the trust[239]; or (c) that the trust purposes were expressed by reference to: (i) an area which has since ceased to have effect for the purpose described expressly or by implication in the trust deed, or (ii) a class of persons or area which has ceased to be suitable or appropriate, having regard to the spirit of the trust deed, or as regards which it has ceased to be practicable to administer the property available under the trust; or (d) that the purposes, in whole or in part, have, since the constitution of the trust, (i) been adequately provided for by other means, or (ii) have ceased to be such as would enable the trust to be recognised as a charity, or (iii) have ceased in any other way to provide a suitable and effective method of using the property available under the trust, having regard to the spirit of the trust deed.[240] Before approving the scheme, the court must be satisfied that the proposed purposes will enable the resources of the trust to be applied to better effect consistently with the spirit of the trust deed, having regard to changes in social and economic conditions since the time when the trust was constituted.[241] The scheme may provide for the transfer of the trust assets to another public trust, with or without a change in the purposes of the other trust or for the amalgamation of the trust with one or more public trusts.[242]

There are two non-judicial routes for small non-charity public trusts. First, where the annual income of the public trust does not exceed £5,000, and a majority of the trustees are of the opinion that any of (a)–(d) above apply in relation to the trust, they may determine that, to enable the resources of the trust to be applied to better effect consistently with the spirit of the trust deed, the trust purposes should be modified or the whole assets should be transferred to another public trust or that the trust should be amalgamated with one or more public trusts.[243] The new purposes must not be so dissimilar in character to the original purposes as to constitute an unreasonable departure from their spirit.[244] Before passing the resolution, the trustees must have regard to the circumstances of any locality to which the trust purposes relate and to achieving economy by amalgamating two or more trusts.[245] Where the trustees have determined that the assets should be transferred, they may pass a resolution that the trust be wound up and that the assets be transferred to another not too dissimilar trust.[246] Before passing the resolution, the trustees must again have regard to the circumstances of any relevant particular locality and ascertain that the trustees of the transferee trust will accept

---

[238] 1990 Act s.9(1); *Mining Institute of Scotland Benevolent Fund Trs, Petitioner*, 1994 S.L.T. 785.

[239] As to the requirements of the 1990 Act s.9(1)(b), see *Mining Institute of Scotland Benevolent Fund Trs, Petitioners*, 1994 S.L.T. 785 at 787, per Lord President Hope (sitting in the Outer House).

[240] As to the requirements of the 1990 Act s.9(1)(d)(iii), see *Mining Institute of Scotland Benevolent Fund Trs, Petitioners*, 1994 S.L.T. 785 at 787; *Inverclyde Council v Dunlop*, 2006 S.C.L.R. 463.

[241] 1990 Act s.9(2).

[242] 1990 Act s.9(3).

[243] 1990 Act s.10(2).

[244] 1990 Act s.10(4).

[245] 1990 Act s.10(5).

[246] 1990 Act s.10(8).

the transfer of the assets.[247] Where the trustees determine that the trust should be amalgamated with another, they may pass a resolution that the trust will be amalgamated with one or more other not too dissimilar trusts.[248] Before passing the resolution the trustees must have regard to the circumstances of any relevant particular locality, and ascertain that the trustees of the other trust or trusts agree to amalgamation.[249] The resolutions cannot be acted upon until after an interval to allow for advertisement, the making of objections by interested persons and notification to the Lord Advocate.[250] The Scottish Ministers (or in practice OSCR) may direct the trust not to proceed with the implementation of the resolution.[251] The second non-judicial method applies to a public trust whose annual income does not exceed £1,000. The trustees may, in certain circumstances, and after following prescribed procedure, expend the capital of the trust notwithstanding any prohibition in the trust deed.[252]

Endowments—Under Pt VI of the Education (Scotland) Act 1980 an "endow- **41.29** ment" means any property (subject to certain exceptions) dedicated to "charitable purposes", in the sense in which that term is defined as part of the charity test in s.7(2) of the Charities and Trustee Investment (Scotland) Act 2005.[253] An "educational endowment" means any endowment which has been applied or is applicable to educational purposes.[254] A public trust which is not registered as a charity with OSCR but whose property meets the definition of endowment may be reorganised under Pt VI of the 1980 Act. Where the property is an educational endowment, the relevant education authority may prepare a draft scheme for its reorganisation, involving, for example, changing its purposes, amalgamating it with another endowment or splitting it into separate endowments.[255] The authority must have regard to the spirit of the founder's intentions, the interests of the locality of the endowment, administrative efficiency and the continuing need for competitive bursaries for advanced education.[256] The draft scheme has to be advertised and if no objections are made the authority can give it effect. Objections are dealt with by a public local enquiry after which the authority can make the scheme in such terms as it thinks fit. Those dissatisfied can then appeal to the Court of Session for its recall or modification.[257] Certain educational endowments are outside the scope of the education authorities' powers of reorganisation but can apply to the Court of Session for approval of a scheme for their future government and management. In giving such a scheme effect, the court must have regard to the same range of issues as an education authority. The trustees of a public trust whose property is a non-educational endowment may also, provided the trust is not registered as a charity with OSCR, make an application to the court for a scheme of reorganisation.[258] The Lord Advocate

---

[247] 1990 Act s.10(9).
[248] 1990 Act s.10(10).
[249] 1990 Act s.10(11).
[250] 1990 Act s.10(12), (13). See also the Public Trusts (Reorganisation) (Scotland) (No.2) Regulations 1993 (SI 1993/2254), made pursuant to s.10(13).
[251] 1990 Act s.10(14).
[252] Law Reform (Miscellaneous Provisions) (Scotland) Act 1990 s.11.
[253] Education (Scotland) Act 1980 (the "1980 Act") s.122.
[254] 1980 Act s.122.
[255] 1980 Act s.105(1A).
[256] 1980 Act s.105(2) and (4A).
[257] 1980 Act s.112.
[258] 1980 Act s.108.

may petition the court to make a scheme of reorganisation for any endowment (educational or non-educational), provided always that the property concerned is not held by a charity registered with OSCR.[259]

41.30 **Cy près**—The Court of Session's cy près jurisdiction covers several different situations. A petition is presented for approval by the court of a proposed scheme for the administration of the trust.[260] The power of sanctioning the settlement of a scheme belongs to the *nobile officium* but a petition may now be presented to a nominated judge of the Court of Session.[261] It must be borne in mind that where a truster's directions are sufficient to enable trustees to prepare a scheme for themselves and where it is not impracticable to carry them out and there is no lack of machinery prescribed by the truster, it is unnecessary for the trustees to apply to the court at all.[262]

The first class of cases concerns public trusts[263] that are in existence but where the intention of the truster can no longer be carried into effect in the precise manner directed. The court may then approve a scheme for the application of the funds in a manner as near as possible to that directed,[264] unless a destination-over is brought into effect by the lapse.[265] Some cases disclose a strict approach to the question whether there has been failure so as to admit of a cy près scheme, and it has been said that it is not a legitimate ground for the application of the doctrine that, through the changing circumstances of society, the administration of a charity has become increasingly arduous and discouraging in its results.[266] On the other hand, the court has shown itself ready to exercise its power in a case of strong expendiency falling short of impossibility of performance, where it is clear that the circumstances of the trust or the arrangements for its administration are such that carrying it out would be seriously hampered unless the means were varied.[267] The use of the cy près jurisdiction for this class of cases has been largely superseded by the statutory provisions for reorganisation in the 1990 and 2005 Acts but sometimes the cy près route may prove more flexible.[268]

The second class of cases relates to bequests for public or charitable purposes which lapse before they take effect. In *Burgess's Trs v Crawford*[269] Lord President Dunedin distinguished between three categories of bequest. The first is where there is a gift for a charitable purpose, but the means by which it is to be carried out are not indicated. Here the court will supply the means so as to enable the

---

[259] 1980 Act s.108A.

[260] For procedure, see *Forrest's Trs v Forrest*, 1960 S.L.T. 88; RCS rr.63.7–63.15.

[261] RCS r.63.8.

[262] *Robertson's Trs*, 1948 S.C. 1; *Galloway v Elgin Magistrates*, 1946 S.C. 353.

[263] Not just charitable trusts: *Anderson's Trs v Scott*, 1914 S.C. 942.

[264] *Clephane v Magistrates of Edinburgh* (1869) 7 M. (HL) 7 at 15; see also *Trs of Carnegie Park Orphanage* (1892) 19 R. 605 and *Grigor Medical Bursary Fund Trs* (1903) 5 F. 1143, per Lord McLaren; *Gibson's Trs*, 1933 S.C. 190.

[265] *Youngs's Trs v Deacons of the Eight Incorporated Trades of Perth* (1893) 20 R. 778; see also *Clarke v Ross*, 1976 S.L.T. (Notes) 62.

[266] *Glasgow Domestic Training School*, 1923 S.C. 892 at 895, per Lord President Clyde; *Scotstown Moor Children's Camp*, 1948 S.C. 630.

[267] *Gibson's Trs*, 1933 S.C. 190; *Glasgow Y.M.C.A.*, 1934 S.C. 452 at 458, per Lord Blackburn; see *Trs of R S Macdonald Charitable Trust Petitioners* [2008] CSOH 116 for a review of the court's change of attitude.

[268] *Mining Institute of Scotland Benevolent Fund Trs, Petitioners*, 1994 S.L.T. 785 see note at end; *Trs of R S Macdonald Charitable Trust Petitioners* [2008] CSOH 116.

[269] *Burgess's Trs v Crawford*, 1912 S.C. 387, following Lord Herschell's opinion in *Re Rymer* [1895] 1 Ch. 19; see also *Cumming's Exr v Cumming*, 1967 S.L.T. 68 at 69, per Lord Avonside.

purpose to be carried out.[270] The second category is where there is a gift to a society or institution which does not exist and never has existed, in which case, from the mere non-existence of the object, there is spelled out a general charitable intention.[271] The third category is that in which the gift is in form made to a particular charitable institution which has ceased to exist, or for a particular purpose which cannot be effected; here the question arises in each case whether, on a fair construction of the deed, there is a general charitable intention with a direction as to the method in which that intention is to be effected,[272] or whether the gift is meant only for that particular institution[273] or that particular purpose.[274] If it is the latter, the doctrine of cy près has no place, and the gift fails with the failure of the institution or purpose. In *Burgess's Trs*[275] the court, applying these rules, held that a bequest for the purpose of establishing an industrial school for females, which had become impossible of fulfilment owing to supervening legislation, lapsed as no intention beyond this particular object was disclosed in the settlement.

II. LIFERENT AND FEE

Nature of liferent—A liferent is a right to use and enjoy property during life **41.31** without destroying or wasting its substance (*salva rei substantia*).[276] Liferents can be either proper liferents[277] or trust (improper) liferents.

In a proper liferent the person who owns the property is called the fiar; he or she has the fee. The liferenter, who must be a natural person, has the subordinate real right of liferent which encumbers the fee. The rights and liabilities of both parties are determined by law.[278] There is no real right intermediate between those of liferent and of fee.[279] The liferenter may possess the property naturally or civilly; in the case of a house the liferenter may live there or let it out. If the subjects should be destroyed or damaged through the fault of another the liferenter is entitled to damages for the loss sustained as a proper liferenter, but cannot also claim damages for the cost of alternative accommodation.[280]

---

[270] e.g. *Ballingall's J.F. v Hamilton*, 1973 S.L.T. 236.

[271] e.g. *Tod's Trs v The Sailors' & Firemen's Orphans' and Widows' Society*, 1953 S.L.T. (Notes) 72; *Pomphrey's Trs v Royal Naval Benevolent Trust*, 1967 S.L.T. 61; *Cumming's Exr*, 1967 S.L.T. 68. Cf. *Mactavish's Trs v St Columba's High Church*, 1967 S.L.T. (Notes) 50, where the expression of intention failed for uncertainty.

[272] e.g. *Macrae's Trs*, 1955 S.L.T. (Notes) 33; *Shorthouse's Trs v Aberdeen Medico Chirurgical Society*, 1977 S.L.T. 148.

[273] e.g. *Connell's Trs v Milngavie District Nursing Association*, 1953 S.C. 230; *Fergusson's Trs v Buchanan*, 1973 S.L.T. 41.

[274] e.g. *Burgess's Trs*, 1912 S.C. 387; *Pennie's Trs v RNLI*, 1924 S.L.T. 520; *Duncan (Tait's J.F.) v Lillie*, 1940 S.C. 534; *Hay Memorial J.F. v Hay's Trs*, 1952 S.C. (HL) 29; *McRobert's Trs v Cameron*, 1961 S.L.T. (Notes) 66.

[275] *Burgess's Trs*, 1912 S.C. 387.

[276] Stair II, 6, 4, Erskine, II, 9, 39.

[277] Erskine, II, 9, 56; *Inland Revenue v Wemyss*, 1924 S.C. 284; *De Robeck v Inland Revenue*, 1928 S.C. (HL) 34, per Lord Dunedin; *Miller v Inland Revenue*, 1930 S.C. (HL) 49, per Lord Dunedin. The date of creation of a proper liferent is dealt with in the Abolition of Feudal Tenure, etc. (Scotland) Act 2000 s.65.

[278] *Ferguson v Ferguson's Trs* (1877) 4 R. 532, per Lord President Inglis; see paras 41.31–41.42 below.

[279] *Cochrane's Exrx v Cochrane*, 1947 S.C. 134; T.B. Smith, *A Short Commentary on the Law of Scotland* (Edinburgh: W. Green, 1962), p.487. As to "fiduciary fee", see Bell, *Principles*, ss.1713–1715; see also the 1921 Act s.8(2).

[280] *MacLennan v Scottish Gas Board*, 1985 S.L.T. 2.

A proper liferent cannot be constituted over fungibles which perish in use, but may be constituted over subjects which, though they wear out in time, yet waste by such slow degrees that they may continue fit for use for the full course of an ordinary life.[281] In *Rogers v Scott*[282] it was held that the effect of a direction to trustees to allow the testator's widow the liferent of his farm and stock was to place on her the obligation to maintain the stock and leave it substantially of the same description, value and extent as it was when she received it. Where a liferent of a house along with its furniture is given, it has been held that the furniture, as an accessory to the possession of the house, cannot be removed from the house and used elsewhere.[283]

Proper liferents were more common in former times. Nowadays trust liferents are preferred because of their inherent flexibility and the trustees being impartial administrators as between the liferenter and the fiar. In a trust liferent the trustees have the real right of ownership of the property; both the liferenter and the fiar have merely a bundle of personal rights against the trustees.[284] Trust liferents are capable of greater flexibility in that the legal rights and liabilities of the liferenter and fiar can be modified by the terms of the trust deed. Thus where the bequest takes the form of a direction to trustees to pay the income of a trust estate to a beneficiary, the terms of the deed may show that the income was intended to comprise either more or less than would have fallen to a proper liferenter.[285] If, however, there is given a liferent simpliciter, it has been laid down that the obligations resting on the liferenter are the same whether the liferent is given directly or through the medium of a trust.[286]

41.32 Annuities and rights of occupancy—A liferent is to be distinguished from an annuity. An annuity is a right to receive from year to year a certain sum, and it is not necessarily limited to the lifetime of the recipient, for it may be given for a number of years or even in perpetuity.[287] A liferenter can claim only the fruits of the subject liferented, whereas an annuitant is entitled to the amount of the annuity, and (unless the deed creating it shows that it is to be charged on income only) can exact payment out of capital if the income falls short.[288]

A right of occupancy is different from a liferent. In *Clark v Clark*[289] a testator directed his trustees to give "the use of" his house to his widow, and it was held that she had not a liferent of, but a right to occupy, the house. Being merely an occupant she had no right to let it but, on the other hand, was liable only for rates and assessments in respect of occupancy and not for those burdens such as repairs or landlord's taxes which fall upon a liferenter. Whether a liferent of a house or this more limited right is given depends on the language used by the testator, but it has been thought to point to a gift of liferent that under the testator's directions no funds are left in the hands of the trustees to meet the annual burdens on the house.[290]

---

[281] Erskine, II, 9, 40; *Miller's Trs v Miller*, 1907 S.C. 833.

[282] *Rogers v Scott* (1867) 5 M. 1078.

[283] *Cochran v Cochran* (1755) Mor.8280; 2 Bell, *Illustrations*, p.141.

[284] See para 41.04, above.

[285] *Miller's Trs v Miller*, 1907 S.C. 833, per Lord McLaren.

[286] *Johnstone v Mackenzie's Trs*, 1912 S.C. (HL) 106 at 109.

[287] *Fleming v Reuther's Exrs*, 1921 S.C. 593; see also *Reid's Exrs v Reid*, 1944 S.C. (HL) 25.

[288] *Kinmond's Trs v Kinmond* (1873) 11 M. 381; *Knox's Trs v Knox* (1869) 7 M. 873; *Colquhoun's Trs v Colquhoun*, 1922 S.C. 32.

[289] *Clark v Clark* (1871) 9 M. 435.

[290] The cases are reviewed in *Johnstone v Mackenzie's Trs*, 1912 SC. (HL) 106; *Milne's Tr. v Milne*, 1920 S.C. 456; see also *Montgomerie-Fleming's Trs v Carre*, 1913 S.C. 1018; and *Countess of Lauderdale*, 1962 S.C. 302.

Creation of liferents by constitution and reservation: Limitations—Liferents **41.33**
may be created by reservation or constitution. A liferent by reservation is that
which a proprietor reserves to himself when conveying the fee to another. In
the case of heritage no title to a reserved liferent requires to be completed, for the
grantor's former title to the land (which included the right to its fruits) still subsists
as to the reserved liferent.[291] A liferent by constitution is one created by the proprietor in favour of another, with or without a grant of the fee to others; familiar
instances of such liferents are those created in testamentary deeds.

Limitation on the creation of liferents—The Law Reform (Miscellaneous **41.34**
Provisions) (Scotland) Act 1968[292] provides that where, by any deed executed on
or after November 25, 1968, there is created a liferent interest in any property, that
interest is converted into a right of fee if anyone of full age becomes entitled to it
who was not living or in utero at the date of the coming into operation of the
deed.[293] In the case of an individual not of full age, the conversion into a right of
fee is postponed until he or she attains majority and is subject to the proviso that
the individual should then still be entitled to the liferent interest. The conversion
does not affect rights created independently of the deed or rights of security
holders. These provisions re-enact with some variations the substance of provisions of the Trusts (Scotland) Act 1921[294] and the Entail Amendment Act 1848[295]
which continue to apply to liferent interests created by deeds executed before
November 25, 1968. Under the 1848 Act—which applies to heritage, whereas the
1921 Act applies to moveables—there is no automatic conversion into a right of
fee but the life-renter is enabled, if he so chooses, to acquire the fee by petitioning
the court for that purpose.[296] The section does not apply to annuities.[297]

Capital or income—The liferenter is entitled to the fruits of the subject but not to **41.35**
anything which is part of the corpus or capital. As between the liferenter and the
fiar, a receipt will fall to, and a charge will be borne by, one or other according as
these are of the nature of capital or of income. Although no general rule can be
laid down, certain tests have been suggested for use in determining to which category a receipt or charge belongs. In *Ross's Trs v Nicoll*[298] Lord McLaren observed:

> "In general I should be disposed to hold that every payment to be made from
> a trust estate which does not involve a diminution of capital ought to be
> regarded as a payment out of income, whether that payment is made yearly
> or half-yearly or periodically at longer intervals. All such payments when
> made to the trust estate are to be regarded as part of the profit as distin-
> guished from the corpus of the estate, and therefore, fall to be made over
> from the estate to the person who is beneficially entitled to the income."

---

[291] Erskine, II, 9, 42.

[292] Law Reform (Miscellaneous Provisions) (Scotland) Act 1968 s.18.

[293] A *mortis causa* deed comes into operation on the death of the testator and the execution or
coming into operation of a special power of appointment is referable to the date of execution or, as the
case may be, coming into operation of the deed creating the power (s.18(5)).

[294] s.9; Conveyancing (Scotland) Act 1924 s.45.

[295] ss.47 and 48; *Earl of Balfour, Petitioner*, 2003 S.C. (HL) 1, liferenter born after date of will but
before date of codicils.

[296] *Crichton-Stuart's Tutrix, Petitioner*, 1921 S.C. 840, per Lord President Clyde; *Earl of Moray,
Petitioner*, 1950 S.C. 281.

[297] *Drybrough's Tr. v Drybrough's Tr.*, 1912 S.C. 939.

[298] *Ross's Trs v Nicoll* (1902) 5 F. 146.

Another suggested criterion (which is only a rough one and not decisive in every case) is

> "that capital expenditure is a thing that is going to be spent once and for all, and income expenditure is a thing that is going to recur every year".[299]

Apart from such general considerations, there is a series of cases regarding timber and minerals which not only rule the right of the liferenter as to these but have been referred to as affording guidance by analogy in questions as to items of receipt or expenditure of a different kind.[300]

41.36 **Rights in timber**—The wood growing on an estate belongs as part of the corpus to the fiar. He has the right to thinnings and to all trees blown down in an "extraordinary storm"; and he may cut wood but not so as to interfere with the amenity and shelter of an estate and thus affect the liferenter's enjoyment of it.[301] The liferenter, on the other hand, is entitled to ordinary windfalls and, in the case of copse-wood cut periodically on reaching maturity, he has the benefit of the cutting when the proper time for it arrives. He may also cut wood at the sight of the fiar for repairing fences and other purposes of the estate.[302]

41.37 **Rights in minerals**—The returns from mineral workings are not strictly fruits of the soil which could be claimed as such by a liferenter, but

> "if the owner of the soil, the fiar, creates a mineral estate by working or letting a particular seam of minerals, he thereby brings the proceeds of the minerals so worked or let within the category of fruits and within the right of usufruct".[303]

Accordingly, it is settled that a gift of liferent or direction to trustees to pay the income of the estate to a beneficiary includes the rents and royalties from mines either worked, or let although not worked, in the lifetime of the grantor or truster. On the other hand, returns from mines opened by the trustees after the truster's death are not included unless the truster directed the trustees to work the minerals.[304]

41.38 **Bonuses and dividends**—Payments in respect of a company's shares may, depending on the circumstances, be treated as income and hence receivable by the liferenter, or as capital so going to the fiar. Normal dividends are income, but if a company, which has power under its constitution to increase its capital, pays a bonus out of accumulated profits which have been carried to reserve, it will depend on the action of the company whether the bonus falls to the liferenter or to the fiar. The accepted rule is that

---

[299] *Vallambrosa Rubber Co v Farmer*, 1910 S.C. 519, per Lord President Dunedin; *British Insulated and Helsby Cables v Atherton* [1926] A.C. 205, per Viscount Cave L.C. and Lord Atkinson.

[300] See, e.g. in *Davidson's Trs v Ogilvie*, 1910 S.C. 294 (copyright royalties).

[301] *Dickson v Dickson* (1823) 2 S. 152; *Tait v Maitland* (1825) 4 S. 247.

[302] *Macalister's Trs v Macalister* (1851) 13 D. 1239.

[303] *Campbell v Wardlaw* (1883) 10 R. (HL) 65, per Lord Watson.

[304] *Ranken's Trs v Ranken*, 1908 S.C. 3; *Naismith's Trs v Naismith*, 1909 S.C. 1380; *Campbell v Wardlaw* (1883) 10 R. (HL) 65.

"when a testator or settlor directs or permits the subject of his disposition to remain as shares or stock in a company, which has the power either of distributing its profits as dividend or of converting them into capital, and the company validly exercises this power, such exercise of its power is binding on all persons interested under him, the testator or settlor, in the shares, and consequently what is paid by the company as dividend goes to the tenant for life,[305] and what is paid by the company to the shareholder as capital, or appropriated as an increase of the capital stock in the concern, enures to the benefit of all who are interested in the capital".[306]

A cash payment out of accumulated profits prima facie belongs to the liferenter.[307] But in cases where a company declares a bonus and at the same time offers its shareholders additional shares to be paid up to an amount equivalent to the bonus, it is a question of fact, looking to the form and substance of the particular transaction, whether the real intention of the company was to distribute cash or to capitalise the profits by effecting a distribution of shares. Unless the fund from which the payment is made has been in fact capitalised the payment is income and falls to the liferenter, and a mere statement by the company that the payment is made as a capital payment will not alter its character.[308]

In the less usual case of companies which have no power to increase their capital, if the company accumulates profits and uses them for capital purposes, it may be regarded as having appropriated the profits to capital, so as to make the distribution of them among the shareholders a distribution of capital.[309]

Shares may be received as a result of a demerger. Whether they are to be treated as capital or income depends on how the demerger is structured.[310]

These rules may be overridden by the trustees exercising powers conferred by the trust deed to allocate payments between income and capital.

Burdens affecting liferent—Liferenters bear the annual and ordinary burdens on the subjects, such as taxes, repairs,[311] the premiums for insurance against fire,[312] and interest on bonds charged on the property.[313] They are not answerable for ordinary wear and tear, nor for loss due to accident or vis major. While ordinary repairs are chargeable against revenue, the cost of extraordinary repairs or of rebuilding or of executing work of a permanent nature the benefit of which will at the expiry of the liferent accrue to the fiars is chargeable against capital.[314] Fiars face considerable difficulties if the proper liferenter neglects or damages the property as they cannot instruct repairs themselves.[315] **41.39**

---

[305] This is the English equivalent of liferenter.

[306] *Sproule v Bouch* (1885) L.R. 29 Ch.D. 635 at 653; *Blyth's Trs v Milne* (1905) 7 F. 799; *Howard's Trs v Howard*, 1907 S.C. 1274; *Hill v Permanent Trustee Corp* [1930] A.C. 720.

[307] *Forgie's Trs v Forgie*, 1941 S.C. 188.

[308] *Re Bates* [1928] Ch. 682; *Hill v Permanent Trustee Corp* [1930] A.C. 720.

[309] *Sproule v Bouch* (1885) L.R. 29 Ch.D. 635.

[310] *Smith's Trs v Graham*, 1952 S.L.T. (Notes) 23 (income); *Sinclair v Lee* [1993] Ch. 497 (capital).

[311] *Johnstone v Mackenzie's Trs*, 1912 S.C. (HL) 106; Erskine, II, 9, 61; Bell, *Principles*, s.1061.

[312] *Brown v Soutar & Meacher* (1870) 8 M. 702; *Glover's Trs v Glover*, 1913 S.C. 115.

[313] *Glover's Trs v Glover*, 1913 S.C. 115.

[314] *Shaw's Trs v Bruce*, 1917 S.C. 169; *Preston v Preston's Trs* (1853) 15 D. 271; *Templeton v Ayr Burgh Council*, 1912 1 S.L.T. 421.

[315] *Stronach's Exs v Robertson*, 2002 S.L.T. 1044.

41.40 Alimentary liferents—A provision for the aliment of an individual is from its nature personal and is not assignable or attachable by creditors.[316] People cannot effectually make an alimentary provision in favour of themselves, for it is against the policy of the law that they should have the beneficial enjoyment of their property and yet put it beyond the reach of creditors.[317] Formerly a woman might in her ante-nuptial marriage contract create an alimentary interest in her own favour in property derived from herself or from her father's estate.[318] This alimentary protection, which continued during the subsistence of the marriage but terminated with the dissolution of the marriage unless the deed effectively provided for its continuation thereafter,[319] cannot be created in any deed executed after July 24, 1984.[320] It is not possible to make a right of fee alimentary.[321] So if trustees are directed to hold a subject or fund for, or to make it over to, a beneficiary in fee, any declaration that it is alimentary is of no effect. But a person may confer on another a liferent or annuity on the condition that it is to be alimentary. The proper mode of effecting this is to declare expressly that what is given is alimentary; but equivalents have been admitted as e.g. where the right was declared to be exclusive of the beneficiary's acts and deeds and the diligence of creditors[322] or for maintenance and support.[323] A mere exclusion of the rights of creditors without any restraint on the beneficiary's power to assign is ineffectual.[324] Further, in order to make the right alimentary, there must be a continuing trust under which the trustees are empowered to retain in their hands the subject out of which the liferent or annuity is given.[325]

An alimentary liferent, once accepted,[326] cannot be assigned or discharged nor can the administration of the trustees in whom the liferented subject is vested be terminated by any act or deed of the liferenter.[327] Moreover, if the liferenter acquires the fee of the subjects, the alimentary liferent does not merge in the fee; but both continue to subsist as separate rights. Hence, where a widower, who had, under his marriage contract, an alimentary liferent in his wife's estate, became

---

[316] J. Graham Stewart, *A Treatise on the Law of Diligence* (Edinburgh: W. Green, 1898), p.93. The protection has been held to apply only to the extent of a reasonable provision for the beneficiary, the excess being open to diligence: *Livingstone v Livingstone* (1886) 14 R. 43.

[317] "That were to impose a condition contrary to law, that a man should at the same time be fiar, and yet not have power to affect the fee.": *Creditors of Primrose v Heirs* (1744) Mor.15501 at 15504; *Kennedy v Kennedy's Trs*, 1953 S.C. 60.

[318] *Dempster's Trs v Dempster*, 1949 S.C. 92; *Sturgis's Tr. v Sturgis*, 1951 S.C. 637; *Martin v Bannatyne* (1861) 23 D. 705; see also *Neame v Neame's Trs*, 1956 S.L.T. 57; *Strange, Petitioners*, 1966 S.L.T. 59.

[319] *Dempster's Trs*, 1949 S.C. 92; *Sturgis's Tr.*, 1951 S.C. 637; *Pearson, Petitioner*, 1968 S.C. 8; *Sutherland, Petitioners*, 1968 S.C. 200.

[320] Law Reform (Husband and Wife) (Scotland) Act 1984 s.5(1)(a).

[321] *Wilkie's Trs v Wight's Trs* (1893) 21 R. 199, per Lord Rutherfurd Clark; *Watson's Trs v Watson*, 1913 S.C. 1133; *Miller v Miller's Trs*, 1953 S.L.T. 225.

[322] *Dewar's Trs v Dewar*, 1910 S.C. 730; see also J. Graham Stewart, *A Treatise on the Law of Diligence* (1898), p.95. An interesting and instructive decision is that in *Textile Pensions Trust v Custodian of Enemy Property*, 1947 S.C. 528.

[323] *Arnold's Trs v Graham*, 1927 S.C. 353; followed in *Miller v Miller's Trs*, 1953 S.L.T. 25.

[324] *Douglas, Gardiner & Mill v Mackintosh's Trs*, 1916 S.C. 125.

[325] *Forbes's Trs v Tennant*, 1926 S.C. 294. As to alimentary rights in a question with creditors, see para.48.04, below.

[326] *Douglas-Hamilton v Duke and Duchess of Hamilton's Trs*, 1961 S.C. 205; as to a testamentary provision, see *Ford v Ford*, 1961 S.C. 122.

[327] *White's Trs v White* (1877) 4 R. 786; *Hughes v Edwardes* (1892) 19 R. (HL) 33; *Cuthbert v Cuthbert's Trs*, 1908 S.C. 967; *Coles, Petitioner*, 1951 S.L.T. 308; *Kennedy v Kennedy's Trs*, 1953 S.C. 60. But see para.41.21, above for judicial variation or discharge.

entitled under her will to the fee it was held that he could not compel the marriage contract trustees to denude in his favour.[328] The court may now, if certain conditions are satisfied, authorise an arrangement varying or revoking an alimentary liferent and making new provision in its place.[329]

Transmission and extinction of liferents—The subordinate real right of a proper **41.41** liferent cannot be transmitted to another person. However, the liferenter may assign the right to enjoy the property and its fruits and profits which the assignee will enjoy during the life of the liferenter.[330] A trust liferent being a *jus crediti* can be assigned in the normal way by the liferenter.[331] Alimentary liferents cannot be assigned.[332]

A liferent is extinguished by the liferenter's death, by consolidation with the fee where the liferent and fee come to be vested in the same individual (unless the liferent is alimentary) and by discharge by the liferenter. Where a deed provides for the destination of the fee on the lapse or expiry of a liferent, failure to take the liferent by the person entitled to it may constitute a lapse.[333]

Apportionment of income—Under the common law, while the interest of money **41.42** and the profits of subjects "arising from continual daily labour" (such as "fishings, collieries, saltworks") were held to vest *de die in diem*, annuities, rents and payments connected with land did not vest until the term of payment arrived.[334] But the common law has been altered by statute. The Apportionment Act 1870 (which superseded an Act passed in 1834), provides that all rents, annuities (which include salaries and pensions), dividends and other periodical payments in the nature of income

> "shall, like interest on money lent, be considered as accruing from day to day, and shall be apportionable in respect of time accordingly".

The Act applies equally to the liability to make, as to the right to receive, such payments.[335] The term "dividend" is comprehensively defined to include all payments made out of the revenue of public companies which are divisible amongst the members, whether as dividends, bonuses or otherwise.[336] Thus, when company shares belonging to a liferented estate are sold in the interval between two dividends, the liferenter is entitled to the portion of the price paid in respect of such part of the future dividend as has accrued at the date of the sale, but this portion is to be estimated in accordance with the dividend expected at the date of the sale and not with the dividend ultimately paid.[337] Independently of the statute it has been

---

[328] *Main's Trs v Main*, 1917 S.C. 660; *Howat's Trs v Howat*, 1922 S.C. 506; *Anderson's Trs, Petitioners*, 1932 S.C. 226.

[329] s.1(4); see para. 41.21, above.

[330] Erskine, II, 9, 41; *Scottish Union & National Insurance Co v Smeaton* (1904) 7 F. 174 per Lord McLaren at 178, and per Lord Kinnear at 179.

[331] *Stair Memorial Encyclopaedia*, Vol.13, at para.1646; Wilson and Duncan, *Trusts, Trustees and Executors* (1995), paras 10.38–10.43.

[332] See para.41.40, above.

[333] *Whitelaw's Trs v Whitelaw's Trs*, 1981 S.L.T. 94.

[334] Erskine, II, 9, 64–96; Bell, *Commentaries*, II, 8; see also *Balfour's Exrs v Inland Revenue*, 1909 S.C. 619.

[335] *Learmonth v Sinclair's Trs* (1878) 5 R. 548.

[336] Apportionment Act 1870 s.5.

[337] *McLeod's Trs v McLeod*, 1916 S.C. 604; *Cameron's Factor v Cameron* (1873) 1 R. 21.

held that where a testator directs his trustees to pay to a liferenter the free income of the *universitas* of a mixed estate, this is to be regarded as equivalent to the gift of the income from a fund and accordingly that the right to the income vests *de die in diem*.[338]

The Act does not apply to sums payable under policies of assurance[339] or to any case in which it is expressly stipulated that no apportionment shall take place.[340] Even where there is no express stipulation an intention not to apportion may be inferred. Thus, where a testator bequeathed shares in a company with the declaration that the dividends should be paid to the legatee as received, apportionment was held to be excluded for the benefit of the legatee.[341]

FURTHER READING

Chalmers, J., *Trusts: Cases and Materials* (Edinburgh: W. Green, 2002).

Dobie, W.J., *Manual of the Law of Liferent and Fee* (Edinburgh, 1941).

Gordon, W.M., *Scottish Land Law*, 2nd edn (Edinburgh: W. Green, 1999).

McLaren, J., *The Law of Wills and Succession*, 3rd edn (Edinburgh: Bell and Bradfute, 1894) and Dykes' supplement (Edinburgh: W. Green, 1934).

Norrie, K. and Scobbie, E.M., *Trusts* (Edinburgh: W. Green, 1991).

Reid, K.G.C., "Patrimony not Equity: the Trust in Scotland" (2000) 8 *European Review of Private Law* 427; Gretton, G.L., "Trusts without Equity" (2000) 49 I.C.L.Q. 599.

Reid, K.G.C., "Constitution of Trust", 1986 S.L.T. (News) 177.

Stair Memorial Encyclopaedia, Vols 13 and 24.

Scottish Law Commission: *Breach of Trust* (The Stationery Office, 2003), Scot. Law Com. Discussion Paper No.123; *Apportionment of Trust Receipts and Outgoings* (The Stationery Office, 2003), Scot. Law Com. Discussion Paper No.124; *Trustees and Trust Administration* (The Stationery Office, 2004), Scot. Law Com. Discussion Paper No.126; *Nature and Constitution of Trusts* (The Stationery Office, 2006), Scot. Law Com. Discussion Paper No.133; *Liability of Trustees to Third Parties* (The Stationery Office, 2008), Scot. Law Com. Discussion Paper No.138; *Accumulation of Income and Lifetime of Private Trusts* (The Stationery Office, 2010), Scot. Law Com. Discussion Paper No.142; and *Supplementary and Miscellaneous Issues Relating to Trust Law* (The Stationery Office, 2011), Scot. Law Com. Discussion Paper No.148.

Scottish Law Commission, *Report on Variation and Termination of Trusts* (HMSO, 2007), Scot. Law Com. No.206 (Session 2006–2007).

Wilson, W.A. and Duncan, A.G.M., *Trusts, Trustees and Executors*, 2nd edn (Edinburgh: W. Green, 1995).

---

[338] *Andrew's Trs v Hallett*, 1926 S.C. 1087, and cases there cited.

[339] Apportionment Act 1870 s.6. In *Inland Revenue v Henderson's Exrs*, 1931 S.C. 681, it was held that the Act did not apply in a question as to income tax.

[340] Apportionment Act 1870 s.7. Most modern testamentary trust deeds exclude apportionment.

[341] *Macpherson's Trs v Macpherson*, 1907 S.C. 1067.

SECTION D: JUDICIAL FACTORS

CHAPTER 42

JUDICIAL FACTORS AND SIMILAR APPOINTMENTS

Judicial factors—A judicial factor is an individual appointed to manage and **42.01**
administer an estate where this is necessary to afford protection against loss or
injustice which cannot be prevented by means of the ordinary legal remedies.
Only one factor may be appointed for an estate. The factor must be a natural
person who has no adverse interest. The factor must be domiciled in Scotland,
but exceptionally the Scottish courts will appoint a foreign domiciliary who
prorogates the jurisdiction.[1]

No limit can be set to the circumstances in which a factor may be appointed[2];
but the more familiar instances of such appointments are: (1) The appointment of
a factor on the estate of a solicitor whose liabilities are believed to exceed assets
or where it is likely that there will be a claim made on the guarantee fund.[3] (2) The
appointment of a factor on a trust estate; for example where there is a total
failure of trustees, or there has been misconduct on their part, or where there is a
deadlock in the administration of the trust.[4] (3) The appointment of a factor on the
estate of a deceased person on the application of a creditor or a person interested
in the succession of the deceased.[5] (4) The appointment of a factor on the application of the Accountant of Court to administer property owned by or due to a child,[6]
or to invest money paid to a child by order of the court.[7] (5) The appointment of a
factor on the estate of a charity on the application of the Office of the Scottish
Charity Regulator.[8] (6) The appointment of a factor *loco absentis* on the property
of an absent person which is in need of management or where the interests of third
parties require that the appointment shall be made.[9] (7) The appointment of a
factor on a partnership estate.[10] (8) The appointment of a factor on property which
is the subject of judicial competition, where circumstances render it expedient that
provision should be made in this way for the custody of the estate pending the

---

[1] *Sim v Robertson* (1901) 3F 1022.

[2] *Leslie's J.F.*, 1925 S.C. 464; *Thurso Building Society's J.F. v Robertson*, 2001 S.L.T. 797.

[3] Solicitors (Scotland) Act 1980 s.41. The application is made by the Council of the Law Society
of Scotland and is heard in chambers by the Inner House.

[4] See, e.g. *Stewart v Morrison* (1892) 19 R. 1009. Another solution is the appointment of new or
additional trustees.

[5] Judicial Factors (Scotland) Act 1889 s.11A (added by the Bankruptcy (Scotland) Act 1985
s.75(1), Sch.7 para.4); Act of Sederunt (Judicial Factors Rules) 1992 (SI 1992/272) Pt II.

[6] Children (Scotland) Act 1995 s.11(2)(g). There cannot now be appointment of a factor *loco
tutoris*: Age of Legal Capacity (Scotland) Act 1991 s.5(4).

[7] Children (Scotland) Act 1995 s.13(2)(a). A personal injury trust may be used instead.

[8] Charities and Trustee Investment (Scotland) Act 2005 s.34.

[9] Stair, IV, 1, 28; Bell, *Principles*, s.2120; *Peterson & Co* (1851) 13 D. 951. See also Presumption
of Death (Scotland) Act 1977 s.2(2)(c), judicial factor on estate of person presumed dead.

[10] *Dickie v Mitchell* (1874) 1 R. 1030; *Carabine v Carabine*, 1949 S.C. 521. For appointment on the
estate of a company, see *Fraser, Petitioner*, 1971 S.L.T. 146; see also *Weir v Rees*, 1991 S.L.T. 345.

issue of litigation. Factors may also be appointed on estates held *pro indiviso* in certain cases where the co-proprietors are unable to agree in regard to its administration,[11] and, on the application of the liferenter and fiduciary fiar, where the fee of the estate has been conveyed to a person in liferent and in fee to persons who are, when the conveyance comes into operation, unborn or incapable of ascertainment.[12] The management of the property and personal welfare of a mentally incapable adult is now undertaken by a guardian appointed under the Adults with Incapacity (Scotland) Act 2000.

A judicial factor ad interim may be appointed where there is an urgent need to safeguard and manage property. The application can be made before the service of the petition for a factor's appointment.[13]

In the Court of Session most petitions for the appointment of judicial factors are heard in the Outer House.[14] The sheriff has concurrent power to appoint most types of judicial factors,[15] but petitions for appointments on the estates of solicitors and charities are reserved to the Court of Session. The petition generally has to be made by a person with a direct interest in the estate.[16]

42.02 Sequestration of estate—As an alternative to appointing a judicial factor, the court may sequestrate the estate. Sequestration is defined by Bell[17] as

> "a judicial assumption by the court of the possession of property which is in competition before it, that it may be placed in the custody of a neutral person, accountable in court for his management, and sufficiently responsible, in order to be preserved and properly managed, for the benefit of those who shall be preferred in the competition".

It may be resorted to in cases where the court deems it necessary that the person in possession of property shall be superseded as regards its custody and management. It can also be used as a method of compelling obedience to a court order.[18]

42.03 Administrators—An administrator can be appointed under: the Criminal Justice (Scotland) Act 1987 over realisable property which is the subject of a restraint order or a confiscation order[19]; the Proceeds of Crime (Scotland) Act 1995 on the application of the prosecutor to realise the property over which an order (confiscation order, restraint order or suspended forfeiture order) has been made[20]; the Proceeds of Crime Act 2002 for the appointment of management administrators where a restraint order has been made[21]; and the Terrorism Act 2000 to take

---

[11] *Bailey v Scott* (1860) 22 D. 1105; *Allan* (1898) 36 S.L.R. 3; (1898) 6 S.L.T. 152.

[12] Trusts (Scotland) Act 1921 s.8(2); *Napier v Napiers*, 1963 S.L.T. 143; see also *Gibson*, 1967 S.L.T. 150.

[13] *McGuiness v Black*, 1990 S.C. 21.

[14] Act of Sederunt (Rules of the Court of Session 1994) 1994 (SI 1994/1443) ("RCS") 14.2, but see fn.2 above.

[15] Judicial Factors (Scotland) Act 1880 s.4 (amended by the Law Reform (Miscellaneous Provisions) (Scotland) Act 1980 s.14(1)(b)); Act of Sederunt (Judicial Factors Rules) 1992 (SI 1992/272) (as amended).

[16] D. Addison, *Judicial Factors* (Edinburgh: W. Green, 1995), para.22.1.

[17] *Commentaries*, II, 244.

[18] *Edgar v Fisher's Trs* (1893) 21 R. 59 and (1894) 21 R. 1076; sequestration awarded for failure to hand over a child.

[19] Criminal Justice (Scotland) Act 1987 s.13, as amended by the Criminal Justice (Scotland) Act 1995.

[20] Proceeds of Crime (Scotland) Act 1995 Sch.1.

[21] Proceeds of Crime Act 2002 s.125.

possession and realise forfeited property. Administrators are dealt with by the Accountant of Court in much the same way as judicial factors.[22]

Duties of factors—A judicial factor is an officer of court, not subject to the **42.04** control of parties,[23] whose duties are largely regulated by statutes and Acts of Sederunt.[24] Judicial factors owe fiduciary duties to those interested in the estate. They must therefore avoid any conflict between their interests as factors and their personal interests.[25] A transaction in breach of fiduciary duty is reducible by those with an interest in the estate and may ground a claim of damages, and any personal profits may have to be accounted for to the estate. The factor must find caution for the due performance of the office, and must within 6 months thereafter lodge with the Accountant of Court a rental of the lands and an inventory of the moveable property belonging to the estate. The factor administers the estate under the superintendence of the Accountant, who may make such orders as seem proper,[26] and with whom the factor must lodge an annual report and accounts.[27] Factors are remunerated by way of commission fixed by the Accountant on the basis of the work they have done during the year. Apart from this commission, factors may claim only outlays against the estate.[28] The Accountant of Court also provides assistance and advice to factors.[29]

Judicial factors must not hold more than £500 in cash or in a non-interest bearing account for more than 10 days.[30] The money is to be placed in an interest bearing account. Factors are under a duty to invest unless the estate is to be disposed of shortly. They may make any kind of investment and buy heritable property for investment or otherwise provided it is not at variance with the terms and purposes of the judicial factory. The factor has to obtain and consider proper advice and bear in mind the need to diversify investments and whether the investment is suitable.[31] Finally, the Accountant of Court has to consent to the factor's proposed investments.[32]

Powers of factors—Factors are appointed with the "usual powers", i.e. the power **42.05** to do ordinary acts of management. By virtue of the definitions of "trustee" and "judicial factor" in the Trusts (Scotland) Act 1921,[33] as amended by the Trusts (Scotland) Act 1961,[34] the provisions of these Acts extend to any person holding a judicial appointment as a factor on another person's estate.[35] But judicial factors

---

[22] Addison, *Judicial Factors* (1995), paras 48.1–48.3.

[23] *McCulloch v McCulloch*, 1953 S.C. 189.

[24] Act of Sederunt, February 13, 1730; Judicial Factors Act 1849 (Pupils Protection Act); Judicial Factors (Scotland) Act 1880; Judicial Factors (Scotland) 1889; Trusts (Scotland) Act 1921; Trusts (Scotland) Act 1961; Charities and Trustee Investment (Scotland) Act 2005; RCS Ch.61; Act of Sederunt (Appointment of Judicial Factors) 1967.

[25] *Lord Gray* (1856) 19 D. 1; *Stair Memorial Encyclopaedia*, Vol.24, para.246.

[26] Judicial Factors Act 1849 ss.19 and 20. The Accountant will report failure to obtemper such orders to the court which appointed the factor.

[27] Interim factors must report monthly.

[28] *Sleigh v Sleigh's J.F.*, 1908 S.C. 1112.

[29] Addison, *Judicial Factors* (1995), para.1.4.

[30] Judicial Factors Act 1849 s.5.

[31] Trusts (Scotland) Act 1921 ss.4(1)(ea), (eb) and 4A added by the Charities and Trustee Investment (Scotland) Act 2005 s.93.

[32] Judicial Factors Act 1849 s.13.

[33] Trusts (Scotland) Act 1921 s.2.

[34] Trusts (Scotland) Act 1921 s.4.

[35] Trusts (Scotland) Act 1921 ss.2, 4, 5; Trusts (Scotland) Act 1961 ss.2, 4.

may exercise the general powers conferred on trustees by s.4 of the 1921 Act only where such an exercise would not be at variance with the terms or purposes of the judicial factory. Where the factor desires to do something which would be at variance with those terms or purposes, an application under s.5 may be made to the court for authority to exercise that power.[36] Special powers may also be sought under s.7 of the Judicial Factors Act 1849.[37] The *nobile officium* is available to authorise retrospectively acts that were outwith the factor's powers.[38] The fact that factors are included in the definition of trustees for the purposes of the 1921 and 1961 Acts does not mean that they are trustees generally.[39] Thus factors are, unlike trustees, the managers rather than the owners of the estate under their charge. However, they are able to complete title in their own name to all or some of the assets of the estate.[40]

The powers of a judicial factor depend on the duties which in turn depend on the purpose of the appointment. In many cases the function of a judicial factor is to conserve and manage the estate, and this is particularly true for factors appointed ad interim. But even this does not preclude active steps being taken to preserve value or prevent loss. Some factors on the other hand are appointed to distribute the estate, e.g. a factor on a deceased bankrupt's estate. It may therefore not be easy to decide whether the exercise of a particular power, e.g. to sell or purchase heritage, would be at variance with the appointment. Each case must be decided on its own facts, and in a case of doubt a petition for authority or special powers would be justified.[41] In the case of the powers specified in s.2(1) of the Trusts (Scotland) Act 1961 (selling property, leasing property, borrowing money, granting security over the estate, making investments and buying heritable property) the factor can apply to the Accountant of Court for consent to an act which might be at variance with the appointment.[42] The Accountant can grant consent, unless the factor is expressly prohibited from doing the act by the terms of the appointment, if it appears to be in the best interests of the owner of the factory estate and no objections were made by those interested in the estate. The Accountant can, in limited circumstances, also authorise encroachment upon capital.[43] Section 2 of the 1961 Act, which guarantees the validity of any title acquired by a person who enters into a transaction with trustees purporting to act under s.4 of the 1921 Act, extends to judicial factors. A purchaser of heritage from a factor therefore need not enquire whether or not the sale is at variance with the terms or purposes of the judicial factory.[44]

---

[36] *Tennent's J.F. v Tennent (No.1)*, 1954 S.C. 215.

[37] The factor first applies to the Accountant who issues a report which the factor then lodges with the application to the court, RCS r.61.15.

[38] *Stair Memorial Encyclopaedia*, Vol.24, para.263; *Gilray* (1876) 3 R. 619.

[39] *Inland Revenue v McMillan's C.B.*, 1956 S.C. 142.

[40] Titles to Land Consolidation (Scotland) Act 1868 s.24, Trusts (Scotland) Act 1921 s.21 and Conveyancing Amendment (Scotland) Act 1938 s.1. There is also s.13 of the Judicial Factors (Scotland) Act 1889 but this may simply give title to manage.

[41] *Cunningham's Tutrix*, 1949 S.C. 275; *Bristow*, 1965 S.L.T. 225; see also *Murray's J.F. v Thomas Murray & Sons (Ice Merchants) Ltd*, 1992 S.L.T. 824 at 830 and 835I–836B, per Lord Justice-Clerk Ross and Lord Cullen respectively.

[42] Trusts (Scotland) Act 1961 s.2(3)–(6) (added by Law Reform (Miscellaneous Provisions) (Scotland) Act 1980 s.8).

[43] *Broadfoot's C.B., Noter*, 1989 S.L.T. 566.

[44] See further, para.41.09, above.

Liability of factor—Judicial factors must act with skill, care and diligence and **42.06** will be liable for losses arising from failure so to act.[45] They are also liable if they act outwith their powers or in breach of their fiduciary duties to those interested in the estate. No personal liability for debts incurred in the course of administration will be incurred unless the factor committed a breach of duty.[46] A factor may also be fined or ordered to forfeit any commission by the court.[47]

Acts of factor—The voluntary acts of a judicial factor in the administration of the **42.07** estate, as, for example, the sale of heritage, do not affect the rights of succession to the estate, unless the act was a necessary one.[48] In the case of a trust estate, the judicial factor takes the place of the trustees and administers the estate in accordance with the provisions of the trust[49] and has no higher powers than those allowed by the truster to the trustees.[50] The factor may do what the truster has directed shall be done,[51] and may even in certain cases exercise discretionary powers conferred on the trustees.[52]

Resignation, removal and discharge—A judicial factor cannot resign. The **42.08** factor has to petition the court for the recall of the appointment and to be discharged and for another factor to be appointed.[53] A judicial factor who is unsatisfactory may be replaced.[54] At the conclusion of the administration, the judicial factor may obtain a discharge on presenting a petition for that purpose to the court.[55] There is an alternative administrative procedure available where the factory has terminated by its recall or the death or coming of age of the owner of the estate or by reason of the exhaustion of the estate. In these circumstances the factor can be discharged by obtaining a certificate from the Accountant of Court.[56] The Accountant can also simply write off the factory if the factor takes no steps.[57]

FURTHER READING

Addison, D., *Judicial Factors* (Edinburgh: W. Green, 1995).
Irons, C., *Law and Practice in Scotland Relative to Judicial Factors* (Edinburgh: W. Green, 1908).

---

[45] *Annan's C.B. v Annan* (1898) 25 R. (HL) 23.

[46] *Scottish Brewers Ltd v J. Douglas Pearson & Co*, 1996 S.L.T. (Sh. Ct) 50.

[47] Judicial Factors Act 1849 s.6.

[48] *Moncrieff v Miln* (1856) 18 D. 1286; *Macfarlane v Greig* (1895) 22 R. 405; *Macqueen v Tod* (1899) 1 F. 1069; *McAdam's Exr v Souters* (1904) 7 F. 179; *Macfarlane's Trs v Macfarlane*, 1910 S.C. 325.

[49] *Orr Ewing v Orr Ewing's Trs* (1884) 11 R. 600 at 627, per Lord President Inglis; *Browning's Factor* (1905) 7 F. 1037, per Lord Johnston.

[50] A factor does not have the powers of investment conferred on the trustees; *Carmichael's J.F., Noter*, 1971 S.C. 295. This is of little importance as factors have, since 2006, wide statutory powers of investment, see para.43.04 above.

[51] *Stirling's J.F.*, 1917 1 S.L.T. 165.

[52] *Leith's J.F. v Leith*, 1957 S.C. 307.

[53] *Stair Memorial Encyclopaedia*, Vol.24, para.267; *Halliday's C.B.*, 1912 S.C. 509.

[54] Judicial Factors Act 1849 s.6.

[55] Judicial Factors Act 1849 s.34; *Campbell v Grant* (1870) 8 M. 988; for procedure, see *Divers' J.F.*, 1966 S.L.T. 181; RCS r.61.33.

[56] Judicial Factors Act 1849 s.34A (inserted by Law Reform (Miscellaneous Provisions) (Scotland) Act 1990 s.67); RCS rr.61.31(1)–61.32.

[57] Addison, *Judicial Factors* (1995), para.29.2.

Scottish Law Commission, *Judicial Factors* (The Stationery Office, 2010), Scot. Law Com. Discussion Paper No.146.

Thoms on Judicial Factors, edited by Fraser, H.G.E., 2nd edn (Edinburgh: Bell and Bradfute, 1881).

Walker, N.M.L., *Judicial Factors* (Edinburgh: W. Green, 1974).

PART IV

PERSONS

CHAPTER 43

CAPACITY

Introductory—Every person who has attained the age of legal capacity and is **43.01** able to manage his affairs has a natural right to do so, and before he can be deprived of that right some procedure is necessary for the purpose of establishing that he is not in a condition properly to exercise it. This chapter considers the legal capacity of those who have not attained the age of majority and those who are adult, but whose mental capacity is in some way impeded. A statutory framework of intervention orders and guardianship has been enacted to cover all situations where appointment of another person to manage the affairs of those under mental disability is required. Most of the relevant provisions[1] of the Adults with Incapacity (Scotland) Act 2000 came into force on April 1, 2002 and the significant provisions relative to appointments under that legislation are outlined below. Reference is also made to the Mental Health (Care and Treatment) Act 2003 which deals with the use of compulsory measures in mental health care. While the system of state intervention in cases of mental illness is essentially outwith the scope of this work, limited key provisions of the legislation merit notice as outlined.

Legal capacity of children—The age of majority in Scots law is 18.[2] Formerly, a **43.02** two-tier system regulated the status and capacity of those persons under the age of 18. The status of pupillarity applied to girls until they attained the age of 12, when they became minors. In boys, pupillarity lasted until the age of 14. Substantial reform of the law was, however, effected by the Age of Legal Capacity (Scotland) Act 1991 (the "1991 Act").[3] The status of minority has not been abolished; the effect of existing rules of law relating to minors and pupils which are not inconsistent with the provisions of the Act is preserved.[4] The introduction of the rules governing capacity, however, has rendered the distinction of little practical importance.

By s.1(1) of the 1991 Act, a general rule is provided, that persons under the age of 16 have no legal capacity to enter into any transaction whereas persons of 16 or over have legal capacity to enter into any transaction. Transaction is defined in s.9 of the Act as any transaction having legal effect, and includes unilateral transactions, the exercise of testamentary capacity or of a power of appointment, the giving of any consent having legal effect and the taking of any step in civil proceedings. Any reference in an existing enactment to pupils or to persons under legal disability by reason of age is to be construed as a reference to a person under 16,[5] and any

---

[1] The provisions for continuing powers of attorney and welfare powers of attorney came into force on April 1, 2001. See para.43.08, below.

[2] Age of Majority (Scotland) Act 1969.

[3] See D. Nichols, "Can they or can't they? Children and the Age of Legal Capacity (Scotland) Act 1991", 1991 S.L.T. (News) 395 and A. Barr and L. Edwards, "Age of Legal Capacity: Further Pitfalls (I)" and "Age of Legal Capacity: Further Pitfalls", 1992 S.L.T. (News) 77 and 91.

[4] As a consequence of the Age of Legal Capacity (Scotland) Act 1991 (the "1991 Act") s.1(4).

[5] 1991 Act s.1(2).

reference in any rule of law, enactment or document to the tutor or tutory of a pupil child is to be construed as a reference to the guardian or guardianship of a person under 16.[6] The Act does not affect transactions entered into before the commencement of the Act on September 25, 1991,[7] nor the delictual or criminal responsibility of any person.[8] Statutory age limits for particular purposes are unaffected,[9] as is the capacity of persons under 16 to receive or hold any right, title or interest.[10] Existing rules of law or practice permitting the bringing or defending of any civil proceedings, or taking steps therein, in the name of persons under 16 and relating to the appointment of curators ad litem and curators bonis, are unaffected.[11]

The general rule concerning capacity suffers various important exceptions, most of which are contained in s.2 of the Act; transactions by persons under 16 not falling within the exceptions are void.[12] Validity is conferred on a transaction entered into by a person under 16 if it is of a type commonly entered into by a person of his age and circumstances, and the terms are not unreasonable.[13] Persons of 12 or over are to have testamentary capacity[14] and the consent of a person of 12 or over to an adoption order or to an order freeing him for adoption is required.[15] Where he appears to a qualified medical practitioner to have sufficient understanding of what is involved, a person under 16 can consent to medical and similar procedures or treatment.[16] Where the child has such capacity to consent, the parents' or guardians' capacity to consent on his behalf is negated and the child's consent may not be overruled by them.[17] Further, those under 16 have legal capacity to instruct a solicitor and to sue or defend any civil matter, where they have a general understanding of what it means to do so, with a presumption that a person 12 years of age or more is of sufficient age and maturity to have such understanding.[18] They may, however, consent to be represented by any person who would have been their legal representative had they lacked such capacity.[19] A child of sufficient maturity may seek to enter a process in which he has an interest, notwithstanding that a curator ad litem has also been appointed, but whether he is permitted such entry is at the discretion of the first instance judge.[20] At common law a child's capacity to give evidence in court proceedings was not the subject of a statutory rule and depended on the individual's ability to understand the duty to give a truthful account.[21] Hearsay evidence of statements made by children was admissible without any need to establish that the child, if called, would be a

---

[6] 1991 Act s.5(1).

[7] 1991 Act s.1(3)(a).

[8] 1991 Act s.1(3)(c).

[9] 1991 Act s.1(3)(d). Examples of such age limits include obtaining a provisional driving licence at age 17 (Road Traffic Act 1988 s.101) and voting at age 18 (Representation of the People Act 1983 s.1(1)(c)).

[10] 1991 Act s.1(3)(e).

[11] 1991 Act s.1(3)(f), as amended by the Children (Scotland) Act 1995. For appointments of curators ad litem see para.43.05, below.

[12] 1991 Act s.2(5).

[13] 1991 Act s.2(1).

[14] 1991 Act s.2(2).

[15] 1991 Act s.2(3); for adoption, see paras 44.49–44.50, below.

[16] 1991 Act s.2(4).

[17] 1991 Act s.15(5) and see *Houston, Applicant*, 1996 S.C.L.R. 943.

[18] 1991 Act s.2(4A) and (4B), inserted by the Children (Scotland) Act 1995 s.105(4) and Sch.4 para.53(3).

[19] Children (Scotland) Act 1995 s.15(6).

[20] See *B v B* [2011] Fam. L.R. 141.

[21] *Rees v Lowe* [1989] S.C.C.R. 664, followed in *Kelly v Docherty*, 1991 S.L.T. 419.

competent witness.[22] That rule is abolished by the provisions of the Vulnerable Witnesses (Scotland) Act 2004.[23] A parent who is under the age of 16 may register his child's birth and any change to his own name.[24]

Some protection against transactions to their detriment is afforded to persons of 16 or 17; until they reach the age of 21 they may apply to court to have a prejudicial transaction set aside.[25] A transaction is prejudicial if an adult exercising reasonable prudence would not have entered into it in the circumstances of the young person at the time, and it has caused or is likely to cause substantial prejudice to the young person.[26] In one application a contributor to a television documentary who was 17 at the time of filming succeeded in persuading a judge that interim interdict was appropriate to prohibit the programme being broadcast pending her claim to have it set aside on grounds that she had been intoxicated when consent was given, that she was dyslexic and had not been in receipt of legal advice when she signed an agreement consenting to her participation.[27] Certain types of transaction are excluded from this provision. Testamentary acts, consent to an adoption order or to medical treatment, initiating, defending or taking steps in civil proceedings, transactions entered into in the course of the young person's trade or business, or induced by his fraudulent misrepresentation as to his age or other material fact, and transactions ratified by the young person or the court cannot be set aside.[28] There are no statutory provisions defining ratification by the young person, but before the right to apply to have the transaction set aside is excluded he must have been aware of his right so to apply.[29] Ratification by the court is available only in respect of proposed transactions by persons of 16 or 17 and will not be granted if it appears that an adult exercising reasonable prudence in the circumstances of the young person would not enter into the transaction.[30] Ratification must be sought in the sheriff court and the sheriff's decision is final.[31]

The Act also introduced a statutory rule for determining age; a person now attains a particular age at the beginning of the relevant anniversary of his birth.[32] In non-leap years, the relevant anniversary for a person born on February 29 is March 1.[33]

Adult capacity to contract—In contrast to adults with full capacity, an insane person has no power to contract and contracts into which he enters are void.[34] If necessaries are sold and delivered to him, he must pay a reasonable price for them.[35] Generally his contracts are void, even although the other party may not have known that he was dealing with a person of unsound mind.[36] But continuing contracts, into which a party has entered while he was sane, are not necessarily

43.03

---

[22] *T v T*, 2000 S.L.T. 1442.

[23] See para.43.04, below.

[24] Registration of Births, Deaths and Marriages (Scotland) Act 1965 ss.14 and 18 (as amended by the Children (Scotland) Act 1995 s.90).

[25] 1991 Act s.3(1).

[26] 1991 Act s.3(2).

[27] *X v British Broadcasting Corporation*, 2005 S.L.T. 796.

[28] 1991 Act s.3(3).

[29] 1991 Act s.3(3)(h).

[30] 1991 Act s.4(1) and (2).

[31] 1991 Act s.4(3).

[32] 1991 Act s.6(1).

[33] 1991 Act s.6(2).

[34] Stair, I, 10, 3; Erskine, III, 1, 16; *Gall v Bird* (1855) 17 D. 1027.

[35] Sale of Goods Act 1979 s.3.

[36] *John Loudon & Co v Elder's C.B.*, 1923 S.L.T. 226.

avoided by his supervening insanity. Thus partnership is not dissolved merely by the insanity of a partner, though that is a ground on which its dissolution may be decreed by the court.[37] A factory and commission or power of attorney does not fall by virtue of the supervening insanity of the granter.[38] Drunkenness is not a ground for the avoidance of a contract unless it reaches a stage where the party no longer knows what he is doing and can give no true consent. Alcoholic overindulgence short of intoxication might render a person facile and present an opportunity to have it reduced on the ground of facility and circumvention.[39] An obligation undertaken in a drunken condition is voidable, provided that the party takes steps to avoid as soon as he recovers his senses and knows what he has done.[40] Some special rules apply to the ability of foreign nationals to contract here. Under the Rome I Regulation, a contract made during a period of residence in Scotland cannot be set aside on the ground that one of the parties was an alien who lacked contractual capacity under his or her own legal system, unless it is proved that the other party knew of the incapacity or was negligently unaware thereof.[41] The contractual capacity of aliens who are party to contracts to which the Rome I Regulation does not apply is subject to the proper law of the contract.[42] The only natural persons qualified to own a British ship, other than a fishing vessel, are[43]: British citizens, or nationals of an EU Member State; British Dependent Territories citizens; British Overseas citizens; British subjects under the British Nationality Act 1981; British Nationals (Overseas) citizens[44]; and citizens of the Republic of Ireland. In addition, a British ship may be owned by a company incorporated in the EU; or by a company incorporated in a British possession and having its principal place of business in Britain; or by a European Economic Interest Grouping.[45] Ownership of fishing vessels registered in the UK by nationals of any EU Member State is now competent.[46]

During wartime, any contract with an alien enemy is illegal[47] and an offence unless a licence from the Crown has been obtained.[48] There is a distinction to be observed between war and armed hostilities[49]: it is only when a state of war exists that the capacity of an alien may be affected.[50] Status as an alien enemy is determined, not by nationality or allegiance, but by voluntary residence in either an enemy state or enemy-occupied territory.[51] The degree of control exercised by

---

[37] Partnership Act 1890 s.35.

[38] Law Reform (Miscellaneous Provisions) (Scotland) Act 1990 s.71(1).

[39] *Jackson v Pollock* (1900) 8 S.L.T. 267.

[40] *Pollok v Burns* (1875) 2 R. 497.

[41] Regulation (EC) No. 593/2008 of the European Parliament and of the Council of 17 June 2008 on the law applicable to contractual obligations (Rome I) art.13.

[42] P. Beaumont and P. McEleavy, *Anton's Private International Law*, 3rd edn (Edinburgh: W. Green, 2011), pp.490–491. See art.1(2) of the Rome I Regulation for contracts excluded from its ambit.

[43] Merchant Shipping Act 1995 s.10, and Merchant Shipping (Registration of Ships) Regulations 1993 (SI 1993/3138) reg.7.

[44] Under the Hong Kong (British Nationality) Order 1986 (SI 1986/948).

[45] Merchant Shipping (Registration of Ships) Regulations 1993 (SI 1993/3138) reg.7.

[46] Merchant Shipping (Registration of Ships) Regulations 1993 regs 12–17. Note also *R. v Secretary of State for Transport, Ex p. Factortame Ltd* [1991] 1 A.C. 603.

[47] Trading with the Enemy Act 1939, as amended by the Emergency Laws (Miscellaneous Provisions) Act 1953 s.2.

[48] The procedure for obtaining a licence is found in A. McNair and A. Watts, *The Legal Effects of War*, 4th edn (Cambridge: Cambridge University Press, 1966), p.108.

[49] *Blomart v Roxburgh* (1664) Mor.16091.

[50] Armed hostilities may, however, amount to frustration of contract.

[51] *Janson v Driefontein Mines* [1902] A.C. 484; *Sovfracht (V/O) v Gebr. Van Udens Scheepvaart en Agentuur Maatschappij* [1943] A.C. 203.

occupying forces over the occupied territory is relevant to the status of residents there.[52] A British prisoner of war held in enemy territory is not an alien enemy.[53] A national of an enemy or enemy-occupied state residing in Scotland does not lose the power to contract,[54] nor his right to resort to the Scottish courts.[55]

Capacity to give evidence—The common law relative to capacity of children **43.04** and adults with restricted capacity to give evidence has been replaced by the provisions of the Vulnerable Witnesses (Scotland) Act 2004.[56] A programme of implementation of the legislation, which covers both criminal and civil litigation commenced in 2005 and was completed in 2008.[57] At common law a person with a mental disorder was presumed to be a competent witness, unless there was evidence to the contrary. Similarly, a child's capacity depended upon the individual's capacity to understand the duty to give a truthful account. The 2004 Act has abolished the competency test for all witnesses[58] and provides that all courts are to take steps to identify those witnesses who are vulnerable and consider what provision should be made for them. All children under the age of 16 at the date of commencement of the proceedings are included in the definition of vulnerable witnesses.[59] Where any child is to give evidence there is a requirement that the court make an order, prior to the hearing at which the child is to give evidence, either authorising or refusing the use of "special measures", which include the taking of the evidence by a Commissioner or through a live television link, placing a screen in the courtroom or enlisting a supporter for the witness.[60] Adult witnesses are assumed to be capable of giving evidence without such special measures unless there is a significant risk that mental disorder or fear and distress in connection with giving evidence in the proceedings will affect the quality of the person's evidence to the Court.[61] In identifying whether a witness is vulnerable for this purpose the court must take into account the nature of the proceedings and of the evidence, the relationship between the witness and any party to the case, the witnesses' age and maturity, their social and cultural background, their domestic and employment circumstances and any physical disability.[62] Where a party perceives a witness as vulnerable, he must make an application for special measures prior to the commencement of the diet of proof. In determining the application, the court will have regard to the possible effect on the witness of being required to give evidence without special measures and consider whether the witness is likely to be able to give evidence with such measures in place.[63]

---

[52] *Sovfracht v Van Udens* [1943] A.C. 203; *Re Anglo-International Bank* [1943] 1 Ch. 233.

[53] *Vandyke v Adams* [1942] Ch. 155.

[54] *Schulze Gow & Co v Bank of Scotland*, 1914 2 S.L.T. 455.

[55] *Schulze*, 1917 S.C. 400; *Weiss v Weiss*, 1940 S.L.T. 447.

[56] Vulnerable Witnesses (Scotland) Act 2004 (asp 3) (the "2004 Act").

[57] A total of seven Commencement Orders was required. See in particular the Vulnerable Witnesses (Scotland) Act 2004 (Commencement) Order 2005 (SSI 2005/168) and the Vulnerable Witnesses (Scotland) Act 2004 (Commencement No.5, Savings and Transitional Provisions) Order 2007 (SSI 2007/329). The other instruments are SSI 2005/590, SSI 2006/59, SSI 2007/101, SSI 2007/447 and SSI 2008/57.

[58] 2004 Act s.24, which specifically prohibits taking steps, prior to the witness giving evidence, to establish the level of his understanding or ability to tell the truth.

[59] 2004 Act s.11(1)(a) and (3).

[60] 2004 Act ss.12(3), 18 and 22.

[61] 2004 Act s.11(1)(b). Section 11(4) defines quality of evidence as including completeness, coherence and accuracy.

[62] 2004 Act s.11(2).

[63] 2004 Act s.12(7).

A separate hearing on the application may be required.[64] Account must be taken of the views of the witness and regard given to their best interests.[65] There is no provision for appealing the court's decision on special measures,[66] but there are procedures for review of any arrangements made.[67] The needs of the witness must be kept under review during the proceedings and any special measures may be cancelled if (i) the witness chooses, appropriately, to give evidence without the measures, or (ii) the use or continued use of the measures would significantly risk prejudicing the fairness of the proceedings or the interests of justice where such prejudice significantly outweighs the possible prejudice to the interests of the vulnerable witness.[68]

43.05 Curators ad litem—A curator ad litem is a guardian appointed as an officer of the court to safeguard the interests of a party lacking full capacity in a litigation. While a child under 16 may have legal capacity to initiate and defend civil proceedings on his own behalf,[69] a curator ad litem may be appointed to him where appropriate.[70] Where an action involving a claim on behalf of a child under 16 has been raised in the name of a parent, a curator ad litem may be appointed if it is apparent that there is a conflict of interest between the parent and child, or if such an appointment is necessary to secure a determination of the matters in issue.[71] In such cases the curator will often investigate issues of fact and report to the court. The UK Supreme Court has now clarified that it will be inappropriate for a curator ad litem to conduct a proof in person where it concerns matters in which he has been personally involved and in relation to which he might require to give evidence. The curator ad litem is the *domins litis* and as such will often require legal advice and to instruct legal representation.[72] Curators ad litem may be appointed to adults under legal disability, such as insane persons, in certain family actions.[73] In other cases, the proper course is to apply for a guardianship order.[74] An action against a person who lacks legal capacity and has a guardian should be brought against the guardian; if the defender has no guardian, the action may be raised against the defender and then sisted until one is appointed. An action raised in the name of a person who lacks sufficient mental capacity is incompetent, and the incompetency cannot be cured by the appointment of a curator ad litem during the action.[75] In all cases brought under the Adults with Incapacity (Scotland) Act 2000, the sheriff must consider whether it is necessary to appoint a safeguarder to represent the interests of the adult concerned, but a curator ad litem may be appointed in place of or in addition to such a safeguarder,

---

[64] See Act of Sederunt (Rules of the Court of Session 1994) (SI 1994/1443) ("RCS") r.35A.5; Act of Sederunt (Sheriff Court Ordinary Cause Rules) (SI 1993/1956) ("OCR") r.45.5. Chapter 35A RCS sets out all the procedural rules applying to vulnerable witness applications in the Court of Session. For the sheriff court these are contained in OCR Ch.45.

[65] 2004 Act s.15.

[66] 2004 Act s.12(6).

[67] RCS rr.35A.6–8; OCR rr.45.6–45.8.

[68] 2004 Act s.13.

[69] See the Age of Legal Capacity (Scotland) Act 1991 s.2(4A) and (4B)—a child aged 12 or over is presumed to have such capacity, but a younger child may be sufficiently mature to understand the proceedings and therefore to give instructions by himself.

[70] This existing practice is preserved by the 1991 Act s.1(3)(f)(ii). See *Ward v Walker*, 1920 S.C. 80.

[71] *Brianchon v Occidental Petroleum (Caledonia) Ltd*, 1990 S.L.T. 322.

[72] *NJDB v JEG* [2012] UKSC 21.

[73] Divorce (Scotland) Act 1976 s.11. See also RCS r.49.17 and OCR r.33.

[74] See para.43.12, below.

[75] *McGaughey v Livingstone*, 1992 S.L.T. 386.

or a second safeguarder may be appointed to advise specifically on the adult's views on the application.[76] The Mental Health Tribunal for Scotland also has powers to appoint curators ad litem if (i) a party to the proceedings lacks the capacity to instruct a legal representative, (ii) the tribunal has withheld documents from the party and he does not have a legal representative, or (iii) if the party is excluded from the hearing and does not have a legal representative.[77] In the absence of a statutory right of appeal, it would in principle be open to such a curator ad litem to bring proceedings for judicial review to challenge an unlawful, unfair or unreasonable decision of the Tribunal.[78]

Tutors dative and curators bonis appointments—Prior to the implementation **43.06** of the Adults with Incapacity (Scotland) Act 2000 it remained competent to seek the appointment of any suitable person as tutor dative to a person under mental disability[79] and appointments made prior to April 2002 remain effective but as guardianship orders under the new legislation.[80] Similarly, fresh petitions for appointment of a curator bonis to manage the financial affairs of an incapacitated adult are no longer competent and existing appointments are treated as guardianship orders.

Adults with Incapacity (Scotland) Act 2000—The Adults with Incapacity **43.07** (Scotland) Act 2000 (the "2000 Act"),[81] as now amended by the Adult Support and Protection (Scotland) Act 2007 (the "2007 Act"),[82] has replaced all of the common law procedures for applications to take decisions on the part of an adult with mental illness or learning disability. An adult for this purpose is anyone who has attained the age of 16 years. Part I of the Act lays down four principles which govern decision making under the legislation. These are: (1) that there shall be no intervention in the affairs of an adult[83] unless it is necessary and for his benefit[84]; (2) where intervention is to be made, the least restrictive option in relation to the freedom of the adult, consistent with the purpose of the intervention, shall be taken[85]; (3) the wishes of the adult appropriately ascertained, and the view of others closely related to or otherwise involved with, the adult concerned, shall be taken into account so far as it is reasonable and practicable to do so[86]; and (4) those appointed under the Act to intervene in the affairs of an adult shall encourage

---

[76] Adults with Incapacity (Scotland) Act 2000 s.3(4) and (5) and see para.43.12, below.

[77] Mental Health Tribunal for Scotland (Practice and Procedure) Rules 2005 (SSI 2005/420) rr.47(9), 68(8) and 69(6). See also para.43.16, below.

[78] *Black v The Mental Health Tribunal for Scotland* [2011] CSIH 83.

[79] H.L. MacQueen et al (eds), *Gloag and Henderson: The Law of Scotland*, 11th edn (Edinburgh: W. Green, 2001), para.48.51.

[80] Adults with Incapacity (Scotland) Act 2000 s.88 and Sch.4. For a summary of the superseded common law see the 11th edition of this book.

[81] Adults with Incapacity (Scotland) Act 2000 (asp 4) (the "2000 Act").

[82] Adult Support and Protection (Scotland) Act 2007 (asp 10) (the "2007 Act"), the relevant parts amending the 2000 Act came into force by October 5, 2007. See the Adult Support and Protection (Scotland) Act 2007 (Commencement No.1, Transitional Provision and Savings) Order 2007 (SSI 2007/334).

[83] Defined in s.1(6) as a person who has attained the age of 16 years.

[84] 2000 Act s.1(2).

[85] 2000 Act s.1(3).

[86] 2000 Act s.1(4) and s.3(5A), inserted by the 2007 Act s.55, imposes a specific requirement on a sheriff determining any application under the Act, without prejudice to the generality of s.1(3), to take account of the wishes and feelings of any adult who is the subject of the proceedings so far as those views are expressed by someone providing independent advocacy services.

him in the exercise and development of skills.[87] For the purposes of the legislation, incapable includes incapable of acting, of making decisions, of communicating decisions, understanding decisions or retaining the memory of decisions through mental disorder or physical disability leading to an inability to communicate.[88] Mental disorder in this context includes mental illness, learning disability or personality disorder, subject to the exclusions set out in the Mental Health (Care and Treatment (Scotland) Act 2003.[89]

43.08 **Powers of attorney**—The 2000 Act introduced[90] a system of continuing powers of attorney and welfare powers of attorney, the former power regulating the practice by which an individual grants a power of attorney relating to his property or financial affairs. Such a power of attorney continues to have effect in the event of the granter becoming incapable in relation to decisions about those matters to which it relates.[91] A welfare power of attorney is a similar power granted where an individual wishes to make provision relative to his personal welfare.[92] Both powers of attorney require to be created in a written document in prescribed form,[93] and registered by the Public Guardian.[94] The Public Guardian's decision on registration is subject to appeal to the sheriff, whose decision is final.[95] Applications may be made to the sheriff court for specified orders where these are necessary to safeguard or promote the interest of the granter of the power of attorney.[96] An attorney must keep a record of his actions[97] and is not obliged to do anything within his powers if it would be unduly burdensome or expensive relative to the possible benefits to the adult.[98] An attorney under a continuing power of attorney or a welfare power of attorney who wishes to resign must give 28 days' notice to the Public Guardian and must also inform, in writing, the granter of the power of attorney, the granter's guardian or carer and the local authority, of his intention to resign.[99] Both powers of attorney come to an end on the termination, by permanent separation or divorce, of marriage, or dissolution of civil partnership by permanent separation or divorce, where the granter and the attorney are spouses or civil partners.[100] There is now provision for the granter of a continuing or welfare power of attorney to revoke the power of attorney or any of the powers granted by it after it has been registered by giving a revocation notice in prescribed form to the Public Guardian.[101] The authority of a continuing or welfare attorney also terminates on the appointment of a guardian under the legislation, to

---

[87] 2000 Act s.1(5).

[88] 2000 Act s.1(6).

[89] 2000 Act s.87(1) (as amended by the Mental Health (Care and Treatment) (Scotland) Act 2003 Sch.4 para.9(5)).

[90] The provisions relative to continuing powers of attorney and welfare powers of attorney came into force on April 1, 2001.

[91] 2000 Act s.15, as now amended by the 2007 Act s.57(1).

[92] 2000 Act s.16, as now amended by the 2007 Act s.57(2).

[93] 2000 Act ss.15(3) and 16(3). Section 16(A), inserted by the 2007 Act provides for a single certificate where a document confers both a continuing power of attorney and a welfare power of attorney.

[94] 2000 Act s.19, as now amended by the 2007 Act s.57(4). The functions of the Public Guardian, who is the Accountant of Court, are set out in ss.6 and 7.

[95] 2000 Act s.19(6)

[96] 2000 Act s.20, as now amended by the 2007 Act s.57(5).

[97] 2000 Act s.21.

[98] 2000 Act s.17.

[99] 2000 Act s.23, as now amended by the 2007 Act s.57(8).

[100] 2000 Act s.24, as amended by the Family Law (Scotland) Act 2006 s.36.

[101] 2000 Act s.22A, inserted by the 2007 Act s.57(7).

the extent that the guardian has powers relating to a matter covered by the power of attorney.[102] A continuing power of attorney ends on the bankruptcy of the grantor or the attorney.[103]

Intromission with incapable adult's funds—Part 3 of the 2000 Act introduced **43.09** a scheme for the withdrawal of money by a named individual from an incapable adult's bank account for authorised purposes, but this was replaced by a more detailed scheme inserted by the 2007 Act[104] An application to the Public Guardian may be made in relation to an incapable adult in relation to decisions about certain funds.[105] The Public Guardian may authorise intromission with the adult's funds for specified purposes and may authorise those who hold funds of an adult to divulge information about those funds.[106] Authority may also be given to open an account to receive and hold funds for an incapable adult so that these can be administered[107] and applications can be made to intromit with designated accounts by way of a withdrawal certificate,[108] valid for three years.[109] There is scope for adding a reserve withdrawer who may act in the event of the main withdrawer becoming unable to act[110] and withdrawal certificates may be varied but not so as to alter the period of validity.[111] Procedures for applications in relation to such funds require a countersignature from an independent third party and must be accompanied by a certificate from a medical practitioner in prescribed form.[112] The Public Guardian may grant the application or remit it to the sheriff for determination.[113] Decisions taken by the Public Guardian in relation to the various applications relative to an adult's funds may be appealed to the sheriff, whose decision is final.[114] There are also detailed provisions for the management of the finances of residents in various hospitals, nursing homes and similar establishments[115] and for the authority of those responsible for the medical treatment of incapable adults.[116]

Intervention and guardianship orders—Part 6 of the 2000 Act has introduced **43.10** an entirely new scheme of intervention and guardianship orders, which as indicated has replaced the previous law of the appointment of curators bonis, tutors-at-law and tutors dative. It is incompetent to appoint a curator bonis, tutor dative or tutor-at-law in any proceedings commenced after April 2, 2002.[117]

---

[102] 2000 Act s.24.

[103] 2000 Act s.15(5) inserted by the 2007 Act s.57(1)(d), which clarifies and declares that this is and has been since the 2000 Act came into force, an existing rule of the law of agent and principal.

[104] The original 2000 Act provisions have been substituted by a new Pt 3 of that Act inserted by the 2007 Act s.58. The new provisions give greater details as to the powers that can be authorised by the Public Guardian.

[105] 2000 Act s.24B.

[106] 2000 Act ss.24A and 24C.

[107] 2000 Act s.24D

[108] 2000 Act ss.25, 26 and 26A.

[109] 2000 Act s.31

[110] 2000 Act ss.26D and 26E

[111] 2000 Act s.26F.

[112] 2000 Act s.27, the detail in ss.27A–G having been inserted by the 2007 Act.

[113] 2000 Act ss.27D–F.

[114] 2000 Act s.31D

[115] 2000 Act Pt 4, ss.35–46.

[116] 2000 Act Pt 5, ss.47–52.

[117] 2000 Act s.80.

Appointments of curators bonis, tutors dative and tutors-at-law made prior to that date are effective but as guardianship orders.[118]

43.11 Intervention orders—Intervention orders may be granted by a sheriff on an application by any person claiming an interest in the property, financial affairs or personal welfare of an incapable adult, including the adult himself.[119] The order may direct the taking of specified action or may authorise the appointee to take specified action or make a specified decision, relative to the personal welfare or property or financial affairs, or both, of the adult concerned.[120] Intervention orders may be made ad interim[121] and may be varied or recalled by the sheriff.[122] The scope of intervention orders is limited only by the exclusion of matters where the procedures of the Mental Health (Care and Treatment) (Scotland) Act 2003 will prevail,[123] but the principle of taking the least restrictive alternative requires an applicant to seek only the powers necessary to protect the interests or property of the adult concerned.[124] This requires consideration of the benefit, if any, to the adult in making the order.[125] A person authorised under an intervention order is required to keep records of the exercise of his powers[126] and notify the Public Guardian of any changes in his or the incapable adult's address.[127] Intervention orders terminate on the death of the adult concerned.[128]

43.12 Guardianship orders—By s.57[129] of the 2000 Act, any person claiming an interest (including the adult himself) may make an application for an order ("Guardianship Order") appointing an individual or office holder as guardian in relation to the property, financial affairs or personal welfare of an adult. Guardianship orders may be made in relation to a child who will become an adult within three months of the date of the order, in which event the order does not have effect until the child attains the age of 16 and becomes an adult.[130] There are provisions that permit joint applications[131] and the substitution of a new guardian where the initial appointee has become unable to act.[132] The application requires to be supported by the reports of at least two relevant medical practitioners[133] following an examination and assessment carried out usually not more than 30 days before the lodging of the application, with an additional report relative to the appropriateness of the order sought and the suitability of the proposed guardian.[134] An interim appointment

---

[118] 2000 Act s.88 and Sch.4, as amended by the 2007 Act s.60(17).

[119] 2000 Act s.53(1).

[120] 2000 Act s.53(5).

[121] 2000 Act s.3(2)(d).

[122] 2000 Act s.53(8).

[123] 2000 Act s.64(2).

[124] 2000 Act s.53(2) and (3).

[125] See, e.g. *M, Applicant*, 2007 S.L.T. (Sh. Ct) 24; *A's Guardian, Applicant*, 2007 S.L.T. (Sh. Ct) 69 and *M, Applicant*, 2009 S.L.T. (Sh. Ct) 185.

[126] 2000 Act s.54.

[127] 2000 Act s.55.

[128] 2000 Act s.77.

[129] As now amended by the 2007 Act s.60.

[130] 2000 Act s.79A, inserted by the 2007 Act s.60(16).

[131] 2000 Act s.62.

[132] 2000 Act s.63.

[133] 2000 Act s.57(6B) and (7).

[134] 2000 Act s.57(3) as enacted did not allow variation of the 30 day rule—see *Stork, Pursuer*, 2004 S.C.L.R. 513. It was amended by the 2007 Act s.60(1)(b), which inserts provisions allowing a sheriff to consider an application where the examination and assessment was carried out more than 30 days

may be made for a period of three months, or until the earlier appointment of a guardian.[135] Where the sheriff is satisfied that the adult is and is likely to continue to be incapable of making decisions relative to his property, financial affairs or personal welfare and that there are no other means in terms of the legislation sufficient to enable the adult's said interests to be safeguarded or promoted, he may grant the application.[136] The court should acknowledge that where the adult concerned is compliant with the care regime in place, but is legally incapable of consenting to or disagreeing with it, that adult is deprived of his liberty in breach of art.5 ECHR and that steps should not be taken without an express statutory authority, which will prescribe the least restrictive option available.[137] In this context, a Guardianship Order may be less restrictive than the alternative of an application by a local authority for a community care service.[138] The court also requires to be satisfied that the individual is aware of the adult's circumstances and condition and the needs arising therefrom and of the functions of a guardian.[139]

Duration of guardianship order—The maximum initial duration of a guardian- **43.13** ship order is three years, unless cause is shown for some other period.[140] An individual appointed as guardian relative to property or financial affairs will, unless the sheriff is satisfied that someone unable to find caution is nevertheless suitable to be authorised under the order, be required to find caution.[141] The Public Guardian is required to keep certain registers,[142] including one containing prescribed particulars of all guardianship orders.[143] An application for renewal of a guardianship order may be made at any time before its expiry, and an existing order continues to have effect pending determination of such an application for renewal.[144] Where a guardianship order vests a right to deal with, convey or manage any interest in heritable property recorded, registered or capable of being recorded or registered

---

previously but there has been no change in the circumstances relevant to the report—see s.57(3A) and (3B). For the prescribed form of the reports see the Adults with Incapacity (Reports in Relation to Guardianship and Intervention Orders) (Scotland) Regulations 2002 (SSI 2002/96).

[135] 2000 Act s.57(5) and (6). See s.64(8) for the reporting obligations of an interim guardian.

[136] 2000 Act s.58(1).

[137] See the discussion in *Muldoon, Applicant*, 2005 S.L.T. (Sh. Ct) 52, followed in *M, Applicant*, 2009 S.L.T. (Sh. Ct) 185. The discussion was focused by the decision of the European Court of Human Rights in *HL v UK* (2005) 40 E.H.R.R. 32 ("the *Bournewood* case"). The Scottish Law Commission published a Discussion Paper on the subject in July 2012: Scottish Law Commission, *Adults with Incapacity* (HMSO, 2012), Scot. Law Com. DP No.156.

[138] Inserted as s.13ZA of the Social Work (Scotland) Act 1968 by s.64 of the 2007 Act, this provision allows the local authority to move an incapable adult to residential accommodation if they consider it would help that adult to benefit from the service. See the excellent critique by Adrian Ward in "Adult Incapacity and the Social Work (Scotland) Act 1968", 2011 S.L.T. (News) 21.

[139] 2000 Act s.59(3). The individual appointed is not restricted to the applicant—see *Application in respect of Mrs M.A.* Unreported December 2004, Glasgow Sheriff Court, Sheriff J. Baird (Case Ref. AW14/04).

[140] 2000 Act s.58(4).

[141] 2000 Act s.58(6), as amended by the 2007 Act s.60(2). For the caution provisions relative to intervention orders see s.53(7).

[142] Listed in 2000 Act s.6(2)(b).

[143] 2000 Act s.6(2)(b)(iv). The sheriff clerk will send a copy of the interlocutor containing the guardianship order to the Public Guardian for this purpose: s.58(7).

[144] 2000 Act s.60, as amended by the 2007 Act s.60(3), which introduces certain requirements in relation to the documents to be lodged in support of such an application. For the procedure relating to a renewal application–see OCR Ch.14. See also the discussion in *G's Guardian, Applicant*, 2009 S.L.T. (Sh. Ct) 153.

in the General Register of Sasines or the Land Register, the interlocutor containing the order is registered or the title sheet updated, as appropriate.[145]

43.14 Powers of guardian—The powers which may be conferred on a guardian extend to all aspects of the property, financial affairs or personal welfare of the adult concerned, including the power to pursue or defend actions of divorce, separation, dissolution of civil partnership or nullity of marriage in the name of the adult,[146] but the Scottish Ministers may define further the particular scope of those general powers and the conditions under which they shall be exercised.[147] A guardianship order renders the adult concerned incapable of entering into any transaction in relation to a matter within the scope of the guardian's authority.[148] The guardian is required to keep records of the exercise of his powers[149] and there are restrictions on making gifts out of the adult's estate.[150] A guardian is entitled to reimbursement for outlays out of the adult's estate[151] and to remuneration therefrom in respect of the exercise of functions relative to the property or financial affairs of the adult, unless the sheriff otherwise directs.[152] Special cause requires to be shown for remuneration from the estate for the exercise of functions relative to the adult's personal welfare.[153]

43.15 Variation and termination of guardianship orders—There are provisions for the replacement or removal of a guardian or recall of a guardianship order by the sheriff.[154] The Public Guardian has authority to recall the powers of guardian in certain circumstances.[155] Guardianship orders may be varied,[156] and a notice in writing of an intention to resign is required.[157] Guardianship orders terminate on the death of the adult concerned,[158] but the appointment of a substitute guardian can be certified by the Public Guardian, who must be notified of the death.[159] Appeals against decisions taken by the sheriff under the Act are to the sheriff principal and thereafter, where leave is granted, to the Court of Session.[160]

43.16 Mental Health (Care and Treatment) (Scotland) Act 2003—The 2003 Act[161] has replaced the Mental Health (Scotland) Act 1984 and deals primarily with compulsory measures in mental health care. It also contains provisions for support and access to services for those who are not subject to compulsory measures. The role and duties of the Mental Welfare Commission for Scotland are now governed

---

[145] 2000 Act s.61. Identical provisions for the registration of intervention orders relating to heritable property are contained in s.56.

[146] 2000 Act s.64(1).

[147] 2000 Act s.64(11).

[148] 2000 Act s.67.

[149] 2000 Act s.65.

[150] 2000 Act s.66.

[151] 2000 Act s.68(1).

[152] 2000 Act s.68(4)(b). See also s.68(5).

[153] 2000 Act s.68(4)(a).

[154] 2000 Act s.71, as amended by the 2007 Act s.60(9)

[155] See s.73 and s.73A, inserted by the 2007 Act s.60(12), which now makes specific provisions applying to recall where a local authority's chief social worker is the appointed guardian.

[156] 2000 Act s.74, as amended by the 2007 Act s.60(13).

[157] 2000 Act s.75, as amended by the 2007 Act s.60(14).

[158] 2000 Act s.77.

[159] 2000 Act s.75A, inserted by the 2007 Act s.60(15).

[160] 2000 Act ss.2(3) and 5.

[161] Mental Health (Care and Treatment) (Scotland) Act 2003 (asp 13) (the "2003 Act").

by the 2003 Act and the legislation also establishes the Mental Health Tribunal for Scotland.

General principles—Part 1 of the Act enunciates the general principles under- **43.17**
lying the legislation. These are: (1) a person exercising functions under the Act must have regard to the wishes and feelings, past and present, of the person (the "named person") about whom decisions are being made[162]; (2) the views of the named person must be considered along with those of any carer or welfare guardian or attorney provided it is reasonably practicable to do so[163]; (3) those carrying out duties under the legislation should do so in the least restrictive manner necessary in the circumstances, having regard to the other principles, the needs of any carer, the duty of reciprocity and any other considerations[164]; (4) those caring out duties under the Act should consider how to provide maximum benefit to the named person[165]; (5) all those with duties under the legislation should consider how to ensure that a patient's treatment is no worse than that which would be received in a similar situation by someone who is not a patient, unless the circumstances justify different treatment[166]; and (6) the principle of reciprocity provides that if someone has been or is subject to an order under the legislation, those acting under the Act must have regard to the importance of providing appropriate services to him or her, including continuing care when the person is no longer subject to the order.[167]

Grounds and procedures—Compulsory measures under the 2003 Act are avail- **43.18**
able where the named person has a mental disorder, including mental illness, personality disorder or learning disability[168] and where treatment is available that would benefit the person and without which there will be a significant risk to that person's health, safety or welfare or to the safety of other people. The named person's ability to take decisions about the treatment must be significantly impaired and the order must be necessary.[169] Short-term detention for 28 days under the Act can be authorised by a detention certificate granted by a single approved psychiatrist, who should seek the consent of a mental health officer.[170] There are separate procedures for emergency detention.[171] On the expiry of such a certificate, if the responsible medical officer considers that a patient requires to remain subject to compulsory measures, he can request that the mental health officer make an application to the Mental Health Tribunal for Scotland ("the Tribunal") for a compulsory treatment order. The case must be heard within five working days of the expiry of the short-term certificate, during which period the authority to detain continues.[172] Two medical practitioners with no conflict of

---

[162] 2003 Act s.1(3)(a).
[163] 2003 Act s.1(3)(b).
[164] 2003 Act s.1(3)(e). The duty of reciprocity is contained in s.1(6).
[165] 2003 Act s.1(3)(f).
[166] 2003 Act s.1(3)(g).
[167] 2003 Act s.1(6).
[168] For the definition and exclusions see s.328.
[169] The grounds are set out in s.64 of the Act.
[170] 2003 Act s.44.
[171] 2003 Act ss.36–38.
[172] 2003 Act ss.68 and 69 and the Mental Health Tribunal for Scotland (Practice and Procedure) Rules 2005 (SSI 2005/420) reg.8. The failure to arrange hearings within the prescribed period has been challenged by judicial review—*Petition for Judicial Review of John Smith, Mental Health Officer for Fife Council* [2006] CSOH 44.

interest[173] must examine the person and provide a report in relation to the application for a compulsory treatment order, certifying that the order sought is necessary.[174] The mental health officer interviews the person and provides a report to the tribunal, with an accompanying care plan as part of his application.[175]

43.19 Compulsory treatment orders—The tribunal may grant a compulsory treatment order for a period of up to six months or an interim 28-day compulsory treatment order, which automatically revokes the short-term detention certificate.[176] Compulsory treatment orders can be community based or they may authorise detention in hospital.[177] A right of appeal on a point of law or procedural irregularity is available to the sheriff and sheriff principal.[178] Where an appeal raises an important or difficult question of law it may appropriately be remitted to the Court of Session. All those subject to compulsory treatment orders must have a responsible medical officer assigned to them, who must prepare a care plan and fulfil a number of related duties.[179] The local authority must also appoint a mental health officer to the person.[180] A first review of the need for compulsory treatment must be carried out within two months before the end of the period of the order[181] and thereafter at 12-monthly intervals.[182] There are provisions for extension and variation[183] of compulsory treatment orders on application to the tribunal.[184] In addition to modification and extension, the powers of the tribunal extend to revocation of the order with immediate effect.[185] Applications to vary or discharge a compulsory treatment order may be made by or on behalf of the person subject to it on the expiry of three months from the making of the order.[186] Parts 8–10 of the 2003 Act make provisions for the treatment of mentally disordered persons in criminal proceedings, with which this work is not concerned.

FURTHER READING

Patrick, H., *Mental Health, Incapacity and the Law in Scotland* (Tottel, 2006).
Scottish Law Commission, *Discussion Paper on Adults with Incapacity* (HMSO, 2012), Scot. Law Com. DP No.156.
Ward, A., *Adult Incapacity* (Edinburgh: W. Green, 2003).
Ward, A., *Adults with Incapacity Legislation* (Edinburgh: W. Green, 2008).

---

[173] 2003 Act s.58(5).
[174] 2003 Act s.57.
[175] 2003 Act ss.61 and 62.
[176] 2003 Act ss.65(2) and 70 and the Mental Health Tribunal for Scotland (Practice and Procedure) Rules 2005 r.8.
[177] 2003 Act s.67.
[178] 2003 Act ss.320 and 324(2).
[179] 2003 Act s.320(4).
[180] 2003 Act ss.65(2), 76 and 230.
[181] 2003 Act s.229.
[182] 2003 Act s.77.
[183] 2003 Act s.78.
[184] 2003 Act ss.84–86.
[185] 2003 Act ss.90–92.
[186] The powers of the tribunal are set out in 2003 Act ss.103–110.

CHAPTER 44

FAMILY LAW

I. MARRIAGE AND CIVIL PARTNERSHIP

Marriage—Marriage is said by Erskine[1] to be truly a contract; but although this **44.01** is true in the sense that it is founded on the consent of the parties, it is much more than a contract. It differs in many important respects from other contracts. Thus, the conditions of marriage, and the rights and duties created by it, are not left to be regulated by the parties, nor can it be dissolved at their pleasure; and it affects the status both of the parties and of their issue. Hence it has always been recognised that the general rules of the law of contract cannot be applied indiscriminately to the relationship of marriage.[2]

Civil partnership—Civil partnership is a purely statutory creation,[3] designed to **44.02** provide parity of treatment with married couples for those who choose to register a same-sex partnership. For many purposes civil partnership rights have been incorporated into the existing legal framework for spouses, for example in relation to financial provision on divorce[4] and succession.[5] The provisions for formation and registration of civil partnerships differ from those of marriage and will be referred to separately.

Legal impediments to marriage—In Scots law, marriage is a union between a **44.03** man and a woman.[6] There can be no marriage between two individuals of the same sex.[7] However, transgendered persons may secure legal recognition of their new, acquired gender and marry accordingly.[8] Men and women of marriageable age have the right to marry and found a family,[9] but the application of this funda-

---

[1] Erskine, I, 6, 2; and see F.P. Walton, *A Handbook of Husband and Wife according to the Law of Scotland*, 3rd edn (Edinburgh, 1951), Ch.1.

[2] *Lang v Lang*, 1921 S.C. 44; and see *Scott v Kelly*, 1992 S.L.T. 915, where averments of facility and circumvention and of undue influence were held irrelevant in an action of declarator of nullity of marriage.

[3] Introduced by the Civil Partnership Act 2004, a statute of the UK Parliament. Part 3 of the Act contains the main provisions applicable to Scotland.

[4] See paras 44.28 and 44.29, below.

[5] See Ch.38, above.

[6] Stair, I, 4, 1– I, 4, 6; Erskine, I, 6, 1; Marriage (Scotland) Act 1977 s.5(4)(e).

[7] Sex is determined at birth registration; *X, Petitioner*, 1957 S.L.T. (Sh. Ct) 61. It cannot be altered by sex realignment surgery; *Corbett v Corbett* [1971] P. 83. The requirement for parties to a marriage to be of opposite sexes is not at present considered to be contrary to ECHR, see *Wilkinson and Kitzinger* [2006] EWHC 2022 (Fam).

[8] Gender Recognition Act 2004 s.9.

[9] art.12, European Convention on Human Rights (Human Rights Act 1998 Sch.1).

mental human right in Scotland has been restricted by a number of prohibitions, constituting legal impediments to marriage.

44.04 Forbidden degrees of relationship—Marriage is prohibited where one party is within certain degrees of relationship to the other party. For all marriages contracted after January 1, 1978, these are defined by the Marriage (Scotland) Act 1977,[10] which includes an exhaustive list of relationships within which parties may not marry.[11] Relationships by consanguinity within the forbidden degrees include those with a parent, grandparent or great-grandparent; a child, grandchild or great-grandchild; a brother, sister, nephew, niece, uncle or aunt. No distinction is made in consanguineous relationships between the full blood and the half blood.[12] In certain circumstances involving assisted reproduction, relationships will be treated as consanguineous where there is no genetic relationship.[13] The only marriages now prohibited by affinity are those to the child or grandchild of a former spouse; the parent or grandparent of a former spouse; the former spouse of a parent or grandparent; the former spouse of one's child.[14] In certain circumstances, however, such marriages may be allowed. Marriage with the former spouse of a parent or grandparent, or with the child or grandchild of a former spouse, is permitted if both parties are aged 21 or over at the time of the marriage and the younger party has not, at any time before attaining the age of 18, lived in the same household as the other party and been treated by him as a child of his family.[15] Marriage with the parent of a former spouse or the former spouse of a child could, until repeal of the rule by the Family Law (Scotland) Act 2006, only take place if both parties were 21 or over and, in the case of marriage with the parent of a former spouse, both the former spouse and the other parent of the former spouse had died or, in the case of marriage with the former spouse of a child, both the child and the other parent of the child had died. There is now no restriction on such marriages.[16] Both in consanguinity and affinity the relationship exists although traced through or to any person whose parents were not married to one another.[17] The only prohibitions based on relationships by adoption are that marriage with an adoptive parent or former adoptive parent, or with an adopted child or former adopted child, is forbidden.[18]

44.05 Subsisting prior marriage—A marriage with one who is at the time married to a third party is *ipso jure null*, even where either, or both, of the contracts are voidable.[19]

---

[10] The pre-1978 law, which would still govern any question of validity of a marriage contracted prior to that date, was not materially different in its prohibitions; see E.M. Clive, *Law of Husband and Wife in Scotland*, 4th edn (Edinburgh: W. Green, 1997), Ch.7, pp.76–77.

[11] Marriage (Scotland) Act 1977 (the "1977 Act") ss.2 and 27(3). Sch.1 (as amended by the Marriage (Prohibited Degrees of Relationship) Act 1986 and the Family Law (Scotland) Act 2006) contains the complete list of the forbidden relationships.

[12] 1977 Act s.2(2)(a).

[13] See s.29 of the Human Fertilisation and Embryology Act 1990 and para.44.40, below.

[14] 1977 Act s.2(1A) and Sch.1 para.2, as amended by the Marriage (Prohibited Degrees of Relationship) Act 1986.

[15] 1977 Act s.2(1A).

[16] 1977 Act s.1(a) of the Family Law (Scotland) Act 2006 repealed the rule contained in s.2(1B) of the 1977 Act with effect from May 4, 2006.

[17] 1977 Act s.2(4).

[18] 1977 Act s.2 and Sch.1 para.3.

[19] See Clive, *Law of Husband and Wife in Scotland* (1997), p.21; 1977 Act s.2(3)(b).

Impotency—Where either of the parties, being of suitable age, is incapable of **44.06** sexual intercourse, the marriage may be declared null.[20]

It is not essential that there should be structural incapacity; invincible repugnance may amount to impotency. Impotency is not, however, an absolute bar to marriage, but only affords ground on which it may be annulled[21]; and there may be circumstances which so plainly imply a recognition of the existence and validity of the marriage by the complaining spouse as to make it inequitable and contrary to public policy that he or she should be permitted to impugn it.[22] The defender in the action is entitled to an opportunity of undergoing remedial medical treatment.[23] The action may be brought by the impotent spouse on the ground of his own irremediable impotency.[24] It has been held that an action of declarator of nullity on the ground of impotency was not out of time 24 years after the pretended marriage.[25]

Nonage—Under the common law a pupil child could not marry, although if the **44.07** married pair cohabited after puberty this gave force to the marriage.[26] The Age of Marriage Act 1929 first enacted that a marriage between persons either of whom is under the age of 16 is void. That Act was repealed and replaced by the Marriage (Scotland) Act 1977, which retains the rule for all marriages solemnised in Scotland.[27]

Invalid consent—At common law there could be no valid marriage if either **44.08** party did not understand the nature of the ceremony of marriage or was otherwise incapable of giving consent to it, for example through mental illness,[28] severe learning difficulty[29] or intoxication.[30] The *tempus inspiciendum* for testing capacity at common law was the time of contracting the marriage,[31] though statute now imposes a capacity requirement at the preliminary stages of a regular marriage.[32] Lack of true consent could void the marriage in a number of ways.[33] Error as to the identity of the other party or as to the nature of the ceremony

---

[20] *G. v G.*, 1924 S.C. (HL) 42. See discussion in Clive, *Law of Husband and Wife in Scotland* (1997), pp.95–100. As to what does and does not constitute physical consummation, see *Baxter v Baxter* [1948] A.C. 274; *Cackett v Cackett* [1950] P. 253; *W v W* [1967] 1 W.L.R. 1554 and *J v J*, 1978 S.L.T. 128.

[21] See *Administrator of Austrian Property v Von Lorang*, 1926 S.C. 598, per Lord President Clyde at 616; 1927 S.C. (HL) 80; *SG v WG*, 1933 S.C. 728; as to onus, see *M v W or M*, 1966 S.L.T. 152.

[22] *C.B. v A.B.* (1885) 12 R. (HL) 36, per Lord Selbourne L.C. at 38, Lord Watson at 45; *L v L*, 1931 S.C. 477; *A.B. v C.B.*, 1961 S.C. 347. Artificial Insemination by the Husband (A.I.H) and adoption of children generally have this effect (see Clive, *The Law of Husband and Wife in Scotland* (1997), pp.103–104).

[23] *W.Y. v A.Y.*, 1946 S.C. 27.

[24] *F v F*, 1945 S.C. 202; *H v H*, 1949 S.C. 587.

[25] *Allardyce v A*, 1954 S.C. 419. See this case too on the subject of expenses in an action of nullity.

[26] Erskine, 1, 6, 3; Fraser, I, 53.

[27] 1977 Act s.1 and s.5(4). For those born after the commencement of the Age of Legal Capacity (Scotland) Act 1991, the age of 16 is attained on the first moment of the sixteenth birthday. See s.6 of the 1991 Act.

[28] Erskine, 1, 6, 2; *Park v Park*, 1914 1 S.L.T. 88; *Calder v Calder*, 1942 S.N. 40.

[29] See *Long v Long*, 1950 S.L.T. (Notes) 32, where the defender was held to have the necessary capacity, albeit that he was mentally defective.

[30] *Johnson v Brown* (1823) 2 S. 495; *Gall v Gall* (1870) 9 M. 177.

[31] *McAdam v Walker* (1813) 1 Dow 148.

[32] 1977 Act s.5(4)(d).

[33] For a fuller discussion of the common law on lack of true consent see Clive, *The Law of Husband and Wife in Scotland* (1997), pp.80–92

rendered a marriage void.[34] Less fundamental error as to the position or qualities of the other party or the lifestyle in which the marriage will result did not vitiate consent, even if the error was induced by the other party's fraudulent misrepresentation.[35] Fraud invalidated a marriage only if it produced the appearance without the reality of consent.[36] Where parties underwent a marriage ceremony without the intention of entering the married state and solely to achieve some other purpose, the marriage could be regarded as a sham to which no matrimonial consent had been given.[37] Consent given through force or fear could render the marriage void[38] and in this context family pressure could be of such force as to amount to duress excluding consent.[39] The fact that one party was disabled by a rule of his religion from entering into the marriage did not render it void.[40] If consent is given, marriage is thereby perfected although the parties may never cohabit; *consensus non concubitus facit matrimonium*. Grounds for nullity of marriage arising from defective consent to marriages solemnised in Scotland have now been put on a statutory footing.[41] Consent continues to be vitiated by duress or error[42] and lack of capacity to consent,[43] but tacit withholding of consent to enter the married state no longer renders the marriage void, so lack of matrimonial intent at the time of the ceremony will not invalidate the formal consent given.[44] Some protection for those forced to enter into a marriage to which they do not consent is now provided by the Forced Marriage etc. (Protection and Jurisdiction) (Scotland) Act 2011.[45] The court may make an order, either on an application being made[46] or in some circumstances without the need for an application[47], for the purpose of protecting a person ("the protected person") who is being forced into marriage or from an attempt to do so or to protect those who have already been forced into marriage.[48] The force required includes coercion by physical, verbal or psychological means, threatening conduct and harassment and knowingly taking advantage of a person's incapacity to consent to marriage or to understand the nature of the marriage.[49] There is considerable flexibility in relation to the content of any protective order and third parties may be ordered to take steps to protect the person at risk of forced marriage. In particular, the order may require a person to take the protected person to a place of safety, to bring him or

---

[34] Stair, I, 9, 9; *S.G. v W.G.*, 1933 S.C. 728.

[35] Thus, in *Lang v Lang*, 1921 S.C. 44, where a man was induced to marry on the basis of the fraudulent statement of a woman that her pregnant condition was due to him, he was unsuccessful in his application to have the marriage declared null. See also *MacDougall v Chitnavis*, 1937 S.C. 390.

[36] *Lang v Lang*, 1921 S.C. 44 at 49–50.

[37] See *McLeod v Adams*, 1920 1 S.L.T. 229; *Orlandi v Castelli*, 1961 S.C. 113; *Mahmud v Mahmud*, 1977 S.L.T. (Notes) 17; *Akram v Akram*, 1979 S.L.T. (Notes) 87 and *SH v KH*, 2005 S.L.T. 1025.

[38] Stair, I, 4, 1; Fraser, I, 444.

[39] *Mahmood v Mahmood*, 1993 S.L.T. 589; *Mahmud v Mahmud*, 1994 S.L.T. 599; *Sohrab v Khan*, 2002 S.C. 382.

[40] *MacDougall v Chitnavis*, 1937 S.C. 390.

[41] 1977 Act s.20A, as inserted by the Family Law (Scotland) Act 2006 s.2.

[42] 1977 Act s.20A(1) and (2). Error includes error as to the nature of the ceremony or as to identity of the other party: subs.(5).

[43] 1977 Act s.20A(1) and (3).

[44] 1977 Act s.20A(4).

[45] Forced Marriage etc. (Protection and Jurisdiction) (Scotland) Act 2011 (asp 15) (the "2011 Act").

[46] 2011 Act s.3.

[47] 2011 Act s.4. There must be proceedings (either civil or criminal) before the court before such an order can be made without an application.

[48] 2011 Act s.1(1).

[49] 2011 Act s.1(6).

her to court and may prohibit specific conduct.[50] There is provision for the making of interim forced marriage protection orders.[51]

Constitution of marriage: Regular marriage—A marriage is regular or irreg- **44.09** ular according to its mode of constitution. A regular marriage may be either a religious or a civil marriage.[52] In either case each party to the marriage must submit to the registrar of the district in which the marriage is to be solemnised, a notice of intention to marry, accompanied by a birth certificate, and where either party has previously been married, evidence of the dissolution of the previous marriage.[53] There are special provisions where a party to a marriage intended to be solemnised in Scotland is residing in another part of the United Kingdom or is not domiciled in any part of the United Kingdom and also for marriages outside Scotland where a party resides in Scotland.[54] After receipt of the notice, the registrar, if satisfied that there is no legal impediment, or if so informed by the Registrar General, issues a marriage schedule which is the authority for the solemnisation of the marriage.[55] The schedule may not, however, be issued before the expiry of 14 days from receipt of the notice unless on the written request of a party to the marriage and with the authority of the Registrar General.[56]

At any time before the solemnisation of a marriage any person may submit an objection in writing to the registrar.[57] Where the objection relates to a matter of misdescription or inaccuracy the registrar may, with the approval of the Registrar General, make any necessary correction. In any other case he must, pending consideration of the objection by the Registrar General, suspend the completion or issue of the marriage schedule or, if a marriage schedule has already been issued for a religious marriage, notify the celebrant of the objection and advise him not to solemnise the marriage.[58] If the Registrar General is satisfied that, on consideration of an objection, there is a legal impediment to the marriage he must direct the registrar to take all reasonable steps to ensure that the marriage does not take place. If, on the other hand, he is satisfied that there is no legal impediment, he must so inform the registrar and the marriage schedule may then be completed and issued, if that has already not been done, so that the marriage may proceed.[59] There is a legal impediment for this purpose where the parties to the marriage are within the forbidden degrees of relationship or are of the same sex or where either of them (a) is already married, (b) will be under the age of 16 on the date of the solemnisation of the intended marriage, (c) is incapable of understanding the nature of a marriage ceremony or of consenting to marriage, or (d) is not domiciled in Scotland and his marriage in Scotland to the other party would be void ab initio according to the law of his domicile.[60]

A religious marriage may be solemnised by a minister of the Church of Scotland, a minister, clergyman, pastor or priest of a religious body prescribed by

---

[50] 2011 Act s.2(3) has a list of what may be included in a forced marriage protection order but it is not exhaustive.

[51] 2011 Act s.5.

[52] 1977 Act s.8.

[53] 1977 Act s.3(1).

[54] 1977 Act s.3(4), (5) and (7).

[55] 1977 Act s.6.

[56] 1977 Act s.6(4).

[57] 1977 Act s.5(1).

[58] 1977 Act s.5(2).

[59] 1977 Act ss.5(3) and 6(1).

[60] 1977 Act s.5(4).

regulations, or other approved celebrant.[61] The marriage schedule must be produced to the celebrant and the parties to the marriage and two witnesses (who must be persons professing to be 16 years or over) must be present. Where the celebrant belongs to the Church of Scotland or a prescribed religious body, the marriage must be in accordance with a form recognised as sufficient by the church or body to which the celebrant belongs.[62] In any other case, the statutory requirement is that the form of solemnisation must include a declaration by the parties, in the presence of each other, the celebrant and the witnesses, that they accept each other as husband and wife and a declaration thereafter by the celebrant that they are husband and wife.[63]

A civil marriage is solemnised by an authorised registrar. No form is prescribed.[64] A marriage schedule must be available and the parties and witnesses must be present.[65]

It is an offence for anyone, who is not within the classes of persons authorised under the Act to solemnise marriages, to conduct a marriage ceremony in such a way as to lead the parties to believe that he is solemnising a valid marriage, or for the celebrant of a religious marriage to solemnise it without at the time having the marriage schedule available to him, or for either the celebrant of a religious marriage or an authorised registrar to solemnise a marriage without both parties being present.[66] Provided both parties were present at the marriage ceremony and the marriage has been registered, its validity is not to be questioned in any legal proceedings on the ground of failure to comply with a requirement or restriction imposed by the Act.[67] This provision does not save a marriage which has not been registered; thus, where parties had failed to comply with the necessary formalities, with the consequence that no schedule was available and registration could not take place, the marriage was void.[68] And even where registration had occurred but the purported schedule gave details of a ceremony that had not taken place, it was held that registration could not validate the fiction.[69]

44.10 Irregular marriage—Two of the three ancient forms of irregular marriage having been abolished in 1940,[70] only marriage by cohabitation with habit and repute remains valid. That form is now also being abolished to the extent that no new marriages may be constituted by fulfilment of its requirements,[71] but declaratory actions may still be brought for subsisting qualifying relationships.[72] For those relationships, a presumption of tacit consent to marriage is constituted by the

---

[61] 1977 Act s.8(1). See also Marriage (Prescription of Religious Bodies) (Scotland) Regulations 1977 (SI 1977/1670).

[62] 1977 Act s.14(a).

[63] 1977 Act ss.14(b) and 9(3).

[64] 1977 Act s.8(1).

[65] 1977 Act s.19(2).

[66] 1977 Act s.24.

[67] 1977 Act s.23A as inserted by the Law Reform (Miscellaneous Provisions) (Scotland) Act 1980 s.22(1)(d).

[68] *Saleh v Saleh*, 1987 S.L.T. 633.

[69] *Sohrab v Khan*, 2002 S.C. 382.

[70] Marriage (Scotland) Act 1939 s.5 now repealed. For a historic account of irregular marriage see Clive, *The Law of Husband and Wife in Scotland* (1997), pp.40–48.

[71] Family Law (Scotland) Act 2006 s.3.

[72] Family Law (Scotland) Act 2006 s.3(2)–(4).

cohabitation, as man and wife,[73] in Scotland,[74] of a couple, free to marry, who are generally reputed to be husband and wife.[75] The presumption is rebuttable.[76]

Cohabitation must be for a considerable time,[77] although it has now been established that there is no minimum period.[78] The repute must be general and consistent, so preponderating as to leave no substantial doubt.[79] Divided repute has been a determinative factor against declarator being granted.[80] The fact that the cohabitation was at the outset adulterous does not preclude the constitution of marriage by continuance of the cohabitation with repute after the parties become free to marry[81]; though circumstances after the removal of the impediment must be sufficient in themselves to establish the inference of tacit consent.[82] A lack of intention to be married at the outset of cohabitation is not fatal.[83] Consent to marriage may be proved by cohabitation with habit and repute where spouses have previously been married to one another and divorced.[84] A Declarator is required before the legal rights and obligations that attach to marriage will apply to a marriage constituted by consent following relevant cohabitation with habit and repute.[85]

Formation of civil partnership by registration—Civil partnership is formed by **44.11** two people of the same sex signing a civil partnership schedule in the presence of each other, two witnesses with legal capacity and the authorised registrar.[86] The witnesses and registrar must also sign the schedule, in the presence of the couple.[87] Ineligibility to enter a civil partnership effectively mirrors the statutory legal impediments to marriage, with the fundamental exception of the requirement to be of the same sex rather than opposite sexes.[88] Thus the parties of the same sex

---

[73] As distinct from cohabitation as cohabitants; see *Walker v Roberts*, 1998 S.L.T. 1133 at 1135; *Ackerman v Blackburn (No.1)*, 2000 Fam. L.R. 35; 2001 G.W.D. 18–70.

[74] To satisfy the *lex loci celebrationis; Dysart Peerage Case* (1881) 6 App. Cas. 489; *Walker v Roberts*, 1998 S.L.T. 1133 at 1134.

[75] Erskine, 1, 6, 6. See the discussion of the development of the present law in Clive, *The Law of Husband and Wife in Scotland* (1997), pp.48–65.

[76] *Lapsley v Grierson* (1845) 8 D. 34 at 47 and 49; *Campbell v Campbell* (1866) 4 M. 867 at 925; in *Nicol v Bell*, 1954 S.L.T. 314, the male defender attempted to rebut the presumption by denying matrimonial intention but was unsuccessful through a lack of credibility.

[77] There was no uniformity of interpretation of this general requirement; contrast *Campbell v Campbell* (1866) 4 M. 867 at 926 (one year said to be insufficient) with *Wallace v Fife Coal Co*, 1909 S.C. 682 (10 months not enough) and *Shaw v Henderson*, 1982 S.L.T. 211 (10 months and 23 days was sufficient).

[78] See *Kamperman v MacIver*, 1994 S.L.T. 763, where the Second Division refused to affirm that a period of six-and-a-half months after the removal of an impediment was insufficient.

[79] See *Petrie v Petrie*, 1911 S.C. 360, per Lord Johnston at 367; *Hamilton v Hamilton* (1839) 2 D. 89, per Lord Fullerton; *Dewar v Dewar*, 1995 S.L.T. 467; cf. *Donnelly v Donnelly's Ex*, 1992 S.L.T. 13, where there was some division in the repute.

[80] *Walker v Roberts*, 1998 S.L.T. 1133; *Ackerman v Blackman*, 2000 Fam. L.R. 35.

[81] *Campbell v Campbell* (1867) 5 M. (HL) 115; *De Thoren v Wall* (1876) 3 R. (HL) 28.

[82] *Low v Gorman*, 1970 S.L.T. 356; *Walker v Roberts*, 1998 S.L.T. 1133 at 1135.

[83] *Hendry v Lord Advocate*, 1930 S.C. 1027; see also *A.B. v C.D.*, 1957 S.C. 415, cohabitation after void marriage.

[84] *Mullen v Mullen*, 1991 S.L.T. 205.

[85] In modern practice, the declarator has fixed a date for the marriage. See *Dewar v Dewar*, 1995 S.L.T. 467 at 473; *Donnelly v Donnelly's Exr*, 1992 S.L.T. 13 at 15. Jurisdiction to grant declarator, previously privative to the Court of Session, has been extended to the sheriff court by the Family Law (Scotland) Act 2006 s.4.

[86] Civil Partnership Act 2004 (the "2004 Act") s.85(1).

[87] 2004 Act s.85(2).

[88] 2004 Act s.86.

must (i) not be related in a forbidden degree, (ii) have attained the age of 16, (iii) be free to marry or enter a civil partnership, and (iv) be capable of understanding the nature of civil partnership and of giving consent. In order to register as civil partners, a notice in prescribed form must be submitted by each intended civil partner to the district registrar,[89] together with a fee, the relevant birth certificates and, where either party has previously been married or in a civil partnership, evidence of the dissolution of the previous marriage or partnership must be produced.[90] The district registrar enters prescribed details from the notice in the "civil partnership book"[91] and publicises, at least 14 days before the proposed registration, the names of the intended partners and the date of the proposed registration, while also sending that "relevant information" to the Registrar General, who must also publicise it.[92] At any time before the registration of a civil partnership, any person may submit an objection in writing to the district registrar.[93] Where the objection relates to a matter of misdescription or inaccuracy the district registrar may, with the approval of the Registrar General, make any necessary correction.[94] In any other case he must, pending consideration of the objection by the Registrar General, suspend the completion or issue of the civil partnership schedule.[95] If the Registrar General is satisfied that, on consideration of an objection, there is a legal impediment to registration of the civil partnership, he must direct the district registrar not to register the intended civil partners and to notify them accordingly.[96] If, on the other hand, he is satisfied that there is no such impediment, he must inform the district registrar to that effect.[97] On expiry of the 14 days after publication, but no more than three months after initial receipt of the notices, and if satisfied that there is no legal impediment to registration, the district registrar is to complete a civil partnership schedule in the prescribed form.[98] After the schedule has been checked and signed by the civil partners, the particulars of the civil partnership are registered in the "civil partnership register".[99] Registration of civil partnership may take place either at a registration office or at such other place as may be agreed with the local registration authority,[100] but there is a prohibition on using premises used solely or mainly for religious purposes as a place of registration.[101] Provision is made for expedited civil partnership registration with a former spouse, where one party to the previous marriage has obtained a full gender recognition certificate and a notice of intention to enter a civil partnership has been submitted within 30 days of the gender recognition certificate being issued.[102] A number of statutory offences are introduced in relation to civil partnerships, including registering a civil partnership knowing that either or both of the purported civil partners are married or

---

[89] 2004 Act s.88(1). Section 88(5) and (6) require the notice to contain a signed declaration that it is believed that the intended civil partners are eligible to be in civil partnership with each other.

[90] 2004 Act s.88(2).

[91] 2004 Act s.89.

[92] 2004 Act s.90.

[93] 2004 Act s.92(1).

[94] 2004 Act s.92(4)(a).

[95] 2004 Act s.92(4)(b).

[96] 2004 Act s.92(5)(a).

[97] 2004 Act s.92(5)(b).

[98] 2004 Act s.94.

[99] 2004 Act s.95.

[100] 2004 Act s.93(1). Section 93(2) permits registration taking place outside the district of the authorised registrar carrying out the registration, if the approval of the Registrar General is obtained.

[101] 2004 Act s.93(3).

[102] 2004 Act s.96.

in a civil partnership with someone other than the other party to the purported partnership, forging relevant civil partnership documents, purporting to register a civil partnership without a civil partnership schedule, wrongfully holding oneself out as an authorised registrar, purporting to register a civil partnership without both parties thereto being present and purporting to register two people in a place other than a registration office or a place agreed under s.93.[103]

Registration of marriages—In the case of religious marriages there is a statutory **44.12** provision requiring that the marriage schedule be signed by the parties, the witnesses and the celebrant and transmitted to the district registrar within three days of the marriage. The registrar must then cause particulars of the marriage to be entered in the register of marriages.[104] Similar provisions apply to a civil marriage.[105] Irregular marriages are registered following intimation to the Registrar General by the Principal Clerk of Session of the decree of declarator.[106]

Recognition of marriages contracted abroad—In determining the validity of a **44.13** marriage contracted abroad, a distinction must be drawn between questions of formal validity and those involving capacity.[107]

It is well settled that the *lex loci celebrationis* governs formal validity.[108] Where a marriage constituted by mutual consent given on the telephone with one party in Pakistan and the other in Scotland was acknowledged to be validly constituted in Pakistan, the court refused to grant declarator of nullity in Scotland.[109] A recognised exception to the general rule is provided for marriages celebrated under the Foreign Marriage Acts 1892–1988.[110] Questions of a party's capacity to marry are, by contrast, determined by the law of his domicile and this is now the subject of a statutory rule.[111] Similarly, the law governing consent to marry is that of the domicile of the party claiming lack of consent.[112] Thus a domiciled Scot who

---

[103] 2004 Act s.100. Summary proceedings must be brought within three months after evidence sufficient to justify the proceedings comes to the knowledge of the Lord Advocate or within 12 months after the offence is committed, whichever is later.

[104] 1977 Act s.15.

[105] 1977 Act s.19(3) and (4).

[106] 1977 Act s.21.

[107] In this context the term "essential validity" is sometimes used to refer to all matters relating to capacity, impotency and defects of consent. For a more comprehensive discussion of the issues see P. Beaumont and P. McEleavy, *Anton's Private International Law*, 3rd edn (Edinburgh: W. Green, 2011), paras 15.30–15.50; Clive, *The Law of Husband and Wife in Scotland* (1997), pp.121–135.

[108] 1977 Act s.82(1)(b). Both this provision and that in s.82(1)(a) above will subsist until the child attains the age of 18 (for the parental responsibility of guidance) or 16 (for the parental right to regulate residence): see s.82(2).

[109] *A v K* [2011] CSOH 101.

[110] These provide for the solemnisation by the British Authorities abroad of marriage between couples where at least one party is a UK national. For a full list of the Acts and their provisions, see Clive, *The Law of Husband and Wife in Scotland* (1997), pp.118–121.

[111] See Family Law (Scotland) Act 2006 s.38(2) and the discussion in Beaumont and McEleavy, *Anton's Private International Law* (2011), paras 15.19–15.20. The common law position is enunciated in *Lendrum v Chakravarti*, 1929 S.L.T. 96 at 103; *MacDougall v Chitnavis*, 1937 S.C. 390 at 406; *Bliersbach v MacEwen*, 1959 S.C. 43. For a practical application of the rule see *Rojas, Petitioner*, 1967 S.L.T. (Sh. Ct) 24. The 2006 Act followed the Scottish Law Commission Report which recommended that capacity should continue to be governed by the law of each party's domicile immediately prior to marriage. See Scottish Law Commission, *Report on Family Law* (HMSO, 1992), Scot. Law Com. No.135, paras 14.5, 14.6 and 14.22.

[112] *Singh v Singh*, 2005 S.L.T. 748, where the obiter dicta in *Di Rollo v Di Rollo*, 1959 S.L.T. 278 suggesting that the *lex loci celebrationis* would determine such an issue was not followed.

marries abroad will require to have attained the age of 16,[113] be within the accepted degrees of relationship,[114] have no prior subsisting marriage,[115] and give full and free consent to the marriage.[116] The validity of a marriage contracted abroad where one of the parties is impotent may be governed by the law of the forum in which there is a subsequent challenge to it.[117]

44.14 Validity of civil partnerships registered outside Scotland—Statutory rules govern the validity of civil partnerships registered in other parts of the United Kingdom or who register an apparent or alleged overseas relationship. For partnerships registered in England and Wales and Northern Ireland, the *lex loci celebrationis* governs validity; the civil partnership is void if it would be void in the part of the United Kingdom in which registration took place and voidable if it would be voidable there.[118] Civil partnerships registered at a British Consulate abroad or by armed forces personnel must comply with the statutory conditions and requirements for registration or they will be void,[119] and again they are voidable if they would be voidable in the appropriate part of the United Kingdom.[120] For a partnership registered overseas, the relevant law of the country or territory where the overseas relationship was registered, including its rules of private international law, will govern validity.[121] Legal relationships validly registered under the law of a country or territory outwith the United Kingdom will be recognised without any requirement to register in this jurisdiction as well on condition that the foreign registered relationship meets the meets the requirements of the Civil Partnership Act 2004.[122]

44.15 Legal effects of marriage and civil partnership: General—Under the common law, marriage had substantial consequences for a spouse in relation to contract,[123] delict, evidence,[124] nationality,[125] property rights[126] and other financial matters.

---

[113] 1977 Act s.1(1).

[114] 1977 Act s.2(1)(b); para.44.04, above.

[115] 1977 Act s.2(3)(b). However, a divorced party can now remarry in any part of the United Kingdom even if the law of their domicile does not recognise the divorce, so long as it is recognised in the jurisdiction of the marriage. See s.50 of the Family Law Act 1986.

[116] Prior to the decision in *A v K* [2011] CSOH 101 there was no Scottish authority directly on this point, but the Scottish Law Commission had recommended that Scots law follow the English position that consent follows the law of the domicile. See Scottish Law Commission, *Report on Family Law*, para.14.5.

[117] See Clive, *The Law of Husband and Wife in Scotland* (1997), pp.131–133.

[118] 2004 Act s.124(1) and (2).

[119] 2004 Act s.124(4)(a).

[120] 2004 Act s.124(4)(b).

[121] 2004 Act s.124(7)–(11).

[122] 2004 Act ss.212–218 and Sch.20 to the Act, which has a growing list of countries or territories together with the specified relationships that qualify for recognition.

[123] For example, a husband was liable for his wife's contracts where these arose as a result of the presumption that he had given her authority to deal with his domestic affairs (*praepositura negotiis domesticis*). This common law rule was ultimately abolished by s.7 of the Law Reform (Husband and Wife) (Scotland) Act 1984.

[124] At common law the spouse of a party was not a competent witness until the rule was altered by s.3 of the Evidence (Scotland) Act 1853.

[125] The rule that a woman's nationality followed that of her husband, enacted by s.16 of the Aliens Act 1844 and s.10(1) of the Naturalistion Act 1870, was finally abolished by the British Nationality Act 1948.

[126] Marriage had the effect at common law of an assignation to the husband of the whole moveable estate belonging to the wife at the date of the marriage or which she might acquire during its subsistence. Known as the *jus mariti*, this was abolished in the case of marriages contracted after July 18,

A series of statutes has limited the legal consequences of marriage,[127] and while the marriage contract continues to create a considerable number of mutual rights and related remedies, there are now few rights and duties in relation to third parties particular to a spouse. Civil partners are likely to be given parity of treatment with spouses in this context. The law formerly refused an action of reparation by one spouse against the other on the ground of the intimate relationship between them, but each may now sue the other in respect of a wrongful or negligent act or omission[128]; and a spouse may sue the other's employer for damages on the basis of vicarious liability.[129] An action of removing by one spouse against the other is competent, if they stand in the relation of landlord and tenant,[130] and an action based on contract is also competent.[131] The duty of adherence remained, but only to the extent that a refusal to live with one's spouse was regarded as desertion in divorce proceedings, prior to desertion as a basis for divorce being removed.[132] Actions for adherence have been abolished.[133]

Aliment—The obligation to aliment represents one of the most significant legal **44.16** consequences of marriage and now also of civil partnership. At common law a husband was bound to aliment his wife if she was willing to live with him.[134] The amount of aliment which would be awarded by the court depended on the rank and manner of life of the spouses.[135] Legislation first imposed a limited reciprocal obligation of aliment on a wife of sufficient means in 1920.[136] Aliment of spouses and civil partners is now regulated by the Family Law (Scotland) Act 1985 under which each spouse or civil partner owes an obligation of aliment to the other.[137] The obligation is to provide such support as is reasonable in the circumstances

---

1881, by the Married Women's Property (Scotland) Act 1881, although a husband retained its consequential liability for at least some of his wife's moveable debts until relieved of this by s.6 of the Law Reform (Husband and Wife) (Scotland) Act 1984. The common law had the further effect that where a wife was able to contract with property, such as heritage, she was obliged, by the *jus administrationis* to obtain the consent of her husband, her "curator", before disposing of it. This rule was abolished by s.2 of the Married Women's Property (Scotland) Act 1920 for women over 18 years of age and ultimately for all wives by s.3 of the 1984 Act.

[127] The most important legislative changes this century include the Married Women's Property (Scotland) Act 1920, the Law Reform (Husband and Wife) (Scotland) Act 1984 and the Family Law (Scotland) Act 1985. For a good historical summary of the statutory development of matrimonial property law, see Clive, *The Law of Husband and Wife in Scotland* (1997), pp.219–223.

[128] The common law rule was replaced by the Law Reform (Husband and Wife) Act 1962 s.2, but the court retained a discretion to dismiss the proceedings if it appeared there would be no substantial benefit to either party. The 1962 Act has been repealed by the Family Law (Scotland) Act 2006 Sch.3, but the common law does not revive—see Interpretation Act 1978 s.16.

[129] *Webb v Inglis*, 1958 S.L.T. (Notes) 8.

[130] *Millar v Millar*, 1940 S.C.56; see *Labno v Labno*, 1949 S.L.T. (Notes) 18 in relation to ejection.

[131] *Horsburgh v Horsburgh*, 1949 S.C. 227.

[132] By the Family Law (Scotland) Act 2006 s.12, repealing para.(c) of s.1(2) of the Divorce (Scotland) Act 1976. See para.44.26.

[133] Law Reform (Husband and Wife) (Scotland) Act 1984 s.2(1).

[134] *Beveridge v Beveridge*, 1963 S.C. 572.

[135] Erskine, Inst., 1, vi, 19; *Thomson v Thomson* (1890) 17 R. 1091; *Scott v Scott* (1894) 21 R. 853; and see *Alexander v Alexander*, 1957 S.L.T. 298, where the husband's regular expenditure of capital was taken into account.

[136] Married Women's Property (Scotland) Act 1920 s.4.

[137] Family Law (Scotland) Act 1985 (the "1985 Act") s.1(1), as amended by the 2004 Act Sch.28 to insert s.1(1)(bb) which provides for the mutual obligation of civil partners to support each other.

having regard to the needs and resources of the parties,[138] their earning capacities, and all the circumstances of the case.[139] As tax relief is effectively no longer available to those paying aliment,[140] it is more appropriate when computing their resources to consider income net of tax.[141] Among the circumstances of which the court may, if it thinks fit, take account is any support, financial or otherwise, which an obligant gives, whether or not under an alimentary obligation, to a person whom he maintains as a dependant in his household.[142] On the other hand, no account is to be taken of any conduct of a party unless it would be manifestly inequitable to leave it out of account.[143] The parents of a person under 18 years of age or, in some circumstances, under 25, have an obligation of aliment which, if that person be married, is concurrent with the obligation owed by his or her spouse.[144] There is no fixed order of liability in such cases but the court, in deciding the amount of any aliment to be paid by one of the obligants is to have regard, among the other circumstances of the case, to the obligation owed by the others.[145]

Proceedings for aliment only may be brought by a spouse or civil partner in the Court of Session or in the sheriff court.[146] A claim for aliment may also be made,[147] within proceedings for divorce, dissolution of civil partnership, separation or declarator of marriage or of nullity, or relating to orders for financial provision or concerning parental responsibilities or parental rights,[148] guardianship, parentage, legitimacy or in any other proceedings where the court considers it appropriate to include a claim for aliment.[149] Where any claim for aliment is made, the court also has power to award interim aliment.[150] In that context, the award will normally be made on the basis of reasonable need. It has been accepted that need is relative to the lifestyle enjoyed by the parties during the marriage, subject to the payer's present ability to continue to fund that lifestyle.[151] An action or claim is competent although the claimant is living in the same household as the defender.[152] It is a defence that the defender has made an offer, which it is

---

[138] Defined in s.27 of the Act as being "present and foreseeable" needs and resources. The provision of benefits in kind by an employer amounts to a resource of the employee, but not to a cash sum equivalent; *Semple v Semple*, 1995 S.C.L.R. 569.

[139] 1985 Act ss.1(2) and 4. For example the court may require to assess the extent of income that a self employed person could have at his disposal, where he chooses not to draw available profit from a business—*B v B*, 1999 Fam. L.R. 74.

[140] The limited tax relief allowed by the Income and Corporation Taxes Act 1988 s.347B, was withdrawn from 2000–2001, except where one party to the marriage was aged 65 or over at April 5, 2000.

[141] As it was from the time all payments of a "maintenance" were effectively taken out of the tax system by the Income and Corporation Taxes Act 1988; *Wiseman v Wiseman*, 1989 S.C.L.R. 757; *Pryde v Pryde*, 1991 S.L.T. (Sh. Ct) 26; cf. *MacInnes v MacInnes*, 1990 G.W.D. 13–690.

[142] 1985 Act s.4(3)(a). See *Pryde v Pryde*, 1991 S.L.T. (Sh. Ct) 26 and *Munro v Munro*, 1986 S.L.T. 72.

[143] 1985 Act s.4(3)(b); *Walker v Walker*, 1991 S.L.T. 649.

[144] 1985 Act s.1(1). See para.44.41, below.

[145] 1985 Act s.4(2).

[146] 1985 Act s.2(1). The provision is not limited to spousal aliment, but relates to claims "against any person owing an obligation of aliment".

[147] "unless in any particular case the Court considers it inappropriate"—s.2(2).

[148] The opportunity to resolve all such issues in one action is now restricted by the provisions of the Child Support Act 1991. See para.44.42.

[149] 1985 Act s.2(2).

[150] 1985 Act s.6(1).

[151] In *McGeoch v McGeoch*, 1998 Fam. L.R. 130, the Lord Ordinary accepted that, for assessment of aliment at an interim stage only, this approach could be adopted, under reference to the English decision of *F. v F.* [1995] 2 F.L.R. 45. See also *B v B*, 1999 Fam. L.R. 74.

[152] 1985 Act s.2(6).

reasonable to expect the person concerned to accept, to receive that person into his household and to fulfil the obligation of aliment.[153] In considering the reasonableness of an offer, the court is to have regard to any conduct, decree or other circumstances which appear to be relevant but an agreement by husband and wife or civil partners to live apart is not of itself to be regarded as making it unreasonable to expect an offer to be accepted.[154]

In granting decree in an action for aliment, the court will usually order the making of periodical payments, for a definite or indefinite period.[155] The making of alimentary payments of an occasional or special nature may also be made, if the court thinks fit.[156] An award of aliment may be backdated to the date of bringing the action or even earlier on special cause shown,[157] although the power to back-date to a time which precedes the raising of proceedings is to be used sparingly.[158] The provisions for backdating do not apply to awards of interim aliment.[159] A decree for aliment may be varied or recalled if there has been a material change of circumstances.[160] Such changes may relate, for example, to the needs and resources of one or both of the parties or the commencement of cohabitation by one of the spouses or civil partners with a third party.[161] Demonstrating that an earlier award was made on information which turned out to be incorrect or incomplete does not constitute a relevant change.[162] On a material change of circumstances a person who has entered into an agreement to pay aliment may apply to the court for variation of the amount or termination of the agreement.[163] Before such an application can be made, however, an obligation of aliment must continue to be owed under the Act; the right to seek a variation does not extend to couples who are cohabiting or are divorced.[164] Variations of awards, including those made in actions brought before the commencement of the 1985 Act, may be backdated, but the power to backdate variations does not extend to variation of awards of interim aliment.[165] The previous inability to backdate a variation of an agreement on interim aliment[166] or to make interim orders in such an application, has been rectified.[167] Any provision in an agreement which purports to exclude liability for future aliment or restrict the right to claim aliment is of no effect unless it was fair and reasonable in all the circumstances of the agreement when it was entered into.[168] An award of aliment to a spouse or civil partner will cease

---

[153] 1985 Act s.2(8).

[154] 1985 Act s.2(9).

[155] 1985 Act s.3(1)(a).

[156] 1985 Act s.3(1)(b).

[157] 1985 Act s.3(1)(c). The remedy is an exceptional one and is rarely granted. See *Buchan v Buchan*, 1993 S.C.L.R. 158.

[158] *Hannah v Hannah*, 1988 S.L.T. 82; *Adamson v Adamson*, 1995 S.L.T. (Sh. Ct) 45.

[159] *McColl v McColl*, 1993 S.C. 276. This is thought to be a defect in the legislation (see Clive, *The Law of Husband and Wife in Scotland* (1997), p.173) but was not remedied by the Family Law (Scotland) Act 2006.

[160] 1985 Act s.5(1).

[161] *Kavanagh v Kavanagh*, 1989 S.L.T. 134; *Munro v Munro*, 1986 S.L.T. 72.

[162] *Walker v Walker*, 1991 S.L.T. 649.

[163] 1985 Act s.7(2).

[164] *Drummond v Drummond*, 1995 S.C. 321.

[165] *McColl v McColl*, 1993 S.C. 276.

[166] See *Ellerby v Ellerby*, 1991 S.C.L.R. 608.

[167] By the insertion of subss.(2ZA)–(2ZC) into s.7(2) of the 1985 Act by the Family Law (Scotland) Act 2006 s.20(2). In backdating a variation, the court may also order any sums paid under the agreement to be repaid.

[168] 1985 Act s.7(1).

to have effect if the obligation to aliment is terminated by death, divorce, or dissolution of civil partnership.[169]

44.17　Matrimonial Homes (Family Protection) (Scotland) Act 1981 and Civil Partnership Act 2004: Occupancy rights and ancillary remedies—These legislative provisions, in creating rights of occupancy in the matrimonial (or family) home, represent a radical departure from the common law rule that the legal owner or tenant of a property had a right to its exclusive use, to the extent that he could insist on the departure from the property of his spouse.[170] The 1981 Act confers occupancy rights, together with various subsidiary and ancillary rights and remedies,[171] on a spouse who is not the owner or tenant of the matrimonial home, referred to as a "non-entitled spouse."[172] The spouse who owns, is the tenant of, or who is permitted by a third party to occupy the property, is the "entitled spouse".[173] The mirror provisions of the 2004 Act use the language of "family home", "entitled partner" and "non entitled partner" in conferring identical rights, subsidiary and ancillary rights and remedies for civil partners.[174] Wide definitions of matrimonial home and family home include any house, caravan, houseboat or other structure provided or made available by one or both of the spouses or civil partners as a family residence (or which, having been provided or made available by one or both of the spouses or civil partners, has become a family residence).[175] It does not include a home provided by one spouse or civil partner as his separate residence.[176] However, a spouse ordered by the court to sell his interest in the matrimonial home to the other spouse was found to have a continuing right to occupy the property in the absence of divorce or grounds for an exclusion order.[177] Occupancy rights include the right to continue in an existing occupation and to enter into and occupy the home where the non-entitled spouse or civil partner is not already in occupation.[178] The rights may be exercised together with any child of the family.[179] A non-entitled spouse or civil partner may renounce his or her rights but only in relation to a particular matrimonial or family home or intended matrimonial or family home and only by swearing or affirming before a notary public that the renunciation is made freely and without coercion

---

[169] It should be noted, however, that an independent claim for aliment can be brought against the estate of a deceased spouse; see Clive, *The Law of Husband and Wife in Scotland* (1997), pp.602–603; and an appellate court may award interim aliment to a spouse after divorce pending outcome of the appeal or reclaiming motion as the divorce itself is suspended—see *Lessani v Lessani*, 2007 Fam. L.R. 81.

[170] *MacLure v MacLure*, 1911 S.C. 200. The rule applied equally to female proprietors; see *Millar v Millar*, 1940 S.C. 56.

[171] Some of these affect a spouse's ability to enter into property transactions. See para.44.20, below.

[172] Matrimonial Homes (Family Protection) (Scotland) Act 1981 (the "1981 Act") s.1(1).

[173] 1981 Act s.1(2) clarifies that permission by a third party to occupy a home renders the spouse "entitled" only if the third party has waived his or her right of occupation in favour of the entitled spouse. See *Murphy v Murphy*, 1992 S.C.L.R. 62.

[174] 2004 Act ss.101–104.

[175] 1981 Act s.22 (as amended by the Family Law (Scotland) Act 2006 s.9 and the 2004 Act s.135(1)). The definition also includes garden, grounds or buildings attached or ancillary to the use of the home itself.

[176] 1981 Act s.22; 2004 Act s.135(1).

[177] *Adams v Adams* [2010] Fam. L.R. 30.

[178] 1981 Act s.1(4) and paras (a) and (b) of s.1(1); 2004 Act s.101(1).

[179] 1981 Act s.1(1A); 2004 Act s.101(2). "Child of the family" is defined as including any child or grandchild of either spouse or civil partner, and any person who has been brought up, or accepted by either spouse or treated by either civil partner as if he or she were a child of that spouse or partner, whatever the age of such a child, grandchild or person—see 1981 Act s.22; 2004 Act s.101(7).

of any kind.[180] A non-entitled spouse or civil partner who has been refused entry to the matrimonial or family home by the entitled spouse or partner, may exercise the right to enter and occupy the home only with leave of the court.[181] Either spouse or civil partner may apply to the court for an order declaring, enforcing or restricting occupancy rights or regulating their exercise or protecting the rights of the applicant spouse or civil partner in relation to the other spouse or civil partner.[182] If it appears to the court that the application relates to a matrimonial or family home, then, if requested, an order must be made declaring the rights of the applicant spouse or civil partner.[183] In relation to orders enforcing, restricting, regulating or protecting occupancy rights, the court has a discretion to make such order as it considers just and reasonable.[184] In that determination, it is directed to have regard to all the circumstances of the case including the conduct of the spouses or civil partners, their respective needs and financial resources, the needs of any child of the family, the use of the matrimonial or family home in relation to any trade, business or profession of either spouse or civil partner,[185] and whether the entitled spouse or civil partner has offered suitable alternative accommodation to the non-entitled spouse or civil partner.[186] There is provision for interim orders pending a decision on regulation of occupancy rights.[187] The court also has power to grant to a non-entitled spouse or civil partner the possession or use of furniture and plenishings in the matrimonial or family home where these are owned or hired by the entitled spouse or civil partner.[188] An order enforcing, restricting, regulating or protecting occupancy rights is not to have the effect of excluding the non-applicant spouse or civil partner from the matrimonial or family home.[189]

The Act grants a non-entitled spouse or civil partner various practical subsidiary rights to enable him or her to secure occupancy in the matrimonial or family home. These include a right to make payment of outgoings[190] and to perform obligations incumbent on the entitled spouse or civil partner (other than non-essential repairs and improvements),[191] to enforce performance of an obligation given by a third party to the entitled spouse or civil partner,[192] to carry out essential repairs and to take other steps to protect his or her occupancy rights.[193] A non-entitled spouse or civil partner who wishes to carry out non-essential repairs or improvements must

---

[180] 1981 Act s.1(6); 2004 Act s.101(5) and (6).

[181] 1981 Act s.1(3); 2004 Act s.101(4).

[182] 1981 Act s.3(1); 2004 Act s.103(1).

[183] 1981 Act s.3(3); 2004 Act s.101(3). The opinion expressed in *Welsh v Welsh*, 1987 S.L.T. (Sh. Ct) 30 that a declarator under s.3(1) is a necessary precondition for the obtaining of the other orders listed in s.3 has been doubted. See Clive, *The Law of Husband and Wife in Scotland* (1997), p.269.

[184] 1981 Act s.3(3); 2004 Act s.103(3).

[185] In *Cowie v Cowie*, 1986 G.W.D. 2–33, the First Division was not prepared to refuse the order where the husband argued that he used the matrimonial home for his work, this being only one of many factors to be taken into account.

[186] 1981 Act s.3(3)(a)–(e); 2004 Act s.103(3)(a)–(e) It has been held that relevant conduct in terms of s.3(3)(a) must be related primarily to the conduct of the spouses in relation to the matter of occupancy of the matrimonial home; see *Berry v Berry*, 1988 S.L.T. 650.

[187] 1981 Act s.3(4); 2004 Act s.101(4).

[188] 1981 Act s.3(2); 2004 Act s.103(2). The remedy extends to items that the entitled spouse or civil partner is acquiring under a hire purchase or conditional sale agreement.

[189] 1981 Act s.3(5).

[190] 1981 Act s.2(1)(a); 2004 Act s.102(1)(a). Payment of rent, rates, secured loan instalments, interest or other outgoings other than repairs or improvements has effect in relation to the rights of a third party as if made by the entitled spouse or civil partner. See 1981 Act s.2(2) and 2004 Act s.102(2).

[191] 1981 Act s.2(1)(b) and (2); 2004 Act s.102(1)(b) and (2).

[192] 1981 Act s.2(1)(c) and (2); 2004 Act s.102(1)(c) and (2).

[193] 1981 Act s.2(1)(d) and (f); 2004 Act s.102(1)(d) and (f).

seek authorisation from the court.[194] There is further provision for the court to apportion expenditure on anything relating to the matrimonial or family home as between the entitled spouse or civil partner and the non-entitled spouse or civil partner.[195] Where both spouses or civil partners are entitled in respect of the matrimonial or family home, provision is made to enable non-essential repairs to be carried out and for the court to apportion expenditure in respect thereof.[196] Occupancy rights conferred as a result of the status of marriage or civil partnership normally terminate on divorce or dissolution of civil partnership, but non-entitled spouses or partners will also lose these rights after two years' absence from the home coupled with non-cohabitation with the entitled spouse or civil partner during that period.[197]

44.18 **Exclusion orders**—Either spouse or civil partner, whether or not in occupation, may apply to the court for an exclusion order suspending the occupancy rights of the other spouse or civil partner.[198] The court is required to make such an order if that is necessary for the protection of the applicant or any child of the family from any conduct or threatened or reasonably apprehended conduct of the non-applicant spouse or civil partner which would be injurious to the physical or mental health of the applicant or child unless it appears to the court that the making of an order would be unjustified or unreasonable having regard to all the circumstances.[199] There is provision for interim suspension of occupancy rights pending the making of an exclusion order, subject to the opportunity being afforded to the non-applicant spouse or civil partner to contest the application.[200] When the provisions of the 1981 Act relating to exclusion orders were enacted, they represented a radical innovation in this area of law and the courts initially took a restrictive view of the necessity test.[201] It remains necessary to satisfy the court that the lesser protection of an interdict would be insufficient[202] or inappropriate.[203] A desire to be free of the tension involved in residing with an estranged spouse (or civil partner) does

---

[194] 1981 Act s.2(1)(e); 2004 Act s.102(1)(e).

[195] 1981 Act s.2(3); 2004 Act s.102(3). The court must have regard to the respective financial circumstances of the parties in determining an application for apportionment. See *Porter v Porter*, 1990 S.C.L.R. 752. Rights to make payments in respect of furniture and plenishings and to apply for orders apportioning expenditure on same as between the entitled and non-entitled spouses or civil partners are contained in the 1981 Act s.2(5) and the 2004 Act s.102(5).

[196] 1981 Act s.2(4); 2004 Act s.102(4).This extends the common law right of co-owners to carry out only essential repairs without the other party's consent.

[197] 1981 Act s.1(7) and (8) added by the Family Law (Scotland) Act 2006 s.5; 2004 Act s.101(7) and (8), added by the 2006 Act Sch.1 para.3.

[198] 1981 Act s.4(1); 2004 Act s.104(1).

[199] 1981 Act s.4(2) and (3); 2004 Act s.104(2) and (3). The circumstances to be considered include the various matters noted above in relation to orders enforcing or restricting occupancy rights—1981 Act s.3(3)(a)–(e); 2004 Act s.103(3)(a)–(e). Further qualifications apply where the matrimonial or family home is an agricultural holding or is a tied house—1981 Act s.4(3)(b); 2004 Act s.104(3)(b).

[200] 1981 Act s.4(6); 2004 Act s.104(6). See *Armitage v Armitage*, 1993 S.C.L.R. 173. The test for an interim order is that in the 1981 Act s.4(2) and (3) and the 2004 Act s.104(2) and (3).

[201] The statements in *Bell v Bell*, 1983 S.L.T. 224 suggesting that there must be a risk of serious injury or immediate danger were later criticised in *McCafferty v McCafferty*, 1986 S.L.T 650 at 655, where it was confirmed that the statutory test must be applied without additional conditions being implied.

[202] *Ward v Ward*, 1983 S.L.T. 472; *Colagiacomo v Colagiacomo*, 1983 S.L.T. 559; *Brown v Brown*, 1985 S.L.T. 376; *McCafferty*, 1986 S.L.T 650 at 656; *Nasir v Nasir*, 1993 G.W.D. 30–1909 and *Pryde v Pryde*, 1996 G.W.D. 39–2245.

[203] See *Roberton v Roberton*, 1999 S.L.T. 38, where the First Division, in refusing an appeal by the husband against an interim exclusion order, commented that an interdict would have been impractical and difficult to frame in the particular circumstances of the unreasonably intrusive and jealous behaviour of the husband.

not justify the protection.[204] The court is required to make further orders on granting an exclusion order. It must grant an interdict prohibiting the excluded spouse or civil partner from entering the matrimonial or family home without the express permission of the applicant.[205] The court is also directed to grant a warrant for summary ejection of the non-applicant spouse or civil partner from the home and an order prohibiting the removal of furniture or plenishings therefrom without written consent or order of court on request by the applicant spouse or civil partner, unless satisfied by the other spouse or civil partner that the remedy sought is unnecessary.[206] A number of further ancillary orders may be granted at the discretion of the court.[207] An exclusion order ceases to have effect on the termination of marriage or civil partnership by death, divorce or dissolution, or when one or both spouses or civil partners ceases to be entitled or permitted to occupy the home.[208]

Interdicts—The existing common law remedy of interdict has been strengthened **44.19** by the introduction through legislation of particular "matrimonial interdicts" for spouses and "relevant interdicts" for civil partners. These terms are now used to denote interdicts which (a) restrain or prohibit any conduct of one spouse or civil partner towards the other spouse or civil partner or a child of the family, or (b) prohibit a spouse or civil partner from entering or remaining in a matrimonial or family home, any other residence occupied by the applicant, any place of work of the applicant or any school attended by a child in the permanent or temporary care of the applicant.[209] The second described matrimonial or relevant interdict cannot be used as a method of removing a spouse or civil partner from the matrimonial or family home, which can be achieved only by an exclusion order or where the court refuses leave to exercise occupancy rights.[210] Powers of arrest can be attached to matrimonial and relevant interdicts. The provisions on powers of arrest are now contained within the Protection From Abuse (Scotland) Act 2001.[211] That Act requires a power of arrest to be attached to matrimonial and relevant interdicts where an application to attach such a power is made and the applicant requires protection from a risk of abuse in breach of the interdict.[212] There is no discretion to refuse to attach a power of arrest to any matrimonial interdict ancillary to an exclusion order.[213] Intimation of a power of arrest requires to be

---

[204] *Matheson v Matheson*, 1986 S.L.T. (Sh. Ct) 2; *Raeburn v Raeburn*, 1990 G.W.D. 8–424; *Davidson v Davidson*, 1991 G.W.D. 34–2088.

[205] 1981 Act s.4(4)(b); 2004 Act s.104(4)(b).

[206] 1981 Act s.4(4)(a) and (c); 2004 Act s.104(4)(a) and (c). A summary ejection warrant may be refused, for example, if the exclusion order is suspended to allow the non applicant spouse (or civil partner) time to organise a removal. See *Mather v Mather*, 1987 S.L.T. 565.

[207] 1981 Act s.4(5); 2004 Act s.104(5).

[208] 1981 Act s.5(1)(a), (b) and (c); 2004 Act s.105(2)(a), (b) and (c).

[209] 1981 Act s.14(2) (as amended by the Family Law (Scotland) Act 2006 s.10(2)); 2004 Act s.113(2) (as amended by the Family Law (Scotland) Act 2006 s.33). Section 14(1) and s.113(1) make clear that the application can competently be made while the parties are living together as husband and wife or civil partners.

[210] 1981 Act s.14(3), (4) and (5) (as added by the Family Law (Scotland) Act 2006 s.10(3)); 2004 Act s.113(3), (4) and (5) (as added by the Family Law (Scotland) Act 2006 s.33). This clarifies the position discussed in *Tattersall v Tatersall*, 1983 S.L.T. 506 but not followed in *Mazur v Mazur*, 1990 G.W.D. 35–2017.

[211] Protection From Abuse (Scotland) Act 2001 (asp 14). For spouses the original power to attach a power of arrest was contained in ss.15–17 of the 1981 Act. The Family Law (Scotland) Act 2006 completed a process of transferring all power of arrest provisions to the 2001 Act.

[212] Protection from Abuse (Scotland) Act 2001 s.1(2).

[213] Protection from Abuse (Scotland) Act 2001 s.1(1A), inserted by the Family Law (Scotland) Act 2006 s.32 (this was also the position previously under s.15(1)(a) of the 1981 Act).

made to the police, after which any police officer may arrest the non-applicant spouse without warrant on having reasonable cause to suspect a breach of the interdict.[214] Previously a power of arrest continued to have effect until the termination of the marriage, but a specified duration and expiry date are now fixed, with provision for extension where necessary.[215]

44.20 Protection against property dealings and transfer of tenancy orders—As a general rule, the continued exercise by a non-entitled spouse or civil partner of his occupancy rights is not to be prejudiced by reason only of any dealing by the entitled spouse or civil partner relating to the home and a third party is not by reason of such dealings entitled to occupy the matrimonial or family home or any part of it.[216] Relevant dealings include the sale or lease of a home, the grant of a heritable security over it, and the creation of a trust.[217] There are certain situations in which this general protection does not apply. If the entitled spouse or civil partner occupies the home by permission of a third party, or along with a third party, there is no protection.[218] The rule against dealings does not apply where the non-entitled spouse or civil partner has, in the required form, consented to the dealing or renounced his or her occupancy rights.[219] The court has power to make an order dispensing with the consent of the non-entitled spouse or civil partner to the dealing, where such consent is being unreasonably withheld, or where it cannot be given through disability, non-age or disappearance.[220] Dispensation with the consent of a non-entitled spouse or partner must relate to a specific proposed dealing.[221] The general protective rule is also excluded where a sale to a third party has occurred, the third party has acted in good faith and there was exhibited to him by the seller either an affidavit or written declaration that, at the time of the dealing, the property was not a matrimonial or family home in relation to which a spouse or civil partner of the seller had occupancy rights, or an ex facie valid renunciation or consent by the non-entitled spouse or partner.[222] Where both spouses or civil partners are entitled spouses or civil partners, the rights of each are also protected[223] and the court has power to refuse division and sale of the matrimonial or family home. In deciding whether or not to exercise the discretion so to refuse, the court must have regard to all the circumstances of the case including the matters specified as relevant to the regulation of occupancy rights and must also consider whether the spouse or partner bringing the action offers or has offered to make available to the other any suitable alternative accommodation.[224]

---

[214] Protection from Abuse (Scotland) Act 2001 ss.2(1) and 3(1).

[215] s.15(2) of the 1981 Act, which provided for termination on divorce, has been replaced by s.2(3) and s.40 of the Protection from Abuse (Scotland) Act 2001, as now amended by the Family Law (Scotland) Act 2006.

[216] 1981 Act s.6(1); 2004 Act s.106(1).

[217] 1981 Act s.6(2); 2004 Act s.106(2).

[218] 1981 Act s.6(2); 2004 Act s.106(2).

[219] 1981 Act s.6(3)(a); 2004 Act s.106(3)(a). The form of consent for spouses is prescribed by the Matrimonial Homes (Form of Consent) (Scotland) Regulations 1982 (SI 1982/971).

[220] 1981 Act s.7(1); 2004 Act s.107(1). A motive for refusing consent which does not relate to the protection of occupancy rights is unreasonable; see *O'Neill v O'Neill*, 1987 S.L.T. (Sh. Ct) 26.

[221] See *Longmuir v Longmuir*, 1985 S.L.T. (Sh. Ct) 33; *Fyfe v Fyfe*, 1987 S.L.T. (Sh. Ct) 38.

[222] 1981 Act s.6(3); 2004 Act s.106(3)(e). The written declaration may be signed by a person acting on behalf of the seller or non entitled spouse or partner under a power of attorney or as a guardian under the Adults with Incapacity (Scotland) Act 2000.

[223] 1981 Act s.9; 2004 Act s.109.

[224] 1981 Act s.19, see e.g. *Edwards v Edwards*, 2001 G.W.D. 6–228; *Berry v Berry*, 1988 S.L.T. 650 and *Bathgate v Bathgate*, 2003 G.W.D. 19–588; 2004 Act s.110.

Where a matrimonial or family home is occupied under a lease the court has power, on an application by a non-entitled spouse or civil partner, to make an order transferring the tenancy of the matrimonial or family home to that spouse or partner. The order may provide for the payment of such compensation to the entitled spouse or partner as seems just and reasonable in all the circumstances of the case.[225] In addition to the factors relevant to orders regulating occupancy rights, the suitability of the applicant and his or her ability to perform the obligations under the lease require to be considered.[226] The landlord of the property must be given an opportunity to contest the application for transfer and will in any event be notified of any order made.[227]

Property—Following the abolition of the husband's rights over the property of **44.21** his wife, marriage came to have little effect on the property rights of spouses until death or divorce when certain rights would emerge. The general rule of separate property of spouses and civil partners is now contained in the Family Law (Scotland) Act 1985 (the "1985 Act")[228] which provides that marriage or civil partnership shall not of itself affect the respective rights of the relevant parties in relation to their property nor shall it affect their legal capacity. Each spouse or civil partner remains owner of his or her estate including any property acquired after marriage or civil partnership unless they choose to create joint property rights. In addition to the modifications to this rule imposed by the Matrimonial Homes (Family Protection) (Scotland) Act 1981 and the Civil Partnership Act 2004, the general rule is subject to several other exceptions.[229] For example, there is a statutory rebuttable presumption that each spouse or civil partner has a right to an equal share in any household goods obtained in prospect of or during the marriage or civil partnership, other than by gift or succession from a third party.[230] Further, there is a statutory rule on property derived from housekeeping allowances. If any question arises between spouses or civil partners (whether during or after a marriage or civil partnership) as to the right of one of the parties to money derived from any allowance made by either party for their joint household expenses or for similar purposes, or to any property acquired out of such money, the money or property shall, in the absence of agreement to the contrary, be treated as belonging to each party in equal shares.[231]

An exception to the rule that an insurance policy taken out for a third party will not give that third party any rights under it unless delivery or some adequate equivalent takes place continues to be provided by the Married Women's Policies of Assurance (Scotland) Act 1880.[232] Thus a policy, effected by a man or woman

---

[225] 1981 Act s.13(1); 2004 Act s.112(1).

[226] 1981 Act s.13(3); 2004 Act s.112(3). Examples include *McGowan v McGowan*, 1986 S.L.T. 112 and *Guyan v Guyan*, 2001 Fam. L.R. 99. See also *Souter v McAuley* Unreported March 31, 2010 Dundee Sheriff Court, involving same sex cohabitants.

[227] 1981 Act s.13(4) and (6); 2004 Act s.112(4) and (7). See also para.44.20, above on transfer of tenancy and the matrimonial home.

[228] 1985 Act s.24 (as amended by the 2004 Act Sch.28).

[229] The 1981 and 2004 Acts insofar as they relate to occupancy rights are dealt with above at paras 44.17–44.19. For a comprehensive analysis of the effect of marriage on the property rights of spouses, see Clive, *Law of Husband and Wife in Scotland* (1997), Ch.14.

[230] 1985 Act s.25 (as amended). Section 25(3) defines household goods as anything kept or used at any time during the marriage or civil partnership for the joint domestic purposes of the parties, under exception of money or securities, road vehicles or domestic animals.

[231] 1985 Act s.26 (as amended by the 2004 Act Sch.28).

[232] s.2 of the 1880 Act, as amended by the Married Women's Policies of Assurance (Scotland) (Amendment) Act 1980.

on his or her own life and expressed on the face of it to be for the benefit of his or her spouse or children or both, shall be deemed a trust for these. "Children" includes adopted children.[233] The provision also now applies to a policy of assurance effected by a civil partner on his own life and expressed to be for the benefit of his or her civil partner, his children or his partner and children.[234] As soon as the policy is effected,[235] it vests in the spouse or civil partner and his or her representatives, or any other trustee nominated, in trust for the purposes so expressed,

> "and shall not otherwise be subject to his or her control, or form part of his or her estate, or be liable to the diligence of his or her creditors, or be revocable as a donation, or reducible on any ground of excess or insolvency".

If, however, the policy was effected with intent to defraud creditors, or if the person insured is made bankrupt within two years from its date, the creditors are entitled to repayment of the premiums out of the proceeds of the policy.[236] Any right to bring a statutory challenge of a gratuitous alienation is expressed to be without prejudice to the operation of s.2.[237] The 1880 Act has been held to apply to a policy taken out by a widower for behoof of his children,[238] and to an endowment policy under which the sum was payable at a fixed date to the husband, whom failing his widow, where the husband had predeceased that date.[239] The trust is for the interest of the wife or children as that interest is expressed in the policy; it may be an interest vesting at once in the beneficiaries or, on the other hand, contingent on their surviving the husband.[240] If the interest has vested in the wife, then although she predeceases her husband, the proceeds of the policy on his death will form part of her estate,[241] but his estate is entitled to receive out of the proceeds of the policy repayment of the amount of the premiums paid since the wife's death.[242] The policy may be surrendered by the trustee with, and it may be even without, the consent of the beneficiary,[243] but the trust created by the policy cannot *stante matrimonio* be revoked or put an end to by the husband even with the consent of his wife and children.[244] By the Married Women's Policies of Assurance (Scotland) (Amendment) Act 1980 trustees are given wide powers of dealing with the policy so far as not at variance with the terms or purposes of the trust[245] and beneficiaries are empowered, subject to the terms of the policy to assign their interest or renounce it.[246] The powers of approval and authorisation of trust variation given to the court by the Trusts (Scotland) Act 1961 are

---

[233] Adoption (Scotland) Act 1978 s.39.

[234] 2004 Act s.132.

[235] *Jarvie's Trs v Jarvie's Trs* (1887) 14 R. 411 confirms that there is no requirement for delivery.

[236] Married Women's Policies of Assurance (Scotland) Act 1880 s.2 (as amended).

[237] Bankruptcy (Scotland) Act 1985 s.34(7).

[238] *Kennedy's Trs v Sharpe* (1895) 23 R. 146. It does not apply to a policy taken out by an unmarried man for his future wife on the eve of his marriage: *Coulson's Trs v Coulson* (1901) 3 F. 1041, per Lord Justice-Clerk Macdonald.

[239] *Chrystal's Trs v Chrystal*, 1912 S.C.1003.

[240] *Chrystal's Trs v Chrystal*, 1912 S.C.1003, per Lord Johnston.

[241] *Cousins v Sun Life Assurance Sun Life Assurance Society* [1933] Ch.126.

[242] *Bilham v Smith* [1937] Ch.636.

[243] *Schumann v Scottish Widows' Fund* (1886) 13 R. 678; Married Women's Policies of Assurance (Scotland) (Amendment) Act 1980 s.2(2)(f).

[244] *Scottish Life Assurance Co v Donald* (1901) 9 S.L.T. 348; *Edinburgh Life Assurance Co v Balderston*, 1909 2 S.L.T. 323; cf. *Barras v Scottish Widows' Fund* (1900) 2 F. 1094.

[245] Married Women's Policies of Assurance (Scotland) (Amendment) Act 1980 s.2(2).

[246] Married Women's Policies of Assurance (Scotland) (Amendment) Act 1980 s.3.

exercisable in relation to any trust constituted by s.2 of the 1880 Act[247] and the terms of settlement of the policy may now be varied or set aside by the court on divorce or dissolution of civil partnership.[248] There are some statutory modifications of the separate property rule in relation to certain tenancies. Where one spouse or civil partner is the tenant of a matrimonial or family home, but leaves the home, thus ceasing to "retain possession" of it, statute now provides that the tenancy is treated as continuing by virtue of the possession of the other spouse or civil partner.[249] The Rent (Scotland) Act 1984 gives a spouse or civil partner a right to succeed as a statutory tenant on the death of the original tenant so long as he or she retains possession of the dwelling house without being entitled to do so under a contractual tenancy.[250] Public sector tenancies can also pass to a spouse or civil partner on the death of the tenant.[251] The surviving spouse or partner will be entitled to apply to purchase the property if the deceased would have qualified for such an application.[252]

II. TERMINATION OF MARRIAGE AND CIVIL PARTNERSHIP

Separation—Informal separation has little impact on the legal effects of marriage **44.22** or civil partnership.[253] The parties may choose to formalise the arrangements for their separation in a separation agreement.[254] However, a separation agreement can be revoked at any time[255] prior to the death of one of the spouses or civil partners[256] and is generally superseded by a decree of divorce or dissolution of civil partnership, unless there are terms specifically designed to survive the termination of the marriage or civil partnership.[257]

Judicial separation, a decree for which ordains the defender to separate from the pursuer and permits the pursuer to live apart from the defender, remains available to a spouse and also now to a civil partner[258] who wishes formal recognition of his or her separated state. It is now seldom used and cannot resolve the issue of financial provision.[259] The grounds justifying judicial separation are now equiparated with the grounds for divorce or dissolution of civil partnership.[260]

---

[247] Married Women's Policies of Assurance (Scotland) (Amendment) Act 1980 s.4.

[248] 1985 Act s.14(2)(h) and (6), as amended by the 2004 Act Sch.28.

[249] 1981 Act s.2(8), which reverses the decision in *Temple v Mitchell*, 1956 S.C. 267; 2004 Act s.102(8).

[250] Rent (Scotland) Act 1984 Sch.1 para.2, as amended by the 2004 Act Sch.28.

[251] Housing (Scotland) Act 1987 s.52(2), as amended by the 2004 Act Sch.28

[252] s.61(2)(c) and 61(10), as amended by the 2004 Act Sch.28.

[253] There are consequences for tax and social security matters (for which see Clive, *Law of Husband and Wife in Scotland* (1997), pp.336–338 and 340–341), but there is no alteration in status or the obligations created by marriage and civil partnership discussed at paras 44.15–44.21, above.

[254] As distinct from an agreement intended to resolve all matters of financial provision on future divorce or dissolution, for which see para.44.32.

[255] This is recognised for the purpose of a defence to a claim for aliment by 1985 Act s.2(8) and (9).

[256] *Palmer v Bonnar*, January 25, 1810, F.C.

[257] *McKeddie v McKeddie* (1902) 9 S.L.T. 381; *Mackenzie v Mackenzie*, 1987 S.C.L.R. 671.

[258] 2004 Act s.120.

[259] As there are no legal consequences of a decree for judicial separation, relative to status or finance, the Scottish Law Commission recommended its abolition—*Report on Family Law* (HMSO, 1992), Scot. Law Com. No.135, para.12.19, but that recommendation was not followed when the Family Law (Scotland) Act 2006 was enacted.

[260] Divorce (Scotland) Act 1976 (the "1976 Act") s.4 and s.117 of the 2004 Act, both amended by the Family Law (Scotland) Act 2006.

44.23 Divorce and dissolution of civil partnership—By the law of Scotland, marriage and civil partnership cannot be terminated until death, except by divorce or dissolution respectively. The Divorce (Scotland) Act 1976 and the Civil Partnership Act 2004 now provide that there are only two grounds for divorce or dissolution of civil partnership, namely (i) a recognised gender change of either party, and (ii) the irretrievable breakdown of the marriage or civil partnership.[261] The question of jurisdiction in divorce, dissolution of civil partnership and other consistorial causes has already been considered.[262] In such actions, if the defender cannot be found, there must be service by advertisement and also service on children of the marriage or civil partnership who have attained the age of 16 and on one of the next of kin, if these are known.[263] In divorce or dissolution proceedings, as in any family action,[264] a person with a relevant interest may apply for leave to lodge defences.[265] Decree will not normally be granted if there is collusion between the parties,[266] but the bar on granting decree of divorce where collusion is established has been abolished,[267] the grant or refusal of decree in such a situation now being within the discretion of the court. Collusion means "permitting a false case to be substantiated or keeping back a just defence".[268] "Mutual desire that a decree . . . should be obtained, and mutual action to facilitate this end are not collusion, if there be no fabrication or suppression".[269] In family actions involving status the facts must be proved.[270] The evidence must consist of or include evidence other than that of a party to the marriage or civil partnership,[271] unless the action satisfies the criteria for a "simplified" divorce or dissolution, namely where the basis is non-cohabitation, there are no children under 16 and no financial claims are made.[272] In proof of adultery, although a confession by a wife, supported by an extract birth certificate purporting to be signed by herself and a paramour, has been held insufficient,[273] and the practice of leading evidence from only the defender and his paramour has been disapproved,[274] the evidence of the defender

---

[261] 1976 Act s.1(1) (s.1(1)(b) added by the Gender Recognition Act 2004 Sch.2 para.6); 2004 Act s.117(2).

[262] See Ch.2, "Courts and Jurisdiction", above.

[263] Act of Sederunt (Rules of the Court of Session 1994) (SI 1994/1443) ("RCS") rr.49.12 and 49.8(1)(a); Act of Sederunt (Sheriff Court Ordinary Cause Rules) (SI 1993/1956) ("OCR") rr.5.6, 33.7(1)(a).

[264] Family actions include divorce or dissolution proceedings, relative financial provision proceedings, declarator of marriage or nullity of marriage, proceedings under the Matrimonial Homes (Family Protection) (Scotland) Act 1981 and various proceedings relating to children. See RCS r.49.1(1) and OCR r.33.1(1).

[265] RCS r.49.16; OCR r.13.1.

[266] See *Cooper v Cooper*, 1987 S.L.T. (Sh. Ct) 37; cf. *Sinclair v Sinclair*, 1986 S.L.T. (Sh. Ct) 54.

[267] Family Law (Scotland) Act 2006 s.14.

[268] *Walker v Walker*, 1911 S.C. 163; *Fairgrieve v Chalmers*, 1912 S.C. 745.

[269] *Administrator of Austrian Property v Von Lorang*, 1926 S.C. 598, per Lord Sands at 628; 1927 S.C. (H.L.) 80. See also *Riddell v Riddell*, 1952 S.C. 475.

[270] Civil Evidence (Scotland) Act 1988 s.8(1), as amended by the 2004 Act Sch.28 and the Family Law (Scotland) Act 2006 Sch.3. The provision applies to actions for divorce or declarator of marriage, nullity of marriage or civil partnership, dissolution of civil partnership, separation of spouses or civil partners and parentage or non-parentage, albeit that actions for separation have no real effect on status.

[271] Civil Evidence (Scotland) Act 1988 s.8(3) as amended by the 2004 Act Sch.28.

[272] Set out in the Evidence in Divorce Actions (Scotland) Order 1989 (SI 1989/582) for divorces and by the introduction of relative rules of court; RCS r.49.72 and OCR r.33.73 and for dissolution by the insertion of RCS r.49.80A, added by the Act of Sederunt (Rules of the Court of Session Amendment No. 9) (Civil Partnership Act 2004 etc.) 2005 (SSI 2005/632).

[273] *Mackay v Mackay*, 1946 S.C.78.

[274] *Cooper v Cooper*, 1987 S.L.T. (Sh. Ct) 37.

and his paramour,[275] or even of the paramour alone,[276] can be sufficient. A finding of adultery in any previous proceedings and, in relation to the other bases for divorce, an extract decree of separation if granted to the pursuer on substantially the same facts, may afford sufficient proof provided the evidence of the pursuer is also received.[277]

While the Divorce (Scotland) Act 1976 and Civil Partnership Act 2004 provide only two grounds for divorce, each statute provides that in respect of the irretrievable breakdown ground, on proof of any one of a series of matters, the marriage or civil partnership is to be taken to have broken down irretrievably with the result that irretrievable breakdown as such does not require to be proved. Each of these matters is, therefore, in effect, a distinct basis for divorce or civil partnership For divorce, the matters so considered are the adultery of the defender, behaviour of the defender of such a kind that the pursuer cannot reasonably be expected to cohabit with him/her, non-cohabitation for a period of one year combined with the defender's consent to divorce and non-cohabitation for a period of two years.[278] For divorce actions raised after May 4, 2006, desertion is no longer a competent basis for establishing irretrievable breakdown of marriage.[279] For dissolution of civil partnership the matters are identical, save for the exclusion of adultery as a statutory basis therefor.[280]

If, at any time before granting decree in an action of divorce or dissolution of civil partnership, it appears to the court that there is a reasonable prospect of reconciliation it must continue the action to enable reconciliation to be attempted. Cohabitation during such a continuation is not to be taken into account for the purposes of the action.[281] In divorce actions such cohabitation does not therefore constitute condonation of adultery. Any basis for divorce or dissolution of civil partnership may be established by proof on a balance of probabilities.[282] Such actions may still be dismissed if the averments are irrelevant.[283]

Divorce for adultery—Sexual intercourse is necessary to constitute adultery. **44.24** Artificial insemination by a donor is not adultery.[284] The court will not order a wife or child to submit to blood tests for the purpose of obtaining evidence relevant to allegations of adultery.[285] A request for a sample of blood or other body fluid may be made by the court for that purpose, however, and an adverse inference relevant to the allegation may be drawn on a party's failure to accede to that

---

[275] *Sinclair v Sinclair*, 1986 S.L.T. (Sh. Ct) 54.

[276] Civil Evidence (Scotland) Act 1988 s.8, as read with s.1(1).

[277] Law Reform (Miscellaneous Provisions) (Scotland) Act 1968 s.11; Divorce (Scotland) Act 1976 s.3 and Sch.I para.4.

[278] 1976 Act s.1(2) as amended by the Family Law (Scotland) Act 2006 ss.11 and 12.

[279] Family Law (Scotland) Act 2006 s.12 and Sch.3. Actions raised prior to that date can be concluded—see Family Law (Scotland) Act 2006 (Commencement, Transitional Provisions and Savings) Order 2006 (SSI 2006/212) para.4. For a summary of the issues relative to desertion see the 11th edition of this text, at para.48.24. For a more comprehensive discussion see Clive, *Law of Husband and Wife in Scotland* (1997), pp.386–398.

[280] 2004 Act s.117(3), as amended by the Family Law (Scotland) Act 2006 Sch.1 para.9 and Sch.3.

[281] 1976 Act s.2(1); 2004 Act s.118.

[282] 1976 Act s.1(6); 2004 Act s.117(8).

[283] *Smith v Smith*, 1994 S.C.L.R. 244.

[284] *MacLennan v MacLennan*, 1958 S.C.105. The case contains a useful discussion of the physical requirements of adultery.

[285] *Whitehall v Whitehall*, 1958 S.C. 252.

request.[286] It is no defence to an action of divorce for adultery that there has been adultery on the part of the pursuer: cross actions of divorce are competent.[287] Condonation or forgiveness of the offence by the aggrieved spouse is, however, a good defence.[288] In order that there may be condonation there must have been genuine belief that the adultery alleged to have been condoned has been committed.[289] Mere suspicion of infidelity will not found the plea.[290] Condonation will not be inferred from anything less than cohabitation, by which is meant living together as man and wife.[291] Verbal forgiveness or even sexual intercourse will not alone suffice. It is not essential to the plea of condonation that the spouses should have shared the same bed.[292] Provided the cohabitation is confined to a period of three months from the date of continuation or resumption, continuation or resumption of cohabitation after knowledge of adultery does not amount to condonation.[293] A condition attached to condonation is inept. If the adultery is condoned, it can never thereafter be founded on as a ground of divorce but, if there is alleged to have been subsequent adultery, it may be used in evidence as throwing light on suspicious conduct with the same, or even a different, paramour.[294]

Another plea in defence to an action of divorce for adultery is *lenocinium* or connivance.[295] If a husband gives facilities, and creates opportunities, for adultery by his wife, he cannot obtain divorce for the offence at which he has thus connived. But this plea will not be applicable if the husband has done no more than refrain from dissuading his wife: there must be active facilitation of, or encouragement to commission of, the adultery.[296] Delay, however long, to take proceedings will not, without other circumstances pointing to acquiescence or condonation, operate as a bar to an action for divorce on the grounds either of adultery.[297]

44.25 Divorce or dissolution for behaviour justifying non-cohabitation—The first of the matters common to the breakdown of marriage and civil partnership is that, since the date of the marriage or civil partnership, the defender has at any time behaved (whether or not as a result of mental abnormality and whether such behaviour has been active or passive) in such a way that the pursuer cannot reasonably be expected to cohabit with the defender.[298] The test requires an assessment of what is reasonable

---

[286] Law Reform (Miscellaneous Provisions) (Scotland) Act 1990 s.70(1); *Petrie v Petrie*, 1993 S.C.L.R. 391; *Smith v Greenhill*, 1993 S.C.L.R. 776.

[287] see e.g. *Connell v Connell*, 1950 S.C. 505.

[288] 1976 Act s.1(3). As to onus of proof, see *Andrews v Andrews*, 1961 S.L.T. (Notes) 48; also *Mitchell v Mitchell*, 1947 S.L.T. (Notes) 8.

[289] *Paterson v Paterson*, 1938 S.C. 251; as to knowledge of the extent of the adultery, see *Ralston v Ralston* (1881) 8 R. 371, and *Steven v Steven*, 1919 2 S.L.T. 239.

[290] *Collins v Collins* (1882) 10 R. 250; and (1884) 11 R. (H.L.) 19.

[291] 1976 Act ss.1(3) and 13(2).

[292] *Edgar v Edgar* (1902) 4 F. 632, per Lord McLaren at 635.

[293] 1976 Act s.2(2). The purpose of this provision is to encourage reconciliation.

[294] *Collins v Collins* (1882) 10 R. 250; *Robertson v Robertson* (1888) 15 R. 1001; also *Nicol v Nicol*, 1938 S.L.T. 98.

[295] 1976 Act s.1(3).

[296] *Wemyss v Wemyss* (1866) 4 M. 660; *Thomson v Thomson*, 1908 S.C. 179. See also *Gallacher v Gallacher*, 1928 S.C. 586; 1934 S.C. 339; *Hannah v Hannah*, 1931 S.C. 275; *Lenocinium* has been regarded as attributable to a wife: *Riddell v Riddell*, 1952 S.C. 475.

[297] *Johnstone v Johnstone*, 1931 S.C. 60; *Macfarlane v Macfarlane*, 1956 S.C. 472 at 476. As to delay in bringing nullity proceedings, see *Allardyce v Allardyce*, 1954 S.L.T. 334.

[298] 1976 Act s.1(2)(b); 2004 Act s.117(2).

for the couple involved, taking account of their particular circumstances rather than applying an objective test of reasonableness.[299] While there is no requirement in the legislation that the behaviour should be culpable or deliberately disruptive of the relationship, a lack of culpability may well lead to a failure to establish the necessary causal link between the behaviour and the reasonable expectation that the pursuer should continue cohabitation.[300] An association by a spouse or civil partner with another member of the opposite sex, without evidence of infidelity, can amount to unreasonable behaviour.[301] Unfounded allegations by a defender of infidelity and incest on the part of the pursuer even if unlikely to be repeated, may be sufficient.[302] While it is competent to found on behaviour at any time since the date of the marriage or civil partnership, that behaviour must be such that the pursuer cannot, at the date of the proof, reasonably be expected to cohabit with the defender. Accordingly, behaviour in the remote past, especially if followed by continued cohabitation, will normally be relevant only in so far as it is part of, or throws light on, more recent conduct. In assessing whether it is reasonable to expect the pursuer to cohabit with the defender, however, the court may take into account events occurring since the separation of parties, such as a new association formed by the pursuer with a third party, provided such events can be seen as causally connected with the defender's behaviour.[303] There is no requirement that the behaviour should be extensive in time, and a single serious incident may suffice.[304] Behaviour suggests something more than a state of affairs or a mental or physical condition[305] but, as the behaviour may be passive, it may consist in neglect or inactivity. It is immaterial that the defender's conduct is conditioned by insanity or mental deficiency, but a purely automatic reaction or an action or state of inactivity which is determined by unavoidable physical constraint is probably not behaviour for the purposes of the Acts.

Divorce or dissolution for desertion—Prior to the coming into force of the **44.26** Family Law (Scotland) Act 2006, another matter which could establish the irretrievable breakdown of marriage or civil partnership was where the defender had wilfully and without reasonable cause deserted the pursuer and (1) during a continuous period of two years thereafter the parties have not cohabited, and (2) the pursuer has not refused a genuine and reasonable offer by the defender to adhere. Actions on this basis were rare, but may still proceed to decree if raised prior to May 4, 2006.[306]

Divorce or dissolution for non-cohabitation with consent—The second of the **44.27** matters which will now establish the irretrievable breakdown of either marriage

---

[299] *Taylor v Taylor*, 2000 S.L.T. 1419.

[300] *Smith v Smith*, 1994 S.C.L.R. 244; *Ross v Ross*, 1997 S.L.T. (Sh. Ct) 51.

[301] *Stewart v Stewart*, 1987 S.L.T. (Sh. Ct) 48.

[302] *Hastie v Hastie*, 1985 S.L.T. 146.

[303] *Findlay v Findlay*, 1991 S.L.T. 457; *Knox v Knox*, 1993 S.C.L.R. (Sh. Ct) (Notes) 381.

[304] Although see *Gray v Gray*, 1991 G.W.D. 8–477 where a single incident was held, in the circumstances, to be insufficient.

[305] See *Katz v Katz* [1972] 1 W.L.R. 955, per Sir George Baker P. at 960; cf. *Thurlow v Thurlow* [1975] 2 All E.R. 979; *H. v H.*, 1968 S.L.T. 40; *Grant v Grant*, 1974 S.L.T. (Notes) 54.

[306] s.12 and Sch.3 of the Family Law (Scotland) Act 2006 repeal s.1(2)(c) of the 1976 Act, thus removing desertion as a ground of divorce; the ability to conclude existing actions is found in the Family Law (Scotland) Act 2006 (Commencement, Transitional Provisions and Savings) Order 2006 (SSI 2006/112) art.4. For a full discussion of the legal requirements to prove desertion see Clive, *Law of Husband and Wife in Scotland* (1997), pp.386–398. Section 117(3)(b) of the 2004 Act, which introduced desertion as a basis for dissolution of civil partnership, was also repealed by the 2006 Act.

or civil partnership is, for actions raised after May 4, 2006, the non-cohabitation of the parties to the marriage or civil partnership at any time during a continuous period of one year after the date of the marriage or civil partnership and immediately preceding the bringing of the action and the consent of the defender to the granting of decree of divorce or dissolution.[307] For actions raised prior to May 4, 2006, the period of non-cohabitation required in such a consent to divorce or dissolution case was two years. The date of bringing the action has been deemed to be the date when a Minute of Amendment altering the basis of the action from unreasonable behaviour to non-cohabitation with consent.[308] Consent must be indicated in the prescribed manner and may be withdrawn at any time before decree is granted.[309] The motive for withdrawal of consent is irrelevant.[310] Failure to defend or even known absence of objection is not enough. There is no provision for dispensation with consent, and so this basis for divorce or dissolution is not available where the defender lacks capacity. The period of non-cohabitation is calculated and allowance made for intervening periods of cohabitation on the same principle as described in the next paragraph.

44.28 **Divorce or dissolution for non-cohabitation for two years or more**—The final matter on which an action for divorce or dissolution of civil partnership may be based is where, in actions commenced after May 4, 2006, there has been no cohabitation between the parties at any time during a continuous period of two years after the date of the marriage or civil partnership and immediately preceding the bringing of the action.[311] The right to bring an action emerges on the day after the second anniversary of the separation.[312] For actions raised prior to May 4, 2006, the period of non-cohabitation required in such a non-cohabitation case was five years. Periods of cohabitation not exceeding six months in all do not interrupt the continuity of the non-cohabitation but are left out of account in measuring its length.[313] Cohabitation means that the parties are in fact living together as man and wife or as civil partners.[314] It is undecided whether a mental element is required for non-cohabitation, so as to exclude cases where the separation is involuntary or without intention of breaking the consortium, as in absence because of imprisonment, illness or the exigencies of military, professional or other duties.[315] Prior to the passing of the Family Law (Scotland) Act 2006 the court had a discretion to refuse decree in an action on this ground, if to grant it would result in grave financial hardship to the defender but that provision has now been repealed.[316] There are conflicting decisions on whether or not a defender who fails

---

[307] 1976 Act s.1(2)(c), as amended by the Family Law (Scotland) Act 2006 s.11; 2004 Act s.117(3) (d), as amended by the 2006 Act Sch.1 para.9. On the meaning of cohabitation and whether or not a mental element is required, see para.44.28 and fn.315, below.

[308] *Duncan v Duncan*, 1987 S.L.T. 17.

[309] 1976 Act s.1(4); 2004 Act s.117(4); RCS r.49.19(2); OCR r.33.18(4).

[310] See *Boyle v Boyle*, 1977 S.L.T. (Notes) 69, where a husband was held entitled to refuse to consent unless his wife agreed not to seek any financial orders against him.

[311] 1976 Act s.1(2)(e); 2004 Act s.117(3)(d).

[312] i.e. by the *civilis computatio*; the position in England is different: see *Warr v Warr* [1975] 1 All E.R. 85.

[313] 1976 Act s.2(4); 2004 Act s.119(3).

[314] 1976 Act s.13(2). There is no parallel provision in the 2004 Act, but it seems likely that cohabitation would be similarly defined.

[315] cf. *Santos v Santos* [1972] Fam. 247. The 1976 Act is, however, stronger against a mental element in non-cohabitation than was the corresponding wording of the Divorce Reform Act 1969 in England and Wales.

[316] 1976 Act s.1(5), repealed by the 2006 Act s.13.

to oppose the grant of decree can advance at appeal reasons which would have justified refusal of decree by the court.[317]

III. FINANCIAL PROVISION ON DIVORCE OR DISSOLUTION

Pre-1985 Act divorce cases—The Succession (Scotland) Act 1964 introduced **44.29** the modern concept of financial provision on divorce[318] by permitting the pursuer in a divorce action to apply for a periodical allowance or a capital sum or both. The court was empowered to make such order, if any, as it thought fit, having regard to the means of the parties and to all the circumstances of the case.[319] Those provisions were replaced by s.5 of the Divorce (Scotland) Act 1976, which differed only insofar as it entitled either party to the proceedings to make such claims. Section 5 was repealed by the Family Law (Scotland) Act 1985 so far as actions of divorce raised after the commencement of that Act are concerned but remains in operation in relation to earlier actions.[320] The section therefore continues to apply to applications made in connection with such actions for variation or recall of orders for a periodical allowance or for the making of such an order subsequent to divorce. In contrast to the 1985 Act,[321] the 1976 Act does not confer upon the court any power to backdate the variation of an award of periodical allowance; to seek to backdate the variation of an award made under the 1976 Act is therefore incompetent.[322] The 1985 Act does, however, confer upon the court the power to make or to vary an award under the 1976 Act for a definite or indefinite period, or until the happening of a specified event.[323] The power to impose a time limit does not amount to a power to terminate periodical allowance,[324] although it is competent to vary both the level and duration of an award at the same time.[325] A time limit may itself be varied or revoked on a subsequent change of circumstances.[326] In varying awards made under the 1976 Act, the court should not have regard to the principles governing the award of financial provision under the 1985 Act.[327] An application for an order for a periodical allowance under the 1976 Act may be made after decree of divorce only if there has been a change in the circumstances of either party.[328] An order already made is subject to variation or recall by the court on a change of circumstances.[329] In determining the application the court must assume that the existing award was appropriately made and consider only the effect of changes in circumstances since

---

[317] *Colville v Colville*, 1988 S.L.T. (Sh. Ct) 23 and *Norris v Norris*, 1992 S.L.T. (Sh. Ct) 51.

[318] Prior to that the effect of a decree of divorce on any ground other than incurable insanity was to entitle the innocent spouse to legal rights and marriage contract provisions as if the other spouse had died. This was the common law rule for adultery, applied to divorce on other grounds by s.2 of the Divorce (Scotland) Act 1938.

[319] Succession (Scotland) Act 1964 ss.24 and 25.

[320] 1985 Act s.28(3).

[321] 1985 Act s.13(4)(b).

[322] *Abrahams v Abrahams*, 1989 S.L.T. (Sh. Ct) 11; *Wilson v Wilson*, 1992 S.L.T. 664.

[323] 1985 Act s.28(3).

[324] *Wilson v Wilson*, 1987 S.L.T. 721.

[325] *Mitchell v Mitchell*, 1993 S.L.T. 419. See also *Capaldi v Capaldi*, 1996 G.W.D. 17–1004 where the award was varied to nil but the variation postponed for a period of six months.

[326] *Macpherson v Macpherson*, 1989 S.L.T. 231.

[327] *Wilson v Wilson*, 1987 S.L.T. 721; *Collins v Collins*, 1989 S.L.T. 194; *Gray v Gray*, 1999 Fam. L.R. 135.

[328] 1976 Act s.5(3).

[329] 1976 Act s.5(4).

that time.[330] An order for periodical allowance made under and in terms of the 1976 Act may be enforced under the Maintenance Orders Act 1950,[331] and terminates on the remarriage or death of the person in whose favour it was made.[332]

44.30 Family Law (Scotland) Act 1985: Orders for financial provision—Financial provision on divorce and dissolution of civil partnership is now governed by the Family Law (Scotland) Act 1985.[333] The relevant provisions of the legislation apply equally to actions for declarator of nullity of marriage or civil partnership and references to an action for divorce or dissolution of civil partnership include an action for declarator of nullity throughout.[334] Section 8(1)[335] of the Act entitles either party to the marriage or civil partnership to apply, in divorce or dissolution proceedings, for one or more of the following orders:

(1) an order for the payment of a capital sum[336];
(2) an order for the transfer of property[337];
(3) an order for a periodical allowance[338];
(4) a pension sharing order[339];
(5) a pension compensation sharing order[340];
(6) an order under s.12B(2)[341];
(7) an "earmarking order" under s.12A(2) or (3) of the Act[342]; and
(8) an incidental order within the meaning of s.14(2) of the Act.[343]

These orders for financial provision can generally[344] only be made by the court on granting decree of divorce or within a period specified by the court on granting decree of divorce.[345] The court is directed, where an application for financial provision has been made, to make such order, if any, as is (a) justified by the principles set out in s.9 of the Act, and (b) reasonable having regard to the parties' resources.[346] A capital sum is due and enforceable on decree of divorce or dissolution being extracted, unless the court defers payment to a specified future date.[347]

---

[330] *Macpherson*, 1989 S.L.T. 231 at 234–5.

[331] 1976 Act Sch.1 para 1.

[332] 1976 Act s.5(5)(b).

[333] As amended to include civil partners by the Civil Partnership Act 2004.

[334] 1985 Act s.17, as amended by the 2004 Act Sch.28.

[335] As amended by the 2004 Act Sch.28.

[336] 1985 Act s.8(1)(a), as amended by the Law Reform (Miscellaneous Provisions) (Scotland) Act 1990 Sch.8 para.34 and Sch.9.

[337] 1985 Act s.8(1)(aa), inserted by the Law Reform (Miscellaneous Provisions) (Scotland) Act 1990 Sch.8 para.34.

[338] 1985 Act s.8(1)(b).

[339] 1985 Act s.8(1)(baa), inserted by the Welfare Reform and Pensions Act 1999 s.20.

[340] 1985 Act s.8(1)(bab), inserted by the Pensions Act 2008 ss.107–120 and Sch.7 para.2.

[341] 1985 Act s.8(1)(bb), inserted by the Pensions Act 2008 s.120 and Sch.7 paras 2 and 6.

[342] 1985 Act s.8(1)(ba), inserted by the Pensions Act 1995 s.167(1).

[343] 1985 Act s.8(1)(c).

[344] There are two exceptions. First, periodical allowance can be applied for after divorce or dissolution where no order was made at the time and there has been a change of circumstances since the date of the decree—s.13(1)(c). Secondly, 8 of the 10 incidental orders may be made before, on or after decree of divorce or dissolution is granted or refused—s.14(1) and (3); cf. *Amin v Amin*, 2000 S.L.T. (Sh. Ct) 115.

[345] 1985 Act s.12(1); *Mackin v Mackin*, 1990 S.C.L.R. 728. See *Leaper v Leaper*, 1997 S.C.L.R. 757, where the failure to specify a date in the decree was later used as a ground of reduction.

[346] 1985 Act s.8(2). See para.44.31, below.

[347] 1985 Act s.12(2). See *Little v Little*, 1990 S.L.T. 785; *Bannon v Bannon*, 1993 S.L.T. 999; *Sweeney v Sweeney (No.2)*, 2006 S.C. 82.

The court is also empowered to order a capital sum to be paid by instalments.[348] An order directing the trustees of pension scheme to pay all or part of a lump sum due to the member, known as an "earmarking order", can only be made by the court on making a capital sum award and will satisfy, at least in part, the amount so ordered.[349] The level of a capital sum is fixed at divorce or dissolution and cannot subsequently be varied, although there is power to alter the date and method of payment after divorce or dissolution.[350] A transfer of property order takes the form of a direction to one party to transfer his or her interest in the property to the other spouse or civil partner. Failure to comply may result in a further order authorising the clerk of court to execute the necessary documents of transfer.[351] Where the consent of a third party is necessary under any obligation, enactment or rule of law such consent requires to be obtained before the court can make a transfer of property order.[352] For divorce or dissolution proceedings initiated after May 4, 2006, the appropriate valuation date for property being transferred will normally be the date of divorce.[353] In divorce proceedings commenced on or after December 7, 2000 and in any dissolution of civil partnership proceedings a pension sharing order can provide that one spouse or civil partner's rights under a specified pension arrangement or state scheme rights[354] shall be subject to pension sharing for the benefit of the other spouse or civil partner and will specify the percentage value, or the amount, to be transferred.[355] Unlike earmarking orders, pension sharing can be activated by the parties themselves if they enter into a formal agreement in prescribed form and give intimation to the trustees or managers of the scheme after decree of divorce or dissolution.[356] The effect of a pension sharing order is to split the value of the pension rights between the parties as at the date of the order or provision. The actual benefits ultimately received by the two parties will be derived from the distinct parts.[357] A pension compensation sharing order is one made to share compensation from the Pension Protection Fund ("PPF") and may be a specified amount or a percentage of the compensation due to the other spouse or partner.[358] As an alternative[359] to a pension compensation sharing order the court may make an order, additional to a capital sum order, requiring the PPF Board, if at any time any payment in respect of PPF

---

[348] 1985 Act s.12(3). See *Sweeney v Sweeney (No.2)*, 2006 S.C. 82.

[349] 1985 Act s.12A(2).

[350] 1985 Act s.12(4). There is an exception to the rule against variation where the payer is sequestrated within five years of the date of the order; see Bankruptcy (Scotland) Act 1985 s.35.

[351] 1985 Act s.14(2)(k); see also Sheriff Courts (Scotland) Act 1907 s.5A, which is restricted to documents required to convey heritable property. Deeds relating to moveable property can now be executed by the sheriff clerk also. See 1985 Act s.14(2)(ja) as inserted by the Family Law (Scotland) Act 2006 s.18.

[352] 1985 Act s.15(1). If the consent of a third party whose consent is required has not been sought, the order for transfer cannot competently be made—*MacNaught v MacNaught*, 1997 S.C.L.R. 151. A creditor with an interest in such an order must receive intimation that it is being sought: s.15(2).

[353] 1985 Act s.10(3A) as inserted by the Family Law (Scotland) Act 2006 s.16. For a summary of the previous rule and the new provision see para.44.31.

[354] See 1985 Act s.27(1) as amended by the Welfare Reform and Pensions Act 1999 for the definition of qualifying pension arrangements.

[355] 1985 Act s.8(1)(baa), as inserted by the Welfare Reform and Pensions Act 1999 s.20 and implemented by the Welfare Reform and Pensions Act 1999 (Commencement No.4) Order (SI 2000/1047).

[356] Welfare Reform and Pensions Act 1999 s.28(1)(f).

[357] Welfare Reform and Pensions Act 1999 s.29.

[358] The compensation can be shared through a qualifying agreement made by the parties rather than an order; Pensions Act 2008 s.110(1); 1985 Act s.8(10) (as amended by the Pensions Act 2008).

[359] 1985 Act s.8(8), inserted by the Pensions Act 2008 Sch.7 para.2, expressly prevents the court from making both orders.

compensation becomes due to the liable person under the decree, to pay the whole or part of that payment to the other party.[360] An award of periodical allowance is restricted to situations where a party's claims cannot appropriately or sufficiently be met by an order for payment of a capital sum or for transfer of property.[361] It is an order for ongoing support not intended to be used as a method of dividing the parties' capital.[362] Periodical allowance may be awarded for a definite or indefinite period,[363] but in any event ceases to have effect on the payee remarrying, entering into a civil partnership or dying.[364] The order may be varied or recalled on a material change of circumstances since the date it was made.[365] While the death, entering into a civil partnership or remarriage of the payer does not terminate the award, the former at least is likely to constitute a material change of circumstances justifying a variation.[366] Incidental orders, while included within the definition of orders for financial provision, cover a wide range of matters, with the court being empowered to make 8 of the 11 available orders before, on or after divorce or dissolution.[367] Thus an order for the sale of property may obviate the need for division and sale proceedings in relation to a jointly owned home,[368] although its application is not restricted to joint property. Orders for the valuation of property and orders determining any dispute between the parties to the marriage or civil partnership as to their respective property rights may be of assistance during the progress of the divorce proceedings,[369] while the regulation of occupancy and liability for outgoings relative to the matrimonial or family home after divorce or dissolution can be ordered only on or after the granting of decree of divorce or dissolution.[370] The power to order security to be given for any financial provision has been used to direct a party to grant a standard security over heritable property to secure future payment of a deferred capital sum.[371] Provision is also made for the payment or transfer of money or property to those entrusted with the estate of an incapax,[372] and the court has the ability to set aside or vary the provisions of antenuptial or postnuptial marriage settlements or corresponding

---

[360] 1985 Act s.12B(2), inserted by the Pensions Act 2008 Sch.7 para.2. Payment in terms of the order discharges the liabilities of the PPF in an amount corresponding to the amount of the payment and in turn that amount is treated, for all purposes, towards discharge of the payer's obligation to pay the capital sum.

[361] 1985 Act s.13(2)(b). See *Mackenzie v Mackenzie*, 1991 S.L.T. 461; *McConnell v McConnell (No.2)*, 1997 Fam. L.R. 108.

[362] 1985 Act s.13(2)(a). The order must be justified by a principle set out in paras (c), (d) or (e) of s.9(1) of the Act. See para.44.31, below.

[363] 1985 Act s.13(3), as amended by the 2004 Act Sch.28.

[364] 1985 Act s.13(7), as amended by the 2004 Act Sch.28.

[365] 1985 Act s.13(4). The discovery that an award was made on the basis of incorrect or incomplete information does not constitute a material change for this purpose. See *Walker v Walker*, 1995 S.L.T. 375; *Bye v Bye*, 1999 G.W.D. 33–1591. For the correct approach see *Macpherson v Macpherson*, 1989 S.L.T. 231 and *Haugan v Haugan*, 2001 G.W.D. 16–641.

[366] 1985 Act s.13(7)(a) and 13(4), as amended by the 2004 Act Sch.28.

[367] 1985 Act s.14(1) and (3); cf. *Amin v Amin*, 2000 S.L.T. (Sh. Ct) 115.

[368] 1985 Act s.14(2)(a); *Jacques v Jacques*, 1995 S.L.T. 963; *Rae v Rae*, 1991 S.L.T. 454. An order prior to divorce may prejudice one party's claims and may be refused, see *P v P*, 2007 Fam. L.B. 90–6 (OH).

[369] 1985 Act s.14(2)(b) and (c); *Demarco v Demarco*, 1990 S.C.L.R.635.

[370] 1985 Act s.14(2)(d) and (e), as restricted by s.14(3). Prior to divorce or dissolution, the regulation of occupancy and liability for outgoings can be the subject of orders of court in terms of the Matrimonial Homes (Family Protection) (Scotland) Act 1981 or the Civil Partnership Act 2004. See paras 44.15–44.17.

[371] 1985 Act s.14(2)(f); *Macdonald v Macdonald*, 1995 S.L.T. 72; *Murley v Murley*, 1995 S.C.L.R. 1138. Cf. *Trotter v Trotter*, 2001 S.L.T. (Sh. Ct) 42.

[372] 1985 Act s.14(2)(g).

settlements in respect of the civil partnership where this would be justified and reasonable.[373] It has been held that a contract of co-partnery entered into between a married couple in business together cannot be construed as a "settlement" in this context.[374] A further power is bestowed on the court to make an order as to the date from which any interest on any amount awarded shall run.[375] Where appropriate, therefore, interest can be awarded on a sum from a date prior to the making of the award or the raising of the action, such as the date of separation. It has been suggested that an appropriate situation for the award of interest from such an early date may be the sole use of matrimonial assets by one spouse for the period from separation until divorce where this has deprived the other party of the use of his or her capital,[376] though the power has been used sparingly.[377] Finally, a general power is conferred on the court to make any ancillary order that is expedient to give effect to the principles of the legislation[378] or to any order for financial provision.[379] An incidental order, whenever granted, may subsequently be varied or recalled on cause shown.[380] The court will not normally make an order for financial provision if a party has not included such a claim in his pleadings.[381]

Family Law (Scotland) Act 1985: Principles—In determining which, if any, of **44.31** the applications for financial provision made should be granted, the court is required to apply the following five governing principles enunciated in s.9[382]:

(a) the net value of the matrimonial property or partnership property should be shared fairly between the parties to the marriage or civil partnership;

(b) fair account should be taken of any economic advantage derived by either party from contributions by the other, and of any economic disadvantage suffered by either party in the interests of the other party or of the family;

(c) any economic burden of caring, after divorce or dissolution, for a child under the age of 16 years and being a child of the marriage or accepted by both partners to a civil partnership as a child of the family should be shared fairly between the parties;

(d) support of the other party should be awarded such financial provision as is reasonable to enable him to adjust, over a period of not more than three years from the date of the decree of divorce or dissolution, to the loss of that support on divorce or dissolution;

(e) a party who at the time of the divorce seems likely to suffer serious financial hardship as a result of the divorce or dissolution should be

---

[373] 1985 Act s.14(2)(h), read with s.9(1). Such settlements cannot be adjusted or set aside if this would affect the rights of third parties, such as children. S.14(6) confirms that "settlements" include those by way of a policy of assurance to which S.2 of the Married Women's Policies of Assurance (Scotland) Act 1880 relates. See para.44.21, above.

[374] *Robertson v Robertson*, 2003 S.L.T. 208.

[375] 1985 Act s.14(2)(h).

[376] *Geddes v Geddes*, 1993 S.L.T. 494.

[377] *Welsh v Welsh*, 1994 S.L.T. 828 is one of the few examples of interest being awarded from separation. For a more recent discussion of what might be required to justify such a claim see *Watt v Watt*, 2009 S.L.T. 931.

[378] That is, the principles enunciated in s.9(1) of the Act. See para.44.31, below.

[379] 1985 Act s.14(2)(k).

[380] 1985 Act s.14(4).

[381] *Muir v Muir*, 1994 S.C.L.R. 178. But see *Murdoch v Murdoch* [2012] CISH 002.

[382] As amended by the 2004 Act Sch.28.

awarded such financial provision as is reasonable to relieve him of hardship over a reasonable period.[383]

So far as the first principle is concerned, the court has a duty to apply it and also to apply whichever of the other specified principles are relevant in light of the established facts.[384] The first step is to ascertain and value the net matrimonial property or partnership property so that it can be shared fairly. Matrimonial property includes all property belonging to the parties or either of them at the relevant date and which was acquired (other than by way of gift or succession from a third party) either (i) before the marriage for use as a family home or as its furniture or plenishings, or (ii) during the marriage but before the relevant date.[385] Partnership property is defined as all property belonging to the civil partners or either of them at the relevant date and which was acquired (other than by way of gift or succession from a third party) either (i) before the registration of partnership for use by them as a family home or as furniture and plenishings for such a home, or (ii) during the partnership but before the relevant date.[386] The relevant date is defined as whichever is the earlier of the date on which the parties ceased to cohabit and the date of service of the summons for divorce or dissolution of civil partnership.[387] Where parties cease to cohabit for a continuous period of 90 days or more, then resume cohabitation for a period or periods of less than 90 days in total, the earliest date on which they ceased to cohabit will remain as the relevant date.[388] Where there is a dispute as to the relevant date, an examination of all relevant features of the parties' relationship will be required.[389] The definition of matrimonial property has been seen to include a claim for damages for personal injuries sustained during the marriage,[390] a potential claim against dismissal from employment,[391] a claim for criminal injuries compensation,[392] fishing quotas[393] and single farm payments.[394] A house acquired for use as a family home prior to a previous marriage between the same parties was regarded as matrimonial property of their second marriage.[395] An item that is gifted to a spouse or civil partner or inherited by him or her during the marriage or partnership will only be excluded from the definition of matrimonial or partnership property at separation if it has retained its original property characteristics.[396] The sale of non-matrimonial property or non-partnership property during the marriage or partnership and the purchase of new property with the proceeds thereof, will result in the new property being classified as matrimonial or partnership property where it is still

---

[383] 1985 Act s.9(1)(a)–(e).

[384] *Cunniff v Cunniff*, 1999 S.C. 537 at 539.

[385] 1985 Act s.10(4).

[386] 1985 Act s.10(4A).

[387] 1985 Act s.10(3). See *Buczynska v Buczynska*, 1989 S.L.T. 558; *Brown v Brown*, 1998 Fam. L.R. 81.

[388] 1985 Act s.10(7).

[389] *Banks v Banks*, 2005 Fam. L.R. 116; *Bain v Bain*, 2008 Fam. L.R. 81; *Carrick v Carrick*, 2008 G.W.D. 28–437.

[390] *Skarpaas v Skarpaas*, 1991 S.L.T. (Sh. Ct) 15; 1992 S.L.T. 343.

[391] *Loudon v Loudon*, 1994 S.L.T. 381.

[392] *McGuire v McGuire's Curator Bonis*, 1991 S.L.T. (Sh. Ct) 76.

[393] *Watt v Watt*, 2009 S.L.T. 931.

[394] See *Simpson v Simpson*, 2007 S.L.T. (Sh. Ct) 43.

[395] *Mitchell v Mitchell*, 1995 S.L.T. 426.

[396] See *Whittome v Whittome (No.1)*, 1994 S.L.T. 114 and the discussion of company reconstructions and bonus issues in Clive, *Law of Husband and Wife in Scotland* (1997), pp.450–452.

held at the relevant date.[397] However, the sale proceeds of a non-matrimonial asset, simply held in cash at the relevant date rather than used to acquire a new asset were in one case held not to constitute matrimonial property.[398] There is specific provision for including as matrimonial property or partnership property the proportion of a party's rights or interests under a life policy or similar arrangement and benefits under a pension arrangement referable to the period of the marriage or civil partnership prior to the relevant date.[399] Where the policy or pension arrangement was entered into prior to marriage or civil partnership, this provision represents an exception to the now established rule[400] that increases in value during the marriage or partnership of non matrimonial property or non partnership property do not themselves constitute matrimonial property. However, a division of the value of the pension that excludes entirely the pre-marriage element has been regarded as fair.[401] A refund of income tax paid by one party during the marriage will constitute matrimonial property even if the refund is paid after the relevant date,[402] although a redundancy payment received after the relevant date will not be so classified.[403] It is the net value of the matrimonial or partnership property after deduction of debts incurred by one or both of the parties during the marriage or partnership and outstanding at the relevant date that requires to be shared.[404] A tax liability relative to a period prior to separation but not assessed or demanded until subsequently can probably fall within the definition of "matrimonial debt".[405] In contrast, a notional liability to tax contingent upon the sale of an asset still held at the relevant date cannot be regarded as a deductible matrimonial (or partnership) debt.[406] Generally, the date at which the value of the matrimonial or partnership property must be ascertained is the relevant date. In *Wallis v Wallis*,[407] the House of Lords confirmed that any increase or decrease in the value of the matrimonial property between the relevant date and the date of divorce had to be left out of account in determining what amounts to fair sharing of the net value of the matrimonial property. That rule applied equally to all matrimonial property, whether in the ownership of the parties jointly or by one of them alone.[408] Its rigidity was perceived as causing considerable unfairness, where one party received the whole benefit of the increase in value between separation and divorce by obtaining a transfer of property order, which had the effect of overriding the transferor's common law property rights.[409] Where title to property is held in joint names, the potential unfairness of the rule could sometimes be avoided by a sale

---

[397] *Davidson v Davidson*, 1994 S.L.T. 506. But the non-matrimonial source of funding may justify an unequal division of value of the new property.

[398] *Wilson v Wilson*, 2009 Fam. L.R. 18.

[399] 1985 Act s.10(5), as amended by the Pensions Act 1995 and the Welfare Reform and Pensions Act 1999.

[400] See *Whittome v Whittome (No.1)*, 1994 S.L.T. 114; *Wilson v Wilson*, 1999 S.L.T. 249.

[401] *B v B*, 2012 CSOH 21.

[402] *MacRitchie v MacRitchie*, 1994 S.L.T. (Sh. Ct) 72.

[403] *Smith v Smith*, 1989 S.L.T. 668 and *Tyrell v Tyrell*, 1990 S.L.T. 406.

[404] 1985 Act s.10(2).

[405] *Buchan v Buchan*, 1992 S.C.L.R. 766; *McConnell v McConnell*, 1997 Fam. L.R. 97 at 105–6; cf. *McCormick v McCormick*, 1994 S.C.L.R. 958.

[406] *Sweeney v Sweeney (No.1)*, 2004 S.C. 372.

[407] *Wallis v Wallis*, 1993 S.C. (HL) 49.

[408] *Wallis v Wallis*, 1993 S.C. (HL) 49, per Lord Keith of Kinkel at 55.

[409] In *Wallis*, 1993 S.C. (HL) 49, the wife, who was joint title holder, was deprived of her common law right to share in one half of the current value of the property, and in *Dible v Dible*, 1997 S.C. 134 the husband, who held sole title to the matrimonial home, lost his right to the whole increase in value by virtue of a transfer of property order made in favour of his wife.

of the property, either voluntarily or by order of court.[410] The absolute rule that property must transfer at relevant date value has been superseded by amendments to the 1985 Act for actions commenced after May 4, 2006. Where the court makes an order for transfer of property, the "appropriate valuation date" for the property that is the subject of the transfer is the date of the order, unless the parties otherwise agree. In exceptional circumstances the court may use another date, but it must be a date "as near as may be" to the date of the order.[411] Matrimonial or partnership property continues to be valued as at the relevant date in the first instance. Current value is used only to calculate the value for the transfer at the time of divorce. Thus, where title to a property is held by the parties in *pro indiviso* shares, only the share being transferred will be valued as at the date of the order.[412]

The Act does not give any guidance as to how value of an item of matrimonial property or partnership property is to be ascertained,[413] although the construct of a hypothetical willing buyer is almost invariably used.[414] Provision has now been made for the method of calculating and verifying the value of pension benefits.[415]

A method of apportioning the value of the benefits attributable to the period of the marriage or civil partnership is also prescribed.[416] Where pre-marriage pension benefits have been subsumed into new arrangements during the course of the marriage, an exclusion of the pre-marriage value can be achieved at the stage of deciding the proportions in which value will be shared.[417] The approach of the court to the valuation of business assets is not uniform, but is restricted only in that it must not involve assumptions that are inconsistent with the terms and policy of the Act.[418] In some cases it may be fair to examine and adjudicate upon individual assets according to their nature rather than valuing each and every asset

---

[410] See the Inner House decision in *Jacques v Jacques*, 1995 S.C. 327 at 331–332.

[411] 1985 Act s.10(3A), as inserted by Family Law (Scotland) Act 2006 s.16. See also Family Law (Scotland) Act 2006 (Commencement, Transitional Proceedings and Savings) Order 2006 (SSI 2006/212) art.4.

[412] *Watt v Watt*, 2009 S.L.T. 931.

[413] The term "value" is not defined in the legislation and may not always be equiperated, for example, with "market value".

[414] *Sweeney v Sweeney*, 2004 S.C. 372 at 380.

[415] For divorce proceedings raised between August 19, 1996 and December 1, 2000, the Divorce etc. (Pensions) (Scotland) Regulations 1996 (SI 1996/1901) as amended by the Divorce etc. (Pensions) (Scotland) Amendment Regulations 1997 (SI 1997/745) apply. There was some doubt as to whether the court was obliged, in terms of those regulations, to use the "cash equivalent" figure in valuing benefits at the relevant date where this could be ascertained: compare *Miller v Miller*, 2000 Fam. L.R. 19 with *Stewart v Stewart*, 2001 S.L.T. (Sh. Ct) 114. For all divorce actions commenced after December 1, 2000, it is clear that it is the cash equivalent value which should be verified: see the Divorce etc. (Pensions) (Scotland) Regulations 2000 (SI 2000/112).

[416] See the Divorce etc. (Pensions) (Scotland) Regulations 1996 (as amended) and the Divorce etc. (Pensions) (Scotland) Regulations 2000 regs 3(3) and 4 respectively. The correct approach to interpretation of s.10(5) when read in conjunction with the time apportionment formula contained in the 1996 Regulations was set out in *Jackson v Jackson*, 1999 Fam. L.R. 108. The formula in the 2000 Regulations is in all material respects identical.

[417] *B v B*, 2012 CSOH 21.

[418] See *McConnell v McConnell*, 1997 Fam. L.R. 97 at 104–105, where the method of capitalising the future maintainable profits of the husband's business was rejected as inconsistent with the policy of the Act as it was dependent on the continuing future involvement of the husband post separation and no alternative earnings based approach had been offered. An assets based valuation was thus adopted. Other decisions involving a discussion of the methodology used to value interests in limited companies or partnerships for the purpose of the 1985 Act include *Brown v Brown*, 1998 Fam. L.R. 81; *Fulton v Fulton*, 2000 Fam. L.R. 8; *Larsen v Larsen*, 2003 Fam. L.R. 101; and *Watt v Watt*, 2009 S.L.T. 931.

to arrive at a global sum for division.[419] The court may leave an asset out of account completely if no evidence of value has been adduced.[420]

The net value of the matrimonial property and now also partnership property is to be taken as shared fairly if it is shared equally or in such other proportions as are justified by special circumstances.[421] In *Jacques v Jacques*,[422] the House of Lords confirmed that these provisions should be interpreted as raising a presumption of equal sharing, and that proof of the existence of special circumstances per se is insufficient to rebut that presumption.[423] A decision as to whether or not proven special circumstances will justify an unequal division of the value of the matrimonial or partnership property is a matter within the unfettered discretion of the court of first instance.[424] The Act provides a list of possible special circumstances, but these have no technical meaning and the list is not exhaustive.[425] The list includes (a) the terms of any agreement on ownership or sale, (b) the source of funds or assets used to acquire the property if not derived from the income or efforts of the parties during the marriage, (c) any destruction, dissipation or alienation of property by either party, (d) the nature of the property and the use made of it and the extent to which it is reasonable to expect it to be realised or divided or used as security, and (e) actual or prospective liability for expenses of valuation or transfer in connection with the divorce.[426] An agreement to hold title to heritage in joint names might support the presumption of equal sharing, but is not a special circumstance.[427] The possibility that a contingent liability to capital gains tax might in some cases constitute special circumstances such as to justify a departure from the principle of equal sharing has not been excluded, but much will depend on whether the liability eventually arises and the impact of it being paid on the resources available to fund financial provision on divorce.[428] The provision relative to non-matrimonial source of funding of matrimonial property or partnership property represents a potential exception to the policy of non-tracing contained within the definition of matrimonial property. There is a clear tendency to exercise discretion in favour of an unequal division of the value of the matrimonial property where an easily identifiable and substantial non-matrimonial source of funding is established,[429] although the proportions may deviate only marginally from the norm of equal sharing where the non-matrimonial contribution was historic and of low value relative to the matrimonial property as a whole.[430] A

---

[419] *Little v Little*, 1990 S.L.T. 785.

[420] *George v George*, 1991 S.L.T. (Sh. Ct) 8; *Pryde v Pryde*, 1991 S.L.T. (Sh. Ct) 26. Cf. *Chaudry v Chaudry*, 2005 G.W.D. 5–65.

[421] 1985 Act ss.9(1)(a) and 10(1).

[422] *Jacques v Jacques*, 1997 S.C. (HL) 20.

[423] *Jacques v Jacques*, 1997 S.C. (HL) 20, per Lord Clyde at 24. See also *Cunningham v Cunningham*, 2001 Fam. L.R. 12.

[424] *Jacques v Jacques*, 1997 S.C. (HL) 20, per Lord Jauncey of Tullichettle at 22, under reference to *Little v Little*, 1990 S.L.T. 785 at 787.

[425] *Jacques v Jacques*, 1997 S.C. (HL) 20, per Lord Clyde at 24. See also *Cunniff v Cunniff*, 1999 S.C. 537 at 540.

[426] 1985 Act s.10(6)(a)–(e).

[427] See *Cunningham*, 2001 Fam. L.R. 12.

[428] *Sweeney v Sweeney (No.2)*, 2006 S.C. 82.

[429] *Davidson v Davidson*, 1994 S.L.T. 506; *MacLean v MacLean*, 1996 G.W.D. 22–1278; *Robertson v Robertson*, 2000 Fam. L.R. 43; *Cunningham v Cunningham*, 2001 Fam. L.R. 12; *Campbell v Campbell*, 2008 Fam. L.R. 115 and *B v B*, 2012 CSOH 21. Cf. *Jacques v Jacques*, 1997 S.C. (HL) 20.

[430] The Lord Ordinary (Kingarth) in *Sweeney v Sweeney* Unreported October 15, 2002 decided upon a 52:48 division in favour of the husband in relation to the business assets which had started in a different and very modest form prior to a lengthy marriage. That part of the decision was not challenged in the Inner House (2006 S.C. 82). A similar approach was taken in *Watt v Watt*, 2009 S.L.T. 931.

possible exception exists where the non-matrimonial funds have been invested in the family home.[431] The pattern of justifying such an unequal division is less clear in relation to the establishment of the other examples of special circumstances.[432]

In addition to achieving a fair division of the value of the matrimonial or partnership property, the court must apply the second principle. It requires a balancing of any economic advantages gained and disadvantages suffered by either of the parties before or during the marriage or civil partnership as a result of their contributions and consideration of whether any resulting imbalance has been or will be corrected by a sharing of the value of the matrimonial or partnership property.[433] The advantages and disadvantages can involve capital, income and earning capacity and contributions include indirect and non-financial contributions such as those made by looking after the family home or caring for the family.[434] Where the division of matrimonial or partnership property will not correct any resulting imbalance, or where there is no matrimonial or partnership property to divide and the balance of advantages and disadvantages is being assessed in isolation, the court has a further broad discretion to award financial provision to the disadvantaged spouse under this principle.[435] The principle was invoked to make a stand-alone award of £100,000 to a wife, in addition to a capital sum based on the equal division of matrimonial property, where her husband had retained profits earned during the marriage in a company incorporated by him prior to marriage and thus excluded from the definition of matrimonial property.[436] The wife's contributions in running the family home and bringing up the parties' children had not been rewarded by the affluent lifestyle the retained profits would have justified and she had thus been deprived of a share of some of the wealth accumulated during the marriage.[437] It seems likely that the principle can be used to rectify future economic disadvantage where this can be ascertained at the time of the divorce and is related to contributions made during the parties' relationship.[438]

The third principle, requiring a fair sharing of the economic burden of caring for children of the marriage or civil partnership under the age of 16 after divorce or dissolution, is not satisfied simply by satisfactory arrangements being made for alimentary provision for such children. The particular educational, financial needs of the child or children also require to be considered, together with issues of

---

[431] *Cunningham v Cunningham*, 2001 Fam. L.R. 12.

[432] For s.10(6)(c) compare *Park v Park*, 1988 S.C.L.R. 584 with *Short v Short*, 1994 G.W.D. 21–1300. S.10(6)(d) has been used, at least in part, to produce radical results—see *Cuniff v Cuniff*, 1999 S.L.T. 999; *Peacock v Peacock*, 1994 S.L.T. 40—but has not justified any unequal division in others—see *Jacques*, 1997 S.C. (HL) 20 and *Adams v Adams (No.1)*, 1997 S.L.T. 144. Compare also the outcomes of *Skarpaas v Skarpaas*, 1991 S.L.T. (Sh. Ct) 15; 1993 S.L.T. 343 and *McGuire v McGuire's C.B.*, 1991 S.L.T. (Sh. Ct) 76. S.10(6)(e) has had no significant practical application.

[433] 1985 Act ss.9(1)(b) and 11(2). For an analysis of how the second principle interrelates with the first, see *Coyle v Coyle*, 2004 Fam. L.R. 2.

[434] 1985 Act s.9(2).

[435] Thus in *De Winton v De Winton*, 1998 Fam. L.R. 110, where there was no matrimonial property left to divide, an award of £30,000 was made against a husband who had benefited from the contribution of his wife's non matrimonial funds. In *Louden v Louden*, 1994 S.L.T. 381, s.(9)(1)(b) was utilised to effect an unequal division of matrimonial property in the wife's favour. See also *B v B*, 2011 Fam. L.R. 91 for a more recent application of the principle.

[436] *Wilson v Wilson*, 1999 S.L.T. 249.

[437] *Wilson v Wilson*, 1999 S.L.T. 249 at 254.

[438] *Cahill v Cahill*, 1998 S.L.T. (Sh. Ct) 96; *Coyle v Coyle*, 2004 Fam. L.R. 2; cf. *Dougan v Dougan*, 1998 S.L.T. (Sh. Ct) 27.

health, accommodation and the cost of suitable child care facilities.[439] While the scope and importance of the third principle has been substantially reduced by the implementation of the Child Support Act 1991,[440] it is still occasionally used to justify an additional capital sum payment[441] or a transfer of property order.[442] The principle can also be used to justify an award of periodical allowance, but only if an order for payment of a capital sum or for transfer of property would be inappropriate or insufficient.[443]

The fourth principle, in directing the court to award to a party who has been substantially dependent on the financial support of the other spouse or civil partner reasonable financial provision for a maximum of three years from divorce or dissolution, can again only be used to justify an award of periodical allowance where an order for payment of a capital sum or for transfer of property would be inappropriate or insufficient.[444] In applying the principle, the court must have regard to the age, health, earning capacity and level of dependence of the party making the claim, together with any intention he or she has to undergo a course of education or training and the needs and resources of the parties.[445] Even if an award of periodical allowance is justified, such factors may affect the period of time during which it will be payable.[446] A failure to consider the length of time during which periodical allowance would be required having regard to the use that could be made of orders for transfer of property and a capital sum was remedied on appeal by a reduction of the duration of the award from three years to six months.[447] Where the circumstances justify ongoing support for a specified period or periods exceeding three years, separate awards may be made under both the fourth and fifth principles.[448]

The fifth principle requires the court to award such financial provision as is reasonable to relieve a party of serious financial hardship where that is a likely consequence of divorce or dissolution of civil partnership. It can be used to justify an order for periodical allowance for a specified reasonable period[449] or without limit of time where capital-based orders would be insufficient or inappropriate for that purpose.[450] The factors to be taken into account in applying this principle indicate that financial hardship is to be understood as a relative concept and that the length of the marriage or civil partnership is a relevant consideration.[451] While the principle emphasises that likely hardship must be a consequence of the divorce

---

[439] 1985 Act s.11(3) provides the list of factors to which the court must have regard in applying s.9(1)(c).

[440] See para.44.42, below.

[441] *Maclachlan v Maclachlan*, 1998 S.L.T. 693; *B v B* [2012] CSOH 21.

[442] In *Cunniff v Cunniff*, 1999 S.L.T. 999, it was used together with principles 9(1)(a) and (b) to achieve this end.

[443] 1985 Act s.13(2).

[444] 1985 Act ss.9(1)(d) and 13(2).

[445] 1985 Act s.11(4)(a)–(d) although all other circumstances of the case will be relevant; s.11(4)(e).

[446] see e.g. *Sheret v Sheret*, 1990 S.C.L.R. 799; *Loudon v Loudon*, 1994 S.L.T. 381; *Wilson v Wilson*, 1999 S.L.T. 249.

[447] *McConnell v McConnell*, 1997 Fam. L.R. 108.

[448] *Smith v Smith*, 2010 S.L.T. 372.

[449] *Smith v Smith*, 2010 S.L.T. 372.

[450] 1985 Act ss.(1)(e) and 13(2). Examples of its application include *Mackenzie v Mackenzie*, 1991 S.L.T. 461; *Haugan v Haugan*, 1996 S.L.T. 321 OH and *Smith v Smith*, 2010 S.L.T. 372.

[451] 1985 Act s.11(5)(a)–(d). In addition to the issues of age, health, earning capacity and needs and resources relevant also in considering principle 9(1)(d), directs the court to have regard to the duration of the marriage or civil partnership and the standard of living of the parties during it. Again all other circumstances of the case should be considered—s.11(5)(e).

or dissolution, it has been held that the spouse seeking the award does not require to be reliant on the other party for financial support at the time of decree,[452] as the prospect of future hardship on a loss of the right to aliment is sufficient to meet the test.[453]

Following application of the principles to determine what award or awards they justify in any particular case, the court must consider whether such an award or awards would be reasonable having regard to the parties' respective resources at the time of divorce or dissolution, including resources reasonably foreseeable at that time.[454] It is thought that this last part of the test cannot be used to increase a justifiable award, only to reduce it.[455] The provision can operate to take account of significant loss of wealth during the period between the relevant date and divorce or dissolution, to avoid an award being made on relevant date values that cannot now be satisfied.[456]

The conduct of either party to the marriage or civil partnership must not be taken into account in applying the first three principles of s.9 unless it has adversely affected relevant financial resources.[457] In applying s.9(1)(d) or (e), however, the court may, in addition to its effect on resources, consider a party's conduct where it would be manifestly inequitable to leave it out of account.[458]

The court is empowered by the legislation to set aside transactions with the actual or likely effect of defeating a claim for aliment or financial provision.[459] An intention so to defeat a spouse or civil partner's claims is not strictly required. A relevant application must be made not later than one year from the date of disposal of a party's claim. In an unusual case the provision was used not to return the funds to the transferor but to order payment of a capital sum by the transferee to the claimant spouse. The transferee was a trustee company into which monies had been placed by one spouse prior to the relevant date, where the company was convened as an additional defender in the divorce and the transferor spouse had little or no realisable resources by the time of divorce.[460] An order for interdict may be used to prevent a party effecting such a transaction.[461]

44.32 **Agreements as to financial provision on divorce or dissolution**—While the parties to a marriage or civil partnership are in general free to reach agreement between themselves as to the regulation of their financial affairs on divorce or dissolution, the 1985 Act empowers the court to set aside or vary an agreement as to financial provision on divorce or dissolution or any term of it where the agreement was not fair and reasonable at the time it was entered into.[462] In considering

---

[452] *Haugan v Haugan*, 2002 S.C. 631; cf. *Barclay v Barclay*, 1991 S.C.L.R. 205.

[453] *Haugan v Haugan*, 2002 S.C. 631.

[454] 1985 Act ss.8(2)(b) and 27(1).

[455] *Welsh v Welsh*, 1994 S.L.T. 828.

[456] *M v M and W Estate Trustees Ltd*, 2011 Fam. L.R. 24. If the court were to make an award that rendered the payer absolutely insolvent, a trustee in sequestration could seek to have it set aside—Bankruptcy (Scotland) Act 1985 s.35.

[457] 1985 Act s.11(7)(a). Examples of conduct affecting financial resources were seen in *Skarpaas v Skarpaas*, 1991 S.L.T. (Sh. Ct) 15; 1993 S.L.T. 343 and *Short v Short*, 1994 G.W.D. 21–1300.

[458] 1985 Act s.11(7)(b).

[459] 1985 Act s.18(1)(a) and (b); *Tahir v Tahir (No. 2)*, 1995 S.L.T. 451. The provision also relates to a relevant application for variation or recall of such orders: s.18(1)(c).

[460] *M v M and W Estate Trustees Ltd* [2011] Fam. L.R. 24.

[461] 1985 Act s.18(1)(ii). See *Morrison v Morrison and Ward Estates Trustees Ltd*, 2009 S.L.T. 750.

[462] 1985 Act s.16(1)(b) and (2)(b), as amended by the2004 Act Sch.28 and the Family Law (Scotland) Act 2006 Sch.2.

an application to set aside such an agreement the court should consider the following five guidelines[463]:

(i) the contract should be assessed from the perspective of both fairness and reasonableness, (although either unfairness or unreasonabless alone is sufficient to have the agreement set aside[464]);

(ii) all relevant circumstances leading up to and prevailing at the time of execution of the agreement should be examined, including the nature and quality of any legal advice given;

(iii) an unfair advantage taken by one spouse during negotiations may have a cogent bearing on the matter;

(iv) the court should not be unduly ready to overturn agreements validly entered into; and

(v) the mere fact that an agreement turns out to be more advantageous to one party does not mean that it is unfair or unreasonable.[465]

A failure to seek independent legal advice will not per se result in a setting aside order, particularly if the aims of the party so refusing were achieved by the terms of the agreement,[466] whereas a failure by one party to disclose a matrimonial asset when negotiating the contract led to an agreement which was otherwise fair being set aside.[467] The inability of a spouse to make appropriate decisions and negotiate due to a poor mental and emotional state was one of several factors justifying an order setting aside the agreement she had entered into,[468] whereas the subsequent realisation that a signed agreement was over generous to the other party did not form a sufficient basis for such an order.[469] Where an agreement as to financial provision is contained in a joint minute, the parties are bound by it, but an application to set it aside as unfair and unreasonable at the time it was entered into is competent until decree of divorce (or dissolution) is pronounced.[470]

The court may also set aside or vary a term relating to periodical allowance if the agreement expressly provides that that may be done.[471] Further, a particular power is given to the court to set aside or vary any term of an agreement as to periodical allowance in one of three specified examples of bankruptcy on the part of the party by whom any periodical allowance is payable.[472] Finally, there is also now a statutory basis for variation or setting aside any term of such an agreement when, by virtue of the making of a maintenance assessment under the Child Support Act 1991, child support maintenance has become payable by either party to the agreement with respect to a child to whom or for whose benefit periodical allowance is paid under the agreement.[473]

---

[463] These were formulated in the leading case of *Gillon v Gillon (No.3)*, 1995 S.L.T. 678.

[464] This is a possible addition later suggested in *Clarkson v Clarkson*, 2008 S.L.T. (Sh. Ct) 2; cf. *Hanif v Hanif*, 2011 G.W.D. 20–471.

[465] *Gillon v Gillon (No.3)*, 1995 S.L.T. 678 at 681.

[466] *Inglis v Inglis*, 1999 S.L.T. (Sh. Ct) 59.

[467] *McKay v McKay*, 2006 S.L.T. (Sh. Ct) 149.

[468] *Short v Short*, 1994 G.W.D. 21–1300.

[469] *Anderson v Anderson*, 1989 S.C.L.R. 475.

[470] *Horton v Horton*, 1992 S.L.T. (Sh. Ct) 37; *Young v Young (No.2)*, 1991 S.L.T. 869; *Jongejan v Jongejan*, 1993 S.L.T. 595 at 599.

[471] 1985 Act s.16(1)(a) and (2)(a); *Ellerby v Ellerby*, 1991 S.C.L.R. 608.

[472] 1985 Act s.16(3)(a)–(c).

[473] 1985 Act s.16(3)(d). This provision, added to s.16 by the Child Support (Amendments to Primary Legislation) (Scotland) Order 1993 (SI 1993/660), may have little practical application, as periodical allowance is rarely, if ever, provided for the benefit of a child. See Clive, *Law of Husband and Wife in Scotland* (1997), pp.489–490.

Enforceable agreements as to financial provision on divorce may be entered into at any time during the marriage or even prior to it.[474] It seems likely, however, that the terms of an ante-nuptial contract are susceptible to the statutory setting aside provision if they were not fair and reasonable at the time they were entered into.[475]

44.33 Recognition of foreign divorces, dissolution of civil partnerships and orders for financial provision—The law relative to the recognition of foreign divorces, dissolutions of civil partnerships, annulments and legal separations is now contained in various statutory provisions.[476] As a general rule, the relevant provisions apply to any divorce, dissolution, annulment or legal separation, whenever obtained.[477] In relation to decrees of a court of civil jurisdiction granted in any part of the British Islands, these shall be recognised throughout the United Kingdom,[478] unless there was no subsisting marriage or civil partnership according to the rules of the part of the United Kingdom in which recognition is sought,[479] or where the decree is irreconcilable with a previous decision on the subsistence or validity of the marriage or civil partnership given in a court of or recognised by that part.[480] Divorces, dissolutions of civil partnerships, annulments and legal separations granted outside the British Islands are divided into those obtained by judicial or other proceedings and those not obtained by such proceedings. A decree obtained by means of proceedings[481] will be given recognition if it is effective under the law of the country in which it was obtained and if, at the date of the commencement of the proceedings, either party to the marriage was (a) habitually resident in the country in which it was obtained, (b) domiciled in that country, or (c) a national of that country.[482] Recognition of a decree which complies with these provisions may however be refused if there has been procedural unfairness in the foreign proceedings, such as a lack of proper notice or ability to participate, or where recognition would be manifestly contrary to public policy.[483] An overseas divorce, dissolution of civil partnership, annulment or legal separation not obtained by judicial or other proceedings[484] will be recognised in Scotland if it is effective under the law of the country in which it was obtained and if, at the date on which it was obtained (a) each party to the marriage was domiciled in that country, or (b) either party to the marriage was domiciled in that country and

---

[474] Ante-nuptial contracts entered into by adults of sound mind have always been valid and enforceable in Scotland; *Thomson v Thomson*, 1982 S.L.T. 521. In England, the previous antipathy towards such contracts on public policy grounds has all but disappeared—*Radmacher v Granatino*, 2010 2 F.L.R. 1900.

[475] *Kibble v Kibble*, 2010 S.L.T (Sh. Ct) 5.

[476] Family Law Act 1986 (the "1986 Act") Pt II ss.44–54; 2004 Act Pt 5 ss.233–238.

[477] 1986 Act s.54(1) defines "annulment" as including any decree or declarator of nullity of marriage, however expressed.

[478] 1986 Act s.44(1) and (2); 2004 Act s.233(2).

[479] 1986 Act s.51(2); 2004 Act s.233(4).

[480] 1986 Act s.51(1); 2004 Act s.233(3). Cf. *Vervaeke v Smith* [1983] 1 A.C. 145.

[481] See *El Fadl v El Fadl*, 2000 Fam. L.R. 175, where a Lebanese Talaq divorce was held to have been obtained by proceedings due to the requirement that it be recorded with the Sharia court.

[482] 1986 Act s.46(1) and (3); 2004 Act s.235(1). See *H v H (Queen's Proctor intervening) (validity of Japanese divorce)* [2007] 1 F.L.R. 1318.

[483] 1986 Act s.51(3)(a) and (c); 2004 Act s.236(3)(a) and (c). See *Chaudhary v Chaudhary* [1984] 3 All E.R. 1017.

[484] In *Chaudhary v Chaudhary* [1984] 3 All E.R. 1017, it was held under a previous provision on the same issue that a simple Talaq, being a private and informal act involving no outside agency, did not constitute "other proceedings".

the other party was domiciled in a country under whose law the divorce, annulment or legal separation is recognised as valid.[485] There is a further requirement that neither party to the marriage was habitually resident in the United Kingdom throughout the period of one year immediately preceding the date on which the divorce, annulment or separation was obtained.[486] Again, there are grounds for refusal of recognition at the discretion of the court. These include an absence of an official document certifying effectiveness of the foreign order, where either party is domiciled in another country an absence of an official document certifying the order's validity, or where recognition would be manifestly contrary to public policy.[487] For civil partners, provision has also now been made for recognition of an overseas dissolution, annulment or separation secured by proceedings in one country where the party seeking the order was habitually resident or domiciled in another jurisdiction which does not recognise same sex relationships in law.[488]

There are now certain restricted grounds upon which recognition of a decree of divorce, legal separation or annulment secured in one EU Member State can be refused in another State. These include circumstances in which recognition would be manifestly contrary to public policy, a lack of proper service of opportunity to prepare a defence to the proceedings in the other jurisdiction and irreconcilability with an earlier judgement.[489] There is no opportunity to review the substance of the other court's decision or to question its jurisdiction to make the order.[490] There are separate statutory rules for the refusal to recognise the validity of a judgement of a Member State on dissolution, annulment or legal separation of a civil partnership.[491]

One consequence of recognition of an overseas divorce, dissolution of civil partnership or annulment is that the parties are free to marry or enter into a civil partnership again.[492] Further, certain powers are conferred upon the Scottish courts to make orders for financial provision following an overseas divorce or dissolution of civil partnership that is recognised in this jurisdiction.[493] Such applications must be made within five years of the date of the divorce or dissolution, which requires to have been at the instigation of the other party.[494] It is also necessary that a court in Scotland would have had jurisdiction to entertain the divorce or dissolution of civil partnership had it been initiated here at the time; the marriage or civil partnership must have had a substantial connection with

---

[485] 1986 Act s.46(2)(a) and (b); 2004 Act s.235(2). The 1986 Act s.46(5) and 2004 Act s.237(1) confirm that domicile includes either domicile according to the law of the overseas country involved or according to the law of the part of the United Kingdom in which the question of recognition arises.

[486] 1986 Act s.46(2)(c); 2004 Act s.235(2)(c).

[487] 1986 Act s.51(3)(b) and (c); 2004 Act s.236(3)(b) and (c).

[488] 2004 Act s.235(1A), inserted by the Civil Partnership (Supplementary Provisions relating to the Recognition of Overseas Dissolutions, Annulments or Separations) (Scotland) Regulations 2005 (SSI 2005/567).

[489] EU Regulation 2201/2003 of the Council of 27 November 2003 concerning jurisdiction and the recognition and enforcement of judgments in matrimonial matters and the matters of parental responsibility, art.22.

[490] Regulation 2201/2003 arts 24 and 26.

[491] 2004 Act s.219 and the Civil Partnership (Jurisdiction and Recognition of Judgments) (Scotland) Regulations 2005 (SSI 2005/629).

[492] 1986 Act s.50; 2004 Act s.238.

[493] Matrimonial and Family Proceedings Act 1984 (the "1984 Act") s.28; 2004 Act s.125 and Sch.11. See *Tahir v Tahir*, 1993 S.L.T. 194.

[494] 1984 Act s.28(3)(a) and (b); 2004 Act Sch.11 para.2(3)(a) and (b).

Scotland and both parties must be alive at the time of the application.[495] Jurisdictional requirements relative to the time of the application provide that the applicant must be domiciled or habitually resident in Scotland when it is made, and that the other party must also (i) be so domiciled or habitually resident, or (ii) have been so domiciled or habitually resident when the parties last lived together as husband and wife or civil partners, or (iii) be an owner, tenant, or otherwise have a beneficial interest in a property in Scotland which was at some time a matrimonial or family home of the parties.[496] Where the requirements are satisfied, the court has power to make any of the orders for financial provision specified in s.8(1) of the Family Law (Scotland) Act 1985.[497] The court should aim, so far as reasonable and practicable to place the parties in the same position as they would have been in had they proceeded to divorce or dissolution of civil partnership in Scotland on the date the foreign decree took effect. In this context account must be taken of the parties' present and foreseeable resources at the time of disposal of the application, together with any financial provision orders made by the foreign court.[498] There is also provision for the making of an interim periodical allowance order where financial provision is likely to be made at the end of the application and it is necessary to avoid hardship,[499] but where the only basis for jurisdiction is a property in Scotland, only orders relative to that property and its value can be made and there is no jurisdiction to award any other form of financial provision.[500]

44.34 Dissolution of marriage or civil partnership on presumed death of spouse or civil partner—Where a person who is missing is thought to have died or has not been known to be alive for a period of at least seven years, any person having an interest, including a spouse or civil partner of the missing person, may raise an action of declarator of his death.[501] Decree in such an action will be effective for all purposes including the dissolution of a marriage or civil partnership to which the missing person was a party.[502] The marriage or civil partnership is not revived if the decree is subsequently recalled or varied, or if it appears that the missing person was in fact alive.[503]

IV. COHABITATION WITHOUT MARRIAGE

44.35 Couples who live together openly as cohabitants, rather than holding themselves out as man and wife or as civil partners are now recognised in law for certain statutory purposes.[504] However, there is no obligation to aliment a cohabitant.[505]

---

[495] 1984 Act s.28(3)(c), (d) and (e); 2004 Act Sch.11 para.2(3)(c), (d) and (e).

[496] 1984 Act s.28(2)(a) and (b)(i)–(iii); 2004 Act Sch.11 para.2(2).

[497] 1984 Act s.30; 2004 Act Sch.11 para.4.

[498] 1984 Act s.29; 2004 Act Sch.11 para.3.

[499] 1984 Act s.29(4); 2004 Act Sch.11 para.4.

[500] 1984 Act s.29(5); 2004 Act Sch.11 para.5. Thus in such circumstances neither periodical allowance or interim periodical allowance can be awarded.

[501] Presumption of Death (Scotland) Act 1977 s.1, as amended by the 2004 Act Sch.28.

[502] Presumption of Death (Scotland) Act 1977 s.3(1), as amended.

[503] Presumption of Death (Scotland) Act 1977 s.3(4), as amended.

[504] See e.g. Social Security Administration Act 1992 s.78; Local Government Finance Act 1992 ss.75 and 77; Housing (Scotland) Act 1987 s.52; Housing (Scotland) Act 1988 s.31; Mortgage Rights (Scotland) Act 2001 ss.1 and 2; Administration of Justice Act 1982 ss.8 and 9.

[505] There is no such common law duty and s.1 of the 1985 Act confirms the obligations of spouses and parents, but not cohabitants.

An individual's property rights are generally unaffected by cohabitation, and a cohabitant who owns the family home outright is not restricted from selling or otherwise dealing with it.[506] But a cohabitant without any right to occupy the home in which the couple resides may apply to the court for occupancy rights therein.[507] The duration of the order available to cohabitants is limited to an initial specified period of up to six months and for further periods each not exceeding that,[508] and no provision is made for the grant of interim occupancy rights. The parties require to have been living together "as husband and wife" or as civil partners at the time of the conduct giving rise to the application.[509] Applications for exclusion orders and ancillary remedies are available to cohabitants where they are jointly entitled or permitted to occupy the property, or where the non-entitled cohabiting partner has been granted occupancy rights by the court.[510] Matrimonial interdicts were previously unavailable to cohabitants, but the Family Law (Scotland) Act 2006, introduced a new category of "domestic interdicts", which applies specifically to cohabitants.[511] Powers of arrest can be attached to domestic interdicts in terms of the Protection from Abuse (Scotland) Act 2001.[512] Transfer of tenancy orders may be sought by cohabitants who are entitled by title or by grant of the court to occupy the home.[513] Cohabitants can seek reparation for their loss on the death of their partners as a result of personal injuries in much the same way as those who are widowed.[514] Homosexual cohabitation has now been recognised in law. Initially this was for the limited purpose of including a stable homosexual partnership within the definition of "family life" for the purpose of a specific statutory provision relative to succession of tenancies.[515] The Family Law (Scotland) Act 2006 has extended that recognition to all cohabitation provisions.

Breakdown of cohabitation without marriage—Although cohabitation per se **44.36** has no legal status and thus fewer legal effects than marriage or civil partnership, a limited statutory regime for financial claims following the breakdown of a cohabiting relationship has now been created by the provisions of the Family Law (Scotland) Act 2006, which apply to cohabitants who ceased to cohabit on or after May 4, 2006.[516] A cohabitant is defined as someone living with another as if they were husband and wife or civil partners.[517] No minimum period of cohabitation is specified, but in order to determine whether or not a party qualifies as a cohabitant, regard must be had to the length of time during which cohabitation is said to have taken place, the nature of the parties' relationship during that period and the nature and extent of any financial arrangements between them while

---

[506] ss.6–12 and 19 of the 1981 Act, which restrict any dealing with, or sale of, a matrimonial home where there is a spouse, do not apply to cohabitants.

[507] 1981 Act s.18 as amended by the Family Law (Scotland) Act 2006 to include cohabitants of the same sex.

[508] 1981 Act s.18(1).

[509] *Armour v Anderson*, 1994 S.C. 488; 1994 S.L.T. 1127.

[510] 1981 Act s.18(3). See paras 44.17 and 44.18, above, for the test to be applied.

[511] 1981 Act ss.18A and 18B, as inserted by the Family Law (Scotland) Act 2006 s.31(3).

[512] Protection from Abuse (Scotland) Act 2001 s.1(2), as amended by the Family Law (Scotland) Act 2006 s.32 and Sch.3.

[513] 1981 Act ss.13 and 18(3)(b).

[514] Damages (Scotland) Act 1976 s.10 and Sch.1 (as amended). See also s.13(1)(b) of the Administration of Justice Act 1982.

[515] *Fitzpatrick v Sterling Housing Association* [1999] 3 W.L.R. 1113.

[516] 2006 Act s.28 and para.6 of the Family Law (Scotland) Act 2006 (Commencement, Transitional Provisions and Savings) Order 2006 (SSI 2006/212).

[517] 2006 Act s.25(1).

living together.[518] For qualifying cohabitants there is now a statutory rebuttable presumption to an equal share in household goods acquired (other than by gift or succession from a third party) during the period of cohabitation.[519] There is an important innovation in relation to (a) money derived from any allowances made by either cohabitant for the couple's joint household expenses or for similar purposes, and (b) any property acquired out of such money. That money or property shall be treated as belonging to each cohabitant in equal shares.[520] However, the sole or main residence of the couple is excluded from the rule[521] and there is no general matrimonial or community property regime for cohabitants. A claim for financial provision must be made within one year of the cessation of cohabitation[522] and the action can be raised in either the Court of Session or the sheriff court, with the jurisdictional bases being those for divorce or dissolution of civil partnership.[523] Proof to resolve any dispute as to the date on which the parties ceased to cohabit may be required to resolve an issue of time bar and the same considerations as those taken into account in ascertaining whether husband and wife have ceased cohabitation will be relevant.[524]

The financial provision that may be awarded under s.28 of the Family Law (Scotland) Act 2006 is wholly discretionary, but the court must have regard to certain factors, namely (a) whether (and, if so, to what extent) the defender has derived economic advantage from contributions made by the applicant; and (b) whether (and, if so, to what extent) the applicant has suffered economic disadvantage in the interests of the defender or any "relevant child".[525] Contributions cover indirect and non-financial contributions, including looking after a relevant child. Economic advantage includes gains in capital, income and earning capacity and the corresponding economic disadvantage includes losses in those aspects of wealth.[526] The only orders that can be made on such an application are for a capital sum or payment in respect of the economic burden of caring for a child of the parties.[527] Payment can be ordered to be made on a specified date or in instalments,[528] and the provision for interim orders includes the ability, in contrast to divorce and dissolution cases, to order financial provision ad interim.[529] Following different and sometimes contradictory views being expressed on how the matter of how the provisions should be applied,[530] the correct approach to the treatment of such claims has now been clarified by the Supreme Court in the case

---

[518] 2006 Act s.25(2).

[519] 2006 Act s.26(1)–(3). The definition of "household goods" is almost identical to that used in the presumption of joint ownership of household goods for spouses (1985 Act s.25), with money, securities, motor vehicles and domestic animals being excluded—see s.26(4).

[520] 2006 Act s.27(1) and (2).

[521] 2006 Act s.27(3).

[522] 2006 Act s.28(8).

[523] 2006 Act s.28(2) and (9).

[524] *Fairley v Fairley* [2008] Fam. L.R. 112.

[525] 2006 Act s.28(3). A "relevant child" is there defined as a child of the cohabitants or one accepted by them as a child of the family.

[526] 2006 Act s.28(9). The factors referred to all seem reflective of principle 9(1)(b) of the Family Law (Scotland) Act 1985. See para.44.31, above.

[527] 2006 Act s.28(2).

[528] 2006 Act s.28(7).

[529] 2006 Act s.28(2) provides that the court can make such interim order as it thinks fit.

[530] See e.g. *M v S*, 2008 S.L.T. 71; *Jamieson v Rodhouse* [2009] Fam. L.R. 34; *Lindsay v Murphy* [2010] Fam. L.R. 156.

of *Gow v Grant*.[531] The provisions of s.28 should be read broadly rather than narrowly, bearing in mind that the principle in s.9(1)(b) of the Family Law (Scotland) Act 1985 which they adopt was designed to correct imbalances arising out of a non commercial relationship where parties are quite likely to make contributions or sacrifices without counting the cost or bargaining for a return. As with s.9(1)(b), a broad approach enabling fair compensation to be awarded, on a rough and ready valuation, is required in cases where otherwise none could be claimed.[532] Intention to benefit the other party is not required, it being the effect of a transaction rather than its intention that should be considered.[533] A transaction that has benefitted both parties may well provide the basis for an award, provided that disadvantage has been suffered in the interests of the defender to some extent.[534] Thus the party who had sold her home such that she, unlike the defender, had no home at the end of the cohabitation, was entitled to compensation for that disadvantage despite having received benefit herself from the proceeds of sale when she sold her home.[535]

For those who are in a committed relationship but do not qualify as cohabitants within the 2006 Act regime, no family law remedies are available, although monies spent by one party to the relationship on the other party's property in contemplation of marriage may be recoverable under the principle of *condictio causa data causa non secuta*.[536] Where no future marriage was contemplated there may still be circumstances in which the principles of unjustified enrichment can be applied.[537]

Provision for a survivor on the death of their cohabitant—The rights on intes- **44.37** tacy afforded to a surviving spouse[538] do not extend to cohabitants. The Family Law (Scotland) Act 2006 introduced a limited right to apply for provision from a deceased cohabitant's estate in such a situation.[539]

V. CHILDREN

Introductory—Formerly, the concept of parent and child was a straightforward **44.38** one, with no difficulty in identifying the person in law entitled to be regarded as the mother of a child and certain rules for establishing who the father was. The development of alternative scientific techniques of reproduction has, however, rendered necessary the enactment of provisions identifying the parents of children born as a result of the use of such techniques.[540] Where relationships are established, both children and the adults involved with them now have a statutorily

---

[531] *Gow v Grant* [2012] UKSC 29, overturning the decision of the Second Division of the Inner House (see 2011 S.C. 618).

[532] *Gow v Grant* [2012] UKSC 29 at [33] and [36], per Lord Hope.

[533] *Gow v Grant* [2012] UKSC 29 at [37]–[38].

[534] *Gow v Grant* [2012] UKSC 29 at [38].

[535] *Gow v Grant* [2012] UKSC 29 at [40].

[536] *Shilliday v Smith*, 1998 S.C. 725.

[537] *Gray v Kerner*, 1996 S.C.L.R. 331; *Christie v Armstrong*, 1996 S.C.L.R. 745; *Satchwell v McIntosh*, 2006 S.L.T. (Sh. Ct) 117; *McKenzie v Nutter*, 2007 S.L.T. (Sh. Ct) 17. See further above, para.24.13.

[538] Succession (Scotland) Act 1964 ss.8 and 9.

[539] 2006 Act s.29. Again the provisions apply to both homosexual and heterosexual cohabitants. The detail of the provisions is set out at para.39.17 as they form part of the law of succession.

[540] Human Fertilisation and Embryology Act 1990. See para.44.40, below.

protected right to respect for their family life that must be balanced in any decisions affecting the upbringing of the children.[541] These developments now
permeate the whole range of matters with which the law of Scotland relating to
children is concerned.

44.39 **Legal equality of children: Legitimacy and illegitimacy**—At common law a
distinction in status was made between legitimate and illegitimate children. That
distinction was of fundamental importance in determining the legal incidents of the
relationship of parent and child and in questions of succession and of legal rights
on a parent's death.[542] Modern statute has shown a progressive trend to modify or
eliminate the remaining points of distinction and this has now culminated in a
formal abolition of the status of illegitimacy with effect from May 4, 2006. The
Law Reform (Parent and Child) Act 1986, as now amended,[543] makes specific
provision that no person whose status is governed by Scots Law shall be illegitimate and that, accordingly, the fact that a person's parents are not or have not been
married to one another must be left out of account in (a) determining the person's
legal status, and (b) establishing the legal relationship between that person and any
other person.[544] In any enactment or deed any reference to a relative, however
expressed, is, unless the contrary intention appears, to be construed in accordance
with that principle.[545] The rule is subject to exceptions for pre-existing statutory
provisions, deeds executed before commencement of the 2006 Act and references
to legitimate and illegitimate persons and relationships in post-commencement
deeds.[546] Subject to one limited exception relating to hereditary titles,[547] no action
for declarator of legitimacy, legitimation or illegitimacy can competently be raised
after May 4, 2006.[548] The previous distinction between legitimate and illegitimate
children for the purpose of ascertaining their domicile of origin has also been abolished.[549] Section 22 of the 2006 Act now provides that a child shall be domiciled in
the same country as his parents if they are domiciled in the same country as each
other and the child has a home with them or either of them.[550] Where that provision
is inapplicable, the child shall be domiciled in the country with which he has for the
time being the closest connection.[551] Three potentially significant legal differences
between children born inside and outwith marriage are retained notwithstanding
the general rule abolishing illegitimacy. These are: (i) the principle of legal equality
of children does not apply to the succession of titles, coats of arms, honours and
dignities transmissible on the death of the holder and the functions of the Lord
Lyon King of Arms are accordingly unaffected by the rule[552]; (ii) rights of

---

[541] European Convention on Human Rights art.8 (Human Rights Act 1998 Sch.1).

[542] For a discussion of the old common law on legitimacy and illegitimacy see *Kerr v Martin* (1840)
2 D. 752 and *McNeill v McGregor* (1901) 4 F. 123.

[543] By the Family Law (Scotland) Act 2006 s.21.

[544] Law Reform (Parent and Child) Act 1986 s.1(1), as amended by the 2006 Act s.21(4)(a).

[545] Law Reform (Parent and Child) Act 1986 s.1(2).

[546] Law Reform (Parent and Child) Act 1986 s.1(4).

[547] Law Reform (Parent and Child) Act 1986 s.9(1)(c) as amended by the 2006 Act s.21(4)(a).
Section 7 of the 1986 Act has been retained to govern any such action.

[548] Law Reform (Parent and Child) Act 1986 s.1(6), inserted by the 2006 Act s.21(2)(c).

[549] s.9(1)(a) of the 1986 Act, which preserved the old common law rule that a legitimate child's
domicile of origin followed that of the father but an illegitimate child took the mother's domicile, was
repealed by the 2006 Act Sch.3.

[550] 2006 Act s.22(1) and (2).

[551] 2006 Act s.22(3).

[552] Law Reform (Parent and Child) Act 1986 s.9(1)(c) and (ca), the latter provision inserted by the
2006 Act s.21(4).

succession to the estates of those who died before the commencement of the 1986 Act are exempt from its application[553]; and (iii) the law on adoption of children is unaffected by the general rule.[554] In addition to these exceptions, in some disputes about children, the legal relationship between father and child continues to be affected by the marital status of the parents.[555] Parental rights and responsibilities in relation to his child are still only conferred automatically on a father who was married to the mother at the time of the child's conception or subsequently, although registration as the child's father has been, from May 4, 2006, sufficient to confer such rights and responsibilities.[556] Provisions remain in force to ensure the legitimacy of a child whose parents' marriage is subsequently declared null.[557]

Parentage: Presumptions and related provisions—At common law, the **44.40** husband of a woman who gave birth during the subsistence of the marriage was presumed to be the child's father, in accordance with the maxim *pater est quem nuptiae demonstrant.*[558] The Law Reform (Parent and Child) (Scotland) Act 1986 now provides that a man is presumed to be the father of a child if he was married to the mother at any time beginning with the conception and ending with the birth of the child,[559] even if the marriage is void, voidable or irregular.[560] Where the presumption arising from marriage does not apply, a man is presumed to be the father of a child if both he and the mother have acknowledged his paternity and he has been registered as the father in any register of births kept under statutory authority in any part of the United Kingdom.[561] These statutory presumptions of paternity are rebuttable by proof on a balance of probabilities.[562] Where assisted reproduction has taken place, the Human Fertilisation and Embryology Act 1990 provides rules to establish parentage in law. Unless a child is adopted, the mother is the woman who is carrying or has carried a child as a result of the placing in her of an embryo or of sperm and eggs.[563] Where, after the commencement of the 1990 Act,[564] a pregnancy results, in the course of treatment services provided for a heterosexual couple together,[565] from the placing in a married woman of an embryo or of sperm and eggs, or from her artificial insemination, but her husband is not the genetic father of the child, he alone will nevertheless be treated as the father unless it is shown that he did not consent to the procedure.[566] Similar rules

---

[553] Law Reform (Parent and Child) Act 1986 s.9(1)(d).

[554] Law Reform (Parent and Child) Act 1986 s.9(1)(b). Thus the agreement of an unmarried father without parental responsibilities and rights is not strictly required in connection with the adoption of his child, subject to any argument about his having had family life with that child. See paras 44.49–44.50.

[555] See para.44.44, below.

[556] Children (Scotland) Act 1995 s.3(1) expressly qualifies the rule in s.1(1) of the 1986 Act in this respect. Section 3(1)(b)(ii), which provides the rule that registration as father is sufficient to confer parental rights, was inserted by the 2006 Act s.23(2).

[557] Law Reform (Miscellaneous Provisions) Act 1949 s.4(1).

[558] Stair III, 3, 42; Erskine I, 6, 49; Bell, *Principles*, s.1626. A marriage subsequent to the birth did not raise any presumption that the husband was the father of the child; *Brooke's Exrx v James*, 1971 S.C. (HL) 71.

[559] Law Reform (Parent and Child) Act 1986 s.5(1)(a).

[560] Law Reform (Parent and Child) Act 1986 s.5(2).

[561] Law Reform (Parent and Child) Act 1986 s.5(1)(b).

[562] Law Reform (Parent and Child) Act 1986 s.5(4).

[563] Human Fertilisation and Embryology Act 1990 (the "1990 Act") s.27.

[564] 1990 Act s.49(3) makes clear that it is the treatment that must take place after the Act came into force. See *Re M (Child Support Act: parentage)* [1997] 2 F.L.R. 90.

[565] See fn.572, below.

[566] 1990 Act s.28(1) and (2).

apply where treatment is provided to an unmarried heterosexual couple together.[567] The House of Lords held that it is necessary for a couple to be "together" both at the time when treatment began and at the time of the successful implantation of the embryo for the man to be treated as the father in terms of the provisions.[568] These statutory rules regarding paternity do not apply, however, where by virtue of another enactment or rule of law the child is to be treated as the child of the parties to a marriage,[569] or where the child is subsequently adopted.[570] There is also provision to exclude entitlement in respect of succession to titles, coats of arms, honours or dignities transmissible on death through being treated as a parent under the Act.[571] The final exception is that a man cannot be treated as the father of a child where his sperm was used after his death to bring about a pregnancy that resulted in the birth of that child,[572] although the fact of paternity can be recorded on the birth certificate.[573] Where a child is the genetic child of one or both of the parties to a marriage but was carried by a woman other than the wife, and certain other statutory requirements, including consent[574] of those who would otherwise be the parent or parents as a matter of law, are fulfilled, a court may make a "parental order", declaring that the child is the child of the married couple.[575] An important consideration is that such surrogacy arrangements must not be for financial gain, other than where payment has been authorised by the court.[576] The Human Fertilisation and Embryology Act 2008 has introduced provisions for a female couple who are civil partners and undergo fertility treatment resulting in the birth of a child.[577] The effect is that the mother's[578] civil partner will be deemed to be the other parent of the child unless she did not consent to the mother's treatment.[579] A female cohabitant may also qualify to be a "parent" in these circumstances.[580] A challenge to any of these presumptions or statutory rules may be taken in an action for declarator of parentage or non-parentage raised in either the Court of Session or the sheriff court.[581] A party to such proceedings can be requested to provide a sample of blood or other fluid, or body tissue, for testing; if such a request is refused, the Court has a discretion to draw such inference, if any, as is appropriate.[582] A relative of the alleged father sued in a representative capacity can still be a party to the proceedings and, therefore, requested to

---

[567] 1990 Act s.28(3).

[568] In *re D (a child appearing by her guardian ad litem) (Respondent)* [2005] A.C. 621.

[569] 1990 Act s.28(5)(b).

[570] 1990 Act s.28(5)(c).

[571] 1990 Act s.29(5)(a).

[572] 1990 Act s.28(6)(b).

[573] Human Fertilisation and Embryology (Deceased Fathers) Act 2003 s.1.

[574] See *C v S*, 1996 S.L.T. 1387 where the surrogate refused to consent and litigation ensued as to who should have parental responsibility for the child.

[575] 1990 Act s.30. See the Parental Orders (Human Fertilisation and Embryology) (Scotland) Regulations 1994 (SI 1994/2804), which govern the applications for the making and registration of such orders.

[576] 1990 Act s.30(7). In *C v S*, 1996 S.L.T. 1387, the Inner House indicated that, had it been necessary to do so, it would have authorised the payment of £8,000 to the surrogate under the similar provision in the Adoption (Scotland) Act 1978.

[577] Human Fertilisation and Embryology Act 2008 ss.42–44.

[578] The mother will be the woman who has carried the child. See s.33(1), which is consistent with the rule in the 1990 Act s.27(1).

[579] Human Fertilisation and Embryology Act 2008 s.44(1).

[580] Human Fertilisation and Embryology Act 2008 ss.43–44.

[581] Law Reform (Parent and Child) (Scotland) Act 1986 s.7.

[582] Law Reform (Miscellaneous Provisions) (Scotland) Act 1990 s.70, which applies to "any civil proceedings". See *Smith v Greenhill*, 1994 S.L.T. (Sh. Ct) 22.

provide a sample; in cases of doubt as to the course to be followed, the child's best interests should rule.[583]

Aliment court proceedings—A father is under a natural obligation to support his **44.41** child and at common law his was the primary obligation.[584] The liability of the mother and others on whom the common law imposed an alimentary obligation was postponed to his, except only that in the case of a married daughter the obligation of her husband might take precedence. The whole common law rules on aliment, with the exception of those relating to the transmission of alimentary claims against the estate of a deceased person, were superseded by the Family Law (Scotland) Act 1985. Under that Act an obligation of aliment is owed by, and only by (a) a husband to his wife, (b) a wife to her husband, (bb) civil partners to each other, (c) a father or mother to his or her child, and (d) a person to a child (other than a child boarded-out by a public authority or voluntary organisation) who has been accepted by him as a child of his family.[585] Where children are concerned, however, the jurisdiction of the courts has, for some time, largely been superseded, except in limited situations, by the Child Support Act 1991, which provides a mechanism for the assessment and collection of maintenance from parents. The courts continue to retain jurisdiction to deal with the maintenance of children in particular cases. These include claims: (i) by children against step-parents or against adults who have accepted them as children of their family[586]; (ii) for aliment additional to child support maintenance assessed by the Child Support Agency[587]; (iii) for the expenses of education or training[588]; (iv) for expenses incurred in connection with a child's disability[589]; (v) for aliment claimed by children against the parent with care of them[590]; (vi) where the child or one of the parents is habitually resident outside the United Kingdom[591], although UK civil servants, diplomats and forces personnel habitually resident abroad, together with those working out of the country but for a company registered in one of the UK jurisdictions or with payroll arrangements here will be liable to Child Support Agency maintenance assessments rather than court awarded aliment[592]; (vii) by children aged 19 or over[593]; (viii) for aliment claimed by children between the ages of 16 and 19 who are not undergoing recognised full-time education[594] and by others between the ages of 16 and 18 where certain

---

[583] *Mackay v Murphy*, 1995 S.L.T. (Sh. Ct) 30.

[584] Stair, I, iii, 3, and I, ix, 1 and Erskine, III, i, 9, speak of this as an "obediential", i.e. a natural obligation; *Fairgrieves v Hendersons* (1885) 13 R. 98; *Dickinson v Dickinson*, 1952 S.C. 27. See too National Assistance Act 1948 s.42.

[585] s.1(1)(a)–(d), with s.1(1)(bb) having been inserted by the 2004 Act Sch.28. For comment on what constitutes "acceptance" as a child of the family see *Watson v Watson*, 1994 S.C.L.R. 1097 and *Inglis v Inglis*, 1987 S.C.L.R. 608.

[586] Child Support Act 1991 (the "1991 Act") s.3(1).

[587] 1991 Act s.8(6).

[588] 1991 Act s.8(7). See e.g *Lavelle v Lavelle*, 2001 G.W.D. 4–144.

[589] 1991 Act s.8(8) and (9).

[590] 1991 Act s.8(10).

[591] 1991 Act ss.8(3) and 44. The parents are characterised in the amended legislation as the "parent with care" and the "non resident parent". See para.44.42, below.

[592] 1991 Act s.44(2A), inserted by the Child Support, Pensions and Social Security Act 2000 s.22 and the Child Support (Maintenance Arrangements and Jurisdiction) Regulations 1992 (SI 1992/2645), as amended by SI 2009/2909.

[593] 1991 Act ss.8(3) and 55(1).

[594] 1991 Act ss.8(3) and 55(1)(b).

prescribed conditions are satisfied[595]; and (ix) by children who are or have been married.[596] The remainder of this paragraph deals with the assessment and recovery of aliment through the courts in such cases. The general scheme of the Child Support legislation is considered in the ensuing paragraph.

There is no order of liability where two or more persons owe an obligation of aliment to another, but the court in deciding how much, if any, aliment is to be paid by any obligant is to have regard to the obligation owed by any other person.[597] No distinction is made between children born of married parents and those of unmarried parents either in respect of the nature and extent of the obligation or in respect of the persons on whom the obligation rests.[598] In a claim based on acceptance of a child into a family, there must have been knowledge of the truth; where a man has treated a child as his own in the belief that he is the father but then discovers that he is not, he will not be held to have accepted the child merely because of his conduct whilst so mistaken.[599] The obligation of parents to aliment their children survived a parental responsibilities order being made in respect of the child in favour of a local authority.[600] That obligation is to provide such support as is reasonable in the circumstances having regard to the needs, resources and earning capacities of the parties and all the circumstances of the case.[601] Needs are to some extent relative to existing lifestyle, at least where resources are sufficient for its continued maintenance.[602] An award may include reasonable provision for the expenses of a parent with care of the child wholly or partly incurred for the purpose of caring for that child.[603] The court will have regard to the level of aliment provided by a defender for his other children or step-children in determining the needs and relative entitlement of one such child.[604] The conduct of a party is not to be taken into account unless it would be manifestly inequitable not to do so.[605] The obligation may be owed to a child until he reaches majority or, if he is reasonably and appropriately undergoing instruction at an educational establishment or is training for employment or for a trade, profession or vocation, until he reaches the age of 25.[606] It is, no doubt, still the law that neglect by the mother of contraceptive precautions cannot be assimilated to contributory negligence and is irrelevant in determining the level of aliment to be paid by the father.[607]

A claim for aliment may be brought in the Court of Session or the sheriff court and, unless the court considers it inappropriate, may be raised as an ancillary matter where appropriate in a variety of proceedings.[608] A claim in respect of a child may be brought (i) by the child himself where he is aged 16 or over,[609] or

---

[595] 1991 Act ss.8(3) and 55(1)(c) and the Child Support (Maintenance Calculation Procedure) Regulations 2000 (SI 2001/157) Sch.1 para.1.

[596] 1991 Act ss.8(3) and 55(2), which makes clear that void and voidable marriages are included.

[597] 1985 Act s.4(2).

[598] 1985 Act s.27(1).

[599] *Watson v Watson*, 1994 S.C.L.R. 1097.

[600] Children (Scotland) Act 1995 s.86. For permanence orders which have replaced the system of parental responsibilities orders see para.44.51, below.

[601] Family Law (Scotland) Act 1985 ss.1(2) and (4). Section 27(1) of the Act defines resources as including both present and foreseeable resources.

[602] *McGeoch v McGeoch*, 1998 Fam. L.R. 130.

[603] 1985 Act s.4(4), added by the Child Support Act 1991 Sch.5 para.5.

[604] *Ahmed v Ahmed*, 2004 S.C.L.R. 247.

[605] 1985 Act s.4(3); see *Walker v Walker*, 1991 S.L.T. 649.

[606] 1985 Act s.1(5).

[607] *Bell v McCurdie*, 1981 S.C. 64.

[608] 1985 Act s.2(1) and (2).

[609] 1985 Act s.2(4)(a); Age of Legal Capacity (Scotland) Act 1991 s.1(1)(b). See, e.g. *Hay v Hay*, 2000 S.L.T. (Sh. Ct) 95.

younger if he is capable of instructing a solicitor, there being a presumption in favour of such capacity once he attains the age of 12 years,[610] (ii) by his parent or guardian, by anyone with whom he lives or who is seeking a Residence Order[611]in respect of him and, (iii) if he is incapax, by his curator bonis.[612] A woman, whether married or not, may bring an action in respect of her unborn child but no such action can be heard or disposed of until the child is born.[613] An order may be made for the making of alimentary payments of an occasional or special nature, including payments in respect of inlying, funeral or educational expenses.[614]

Where the person to be alimented is living in the same house as the defender it is a defence to the action for aliment that the defender is thereby fulfilling his alimentary obligation and intends to continue doing so[615]; and it is also a defence that the defender is making an offer, which it is reasonable to expect the person concerned to accept, to receive that person into his household and thereby fulfil his obligation of aliment.[616] That defence is not, however, open in the case of aliment for a child under 16.[617] The residence of such a child, if disputed, may be regulated by court order. Awards of aliment and agreements to pay aliment may be varied or terminated on a material change of circumstances.[618] A change of circumstances cannot be established merely by demonstrating that the earlier award was made in reliance on inaccurate or incomplete information,[619] but the making of a maintenance assessment with respect to the child concerned will itself constitute such a material change.[620] An award may be backdated, and variation of an award contained in an interlocutor may also be backdated.[621] There was no power in the legislation to backdate a variation of aliment contained within an agreement. This defect has been rectified by amendment with effect from May 4, 2006.[622] Periodical payments of interim aliment may be awarded in the course of proceedings for aliment of children but the provisions for backdating do not apply to orders for interim aliment or to variations thereof.[623] Agreements to exclude future liability for aliment or restrict rights of action in that respect are of no effect unless in all the circumstances they were fair and reasonable when entered into.[624] A general discharge by a woman of her right to claim aliment from the father of her child does not discharge either her specific right to claim aliment

---

[610] 1991 Act s.2(4A)–(4C), inserted by the Children (Scotland) Act 1995 Sch.4 para.53.

[611] Within the meaning of s.11(2)(c) of the Children (Scotland) Act 1995. See para.44.45, below.

[612] 1985 Act s.2(4). See Ch.44 for provisions relative to capacity generally.

[613] 1985 Act s.2(5).

[614] 1985 Act s.3(1)(b). Such an order requires to make or secure the making of periodical payments for educational or training expenses: 1991 Act s.8(7)(b). Thus a school fees order of the type approved in *Macdonald v Macdonald*, 1995 S.L.T. 72 would require to be adapted to comply with that provision. See also *Lavelle v Lavelle*, 2001 G.W.D. 4–144.

[615] 1985 Act s.2(7).

[616] 1985 Act s.2(8).

[617] 1985 Act s.2(8).

[618] 1985 Act ss.5(1) and 7(2).

[619] *Walker v Walker*, 1995 S.L.T. 375.

[620] 1985 Act ss.5(1A) and 7(2A).

[621] 1985 Act ss.3(1)(c) and 5(2). Special cause is required to backdate an order to before the date of the action or application. See *Abrahams v Abrahams* [1989] S.C.L.R. 102. It is incompetent to back-date further than the original decree or last variation: *Walker v Walker*, 1991 S.L.T. 649.

[622] 1985 Act s.7(2ZA)–(2C), inserted by the Family Law (Scotland) Act 2006 s.20(2).

[623] 1985 Act s.6; *McColl v McColl*, 1993 S.C. 276.

[624] 1985 Act s.7(1).

for the child, or the child's own right to pursue such a claim.[625] The court is also empowered to pronounce a decree for aliment for children to give effect to the terms of a written agreement, if the decree is in all material respects in the same terms as the agreement.[626] It is not competent to defend such an application on the basis that the amount in the agreement has become excessive or to counter-claim to that effect.[627] It is now clear that any agreement registered in the Books of Council and Session will be treated as a court order,[628] thus ousting the jurisdiction of the Child Support Agency, but only for a year, after which either parent may apply for a maintenance assessment.[629] Further, in actions where spousal aliment is sought prior to a child support assessment being made, the court may take into account the lack of support for the children in determining the level of aliment for the wife, at least on an interim basis.[630]

The statutory formulation of the circumstances in which an obligation of aliment is owed does not affect the common-law rules

> "by which a person who is owed an obligation of aliment may claim aliment from the executor of a deceased person or from any person enriched by the succession to the estate of a deceased person".[631]

Such claims are open where the deceased person owed an obligation of aliment at common law or under statutory modifications of the common law prior to the 1985 Act. As the liability is of a representative character it is thought, however, that it can only arise if the deceased also had an obligation of aliment under the present law. It is not clear whether the liability of persons who before the 1985 Act would have had no obligation of aliment (certain cases of acceptance of a child as a child of the obligant's family) transmits against the obligant's executors and persons enriched by succession to his estate. It appears that the provisions of the Act on determining the amount of aliment and on the absence of any order of liability where there are two or more obligants apply to representational as they do to other claims.[632] A parent's obligation will be transmitted with his estate, and if one child takes the estate he does so with the corresponding liability to aliment his brothers and sisters out of that estate. There will be no such liability, however, if in the division of the estate among the children, equality or substantial equality has been observed.[633] It is also not appropriate to grant aliment where a child's claim for legal rights against the estate of the deceased parent is sufficient to satisfy his alimentary needs.[634] The resources of the surviving parent may also be taken into account.[635]

---

[625] *H v H*, 2004 Fam. L.R. 30.

[626] 1991 Act s.8(5); the Child Support (Written Agreements) (Scotland) Order 1997 (SI 1997/2943).

[627] *Otto v Otto*, 2002 Fam. L.R. 95.

[628] Child Maintenance and Other Payments Act 2008 s.35. This has resolved the tension between the finding to that effect in the *Child Support Agency Commissioner's Case CSCS/5/97* [1999] Fam. L.R. 39 which had been doubted in *Woodhouse v Wright Johnston and Mackenzie*, 2004 S.L.T. 911.

[629] Child Support, Pensions and Social Security Act 2000 s.2.

[630] *Stokes v Stokes* [1999] S.C.L.R. 327.

[631] 1985 Act s.1(4).

[632] 1985 Act s.4.

[633] *Mackintosh v Taylor* (1868) 7 M. 67; *Beaton v Beaton's Trs*, 1935 S.C. 187; *Hutchison v Hutchison's Trs*, 1951 S.C. 108.

[634] *Russell v Wood's Trs*, 1987 S.L.T. 503.

[635] *Russell v Wood's Trs*, 1987 S.L.T. 503.

If a child has separate estate and is alimented by a parent, the latter is entitled to be reimbursed out of the income of that estate.[636] Indeed, in a proper case a parent, although of ample means, may be entitled to be recompensed for the maintenance and education of children out of the capital belonging to those children.[637]

Aliment: Child Support Act 1991—This Act has not altered the substantive law **44.42** regarding the persons on whom obligations of aliment lie. Rather, it has provided a new mechanism for the assessment and enforcement of the contribution of an absent or non-resident parent[638]or parents towards the maintenance of a child. The Act came into force on April 5, 1993 and was subsequently amended by the Child Support Act 1995, the Child Support, Pensions and Social Security Act 2000 and now the Child Maintenance and Other Payments Act 2008.[639] Where there is in force either a maintenance agreement entered into prior to April 5, 1993 or a maintenance order made after March 3, 2003 that has been in force for less than a year, or where social security benefit is being paid to a parent with care of a child or children, no application for child support maintenance may be made with respect to that child or any of those children by either parent.[640] The court's jurisdiction to vary existing orders and agreements is retained in those circumstances.[641] Otherwise, orders made under the Family Law (Scotland) Act 1985 cease to have effect, and maintenance agreements become unenforceable, when a maintenance assessment is made under the Act.[642] What follows is a summary of the principal provisions of the Act; for many details of the scheme it is necessary to consult Regulations, which are referred to in outline where relevant.

The system has been administered by the Child Support Agency, run by child support officers who are civil servants, based in three main administrative areas across Great Britain. Since the creation of the Child Maintenance and Enforcement Commission many of the functions of the Child Support Agency have been transferred to the Commission, a body that replaces the Child Support Agency.[643] Where the person with care of a child makes a claim for certain social security benefits, that person may be required by the Secretary of State for Social Security to authorise the taking of action in respect of a non-resident parent,[644]

---

[636] *Ker's Trs v Ker*, 1927 S.C. 52; *Duke of Sutherland, Petitioner* (1901) 3 F. 761; *Hutcheson v Hoggan's Trs* (1904) 6 F. 594.

[637] *Polland v Sturrock's Exrs*, 1952 S.C. 535.

[638] The term "absent parent" was replaced by "non resident parent" by amendment to the 1991 Act by the Child Support, Pensions and Social Security Act 2000 s.26, Sch.3 para.11.

[639] The original legislation and the formula for assessing child maintenance there set out was first amended by the Child Support (Miscellaneous Amendments and Transitional Provisions) Regulations 1994 (SI 1994/227), then by the Child Support (Miscellaneous Amendments) Regulations 1995 (SI 1995/123), prior to the provision for departures from the formula introduced by the 1995 Act. The formula was altered again by the Child Support, Pensions and Social Security Act 2000 Sch.1 Pt I para.2 and regulations made thereunder, in particular the Child Support (Maintenance Calculations and Special Cases) Regulations 2000 (SI 2001/155). The Child Maintenance and Other Payments Act 2008 (c.6) will be implemented in stages.

[640] 1991 Act ss.4(10) and 7(10), inserted by the Child Support Act 1995 s.18(1) and (2) and subsequently amended by the Child Support Pensions and Social Security Act 2000 Sch.3 para.11(4).

[641] 1991 Act s.8(3A), inserted by the Child Support Act 1995 s.18(3).

[642] 1991 Act s.10(1) and (2); SI 1992/2645, as amended by SI 1993/913 and SI 1995/123.

[643] Child Maintenance and Other Payments Act 2008 s.13 provides that all but six limited matters will be transferred to the Commission. The date for full implementation is not known at the time of writing, but see SI 2012/2523 for a list of the provisions now in force.

[644] 1991 Act s.6.

with sanctions for non-compliance with this request in the form of a reduction of benefit.[645] Otherwise, utilisation of the system is on the application of the parties involved,[646] but where child support officers would have jurisdiction under the Act, the courts can make, vary or revive maintenance orders only in specified limited situations.[647] Child support officers have jurisdiction to make a maintenance calculation only if both the person against whom the assessment is made and the child are habitually resident in the United Kingdom, although those habitually resident abroad may be subject to an assessment by the Agency if they are in the civil and diplomatic services or armed forces, or employed by a UK company with payment arrangements being made from this country.[648] No agreement to oust the jurisdiction of child support officers is valid.[649]

For the purposes of the Act, each parent of a qualifying child is responsible for the maintenance of the child, the responsibility being met by payment of the amounts assessed in terms of the Act.[650] A child is defined as a person under 16, or under 19 and in full-time education,[651] or a person under 18 who fulfils certain criteria.[652] Persons who are or have been married do not fall within the definition.[653] A qualifying child is a child having a non-resident parent or parents.[654] A non-resident parent is a parent not living in the same household as the child, where the child is living with a person with care.[655] A person with care is a person with whom the child has his home, who provides day-to-day care of the child and who does not fall within certain prescribed categories.[656] There may be more than one person with care.[657] A person with care does not require to be an individual, thus a parent can be found liable to contribute to the maintenance of a child in the care of a voluntary agency, although no assessment can be levied against an agency.[658] The procedure may be initiated by an application for a maintenance calculation made to the Secretary of State by the person with care, or by the non-resident parent.[659] In provisions restricted to Scotland, an application may also be made by the child himself if he is over 12.[660]

Applications and related functions under the Act are the responsibility of the Secretary of State, who delegates various activities to the child support officers.[661] The person applying can subsequently request that action cease.[662] Where persons

---

[645] 1991 Act s.46 and the Child Support (Maintenance Assessment Procedure) Regulations 1992 (SI 1992/1813) regs 35–49.

[646] Those who are not in receipt of state benefits and who choose to apply are charged an annual fee. See Child Support Fees Regulations 1992 (SI 1992/3094) reg.4.

[647] 1991 Act s.8 and see para.44.41, above.

[648] 1991 Act s.44, as amended by the Child Support, Pensions and Social Security Act 2000 s.22. See also *A v Secretary of State for Work and Pensions*, 2004 S.C.L.R. 840.

[649] 1991 Act s.9(4).

[650] 1991 Act s.1.

[651] Not advanced education. Advanced and full-time education are defined in Sch.1 to SI 1992/1813.

[652] 1991 Act s.55(1). The criteria are set out in Sch.1 to SI 1992/1813.

[653] 1991 Act s.55(2).

[654] 1991 Act s.3(1).

[655] 1991 Act s.3(2).

[656] 1991 Act s.3(3). The categories are prescribed in SI 1992/1813, reg.51, and cover local authorities and their carers.

[657] 1991 Act s.3(5).

[658] 1991 Act s.44(2).

[659] 1991 Act s.4(1).

[660] 1991 Act s.7.

[661] The Social Security Act 1998 s.1 transferred the functions of child support officers previously appointed under s.13 of the 1991 Act to the Secretary of State.

[662] 1991 Act ss.4(5) and 7(6).

claiming benefit are concerned, the discretion of the Secretary of State to require the parent of a qualifying child to authorise him to proceed is fettered only by a provision that a requirement should not be made if the Secretary of State has reasonable grounds to think that either the requirement or the giving of authorisation would risk the person with care or a child living with her suffering harm or undue distress.[663] There is also a general requirement in the Act that in taking any decision under the Act, the Secretary of State officer shall have regard to the welfare of any child likely to be affected.[664] Once the procedure has been initiated, an interim assessment can be made.[665] There are provisions requiring the disclosure of information needed to trace the non-resident parent, to assess amounts and to recover maintenance.[666]

The formulae by which the calculations are made are contained in Sch.1 to the Act and associated regulations.[667] The amount computed under the original formula included a basic element, known as the maintenance requirement, and could include an additional element. It reflected both the amount that the maintenance of the child was deemed to require and the relative wealth of the parents. Provision was made for a protected income level, although this was subject to the power of the Secretary of State to prescribe a minimum amount which was to be paid in respect of a child.[668] A fixed upper limit was introduced to restrict the amount which a parent was liable to contribute by way of additional element.[669] Regulations also enumerated "special cases", to which the usual method of maintenance assessment did not apply.[670] An application for a departure from the formula could be made by either party, in the form of a departure direction relative to an existing maintenance assessment, introduced by the Child Support Act 1995.[671] Determination of the application is made either by the Secretary of State officer or by a child support appeal tribunal on a referral.[672] There is discretion as to whether to grant a departure direction in a suitable case, having regard to specified general principles and factors.[673] The current formula is based primarily on the non-resident parent's net income, with no consideration of his or her housing costs and without regard to the income of the parent with care. The basic rate applies in all cases where the non-resident parent has a net weekly income of £800 or less. Where he or she has no relevant other children, the rate is 12 per cent of net income for one qualifying child, 16 per cent of net income for two qualifying

---

[663] 1991 Act s.6(2).

[664] 1991 Act s.2, as amended by the Social Security Act 1998. Note that there is no provision requiring that the welfare of the child be seen as paramount.

[665] 1991 Act s.12 and SI 1992/1813.

[666] 1991 Act ss.4(4), 6(9), 7(5) and 14 and Child Support (Information, Evidence and Disclosure) Regulations 1992 (SI 1992/1812).

[667] Child Support (Maintenance Assessments and Special Cases) Regulations 1992 (SI 1992/1815), as amended by SIs 1993/913 and 925, 1994/227 and 1995/1045 for applications made prior to March 3, 2003. For applications made after March 3, 2003, the Child Support (Maintenance Calculation Procedures) Regulations 2001 (SI 2001/157) applies. The new rates are fixed by Sch.4 of the 2008 Act which amends Sch.1 of the 1991 Act.

[668] The minimum maintenance assessment figure is prescribed by SI 1992/1815 reg.13 (amended by SI 1996/481).

[669] 1991 Act Sch.1 para.4(3) and SI 1992/1815 regs 6(2)(a), 11(6) (added by SI 1995/1045 reg.46(6)) and 11(6A) (added by SI 1996/1945 reg.20(3)).

[670] 1991 Act s.42. The list of specified special cases can be found in SI 1992/1815 regs 19–27.

[671] Provision for departure directions is contained in the 1991 Act s.28A–I, added by the Child Support Act 1995, which continues to apply to assessments made under the old formula.

[672] 1991 Act s.28D (added by the Child Support Act 1995 s.4).

[673] ss.28E and 28F (added by the Child Support Act 1995 ss.5 and 6(1) respectively). The cases suitable for a departure direction application are listed in the 1991 Act Sch.4B (added by the Child Support Act 1995 s.6(2), Sch.2).

children and 19 per cent of net income for three or more such children.[674] For those on higher incomes, a lower rate on the part that exceeds £800 per week is applicable.[675] There is provision for variations from the calculation in certain circumstances, replacing the old departures scheme.[676]

The Act contains provisions dealing with the termination of maintenance assessments,[677] and with the means of obtaining a review of a maintenance assessment. Initially, the legislation provided for the periodic review of maintenance assessments.[678] 2 This has been substituted by a general discretion vested in the Secretary of State to revise any decision in relation to maintenance assessments, interim maintenance assessments or changes in circumstances.[679] The original system for a review of a maintenance assessment[680] has also been replaced. Any decision on a maintenance assessment or interim maintenance assessment or calculation and decisions of a child support appeal tribunal or Child Support Commissioner can now be superseded by a decision of the Secretary of State.[681] A supersession decision may take effect from the date of the original decision, or from an alternative date where prescribed.[682] Appeals from the decisions of child support officers acting for the Secretary of State lie to the Child Support Appeal Tribunal,[683] from there, on a point of law and with leave, to a Child Support Commissioner,[684] and from the Commissioner, again on a point of law and with leave, to the court.[685] Remarkably, the appropriate court for Scottish appeals is the English Court of Appeal, unless the Child Support Commissioner directs that in the circumstances of the case, and taking into account the convenience of the parties to the appeal, the appropriate court is the Court of Session.[686]

Where a dispute arises concerning parentage, no maintenance calculation can be made unless the case falls within one of the six cases where parentage is assumed, as set out in s.26.[687] If a child support officer is not satisfied that the dispute falls within one of the six cases, the Secretary of State may bring an action for declarator of parentage,[688] and any action by the alleged parent seeking declarator of non-parentage may also be defended.[689]

---

[674] 1991 Act Sch.1 (as amended).

[675] 1991 Act Sch.1 (as amended).

[676] See the 1991 Act ss.28A–28F.

[677] Child Support, Pensions and Social Security Act 2000 Sch.1 Pt II para.16.

[678] 1991 Act s.16(1) and SI 1992/1813 reg.17(1), amended by SI 1995/1045 reg.34.

[679] 1991 Act s.16, as substituted by the Social Security Act 1998 s.40 and subsequently amended by the Child Support, Pensions and Social Security Act 2000 s.8.

[680] 1991 Act s.17.

[681] 1991 Act s.17(1), as substituted by the Social Security Act 1998 s.41, and subsequently amended by the 2000 Act s.9(2).

[682] 1991 Act s.17(4) and (5), as substituted by the Social Security Act 1998 s.41.

[683] 1991 Act s.20, as substituted by the Social Security Act 1998 s.42. See also the Social Security and Child Support (Decisions and Appeals) Regulations 1999 (SI 1999/991). There is one exception where the appeal is on a question of parentage, it is made to a court: SI 1993/961.

[684] 1991 Act s.24(1) and (6). See also the Child Support Commissioners (Procedure) Regulations 1992 (SI 1992/2640).

[685] 1991 Act s.25(1) and (2).

[686] 1991 Act s.25(4).

[687] These include cases where the alleged parent has adopted the child, is a parent by virtue of a parental order in terms of s.30 of the Human Fertilisation and Embryology Act 1990, is the subject of a declarator of paternity or has been found in any other court proceedings to be the father without subsequent adoption of the child by another, or has registered the child's birth together with the mother.

[688] 1991 Act s.28(1). The action is brought under s.7 of the Law Reform (Parent and Child) (Scotland) Act 1986.

[689] 1991 Act s.28(2).

The Act also confers powers to arrange collection of maintenance.[690] The amounts assessed in terms of the Act may be recovered by deduction from earnings[691] or from benefit.[692] Where income or assets are shown to have been diverted during assessment, penalties including criminal fines[693]or a period of imprisonment may now be imposed.[694] If an earnings order is inappropriate, the Secretary of State or his official[695] 9 can apply to the sheriff for a liability order[696]which enables diligence to be carried out[697] and, ultimately, disqualification from driving or civil imprisonment sought.[698] When arrears are recovered, they may be retained against benefit paid.[699] A sanction of interest charges has been abandoned in favour of discretionary financial penalties of up to 25 per cent of the amount owed.[700]

Parental responsibilities and parental rights—Prior to the enactment of the **44.43** Children (Scotland) Act 1995, the focus of the law in this area was on parental rights and authority. At common law parental authority over a legitimate child belonged exclusively to the father. He held the general right to govern the person of a child and to order his or her upbringing. Accordingly, he was entitled to custody of his children, subject to control by the Inner House of the Court of Session in the exercise of the *nobile officium*.[701] The Court did not, however, interfere with the father's right unless it could be shown that the child's health or morals would be endangered by his remaining in the father's custody.[702] In the case of an illegitimate child it was the mother who was, in general, entitled to custody. In 1973 legislation first provided that the rights and authority of married parents over their children should be equal and exercisable by either without the other.[703] That provision was replaced by the Law Reform (Parent and Child) (Scotland) Act 1986, which regulated parental rights, whether or not the parents were married, up until November 1, 1996, and continued to govern applications for parental rights commenced prior to that date.[704] Parental rights included guardianship, custody, access and any other right or authority relating to the welfare or upbringing of a child conferred on a parent by law.[705] The 1986

---

[690] 1991 Act s.29, and the Child Support (Collection and Enforcement) Regulations 1992 (SI 1992/1989), as amended by SI 1993/913 and SI 1994/227.

[691] 1991 Act ss.31 and 32, and SI 1992/1989 regs 8–25, as so amended.

[692] 1991 Act s.43.

[693] 1991 Act s.14(A) (inserted by the Child Support, Pensions and Social Security Act 2000 s.13).

[694] 1991 Act s.40(A), inserted by the Child Support, Pensions and Social Security Act 2000 s.17. This replaced the previous system of departure directions in such circumstances.

[695] *Secretary of State for Social Security v Love*, 1996 S.C.L.R. 535.

[696] 1991 Act s.33. Any appeal to the child support tribunal can be ignored in considering a liability order application: *Secretary of State of State for Social Security v Nicol (No.2)*, 1996 S.C.L.R. 974.

[697] 1991 Act s.38.

[698] 1991 Act s.39A, inserted by the Child Support, Pensions and Social Security Act 2000 s.16 with effect from April 2, 2001 (disqualification from driving) and s.40(A) and (B) inserted by the 2000 Act s.17.

[699] 1991 Act s.41(2).

[700] 1991 Act s.41A, added by the Child Support, Pensions and Social Security Act 2000 s.18.

[701] *Craig v Greig and McDonald* (1863) 1 M. 1172.

[702] *Lang v Lang* (1869) 7 M. 445; *Nicholson v Nicholson* (1869) 7 M. 1118.

[703] Guardianship Act 1973 s.10(1).

[704] Pt I of the Children (Scotland) Act 1995 came into force on November 1, 1996. Section 15(2) of the Act confirms that the legislation does not apply to proceedings raised prior to that date, but that applications in pre-1995 Act proceedings for variation or recall of existing custody, access or other parental rights orders are governed by the provisions of the 1995 Act. This provision has become moribund with the passage of time.

[705] Law Reform (Parent and Child) (Scotland) Act 1986 s.8.

Act provided that a child's mother had full parental rights whether or not she was married to the child's father.[706] A child's father had full parental rights only if he was married to the mother at the time of conception or subsequently.[707] Any person claiming an interest could apply to the court for an order relating to parental rights.[708] In any dispute relating to parental rights the child's welfare was to be the paramount consideration and no order was to be made unless the court was satisfied that to do so would be in the interests of the child.[709] All other factors, including the rights of a natural parent in a conflict with a carer unrelated to the child, required to yield to the welfare principle.[710] While the mother of a child of tender years continued to be perceived as better able to cater for the child's needs,[711] there was an onus on a father without parental rights to satisfy the court, in seeking parental rights, that the order would be in the interests of the child.[712] An order could be made giving custody to one party de jure on the understanding that de facto control would be exercised by another,[713] and awards of joint custody were competent, though rare.[714] Unlike an award of access,[715] a custody order could be made in favour of someone who could not in practice exercise the right for the time being.[716]

44.44 Parental responsibilities and parental rights under the Children (Scotland) Act 1995—The law relating to parental rights was completely reformulated by the 1995 Act. Parents are now entrusted with statutory responsibilities towards children, and parental rights are given only to enable them to discharge those parental responsibilities. The general statutory responsibilities imposed are (a) to safeguard and promote the child's health, development and welfare, (b) to provide direction and guidance in a manner appropriate to the stage of development of the child, (c) if the child is not living with the parent, to maintain personal relations and direct contact with the child on a regular basis, and (d) to act as the child's legal representative.[717] A parent's corresponding rights are (a) to have the child living with him or otherwise to regulate the child's residence, (b) to control, direct or guide, in a manner appropriate to the stage of development of the child, the child's upbringing, (c) if the child is not living with him, to maintain personal relations and direct contact with the child on a regular basis, and (d) to act as the child's legal representative.[718] These responsibilities and rights supersede any

---

[706] Law Reform (Parent and Child) (Scotland) Act 1986 s.2(1)(a).

[707] Law Reform (Parent and Child) (Scotland) Act 1986 s.2(1)(b). In the case of certain purported marriages, there was provision for him to be deemed to have been married for this purpose.

[708] Law Reform (Parent and Child) (Scotland) Act 1986 s.3(1), interpreted as including those other than parents in *F v P*, 1991 S.L.T. 357, but excluding a parent whose child had been freed for adoption or the subject of an adoption order in *D v Grampian RC*, 1995 S.L.T. 519.

[709] Law Reform (Parent and Child) (Scotland) Act 1986 s.3(2).

[710] *Osborne v Matthan (No.3)*, 1998 S.C. 682.

[711] *Brixey v Lynas (No.1)*, 1994 S.L.T. 847; sub nom. *B v L (No.1)*, 1997 S.C. (HL) 1.

[712] *Sanderson v McManus*, 1996 S.L.T. 750; 1997 S.C. (HL) 55.

[713] *Robertson v Robertson*, 1981 S.L.T. (Notes) 7.

[714] *McKenzie v Hendry*, 1984 S.L.T. 322; *McKechnie v McKechnie*, 1990 S.L.T. (Sh. Ct) 75.

[715] An order for access was categorised as an infringement of custody and had to be physically operable at the instant of time, unlike the legal right of custody itself, see *Dewar v Strathclyde RC*, 1985 S.L.T. 114.

[716] *Aitken v Aitken*, 1978 S.L.T. 183. In *F v P*, 1991 S.L.T. 357, it was said that this would seldom be an appropriate course.

[717] Children (Scotland) Act 1995 (the "1995 Act") s.1(1)(a)–(d).

[718] 1995 Act s.2(1)(a)–(d).

analogous rights and duties imposed on parents at common law.[719] Parental responsibilities and rights are extinguished when the child attains the age of 16 years, with the exception of the responsibility to give guidance, which subsists until he or she is 18.[720] While a mother has statutory parental responsibilities and parental rights in relation to her child whether or not she is or has been married to his father,[721] the father does not automatically have such responsibilities and rights unless married to the mother at the time of the child's conception or subsequently.[722] This discrimination on the ground of a parent's sex was regarded as justifiable notwithstanding the incorporation of arts 8 and 14 of the European Convention of Human Rights into domestic law.[723] However, an unmarried father has been able, from May 4, 2006, to acquire parental rights and responsibilities by registering the child's birth together with the mother.[724] If not so registered, he can acquire parental rights only by agreement or court order.[725]

To be effective, an agreement providing that, from the appropriate date, a father shall have the parental rights and responsibilities he would have if married to the mother, requires to be in prescribed form and registered in the Books of Council and Session.[726] Once registered, such an agreement can only be revoked by the court.[727] There is a specific prohibition on removal from or retention outwith the United Kingdom of a child habitually resident in Scotland without the consent of a person who has and is exercising a right of residence or contact to that child. Where both parents are exercising such parental rights, the consent of both of them is required before the child can be removed from or retained outside Scotland.[728] A measure of responsibility is imposed on those without parental responsibilities who are entrusted with the care and control of a child, with the ability to consent to surgical, medical or dental treatment where the child cannot do so and it is not known that the parent would refuse such consent.[729] In reaching any major decision, those entrusted with the care and control of children and those exercising parental responsibilities and rights are now required by statute to have regard so far as practicable to the views (if he wishes to express them) of the child concerned.[730] Account must be taken of the age and maturity of the particular child, but there is a rebuttable presumption that a child of 12 years of age or more is of sufficient age and maturity to form such views. This constitutes a significant departure from the previous emphasis on parental authority and represents an attempt to comply with art.12 of the UN Convention on the Rights of the Child. The statute also requires that children are given the opportunity of having their views considered in court proceedings affecting them,[731] which is considered in more detail below. Transactions entered into by a child's legal representative with

---

[719] 1995 Act ss.1(4) and 2(5).

[720] 1995 Act ss.1(2) and 2(7).

[721] 1995 Act s.3(1)(a), which is effectively a re-enactment of s.2(1)(a) of the Law Reform (Parent and Child) (Scotland) Act 1986.

[722] 1995 Act s.3(1)(b), which restates the earlier provision contained in s.2(1)(b) of the 1986 Act.

[723] *McMichael v UK* (1995) 20 E.H.R.R. 205; *B v UK* [2000] F.L.R. 1.

[724] 1995 Act s.3(1)(b)(ii), inserted by the Family Law (Scotland) Act 2006 s.23(2).

[725] 1995 Act ss.4 and 11.

[726] The appropriate date is the date of registration of the agreement: s.4(3). The form of agreement is prescribed by the Parental Rights Agreements (Scotland) Regulations 1996 (SI 1996/2549).

[727] 1995 Act ss.4(4) and 11(11).

[728] 1995 Act s.2(3) and (6). This provision is an avoidance measure against international child abduction, for which see para.44.48, below.

[729] 1995 Act s.5.

[730] 1995 Act s.6(1).

[731] 1995 Act ss.11(7) and 16(2).

a third party in good faith remain valid even if that representative has failed to consult, or have regard to the views of, the child.[732] The 1995 Act makes specific provision for the appointment by a parent of a guardian or guardians for the child in the event of the parent's death. The appointment must be in writing and signed by a parent entitled to act as the child's legal representative.[733] A guardian who accepts such an appointment has full parental rights and responsibilities in respect of the child concerned, and may appoint a person to take his place as guardian in the event of his own death.[734] The appointment of a guardian under the Act is presumed to revoke an earlier such appointment, unless the contrary is clearly intended.[735] Any appointment made can be revoked in writing or by the destruction of the document making the appointment. Once effective, the appointment of a guardian can be terminated only on the child attaining the age of 18 years, on the death of the child or guardian, or by court order.[736] Detailed provisions are also made for the administration of property owned by, or owed to, a child by someone other than his parent or guardian.[737] Those holding the property may apply to the Accountant of Court for directions as to its administration, but there is no requirement to do so unless the value of the property exceeds £20,000 and is held by an executor or trustee.[738] The Accountant of Court may apply to the court for the appointment of a judicial factor in addition to, or in place of, making specific directions and conditions relative to the administration of the property.[739] Where a child's legal representative is administering the property of the child, he is entitled to do anything which the child, if of full age and capacity, could do with it, subject to a general statutory obligation to act as a reasonable and prudent person would act on his own behalf.[740] The legal representative has no liability to account for funds used in the proper discharge of the responsibility to safeguard and promote the child's health, development and welfare.[741] Where an award of damages is made in favour of a child by the court, separate rules apply, involving a decision as to whether the funds will be administered by a judicial factor, the sheriff clerk or Accountant of Court, or the parent or guardian of the child.[742]

44.45 Court orders relating to parental responsibilities and parental rights— Section 11 of the Children (Scotland) Act 1995 provides that in any proceedings in either the Court of Session or the sheriff court, orders for parental responsibilities and parental rights, guardianship or the administration of a child's property ("s.11 orders"), may be made, in "relevant circumstances".[743] However, as jurisdiction in actions relating to parental rights and responsibilities is now governed principally by Council Regulation EC 2201/2003 ("Brussels II bis),[744]

---

[732] 1995 Act s.6(2).

[733] 1995 Act s.7(1).

[734] 1995 Act s.7(2) and (5).

[735] 1995 Act s.8(1)

[736] 1995 Act s.8(2)–(5).

[737] 1995 Act s.9(1).

[738] 1995 Act s.9(2) and (3). The provisions do not apply to a defender in a reparation action who is liable to pay damages to a child: *I v Argyll & Clyde Health Board*, 2003 S.L.T. 231.

[739] 1995 Act s.9(5)–(6).

[740] 1995 Act s.10(1).

[741] 1995 Act s.10(2).

[742] 1995 Act s.13.

[743] 1995 Act s.11(1).

[744] Regulation EC 2201/2003 of the Council of 27 November 2003 concerning jurisdiction and the recognition and enforcement of judgments in matrimonial matters and the matters of parental responsibility, OJ L 338 23.12.2003, pp.1–29.

the court cannot make any order under s.11 if this would conflict with the jurisdictional provisions of the Regulation.[745] Prior to the coming into force of the relevant provisions of the Adoption and Children (Scotland) Act 2007 there were three categories of applicants who could create the relevant circumstances.[746] Now there are four, namely: (i) those not having, and never having had, parental rights and responsibilities in relation to the child; (ii) those who have parental rights and responsibilities in relation to the child; (iii) those whose parental responsibilities and parental rights in relation to the child were extinguished on the making of an adoption order but who are now applying for a contact order; and (iv) those applying for an order (other than a contact order) who have had, but no longer have, parental responsibilities and rights, unless those rights were extinguished or transferred as a result of a specified reason.[747] There were four such reasons specified prior to September 28, 2009 which excluded future applications for parental responsibilities and rights by those losing parental responsibilities or rights as a result of (a) the making of an adoption order,[748] (b) the making of an order declaring the child free for adoption,[749] (c) the making of a parental order under the Human Fertilisation and Embryology Act 1990 or the Human Fertilisation and Embryology Act 2008,[750] or (d) the making of a parental responsibilities order.[751] The second and fourth reasons were deleted following the replacement of freeing for adoption orders and parental responsibilities orders by the new permanence orders regime, and a provision enacted to preclude those whose parental responsibilities and rights have vested in a local authority from applying.[752] Even without a formal application by any of those entitled to do so, the court can make an order *ex proprio motu*, or on request.[753] The existence of a supervision requirement in relation to a child does not prevent the making of a s.11 order, but an order that would be in direct conflict with such a requirement would be inappropriate and could therefore be regarded as incompetent.[754] Where relevant circumstances exist, the court is empowered to make such s.11 orders as it thinks fit, but various types of orders are specified without prejudice to that generality. These are: (a) an order depriving a person of some or all of his parental responsibilities or parental rights in relation to a child; (b) an order imposing such responsibilities or giving such rights to someone over 16 years of age or to a person under that age who is a parent[755]; (c) a Residence Order, which regulates the arrangements as to the person with whom a child is to live, or the persons with whom he is to live alternatively or periodically; (d) a Contact Order, which regulates the arrangements for maintaining personal relations and direct contact

---

[745] 1995 Act s.14(5), inserted by the European Communities (Matrimonial and Parental Responsibility Jurisdiction and Judgments) (Scotland) Regulations 2005 (SSI 2005/42) para.5(2).

[746] s.107 of the Adoption and Children (Scotland) Act 2007 has, with effect from September 28, 2009, amended s.11 of the Children (Scotland) Act 1995 to allow those whose parental responsibilities and parental rights have been extinguished by way of an adoption order to apply, with leave of the court for a post adoption contact order. The three categories prior to that date did not include such persons, consistent with the position ultimately reached prior to the 1995 Act in *D v Grampian RC*, 1995 S.C. (HL) 1.

[747] 1995 Act s.11(3)(a)(i)–(ii), (aa) and (ab).

[748] 1995 Act s.11(4)(a). See paras 44.49–44.50, below.

[749] 1995 Act s.11(4)(b), repealed with effect from September 28, 2009. See para.44.51, below.

[750] 1995 Act s.11(4)(c); 2008 Act s.54.

[751] 1995 Act s.11(4)(d), repealed with effect from September 28, 2009.

[752] 1995 Act s.11A. See also para.44.51, below.

[753] 1995 Act s.11(3)(b). It can only do so in the context of competent proceedings, however, see *McEwen v McEwen* [2000] Fam. L.R. 116.

[754] 1995 Act s.3(4); *P v P*, 2000 S.L.T. 781.

[755] This can be sought on its own, without any specific orders: *T v A*, 2001 G.W.D. 15–567.

between a child and a person with whom he is not, or will not be, living; (e) a Specific Issue Order, which regulates any specific question which has arisen, or may arise in connection with parental responsibilities, parental rights, guardianship or the administration of a child's property; (f) an interdict prohibiting the taking of any step specified therein in the fulfilment of parental responsibilities or the exercise of parental rights relating to a child or in the administration of a child's property; (g) an order appointing a judicial factor to manage a child's property or remitting that matter to the Accountant of Court; and (h) an order appointing or removing a person as guardian of the child.[756] All of these orders can be made ad interim, varied and discharged by the court.[757] Where two parents have parental responsibilities and parental rights, the granting of any of the specified orders will inhibit the exercise of those responsibilities and rights only to the extent provided for in the order.[758] All other rights may continue to be exercised by either parent without the consent of the other.[759] Thus, a Residence Order providing that a child will live with one parent does not affect the right of the other parent with such responsibilities and rights to take decisions relative to health education and welfare of the child, either alone, or together with the parent with whom the child lives, unless parental responsibilities and rights have been removed from him by court order. A blanket order removing all parental rights and responsibilities from a parent is unusual and should not be made without careful consideration.[760] A Residence Order should not be granted unless it is intended that the child will have a home or homes with the person or persons stated in the order; provision for him to stay regularly somewhere other than his home can where necessary be made by a Contact Order.[761] The parental right to and responsibility to maintain contact with a child exists independently of any order of court, the purpose of such an order being only to regulate the arrangements for exercising that right in the event of a dispute.[762] The parent with whom the child lives has a responsibility to encourage contact between the child and the other parent in terms of a Contact Order,[763] which may provide for direct, physical contact or indirect contact such as by telephone or letter.[764] Even where the court has decided that no ongoing direct contact between a child and a parent with parental responsibilities would, for the time being, be in the interests of a child, the obligation of the other parent to acknowledge the non-resident parent's responsibilities to the child continues.[765] Specific Issue Orders have been sought by parents wishing to remove children from the jurisdiction where they have been unable to obtain the consent of the

---

[756] 1995 Act s.11(2)(a)–(h).

[757] 1995 Act s.11(13).

[758] 1995 Act ss.3(4) and 11(11).

[759] 1995 Act s.2(2), with the specific exception in s.2(3) and (6) of removing from, or retaining outwith, the United Kingdom, a child who is habitually resident in Scotland without the consent of the other parent.

[760] In *T v T*, 2000 S.L.T. 1442 at 1454 (5 judges), the sheriff of first instance was criticised for making such a blanket order as he had failed to address a submission that he should specify each of the responsibilities and rights he intended to deprive the father of in a difficult case of sexual abuse allegations.

[761] *McBain v McIntyre*, 1997 S.C.L.R. 181. It is clear from the terms of s.11(2)(c), however, that a child may have two homes for the purpose of a Residence Order.

[762] *P v P*, 2000 S.L.T. 781.

[763] The parent with care is to that extent in the position of one who had custody in terms of previous legislation; see *Blance v Blance*, 1978 S.L.T. 74; *Perendes v Sim*, 1998 S.L.T. 1382.

[764] *A v M* [1999] Fam. L.R. 42.

[765] *NJDB v JEG and Andrew* [2010] CSIH 83, upheld in [2012] UKSC 21.

other parent,[766] but can be used to regulate any specific parental rights issue other than those covered by other orders. Disputes relative to changing a child's surname,[767] sanctioning medical treatment in the face of opposition from the other parent and choice of school[768] are all matters that might involve an application for a Specific Issue Order. All parental rights and responsibilities orders can be made ad interim.[769] However, where a mother sought a Specific Issue Order ad interim to permit her daughter to take up a scholarship that would involve moving from a day school in Scotland to a boarding school in England, the interim order in her favour was successfully appealed by the father on the basis that it would be unfair to disturb the status quo potentially irreparably pending proof.[770] If the proceedings before the court are matrimonial proceedings where there is a child of the family under the age of 16, the court is required to consider, in the light of any information before it, whether to make a s.11 order or to refer the matter to the Principal Reporter specifying the basis upon which compulsory measures of supervision may be required. In exceptional circumstances, where it is likely that one of those orders will be made, decree may be postponed while the court gives the matter further consideration.[771]

The welfare principle and the views of the child—In considering whether or **44.46** not to make a s.11 order, the court is required to have regard to two distinct principles. First, it "shall regard the welfare of the child concerned as its paramount consideration".[772] This principle, enshrined in similar form in previous legislation, has been interpreted as requiring the court to identify what the welfare of the child demands, and then to follow that course.[773] As part of that exercise the court is enjoined not to make any s.11 order unless it considers that it would be better for the child that the order be made than that none should be made at all.[774] This initial presumption against making an order is effectively a statutory formulation of the previous law, under which unnecessary orders were already refused.[775] The principle that the welfare of the child is paramount applies to all applications for orders relating to children. Potentially controversial guidance from the English Court of Appeal to the effect that as a rule the court should place emphasis on the reasonable proposals of a parent with residence requesting to relocate with the

---

[766] *Fourman v Fourman* [1998] Fam. L.R. 98; *M v M* [2000] Fam. L.R. 84; *Shields v Shields*, 2002 S.C. 246. See also *H v H*, 2010 S.L.T. 395, where a residence order was granted but on the basis that the father with the order would return to Australia to live with the child.

[767] *Dawson v Wearmouth* [1999] 2 A.C. 308; *M v C*, 2002 S.L.T. (Sh. Ct) 82.

[768] 1995 Act s.11(2)(e) gives a statutory basis for applications about choice of school but these were previously competent, see *Clayton v Clayton*, 1995 G.W.D. 18–1000.

[769] 1995 Act s.11(13).

[770] *G v G*, 2002 Fam. L.R. 120.

[771] 1995 Act s.12. This provision replaces ss.8 and 10 of the Matrimonial Proceedings (Children) Act 1958, which specifically obliged the court to consider the arrangements for the care and upbringing of the children. The necessity which flowed from the 1958 Act for the party seeking decree to produce such information in every case does not exist under the 1995 Act provision.

[772] 1995 Act s.11(7)(a).

[773] Law Reform (Parent and Child) (Scotland) Act 1986 s.3(2), as interpreted in *Osborne v Matthan (No.3)*, 1998 S.C. 682.

[774] 1995 Act s.11(7)(a).

[775] s.3(2) directed the court not to make any order unless it was satisfied that to do so would be in the interests of the child. See, e.g. *Clayton v Clayton*, 1995 G.W.D. 18–1000; *Ross v Ross*, 1997 S.L.T. (Sh. Ct) 51.

child[776] forms no part of the law of Scotland.[777] From May 4, 2006, the Court is required, as part of its duties in applying the welfare principle, to have regard to (a) the need to protect the child from any abuse or the risk of any abuse which affects or might affect him, (b) the effect such abuse or the risk of it may have on the child, (c) the ability of a person who has carried out or might carry out such abuse to care or meet the needs of the child, and (d) the effect any abuse or risk of it might have on the carrying out of child welfare responsibilities by someone who has, or would have those responsibilities.[778]Abuse includes violence, harassment, threatening conduct and any conduct giving rise to physical or mental injury, fear, alarm or distress, abuse of a person other than the child and domestic abuse.[779] Further, the court is now obliged to consider whether it would be appropriate to make a parental rights order where a person who does not have parental responsibilities and rights would in consequence of the order have to co operate with a person who has such responsibilities and rights.[780] Secondly, the Act innovates the principle that the court must (i) give a child of sufficient age and maturity the opportunity to express views on the issue under consideration, if he wishes to do so, and (ii) have regard to such views as he may express.[781] While the welfare principle does not of itself import any strict legal onus on the party seeking the parental rights order,[782] it has been emphasised that:

"... [A] party who seeks to alter the status quo must have some liability to furnish the court with material potentially capable of justifying the making of a relevant order."[783]

The court's task is "to consider all the relevant material and decide what would be conducive to the child's welfare".[784] There is no exhaustive list of factors relevant to welfare, which is concerned with physical, emotional, spiritual and material needs. The factors previously of significance in custody and access disputes continue to be of interest in issues relating to residence and contact.[785] These include, inter alia, the maintenance of the status quo in a child's life,[786] the desirability of contact with both parents[787]and with other family members,[788] the need to understand one's racial or ethnic origin,[789] and respect for religious

---

[776] *Payne v Payne* [2001] Fam. 473.

[777] *SM v CM* [2011] CSIH 65.

[778] 1995 Act s.11(7A) and (7B), as inserted by the Family Law (Scotland) Act 2006 s.24.

[779] 1995 Act s.11(7C), also inserted by the 2006 Act s.24. Section 11(7C) also gives "conduct" is a similarly wide definition.

[780] 1995 Act s.11(7D)–(7E), also inserted by the 2006 Act s.24. It may be difficult to reconcile these provisions with the requirement to treat the child's welfare as the paramount consideration.

[781] 1995 Act s.11(7)(b).

[782] *White v White*, 2001 S.C. 689. The onus was on the applicant under s.3(2) of the 1986 Act; *Sanderson v McManus*, 1997 S.C. (HL) 55.

[783] *MS v SS* [2012] CSIH 17, citing *Sanderson v McManus*, 1997 S.C. (HL) 55 in support. See also *SM v CM* [2011] CSIH 65 where that duty is articulated more in terms of an onus, albeit an evidential one.

[784] *White v White*, 2001 S.C. 689.

[785] For a full analysis of the various relevant factors, see A.B. Wilkinson and K.N. Norrie, *Parent and Child*, 2nd edn (Edinburgh: W. Green, 1999), Ch.10.

[786] *J v C* [1970] A.C. 668; *Whitecross v Whitecross*, 1977 S.L.T. 225; *Breingan v Jamieson*, 1993 S.L.T. 186; *Brixey v Lynas (No.1)*, 1994 S.L.T. 847; sub nom. *B v L (No.1)*, 1997 S.C. (HL) 1.

[787] *Sanderson v McManus*, 1997 S.C. (HL) 55.

[788] *MacInnes v Highland RC*, 1982 S.C. 69; *Early v Early*, 1989 S.L.T. 114; 1990 S.L.T. 221.

[789] *Perendes v Sim*, 1998 S.L.T. 1382 at 1384.

convictions.[790] The sexual orientation of an applicant seeking parental rights is relevant only if it directly affects the child's welfare.[791] The welfare principle has been held to be compliant with art.8 of the European Convention on Human Rights, by making provisions consistent with the respect for family life and by balancing the competing interests of family members.[792] It is assumed that a child will benefit from continuing contact with a natural parent.[793] In relation to the views of the child, there is no minimum age limit,[794] although there is a presumption that a child of 12 years of age or more is of sufficient age and maturity to express a view on the order under consideration.[795] Where a view is expressed, no order will be made without due weight being given to it.[796] A child who wishes to express a view may be legally represented, although there is no requirement to that effect.[797] A child wishing the court to have regard to his expressed views will be unable to prevent disclosure of those views to all parties to the action unless that would involve a real possibility of his suffering significant harm.[798] The views of the sufficiently mature child are likely to prevail if they are reasonable, and coincide with his best interests,[799] whereas the wishes of younger children may well require to yield to the welfare principle.[800] Undue influence by one of the parties over a child may lead to less significance being attached to that child's expressed views.[801] The duty to consult the child one that continues throughout the proceedings. Thus, a failure to elicit the views of a child who was only seven when an application by his mother to relocate to Australia for career reasons commenced, resulted in lower court decisions to allow her to do so being overturned when a report two years later elicited that he did not wish to leave Scotland.[802]

Child abduction within the United Kingdom—There has long been power at **44.47** common law, where a child was withheld from the person having right to his custody, for the court to order the delivery to him of the child.[803] By ss.51 and 52 of the Children Act 1975, where an application for a Residence Order is pending and the applicant has had the care and possession of the child for at least three years, it is an offence to remove the child from his care and the court may order the return of the child. An order for delivery of a child in order to exercise

---

[790] Refusal of parental rights due to the parent's religious affiliations amounts to a breach of the European Convention on Human Rights; *Hoffmann v Austria* (1994) 17 E.H.R.R. 293.

[791] *T, Petitioner*, 1997 S.L.T. 724. Discrimination against an applicant for parental rights on the basis of sexual orientation has also now been held to breach the European Convention on Human Rights, see *Salgueiro da Silva Mouta v Portugal*, 2001 Fam. L.R. 2.

[792] *White v White*, 2001 S.C. 689, under reference to *Elsholz v Germany* [2000] F.L.R. 486.

[793] *White v White*, 2001 S.C. 689. See also *J v J*, 2004 Fam. L.R. 21.

[794] Pre-1995 Act decisions where the views of young children were considered are still, therefore, of interest. See, e.g. *Pow v Pow*, 1931 S.L.T. 485; *Russell v Russell*, 1991 S.C.L.R. 429.

[795] 1995 Act s.11(10).

[796] RCS r.49.20; OCR r.33.19.

[797] 1995 Act s.11(9).

[798] See *McGrath v McGrath*, 1999 S.L.T. (Sh. Ct) 90, where the approach of the House of Lords in *Re D (minors) (adoption reports: confidentiality)* [1995] All E.R. 385 was followed.

[799] *Cosh v Cosh*, 1979 S.L.T. (Notes) 72; *Fourman v Fourman*, 1998 Fam. L.R. 98.

[800] *Ellis v Ellis* [2003] Fam. L.R. 77; *J v J* [2004] Fam. L.R. 20.

[801] *Hastie v Hastie*, 1985 S.L.T. 146; *Perendes v Sim*, 1998 S.L.T. 1382; cf. *Russell v Russell*, 1991 S.C.L.R. 429.

[802] *Shields v Shields*, 2002 S.C. 246.

[803] *Leys v Leys* (1886) 13 R. 1223; *Campbell v Campbell*, 1920 S.C. 31; *Begbie v Nichol*, 1949 S.C. 158.

statutory rights and responsibilities in respect of him, rather than to implement a court order, can be sought under the Family Law Act 1986,[804] and courts dealing with parental rights applications may order anyone who has relevant information to disclose the whereabouts of a child.[805] The 1986 Act contains a number of provisions that set out a uniform system of jurisdiction for the United Kingdom in cases involving parental rights and responsibilities orders, although the provisions are all now subject to Brussels II bis, although it is unclear whether the Regulation governs inter-UK disputes as well as those between Member States.[806] The following provisions of the 1986 Act will govern those cases to which the Council Regulation does not apply. Court orders relating to children's care should usually be determined in the jurisdiction of habitual residence.[807] Accordingly, provision is made to avoid that objective being frustrated by the abduction of children within the United Kingdom. Section 41 provides that if a child is removed from, or retained outside a part of the United Kingdom in which he was habitually resident before that change, either (a) without the agreement of anyone else having the right to determine where the child should reside, or (b) in contravention of an order made by a court in the United Kingdom, then that child shall be treated as continuing to be habitually resident in that part of the United Kingdom for a period of one year from the date of the removal or retention.[808] However, the change of residence will be accepted by the court if, during that year, the child attains the age of 16 years, or consent is given by the person whose agreement to the change of residence was not obtained initially, where that does not contravene a UK court order.[809] It has been recognised that there is a tension between the rule that the habitual residence of a child cannot be changed without the consent of a parent with parental rights and the terms of s.41.[810] The provision appears to assume that, at least within the constituent parts of the United Kingdom, a unilateral change of the habitual residence of a child may be achieved, subject to the one year moratorium.[811] The 1986 Act also makes provision for the cross-border recognition and expeditious enforcement of such orders made in one part of the United Kingdom in the other parts.[812] An order is to be recognised in another part of the United Kingdom as if it had been made by the appropriate court in that part.[813] Enforcement proceedings can only be taken if the order is registered[814] but, once registered, the order can be enforced by the registering court as if it had

---

[804] 1995 Act s.17(1).

[805] 1986 Act s.33.

[806] 1986 Act s.17A, inserted by the European Communities (Matrimonial and Parental Responsibility Jurisdiction and Judgements) (Scotland) Regulations 2005 (SSI 2005/42) reg.4(3). See also *S v D*, 2007 S.L.T. (Sh. Ct) 37, a decision based on the presupposition that art.66 of Brussels II bis is intended to deal with inter-UK disputes and not just those between one of the jurisdictional territories of the United Kingdom and another Member State, something that has not been authoritatively determined.

[807] Brussels II *bis* art.8; 1986 Act s.9. The meaning of habitual residence in this context is that given in international private law. See para.44.48, below.

[808] 1986 Act s.41(1) and (2); *Rellis v Hart*, 1993 S.L.T. 738; *Morris v Morris*, 1993 S.C.L.R. 144.

[809] 1986 Act s.41(3).

[810] *B v B*, 2008 S.L.T. 355.

[811] *B v B*, 2008 S.L.T. 355 at [15].

[812] Ch.V of Pt 1, ss.25–30.

[813] 1986 Act s.25(1).The appropriate court for Scotland is the Court of Session: s.32.

[814] 1986 Act s.25(3). Registration must proceed in accordance with the administrative requirements of s.27. See Act of Sederunt (Rules for the Registration of Custody Orders of the Sheriff Court) 1988 (SI 1988/613) (amended by SI 1991/2205); RCS rr.71.3 and 71.4.

made the order itself.[815] While a parent who has removed a child will be given the opportunity to be heard,[816] the court will refuse the primary purpose of enforcement only in exceptional circumstances; it will be slow to grant a sist of the application to enable the abducting parent to seek a variation of the original order at their leisure.[817]

International child abduction—The extent to which the exercise of parental **44.48** rights can be defeated by removing a child to another country is now limited by three international instruments, all of which are part of domestic law,[818] on the abduction of children and on recognition of foreign custody or other parental rights orders. These are: (1) the Hague Convention on the Civil Aspects of International Child Abduction ("the Hague Convention"); (2) the European Convention on Recognition and Enforcement of Decisions concerning, and the Restoration of, Custody of Children ("the European Convention"); and (3) Council Regulation (EC) 2201/2003 concerning jurisdiction and the recognition and enforcement of judgements in matrimonial matters and the matters of parental responsibility[819] ("Brussels II *bis*"). The first two Conventions are introduced into the law of the United Kingdom by the Child Abduction and Custody Act 1985, in the Schedules to which they are set out. The recognition and enforcement of orders relating to parental responsibility pronounced in the courts of Member States of the European Community is contained in Ch.III, Brussels II *bis* and has direct effect in the United Kingdom.[820] Brussels II *bis* supersedes the European Convention in relation to matters with which that Convention is concerned for children habitually resident in any Member State other than Denmark. It provides that judgments relating to parental responsibility pronounced and certified in one Member State are entitled to recognition in the other Member States without the requirement for any special procedure.[821] Any interested party may, however, apply to the court for a decision that such a judgment should or should not be recognised.[822] The grounds for non-recognition are that recognition would be manifestly contrary to public policy, that it was given (save in cases of urgency) without the child or the person whose parental responsibilities are infringed by the order having an opportunity to be heard, that the document instituting the proceedings was not properly served with the result that no defence was entered, or that the order it is irreconcilable with a later judgment relative to the child.[823] No review as to substance is possible.[824] Generally, for a parental rights judgment covered by Brussels II *bis* to be enforced in Scotland, it must first be registered for enforcement in the Court of Session.[825]

---

[815] 1986 Act s.29(1).

[816] *Woodcock v Woodcock*, 1990 S.L.T. 848.

[817] Family Law Act 1986 s.30, as interpreted in *Cook v Blackley*, 1997 S.C. 45.

[818] The United Kingdom is also a signatory to the Hague Convention of October 19, 1996 on jurisdiction, applicable law, recognition, enforcement and co-operation in respect of parental responsibility and measures for the protection of children ("The Hague Convention on Children 1996"), but has not yet introduced that Convention into domestic law.

[819] Repealing Council Regulation (EC) 1347/2000 ("Brussels II"), which was in force from March 1, 2003 and was far less extensive in its application to parental rights issues. Article 64 of Brussels II bis has transitional provisions to deal with actions raised under Brussels II.

[820] Council Regulation (EC) 2201/2003. For the jurisdiction provisions of the Regulation, see Ch.2 of this book.

[821] Council Regulation (EC) 2201/2003 art.21(1) and (2).

[822] Council Regulation (EC) 2201/2003 art.21(3).

[823] Council Regulation (EC) 2201/2003 art.23.

[824] Council Regulation (EC) 2201/2003 art.26.

[825] Council Regulation (EC) 2201/2003 art.28(2).

Where the procedural requirements are met, an application for enforcement may be refused only on the grounds for non-recognition listed above,[826] although proceedings to recognise or enforce may be "stayed" pending appeal in the Member State of Origin.[827] A decision to grant or refuse a declaration of enforceability can be appealed.[828] There are two types of orders that can be enforced without any need for a declaration of enforceability, namely an order for return of a child to another Member State after a Hague Convention application has been refused and an order conferring rights of access.[829] In those situations, the court making the order itself issues a certificate that enables direct enforcement, so long as the certificate confirms that certain requirements of natural justice and the need to give the child an opportunity to express a view have been met.[830]

Brussels II bis also introduces provisions to avoid international child abduction between Member States which dovetail with the provisions of the Hague Convention. Article 10 prevents any change in jurisdiction from the courts of a child's habitual residence to a proposed new habitual residence before (a) each person, institution or other body with "rights of custody" has acquiesced in the removal or retention of the child, or (b) the child has lived in the new Member State for one year after such a person has had or should have had knowledge of the whereabouts of the child and the child is settled in the new environment and at least one of the conditions to avoid a conflict with relevant court proceedings is met.[831] Article 11 adds specific new provisions to the operation of the Hague Convention as between Member States. These include: (1) a requirement to give the child an opportunity to be heard during Hague Convention proceedings unless that would be inappropriate having regard to his age and maturity[832]; (2) a reiteration of the requirement to act expeditiously in such proceedings and to take a decision within six weeks save in exceptional circumstances[833]; (3) a prohibition on refusing to return a child on the basis of art.13b of the Hague Convention where it is established that adequate arrangements have been made to secure the protection of the child after his or her return[834]; (4) a requirement to give the person seeking return an opportunity to he heard before making any order refusing that return[835]; (5) a requirement to transmit the order and any transcript of the hearing to the authority of the requesting Member State immediately on making an order refusing to return the child, and an obligation on the courts of that Member State to send those documents to the parties and invite them to make submission within three months[836]; and

---

[826] Council Regulation (EC) 2201/2003 arts 31(2) and 23.

[827] Council Regulation (EC) 2201/2003 arts 27 and 35.

[828] Council Regulation (EC) 2201/2003 arts 33 and 34.

[829] Council Regulation (EC) 2201/2003 art.40. The term access rather than contact is used in both the Council Regulation and the Hague Convention, but they should be treated as synonymous.

[830] Council Regulation (EC) 2201/2003 art.41. The relevant forms are produced in Annexes I and II of Brussels II *bis*. Requests for certificates are made of the Deputy Principal Clerk of Session or the Sheriff Clerk as appropriate. See RCS r.62.78 and SSI 2006/397 para.10 respectively.

[831] The conditions are that (i) no request for return has been lodged within the year to the competent court of the Member State to which the child has been removed, (ii) such a request for return has been withdrawn and no new request made within the year, (iii) a case before the court of the original Member State has been closed pursuant to art.11(7), or (iv) a judgment on custody has been made by the court of the original Member State that does not require the child's return there.

[832] Council Regulation (EC) 2201/2003 art.11(2).

[833] Council Regulation (EC) 2201/2003 art.11(3).

[834] Council Regulation (EC) 2201/2003 art.11(4). The provisions of art.13b of the Hague Convention are discussed below.

[835] Council Regulation (EC) 2201/2003 art.11(5).

[836] Council Regulation (EC) 2201/2003 art.11(6) and (7). If no submissions are received by the court within the three-month time limit, the case shall be closed.

(6) a provision that a subsequent order to return a child can be made under Brussels II bis can be made in appropriate circumstances notwithstanding an order under art.13 having been made that refuses to return the child.[837]

Under both the Hague Convention and the European Convention, responsibilities are imposed in relation to co-operation and assistance on the central authorities of states and, in relation to enforcement, on the courts. The Scottish Ministers constitute the appropriate authority in Scotland, the functions of which are delegated through the Justice Department.[838] The appropriate court is the Court of Session.[839] The objective of the Hague Convention is to secure the expeditious return of abducted children to the country of their habitual residence. The removal or retention[840] of a child under the age of 16, in breach of custody rights existing and exercised under the law of the state in which the child was habitually resident, is wrongful.[841] In this context, rights of custody include rights relating to the care of the person of the child and, in particular, the right to determine the child's place of residence.[842] An interim residence order in the home state may be sufficient to supersede a request for return.[843] A court may be regarded as an "other body" having rights of custody when there is an action relative to parental rights pending before it.[844] The question of whether a child is or is not habitually resident in a specified country is a question of fact to be decided by reference to all the circumstances of the case.[845] No minimum period is necessary to establish the acquisition of a new habitual residence; it is sufficient if there is actual presence, coupled with an intention to reside there for an appreciable period.[846] Where the court has determined that there has been a wrongful removal or retention, an order for return of the child is mandatory, unless the person opposing the return establishes one or more of the limited exceptions justifying refusal of the order.[847] The court may, in the exercise of its discretion, order a return notwithstanding that it has found a ground for refusal established. Normally it will be only at this stage that general considerations of the child's welfare form part of the decision.[848] The European Court of Human Rights has expressed the view that the best interests of the child must be assessed in detail in every case in which a return is sought under the Hague

---

[837] Council Regulation (EC) 2201/2003 art.11(8). The subsequent order would require to be in accordance with the provisions of s.4 of Ch.III of Brussels II *bis*.

[838] See ss.3 and 14 of the 1985 Act.

[839] 1985 Act ss.4 and 27(2).

[840] See *Kilgour v Kilgour*, 1987 S.L.T. 568, approved by the House of Lords on *Re H* [1991] 2 A.C. 476, regarding the concept of retention.

[841] Child Abduction and Custody Act 1985 Sch.1 art.3.

[842] Child Abduction and Custody Act 1985 Sch.1 art.5.

[843] *Petition of ERG* [2011] CSOH 126.

[844] In *Re H (Abduction: Rights of Custody)* [2000] 2 A.C. 291; cf. *Seroka v Bellah*, 1995 S.L.T. 204, where doubts were expressed about such a proposition. For further consideration of whether an individual could be described as exercising custody rights in particular circumstances see *Bordera v Bordera*, 1995 S.L.T. 1176 and *McKiver v McKiver*, 1995 S.L.T. 790. See also *Z, Petitioner*, 2010 S.L.T. 285 where a Dutch Welfare Organisation failed to show that they had the requisite custody rights over a youth in their care, thus a Petition for his return was dismissed.

[845] *Re J (A Minor) (Abduction: Custody Rights)* [1990] 2 A.C. 562; *Dickson v Dickson*, 1990 S.C.L.R. 692; *Findlay v Findlay (No.2)*, 1995 S.L.T. 492; *D v D*, 2001 G.W.D. 22–823.

[846] *Cameron v Cameron (No.1)*, 1996 S.C. 17; 1996 S.L.T. 306. A view that at least three months residence is required before a new habitual residence can be established was expressed in *M Petitioner*, 2005 S.L.T. 2. For examples of the circumstances in which it has been held that a new habitual residence has lawfully been acquired, see *Moran v Moran*, 1997 S.L.T. 541 and *Watson v Jamieson*, 1998 S.L.T. 180.

[847] Child Abduction and Custody Act 1985 Sch.1 arts 12 and 13.

[848] Child Abduction and Custody Act 1985 Sch.1 art.18. See *Singh v Singh*, 1998 S.C. 68; *T v T*, 2003 G.W.D. 34–952 (IH).

Convention, to avoid a breach of art.8 ECHR.[849] However, the UK Supreme Court has now clarified that as the Hague Convention was designed with the best interests of the child as a primary consideration, its application will not breach any international obligations.[850] The court will not return any child "automatically and mechanically", but a full-blown examination of the child's future is unlikely to be required and there is no need to depart from the normal summary process through which Hague applications are decided.[851] The exceptions for refusing a return remain limited. These include provision for refusing a return where over a year has elapsed from the date of the removal or retention and the child has become settled in his new environment.[852] It can be more difficult to show that a very young child has "settled"[853]and a child whose parent has hidden from authority and moved around to avoid detection is not likely to be so regarded.[854] Consent to, or subsequent acquiescence in, the removal or retention may also lead to a court refusing to order return of the child.[855] Consent and acquiescence[856]can both be express or implied, but where acquiescence is to be inferred either from conduct or inactivity, the subjective intention of the wronged parent claimed to have so acquiesced requires to be proved by the abducting parent.[857] There are further grounds for refusing the order sought by the wronged parent if there is a grave risk of physical or psychological harm or other intolerable situation for the abducted child on his return, or where a sufficiently mature child objects to being returned to the country of habitual residence.[858] Where a grave risk or intolerable situation defence is pled, the court will not explore the merits of the alleged risk and will usually assume that, while some short term emotional difficulties may arise in consequence of a return, the state of habitual residence will take appropriate action to protect the child.[859] It is now obliged to make such an assumption in cases involving EU Member States.[860] Undertakings that will ensure the child is not placed in an intolerable situation on his return are often elicited from the parent seeking return and recorded by the court.[861] However, if the courts of the country from which the child was abducted are unwilling or unable to protect the child from the alleged risk, the exceptional course of refusing the order for return may be taken.[862] A decision that will inevitably separate mother and child or siblings may be intolerable, but much will depend on the circumstances that await the child on a return to the state of habitual residence.[863] There is no presumption relative to the age at which a child will be sufficiently mature to object to a return; the reason for the objection must

---

[849] *Neulinger and Shuruk v Switzerland* [2011] 1 F.L.R. 122.

[850] *E (Children) (FC)* [2012] 1 A.C. 144, esp at [52].

[851] *E (Children) (FC)* [2012] 1 A.C. 144 at [26] and [52].

[852] Sch.1 art.12.

[853] *Perrin v Perrin*, 1995 S.L.T. 81; *Soucie v Soucie*, 1995 S.L.T. 414.

[854] *P. v S. and A. and West Lothian Council* Unreported June 2, 2000 Extra Division, Inner House.

[855] Sch.1 art.13(a).

[856] For examples of the consent ground being argued see *Zenel v Haddow*, 1993 S.L.T. 975 and *Findlay v Findlay (No.2)*, 1995 S.L.T. 492. The extent to which knowledge on the part of the wronged party of his Convention rights bears upon the question of acquiescence was explored in *Soucie v Soucie*, 1995 S.L.T. 414, and *Robertson v Robertson*, 1998 S.L.T. 468.

[857] *Re H (Minors) (Abduction: Acquiescence)* [1998] A.C. 72.

[858] Sch.1 art.13(b) and second paragraph.

[859] *Friedrich v Friedrich*, 78 F. 3d. 1060 (1996); *McCarthy v McCarthy*, 1994 S.L.T. 743; *Starr v Starr*, 1999 S.L.T. 335

[860] Brussels II *bis* art.11(4).

[861] See, e.g. *H v H*, 2006 Fam. L.R. 59.

[862] *Q, Petitioner*, 2001 S.L.T. 243.

[863] *Urness v Minto*, 1994 S.C. 249; *Singh v Singh*, 1998 S.C. 68.

relate to the country of habitual residence rather than the parent who resides there.[864] The court must first decide whether the child is of an age and maturity to express an opinion and, if so, then to assess the validity of the views expressed, the reason for the child objecting to the return, the purpose of the Convention and the child's welfare before determining the issue.[865] In cases involving EU Member States, greater emphasis requires to be placed on eliciting the views of the child whenever a defence to a return is being considered.[866] The Hague Convention also attempts to ensure the recognition and respect of both custody and access orders between contracting states.[867] Access rights made in another state can be enforced by the Court of Session, although welfare considerations are more likely to have to be considered and existing orders adapted to suit the changed circumstances.[868]

Under the European Convention, application may be made to have a custody order recognised or enforced in another Contracting State.[869] Duties to take positive steps are imposed on the central authority in the state to which application is made.[870] Recognition and enforcement are again, in general, mandatory,[871] but the listed exceptions are wider in scope than under the Hague Convention. A procedure of registration in the Court of Session prior to enforcement is required in terms of the 1985 Act.[872] Registration will be refused if the order is unenforceable in the state in which it originated, if there is an overlap with proceedings under the Hague Convention, or if one of the exceptions to recognition and enforcement set out in the Convention is satisfied.[873] These include failure to serve properly the documents instituting the proceedings or give time to arrange a defence; the making of certain orders in the absence of the defendant, and incompatibility of the order with another order enforceable in the state addressed or with fundamental principles of family law there.[874] Recognition and enforcement may also be refused if changes in circumstances including the passage of time render the original decision manifestly no longer in accordance with the welfare of the child, or if the order was made when the child had a stronger connection with the state later addressed.[875] Once an order has been registered by a court in the United Kingdom, that court has the same powers to grant or refuse enforcement it would have if it had made the order,[876] but not, it would appear, to vary the original decision to take account of a change in circumstances.[877]

---

[864] *Urness v Minto*, 1994 S.C. 249.

[865] *M Petitioner*, 2005 S.L.T. 2; cf. *W v W*, 2003 S.L.T. 1253.

[866] Brussels II *bis* art.11(2).

[867] Child Abduction and Custody Act 1985 Sch.1 art.21.

[868] RCS r.70.5(2). See the discussion about appropriate procedure in *Donofrio v Burrell*, 2000 S.L.T. 1051. The English Courts have rejected the proposition that art.21 may be used to apply direct to them for a contact order: *Re G (A Minor) (Enforcement of Access Abroad)* [1993] 3 All E.R. 657.

[869] Sch.2 art.4, which should be read together with art.13 and ss.14, 22 and 23(1) of the 1985 Act.

[870] Sch.2 art.5.

[871] Sch.2 art.7.

[872] 1985 Act ss.15 and 16.

[873] 1985 Act s.16(4).

[874] Sch.2 arts 9(1)(a)–(c) and 10(1)(d). A successful defence under art.10(1)(d) was made out in *Campins-Coll, Petitioner*, 1989 S.L.T. 33, although the interpretation of that exception in the case is difficult to square with art.9(1)(c).

[875] Sch.2 art.10(1)(b), subject to arts 15 and 10(1)(c). See *Campins-Coll, Petitioner*, 1989 S.L.T. 33.

[876] 1985 Act s.18.

[877] *Dehn v Dehn*, 1998 G.W.D. 2–59.

44.49 Adoption of children—The contract of adoption was not recognised at common law in Scotland.[878] It is a purely statutory process, introduced by the Adoption of Children (Scotland) Act 1930 and then consolidated in the Adoption (Scotland) Act 1978[879]. With effect from September 28, 2009, the Adoption and Children (Scotland) Act 2007[880] has effectively repealed the whole of the 1978 Act and provides a new comprehensive statutory framework, further consolidating the existing rules but also introducing some significant changes to the law and practice of adoption law in Scotland. Where relevant, the old 1978 Act statutory provisions are noted. Adoption is effected not by contract but by order of the court.[881] Unless the proposed adopter is a relative of the child, it is an offence for any person other than an adoption agency[882] to make arrangements for a child's adoption.[883] It is the duty of every local authority to establish and maintain adoption service to meet the needs of all those who are or may be affected by adoption. The decision of the children's hearing determining a child's placement with prospective adopters as a condition of a supervision requirement is not regarded as making such arrangements.[884] An adoption agency is prohibited from making arrangements for the adoption of a child if a better, practicable alternative exists.[885] That requirement is mirrored in the court's duty not to make an adoption order if it would be better for the child for it to be made than not.[886] Adoption necessarily interferes with the natural parents' right to respect for family life in terms of art.8 of the European Convention on Human Rights,[887] particularly where it has the effect of severing contact between natural parent and child.[888] However, it may, in appropriate cases, be justified as necessary where it is the only means available to pursue the legitimate aim of protecting the welfare of the child.[889] A challenge to the ECHR compatibility of the new "welfare" condition for adoption in the 2007 Act has been rejected by the Supreme Court and the criterion of a whole of life welfare test in adoption held to be Convention compliant.[890] Provided various statutory requirements referred to in the ensuing paragraph are met, an adoption order may be made extinguishing the parental responsibilities and parental rights

---

[878] *Kerrigan v Hall* (1901) 4 F. 10.

[879] As amended by the Children (Scotland) Act 1995.

[880] Adoption and Children (Scotland) Act 2007 (the "2007 Act") (asp 4). Most of the provisions were brought into force by the Adoption and Children (Scotland) Act 2007 (Commencement and Savings Provisions) Order 2009 (SSI 2009/267), which also provides the transitional rules.

[881] *J & J v C's Tutor*, 1948 S.C. 636.

[882] Adoption agencies are either local authorities or registered adoption services. See the 2007 Act ss.1 and 2(1).

[883] 2007 Act s.75. In addition to direct relatives the other member of a "relevant couple" may adopt with the natural parent without the involvement of an adoption agency. Section 29(3) of the Act provides that homosexual and heterosexual married and unmarried couples are "relevant couples" for this purpose.

[884] 2007 Act s.119(7), which replaced the provision in the 1978 Act, namely s.65(3) (as amended). The Adoption (Scotland) Act 1978 amended provision had reversed the effect of *R v Children's Hearing for Borders Region*, 1984 S.L.T. 65.

[885] 2007 Act s.14(6) and (7).

[886] 2007 Act ss.28(2) and 83(1)(d).

[887] Human Rights Act 1998 Sch.1.

[888] *Johansen v Norway* (1997) 23 E.H.R.R. 33.

[889] See, e.g. *Soderback v Sweden*, 1999 Fam. L.R. 104; *Scott v United Kingdom*, 2000 Fam. L.R. 102; *Re B (A Child) (Adoption: Natural Parent)* [2002] 1 W.L.R. 258; *Aberdeen City Council v R*, 2003 Fam. L.R. 59 and *Dundee City Council v K*, 2006 S.L.T. 63.

[890] *ANS v ML* [2012] UKSC 30, upholding the First Division in *S v L*, 2011 S.L.T. 1204. See para.44.50, below.

of the natural parents and vesting them in the adopters.[891] An adoption order may be made subject to such terms and conditions as the court thinks fit.[892] These might enable the child to maintain links with his natural family. Thus, a condition was imposed requiring adoptive parents to raise children with an understanding of their own ethnic origins and traditions[893] and, in an unusual case where both natural parents suffered from Huntingdon's Disease, a condition of contact was inserted in the adoption order.[894] However, prior to the 2007 Act, ongoing direct contact with the natural parent was normally regarded as constituting an interference with the responsibilities and rights of the adoptive parents and as there was no mechanism for varying an adoption order on a change of circumstances, contact conditions were used only exceptionally.[895] Since the coming into force of the 2007 Act, it is now possible to make a contact order not just at the time of adoption but also after a parent's rights and responsibilities in respect of his or her child have been extinguished on the making of an adoption order. However, a system of leave to apply has been implemented, so that there is no automatic retention of title and interest to claim such a right.[896] Once an adoption order has been made, the child is treated in law as if he had been born as a legitimate child of the adopter or adopters.[897] Accordingly, he has the same rights of aliment and to sue for damages for the death of an adoptive parent as any child born to the adopters would have, and the adopters have corresponding rights. Adoption, however, affects the prohibited degrees of relationship for the purposes of the crime of incest and the law relating to marriage only in that the adopted child and the adopters are deemed for all time coming to be within the prohibited degrees.[898] An adopted person is treated as the child of the adopter or adopters and not of any other person for all purposes relating to the succession of a deceased person and the disposal of property under an inter vivos deed.[899] The adopted person loses all rights in the estate of his natural parents,[900] and any reference in a deed to the child or children of the adopter is construed as including a reference to the adopted person.[901] When an adoption order is made, the child adopted becomes a British citizen if the adopter, or one of two adopters, is a British citizen.[902] The benefits to the child of acquiring British citizenship should not, however, be taken into account in deciding whether

---

[891] 2007 Act s.35(2) (previously s.12 of the Adoption (Scotland) Act 1978). Where a parent and a step-parent adopt the parent's natural child, his or her parental responsibilities and rights are not extinguished by the adoption: 2007 Act s.35(1)(a) (previously s.12(3A) of the Adoption (Scotland) Act 1978).

[892] 2007 Act s.28(3) (previously s.12(6) of the Adoption (Scotland) Act 1978).

[893] *A.H. & P.H. Petitioners*, 1997 Fam. L.R. 4.

[894] *B v C*, 1996 S.L.T. 1370, where the English authority of *Re C (A Minor; Adoption Conditions)* [1989] A.C. 1 was followed.

[895] In *B v C*, 1996 S.L.T. 1370, an extract of the adoption order was issued to all parties so that they could return to court if future variation was required.

[896] See Children (Scotland) Act 1995 s.11(3)(aa) and (ab), inserted by the 2007 Act s.107.

[897] Adoption (Scotland) Act 1978 s.39, which has not been repealed by the 2007 Act. See also 2007 Act s.40. On the death of the adoptive parent the obligation to aliment transmits as in the case of any other child.

[898] 2007 Act s.41(1) (previously s.41 of the 1978 Act).

[899] s.23(1) of the Succession (Scotland) Act 1964, preserved by the Adoption (Scotland) Act 1978 and now by the 2007 Act s.44. See para.38.02, above.

[900] Other than in situations where the transitional provisions of the Law Reform (Miscellaneous Provisions) (Scotland) Act 1966 s.5, which provide that if the adopters died before 1964 the adopted child still has rights in the estates of the birth parents, might still apply.

[901] Succession (Scotland) Act 1964 s.23(2).

[902] British Nationality Act 1981 s.1(5).

or not to grant an adoption order.[903] An adopted children register (with an index) is maintained in which entries, as directed by adoption orders, are made, and the word "adopted" is inserted in the register of births.[904]

44.50 **Applications for adoption**—Any person who has not attained the age of 18 when the application for adoption is made and who is not and has not been married or a civil partner, may be adopted.[905] Under the 1978 Act, an adoption order could only be made on the application either of a married couple[906] or of one person.[907] A step-parent wishing to adopt the natural child of his spouse could apply either alone, or together with the child's parent.[908] That exception apart, there were considerable restrictions on sole applicants,[909] and on homosexual cohabitants.[910] The 2007 Act has extended the categories of people who may apply to adopt. Couples are characterised as "relevant couples" who may adopt if they are married to each other, civil partners of each other, living together as if husband and wife in an enduring relationship or living together as if civil partners in an enduring relationship.[911] The provisions for sole applicants have also been extended to include those who are civil partners, homosexual or heterosexual cohabitants as well as those who are married where the applicant's spouse, civil partner or cohabitant cannot be found, is permanently separated from the applicant or is incapable of applying for an adoption order.[912] Adopters must be 21 or over,[913] except that an application by a married couple may proceed where one spouse is a natural parent of the child and is 18 or over, and the other spouse is 21 or over.[914] There are provisions forbidding adoption by the mother or father of the child alone unless, where there is another parent,[915] he is dead or cannot be found or there is some other reason justifying his exclusion.[916] The Act imposes a probationary period, usually 13 weeks, during which the child should at all times have had his home with the applicants, or one of them.[917] An application for adoption of a child is initiated by a petition to either the Court of Session or the sheriff court.[918] A curator ad litem to the child and a reporting officer, both independent of the

---

[903] *Re K (A Minor) (Adoption Order: Nationality)* [1995] Fam. 38.

[904] 2007 Act s.53 (previously Adoption (Scotland) Act 1978 s.45).

[905] 2007 Act s.119(1) and 28(4) and (7) (previously Adoption (Scotland) Act 1978 ss.65(1) and 12(1) and (5)).

[906] Adoption (Scotland) Act 1978 s.14.

[907] Adoption (Scotland) Act 1978 s.15.

[908] Adoption (Scotland) Act 1978 ss.14(1B) and 15(1)(aa). Those provisions had been inserted by the Children (Scotland) Act 1995, prior to which a step-parent could only apply to adopt a child by joint application with the natural parent, who are thereby required to relinquish their parental rights and responsibilities in relation to the child.

[909] Adoption (Scotland) Act 1978 s.15(1)(b).

[910] See *T, Petitioner*, 1997 S.L.T. 724.

[911] 2007 Act s.29(1) and (3).

[912] 2007 Act s.30(1)–(5).

[913] 2007 Act ss.29(1) and 30(1) (previously Adoption (Scotland) Act 1978 ss.14(1A) and 15(1)).

[914] 2007 Act s.30(3), which has again extended "relevant couples" for this purpose to civil partners, homosexual cohabitants and heterosexual cohabitants.

[915] Where artificial reproductive methods have been used, it is recognised that, by virtue of s.28 of the Human Fertilisation and Embryology Act 1990, there might not, in law, be any other parent.

[916] 2007 Act s.30(1)(d) and (7) (previously Adoption (Scotland) Act 1978 s.15(3)).

[917] 2007 Act s.15(1)–(3) (previously Adoption (Scotland) Act 1978 s.13). In a non adoption agency placement, if the prospective adopter is not a relative of the child, the period is 12 months: 2007 Act s.15(4).

[918] 2007 Act s.118. The procedural rules are contained in RCS Ch.67 for Court of Session petitions and in the Act of Sederunt (Sheriff Court Rules Amendment) (Adoption and Children (Scotland) Act 2007) 2009 (SSI 2009/ 284) for sheriff court applications.

adoption agency, must be appointed.[919] The consent of a child aged 12 or over to his adoption is required.[920] Children younger than that are given an opportunity to express views on the application. The court hearing the application is required to have regard, so far as practicable, (i) to any views expressed, taking account of the child's age and maturity, and (ii) to the child's religious persuasion, racial origin and cultural and linguistic background.[921] The 2007 Act will also require the court to have regard to the value of a stable family unit in the child's development and the likely effect on the child, throughout his life, of the making of an adoption order.[922] The child's views may initially be given confidentially, but the applicants will be able to access them other than where that would involve a real possibility of significant harm to the child.[923] Unless a child is free for adoption by virtue of an order to that effect, or, under the 2007 Act, unless a permanence order is in force,[924] the agreement (which must be in writing) of each parent or guardian of the child is required.[925] A natural father who does not have parental rights and responsibilities is not a parent of the child for this purpose, and his agreement to an adoption of the child is not required.[926] The agreement of a parent or guardian must be with full understanding of what is involved.[927] Unlike the 1978 Act, the 2007 Act does not state in terms that such consent must be unconditional and given freely, perhaps as it is axiomatic that both requirements are implied for consent.[928] It is not necessary for this purpose that the parent or guardian should know the identity of the applicants, a rule now given statutory force.[929] The court may dispense with the agreement of a child aged 12 or over who is to be adopted only if it is satisfied that he is incapable of giving his consent.[930] Under the 2007 Act, the court may not make an adoption order unless one of five conditions is met. The first condition is that either consent by the parent or guardian is given, as narrated above, or that such consent should be dispensed with.[931] The grounds for dispensing with consent of a parent or guardian have been almost completely altered from those in the 1978 Act.[932] The 2007 Act

---

[919] 2007 Act s.108. For the duties of the curator ad litem see RCS r.67.12 (Court of Session) and SSI 2009/284 r.12 (sheriff court).

[920] 2007 Act s.32(1) (previously Adoption (Scotland) Act 1978 s.12(8)).

[921] 2007 Act s.14(4)(b) and (c) (previously Adoption (Scotland) Act 1978 s.6(1)(b)). An adoption order may be refused if its effect would be to deprive the child of the advantages involved in an upbringing by adults of the same racial origin: *Re P (A Minor) (Adoption)* [1990] 1 Fam. L.R. 96. See also *AH and PH, Petitioners* [1997] Fam. L.R. 84.

[922] 2007 Act s.14(4)(a) and (d).

[923] *Re D (Minors) (Adoption Reports: Confidentiality)* [1995] 4 All E.R. 385.

[924] 2007 Act s.31(1) and (5)(a).

[925] 2007 Act s.31(1) and (2)(a) (previously Adoption (Scotland) Act 1978 s.16(1)). For permanence orders, see para.44.51, below.

[926] 2007 Act s.31(2) and (15). For the methods of acquisition of parental rights by fathers, see para.44.45, above; for the significance of a registered agreement bestowing parental responsibilities and parental rights on a man in this context, see *J v Aberdeen City Council*, 1999 S.C. 404.

[927] 2007 Act s.31(2)(a).

[928] For the previous more detailed provision see the Adoption (Scotland) Act 1978 s.16(1)(b)(i).

[929] 2007 Act s.31(2)(a). See also *A, Petitioner*, 1936 S.C. 255. The procedural rules are designed to protect the anonymity of the prospective adopters, at least in unopposed petitions: see RCS rr.67.10–67.14; SSI 2009/284 r.10.

[930] 2007 Act s.32(2) (previously Adoption (Scotland) Act 1978 s.12(8)).

[931] 2007 Act s.31(2)(a) and (b).

[932] Those grounds were that the parent or guardian was (a) not known, could not be found or was incapable of giving agreement, (b) was withholding agreement unreasonably, (c) had persistently failed without reasonable cause to fulfil either the responsibility to safeguard and promote the child's health developments and welfare or, if the child was not living with him to maintain personal relations and direct contact with the child on a regular basis or (d) had seriously ill-treated the child, whose

now provides that on one or more of five grounds being established, the court may dispense with the agreement of a parent or guardian. The grounds are, that the parent or guardian: (a) is dead[933]; (b) cannot be found or is incapable[934] of giving consent[935]; (c) who has parental responsibilities or parental rights (other than those relating to maintaining personal relations and direct contact) is unable satisfactorily to discharge those responsibilities or exercise those rights[936]; (d) who has no parental responsibilities or parental rights by virtue of the making of a permanence order (without authority to adopt) and it is unlikely that such responsibilities will be imposed on, or rights given to him.[937] The fifth ground, (e), is that where neither (c) nor (d) above applies, the welfare of the child otherwise requires the consent to be dispensed with.[938] This last ground, which permits the court to dispense with consent on the basis only of what the welfare of the child requires, is a new and controversial one. It has been the subject of a competency challenge on the basis that it is ECHR-incompatible.[939] The challenge failed,[940] both before the First Division and the Supreme Court. It is clear that decisions made under the provision have as their legitimate aim the protection of the welfare of children. In that context there must be an overriding requirement that adoption should proceed, for the sake of the child's welfare and that nothing less than adoption ill suffice. The likely effect on the child of ceasing to be a member of his original family will be taken into account in assessing the overall proportionality of an order. Properly interpreted, the provision meets the requirements of art.8 and the legislative provision was competently made.[941] The second condition for the making of an adoption order is that a permanence order granting authority for the child to be adopted is in force.[942] The third condition is that each parent or guardian has consented to adoption in advance under the relevant English legislation, has not withdrawn the consent and does not oppose the making of the adoption order.[943] The fourth condition is that the child has been placed for adoption by an adoption agency under the said English legislation with the prospective adoptive parents either with the consent of each parent or guardian or under a placement order and that no parent or guardian now opposes the making of an adoption order.[944] The fifth condition is that an order under the relevant Northern Ireland Order declaring the child free for adoption is in force.[945] Where a natural parent or guardian is opposed to adoption, the court, in reaching the

---

re-integration into the same household as the parent or guardian was, because of the serious ill treatment, or for other reasons, unlikely; Adoption (Scotland) Act 1978 s.16(2)(a)–(d).

[933] 2007 Act s.31(3)(a).

[934] 2007 Act s.31(3)(b). This ground is almost the same as that in s.16(2)(a) of the Adoption (Scotland) Act 1978. See *S v M*, 1999 S.L.T. 571.

[935] Where capacity to consent is in doubt, a curator ad litem may be appointed: *Strathclyde RC, Petitioners*, 1996 S.C.L.R. 109.

[936] 2007 Act s.31(3)(c) and (4).

[937] 2007 Act s.31(3)(c) and (5). The provision refers to a "relevant order", which is defined in s.31(6) as a permanence order which does not include provision granting authority for the child in question to be adopted.

[938] 2007 Act s.31(3)(d).

[939] The case was referred to the Inner House by the sheriff at Dumbarton hearing the adoption for a ruling on the issue and from there it was appealed to the Supreme Court.

[940] *S v L*, 2011 S.L.T. 1204 (Inner House); *ANS v ML* [2012] UKSC 30.

[941] *ANS v ML* [2012] UKSC 30 at [43].

[942] 2007 Act s.31(7). See para.44.51, below.

[943] 2007 Act s.31(8). The English legislation referred to is the Adoption and Children Act 2002.

[944] 2007 Act s.31(9).

[945] 2007 Act s.31(10).

decision whether or not to make the order sought must indulge in a balancing exercise, but has a duty to "regard the need to safeguard and promote the welfare of the child throughout the child's life as the paramount consideration".[946] Some of the issues on the approach to be taken by the court under the previous legislation remain relevant. The decision is thought to involve the same two-stage process as under the 1978 Act, namely (i) has a ground on which the parent's agreement may be dispensed with been made out and, (ii) if so, and having regard to all the relevant circumstances required by the provisions in the Act,[947] should the order be made?[948] As part of that exercise, the court is also enjoined not to make an adoption order unless it considers that it would be better for the child that it should do so than it should not.[949] Under the 1978 Act, the benefits of continued contact between parent and child required to be balanced against the benefits for the child of being adopted[950]; but this has become less important under the 2007 Act given the ability of the parent to apply post adoption, with leave of the court, for a contact order in appropriate circumstances.[951] The court will put the welfare of the child before a public policy argument stemming from an irregularity in the placing of the child for adoption.[952] The test for considering whether consent was being withheld unreasonably under the 1978 Act was an objective one; a reasonable parent would have the rights and interests of all parties, the child, the birth parents and the prospective adopters in mind.[953] The question in each case was not whether the refusal of consent is correct or mistaken, but whether it came within the range of possible reasonable decisions.[954] These decisions may continue to be of interest as the unreasonableness or otherwise of a parent's refusal to give consent can be one of many factors used to determine whether the welfare of the child requires their consent to be dispensed with under the 2007 Act.[955] For the previous ground of persistent failure to discharge parental rights and responsibilities under the 1978 Act, the failure did not require to be deliberate, but must have subsisted over a period of time.[956] The inability of a parent to satisfactorily discharge parental rights and responsibilities under the 2007 Act may also be interpreted as requiring a history of such inability.[957] The court may, in refusing an adoption application, direct that the general provision against the same person or couple reapplying in respect of the same child shall not apply. Even where no such direction is made, such an application after a refusal may proceed if it appears to

---

[946] 2007 Act s.14(3) (previously Adoption (Scotland) Act 1978 s.6(1)(a)).

[947] The previous provisions in s.6 of the Adoption (Scotland) Act 1978 have been replaced by s.14 of the 2007 Act. The new provisions require consideration of the value of a stable family unit in the child's development where practicable and the likely effect on him of an adoption order being pronounced, in addition to the factors in the previous legislation of the child's views where expressed and his religious background and ethnic origin.

[948] *Lothian RC v A*, 1992 S.L.T. 858, following *L v Central RC*, 1990 S.L.T. 818. These cases concerned freeing orders, where the same approach applied as in the making of an adoption order.

[949] In the 2007 Act, the "no order" principle is contained in s.28(2) and consideration of whether there is a better practicable alternative to adoption must be given by the court or adoption agency in carrying out their duties, see s.14(6).

[950] *Edinburgh City Council v N B*, 1999 S.C.L.R. 694.

[951] s.11(3)(aa) and (ab) of the Children (Scotland) Act 1995 as inserted by the 2007 Act s.107, referred to at para.44.49, above.

[952] *D & D v F*, 1994 S.C.L.R. 417.

[953] *A v B and C*, 1971 S.C. (HL) 129.

[954] *Re W (An Infant)* [1971] A.C. 682; *D v F*, 1994 S.C.L.R. 417.

[955] 2007 Act s.31(2)(b) and (3)(d).

[956] *Re D (Minors)* [1973] 3 All E.R. 1001; *G v M*, 1999 S.C. 439.

[957] 2007 Act s.31(2)(b) and (4).

the court that, because of a change in circumstances, or for any other reason, it is proper to hear the application.[958] It may also grant any order relating to parental responsibilities and parental rights when making or refusing an adoption application.[959]

44.51 **Freeing for adoption under the Adoption (Scotland) Act 1978 and permanence orders under the Adoption and Children (Scotland) Act 2007**—Under the 1978 Act, as a preliminary to adoption, an application could be made, by an adoption agency which is a local authority, declaring the child free for adoption.[960] The previous law remains of interest, not least because there has been dubiety about the interpretation of provisions allowing freeing for adoption petitions commenced during the transitional period to be concluded.[961] Since September 28, 2009 no new freeing applications can be raised but it seems that those started before that date can continue under the previous legislation without limit of time.[962] The following is a summary of the previous requirements for a freeing for adoption application. Where the local authority had decided to make arrangements for the adoption of a child and the parent or guardian did not agree with that decision, it was required to make such an application, unless an application for an adoption order in relation to the child had been initiated.[963] As with adoption applications, in the absence of consent to the order by each parent or guardian, the application also required to seek to dispense with parental agreement to adoption.[964] The court then required to be satisfied either that the parent or guardian agrees to the making of an adoption order or that agreement could be dispensed with on one of the specified grounds.[965] Before dispensing with agreement the court also required to be satisfied that the child is already placed for adoption or is likely to be placed.[966] As with a decision whether or not to make an adoption order under the 1978 Act, where a parent did not consent to a freeing order, the court required to approach the decision in two stages. First, it had to decide whether or not a ground set out in the Act for dispensing with consent had been made out and, if it had, and bearing in mind the principles set out in s.6 of the Act, whether or not the order should be made.[967] Again, the court was prohibited from making the order unless it would be better for the child that it should do so than that it should not.[968] An order declaring the child free for adoption could then be made. The result of such an order was that parental rights and duties vest in the adoption agency, parental agreement to adoption was no longer required and an adoption

---

[958] 2007 Act s.33.

[959] Children (Scotland) Act 1995 s.11; see *G v M*, 1999 S.C. 439.

[960] Adoption (Scotland) Act 1978 s.18, now repealed.

[961] See regs 16 and 17 of the transitional provisions of the Adoption and Children (Scotland) Act 2007 (Commencement No.4, Transitional and Savings Provisions) Order 2009 (SSI 2009/267).

[962] *IO and LO v Aberdeen City Council* [2011] CSIH 43 where the Second Division approved an interpretation of reg.17 of the 2009 Order that involved reading in words to allow freeing for adoption applications not concluded by September 28, 2010, the end of the transitional period, to continue.

[963] The Adoption Agencies (Scotland) Regulations 1996 (SI 1996/3266) r.16. A different process is undertaken if the child is already subject to a supervision requirement, but if the children's hearing approve the local authority's decision, again an application for a freeing order must be made: r.18.

[964] Adoption (Scotland) Act 1978 s.18(1) and (2).

[965] Adoption (Scotland) Act 1978 s.18(1).

[966] Adoption (Scotland) Act 1978 s.18(3). See *Edinburgh City Council v B*, 1999 S.C.L.R. 694; *Edinburgh City Council v S*, 2000 S.C.L.R. 605.

[967] *Lothian RC v A*, 1992 S.L.T. 858. See para.44.50, above.

[968] Adoption (Scotland) Act 1978 s.24(3).

application may proceed accordingly.[969] A father without parental responsibilities and rights was not a parent whose consent was required or required to be dispensed with before a freeing order could be made. But provisions peculiar to freeing for adoption required the court to be satisfied, in relation to any person claiming to be the father: (a) that he had no intention of applying for, or, if he did so apply, that it was likely he would be refused, an order relating to parental responsibilities and parental rights; and (b) that he had no intention of entering into a registered parental rights agreement with the mother of the child or, if he had such an intention, that no such agreement was likely to be made.[970] Where a father without parental rights had been involved in the child's family life, he had a right to enter the process as a party; in some cases the freeing process could be delayed to enable such a father to apply for parental rights and responsibilities.[971] A father without parental rights was not precluded from seeking orders relative to his child after a freeing order was made.[972] As in the case of adoption, a freeing order could not be made without the consent of a child under 12 unless he is incapable of giving that consent.[973] Each parent or guardian of the child who could be found was entitled to be given the opportunity to make a declaration that he did not wish to be involved in further questions concerning the adoption of the child.[974] If he had not made such a declaration, he was entitled to receive reports on the progress of the adoption,[975] and to apply to the court, at any time more than 12 months after the making of the freeing order, for revocation of the order on the ground that he wished to resume his parental rights and duties.[976] An adoption agency could also apply to the court for revocation of the freeing order. Applications for revocation either by the parent or the agency could, however, be made only if at that time no adoption order had been made and the child had not been placed for adoption.

The system of freeing for adoption was criticised for its inflexibility and interference with the right to family life in a manner that could in some cases go beyond legitimate interference to meet an overriding requirement pertaining to the child's best interests.[977] It has been abolished by the 2007 Act. Both freeing for adoption and the provisions for local authorities to be granted parental responsibilities orders[978] have been replaced by a system of Permanence Orders, which are inherently flexible and are designed to be as limited or far reaching as the circumstances of the particular case demand.[979] Existing freeing orders and parental responsibilities orders are now deemed to be permanence orders.[980] The Court of Session or the sheriff court[981] may, on the application of a local authority,

---

[969] Adoption (Scotland) Act 1978 ss.18(5) and 16(1)(a).

[970] Adoption (Scotland) Act 1978 s.18(7). For the issues involved in applications for parental responsibilities and parental rights orders and registered parental rights agreements, see paras 44.44–44.46, above.

[971] *G v Edinburgh City Council*, 2002 S.L.T. 828.

[972] As he has never had parental rights and responsibilities: Children (Scotland) Act 1995 s.11(1) and (3)(a)(i). Under the 2007 Act, parents who have lost parental rights and responsibilities orders will be able to seek leave to apply for a contact order only. See para.44.45, above.

[973] Adoption (Scotland) Act 1978 s.18(8).

[974] Adoption (Scotland) Act 1978 s.18(6).

[975] Adoption (Scotland) Act 1978 s.19.

[976] Adoption (Scotland) Act 1978 s.20.

[977] *West Lothian Council v McG*, 2002 S.C. 411; *Dundee City Council v K*, 2006 S.L.T. 63.

[978] These were made in terms of the Children (Scotland) Act 1995 ss.86–89. See para.44.52, below.

[979] The provisions relative to the making of permanence orders are contained in Pt 2 of the 2007 Act ss.80–104.

[980] See arts 13–17 of SSI 2009/267.

[981] For the applicable court rules see RCS Ch.67 as amended by the Act of Sederunt (Rules of the

make a permanence order respect of a child,[982] including an adopted child, but not one who is or has been married or a civil partner.[983] Such an order always contains the mandatory provision of vesting in the local authority both the parental responsibility to provide guidance appropriate to the child's stage of development in relation to the child and the parental right to regulate the child's residence.[984] The making of an order always extinguishes permanently the natural parent or guardian's right to regulate their child's residence.[985] The order subsists until the child attains the age of 18 so far as the guidance responsibility is concerned and in relation to regulating the right to reside until he is 16.[986] A permanence order may also contain such of the ancillary provisions as the court thinks fit. These include provisions (a) vesting in the local authority such other parental responsibilities and rights in relation to the child as the court considers appropriate,[987] (b) vesting in a person other than the local authority such parental rights and responsibilities as the court thinks fit (other than the right to regulate residence),[988] (c) extinguishing any parental responsibilities which vested in a parent or guardian immediately before the making of the order but which, by virtue of the order, vest either in the local authority by virtue of the mandatory provision or in a person other than the local authority,[989] (d) extinguishing any parental rights which vested in a parent or guardian immediately before the making of the order but which, by virtue of the order, vest either in the local authority by virtue of the mandatory provision or in a person other than the local authority,[990] (e) specifying such arrangements for contact between the child and any other person as the court considers appropriate and to be in the best interests of the child,[991] and (f) determining any question which has arisen in connection with any parental responsibilities or rights or any other aspect of welfare relative to the child.[992] Thus, with the exception of the right to regulate residence, parental rights and responsibilities may be held both by the local authority and the parent or guardian, or between the local authority and another party, but the prospect of multiple parties holding parental rights and responsibilities concurrently is ruled out by the legislation It is made clear that where two or more "persons" hold parental rights and responsibilities by virtue of a permanence order, each person may exercise those rights without the consent of the other or others, unless the order vesting the right or regulating its exercise provides otherwise.[993] A permanence order may also make provision granting authority for the child to be adopted if certain conditions are met.[994] The local authority must request that the order includes such authority and the court must be

---

Court of Session Amendment No.7) (Adoption and Children (Scotland) Act 2007) 2009 (SSI 2009/283) and the Act of Sederunt (Sheriff Court Rules Amendment) (Adoption and Children (Scotland) Act 2007) 2009 (SSI 2009/284).

[982] 2007 Act s.80(1).

[983] 2007 Act s.85.

[984] 2007 Act ss.80(2)(a) and 81.

[985] 2007 Act s.87.

[986] 2007 Act s.87.

[987] 2007 Act s.82(1)(a).

[988] 2007 Act s.82(1)(b). Both this provision and that in s.82(1)(a) above subsist until the child attains the age of 18 (for the parental responsibility of guidance) or 16 (for the parental right to regulate residence): see s.82(2).

[989] 2007 Act s.82(1)(c).

[990] 2007 Act s.82(1)(d).

[991] 2007 Act s.82(1)(e).

[992] 2007 Act s.82(1)(f).

[993] 2007 Act s.91.

[994] 2007 Act s.80(2)(c).

satisfied that the child has been, or is likely to be, placed for adoption.[995] Otherwise, the conditions are identical to those required to make an adoption order with the consent of a parent or guardian or by dispensing with such consent.[996] A permanence order may not be made in respect of a child who is aged 12 or over unless the child consents, or is incapable of giving such consent.[997] The "no order principle" that it must be better for the child that the order is made than that no order is made at all applies[998] and the court must regard the need to safeguard and promote the welfare of the child throughout childhood as the paramount consideration.[999] Before making a permanence order the court is required: (a) having taken account of the child's age and maturity, so far as reasonably practicable, give the child an opportunity to express any views should he wish to do so[1000]; (b) to have regard to (i) any such views expressed by the child, (ii) the child's religious persuasion, racial origin and cultural and linguistic background, and (iii) the likely effect on the child of the making of the order[1001]; and (c) be satisfied that there is no person who has the right to have the child living with him or otherwise to regulate the child's residence, or where there is such a person that the child's residence with the person is, or is likely to be, seriously detrimental to the welfare of the child.[1002] The no order principle, the paramountcy of the welfare of the child, and the provisions noted as (a)–(c) above impose separate requirements and while each has a bearing on whether the order should be made, there is no hierarchy between them.[1003] In applications for a permanence order with authority to adopt, the court should consider both the need to safeguard and promote the child's welfare throughout childhood and throughout life.[1004] In any proceedings relating to an application for a permanence order the court must permit any person who wishes to make representations to do so, such "persons" being the local authority, the child or his representative, any person with parental responsibilities and rights in respect of the child and any other person who claims an interest.[1005] A permanence order revokes existing orders in respect of a child, including existing permanence orders and s.11 orders,[1006] but a supervision requirement in respect of a child will only cease to have effect when a permanence order is made if the court is satisfied that it is no longer necessary and makes provision on the making of the permanence order for it to cease to have effect.[1007] Where a supervision requirement or other court order relating to the child remains in force after the making of a permanence order, the local authority must not act in any way that would be incompatible therewith.[1008] There is provision for future variation of the ancillary provisions of a permanence order[1009] on a material change of

---

[995] 2007 Act s.83(1)(a) and (b).
[996] 2007 Act s.83(1)(c) and (2)–(4). See para.44.49, above for the circumstances in which the court can dispense with parental consent to adoption.
[997] 2007 Act s.84(1) and (2).
[998] 2007 Act s.84(3).
[999] 2007 Act s.84(4).
[1000] 2007 Act s.84(5)(a).
[1001] 2007 Act s.84(5)(b).
[1002] 2007 Act s.84(5)(c).
[1003] *TW and JW v Aberdeenshire Council* [2012] CSIH 37 at [12].
[1004] *Inverclyde Council v MT and MS* [2011] CSOH 27.
[1005] 2007 Act s.86.
[1006] 2007 Act s.88.
[1007] 2007 Act s.89. See para.44.52, below re supervision requirements.
[1008] 2007 Act s.90.
[1009] 2007 Act ss.92 and 94.

circumstances or for any other proper reason[1010] and to amend it to grant authority for the child to be adopted on the conditions relating to consent or dispensing with consent being met.[1011] Permanence orders may be revoked on a material change in the circumstances directly relating to the order's provisions or on any wish by the parent or guardian of the child to have any parental rights or responsibilities extinguished by the order reinstated and the test for revocation is effectively the same as that for the making of a permanence order.[1012] Where it is clear to the local authority that a material change in consequence of which the order should be varied or revoked has occurred, it is under an obligation to make the appropriate application.[1013] A permanence order ceases to have effect on the making of an adoption order.[1014]

44.52   Child protection—Part II of the Children (Scotland) Act 1995 enacts a substantial number of public law provisions relative to the promotion of children's welfare by local authorities and children's hearings.[1015] The detailed rules will be changed by the provisions of the Children's Hearings (Scotland) Act 2011 once implemented,[1016] but the principles of the system will not alter. Though consideration of the law relative to the protection of children by local authorities and under the children's hearing system is effectively beyond the scope of this work,[1017] there are certain key aspects of it which merit notice here. Proceedings before the children's hearing are initiated by the Principal Reporter, who refers the case of any child in respect of whom he is satisfied that compulsory measures of supervision are necessary and at least one of specified grounds of referral is established.[1018] Where the specified grounds are disputed by the child or any "relevant person",[1019] or are not understood by the child, the matter is referred to the sheriff for a finding on whether the grounds are established.[1020] The term "relevant person" has been read down to include both fathers with no parental responsibilities or parental rights but who have contact with the child regulated in terms of a contact order[1021] and those who appear to have established family life with the child with which the decision of a children's hearing may interfere.[1022]

[1010] 2007 Act s.94(5).

[1011] 2007 Act s.93.

[1012] 2007 Act s.98. If it revokes the order, the court must consider whether to make any s.11 order, see s.100.

[1013] 2007 Act s.99.

[1014] 1995 Act s.102.

[1015] 1995 Act ss.16–93. The previous statutory framework was contained in the Social Work (Scotland) Act 1968. See para.2.16, above.

[1016] Children's Hearings (Scotland) Act 2011 (asp 1) ("CH(S)A 2011"). The main provisions of the Act will take effect in 2013. The relevant provisions are noted in parentheses.

[1017] For a detailed discussion of the substantive law in this area, see B. Kearney, *Children's Hearings and the Sheriff Court*, 2nd edn (Butterworths, 2000) and Wilkinson and Norrie, *Parent and Child* (1999), Ch.19.

[1018] 1995 Act s.65(1). The specified grounds, or conditions, for referral are contained in s.52(2) (CH(S)A 2011 s.67(2)).

[1019] Defined in Children (Scotland) Act 1995 s.93(2)(b), the term includes those with parental rights and responsibilities and anyone having care and control of the child. An unmarried father who has not acquired parental rights and responsibilities may apply to the court for a s.11 order so that he can acquire the status of a relevant person. Such orders can be granted whether or not a supervision requirement is in force, see *P v P*, 2000 S.C.L.R. 477.

[1020] 1995 Act s.65(7), (8) and (9). The provisions relative to the hearing before the sheriff are contained in s.68 (CH(S)A 2011 s.93).

[1021] *Authority Reporter v S*, 2010 S.C. 531.

[1022] *Principal Reporter v K* [2011] 1 W.L.R. 18.

Either the children's hearing or the sheriff may appoint a person to safeguard the interests of the child.[1023] If the grounds are established, the children's hearing has power to make a supervision requirement (a compulsory supervision order under the CH(S)A 2011) where satisfied that compulsory measures of supervision are necessary.[1024] A supervision requirement or order may require the child to reside at a specified place or places and to comply with any number of conditions.[1025] The courts are not prevented from making orders of parental rights and responsibilities in respect of a child subject to a supervision requirement unless the order sought would be in direct conflict with the requirement or its conditions.[1026] Where a children's hearing or court determines any matter with respect to a child under Pt II of the Children (Scotland) Act 1995 (and in future under the CH(S)A 2011), the paramount consideration must be the welfare of that child throughout childhood.[1027] The rule does not, however, apply to issues such as the question of the extent of the jurisdiction of the hearing or other competency issues.[1028] The views of the child concerned are taken into account so far as practicable, as with orders of parental responsibilities and parental rights and in adoption.[1029] A supervision requirement should not remain in force longer than is necessary in the interests of the child, which, unless it is renewed, cannot be more than a year.[1030] It is clear that proceedings before children's hearings involve the determination of civil rights and obligations, and that the hearing constitutes an independent tribunal, all in terms of art.6(1) of the European Convention on Human Rights,[1031] one consequence of which is that documentary information used in the decision-making process must be distributed to all parties, including the child.[1032] The decision of a children's hearing is subject to appeal at the instance of a child or a relevant person.[1033] The 1995 Act also allows local authorities to apply to the sheriff for a child assessment order where it is suspected that a child is being treated in such a way that he is suffering or may suffer significant harm, in order to establish whether there is reasonable cause to believe that he is being so treated.[1034] Where there is an urgent need to protect a child pending enquiry into the steps that may be taken to protect his welfare, local authorities and others may apply to the sheriff for a child protection order, which may authorise removal of the child and his keeping at a place of safety.[1035] In appropriate circumstances and where the urgency is not immediate, the Sheriff may hear representations from interested parties, such as the parents.[1036] There is also provision for the local authority to apply to the sheriff for an exclusion order, in terms of which a person in a household causing or likely to cause a child to suffer

---

[1023] 1995 Act s.41(1).

[1024] 1995 Act s.70 (CH(S)A 2011 s.83). The children's hearing is not limited to considering information strictly relevant to the stated ground of referral: *O v Rae*, 1993 S.L.T. 570.

[1025] 1995 Act s.70(3) (CH(S)A 2011 s.83). Conditions must be expressly specified and in relevant form: *Kennedy v M*, 1995 S.L.T. 717.

[1026] *P v P*, 2000 S.C.L.R. 477.

[1027] 1995 Act s.16(1).

[1028] *S v Proudfoot*, 2002 S.L.T. 743.

[1029] 1995 Act s.16(2) and see para.44.46, above.

[1030] 1995 Act s.73 (CH(S)A 2011 s.83).

[1031] *S v Miller (No.1)*, 2001 S.L.T. 531.

[1032] This was conceded by the Principal Reporter in *S v Miller*, 2001 S.L.T. 531 at 542 and 560.

[1033] 1995 Act s.51(1) (CH(S)A 2011 s.154).

[1034] 1995 Act s.55 (CH(S)A 2011 s.35).

[1035] 1995 Act ss.57–60 (CH(S)A 2011 ss.37–54).

[1036] *C, Petitioner*, 2002 Fam. L.R. 42.

significant harm may be removed from the family home for up to six months.[1037] Where an interim exclusion order is granted, the six month period will begin on that date. Thus if the interim order lapses before the final determination of the application, the application itself falls, but a fresh application can properly be made.[1038] Sections 86 to 89 of the 1995 Act made provision for parental responsibilities orders, in terms of which "appropriate parental rights and responsibilities" could be transferred from a relevant person[1039] to the local authority.[1040] The conditions that had to be established before the order could be made were identical to those under which the court could dispense with parental agreement to adoption under the 1978 Act.[1041] The sheriff could attach such conditions to a parental responsibilities order as he considers appropriate.[1042] Sections 86 to 89 have been repealed by the Adoption and Children (Scotland) Act 2007 which introduced the system of permanence orders.[1043]

FURTHER READING

Bennett, S.A., *Divorce and Dissolution of Civil Partnership in the Sheriff Court*, 8th edn (Barnstoneworth Press, 2007).

Clive, E.M., *Law of Husband and Wife in Scotland*, 4th edn (Edinburgh: W. Green, 1997).

Kearney, B., *Children's Hearings and the Sheriff Court*, 2nd edn (Butterworths, 2000).

McNeill, P. and Jack, M., *Adoption of Children in Scotland*, 4th edn (Edinburgh: W. Green, 2010).

Scottish Family Law Service (Edinburgh: Butterworths).

Sutherland, E., *Child and Family Law*, 2nd edn (Edinburgh: W. Green, 2008).

Thomson, J., *Family Law in Scotland*, 6th edn (Bloomsbury Professional, 2011).

Wilkinson, A.B. and Norrie, K.N., *The Law Relating to Parent and Child in Scotland*, 2nd edn (Edinburgh: W. Green, 1999).

[1037] 1995 Act s.76. See *Russell v W*, 1998 Fam. L.R. 25.

[1038] *Glasgow City Council v H*, 2003 S.L.T. 948.

[1039] 1995 Act s.86(4) defines relevant person for this purpose as a parent of the child or a person who for the time being has parental responsibilities and parental rights.

[1040] 1995 Act s.86(1).

[1041] 1995 Act s.86(2)(b). See *Glasgow City Council v M*, 1999 S.L.T. 989 and para.44.51, above.

[1042] 1995 Act s.86(5).

[1043] See para.44.51, above.

CHAPTER 45

PARTNERSHIP

Statutory law—The general law of partnership was codified by the Partnership **45.01**
Act 1890.[1] Except in minor details it made no change in the existing law. There is
a general provision that the rules of common law prevail except so far as they are
inconsistent with the express provisions of the Act.[2] The Corporate Manslaughter
and Corporate Homicide Act 2007 applies to partnerships.[3] In 2000 the Scottish
Law Commission and the Law Commission in England and Wales produced a
joint consultation paper on partnership law with a view to reform, followed by a
joint report in 2003, but no progress on the matter has been made since that date.[4]
It should be emphasised that despite having the word "partnership" in common,
partnerships are legal entities different from limited partnerships (governed by the
Limited Partnerships Act 1907) and limited liability partnerships (governed by
the Limited Liability Partnerships Act 2000).

Joint adventure—It would appear that under the provisions of the Partnership **45.02**
Act there is no general distinction between an ordinary partnership and a partnership for one particular transaction (now commonly known as a joint venture[5])
except that in the latter case the implied authority of each partner is more limited,
and further that, in the absence of any provision to the contrary, the partnership is
dissolved by the completion of the transaction in question.[6] A joint adventure
is simply one type of partnership, differentiated by its limited purpose and
duration (which necessarily affect the extent of the rights and liabilities flowing
from the relationship), but in all other essential respects indistinguishable
from partnership.[7]

---

[1] For an interesting discussion of Sir Frederick Pollock's drafting of the Act, see *Duncan v MFV Marigold PD 145*, 2006 S.L.T. 975; 2007 S.C.L.R. 155. See also the *Stair Memorial Encyclopaedia*, Vol.16, "Partnership".

[2] Partnership Act 1890 (the "1890 Act") s.46.

[3] See para.46.03, below.

[4] Scottish Law Commission, *Partnership Law: A Joint Consultation Paper* (HMSO, 2000), Scot. Law Com. No.111; Law Commission, *Report on Partnership Law* (HMSO, 2003), Law Com. No.159; the Law Commission and the Scottish Law Commission, *Partnership Law* (HMSO, 2003), Law Com. No.283 and Scot. Law Com. No.192. In April 2012 the Office of the Attorney General for Scotland began consulting on the criminal liability of partnerships, a matter discussed within the Report. For the consultation, see *http://www.scotlandoffice.gov.uk/scotlandoffice/files/ConDoc-Unincorporated-Associations-and-Partnerships.pdf* [Accessed July 26, 2012].

[5] Formerly known as a "joint adventure", Bell, *Principles*, s.392; Bell, *Commentaries*, II, 538; and, as distinct from a contract of service, *Parker v Walker*, 1961 S.L.T. 252.

[6] 1890 Act s.32. See para.45.25, below.

[7] *Mair v Wood*, 1948 S.C. 83 at 86, per Lord President Cooper.

I: PARTNERSHIPS

45.03 **Definition**—Partnership is defined (s.1) as, "the relation which subsists between persons carrying on a business in common with a view of profit." "Person" includes every person recognised as a person in law, so a partnership could be formed between a natural person and a limited company. "Business" includes every trade, occupation or profession.[8] The relationship of the members of a company or association, registered under the Companies Acts, or formed or incorporated under any other Act of Parliament, Royal Charter or letters patent, is expressly excluded.[9] From the definition it is clear that there must be at least two persons to form a partnership, though there is no specified maximum number of partners. A business carried on by one person alone, though in a name indicating a firm, is not a partnership,[10] though it is probably included under the term "firm" in certain sections of the Act.[11] Apart from that, in most respects the words "firm" and "partnership" are interchangeable. Associations formed for purposes other than profit (e.g. clubs) do not fall within the Act.[12] The proposed business or activity to be carried out by the partnership must not be illegal.[13] Although s.1 refers to "a view of profit" there is no obligation to make a profit: it is sufficient that the partners hope to make a profit.

45.04 **Constitution of partnership**—A partnership may be constituted orally, or in writing, or may be inferred from the relationship of the parties. It is a question of their intention, to be gathered from the whole circumstances of the case.[14] There is no simple or single test which can be applied in every case,[15] and an agreement to set up a business and carry it on as a partnership does not establish a partnership any more than statements by the parties that they are partners.[16] In questions of liability for the debts of a business, a person may be held to be a partner, and therefore liable, if he be judged to have intended to assume the position, in relation to that business, from which the law infers partnership, although he may not have regarded himself as a partner, or may have expressly disclaimed that position.[17] So a partnership may be held to have been created when the question is with creditors, although, on the same facts, it would be held that there was no partnership in a question between the alleged partners themselves.[18] The question whether the relationship of parties involves partnership, and consequent liability for debts, where there is no express agreement for partnership, has generally arisen in relation to agreements to share profits. The tendency of the earlier authorities to hold that everyone who in any way shared in the profits of a

---

[8] 1890 Act s.45.

[9] 1890 Act s.1(2).

[10] For the use of the term "sole partner", see *Allen & Son v Coventry* [1980] I.C.R. 9 at 12, per Lord McDonald in an English appeal to the EAT.

[11] e.g. 1890 Act ss.14, 17, 18.

[12] As to such associations, see Ch.47.

[13] *Michael Jeffery & Co v Bamford* [1921] 2 K.B. 351; *Foster v Driscoll* [1929] 1 K.B. 470, CA; *Lindsay v Inland Revenue*, 1933 S.C. 33; 1933 S.L.T. 57.

[14] See *Morrison v Service* (1879) 6 R. 1158.

[15] *Dollar Land (Cumbernauld) Ltd v C.I.N. Properties*, 1996 S.L.T. 186; *Pine Energy Consultants Ltd v Talisman Energy (UK) Ltd* [2008] CSOH 10.

[16] *Khan v Miah* [1998] 1 W.L.R. 477, CA.

[17] *McCosh v Brown's Tr.* (1899) 1 F. (HL) 86; *Adam v Newbigging* (1888) L.R. 13 App. Cas. 308 at 315, per Lord Halsbury L.C.; *Charlton v Highet*, 1923 S.L.T. 493.

[18] Bell, *Commentaries*, VII, 2, 1.2; *Clippens Co v Scott* (1876) 3 R. 651; *Walker v Hirsch* (1884) L.R. 27 Ch.D. 460.

business must be liable for all its debts was checked by the decision in *Cox v Hickman*,[19] where it was held that a committee of creditors, who had appointed a manager to carry on their debtor's business, with a provision that all profits should go to meet their debts, were not liable as partners in the business. The Partnership Act 1865, commonly known as Bovill's Act, dealing with the inference of partnership to be drawn from certain specified relationships, was repealed by the Partnership Act, but was substantially re-enacted by s.2. The section is printed below.[20] In the last two cases ((d) and (e)) the lender or seller of goodwill is, in the event of bankruptcy, postponed to all other creditors, whether the contract is in writing or not.[21]

The statutory rules, and the decisions,[22] seem to justify the following statements: (1) an agreement may create a partnership in a question of liability for the debts of a business but not in a question between the parties themselves[23]; (2) a lender who stipulates for nothing more than a share in the profits is not a partner[24]; (3) a right to a share in profits, and in addition a right, absolute or conditional, to receive or dispose of the partnership assets, involves partnership[25]; (4) where a right to a share in the profits is coupled with a power to control the method by which the business is carried on, it is a question depending upon the degree of control whether partnership is involved or not[26]; (5) creditors appointing a

---

[19] *Cox v Hickman* (1860) 8 H.L. Cas. 268.

[20] Rules for determining existence of partnership. In determining whether a partnership does or does not exist, regard shall be had to the following rules:

(1) Joint tenancy, tenancy in common, joint property, common property, or part ownership does not of itself create a partnership as to anything so held or owned, whether the tenants or owners do or do not share any profits made by the use thereof.

(2) The sharing of gross returns does not of itself create a partnership, whether the persons sharing such returns have or have not a joint or common right or interest in any property from which or from the use of which the returns are derived.

(3) The receipt by a person of a share of the profits of a business is prima facie evidence that he is a partner in the business, but the receipt of such a share, or of a payment contingent on or varying with the profits of a business, does not of itself make him a partner in the business; and in particular:

(a) The receipt by a person of a debt or other liquidated amount by instalments or otherwise out of the accruing profits of a business does not of itself make him a partner in the business or liable as such;

(b) A contract for the remuneration of a servant or agent of a person engaged in a business by a share of the profits of the business does not of itself make the servant or agent a partner in the business or liable as such;

(c) A person being the widow or child of a deceased partner, and receiving by way of annuity a portion of the profits made in the business in which the deceased person was a partner, is not by reason only of such receipt a partner in the business or liable as such;

(d) The advance of money by way of loan to a person engaged or about to engage in any business on a contract with that person that the lender shall receive a rate of interest varying with the profits, or shall receive a share of the profits arising from carrying on the business, does not of itself make the lender a partner with the person or persons carrying on the business or liable as such. Provided that the contract is in writing and signed by or on behalf of all the parties thereto;

(e) A person receiving by way of annuity or otherwise a portion of the profits of a business in consideration of the sale by him of the goodwill of the business is not by reason only of such receipt a partner in the business or liable as such.

[21] 1890 Act s.3; *Re Fort* [1897] 2 Q.B. 495.

[22] Reviewed in *Dollar Land (Cumbernauld) Ltd v C.I.N. Properties Ltd*, 1996 S.L.T. 186.

[23] See fn.18, above.

[24] *Laing Bros Tr. v Low* (1896) 23 R. 1105. This may be doubtful if the agreement was not in writing.

[25] *McCosh v Brown's Tr.* (1899) 1 F. (HL) 86; *Charlton v Highet*, 1923 S.L.T. 493.

[26] *Stewart v Buchanan* (1903) 6 F. 15; *Re Young* [1896] 2 Q.B. 484.

manager to carry on their debtor's business, under an arrangement by which the profits are to go to meet their debts, are not partners in the business[27]; (6) persons registered as owners of shares in a ship[28] or employed on board and remunerated by a share in the earnings,[29] are not, merely from their ownership or their method of remuneration, to be deemed partners.

Unlike a registered company, there is no requirement for a partnership publicly to register its existence, save with Her Majesty's Revenue and Customs, and there is no requirement for it to publish either its accounts or any other documentation.

45.05   **Holding out**—A person who is not a partner may be liable for the debts of a business on the ground that he has, by words or conduct, held himself out as a partner, or knowingly suffered himself to be so held out.[30] A retiring partner does not knowingly suffer himself to be held out merely because the remaining partner uses notepaper belonging to the partnership which, contrary to an arrangement between the partners, has not been destroyed upon the dissolution of the partnership.[31] The liability involved in holding out rests on the principle of personal bar, and is not incurred to persons who have notice of the actual facts. So a trustee in the sequestration of a firm has no title to sue a party alleged to have held himself out as a partner, because he represents all the creditors, some of whom may have had notice.[32] A person may incur liability by holding out either when, having been a partner and known as such, he has retired from the firm without giving notice,[33] or by allowing his name to appear in a business of which he is not a partner.[34] A person whose name is so used without his consent has a title to interdict.[35]

45.06   **The partnership's name**—The Companies Act 2006 contains various provisions in connection with the names of businesses, including partnerships.[36] Partnerships may trade either under a business name, or use a name comprising all the partners' own surnames, e.g. "Smith Jones & Brown".[37] Permissible additions to surnames are (1) the forenames or initials of the forenames of the individual partners, e.g. "Alan Smith, B. Jones & C. Brown," (2), when two or more partners have the same surname, just the letter "s", e.g. "Smith & Browns", or (3) an indication that the business is carried on in succession to a former owner.[38]

A partnership to which the Companies Act applies may not, without the Secretary of State's approval, use any name which is likely to give the impression that the business is connected with Her Majesty's Government or local

---

[27] *Cox v Hickman* (1860) 8 H.L.C. 268; *Gosling v Gaskell* [1897] A.C. 575; *Stott v Fender* (1878) 5 R. 1104; *Alna Press v Trends of Edinburgh*, 1969 S.L.T. (Notes) 91.

[28] *Sharpe v Carswell*, 1910 S.C. 391.

[29] *Jamieson v Clark*, 1909 S.C. 132; contrast *Scottish Insurance Commissioners v McNaughton*, 1914 S.C. 826.

[30] 1890 Act s.14(1).

[31] *Tower Cabinet Co v Ingram* [1949] 2 K.B. 397.

[32] *Mann v Sinclair* (1879) 6 R. 1078.

[33] See para.45.13, below.

[34] See *Brember v Rutherford* (1901) 4 F. 62.

[35] *Walter v Ashton* [1902] 2 Ch. 282.

[36] The rules relating to partnership and company names also apply to sole traders (see Companies Act 2006 Pt 41).

[37] Companies Act 2006 (the "2006 Act") s.1192(2).

[38] 2006 Act s.1192(3).

government.[39] If a partnership wishes to have a name that suggests a connection between some branch of national or local government, it must write beforehand to the relevant government department or other body requesting it to indicate whether, and if so why, it has any objections to the proposed partnership name.[40] The letter and the response need to be submitted for approval to the Secretary of State, and if this is not done, the application for the proposed name may not be considered.[41] Approval may also subsequently be withdrawn.[42] Other regulations prohibit "sensitive" names not deemed suitable for any business.[43] There are also regulations prohibiting someone from carrying on a business with a misleading name consisting of or containing specified words or expressions associated with particular types of company or organisation[44] or likely to cause harm to the public.[45] The partnership must state certain details on all its business letters, written orders for goods or services, invoices, receipts and written demands for payment of debts.[46] Those details are the partnership's trading name (if any), the name of each partner[47] and an address in the United Kingdom for service on him of any document relating to the business.[48] In its business premises, where customers or suppliers have access, the firm must display a notice with the partners' names and addresses.[49] A person doing or discussing business with the firm must be given written notice of the names and addresses on request.[50]

Failure without reasonable excuse to comply with these obligations constitutes a criminal offence,[51] but a breach may also affect the firm's right to take legal proceedings.[52] If, when it enters a contract, the firm is in breach of its obligations under the Act, any action taken by the firm to enforce a right arising out of the contract will be dismissed if the defender can show either that he has a claim against the firm which he has been unable to pursue because of the firm's breach of those obligations or that he has suffered some financial loss in connection with the contract by reason of that breach, unless the court is satisfied that it is just and equitable to permit the proceedings to continue.[53] Failure to comply with the relevant obligations does not affect the firm where it is the defender in an action and would not prevent the firm from counter-claiming in an action brought against it.[54]

---

[39] 2006 Act s.1193(1).

[40] 2006 Act s.1195(1), (2). See the Company, Limited Liability Partnership and Business Names (Public Authorities) Regulations (SI 2009/2982).

[41] 2006 Act s.1195(4).

[42] 2006 Act s.1196.

[43] 2006 Act s.1194. See the Company, Limited Liability Partnership and Business Names (Sensitive Words and Expressions) Regulations (SI 2009/2615). Words like "Scottish", "Royal", "nurse" and "abortion" are unacceptable.

[44] See the Business Names (Miscellaneous Provisions) Regulations (SI 2009/1085). This prohibits the use of words suggesting limited liability or otherwise giving a misleading impression of the partnership's status.

[45] 2006 Act s.1198.

[46] 2006 Act s.1202.

[47] For firms with more than 20 partners, a list of the partners' names may instead be available at the firm's place of business, rather than having to be printed on the headed paper (s.1203).

[48] 2006 Act s.1201.

[49] 2006 Act s.1203.

[50] 2006 Act s.1205.

[51] 2006 Act s.1206.

[52] The wording of the section shows that it does not apply to arbitrations or tribunals, but only to proceedings in court.

[53] 2006 Act s.1206(2).

[54] 2006 Act s.1206(4).

45.07 Firm: Firm name—Section 4 of the Partnership Act 1890 provides:

> "Persons who have entered into partnership with one another are for the purposes of this Act called collectively a firm, and the name under which their business is carried on is called the firm name."

The section expressly preserves the rule of Scots law that a firm is a legal personality distinct from the persons who compose it.[55] The recognition of the firm as a separate legal personality is particularly significant in the matters of actions, diligence, prescription,[56] ranking in bankruptcy,[57] questions of compensation between debts of the firm and debts of the partners, and criminal matters.[58]

45.08 Actions by firm—As the firm is a separate legal personality, an individual partner has no title to sue for the enforcement of firm obligations. An action by all the partners is good, provided that there is an indication that they are suing for a firm debt.[59] A firm cannot sue for loss of profit arising out of personal injury to a partner caused by the negligence of an outsider,[60] but the injured partner may sue for his loss of profit.[61] If the firm name be descriptive, e.g. the Antermony Coal Co, it is not a sufficient instance without the addition of the names of three partners, or of all the partners, if less than three.[62] If the firm name consists of the names of individuals, action in the firm name alone is competent, even if the names may not be those of the existing partners.[63]

The same rules hold with regard to the method by which a firm may be sued; it is not competent to sue an individual partner, even though the firm be dissolved.[64]

45.09 Diligence—When decree has been obtained against a firm, diligence may proceed against any individual partner, without any further judicial procedure, whether he be named in the decree or not.[65] A party who is charged for payment, and is prepared to maintain that he is not a partner, has his remedy by suspension, and may claim damages. A charge against a party who is not a partner is not justified by proof that he is liable for the firm's debts on the ground that he has held himself out as a partner.[66] A protested bill, signed by all the partners, and followed by a charge against each of them, was a warrant for poinding the assets of the firm.[67]

45.10 Authority of partners—In matters of contract the authority of any partner to bind the firm may, in a question between the partners themselves, be regulated by

---

[55] *Jardine-Paterson v Fraser*, 1974 S.L.T. 93.

[56] *Highland Engineering Ltd v Anderson*, 1979 S.L.T. 122.

[57] See para.45.17, below.

[58] *Balmer v HMA*, 2008 S.L.T. 799. See para.45.12, below.

[59] *Plotzker v Lucas*, 1907 S.C. 315.

[60] *Gibson v Glasgow Corp*, 1963 S.L.T. (Notes) 16.

[61] *Vaughan v Glasgow P.T.E.*, 1984 S.C. 32.

[62] *Antermony Coal Co v Wingate* (1866) 4 M. 1017; *Hutcheon & Partners v Hutcheon*, 1979 S.L.T. (Sh. Ct) 61. By r.57 in Sch.1 to the Sheriff Courts (Scotland) Act 1907, as substituted by the the Act of Sederunt (Sheriff Court Ordinary Cause Rules) 1993, a firm may sue and be sued in the sheriff court by its trading or descriptive name alone. There are no equivalent rules in the Court of Session.

[63] *Forsyth v Hare* (1834) 13 S. 42; *Brims & Mackay v Patullo*, 1907 S.C. 1106.

[64] *McNaught v Milligan* (1885) 13 R. 366.

[65] 1890 Act s.4(2); *Ewing v McClelland* (1860) 22 D. 1347.

[66] *Brember v Rutherford* (1901) 4 F. 62.

[67] *Rosslund Cycle Co v McCreadie*, 1907 S.C. 1208. The same principle could be used for attachment.

the partnership deed. In questions with third parties every partner is an agent of the firm and of the other partners, and his acts in carrying on in the usual way the business of the partnership,[68] and his signature in the firm name to obligatory documents, bind the firm, unless he had in fact no authority and the person with whom he deals knows this or does not know or believe that he is a partner.[69] A partner's admission is evidence against the firm,[70] and notice on matters connected with the firm's affairs to any partner who habitually acts in those affairs is notice to the firm, except in the case of a fraud on the firm committed by or with the consent of that partner.[71] The giving of false information to a partner does not, however, necessarily mean that a partner acting in good faith on the basis of that information makes his firm liable for a false representation made neither negligently nor fraudulently.[72] The extent of the implied authority of a partner as an agent for the firm depends upon the nature of the business.[73] The firm is not bound by an undertaking in the firm name which is known to be granted in the private interests of the partner. Thus, while an obligation to clear the record of burdens on a subject disponed in security used to be within the implied authority of a partner in a firm of law agents, the firm was not bound by such an obligation when granted by a partner in connection with a loan to himself.[74] And where there are exceptional terms the other party should inquire whether the partner has in fact authority, as where a partner in a firm of builders signed the firm name to a promissory note in terms involving interest at 40 per cent.[75] An obligation in the firm name which is beyond the real or ostensible authority of a partner, and is therefore not binding on the firm, is binding on the partner as an individual.[76]

Liability of firm for wrongs—Under s.10 of the Act the firm is liable for any **45.11** wrongful act or omission of any partner acting in the ordinary course of its business,[77] or with the authority of his co-partners,[78] to the same extent as the partner himself,[79] except that it is not liable to any partner for an injury negligently

---

[68] 1890 Act s.5; *Mann v D'Arcy* [1968] 1 W.L.R. 893; *Mercantile Credit Co v Garrod* [1962] 3 All E.R. 1103 (a sale of a car by a partner of firm mainly concerned with lock-up garages and repairs was held valid, although excluded by a term of the partnership agreement).

[69] 1890 Act ss.5, 6. For the signing of partnership documents see the Requirements of Writing (Scotland) Act 1995 s.7(7) and Sch.2 para.2. For authority to sign guarantees see *Bank of Scotland v Henry Butcher & Co* [2003] All E.R. (D) 181 (Feb).

[70] 1890 Act s.15.

[71] 1890 Act s.16. See G. Brough and J. Miller, *Miller on Partnership*, 2nd edn (Edinburgh: W. Green, 1994), p.219; *Campbell v McCreath*, 1975 S.C. 81. As to notice by one partner, in a case of joint tenancy, see *Graham v Stirling*, 1922 S.C. 90; *Walker v Hendry*, 1925 S.C. 855; *Tait v Brown & McRae*, 1997 S.L.T. (Sh. Ct) 63).

[72] 1890 Act s.16; *Zurich GSG Ltd v Gray & Kellas*, 2007 S.L.T. 917.

[73] Illustrative cases are *Bryan v Butters* (1892) 19 R. 490; *Mains & McGlashan v Black* (1895) 22 R. 329; *Ciceri v Hunter* (1904) 12 S.L.T. 293; *Cooke's Circus v Welding* (1894) 21 R. 339.

[74] *Walker v Smith* (1906) 8 F. 619.

[75] *Paterson Bros v Gladstone* (1891) 18 R. 403.

[76] *Fortune v Young*, 1918 S.C. 1.

[77] *ADT v Binder Hamlyn* [1996] B.C.C. 808 QBD. For a discussion of the cases on "the ordinary course of business" see Lord Denning's judgment in *Morris v C W Martin & Sons Ltd* [1966] 1 Q.B. 716 at 724; and Lord Millet in *Lister v Hesley Hall Ltd* [2002] 1 A.C. 215 at 245 and Lord Steyn at 223–224 and 230. See also *Dubai Aluminium Co Ltd v Salaam* [2002] UKHL 48; [2003] 2 A.C. 366 and *McHugh v Kerr* [2003] EWHC 2985 (Ch).

[78] Meaning "control, direction or knowing approval of the action or actions in question": *Kirkintilloch Equitable Co-operative Society v Livingstone*, 1972 S.C. 111 at 122, per Lord Cameron.

[79] *Scarborough Building Society v Howes Percival (A Firm)* [1998] EWCA Civ 407 (March 5, 1998); to act as the secretary of a company is not part of the ordinary business of a firm of law agents, even although the partnership deed provides that any salary thence derived is part of the firm's assets,

done to him by another partner acting on the firm's behalf.[80] The question whether a partner can act as a servant of his firm has been raised but not decided.[81] Each partner is liable jointly and severally.[82] The firm is also liable when one partner, acting within his apparent authority, receives the money or property of a third party and misapplies it, or when a firm, in the course of its business, receives the money or property of a third party, and it is misapplied by a partner.[83] The firm may also be liable on the ground that it has gratuitously profited by the wrongful act of a partner, as when a partner, obtaining money by fraud, applies it in meeting debts due by the firm.[84] Where a partner who is a trustee improperly employs trust property in the business or on the account of the partnership, the other partners are not liable unless they had notice of the breach of trust, but the trust money can be followed and recovered from the firm if still in its possession or control.[85]

45.12 **Liability of partners**—Every partner is liable jointly and severally for all the debts of the firm, and the estate of a deceased partner is also liable,[86] but the debt must be constituted against the firm.[87] As between themselves, a partner who has paid the firm debts is entitled to pro rata relief from the other partners.[88] A partner may be liable to the other partners for loss occasioned in the firm business by his lack of care or skill.[89] A partner who has retired does not cease to be liable for all debts or obligations incurred while he was a partner,[90] and no arrangement between him and the other partners is of any avail against creditors. He may avoid liability by an arrangement between himself and the firm as newly constituted, and the creditor.[91] Such an arrangement may be inferred from a course of dealing between the firm as newly constituted and the creditor,[92] but the decisions establish that the inference is not easy, and that acceptance of interest or part payment from a new firm, or ranking in their bankruptcy, is not sufficient.[93]

45.13 **Liability of retired partner: Notice**—A partner who has retired and has failed to give adequate notice of the fact may be liable on obligations incurred subsequent to his retirement.[94] A partner who has become bankrupt, or the representatives of one who has died, are not in any event liable for obligations subsequently incurred

---

and therefore the firm is not liable for the fraudulent act of a partner in his capacity as secretary: *New Mining Syndicate v Chalmers*, 1912 S.C. 126. Cf. *Kirkintilloch Equitable Coop Society v Livingstone*, 1972 S.C. 111.

[80] *Mair v Wood*, 1948 S.C. 83.

[81] *Fife County Council v Minister of National Insurance*, 1947 S.C. 629.

[82] 1890 Act s.12. For what is meant by "joint and severally liable" see the Law Reform (Miscellaneous Provisions) (Scotland) Act 1940 s.3 and *Farstad Supply AS v Enviroco Ltd and Asco UK Ltd* [2010] UKSC 18; 2010 S.C. (U.K.S.C.) 87; 2010 S.L.T. 994.

[83] 1890 Act s.11.

[84] *New Mining Syndicate v Chalmers*, 1912 S.C. 126.

[85] 1890 Act s.13. See *Walker v Stones* [2001] Q.B. 902; [2001] 2 W.L.R. 623.

[86] 1890 Act s.9.

[87] *Highland Engineering Ltd v Anderson*, 1979 S.L.T. 122.

[88] 1890 Act s.4. See *Primary Healthcare Centres (Broadford) Ltd v Dr Alan William Humphrey* [2010] CSOH 129.

[89] *Blackwood v Robertson*, 1984 S.L.T. (Sh. Ct) 68; *Ross Harper & Murphy v Banks*, 2000 S.L.T. 699. Much depends on the exact wording of the partnership agreement: *Forster v Ferguson & Forster*, 2010 S.L.T. 867.

[90] 1890 Act s.17(2). See *Welsh v Knarston*, 1973 S.L.T. 66.

[91] 1890 Act s.17(3).

[92] 1890 Act s.17(3).

[93] *Morton's Trs v Robertson's J.F.* (1892) 20 R. 72; *Smith v Patrick* (1901) 3 F. (HL) 14.

[94] 1890 Act s.36.

by the firm, and in these cases no notice is required.[95] Similarly, a retired partner who was not known to the person dealing with the firm to be a partner, is not liable for partnership debts contracted after his retirement, and does not have to give notice.[96] This provision includes apparent as well as dormant partners, and operates from the date of the dissolution of the partnership.[97] In other cases the Act provides that a Gazette advertisement is notice to all persons who had no prior dealings with the firm.[98] With regard to persons who have had dealings, a mere Gazette or newspaper advertisement is not sufficient, unless knowledge of it can be brought home to the particular creditor. Intimation by circular, or by an obvious change in the firm name, is required.[99]

Liability of a partner who has retired, but failed to give notice, for obligations subsequently incurred by the firm as re-constituted after his retirement, rests on the principle of holding out or personal bar.[100] It would appear that in Scotland it is a joint and several, not an alternative, liability. This proceeds on the principle that, as the retired partner, by his failure to give notice, has held himself out to be a member of the new firm so far as the creditor is concerned, he must be regarded as if he were such a member.[101] But he has a right of relief against the actual members of the new firm.[102]

Liability of new partner—The Act provides at s.17(1):   **45.14**

> "A person who is admitted as a partner into an existing firm does not thereby become liable to the creditors of the firm for anything done before he became a partner."

Where the whole assets of a going concern are handed over to a new partnership and the business is continued on the same footing as before, the presumption is that the liabilities are taken over with the stock but the presumption may be rebutted if the new partner pays in a large sum as capital and the other partners contribute merely their shares of the going concern.[103]

Effect of change in firm on contracts—The Act does not decide the question   **45.15** whether a change in the personnel of a firm has any effect on continuing contracts which involve the element of *delectus personae*. It is expressly provided that a continuing guarantee or cautionary obligation given either to a firm or to a third person in respect of the transactions of a firm is, in the absence of agreement to the contrary, revoked as to future transactions by any change in the constitution of

---

[95] 1890 Act s.36(3).

[96] 1890 Act s.36(3).

[97] *Tower Cabinet Co v Ingram* [1949] 2 K.B. 397. See also s.4.

[98] 1890 Act s.36(2).

[99] Bell, *Principles*, s.384; 1890 Act s.36(2). In practice any potential liability for the retiring partner is dealt with either by a well drafted partnership agreement or by terms of disengagement for the partner retiring from the firm.

[100] *Black v Girdwood* (1885) 13 R. 243 (in which *Scarf v Jardine* (1882) L.R. 7 App. Cas. 345, to the opposite effect, was discussed and disapproved by a majority of the Second Division: but the question was obiter).

[101] *Black v Girdwood* (1885) 13 R. 243 at 249, per Lord Young.

[102] *Mann v Sinclair* (1879) 6 R. 1078; *Black v Girdwood* (1885) 13 R. 243 at 249, per Lord Young.

[103] *Thomson & Balfour v Boag & Son*, 1936 S.C. 2; *Miller v John Finlay MacLeod & Parker*, 1973 S.C. 172. See also Lord Hodge's decision in *Sim v Howat and MacLaren* [2011] CSOH 115 which comprehensively reviews the Scottish case law on this point.

the firm to which, or of the firm in respect of the transactions of which, the guarantee or obligation was given.[104] Contracts of service are not dissolved by a mere change in the constitution of the firm of employers,[105] except where by the death of one of the partners the partnership necessarily comes to an end.[106] The retirement of one of the partners, or the adoption of a new partner, has no such effect.[107]

45.16   Partnership property—Money or property originally brought into the partnership stock or acquired on account of the firm, or for the purposes and in the course of the partnership business, becomes partnership property, and must be held exclusively for the purposes of the partnership and in accordance with the partnership agreement.[108] Unless the contrary intention appears, property bought with money belonging to the firm is deemed to have been bought on account of the firm.[109] The interest of each partner is a right to a *pro indiviso* share of the firm's assets, with the results: (1) that his interest is moveable in his succession, though the property actually held may be heritable[110]; (2) that the proper diligence to attach a partner's interest is arrestment in the hands of the firm, and not attachment of the particular assets.[111] The mere contract under which a partner agrees to contribute property to the firm does not complete the firm's title, or remove the property, as a separate asset, from the diligence of the partner's creditors; a conveyance, in the manner appropriate to the particular property in question, is required.[112] Partnership property may now be held in the name of the firm.[113]

45.17   Ranking in bankruptcy—In bankruptcy the creditors of the firm rank on the firm's estate to the exclusion of the creditors of an individual partner.[114] Where a creditor ranks on the firm's estate for payment of a firm debt, he need not deduct the estimated value of any claim against the estates of the individual partners,[115] since the liability of the firm is the primary liability. Conversely, when a creditor claims for a firm debt against the estate of one of the partners, he must make a deduction in respect of the liability of the firm. The deduction varies according to whether or not the firm's estate has been sequestrated. Where the estate of the firm has not been sequestrated, the creditor must estimate and deduct the value of the debt due to him from the firm's estate. Where the estate of the firm has been sequestrated, he must estimate and deduct the value of his claim in the firm's

---

[104] 1890 Act s.18, re-enacting s.7 of the Mercantile Law Amendment Act Scotland 1856.

[105] *Campbell v Baird* (1827) 5 S. 335. See now the Employment Rights Act 1996 s.218(1)–(5).

[106] *Hoey v MacEwan & Auld* (1867) 5 M. 814. In practice, most partnership agreements allow for the continuation of the partnership notwithstanding the death of a partner.

[107] *Berlitz Schools v Duchene* (1903) 6 F. 181 at 186, per Lord McLaren. See, however, *Garden, Haig-Scott & Wallace v Prudential Society*, 1927 S.L.T. 393. In any event, the Transfer of Undertaking (Protection of Employment) Regulations 2006 (SI 2006/246) would protect the position of employees under such circumstances.

[108] 1890 Act s.20.

[109] 1890 Act s.21; *Marshall v Marshall*, 2007 Fam. L.R. 48; 2007 G.W.D. 10–188; *Longmuir v Moffat*, 2009 S.C. 329; 2009 G.W.D. 10–166.

[110] 1890 Act s.22; Bell, *Commentaries*, II, 501; *Minto v Kirkpatrick* (1833) 11 S. 632 (*legitim*).

[111] Erskine, III, 3, 24; *Parnell v Walter* (1889) 16 R. 917.

[112] Bell, *Commentaries*, II, 501.

[113] Abolition of Feudal Tenure etc (Scotland) Act 2000 s.70.

[114] H. Goudy, *Bankruptcy*, 4th edn (1914), pp.578–579.

[115] Bell, *Commentaries*, II, 550.

sequestration.[116] If the trustee in sequestration does not accept the creditor's valuation, he may reject the claim.[117]

Fiduciary element in partnership[118]—Partnership is a contract which involves **45.18** fiduciary duties. A partner must be honest in his accounts with his partners and in his dealings with third persons.[119] He must render to a fellow partner or his legal representatives true accounts and full information on all things affecting the firm.[120] If a partner, without the consent of the others, carries on any business of the same nature as, and competing with, that of the firm he must account for and pay over to the firm all profits made in that business.[121] Where a partner has breached the duty to account the firm should raise an action of accounting for all sums obtained in breach of the duty.[122] Fiduciary duties are owed by partners who are leaving the firm: when three partners resigned from a solicitors' partnership, taking a large number of clients' files with them to open a competing firm, they were held to have breached their duty not to damage the interests of the partnership they were leaving.[123] Each partner must also

> "account to the firm for any benefit derived by him without the consent of the other partners from any transaction concerning the partnership, or from any use by him of the partnership property, name, or business connection".[124]

So if a partner supplies goods to the firm without disclosing that they are his, he acts as an agent and must account for any profit on the transactions.[125] A partner must account for benefits derived from information obtained in connection with the firm or in the course of its business,[126] but a third party to whom the information has been passed cannot be prevented from using it.[127] This rule applies also, in the case of a firm dissolved by the death of a partner, to any transactions either by the surviving partners, or by the representatives of the deceased partner, before the affairs of the partnership are completely wound up.[128] Though it is not expressly stated in the Act, the rule also applies to the case where a partner, having the right to do so, dissolves the partnership in order to secure for his private advantage some contract which the firm was about to obtain.[129] The phrase, "transaction concerning the partnership" does not include the purchase, by one of three partners, of the interest of another in the partnership assets, without the knowledge or consent of the third. He is under no obligation to account for his

---

[116] Sch.1 para.6 to the Bankruptcy (Scotland) Act 1985 applied to the submission of claims for a dividend by ss.48(7) and 22(9).

[117] Bankruptcy (Scotland) Act 1985 s.49(2).

[118] *Adam v Newbigging* (1888) 13 App. Cas 308; *Roxburgh Dinardo & Partners' J.F. v Dinardo*, 1993 S.L.T. 16.

[119] *Carmichael v Evans* [1904] 1 Ch. 486.

[120] 1890 Act s.28. *Ferguson v Mackay*, 1985 S.L.T. 94.

[121] 1890 Act s.30; see as illustrations of this section, *Stewart v North* (1893) 20 R. 260; *Pillans Bros v Pillans* (1908) 16 S.L.T. 611; *Trimble v Goldberg* [1906] A.C. 494.

[122] *Smith v Barclay*, 1962 S.C. 1.

[123] *Finlayson v Turnbull (No.1)*, 1997 S.L.T. 613.

[124] 1890 Act s.29(1).

[125] *Kuhlirz v Lambert Bros* (1913) 18 Com. Cas. 217 at 226, per Scrutton J.

[126] *Aas v Benham* [1891] 2 Ch. 244; *Boardman v Phipps* [1967] 2 A.C. 46.

[127] *Roxburgh v Seven Seas Engineering*, 1980 S.L.T. (Notes) 49.

[128] 1890 Act s.29(2).

[129] Erskine, III, 25, 4; Bell, *Commentaries*, II, 522; *Featherstonhaugh v Fenwick* (1810) 17 Ves. 298; *McNiven v Peffers* (1868) 7 M. 181—both cases of leases.

profit to the firm.[130] And where one partner owed a directorship to his connection
with the firm, but the business in which he was a director did not compete with
that of the firm, it was held that there were no grounds on which the other partner
could claim a share of the director's fees.[131] The rights of a person who is not a
partner, but has lent money on profit-sharing terms, are purely contractual, and no
fiduciary duties are owed to him.[132]

45.19   Assignation—As partnership is a contract involving *delectus personae*, no partner,
without the consent of the others, may assign his interest so as to make the assignee
a partner in the firm,[133] except under the provisions of the Limited Partnerships
Act 1907.[134] The interest of a partner is, however, assignable, absolutely or in
security. The assignee has no right to interfere in the administration of the firm, to
require any accounts, or to inspect the partnership books. He had, therefore, it was
held, no right to object to a resolution by which the partners arranged that they
should receive salaries for attending to the partnership business.[135] He is only entitled, while the firm is a going concern, to the share of the profits to which the
cedent has right, and must accept the account of profits to which the partners have
agreed.[136] An assignee has no power to dissolve the firm, but on its dissolution is
entitled to receive the share of the partnership assets to which the cedent is entitled
as between himself and the other partners, and, for the purpose of ascertaining that
share, to an account as from the date of the dissolution.[137]

45.20   Rights of partners *inter se*—The interests and rights of partners may be regulated by an agreement, express or implied. The Act provides (s.19):

> "The mutual rights and duties of partners, whether ascertained by agreement
> or defined by this Act, may be varied by the consent of all the partners, and
> such consent may be either express or inferred from a course of dealing".

But it is conceived that if the partnership agreement were in writing, a merely oral
consent to alter its terms would not be binding, unless it had been acted upon.[138]
In the absence of any agreement to the contrary, the undernoted rules are provided
by s.24 as regulating the relations of partners.[139]

---

[130] *Cassels v Stewart* (1881) 8 R. (HL) 1.
[131] *Aas v Benham* [1891] 2 Ch. 244.
[132] *Teacher v Calder* (1899) 1 F. (HL) 39.
[133] 1890 Act s.31(1).
[134] Limited Partnership Act 1907 s.6(5)(b).
[135] *Re Garwood's Trusts* [1903] 1 Ch. 236.
[136] 1890 Act s.31(1).
[137] 1890 Act s.31(2).
[138] *Barr's Trs v Barr & Shearer* (1886) 13 R. 1055; *Starrett v Pia*, 1968 S.L.T. (Notes) 28.
[139] (1) All the partners are entitled to share equally in the capital and profits of the business, and
must contribute equally towards the losses, whether of capital or otherwise, sustained by the firm
(*Garner v Murray* [1904] 1 Ch. 57; the rule has been held to apply even where there is a substantial difference between the amount of capital contributed by partners, see *Popat v Shanchhatra*
[1997] 1 W.L.R. 1367).
(2) The firm must indemnify every partner in respect of payments made and personal liabilities
incurred by him:
    (a) in the ordinary and proper conduct of the business of the firm; or
    (b) in or about anything necessarily done for the preservation of the business or property of the
firm (*Stroyan v Milroy*, 1910 S.C. 174).

Expulsion of partner—No majority can expel a partner, unless power to do so is   **45.21**
conferred by express agreement.[140] Clauses in a deed of partnership giving power
to expel a partner are construed strictly, and the court has power, on English
authority, to refuse to give effect to them if satisfied that the expulsion is not in the
interests of the firm but for some private reasons.[141] A power of expulsion can
continue in a partnership at will.[142]

Retirement of partner—Where the partnership is at will, i.e. not for any fixed   **45.22**
term, any partner may determine the partnership by giving notice to all the other
partners of his intention to do so.[143] In the absence of agreement to the contrary
the notice may take immediate effect. There is nothing in the Act to preclude a
partner from retiring without dissolving the firm, and its competency is recognised at common law, subject to the condition that a provision to that effect has
been made in the partnership deed, or that all the partners consent.[144]

Tacit relocation—Where a partnership is for a fixed term, which has expired, and   **45.23**
the business is carried on without any express agreement by such of the partners
as habitually acted in the affairs of the firm, the law will infer continuance of the
relationship as a partnership at will. The terms of the partnership which has
expired will prevail, in so far as is consistent with a partnership at will.[145] In order
that a partnership may be continued by tacit relocation there must be at least two
partners surviving at the expiry of the fixed date. It is not enough that one surviving
partner continues the business.[146] From the same case it appears that the business
must be carried on for some period long enough to justify the inference that
continuance was intended; no inference can be drawn from acts done on a single
day. A right of pre-emption conferred on one of the partners and exercisable at the
expiry of a fixed period has been held to survive as a condition of a subsequent
partnership by tacit relocation[147]; but a clause under which certain rights depended
on notice being given three months before the expiry of the partnership was held

---

(3) A partner making, for the purpose of the partnership, any actual payment or advance beyond
the amount of capital which he has agreed to subscribe, is entitled to interest at the rate of 5 per
cent per annum from the date of the payment or advance.
(4) A partner is not entitled, before the ascertainment of profits, to interest on the capital
subscribed by him.
(5) Every partner may take part in the management of the partnership business.
(6) No partner shall be entitled to remuneration for acting in the partnership business (*Pender
v Henderson* (1864) 2 M. 1428).
(7) No person may be introduced as a partner without the consent of all existing partners.
(8) Any difference arising as to ordinary matters connected with the partnership business may
be decided by a majority of the partners, but no change may be made in the nature of the partnership business without the consent of all existing partners.
(9) The partnership books are to be kept at the place of business of the partnership (or the principal place, if there is more than one), and every partner may, when he thinks fit, have access to
and inspect and copy any of them. (As to inspection by an accountant or solicitor, see *Cameron
v McMurray* (1855) 17 D. 1142; *Bevan v Webb* [1910] 1 Ch. 724).
[140] 1890 Act s.25.
[141] *Blisset v Daniel* (1853) 10 Hare 493; *Green v Howell* [1910] 1 Ch. 495; cf. *Re Westbourne
Galleries* [1973] A.C. 360 at 380, per Lord Wilberforce.
[142] *Walters v Bingham* [1988] F.T.L.R. 260 at 268.
[143] 1890 Act s.26.
[144] Bell, *Commentaries*, II, 522 and see s.32.
[145] 1890 Act s.27.
[146] *Wallace v Wallace's Trs* (1906) 8 F. 558.
[147] *McGown v Henderson*, 1914 S.C. 839.

inconsistent with a partnership at will, in respect that there was no time from which the three months could be computed.[148]

45.24 Rescission for fraud: Misrepresentation—Like other contracts, partnership may be rescinded on the ground that it was induced by fraud or misrepresentation.[149] As it is a contract uberrimae fidei (of utmost good faith), proof of the concealment of material facts will justify rescission,[150] and will, where fraud or negligence is proved, found a claim for damages.[151] While no claim of damages can be founded on an innocent and non-negligent misrepresentation, the Act provides at s.41 that the party entitled to rescind shall have the following rights, whether fraud be proved or not: (a) to a lien on, or right of retention of, the surplus of the partnership assets, after satisfying the partnership liabilities, for any sum of money paid for the purchase of a share in the partnership and for any capital contributed; (b) to stand in the place of the creditors of the firm for any payments made by him in respect of the partnership liabilities; (c) to be indemnified by the person guilty of the fraud or making the representation against all the debts and liabilities of the firm.[152] Where a partner had systematically embezzled clients' funds, resulting in his conviction and imprisonment, it was held that his breach of the terms of the partnership agreement entirely justified the partnership's retention of sums, otherwise payable to him by way of a pension, in order to cover the loss occasioned to the partnership by his behaviour.[153]

45.25 Dissolution of partnership—The Act provides at s.32:

"Subject to any agreement between the partners,[154] a partnership is dissolved—

(a) if entered into for a fixed term,[155] by the expiration of that term[156];
(b) if entered into for a single adventure or undertaking, by the termination of that adventure or undertaking[157];
(c) if entered into for an undefined time,[158] by any partner giving notice[159] to the other or others of his intention to dissolve the partnership.

In the last-mentioned case the partnership is dissolved as from the date mentioned in the notice as the date of dissolution, or, if no date is so mentioned, as from the date of the communication of the notice."

It has been held that s.32(c) does not apply to a partnership at will arising after the expiry of a fixed term.[160] A partnership is also dissolved by agreement, whether express or to be inferred from the partners' actings,[161] in the absence of

---

[148] *Neilson v Mossend Iron Co* (1886) 13 R. (HL) 50.

[149] See paras 7.13–7.18 and 7.33–7.35, above.

[150] *Ferguson v Wilson* (1904) 6 F. 779.

[151] Law Reform (Miscellaneous Provisions) (Scotland) Act 1985 s.10.

[152] The section is mainly founded on *Adam v Newbigging* (1888) L.R. 13 App. Cas. 308.

[153] *Forster v Ferguson & Forster*, 2010 S.L.T. 867.

[154] For a case where a contractual right to dissolve could not be exercised by partners in breach of the partnership contract, see *Hunter v Wylie*, 1993 S.L.T. 1091.

[155] *Walters v Bingham* [1988] 1 F.T.L.R. 260 at 266.

[156] See, as to continuance by tacit relocation, para.45.23, above.

[157] See *Gracie v Prentice* (1904) 42 S.L.R. 9; *Millar v Strathclyde RC*, 1988 S.L.T. (Lands Tr.) 9.

[158] Such a partnership is known as a "partnership at will".

[159] For the effect of bad faith see *Walters v Bingham* [1988] 1 F.T.L.R. 260 at 267.

[160] *Maillie v Swanney*, 2000 S.L.T. 464.

[161] *Jassal's Exx v Jassal's Trs*, 1988 S.L.T. 757 (not reclaimed).

any agreement to the contrary, by the death or bankruptcy of any partner[162] and, irrespective of agreement, by the happening of any event which makes it unlawful for the business of the firm to be carried on or for the members of the firm to carry it on in partnership.[163] So where, on the declaration of war, one of the partners became an alien enemy, it was held that, as partnership with an alien enemy was illegal, the result was necessarily the instant dissolution of the firm.[164]

Dissolution by court—Under s.35 a partnership may be dissolved by the court,[165] **45.26** on application by a partner, on the following grounds: (a) that a partner is of permanently unsound mind; (b) that a partner, other than the partner suing, is permanently incapable of performing his part under the partnership contract; (c) that a partner, other than the partner suing, has been guilty of such conduct as, regard being had to the nature of the business, is calculated prejudicially to affect the carrying on of the business[166]; (d) where a partner, other than the partner suing, wilfully or persistently commits a breach of the partnership agreement, or otherwise so conducts himself in matters relating to the partnership business that it is not reasonably practicable for the other partners to carry on the business in partnership with him[167]; (e) when the business of the partnership can be carried on only at a loss; (f) whenever, in any case, circumstances have arisen which render it just and equitable that the partnership be dissolved.[168]

Effects of dissolution—On dissolution the general authority of each partner to **45.27** bind the firm is determined. But each partner (unless he is bankrupt) retains authority to bind the firm, in so far as may be necessary to wind up the affairs of the partnership, and to complete transactions begun but unfinished at the date of dissolution.[169] So where trust money was lodged with a bank on consignation receipt, payable to a firm of law agents, it was held that the bank was justified in accepting the signature of the firm name by one of the partners, some years after the firm had been dissolved, on the ground that the uplifting of the money was the completion of a transaction left unfinished at the date of the dissolution of the partnership.[170]

On dissolution, the winding up of the partnership affairs is primarily with the surviving partner or partners. Any partner may apply to the court to wind up the business and affairs of the firm,[171] but the court will not readily, or merely on

---

[162] 1890 Act s.33; *William S. Gordon & Co v Mrs Mary Thomson Partnership*, 1985 S.L.T. 122. In practice most partnership agreements provide for the continuity of the partnership after the death or bankruptcy of a partner.

[163] 1890 Act s.34; *Hudgell Yeates & Co v Watson* [1978] Q.B. 451.

[164] *Hugh Stevenson & Sons v Cartonnagen-Industrie* [1918] A.C. 239.

[165] For the scope of arbitration, see *Roxburgh v Dinardo*, 1981 S.L.T. 291.

[166] e.g. a conviction for dishonesty, though not a matter affecting the firm, *Carmichael v Evans* [1904] 1 Ch. 486.

[167] *Mullins v Laughton* [2003] Ch.250; [2003] W.L.R. 1006.

[168] As to the construction of "just and equitable", in similar company cases, see *Elder v Elder & Watson*, 1952 S.C. 49; *Re Westbourne Galleries* [1973] A.C. 360 and para.46.51, below.

[169] 1890 Act s.38. See *Welsh v Knarston*, 1973 S.L.T. 66. See also *Inland Revenue v Graham's Trs*, 1971 S.C. (HL) 1; *Jardine-Paterson v Fraser*, 1974 S.L.T. 93; *Lujo Properties Ltd v Green*, 1997 S.L.T. 225; *Moray Estates Development Co v Butler*, 1999 S.L.T. 1338; *Duncan v MFV Marigold PD 145*, 2006 S.L.T. 975.

[170] *Dickson v National Bank of Scotland*, 1917 S.C. (HL) 50.

[171] See 1890 Act s.39; but where the appointment of a judicial factor is sought, this is only available from the Court of Session, not from the sheriff court: *Pollock v Campbell*, 1962 S.L.T. (Sh. Ct) 89.

averments that differences have arisen between the partners, accede to the application by one partner for the appointment of a judicial factor.[172]

Merely because the partnership has been dissolved does not necessarily mean the partners are no longer responsible for obligations entered into before the dissolution. Following the dissolution of a partnership occupying rented premises, the landlord was still entitled to be paid the rent by the partners personally for the unexpired term of the lease.[173]

If a premium has been paid for entering into a partnership for a fixed term, and the partnership has been dissolved before the expiration of that term otherwise than by the death of a partner (e.g. by supervening illegality) the court may order repayment of the whole or part of the premium. This does not apply to the case where the dissolution is due wholly or chiefly to the misconduct of the partner who paid the premium, or where the firm is dissolved by an agreement containing no provision for the return of the premium.[174]

45.28 Carrying on business after dissolution—When any member of a firm has died or ceased to be a partner, and the other partners carry on the business of the firm with its capital or assets without any final settlement of accounts, then, unless there is an agreement to the contrary, or an option to purchase the share of the deceased or outgoing partner has been exercised,[175] he or his estate has the option of claiming such share of the profits made after the dissolution as the court may find to be attributable to the use of his share of the partnership assets, or 5 per cent interest on the amount of his share of the partnership assets.[176] So where a partnership was dissolved on the declaration of war on the ground that one partner had become an alien enemy, and the other partners had carried on the business, it was held that a share of the profits, so far as attributable to the use of the enemy partner's share of the assets, must be set aside for him, and would become payable on the conclusion of peace.[177]

45.29 Settling accounts—In the absence of any agreement to the contrary the following rules[178] hold in settling accounts on the dissolution of a partnership:

(a) Losses, including losses and deficiencies of capital, shall be paid first out of profits, next out of capital, and lastly, if necessary, by the partners individually in the proportion in which they were entitled to share profits.

(b) The assets[179] of the firm, including the sums, if any, contributed by the partners to make up losses or deficiencies of capital, shall be applied in the following manner and order:

---

[172] *Schulze v Gow* (1877) 4 R. 928; *Elliott v Charles W Cassils & Co* (1907) 15 S.L.T. 190; *Allan v Gronmayer* (1891) 18 R. 784. A judicial factor was appointed in *Carabine v Carabine*, 1949 S.C. 521, and in *McCulloch v McCulloch*, 1953 S.C. 189, where observations were made on the duties of the factors.

[173] *Lujo Properties Ltd v Green*, 1997 S.L.T. 225.

[174] 1890 Act s.40.

[175] 1890 Act s.42(2).

[176] 1890 Act s.42(1). See also *Hopper and Anr. V Hopper*, 2008 CA 12 Dec 2008; *Purewall v Purewall*, 2010 S.L.T. 120

[177] *Hugh Stevenson & Sons v Cartonnagen-Industrie* [1918] A.C. 239.

[178] 1890 Act s.44. *Duncan v MFV Marigold PD 145*, 2006 S.L.T. 975. For interest see *Roxburgh Dinardo & Partners' J.F. v Dinardo*, 1993 S.L.T. 16.

[179] For the distinction between a firm's assets and its capital, see *Noble v Noble*, 1983 S.L.T. 339 (Appendix), and *Thom's Exx v Russel & Aitken*, 1983 S.L.T. 335.

1. In paying the debts and liabilities of the firm to persons who are not partners therein.
2. In paying to each partner rateably what is due from the firm to him for advances as distinguished from capital.
3. In paying to each partner rateably what is due from the firm to him in respect of capital.[180]
4. The ultimate residue[181] if any, shall be divided among the partners in the proportion in which profits are divisible. In the absence of agreement to the contrary, where rights in capital fall to be determined by reference to accounts or balance sheets, assets should be entered at their fair market value.[182]

II: LIMITED PARTNERSHIPS

Limited Partnerships Act 1907—This Act[183] makes provision for a partnership **45.30** with a combination of limited and unlimited liability. A limited partnership requires the existence of one or more partners, called general partners, who run the business and are responsible for all debts, and one or more limited partners (who may be corporate bodies[184]), who are inactive in the business and are liable only to the extent of the amount they have contributed to the firm.[185] To secure this limitation of liability, registration with the Registrar of Companies is essential.[186] An application for registration must state the firm name, the general nature and principal place of business, the full name of each partner, the terms, if any, of the partnership, and the date of commencement, a statement that the partnership is limited and which are the limited partners, and the sum contributed by each limited partner and how it was contributed.[187] Any change in these particulars must, under penalties exigible from the general partners, also be registered.[188] There is no provision for de-registering limited partnerships.[189]

---

[180] *Garner v Murray* [1904] 1 Ch. 57.

[181] *Rowella Pty Ltd v Abfam Nominees Pty Ltd* (1989) 168 C.L.R. 301, H.Ct. Aust.

[182] *Noble v Noble*, 1983 S.L.T. 339 (Appendix); *Shaw v Shaw*, 1968 S.L.T. (Notes) 94; *Clark v Watson*, 1982 S.L.T. 450; *Thom's Exx*, 1983 S.L.T. 335; *Wilson v Dunbar*, 1988 S.L.T. 93. Where, as in calculating remuneration, adjustment to fair market value would cause injustice, the general rule should not be applied: *Lindsay v High* Unreported May 9, 1984 OH (decision of Lord Davidson). There is no presumption that the rule applies in the context of family partnerships; *White v Minnis* [2001] Ch.393.

[183] See, as to the nature of a limited partnership, *Re Barnard* [1932] 1 Ch. 269. See also, generally, Brough and Miller, *Miller on Partnership* (1994), Ch.XIV and R. Banks, *Lindley and Banks on Partnership*, 19th edn (London: Sweet and Maxwell, 2010), Pt 6.

[184] Limited Partnerships Act 1907 s.4(4). Unhelpfully, this states that a body corporate may be a limited partner, but does not state that a body corporate may also be a general partner. However, Companies House is willing to register limited companies as general partners, provided no body corporate is both a limited partner and a general partner in the same limited partnership. For a review of the Act, see the Law Commission and the Scottish Law Commission *Joint Report on Partnership Law*.

[185] Limited Partnerships Act 1907 s.4(2).

[186] Limited Partnerships Act 1907 s.5. The Registrar must keep an index of the names of limited partnerships: Companies Act 2006 s.1061.

[187] Limited Partnerships Act 1907 s.8. Use form LP5 at Companies House.

[188] Limited Partnerships Act 1907 s.9. Use form LP6. This must be sent in within seven days of the change.

[189] Companies House will accept a form LP6 indicating the limited partnership's dissolution but the limited partnership will still remain on the register.

A limited partner has no right to withdraw any portion of the capital he has contributed, and if he does so remains liable for the full amount of the original sum. He may inspect the books but cannot bind the firm, and is not entitled to intervene in the management of the business. Should he do so he incurs liability for all debts incurred during the period while he was intervening.[190]

The main distinctions between a limited partnership and an ordinary partnership are as follows: the death or bankruptcy of a limited partner does not dissolve the firm; his insanity is not a ground for an application to the court for dissolution; only the general partner can wind up the affairs of the firm on its dissolution, unless the court orders otherwise.[191] But there may be circumstances in which a limited partner will have to apply to the court to wind up the affairs of the firm, as for instance where the only general partner in the firm dies.[192] In the absence of any agreement to the contrary, the death or bankruptcy of a general partner will dissolve the partnership as to all the partners.[193] Applications for winding up should be made either by means of sequestration under the Bankruptcy (Scotland) Act 1985[194] or by the appointment of a judicial factor.[195]

The relationship between general and limited partners may be settled by their contract, express or implied. In the absence of any such contract the general partners may decide all ordinary matters of business, and may introduce a new partner without the limited partner's consent. A limited partner is not entitled to dissolve the firm by notice.[196] A limited partner may, with the consent of the general partners, assign his share, when the assignee becomes a limited partner with all the rights of the assigner. Notice of the assignation must be made in the Gazette.[197] A limited partnership is not obliged to send in its accounts to the Register of Companies. A limited partnership may be sequestrated in the same manner as a partnership under the Bankruptcy (Scotland) Act 1985.[198] A particular use of limited partnerships recently is to take account of the separate legal personality of a limited partnership in Scotland, something not available in England. This means that it can be an intermediate holding entity in a group for tax purposes, it can be a member at Lloyds, and it can be the main fund vehicle for a venture capital fund investing in a new business.

III: LIMITED LIABILITY PARTNERSHIPS

45.31 **Limited Liability Partnerships Act 2000**—This legislation, in force from April 6, 2001, provides for the creation of a body corporate with separate legal persona and unlimited capacity, in which the members have liability for its debts only to the extent of their financial interests in it, subject to an additional liability to contribute to its assets on a winding up.[199] The general law relating to partnerships

---

[190] Limited Partnerships Act 1907 s.6(1).

[191] Limited Partnerships Act 1907 s.6(2) and (3).

[192] See Banks, *Lindley and Banks on Partnership* (2010), pp.767–768.

[193] Brough and Miller, *Miller on Partnership* (1994), p.623.

[194] Limited Partnerships Act 1907 s.6(1) and (7); cf. *Royal Bank of Scotland v J. & J. Messenger*, 1991 S.L.T. 492.

[195] cf. *Muirhead v Borland*, 1925 S.C. 474.

[196] Limited Partnerships Act 1907 s.6(5)(e).

[197] Limited Partnerships Act 1907 ss.6(5)(b) and 10.

[198] Bankruptcy (Scotland) Act 1985 s.6(1)(d).

[199] Limited Liability Partnerships Act 2000 (the "2000 Act") s.1. See also the Limited Liability Partnerships Regulations 2001 (SI 2001/1090) and the Limited Liability Partnership (Scotland) Regulations 2001 (SI 2001/128).

does not apply to these statutorily created entities.[200] A limited liability partnership ("LLP") is formed by the subscription, followed by delivery to the Registrar of Companies, of an incorporation document.[201] The document must be subscribed by two or more persons associated for carrying on a lawful business with a view to profit, and a statement by either a solicitor involved in the formation or one of the subscribers, confirming that the subscription requirements have been complied with, must also be registered.[202] Where these requirements have been met, the registrar has a duty to register the LLP and issue a certificate of incorporation.[203] The name of an LLP must end with the expression "limited liability partnership" or the abbreviation "llp" or "LLP", which expression or abbreviation cannot appear in the name other than at the end.[204] Names already used by a registered company or another limited liability partnership are prohibited, and any change of name must be registered.[205]

While the initial members of an LLP are those who subscribed the incorporation document, any person can become a member or cease to be a member thereafter by agreement with the existing members.[206] A member is not an employee of the LLP unless, if it were a partnership, he would be regarded as such.[207] The rights and duties of the members of an LLP inter se and as between the members and the LLP may be governed by agreement (including a pre-incorporation agreement) between the members, or in the absence of agreement, by regulations.[208] A member of an LLP may be a natural person or a body corporate. A body corporate need not be registered in the United Kingdom. Only the member's service address is disclosed to the public although the member's residential address still needs to be disclosed to the Registrar of Companies.

Section 6 of the Act provides that every member of an LLP is an agent thereof, but that an LLP is not bound by the actions of a member who has no authority to act for the LLP and provided the person dealing with him knows that he has no such authority or does not know or believe him to be a member of the LLP. The agency of a member survives the termination of his membership until notice is given.[209]

There is provision in s.8 for designated members who will generally undertake the formal administrative responsibilities of the LLP. Regulations may impose specific duties that fall to be carried out by designated members.[210] The number of designated members may not fall below two and on appropriate notice being

---

[200] 2000 Act s.1(5). However, much company law does apply. See s.15 and fn.208.

[201] 2000 Act s.2. Use form LLIN01 available from Companies House.

[202] 2000 Act s.2(3) renders the making of a false statement in this connection a criminal offence.

[203] 2000 Act s.3.

[204] 2000 Act s.1(6), Sch. Pt 1 para.2.

[205] See 2000 Act Sch. Pt 1 paras 3–8 for the detailed provisions on use and change of name of limited liability partnerships.

[206] 2000 Act s.4(1)–(3). Section 4(3) makes clear that membership also ceases by death or dissolution. Section 7 also identifies sequestration, the granting of a trust deed for the benefit of creditors and assignation of an interest as events that terminate a member's participation in an LLP.

[207] 2000 Act s.4(4).

[208] 2000 Act ss.5 and 15(c) and the Limited Liability Partnerships Regulations 2001 (SI 2001/1090) regs 7 and 8.

[209] 2000 Act s.6(3). For liability of the LLP to third parties arising from the wrongful acts or omissions of a member, see s.6(4).

[210] SI 2000/1090. Regulation 4 and Schs 1 and 2 thereof apply, with modifications, a large number of specified provisions of the Companies Act 1985 and of the provisions of the Company Directors Disqualification Act 1986 to LLPs. Numerous duties, including the approval and signing of accounts, are to be undertaken on behalf of members by a designated member.

given to the registrar, all of the members of an LLP may be designated members.[211] Notification of changes to the membership of an LLP must be delivered to the registrar: within 14 days where a person ceases to be a member or designated member and within 28 days for a change to a member's name or address.[212]

A trade, profession or business carried on by an LLP with a view to profit is to be treated for the purposes of the Taxes Acts as carried on in partnership by its members and the property of an LLP is thus to be treated for tax purposes as partnership property.[213]

LLPs must publish their accounts in the same manner as companies, but the capital maintenance rules do not apply to LLPs as there is no share capital. LLPs may grant floating charges.[214] LLPs are not obliged to have general meetings of their members, but may do so if they wish. LLPs must file an annual return in the same manner as registered companies.[215]

The winding up of a LLP is regulated by the Insolvency Act 1986, and there are special provisions applicable where the members have been making excessive withdrawals in the period of two years before the outset of insolvency.[216]

FURTHER READING

Bennet, D., *Introduction to the Law of Partnership in Scotland* (Edinburgh: W. Green, 1995).

Banks, R., *Lindley and Banks on Partnership*, 19th edn (London: Sweet and Maxwell, 2010).

Brough and Miller, *Miller on Partnership in Scotland*, 2nd edn (Edinburgh: W. Green, 1994).

Hardy Ivamy, E.R., *Underhill, Partnership*, 12th edn (London: Butterworths, 1986).

Law Commission and Scottish Law Commission, *Joint Report on Partnership Law* (HMSO, 2003), Scot. Law Com. No.192, Law Com. No.283.

Morse, G., *Partnership Law*, 7th edn (Oxford: Oxford University Press, 2010).

Scottish Law Commission, *Report on the Criminal Liability of Partnerships* (HMSO, 2011), Scot. Law Com. No.224.

---

[211] 2000 Act s.8(4).

[212] 2000 Act s.9(1). Use form LL CH01 or 02 if a corporate member.

[213] Income and Corporation Taxes Act 1988 s.118Z(A–D), added by the Limited Liability Partnerships Act 2000 s.10(1); Taxation of Chargeable Gains Act 1992 ss.59A, 156A, added by the 2000 Act s.10(3). See also Inheritance Tax Act 1984 s.267A, added by the 2000 Act s.11.

[214] These need to be registered (as do fixed charges) using form LL MG01s.

[215] Use form LL AR01.

[216] See Insolvency Act 1986 s.214A.

CHAPTER 46

COMPANY LAW

The purpose of incorporation—Originally the word "company", in commercial **46.01** terms, was a group of merchants or businessmen working together in a common trade or profession. As indicated in the next paragraph, over time it became possible for some companies to obtain the benefit of incorporation, usually by means of a royal charter. Incorporation gave the company an existence in its own right, separate from those who work for it, manage it, or own it. The benefit of its own legal identity was, and still is, that the company was able to undertake in its own name and at its own risk commercial adventures that might be too financially uncertain for any investor, or even group of investors, to take on personally. This means that a company is more likely to embark on speculative enterprises than individual investors would; and thus companies promote commerce. Provided the company is a company limited by shares, investors' liability to the company is limited to the amount the investors have undertaken to pay to the company for their shares, and once each share has been paid up to its nominal value, plus any premium if required, there is no further sum payable to the company by the investors[1] even if the company later becomes insolvent and cannot pay its debts.[2] The effect of incorporation is therefore that the risk of dealing with the company is transferred away from the investors to the creditors, and for this reason it is necessary to have mechanisms to protect creditors' interests. However, investors also need protection, not so much from creditors, but from directors who may be tempted to exploit their informational advantage in the management of the company to their own, rather than the investors' benefit. Much of the legislation applicable to companies therefore addresses these two points.

The legislation applicable to companies—It is possible, but rare nowadays, for **46.02** companies to be incorporated by charter or letters patent from the Crown or by a Private Act of Parliament. Certain older enterprises, including some Scottish banks, were incorporated in this manner. However, the usual method of incorporation nowadays is by registration under the principal legislation applicable to companies, the Companies Act 2006 ("CA 2006"). Other important statutes applicable to companies are the Company Directors Disqualification Act 1986 ("CDDA") and the Financial Services and Markets Act 2000. CA 2006 remains the principal statute dealing with the establishment, financing, management and general administration of companies. Winding up, receivership, administration and voluntary arrangements are dealt with in the Insolvency Act, 1986 ("IA 1986") as amended by the Enterprise Act 2002. Insider dealing is dealt with in Pt V of the Criminal Justice Act 1993. Much UK company law is derived from

---

[1] Unless they have guaranteed the company's debts.

[2] Even if the company alters its articles to this effect, the shareholders cannot be made to pay any more (Companies Act 2006 ("CA 2006") s.25).

various EU directives as part of a continuing process of harmonising company law throughout the European Union.

46.03 Company distinct from members—A company, once incorporated,[3] is a legal personality distinct from its shareholders.[4] In the landmark case *of Salomon v A. Salomon & Co Ltd*,[5] the then requirements for the incorporation of A. Salomon & Co Ltd were fully complied with. Salomon, who was the managing director and principal shareholder, in his personal capacity held debentures granted by the company in his favour. It was held, in liquidation, that despite Salomon's position and shareholding, there were no grounds on which Salomon could be made personally liable for the trade debts of the company and that he was fully entitled to claim in liquidation on his debentures. Similarly, where an individual was controlling shareholder and governing director of a company, he was not precluded from having a contractual relationship, as employee, with that company: it was a logical consequence of Salomon's case that one person might function in the dual capacities of agent (i.e. a director) and employee of the company.[6] On the same principle, no shareholder has an insurable interest in any asset belonging to the company[7] and the owner of shop premises which were acquired compulsorily by a local authority and which were occupied not by him but by a company of which he was the principal shareholder was held not to be personally entitled to compensation for disturbance.[8] Where, for example, a firm of solicitors had advised the liquidator of a company, it was the liquidator as agent for the company and not its individual members who had a right to challenge the firm's account for professional fees.[9]

By a legal metaphor, the imaginary barrier that separates the company from its members, or its directors, is known as the corporate veil. Since the whole point of company law is that the company is not the same as its members or directors, the courts are in general reluctant to lift or pierce the veil, and thus make the members or directors liable for the company's debts. However, under statute the veil will on occasion be lifted in order to make the members[10] or the directors[11] or occasionally anyone else dealing with the company[12] liable for the company's debts. Sometimes the veil is lifted in cases where the control of the company is in issue, as may arise in connection with the taxation of companies[13] or under the law relating to trading with the enemy,[14] or where the device of incorporation has been used for some illegal or improper purpose.[15] This is certainly the case where fraud

---

[3] Prior to incorporation a company has no legal existence: see *F.J.Neale (Glasgow) v Vickery*, 1973 S.L.T. (Sh. Ct) 88.

[4] A subsequent change of name does not affect this: *Vic Spence Associates v Balchin*, 1990 S.L.T. 10.

[5] *Salomon v A. Salomon & Co Ltd* (1887) A.C. 22

[6] *Lee v Lee's Air Farming* [1961] A.C. 12.

[7] *Macaura v Northern Insurance Co* [1925] A.C. 619; *Cowan v Jeffrey Associates*, 1998 S.C. 496.

[8] *Woolfson v Strathclyde Regional Council*, 1978 S.C. (HL) 90.

[9] *Davidson & Syme, W.S. v Kaye*, 1970 S.L.T. (Notes) 65.

[10] For example, Insolvency Act 1986 ("IA 1986") ss.74, 213. For the latter see *Morris v Banque Arabe Internationale d'Investissement SA (No.2)* [2002] B.C.C. 407.

[11] For example, the failure by the directors of a public company to obtain a trading certificate before the company trades or borrows (CA 2006 s.767).

[12] IA 1986 s.213; *Morris v Bank of India* [2003] B.C.C. 735; 2 [2004] B.C.L.C. 236.

[13] *S. Berendsen v I.R.C.* [1958] Ch.1; *Re Nadler Enterprises Ltd* [1981] 1 W.L.R. 23; *R. v Bassam Omar* [2005] 1 Cr. App. R. (S.) 86.

[14] *Continental Tyre Co v Daimler* [1916] 2 A.C. 307.

[15] *Trustor A.B. v Smallbone* [2001] 3 All E.R. 987; *Kensington International Ltd v Congo* [2006] 2 B.C.L.C. 296.

is involved. Where a director, through his company, instructed the false dating of a bill of lading, he was treated as a joint tortfeasor of the fraud, along with his company, and therefore became personally liable.[16] The general rule, however, is that the courts are slow to lift the veil, even when there is much to suggest that the benefits of incorporation have been abused,[17] and will only do so where special circumstances exist indicating that the company is a mere "façade concealing the true facts".[18] Victims of negligent acts perpetrated by the company may therefore have difficulty obtaining redress, since there may be no right of action against either the members[19] or the directors[20] while the company itself may not be worth suing. A holding company is not liable for the debts of its subsidiaries.[21]

As a general rule, a company cannot be guilty of a criminal offence which it, unlike its human agents, is incapable of committing as an entity. It cannot, for example, be charged with perjury or, while the crime existed, shameless indecency, or an offence for which imprisonment is the only penalty.[22] Although it was formerly held incompetent to charge a company with a common law offence involving mens rea,[23] the Corporate Manslaughter and Corporate Homicide Act 2007 permits a company to be convicted of corporate homicide where the ways in which the company's affairs are managed or organised cause a person's death and amount to a gross breach of a duty of care owed by the company to the victim.[24] The duty of care is the duty of care owed by the company to the victim under the law of negligence.[25] A "gross" breach of that duty is where the conduct amounting to the breach falls far below what can reasonably be expected of the organization in the circumstances.[26] The company will be liable if the way in which its activities are managed or organized by its senior management is a substantial element in the breach.[27] It is for the judge to decide whether there has been a breach of the duty of care, but for the jury to decide if it has been a "gross" breach of that duty.[28] A court may make a remedial order requiring the company to remedy the breach and any other matter or defect in the organisation's policies.[29] On conviction, the company may be fined.[30]

---

[16] *Standard Chartered Bank v Pakistan National Shipping Corporation (No.2)* [2002] 3 W.L.R. 1547; *Daido Asia Japan Co Ltd v Rothen* [2002] B.C.C. 589.

[17] *Yukong Line Ltd v Rendsburg Investment Corporation of Liberia* [1998] 2 B.C.L.C. 485.

[18] *Woolfson v Strathclyde R.C.*, 1978 S.C. (HL) 90 at 95, per Lord Keith of Kinkel; *Glasgow District Council v Hamlet Textiles Ltd*, 1986 S.L.T. 415.

[19] *Adams v Cape Industries Plc* [1990] Ch.433. In this case a holding company was not liable for the torts of its subsidiary.

[20] *Williams v Natural Life Health Foods Ltd* [1998] 1 W.L.R. 830.

[21] per Lord Templeton in *Re Southard & Co Ltd* [1979] 3 All E.R. 556 and 565; [1979] 1 W.L.R. 1198 at 1208.

[22] *R. v I.C.R. Haulage Ltd* [1944] K.B. 551; *D.P.P. v Kent and Sussex Contractors Ltd* [1944] K.B. 146; *Dean v John Menzies (Holdings) Ltd*, 1981 J.C. 23 and 31, per Lord Cameron; *Richmond-on-Thames B.C. v Pinn & Wheeler Ltd* [1989] R.T.R. 354. The crime of shameless indecency was abolished in *Webster v Dominick*, 2005 J.C. 65; 2003 S.L.T. 975; 2003 S.C.L.R. 525.

[23] *Transco Plc v HM Advocate (No.1)*, 2004 J.C. 29.

[24] Corporate Manslaughter and Corporate Homicide Act 2007 s.1(1)(a); *HSE v Cotswold Geotechnical (Holdings) Ltd* February 17, 2011 Winchester Crown Court; [2011] EWCA Crim 1337; [2012] 1 Cr. App. R. (S.) 26;

[25] Corporate Manslaughter and Corporate Homicide Act 2007 s.2.

[26] Corporate Manslaughter and Corporate Homicide Act 2007 s.1(4)(b).

[27] Corporate Manslaughter and Corporate Homicide Act 2007 s.1(3).

[28] Corporate Manslaughter and Corporate Homicide Act 2007 s.8.

[29] Corporate Manslaughter and Corporate Homicide Act 2007 s.9.

[30] Corporate Manslaughter and Corporate Homicide Act 2007 s.1(6); *HSE v Cotswold Geotechnical (Holdings) Ltd* February 17, 2011 Winchester Crown Court.

46.04 **Types of company**—A company incorporated under the Companies Act may take a variety of forms. The three basic types of company are those with liability limited by shares, those with liability limited by guarantee and those whose liability is unlimited.[31] Although there are some older companies which are guarantee companies with a share capital, it is no longer possible to set up a company as a guarantee company with a share capital.[32] Any company that is not a public company is a private company.[33] Single member companies may be either private or public.[34] There are special provisions for community interest companies.[35] The Act also provides for the registration of certain companies not formed under the Companies legislation such as joint stock companies[36] and of companies incorporated outside the United Kingdom but with an established place of business in United Kingdom,[37] known as overseas companies.[38] A subsidiary company broadly speaking is one where a holding company either has most of the shares or most of the control rights in the subsidiary.[39] A dormant company is one where the company has no significant accounting transaction.[40]

46.05 **European economic interest grouping ("EEIG")**—This type of business grouping is intended to facilitate collaborative ventures between companies, partnerships, trades unions and others located in the European Community.[41] An EEIG must be registered with the Registrar of Companies[42] but it is not a company in the normal sense of the word and its members are liable jointly and severally if it cannot meet its debts. An EEIG cannot be formed for the purpose of making profits but to "facilitate or develop the economic activities of its members".[43]

46.06 *Societas Europaea*—This type of company, also known as a European Company, is effectively a pan-European company. They are registered under the applicable regulations.[44] If such a company is set up, it can simultaneously exist in several different European countries, avoiding the necessity of setting up subsidiaries in each country, and thus reducing costs. A notable feature of SEs is the requirement of worker consultation.[45]

---

[31] CA 2006 ss.3–5.
[32] CA 2006 s.5(1).
[33] CA 2006 s.4(1).
[34] CA 2006 s.7.
[35] CA 2006 s.6.
[36] CA 2006 s.1040. Joint stock companies are generally companies formed before 1862 or companies set up by Act of Parliament.
[37] CA 2006 ss.1044–1059.
[38] As defined in s.1044.
[39] A closer definition of "subsidiary" is to be found in CA 2006 ss.1159–1162 and Schs 6 and 7.
[40] CA 2006 s.1169.
[41] Regulation (EEC)/2137/85 of the Council of 25 July 1985 on the European Economic Interest Grouping (EEIG) [1985] OJ L199, implemented by the European Economic Interest Grouping Regulations 1989 (SI 1989/638). They are little used in the United Kingdom but are successfully used in Austria and Germany. See the chapter by R. Mackay on EEIGs in *Corporate Law: The European Dimension* (London: Butterworths, 1991).
[42] European Economic Interest Grouping Regulations 1989 (SI 1989/638) regs 3, 9.
[43] Council Regulation /2173/85 art.3.
[44] European Public Limited Liability Company Regulations 2004 (SI 2004/2326) and European Public Limited Company (Amendment) Regulations 2009 (SI 2009/2400). See also Council Regulation (EC) 2001/2157 of 8 October 2001 on the Statute for a European Company [2001] OJ L294.
[45] Council Directive 2001/86/EC of 8 October 2001 supplementing the Statute for a European company with regard to the involvement of employees.

Limited and unlimited liability—A company which is formed with the liability of **46.07** its members limited to the amount, if any, unpaid on the shares respectively held by them is known as a company limited by shares.[46] When the liability of the members is limited to such amount as the members respectively undertake to contribute to its assets in the event of its being wound up, it is known as a company limited by guarantee.[47] A company not having any limit on the liability of its members is known as an unlimited company.[48] A company limited by shares must, by definition, have share capital. Unlimited companies may be formed with or without share capital. As a general rule the name of a company limited by shares or by guarantee, not being a public company, must end with "limited" or "Ltd",[49] and the name of a public company must end with "public limited company" or "Plc".[50] A company which is registered as limited may be re-registered as unlimited, and vice versa.[51]

Certain private companies are exempt from the requirements relating to the use of "limited" as part of the company name.[52] These are generally companies set up for charitable purposes.[53] A company which is exempt from the use of the word "limited" as part of its name is still required to state in all business letters and order forms of the company the fact that it is a limited company.[54] In an unlimited company each shareholder is potentially liable for all the debts of the company.[55] In a company limited by guarantee, the liability of each member is limited to the amount he undertakes to contribute in the event of the company being wound up.[56] In a company limited by shares each member is liable only up to the nominal value of each share that he has agreed to take (plus any premium), the time for payment depending on the articles of the particular company. The liquidator of a company may demand that any shareholder who owns shares of which the nominal value is only partly paid must pay up the outstanding amount on each share.[57] In practice nowadays it is rare to have partly paid shares.

Public and private companies—A company having share capital may be **46.08** registered as a private company or as a public company. A public company is a company limited by shares or limited by guarantee and having a share capital,[58] the certificate of incorporation of which states that it is to be a public company and which has been registered in compliance with the requirements of the Act as to the registration or re-registration of a company as a public company. These include the requirements that the name under which it is registered or re-registered must end with the words "public limited company" or "Plc" and that the amount

---

[46] CA 2006 s.3(2).

[47] CA 2006 s.3(3).

[48] CA 2006 s.3(4).

[49] CA 2006 s.59(1).

[50] CA 2006 s.58(1). This section refers to "p.l.c." but it is as common to see "PLC" or "Plc".

[51] CA 2006 ss.102–111.

[52] CA 2006 s.60.

[53] CA 2006 s.60–64.

[54] CA 2006 s.82. See the Companies (Trading Disclosures) Regulations 2008 (SI 2008/495) and the Companies (Trading Disclosures) Regulations (Amendment) Regulations 2009 (SI 2009/218). There are penalties for non-compliance (ss.83, 84).

[55] CA 2006 s.3(4).

[56] See, as to companies limited by guarantee, IA 1986 ss.74(3), 75 and *Robertson v British Linen Co* (1891) 18 R. 1225.

[57] IA 1986 s.74(2)(d). Under exceptional circumstances a past member who has transferred a partly paid share may be liable for the outstanding amount on a shares where the transferee has failed to pay the outstanding amount (s.74(2)(a)–(c)).

[58] CA 2006 s.4(2).

of the share capital stated in the statement of capital must not be less than the authorised minimum.[59] There is no minimum prescribed for the share capital of a private company, and its shares need not be paid up. A private company must not offer any shares to the public or agree to allot any shares with a view to them being offered to the public.[60]

A company which is registered as a Plc may not do business or exercise any borrowing powers unless the Registrar has issued it with a certificate, commonly called a trading certificate, stating that he is satisfied that the nominal value of the company's allotted share capital is not less than the authorised minimum.[61]

The trading certificate issued by the Registrar is conclusive evidence that the company is entitled to do business and to exercise any borrowing powers.[62] A third party who does business with a plc before a trading certificate has been issued to it is protected. The transaction is valid as against the company, but the directors of the company are jointly and severally liable to indemnify the third party for any loss or damage which he suffers in consequence of the company's failure to comply with its obligations.[63] A private company does not require a trading certificate before it does business or exercises any borrowing powers.

A Plc must have at least two directors but a private company is required only to have at least one.[64] A private company is not obliged to have a company secretary,[65] but a Plc must have one.[66] The company secretary of a Plc must be properly qualified to practise as such.[67]

46.09 **Registration of company**—A company, whether public or private, is brought into existence as a corporation by the registration with the Registrar of its memorandum of association,[68] its registration application,[69] (including its statement of compliance)[70] and its articles of association if a default set of model articles is not used.[71] The memorandum must be subscribed by one or more persons, indicating their intention to form a company.[72] The registration application contains information as to the company's name, the country (within the United Kingdom) of its registered office, the limit of the liability of the members (by shares, guarantee or without limit), whether the company is private or public, a statement of capital[73]

---

[59] CA 2006 s.761. At present the authorised minimum is £50,000 (s.763) but this figure may be altered by statutory instrument. A minimum of 25% of the allotted share capital must be paid up plus any premium (s.761(3)).

[60] CA 2006 ss.765–760.

[61] CA 2006 ss.761, 762, 767. If the company has previously been trading as a private company, there is no need for a trading certificate when it reregisters as a Plc.

[62] CA 2006 s.761(4).

[63] CA 2006 s.767(3).

[64] CA 2006 s.154. If there is only director, that director must be a natural person (s.155(1)).

[65] CA 2006 s.270. A private company may have a company secretary if it wishes to do so. The company secretary need not have any qualifications to hold office.

[66] CA 2006 s.271.

[67] CA 2006 s.273.

[68] CA 2006 s.7(1)(a). See Companies House *pro formas* available on *http://www.companieshouse. gov.uk/forms/formsOnline.shtml* [Accessed August 9, 2012].

[69] CA 2006 s.9–12. See also Companies House form IN01 on the above website.

[70] CA 2006 s.13. The statement itself is contained with form IN01.

[71] CA 2006 s.20.

[72] CA 2006 s.8. See Schs 1 and 2 of the Companies (Registration) Regulations 2008 (SI 2008/3014) for the recommended wording of memoranda.

[73] CA 2006 s.10. This shows the total number of shares taken by the subscriber or subscribers, the aggregate nominal value of the shares, the class or classes of share applicable, the rights attaching to each shares, the nominal value of each share and the extent to which each share is paid up.

or statement of guarantee,[74] a statement of the company's proposed officers and the intended address of the registered office. The statement of the proposed officers gives the details of the first director or directors and the first secretary (if any) or joint secretaries.[75] The officers need to give their consent to act. Each director who is a natural person (and every company must have at least one director who is a natural person[76]) must give a service address.[77] The company is obliged to give the directors' residential addresses to the Registrar of Companies, but the directors' residential addresses are protected and not disclosed to the general public.[78]Assuming all the forms are completed correctly, the statutory fee paid and the company set up for a lawful purpose,[79] the company will be registered. On the registration of the company the Registrar issues a certificate that the company is incorporated.[80] The certificate of incorporation is conclusive evidence that the requirements of the Act in respect of registration have been complied with, the company properly registered,[81] the directors (and secretary, where applicable) appointed and the company capable of exercising all its requisite functions.[82] Formerly, a company was required to state in its memorandum what its authorised capital was. This is no longer necessary, though a company may insert such information into its articles if it wishes to do so.

Name of a company—No company may be registered under a name which is the **46.10** same as a name appearing in the Registrar's index of company names,[83] or the use of which in the opinion of the Secretary of State would constitute a criminal offence or which in his opinion is offensive.[84] A company may not have a name that suggests a connection with any part of the Government, any local authority, or any public authority without the consent of the Secretary for State.[85] The approval of the Secretary of State is also required for "sensitive" names not deemed suitable for a company.[86] If a company wishes to have a name that suggests a connection between some branch of national or local government, or to use a sensitive name, it must write beforehand to the relevant government department or other body requesting it to indicate whether, and if so why, it has any

---

[74] CA 2006 s.11. This states the extent of the guarantee to be paid by each member if called upon to do so.

[75] CA 2006 s.12.

[76] CA 2006 s.155. Directors must also be over the age of 16 (s.157).

[77] The director's service is address is what is displayed at Companies House, but the company itself will keep a register of all the directors' residential addresses (s.165). The information about the director's residential address is to be protected by the company and not made available to anyone without the consent of the director or a court order (s.241(2)). The service address may be the same as the residential address.

[78] CA 2006 s.242. Under limited circumstances, the addresses disclosed may be disclosed by the Registrar of Companies with or without a court order (ss.243–246).

[79] CA 2006 s.7(2). For an enterprising but unlawful purpose, see *R. v Registrar of Companies Ex p. Att Gen* [1991] B.C.L.C. 476.

[80] CA 2006 s.15.

[81] CA 2006 s.15(4).

[82] CA 2006 s.16.

[83] CA 2006 s.66

[84] CA 2006 s.53. An example of a criminal name would be one that was contrary to the Equality Act 2010. As to the requirement to include the words "limited" or "public limited company" as the case may be, see ss.58, 59.

[85] CA 2006 s.54.

[86] CA 2006 s.55. The Companies, Limited Liability Partnerships and Business Names (Sensitive words and expressions) Regulations 2009 (SI 2009/2615).

objections to the proposed company name.[87] The letter and the response need to be submitted to the Secretary of State.[88] The same rules apply to change of name.[89]

There are specific regulations prohibiting someone from carrying on a business with a potentially misleading name consisting of or containing specified words or expressions associated with particular types of company or organisation[90] or likely to cause harm to the public.[91] A company may change its name by special resolution or other procedure indicated in the company's articles[92] or it may be required to change its name by the Secretary of State on loss of any exemption from use of the word "limited",[93] on being required by the company names adjudicator to adopt a new name,[94] by the court,[95] or on its restoration to the register.[96] It may also be required to change its name if the name by which the company is registered is too like a name appearing in the list of registered companies or which should have appeared in that list.[97] If its name is the same or similar to that of a name in which a person has goodwill, or is sufficiently similar to suggest that within the United Kingdom its use might mislead by suggesting a connection between the company and that person, that person ("the applicant") may apply to a company names adjudicator to have the company name changed. It is for the respondent company to show in its defence that it has registered its name before the applicant commenced such activities as generated the goodwill he seeks to protect; that the company is operating under that name or is proposing to do so and has incurred start-up costs or was formerly operating under the name and is now dormant; that the name was registered in the ordinary course of business and the company is available for sale to the applicant; that the name was adopted in good faith; or that the interests of the applicant are not adversely affected to any significant extent.[98] Where the company's main purpose in taking the name was to obtain money from the applicant or to prevent him from registering it, the applicant's objection will be upheld.[99] The adjudicator may direct the name to be changed.[100] There is an appeal to the courts.[101] If it appears to the Secretary of State that misleading information had been given for the purposes of having a company registered under a particular name, or that an undertaking or assurance had been given which had not been fulfilled, the Secretary of State may direct the company to change its name.[102] Likewise, where the chosen name gives so misleading an indication of the nature of its activities that it might mislead the public, the Secretary of State may direct that the company change its name.[103]

---

[87] CA 2006 s.56(1), (2).

[88] CA 2006 s.56(3).

[89] CA 2006 s.56(4).

[90] The Companies, Limited Liability Partnerships and Business Names (Sensitive words and expressions) Regulations 2009 (SI 2009/2615). The list of sensitive words and expressions is available on the Companies House website.

[91] CA 2006 s.1198.

[92] CA 2006 ss.77(1), 78, 79.

[93] CA 2006 s.64.

[94] CA 2006 s.73.

[95] CA 2006 s.74.

[96] CA 2006 s.1033.

[97] CA 2006 s.67.

[98] CA 2006 s.69(4).

[99] CA 2006 s.69(5).

[100] CA 2006 s.73.

[101] CA 2006 s.74.

[102] CA 2006 s.75.

[103] CA 2006 s.76.

Where a company changes its name the Registrar is required to enter the new name in the register in place of the former name and to issue an altered certificate of incorporation, and the change of name has effect from the date on which the altered certificate is issued.[104] A change of name by the company does not affect any rights or obligations of the company and does not affect or interrupt its corporate existence.[105] A contract is valid if entered into in the new name even before the altered certificate of incorporation has been issued.[106]

There is a prohibition against a director being involved with a business (whether a company or not) using, within a period of five years, the name (or a very similar name) of a company which went into insolvent liquidation and of which he was a director in the period of twelve months before the company's liquidation.[107] However, if permission is sought from the courts for the use of the prohibited name, usually following the consent of the creditors,[108] the name, or a similar name, may be used.[109] It may also be used if a period of five years has elapsed since the liquidated company went into insolvent liquidation.[110] There are also further rules for granting permission to be found in the Insolvency (Scotland) Rules 1986 Pt 4 Ch.13.[111]

Every company is required, subject to certain penalties,[112] to display certain information about itself at specified locations. A company is required to display its name in legible characters outside every office or place in which its business is carried on, on its seal and on all business letters, official publications, invoices, etc. of the company.[113] It is also required to mention in legible characters on all business letters and order forms of the company the place of registration and the number with which it is registered, and the address of its registered office.[114] A company may do business under a name other than the one it is registered with.[115]

A company's objects clause—Under CA 2006 the memorandum of association **46.11** of a company is merely a record of the intention of the first subscribers to set up the company and there is no opportunity for an objects clause within the memo-randum as used to be the case. CA 2006 significantly reduces the significance of objects clauses. Consequently much of the previous law relating to objects clauses and the ultra vires rule is redundant except to some extent for charities. However,

---

[104] CA 2006 s.87. It is now permissible to have the change of name dependent on the occurrence of an event, in which case the Registrar will issue the new certificate on intimation of the event taking place (s.780(1)).

[105] CA 2006 s.81(2).

[106] *Lin Pac (Containers) Scotland) v Kelly*, 1982 S.C. 50.

[107] IA 1986 s.216(3). *Ricketts v Ad Valorem Factors Ltd* [2004] 1 All E.R. 894; [2004] B.C.C. 164; [2004] 1 B.C.L.C. 1. The effect of this is to penalise the director, either by criminal sanctions (s.216(4)) or civil liability for the new company's debts if the new company is using a prohibited name (s.217). These provisions do not necessarily preclude the use of the name in general, but not by that particular director.

[108] *Re Bonus Breaks Ltd* [1991] B.C.C. 546.

[109] IA 1986 s.216(3).

[110] IA 1986 s.216(3).

[111] Insolvency (Scotland) Rules 1986 (SI 1986/1915). For an English case on the very similar rules and the required notice, see *First Independent Factors & Finance Ltd v Churchill* [2007] B.C.C. 45.

[112] CA 2006 ss.83, 84.

[113] The Companies (Trading Disclosures) Regulations 2008 (SI 2008/495) and the Companies (Trading Disclosures) Regulations 2009 (SI 2009/218).

[114] IA 2006 s.82.

[115] IA 2006 s.82. The Companies (Trading Disclosures) Regulations 2008 (SI 2008/495) and the Companies (Trading Disclosures) Regulations 2009 (SI 2009/218).

if a company formed under CA 2006 wishes to have some equivalent of an objects clause in its constitution, it must put it in the articles, but in the absence of such a provision a company's objects are unrestricted.[116] If a company does have a statement of its objects, whenever those objects are altered, the Registrar must be notified, but the change of the company's objects does not alter the company's obligations or rights or make any difference to proceedings raised by or against it.[117] If the company is a Scottish charity, which would mean that it would be likely to have an objects clause, any change to the objects clause must be intimated to and receive the approval of the Office of the Scottish Charities Regulator.[118] If the objects clause is entrenched in the articles, further special rules need to be followed.[119]

46.12 The continuing limited effect of the ultra vires rule—Part of the former law relating to the objects clause was that a company would not be liable for any act not authorised under the objects clause. This is no longer the case, and it is not possible for a company to avoid liability for an act done by that company on the ground that its constitution does not give it the capacity to carry out that act.[120] The word "act" means not just a commercial transaction but any undertaking by the company including gifts and guarantees: the word "constitution" covers the company's articles and any special resolutions or court orders altering the articles, or any agreement between the members of the company or of any class of shareholders.[121] A company's articles may specifically impose restrictions on the directors, or others authorised by the directors, from carrying out certain acts. Even so, under s.40, any person dealing with the company, in good faith, is entitled to assume that the power of the directors to bind the company, or authorise others to do so, is free of any limitation under the company's constitution.[122] That person is not required to enquire as to any limitation on the restrictions on the powers of the directors to bind the company or authorise others to do so, is presumed to have acted in good faith unless the contrary is shown, and is not to be regarded as acting in bad faith even if he knows that an act being carried out by the directors or their authorisees is beyond the powers of the directors under the company's constitution.[123] Although a member may obtain an interdict to prevent his company undertaking or repeating an unauthorised act, no interdict may be effective where the company has already entered a legal obligation to carry out that act.[124] This provision does not prevent a director or any other person from being liable for the unauthorised act of the company.

Notwithstanding the above, where the person dealing with the company is himself a director, or a person associated with a director, he loses the protection of s.40 on the grounds that the director (or his associate) is well placed to know the limits to his and his fellow directors' own authority. If, therefore, the director or his associate enters a transaction with the company in breach of his authority

---

[116] CA 2006 s.31(1).
[117] CA 2006 s.31(3).
[118] Charities and Trustee Investment (Scotland) Act 2005 s.10(6).
[119] See para.46.15.
[120] CA 2006 s.39.
[121] CA 2006 s.40(3).
[122] CA 2006 s.40(1).
[123] CA 2006 s.40(3).
[124] CA 2006 s.40(4). The legislation uses the word "proceedings" for what in practice in Scotland would be an interdict.

under the constitution, the transaction is voidable at the instance of the company, and the director, his associate, and any other director who authorised the transaction is liable to account to the company for any gain he made or to indemnify the company for any loss it suffers.[125] The transaction will cease to be voidable where: (1) restitutio in integrum cannot be made; (2) the company has been indemnified in respect of any loss caused by the transaction; (3) rights have been acquired by a bona fide purchaser who is ignorant of the circumstances rendering the original transaction voidable; and (4) the transaction has been ratified in the appropriate manner.[126] The court has power to affirm, sever or set aside the transaction.[127] It would also be open to the members to pass a special resolution to ratify the director's action, but in such an event, the director's own votes, and those of any member connected[128] with him, should not cause the resolution for ratification to be passed[129] unless the vote in his favour is unanimous.[130]

Charities—The law is somewhat different for charitable companies. An ultra **46.13** vires act by such a company is unenforceable except in favour of a third party who (1) gives full consideration for it, and (2) is either unaware that it is not permitted by the company's constitution or that it is beyond the directors' powers or does not appreciate at the time that the company is a charity.[131] The onus of proof rests on the party alleging such lack of awareness by the third party.[132] This burden may be relatively easy to discharge since even if the words "charity" or "charitable" are omitted from the company name, its business stationery, invoices and receipts, etc. still must state that it is a charity.[133] Where property is sold or transferred ultra vires the charitable company's powers, or beyond the directors' powers, a subsequent purchaser's title thereto cannot be disturbed so long as he did not know that the original transaction was ultra vires.[134]

Articles of association—The articles of association are the major part of the **46.14** constitution of the company. Each of the major Companies Acts up to the Companies Act 1985 introduced a model set of articles which might be adopted in its entirety by the members of the company, or might be adopted subject to such modifications as the members wish. The former model set is known as Tables A–F and many extant companies will have adopted, either wholly or partially, the 1948 Table A or, for post-1985 and pre-2009 companies, the 1985 Table A.[135] The wording of articles of association remains in place until such time as they are altered. A company incorporated after October 1, 2009 must use one of the new default set of articles under CA 2006 as its default set, though, as before, the members may make such modifications to the articles as they see fit.[136] Unless

---

[125] CA 2006 s.41(3).

[126] CA 2006 s.41(4).

[127] CA 2006 s.41(6). For an example of the court affirming a transaction, see *Hunt v Edge and Ellison Trustees Ltd* [1999] 2 B.C.L.C. 605.

[128] For the meaning of "connected" see s.252.

[129] CA 2006 s.239(4).

[130] CA 2006 s.239(6).

[131] Companies Act 1989 s.112(3). The charity must be entered in the Scottish Charity Register.

[132] Companies Act 1989 s.112(5).

[133] Companies Act 1989 s.112(6).

[134] Companies Act 1989 s.112(4).

[135] There were various transitional versions while CA 2006 was gradually being implemented.

[136] CA 2006 ss.19, 20. For the wording of the new model articles, see the Companies (Model Articles) Regulations 2008 (SI 2008/3229).

one of the model default sets is used in its entirety, articles of association have to be registered. Articles regulate the management of the company and once registered, form a tripartite contract between the shareholders, the company,[137] and, depending on the wording, the directors or anyone else given rights in the articles.[138] If articles prescribe a certain course of action to be followed, it must be followed,[139] and if a member is dissatisfied with the articles, his only realistic remedy is to persuade enough other members to agree that they should be changed.[140] However, in order to enforce the provisions of the articles, it is necessary to sue in the capacity of a member and in no other capacity. A solicitor, who had drafted the articles to contain a provision that he should be the company's solicitor, was unable, in his potential capacity as the company's solicitor, to enforce a clause in the articles providing that he should be so employed.[141] If a provision contained in the articles is contrary to public policy it does not bind the members and will not be enforced by the court.[142] If the articles are poorly drafted, the court will try to give commercial effect to what was meant to have been stated,[143] but if the articles omitted something that was meant to be present, but was overlooked, the courts will not remedy the error by altering the articles.[144] The articles are a public document, both an expression of the terms between the principal actors in the company and an advertisement to potential investors in the company, and as such, extrinsic rules, if not statutorily required, have no bearing on the members' expectations of their entitlements in terms of the articles.[145] Merely because some shareholders have a majority of the shares, albeit not enough to pass a special resolution, does not entitle those shareholders to override the provisions of the articles.[146]

46.15 Alteration of articles—A company has power, by special resolution,[147] but without requiring confirmation by the court, to alter or add to its articles.[148] The power cannot be excluded by any provision in the articles themselves,[149] nor can it be excluded by contract with a third party.[150] Apart from charity companies, there are few limits to the power to alter the articles, but, by the decisions, a resolution to alter is reducible if it is made in the interest of individual

---

[137] CA 2006 s.33. *Hickman v Kent & Romney Marsh Sheepbreeders' Association* [1915] 1 CH. 881; *Alexander Ward & Co. v Samyang Navigation Co*, 1975, S.C. (HL) 26.

[138] *Southern Foundries (1926) Ltd v Shirlaw* [1940] A.C. 701.

[139] *Hickman v Kent & Romney Marsh Sheepbreeders' Association* [1915] 1 CH. 881.

[140] This would need a special resolution (approval by 75% of the members voting and entitled to vote) (s.21).

[141] *Eley v Positive Government Security Life Assurance Co Ltd* (1875–76) L.R. 1 Ex.D. 88; see also *Alexander Ward & Co. v Samyang Navigation Co*, 1975, S.C. (HL) 26 at 36, per Lord Fraser.

[142] *St Johnstone FC v Scottish Football Association*, 1965 S.L.T. 171.

[143] *Folkes Group Plc v Alexander* [2002] 2 B.C.L.C. 254.

[144] *Bratton Seymour Service Co Ltd v Oxborough* [1992] B.C.L.C. 693.

[145] *Re Astec (BSR) Plc* [1998] 2 B.C.L.C. 556.

[146] *Breckland Group Holdings Ltd v London and Suffolk Properties* [1989] B.C.L.C. 100.

[147] For special resolutions, see s.283. Strictly speaking a Plc should have a meeting to change its articles, but following the case of *re Duomatic Ltd* [1969] 2 Ch.365, an agreement between all the members acting together and representing their unanimous will will be held to be effective to alter the company's articles even though there was neither a meeting nor a resolution in writing. CA 2006 s.281(4) also allows for this.

[148] CA 2006 s.21. If the company is a Scottish charity, the change needs to be intimated to the Office of the Scottish Charity Regulator (s.21(3)).

[149] *Malleson v National Insurance Corp* [1894] 1 Ch. 200; *Russell v Northern Bank Development Corp Ltd* [1992] 3 All E.R. 161 (HL).

[150] *Russell v Northern Bank Development Corp Ltd* [1992] 3 All E.R. 161 (HL).

shareholders or classes of shareholders and not bona fide for the benefit of the company as a whole.[151] Where purchasers of policies with a guaranteed annuity rate from an insurance company accepted terms that were beneficial to the purchasers, but later became disadvantageous to the company, the company's directors were not permitted to use a new discretion (granted to them under new altered articles that were not in force at the time of the purchasers' acquisition of the policies) to vary the purchasers' terms to the purchasers' disadvantage where this would not have been within the reasonable expectations of both parties at the time when the policies were purchased.[152] Accrued rights, such as the right to have a transfer registered, may not be affected.[153] By s.25 of CA 2006 no member of a company, unless he agree in writing, is bound by an alteration of articles made after he became a member, if it in any way increases his liability to subscribe for shares, to contribute to the share capital or to pay money to the company. Where the articles are altered the company is required to send a copy of the articles as altered to the Registrar.[154] In the rare event that the company's articles are altered by enactment, such as by private Act of Parliament, or the courts, this fact must be notified to the Registrar.[155] Any resolution affecting the company's constitution, whether a special resolution, unanimous resolution, or any other type of resolution or agreement that binds all the members, must also sent to the Registrar within 15 days of the date of it being passed or made.[156]

Normally articles will be amended by special resolution[157] but it is possible for companies to have "entrenched" clauses, which means that more restrictive procedures need to be followed, or conditions complied with (these procedures or conditions being known as "provision for entrenchment"), before either the articles as a whole, or certain clauses within the articles, may be changed.[158] Even where there is provision for entrenchment in place, the existence of that provision does not preclude amendment of the relevant clause, by agreement of all the members of the company[159] or by the court or other authority, such as the Office of the Scottish Charities Regulator.[160] Where a company has been formed with provision for entrenchment, or the articles are amended to have such provision, or where the company's articles are altered by the court or other authority in order to restrict or exclude the power of the company to amend its articles, this fact must be notified to the Registrar of Companies.[161] Similar notification is required if the provision for entrenchment is removed.[162] When a company amends its articles,

---

[151] *Sidebotham v Kershaw* [1920] 1 Ch. 154; *Greenhalgh v Arderne Cinemas* [1951] 1 Ch. 286, especially at 291, per Lord Evershed M.R. Such behaviour would generally now be grounds for a minority protection petition under s.994.

[152] *Equitable Life Assurance Society v Hyman* [2000] 3 All E.R. 961; [2000] 3 W.L.R. 529 (HL). For a thoughtful discussion of this case, see A. Berg "*Equitable Life Assurance Society v Hyman*—the extrinsic facts issue", 2002 J.B.L. 570–7.

[153] *Liquidator of W & A McArthur v Gulf Line*, 1909 S.C. 732.

[154] CA 2006 s.26.

[155] CA 2006 ss.34, 35.

[156] CA 2006 ss.29, 30.

[157] CA 2006 s.21.

[158] CA 2006 s.22. Entrenchment is not common nowadays, though it is not unusual in companies set up for charitable purposes. Subsection (2) is not yet in force because of the difficulty in dealing with class rights enshrined in the articles. The Department of Business, Information and Skills is therefore reviewing this subsection (see SI 2009/2476).

[159] CA 2006 s.22(3)(a).

[160] CA 2006 s.22(3)(b).

[161] CA 2006 s.23(1).

[162] CA 2006 ss.23(2).

either by exercising the provision for entrenchment, or by order of the court, a statement of compliance, together with the amended articles, must be completed and sent to the Registrar.[163] Where an existing company, formed before CA 2006, has entrenched clauses in its memorandum, those clauses are with effect from the date of implementation of the CA 2006 to be treated as if they were in the articles.[164] This means that they will normally be alterable by special resolution, unless those clauses were entrenched in the old memorandum and have a particularly restrictive provision for entrenchment. In that case, the clauses themselves, together with their own particular provision for entrenchment, may only be amended by unanimous approval or by court order,[165] followed by notice to the Registrar that this has taken place.[166]

46.16 Company contracts—A contract (or any other document) is signed by a company if signed on its behalf by a director or the company secretary, or by a person authorised to sign on its behalf.[167] Where a contract (or any other document) appears to have been subscribed by a director, or by the company's secretary, or by anyone bearing to have been authorised to subscribe on the company's behalf, and, further, bears to have been signed by a person as witness to such subscription, and there is nothing in the contract (or document) or in any testing clause contained therein to indicate that it was not subscribed or witnessed, there is a presumption that it was subscribed by the subscriber and by the company.[168] The presumption also applies where a deed has been signed by two directors, by a director and a secretary of the company, or by two persons authorised to subscribe on behalf of the company, without a witness.[169] There is no presumption, however, that the person subscribing as a director or secretary was truly such, nor that someone signing as a person authorised to do so, was really so authorised.[170] Similar provisions apply in respect of alterations made to a document after it has been subscribed.[171] All that is required for the valid drawing, acceptance or indorsement of bills of exchange and promissory notes is the signature of someone authorised by the company.[172] Companies are not obliged to have a company seal but may use one if they wish to do so.[173] Where a director of a company which has yet to be formed purports to make a contract on behalf of his company, subject to any agreement to the contrary, he will be personally liable on that contract.[174]

46.17 Register of shareholders and information about shareholders—A company is bound, under penalties, to keep a register of members[175] either at its registered office or, if the work of making it up is done at another office, at that office.[176] If there are more than 50 members the company must keep an index of the

---

[163] CA 2006 ss.24, 26.
[164] CA 2006 s.28(1).
[165] CA 2006 s.28(2)
[166] CA 2006 s.28(3).
[167] Requirements of Writing (Scotland) Act 1995 Sch.2 para.3(1); CA 2006 s.48.
[168] Requirements of Writing (Scotland) Act 1995 s.3(1).
[169] Requirements of Writing (Scotland) Act 1995 s.3(1A).
[170] Requirements of Writing (Scotland) Act 1995 Sch.2 para.3(5)(a).
[171] Requirements of Writing (Scotland) Act 1995 s.5(8), Sch.1 para.1(1).
[172] CA 2006 s.52; *Brebner v Henderson*, 1925 S.C. 643.
[173] CA 2006 s.48(2).
[174] CA 2006 s.51; *Phonogram Ltd v Lane* [1982] Q.B. 938, CA.
[175] CA 2006 s.113.
[176] CA 2006 s.114. The Registrar of Companies needs to be informed of this. Use form AD02.

members.[177] The register and the index must be open to inspection by any member without charge, and to others on payment of a fee. A copy of the register may be obtained. Those who wish either to inspect or copy the register must make a request to this effect to the company and supply their names and addresses, the organisation (if any) they represent, the purpose for which the information will be used, and whether the information will be disclosed to any one else.[178] The company must within five working days then comply with the request or apply to court not to comply with the request on the grounds that that the inspection or copy is not being sought for a proper purpose.[179] While it is an offence on the company's part (or its directors') not to comply with the request unless the court grants permission not to comply with the request,[180] it is also an offence to supply misleading information in order to be able to inspect or obtain a copy of the register or index.[181] Where membership of a private company limited by shares or guarantee falls to one this fact must be recorded in the register of members and, should it rise again, the register must be amended accordingly.[182] By s.126 no notice of any trust may appear on the register of a company in England, but this section does not apply to Scotland, where the usual practice is to register trustees as such. A person registered as a holder of shares in trust incurs the same liability as a person holding them for his own behoof.[183] Any person whose name is, without sufficient cause, entered in or omitted from the register may apply to the court for its rectification.[184] The same remedy is open when unnecessary delay occurs in entering on the register the fact that a person has ceased to be a member. The application may be made by the person aggrieved, by any member of the company, or by the company.[185]

A subsidiary company is not allowed to be a member of its holding company, though a subsidiary may hold shares in the holding company when it is acting as trustee for another or when is it acting as an authorised dealer in securities.[186]

A shareholder of shares in a company whose shares are traded on a regulated market may nominate another person to receive "information rights".[187]

A Plc, or its members,[188] may wish to know who has an interest[189] in its shares. There are provisions to require any person who the company knows has, or has reasonable cause to believe to have, an interest in its shares to confirm the fact or to provide further information about his present or past interest, and in particular to disclose whether he represents any other interests, beneficial or otherwise, in

---

[177] CA 2006 s.115.

[178] CA 2006 s.116.

[179] CA 2006 s.117. The intention of the legislation is to make it difficult for protest organisations to obtain lists of members to enable them to write to and intimidate those members. "Proper purpose" has been left for the courts to decide.

[180] CA 2006 s.118.

[181] CA 2006 s.119.

[182] CA 2006 s.123.

[183] *Muir v City of Glasgow Bank*, (1879) 6 R. (HL) 21.

[184] CA 2006 s.125; *Re Thundercrest Ltd* [1994] B.C.C. 857; *New Celos Engineering Co Ltd* [1994] 1 B.C.L.C. 797.

[185] CA 2006 s.125(1); *Re Transatlantic Life Assurance* [1980] 1.W.L.R. 79.

[186] CA 2006 s.136.

[187] CA 2006 s.146. This is to enable those whose shares are held on their behalf by nominees (such as stockbrokers) to receive information on their shares.

[188] CA 2006 s.803. Members have the power to force the company to establish who has an interest in its shares.

[189] "Interest" is widely defined. See CA 2006 ss.820–825.

the shares.[190] If the person refuses to co-operate in these matters, the company may apply to court for an order under s.797 to render any transfer of shares by that person void, to prevent voting in respect of those shares, to prevent him receiving a rights offer or any other share offer from the company, and, save in liquidation, to prevent him receiving any dividends or returns of capital. If necessary the shares in question may be sold following an application to court by the company.[191] The information collected in response to the investigations into interests must be reported to the members[192] and must be kept in a register maintained by the company.[193]

46.18 **Share certificates and certificates of transfer**—A share certificate is under English law prima facie evidence of a shareholder's entitlement to his shares[194]; and under Scots law, a certificate under the common seal of the company specifying the number of shares held by the member or a certificate specifying the shares held by the member and subscribed by the company in accordance with the Requirements of Writing (Scotland) Act 1995 is, unless evidence to the contrary is shown, sufficient evidence of title.[195] Share certificates, and indeed debenture stock certificates, must be issued within two months of allotment[196] or transfer.[197] If regularly issued, a share certificate is conclusive against the company, and therefore if a company, deceived by a forged transfer, issues a certificate, it is barred from denying the title of a bona fide transferee, and is liable to him in the value of the shares.[198] When a company, either owing to a mistake or to fraud on the part of its officials, issued certificates stating, falsely, that the shares were fully paid up, the company became liable to a person who was induced to advance money on the faith of the certificates.[199] But a company was not bound by the issue of share certificates fraudulently issued by the secretary on which the signatures of directors had been forged.[200] Anyone who sends a transfer for registration impliedly contracts that he will relieve the company of any liability. So where a banker sent for registration a transfer of corporation stock to which the name of the holder had been forged, and the company registered the transfer and issued new certificates to transferees, with the result that it was bound to recognise the right both of holder and of the transferees, it was held that it had a right of relief from the banker.[201] Similarly, where a registrar of a company was induced to issue a new share certificate by fraud, the new share certificate was still valid and the issuing registrar could not disown it, but those who acted on behalf of the fraudster were liable to the issuing registrar because by instructing the transfer of the newly issued share certificate they had impliedly warranted to undertake to indemnify the issuing registrar for any loss sustained, and had also impliedly

---

[190] CA 2006 s.793.

[191] CA 2006 s.801.

[192] CA 2006 s.806.

[193] CA 2006 s.808.

[194] CA 2006 s.768(1); *Re Bahia San Francisco Railway Co Ltd,* (1868) L.R. 3 Q.B.; *Bloomenthal v Ford* [1897] A.C. 156.

[195] CA 2006 s.768(2).

[196] CA 2006 s.769. This provision does not apply where the allottee is a financial institution (s.778).

[197] CA 2006 s.776. This provision again does not apply where the allottee is a financial institution (s.778).

[198] *Balkis Co v Tomkinson* [1893] A.C. 396.

[199] *Clavering v Goodwin, Jardine & Co,* (1891) 18 R. 652; *Penang Co v Gardiner,* 1913 S.C. 1203.

[200] *Ruben v Great Fingall Consolidated Co* [1906] A.C. 439.

[201] *Sheffield Corporation v Barclay* [1905] A.C. 1892.

warranted that the transfer form was genuine.[202] The transfer of shares and debentures may not be registered unless a proper instrument of transfer has been delivered.[203] On receipt of the instrument of transfer the company must register the transfer or give its reasons for its refusal within two months.[204] Shares in a company must be transferred in the manner prescribed in the articles,[205] which may, or may not, provide that the directors should have a power to decline transfers of which they do not approve,[206] or, as is common in the case of private companies, that the shares should not be transferred to an outsider before first being offered to the other members.[207] If not, the shareholder has an absolute right to transfer his shares to anyone he pleases, and thereby to escape liability for calls,[208] unless the transfer is presented on the eve of liquidation, when the directors are entitled to refuse registration.[209] The fact that the transferee was induced by fraud to accept the shares cannot be founded on by the company or by its liquidator.[210] The result of a valid refusal by the directors to transfer the shares is that the transferor may avoid the contract on repaying the price; if he does not choose to do so he must regard himself as a trustee for the transferee, bound to receive dividends and hand them on.[211] In the event of refusal, the company must provide the transferee with such information about the refusal as he may reasonably request, but the company does not need to include copies of minutes of directors' meetings.[212] Where a company issues share warrants, on their surrender for cancellation, the company must produce within two months the share certificates for the shares specified in the warrants.[213]

Transparency obligations—Following the Transparency Obligations Directive[214] **46.19** various amendments were made to the Financial Services and Markets Act 2000[215] ("FSMA 2000") to enable the Financial Services Authority (the "FSA"), acting in its capacity as the UK Listing Authority, to make rules to implement the Directive.[216] The Transparency Directive covers issuers whose securities are traded on regulated markets and persons who hold voting rights attached to shares in those issuers. The rules implemented the Transparency Directive by requiring

---

[202] *Royal Bank of Scotland v Sandstone Properties Ltd* [1998] 2 B.C.L.C. 429.

[203] This will normally be a stock transfer form.

[204] CA 2006 s.771(1).

[205] CA 2006 s.543(1).

[206] *Re Smith and Fawcett Ltd* [1942] Ch.304, CA. Nowadays directors have to give their reasons for refusal (s.771(2)).

[207] *Borland's Tr. v Steel Bros & Co*, [1901] 1 Ch. 279; *Rayfield v Hands* [1960] Ch.1.

[208] *Re Discoverer's Finance Corp (Lindlar's Case)* [1910] 1 Ch. 312; see also *Re Swaledale Cleaners* [1968] 1 W.L.R. 1710. A "call" is a demand by the directors or liquidator to pay the unpaid portion of a partly paid share.

[209] *Dodds v Cosmopolitan Insurance Co*, 1915 S.C. 992; cf. *Lindlar's Case* [1910] 1 Ch. 312 at 318, per Buckley L.J.

[210] *McLintock v Campbell*, 1916 S.C. 966.

[211] *Stevenson v Wilson*, 1907 S.C. 445.

[212] CA 2006 s.771(2). This replaces the former rule whereby if the articles so provided directors were under no obligation to explain their refusal to register a transfer of shares.

[213] CA 2006 s.780. This does not apply if the company's articles provide otherwise.

[214] Directive 2004/109 EC of the European Parliament and of the Council of 15 December 2004 on the harmonisation of transparency requirements in relation to information about issuers whose securities are admitted to trading on a regulated market and amending Directive 2001/34/EC.

[215] CA 2006 s.1266 provided for the insertion of ss.89A–89O to the FSMA 2000.

[216] These rules may be found in the FSA Handbook within the section "Listing, Disclosure and Prospectus" under the heading of "Disclosure Rules and Transparency Rules". The Handbook itself is available online at *http://fsahandbook.info/FSA/html/handbook* [Accessed August 9, 2012].

holders of votes attached to shares in issuers to disclose their holdings at certain thresholds; requiring issuers to make public their annual accounts and reports, together with half-yearly and interim management statements prepared in accordance with the EU International Accounts Standards Regulation[217]; requiring issuers to notify their use of voting rights held by themselves in respect of their own voting shares; and requiring issuers to notify the FSA and the market of any proposed change to their constitution. The rules also provide for conformity between the rules of the Takeover Panel and the requirements of the Transparency Directive, allow the FSA powers to call for information from all those involved in dealing with securities on regulated markets, gives the FSA sanctions to exercise against those that do not comply with its rules, and gives the FSA power to issue rules about corporate governance.

46.20 Issue and trading of shares—Public and private companies may issue securities[218] in accordance with each company's articles of association and company legislation.[219] The principal reason for issuing securities is, generally,[220] to raise capital for the company. Companies whose securities are to be offered to or traded by the public[221] on a recognised market must comply with the FSA's regulatory regime relating to that market. The principal market for transferable securities in the United Kingdom is the main market of the London Stock Exchange. Securities traded there have to comply with a rigorous process of scrutiny before they may be admitted to listing on that market.[222] Securities which do not conform to the listing requirements may be issued on other markets such as the Alternative Investment Market ("AIM") or PLUS. Securities so traded are known as "unlisted securities" and the requirements for admission are less onerous. The issue of securities in companies whose securities are to be publicly traded and thereby transferable is regulated by FSMA 2000. Common types of issue by public companies include: (a) issue of securities which are to be admitted to the London Stock Exchange or other recognised investment exchanges; (b) issues of securities on the occasion of their admission to dealings on other markets; (c) an offer of securities which is a direct offer to the public by the company (usually accompanied by a prospectus); (d) offers for sale in which an issuing house, which has subscribed to take the whole issue of securities from the company, sells the securities on its own behalf to the public; and (e) a rights issue (in which existing holders of the company's securities are given a prior right to subscribe for the new securities).

---

[217] EC Regulation 1606/2002.

[218] "Securities" predominantly covers shares, but also includes debentures, bonds, warrants and other financial instruments.

[219] CA 2006 ss.549–616 describe the process of issue of shares in particular. See also para 46.21.

[220] The issue of bonus shares converts retained profits into further capital.

[221] Such companies must be Plcs: private companies, except within certain narrow exceptions, are prohibited from offering their shares or debentures to the general public (CA 2006 s.755).

[222] See FSMA 2000 ss.79–82. The FSA Handbook contains the rules that need to be followed. Where transferable securities are being offered to the public, it is obligatory to supply the details of the offer in a prospectus (FSMA 2000 s.85) unless specified exemptions (mostly to be found in FSMA 2000 Sch.11A and in the Prospectus Rules (see r.1.2.2) issued by the FSA in its Handbook) apply. Securities admitted to listing in the United Kingdom are eligible for listing on other similar markets elsewhere within the EU.

Liability for misleading and untrue statements—There is an expectation that **46.21** in all documentation about companies whose securities are listed the listing particulars and other documentation are accurate, and contain all such information as investors and their professional advisers would reasonably require and reasonably expect to find in order to make an informed assessment of the company's assets, liabilities, financial position etc.[223] Civil liability under statute for omitted, untrue or misleading statements in listing particulars and prospectuses is to be found at s.90 of FSMA 2000. A person acquiring securities on the strength of such statements may be able to claim compensation from anyone responsible for the listing particulars or prospectus.[224] To succeed, the pursuer must prove that he suffered loss as a result of the misstatement or omission.[225] The persons responsible for listing particulars or the prospectus are: (a) the issuer of the securities to which the particulars or prospectus relate; (b) where the issuer is a body corporate, each person who is a director of that body at the time when the particulars were submitted or the prospectus registered; (c) where the issuer is a body corporate, each person who has authorised himself to be named, and is named, in the particulars or prospectus as a director or as having agreed to become a director of that body either immediately or at a future time; (d) each person who accepts, and is stated in the particulars or prospectus as accepting, responsibility for, or for any part of, the particulars; (e) each person not falling within any of the foregoing paragraphs who has authorised the contents of, or any part of, the particulars.[226]

There are several defences available to those responsible for these documents: (a) that there were reasonable grounds for believing that the statements made therein were true or that the omission was proper; (b) that the statement purported to be made by or on the authority of an expert and that the responsible parties reasonably believed, and continued to believe until the time when the securities were acquired, that the expert was competent to make or authorise the statement and had consented to its inclusion in the form and context in which it appeared; (c) that a correction, or statement that an expert was either not competent or had not given his consent, was published in a fashion calculated to draw it to the attention of likely acquirers of securities or that the parties responsible took all reasonable steps to publish these and reasonably believed this to have been done before any securities were acquired; (d) that the offending statement was an accurate and fair reproduction of one made by a public official or contained in an official document; (e) that the party who suffered the loss knew that the statement was misleading or untrue or that something had been omitted.[227] There are also some exemptions from disclosure of certain information under s.82 for listing particulars and s.87B for prospectuses, providing for circumstances where disclosure is not needed in the public interest, where it would be seriously detrimental to the issuer, or where it is unnecessary for the persons expecting to buy or deal in the securities.

---

[223] FSMA 2000 s.80. As regards prospectuses, see FSMA ss.87A, 87B.

[224] FSMA 2000 s.90(1). There are exceptions for experts acting in good faith etc. See Sch.10 to the Act. See also the Financial Services and Markets Act 2000 (Official Listing of Securities) Regulations 2001 (SI 2001/2956) reg.6.

[225] FSMA 2000 s.90(4).

[226] For listing particulars, see Pt 3 of the Financial Services and Markets Act 2000 (Official Listing of Securities) Regulations 2001 (SI 2001/2956); for prospectuses see Financial Services Authority Handbook Prospectus r.5.5.

[227] FSMA 2000 Sch.10.

Although it would now be unusual to use the common law to seek a remedy for misrepresentation in listing particulars or a prospectus, a person, acquiring securities in reliance on a fraudulent or negligent misrepresentation concerning the issue of those securities, is entitled to rescind his contract to acquire the securities.[228] After the commencement of the winding up of a company, the right to rescind cannot be exercised.[229]

Similar rules apply under s.90A of FSMA 2000 as regards continuing reports and statements about listed companies, such as the directors' report and in particular the matters referred to in the Transparency Directive arts 4, 5 and 6, these being the provision of regular periodic accounts, information about voting and changes to companies' constitutions: where information that is or ought to be provided in a statement or report about a company is misleading, inaccurate or omitted, as a result of which investors, relying on that statement or report, suffered loss, the company will have to make good the loss to the investor, but only if a person discharging managerial responsibilities within the company knew the statement was untrue or misleading or was reckless as to whether it was untrue or misleading, or knew the omission to be dishonest[230] concealment of a material fact.

46.22 Shares: Shareholders—The shares or other interest of any member in a company are moveable property.[231] Unless all the issued shares, or all the issued shares of a particular class, are fully paid and rank pari passu, each share must be distinguished by its appropriate number.[232] Although most companies, adopting Table A or the new model article for private limited companies, have only one class of ordinary shares, some companies have many different classes of shares, such as founders', employees', redeemable, preference, non-voting, deferred shares—a matter to be regulated by the articles. If a company wishes to create a new class of shares at any stage after the company's incorporation, the company will need to amend the company's articles by special resolution and send in the amended articles (with the terms relating to the new class of shares) to the Registrar of Companies.[233] As regards preference shares, the terms of the articles under which preference shares are issued are exhaustive of the rights of holders of these shares, and, unless otherwise provided, they have no right to any surplus assets which may remain, in liquidation, after all capital has been repaid.[234] In the absence of any provision to the contrary, preference shares are cumulative; if the full dividend has not been paid in any one year the arrears must be paid before any dividend is declared on the ordinary shares.[235]

Each of the subscribers of the memorandum is deemed to have agreed to become a member of the company, and is a shareholder for the number of shares which he thereby agrees to take.[236] Other persons are members of the company if

---

[228] *Mair v Rio Grande Rubber Estates Ltd*, 1913 SC (HL) 74; *Liverpool Palaces of Varieties Ltd v Miller* (1896) 4 S.L.T. 153.

[229] *Addie v Western Bank* (1867) 5 M. (HL) 80; as to the commencement of winding up, see para.46.51.

[230] For the meaning of "dishonest" in this context see FSMA 2000 Sch.10A para.6, namely being regarded as dishonest by people regularly trading on the securities market in question and the "dishonest" person being aware that it was so regarded.

[231] CA 2006 s.541.

[232] CA 2006 s.543.

[233] CA 2006 ss.21, 26.

[234] *Wilsons and Clyde Co v Scottish Insurance Corp*, 1949 S.C. (HL) 90.

[235] *Partick Gas Co v Taylor* (1888) 15 R. 711; *Ferguson and Forrester v Buchanan*, 1920 S.C. 154.

[236] CA 2006 s.112(1).

they have agreed to be so, and if their names are entered in its register of members.[237] A statement of willingness to take shares will not readily be construed as an application.[238] In the ordinary case an application for shares, where there is no prior obligation on either party, is merely an offer, which must be accepted by the company, and may be withdrawn by the applicant.[239] But an application is in substance the acceptance of an offer and cannot be withdrawn if it is made in response to an undertaking by the company to allot a certain number of shares if applied for,[240] or in pursuance of a prior agreement to underwrite the shares.[241] The power of a company to allot shares may be conferred on the directors by the company's articles or by the company in general meeting,[242] normally for a period of up to five years,[243] but when there is only one class of shares, there is no need for the directors to seek the prior approval of the members (unless the articles say otherwise) or have the power to allot shares specified in the articles.[244] The restriction on public offers or allotments by private companies has been noted.[245] There are particular provisions dealing with allotments of share capital of a Plc where the issue is not fully subscribed.[246] An allotment made in contravention of these provisions is voidable, at the instance of the applicant, within one month of the allotment, and not later, and it is voidable whether or not the company is in liquidation.[247] All allotments of shares must be registered with the Registrar within one month of allotment.[248] Allotment gives the acquirer of the shares the unconditional right to be included in the company's register of members in respect of those shares.[249] Before any allotment takes place, the directors must consider the significance of members' pre-emption rights. Pre-emption rights entitle existing shareholders to subscribe for a proportion of the newly allottable shares relative to their current shareholding within their companies.[250] The purpose of pre-emption rights is to enable existing shareholders to maintain their proportion of the equity of the company. Pre-emption rights do not, however, apply where: (a) bonus shares are being issued[251]; (b) shares are being allotted wholly or partly for non-cash consideration[252]; (c) where the shares in question are those within an employees' share scheme[253]; (d) where pre-emption rights are excluded under the

---

[237] CA 2006 s.112(2). *Farstad Supply A/S v Enviroco Limited* [2011] UKSC 16; [2011] 1 W.L.R. 921 confirms that a member named on the register is deemed to be a member of the company, even if it is only holding the shares on behalf of a nominee or as a result of having had shares pledged to it in security for some other obligation.

[238] *Mason v Banhar Coal Co* (1882) 9 R. 883; *Todd v Millen*, 1910 S.C. 868.

[239] *Mason* (1882) 9 R. 883; *Chapman v Sulphite Paper* Co (1892) 19 R. 837.

[240] *Todd v Millen*, 1910 S.C. 868.

[241] *Premier Briquette Co v Gray*, 1922 S.C. 329.

[242] CA 2006 s.551.

[243] CA 2006 s.551(3). This power may be renewed or revoked as necessary.

[244] CA 2006 s.550.

[245] CA 2006 s.755. See para.46.08.

[246] CA 2006 s.578.

[247] CA 2006 s.579. However, proceedings to recover loss or damage may not commence more than two years from the date of allotment: s.579(4).

[248] CA 2006 s.555(2).

[249] CA 2006 s.558. The distinction between issue and allotment has not been clarified in statute, but following *National Westminster Bank v IRC* [1994] 2 B.C.L.C. 239 (HL) allotment precedes issue, and issue is when the member's name is inserted in the register of members. In many respects the words are treated as synonymous.

[250] The period within which to take up the pre-emption right offer must be at least 15 days.

[251] CA 2006 s.564.

[252] CA 2006 s.565.

[253] CA 2006 s.566.

company's articles[254] either generally[255] or for particular allotments[256]; (e) where the members decline to exercise their pre-emption rights (but only as regards those particular members who so decline)[257]; (f) where the company has only one class of shares and the articles provide for no pre-emption rights[258]; (g) where the directors are authorised by the articles or special resolution to ignore the pre-emption rights[259]; or (h) where the members pass a special resolution to dispense with pre-emption rights for a particular allotment.[260] When the shares in question are treasury shares,[261] the directors may be given the authority to allot shares without considering the pre-emption rights.[262] Where directors fail to take account of the provisions of a company's pre-emption rights (where they exist) the directors are jointly and severally personally liable to compensate any person to whom the pre-emption offer should have been made and who suffered loss as a result.[263]

46.23 Liability on shares—A shareholder is liable to pay the amount for the time being unpaid on his shares up to the nominal amount of his shares when called upon to do so, or ultimately on its liquidation. Shares may be allotted as fully or partly paid up[264] otherwise than in cash in return for goods, services or other consideration, but the company must in all cases, within one month, lodge with the Registrar the statement of capital indicating the number of the shares, the aggregate nominal value of those shares, and the amount paid up on those shares.[265] Failure renders the officers of the company liable to penalties, but it is possible, on application to the court, to apply to the court for relief where the omission was accidental or inadvertent or where it is just and equitable to afford relief.[266] The issue of shares at a discount is expressly prohibited.[267] However, a private company, in the absence of fraud, may issue shares for what turns out to be less than full value[268] though there does need to be genuine and present consideration.[269] For Plcs, not only must the subscriber shares be paid in cash[270] but a public company may not accept undertakings to do work or perform services in exchange for shares,[271] accept an undertaking to be performed in more than five years' time in exchange

---

[254] CA 2006 s.567(1)(a).

[255] CA 2006 s.567(2)(a).

[256] CA 2006 s.567(2)(b).

[257] CA 2006 s.561(1)(b).

[258] CA 2006 s.569.

[259] CA 2006 s.570.

[260] CA 2006 s.571. In this case the directors must explain beforehand the significance of the resolution to the members. The directors will suffer criminal penalties for any matter that is false or misleading in their explanations (s.572).

[261] Treasury shares are commonly shares bought back by the company and available for re-issue without the requirement to go through the entire allotment procedure again.

[262] CA 2006 s.573.

[263] CA 2006 s.568(4).

[264] All shares in Plcs must be paid up to at least one quarter of their nominal value plus any premium (s.586).

[265] CA 2006 s.555.

[266] CA 2006 s.557(3).

[267] CA 2006 ss.552, 580. See *Klenck v East India Mining Co* (1886) 16 R. 271; *Ooregum Gold Mining Co v Roper* [1982] A.C. 125.

[268] *Re Wragg Ltd* [1897] 1 Ch. 796, CA.

[269] *Hong Kong and China Gas Coal Ltd v Glen* [1914] 1 Ch. 527.

[270] CA 2006 s.584.

[271] CA 2006 s.585.

for shares[272] or accept non-cash consideration for shares without the non-cash consideration being independently valued before the allotment is made.[273] In each case the penalty lies with the allottee who is required to pay the proper cash amount together with interest on the sum due at the rate of 5 per cent.[274] Subject to power contained in the articles and notice in any prospectus, a commission (within certain limits) may be paid by the company to any person in consideration of his subscribing or agreeing to subscribe for shares in the company or procuring subscriptions.[275] Unless these conditions are satisfied the company is prohibited from applying any of its shares or capital money in this way.[276]

Provisions as to shares: Alteration and reduction of capital—A company **46.24** may alter its issued share capital[277] of the company in the following respects[278]: (1) the increase of its share capital by the allotment and issue of new shares; (2) consolidation and division of its share capital into shares of larger amount[279]; (3) subdivision of shares into shares of smaller amount[280]; (4) reconversion of stock into shares[281]; (5) redenomination of shares from one currency to another.[282] The process of allotment and issue is explained above.[283]

A private company having a share capital may reduce its share capital by special resolution preceded by a solvency statement which must be signed by all the directors no more than fourteen days before the special resolution.[284] A private company does not now need to have authority in its articles to reduce its capital. There must be at least one member of the company in existence after the reduction.[285] The solvency statement must indicate that each director is of the opinion that as at the date of the statement the company can meet its debts as they fall due or, if the company is to be wound up within the next twelve months, that it could pay all its debts within twelve months of the company's winding up.[286] In forming their opinion, the directors must take into account all the company's liabilities, including both prospective and contingent liabilities.[287] The resolution, directors' solvency statement and the required statement of capital must be registered with the Registrar.[288] Public companies must, and private companies may, use the court procedure for reduction of capital under s.645. This requires the company to apply to the court, having previously passed a special resolution, for confirmation of the

---

[272] CA 2006 s.587.

[273] CA 2006 ss.593–609.

[274] CA 2006 s.591.

[275] CA 2006 s.553(1),(2).

[276] CA 2006 s.552.

[277] As authorised share capital is no longer required under CA 2006, there is no provision in the Act for its alteration.

[278] CA 2006 s.617.

[279] CA 2006 s.618.

[280] CA 2006 s.618.

[281] CA 2006 ss.620, 621.

[282] CA 2006 ss.622–628.

[283] At para.47.22.

[284] CA 2006 s.642.

[285] That member must not hold redeemable shares (s.641(2)).

[286] CA 2006 s.643(1). If a director refuses to make this statement, the company will have to use the court procedure instead.

[287] CA 2006 s.643(2). If the directors do not have reasonable grounds for their opinions, and the statement is delivered to the Registrar of Companies, the directors commit an offence punishable by up to two years in prison (s.643(4),(5)).

[288] CA 2006 s.644(1).

reduction.[289] The court must be satisfied[290] that the terms are just and equitable as between the various classes of shareholders,[291] and as between creditors.[292] There is no limit to the power of a company to reduce its capital, which it may exercise in any way.[293] It may extinguish or reduce the liability on any of its shares in respect of capital not paid up, cancel any paid-up share capital which is lost or unrepresented by available assets and pay off any paid-up share capital which is in excess of the company's wants.[294] It may convert issued shares into redeemable shares with a postponed redemption date,[295] or cancel a share premium account to use the released funds for other purposes.[296] Again, the court order, the special resolution and the statement of capital need to be sent to the Registrar of Companies.[297]

If a company has issued redeemable shares,[298] they may be redeemed if they are fully paid and paid for on redemption, but payment may be made only out of distributable profits of the company or the proceeds of a fresh issue of shares made for the purposes of the redemption,[299] or, exceptionally, by a private company, following complex rules, out of capital.[300] A company may also acquire its own shares, following the "market" procedure[301] or the "off-market" procedure.[302] The market purchase procedure is used in the case of shares purchased on a recognised investment exchange in the open market. It requires an ordinary resolution to give the directors authority to purchase a maximum number of shares at a price or within a range of prices.[303] The off-market procedure is used for shares purchased otherwise than on a recognised investment exchange, or where they are on a recognised investment exchange but are not subject to a marketing arrangement.[304] The off-market purchase requires a special resolution to give the directors the authority to purchase the shares in terms of a contract (or memorandum) for the purchase.[305] The contract must be exhibited to the members at least fifteen days before the meeting at which the resolution is to be approved, or sent out with the copy of the written resolution approving the purchase.[306] Shares

---

[289] CA 2006 s.641(1)(b).

[290] The court will generally appoint a reporter, commonly a solicitor with expertise in company law, to report back and confirm that the requirements of the legislation have been fully complied with.

[291] *Balmenach Glenlivet Distllery v Croall* (1906) 8 F. 1135; *Caldwell v Caldwell*, 1916 S.C. (HL) 120; *Wilsons and Clyde Coal Co v Scottish Insurance Corp*, 1949 S.C. (HL) 90.

[292] CA 2006 s.646; *Westburn Sugar Refineries*, 1951 S.C. (HL) 57; *Anderson, Brown and Co*, 1965 S.C. 81; *Lawrie & Symington*, 1969 S.L.T. 221. A creditor who wishes to object to the reduction have to be able to prove that there is a real likelihood that the company would be unable to pay his debt or claim when it falls due (s.646(1)).

[293] CA 2006 s.641(3). This is subject to the requirement that after the reduction in capital, there must still be some shares in the company in existence, and to the requirements of any terms to the contrary in the company's articles.

[294] CA 2006 s.641(4).

[295] *Forth Wines Ltd, Petitioners*, 1993 S.L.T. 170.

[296] *Re Ratners Group Plc* [1988] B.C.L.C. 685; *Quayle Munro Ltd, Petitioners*, 1992 S.C. 24.

[297] CA 2006 s.649.

[298] A redeemable share is one that is issued with the expression intention that it should be taken back by the company at a later date on which occasion the shareholder's capital is returned to him (s.684).

[299] CA 2006 ss.685–687.

[300] CA 2006 ss.709–723.

[301] CA 2006 s.693(2).

[302] CA 2006 s.693(1).

[303] CA 2006 s.701.

[304] CA 2006 s.693(2), (3).

[305] CA 2006 s.694.

[306] CA 2006 s.695.

which are redeemed or purchased by the company are treated as cancelled, unless they are retained as treasury shares to be re-issued at a later date,[307] and the amount of the company's issued share capital is diminished by the nominal value of the shares.[308] To the extent that the diminished capital is not replenished by new capital from a new allotment of shares made for the purposes of the redemption or repurchase, a capital redemption reserve must be created, equal in value to the aggregrate nominal value of the redeemed or repurchased shares.[309]

Financial assistance for the acquisition of shares—Financial assistance means **46.25** the direct or indirect giving or lending of funds by a company to a purchaser, or providing security, an indemnity or a guarantee, or any form of assistance whereby the net assets of the company are reduced to a material extent (or where the company has no net assets), for a purchaser, to enable that purchaser to acquire shares in that company or its holding company.[310] This is prohibited,[311] subject to certain exceptions. Financial assistance by any company to enable a purchaser to acquire shares in that company, or one of its subsidiaries, is permissible for the payment of dividends, a distribution in a winding up, the issue of bonus shares, a reduction of capital, a permitted redemption or repurchase of shares, and anything done under the order of the court.[312] The following are also permissible where the company providing the assistance is a free-standing private company (i.e. a private company that is not a subsidiary or the holding company of a public company)[313]: the lending of money in the ordinary course of business; the provision of assistance for an employees' share scheme or for employees and their families to enable the scheme or the employees to buy shares in their employer; or the provision of loans to enable employees to buy shares in their employer.[314] Where the company is a public company this second set of permitted forms of financial assistance is only available where the net assets of the company are not reduced by the giving of the assistance, or to the extent that those assets are reduced, the assistance is provided out of distributable profits.[315] It is also permissible to give financial assistance for the purchase of shares in a company or its holding company if the company's principal purpose in giving the assistance is not to give it for the purpose of any such acquisition, or the giving of that assistance for that purpose is only an incidental part of some larger purpose of the company, and the assistance is given in good faith in the interests of the company.[316] This impenetrable wording is not without its difficulties and CA 2006 has not resolved them. The wording was extensively discussed in *Brady v Brady*[317] and in that case was given a very restricted interpretation. Outside the permitted exceptions, financial assistance is unlawful: a criminal offence is committed by the company and by any officer in

---

[307] CA 2006 ss.724–732.
[308] CA 2006 s.706.
[309] CA 2006 s.733.
[310] CA 2006 s.677.
[311] CA 2006 s.678(1).
[312] CA 2006 s.681.
[313] CA 2006 ss.678(1), 679(1)
[314] CA 2006 s.682.
[315] CA 2006 s.682(1).
[316] CA 2006 s.678(2).
[317] *Brady v Brady* [1989] A.C. 755, HL; [1988] B.C.L.C. 20, CA, followed in *Plaut v Steiner* (1989) 5 B.C.C. 352. Broadly speaking, it would appear that financial assistance is acceptable provided the assistance plays a relatively insignificant part within some wider restructuring or operation undertaken by the company.

default.[318] Private companies, provided they are not subsidiaries of public companies[319] or holding companies with subsidiaries which are public companies,[320] are not bound by the prohibition on financial assistance.[321] The prohibition does not extend to foreign subsidiaries.[322] If the company providing the financial assistance is a private company at the time of the assistance, even if it previously was a public company and subsequently returns to being a public company, the company avoids the sanctions applicable to financial assistance.[323]

46.26 Resolutions—Certain acts are required, either by statute or under the articles, to be done not by the directors or others to whom the management of the business of the company may have been delegated, but only by the members acting collectively as the company. The company acts by resolutions of its members passed at a general meeting, or in the case of private companies only, by written resolutions. Resolutions are now of two kinds, namely ordinary and special. An ordinary resolution is one passed by a bare majority, either at a general meeting or as a written resolution.[324] Certain ordinary resolutions, such as for the removal of an auditor or director, require "special notice" of 28 days before the meeting at which the resolution is to be moved to have been given to the company.[325] A special resolution is one passed by a three-quarters majority, and where it is passed at a general meeting, the notice of the meeting must have included the text of the resolution and specified the intention to propose the resolution as a special resolution.[326] A written resolution is the common means of passing resolutions in private companies, except in the case of the resolution to remove a director under s.168 or an auditor under s.510.[327] Where written resolutions are used, such resolutions may be proposed either by the directors or the members.[328] If the directors wish to propose a written resolution, a copy of it must be sent to every member, either in electronic copy or in hard copy, together with an indication of how to assent to it, and the date by which assent must be given, that date being the date 28 days after the circulation date.[329] If insufficient assent is given by the

---

[318] CA 2006 s.680; *Heald v O'Connor* [1971] 1 W.L.R. 497; *Re Hill and Tyler Ltd* [2005] 1 B.C.L.C. 41; *Neilson v Stewart*, 1991 S.C. (HL) 22. It may also be grounds for disqualification as a director: *Re Continental Assurance Co of London Plc* [1997] 1 B.C.L.C. 48.

[319] CA 2006 s.678(1).

[320] CA 2006 s.679(1).

[321] This is not to say that lenders may not insist on some procedure, similar to the former (and now no longer required) "whitewash" procedure, being required of the company's directors where financial assistance is taking place. In any event directors need to be satisfied that the financial assistance is likely to promote the success of the company in terms of CA 2006 s.172.

[322] *Arab Bank Plc v Mercantile Holdings Ltd* [1994] 1 B.C.L.C. 330.

[323] CA 2006 s.678(1) and (3).

[324] CA 2006 s.282. The former 14 days' notice is no longer required. The only significant ordinary resolutions which need to be intimated to the Registrar of Companies are a resolution to give directors authority to allot shares and a resolution to wind up the company.

[325] CA 2006 s.312. This is to allow time for the auditor or director to prepare a statement to be issued to the members of the company. The words "special notice" are supposed to alert the members to the significance of the resolution.

[326] CA 2006 s.283. Copies of all special resolutions must be sent to the Registrar of Companies within 15 days of being passed.

[327] CA 2006 s.288(2). These two resolutions must be passed at a general meeting and cannot be passed by written resolution.

[328] CA 2006 s.288(3).

[329] CA 2006 s.297. The circulation date is the day the letter or email with the resolution is sent out to the members. A company may have a longer or lesser period than 28 days if so stated in the articles (s.297(1)).

required date the resolution will lapse.[330] The day that the required majority[331] has assented to the written resolution, whether in writing or electronically, is the day the written resolution is passed.[332] If members representing 5 per cent[333] of the voting rights wish to propose a resolution they may do so, but the company is not compelled to circulate it if the proposed written resolution would be ineffective, is defamatory of any person, is frivolous or is vexatious.[334] Assuming the resolution is acceptable, the members may require the company to accompany the resolution with a statement not more than 1,000 words long.[335] The same procedures that apply to assent to directors' resolutions apply to members' resolutions.[336] The expenses of the circulation are to be borne by the members proposing the resolution and the company may insist on funds being paid to cover the circulation costs.[337] During the time for assent, the resolution must remain visible on the company's website.[338]

Public companies may not pass written resolutions,[339] and in the case of a public company, a resolution may only be passed at a general meeting which has been duly convened and has followed the procedures outlined in ss.301–335, explained shortly.

Where a company, private or public, wishes to hold general meetings, the meetings may either be called by the directors[340] or the members.[341] Most general meetings are called by the directors, but the directors are required to convene a meeting properly requested by the members within 21 days of the date of the request, and directors may not convene the meeting for a date more than 28 days after the date of the notice convening the meeting.[342] The members' request must indicate the general nature of the business to be held at the meeting and include the text of any resolution to be moved at the meeting.[343] Any resolution proposed by the members at such a general meeting must not be ineffective, defamatory, frivolous or vexatious.[344] If the directors fail to convene the general meeting, the members themselves may call the meeting at the company's expense, and the costs thereof to the company must be reimbursed out of the directors' fees or other remuneration.[345] The court can also order the holding of a meeting.[346]

General meetings require at least 14 days' notice, and annual general meetings require at least 21 days' notice.[347] Articles may prescribe longer periods if desired.

---

[330] CA 2006 ss.291(4), 297.
[331] This will depend on whether it is a special or an ordinary resolution.
[332] CA 2006 s.296(4).
[333] Or such lesser figure as is stated in the articles (s.292(5)).
[334] CA 2006 s.292(2).
[335] CA 2006 s.292(3).
[336] CA 2006 s.293.
[337] CA 2006 s.294.
[338] CA 2006 s.299.
[339] CA 2006 ss.281(2) and 288(1).
[340] CA 2006 s.302.
[341] CA 2006 s.303. This is only permissible where the members representing at least 10% of the voting rights or 10% of the capital (and having voting rights) request the directors to call a meeting (s.303(2), (3)). Under certain circumstances the percentage is reduced to 5% (s.303(3)).
[342] CA 2006 s.304.
[343] CA 2006 s.303(4).
[344] CA 2006 s.303(5).
[345] CA 2006 s.305.
[346] CA 2006 s.306.
[347] CA 2006 s.307(1), (2). Section 360 explains that in all these notices, the "clear day" rule applies whereby the day of the meeting and the day of the notice of the meeting are excluded from the period of 21 days.

The members may agree to accept a lesser period of notice for general meetings, this being known as consent to short notice. For short notice for a private company, at least 90 per cent of the members must consent, and for a public company, at least 95 per cent of the members must consent.[348] Notice of the meeting must be given in hard copy, electronically or on a website, or by a combination of these means.[349] Every member is entitled to receive notice of the meeting,[350] and the notice must contain the date, time, place and general nature of the business to be discussed at the meeting.[351] Members with the required number or percentage of voting rights[352] may require a statement of not more than 1,000 words about any matter to be circulated to the members,[353] the cost normally to be borne by the members requesting its circulation unless the company resolves otherwise or the company is a public company, the statement relates to an annual general meeting of that company, and sufficient members request its circulation.[354]

When a meeting is held, two members, unless the articles say otherwise, will be a quorum, except when the company is a single member company in which case that one person will be a quorum.[355] Normally decisions may be made by a show of hands[356] and a declaration by the chairman that the resolution has been carried is conclusive evidence of the fact, unless a poll be demanded,[357] when reference must be had to the number of votes to which each shareholder is entitled.[358]

A member who cannot attend a general meeting may appoint a proxy, who may attend, speak and vote at the meeting.[359] Members that are companies may send corporate representatives.[360] These rules all apply, with suitable modifications, to any meetings of classes of shares within a company.[361] Public companies have additional requirements in that they must hold their annual general meetings within six months of their accounting reference date,[362] and consent to short notice may only be given if there is unanimous approval of this.[363] There are provisions, very similar to those for general meetings above, for the circulation of members' resolutions at annual general meetings[364] although the costs of such circulation must be tendered earlier than is the case for ordinary general meetings.[365] There are also special provisions for quoted companies requiring the publication of poll

---

[348] CA 2006 s.307. This provision only applies to extraordinary general meetings of public companies.

[349] CA 2006 s.308. "Electronic Form" includes text messages.

[350] CA 2006 s.310.

[351] CA 2006 s.311.

[352] See CA 2006 s.314(2).

[353] CA 2006 s.314.

[354] CA 2006 s.316. This section is designed to allow members the opportunity to have a statement about a resolution they wish to move circulated to the other members. There are provisions to prevent its circulation if the court is satisfied that the right to have the statement circulated is being abused (s.317). For the number of members who may request the circulation, see s.314(2).

[355] CA 2006 s.318(1), (2).

[356] CA 2006 s.320.

[357] CA 2006 s.321.

[358] CA 2006 s.320. *Graham's Morocco Co*, 1932 S.C. 269.

[359] CA 2006 s.324. There are detailed provisions for the appointment and rights of proxies (ss.324–331).

[360] CA 2006 s.323.

[361] CA 2006 s.334.

[362] CA 2006 s.336.

[363] CA 2006 s.337.

[364] CA 2006 ss.338, 339.

[365] CA 2006 s.340. However, if the required number or proportion of shareholders (as shown in s.338(3)) manage to make their request for the circulation of a resolution before the end of the financial year preceding the meeting, the costs of circulation are borne by the company (s.340(1)).

results on their websites[366] and extensive provisions for independent reports on any polls.[367]

A public company must lay before a general meeting the company's annual accounts, the directors' report and the report of the auditors on the annual accounts.[368] Quoted companies must lay the directors' remuneration report before the members to be approved by ordinary resolution.[369] Records of all meetings must be properly kept,[370] even in single member limited companies,[371] and made available for inspection.[372]

Majority and minority rights—By his contract with the company, each individual member undertakes to accept as binding upon him the decision of the majority of the shareholders, provided that it is arrived at in accordance with the law and the articles of association. This principle is often referred to as the common law rule in *Foss v Harbottle*.[373] In that case, a minority of the shareholders alleged that the company had a claim of damages against certain of its directors, but at a general meeting the majority, who happened also to be the directors, resolved that no action should be taken against them. An action against the directors by the minority was dismissed, on the ground that the acts of the directors were capable of confirmation by a majority of the members, and that it was not for the court to interfere with the majority's decision as to what was for the benefit of the company. Under the common law a limited number of exceptions arose to this principle, but unless the circumstances of the case fell within those exceptions, a minority's chances of success were slim. Consequently the use of the common law to protect minority interests was rare.[374] As a further point, in general the courts were, and indeed still are, very reluctant to interfere with commercial decisions made by those managing the company, whether or not the managers are the majority.[375]

An aggrieved minority shareholder may nevertheless avail himself of certain statutory remedies. If the majority of the shareholders act in oppression of the minority, the minority may apply to the court for the winding up of the company, on the ground that it is just and equitable to do so,[376] or, in exceptional cases, for the appointment of a judicial factor.[377] The court cannot make a winding-up order on the ground that it is just and equitable to do so, if those who are petitioning are contributories, as defined by s.76, if the court is of the opinion that some other remedy is available to the petitioners, or that the petitioners are acting

46.27

---

[366] CA 2006 s.341.

[367] CA 2006 ss.342–351.

[368] CA 2006 ss.437, 495.

[369] CA 2006 s.439.

[370] CA 2006 s.355.

[371] CA 2006 s.357; *Neptune (Vehicle Washing Equipment) Ltd v Fitzgerald (No.2)* [1995] B.C.C. 1000 Ch.D.

[372] CA 2006 s.358.

[373] *Foss v Harbottle* (1843) 2 Hare 461; see G. Morse, *Palmer's Company Law* (Sweet and Maxwell), para.2.1112. The rule in *Foss* has been applied by the House of Lords in a Scottish appeal: see, e.g. *Orr v Glasgow, Airdrie and Monklands Junction Railway Co* (1860) 3 Macq. 799.

[374] *Wilson v Inverness Retail and Business Park Ltd*, 2003 S.L.T. 301 contains a useful discussion of the common law position in Scotland.

[375] *Re Saul Harrison and Sons Plc* [1994] B.C.C. 475.

[376] IA 1986 s.122(1)(g); *Ebrahimi v Westbourne Galleries* [1973] A.C. 360; *Lewis v Haas*, 1971 S.L.T. 57; *Teague, Petr*, 1985 S.L.T. 469; *Jesner v Jarrad Properties*, 1994 S.L.T. 83.

[377] See *Fraser, Petitioner*, 1971 S.L.T. 146. Note also *McGuinness v Black (No.2)*, 1990 S.L.T. 461; *Weir v Rees*, 1991 S.L.T. 345.

unreasonably in seeking to have the company wound up instead of pursuing that other remedy.[378]

The more common statutory remedy is under s.994.[379] Any member of a company who complains that the company's affairs are being or have been conducted in a manner which is unfairly prejudicial to the interests of its members generally or of some part of the members including at least himself, or that any actual or proposed act or omission of the company is or would be so prejudicial, may apply to the court for relief. If the court is satisfied that the application is well founded, it may make such order as it thinks fit for giving relief in respect of the matters complained of.[380] The court has unrestricted powers in this regard, but four possible ways[381] in which it may provide relief are to pronounce an order (a) regulating the conduct of the company's affairs in the future, (b) requiring the company to refrain from doing or continuing to do an act complained of or to do an act which the petitioner has complained it has omitted to do,[382] (c) authorising civil proceedings to be brought in the name and on behalf of the company by such person or persons on such terms as the court may direct, or (d) providing for the purchase of the shares of any member of the company by other members of the company or by the company itself.[383] This last remedy is in practice by far the commonest. What constitutes "unfairly prejudicial" conduct is not defined by statute but it requires both unfairness and prejudice and where either of these is not present the case for unfair prejudice will not have been made.[384] A member of a company will not ordinarily be entitled to complain of unfairness unless there has been some breach of the terms on which the member agreed that the affairs of the company should be conducted and unless the member is litigating in his capacity as a member as opposed to any other capacity.[385] However, equitable considerations will temper this when it would be unfair for those conducting the affairs of the company to rely upon their strict legal powers. For example, an order was granted prohibiting a rights issue, because the majority shareholder knew that the petitioner could not find the money to take up his shares.[386] Relief is available to a person who is not a member of a company but to whom shares in the company have been transferred or transmitted by operation of law,[387] such as the executors of a deceased shareholder or his trustee in bankruptcy. It is not limited to persons who hold minority interests in the company, and is therefore available to majority shareholders who can claim to have suffered unfair prejudice as a result of the exercise of their rights by a minority.[388]

A further statutory remedy is introduced by CA 2006 s.265. This introduced into the law of Scotland by statute a derivative claim, which confers on a member the right to raise proceedings against a director in circumstances where there is an

---

[378] IA 1986 s.125(2); *Gammack v Mitchells (Fraserburgh) Ltd*, 1983 S.C. 39.

[379] This was formerly s.459 of the Companies Act 1985.

[380] CA 2006 s.996(1).

[381] CA 2006 s.996(2).

[382] e.g. *Whyte, Petitioner*, 1984 S.L.T. 330; *Re H.R. Harmer Ltd* [1959] 1 W.L.R. 62.

[383] e.g. *Re Bird Precision Bellows Ltd* [1986] Ch. 658; *Re London School of Electronics* [1986] Ch. 211; see also *Meyer v Scottish Cooperative Wholesale Society*, 1958 S.C. (HL) 40; *Ferguson v MacLennan Salmon Co Ltd*, 1990 S.L.T. 658.

[384] *Re Saul Harrison and Sons Plc* [1994] B.C.C. 475.

[385] *O'Neill v Phillips* [1999] 1 W.L.R. 1092.

[386] *Re Cumana Ltd* [1986] B.C.L.C. 430. For a slightly similar Scottish case, see *Pettie v Thomson Pettie Tube Products Ltd*, 2001 S.C. 431.

[387] CA 2006 s.994(2).

[388] CA 2006 s.994(1)(a).

actual or proposed act or omission, involving negligence, default, breach of duty or breach of trust.[389] The aggrieved member will raise the proceedings in order to protect the interests of the company and to obtain a remedy, not on his own behalf, but on behalf of the company and for its benefit.[390] The term "director" covers present and past directors and shadow directors, and the term "member" covers those to whom shares have passed by operation of law.[391] Under s.266 the member may only bring the derivative proceedings with the leave of the court, and in applying for leave, must specify the cause of the action and the facts of the matter.[392] If the application and the evidence in its support do not support a prima facie case for granting such leave, the court must refuse the application and make any necessary consequential order.[393] If the application is not refused, the applicant must serve the application on the company and the court must make an order requiring the company to produce its evidence on the matter or may adjourn the proceedings for the obtaining of evidence,[394] and the company will then be entitled to take part in any further proceedings. The court may then have a hearing at which the application may or may not be granted, or the proceedings further adjourned, perhaps for a meeting of the shareholders to consider the position.

Under s.267, if a company has raised proceedings, and those proceedings are in respect of an act or omission which could be the basis for a derivative action, a member may apply to the court to be substituted for the company, and for the proceedings to continue as derivative proceedings because (i) the way in which the company has been conducting its own proceedings amounts to an abuse of the process of court, (ii) the company has not been diligent in prosecuting its own proceedings, or (iii) it is appropriate for the member to take over the proceedings instead.[395] Again, if it appears to the court that the evidence in support of the application does not amount to a prima facie case, the court must refuse the application; and where it does amount to a prima facie case, the company may be asked to produce its own evidence and to take part in the further proceedings.

The court must refuse leave to raise derivative proceedings under s.266 or the application under s.267 if it is satisfied that a person (generally a director) acting in accordance with s.172 of CA 2006[396] would not seek to raise or continue the proceedings, or, where the matter in question is an act or omission which has already occurred, the act or omission has been previously authorised or ratified.[397] Where the court is not obliged to refuse leave, but is considering whether or not

---

[389] At the time of writing there have been concerns that these provisions may expose directors to unwelcome litigation from opportunistic litigants. For this reason, the two-stage court process has been introduced with the intention that this should ensure that only serious cases proceed. For consideration of the purposes of these provisions, see *Wishart, Petitioner*, first heard at 2010 S.L.T. 371 by Lord Glennie, and subsequently appealed to the Inner House at 2010 S.C. 16; 2009 S.L.T. 812; [2010] B.C.C. 161. See also D. Cabrelli, "Statutory derivative proceedings: the view from the Inner House", Edin. L.R. 2010, 14(1), 116–121 and A. Keay and J.M. Loughrey, "Derivative proceedings in a brave new world for company management and shareholders", 2010 J.B.L. 151–178.

[390] If the member wishes to raise proceedings on his own behalf, s.994 would be the better remedy.

[391] CA 2006 s.265(7).

[392] CA 2006 s.266(2).

[393] CA 2006 s.266(3). The purpose of this first stage in the proceedings is to weed out the cases that clearly are frivolous, vexatious or otherwise without merit. For consideration of what is meant by a prima facie case, see *Gillespie v Toondale Ltd*, 2006 S.C. 304

[394] It is thought that during the adjournment the company may take the opportunity to convene a meeting to ratify the director's acts or omissions, or alternatively disown those acts or omissions.

[395] CA 2006 s.267(2).

[396] This is the duty to promote the success of the company.

[397] CA 2006 s.268(1).

to do so, under s.268(2) the court must take into account such matters as whether the applicant was acting in good faith,[398] the importance that a person acting in accordance with s.172 would attach to the raising or continuing of the action or the application, the likelihood of authorisation by the members of the act or omission before it occurs or ratification after it occurs, whether the company has decided not to raise proceedings or to persist in the proceeding, or whether the member would be better pursuing the matter in his own right.[399] In particular, the court should pay particular regard to the views of the members who have no personal interest, direct or indirect, in the matter.[400] It is also possible for a further member to seek the court's leave to stand in place of the member pursuing the derivative action.[401]

The remedies referred to in the previous paragraph may be exercised by any individual member of the company. Certain other rights are conferred by the Act on a minority of the members, and may be exercised despite the wishes of the majority. These include the right of the minority of not less than one-tenth of the paid-up capital to requisition the holding of an extraordinary general meeting,[402] of a specified minority to demand a poll,[403] and of 15 per cent of the holders of special classes of shares to object to a variation of the rights attached to that class.[404]

46.28 Accounts and balance sheet: Directors' report—Every company must keep accounting records sufficient to show and explain its transactions. These require to disclose with reasonable accuracy at any time the financial position of the company at that time, and to enable the directors to ensure that any balance sheet and profit and loss account which are prepared comply with the requirements of the Act.[405] In particular, accounting records must contain daily receipts and expenditure and record the company's assets and liabilities.[406] Directors are responsible for the annual preparation of a balance sheet and profit and loss account. Both must give a true and fair view of the company's state of affairs and profit or loss respectively.[407] Additionally, they must submit a Directors' Report presenting a fair view of the company's business development during the financial year and its position at its close.[408] In particular, unless the company is a small company, part of the Report should include a business review which should contain a fair review of the company's business and a description of the principal risks and uncertainties facing the company. Further information is required of quoted companies on environmental matters, the company's employees and social

---

[398] For an exploration of the extent of the necessary good faith, see *Iesini v Estrip Holdings Ltd* [2009] EWCH 2526.

[399] Under the equivalent English legislation, in *Franbar Holdings Ltd v Patel* [2009] 1 B.C.L.C. 1, *Mission Capital Plc v Sinclair* [2008] EWHC 1339 (Ch), and *Kleanthous v Paphitis* [2011] EWHC 2287 (Ch) the claimants were required to use the s.994 procedure instead of the derivative claim.

[400] CA 2006 s.268(3). There are concerns that these considerations may effectively amount to the courts being required to revisit commercial decisions legitimately made by the directors in the course of business.

[401] CA 2006 s.269.

[402] CA 2006 s.303.

[403] CA 2006 s.321(2).

[404] CA 2006 s.633.

[405] CA 2006 s.386(2).

[406] CA 2006 s.386(3).

[407] CA 2006 s.393. The degree of information required in the accounts varies between small companies, medium-sized companies, quoted companies and unquoted companies.

[408] CA 2006 s.416.

and community issues and the effectiveness of the company on these matters.[409] If the accounts are audited (and small companies' accounts do not need to be audited) the accounts must also be accompanied by the auditors' report stating whether or not, in their opinion, those accounts give a true and fair view of the company's finances.[410] The accounting records are to be kept at the registered office of the company or such other place as the directors think fit, and are to be at all times open to inspection by the officers of the company.[411]

A private company must send a copy of its accounts to the members at the end of the period for filing accounts or, if earlier, the date on which it actually delivers its accounts and report to the Registrar.[412] Public companies must deliver a copy of the accounts to the members 21 days before a general meeting of the company.[413] A copy of the accounts and directors' report must be delivered to the Registrar within six months after the ending of its financial year in the case of a public company, or nine months for private companies.[414] The accounts themselves must comply with the detailed requirements of CA 2006 and it is beyond the scope of this book to deal with these accounting matters. Each year a company must also lodge with the Registrar an annual return indicating the current directors and shareholders[415]: there are severe penalties for late returns.[416]

Dividends and distributions—A company is prohibited from making any distri- **46.29** bution except out of profits available for the purpose.[417] "Distribution" for this purpose means any form of distribution of a company's assets to its members whether in cash or otherwise, except for the issue of bonus shares, the redemption of redeemable shares or purchase by a company of its own shares, the reduction of share capital and a distribution of assets to members of the company on its winding up.[418] A company's profits available for distribution are defined as being its accumulated, realised profits so far as not previously utilised by distribution or capitalisation, less its accumulated, realised losses, so far as not previously written off in a reduction or re-organisation of capital duly made.[419] A public company may only make a distribution if the amount of the net assets is not less than the aggregate of its called up share capital and undistributable reserves, but a distribution may only be made to the extent that the distribution does not reduce the amount of those assets to less than that aggregate.[420] A profit which has not been realised is not available for distribution, nor may it be applied in paying up debentures or any amounts unpaid on the company's issued shares.[421] There are provisions made as to how "realised profits" and "realised losses" are to be calculated in particular circumstances such as when assets are revalued or distributions in kind are made.[422] If an unlawful distribution is made to a shareholder

---

[409] CA 2006 s.417.
[410] CA 2006 s.475.
[411] CA 2006 s.388.
[412] CA 2006 s.423.
[413] CA 2006 s.424.
[414] CA 2006 s.442.
[415] CA 2006 ss.854–857.
[416] CA 2006 s.858.
[417] CA 2006 s.830.
[418] CA 2006 s.829.
[419] CA 2006 s.830.
[420] CA 2006 s.831(1).
[421] CA 2006 s.849.
[422] CA 2006 ss.841–844.

who knew or had reasonable grounds for believing that it was unlawful, he is liable to repay it or a sum equal to its value to the company.[423] At common law, directors who were parties to the payment of a dividend which was unlawful were liable jointly and severally to repay the amount,[424] and this rule has been preserved in statute.[425] When the articles provide for payment of dividends in a certain event—provided that event does not amount to a contravention of the rules discussed above—a shareholder, or one class of shareholders may enforce compliance.[426]

46.30 Promoters—The term "promoter" has been judicially referred to as

> "a term not of law but of business usefully summing up in a single word a number of business operations familiar to the commercial world by which a company is generally brought into existence".[427]

The term is probably too vague to admit of an exact definition.[428]

A promoter is neither an agent nor a trustee for the company which he brings into existence.[429] Thus—subject to the necessity of full disclosure of the facts—a sale by a promoter to his company is valid.[430] It has been held that a promoter

> "must put himself in the position of an agent for the company which he has promoted, and must regulate his relations towards the company according to the duty of an agent".[431]

He stands in a fiduciary position to the company and must disclose all material facts.[432] The principle is not that it is illegal for a promoter to make a profit, but that the nature and source of his profit must be disclosed; and they must be disclosed to the shareholders, not merely to the directors who may be his nominees.[433] So while someone may purchase a property for £10,000 and sell it next day for £20,000, he may not do so without disclosure of the facts, if he is a promoter and the company the purchaser.[434] The company has in such cases the right, resting on general principles of law and not on any express provision of the Companies Acts, either to avoid the contract or to recover from the promoter any benefit he, or a firm of which he is a partner, may have gained.[435] To justify such

---

[423] CA 2006 s.847; *It's a Wrap (UK) Ltd (In Liquidation) v Gula* [2006] B.C.C. 626.

[424] *Flitcroft's Case* (1882) L.R. 21 Ch.D. 519; *Moxham v Grant* [1900] 1 Q.B. 88; *Liquidators of City of Glasgow Bank v Mackinnon* (1882) 9 R. 535; *Bairstow v Queen's Moat Houses Plc* [2002] B.C.C. 1025.

[425] CA 2006 s.847(3).

[426] *City Property Inv Co v Thorburn* (1897) 25 R. 361; *Paterson v Paterson*, 1917 S.C. (HL) 13.

[427] *Whaley Bridge Co v Green* (1879) L.R. 5 Q.B.D. 109 at 111, per Bowen L.J.

[428] See *Lydney Co v Bird* (1886) L.R. 33 Ch.D. 85; *Jubilee Cotton Mills v Lewis* [1924] A.C. 958.

[429] *Omnium Electric Palaces Ltd v Baines* [1914] 1 Ch. 332; *Tinnevelly Sugar Refining Co Ltd v Mirrlees* (1894) 21 R. 1009.

[430] *Lagunas Nitrate Co v Lagunas Syndicate* [1899] 2 Ch. 392.

[431] *Edinburgh Northern Tramways Co v Mann* (1896) 23 R. 1056, per Lord McLaren at 1066.

[432] *Erlanger v New Sombrero Phosphate Co* (1878) L.R. 2 App. Cas. 1218.

[433] *Mann v Edinburgh Northern Tramways Co* (1891) 18 R. 1140, affd 20 R. (HL) 7; *Erlanger v New Sombrero Phosphate Co* (1878) L.R. 2 App. Cas. 1218; *Re Lady Forrest Mine* [1901] 1 Ch. 582. It may be otherwise if the board of directors is truly independent.

[434] See opinion of Lord Blackburn in *Erlanger* (1878) L.R. 2 App. Cas. 1218.

[435] *Henderson v Huntingdon Copper Co* (1877) 4 R. 294, affd 5 R. (HL) 1; *Scottish Pacific Coast Mining Co v Falkner* (1888) 15 R. 290; *Mann v Edinburgh Northern Tramways Co* (1891) 18 R. 1140.

a claim it is not necessary that the promoter has obtained something from the company, or at its expense. Where what he obtained were debentures, irregularly issued, and in reality valueless, it was held that the company could recover from him the price at which he had fraudulently sold them to a third party.[436]

Directors: Appointment—Every public company must have at least two direc- **46.31** tors but a private company need only have one.[437] At least one director must be a natural person.[438] Directors must be over the age of 16, but if a director under the age of 16 purports to act as a director, he may not avoid liability for his actions because of his age.[439] In a public company each director must be voted for individually by the members.[440] Even if a director turns out to be invalidly appointed, his acts as a director are still treated as valid.[441] A register of the company's directors must normally be kept at the company's registered office,[442] and the register is open to inspection by the members without charge or by others on payment of a fee.[443] Separately, but not available to the public, a company must keep a register of directors' residential addresses.[444] All appointments of directors, along with changes to directors' particulars, such as ceasing to be a director, must be intimated to the Registrar.[445] There is no general rule that a director must be a shareholder in the company, but it is sometimes provided in articles that every director must hold one or more shares, commonly referred to as qualification shares.

The duration of a company director's appointment, and any methods of re-appointment, are commonly specified in the company's articles. The members of the company may increase or reduce the number of directors by ordinary resolution, subject to any minimum for the number of directors which may be set by the articles and statute. A director (notwithstanding anything in the articles or in any agreement with the company) may be removed by the company during his term of office by means of an ordinary resolution with special notice.[446] The director is allowed the right to protest against his removal and to make representations to the members in writing, and at the meeting itself, unless the representations suggest that he is abusing his right of protest.[447] Every company must keep and make available for inspection by its members free of charge a record of the terms of the contract of service of each director.[448] A director may not have a provision in a contract of employment with his company which allows him a guaranteed term of

---

[436] *Jubilee Cotton Mills v Lewis* [1924] A.C. 958.

[437] CA 2006 s.154.

[438] CA 2006 s.155.

[439] CA 2006 s.157.

[440] CA 2006 s.160.

[441] CA 2006 s.161.

[442] They may also be kept elsewhere along with all the other company records, but if so, that address must be intimated to the Registrar of Companies on Form AD02 (s.162(3)(b) and s.1136). The information required to be shown on the register is indicated in ss.163 and 164.

[443] CA 2006 s.162.

[444] CA 2006 s.165.

[445] CA 2006 s.167. See the Companies House website for the various forms which should be used to intimate these appointments etc. Although a director's residential address is disclosed to the Registrar of Companies, the address itself is not made available to the public (s.242). Under limited circumstances, the addresses may be disclosed by the Registrar of Companies, with or without a court order (ss.243–246).

[446] CA 2006 s.168.

[447] CA 2006 s.169.

[448] CA 2006 ss.228, 229.

employment in excess of two years unless that provision has been approved by the members.[449] A guaranteed term is one where the employment is to continue otherwise than at the instance of the company, and cannot be terminated by notice by the company or can only be terminated in specified circumstances.[450] There are provisions to prevent evasion of these rules[451] and where the rules are not followed, the terms in the contract are void to the extent of any contravention and the contract is deemed to contain a term entitling the company to terminate the contract at any time with reasonable notice.[452]

46.32 Powers of directors—The powers delegated to its directors by a company are set out in its articles and usually give the directors the authority to deal with the general management of the company. So long as they do not exceed the powers given to them, the directors cannot be prevented by members' resolutions from exercising those powers.[453] Directors are under a duty to exercise their powers in conformity with the constitution of the company,[454] though if directors exceed those powers the members may ratify the directors' actions by special resolution.[455] Section 40 protects third parties dealing with companies by deeming the power of the board of directors to bind the company (or to authorise others to bind it) to be free of any limitation in the company's constitution.[456] The powers enjoyed by the directors may, however, be restrained in several ways: the directors may only exercise such powers as they have for the purposes for which they are conferred.[457] For example, the members have power to alter the articles[458] and thereby to restrain the directors, or to remove a director at any time,[459] or to bring a derivative claim against the directors under ss.266 or 267.[460]

46.33 The general duties of directors—The CA 2006 codified the common law on certain directors' duties, renaming them "general duties". In order to maintain the benefits of the continuing common law approach to these duties, the statute requires that "regard must be had to the corresponding common law rules and equitable principles in interpreting and applying the general duties".[461] The general duties are to be found in ss.171–177, and are the duty to act in accordance with the company's constitution,[462] the duty to promote the success of the company,[463] the duty to exercise independent judgement,[464] the duty to use

---

[449] CA 2006 s.188(1), (2).
[450] CA 2006 s.188(3).
[451] CA 2006 s.188(4).
[452] CA 2006 s.189.
[453] *Quin & Axtens v Salmon* [1909] A.C. 442; *Alexander Ward & Co v Samyang Navigation Co*, 1975 S.C. (HL) 26; *Lord Duncan Sandys v House of Fraser*, 1985 S.L.T. 200.
[454] CA 2006 s.171(a).
[455] CA 2006 s.239. For the details of the voting on the resolution, see the next para.
[456] See para.27.12.
[457] CA 2006 s.171(b); *Howard Smith Ltd v Ampol Petroleum Ltd* [1974] A.C. 821; [1974] 2 W.L.R. 689.
[458] CA 2006 s.21.
[459] CA 2006 s.168.
[460] See para.47.24.
[461] CA 2006 s.170(4).
[462] CA 2006 s.171.
[463] CA 2006 s.172.
[464] CA 2006 s.173.

reasonable skill, care and diligence,[465] the duty to avoid conflicts of interest,[466] the duty not to accept benefits from third parties,[467] and the duty to declare an interest in any proposed transaction or arrangement.[468] These general duties are solely owed to the company, not to the bodies themselves whose interests are included within the general duties.[469] Each general duty will now be examined in turn.

Directors are under a duty to exercise their powers in conformity with the constitution of the company.[470] So long as they do not exceed these powers, the directors cannot be prevented by members' resolutions from exercising them.[471] The directors may only exercise such powers as they have for the purposes for which they are conferred and for no other ulterior purpose.[472]

The duty to promote the success of the company requires the director to act in the way he considers in good faith would be most likely to promote the success of the company for the benefit of its members as a whole, and in so doing to have regard (amongst other matters) to the likely consequence of any decision in the long term, the interests of the company's employees, the need to foster the company's business relationships with suppliers, customers and others, the impact of the company's operations on the community and the environment, the desirability of the company maintaining a reputation for high standards of business conduct and the need to act fairly as between members of the company.[473] If the company were set up to have purposes other than benefiting the members, the same duty applies to the pursuit of those purposes as it would towards benefiting the members.[474] The duty is nevertheless subject to any rules requiring directors to consider the interests of creditors, as for example under the Insolvency Act 1986 s.234.[475]

The duty to exercise independent judgement does not preclude a director adhering to an agreement entered into by the company whereby he agrees to fetter his judgment or where he is acting in a way authorised by the company's constitution.[476]

The duty to exercise reasonable care, skill and diligence is the same two-fold skill indicated in the Insolvency Act 1986 s.214(4), namely a general skill for ordinary directors and a further higher standard of skill expected of experienced directors.[477]

---

[465] CA 2006 s.174.

[466] CA 2006 s.175.

[467] CA 2006 s.176.

[468] CA 2006 s.177.

[469] CA 2006 s.170(1). This means that it is only if the collective body of shareholders, acting as the company, feels strongly about the directors' dereliction of their duties is it likely that action will be taken against the directors by the company.

[470] CA 2006 s.171. In *West Coast Capital (Lios) Ltd* [2008] CSOH 72, the court confirmed that this section set out the pre-existing law on the matter.

[471] *Quin & Axtens v Salmon* [1909] A.C. 442; *Alexander Ward & Co v Samyang Navigation Co*, 1975 S.C. (HL) 26; *Lord Duncan Sandys v House of Fraser*, 1985 S.L.T. 200.

[472] CA 2006 s.171(b); *Howard Smith Ltd v Ampol Petroleum Ltd* [1974] A.C. 821; [1974] 2 W.L.R. 689.

[473] CA 2006 s.172(1). It is anticipated that directors' minutes should therefore always formally indicate that the directors duly considered these matters.

[474] CA 2006 s.172(2). This would particularly apply where the company was a charity or set up for some other benevolent purpose.

[475] CA 2006 s.172(3).

[476] See *Dawson International Plc v Coats Paton Plc* [1989] 5 B.C.C. 405; *Fulham Football Ltd v Cabra Estates Plc*, 1994 1 B.C.L.C. 363.

[477] For examples of these two levels of skill, see respectively *Re D'Jan of London Ltd* [1994] 1 B.C.L.C. 561 and *Dorchester Finance Co Ltd v Stebbing* [1989] B.C.L.C. 498. In *Gregson v HAE Trustees Ltd* [2008] 2 B.C.L.C. 542 the court indicated that this section set out the existing common law duty of care, skill and diligence.

The duty to avoid conflicts of interest requires the director not to put himself in a position where he wishes to exploit any property, information or opportunity arising from his position within the company.[478] However, the duty is not infringed where the director is involved in a "transaction or arrangement" with the company personally,[479] where the situation cannot reasonably be regarded as giving rise to a conflict of interest, or if the matter has been authorised by the directors.[480] In that last instance, the directors of private companies may authorise such a matter unless the articles say otherwise[481] but public companies' directors may only authorise such matters where the company's constitution allows them to do so.[482] Where the directors vote on such a matter, the meeting must be quorate without including the interested directors and the interested directors' votes must not cause the resolution to be passed.[483] This section applies to past directors as well.[484]

The duty not to accept benefits from third parties is strict.[485] If benefits are offered, they may only be accepted if the acceptance of the benefits cannot reasonably be regarded as likely to give rise to a conflict of interest.[486] This section applies to past directors as well.[487]

Subject to certain limited exceptions,[488] the duty to declare an interest in a proposed transaction or arrangement requires the director to tell the other directors of the nature and extent of his interest before the company enters into the transaction or arrangement.[489] Members' consent is therefore not necessary.

Subject to certain limited exceptions, to ensure that the duty to declare an interest in transactions and arrangements is taken seriously, there are criminal penalties for a director if he does not declare his interest in an existing transaction or arrangement[490] unless he has previously declared it for a proposed transaction or arrangement.[491]

If a director breaches any of the general duties, the company may require him to reimburse the company for any loss it has suffered, indemnify the company for any expenses, hand over any profit which he has obtained and which rightfully should be the company's, and return to the company any assets which he has misappropriated. The court may reduce any contract where the director failed to declare his interest.[492] The director may be able to persuade the company to ratify his actions under s.239, but if so, if the company is a private company, and the vote is by means of a written resolution, the director, and those who are connected

---

[478] CA 2006 s.175. For example of conflict of interest, see *Industrial Development Consultants Ltd v Cooley* [1972] 1 W.L.R. 443; *Item Software (UK) Ltd v Fassihi* [2004] B.C.C. 994; [2005] 2 B.C.L.C. 91; *West Coast Capital (LIOS) Ltd, Petitioner*, 2008 CSOH 72; *Commonwealth Oil and Gas Co Ltd v Baxter*, 2010 S.C. 156.

[479] CA 2006 s.175(3). A transaction or arrangement would be, say, where the director sells an asset to his company or offers some particular service to his company. How transactions and arrangements should be dealt with is spelled out in s.177.

[480] CA 2006 s.175(4)(a), (b).

[481] CA 2006 s.175(5)(a).

[482] CA 2006 s.175(5)(b).

[483] CA 2006 s.175(6).

[484] CA 2006 s.170(2)(a).

[485] CA 2006 s.176.

[486] CA 2006 s.176(4).

[487] CA 2006 s.170(2)(b).

[488] CA 2006 s.177(4)–(6).

[489] CA 2006 s.177.

[490] CA 2006 s.183.

[491] CA 2006 s.182(1).

[492] CA 2006 s.178.

with him in terms of s.252, are not eligible to vote on the matter.[493] If the vote on ratification takes place at a general meeting, the resolution may only be passed if the necessary majority voted in favour, disregarding the votes of the director and the votes of those connected with him. The director may still be counted as part of any quorum and speak at the meeting.[494] Whether by written resolution or by resolution passed at a meeting, if the vote is unanimously in his favour, the resolution is validly passed.[495] In addition, the courts may forgive a breach where having regard to all the circumstances of the case, in their opinion the director has acted honestly and reasonably.[496]

Existing statutory liabilities of directors—While the general duties were new to CA 2006, CA 2006 also incorporates a number of duties from previous legislation. These are now addressed.   **46.34**

Directors' service contracts—Directors' service contracts or a memorandum of their terms must be available for inspection at the company's registered office or at a place specified under the regulations under s.1136.[497] Any member is entitled to inspect or obtain a copy of a director's contract or a memorandum of its terms.[498] Any term of a director's contract which provides that the contract is to continue for a period in excess of two years and which may be terminated at the director's instance, but not the company's, or may be terminated by the company under specified circumstances, will only be valid if the contract with the offending term has been approved by the members first.[499] Any term contravening this will be void and the company is deemed to be allowed to terminate the contract at any time with reasonable notice.[500] The overlapping of directors' service contracts in an attempt to avoid these rules is also forbidden.[501]   **46.35**

Substantial property transactions—Members must give approval to the direc-tors[502] for the sale by the director of an asset to his company, or the purchase by a director of a company asset, if that asset is either worth more than £100,000 or more than 10 per cent of the company's net asset value, subject to a de minimis exception where the asset is less than £5,000 in value.[503] If the director fails to obtain such approval, the transaction is voidable at the instance of the company,[504] and the asset, provided it is not in the hands of a third party who has acquired it in good faith and for value, or its value, must be returned to the company unless the members have affirmed the transaction within a reasonable period of time.[505] Failing such affirmation, the director in question are liable to account to the   **46.36**

---

[493] CA 2006 s.239(3).
[494] CA 2006 s.239(4).
[495] CA 2006 s.239(6)(a).
[496] CA 2006 s.1157; *Re Simmon Box (Diamonds) Ltd* [2002] 2 B.C.C. 82; [2001] 1 B.C.L.C. 176. This provision applies to any breach of duty by the director to his company, not just the general duties.
[497] CA 2006 s.228. This now includes the contracts of directors outside the United Kingdom.
[498] CA 2006 s.229.
[499] CA 2006 s.188.
[500] CA 2006 s.189.
[501] CA 2006 s.188(4).
[502] This includes shadow directors (s.223(1)(b)).
[503] CA 2006 s.191(2). Conditional approval from the members is permissible (s.190(1)). There are also provisions for the aggregation of transactions (s.190(5)).
[504] CA 2006 s.195(2). See also *Re Duckwari Plc (No. 1)* [1997] 2 B.C.L.C. 713.
[505] CA 2006 s.196.

company for any gain he has made, or must indemnify the company for any loss.[506] It is acceptable to take a subjective valuation of the asset.[507] This requirement is inapplicable when the transaction in question is with a member (rather than a director) or another company in a group,[508] when the company is being wound up (unless it is a members' voluntary winding up) or in administration[509] or when the transaction takes place on a recognised investment exchange.[510]

46.37 Loans, quasi-loans, and credit transactions—A private company or a Plc may make an ordinary loan of any amount to its director or to a director of its holding company, or give a guarantee, or provide any form of security for a loan made by someone to such a director, provided the transaction[511] has been approved by the members,[512] unless the loan is for less than £10,000, in which case approval is unnecessary.[513] If the director is a director of the company's holding company, the holding company's members must also approve the loan.[514] Members must be given a memorandum outlining the terms of the transaction and may then vote on the matter.[515]

A private company, but not a Plc nor a private company associated[516] with a Plc,[517] may make a quasi-loan[518] of any amount to its director or to a director of its holding company, or give a guarantee, or provide a security for a quasi-loan made by someone to such a director: no members' approval is required. A Plc, or a private company associated with a Plc, may grant a director a quasi-loan, or give a guarantee, or provide any form of security for a quasi-loan, without members' approval provided it is under £10,000[519]; if the quasi-loan is greater than £10,000, the members must approve it,[520] and the same rules apply or if the recipient of the quasi-loan is connected[521] with the director[522] or if the director is a director of the company's holding company, in which case the holding company's members must also approve the quasi-loan.[523]

A private company, but not a Plc nor a private company associated[524] with a Plc,[525] may enter into a credit transaction of any amount with its director or with

---

[506] CA 2006 s.195(3); *Re Duckwari Plc (No. 2)* [1999] Ch. 253; [1998] 3 W.L.R. 913; [1999] B.C.C. 11; [1998] 2 B.C.L.C. 315.

[507] *Micro Leisure Ltd v County Properties and Developments Ltd*, 1999 S.L.T. 1428; [2000] B.C.C. 872.

[508] CA 2006 s.192.

[509] CA 2006 s.193.

[510] CA 2006 s.194.

[511] The term "transaction" covers the words "loan", "guarantee" and "security".

[512] CA 2006 s.197(1).

[513] CA 2006 s.207(1).

[514] CA 2006 s.197(2).

[515] CA 2006 s.197(3), (4). No vote is needed if the lending company is not a UK registered company or if the company is a wholly owned subsidiary of some other registered company (s.197(5)).

[516] CA 2006 s.256. "Associated" in essence means a holding company, subsidiary company, or another company that is also a subsidiary of the same holding company.

[517] CA 2006 s.198(1).

[518] A quasi-loan is a loan funded by a credit facility extended to the company, such as a company credit card.

[519] CA 2006 s.207(1).

[520] CA 2006 s.198(4)–(6).

[521] As defined in ss.252–255.

[522] CA 2006 s.200.

[523] CA 2006 s.198(3).

[524] CA 2006 s.256.

[525] CA 2006 s.198(1).

a director of its holding company, or with anyone connected[526] either with its director or with a director of its holding company, or give a guarantee, or provide any form of security for the credit transaction entered into by someone for the benefit of such a director or person connected with the director, and no members' approval is needed. A Plc, or a private company associated with a Plc, may enter into a credit transaction, or give a guarantee, or provide any form of security for the credit transaction, with such a director, or person connected[527] with such director, without members' approval provided the credit transaction is under £15,000[528]; but where the credit transaction is greater than £15,000, the members must approve it in the manner previously indicated.[529] If the recipient of the credit transaction is a director of the company's holding company, or a person connected with him, the holding company's members must also approve the credit transaction.[530] The term "credit transaction" is explained in s.202, and allows a director (or person connected with him) to defer payment for goods or land because the company, on a hire purchase agreement or a conditional sale agreement, acquires the goods for him on the understanding that he will ultimately repay the company. The term applies where the company leases or hires any land or goods for the benefit of the director (or person connected with the director).[531] But if the credit transaction is in the ordinary course of business and the terms of the credit transaction are no different from the terms that would be offered to anyone who was not involved in the company, there is no need for members' approval.[532]

There are various complex anti-evasion provisions for the rules relating to these transactions[533] and special exemptions for associated companies.[534] Companies may lend money to their directors to meet expenditure on behalf of the company or to carry out their duties[535] provided the sums involved are less than £50,000.[536] There are special exemptions for money-lending companies.[537] If a company makes an unapproved loan, quasi-loan or credit transaction, the loan, quasi-loan or credit transaction is voidable at the instance of the company and the director or connected person is required to account to the company for any gain made directly or indirectly, and jointly and severally with anyone else involved, to indemnify the company for any loss.[538] The loan, quasi-loan or credit transaction will not be voidable if restitution is impossible, if the company has already been indemnified for any loss, or rights in the subject matter of the loan, quasi-loan or credit transaction have been acquired by a third party for value in good faith and without notice of the lack of authorisation.[539] A director will be free from liability if he took all reasonable steps to obtain authorisation,[540] and neither a connected person nor a director who authorised the loan, quasi-loan or credit

---

[526] As defined in ss.252–255.
[527] CA 2006 ss.252–255.
[528] CA 2006 s.207(2).
[529] CA 2006 s.201(4)–(6).
[530] CA 2006 s.198(3).
[531] CA 2006 s.202(1)(b).
[532] CA 2006 s.207(3).
[533] CA 2006 s.203.
[534] CA 2006 s.208(1), (2).
[535] CA 2006 s.204(1).
[536] CA 2006 s.204(2).
[537] CA 2006 s.209(2).
[538] CA 2006 s.213.
[539] CA 2006 s.213(2).
[540] CA 2006 s.213(6).

transaction will be liable if he was unaware of all the relevant circumstances.[541] All the provisions relating to these matters also apply to shadow directors.[542] If a loan, quasi-loan or credit transaction is unapproved, but the members affirm it within a reasonable time, it will no longer be voidable.[543]

46.38 Payments on loss of office, transfer of property or transfer of shares—If a director is offered a payment for loss of office or retirement,[544] that payment should be disclosed to and approved by the members first, failing which the company may claim it from the director.[545] If a director is offered a payment on the occasion of the transfer of some or all of the company's property or undertaking,[546] that payment should be disclosed to and approved by the members[547]; if he receives such payment without approval he is to hold it in trust for the company.[548] Similar rules apply under section 219 where a director obtains payment for loss of office following the sale of all or part of the company's shares on a takeover,[549] with the like consequences for unapproved payments.[550] There is a de minimis exception for payments of up to £200,[551] and if the payments are being made in good faith as a discharge of some legal obligation, damages for breach of that obligation, a settlement of a claim or pension, approval from the members is not required.

46.39 Contracts with sole members who are also directors—Any contracts between a single member company and its single member who is also a director of the company must either be in writing, set out in a memorandum or recorded in the minutes of the first meeting of the company after making the contract.[552]

46.40 Clauses protecting directors from liability—A company may not have articles or any other contract that relieves a director from liability to his company for any negligence, default, breach of duty or breach of trust in relation to his company. Any such provision would be void,[553] as would be the provision of any indemnity to a director for any of the above.[554] It is permissible for a company to provide the director with insurance, certain types of third party indemnity and certain types of pension scheme provision indemnity.[555] A company may pay the premiums for an insurance policy to cover a claim by the company against

---

[541] CA 2006 s.213(7).

[542] CA 2006 s.223(1)(c).

[543] CA 2006 s.214.

[544] CA 2006 s.215. This includes any form of employment with the company.

[545] *Lander v Premier Pict Petroleum Ltd*, 1997 S.L.T. 1361.

[546] CA 2006 s.218.

[547] CA 2006 s.217. If the payment is to a director of a holding company, the approval of the holding company's members is necessary as well. The approval is in the same manner as the approval for loans indicated above.

[548] CA 2006 s.222.

[549] However, in this case, the person making the takeover, and anyone associated with him, may not vote to approve the resolution (s.219(4)).

[550] CA 2006 s.222.

[551] CA 2006 s.221.

[552] CA 2006 s.231. See also *Re Neptune (Vehicle Washing Equipment) Ltd (No. 2)* [1995] B.C.C. 1000. This section applies to shadow directors (s.231(5)).

[553] CA 2006 s.232(1).

[554] CA 2006 s.232(2).

[555] CA 2006 s.232(2).

the director personally.[556] It may pay the premiums for an insurance policy to cover a claim by third parties against the director personally, but in this case, the policy will not underwrite the liability of the director if he has to pay a fine following criminal proceedings, pay a penalty to a regulatory authority, pay his court costs for his unsuccessful defence in a criminal prosecution, his unsuccessful defence in any civil proceedings against him, or any unsuccessful application for relief either under s.661[557] or s.1157.[558] The company may also pay the premiums for an insurance policy to cover any claim by the company's pension scheme against the director personally when acting as a trustee for the company's pension scheme.[559] The terms of all these policies need to be disclosed in the directors' report[560] and be available for inspection by the members.[561]

Statutory liabilities of directors on insolvency—In addition to the liabilities **46.41** referred to above, in the course of winding up of a company, under s.212[562] of the IA 1986, where the director has misapplied or retained, or become accountable for, any money or other property of the company, or has been guilty of any misfeasance or breach of any fiduciary or other duty in relation to the company, he will be liable to make good the loss to the company or compensate it for its loss to the company.[563] A director may be relieved of liability in respect of negligence, default, breach of duty or breach of trust if he has acted honestly and reasonably and, having regard to all of the circumstances, he ought fairly to be excused.[564] Under s.213, where in the course of winding up of a company it appears that any business of the company has been carried out with the intent to defraud creditors of the company, creditors of another person, or for any fraudulent purpose, the court, on the application of the liquidator, may make anyone knowingly party to the carrying on of that business with the intent to the defraud liable to contribute to the company's assets.[565] This applies not only to members and officers of the company, but also to people[566] or other businesses[567] not part of the company but nevertheless part of the fraud.[568] Following a liquidator's application to the court, a person who is or was a director of a company which subsequently goes into insolvent liquidation may be made liable to contribute to the company's assets if at any time before the commencement of the winding up of the company, that person knew or ought to have concluded that there was no reasonable prospect that the company would avoid going into insolvent liquidation and the person was

---

[556] CA 2006 s.233.

[557] This deals with the power of court to grant relief in the case of acquisition of shares by an innocent nominee.

[558] This deals with the power of court to grant relief where a director has acted honestly and reasonably in all the circumstances.

[559] CA 2006 s.235.

[560] CA 2006 s.236.

[561] CA 2006 ss.237, 238.

[562] IA 1986 s.212 is generally known as the misfeasance provision.

[563] *Re D'Jan of London Ltd* [1993] B.C.C. 646; *Bairstow v Queens Moat Houses Plc* [2000] 1 B.C.L.C. 549.

[564] CA 2006 s.1157; *Re D'Jan of London Ltd* [1993] B.C.C. 646; *Coleman Taymar Ltd v Oakes* [2001] 2 B.C.L.C. 749.

[565] IA 1986 s.213. This is generally known as the fraudulent trading provision.

[566] *Morris v Banque Internationale d'Investissement SA (No.2)* [2002] B.C.C. 407.

[567] *Morris v Bank of India* [2005] B.C.C. 739.

[568] For an important discussion of the difficulties of using s.213 and in particular the importance of proving actual dishonesty, see *Re Patrick and Lyon Ltd* [1933] Ch. 786.

a director of that company at that time.[569] The court will not grant such an application if the person at that time took every step with a view to minimising the potential loss to the company's creditor as he ought to have taken, assuming he was aware that there was no reasonable prospect that the company would avoid going into insolvent liquidation.[570] In such circumstances the director is expected to act as a reasonably diligent person having the general knowledge, skill and experience as may reasonably be expected of that director for that company plus, where appropriate, the general knowledge, skill and experience that that director has.[571] Merely because a director plays little part in the management of the company is no excuse.[572] It is possible for a director to be liable under both s.213 (fraudulent trading) and s.214 (wrongful trading),[573] or for both s.212 (misfeasance) and s.214 (wrongful trading).[574] Being found liable for wrongful or fraudulent trading is grounds for disqualification as a director under s.6 of the CDDA 1986. Phoenix trading, which is the prohibited practice of setting up without authority from the court a new business with a name the same as or similar to that of a company which has gone into insolvent liquidation within the period of 12 months beforehand,[575] may make the director[576] of the new business jointly and severally liable for the debts of the new business with the same or the similar name as the liquidated company's name.[577] Any other directors or managers who were aware of the director's misuse of the name will also be liable for those debts on the same basis.[578]

46.42 The Company Directors Disqualification Act 1986 ("CDDA 1986")—The court has power to order that a person must not be a director of a company, act as a receiver of a company's property or in any way, either directly or indirectly, be concerned or take part in the promotion, formation or management of a company, without leave of the court, or to be an insolvency practitioner.[579] CDDA 1986 is also directed at those acting as de facto and shadow directors.[580] There is further provision for disqualification consequent upon conviction for an indictable offence,[581] persistent default under the companies legislation,[582] or if the person is

---

[569] IA 1986 s.214(1). This is generally known as the wrongful trading provision.

[570] IA 1986 s.214(2). *Re Produce Marketing Consortium Ltd (No.2)* [1989] B.C.L.C. 520.

[571] *Re D'Jan of London Ltd* [1993] B.C.C. 646.

[572] *Re Brian D. Pierson (Contractors) Ltd* [1999] B.C.C. 26.

[573] IA 1986 s.214(8).

[574] *Re DKG Contractors Ltd* [1990] B.C.C. 903.

[575] IA 1986 s.216(2).

[576] *Ricketts v Ad Valorem Factors Ltd* [2004] 1 All E.R. 894; [2004] B.C.C. 164; [2004] 1 B.C.L.C. 1. Strictly speaking, the legislation is not restricted to directors: it also covers anyone involved in the promotion, formation or management of the company, thus catching shadow directors (IA 1986 s.217(1)). The director must also have been a director of the liquidated company within the period of 12 months before the company went into liquidation. Phoenix trading is also a criminal offence (IA 1986 s.216(4)).

[577] IA 1986 s.217(1)(a).

[578] IA 1986 s.217(1)(b); *Glasgow City Council v Craig and Moccia* [2008] CSOH 171.

[579] Company Directors Disqualification Act 1986 s.1(1)(a). "Insolvency practitioner" is defined in s.388(1) of IA 1986.

[580] Company Directors Disqualification Act 1986 s.22(4), (5). For a discussion of the meaning of de facto director, see *Secretary of State for Trade and Industry v Hall* [2009] B.C.C. 190. For the meaning of "shadow director", see *Secretary of State for Trade and Industry v Deverell* [2000] 2 B.C.L.C. 133 at [24] et seq.

[581] CDDA 1986 s.2; *Re Georgiou* (1988) 4 B.C.C 322; *R. v Goodman* [1994] B.C.L.C. 349.

[582] CDDA 1986 s.3; *Re Arctic Engineering Ltd* [1986] 1 W.L.R. 686.

guilty[583] of the offence of fraudulent trading[584] or of any other fraud or breach of duty in relation to the company while an officer, liquidator or administrative receiver or a receiver of the company's property.[585] Under s.6, the court is obliged to disqualify a director where the company of which he is or was a director has gone into insolvency and where his conduct, either in that company or any other company (whether insolvent or not), renders him unfit to be a director.[586] "Insolvency" for the purposes of s.6 means insolvent liquidation, receivership or administration.[587] Guidance as to what is meant by "unfitness" to be a director is given in s.9 which in turn refers to Sch.1 to CDDA 1986. If a director has committed a breach of competition law, he may be liable for a competition disqualification order.[588] When a director is disqualified, he may be banned from being a director from between 2 to 15 years, depending on the heinousness of his conduct,[589] though there have been occasions when the director has simultaneously been banned as a director of one company but also been given leave, subject to certain conditions, to continue acting as a director of certain other companies.[590] Disqualification may also be imposed after a statutory investigation of a company's affairs.[591] An undischarged bankrupt is disqualified from acting as a director of, or directly or indirectly taking part in or being concerned in the promotion, formation, or management of, a company except with leave of the court.[592] It is competent for the Secretary of State to accept an undertaking in lieu of seeking a disqualification order from the court.[593] An application for disqualification must, ordinarily,[594] be made within two years of the date upon which the company became insolvent.[595] A person subject to a disqualification order may subsequently apply to the court for leave to be concerned with a specific company or companies.[596] A person who has given a disqualification undertaking may apply to the court for a variation.[597] It must be noted, however, that the acts of a director or manager are valid notwithstanding any defect that may afterwards be discovered in his appointment or qualification.[598] A company that is a director may be disqualified.[599]

---

[583] Liability under either s.4(1)(a) or (b) is not dependent upon a conviction under CA 2006 s.993.

[584] CA 2006 s.993; CDDA 1986 s.4(1)(a).

[585] CDDA 1986 s.4(1)(b).

[586] CDDA 1986 s.6.

[587] CDDA 1986 s.6(2).

[588] CDDA 1986 s.9A.

[589] *Re Sevenoaks Stationers Ltd* [1991] B.C.L.C. 325.

[590] *Re Majestic Recording Studios Ltd* [1989] B.C.L.C. 1; *Secretary of State for Trade and Industry v Rosenfield* [1999] B.C.C. 413.

[591] CDDA 1986 s.8.

[592] CDDA 1986 s.11(1). Ignorance of one's own bankruptcy is no excuse: *R. v Brockley* [1994] 1 B.C.L.C. 606.

[593] CDDA 1986 s.1A. An undertaking is when a director accepts that he has erred and prefers to avoid court proceedings, usually in exchange for a reduced period of disqualification.

[594] There is provision to seek leave from the court to commence proceedings outwith the statutory two-year time limit: s.7(2).

[595] CDDA 1986 s.7(2); *Secretary of State for Trade and Industry v Josolyne*, 1990 S.L.T. (Sh. Ct) 48; *Secretary of State for Trade and Industry v Normand*, 1994 S.L.T. 1249; and *Secretary of State for Trade and Industry v Campleman*, 1999 S.L.T. 787.

[596] CDDA 1986 s.17.

[597] CDDA 1986 s.8A.

[598] CA 2006 s.161(b); *Morris v Kanssen* [1946] A.C. 459; see *Freeman & Lockyer v Buckhurst Park Properties* [1964] 2 Q.B. 480.

[599] *Official Receiver v Brady* [1999] B.C.C. 258.

46.43 **Auditor**—A company's annual accounts must be audited each year unless the company is a small company,[600] a dormant company[601] or is a non-profit making company[602] subject to public sector audit[603] in which case it is not obliged to have an audit. There are provisions to enable the members of an unaudited company to insist on an audit taking place.[604] For a private company which is to be audited, the company must appoint its auditor before the end of the period of 28 days beginning with the end of the time allowed for sending out copies of the company's annual reports and accounts[605] or, if earlier, the day on which the copies of the company's annual reports and accounts are sent out to the members under s.423.[606] Auditors are appointed for a period of one financial year, whereupon they will normally be reappointed for a further year.[607] With public companies, each company must at each general meeting before which accounts are laid appoint an auditor or auditors to hold office until the next such general meeting,[608] and if no appointment is made, the Secretary of State may appoint a person to fill the vacancy.[609] Auditors are regulated under Pt 42 and Schs 10–14 of CA 2006, and in essence an auditor must be suitably professionally qualified[610] by being a member of recognised supervisory body[611] and must be independent of the company.[612] Auditors must sign and date their report, and where the auditor is a firm, the senior statutory auditor must append his own signature on behalf of his firm.[613] Auditors who knowingly cause an audit report to be misleading, false, or deceptive in a material particular may be prosecuted.[614]

The auditor is bound to make a report to the members on the annual accounts to be laid before the company in general meeting or sent to the members as the case may be.[615] The report must state whether in the auditor's opinion the annual accounts have been properly prepared in accordance with the provisions of CA 2006 and the relevant financial reporting framework, and whether in his opinion a true and fair view is given, in the case of an individual balance sheet, of the company's affairs at the end of its financial year; in the case of an individual profit and loss account, of the profit or loss for the year; and in the case of group accounts of the state of affairs and profit or loss of the company and its subsidiaries thereby, so far as concerns members of the company.[616] The report must be unqualified or qualified, and must include any matters to which the auditor wishes to draw attention by way of emphasis without qualifying the report.[617] The auditor should

---

[600] At the time of writing, a small company is one with a turnover of £6.5 million, a balance sheet of not more than £3.26 million and not more than 50 employees (s.477). Certain companies, such as private company subsidiaries of public companies, are not eligible to be small companies.

[601] CA 2006 ss.480–481 gives the requirements for dormant companies not to have auditors.

[602] CA 2006 s.483.

[603] CA 2006 s.475.

[604] CA 2006 s.476.

[605] CA 2006 s.424.

[606] CA 2006 s.485.

[607] Subject to certain exceptions (s.487(2), (3)).

[608] CA 2006 s.489.

[609] CA 2006 s.490.

[610] CA 2006 s.1219.

[611] CA 2006 s.1212. An example would be the Institute of Chartered Accountants of Scotland.

[612] CA 2006 s.1214.

[613] CA 2006 ss.503, 504.

[614] CA 2006 s.509.

[615] CA 2006 s.495.

[616] CA 2006 s.495(3).

[617] CA 2006 s.495(4).

consider whether the directors' report is consistent with the picture revealed by the annual accounts and, if it is not, this should be noted in his report.[618] It is the duty of the auditor in preparing his report to carry out such investigations as will enable him to form an opinion as to whether proper accounting records have been kept by the company and proper returns adequate for their audit have been received from branches not visited by him, and whether the company's balance sheet and profit and loss account are in agreement with the books of account and returns. If the auditor is of the opinion that accounting records have not been kept, or that proper returns have not been received, if the balance sheet and profit and loss account are not in agreement with the accounting records and returns, or if he fails to obtain all the information and explanations which to the best of his knowledge and belief are necessary for the purposes of his audit, he must state that fact in his report.[619] The auditor has a right of access at all times to the company's books, accounts and vouchers and is entitled to require from the officers of the company and from subsidiary companies and their auditors such information and explanations as he thinks necessary.[620] Failure to provide information, or to provide information that is misleading, false or deceptive in a material particular is a criminal offence.[621] He has the right to attend any general meeting of the company and to be heard on any part of the business of the meeting which concerns him as auditor.[622]

There are complex provisions for the removal, resignation and retiral of auditors, designed to ensure that members appreciate the significance of and the reasons for the auditor's departure. An auditor may be removed by the members by an ordinary resolution with special notice, subject to the auditor's right to make representations to the members.[623] There are provisions to deal with the appointment of a new auditor in place of an auditor whose period of appointment is expired.[624] Where an auditor ceases to hold office in an unquoted company, he must deposit at the company's registered office a statement of the circumstances connected with his ceasing to hold office, unless he considers that there are no circumstances which need to be brought to the attention of the members or creditors of the company.[625] Where the company is quoted, he must deposit a statement of the circumstances connected with his ceasing to hold office even if there is nothing sinister concerning his cessation of office.[626] Where he does make such a statement it must be sent to all the members[627] and to the Registrar of Companies[628] unless the company obtains an order from the court to the contrary. The auditor must also inform the relevant audit authority[629] as must the company[630] where the

---

[618] CA 2006 s.496.
[619] CA 2006 s.498.
[620] CA 2006 s.499.
[621] CA 2006 s.501.
[622] CA 2006 s.502.
[623] CA 2006 s.511.
[624] CA 2006 ss.514, 515.
[625] CA 2006 s.519(1), (5).
[626] CA 2006 s.519(3).
[627] CA 2006 s.520.
[628] CA 2006 s.521.
[629] CA 2006 s.522.
[630] CA 2006 s.523.

audit is a "major audit".[631] The members have the right to raise audit concerns at accounts meetings.[632]

46.44 Auditors' liability—As a statement of general principle an auditor who is negligent in the preparation of the company's accounts and his report owes a duty of care to the company and may be liable in damages to the company should his negligence result in it suffering loss.[633] Auditors owe no such duty to individual investors, as distinct from the company.[634] If an investor can demonstrate that the auditors know that the accounts and their report will be shown to that investor (or an identifiable class to which an investor belongs), and that such an investor is likely to rely on these in deciding whether or not to invest in the company, then a "special relationship" exists between auditor and investor and creates a duty of care on the auditor's part.[635] Such a special relationship would include the holding company of any audited company[636] or where the auditors are put on notice that a particular investor will be relying on the audit.[637] Auditors in practice normally draft their terms on engagement restrictively to limit the possibility of such special relationships arising.[638] Following CA 2006, auditors may not exclude their liability to the companies for which they carry out audits, except where permitted under statute, namely s.533 (indemnity for costs of successfully defending proceedings) and ss.534–536 (liability limitation agreements). A liability limitation agreement is one that limits the liability of the auditor to the company, but only for one year at a time,[639] where authorised by the members,[640] where the limitation is to an amount that is fair and reasonable in all the circumstances, and where the company and auditor have complied with the relevant regulations on this matter.[641]

46.45 Investigations[642]—The Secretary of State may on the application of the company or of a proportion of its members, or, if he suspects fraud or the withholding of information from its members, on his own initiative, appoint inspectors to investigate the affairs of a company and report on them in such manner as he may direct.[643] He is bound to do so if the court declares that the company's affairs ought to be investigated.[644] He also has power to require a company to produce

---

[631] A major audit is an audit of a listed company or a company in which there is a major public interest (s.525(2)).

[632] CA 2006 s.527. These concerns must be posted on the website of the company in question.

[633] *Re Thomas Gerrard & Son Ltd* [1968] Ch. 455; *Sasea Finance Ltd (In Liquidation) v KPMG (No.2)* [2000] 1 B.C.L.C. 236.

[634] *Caparo Industries Plc v Dickman* [1990] 2 A.C. 605. Note also *James McNaughton Paper Group v Hicks Anderson & Co* [1991] 2 Q.B. 113.

[635] *Caparo Industries Plc v Dickman* [1990] 2 A.C. 605 at 621, per Lord Bridge. Note also *Morgan Crucible & Co v Hill Samuel & Co* [1991] Ch. 295.

[636] *Barings Plc v Coopers and Lybrand* [1997] 1 B.C.L.C. 427; [1997] B.C.C. 498.

[637] *ADT Ltd v Binder Hamlyn* [1996] B.C.C. 808.

[638] See *Royal Bank of Scotland v Bannerman, Johnstone Maclay*, 2003 S.C. 125; *Precis (521) Plc v William M Mercer Ltd* [2004] EWHC 838 (ChD).

[639] CA 2006 s.535.

[640] CA 2006 s.536.

[641] CA 2006 ss.535(2) and 538. There has been little enthusiasm for such agreements.

[642] The rules on investigations are to be found in the CA 1985 and have not been consolidated into CA 2006, although the Secretary of State now has power under CA 2006 ss.1035–1039 to give directions to the inspectors.

[643] CA 1985 ss.431, 432(2). For powers of inspectors, see CA 1985 ss.433–434, 437.

[644] CA 1985 s.432(1).

such documents as he may specify at any time if he thinks there is good reason so to do.[645] Failing production by a company when so required, its premises may be entered and searched, and there are penalties for the destruction, mutilation or falsification of a document affecting or relating to the property or affairs of a company.[646] The Secretary of State has power, in the light of the inspectors' report or of any information obtained by them under these provisions, to bring civil proceedings on behalf of any body corporate.[647]

Arrangements and reconstructions—A compromise or arrangement between a **46.46** company and its creditors,[648] or any class of them, or between the company and its members,[649] or any class of them, is binding if approved (a) by a majority of three-fourths in value of the creditors or members concerned present and voting either in person or by proxy at a meeting called by order of the court, and (b) if it is sanctioned by the court.[650] Before the meeting, the creditors or members concerned must be given an explanation of the effect of the compromise or arrangement and of the material interests of the directors and the effect of the scheme on their interests.[651] Where the compromise or arrangement is proposed in connection with the reconstruction of a company or the amalgamation of companies and under the scheme property is to be transferred from one company to another the court may provide for, inter alia, the transfer or allotment of shares.[652] The court may provide for those who dissented from the proposed compromise or arrangement and for the acquisition of the shares of the dissenters.[653] But it may refuse to sanction an arrangement or compromise on the application of a dissenting shareholder.[654] Where a proposed compromise or arrangement has as its purpose (or is connected with) the reconstruction of a company (or companies) or the amalgamation of companies, and would involve the transfer of the undertaking, property and liabilities of one public company to another, or to any company formed for the purposes of the scheme, the court cannot sanction it unless: (a) there is a three-quarters majority of each class of shareholder of all the pre-existing companies in favour of the scheme; (b) draft terms of the scheme have been drawn up and adopted by all the directors of the transferor and pre-existing transferee companies involved in the scheme and copies of these sent to the Registrar who must publish a notice of their receipt in the Edinburgh Gazette; and (c) detailed

---

[645] CA 1985 s.447(2).

[646] CA 1985 ss.448, 450.

[647] CA 1985 s.438.

[648] "Creditors" does not include beneficiaries under trust arrangements: *Re Lehman Bros International (Europe)* [2009] EWCH (Civ) 1161. Creditors whose interests will not be adversely affected need not be party to the scheme of arrangement: *Sea Assets Ltd v Pereroan etc Garuda Indonesia* [2001] EWCA Civ 1696; *In re British & Commonwealth Holdings Plc* [1992] 1 WLR 672; *Re Bluebrook Ltd* [2009] EWCH 2214 (Ch).

[649] See *Singer Manufacturing Co v Robinow*, 1971 S.C. 11. If the members have no economic interest in the scheme, they do not need to be consulted: *Re Tea Corporation Ltd* [1904] 1 Ch 12.

[650] CA 2006 s.899. See *B.T.R. Plc* [2000] 1 B.C.L.C. 740.

[651] CA 2006 s.897; the requirements of this section as to the giving of information about the scheme, including the notice to be given by advertisement, must be strictly complied with: see *Coltness Iron Co*, 1951 S.C. 476; *City Property Investment Trust Corp*, 1951 S.C. 570; *Second Scottish Investment Trust Co, Petitioners*, 1962 S.L.T. 392; *Scottish Eastern Investment Trust, Petitioners*, 1966 S.L.T. 285.

[652] CA 2006 s.900.

[653] CA 2006 s.900(2)(e); *Nidditch v Calico Printers' Association*, 1961 S.L.T. 282; *Standard Property Investment Co v Dunblane Hydropathic* (1884) 12 R. 328.

[654] *Re Hellenic & General Trust Ltd* [1975] 3 All E.R. 382.

reports by the directors of the transferor company and independent experts have been made available for inspection by the shareholders.[655]

46.47 **Takeovers**—The practice of takeovers is a large and complex one beyond the ambit of a book of this nature, but in essence CA 2006 puts the Takeover Panel on a statutory basis, even though the Code that it operates is in itself non-statutory. The Takeover Code regulates the practice of the takeovers of listed companies[656] of which one of the best known requirements is the mandatory bid for the rest of a target company's shares by the bidder when the bidder has acquired 30 per cent of the company's shares. CA 2006 also puts on a statutory basis the requirements of the Takeover Directive,[657] in particular setting out the rules when a target company may take frustrating action to prevent a takeover of that company taking place,[658] and providing compensation to anyone whose rights may be adversely affected by the denial of the opportunity to take frustrating action.[659] The legislation also provides for the right of minority shareholders to be bought out at a proper price rather than a discounted price, and for the right of shareholders who have 90 per cent of the shares or of the control rights to acquire the remaining shares in the company where the remaining shareholders are unwilling to sell.[660]

46.48 **Insider dealing and market abuse**—Insider dealing is the misuse of confidential information about a company to take advantage of that information before others can do so. It is forbidden under the Criminal Justice Act 1993 ss.52–65. It only applies to the illegal dealing in securities on a regulated market, and arises where an insider (someone who has the benefit of inside information) deals in price-affected securities using inside information specific to the securities in question while knowing that it came from an inside source. An insider dealer, when prosecuted, has to show that one of the permitted defences is available to him,[661] these being in general that the insider was unaware that the information was inside information, that the information was in the public domain, or that the insider would have dealt anyway even if he had not had the inside information.[662] There are also special defences open to market makers or other professionals dealing without the intention of taking advantage of any inside information they might happen to have. If insider dealing takes place, there must be proper corroboration of the provision of the inside information.[663] Market abuse is the manipulation of the market price of securities by spreading false or misleading information about securities or action or behaviour which causes a false market in securities.[664] While insider dealing is a criminal matter, market abuse can be civil or criminal in its legal effects, and can apply to businesses as well as individuals.

46.49 **Charges, their registration, receivers and administrators**—The reasons for and the practicalities of registration of company charges is addressed in Ch.36,

---

[655] CA 2006 s.902. Sections 904–941 deal with the details of such mergers and divisions.

[656] It may be viewed at *http://www.thetakeoverpanel.org.uk* [Accessed August 9, 2012].

[657] Directive 2004/25/EC of the European Parliament and of the Council of 21 April 2004 on takeover bids [2004] OJ L 142.

[658] CA 2006 ss.966–970. These are known as the opting-in and opting-out provisions.

[659] CA 2006 s.968.

[660] CA 2006 ss.974–991. These are known as the squeeze-out and sell-out provisions.

[661] Criminal Justice Act 1993 s.53.

[662] As might happen, say, if a person had to liquidate all his assets to pay a debt.

[663] *Mackie v HM Advocate*, 1994 J.C. 132; 1994 S.C.C.R. 277.

[664] FSMA 2000 s.118.

"Rights in Security", paras 36.05–36.06, while paras 36.33–36.36 deal with the invalidity of certain floating charges, receivership and administration.

Compulsory winding up by the court[665]—A company registered in Scotland **46.50** may be wound up by the court by petition presented to the Court of Session, or to the sheriff court.[666] An unregistered company which is dissolved or has ceased to carry on business may also be wound up by the court in Scotland if there are or may be assets in this country belonging to the company and at least one person in Scotland is interested in the distribution of the assets of the company.[667] The title to petition rests with the company, its directors, any creditor (including a contingent or prospective creditor[668]), or any contributory,[669] and in certain situations in the public interest, with the Secretary of State,[670] or the supervisor of a voluntary arrangement.[671]

A company may be wound up by the court on any one or more of the following grounds[672]: (a) that the company has by special resolution, resolved that the company be wound up by the court; (b) that the company, being a public company, has failed to obtain a trading certificate under CA 2006 s.761, has failed to comply with the statutory requirements for minimum capital[673] and more than a year has expired since it was registered; (c) that the company has not commenced business within a year from its incorporation, or has suspended business for a year; (d) that the company is unable to pay its debts; (e) that at the time that a moratorium under s.1A of the Insolvency Act 1986 comes to an end no company voluntary arrangement under Pt 1 of that Act has been approved; (f) that the court is of opinion that it is "just and equitable" that the company should be wound up. A company which the Court of Session has jurisdiction to wind up may also be wound up by the court on the ground that the security of the creditor entitled to the benefit of an old style floating charge over property comprised in the company's property and undertaking is in jeopardy.[674] The construction of the term "just and equitable" has been that it is not confined to cases with the grounds of petition set out in s.122, but covers such cases as the loss of the substantial part of the company's business or abandonment of its objects or impossibility of carrying them out, i.e. what is referred to as the disappearance of the "substratum of the company",[675] persistent disregard by the directors of the provisions of the Acts or other circumstances sufficient to warrant the inference that there has been an unfair abuse of power and an impairment of confidence in the probity with which the affairs of

---

[665] For detailed discussion of the process of winding up in Scotland, see Morse, *Palmer's Company Law*, Vol.I, paras 15.601 et seq.

[666] See, generally, IA 1986 s.120. The sheriff court is appropriate where the paid up share capital of the company does not exceed £120,000.

[667] *Inland Revenue v Highland Engineering*, 1975 S.L.T. 203.

[668] For a definition of contingent and prospective creditors, see *Stonegate Securities Ltd v Gregory* [1980] All E.R. 241, per Buckley L.J. at 243.

[669] IA 1986 s.124(1).

[670] IA 1986 s.124(4); the bases upon which the Secretary of State may do so are set out in s.124A.

[671] IA 1986 s.7(4)(b).

[672] IA 1986 s.122(1)(a)–(g).

[673] At present, £50,000.

[674] IA 1986 s.122(2); for this purpose the creditor's security is deemed to be in jeopardy if the court is satisfied that events have occurred or are about to occur which render it unreasonable in the creditor's interests that the company should retain the power to dispose of the property which is subject to the floating charge.

[675] *Re German Date Coffee Company Ltd* (1882) L.R. 20 Ch.D. 169. Given the demise of the objects clause it is unlikely that this will still be a good ground for winding up a company.

the company are being conducted[676] or illegality of operation[677]; or, in a private company which is in substance a partnership, a division between the directors which brings the affairs of the company to a deadlock[678] or the unjustified exclusion of one of the parties from its affairs.[679] The usual ground for a petition for winding up is, however, that afforded by (d), namely the company's inability to pay its debts. By s.123(1) of the 1986 Act a company is deemed unable to pay its debts when: (1) a creditor, to whom a debt exceeding £750[680] is due, has served on the company a demand to pay, and the company has for three weeks neglected to pay, or to compound or secure the debt to the satisfaction of the creditor; (2) the *induciae* of a charge for payment on an extract decree, or an extract registered bond, or an extract registered protest, has expired without payment, even although the debt be less than £750[681]; (3) when it is proved to the satisfaction of the court that the company is unable to pay its debts as they fall due.[682] The court will refuse a petition on this ground where the whole debt is the subject of a genuine dispute with the company[683] but will not necessarily refuse it when only some of the debt is disputed.[684] Section 123(2) provides a second definition of a company's inability to pay its debts if it is proved to the satisfaction of the courts that the value of the company's assets is less than the value of its liabilities, taking into account its contingent and prospective liabilities.[685]

The court has a discretion to grant or refuse a petition for winding up, but will not readily refuse the application of a creditor,[686] and is directed not to refuse it merely on the ground that the company has no assets.[687] Where the application is made by members of the company as contributories[688] on the ground that it is just and equitable that the company should be wound up, the court is not entitled to make a winding-up order if it is of the opinion that some other remedy is available to the petitioners and that they are acting unreasonably in seeking to have the company wound up instead of pursuing that other remedy.[689] An alternative remedy to winding up in cases of prejudice being suffered by the minority is provided by CA 2006 s.994.[690]

---

[676] *Loch v John Blackwood Ltd* [1924] A.C. 783; *Elder v Elder & Watson*, 1952 S.C. 49 at 55, per Lord President Cooper; *Levy v Napier*, 1962 S.C. 468; *Re Westbourne Galleries* [1973] A.C. 360; *Todd v Todd*, 2008 S.L.T. (Sh. Ct) 26.

[677] *Re Thomas Brinsmead & Sons Ltd* [1897] 1 Ch. 45.

[678] *Re Yenidje Tobacco Co Ltd* [1916] 2 Ch. 426; *Baird v Lees*, 1924 S.C. 83; *Lewis v Haas*, 1971 S.L.T. 57.

[679] *Re Lundie Bros* [1965] 1 W.L.R. 1051; *Re Fildes Bros* [1970] 1 W.L.R. 592.

[680] This amount is subject to alteration by statutory instrument: IA 1986 s.123(3).

[681] *Speirs v Central Building Co*, 1911 S.C. 330.

[682] IA 1986 s.123(1)(e); *Blue Star Security Services (Scotland) Ltd, Petitioners*, 1992 S.L.T. (Sh. Ct) 80; *Macplant Services Ltd v Contract Lifting Services (Scotland) Ltd* [2008] CSOH 158.

[683] *Cuninghame v Walkinshaw Oil Co Ltd* (1886) 14 R. 87; *Re Janeash Ltd* [1990] B.C.C. 250.

[684] *Macplant Services Ltd v Contract Lifting Services (Scotland) Ltd* [2008] CSOH 158.

[685] *BNY Corporate Trustee Services Ltd v Eurosail 3BLL Plc* [2011] EWCA Civ. 227. This case suggests that a common sense approach should be taken into account when valuing assets and liabilities.

[686] *Gardner v Link* (1894) 21 R. 969; cf. *Foxall v Gyle Nurseries*, 1978 S.L.T. (Notes) 29.

[687] IA 1986 s.125(1); *Spiers v Central Building Co*, 1911 S.C. 330.

[688] As to the meaning of "contributory", see s.79 and para.46.55.

[689] IA 1986 s.125(2).

[690] See para.46.27, above; *Gammack, Petitioner*, 1983 S.C. 39; *Re A Company* [1983] 1 W.L.R. 927; *Virdi v Abbey Leisure* [1990] B.C.L.C. 342; *Hyndman v R.C. Hyndman Ltd*, 1989 S.C.L.R. 294.

Consequences of winding up—If the court grants an order for the winding up of **46.51** the company, the winding up is deemed to have commenced at the time of the presentation of the petition.[691]

Thereafter, no action or proceeding against the company or its property can be commenced or proceeded with without leave of the court,[692] and any disposition of the company's property, or transfer of shares, is void, unless the court otherwise directs.[693] Any person who has at any time mishandled or appropriated property belonging to a company which is being wound up, including a director, manager or liquidator, may be compelled to repay or restore or account for the money or property or to contribute such sum to the company's assets as the court thinks fit.[694] The winding up confers on creditors who are creditors by virtue of a debt incurred on or before its commencement and on the liquidator the same rights as are given in bankruptcy to challenge gratuitous alienations,[695] and unfair preferences.[696] A liquidator may also challenge extortionate credit transactions[697] and certain floating charges.[698]

Liquidation has the same effect as sequestration with regard to the equalisation of diligences,[699] and it is equivalent to a decree of adjudication over the company's heritage, arrestment in execution and decree of furthcoming, an arrestment in execution and warrant of sale and an attachment in favour of the creditors according to their respective entitlements.[700] The property of a company in liquidation does not vest in the liquidator.[701] The custody and control of its property are transferred from the company and its directors to the liquidator over whom the company has no control, but the company remains the legal owner of all its assets and interests.[702] A liquidator is merely a manager, taking the place of the directors, for the special purpose of dividing the company's assets among the creditors and any balance among the contributories.[703] The court has power to appoint a

---

[691] IA 1986 s.129(2). See also *John Haig & Co Ltd v Lord Advocate*, 1976 S.L.T. (Notes) 16. If the company has already passed a resolution for voluntary winding up, the date of commencement is the date of the passing of the resolution (s.129(1)). If a company is already in administration and is then being put into the liquidation, the date of commencement is the date of the making of the order (s.129(1A)).

[692] IA 1986 s.130(2).

[693] IA 1986 s.127; *United Dominions Trust*, 1977 S.L.T. (Notes) 56; *Site Preparations v Buchan Development Co*, 1983 S.L.T. 317; *Hollicourt (Contracts) Ltd (in Liquidation) v Bank of Ireland* [2000] 1 W.L.R. 895.

[694] IA 1986 s.212.

[695] IA 1986 s.242. *Nova Glaze Replacement Windows Ltd v Clark Thomson & Co*, 2001 S.C. 815; *John E Rae (Electrical Services) Linlithgow Ltd v Lord Advocate*, 1994 S.L.T. 788; *McLuckie Bros Ltd v Newhouse Contracts Ltd*, 1993 S.L.T. 641. For a rare common law case on the same point of gratuitous alienations, see *Stuart Eves Ltd (In Liquidation) v Smiths Gore*, 1993 S.L.T. 1274.

[696] IA 1986 s.243; *Craiglaw Developments Ltd v Gordon Wilson & Co*, 1997 S.C. 356; *Nicoll v Steelpress (Supplies) Ltd*, 1992 S.C. 119; *Baillie Marshall Ltd (In Liquidation) v Avian Communications Ltd*, 2002 S.L.T. 189.

[697] IA 1986 s.244.

[698] IA 1986 s.245. *Power v Sharp Investments Ltd* [1993] B.C.C. 609.

[699] IA 1986 s.185(1), applying Bankruptcy (Scotland) Act 1985 s.37(1).

[700] Bankruptcy (Scotland) Act 1985 s.37(1). Adjudication may potentially be abolished and replaced by land attachment under the Bankruptcy and Diligence etc. (Scotland) Act 2007.

[701] IA 1986 s.145 permits the court to vest the liquidator in the company's assets, but this provision is rarely used.

[702] *Clark v West Calder Oil Co* (1882) 9 R. 1017 at 1025, per Lord President Inglis, and Lord Shand at 1030.

[703] *Smith v Lord Advocate (No.1)*, 1978 S.C. 259 at 271, per Lord President Emslie. For a discussion of the effects of the statutory scheme, see *Ayerst v C. & K. (Construction)* [1976] A.C. 167, per Lord Diplock.

provisional liquidator,[704] and, on an application by the liquidator or provisional liquidator, to appoint a special manager of the business or property of the company.[705] Where a liquidator and a receiver have both been appointed to a company the rights of the receiver take precedence over those of the liquidator irrespective of whether he was appointed before or after the commencement of the winding up, and the liquidator is bound to deliver to the receiver the property which is covered by the floating charge.[706] If he does so the receiver is primarily liable for the payment of the secured creditors and those who have preferential claims against the company, although otherwise this would be the task of the liquidator.

46.52 **Liquidators**—When an order for winding up is pronounced, an interim liquidator is appointed by the court.[707] His function is to summon separate meetings of the company's creditors and contributories for the purpose of choosing a person, who may be the interim liquidator, to be the liquidator of the company in his place.[708] The liquidator is the person nominated by the creditors, or if no person is so nominated, the person, if any, nominated by the contributories.[709] The court may, however, appoint a person as liquidator of a company where he has been acting as administrator under an administration order which has been discharged or as the supervisor of a voluntary arrangement.[710] A person who has been appointed as liquidator is described by the style of "the liquidator" of the company concerned and not by his individual name.[711] A person who acts as the liquidator of a company must be qualified to do so, which means that he must be permitted to act as an insolvency practitioner by or under the rules of a recognised professional body or authorised so to act, that he must have furnished the proper caution for the performance of his functions and not been disqualified from acting on grounds such as that he is an undischarged bankrupt or is mentally incapable of managing his own affairs.[712] A person who is not an individual is not qualified to act as an insolvency practitioner, so it is not competent to appoint a partnership or company to the office of liquidator.[713]

The general function of the liquidator is to ensure that the assets of the company are got in, realised and distributed to the company's creditors and, if there is a surplus, to the persons entitled to it.[714] A committee of creditors and contributories may be appointed to act with him by the meetings of creditors and contributories at which he is appointed, or by separate meetings of the creditors and contributories called by the liquidator for the purpose of determining whether such a committee should be established.[715] Its members have no claim to

---

[704] IA 1986 s.135; see *Levy v Napier*, 1962 S.C. 468.

[705] IA 1986 s.177.

[706] *Manley, Petitioner*, 1985 S.L.T. 42. Note also *McGuiness v Black*, 1990 S.L.T. 156 regarding the position of a judicial factor and a provisional liquidator.

[707] IA 1986 s.138(1); Insolvency (Scotland) Rules 1986 (SI 1986/1915) r.4.18(2).

[708] IA 1986 s.138(3); Insolvency (Scotland) Rules 1986 (SI 1986/1915) r.4.12.

[709] IA 1986 s.139.

[710] IA 1986 s.140.

[711] IA 1986 s.163.

[712] IA 1986 ss.230, 390.

[713] IA 1986 s.390(1).

[714] IA 1986 s.143(1). For an example of distribution of the surplus to some members in circumstances where others could not be traced, see *Joint Liquidators of Automatic Oil Tools Ltd, Noters*, 2001 S.L.T. 279.

[715] IA 1986 s.142. Note that a committee should consist of more than one individual: *Souter, Petitioner*, 1981 S.L.T. (Sh. Ct) 89. See also Insolvency (Scotland) Rules 1986 (SI 1986/1915) Pt 4 Ch.7.

remuneration.[716] The powers of a liquidator in a winding up are set out in Sch.4 to the 1986 Act. Some of these powers may only be exercised by him with the sanction of the court or of the committee,[717] and he is subject to the control of the court in the exercise of all of them.[718] He may ratify acts or proceedings done or started in the name of the company without proper authority.[719] It is his duty to summon a final meeting of the company's creditors when the winding up is complete, and he vacates office as soon as he has given notice to the court and the Accountant in Bankruptcy that the final meeting has been held, and of the decisions, if any, which it took.[720] A liquidator may be removed or released from office in various circumstances before the winding up is complete.[721]

Voluntary winding up—Voluntary liquidation is a step often taken when it is **46.53** proposed to reconstitute the company with wider powers, when two companies propose to amalgamate, or where for any reason it is desired to bring a company to an end. It is competent in the following cases: (1) when the period (if any) fixed for the duration of the company by its articles has expired, or the event (if any) occurs, on the occurrence of which the articles provide that the company is to be dissolved, and the company in general meeting has passed a resolution requiring the company to be wound up voluntarily; (2) if the company resolves by special resolution that it be wound up voluntarily.[722] If the company has granted a floating charge, the floating charge holder must be given five days notice before the meeting at which the resolution for the winding up of the company is to be moved, unless the floating charge holder consents to the passing of the resolution.[723] A voluntary winding up is deemed to commence at the date of the resolution to wind up.[724] The company is bound to give notice of the resolution by advertisement in the Edinburgh Gazette.[725]

When a company is wound up voluntarily it must cease to carry on business from the commencement of the winding up, except in so far as may be required for its beneficial winding up.[726] Any subsequent transfer of shares, without the sanction of the liquidator, is void.[727] The resolution does not bar an action being commenced or proceeded with against the company, but the liquidator may apply to the court to direct that no action or proceeding may be commenced or proceeded with.[728] It is no bar to an application for winding up by the court,[729] but where a majority of the creditors favours a voluntary winding up, the court as a rule has regard to its views.[730]

A voluntary winding up may be either a members' or a creditors' voluntary winding up.[731] It is the former if the directors, or at least a majority of the

---

[716] *Liquidator of Pattisons* (1902) 4 F. 1010.

[717] IA 1986 s.167(1).

[718] IA 1986 s.167(3).

[719] *Alexander Ward & Co v Samyang Navigation Co*, 1975 S.C. (HL) 26 at 36, per Lord Fraser.

[720] IA 1986 s.172(8); Insolvency (Scotland) Rules 1986 (SI 1986/1915) r.4.31.

[721] IA 1986 ss.172, 174; Insolvency (Scotland) Rules 1986 (SI 1986/1915) rr.4.23–4.30.

[722] IA 1986 s.84.

[723] IA 1986 s.84(2A), (2B).

[724] IA 1986 s.86.

[725] IA 1986 s.85.

[726] IA 1986 s.87.

[727] IA 1986 s.88.

[728] IA 1986 s.113.

[729] IA 1986 s.116.

[730] *Bouboulis v Mann, Macneal & Co*, 1926 S.C. 637; *Re Home Remedies* [1943] Ch. 1.

[731] Where there is a members' voluntary winding up the company is assumed still to be solvent: where there is a creditors' winding up, the company is unlikely to be solvent.

directors, at a meeting held before the notices for the meeting at which the resolution to wind up is to be proposed are sent out, make, and deliver to the Registrar of Companies,[732] a declaration, termed a declaration of solvency, to the effect that they have made a full inquiry into the affairs of the company, and that, having done so, they have formed the opinion that the company will be able to pay its debts, with interest, in full, within a period, not exceeding 12 months from the commencement of the winding up.[733] This declaration must be made no more than five weeks before the passing of the resolution to wind the company up.[734] If no such declaration is made and delivered to the Registrar, it is a creditors' voluntary winding up.[735] The declaration must embody a statement of the company's assets and liabilities as at the latest practicable date before the making of the resolution. If a director makes the declaration without having reasonable grounds for his opinion concerning the company's ability to pay its debts, he renders himself liable to imprisonment or a fine.[736] In a members' winding up the liquidator is appointed by the company in general meeting.[737] Provisions may be made for the sale, or transfer to another company, of the company's business,[738] and for its dissolution.[739]

In a creditors' voluntary winding up the company must call a meeting of its creditors for a day not later than the fourteenth day after the day when the meeting at which the resolution for voluntary winding up is to be proposed.[740] One of the directors must be appointed to preside at the meeting.[741] The liquidator in a creditors' voluntary winding up is the person nominated by the creditors or, where no person has been nominated by them, the person, if any, nominated by the company.[742] A committee of not more than five persons may be appointed by the creditors to act in the liquidation.[743] The company has the right to appoint no more than five other persons to act as members of that committee.[744] On the appointment of a liquidator, all the powers of the directors cease, except in so far as the committee, or, if none, the creditors, sanction their continuance.[745]

46.54 Ranking of creditors—Except in a members' voluntary winding up, a creditor claiming to vote at meetings and to be entitled to payment of a dividend must submit a claim in the prescribed form to the liquidator together with an account or voucher as evidence of his debt.[746] In calculating the amount of his claim he must deduct the value of any security.[747] Priority is given to the payment of preferential

---

[732] IA 1986 s.89.

[733] IA 1986 s.89(1).

[734] IA 1986 s.89(2).

[735] IA 1986 s.90; see also s.95.

[736] IA 1986 s.89(4).

[737] IA 1986 s.91. In a creditors' voluntary winding up, the creditors may choose the liquidator.

[738] IA 1986 s.110.

[739] IA 1986 s.201.

[740] IA 1986 s.98.

[741] IA 1986 s.99(1). It has been held in England that the meeting is not invalid because none of the directors are present: *Re Salcombe Hotel Development Co Ltd* [1991] B.C.L.C. 44.

[742] IA 1986 s.100.

[743] IA 1986 s.101(1); for the proceedings of the committee, see Insolvency (Scotland) Rules 1986 (SI 1986/1915) rr.4.40–4.59A.

[744] IA 1986 s.101(2).

[745] IA 1986 s.103.

[746] Insolvency (Scotland) Rules 1986 rr.4.15, 7.30.

[747] Bankruptcy (Scotland) Act 1985 s.22(9), Sch.1, as applied by r.4.16 of the Insolvency (Scotland) Rules 1986.

debts, which rank equally among themselves and must be paid in full unless the assets are insufficient to meet them in which case they abate in equal proportions.[748] Preferential debts have priority over the holder of a floating charge.[749] Questions as to the liabilities and rights of co-obligants, including cautioners, are dealt with according to the same rules as apply in sequestration.[750] The funds are distributed by the liquidator in the following order[751]: (a) the expenses of liquidation[752]; (b) the expenses of any voluntary arrangement in force at the time when the petition for winding up was first presented; (c) the preferential debts; (d) ordinary debts, i.e. debts neither secured nor falling under (a), (b), (c) or (f); (e) interest at 15 per cent on (i) the preferential debts, (ii) the ordinary debts, between the commencement of the winding up and payment; (f) any postponed debt, i.e. a creditor's right to any alienation which has been reduced or restored to the company's assets or to the proceeds of the sale of such alienation. Debts within the same category have the same priority and abate in equal proportions.[753]

Contributories—Should the assets of the company in liquidation be insufficient **46.55** to meet its liabilities, calls may be made on the shareholders as contributories in so far (in a limited company) as the shares are not fully paid up.[754] The primary liability rests on the existing holders of the shares, but should it appear to the court that they are unable to meet their liabilities, calls may be made on those prior shareholders who have held the shares during the 12 months preceding the liquidation.

A director may also be a contributory where the directors have arranged a payment out of capital for the redemption or repurchase of their company's shares and the company has subsequently gone into liquidation with insufficient funds to pay its debts.[755]

Company voluntary arrangements—This procedure is available to a liquidator **46.56** in the course of a winding up or to an administrator while an administration order is in force[756] or at any other time when the directors may think it appropriate. The directors may not, however, propose a voluntary arrangement where the company is already in liquidation or where an administration order is in force.[757] It provides a simple procedure whereby a company may conclude an arrangement with its creditors which will be binding on both the company and those of its creditors who have had notice of it, and may enable a company which is nearly or actually insolvent to rationalise its affairs more speedily and with less formality than if a winding up had to be carried through to its conclusion, which is normally the dissolution of the company. The essential elements are the making of a proposal to the company and its creditors for a composition in satisfaction of its debts or a scheme of arrangement of its affairs, which provides for a nominee, who must be

---

[748] IA 1986 s.175; see Sch.6 for a list of preferential debts; cf. Bankruptcy (Scotland) Act 1985 s.51(1)(e), Sch.3.

[749] IA 1986 s.175(2)(b).

[750] Bankruptcy (Scotland) Act 1985 s.60, as applied by r.4.16 of the Insolvency (Scotland) Rules 1986.

[751] Insolvency (Scotland) Rules 1986 r.4.66.

[752] See Insolvency (Scotland) Rules 1986 r.4.67.

[753] Insolvency (Scotland) Rules 1986 r.4.66(4).

[754] IA 1986 s.74. It is now very rare for this to happen.

[755] IA 1986 s.76(1).

[756] IA 1986 s.1(3).

[757] IA 1986 s.1(1).

an insolvency practitioner,[758] to act as trustee or otherwise for the purpose of supervising its implementation. The proposal is made by the liquidator, the administrator or the directors of the company as the case may be.[759] The nominee, where he is not the liquidator or administrator, is required to submit a report to the court within 28 days as to whether in his opinion meetings of the company and of its creditors should be summoned to consider the proposal.[760] Such a nominee must state whether, in his opinion, the proposal voluntary arrangement has a reasonable prospect of being approved and implemented.[761] If he reports favourably on the scheme he is required to summon the meetings for the time, date and place proposed in his report unless the court directs otherwise.[762] The contents of a proposal made by either the liquidator or administrator and proposing either himself or another insolvency practitioner as nominee are the same as where the proposal is made by the directors,[763] except that in the former case the proposal should also include anything he thinks appropriate to enable members and creditors to reach an informed decision.[764] He may also summon a meeting of these to consider his proposal wherever and whenever he thinks fit.[765] If the composition or scheme is approved by the company and its creditors at these meetings, with or without modifications, it takes effect as if made by the company at the creditors' meeting and binds every person who had notice of and was entitled to vote at that meeting as if he were a party to it.[766] Provision is made for the implementation and supervision of the composition or scheme and for the sisting or other conduct of any proceedings for the winding up or administration of the company so as to enable the composition or scheme to be implemented.[767] A composition or scheme may be challenged on the ground of unfair prejudice or of some material irregularity at or in relation to either of the meetings.[768]

It is also possible for directors of an eligible company[769] subject to a company voluntary arrangement to obtain a moratorium for the company in respect of hostile steps taken against it.[770] The main effects of the moratorium during its currency are to preclude the presentation of petitions for a winding up or an administration order in relation to the company, the passing of a resolution to wind up the company, the appointment of an receiver, the taking of any steps to enforce any security over the company's prospects without the leave of the court, or commencing or continuing any proceedings against the company without the leave of the court.[771] The breathing space arising from the moratorium may allow

---

[758] Note that it is a criminal offence for a person to act as liquidator or administrator in relation to a company or supervisor of a voluntary agreement when he is not qualified to do so: IA 1986 s.389.

[759] IA 1986 s.1. In the case of the directors, a resolution of the board proposing a voluntary arrangement is probably sufficient: *Re Equiticorp International Plc* [1989] 1 W.L.R. 1010.

[760] IA 1986 s.2. See Act of Sederunt (Rules of the Court of Session 1994) (SI 1994/1443) rr.74.01–74.09.

[761] IA 1986 s.2(2)(a).

[762] IA 1986 s.3(1).

[763] Insolvency (Scotland) Rules 1986 rr.1.3, 1.10 and 1.12(3).

[764] Insolvency (Scotland) Rules 1986 r.1.10(b).

[765] IA 1986 s.3(2).

[766] IA 1986 s.5; Insolvency (Scotland) Rules 1986 rr.1.13–1.17.

[767] IA 1986 ss.7, 5(3); Insolvency (Scotland) Rules 1986 rr.1.18–1.24.

[768] IA 1986 s.6.

[769] Defined in para.3 of Sch.A1 to the IA 1986, and excluding from eligibility a number of either large companies or companies involved in the money markets. For the list of excluded companies see paras 4–4K.

[770] The procedure for this is given in IA 1986 Sch.A1 paras 6–11.

[771] See para.12 of Sch.A1 to the IA 1986.

the company time to sort out its affairs in a way that allows the company and its business to be saved. It is especially useful when a company has been beset by unfortunate events which are unlikely to arise again, and where the creditors see the continued benefit of an arrangement rather than the cessation of business following a liquidation.

Dissolution of a company—A company is dissolved automatically on the expira- **46.57** tion of three months from the date of registration of a notice by the liquidator that a final general meeting of the company has been held. The procedure is the same in the case of a compulsory winding up[772] as for a voluntary liquidation.[773] The liquidator vacates office as soon as he has given notice to the Registrar, and to the court if it was a compulsory winding up or he was appointed by the court, that the meeting has been held and of the decisions if any at that meeting.[774] A liquidator appointed by the court who finds, after meetings of the creditors and contributories have been held, that the realisable assets of the company are insufficient to cover the expenses of the winding up may apply to the court for an early dissolution of the company.[775] In all these cases the court may, on the application of any person who appears to the court to have an interest, order that the date at which the dissolution of the company is to take effect shall be deferred for such period as it thinks fit.[776] At any time within six years of the dissolution of a company, the court, on the application of the liquidator or of any person interested,[777] may make an order to have the company restored to the register, and thereafter such proceedings may be taken as might have been taken if the company had not been dissolved.[778] The court has power, under its *nobile officium*, to declare the dissolution to have been void in a case where the company has failed or omitted to grant a conveyance of property sold,[779] but will not exercise this power if there are other means of completing the title.[780]

While a winding up is the normal process by which a company is dissolved, the Registrar of Companies may take steps which will result in striking a company off the register if he has reasonable cause to believe that it is not carrying on business or in operation.[781] The company itself may apply to be struck off.[782] If the company was struck off by the Registrar of Companies (but not by the court or at the company's own request) there is a procedure to allow companies to be restored to the Register within six years of dissolution but without application to court.[783] This is known as administrative restoration. It requires the consent of the Queen's Lord Treasurer and Remembrancer as representing the Crown's interest in bona vacantia.

---

[772] IA 1986 s.205.

[773] IA 1986 s.201.

[774] IA 1986 s.172(8).

[775] IA 1986 s.204; *Redmount Properties Ltd* Unreported December 11, 2009; *http://www.scotcourts.gov.uk/opinions/L72_04.html* [Accessed August 9, 2012].

[776] IA 1986 ss.201(3), 204(5), 205(5).

[777] CA 2006 s.1029(2).

[778] CA 2006 s.1030. If the restoration to the register is to enable proceedings against the company for damages for personal injury to take place the application may be made at any time, subject to any other limits applicable to the actual proceedings (s.1030(2)).

[779] *Collins Bros, Petitioners*, 1916 S.C. 620.

[780] *Lord Macdonald's Curator*, 1924 S.C. 163; *Forth Shipbreaking Co*, 1924 S.C. 489.

[781] CA 2006 s.1000.

[782] CA 2006 s.1003. See also the Register of Companies and Applications for Striking Off Regulations 2009 (SI 2009/1803) and associated advice on the Companies House website.

[783] CA 2006 ss.1024–1028. Companies House form RT01 is required.

When a company is dissolved, and not resuscitated, in the absence of any other person having right thereto, all property and rights vested in, or held in trust for the company immediately before its dissolution, are deemed to be bona vacantia, and belong to the Crown.[784]

FURTHER READING

Boyle, A.J. and Birds, J., *Boyle and Birds' Company Law*, 8th edn (Jordans, 2011).
Cabrelli, D., "Statutory derivative proceedings: the view from the Inner House", 2010 Edin. L.R. 14(1), 116–121.
Flint, D., *Scottish Liquidation Handbook*, 4th edn (Edinburgh: W. Green, 2010).
Grier, N., *Company Law*, 3rd edn (Edinburgh: W. Green, 2009).
Keay, M. and Loughrey, J.M., "Derivative proceedings in a brave new world for company management and shareholders", 2010 J.B.L. 151–178.
Lowry, J. and Reisberg, A., *Pettet's Company Law: Company Law and Corporate Finance*, 4th edn (Pearson, 2012).
Mayson, S., French, D., and Ryan, C., *Company Law* (Oxford: Oxford University Press) (updated each year).
Morse, G., *Palmer's Company Law* (Sweet and Maxwell) (continually updated).
Scottish Law Commission, *Report on Registration of Rights in Security by Companies* (HMSO, 2004), Scot. Law Com. No.197 (Background to Bankruptcy and Diligence etc. (Scotland) Act 2007).
St Clair, J. and Drummond Young, J.E., *The Law of Corporate Insolvency in Scotland*, 4th edn (Edinburgh: W. Green, 2011).
Tolley's Company Law Service (LexisNexis) (continually updated).

The monthly journal, *Company Lawyer*, has a wide range of articles on all aspects of company law. It is available on Westlaw.

---

[784] CA 2006 s.1012; as to any Crown disclaimer, see ss.1020–1022.

CHAPTER 47

ASSOCIATIONS

Legal position—Unincorporated associations, commonly referred to as volun- **47.01** tary associations, occupy an anomalous and unsatisfactory position in the eye of the law. Corporate bodies[1] and, in Scotland, partnerships or firms,[2] are recognised as possessing legal personality; but, although the courts will adjudicate on matters relating to a voluntary association, a voluntary association is not regarded as having a legal existence distinct from that of its members. Hence, at least in the higher courts, such an association cannot at common law sue or be sued in its collective name alone; the names either of all the members, or of responsible members such as office bearers, must be added.[3] In the sheriff court an association carrying on business under a trading or descriptive name may sue or be sued in its trading or descriptive name alone, and an extract of a decree pronounced against it under its trading or descriptive name is a valid warrant for diligence against it.[4] Associations have difficulty owning property, it not always being clear whether the office-bearers should act as trustees for the association, and if they do perform that function, unless there is prior agreement, they may only have a right of indemnity to the extent of the association's funds.

The court does not take any concern with the actions or resolutions of associations except for the following matters: the court's exercise of their supervisory jurisdiction to review any ultra vires decisions[5] and the court's right to provide a remedy for the loss of associations' members' patrimonial interests or civil rights (such as, for example, unwarranted loss of status[6] or infringement of the requirements of natural justice[7]). Unless these matters are involved, an action for determining questions between a member and the association will not be entertained.[8]

---

[1] See *J.H. Rayner (Mincing Lane) Ltd v Department of Trade and Industry* [1990] 2 A.C. 418.

[2] See para.45.07, above; Partnership Act 1890 s.4(2).

[3] *Somerville v Rowbotham* (1862) 24 D. 1187; *Renton Football Club v McDowall* (1891) 18 R. 670; *Pagan v Haig*, 1910 S.C. 341; *Bridge v South Portland Street Synagogue*, 1907 S.C. 1351; *Harrison v West of Scotland Kart Club*, 2004 S.C. 615.

[4] Sheriff Courts (Scotland) Act 1907 Sch.1 r.5.7 (as substituted by the Act of Sederunt (Sheriff Court Ordinary Cause Rules) (SI 1993/1956) as amended by the Act of Sederunt (Sheriff Court Ordinary Cause Rules Amendment) (Miscellaneous) (SI 1996/2445)).

[5] *Gardner v McClintock* (1904) 11 S.L.T. 654; *Ellice v Invergarry and Fort Augustus Railway Co*, 1913 S.C. 849; *Gunstone v Scottish Women's Amateur Athletic Association*, 1987 S.L.T. 611; *Graham v Ladeside of Kilbirnie Bowling Club*, 1990 S.C. 365; *Crocket v Tantallon Golf Club*, 2005 S.L.T. 663.

[6] *Gunstone v Scottish Women's Amateur Athletic Association*, 1987 S.L.T. 611.

[7] *McDonald v Burns*, 1940 S.C. 376; *Brown v Executive Committee of the Edinburgh District Labour Party*, 1985 S.L.T. 985; *Lennox v Scottish Branch of the British Show Jumping Association*, 1996 S.L.T. 353; *Irvine v Royal Burgess Golfing Society of Edinburgh*, 2004 S.C.L.R. 386; *Smith, Petitioner*, 2007 S.L.T. 909.

[8] *Forbes v Eden* (1867) 5 M. (HL) 36; *Skerret v Oliver* (1896) 23 R. 468; *Drennan v Associated Ironmoulders of Scotland*, 1921 S.C. 151, per Lord Dundas; *Marshall v Cardonald Bowling Club*, 1971 S.L.T. (Sh. Ct) 56; *Bell v The Trustees*, 1975 S.L.T. (Sh. Ct) 60.

47.02 Classes of Associations—Unincorporated associations[9] include bodies such as social clubs and societies formed for charitable, religious or scientific purposes. There is a broad distinction between the two types of association. In the case of social clubs the funds are contributed by the members and are to be applied primarily for their benefit. Any questions which may arise are solved, therefore, by the application of the law of contract and joint property. The other type of association exists for the promotion of some further purpose or object. Here the element of trust is present, and the general principles of trust law will control the application of the funds contributed or subscribed.

47.03 Clubs—Most clubs are governed by rules or a constitution drawn up by the members, and any member who joins is understood to agree to be bound by those rules; they form part of a contract between him and the other members.[10] The contract is unusual in that a member of the club may be unaware of the other parties to the contract, and the contract may allow the membership of the association to change from time to time in accordance with the rules of the association. Normally the rules will provide that the members authorise office bearers to act or to take decisions on their behalf, on the basis that the members will be bound by those office bearers' acts and decisions provided the office bearers stay within the terms of their authority.

If the association's rules contain a provision for their alteration, any alteration made bona fide and in accordance with the rules is binding on all the members unless the alteration is incompatible with the fundamental purpose of the association.[11] An alteration of the rules of a club to allow for its dissolution will not be in conflict with its fundamental objects, since any club can be dissolved by the unanimous will of its members.[12] But where the rules make no provision for their alteration they cannot be altered without the consent of all the members.[13]

Unless the club rules say otherwise, the property of the club belongs to all the members, each member having a right with all the other members.[14]

> "The right of a member of a club in the property of the club is of a peculiar description. While the club exists as a going concern he is not entitled to insist on a sale and a division of the price. When he dies his right, such as it is, does not pass to his representatives, and if he retires from the club his whole interest therein ceases. But as long as he remains a member of the club his right is one of common property."[15]

Hence it has been held that, while the wish of the majority of the members will rule in the ordinary administration of the property of the club, it is not competent for the

---

[9] In *Graham v Hawick Common Riding Committee*, 1998 S.L.T. (Sh. Ct) 42 the court would not accept that the whole residents of a town constituted an unincorporated association.

[10] *Lyttleton v Blackburne* (1875) L.J. Ch. 219.

[11] *Thellusson v Viscount Valentia* [1907] 2 Ch. 1; *Morgan v Driscoll* (1922) 38 T.L.R. 251.

[12] *Blair v Mackinnon*, 1981 S.L.T. 40. Note, however, that unless there is a provision in the rules to this effect a club cannot be dissolved by a majority of its members against the wishes of a minority: *Gardner v McLintock* (1904) 11 S.L.T. 654.

[13] *Harington v Sendall* [1903] 1 Ch. 921; *Dawkins v Antrobus* (1881) 17 Ch.D. 615, per Jessel M.R. But see the observations of Lords Guthrie and Skerrington in *Wilson v Scottish Typographical Association*, 1912 S.C. 534. See also *Martin v Scottish Transport and General Workers Union*, 1952 S.C. (HL) 1.

[14] *Graff v Evans* (1881) L.R. 8 Q.B.D. 373.

[15] *Murray v Johnstone* (1896) 23 R. 981 at 990, per Lord Moncreiff.

majority gratuitously to alienate club property against the protest of a minority where there is nothing in the constitution of the club giving such a power.[16] If the club comes to an end the property remaining after all the debts and liabilities have been met is distributable among the members at the time in accordance with the terms of the club's rules.[17] Where a club omits or forgets to follow its own rules or adhere to its own previous decisions properly made, litigation may follow.[18]

No member of the club, as such, is liable to pay to it or to anyone else any money beyond his subscription or what is allowed for in the club's constitution[19]; and if he is personally to be made liable by a creditor of the club, his liability must be established on the ground that he has undertaken liability or has so acted as to render himself liable under the ordinary rules of the law of agency.[20] If the rules contain no provision as to resignation, he has the unilateral right, not dependent on acceptance by the club, to resign his membership at any time.[21]

A member who has been expelled from a club may apply to the court to have the resolution of the club set aside; and the court will entertain the action if the club possesses property, for the effect of the expulsion is to deprive the member of his right in that property. The court will not, however, review the merits of the club's decision, and will interfere only if it is not authorised by the rules, or if it is contrary to natural justice (as for example if no opportunity were afforded to the member of defending himself against the charge on which the decision is founded), or if the decision was not arrived at in good faith.[22]

It has been held that a member of a club cannot sue the club (or its office bearers as such) in delict for injury sustained by him while participating in club activities, since to do so would amount to suing himself.[23]

Other associations—Where subscriptions are contributed to an association or **47.04** society formed for the promotion of a certain object, the sums so contributed are held in trust for that object.[24] If that object is charitable within the meaning of the Charities and Trustee Investments (Scotland) Act 2005, the association will need to be registered with the Office of the Scottish Charity Regulator in the Scottish Charity Register. If the object is not charitable within the terms of that Act[25] it does not need to be so registered. Every contribution is an irrevocable appropriation of

---

[16] *Murray v Johnstone* (1896) 23 R. 981; *Gardner v McLintock* (1904) 11 S.L.T. 654. Cf. *Hopwood v O'Neill*, 1971 S.L.T. (Notes) 53.

[17] *Baird v Wells* (1890) L.R. 44 Ch.D. 661, per Stirling J.; cf. *Re Sick and Funeral Society of St John's Sunday School v Golcar* [1973] Ch. 51; *G.K.N. Bolts and Nuts (Automative Division) Birmingham Works Sports and Social Club* [1982] 1 W.L.R. 774. These rules do not, however, apply to a proprietary club, that is, one in which the club premises and what is necessary for the members belong to and are provided by the proprietor, who receives the fees of the members. In this case the members have no right in the property.

[18] *Fletcher v Royal Automobile Club Ltd* [2000] 1 B.C.L.C. 331.

[19] *Wise v Perpetual Trustee Co* [1903] A.C. 139.

[20] *Thomson v Victoria Eighty Club* (1905) 43 S.L.R. 628; *Flemyng v Hector* (1836) 2 M. & W. 172; *Todd v Emly* (1841) 7 M. & W. 427; *Cromarty Leasing Ltd v Turnbull*, 1988 S.L.T. (Sh. Ct) 62.

[21] *Finch v Oake* [1896] 1 Ch. 409.

[22] *Anderson v Manson*, 1909 S.C. 838, per Lord Dundas; *Dawkins v Antrobus* (1881) 17 Ch.D. 615; *Burn v National Amalgamated Labourers Union* [1920] 2 Ch. 364; *Young v Ladies Imperial Club* [1920] 2 K.B. 523; *McLean v Workers' Union* [1929] 1 Ch. 602; *Bell v The Trustees*, 1975 S.L.T. (Sh. Ct) 60; *Crocket v Tantallon Golf Club*, 2005 S.L.T. 663; *Wiles v Bothwell Castle Golf Club*, 2005 S.L.T. 785.

[23] *Mair v Wood*, 1948 S.C. 83; *Carmichael v Bearsden & District Rifle and Pistol Club*, 2000 S.L.T. (Sh. Ct) 49; *Harrison v West of Scotland Kart Club*, 2001 S.L.T. 1171.

[24] *Ewing v McGavin* (1831) 9 S. 622; *Connell v Ferguson* (1857) 19 D. 482, per Lord Deas.

[25] As, for example, a charity set up to support a political organisation.

the donor's money to the purposes of the association, and, so long as these purposes are capable of being effected, the donor is not entitled to repayment of his contribution.[26] Unless it is otherwise provided in the rules of the association or the terms on which subscriptions were invited, the purposes to which the money is to be applied cannot be altered without the consent of all the subscribers.[27]

A well-drafted constitution should provide for the situation where it becomes impossible to carry out the purpose for which the subscriptions were given. The disposal of the funds of the association may present great difficulty. Where that purpose is of a public or charitable nature, it would appear from the decision in *Anderson's Trs v Scott*[28] that the proper course is that a scheme should be prepared by the court in the exercise of the jurisdiction which it possesses in regard to such public trusts.[29] Otherwise the funds would apparently fall, as a rule, to be repaid to the subscribers.

> "Where parties join in a subscription to effect a particular object, and place the money subscribed in the hands of certain persons to carry out that object, I think the quasi trust, thereby created, is for the alternative purpose of either carrying out the object of the subscription, or, if that cannot be done, of paying back the money."[30]

There may be great practical difficulties in this course: and if a subscriber could not be traced it is possible that his share would fall to the Crown as bona vacantia.[31]

The terms on which the funds were contributed may, however, be such as to negative any quasi-trust as, for example, where the contributions are not purely gratuitous but have been finally paid over by the contributors as the consideration for benefits to be received by them, and in that case they would have no claim for the return of their contributions.[32]

In the case of a dissenting church, the funds contributed to it are held in trust, and in case of division among its members any question as to the right to these funds is determined by inquiring which of the parties is adhering to the original principles professed by the church. The constitution of the church may provide for the disposal of the property in the event of a schism or may give the church the power of altering its principles; but, in the absence of such provisions, where the property is claimed by different sections of those who formed the church, the property will be held to belong to those who adhere to those principles.[33]

---

[26] *Ewing v McGavin* (1831) 9 S. 622; *Peake v Association of English Episcopalians* (1884) 22 S.L.R. 3.

[27] *McCaskill v Cameron* (1840) 2 D. 537; *Steedman v Malcolm* (1842) 4 D. 1441.

[28] *Anderson's Trs v Scott*, 1914 S.C. 942; see also *Gibson* (1900) 2 F. 1195; *Davidson's Trs v Arnott*, 1951 S.C. 42.

[29] Law Reform (Miscellanous Provisions) (Scotland) Act 1990 s.9. See also the Charities and Trustee Investment (Scotland) Act 2005.

[30] per Lord Deas in *Connell v Ferguson* (1857) 19 D. 482, and *Mitchell v Burness* (1878) 5 R. 954; *Bain v Black* (1849) 11 D. 1287 at 1307, per Lord Mackenzie, and at 1310, per Lord Fullerton, affd 6 Bell's App.317; *Re British Red Cross Balkan Fund* [1914] 2 Ch. 419.

[31] This was the decision of the Lord Ordinary (Cullen) in *Anderson's Trs v Scott*, 1914 S.C. 942; see also Lord President Dunedin's opinion in *Incorporation of Maltmen of Stirling*, 1912 S.C. 887, and Lord Sands' opinion in *Caledonian Employees' Benevolent Society*, 1928 S.C. 633.

[32] *Smith v Lord Advocate* (1899) 1 F. 741; *Cannock v Edwards* [1895] 1 Ch. 489.

[33] *Free Church of Scotland v Lord Overtoun* (1904) 7 F. (HL) 1; *Free Church of Scotland v General Assembly of the Free Church of Scotland*, 2005 1 S.C. 396; *Smith v Morrison*, 2011 CSIH 52. See also M. Gretason, "When club members fall out: the changing law on religious trusts" (2006) *Law & Justice* 157, 29–38 and Lord Rodger, *The Courts, the Church and the Constitution* (Edinburgh University Press, 2008).

If a clergyman wrongfully expelled from a church or a member from an association applies to the court for redress he must show that he has suffered some patrimonial loss; but under such loss is included the deprivation through the expulsion of some particular status, i.e. the capacity to perform certain functions or to hold certain offices.[34] The court will award damages for any wrong done in this way, but will not pronounce decree ordaining the church or association to re-admit the expelled member.[35] The court will not interfere with the judgments of an ecclesiastical tribunal, unless the tribunal has acted clearly beyond its constitution and has affected the civil rights and patrimonial interests of a church member, or its proceedings have been grossly irregular or contrary to natural justice.[36]

Liability of committee members and liability of other members—The essential difficulty with clubs is that they have no legal existence. This means that when an action is raised against a club, in the absence of the club's legal existence, a creditor is entitled to claim against those who apparently represent the club, namely its committee members, and specifically those who purport to sign any contract or accept any responsibility for the club's actions. Most clubs have a committee which is authorised by the members of the club to run the club and to purchase what is necessary for the club using club funds, and where there are such committee members, while they may not be agents of the club, they may be agents for the generality of the members.[37] Where through incompetence a committee member has failed to take account of a recognised danger or employed someone unsuitable, he may be liable,[38] though he may have the benefit of an indemnity from the club itself. However, from the point of view of a creditor, it is not for the creditor to concern himself with the internal arrangements of the club. Under English law, it would appear to be the case that committee members contracting or appearing to contract on behalf of a club may incur personal liability, either because of the terms of the contract, or because by making the contract they are acting in excess of their authority. If those committee members contract in their own right, they are prima facie personally liable, without the requirement to sue the other members of the club, even though they may have been duly authorised to enter the contract on behalf of the members generally. If the committee members were so authorised, the other contracting party may elect to sue either them, as having contracted personally, or to sue the club members collectively, as the principals on whose behalf the contract was made.[39] A well drawn-up constitution should permit a committee member to be indemnified by the club's members collectively for his actions in the proper course of his business as a committee member. If there is no such power in the club's constitution to indemnify the committee members, it would appear that although the committee cannot pledge members' credit,[40] the committee may nevertheless employ staff and pay staff

47.05

---

[34] *Skerret v Oliver* (1896) 23 R. 468, per Lord Kincairney; *Bell v The Trustees*, 1975 S.L.T. (Sh. Ct) 60.

[35] *Gall v Loyal Glenbogie Lodge of the Oddfellows' Friendly Society* (1900) 2 F. 1187, per Lord Trayner.

[36] *McDonald v Burns*, 1940 S.C. 376; *Brentnall v Free Presbyterian Church of Scotland*, 1986 S.L.T. 471.

[37] *Cromarty Leasing Ltd v Turnbull*, 1988 S.L.T. (Sh. Ct) 62 at 63J.

[38] *Brown v Lewis* (1896) 12 T.L.R. 455, DC.

[39] *Michael John Construction Ltd v Golledge* [2006] EWHC 71 (TCC); [2006] T.C.L.R. 3; 2006 W.L. 316091 and *Marston Thompson & Evershed Plc v Benn* [2007] W.T.L.R. 315; 1997 W.L. 1104740.

[40] *Flemyng v Hector* (1836) 2 M. & W. 172; *Hawke v Cole* (1890) 62 L.T. 658.

redundancy payments etc. and be indemnified by the club for their actions.[41] However, even if there is an indemnity in place, if the club has no funds, the committee members may still find themselves personally liable for the debts of the club without recourse against the members.[42] Where the committee members sign a contract in their own name, without any designation of their position as committee members, they are taken to have accepted responsibility for the club's debts themselves.[43] It is therefore in a committee member's interest to insist, where a creditor is willing to accept it, in contracts and other obligations that the contracting party may only claim against the club to the extent of the club's funds and not the committee members personally. Merely because a club does not have any legal existence does not mean that it cannot be sued, but that those who represent it may be liable in the absence of the club's ability to satisfy the debt in the absence of any terms avoiding liability. This presents difficulties for creditors seeking to effect diligence against the club itself or its office-bearers.

The duty of a member is usually only to pay his subscription and depending on the club's constitution he may be liable to the club for arrears or penalties on delay. Much depends on the precise wording of the constitution or rules of the club or any agreement between the members of the club, or, in the absence of specific adherence to any particular set of rules, on the established practice of the club. But in the absence of any provision, statutory or otherwise, imposing liability on the members, or the members' ratification of some liability incurred by the committee members, the individual members are not liable.[44] If the members are to be liable for any reason, the extent of each member's liability will depend on whether the members are jointly and severally liable for the debt or merely liable pro rata; and ideally this should be evident from the club's constitution. Normally the victim of a delict can claim against the club,[45] but only exceptionally against its members.[46] In practice most clubs will have insurance, thus minimising the likelihood of personal liability against the members. Another practical solution is for the club to be registered as a limited company. There is a potential liability of members of a club towards third parties where a club owns premises, as the Occupiers' Liability (Scotland) Act 1960 gives third parties the right to sue the members personally on the grounds that they own the premises collectively.[47] Where the club's agents or servants acting within the scope of their authority or employment act negligently or create a nuisance or suffer injury, the members collectively who were members at the time of the incident may collectively incur liability for that negligence or nuisance or injury.[48]

---

[41] *Todd v Emly* (1841) 7 M. & W. 427 at 434.

[42] Giving a tradesman a copy of the club rules does not remove the committee member's liability: *Steele v Gourlay and Davis* (1888) 3 T.L.R. 118; *Overton v Hewett* (1886) 3 T.L.R. 246.

[43] *Cromarty Leasing Ltd v Turnbull*, 1988 S.L.T. (Sh. Ct) 62.

[44] *Wise v Perpetual Trustee Co* [1903] A.C. 139; *Thomson and Gillespie v Victoria Eighty Club* (1905) 13 S.L.T. 399, OH.

[45] *Bolton v Stone* [1951] A.C. 850; *Miller v Jackson* [1977] Q.B. 966; [1977] 3 All E.R. 338, CA.

[46] *Murdison v Scottish Football Union* (1896) 23 R. 449. This was an action of defamation against the club and some of its members: no objection was taken to the action against the members themselves since they were the ones alleged to have been defaming the pursuer.

[47] Occupiers' Liability (Scotland) Act 1960 s.1 See also *McQueen v Ballater Golf Club*, 1975 S.L.T. 160, OH, where no exception was taken to the raising of the action against the club per se. However, in *McCall v Dumfries and Galloway Rugby Football Club*, 1999 S.C.L.R. 977 a member of the club injured on the club's premises was unable to raise an action against his own club.

[48] *Ellis v National Free Labour Association* (1905) 7 F. 629; *Campbell v Thompson* [1953] 1 Q.B. 445.

Should a member wish to avoid liability for any of the club's obligations he must resign from the club, but in the absence of express agreement to the contrary he would remain potentially liable for all obligations arising during his membership.[49]

Societies Regulated by Statute—There are certain associations which hold an **47.06** intermediate position between corporate and unincorporated bodies. They have no corporate existence, but the legislature has intervened for their regulation and assistance. The most important of these are trade unions.[50]

At common law a trade union, if its rules and objects were open to objection as being in restraint of trade, was an illegal association in the sense that it could not sue or enforce contracts,[51] or be sued in respect of an alleged breach of contract with a member.[52] By the Trade Union Act 1871[53] it was enacted that the purposes of any trade union should not be illegal on this ground so as to render any member liable to criminal prosecution, or any agreement or trust void or voidable. This dispensation has been preserved in subsequent legislation,[54] and extended so as to cover any rule of a trade union. Any such rule is not to be held to be unlawful or unenforceable by reason only that it is in restraint of trade.[55] Trade unions and employers' associations within the meaning of the Trade Union and Labour Relations (Consolidation) Act 1992 have, however, certain attributes and privileges in consequence of which, although unincorporated, they may be said to have a legal entity.[56] For instance they are capable of making contracts and, subject to certain immunities, of suing and being sued in their own name, and any judgment, order or award made against them is enforceable against any property held in trust for them as if they were bodies corporate.[57] Statutory rights[58] not to be excluded or expelled from a trade union by way of arbitrary or unreasonable discrimination have been repealed[59] but in some circumstances protection may be afforded at common law[60] and in the case of any employment in which it is the practice, in accordance with a union membership agreement, for employees to belong to a specified trade union or one of a number of specified trade unions, anyone who is or seeks to be in such employment has a right not to have an application for trade union membership unreasonably refused and not to be unreasonably expelled from membership.[61] A member of a trade union has the right, on giving reasonable notice and complying with any reasonable conditions, to terminate his membership.[62] He also has rights

---

[49] *Howells v Dominion Insurance Co Ltd* [2005] EWHC 552.

[50] Building societies are incorporated under the Building Societies Act 1986. Societies regulated by the Industrial and Provident Societies Act 1965 are incorporated on registration (s.3).

[51] *Wilkie v King*, 1911 S.C. 1310, per Lord Dunedin; *Shanks & McKernan v United Operative Masons Society* (1874) 1 R. 453 and 823. Not all trade unions were illegal: *Russell v Amalgamated Society of Carpenters and Joiners* [1910] 1 K.B. 506.

[52] *Bernard v National Union of Mineworkers*, 1971 S.C. 32.

[53] Trade Union Act 1871 ss.2 and 3.

[54] See Industrial Relations Act 1971 s.135; Trade Union and Labour Relations Act 1974 s.2(5).

[55] Trade Union and Labour Relations (Consolidation) Act 1992 s.11; see *Faramus v Film Artistes' Association* [1964] A.C. 925; *Edwards v Society of Graphical and Allied Trades* [1971] Ch. 354.

[56] *Taff Vale Rly Co v Amalgamated Society of Railway Servants* [1901] A.C. 426; *Bonsor v Musicians Union* [1956] A.C. 104.

[57] Trade Union and Labour Relations (Consolidation) Act 1992 ss.10, 12.

[58] Trade Union and Labour Relations Act 1974 s.5.

[59] Trade Union and Labour Relations (Amendment) Act 1976 s.1.

[60] e.g. on grounds of natural justice, of ultra vires or of a public policy against arbitrary exclusion: *Nagle v Fielden* [1966] 2 Q.B. 633; *McGregor v NALGO*, 1979 S.C. 401.

[61] Trade Union and Labour Relations (Consolidation) Act 1992 ss.174–177.

[62] Trade Union and Labour Relations (Consolidation) Act 1992 s.69.

that there will be a ballot before industrial action, that he is not denied access to the courts and that he will not be unjustifiably disciplined.[63]

47.07 Friendly Societies—Friendly Societies are, broadly speaking, constituted for the maintenance and relief of members and their families in sickness or old age and distress and to a limited extent for certain methods of insurance. The Friendly Societies Act 1974, a consolidation statute, contained provisions whereby societies could register and obtain certain privileges and duties. Under the Friendly Societies Act 1992, societies fulfilling prescribed conditions can be registered and on registration become incorporated.[64] The permissible purposes and powers of incorporated friendly societies are extended and they may form subsidiaries.[65] They are subject to supervision by the Friendly Societies Commission.[66]

47.08 Building Societies—A building society is not a company but it must have a memorandum and rules and it may raise funds by issuing shares, including deferred shares at a premium, to its members.[67] The principal purpose of a building society is secured lending on land bought for residential use[68] but it can also provide other financial services (e.g. banking, estate agency, insurance, and investment) so long as lending is not made conditional on the borrower being restricted to making use only of the financial services offered by the lender.[69] A building society may, subject to satisfying requirements laid down by the 1986 Act,[70] transfer its business to either an existing public company limited by shares or such a company specifically formed for the purpose of taking over and running its existing business.[71] Both borrowing members' and shareholders' special resolutions must be passed approving such a transfer. Where the proposed transfer is to an existing company, there is a requirement that the shareholders' resolution must be passed either by not less than 50 per cent of those qualified to vote or by those holding a minimum of 90 per cent of the total value of the shares. Where the proposed transfer is to a company formed in order to take over the society's business, the resolution must be passed on a poll of which not less than 20 per cent of the members of the society qualified to vote have voted.[72]

47.09 Reform—The Scottish Law Commission published a report on unincorporated associations in November 2009.[73] This eloquently discusses the many anomalies, impracticalities and inconsistencies in the law relating to associations and suggests the setting up of a free-standing legal entity. To some extent its concerns have been met, at least as far as charities are concerned, by the creation of Scottish

[63] Trade Union and Labour Relations (Consolidation) Act 1992 ss.62–67.
[64] Friendly Societies Act 1992 ss.5–6.
[65] Friendly Societies Act 1992 ss.7–17.
[66] Friendly Societies Act 1992 Pt V.
[67] Building Societies Act 1986 s.5, Sch.2, s.7(1), (2A). Subs.(2A) was added by the Deregulation and Contracting Out Act 1994 s.15.
[68] Building Societies Act 1986 s.5(1).
[69] Building Societies Act 1986 ss.34, 35, Sch.8 Pt 1.
[70] Building Societies Act 1986 ss.97–102.
[71] Building Societies Act 1986 s.97.
[72] Building Societies Act 1986 s.97(4), Sch.2 para.30.
[73] Scottish Law Commission, *Report on Unincorporated Associations* (HMSO, 2009), Scot. Law Com. No.217. This report underlies the Scotland Office's consultation on reforming the law on unincorporated associations, April 2012, to be found at *http://www.scotlandoffice.gov.uk/scotlandoffice/files/ConDoc-Unincorporated-Associations-and-Partnerships.pdf* [Accessed July 26, 2012].

Charitable Incorporated Organisations ("SCIO") which arose out of the Charities and Trustee Investment (Scotland) Act 2005.[74]

Scottish Charitable Incorporated Organisations—SCIOS are slightly akin to **47.10** trusts but have the benefit of separate legal identity and are subject to sequestration procedures on insolvency. SCIOs can hire staff, own property, can sue and be sued. The members of a SCIO are not liable to contribute to its assets if it is wound up, and the SCIO's trustees' liability is on the whole limited. It is anticipated that many smaller charities, industrial and provident societies, friendly societies, and other benevolent associations will convert into SCIOs. The Office of the Scottish Charities Regulator provides much helpful guidance on SCIOs.[75] For not-for-profit associations that are not necessarily charitable in purpose, nor mercantile, the current difficulties with the law are likely to remain in place.

FURTHER READING

Ashton, D. and Reid, P., *Ashton and Reid on Club Law* (Jordan Publishing Ltd, 2005).
Scottish Law Commission, *Report on Unincorporated Associations* (HMSO, 2009), Scot. Law Com. No.217.
Stair Memorial Encyclopedia, Vol.2, "Associations and Clubs".

---

[74] See also the applicable regulations at the Scottish Charitable Incorporated Organisations Regulations 2011 (SSI 2011/44) and the Scottish Charitable Incorporated Organisations (Removal from Register and Dissolution) Regulations 2011 (SSI 2011/237).

[75] See *http://www.oscr.org.uk* [Accessed July 26, 2012].

PART V

DEBT ENFORCEMENT AND INSOLVENCY

CHAPTER 48

DILIGENCE

Meaning and forms of diligence—Diligence[1] has been defined as   **48.01**

> "the legal procedure by which a creditor attaches the property or person of his debtor, with the object of forcing him either (1) to appear in court to answer an action at the creditor's instance, or (2) to find security for implement of the judgment which may be pronounced against him in such an action, or (3) to implement a judgment already pronounced."[2]

This definition does not entirely cover the other occasions when diligence may be used, such as where a debtor consents to diligence being used against him without an action being raised in court, provided the appropriate documents have been properly registered ("summary diligence"). Although diligence involves the forcible removal of a debtor's property, the law is anxious to balance the needs of creditors to receive what is rightfully due to them against the difficulties some debtors have in meeting their creditors' demands. Diligence has for some time been under some political scrutiny and been the subject of various Scottish Law Commission reports.[3] As a result, the Debt Arrangement and Attachment (Scotland) Act 2002 (the "2002 Act") and the Bankruptcy and Diligence etc. (Scotland) Act 2007 (the "2007 Act") were passed. The former Act abolished poindings[4] and replaced them with attachment, a similar but less draconian method of enforcing payment from debtors by seizing and ultimately selling debtors' assets, and also set up a scheme, in many respects similar to protected trust deeds, known as the debt arrangement scheme,[5] to enable debtors to repay their creditors and to keep diligence at bay. The 2007 Act also abolished some of the old and little used forms of diligence and introduced new ones more appropriate to modern commercial practice. The 2007 Act introduced statutory provisions for much (but not all) of what had been governed by the common

---

[1] All diligence is subject to the provisions of the Reserve and Auxiliary Forces (Protection of Civil Interests) Act 1951 ss.7–9.

[2] J.G. Stewart, *A Treatise on the Law of Diligence* (Edinburgh: W. Green, 1898), p.1. Note that the phrase "due diligence" is a separate matter entirely, being the phrase used to describe the process whereby a purchaser of a business instructs solicitors and accountants to check the seller's business records to ascertain that the seller is not trying to mislead the purchaser.

[3] Scottish Law Commission, *Report on Statutory Fees for Arrestees* (HMSO, 1992), Scot. Law Com. No.133; *Report on Diligence on the Dependence and Admiralty Arrestments* (HMSO, 1998), Scot Law Com. No.164; *Report on Poinding and Warrant Sale* (HMSO, 2000), Scot Law Com. No.177; *Report on Diligence* (HMSO, 2001), Scot Law Com. No.183.

[4] Poinding (pronounced "pinding") was a former method of seizing the debtor's property and having it sold at a roup or auction, known as a warrant sale, sometimes, at least historically and humiliatingly, held in the debtor's own home. What was not sold became the creditor's property. See *MacIntyre v Sheridan*, 1993 S.L.T. 412.

[5] See para.48.53, below.

law of diligence, and made significant amendments to the Debtors (Scotland) Act 1987 (the "1987 Act"). Some parts of the 2007 Act have not been brought into force, in particular those parts relating to land attachment and residual attachment, the former of which has attracted some political controversy. At the time of writing, it is not clear when, if ever, land attachment will be brought into force, and until it is brought into force, residual attachment cannot be brought into force either. This chapter is written on the basis that land attachment and residual attachment will eventually be brought into force, but at the time of writing there are no statutory instruments to flesh out the detail of the operation of these two diligences. Land attachment has been designed to replace adjudication for debt, but as at the time of writing adjudication for debt is still being used, so for that reason, the details of adjudication are included within this chapter. If the 2007 Act is brought fully into force, leaving aside admiralty matters, the available diligences will be civil imprisonment, arrestment, earnings arrestment orders, current maintenance arrestment, attachment, inhibition, land attachment, attachment of money and residual attachment. Adjudication and maills and duties would be abolished though they still exist at the time of writing. Sequestration for rent has already been abolished[6] but the landlord's hypothec still exists, in a truncated form.[7] Effective methods of stopping diligence are sequestration[8] (or liquidation for companies), debt payment programmes under the 2002 Act, and time to pay orders and time to pay directions, all discussed later.

Diligence may competently proceed only on a lawful warrant therefor, namely a decree or a document of debt.[9] A decree for payment is warrant for any of the above diligences.[10] Most diligences proceed on a decree or warrant obtained. Warrant may be obtained to arrest or inhibit on the dependence of proceedings in Scotland[11] or in certain other jurisdictions.[12] Two particular procedures for obtaining warrant to execute diligence should be noted:

(1) Summary warrant procedure. This is a special procedure available for enforcement of certain public debts, being rates, taxes, fines etc.[13] A certificate of non-payment from the creditor is presented to a sheriff, who must give summary warrant for diligence without the debt having been constituted by decree.[14] Where the summary warrant is for attachment or arrestment, following the 2007 Act, a charge for payment is now required to be served on the debtor (where the debtor is a natural person) first.[15]

---

[6] With effect from April 1, 2008.
[7] Bankruptcy and Diligence etc. (Scotland) Act 2007 (the "2007 Act") s.208.
[8] See Ch.49.
[9] As defined in the 2007 Act s.221.
[10] Debtors (Scotland) Act 1987 (the "1987 Act") s.87; see also ss.88, 91.
[11] For the procedure, see paras 48.13 and 48.32.
[12] Civil Jurisdiction and Judgments Act 1982 s.27.
[13] See the definition of "summary warrant" in the 1987 Act s.106 and Sch.4.
[14] 1987 Act s.74, Sch.4. The words "summary warrant" mean that there is no requirement to have a court hearing first. Provided the debtor has failed to make payment within the required period following notice, the creditor may proceed directly to such form of diligence as is appropriate and permissible. In practice it is common for the creditor to apply to the court in order to allow the debtor the chance to make his own representations in court if necessary, or at least to consult a solicitor beforehand.
[15] For attachment, the 2007 Act s.209(1) repeals s.10(4) of the 2002 Act; for arrestment, the 2007 Act s.206, inserts 1987 Act s.73A(2). In each case the effect is to require a charge before attachment or arrestment.

(2) Summary diligence. Summary diligence is diligence proceeding on registration of a document in the appropriate public register. Summary diligence is available in the following cases: (a) the holder of a dishonoured bill of exchange or promissory note (but not a cheque) may register a notarial instrument of protest in the Register of Protests or the Sheriff Court Books and proceed to do diligence on an extract thereof[16]; (b) where a deed imposing an obligation contains the debtor's consent to registration for execution, the deed may be registered in the Books of Council and Session or in the Sheriff Court Books and the creditor may do diligence on the basis of an extract thereof.[17] The parties to arbitration agreements often agree that the arbiter's award will be registrable for execution. The decisions of certain tribunals are by statute registrable for execution,[18] while the decisions of others are enforceable as if they were extract registered decrees arbitral.[19] Summary diligence is specifically not available to creditors in regulated agreements governed by the Consumer Credit Act 1974.[20]

In granting decree against a debtor for payment of certain types of debt, on application by the debtor, the court may make a "time to pay direction" to the effect that the sum will be payable by instalments or in a lump sum after a specified interval.[21] Time to pay directions are not available for certain debts, in particular debts over £25,000, fines, child support payments, tax, etc.[22] In granting or refusing the application, the court should have regard to the nature and reasons for the debt to which decree is granted, any action taken by the creditor to assist the debtor in paying the debt, the debtor's financial position, the reasonableness of any proposal by the debtor to pay the debt and the reasonableness of any refusal or objection by the creditor to the debtor's proposals for paying the debt.[23] Once diligence has commenced, the court may make a "time to pay order" to the same effect,[24] and with the same opportunities for the debtor to apply to the court as in a time to pay direction.[25] While a direction or order is in force, it is not competent to serve a charge for payment or to commence or execute an arrestment and furthcoming, an attachment, an earnings arrestment, or an adjudication for debt to enforce payment of the debt concerned.[26]

---

[16] Bills of Exchange Act 1681; Inland Bills Act 1696; Bills of Exchange (Scotland) Act 1772; *Glickman v Linda*, 1950 S.C. 18.

[17] 1987 Act s.87; see also ss.88, 91. An "extract" is a certified copy of the relevant registered deed.

[18] e.g. the Lands Tribunal for Scotland: Conveyancing and Feudal Reform (Scotland) Act 1970 s.50(2).

[19] e.g. Employment Tribunals and the Employment Appeal Tribunal: Employment Tribunals Act 1996 ss.15(2), 56(2).

[20] Consumer Credit Act 1974 s.93A.

[21] 1987 Act ss.1–4.

[22] 1987 Act ss.1(5) and 15. Note that the 2007 Act s.209(2) now permits time to pay directions for rates, community charge, community water charge, council tax or council water charge. Time to pay directions would not be available for diligence arising from deeds registrable in the Books of Council and Session or the Sheriff Court Books (1987 Act s.1).

[23] 1987 Act s.1A.

[24] 1987 Act ss.5–11. The same debts as are excluded in s.1(5) (as amended) are also excluded here. It is permissible to obtain a time to pay order against diligence commenced out of enforcement of a deed registrable in the Books of Council and Session or the Sheriff Court Books (1987 Act s.5).

[25] 1987 Act s.2A.

[26] 1987 Act ss.2(1), 9(1).

The practicalities of diligence require solicitors, sheriff officers and messengers at arms to serve on debtors certain forms and provide various reports for the courts. Although there is some commonality between the forms and procedure in the Court of Session and the Sheriff Court in respect of Ordinary Causes, Summary Causes and Small Claims, to list each form and detail the particular procedure for each type of court is beyond the reach of a book of this nature and the reader is referred for these matters to the Rules of the Court of Session and the Sheriff Court Rules.

I. CIVIL IMPRISONMENT

48.02 **Imprisonment**—Civil imprisonment, competent at common law, has been considerably restricted in its availability by statute.[27] Imprisonment remains competent in respect of failure to pay aliment to the extent allowed by the Civil Imprisonment (Scotland) Act 1882. Under this Act, a sheriff or sheriff principal may inflict imprisonment for a period of not more than six weeks for wilful failure to pay arrears of aliment and expenses.[28] Civil imprisonment is competent under the Child Support Act 1991, where the failure to support is treated as a failure to pay a sum decerned for aliment.[29] Failure to pay is deemed to be wilful unless the debtor proves want of means, but a warrant for imprisonment may not be granted where the sheriff is satisfied that the debtor has not possessed or been able to earn the means of paying the sum in question since the commencement of the action in which the decree was pronounced.[30] Imprisonment under this provision is not competent in respect of: (a) a sum decerned for as periodical allowance on divorce[31]; (b) aliment due under a registered bond or agreement[32]; (c) a claim by a public authority for reimbursement of money expended in aliment[33]; or (d) a claim by a parent for reimbursement of sums expended in aliment of a child after the duty to aliment has ceased.[34] Imprisonment does not operate as a satisfaction or extinction of the debt or interfere with the creditor's other rights and remedies for its recovery.[35] The abolition of imprisonment for debt leaves untouched the power of the court to imprison for failure to implement a decree *ad factum praestandum*.[36] By the Law Reform (Miscellaneous Provisions) (Scotland) Act

---

[27] Debtors (Scotland) Act 1880 s.4; the 1987 Act ss.74(3), 108, Schs 6, 8. Imprisonment remains competent in respect of fines imposed for contempt of court or under s.45 of the Court of Session Act 1988: Debtors (Scotland) Act 1880 Act s.4 as amended by the 1987 Act s.108(1), Sch.6.

[28] Civil Imprisonment (Scotland) Act 1882 s.4, as amended by Sheriff Courts (Scotland) Act 1971 s.4. There is no right of appeal against the sheriff's exercise of this discretion: *Strain v Strain* (1886) 13 R. 1029; *Crosbie v Crosbie* (1902) 4 F. 945; *Macdonald v Denoon*, 1929 S.C. 172.

[29] Child Support Act 1991 ss.40(13), (14) and 40A(1). See *Secretary of State for Work and Pensions Child Support Agency v MacNamara* Unreported October 12, 2005, 2005 ScotSC 70.

[30] Civil Imprisonment (Scotland) 1882 Act s.4(3); e.g. *Strain v Strain* (1886) 13 R. 1029; *Cassells v Cassells*, 1955 S.L.T. (Sh. Ct) 41; *McWilliams v McWilliams*, 1963 S.C. 259; *Gray v Gray*, 1993 S.C.L.R. 580.

[31] *White v White*, 1984 S.L.T. (Sh. Ct) 30.

[32] *McGeekie v Cameron* (1897) 13 Sh. Ct Rep. 357.

[33] *Tevendale v Duncan* (1882) 10 R. 852; *Mackay v P.C. of Resolis* (1899) 1 F. 521.

[34] *Glenday v Johnston* (1905) 8 F. 24.

[35] 1882 Act s.4(5); but an obligation *ad factum praestandum* in a document registered in the Books of Council and Session or Sheriff Court Books is not by virtue of registration enforceable by imprisonment: 1987 Act s.100(1).

[36] Debtors (Scotland) Act 1880 Act s.4.

1940,[37] however, no person may be imprisoned on account of his failure to comply with a decree *ad factum praestandum* unless the court is satisfied that he is wilfully refusing to comply with the decree.[38] The term of imprisonment is limited to six months, but the court is required to order immediate liberation if satisfied that the person undergoing imprisonment has complied or is no longer wilfully refusing to comply with the order.[39] Such imprisonment does not operate to extinguish the obligations imposed by the decree on which the application for imprisonment proceeds.[40] The court has power, in lieu of granting warrant for imprisonment, to recall the decree on which the application proceeds and to make an order for payment of a specified sum or such other order as to the court appears just and equitable.[41]

II. ARRESTMENT AND FURTHCOMING

Nature of arrestment—Arrestment is a diligence against a debtor's moveable **48.03** property which is in the custody of a third party.[42] Subject to certain exceptions, it is available against incorporeal moveable rights.[43] If the property is in the debtor's own custody, attachment is the appropriate diligence, except in the case of a ship.[44] Arrestment is effected by service of a schedule of arrestment on the person who owes the debt to the arresting creditor's debtor or who has possession of the debtor's corporeal moveable property ("the arrestee").[45] It operates not in rem but in personam, amounting to a prohibition against the arrestee from parting with the property and rendering him liable to a penalty if he does so.[46] In order to complete the diligence it is necessary that the arrestment be followed either by automatic release under the 1987 Act s.73J or by a process of furthcoming in which the arrestee is ordained to pay the debt directly to the arresting creditor or the property arrested is sold and the proceeds paid to the creditor.[47] Alternatively, the debtor signs a mandate authorising the arrestee to release the arrested items to the creditor.[48] Arrestment may be used either on the dependence of an action (so that the debtor's property may be secured for the benefit of the creditor before judgment is obtained) or in execution.

Subjects arrestable—It has been said that the subject attachable by arrestment is **48.04** "an obligation to account".[49] This includes debts, funds held by a bank in name of

---

[37] Law Reform (Miscellaneous Provisions) (Scotland) Act 1940 s.1; see *Retail Parks Investment Ltd v The Royal Bank of Scotland Plc (No.2)*, 1996 S.C. 227.

[38] See *Nelson v Nelson*, 1988 S.C.L.R. 663.

[39] Law Reform (Miscellaneous Provisions) (Scotland) Act 1940 s.1(1)(ii).

[40] Law Reform (Miscellaneous Provisions) (Scotland) Act 1940 s.1(1)(iii).

[41] Law Reform (Miscellaneous Provisions) (Scotland) Act 1940 s.1(2).

[42] Stewart, *A Treatise on the Law of Diligence* (1898), p.105.

[43] For subjects arrestable, see para.48.04, below; see also in relation to arrestment on the dependence, para.48.13, below.

[44] *Clan Line Steamers v Earl of Douglas S.S. Co*, 1913 S.C. 967.

[45] For more detail of the forms and procedure required for this, see the Diligence (Scotland) Regulations 2009 (SSI 2009/68).

[46] Stair, III, 1, 25–26.

[47] See *Lord Advocate v Royal Bank of Scotland*, 1977 S.C. 155.

[48] See the Diligence (Scotland) Regulations 2009 (SSI 2009/68) Sch.9.

[49] Bell, *Commentaries*, II, 71; *Shankland v McGildowny*, 1912 S.C. 857; *Agnew v Norwest Construction Co*, 1935 S.C. 771; *McNairn v McNairn*, 1959 S.L.T. (Notes) 35.

the debtor,[50] shares in a company,[51] interests in a trust estate,[52] a policy of insurance, although premiums may have to be paid upon it before it becomes due,[53] and corporeal moveable property belonging to the debtor which is in the hands of an independent third party.[54] Assuming there is an obligation to account, it is no objection that the debt is contingent and that it may turn out that nothing is due by the arrestee to the debtor.[55] But if there is no general obligation to account, an arrestment will attach only funds currently held by the arrestee or debts currently due by the arrestee to the debtor.[56] Thus an arrestment in the hands of an agent on the dependence of a claim against the principal does not attach funds which come into the agent's hands after execution of the arrestment.[57] And a collecting bank has no arrestable obligation to account in respect of its customer's cheque which it has presented for payment before it has received the funds.[58] It has been held that a claim of damages for wrongful dismissal might be arrested, although at the time of the arrestment the debtor had neither raised an action nor asserted a claim.[59] In principle it would appear that a claim of damages, whether arising from breach of contract or delict, is not arrestable until it has been asserted and thus made the subject of a claim by the injured party.[60] A debt payable in future (e.g. instalments of rent or interest not yet due) cannot be arrested, because there is no present obligation either to pay or to account.[61] Bills of exchange cannot be arrested[62]; any goods or other moveables may be, unless they are in the hands of the debtor himself (or held by somebody, e.g. a bank, on his behalf for safekeeping only, with no right of lien over them) when attachment is the proper diligence.[63] Private books and papers, of no commercial value, cannot be arrested, either in execution or to found jurisdiction.[64]

It is a general principle of Scots law that funds held for a debtor are not arrestable to the extent that they are alimentary.[65] A debt may be alimentary either by some rule of law or by express provision. Subject to the conditions that the capital must be vested in trustees,[66] and must be provided by some person other

---

[50] Sums in the creditor's deposit account with the National Savings Bank may be arrested: Law Reform (Miscellaneous Provisions) (Scotland) Act 1985 s.49. Note that s.73F of the 1987 Act protects a minimum bank balance for individuals.

[51] *American Mortgage Co v Sidway*, 1908 S.C. 500.

[52] *Learmont v Shearer* (1866) 4 M. 540.

[53] *Bankhardt's Trs v Scottish Amicable* (1871) 9 M. 443.

[54] *Inglis v Robertson & Baxter* (1898) 25 R. (HL) 70.

[55] *Boland v White Cross Insurance Co*, 1926 S.C. 1066; *Park, Dobson & Co v William Taylor & Son*, 1929 S.C. 571.

[56] *Royal Bank of Scotland v Sievewright*, 1995 S.C. 508; *McLaughlin v Allied Irish Bank*, 2001 S.C. 485.

[57] *Royal Bank of Scotland v Sievewright*, 1995 S.C. 508.

[58] *McLaughlin v Allied Irish Bank*, 2001 S.C. 485.

[59] *Riley v Ellis*, 1910 S.C. 934.

[60] *Caldwell v Hamilton*, 1919 S.C. (HL) 100 at 109, per Lord Dunedin; *Shankland v McGildowny*, 1912 S.C. 857, per Lord Kinnear at 867.

[61] *Smith & Kinnear v Burns* (1847) 9 D. 1344; *Kerr v R&W Ferguson*, 1931 S.C. 736.

[62] Bell, *Commentaries*, II, 68.

[63] Stewart, *A Treatise on the Law of Diligence* (1898), pp.107–9. But some goods are exempted: 1987 Act s.99(2). Attachment of money could also be used: see para.48.42.

[64] *Trowsdale's Tr. v Forcett Ry* (1870) 9 M. 88.

[65] In *North Lanarkshire Council v Crossan*, 2007 S.L.T. (Sh. Ct) 169, the debtor received social security benefits that were alimentary in nature. However, once paid into her bank account, they were nevertheless arrestable and could be subject to an action of furthcoming.

[66] *Forbes's Trs v Tennant*, 1926 S.C. 294.

than the liferenter or annuitant himself,[67] a liferent or annuity may be declared to be alimentary. The effect of such a declaration is that the liferent or annuity is protected from the diligence of creditors in so far as it is a reasonable provision in relation to the beneficiary's station in life.[68] But it remains arrestable in virtue of alimentary debts, such as rent, food and clothing suitable to the debtor's condition in life.[69] It is no objection that the debt was incurred before the instalment of the alimentary fund which is arrested became due.[70] Arrears of an alimentary fund are arrestable.[71] By statute, wages, salaries and pensions are not subject to ordinary arrestment.[72]

Arrestment in execution—Arrestment in execution is now governed by s.73A of **48.05** the 1987 Act. It may proceed: (1) on an extract of a decree of any court[73]; (2) on an extract of a document of debt,[74] being a document by registration or a document stated by statute to be enforceable by registration; and (3) on a summary warrant for the recovery of rates or taxes obtained on application to the sheriff, a charge having been served first and the period for payment specified in the charge having expired without payment having been made.[75] A schedule of arrestment is served on the arrestee.[76] Under the former common law, when the arrestee is a body of trustees a schedule should be served on each trustee[77]; in the case of a corporate body, service at its place of business is sufficient.[78] If the arrestee has no liability to account to the debtor at the date when the arrestment is served on him, the arrestment will fall.[79]

Warrants for arrestment emanating from the Court of Session must be executed by messengers at arms or sheriff officers, who are duly authorised to carry out this task.[80] Warrants for arrestment in execution emanating from the sheriff court must also be executed by messengers at arms or sheriff officers.[81] The same applies to warrants for arrestment on the dependence granted by a sheriff.[82] It is competent to serve schedules of arrestment proceeding on any warrant or decree of the sheriff in a summary cause by registered post or by recorded delivery.[83] A messenger at

---

[67] *Lord Ruthven v Drummond*, 1908 S.C. 1154.

[68] *Cuthbert v Cuthbert's Trs*, 1908 S.C. 967; see also *Weir v Weir*, 1968 S.C. 241.

[69] *Lord Ruthven v Pulford*, 1909 S.C. 951.

[70] *Lord Ruthven v Pulford*, 1909 S.C. 951.

[71] *Muirhead v Miller* (1877) 4 R. 1139.

[72] 1987 Act ss.46, 73(2); for diligence against earnings see para.48.14, below.

[73] 1987 Act s.73A(1)(a) and (4).

[74] 1987 Act s.73A(1)(b) and (4).

[75] 1987 Act s.73A(2); Local Government (Scotland) Act 1947 s.247(2) and (3); Taxes Management Act 1970 s.63. Local Government Finance Act 1992 s.97(5), Sch.8. Formerly a charge was not necessary for summary warrants for arrestments but following the 2007 Act it is. The period for a charge is 14 days where the debtor is within the United Kingdom or 28 days if he is out of UK jurisdiction.

[76] 1987 Act s.73B.

[77] *Gracie v Gracie*, 1910 S.C. 899. The capacity in which the subject is held by the arrestee need not be specified in the schedule, although it is normal practice to do so: see *Huber v Banks*, 1986 S.L.T. 58.

[78] *Campbell v Watson's Tr.* (1898) 25 R. 690; *Abbey National Building Society v Strang*, 1981 S.L.T. (Sh. Ct) 4.

[79] See para.48.08, below.

[80] Execution of Diligence (Scotland) Act 1926 s.1. See also the 2007 Act s.60(3).

[81] 1987 Act s.91(1)(a), (b), (2). See also 2007 Act s.60(3).

[82] 1987 Act s.91(1)(d), (2).

[83] Execution of Diligence (Scotland) Act 1926 s.2 as amended by Sheriff Courts (Scotland) Act 1971 Sch.1; Recorded Delivery Service Act 1962 s.1 and 2007 Act Sch.5 para.7.

arms or sheriff officer must not act in a case in which he has a personal interest.[84] If the sheriff is satisfied that no messenger at arms or sheriff officer is reasonably available to execute an extract decree or warrant, he may grant authority to any person whom he may deem suitable to execute such decree or warrant, and the person so authorised has all the powers of a messenger at arms or sheriff officer as regards any diligence or execution competent on such decree.[85]

48.06 Arresting creditor's right—The service of the schedule of arrestment confers on the arrester a personal right to the subject arrested preferable, where there is no question of bankruptcy, to an inchoate right granted by the debtor, such as an unintimated assignation[86] or a delivery order for goods in a store not completed by intimation to the storekeeper.[87] The rights of the debtor are transferred to the arresting creditor, so that, in the case of the arrestment of an illiquid claim, the creditor may vindicate it by action.[88] An arrestment prescribes in three years from its date, if not pursued or insisted on within that time or, in the case of the arrestment of a future or contingent debt, from the date when the debt became due or the contingency was purified.[89]

48.07 Extent of arrestment—In order not to prejudice a debtor, there are now limits on the extent of the arrestment of a debtor's property in the hands of the arrestee. Where a creditor has not used an arrestment on the dependence, but is arresting in execution of a decree or a document of debt, and where the funds arrested in the hands of the arrestee are ascertainable (irrespective of any other moveable property of the debtor's held by the arrestee), the funds that may be arrested are limited to the lesser of (a) the sums due by the arrestee to the debtor, or (b) the aggregate of the principal sum owed by the debtor to the creditor, any judicial expenses, the expenses of executing the arrestment, interest on the principal sum up to the date of service of the arrestment, interest on the principal sum arising after the date of service of the arrestment, any interest on the expenses of serving the arrestment, plus a further sum in recognition of any likely charges arising in an action of furthcoming.[90] Where the arrestee holds both funds and other moveable property belonging to the debtor, and where the aggregate sum (b) above is greater than the funds in (a), the arrestment may attach all the moveable property in addition to the funds in (a).[91] Where the funds arrested are sufficient to cover the aggregate sum (b), the arrestment will not attach any other moveable property belonging to the debtor. The creditor cannot unnecessarily attach extra funds relating to any unascertainable debts due to the debtor, except to the extent that the funds arrested in (a) are insufficient to meet the debt, interest and expenses owed to the creditor.[92]

In addition, the 2007 Act prevents a creditor evacuating a debtor's bank or building society account. If a creditor arrests funds in a bank or other financial institution either on the dependence of an action or in execution of a decree or a

---

[84] *British Relay v Keay*, 1976 S.L.T. (Sh. Ct) 23.

[85] Execution of Diligence (Scotland) Act 1926 s.3.

[86] *Gracie v Gracie*, 1910 S.C. 899.

[87] *Inglis v Robertson & Baxter* (1898) 25 R. (HL) 70.

[88] *Boland v White Cross Insurance Co.*, 1926 S.C. 1066.

[89] Debtors (Scotland) Act 1838 s.22 as amended by the 1987 Act Sch.6 para.3; *Jameson v Sharp* (1887) 14 R. 643.

[90] 1987 Act s.73E(2).

[91] 1987 Act s.73E(4).

[92] 1987 Act s.73E(6).

document of debt, and where the debtor is an individual, the creditor may only arrest such funds as are in excess of the sum of £415.[93] This should leave a minimum balance in the account which should be available to aliment the debtor's family.

Breach of arrestment—Arrestments which have been regularly executed render **48.08** the property arrested litigious, so far as the arrestee and other parties who have knowledge of the arrestment are concerned.[94] The arrestee is under a duty to tell the arresting creditor the extent and value of the property arrested.[95] The debtor must also be informed.[96] Where the arrestee fails without reasonable excuse to send the prescribed form about the arrestment to the creditor and debtor, the sheriff may make the arrestee pay the creditor the sum due to the creditor by the debtor, or the excess in the debtor's bank account above the figure of £415, which-ever be the lesser.[97] The arrestee is prohibited from parting with the arrested subjects to the prejudice of the arresting creditor,[98] but he is under no duty to invest the arrested funds and is not liable to pay interest to the debtor in the event of their being released from the arrestment.[99] If an arrestee in the knowledge of an arrestment parts with the funds or subjects arrested to the prejudice of the arresting creditor, he is liable to the creditor for the value of the funds or subjects arrested up to the limit of the amount secured by the arrestment, or, if the value of the funds or subject cannot be ascertained, for payment of the amount of the debt owed to the arresting creditor.[100] A party to an action who had received payment of funds from an arrestee in breach of an arrestment on the dependence of the action was ordained to repay the funds to the arrestee, on the ground that it had accepted the funds in the knowledge of the arrestment and to the prejudice of the arresting creditor.[101] An arrestee who acts in breach of an arrestment is also theoretically in contempt of court and liable to a fine or imprisonment.[102]

Automatic release of arrested funds—Under the common law, in order for the **48.09** creditor to have the arrested assets made over to him, it was necessary to raise an action of furthcoming. While this remains extant, the 2007 Act provides for a new procedure whereby provided the creditor has obtained a final decree on the dependence of which he had executed an arrestment or he had arrested in execu-tion of a decree of document of debt, and provided the arrestment had attached funds, the arrestee must release those funds to the creditor at the expiry of a period of 14 weeks beginning with the date of service of the copy of the final decree on the debtor or the date of service of the schedule of arrestment on the debtor.[103] The

---

[93] 1987 Act s.73F. This figure is increased from time to time. The Accountant in Bankruptcy website always displays the current figure.

[94] Stewart, *A Treatise on the Law of Diligence* (1898), p.127; see also *High-Flex (Scotland) v Kentallen Mechanical Services Co*, 1977 S.L.T. (Sh. Ct) 91.

[95] 1987 Act s.73G(4). There is no requirement to send in a "nil" return if nothing is arrested.

[96] 1987 Act s.73G(5).

[97] 1987 Act s.73H. There are further provisions to deal with the failure of the arrestee to send the required form intimating the arrestment. The figure of £415 may also be revised from time to time (s.73F(4)).

[98] Breach of Arrestment Act 1581; see *McSkimming v Royal Bank of Scotland Plc*, 1997 S.L.T. 515.

[99] *Glen Music Co Ltd v City of Glasgow DC*, 1983 S.L.T. (Sh. Ct) 26.

[100] Stewart, *A Treatise on the Law of Diligence* (1898), p.222.

[101] *High-Flex (Scotland) v Kentallan Mechanical Services Co*, 1977 S.L.T. (Sh. Ct) 91.

[102] See *Inglis & Bow v Smith* (1867) 5 M. 320.

[103] 1987 Act s.73J.

funds that may be released are the least of the following: the sum attached by the arrestment; the sum due by the arrestee to the debtor; or the aggregate of the principal sum sued for, any judicial expenses by virtue of the decree, the expenses of executing the arrestment, interest on the principal sum up to the date of arrestment, interest on the principal sum after arrestment, and any interest on the expenses of executing the arrestment.[104] There are provisions to enable those objecting to the automatic release to apply to the sheriff for a hearing[105] to prevent the release or for a multiplepoinding of the funds to take place.[106] Where the arrestee releases the funds in good faith, but it turns out that the warrant for execution was invalid, or the arrestment was incompetently or irregularly executed, the arrestee is not liable to the debtor or anyone for patrimonial loss caused by the release of the funds.[107] It should be noted that these particular statutory procedures only apply to funds and do not apply to the arrestment of other moveable assets, corporeal or incorporeal, or funds that are future or contingent,[108] where the common law remains in force and an action of furthcoming remains necessary.

Should the debtor consider that the release of the funds, or any of the debtor's moveable property, would be "unduly harsh" to the debtor or anyone closely connected with the debtor,[109] the debtor may apply to the court to have the arrestment lifted and the funds or property released to the debtor.[110] There would then be a hearing on the matter,[111] and the sheriff would take into account such matters as the source of the funds and whether or not the funds include earnings subject to earnings arrestment, current maintenance arrestment or a conjoined arrestment order.[112] The sheriff may then delay the release of the funds until a later date.[113] In practice, it is common for the debtor to consent to the release of the funds and the 2007 Act provides for mandates to be used for this purpose.[114]

48.10 Action of furthcoming—Under the common law, an arrestment is not a perfected diligence, and does not give the arrester a complete right to the subject arrested unless it is followed by decree in an action of furthcoming. Where a liquid debt has been arrested, and where the new statutory procedures for automatic release are inapplicable, an action of furthcoming may proceed as soon as the arrestments are laid; if the debt is future or contingent the furthcoming, if brought, will be sisted until the debt becomes liquid.[115] The purpose of the action is to ascertain precisely the nature and extent of the obligation to account which has been arrested and to adjudge to the arrester so much as may be required to make payment to him of the principal debt with interest and expenses.[116] Where the subjects are not a debt but consist of corporeal moveable property or incorporeal moveable property

---

[104] 1987 Act s.73K.

[105] 1987 Act s.73N.

[106] 1987 Act ss.73L, 73M. Multiplepoinding is where all those asserting an interest in the funds place their claims before the court which then decides who may be entitled, and to what extent, to any of those funds.

[107] 1987 Act s.73P.

[108] 1987 Act s.73J(4). Section 73J only refers to funds and so automatic release is not available to other types of arrested property.

[109] In terms of 1987 Act s.73R(4).

[110] 1987 Act s.73Q.

[111] 1987 Act s.73R.

[112] 1987 Act s.73Q(3).

[113] 1987 Act s.73R.

[114] 1987 Act s.73S.

[115] *Boland v White Cross Insurance Co*, 1926 S.C. 1066.

[116] Bell, *Commentaries*, II, 63.

such as rights under an insurance policy or shares, the arresting creditor may conclude for a sale of the property and payment out of the proceeds.[117] If there are competing claims on the same fund an action of multiplepoinding may be necessary.[118] In a question with the arrestee the arrester takes no higher right than the debtor, and any defence available against the debtor may be pleaded against the arrester in an action of furthcoming.[119]

Preference secured by arrestment—Arrestments, whether in security or in **48.11** execution, are preferred *inter se* according to their date of service,[120] the date of any decree of furthcoming being irrelevant for this purpose.[121] Where two or more arrestments are served on the same date they rank *pari passu*.[122] In order to secure a preference to the arresting creditor in competition with an attachment the arrestment must have been followed by automatic release under the 1987 Act, s.73J or by a decree of furthcoming prior in date to the completion of the attachment.[123] Arrestments used within 60 days prior to the constitution of the apparent insolvency of the debtor or within four months thereafter are ranked *pari passu* as if they had all been used on the same date.[124] Arrestments executed within 60 days of sequestration or the commencement of a winding up are ineffectual to secure any preference to the arresting creditor in competition with other creditors.[125] Where an arrestment on the dependence of funds held by an arrestee took place more than 60 days before the sequestration of the debtor, the arresting creditor (assuming there had been no delay) was entitled to a preference in ranking by the trustee in sequestration.[126] Arrestments used more than 60 days before the commencement of a winding up are effectual to secure the preference to the arresting creditor, even if at the time of winding up furthcoming had not taken place.[127] The difference between liquidation and sequestration in this respect is that the liquidator's rights to the arrested assets are postponed to the arresting creditor's rights irrespective of whether or not furthcoming has taken place, and the arrestee is bound to make over the assets to the arresting creditor[128]; but in a sequestration, the trustee is vested in the debtor's assets, and the arresting creditor must claim against the trustee for the assets he would otherwise have received directly from the arrestee.[129]

---

[117] *Lucas's Trs v Campbell* (1894) 21 R. 1096; cf. *Stenhouse London v Allwright*, 1972 S.C. 209.

[118] Stewart, *A Treatise on the Law of Diligence* (1898), pp.140–1.

[119] *Chambers' Trs v Smith* (1878) 5 R. (HL) 151.

[120] Stair, III, i, 46; Erskine, III, vi, 18; *Hertz v Itzig* (1865) 3 M. 813.

[121] *Wallace v Scot* (1583) M 807.

[122] Bankton, III, i, 41; *Sutie v Ross* (1705) M 816.

[123] Erskine, III, 6, 21; Stewart, *A Treatise on the Law of Diligence* (1898), p.159. The references are to poinding, but the principle remains the same.

[124] Bankruptcy (Scotland) Act 1985 (the "1985 Act") Sch.7 para.24; *Stewart v Jarvie*, 1938 S.C. 309.

[125] 1985 Act s.37(4); Insolvency Act 1986 s.185.

[126] *Mitchell v Scott* (1881) 8 R. 875; *James Gilmour (Crossford) Ltd v John Williams (Wishaw) Ltd*, 1970 S.L.T. (Sh. Ct) 6.

[127] *Commercial Aluminium Windows Ltd v Cumbernauld Development Corporation*, 1987 S.L.T. (Sh. Ct) 91; *Granite Properties v Edinburgh City Council*, 2002 S.L.T. (Sh. Ct) 79. For the historical position in sequestration, see *Gordon v Millar* (1842) 4 D. 352. This seems to be inconsistent with Insolvency Act 1986 s.185 which specifically refers to the 1985 Act s.37(4) for its terms.

[128] This is because the liquidator is not vested in the company's assets, though a liquidator could choose to obtain an order from the court vesting him in the company's assets if necessary under Insolvency Act 1986 s.145.

[129] *Granite Properties v Edinburgh City Council*, 2002 S.L.T. (Sh. Ct) 79.

Where a creditor arrested an item of a company's property and the company subsequently granted a floating charge, a receiver later appointed by the floating charge holder was unable to seize that item since it was litigious.[130] On the other hand, where a company had granted a floating charge, and a creditor later arrested in the hands of a third party an asset of that company's, but failed to carry out an action of furthcoming before the appointment of a receiver under the floating charge, the receiver successfully took possession of the asset on the grounds that an arrestment not followed up by an action of furthcoming was not "effectually executed diligence".[131] Furthermore a receiver's appointment has effect as if an assignation to the holder of the floating charge of all debts owed to the company which are subject to the charge has been duly intimated to the company's debtors on the date of the appointment, with the result that such debts are no longer capable of arrestment.[132]

No arrestment may be "instituted or continued" once an administrator has been appointed by a qualifying floating charge-holder (or any other person entitled to appoint an administrator in terms of Sch.B1 of the Insolvency Act 1986) except with the consent of the administrator or the court.[133] If the company has granted a qualifying floating charge under which the administrator was appointed, the administrator is entitled to dispose of or take action relating to any property subject to the floating charge.[134] The creditor does not lose his right to repayment but he does lose his right to obtain the arrested property.

48.12   Arrestment of ships[135]—There are five types of arrestment of ships: (1) arrestment to found jurisdiction[136]; (2) arrestment in rem in an Admiralty action[137] in rem to enforce a maritime lien[138]; (3) arrestment in rem under s.47(3)(b) of the

---

[130] *Iona Hotels Ltd, Petitioners*, 1991 S.L.T. 11.

[131] Insolvency Act 1986 s.55, Sch.2; *Gordon Anderson (Plant) Ltd v Campsie Construction Ltd and Anglo Scottish Plant Ltd*, 1977 S.L.T. 7; *Lord Advocate v Royal Bank of Scotland Ltd*, 1977 S.C. 155. This decision is generally considered to be wrong, being based on a misunderstanding of what was meant by "effectually executed diligence", but has not been overturned. To confuse the position further, Insolvency Act 1986 ss.61(1) and 61(1A) refer to "effectual diligence", while s.61(1B), designed to clear up what is meant by this phrase, is not yet in force at the time of writing. For a critique of the case, see S. Wortley, "Squaring the circle: revisiting the receiver and 'effectually executed diligence'", 2000 Jur. Rev. 5, 325–46.

[132] Insolvency Act 1986 s.53(7); *Forth & Clyde Construction Co Ltd v Trinity Timber and Plywood Co Ltd*, 1984 S.C. 1, per Lord President Emslie at 10.

[133] Insolvency Act 1986 Sch.B1 para.43(6).

[134] Insolvency Act 1986 Sch.B1 para.70.

[135] See generally, Scottish Law Commission, *Diligence on the Dependence and Admiralty Arrestments* (HMSO, 1989), Scot. Law Com. Discussion Paper No.84; *Report on Diligence on the Dependence and Admiralty Arrestments* (HMSO, 1998), Scot. Law Com. No.164. The special rules applicable to ships are not, in general, applicable to aircraft: *Emerald Airways Ltd v Nordic Oil Services Ltd*, 1996 S.L.T. 403. The 2007 Act Sch.4 introduces various changes to admiralty actions and the arrestment of ships: these bring Scots maritime law more into line with the law elsewhere in the United Kingdom.

[136] Arrestment to found jurisdiction does not give a nexus over the ship arrested (*Craig v Burnsgaard Kjosternd & Co*, 1896 23 R. 500, per Lord McLaren at 503). If the creditor wishes to have a security over the arrested ship or its cargo he will need to arrest on the dependence as well.

[137] For Admiralty actions see Act of Sederunt (Rules of the Court of Session 1994) 1994 (SI 1994/1443) ("RCS") Ch.46. An admiralty action is defined as an action having a conclusion appropriate for the enforcement of any of the claims in s.47(2) of the Administration of Justice Act 1956 (the "1956 Act" s.47(2A), as amended by the 2007 Act Sch.4 para.4); *Stephen v Simon Mokster Shipping AS*, 2008 S.L.T. 743.

[138] A maritime lien is an international term meaning a hypothec (a non-possessory security) over a ship, cargo or other maritime property (s.48(2) of the 1956 Act as amended by the 2007 Act Sch.4 para.3).

Administration of Justice Act 1956 in an Admiralty action in personam to enforce one of the types of claim specified in paras (p)–(s) of s.47(2) of the 1956 Act; (4) arrestment on the dependence of an action; and (5) arrestment in execution. Exceptionally, a ship may be arrested in the hands of its owners. Unlike the other types of arrestment mentioned, arrestment to found jurisdiction[139] does not prevent the ship from sailing.[140] Arrestment in rem is a necessary part of the working out of a maritime lien in an Admiralty action in rem. The power to arrest a ship or other maritime property which is not cargo on the dependence of an action is restricted by statute. No warrant to arrest on the dependence authorises detention of a ship unless the conclusion in respect of which the warrant is issued is appropriate for the enforcement of a claim to which s.47 of the 1956 Act applies and either the ship is the ship with which the action is concerned and the defender against whom the conclusion is directed owns at least one share in it or is the demise charterer[141] of the ship or all the shares in the ship are owned by the defender.[142] A warrant for the arrestment in rem of a ship, cargo or other maritime property granted by the sheriff may be exercised within the sheriffdom in which the warrant was granted, or where the ship, cargo or other maritime property was situated within that sheriffdom when the warrant was granted, anywhere in Scotland.[143] Where a warrant to arrest on the dependence a ship or other maritime property which is not cargo has been executed, no further warrant may be granted to arrest on the dependence the subjects of the initial arrestment or, while the initial arrestment continues to have effect, any other ship in which the defender owns at least one share, unless cause is shown why a further ship should be arrested.[144] The pursuer is entitled to his expenses in obtaining any warrant for arrest on the dependence or in execution except where the court is satisfied that the pursuer has been acting unreasonably, in which case the expenses may be refused or modified as necessary.[145]

The claims to which s.47 applies are set out in s.47(2) of the Act and include (among other maritime claims) claims arising out of damage done or received by any ship, personal injury sustained in consequence of defects in the ship or wrongful acts related to the use of the ship by the owners and others connected with the ship, salvage, as well as any agreement relating to the use or hire of any ship and to the carriage of goods in any ship.[146] These claims are now known as admiralty actions.[147] Should it be apprehended that the ship will sail in disregard of the arrestment, a warrant to dismantle the ship, by removing some necessary part of her equipment, may be obtained.[148] It is not competent for the court to

---

[139] *Ladgroup Ltd v Euroeast Lines S.A.*, 1997 S.L.T. 916.

[140] cf. in respect of arrestments in rem under s.47(3)(b) of the 1956 Act s.47(5). If the only basis for jurisdiction against the defender is an arrestment to found jurisdiction, this must be executed before any arrestment on the dependence: *Dramgate Ltd v Tyne Dock Engineering Ltd*, 2000 S.C. 43.

[141] A demise charterer is one who hires the entire ship and crew for the duration of a particular time, and while not the owner of the ship, in practice takes on many of the responsibilities of an owner.

[142] 1956 Act s.47(1); see *Interatlantic (Namibia) (Pty) Ltd v Okeanski Ribolov Ltd*, 1996 S.L.T. 819.

[143] 1956 Act s.47A (as amended by the 2007 Act Sch.4 para.6).

[144] 1956 Act s.47(1A) (as amended by the 2007 Act Sch.4 para.7). This is because if the first warrant caught a ship of low value to the pursuer's claim, the pursuer would be prejudiced by not being allowed to arrest a further ship to secure his claim more satisfactorily.

[145] 1956 Act s.47B (as amended by the 2007 Act Sch.4 para.8).

[146] *West of Scotland Ship Owners' Mutual Protection and Indemnity Association (Luxembourg) v Aifanourios Shipping S.A.*, 1981 S.L.T. 233; *Gatoil International Inc v Arkwright-Boston Manufacturers Mutual Insurance Co*, 1985 S.C. (HL) 1.

[147] 1956 Act s.47(2A) (as amended by the 2007 Act Sch.4 para.4).

[148] RCS rr.13.6A(1)(c)(iv), 13.8A(1)(b)(iv).

authorise the seizure of a ship or cargo on board a ship while it is in on passage in the open sea, even if it is within the jurisdiction of the Scottish court,[149] but it is competent to execute an arrestment of ship, cargo or other maritime property if the ship or other maritime property is on non-tidal or tidal waters or on land.[150] It is not competent to execute an arrestment of cargo unless the cargo is on board a ship at the time of the arrestment, but it is competent to execute an arrestment of cargo where the cargo is in the possession of the defender or of someone acting on behalf of the defender.[151] Where cargo is arrested the ship is also treated as arrested until the cargo is unloaded.[152]

Where a ship is arrested on the dependence of an admiralty action against the demise charterer of the ship and the pursuer obtains decree against the demise charterer, the arrestment will cease to have effect if the demise charterer or the owner of the ship pays the sum due to the pursuer, or if he offers a tender which is not accepted by the pursuer within a reasonable time. In the absence of payment or tender, the pursuer may apply to court for an order to sell the ship. Where a sale takes place, an arrestment of the ship (or a share of the ship) executed by a creditor of the owner of the ship (or share) before the sale will rank in preference over any arrestment of the ship executed on the dependence of an admiralty action against the demise charterer of the ship.[153] Where there is an arrestment of a ship on the dependence of an admiralty action against the demise charterer of a ship, and the owner of the ship is subsequently sequestrated or wound up, the creditor effecting the arrestment is entitled to rank on the proceeds of any sale of the ship resulting from the sequestration or winding up. Any arrestment carried out 60 days before the date of sequestration or winding up or four months thereafter is subject to the normal rules for equalisation of diligence.[154]

48.13 Arrestment on the dependence—Following the 2007 Act, arrestment on the dependence of an action[155] is competent only if there are conclusions for payment of money, other than the conclusion for expenses.[156]

It is competent for the Court of Session to grant warrant for arrestment on the dependence of a petition but only where the petition contains a prayer for payment of a sum other than expenses.[157] Arrestment on the dependence of an action[158] for payment of a contingent or future debt is competent.[159] A debt is not contingent for these purposes merely because a dispute about it falls to be determined by arbitration.[160] It is not competent to arrest on the dependence of an action any earnings or any pension.[161] For this purpose "earnings" means any sums payable by way of wages or salary, and "pension" includes any annuity in respect of past

---

[149] *The Grey Dolphin*, 1982 S.C. 5; 1956 Act s.47(6) (as amended by the 2007 Act Sch.4 para.10).
[150] 1956 Act s.47(5A) (as amended by the 2007 Act Sch.4 para.10).
[151] 1956 Act s.47C (as amended by the 2007 Act Sch.4 para.9).
[152] 1956 Act s.47D (as amended by the 2007 Act Sch.4 para.12).
[153] 1956 Act s.47F (as amended by the 2007 Act Sch.4 para.9).
[154] See para.48.11.
[155] In the Court of Session or in the sheriff court, including a summary cause, a small claim and a summary application (1987 Act s.15A(3)).
[156] 1987 Act s.15A(2)(a).
[157] 1987 Act s.15B(2)(a).
[158] "Action" covers actions and petitions (s.15B(3)).
[159] 1987 Act s.15C(1). Examples of future or contingent debts include aliment or a capital sum paid on a divorce.
[160] *Rippin Group Ltd v IPT Interpipe S.A.*, 1995 S.C. 302.
[161] Law Reform (Miscellaneous Provisions) (Scotland) Act 1966 s.1.

services and any pension or allowance payable in respect of disablement or disability.[162] There are restrictions on the circumstances in which a ship may be arrested on the dependence of an action.[163] The process of applying to the court for grant of warrant of arrestment on the dependence may be done at any time while the action is in dependence[164] but any such application must be intimated to the debtor and to any other person having an interest, unless the application is for a grant without a hearing under s.15E, in which case intimation is not necessary. In an action in the Court of Session application for a warrant for arrestment on the dependence should be inserted in the summons before it is signeted[165]; in the sheriff court it should be craved in the initial writ.[166] Pursuers in certain foreign actions, which have been commenced but not concluded, may apply by petition to the Court of Session for warrant to arrest assets situated in Scotland.[167] An arrestment on the dependence is executed by serving a schedule of arrestment on the arrestee.[168] A high degree of precision and accuracy is required if the arrestment is to be valid,[169] and if the action is raised using the wrong name the arrestment is liable to be recalled.[170] An order under a s.15E application (i.e. where the debtor is not immediately given the opportunity of a hearing) is available to the creditor only where the following provisions apply: (a) when the creditor has a prima facie case on the merits of the action[171]; (b) when there is a real and substantial risk that enforcement of a decree in favour of the creditor would be defeated or prejudiced by the debtor being insolvent or verging on insolvency or being likely to remove, dispose of, burden, conceal or otherwise deal with all or some of his assets unless diligence was not granted in advance of the hearing; and (c) when it is reasonable in all the circumstances, including the effect granting the warrant may have on any other person having an interest, to do so.[172] The onus is on the creditor to satisfy the court that the s.15E order should be made, but if the court does make such an order, the court must fix a hearing under s.15K[173] and the creditor must intimate as much to the debtor and anyone else with an interest.[174] If the court will

---

[162] Law Reform (Miscellaneous Provisions) (Scotland) Act 1966 s.1(2).

[163] See para.48.12, above.

[164] 1987 Act s.15D(1)(a).

[165] RCS r.13.6A. A warrant for arrestment on the dependence may also be obtained by motion or on a counter-claim or a third party notice in the Court of Session: RCS rr.13.8A, 25.2, 26.3 (as to which see *Chartwell Land Investments Ltd v Amec Construction Scotland Ltd*, 2001 S.L.T. 732).

[166] Act of Sederunt (Sheriff Court Ordinary Cause Rules) 1993 (SI 1993/1956) ("OCR") rr.3.1, 3.3, 3.5, 5.1; Act of Sederunt (Summary Cause Rules) 2002 (SSI 2002/132) ("Summary Cause Rules") r.3(2); Act of Sederunt (Small Claims Rules) 1988 (SI 1988/1976) r.3(6); for counter-claims, see OCR r.19.2, Summary Cause Rules r.21(4); for third party notices, see OCR r.20.3.

[167] Civil Jurisdiction and Judgments Act1982 s.27; see *Clipper Shipping Co Ltd v San Vincente Partners*, 1989 S.L.T. 204; *Stancroft Securities Ltd v McDowall*, 1990 S.C. 274.

[168] For the form of a schedule of arrestment see RCS Form 16.15-B and for a ship 16.15-BB. For methods of execution see RCS r.16.12; OCR r.6.1.

[169] *Anglo-Dutch Petroleum International Inc v Ramco Energy Plc*, 2006 S.L.T. 334.

[170] *Richards & Wallington (Earthmoving) Ltd v Whatlings Ltd*, 1982 S.L.T. 66.

[171] As to what is meant by a prima facie case, see *Barry D Trentham Ltd v Lawfield Investments Ltd*, 2002 S.C. 401; *Gillespie v Toondale Ltd*, 2006 S.C. 304.

[172] 1987 Act s.15E(2). This replaces the former common law requirement that the debtor be *vergens ad inopiam* or *in meditatione fugae* (verging on insolvency or considering flight (of himself or of his property) from the country).

[173] 1987 Act s.15E(4)(a). Section 15K provides for recall or restriction of diligence granted on the dependence. This provision takes account of the requirement under the Human Rights Act 1998 that owners of property should not be deprived of peaceful enjoyment of their property without proper process. See also *Karl Construction Ltd v Palisade Properties Plc*, 2002 S.C. 270.

[174] 1987 Act s.15E(4).

not make a s.15E order, but the creditor still insists on seeking a warrant for diligence on the dependence, the court may grant a hearing under s.15F, which requires intimation to the debtor and anyone else with an interest.[175] A s.15F application specifically involves intimation to the debtor and to anyone who has an interest the opportunity for a hearing before any order for warrant for diligence on the dependence is granted. With a s.15F application and after the hearing, the court may grant the order for warrant of arrestment on the dependence where the same provisions (a), (b) and (c) above, as in a s.15E application, are satisfied,[176] but if the court refuses the creditor a grant of warrant for arrestment, the court may instead impose such conditions on the debtor as it sees fit, including requiring the debtor to consign money into court or finding caution or other security.[177] Having obtained the warrant for diligence on the dependence, the creditor will then instruct messengers at arms or sheriff officers, as the case may be, to execute the arrestment.

Assuming arrestment on the dependence is duly executed, if the summons is not served within 21 days from the date of execution, the arrestment will be invalid, though that period may be extended for good reason.[178] The maximum extent of the property that may be arrested is equivalent to the aggregate of 120 per cent of the principal sum concluded for, one year's interest on the principal sum at the judicial rate and such a sum as should cover expenses.[179]

Arrestment on the dependence may be recalled or restricted under s.15K where the warrant was invalid or the arrestment incompetent, irregular or ineffective, or where the provisions in ss.15E and 15F no longer apply.[180] The onus is on the creditor to satisfy the court that the order for recall or restriction should not be granted.[181] Recall extinguishes the arrestment; restriction limits the amount of the claim which the arrestment secures.[182] In the absence of many reported cases on the new statutory provisions, the common law may still provide guidance as to the operation of s.15K. Arrestments on the dependence have in the past been recalled or restricted in the following circumstances: (a) where there has been some irregularity in the execution of the arrestment[183]; (b) where the arrestment is incompetent, as there are no averments of debtor verging on insolvency or considering flight[184]; (c) where the property arrested does not belong to the defender[185]; (d) where the diligence has been used oppressively (e.g. where the purpose is to embarrass the defender)[186]; (e) where adequate caution or security is offered;

---

[175] 1987 Act s.15E(6).

[176] *Bain v The Rangers Football Club Plc* [2011] CSOH 158

[177] 1987 Act s.15F(6), (7).

[178] 1987 Act s.15G.

[179] 1987 Act s.15H.

[180] Namely the provisions in (a), (b) and (c) referred to above apply (s.15K(8), (9)); *MRK-1 Ltd v Sakur* [2008] CSOH 176; *Fish & Fish Ltd v Sea Shepherd UK* [2011] CSOH 122; 2012 S.L.T. 156.

[181] 1987 Act s.15K(10).

[182] *McCormack v Hamilton Academicals Football Club*, 2009 S.C. 313.

[183] e.g. *Richards & Wallington (Earthmoving) Ltd v Whatlings Ltd*, 1982 S.L.T. 66.

[184] e.g. *Costain Building and Civil Engineering Ltd v Scottish Rugby Union*, 1993 S.C. 650. The wording *in meditatione fugae* does not wholly equiparate with that in s.15E(b)(ii) or s.15F(3)(b)(ii).

[185] e.g. *Blade Securities Ltd, Petitioners*, 1989 S.L.T. 246. Such a matter will be decided on a motion for recall only if the matter can be resolved without proof: *William Batey (Exports) Ltd v Kent*, 1987 S.L.T. 557.

[186] e.g. *Levy v Gardiner*, 1964 S.L.T. (Notes) 68; *West Cumberland Farms Ltd v Ellon Hinengo Ltd*, 1988 S.L.T. 294; *Matheson v Matheson*, 1995 S.L.T. 765; *Hydraload Research & Developments Ltd v Bone Connell & Baxters Ltd*, 1996 S.L.T. 219.

(f) where the pursuer has not made out a prima facie case.[187] Equally there have been occasions when recall or restriction was refused: where the amount of caution or security was insufficient,[188] or when a ship unsuccessfully claimed state immunity.[189] There are opportunities open to the debtor to apply for variation or removal of any conditions imposed on the debtor in connection with the refusal of an order for grant of warrant or a restriction of arrestment.[190] The creditor is entitled to the expenses of the arrestment on the dependence unless the creditor was acting unreasonably in applying for the warrant, or the court is satisfied that the refusal or modification of expenses is reasonable in all the circumstances and having regard to the outcome of the action.[191] An arrestment on the dependence prescribes three years after the date of the interlocutor in favour of the creditor where an action is raised, or three years from the date of execution of the arrestment in execution of an extract decree or other extract registered document, subject to provisions for time to pay directions and time to pay orders.[192]

If an arrestment on the dependence is duly executed, and decree in the action is ultimately obtained, the creditor must as soon as reasonably practicable serve a copy of that final decree on the arrestee.[193] The creditor has a preferable right over the subjects arrested, even although the debtor may have been sequestrated before the decree was obtained, provided that the arrestment was used more than 60 days before sequestration[194] and that the action was carried on without undue delay.[195]

III. DILIGENCE AGAINST EARNINGS AND PENSIONS

Earnings arrestments—In execution, instead of arrestment and furthcoming, the **48.14** appropriate diligences against a debtor's earnings are an "earnings arrestment", a "current maintenance arrestment" or a "conjoined arrestment order".[196] "Earnings" for this purpose includes salary, wages, fees, bonuses, commission, many types of pension payments and statutory sick pay but not a disablement pension or a social security or redundancy payment.[197] In addition, a deduction from earnings order may be made under the Child Support Act 1991. The debtor must have been served with a debt information and advice package no earlier than 12 weeks before the date of service of the earnings arrestment schedule, current maintenance arrestment or conjoined arrestment order as the case may be.[198]

An earnings arrestment may proceed on a decree for payment, including a decree of registration, or on a summary warrant for recovery of rates or taxes.[199]

---

[187] *Advocate General v Taylor*, 2004 S.C. 339; *Gillespie v Toondale Ltd*, 2006 S.C. 304.

[188] *Marie Brizzard et Roger International S.A. v William Grant & Sons Ltd (No.1)*, 2002 S.L.T. 1359.

[189] *Coreck Maritime GmbH v Sevrybokholodflot*, 1994 S.L.T. 893.

[190] 1987 Act s.15L.

[191] 1987 Act s.15M.

[192] 1987 Act s.95A.

[193] 1987 Act s.73C. Note that at the time of writing, s.73D, the requirement to supply a debt advice and information package, is not yet in force.

[194] 1985 Act s.37(4); see Ch.49, "Bankruptcy", below. For the operation of the same principle in liquidation, see the Insolvency Act 1986 s.185.

[195] *Mitchell v Scott* (1881) 8 R. 875; *Benhar Coal Co v Turnbull* (1883) 10 R. 558 (liquidation).

[196] 1987 Act s.46; Act of Sederunt (Proceedings under the Debtors (Scotland) Act 1987) 1988 (SI 1988/2013) Pt IV.

[197] 1987 Act s.73; see *GUD Pensions Trustee v Quinn*, 1994 S.C.L.R. 1105.

[198] 1987 Act ss.47(3), (4), 51(2A), 60(3A) as amended by the 2007 Act s.201.

[199] 1987 Act s.87. Local Government (Scotland) Act 1947 s.247(2) and (3); Taxes Management Act 1970 s.63; Local Government Finance Act 1992 s.97(5), Sch.8; Finance Act 1997 s.52.

An earnings arrestment is appropriate to enforce payment of any debt other than current maintenance which is due as at the date of execution of the diligence. It must be preceded by a charge even if it proceeds on a summary warrant.[200] It is executed by service of an earnings arrestment schedule on the employer, and the creditor must take all reasonably practicable steps to serve a copy of the schedule on the debtor.[201] The earnings arrestment requires the employer, while the arrestment is in effect, to deduct a sum from the employee's net earnings on every pay-day, the sum being calculated in accordance with a statutory table.[202] Where a debtor has holiday pay, there are special provisions for the deductions from that holiday pay.[203] The employer must pay the sum deducted to the creditor as soon as is reasonably practicable and he is entitled to deduct a fee for each payment from the balance of the debtor's earnings.[204] The employer must also inform the debtor of the date and amount of the first deduction[205] and provide information to the sheriff clerk or the creditor regular details of the debtor's payments and the name and address, so far as is known, of any new employer of the debtor.[206] The creditor must also regularly tell the sheriff clerk or, as the case may be, the employer how much he has received.[207] The earnings arrestment remains in effect until the debt is paid or otherwise extinguished, the employment ceases, the arrestment is recalled or abandoned or has for any other reason ceased to have effect, the debtor is sequestrated or a time to pay order or a conjoined arrestment order is made.[208] While it is in effect, any other earnings arrestment against the earnings of the debtor payable by the same employer is not competent but one earnings arrestment and one current maintenance arrestment may be in effect simultaneously against the same earnings. Formerly the earnings arrestment was given priority, but following s.199 of the 2007 Act, where the debtor's net earnings are insufficient to pay both arrestments, the two arrestments rank equally in the deductions from his earnings.[209] If the employer fails to comply with the earnings arrestment, he is liable to the creditor for the amount he should have deducted and he cannot recover from the debtor the sums paid in contravention of the arrestment. An employer can execute an earnings arrestment in his own hands to recover a debt due to him by the employee.[210] An earnings arrestment does not constitute seizure of moveable property in terms of the Bankruptcy (Scotland) Act 1985 s.7(1)(c)(iii) and is not one of the qualifications for a debtor's apparent insolvency.[211]

---

[200] 2007 Act s.209(5)(c) abolishes the former rule that no charge was required with a summary warrant.

[201] 1987 Act s.70; for the effect of deviations from the prescribed form see *Scobie v Dumfries & Galloway RC*, 1991 S.L.T. (Sh. Ct) 38; for the effect of errors in designation of the debtor, see *Clydesdale Bank Plc v Scottish Midland Cooperative Society Ltd*, 1995 S.C.L.R. 1151.

[202] 1987 Act ss.47(1), 49, Sch.2.

[203] 1987 Act s.49A, as amended by 2007 Act s.200(3).

[204] 1987 Act s.71. The figures are updated from time to time.

[205] 1987 Act s.70(4A), (4B).

[206] 1987 Act s.70A. Failure to provide this information with reasonable excuse could make the employer liable to the creditor for twice the sum which the employer would otherwise have had to deduct on the debtor's next payday (s.70B).

[207] 1987 Act s.70C.

[208] 1987 Act ss.9(2), 47(2), 60(3), 72.

[209] 1987 Act s.58 as amended by 2007 Act s.199.

[210] *Scobie v Dumfries & Galloway RC*, 1991 S.L.T. (Sh. Ct) 33; *Slater v Grampian RC*, 1991 S.L.T. (Sh. Ct) 72.

[211] *Mackay Petitioner*, 1996 S.C.L.R. 1091.

Current maintenance arrestment—A current maintenance arrestment is used **48.15** to enforce payment of aliment or a periodical allowance on divorce.[212] After intimation to the debtor of the court order and the lapse of four weeks, a current maintenance arrestment schedule is served on the employer who must then make deductions from the debtor's net earnings related to the daily rate of maintenance specified in the schedule. Only one current maintenance arrestment may be in effect against the earnings of the debtor from one employer.

Conjoined arrestment order—A conjoined arrestment order is appropriate where **48.16** there is more than one creditor entitled to proceed against the earnings of the debtor.[213] It has the effect of recalling any prior earnings arrestment or current maintenance arrestment. The employer must pay the sums deducted to the sheriff clerk who pays to each creditor an amount in proportion to the amount of his debt. An employer may carry out a conjoined arrestment order against one of its own employees.[214]

Deduction from earnings order—The Secretary of State may make a deduction **48.17** from earnings order against anyone liable to pay child support under a maintenance arrestment made under the Child Support Act 1991.[215] The order operates as intimation to the employer to make deductions from the liable person's earnings and to pay them to the Secretary of State.[216]

IV. ATTACHMENT

The Debt Arrangement and Attachment Act 2002 abolished the former diligence **48.18** of poinding,[217] which involved the forcible sale of the debtor's corporeal moveable assets in satisfaction of debts due to a creditor. In that Act poinding was replaced by a new, albeit similar, diligence, known as attachment, which provides greater safeguards for the wellbeing of the debtor and his family. In particular, it requires that attachment should initially be carried out against a debtor's business assets rather than his domestic assets, and only exceptionally, by means of an "exceptional attachment order", should a creditor be able to proceed to attach a limited range of the debtor's domestic assets. Furthermore, the range of attachable assets is carefully restricted,[218] with further provisions for exceptional attachment.[219]

Until followed by a sale of the attached effects, attachment, like arrestment, is an inchoate or incomplete diligence. It confers on the creditor no real security in the debtor's assets, but prohibits the debtor from parting with them to the prejudice of the creditor. Following the 2007 Act it is competent to carry out interim attachment.[220] Attachment may take place following a liability order under the

---

[212] 1987 Act ss.51–56.

[213] 1987 Act ss.60–66, Sch.3.

[214] *Glasgow City Council, Applicants*, 2001 S.L.T. (Sh. Ct) 85.

[215] Child Support Act 1991 s.31.

[216] Child Support Act 1991 s.31; see generally Child Support (Collection and Enforcement of Other Forms of Maintenance) Regulations 1992 (SI 1992/2643); Child Support (Collection and Enforcement) Regulations 1992 (SI 1992/1989).

[217] 2002 Act s.58.

[218] 2002 Act s.11.

[219] 2002 Act Sch.2.

[220] 2007 Act s.2A(1). For the details of interim attachment, see para.48.23, below. Even if the creditor is subsequently successful in the case raised against the debtor, whose assets have been subject to interim attachment, the creditor still needs to carry out a further attachment in execution of the decree.

Child Support Act 1991, a decree from the court or a document of debt.[221] An extract decree of the Court of Session or sheriff court is itself sufficient warrant to charge and attach,[222] as is an extract from the Books of Council and Session or sheriff court books in which has been registered either a deed containing a clause consenting to registration and execution or a protest by a notary public of a bill for non-payment.[223]

48.19 Charge for payment—An attachment must, if it proceeds on a summary warrant, be preceded by a charge,[224] or formal requisition for payment. It must also, no earlier than 12 weeks before taking any steps to execute the attachment, be preceded by the provision to the debtor of a debt advice and information package.[225] The charge, in the prescribed form, is executed by service of a schedule of charge by a judicial officer.[226] After the charge has been given, certain days of charge within which payment may be made, known as *induciae*, must elapse before the attachment is executed. The period for payment specified in any charge in pursuance of a warrant for execution is 14 days if the debtor is within the United Kingdom and 28 days if he is outside the United Kingdom or his whereabouts are unknown.[227] The attachment must be executed within two years after service of the charge.[228] The right to attach can be reconstituted by service of a further charge.[229] A debtor who has already satisfied in full the decree upon which the charge proceeds may seek suspension of the charge.[230] As with arrestment, where attachment is taking place by means of summary diligence proceeding from a registered document of debt, a charge is not necessary.

48.20 Execution of attachment—On the expiry of the days of charge (assuming a charge is used), if no payment is offered, the attachment may be executed by the sheriff officer or messenger at arms, as the case may. The execution must normally take place between 8am and 8pm and may not take place on a Sunday or public holiday.[231] The sheriff officer or messenger at arms, accompanied by one witness, exhibits to any person present the warrant to attach and the certificate of execution of the charge relating thereto; he then demands payment of the sum recoverable from the debtor, if he is present, or from any person appearing to be authorised to act for the debtor, and makes inquiry of any person present as to the ownership of the goods proposed to be attached.[232] He is entitled to presume that the assets about to be attached are the debtor's, or owned in common between the debtor and another person, but if he knows or ought to know that they are not the debtor's, he may not proceed on that assumption.[233] He may open shut and lockfast places to

---

[221] For the full definition of "decree" and "document of debt" see 2002 Act s.10(5).

[222] 1987 Act s.87.

[223] Writs Execution (Scotland) Act 1877 s.3; Conveyancing (Scotland) Act 1924 s.10(5).

[224] See para.48.01, above; s.209(1) of the 2007 Act repeals s.10(4) of the 2002 Act.

[225] 2002 Act s.10(3)(b). This only applies to human debtors, not corporate debtors.

[226] 1987 Act s.90.

[227] 1987 Act s.90(3).

[228] 1987 Act s.90(5).

[229] 1987 Act s.90(6).

[230] *Dickson v United Dominions Trust Ltd (No.2)*, 1983 S.L.T. 502; the suspension of charges on decrees granted by the Sheriff may be applied for in the sheriff court: 1907 Act s.5(5) as amended.

[231] 2002 Act s.12.

[232] 2002 Act s.13.

[233] 2002 Act s.13.

attach assets therein but not where those places are dwelling-houses.[234] He must value the attached assets at their market value and if necessary obtain a professional valuation.[235] He is not permitted to attach certain assets, these being the tools of the debtor's trade (not exceeding £1,000 in value), a vehicle used by the debtor and not worth more than £1,000, a mobile home which is the debtor's only residence, and the debtor's garden tools with which to keep his garden or yard in good order.[236] He must prepare a schedule of attachment and give a copy to the debtor. The date of the attachment is the date a copy of the schedule is given to the debtor or someone present at the place of attachment.[237] There are special provisions for the attachment of mobile homes not occupied by the debtor.[238] The sheriff officer or messenger at arms then prepares a report for the sheriff, specifying the identity of the debtor and the creditor, the articles attached and their respective values, the sum recoverable and the place where the attachment was executed.[239] The debtor may redeem any article at its specified value within 14 days.[240] The attached articles may be removed if they need to be taken to a place of security or may be immediately sold if they are perishable,[241] but otherwise will be removed under the supervision of the sheriff officer or messenger at arms and taken to an auction house at least seven days later.[242] Where articles need to be removed urgently, it is possible to do so without notice if it is necessary for the security or preservation of the articles.[243] Only sufficient articles may be uplifted for auction as will in value cover the debt and expenses due to the creditor.[244] Removal, damage or destruction of the articles by the debtor or anyone who knows they have been attached is a breach of the attachment[245] and may be dealt with as contempt of court.[246] If the valuation put on the articles is unrealistically low, the attachment may be stopped by the sheriff.[247] Attachment normally endures for the lesser of a period of six months from the date of attachment or 28 days from the date the attached article is removed by the sheriff officer or messenger of arms.[248] There are provisions to enable a vehicle worth less than £1,000 to be released from attachment where the attachment of the vehicle would be unduly harsh to the debtor.[249] Where one attachment has already taken place a second attachment may not take place except where new articles, since the first arrestment, have been moved to that place.[250] The auction of the arrested articles is organised by the sheriff officer or messenger at arms and generally must take place in an auction room, following an advertisement to the public. There must be intimation to the debtor[251] and the auction may be cancelled if agreement is

---

[234] 2002 Act s.15(1). For the definition of dwelling-house, see the 2002 Act s.45.
[235] 2002 Act s.15(2), (3).
[236] 2002 Act s.11.
[237] 2002 Act s.13.
[238] 2002 Act ss.14, 16.
[239] 2002 Act s.17.
[240] 2002 Act s.18.
[241] 2002 Act s.20.
[242] 2002 Act s.19.
[243] 2002 Act s.19A.
[244] 2002 Act s.19(4).
[245] 2002 Act s.21.
[246] 2002 Act s.21(9).
[247] 2002 Act s.23.
[248] 2002 Act s.24.
[249] 2002 Act s.22.
[250] 2002 Act s.25.
[251] 2002 Act s.27.

reached between the debtor and creditor.[252] An article may be purchased by the creditor or by any other creditor or by a person who owns the article in common with the debtor.[253] If the sum recoverable has not been realised by the sale, ownership of unsold articles passes to the creditor provided the creditor uplifts them within three working days and the debtor is credited with the specified value of the article.[254] If an auctioned article is sold at a price below the valuation, the difference between the actual price and the value is credited against the sum recoverable from the debtor.[255] Where in the process of attachment and auction an article is damaged through no fault of the debtor's, any downwards revaluation (taking account of the damage) is disregarded for the purpose of crediting the value against the sum recoverable from the debtor.[256] The sheriff officer or messenger at arms pays to the creditor the proceeds of sale so far as necessary to meet the sum recoverable and any surplus is paid to the debtor.[257] The sheriff officer or messenger at arms must make a report of the sale to the sheriff within 14 days[258] and the report is taxed by the auditor of court.[259] If a third party satisfies the sheriff before the sale that an attached article belongs to him, an order is made releasing the article from the attachment.[260] An article owned in common by the debtor and a third party may be released from the attachment before the sale if the third party pays the officer a sum equal to the value of the debtor's interest in the article or if the sheriff is satisfied that the continued attachment of the article would be unduly harsh to the third party.[261] There are provisions to safeguard the third party's entitlement to the sale proceeds of an article owned in common but still sold at auction.[262] The creditor is entitled to the expenses of the whole process but only through attachment and no other legal process.[263]

48.21 **Exceptional attachment**—The process in the paragraph above does not permit the attachment of articles in dwelling-houses.[264] In order to be able to attach articles in a dwelling-house, it is necessary to obtain an exceptional attachment order.[265] This permits the attachment, removal and ultimate auction of "non-essential assets".[266] Non-essentials assets comprise the same items as in ordinary attachment,[267] but with the exclusion of clothing for the debtor and his household, medical aids, books and articles for education and training (not above £1,000 in value), children's toys, tables and chairs, household linen, kitchen furniture and white goods, computers, televisions, telephones etc., whether owned or used by the debtor or by members of his household. If the creditor can persuade the sheriff that there are exceptional circumstances, the sheriff may award an exceptional attachment order. Exceptional circumstances are shown in s.48. The sheriff must

---

[252] 2002 Act s.29.
[253] 2002 Act s.30.
[254] 2002 Act s.31.
[255] 2002 Act s.31(1A).
[256] 2002 Act s.31(1B).
[257] 2002 Act s.38.
[258] 2002 Act s.32.
[259] 2002 Act s.33.
[260] 2002 Act s.34.
[261] 2002 Act s.35.
[262] 2002 Act s.36.
[263] 2002 Act s.40.
[264] For the definition of dwelling-house, see the 2002 Act s.45.
[265] 2002 Act s.47.
[266] Non-essential assets are shown in Sch.2 to the 2002 Act.
[267] 2002 Act s.11.

be satisfied that the creditor has taken reasonable steps to negotiate a settlement, or used or tried to use other forms of diligence first, rather than resorting to exceptional attachment, and that there would be assets available at least to satisfy the creditor's expenses plus the sum of £100. In considering whether to make the order, the sheriff must have regard to the nature of the debt (particularly tax or duty arising from the debtor's business), whether the debtor carries on business at the dwelling-house, whether the debtor has received money advice, whether any time to pay order or direction has elapsed, any agreements between the debtor and the creditor, the state of any debt payment programme undertaken by the debtor, and any statements or documents about the debtor's non-essential assets, their value and the debtor's own financial circumstances.[268] As before, the sheriff officer or messenger at arms, once the exceptional attachment order has been granted, is entitled to enter shut and lockfast premises to attach non-essential assets[269] and the debtor must not deal with or dispose of those assets once that order has been granted.[270] The sheriff officer or messenger at arms may not execute the order against any articles which the officer considers to be likely to be of sentimental value to the debtor.[271] If articles are attached, they must be immediately removed[272] (for subsequent auction in the same manner as auction of attached articles), valued[273] or on application to the sheriff where the removal would be unduly harsh, returned to the debtor.[274] They may also be redeemed.[275]

Preference secured by attachments—As with arrestments, attachments used **48.22** within 60 days prior to the constitution of the apparent insolvency of the debtor and within four months thereafter are ranked pari passu as if they had all been used on the same date.[276] Sequestration or the winding up of a company is equivalent to a completed attachment, and attachment executed on or within 60 days prior to the date of the sequestration or winding up is ineffectual to secure any preference to the attaching creditor except for the expenses incurred by him in using the diligence.[277] The preference of attaching in competition with a completed diligence depends upon the date when the attachment has been completed by a sale or the handing over of the goods to the creditor.[278] In competition with other inchoate diligences it is determined by priority in date of execution. An attachment which has not been completed by sale or the handing over of goods to the creditor before the appointment of a receiver will not be effective so as to exclude the power of the receiver to take possession of the property of the company[279] unless the attachment was executed prior to the registration of the floating charge.[280] No attachment may be "instituted or continued" once an administrator has been appointed by a qualifying floating charge-holder (or any other person

---

[268] 2002 Act s.47(4).
[269] 2002 Act s.49.
[270] 2002 Act s.50.
[271] 2002 Act s.52. This exception only applies where there the article or articles are worth less than £150 in total.
[272] 2002 Act s.53.
[273] 2002 Act ss.51, 54.
[274] 2002 Act s.55.
[275] 2002 Act s.56.
[276] Bankruptcy (Scotland) Act 1985 Sch.7 para.24.
[277] 1985 Act s.37(5); Insolvency Act 1986 s.185.
[278] Stewart, *A Treatise on the Law of Diligence* (1898), p.365; see also para.48.11, above.
[279] Insolvency Act 1986 s.55(3); *Lord Advocate v Royal Bank of Scotland*, 1977 S.C. 155.
[280] *Iona Hotels Ltd*, 1991 S.L.T. 11.

entitled to appoint an administrator in terms of Sch.B1 of the Insolvency Act 1986) except with the consent of the administrator or the court.[281] If the company has granted a qualifying floating charge under which the administrator was appointed, the administrator is entitled to dispose of or take action relating to any property subject to the floating charge.[282] The attaching creditor does not lose his right to repayment but he does lose his right to obtain the attached property or the proceeds thereof.

48.23 Interim attachment—This was introduced in the 2007 Act.[283] The court may grant warrant for interim attachment, but only where an action contains a conclusion for payment of a sum other than expenses.[284] For the purposes of this paragraph, the term "action" includes a petition in the Court of Session.[285] Interim attachment is not available for any article in a dwelling-house, any article incompetent in terms of s.11,[286] a mobile home which is the only or principal residence of a person other than the debtor, an article of a perishable nature, any article acquired by the debtor (where the debtor is engaged in trade) to be sold by debtor, with or without adaptation, nor a material for a process of manufacturing for sale by the debtor in the course of business.[287] The creditor may apply for a warrant for interim attachment at any time while the action is in dependence with intimation to the debtor, and anyone else having an interest, of a hearing on the matter under s.9E.[288] It is possible to apply for a warrant without intimation where a warrant for interim attachment is sought without a hearing first (a s.9D order).[289] If the creditor can persuade the court of the following provisions: (a) that he has a prima facie case on the merits of the action; (b) that there is a real and substantial risk that enforcement of a decree in favour of the creditor would be defeated or prejudiced by the debtor being insolvent or verging on insolvency or being likely to remove, dispose of, burden, conceal or otherwise deal with all or some of his assets unless interim attachment was not granted in advance of the hearing; and (c) that it is reasonable in all the circumstances, including the effect granting the warrant may have on any other person having an interest, to do so,[290] an order under s.9D (i.e. without a hearing) may be so made, but the onus is on the creditor to satisfy the court that the s.9D order should be made. Where the court does make such an order, the court must nevertheless fix a hearing under s.9M[291] and the creditor must intimate as much to the debtor and anyone else with an interest.[292] Where the court does not make the order without a hearing, but the creditor insists on the application, the court must fix a date for the hearing in terms of s.9E.[293] The

---

[281] Insolvency Act 1986 Sch.B1 para.43(6).

[282] Insolvency Act 1986 Sch.B1 para.70.

[283] 2007 Act s.173. This introduces new ss.9A–9S into the 2002 Act. The provisions for interim attachment closely mirror the provisions for arrestment on the dependence referred to above.

[284] 2002 Act s.9A(2).

[285] 2002 Act s.9A(3).

[286] See para.48.18, above.

[287] 2002 Act s.9B.

[288] 2002 Act s.9C.

[289] 2002 Act s.9C(3).

[290] 2002 Act s.9D(2). For guidance on these provisions see para.48.13, above.

[291] 2002 Act s.9M provides for recall or restriction of attachment granted on the dependence. This provision takes account of the requirement under the Human Rights Act 1998 that owners of property should not be deprived of peaceful enjoyment of their property without proper process. See also *Karl Construction Ltd v Palisade Properties Plc*, 2002 S.C. 270.

[292] 2002 Act s.9D(4).

[293] 2002 Act s.9D(6).

court will not grant a s.9E order until the debtor and anyone else having an interest has had an opportunity to be heard. A hearing having been held, the court may grant the order for warrant of attachment where the same provisions as in a s.9D application are satisfied (namely, (a), (b) and (c) above) but where the court refuses the creditor a grant of warrant for interim attachment, the court may instead impose such conditions as it sees fit, including requiring the debtor to consign money into court or finding caution or some other security.[294]

Assuming interim attachment is duly granted and subsequently executed, if the summons is not served within 21 days from the date of execution, the attachment will be invalid, though that period may be extended for good reason.[295] When the execution of the interim attachment takes place, the same rules as apply to attachment will apply to interim attachment.[296] The sheriff officer or messenger at arms executing the interim attachment must complete a schedule of attachment of the attached goods, indicating the articles attached and their value, with a copy given to the debtor or anyone else present.[297] If necessary, the attached articles may be taken to a secure place.[298] Once attached, the articles may not be moved by the debtor.[299] There are provisions to protect the rights of any third parties who may have an interest in the attached articles.[300] Interim attachment endures (a) for a period of six months after the disposal of the action, provided the creditor obtains a final interlocutor in his favour in the action on the dependence of which the warrant for interim attachment was granted, or, even if the debtor is assoilzied, or the action dismissed, there is an award of expenses against the debtor,[301] (b) until the debtor is assoilzied or the action dismissed with no award of expenses against the debtor,[302] or (c) the creditor consents to the release of the attachment of all the attached assets.[303] It is open to the creditor to release selected attached assets[304] or to apply to have the period of attachment extended if necessary.[305] There are further provisions to allow for the six-month period to be put in abeyance where time to pay directions and time to pay orders are in place.[306] Interim attachment may be recalled or restricted under s.9M where the warrant was invalid or the interim attachment incompetent, irregular or ineffective, or where the provisions in ss.9D and 9E no longer apply. The onus is on the creditor to satisfy the court that the order for recall or restriction should not be granted.[307] Recall extinguishes the interim attachment. Restriction limits the amount of the claim which the interim attachment secures. There are opportunities open to the debtor to apply for variation or removal of any conditions imposed on the debtor in connection with the refusal of an order for grant of warrant or a restriction of interim attachment.[308] The creditor is entitled to the expenses of the interim

---

[294] 2002 Act s.9E(6), (7).
[295] 2002 Act s.9G.
[296] In particular, see ss.12, 13, 15 and 17.
[297] 2002 Act s.9F.
[298] 2002 Act s.9H.
[299] 2002 Act s.9J, repeating the provisions of s.21.
[300] 2002 Act s.9K.
[301] 2002 Act s.9L(1)(a).
[302] 2002 Act s.9L(1)(b).
[303] 2002 Act s.9L(1)(c).
[304] 2002 Act s.9L(3).
[305] 2002 Act s.9L(4)–(7).
[306] 2002 Act s.9L(8).
[307] 2002 Act s.9M(10).
[308] 2002 Act s.9N.

attachment unless the creditor was acting unreasonably in applying for the warrant, or the court is satisfied that the refusal or modification of expenses is reasonable in all the circumstances and having regard to the outcome of the action.[309] The debtor remains liable for these expenses even if the actual interim attachment is recalled by virtue of a time to pay direction or order, sequestration, the appointment of an administrator, the appointment of a receiver, winding up, or the debtor entering into a composition contract or trust deed for creditors, unless those expenses are themselves discharged by virtue of any of the above.

While interim attachment is in effect, any sums paid to reduce the sums payable by the debtor will be applied first to the payment of the expenses of the interim attachment, the interest on the sum sued for up to the date of granting of warrant for interim attachment, and thereafter the principal sum sued for and interest on that sum. Finally, an interim attachment is to be treated as if it were an attachment on the property in terms of s.10 of the 2002 Act, executed when the interim attachment was executed.

The practical effect of interim attachment is that it prevents the debtor alienating the attached assets for the duration of the interim attachment. If the creditor is successful in the action raised against the debtor, the interim attachment acts as a security in the creditor's favour, but falls on the day six months after the pronouncement of the final interlocutor in the creditor's favour.[310] If the successful creditor wishes to proceed to auction the debtor's assets, he still needs to carry out a normal attachment, to have the debtor's assets valued and to give the debtor the opportunity to redeem the debt, all as in the manner described above. Interim attachment over a particular item ceases once attachment takes place.

V. INHIBITION

48.24 Nature of inhibition—Inhibition used to be defined as

> "a personal prohibition, prohibiting the party inhibited to contract any debt, or grant any deed by which any part of his lands may be alienated, or carried off, to the prejudice of the creditor inhibiting".[311]

The effect of inhibition is to render voidable at the inhibiting creditor's instance any voluntary acts by the debtor after the date of inhibition.[312] In practical terms, this means that the debtor cannot sell his land, or grant any security over it, unless the inhibiting creditor permits him to do so. Inhibition is only a negative or prohibitory diligence; it inconveniences the debtor but it has no positive effect in giving the inhibitor any real right in any part of the debtor's estate. Its effect is to preserve the heritable property as part of the debtor's estate, and therefore attachable if necessary by the inhibitor by adjudication or, possibly, land attachment.

Part V of the 2007 Act has put much of the previous common law on inhibition onto a statutory basis.[313] Inhibition may be obtained in execution of any decree, or

---

[309] 2002 Act ss.9P, 9Q.

[310] 2002 Act s.9L(1)(a).

[311] Erskine, II, 11, 2.

[312] Technically, the debtor may still, say, validly sell heritage, but the inhibiting creditor may reduce the transaction and so no prudent purchaser would take the risk.

[313] For the detailed rules and forms that apply to inhibitions, see the Diligence (Scotland) Regulations 2009 (SSI 2009/68).

on the basis of a document of debt.[314] It is also competent to enforce an obligation to perform a particular act (other than payment)[315] in a decree, but only if that decree is a decree in an action that contained an alternative conclusion or crave for payment of a sum other than by way of expenses, or is a decree for specific implement of an obligation to convey heritable property to the creditor and to grant in favour of the creditor a heritable security or some other right over the debtor's property.[316] Extract decrees and documents of debt will henceforth automatically be deemed to carry a warrant for inhibition.[317] Registration of an inhibition is no longer by letters of inhibition to the Court of Session[318] but instead is carried out by registering the schedule of inhibition and the certificate of execution of the inhibition in the Register of Inhibitions and Adjudications.[319]

The date on which an inhibition has effect is from the beginning of the day it is registered in that Register, unless a notice of inhibition is registered in the Register, the schedule of inhibition is served on the debtor and the inhibition is registered within 21 days beginning with the date on which the notice is registered. Under those latter circumstances, the inhibition has effect from the beginning of the day on which the schedule of inhibition is served on the debtor,[320] this potentially being earlier than the actual date of registration of the inhibition. Where the debtor about to be inhibited is an individual, and the creditor is seeking a decree for payment or a decree to perform a particular act other than the conveyance of heritage or a grant of security over heritage, the debtor must be supplied with a copy of the debt advice and information package.[321] Any heritable property that the debtor owns or acquires may be affected by the inhibition, and for the avoidance of doubt, a person acquires property at the beginning of the day on which the deed conferring a real right in the acquired property is delivered to that person.[322] This means that if a deed of conveyance is delivered to an acquirer of heritage, and later that day the acquirer is inhibited, the acquirer is barred from transferring the heritage to which the deed relates. However, if a debtor is already inhibited, but receives property after he is inhibited, he is not inhibited in respect of that newly acquired property.[323] Where a decree requires performance of a particular act but has an alternative conclusion or crave of payment, and if decree is granted in terms of the conclusion or crave for payment, the inhibition is still valid for the purposes of enforcing payment of the debt referred to in the decree.[324]

---

[314] 2007 Act s.146(1)(a). Decrees and documents of debt are defined in s.221 of the 2007 Act. Summary warrants (for tax, rates, etc.) are included within this definition of "decree".

[315] This is the current form of the phrase *ad factum praestandum*.

[316] 2007 Act s.146(2). In this event, when decree is granted, any inhibition executed to enforce the decree is limited to the property to which the decree relates (s.153).

[317] 2007 Act s.146(3), (4) and (5).

[318] 2007 Act s.146(6).

[319] 2007 Act s.128.

[320] 2007 Act s.149, inserting a new s.155 in the Titles to Land Consolidation (Scotland) Act 1868. Note that while formerly the inhibition was "backdated" to the date of the notice, it is now only backdated to the date of serving of the schedule of inhibition on the debtor. Note the use of the word "beginning of the day"—this was designed to deal with the problem in *Park Petitioners*, 2008 S.L.T. 1206.

[321] 2007 Act s.147. As the wording of the statute uses the word "must", failure to supply the package renders the whole inhibition incompetent.

[322] 2007 Act s.150. Note the requirement of delivery, rather than registration in the Register of Sasines or Land Register. Note also that inhibition now only applies to heritage and no other property (s.150(2)).

[323] 2007 Act s.150(3). This is derived from s.157 of the Titles to Land Consolidation (Scotland) Act 1868.

[324] 2007 Act s.151.

48.25 Termination and ineffectuality of inhibition—An inhibition prescribes in five years from the date when it takes effect.[325] An inhibition is terminated or "purged" by payment of the full amount owing, which means the debt, interest on the debt, the expenses of the inhibition and the expenses of discharging the inhibition,[326] or, where the inhibition was executed to enforce an obligation to perform a particular act contained in a decree, on compliance with that decree.[327] An inhibition may be in place but treated as having no effect if an acquirer acquires property, or a right in the property, from an inhibited debtor (or any other person who acquired the property from the inhibited debtor[328]) in good faith and for adequate consideration. In these circumstances, acquisition means the delivery to the acquirer of the deed of conveyance of the property or the right in the property, and the acquirer is presumed to have acted in good faith if he is unaware of the inhibition and has taken all reasonable steps to discover the existence of any inhibition affecting the property.[329] "Reasonable steps" would appear to mean such matters as searching in the Register of Inhibitions and Adjudications against the seller and any previous owners against whom a diligence might be in force, and the search failing to disclose the presence of any inhibition.

48.26 Breach of inhibition—This takes place when an inhibited debtor delivers a deed conveying or otherwise granting a right in property over which the inhibition has effect to someone other than the inhibiting creditor.[330] Should this happen, the inhibiting creditor has 20 years in which to reduce a deed granted in breach of the inhibition,[331] though such reduction will not be available where the acquirer has acquired the property in good faith and for valuable consideration as stated above. Where a pursuer raises an action of reduction of conveyance or deed granted in breach of inhibition, a notice of the signeted summons, this being a notice of litigiosity, must be registered in the Register of Inhibitions and Adjudications in accordance with s.159 of the Titles to Land Consolidation (Scotland) Act 1868 and a copy in the Land Register of Scotland or the Register of Sasines.[332] Where an inhibited debtor grants a lease of more than five years in duration, or with at least five years to run before it comes to an end, it may also be reduced; leases for lesser periods may also be reduced if the Court of Session is satisfied that it would be fair and reasonable to reduce them.[333] Where a property or a right in property has been transferred or created in breach of any inhibition, the Keeper will enter it on the title sheet when registering an interest in the land in question.[334]

48.27 The expenses of inhibition and ascription—The expenses of inhibition are chargeable against the debtor. If land attachment and residual attachment are ever

---

[325] Conveyancing (Scotland) Act 1924 s.44(3)(aa) as inserted by the 2007 Act s.156. As to the date of effect, see above.

[326] 2007 Act s.157. The common law only required payment of the debt alone. This section does not apply to an inhibition on the dependence of an action.

[327] 2007 Act s.158. The formerly inhibited debtor will need to record the discharge of the inhibition in the Register of Inhibitions and Adjudications.

[328] This other person need not himself have acquired the property in good faith or for value (s.159(3)).

[329] 2007 Act s.159(4).

[330] 2007 Act s.160.

[331] 2007 Act s.161.

[332] 2007 Act s.162, inserting s.159A into the Titles to Land Consolidation (Scotland) Act 1868. There are also provisions for the discharge of the notice of litigiosity should the pursuer's action fail.

[333] 2007 Act s.163.

[334] 2007 Act s.167.

brought into force, those two methods will be the only diligences that may be used to enforce payment of the expenses, but at the time of writing the relevant subsection is not yet in force.[335] Although the creditor may re-inhibit the debtor at the end of each five-year period, the debtor is only liable for one further set of inhibition expenses.[336] If the debtor, being inhibited, makes payment to account in respect of his debt, the sums paid are applied in the following order: the expenses of any diligence (other than inhibition), the inhibition expenses, interest due on the sum at the time the inhibition came into force, the debt itself and any interest after the inhibition came into force.

Ranking of inhibitions—Bell's Canons of Ranking, to be found in his **48.28** *Commentaries,*[337] were a complex method[338] of ensuring fairness to pre-inhibition, inhibiting and post-inhibition creditors seeking repayment out of the proceeds of a debtor's heritable estate.[339] Section 154 of the 2007 Act removes the inhibiting creditor's preference in ranking in competition with post-inhibition creditors, thereby dispensing with all these previous rules.

Inhibition and sequestration or liquidation—If the debtor is sequestrated, the **48.29** award of sequestration has the effect of an adjudication for the benefit of all creditors, including the inhibitor.[340] Inhibition gives no preference to the inhibiting creditor in sequestration of the debtor or any other insolvency proceedings, including the sale of heritage by the secured creditor.[341] The exercise by the trustee in sequestration of his powers in respect of the heritable estate is not challengeable on the ground of any prior inhibition.[342] Where there is an inhibition on the estate of the debtor which takes effect within 60 days before the date of sequestration a right to challenge the inhibition vests in the trustee,[343] as do the right of the inhibitor to receive payment for the discharge of the inhibition and the right in terms of the inhibition to challenge any deed voluntarily granted by the debtor.[344] A liquidator in a compulsory winding up by the court has the same powers as a trustee in sequestration[345] which would include the ability to sell any heritable estate of a company even if there is a prior inhibition.[346] A liquidator appointed under a creditors' voluntary winding up may also dispose of any heritage owned by the company notwithstanding the existence of an inhibition against that company.[347]

---

[335] 2007 Act s.165(2). See the Bankruptcy and Diligence etc. (Scotland) Act 2007 (Commencement No.4, Savings and Transitionals) Order 2009 (SSI 2009/67), para.3(1)(a).

[336] 2007 Act s.165.

[337] Bell, *Commentaries*, 2.413.

[338] See G.L. Gretton, *Law of Inhibition and Adjudication*, 2nd edn (Edinburgh: W. Green, 1996).

[339] The complexity of the rules ensured that there were very few recent cases on the matter, *Halifax Building Society v Smith*, 1985 S.L.T. (Sh. Ct) 25 being one of the few.

[340] 1985 Act s.37(1); see the Insolvency Act 1986 s.185, as regards the winding up of a company. For the effect of an inhibition in the event of the debtor being adjudged bankrupt in England, see *Morley's Tr. v Aitken*, 1982 S.C. 73.

[341] 2007 Act s.154.

[342] 1985 Act s.31(2). The phrase "any prior inhibition" in this subsection is thought to refer to any inhibition prior to the date of sequestration.

[343] 1985 Act s.37(2).

[344] 1985 Act s.37(2), (3).

[345] Insolvency Act 1986 s.169(2) which refers to the powers of the trustee in sequestration in the 1985 Act.

[346] 1985 Act s.31(2), subject to the provisions of 2007 Act s.154(1).

[347] Insolvency Act 1986 s.166(1A) as inserted by the 2007 Act s.155(3).

48.30 Inhibition when company put into receivership or administration—Inhibition gives no preference to the inhibiting creditor in the receivership or administration of the company.[348] Should a creditor inhibit a debtor company after that company has created a floating charge but before it is put into receivership, the inhibition is not deemed to be an effectual diligence and the receiver neither needs the consent of the inhibiting creditor nor court approval to sell or dispose of the company's heritage.[349] As regards administration, no inhibition may be "instituted or continued" once an administrator has been appointed by a qualifying floating charge-holder (or any other person entitled to appoint an administrator in terms of Sch.B1 of the Insolvency Act 1986) except with the consent of the administrator or the court.[350] If the company has granted a qualifying floating charge under which the administrator was appointed, the administrator is entitled to dispose of or take action relating to any property subject to the floating charge.[351] The inhibiting creditor does not lose his right to repayment, but he has no power to prevent the administrator disposing of the debtor company's property.

48.31 Recall of inhibition—An application may be made for recall or restriction of an inhibition on the same grounds as are applicable to arrestments.[352] When the debt on which the inhibition is used has been paid the creditor is bound, at the debtor's expense, to clear the record by recording a discharge. Should he refuse to do so, the party inhibited may present an application for recall, and the creditor will be liable for the expenses of the application and for all expenses necessarily incurred in having the inhibition completely removed.[353]

An inhibition may be recalled, with or without caution, if the court is satisfied that in the circumstances its use is nimious or oppressive.[354] The partial recall of an inhibition is also competent.[355]

48.32 Inhibition on the dependence—Following the 2007 Act, inhibition on the dependence of an action[356] is competent only if there are conclusions for payment of money, other than the conclusion for expenses.[357] It is competent for the Court of Session to grant warrant for inhibition on the dependence of a petition but only where the petition contains a prayer for payment of a sum other than expenses.[358] Inhibition on the dependence of an action[359] for payment of a contingent or future debt is competent.[360] A debt is not contingent for these purposes merely because a dispute about it falls to be determined by arbitration.[361] The process of applying to

---

[348] 2007 Act s.154.

[349] Insolvency Act 1986 s.61(1A) as inserted by the 2007 Act s.155(2).

[350] Insolvency Act 1986 Sch.B1 para.43(6).

[351] Insolvency Act 1986 Sch.B1 para.70.

[352] The 2007 Act makes no changes to the previous process of recall of inhibitions; RCS r.13.10; *Allied Irish Banks Plc v Gpt Sales & Services Ltd*, 1995 S.L.T. 163; 1993 S.C.L.R. 778.

[353] *Robertson v Park, Dobson & Co* (1896) 24 R. 30; *Milne v Birrell* (1902) 4 F. 879.

[354] *Mackintosh v Miller* (1864) 2 M. 452; *Burns v Burns* (1879) 7 R. 355; *MT Group v Howden Group Plc*, 1993 S.L.T. 345; *Stratmil Ltd v D & A Todd (Building Contractors) Ltd*, 1990 S.L.T. 493; 1990 S.C.L.R. 147; *Rodger v Maracas Ltd*, 1990 S.L.T. 45.

[355] *McInally v Kildonan Homes Ltd*, 1979 S.L.T. (Notes) 89.

[356] Both in the Court of Session and in the sheriff court (1987 Act s.15A(3)).

[357] 1987 Act s.15A(2)(a).

[358] 1987 Act s.15B(2)(a).

[359] "Action" hereafter covers both actions and petitions (1987 Act s.15B(3)).

[360] 1987 Act s.15C(1). Examples of future or contingent debts include aliment or a capital sum paid on a divorce.

[361] *Rippin Group Ltd v IPT Interpipe S.A.*, 1995 S.C. 302.

the court for grant of warrant of inhibition on the dependence may be done at any time while the action is in dependence[362] but any such application must be intimated to the debtor and to any other person having an interest unless the application is for a grant without a hearing under s.15E, in which case intimation is not necessary. Pursuers in certain foreign actions, which have been commenced but not concluded, may apply by petition to the Court of Session for warrant to inhibit in Scotland.[363] An inhibition on the dependence is executed by serving a schedule of inhibition on the debtor.[364] An order under a s.15E application (i.e. where the debtor is not immediately given the opportunity of a hearing) is available to the creditor only where the following provisions apply: (a) when the creditor has a prima facie case on the merits of the action[365]; (b) when there is a real and substantial risk that enforcement of a decree in favour of the creditor would be defeated or prejudiced by the debtor being insolvent or verging on insolvency or being likely to remove, dispose of, burden, conceal or otherwise deal with all or some of his assets unless inhibition was not granted in advance of the hearing; and (c) when it is reasonable in all the circumstances, including the effect granting the warrant may have on any other person having an interest, to do so.[366] The onus is on the creditor to satisfy the court that the s.15E order should be made, but where the court does make such an order, the court must fix a hearing under s.15K[367] and the creditor must intimate as much to the debtor and anyone else with an interest.[368] Where the court does not make the order without a hearing, but the creditor insists on the application, the court must instead fix a date for the hearing in terms of s.15F.

A s.15F application specifically involves a hearing and the court will not grant any order under this section until the debtor and anyone else having an interest has had an opportunity to be heard. The court may grant the order for warrant of inhibition on the dependence where the same provisions as in a s.15E application are satisfied, namely (a), (b) and (c) above, but where the court refuses the creditor a grant of warrant for inhibition, the court may impose such conditions as it sees fit, including requiring the debtor to consign money into court or finding caution or some other security.[369]

Assuming inhibition on the dependence is duly executed, if the summons is not served within 21 days from the date of execution, the inhibition will be invalid, though the 21-day period may be extended for good reason.[370] The court has discretion to limit the amount of the debtor's property to be inhibited, and where an action is brought for specific implement of an obligation to convey heritable property to the creditor, to grant a real right in security over that property in favour

---

[362] 1987 Act s.15D(1)(a).

[363] Civil Jurisdiction and Judgments Act 1982 s.27.

[364] For the practicalities of this, see RCS rr.13.6–13.9. There are equivalent rules for the various sheriff courts.

[365] *Advocate General v Taylor*, 2004 S.C. 339; *Gillespie v Toondale Ltd*, 2006 S.C. 304.

[366] 1987 Act s.15E(2). This replaces the former common law requirement that the debtor be *vergens ad inopiam* or *in meditatione fugae* (verging on insolvency or considering flight (of himself or of his property) from the country).

[367] 1987 Act s.15E(4)(a). Section 15K provides for recall or restriction of diligence granted on the dependence. This provision takes account of the requirement under the Human Rights Act 1998 that owners of property should not be deprived of peaceful enjoyment of their property without proper process. See also *Karl Construction Ltd v Palisade Properties Plc*, 2002 S.C. 270; 2002 S.L.T. 312.

[368] 1987 Act s.15E(4).

[369] 1987 Act s.15F.

[370] 1987 Act s.15G.

of the creditor, or to grant some other right over the property, the court may limit the property inhibited to that particular property.[371] Inhibition on the dependence may be recalled or restricted under s.15K where the warrant was invalid or the inhibition incompetent, irregular or ineffective, or where the provisions in ss.15E and 15F no longer apply.[372] The onus is on the creditor to satisfy the court that the order for recall or restriction should not be granted.[373] When an inhibition is used on the dependence of an action, and the defender is ultimately assoilzied, the court may grant an order to have the inhibition marked as recalled.[374] On the assumption that the common law may provide guidance as to the interpretation of s.15K in the context of inhibitions, inhibitions on the dependence have in the past been recalled or restricted in the following circumstances: (a) where the inhibition is incompetent as there are no averments of debtor verging on insolvency or considering flight[375]; (b) where the defender successfully entered a plea of *lis alibi pendens*[376]; (c) where the diligence has been used oppressively[377]; (d) where the pursuer has not made out a prima facie case.[378] There are opportunities open to the debtor to apply for variation or removal of any conditions imposed on the debtor in connection with the refusal of an order for grant of warrant or a restriction of inhibition.[379] The creditor is entitled to the expenses of the inhibition on the dependence unless the creditor was acting unreasonably in applying for the warrant, or the court is satisfied that the refusal or modification of expenses is reasonable in all the circumstances and having regard to the outcome of the action.[380]

Where a creditor obtains a decree in proceedings for payment of all or part of a principal sum concluded or craved for, and had obtained warrant for inhibition on the dependence therefor, and where the warrant was restricted to specified property of the debtor's, any inhibition in execution of the actual decree is not restricted to that specified property.[381]

VI. ADJUDICATION FOR DEBT

48.33   Adjudication for debt—Adjudication is a diligence against heritable property. Although the 2007 Act would have abolished it and replaced it with land attachment,[382] at the time of writing land attachment has not been brought into force, and adjudication is still extant, even if little used. It is obtained by way of an action of adjudication in the Court of Session. The service of a summons of

---

[371] 1987 Act s.15J.

[372] *Beaghmor Property Ltd v Station Properties Ltd* [2009] CSOH 133; *MRK -1 Ltd v Sakur* [2008] CSOH 176.

[373] 1987 Act s.15K(10); *McCormack v Hamilton Academicals Football Club*, 2009 S.C. 313. This case concerns arrestment but explains the proper use of s.15K.

[374] *Barbour's Trs v Davidsons* (1878) 15 S.L.R. 438.

[375] e.g. *Stratmil Ltd v D & A Todd (Building Contractors) Ltd*, 1990 S.L.T. 493; 1990 S.C.L.R. 147. The wording *in meditatione fugae* does not wholly equiparate with that in s.15E(b)(ii) or s.15F(3)(b)(ii).

[376] *Stratmil Ltd v D & A Todd (Building Contractors) Ltd*, 1990 S.L.T. 493.

[377] *Rodger v Maracas Ltd*, 1990 S.L.T. 45.

[378] *Advocate General v Taylor*, 2004 S.C. 339; 2004 S.L.T. 1340; *Gillespie v Toondale Ltd*, 2006 S.C. 304.

[379] 1987 Act s.15L.

[380] 1987 Act s.15M.

[381] 2002 Act s.152.

[382] 2007 Act s.79.

adjudication, if followed by a registration of a notice in statutory form in the Register of Inhibitions and Adjudications[383] renders the subject litigious, that is to say, it impliedly prohibits voluntary alienation, and any disponee takes subject to the diligence. The recording of an extract decree of adjudication in the Register of Sasines or in the Land Register[384] has the effect of a heritable security in favour of the adjudicating creditor, who is known as the "adjudger". The adjudger takes the subjects *tantum et tale* as they are vested in the debtor, and subject to the real rights of third parties[385] and the debtor's right of redemption. The adjudger has, in general, the same rights as other heritable creditors apart from a power of sale.[386] If the debtor is in possession the adjudger may take proceedings to remove him.[387] If the subjects are let, the adjudger may, by way of an action of mails and duties,[388] require the rents to be paid to him.[389] If the debt still remains unsatisfied after a period of ten years, known as the "legal", the adjudger may acquire ownership in an action of declaratory of the expiry of the legal.[390]

During the legal, the adjudger may grant leases of up to seven years, and longer on a warrant from the sheriff.[391] In a competition between adjudgers all adjudications prior to that first made effectual, i.e. by recording in the General Register of Sasines or the Land Register as the case may be, and all those subsequently led within a year and a day rank pari passu.[392] Those outwith the year and a day rank according to the date of the recording of the decree. Sequestration is equivalent to a decree of adjudication of the debtor's heritable estate which has been duly recorded on the date of sequestration, and any adjudications which have not been made effectual more than a year and a day before that date confer no preference on the adjudger.[393]

VII. LAND ATTACHMENT

Nature of land attachment—Land attachment is a diligence against heritable **48.34**
property and if brought into force will replace adjudication for debt.[394] The part of the chapter explains land attachment on the assumption that it will be brought into effect in due course. It remains to be seen if it is brought into force. There are as yet no statutory instruments to provide the detail of the procedure.

Grounds for land attachment—Land attachment gives the creditor a subordinate **48.35**
real right in the land in security of the sum owed to the creditor, together with

---

[383] Titles to Land Consolidation (Scotland) Act 1868 s.159; Conveyancing (Scotland) Act 1924 s.44; Law Reform (Miscellaneous Provisions) (Scotland) Act 1985 Sch.2 paras 4–5.

[384] Conveyancing (Scotland) Act 1924 s.44(5); Land Registration (Scotland) Act 1979 s.29(2).

[385] Stewart, *A Treatise on the Law of Diligence* (1898), p.620.

[386] Heritable Securities (Scotland) Act 1894.

[387] Heritable Securities (Scotland) Act 1894 s.5.

[388] This too is due to be abolished under the 2007 Act. It is an action that allows a heritable creditor to receive rent directly from the debtor's tenants, rather than the rent being paid to the debtor. Such actions are even rarer than adjudications.

[389] Heritable Securities (Scotland) Act 1894 s.3.

[390] The declaratory power of the court should be tempered by the court to prevent any unfairness to the debtor: *Hull v Campbell* [2011] CSOH 24; 2011 S.L.T. 881.

[391] Heritable Securities (Scotland) Act 1894 ss.6, 7.

[392] Diligence Act 1661 (c.62); Adjudication Act 1672 (c.45).

[393] 1985 Act s.37(1); for liquidations see the Insolvency Act 1986 s.185.

[394] 2007 Act s.79.

interest and expenses.[395] Land attachment is competent to enforce payment of a debt, but only if the debt is constituted by a decree or a document of debt,[396] the debtor has been charged to pay the debt, the *induciae* of the charge has expired[397] and, where the debtor is an individual, the debtor has received from the creditor, no earlier than 12 weeks before the registration of the notice of land attachment, a debt advice and information package.[398] The debt itself must be of £3,000 or more.[399] The notice of land attachment needs to be registered both in the appropriate property register for the land in question[400] and in the Register of Inhibitions.[401]

A copy of the notice is then served on the debtor, any person who owns the land, and any tenant under a long lease.[402] Service of the copy of the notice must be carried out within 28 days of the registration of the notice, and the creditor must then register the certificate of service both in the appropriate property register for the land in question and in the Register of Inhibitions.[403] Failure to register the certificate renders the notice void.[404] During the period of 28 days after registration and during which time the debtor must be served the copy of the notice, the notice acts as if it were an inhibition registered against the debtor in the Register of Inhibitions, but is restricted to the property described in the notice.[405]

Assuming the certificate is duly registered and the sum not paid, the land attachment itself is created either (a) at the beginning of the day which falls immediately after the expiry of a period of 28 days after the day on which the notices of land attachment are registered, or (b) should the notices be registered on separate days, at the beginning of the day which falls immediately after the period of 28 days after the later of the two dates of registration of the notices of land attachment.[406]

The property that is covered by land attachment is land (buildings, structures and land covered by water) owned by the debtor and a long lease of land where the debtor is the tenant.[407] It is not possible to attach land that has never been registered,[408] land to which the debtor does not have a registered title, a proper liferent where the debtor is the liferenter, nor a non-assignable long lease.[409] If a debtor has granted a standard security over his land, but a notice of land attachment over his land is registered and a copy thereof served on the standard security holder, and a land attachment subsequently created on the expiry of the 28-day

---

[395] 2007 Act s.81(5).

[396] For the definition of these terms see 2007 Act s.221.

[397] 14 days within the United Kingdom, 28 days otherwise. See 1987 Act s.90(3).

[398] 2007 Act s.81(2). A time to pay order or direction will prevent land attachment taking place.

[399] 2007 Act s.83(3). This figure may be increased from time to time, and on promulgation attracted criticism on the grounds that it is a relatively small sum of money for which someone could lose his home.

[400] The Land Register or the Register of Sasines.

[401] 2007 Act s.83(1). The style of notice is yet to be devised.

[402] 2007 Act s.83(5).

[403] 2007 Act s.83(7). If land attachment is brought into force, adjudication would be abolished, and the register would then be the "Register of Inhibitions".

[404] 2007 Act s.83(6).

[405] 2007 Act s.81(4).

[406] 2007 Act s.81(3). Although generally the registration in the property register and the Register of Inhibitions will take place on the same day, it is possible that there may be a gap between the two registrations, in which case the land attachment starts from 28 days after the latter of the two registrations.

[407] 2007 Act s.82(1).

[408] Such as certain old churches and buildings such as the Advocates Library.

[409] 2007 Act s.82(2). Where a lease is assignable only with the consent of the landlord, the lease is attachable (s.82(3)).

period, the standard security holder will thereafter be precluded from lending further sums to the debtor except to the extent that those further sums are postponed to the attaching creditor's claim.[410] Where a debtor, or a tenant of the debtor, creates a lease of the land specified in the registered notice of land attachment during the 28-day period, and where subsequently the land attachment is created, the creditor may reduce that lease.[411] The land attachment assigns to the creditor all the title deeds to the attached land and on a subsequent sale of the land he may assign those title deeds to the purchaser.[412] It is permissible to assign the right to a land attachment.[413] If a debtor, against whose property a creditor has taken steps to register the notice of land attachment, dies before the land attachment is created, such steps as have been taken are void but the creditor is not barred from proceeding against the debtor's executor,[414] but where the debtor dies after the land attachment has been created, the land attachment continues to have effect.[415] Where a purchaser has entered into a contract (missives) to purchase land from the debtor and ownership has not been transferred to that purchaser, the purchaser may register in the Register of Inhibitions a caveat. This will enable the potential purchaser to be informed of any action by the creditor, to lodge objections to the sale and if necessary to complete title to the attached land.[416]

Warrant for sale—Having attached the land, the creditor may wish to apply to **48.36** the sheriff for a warrant to sell the land, if (a) the land attachment is in effect, (b) he has not yet been paid and the sum recoverable and outstanding is still greater than £3,000, and (c) the period of six months from the date of registration of the notice has expired.[417] In this event, he applies on the requisite form which will specify the attached land to be sold and a solicitor willing to execute the warrant for sale,[418] and which will be accompanied by a report on searches in the appropriate property register and the Register of Inhibitions and a copy of the land attachment, a copy of the certificate of service and the solicitor's declaration.[419] The application must be served on the debtor and anyone having an interest in the property,[420] with a special notice for the local authority if the attached land comprises a dwelling-house.[421] These persons (except the local authority) may lodge objections to the application.[422] The sheriff must then hold a preliminary hearing and if satisfied that the application is in order, fix a date for the full hearing and appoint a chartered surveyor to value the land specified in the application,[423] and require any holders of any prior securities or anyone effecting diligence over

---

[410] s.13A of the Conveyancing and Feudal Reform (Scotland) Act 1970 as inserted by s.85 of the 2007 Act.

[411] 2007 Act s.86.

[412] 2007 Act s.87.

[413] 2007 Act s.88.

[414] 2007 Act s.89.

[415] 2007 Act s.90.

[416] 2007 Act s.91.

[417] 2007 Act s.92(1). The figure of £3,000 may be altered.

[418] Assuming this solicitor is appointed to carry out the sale, he, or someone in his place, will be known as the "appointed person" (s.97(2)). He has to make a declaration that he is willing to execute the sale.

[419] 2007 Act s.92(4).

[420] 2007 Act s.92(5). This includes heritable creditors or creditors effecting diligence on the property, any occupier of the land and anyone owning the land in common with the debtor.

[421] 2007 Act s.93. This is because the debtor may be made homeless.

[422] 2007 Act s.92(6).

[423] 2007 Act s.94(3)(c).

the land to disclose the debt outstanding on those securities or diligences.[424] At the full hearing the sheriff must give every person who has lodged objections an opportunity to be heard.[425] The sheriff has various options available to him as regards the sale of the property: he may grant the warrant for sale, but must specify the period within which the attached land is to be sold, and may grant warrant for only part of the land to be sold or for it to be sold in lots[426]; alternatively, if the warrant for sale would be unduly harsh, he may agree to let the sale take place, but suspend it for up to a year or not grant the order at all.[427] He must refuse it under certain circumstances, such as the invalidity of the land attachment, the sum recoverable being less than £3,000, the property being sold by another creditor including a heritable creditor etc.[428] In addition, the sheriff must refuse a warrant for sale if the likely net sale proceeds would not exceed that figure which is the aggregate of the expenses of the land attachment, and whichever is the lesser of the sum of £1,000 and the sum equal to 10 per cent of the sum (or the outstanding amount) which the debtor was charged to pay.[429] There are further provisions for the sheriff to take into account when the property is a dwelling-house[430] and the sole or main residence of the debtor or the spouse, partner, civil partner or the debtor's or his or her partner's child,[431] having regard to the nature and reasons the for the debt secured by the land attachment, the debtor's ability to pay, any action taken by the creditor to assist in paying the debt, and the ability of those dwelling in the dwelling-house to find alternative accommodation.[432] In these cases the sheriff may suspend the effect of the warrant for up to one year.[433]

48.37 Protection for purchaser and others—In addition to the safeguards for the protection of the debtor, there are safeguards to protect the position of purchasers who are attempting to purchase attached land. The purchaser may lodge objections to the application for the sale by the creditor and have the application sisted, or require the purchaser to pay the price to the creditor, the sheriff being satisfied that the purchaser was not attempting to defeat the rights of the creditors of the debtor.[434] Once the warrant for sale has been granted, there are further opportunities to protect the purchaser, such as by means of having the sale delayed for a year or having the purchaser pay the price to the creditor.[435] There are provisions to protect the position of a third party who owns the attached land in common with the debtor.[436] Equally, there are provisions to allow a creditor to try again to apply for a warrant to sell the attached land where that has been previously refused.[437] Where an order has been made for a warrant of sale, the creditor may serve on the debtor and anyone else deriving a right from the debtor a notice requiring the debtor (and such other persons) to terminate their occupation of the

---

[424] 2007 Act s.94(3)(d).
[425] 2007 Act s.97(1).
[426] 2007 Act s.97(4).
[427] 2007 Act s.97(3).
[428] 2007 Act s.97(6).
[429] 2007 Act s.97(6)(g), (7). This is known as the "not worth it test".
[430] For the definition of a dwelling-house, see 2002 Act s.45.
[431] 2007 Act s.98(1)–(3).
[432] 2007 Act s.98(5).
[433] 2007 Act s.98(7).
[434] 2007 Act s.99.
[435] 2007 Act s.100.
[436] 2007 Act s.102.
[437] 2007 Act s.105.

attached land.[438] This places the creditor in the position of a heritable creditor of the attached land, in a manner similar to that of s.20(5) of the Conveyancing and Feudal Reform (Scotland) Act 1970, enabling the creditor to receive rent, and, if necessary, applying to the sheriff for an order allowing him to carry out works of reconstruction, alteration or improvement if these are necessary to preserve the market value of the land and to recover from the debtor the expenses of so doing.[439]

Process of sale—As regards the sale of the attached land, the appointed person **48.38** (normally the solicitor asked to sell the land) must follow the directions of the statute, the sheriff and any further requirements yet to be specified by the Scottish Ministers,[440] and will be liable to the creditor, the debtor, any person who owns the land in common with the debtor and any secured creditor for any patrimonial loss incurred by his negligence in handling the sale.[441] The sale itself should be sold by private bargain or by auction.[442] The appointed person has authority under the sheriff's warrant to grant a disposition on behalf of the creditor in favour of the purchaser. Any legal incapacity or disability of the debtor will not affect the title acquired by the purchaser,[443] and should there be irregularities in the execution of the land attachment, or in the continued effect of the land attachment, but provided the purchaser acted in good faith and the appointed person has given him a certificate (as required by Act of Sederunt) confirming that the land attachment was regularly executed, the purchaser's title will be secure.[444] Once sold, the formerly attached land is disburdened of the land attachment, and of any heritable security or any diligence ranking pari passu with or after the land attachment.[445]

Thereafter, the appointed person must lodge a report of the sale with the sheriff clerk,[446] to be forwarded to the auditor of court,[447] who will tax the expenses, certify the balance due to or by the debtor and report to the sheriff. The sheriff considers and approves (or not as the case may be) the sale.[448] If he does not approve it, because of some substantial irregularity, the sheriff may declare the entire land attachment void and make any necessary consequential order.[449] As regards the proceeds of sale, the proceeds are used to pay the attaching creditor's expenses of the land attachment, to pay any creditor holding a security or diligence over the attached land, to pay the sums due to the attaching creditor, to pay any creditor ranking pari passu with the attaching creditor, any postponed creditor and finally to pay any balance due to the debtor.[450]

Foreclosure—Instead of sale, it may be necessary to foreclose, particularly where **48.39** the appointed person has exposed the land in the warrant for sale and failed to find a purchaser or succeeded in only selling part of the land at a price less than the sum secured by the land attachment and any prior or pari passu security or

---

[438] 2007 Act s.106.
[439] 2007 Act s.107.
[440] 2007 Act s.108.
[441] 2007 Act s.108(5).
[442] 2007 Act s.109.
[443] 2007 Act s.110.
[444] 2007 Act s.111.
[445] 2007 Act s.112. This does not include any real right or preference ranking prior to it.
[446] 2007 Act s.113.
[447] 2007 Act s.114.
[448] 2007 Act s.115.
[449] 2007 Act s.115(1)(b).
[450] 2007 Act s.116(1).

diligence. There are careful procedures[451] to ensure that all those with an interest in the property are made aware of the application for foreclosure to the sheriff and allowing those with an interest the opportunity to make representations and to allow the debtor a further period of up to three months in which to pay the sum recoverable.[452] A valuer may be appointed to sell the land subject to the warrant at an auction, but if still unsold, the sheriff may grant decree of foreclosure.[453] The decree of foreclosure needs to be registered in the appropriate property register and the creditor is thereupon vested in the land, the land is disburdened of the land attachment, and the creditor may redeem any prior ranking security or diligence over the property.[454]

48.40　Ascription and recall—Where sums are recovered by land attachment, they are first applied to the creditor's expenses of the land attachment, interest up to the date of the registration of the notice of the land attachment, the principal sum sued for and interest from the date of registration of the notice.[455] The expenses of land attachment are payable by the debtor but may only be recovered, in the absence of payment, by land attachment. Where the debtor pays the sums due before the expiry of the 28-day period in s.81(3),[456] the land attachment is not created and the notice of land attachment is of no effect,[457] and it is of no effect if the full sum is paid before warrant for sale is granted, a contract for sale of the land is concluded, or an extract decree of foreclosure is registered.[458] Where the notice of land attachment or the land attachment ceases to be of effect, the creditor must discharge the notice of land attachment or the land attachment, once payment of expenses has been made.[459] The debtor or anyone having an interest may recall or restrict the land attachment for good cause shown.[460] Land attachment endures for five years from the date or registration of the notice of land attachment, though this period may be extended.[461] Where a debtor has granted a deed to a third party in breach of an inhibition, and that deed has been reduced by the inhibiting creditor, it is competent for the inhibiting creditor to register a notice of land attachment in respect of the land to which the reduced deed relates.[462] Once a land attachment (following the notice) is established, it will enjoy preference in ranking over any security in favour of the third party granted over the land and any land attachment over the land executed by a creditor of the third party.[463] Finally, for the avoidance of doubt, a land attachment is not a heritable security for the purposes of the Heritable Securities (Scotland) Act 1894.[464]

48.41　Preference secured by land attachment—This matter is not dealt with in the existing legislation and ideally would be clarified in subordinate legislation. It is

---

[451] Under the 2007 Act s.117.
[452] 2007 Act s.117(5)(b).
[453] 2007 Act s.117(8).
[454] 2007 Act s.118(1).
[455] 2007 Act s.119.
[456] See para.48.35.
[457] 2007 Act s.121.
[458] 2007 Act s.121(3).
[459] 2007 Act s.122.
[460] 2007 Act s.123.
[461] 2007 Act s.124.
[462] 2007 Act s.125(1).
[463] 2007 Act s.125(2).
[464] 2007 Act s.127.

suggested that in the absence of subordinate legislation it could be set aside on the same basis as attachment or arrestment.

VII. ATTACHMENT OF MONEY

Need for attachment of money—Until the 2007 Act it was not possible for a **48.42** creditor to attach money or banking instruments. This could mean that the debtor could have substantial amounts of cash on his premises which could be used to satisfy a creditor but which could not be seized by the creditor. Once money had been banked it could be arrested, but while it was still in the hands of its owner it could not be removed. With effect from November 23, 2009 this is now changed.[465]

Money attachment is competent to enforce payment of a debt if the debt is constituted by decree or an instrument of debt,[466] the debtor has been charged to pay the debt, the period of the *induciae* of the charge has expired without payment having been made,[467] and, where the debtor is an individual, the creditor has provided the debtor with a debt advice and information package no earlier than 12 weeks before executing the money attachment.[468] Money attachment is neither competent in a dwelling-house[469] nor where arrestment would be competent.[470]

Money is defined as cash,[471] banknotes in any currency and banking instruments (cheques, banker's drafts, government cheques, promissory notes, other negotiable instruments, money orders and postal orders).

Execution of money attachment—Money attachment is carried out by sheriff **48.43** officers or messengers at arms. They must not without the prior authority of the sheriff attempt the execution of money attachment between 8pm and 8am, or continue any money attachment after 8pm.[472] It is not competent to execute a money attachment on Sunday, on a public holiday or such other day as may be prescribed by Act of Sederunt.[473] Once a money attachment has been executed, it is not competent to attach other money at the same address for the same debt unless that other money is brought to that address after the first execution[474] unless the first money did not belong to the debtor, in which case it is competent to attach other money belonging to the debtor at the same address.[475] Money attached by a money attachment may not be re-attached if the first attachment ceases to have effect in relation to that money.[476]

---

[465] See the Bankruptcy and Diligence etc. (Scotland) Act 2007 (Commencement No.5 and Transitional) Order 2009 (SSI 2009/369). The specific rules and forms relating to money attachment may be found at Act of Sederunt (Money Attachment) Rules 2009 (SSI 2009/382).

[466] For the definition of a decree or an instrument of debt, see s.221. The definition includes a summary warrant.

[467] 14 days within the United Kingdom, 28 days otherwise. See 1987 Act s.90(3).

[468] 2007 Act s.174(2).

[469] A dwelling-house is as defined in s.45 of the 2002 Act.

[470] 2007 Act s.172(3).

[471] This definition is intended to catch ordinary cash, not valuable coins collected for numismatic purposes—those being attachable but not by money attachment (s.175(1)).

[472] 2007 Act s.176(2).

[473] 2007 Act s.176(1).

[474] 2007 Act s.176(3).

[475] 2007 Act s.176(3).

[476] 2007 Act s.176(4).

The sheriff officer or messenger at arms must attach, and remove from the place where it is found, enough money which in his opinion will not exceed the sum for which the charge was served, together with interest and expenses.[477] Where the money is not sterling, he must as soon as reasonably practical afterwards convert it into sterling at the best rate possible. He must then deposit it in a bank account.[478] He is not obliged to attach any banking instruments other than cheques unless instructed by the creditor to do so, and is not liable to the creditor for any loss caused by the failure to attach any such instruments.[479] Where he does attach instruments, he must value them at the price they would fetch on the open market unless professional valuation is needed.[480] He is entitled to assume that the money found in the place of attachment is the debtor's, but must make enquiries as to its ownership. He may not make that assumption where he knows or ought to know that the money is not the debtor's, but he is not precluded from relying on the assumption just because someone says that the money is not the debtor's.[481] Having executed the money attachment, the judicial officer must serve on the debtor, whom failing a person present at the place of attachment, a schedule of money attachment in the relevant form.[482] The date of giving a copy of the schedule to the debtor is the date of execution of the money attachment.[483] Once the money has been attached, the creditor, the sheriff officer, the messenger at arms or the debtor may at any time apply to the sheriff for an order that the money be immediately realised if it is likely to deteriorate substantially and rapidly in value. This would be appropriate if the money was in a rapidly devaluing foreign currency. The sheriff officer or messenger at arms is authorised to act as the irrevocable agent of the debtor in relation to the money, thus allowing him to negotiate any banking instruments.[484] Within 14 days of the date of execution of the money attachment, he must make a signed report to the sheriff.[485] The report will specify the money attached, its value, its ownership,[486] the extent to which it may already have been realised in the case of deterioration, and the extent to which has been released under a payment order.[487] It is important that it be properly signed and the sheriff may refuse to receive the report if it does not conform with the statutory requirements. If it is refused, the money attachment ceases to have effect, the money must be returned whence it came and the sheriff clerk must intimate the refusal to all those with an interest in the matter.[488] If the report is accepted, the date of the report of the money acceptance is the date it is received by the sheriff.[489]

48.44 Creditor's application for payment order—The creditor, having successfully had the debtor's money attached, may next make an application for a payment

---

[477] 2007 Act s.177(1).

[478] 2007 Act s.177(3), (4).

[479] 2007 Act s.177(6).

[480] 2007 Act s.180.

[481] 2007 Act s.178.

[482] 2007 Act s.179.

[483] 2007 Act s.179(3).

[484] 2007 Act s.181.

[485] See the Schedule to the Act of Sederunt (Money Attachment) Rules 2009 (SSI 2009/382) for the required form.

[486] There may have been an assertion that the money was not the debtor's or that it was owned in common with another person.

[487] 2007 Act s.182(1)–(3).

[488] 2007 Act s.182(6).

[489] 2007 Act s.182(7).

order authorising payment to the creditor of the sum due to the creditor out of the attached money. The application must be in the required form,[490] and made within 14 days of the day on which the report of the money attachment was made.[491] Following intimation to all those with an interest, and provided there is no opposition to it, the sheriff must grant the payment order.[492] Where there is opposition, the sheriff may not make a payment order without having a hearing first, and where the debtor or another person asserts that the money is not the debtor's money, it is for the debtor to prove this fact.[493] Where the sheriff is satisfied that there has been a material irregularity in the execution or that the attached money was not the debtor's, he must make an order declaring that the money attachment is of no effect and requiring repayment to the debtor or the person who owned the money. If the money to be returned did not belong to the debtor, but to someone else, the creditor is still entitled to attempt a second time to attach money belonging to the debtor.[494]

Effect of the payment order—The payment order authorises the sheriff officer **48.45** or messenger at arms to realise the value of the money attached and, subject to the equalisation of diligence rules in the Bankruptcy Scotland Act 1985 s.37, pay the sheriff officer or messenger at arms his own fees and expenses, pay the creditor what he is due and pay the debtor any surplus remaining.[495] In so doing, the sheriff officer or messenger at arms is authorised to act as the irrevocable agent of the debtor in relation to any banking instruments, to present the instrument for payment, to sue for non-payment of the instrument, to negotiate the instrument for value or to the creditor to reduce the sum due to the creditor from the debtor or carry out any other steps in relation to the instrument that the debtor could have taken before the money attachment.[496]

The debtor may apply to the sheriff before the payment order is made, or before the money attachment takes place, for an order that the money attachment should not have effect or have only partial effect, and requiring the sheriff officer or messenger at arms to return the money to the debtor.[497] The sheriff must grant such an order if he is satisfied that the money attachment is unduly harsh,[498] but where the value of the attached money is greater than £1,000 he may release that sum to the debtor, with the balance being retained for the creditor. If at any time before a payment order is made or the money attachment ceases to have effect the sheriff is satisfied that there has been a material irregularity in the execution of the money attachment, or that the money does not belong the debtor, he must make an order declaring that the money attachment ceases to have effect and requiring the attached money to be returned to the debtor or any other interested person. This order may be made at the behest of the debtor, the creditor, the sheriff officer or messenger at arms, a third party claiming an interest or at the sheriff's own initiative, but in each case there must be a hearing first on the matter.[499]

---

[490] See the Schedule to the Act of Sederunt (Money Attachment) Rules 2009 (SSI 2009/382) for the required form.
[491] 2007 Act s.183(3).
[492] 2007 Act s.183(5).
[493] 2007 Act s.183(9).
[494] 2007 Act s.183(12)(b).
[495] 2007 Act s.184(1).
[496] 2007 Act s.184(2), (3).
[497] 2007 Act s.185(1), (2). This is known as release of money.
[498] 2007 Act s.185(3).
[499] 2007 Act s.186.

48.46 Termination of money attachment—A money attachment ceases to have effect on expiry of 14 days beginning with the date on which the report of the money attachment was made unless the creditor applies for a payment order and sends a copy of the application to the sheriff officer or messenger at arms.[500] A money attachment also ceases to have effect if the sums recoverable by the money attachment are paid to the creditor, the sheriff officer or messenger at arms or any agent of the creditor, or if the sum is tendered to any of those persons but not accepted within a reasonable time.[501] It is open to the debtor to redeem any banking instrument attached by the money attachment, but this must be done within 14 days from the date on which the report of the money attachment was made. The sheriff officer or messenger at arms, on receiving payment from the debtor for the redeemed instrument, must furnish the debtor with a receipt and inform the sheriff as soon as possible. This also terminates money attachment in respect of the banking instrument.[502] Within 14 days after the later of (a) the sheriff officer or messenger at arms making payment to the creditor under a payment order, or (b) the money attached being returned to the debtor or interested third party, the sheriff officer or messenger at arms must give a statement on the required form[503] to the sheriff detailing the bank instruments, their values, the sums paid to the creditor's account, any chargeable expenses, the sums paid to the creditor, the instruments or surplus (if any) returned to the debtor, and any balance due or by the debtor. This must be accompanied by a declaration by the sheriff officer or messenger at arms and delivered timeously by the sheriff officer or messenger at arms.[504] The sheriff must remit the statement to the auditor of court who will tax the expenses, certify the balance due or by the debtor, and make a report to the sheriff who will grant an order declaring the sum due or by the debtor, declaring the balance after any modifications following the auditor's inspection, or, where there has been a material irregularity, declaring the attachment void.[505] There are provisions for dealing with the situation where the money under money attachment is in common ownership, whereby the other owner may buy out the debtor's interest, or, where the money attachment is unduly harsh to the other owner, the sheriff may order that the money attachment should cease to have any effect.[506] A breach of the money attachment is contempt of court.[507] The creditor's expenses[508] are only recoverable, if they are not already paid, by money attachment and no other means of diligence, but if they are not recovered by the time the proceeds of the money attachment are disposed of, they cease to be chargeable against the debtor.[509] Sums recovered from the debtor by means of the money attachment are applied first against the creditor's expenses, then interest up to the date of execution of the money attachment, and finally the principal sum plus interest from the date of execution of the money attachment.[510]

---

[500] 2007 Act s.187(1).
[501] 2007 Act s.186(2), (3).
[502] 2007 Act s.188.
[503] Yet to be devised.
[504] 2007 Act s.189.
[505] 2007 Act s.190.
[506] 2007 Act s.191.
[507] 2007 Act s.193.
[508] 2007 Act Sch.3.
[509] 2007 Act s.195(2).
[510] 2007 Act s.197.

Preference secured by attachments—As with ordinary attachment, money **48.47** attachments used within 60 days prior to the constitution of the apparent insolvency of the debtor and within four months thereafter are ranked pari passu as if they had all been used of the same date.[511] Sequestration or the winding up of a company is equivalent to a completed attachment, and money attachment executed on or within 60 days prior to the date of the sequestration or winding up is ineffectual to secure any preference to the attaching creditor except for the expenses incurred by him in using the diligence.[512] In competition with other inchoate diligences it is probably determined by priority in date of execution, this being the case for other diligences. A money attachment which has not been completed before the appointment of a receiver will not be effective so as to exclude the power of the receiver to take possession of the property of the company[513] unless the attachment was executed prior to the registration of the floating charge.[514] No money attachment may be "instituted or continued" once an administrator has been appointed by a qualifying floating charge-holder (or any other person entitled to appoint an administrator in terms of Sch.B1 of the Insolvency Act 1986) except with the consent of the administrator or the court.[515] If the company has granted a qualifying floating charge under which the administrator was appointed, the administrator is entitled to dispose of or take action relating to any property, including money, subject to the floating charge.[516] The money-attaching creditor does not lose his right to repayment but he does lose his right to obtain the attached money.

IX. RESIDUAL ATTACHMENT

Purpose of residual attachment—At the time of writing this attachment is not **48.48** yet in force: it is likely to be brought into force only once land attachment is in force. On the assumption that it may be brought into force at some stage, the outlines of the legislation are here explained. Residual attachment is designed to catch those assets that are within no other category of diligence. At the time of writing there are no regulations either as to the precise description or class of the heritable and moveable property residual attachment should attach[517] or as to the detail of some of the proposed procedure for residual attachment,[518] but it is likely that the sort of assets that residual diligence should be able to catch are assets such as, for example, the right to grant a licence to use copyright material, the right to demand a fee for access to land or fishing rights, the right to charge for admission to premises, the right to charge a stud fee, or the right to demand payment for not exercising a right which the debtor is entitled to exercise. These assets must be transferable but must not be attachable by or exempt from any other diligence.[519] They specifically do not include the right of a debtor as tenant of a dwelling-house which is the debtor's sole or main residence or the right of a debtor as the tenant

---

[511] 1985 Act Sch.7 para.24.
[512] 1985 Act s.37(5); Insolvency Act 1986 s.185.
[513] Insolvency Act 1986 s.55(3); *Lord Advocate v Royal Bank of Scotland*, 1977 S.C. 155.
[514] *Iona Hotels Ltd (In Receivership), Petitioners*, 1991 S.L.T. 11.
[515] Insolvency Act 1986 Sch.B1 para.43(6).
[516] Insolvency Act 1986 Sch.B1 para.70.
[517] 2007 Act s.129(2).
[518] 2007 Act s.129(7), (8).
[519] 2007 Act s.129(3).

of a croft.[520] Residual attachment is not available on the dependence of an action, since it is only available in execution.[521] What follows is a synopsis of the main statutory provisions in the absence at this stage of any detailed legislation.

48.49 **Application for residual attachment order**—A residual attachment order is competent to enforce payment of a debt if the debt is constituted by decree or an instrument of debt,[522] the debtor has been charged to pay the debt, the period of the *induciae* of the charge has expired without payment having been made,[523] and, where the debtor is an individual, the creditor has provided the debtor with a debt advice and information package no earlier than 12 weeks before executing the residual attachment.[524] The application itself must be in a form yet to be devised, must specify the property it will attach, must state how the value of the property will be realised, and that doing so would result in payment of the debt for which the charge was made, together with interest and expenses. The application must be intimated to the debtor and any other person having an interest.[525] Those persons then have 14 days from the date of intimation in which to lodge objections to the application. Once intimation has taken place, the debtor must not dispose of, burden, license, or enter into an agreement to carry out those acts, within the period from the date of intimation until the day of the court order granting the application or dismissing the application. Any disposition, burden or licence so granted is void and may render the debtor or any other person with an interest in contempt of court.[526]

The court will not grant a residual attachment order without giving an opportunity to those who have lodged objections to be heard in court. On hearing the objections, the court may grant the order, or grant any other order it sees fit.[527] The court may also provide in the order such other requirements as may be necessary to make the residual attachment order of practical effect.[528] The order must be intimated to the debtor and anyone else with an interest.[529]

The order may instead be refused if the property is not capable of being attached by the order, if it would not result in the value of the property being realised, or even if it were realised it would still not result in the sum recoverable by the creditor from the debtor being paid off or reduced.[530] If the order is granted, the creditor must serve on the debtor a schedule or residual attachment on the debtor and anyone else with an interest.[531] The residual attachment order is created at the beginning of the day after the day the schedule is served on the debtor.[532] The residual attachment order confers on the creditor a right in security over the attached property and secures the sum for which the charge was made, together with interest and expenses.[533]

---

[520] 2007 Act s.129(4).
[521] 2007 Act s.130.
[522] For the definition of a decree or an instrument of debt, see s.221. The definition includes a summary warrant.
[523] 14 days within the United Kingdom, 28 days otherwise. See 1987 Act s.90(3).
[524] 2007 Act s.130(1).
[525] 2007 Act s.130.
[526] 2007 Act s.131.
[527] 2007 Act s.132(2).
[528] 2007 Act s.132(5).
[529] 2007 Act s.132(3).
[530] 2007 Act s.132(4).
[531] 2007 Act s.133. The form of the schedule is yet to be devised.
[532] 2007 Act s.134(1).
[533] 2007 Act s.134(2), (3).

Satisfaction orders—It is then open to the creditor to apply for a satisfaction **48.50**
order using the required form, specifying the attached property, how it is to be
realised, and how doing so would result in payment of the sum recoverable by the
residual attachment being paid off or reduced. The application must be intimated
to the debtor and anyone else with an interest. These persons then have 14 days in
which to object to the application.[534] At the hearing for the satisfaction order, the
court may not make any order without giving those objecting to the satisfaction
order the opportunity to be heard.[535] If the court is satisfied that the application is
in order, it will grant the satisfaction order or any other order it sees fit.[536] If
granted, the satisfaction order must be intimated to the debtor and anyone else the
court specifies.[537] The order may permit the creditor to sell the property, transfer
the ownership of the property to the creditor, transfer the income derived from the
property to the creditor, or permit the creditor to "lease or license" the property.[538]
If the court authorises the sale of property, it must appoint a suitably qualified
person willing to execute the order to sell the property, and specify the period
within which it must be sold. The court may also appoint a suitably qualified
person to value the property.[539] The court may refuse the order if the residual
attachment is invalid, if the residual attachment has ceased to have effect, if even
were the order made it would not result in the value of the property being realised,
or if, even were the value realised, the sum recoverable by the residual attachment
would not be paid off or reduced.[540] The court may, if it is of the view that the
residual attachment order would be unduly harsh to the debtor or anyone else with
an interest, make a satisfaction order but suspend its effect for a year, or may
refuse the application.

Where a satisfaction order is made, the creditor must intimate as much to the
debtor and anyone else required by the court, including, where relevant, the person
appointed to sell the property. Where the order is refused, the court must intimate
as much to the debtor and anyone else having an interest.[541] Where the order is
refused on the grounds that the order would not result in the value being realised
or the sum recoverable being paid off or reduced, the residual attachment remains
in place, even if the satisfaction order is not available, and the creditor may try
again at a later date.[542] The residual attachment ceases to be of effect where the
full sum recoverable by the residual attachment is either paid to the creditor, the
person appointed to sell the property, a sheriff officer, messenger at arms, or any
other agent of the creditor. This does not apply unless the sum is paid or tendered
before a contract for the sale of attached property (following the satisfaction
order) is concluded or in any other case, the attached property is otherwise
disposed of.[543]

---

[534] 2007 Act s.135.
[535] 2007 Act s.136(1).
[536] 2007 Act s.136(2).
[537] 2007 Act s.136(3).
[538] It is submitted that the legislation meant to say that the creditor may let, or grant licences over,
the property, rather than becoming a tenant of the property or holding it on a licence.
[539] 2007 Act s.136(4), (5).
[540] 2007 Act s.136(6), (7).
[541] 2007 Act s.137.
[542] 2007 Act s.138.
[543] 2007 Act s.139.

48.51 Recall of residual attachment—The debtor or anyone else with an interest may apply to have the residual attachment recalled or restricted.[544] If the court is satisfied that the residual attachment is invalid, was executed incompetently or irregularly or has ceased to have effect, the residual attachment may be recalled.[545] It may also be restricted if more property is subject to the attachment than is necessary, and it is reasonable to do so.[546] Residual attachment endures for a period of five years beginning with the day the schedule of the residual attachment was served on the debtor. It may be extended if necessary.[547] Where a creditor has taken steps to obtain a residual attachment order against a debtor, but has not served the schedule of residual attachment on the debtor before his death, any steps so taken cease to have effect and any residual attachment order is void on his death. But where a residual attachment order is created before the death of the debtor, the order continues to have effect in relation to the attached property after his death.[548] The expenses of residual attachment are payable by the debtor, and may be recovered by residual attachment but by no other form of diligence. Where they are not recovered by the time the residual attachment is completed, the expenses cease to be recoverable.[549] Sums recovered from the debtor by means of the residual attachment are applied first against the creditor's expenses, then interest up to the date of execution of the residual attachment, and finally the principal sum plus interest from the date of execution of the residual attachment.[550]

48.52 Preference secured by residual attachment—This matter is not dealt with in the existing legislation and ideally would be clarified in subordinate legislation. It is suggested that in the absence of subordinate legislation it could be set aside on the same basis as attachment or arrestment.

48.53 Debt arrangement programmes—In order to give debtors, in receipt of a regular income, some means other than a protected trust deed of repaying their creditors, the 2002 Act set up the Debt Arrangement Scheme.[551] This enables a debtor to set up, in consultation with a money adviser, a debt payment programme, which when once approved, requires the debtor to transfer a proportion of his income to a payments distributor who each week or month divides up that proportion between his various creditors. Once a debtor has entered a debt payment programme it is not competent for a creditor to serve a charge upon him,[552] and for this reason a debt payment programme is sometimes known, along with sequestration, as a "diligence stopper", since once the programme is running, and, indeed while it is being applied for, creditors may not enforce payment by diligence.[553] In particular, a debt payment programme enables interest, fees, penalties and other charges to be written off in accordance with the relevant rules.[554]

---

[544] 2007 Act s.140(1). The form for this is yet to be devised.
[545] 2007 Act s.140(3).
[546] 2007 Act s.140(4).
[547] 2007 Act s.141.
[548] 2007 Act s.142.
[549] 2007 Act s.143.
[550] 2007 Act s.197.
[551] See the helpful website at *http://dasscotland.gov.uk/home* [Accessed July 22, 2012]. For the current applicable rules, see the Debt Arrangement Scheme (Scotland) Regulations 2011 (SSI 2011/141).
[552] 2002 Act s.4(2)(a).
[553] 2002 Act s.4(2)(b).
[554] The Debt Arrangement Scheme (Interest, Fees, Penalties and Other Charges) (Scotland) Regulations 2011 (SSI 2011/238).

FURTHER READING

Cowan, S., *Scottish Debt Recovery—a practical guide* (Edinburgh: W. Green, 2011).

Fordyce, J., "Diligence on the dependence—a return to the old regime?", 2009 S.L.T. 13, 71–74.

Gretton, G.L., *The Law of Inhibition and Adjudication*, 2nd edn (Edinburgh: W. Green, 1996).

Maher, G., *The Law and Practice of Diligence*, 2nd edn (London: Bloomsbury Professional, 2011).

Stewart, J.G., *A Treatise on the Law of Diligence* (Edinburgh: W. Green, 1898).

Stewart, W., "Reconsidering economic loss arising out of Breach of Arrestment", 2009 Jur. Rev. 3.

CHAPTER 49

BANKRUPTCY

The law relating to bankruptcy and personal insolvency at present is governed by **49.01** the Bankruptcy (Scotland) Act 1985 (the "1985 Act") as substantially amended by the Bankruptcy and Diligence etc. (Scotland) Act 2007.[1] At the time of writing a new consolidated Bankruptcy Bill is being considered.[2] The practicalities of sequestration, for the benefit of debtors and practitioners alike, are well explained on the website of the Accountant in Bankruptcy.[3] The chief advantage of being made bankrupt is that once this has been formally established, creditors cannot effect any further diligence against the bankrupt, and responsibility for sorting out the bankrupt's financial difficulties passes to his trustee (as explained in the next paragraph). Normally after a one year period of bankruptcy, the bankrupt may start afresh in business.

In Scotland, "bankruptcy" has no technical meaning. Its proper term in Scotland is "sequestration" and the person generally known elsewhere as the "bankrupt" is known in Scotland as the "debtor", and will be referred to by this term hereafter. Debtors for the purposes of the 1985 Act include individuals, partnerships, trusts, certain bodies corporate not registered under the Companies Acts, clubs and other unincorporated associations, Scottish charitable incorporated organisations and limited partnerships, but do not include registered companies, unregistered companies for which sequestration is unavailable, or limited liability partnerships.[4] The person who looks after a debtor's affairs during his period of sequestration is known as the "trustee in sequestration". The collective body of the debtor's assets is known as the "trust estate". A "trust deed for creditors" arises when some or all of the debtor's assets are transferred into a trust, whose trustee administers the income therefrom for the benefit of the debtor's creditors. Under certain circumstances the trust deed may be a "protected trust deed", as explained at the end of this chapter.

Insolvency—Insolvency may mean that at a particular date the debtor's assets, if **49.02** realised, are less than his liabilities, although he may be able to meet all debts which are presented for payment; or it may mean the debtor's inability to pay his debts as they fall due, even though when his assets are realised, they may exceed his liabilities.

The first of these two meanings is known as absolute insolvency, sometimes known as the balance sheet test, and may bar the insolvent debtor from entering into or remaining in a contract. For example, it may affect the rights and

---

[1] Throughout this chapter references to the Bankruptcy (Scotland) Act 1985 (c.66) (the "1985 Act") will be to the Act as amended by the Bankruptcy and Diligence etc. (Scotland) Act 2007 except where specifically indicated otherwise.

[2] For further details, see *http://www.scotlawcom.gov.uk/news/making-bankruptcy-law-accessible/* [Accessed July 23, 2012].

[3] *http://www.aib.gov.uk/* [Accessed July 23, 2012].

[4] 1985 Act s.73(1).

obligations of parties to certain contracts such as those of sale, loan, employment or partnership which may according to their terms be altered or terminated once insolvency has occurred. An unpaid seller may exercise the right of stoppage in transit against a buyer who has become insolvent,[5] and insolvency may give rise to an irritancy under a lease.[6] Where an executor of a deceased's estate knows or ought to have known that the estate is absolutely insolvent and should within a reasonable period of time be sequestrated or have a judicial factor appointed over it, his intromissions will be deemed to be intromissions without title and he may therefore be liable for them.[7]

The second of these meanings is now known as "apparent insolvency", sometimes known as the cash flow test. Apparent insolvency is one of the grounds under which a debtor may be sequestrated.[8]

As a general rule, apparent insolvency does not affect the capacity or the rights and duties of the debtor or terminate any legal relations which may have arisen from a contract with him. In itself it is not a bar to a debtor pursuing or defending an action, although he may in certain cases be required to find caution for expenses. It does not necessarily prevent a debtor from entering into contracts or from continuing with his business with the purpose and intention of recovering his commercial position.[9]

49.03 **Apparent insolvency**—Apparent insolvency is constituted[10] whenever (a) the debtor's estate is sequestrated, or he is adjudged bankrupt in England or Wales or Northern Ireland; or (b) not being a person whose property is for the time being affected by a restraint order[11] or subject to a confiscation, or charging,[12] order, he gives written notice to his creditors that he has ceased to pay his debts in the ordinary course of business; (c) he becomes subject to main proceedings in a Member State other than the United Kingdom[13]; (d) any of the following circumstances occurs, namely, (i) he grants a trust deed for the benefit of his creditors, (ii) a charge for payment is served on him followed by the expiry of the days of charge without payment, (iii) a decree of adjudication of any part of his estate is granted, (iv) a debt payment programme under the Debt Arrangement and Attachment (Scotland) Act 2002 is revoked, unless it is shown that in respect of (i) to (iv) the debtor was able and willing to pay his debts as they became due or that but for his property being affected by a restraint order or subject to a confiscation, or charging, order he would be able to do so; (e) a creditor in respect of a liquid[14] debt of not less than £3,000[15] has served on the debtor personally a demand requiring him

---

[5] Sale of Goods Act 1979 s.44.

[6] See paras 35.23 and 35.26, above.

[7] 1985 Act s.8(4).

[8] 1985 Act s.5.

[9] *Ehrenbacher & Co v Kennedy* (1874) 1 R. 1131.

[10] See the full definition of "apparent insolvency" at 1985 Act s.7.

[11] A restraint order or compensation order means a restraint order or confiscation order made under Pts 2, 3 or 4 of the Proceeds of Crime Act 2002.

[12] A charging order has the meaning assigned by s.78(2) of the Criminal Justice Act 1988 or by s.27(2) of the Drug Trafficking Act 1994.

[13] Cross Border Insolvency Regulations 2006 (SI 2006/1030) Sch.3 Pt 1; this means proceedings opened in accordance with art.3(1) of the Council regulation (EC) No 1346/2000 of 29 May 2000 on insolvency proceedings ("EC Insolvency Regulations") and falling within the definition of insolvency proceedings in art.2(a) of the EC Insolvency Regulations.

[14] The term "liquid debt" does not include a sum payable under a confiscation order (s.7(1)(d)).

[15] This figure may be increased at a later date.

either to pay the debt or to find security for its payment[16] and within three weeks the debtor has not either complied with the demand or intimated to the creditor by recorded delivery to the court that he denies that there is a debt or that the sum claimed is immediately payable. The condition of apparent insolvency continues until, if he has been sequestrated or adjudged bankrupt, he is discharged, and in other cases until he becomes able to pay his debts and pays them as they become due[17] or until main proceedings have ended.[18] A partnership may be constituted as apparently insolvent if any of the partners of that partnership is apparently insolvent for a debt of the partnership, and likewise an unincorporated body may be constituted apparently insolvent if a person representing the body, or a person holding property for the body, is apparently insolvent for a debt of that body.[19]

Apparent insolvency is one of the preconditions before a petition for a debtor's sequestration may be presented by a creditor or a debtor application made by the debtor.[20] Apparent insolvency is relevant for the timing of a petition for sequestration by a qualified creditor of a living debtor's estate or of a deceased debtor's estate, since in the former case the apparent insolvency must have been constituted within four months before the presentation of the petition,[21] and in the latter case, where the apparent insolvency was constituted within four months before the debtor's death, the presentation may be at any time.[22]

Effect of apparent insolvency on diligence—Apparent insolvency, in addition **49.04** to providing the basis for a petition for sequestration by a creditor or a debtor application for sequestration, has the effect of equalising diligence, thereby denying the claims of creditors effecting diligence priority over the claims of creditors who had not effected diligence, except to the extent of their expenses. Arrestments and attachments[23] executed within 60 days prior to the constitution of apparent insolvency, and within four months thereafter, rank pari passu as if they had all been executed on the same date; and any creditor judicially producing in a process relative to the subject of such arrestment or attachment liquid grounds of debt or decree of payment, is entitled to rank as if he too had executed an arrestment or an attachment.[24] This means that if sequestration occurs within four months after apparent insolvency any arrester or attacher within the period of 60 days before or four months after apparent insolvency ranks pari passu with all the other creditors.[25] Diligence effected before the period of 60 days before

---

[16] For the current form of the demand see Bankruptcy (Scotland) Regulations 1985 (SI 1985/1925) Form 1; for the effect of a failure to serve a valid statutory demand see *Lord Advocate v Thomson*, 1995 S.L.T. 56.

[17] 1985 Act s.7(2).

[18] 1985 Act s.7(2)(c).

[19] 1985 Act s.7(3).

[20] 1985 Act s.5(2B)(c)(i).

[21] 1985 Act s.8(1)(b).

[22] 1985 Act s.8(3)(b).

[23] Including money attachment.

[24] 1985 Act Sch.7 para.24; *Clark v Hinde, Milne & Co* (1884) 12 R. 347. This does not apply to diligence against earnings: 1985 Act Sch.7 para.24(8). Note that this provision only applies to diligence in the context of apparent insolvency: diligence in the context of sequestration (which is in practice much more common) is dealt with under s.37.

[25] *Stewart v Jarvie*, 1938 S.C. 309; in this case an arrestment took place about 45 days before apparent insolvency. Sequestration took place six weeks after apparent insolvency. Because sequestration was still within the four-month period after apparent insolvency, equalisation of diligence applied to the arrestment since the arrestment was within the 60-day period prior to apparent insolvency. The arresting creditor thus had to be treated pari passu with all the other creditors and obtained no priority over those other creditors.

apparent insolvency remains unaffected by equalisation and the creditor is entitled to retain such assets of the debtor's as he has already lawfully obtained.[26]

49.05 **Sequestration and its administration**—The 1985 Act makes provision for the sequestration of the estates of persons who are subject to the jurisdiction of the Courts of Scotland, and for the administration of bankruptcy generally. The administration of sequestration and personal insolvency is subject to the supervision of the Accountant in Bankruptcy,[27] whose duties consist of the supervision of the performance by trustees and commissioners of their functions under the 1985 Act and the maintenance and publication of records and statistics relating to insolvencies. In particular, following the 2007 Act the Accountant in Bankruptcy determines debtor applications for awards of sequestration.[28] In many cases, and in particular in debtor applications, the trustee in sequestration will be the Accountant in Bankruptcy, who either, through officials,[29] acts as the actual trustee in the sequestration, or delegates the task to one of a panel of insolvency practitioners who act as trustees on behalf of the Accountant in Bankruptcy.[30] It is nevertheless open to a debtor in a debtor application to the Accountant in Bankruptcy, or a creditor or trustee acting under a trust deed petitioning the sheriff, to nominate a particular insolvency practitioner other than the Accountant in Bankruptcy to be the debtor's trustee, and provided the Accountant in Bankruptcy is satisfied with that insolvency practitioner, he may be appointed as trustee to that debtor.[31] If no specific trustee is nominated, the Accountant in Bankruptcy will be the trustee.[32] Exceptionally, an interim trustee may be appointed by the sheriff prior to sequestration on a petition by a creditor, or a trustee acting under a trust deed, if the debtor consents to such interim appointment or if any creditor or the trustee acting under the trust deed shows cause.[33] Where the interim trustee appointed is not the Accountant in Bankruptcy, the interim trustee's functions are to safeguard the debtor's estate pending the determination of the petition for sequestration.[34] Following the grant of the award of sequestration, the interim trustee, if not already the Accountant in Bankruptcy, may be appointed the trustee, and, if so, he must be a qualified insolvency practitioner and be willing to be the trustee.[35] The functions of the trustee, in whom the whole of the debtor's estate vests as at the date of sequestration,[36] are to recover, manage and realise the debtor's estate and to distribute it among the debtor's creditors according to their entitlements. He must also make his own inquiries as to the reasons for the debtor's insolvency and the state of his liabilities and assets, and is required to have regard to advice offered to him by commissioners, if any, in performing his functions under the Act. The general function of commissioners, if elected, is

---

[26] For the position of equalisation of diligence following sequestration, as opposed to apparent insolvency, see 1985 Act s.37 and para.49.29.

[27] 1985 Act s.1A. The Accountant in Bankruptcy maintains the public Register of Insolvencies.

[28] 1985 Act s.1A(1)(aa).

[29] 1985 Act s.1B(1).

[30] 1985 Act s.1B(2).

[31] 1985 Act s.2(1A).

[32] 1985 Act s.2(1B), (2).

[33] 1985 Act s.2(5). There is no provision for an interim trustee in a debtor application.

[34] 1985 Act s.2(6A).

[35] 1985 Act s.2(2A), (2B), (2C) and (3). It is permissible to appoint someone other than the interim trustee to be the trustee.

[36] 1985 Act s.31.

to supervise the intromissions of the trustee with the sequestrated estate.[37] The creditors may if they wish elect one or more but not more than five commissioners from among the creditors or their mandatories at the statutory meeting or at any subsequent meeting of creditors, but the election of commissioners by them is not compulsory.[38]

Methods of sequestration 1: Debtor applications for living debtors—There **49.06** are two main methods of sequestrating a debtor. The first method, introduced by the 2007 Act, and in respect of living debtors only, is a debtor application for sequestration to the Accountant in Bankruptcy,[39] who, since the implementation of the 2007 Act, has been authorised to determine such awards of sequestration.[40] The second method is by petition to the sheriff and is discussed shortly. Debtor applications come in three forms: the standard debtor application[41]; a low income low asset debtor application[42]; and the certification debtor application.[43]

A standard debtor application may be made by the debtor himself using a "debtor application pack"[44] provided the following conditions are satisfied: (a) the total amount of his debts (including interest) at the date of the petition is not less than £1,500; (b) an award of sequestration has not been made against the debtor in the preceding five years; and either (c) the debtor is apparently insolvent or is unable to pay his debts, or (d) he has granted a trust deed and the trustee has been unable to have that trust deed protected by reason of the requisite majority of creditors objecting to the trust deed and not wishing to accede to it[45]; for the purposes of these latter two conditions, neither the granting of a trust deed nor giving of notice to creditors that he has ceased to pay debts constitutes apparent insolvency.[46]

A low income low asset application (sometimes known as a LILA application) is the same as a standard debtor application except that instead of (c) or (d) above applying, the debtor satisfies the requirements of s.5A of the 1985 Act. These requirements are that the debtor's weekly income (if any) on the date the debtor application is made does not exceed 40 times the national minimum wage from time to time, the debtor does not own any land, and that the total value of the debtor's assets (leaving out of account any liabilities) on the date the debtor application is made does not exceed £10,000, with no one asset being worth more than £1,000.[47]

A certification debtor application merely requires that the debtor obtains a certificate from an insolvency practitioner or other authorised official[48] certifying

---

[37] 1985 Act ss.4, 30; see also para.49.19, below.

[38] 1985 Act s.30.

[39] 1985 Act s.5(2)(a).

[40] 1985 Act s.1A(1)(aa).

[41] 1985 Act s.5(2).

[42] 1985 Act s.5A.

[43] 1985 Act s.5(2B)(c)(ib).

[44] This is available from the website of the Accountant in Bankruptcy. The fee is £100.

[45] The trust deed will be deemed to be acceded to by the notified creditors, unless within the relevant period the trustee has received notification in writing from a majority in number or not less than one third in value of those creditors that they object to the trust deed (the Protected Trust Deed (Scotland) Regulations 2008 (SSI 2008/143) reg.9(2).

[46] 1985 Act s.5(2A), (2B), Sch.5 para.5.

[47] The Bankruptcy (Scotland) Act 1985 (Low Income, Low Asset Debtors etc.) Regulations 2008 (SSI 2008/81).

[48] For example, money advisers in Citizens Advice Bureaux. See the Bankruptcy (Certificate for Sequestration) (Scotland) Regulations 2010 (SSI 2010/397) reg.3(1)(b).

that the debtor has had the significance of his sequestration explained to him and that he is unable to pay his debts as they fall due. The certificate is valid for 30 days and must be sent to the Accountant in Bankruptcy within that period.[49]

Except in the case of the certification debtor application, the debtor must send a statement of his assets and liabilities to the Accountant in Bankruptcy along with his application[50] and failure to do this without a reasonable excuse will result in criminal penalties.[51] A debtor application may be made at any time[52] and the making of an application interrupts the periods of prescription or limitations of the debtor's debts.[53] Where a debtor application is made, the debtor must state in the application whether or not the debtor's centre of main interests is situated in the United Kingdom or in another Member State and whether or not the debtor possesses an establishment in the United Kingdom or in any other Member State. If, to the debtor's knowledge, there is a Member State liquidator appointed in main proceedings in relation to the debtor, the debtor must send a copy of the debtor application to that Member State liquidator.[54]

49.07 **Methods of sequestration 2: Petitions to the sheriff**—The second method of sequestration is by petition to the sheriff court.[55] Only the sheriff court now has jurisdiction in petitions for sequestration petitions.[56] The petitioner must send copies of the petition to the Accountant in Bankruptcy.[57] A petition for the sequestration of a debtor may be presented by (a) one or more qualified creditors owed not less than £3,000 by the debtor, but in this case there is the additional requirement that the debtor must be apparently insolvent,[58] (b) a temporary administrator,[59] (c) a Member State liquidator appointed in main proceedings,[60] or (d) the trustee appointed under a voluntary trust deed granted by or on behalf of the debtor for the benefit of his creditors but only if the debtor has failed to comply with his obligations under the trust deed or with the trustee's reasonable instructions or requirements or if the trustee avers that it would be in the best interests of the creditors that an award of sequestration be made.[61] No petition may be presented by a qualified creditor unless the qualified creditor has previously provided the debtor with a debt advice and information package.[62] In the case of a deceased debtor, those who may petition for the sequestration of his estate are his executor, or a person entitled to be appointed his executor, one or more qualified creditors, a temporary administrator, a Member State liquidator appointed in main proceedings or the trustee acting under his trust deed.[63] Apparent insolvency

---

[49] The Bankruptcy (Certificate for Sequestration) (Scotland) Regulations 2010 (SSI 2010/397).

[50] 1985 Act s.5(6A).

[51] 1985 Act s.5(8), (9).

[52] 1985 Act s.8A(1).

[53] 1985 Act s.8A(3). See also the Prescription and Limitation (Scotland) Act 1973 s.9(1)(b).

[54] 1985 Act s.6B.

[55] For forms of petition see the Act of Sederunt (Sheriff Court Bankruptcy Rules) 1996 (SI 1996/2507) Forms 1–4.

[56] 1985 Act s.9.

[57] 1985 Act s.5(6).

[58] 1985 Act s.5(2)(b)(i). A single petition to sequestrate spouses who are not in partnership is not competent: *Campbell v Dunbar*, 1989 S.L.T. (Sh. Ct) 29.

[59] 1985 Act s.5(2)(b)(ii). A temporary administrator is one appointed under art.38 of the EC Insolvency Regulations.

[60] 1985 Act s.5(2)(b)(iii).

[61] 1985 Act s.5(2)(b)(iv) and (2C).

[62] 1985 Act s.5(2D).

[63] 1985 Act s.5(3).

is not required in any case where the debtor is deceased, but the existence or absence of apparent insolvency is relevant to the time limits within which a creditor's application may be made.[64] A petition at the instance of creditors may be presented during the debtor's lifetime only if the apparent insolvency founded on in the petition was constituted within four months before the petition is presented.[65] Where the debtor is deceased his creditors may present the petition at any time if the apparent insolvency of the debtor was constituted within four months before his death, but in any other case a petition by them may not be presented earlier than six months after the debtor's death.[66] The presentation of a petition for sequestration has the effect of interrupting the prescription of the debt of those creditors who petition.[67] In all cases a petitioning creditor or concurring creditor must produce an oath made by him or on his behalf in the prescribed form and an account or voucher which constitutes prima facie evidence of the debt,[68] and a petitioning creditor must in addition produce such evidence as is available to him to show the apparent insolvency of the debtor.[69] There are special provisions to take account of the situation where either the debtor dies[70] or the creditor dies.[71]

Other estates which may be sequestrated—In addition to the estates of living or **49.08** deceased individuals, the estates belonging to or held for or jointly by the members of various other entities may be sequestrated. These are a trust in respect of debts incurred by it,[72] a partnership including a dissolved partnership,[73] a body corporate or unincorporated body but not a company incorporated under the Companies Acts,[74] a Scottish charitable incorporated organisation,[75] and a limited partnership including a dissolved partnership within the meaning of the Limited Partnerships Act 1907.[76] It is not competent, however, to sequestrate an entity in respect of which an enactment provides either expressly or by implication that sequestration is incompetent,[77] for example registered companies,[78] friendly societies[79] and insurance companies.[80] A trust estate may be sequestrated by debtor application made by a majority of the trustees to act on behalf of the body, with the concurrence of a qualified creditor or qualified creditors; or it may

---

[64] 1985 Act s.8(3).

[65] 1985 Act s.8(1)(b); see *Burgh of Millport, Petitioners*, 1974 S.L.T. (Notes) 23.

[66] 1985 Act s.8(3)(b).

[67] 1985 Act s.8(5); see also Prescription and Limitation (Scotland) Act 1973 s.9(1)(b).

[68] 1985 Act s.11(1), (5); *Ballantyne v Barr* (1867) 5 M. 330; *Blair v North British and Mercantile Insurance Co* (1889) 16 R. 325; *Lord Advocate v Thomson*, 1995 S.L.T. 56; *Clydesdale Bank Plc v Grantly Developments*, 2000 S.L.T. 1369. Failure in this regard may be remedied by an application under s.63: *Bell v McMillan (No.1)*, 1999 S.L.T. 947. If the debt has been assigned, the evidence of assignation must be produced too: *Liandu v Go Debt Ltd*, 2010 G.W.D. 33–674.

[69] 1985 Act s.11(5); *Drummond v Clunas Tiles & Mosaics Ltd*, 1909 S.C. 1049.

[70] 1985 Act s.5(7), (7A).

[71] 1985 Act s.5(8), (8A).

[72] 1985 Act s.6(1)(a).

[73] *Clydesdale Bank Plc v Grantly Developments*, 2000 S.L.T. 1369.

[74] 1985 Act s.6(1)(c). Limited liability partnerships are, like registered companies, wound up under the Insolvency Act 1986 (Limited Liability Partnership Act 2000 s.14) and therefore cannot be sequestrated.

[75] The Scottish Charitable Incorporated Organisations (Removal from Register and Dissolution) Regulations 2011 (SSI 2011/237).

[76] 1985 Act s.6(1)(d), (2).

[77] 1985 Act s.6(2).

[78] 1985 Act s.6(2)(a).

[79] Friendly Societies Act 1992 s.19.

[80] Insurance Companies Act 1982 s.55.

be sequestrated on the petition of a temporary administrator, a Member State liquidator appointed in main proceedings, or a qualified creditor or qualified creditors, if the trustees (in their capacity as trustees) are apparently insolvent.[81] The estate of a partnership may be sequestrated by debtor application by the partnership with the concurrence of a qualified creditor or qualified creditors; or it may be sequestrated on the petition of a temporary administrator, a Member State liquidator appointed in main proceedings, or a qualified creditor or qualified creditors, if the partnership is apparently insolvent.[82] Where a qualified creditor petitions for the sequestration of the estate of an apparently insolvent partnership, the petition may be combined with a petition for the sequestration of the estate of any partner who is also apparently insolvent,[83] although a single award of sequestration is inappropriate.[84] The estate of a body corporate or unincorporated body may be sequestrated by debtor application by someone with the authority to act on behalf of the body, with the concurrence of a qualified creditor or qualified creditors; or it may be sequestrated on the petition of a temporary administrator, a Member State liquidator appointed in main proceedings, or a qualified creditor or qualified creditors, if the body is apparently insolvent.[85] A petitioner for sequestration of a debtor's estate must, insofar as it is within the petitioner's knowledge, state in the petition whether or not the debtor's centre of main interests is situated in the United Kingdom or in another Member State, and whether or not the debtor possesses an establishment in the United Kingdom or in any other Member State. If, to the petitioner's knowledge, there is a Member State liquidator appointed in main proceedings in relation to the debtor, the petitioner must send a copy of the petition to that Member State liquidator.[86] The petitioner must send a copy of the petition to the Accountant in Bankruptcy[87] and there are provisions to deal with the situation of the debtor or a creditor dying.[88]

49.09 Jurisdiction—The Accountant in Bankruptcy has jurisdiction in respect of a debtor application for the sequestration of the estate of a living debtor throughout Scotland if the debtor had an established place of business in Scotland or was constituted or was habitually resident there at the relevant time.[89] Where there is a petition for the sequestration of an estate of a living or deceased debtor, the sheriff will have jurisdiction if the debtor had an established place of business in the sheriffdom or was habitually resident there at the relevant time.[90] In both cases the relevant time for these purposes is any time within the year immediately preceding the date of presentation of the petition or the date of death, as the case may be.[91] In the case of a debtor application for the sequestration of other entities, the requirements are that the entity had an established place of business in Scotland at the relevant time, or that the entity was constituted or formed under Scots law and at any time carried on business in Scotland.[92] In the case of a petition for

---

[81] 1985 Act s.6(3).
[82] 1985 Act s.6(4).
[83] 1985 Act s.6(5).
[84] *Royal Bank of Scotland v J & J Messenger*, 1991 S.L.T. 492.
[85] 1985 Act s.6(6).
[86] 1985 Act s.6A.
[87] 1985 Act s.6(8).
[88] 1985 Act s.6(8).
[89] 1985 Act s.9(1A).
[90] 1985 Act s.9(1).
[91] 1985 Act s.9(5).
[92] 1985 Act s.9(2A); see the definition of "business" in s.73(1).

sequestration of other entities, the requirements are that they had an established place of business in the sheriffdom at the relevant time, or that the entity was constituted or formed under Scots law and at any time carried on business in the sheriffdom.[93] For both debtor applications and petitions for sequestrations of an entity, the habitual residence requirement is not necessary. Should any proceedings either relating to a debtor application or the sequestration of a debtor's estate following a debtor application need to come before a sheriff, the appropriate sheriff would be the sheriff within whose jurisdiction a petition for the debtor's sequestration could have been made.[94] Provision is made for the possibility that other insolvency proceedings[95] are already before a court or the Accountant in Bankruptcy for sequestration or an analogous remedy[96] affecting the same debtor or his estate. It is the duty of the petitioner promptly to bring the existence of such proceedings of which he is aware to the sheriff court where the petition was raised,[97] which has power to take appropriate steps to deal with the situation. Likewise, it is the duty of the debtor or any creditor concurring in a debtor application promptly to bring the existence of such proceedings to the Accountant in Bankruptcy.[98] In the case of a petition, the sheriff or indeed the Court of Session may then, on his or its own motion, allow the petition or application to proceed, or may sist or dismiss it[99]; in the case of a debtor application, the Accountant in Bankruptcy may determine or dismiss the application.[100] An order made by a court in any part of the United Kingdom in the exercise of jurisdiction in relation to insolvency law is enforceable in any other part of the United Kingdom as if it were made by a court exercising the corresponding jurisdiction there, and courts having jurisdiction in relation to insolvency law in any part of the United Kingdom are required to assist the courts having jurisdiction in any other part of the United Kingdom, the Channel Islands or the Isle of Man, or any country or territory designated by statutory instrument.[101]

Award of sequestration—Where a debtor application is presented to the **49.10** Accountant in Bankruptcy, sequestration must be awarded forthwith if the Accountant in Bankruptcy is satisfied that the application has been presented in accordance with the provisions of the Act.[102] Where a petition to the sheriff court is by a creditor or by a trustee acting under a trust deed, the court will grant an order for warrant to cite the debtor to appear before the court to show cause why sequestration should not be awarded.[103] The warrant should require appearance by the debtor on a specified date not less than six or more than 14 days after the date

---

[93] 1985 Act s.9(2); see the definition of "business" in s.73(1).

[94] 1985 Act s.9(3A).

[95] Under 1985 Act s.10(2)(a)–(d). This covers sequestrations, debtor applications, petitions for judicial factors, winding up of a registered or unregistered company or the bankruptcy or sequestration of an individual carrying on a regulated activity in terms of the Financial Services and Markets Act 2000.

[96] An analogous remedy is a bankruptcy order, individual voluntary arrangement or an administration order in England and Wales, and analogous remedies in Northern Ireland (s.10(7)).

[97] 1985 Act s.10(3)(a).

[98] 1985 Act s.10(3)(b).

[99] 1985 Act s.10A(1), (2).

[100] 1985 Act s.10A(4), (6).

[101] Insolvency Act 1986 s.426; the Co-operation of Insolvency Courts (Designation of Relevant Countries and Territories) Order 1986 (SI 1986/2123); the Co-operation of Insolvency Courts (Designation of Relevant Countries) Order 1996 (SI 1996/253); the Co-operation of Insolvency Courts (Designation of Relevant Country) Order 1998 (SI 1998/2766).

[102] See para.49.06, above.

[103] 1985 Act s.12(2).

of citation.[104] On the expiry of the *induciae*, if the court is satisfied that there has been proper citation of the debtor, that the petition has been presented in accordance with the provisions of the Act, that a copy of the petition has been sent to the Accountant of Bankruptcy,[105] that the requirements as to apparent insolvency are satisfied (or, in the case of a petition by a trustee under a trust deed, that his averments as to the debtor's conduct or the interests of creditors are true) sequestration must be awarded forthwith[106] unless cause is shown why it cannot competently be awarded[107] or the debtor forthwith pays or satisfies, or produces written evidence of payment or satisfaction of, or gives or shows that there is sufficient security for the payment of the debt in respect of which he became apparently insolvent and any other debt due to the petitioner and any concurring creditor.[108] Where the sheriff is satisfied that the debtor will, before the expiry of a period of 42 days beginning with the day on which the debtor appears before the sheriff, pay or satisfy the debt in respect of which the debtor became apparently insolvent and any other debt due by the debtor to the petitioner and any creditor concurring in the petition, the sheriff may continue the petition for a period of no more than 42 days.[109] Where the sheriff is satisfied that a debt payment programme relating to the debt in respect of which the debtor became apparently insolvent and any other debt due by the debtor to the petitioner and any creditor concurring in the petition, has been applied for and has not yet been approved or rejected, or that such a debt payment programme will be applied for, the sheriff may continue the petition for such period as he thinks fit.[110] The actual date of sequestration is in the case of a debtor application the date on which sequestration is awarded by the Accountant in Bankruptcy,[111] and in the case of a petition the date of the order for warrant to cite the debtor, if the petition is presented by a creditor or a trustee acting under a trust deed, or the date of the first such warrant if there is more than one.[112]

49.11 Appointment of interim trustee—An interim trustee[113] may be appointed before sequestration is awarded, where the petition is by a creditor or a trustee acting under a trust deed, if the debtor consents or if the trustee or any creditor shows cause for the making of a provisional appointment at this stage[114]: if the petition nominates as interim trustee an eligible person who has given a written

---

[104] 1985 Act s.12(2). See *Hill v Hill*, 1984 S.L.T. (Sh. Ct) 21; *Hodgson v Hodgson's Tr.*, 1984 S.L.T. 97.

[105] *Scottish & Newcastle Breweries Plc v Harvey-Rutherford*, 1994 S.C.L.R. 131.

[106] 1985 Act s.12(3).

[107] See, e.g. *Racal Vodac Ltd v Hislop*, 1992 S.L.T. (Sh. Ct) 21; *Unity Trust Bank Plc v Ahmed*, 1993 S.C.L.R. 53.

[108] 1985 Act s.12(3), (3A); *Clydesdale Bank Plc v Grantly Developments*, 2000 S.L.T. 1369; *Advocate General v Zaoui*, 2001 S.C. 448; *Advocate General v Dickie*, 2010 G.W.D. 31–650. The use of the words "or shows" in the wording of s.12(3A)(b) of the 1985 Act is to indicate that a pre-existing security suffices.

[109] 1985 Act s.12(3AA).

[110] 1985 Act s.12(3B).

[111] 1985 Act s.12(4)(a).

[112] 1985 Act s.12(4)(b); see *Sutherland v Inland Revenue*, 1999 S.C. 104.

[113] Note that, following the Bankruptcy and Diligence etc (Scotland) Act 2007, the former practice of an interim trustee being appointed on sequestration, and a permanent trustee being appointed at the creditors' meeting, is changed. An interim trustee is now only appointed on an emergency basis to safeguard the debtor's assets up to the award of sequestration.

[114] 1985 Act s.2(5).

undertaking to act as interim trustee,[115] the court may appoint that person[116]; otherwise the Accountant in Bankruptcy is appointed.[117] The role of the interim trustee is to safeguard the debtor's estate on an interim basis pending the determination of the award of sequestration.[118] In this regard he may give general or particular directions to the debtor relating to the management of the estate,[119] and although he is not vested in the estate[120] he has power to require the debtor to deliver up to him any money or valuables or documents relating to his business or financial affairs and to place them in safe custody, to require him to deliver up to him any perishable goods and arrange for their sale or disposal, to make up an inventory of any property belonging to the debtor, to require the debtor to implement any transaction entered into by him, to effect insurance policies in respect of the debtor's business or property, and to carry on the debtor's business or borrow money in so far as is necessary to safeguard the estate.[121] Additional powers may be given to the interim trustee by the court.[122] These may include power to enter the debtor's house and business premises and to search for and take possession of any money, valuables, documents and perishable goods which the trustee is entitled to require the debtor to deliver up to him. A debtor who fails without reasonable excuse to comply with the interim trustee's directions or requirements or obstructs the interim trustee in the exercise of a power of search commits an offence.[123] The interim trustee may resign office if authorised to do so by the court.[124] The court has power on the application of the Accountant in Bankruptcy to remove from office an interim trustee who has failed to perform a duty imposed on him without reasonable excuse,[125] and it may replace an interim trustee by appointing another interim trustee to act in his place in various other circumstances including the inability of the interim trustee to act from any cause whatsoever.[126] The interim trustee appointed pursuant to a petition by a creditor or trustee acting under a trust deed is required to notify the debtor as soon as practicable after the date of his appointment.[127]

Appointment of trustee—Provided no interim trustee has been appointed, where **49.12** a sheriff awards sequestration of the debtor's estate following a petition for sequestration, and the petition for the sequestration nominates a trustee, states that the nominated trustee satisfies the required conditions under s.2(3) of the 1985 Act, namely that that he is an insolvency practitioner and willing to act as trustee,

---

[115] For the form of undertaking see Act of Sederunt (Sheriff Court Bankruptcy Rules) 1996 (SI 1996/2507) Form 5.
[116] 1985 Act s.2(6)(a).
[117] 1985 Act s.2(6)(b).
[118] 1985 Act s.2(6A) and s.18.
[119] 1985 Act s.18(1).
[120] Unlike the trustee: see para.50.20, below.
[121] 1985 Act s.18(2). Note that the supplier of gas, electricity and water and telecommunication services may make it a condition of supply that the interim trustee personally guarantees payment of any charges in respect of the supply; s.70.
[122] 1985 Act s.18(3). See as to power to sell heritage, *Clark's Tr.*, 1993 S.L.T. 667.
[123] 1985 Act s.18(5), (6). The debtor may apply to the court under s.18(4) to have a direction set aside but, in the absence of any interim order, must comply with the direction pending the court's decision.
[124] 1985 Act s.13(3).
[125] 1985 Act s.1A(2).
[126] 1985 Act s.13(2).
[127] 1985 Act s.2(7).

and has annexed to the petition a copy of the undertaking confirming as much,[128] the sheriff may, if satisfied by these requirements, appoint the nominated trustee to be the trustee in the sequestration.[129] Where there is no nominated trustee in the petition, and there is no interim trustee, the sheriff must appoint the Accountant in Bankruptcy.[130] Where there is an interim trustee, the sheriff may either appoint the interim trustee as trustee[131] or some other nominated person to be the trustee, in which case that person must have satisfied the above conditions of s.2(3) of the 1985 Act.[132] If neither the interim trustee nor the nominated trustee is appointed by the sheriff, the sheriff must appoint the Accountant in Bankruptcy as trustee.[133] There are procedures for replacement of the interim trustee,[134] the termination of his functions where he is not appointed as trustee[135] and the termination of the functions of the Accountant in Bankruptcy as interim trustee where he is not appointed as trustee.[136]

49.13 Registration of award or court order and their effect—Where there is a successful debtor application, the Accountant in Bankruptcy must forthwith after the date of sequestration send a copy of the determination of the application to the keeper of Register of Inhibitions and Adjudications.[137] Where there is a successful petition for sequestration, the clerk of the court which awards sequestration is required to send forthwith after the date of sequestration a certified copy of the order of the sheriff granting warrant to cite the debtor under s.12(2) of the 1985 Act to the keeper of the Register of Inhibitions and Adjudications for recording in that register. A copy of the order must also be sent to the Accountant in Bankruptcy.[138] In either case there will be notice of the award of sequestration in the Register of Insolvencies maintained by the Accountant in Bankruptcy.[139] The recording of the certified copy of the court order in the Register of Inhibitions and Adjudications has the effect, as from the date of sequestration,[140] of an inhibition at the instance of the creditors who subsequently have claims in the sequestration which are accepted by the permanent trustee.[141] The debtor must tell the trustee, either before or after sequestration, if he may derive benefit from some another estate, such as an executry, and if he fails to do this, he commits a criminal offence.[142]

49.14 Recall of sequestration—A petition for recall of the award of sequestration may be presented to the sheriff by the debtor, any creditor or any other person having

---

[128] As required by 1985 Act s.2(3).

[129] 1985 Act s.2(1).

[130] 1985 Act s.2(2).

[131] 1985 Act s.2(2A)(a).

[132] 1985 Act s.2(2B).

[133] 1985 Act s.2(2C).

[134] 1985 Act s.13.

[135] 1985 Act s.13A.

[136] 1985 Act s.13B.

[137] 1985 Act s.14(1A). If adjudication is ultimately abolished, as may be the case if land attachment ever comes into force, the register will merely be the Register of Inhibitions.

[138] 1985 Act s.14(1). The effect expires after three years (if not earlier by virtue of an order of the Court of Session unless renewed by the trustee): s.14(3), (4); *Tewnion's Tr., Noter*, 2000 S.L.T. (Sh. Ct) 37.

[139] The requirement to publish the sequestration in the Edinburgh Gazette has been abolished (Bankruptcy (Scotland) Amendment Regulations 2010 (SSI 2010/367) para.3(3)).

[140] See 1985 Act s.12(4).

[141] 1985 Act s.14(2).

[142] 1985 Act s.15(8), (9).

an interest notwithstanding that any of these persons was a petitioner or concurred in the petition for sequestration, or by the interim or permanent trustee or the Accountant in Bankruptcy.[143] The court is given a wide discretion as to the grounds upon which an award of sequestration may be recalled and as to what further orders should be made in the circumstances,[144] but three particular grounds which are provided by the Act[145] are (a) that the debtor has paid his debts in full or given sufficient security for their payment,[146] (b) that a majority in value of the creditors reside in a country other than Scotland and that it is more appropriate for the debtor's estate to be administered in that other country, and (c) that one or more other awards of sequestration of the estate or analogous remedies have already been granted. A defect in the procedure leading up to sequestration may also provide a proper basis for recall,[147] but the court has discretion in the matter and may decline to recall the sequestration especially if the defect is trivial and a recall would prejudice creditors,[148] or if there has been a failure to proceed with recall expeditiously.[149] The petition may be presented at any time if it is presented on any of the particular grounds provided by the Act which are mentioned above[150] but otherwise must be presented within 10 weeks of the date of the award of sequestration.[151] Special rules apply where the application is made by the non-entitled spouse who has occupancy of a matrimonial home.[152] Publication of an application for recall must be made by notice in the Edinburgh Gazette, and any person having an interest as well as those on whom the petition is served may lodge answers to the petition.[153] The effect of a recall of the award of sequestration should be, so far as possible, to restore the debtor to the position he would have been if the sequestration had not been awarded.[154]

The debtor's statement of assets and liabilities—One of the functions of the **49.15** trustee is to ascertain the state of the debtor's liabilities and assets.[155] If the debtor has made a debtor application he must, not later than seven days after the trustee's appointment (assuming the trustee is not the Accountant in Bankruptcy), send to

---

[143] 1985 Act s.16(1); a petition for recall may be presented by a non-entitled spouse of the debtor where the purpose of the sequestration was to defend her occupancy rights in the matrimonial home: see s.41.

[144] 1985 Act s.17(1), (3); *Button v Royal Bank of Scotland Plc*, 1987 G.W.D. 27–1019; *Wright v Tennent Caledonian Breweries Ltd*, 1991 S.L.T. 823; *Archer Car Sales (Airdrie) Ltd v Gregory's Tr.*, 1993 S.L.T. 223; *Mowbray v Valentine*, 1998 S.C. 424; *Ritchie v Dickie*, 1999 S.C. 593; *Crawford's Tr. v Crawford*, 2002 S.C. 464; *Sutherland v Advocate General for Scotland*, 2006 S.C. 682.

[145] 1985 Act s.17(1)(a)–(c). If the petition is presented more than 10 weeks after the date of the award of sequestration it must proceed on one of these grounds: *Martin v Martin's Tr.*, 1994 S.L.T. 261.

[146] See *Martin v Martin's Tr.*, 1994 S.L.T. 261.

[147] *Ballantyne v Barr* (1867) 5 M. 330; *Hodgson v Hodgson's Trs*, 1984 S.L.T. 97; *Lord Advocate v Thomson*, 1995 S.L.T. 56; *Liandu v Go Debt Ltd*, 2010 G.W.D. 33–674.

[148] *Nakeski-Cumming v Gordon*, 1924 S.C. 217.

[149] *Van Overwaele v Hacking and Paterson (No. 1)*, 2002 S.C. 62

[150] 1985 Act s.16(4); the grounds are those set out in s.17(a)–(c); see *Martin v Martin's Tr.*, 1994 S.L.T. 261.

[151] 1985 Act s.16(4); for the date of presentation see *Ritchie v Dickie*, 1999 S.C. 593.

[152] 1985 Act s.41(1)(b).

[153] 1985 Act s.16(3).

[154] 1985 Act s.17(4).

[155] 1985 Act s.2(4)(c). For the procedure which should be adopted if the Accountant in Bankruptcy discovers that the debtor uses more than one name, see *Accountant in Bankruptcy v Dobbin*, 1997 S.C.L.R. 543.

the trustee the statement of assets and liabilities[156] which was lodged with the debtor application[157]; in other cases, where the award of sequestration followed a petition by a creditor or a trustee acting under a trust deed, the debtor must, not later than seven days after the trustee has notified him of his appointment, send to the trustee a statement of assets and liabilities containing a list of assets and liabilities.[158] Failure by the debtor to provide the statement attracts criminal penalties.[159] The trustee must then prepare a statement of the debtor's affairs so far as within his knowledge and indicate therein whether, in his opinion, the debtor's assets are unlikely to be sufficient to pay any dividend in respect of preferred, ordinary and postponed debts.[160] Not later than four days before the date of the statutory meeting (referred to in the next paragraph), or, where the trustee does not intend to hold such a meeting, not later than 60 days after sequestration is awarded, he must send to the Accountant in Bankruptcy the statement of assets and liabilities, a copy of the statement of affairs and his written comments indicating what in his opinion are the causes of the insolvency and to what extent the conduct of the debtor may have contributed to the insolvency.[161] Where the Accountant in Bankruptcy is already the trustee this task is not required.

49.16 Statutory meeting of creditors—The trustee, whether the Accountant in Bankruptcy or any other trustee, must, within 60 days of the date of sequestration, or such longer period as the sheriff may allow, give notice to the creditors of whether or not he intends to call a statutory meeting: he must call a meeting at the request of not less than one-quarter in value of the creditors.[162] If the trustee does give notice that he intends to call the statutory meeting, the meeting must be held within 28 days of that notice.[163] He is required to give not less than seven days' notice of the date, time and place of the meeting to every creditor known to him, and to invite the submission of such claims as have not already been submitted to him and inform them of his duties as regards providing them with information as to the debtor's affairs[164]; the creditors have power to continue the statutory meeting to a date not later than seven days after the end of the period within which it requires to be held.[165] For the purposes of voting at the statutory meeting each creditor must submit a claim to the trustee either at or before the meeting.[166] This is done by producing to the trustee a statement of claim in the prescribed form and an account or voucher, according to the nature of the debt, which constitutes prima facie evidence of it.[167] The trustee may allow a creditor who neither resides

---

[156] The statement of assets and liabilities in defined in s.73 as a list of the debtor's assets and liabilities, a list of his income and expenditure and such other information as may be prescribed.

[157] 1985 Act s.19(1).

[158] 1985 Act ss.19, 73(1). The form of the statement is prescribed: Bankruptcy (Scotland) Regulations 1985 (SI 1985/1925) reg.5, Form 4.

[159] 1985 Act s.19(3), (4).

[160] 1985 Act s.20(1).

[161] 1985 Act s.20(2). Where the Accountant in Bankruptcy already has received a copy of the debtor's inventory and valuation under s.38(1)(c) of the Act, it is not necessary to send the statement of affairs to him.

[162] 1985 Act s.21A.

[163] 1985 Act s.21A(6).

[164] 1985 Act s.21A(7).

[165] 1985 Act s.21A(8).

[166] 1985 Act s.22(1).

[167] 1985 Act s.22(2); he may submit a different statement of claim specifying a different amount from his claim at any time before the statutory meeting: see s.22(4); for the form see Bankruptcy (Scotland) Regulations 1985 (SI 1985/1925) reg.5, Form 5.

nor has a place of business in the United Kingdom to submit an informal claim in writing.[168] At the commencement of the statutory meeting the trustee is required to accept or reject in whole or part the claim of each creditor in order to determine the creditor's entitlement to vote[169] and to arrange for a record to be made of the proceedings.[170] He is also required to invite the creditors thereupon to elect one of their number as chairman in his place and to preside over the election, but if a chairman is not elected he must remain the chairman throughout the meeting.[171] Thereafter his duties at the meeting are to make the debtor's statement of assets and liabilities and his own statement of the debtor's affairs (which he may revise at, or as soon as possible after, the meeting) available for inspection by the creditors and to answer to the best of his ability any question and consider any representations put to him by them relating to the debtor's assets, business or financial affairs or his conduct in relation thereto and to indicate whether in his opinion the debtor's assets are unlikely to be sufficient to pay any dividend.[172] The meeting then proceeds to the confirmation of the original trustee or replacement of the trustee,[173] and it may also elect commissioners.[174] The debtor has no right to attend or address the meeting.

Where the trustee does not intend to call a statutory meeting and no request for one has been received from a creditor, the trustee (unless he is the Accountant in Bankruptcy) must make a report to the Accountant in Bankruptcy of the circumstances of the sequestration.[175]

Confirmation or replacement of the trustee—The trustee is either confirmed **49.17** or replaced by the creditors at the statutory meeting at the conclusion of the proceedings for the provision of information by the original trustee.[176] The result of the trustee vote is determined by a majority in value of such creditors or their mandatories as vote on the question; creditors who acquired a debt due by the debtor after the date of sequestration other than by succession are not entitled to vote in the election, and no creditor is entitled to vote to the extent that his debt is a postponed debt.[177] A person must be qualified to act as an insolvency practitioner in order to be eligible for election as replacement trustee; the debtor himself is not eligible, and neither is a person who holds an interest opposed to the general interests of the creditors nor a person who has not given an undertaking, in writing, to act as replacement trustee.[178] The Accountant in Bankruptcy may not be the replacement trustee.[179] The election of the replacement trustee by the creditors requires to be approved by the sheriff.[180] An opportunity is given to the debtor, the creditors, the original trustee, the replacement trustee and the Accountant in

---

[168] 1985 Act s.22(3).

[169] 1985 Act s.23(1)(a), (2).

[170] 1985 Act s.23(1)(c). For further provisions as to the procedure to be followed at the meeting see Sch.6 Pt II.

[171] 1985 Act s.23(1)(b).

[172] 1985 Act s.23(3).

[173] 1985 Act s.24.

[174] 1985 Act s.30.

[175] 1985 Act s.21B.

[176] 1985 Act s.24(1).

[177] 1985 Act s.24(3), Sch.6 paras 11 and 13.

[178] 1985 Act s.24(2). It is incompetent to elect two persons jointly: *I.R.C. v MacDonald*, 1988 S.L.T. (Sh. Ct) 7.

[179] 1985 Act s.24(2)(f).

[180] 1985 Act s.25.

Bankruptcy to object to any matter connected with the election within four days after the statutory meeting and to be heard thereon. If there is no timeous objection, the sheriff must forthwith declare the elected person to be the trustee. If there is a timeous objection which the sheriff sustains, a new meeting for the election of a replacement trustee must be held.[181]

Where the Accountant in Bankruptcy is the original trustee, if no creditor entitled to vote in the trustee vote attends the statutory meeting or no replacement trustee is elected, the Accountant in Bankruptcy must report the proceedings to the sheriff and must continue to act as trustee.[182] Where the Accountant in Bankruptcy is not the original trustee, and if no creditor entitled to vote in the trustee vote attends the statutory meeting, or if no replacement trustee is elected, the original trustee must forthwith notify the Accountant in Bankruptcy, report the proceedings to the sheriff and must continue to act as the trustee.[183] The appointment of a replacement trustee marks the end of the functions of the original trustee, who must hand over to the replacement trustee everything in his possession which relates to the sequestration and cease to act as trustee.[184] Provision is made for the death, resignation and removal from office of the replacement trustee.[185]

49.18 Election and removal of commissioners—The creditors may elect up to a maximum of five commissioners to act in the sequestration, but the election of commissioners is not compulsory.[186] The election may be made either at the statutory meeting or at any subsequent meeting of creditors, but creditors who acquired a debt due by the debtor after the date of sequestration other than by succession are not entitled to vote in this matter and no creditor is entitled to vote to the extent that his debt is a postponed debt. The debtor himself is not eligible for election as a commissioner, and neither is a person who holds an interest opposed to the general interests of the creditors nor a person who is an associate of the debtor or the trustee.[187] A commissioner may resign office at any time, and may be removed from office by the creditors at a meeting called for the purpose; if he is a mandatory of a creditor he may be removed from office by the creditor recalling the mandate and intimating its recall to the trustee.[188] The general functions of the commissioners are to supervise the intromissions of the trustee with the sequestrated estate and to advise him.[189]

49.19 Vesting of estate in trustee—The whole estate of the debtor, by virtue of the trustee's appointment, vests as at the date of sequestration in the trustee for the benefit of the creditors.[190] The whole estate of the debtor for this purpose means his whole estate, heritable and moveable, at the date of sequestration,[191] wherever

---

[181] 1985 Act s.25(4).
[182] 1985 Act s.24(3A).
[183] 1985 Act s.24(4).
[184] 1985 Act s.26.
[185] 1985 Act ss.28, 28A, 29.
[186] 1985 Act s.30.
[187] 1985 Act s.30(2).
[188] 1985 Act s.30(3), (4).
[189] 1985 Act s.4.
[190] 1985 Act s.31(1). For the meaning of the expression "date of sequestration" see s.12(4) and para.49.10, above.
[191] 1985 Act s.31(8).

situated,[192] including any income or estate vesting in the debtor on that date and the capacity to exercise all such powers in, over or in respect of any property as might have been exercised by the debtor for his own benefit as at or on the date of sequestration, such as the exercise of a right to vote in respect of shares held by him, the claiming of legal rights or completing title to heritage.[193] For the avoidance of doubt, it also includes any property which has been conveyed by the debtor to another person and title to which has not been completed by that other person,[194] subject to the provisions of s.32(9ZA), to be discussed shortly. However, as regards heritage, it is not competent for the trustee or anyone deriving title from the trustee to complete title to any heritable estate in Scotland vested in the trustee before the expiry of a period of 28 days beginning with the day on which either the certified copy of the order of the sheriff granting warrant to cite the debtor[195] or the certified copy of the determination of the Accountant in Bankruptcy[196] is recorded in the Register of Inhibitions and Adjudications.[197] The trustee is not affected by any prior inhibition in the exercise of any powers which he is given by the 1985 Act in relation to the heritable estate.[198] The effect of these provisions is to give, after the 28-day period, the trustee a personal right to the heritage, which he may complete by registration in the Land Register for Scotland using his appointment as a link in title in order to obtain a real right.[199] By contrast, any moveable property which normally would require delivery, possession or intimation of its assignation in order to complete title to it vests in the trustee as at the date of sequestration without either the normal required delivery, possession, 28-day delay, or intimation.[200] Likewise any non-vested contingent interest of the debtor's vests in the trustee as if assignation and intimation had been made at the date of sequestration.[201] If any such moveable property is still vested in the trustee at the time of the debtor's discharge, it is then automatically reinvested in the debtor at the date of discharge.[202]

---

[192] The Insolvency Act 1986 s.426 provides for co-operation between courts in the United Kingdom in relation to insolvency law.

[193] 1985 Act s.31(3); *Aikman* (1893) 30 S.L.R. 804; *Cumming's Tr. v Glenrinnes Farms Ltd*, 1993 S.L.T. 904. As to claims for *solatium* see *Watson v Thomson*, 1991 S.C. 447; *Coutts' Trs v Coutts*, 1998 S.C. 798.

[194] 1985 Act s.31(8)(c) This is to get round the difficulties raised by the case of *Burnett's Tr. v Grainger*, 2004 S.C. (HL) 19 which eventually established that the principle of "beneficial ownership" introduced into the law relating to receivership in *Sharp v Thomson*, 1997 S.C. (HL) 66 is limited to receivership alone.

[195] In terms of 1985 Act s.14(1)(a).

[196] In terms of 1985 Act s.14(1A).

[197] 1985 Act s.31(1B) This means that a purchaser acting in good faith has 28 days in which to register his title, but if he fails to do so within that period, and the trustee then completes title to the heritage, the purchaser loses his opportunity to register the title himself.

[198] 1985 Act s.31(2).

[199] See also 1985 Act s.31(3), by which the trustee is enabled to complete title to any heritable estate in Scotland to which the debtor had an incomplete title. The trustee may prefer to dispone the property using the appointment as a link in title: see W.W. McBryde, *Bankruptcy*, 2nd edn (Edinburgh: W. Green, 1995), pp.190–2. For special destinations see *Fleming's Tr. v Fleming*, 2000 S.C. 206.

[200] 1985 Act s.31(4). Note, however, that by s.32(9ZA), any incorporeal moveable property (such as shares or a right to receive income), or the creation, transfer, variation or extinguishing of a real right in heritable property, the dealing of which would require the delivery of a deed, and which is conveyed to a third party for adequate consideration within a period of seven days from the date of registration of the sequestration, is an exception to s.31(4).

[201] 1985 Act s.31(5). Such a contingent interest might be a *spes successionis.*

[202] 1985 Act s.31(5A). This would mean that a right to a legacy which vested in the trustee up to the time that the debtor was discharged is reinvested in the debtor on his discharge.

Any property other than income acquired by the debtor after the date of sequestration and before the date of his discharge vests also in the trustee, although if a person has transferred that property to the debtor or to a third party on the instructions of the debtor, the transferor incurs no liability to the trustee except to the extent of any proceeds in his hands, and the transfer is without prejudice to any right or interest acquired in the property in good faith and for value by that third party.[203] Once sequestrated, the debtor is no longer able to deal with his property (both that which vests in the trustee at the date of sequestration and any property that comes into the hands of the debtor but is passed to the trustee) and any dealings by the debtor may be reduced at the instance of the trustee.[204] However, where: (a) the trustee has abandoned to the debtor the property to which the dealing relates, has expressly or impliedly authorised the dealing, or is otherwise personally barred from challenging the dealing[205]; (b) where the dealing is the performance of an obligation undertaken before the date of sequestration by a person obliged to the debtor in the obligation, the purchase from the debtor of goods for which the purchaser has given value to the debtor or is willing to give value to the trustee, or a banking transaction in the ordinary course of business between the banker and the debtor; or (c) where the dealing satisfies certain conditions, provided that the person dealing with the debtor was, at the time when the dealing occurred, unaware of the sequestration and had at that time no reason to believe that the debtor's estate had been sequestrated or was the subject of sequestration proceedings, the trustee may not reduce the dealing with or by the debtor.[206] The conditions (to be found at s.32(9ZA)) referred to in (c) above are that the dealing is either the transfer of incorporeal moveable property, or the creation, transfer, variation or extinguishing of a real right in heritable property, in either case for which the person dealing with the debtor has given adequate consideration to the debtor, or is willing to give adequate consideration to the trustee; the dealing requires the delivery of a deed; and the delivery of that deed occurs during the period beginning with the date of sequestration[207] and ending on the day which falls seven days after the day on which the certified copy of the order of the sheriff granting warrant to cite the debtor is recorded[208] or the certified copy of the determination of the Accountant in Bankruptcy awarding sequestration is recorded[209] in the Register of Inhibitions and Adjudications.[210]

If the debtor acquires any assets or has any substantial change in his financial circumstances, he is required to tell the trustee and failure to do so incurs criminal sanctions.[211] Any income arising from the estate which is vested in the trustee

---

[203] 1985 Act s.32(6).

[204] 1985 Act s.32(8).

[205] Where this takes place, and the property is heritable property, a notice of abandonment must be lodged by the trustee in the Register of Inhibitions so as to make it clear that the property is still vested in the debtor (s.32(9A), (9B)). This is also of relevance where the trustee fails to sell the family home within three years in terms of s.39A.

[206] 1985 Act s.32(9)(b)(iv).

[207] See 1985 Act s.12(4).

[208] Under 1985 Act s.14(1)(a).

[209] Under 1985 Act s.14(1A).

[210] The point of this provision is to give protection to someone who had, say, acquired for proper consideration by deed of assignation the debtor's rights under a patent with the assignee being genuinely unaware of the debtor's sequestration at the time of the assignation. The assignee has a window of opportunity lasting from the date of sequestration and seven days after the recording of the sequestration in which to have the deed of assignation delivered to him. It is the duty of the sheriff clerk or the Accountant in Bankruptcy (as the case may be) to record the sequestration "forthwith", so in practice the window of opportunity will be slender indeed.

[211] 1985 Act s.32(7).

vests in the trustee, but any other income vests in the debtor[212] subject to the right of the trustee to apply to the sheriff for payment to him of the excess over a suitable amount to allow for the aliment of the debtor and for any obligations of aliment or to pay periodical allowance or child support maintenance which may be owed by him.[213] No application to this effect may be made after the date on which the debtor's discharge becomes effective,[214] but any order (known as an "income payment order") made by the sheriff may specify that the obligation by the debtor to pay the trustee may continue up to three years from the date of the order, even after the date of discharge if necessary.[215] Any order as to what is a suitable amount of income for this purpose may be varied on change of circumstances.[216] The sheriff may also direct that a third person make the payment to the trustee.[217] This could mean that employers could be required to make the payments out of the debtor's income. The debtor may also voluntarily undertake to make a regular payment (known as an "income payment undertaking") to the trustee or arrange for a third person to do so.[218] After each period of six months, while the income payment order or undertaking is in force, the debtor must provide the trustee with a statement of his current state of affairs, with a view, if necessary, of altering the payments.[219]

Property not vested in the trustee—Property which is exempted from attach- **49.20** ment for the purpose of protecting the debtor and his family[220] and property held on trust by the debtor for any person[221] do not vest in the trustee. Rights of the debtor under an approved pension arrangement are excluded from his estate.[222] Overpayments, repayments from social funds and sums recovered from compensation but repayable to the Government all in terms of the Social Security Administration Act 1992 ss.71(10B), 78(3B) and 89(2) do not pass to the trustee, along with benefits (as defined in s.122 of the Social Security Contributions and Benefits Act 1992), income-related benefits, jobseeker's allowance and child benefit.[223] The deduction to be made from injury compensation awards in respect of social security benefits does not form part of the estate[224]; and neither does a statutory criminal injuries compensation award.[225] The interest of the debtor under an assured, protected or secure tenancy does not pass to the trustee unless and

---

[212] In particular, note the specific provisions in respect of pensions and social security benefits (s.32(2A)).

[213] 1985 Act ss.32(1)–(3); e.g. *Brown's Tr. v Brown*, 1995 S.L.T. (Sh. Ct) 2.

[214] 1985 Act s.32(2WA).

[215] 1985 Act s.32(2XA).

[216] 1985 Act s.32(4).

[217] 1985 Act s.32(YA).

[218] 1985 Act s.32(4A).

[219] 1985 Act s.43A.

[220] 1985 Act s.33(1)(a), (aa): see Ch.48, "Diligence", above.

[221] 1985 Act s.33(1)(b). Funds in a solicitor's client account do not vest in the solicitor's trustee in sequestration: *Council of the Law Society of Scotland v McKinnie*, 1993 S.L.T. 238.

[222] Welfare Reform and Pensions Act 1999 ss.11, 13; for unapproved schemes see s.12; there are provisions designed to deal with a case where contributions to a pension arrangement have unfairly prejudiced the debtor's creditors: ss.36A, 36B, 36C.

[223] Social Security Administration Act 1992 ss.187, 191, as amended by the Jobseekers Act 1995; on the interaction between social security legislation and sequestration see *Mulvey v Secretary of State for Social Security*, 1997 S.C. (HL) 105.

[224] Social Security Administration Act 1992 s.89(2).

[225] Criminal Justice Act 1988 s.117.

until he serves notice on the debtor to that effect.[226] Under the Proceeds of Crime Act 2002[227] any property of the debtor's subject to a restraint order, receivership or administration order, or confiscation order is excluded from the debtor's estate except to the extent that where the relevant order is satisfied or discharged, any excess of the property in the hands of the appropriate receiver, administrator or other official vests in the trustee, and where the relevant order is quashed, again any formerly confiscated property vests in the trustee.[228] However, as regards heritage, a restraint order must be registered in the Land Register before the date of sequestration if it is to be excluded from the debtor's estate.[229] The vesting of the estate does not prejudice the right of any secured creditor which is preferable to the rights of the trustee.[230]

Any person claiming a right to any estate claimed by the trustee may apply to the court for the estate to be excluded from vesting under these provisions.[231] Any property held on trust by the debtor for any other person is specifically excluded by the Act from vesting in the trustee.[232] If the debtor has paid money held by him in trust into an account which is not earmarked with the trust, and also keeps money of his own in the same account, the court will, if it can, disentangle the account, separate the trust funds from the private moneys and award the former specifically to the beneficiaries.[233] A trust may be held to have been created by the debtor over incorporeal moveables such as debts owed to him in the course of his business, but it is necessary for this purpose that there should have been an unequivocal declaration of trust by the debtor over such assets together with delivery or its equivalent in order to constitute the trust.[234] The common law rule remains that the trustee takes the estate *tantum et tale* as it stood in the debtor,[235] and that he cannot maintain a right to property which is reducible on the ground of the debtor's fraud.[236] In the absence of fraud, however, there is no rule in Scotland that the trustee cannot assert a claim which it would have been dishonourable for the debtor to make.[237]

49.21 **Safeguarding of interests of creditors**—Although insolvency does not in itself prevent a person from entering into contracts or incurring obligations, insolvency has important effects on transactions by debtors before their sequestration, particularly where those transactions may have prejudiced the interests of the debtor's creditors. A gratuitous alienation is the voluntary disposition of an asset of

---

[226] 1985 Act s.31(9), (10).

[227] Proceeds of Crime Act 2002 s.420(2).

[228] 1985 Act ss.31A, 31B and 31C. The administrator referred to here is an administrator appointed under the Proceeds of Crime Act 2002, not the Enterprise Act 2002.

[229] Proceeds of Crime Act 2002 s.420(3).

[230] 1985 Act s.33(3); *Berry v Taylor*, 1993 S.L.T. 718; *Abbey National Plc v Arthur (No.2)*, 2000 S.L.T. 103.

[231] 1985 Act s.31(6); *Smith v Berry's Tr.*, 1996 S.L.T. (Sh. Ct) 31.

[232] 1985 Act s.33(1)(b).

[233] *Macadam v Martin's Tr.* (1872) 11 M. 33; *Smith v Liquidator of James Birrell Ltd (No.2)*, 1968 S.L.T. 174.

[234] *Allan's Trs v Lord Advocate*, 1971 S.C. (HL) 45; *Tay Valley Joiners Ltd v C.F. Financial Services Ltd*, 1987 S.L.T. 207. See also Gretton, "Debt factoring and floating charges (Scotland)", 1987 J.B.L. 390–2.

[235] *Davidson v Boyd* (1868) 7 M. 77.

[236] *Colquhoun's Tr. v Campbell's Trs* (1902) 4 F. 739; *AW Gamage v Charlesworth's Tr.*, 1910 S.C. 257.

[237] *Liqr. of Clyde Marine Insurance Co v Renwick*, 1924 S.C. 113.

the debtor's by the debtor to another person for no or less than full value.[238] A fraudulent or unfair preference is the conferring of a voluntary and unfair preference on a creditor at the expense of the other creditors, usually by ensuring that creditor is repaid first or given some security over the debtor's assets to ensure that he is advantaged compared to the other creditors.[239] Both gratuitous alienations and fraudulent or unfair preferences are provided for under both common law and by statute. The general principle of the common law is that from the moment of insolvency a debtor is bound to act with regard to the interests of his creditors.[240] He ceases to be entitled secretly to set his funds apart for his own use, and is no longer entitled to alienate them voluntarily whether by giving away his assets gratuitously and voluntarily to third parties or by conferring a preference upon a particular creditor which is voluntary.[241] The common law remains extant if little used: in practice the 1985 Act provides a simpler and clearer framework for challenging gratuitous alienations and unfair preferences.[242]

Gratuitous alienations at common law[243]—As has just been noted, it is a general **49.22** principle at common law that from the moment of his insolvency a debtor is bound to administer his estate for the benefit of his creditors. While he may continue with his trade with the intention of making gain for his creditors and for himself, his funds are no longer his own to give away as caprice or affection may dictate.[244] Accordingly, every voluntary alienation of property by a debtor for no consideration or for inadequate consideration, while in a state of insolvency to the prejudice of his creditors, is fraudulent and may be the subject of challenge at common law. Thus, an alienation of goods or money, if it was in the nature of a gift,[245] or a gratuitous surrender of rights,[246] or a purchase at an exorbitant price[247] is reducible either at the instance of creditors, prior or posterior,[248] or of the trustee in the debtor's subsequent sequestration or by the trustee acting under a protected trust deed or by a judicial factor appointed under s.11A of the Judicial Factors (Scotland) Act 1889 on the estate of a person deceased.[249] It is for the challenger to prove that the transaction was gratuitous and that the debtor was insolvent at the date of the alienation. In practice, this can be difficult for the challenger to establish without access to the debtor's financial records.[250] It is not, however, necessary to prove that the alienation was made with fraudulent intention. A presumption of fraud, in the sense of breach of trust, is created by proof that the alienation was

---

[238] In England this is known as a transaction at an undervalue (Insolvency Act 1986 s.339).

[239] At common law, an unfair preference is known as a fraudulent preference. In England the equivalent term is a preference (Insolvency Act 1986 s.340).

[240] Bell, *Commentaries*, II, 170.

[241] *Nordic Travel Ltd v Scotprint Ltd*, 1980 S.C. 1 at 10, per Lord President Emslie.

[242] Donna McKenzie Skene, "Gratuitous alienations and unfair preferences in insolvency", 1993 J.L.S.S. 38(4), 141–5.

[243] See generally McBryde, *Bankruptcy* (1995), Ch.12.

[244] Bell, *Commentaries*, II, 170; H. Goudy, *A Treatise on the Law of Bankruptcy in Scotland*, 4th edn (Edinburgh: T&T Clark, 1914), p.22. See also *Nordic Travel Ltd v Scotprint Ltd*, 1980 S.C. 1, per Lord President Emslie at 10, Lord Cameron at 24.

[245] Bell, *Commentaries*, II, 184; *Wink v Speirs* (1867) 6 M. 77; *Main v Fleming's Trs* (1881) 8 R. 880; *Boyle's Tr. v Boyle*, 1988 S.L.T. 581.

[246] *Obers v Paton's Trs* (1897) 24 R. 719; *Thomson v Spence*, 1961 S.L.T. 395.

[247] *Abram S.S. Co v Abram*, 1925 S.L.T. 243.

[248] *Wink v Speirs* (1867) 6 M. 77, per Lord Justice-Clerk Patton at 80.

[249] 1985 Act s.34(8).

[250] This is the principal reason that challenges at common law are rare.

made without onerous consideration when the debtor was insolvent.[251] A significant advantage of the right to challenge a transaction as a gratuitous alienation at
common law is that the right is not subject to time limits, and remains available
until it has been cut off by the negative prescription.

It is a good answer to a reduction at common law that the deed in question was
granted for some true, just and necessary cause. The fulfilment of an obligation,
undertaken during solvency, is not struck at.[252] Provisions in ante-nuptial marriage
contracts made for the purpose of securing the party to be benefited against the
financial risks of marriage were formerly regarded as having been made for a true
and just cause, but marriage is no longer regarded as an onerous consideration[253]
so that it is a question of fact in each case whether the transfer was onerous.[254]

49.23 Gratuitous alienations: Statute—Gratuitous alienations are also challengeable,
within certain time limits, under 1985 Act.[255] The statutory right of challenge is
available only where (i) the debtor's estate has been sequestrated, (ii) he has
granted a trust deed which has become a protected trust deed, (iii) he has died and
his estate has been sequestrated within 12 months after his death, or (iv) he has
died and a judicial factor has been appointed under s.11A of the Judicial Factors
(Scotland) Act 1889 to administer his estate within 12 months of his death and the
estate was absolutely insolvent at the date of death.[256] The title to challenge is
given to any creditor who is a creditor by virtue of a debt incurred on or before the
date of sequestration[257] or before the granting of the trust deed or the debtor's
death as the case may be, to the trustee, to the trustee acting under a trust deed or
to a judicial factor.[258] Under the statute a challenge may be mounted to an alienation by the debtor whereby any of the debtor's property has been transferred or
any claim or right of the debtor has been discharged or renounced[259] if the alienation became effectual on a day not earlier than two years before (i) the date of
sequestration, (ii) the granting of the trust deed or (iii) the debtor's death as the
case may be, except that this time limit is extended to five years if the alienation
was to an associate of the debtor.[260] An associate of the debtor for this purpose
is, if the debtor is an individual, a husband, wife, civil partner or other close
relative.[261] A person is an associate of a person with whom he is in partnership and
of an associate of any person with whom he is in partnership, and a firm is an
associate of any person who is a member of a firm.[262] A person is also an associate
of any person whom he employs or by whom he is employed, any directors or
other officers of a company being treated as employed by the company.[263] A
company may also be an associate if the debtor or his associates have control of

---

[251] *McCowan v Wright* (1852) 14 D. 901.

[252] *Pringle's Tr. v Wright* (1903) 5 F. 522.

[253] *McLay v McQueen* (1899) 1 F. 804; *Gilmour Shaw & Co's Tr. v Learmonth*, 1972 S.C. 137; Law
Reform (Husband and Wife) (Scotland) Act 1984 s.5(1)(b); as to post-nuptial arrangements see
Dunlop v Johnston (1865) 3 M. (HL) 22; *Robertson's Tr. v Robertson* (1901) 3 F. 359.

[254] cf. *Henderson v McManus*, 1981 S.C. 233.

[255] 1985 Act s.34.

[256] 1985 Act s.34(2)(b).

[257] For the meaning of this expression, see s.12(4) and para.49.10, above.

[258] 1985 Act s.34(1); e.g. *Thoar's J.F. v Ramlort Ltd*, 1998 S.C. 887.

[259] e.g. *Ahmed's Tr. v Ahmed (No.2)*, 1993 S.L.T. 651.

[260] 1985 Act s.34(2)(a), (c), (3).

[261] 1985 Act s.74(1), (2), (4); *Ahmed's Tr. v Ahmed (No.2)*, 1993 S.L.T. 651. See also the Civil
Partnership Act 2004.

[262] 1985 Act s.74(1), (3), (4); Bankruptcy (Scotland) Regulations 1985 reg.11.

[263] 1985 Act s.74(5).

it.[264] The onus lies on the person who seeks to uphold the alienation (who will generally be the debtor or the recipient of the alienation) to establish either that immediately or at any other time after the alienation the debtor's assets were greater than his liabilities,[265] or that the alienation was made for adequate consideration[266] or that it was a birthday, Christmas or other conventional gift or a gift made for a charitable purpose to someone who was not an associate and which it was reasonable for the debtor to make.[267] If any one or more of these matters is not established, the remedy to be granted by the court is that of reduction or restoration of property to the debtor's estate or such other redress as may be appropriate,[268] but a third party who acquired any right or interest in good faith and for value from the transferee in the transaction is protected.[269] The words "such redress as may be appropriate" do not provide a general discretion to the court to decide the matter on equitable principles, but enable the court to make an appropriate order where reduction or restoration of the property is not otherwise possible.[270] If the recipient of the gratuitous alienation has sold on the property, so that it is therefore unrecoverable, the recipient still will have to pay the trustee the value of the property.[271] Where the recipient has paid the debtor some money for the property but nevertheless has been required to return the property or its value to the trustee, the recipient may be able to claim as a postponed creditor (to the extent of the money paid to the debtor) against the debtor's estate.[272]

Unfair preferences—Transactions entered into by a debtor which have the effect **49.24** of creating a preference in favour of a creditor to the prejudice of the general body of creditors are known as "unfair preferences" and are challengeable under the 1985 Act.[273] The right to challenge such transactions under statute is available where the preference was created not earlier than six months before the date of sequestration[274] of the debtor's estate, or the granting by him of a trust deed which has become a protected trust deed[275] or his death where within 12 months after his death his estate has been sequestrated or a judicial factor has been appointed under s.11A of the Judicial Factors (Scotland) Act 1889 to administer his estate and his estate was absolutely insolvent at the time of his death.[276] As in the case

---

[264] 1985 Act s.74(5A)–(5C).

[265] 1985 Act s.34(4)(a). See *Lombardi's Tr. v Lombardi*, 1982 S.L.T. 81; *Hunt's Tr. v Hunt*, 1984 S.L.T. 169; *Bank of Scotland v Reid*, 2000 G.W.D. 22–858.

[266] 1985 Act s.34(4)(b). See also *Matheson's Tr. v Matheson*, 1992 S.L.T. 685; *John E Rae (Electrical Services) Linlithgow Ltd v Lord Advocate*, 1994 S.L.T. 788; *Lafferty Construction v McCombe*, 1994 S.L.T. 858; *MacFadyen's Tr. v MacFadyen*, 1994 S.L.T. 1245; *Cay's Tr. v Cay*, 1997 S.C.L.R. 556; *Kerr v Aitken* [2000] B.P.I.R. 278; *Bank of Scotland v Reid*, 2000 G.W.D. 22–858; *Nottay's Tr. v Nottay*, 2001 S.L.T. 769. There cannot be adequate consideration on facts which show that no consideration was given.

[267] 1985 Act s.34(4).

[268] 1985 Act s.34(4). See *Short's Tr. v Chung (No.1)*, 1991 S.L.T. 472; *Short's Tr. v Chung (No.2)*, 1999 S.C. 471; *Nottay's Tr. v Nottay*, 2001 S.L.T. 769.

[269] 1985 Act s.34(4); *Liquidator of Letham Grange Development Co Ltd v Foxworth Investments Ltd and 3052775 Nova Scotia Developments Ltd* [2011] CSOH 66.

[270] *Short's Tr. v Chung (No.1)*, 1991 S.L.T. 472 at 476K.

[271] *Nottay's Tr. v Nottay*, 2001 S.L.T. 769.

[272] 1985 Act s.51(3)(c).

[273] 1985 Act s.36. There are special rules dealing with pension contributions which have unfairly prejudiced creditors: ss.36A, 36B, 36C.

[274] For the meaning of this expression, see s.12(4) and para.49.10, above.

[275] Note that the trust deed must have become protected, but that the time limit runs from the date of the granting of the trust deed.

[276] 1985 Act s.36(1).

of gratuitous alienations, the title to challenge is given to any creditor who is a creditor by virtue of a debt incurred on or before the date of sequestration or before the granting of the protected trust deed or the debtor's death as the case may be, and to the trustee, the trustee acting under the trust deed or the judicial factor.[277] The remedy to be granted by the court, if satisfied that the transaction is one to which the section applies, is that of reduction or restoration of property to the debtor's estate or such other redress as may be appropriate, but this is without prejudice to any right or interest acquired by a third party in good faith and for value from or through the creditor in whose favour the preference was created.[278]

The only other requirement under statute is that the transaction should have had the effect of creating a preference in favour of a creditor to the prejudice of the general body of creditors. This description is so broad as to cover every form of alienation by which a right to heritable or moveable property may be transferred from one person to another, whether directly or indirectly. Such transactions might include, for example, the delivery or disposition of property in security of a prior debt,[279] the indorsation of a bill or cheque for a payment not yet due[280] and an arrangement with a debtor to pay a creditor direct.[281] Any transaction which results in giving a creditor, or it would seem a class of creditors, until then unsecured or imperfectly secured, a security for his or their debt is reducible.[282]

A mere acknowledgement of an existing debt, which enables a creditor to obtain no more than an ordinary ranking, and does not confer on him any preference, is not struck at by the Act.[283] Nor is the substitution for an existing security of another of equivalent value.[284] It is specifically provided that the right of challenge does not apply to four classes of transactions. These are: (1) a transaction in the ordinary course of trade or business; (2) a payment in cash for a debt which when it was paid had become payable, unless the transaction was collusive[285] with the purpose of prejudicing the general body of creditors; (3) a transaction whereby the parties thereto have undertaken reciprocal obligations, unless the transaction was collusive[286]; and (4) the granting of a mandate by a debtor authorising an arrestee to pay over arrested funds or part thereof to the arrester, provided there has been a decree for payment or a summary warrant for diligence which was

---

[277] 1985 Act s.36(4).

[278] 1985 Act s.36(5); *Short's Tr. v Chung (No.1)*, 1991 S.L.T. 472; *Short's Tr. v Chung (No.2)*, 1998 S.C. 105.

[279] *Stiven v Scott and Simson* (1871) 9 M. 923; *T v L*, 1970 S.L.T. 243.

[280] *Blincow's Tr. v Allan* (1828) 7 S. 124; *Carter v Johnstone* (1886) 13 R. 698, distinguished in *Whatmough's Tr. v British Linen Bank*, 1934 S.C. (HL) 51; *Raymond Harrison & Co's Tr. v North West Securities*, 1989 S.L.T. 718; *Balcraig House v Roosevelt Property Services Ltd*, 1994 S.L.T. 1133.

[281] *Newton & Sons' Tr. v Finlayson & Co*, 1928 S.C. 637.

[282] *McCowan v Wright* (1852) 14 D. 901; *Thomas v Thomson* (1866) 5 M. 198; *Mackenzie v Calder* (1868) 6 M. 833.

[283] *Matthew's Tr. v Matthew* (1867) 5 M. 957. This case was heard under the Bankruptcy (Scotland) Act 1696 but the relevant provisions were re-enacted under later legislation.

[284] *Roy's Tr. v Colville* (1903) 5 F. 769.

[285] As to the meaning of collusion, see *Nordic Travel Ltd v Scotprint Ltd*, 1980 S.C. 1 at 19, per Lord President Emslie.

[286] *Nicoll v Steelpress (Supplies) Ltd*, 1992 S.C. 119. This case was decided under the equivalent provisions of the Insolvency Act 1986 but is still applicable to sequestration. It is important that the reciprocal obligations are of equal value so that the debtor's estate is not diminished by the transaction. An example would be the grant by a debtor of a new heritable security to a creditor to secure new loans made by that creditor to the debtor (*Thomas Montgomery and Sons v Gallacher*, 1982 S.L.T. 138).

preceded by an arrestment on the dependence of the action or followed by an arrestment in execution.[287]

Fraudulent preferences at common law—Although a creditor has a legal claim **49.25** on the debtor, it is the duty of the debtor once he is insolvent to abstain from any act which interferes with the preferences or rights of the creditors inter se.[288] Accordingly any transactions by an insolvent debtor which have the effect, whether directly or indirectly, of conferring a benefit on one creditor in preference to others are challengeable as frauds at common law and known as "fraudulent preferences". Creditors, the trustee, the trustee appointed under a protected trust deed and a judicial factor appointed under s.11A of the 1889 Act all may challenge fraudulent preferences at common law.[289] The difficulty of the common law challenge, as compared to the statutory challenge, is that it is necessary for the challenger at common law to prove that the debtor was absolutely insolvent at the time of the transaction or as a consequence of it and was also absolutely insolvent at the time of challenge.[290] Under the common law there is no time limit within which the transaction must have taken place, but under the statute it is necessary to prove that the day on which the transaction became effectual was within the previously explained six month period.[291] Examples of transactions challengeable at common law are where during his absolute insolvency a debtor gives security for what was formerly an unsecured debt or an obligation to grant a security is undertaken,[292] or where he facilitates a creditor's efforts to exercise diligence or to obtain a decree against him.[293] Once it has been proved that the transaction was entered into voluntarily, during absolute insolvency and while the debtor was conscious of his insolvency, fraud is presumed and it is unnecessary for the challenger to prove an intention of fraud on the debtor's part or any collusion or concert on the part of the favoured creditor.[294] The debtor must also be shown to be absolutely insolvent at the time when the transaction is challenged.[295] Once these requirements are satisfied, all such voluntary transactions are liable to be reduced unless they fall within one or other of the following classes: (1) payments in cash of debts due and payable; (2) transactions in the ordinary course of trade; and (3) *nova debita* or transferences for a consideration given at the time.[296]

A payment in cash includes, besides currency, cheques drawn by the debtor on his banker.[297] As a general rule payment of a debt before it is due is not protected.[298]

---

[287] 1985 Act s.36(2). Note following the Bankruptcy and Diligence etc. (Scotland) Act 2007 s.206 the reference to automatic release of funds (or consent to payment of funds) within 14 weeks after arrestment pursuant to mandates, as indicated in the 1985 Act s.73J(2)(b).

[288] Bell, *Commentaries*, II, 226; *McEwen v Doig* (1828) 6 S. 889.

[289] 1985 Act s.36(6).

[290] *McCowan v Wright* (1853) 15 D. 494; Goudy, *A Treatise on the Law of Bankruptcy in Scotland* (1914), p.41.

[291] 1985 Act s.36(1), (3).

[292] *McCowan v Wright* (1853) 15 D. 494; *Thomas v Thomson* (1866) 5 M. 198.

[293] *Lauries' Tr. v Beveridge* (1867) 6 M. 85.

[294] *McCowan v Wright* (1853) 15 D. 494, per Lord Justice-Clerk Hope at 504; *Whatmough's Tr. v British Linen Bank*, 1932 S.C. 525 at 543, per Lord President Clyde; see also *MacDougall's Tr. v Ironside*, 1914 S.C. 186; *Nordic Travel Ltd v Scotprint Ltd*, 1980 S.C. 1.

[295] *McCowan v Wright* (1853) 15 D. 494; Goudy, *A Treatise on the Law of Bankruptcy in Scotland* (1914), p.41.

[296] Bell, *Commentaries*, II, 201.

[297] *Horsburgh v Ramsay* (1885) 12 R. 1171.

[298] *Blincow's Tr. v Allan* (1828) 7 S. 124; *Whatmough's Tr.*, 1932 S.C. 525, per Lord Thankerton at 59; Goudy, *A Treatise on the Law of Bankruptcy in Scotland* (1914), p.85.

Payment in cash of a debt which is due is reducible only if collusion or consent between the debtor and the favoured creditor (with the object of defrauding the equal rights of the debtor's other creditors) is proved.[299] The fact that both parties were aware of the insolvency or impending bankruptcy does not, by itself, infer collusion[300]; the decisions leave it in doubt what further evidence is necessary.[301]

Transactions in the ordinary course of trade include payments for goods supplied on credit, or delivery of goods already paid for,[302] if, in the latter case, the transfer is in fulfilment of a definite obligation, and does not amount to an attempt to complete a security under which the creditor had no real right.[303] In general, direct payments in cash are in the ordinary course of trade or business when they are made by a party who is still in the administration of his estate and in funds, in discharge of debts past due.[304]

Nova debita include transactions where the debtor and the party whose right is challenged incurred reciprocal obligations at the same time, or with an interval so short as to admit of the application of the term.[305] To these, though the party may have been insolvent at their date, the common law does not take any objection. So a party lending money, and taking a security for it in return which is duly completed in the way appropriate to the particular subject, obtains a good security, although he may have known that the borrower was insolvent.[306]

49.26 Capital sum on divorce—Provision is made by the 1985 Act for the recall of an order by the court for the payment by the debtor of a capital sum on divorce or for the transfer of property by him on divorce.[307] It is a requirement of the right to apply for the recall of such an order that the debtor was absolutely insolvent at the date of the making of the order, or was rendered so by implementation of it.[308] It is also necessary that within five years after the making of the order the debtor's estate has been sequestrated other than after his death, or that he has granted a trust deed which became a protected trust deed, or that he has died and within 12 months after his death his estate has been sequestrated or a judicial factor has been appointed under s.11A of the Judicial Factors (Scotland) Act 1889 to administer his estate.[309] The only parties who are entitled to apply for a recall of the

---

[299] *Whatmough's Tr.*, 1932 S.C. 525 at 543, per Lord President Clyde.

[300] *Coutts' Tr. & Doe v Webster* (1886) 13 R. 1112; *Pringle's Tr. v Wright* (1903) 5 F. 522; *Nordic Travel Ltd v Scotprint Ltd*, 1980 S.C. 1, per Lord President Emslie at 19, Lord Cameron at 27.

[301] See *Jones' Tr. v Jones* (1888) 15 R. 328; *Craig's Tr. v Macdonald, Fraser & Co* (1902) 4 F. 1132; *Newton & Son's Tr. v Finlayson*, 1928 S.C. 637, where the payment was reduced; *Crockart's Tr. v Hay*, 1913 S.C. 509; *Angus' Tr. v Angus* (1901) 4 F. 181; *Whatmough's Tr. v British Linen Bank*, 1932 S.C. 525.

[302] *Taylor v Farrie* (1855) 17 D. 639.

[303] *Jones & Co's Tr. v Allan* (1901) 4 F. 374.

[304] *Nordic Travel Ltd v Scotprint Ltd*, 1980 S.C. 1, per Lord President Emslie at 20; as to the meaning of "ordinary course", see also Lord Cameron at 29.

[305] See *Cowdenbeath Coal Co v Clydesdale Bank* (1895) 22 R. 682. In *Robertson's Trs v Union Bank of Scotland*, 1917 S.C. 549, the debtor granted the bank an assignation in security to cover its overdraft 60 days before the debtor's bankruptcy. The debtor then repaid the overdraft but using the existing security obtained a new advance. It was held (using the then rules under the Bankruptcy (Scotland) Act 1696) that the assignation in security was still valid for the new advance despite the subsequent bankruptcy.

[306] *Price & Pierce v Bank of Scotland*, 1910 S.C. 1095, affd 1912 S.C. (HL) 19; *Thomas Montgomery & Sons v Gallacher*, 1982 S.L.T. 138.

[307] 1985 Act s.35.

[308] 1985 Act s.35(1)(b). Note that there is no presumption as to insolvency in this case, so this must be proved by the party who seeks recall.

[309] 1985 Act s.35(1)(c).

order are the trustee, a trustee acting under the trust deed or the judicial factor,[310] no right of application being given in this instance to any creditor. The court has a discretion as to whether or not to make an order for recall, having regard to all the circumstances including those of the person against whom the order for recall would be made,[311] who will normally be the debtor's former spouse.

Recovery of excessive pension contributions—The trustee under ss.36A–36F **49.27** may apply to the courts to recover sums from the debtor's pension scheme if the sheriff is satisfied that the debtor's payments into his pension schemes have unfairly prejudiced the debtor's creditors. The sheriff may make such order as he sees fit to restore the debtor's estate to what it would have been had the excessive contributions not been made,[312] particularly if any of the contributions were made in order to put the debtor's assets beyond the reach of his creditors or were excessive in view of the debtor's circumstances at the time he made them.[313]

Effect of sequestration on diligence—The order of the court awarding sequestra- **49.28** tion, or the determination of a debtor application by the Accountant in Bankruptcy has the effect, as from the date of sequestration,[314] in relation to diligence done, whether before or after that date, in respect of any part of the debtor's estate of a decree of adjudication of the heritable estate which has been duly recorded in the Register of Inhibition and Adjudications on that date,[315] an arrestment in execution and decree of furthcoming, an arrestment in execution and warrant of sale and an attachment in favour of the creditors according to their respective entitlements.[316] No arrestment or attachment[317] of the debtor's estate executed within 60 days before the date of sequestration or on or after that date is effectual to create a preference for the arrester or attaching creditor, who is thus deprived of his diligence, to payment of his expenses.[318] Although at the time of writing land attachment in terms of the Bankruptcy and Diligence etc (Scotland) Act 2007 has yet to be brought into force,[319] a creditor who creates a land attachment of the debtor's heritable property within a period of six months before the date of sequestration will be unable to obtain a preference,[320] but if he has created a land attachment, he will be entitled to the expenses of creating that land attachment.[321] Where the

---

[310] 1985 Act s.35(2).

[311] 1985 Act s.35(2).

[312] 1985 Act s.36A(2).

[313] 1985 Act s.36A(6).

[314] For the meaning of this expression, see s.12(4) and para.49.10, above.

[315] 1985 Act s.37(1)(a). The Bankruptcy and Diligence etc (Scotland) Act 2007 would have abolished adjudication but at the time of writing adjudication is still available.

[316] 1985 Act s.37(1). Note that the provisions of s.37 only apply to diligence in the context of sequestration. The slightly similar rules in Sch.7 para.24 specifically refer to diligence in the context of apparent insolvency. See also para.49.04.

[317] Note that this now includes money attachment (s.37(4)).

[318] 1985 Act s.37(4), (5). Under s.37(5A) this does not apply to earnings arrestment, a current maintenance arrestment, a conjoined arrestment order or a deduction from earnings order under the Child Support Act 1991. This means that payments under the Child Support Act 1991 override the rights of the trustee. Where an arrestment executed prior to the 60-day period still subsists at the date of sequestration the fund vests in the trustee but he must give effect to the preference: *Berry v Taylor*, 1992 S.C.L.R. 910.

[319] This paragraph is written on the assumption that land attachment (in terms of the 2007 Act) is eventually brought into force. It remains to be seen if this is the case.

[320] 1985 Act s.37(5B).

[321] 1985 Act s.37(5C)(a).

creditor has also registered a decree of foreclosure within that period, he must convey the heritable property to the trustee on receiving payment of his expenses in respect of the land attachment and decree of foreclosure.[322] Land attachment carried out by a creditor against the debtor's heritable property after the date of sequestration will be of no effect,[323] and likewise where the land attachment was created more than six months before the date of sequestration but has not proceeded to a warrant for sale, the creditor may no longer insist in that land attachment.[324] Where the land attachment has proceeded to the execution of a warrant for sale, and a contract to sell the land has been concluded, the trustee will have to concur in and ratify the deed implementing the contract, and receive that part of the proceeds of sale that would, but for the sequestration, have gone to the debtor.[325] However, this will not apply if the deed implementing the contract is not registered within the period of 28 days beginning on the date of recording of the certified copy order of the sheriff granting warrant to cite the debtor,[326] or the date of recording of the determination of the Accountant in Bankruptcy in a debtor application,[327] in each case in what would be the Register of Inhibitions. Where a decree of foreclosure has been granted, but the extract therefore has not been registered, the creditor may register title to it provided he does so within the same 28-day period.[328]

The order awarding sequestration also affects inhibitions, it being provided that where there is an inhibition on the estate of the debtor which takes effect within 60 days before the date of sequestration a right to the challenge the inhibition vests in the trustee,[329] as do the right of the inhibitor to receive payment for the discharge of the inhibition and the right in terms of the inhibition to challenge any deed voluntarily granted by the debtor.[330] These provisions apply also to the estate of a deceased debtor which has been sequestrated within 12 months after his death or which was absolutely insolvent at the date of death and to which within 12 months a judicial factor has been appointed under s.11A of the Judicial Factors (Scotland) Act 1889.[331]

49.29 Effect of sequestration on personal rights—Sequestration does not, as such, affect the validity of personal obligations undertaken by the debtor, except to the extent that any such obligation should, by virtue of its terms or nature, be extinguished upon the debtor's sequestration. The creditor may call on the trustee to adopt the contract. If he declines to do so, the creditor's remedy is a claim for damages against the sequestrated estate, for which he will rank in the sequestration.

49.30 Administration by trustee—The principal functions of the trustee are to recover, manage and realise the debtor's estate so far as vesting in him under the Act, and to distribute it among the debtor's creditors according to their entitlements.[332] He

---

[322] 1985 Act s.37(5C)(b).
[323] 1985 Act s.37(8A).
[324] 1985 Act s.37(8B).
[325] 1985 Act s.37(8C).
[326] 1985 Act s.37(8D)(a).
[327] 1985 Act s.37(8D)(b).
[328] 1985 Act s.37(8E).
[329] 1985 Act s.37(2).
[330] 1985 Act s.37(2), (3).
[331] 1985 Act s.37(7).
[332] 1985 Act s.3(1)(a), (b); see also s.38.

is required to make up and maintain an inventory and valuation of the estate, to maintain a sederunt book for the purpose of keeping an accurate record of the sequestration process and to keep regular accounts of his intromissions with the debtor's estate.[333] He is entitled to have access to all documents relating to the debtor's assets, business or financial affairs which may be sent by or on behalf of the debtor to a third party and to make copies of any such documents.[334] He is also entitled to require delivery to him of any title deed or other document of the debtor notwithstanding that a right of lien is claimed over it, but this is without prejudice to any preference to which the holder of the lien may be entitled.[335] A right of lien is a security within the meaning of the Act and the holder of it is a secured creditor,[336] who is entitled to a preferential ranking on the estate.[337] Where the trustee is not the Accountant in Bankruptcy,[338] as soon as possible after his confirmation in office the trustee must consult with the commissioners, or, if there is none, with the Accountant in Bankruptcy, concerning the exercise of his functions with regard to the management and realisation of the estate, and he is required to comply with any general or specific directions given to him in this regard by the creditors, by the court on the application of the commissioners or by the Accountant in Bankruptcy, except in the case of the sale of perishable goods.[339] Various powers (including carrying on a business of the debtor, borrowing money, taking out insurance, bringing, defending or continuing legal proceedings and creating securities) may be exercised by him if he considers that their exercise would be beneficial for the administration of the estate.[340] He may obtain supplies of gas, electricity, water and telecommunication services for the purposes of any business which has been carried on by the debtor or on his behalf, although the supplier may insist that the trustee personally guarantees payment of any charges in respect of the supply.[341] The trustee has power to adopt any contract entered into by the debtor before the date of sequestration where he considers that this would be beneficial to the administration of the debtor's estate, unless its adoption is precluded by the express or implied terms of the contract.[342] Special rules apply to the sale by the trustee of any part of the debtor's estate over which a heritable security is held by a creditor or creditors.[343] These entitle the trustee to sell the heritable property, though where there is a heritable security, he must take the heritable creditor's interest into account, and in practice, it will be in both the heritable creditor's interest and the trustee's interest to sell the heritable property, with the heritable creditor entitled to the payment of any sums due to him first before the balance of the proceeds of sale is handed to the trustee. Where the trustee proposes to sell or dispose of any right or interest in the debtor's family home, the trustee must obtain the consent from the debtor's spouse or civil partner to do so, and where that is not forthcoming, the trustee may apply to the sheriff for

---

[333] 1985 Act ss.3(1)(e), (f) and 38(1); see also s.62.

[334] 1985 Act s.38(2).

[335] 1985 Act s.38(4).

[336] 1985 Act s.73(1).

[337] *Adam & Winchester v White's Tr.* (1884) 11 R. 863; *Findlay v Waddell*, 1910 S.C. 670; *Pattullo v Accountant in Bankruptcy*, 2010 G.W.D. 18–360.

[338] 1985 Act s.39(1).

[339] 1985 Act s.39(1), (6).

[340] 1985 Act s.39(2).

[341] 1985 Act s.70.

[342] 1985 Act s.42; any party to a contract by the debtor may require the trustee to take a decision on this matter within 28 days: s.42(2).

[343] See s.39(4). See also para 49.36, below.

permission to sell.[344] The sheriff, when deciding whether or not to grant that permission, will take into account the needs and financial resources of the debtor's spouse or civil partner, the debtor's children, the interest of the creditors and the length of the period the family home was used as a residence.[345] The sheriff may refuse to grant the sale or postpone the sale for a period of up to three years.[346] There are further provisions designed to permit a non-entitled spouse or partner the opportunity to apply to the sheriff under s.16 of the 1985 Act to recall the sequestration or to protect the occupancy rights of the spouse or partner (as the case may be) if the purpose of the petition or debtor application for sequestration was wholly or mainly to defeat the occupancy rights of the non-entitled spouse or partner within the meaning of the Matrimonial Homes (Family Protection) (Scotland) Act 1981.[347] If the trustee does intend to sell the debtor's family home, he must do so within three years beginning with the date of sequestration, failing which it will revert to the debtor.[348]

All money received by the trustee in the exercise of his functions must be deposited by him in the name of the debtor's estate in an appropriate bank or institution.[349] He may also obtain an order from the court with respect to any transaction for, or involving the provision of, credit to the debtor if that transaction is or was extortionate and was not entered into more than three years before the date of sequestration.[350] The order may provide for the setting aside of any obligation created by the transaction in whole or part, for varying the terms of the transaction or the terms on which any security for it is held, for the payment by any party to the transaction to the trustee of any sums paid to that party by the debtor by virtue of the transaction or for the surrender to the trustee of any property held as security for the transaction.[351]

49.31 Examination of the debtor—Among the general functions of the trustee are those of ascertaining the reasons for the debtor's insolvency and the circumstances surrounding it, and to ascertain the state of the debtor's liabilities and assets.[352] To enable him to perform these functions he may request the debtor or the debtor's spouse or any other person who he believes can give such information to appear before him and give information relating to the debtor's assets, his dealings with them or his conduct in relation to his business or financial affairs.[353] If necessary he may apply to the sheriff for an order for a private examination of these persons to be held before the sheriff,[354] and he may also, and must if requested to do so by the Accountant in Bankruptcy, or the commissioners, or one-quarter in value of the creditors, apply to the sheriff for an order for a public examination.[355] Unlike

---

[344] 1985 Act s.40(2); see also para.49.33, below.

[345] 1985 Act s.40(2); *Salmon's Tr. v Salmon*, 1989 S.L.T. (Sh. Ct) 49; *Simpson's Tr. v Simpson*, 1993 S.C.L.R. 867; *Gourlay's Tr. v Gourlay*, 1995 S.L.T. (Sh. Ct) 7; *McMahon's Tr. v McMahon*, 1997 S.L.T. 1090.

[346] 1985 Act s.40(2)(d) (as amended by the Home Owner and Debtor Protection (Scotland) Act 2010 s.11); *McMahon's Tr. v McMahon*, 1997 S.L.T. 1090; *Stewart's Tr. v Stewart*, 2011 G.W.D. 31–671.

[347] 1985 Act s.41.

[348] The word "family home" is defined in s.40(4)(a). S.39A provides for certain exceptions to the three year rule.

[349] 1985 Act s.43.

[350] 1985 Act s.61; note the provisions of s.61(3) as to the meaning of "extortionate" in this context.

[351] 1985 Act s.61(4).

[352] 1985 Act s.3(1)(c), (d).

[353] 1985 Act s.44(1).

[354] 1985 Act s.44(2); on appeals see *Gupta's Tr. v Gupta*, 1996 S.C. 82.

[355] 1985 Act s.45.

a private examination, a public examination is held in open court and notice of it requires to be published in the Edinburgh Gazette, and given to every creditor known to the trustee. Provision is made for the granting of warrants to require the attendance of the debtor or other persons for examination before the sheriff and for the appointment of an examining commissioner if the debtor is for any good reason unable to attend.[356] The examination before the sheriff or examining commissioner is taken on oath or affirmation.[357] The 1985 Act lays down rules as to who may ask questions at the examination and limits the scope of these questions to matters relating to the debtor's assets, his dealings with them and his conduct in relation to his business or financial affairs.[358] No such rules apply to any attendances by the debtor or other person at the request of the trustee to give information to him privately.

Duties and position of debtor and his spouse and family—The debtor is under **49.32** a general duty to take every practicable step, and in particular to execute any document which may be necessary to enable the trustee to perform the functions conferred on him by the Act.[359] If necessary, the trustee may apply to the sheriff for an order on the debtor to do so, and the sheriff may authorise the sheriff clerk to execute any documents which the debtor has failed to execute with the like force and effect in all respects as if the document had been executed by the debtor himself.[360] The debtor commits an offence if he makes a false statement in relation to his assets or his business and financial affairs to any creditor, or any person concerned in the administration of his estate such as the trustee, after his sequestration unless he shows that he neither knew nor had reason to believe that the statement was false. He also commits an offence if he, or any other person acting in his interest, whether with or without his authority, destroys, damages, conceals, disposes of or removes from Scotland any part of the debtor's estate or any document relating to his assets or business unless he can show that this was not done with intent to prejudice creditors.[361] The period during which these offences may be committed is the period commencing one year immediately before the date of sequestration and ending with the debtor's discharge.[362] The Act makes provision for various other offences in relation to the failure of a debtor who is absent from Scotland to come to Scotland for any purpose connected with the administration of his estate when required to do so by the court, the falsification of documents by the debtor or any other person acting in his interest and the failure of the debtor to report any falsifications of which he is aware to the trustee, and also the making of transfers for inadequate consideration or the granting of unfair preferences to any creditor by a person who is absolutely insolvent.[363] It is also an offence for a person whose estate has been sequestrated, who has been adjudged bankrupt in England and Wales or Northern Ireland, who is subject to an bankruptcy restrictions order or bankruptcy restrictions undertaking in England, Wales, or Scotland, and who has not been discharged, to obtain, either alone or

---

[356] 1985 Act s.46.
[357] See Interpretation Act 1978 Sch.1.
[358] 1985 Act s.47; see *Holmes, Petitioner*, 1988 S.L.T. (Sh. Ct) 47 on the role of the witness's legal representatives.
[359] 1985 Act s.64.
[360] 1985 Act s.64(2).
[361] 1985 Act s.67(1), (2).
[362] 1985 Act s.67(11).
[363] See generally, 1985 Act s.67.

jointly with others, credit to the extent of £500 (excluding sums owed by way of council tax or to utilities) or more without giving the person from whom he obtains it information about his status as an undischarged bankrupt.[364] If the debtor already has debts of over £1,000 (excluding sums owed by way of council tax and utilities) obtaining credit of any amount is also a criminal offence.[365]

The trustee must report any offences of which he is aware to the Accountant in Bankruptcy, who is under a duty to report them to the Lord Advocate with a view to prosecution.[366] A debtor whose estate has been sequestrated is disqualified from sitting or voting in Parliament, from being elected a member of the House of Commons or any local authority and from holding certain specified offices.[367] He commits an offence if, prior to his discharge, he acts as director or liquidator of, or directly or indirectly takes part in or is concerned in the promotion, formation or management of, a company.[368] He is disqualified from acting as an insolvency practitioner[369] and, if he is a solicitor, his practising certificate ceases to have effect.[370]

49.33 Submission and adjudication of claims—A creditor who wishes to vote at a meeting of creditors other than the statutory meeting or to draw a dividend out of the debtor's estate for any accounting period must submit a claim to the trustee for adjudication, together with any further evidence which the trustee may require to satisfy himself as to the amount or validity of the claim.[371] It is not competent to refer to the oath of the debtor for this purpose,[372] and a written acknowledgement by him if dated after the date of sequestration is not competent as proof of a loan.[373]

The claim must be submitted at or before the meeting in order to entitle the creditor to vote, or not later than eight weeks before the end of the accounting period to entitle him to draw a dividend in respect of it. A claim submitted to and accepted by the trustee at or before the statutory meeting or submitted to the trustee and accepted by him for the purpose of voting or drawing a dividend is deemed to have been re-submitted to the trustee for the purpose of any subsequent meeting or accounting period,[374] but the creditor is free at any time to submit a further claim specifying a different amount.[375] The trustee is required to accept or reject the claim of each creditor at the commencement of every meeting for the purposes of the creditor's right to vote at it, and to accept or reject any claim submitted or deemed to have been re-submitted to him not later than four weeks before the end of each accounting period. He is not bound by any decisions or any adjudications which he may have made for the purposes of earlier meetings or accounting periods.[376] Reasons must be given to the creditor by the trustee when

---

[364] 1985 Act s.67(9), (9A), (10).

[365] 1985 Act s.67(9)(b).

[366] 1985 Act ss.3(3), 1A(3).

[367] Local Government (Scotland) Act 1973 s.31; Insolvency Act 1986 s.427; Criminal Proceedings etc (Scotland) Act 2007 s.73.

[368] Company Directors Disqualification Act 1986 s.11.

[369] Insolvency Act 1986 s.390.

[370] Solicitors (Scotland) Act 1980 s.18(1)(c); see also s.19.

[371] 1985 Act s.48(1), (5); for the form of claim see Bankruptcy (Scotland) Regulations 1985 (SI 1985/1925) reg.5, Form 5.

[372] *Adam v Maclachlan* (1847) 9 D. 560.

[373] *Carmichael's Tr. v Carmichael*, 1929 S.C. 265.

[374] 1985 Act s.48(2).

[375] 1985 Act s.48(4).

[376] 1985 Act s.49(1), (2).

he rejects a claim, and the debtor or creditor may appeal to the sheriff against the acceptance or rejection of any claim within certain time limits,[377] though the debtor may only appeal where he has a pecuniary interest in the outcome.[378] He must as soon as reasonably possible send a list of every accepted and rejected claim to the debtor and the creditors.[379] In calculating the amount of his claim for the purposes of these rules a secured creditor must deduct the value of any security as estimated by him or the amount, less expenses, which he has received or is entitled to receive on the realisation of his security.[380] As regards the balancing of accounts between creditor and debtor, debts arising before insolvency may be set off against each other, but a debt which arises before insolvency may not be set off against a debt arising after insolvency.[381] Provided the debts arose from obligations existing before insolvency, an illiquid claim may be set off against a liquid claim, illiquid claims including future and contingent debts[382] but not certain illiquid claims for damages.[383] There must be *concursus debiti et crediti* so that debtor and creditor alike must claim against each other in the same capacity. There is no requirement that the two claims must arise out of the same contract.[384]

Entitlement to vote and draw dividend—A creditor who has had his claim **49.34** accepted in whole or in part by the trustee, or on appeal to the sheriff, may vote on any matter at the meeting of creditors for the purpose of which the claim is accepted.[385] The acceptance of his claim in whole or in part in respect of an accounting period entitles him to payment out of the debtor's estate of a dividend for that accounting period in so far as the estate has funds available to make the payment, having regard to his position in the order of priority for distribution.[386]

Distribution of the debtor's estate—The trustee is required to make up accounts **49.35** of his intromissions with the debtor's estate in respect of periods of 12 months, the first period commencing with the date on which sequestration is awarded,[387] until the funds of the estate are exhausted. He has power with, where relevant, the consent of the commissioners or the Accountant in Bankruptcy to shorten the length of any accounting period other than the first, if he considers that it would be expedient to accelerate payment of any dividend, and he also has power to postpone payment of a dividend to the next accounting period.[388] Within two weeks after the end of an accounting period he must submit to the commissioners, or if there be none to the Accountant in Bankruptcy, his accounts of his intromissions with the debtor's estate for audit, together with a scheme of division of the divisible funds and a claim for his outlays and remuneration.[389] Provision is made

---

[377] 1985 Act s.49(4), (6). There is provision for submitting claims to arbitration: s.65.

[378] 1985 Act s.49(6A).

[379] 1985 Act s.49(2A).

[380] 1985 Act Sch.1 para.5.

[381] As per Lord McLaren in *Asphaltic Limestone Company Ltd v Corporation of Glasgow*, 1907 S.C. 463 at 474.

[382] *Smith v Lord Advocate (No.2)*, 1980 S.C. 227

[383] W.M. Gloag, *The Law of Contract*, 2nd edn (Edinburgh: W. Green, 1929), p.626 suggests that some damages claims, such as a claim for defamation, might stand a less successful chance of being validly set off.

[384] Bell, *Commentaries*, ii, 122.

[385] 1985 Act s.50(a).

[386] 1985 Act s.50(b).

[387] 1985 Act s.52(2) For the meaning of this expression, see s.12(4) and para.49.10, above.

[388] 1985 Act s.52(5).

[389] 1985 Act s.53(1).

for the taxation of accounts for legal expenses, and for the audit and determination of the trustee's outlays and remuneration by the commissioners or the Accountant in Bankruptcy, and also for appeal not later than eight weeks after the end of an accounting period against their determination in fixing these amounts.[390] After these procedures have been completed, the trustee must pay to the creditors their dividends in accordance with the scheme of division.[391] Any dividend which is not cashed or uplifted must be deposited by him in an appropriate bank or institution, and the same procedure is followed if the trustee has decided to exercise his power to set aside an amount for a creditor pending the production of evidence in support of his claim.[392] Certain outlays and expenses may be paid by the trustee at any time, as also may the preferred debts with the consent of the commissioners or the Accountant in Bankruptcy.[393] Where the Accountant in Bankruptcy is the trustee, there are slight modifications to the above procedures to take account of the absence of the need for auditing of the accounts.[394]

49.36 Order of priority—The order of priority in the distribution is as follows[395]: (a) the outlays and remuneration of the interim trustee (where applicable); (b) the outlays and remuneration of the trustee; (c) where the debtor is a deceased debtor, deathbed and funeral expenses reasonably incurred and expenses reasonably incurred in administering the estate; (d) the expenses reasonably incurred by a creditor who is a petitioner for sequestration; (e) preferred debts,[396] excluding interest accrued to the date of sequestration; (f) ordinary debts, that is, debts which are neither secured debts nor any of the debts mentioned in any other heading of this sentence; (g) interest on the preferred debts and the ordinary debts between the date of sequestration and the date of payment[397]; and (h) any postponed debt,[398] such as a loan made to the debtor by his spouse or a loan made to the debtor in consideration of a share of the profits in his business, which is postponed by s.3 of the Partnership Act 1890 to the claims of other creditors. Any debt falling within any of the heads (c)–(h) has the same priority as any other debt falling under the same head, and where the funds of the estate are inadequate to enable them to be paid in full they abate in equal proportions.[399] Any surplus, other than an unclaimed dividend, which remains after all these debts have been paid in full, falls to be made over to the debtor or to his successors or assignees.[400]

The rights of secured creditors whose rights are preferable to those of the trustee and the preference of the holder of a lien over a title deed or other document required to be delivered to the trustee are not affected by these rules.[401] A secured creditor whose rights are preferable to those of the trustee is in a

---

[390] 1985 Act s.53(2), (6).

[391] 1985 Act s.53(7).

[392] 1985 Act s.53(8); see also s.52(8).

[393] 1985 Act s.52(4).

[394] 1985 Act s.53A.

[395] 1985 Act s.51(1).

[396] For the meaning of preferred debts, see Sch.3 and para.49.37, below.

[397] As to the rate of interest, see s.51(7). The prescribed rate of interest is 8% per annum, in terms of reg.8 of the Bankruptcy (Scotland) Regulations 1985 (SI 1985/1925), but the rate applicable to the debt apart from the sequestration prevails if it is higher than the prescribed rate.

[398] For the meaning of postponed debts, see s.51(3). A recipient of a gratuitous alienation who has had to return the alienated asset to the trustee may claim as a postponed creditor for any sums he may have paid the debtor.

[399] 1985 Act s.51(4).

[400] 1985 Act s.51(5).

[401] 1985 Act s.51(6). As to the position of the holder of a lien, see para.49.31, above.

position at the outset of the sequestration to enforce the security to obtain a payment of his debt, subject to special procedures whereby the trustee may take the initiative and require any part of the debtor's heritable estate which is subject to such a security to be sold.[402] At any time after the expiry of 12 weeks from the date of sequestration the trustee may require a secured creditor to discharge the security at the expense of the debtor's estate irrespective of whether it relates to heritage or moveables or to convey or assign it to the trustee on payment to the creditor of the value specified by the creditor, whereupon the amount in respect of which the creditor is entitled to claim in the sequestration is any balance of his debt remaining after receipt of such payment.[403]

Preferred debts—Preferred debts are those listed in Sch.3 to the Act,[404] all of which rank equally inter se.[405] These comprise: (a) contributions to occupational pension schemes and state scheme premiums[406]; (b) amounts owed by the debtor by way of remuneration or accrued holiday remuneration to any person who is or has been his employee in respect of the whole or any part of four months before the date of sequestration or death, not exceeding £800[407]; (c) so much of any sum owed in respect of money advanced for the purpose as has been applied for the payment of a debt which, if it had not been paid, would have been a debt falling within (b) above; (d) sums for members of the reserve forces[408] under the Reserve Forces (Safeguard of Employment) Act 1985; (e) sums due in respect of levies on coal and steel production.[409] Since the Enterprise Act 2002, debts due to HM Revenue and Custom are no longer preferred debts. **49.37**

Co-obligants—Special provision is made by the Act with regard to the liabilities and rights of co-obligants of the debtor including his cautioners.[410] First, the co-obligant or cautioner is not freed or discharged from his liability for the debt by reason of the discharge of the debtor or by virtue of the creditor's voting or drawing a dividend or assenting to or not objecting to the discharge of the debtor or any composition.[411] In these respects, therefore, the creditor's position in a sequestration is protected against any results which might otherwise have flowed from these actings under the common law.[412] Secondly, where a creditor has had a claim accepted in whole or in part and a co-obligant of the debtor or his cautioner holds a security over any part of the debtor's estate, the co-obligant or cautioner must account to the trustee so as to put the estate in the same position as if he had paid the debt to the creditor and thereafter had his own claim accepted in whole or in part in the sequestration after deduction of the value of his security.[413] This means that the co-obligant or cautioner is not entitled to the benefit of his security unless the creditor claims against him in the first instance and not in the sequestration. **49.38**

---

[402] See 1985 Act s.39(4).
[403] 1985 Act Sch.1 para.5(2).
[404] 1985 Act s.51(2).
[405] 1985 Act s.51(4).
[406] Under the Pension Schemes Act 1993.
[407] Bankruptcy (Scotland) Amendment Regulations 1986 (SI 1986/1914), adding reg.14 to Bankruptcy (Scotland) Regulations 1985 (SI 1985/1925).
[408] Such as the Royal Naval Reserve and the Territorial Army.
[409] Insolvency (E.C.S.C. Levy Debts) Regulations 1987 (SI 1987/2093).
[410] 1985 Act s.60.
[411] 1985 Act s.60(1).
[412] See Ch.16, above.
[413] 1985 Act s.60(2).

Thirdly, the co-obligant or cautioner is entitled to require and obtain at his own expense from the creditor an assignation of the debt on payment of the amount thereof in full, and thereafter to submit a claim, vote and draw a dividend on that debt if otherwise legally entitled to do so.[414]

49.39 Rule against double ranking—The common-law rule that no debt can be ranked twice on a sequestrated estate is of practical importance in the case where a principal debtor and cautioner are both bankrupt. The creditor may then rank on each estate; but the cautioner's estate has no ranking on the estate of the principal debtor. To allow such a ranking would mean that a higher dividend would be paid on the debt in question than is paid on the other debts. Nor can the cautioner's estate obtain the result of a ranking by deducting the amount paid from separate claims in which the principal debtor was a creditor of the cautioner.[415] The rule rests on the theory that when a debt is ranked in sequestration it is, so far as the sequestrated estate is concerned, to be treated as paid. It does not apply where the principal debtor is not sequestrated but compounds with his creditors.[416]

49.40 Automatic discharge of the debtor—Subject to the provisions of s.54 of the 1985 Act the debtor is automatically discharged on the expiry of one year from the date of sequestration.[417] His discharge is however subject to any application, by the trustee or any creditor, to the sheriff for deferment of the discharge.[418] An application for deferment must be made no later than nine months after the date of sequestration[419] and the sheriff has power to defer the discharge for a maximum of two years.[420] When an application for deferment is made timeously, discharge does not occur until the court pronounces an order under s.54.[421] The trustee or any creditor may apply for further deferments provided the application is made not later than three months before the end of the current period of deferment.[422] A discharged debtor may apply to the Accountant in Bankruptcy for a certificate that he has been discharged, in order to obtain evidence of this fact.[423] A debtor whose discharge has been deferred may petition the sheriff for his discharge at any time thereafter, and the question whether or not he should be granted his discharge will then be considered in the light of the debtor's declarations to the effect that he has made a full and fair surrender and disclosure of his estate, a report by the trustee and any representations by the debtor, the trustee or any creditor.[424] The effect of the discharge is that the debtor is discharged within the United Kingdom of all debts and obligations contracted by him, or for which he was liable, at the date of sequestration.[425] There are some exceptions, however: he is not discharged from the following: liability to pay a fine or other penalty due to the Crown or to forfeiture of any bail; any liability for compensation for any injury, loss or damage

---

[414] 1985 Act s.60(3); cf. Ch.16, above.
[415] *Anderson v Mackinnon* (1876) 3 R. 608.
[416] *Mackinnon v Monkhouse* (1881) 9 R. 393.
[417] 1985 Act s.54(1).
[418] *Clydesdale Bank Plc v Davidson*, 1993 S.C. 307; *Accountant in Bankruptcy v Campbell*, 2012 S.L.T. (Sh. Ct) 35
[419] 1985 Act s.54(3); see *Hooke, Noter*, 2000 S.L.T. 1028.
[420] 1985 Act s.54(4), (6); *Pattison v Halliday*, 1991 S.L.T. 645.
[421] *Clydesdale Bank Plc v Davidson*, 1993 S.C. 307.
[422] 1985 Act s.54(9).
[423] 1985 Act s.54(2).
[424] 1985 Act s.54(8).
[425] 1985 Act s.55(1); *Grimshaw v Bruce* [2011] CSOH 212.

arising from an offence under which he was convicted; any liability incurred by reason of fraud or breach of trust; any obligation to pay aliment under any enactment or rule of law or periodical allowance on divorce[426]; any obligation to pay child maintenance; his obligation to co-operate with the trustee in the performance of his functions under the Act[427]; or a student loan.[428] The discharge removes the disability of the debtor from holding public or other offices, and he is once more enabled to acquire estate without that estate vesting in the trustee.[429]

Bankruptcy restrictions orders and undertakings—Bankruptcy restrictions **49.41** orders and undertakings have been adapted from the law on bankruptcy in England and Wales. They are a way of ensuring some restraints on debtors' activities even after the debtors' discharge, relative to the debtors' conduct before and during the period of sequestration. A bankruptcy restrictions order ("BRO") is one imposed by the sheriff, who may grant such an application if he thinks it appropriate having regard to the conduct of the debtor,[430] while a bankruptcy restrictions undertaking ("BRU") is one that is offered by the debtor to the Accountant in Bankruptcy as a form of acknowledgement by the debtor that his conduct may have been in some respects unsatisfactory. The Accountant in Bankruptcy maintains a register of BROs and BRUs.[431] Where a debtor is subject to a BRO or a BRU, not only will he have to disclose the fact on pain of criminal penalties[432] but such a debtor is disqualified from being a receiver,[433] and from holding office as a member of a local authority.[434] The Scottish Ministers have the power to extend the range of positions for which someone subject to a BRO or a BRU may be disqualified.[435]

The grounds under which a sheriff may make an order are outlined in s.56B, and cover the following, whether before or after the date of sequestration: failure to keep property or business records for two years before the date of presentation of the petition or application for sequestration; failure to produce property or business records to the Accountant in Bankruptcy or the trustee; gratuitous alienations; unfair preferences; excessive pension contributions; failing to supply goods or services already paid for; trading while unable to meet one's debts; incurring debts with no reasonable expectation of being able to pay them; failure to account for loss of property to the sheriff, the Accountant in Bankruptcy or the trustee; gambling, speculation or extravagance; neglect of business affairs; fraud or breach of trust; failure to co-operate with the Accountant in Bankruptcy, or the trustee; and any previous history of sequestration. If the Accountant in Bankruptcy wishes to apply for a BRO, the application must be within the period beginning with the date of sequestration and ending with the date of the debtor's discharge.[436] The minimum

---

[426] *Lessani v Lessani*, 2007 Fam. L.R. 81.

[427] 1985 Act s.55(2). The discharge does not affect any right of a secured creditor to enforce his security for payment of a debt and any interest due and payable thereon until the debt is paid in full: s.55(3).

[428] Education (Student Loans) Act 1990 Sch.2 para.6.

[429] 1985 Act s.32(6), (10).

[430] 1985 Act s.56B(1).

[431] 1985 Act s.1A(1)(b).

[432] 1985 Act ss.56C and 56H, amending s.67(10)(c)(i).

[433] 2007 Act s.3, amending the Insolvency Act 1986 s.51. Insolvency practitioners are in any event disqualified if they are bankrupt: Insolvency Act 1986 s.390.

[434] 2007 Act s.4 amending the Local Government (Scotland) Act 1973 s.31.

[435] 1985 Act s.71B.

[436] 1985 Act s.56D.

duration of the BRO is two years and the maximum 15 years.[437] It is open to the debtor to apply for the BRO to be annulled or varied.[438] It is also possible to obtain an interim BRO if the sheriff thinks that the subsequent application for a BRO will be successful and that it is in the public interest to make one.[439] By contrast, a BRU is offered by the debtor to the Accountant in Bankruptcy[440] who when determining whether or not to accept it will have regard to the same matters as are considered by the sheriff above. A BRU also endures for a minimum of two and a maximum of 15 years[441] and may be varied on application to the sheriff by the debtor.[442] When a debtor has his award of sequestration recalled under s.17, the sheriff may at the same time annul any existing BRO or BRU, and if he does not do so, the debtor has a right of appeal to the sheriff principal whose decision is final.[443] Even after a debtor is discharged from his sequestration any extant BRO or BRU will remain in place unless it is specifically discharged by the sheriff, but after the date of discharge no application for a BRO may be made.[444]

49.42 Discharge of the debtor on composition—The debtor may obtain his discharge at any time after the sheriff has appointed the trustee, or the Accountant in Bankruptcy appointed a trustee, by making an offer, known as a composition, to the trustee in respect of his debts and specifying the caution or other security to be provided for its implementation.[445] If such an offer is made the trustee (where he is not the Accountant in Bankruptcy) must submit the offer along with a report thereon to the commissioners or, if there be none, to the Accountant in Bankruptcy. It is then for the commissioners or the Accountant in Bankruptcy to decide whether the offer should be placed before the creditors. If they consider that the offer will be timeously implemented and that its implementation would secure payment of a dividend of at least 25p in the pound in respect of the ordinary debts and are satisfied with the caution or other security specified in the offer, they are required to recommend that a copy of it should be placed before the creditors, and it is then for the trustee to arrange for this to be done. The trustee must publish a notice in the Edinburgh Gazette stating that an offer of composition has been made and where its terms may be inspected. The trustee must invite every creditor known to him, to whom he must send a report on the matter, to accept or reject the offer within a period of five weeks. If within that period the trustee has not received notification in writing from a majority in number and not less than one-third in value of the creditors that they reject the offer of composition, the offer must be approved by the trustee. If he does receive the requisite notification of rejection he must reject the offer. A creditor who has received a copy of the offer and has failed to notify the trustee that he rejects the offer is deemed to have accepted it.

If it is approved, and once steps have been taken for payment of or provision for all necessary charges in connection with the sequestration and for lodging the debtor's bond of caution or other security with the sheriff clerk, the Accountant in Bankruptcy will make an order discharging the debtor and the trustee. The order

---

[437] 1985 Act s.56E.
[438] 1985 Act s.56E(3).
[439] 1985 Act s.56F.
[440] 1985 Act s.56G(1).
[441] 1985 Act s.56G(1).
[442] 1985 Act s.56G(5).
[443] 1985 Act s.56J.
[444] 1985 Act s.56K.
[445] 1985 Act s.56; the whole procedure is set out in Sch.4 (as amended by the 2007 Act s.21).

approving the offer of composition and discharging the debtor and trustee may be recalled by the Court of Session if it is satisfied that there has been or is likely to be default in payment of the composition or any instalment thereof, or that for any reason it cannot be proceeded with or cannot be proceeded with without undue delay or injustice to the creditors. The effect of a recall is to revive the sequestration and, if the trustee has been discharged, the Court of Session may appoint a judicial factor to administer the estate. Where an offer of composition is made the sequestration must nevertheless proceed for the time being as if no such offer had been made until the discharge of the debtor becomes effective. A debtor may make two, but not more than two, offers of composition in the course of a sequestration.

Discharge of trustee in the absence of composition—After the trustee has made **49.43** a final division of the debtor's estate and has inserted his final audited accounts in the sederunt book he may take steps to obtain his discharge.[446] He must deposit any unclaimed dividends and any unapplied balances in an appropriate bank or institution. Once this has been done he must send to the Accountant in Bankruptcy the sederunt book, a copy of the audited accounts and a receipt for the deposited moneys, and at the same time apply to him for a certificate of discharge. An opportunity is given to the debtor and to all the creditors known to the trustee to make representations on his application within 14 days to the Accountant in Bankruptcy. On the expiry of that period the Accountant in Bankruptcy must, after examining the documents sent to him and considering any representations duly made to him, grant or refuse to grant the certificate of discharge. There is a right of appeal to the sheriff against his decision. The effect of the grant of a certificate of discharge is to discharge the trustee from all liability, other than liability arising from fraud, to the creditors or to the debtor in respect of any act or omission by him in exercising the functions conferred on him by the Act. The same rights of application for a discharge are given to the executor of a trustee who has died and to a trustee who has resigned office.[447]

Voluntary trust deeds for creditors—The estates of a party who is insolvent **49.44** may be wound up by some private arrangement with his creditors without resorting to sequestration, of which the best known, other than a composition, are trust deeds and protected trust deeds. The advantage of a protected trust deed is that it may become protected against the possibility of being superseded by a sequestration.[448]

A trust deed for creditors is carried out by a conveyance by the debtor to a trustee, with the accession of some, or all, of the creditors. Under the 1985 Act a "trust deed" means a voluntary trust deed granted by or on behalf of the debtor whereby his estate (other than such of his estate as would not vest in the trustee if his estate were sequestrated)[449] is conveyed to the trustee for the benefit of his creditors generally.[450] Such a trustee has no statutory title, and must complete his right to the various subjects conveyed to him by the appropriate methods. He may register a notice of inhibition in the Register of Inhibitions and Adjudications at any time after the trust deed has been delivered to him, which has the same effect

---

[446] 1985 Act s.57. If the trustee is the Accountant in Bankruptcy his discharge is governed by s.58A.
[447] 1985 Act s.57(7).
[448] See para.49.45.
[449] See para.49.20, above.
[450] 1985 Act s.5(4A).

as the recording of letters of inhibition against the debtor.[451] Should the trustee fail to take these steps, the subjects left in the debtor's possession may be attached by diligence at the instance of creditors who have not acceded to the trust deed or of creditors to whom the debtor may have subsequently become indebted.[452] When the trustee has completed his title nothing is left with the debtor that can be attached by diligence. The granting of a trust deed is, subject to the restrictions applicable in the case of protected trust deeds,[453] no bar to sequestration, which may still be applied for at any time by a non-acceding creditor[454]; by the debtor, with concurrence of a non-acceding creditor[455]; or by a creditor who has acceded, in the event of non-acceding creditors taking proceedings which might result in giving them preferential rights.[456] The trustee himself may also present a petition for the debtor's sequestration at any time.[457] The act of granting a trust deed for his creditors renders the debtor apparently insolvent, thus opening the way for a petition for his sequestration by any of his creditors whose debts exceed £3,000 if they wish to proceed in this way.[458] Where sequestration is awarded, the trust deed falls without any reduction, the estate must be wound up by the trustee in the sequestration, and any rights acquired under the private trust deed must be asserted in the sequestration proceedings.[459] The trustee under the private trust deed has, in the event of sequestration, a lien for any expenses he may have incurred.[460] But, like other liens, this requires possession; where the trustee in a private trust deed granted by a farmer had advanced money for the administration of the farm, but had not obtained a completed assignation of the debtor's lease, it was held that as he had no possession he had no lien, and that there were no grounds on which he could claim any preferential ranking in the ensuing sequestration.[461]

In dividing the estate the trustee in a trust deed for creditors is bound to provide for all claims intimated to him. He was held personally liable when he rejected a claim which the creditor was able to prove to be well founded.[462] Unless the trust deed otherwise provides, the provisions of Sch.1 to the 1985 Act must be applied for the purposes of determining the amount of each creditor's claim.[463] The submission of a claim by a creditor to the trustee acts as a bar to the effect of any enactment or rule of law relating to limitation of actions in any part of the United Kingdom.[464] Even although a particular creditor may not have acceded to the trust deed, he is entitled to be ranked in the distribution of the estate.[465] The trustee under a private trust deed has no title at common law to challenge illegal prefer-

---

[451] 1985 Act Sch.5 para.2. The form of notice (no.8) to be recorded may be found on the Scottish Court Service website at *http://www.scotcourts.gov.uk/library/publications/docs/Bankruptcy RulesForms.pdf* [Accessed September 30, 2012].

[452] *Gibson v Wilson* (1841) 3 D. 974.

[453] See para.49.45, below.

[454] *Kyd v Waterson* (1880) 7 R. 884.

[455] *Macalister v Swinburne* (1874) 1 R. 958; *Salaman v Rosslyn's Trs* (1900) 3 F. 298. As there is no longer a statutory provision for an application by a debtor with a concurring creditor (s.2A of the 1985 Act having been repealed) it is not clear whether this method would still be possible.

[456] *Jopp v Hay* (1844) 7 D. 260. See *Munro v Rothfield*, 1920 S.C. (HL) 165.

[457] 1985 Act s.8(1)(a).

[458] 1985 Act s.5(3), (4).

[459] *Salaman v Rosslyn's Trs* (1900) 3 F. 298.

[460] *Thomson v Tough's Tr.* (1880) 7 R. 1035.

[461] *Mess v Sime's Tr.* (1898) 1 F. (HL) 22.

[462] *Cruickshank v Thomas* (1893) 21 R. 257.

[463] 1985 Act Sch.5 para.4.

[464] 1985 Act Sch.5 para.3.

[465] *Ogilvie v Taylor* (1887) 14 R. 399.

ences granted by the debtor, unless a creditor entitled to challenge has acceded to the trust, and has assigned his title to sue to the trustee.[466] The debtor, the trustee or any creditor may at any time before the final distribution of the debtor's estate among the creditors have the trustee's accounts audited by and his remuneration fixed by the Accountant in Bankruptcy.[467] The trustee under a private trust deed has the same power as the trustee in a sequestration to obtain supplies of utilities for the purposes of any business which has been carried on by the debtor or on his behalf, on condition that he personally guarantees payment of any charges in respect of the supply.[468]

Protected trust deeds—Private trust deeds are not common because of the **49.45** limited protection they afford the debtor. A debtor may be protected against the possibility of sequestration, and indeed from diligence, by granting a trust deed that is made a protected trust deed.[469] A protected trust deed is only available to individuals, and not to any individual who is already in an approved debt payment programme in terms of the Debt Arrangement Scheme.[470] Until recently the debtor was required to transfer all his estate to the trust[471] but following s.10 of the Home Owner and Debtor Protection (Scotland) Act 2010 it is permissible to exclude the debtor's dwelling-house[472] from the estate when there is a standard security over it and the standard security holder has agreed beforehand that it will not claim under the trust deed for any of the debt for which the security was given.[473] In order to obtain this benefit of a protected trust deed it is necessary that the deed should comply with the statutory definition of a trust deed,[474] that the trustee would not be disqualified from acting as trustee if the debtor's estate were being sequestrated,[475] that after the delivery to him of the trust deed, the trustee should have published a notice in the Edinburgh Gazette and within one week have sent to every creditor known to him a copy of the trust deed, a copy of the notice and other prescribed information and that within the period of five weeks from the publication of the notice, the trustee has not received notification in writing from a majority in number or not less than one-third in value of the creditors that they object to the trust deed and do not wish to accede to it.[476] If these requirements are satisfied the trustee must immediately send a copy of the trust deed to the Accountant in Bankruptcy for registration together with a certificate that he has not received such notification from the creditors. The trust deed is then protected and the protected trust deed is recorded in the Register of Insolvencies. Any creditor who has received a copy of the trustee's notice and has not notified the trustee that he objects to it is treated as if he has acceded to the trust deed.[477] Once the

---

[466] *Fleming's Trs v McHardy* (1892) 19 R. 542; in relation to challenges under statute, see ss.34(1), 36(1).

[467] 1985 Act Sch.5 para.1.

[468] 1985 Act s.70.

[469] 1985 Act Sch.5 para.5(1).

[470] Protected Trust Deed (Scotland) Regulations 2008 (SSI 2008/143) (the "2008 Regulations") reg.4.

[471] 2008 Regulations reg.6(1).

[472] As defined in the 1985 Act s.5(4AA),(4AB), as inserted by s.10 of the Home Owner and Debtor Protection (Scotland) Act 2010.

[473] 1985 Act s.5(A)(b), as inserted by s.10 of the Home Owner and Debtor Protection (Scotland) Act 2010.

[474] 1985 Act s.5(1)(a).

[475] 2008 Regulations reg.5

[476] 2008 Regulations reg.10.

[477] 2008 Regulations reg.9.

trust deed is protected, a creditor who has not been sent a copy of the trustee's notice or who has notified the trustee of his objection to the deed has no higher right to recover his debt than a creditor who has acceded to the deed and an application for sequestration by the debtor may not be made while the trust deed subsists.[478] A creditor who has not been sent a copy of the trustee's notice or who has notified the trustee of his objection loses the right to petition for sequestration after six weeks have elapsed from the date of publication of the notice inviting accession unless he avers that distribution of the estate is or is likely to be unduly prejudicial to a creditor or class of creditors, and the court may award sequestration in these circumstances only if it is satisfied that the averment is correct.[479] A creditor may also object to the trustee's discharge if he satisfies the sheriff that the trustee's intromissions with the estate have been so unduly prejudicial to his claim that he should not be bound by the trustee's discharge.[480] In addition to the benefits mentioned above, the fact that a trust deed has become a protected trust deed enables the trustee acting under it to challenge gratuitous alienations,[481] capital sums payable on divorce,[482] and unfair preferences[483] without resorting to sequestration.[484] Protected trust deeds are also subject to the supervision of the Accountant in Bankruptcy[485] and are sent to him for registration. Trustees acting under such trust deeds have to send their accounts and reports to him regularly.[486] Trustees are entitled to be remunerated out of the debtor's estate.[487] Assuming the trustee is able to deal with the debtor's affairs successfully and the debtor complies with the terms of the protected trust deed, the debtor will eventually be discharged.[488]

49.46 Composition contracts—At common law, an insolvent estate may be wound up without depriving the debtor of his estates, through the medium of a composition contract. Such contracts are extremely rare since they provide no protection at all for the debtor. Under its usual form the debtor agrees to pay so much in the pound to each creditor, and grants bills payable in instalments for that amount thereby conferring on each creditor, in the event of failure in payment, a liquid debt on which diligence may at once proceed. In the absence of any provision to the contrary, the full debt revives on failure in payment of any instalment.[489] As the debtor under the process is not deprived of his estate it remains open to the diligence of any creditor who is not barred by his accession to the composition contract. Each creditor who accedes does so on the implied condition that the accession of all is obtained.[490]

---

[478] 2008 Regulations reg.11.
[479] 2008 Regulations reg.12.
[480] 2008 Regulations regs 13,14.
[481] 1985 Act s.34(1)(b).
[482] 1985 Act s.35(2).
[483] 1985 Act s.36(4)(b).
[484] It is not clear whether excessive pension contributions under s.36A(1) may also be challenged by the trustee under a protected trust deed. S.36A(1) refers to a "trustee" without saying "trustee under a protected trust deed" as it does elsewhere.
[485] 2008 Regulations reg.15.
[486] 2008 Regulations reg.17.
[487] 2008 Regulations reg.18.
[488] 2008 Regulations reg.19. Note that student loans may still be recovered from the debtor notwithstanding the debtor's discharge (reg.20).
[489] Bell, *Commentaries*, II, 400.
[490] Bell, *Commentaries*, II, 395, 400.

FURTHER READING

Adams, R., "Sequestration and divorce: Some reflections", 2011 Fam. L.B. 112–2.

Adie, A., *Bankruptcy* (Edinburgh: W. Green, 1995).

Junor, G., "A bankrupt's "radical right" in his sequestrated estate—suing the trustee?", 2007 S.L.T. 215.

Junor, G., "Creditors' rights in bankruptcy", 2009 S.L.T. 231.

McBryde, W.W., *Bankruptcy*, 2nd edn (Edinburgh: W. Green, 1995).

McKenzie-Skene, D.W., "Gratuitous alienations and unfair preferences in insolvency", 1993 J.L.S.S. 38(4), 141–5.

McKenzie-Skene, D.W., *Insolvency Law in Scotland* (Edinburgh: T. & T. Clark, 1999).

McKenzie-Skene, D.W., "The reform of bankruptcy law in Scotland", 2009 Insolv. Int. 22(2), 17–25.

Scottish Law Commission, *Consultation Paper on the Consolidation of Bankruptcy Legislation in Scotland* (HMSO, 2011), available at *http://www. scotlawcom.gov.uk/news/making-bankruptcy-law-accessible/* [Accessed July 23, 2012].

The Accountant in Bankruptcy maintains an excellent website at *http://www.aib. gov.uk/* [Accessed July 24, 2012] which provides detailed information for debtors, creditors and insolvency practitioners. It has up to date versions of all the relevant statutes and regulations. The Register of Insolvencies is also available from this website.

INDEX